NORWEGIAN DICTIONARY

NORWEGIAN DICTIONARY

Norwegian–English English–Norwegian

With a supplement by Kari Bråtveit

London and New York

First published 1990
by J.W. Cappelens Forlag A-S, Oslo
Second edition published 1994
by Routledge
11 New Fetter Lane, London EC4P 4EE

Simultaneously published in the USA and Canada
by Routledge
29 West 35th Street, New York, NY 10001

Printed and bound in Great Britain by
TJ Press Ltd, Padstow, Cornwall

Printed on acid-free paper

British Library Cataloguing in Publication Data
A catalogue record for this book is available from the British Library

Library of Congress Cataloging in Publication Data
Norwegian dictionary: Norwegian–English, English–Norwegian
p. cm.
ISBN 0–415–10801–2
1. Norwegian language—Dictionaries—English. 2. English language—Dictionaries—Norwegian.
PD2691.N58 1994
439.8′231—dc20
93-48842
CIP

ISBN 0–415–10801–2

CONTENTS

ABBREVIATIONS

adj	adjectiv (adjective)
adv	adverb (adverb)
anat	anatomi, anatomisk (anatomy, anatomical)
art	artikkel (article)
best	bestemt (definite)
bibl	bibelsk (biblical)
biol	biologi, biologisk (biology, biological)
bl.a.	blant annet (among other things)
bokl	boklig (literary)
bot	botanikk, botanisk (botany, botanical)
dgl	dagligtale, i daligtalen (everyday language)
dial	dialekt, dialektisk (dialect, dialectal)
dvs	det vil si (that means, i.e.)
egtl	egentlig (real, actual)
e.l.	eller lignende (or similar)
el	eller (or)
elek	elektristet, elektrisk (electricity, electrical)
ent	entall (singular)
etc	et cetera
f.eks.	for eksempel (for example, e.g.)
fig	figurlig, i figurlig/overfort betydning (figurative, figurative meaning)
fl	flertall (majority)
fork	forkortelse, forkortet (abbreviation, abbreviated)
fys	fysikk, fysisk (physics, physical)
GB	Great Britain, britisk, i britisk-engelsk språkbruk (Great Britain, British, in British-English usage)
gml	gammel, i gammelsdags språkbuk (old, in old-fashioned usage)
gram	grammatikk, grammatisk (grammar, grammatical)
hist	historie, historisk (history, historical)
hum	humoristisk (humoristic)
inf	infinitiv (infinitive)
int	interjeksjon (interjection)
intr	intransitivt (intransitive)
iron	ironisk (ironical)
jf	jamfor, sammenlign (compare, cf.)
jur	juridisk (in legal terms)
koll	kollektiv(t), som kollektiv-(ord) (collective, as collective word)

komp	komparativ (comparative)
konj	konjunksjon (conjunction)
mat	matematikk, matematisk (mathematics, mathematical)
med	medisin, medisinsk (medicine, medical)
mek	mekanikk, mekanisk; teknikk, teknisk (mechanics, mechanical; technique, technical)
merk	merkantilt, i forretningsspråket (commercial, in business usage)
mht	med hensyn til (as regards)
mil	militært, i militær språkbruk (military, in military usage)
mots	motsatt, i motsetning til (opposite, in contrast to)
mus	musikk (music)
m.v.	med videre (and so forth)
neds	nedsettende (derogatory)
o.a.	og annet, og andre (et al.)
o.l.	og lignende (and similar, etc.)
oppr	opprinnelig (original)
osv	og så videre (and so forth, etc.)
part	partissip (participle)
pers	personlig (personal)
pga	på grunn av (because of)
pkt	punkt (point)
poet	poetisk (poetic)
pol	politikk, politisk (politics, political)
p.p.	perfektum partisipp (perfect participle)
pref	prefiks, forstavelse (prefix)
prep	preposisjon (preposition)
pres	presens (present)
pret	preteritum (preterite)
pron	pronomen (pronoun)
rel	religion, i religios språkbruk (religion, in religious usage)
sb	substantiv (noun)
sl	slang
spes	spesiell, spesielt (special, specially)
suff	suffiks, endelse (suffix, ending)
sup	superlativ (superlative)
teat	teater (theatre)
tilsv	tilsvarende (corresponding)
trans	transitivt (transitive)
TV	televisjon, fjernsyn (television)
ubest	ubestemt (indefinite)
US	United States (of Amerika), i amerikansk språkbruk (United States, in American usage)
vb	verb
vi	intrasitivt verb (intransitive verb)

vr	refleksivt verb (reflexive verb)
vt	transitivt verb (transitive verb)
vulg	vulgært, i vulgær språkbruk (vulgar, in vulgar usage)
zo	zoologi, zoologisk (zoology, zoological)

A

a *(bokstaven a)* a.

à *2 kasser à 25 flasker* two cases of 25 bottles; *to flasker à 50 pence* two bottles at 50p each; *2 à 3 dager* two or three days.

abbed *sb* abbot. **abbedi** *sb* abbey. **abbedisse** *sb* abbess.

abbor *sb* perch.

abc, abc-bok *sb* ABC book; spelling-book.

abdikasjon *sb* abdication. **abdisere** *vb* abdicate.

aber *sb* **1** *(ulempe)* drawback; **2** *(hake)* catch, snag.

abnorm *adj* abnormal. **abnormitet** *sb* abnormity.

abonnement *sb* subscription. **abonnent** *sb* subscriber; *fast* ~ regular subscriber. **abonnere** *vb* subscribe; ~ *på en avis* subscribe to a paper.

abort *sb* abortion, miscarriage; *fremkalle (en)* ~ induce an abortion. **abortere** *vb* have an abortion.

absolutt **1** *adj* absolute *(også data)*; **2** *adv* absolutely, completely; ~ *ikke* by no means; certainly not; not at all; ~ *nødvendig* absolutely necessary.

absorbere *vb* absorb. **absorbering, absorbsjon** *sb* absorption.

abstraksjon *sb* abstraction. **abstrakt** *adj* abstract.

absurd *adj* absurd. **absurditet** *sb* absurdity.

acetylen *sb* acetylene.

adams | drakt *sb: i* ~ ~ in one's birthday suit; in the altogether. **~eple** *sb* Adam's apple.

addend *sb* addend. **addere** *vb* add up; do an addition. **addisjon** *sb* addition.

adel *sb* nobility. **adelig** *adj* noble; of noble birth. **adels|mann** *sb* nobleman. **~stand** *sb* nobility, peerage.

adgang *sb* **1** *(vei til)* access, approach; ~ *til sjøen* access to the sea; **2** *(tillatelse til å komme inn etc)* admission, admittance; ~ *forbudt* no admittance.

adjektiv *sb* adjective. **adjektivisk** *adj* adjectival.

adjø *interj, sb* good-bye; ~ *så lenge* good-bye for now (till then/till next time); *også* so long.

adle *vb* **1** *(opphøye i adelsstanden)* raise to the peerage; **2** *(slå til ridder)* knight; **3** *(foredle)* ennoble.

adlyde *vb* obey; *han adlød sin mor* he obeyed his mother; *ikke* ~ disobey.

administrasjon *sb* administration, management. **administrasjonsomkostninger** *sb fl* overhead costs/charges. **administrativ** *adj* administrative. **administrator** *sb* administrator. **administrere** *vb* administer. **administrerende direktør** *sb* managing director.

admiral *sb* admiral.

adopsjon *sb* adoption. **adoptere** *vb* adopt. **adoptiv|barn** *sb* adopted child. **~far** *sb* adoptive father. **~mother** *sb* adoptive mother.

adressat *sb* addressee. **adresse** *sb* address; *data også* address reference. **adresse|buss** *sb data* address bus. **~katalog** *sb data* directory. **~liste** *sb data* load map. **~område** *sb data* address space. **adresserbar** *adj data* addressable. **adressere** *vb* address *(også data)*.

ad undas: *gå* ~ ~ go to pot/to rack and ruin.

advare *vb* caution, warn; *jeg advarte henne mot (å gjøre) det* I warned her against (doing) it. **advarsel** *sb* caution, warning; *vi slapp med en advarsel* we were let off with a caution.

advent *sb* Advent.

adverbiell *adj* adverbial. **adverb(ium)** *sb* adverb.

advokat *sb* lawyer, solicitor; *(prosederende ~)* barrister; *(i retten ofte kalt)* counsel; *US* attorney. *Se også sakfører.*

aerogram *sb* air letter.

affeksjonsverdi *sb* sentimental value. **affekt** *sb* excitement, passion; *komme i* ~ get excited. **affektasjon** *sb* affectation. **affektert** *adj* affected, conceited. **affisere** *vb: uten å la seg* ~ without batting an eyelid/turning a hair.

affære *sb* affair, matter.

aften *sb* **1** *(tidlig aften)* evening; **2** *(sen aften)* night; **3** *(dagen før spesiell begivenhet, helg etc)* eve; **4** *god* ~ good evening; *i* ~ tonight; this evening; *i morgen* ~ tomorrow evening/night; *i går* ~ last night; *om aftenen* at night; in the evening; *om aftenen den 9. April* on the evening of April 9th. **aftens** *sb (aftensmat)* supper; *spise* ~ have supper.

age *sb* awe, respect; *holde i* ~ keep in check.

agent *sb* **1** *(representant)* agent, representative; **2** *(spion)* agent, spy. **agentur** *sb* agency. **agere** *vb* act, play; pose as.

agg *sb* grudge; *ha et* ~ *til* bear/have a grudge against.

aggresjon *sb* agression. **aggressiv** *adj* aggressive.

12. Svenkerud: Ordbok.

agitasjon *sb* propaganda; *(pol etc husagitasjon)* canvassing. **agitator** *sb* propagandist. **agitatorisk** *adj* propagandist. **agitere** *vb* make propaganda; *pol også* canvass.

agn *sb* bait; *fisken tok ~et* the fish took the bait. **agne** *vb* bait; *~ kroken med mark* bait the hook with a worm.

agner *sb fl (som avfall)* chaff.

agnostiker *sb* agnostic.

agronom *sb* agronomist.

agurk *sb* cucumber.

à jour *adv* up to date; *bringe ~ ~* update; bring up to date; *holde seg ~ ~ (med)* keep up to date (with); *komme ~ ~ med* catch up with.

akademi *sb* academy. **akademiker** *sb* academic; university man/woman. **akademisk** *adj* academical; *(i betydningen teoretisk)* academic.

ake *vb* sledge, toboggan.

akilles|hæl *sb* Achilles' heel; heel of Achilles. **~sene** *sb* Achilles tendon.

akk *interj* ah, alas.

akklamasjon *sb* acclamation; *vedta med ~* carry by/with acclamation; *valgt med ~* elected by/with acclamation.

akklimatisere *vb: akklimatisere seg, bli akklimatisert* become acclimatized. **akklimatisering** *sb* acclimatization.

akkompagnement *sb* accompaniment. **akkompagnere** *vb* accompany.

akkord *sb* **1** *(om arbeid)* piece-work contract; *arbeide på ~* do piece-work; **2** *mus* chord; *hun slo an en ~* she struck a chord.

akkumulator *sb* accumulator.

akkurat **1** *adj (nøyaktig)* accurate, exact; **2** *adv a)* accurately, exactly; *i ~ seks uker* for exactly six weeks; *b) (nettopp)* exactly, just; *~ det jeg sa* just what I said.

akkusativ *sb* accusative.

akrobat *sb* acrobat. **akrobatisk** *adj* acrobatic.

aks *sb* ear.

akse *sb* axis; *jordaksen* the axis of the earth. **aksel** *sb* **1** *(hjulaksel)* axle; **2** *(drivaksel)* shaft; **3** *(skulder)* shoulder.

akselerasjon *sb* acceleration. **akselerere** *vb* accelerate; *akselererende hastighet* increasing speed.

akseltrykk *sb* axle load.

aksent *sb* accent; *snakke med ~* speak with an accent.

akseptabel *adj* acceptable. **akseptere** *vb* accept.

aksess *sb data* access. *Se også tilgang.*

aksiom *sb* axiom.

aksje *sb* share. **aksje|eier, -innehaver** = *aksjonær.* **~kapital** *sb* share capital. **~majoriteten** *sb* the majority holding; the bulk of the shares; *US* the controlling interest. **~megler** *sb* stockbroker. **~selskap** *sb* limited company (*fork* Ltd); joint-stock company; *US* corporation. **~utbytte** *sb* dividend.

aksjon *sb* action; *gå til ~* take action. **aksjons|komité** *sb* action committee. **~radius** *sb* range.

aksjonær *sb* shareholder.

akt *sb* **1** *(del av skuespill)* act; *første ~* act one; the first act; **2** *(nakenmodell)* nude; **3** *(oppmerksomhet)* attention; *vi gav nøye ~ på hva de sa* we paid close attention to what they were saying; **4** *(hensikt)* intention, purpose. **akte** *vb* **1** *(ha til hensikt)* intend, mean; **2** *(respektere, ære)* respect. **aktelse** *sb* esteem, regard, respect; *ha ~ for* respect; *hun vant alles ~* she won everybody's respect.

akter *adv* aft, abaft, astern. **akters:** *det gikk til ~ med dem* they came down in the world. **akter|speil** *sb* stern. **~stavn** *sb* sternpost; *(akterende)* stern. **~ut** *adv: sakke ~ut* lag behind.

aktet *adj* respected.

aktiv **1** *adj (virksom)* active; *han tok ~t del i arbeidet* he took an active part in the work; **2** *sb gram* the active (voice). **aktiva** *sb (fl av aktivum)* assets; *~ og passiva* assets and liabilities. **aktivere** *vb* activate *(også data)*. **aktivisere** *vb* activate; set to work. **aktivitet** *sb* activity. **aktivum** *sb* asset; *god helse er et stort ~* good health is a great asset.

aktor *sb* counsel for the prosecution.

aktpågivende *adj* attentive, watchful. **aktsom** *adj* careful, cautious; attentive. **aktsomhet** *sb* attention, care.

aktstykke *sb* document.

aktualitet *sb* **1** current interest; news value; *det har ~ens interesse* it is of topical interest; **2** *data* currency. **aktuell** *adj* **1** of current/topical interest; of immediate importance; relevant, topical; *~e spørsmål* questions of current/topical interest; outstanding questions of the day. [Det engelske ordet *actual*, jf den engelsk-norske delen, kan sjelden brukes i betydningen *aktuell*]; **2** *data* current.

aktverdig *adj* respectable.

akustikk *sb* acoustics; *~en i kirken vår er ikke god* the acoustics of our church are not good. **akustisk** **1** *adj* acoustic; **2** *adv* acoustically. **akustisk | lager** *sb data* acoustic storage. **~ logg** *sb petro* acoustic log. **~ pigg** *sb petro* acoustic pig.

akutt *adj* acute.

akvarell *sb* water-colour (painting). **akvarellmaler** *sb* watercolour painter. **akvarium** *sb* aquarium.

alarm *sb* alarm; *hun slo ~* she gave the alarm. **alarmerende** *adj* alarming.

albino *sb* albino.

albue **1** *sb* elbow; **2** *vb: ~ seg frem* elbow one's way.

album *sb* album.

aldeles *adv* completely, quite; *~ ikke* not at all.

alder *sb* **1** *(persons alder)* age; *hun er på min ~* she is my age; *i en ~ av 5 år* at an age of five years; *være liten for ~en (eller sin ~)* be small for one's age; **2** *(tidsalder)* age; *middelalderen* the Middle Ages; *steinalderen* the Stone Age. **alderdom** *sb* old age. **alders|forskjell** *sb* difference in age. **~trygd** *sb* old age (*eller:* retirement) pension. **aldrende** *adj* ageing.

aldri *adv* never; *~ mer* never again; no more; *nesten ~* hardly ever; *~ så snart så han meg før han sa* no sooner did he see me than he said; *om vi strever ~ så mye* however hard we try.

alene *adv* alone; by oneself.

ale opp *vb* breed, raise.

alfabet *sb* alphabet. **alfabetisk** *adj* alphabetic(al). **alfabetisk | streng** *sb data* alphabetic string. ~ **tegn** *sb data* alphabetic character. ~ **tegnsett** *sb data* alphabetic character set. **alfanumerisk** *adj data* alphanumeric.

alge *sb* alga.

algebra *sb* algebra. **algebraisk** *adj* algebraic.

algoritme *sb* algorithm *(også data)*. **algoritmespråk** *sb data* algorithmic language.

alias *sb* alias.

alibi *sb* alibi.

alke *sb* auk.

alkohol *sb* alcohol. **alkoholiker** *sb* alcoholic; *Anonyme Alkoholikere* Alcoholics Anonymous.

all *adj, pron* **1** *(foran sb)* all; *~ maten* all the food; **2** *(enhver)* every; *vi har ~ grunn til å tro at* we have every reason to believe that. *Se også alle, alt.* **alle** *adj, pron* **1** *(uten etterfølgende sb)* all, everybody, everyone; *~ er enige (om at)* all agree (that); *~ kjenner henne* everybody knows her; *~ andre* everybody else; *~ de andre* all the others; *de var ~ gamle* all of them were old; *~ sammen* everybody; all (of them, us, you); *de var hjemme, ~ sammen* all of them were at home; *god natt, ~ sammen* good night, everbybody; **2** *(alle og enhver)* anybody; *jeg trodde ~ visste det* I thought anybody knew/would know that; *~ andre ville ha sagt ja* anybody else would have said yes.

allé *sb* avenue.

allegori *sb* allegory. **allegorisk** *adj* allegoric(al).

allemannseie *sb* common property.

aller *adv* by far; of all; *~ best* best of all; by far the best; *også* the very best; *~ helst vil jeg ha kaffe* I should like coffee best; *~ minst vil jeg du skal tro at* least of all do I want you to think that; *den ~ første dagen* the very first day; *han kom ~ sist* he came last of all; *jeg liker henne aller best* I like her best of all; *vi kom ~ først* we came first of all.

allerede *adv* **1** *(om tiden)* already, even; as early as; *~ nå* even now; *han har ~ vært her to ganger* he has already been here twice; *~ som gutt kunne han gjøre det* even as a boy he could do it; *~ i det tredje århundre* as early as the third century; **2** *(endog)* even.

allergi *sb* allergy. **allergisk** *adj* allergic (*mot* to).

allesteds *adv* everywhere. **allestedsnærværende** *adj* omnipresent, ubiquitous.

allfarvei *sb* public highway.

allianse *sb* alliance. **alliere** *vb: ~ seg med* ally oneself with. **alliert** *adj* allied; *de allierte (hist, pol)* the Allies.

alligator *sb* alligator.

allikevel = *likevel.*

allmakt *sb* omnipotence. **allmannamøte** *sb* mass meeting. **allmektig** *adj* almighty, omnipotent. **allmenn** *adj* general; common, public; universal. **allmenngyldig** *adj* generally accepted. **allmenning** *sb* common. **allsidig** *adj* all-round, versatile; *en ~ idrettskvinne* an all-round sportswoman; *et allsidig intellekt* a versatile mind. **allslags** all kinds/sorts of; of all kinds.

alltid *adv* always.

allting *pron* everything.

allusjon *sb* allusion; hint, innuendo.

allvitende *adj* omniscient. **allvitenhet** *sb* omniscience.

alm *sb* elm.

almanakk *sb* almanac.

alminnelig *adj* **1** *(ikke sjelden)* common; *denne planten er ~ i Norge* this plant is common in Norway; **2** *(felles for alle eller nesten alle)* general; **3** *(vanlig)* common, ordinary, usual; *~ mannesker* ordinary people; **4** *(dagligdags)* plain. **alminnelighet** *sb: i ~* generally.

almisse *sb* alms.

alpelue *sb* beret.

Alpene *fl* the Alps.

alskens *adj* various; of all kinds.

alt *adj, pron* **1** *(uten sb etter)* all, everything; *~ er nytt* everything is new; *~ det andre* everything else; *~ (det) du ser* all (that) you see; *ta det, ~ sammen* take it all; take all of it; *fremfor ~* above all; *når ~ kommer til ~* after all; when all is said and done; **2** *(hva som helst)* anything; *hun kan ~* she can do anything; *hun er ~ annet enn dum* she is anything but stupid; **3** *adv (allerede)* already, even; *han har ~ vært her to ganger* he has already been here twice. *Se også all, alle.*

alt *sb (stemme)* alto, contralto; *en ~sanger* an alto singer; *hun synger ~* she sings alto.

altan *sb* balcony.

alter *sb* altar.

alternativ *sb* alternative.

altertavle *sb* altar piece.

altetende *adj* omnivorous.

altfor *adv* too; all too; much too.

altmuligmann *sb* jack-of-all-trades.

altruisme *sb* altruism. **altruistisk** *adj* altruistic.

altså *adv* so; accordingly, therefore.

aluminium *sb* aluminium; *US* aluminum.

alv *sb* elf, fairy.

alvor *sb* **1** gravity, seriousness; *sakens ~* the seriousness of the matter; **2** *(iver)* earnestness; *det er mitt ~* I am in earnest; *gjøre ~ av* realize; carry out. **alvorlig I** *adj* **1** serious; *en ~ ung mann* a serious young man; *en ~ sykdom* a serious illness; **2** *(ivrig)* earnest; *et ~ forsøk* an earnest attempt; **3** *(svært alvorlig, streng)* grave; *vi var i ~ fare* we were in grave danger; **II** *adv* gravely, seriously; earnestly; in earnest.

amasone *sb* amazon.

amatør *sb* **1** *(ikke profesjonell)* amateur; **2** *(nedsettende: fusker i faget)* dilettante.

ambassade *sb* embassy. **ambassadør** *sb* ambassador.

ambisiøs *adj* ambitious. **ambisjon** *sb* ambition.

ambolt *sb* anvil.

ambulanse *sb* ambulance.

amen *interj, sb* amen.

amfi *sb: sitte i ~* sit up in the gods. **amfiteater** *sb* amphitheatre.

amme 1 *sb* (wet) nurse; **2** *vb* breast-feed.

ammoniakk *sb* ammonia.

ammunisjon *sb* ammunition.

amnesti *sb* amnesty; *gi ~* grant an amnesty.

amok: *gå ~* run amuck.

amoralsk *adj* amoral.

Amor Cupid.

amortisering *sb* amortization. **amortisere** *vb* amortize.

amper *adj* fretful, peevish.

amputasjon *sb* amputation. **amputere** *vb* amputate.

amulett *sb* amulet, charm.

amøbe *sb* amoeba.

an, *se gå, komme.*

anakronisme *sb* anachronism. **anakronistisk** *adj* anachronistic.

analfabet *sb* illiterate (person). **analfabetisme** *sb* illiteracy.

analog *adj* **1** analogous; **2** *data* analog. **analog|adderer** *(~dividerer, ~multiplikator) sb data* analog adder (~ divider, ~ multiplier). **~data** *sb fl data* analog data. **analogi** *sb* analogy. **analogmaskin** *sb data* analog computer.

analyse *sb* analysis. **analysere** *vb* analyse. **analytiker** *sb* analyst. **analytisk** *adj* analytic(al).

ananas *sb* pineapple.

anarki *sb* anarchy. **anarkist** *sb* anarchist. **anarkistisk** *adj* anarchist.

anatomi *sb* anatomy. **anatom** *sb* anatomist.

anbefale *vb* recommend; *kan De ~ en dyktig lege?* can you recommend me a good doctor? **anbefaling** *sb* recommendation.

anbringe *vb* put, place; *(om penger)* invest.

anbud *sb* tender; *gi ~ på* make/put in a tender for.

and *sb* duck.

andakt *sb* **1** *(oppbyggelse)* prayers; **2** *(andektighet)* devotion. **andektig** *adj* devout.

andel *sb* share; *~ i utbyttet* share of the profits.

andpusten *adj* breathless; out of breath.

andragende *sb* application.

andre 1 *pron* others; other people; *alle ~* everybody else; *blant ~* among others; *hvem ~* who else; *ingen ~* nobdy else; *alle ~ enn hun* anybody/everybody but she; *hvem ~ så du enn ham* who did you see other than him; *vi ~* the rest of us; **2** *(ordenstall)* second; *for det ~* secondly; in the second place. *Se også annen, annet.*

andunge *sb* duckling; *Den stygge andungen* the Ugly Duckling.

ane A *vb* guess, suspect; *det ~r jeg ikke* I have no idea; **B** *sb: se aner.*

anekdote *sb* anecdote.

anemi *sb* anaemia. **anemisk** *adj* anaemic.

anelse *sb* **1** *(forutfølelse)* presentiment; hunch, inkling; **2** *(svak forestilling)* suspicion; (vague) idea; notion; *jeg har ikke den fjerneste/ringeste) ~* I haven't the faintest notion.

aner *sb fl (forfedre)* ancestors, ancestry.

anerkjenne *vb* **1** *(erkjenne, innrømme)* acknowledge, admit; **2** *(godkjenne)* approve, recognize; **3** *(rose)* appreciate. **anerkjennelse** *sb* acknowledgement, recognition.

anfall *sb* **1** attack, fit; *et ~ av influensa* an attack of (the) influenza/*dgl* of the flu; **2** *(plutselig angrep)* assault. **anfalle** *vb* assault, attack.

anføre *vb* **1** *(ha kommandoen over)* command; **2** *(lede)* lead; **3** *(nevne, si)* mention, say, state. **anfører** *sb* leader. **anførsel** *sb: under ~ av* commanded/led by. **anførselstegn** *sb fl* quotation marks; *også* inverted commas.

angelsakser *sb*, **angelsaksisk** *adj* Anglo-Saxon.

anger *sb* repentance, self-reproach.

angi *vb* **1** *(melde, røpe)* inform (upon); *hans medfange angav ham (til politiet)* his fellow-prisoner informed upon him; **2** *(nevne)* state; *~ som grunn* give/state as a reason. **angivelig 1** *adj* alleged; **2** *adv* allegedly. **angiver** *sb* informer.

anglikansk *adj* Anglican.

angre *vb* repent, regret; be sorry about/for; *hun ~t sine synder* she repented (of) her sins; *han ~angret (på) at han hadde gjort det* he regretted having done it; *jeg ~r på det nå* now I am sorry about/for it. **angrende** *adj* repentant.

angrep *sb* **1** attack; *(voldsomt ~)* assault; *de rettet et ~ mot ham* they attacked him/made an attack on him; **2** *(om sykdom)* attack, fit.

angretast *sb data* cancel/undo key.

angripe *vb* attack. **angriper** *sb* attacker; *om stat især* aggressor.

angst *sb* **1** *(engstelse)* anxiety; **2** *(frykt, redsel)* alarm, fear.

angå *vb* concern; *det ~r ikke meg* it does not concern me; it is none of my business; *hva det ~r* as for/to that; for that matter. **angående** *prep* about, concerning; regarding; with regard to.

anholde *vb* **1** *(arrestere)* arrest; **2** *~ om hennes hånd* ask for her hand (in marriage). **anholdelse** *sb* arrest; *foreta en ~* make an arrest.

animalsk *adj* animal; *~ føde* animal food.

anke *sb, vb* appeal. **ankemål** *sb* complaint, grievance.

ankel *sb* ankle.

anker *sb* **1** *(skipsanker)* anchor; *kaste ~* cast/drop anchor; *lette ~* weigh anchor; **2** *(kagge, tønne)* barrel, cask, keg; *et ~ vin* a cask of wine. **anker|pæl, ~påle** *sb petro* anchor pile. **ankrings|båt** *sb petro* anchor-handling boat. **~system** *sb petro* anchoring system.

anklage 1 *sb* accusation, charge; **2** *vb* accuse (*for* of); charge (*for* with); *hun ble ~t for mord* she was accused of/charged with murder. **anklager** *sb* accuser; *(i retten)* counsel for the prosecution.

ankomme *vb* arrive; *~ til (sted, mindre by)* arrive at; *~ til (land, større by)* arrive in; *vi ankom til Oxford* we arrived at Oxford; *de ankom til London* they arrived in London. **ankomst** *sb* arrival; *ved vår ~* on our arrival.

ankre (opp) *vb* anchor; cast/drop anchor.

anlagt *adj: hun er praktisk ~* she is practical (or: of a practical turn); *melankolsk ~* of a melancholy disposition.

anledning *sb* **1** *(hendelse, tidspunkt)* occasion; *i/ved den ~* on that occasion; **2** *(sjanse)* chance, opportunity; *benytte ~* take the opportunity; *la en ~ gå fra seg* miss an opportunity.

anlegg *sb* **1** *(bygging)* construction; *en jernbane under ~* a railway under construction; **2** *(fabrikk etc)* plant, works; factory; **3** *(parkanlegg)* park; **4** *(disposisjon)* tendency; *~ for fedme* tendency to stoutness; **5** *(medfødt evne)* gift, talent; *han har ~ for musikk* he has a talent for music. **anleggs|arbeider** *sb* navvy. **~gartner** *sb* landscape gardener. **~sjef** *sb petro etc* superintendent.

anliggende *sb* affair, business, matter.

anløpe *vb* **1** *(om skip)* call (*eller:* put in) at; *skipet anløp Malta* the ship called at Malta; **2** *(irre, ruste etc)* be oxidized/tarnished.

anmarsj *sb: i ~* approaching; on the way.

anmelde *vb (~ bok etc)* review. **anmeldelse** *sb (av bok etc)* review.

anmerkning *sb* **1** *(forklarende opplysning)* comment, note; **2** *gi en gutt en ~* put a boy's name down.

anmode *vb* ask (*om* for); request; *de ~t om hjelp* they asked for help; *gjestene ~s om å benytte den andre heisen* the guests are requested to use the other elevator. **anmodning** *sb* request; *etter ~* by request; *på hennes ~* at her request.

anneksjon *sb* annexation. **annektere** *vb* annex.

annen 1 *adj* other, another; *en ~ dag* another day; *en eller ~ dag* some day (or other); *en ganske ~ mann* quite a different man; **2** *(pron) hun traff en ~* she met somebody else; she met another (person); *den ene etter den ~ (om to)* one after the other; *(om flere enn to)* one after another; *en eller ~* somebody; *enhver ~* anybody else; *hvem ~* who else; *ingen ~* nobody else; *ingen ~ enn han kunne gjøre det* no one but he could do it; *en ~s hatt* somebody else's hat; **3** *(ordenstall)* second. *Se også andre, annet.* **annen|gradsligning** *sb* quadratic equation. **~hver** *adj* every other (*eller:* second); *~hver dag* every other day. **~rangs** *adj* second-rate. **~steds,** *se annetsteds.*

annerledes 1 *adj* different; *den bilen er ~ enn de andre* that car is different from the others; **2** *adv (på en annen måte)* otherwise; in another way.

annet 1 *pron: jeg kan gjøre alt ~* I can do everything else; *han er alt ~ enn pen* he is anything but good-looking; *blant ~* among other things; *et eller ~* something (or other); *hva ~* what else; *ingenting/ikke (noe) ~* nothing else; *hva ~ kunne en vente* what else could you expect; *det var ikke ~ å få enn brød* there was nothing but bread to be had; *det er ikke ~ å gjøre enn å betale* there is nothing for it but to pay; *noe ~* anything/something) else; *det er noe ganske ~* that is something quite different; **2** *(ordenstall)* second. *Se også andre, annen.* **annetsteds** *adv* somewhere else.

anno: *~ 1880* in the year 1880; *også* A.D. 1880.

annonse *sb* advertisement. **annonsere** *vb* advertise.

annullasjon *sb* annulment, cancellation. **annullere** *vb* annul, cancel. **annulleringstegn** *sb data* cancel/ignore character.

anonym *adj* anonymus; *et ~t brev* an anonymous letter; *boken ble utgitt ~t* the book was published anonymously. **anonymitet** *sb* anonymity.

anorakk *sb* anorak, parka.

anorganisk *adj* inorganic.

anrette *vb* **1** *(forårsake)* cause; *stormen ~t stor skade* the gale caused great damage; **2** *(om mat)* serve.

anrike *vb* enrich; concentrate, strengthen. **anriket råolje** *sb petro* spiked crude.

anrop *sb* call, challenge; *sjø især* hail. **anrope** *vb* call, challenge; *sjø især* hail; *også data* invoke.

ansatt 1 *pp* employed, engaged; *~ hos* in the employ of; *fast ~* permanently employed; on the permanent staff of; **2** *som sb* employee; *de ~e* the employees; the staff.

anse *vb: ~ for* consider; look upon/regard as; *jeg ~r ham for en tosk* I consider him a fool. **anseelse** *sb* reputation; *hun nøt stor ~* she was highly regarded/respected. **anselig** *adj* considerable; *stundom* important. **ansett** *adj* distinguished.

ansette *vb* **1** *(utnevne)* appoint; **2** *(gi arbeid)* employ, engage; *hun ansatte to sekretærer* she engaged two secretaries. **ansettelse** *sb* appointment; employment, engagement; *fast ~* permanent appointment/job; *søke ~ hos dem* apply for a job with them.

ansiennitet *sb* **1** ≈ seniority; *det går etter ~* it goes by seniority; **2** *(tjenestetid)* time of service.

ansikt *sb* face. **ansikts|farge** *sb* complexion. **~løftning** *sb* face lift. **~trekk** *sb* feature.

ansjos *sb* anchovy.

anskaffe (seg) *vb* buy, purchase; provide oneself with. **anskaffelse** *sb* purchase.

anskueliggjøre *vb* illustrate; make clear. **anskuelsesundervisning** *sb* object lesson(s)/teaching.

anslå *vb* **1** *(vurdere)* estimate; **2** *(~ tone)* strike (a note).

anspent *adj* **1** intense, tense; **2** *(oppspilt)* keyed up.

anstalt *sb* **1** institution; **2** *gjøre ~er* make a fuss. **anstalt|maker** *sb* fussy person. **~makeri** *sb* fuss.

anstendig *adj* **1** *(skikkelig)* decent, proper; **2** *(aktverdig)* respectable. **anstendighet** *sb* decency, propriety.

anstrenge *vb* **1** *(trette ut)* tire (out); **2** *~ seg* endeavour; *hun anstrengte seg for å gjøre et godt inntrykk* she endeavoured to make a good impression. **anstrengelse** *sb* effort; *han gjorde store ~r* he made great efforts. **anstrengende** *adj* fatiguing, tiring. **an-**

strengt *adj* **1** *(anspent)* intense; **2** *(forsert)* forced; **3** *(trett)* tired.

anstrøk *sb* **1** *(fargeskjær)* tinge; **2** *(svak antydning)* touch; suspicion, tinge; *et ~ av ironi* a touch of irony.

anstøt *sb* offence; *vekke ~* give offence; *ta ~ av* take offence at. **anstøtelig** *adj* offensive.

ansvar *sb* responsibility; *han har ~et* the responsibility is his; he is responsible for it; *hun ble trukket til ~* she was called to account. **ansvarlig** *adj* responsible. **ansvarsløs** *adj* irresponsible.

ansøkning *sb* application.

anta *vb* **1** *(tenke seg)* assume, suppose; *jeg ~r de vet det* I suppose they know (it); **2** *(godta)* accept; approve; *forslaget ble ~tt* the proposal was accepted. **antakelig** *adv* **1** *(sannsynligvis)* probably; very likely; **2** *(som kan godtas)* acceptable. **antakelse** *sb* **1** assumption, supposition; **2** acceptance.

antall *sb* number.

Antarktis Antarctica. **antarktisk** *adj* antarctic.

antenne A *sb* aerial *[NB: Det engelske ordet* antenna *brukes især i betydningen* følehorn*]*; **B** *vb (tenne på)* set fire to.

anti|biotikum *sb* antibiotic. **~biotisk** *adj* antibiotic.

antikk *adj* antique. **antikken** *sb* Antiquity. **antikvarbokhandel, antikvariat** *sb* second-hand bookshop. **antikvarisk** *adj* second-hand. **antikvitet** *sb* antique.

anti|luftskyts *sb* anti-aircraft gun; ack-ack gun. **~pati** *sb* antipathy. **~podene** *sb fl* the antipodes. **~semitt** *sb* anti-Semite. **~semittisk** *adj* anti-Semitic. **~semittisme** *sb* anti-Semitism. **~septisk** *adj* antiseptic.

antologi *sb* anthology.

antrekk *sb* attire, dress; *daglig ~* informal dress; *~ galla* dress formal.

anvende *vb* employ, use. **anvendelig** *adj* applicable; of use; *meget ~* very useful. **anvendelse** *sb* employment, use; *også data* application. *Se også bruk, brukbar og bruke.*

anvise *vb* **1** *(angi, vise)* indicate; point out; show; **2** *(om penger) ~ til utbetaling* order to be paid out; pass for payment. **anvisning** *sb* **1** *(veiledning)* direction(s), instructions; **2** *(av penger)* bank draft; money--order.

ap *sb: drive ~ med* make fun of.

apanasje *sb* civil list.

apati *sb* apathy. **apatisk** *adj* apathetic.

ape I *sb* **1** *(menneskeape)* ape; **2** *(apekatt)* monkey; **II** *vb: ~ etter* imitate, mimic. **apekatt** *sb* monkey.

apostel *sb* apostle.

apostrof *sb* apostrophe.

apotek *sb* chemist's (shop); *US* drugstore, pharmacy. **apoteker** *sb* dispensing (*eller:* pharmaceutical) chemist; pharmacists; *US også* druggist.

apparat *sb* apparatus; *stundom* instrument.

appell *sb* appeal. **appellere** *vb* appeal.

appelsin *sb* orange. **appelsinskall** *sb* orange peel.

appetitt *sb* appetite. **appetittlig** *adj* appetizing. **appetittvekker** *sb* appetizer.

applaudere *vb* applaud. **applaus** *sb* applause.

approbasjon *sb* approbation, sanction. **approbere** *vb* approve of; sanction.

aprikos *sb* apricot.

april April; *(den) første ~* the first of April; *også* All Fools' Day; *narre en ~* make somebody an April Fool. **aprilsnarr** *sb* April Fool.

apropos *adv* by the way.

araber *sb* Arab. **arabisk 1** *adj* Arab, Arabian; **2** *sb (om språket)* Arabic.

arbeid *sb* **1** work; *gå på ~* go to work; *være på ~* be at work; *hardt ~* hard work; *være uten ~* be out of work; **2** *(anstrengelse, slit)* labour; *US* labor; **3** *(sysselsetting)* employment; **4** *(pålagt arbeid)* task; **5** *(om utførelsen)* workmanship; *det er godt ~* it is fine workmanship. **arbeide** *vb* **1** work; *hun ~r godt* she works well; she is a good worker; **2** *(arbeide hardt, slite)* labour; *US* labor, toil. **arbeider** *sb* worker, hand; *(på oljeplattform)* roustabout; *fag~, faglært ~* skilled worker; *ufaglært ~* unskilled worker; labourer. **arbeiderklassen** *sb* the working class(es). **Arbeiderpartiet** *(det britiske)* the Labour Party; *dgl også* Labour. **arbeids|besparende** *adj* labour-saving. **~byrde** *sb* workload. **~dag** *sb* **1** *(daglig arbeidstid)* hours; working day; *ha lang ~* work long hours; **2** *(hverdag)* weekday; working day. **~deling** *sb* division of labour. **~dyktig** *adj* able-bodied; fit (for work). **~evne** *sb* working capacity. **~fil** *sb data* work file. **~fred** *sb* industrial peace. **~giver** *sb* employer. **~klær** *sb* working clothes. **~kraft** *sb* **1** *(arbeidsevne)* working capacity/power. **2** *(arbeidere)* labour. **~leder** *sb* **1** supervisor; *dgl* boss, chief; **2** *petro* roustabout pusher. **~lønn** *sb (ukelønn)* wages *fl.* **~løs** *adj* unemployd; out of work; *de ~e* the unemployed. **~løshet** *sb* **1** unemployment; **2** *(ved innskrenkninger etc)* redundancy. **arbeidsom** *adj* hard-working, industrious. **arbeids|område** *sb data* working area/space. **~sky** *adj* work-shy. **~stasjon** *sb data* work (*eller:* data processing) station. **~taker** *sb* employee. **~tid** *sb* (working) hours; *etter ~tid* after hours. **~tillatelse** *sb* labour permit. **~ufør** *adj* disabled. **~uførhet** *sb* disablement. **~villig** *adj* willing to work.

areal *sb* area.

arena *sb* arena; *opptre på ~en* appear on the scene.

arg *adj (sint)* angry.

argument *sb* argument *[NB: Det engelske ordet* argument *brukes ofte i betydningen* uoverensstemmelse; krangel, trette*]*. **argumentasjon** *sb* argumentation. **argumentere** *vb* argue, reason.

aristo|krat *sb* aristocrat. **~krati** *sb* aristocracy. **~kratisk** *adj* aristocratic.

aritmetikk *sb* algebra. **aritmetisk** *adj* algebraic(al), arithmetic(al). **aritmetisk | operasjon** *sb data* arithmetic operation. **~ rekke** *sb* arithmetical progression.

ark *sb* **1** *(papir)* sheet; **2** *(på hus)* attic.

arkeo|log *sb* archaeologist. **~logi** *sb* archaeology. **~logisk** *adj* archaeological.

arkitekt *sb* architect. **arkitektur** *sb* architecture. **arkitektonisk** *adj* architectonic, architectural.

arkiv *sb* archive(s); *(på kontor etc også)* file(s). **arkivar** *sb* archivist. **arkivere** *vb* **1** file (away); **2** *data* archive, save. **arkivering** *sb* **1** filing; **2** *data* archiving.

arkmater *sb data* sheet feeder.

Arktis *geogr* the Arctic. **arktisk** *adj* Arctic *[NB: I betydningen* sprengkald *brukes fortrinnsvis liten forbokstav]*.

arm A *adj (fattig, stakkars)* poor; **B** *sb (legemsdelen)* arm. **arm|bind** *sb* armlet. **~bånd** *sb* bracelet. **~båndsur** *sb* wristwatch.

armé *sb* army.

armert *adj* **1** *(beskyttet, pansret)* armoured; **2** *(forsterket)* reinforced; *~ betong* reinforced concrete.

arm|hule *sb* armpit. **~lene** *sb* arm, armrest.

armod *sb* (great) poverty.

aroma *sb* aroma. **aromatisk** *adj* aromatic.

arr *sb (etter sår)* scar.

arrangement *sb* arrangement. **arrangere** *vb* arrange, organize. **arrangør** *sb* organizer.

arrest *sb* **1** *(anholdelse)* custody *(jf arrestere)*; detention; **2** *(arrestlokale)* gaol, *US* jail; prison. **arrestant** *sb* prisoner. **arrestasjon** *sb* arrest. **arrestere** *vb* arrest; take into custody. **arrestordre** *sb* warrant (for an arrest); *utstede en ~ mot* issue a warrant against.

arrig *adj* cross; ill-tempered.

arroganse *sb* arrogance. **arrogant** *adj* arrogant.

arsenal *sb* arsenal.

arsenikk *sb* arsenic.

art *sb* **1** *(slags)* kind, type; *dgl* sort; **2** *(i biologien)* species *(både entall og flertall)*. **arte seg** *vb* **1** *(utvikle seg)* develop; **2** *(falle ut)* turn out. **artig** *adj* **1** *(interessant)* interesting; **2** *(rar, snodig)* funny, odd, quaint, queer.

artikkel *sb* **1** article; **2** *den bestemte/ubestemte ~* the definite/indefinite article.

artikulasjon *sb* articulation. **artikulere** *vb* articulate.

artilleri *sb* artillery.

artist *sb* artiste *[NB:* artist, *uten -e =* kunstner*]*. **artistisk** *adj* artistic.

arv *sb* heritage, inheritance; *~en fra fortiden* the heritage from the past; *gården tilfalt dem ved ~* the farm came to them by inheritance; *hun fikk en stor ~* she was left a large fortune. **arve** *vb* inherit; succeed to; *~ etter* inherit from; *hun ~t en formue* she inherited *(eller:* came into) a fortune; *han ~t tronen* he succeeded to the throne. **arve|anlegg** *sb* gen. **~avgift** *sb* death duty. **~fiende** *sb* archenemy; inveterate enemy. **~følge** *sb* order of succession. **arvelig** *adj* hereditary. **arvelighet** *sb* heredity. **arve|lott** *sb* **1** *(arv)* inheritance; **2** *(del av arv)* share of (an) inheritance. **~lov** *sb* **1** *jur* Inheritance Act; **2** *biol* law of heredity. **~rett** *sb* right of inheritance; succession. **~synd** *sb* original sin. **arving** *sb* heir; *(om kvinne)* heiress.

asfalt *sb* asphalt; *som veidekke ofte ≈* tarmac; *petro også* bitumen. **asfaltbelegg** *sb petro* asphalt enamel. **asfaltere** *vb* asphalt.

asjett *sb* side-plate, tea-plate; small plate.

ask *sb bot* ash.

aske *sb* **1** ashes *fl*; **2** *(bestemt slags ~)* ash; *sigar~* cigar ash. **askebeger** *sb* ash-tray.

askese *sb* asceticism. **asket** *sb* ascetic. **asketisk** *adj* ascetic.

asp *sb* aspen.

asparges *sb* asparagus.

aspirant *sb* aspirant, candidate.

assembler *sb data* assembler; assembly program. **assemblere** *vb data* assemble. **assemblerings|tid** *sb data* assembly time. **~trinn** *sb data* assembly phase. **assemblerspråk** *sb data* assembly language.

assimilasjon *sb* assimilation. **assimilere** *vb* assimilate.

assistanse *sb* assistance, help. **assistent** *sb* assistant. **assistere** *vb* assist, help. **assisterende | borer** *sb petro* assistant driller. **~ boresjef** *sb petro* drilling section leader assistant.

assosiasjon *sb* association. **assosiativt lager** *sb data* associative/content-addressed storage. **assosiere** *vb* associate.

assuranse *sb* **1** *(især om livsforsikring)* assurance; **2** *(især om skadeforsikring)* insurance. **assurere** *vb* insure.

asters *sb bot* aster.

astma *sb* asthma. **astmatiker** *sb* asthmatic. **astmatisk** *adj* asthmatic.

astro|log *sb* astrologer. **~logi** *sb* astrology. **~logisk** *adj* astrological. **astronaut** *sb* astronaut; space traveller. **astro|nom** *sb* astronomer. **~nomi** *sb* astronomy. **~nomisk** *adj* astronomic(al).

asyl *sb* **1** *(sinnssykehus)* mental hospital; **2** *(politisk ~)* asylum.

at *konj* **1** that; *jeg vet (at) det er umulig* I know (that) it is impossible *[NB:* that *kan utelates, akkurat som* at *på norsk]*; **2** *(omskrivning med* -ing-*form etter preposisjon) det hadde vært mye snakk om at de kom til London* there had been much talk of their coming to London; **3** *(at + setning skrives om med infinitiv) jeg sa at han skulle hente boken* I told him to fetch the book.

ate|isme *sb* atheism. **~ist** *sb* atheist. **~istisk** *adj* atheistic.

atelier *sb* studio.

atferd *sb (oppførsel)* behaviour; *US* behavior.

Atlanterhavet *geogr* the Atlantic (Ocean).

atlas *sb* atlas.

atmo|sfære *sb* atmosphere. **~sfærisk** *adj* atmospheric.

atom *sb* atom. **atom|bombe** *sb* atom(ic) bomb. **~energi** *sb* atomic energy. **~forsker, ~fysiker** *sb* nuclear physicist. **~fysikk** *sb* nuclear physics.

~kjerne *sb* nucleus of an atom. **~krig(føring)** *sb* atomic/nuclear war(fare). **~reaktor** *sb* atomic/nuclear reactor. **~ubåt** *sb* nuclear submarine. **~våpen** *sb* atomic/nuclear weapon.

atskille *vb* separate. **atskillelse** *sb* separation; *etter mange års ~* after many years' separation. **atskillig** *adj* several; a good deal; *for ~e år siden* several years ago; *det gav oss ~ bry* it gave us a good deal of trouble. **atskilt** *adj* separate, apart; *to ~e grupper* two separate groups. **atspredt** *adj (distré, åndsfraværende)* absent--minded.

attentat *sb* attempted murder.

atter *adv* again; once more; *~ og ~* again and again.

attest *sb* certificate, testimonial; *om arbeidsforhold også* references *fl.* **attestere** *vb* certify.

attpå, attpåtil *adv* besides; in addition; into the bargain.

attraksjon *sb* attraction.

attributt *sb* attribute *(også data)*.

au *interj* oh! ouch!

audiens *sb* audience; *få ~ hos* obtain an audience of/with.

auditorium *sb* **1** *(om rommet)* lecture hall/room; **2** *(om forsamlingen)* audience.

august August; *den første ~* the first of August; Aug. 1st.

auksjon *sb* auction (sale); public sale. **auksjonere** *vb* auction; sell by auction.

aula *sb* aula; great hall.

aust etc se *øst etc.*

autentisk 1 *adj* authentic; **2** *adv* authentically.

autodidakt *sb* self-taught person. **autograf** *sb* autograph.

automasjon *sb* automation *(især data)*. **automat** *sb* **1** *(salgsautomat)* slot machine; **2** *(telefonautomat)* pay (tele)phone; slot telephone. **automatisere** *vb* automate *(også data)*. **automatisering** *sb* automation. **automatisk 1** *adj* automatic(al); **2** *adv* automatically. **automatisk | databehandling** *sb data* automatic data processing (ADP). **~ innrykk** *sb data* indent. **~ kontroll** *sb* automatic check *(også data)*. **~ omstart** *sb data* automatic restart. **~ programmering** *sb data* automatic coding/programming.

autorisasjon *sb* authorization. **autorisere** *vb* authorize. **autoritet** *sb* authority.

av *prep* **1** *(om materiale)* of; *en kjole av silke* a dress of silk; *dette huset er (bygd) av murstein* this house is built of brick(s); **2** *(om del av mengde)* of; *en av guttene* one of the boys; *en venn av meg* a friend of mine; **3** *(om opprinnelse)* from; *vin er laget av druer* wine is made from grapes; **4** *(om årsak)* of, for, from, with; *dø av sult* die of hunger; *synge av glede* sing for joy; *skjelvende av frykt* trembling with fear; **5** *(ved passiv)* by; *hunden ble overkjørt av en bil* the dog was run over by a car.

avanse *sb* profit. **avansere** *vb* **1** *(gå fremover)* advance; **2** *(bli forfremmet)* be promoted. **avansement** *sb (forfremmelse)* promotion.

avantgarde *sb* vanguard.

avbestille *vb* cancel. **avbestilling** *sb* cancellation.

avbetale *vb* pay by/in instalments. **avbetaling** *sb* **1** *(om avdraget)* instalment; **2** *(om betalingsmåten)* hire-purchase (*eller:* H.P.) plan/system; *på ~* by instalments; *dgl* on the never-never.

avbilde *vb* depict, portray; *også data* map. **avbildet buffer** *sb data* mapped buffer.

avblåse *vb* call off; *streiken ble avblåst* the strike was called off.

avbrennings|bom *sb petro* burner/flare boom. **~plattform** *sb petro* flare platform. **~tårn** *sb petro* flare stack/tower.

avbrudd *sb* interruption; *data også* interrupt. **avbrudds|sikker** *adj data* enabled, interruptible. **~tast** *sb data* attention key. **avbryte** *vb* **1** *(midlertidig)* interrupt; *taleren ble avbrutt* the speaker was interrupted; **2** *(for godt)* break off; **3** *(data, om program)* abend, abort. **avbrytelse** *sb* **1** interruption; **2** *(opphold, stans)* break.

avbud *sb: sende ~* send a letter of excuse.

avdeling *sb* **1** *(del)* part, section; **2** *(av forretning eller større foretagende)* department, division; **3** *(av sykehus etc)* ward; *i fengsel også* block; **4** *(gruppe personer, især mil)* detachment, unit. **avdelingssjef** *sb* head of department *[ofte en sammensetning med* manager, *f.eks.* sales manager*]*; *(på oljerigg etc)* superintendent.

avdrag *sb (nedbetaling)* instalment, part-payment; *renter og ~* interest and repayment.

avdrift *sb* drift *(også data)*.

avduke *vb* unveil.

avdød *adj* deceased; *den ~e* the deceased; *min ~e mann* my late husband.

aversjon *sb* aversion, dislike.

avertere *vb* advertise; *~ etter* advertise for. **avertissement** *sb* advertisement.

avfall *sb* **1** *(rester)* refuse, waste; **2** *(skrap, søppel)* garbage, rubbish. **avfalls|bøtte** *sb* refuse/rubbish bin; *(især US)* garbage can. **~dynge** *sb* rubbish/refuse heap. **~kvern** *sb* waste disposer. **~olje** *sb petro* spill oil; waste oil. **~paper** *sb* waste paper. **~plass** *sb* refuse dump, tip. **~spann** = *~bøtte.*

avfeie *vb* **1** *(~ en person)* snub; **2** *(~ en innvending)* brush aside.

avfeldig *adj* decrepit, infirm.

avførende *adj* aperient, laxative; *~ middel* aperient, laxative. **avføring** *sb* **1** *(tømming av tarmen)* (bowel) movement; evacuation; **2** *(eksrementer)* faeces, stools. **avføringsmidler** *sb fl* laxatives, purgatives.

avgang *sb* **1** *(om kommunikasjonsmidler)* departure; *klar til ~* ready for departure/start; **2** *(fra stilling)* retirement. **avgangs|eksamen** *sb* school-leaving examination. **~klasse** *sb* final-year class/form; top form. **~vitnemål, ~vitnesbyrd** *sb* school-leaving certificate.

avgi *vb: ~ en erklæring* make a statement. **avgift** *sb*

1 *(på f.eks. tobakk og drikkevarer)* excise; **2** *(toll)* duty, tax; **3** *(gebyr for f.eks. lisens, pass etc)* fee; **4** *(bompenger etc)* toll.

avgjort *adj* **1** *(brakt i orden)* settled; **2** *(desidert)* decided, definite; *en ~ fordel* a decided/definite advantage; **3** *adv* decidedly; *hun er/har det ~ bedre* she is decidedly better. **avgjøre** *vb* **1** *(bestemme)* decide, settle; *det må du selv ~* that is for you to decide; you must decide that for yourself; **2** *(bilegge, bringe i orden)* settle; *det avgjør saken* that settles the matter; **3** *(bli klar over)* make out; *jeg kan ikke ~ om han er engelsk eller amerikansk* I cannot make out whether he is English or American. **avgjørelse** *sb* **1** *(bestemmelse)* decision; **2** *(ordning)* settlement. **avgjørende** *adj* **1** *(utslagsgivende)* decisive; **2** *(endelig)* final.

avgrunn *sb* abyss.

avgud *sb* idol.

avgå *vb* **1** *(om tog)* leave; *(om skip også)* sail; **2** *~ ved døden* die; pass away.

av gårde, *se av sted.*

avhandling *sb* paper; dissertation, thesis, treatise.

avhende *vb* dispose of; sell.

avhenge *vb: ~ av* depend on; *det ~r av været* that depends on the weather. **avhengig** *adj* dependent; *være ~ av* be dependent on; *(i forbindelse med rusmidler)* be addicted to.

avhjelpe *vb* relieve, remedy; set right; *~ et behov* meet/supply a want.

avholdende *adj* abstinent. **avholds|folk** *sb* teetotallers. **~lag** *sb* temperance society. **~mann** *sb* teetotaller. **~saken** *sb* teetotalism.

avholdt *adj* popular; well liked; *hun er meget ~ av sine elever* she is very popular with her pupils.

avhøre *vb* examine; *~ et vitne* examine a witness.

avis *sb* (news)paper; *~en for i dag* today's paper. **avis|artikkel** *sb* (newspaper) article. **~utklipp** *sb* newspaper/press cutting(s).

avkall *sb: gi ~ på* give up.

avkastning *sb* **1** *(utbytte)* return, yield; proceeds *fl*; **2** *(fortjeneste)* profit.

avkjøle *vb* cool.

avklare *vb* clarify.

avkobling *sb* relaxation.

avkom *sb* offspring, progeny; *jur også* issue.

avkreftet *adj* weakened.

avkrok *sb* remote place; *også* backwoods.

avkutte *vb data* truncate. **avkutting** *sb data* truncation. **avlang** *adj* oblong.

avlaste *vb* relieve. **avlastning** *sb* relief. **avlastningsbrønn** *sb petro* relief well.

avlat *sb* indulgence. **avlats|brev** *sb* letter of indulgence. **~handel** *sb* sale of indulgences. **~handler** *sb* pardoner.

avle *vb* **1** *(dyrke)* grow, raise; **2** *(gml: avle barn)* beget.

avlede *vb* **1** *(lede bort)* divert; *~ oppmerksomheten* divert the attention; **2** *(utlede)* derive; *mange engelske ord er ~t av latin* many English words are derived from Latin.

avlegge *vb* **1** *~ et besøk* pay a visit; **2** *~ et løfte* make a promise; **3** *~ (og bestå) en prøve* pass a test; **4** *~ regnskap* give an account; **5** *~ ed* take the oath. **avlegger** *sb* cutting. **avleggs** *adj* antiquated, dated, obsolete; out of date.

avleiring *sb* deposit.

avlese *vb* read.

avlevere *vb* deliver.

avling *sb* crop.

avlive *vb* kill; put to death.

avlukke *sb* box, compartment, cubicle.

avluse *vb* delouse; *data* debug; check out.

avlyse *vb* call off; cancel; *møtet ble avlyst* the meeting was called off.

avløp *sb* **1** *(for væsker etc)* outlet; *(avløpsrør)* drain; **2** *(om følelser)* vent; *få/gi avløp for* give vent to.

avløse *vb* **1** *(i et arbeid, på en post)* relieve; *hvem skal ~ deg?* who is relieving (*eller:* to relieve) you? **2** *(erstatte, følge etter)* replace, succeed. **avløsning** *sb* relief.

avmagret *sb* emaciated.

avmarsj *sb* marching off; departure, start.

avmektig *sb* impotent, powerless; *~ raseri* impotent rage.

avmerke *vb* mark.

avmønstre *vb* sign off.

avmålt *adj* **1** measured; **2** *(fig: reservert, stiv)* reserved.

avpasse *vb: ~ etter* adapt/adjust to.

avreise *sb* departure, start; *hennes ~ til London* her departure for London.

avrunde *vb* round off (*data ofte bare* round). **avrundingsfeil** *sb data* rounding error.

avsats *sb* **1** *(trappeavsats)* landing; **2** *(berghylle etc)* ledge.

avse *vb: ~ tid til* find time to.

avsender *sb* sender.

avsetning *sb* sale. **avsette** *vb* **1** *(avskjedige)* dismiss; *han ble avsatt* he was dismissed; **2** *(om konge)* dethrone.

avsi *vb: ~ dom over* pass sentence upon.

avsides *adj* out-of-the-way; remote.

avsindig *adj* mad; *dgl* crazy. *[NB: Især på amerikansk engelsk brukes* mad *i betydningen* sint*]*.

avskaffe *vb* abolish; do away with; *slaveriet ble ~t* slavery was abolished. **avskaffelse** *sb* abolition.

avskjed *sb* **1** *(farvel)* leave; *han tok ~ med meg* he took leave of me; **2** *(det å skilles)* parting; *~en mellom dem* their parting; **3** *(avskjedigelse)* discharge, dismissal; *hun fikk ~* she was dismissed (*dgl* fired/sacked). **avskjedige** *vb* dismiss; *dgl* fire; give the sack; sack.

avskjære *vb: ~ tilbaketoget* cut off the retreat.

avskrekkende *adj* deterrent, discouraging; *ha en ~ virkning* have a deterrent effect.

avskrift *sb* copy; *ta en ~ av* make a copy of.

avsky 1 *sb* disgust, dislike; *få ~ for* take a dislike to; *også* come to hate; *vende seg bort med ~* turn away in disgust; **2** *vb* detest, loathe; hate. **avskyelig** *adj* abominable, detestable; hateful; nasty, odious.

avslag *sb* **1** *(nekting)* refusal; *vi fikk avslag* we were refused; we were met with a refusal; **2** *(prisreduksjon)* discount, reduction.

avslapning *sb* relaxation.

avslutning *sb* finish, termination; conclusion. **avslutnings-** *adj* final, terminal; closing, concluding. **avslutte** *vb* finish, terminate.

avsløre *vb* **1** *(røpe)* reveal; *~ en hemmelighet* reveal a secret; **2** *(avduke)* unveil. **avsløring** *sb* disclosure; *(av misligheter især)* exposure.

avslå *vb* decline; refuse; turn down; *~ en anmodning* refuse a request; *hun avslo innbydelsen* she declined the invitation.

avsmak *sb* distaste; *få ~ for/på* acquire a distaste for.

avsnitt *sb* **1** *(del, parti)* section; **2** *(av tekst)* paragraph; **3** *(tidsrom)* period.

avspeile *vb* mirror, reflect.

avsperret *adj* barred, blocked; roped off; *data* intercepted.

avspise *vb: ~ med* put off with; *vi ble avspist med 50 pund* we were put off with £50.

avspore *vb* derail. **avsporing** *sb* derailing; *fig også* derailment.

avstamning *sb* descent.

avstand *sb* distance; *i en ~ av to kilometer* at a distance of two kilometres; *på ~* at a distance.

av sted *adv* along, away, off.

avstemme *vb* **1** attune, harmonize; **2** *data* reconcile. **avstemning** *sb* vote, voting; *(i parlamentet)* division; *foreta/holde ~* take a vote; *hemmelig ~* voting by ballot.

avstikker *sb* detour.

avstraffe *vb* punish. **avstraffelse** *sb* punishment.

avstumpet *adj* blunt, blunted, obtuse.

avstå *vb* **1** *(unnlate)* refrain from; *jeg avstod fra å gjøre det* I refrained from doing it; **2** *(gi fra seg)* give up; surrender. **avståelse** *sb* surrender.

avsvekke *vb* weaken.

avsverge *vb* abjure, renounce.

av syne *adv* out of sight.

avsøke *vb* scan *(også data)*. **avsøker** *sb* scanner. **avsøking** *sb* scanning.

avta *vb* decrease; go down. **avtagende | måne** *sb* waning moon. **~ rekkefølge** *sb* descending order.

I avtale *sb* **1** *(overenskomst)* agreement, arrangement; *bryte/holde en ~* break/keep an agreement; **2** *(avtale om å møtes)* appointment; *jeg har truffet en avtale med henne om å møtes kl. 6* I have made an appointment to meet her at 6 o'clock. **II avtale** *vb* arrange, agree; *vi avtalte å dra til Bergen* we agreed to go to Bergen. **avtalt** *adj* arranged; agreed upon; *det ~e tidspunkt* the time (of day) agreed upon.

avtjene *vb: ~ verneplikt* serve as a soldier.

avtrykk *sb* **1** *(spor etc)* imprint, print; **2** *(trykt gjengivelse)* copy, print.

avvei *sb: komme på ~e* go astray.

avveie *vb* weigh.

av veien *adv* out of the way; *det ville ikke ha vært ~ ~ med en pause* I (we etc) could do with a break; *han går ikke ~ ~ for noe* he is not afraid of anything; *dgl* he sticks at nothing.

avveksling *sb: til en ~* for a change; *trenge til ~* need a change.

avvente *vb* await; wait for. **avverge** *vb* avert.

avvike *sb: avvike fra normen* deviate from the norm.

avvikle *vb (avslutte)* wind up.

avviksliste *sb data* discrepancy report.

avvise *vb* **1** *(nekte adgang)* refuse; turn away; **2** *(avslå, si nei til)* decline, refuse; *han avviste tilbudet* he declined the offer; **3** *(forkaste)* reject; *planen min ble avvist* my plan was rejected.

avvæpne *vb* disarm. **avvæpning** *sb* disarmament, disarming.

B

b *(bokstaven)* b.

babord *sb* port.

baby *sb* baby.

bacon *sb* bacon; *en skive ~* a rasher.

bad *sb* **1** *(innendørs)* bath; *hun tar et ~ hver morgen* she has/takes a bath every morning; **2** *(utendørs)* bathe, swim; **3** *(badeværelse)* bath, bathroom; *et værelse med ~* a room with a bath. **bade 1** *vb* have/take a bath; *(utendørs)* bathe; go bathing; go for a swim; **2** *vb (skylle, vaske)* bathe. **bade|bukse(r)** *sb* (bathing-)trunks. **~drakt** *sb* bathing|costume, -suit; swim-suit. **~hette** *sb* bathing-cap. **~hotell** *sb* seaside hotel. **~kar** *sb* bathtub. **~kåpe** *sb* bathrobe. **~plass** *sb* bathing beach/place. **~sted** *sb* seaside resort. **~strand** *sb* bathing beach. **~værelse** *sb* bathroom. **bading** *sb* bathing; *drukne under ~* be drowned while bathing. **badstubad, badstue** *sb* sauna, Finnish steam bath.

bagasje *sb* luggage; *US* baggage. **bagasje|brett** *sb (på sykkel)* (luggage) carrier. **~hylle, ~nett** *sb* luggage rack. **~rom** *sb (i bil)* luggage locker, boot.

bagatell *sb* trifle. **bagatellisere** *vb* minimize, make light of. **bagatellmessig** *adj* trifling.

bajas *sb* clown.

bajonett *sb* bayonet.

bak I *prep* behind; at the back of; *han stod ~ meg* he stood behind me; *hagen lå ~ huset* the garden was at the back of the house; **II** *sb* **1** *(bakende)* behind, bottom; **2** *(buksebak)* seat. **bak|bein** *sb* hind leg. **~dør** *sb* back door.

bake *vb* bake; *han bakte en kake* he baked/made a cake.

bakenfor *prep* behind; at the back of.

bakepulver *sb* baking-powder. **baker** *sb* baker; *vi gikk til ~en* we went to the baker's. **bakerbutikk** *sb* baker's shop. **bakeri** *sb* bakery, bakehouse. **bakerovn** *sb* oven.

bakerst 1 *adj, adv* back; *~e rekke* the back row; *de (som befinner seg) ~* those at the back; **2** *prep* at the back; *~ i salen* at the back of the hall. **bak|etter** *adv* **1** *(lenger bak)* behind; *de kom (gående) ~* they came walking behind; **2** *(senere)* afterwards. **~evje** *sb* backwater. **~fra** *adv* from behind; *sett ~* seen from behind. **~gate** *sb* (back) alley; back street. **~grunn** *sb* background. **~hjul** *sb* rear wheel. **~hold** *sb* ambush; *ligge i ~ for* be/lie in ambush for. **~hun** *sb* slab. **~hånd** *sb: ha i ~hånd* have in reserve; *(om noe hemmelig el overraskende)* have something up one's sleeve. **baki, bak i** *prep* in/at the back (of).

bakke A *sb* **1** *(haug, stigning)* hill; rising ground; *se også oppover, nedover*; **2** *(mark)* ground; *på bar ~* at the end of one's resources; **B** *vb (rygge)* back; *(om maskin, skip etc også)* reverse. **bakket** *adj* hilly.

bak|lekse *sb: være/komme i bakleksa (med)* be/fall behind (in/with). **~lengs** *adv* backwards. **~lomme** *sb* hip pocket. **~lykt** *sb* rear light. **~lås** *sb: døren er gått i baklås* the lock has jammed. **~om** *prep* behind; at the back of. **~over** *adv* backwards. **bakre** *adj* hinder, rear. **bakrus** *sb: være i ~* have a hangover.

bakse *vb* struggle; manoeuvre.

bak|sete *sb* rear seat; *(på motorsykkel)* pillion. **~side** *sb* back; *på ~n av konvolutten* on the back of the envelope.

bakst *sb* baking.

bak|stavn *sb* stern. **~strev** *sb* reaction. **~tale** *vb* malign, slander; speak ill of somebody behind his back. **~tanke** *sb* ulterior motive.

bakterie *sb* bacterium; *dgl også* germ.

bak|trapp *sb* back stairs. **~tropp,** *sb: danne ~-troppen* bring up the rear. **~vei** *sb* back way; *gå bakveien (dvs bruke lureri)* use underhand means. **~vendt** *adj, adv* **1** *(snudd)* backwards; turned the wrong way; **2** *(upraktisk)* awkward.

bakverk *sb: (kaker)* cakes, pastry.

bakværelse *sb* back room.

balanse *sb* balance; *hun mistet ~n* she lost her balance. **balansere** *vb* balance.

bale *vb* toil, struggle.

balje *sb* tub.

balkong *sb* balcony; *(i teater)* dress circle.

ball *sb* **1** ball; *spille ~* play ball; **2** *(dans)* dance; *(større)* ball; *på et ~* at a dance.

ballade *sb* **1** *(vise)* ballad; **2** *(spetakkel)* row; *han laget ~* he kicked up a row.

ballast *sb* ballast.

balle *sb (med varer)* bale; *en bomullsballe* a bale of cotton.

ballett *sb* ballet. **~danser(inne)** *sb* balletdancer.

ballong *sb* balloon.

ballsal *sb* ball-room.

balsam *sb* balsam, balm.

balsamere *vb* embalm.

balustrade *sb* balustrade.

bambus *sb* bamboo. **~stokk** *sb* cane.

bamse *sb* **1** *(bjørn)* bear; **2** *(leketøys~)* teddy bear.

banal *adj* banal, commonplace. **banalitet** *sb* commonplace.

banan *sb* banana. **~skall** *sb* banana skin.

band *sb* **1** *se bånd*; **2** *(danseorkester)* band. **bandasje** *sb* bandage. **bande** *sb* gang. **banditt** *sb* bandit, gangster; crook. **bandolær** *sb* bandoleer (bandolier).

bane I *sb* **1** *(vei)* course, path; **2** *(jernbane)* railway; *US* railroad; **3** *a) (idrettsbane)* ground, field; *b) (løpebane på idrettsplass)* track; **4** *(galoppbane, travbane)* racecourse, turf; **5** *(livsløp)* career; **6** *(planets, satelitts bane)* orbit; **7** *bringe noe på ~* bring up a subject; **II** *vb: han bante seg vei* he made his way; *(ved motstand)* he forced his way. **banebrytende** *adj* epoch making; *~ arbeid* pioneer work. **banebryter** *sb* pioneer. **banesår** *sb* fatal/mortal wound.

bange *adj* afraid, scared; uneasy. **bange anelser** *sb fl* misgivings.

banjo *sb* banjo.

bank A *sb (sparebank etc)* bank; *sette penger i banken* pay money into the bank; *jeg skal i banken* I am going to the bank; **B** *sb (juling)* a beating/hiding. **bank|direktør** *sb se ~sjef.*

banke A *sb (fiskebanke, skybanke, tåkebanke)* bank; **B** *vb* **1** *(slå)* beat, knock; *(ganske lett)* tap; *det ~r (på døren)* somebody is knocking; *vi ~t på døren* we knocked at the door; *~ i bordet!* touch wood! **2** *(denge)* beat, thrash; **3** *(om hjerte)* beat; *med bankende hjerte* with a beating heart.

bankerott *adj* bankrupt; *gå ~* go bankrupt; **bankerott** *sb* bankruptcy; failure.

bankett *sb* banquet.

bankier *sb* banker. **bankierfirma** *sb* banking firm. **bank|innskudd** *sb* bank deposit. **~konto** *sb* bank account. **~rente** *sb* interest. **~sjef** *sb* bank manager. **~vesen, ~virksomhet** *sb* banking.

bann excommunication; *sette i ~* excommunicate. **banne** *vb* swear; curse.

banner *sb* banner.

bannlyse *vb* **1** *(sette i bann)* excommunicate; **2**

(forvise) banish; **3** *(forby)* ban, forbid. **bannstråle** *sb* anathema.

baptist *sb* Baptist.

bar I *adj* **1** bare; *det er ~t (ute)* there is no snow (outside); the snow is gone; **2** *(uten fjær, hår etc)* bald; **II** *sb* **A** *(skjenkedisk)* bar; **B** *(på trær) se furubar, granbar.*

barbar *sb* barbarian. **barbari** *sb* barbarism. **barbarisk** *adj* **1** *(usivilisert)* barbarian; **2** *(grusom)* barbarous.

bar|beint 1 *adj* barefoot, barefooted; **2** *adv* barefoot; *gå ~* go/walk barefoot.

barber *sb* barber, hairdresser. **barbere** *vb* shave; *~ seg* shave. **barber|blad** *sb* razor blade. **~høvel** *sb* safety-razor. **~kniv** *sb* razor. **~maskin** *sb (elektrisk)* electric shaver/razor.

bardun *sb* stay; rope, wire.

bardus *adj, adv* suddenly, unexpected.

bare *adv* only, just; *~ én gang* just once; *~ for moro skyld* just for (the) fun (of it); *~ han ikke er kommet til skade* I hope he isn't hurt; *for ~ livet* for dear life; *om ~ far gir meg lov* if only father allows it; *som ~ det* like everything.

barfrost *sb* black frost. **barhodet** *adj* bare-headed.

bark *sb* **A** *(på trær)* bark; **B** *(skip)* bark. **barket** *adj* **1** *(brun, værbitt)* tanned, weather-beaten; **2** *(hard)* callous, horny.

barlind *sb* yew.

barm *sb (bryst)* bosom. **barmhjertig** *adj* **1** *(det motsatte av hard og nådeløs)* merciful; **2** *(godgjørende)* charitable; **3** *(medlidende)* compassionate. **barmhjertighet** *sb* mercy; *han viste dem ~/hadde ~ med dem* he showed them mercy.

barn *sb* child; *(spedbarn)* baby; *de har mange ~* they have a large family; *han har kone og ~* he has a wife and family. **barnaktig** *adj* childish. **barndom** *sb* childhood; *fra barndommen av* from childhood. **barndomsvenn(inne)** *sb* childhood friend. **barne|barn** *sb* grandchild. **~begrensning** *sb* family planning; birth control. **~billett** *sb* half (ticket). **~hage** *sb* kindergarten. **~hjem** *sb* orphanage; children's home. **~lek** *sb* children's play. **~mat** *sb: det er bare ~mat* that is child's play. **~oppdragelse** *sb* education/bringing up of children. **~pike, ~pleierske** *sb* nurse. **~regle, ~rim** *sb* nursery rhyme. **~seng** *sb* cot. **~streker** *sb fl* childish pranks. **~trygd** *sb* family allowance. **~vakt** *sb* babysitter. **~vogn** *sb* pram. **~værelse** *sb* nursery. **barnlig** *adj* **1** childlike; **2** *(i forhold til foreldrene)* filial. **barnløs** *adj* childless. **barnløshet** *sb* childlessness. **barnsbein** *sb: fra ~ (av)* from a child; from childhood. **barnslig** *adj* childish. **barnslighet** *sb* childishness.

barometer *sb* barometer.

baron *sb* baron. **baronesse** *sb* baroness.

barriere *sb* barrier.

barrikade *sb* barricade. **barrikadere** *vb* barricade.

barsel *sb* childbirth, confinement. **barsel|pleie** *sb* maternity work. **~seng** *sb* childbed; *dø i ~* die in childbirth.

barsk *adj* **1** *(om vesen)* harsh, stern, rough; *~e ord* harsh words; **2** *(om blikk og utseende)* fierce, stern; *(om smil ofte)* grim; **3** *(om klima)* severe, rough.

barskog *sb* fir and spruce forest; coniferous forest.

bart *sb* moustache.

bartre *sb* conifer.

bas *sb (i arbeidslag)* foreman.

basar *sb* bazaar.

base *sb (støttepunkt)* base. **baseolje** *sb petro* base oil. **basere** *vb* base (*på* (up)on).

basill *sb* bacillus.

basis *sb* basis.

baske *vb (bakse, kave)* struggle. **basketak** *sb* fight, struggle.

bass *sb* bass; *synge ~* sing bass.

basseng *sb* **1** *(havnebasseng)* basin; **2** *(større vannsamling)* reservoir; **3** *(svømmebasseng) (a) utendørs)* swimming-pool; *b) (innendørs)* swimming-bath.

bast *sb* bass, bast.

basta *adv: og dermed ~!* and that's flat! **bastant** *adj* **1** *(svær)* good-sized; **2** *(håndfast)* solid, heavy-handed.

bastard *sb* **1** *(krysning)* hybrid, crossbreed; **2** *(kjøter)* mongrel.

baste *vb: bastet og bundet* tied and bound.

basun *sb* trombone.

batalje *sb* fight. **bataljon** *sb* battalion.

batteri *sb (elektrisk, militært)* battery.

baufil *sb* hacksaw.

baug *sb* bow.

baut *sb sjø: gå ~* tack; go about.

bautastein *sb* stone monument.

baute *vb sjø* tack; go about.

bavian *sb* baboon.

be *vb* **1** *(anmode)* ask; *(især bønnfallende)* beg; *hun bad meg (om å) komme* she asked me to come; *de bad meg om hjelp* they asked me for help; **2** *a) (oppfordre)* tell; *be henne komme hit bort* tell her to come over here; *b) (mer inntrengende også)* implore; **3** *(be til Gud)* pray; say one's prayers; *han bad (til) Gud om hjelp* he prayed to God for help; **4** *(invitere)* ask, invite.

• **bearbeide** *vb* **1** *(med hender eller maskiner)* process, work; **2** *(tillempe)* adapt; *~t for radio* adapted for broadcasting/radio; **3** *(om musikk)* arrange; **4** *fig* press; manipulate. **bearbeidelse** *sb* processing, working; adaption.

bebo *vb* occupy; live in. **bebodd** *adj* **1** *(om hus, leilighet)* occupied; **2** *(om land)* inhabited. **beboelig** *adj* **1** *(om hus, leilighet)* fit to live in; habitable; **2** *(om land)* inhabitable. **beboer** *sb* **1** *(av hus, leilighet)* occupant; **2** *(av land, by)* inhabitant.

bebreide *vb* reproach. **bebreidelse** *sb* reproach.

bebude *vb* announce.

bebyggelse *sb* **1** *(bygninger)* buildings, houses; **2** *(bebygd område)* built-up area.

bebyrde *vb* burden, trouble.

bed *sb* bed; *et rosen~* a rose bed.

bedehus *sb* chapel.

bedra *vb* **1** cheat, swindle; *han bedrog meg for mange penger* he cheated/swindled me out of a lot of money; **2** *(i kjærlighet)* deceive. **bedrager** *sb* swindler. **bedrageri** *sb* imposture, swindle; fraud.

bedre I *adj, adv* better; *bli ~* be/become better; improve; *gjøre ~* make better; improve; *en ~ middag* a very good dinner; *han har det ~ i dag* he is better today; *min bil er ~ enn din* my car is better than yours; **II** *vb: ~ seg* improve; get better.

bedrift *sb* **1** *(dåd)* achievement, exploit, feat; **2** *(industri~)* industrial company/concern, works.

bedring *sb* **1** improvement; change for the better; **2** *(helbredelse)* recovery; *god ~!* I hope you will soon be better.

bedrøvelig *adj* **1** *(trist)* sad; **2** *(ynkelig)* miserable. **bedrøvet** *adj* sad, sorrowful; grieved; *han ble dypt bedrøvet ved å høre om ulykken* he was deeply grieved/ distressed to hear of the accident.

bedømme *vb* judge; *(~ skolearbeid)* mark. **bedømmelse** *sb* judgement; *(~ av skolearbeid)* marking.

bedøve *vb* **1** *(under legebehandling)* give an anaesthetic; **2** *(ved narkotika)* drug; **3** *(ved slag, støy)* stun. **bedøvelse** *sb* anaesthesia, narcosis.

bedåre *vb* charm, fascinate. **bedårende** *adj* charming.

befal *sb koll* officers. **befale** *vb (gi ordre)* command, order; *~ over* command; *han befalte meg å gjøre det* he ordered me to do it. **befaling** *sb* command, order; *etter/på hans ~* by his orders/at his command.

befatte *vb: ~ seg med* have to do with; occupy oneself with.

beferdet *adj* busy, crowded, frequented; *sterkt ~* very busy.

befeste *vb* fortify; *en ~t by* a fortified town. **befestning** *sb* fortification.

befinne seg *vb* **1** *(holde til, være)* bo; *jeg vet ikke hvor han ~r seg* I do not know where he is; **2** *(ha det, trives)* be, feel; *jeg ~r meg ganske bra* I feel quite well. **befinnende** *sb: jeg spurte etter hans ~* I asked after his health/how he was.

befolke *vb* people, populate; *tett ~t* densely populated. **befolkning** *sb* population.

befri *vb* **1** *(sette i frihet)* free; set free; release; *vi ~dde fangene* we set the prisoners free; **2** *(ved beleiring)* relieve. **befrielse** release, relief; *det føltes som en ~* it was felt as a relief.

befrukte *vb* fertilize, fecundate; *(fig)* inspire, stimulate. **befruktning** *sb* fertilization, fecundation; *kunstig ~* insemination.

begavelse *sb* **1** *(evner, talent)* gifts, powers, talent(s); **2** *(begavet person)* gifted person. **begavet** *adj* gifted, talented; *høyt ~* brilliant; *svakt ~* backward.

begeistret *adj* enthusiastic, keen; *hun ble ~ for tanken* she became enthusiastic about the idea; *han var ikke særlig ~ for det* he did not think much of it. **begeistring** *sb* enthusiasm.

beger *sb* cup; *~et er fullt* the cup is full.

begge *pron* both; *(hver især av to)* either; *~ to* both of them; either of them; *~ (de to) jentene er flinke nok til å greie eksamen* either of the girls is clever enough to pass the exam; *de er ~ døde* both of them are dead; they are both dead; *vi gikk ~* both of us went; we both went; *to menn som ~ var sjøfolk* two men who were both sailors/both of whom were sailors.

begi *vb: ~ seg til* go to; *~ seg av sted* set out; *~ seg på vei* set out; start. **begivenhet** *sb* event, happening; occurence; *en tilfeldig ~* an incident; *dagens ~er* the events of the day. **begivenhetsrik** *adj* eventful.

begjærlig *adj* **1** *(oppsatt på)* eager; *han var ~ etter ros* he was eager for praise; **2** *(grisk)* greedy; *~ etter gull* greedy for gold. **begjærlighet** *sb* **1** *(sterkt ønske)* desire, eagerness; **2** *(griskhet)* greed, greediness; *med ~* eagerly, greedily.

begrave *sb* bury; *han ble ~t i hjembyen (sin)* he was buried in his native town. **begravelse** *sb* **1** *(det å begrave)* burial; **2** *(høytideligheten)* funeral. **begravelses|byrå** *sb* (firm of) undertakers. **~plass** *sb* **1** *(gravsted)* grave; **2** *(gravlund)* cemetry.

begrense *vb* limit, confine. **begrenset** *adj* limited, restricted. **begrensning** *sb* limitation; *kjenne sin ~* know one's limitations.

begrep *sb* concept, idea; notion. **begripe** *vb* grasp, understand; *det er ikke til å ~* it is incomprehensible.

begrunne *vb* state the reasons for. **begrunnelse** *sb* grounds, reasons.

begunstige *vb* favour. **begunstigelse** *sb* favour.

begynne *vb* begin, start; commence; *de begynte å le* they began laughing/to laugh; *det ~r å bli mørkt* it is getting dark; *til å ~ med* to begin with/at first. **begynnelse** *sb* beginning, start; outset; *fra begynnelsen* from the outset/the very start; *i ~n* at the beginning. **begynnelsesbokstav** *sb* initial. **begynner** *sb* beginner. **begynnerbok** *sb* primer.

begå *vb* commit, make; *~ en feil* make a mistake; *~ en forbrytelse* commit a crime.

behag *sb* pleasure; *etter ~* at pleasure; as you like. **behagelig** *adj* **1** pleasant, agreeable; *en ~ overraskelse* an agreeable/a pleasant surprise; **2** *(tiltalende)* attractive; **3** *(bekvem)* comfortable; *en ~ stol* a comfortable chair; **4** *adv* pleasantly, agreeably.

behandle *vb* **1** treat; *de ~t meg godt/dårlig* they treated me well/badly; **2** *(håndtere)* handle; *om verktøy etc også* wield; **3** *data* process. **behandling** *sb* treatment.

behendig *adj* **1** *(smidig)* agile; **2** *(fingerferdig)* dexterous. **behendighet** *sb* agility, dexterity; cleverness, ingenuity.

beherske *vb* **1** *(regjere over)* govern, rule; **2** *(være herre over)* control; *han klarte ikke å ~ seg* he could not control himself; **3** *(mestre)* master; *hun ~t emnet* she mastered the subject. **behersket** *adj (rolig, sindig)* controlled, restrained; moderate.

behjelpelig *adj: være ~* help, assist.

behold *sb: i ~* intact, safe; *vi kom hjem i god ~* we came home safe and sound; *varene ankom i god ~* the goods arrived in good condition. **beholde** *vb* keep; *kan jeg ~ denne boken* may I keep this book; *vi beholdt klærne på hele natten* we kept our clothes on all night; *de lot ham ~ livet* they spared his life. **beholder** *sb* container; *(tank)* tank. **beholdning** *sb* **1** *(forråd)* supply, supplies; **2** *(lager)* stock; **3** *(penger)* cash.

behov *sb* **1** need(s), requirement(s); **2** *(etterspørsel)* demand; *det er stort ~ for det* there is a great demand for it. **behøve** *vb* **1** *(trenge til)* need, want; require; *har du/dere alt du/dere ~r?* have you got everything you want? **2** *(være nødt til)* need; have (got) to; *~r jeg å fortelle deg alt?* need I tell you everything? *du ~r ikke å betale* you need not pay; *~r han å betale?* need he pay; does he need to pay? *det ~s ikke* it is not necessary; *om det ~s* if (it is) necessary; in case of need.

behå *sb* bra, brassiere.

beige *adj, sb* beige.

bein A *adj = ben*; **B** *sb* **1** *(knokkel)* bone; *han er bare skinn og ~* he is all skin and bone; **2** *(mellom hofte og ankel)* leg; *jeg brakk ~et* I broke my leg; **3** *(fot)* foot; *han var kald på ~a* his feet were cold; **4** *(på møbler etc)* leg.

beis *sb* stain. **beise** *vb* stain.

beist *sb* **1** *(om både dyr og mennesker)* beast; **2** *(om mennesker)* brute.

beit *sb: være i ~* be in a tight place; *i ~ for* in need of.

beite 1 *sb* pasture; **2** *vb* graze.

bek *sb* pitch.

bekjempe *vb* fight, oppose. **bekjempelse** *sb* fight; *~n av sykdom* the fight against disease.

bekjenne *vb* **1** *(innrømme)* admit; **2** *(tilstå)* confess; *han bekjente sine synder* he confessed his sins. **bekjennelse** *sb* **1** confession; *gå til ~* confess/make confession; **2** *(tros~)* creed.

bekjent I *adj* **1** *(alminnelig kjent, omtalt)* well-known; **2** *(berømt)* famous; **II** *sb* acquaintance, friend. **bekjentgjøre** *vb* announce; make known/public. **bekjentgjørelse** *sb* announcement, advertisement. **bekjentskap** *sb* acquaintance; *jeg stiftet ~ med hele familien* I became acquainted with the whole family. **bekjentskapskrets** *sb* (circle of) acquaintances.

bekk *sb* brook, brooklet; *US* creek.

bekken *sb* **1** *(legemsdel)* pelvis; **2** *(musikkinstrument)* cymbal; **3** *(sykebekken)* bedpan. **bekkenpartiet** *sb* the pelvic region.

beklage *vb* **1** *(være lei for)* regret, be sorry; *jeg ~r at jeg ikke kan hjelpe Dem* I regret/am sorry (that) I cannot help you; *jeg ~r det som er skjedd* I am sorry that this should have happened; **2** *~ seg over* complain of/about; *han ~t seg til meg over gutten* he complained to me about the boy; **3** *(synes synd på)* pity; be sorry for; *hun er meget å ~* she is greatly to be pitied. **beklagelig** *adj* deplorable, unfortunate; *en ~ hendelse* a deplorable incident. **beklagelse** *sb* **1** *jeg hører til min ~ at Deres kone er syk* I hear with regret that your wife is ill; **2** *(klage)* complaint.

bekle *vb: ~ et embete* hold an office. **bekledning** *sb* clothing.

bekmørk *adj* pitch-dark.

bekomst *sb: få sin ~ (dvs den medfart en fortjener)* be served/paid out.

bekoste *vb* pay for. **bekostning** *sb* expense; *på min ~* at my expense; *på ~ av* at the expense of.

bekrefte *vb* **1** *(bevitne riktigheten av)* attest, verify; **2** *(stadfeste)* confirm. **bekreftelse** *sb* confirmation.

beksel *sb* **1** *(munnbitt)* bit; **2** *(hodelag)* headstall.

beksvart *adj* pitch-black.

bekvem *adj* comfortable.

bekymre *vb* **1** worry, trouble; *jeg er ~t for fremtiden* I am anxious/worried about the future; **2** *~ seg* worry, care; *det ~r jeg meg ikke om* I don't let that worry me; *hvem ~r seg (vel) om det?* who cares (about that)? **bekymret** *adj* anxious, worried; concerned. **bekymring** *sb* worry, anxiety.

belage *vb: ~ seg på* prepare (oneself) for.

belastet *adj: han er arvelig ~* he comes of a tainted stock. **belastning** *sb* strain; *arvelig ~* hereditary taint.

belegg *sb* coat, coating. **belegge** *vb: ~ sine ord* choose one's words carefully.

beleilig *adj* convenient.

beleire *vb* besiege. **beleiring** *sb* siege.

belesse *vb* load; *tungt ~t* heavily loaded.

beleven *adj* courteous.

belg|mørk *adj* pitch-dark. **~mørke** *sb* pitch-darkness.

beliggende *adj* situated; *~ ved en elv* situated on a river. **beliggenhet** *sb* situation; position.

belje *vb* bellow, roar.

belje *vb: ~ i seg* gulp down; swill.

belte *sb* belt, girdle. **belte|bil** *sb* caterpillar tractor; weasel. **~sted** *sb: under ~stedet* below the belt.

belyse *vb* **1** *(lyse på)* illuminate; light up; **2** *(forklare, kaste lys over)* illustrate; throw light on. **belysning** **1** lighting; **2** *(forklaring)* illustration.

belønne *vb* reward. **belønning** *sb* reward; *utlove en ~* offer a reward.

beløp *sb* amount; *hele ~et* the total amount. **beløpe** *vb: ~ seg til* amount to.

bemanne *vb* man.

bemektige *vb: ~ seg* take possession of; seize (upon).

bemerke *(si, ytre)* observe, remark. **bemerkelsesverdig** *adj* remarkable. **bemerkning** *sb (nøytral ~)* remark; *(kritisk ~)* comment.

bemyndige *vb* authorize. **bemyndigelse** *sb* authorization; *gi ~* authorize.

ben 1 *adj* straight; *bent frem* straight on; **2** *sb se bein.*

bende *vb* bend.

bendel|bånd *sb* tape. **~orm** *sb* tapeworm.

benekte *vb* deny. **benektende 1** *adj* negative; *et ~ svar* a negative answer; **2** *adv* in the negative; *hun svarte ~* she answered in the negative.

benk *sb* bench; *(uten rygg også)* form.

bensin *sb* **1** *(til bilmotor etc)* petrol; *US* gasoline, gas; **2** *(til rensing)* benzine. **bensin|motor** *sb* petrol motor. **~stasjon** *sb* filling station; *også* garage. **~tank** *sb* petrol tank.

benytte *vb* use; make use of; **~** *anledningen* take the opportunity; **~** *seg av* avail oneself of; take advantage of. **benyttelse** *sb* use.

benåde *vb* pardon; *ved dødsstraff* reprieve. **benådning** *sb* mercy, pardon; *ved dødsstraff* reprieve.

beordre *vb* order.

beplante *vb* plant. **beplantning** *sb* **1** *(beplantet område)* plantation; **2** *(det å plante)* planting.

beramme *vb* fix.

beredskap *sb* preparedness; *i* **~** in readiness. **beredskapsflamme** *sb petro* pilot flame. **beredt** *adj* prepared, ready. **beredvillig** *adj* ready, willing.

beregne *vb* **1** *(regne ut)* calculate; **2** *(forlange som pris)* charge; *vi* **~***r oss 10%* we charge 10 per cent. **beregning** *sb* calculation.

bereist *adj* travelled; *han er meget* **~** he has travelled widely.

beretning *sb* **1** report, account; *han avla en* **~** *om sin reise* he gave an account of his journey; **2** *(fortelling)* narrative. **berette** *vb* tell, relate.

berettiget *adj: være* **~** *til* have a right to; be entitled to.

berg *sb* mountain.

berge *vb* rescue, salvage; save.

berg|art *sb* rock-type. **~verk** *sb* mine. **~verksdrift** *sb* mining.

berike *vb* enrich.

berme *sb* dregs *fl*; *samfunnets* **~** the dregs of society.

bero **1** *sb: stille saken i* **~** let the matter rest; **2** *vb:* **~** *på (skyldes)* be due to; *(komme an på)* depend on.

berolige *vb* calm (down); quiet, soothe. **beroligende** *adj* soothing; **~** *middel* sedative.

berserk(er)gang *sb: gå* **~** run amuck.

beruse *vb* intoxicate; *bli beruset av* get drunk on. **beruselse** *sb* intoxication.

beryktet *adj* notorious.

berømmelse *sb* **1** fame; **2** *(ros)* praise. **berømt** *adj* famous; renowned, well-known; celebrated. **berømthet** *sb (***~** *person)* celebrity.

berøre *vb* **1** *(røre ved)* touch; **2** *(angå, påvirke)* affect; *det* **~***r meg personlig* it affects me personally; **3** *(omtale)* touch on; *han berørte ikke den siden av saken* he did not touch on that side of the matter. **berøring** *sb* touch, contact. **berøringsskjerm** *sb data* touch screen.

berøve *vb* deprive of.

besatt *adj* **1** *(okkupert)* occupied; **2** *(om stilling)* filled; *stillingen er* **~** the position has been filled; **3** *(forhekset, oppslukt)* obsessed/possessed (*av* by).

bese *vb* view; **~** *seg* see the sights; have a look (a)round.

besegle *vb* seal; *deres skjebne var* **~***t* their fate was sealed.

beseire *vb* beat, defeat; conquer.

besetning *sb* **1** *(på skip)* crew; **2** *(mil)* garrison; **3** *(husdyr)* livestock; **4** *(pynt på klær)* trimming(s). **besette** *vb (mil etc: okkupere)* occupy. **besettelse** *sb* **1** *(mil)* occupation; **2** *fig* obsession (jf *besatt*).

besindig *adj* cool; calm, steady.

besitte *vb* have, possess. **besittelse** *sb* possession; *komme i* **~** *av* come into the possession of; *ta i* **~** take possession of; *også* occupy.

besk *adj* acrid, bitter.

beskadige *vb* damage; *bildene ble* **~***t under brannen* the pictures were damaged by the fire. **beskadigelse** *sb* damage; *om mennesker* injury.

beskaffenhet *sb* character, nature.

beskatning *sb* taxation. **beskatte** *vb (skattelegge)* tax.

beskjed *sb* **1** *(bud)* message; *det er (en)* **~** *til deg (her)* there is a message for you; *jeg fikk* **~** *om å gjøre det* I was told to do it; **2** *(opplysning)* information.

beskjeden *adj* modest. **beskjedenhet** *sb* modesty.

beskjeftige *vb* **1** *(sysselsette)* employ; **2** *(holde beskjeftiget)* engage; *travelt* **~***t med å skrive brev* busily engaged (in) writing letters; **~** *seg med* occupy oneself with.

beskjeftigelse *sb* occupation, work; *uten* **~** with nothing to do; *(arbeidsløs)* out of work; unemployed.

beskjære *vb (f.eks. trær)* prune.

beskrive *vb* describe. **beskrivelse** *sb* description.

beskylde *vb:* **~** *en for noe* accuse somebody of something; *han beskyldte gutten for tyveri* he accused the boy of (a) theft. **beskyldning** *sb* accusation.

beskytte *vb* **1** protect; **~** *mot* protect from/against; **2** *(gi ly)* shelter. **beskyttelse** *sb* **1** protection; **2** *(ly)* shelter.

beslag *sb* **1** *(av metall)* (metal) fitting(s); **2** *legge* **~** *på (oppta)* occupy; take up; *arbeidet la* **~** *på all hans tid* the work took up all his time; **3** *(det å beslaglegge)* confiscation. **beslaglegge** *vb (konfiskere)* confiscate.

beslektet *adj* related (*med* to).

beslutning *sb* decision, resolution; *fatte/ta en* **~** make up one's mind. **beslutningsdyktig** *adj: et* **~** *antall* a quorum; *være* **~** form a quorum. **beslutte** *vb* decide, resolve; make up one's mind. **besluttsom** *adj* resolute. **besluttsomhet** *sb* resolution, resoluteness.

besparelse *sb* economy, entrenchment.

bespottelig *adj* blasphemous.

best A *adj, sb* best; *det* **~***e du kan gjøre* the best thing you can do; *du gjør* **~** *i å bli* you had better stay; *hun er den* **~***e* she is the best (woman); *jeg håper det* **~***e* I hope for the best; **B** *sb = beist.*

bestand *sb (av dyr)* population. **bestanddel** *sb* part; component, element. **bestandig** *adv* **1** *(alltid)* always; **2** *(stadig)* constantly; **3** *for* **~** for good/for ever.

beste *ab (gagn)* advantage, benefit, good; *det er til ditt eget* **~** it is for your own good. **beste|borger** *sb* bourgeois. **~far** *sb* grandfather. **~foreldre** *sb* grandparents.

bestemme *vb* **1** decide, determine; make up one's mind; *det må du* ~ that is for you to decide; *hun har bestemt seg for å reise* she has made up her mind to leave; *vi har bestemt oss for den lille bilen* we have decided on the small car; **2** *(fastsette)* fix; *han bestemte prisen* he fixed the price. **bestemmelse** *sb* **1** *(avgjørelse)* decision; **2** *(påbud)* regulation. **bestemmelsessted** *sb* destination.

bestemor *sb* grandmother.

bestemt *adj* **1** *(energisk, viljesterk)* determined; **2** *(spesiell)* specific; *i en* ~ *hensikt* for a specific purpose; **3** *(gram)* definite; ~ *artikkel/pronomen* definite article/pronoun; **4** *(viss, nærmere omtalt)* certain; *på* ~*e dager* on certain days; **5** *jeg vet (det) ikke* ~ I don't know for certain; *jeg tror* ~ *at de kommer* I am certain they are coming. **bestemthet** *sb* **1** *(fasthet)* firmness; **2** *(visshet)* certainty.

bestialsk *adj* bestial.

bestige *vb* climb, mount; ascend; ~ *et fjell* climb a mountain; ~ *tronen* ascend the throne.

bestikk *sb (spise~)* cutlery.

bestikke *vb (bruke bestikkelser)* bribe. **bestikkelig** *adj* corrupt; open to bribery. **bestikkelse** *sb* bribery.

bestille *vb* **1** *(tinge)* order; ~ *billett(er)* book; *han bestilte en dress* he ordered a suit; **2** *(gjøre, utføre)* do; *jeg hadde ingenting å* ~ I had nothing to do. **bestilling** *sb (ordre)* order; *etter/på* ~ to order.

bestjålet *adj, pp: jeg er blitt* ~ I have been robbed.

bestrebe *vb:* ~ *seg for/på* endeavour; try/work hard; *hun* ~*t seg for å hjelpe meg* she endeavoured to help me. **bestrebelse** *sb* effort, endeavour.

bestride *vb* deny, dispute.

bestyre *vb* manage; be in charge of; *hun* ~*r butikken* she is in charge of the shop. **bestyrer** *sb* manager; *om kvinne* manageress.

bestyrke *vb* confirm, strengthen; *dette* ~*t vår oppfatning* this confirmed our opinion.

bestyrtelse *sb* consternation, dismay. **bestyrtet** *adj* dismayed; amazed.

bestå *vb* **1** ~ *av* consist of; *bronse* ~*r av kobber og tinn* bronze consists of copper and tin; *det* ~*ende samfunn* the established order; **2** *(greie eksamen)* pass; *hun bestod eksamen* she passed the examination.

besvare *vb* answer, reply to; *jeg besvarte alle brevene* I answered all the letters. **besvarelse** *sb* **1** *(oppgavesvar)* paper; **2** *(løsning)* solution.

besvime *vb* faint, swoon. **besvimelse** *sb* faint; fainting fit; swoon.

besvær *sb* **1** *(anstrengelse)* effort; *uten* ~ without effort; **2** *(uleilighet)* trouble, inconvenience; *var det til mye* ~ *for deg?* did it give you much trouble? **3** *(vanskelighet)* difficulty; *jeg hadde noe* ~ *med å lese brevet* I had some difficulty in reading the letter. **besværlig** *adj* **1** *(trettende)* tiresome; **2** *(ubehagelig)* troublesome; **3** *(vanskelig)* difficult, hard. **besværlighet,** *se besvær*.

besynderlig *adj* strange; odd, queer; curious; ~ *nok* oddly enough.

besøk *sb* visit; *et* ~ *i England* a visit to England; *jeg avla ham et* ~ I paid him a visit; *(om kortere visitt)* I called on him. **besøke** *vb* **1** visit; pay a visit to; *vi besøkte Tower* we paid a visit to the Tower; **2** *(~ person, ofte i et bestemt ærend)* (come to) see; *når kommer du og* ~*r meg* when are you coming to see me; **3** *(om kortere visitt)* call on; *jeg har nettopp besøkt (= sett til) min gamle tante* I have just called on my old aunt. **besøkende** *sb* visitor.

besørge *vb* see to; *jeg skal nok* ~ *det* I'll see to it.

beta *vb* **1** *(imponere)* impress; *vi var sterkt* ~*tt av utsikten* we were deeply impressed by the view; **2** *(fig: bevege, gripe)* move, stir; thrill. **betagende** *adj* moving, stirring; impressive.

betakke *vb:* ~ *seg* decline, refuse.

betale *vb* pay; ~ *for* pay for; *jeg betalte for boken* I paid for the book; *hun betalte meg for å gjøre det* she paid me to do it; *hvor mye blir/er det å* ~*?* how much is it? **betaling** *sb* **1** payment; *han fikk en sjekk som* ~ *for sine tjenester* he got a cheque in payment of his services; **2** *(lønn)* pay.

betatt *adj, pp* fascinated; *(forelsket)* infatuated.

bete *se bit(e)*.

betegne *vb* **1** *(bety)* denote; stand for; *tegnet x betegner en ukjent størrelse* the sign x denotes an unknown quantity; **2** *(markere)* mark. **betegnelse** *sb* name. **betegnende** *adj* characteristic; ~ *nok* characteristically.

betenke *vb* **1** *(overveie)* consider; ~ *seg* think it over; **2** *(nøle)* hesitate; *hun betenkte seg på å gjøre det* she hesitated to do it; *uten å* ~ *seg* without hesitation. **betenkelig** *adj* alarming; critical, serious; dangerous. **betenkelighet** *sb* doubt, hesitation; scruple. **betenkning** *sb* **1** *(overveielse)* consideration, reflection; **2** *(betenkelighet)* hesitation; scruple. **betenkningstid** *sb: en ukes* ~ a week to think the matter over. **betenkt** *adj (bekymret)* uneasy.

betennelse *sb* inflammation. **betent** *adj* inflamed.

betinge *vb:* ~ *seg at* make it a condition that. **betingelse** *sb* condition, term; *de godtok/gikk med på mine betingelser* they accepted my terms; *på* ~ *av at* on condition that.

betjene *vb* **1** *(maskiner etc)* operate, run; **2** *(ekspedere)* attend, serve; *kunden ble betjent av en ung mann* the customer was attended to/served by a young man. **betjening** *sb* (serving) staff. **betjent** *sb* **1** ≈ attendant, servant; **2** *(politi~)* policeman.

betong *sb* concrete. **betongblander** *sb* concrete mixer.

betrakte *vb* **1** *(se på)* look at; regard, view; **2** ~ *som* look upon as; consider (to be); regard as; *jeg betrakter ham som min beste venn* I look upon him/regard him as my best friend. **betraktelig** *adj* considerable. **betraktning** *sb (overveielse)* consideration; *alt tatt i* ~ all things considered; *i* ~ *av at de er så unge* considering that they are so young; *når alt tas i* ~ when everything is taken into consideration; *sette ut av* ~ leave out of account/consideration.

betro *vb* **1** *(meddele)* ~ *en noe* confide something to somebody; *han betrodde meg sine vanskeligheter* he confided his troubles to me; **2** *(overlate en noe)* entrust something to somebody; entrust somebody with something. **betrodd** *adj: en ~ tjener* a confidential servant; *en ~ stilling* a responsible post.

betryggende *adj* safe; *på ~ avstand* at a safe distance.

betuttet *adj* perplexed, confused.

betvile *vb* doubt.

bety *vb* **1** *(ha som betydning)* mean; *hva ~r dette ordet* what does this word mean; *hva skal dette ~* what is the meaning of this; **2** (være betydningsfull) matter, mean; *det har ikke noe å ~* it does not matter; *ditt vennskap ~r mye for meg* your friendship means a great deal to me. **betydelig** *adj* considerable; *et ~ (penge)beløp* a considerable sum of money; *~ større* considerably larger. **betydning** *sb* **1** *(mening)* meaning, sense; *~en av et ord* the meaning/sense of a word; *i en viss ~* in a sense; **2** *(viktighet)* importance; *oppfinnelsen var av stor ~ for jordbruket* the invention was of great importance to agriculture; *uten ~* of no importance; without importance. **betydnings|full** *adj* **1** *(viktig)* important; **2** *(megetsigende)* meaning, significant. **~løs** insignificant, unimportant; indifferent.

beundre *vb* admire. **beundrer** *sb* admirer. **beundring** *sb* admiration. **beundringsverdig** *adj* admirable.

bevandret *adj: ~ i* familiar with; versed in.

bevare *vb* keep, preserve; *den gamle bygningen er godt bevart* the old building has been well preserved; *Gud ~ dronningen* God save the Queen; *er du ikke vel bevart* are you out of your mind.

bevege *vb* **1** move, stir; *fig også* touch; *~ seg* move, stir; *~ seg omkring* move about; *den triste historien ~t oss sterkt* the sad story moved/touched us deeply; **2** *(formå, overtale)* induce, persuade. **bevegelig** *adj* mobile, movable. **bevegelighet** *sb* mobility. **bevegelse** *sb* **1** *(enkelt ~)* movement; *han gjorde en plutselig ~* he made a sudden movement; **2** *(tilstand av ~)* motion; *sette seg i ~* start; *være i ~* be in motion; **3** *(hånd~)* gesture; **4** *fig a) (åndelig etc ~)* movement; *b) (sinns~)* excitement. **bevegelsesfrihet** *sb* freedom of movement. **beveget** *adj* **1** *(rørt)* moved; stirred; *han var ~ til tårer* he was moved to tears; **2** *(begivenhetsrik)* dramatic, eventful; *et ~ liv* an eventful life. **beveggrunn** *sb* motive.

beven *sb: med frykt og ~* in/with fear and trembling.

bever *sb* beaver.

beverte *vb* entertain, treat. **bevertning** *sb* **1** *(det å beverte)* entertainment; **2** *(mat og drikke)* food and drink(s); **3** = **bevertningssted** *sb* restaurant.

bevilge *vb* grant. **bevilgning** *sb* grant.

bevilling *sb* licence.

bevinget *adj: bevingede ord* familiar quotations.

bevirke *vb* cause, effect; bring about.

bevis *sb* **1** *(avgjørende ~)* proof (*på* of); **2** *(vitnesbyrd)* evidence (*om* of); *et ~* a piece of evidence. **bevisbyrde** *sb* burden of proof. **bevise** *vb* prove; show. **bevis(e)lig** *adj* provable, demonstrable. **bevis|førsel** *sb* argumentation. **~kraft** *sb* weight (as evidence). **~materiale** *sb* evidence.

bevisst *adj* **1** *(ved bevissthet)* conscious; **2** *(overlagt)* deliberate; *en ~ løgn* a deliberate lie. **bevissthet** *sb* consciousness; *ved ~* conscious; *miste ~en* lose consciousness; become unconscious; *komme til ~* regain consciousness; *dgl* come to. **bevisstløs** *adj* unconscious. **bevisstløshet** *sb* unconsciousness.

bevitne *vb* attest, certify; *herved ~s at* this is to certify that; *jeg kan ~ at* I can certify that. **bevitnelse** *sb* attestation.

bevokst *adj: ~ med skog* covered with forest(s).

bevokte *vb* guard, watch. **bevoktning** *sb* guard, watch; *under streng ~* closely guarded.

bevæpne *vb* arm. **bevæpning** *sb* armament, arms.

beære *vb* honour, favour; *jeg følte meg beæret* I felt/was honoured.

bi *adv: legge ~* lay to; *stå ~* assist; stand by; *lykken står den kjekke/tapre ~* fortune favours the brave. **biapparat** *sb (telefonisk)* extension.

bibel *sb* Bible. **bibel|historie** *sb* biblical history; *(som skolefag)* scripture. **~ord** *sb se ~sted.* **bibelsk** *adj* biblical. **bibelsted** *sb* Bible passage; text. **bibliofil** *adj* bibliophile. **biblio|graf** *sb* bibliographer. **~grafi** *sb* bibliography. **~grafisk** *adj* bibliographic. **biblio|tek** *sb* library. **~tekar** *sb* librarian.

bidra *vb* contribute. **bidrag** *sb* contribution; *gi (levere, yte etc) sitt ~ til* contribute/make one's contribution to.

bidronning *sb* queen bee. **bie A** *sb (insekt)* bee; **B** *vb (vente)* wait; *bi litt* wait a bit.

bielv *sb* tributary.

bifall *sb* **1** *(applaus)* applause; *(bifallsrop)* cheers; *stormende ~* a storm of applause; **2** *(samtykke)* approval; *han gav saken sitt ~* he approved of the cause. **bifalle** *vb* approve of; agree/consent to.

biff *sb* beefsteak; *~ med løk* steak and onions.

bigami *sb* bigamy. **bigamist** *sb* bigamist.

bi|hensyn *sb* secondary consideration. **~hule** *sb* sinus. **~hulebetennelse** *sb* sinusitis. **~inntekt** *sb* side/supplementary income.

bikkje *sb* dog.

bikube *sb* beehive.

bil *sb* car, motor-car; *US* automobile; *(drosje)* taxi; *kjøre ~* drive a car; *også* motor.

bilag **1** *(til brev)* enclosure; **2** *(til regnskap)* voucher.

bilbølle *sb* road-hog.

bilde *sb* **1** *(maleri, tegning etc)* picture; *også fig* image; *hunden på ~t* the dog in the picture; *et ~ av jomfru Maria* an image of the Virgin Mary; *for å tale i ~r* to speak in images; **2** *(fotografi)* photo, photograph; **3** *(portrett)* portrait; **4** *data* screen image; **5** *(skildring)* picture. **bildebok** *(og andre sammensetninger med bilde-) se billed-.*

bildekk *sb* (motor-car) tyre.

bildende *adj:* ~ *kunst* the visual arts.

bile *vb* gå by car; motor.

bilegge *vb* settle.

bil|ferje *sb* car ferry; motor ferry. **~fører** *sb* driver. **~holdeplass** *sb* cab/taxi rank. **~horn** *sb* motor horn. **bilist** *sb* motorist.

biljard *sb* billiards.

bil|kart *sb* road map. **~kjøring** *sb* motoring.

bille *sb* beetle.

billed|bok *sb* picture-book. **~element** *sb data* picture element; pixel. **~flate** *sb data* screen. **~hugger** *sb* sculptor. **~hugger|arbeid** *sb* sculpture. **~kunst** *sb* (art of) sculpture. **billedlig** *adj* figurative; ~ *talt* figuratively speaking; ~ *uttrykk* metaphor. **billed|rør** *sb data etc* display tube. **~skjerm** *sb data* graphic display device. **~støtte** *sb* statue.

billett *sb* ticket; *kjøpe* ~ *til New York* book a passage to/for New York; *kjøpe* ~ *(til konsert, teaterforestilling etc)* book a seat; *en* ~ *til »Hamlet»* a seat for »Hamlet». **billett|kontor** *sb* booking-office; *(i teater)* box office. **~luke** *sb* booking/box office; ticket window. **~pris** *sb* **1** *(inngangspenger)* entrance fee; (price of) admission; **2** *(reisepenger)* fare. **billettør** *sb (på buss, trikk)* conductor; *om kvinner* conductress.

billig *adj* **1** *(om pris)* inexpensive; *også fig* cheap; *reise på ~ste måte* travel by the cheapest route; *vi slapp* ~ *fra det* we got off cheap(ly). **billigbok** *sb* paperback; pocket-book.

billige *vb* approve of; sanction.

billion *sb* billion; *US* trillion.

bil|lys *sb* headlight. **~panser** *sb* bonnet; *US* hood. **~slange** *sb* inner tube. **~sport** *sb* motoring. **~trafikk** *sb* motor traffic. **~tur** *sb* (motor) drive; *(lengre)* excursion (tour, trip etc) by car. **~uhell, ~ulykke** *sb* motor-car accident. **~verksted** *sb* garage; repair shop.

bind *sb* **1** *(bok)* volume; *et verk i seks* ~ a work in six volumes; **2** *(innbinding)* binding; **3** *(varebind)* dust jacket; **4** *(fasle)* sling; **5** *(forbinding)* bandage; **6** *(sanitetsbind)* sanitary napkin/towel. **binde** *vb* **1** *(binde fast)* bind; tie (up); *han bandt hunden* he tied up the dog; *beina til fangen var bundet sammen* the prisoner's legs were bound together; **2** *(knytte)* tie; *han bandt en hyssing om pakken* he tied the parcel up with a string; **3** *(~ inn)* bind; *boken er bundet inn i blå sjirting* the book is bound in blue cloth; **4** *(forplikte)* bind; *jeg er bundet av mitt løfte* I am bound by my promise; *et bindende løfte* a binding promise. **bindeledd** *sb* link. **binders** *sb* paper-clip. **bindestrek** *sb* hyphen.

binge *sb* **1** *(til korn etc)* bin; **2** *(til griser)* (pig)sty; **3** *(til andre dyr)* pen.

binne *sb* she-bear.

binær *adj data etc* binary. **binærsiffer** *sb data* = *bit.*

biograf *sb* biographer. **biografi** *sb* biography. **biografisk** *adj* biographical. **biolog** *sb* biologist. **biologi** *sb* biology. **biologisk** *adj* biological.

biperson *sb* minor character.

bi|røkt *sb* bee-keeping. **~røkter** *sb* bee-keeper.

bisak *sb* minor matter; side issue.

bisam|pels *sb* musk-rat coat. **~rotte** *sb* muskrat.

bisetning *sb* (subordinate) clause.

bisettelse *sb* funeral service. *Se også begrave, begravelse.*

bisk *adj* fierce.

biskop *sb* bishop.

bisonokse *sb* bison.

bisp *sb* bishop. **bispedømme** *sb* bishopric, diocese.

bissel *sb se beksel.*

bistand *sb* assistance, help.

bister *sb* fierce, grim, gruff.

bistå *vb* assist, aid.

bit *sb data* binary digit; bit.

bit(e) *sb (lite stykke)* bit; (small) piece; morsel; *en brød~* a morsel of bread. **bite** *vb* bite; ~ *tennene sammen* clench one's teeth; *han bet seg i leppen* he bit his lip; *hunden bet meg i beinet* the dog bit my leg. **bitende** *adj* biting; ~ *kaldt* bitterly cold. **bitt** *sb* bite.

bitte liten *adj* tiny; very small.

bitter *adj* **1** bitter (også *fig*); *han var* ~ *på meg* he felt bitter towards me; **2** *(om smak)* acrid. **bitterhet** *sb* bitterness. **bitterlig** *adv* bitterly.

bivåne *vb* attend; be present at.

bjeff *sb* yelp. **bjeffe** *vb* yelp.

bjelke *sb* beam; *(stor ~)* balk; *(jern~)* girder.

bjelle *sb* bell.

bjerk *sb* birch.

bjørn *sb* bear. **bjørne|bær** *sb* blackberry. **~jakt** *sb* bear-hunting. **~skinn** *sb* bear's skin. **~tjeneste** *sb* disservice. **~unge** *sb* bear's cub.

bla *vb:* ~ *i en bok* turn over the leaves of a book; ~ *om* turn over. **blad** *sb* **1** *(i bok, plante etc)* leaf; **2** *(på kniv, åre etc)* blade; **3** *(avis, ukeblad etc)* (news)paper; magazine; periodical.

blaff *sb (vindpust)* breath/puff of wind. **blaffe** *vb se blafre.* **blaffen** *sb: jeg gir* ~ I don't care a pin. **blafre** *vb* **1** *(om lys)* flicker; **2** *(om flagg etc)* flap.

blakk *adj* **1** *(om hest)* dun; **2** *(pengelens)* hard up; broke.

blamere seg *vb* make a fool/an exhibition of oneself; put one's foot in it.

blande *vb* mix, mingle; *(om varesorter ofte)* blend; ~ *seg i andre folks saker* meddle/interfere with other people's business; ~ *sammen (dvs forveksle)* mix up; confuse; *bland ikke sammen verbene »lie» og »lay»* do not confuse the verbs »lie» and »lay». **blanding** *sb (det som er blandet)* blend, mixture; *lufta er en* ~ *av gassarter* the air is a mixture of gases. **blandingsrase** *sb* mixed breed; hybrid race; *(av husdyr især)* cross-breed.

blank *adj* bright; shining, shiny; glossy; *(ubeskrevet)* blank; *la en side stå* ~ leave a page blank. **blankett** *sb* form; *US* blank; *fylle ut en* ~ fill in/out a form. **blankettmating** *sb data* form feed. **blankpusse** *vb* polish.

blant *prep* among; from among; ~ *andre* among others; ~ *annet* among other things; *hun ble valgt (ut)* ~ *elevene på skolen* she was chosen from among the pupils of the school.

blasert *adj* blasé.

blasfemi *sb* blasphemy. **blasfemisk** *adj* blasphemous.

blass *adj* pale, colourless.

blei *sb* **1** *(kile)* wedge; **2** *(hoven fyr)* arrogant (snooty/stuck-up) fellow. **bleie** *sb* (baby's) napkin/ nappy; *US* diaper.

blek *adj* **1** pale; *han ble* ~ *av skrekk* he turned pale with horror; **2** *(lik~)* pallid, white; **3** *(sykelig ~)* wan. **bleke** *vb* bleach. **blekemiddel** *sb* bleaching agent. **blekfet** *adj* pasty.

blekhet *sb* paleness. **blekne** *vb* turn pale; *(falme)* fade.

blekk *sb* **A** ink; *skrevet med rødt* ~ written in red ink; **B** *(metall) se blikk*. **blekk|flaske** *sb* ink-bottle. **~hus** *sb* ink|-pot, -stand. **~flekk, ~klatt** *sb* ink-stain. **blekksprut** *sb* cuttle-fish; *(åttearmet)* octopus.

blekne *vb* **1** turn pale; **2** *(falme)* fade.

blemme *sb* blister.

blende *vb* **1** *(om sterkt lys)* dazzle (også *fig*); **2** *(dekke til)* darken; ~ *frontlysene (på en bil)* dip the headlights. **blendende** *adj* dazzling. **blender** *sb foto* **1** *(selve blenderen)* diaphragm; **2** *(blenderåpning)* stop. **blending** *sb* black-out. **blendverk** *sb* delusion, mirage, phantom.

blest *sb* wind.

bli *vb* **1** *(i passiv)* be; *de ble drept alle sammen* they were all killed; **2** *a) (~ + adj/sb om varig forandring)* become; *hun ble lege (rik, berømt etc)* she became a doctor (rich, famous etc); *b) (~ + adj, især om noe kortvarig)* get; *han ble sint (opphisset, våt etc)* he got angry (excited, wet etc); **3** *(~ litt etter litt)* grow; *han ble gammel* he grew old; **4** *(~ plutselig, især om farge)* turn; *hun ble blek/rød* she turned pale/red; **5** *(~ + adj/sb: vise seg å ~, ~ i fremtiden)* be; turn out; *det ble en suksess* it was/it turned out (to be) a success; *det ~r (dvs vil ~) vanskelig* it will be difficult; *jeg vil ~ sjømann* I will be a sailor; *det ~r torden(vær)* there will be a thunderstorm; **6** *(om alder, pris)* be; *han ~r 25 i morgen* he will be/is 25 tomorrow; *hvor mye ~r det? det ~r £5.* how much is it/will it be? that is/will be £5; **7** *(~ værende, oppholde seg)* stay; *vi ble i fire dager* we stayed for four days; **8** *(for~, fortsette å være)* remain; *jeg ble (igjen), de andre gikk* I remained (there), the others left; **9** *(uttrykk) hva skal det ~* **av** *ham?* what is to become of him? *vi kan ikke ~* **av med** *dem* we cannot get rid of them; *det ble ikke til noe* nothing came of it/it came to nothing; ~ **ved med** *å (om virkelig handling)* go on; *(uavlatelig)* go on; keep (on); *(om stilling og tilstand)* continue; remain, stay.

blid *adj* **1** *(smilende)* smiling, cheerful; **2** *(mild)* gentle, mild; **3** *(elskverdig)* kind.

blikk *sb* **A** *(øyekast)* look, glance; *han kastet et ~ på det* he had/took a look at it; he glanced at it; *hun sendte ham et sint ~* she gave him an angry look; *med et eneste ~* at a glance; **B** *(metall)* sheet iron; sheet metal. **blikkboks** tin; *US* can. **blikk|fang** *sb* eye-catcher. **~stille** *adj* dead calm.

blind *adj* blind; ~ *på det ene øyet* blind in one eye; *den ~e* the blind person; *de ~e* the blind; *han ble ~* he went/became blind. **blinde 1** *sb: i ~* blindfold; in the dark; **2** *vb* blind. **blinde|bukk** *sb* blindman's buff. **~mann** *sb (i kortspill)* dummy. **~skrift** *sb* braille; Braille alphabet. **blind|gate** *sb* blind alley, cul-de-sac. **~het** *sb* blindness. **blind|passasjer** *sb* stowaway. **~tarm** *(dvs vedhenget)* appendix. **~tarmsbetennelse** *sb* appendicitis.

blingse *sb vulg* squint. **blingset** *adj vulg* cross-eyed, squint-eyed.

blink *sb* **1** *(glimt)* flash; *(fjernt, svakt)* gleam; **2** *(~ i øyet)* twinkle; **3** *(på skyteskive)* bull's eye. **blinke** *vb* **1** *(glimte)* gleam, twinkle; *stjernene ~r* the stars are twinkling; **2** *(for hugst)* mark, blaze.

blitz *sb foto* flash-light, flash-lamp.

blivende *adj* lasting, permanent.

blod *sb* blood; *med kaldt ~* in cold blood. **blod|appelsin** *sb* blood orange. **~bad** *sb* massacre, slaughter. **~fattig** *adj* anaemic. **~forgiftning** *sb* blood poisoning. **~giver** *sb* blood donor. **~hevn** *sb* blood revenge/vengeance; vendetta. **~hund** *sb* blood-hound. **blodig** *adj (blødende, blodflekket)* bleeding; blood-stained; stained with blood *(NB: Det engelske ordet* bloody *er et grovt banneord)*; *en ~ nese* a bleeding nose. **blod|kar** *sb* blood vessel. **~legeme** *sb* blood corpuscle; *hvitt ~legeme* leucocyte; *rødt ~legeme* red blood corpuscle, erythrocyte. **~mangel** *sb* anaemia. **~omløp** *sb* circulation (of the blood). **~overføring** *sb* blood transfusion. **~propp** *sb* blood clot. **~pølse** *sb* black pudding. **~senkning** *sb* (blood) sedimentation. **~skam** *sb* incest. **~suger** *sb* bloodsucker, vampire. **~trykk** *sb* blood pressure. **~tørstig** *adj* bloodthirsty. **~åre** *sb* vein.

blokade *sb* blockade.

blokk *sb* **1** *(kloss)* block; **2** *(bolig~)* block; **3** *(skrive~)* pad. **blokkere** *vb* **1** *mil etc* blockade; **2** *(sperre)* bar; block up. **blokkfløyte** *sb* recorder.

blom|karse *sb* Indian cross; climbing nasturtium. **~kål** *sb* cauliflower.

blomst *sb* flower; *(især på frukttrær)* blossom; *(~ring)* bloom; *avskårne ~er* cut flowers; *være/stå i ~* be in flower/bloom; *(om frukttrær)* be in blossom. **blomster|bed** *sb* flower-bed. **~bukett** *sb* bunch of flowers; nosegay, posy. **~forretning** *sb* florist's (shop). **~gartner, ~handler** *sb* florist. **~potte** *sb* flowerpot. **~plante** *sb* flowering plant. **blomstre** *vb* (be in) flower/bloom; *fig* flourish. **blomstringstid** *sb* flowering time.

blond *adj* blond; *(om hår især)* fair(-haired), light. **blonde(r)** *sb (fl)* lace. **blondine** *sb* blonde.

blott *adv gml* only; *med det ~e øye* with the naked eye. **blotte** *vb* bare, denude; lay bare; ~ *sitt hode* uncover (one's head). **blottende** *adv: ~ ung* very young.

blotter *sb* exhibitionist. **blottet** *adj: ~ for* without; devoid of.

bluferdig *adj* bashful, shy, modest. **bluferdighet** *sb* bashfulness, modesty.

blund *sb* doze, nap; *ikke få ~ på øynene* not bat an eyelid. **blunde** *vb* doze; take a nap.

blunk *sb: på en/et ~* in the twinkling of an eye; in a flash/a jiffy. **blunke** *vb* blink; *~ til* wink at.

bluse *sb* blouse.

bluss *sb* **1** *(flamme)* flame, blaze; **2** *(bål)* fire. **blusse** *vb* **1** *(brenne)* blaze; *~ opp* blaze up; burst into flame; **2** *(rødme)* blush. **blussende** *adj* flushed; *han ble ~ rød* he turned scarlet.

bly *sb* lead; *av ~* leaden.

blyant *sb* pencil; *skrevet med ~* written in pencil; *han skrev med ~* he wrote with a pencil. **blyfri** *adj* unleaded; *petro også* clear.

blyg *adj* bashful, shy; modest. **blyghet** *sb* bashfulness, shyness; modesty.

blære I *sb* **1** *(luft~)* bubble; **2** *(vable)* blister; **3** *(galle~, urin~)* bladder; **4** *(overlegen person)* windbag; **II** *vb: ~ seg* put on airs.

blø *vb* bleed; *han blødde (seg) i hjel* he bled to death. **bløder** *sb* bleeder.

blødme *sb* foolish/silly joke.

bløff *sb* bluff. **bløffe** *vb* bluff.

bløt I *adj* **1** *(myk)* soft; **2** *(våt)* wet; **II** *sb: legge i ~* put on soak; *legge hodet i ~* rack one's brains; *ligge i ~* soak. **bløt|aktig** *adj* soft, effeminate. **~aktighet** *sb* softness, effeminacy. **~gjøre** *vb* soften. **~kake** *sb* cream-cake, layer-cake. **~kokt** *vb* soft-boiled. **bløyt** *sb se bløt II.* **bløyte** *vb* soak.

blå *adj* blue. **blå|bær** *sb* bilberry; *US også* blueberry, huckleberry. **~frossen** *adj* blue with cold. **~grønn** *adj* bluish green. **~klokke** *sb* harebell; *skotsk* bluebell. **~papir** *sb* carbon paper. **~rev** *sb* blue fox.

blåse *vb* blow; *det ~r* it is windy/there is a wind; *det blåste sterkt* it/the wind was blowing hard; there was a strong wind; *hatten (min) blåste av meg* my hat blew off; *~ (på) trompet (om et enkelt trompetstøt)* blow the trumpet; *(om å spille)* play the trumpet; *blås i det!* never mind! *det ~r jeg i* I couldn't care less (about it). **blåsende** *adj* windy. **blåst** *vb* wind; windy weather.

blå|veis *sb* blue anemone. **~øyd** *adj* blue-eyed; *fig også* simple, artless.

bo I *sb* property, estate; **II** vb **1** *(fast)* live, reside; **2** *(for kortere tid)* stay; *hvor ~r du? (fast)* where do you live? *(midlertidig)* where are you staying?

boble *sb/vb* bubble.

bod *el* **bu** *sb* **1** *(skur)* shed; **2** (markeds~) booth, stall; **3** *(butikk)* shop.

bog *sb* shoulder.

boggi *sb* bogie. **boggivogn** *sb* bogie carriage/wagon.

bohem *sb* Bohemian.

boikott *sb* boycott. **boikotte** *vb* boycott.

bok *sb* book. **bok|bind** *sb* binding, cover. **~binder** *sb* bookbinder.

bokfink *sb* chaffinch.

bok|føre *vb* enter, book. **~føring** *sb* book-keeping. **~handel** *sb* bookshop. **~handler** *sb* bookseller. **~holder** *sb* book-keeper. **~holderi** *sb* book-keeping. **~hylle** *sb* bookshelf; *(reol)* bookcase. **boklig** *adj: ~ lærdom* book learning; *~e sysler* literary occupation. **bok|merke** *sb* book-mark(er). **~reol** *sb* bookcase, bookshelves.

boks *sb* **1** box; *(med lokk)* canister; *(til te også)* caddy; *hermetikk~* tin; *US* can.

boksamling *sb* book collection; library.

bokse *vb* box. **boksekamp** *sb* boxing-match. **bokser** *sb* **1** boxer; *(profesjonell ~ også)* prize-fighter; **2** *(hunderase)* boxer.

bokstav *sb* letter; *stor ~* capital (letter); *stum ~* silent letter; *et ord på fem ~er* a word of five letters. **bokstavelig** *adj* literal; *adv* literally; *~ talt* literally. **bokstav|rim** *sb* alliteration. **~tast** *sb data* alphabetic key.

boksåpner *sb* tin opener; *US* can opener.

bok|trykker *sb* printer. **~trykkeri** *sb* printing office/house.

bolig *sb* **1** *(hus)* house; *(især om stort hus)* residence; **2** *(leilighet)* flat; **3** *(losji)* lodgings. **bolig|dekk** *sb petro* accommodation deck. **~forhold** *sb* housing situation. **~lekter** *sb petro* accommodation barge. **~nød** *sb* housing famine/shortage. **~plattform** *sb petro* accommodation platform; *også* flotel.

bolle *sb* **1** *(kar)* basin, bowl; **2** *(bakt ~)* bun, muffin; **3** *(fiske~, kjøtt~)* ball.

bolt *sb* bolt.

boltre *vb: ~ seg* disport oneself; frisk, romp; frolic.

bolverk *sb fig* bulwark.

bom *sb* **A 1** *(veisperring)* bar; *(på bomvei)* toll-bar, tollgate; turnpike; **2** *(jernbane~)* gate; **3** *(gymnastikk~)* boom; **B** *(bomskudd)* miss; *skyte ~* miss (the mark).

bombardement *sb* bombardment. **bombardere** *vb* **1** *(med bomber)* bomb; **2** *(med granater)* shell; **3** *(med spørsmål)* bombard.

bombastisk *adj* bombastic.

bombe *sb* bomb.

bomme *vb* **A** *(tigge)* beg, sponge; *han ~r meg bestandig for sigaretter* he is always sponging on me for cigarettes; **B** *(ikke treffe)* miss (the mark). **bommert** *sb* blunder; *(latterlig ~)* howler; *hun begikk en ~* she made a blunder/howler.

bompenger *sb* toll.

bomull *sb* cotton. **bomullsspinneri** *sb* cotton mill.

bomvei *sb* toll road; turnpike road.

bonde *sb* farmer; *(småbonde)* peasant; *(i sjakk)* pawn. **bonde|gård** *sb* farm; *(om bygningene)* farmstead. **~kone** farmer's wife. **bondsk** *adj* churlish, rustic.

bone *vb* polish, wax. **bonevoks** *sb* floor-polish.

bopel *sb* (place of) residence; address; *fast ~* permanent address. *Se også bolig.*

bor *sb (til borvinde)* (brace) bit; *(vri~)* gimlet; *(stort vri~)* auger; *(drill~, tannlege~)* drill.

bord *sb* **A** *(møbel)* table; *bank i ~et!* touch wood! *dekke ~et* lay the table; *gå til ~s* sit down to dinner/lunch etc; *ha til ~s* have as one's table companion; *ta av ~et* clear the table; *ved ~et (under måltidet)* at table; *vi var tretten til ~s* we were thirteen at table; **B** *(treplanke)* board; **C** *(skipsside)* board; *gå fra ~e* disembark; go on shore; *gå om ~* embark; go on board; *om ~* on board; *om ~ på et skip* on board a ship; *over ~* overboard; **D** *sb (kant)* border, edging. **bord|bein** *sb* table-leg. **~bønn** *sb* grace; *be ~bønn* say grace. **~dame** *sb* dinner partner. **borde** *vb (entre)* board.

bordell *sb* brothel.

bord|kavaler *sb* dinner partner. **~tennis** *sb* table--tennis, ping-pong.

bore *vb* bore, drill; *~ etter olje* bore for oil. **bore|assistent** *sb petro* assistant driller. **~avdelingssjef** *sb petro* drilling superintendent. **~dekk** *sb petro* drill floor. **~dekksarbeider** *sb petro* drill floor crew; *dgl* roughneck. **~entreprenør** *sb petro* drilling contractor. **~fartøy** *sb petro* drilling vessel. **~gjeng** *sb petro* roughnecks. **~gulv** *sb petro = ~dekk.* **~hastighet** *sb petro* rate of penetration. **~hull** *sb petro* bore hole; well. **~hullslogg** *sb petro* well log. **~ingeniør** *sb petro* drilling engineer. **~lekter** *sb petro* drilling barge. **~mast** *sb petro* drilling mast. **~olje** *sb petro* boring oil. **~operasjonsleder** *sb petro = ~avdelingssjef.* **~plass** *sb petro* drilling site. **~plattform** *sb petro* drilling platform. **~rigg** *sb petro* (drilling) rig. **~rør** *sb petro* drill(ing) pipe. **~sjef** *sb petro* drilling section leader; *dgl* tool pusher. **~skaft** *sb petro* drill(ing) shaft. **~skip** *sb petro* drill(ing) ship. **~slam** *sb petro* drilling mud. **~stans** *sb petro* down time. **~start** *sb petro* spudding-in. **~streng** *sb* drill column (stem *el* string). **~tårn** *sb petro* derrick. **~vaier** *sb petro* drill(ing) line. **boring** *sb petro etc* drilling.

borg *sb* **A** *(slott)* castle; **B** *(kreditt)* credit; *ta på ~* take on credit. **borge** *vb (ta på borg)* take on credit.

borger *sb* **1** citizen; *(by~ også)* townsman; **2** *(borgerlig person)* commoner. **borgerkrig** *sb* civil war. **borgerlig** *adj (motsatt militær eller kirkelig)* civil; *~ ekteskap* civil marriage; **2** *a) (middelstands)* middle-class; *b) (jevn)* plain, simple; **3** *(ikke-sosialistisk)* non--Socialist. **borger|mester** *sb* mayor; *(i London og enkelte andre* cities*)* Lord Mayor. **~plikt** *sb* civic duty. **~rett** *sb (statsborgerskap)* nationality; *US* citizenship. **~skap** *sb (borgerne)* citizens; middle classes. **~standen** *sb* the middle classes.

bor|krone *sb petro etc* bit; drill(ing) bit. **~kronelager** *sb petro* bit bearing. **~kroneskaft** *sb petro* shank.

borre *sb* burdock, bur(r); *(blomsterhodet på planten)* bur(r).

bort *adv* away, off; *gå ~ a) (fjerne seg)* go away/off; leave; *b) (dø)* die; pass away; *langt ~* far away. **borte** *adv a) (ikke til stede)* away; *hun var bare ~ i ti minutter* she was only gone for ten minutes; *jeg så dem et stykke ~* I saw them at a distance; *b) (forsvunnet)* gone; *c) (savnet)* missing. **borte|bane** *sb* away ground; *de spiller på ~bane* they are playing away. **~kamp** *sb* away match. **bortenfor** *adv* beyond. **bortest** *adj, adv* farthest, furthest; farthermost, furthermost; *(av to)* farther, further. **bort|forklare** *vb* explain away. **~forpakte** *vb* farm out; (let on) lease. **~føre** *vb* carry off; kidnap. **~gang** *sb (død)* death. **borti** *adv* **1** against; *komme ~* brush against; **2** *(borte i)* (over) in. **bortimot** *adv* **1** towards; **2** *(nesten)* almost; close to. **bort|kastet** *adj* thrown away, wasted. **~kommen** *adj* lost. **~over** *adv* along. **bortre** *adj, adv* farther, further. **bort|reist** *adj* away, out of town. **~sett fra** *prep* apart from.

borvann *sb* boric acid solution.

borvinde *sb* brace.

bo|satt *adj: hun er ~satt i Tromsø* she lives in Tromsø. **~setning** *sb* settlement. **~sette seg** *vb* settle; set up; *vi ~satte oss i Canada* we settled in Canada. **~sted** *sb* place of residence; address.

bot *sb* **A** *(lapp)* patch; **B** *(mulkt)* fine, penalty; *en bot på 100 pund* a fine of £100; *hun fikk/ble idømt en ~ på 100 pund* she was fined £100; **3** *(uttrykk) gjøre ~* do penance; *love ~ og bedring* promise to reform/to turn over a new leaf; *råde ~ på* remedy.

botaniker *sb* botanist. **botanikk** *sb* botany. **botanisere** *vb* botanize. **botanisk** *adj* botanical.

botemiddel *sb* remedy. **botsfengsel** *sb* penitentiary.

bra *adj, adv* **1** *(god, godt)* fine, good; well; all right; satisfactory; excellent; *ganske ~* not at all bad; *(det var) ~!* (that is) fine/good! *et ~ resultat* a satisfactory result; *ha det ~!* take care of yourself! *jeg har det ~* I am all right/fine; **2** *(frisk)* well; *(hvordan står det til?) takk ~* (how are you?) I am quite well, thank you; *ikke helt ~* not quite well; out of sorts; *jeg håper du snart blir ~ (igjen)* you will soon get well (again), I hope; **3** *(hederlig, skikkelig)* honest, respectable; good.

bragd *sb* feat, exploit.

brak *sb* bang, crash; noise; *(om torden)* peal. **brake** *vb* crash; *(tordne)* thunder; roar.

brakk *adj* **1** *(om jord)* fallow; *ligge ~* lie fallow; **2** *(om vann)* brackish.

brakke *sb* barrack(s).

brakkmark *sb* fallow (field).

brann *sb* **1** fire; *(stor ~)* conflagration; *huset stod i ~* the house was on fire; *høyet kom i ~* the hay caught fire; **2** *(brennende trestykke)* firebrand. **brann|alarm** *sb* fire alarm. **~assuranse** *sb = ~forsikring.* **~bil** *sb* fire engine. **~bombe** *sb* incendiary (bomb); fire-bomb. **~fakkel** *sb fig* firebrand. **~farlig** *adj* combustible, inflammable. **~folk** *sb* firemen; fire brigade. **~forsikring** *sb* fire insurance. **~konstabel, ~mann** *sb* fireman. **~melding** *sb* fire alarm. **~mur** *sb* fire-proof wall. **~polise** *sb* fire (insurance) policy. **~sikker** *adj* fire-proof. **~slange** *sb* fire hose. **~slokningsapparat** *sb* extinguisher. **~sprøyte** *sb* fire-engine. **~stasjon** *sb* fire-station. **~stiftelse** *sb* arson, fire-raising. **~stifter**

sb incendiary. **~stige** *sb* fire-escape. **~sår** *sb* burn. **~tau** *sb* rescue rope. **~utrykning** *sb* fire-brigade turn-out. **~vern** *sb* fire protection. **~vesen** *sb* fire service; *(konkret)* fire brigade.

bransje *sb* trade; line of business.

brase *vb* **1** *(sprake, steke)* frizzle; **2** *(fare)* rush; *~ inn i* crash into.

brasene *sb fl: klare ~* weather the storm; pull/bring it off.

brask *sb: med ~ og bram* ostentatiously.

bratsj *sb* viola.

bratt *adj* steep; *(stup~)* precipitous.

braute *vb* swagger, brag.

bravo! *interj* bravo! **bravorop** *sb* bravo, cheer.

bre A *sb* glacier; **B** *vb* **1** *(spre)* spread; *~ seg (vinne utbredelse)* spread; *nyheten/epidemien ~dte seg* the news/the epidemic spread; **2** *(bli bredere)* broaden; spread, widen; **3** *(tjære~)* tar. **bred** *adj* broad, wide; *60 fot ~* sixty feet broad/wide; *se også bredt.*

bredd *sb* bank; *(strand~)* shore; *den annen ~* the opposite bank; *gå over sine ~er* overflow its banks.

bredde *sb* **1** breadth, width; *fem fot i ~n* five feet across/broad/in width; *de marsjerte fire i ~n* they marched four abreast; **2** *(astronomisk, geografisk)* latitude. **bredde|grad** *sb* degree of latitude; parallel. **~steg** *sb data* horizontal step. **breddfull** *adj* brimful. **bred|side** *sb* broadside. **~skuldret** *adj* broad-shouldered. **~sporet** *adj* broad-gauge. **bredt** *adv* broadly, widely; *vidt og ~* far and wide; *han talte vidt og ~ om saken* he spoke at great length on the subject.

bregne *sb* bracken, fern.

brei, breie etc *se bred, bre etc.*

breke *vb* bleat.

brekk, brekkasje *sb* breakage. **brekke** *vb* **1** break; *stokken brakk i to* the stick broke in two; **2** *~ seg* retch; *(kaste opp)* vomit. **brekk|jern, ~stang** *sb* jemmy, crowbar.

brem *sb (på hatt)* brim.

brems *sb (insekt)* gadfly, botfly.

brems(e) **1** *sb (på hjul eller maskin)* brake; **2** *vb* brake; put on the brake; *hun bremset* she put on the brake.

brennbar *adj* combustible, inflammable. **brenne** *vb* burn; *~ inne (dvs omkomme ved brann)* perish in the flames; *~ inne med a) (ikke bli av med)* be left with on one's hands; *b) (ikke få sagt)* not get the chance to say/tell; *~ seg* burn oneself; *han brente fingrene (sine)* he burnt his fingers; *huset brant (dvs stod i brann)* the house was on fire; *huset brant (ned)* the house burned/was burnt down; *lyset brant* the light was on; *papiret begynte å ~* the paper caught fire. **brennemerke** *vb* stigmatize, brand. **brennende** *adj* burning; *fig også* ardent, fervent; *et ~ spørsmål* a burning question. **brennesle** *sb* (stinging) nettle, **brenner** *sb (i lampe etc)* burner. **brenneri** *sb* distillery. **brennevin** *sb* liquor, spirits *fl*; *US* hard liquor. **brenning** *sb* breakers *fl*; surf. **brenn|manet** *sb* sea nettle; stinging jelly-fish. **~punkt** *sb* focus. **~sikker** *adj* dead certain. **~stoff** *sb* fuel. **~verdi** *sb petro* burning property. **brensel** *sb = brennstoff.*

bresje *sb* breach; *gå i bresjen for* make a stand for; stand up for.

brett *sb* **A** *(serverings~ etc)* tray; **B** *(foldet stripe etc)* crease, fold; *(oppbrett)* turned-up edge; *legge ~ på* lay stress on. **brette** *vb* fold; *~ sammen* fold (up).

brev *sb* letter; *(mindre ~)* note. **brev|due** *sb* carrier pigeon. **~kort** *sb* postcard. **~veksle** *vb* correspond. **~veksling** *sb* correspondence. **~vekt** *sb* letter balance.

brigade *sb* brigade.

brikett *sb* briquette.

brikke *sb* **1** *(brodert, heklet etc)* mat, doily; **2** *(til spill)* piece; **3** *(med integrerte kretser) data* chip.

briks *sb* bunk.

briljant *adj/sb* brilliant. **briljere** shine.

briller *sb fl* spectacles, glasses; *et par ~* a pair of spectacles/glasses; *gå med/bruke ~* wear spectacles/glasses.

bringe A *sb (bryst)* breast, chest; **B** *vb (hente, ta hit, ta med tilbake)* bring, fetch; *(ta med til andre)* carry, take; *varene ble brakt* the goods were delivered.

bringebær *sb* raspberry.

bris *sb* breeze; *lett ~* gentle breeze.

brisk *sb (einer)* juniper.

briske *vb: ~ seg* swagger; show off.

brisling *sb* brisling, sprat.

brist *sb* **1** *(sprekk)* crack; **2** *(lyte, mangel)* flaw, defect. **briste** break, burst; *jeg brast i gråt* I burst into tears/out crying; *det får ~ eller bære* it is neck or nothing; *håpet brast* his/her/our hopes were wrecked. **briste|ferdig** *adj* bursting; ready to burst. **~punkt** *sb* breaking point.

brite *sb* Briton. **britisk** *adj* British; *De britiske øyer* the British Isles.

bro *sb* bridge; *vi gikk/kjørte over en ~* we crossed a bridge; *gå (ned) i ~* do backwards.

brodd *sb* sting.

brodere *vb* embroider. **broderi** *sb* embroidery. **broderiforretning** *sb* needlework shop.

broderlig *adj* brotherly, fraternal.

broket *adj* **1** *(mangefarget)* multi-coloured, parti--coloured; motley; **2** *(uensartet)* varied, variegated; motley; *en ~ forsamling* a motley crowd; **3** *(rotet)* confused, tangled; *en ~ blanding* a confused/tangled mixture.

brokk *sb* hernia, rupture.

brokke *sb* bit, fragment.

bro|legge *vb* pave. **~legning** *sb* pavement.

bronkier *sb fl* bronchi. **bronkitt** *sb* bronchitis.

bronse *sb* bronze. **bronsealderen** *sb* the Bronze Age.

bror *sb* brother; *brødrene Smith* the brothers Smith/the Smith brothers; *(som firmanavn)* Smith Brothers/Smith Bros. **bror|datter** *sb* niece; brother's daughter. **~parten** *sb* the lion's share. **~sønn** *sb* nephew; brother's son.

brosje *sb* brooch.

brosjyre *sb* folder, leaflet; brochure; *(større)* prospectus.

brostein *sb koll* cobbles; paving-stones.

brottsjø *sb* breaker.

bru etc *sb se bro etc.*

brud *sb* bride.

brudd *sb* **1** break, breaking; ~ *på vannledningen* break in the water-pipe; ~ *på sammenhengen* break of continuity; **2** *(åpning, revne; overtredelse)* breach; ~ *på disiplinen* breach of discipline; **3** *(knokkel~)* fracture; **4** *(brudd på vennskap)* break, rupture; *det kom til ~ mellom dem* there was a break/rupture between them; they fell/have fallen out. **bruddstykke** *sb* fragment.

brude|kjole *sb* wedding dress. **~par** *sb* bridal couple; newly-married couple. **~pike** *sb* bridesmaid. **~slør** *sb* bridal veil. **brudgom** *sb* bridegroom.

brudulje *sb* row.

bruk *sb* **A 1** use; employment; *et rom til ~ for skolelegen* a room for the use of the school doctor; *det gikk (ut) av ~* it went out of use; *jeg har ikke ~ for deres hjelp* I do not want/need their help; **2** *(forbruk)* consumption; *~en av kaffe i England* the consumption of coffee in England; **3** *(skikk)* custom; *det er skikk og ~ her i landet* it is the custom of this country; it is customary in this country; **B 1** *(gårdsbruk)* farm; **2** *(bedrift, virksomhet)* mill, works; factory. **brukbar** *adj* fit for use; usable, useful; *i ~ stand* in working condition/order. **brukbarhet** *sb* fitness for use; usefulness. **bruke** *vb* **1** *(benytte)* use; make use of; employ; *han brukte all sin sjarm for å* he employed/used all his charm to; **2** *(anvende)* spend; *hun brukte over 100 pund på bøker* she spent more than £100 on books; *han brukte sin tid til å lese* he spent his time reading; **3** *(utnytte)* use; make use of; ~ *tiden* make the most of one's time; **4** *(gå med, om klær etc)* wear; *han brukte briller* he wore spectacles. **bruker|håndbok** *sb* reference manual; user manual. **~program** *sb data* application program. **~programvare** *sb data* application software. **~snitt** *sb data* user interface. **~terminal** *sb data* user terminal. **~tilpasse** *vb data* customize. **~veiledning** *sb* user/user's guide. **~vennlig** *adj* user-friendly. **bruks|anvisning** *sb* directions (for use). **~gjenstand** *sb* article for everyday use. **~kunst** *sb* applied art. **~verdi** *sb* utility value. **brukt** *adj* used, second-hand; *~biler* second-hand/used cars; *~e frimerker* cancelled stamps; *håndkledet var ~* the towel was soiled; *jeg kjøpte bøkene ~* I bought the books second-hand.

brumme *vb* **1** *(summe)* hum, buzz; **2** *(mumle)* mumble, mutter; *(protestere, gi vondt fra seg)* grumble.

brun *adj* brown; *(etter soling)* tanned. **brune** *vb* brown; *(ved soling)* bronze, tan. **brunette** *sb* brunette. **brun|aktig** *adj* brownish. **~het** *sb (etter soling)* sun-tan. **~rød** brownish red.

brunst *sb (hos hanndyr)* rut; *(hos hunndyr)* heat.

brunstekt *adj* done brown.

brus *sb* **1** *(sterk lyd)* roar; *(svakere)* murmur; rustle; **2** *(drikk)* pop, lemonade. **bruse** *vb* **1** *(sterkt)* roar; *(svakere)* murmur; rustle; *(om musikk)* sound; **2** *(perle, skumme)* fizz.

brusk *sb* cartilage, gristle.

brutal *adj* brutal; *han var ~ mot gutten* he bullied the boy. **brutalitet** *sb* brutality.

brutto *adj, adv* gross. **brutto|beløp** *sb* gross amount. **~vekt** *sb* gross weight.

bry I *sb* inconvenience, trouble; *skaffe ~* give/put to trouble; *vil det være (til) mye ~ for Dem* will it be much trouble for you; *det er ikke ~et verdt* it isn't worthwhile; **II** *vb* **1** *(uleilige)* inconvenience, trouble; *jeg beklager at jeg ~r Dem* I am sorry to trouble you; **2** *~ seg om a) (like, ønske)* care to; *~r De Dem om å komme?* would you care to come? *b) (like, være glad)* like, love; care for; *~r hun seg om ham i det hele tatt?* does she care for him at all? **3** *ikke ~ seg om (dvs ikke ta hensyn til)* not mind; *det er ikke noe å ~ seg om* never mind; *ikke ~ deg om meg* don't mind me; **4** *~ seg (dvs legge seg opp i andres saker)* meddle; *ikke ~ deg med mine saker* don't meddle in my affairs; *ikke ~ deg!* mind your own business! **bryderi** *sb* trouble. *Se også bry.*

brygg *sb* brew. **brygge** *sb* **A** *(kai)* quay, wharf; landing stage; **B** *vb* brew. **bryggeri** *sb* brewery. **bryggesjauer** *sb* docker.

bryllup *sb* wedding; *ha/holde ~* marry; be married; *hun var i ~et deres* she was present at their wedding. **bryllupsreise** *sb: de drog på ~ til Spania* they went to Spain for their honeymoon.

bryn *sb* **1** *(øyen~)* brow; *rynke brynene* knit one's brows; *(i sinne)* frown; **2** *(skog~)* edge, fringe. **bryne** **1** *sb* whetstone, hone; **2** *vb* sharpen, whet, hone.

brysk *adj* blunt, brusque, gruff.

brysom *adj* troublesome.

bryst *sb* breast; *(brystkasse)* chest; *han hadde smerter i brystet* he had a pain in the chest. **bryst|bilde** *sb* half-length portrait. **~kasse** *sb* chest. **~nål** *sb* brooch. **~svømming** *sb* breast stroke. **~vorte** *sb (på mennesker)* nipple; *(på dyr)* teat.

bryte *vb* **1** break; *han brøt sitt løfte* he broke his promise; *hun brøt forlovelsen* she broke off their engagement; ~ *igjennom (fig)* come to the fore; ~ *i stykker* break up; ~ *(seg) inn i* break into; ~ *(løpet)* drop out; *to av løperne brøt* two of the runners dropped out; ~ *med* break with; *han brøt med familien (sin)* he broke with his family; ~ *mot* break against; ~ *opp a) (åpne med makt)* break open; *de brøt opp døren* they broke open the door; *b) (starte)* leave, start; ~ *sammen* break down; collapse; *han brøt sammen da vi fortalte ham nyheten* he broke down when we told him the news; ~ *(seg) ut* break out; *det brøt ut krig* war broke out; **2** *(om lysstråler)* refract. **brytekamp** *sb* wrestling match. **bryter** *sb* **1** *elek etc* switch; **2** *sport* wrestler. **bryte(s)** *vb* **1** wrestle; **2** *(om lys)* be refracted.

brød *sb* **1** *(som næringsmiddel)* bread; **2** *(om det enkelte brød)* loaf (of bread); *en skive/et stykke ~* a piece/slice of bread; *hun tjente sitt ~ som kranfører* she earned her living as a crane operator.

brøde *sb* guilt.

brød|fø *vb: Norge kan ikke ~ seg* Norway does not produce enough corn for its own needs. **~rister** *sb* toaster. **~skalk** *sb* first cut; outside slice; *US* heel (of a loaf). **~skive** *sb* slice of bread. **~skorpe** *sb* bread crust. **~smule** *sb* bread crumb.

brøk *sb* fraction. **brøkstrek** *sb* fraction line.

brøl *sb* roar. **brøle** *vb* roar.

brønn *sb* well; *petro også* bore hole. **brønn|erosjon** *sb petro* cave-in. **~hode** *sb petro* wellhead. **~hodetrykk** *sb petro* wellhead pressure. **~hodeutstyr** *sb petro* wellhead equipment. **~kapasitet** *sb petro* well capacity. **~klynge** *sb petro* well cluster.

brøyte *vb (med snøplog)* clear the road of snow. **brøytebil** *sb* snow-plough.

brå *adj, adv (plutselig)* sudden, abrupt; *en ~ død* a sudden death; *møtet fikk en ~ slutt* the meeting came to an abrupt end; *veien dreide ~tt til venstre* the road took a sharp turn/turned sharply to the left; *han stanset ~tt* he stopped short. **brå|bremse** *vb* slam on the brakes. **~hast** *sb* hot hurry.

bråk *sb* noise; *lage ~* = **bråke** *vb* make a noise; kick up a row. **bråket(e)** *adj* noisy.

bråkjekk *adj* cocky.

bråkmaker *sb* troublemaker.

bråne *vb* melt.

brå|sinne *sb* flare-up. **~sint** *adj* quick-tempered. **~snu** *vb* turn short. **~stanse** *vb* stop short.

bråte *sb* **1** *(mengde)* lot; *en ~ (med) brev* a lot of letters; **2** *brenne ~* make a bonfire. **bråtebrann** *sb* bonfire.

brått *adv se brå.*

brå|vende *vb* = *~snu.* **~vending** *sb: i en ~vending* in a jiffy/a trice.

bu *sb se bod.*

bud 1 *(beskjed, melding)* message, word; *sende ~ etter/på* send for; *det ble sendt ~ etter legen* the doctor was sent for; **2** *(befaling)* command; *vi gjorde det på deres ~* we did it at their command; **3** *(påbud) de ti ~* the ten commandments; **4** *(tilbud)* offer; *(på auksjon)* bid; *gi et ~ på* make an offer/a bid for; **5** *(sendebud)* messenger. **bud|bringer, ~bærer** messenger.

budeie *sb* milkmaid, dairymaid.

budsende *vb* send for.

budsjett *sb* budget.

budskap *sb* message, news.

bue *sb* **1** *(skytevåpen)* bow; **2** *a) (sirkelbue)* arc; *b) (krum linje)* curve; **3** *a) (buegang)* arch; *b) (hvelving)* vault; **4** *(fiolin~)* bow, fiddle-stick. **bue|skytning** *sb* archery. **~skytter** *sb* archer.

buffer *sb* buffer (også *data*). **buffer|lager** *sb data* buffer storage. **~område** *sb data* buffer pool. **~stat** *sb* buffer state.

buffet *sb* **1** *(spisestuemøbel)* buffet, sideboard; **2** *(disk i restaurant)* buffet.

bufre *vb data* buffer.

bugne *vb: ~ av* abound in/with; be full of/heavy with.

buk *sb* **1** *(mave)* belly, stomach; **2** *(underliv)* abdomen.

bukett *sb* bunch, bouquet; *en ~ blomster* a bunch of flowers.

bukk A *sb* **1** *(geite~)* billy-goat, he-goat; **2** *(rå~)* buck; **3** *(kuskesete)* box; **4** *(turnapparat)* buck; *hoppe ~* (play) leap-frog; **B** *(bøyning)* bow. **bukke** *vb* **1** *(gjøre et bukk)* bow; *han bukket dypt for meg* he made a low bow to me; **2** *~ under (for)* succumb (to). **bukkebein** *sb: sette ~* dig in one's heels.

bukse *se bukser.* **bukse|bak** *sb* trouser seat. **~lomme** *sb* trouser pocket. **bukser** *sb* **1** *(lang~)* trousers *fl*; *US* pants; *et par ~* a pair of trousers/pants; **2** *(kort~)* shorts, breeches.

buksere *vb* tow, haul.

bukse|seler *sb fl* braces; *US* suspenders. **~smekk** *sb* fly.

bukt *sb* **1** *(på tau)* loop, bight; **2** *a) (hav~)* bay; *b) (vik)* creek; **3** *(uttrykk) han fikk ~ med sin motstander* he got the better of his opponent; *hun fikk ~ med vanskelighetene* she overcame her difficulties. **bukte seg** *vb* wind; *(især om elv)* meander. **buktning** *sb* curve, winding.

bulder *sb* rumble, rumbling; din, roar. **buldre** *vb* rumble, thunder.

bule *sb* **1** *(kneipe)* dive; **2** *(bulk)* dent; **3** *(kul)* bulge; *(i pannen)* swelling, lump.

buljong *sb* beef tea; bouillon.

bulk *sb* **1** *(søkk)* dent; **2** *(kul)* bulge. **bulket** *adj* dented. **bulkolje** *sb petro* bulk oil.

bull|dogg *sb* bulldog. **~doser** *sb* bulldozer.

bulletin *sb* bulletin.

bulne *vb* swell; *~ ut* bulge.

bumerang *sb* boomerang.

bums 1 *adv* bump; **2** *interj* bang!

bunad *sb (nasjonaldrakt)* national costume.

bunke *sb* pile.

bunkers *sb* bunkers, bunker coal. **bunkre** *vb* bunker.

bunn *sb* bottom; *i ~ og grunn* actually, virtually; entirely, totally; *komme til ~s i* get to the bottom of; *med ~en i været* upside down; *på ~en av havet* at the bottom of the sea; *skipet gikk til ~s* the ship went down. **bunne** *vb* touch bottom; *~ i* be rooted in; be due to; be the result of. **bunn|fall** *sb* sediment, deposit, residuum; *(grums)* dregs, lees. **~felle** *vb* deposit. **~installasjoner** *sb fl petro* subsea completion. **~løs** *adj* bottomless, unfathomable; *i ~ gjeld* head over ears in debt. **~marg** *sb data etc* bottom margin. **~tekst** *sb data* footer.

bunt *sb* bunch, bundle; *en ~ gulrøtter* a bunch of carrots. **bunte** *vb: ~ sammen* bunch up; bundle together.

buntmaker *sb* furrier.

buorm *sb* grass snake.

bur *sb* cage; *(til kaniner etc)* hutch, coop; *sette i ~* put in a cage.

burde *vb (i pres og pret)* ought to; should; *du ~ gjøre* *det* you ought to do it; *du ~ ikke si den slags så ungene hører det* you should not say things like that in front of the children.

bureiser *sb* pioneer, settler.

bursjoasi *sb* buorgeoisie; upper middle class.

buse *vb* **1** *(fare)* rush; **2** *~ ut med* blurt out. **busemann** *sb* bugbear, bogey.

busk *sb* bush.

buskap *sb* herd; cattle, livestock.

buskas *sb* brush, thicket. **buske** *sb = busk.* **busket** *adj* bushy.

buss *sb* bus (også *data*); *vi kom med ~en* we came by bus. **busse** *vb* bus; go by bus.

busser *sb fl: de er gode ~* they are great chums.

buss|holdeplass *sb* bus stop. **~rute** *sb* bus route. **~tur** *sb* bus ride.

bust *sb* bristle; *reise ~* bristle up. **bustet** *adj* dishevelled.

butan *sb* butane.

butikk *sb* shop; *US* store; *gå i ~en/~er* go shopping. **butikk|betjent, ~ekspeditør** *sb* shop assistant. **~senter** *sb* shopping centre. **~vindu** *sb* shop window.

butt *adj* blunt.

buttet *adj (lubben)* chubby.

by A *sb* town; *(US, og i GB om større byer og om viktige byer utenfor GB)* city; *vi bor i ~en (i motsetning til på landet)* we live in town; **B** *vb* **1** *(påby)* command, order; **2** *(tilby)* offer; *han bød meg en sigar* he offered me a cigar; **3** *(på auksjon)* bid; *jeg bød 130 pund for det gamle gulvuret* I bid £130 for the old grandfather clock; **4** *(~ velkommen, farvel etc)* bid; *de bød oss velkommen* they bade us welcome. **bybefolkning, byfolk** *sb* townspeople.

bygd *sb* rural district; parish.

byge *sb* shower. **byget** *adj* showery. **bygevær** *sb* showery weather.

bygg *sb* **I 1** *(hus under oppføring)* building under construction; **2** *(byggverk)* building, edifice; **II** *(kornslaget)* barley. **bygge** *vb* build; *~ at hus/en bro/et rede* build a house/a bridge/a nest; *~ på a) (stole på)* rely on; *b) (støtte seg til)* build upon; *vi ~r på forfedrenes erfaring* we build upon the experience of our forefathers. **bygge|klosser** *sb fl* building blocks. **~plass** *sb* site. **bygg|herre** *sb* builder. **~mester** *sb* master builder. **~verk** *sb* building, edifice. **bygning** *sb* **1** building, house; **2** *(kropps~)* build. **bygningssnekker** *sb* joiner.

bygselmann *sb* leaseholder. **bygsle** *vb* lease.

byks *sb* bound, leap. **bykse** *vb* bound, leap; jump.

byll *sb* abscess, boil.

bylt *sb* bundle.

bymessig *adj* urban; *~messig bebyggelse* built-up area.

byrd *sb* birth, descent; parentage.

byrde *sb* burden, load, weight. **byrdefull** *adj* burdensome.

byrå *sb* office, bureau. **byrå|krat** *sb* bureaucrat. **~krati** *sb* bureaucracy; *dgl ofte* red tape. **~kratisk** *adj* bureaucratic.

bysse A *sb sjø* galley; **B** *vb* lull; *~ i søvn* lull to sleep.

byste *sb* bust. **bysteholder** *sb* bra, brassiere.

bystyre *sb* city/town council. **bystyremedlem** *sb* councillor.

bytte I *sb* **1** *(ombytning)* exchange; *hva fikk du i ~ for den/det* what did you receive in exchange for it; **2** *(erobret gods)* booty, spoils; plunder; **3** *(vergeløst offer, villdyrs ~)* prey; *han ble et lett ~ for dem* he fell an easy prey to them; **II** *vb* **1** change, exchange; *han ~t bort hesten sin for en ku* he exchanged his horse for a cow; *jeg ~t plass med ham* I changed seats *(OBS fl)* with him; **2** *(byttehandle)* barter. **byttehandel** *sb* barter, exchange. **bytting** *sb* **1** *(byttehandel)* exchange; **2** *(forbyttet person)* changeling.

bæ *interj, sb* baa.

bær *sb* berry. **bærtur** *sb: dra på ~* go berry-picking.

bærbar *adj* portable; *data også* lap-top. **bære** *vb* **1** carry; *han bar (på) en kurv* he carried a basket (in his hand); **2** *(holde oppe)* carry, support; *beina nektet å ~ henne lenger* her legs refused to carry her further; **3** *(holde ut, tåle)* bear; *han bar sin sorg tålmodig* he bore his sorrow patiently; **4** *(fig: ha)* bære; *hun ~r et stolt navn* she bears a proud name; **5** *(uttrykk) ~ over med* bear with; make allowances for; *~ seg (dvs klage)* carry on; *hun bar seg over levekostnadene* she carried on about the cost of living; *~ seg at a) (oppføre seg)* behave; *b) ~ seg at med* go/set about; *han visste ikke hvordan han skulle ~ seg at med det* he did not know how to set about it. **bærer** *sb* carrier; *(på hotell, jernbane etc)* porter.

bøddel *sb* executioner, hangman.

bøffel *sb* buffalo.

bøk *sb* beech.

bøkker *sb* cooper.

bølge 1 *sb* wave; *stor ~* sea; **2** *vb* wave; *(gå i bølger)* undulate. **bølge|blikk** *sb* corrugated iron. **~kam** *sb* crest (of a wave). **bølget** *adj* wavy; *~ hår* wavy hair.

bøling *sb* herd, livestock.

bølle *sb* hooligan, rough.

bønn *sb* **1** *(anmodning)* request; *(innstendig ~)* appeal, entreaty; *hun gjentok sin ~ om hjelp* she repeated her appeal/request for help; **2** *(til Gud)* prayer; *(bord~)* grace; *han bad en ~ for henne* he said a prayer for her.

bønne *sb* bean.

bønn|falle *vb* entreat, implore; *hun ~falt ham om å vise medlidenhet* she implored/entreated him to show mercy. **~høre** *vb* grant, hear; lend an ear to. **~lig** *adj* appealing, imploring. **~skriv** *sb* petition.

bør *sb* **1** *(byrde)* burden, load, weight; **2** *(medvind)* fair wind.

børs *sb* exchange.

børse *sb* gun. **børse|kolbe** *sb* butt-end of a gun. **~løp, ~pipe** *sb* gun-barrel.

børste *sb/vb* brush.

bøss *sb (oppsop, søppel)* sweepings; *ikke det* ~ not a bit.

bøsse *sb* **1** *(til pepper, salt etc)* castor; **2** *(spare~)* moneybox.

bøte *vb (reparere)* mend, repair; *(lappe også)* patch; ~ *for* pay/suffer for; ~ *på* remedy; ~ *på en mangel* remedy a defect. **bøtelegge** *vb* fine.

bøtte *sb* bucket, pail.

bøye A *sb (liv~ etc)* buoy; **B** *vb* **1** bend, bow; ~ *av* turn off; *han bøyde hodet/nakken* he bowed his head/neck; *hun bøyde knærne* she bent her knees; **2** *gram:* ~ *et substantiv* decline a noun; ~ *et verb* conjugate a verb; **3** ~ *seg* bend; *(fig: gi etter)* give in; yield; *han bøyde seg frem* he bent forward; *hun bøyde seg (ned) for å ta opp blomsten* she bent down/stooped to pick up the flower. **bøyelig** *adj* flexible, pliant. **bøyelighet** *sb* flexibility, pliancy.

bøyle *sb* hoop.

bøyning *sb gram* inflection; *av sb* declension; *av vb* conjugation.

både *konj:* ~ ... *og* both ... and *(bare om to)* ~ *England og Frankrike* both England and France; ~ *England, Frankrike og Italia forsøkte* England, France, and Italy, all tried.

bål *sb* fire; *sankthans~* bonfire; *(som middelaldersk straff)* the stake; *hun døde på ~et* she died at the stake.

bånd *sb* **1** *(snor)* string; **2** *(til hund)* lead, leash; *hunder skal føres/holdes i* ~ *i parken* dogs must be kept on a lead/leash in the park; **3** *(til pynt)* ribbon; *det var et blått* ~ *rundt konfektesken* there was a blue ribbon round the box of chocolates; **4** *(lim~, magnet~ etc)* tape; **5** *fig: vennskaps~* bonds/ties of friendship. **bånd|drev** *sb data* tape drive. **~kassett** *sb* (tape) cartridge/cassette. **~lager** *sb data* tape storage. **~opptaker** *sb* tape recorder. **~skriver** *sb data* band printer. **~stasjon** *sb data* tape station.

båre 1 *(syke~)* stretcher; **2** *(lik~)* bier.

bås *sb (i fjøs)* box, stall.

båt *sb* boat; *de gikk i ~ene* they took to the boats; *med* ~ by boat. **båt|hvelv** *sb* overturned bottom. **~lengde** *sb* boat's length. **~rip(e)** *sb* gunwale. **båts|-hake** *sb* boathook; *(til tømmerfløting)* pike pole. **~mann** *sb* boatswain.

C

c *(bokstaven)* c.

C *fork* for *celsius*. **c., ca.** *fork* for *cirka)*.

camping *sb* camping. **~bil** *sb* motor-caravan; *US* camper. **~plass** *sb* camping ground/site. **~stol** *sb* camping stool. **~tur** *sb* camping trip; *dra på ~tur* go camping. **~tilhenger, ~vogn** *sb* caravan, trailer.

celeber *adj* celebrated, distinguished. **celebritet** *sb* celebrity.

celle *sb* cell. **celle|kjerne** *sb* nucleus. **~vev** *sb* cellular tissue.

cellist *sb* cellist. **cello** *sb* cello.

cellofan *sb* cellophane. **celluloid** *sb* celluloid. **cellulose** *sb* cellulose.

celsius *sb* centigrade; *20 grader* ~ 20 degrees centigrade.

centi- *pref* centi-. **centi|liter** *sb* centilitre. **~meter** *sb* centimetre.

cerebral parese *sb* cerebral palsy.

champagne *sb* champagne; *dgl* fizz.

champignon *sb* (edible) mushroom.

champion *sb* champion.

charme etc *se sjarm etc.*

charter|fly *sb* chartered aircraft. **~reise, ~tur** *sb* charter flight/trip. **chartre** *vb* charter.

chassis *sb* chassis.

chic *adj* chic, smart, stylish.

choke *sb/vb* choke.

cirka *adv* about, circa.

clutch *sb* clutch.

cockpit *sb* cockpit.

cocktail *sb* cocktail.

computer *sb data* computer, datamaskin. **computerstyrt** *adj* computer-controlled.

container *sb* **1** *(beholder)* container; **2** *(søppel~)* skip.

crawl *sb* crawl. **crawle** *vb* crawl; do/swim the crawl.

cup *sb* cup. **cup|finale** *sb* cup final; **~kamp** *sb* cup tie..

C-vitamin *sb* vitamin C.

D

d *(bokstaven)* d.

da I *adv* **1** *(den gang, på den tiden)* then; at that time; *~ var vi ennå unge* then we were still young; *nå og ~* now and then; now and again; **2** *(deretter, så)* then; *~ kom far tilbake* then my father came back; **3** *(i så fall)* then; if so; *~ bør du heller bli hjemme* then you had better stay at home; **4** *(altså)* then; *du vil gå ~* you want to go, then; **5** *(annen bruk) det var ~ deilig!* o, wasn't it wonderful! *du ~!* go on! *du kan ~ si det til meg* you may tell me, you know; *hun håper ~ å bli frisk* she does hope to recover; *ja ~, nei ~* oh yes, oh no; *nå~?* well? *vær stille ~!* do be quiet! **II** *konj* **1** *(dengang da)* when; *~ we were unge* when we were young; **2** *(nettopp da)* (just) as; *(akkurat) ~ vi skulle til å gå* (just) as we were about to start; **3** *(fordi) a)* as, since; *~ det var sent, skyndte vi oss* as it was late, we made haste; **4** *b) (i skrift brukes gjerne omskriving med -ing-form) ~ de hadde brukt opp alle pengene sine, måtte de gå hjem* having spent all their money they had to walk home; **5** *(etter nå) nå ~ han er frisk* now that he is well.

dabbe av *vb* flag; *interessen hans dabbet av* his interest was flagging.

dadda *sb* nanny, nurse.

daddel *sb* **1** *(frukt)* date; **2** *(kritikk)* blame. **dadle** *vb (klandre, kritisere)* blame.

dag *sb* day; *en ~ (i fortiden)* one dag; *en ~ (i fremtiden)* some day; *~ etter ~* day after day; *~ for ~* day by day; *~ ut og ~ inn* day after day; day in, day out; *~en derpå (etter rangel)* the morning after (the day before); *~en etter* the next day; the following day; *en vakker ~* one of these days; *etter to ~er* after two days; *fjorten ~er* a fortnight; *forleden ~* the other day; *fra ~ til ~* from day to day; *jeg gir en god ~* I do not care a fig; *i ~* today; *i ~ om åtte ~er* this day week; *i gamle ~er* in former times; in the old days; *i tre ~er* for three days; *i våre ~er* in our day; nowadays; *komme for en ~* come to light; *legge for ~en* demonstrate, show; *midt på ~en* at noon; in the middle of the day; *nå til ~s* nowadays; *om ~en* by day; in the daytime; *tolv pund (om) ~en* £12 a day; *om tre ~er* in three days; *på hennes gamle ~er* in her old age; *sent/tidlig på ~en* late/early in the day; *ved høylys ~* in broad daylight.

dag|blad *sb* newspaper, daily. **~bok** *sb* **1** diary; **2** *(regnskapsbok)* journal; **3** *(på skole)* class/form register. **~driver** *sb* idler; loafer. **~drøm** *sb* day-dream. **dagevis** *adv: i ~* for days (on end). **dag|gry** *sb* dawn, daybreak; *ved ~gry* at dawn/daybreak. **~hjelp** *sb* daily. **~hjem** *sb* day nursery. **daglig** *adj, adv* **1** *(som skjer hver dag)* daily; every day; *min ~e (spaser)tur* my daily walk; *tre ganger ~* three times a day; *den ~e tralten* the daily routine; the old rut; **2** *(alminnelig, dagligdags)* everyday; *~ antrekk* daily/ordinary clothes. **daglig|dags** *adj* everyday; *en ~ hendelse* an everyday occurence; *~dags ord/uttrykk* colloquial word/phrase. **~liv** *sb* everyday life. **~stue** *sb* living-room, sitting-room; *også* drawing-room. **daglønn** *sb* day's wage(s). **dags|aktuell** *adj* of current interest. **~arbeid** *sb* day's work. **~avis** *sb* daily. **~lys** *sb* daylight; *i fullt ~lys* in broad daylight. **~marsj** *sb* day's march. **~nytt** *sb* news (of the day); *vi får ~* here is the news. **~orden** *sb* agenda. **~presse** (*sb* daily) press. **~reise** *sb* day's journey. **~tur** *sb* day's outing. **dagstøtt** *sb* every day. **dagsverk** *sb* day's work. **dagtog** *sb* day train.

dakapo *sb (~nummer)* encore.

dal *sb* valley.

dale *vb* **1** *(senke seg jevnt)* go down; sink; *~ ned på* descend on; **2** *(avta)* decline, decrease; wane.

dalevende *adj* contemporary; then living.

dam *sb* **A 1** *(demning)* dam; **2** *(basseng etc)* reservoir; **3** *(mindre ~)* pond; **4** *(pytt)* pool; **B** *(spill)* draughts *(fl)*. **dam|brett** *sb* draughtboard. **~brikke** *sb* draughtsman.

dame *sb* **1** lady; *~nes vals* ladies' choice; *mine ~r (og herrer)!* ladies (and gentlemen)! **2** *(bord~, dansepartner)* partner. Se også *kvinne*. **dame|bekjentskap** *sb* lady friend. **~bind** *sb* sanitary napkin/towel. **~frisør** *sb* ladies' hairdresser. **~garderobe** *sb* ladies' cloakroom. **~selskap** *sb* ladies' party; *i ~selskap* in the company of ladies. **~skredder** *sb* ladies' tailor. **~toalett** *sb* Ladies. **~underbukser** *sb fl* knickers. **~undertøy** *sb koll* ladies' underwear, lingerie.

damp *sb* vapour; *(vann~ især)* steam; *for full ~* at full speed. **damp|bad** *sb* steam bath. **~båt/~skip** *sb* steamship, steamer. **dampe** *vb* steam; *~ på (pipe o.l.)* puff at. **damper** *sb* steamer, steamship. **damp|fløyte** *sb* hooter. **~kjel(e)** *sb* (steam-)boiler. **~koke** *vb* steam. **~maskin** *sb* steam-engine. **~trykk** *sb* steam pressure. **~turbin** *sb* steam turbine. **~veivals** *sb* steam roller.

dank *sb: drive ~* idle about; dawdle, loaf.

danne *vb* **1** form; make (up); frame, shape; *det ble ~t (en) ny regjering* a new government was formed; **2** *(utvikle seg)* develop. **dannelse** *sb* **1** *(tilblivelse)* formation; *under ~* in the process of formation; **2** *(kultur)* culture, education; refinement. **dannet** *adj* **1** *(i det ytre)* well-behaved, well-mannered; polite; **2** *(kultivert)* cultured, well-bred; *~ fremtreden* good manners; *dannede mennesker* people of culture/cultured people.

dans *sb* **1** dance; *en ~ på roser* a bed of roses; *gå på ~* go to a dance; *ut/ute av ~en* out of the running; **2** *(det å danse)* dancing; *etter middagen var det ~* there was dancing after dinner. **danse** *vb* dance; *~ etter hennes pipe* dance to her pipe/tune; *~ vals* dance the waltz; dance waltzes; *han danser dårlig/godt* he is a poor/good dancer. **danser(inne)** *sb* dancer. **danse|-sal** *sb* ballroom. **~sko** *sb* dancing shoe; pump. **~skole** *sb* dancing school.

dask *sb* slap. **daske** *vb* slap.

data *sb fl* data.

data|bank *sb data* data bank. **~base** *sb data* data base. **~behandling** *sb data* data processing. **~buss** *sb data* data bus. **~kommunikasjon** *sb data* data communication. **~kraft** *sb data* computer/data utility. **~maskin** *sb data* computer. **~nett** *sb data* (data) network. **~operatør** *sb data* key punch operator. **~overføring** *sb data* data transfer/transmission. **~program** sb data computer program. **~registrering** *sb data* data recording. **~samband** *sb data* data circuit. **~sanering** *sb data* garbage collecting; shuffling. **~senter** *sb data* data (processing) center. **~sikkerhet** *sb data* data safety. **~sikring** *sb data* data protection. **~skilletegn** *sb data* unit separator. **~skjerm** *sb data* display device; visual display unit (VDU). **~snok** *sb data* hacker, snooper. **~tabell** *sb data* arra, **~vern** *sb data* data security.

datere *vb* date; *et brev (som var) datert 2. mars* a letter dated March 2nd.

datid *sb: en av datidens (dvs sin tids) største kvinner* one of the greatest women of that (of her) age/time.

dato *sb* date; *(om dag i måneden også)* day of the month; *hvilken ~ er det i dag* what's the date today; what day of the month is today; *av ny ~* recent; of recent date; *dags ~* this date; today's date; *fra ~* from date.

datter *sb* daughter; *hun er ~ av Mr S.* she is the daughter of Mr S. **~datter** *sb* granddaughter. **~sønn** *sb* grandson.

dau *adj dgl* **1** *(kjedelig)* dull; **2** *(slapp)* limp, listless; **3** se *død.*

daværende *adj* of that time; then; *(den) ~ eier* the then owner.

de I *pron* **1** *(personlig) a)* they; *b) (De i tiltale)* you; **2** *(påpekende)* those; the; *~ som* those who; *~ bøkene (der)* those books; *~ bøkene du kjøpte* the books you bought; **II** *(art foran adj)* the, those; *~ gamle bøkene* the old books; *~ innbudte* those invited; *~ rike* the rich; *~ tilstedeværende* those present.

debatt *sb* debate, discussion. **debattere** *vb* debate, discuss.

debet *sb* debit; *føre til (Deres) ~* place to (your) debit. **debitere** *vb* debit. **debitor** *sb* debtor.

debut *sb* début. **debutere** *sb* make one's début.

decennium *sb (tiår)* decade.

dedikasjon *sb* dedication. **dedisere** *vb* dedicate.

defaitisme *sb* defeatism.

defensiv *adj* defensive.

definerbar *adj* definable. **definere** *vb* define. **definisjon** *sb* definition.

deflasjon *sb* deflation.

De forente nasjoner the United Nations. **De forente stater** the United States.

degenerasjon *sb* degeneration. **degenerere** *vb* degenerate. **degenerert** *adj* degenerate.

degge for *vb* coddle, cosset, pamper, pet.

deig *sb* dough; *kake~ (også)* paste; *sette ~* prepare the dough.

deilig *adj* **1** *(vakker)* beautiful, lovely; *en ~ dag* a beautiful/lovely day; **2** *(herlig, vidunderlig)* lovely, wonderful; *~ vær* lovely/wonderful weather; **3** *(vel/-luktende, -smakende)* appetizing, delicious; *en ~ kake* a delicious cake.

deise *vb* **1** *~ ned* tumble down; **2** *~ til en* deal somebody a blow.

dekk *sb* **1** *(skips~)* deck; **2** *(bil~, sykkel~)* tyre; *US* tire. **dekke** *sb* **1** cover, covering; *under ~ av mørket* under cover of darkness; **2** *jf veidekke.*

dekke *vb* **1** *a)* cover; *snø ~t bakken* snow covered the ground; *krigsskip ~t landsettingen av invasjonsstyrken* warships covered the landing of the invading force; *sjekken ~r så vidt utgiftene mine* the cheque will just cover my expenses; *b) ~ bordet* lay the table; *det var dekket til tolv* covers were laid for twelve; **2** *(~ over, f.eks. feil)* gloss over; *~ til* cover up. **dekketøy** *sb koll* table linen.

dekorasjon *sb* **1** *(orden)* decoration; **2** *(utsmykning)* decoration; **3** *(dekorativ gjenstand)* ornament. **dekorativ** *adj* decorative, ornamental. **dekorere** *vb* decorate, ornament. Se også *pynte.*

del *sb* **1** *(av det hele)* part; *ved utdeling også* portion; *en ~ av det* part of it; *en ~ av historien er sann* part of the story is true; **2** *(andel, det som tilkommer en)* share; *min ~ av utgiftene* my share of the expenses; **3** *(ubestemt mengde) en ~* some; *en ~ gjester* some guests; *en ~ av gjestene* some of the guests; *for en ~ år siden* some years ago; **4** *en god/hel ~ a) (uten sb)* a good deal; (quite) a lot; *hun leser en god ~* she reads a good deal/quite a lot; *b) ~ (foran entallsord)* a great/good deal of; a lot of; *en god ~ smør* a great deal of butter; a lot of butter; *c) (foran flertallsord)* a great/good many; a number of; a lot/lots of; *en god ~ bøker* a great many books/quite a number of books; **5** *en av ~ene* one or the other; *for all ~* by all means; *for en ~* to some extent; in part; partly; *for min ~* as far as I am concerned; for my part; *i alle ~er* in every respect/way; *ingen av ~ene* neither (the one nor the other); *ha ~ i* have a share in; *ta ~ i* take part in; join in; *hun tok ~ i samtalen* she joined in the conversation; *jeg tok ~ i leken* I took part in the game. **delaktig** *adj: gjøre en ~ i en hemmelighet* let somebody into a secret; *være ~ i* be a party to. **delaktighet** *sb* participation; share; *(i forbrytelse)* complicity. **dele** *vb* **1** divide; *~ opp* cut into pieces; divide; *hun delte kaken i flere stykker* she divided the cake into several parts; *30 delt med 5 er 6* 30 divided by 5 is 6; *vi delte pengene likt mellom oss* we divided the money equally among/between us; **2** *~ ut a)* distribute; hand round/out; *læreren delte ut bøkene* the teacher distributed the books; *b) ~ ut i små porsjoner* dole out; **3** *(ha felles/sammen)* share; *vi delte værelse* we shared a room.

delegasjon *sb* delegation. **delegere** *vb* delegate. **delegert** *sb* delegate, deputy, representative.

delelig *adj* divisible.

delfin *sb* dolphin.

delikat *adj* **1** *(lekker)* delicious, tasty; *en ~ kake* a delicious cake; **2** *(vanskelig)* delicate; *en ~ sak* a delicate matter. **delikatesse** *sb* delicacy, dainty. **delikatesse|butikk, ~forretning** *sb* delicatessen; *US dgl* deli.

deling *sb* **1** *(det å dele)* dividing, sharing; **2** *(inndeling, oppdeling)* division, partition; *~en av Polen* the partition of Poland.

delje *vb: ~ til en* deal someone a blow.

dels *adv* in part; partly; *~ ved makt, ~ ved overtalelse* partly by force, and partly by persuasion; *~ på grunn av sykdom, ~ på grunn av fattigdom* what with illness and what with poverty. **delta** *vb* participate; take part; *han deltok i samtalen* he took part in the conversation; *hun deltok i et kurs* she attended a course; *vi deltok i leken* we joined in the game. **deltakelse** *sb* **1** *(medvirkning)* participation; **2** *(medfølelse)* concern, sympathy; *alle var fulle av ~* everybody was full of concern. **deltakende** *adj* **1** *(medvirkende)* participating; **2** *(medfølende)* sympathetic; *adv* sympathetically. **deltaker** *sb* **1** *(i en forretning)* partner; **2** *(i fest, møte etc)* participant; **3** *(i konkurranse)* competitor; **4** *(i reise, tur etc)* member of the party. **deltid** *sb* part-time. **deltidsarbeid** *sb* part-time work. **delvis** *adv* in part; partly.

demagog *sb* demagogue. **demagogi** *sb* demagogy. **demagogisk** *sb* demagogic.

demarkasjonslinje *sb* line of demarkation.

dementere *vb* deny, disavow. **dementi** *sb* disavowal; official denial; *sende ut et ~* issue a denial.

demme *vb (~ opp)* dam, stem. **demning** *sb* **1** *(dam)* dam; **2** *(langs elv)* embankment; **3** *(mot sjøen)* dike.

demokrat *sb* democrat. **demokrati** *sb* democracy. **demokratisk** *adj* democratic.

demon *sb* demon. **demonisk** *adj* demoniac, demoniacal.

demonstrant *sb* demonstrator. **demonstrasjon** *sb* demonstration. **demonstrasjonstog** *sb* demonstration march. **demonstrativ** *adj* demonstrative. **demonstrere** *vb* demonstrate; *stundom* picket.

dempe *vb* calm, moderate, subdue; *~t lys* dim/subdued light; *han ~t stemmen* he lowered his voice.

demre *vb* dawn; *det demrer for meg* it dawns on me. **demring** *sb (grålysning)* dawn.

den, det *pron* **I** *(personlig)* it; *(om dyr, når kjønnet er kjent, ofte)* he, she; **II** *(påpekende)* **1** that; the; *se på den mannen/det treet* look at that man/that tree; *den idioten!* the idiot! **2** *(foran sb med relativsetning etter)* the; *den boken (som) du kjøpte* the book you bought; *den som a) (om personer)* the boy (girl, man, woman, person etc) who; the one who; *bokl* he/she who; *jeg gav boken til den som kom først* I gave the book to the boy/girl who came først; *han bad den som kom sist lukke døren* ha asked the one who came last to close the door; *b) (om ting)* the one that; *denne boken er ikke den jeg så i går* this book is not the one (that) I saw yesterday; **3** *(foran adj)* the; *det gamle huset* the old house.

denaturert *adj: ~ sprit* methylated spirit.

dengang se *da* og *gang*.

denge *vb* beat; thrash, whip; lick.

denne, dette *pron* **1** *(etterfulgt av sb)* this; *denne veien)* this way; *dette eplet* this apple; **2** *(uten sb) a) om personer)* he, she; *(den sistnevnte)* the latter; *b) (om ting)* this one; *hvilken bok/hvilket eple vil du ha? Jeg vil ha denne/dette* what book/what apple will you have? I will have this one.

departement *sb* ministry, office; department; *landbruksdepartementet* ≈ (the) Ministry of Agriculture; *utenriksdepartementet* ≈ the Foreign Office; *US* (the) State Department.

deponere *vb* deposit. **depositum** *sb* deposit.

der *adv* **1** there; *~ bort(e)* over there; *~ inn(e)* in there; *~ ned(e)* down there; *~ opp(e)* up there; *~ ut(e)* out there; **2** *den/det ~* that; *den boken ~* that book; **3** *de ~* those; *de bøkene ~* those books; **4** *(der hvor)* where; *jeg fant bøkene ~ jeg la dem* I found the books where I left them.

dere *pron* you. **deres** *pron* **I** *(som dere eier/har)* **1** *(foran sb)* your; *bøkene ~* your books; **2** *(stående alene)* yours; *bøkene er ~* the books are yours; **II** *(som de eier/har)* **1** *(foran sb)* their; *~ hus* their house; **2** *(stående alene)* theirs; *huset er ~* the house is theirs. **Deres** *pron* your, yours (brukes på samme måte som *deres I*).

deretter *adv* **1** *(etterpå)* afterwards; after that; *~ gikk vi vår vei* after that/which we walked away; *året ~* the next/following year; the year after that; *kort ~* soon/shortly afterwards; **2** *(i samsvar med det)* accordingly; *han handlet ~* he acted accordingly; *resultatet ble ~* the result was as might be expected.

derfor *adv* **1** *(av den grunn)* so, therefore; that's why; *han var ikke hjemme, (og) ~ gikk jeg igjen* he was not at home, and so/therefore I went away again; *det var ~ jeg gjorde det* that was why I did it; **2** *(likevel, til tross for)* still; for all that; *~ kan det (jo) godt være sant* it may be true for all that.

derfra *adv* from there; *det er 50* miles *~ til London* it is 50 miles from there to London; *vi gikk ~ klokken ett* we left there at one o'clock.

derimot *adv* on the other hand.

deriblant, derimellom *adv* among them; including.

dermed *adv* **1** *(med det) ~ basta!* and that is that! *~ var det forbi* that was the end of it; *~ var saken avgjort* that settled the matter; **2** *(med disse ord)* so saying; *~ forlot han værelset* so saying he left the room.

dernest *adv* next, then; in the next place.

derom *adv: ~ tier historien* that is not on record.

deromkring *adv* **1** *(der i nærheten)* somewhere near there; *i Oxford eller ~* at Oxford or somewhere near there; **2** *(omtrent)* thereabout(s); more or less; *klokken to eller ~* at two o'clock or thereabout(s); *20 pund eller ~* £20 more or less.

derpå *adv* after that; then, next; *dagen ~* the next

day; *(etter rangel)* the morning after (the day before).

dersom *konj* if; in case.

dertil *adv* **1** *(til det)* for that (purpose); *~ kreves penger* for that money is necessary; **2** *(til dit)* there; *herfra og ~* from here to there; **3** *(dessuten)* besides; *~ kommer at det er for dyrt* besides it is too expensive.

derunder *adv* less; *5 pund eller ~* £5 or less.

desavuere *vb* repudiate, disavow.

desember *sb* December; *(den) første ~* the first of December; Dec. 1st.

desentralisere *vb* decentralize. **desentralisering** *sb* decentralization.

desillusjonere *vb* disillusion. **desillusjonering** *sb* disillusion; disillusionment.

desimal *sb* decimal. **desimal|brøk** *sb* decimal fraction. **~komma** *sb* decimal point *(som i engelsktalende land = punktum)*. **~notasjon** *sb data* decimal notation. **~regning** *sb* decimal arithmetic. **~system** *sb* decimal system. **desimeter** *sb* decimetre.

desinfeksjonsmiddel *sb* disinfectant. **desinfisere** *vb* disinfect. **desinfisering** *sb* disinfection.

desorientert *adj* bewildered, confused; perplexed.

desperasjon *sb* desperation. **desperat** *adj* **1** *(fortvilet)* desperate; *en ~ kamp* a desperate struggle; **2** *(rasende)* furious.

despot *sb* despot, tyrant. **despoti** *sb* despotism. **despotisk** *adj* despotic.

dess *adv* se *desto*.

dessert *sb* sweet; *(særlig om frukt)* dessert; *US (om all dessert)* dessert.

destillasjon *sb* distillation. **destillasjons|anlegg** *sb* distillery; *petro etc* distillation plant. **~rest** *sb petro etc* residue. **~tårn** *sb petro* column still; distillation column/tower. **destillere** *vb* distil. **destillering** *sb* distillation.

desto *adv* (all) the; *~ bedre* all the better; *jo ... ~, ~ ... ~ ...* the ... the; *jo større de er, ~ hardere faller de* the bigger they come, the harder they fall; *ikke ~ mindre* nevertheless; none the less.

dessuten *adv* besides, moreover; in addition.

dessverre *adv* unfortunately; I am sorry (to say); I am afraid; *jeg kan ~ ikke komme* I am afraid/I am sorry (to say that) I cannot come; unfortunately, I cannot come; *vi må ~ meddele Dem at* we regret to inform you that.

det A se *den*; **B** *(i andre sammenhenger)* **I** *(svarer til engelsk)* it; **1** *(pers pron, viser til et sb i intetkjønn) hun åpnet brevet og leste ~* she opened the letter and read it; **2** *(ubest pron, om avstand, tid, vær, temperatur etc) ~ er kaldt/sent* it is cold/late; *~ regner* it is raining; **3** *(brukt som foreløpig subjekt når det virkelige subjekt er en infinitiv eller en hel setning) ~ er ikke lett å tilgi sine fiender* it is not easy to forgive our enemies; *~ er en hemmelighet hvor han har vært* it is a secret where he has been; **4** *(brukt til å fremheve et følgende ord i setninger som: ~ er/var jeg etc som...) ~ er ditt råd vi trenger* it is your advice we want; *~ var jeg som gjorde ~* it was I who did it; **II** *(påpekende, (trykksterkt pron)* that, those; *~ visste jeg ikke* I did not know that; *er ~ brødrene dine* are those your brothers; *hvem bor i ~ huset* who lives in that house; **III** *(det som)* what; *han fortalte meg ~ han visste* he told me what he knew; *er ~ sant som de sier* is it true what they say; *gjør ~ du mener er riktig* do what you think is right; **IV** *(svarer til engelsk)* so; **1** *(etter verb som* believe, do, hope, say, suppose, tell, think*) jeg håper ~* I hope so; *jeg sa ~ til ham* I told him so; *jeg tror ~* I think so; **2** *(i setninger av typen: ~ gjør/gjorde ... også) han er glad i idrett, og ~ er jeg også* he loves sport, and so do I; *de har mange bøker, og ~ har vi også* they have many books, and so have we; *hun kan svømme, og ~ kan jeg også* she can swim, and so can I; **V** *(som foreløpig subjekt når det virkelige subjekt er et sb eller et pron, oftest med en form av* to be *eller* appear, need, seem + to be*)* there; *~ er/finnes* there is/are; *~ var/fantes* there was/were; *~ er ingen regel uten unntagelse* there is no rule without an exception; *~ er noen på døren* there is somebody at the door; *~ var en gang en konge* once upon a time there was a king; **VI** *(når ~ egentlig viser tilbake på personer eller på ting i flertall)* he, she, they; *(hvem eier de bøkene?) ~ er mine (bøker)* (whose books are those?) they are my books; they are mine; *(hvem er de guttene?) ~ er brødrene mine* (who are those boys?) they are my brothers; *(hvem er den piken?) ~ er søsteren min* (who is that girl?) she is my sister; **VII** *(svarer til engelsk)* the; **1** *(adjektivets bestemte artikkel)*; *~ gamle huset* the old house; **2** *(foran et sb med en relativsetning etter) her er ~ brevet jeg fortalte deg om* here is the letter I told you of; **VIII** *(oversettes ikke)* **1** *(foreløpig subjekt ved andre verb enn* to be*) ~ brøt ut krig* a war broke out; *~ ble bygd veier og jernbaner* roads and railways were built; **2** *(i svar) er de rike? nei, ~ er de ikke* are they rich? no, they are not; *ser du henne ofte? ja, ~ det gjør jeg* do you often see her? yes, I do; **3** *(om motsetninger) han kom, men ~ gjorde ikke hun* he came, but she did not; **4** *(ved verb som* forget, know, remember, tell *etc) ~ visste jeg ikke* I didn't know; *han har fortalt meg ~* he has told me; **5** *(ved en del upersonlige uttrykk) ~ lyktes (for) meg* I succeeded; *~ er best jeg går* I had better go; *~ gleder meg å høre* I am glad to hear that.

detalj *sb* detail; *beskrive/forklare i ~er* describe/explain in detail; *gå i ~er* gå/enter into details; *selge i ~* sell (by) retail. **detaljert** *adj, pp* detailed; *en ~ beskrivelse* a detailed description. **detalj|handel** *sb* retail trade. **~handler, detaljist** *sb* retail dealer, retailer. **~pris** *sb* retail price.

detektiv *sb* detective. **~roman** *sb* detective novel.

detronisere *vb* dethrone.

dette, se *denne*.

devaluere *vb* devalue. **devaluering** *sb* devaluation.

diabolsk *adj* diabolic(al).

diadem *sb* diadem.

diagnose *sb* diagnosis; *stille ~* diagnose; make a diagnosis. **diagnostisere** *vb* diagnose.

diagonal *adj, sb* diagonal. **diagonalt** *adv* diagonally.

diagram *sb* diagram, figure, graph.

diakon *sb* male nurse. **diakonisse** *sb* nursing sister.

dialekt *sb* dialect. **dialektisk** *adj* dialectal.

dialog *sb* dialogue. **dialogform** *sb data* conversational mode; interactive mode.

diamant *sb* diamond.

diameter *sb* diameter. **diametral** *adj* diametrical; *en ~ motsetning* a diametrical contrast. **diametralt** *adv* diametrically; *et ~ motsatt syn* a diametrically opposite view.

diaré *sb* diarrhoea.

die 1 *sb: gi ~* suckle, nurse; **2** *vb* suckle; nurse. Jf *amme 2.*

diesel|motor *sb* diesel engine. **~olje** *sb* diesel oil.

diett *sb* **1** *(spesialkost)* diet; *holde/være på ~* be on a diet; *sette på ~* put on a diet; *streng ~* strict diet; **2** *(kostpenger)* (daily) allowance.

differanse *sb* difference.

diffus *adj* diffuse.

difteri *sb* diphtheria.

diftong *sb* diphthong.

diger *adj* big, bulky, enormous, huge; *en ~ skrøne* a corker.

digital *adj data etc* digital. **digitalisere** *vb data etc* digitize.

digresjon *sb* digression; *fortape seg i ~er* digress, meander.

dike *sb (demning, grøft)* dike. Se også *demning.*

dikkedarer *sb fl* fuss.

dikt *sb* poem; *koll* poetry, verse. **diktafon** *sb* dictaphone. **diktat** *sb* **1** dictation; *skrive ~* write dictation; **2** *(påbud)* dictate. **diktator** *sb* dictator. **diktatorisk** *adj* dictatorial; *adv* dictatorially. **diktatur** *sb* dictatorship. **dikte** *vb* compose, write; *(skrive vers)* write poetry; *~ opp* fabricate, invent. **dikter 1** *(lyriker)* poet; **2** *(forfatter)* writer, author. **diktere** *vb* dictate. **diktning** *sb* **1** *(det å dikte)* writing, composition; **2** *(dikterverker)* works; **3** *(diktekunst)* literature; *fortellende ~* fiction; *lyrisk ~* poetry; **4** *(oppdiktning)* fabrication, fiction.

dilemma *sb* dilemma, quandary.

dilettant *sb* amateur, dabber; *(især nedsettende)* dilettante. **dilettantisk** *adj* amateurish.

diligence *sb* stage-coach.

dill *sb* **1** *(krydderurt)* dill; **2** *(tøys)* nonsense.

dilla *sb* delirium tremens; *dgl* the jim-jams.

dilt *sb* trot, jogtrot. **dilte** *vb* trot; jogtrot.

dimensjon *sb* dimension.

diminuitiv *adj* diminutive.

din, ditt, dine *pron* **1** *(foran sb)* your; *sykkelen ~* your bicycle/bike; **2** *(uten sb etter)* yours; *sykkelen er ~* the bicycle/bike is yours; **3** *~ tosk!* you fool!

dingle *vb* dangle, swing.

dings *sb* gadget, contraption; what d'you-call-it.

diplom *sb* diploma. **diplomat** *sb* diplomat, diplomatist. **diplomati** *sb* diplomacy. **diplomatisk** *adj* diplomatic.

direksjon *sb* board of directors; directorate, management.

direkte I *adj* direct; *~ skatter* direct taxes; *en ~ etterkommer* a direct descendant; *i ~ linje* in a direct line; **II** *adv* **1** *(umiddelbart)* directly; *~ avhengig av* directly dependent on; *bli ~ påvirket av* be directly influenced by; **2** *(uten omvei eller stans)* direct, straight; *hun drog ~ til Liverpool* she went direct/straight to Liverpool. **direkte|fil** *sb data* random file. **~lager** *sb data* random access memory (RAM)/storage.

direktør *sb* **1** *(i offentlig institusjon, medlem av styre)* director; **2** *(i privat selskap)* manager; *administrerende ~* managing director.

dirigent *sb* **1** *(orkester~)* conductor; *(jazzorkester~)* leader; *(militær~)* bandmaster; **2** *(på et møte)* chairman; *hun var ~* she took the chair; she was in the chair. **dirigere 1** *(musikk)* conduct; **2** *(være møteleder)* be in the chair; take the chair; **3** *(lede, styre)* direct; *politimannen dirigerte trafikken* the policeman directed the traffic; **4** *data* route.

dirk *sb* picklock.

dirre *vb* quiver, vibrate.

dis *sb (tåke)* haze.

disharmoni *sb* discord, discordance. **disharmonisk** *adj* discordant, dissonant.

disig *adj* hazy, misty.

disiplin *sb* **1** *(orden, tukt)* discipline; *holde ~* maintain discipline; **2** *(fagområde)* subject. **disiplinert** *adj* disciplined. **disippel** *sb* disciple.

disk *sb* **1** *(bord, skranke etc)* counter; **2** *data* disk, diskette. **diske** *vb* **1** *~ opp med* serve; place on the table; **2** *dgl = diskvalifisere.* **diskett** *sb data* diskette. **diskett|klaff** *sb data* drive door. **~konvolutt, ~omslag** *sb data* diskette cover. **~stasjon** *sb data* diskette drive. **~åpning** *sb data* slot.

diskontere *vb* discount. **diskonto** *sb* bank rate; *forhøye/sette ned diskontoen* increase/reduce the bank rate.

diskos *sb* discus; *kaste ~* throw the discus. **diskoskast(ing)** *sb sport* the discus throw.

diskotek *sb* **1** *(platesamling)* record library; **2** *(med dans)* discotheque.

diskresjon *sb* **1** *(takt)* tact; **2** *(taushet)* secrecy; *man kan stole på hennes ~* you can rely on her secrecy. **diskret** *adj* discreet, tactful; *(om farger)* quiet.

diskriminere *vb* discriminate against. **diskriminerende** *adj* discriminating. **diskriminering** *sb* discrimination.

diskusjon *sb* **1** *(uenighet)* argument, dispute; **2** *(drøfting, samtale)* discussion; **3** *(offentlig debatt)* debate. **diskutere** *vb* **1** *(utveksle meninger)* argue; **2** *(drøfte uten strid)* discuss; **3** *(offentlig)* debate.

diskvalifikasjon *sb* disqualification. **diskvalifisere** *vb* disqualify.

dispensasjon *sb* exemption; *vi fikk ~* we were granted an exemption; *jeg søkte om ~* I applied for an exemption.

disponent *sb* manager.

disponere *vb* **1** *(ha til rådighet)* ~ *over* have at one's disposal; have the disposal of; **2** *(bruke)* use; make use of; **3** *(ordne stoff i artikkel, foredrag etc)* arrange; organize, plan; **4** *(~ for sykdom)* make susceptible. **disponibel** *adj* free, available; at one's disposal. **disposisjon** *sb* **1** *(rådighet)* disposal; *til din* ~ at your disposal; **2** *(arrangement)* arrangement; *treffe disposisjoner* make arrangements; take steps; **3** *(ordning av stoff i artikkel, foredrag etc)* arrangement, framework, plan; **4** *(anlegg for)* predisposition to.

disse *pron* these; *(især om de sist nevnte)* the latter.

dissens *sb* dissent, disagreement; *under* ~ with dissenting votes. **dissenter** *sb* nonconformist. **dissenter|kirke** *sb* **1** *(menighet)* Free Church; Nonconformist Church; **2** *(bedehus)* chapel. **~prest** *sb* minister.

dissonans *sb* discord, dissonance.

distanse *sb* distance. **distansere** *vb (gå, løpe fortere enn)* outdistance, outstrip.

distingvert *adj* distinguished, distinguished-looking. **distinksjon** *sb (på uniform)* badge (of rank); *(på ermet)* chevron, stripe(s). **distinkt** *adj* distinct.

distrahere *vb* distract. **distraksjon** *sb* absence of mind, absentmindedness. **distré** *adj* absent-minded.

distribuere *vb* distribute. **distribuering, distribusjon** *sb* distribution.

distrikt *sb* district, area; neighbourhood, region.

dit *adv* there; *jeg gikk ~ i går* I went there yesterday; *det var ~ jeg ville* it was where I wanted to get to.

ditt *pron: ~ og datt* this and that; this, that and the other; one thing and another. Jf *din.*

ditto *adv* ditto; the same.

divan *sb* couch, divan.

divergere *vb* diverge.

diverse *adj* sundry, various; ~ *saker/utgifter* sundries; *av ~ grunner* for various reasons; *ved ~ anledninger* on sundry occasions.

dividende *sb* dividend. **dividere** *vb* divide; *ti dividert med fem er to* ten (divided) by five is two; five into ten is two. **divisjon** *sb* division. **divisor** *sb* divisor.

djerv *adj* bold, brave, fearless. **djervhet** *sb* boldness, courage.

djevel *sb* devil, fiend; *djevelen* the Devil; Satan. **djevelsk** *adj* devilish, diabolic(al), fiendish. Jf *jævlig.* **djevelskap** *sb* devilry, devilment.

do *sb* lavatory; water-closet.

dobbe *sb (på fiskesnøre)* float; *US* bobber.

dobbelt *adj* double, twofold; ~ *så mye/god* twice as much/good; *~vinduer, ~e vinduer* double windows; *det ~e* twice as much; double the amount; *en ~ grunn til å gjøre det* a twofold reason for doing it; *jeg er ~ så gammel som han* I am twice as old as he/twice his age. **dobbelt|gjenger** *sb* double. **~knappet** *adj* double--breasted. **~løpet** *adj* double-barrelled. **~spent** *adj* double-breasted. **~spill** *sb* double-dealing. **doble** *vb (i bridge)* double.

dog *adv* **1** *(likevel)* still, yet; **2** *(imidlertid)* however.

dogg(e) se *dugg(e).*

dogmatisk *adj* dogmatic. **dogmatiker** *sb* dogmatist. **dogme** *sb* dogma.

dokk *sb* dock; *Londons ~er* the London docks.

dokke etc se *dukke etc.*

dokksette *vb* dock.

doktor *sb* doctor. **~grad** *sb* doctor's degree.

doktrine *sb* doctrine. **doktrinær** *adj* doctrinaire.

dokument *sb* document. **dokumentarfilm** *sb* documentary (film). **dokumentarisk** *adj* documentary. **dokumentere** *vb* document; prove. **dokument|mappe** *sb* briefcase; portfolio, attaché case. **~register** *sb data* directory.

dolk *sb* dagger. **dolke** *vb* stab. **dolkestøt** *sb* stab.

dom *sb* **1** *(i kriminalsak)* sentence; *avsi ~ over* pass sentence upon; *fellende ~* conviction; *han fikk en hard ~* he received a heavy sentence; **2** *(i sivilsak)* judg(e)ment; **3** *(mening)* opinion, judg(e)ment. **dom|felle** *vb* pass sentence upon. **~fellelse** *sb* conviction, judg(e)ment. **~felt** *sb* convict.

dominere *vb* **1** *(ha innflytelse/herske over)* dominate; *de sterke ~r de svake* the strong dominate the weak; **2** *(ved vold eller urimelighet)* domineer; *gutter ~r stundom småsøstrene og småbrødrene sine* boys sometimes domineer over their younger sisters and brothers.

domkirke *sb* cathedral.

dommedag *sb* the Day of Judgement. **dommer** *sb* **1** judge; **2** *(i høyere domstoler)* justice; **3** *(freds~)* magistrate; Justice of the Peace; **4** *(i baseball, cricket, golf, tennis)* umpire; **5** *(i fotball)* referee; **6** *(vedkapproing, utstilling, veddeløp)* judge.

dompap *sb* bullfinch.

domprost *sb* dean.

domstol *sb* court (of justice); law-court.

dongeribukser *sb fl* dungarees, jeans.

donkraft *sb* jack.

dorme *vb* doze.

dorsk *adj* sluggish. **dorskhet** *sb* sluggishness.

dose *sb* dose; *for stor ~, over~* overdose.

dossere *vb* bank. **dossering** *sb* bank.

dott *sb* **1** *(hår~, ull~)* flock, tuft; **2** *(høy~, sky~)* wisp; **3** *(person)* weakling.

doven *adj* lazy, idle; *(om drikk)* stale. **doven|peis** *sb* lazybones. **~skap** *sb* laziness. **dovne seg** *vb* laze, idle.

dra *vb* **1** *(hale, trekke)* draw; *~ etter seg (ha til følge)* have the result that; result in; *~ i tvil* question; *~ innpå* gain on; *~ kjensel på* recognize; *~ nytte av* profit by; turn to account; *~ på (gå fort eller fortere)* hurry (on); *~ på (slepe på)* drag, haul; *~ seg unna/vekk* take oneself off; *~ til (slå)* deal/fetch a blow; hit; *~ ut (trekke i langdrag)* drag on; **2** *(reise)* go, leave; *~ hjemmefra* leave home; *~ sin vei* go away; *~ tilbake* go back; return; *~ utenlands* go abroad; **3** *~ seg* idle, loaf; *gå og ~ seg* idle about; loaf; *ligge og ~ seg* idle in bed.

drabantby *sb* satellite town; *også* dormitory town. **drabantbyboer** *sb* commuter.

drabelig *adj* big, colossal, enormous, tremendous.

draft *sb sjø* chart.

drag *sb* **1** *(ånde~)* breath; **2** *(av sigarett etc)* puff; **3**

(slurk) draught; *han tømte glasset i ett* ~ he emptied the glass in/at one draught.

drage *sb* **1** *(fabeldyr)* dragon; **2** *(av papir)* kite.

drakt *sb* **1** suit, clothes; **2** *(dames spaser~)* (tailor-made) suit; coat and shirt; **3** *(nasjonal~, spesiell ~)* costume.

dram *sb* dram, nip.

drama *sb* drama. **dramatiker** *sb* dramatist, playwright. **dramatisere** *vb* dramatize. **dramatisering** *sb* dramatization. **dramatisk** *adj* dramatic.

dranker *sb* drunkard.

drap *sb* manslaughter, murder; *overlagt* ~ wilful murder.

drasse (på) *vb dgl* drag (along).

drastisk *adj* drastic.

dratte ned *vb dgl* flop down.

dreie *vb* **1** *(snu)* turn; *han dreide om hjørnet* he turned the corner; *han dreide seg rundt* he turned round; **2** *hva dreier det seg om?* what is it all about? **3** *(~ på dreiebenk)* turn; **4** *(~ seg om en akse)* turn, revolve; **5** *(om vind)* change, shift. **dreiebenk** *sb* lathe. **dreier** *sb* turner.

drenere *vb* drain. **drenering** *sb* draining, drainage. **drenerings|hull** *sb petro etc* weep hole. **~rør** *sb* drainpipe.

drepe *vb* kill. **drepende** *adj* killing (også *fig*); mortal.

dress *sb* suit.

dressere *vb* train; *han dresserte hunden til å sitte på bakbeina* he trained the dog to sit on its hind legs.

drible *vb* dribble.

drift *sb* **1** *(av fabrikk)* operation, working; *~en av fabrikken* the operation of the factory; *komme i* ~ come into operation; *være i* ~ be working/running; *fabrikken er ute av* ~ the factory is not working/has stopped working; **2** *(~ for vær og vind)* drift; *komme i* ~ *(om skip)* break/go adrift; *være i* ~ be adrift; **3** *(naturgitt trang)* inclination, instinct, urge; *av egen* ~ on one's own initiative. **drifts|bestyrer** *sb* works manager. **~døgn** *sb petro* stream day. **~kapital** *sb* working capital. **~materiell** *sb* plant; *(ved jernbane)* rolling stock. **~omkostninger** *sb* working/operating costs/expenses. **~overskudd** *sb* trading/working profits. **~pause** *sb petro* turnaround. **~sikker** *adj* reliable. **~stans** *sb* shut-down; *(midlertidig forstyrrelse)* breakdown. **~utgifter** *sb fl* = *~omkostninger.*

drikk *sb* **1** *(noe som drikkes)* drink; *appelsinsaft er en deilig* ~ orange juice is a pleasant drink; **2** *(drikkevare)* beverage; **3** *(det å drikke)* drinking. **drikke 1** *sb* drink; *mat og* ~ food and drink; **2** *vb* drink; *drikk opp melken din* drink up your milk; ~ *ens skål* drink somebody's health; ~ *seg full* get drunk; ~ *seg utørst* drink one's fill; ~ *ut* drink up; empty one's glass; *han har drukket opp alle pengene sine* he has spent all his money on drink. **drikkepenger** *sb fl* tip, gratuity; *hun gav servitøren et pund i* ~ she tipped the waiter one pound. **drikkfeldig** *adj* addicted to drinking/drink.

drill *sb* **1** *(til boring)* drill; **2** *(eksersis)* drill; **3** *(i jordbruk)* drill. **drille** *vb* **1** *(bore)* drill; **2** *(eksersere)* drill; **3** *(radså)* drill.

drink *sb* drink.

driste *vb:* ~ *seg til* venture; dare to. **dristig** *adj* bold, daring. **dristighet** *sb* boldness, daring.

driv *sb* push, energy.

drivbenk *sb* hotbed; garden frame.

drive *vb* **1** *(jage)* drive; ~ *krøtter til torgs* drive cattle to market; **2** *(arbeide ivrig; presse til arbeid)* work (hard); *han ~r sine menn altfor hardt* he works his men too hard; **3** *(uttrykk)* ~ *dank* idle (about); loaf about; ~ *det langt/vidt* go far; ~ *en fabrikk* operate/run a factory; ~ *en gård* run/work a farm; ~ *et yrke* carry on a trade; ~ *forretning/hotell* run a business/hotel; ~ *frem* propel; ~ *frem planter* force plants; ~ *idrett* go in for sports; ~ *igjennom* carry/force through; ~ *maskiner (etc)* drive; *drevet med damp* driven by steam; ~ *med vind og strøm* drift, float; *båten drev nedover elven* the boat floated down the river; ~ *prisen i været* force up the price; ~ *på flukt* put to flight; rout; ~ *til fortvilelse* drive to despair; *gå og* ~ *(slentre)* stroll, saunter; *ligge og* ~ be adrift; *drivende kraft* prime mover.

driv|fjær *sb* mainspring. **~garn** *sb* drift-net. **~hjul** *sb* driver; driving-wheel. **~hus** *sb* glasshouse. **~is** *sb* drift-ice. **~kraft** *sb* motive power; driving force. **~stoff** *sb* fuel. **~tømmer** *sb* drift timber. **~ved** *sb* drift-wood. **~verdig** *adj petro* commercial.

drone *sb* drone.

dronning *sb* queen.

drops *sb koll* boiled sweets; drops; *US* hard candy.

drosje(bil) *sb* cab; taxi(-cab). **drosje|holdeplass** *sb* cab|rank, ~stand; taxi | rank, ~ stand. **~sjåfør** *sb* taxi-driver.

drue *sb* grape. **~klase** *sb* cluster of grapes.

drukken *adj* drunk, intoxicated; *(foran sb også)* drunken. **drukkenskap** *sb* drunkenness.

drukne 1 *vt* drown; *han ville* ~ *kattungene* he wanted to drown the kittens; **2** *vi* be drowned; *holde på å* ~ be drowning; *hun falt i vannet og ~t* she fell into the water and (was) drowned/got drowned; *han ~t i mengden* he was lost in the crowd. **drukning** *sb* drowning.

dryg se *drøy*.

drypp *sb* drip, dripping. **dryppe** *vb* drip, drop; *kranen ~r* the tap is dripping.

dryppert *sb* gonorrhoea.

drysse *vb* **1** *(strø)* sprinkle; **2** *(falle som f.eks. snø)* fall.

drøfte *vb* discuss, debate; talk over; *jeg ~t saken med ham* I discussed the matter with him; I talked it over with him; *spørsmålet er ofte blitt ~t* the question has often been debated. **drøftelse** *sb* discussion, debate; *fl også* talks.

drøm *sb* dream; *i ~me* in a dream; *~men gikk i oppfyllelse* the dream came true. **drømme** *vb* dream; *han ~te om å bli dikter* he dreamt of becoming a poet; *jeg ville ikke* ~ *om å gjøre noe slikt* I wouldn't dream of doing such a thing.

drønn *sb* bang, boom, crack, roar; *~et fra fossen* the roar of the waterfall. **drønne** *vb* boom, roar, thunder.

drøv *sb: ~tygge, tygge ~* chew the cud; *(også fig)* ruminate. **~tygger** *sb* ruminant.

drøy *adj* **1** *(som varer lenge)* that goes a long way/ lasts a long time; **2** *(hard, vanskelig)* hard, stiff; *US også* tough; *en ~ jobb* a hard/tough job; **3** *(grov)* coarse; *en ~ spøk* a coarse joke. **drøye** *vb* drag on; last long; *han drøyde med å svare* he was late in answering; it was some time before he answered; *det drøyde en stund før* ... some time passed before ...

dråpe *sb* drop; *en ~ vann* a drop of water. **~vis** *adv* drop by drop.

dublere *vb* double. **dublett** *sb* double, duplicate; copy.

due *sb* pigeon; *fig, poet (turtel~)* dove; *en flokk duer* a flight/flock of pigeons. **duehus** pigeon-house; *(på en stang)* dovecot.

duell *sb* duel. **duellere** *vb* duel; fight a duel/duels.

duett *sb* duet.

duft *sb* **1** *(behagelig)* fragrance, scent; aroma; *en tung ~ av roser* a heavy scent of roses; **2** *(nøytral)* odour. **dufte** *vb* smell (sweet); *det dufter av roser* there is a scent of roses. **duftende** *adj* fragrant, sweet--smelling; aromatic.

duge *vb* be good; be fit; *det ~r ikke* it is no good; it won't do. **dugelig** *adj (svær, diger)* huge; *~ med* plenty of; lots of.

dugg *sb* dew. **dugge** *vb* **1** *det ~er* the dew is falling; **2** *(om vinduer, glass)* become misty; *frontruten ~er* the windscreen is misty.

duk *sb* **1** *(bord~)* (tacle-)cloth; *han la duken på bordet* he spread/laid the cloth; **2** *(seilduk etc)* canvas.

dukke A *sb* **1** doll; **2** *(i dukketeater)* puppet; **3** *(garndukke)* skein. **dukke|stue** *sb* doll's house. **~teater** *sb* marionette theatre. **~teaterforestilling** *sb* puppet show; **B** *vb* duck, dip, plunge; dive; *han ~t hodet* he ducked his head; *han ~t seg* he ducked; *hun ~t ned etter den druknende gutten* she dived in after the drowning boy; *de ~t opp (av vannet)* they came up/ came to the surface; *(kom til syne)* they appeared/ turned up. **dukkert** *sb* plunge, dive.

dulle med *vb* fuss over; coddle, pamper.

dulte *vb* **1** *(puffe lett)* poke; *jeg ~t (til) ham i siden* I poked him in the ribs; **2** *(~ (til) med albuen)* nudge.

dum *adj* **1** *(ubegavet)* stupid; *han var altfor ~ til å lære det* he was too stupid to learn it; **2** *(tankeløs, tåpelig)* foolish, silly; *ikke så ~t* not a bad idea; *jeg har gjort noe ~t* I have done something foolish; **3** *(irriterende)* stupid; **4** *(svært ~)* idiotic. **dumdristig** *adj* foolhardy, rash. **dumdristighet** *sb* foolhardiness, rashness. **dumhet** *sb* **1** stupidity; foolishness, silliness; **2** *(dum handling)* stupid thing; blunder; *begå/ gjøre en ~* do a stupid thing/a blunder; **3** *(dum ytring)* stupid remark. **dumme** *vb: ~ seg ut* make a fool of oneself; put one's foot in it.

dump 1 *adj* dull, hollow; muffled; *en ~ lyd* a thud; **2** *sb* depression; hollow; *(~ i veien)* chuck-hole.

dumpe *vb* **1** *(falle tungt) ~ ned* tumble; *~ oppi* blunder into; *la seg ~ ned* flop down; **2** *(selge til underpris)* dump. **dumping** *sb* dumping.

dumrian *sb* fool, blockhead. **dumsnill** *adj* **1** *(foran sb)* fond; doting; **2** *(som predikatsord)* kind; kind to a fault.

dun *sb* down.

dundre *vb* **1** *(buldre)* rumble, thunder; **2** *(banke, slå)* hammer, thump; bang.

dunk *sb* **A** *(beholder)* keg; (small) cask; *(av metall)* can; **B** *(lyd, slag)* knock, thump. **dunke** *vb* knock, thump.

dunkel *adj* **1** *(mørk)* dark, obscure; *(halvmørk)* dim; *det dunkle skjæret fra et talglys* the dim light of a candle; **2** *(uklar)* dim, vague; *dunkle erindringer/minner* dim memories; *et ~t svar* an obscure answer; **3** *(mystisk)* mysterious; *en ~ hentydning* a mysterious hint.

dunst *sb* fume, vapour; *(stank)* stink. **dunste** *vb* fume, reek.

dupere *vb (bløffe)* impose upon; bluff; take in.

duplikator *sb* duplicator. **duplisere** *vb* duplicate, copy; *data også* reproduce.

dur *sb* **A** *(vedvarende sterk lyd)* din, roar; *(svakere)* drone, hum; **B 1** *(toneart)* major; *C-~* C major; **2** *fig: mer i samme ~* more in the same vein. **dure** *vb* din, roar; *(svakere)* drone, hum.

dusin *sb* dozen; *et halvt ~* half a dozen; *et helt ~* a full dozen; *seks ~ blyanter* six ~ pencils. **dusinvis** *adv: knapper i ~* dozens of buttons.

dusj *sb* **1** *(~bad, ~innretning)* shower (bath); **2** *(dusjing, oversprøyting)* douche. **dusje 1** *(ta dusjbad)* take a shower; **2** *(oversprøyte)* douche.

dusk *sb* tuft; *(til pynt)* tassel.

duskregn *sb* drizzle. **duskregne** *vb* drizzle.

dusør *sb* reward; *han utlovte en ~* he offered a reward.

dvale *sb (vinter~)* hibernation; *ligge i ~* hibernate.

dvele *vb* tarry, linger; *~ ved* dwell on.

dverg *sb* dwarf.

dy *vb: jeg kunne ikke ~ meg for å gjøre det* I could not help doing it.

dybde *sb* depth; *på ti fots ~* at a depth of ten feet.

dyd *sb* virtue. **dydig** *adj* virtuous. **dydsiret** *adj* demure, smug; *dgl* goody-goody.

dykker *sb* diver. **dykker|dekk** *sb petro* diving deck. **~drakt** *sb* diving suit. **~hjelm** *sb* diving helmet. **~klokke** *sb petro etc* diving bell/capsule.

dyktig *adj* **1** *(flink)* good; *en ~ taler/lærer* a good speaker/teacher; **2** *(mer rosende)* capable, competent; *en ~ lege* a capable/competent doctor; **3** *(især teknisk ~)* able, skilful; *en ~ mekaniker* a skilful mechanic; **4** *(som adv) vi ble ~ våte* we got soaked to the skin. **dyktighet** *sb* ability, capability, competence, skill.

dynamisk *adj* dynamic. **dynamitt** *sb* dynamite. **dynamo** *sb* dynamo.

dyne *sb* **1** *(i seng)* eiderdown; quilt; **2** *(sand~)* dune. **dynetrekk** *sb* quilt cover.

dynge *sb* heap, pile. **dynge** *vb:* ~ *opp/sammen* heap/pile up; ~ *seg opp* pile up.

dynn *sb* mire, mud.

dyp 1 *adj* deep; *om tone også* low; *et* ~*t hull/mørke/sår* a deep hole/darkness/wound; *i* ~ *søvn* fast asleep; **2** *sb* depth; *(avgrunn, svelg)* abyss, deep. **dyp|fryse** *vb* (deep)freeze. ~**fryser** *sb* deep-freeze(r); freezer. ~**fryst** *adj, pp* deep-frozen; ~*fryst fisk* deep-frozen fish.

dyppe *vb* dip; *(senke helt nedi)* immerse; *(plutselig)* plunge.

dypt *adv* deep, deeply; *bukke* ~ bow low; *han gravde* ~ he dug deeply/deep; *jeg beklager* ~ I deeply regret; *we gikk* ~ *inn i skogen* we walked deep into the wood.
dypfølt *adj* heartfelt.

dyr 1 *adj (kostbar)* expensive, dear; *(om urimelig høy pris)* high-priced; *betale* ~*t* pay dear; *det faller* ~*t* it is expensive; **2** *sb* **1** animal; *(om større patte*~ *og om* ~ *på gård også)* beast. **dyre|hage** *sb* zoo; zoological garden(s). ~**kjøtt** *sb* venison. ~**liv** *sb* **1** *(dyrs liv)* animal life; **2** *(fauna)* fauna. ~**plager** *sb* tormentor of animals. ~**plageri** *sb* cruelty to animals; *the Royal Society for the Prevention of Cruelty to Animals* ≈ Foreningen til dyrenes beskyttelse; Dyrebeskyttelsen. ~**riket** *sb* the animal kingdom. **dyrisk** *adj* **1** *(som angår dyr)* animal; **2** *(brutal)* brutish, bestial.

dyrkbar *adj* cultivable; arable, tillable. **dyrke** *vb* **1** *(~ jord)* cultivate; **2** *(avle, ~ frem)* grow; *han* ~*r korn og poteter* he grows corn and potatoes; **3** *(tilbe)* worship; *Osiris ble* ~*t i Egypt* Osiris was worshipped in Egypt; **4** *(ha som hobby)* go in for; *hun* ~*r idrett* she goes in for sport. **dyrkelse** *sb (tilbedelse)* worship, cult. **dyrking** *sb (oppdyrking)* cultivation.

dyrlege *sb* veterinary (surgeon); *dgl* vet.

dyrtid *sb* time of high prices; *det var* ~ prices were high.

dysse *vb:* ~ *i søvn* lull to sleep; ~ *ned en skandale* hush up a scandal.

dyster *adj* gloomy, dismal; sombre; *dystre fremtidsutsikter* gloomy/dismal prospects; *en* ~ *mine* a gloomy air; *et* ~*t landskap* a sombre/desolate scenery.

dytt *sb* nudge, poke; push. **dytte** *vb* **1** *(~ til)* poke; *(med albuen)* nudge; *han* ~*t (til) henne i siden* he poked her in the ribs; **2** *(skyve)* push; *ikke* ~*!* don't push! ~ *noe på en* force something upon somebody; **3** *(stoppe igjen)* stop up; stuff; ~ *bomull i ørene* stuff one's ears with cottonwool; ~ *igjen en sprekk/et hull* stop up a chink/crack/hole.

dyvåt *adj* dripping wet; drenched, soaked.

dø *vb* die; ~ **av** *(sykdom etc)* die from/of; ~ *av sult/av et sår* die of/from hunger/a wound; *de* ~*de av kolera* they died of cholera; *de holdt på å* ~ *av latter* they were dying with laughter; ~ **for:** ~ *for egen hånd* die by one's own hand; commit suicide; ~ *for morderhånd* die at the hand of a murderer; *de* ~*de for sitt land* they died for their country; ~ **fra:** *han* ~*de fra kone og tre barn* he died leaving a wife and three children; ~ **hen** die away; *sangen* ~*de hen i det fjerne* the song died away in the distance; ~ **som:** *hun* ~*de som mangemillionær* she died a multi-millionaire; ~ **ut** die out; ~ **ved:** *de* ~*de ved en ulykke* they died in an accident. **død I** *adj* **1** *(avgått ved døden)* died; *hans mor er nettopp* ~ *av kreft* his mother has just died of cancer; *hun var* ~ *dagen før* she had died the day before; **2** *(ikke levende)* dead; *den* ~*e* the dead man/woman etc; *de* ~*e* the dead; *500 døde* 500 dead; ~ *som en sild* dead as a doornail; **3** *fig:* ~*t løp* dead heat/race; **II** *sb* death; *dømme til døden* condemn to death; *kamp på liv og* ~ mortal fight; *ligge for døden* be dying; be on one's deathbed; *sveve mellom liv og* ~ hover between life and death. **dødelig** *adj* **1** *(dødbringende)* deadly; lethal, mortal; fatal; ~ *gift* deadly poison; *et* ~ *sår* a mortal wound; **2** *(som engang skal dø)* mortal; *vi alminnelige* ~*e* we ordinary mortals. **dødelighet** *sb* death-rate, mortality. **dødfødt** *adj* stillborn; *et* ~ *barn* a stillborn child; *en* ~ *plan* an abortive plan. **dødning** *sb* ghost. **dødpunkt** *sb* **1** deadlock, impasse; *forhandlingene har nådd et* ~ the negotiations have reached a deadlock/have arrived at an impasse; **2** *(i maskin)* dead point/centre. **dødsens** *adj* **1** *(sikker på å miste livet)* doomed; *du er* ~ you are a dead man/woman; **2** *fig:* ~ *alvorlig* deadly serious. **døds|fall** *sb* death. ~**fare** *sb: de var i* ~*fare* they were in danger of their lives. ~**fiende** *sb* deadly/mortal enemy. ~**kamp** *sb* agony. ~**leie** *sb* deathbed. ~**stille** *adj* silent as death. ~**straff** *sb* capital punishment. ~**stund** *sb* hour of death. ~**støt** *sb* death blow. ~**syk** *adj* mortally ill. ~**trett** *adj* dead tired; *dgl* dog-tired. ~**årsak** *sb* cause of death. **dødsvekt** *sb* deadweight.

døgenikt *sb* good-for-nothing; ne'er-do-well.

døgn *sb* day and night; ~*et rundt* night and day; round-the clock; *fem* ~ five days and nights; *fem timer i døgnet* five hours a day/in the twenty-four. **døgnrytme** *sb* diurnal rhythm.

dølge *vb* conceal. Se også *gjemme, skjule*.

dømme *vb* **1** *a) (bedømme)* judge; ~ *i en sak* judge/try a case; ~ *mellom* judge between; *(ved voldgift)* arbitrate between; *etter alt å* ~ as far as we can judge; to all appearances; *b) (sport,* ~ *i boksing og fotball)* referee, umpire; **2** *(finne skyldig)* convict; find guilty; **3** *(idømme straff)* condemn, sentence; ~ *til* sentence to; *de ble dømt til døden* they were condemned/sentenced to death; *han ble dømt til seks års fengsel* he was sentenced to six years' imprisonment; **4** *(idømme bot/bøter)* fine; *hun ble dømt til å betale fem pund i bot* she was fined five pounds. **dømmekraft** *sb* judg(e)ment. **dømmende makt** *sb: den* ~ ~ the judiciary. **dømmesyk** *adj* censorious.

døpe *vb* baptize, christen; *hun ble døpt Elizabeth etter sin bestemor* she was christened Elizabeth after her grand-mother. **døpe|font** *sb* font. ~**navn** *sb* Christian name; *US* given name.

dør *sb* door; *jeg banket på* ~*en* I knocked at the door; *stå for* ~*en* be at hand; be near; *vinteren står for* ~*en* winter is at hand. **dør|hank,** ~**håndtak** *sb* door handle.

dørk *sb sjø* deck, floor(ing).

dør|klokke *sb* door-bell. **~matte** *sb* door-mat. **~skilt** *sb* doorplate.

dørslag *sb* colander.

dør|terskel *sb* threshold. **~åpning** *sb* doorway.

døs *sb* doze, drowse. **døse** *vb* doze, drowse. **døsig** *adj* drowsy. **døsighet** *sb* drowsiness.

døv *adj* deaf; *han er ~ på det ene øret* he is deaf in/of one ear; *vende det ~e øre til* turn a deaf ear to. **døv-stum** *adj* deaf-mute; *gml* deaf-and-dumb; *en ~* a deaf-mute (person).

døye *vb (lide, utholde)* suffer, endure.

døyve *vb (lindre)* deaden; *~ smerten* deaden the pain.

dåd *sb* **1** *(bedrift)* achievement; *dristig ~* exploit; **2** *(handling)* act, deed; *med råd og ~* by word and deed.

då|dyr *sb* fallow-deer. **~kalv** *sb* fawn.

dåne *vb* faint, swoon. Se også *besvime*.

dåp *sb* baptism, christening.

dåre 1 *sb* fool; **2** *vb* charm, enchant.

dårlig *adj, adv* **1** *(mangelfull, slett)* bad, poor; *en ~ hukommelse* a poor memory; *en ~ vane* a bad habit; *han er ~ til å danse* he is a poor/bad dancer; **2** *(syk)* ill; *(om legemsdel)* bad; *han ble ~* he was taken ill; **3** *(ikke godt)* badly; *det er ~ betalt* it is poorly/badly paid; *det går ~ for dem* they are doing badly; *ikke (så) ~* not bad. **dårligere** *adj* worse; *hun er ~ stilt enn søsteren* she is worse off than her sister; *pasienten ble ~* the patient grew/got worse. **dårligst** *adj* worst; *han er den dårligste til å synge* he is the worst singer.

dårskap *sb* folly; *en ~* a piece of folly.

E

e *(bokstaven)* e.

ebbe 1 *sb* ebb, ebb-tide; low tide; *ved ~* at low water; **2** *vb: ~ ut* ebb (away); peter out.

ed *sb* **1** oath; *falsk ~* perjury; *avlegge falsk ~* commit perjury; perjure oneself; *han avla ~ på at det var sant* he swore that it was true; *ta i ~* swear (in); *vitnet ble tatt i ~* the witness was sworn (in); *under ~s ansvar* on one's oath; **2** *(bannord, kraftuttrykk)* oath; curse, swearword.

edderkopp *sb* spider.

eddik *sb* vinegar.

edel *adj* **1** noble; *et ~t menneske* a noble character; **2** *edle metaller* precious metals. **edel|modig** *adj* noble-minded, generous. **~modighet** *sb* noble-mindedness, generosity. **~stein** *sb* precious stone; gem, jewel.

Edens Hage the Garden of Eden.

edfeste *vb (ta i ed)* swear (in).

edru, edruelig *adj* sober. **edruelighet** *sb* **1** abstemiousness, abstention; **2** *især fig* sobriety. **edru-skap** *sb* abstemiousness, abstention.

edsvoren *adj* sworn; *~ translatør* a sworn interpreter.

effekt *sb (virkning)* effect. **effekter** *sb fl (løsøre)* belongings, goods; effects. **effektiv** *adj* **1** *(virkningsfull)* effective; **2** *(dyktig)* efficient; *en ~ lærerstab* an efficient staff of teachers. **effektivitet** *sb* **1** *(effektiv virkning)* effectiveness; *om legemiddel* efficacy; **2** *(dyktighet, yteevne)* efficiency. **effektuere** *vb: ~ en bestilling* execute/fill an order.

efter etc se *etter etc*.

eføy *sb* ivy.

egen *adj* **1** *(særegen)* peculiar; **2** *(eiendommelig, sær)* odd; eccentric, queer; *en ~ type* an eccentric; **3** *(egensindig, sta)* stubborn; **4** *(viss)* certain; *en ~ stemning* a certain atmosphere. **egen, eget, egne** *adj* own; of one's own; *vi har eget hus* we have a house of our own; *det er vårt eget hus* it is our own house; *han er sin egen herre* he is his own master; *hun går sine egne veier* she goes her own way; *vi hadde egen bil (også)* vi had a private car. **egen|artet** *adj* peculiar, original. **~hendig** *adj, adv: ~ levert* delivered by hand; *~hendig underskrift* one's own signature. **~het** *sb* **1** *(særegenhet)* peculiarity; **2** *(eiendommelighet, særhet)* foible, oddity; eccentricity; **3** *(egensindighet, stahet)* wilfulness, pigheadedness, stubbornness. **~interesse** *sb* selfinterest. **~kjærlig** *adj* selfish. **~kjærlighet** *sb* selfishness. **~mektig** *adj* high-handed; arbitrary. **~navn** *sb* proper name. **~nytte** *sb* self-interest, selfishness. **~nyttig** *adj* selfish. **~rådig** *adj* wilful, obstinate. **~sindig** *adj* wilful, pigheaded, stubborn.

egenskap *sb* quality; *hun har mange gode ~er* she has many good qualities/good points; *i ~ av* in the capacity of.

egentlig 1 *adj* real, proper; *i ordets ~e betydning* in the true/real sense of the word; *det ~e Norge* Norway proper; **2** *adv* really; strictly speaking; after all; *jeg vet ~ ikke hva som hendte* I really don't know what happened; *hva gjør det ~?* after all, what does it matter?

egen|vekt *sb* specific gravity. **~verdi** *sb* intrinsic value.

eget se *egen etc*.

egg *sb* **A** *(fugle~ etc)* egg; *bløtkokte/hardkokte ~* soft-boiled/hard-boiled eggs; *nylagte ~* fresh eggs; **B** *(på kniv etc)* edge; *en skarp ~* a sharp/keen edge.

egge *vb* incite, urge; egg on; *de ~t ham til å gjøre det* they incited/urged him to do it; they egged him on to do it.

egge|glass *sb* egg-cup. **~hvite 1** *(i egg)* the white of an egg; **2** *(~hvitestoff)* protein. **~krem** *sb* ≈ custard. **~plomme** *sb* (egg) yolk; the yolk of an egg. **~røre** *sb* scrambled eggs. **~skall** *sb* eggshell. **eggstokk** *sb* ovary.

egle *vb: ~ seg inn på* pick a quarrel with.

egn *sb* region; locality, neighbourhood; tract.

egne A *adj* se *egen etc*; **B** *vb: ~ seg for/til* be fit/suited for; *han ~r seg ikke til stillingen* he is not fit for the position; *hun ~r seg godt til stillingen* she is cut out for the job; *klær som ~r seg til vinterbruk* clothes suitable for winter (wear). **egnet** *adj* fit, fitted; suitable.

egoisme *sb* egotism; egoism, selfishness. **egoist** *sb* egotist; egoist. **egoistisk** *adj* egotistic; egoistic(al), selfish.

ei *ubest art*, se *en*.

eid *sb* isthmus; neck of land.

eie 1 *sb bokl* possession; *i offentlig ~* publickly owned; **2** *vb* own, possess; have; *alt jeg ~r* all I have/possess; *han ~r en formue* he has a fortune; *jeg ~r dette huset* I own this house. **eien|deler** *sb fl* belongings, effects. **~dom** *sb* possessions, property; *fast ~dom* real estate; *(jord~)* estate; landed property.

eiendommelig *adj* **1** *(særegen)* characteristic, peculiar; **2** *(merkelig, underlig)* curious, strange; *det er ~ å se* it is curious to see; *~ oppførsel* strange behaviour. **eiendommelighet** *sb* peculiarity; peculiar feature; characteristic.

eiendoms|besitter *sb* (landed) proprietor. **~megler** *sb* estate/house agent; *US* realtor. **~pronomen** *sb* possessive pronoun. **~rett** *sb* proprietary right/title; right of ownership. **~skatt** *sb* property tax; *GB* land tax.

eier *sb* owner; *(av forretning etc)* proprietor; *~en av hotellet* the proprietor of the hotel; *hun ble ~ av huset* she became the owner of the house; *skifte ~* change hands.

eik *sb* oak; *som materiale også* oak-wood.

eike *sb (i hjul)* spoke.

eike|nøtt *sb* acorn. **~tre** *sb* oak(-tree); *som materiale også* oak(-wood).

eim *sb* steam, vapour.

einer *sb* juniper.

einstøing *sb* **1** *(en som lever/står alene)* lone wolf; **2** *(særling)* eccentric.

eiter *sb* venom.

ekkel *adj* disgusting, nasty.

ekko *sb* echo. **ekkolodd** *sb* echo-sounder.

ekorn *sb* squirrel.

eksakt *adj* exact.

eksaltert *adj* exalted; exited, unbalanced.

eksamen *sb* examination; *dgl* exam; *muntlig ~* oral examination; *skriftlig ~* written examination; *gjøre det godt til ~* do well in the exam; *gå opp/være oppe til ~* sit for an examination; *stryke til ~* fail at/in an examination; *stå til ~* pass an examination; *ta ~* pass an examination; *(ved universiteter, US også ved andre læreanstalter)* graduate; take a degree. **eksamens|fest** *sb* end-of-term celebration; *GB* speech day; *US* commencement. **~karakter** *sb* examination marks. **~oppgave** *sb* **1** *(spørsmål)* (question) paper; **2** *(besvarelse)* (examination) paper. **~vitnemål, ~vitnesbyrd** *sb* certificate; diploma.

eksekusjon *sb* execution. **eksekusjonspelotong** *sb* firing-squad.

eksem *sb* eczema.

eksempel *sb* **1** *(illustrerende tilfelle)* example, instance; *for ~* for example/instance *(skrevet* e.g.*)*; *store byer som for ~ Paris* large cities such as for instance Paris; **2** *(forbilde)* example; *et godt ~* a good example; *foregå med et godt ~* set a good example; *følge deres ~* follow their lead. **eksemplar** *sb* **1** *(av avis, bok etc)* copy; *boken ble solgt i over enn 5000 ~er* over 5000 copies of the book were sold; **2** *(av dyreart)* specimen; *jeg har to ~er av denne sommerfuglen* I have two specimens of this butterfly. **eksemplarisk** *adj* exemplary; *~ oppførsel* exemplary conduct.

eksentrisk *adj* eccentric.

eksersere *vb* drill, train. **ekserserplass** *sb* drill ground. **eksersis** *sb* drill, training.

eksil *sb* exile; *gå i ~* go into exile; *leve i ~* live in exile. **~regjering** *sb* exile government.

eksistens *sb* existence. **~minimum** *sb* subsistence level. **eksistere** *vb* exist; *mennesket kan ikke ~ uten mat* man cannot exist without food.

ekskludere *vb (utelukke, utstøte)* expel. **eksklusiv** *adj* exclusive. **eksklusjon** *sb* expulsion.

ekskursjon *sb* excursion.

eksos *sb* exhaust. **~potte** *sb* exhaust box; silencer. **~rør** *sb* exhaust pipe. **~ventil** *sb* exhaust valve.

eksotisk *adj* exotic.

ekspandere *vb* expand. **ekspansiv** *adj* expansive. **ekspansjon** *sb* expansion; increase.

ekspedere *vb* **1** *(besørge, sende)* dispatch, send; *~ et telegram* send a telegram; **2** *(~ kunder)* attend to; serve; *blir De ekspedert?* are you attended to? are you being served? **3** *dgl (drepe)* dispatch. **ekspedering** *sb (av kunder)* attendance, service; *rask/sen ~* quick/slow service. **ekspedisjon** *sb* **1** = *ekspedering*; **2** *(ekspedisjons|lokale, -skranke)* office; counter; *henvend Dem i ekspedisjonen* apply at the counter; **3** *(reise)* expedition; *hun var med på en ~* she took part in an expedition.

ekspeditrise *sb* shop assistant/girl; saleswoman; *US* clerk.

ekspeditt *adj* prompt, quick; expeditious.

ekspeditør *sb* shop assistant; sales|man, ~woman; *US* clerk.

ekspektanseliste *sb* waiting list.

eksperiment *sb* experiment. **eksperimentere** *vb* experiment. **eksperimentering** *sb* experimentation.

ekspert *sb* expert, specialist; *hun er ~ på dette* she is an expert on this/in this field. **ekspertise** *sb* expertise, know-how.

eksplodere *vb* **1** explode; blow up; go off; *bomben eksploderte ikke* the bomb did not explode/go off; **2** *(ved indre trykk)* burst; *kjelen eksploderte* the boiler burst; *de holdt på å ~ av latter* they were ready to burst with laughter. **eksplosiv** *adj, sb* explosive. **eksplosjon** *sb* explosion; bursting; *de omkom ved en ~* they were killed in an explosion. **eksplosjonsmotor** *sb* internal combustion engine.

eksport *sb* **1** *(eksportering)* export; *~ av gull er blitt forbudt* the export of gold has been forbidden; **2** *(eksportvarer)* exports. **eksport|artikkel** *sb* export article; *fl også* exports. **~avgift** *sb* export duty. **exportere** *vb* export. **eksport|forbud** *sb* export prohibition. **~handel** *sb* export trade. **~industri** *sb* export industry. **~marked** *sb* export market. **~overskudd** *sb* excess of exports (over imports). **~vare** *sb = ~artikkel.* **eksportør** *sb* exporter.

ekspress *adj, adv, sb* express. **~brev** *sb* express letter. **~tog** *sb* express (train).

ekspropriasjon *sb* expropriation; compulsory purchase. **ekspropriere** *vb* expropriate.

ekstase *sb* ecstasy; *falle i ~ over* go into/be thrown into ecstasy over. **ekstatisk** *adj* ecstatic.

ekstemporere *vb (improvisere)* extemporize; *(på skolen)* do unseens/an unseen.

eksteriør *sb* exterior.

ekstra *adj* **1** *(ytterligere)* additional; *en ~ kopi/et ~ eksemplar* an additional copy; **2** *adv (usedvanlig)* extra; *~ fin* extra fine. **ekstra|arbeid** *sb* extra/overtime work. **~betaling** *sb* extra pay. **~forpleining** *sb* special food. **~fortjeneste** *sb* extra money.

ekstrakt *sb* extract.

ekstra|nummer *sb* **1** *(av avis)* special (edition); **2** *(på konsert etc)* encore; *han gav tre ~nummer* he gave three encores. **~ordinær** *adj* extraordinary, exceptional.

ekstrem *adj* extreme. **ekstremitet** *sb* extremity.

ekte *adj* genuine, real, true; authentic; *om farger* fast; *en ~ perle* a genuine pearl; *en ~ amerikaner* a real/true American; *dokumentet er ~* the document is authentic. **ekte|felle** *sb* spouse, partner. **~folk** *sb* married couple; husband and wife. **~født** *adj* legitimate; born in wedlock. **~make** *sb = ektefelle.* **~mann** *sb* husband. **~par** *sb* married couple. **~skap** *sb* marriage; married life; matrimony; *gml* wedlock; *borgerlig ~* civil marriage; *lyse til ~* publish the banns. **~skapelig** *adj* matrimonial, conjugal. **ekthet** *sb* genuineness, authenticity.

ekvator *sb* equator.

elastisitet *sb* elasticity. **elastisk** *adj* elastic.

eldes *vb* age; grow old. **eldgammel** *adj* **1** very old; **2** *(fra gammel tid)* ancient. **eldre** *adj* **1** older; *han er ~ enn sin bror* he is older than his brother; *(om familieforhold, foran sb)* elder; *min ~ bror* my elder brother; *jeg har en ~ søster, hun er ti år ~ enn jeg* I have one elder sister, she is ten years older than I; **2** *(nokså gammel)* elderly; elderly lady. **eldst** *adj* **1** oldest; *(av to)* older; *(om familieforhold)* eldest; *(av to)* elder; *hun er ~e datter av min ~ venn* she is the eldest daughter of my oldest friend; *den ~e broren (av to) er i flyvåpenet* the elder brother is in the airforce; **2** *(som sb, i kirkesamfunn)* elder; *den skotske kirke styres av de eldste* the Kirk is governed by Elders.

elefant *sb* elephant.

eleganse *sb* elegance. **elegant** *adj, adv* elegant; neat, smart; *~ kledd* elegantly/smartly dressed.

elektrifisere *vb* electrify. **elektriker** *sb* electrician. **elektrisere** *vb* electrify. **elektrisitet** *sb* electricity. **elektrisitets|måler** *sb* electric meter. **~verk** *sb* power station. **elektrisk** *adj* electric. **elektrisk | lys** *sb* electric light. **~ strøm** *sb* electric current. **elektro|ingeniør** *sb* electrical engineer. **~kjemisk** *adj* electrochemical. **elektron** *sb* electron. **elektronikk** *sb* electronics. **elektronisk** *adj* electronic. **elektronisk | databehandling (EDB)** *sb* electronic data processing. **~ musikk** *sb* electronic music.

element *sb* **1** *(i batteri)* cell; *et batteri på 4 elementer* a four-cell battery; *tørr~* dry battery; **2** *(bestanddel, stoff)* element. **elementær** *adj* elementary.

elendig *adj* miserable; wretched. **elendighet** *sb* misery, wretchedness.

elev *sb* pupil, student.

elevator *sb se heis.*

elevert *adj (opphøyet)* elevated, lofty, *(kultivert også)* noble.

elfenbein *sb* ivory.

elg *sb* elk; *US* moose.

eliminasjon *sb* elimination. **eliminere** *vb* eliminate.

elite *sb* élite; cream, flower; *samfunnets ~* the cream/élite of society; *~en av engelsk ungdom* the flower of English youth.

eller *konj* or; *~ også* or else; *jeg vet ikke om jeg skal kjøpe det ~ ikke* I don't know whether to buy it or not.

ellers *adv* **1** *(i motsatt fall)* or (else); otherwise; *opp med hendene, ~ skyter jeg* hands up or I fire; *pass på ~ faller du* take care or else you will fall; **2** *(for øvrig)* normally, usually; otherwise; *~ er han en stille fyr* normally/usually he is a quiet fellow; *jeg er litt tunghørt, men ~ ganske normal* I am a little hard-of-hearing, but otherwise quite normal; **3** *(forresten)* by the way; you know; *hva synes du ~ om boken min?* by the way, what do you think of my book? *~ takk* thank you/thanks all the same; **4** *(ved pron)* else; *hvem ~?* who else? *ingen ~* no one else; *~ ingenting* nothing else.

ellevill *adj: ~ av glede* overjoyed; mad with joy; *tilhørerne var ~e av begeistring* the audience went into raptures.

ellipse *sb* ellipse. **elliptisk** *adj* elliptic(al).

elsk *sb: legge sin ~ på* take a fancy to. **elske** *vb* **1** *a) (være glad i)* love; *~ høyt* love dearly; *b) (elske intimt)* make love (to); **2** *dgl* adore; *jeg simpelthen ~r den kjolen* I simply adore that dress. **elskelig** *adj* lovable; *et ~ menneske* a lovable person; *en ~ gammel dame* a sweet old lady. **elsker** *sb* lover. **elskerinne** *sb* mistress. **elskverdig** *adj* kind; charming, pleasant; amiable; *det var meget ~ av Dem* it was very kind of you; *vil De* *være så ~ å hjelpe meg* will you be so kind as to help me. **elskverdighet** *sb* kindness.

elv *sb* river; *nedover ~en* downstream; down the river; *oppover ~en* upstream; up the river; *ved ~en* by/near the river; *(om by, hus etc)* on the river; *Stratford ligger ved (~en) Avon* Stratford stands on the river Avon; *et hus ved en ~ (også)* a riverside house. **elve|bredd** *sb* riverbank, riverside. **~leie** *sb* river bed. **~munning, ~os** *sb* the mouth of a river; *(bred ~munning)* estuary. **~stryk** *sb* chute.

emalje *sb* enamel. **emaljere** *vb* enamel.

emballasje *sb* packing. **emballere** *vb* package; pack/wrap up.

emansipasjon *sb* emancipation. **emansipere** *vb* emancipate.

embargo *sb* embargo; *heve ~en* remove/lift the embargo; *legge ~ på* lay an embargo on.

embete *sb* office; (government) post; *ledig ~* vacancy; vacant post; *hun søkte et ~* she applied for a post. **embets|eksamen** *sb* final university examination; *ha ~eksamen* have a university degree. **~kvinne, ~mann, ~person** *sb* civil servant; (government) officer/official. **~standen** *sb* the Civil Service.

emblem *sb* emblem, badge.

emigrant *sb* emigrant. **emigrere** *vb* emigrate; *mange nordmenn emigrerte til Amerika* many Norwegians emigrated from to America.

emissær *sb* evangelist.

emmen *adj* nauseous.

emne *sb* **1** *(for noe som skal lages)* material; **2** *(for samtale etc)* subject, topic; *samtale~/~t for samtalen* the subject of the conversation; *dagens ~r* the topics of the day.

en, ei, et I *ubest art* **1** *a) (foran konsonantlyd)* a; *a man; a yellow cab*; *b) (foran vokallyd)* an; *an apple; an hour*; **2** *(ved ubestemt tidsangivelse)* one; *det hendte en morgen* it happened one morning; **3** *(omtrent)* about, some; *om en tre-fire dager* in about three or four days; *for en åtte-ti år siden* some eight or ten years ago; **4** *(en viss)* a (certain); *en herr Smith* a Mr Smith; **II** *(tallord: én, ei, ett)* **1** one; *en etter en* one by one; *de har bare én datter* they have only one daughter; *den ene - den andre (av to)* one - the other; *(av flere)* one - another; *det ene beinet mitt* one of my legs; *ett er sikkert* one thing is certain; *komme ut på ett* amount to the same thing; *med ett* suddenly; all of a sudden; **2** *(unntak) jeg har vært der én gang* I have been there once; *om en eller to uker* in a week or two; *Roma ble ikke bygd på én dag* Rome was not built in a day; **III** *ubest pron* **1** *(man)* one, you; we; *en kan aldri vite* one never knows; you never can tell; *en kan bare gjøre sitt beste* one can only do one's best; *en vet svært lite om Shakespeares liv* we know very little of Shakespeare's life; *også* little is known of Shakespeare's life; **2** *(en eller annen)* some, somebody, someone; *~ eller annen bok* some book; *det er en som har tatt hatten min* someone has taken my hat; *et eller annet* something; *et eller annet sted* somewhere.

en|akter *sb* one-act play. **~båren** *adj: Guds enbårne sønn* God's only-begotten Son.

enda I *adv* **1** *(fremdeles,* jf *ennå) a)* still; *på den tiden bodde de ~ i Liverpool* at that time they were still living in Liverpool; *b) ved nektelse* yet; *~ aldri* never as yet; *de har ikke gått ~* they haven't gone yet; **2** *(likevel)* still, yet; *det er sant som de sier, men jeg er ~ ikke overbevist* what they say is true, but I am still not convinced/yet I am not convinced; **3** *(foran komparativ)* still; *~ bedre/verre* still better/worse; *~ verre skulle det bli* there was worse to come; **4** *(ytterligere)* more; *~ en* one more; *~ en gang* once more; **5** *(til og med)* even; *det kan ~ et barn forstå* even a child can see that; **6** *(etter hvis/om)* only; *om det ~ ikke hadde regnet* if only it hadn't been raining; **II** *konj (skjønt)* although, though; even (if/though); *~ hun nesten ikke kunne gå, insisterte hun på å få være med* although she could hardly walk, she insisted on coming along.

ende I *sb* **1** end; *begynne i den gale ~n* begin at the wrong end; *brenne sitt lys i begge ~r* burn the candle/one's candle at both ends; *falle over ~* fall over; *for ~n av bordet* at the end of the table; *fra ~ til annen* from one end to the other; *på ~* on end; *sette huset på ~* turn the house upside down; *verdens ~ (langt av gårde)* the ends of the earth; *(fig: dommedag)* the end of the world; **2** *(slutt)* end; *allting har en ~* there is an end to everything; *få en ~ på saken* put an end to the matter; *gjøre ~ på (drepe)* kill; *når enden er god er allting godt* all's well that ends well; *til ~* at an end; **3** *(bak~)* behind, seat; haunches; posterior; **4** *(historie)* yarn; *spinne en ~* spin a yarn; **II** *vb (slutte)* end, finish; close; *hvordan ~r historien* how does the story end; *boken endte godt* the book had a happy ending; *hun endte med å si* she finished by saying.

endefrem *adj* **1** *(liketil)* simple; **2** *(åpenhjertig)* frank, outspoken.

endelig I *adj* **1** *(avgjørende, avsluttende)* final; decisive; *den ~e seier* the decisive victory; *det ~e resultat* the final result; **2** *(ikke uendelig)* finite, limited; *en ~ størrelse* a finite quantity; **II** *adv (omsider)* at length/last; finally; *~ kom hun* at last she came; *de vil ~ at jeg skal komme* they insists on my coming.

endelse *sb* ending.

ende|løs *adj* endless. **~morene** *sb* terminal moraine. **~punkt** *sb* terminal/extreme point. **~rim** *sb* end rhyme. **~stasjon** *sb* terminal (station). **~tarm** *sb* rectum. **~vegg** *sb* end wall. **~vende** *vb* turn upside down; *(gjennomsøke)* ransack.

ending *sb* ending.

endog *adv* even (jf *enda I 5)*.

endre *vb* **1** *(forandre delvis)* alter; *~ kurs* alter one's course; *gjort gjerning står ikke til å ~* what is done cannot be undone; **2** *(om lovforslag)* amend. **endring** *sb* **1** *(delvis forandring)* alteration; **2** *(lov~)* amendment. Se også *forandre, forandring*.

ene *adv: ~ og alene* solely; *~ og alene på grunn av deg* solely because of you. **ene|arving** *sb* sole heir. **~barn** *sb* only child. **~boer** *sb* hermit. **~bolig** *sb* single-

-family house.

enegget *sb: ~ tvilling* identical twin.

ene|herredømme *sb* absolute mastery. **~hersker** *sb* **1** *(fyrste)* absolute monarch; **2** *(ikke fyrstelig person)* dictator; **3** *(eneveldig fyrste eller diktator)* autocrat. **~merker** *sb: trenge seg inn på andres ~* tresspass.

ener *sb* one; *to tiere og fire ~e* two tens and four ones; *jeg fikk 20 poeng i bare enere* I scored twenty all in ones; **2** *(på terning)* ace; **3** *(enestående person)* an exceptional/outstanding person.

enerett *sb* monopoly; sole and exclusive right; *(copyright)* copyright; *få/ha ~* monopolize.

energi *sb* energy. **energikilde** *sb* source of energy. **energisk** *adj* energetic; *adv* energetically.

enerom *sb* **1** *(f.eks. på sykehus)* private room; **2** = *enrom.*

enerverende *adj* nerve-racking; trying; *det virker ~* it gets on your nerves.

eneste *adj* only, single; *de ~ som var til stede* the only ones present; *det ~ hun visste* the only thing she knew; *en ~ gang* just once; once only; *hver ~* every (single); *hver ~ en* every single one; *ikke en ~ gang* not once; not a single time; *ikke en/et ~* not one; not a single; *han kunne ikke et ~ ord engelsk* he did not know one word/a single word of English. **ene|stående** *adj* unique; *adv* exceptionally; *~stående billig* exceptionally cheap. **~tale** *sb* monologue. **~velde** *sb* absolute monarchy; absolutism, autocracy. **~veldig** *adj* absolute, arbitrary; *en ~ hersker* an absolute ruler. **~voldskonge** *sb* absolute monarch. **~voldsmakt** *sb* absolute power. **~værelse** *sb* = *~rom.*

enfold *sb* simplicity. **enfoldig** *adj* simple; *~e sjeler* simple souls. **enfoldighet** *sb* = *enfold.*

eng *sb* meadow.

engang *adv: det er nå ~ sånn* well, that's how it is; well, there it is; *ikke ~* not even. **en gang** *adv (se også gang)* **1** *(i fortiden)* once; on one occasion; one day; *det var ~* once (upon a time) there was; **2** *(i fremtiden)* one day; some day; some time; *~ ~ vil du (komme til å) angre dette* one day/some day you will regret this. **engangs-** *pref* **1** *(som gjelder etc én gang for alle)* once-(-and)-for-all; once-only; **2** *(som kastes etter én gangs bruk)* disposable; non-returnable.

engasjement *sb* engagement. **engasjere** *vb* **1** *(ansette)* engage; **2** *(by opp til dans)* ask for a dance. **engasjert** *adj* **1** *(opptatt)* engaged; **2** *(interessert)* engaged/engrossed (in); committed, involved.

engel *sb* engel.

engelsk *adj, sb* English; *på ~* in English; *hva heter* stol *på ~* what is *stol* in English? **engelsk|mann** *sb* Englishman (NB: om kvinne brukes *Englishwoman*). **~talende** *adj* English-speaking. **~time** *sb* English lesson. **~vennlig** *adj* pro-English; anglophile. **England** **1** England (som ikke omfatter Wales, Skotland og Nord-Irland); **2** *(offisielt ofte)* the United Kingdom; **3** *(dgl og i avisspråk etc)* Britain.

engleaktig *adj* angelic.

en gros *adj, adv* wholesale; wholesale prices; *kjøpe ~* buy wholesale; *selge ~* sell by wholesale.

engstelig *adj* **1** *(bekymret)* anxious, uneasy, troubled; *(sterkere)* alarmed; *han ble ~* he became anxious/he got uneasy; *det gjorde henne ~* it made her anxious/uneasy; *han var ~ for fremtiden* he was uneasy about his future; **2** *(fryktsom)* timid; *hun er ~ av seg* she is timid; **3** *(redd)* afraid. **engstelse** *sb* anxiety; *ingen grunn til ~* no reason for anxiety.

enhet *sb* **1** *(sammensveiset hele)* unity; *nasjonal ~* national unity; **2** *(del av et hele; måle~)* unit; *meter(en) er en lengde~* the metre is a unit of length.

enhver *adj, pron* **1** *(alle)* everybody; every one; *foran sb* every; **2** *(hvilken som helst)* anybody, anyone; *foran sb* any; *alle og ~* everybody, anybody; *~ annen* anybody else; *~ annen enn han* anybody except him/but he.

enig *adj: bli/være ~* agree; *vi er ~e* we are agreed; *vi ble ~e om å hjelpe ham* we agreed to help him; *vi er blitt ~e om en plan* we have agreed upon a plan. **enighet** *sb* agreement; *det ble oppnådd ~ på alle punkter* agreement was reached on all points; *komme til ~* come to terms.

enke *sb* widow; *hun er ~ etter John S.* she is the widow of John S. **enkedronning** *sb* **1** Queen Dowager; **2** *(konges eller regjerende dronnings mor)* Queen Mother.

enkel *adj* plain, simple. **enkelhet** *sb* simplicity; *i all ~* in all simplicity; quite informally. **enkelt** *adj* **1** *(eneste; motsatt dobbelt)* single; *bare en ~* just one; *en ~ gang* once; on one occasion; **2** *(usammensatt)* simple; **3** *(enslig)* solitary. **enkelte** *pron* some; a few; *~ mener det er galt* some (people) think it is wrong; *~ ganger* now and then. **enkelt|het** *sb* detail, particular; *i alle enkeltheter* in every single detail/particular. **~knappet** *adj* = *~spent.* **~person** *sb* individual. **~rom** *sb* single room. **~seng** *sb* single bed. **~spent** *adj* single-breasted. **~sporet** *adj* single-track. **~stående** *adj* isolated; *et ~ stående tilfelle* an isolated instance. **~vesen** *sb* individual. **~vis** *adv* singly; one by one. **~værelse** *sb* = *~rom.*

enke|mann *sb* widower. **~pensjon** *sb* widow's pension, *fl* widows' pensions. **~stand** *sb* widowhood.

en masse *adv: arrestasjoner ~* wholesale arrests; *bøker ~* lots of books; *henrettelser ~* mass executions.

enn *adv, konj* **1** than; *han har mer penger ~ jeg* he has more money than I; **2** *(etter annen/annet/andre)* but, except; *han er alt annet ~ klok* he is anything but clever; **3** *(i uttrykk som hva som ~, hvor ~)* -ever; *hva som ~ skjer* whatever happens; *hvem som ~ gjør det* whoever does it; *hvor de ~ er* wherever they are; *hvor mye jeg ~ leser* however much I read; **4** *(som innledning til spørsmål) ~ du da?* what about you? *~ om det er sant?* suppose it is true? **5** *(uttrykk) ~ si* let alone; still less; *jeg har ikke tid, ~ si penger* I haven't the time, let alone the money; *~ videre* besides, moreover; further.

ennå *adv* (jf *enda*) **1** *(om noe som har vært og fremdeles varer)* still; *han er her ~* he is still here; *hun er opptatt ~* she is still busy; **2** *(om noe som ventes eller er usikkert)* yet; *han er ikke kommet ~* he has not arrived yet; **3** *(foreløpig, hittil)* as yet; *~ har vi ikke lagt noen planer for ferien* as yet we have made no plans for the holidays.

enorm *adj* enormous, huge, immense.

en passant *adv* by the way.

enquete *sb* **1** *(rundspørring blant eksperter)* (newspaper) inquiry (of expert opinion); **2** *(blant publikum)* (public opinion) poll; questionnaire.

enrom *sb: i ~* in private.

ens I *adj* **1** identical; **2** *(bare som predikatsord)* alike; the same; *prisene er ~ overalt* the prices are the same everywhere; *barna går ~ kledt* the children are dressed alike; **3** *(like stor etc)* equal; *ting av ~ størrelse/vekt/verdi* things of equal size/weight/value; **4** *~ ærend* purposely; on purpose; *han kom hit ~ ærend for å låne penger av deg* ha came here on purpose/purposely to borrow money from you; **II** *pron (genitiv av en)* one's. **ensartet** *adj* uniform, homogeneous. **ensartethet** *sb* uniformity, homogeneity.

ense *vb* pay heed/attention to; take notice of.

ens|farget *adj* one-coloured, solid-coloured. **~formet** *adj geom* similar; *ensformede trekanter* similar triangles. **~formig** *adj* monotonous, dull; dreary. **~formighet** *sb* monotony.

en|sidig *adj* **1** *(partisk etc)* one-sided; **2** *(ikke gjensidig)* unilateral. **~sidighet** *sb* one-sidedness. **~sifret** *adj: ~ tall* digit.

enskjønt *konj* though, although.

enslig *adj* **1** *(alene)* single, solitary; **2** *(avsidesliggende)* isolated.

ensom *adj* lonely, solitary; *en ~ mann* a lonely man; *vi følte oss ~me* we felt lonely. **ensomhet** *sb* loneliness, solitude.

ens|rette *vb* unify; standardize. **~retting** *sb* unification; regimentation.

enstemmig *adj* **1** *(med alle stemmer)* unanimous; *~ vedtatt* carried unanimously; **2** *(som med én stemme)* in unison; *synge ~* sing in unison.

enstonig *adj* monotonous.

entall *sb* the singular.

enten *konj* **1** *(sideordnende) ~ ... eller* either ... or; *hun er ~ i Paris eller Berlin* she is either in Paris or Berlin; **2** *(underordnende) ~ ... eller* whether ... or; *vi drar ~ han kommer eller ikke* we shall leave whether he comes or not.

entre *vb* **1** *(borde fiendtlig skip)* board; **2** *(klatre)* climb; *~ riggen* go aloft; mount the rigging.

entré *sb* **1** *(forstue)* hall; **2** *(adgang)* admission; *det er gratis ~* the admission is free.

entreprenør *sb* contractor.

entusiasme *sb* enthusiasm. **entusiast** *sb* enthusiast. **entusiastisk** *adj* enthusiastic; *~ over* enthusiastic about/over.

enveis|drift *sb* **1** one-way operation; **2** *data* simplex operation. **~veisgate** *sb* one-way street. **~kjøring** *sb* one-way traffic. **~regulert gate** *sb* = *~veisgate.*

epidemi *sb* epidemic. **epidemisk** *adj* epidemic.

epigram *sb* epigram.

epilepsi *sb* epilepsy; falling sickness. **epileptiker** *sb* epileptic. **epileptisk** *adj* epileptic.

epilog *sb* epilogue.

episk *sb* epic.

episode *sb* episode, incident.

epistel *sb* epistle.

eple *sb* apple; *stridens ~* the bone of contention. **eple|saft** *sb* apple juice; *US* sweet cider. **~sider 1** *(eplevin)* cider; **2** *US* hard cider.

epoke *sb* epoch, era. **~gjørende** *adj* epoch-making.

epos *sb* epic.

eremitt *sb* hermit.

erfare *vb* **1** *(få vite)* learn; be informed; get to know; **2** *(oppleve)* experience; *jeg har erfart hva det vil si å være fattig* I have learnt what it is to be poor. **erfaren** *adj* experienced; *en ~ lærer* an experienced teacher. **erfaring** *sb* experience; *av egen ~* from personal experience.

ergerlig *adj* **1** *(irriterende)* annoying, irritating; *det ~e var* the annoying thing (about it) was; **2** *(som ergrer seg)* annoyed, irritated; *hun var ~ over at jeg var der* she was annoyed that I was there; *vi var ~e over tapet* we were annoyed at the loss; *han var ~ på meg* he was annoyed with me. **ergre** *vb* annoy, irritate, vex; *~ seg over noe* be annoyed/vexed at something; *det ~r meg* it annoys/vexes me. **ergrelse** *sb* annoyance, vexation; *til min store ~* to my great annoyance/vexation.

erindre *vb* recollect, remember. **erindring** *sb* memory; recollection, remembrance; *gjenkalle i ~en* bring/call to mind. (Se også *huske* og *hukommelse*).

erke|biskop *sb* archbishop. **~engel** *sb* archangel. **~kjeltring** *sb* arch villain; villain of the deepest dye. **~sludder** *sb* absolute nonsense.

erkjenne *vb (innrømme)* admit, own; acknowledge; recognize; *han ~r feilen* he admits the mistake; *jeg ~r at jeg har urett/har tatt feil* I acknowledge/own that I am wrong; *jeg ~r mottakelsen av Deres brev* I acknowledge the receipt of your letter.

erklære *vb* declare; *~ krig (mot)* declare war (on); *~ seg enig* declare oneself in agreement. **erklæring** *sb* declaration, statement; *komme med en ~* give/make a declaration; make a statement.

erme *sb* sleeve; *brette opp ~ne* roll up one's sleeves.

ernære *vb: se fø, forsørge, underholde).* **ernæring** *sb* food, nourishment.

erobre *vb* conquer, capture; *~ nye markeder* capture new markets; *landet ble ~t av fienden* the country was conquered by the enemy. **erobrer** *sb* conqueror. **erobring** *sb* conquest.

erotikk *sb* eroticism, sex. **erotisk** *adj* erotic.

erstatning *sb* **1** *(godtgjørelse)* compensation; *hun fikk full ~* she received full compensation; **2** *(skades~)* damages; *kreve ~ av dem* claim damages against them; **3** *(surrogat)* substitute; *en dårlig ~ for kaffe* a poor substitute for coffee. **erstatte** *vb* **1** *(gi erstatning for)* compensate; make good; make up for; *de ~t tapet* they made good the loss; *ingenting kan ~ tapet av helsen* nothing can compensate/make up for the loss of one's health; **2** *(gi/tre i stedet for)* replace.

ert *sb* **A** *(belgfrukten)* pea; **B** *(erting) hun gjorde det på ~* she did it (on purpose) to tease/annoy me/us/ them etc. **erte** *vb* **1** tease; *de ~t ham med at han var så tykk* they teased him about being so fat; **2** *(om mer godmodig erting)* banter; chaff. **ertekrok** *sb* tease, teaser.

erte|ris *sb* pea straw; *de henger sammen som ~* they are as thick as thieves. **~suppe** *sb* pea-soup.

ertevoren *adj: han er ~* he is a tease. **erting** *sb* teasing; banter, chaff.

erts *sb (malm)* ore.

erverv *vb se yrke.* **erverve** *vb se anskaffe, få.* **ervervet egenskap** *sb* acquired character.

ese *vb (svulme)* swell; *(om deig)* rise.

esel *sb* ass, donkey. **eseløre** *sb (i bok etc)* dog-ear.

esing *sb (båtripe)* gunwale.

eske *sb* **1** box; *en ~ fyrstikker* a box of matches; **2** *(papp~)* carton.

eskimo *sb* In(n)uit; *gml* Eskimo, Esquimau. **eskimohund** *sb* Eskimo dog; husky. **eskimoisk** *adj* In(n)uit; *gml* Eskimo.

eskorte *sb* escort. **eskortere** *vb* escort.

esle *vb* intend, mean; *dette bildet er ~t til deg* this photo is intended/meant for you.

espalier *sb (gitterverk)* espalier, trellis.

ess *sb* **1** *(i kortstokk)* ace; **2** *(ener, overlegent dyktig person etc)* ace; *være i sitt ~* be in one's element; **3** *mus* E flat.

esse *sb (smieavl)* forge; smith's hearth.

essens *sb* essence, extract. **essensiell** *adj* essential.

estetiker *sb* aesthete. **estetikk** *sb* aesthetics. **estetisk** *adj* aesthetic.

et *ubest art,* se *en.*

etablere *vb (grunnlegge)* establish, found; *~ seg* establish oneself/set up in business. **etablissement** *sb* establishment.

etappe *sb* **1** stage; *vi gjorde turen unna i små ~r* we made the trip by easy stages; **2** *(især om del av flytur)* hop, leg; **3** *(i stafettløp)* leg. **etappevis** *adv* stage by stage.

etasje *sb* floor, stor(e)y; *første ~* (the) groundfloor; *US* (the) first floor; *annen/tredje/fjerde ~* (the) first/ second/third floor; *US* (the) second/third/fourth floor; *i første ~* on the groundfloor; *US* on the first floor. **etasjeseng** *sb (køyeseng)* double-decker bed.

etat *sb* department, service; works.

ete *vb* eat.

eter *sb* ether.

etikett *sb* label.

etikk *sb* ethics. **etisk** *adj* ethic; ethical.

etse *vb* **1** burn; eat (into); *med* cauterize; **2** *(med syre)* corrode; **3** *(om kunstteknikk)* etch.

etsteds *adv* somewhere.

ett *tallord,* se *en.*

etter *prep* **1** *(om tid og rekkefølge)* after; *(adv også)* afterwards, later; *~ at hun var gått* after she had left; *~ krigen* after the war; *dagen ~* the next/the following day; *kort/snart ~* soon/shortly afterwards; a little later; *lukk døren ~ deg* shut the door after you; *straks ~* immediately afterwards; **2** *(om formål og hensikt)* for; *han løp ~ hjelp* he ran for help; *hun så etter fotoapparatat sitt* she was looking for her camera; **3** *(om forskjellige forhold)* at, by, from; *~ det/hva jeg har hørt* from what I have heard; *~ min smak* to my taste; *~ ordre* by order; *~ vekt* by weight; *han gjentok ~ hukommelsen* he repeated from memory.

etter|anmeldelse, ~anmeldt person *sb* late entry. **~ape** *vb* imitate, mimic. **~betaling** *sb (av lønn)* back pay. **~datere** *vb* postdate. **~forske** *vb* investigate; inquire into. **~forskning** *sb* investigation, inquiry. **~følge** *vb* succeed, follow. **~følger** *sb* successor. **~gi** *vb* remit. **~givende** *adj* compliant, indulgent. **~givenhet** *sb* compliance, indulgence. **~hvert, ~hånden** *adv* gradually; by degrees. **~komme** *vb* comply with. **~kommer** *sb* descendant. **~krav** *sb* cash on delivery; C.O.D.; *varene ble sendt mot ~* the goods were sent C.O.D. **~late** *vb* leave behind; *~late seg* leave; *hun etterlot seg en formue* she left a fortune; *de etterlatte* the surviving relatives. **~ligne** *vb* imitate. **~ligning** *sb* imitation. **~lyse** *vb* **1** *(noe som er borte)* advertise for; *(i radio)* broadcast an S.O.S. for; **2** *(kalle på over høyttaler)* page; **3** *(~ forbryter etc)* institute a search for; *etterlyst av politiet* wanted by the police. **~mann** *sb* successor.

ettermiddag *sb* afternoon; *i ~* this afternoon; *kl. tre i ~* at three o'clock this afternoon; *om ettermiddagen* in the afternoon; *om ettermiddagen den 23. januar* on the afternoon of January 23rd; *om ettermiddagen samme dag* on the afternoon of the same day.

etter|navn *sb* family name; surname. **~nøler** *sb* **1** *(en som kommer sent)* late-comer; **3** *(en som blir etter)* laggard. **~plaprer** *sb* parrot. **~på** *adv* afterwards; after that. **~påklokskap** *sb* hindsight; wisdom after the event. **~retning** *sb* a piece of information/news; *~er* information, news; *de siste ~er* the latest news. **~retningstjeneste/~vesen** *sb* intelligence service. **~sende** *vb (brev etc)* forward. **~sittende** *adj (om klær)* clinging. **~skrift** *sb* postscript. **~skudd** *sb: i/på ~skudd* in arrears. **~slekt** *sb* posterity. **~slått** *sb* aftermath. **~ som** *konj (etter hvert som)* as. **~som** *konj (da, fordi, siden)* because, since; seeing that. **~sommer** *sb* late summer. **~spurt** *adj* in demand; *meget ~spurt* in great demand. **~spørsel** *sb* demand; *ingen/liten/stor ~spørsel* no/small/great demand. **~syn** *sb (kontroll etc)* inspection; examination; **2** *(overhaling)* overhaul; *foreta ~syn* inspect; examine; overhaul; *ved nærmere ~syn* on (a) closer inspection. **~tanke** *sb* reflection, meditation; *ved nærmere ~tanke* on reflection/second thoughts; now I come to think of it. **~tenksom** *adj* thoughtful. **~tid** *sb* future; *for ~tiden* in future. **~trykk** *sb* **1** *(aksentuering, vekt)* emphasis; *med ~* emphatically; **2** *(av bok)* piracy; *~ forbudt* all rights reserved. **~trykkelig** *adj* emphatic. **~utdannelse** *sb* in-service training. **~virkning** *sb* after-effect, repercussion.

ett|-tall *sb* (the figure) one; *jeg går surr i ett-tallene og sjutallene dine* I mix up your ones and your sevens. **~tid** *sb: ved ~tiden* about one o'clock. **~årig** *adj* **1** one-year; *et ~årig kursus* a one-year course; **2** *(om plante)* annual.

etui *sb* case.

etymologi *sb* etymology. **etymologisk** *adj* etymologic.

evakuere *vb* evacuate. **evakuering** *sb* evacuation.

evangelisk *adj* evangelical. **evangelist** *sb* evangelist. **evangelium** *sb* gospel; *Johannes' ~* the Gospel according to St John.

eventuell *adj* possible; (if) any; *~e mistenkte* any/possible suspects. **eventuelt 1** *adv* possibly; if desired; if necessary; perhaps; *en eller ~ flere biler vil ...* one or possibly/if necessary more cars will ...; *jeg kunne ~ hjelpe deg* I might help you; **2** *sb (post på dagsorden)* a.o.b. (= any other business).

eventyr *sb* **1** *(fortelling)* tale; fairy-tale, folke-tale; **2** *(opplevelse)* adventure. **eventyrer** *sb* adventurer. **eventyr|land** *sb* fairyland, wonderland. **~lig** *adj* fantastic. **~lysten** *adj* adventurous.

evig *adj* **1** eternal; *~ fred* eternal peace; *~ og alltid* always; for ever and ever; *til ~ tid* for ever; **2** *(endeløs)* everlasting, perpetual; *~ ungdom* eternal/perpetual youth; **3** *(uforgjengelig)* immortal, undying; *~ berømmelse/ry* undying fame. **evighet** *sb* eternity; *aldri i ~* never in my life; *det varte en ~ før* it was ages before. **evigvarende** *adj* everlasting, perpetual.

evinnelig *adj = evigvarende.*

evje *sb* backwater.

evne I *sb* **1** faculty; ability; gift, talent; *hun har gode evner* she is a girl/woman of great ability; she is a gifted girl/woman; *han har ~n til lett å skaffe seg venner* he has the faculty of making friends easily; **2** *(økonomisk ~)* means; *de levde over ~* they lived beyond their means; **II** *vb (kunne, makte)* be able (to); be capable (of). **evne|løs** *adj* incapable, incompetent. **~rik** *adj* gifted, talented. **~veik** *adj* backward; mentally retarded.

evolusjon *sb* evolution.

F

f *(bokstaven)* f.

fabel *sb* fable. **fabelaktig 1** *adj* fabulous; **2** *adv* fabulously; *(også)* fantastically; *hun er ~ flink* she is fantastically clever. **fable** *vb* (day)dream; talk wildly; *han ~t om å vinne hele verden* in his (day)dreams he conquered the whole world; he talked wildly of conquering the whole world.

fabrikant *sb* maker, manufacturer. **fabrikasjon** *sb* making; manufacture, manufacturing. **fabrikasjonsfeil** *sb* defect, flaw. **fabrikk** *sb* factory, works; *om papir~, tekstil~, treforedlings~ etc* mill; *ansatt på en ~* employed in a factory. **fabrikk|arbeider** *sb* factory hand/worker, mill hand. **~by** *sb* industrial town. **~drift** *sb* manufacturing industry. **fabrikkere** *vb* make, manufacture.

fabrikk|inspektør *sb* factory inspector. **~merke** *sb* trade mark. **~pipe** *sb* factory chimney. **~pris** *sb: til ~pris* at factory price. **~tilsyn** *sb* factory inspection. **~vare** *sb* manufacture; *fl også* factory-made goods.

fadder *sb* godfather, godmother.

faderlig *adj* fatherly, paternal.

fadervår *sb* the Lord's Prayer.

fadese *sb* blunder; *gjøre ~* blunder.

faen *sb* the devil; Old Nick; *det gir jeg ~ i* I do not care a damn (about it); *gi ~ lillefingeren, og han tar snart hele hånden* give him (the devil) an inch and he will take an ell; *som bare ~* like hell. **faen|ivoldsk** *adj* reckless; devil-may-care. **~skap** *sb* devilment, devilry.

fag *sb* **1** *(skole~)* subject; *hvilke ~ har du på skolen?* what subjects are you taught at school? **2** *(~ som forutsetter større boklig utdannelse)* profession; **3** *(håndverk)* trade. **fag|arbeider** *sb* skilled worker. **~bevegelse** *sb* trade union movement. **~folk** *sb koll* experts, specialists. **~forbund** *sb* federation of trade unions. **~forening** *sb* trade union. **~krets** *sb* **1** *(skoles ~krets)* curriculum; **2** *(elevs/students ~krets)* (range of) subjects. **~kunnskap** *sb* expert knowledge; *teknisk ~kunnskap også* know-how. **faglig** *adj* professional, technical. **fag|litteratur** *sb* **1** special/technical literature; scientific literature; **2** *(motsatt skjønnlitteratur)* non-fiction. **~lærer** *sb* subject teacher. **~lært** *adj* skilled. **~mann** *sb* expert, specialist. **~organisert** *adj: ~organiserte arbeidere* trade unionists. **~skole** *sb* vocational school. **~utdannelse** *sb* vocational training. **~utdannet** *adj = ~lært.*

fajanse *sb* faience.

fakke *vb* catch.

fakkel *sb* torch. **fakkeltog** *sb* torchlight procession.

fakter *sb fl* gestures.

faktisk I *adj* actual, real, virtual; **II** *adv* **1** actually, virtually; as a matter of fact; *jeg kjøpte den* ~ as a matter of fact I bought it; **2** *(brukt forsterkende)* really; *det er* ~ *ingen ting å gjøre med det* there is really nothing to be done about it.

faktor *sb* **1** *mat etc* factor; **2** *(i trykkeri)* compositor, foreman.

faktum *sb* fact.

faktura *sb* invoice.

fakultet *sb* faculty.

fald *sb (på tøy)* hem.

falk *sb* falcon.

fall *sb* **1** *(det å falle)* fall; *hovmod står for* ~ pride goes before a fall; **2** *(tilfelle) i* **alle** ~ = *i hvert* ~; *i* **beste** ~ at best; *i* **hvert** ~ at all events; in any case; at any rate; at least; *i* **motsatt** ~ if not; failing that; *i* **så** ~ if so; if that is the case; *i* **verste** ~ at worst.

falle *vb* **1** drop, fall; *han falt av sykkelen* he fell over/took a spill with his bike; *hun falt så lang hun var* she fell full length; *temperaturen falt* the temperature dropped/fell; **2** *med adv, prep etc* ~ **av** fall from/off; ~ **for:** ~ *for aldersgrensen* retire (on reaching the age limit); ~ *for fristelsen* succumb to the temptation; ~ **fra 1** *(dø)* die; **2** *(svikte)* desert; ~ *fra hverandre* fall apart; fall to pieces; ~ **i fisk:** *planen falt i fisk* the plan was a complete failure; ~ **i grus** collapse; fall in ruins; ~ **i krig** fall; be killed in action; ~ **i smak:** *det* ~*r i min smak* it is to my taste/liking; ~ **i søvn** fall asleep; ~ **i tanker** be lost in thoughts; ~ **i vannet** fall into the water; ~ *en* **inn:** *det har aldri falt meg inn* it never crossed my mind/entered my head; *det kunne ikke* ~ *meg inn* I wouldn't dream of it; ~ **lett** come easy; ~ **over ende** fall/tumble down; fall over; ~ **på:** *det* ~*r på deg* it falls to you; *i år* ~*r 17. mai på en søndag* this year the 17th of May falls on a Sunday; ~ **sammen** *(især om personer)* break down; collapse; se også ~ *i grus*; ~ **som offer** *for* fall a victim to; ~ **til ro** come to rest; calm/settle down; ~ **ut 1** fall out; **2** *fig (ha som resultat)* turn out; *det falt heldig ut* it turned out well; it was a success. **falleferdig** *adj* tumble-down, ramshackle. **fallen** *adj, pp* fallen; *en* ~ *kvinne* a fallen woman; se for øvrig *falt.* **falt** *adj, pp (~ i krig)* fallen; *falne og sårede* killed and wounded; *de falne* those killed in war.

fallent *sb* bankrupt.

fall|gruve *sb* pitfall. **~høyde** *sb* height of drop/fall.

fallitt 1 *adj* bankrupt; *han gikk* ~ he went bankrupt; **2** *sb* bankruptcy, failure.

fall|reip *sb: på ~reipet (like før avreise etc)* on the point of leaving; on the eve of departure.

fallskjerm *sb* parachute. **fallskjerm|hopper** *sb* parachutist. **~soldat** *sb* paratrooper.

falme *vb* fade; *solen har ~t gardinene/fått gardinene til å* ~ the sun has faded the curtains.

falsk I *adj* **1** false; *en* ~ *mynt/venn* a false coin/friend; ~ *ed* perjury; se også *ed;* **2** *(forfalsket)* forged; ~*e penger* forged bank-notes; *et* ~*t pass* a forged passport; **2** *adv* falsely; *han spilte/sang* ~*t* he played/sang out of tune. **falskhet** *sb* falseness. **falskner** *sb* forger. **falskneri** *sb* forgery. **falskspiller** *sb* card-sharper. **falsum** *sb (falsk påstand)* falsehood; untruth.

familie *sb* family; ~*n Nilsen* the Nilsen family; the Nilsens; *min* ~ *(nærmeste)* my people; *(fjernere)* my relations; *han er i* ~ *med meg* he is a relation/relative of mine; ~*n er blitt underrettet (om ulykke)* the next-of-kin have been informed. **familie|far** *sb* father/head of a family. **~fest** *sb* = ~ *reunion.* **~forsørger** *sb* bread-winner. **~hemmelighet** *sb* family secret; *(ubehagelig)* skeleton in the cupboard. **~krets** *sb* family circle. **~likhet** *sb* family likeness. **~liv** *sb* family/home/domestic life. **~sammenkomst** *sb* family reunion.

familiær *adj* familiar.

famle *vb* **1** grope; *vi ~t oss frem gjennom de mørke gatene* we groped our way through the dark streets; **2** *(beføle)* fumble; *hun ~t etter nøklene* she fumbled for her keys. **famlende** *adj (nølende etc)* faltering, hesitating.

fanatiker *sb* fanatic. **fanatisk** *adj* fanatic(al). **fanatisme** *sb* fanaticism.

fanden etc se *faen etc.*

fane *sb* banner; *frihets~* banner of freedom. **~bærer** *sb* standard bearer.

fanfare *sb* flourish.

fang *sb* **1** lap; *på ~et* on one's knee/lap; **2** = **fange A**.

fangarm *sb* tentacle.

fange A *sb (armfull)* armful; *et* ~ *ved* an armful of wood; **B I** *sb* **1** prisoner, captive; *vi tok ham til* ~ we took him prisoner; we captured him; **2** *(straff~)* convict; **II** *vb* catch; *katten ~t en fugl* the cat caught a bird; **2** *(ta til ~)* capture; take prisoner; *han ble tatt til* ~ he was taken prisoner. **fangeleir** *sb* prison camp. **fangenskap** *sb* captivity. **fangevokter** *sb* prison officer; warder. **fangline** *sb* painter. **fangst** *sb* **1** *(av fisk etc)* catch, haul; **2** *(jaktbytte også)* bag; *jegeren fikk en god* ~ the sportsman made a good bag/catch; **3** *(~virksomhet)* hunting, trapping. **fangstfolk** *sb* hunters, trappers.

fant *sb* **1** *(landstryker)* tramp; *US stundom* hobo; **2** *(kjeltring)* knave, rascal; **3** *(lutfattig fyr)* penniless beggar; *han er raka* ~ he is poor as a church mouse.

fantasere *vb (fable, snakke over seg)* rave; be delirious. **fantasi** *sb* imagination; *en livlig* ~ a vivid/lively imagination. **fantastisk 1** *adj* fantastic(al); **2** *adv* fantastically.

fanteri *sb (lureri)* tricks; *hva er det for* ~ *han farer med?* what tricks is he up to? *fusk og* ~ dirty tricks. **fantestrek** *sb* dirty trick.

far *sb* **A** *(opphav)* father; **B** *(spor)* track, trail.

farang *sb (omgangssyke)* epidemic.

farbar *adj* **1** *(om vei)* passable; *ikke* ~ impassable; **2** *(seilbar)* navigable; *en* ~ *elv* a navigable river.

farbror *sb* uncle.

fare A *sb* **1** danger; ~ **for:** *en* ~ *for helsen* a danger to health; *en* ~ *for skipsfarten* a danger to navigation; **i**

~: *livet hennes er i* ~ her life is in danger; **uten ~** without any danger; **utenfor ~** out of danger; *han har vært svært syk, men er nå utenfor* ~ he has been very ill, but is now out of danger; **2** *(stor ~)* peril; **3** *(risiko)* risk; **~ for** danger/risk of; *det er ~ for krig* there is a danger/risk of war; *stå* **i ~ for** be in danger of; *vi stod i ~ for å miste pengene våre* we were in danger of losing our money; **med ~ for** at the risk of; *med ~ for livet* at the risk of one's life; **B** *vb* **1** *(dra, reise)* go, travel; *(om skip)* sail; **~ frem** *(opptre)* act, behave, proceed; **~ med** *løgn* tell lies; *han har ikke stort å ~ med* he is not likely to set the Thames on fire; **~ over** *(med en harelabb)* pass lightly over; **~ vill** go astray; lose one's way; *(ta feil)* be mistaken; err; **2** *(styrte)* rush, tear; dart; dash; *en bil for forbi oss* a motor-car dashed past us; **~ igjennom** flash through; **~ løs på** rush at; *oksen for løs på ham* the bull rushed at him; **~ opp** jump/start up; jump to one's feet; *~ opp i sinne* flare up; fly into a temper; **~ på** se *~ løs på*; **~ sammen** *(rykke til)* start; give a start. **fare|full** *adj* dangerous. **~truende** *adj* menacing.

farfar *sb* grandfather.

farge I *sb* **1** colour; *hvilken ~ har den?* what colour is it? **2** *(~stoff)* dye; **3** *(i kortstokk)* suit; **II** *vb* **1** *(~legge)* colour; **2** *(~ hår, tøy etc)* dye. **farge|blind** *adj* colour-blind. **~blyant** *sb* crayon. **~ekte** *adj* colourfast, fast. **~film** *sb* colour film; *(om kinofilm sies ofte)* Technicolor. **~handel** *sb* oil and colour shop. **~lagt** *adj* coloured. **~løs** *adj* colourless. **~rik** *adj* colourful. **~skrin** *sb* paint-box. **~stift** *sb* = *~blyant*. **farget 1** *(også om raser)* coloured; **2** *(om hår/tøy)* dyed.

farin *sb* castor sugar.

fariseer *sb* Pharisee. **fariseisk** *adj* pharisaic(al).

farkost *sb* boat, craft, vessel.

farlig *adj* **1** *(som medfører fare)* dangerous; *en ~ sykdom* a dangerous disease/illness; *det er ikke (så) ~ (dvs spiller liten rolle)* it does not matter (much); **2** *(risikabel)* risky.

farmasøyt *sb* pharmacist. Se også *apoteker*.

farmor *sb* grandmother.

farse *sb* **1** *(fiske~, kjøtt~)* forcemeat; **2** *(muntert lystspill)* farce.

farskap *sb* fatherhood, paternity.

farsott *sb* epidemic; *(pest)* plague, pestilence.

fart *sb* **1** *(hastighet)* speed; rate; *for/i full (halv etc) ~* at full (half etc) speed; *i ~en: i ~en glemte vi det* in our hurry we forgot it; *jeg kan ikke komme på det i ~en* I cannot think of it at the monemt; *med en ~ av 50 miles i timen* at the speed/rate of 50 miles an/per hour; *med liten (stor etc) ~* at a low (high etc) speed; *sette ned ~en* slow down; *sette opp ~en* accelerate; speed up; **2** *(trafikk, seilas)* navigation, trade; *gå i ~ på (om skip)* trade to; **3** *(tempo, virksomhet etc)* pace; *bestemme ~en* set the pace; *på ~en* on the run/go/move.

farte *vb: ~ omkring* gad about; go places.

fartøy *sb* craft, vessel; boat.

farvann *sb* water(s); *de er i ~et* they are on their way.

farvel *interj, sb* **1** *(især når det ikke regnes med snarlig gjensyn)* good-bye; *si ~ til* say good-bye to; take leave of; **2** *dgl a)* good morning/afternoon/evening/night; *b) (mellom venner)* cheerio; so long; **3** *mer formelt (f.eks. i butikker)* good day; **4** *høytidelig* farewell.

fasade *sb* front, façade. **fasadeklatrer** *sb* cat burglar.

fasan *sb* pheasant.

fascisme *sb* Fascism. **fascist** *sb* Fascist. **fascistisk** *adj* Fascist.

fase *sb* phase.

fasit *sb* **1** *(resultat)* answer; **2** *(~liste)* answers, key.

fasle *sb* se *fatle*.

fasong *sb* form, shape; make.

fast I *adj* **1** *(ubevegelig)* firm; immovable; *en ~ hånd/stemme* a firm hand/voice; *en ~ karakter* a strong character; *ha ~ grunn under føttene* be on firm ground; **2** *(~ tilkoblet etc)* attached; **3** *(motsatt flytende)* solid; *~ føde* solid food; **4** *(etablert, mer el. mindre permanent)* fixed, permanent; regular; *~ adresse* permanent address; *~ arbeid* a permanent job; *~e priser* fixed prices; *~e utgifter* overhead expenses; overheads; *~ kunde* a regular customer; *~ lønn* a fixed salary; *de har ~ følge* they go steady; **II** *adv* firmly (etc, jf *fast I*); *han er ~ ansatt* he is on the permanent staff; *de sov ~* they were fast/sound asleep; *kjøre seg ~* get stuck; *sette seg ~, sitte ~* stick; *bussen satt~ i gjørmen* the bus stuck in the mud.

fastboende *adj* **1** *(ikke tilreisende)* resident; **2** *(ikke nomader)* settled.

faste *sb, vb* fast. **fastelavn** *sb* Shrovetide. **fasten** *sb (fastetiden)* the Lent. **fastende** *adj* fasting; *på ~ hjerte* on an empty stomach.

fast|het *sb* firmness, solidity; permanence. **~kjørt** *adj data* = *~låst*. **~land** *sb* mainland; *(større ~land, verdensdel)* continent. **~låst** *adj data* wedged. **~sette** *vb* fix, settle (on); *vi fastsatte møtet til fredag* we fixed the meeting for Friday.

fat *sb* **1** *(mat~ etc)* dish; *hun fylte ~ene* she filled the dishes; **2** *(vaskevanns~)* basin; **3** *(tønne)* barrel, cask; *et ~ med vin* a cask of wine.

fatle *sb* sling.

fatning *sb* composure.

fattbar *adj* conceivable; comprehensible, intelligible.

fatt *adv* **1** *få ~ i* get/catch hold of; *hun fikk ~ i en gren* she caught hold of a branch; *de tok ~ på arbeidet* they set to work; **2** *hvordan er det ~ med deg?* how are you (feeling)? how are things with you? **fatte** *vb* **1** *(gripe)* catch (hold of); grasp, seize; **2** *(forstå)* grasp, understand; *jeg tror ikke han ~t meningen* I don't think he grasped/understood the meaning; **3** *(om følelse, plan)* conceive; *~ håp* conceive a hope; *~ mistanke* suspect; *~ mot* take courage/heart; *~ seg i korthet* be brief; *han fattet en beslutning* he made up his mind. **fattelig** se *fattbar*. **fatteevne** *sb* grasp, comprehension. **fattet** *adj* calm, selfpossessed; *blek, men ~* pale but resolute.

fattig *adj* poor; *~ på* poor in; *vi er ~e på jordisk gods* we are poor in wordly goods. **fattig|dom** *sb* poverty. **~folk** *sb* poor people; the poor. **~forsorg, ~understøttelse, ~vesen** *sb hist* poor relief.

favn *sb* **1** *(åpen ~)* arms; *ta i ~* take into one's arms; embrace; **2** *(sluttet ~) med ~en full av blomster* carrying an armful of flowers; **3** *(armfull etc) en ~ ved* a cord of wood; **4** *(lengdemål)* favn (som lengdemål, se midtsidene); *på ni ~er vann* in nine fathoms of water. **favne** *vb* embrace, hug; *(dekke, omfatte)* cover. **favntak** *sb* embrace, hug.

favorisere *vb* favour. **favoritt** *sb* favourite. **favør** *sb* favour; *i vår ~* in our favour.

fe *sb* **A** *(eventyrskikkelse)* fairy; **B 1** *(koll: kveg)* cattle; **2** *(tosk)* fool. **feavl** *sb* cattle breeding.

feber *sb* **1** *(for høy temperatur)* temperature; *han har ~* he has/he is running a temperature; he is feverish; **2** *(~sykdom)* fever. **feberfantasier** *sb* delirium. **febril** *adj* feverish. **febrilsk** *adj* feverish; feverish haste.

februar February; *første ~* the first of February; Febr. 1st.

fedd *sb (av garn)* skein.

fedme *sb* fatness, obesity.

fedreland *sb* (native) country. **fedrelands|kjærlighet** *sb* patriotism. **~sang** *sb* patriotic song.

fedrift *sb* **1** *(avl)* cattle breeding; **2** *(bøling)* drove of cattle.

fei *sb: i en ~* in a jiffy; in less than no time.

feide *sb* feud.

feie *vb* sweep; *~ gulvet* sweep the floor; *~ for (sin) egen dør* sweep before one's own door; *nye koster ~r best* new brooms sweep clean; *mine bemerkninger ble feid til side* my remarks were brushed aside. **feie|brett** *sb* dustpan. **~kost** *sb* dust-brush; *(langskaftet)* broom. **feiende** *adv: ~ flott* dashing. **feier** *sb* chimney-sweep.

feig *adj* **1** *(ikke modig)* cowardly; *han er ~* he is a coward; **2** *(som snart skal dø)* doomed to die. **feighet** *sb* cowardice. **feiging** *sb* coward.

feil I *adj (feilaktig, uriktig)* wrong, incorrect; *oppgi ~ adresse* give a wrong address; *slå ~ nummer* dial the wrong number; **II** *adv* **1** wrong, wrongly; *gå ~* go wrong; go/take the wrong way; *slå ~ (dvs mislykkes)* go wrong; *ta ~* be mistaken/wrong; make a mistake; *du tar fullstendig ~* you are quite mistaken/wrong; *ta ~ av veien* go wrong/the wrong way; *jeg tok ~ av ham og hans bror* I mistook him for his brother; **2** *som forstavelse til vb* mis-; *~(be)regne* miscalculate; *~datere ~* misdate; *~plassere* misplace; *~sitere* misquote; *~tolke* misinterpret; **III** *sb* **1** *(~takelse)* fault; error, mistake; *(liten ~, slurve~)* slip; *(stor ~, tabbe)* blunder; *begå/gjøre en ~* make a mistake etc; commit a fault/an error; **2** *(~ en har, skyld)* fault; *det er ikke min ~* it is not my fault; **3** *(lyte, mangel)* defect, fault; *jeg elsker ham til tross for hans ~* I love him in spite of his faults; **4** *(brist, svakt punkt)* flaw; **5** *(ulempe)* drawback(s); *~en ved skolesystemet vårt* the drawbacks of our educational system. **feilaktig** *adj* se *feil I*. **feilbar** *adj* fallible. **feile** *vb* **1** *(begå feil)* err; make mistakes/a mistake; **2** *(være i veien med): hva ~r det deg?* what is the matter with you? *det ~r ikke henne noe* there is nothing wrong with her. **feilfri** *adj* faultless, correct; *et ~tt svar* a correct answer; *hun snakker engelsk ~tt* her English is faultless. **feiltakelse** *sb* mistake; *jeg gjorde det ved en ~* I did it by mistake.

feire *vb* **1** *(en begivenhet)* celebrate; *de ~t sølvbryllup* they celebrated their silver wedding; **2** *(en person)* fête; *hun ble ~t overalt hvor hun kom* she was fêted wherever she went. **feiring** *sb* celebration.

feit etc se *fet etc.*

fekte *vb* **1** *(med kårde etc)* fence; **2** *(med armene)* gesticulate.

fele *sb* fiddle; *spille ~* fiddle. **felespiller** *sb* fiddler.

felg *sb (hjulring)* rim.

fell *sb (skinn~)* fur; fell, pelt.

felle A *sb* trap, pitfall; **B** *vb* **1** *(~ trær)* fell; cut down; **2** *(~ fiende)* kill, slay; **3** *(~ dom)* pass (judgement/sentence); **4** *(~ fjær)* moult; *(~ hår)* shed; *~ tenner* cut one's second teeth; *~ tårer* shed tears; **5** *(i strikking)* cast off.

felles *adj* common, joint; *de har ~ interesser* they have common interests; *de har ingenting (til) ~* they have nothing in common; *til ~ bruk* to the common advantage; *ved ~ anstrengelser* by joint efforts. **felles|eie** *sb* **1** *(det å eie noe sammen)* joint ownership; **2** *(det som eies sammen)* joint property. **~lager** *sb data* shared memory. **~navn** *sb* common name/noun. **~nevner** *sb* common denominator. **~skap** *sb* community; *opptre i ~skap* act jointly/together; make common cause.

felt *sb* **1** *(område)* field, line, province, sphere; **2** *(kjøre~ etc)* lane; **3** *(mil)* field; *i ~en* in the field; *dra til ~s mot* take up arms against. **felt|herre** *sb* commander, general. **~seng** *sb* camp bed; folding bed. **~tog** *sb* campaign.

fem *tallord* five; *han er ikke ved sine fulle ~* he is not all there.

feminin *adj (kvinnelig)* feminine; *(sagt om menn)* effeminate.

fem|kamp *sb* pentathlon. **~kant** *sb* pentagon. **~tall** *sb* five.

fenge *vb* catch fire. **fengende** *adj* catchy; *en ~ melodi* a catchy tune. **fenghette** *sb* percussion cap.

fengsel *sb (om bygningen)* prison; goal, jail; *(om straffen)* imprisonment; *komme i ~* be imprisoned; be sent to prison; go to jail; *sette i ~* imprison; put in prison; *sitte i ~* be in prison; *livsvarig ~* imprisonment for life; *tre års ~* three years' imprisonment. **fengsels|betjent** *sb* prison officer/guard. **~direktør** *sb* (prison) governor; *US* warden. **~vesen** *sb* prison administration. **fengsle** *vb* **1** imprison; **2** *(arrestere)* arrest; **3** *(virke fengslende)* fascinate.

fenomen *sb* phenomenon. **fenomenal** *adj* phenomenal.

ferd *sb* **1** *(reise)* expedition; **2** *(fremferd, oppførsel)* conduct; behaviour; **3** *(uttrykk) det er noe galt på ~e* there is something wrong (going on); *han var tidlig på ~e* he was up and about early; *hva er på ~e?* what is going on here? *også* what is the matter? *være i ~ med å (skulle til å)* be about to; *(holde på med)* be ...ing; *hun var i ~ med å lese* she was reading. **ferdes** *vb* travel.

ferdig *adj* **1** *(parat)* ready; *vi er ~ til å begynne* we are ready to begin; **2** *(fullført)* done, finished; *arbeidet er ~* the work is done/finished; *er du ~ med boken/med å snakke?* have you finished the book/finished speaking? *gjøre ~* finish; make ready; *(avslutte)* terminate; *lage/ skrive ~* finish; **3** *(utkjørt) jeg er helt ~* I am exhausted/done up.

ferdighet *adj* proficiency, skill; *(behendighet)* dexterity.

ferdig|laget, ~sydd *adj* ready-made.

ferdsel *sb* traffic. Se for øvrig *trafikk*.

ferie *sb* holidays; leave, vacation *(især om embetsmenn og universitetsfolk og i US); (hvileperiode)* holiday; *hun trenger ~* she needs a holiday; *vi drog til Danmark i ~n* we went to Denmark for the holidays. **ferie|dag** *sb* holiday; *også* day off. **~gjest** *sb* holiday-maker. **feriere** *vb* be on holiday. **ferie|reise** *sb* se *~tur*. **~sted** *sb* holiday resort. **~tur** *sb* holiday trip. **~vikar** *sb* holiday/leave substitute.

ferje 1 *sb* ferry; *(mindre)* ferry-boat; **2** *vb* ferry. **~sted** *sb* ferry.

ferniss *sb* varnish. **fernissere** *vb* varnish.

fersk *sb* fresh; *~ fisk/kjøtt* fresh fish/meat; *han ble tatt på ~ gjerning* he was caught red-handed/in the (very) act.

fersken *sb* peach.

ferskvann *sb* fresh-water.

fest *sb* **1** *(privat selskap)* celebration; *vi skal ha en liten ~ i kveld* we are having a little celebration tonight; **2** *(~middag)* feast, banquet; **3** *(~ med dans)* dance; **4** *(løssluppen ~)* revelry; **5** *(offentlig ~)* festival; celebration, function. **fest|antrekk** *sb* full dress; gala (dress); *(kjole og hvitt)* evening dress. **~dag** *sb* public holiday.

feste *vb* **A 1** *(holde fest)* celebrate; **2** *(rangle)* revel; **B** *(gjøre fast)* fasten; attach, fix; *det var ~t en krok til tauet* a hook was attached to the rope; *han ~t blikket på meg* he fixed his eyes on me; *~ oppmerksomheten på/ved* fix one's attention on; *~ seg ved* pay attention to; take notice of.

festlig *adj* festive; *~e anledninger* festive occasions; *~ smykket* gaily decorated; *vi hadde det ~* it was great fun. **festligheter** *sb fl* festivities.

festning *sb* fort, fortress.

fet *adj* **1** fat; **2** *(om mat)* rich; rich cakes. **fett** *sb* **1** fat; **2** *(smøre~)* grease; **3** *(steke~)* cooking fat; lard; **4** *det er ett ~* it is all the same; it does not matter.

fetter *sb* (male) cousin.

fettet(e) *adj* greasy.

fiasko *sb* failure; *(sterkere)* fiasco; *stykket var en ~* the play was a failure.

fiende *sb* enemy. **fiendskap** *sb* enmity, hostility. **fiendtlig** *adj* **1** *(~sinnet)* hostile; *~ holdning* hostile attitude; **2** *(som tilhører fienden)* enemy; *~e fly* enemy aircraft. **fiendtlighet** *sb* hostility.

fiffig *adj* astute, cunning, sly.

figur *sb* figure. **figurlig** *adj* figurative.

fiken *sb* fig.

fikle *vb: ~ med* fumble with.

fiks *adj* chic, smart; *~ og ferdig* all ready; *en ~ idé* a bee in one's bonnet; a fixed idea. **fikse** *vb* **1** *(reparere)* fix, mend, repair; *jeg skal ~ den klokka di* I'll fix that watch of yours; *~ på (pusse opp)* smarten up; **2** *(arrangere)* arrange; fix (up). **fiksstjerne** *sb* fixed star.

fil *sb* **A** *(verktøy)* file; **B** *(kjøre~)* lane.

filantrop *sb* philanthropist. **filantropi** *sb* philanthropy. **filantropisk** *adj* philanthropic.

filateli *sb* philately; stamp collecting. **filatelist** *sb* philatelist; stamp collector. **filatelistisk** *adj* philatelist.

file *vb* file.

filet *sb* fillet.

filial *sb* branch.

filipens *sb* pimple.

fille *sb* rag. **fillet(e)** *adj* ragged, tattered.

film *sb* film; *kjøre en ~* run a film. **film|apparat** *sb* **1** *(fremviser)* film projector; **2** *(kamera)* film camera. **~avis** *sb* newsreel. **filme** *vb* **1** *(opptre i film)* act in a film/in films; **2** *(ta opp film)* film; make/take a film. **film|fremviser, ~kamera** *sb* = *~apparat*. **~rull** *sb* a roll/*US* spool of film. **~skuespiller** *sb* film actor. **~skuespillerinne** *sb* film actress. **~star** *sb* film star.

filolog *sb* philologist; *stundom* scholar. **filologi** *sb* philology; *hun studerer ~* she is an arts student. **filologisk** *adj* philological. **filosof** *sb* philosopher. **filosofere** *vb* philosophize. **filosofi** *sb* philosophy. **filosofisk** *sb* philosophic.

filt *sb* felt. **filthatt** *sb* felt hat.

filter *sb* filter, strainer. **filterkake** *sb petro* wall-cake. **filtrere** *vb* filter, filtrate; strain.

fin *adj* fine; *~ sand* fine sand; *~e klær* fine clothes; *det er ~t vær* it is a fine day; *de var fine venner* they were great friends.

finale *sb (sluttkamp)* final(s); *de var med i ~n* they were in the finals.

finansdepartementet *sb* the Ministry of Finance; *GB* the Treasury; *US* the Treasury Department. **finanser** *sb fl* economics, finances. **finansiell** *adj* financial. **finansiere** *vb* finance. **finans|mann** *sb* financier. **~minister** *sb* Minister of Finance; *GB* Chancellor of the Exchequer; *US* Secretary of the Treasury.

finer *sb* veneer; *kryss~* plywood. **finerplate** *sb* veneer/plywood sheet.

finesse *sb* fine point; subtlety.

fin-fin *adj* first-rate, first-class, superfine; tip-top.

finfølelse *sb* delicacy, tact.

finger *sb* finger; *fingrene av fatet!* hands off! *det er ikke noe å sette ~en på* there is nothing you can put your finger on; *en ~ med i spillet* a finger in the pie; *han kan det på fingrene* he has it at his fingers' ends; *hun løftet ikke en ~ for å hjelpe ham* she did not lift/stir a finger to help him; *ikke legge fingrene imellom* be relentless; *se gjennom fingrene med* shut one's eyes to, connive/wink at. **finger|avtrykk** *sb* finger-print. **~bøl, ~bør** *sb* thimble. **~ferdighet** *sb* legerdemain. **~smokk** *sb* fingerstall. **~språk** *sb* manual alphabet.

fingert *adj* feigned, fectitious, invented.

fingre *vb* finger.

finne *sb (på fisk)* fin.

finne *vb* find; **~ for godt** think fit; **~ frem** find one's way; **~ hjem** find one's way home; **~ hverandre** *(møtes i gjensidig interesse/sympati)* meet; *de fant hverandre i (en felles) kjærlighet til musikken* they met in a common love of music; **~ på** *(tenke ut)* hit upon; think of; invent; *jeg kunne ikke ~ på noe å si* I could not think of anything to say; *(dikte opp)* invent, manufacture; **~ seg i** put up with; resign oneself to; *det må du (bare) ~ deg i* you will (just) have to put up with that; *han fant seg i sin skjebne* he resigned himself to his fate; **~ seg til rette** find one's feet; feel at home; **~ sted** take place; **~ ut** find out; **~ ut av:** *jeg ~r ikke/kan ikke ~ ut av det* I cannot make it out. **finne(r)lønn** *sb* reward. **finnes** *vb* **1** *(bli funnet)* be found; **2** *(forekomme, være til)* be, exist; *~ det liv på planetene?* does life exist on the planets?

finpusse *vb* finish, polish.

fintfølende *adj* delicate, sensitive.

fiol *sb* violet. **fiolett** *adj, sb* violet.

fiolin *sb* violin; *spille ~* play the violin. **fiolinbue** *sb* violin bow. **fiolinist** *sb* violinist. **fiolinkasse** *sb* violin case.

fire *tallord* four; *gå på ~* walk on all fours; *under ~ øyne* in private.

fire *vb* **1** *(heise ned)* lower; *~ en båt* lower a boat; **2** *(gi etter)* give way; budge; yield; *jeg ~r ikke en tomme* I won't budge an inch.

firfisle *sb* lizard. **firkant** *sb* quadrangle; *(kvadrat)* square. **firkantet** *adj* quadrangular; *(kvadratisk)* square.

firma *adj* firm.

fisk *sb* fish (også som *koll* og stundom i *fl*); *han fikk bare to ~er* he only caught two fish(es); *falle i ~* go wrong (to pieces, to pot); *frisk som en ~* fit as a fiddle; *som ~en i vannet* in one's element; *verken fugl eller ~* neither fish, flesh, nor fowl/good red herring. **fiske I** *sb (fisking)* fishing, fishery; **II** *vb* **1** fish; *de ~t laks* they fished salmon; **2** *(om stang~ især)* angle; *hun ~t (etter) ørret* she fished/angled for trout; **3** *~ i rørt vann* fish in troubled waters. **fiske|bolle** *sb* fish ball. **~båt** *sb* fishing-boat. **~garn** *sb* fishing-net. **~handler** *sb* fish-monger. **~hermetikk** *sb* tinned/*US* canned fish. **~kake** *sb* fish cake. **~kort** *sb* fishing permit/licence. **~krok** *sb* fish-hook. **fisker** *sb* **1** fisherman; **2** *(sports~, stang~)* angler, sportsman. **fiske|redskap** *sb* fishing-tackle. **~rett** *sb* **1** *(rett til fiske)* fishing right/rights; **2** *(matrett)* fish course/dish. **fiskeri** *sb* (jf *fiske I*). **fiske|snøre** *sb* fishing-line. **~stang** *sb* fishing-rod. **~stim** *sb* shoal of fish. **~torg** *sb* fishmarket. **~tur** *sb* fishing trip; *de er på ~tur* they are out fishing. **~yngel** *sb* fry.

fjas *sb* **1** *(sludder)* foolery, nonsense; **2** *(flørt)* dalliance, flirtation. **fjase** *vb* **1** talk (pleasant) nonsense; crack silly jokes; **2** *(flørte)* dally, flirt.

fjel *sb* board.

fjell *sb* mountain; *(især grunn~)* rock; *fast som ~* firm as (a) rock; *på ~et* in the mountains; *til ~s (opp på ~et)* into the mountains; *høyt til ~s* high (up) in the mountains. **fjell|kjede** *sb* mountain range; range of mountains. **~klatrer** *sb* mountaineer. **~klatring** *sb* mountaineering. **~land** *sb* mountainous country. **~overgang** *sb* mountain pass. **~rik** *sb* mountainous. **~topp** *sb* mountain top.

fjern *adj* distant, far-off; *~e land* distant/far-off countries; *en ~ slektning* a distant relative; *Det ~e østen* the Far East; *i det ~e* in the distance, far away, far off. **fjerne** *vb* remove. **fjernsyn** *sb* television, TV; *dgl* telly; *se ~* watch TV. **fjernsynsapparat** *sb* TV-set.

fjes *sb* face; *slang* mug.

fjetre *vb* paralyse. **fjetret** *adj* spellbound.

fjollet(e) *adj* foolish, silly. **fjols** *sb* fool, idiot; silly creature.

fjord *sb* inlet; *(i Norge)* fiord; *(i Skottland)* firth.

fjorten *tallord* fourteen; *~ dager* a fortnight; *hver ~de dag* once a fortnight/every fortnight.

fjær *sb* **1** *(fugle~)* feather; **2** *(stål~)* spring. **fjære A** *sb* **1** *(motsatt flo)* ebb(-tide); **2** *(strandkant)* seaboard; **B** *vb* be springy/elastic/resilient. **fjærende** *adj* springy; resilient; elastic. **fjærfe** *sb koll* poultry. **fjæring** *sb* resilience, give.

fjøl *sb* se *fjel.*

fjøs *sb* cowshed.

flagg *sb* flag; *data* sentinel. **flagge** *vb* fly a flag; *de ~t for kongen* they flew the flag in honour of the King.

flaggermus *sb* bat.

flaggstang *sb* flagstaff.

flagre *vb* **1** *(vimse, vingle)* flutter, flit; **2** *(flakse)* flap.

flak *sb* flake; *is~* floe.

flakke *vb (vandre omkring)* roam, wander; *med ~nde blikk* shifty-eyed.

flaks *sb (hell)* good luck; *ha ~* be in luck.

flakse *vb* flap, flutter; *fuglen ~t med vingene* the bird flapped/fluttered its wings.

flamme 1 *sb* flame; *huset stod i ~r* the house was in flames; **2** *vb* blaze; *~nde ild* blazing fire; *~ opp* flare up; burst into flame(s). **flamme|bro, ~vegg** *sb petro* bridge wall.

flanell *sb* flannel.

flanke *sb* flank.

flaske *sb* bottle; *en ~ vin* a bottle of wine; *felt~, lomme~* flask. **flaske|barn** *sb* bottle-fed baby. **~hals** *sb* bottleneck.

flass *sb (i håret)* dandruff, scurf. **flasse** *vb: ~ av* flake/peel off.

flat *adj* **1** flat, level; *~t tak* (a) flat roof; **2** *(flau)* abashed, crestfallen. **flate** *sb* **1** *(flatt land)* plain; **2** *(over~)* surface; *en plan ~* a plane; a flat/level surface. **flateinnhold** *sb* area; *(~ av jord målt i acres)* acreage; *~et i en trekant* the area of a triangle.

flattere *vb* flatter; *et ~nde portrett* a flattering portrait.

flau *adj* **1** *(skamfull: bare som predikatsord)* ashamed; *hun var ~ over at hun hadde vært så dum* she was ashamed of having been so stupid; *jeg var ~ over det* I was ashamed about/of it; **2** *(pinlig berørt)* embarrassed, sheepish; awkward; **3** *(pinlig: om situasjonen)* awkward, embarrassing; **4** *(om smak)* flat, insipid, tasteless; stale, vapid; **5** *(om vits)* feeble, pointless; **6** *(om vindstyrke) ~ vind* light air. **flause** *sb* **1** *(fadese)* blunder, gaffe; **2** *(flau vits)* feeble/pointless joke.

flegmatisk *adj* phlegmatic.

fleip *sb* **1** flippancy; flippant remarks; **2** *(~et person)* wisecracker; smart aleck/smart-alec. **fleipe** *vb* talk flippantly; make flippant remarks. **fleipet(e)** *adj* flippant.

flekk *sb* stain, spot; *en ~ på duken* a stain on the tablecloth; *en ~ på hennes rykte* a stain/spot on her character; *han rørte seg ikke av ~en* he did not budge/ stir an inch. **flekket(e)** *adj* dirty, stained; *(full av flekker)* spotted; with specks.

fleksibel *adj* flexible.

fleng: *i ~ (adv)* at random; indiscriminately.

flenge I *sb* **1** tear; **2** *(gapende sår)* gash; **3** *(avrevet stykke)* shred; **II** *vb* tear, slash; *~nde kritikk* slashing criticism.

flere *adj, pron* **1** *(ved sammenligning)* more; *du har ~ bøker enn jeg* you have more books than I; **2** *(atskillige)* several; *~ hundre* several hundred; *en eller ~* one or more; *jo ~ jo bedre* the more the better; **3** *(i spørsmål og ved nekting)* any other(s); *har du ~ bøker å vise meg? Nei, jeg har ikke ~* have you got any books to show me? No, I have not got any others. **fler|farget** *adj* multicoloured. **~koneri** *sb* polygamy. **~stemmig** *adj: ~stemmig sang* part singing. **~tall** *sb* **1** *(majoritet)* majority; *et knapt ~* a bare majority; *hun ble valgt med et ~ på 3000* she was elected by a majority of 3000; *to tredjedels ~* a two-thirds majority; *være i ~* be in majority; **2** *(i grammatikk)* the plural; *sette i ~* put in the plural.

flesk *sb* **1** pork; **2** *(saltet og røykt)* bacon. **fleskesvor** *sb* rind (of bacon). **flesket(e)** *adj* fat, obese.

flest *adj, pron* most; *de ~e av dem* most of them; *de ~e sier* most people say; *i de ~e tilfeller* in most cases.

flette I *sb* plait, braid; *(muse~)* pigtail; **II** *vb (~ hår)* plait, braid; **2** *(~ kurver, matter etc)* weave; *~ sammen* interweave, interlace, intertwine.

flid *sb* diligence; *(arbeidsomhet)* industry; *han gjorde seg stor ~ med arbeidet (sitt)* he took great pains over his work.

flikk *sb (lapp)* patch. **flikke** *vb* patch, mend; *(~ sko)* cobble.

flimre *vb* flicker, shimmer; *det ~r for øynene mine* everything is swimming before my eyes.

flink *adj* good, clever; *en ~ elev* a good pupil; *~ til å danse/regne* good at dancing/arithmetic; *de er ~e i språk* they are clever at languages.

flint *sb* flint; *fly i ~* fly into a passion; *hard som ~* hard as flint.

flir *sb* **1** (silly/scornful) laughter; **2** *(bredt smil)* grin; **3** *(hånsmil)* sneer. **flire** *vb* **1** laugh, grin; **2** *(~ hånlig)* jeer, sneer.

flis *sb* **1** chip; **2** *(høvelfliser etc)* shavings; **3** *(stein~, helle)* flag, flagstone; **4** *(til gulv, vegg)* tile. **flisespikkeri** *sb* hairsplitting, quibble.

flittig *adj* **1** hard-working, industrious, diligent; *han arbeidet ~ (også)* he worked hard; **2** *(ved boklig arbeid)* studious; **3** *en ~ gjest* a frequent guest/visitor.

flo *sb (høyvann)* high tide/water; flood.

flodhest *sb* hippopotamus; *dgl* hippo.

floke *sb* tangle; *en håpløs ~* a hopeless tangle; *løse en ~* unravel a tangle. **floket** *adj* tangled.

flokk *sb* **1** *(om mennesker)* crowd, group, party; *en ~ (med) reisende* a group of travellers; *en ~ (med) turister* a party of tourists; **2** *(om storfe)* herd; **3** *(om småfe)* flock; **4** *(om fugler)* flock, flight. **flokke seg** *vb* crowd, flock, gather; *elevene ~t seg om læreren* the pupils crowded/flocked round the teacher. **flokkevis** *adv* in groups.

flokse *sb* flirt, gadabout.

flom *sb* flood(s); *det er ~* the floods are out; *det er ~ i elven* the river is in flood; *en ~ av ord* a flood of words; *regnet førte til ~ i de lavereliggende delene av byen* the rainfall caused floods in the low-lying parts of the town. **flom|belyse** *vb* flood-light. **~belysning** *sb* flood lighting; flood lights. **flomme** *vb (strømme rikelig)* flow, stream; *~ over* overflow; *elven ~t over sine bredder* the river overflowed its banks.

flor *sb* **1** *(blomstring)* bloom, flowering; blossom; *rosene stod i fullt ~* the roses were in full bloom; **2** *(gasvevd stoff)* gauze; *(sørgeflor)* crape. **flora** *sb (planteliv, plantebok)* flora. **florere** *vb* flourish.

floskel *sb (frase)* empty phrase; platitude.

flott *adj* **1** *(raus, rundhåndet)* generous; **2** *(ødsel)* extravagant; **3** *(elegant)* elegant, smart; *~e vaner* expensive habits. **flotte seg** *vb* be extravagant. **flotthet** *sb* extravagance, lavishness.

flue *sb* fly; *de døde som ~r* they died like flies; *slå to ~r i en smekk* kill two birds with one stone.

flukt *sb* **1** *(det å fly/flykte)* flight; *på ~* on the run; *de jaget fienden på ~* they put the enemy to flight; **2** *(rømming)* escape; *fangenes ~ fra Dartmoor* the prisoner's escape from Dartmoor; **3** *i ~ med* flush with. **fluktforsøk** *sb* attempted escape. **fluktstol** *sb* deck-chair.

flunkende *adv: ~ ny* brand-new.

flust *adj (rikelig)* abundant, plentiful.

fly I *sb* plane, aeroplane; *US* airplane; aircraft; *~et landet/lettet* the plane landed/took off; *reise med ~, ta ~* go by air/by plane; **II** *vb* **1** fly; *han var fløyet til Paris* he had flown to Paris; **2** *(fare, styrte)* dash, fling, fly, rush; *han fløy på dør* he rushed out of the room; **3** *(rømme)* se *flykte*. **fly|alarm** *sb* air-raid warning, alert. **~angrep** *sb* air raid. **~båren** *adj* airborne. **~fille** *sb* gadabout, hussy. **~forbindelse** *sb* airline; air service. **flyge** *vb = fly II*. **flyge|blad** *sb* flysheet. **~fisk** *sb* flying-fish. **~idé** *sb* (passing) whim.

flygel *sb* grand piano.

flyger *sb* **1** airman, aviator; **2** *(fører av fly)* pilot. **flygersertifikat** *sb* pilot's certificate. **flyging** *sb* flying; aviation. **fly|kaprer** *sb* hijacker. **~kapring** *sb* hijacking. **~korridor** *sb* air lane.

flykte *vb* **1** run away; take flight; *(mer boklig)* flee; *~ for* run away/flee before; *de ~t for fienden* they ran away/fled before the enemy; **2** *(komme unna)* escape; *to av fangene ~t* two of the prisoners escaped; *~ fra* run away/escape from. **flyktig** *adj* fleeting, passing; *et ~ blikk* a fleeting glance; *en ~ tanke* a passing thought. **flyktning** *sb* refugee; *politiske ~er* political refugees.

flymekaniker *sb* aircraft mechanic.

flyndre *sb* **1** *(flyndrefisk)* flatfish; **2** *(gullflyndre, rødspette)* plaice; **3** *(skrubbflyndre)* flounder.

fly|plass *sb* **1** *(lufthavn)* airport; **2** *(mindre)* airfield; aerodrome; **3** *(~stripe)* landing-field, landing-strip. **~post** *sb* air mail; *med ~post* by air mail. **~rute** *sb* airline, airway. **~selskap** *sb* airline company; airlines, airways.

flyt *sb* **1** *(~ i talen)* fluency; **2** *(~ i trafikken) det er ~ i trafikken* traffic is flowing smoothly. **flyte** *vb* **1** *(renne)* flow, run; *~ over* overflow; run over; **2** *(~ på væske)* float; *båten fløt nedover elven* the boat floated down the river; **3** *(ligge uordentlig)* lie about.

flyteknikk *sb* aeronautics.

flytende *adj* **1** *(rennende)* flowing, running; **2** *(om tale)* fluent; *hun snakker ~ engelsk* she speaks fluent English/she speaks English fluently; **3** *(motsatt fast/gassformig)* liquid; *~ brensel* liquid fuel; **4** *(~ på væske)* afloat, floating; *holde ~* keep afloat.

flytning *sb (skifte av bopel)* move, removal; change of address.

flytrafikk *sb* air traffic.

flytskjema *sb data* chart.

flyttbar *adj* movable. **flytte** *vb* **1** move; *(skifte bopel også)* move house; *familien har ~t* the family has moved/moved house; *~* **fra** move from; leave; *han ~t fra byen* he left the town; *de ~t fra hverandre* they moved apart; they separated; *~* **ned** *(en elev)* move (a pupil) down a class; *~* **opp** move up; *~* **på** remove; take away; *~* **seg** move; get out of the way; **2** *data* relocate; **3** *(fjerne)* remove; *statuen ble ~t fra torget* the statue was removed from the market place. **flytte|bil** *sb* removal van. **~byrå** *sb* (furniture) removers. **~folk** *sb koll* removers. **~lass** *sb* vanful of furniture, removal load. **flyttfugl** *sb* bird of passage, migratory bird. **flytting** *sb* removal.

fly|tur *sb* flight. **~ulykke** *sb* air crash; *(mindre)* flying accident. **~vertinne** *sb* air hostess; stewardess. **~våpen** *sb* air force.

flø *vb: det flør* the tide is coming in.

flømme se *flomme.*

flørt *sb* **1** *(flørting)* flirtation; **2** *(en som flørter)* flirt. **flørte** *vb* flirt.

fløte A *sb* cream; *skumme ~n av* skim/take the cream off; *fig især* take all the plums; **B** *vb (~ tømmer etc)* float, raft. **fløte|krem** *sb* whipped cream. **~mugge** *sb* cream jug. **fløter** *sb* floater, raftsman. **fløt(n)ing** *sb* floating, rafting.

fløy *sb* **1** *(vindfløy)* vane; **2** *(av bygning)* wing; **3** *(av hær)* wing, flank.

fløyel *sb* velvet.

fløyt *sb* whistle. **fløyte I** *sb* **1** *(tverr~)* flute; *spille på ~* play the flute; **2** *(signal~)* whistle; **3** *(damp~)* steam whistle; **4** *(fabrikk~)* hooter; **II** *vb* whistle; pipe.

flå *vb* **1** skin, flay; *de ~dde skinnet av bjørnen* they skinned the bear; **2** *(utplyndre)* fleece, flay; bleed; *~ til skinnet* bleed white.

flåkjefta, flåset(e) *adj* flippant.

flåte *sb* **1** *(samling av skip/fly)* fleet; *en ~ på femti skip* a fleet of 50 ships; *(handelsflåten)* the merchant marine/navy; *(marinen)* the navy; **2** *(tømmer~ etc)* raft.

FN *(De forente nasjoner)* UN (the United Nations); *FN-pakten* the Charter of the United Nations.

fnise *vb* titter; giggle. **fnising** *sb* titter, tittering; giggle, giggling.

fnugg *sb* **1** *(~fnugg)* flake; **2** *(av ull)* flock; **3** *(av dun)* fluff, down; **4** *(støv~)* mote/speck (of dust); *ikke et ~* not an atom/a jot/a particle.

fnyse *vb* snort; *~ av raseri* snort with rage.

fob f.o.b. (free on board).

fokk *sb* **1** *(snø~)* drifting snow; **2** *(seil)* foresail.

fokus *sb* focus.

fold *sb* **1** fold; *legge ansiktet i de rette ~er* straighten one's face; **2** *(legg)* fold, pleat. **folde** *vb* fold; *~ hendene* clasp/fold one's hands; *blomsten begynte å ~ seg ut* the flower began to unfold; *han ~et avisen sammen* he folded up the paper; *hun ~et den ut* she unfolded it. **folder** *sb* folder.

fole *sb, vb* foal.

folie *sb* foil.

folio *sb* folio. **folio|ark, ~format** *sb* folio, foolscap.

folk *sb* **1** *(~eslag, nasjon)* people, *fl* peoples; *Europas ~* the peoples of Europe; **2** *(mennesker)* people; *~ flest* most people; *~ene på stedet* the locals; *det var mange folk der* there were many people there; **3** *(arbeidere)* men; *de hadde mange ~ i sitt arbeid* they employed many men. **folke|avstemning** *sb* plebiscite; *(om lovforslag)* referendum. **~bibliotek** *sb* public library. **~dans** *sb* folk-dance. **~eventyr** *sb* folk-tale. **~forlystelse** *sb* popular entertainment. **~forsamling** *sb* popular assembly; assembly of the people. **~front** *sb* popular front. **~fører** *sb* leader of the people. **~gruppe** *sb* ethnic group; *(minoritet)* minority. **~gunst** *sb* popularity; popular favour. **~helse** *sb* public health. **~karakter** *sb* national character. **folkelig** *adj* popular; *(liketil)* simple. **folke|masse** *sb* mass, crowd. **~mengde** *sb* **1** *(~masse)* crowd; **2** *(innbyggertall)* population. **~mening** *sb* public opinion. **~minner** *sb fl* folklore. **~minnegransker** *sb* folklorist. **~minnegranskning** *sb* folklore. **~mord** *sb* genocide. **~munne** *sb: komme på ~* have one's name bandied about. **~opplysning** *sb* general education. **~reisning** *sb* popular rising. **~rett** *sb* international law. **~rik** *sb* populous; thickly populated. **~sagn** *sb* legend. **~skikk** *sb* good manners; decorum; *han eier ikke ~skikk* he has no manners. **~skole** *sb* primary school; *US* grade school. **~sky** *adj* retiring. **~slag** *sb* people, nation. **~snakk** *sb* talk, gossip, scandal. **~styre** *sb* government by the people; democracy. **~telling** *sb* census. **~tom** *adj* deserted. **~trygd** *sb* national insurance. **~vandring** *sb* migration. **~vise** *sb* ballad, folk-song.

fomle *vb* fumble.

fond *sb* **1** *(kapital, rikdom)* fund; *han har et ~ av kunnskaper* he has a fund of knowledge; **2** *(legat)* foundation.

fonetiker *sb* phonetician. **fonetikk** *sb* phonetics. **fonetisk** *adj* phonetic.

fonn *sb* drift (of snow); snowdrift.

fontene *sb* fountain.

for *adv, konj, prep* **1 a)** *(til gunst/ugunst ~)* for; *hva kan jeg gjøre ~ Dem?* what can I do for you? *røyking er skadelig ~ helsen* smoking is bad for your health; **b)** *(som vederlag ~)* for; *jeg kjøpte bilen ~ 1500 pund og solgte den året etter ~ 500* I bought the car for £1500 and sold it next year for £500; **c)** *(på grunn av)* for; *hun er mislikt ~ sin uhøflighet* she is disliked for her rudeness; **d)** *(om tidsrom)* for; *vi leide rommet ~ to uker* we took the room for a fortnight; **2** *(foran)* before; *rett ~ øynene på meg* before my very eyes; **3** *(altfor)* too; *du snakker ~ lavt* you speak too low; **4** *(ved oppregning etc)* by; *ord ~ ord* word by word; **5** *(i andre tilfeller)* to; *det er viktig ~ meg* it is important to me; *det var felles ~ dem alle* it was common to them all; *skal jeg lese det ~ deg?* shall I read it to you? **6 ~ å** *(+ infinitiv)* to; in order to; *hun gjorde det ~ å glede dem* she did it (in order) to please them; **~ å** *(+ setning)* in order that; so that; *jeg gjemte boken ~ at de ikke skulle finne den* I hid the book so that they should not find it; **7 ~ ... siden** ago; *~ tre dager siden* three days ago; **8 ~ ... skyld** for ... sake; *for Guds skyld* for God's sake; **9** *~ at, ~ så vidt* se *egne oppslag.*

fôr *sb* **A** *(i klær)* lining; *jeg satte ~ i frakken* I lined the coat; **B** *(dyremat)* fodder, forage.

forakt *sb* contempt. **forakte** *vb* despise; *ikke å ~* not to be despised. **foraktelig** *adj* **1** *(som fortjener forakt)* contemptible; *en ~ liten kjeltring* a contemptible little scoundrel; **2** *(som viser forakt)* contemptuous; *en ~ bemerkning* a contemptuous remark.

foran *prep* in front of; ahead of; before.

foranderlig *adj* changeable. **forandre** *vb (~ litt)* alter; *(~ mye)* change; *~ seg til* change into; *~ seg til det bedre/verre* change for the better/worse; *det ~r saken* that alters the case; *tidene har ~t seg* times have changed. **forandring** *sb* **1** change; *(mindre endring)* alteration; *~ fryder* ≈ variety is the spice of life; *til en ~* for a change; *vi trenger alle ~ av og til* we all need a change now and then.

foranledige *vb* bring about; cause. **foranledning** *sb* cause, occasion; *på ~ av* at the request of.

foranstalte *vb* arrange, organize. **foranstaltning** *sb* arrangement, organization; *treffe ~er* make arrangements.

forarge *sb* offend; scandalize, shock. **forargelig** *adj* **1** *(som vekker forargelse)* offensive, scandalous; **2** *(ergerlig)* annoying, irritating.

for at *konj* that; in order that; so that; *han snakket lavt ~ ~ barna ikke skulle høre det* he spoke low, so that the children should not hear it.

forbanne *vb* curse, damn. **forbannelse** *sb* curse. **forbannet** *adj* accursed, cursed, damned; *~ på* mad at.

forbarme *vb: ~ seg over* take pity on; have mercy on.

forbasket *adj* blasted, confounded.

forbause *vb* **1** *(gjøre ~)* astonish; **2** *(overraske)* surprise; **3** *(forbløffe)* amaze. **forbauselse** *sb (jf forbause)* astonishment; surprise; amazement. **forbauset** *adj (jf forbause)* astonished; surprised; amazed; *~ over* surprised/astonished/amazed at; *~ over at* surprised/astonished/amazed that; *jeg var ~ over at han kunne gjøre det* I was surprised that he could do it.

forbedre *vb* improve; make better; *~ seg* improve. **forbedring** *sb* improvement. **forbedringsanstalt** *sb* reformatory.

forbehold *sb* reservation; *uten ~* without reservation; unconditionally; *ta ~* make a reservation/reservations. **forbeholde seg** *vb* reserve (for oneself); *~ seg retten til (å)* reserve (for oneself) the right to. **forbeholden** *adj* reserved.

forberede *vb* prepare; *hun forberedte seg til en eksamen* she prepared (herself) for an exam, *vi er forberedt på det verste* we are prepared for the worst. **forberedelse** *sb* preparation. **forberedende** *adj* preparatory, preliminary. **forberedt** *adj* prepared, ready.

forbi *adv, prep* **1** by, past; *jeg gikk ~/~ huset deres hver dag* I walked past/by their house every day; *han skyndte seg ~ uten et ord* he hurried by without a word; *det er ikke til å komme ~ (at)* one cannot ignore/there is no getting away from (the fact that); **2** *gjøre det ~ (heve forlovelse etc)* break it off; *det er ~ mellom dem* all is over between them; **3** *(om tid)* over; *krigen/timen er ~* the war/the lesson is over. **forbi|gå** *vb (ved ansettelse)* pass over; *~ i taushet* pass by/over in silence. **~gående** *adj: i ~gående* in passing. **~kjøring** *sb* overtaking; *~kjøring forbudt!* no overtaking!

forbilde *sb* **1** *(eksempel)* example; **2** *(ideal)* ideal; **3** *(mønster)* model, pattern.

forbinde *vb* **1** *(knytte sammen)* connect, link; *de to byene er forbundet med en jernbane* the two towns are linked by a railway; **2** *(forene)* combine, unite; **3** *(legge forbinding på)* bandage, dress; *de forbandt fingeren hennes* they bandaged her finger. **forbindelse** *sb* **1** connection, connexion; contact; *i den/denne ~* in that/this connection; *kommme i ~ med* come into contact with; *sette seg i ~ med* contact; get in touch with; *stå i*

~ *med* be connected with; be in touch with; **2** *(trafikkmidler)* communication(s); *all ~ mellom de to landene er brutt* all communications between the two countries have been broken off; *det er daglig ~ i begge retninger* there is a daily service in both directions. **forbindelseslinje** *sb* connection; line of communication. **forbinding** *sb* **1** *(det å forbinde)* bandaging, dressing; **2** *(bandasje)* bandage. **forbindingssaker** *sb* dressing materials.

forbipasserende *sb ent* passer-by; *fl* passers-by.

forbitrelse *sb* indignation; ~ *over* indignation at. **forbitret** *adj* indignant; ~ *over* indignant at/about; ~ *på* indignant with; *en ~ kamp* a furious struggle.

forbli *vb* remain.

forblinde *vb* blind.

forblø *vb* bleed to death.

forbløffe *vb* amaze, astound; *(sterkere)* dumbfound, nonplus. **forbløffelse** *sb* amazement. **forbløffet** *adj* amazed; taken aback.

forbokstav *sb* initial (letter).

forbrenne *vb* burn. **forbrenning** *sb* **1** combustion; **2** *(brannsår)* burn. **forbrennings|anlegg** *sb petro etc* combustion plant. **~motor** *sb* (internal) combustion engine.

forbruk *sb* consumption; *~et av tobakk* the consumption of tobacco. **forbruker** *sb* consumer.

forbrytelse *sb* **1** crime; *hans mor hadde begått en ~* his mother had committed a crime; **2** *(mindre forseelse)* offence. **forbryter** *sb* **1** criminal; *en farlig ~* a dangerous criminal; **2** *(skyldig i mindre, ikke-kriminell forseelse)* offender. **forbryter|bande** *sb* gang of criminals. **~bane** *sb* course of crime; *slå inn på ~banen* enter upon a course of crime. **forbrytersk** *adj* criminal.

forbud *sb* prohibition; ~ *mot import av silke* prohibition on the import of silk; *nedlegge ~ mot* prohibit, ban. **forbudt** *adj* forbidden, prohibited; *adgang ~* No Admittance; *(til eiendom især)* Private. Trespassers will be Persecuted; *røyking ~* No Smoking.

forbund *sb* alliance, union; association, league; *inngå ~ med* ally oneself with; enter into a union etc with. **forbunds|felle** *sb* ally. **~stat** *sb* federation.

forby *vb (jf forbudt)* forbid; *(mer offisielt)* prohibit; *forbuden frukt smaker best* forbidden fruit is sweet.

forbønn *sb* intercession; *gå i ~ for (hos)* intercede for somebody (with).

fordektig *adj* suspicious.

fordel *sb* advantage; *~ fremfor* advantage over; *~er og ulemper* advantages and disadvantages; *dra (ha, høste etc) ~ av* gain/derive advantage from; benefit by; *han har ~en av en god utdannelse* he has the advantage of a good education; *til hennes ~* to her advantage/in her favour. **fordelaktig** *adj* **1** *(gunstig)* advantageous; favourable; **2** *(innbringende)* profitable. **fordele** *vb* distribute, divide; *likelig fordelt* equally divided.

fordervet *adj* **1** *(moralsk ødelagt)* corrupt; debauched, depraved; **2** *le seg ~* nearly die laughing; split (one's sides) with laughter; *slå seg ~* be badly hurt/gravely injured.

fordi *konj* **1** because; *folk liker ham ikke ~ han er så egoistisk* people dislike him because he is so selfish; **2** *(ettersom)* as; *~ det regnet, gikk vi ikke* as it was raining, we didn't go; **3** *(med omskrivning) ~ hun hadde brukt opp alle pengene sine, måtte hun gå* having spent all her money she had to walk.

fordoble *vb* double.

fordom *sb* prejudice, bias; *en inngrodd ~* a rooted prejudice. **fordomsfri** *adj* unprejudiced, unbiassed; open-minded. **fordomsfritt** *adv* without prejudice/bias. **fordomsfrihet** *sb* freedom from prejudice; open-mindedness. **fordomsfull** *adj* prejudiced, biassed, narrow-minded.

fordra *vb: jeg kan ikke ~ det/ham* I cannot stand it/him; *jeg ~r ikke/kan ikke ~ å legge meg tidlig* I hate going/to go to bed early.

fordre *vb* **1** *(forlange)* demand, require; *jeg ~r omgående betaling* I demand immediate payment; **2** *(sette frem begrunnet krav)* claim.

fordreie *vb* **1** *(forvrenge)* contort, distort, twist; *fordreid av smerte* contorted/twisted with pain; distorted by pain; *~ hodet på en* turn somebody's head; **2** *(forvanske)* distort, twist; *~ sannheten* distort/twist the truth.

fordring *sb* **1** demand, requirement; *de stilte store ~er til oss* they made great demands on us; *hans ~er (til livet) var få* his requirements were few; **2** *(begrunnet krav)* claim. **fordringsfull** *(kravstor)* pretentious.

fordrive *vb* **1** *(jage bort)* drive away; **2** *(landsforvise)* banish, exile; **3** *~ tiden* pass (away) the time; while away (the) time.

fordufte *vb (stikke av)* beat it; make oneself scarce.

fordums *adj* former, sometime.

for|dype *vb: ~ dype seg i* lose/bury oneself in; *~dypet i* absorbed (buried or engrossed) in. **~dypning** *sb* **1** *(mindre)* depression; **2** *(større)* hollow.

fordyre *vb* make more expensive; increase the price of.

for|dømme *vb* **1** condemn; **2** *(i religiøs betydning)* damn. **~dømt** *adj* damned; confounded; *vulg* bloody.

for|døye *vb* digest. **~døyelig** *adj* digestible; *lett/tungt ~døyelig* easy/hard to digest. **~døyelse** *sb* digestion; *dårlig ~døyelse* indigestion.

fore *(adv): ha ~ (være opptatt med)* be occupied with; *(ha planer om)* plan; *sette seg ~* make up one's mind.

fôre *vb* **1** *(forsyne klær med fôr)* line; *~t med silke* lined with silk; *(~ med pelsverk)* fur; **2** *(gi fôr)* feed.

fore|bygge *vb* prevent; *ulykker bør ~bygges* accidents should be prevented. **~byggelse** *sb* prevention; *~byggelse er bedre enn helbredelse* prevention is better than cure. **~byggende** *adj* preventive.

for|edle *vb* **1** *(gjøre edel)* ennoble, refine; **2** *(om råvarer)* process, refine; work up; **3** *(om dyr og planter)* improve; *(om husdyrraser)* grade (up). **~edling** *sb* processing, refinement; improvement.

foredrag *sb* lecture, talk; *hun holdt ~ om Kina* he gave a lecture on China. **foredragsholder** *sb* lecturer.

foregangs|kvinne, -mann, -person *sb* pioneer.

foregi *vb* pretend. **foregivende** *sb* pretext; *under ~*

av å være syk under the pretext of being ill.

foregripe *vb* anticipate, advance; *vi ~r begivenhetenes gang* we are advancing matters.

foregå *vb* **1** *(finne sted)* go on; happen; take place; *når foregikk innbruddet?* when did the burglary take place? *vi visste ikke hva som hadde foregått* we did not know what had happened; **2** *hun foregikk ham med et godt eksempel* she set him a good example. **foregående** *adj* preceding, previous; *i (det) foregående kapittel* in the preceding chapter; *i et ~ kapittel* in a previous chapter.

forekomme *vb* **1** *(inntreffe)* happen, occur; **2** *(finnes)* be found; *denne planten ~r ikke i Norge* this plant is not (to be) found in Norway; **3** *(synes)* appear, seem; *det ~r meg at jeg har hørt det* I seem to have heard it. **forekommende** *adj (elskverdig)* kind, obliging. **forekomst** *sb* **1** occurence, existence; **2** *(utbredelse)* incidence; **3** *(av malm etc)* deposit.

foreldes *vb* become obsolete. **foreldet** *adj* dated, obsolete; antiquated, old-fashioned.

foreldre *sb fl* parents. **foreldreløs** *adj* orphant; *et ~t barn* an orphan; *han ble ~* he was left an orphan.

fore|legge *vb: ~legge noe for en* submit something to somebody; place/put/lay something before somebody; *hun ~la planen (sin) for komiteen* she submitted her plan to the committee. **~lese** *vb* lecture; *~lese om/over* lecture on. **~lesning** *sb* lecture. **~ligge** *vb* **1** *(eksistere)* be (available); exist; *det ~ligger en misforståelse* there is a mistake; *nærmere enkeltheter ~ligger ikke* no further details are available; **2** *(~ligge til behandling)* be at issue; be under consideration; *hvilken sak ~ligger i dag?* what is the point at issue today? *den ~liggende sak* the present case.

forelske *vb: ~ seg i* fall in love with. **forelskelse** *sb* love; *~ i* love for; *blind ~* infatuation. **forelsket** *adj* in love; *bli ~ i* fall in love with; *være ~ i* be in love with; *vilt ~ i* infatuated with.

foreløpig *adj* **1** temporary; *~ beskjeftigelse* temporary employment; **2** *adv* temporarily; for the present; so far; *~ er det blitt utsatt* it has been temporarily postponed; *~ har jeg ikke sett stort til ham* so far I have not seen much of him.

forene *vb* join, unite; combine; *~ det nyttige med det behagelige* combine business with pleasure; *De forente nasjoner* the United Nations; *De forente stater* the United States; *med forente anstrengelser* by our (their etc) united efforts; *Sverige og Norge ble forent i 1814* Sweden and Norway were united in 1814. **foren(e)lig** *sb* compatible, consistent (*med* with). **forening** *sb* **1** *(~ av medlemmer)* association; **2** *(finere)* society; **3** *(mindre)* club; **4** *(politisk sammenslutning)* union.

forenkle *vb* simplify. **forenkling** *sb* simplification.

forenlig se *forenelig*.

foresatt *sb* **1** *(overordnet)* superior; **2** *(som er i foreldres sted)* guardian.

foreskrive *vb* prescribe, order.

foreslå *vb* **1** propose, suggest; *jeg foreslo å gå en tur* I proposed/suggested that we should take a walk; **2** *(legge frem forslag)* move, propose; *jeg ~r at møtet blir hevet* I move that the meeting be adjourned.

forespeile *vb* hold out (to); *hun sa hun kunne ikke ~ meg noen lønnsforhøyelse* she said she could not hold out to me a rise of salary.

fore|spørre *vb* inquire. **~spørsel** *sb* inquiry, question.

forestille *vb* **1** *(presentere)* introduce; *må jeg få ~ Mr. Smith for Dem?* may I introduce Mr Smith (to you)? **2** *(gjengi)* represent; *dette bildet ~r Mr S* this picture represents Mr S; *hva skal dette ~?* what does this mean? **3** *~ seg* imagine; *~ deg min forbauselse!* imagine my surprise! **forestilling** *sb* **1** *(på scene etc)* performance; *~en begynner klokken 8* the performance begins at 8; **2** *(tanke)* idea, notion.

forestå *vb (nærme seg, være ~ende)* be approaching; be at hand.

foreta *vb* do, make, undertake; carry out; *~ seg noe* do something; *vi foretok en reise* we made/undertook a journey; *hun foretok seg ingen verdens ting* she did absolutely nothing. **foretagende** *sb* **1** *(arbeid, virksomhet)* enterprise, undertaking; **2** *(dristig ~)* venture; **3** *(ingeniør~, større ~)* project; **4** *(plan)* plan; **5** *(forretningsvirksomhet)* concern, firm. **foretaksom** *adj* enterprising. **foretaksomhet** *sb* enterprise, initiative; energy.

foreteelse *sb* phenomenon.

foretrekke *vb* prefer; *takk, jeg ~r å vente* I prefer to wait, thank you; *jeg ~r te for kaffe* I prefer tea to coffee; *jeg ~r å sykle fremfor å gå* I prefer cycling to walking; I would rather cycle than walk.

forfall *sb* **1** *ha ~* be prevented from meeting; **2** *(nedgang)* decline; *Romerrikets ~* the decline of the Roman Empire; **3** *(oppløsning)* decay; *en bygning i ~* a building in decay; **4** *merk (forfallstid) ved ~* when due; on the due date; on maturity. **forfalle** *vb* **1** *(ødelegges)* decay; fall into decay/disrepair; become delapidated; **2** *merk (~ til betaling)* be/fall due; mature; *vekselen ~r den 1. juni* the bill is due (falls due, matures) on June 1; **3** *(henfalle)* become addicted. **forfallen** *adj* **1** *(skrøpelig)* dilapidated; in a state of disrepair; **2** *(~ til betaling)* (fallen) due; **3** *(henfallen)* addicted/given to.

forfalske *vb* fake, falsify; *(~ dokumenter)* forge. **forfalskning** *sb* **1** *(det å forfalske)* faking, falsification; forgery; **2** *(noe forfalsket)* fake; forgery; imitation.

forfatning *sb* **1** *(tilstand)* condition; *i god ~* in a good condition; **2** *(stats~)* constitution.

forfatte *vb* write, compose. **forfatter** *sb* writer; *(~ av større, betydelige verker)* author; *om kvinne også* authoress. **forfatter|honorar** *sb* author's fee; *(i prosenter av salget)* royalties. **~navn** *sb (psevdonym)* pen-name. **~skap** *sb* **1** *(det å være ~)* authorship; **2** *(litterær produksjon)* work(s).

forfedre *sb fl* ancestors, forefathers.

forfengelig *adj* vain. **forfengelighet** *sb* vanity.

forferde *vb* **1** terrify; **2** *(især moralsk)* shock. **forferdelig I** *adj* **1** *(skrekkelig)* terrible; awful, dreadful, frightful; *en ~ ulykke* an awful/a dreadful etc accident; **2** *dgl (umåtelig stor)* awful, terrible; *en ~ tosk* an awful/a terrible fool; **II** *adv* **1** dreadfully, horribly; *~ redd* dreadfully frightened; **2** *(dgl: veldig)* awfully, frightfully, terribly; *det var ~ snilt av Dem* that was awfully kind/nice of you. **forferdelse** *sb* **1** horror, terror; **2** *(særlig over egen fare)* dismay. **forferdet** *adj* **1** horrified, terrified; *hun var ~ over å høre* she was horrified to hear; *vi var ~ over mordet* we were horrified at the murder; **2** *(bare som predikatsord)* aghast; **3** *(især moralsk)* shocked.

forfinet *adj* refined.

forfjamselse *sb* confusion, flurry. **forfjamset** *adj* confused; flurried, flustered.

forflytte *vb* transfer. **forflytning** *sb* transfer.

forfordele *vb* not give a fair deal; treat unfairly..

forfra *adv* **1** *(fra forsiden)* from the front; *~ ser huset nytt ut* from the front the house looks new; **2** *(fra begynnelsen)* from the beginning; *jeg måtte begynne ~ igjen* I had to start all over again.

forfremme *vb* promote; *han ble ~t til kaptein* he was promoted captain/to be a captain. **forfremmelse** *sb* promotion.

forfriske *vb* refresh; *en ~nde bris* a refreshing breeze. **forfriskning** *sb* refreshment.

forfrossen *adj* **1** *(gjennomfrossen)* chilled, freezing; **2** *(frostskadd)* frost-bitten. **forfrysning** *sb* frostbite.

forfølge *vb* **1** *(jage noe flyktende)* pursue; *han ble forfulgt av en okse* he was pursued by a bull; **2** *(~ på grunn av tro etc)* persecute; *de første kristne ble forfulgt* the early Christians were persecuted; **3** *(være etter for å plage)* persecute; *alle lærerne ~r meg* all my teachers persecute me. **forfølgelse** *sb* pursuit; persecution. **forfølger** *sb* pursuer; persecutor.

forføre *vb* seduce. **forfører** *sb* seducer.

forgasser *sb* carburettor, carburetter; *US* carburetor, carbureter.

forgifte *vb* poison; *en ~t pil* a poisoned arrow. **forgiftning** *sb* poisoning.

forgjeldet *adj* in debt.

forgjengelig *adj* perishable. **forgjengelighet** *sb* perishableness.

forgjenger *sb* predecessor.

forgjeves *adj, adv* **1** *(især foran sb)* vain; et ~ forsøk a vain attempt; **2** *(bare som adv og predikatsord)* in vain; *alt var ~* everything was in vain.

forglemmegei *sb* forget-me-not. **forglemmelse** *sb* forgetfulness, oversight.

forgodtbefinnende *sb: etter ~* at pleasure.

forgrene seg *vb* branch off. **forgrening** *sb* ramification.

forgrunn *sb* foreground; *i ~en* in the foreground; *i ~en (av scenen)* at the front (of the stage); *komme i ~en* come to the front.

forgude *vb* idolize.

forgylle *vb* gild. **forgylling** *sb* gilding, gilt. **forgylt** *adj* gilt.

forgå *vb* perish; *de holdt på å ~ av sult* they were perishing with hunger; they were starving.

forhale *vb (trekke ut)* obstruct; *US (trekke politisk debatt i langdrag og derved ~ saken)* filibuster. **forhalingstaktikk** *sb* delaying tactics; policy of obstruction; *US* filibustering.

forhandle *vb* **1** *(handle med)* deal in; **2** *(underhandle)* negotiate; **3** *(diskutere)* debate, discuss. **forhandler** *sb* **1** *(handlende)* dealer, distributor; **2** *(underhandler)* negotiator. **forhandling** *sb (underhandling)* negotiation; *lede ~ene* take the chair.

forhaste *vb: ~ seg* be in too great a hurry. **forhastet** *adj* over-hasty, rash; hasty; *trekke forhastede slutninger* jump to conclusions.

forhatt *adj* hated, detested.

forhekse *vb* bewitch, charm; put a spell on.

forheng *sb* curtain.

forhenværende *adj* **1** former; *han er ~ rektor* he is a former headmaster/he used to be a headmaster; **2** *(om avdød)* late.

forherde *vb* harden; *en ~t forbryter* a hardened criminal. **forherdet** *adj* callous, hardened.

forherlige *vb* glorify. **forherligelse** *sb* glorification; glory.

forhindre *vb* prevent; *vi var ~t fra å møte* we were prevented from meeting. **forhindring** *sb* hindrance, obstacle; *stundom* difficulties.

forhippen *adj: ~ på* bent on; keen on.

forhistorie *sb* previous history; *(særlig om en persons ~)* antecedents. **forhistorisk** *adj* prehistoric; *i ~ tid* in prehistoric times.

forhjul *sb* front wheel.

forhold *sb* **1** *(tilstand)* conditions; *~ene i Irland* conditions in Ireland; **2** *(omstendigheter)* circumstances; *~ene er forandret/har forandre seg* circumstances have changed; *som ~ene nå engang er* as things go; *under ellers like ~* other things being equal **3** *(innbyrdes ~)* relation, relationship; *~t mellom lønninger og priser* the relation between wages and prices; **4** *(~ mellom mennesker)* relations, terms; *~et mellom barn og lærere* the relations between children and teachers; *det er et godt ~ mellom dem* they are on good terms; **5** *(matematisk ~)* ratio; *~et mellom utsalgspris og kostpris er 3 til 1* the ratio between selling price and cost price is 3 to 1; *ikke i noe ~ til* out of all proportion to; **6** *(kjensgjerning, sak)* fact, matter; *~et er (det) at ...* the fact is that ...; *det er et ~ jeg ikke vet noe om* that is something/a matter I know nothing about. **forholde seg** *vb* be, remain; *hun forholdt seg rolig* she was/remained quiet; **2** *saken ~er seg slik* the fact is this. **forholds|messig** *adj* proportional. **~regel** *sb* measure; *ta ~regler mot* provide/take steps against. **~vis** *adv* **1** comparatively; **2** *(temmelig)* rather; *~vis stor* rather big.

forhør *sb* **1** *holde ~* hold an inquiry; **2** *(utspørring)* examination, interrogation, questioning; *hun ble tatt i ~* she was interrogate (examined, questioned). **forhøre** *vb* examine, interrogate; question; *~ seg* inquire, ask.

forhøye *vb* increase, raise; *~ virkningen av* heighten the effect of; *prisen ble ~t med 5 prosent* the price was increased/raised by 5 per cent. **forhøyelse** *sb* increase, rise; *en ~ av lønnen på 15 pund i uken* an increase/a rise in wages of £15 a week. **forhøyning** *sb* **1** *(i terrenget)* high ground; rise; **2** *(på gulvet)* raised platform.

forhånd *sb: på ~* in advance; beforehand.

forhåne *vb* mock; mock (sneer, scoff) at.

forhåpentlig *adv* I/we hope; let us hope; it is to be hoped; *stundom* hopefully. **forhåpning** *sb* hope; *gjøre seg ~er* hope; have hopes; *vekke ~er* raise hopes. **forhåpningsfull** *adj* hopeful.

fôring *sb* **1** *(av dyr)* feeding; **2** *(i f.eks. klesplagg)* lining. **fôringsrør** *sb petro* casing.

forkaste *vb* reject; *tilbudet/forslaget ble ~t* the offer/proposal was rejected. **forkastelig** *adj* objectionable, reprehensible, vicious.

forkavet *adj* flurried, hectic.

forkjemper *sb* champion; *en ~ for frihet* a champion of liberty.

forkjæle *vb* spoil, coddle; *et forkjælt barn* a spoilt child. **forkjærlighet** *sb: ~ for* preference (predilection or partiality) for.

forkjølelse *sb* cold. **forkjølet** *adj: bli ~* catch (a) cold; *være ~* have a cold.

forkjøp *sb: komme i ~et* forestall; get (in) ahead of; steal a march on. **forkjøpsrett** *sb: ~ til* option (on); the first refusal (of); right of preemption (to).

forkjørsrett *sb* right of way.

forklare *vb* **1** *(gjøre forståelig)* explain; *kan du ~ dette for meg?* can you explain this to me? **2** *(gjøre greie for)* account for; *hvordan ~r du forskjellen?* how do you account for the difference. **forklaring** *sb* explanation; *~ på* explanation of; *som ~ på* in explanation of. **forklarlig** *adj* explicable.

forkle *sb* **1** apron; *(især om barne~)* pinafore; *(erme~)* overall; **2** *(fig: anstandsdame)* chaperon.

forkle *vb (gjøre ukjennelig)* disguise; *~dd som bonde* disguised as a peasant. **forkledning** *sb* disguise.

forkleinelse *sb* belittlement, disparagement; *uten ~ for* without disparaging.

forknytt *adj* **1** *(forsagt)* timid; **2** *(nedslått)* dejected, dispirited.

forkommen *adj* in a miserable condition.

forkorte *vb* **1** shorten; **2** *(~ et ord)* abbreviate; *centimeter ~s til cm* centimetre is abbreviated to cm; **3** *(~ bok)* abridge; *en ~t utgave* an abridged edition; **4** *(~ en brøk)* reduce. **forkortelse** *sb* abbreviation; *BC er en (engelsk) ~ for Before Christ (før Kristi fødsel)* B.C.is an abbreviation of Before Christ. **forkorting** *sb* reduction, shortening; abridgement; *perspektivisk ~* foreshortening.

forkrøplet *adj* crippled; dwarfed, stunted; scrubby.

forkulle *vb* char; *~de rester* charred remains.

forkunnskaper *sb* previous knowledge/training.

forkvakle *vb* **1** *(spolere)* bungle; **2** *(gjøre forskrudd)* warp; *en ~t tankegang* a warped mind.

forkvinne *sb* chairwoman, leader. Se også *formann.*

forkynne *vb* **1** *(kunngjøre)* announce, proclaim; **2** *(preke)* preach; *~ evangeliet* preach the gospel.

forlag *sb* publisher(s); publishing house; *utsolgt fra ~et* out of print. **forlagsrett** *sb* copyright.

forlange *vb* **1** *(kreve)* demand; *(mer formelt)* request, require; *(~ bestemt)* insist; *de forlangte (et) omgående svar* they demanded/requested an immediate answer; *jeg ~r omgående betaling* I insist on being paid at once; **2** *(kreve sin rett)* claim; *vi forlangte erstatning* we claimed damages; **3** *(~ som betaling etc)* ask for; charge, demand; want; *det er for mye forlangt* that is asking too much; *han ~r 10 pund i uken* he is asking for £10 a week; *legen forlangte 15 dollar* the doctor charged $15; **4** *(bestille)* order; *hun forlangte en flaske hvitvin* she ordered a bottle of white wine. **forlangende** *sb* demand; *(mer formelt)* request; *etter/på ~* on demand; *etter/på hennes ~* at her request.

forlate *vb* **1** *(gå bort fra)* leave; *vi forlot huset* we left the house; **2** *(svikte)* desert; *vennene (hans) forlot ham i nødens stund* his friends deserted him in the hour of need; **3** *(oppgi)* abandon; *skipet måtte ~s* the ship had to be abandoned; **4** *(tilgi)* forgive. **forlatelse** *sb* pardon; *om ~!* (I beg your) pardon! (I am) sorry! *han bad sin far om ~* he asked his father's pardon.

forlatt *adj: ene og ~* lonely.

forlede *vb* lead astray; *(forføre)* seduce; *~ til* seduce to.

forleden *adj* the other; *~ dag* the other day.

forlegen *adj* **1** *(sjenert)* self-conscious, shy; **2** *(~ på grunn av noe)* embarrassed. **forlegenhet** *sb* **1** *(sjenerthet)* self-consciousness, shyness **2** *(i den enkelte situasjon)* embarrassment.

forlegger *sb* publisher.

forlenge *vb* **1** *(i rom)* lengthen, prolong; extend; **2** *(i tid)* extend, prolong. **forlengelse** *sb* extension, prolongation.

for lengst *adv* long ago; long since.

forlik *sb* compromise; *slutte ~ med* come to terms with. **forlike** *vb: ~ seg med* become reconciled with; come to terms with. **forlikes** *vb* agree; *de kunne ikke ~* they could not agree. **forlikt** *adj, pp: bli ~ med* become reconciled/come to terms with; *de var venner og vel ~e* they got on well together; they were on good terms (with each other).

forlis *sb* shipwreck. **forlise** *vb* be (ship-)wrecked.

forlove seg *vb* become engaged (to be married); *han ble ~t med henne* he became/got engaged to her; *hans forlovede* his fiancée; *hennes forlovede* her fiancé. **forlovelse** *sb* engagement; *~ med* engagement to; *heve ~n* break off the engagement. **forlover** *sb (brudens)* maid of honour; *(brudgommens)* best man.

forlystelse *sb* amusement, entertainment. **forlystelsessyk** *adj* pleasure-seeking.

forløp *sb: etter en tids/en måneds ~* after some time/a month. **forløpe seg** *vb* forget oneself. **forløper** *sb* forerunner/precursor (*for* of).

form *sb* **1** *(fasong etc)* form, shape; *~en på kysten/skoen* the shape of the coast/of the shoe; *forskjellige ~er for sport* various forms of sport; **2** *(støpe~)* mould; *(kake~)* (baking) tin; **3** *(fysisk ~, kondisjon)* condition, form;

fitness; **4** *(norm for opptreden)* etiquette, form; ceremony; *holde på ~ene* stand on ceremony. **formalitet** *sb* formality; matter of form.

formane *vb* admonish, exhort; *~ til ikke å* warn against; *jeg formante henne til ikke å arbeide for hardt* I warned her against working too hard. **formaning** *sb* admonition, exhortation; warning.

formann *sb* **1** *(arbeids~)* foreman, leader; **2** *(~ i forening)* president, secretary; **3** *(~ i komité, styre etc)* chairman, leader. Se også *forkvinne.*

formasjon *sb* formation.

formastelig *adj* presumptuous.

format *sb* **1** size; *data etc* format; **2** *(målestokk)* scale. **formatere** *vb* format. **forme** *vb* form, shape. **formel** *sb* formula. **formelig** *adv* actually, positively, downright. **formell** *adj* formal.

formere seg *vb* breed, propagate; *~ ~ sterkt* multiply.

formiddag *sb* morning; *i ~* this morning; *i går ~* yesterday morning. **formiddagsmat** *sb* lunch.

formilde *vb* mollify; *~nde omstendigheter* extenuating circumstances.

forminske *vb* diminish, reduce; *i ~t målestokk* on a reduced scale.

formode *vb* presume, suppose; guess. **formodentlig** *adv* presumably, probably; most likely. **formodning** *sb* **1** *(forventning)* expectation; **2** *(gjetning)* guess, conjecture.

form|sak *sb* matter of form. **~sans** *sb* sense of form.

formue *sb* **1** *(mange penger)* fortune; *en ~ på 10 000 pund* a fortune of £10,000; *han tjente en ~* he made a fortune; **2** *(eiendeler)* property; **3** *(motsatt inntekt)* capital. **formueskatt** *sb* property tax.

formular *sb* formula. **formulere** *vb* formulate, phrase, word.

formynder *sb* guardian. **formynder|skap** *sb* guardianship. **~regjering** *sb* regency.

formørke *vb* darken, obscure. **formørkelse** *sb (av sol og måne)* eclipse.

formål *sb* end, purpose; aim; *~et med besøket hans* the purpose of his visit; *med det ~ å finne søsteren* with the purpose of finding the sister.

fornavn *sb* Christian name; first name; *US* given name.

fornekte *vb* **1** disown, renounce, repudiate; **2** *hennes gode humør ~t seg ikke* her cheerfulness did not fail her.

fornem *adj* **1** *(om rang og stilling)* distinguished; of distinction; **2** *(om utseende)* distinguished-looking; **3** *(tilhørende den fine verden)* fashionable.

fornemme *vb (føle)* perceive. **fornemmelse** *sb* sensation. Se også *følelse.*

fornuft *sb* reason; *sunn ~* common sense; *han ville ikke ta imot ~* he refused to listen to reason. **fornuftig** *adj* **1** reasonable, sensible; *~ mennesker* sensible people; *en ~ grunn/plan* a reasonable cause/plan; *en ~ bemerkning* a sensible remark; **2** *adv* reasonably, sensibly. **fornuftstridig** *adj* absurd, irrational.

fornye *vb* **1** renew; **2** *(skifte ut)* replace; *bildekkene ble ~t* the tyres of the car were replaced/renewed. **fornyelse** *sb* renewal.

fornærme *vb* offend; *(sterkere)* insult. **fornærmelig** *adj* insulting; *(sterkere)* offensive. **fornærmelse** *sb* **1** *(ord, handling)* insult; *en ~ mot publikum* an insult to the public; **2** *(fornærmethet)* resentment. **fornærmet** *adj* offended; *han ble/var ~ på meg* he was offended with me; *han ble ~ over mine bemerkninger* he was offended at/by my remarks.

fornøyd *adj* **1** *(glad)* delighted, pleased; happy; **2** *(tilfreds)* content, satisfied; *~ med* content/satisfied with; **3** *(bare som predikatsord)* contented. **fornøyelig** *adj* amusing, delightful, pleasant. **fornøyelse** *sb* **1** *(glede)* delight, pleasure; *det skal være meg en stor ~ å komme* I shall be very pleased to come; **2** *(forlystelse)* entertainment; *(morskap)* amusement; *god ~!* have a good time! **fornøyelses|park** *sb* amusement park. **~syk** *adj* pleasureseeking.

forord *sb* preface; *(især skrevet av en annen person enn forfatteren)* foreword.

forover *adv* ahead; *full fart ~* full speed ahead.

forpakte *vb* farm, rent; take a lease of. **forpakter** *sb* tenant; tenant farmer.

forpeste *vb* poison, infect.

forpint *adj* anguished; harassed; tortured; *~ av latter* bursting/dying with suppressed laughter.

forplante seg *vb* **1** *(formere seg)* breed, propagate; **2** *(bre seg)* spread; *brannen ~t seg til nabohuset* the fire spread to the next house; **3** *(om lys, lyd)* travel; *lyset ~r seg fortere enn lyden* light travels faster than sound. **forplantning** *sb* procreation, reproduction; propagation. **forplantnings|dyktig** *adj* procreative; capable of reproduction. **~evne** *sb* power of reproduction.

forpleining *sb (kost)* board, food.

forplikte seg *vb: ~ ~ til* bind/pledge oneself to. **forpliktelse** *sb* obligation; *økonomiske ~r* debts, liabilities. **forpliktende** *adj* binding. **forpliktet** *adj: ~ til* bound to; under an obligation to; *føle seg ~ til* feel under an obligation to; *moralsk ~* in honour bound.

forpost *sb* outpost.

forpurre *vb* frustrate, thwart; baffle.

forpustet *adj* breathless; out of breath.

forrang *sb* precedence; *ha ~en for* take precedence of/over.

forranglet *adj* dissipated, debauched.

forregne seg *vb* **1** *(regne feil)* miscalculate; **2** *(ta feil)* be mistaken.

forrente *vb: ~ et lån* pay interest on a loan; *~ seg* yield interest; *(lønne seg)* pay.

forrest 1 *adj* foremost, front; *han var blant de ~e* he was among the foremost; *i ~e rekke* in the front rank; **2** *adv* in front; first; *hun gikk ~* she went first/walked in front.

forresten *adv* **1** come to think of; *jeg har ~ truffet Dem før* come to think of it, I have met you before; **2** *(apropos)* by the way; talking of that; that reminds me; *har du ~ lest Times for i dag?* by the way/talking of that - have you read today's Times? *hva gjorde du ~ med pak-*

ken? that reminds me, what did you do with the parcel? **3** *(i virkeligheten)* as a matter of fact; *han kom ~ tilbake dagen etter* as a matter of fact he returned the next day; **4** *(for den saks skyld)* for that matter; *det var ~ ikke noe dårlig hus* it was not a bad house, for that matter.

forretning *sb* **1** *(handelsvirksomhet)* business; *(enkelt kjøp eller salg)* bargain; *en innbringende ~* a profitable business; *han gjorde en god ~* he made a good bargain; *vi er her i ~er* we are here on business; **2** *(firma)* business, firm, house; *de har en god ~* they have a good business; **3** *(butikk)* shop; *US* store; *hun driver en liten ~* she has/runs a little shop. **forretnings|brev** *sb* business letter. **~forbindelse** *sb* business connection. **~gård** *sb* business premises. **~kvinne** *sb* business woman. **~liv** *sb* business life. **~mann** *sb* business man. **~messig** *adj* business-like. **~ministerium** *sb* caretaker ministry. **~reise** *sb* business trip.

forrett *sb* **1** *(matrett)* first course; **2** *(forrang, førsterett)* priority; **3** *(særrett)* privilege.

forrette *vb* execute, perform; *(om prester)* officiate.

forreven, forrevet *adj* **1** *(om landskap)* rugged; **2** *(om skyer)* ragged.

forrige *adj* **1** *(tidligere)* former, previous; *den ~ eieren* the former/previous owner; **2** *(sist forløpne)* last; *~ år/måned* last year/month.

forringe *vb* **1** *(~ i verdi)* depreciate, **2** *(forkleine)* disparage. **forringelse** *sb* depreciation, disparagement; deterioration. **forringes** *vb* deteriorate.

forrykende *adj: en ~ storm* a howling gale; *i ~ fart* at breakneck speed.

forrykt *adj* crazy, mad.

forræder *sb* traitor. **forræderi** *sb* treachery; *(lands~)* treason. **forrædersk** *adj* treacherous.

forråd *sb* **1** *(opplag)* store, supply; *~et deres holdt på å ta slutt* they were running out of stores; **2** *(lager)* stock.

forråde *vb* betray.

forråe *vb* brutalize.

forråtnelse *sb* putrefaction; *gå i ~* putrefy, rot.

forsagt *adj* timid, diffident.

forsamle *vb* assemble; gather (together). **forsamles** *vb* assemble, meet. **forsamling** *sb* **1** *(møte, også om deltakerne)* assembly; **2** *(litt uformelt)* gathering; **3** *(tilhørere)* audience. **forsamlingslokale** *sb* meeting hall.

forse *sb* forte; strong point.

forseelse *sb* *(lovovertredelse)* offence.

forsegle *vb* seal (up); sealed orders.

forsendelse *sb* **1** *(sending av varer etc)* forwarding; **2** *(vareparti)* consignment.

forsere *vb* force; *et forsert smil* a forced smile.

forsete *sb* **1** *(forreste sete)* front seat; **2** *(ledelse)* chairmanship, presidency; *under ~ av Ms Smith* with fr Smith in the chair.

forsett *sb* purpose, intention; *han gjorde det med ~* he did it on purpose; *med det ~ å legge seg tidlig* with the intention of going early to bed; *veien til helvete er brolagt med gode ~er* hell is paved with good intentions.

forside *sb* **1** front, face; **2** *(av avis)* front page.

forsikre *vb* **1** *(erklære, påstå)* assure *(alltid fulgt av omsynsledd) han ~t at jeg tok feil* she assured me that I was wrong; *hun forsikret meg om sitt vennskap* she assured me of her friendship; **2** *(assurere)* insure; *~t mot brann* insured against fire. **forsikring** *sb* **1** *(erklæring, påstand)* assurance; *jeg trodde ikke på ~ene deres* I did not believe in their assurances; **2** *(assuranse)* insurance; *~en dekker tapet* the insurance covers the loss; *(livs~)* assurance. **forsikrings|selskap** *sb* insurance company. **~taker** *sb* insured; policy holder.

forsiktig *adj* **1** *(omhyggelig)* careful; **2** *(varsom, ~ i fare)* cautious; *~ med penger* cautious about money; *en ~ bemerkning* a cautious remark; *Forsiktig!* Caution! **forsiktighet** *sb* **1** *(omhu)* care; *med ~* with care; **2** *(varsomhet, ~ i fare)* caution, cautiousness; *med ~* cautiously. **forsiktighetsregel** *sb* precaution.

forsinke *vb* delay; *snøen ~t toget to timer* the snow delayed the train for two hours. **forsinkelse** *sb* delay; *med to dagers ~/en ~ på to dager* with a delay of two days. **forsinket** *adj: to timer ~* two hours behind time; to hours late

forskanse *vb* entrench. **forskansning** *sb* entrenchment.

forske *vb* carry on research; do research work. **forsker** *sb* researcher; research worker. **forsking** se *forskning.*

forskjell *sb* difference, distinction; *~ i pris* difference in price; *~ mellom/på* difference between; *~en mellom mord og drap* the distinction between murder and manslaughter; *det er stor ~ mellom/på dem* there is a great difference between them; *en ~ på to tommer* a difference of two inches; *se ~ på* see a difference between; distinguish; tell (the difference); *jeg ser ikke/kan ikke se ~ på tvillingene* I cannot see any difference between the twins; *bare med den ~ at* with the sole difference that; *gjøre ~;* be unfair; have favourites; *(ikke behandle likt)* discriminate between; *til ~ fra* unlike; as distinct from; in contradistinction to; *uten ~* without distinction; indiscriminately. **forskjellig** *adj* **1** different, unlike; *hun er svært ~ fra søsteren (sin)* she is very unlike her sister; *være ~ (også)* differ; *smaken er ~* tastes differ; *være ~ fra* differ from; **2** *(atskillige)* various, several.

forskjærkniv *sb* carving knife; carver.

forskning *sb* research; *drive ~* carry on research.

forskole *sb* preparatory school.

forskrekke *vb* **1** *(gjøre ~t)* frighten; *hun ble/var ~t over ordene hans* she was frightened at/by his words; *ordene hans gjorde henne ~t* his words gave her a fright; **2** *(skremme)* scare. **forskrekkelig** *adj* awful, dreadful, frightful. **forskrekkelse** *sb* fright; *vi fikk (oss) en ordentlig ~* we had a shock/a thorough fright. **forskrekket** *adj* frightened, scared. **forskremt** *adj* afraid; frightened, scared.

forskrift *sb* **1** *(bestemmelse, regel)* regulations, rule; **2** *(rettesnor)* precept, directions, instructions. **forskriftsmessig** *adj, adv* in due form; according to the regulations.

forskrudd *adj* eccentric, cranky.

forskudd *sb* advance; *betale (på) ~* pay in advance;

de gav henne en ukes gasje på ~ they advanced her a week's salary; *ta på ~* anticipate; *ta sorgene på ~ (også)* meet trouble half-way. **forskuttere** *vb* advance.

forslag *sb* **1** proposal; *gå med på et ~* accept a proposal; **2** *(henstilling, råd)* suggestion; *komme med/sette frem et ~* make a proposal/suggestion; **3** *(resolusjons~)* motion; **4** *(lov~)* bill; *komme med/sette frem et ~* put a motion/bring in a bill; *~et ble vedtatt/forkastet* the motion/bill was carried/rejected. **forslagsstiller** *sb* proposer, mover.

forslitt *adj (banal)* hackneyed, stale; *~ uttrykk* hackneyed phrase; commonplace.

forsluken *adj* greedy, ravenous, voracious.

forslå *vb: så det ~r* **1** *(flust)* enough and to spare; *også* galore; **2** *(som bare det)* with a vengeance; **3** *det ~r ikke* that won't do.

forslått *adj* bruised, battered.

forsmak *sb: en ~ på* a foretaste of.

forsnakke seg *vb* **1** *(snakke galt)* make a slip of the tongue; **2** *(si for mye)* give oneself away; give a secret away. **forsnakkelse** *sb* a slip of the tongue.

forsommer *sb* early summer.

forsone *vb* **1** *(forlike)* reconcile; *bli ~t med (noen)* become reconciled with (somebody); *~ seg med (noe)* reconcile oneself to (something); *et forsonende trekk* a redeeming feature. **forsoning** *sb* reconciliation. **forsonlig** *adj* **1** *(fredelig)* conciliatory; **2** *(medgjørlig)* placable.

forsove seg *vb* oversleep (oneself). **forsovelse** *sb* oversleeping.

forspill *sb* prelude.

forspille *vb* forfeit; lose; throw away; *~ sjansen* miss the chance.

forspise seg *vb* overeat (oneself).

forsprang *sb* lead, start; *du må gi meg et ~* you must give me a start; *et ~ på ti yards* a lead of ten yards.

forstad *sb* suburb.

forstand *sb* **1** *(klokskap)* intelligence; **2** *(fornuft)* reason; *han mistet ~en* he lost his reason; **3** *(motsatt sinnsykdom)* sanity; *jeg tviler på hennes ~* I doubt her sanity; **4** *(evne til å tenke og forstå)* intellect; *den menneskelige ~* the human intellect; *jeg har ingen ~ på biler* I know nothing about cars; **5** *(betydning)* meaning, sense; *i god ~* in a good sense.

forstander *sb* director, principal, superintendent; *(menighets~)* elder, pastor, reverend. **forstanderskap** *sb* board (of directors); direction, management.

forstandig *adj* intelligent, sensible.

forstavelse *sb* prefix.

forstavn bow(s), stem.

forsteine *vb* petrify. **forsteining** *sb* petrification; *(fossil også)* fossil.

forsterke *vb* strengthen, fortify, reinforce. **forsterker** *sb (i radio etc)* amplifier. **forsterkning** *sb* strengthening, reinforcement; *(i radio etc)* amplification.

forst|kandidat *sb* Master of Forestry. **~mann** *sb* forester.

forstokket *adj* obdurate.

forstoppelse *sb* constipation. **forstoppet** *adj* constipated.

forstue *vb* sprain. **forstuing** *sb* sprain.

forstumme *vb* **1** become silent; **2** *(dø hen)* cease, stop; die down.

forstvesen *sb* forestry.

forstyrre *vb* **1** *(uroe)* disturb; *jeg vil ikke bli ~t* I do not want to be disturbed; *jeg håper jeg ikke ~r* I hope I am not disturbing; **2** *(avbryte)* interrupt; *han ~t henne stadig i arbeidet (hennes)* he kept interrupting her work; **3** *(bringe i uorden)* upset; **4** *(komme til uleilighet)* intrude on. **forstyrrelse** *sb* disturbance, interruption. **forstyrret** *adj* **1** *(forvirret)* confused; **2** *(nervøs, rystet)* upset; **3** *(forrykt)* crazy.

forstørre *vb* enlarge, magnify; *(~ fotografi)* enlarge. **forstørrelse** *sb* enlargement. **forstørrelses|apparat** *sb* enlarger. **~glass** *sb* magnifying glass.

forstå *vb* **1** understand; *~r du hva jeg sier?* do you understand what I am saying? **2** *(innse)* realize, see; *jeg ~r fullt ut at ...* I quite realize that ...; *jeg ~r ikke hva det skal være til* I do not see what use it is; **3** *(ha lært, kunne)* know; *hun ~r seg på biler* she knows about cars; **4** *(uttrykk) ~ spøk* take a joke; *ikke så å ~ at* I do not mean to imply that; not that; *jeg forstod på ham at* he gave me the impression/gave me to understand that. **forståelig** *adj* **1** *(begripelig)* comprehensible, intelligible; *lett ~* easy to understand; *de kunne ikke gjøre seg ~* they could not make themselves understood; **2** *(unnskyldelig)* understandable, pardonable. **forståelse** *sb* **1** understanding; **2** *(enighet)* agreement; **3** *(sympati)* sympathy; *han fant ingen ~ hos dem* he met with no sympathy from them; *hun hadde ingen ~ for deres vanskeligheter* she did not understand their difficulties. **forståelsesfull** *adj* understanding, sympathetic. **forståsegpåer** *sb* know-all, wiseacre.

forsvar *sb* defence; *til deres ~* in their defence. **forsvare** *vb* defend. **forsvarer** *sb* defender; *jur* counsel for the defence. **forsvarlig I** *adj* **1** *(som kan forsvares)* defensible; **2** *(ordentlig)* proper; *på en ~ måte, på ~ vis* in a proper manner; *i ~ stand* in a good condition; **II** *adv (sikkert)* securely; *~ låst* securely locked. **forsvars|beredskap** *sb* military preparedness. **~departement** *sb* Ministry of Defence; *US* Defence Department; the Pentagon. **~krig** *sb* defensive war. **~løs** *adj* defenceless. **~minister** *sb* Minister of Defence. **~skrift** *sb* apology, defence. **~tale** *sb* plea; *jur* speech for the defence. **~utgifter** *sb fl* defence expenditure. **~vitne** *sb* witness for the defence. **~våpen** *sb* defensive weapon.

forsvinne *vb* disappear; *(især plutselig eller mystisk)* vanish. **forsvinnende** *adj, adv: ~ liten* negligible, infinitesmal. **forsvunnet** *adj* gone, vanished; lost; *den forsvunne* the missing person.

forsyn *sb* providence; *forsynet* Providence.

forsyne *vb* **1** *(levere til)* supply; *de ~r oss med kjøtt* they supply us with meat; **2** *(~ en med)* provide; *skolen ~r barna med bøker* the school provides the children with books; **3** *(utstyre med)* equip; **4** *(~ ved bordet)* help; *han forsynte seg med poteter* he helped himself to potatoes; *(bare) forsyn Dem!* just help yourself! *takk, jeg er forsynt* I have had quite enough, thank you; **5** *~ meg!* indeed! by Jove! **forsyning** *sb* **1** supply; **2** *(særlig om mat~)* provisions. **forsyningsskip** *sb* supply | boat, ~ vessel.

forsøk *sb* **1** *(prøve)* attempt; *vi gjorde et ~ på å lande* we made an attempt to land/at landing; **2** *(eksperiment)* experiment; *et kjemi~* an experiment in chemistry; *det er ~et verdt* it is worth trying. **forsøke** *vb* attempt, try. **forsøks|kanin** *sb (prøveklut)* guinea-pig. **~vis** *adv* by way of experiment; experimentally, tentatively.

forsølve *vb* silver, silver-plate.

forsømme *vb* **1** *(vanskjøtte)* neglect; *bli forsømt* fall into neglect; *hun forsømte barna sine* she neglected her children; **2** *(ikke møte frem etc)* miss; *han forsømte skolen (f.eks. på grunn av sykdom)* he missed his lessons; **3** *(skulke)* play truant. **forsømmelse** *sb* **1** *(vanskjøtsel)* neglect; **2** *(uteblivelse)* absence. **forsømmelig** *adj* negligent.

forsørge *vb* support; provide for; *hun ~r en stor familie* she supports a large family. **forsørger** *sb* bread-winner, supporter.

for så vidt *adv* as far as it goes; in a way/a sense; *det er ~ ~ ~ greit nok* that is all right as far as it goes; *Kjenner du ham? Ja, ~ ~ ~.* Do you know him? Yes, in a way. **for så vidt som** adv in so far as; *Snakker han engelsk? Ja, ~ ~ ~ ~ han kan gjøre seg forstått.* Does he speak English? Yes, in so far as he can make himself understood.

fort I *adj* fast, quick, rapid *(jf hurtig, rask)*; **II** *adv* **1** *(med stor fart)* fast, quickly; *du snakker for ~* you speak too fast; *jeg løp så ~ jeg kunne* I ran as fast/quickly as I could; **2** *(uten å somle)* quick; *kom så fort du kan* come as quick as you can; **3** *(raskt, i løpet av kort tid)* quickly; *det er ~ gjort* that is quickly done; **III** *sb (befestning)* fort, fortress.

fortann *sb* front tooth; incisor.

fortapt *adj* lost; *en ~ sjel* a lost soul; *vi er ~* we are lost; *den ~e sønn* the Prodigal Son.

fortau *sb* pavement; *især US* sidewalk. **fortaus|-kafé** *sb* pavement café. **~kant** *sb* curb, kerb.

fortegn *sb* **1** *mat* sign; **2** *data* sign character; **3** *mus* signature.

fortegnelse *sb* list; *en alfabetisk ~* an alphabetical list.

fortelle *vb* **1** tell; *han fortalte at ...* he told me (her, him, them, us etc) that ...; *det ~s at* rumour has it that; **2** *(berette, ~ om)* relate; *hun fortalte om sine opplevelser* she related (told us etc about) her experiences. **fortellende** *adj* narrative (style/poem). **forteller** *sb* narrator, story-teller. **forteller|evne** *sb* narrative skill. **~talent** *sb* gift for storytelling. **fortelling** *sb* story, narrative; *(oppdiktet også)* tale.

fortid *sb* **1** past; *vi vet ingenting om deres ~* we know nothing of their past; **2** *(i grammatikk)* the past (tense); **3** *(historisk ~)* early history; *Norges ~* the early history of Norway. **fortids|levninger, ~minnesmerker** *sb fl* antiquities.

fortie *vb* be silent about; keep secret.

fortjene *vb* deserve. **fortjeneste** *sb* **1** *(inntekt)* earnings; **2** *(avanse)* profit, gain; *en ~ på 150 pund* a profit of £150; *vi solgte gården med ~* we sold the farm at a profit. **fortjent** *adj: gjøre seg ~ til* deserve, merit.

fortolle *vb* **1** *(oppgi til fortolling)* declare; *har De noe å ~* have you anything to declare? **2** *(betale toll for)* pay duty on.

fortreffelig *adj* excellent, splendid.

fortrenge *vb* **1** *(erstatte)* supersede; **2** *(~ fra bevisstheten)* repress; *fortrengte følelser* repressed feelings. **fortrengning** *sb* repression.

fortrinn *sb* merit. **fortrinnsberettiget** *adj* privileged; having a right to preferential treatment. **fortrinnsrett** *sb* priority; preference; preferential claim.

fortrolig *adj* **1** *(om opplysninger etc)* confidential; **2** *(om personer)* familiar, intimate; *~e venner* intimate friends; *~ med engelsk* familiar with the English language. **fortrolighet** *sb* **1** *(tillit)* confidence; *i all ~* in confidence; **2** *(inngående kjennskap)* intimate knowledge; *hennes ~ med engelsk* her intimate knowledge of English; **3** *(meget høy grad av ~)* intimacy.

fortropp *sb* vanguard.

fortryllelse *sb* charm, fascination. **fortryllende** *adj* charming.

fortsette *vb* continue, proceed; go (carry, keep) on; *vi fortsatte å synge* we continued to sing; we continued/went on singing; *han fortsatte med sitt arbeid* he carried on/continued with his work. **fortsettelse** *sb* continuation.

fortumlet *adj* confused, perplexed.

fortvile *vb* despair. **fortvilelse** *sb* **1** *(håpløshet)* despair; *de drev hverandre til ~* they drove each other to despair; **2** *(vill ~)* desperation. **fortvilet** *adj* **1** desperate; *en ~ kamp* a desperate struggle; **2** *(motløs)* disconsolate; in despair; *han var ~* he was in despair.

fortynne *vb* dilute.

fortære *vb* **1** *(spise)* consume, eat; **2** *(ødelegge)* consume, destroy.

fortøye *vb* moor; *(~ ved kai)* berth; *(om båt også)* make fast. **fortøyninger** *sb* moorings.

forulempe *vb* molest; annoy, trouble.

forunderlig *adj* odd, strange. **forundre seg** *vb: ~ ~ over* marvel/wonder at; be surprised at. **forundret** *adj* surprised. **forundring** *sb* wonder; astonishment, surprise.

forurense *vb* pollute; contaminate, foul. **forurensing** *sb* pollution; contamination.

forurette *vb* wrong; injure; *føle seg ~t* be aggrieved.

forurolige *vb* alarm, disquiet; *~nde nyheter* alarming news.

forut *adv* **1** *(på skip)* forward; **2** *(foran skip)* ahead; **3** *~ for* previous to; *~ for sin tid* ahead of/in advance of/before one's time/age. **forutanelse** *sb* presentiment.

foruten *prep* besides; *det var to gjester ~ meg* there were two guests besides me.

forut|fattet *adj* preconceived. **~følelse** *sb* presentiment. **~gående** *adj* preceding, previous. **~inntatt** *adj: ~ mening* prejudice. **~satt** se *~sette*. **~se** *vb* foresee; anticipate. **~seende** *adj* provident. **~setning** *sb* **1** *(antakelse)* assumption; **2** *(betingelse)* condition; *under den ~ at* on the assumption that; on condition that; **3** *(kvalifikasjon)* qualification; *falske ~er* false pretences. **~sette** *vb* assume, presuppose; take for granted; *~satt at* provided that. **~si** *vb* foretell, predict; prophesy. **~sigelse** *sb* prediction.

for|valte *vb* manage; administer. **~valtning** *sb* management; administration.

forvandle *vb* change, transform; *larver ~r seg til sommerfugler* caterpillars change into butterflies. **forvandling** *sb* change.

for|vanske *vb* corrupt, distort. **~vansking** *sb* corruption, distortion.

forvaring *sb: ta i ~ (arrestere)* arrest; take into custody.

forveien: *i ~ (adv)* **1** *(om tid)* before, beforehand; *vite i ~* know beforehand; **2** *(om sted)* ahead; *vi løp i ~* we ran on ahead.

forveksle *vb* mistake; mix up; confuse; *han ~t navnene deres* he mixed up their names; *jeg ~r henne alltid med søsteren (hennes)* I always mistake her for her sister. **forveksling** *sb* mistake; *ved en ~* by (a) mistake.

forvente *vb* expect; look forward to. **forventning** *vb* expectation.

for|verre *vb* make worse. **forverres** *vb* deteriorate; grow worse. **~verring** *sb* worsening.

forvirre *vb* confuse, perplex; baffle, puzzle. **forvirret** *adj* confused. **forvirring** *sb* confusion, disorder; *i vill ~* in disorder.

forvise *vb* banish; *lands~* exile.

forvisse *vb: ~ seg om* make sure of; satisfy oneself that; ascertain.

for|vitre *vb* crumble, disintegrate. **~vitring** *sb* crumbling, disintegration.

for|vrenge *vb* distort, misrepresent. **~vrengning** *sb* distortion, misrepresentation.

forværelse *sb* ante-room. **forværelsesdame** *sb* receptionist.

forynge *vb* rejuvenate. **foryngelse** *sb* rejuvenation.

forære *vb: ~ en noe* give someone something; make someone a present (of something). **foræring** *sb* present; *(sjeldnere, i skrift)* gift.

forøke *vb* increase. **forøkelse** *sb* increase.

for øvrig *adv* **1** *(hva resten angår)* for the rest; **2** *(ellers)* otherwise; in other respects.

forårsake *vb* bring about; cause; *stormen ~t en god del skade* the gale caused a good deal of damage.

fosfat *sb* phosphate. **fosfor** *sb* phosphorus.

foster *sb* **1** *(på tidlig stadium)* embryo; **2** *(temmelig utviklet)* foetus, fetus.

foss *sb* waterfall. **fosse** *vb* **1** gush; *det ~t vann fra røret* water gushed out of the pipe; **2** *(om regn)* pour; *regnet ~t ned* the poured dowm. **fossekraft** *sb* water-power.

fossil *sb* fossil.

fot *sb* foot (som lengdemål, se midtsidene); *~ for ~* foot by foot; *hjelpe en på ~e* set somebody on his feet/legs; *komme på ~e igjen* pick up; recover; *på like ~ med* on the same/on an equal footing with; *konkurrere på like ~* compete on equal terms; *på stående ~* on the spur of the moment; offhand; *sikker på ~en* footsure; *stå på god ~ med* be on good terms with; *så lett som ~ i hose* plain sailing; as easy as falling off a log; *til ~s* on foot; *ved ~en av bakken* at the foot of the hill. **football** *sb* football; *(i motsetning til Rugby)* association football; *dgl* soccer. **fotball|bane** *sb* football ground. **~kamp** *sb* football match. **~lag** *sb* football team. **~spiller** *sb* footballer; football player.

fot|brems *sb* foot brake. **~feste** *sb* foothold, footing; *han mistet ~festet* he lost his footing. **~folk** *sb koll* infantry, foot; *500 ~* 500 foot. **~gjenger** *sb* pedestrian. **~gjengerovergang** *sb* crossing; zebra crossing. **~note** *sb* footnote.

foto *sb* photo. **fotograf** *sb* photographer. **fotografere** *vb* photograph. **fotografering** *sb* photography. **fotografi** *sb (bilde)* photograph. **fotografiapparat** *sb* camera. **fotografisk** *adj* photographic.

fot|pleie *sb* pedicure. **~sid** *adj: ~ kjole* full-length dress. **~spor** *sb* foot-print; *i hans ~spor* in his path. **~trinn** *sb: lyden av ~trinn* fotfall. **~tur** *sb* hike; *gå på ~* hike. **~turist** *sb* hiker.

foxterrier *sb* fox-terrier.

fra **1** *prep* from; *han kommer ~ London* he comes from London; **2** *konj* since; *~ jeg var fire år* since I was four years; **3** *(uttrykk)* **~ da av** from that time; since then; **~ nå av** from now; *det gjør* **verken ~ eller til** it does not matter; it makes no difference; **~ og med** from and onward; *~ og med femte kapittel* from chapter five and onward; **~ og med - til og med** from - to - inclusive; *~ og med 1. juli til og med 7. august* from July 1 to August 7 inclusive; *dra/reise ~* leave; *dra ~ landet* leave the country; *være ~* **seg** *(~ vettet, ~ forstanden)* be out of one's mind; be beside oneself.

fradrag *sb* deduction; *skattefritt ~* (tax-free) allowance.

fragment *sb* fragment. **fragmentarisk** *adj* fragmentary.

frakk *sb* coat, topcoat.

fraksjon *sb* **1** *(av f.eks. politisk parti)* section, wing; **2** *petro etc (ved destillering)* cut.

frakt *sb* **1** *((sjø)transport, betaling for transport)* freight; **2** *(last)* freight, cargo. **~brev** *sb* consignment note; *(konossement)* bill of lading. **frakte** *vb* carry, convey, transport. **frakt|fart** *sb* tramp trade. **~fritt** *adv* carriage free/paid.

fralandsvind *sb* off-shore wind.

fram etc se *frem etc.*

frarå(de) *vb* dissuade; advise not to; *jeg ~t ham å gjøre det* I dissuaded him from doing it.

frase *sb* (empty) phrase; *tomme ~r* cant, froth. **frase|maker** *sb* phrasemonger. **~makeri** *sb* cant.

fraskilt *adj* divorced; *en ~* a divorced person.

frastøtende *adj* repulsive, forbidding; *et ~ utseende/ytre* a repulsive/forbidding appearance.

fravær *sb* absence; *etter flere års ~* after several years' absence. **fraværende** *adj* absent.

fred *sb* peace; *de sluttet ~* they made peace; *la meg få ~/la meg være i ~* leave me alone; leave me in peace.

fredag *sb* Friday.

fredelig *adj* **1** *(fredsommelig)* peaceable; *en ~ person* a peaceable person; **2** *(fredfylt)* peaceful; *en ~ aften* a peaceful evening; **3** *(om dyr)* harmless. **fredløs** *adj: gjøre/lyse ~* outlaw; *han var ~* he was an outlaw. **fredsommelig** *adj* peaceful. **freds|slutning** *sb* conclusion of peace. **~traktat** *sb* peace treaty. **~vilkår** *sb* peace term.

fregatt *sb* frigate.

fregne *sb* freckle. **fregnet** *adj* freckled.

freidig *adj* **1** *(ubekymret)* cheerful, confident; bold; **2** *(utvungen)* free and easy; **3** *(frekk)* cheeky, cool; bold. **freidighet** *sb* cheerfulness, confidence; boldness.

frekk *adj* impudent; barefaced, cheeky; *(især om kvinner)* bold; *en ~ person* an impudent person; *en ~ løgn* a barefaced lie; *hun var ~ nok til ...* she had the nerve/face to ... **frekkhet** *sb* impudence, audacity; *en ~* a piece of impudence.

frelse 1 *sb* salvation; *(berging)* rescue; **2** *vb (jf redde)* save; *(berge)* rescue. **frelser** *sb* saviour; *Vår Frelser* our Saviour. **Frelsesarmeen** the Salvation Army.

frem el **fram** *adv* **1** *(~over)* forward, on; *han gikk ~* he stepped forward; *hun arbeidet seg ~* she worked her way forward; **2** *(~ i dagen)* out; *de kom ~ fra buskene* they came out of the bushes; *jeg tok ~ lommebokan* I took out my wallet; *~ med det!* out with it! **3** *(~ til bestemmelsesstedet) komme/nå ~* arrive; *de kom ~ i god behold* they arrived safely/in safety; **4** *(lenger fremme) to år ~ i tiden* two years ahead; **5** *(~ og tilbake) han gikk ~ og tilbake* he walked backward(s) and forward(s)/up and down/to and fro. **frem|bringe** *vb* make, produce. **~brudd** *sb: dagens ~* daybreak; *nattens ~* nightfall. **~deles** *adv* still. **~for** *prep* **1** *(foran)* before; in front of; **2** *(heller enn, mer enn)* above; *~ alt* above all; *foretrekke ~for* prefer to; *jeg foretrekker å spille kort ~for å lese* I prefer playing cards to reading. **~gang** *sb* **1** *(fremskritt)* progress, advance; *soldatenes ~gang ble stanset* the advance of the soldiers was stopped; **2** *(medgang)* success. **~gangsmåte** *sb* method, procedure; course/line of action. **~kalle** *vb* **1** *(forårsake)* cause; bring about; call forth; produce; **2** *(~ film)* develop. **~kalling** *sb (av film)* development. **~kommelig** *adj* passable. **~komst** *sb* arrival; *ved ~komsten* on arrival. **~komstmiddel** *sb* conveyance; means of communication.

fremme el **framme** *adv* **1** *(foran)* in front; *de som stod ~* those in front; *lenger ~* further ahead/on; **2** *(synlig, ute)* on view; out; *månen er ~* the moon is out; **3** *(ved målet)* at one's destination; *også* there; *da vi endelig var ~* when at length we were there. **fremme** *vb (hjelpe frem, oppmuntre)* promote; encourage; further; *~ fred og forståelse* promote/further peace and understanding.

fremmed I *adj* **1** *(ukjent)* strange; *en ~ dame* a strange lady; **2** *(utenlandsk)* foreign, alien; *~e land* foreign countries; *en ~ statsborger* an alien citizen/subject; **II** *sb* **1** *(person ukjent på et sted)* stranger; *jeg er ~ her* I am a stranger here; *jeg følte meg som en ~* I felt a stranger; **4** *(utlending)* foreigner; *(utenlandsk statsborger bosatt i landet)* alien. **fremmed|arbeider** *sb* foreign worker. **~artet** *adj* alien, strange. **~bok** *sb* register; visitors' book. **~ord** *sb* foreign word.

fremmelig *adj* forward, precocious.

frem|møte *sb* attendance, turn-out. **~over** *adv* forward, on, ahead; *han bøyde seg ~* he bent forward; *hun så ~* she looked ahead. **~ragende** *adj* eminent, brilliant. **~sette** *vb: ~ forslag (til avstemning)* move; put a motion; *(lovforslag)* bring in (a bill). **~skritt** *sb* progress; *de gjorde ~skritt* they made progress; *store ~skritt* great progress; *det var et stort ~skritt* it was a great step forward.

fremst *adv* foremost, front; *først og ~* first and foremost; first of all.

frem|stille *vb* **1** *(lage)* make, produce; *fremstilt av naturlig frukt (helt)* made from natural fruit; *(delvis)* made with natural fruit; **2** *(forklare, utrede)* explain; *slik de ~stilte det* the way they explained it; **3** *(forestille, gjengi)* represent; **4** *(spille på scene)* act, play. **~stilling** *sb* production; account, explanation; representation; *gi en ~stilling av* give an account of. **~stående** *adj* **1** *(~ragende)* outstanding, prominent; *en ~stående person* a prominent person; **2** *(utstående)* protruding. **~tid** *sb* future; *for ~tiden* in future; *i ~tiden* in (the) future; in times to come. **~tidig** *adj* future. **~tredende** *adj* outstanding, prominent.

fres *sb* **1** *(fresemaskin)* mill; **2** *for full ~* at full/top speed, on top gear. **frese** *vb* **1** *(med fresemaskin etc)* mill, cut; **2** *(om ild)* crackle, sputter; **3** *(visle)* hiss. **fresemaskin, freser** *vb* milling machine.

freskomaleri *sb* mural (painting).

fri A *adj* free; *be seg ~* ask for leave of absence (for a day/evening etc off); *det er ikke fritt (dvs det skal være sikkert etc)* rather; *det står deg fritt å gå etc* you are free to leave etc; *gi fritt løp* give vent to; *gi fritt løp for følelsene sine* give vent to one's feelings; *ha ~* have a holiday/a day off; *ha ~e hender* have free hands; *ha fritt spill* have free play; *ordet er fritt* everyone is free to speak; *sette i ~ (gir)* put in neutral; *sette/slippe ~* release; set free; be released/set free; **B** *vb (foreslå ekteskap)* propose. **fri|areal** *sb* common; *(rundt by)* green belt. **~billett** *sb* free ticket. **~dag** *sb* day off; holiday.

frier *sb* suitor. **frierbrev** *sb* letter of proposal. **frieri** *sb* proposal.

fri|finne *vb* acquit; find not guilty. **~finnelse** *sb* acquittal. **~gi** *vb* release; set free; *fangene ble ~gitt* the prisoners were set free.

frigid *adj* frigid. **frigiditet** *sb* frigidity.

fri|gjort *adj* emancipated. **~gjorthet** *sb* emancipation. **~gjøre** *vb* release; set free; liberate. **~gjøring** *sb* liberation. **~handel** *sb* free trade.

frihet *sb* freedom; *(især om ~ fra tvang)* liberty; *de kjempet for ~en* they fought for freedom. **frihets|bevegelse** *sb* liberation movement. **~helt** *sb* champion of liberty. **~kamp, ~krig** *sb* war of independence; *den amerikanske ~krig* the War of American Independence.

fri|idrett *sb* athletics. **~idrettskvinne, ~idrettsmann** *sb* athlete. **~kirke** *sb* **1** *(om menigheten)* Free Church; nonconformist church; **2** *(om bygningen)* chapel. **~kirkeprest** *sb* minister, pastor. **~kjenne** *vb* acquit; find not guilty. **~kjennelse** *sb* acquittal.

friksjon *sb* friction.

fri|kvarter *sb* break, interval. **~kveld** *sb* evening off.

fr. ufts|liv *sb* outdoor life. **~kvinne, ~mann, ~menneske** *sb* outdoor(s) woman/man/person.

frimerke *sb* stamp; *sette ~ på et brev* stamp a letter; *samle på ~r* collect stamps; *brukt/ubrukt ~* cancelled/uncancelled stamp. **frimerke|album** *sb* stamp album. **~samler** *sb* stamp-collector. **~samling** *sb* stamp-collection.

frimodig *adj* frank, open.

frimurer *sb* freemason. **frimurerlosje** *sb* masonic lodge.

frisérdame *sb* hairdresser. **frisere** *vb: hun friserte seg* she did her hair; *hun ble frisert* she had her hair done. **frisérsalong** *sb* hairdresser's parlour.

frisk *adj* **1** *(ved god helse)* healthy; in good health; *~ som en fisk* fit as a fiddle; **2** *(~ igjen etter sykdom)* well; *bli ~* get well (after an illness); recover (from an illness); **3** *(ny, ubrukt etc)* fresh; *~e blomster* fresh flowers; *~ krefter* renewed vigour; **4** *(forfriskende)* fresh; *~ bris* fresh breeze; *~ luft* fresh air. **friske** *vb: ~ opp (kunnskaper)* brush up (one's knowledge).

frispark *sb* free kick; *dømme ~* award a free kick.

frist *sb* respite; delay; time; *et års ~* a respite of a year; *gi dem en ukes ~* give them a week; *siste ~* deadline. **friste** *vb* tempt. **fristelse** *sb* temptation; *det var en stor ~* it was a great temptation; *jeg falt for ~n* I succumbed to the temptation; *hun motstod ~n* she resisted the temptation.

frisør *sb* hairdresser.

fri|ta *vb* exempt, excuse; *~ for et verv/en oppgave* excuse from a task; *~ for militærtjeneste/skatt* exempt from military service/taxation. **~takelse** *sb* exemption. **~tenker** *sb* free-thinker. **~tid** *sb* leisure (hours/time); spare time. **~tidsbeskjeftigelse** *sb* spare time occupation; hobby.

fritt *adv* **1** freely; *~ oversatt* freely translated; **2** *(gratis)* free. Se også *fri A.* **fritt|liggende, ~stående** *adj* free-standing; *(om hus især)* detached.

frivillig **1** *adj* voluntary; **2** *sb* volunteer, *melde seg (som) ~* volunteer.

frodig *adj* **1** *(om planter)* vigorous; **2** *(om ugress)* rank; **3** *(om jord: fruktbar)* fertile; **4** *(om fantasi)* exuberant, fertile.

frokost *sb* breakfast; *ha til ~* have for breakfast; *spise ~* breakfast; have breakfast.

from *adj* **1** *(gudfryktig)* pious; **2** *(saktmodig)* gentle, meek. **fromhet** *sb* piety.

front *sb* front; *ved ~en* at the front. **front|glass** *sb* windscreen. **~kollisjon** *sb* head-on collision. **~lykt, ~lys** *sb* headlight.

frosk *sb* frog. **froskemann** *sb* frogman.

frossen *adj* frozen; *~t kjøtt* frozen meat; *(frostskadet)* frost-bitten; *frosne poteter* frost-bitten potatoes. **frost** *sb* frost. **frost|fri** *adj* frost-proof. **~skade** *sb* frost-bite. **~skadet** *adj* frost-bitten. **~væske** *sb* anti-freeze (solution).

frotté *sb* terry cloth. **frottéhåndkle** *sb* Turkish towel. **frottere** *vb* rub.

fru *(tittel)* Mrs; *~ Smith* Mrs Smith. **frue** *sb* **1** *(gift kvinne)* married woman; **2** *(hustru)* wife; *husets ~* the mistress/lady of the house.

frukt *sb* fruit. **fruktbar** *adj* **1** fertile; *~ jord* fertile/rich soil; **2** *(som formerer seg sterkt)* prolific; **3** *(fruktbringende)* fruitful; *~t samarbeid* fruitful cooperation. **fruktbarhet** *sb* fertility. **frukt|blomst** *sb* blossom. **~butikk** *sb* fruit shop. **~dyrking** *sb* fruit-growing. **~handler** *sb* fruiterer. **~hage** *sb* orchard. **~saft** *sb* fruit juice.

fruktsommelig *adj* pregnant. **fruktsommelighet** *sb* pregnancy.

frukttre *sb* fruit tree.

fryd *sb* delight, joy, rapture. **fryde** *vb* delight; *det ~t meg* I was delighted; *forandring ~r* variety is the spice of life.

frykt *sb* fear; *av ~ for hunden* for fear of the dog; *av ~ for å gjøre feil* for fear of making a mistake. **frykte** *vb* fear; be afraid of. **fryktelig** *adj* dreadful, horrible, terrible; awful; *~ mange mennesker* an awful lot of people. Se også *forferdelig.* **frykt|inngytende** *adj* formidable. **~løs** *adj* fearless. **~som** *adj* timid.

frynse *sb* fringe. **frynsegoder** *sb fl* fringe benefits. **frynset(e)** *adj* frayed.

fryse *vb* **1** *(føle kulde)* be/feel cold; *(være gjennomfrossen)* freeze; *jeg ~r* I am/feel cold; *jeg ~r på hendene* my hands are cold; *de frøs i hjel* they froze to death; **2** *(bli frostskadet)* be frostbitten; *potetene frøs* the potatoes were frostbitten; **3** *(~ til is)* freeze; *~* til *freeze over; dammen er frosset (til)* the pond is/has frozen over; **4** *(~ matvarer)* freeze, refrigerate; **5** *~ ut* freeze out. **fryse|boks** *sb* deep freeze; freezer. **~punkt** *sb* freezing-point. **fryseri** *sb* cold storage plant.

frø *sb* seed.

frøken *sb* **1** *(tittel)* Miss; **2** *(lærerinne)* teacher.

fråsse, fråtse *vb* gorge oneself; gormandize; *~ i* gorge oneself with. **fråsser, fråtser** *sb* glutton. **fråsseri, fråtseri** *sb* gluttony.

fugl *sb* bird. **fugle|bur** *sb* bird-cage. **~egg** *sb* bird's egg. **~hund** *sb* bird dog. **~nebb** *sb* beak. **~perspektiv** *sb* bird's-eye view. **~rede** *sb* bird's nest. **~sang** *sb* singing of birds. **~skremsel** *sb* scarecrow. **~unge** *sb* young bird.

fuktig *adj* moist; *(klamt, ubehagelig)* damp; *~ vegger* damp walls; *et ~ klima* a moist/damp climate. **fuktighet** *sb* **1** dampness, moistness; **2** *(væte)* moisture.

full *adj, adv* (se også *fullt*) **1** full; *stundom* all; whole; *~ av* full of; *~ storm* whole gale; *~t navn* full name; name in full; *det er å ta munnen for ~* that is saying too much; *for ~e seil* at full sail; (with) all sails set; *for/i ~ fart* at full speed; *ha hendene ~e* have one's hands full; *i ~ gang* at full blast; *i ~t alvor* in all seriousness; *med ~ styrke* at full blast; *månen er ~* the moon is full; **2** *(~t belagt)* full up; *bussen er ~* the bus is full up; **3** *(beruset)* drunken; *som predikatsord* drunk; *bli/drikke seg ~* get drunk.

full|blods *adj* thoroughbred. **~ende** *vb* complete, finish. **~endt** *adj* complete, perfect. **~føre** *vb* complete; carry through; finish; *hun ~førte ikke utdannelsen sin* she did not finish her education. **~god** *adj* adequate, satisfactory. **~kommen** *adj* **1** *(feilfri)* perfect; *ingen (av oss) er ~* none of us are perfect; **2** *(fullstendig)* complete. **~kommenhet** *sb* perfection. **~makt** *sb* authorization; *(skriftlig)* power of attorney; *gi ~ til* authorize to; give the authority to. **~mektig** *sb* **1** *(en som har fullmakt)* authorized agent (person, representative etc); **2** *(på kontor etc)* head clerk; managing clerk. **~stendig** *adj* complete; *(fullkommen)* perfect; *(adv)* completely, perfectly; quite; *han er ~stendig frisk* he is in perfect health; *hun er ~stendig fremmed for meg* she is a complete stranger to me. **fullstendighet** *sb* completeness.

fullt *adv* (se også *full*) completely, fully; quite; *~ ferdig* completely finished; *~ og fast* firmly; *tro ~ og fast* believe firmly; *være ~ og fast bestemt på* be firmly resolved to; *~ og helt* entirely; *~ opp av* plenty of; *~ utviklet* fully developed; full-grown; *ikke ~ en uke* not quite a week; *like ~* all the same; none the less.

full|treffer *sb* direct hit. **~ voksen** *adj* full-grown.

fundament *sb* foundation.

fungere *vb* act; officiate; *(om maskineri og organer)* function, work; *~ som* act as. **fungerende** *adj* acting. **funksjon** *sb* action, function. **funksjonere** *vb* function, work. **funksjons|dyktig** *adj* capable (of functioning). **~hemmet** *adj* handicapped; functionally disable. **~tid** *sb* term of office. **funksjonær** *sb* officer, official, servant; *bank~* bank official; *offentlig ~ (kommune~, stats~)* public servant.

funn *sb* discovery, find; *et stort ~* a great find.

fure I *sb* **1** groove; *(især plogfår)* furrow; **2** *(i ansiktet)* line, wrinkle; **II** *vb* furrow, groove. **furet** *adj* **1** furrowed, wrinkled; **2** *(forrevet)* rugged.

furie *sb* fury, virago.

furte *vb* sulk; be in the sulks. **furten** *adj* sulky. **furting** *sb* sulking, sulks.

furu *sb* (Scots) pine. **furu|bar** *sb* pine sprigs. **~materialer** *sb* (red) deal. **~møbler** *sb* deal furniture.

fusk *sb* cheating. **fuske** *vb* **1** *(i kort, på skolen)* cheat; **2** *(om motor)* misfire. **fusker** *sb: en ~ i faget* a dabbler in the trade.

futteral *sb* case.

futurum *sb (gram)* the future (tense).

fy *interj* ugh!, phew; *~ skam deg!* you ought to be ashamed of yourself! you naughty boy/girl!

fyke *vb* **1** *(om snø, sand)* drift; **2** *(om gnister, støv)* fly; **3** *~ opp (i sinne)* flare up. **fykende** *adj: i ~ fart* quick as lightning.

fyldig *adj* **1** *(tykkfallen)* plump; **2** *(nokså utførlig)* full; *en ~ fremstilling* a full account.

fylke *sb* ≈ county.

fyll *sb* **1** *(drukkenskap)* drinking, drunkenness; *i ~a* in drink; when drunk; **2** *(fyllmasse)* filling; rubbish. **fylle** *vb* **1** fill; *~ glasset* fill the glass; *teatret fyltes raskt* the theatre filled up quickly; *øynene hans fyltes med tårer* his eyes filled with tears; **2** *~* **år:** *hun ~r år i dag* it is her birthday today; *tvillingene ~r sitt tiende år i dag* the twins complete their tenth year today; *jeg ~r ti (år) i morgen* I shall be ten tomorrow; *til man ~r tjue år* until reaching the age of twenty. **fylle|bøtte** *sb* drunkard; boozer, soaker. **~kjører** *sb* drunken driver. **~kjøring** *sb* drunken driving. **~kalk** *sb fig* padding. **~penn** *sb* fountain-pen. **~sjuk** *adj: være ~* have a hangover. **fyllik** *sb = fyllebøtte.*

fyr *sb* **A** *(mann)* chap, fellow; *US* guy; **B** **1** *(ild)* fire; *sette/tenne ~ på* set fire to; set on fire; *ta ~* catch fire; **2** *(sentral~)* furnace; **3** *(~lys)* light; **4** *(~tårn)* lighthouse. **fyrbøter** *sb* stoker. **fyre** *vb* **1** *(tenne ild og holde den ved like)* fire; *~ med kull* burn coal; *~ på peisen* have a fire; **2** *(~ under fyrkjele)* stoke; **4** *(løsne skudd)* fire.

fyrste *sb* prince. **fyrstelig** *adj* princely.

fyrstikk(e) *sb* match. **fyrstikkeske** *sb* matchbox.

fyrstinne *sb* princess.

fyr|tårn *sb* lighthouse. **~verkeri** *sb* fireworks. **~vokter** *sb* lighthouse keeper.

fysiker *sb* physicist. **fysikk** *sb* **1** *(faget)* physics; *en lærebok i ~* textbook of physics; **2** *(kroppsbygning etc)* physique.

fysio|log *sb* physiologist. **~logi** *sb* physiology. **~logisk** *adj* physiological. **~terapeut** *sb* physiotherapist. **~terapi** *sb* physiotherapy.

fysisk *adj* physical.

fæl *adj* awful, horrible; foul, nasty.

færre *adj* fewer; *ikke ~ enn åtte (hele åtte)* no fewer than eight; *(minst åtte)* not fewer than eight. **færrest** *adj* fewest; *de færreste (bare svært få)* only a few.

fø *vb* **1** *(gi mat)* feed, nourish; **2** *(forsørge)* support; **3** *~ opp (husdyr)* breed, raise. **føde** **1** *sb (mat)* food; *(for dyre også)* feed; *vi måtte arbeide hardt for ~n* we had to work hard for a living; **2** *vb (få barn)* bear (se også *født*). **føde|avdeling** *sb* maternity ward. **~by** *sb* native town. **~midler** *sb koll* foodfstuffs, provisions.

føderal *adj* federal. **føderasjon** *sb* federation.

føde|sted *sb* birthplace. **~stue** *sb* delivery room. **~varer** *sb* foodstuffs, provisions. **fødsel** *sb* birth; *hun er engelsk av ~* she is English by birth. **fødsels|dag** *sb* birthday. **~overskudd** *sb* excess of births. **~prosent, ~tall** *sb* birth-rate. **~underskudd** *sb* excess of deaths. **født** *pp* **1** *(være født)* born; *jeg er ~ i 1907* I am born in 1907; *barnet var ~ få dager før* the child had been born a few days before; **2** *(har ~)* borne; *hun har ~ fem barn* she has borne five children; **3** *(ha som pikenavn)* née; *fru Jones ~ Smith* Mrs Jones née Smith. **føflekk** *sb* birthmark, mole.

følbar *adj* palpable, tangible.

føle *vb* feel; *~ seg* feel; *~ seg trett* feel tired; *~ seg frem* feel one's way; *~ seg (være kry)* fancy oneself. **følehorn** *sb* antenna; *især fig* feeler; *trekke ~ene til seg* draw in one's horns. **følelse** *sb* **1** feeling; *(sterk ~)* emotion; *blandede ~r* mixed feelings *vennskapelige ~r* friendly feelings; **2** *(følesans)* sense of touch. **følelses|ladet** *adj* charged with emotions; emotionally charged. **~liv** *sb* emotional life. **~løs** *adj* **1** *(hard, kald)* unfeeling; **2** *(ufølsom)* insensible; **3** *(~løs av kulde)* numb. **~messig** *adj* emotional.

følge I *sb* **1** *(ledsagelse)* company; *ha ~ med (person av motsatt kjønn)* go (about) with; walk out with; *ha fast ~* go steady; *i ~* in company; together; *vi er i ~* we are together; *i ~ med* in company with; in the company of; together with; *i ~ med en dame* in the company of a lady; **2** *(ledsagere)* followers, retinue; **3** *(opptog, prosesjon)* procession, train; *begravelses~* mourners; **4** *(rekke~)* order, succession; **5** *(konsekvens, resultat)* consequence, result; *hva vil ~(e) bli?* what will be the result? *som ~ av* in consequence (of); **II** *vb* **1** *(ledsage)* accompany; come/go with; *~ hjem* see/take home; *kan jeg få ~ deg hjem?* may I take you home? *jeg fulgte min kone på hennes reiser* I accompanied my wife on her travels; **2** *(~ etter, ~ langs etc)* follow; *jeg fulgte etter dem på avstand* I followed them at some distance; *veien ~r kysten* the road follows the coast; **3** *(etter~)* follow, succeed; *Olav 5. fulgte sin far på tronen* Olav 5. succeeded his father to the throne; **4** *(komme som en ~ av)* follow; *av dette ~r at ...* from this follows that ...; *det ~r av seg selv* that follows as a matter of course; that goes without saying; **5** *(fig: ~ regelmessig)* attend, follow; *~ forelesninger* attend lectures; **6** *(rette seg etter)* follow; *jeg fulgte hennes råd* I followed her advice; **7** *(holde tritt med)* keep pace with; keep up with; *~ med (i undervisning etc)* be attentive; *(holde seg à jour)* keep abreast of the events/times; keep oneself posted. **følgelig** *adv* consequently. **følgende** *adj* following; *den ~ dag* the following day.

føll *sb* foal. **følle** *vb* foal.

følsom *adj* sensitive; *(lettbevegelig)* emotional; *(affektert, overfølsom)* sentimental. **følsomhet** *sb* sensitiveness, sensitivity; sensibility.

før 1 *adv* before; *(før i tiden)* formerly; *~ eller senere* sooner or later; *dagen ~* the day before; *jeg hadde aldri sett ham ~* I had never seen him before; *jo ~ han går desto bedre* the sooner he leaves the better; **2** *konj* before; *jeg må få et ord med deg ~ du drar* I must have a word with you before you leave; *ikke ~* not till/until; *han kom ikke ~ middagen var over* he did not come till dinner was over; *ikke ~ ... så* hardly/scarcely ... when; no sooner ... than; *ikke ~ hadde han gått, så begynte det å regne* hardly had he/he had hardly left before/when the rain began; no sooner had he/he had no sooner left than rain began; **3** *prep* before; *han kom ~ meg* he came before me; *ikke ~* not till/until; *han kom ikke ~ klokken to* he did not come till two o'clock.

føre I *sb: det er dårlig ~* it is muddy/the roads are in a bad state; *på glatt ~* when the roads are slippery; *ski~* skiing (snow/surface); *godt (ski)~* good going/skiing; **II** *vb* **1** *(bringe, transportere)* carry; *(især om personer)* take; *han førte oss til hotellet* he took us to the hotel; **2** *(lede)* lead; *denne veien ~r til Oxford* this road leads to Oxford; *kompaniet ble ført av en ung offiser* the company was led by a young officer; **3** *(veilede)* guide; **4** *(~ varer)* stock; *denne butikken ~r alle slags matvarer* this shop stocks all sorts of food; **5** *(uttrykk) ~ bøker/regnskap* keep books/accounts; *~ en samtale* carry on a conversation; *~ inn (i protokoll etc)* enter (in); *(i stilbok)* write out; make a fair copy. **fører** *sb* **1** *(anfører)* leader; **2** *(bil~)* driver; **3** *(turist~)* guide. **førerkort** *sb* driving licence.

førkrigs- *adj* pre-war.

først I *adj* **1** *(tidligst)* early; *de ~e kristne* the early Christians; **2** *(førstnevnte)* former; *for det ~e* first; firstly; in the first place; *han hadde to døtre, Ruth og Ingrid. Den første ble ingeniør, den siste lege* he had two daughters, Ruth and Ingrid. The former became an engineer, the latter a doctor; **II** *adv* **1** *(i begynnelsen)* at first; *jeg kjente ham ~ ikke igjen* I did not recognize him at first; **2** *(som nr én)* first; *hun kom ~* she came first; **3** *~ da* ... not till/until ...; only ...; *jeg hørte det ~ i går* I did not hear it till yesterday; I heard it only yesterday; **III** *ordenstall* first; *~e mai* the first of May; *det ~e de så* the first thing they saw; *noe av det ~e hun sa* one of the first things she said. **første|hjelp** *sb* first aid. **~klasses** *adj* first-class. **~styrmann** *sb* second mate/officer. **først|kommende** *adj* next; next Monday. **førstnevnte** *adj, sb* the former.

føye *vb* **1** *(la få sin vilje)* humour; *er det klokt å ~ et barn?* is it wise to humour a child? *~ seg* comply, yield; *han føyde seg alltid etter sin kones ønsker* he always complied with/yielded to his wife's wishes; **2** *~ sammen* join, connect. **føyelig** *adj* compliant, docile.

få A *adj* few; *en mann av ~ ord* a man of few words; *noen ~* a few; *om noen ~ minutter* in a few minutes; *ikke så ~* not a few; quite a few; **B** *vb* **1** *(motta)* get, have, receive; *jeg har fått brevet ditt* I received your letter; *du skal ~ boken i morgen* you shall have the book tomorrow; **2** *(oppnå)* get, obtain; *han fikk jobben* he got the job; **3** *(~ en sykdom)* get; *(om smittsom sykdom)* catch; **4** *(om mat og måltider)* have; *vi fikk middag klokken åtte* we had dinner at eight; **5** *(~ + pp)* get, have; *han fikk* *klippet håret/reparert sykkelen sin* he had his hair cut/ his bicycle repaired; **6** *(~ til, lykkes med)* manage to; succeed in; *hun fikk arbeidet utført i rett tid* she managed to finish (her work) in time; **7** *(uttrykk) ~ til å* get, make; *jeg fikk ham til å gå hjem* I made him go home/got him to go home; *~ fatt/tak i/på* get hold of; *~ greie på, ~ vite* hear, learn; *vi fikk vite at* ... we were told that ...; *~ seg til å* bring/get oneself to; *~ øye på* catch/get sight of.

få|fengt *adj, adv* useless, vain; *det var ~fengt å tenke på* it was useless to think of; *~fengt strev* vain efforts. **~mælt** *adj* taciturn. **~mælthet** *sb* taciturnity.

får *sb* **A** *(sau)* mutton, sheep; **B** *(plog~)* furrow.

fåre|hund *sb* sheep-dog; *skotsk ~* collie. **~kjøtt** *sb* mutton. **~kotelett** *sb* mutton chop. **~stek** *sb* roast mutton.

få|tall *sb* minority. **~tallig** *adj* few in number.

G

g *(bokstaven)* g.

gabardin *sb* gaberdine.

gadd *vb* se *gidde.*

gaffel *sb* fork.

gagn *sb* **1** *(fordel)* benefit, good; profit; good advantage; *det kan ikke være til stort ~* it cannot do much good; *til ~ for de fattige* for the benefit of the poor; *til ~s* with a vengeance; thoroughly; **2** *(nytte)* use; *gjøre mer skade enn ~* do more harm than good; *hva ~ er det i det?* what is the good/use of it? what use is it? **gagne** *vb* **1** benefit, profit; be good for; **2** *(være nyttig)* be useful/of use to. **gagnlig** *adj* **1** advantageous, profitable; **2** *(nyttig)* useful.

gal *adj* **1** *(sinnssyk)* mad; *bli ~* go mad; *som en ~* like mad; *splitter ~* raving mad; **2** *(skrullet, sprø)* crazy; **3** *(uriktig)* wrong; *på den ~e siden av veien* on the wrong side of the road. Se også *galt.*

galant *adj* courteous.

gale *vb* crow.

galge *sb* gallows.

galla *sb (~antrekk)* full dress.

galle *sb* bile, gall.

galleri *sb* gallery.

gallionsfigur *sb* figurehead.

gallupundersøkelse *sb* Gallup poll.

galning *sb* **1** *(sinnssyk person)* madman; **2** *(skrullet person)* madcap.

galopp *sb* gallop; *i ~* at the gallop; *han satte av sted i full ~* he galloped off at full speed. **galoppere** *vb* gallop.

galskap *sb* madness.

galt *adj, adv* **1** *(feil, uriktig)* wrong; *(foran perf part)* wrongly; *(uttrykkes også ofte med forstavelsen)* mis-; *hun stavet ordet ~* she misspelt the word/spelt the word wrong; *ordet er ~ stavet* the word is misspelt/ wrongly spelt; **2** *(ille)* bad; *aldri så ~ at det ikke er godt for noe* it's an ill wind that blows nobody any good; *det er for ~* it is too bad; *fra ~ til verre* from bad to worse; *gå ~* fail; go wrong; fail; *(om klokke)* be wrong.

galvanisere *vb* galvanize.

gamasjer *sb fl* gaiters, spats.

Gamle-Erik Old Harry, Old Nick.

gamling *sb* old man. **gammel** *adj* **1** old; *(om meget gamle personer også)* aged; *bli ~ (eldes)* get/grow old; *(leve lenge)* live to a great age; live long; *de er like gamle* they are the same age; **2** *(fra ~ tid)* ancient; *de gamle romere* the ancient Romans; *i gamle dager* in former days; in days of old; **3** *(forhenværende)* old; *en av mine gamle elever* an old pupil of mine; **4** *(motsatt av fersk, frisk)* stale; *~t brød* stale bread. **gammel|dags** *adj* old-fashioned. **~norsk** *sb* (Old) Norse.

gamp *sb* farm-horse, work-horse; *fille~* jade.

gane *sb* palate; roof of the mouth.

gang I *sb* **1** se *gange I*; **2** *(gjenge, virksomhet)* running, working; *gå i ~* begin, start; *sette i ~* set to work; *maskinen er i ~* the machine is running/working; **3** *(forløp, utvikling)* course; *begivenhetenes ~* the course of events; **4** *(om tid, gjentakelse)* time; *én ~* once; *to ~er* twice; *to eller tre ~er* two or three times; *fem ~er* five times; *en ~ imellom* sometimes; now and then, *for første/annen ~* for the first/second time; *med en ~* all at once; suddenly; *på en ~ (samtidig)* at a time; *~ på ~* again and again; *to av/om gangen* two at a time; **II** *sb* **1** *(entré)* hall; **2** *(korridor)* passage; **3** *(hage~)* path, walk. **gange 1** *sb (det å gå, ganglag)* walk, walking; *det er ti minutters ~ til stasjonen* it is ten minutes' walk to the station; **2** *vb (multiplisere)* multiply; *~ med 12* multiply by 12. **gangsti** *sb* foot-path.

ganske *adv* **1** *(helt)* quite; perfectly; absolutely, completely; *~ annerledes* completely different; *~ riktig* quite right; *~ umulig* absolutely impossible; *~ uskyldig* perfectly innocent; *ikke ~* not altogether; **2** *(temmelig)* fairly, pretty, quite, somewhat; *~ god* fairly/ pretty good; *~ forbausende* somewhat surprising; *en ~ god middag* quite a good dinner.

gap *sb* **1** *(åpen munn)* (wide open) mouth; **2** *(åpning)* gap, opening; *døren står på vidt ~* the door is wide open; **3** *(kløft)* chasm. **gape** *vb* **1** *(åpne munnen)* open one's mouth; **2** *(måpe)* gape; **3** *(være åpen)* be open; *et ~nde sår* a gaping wound; a gash. **gapestokk** *sb* pillory.

garantere *vb* guarantee; *vi ~r (for) et heldig utfall* we guarantee success. **garanti** *sb* guarantee, warranty; *(især ved lån)* security; *det er fem års ~* there is a five years' guarantee.

garasje *sb* garage.

gard etc *sb se gård etc.*

garde *sb* guard; *Garden* the Guards.

garderobe *sb* **1** *(rom/skap for klær etc)* cloak-room; **2** *(klær)* wardrobe, clothes. **garderobeskap** *sb* wardrobe.

gardin *sb* curtain. **gardin|preken** *sb* curtain lecture. **~trapp** *sb* step-ladder.

gardist *sb* guardsman.

garn *sb* **1** yarn, thread; *(bomulls~)* cotton; *(ull~)* wool; **2** *(fiske~)* net.

garnison *sb* garrison.

garnnøste *sb* clew; ball of yarn.

gartner *sb* gardener. **gartneri** *sb* **1** *(handels~)* market garden; **2** *(planteskole)* nursery (garden).

garve *vb* tan. **garveri** *sb* tannery.

gas *sb* gauze. **gasbind** *sb* surgical gauze.

gasje *sb (især for embetsmenn etc)* salary, stipend; se også *lønn.*

gass *sb* gas; *gi (motoren) ~* step on the gas. **gass|-apparat** *sb* gas-ring. **~kammer** *sb* gas chamber. **~komfyr** *sb* gas range. **~pedal** *sb* accelerator; gas pedal. **~vasker** *sb petro* scrubber. **~verk** *sb* gas-works.

gate *sb* **1** street; *på ~n* in the street; **2** *(større ferdselsåre)* thorough-fare; **3** *(kjørebane)* roadway. **gate|-dør** *sb* **1** *(dør direkte mot gate)* street door; **2** *(ut mot forhage)* front door. **~gutt** *sb* street urchin. **~kryss** *sb* street crossing. **~pike** *sb* street-walker; prostitute.

gauk *sb* **1** *(brennevins~)* bootlegger; **2** se *gjøk.*

gave *sb* **1** *(presang)* gift, present; **2** *(evne)* gift, talent.

gavl *sb* gable.

gavmild *adj* generous, liberal. **gavmildhet** *sb* generosity, liberality.

geberde *sb* gesture.

gebiss *sb* denture; (set of) false teeth.

gebyr *sb* charge, fee.

gehør *sb: spille etter ~* play by ear.

geip *sb* grimace. **geipe** *vb* grimace; make/pull a face/faces.

geistlig *adj* clerical; *en ~* a clergyman. **geistlighet** *sb* clergy.

geit *sb* nanny-goat, (she-)goat. **geitebukk** *sb* billy-goat, he-goat.

gelé *sb* jelly.

geledd *sb* rank.

gelender *sb* railing, rails; *trappe~* banister(s).

gemyttlig *adj* genial; jolly, jovial.

gen *sb (arveanlegg)* gene.

general *sb* general. **generalforsamling** *sb* general meeting.

generalisere *vb* generalize. **general|løytnant** *sb* lieutenant general. **~prøve** *sb* **1** *(på teater)* dress rehearsal; **2** *(ellers)* rehearsel. **~stab** *sb* General Staff. **~streik** *sb* general strike.

generasjon *sb* generation. **generasjons|kløft, ~motsetning** *sb* generation gap.

generell *adj* general. **generelt** *adv (i sin alminnelighet, stort sett)* generally.

geni *sb* genius. **genial** *adj* of genius; *en ~ idé* a stroke of genius; *en ~ maler* a painter of genius; *hun er ~* she is a genius.

genitiv *sb* the genitive (case).

genser *sb* pull-over, sweater.

geograf *sb* geographer. **geografi** *sb* geography. **geografisk** *adj* geographical. **geolog** *sb* geologist. **geologi** *sb* geology. **geologisk** *adj* geologic(al). **geometri** *sb* geometry. **geometrisk** *adj* geometric(al).

gerilja *sb* guer(r)illa. **gerilja|(krig)** *sb* guer(r)illa war. **~krigføring** guer(r)illa warfare.

germaner *sb* Teuton. **germansk** *adj* Germanic, Teutonic.

gesims *sb* cornice.

geskjeftig *adj* bustling, fussy; *~ person* busybody.

gest *sb* gesture. **gestikulere** *vb* gesticulate. **gestus** *sb* gesture.

gevinst *sb* **1** *(fortjeneste)* gain(s), profit; **2** *(i lotteri)* prize; **3** *(i spill)* winnings.

gevær *sb* **1** *(især militært ~)* rifle; *presentere ~* present arms; **2** *(især jakt~)* gun. **geværkule** *sb* bullet.

gi *vb* **1** give; *jeg gav ham den* I gave it to him; **2** *(i kortspill)* deal; *hvem ~r?* who deals? *det er deg til a ~* (it's) your deal; **3** *(uttrykk)* **~ bort** give away; *han gav bort alle pengene sine* he gave all his money away; **~ etter** give way; *isen gav etter* the ice gave way; **~ etter for** give way to; yield to; *hun gav etter for truslene deres* she gave way/yielded to their threats; **~ for:** *hva gav du for den hatten?* what did you give/pay for that hat? **~ fra seg** *(utlevere)* give up; surrender; *han måtte ~ fra seg pistolen* he had to give up/surrender his pistol; **~ igjen** 1 *(gjengjelde)* pay (him, etc her) back in (his, her etc) own coin; 2 *~ igjen på (ved betaling)* give change for; *kan du ~ igjen på en femmer?* can you give me change for a fiver? **~ en inn** *(overhøvle)* give (him/her etc) a piece of one's mind; take (him, her etc) to task; **~ opp** *(~ tapt)* give up; **~ seg** 1 *(~ tapt)* give in, give up; 2 *(minke, bli bedre)* wear off; *det ~r seg med tiden* it will wear off in time; 3 *~ deg litt nå!* oh, come! go along! **~ seg i kast med** embark upon; tackle; **~ seg tid** take (one's) time; **~ seg ut for** *(å være)* pass oneself off as; pretend to be; *han gav seg ut for å være lege* he passed himself off as a doctor; **~ skylden** blame; lay/put the blame on; **~ tilbake** give back; restore, return.

gid *interj* I wish; if only; I hope; *~ jeg kunne se ham nå* I wish I could see him now; if only I could see him now.

gidde *vb* **1** *(orke)* take the trouble to; choose to; *han ~r ikke engang spørre* he does not even take the trouble to inquire; *når hun ~r arbeide* when she chooses to work; **2** *jeg gadd vite/visst* I wonder; I should like to know.

gift *sb* poison; *(slange~ også)* venom.

gift *adj* married; *han er ~ med en engelsk kvinne* he is married to an Englishwoman. **gifte** *vb: ~ bort* marry; *~ seg* marry; be/get married; *hun ~t seg med en fransk-mann* she married a Frenchman. **giftermål** *sb* marriage.

giftig *adj* poisonous, venomous. **gift|slange** *sb* poisonous snake. **~tann** *sb* poisonous fang.

gigant *sb* giant. **gigantisk** *adj* gigantic.

gikt *sb* gout, rheumatism.

gild *adj* fine; capital, excellent.

gips *sb* plaster (of Paris). **gipsbandasje** *sb* plaster cast. **gipse** *vb* plaster.

gir *sb* gear; *første/annet ~* first/second gear; *sette bilen i tredje ~* change into third gear. **gire** *vb* gear. **girkasse** *sb* gearbox.

girlande *sb* festoon.

girstang *sb* gear lever.

gisp *sb* gasp. **gispe** *vb* gasp; *~ etter luft* gasp for breath.

gissel *sb* hostage; *ta gisler* take hostages.

gitar *sb* guitar; *spille (på) ~* play the guitar.

gitt *adj: ta for ~* take for granted.

gitter *sb* grating; *(for cellevindu)* bars.

gjalle *vb* resound, reverberate.

gjedde *sb* pike.

gjel *sb* ravine.

gjeld *sb* debt; *ha ~* be in debt; *stå i ~ til* be indebted to; *stå i ~ til opp over begge ørene* be over head and ears in debt.

gjelde A *vb* **1** *(være gyldig)* be valid; *billetten ~r (for) én måned* the ticket is valid for a month; **2** *(telle med)* count; *dette målet ~r ikke* this goal does not count; **3** *(angå)* apply, concern; *denne regelen ~r ikke lenger* this rule no longer applies; *hans siste tanke gjaldt barna* his last thought was for his children; **4** *(stå på spill, være om å gjøre)* be at stake; *det gjaldt livet* (his/her/etc) life was at stake; it was a matter of life and death; *når det ~r* in case of need; *de løp som om det gjaldt livet* they ran for dear life; **B** *(kastrere)* geld, castrate. **gjeldende** *adj: (de) ~ bestemmelser* the regulations in force; *~ kurs/priser* current rate of exchange/prices; *gjøre ~ et krav* advance a claim; *gjøre seg ~* assert oneself.

gjeldfri *adj* free from debt; out of debt.

gjeller *sb fl (fiske~)* gills.

gjemme *vb* conceal, hide; *~ seg* hide; conceal/hide oneself; *~ seg for* hide from; *hvor gjemte hun seg?* where was she hiding? **gjemme(sted)** *sb* hiding-place. **gjemsel** *sb: leke ~* play hide-and-seek.

gjen|drive *vb* confute, refute. **~døper** *sb* anabaptist. **~ferd** *sb* ghost, apparition. **~finne** *vb data* retrieve. **~finning** *sb data* retrieval. **~fortelle** *vb* retell, reproduce. **~fortelling** *sb* reproduction.

gjeng *sb* **1** *(klikk)* crowd, set; clique; **2** *(arbeidslag, bande)* gang.

gjen|gi *vb* render, reproduce; *~gi galt* misrepresent. **~givelse** *sb* rendering, representation.

gjengjeld *sb* repayment, return; *(hevn)* retaliation; *til ~ a) (som motytelse)* in return; *gjøre ~* repay; do something in return; *b) (på den annen side)* on the other hand; *han er ikke sterk, men til ~ er han tålmodig* he is not strong, but on the other hand he is patient. **gjen|gjelde** *vb* **1** repay; **2** *(hevne seg på)* pay back; **3** *(om følelse)* return. **~gjeldelse** *sb* retaliation, retribution.

gjengs *adj* common, current.

gjen|kalle *vb: ~kalle i erindringen* recall; bring/call to mind. **~kjenne** *vb* recognize. **~kjennelig** *adj* recognizable. **~kjennelse** *sb* recognition. **~klang** *sb* resonance, echo; *vinne ~klang* meet with sympathy. **~levende 1** *adj* surviving; **2** *sb* survivor. **~lyd** *sb* echo, resonance. **~mæle** *sb: ta til ~mæle* retort.

gjennom *prep* through; *~ hele* throughout; all through; through all; *~ tykt og tynt* through thick and thin. **gjennom|bore** *vb* **1** pierce; **2** *(stikke ned)* stab. **~brudd** *sb* **1** *(militært, vitenskapelig etc ~)* breakthrough; **2** *(kunstners etc ~)* turningpoint in one's career. **~føre** *vb* carry out/through; accomplish. **~førlig** *adj* feasible, practicable. **gjennomgangs|billett** *sb* through ticket. **~trafikk** *sb* through traffic. **gjennom|gripende** *adj* thorough, radical; *~gripende reformer* radical reforms. **~gå** *vb* **1** *(lide)* go through; suffer; **2** *(undersøke)* go through; examine; **3** *(forklare trinn for trinn)* go through. **~kjøring** *sb* through traffic; *~kjøring forbudt* no through traffic; no thoroughfare. **~lesning** *sb* **1** *(grundig)* perusal; **2** *(overflatisk)* skimming through. **~reise** *sb: jeg er her på ~reise* I am passing through here. **~rote** *vb* ransack, rummage, search. **~siktig** *adj* transparent. **~siktighet** *sb* transparency. **~skue** *vb* see through. **~snitt** *sb* average; *i ~* on an/the average; *over/under ~* above/below average/the average. **~snittlig** average; *adv* on an/the average. **~stekt** *adj* (well) done. **~syn** *sb* examination, inspection. **~søke** *vb* search; *de ~søkte huset* they searched the house. **~trekk** *sb* draught. **~trengende** *adj* piercing, penetrating. **~våt** *adj* drenched, soaked.

gjen|oppbygge *vb* rebuild. **~opplive** *vb* revive, resuscitate. **~oppliving** *sb* revival, resuscitation. **~opprette** *vb* restore; *data også* recover. **~oppretting** *sb* restoration; *data* recovery. **~sidig** *adj* mutual; *~sidig hjelp* mutual aid/assistance. **~skinn** *sb* reflection. **~stand** *sb* object, thing. **~stridig** *adj* obstinate, stubborn. **~syn** *sb: på ~syn!* see you later! I'll be seeing you! So long! **~ta** *vb* repeat; *~ seg* repeat itself; happen again. **~takelse** *sb* repetition. **~valg** *sb* re-election. **~velge** *vb* re-elect. **~vinne** *vb* regain, recover.

gjerde *sb* fence.

gjerne *adv* **1** *(med glede) a)* gladly, willingly; readily; with pleasure; *ofte brukes omskriving:* be fond of; should/would like; *~ det* with pleasure! *~ for meg!* all right! I have no objection! *hun kjører ~ bil* she is fond of driving; **2** *(bebreidende) du kunne ~ ha sagt det* you might have told me; **3** *(som oftest)* generally, usually; as a rule; *ofte brukes omskriving med* will/would: *om kvelden gikk vi ~ en tur* in the evening we would go for a walk.

gjerning *sb* **1** *(handling)* act, action; deed, turn; work; *en god ~* a good deed/turn; *hun gjorde en god ~ mot ham* she did him a kindness/a good turn; *grepet på fersk ~* caught in the act; caught red-handed; **2** *(virksomhet)* business, work; task. **gjerningsmann** *sb* doer, perpetrator, criminal, culprit.

gjerrig *adj* avaricious, stingy. **gjerrig|het** *sb* avarice, stinginess. **~knark** *sb* miser.

gjespe *sg* gape, yawn.

gjest *sb* **1** *(innbudt ~, restaurant~ etc)* guest; *stam~* patron. **2** *(besøkende, fremmed)* visitor. **gjeste** *vb* visit. **gjeste|bud** *sb* banquet, feast. **~værelse** *sb* guest room; spare bedroom. **gjest|fri** *adj* hospitable. **~frihet** *sb* hospitality.

gjete *vb* herd, tend. **gjeter** *sb* herdsman; *saue~* shepherd.

gjetning *sb* guess, guess-work. **gjette** *vb* guess; make a guess; *~ en gåte* solve a riddle; *han ~t galt/riktig* he guessed wrong/right; he made a wrong/right guess; *jeg ~r på Tom* my guess is Tom.

gjort *perf part: ~ er ~* what is done can't be undone; it is noe use crying over spilt milk.

gjær *sb* yeast. **gjære A** *sb: i ~* brewing; in the windt; **B** *vb* ferment.

gjø *vb* **A** *(fôre opp)* fatten; **B** *(bjeffe)* bark; *hunden ~dde mot meg* the dog barked at me. **gjødning** *sb* fertilizer, manuring. **gjødsel** *sb* manure; *(møkk)* dung; *(kunst~)* fertilizer. **gjødsel|greip** *sb* dung-fork. **~haug** *sb* dunghill. **gjødsle** *vb (med natur- eller kunstgjødsel)* manure; *(med kunstgjødsel)* fertilize.

gjøk *sb* cuckoo.

gjøn *sb* fun; *drive ~ med* make fun of. **gjøne** *vb* make fun.

gjøre *vb* **1** *(handle, utføre etc)* do; *det var ikke annet a ~ enn å* there was nothing to do but; there was nothing for it but to; *det har ikke noe med saken å ~* it is irrelevant; *han vet hva han gjør* he knows what he is doing/what he is about; *hun har gjort godt arbeid* she has done her work well; *jeg visste ikke hva jeg skulle ~* I did not know what to do; **2** *(lage)* make; *de gjorde plass for meg* they made room for me; *han ble gjort til konge* he was made king; *hun gjorde en feil* she made a mistake; **3** *(uttrykk)* **~ av:** *hvor har du gjort av pengene?* what have you done with the money? where have you put the money? *~ av med* 1 *(ta knekken på)* finish; 2 *(drepe)* do away with; kill; **~ for:** *jeg kan ikke ~ for det* I cannot help it; **~ fra eller til:** *det gjør verken fra eller til* it makes no difference; **ha å ~:** *jeg har mye å ~* I have a lot to do; I am very busy; **hva** *gjør (vel) det?* what does it matter? **ikke ~:** *det gjør ikke noe* it does not matter; never mind; **~ en noe** *(vondt)* do harm (to); *han gjorde meg ikke noe* he did me no harm; **la seg** ~ be possible; *det lar seg ikke ~ å hjelpe dem* it is impossible to help them; **~ opp** settle; *~ opp et regnskap* settle an account; *~ opp med* settle accounts with; **~ seg til** put on airs; **~ unna** get done; finish. **gjørlig** *adj* feasible, practicable.

gjørme *sb* mud.

gjørs 1 *sb: på ~* deliberately; on purpose; **2** *vb: ~ på* do on purpose.

glad *adj* **1** *(lykkelig, tilfreds)* happy, pleased; *(sterkere)* delighted; *(især som predikatsord fulgt av at-setning eller infinitiv)* glad; *jeg er ~ for at du kom* I am glad (that) you came; *(sterkere)* I am so happy that you came; **2** *(lystig, munter)* cheerful, merry; *~ latter* merry laughter; **3** *være ~ i* be fond of; like, love.

glane *vb* gape, stare.

glans *sb* gloss, lustre; brightness; *med ~* brilliantly, splendidly; *~en i øynene hennes* the brightness of her eyes.

glass *sb* glass; *(til tabletter)* bottle; *(til syltetøy)* jar, bottle. **glassere** *vb* glaze. **glass|fiber** *sb* fibre glass. **~mester** *sb* glazier. **~rør** *sb* glass tube. **glasskår** *sb fl* broken glass; *et glasskår* a fragment of glass.

glatt *adj* **1** *(uten ujevnheter)* smooth; *en ~ overflate* a smooth surface; *(som adv)* smoothly; *det gikk ~* it went off smoothly; **2** *(sleip)* slippery; *det er ~ føre* the roads are slippery. **glattbarbert** *adj* clean-shaven. **glatte** *vb* smooth; *hun ~t på kjolen (sin)* she smoothed her dress. **glattisen** *sb: lokke en ut på ~* get somebody out on thin ice.

glede 1 *sb* delight, joy, pleasure; *det fylte dem med ~* it filled them with delight/joy/pleasure; *min ~ over å se henne* my joy at seeing her; *hun ville gjøre ham en ~* she wanted to give him pleasure; **2** *vb* please; give pleasure to; make happy; *han gjorde det for å ~ henne* he did it to please her; *det ~r meg å se deg her* I am glad to see you here; *(mer hjertelig)* I am happy to see you here; **~ seg** *(være glad)* be glad/happy/pleased; *jeg ~r meg over det* I am happy about it; **~ seg til** look forward to; *jeg ~r meg til han kommer* I look forward to seeing him. **gledelig** *adj* happy, joyful, pleasant; *en ~ begivenhet* a happy event; *en ~ overraskelse* a pleasant surprise; *~ jul* a merry Christmas.

glemme *vb* **1** *(ikke huske)* forget; *jeg glemte å låse døren* I forgot to lock the door; *jeg har glemt hva han heter* I forget *(OBS presens)* his name; **2** *(~ igjen)* forget, leave; *jeg glemte (igjen) hatten min på toget* I left my hat in the train. **glemmeboka** *sb: gå i ~* be forgotten; sink into oblivion. **glemsel** *sb* forgetfulness, oblivion. **glemsom** *adj* forgetful. **glemsomhet** *sb* forgetfulness.

gli *vb* **1** *(bevege seg jevnt)* glide, slide; *toget gled ut fra stasjonen* the train slid out of the station; **2** *(skli)* slide, slip; *han gled på et bananskall* he slipped on a banana skin; **3** *(skrense)* skid; *bilen gled (tvers) over veien* the car skidded across the road. **glid** *sb: få på ~* set going; *komme på ~* get going. **glide|flukt** *sb* glide, volplane. **glide|fly** *sb* glider. **~flyger** *sb* glider pilot. **~flyging** *sb* gliding; *(om flyturen)* glide. **~lås** *sb* zipper, zip.

glimre *vb* **1** *(skinne)* glitter; *det er ikke gull alt som ~r* all that glitters is not gold; it is not gold all that glitters; **2** *(briljere)* shine; **glimrende** *adj* brilliant, splendid; *en ~ idé* a brilliant idea; *alt går ~* everything is going splendidly.

glimt *sb* **1** *(lys~)* flash, twinkle; **2** *(flyktig syn)* glimpse; *jeg fikk bare et ~ av dem* I only caught a glimpse of them. **glimte** *vb* flash, gleam, twinkle; *(svakt)* glimmer.

glinse *vb* glisten, shine.

glipp *sb: gå ~ av* miss; *vi gikk ~ av den mest spennende delen av filmen* we missed the most exciting part of the film. **glippe** *vb* **A 1** *(løsne, ikke holde)* get/work loose; **2** *(gli)* slip; *kniven glapp, og han skar seg i hånden* the knife slipped and cut his hand; **3** *(mislykkes)* fail; **B** *(med øynene)* blink.

glis *sb* grin. **glise** *vb* grin.

glitre *vb* glitter, sparkle.

glo A *sb* ember *(brukes mest i fl)*; *(kull~ også)* live coal; **B** *vb (glane)* gape; gaze, stare.

global *adj* global, world-wide. **globus** *sb* globe.

gloende *adj (glødende)* red-hot; *~ rød* fiery red.

gloret(e) *adj* garish, gaudy, glaring.

glorie *sb* halo.

glose *sb* word. **glose|bok** *sb* notebook. **~forråd** *sb* vobabulary. **~prøve** *sb* vocabulary test. **glossar** *sb* glossary.

glupende *adj (om apetitt)* ravenous, voracious. **glupsk** *adj* **1** *(grådig)* greedy; **2** *(om dyr)* fierce.

glød *sb (begeistring)* ardour, fervour.

gløde *vb (være gloende)* glow; *kinnene hans ~t* his cheeks glowed. **glødende** *adj* glowing, red-hot; *fig* ardent.

gløgg *adj* bright, quick-witted, smart.

gløtt *sb* **1** *(liten åpning)* rift; *på ~* ajar; *døren stod på ~* the door was ajar; **2** *(skimt)* peep; *et ~ av sjøen over hustakene* a peep of the sea over the roofs; **3** *(glimt)* gleam; *et ~ av sol* a gleam of sunshine. **gløtte på** *vb* **1** *(åpne forsiktig)* open slightly; **2** *(kikke på)* peep at; steal a glance at.

gnage *vb* **1** *(med tennene)* gnaw; *hunden gnagde på et bein* the dog was gnawing (at) a bone; **2** *(smågnage)* nibble; *musene har gnagd av osten* the mice have nibbled the cheese; **3** *(slite/tære på)* fret; **4** *(irritere huden)* chafe; *skoen (min) gnager på hælen* my shoe is chafing my heel; **5** *(gnåle)* nag. **gnager** *sb* rodent. **gnagsår** *sb* chafe; *(blemme)* blister; *(hudløst sår)* raw place.

gni *vb* rub; *han gned seg i hendene* he rubbed his hands. **gnier** *sb* miser, niggard.

gnist *sb* spark. **gnistfanger** *sb (i peis)* fire-guard. **gnistre** *vb* flash, sparkle.

gnål *sb (småskjenning, syting)* fussing; nag, nagging; *det er (et stadig) ~ hele dagen* it is nag, nag all day long. **gnåle** *vb* **1** *(småskjenne, syte)* fret, fuss; nag; **2** *(mase om)* harp on; *han ~r alltid om det samme* he is always harping on the same string/the same subject.

god *adj* good; *holde seg* **for ~ til** *å gjøre det* be above doing it; *være ~* **for** *(greie)* be able to; *(eie)* be good for; *han er ~ for 5000 pund* he is good for £5000; **~ til** se *flink til*. Se også *gode, godt*.

god aften good evening.

god|artet *adj (om sykdom)* benign. **~bit** *sb* dainty.

god dag *(før kl. 12)* good morning; *(etter kl. 12)* good afternoon; *(hele dagen)* hello; *(ved presentasjon)* how do you do; *gi en ~ i* not care a fig for.

gode *sb: det ~* the good; *det ~ ved det* the good thing about it; *et ~* a good thing; *for mye av det ~* too much of a good thing; *være av det ~* be all to the good; **med det ~** *(vennlig)* in a friendly way; *(med lempe)* gently; *ta med det ~* use kindness; **ha til ~:** *han har til ~ fem pund* there are £5 due to him; he has £5 owing to him; *han har fem pund til ~ av meg* I owe him £5. **god|gjørende** *adj* charitable. **~gjørenhet** *sb* charity. **~het** *sb* goodness, kindness. **~hjertet** *adj* kind-hearted. **~kjenne** *vb* approve, sanction. **~kjenning** *sb* approval, sanction.

god kveld good evening; *(især sagt til avskjed)* good night.

god|lag *sb: i ~* in a happy mood. **~modig** *adj* good-natured. **god | morgen** good morning. **~ natt** good night.

gods A *sb fl* **1** *(varer)* goods; **2** *(eiendeler)* property; **B** *ent (herregård)* estate. **godseier** *sb* landowner; landed proprietor.

godslig *adj* good-natured.

godsnakke *vb* speak friendly/gently; *~ for* coax.

gods|tog *sb* goods train; *US* freight train. **~vogn** *sb* goods waggon; *US* freight car; *(åpen ~vogn)* truck; *(lukket ~vogn)* van.

godt I *adv* **1** well; *har du sovet ~?* did you sleep well? **2** (etter *smell* og *taste*) good; *det lukter/smaker ~* it smells/tastes good; **II** *sb* good; *gjengjelde ondt med ~* return good for evil; *hun gjør mye ~* she does a lot of good; **III** *(uttrykk)* **for ~** for good; *hun kom hjem for ~* she came home for good; **~ for:** *hva skal det være ~ for?* what's the idea? *aldri så galt at det ikke er ~ for noe*, se *galt*; **gjøre ~ igjen** make amends; **gå ~** go well; succeed; *jeg håper det går/vil gå ~ med planene våre* I hope our plans will succeed; **gå ~ sammen** *(om mennesker)* get on well together; *(om farger etc)* go well together; mix well; *gult går ~ sammen med brunt* yellow goes well with/mixes well with brown; **ha det ~** be all right; be well; *(økonomisk)* be well off; **ha ~ av:** *du vil ha ~ av en ferie* a holiday would do you good; *(tåle) jeg har ikke ~ av hummer/klimaet* lobster/the climate does not agree with me; *det* **kan ~ være** (it) may be; possibly; **like ~, likså ~** just as soon; just as well; **mene det ~** mean well; **så ~ som** practically; as good as; *så ~ som alle* practically everybody; *så ~ som avgjort* as good as settled.

godta *vb* accept.

godter *sb fl* sweets; *US* candy. **godte seg** *vb* be tickled; *(ondskapsfullt)* gloat (over).

godtgjøre *vb* **1** *(bevise)* prove; **2** *(erstatte)* compensate (for). **godtgjørelse** *sb* **1** *(betaling)* remuneration; **2** *(erstatning)* compensation, damages.

god|troende *adj* credulous, gullible. **~troenhet** *sb* credulity. **~venner** *sb: bli/gjøre seg ~ venner med* chum/pal up with. **~vilje** *sb* good-will. **~villig** *adj* voluntary.

gold *adj* barren, sterile.

golv etc *sb* se *gulv etc.*

gomle *vb* munch.

gomme *sb* gum.

gondol *sb* gondola.

gongong *sb* gong.

gordisk *adj: løse den ~ knute* cut the Gordian knot.

gorilla *sb* gorilla.

goter *sb* Goth. **gotikk** *sb* Gothic. **gotisk** *adj* Gothic.

grad *sb* degree; *i høy ~* in/to a high degree; *i noen ~* to some extent; *til en viss ~* up to a point; *i samme ~ som* in proportion as. **grad|bøye** *vb* compare. **~bøyning** *sb* comparison. **grads|adverb** *sb* adverb of degree. **~forskjell** *sb* difference of/in degree. **gradvis** *adj* gradual; *adv* gradually; by degrees.

grafisk *adj* graphic; *~ fremstilling* graph.

gram *sb* gram(me); *femti ~ sukker* 50 grammes of sugar.

grammatikalsk *adj* grammatical. **grammatikk** *sb* grammar. **grammatisk** *adj* grammatical.

grammofon *sb* gramophone; record player.

grammofon|plate *sb* (gramophone) record. **~stift** *sb* gramophone needle.

gran *sb* spruce; *dgl* fir.

granat *sb* **1** *(til kanon)* shell; **2** *(hånd~)* (hand) grenade.

granbar *sb* sprigs of spruce.

granitt *sb* granite.

grann *sb (smule)* bit, particle.

granne *sb* neighbour.

granske *vb* study.

grapefrukt *sb* grape-fruit.

gras etc se *gress etc.*

grasiøs graceful.

grasrot *sb, især fig* grassroots; *i ~a (dvs blant vanlige folk)* among the grassroots; *på ~nivå* at the grassroots level.

grassat *adv* at a furious speed.

gratis *adj* free, gratuitous; *(som adv)* free of charge; gratuitously; *~ adgang* admission free; *(adv også)* free of charge; *vi sender boken ~* we send the book free of charge. **gratis|billett** *sb* free ticket. **~eksemplar** *sb* free copy; free sample. **~passasjer** *sb* non-paying passenger. **~prøve** *sb* free sample.

gratulant *sb* congratulator. **gratulasjon** *sb* congratulation. **gratulere** *vb* congratulate; *(jeg, vi etc) ~r!* congratulations! *(på fødselsdag)* many happy returns (of the day)! *jeg gratulerte henne med forfremmelsen* I congratulated her on her promotion.

graut se *grøt.*

grav *sb* **1** *(til døde)* grave, tomb; *stå på ~ens rand* have one foot in the grave; **2** *(grop, grøft)* ditch. **grave** *vb* dig; *han gravde etter gull* he dug for gold; *han gravde med skatten* he buried the treasure. **gravemaskin** *sb* excavator; steam navvy, *US* steam shovel. **graver** *sb* grave-digger; *(~ og kirketjener)* sexton.

gravere *vb* engrave. **graverende** *adj* grave, serious; *en ~ feil* a grave/serious mistake.

grav|ferd *sb* funeral, obsequies. **~funn** *sb* grave find. **~haug** *sb* burial mound; barrow.

gravid *adj* pregnant; with child. **graviditet** *sb* pregnancy.

gravitasjon *sb* gravitation.

grav|legge *vb* bury, entomb. **~lund** *sb* cemetry, graveyard. **~mæle** *sb* (sepulchral) monument. **~plass** se *~sted.* **~skrift** *sb* epitaph. **~sted** *sb* burial-place. **~stein, ~støtte** *sb* headstone, tombstone. **~øl** *sb* funeral feast.

gre *vb* comb; *~ håret* comb one's hair.

grei *adj* **1** *(enkel, klar)* clear, plain, simple; **2** *(likefrem, åpen)* artless, guileless; honest; **3** *(hjelpsom, sympatisk)* helpful, kind; lik(e)able; *naboene er ~e* the neighbours are kind and helpful; *en ~ kar* a fine, honest fellow; **4** *(lett) det er ikke ~t å ...* it is no easy matter to ...; **5** *(praktisk)* practical, simple; *en ~ ordning* a practical/simple arrangement.

greie I *sb* **1** *(beskjed, kjennskap)* **få ~ på** get to know; learn; **ha ~ på** have knowledge of; know about; **gjøre ~ for** account for; explain; **2** *(sak)* affair, business, matter; *det(te) er andre ~r* this is ever so much better; *hele greia* the whole affair/business; *ikke rare ~ne* nothing to brag about; **3** *(dings)* contraption, gadget; **II** *vb* **1** *(klare)* be able to; manage; *det ~r seg* that will do; *det var så vidt jeg greide det* I just managed it; *jeg greide ikke å åpne døren* I was not able to open the door; **ikke ~** *(også)* be unable to; *han greide ikke å reise seg* he was unable to get up; **~ seg** manage; get along; *~ seg bra/dårlig* do well/badly; give a good/bad account of oneself; *~ seg med/uten* manage/do with/without; *jeg kan ~ meg med mindre* I can manage with less; *vi ~r oss/kan ~ oss uten deg* we can manage without you; *vi ~r oss ikke uten penger* we can't get along without money; *(~ seg økonomisk, også)* make both ends meet; **2** *(ordne)* arrange; see to; **~ med** arrange for; *jeg skal ~ med det* I'll see to that; **~ ut/opp i** *(noe floket)* disentangle, unravel; **~ ut om** explain; give an account of; **3** *(tåle)* stand; *jeg ~r ikke den fyren* I cannot stand that fellow; **4** (~ håret) se *gre.*

grein se *gren.*

greip *sb* fork.

grell *adj* garish, glaring, loud.

gremme seg *vb* grieve.

gren *sb* branch; *(større ~ på tre)* bough.

grend *sb* hamlet, neighbourhood.

grense I *sb* **1** *(stats~)* frontier; *US* border; *ved ~n* et the frontier; *vi krysset ~n* we crossed the frontier; **2** *(naturlig ~)* boundary; *denne elven danner ~n mellom ditt og mitt land* this river forms a boundary between your country and mine; **3** *(~land)* border; *en by på den skotske ~n* a town on the Scots border; **4** *(ytter~)* limit; *~ne for vår viten* the limits of our knowledge; **II**

vb: ~ *til* border on; *dette* ~*r til vanvidd* this borders on insanity. **grense|boer** *sb* frontiersman, borderer. **~by** *sb* frontier/border town. **~elv** *sb* boundary river. **~episode** *sb* frontier incident. **~linje** *sb* boundary line; *fig også* borderline. **~løs** *adj* boundless, unlimited. **~område** *sb* border district; *fig* borderland. **~pæl** *sb* boundary marker/post; *flytte vitenskapens* ~*pæler* extend the bounds of knowledge. **~snitt** *sb data* interface. **~stridigheter** *sb fl* frontier dispute. **~tilfelle** *sb* border(line) case.

grep *sb* **1** *(tak)* hold; **2** *(håndlag)* knack; *ha* ~*et på det* have the knack of it.

grepa *adj dgl* excellent, splendid; first-rate.

gress *sb* grass; *bite i* ~*et* bite the dust; *mens* ~*et gror, dør kua* while the grass grows, the steed starves. **gress|bevokst** *adj* grass-grown, grassy. **~hoppe** *sb* grasshopper.

gresselig *adj* awful, horrible, shocking.

gress|enke *sb* grass widow. **~enkemann** *sb* grass widower. **~kar** *sb* gourd, pumpkin. **~klipper** *sb* lawn-mover. **~løk** *sb* chive. **~plen** *sb* lawn. **~rot** *sb fig* se *grasrot*. **gresstrå** *sb* blade of grass.

gretten *adj* bad-tempered, ill-tempered; cross, grumpy, irritable.

grev *sb* **1** *(hakke)* hoe; **2** *(på hestesko)* calk.

greve *sb (ikke engelsk)* count; *(svarer i GB til)* earl. **grevinne** *sb* countess.

grevling *sb* badger.

grill *sb* gridiron, grill. **grille A** *sb* fad, freak; *sette* ~*r i hodet på en* turn somebody's head; **B** *vb (~grillsteke)* grill. **grill|rett** *sb* grill. **~steke** *vb* grill.

grimase *sb* grimace; *gjøre/skjære* ~*r* grimace; make grimaces; pull/make a face/faces.

grime *sb* alter.

grimet(e) *adj* grimy.

grind *sb* gate, wicket.

grine *vb* **1** *(gråte)* cry, weep; **2** *(surmule)* scowl; **3** *(gnåle grettent)* grouch, grumble. **grinebiter** *sb* cross-patch, grouch, grumbler. **grinet(e)** *adj* cross, grumbling, peevish.

gripe *vb* **1** *a)* catch, seize; *han grep ballen* he caught the ball; *hun grep ham i armen* she caught/seized him by the arm; *jeg grep etter tauet* I caught at the rope; *vi grep sjansen* we seized the opportunity; *b)* ~ **inn (i)** interfere (in, with); intervene (in); ~ *inn i hverandre* interlock; *fig* interact; ~ **om seg** spread; *ilden grep raskt om seg* the fire spread rapidly; ~ **til:** ~ *til våpen* take up arms; *de visste ikke hva de skulle* ~ *til* they did not know what to do; *grepet* **ut av** *luften* pure imagination; **2** *(snappe, rive til seg)* snatch; **3** *(~ med et fast tak)* grasp, grip; *hun grep om håndtaket* she grasped the handle; **4** *(gjøre inntrykk på)* move, stir; affect; *dypt grepet* deeply moved. **gripende** *adj* moving, stirring.

gris *sb* **A** *(svin)* pig; *en heldig* ~ a lucky dog; **B** *(smørefett)* grease. **grise til** *vb (søle til)* foul; *(rote til)* litter (up); mess up. **grisehus** *sb* pigsty. **griseri** *sb* filth, dirt. **griset(e)** *adj* filthy, dirty.

grisk *adj* greedy. **griskhet** *sb* greed.

grissen *adj* sparse, scattered; thin. **gris(s)grendt** *adj* sparsely populated; with scattered houses.

gro *vb* **1** *(vokse)* grow; **2** *(heles, om sår)* heal.

grom *adj* excellent, fine.

grop *sb* hole, hollow; depression.

grosserer, grossist *sb* wholesale dealer/merchant.

grotesk *adj* grotesque.

grotte *sb* grotto.

grov *adj* coarse; ~*t brød/mel* coarse bread/flour; *en* ~ *feil* a bad mistake; *(sterkere)* a gross blunder; *en* ~ *forbrytelse* a felony; a serious crime; *en* ~ *skrøne* a coarse joke; *en* ~ *stemme* a gruff/coarse voice; *et* ~*t svar* a rude answer; *bruke* ~ *kjeft på en* give somebody the rough side of one's tongue; *i* ~*e trekk* in broad outline; roughly; *være* ~ *i kjeften* be foul-mouthed; use coarse language. **grov|arbeid** *sb (foreløpig arbeid)* spade--work. **~brød** *sb* dark bread. **~het** *sb* **1** coarseness; **2** *(uforskammethet)* rudeness; *(uforskammet bemerkning)* rude remark. **~smed** *sb* blacksmith.

gru *sb* horror.

gruble *vb* meditate (*over* on); ruminate (*over* about/on/over); ponder (*over* over); *(~ mørkt/tungsindig)* brood (*over* on/over). **grubling** *sb* brooding; meditation; pondering.

grue *sb* fire-place.

grue seg for/til *vb* dread; be nervous about; shudder to think of; *jeg* ~*r meg til eksamen* I am nervous about/shudder to think of the examination; *jeg* ~*r meg til å treffe ham* I dread the meeting with him.

grufull *adj* ghastly, horrible, terrible.

grums *sb* **1** *(bunnfall)* dregs, sediment; **2** *(berme)* lees. **grumset(e)** *adj* muddy, turbid.

grundig *adj* thorough; *(omhyggelig)* careful; *svært* ~ *(adv)* most thoroughly; ~ *kjennskap til tysk* a thorough knowledge of German; ~*e forberedelser* careful preparations.

grunn I 1 *adj* shallow; **2** *som adv/sb: gå på* ~ go/run aground; strike ground; *komme av* ~*en, trekke (skip) av* ~*en* get afloat; *skipet står på* ~ the ship has gone aground/struck ground; **II** *sb* **1** *(årsak)* cause, reason; grounds; ~ *til mistanke* grounds for suspicion; ~*en til at* the reason why; *av den* ~ for that reason; *av gode* ~*er* for good reasons; *det er* ~ *til å tro* there is (every) reason to believe; *har du noen* ~ *til å klage?* have you any reason for complaining? *hva var* ~*en til ulykken?* what was the cause of the accident? *på* ~ *av* because of; on account of; owing to; *uten gyldig* ~ without excuse; **2** *(jordbunn)* ground; *fra* ~*en av* radically, thoroughly; *i* ~*en* after all; *(i virkeligheten)* in fact; really; *i bunn og* ~ at bottom; *på fast* ~ on firm ground; *på gyngende* ~ on boggy ground; *vi er på gyngende* ~ we are skating on thin ice. **grunn|brott** ground breaker. **~drag** main feature, essential feature.

grunne I *sb (grunt sted)* shallow, shoal; bank. Se også *grunn I 2*; **II** *vb* **1** *(grunnlegge)* establish, found; lay the foundation of; **2** *(basere)* base; *hva* ~*r du mis-*

tanken din på? what do you base your suspicions on? **3** *(tenke)* meditate/reflect (*over* on); ponder (transitivt el. med preposisjonen *over*).

grunn|eier *sb* landowner. **~farge** *sb* primary colour. **~festet** *adj* deep-rooted, established. **~fjell** *sb* bedrock. **~flate** *sb* base. **~lag** *sb* basis; *danne ~lag(et) for* form the basis of. **~legge** *vb* establish, found; lay the foundation of. **~leggende** *adj* basic, fundamental; essential. **~legger** *sb* founder. **~linje** *sb* base.

grunnlov *sb* constitution; constitutional law; *~givende forsamling* constituent assembly. **grunnlovs|forandring** *sb* amendment (of/to the constitution). **~messig** *adj* constitutional. **~stridig** *adj* unconstitutional.

grunn|løs *adj* groundless, unfounded. **~mur** *sb* base wall; foundation wall. **~riss** *sb* outline. **~skole** *sb* primary school. **~stein** *sb* foundation stone. **~stoff** *sb* element. **~støte** *vb* strike ground; go/run aground. **~tall** *sb* cardinal number. **~tanke** *sb* basic/fundamental idea. **~voll** *sb* basis, foundation; groundwork.

gruppe *sb* group. **gruppere seg** *vb* group.

grus *sb* gravel; *byen ligger i ~* the town is a heap of ruins. **grus|gang** *sb* gravel walk. **~haug** *sb* gravel heap.

grusom *adj* cruel; *~ mot* cruel to. **grusomhet** *sb* cruelty; *en ~* an act of cruelty; an atrocity; *hans ~ mot meg* his cruelty to me.

grus|tak *sb* gravel pit. **~vei** *sb* earth road; gravelled road; *US* dirtroad.

grut *sb* grounds *(fl)*.

gruve *sb* mine, pit; *gull~* gold mine; *kull~* coalpit, colliery; coal mine. **gruvearbeider** *sb* miner; *kull~* collier. **gruve|drift** *sb* mining (industry). **~district** *sb* mining district. **~sjakt** *sb* mine shaft; pit.

gry 1 *sb* dawn, daybreak; **2** *vb* dawn; *dagen ~r* the day dawns/is breaking.

gryn *sb koll* grits, groats; *et ~* a grain.

grynt *sb* grunt. **grynte** *vb* grunt.

gryte *sb* pot; *en ~ med suppe* a pot of soup.

grøde *sb (avling)* crop, produce.

grøft *sb* ditch. **grøfte** *vb* ditch. **grøftegraver** *sb* ditcher.

grønn *adj* green. **grønn|kål** *sb* curly kale. **~saker** *sb fl* vegetables. **~sakhandler** *sb* greengrocer. **~skolling** *sb* greenhorn. **~såpe** *sb* soft soap.

grøsse *vb* shudder. **grøsser** *sb* thriller; *(om skrekkroman også)* Gothic novel.

grøt *sb* **1** porridge; *frukt~* stewed fruit; jelly; *gå som katten om den varme ~en* beat about the bush; **2** *(grøtaktig masse)* mash, mush.

grå *adj* grey; *især US* gray. **grå|blek** *adj* ashen, ashy. **~brun** *adj* greyish-brown; dun.

grådig *adj* greedy. **grådighet** *sb* greed, greediness.

grå|gås *sb* grey goose; greylag. **~håret** *adj* grey-haired. **~kald** *adj* bleak. **~lig** *adj* greyish. **~lysning** *sb* dawn. **gråne** *vb* turn grey. **grå|sprengt** *adj* grizzled. **~spurv** *sb* house sparrow.

gråt *sb* crying, weeping; *(tårer)* tears; *han brast i ~* he burst into tears. **gråte** *vb* cry, weep; *~ sårt* cry/weep bitterly; *hun gråt av glede/smerte* she wept for joy/with pain; *hva ~r du for?* what are you crying for?

gubbe *sb* old man; greybeard.

gud *sb* god; *for Guds skyld* for God's/Heaven's sake; *gud skje lov* thank God; thank goodness; *Gud være med deg* God be with you. **gud|barn** *sb* godchild. **~datter** *sb* goddaughter. **guddom** *sb* deity. **guddommelig** *adj* divine. **gudebilde** *sb* idol. **gudelig** *adj* godly; devout, pious; *(skinnhellig)* sanctimonious. **gude|lære** *sb* mythology. **~sagn** *sb* myth. **gud|far** *sb* godfather. **~fryktig** *adj* godfearing; devout, pious. **~fryktighet** *sb* devoutness, piety. **~inne** *sb* goddess. **~mor** *sb* godmother. **guds|bespottelig** *adj* blasphemous. **~bespottelse** *sb* blasphemy. **~dyrkelse** *sb* worship. **~forlatt** *adj* godforsaken. **~fornekter** *sb* atheist. **~frykt** *sb* fear of God. **~tjeneste** *sb* (divine) service. **gudsønn** *sb* godson.

guffen *adj* disgusting, nasty; *det var ~t gjort* that was a dirty trick.

gufs *sb* gust.

gul *adj* yellow; *bli ~* become/turn yellow; *~t (trafikk)lys* amber light. **gul|aktig** *adj* yellowish. **~brun** *adj* yellowish brown; tawny. **~feber** *sb* the yellow fever.

gull *sb* gold; *ringen er av ~* the ring is made of gold. **gull|bryllup** *sb* golden wedding. **~feber** *sb* gold fever. **~fisk** *sb* goldfish. **~graver** *sb* gold-digger. **~gruve** *sb* gold-mine. **~kantet** *adj: ~kantete papirer* gilt-edged securities. **~smed** *sb* goldsmith, jeweller.

gulne *vb* yellow; turn yellow. **gulrot** *sb* carrot. **gulsott** *sb* jaundice.

gulv *sb* floor. **gulv|lampe** *sb* standard lamp. **~matte** *sb* mat. **~teppe** *sb* carpet.

gummi *sb* rubber. **gummi|ball** *sb* rubber ball. **~hanske** *sb* rubber glove. **~ring** *sb* **1** *(på hjul)* tyre; **2** *(på syltetøyglass)* rubber ring. **~sko** *sb* sneakers *(fl)*; tennis shoe. **~slange** *sb* rubber hose/tube. **~stempel** *sb* rubber stamp. **~strikk** *sb* rubber band. **~støvel** *sb* rubber boot; *~støvler (også)* wellington boots; wellingtons. **~såle** *sb* rubber sole.

gunst *sb* favour; *det taler til deres ~* it is in their favour. **gunstbevisning** *sb* favour. **gunstig** *adj* favourable; *adv* favourably; *havnen ligger ~ for ...* the port is favourably situated for ...

gurgle *vb* gargle; *(gi en gurglende lyd)* gurgle.

gusten *adj* sallow.

gutere *vb* relish; *jeg ~r ikke den slags spøk* I do not relish that kind of jokes.

gutt *sb* boy. **guttaktig** *adj* boyish. **gutte|alder** *sb* boyhood. **~barn** *sb* boy child. **~dager** *sb fl* boyhood. **~skole** *sb* boys' school. **~år** *sb fl* boyhood. **guttunge** *sb* boy, lad.

guvernante *sb* governess. **guvernør** *sb* governor.

gyldig *adj* valid; *om mynt også* current; *billetten er ~ (i) én måned* the ticket is valid for a month. **gyldighet** *sb* validity.

gyllen *adj* golden; *den gylne middelvei* the golden mean; *en ~ regel* a golden rule.

gymnas *(GB)* ≈ (the sixth form of) grammar school; *(US)* ≈ junior college; senior high school. **gymnasiast** *(GB)* ≈ sixth former; *(US)* ≈ junior college student. **gymnassamfunn** *sb* school debating society.

gymnastikk *sb* physical exercise(s)/training; gymnastics. **gymnastikk|lærer** *sb* games master. **~sal** *sb* gymnasium.

gynge 1 *sb (huske)* swing; **2** *vb (i huske)* swing; *(i gyngestol)* rock; *(på bølgene)* rock, roll. **gyngestol** *sb* rocking-chair.

gys *sb (av kulde)* shiver; *(av spenning)* thrill; *(av redsel)* shudder. **gyse** *vb (av kulde)* shiver; *(av spenning)* thrill; *(av redsel)* shudder; *jeg ~r* I shudder/shiver; I am thrilled. **gyselig** *adj* horrible. **gyser** *sb (om bok, film)* thriller; *(om roman også)* Gothic novel.

gyte *vb (legge rogn)* spawn.

gyve *vb: ~ på* fly at; fly in somebody's face.

gæler *sb* Gael. **gælisk** *sb* Gaelic.

gørr *sb* mire, mud; *det er ~ (kjedelig)* it is boring/as dull as ditch-water; *~ lei av* completely fed up with.

gøy *sb* fun; *det var liddelig ~* it was great fun. **gøyal** *adj* funny, amusing.

gå *vb* **1** *(på beina)* walk; *barnet har nettopp lært å ~* the child has just learnt to walk; *vi rakk ikke bussen og måtte ~* we missed the bus and had to walk; **2** *(for øvrig som oftest)* go; *alt gikk bare bra* everything went just well; *barna ~r på skole i byen* the children go to school in town; *de første bilene gikk med damp* the first cars went by steam; *denne veien ~r til Fagernes* this road goes to Fagernes; *går han dit, eller tar han bussen?* Does he walk there, or does he go by bus? **3** *(om tiden)* pass; go by; *det gikk tre uker, tre uker gikk* three weeks passed/went by; **4** *(bryte opp)* go, leave; *de gikk ikke før midnatt* they did not leave till midnight; *jeg må ~ nå* I shall have to go now; **5** *(avgå, om kommunikasjonsmiddel)* leave; *toget ~r klokken seks* the train leaves at six; **6** *(spilles på kino, teater)* be on; be performed; *hvilken film ~ det der i kveld?* what film is on there tonight? **7** *(falle ut, hende)* happen; turn out; *hvordan gikk det?* what happened? how did it turn out? *jeg lurer på hvordan det ~r* I wonder how it will all turn out? **8** *(uttrykk)* **~ an:** *det ~r an* that will do; *det ~r ikke an* it doesn't do; **~ av** *(løsne)* come off; *malingen ~r av* the paint comes off; *(om skudd, skytevåpen)* go off; *geværet gikk av* the gun went off; *(stige av)* get off; get out; *hun gikk av toget på feil stasjon* she got off the train at the wrong station; *(ta avskjed)* retire; *han gikk av da han var seksti* he retired at sixty; *(være i veien med): hva ~r det av deg?* what is the matter with you? **~ bort** go away; leave; *(dø)* die; pass away; *~ seg bort* get lost; lose one's way; **~ etter** *(for å hente)* go for; go to fetch; *det er best du ~r etter doktoren* you (had) better go for the doctor; **~ for seg:** *hva ~r for seg her?* what is going on here? **~ igjennom** *(bli vedtatt)* be carried; pass; *forslaget gikk igjennom* the motion was carried; the proposal was passed; **~ med** *(ha på seg)* wear; *han ~r alltid med svarte sko* he always wears black shoes; *hun ~r med briller* she wears spectacles; **~ ned** *(om solen)* go down; set; the sun set/went down; *(om fly)* come/go down; land; *(om pris, temperatur)* drop, fall; *prisene gikk ned* the prices fell/dropped; **~ opp** *(om dør etc)* open; *døren gikk opp* the door opened; *~ opp for (bli klart for); det gikk opp for meg at* I realized that; it struck me that; **~ over** *(bli bra igjen)* pass (off); *hennes forargelse vil ~ over* her indignation will pass off; **~ på** *(angripe)* charge; *~ en på nervene* get on one's nerves; **~ til** *(foregå)* happen; *hvordan gikk det til* how did it happen; *~ til lege* see a doctor; **~ ut** go out; *vi ~r mye ut* we go out a great deal; *~ ut fra* take for granted; *jeg gikk ut fra at du ville komme* I took for granted that you would come; **~ ut over:** *det kommer til å ~ ut over oss* we will have to pay for it; **~ under** *(om skip)* founder; go down; *(gå til grunne)* be destroyed; perish.

gård *sb* **1** = *gårdsbruk*; **2** *(bygning)* building; *forretnings~* office building; *leie~* block (of flats); **3** *(gårdsrom)* court, yard; courtyard; *US også* dooryard. **gårdbruker** *sb* farmer. **gårds|bruk** *sb* farm. **~gutt** *sb* farm hand.

gås *sb* goose; *det er som å skvette vann på ~a* it runs like water off a duck's back. **gåsegang** *sb* Indian/single file. **gåsehud** *sb* goose flesh. **gåsestek** *sb* roast goose. **gåsunge** *sb* gosling; *(på selje etc)* catkin, pussy-willow.

gåte *sb* **1** *(som skal gjettes)* puzzle, riddle; **2** *(noe gåtefullt)* mystery. **gåtefull** *adj* mysterious, puzzling.

H

h *(bokstaven)* h.

ha *vb* **1** *(som hjelpeverb)* have; *~r du gjort leksene dine?* have you done your homework? *jeg ~r ikke vært der ennå* I haven't been there yet; *om jeg hadde sagt ja, hadde han kommet/ville han ~ kommet som et skudd* if I had said yes, he would have come like a shot; **2** *(eie)* have; have got; *de ~r (et) hus på landet* they have a house in the country; *~r du en kniv?* have you (got) a knife? *~r du hodepine? (nå i øyeblikket)* have you a head--ache? *(ofte, vanligvis)* do you have headaches? **3** *(om farge, helse, kår, form, størrelse etc)* be; *hun ~r det godt* she is well off; *hvilken farge ~r døren?* what colour is the door? *hvordan ~r du det?* how are you? **4** *(uttrykk)* **~ det!** cheerio! so long; **~ det bra:** *jeg ~r det bra* I am all right; **~ det med å** be given to; be in the habit of; *han ~r det med å svare uforskammet* he is given to/is in the habit of answering back; **~ det så godt:** *nå kan du ~ det så godt!* serve you right; **~ etter:** *det ~r hun etter bestemoren sin* she takes after her grandmother in that; she has got/gets that from her grandmother; **~ fore:** *~r du noe fore i kveld?* have you anything on tonight? **~ imot** *(mislike)* dislike; *(ha noe å innvende mot)* mind; *~r De noe imot at jeg røyker?* do you mind my smoking? **~ med** have with one; bring (along); *~r du med deg boken min?* have you brought my book? **ikke ~ noe med:** *det ~r ikke du noe med* that is none of your business; **~ på seg** *(om klær)* have on; wear; *han hadde på seg en gammel jakke* he wore an old jacket; *(om ting)* have on; *~r du en kniv på deg?* have you got a knife on you? *(om penger)* have about one; *jeg ~r ingen penger på meg* I have got no money about me; **ville ~** want; *hva vil du ~?* what do you want?

habil *adj* able, competent.

hage *sb* garden; *(større ~)* gardens, grounds; *(frukt~)* orchard. **hage|by** *sb* garden city; garden suburb. **~gang** *sb* garden path. **~slange** *sb* garden hose.

hagl *sb* **1** *(nedbør)* hail; *(et enkelt ~)* hailstone; **2** *(til haglbørse)* shot. **haglbyge** *sb* hailstorm, hail--shower. **haglbørse, hagle** *sb* shotgun. **hagle** *vb* **1** hail; **2** *(falle tett)* rain; *slagene ~t ned over ham* the blows rained down on him. **hagl|gevær** *sb* shotgun. **~korn** *sb* hailstone. **~ladning** *sb* charge of shot. **~patron** *sb* shot cartridge. **~vær** *sb* hailstorm.

hai *sb* shark.

haike *vb* hitch-hike. **haiker** *sb* hitch-hiker. **haiketur** *sb: vi drog på ~* we went hitch-hiking.

hake *sb (del av ansiktet)* chin.

hake I *sb* **1** *(krok)* hook; **2** *(uheldig omstendighet)* catch; *det er en ~ ved det* there is a catch in it; **II** *vb (feste med hake)* hook; *~ seg fast* hang on. **hake|kors** *sb* swastika. **~parentes** *sb* (square) brackets. **~reim** *sb* chin strap. **~spiss** *sb* point of the chin.

hakk *sb* cut, notch; *et ~ over (bedre)* a cut above. **hakke I** *sb* hoe; **II** *vb* **1** *(med hakke eller grev)* hoe; *(med skarpt redskap)* cut, hack; *fin~, ~ opp* chop, mince; **2** *(med nebb)* peck; *hønen ~t hull på egget* the hen pecked a hole in the egg; **~ på** *(kritisere etc)* nag; carp/pick at; *hun ~t på ham dagen lang* she nagged (at) him all day long; **3** *(stamme)* stutter; hum and haw; **4 ~ tenner:** *han ~t tenner* his teeth chattered. **hakkels(e)** *sb* chaff. **hakkespett** *sb* woodpecker. **hakket(e)** *adj* **1** *(med hakk i)* chipped; **2** *(stammende)* stuttering.

hale 1 *sb* tail; *hunden logret med ~n* the dog wagged its tail; **2** *vb (dra)* haul, pull; *han halte i et tau* he hauled/pulled at a rope; *~ innpå (komme nærmere)* gain on; *~ ut tiden* play for time; drag one's feet; *vi kunne ikke ~ et ord ut av ham* we could not drag/screw a word out of him. **hale|bein** *sb* tail bone. **~fjær** *sb* tail feather. **~tipp** *sb* tip of the tail. **~virvel** *sb* caudal vertebra.

hall *sb* hall; *(i hotell ofte)* lobby, lounge.

hallik *sb* pimp.

hallo *interj* hallo.

halloi *sb (spetakkel)* hubbub, row.

hallomann *sb* announcer.

hallusinasjon *sb* hallucination. **hallusinere** *vb* hallucinate.

halm *sb koll* straw. **halmstrå** *sb* straw; *gripe etter/klamre seg til et ~* catch at a straw.

hals *sb (den ytre ~)* neck; *(innvendig ~)* throat; *han er sår i ~en* he has a sore throat; *hun lo av full ~* she roared with laughter. **hals|brekkende** *adj* breakneck. **~bånd** *sb* **1** *(til hund)* collar; **2** *(~kjede)* necklace. **halse** *vb (gjø)* bark, bay. **hals|hugge** *vb* behead. **~kjede** *sb* necklace. **~linning** *sb* neckband. **~tørkle** *sb* scarf. **~virvel** *sb* cervical vertebra.

halt *adj* lame, limping; *~ på det venstre beinet* lame in the left leg. **halte** *vb* limp; walk with a limp; *sammenligningen ~r* the comparison halts.

halv *adj* half; *en ~ side* half a page; *to og en ~ side* two and a half pages; two pages and a half; *~e århundret* half the century; *en ~ fridag* a half holiday; *klokken er ~ to* it is half past one o'clock. **halvannen** *adj* one and a half; *halvannet år* eighteen months; a year and a half. **halv|automatisk** *adj* semi-automatic. **~bror** *sb* half-brother. **~del,** *se halvpart.* **halvere** *vb* halve; *(i geometrien)* bisect. **halv|fabrikata** *sb koll* semi-manufactures, semi-products. **~flaske** *sb* half-bottle. **~ferdig** *adj (foran sb)* half-done; *(som predikatsord)* half done. **~gal** *adj* half-witted. **~kule** *sb* hemisphere. **~leder** *sb* semi-conductor. **~mørke** *sb* half-light, semi-darkness. **~måne** *sb* crescent; half moon. **~part** *sb* half; *~parten av boken* half the book; (one) half of the book; *jeg forstod ikke ~parten av det han sa* I did not understand (one) half of what he said. **~søvn** *sb: i ~søvne* half asleep. **~såle** *sb, vb* half-sole. **halvt** *adv* half; *han fikk ~ så mange* he received half as many. **halv|tid** *sb (i fotball)* half. **~vei** *sb: på ~veien* half--way; *de møttes på ~veien* they met half-way. **~veis** *adv* half-way; *~veis oppe i bakken* half-way up the hill; *han er ~veis død* he is half dead. **~voksen** *adj* adolescent, teen-age. **~øy** *sb* peninsula. **~åpen** *adj: døren er ~åpen* the door is half open. **~år** *sb* six months. **~årlig** *adj* half-yearly; *adv* every six months.

ham *sb* slough; *skifte ~* cast off/shed the slough/the skin.

hamle *vb: ~ opp med* be a match for.

hammer *sb* **1** *(verktøy)* hammer; **2** *(berg~)* crag.

hamn etc se *havn etc.*

hamp *sb* hemp; *av ~* hempen.

hamre *vb* hammer; ~ *løs på* hammer away at.

hamstre *vb* hoard. **hamstring** *sb* hoarding.

hand se *hånd.*

handel *sb* **1** *(handelsvirksomhet)* trade; *(i stor stil, som næringsvei)* commerce; *~en med utlandet* the foreign trade; *drive ~ med (bestemt varesort)* deal/trade in; *de drev ~ med hvete* they dealt/traded in wheat. **2** *(enkelt kjøp og salg)* bargain, deal; *du kan gjøre en god ~ her* you can make a bargain here. **handels|avtale** *sb* trade agreement. **~brev** *sb* trading licence. **~flåte** *sb* merchant marine/fleet. **~gartner** *sb* market gardener. **~gartneri** *sb* market garden. **~gymnas** *sb* ≈ (higher) commercial school. **~hus** *sb* company, firm, house. **~høyskole** *sb* ≈ commercial college. **~korrespondanse** *sb* business/commercial correspondence. **~mann** *sb (butikkeier)* shopkeeper. **~overskudd** *sb* trade surplus. **~reisende** *sb* commercial traveller; *US* travelling salesman. **~skip** *sb* merchant ship/vessel; merchantman. **~skole** *sb* business school; commercial school. **~traktat** *sb* treaty of commerce; commerce treaty. **~vare** *sb* commodity; *~varer (også)* merchandise.

handi|kap *sb* handicap. **~kappet** *adj* handicapped; disabled, invalid; *de ~pede* disabled persons.

handle *vb* **1** *(drive handel)* deal, trade; *de ~r med England* they trade with England; *vi ~r med hvete* we deal in wheat; **2** *(gjøre innkjøp)* shop; *jeg ~r alltid hos Brown* I always shop at Brown's; *vi har vært ute og ~t* we have been out shopping; **3** *(gjøre, utføre)* act; *vi må ~ raskt* we must act quickly; **4** ~ *om* be about; deal with; *hva ~r denne boken om?* what is this book about? *den ~r om jordbruket i England* it deals with farming in England. **handle|frihet** *sb* freedom of action. **~kraft** *sb* energy. **~kraftig** *adj* energetic, strong; active; *en ~ regjering* a strong government. **handlende** *sb* shopkeeper, tradesman. **handling** *sb* **1** *(noe man gjør)* act, action; *en vennlig ~* an act of kindness; **2** *(i roman etc)* action, story; *(intrige)* plot; **3** *(det å handle)* action; *en ~ens mann* a man of action; *nå er det tid for ~* the time has come for action.

hane *sb* **1** *(hannfugl)* cock; *(bare av høns)* rooster; *(på skytevåpen)* cock; *hun spente ~n på pistolen* she cocked her pistol; **3** *(kran)* tap.

hang *sb: ha ~ til alkohol/narkotika* be addicted to drink/drugs.

hangar *sb* hangar. **hangarskip** *sb* aircraft carrier.

hangle *vb: ~ igjennom* muddle/scrape along/through; *gå og ~* be ailing/failing/poorly.

hank *sb* handle.

hankjønn *sb (i grammatikk)* the masculine (gender). Se også *hannkjønn.* **hankjønnsord** *sb* masculine (noun). **hann** *sb* he, male; *en ~ og tre hunner* a he and three shes; *(om enkelte fugler)* cock; *(om enkelte store dyr)* bull. **hann|dyr** *sb* male. **~kanin** *sb* buck rabbit. **~katt** *sb* tomcat. **~kjønn** *sb* male sex. Se også *hankjønn.* **~plante** *sb* male plant.

hansa|by *sb* Hanseatic town. **~forbundet** *sb* the Hansiatic League. **hanseat** *sb* Hanseatic merchant.

hanske *sb* glove.

hard *adj* **1** hard; *en ~ seng* a hard bed; **2** *(streng)* hard, severe; *~ konkurranse* severe competition; *en ~ herre* a hard master; *han var ~ mot sin sønn* he was hard on his son. **hard|før** *adj* hard, robust; tough. **~hendt** *adj* heavy-handed, rough. **~het** *sb* hardness; *(strenghet)* severity. **~hjertet** *adj* hard-hearted. **~hudet** *adj* callous, thick-skinned (også *fig*). **~kokt** *adj* hard-boiled. **~nakket** *adj* stiff-necked; obstinate. **hardne** *vb* harden. **hardt** *adv* **1** hard; *de arbeidet ~* they worked hard; **2** *(strengt)* severely; **3** *(slemt)* badly; *~ medtatt* severely damaged; *~ såret* badly wounded; *hun trengte ~ til hjelp* she needed help badly.

hare *sb* hare. **harehund** *sb* beagle, harrier.

harem *sb* harem.

hare|mynt *adj* hare-lipped. **~skår** *sb* hare-lip.

harke *sb* hawk.

harm *adj* angry, indignant. **harme** *sb* indignation; *(især over en fornærmelse)* resentment. **harmelig** *adj* annoying. **harmløs** *adj* harmless, innocent; *en ~ spøk* a harmless joke.

harmonere *vb* harmonize. **harmoni** *sb* harmony, concord. **harmonisk** *adj* harmonious.

harnisk *sb* armour; *komme i ~* fly into a rage; *være i ~* be up in arms.

harpe *sb* harp; *spille (på) ~* play the harp.

harpiks *sb* resin; *(til fiolinbue)* rosin. **harpiksaktig** *adj* resinous.

harpun *sb* harpoon. **harpunere** *vb* harpoon.

harselas *sb* banter, raillery. **harselere** *vb: ~ over* poke/make fun at; ridicule.

harsk *adj* rancid.

harv *sb* harrow. **harve** *vb* harrow.

has *sb: få ~ på* get the better of.

hasard *sb* hazard, gamble; *spille ~* gamble. **hasardiøs** *adj* hazardous. **hasard|spill** *sb* gambling. **~spiller** *sb* gambler.

hase *sb* hamstring.

hasj, hasjisj *sb* hashish.

haspe *sb* catch.

hassel, hassel|busk *sb* hazel. **~nøtt** *sb* hazel-nut.

hast *sb* hurry, haste; *det har ingen ~* there is no hurry; *i største ~* in great haste. **haste** *vb* **1** *(om personer)* hasten, hurry; *vi ~t til møtestedet* we hastened/hurried to the meetingplace; **2** *(om ting)* be urgent; *(på brev)* Urgent! *~r det?* is it urgent? *det ~r* it is urgent; there is no time to be lost; *det ~r ikke* there is no hurry. **hastig** *adj* hurried, quick; *et ~ måltid* a hurried meal. **hastighet** *sb* speed, velocity; rate; *lydens ~* the velocity of sound; *med en ~ av* with a speed of; at a rate of. **hastverk** *sb* haste, hurry; *de hadde ~* they were in a hurry; *~verk er lastverk* haste makes waste; more haste, less speed.

hat *sb* hatred; *(især poetisk)* hate. **hate** *vb* hate; *de ~t hverandre* they hated each other. **hatefull, hatsk** *adj* rancorous.

hatt *sb* hat; *(kyseformet dame~)* bonnet; *(skalk)* bowler; *han tok av seg ~en* he took off his hat; *han tok* *av seg ~en for henne* he raised his hat to her; *hun kjøpte en ny ~* she bought a new hat. **hatteforretning** *sb* hat-shop; hatter's (shop); *(for damehatter)* milliner's (shop).

haug *sb* hill; *(mindre)* hillock; *(jord~)* mound; *(grav~)* barrow; *(dynge)* heap; *gammel som alle ~ene* old as the hills; *kaste i ~, samle i ~* heap up. **haugevis av** heaps of.

hauk *sb* hawk.

hav *sb* sea; *(verdens~)* ocean; *et ~ av blomster* a blaze of flowers; *et ~ av vanskeligheter* an ocean of difficulties; *som en dråpe i ~et* like a drop in the ocean/in a bucket; **i** *~et* in the sea; **over** *~flaten/~et* above the sea-level/the level of the sea; **på** *~et* on the sea; *(ute) på ~et* at sea; **til ~s:** *stikke/stå til ~s* put to sea; **ved** *~et* at the sea.

havarere *vb* be damaged; receive/suffer damage; *(bli vrak)* be wrecked. **havari** *sb* average, damage; *(forlis)* shipwreck, wreck. **havarist** *sb* damaged/wrecked ship.

hav|bukt *sb* bay, gulf. **~bunn** *sb* bottom of the sea. **~dybde** *sb* depth of the sea. **~flate** *sb* surface of the sea; *over ~flaten* above the sea-level/the level of the sea. **~fiske** *sb* deep-sea fishing/fishery. **~frue** *sb* mermaid.

havn *sb* **1** *(sjø~)* harbour, port; *(GB ofte)* docks; **2** *(beitemark)* pasture. **havne** *vb* end, land. **havne|arbeider** *sb* docker; *US* longshoreman. **~by** port; sea-port town. **~gang, ~hage** *sb* pasture. **~vesen** *sb* port authority.

havre *sb* oats *(fl)*. **havre|grøt** *sb* (oatmeal) porridge. **~gryn** *sb koll* groats, oatmeal. **~suppe** *sb* (water) gruel.

havskilpadde *sb* turtle.

havsnød *sb: et skip i ~* a ship in distress.

H-bombe *sb* H-bomb.

hedensk *adj* heathen, pagan. **hedenskap** *sb* paganism.

heder *sb* honour, glory. **hederlig** *adj* honest, upright; *~ arbeid* honest work. **hederlighet** *sb* honesty, integrity. **heders|gjest** *sb* guest of honour. **~kvinne** *sb* woman of honour. **~mann** *sb* man of honour. **~plass** *sb* place/seat of honour.

hedning *sb* heathen, pagan; *~ene* the heathen. **hedningmisjon** *sb* mission to the heathen.

hedre *vb* honour.

hefte I *sb* **1** *(liten trykksak)* booklet, pamphlet; **2** *(skrive~ etc)* exercise book; **II** *vb* **1** *(feste, gjøre fast)* fasten, fix; *(med nåler)* pin; *(med binders etc)* clip; *(med heftemaskin)* staple; *(med lim)* stick; **2** *(oppholde, sinke)* delay, detain, keep; **3** *~ seg ved (legge merke til)* notice; *(bry seg om)* care about; *~ seg i/ved en bagatell* strain at a gnat. **heftet** *adj (om bok)* paper-bound, paperbacked.

heftig *adj* violent; *(intens)* acute, intense; *~ lidenskap* intense passion. **heftighet** *sb* intensity, violence.

heftplaster *sb* adhesive plaster, court plaster, sticking-plaster; Band-Aid *(reg. varemerke)*.

hegemoni *sb* hegemony.

hegg, heggebær *sb* bird cherry.

hei *sb* upland heath/moor.

hei *interj* heigh! hey! hello! **heia**! *interj* come on! **heiagjeng** *sb* cheering gang.

heim, heime etc se *hjem, hjemme etc.*

heimevern *sb* militia; *~et* ≈ the Home Guard. **heimevernsoldat** *sb* militiaman.

heis *sb* lift; *US* elevator. **heise** *vb* hoist; they hoisted the flag. **heise|innretning** *vb* hoist, winch. **~kran** crane.

hekk *sb* hedge; *(i hekkeløp)* hurdle.

hekke *vb (om fugler)* nest, brood.

hekkeløp *sb* hurdle-race.

hekle *vb* crochet. **hekle|nål** *sb* crochet-hook. **~tøy** *sb* crochet work.

heks *sb* witch, hag.

hekse|bål *sb* witchburning fire; stake. **~doktor** *sb* witch doctor; medicine man. **~gryte** *sb* (witches') cauldron; *fig også* maelstrom. **~kunst** *sb: det er ingen ~kunst* it is easily done. **hekseri** *sb* witchcraft. **hekseskudd, heksesting** *sb* lumbago.

hekt *sb: det var på ~a* it was a close shave; it was touch and go. **hekte I** *sb* hook; *~ og malje* hook and eye; *komme til ~ene* pick up; **II** *vb* **1** hook; *denne kjolen ~s i ryggen* this dress hooks up the back; *~ opp* unhook; *~ sammen* hook up; **2** *(arrestere)* pinch.

hel *adj* **1** *(ikke i stykker)* whole; *det finnes ikke en ~ tallerken i huset* there is not a whole plate in the house; **2** *(udelt)* complete; entire, whole; *~e byen* the whole town; all the town; *~e London (om byen)* the whole of London; *(om menneskene der)* all London; *~e natten* the whole night; all night; all through the night; *~e året* all the year round; *et ~t år* a whole year; *en ~ del,* se *del*; **3** *(ublandet)* all, pure; *~ ull, ~ull* all/pure wool; **4** *(formelig, likefrem)* quite *(følges alltid av ubest art) en ~ begivenhet* quite an event.

helbred *sb* health; *han er ved god ~* he is in good health. **helbrede** *vb* cure; restore to health; *hun ~t ham for en sykdom* she cured him of a disease; *jeg er fullstendig ~t* I am quite well again; I am completely restored (to health). **helbredelig** *adj* curable. **helbredelse** *sb* **1** *(det å komme seg)* recovery; *~ etter influensa* recovery from influenza; **2** *(det å helbrede)* cure; *legen kan ikke garantere ~* the doctor cannot guarantee a cure.

heldags|jobb, ~post *sb* full-time/whole-time job.

heldig *adj* **1** *(lykkelig)* fortunate; *du er ~ som har så rike foreldre* you are fortunate to have such rich parents; **2** *(som har hell med seg)* lucky; *han er ~ i kortspill* he is lucky at cards; **3** *(som har fremgang)* successful; *et ~ foretagende* a successful enterprise; **4** *(gunstig)* favourable; *under ~e omstendigheter* under favourable conditions. **heldigvis** *adj* fortunately, luckily.

hele A 1 *sb* whole; *danne et ~* form a whole; *det ~* all of it; the whole thing; it all; *er det det ~?* is that all? *det ~ varte en time* the whole thing lasted an hour; *den er svart over det ~* it is black all over; *i det ~ tatt (i det* *store og ~)* on the whole; *(kort sagt)* altogether; se også *hel, helt (adv)*; **2** *vb* = *helbrede*; **B** *vb (drive heleri)* fence; receive (stolen goods). **heler** *sb* fence; receiver (of stolen goods). **heleri** *sb* receiving stolen goods.

helg *sb* **1** *(kirkelig høytid)* church festival; **2** *(søndag)* Sunday; **3** *(ukeslutt)* week-end. **helgedag** se *helligdag*. **helgen** *sb* saint.

helhet *sb* entirety, whole; *i sin ~* in full. **helhetsinntrykk** *sb* general impression.

helikopter *sb* helicopter.

hell *sb* **A 1** *(lykke, skjebne)* luck; good fortune; *et ~* a piece of luck/of good fortune; *for et ~!* what luck! *det var et ~ at du kom* it was fortunate that you came; *til alt ~* fortunately; **2** *(heldig utfall)* success; *vi forsøkte flere ganger, men uten ~* we tried several times, but without success; **B** *(skråning)* slope; *på ~* on the wane; waning.

helle A *sb (til hellelegging)* flag, flagstone; *(større steinhelle)* flat stone; (piece of) flat rock; **B** *vb* **1** *(øse opp)* pour; *hun helte vin på flasken* she poured wine into the bottle; **2** *(stå skjevt)* lean; *veggen ~r mot høyre* the wall leans to the right; **3** *(skråne)* slant, slope; *~ seg bakover/fremover* lean back/forward; *~ seg inn til* lean against; *jeg ~r til den oppfatning at* I am inclined to think that; I incline to the opinion that. **helle|fisk** *sb* halibut. **~legge** *vb* pave (with flagstones).

hellen, hellener *sb* Hellene, Greek. **hellenisme** *sb* Hellenism. **hellenistisk** *adj* Hellenistic. **hellensk** *adj* Hellenic, Greek.

heller *adv* **1** rather, sooner; *~ døden enn trelldom* rather death than slavery; **vil/ville** *~* would/had rather; *jeg vil(le) ~ dø enn gjøre det* I would rather die than do that; *~ ville ha (også)* prefer; **jo før jo** *~* the sooner the better; **2** *(sammen med nektelse)* nor, neither; not ... either; *~* **aldri** nor ... ever; never; *han så henne ~ aldri der* nor did he ever see her there; *~* **ikke** nor; not ... either; neither; *jeg så ham ikke, det gjorde ikke min bror ~* I did not see him, nor did my brother; ... neither did my brother.

hellig *adj* holy, sacred; *Den hellige skrift* the Holy Writ; *Den hellige ånd* the Holy Ghost; *Det ~e land* the Holy Land; *en ~ plikt* a sacred duty; *intet er ~ for dem* nothing is sacred to them. **helligdag** *sb* holiday, Sunday. **hellige** *vb* **1** sanctify; *(innvie, vigsle også)* consecrate, dedicate; **2** *(rettferdiggjøre)* justify; *hensikten ~r midlet* the end justifies the means. **helligholde** *vb: ~ hviledagen* observe the Lord's Day.

helling *sb* slope, inclination.

helmelk *sb* whole milk.

helse *sb* health; *dårlig ~* bad health; *skrantende ~* failing health; *svak ~* delicate/poor health; *ta vare på ~en* look after one's health; *ved god ~* in good health. **helse|attest** *sb* health certificate. **~bot** *sb* cure, remedy. **~direktorat** *sb* ≈ Ministry of Health. **~direktør** *sb* ≈ Minister of Health. **~farlig** *adj* injurious to health; *(om bolig etc)* insanitary, unhealthy. **~lære** *sb* hygiene. **~løs** *adj* broken in health; invalid. **~myndighet** *sb* health authority. **~messig** *adj: av ~messige grunner (personlige)* for reasons of health; *(offentlige)* for sanitary reasons. **~råd** *sb* ≈ health committee; *(i eldre tider)* local board of health. **~sterk** *adj* of strong/robust health. **~svak** *adj* of poor health. **~søster** *sb GB* health visitor; *US* public health nurse. **~vesen** public health service.

hel|skinnet *adj* safe and sound; unhurt. **~skjegg** *sb* full beard.

helst *adv* preferably, rather; *~ ikke* rather not; *~ om formiddagen* preferably in the morning; *det han ~ vil er å ...* what he likes best is to ...; *du bør ~ gå nå* you had better go now; *hva/hvem/hvor/når etc som ~* se *hva/hvem/hvor/når etc*; *jeg vil ~ bli her* I would rather stay here; I (should) prefer to stay here;.

helstøpt *adj: en ~ personlighet* a person of sterling character; *et ~ kunstverk* a perfect work of art.

helsøsken *sb koll* full brothers and sisters.

helt *adv* **1** *(fullt ut)* completely, perfectly; quite; altogether; *~ alene* quite alone; *~ galt* altogether/completely wrong; *det er ~ umulig* it is completely impossible; *noe ~ annet* something quite different; **2** *(foran stedsadv og prep ofte)* all the way; right, *~ fra København* all the way from Copenhagen; *~ igjennom* right/all through; *~ til enden av gaten* right to the end of the road; *~ oppe på toppen* right on the top; **3** *~ fra (om tiden)* ever since; *~ fra guttedagene* ever since I was a boy.

helt *sb* hero. **helte|dyrkelse** *sb* hero worship. **~dåd** *sb* heroic deed. **~modig** *adj* heroic. **~mot** *sb* heroism. **heltinne** *sb* heroine.

helvete *sb* hell.

helårsolje *sb* all-season oil.

hemme *vb* hamper, hinder, impede, retard; *(sjelelig)* inhibit; *~t i veksten* retarded in growth; *hun var noe ~t i sine bevegelser* her movements were somewhat hampered.

hemmelig *adj* secret; *vi holdt det ~ for ham* we kept it (a) secret from him. **hemmelighet** *sb* **1** *(noe hemmelig)* secret; *kan du holde på en ~?* can you keep a secret? **2** *(hemmeligholdelse)* secrecy; *i all ~* secretly; in secret; *i dypeste ~* in deep secrecy. **hemmelighetsfull** *adj* **1** *(mystisk)* mysterious; *en ~ skikkelse* a mysterious figure; **2** *(umeddelsom)* secretive.

hemmet *adj* inhibited. **hemning** *sb* restraint; *(sjelelig)* inhibition. **hemningsløs** *adj* unrestrained, uninhibited.

hemoroider *sb fl* h(a)emorrhoids; *dgl* piles.

hempe *sb (stropp)* loop; *(metall~)* eye.

hen *adv (oversettes vanligvis ikke) hvor skal du ~?* where are you going? Se ellers *bort*.

hende *sb: i ~* to hand; in one's possession.

hende *vb (skje, finne sted)* happen, occur; take place; *~ med* happen to; *det hendte i går* it took place yesterday; *jeg håper det ikke er hendt dem noe* I hope nothing has happened to them.

hendelse *sb* **1** *(hending)* happening, occurence; *(mindre hending)* incident; *(treff)* chance **2** *(større begivenhet)* event.

hendig *adj* handy, neat-handed; deft, dexterous.

hending se *hendelse.*

henfallen *adj:* ~ *til* addicted to.

henge *vb* **1** hang; *før i tiden ble tyver hengt* in former days thieves were hanged; *hun hengte bildet på veggen* she hung the picture on the wall; **2** *(uttrykk)* ~ **fast** stick; ~ **i:** *a)* ~ *i et tau* hang by/from a rope; ~ *i en tråd* hang by a thread; *lampen ~r i taket* the lamp hangs from the ceiling; *b) (arbeide hardt)* keep at it; work hard; *heng i!* go it!; ~ **sammen** stick together; *(ha sammenheng)* be coherent; hang together; *historien deres hang ikke sammen* their story did not hang together/was not coherent; *det ~r slik sammen* the fact of the matter is; *hvordan ~r det sammen?* how can that be? ~ **seg opp i** *en småting* strain at a gnat. **henge|bjerk** *sb* weeping birch. **~bro** *sb* suspension bridge. **~køye** *sb* hammock. **~lampe** *sb* hanging lamp. **~lås** *sb* padlock. **~myr** *sb* quagmire.

hengi *vb:* ~ *seg til* abandon oneself to; indulge in. **hengivelse** *sb* abandonement, devotion. **hengiven** *adj* devoted. **hengivenhet** *sb* devotion, devotedness; affection.

hengsel *sb* hinge. **hengsle** *vb* hinge. **hengslet(e)** *adj* lanky, ungainly.

henhold *sb: i* ~ *til* in accordance/conformity with; with reference to; *i* ~ *til avtale (også)* as per agreement; *i* ~ *til lov av ...* pursuant to the Act of ...

henholdsvis *adv* respectively; *den gamle og den nye bilen kostet* ~ *ett tusen og tre tusen pund* the old car and the new one cost £1000 and £3000 respectively.

henimot *prep* towards. Se også *mot.*

henkastet *adj: en (lett)* ~ *bemerkning* a casual remark.

henlagt *perf part: handlingen er* ~ *til Roma* the scene is laid in Rome.

henrette *vb* execute. **henrettelse** *sb* execution.

henrivende *adj* charming, delightful, lovely.

henrykkelse *sb* delight, rapture. **henrykt** *adj* delighted; ~ *over* delighted at/with.

henseende *sb* regard, respect; *i alle ~r/enhver* ~ in every respect. Se også *sammenheng.*

hensikt *sb* intention, purpose; *det er min* ~ *å ...* it is my intention to...; I intend to ...; *i den* ~ *å drepe dem* with the intention of killing them; *med* ~ on purpose; intentionally; *~en helliger midlet* the end justifies the means. **hensikts|løs** *adj* pointless, purposeless; futile. **~messig** *adj* adequate, suitable; serviceable; *den er ~messig* it serves its purpose.

henslengt *adj* discarded; thrown away. Se også *henkastet.*

hensyn *sb* consideration, regard, respect; **av** ~ **til** *a)* out of consideration/regard for; *av* ~ *til henne (også)* for her sake; *b) (på grunn av)* because of; on account of; **med** ~ **til** as regards; as to; with regard to; **uten** ~ **til** without regard to; regardless of. **hensyns|full** *adj* considerate, thoughtful; ~ *mot ham* considerate to him. **~løs** *adj* inconsiderate, thoughtless; ruthless.

henstille *vb* request, suggest. **henstilling** *sb* request, suggestion; *etter* ~ *fra* et the request/suggestion of. Se også *anmode, be.*

hente *vb* **1** fetch; *(komme etter)* come for; call for; *vi vil* ~ *varene* we will call for the goods; **2** *(møte ved ankomst)* meet; *vi ~t dem på stasjonen* we met them at the station.

hentyde *vb:* ~ *til* allude to; hint at. **hentydning** *sb* allusion, hint.

henvende *vb* **1** ~ *seg* apply, inquire; ~ *seg ved skranken* inquire at the counter; *han henvendte seg til en advokat* he consulted a lawyer; *vi henvendte oss til banken for å få et lån* we applied to the bank for a loan; **2** ~ *seg til* address; *hun henvendte seg til meg* she addressed (herself to) me. Se også *rette, vende.* **henvendelse** *sb* application; *(forespørsel)* inquiry.

henvise *vb:* ~ *til* refer to; *hun ble henvist til spesialist* she was referred to a specialist; *jeg ble henvist til Dem for ytterligere opplysninger* I was referred to you for further information. Se også *vise.* **henvisning** *sb* reference; *under* ~ *til* referring to; with reference to.

her *adv* here; ~ *fra byen* from this town; ~ *i byen* in this town.

herbarium *sb* herbarium.

herberge *sb* hostel; *(for hjemløse også)* shelter *ungdoms~* youth hostel..

herde *vb* harden; ~ *kroppen* harden the body; ~ *seg* make oneself hardy; train oneself to hardiness; ~ *stål* temper. **herdet** *adj* hardened, hardy; *(om stål)* tempered.

her|etter *adj* from now on; in future; *bokl* henceforth. **~fra** *adv* from here. **~i** *adv* in this.

herje *vb* plunder, ravage; harry; *et ansikt ~t av sykdom* a face ravaged by disease; *vikingene ~t England* the Vikings harried England. **herjing** *sb* plunder, plundering; ravage.

herk *sb* junk, rubbish.

herlig *adj* glorious; grand, magnificent; *(om mat etc)* delicious, delightful. **herlighet** *sb* glory.

herme *vb* imitate, mimick; mock.

hermed *adv* herewith; with this. Jf *herved.*

hermelin *sb* ermine.

hermetikk *sb* tinned food; *US* canned food. **hermetikk|boks** *sb* tin; *US* can. **~fabrikk** *sb* cannery. **~industri** *sb* canning industry. **~åpner** *sb* tin opener; *US* can opener. **hermetisere** *vb* can, preserve. **hermetisk** *adj* hermetic; ~ *lukket* hermetically sealed.

heroisk *adj* heroic.

herold *sb* herald.

herr *(i tiltale til overordnede eller ved høflig omgang)* sir; *denne vei, herr ...* this way, sir; *ja vel, herr løytnant (kaptein etc)* yes, sir; *mine ~er!* gentlemen! **herre** *sb* **1** *(mann)* gentleman; **2** *(hersker)* master; *husets* ~ the master of the house; *bli* ~ *over* get under control; *bli* ~ *over ilden* get the fire under control; *være* ~ *over* control, master; keep/have under control; **3** *(Herren, Gud)* the Lord; *Herrens bønn (Fadervår)* the Lord's Prayer; *Vårherre, Vår Herre* Our Lord

herred *sb GB* ≈ rural district; *US* ≈ township. **herredsstyre** *sb* ≈ rural district council.

herre|dømme *sb* mastery; command, rule; control; *hun mistet ~dømmet over bilen* she lost control of the car; *det engelske ~dømme i India* the British rule in India. **~ekviperingsforretning** *sb* gentlemen's outfitter. **~gård** *sb* manor; *(bygningen)* manor-house. **~hanske** *sb* gentleman's glove. **~løs** *adj* ownerless; *en ~løs hund* a stray dog. **~sykkel** *sb* gentleman's bicycle.

herske *vb* **1** *(regjere)* govern, rule; **2** *(råde)* be; *det ~t stor forvirring i landet* there was great confusion in the country. **herskende** *adj* **1** *(regjerende)* governing, ruling; **2** *(rådende)* prevailing, prevalent. **hersker** *sb* ruler, sovereign; master. **herskerinne** *sb* mistress.

hertug *sb* duke. **hertug|dømme** *sb* duchy. **~inne** *sb* duchess.

her|under *adv* among these. **~ved** *adv* hereby; by this; *jeg erklærer ~ at* I hereby declare that; *~ tillater vi oss å meddele Dem that* we beg to inform you at. Jf *hermed.*

hes *adj* hoarse; *en ~ stemme* a hoarse voice. **heseblesende** *adj* panting; breathless; out of breath.

hesje 1 *sb* hay fence; haydrying hurdle/rack; **2** *vb* dry hay on (a) fence/hurdle/rack. **hesjetråd** haywire.

heslig *adj* hideous.

hest *sb* horse; *til ~* on horseback; *en motor på 50 ~er (dvs hestekrefter)* a 50 horsepower engine. **heste|hov** *sb* horse's hoof; *(om planten)* coltsfoot; colt's foot. **~kastanje** *sb* horse chestnut. **~kraft** *sb* horsepower. **~lengde** *sb* horse's length. **~sko** *sb* horseshoe. **~veddeløp** *sb* horse race; race meeting.

het *adj* hot. **hete A** *sb (varme)* heat; **B** *vb (ha som navn)* be called; *hun ~r Ingrid* she is called Ingrid; her name is Ingrid; *hva ~r* eple *på engelsk?* what is the English for *eple? som det ~r hos Byron* as Byron has it. **hete|bølge** *sb* heat wave. **~slag** *sb* heatstroke.

hette *sb* hood.

hevde *sb* **1** *(fremholde, påstå)* assert, maintain; *det er ikke sant, som noen ~r, at ...* it is not true, as some assert, that ...; *han ~t at jorden var flat* he maintained that the earth was flat; **2** *(gjøre gjeldende)* claim; *~ seg* assert oneself; *hun ~r å være rettmessig arving* she claims to be the rightful heir.

heve *vb* **1** raise; *~ seg* rise; *han ~t glasset/stemmen* he raised his glass/his voice; *være ~t over* be above; *hun er ~t over smiger* she is above flattery; *være ~t over tvil* be beyond doubt; **2** *(få utbetalt)* cash, draw; *~ en sjekk* cash a cheque; *hun ~t to hundre pund hver uke* she drew £200 every week; **3** *(oppheve)* raise; *~ en beleiring* raise a siege; *~ forlovelse* break off (an engagement); **4** *~ et møte* close (a meeting); *(for en tid)* adjourn (a meeting); *møtet ble ~t* the meeting was adjourned/ closed. **hevelse** *sb* swelling.

hevn *sb* revenge, vengeance; *~en er søt* revenge is sweet; *få ~ over* be revenged on; *som ~* in revenge; *ta ~ for* take/have one's revenge for. **hevne** *vb* revenge; *(~ med en viss rett)* avenge; *hun ~t seg på ham* she revenged herself on him. **hevngjerrig** *adj* revengeful, vindictive.

hi *sb* den, lair; *(grevling~, reve~)* earth.

hige *vb: ~ etter* aspire to; *(lengte inderlig etter)* yearn after/for; *han ~t etter berømmelse* he aspired to fame.

hikk *sb (hikkestøt)*, **hikke** *sb (hikking)* hiccough, hiccup; *jeg fikk ~* I got the hiccups. **hikke** *vb* hiccough, hiccup.

hikst *sb* gasp. **hikste** *vb* gasp.

hilse *vb* **1** *~ på* say good morning/good evening etc to; pass the time of day with; *(med ord eller tegn)* greet; *(med nikk)* nod to; *(med bukk)* bow to; *(militært etc)* salute; *~ velkommen* bid welcome; welcome; *de ble hilst (velkommen) med hurrarop* they were greeted/ received with cheers; **2** *(sende ~n til): hils din søster fra meg!* remember me to your sister! *hils dem så mye fra meg* give them my best regards; give them my love; *jeg skal ~ fra min bror* my brother sends his compliments; *du kan ~ ham fra meg og si at det er noe vrøvl* tell him from me that it is (all) nonsense; **3** *(møte i forbifarten)* meet; *jeg hilste på ham på bussen i dag* I met him on the bus today; **4** *(avlegge visitt hos): han kom og hilste på oss her om dagen* he called on/dropped in on us the other day. **hilsen** *sb* greeting; *(bukk)* bowing; *(nikk)* nodding; *(militær ~)* salute; *(sendt ~)* greeting, regards; best wishes; *(mer formelt)* compliments; *kjærlig ~* love; *kjærlig ~, Anne* love from Anne; love, Anne; *vennlig ~* kind regards/best wishes; *(i forretningsbrev)* yours faithfully *(dersom man ikke kjenner navnet på adressaten)*; yours sincerely *(dersom man kjenner navnet).*

himmel *sb* **1** *(den synlige)* sky; *klar ~* a clear sky; *på ~en* in the sky; *under åpen ~* in the open; **2** *(Guds ~)* Heaven, heaven(s); *for ~ens skyld* for Heaven's sake; *i ~en* in Heaven; **3** *(uttrykk) som et lyn fra klar ~* like a bolt from the blue; *sette ~ og jord i bevegelse* move heaven and earth. **himmel|blå** *adj* sky-blue, azure. **~bryn** *sb* skyline. **~fallen** *adj* dumbfounded, thunderstruck. **~fart** *sb: Kristi ~fartsdag* Ascension Day. **~hjørne** *sb: de fire ~hjørner* the four quarters (of the heavens). **~hvelv** *sb* firmament. **~legeme** *sb* celestial body. **~rand** = *~bryn.* **~rike** *sb* Heaven, Paradise. **~ropende** *adj: ~ropende skandale* a crying scandal; *~ropende urett* a glaring injustice. **himmelsk** *adj* heavenly, celestial. **himmel|strøk** *sb* zone. **~vid** *adj: ~vid forskjell* all the difference in the world; *de er ~vidt forskjellige* they are poles apart. **himmerike** = *himmelrike.*

hinannen se *hverandre.*

hind *sb (hunnhjort)* hind.

hinder *sb* **1** *(hindring): være til ~* hinder, prevent; *det er ikke noe til ~ for det* there is nothing to prevent it; *det skulle ikke være noe til ~ for det* there can be no objection to that; **2** *(fysisk ~)* obstacle; *(i hinderløp)* fence, hurdle; **3** *(~løp)* the hurdles; *3000 meter ~* 3.000 metres hurdles/steeple-chase. **hinderløp** *sb* obstacle race; *(for hester)* steeple-chase. **hindre** *vb (virke hindrende)* hinder, obstruct; hamper; *(forhindre)* prevent; *snøen ~t våre bevegelser, men ~t oss ikke i å nå målet* the snow hampered/obstructed our movements, but did not prevent us from reaching our objective. **hindring** *sb* hindrance, obstacle; *vi støtte på ~er* we met with obstacles.

hingst *sb* stallion.

hinke *vb* limp, hobble; *(hoppe på ett bein)* hop.

hinne *sb* membrane, coat; *(svært tynn ~)* film.

hipp I *interj: ~, ~, hurra!* hip, hurrah! **II** *sb* **1** *(spydighet)* dig; *det var et ~ til meg* that was a dig at me; **2** *det er/kan bli ~ som happ* it is all the same; it makes no difference.

hisse *vb* **1** *(~ opp)* arouse, excite; work up; *ikke hiss deg opp* don't work yourself up; **2** *(få til å angripe)* set on; *han ~t hundene på meg* he set the dogs on me. **hissig** *adj* **1** *(oppfarende)* hot-tempered; *han ble ~* he lost his temper; **2** *(voldsom)* fierce, severe; heated, hot; *en ~ diskusjon* a fierce/heated/hot debate; *en ~ kamp* a fierce/severe struggle; **3** *(ivrig)* keen; *ikke så ~ nå!* take it easy, now! *jeg er ikke så ~ etter å treffe ham* I am not (all that) keen on meeting him. **hissighet** *sb* hot temper; *i et øyeblikks ~* in the heat of the moment. **hissigpropp** *sb* fire-eater, spitfire.

hist *adv: ~ og her* here and there.

historie *sb* **1** *(som fag)* history; *Englands ~* the history of England; *~bok, lærebok i ~* history-book; **2** *(fortelling)* story; *(svært kort ~)* anecdote; *fortelle en ~* tell a story; *for å gjøre en lang ~ kort* to cut a long story short; **3** *(affære)* business, matter; *det er en annen ~* that's another matter/story. **historiker** *sb* historian. **historisk** *adj* **1** *(som angår historien)* historical; *en ~ roman* a historical novel; **2** *(berømmelig, epokegjørende)* historic.

hit *adv* here; as far as this; *~ og dit* here and there; this way and that; up and down; *kom ~!* come (over) here! *lukten nådde helt ~* the smell reached as far as this; *vi var kommet ~ da ...* we had come/got as far as this when ...

hitte|barn *sb* foundling. **~gods** *sb* lost property. **~godskontor** *sb* lost property office.

hittil *adv* **1** *(til nå)* as yet; till now; so far; *~ har alt vært tilfredsstillende* so far everything has been satisfactory; **2** *(til da)* till then; so far.

hive *vb* **1** *(kaste, slenge)* fling, heave, throw; **2** *(heise opp)* heave (up); hoist; *~ anker (også)* weigh anchor; **3** *~ etter pusten* gasp for breath.

hjelm *sb* helmet; *styrt~* crash helmet.

hjelp *sb* **1** help; aid, assistance; *hun ropte om ~* she cried for help; *jeg bad dem om ~* I asked them for assistance; I asked their aid/assistance; **2** *(unnsetning)* rescue; *de kom til ~* they came to rescue; **3** *(understøttelse)* assistance, support; relief; **4** *(nytte)* help, use; *ved ~ av* by means of; **5** *(hus~)* help. **hjelpe** *vb* **1** help; aid, assist; *de hjalp meg opp* they helped me to get up; *det ~r ikke å prøve* it is no good trying; *han hjalp meg med arbeidet mitt* he assisted me with my work; *jeg hjalp henne (med) å bære kofferten* I helped her (to) carry the trunk; **2** *(uttrykk) ~* **for/mot** be good for; *det ~r for gikt* it is good for the gout; *~* **til** *(gi en håndsrekning)* lend a hand; *~ til i huset* help about the house. **hjelpe|aksjon** *sb* relief action/measures. **~fartøy** *sb petro etc* tender vessel. **~funksjon** *sb data* utility function. **~kilde** *sb* resource. **~klasse** *sb* class for backward children. **~lager** *sb data* auxiliary/secondary storage. **~løs** *adj* helpless. **~løshet** *sb* helplessness. **~mann** *sb* helper, mate; *petro* tender. **~middel** *sb* aid, help; *fl også* facilities; *moderne (tekniske) ~midler* modern (technical) facilities. **~program** *sb data* utility (program).

hjelper *sb* assistant, helper.

hjelpe|rutine *sb data* service/utility routine. **~tropper** *sb* auxiliaries. **~utstyr** *sb* utility equipment. **~verb** *vb* auxiliary (verb).

hjelpsom *adj* helpful; ready/willing to help. **hjelpsomhet** *sb* helpfulness.

hjemle *vb* authorize, justify, warrant.

hjem 1 *adv* home; *jeg vil ~* I want to go home; *vi gikk ~* we walked home; **2** *sb* home. **hjem|by** *sb (fødeby)* native town. **~bygd** *sb* native district. **~komst** *sb* home-coming, return. **~land** *sb* native country. **~lengsel** *sb* homesickness, nostalgia; *ha ~* be homesick. **~lig** *adj* **1** *(som hører til hjemmet)* domestic, home; *(hyggelig)* homelike, nice. **~løs** *adj (uten hjem)* homeless; *(om landstrykere etc)* down and out; *(etc flyktninger etc)* displaced. **hjemme** *adv* at home; *(hjemkommet)* home; *~ hos oss* at home; at our place; *føle seg ~* feel at home; *holde seg ~* stay at home; *høre ~ (ha sin naturlige plass)* belong (in/under); *det hører ingen steder ~* it is neither here nor there; *jeg er glad jeg er ~ igjen* I am glad to be home again; *lat som du er ~!* make yourself at home! **hjemme|bakt** *adj* home-made. **~bane** *sb: spille på ~bane* play at home; *være på ~bane* be in one's element; know the ropes. **~fra** *adv* from home; *brev ~fra* letter from home; *dra ~fra* leave home. **~industri** *sb* domestic industry; home industry. **~kamp** *sb* home match. **~laget** *adj* home-made. **~lekse** *sb* homework.

hjemmelsmann *sb* authority, informant.

hjemme|marked *sb* home market. **~oppgave** *sb* piece of (written) homework. **~seier** *sb* home win; *(i tipping)* home; *fem ~seirer* five homes. **~regning** *sb* home work (in mathematics). **~sitter** *sb (ved valg)* abstainer; *US* non-voter. **~stil** *sb* essay/exercise (written at home). **hjem|over** *adv* homeward; *med kurs ~over* homeward bound. **~reise** *sb (over land)* home journey; *(til sjøs)* homeward passage, home/return voyage. **~vé** = *~lengsel*. **~vei** *sb* way home; *på ~veien* on my/his etc way home.

hjerne *sb* brain; *(forstand)* brains; *legge ~n i bløt* cudgel/rack one's brain; *få på ~n* get on the brain; *bløt på ~n* soft in the head, softheaded. **hjerne|betennelse** *sb* brain fever; inflammation of the brain. **~blødning** *sb* cerebral haemorrhage. **~gymnastikk** *sb* mental gymnastics. **~rystelse** *sb* concussion (of the brain). **~skalle** *sb* cranium, skull. **~vask** *sb* brainwashing. **~vaske** *sb* brainwash.

hjerte *sb* heart; *~t mitt banker/banker sterkt* my heart beats/throbs; *av hele sitt ~* with all one's heart; *av ~ns lyst* to one's heart's content; *ha dårlig ~* have a weak heart; *ha godt ~* have a kind heart; *ha på ~t* have on one's mind; *hun har ikke ~ til å* she has not the heart to; she cannot find it in her heart to; *i ~t av Afrika* in the heart of Africa; *på fastende ~* on an empty stomach. **hjerte|anfall** *sb* heart attack. **~bank, ~banking** *sb* palpitation. **~feil** *sb* organic heart disease. **~knuser** *sb* charmer; *(om mann stundom)* lady-killer. **~lag** *sb* a kind heart. **~lammelse** *sb* heart failure; paralysis of the heart. **~lidelse** *sb* heart trouble/disease. **hjertelig** *adj* heartfelt; *(litt formelt)* cordial; *(mer inderlig)* hearty; *(begeistret)* warm; *(oppriktig)* sincere; *~ lykkønsking* heartfelt/sincere congratulations; *~ hilsen* kindest regards. **hjertelighet** *sb* cordiality. **hjerteløs** *sb* heartless. **hjerter** *sb fl (i kortspill)* hearts; *~ ess* the ace of hearts. **hjerte|skjærende** *adj* heart-breaking; heart-rending. **~slag** *sb* **1** *(pulsslag)* heartbeat; **2** = *~lammelse.* **~transplantasjon** *sb* heart transplant/transplantation. **~venn(inne)** *sb* bosom friend.

hjort *sb* deer; *fl* deer.

hjul *sb* wheel; *være et ~ i maskineriet* be a cog in the machine. **hjul|aksel** *sb* (wheel)axle. **~beint** *sb* bandy-legged, bow-legged. **~spor** *sb* rut; wheel track.

hjørne *sb* corner; *huset ligger på ~t av Mill Street* the house stands at the corner of Mill Street; *han dreide om ~t* he turned the corner. **hjørne|butikk** *sb* corner shop. **~skap** *sb* corner cupboard. **~spark** *sb* corner, corner-kick. **~tann** *sb* canine tooth; *(i overmunnen også)* eye-tooth.

hm! *interhj* hem! ahem!

hobby *sb* hobby.

hockey *sb* hockey.

hode *sb* **1** head; *miste ~t* lose one's heads; **2** *(begavelse)* brains, intelligence; head; *hun har et godt ~* she has got brains; **3** *(uttrykk) alt står på ~t* everything is topsy-turvy; *det gikk over ~t på meg* it was/went over my head; *etter mitt (eget) ~* to my taste/liking; *ha vondt i ~t* have a headache; *han fulgte sitt eget ~* he had his own way; *har du ikke øyne i ~t?* where are your eyes? *henge med ~t* hang one's head; *hårene reiste seg på ~t hans* his hair stood on end; *jeg kan ikke få det inn i ~t* I cannot get it into my head; *legge ~t i bløt* cudgel/rack one's brains; *riste på ~t* shake one's head; *sette tingene på ~t* turn things upside down; *styrte seg på ~t uti* plunge headlong in; *ta seg vann over ~t* bite off more than one can chew; *treffe spikeren ~t* hit the nail on the head. **hode|kulls** *adj, adv: ~kulls flukt* headlong flight. **~kål** *sb* (common) cabbage. **~pine** *sb* headache; *ha ~pine* have a headache. **~plagg** *sb* head-dress, head-gear. **~pute** *sb* pillow. **~regning** *sb* mental arithmetic. **~skalle** *sb* cranium, skull.

hoff *sb* court; *ved ~et* at the Court. **hoff|dame** *sb* lady-in-waiting. **~folk** *sb koll* courtiers. **~mann** *sb* courtier.

hofte *sb* hip. **hofteholder** *sb* girdle; suspender belt.

hogg etc *se hugg etc.*

hokuspokus 1 *adv, interj* (hey) presto! **2** *sb (knep)* hocus-pocus.

hold *sb* **A 1** *(avstand, skudd~)* distance, range; *på kort/langt ~* at short/long range; *på nært/kloss ~* at close quarters; **2** *(kant)* quarter; *fra et annet ~* from another quarter; *fra flere ~* from several quarters; *på høyeste ~* in the highest quarters; **B 1** *(tak)* hold; grasp, grip; **2** *(~ i siden, sting)* stitch. **holdbar** *adj (solid)* durable; *(om påstand)* valid; *(om farge)* fast; *(om matvarer)* that will keep. **holdbarhet** *sb* keeping/wearing quality; durability, keeping. **holde** *vb* **1** hold; *han holdt hånden frem* he held out his hand; *hun holdt boken for ham* she held the book for him; **2** *(ikke gå i stykker)* hold; *hvor lenge holder dette reipet?* how long will this rope hold? **3** *(~ seg, over~)* keep; *eggene vil ~ seg friske i lang tid* the eggs will keep fresh for a long time; *hun holdt sitt løfte/ord* she kept her promise/word; **4** *(vare)* last; *om godværet ~r seg* if the good weather lasts; **5** *~ en avis/et tidsskrift* take in a (news) paper/a magazine; *~ foredrag* give a lecture; *~ møte* hold a meeting; *~ selskap* give a party; *~ tale* make a speech; **6** *(uttrykk)* **~ an** *(stanse)* stop; **~ av** *(være glad i)* be fond of; love; **~ for** *(å være)* consider; regard as; *jeg ~r henne for å være den beste legen her i byen* I regard her as the best doctor in this town; **~ med** *(være enig med)* agree with; side with; **~ opp** *(slutte)* cease, stop; leave off; *han ~r aldri opp med å snakke* he never leaves off talking; **~ på å** *(være i ferd med, på nippet til)* be + *pres part*; be on the point of; *de holdt på å oppgi håpet* they were on the point of giving up hope; **~ på med** be doing; *hva ~r dere på med?* what are you doing? *jeg holdt på å skrive et brev* I was writing a letter; **~ sammen** keep/stick together; **~ til** *(oppholde seg)* live, stay; *(om dyr)* have its/their haunts in; **~ ut** *(greie, tåle)* bear, stand; *jeg ~r det ikke ut lenger* I can stand it no longer; *smerten var nesten ikke til å ~ ut* the pain seemed too great to bear/to be borne.

holden *adj (velstående)* prosperous, well-to-do; *helt og holdent* completely, entirely.

holde|plass *sb (for buss, trikk)* stop; *(for drosjebiler)* cab rank/stand; taxi rank/stand. **~punkt** *sb (grunnlag)* basis; *(spor)* clue; *politiet har ikke noe ~punkt* the police have no clue/nothing to go on.

holdning *sb* **1** *(kroppsføring)* carriage; **2** *(opptreden)* conduct; **3** *(innstilling)* attitude; *regjeringens ~ i saken* the attitude of the ministry in this matter.

holdt *vb imp: holdt!* halt; *han gjorde ~* he halted/he came to a halt.

holme *sb* holm, islet.

holt *sb* grove, wood.

homo|fil *adj* homophile, homosexual. **~gen** *adj* homogeneous. **~genisert** *adj* homogenized. **~seksualitet** *sb* homosexuality. **~seksuell** *adj* homosexual.

honning *sb* honey.

honnør *sb* honour; *gjøre* ~ salute.

honorar *sb* fee; *forfatter~ (i prosent av salget)* royalty. Se også *lønn.*

hop *sb* crowd; *den store* ~ the masses; the multitude. **hope** *vb:* ~ *opp* heap (up); ~ *seg opp* accumulate.

hopp *sb* jump, leap. **hoppbakke** *sb* jumping hill. **hoppe A** *sb (hunnhest)* mare; **B** *vb* jump, leap; *(om fugler)* hop; ~ **av** *(fig: fra politisk parti etc)* defect; ~ **over** *(utelate)* skip; *du ~t over en linje* you skipped a line. **hoppetau** *sb* skipping-rope. **hopp|renn** *sb* jumping competition. **~ski** *sb* jumping ski.

hor *sb* adultery; *(utukt)* fornication.

horde *sb* horde.

hore *sb, vb* whore.

horisont *sb* horizon, skyline; *i ~en* on the horizon. **horisontal** *adj* horizontal.

hormon *sb* hormone.

horn *sb* horn; *han har et* ~ *i siden til meg* he bears me a grudge. **horn|aktig** *adj* horny. **~musikk** *sb* brass music. **~orkester** *sb* brass band.

horoskop *sb* horoscope; *jeg stilte hennes* ~ I cast her horoscope.

hos *prep* with; *(i nærheten av)* by; *hun bor* ~ *oss* she lives with us; *jeg bor* ~ *onkelen min* I live at my uncle's; ~ *oss er det helligdag* with us it is holiday; *jeg satt* ~ *ham* I was sitting by him; *vi var på besøk* ~ *besteforeldrene våre* we were on a visit to our grandparents.

hose *sb* stocking; *så lett som fot i* ~ as easy as falling off a log. **hose|båndsordenen** *sb* the Order of the Garter. se for øvrig *strømpe etc.*

hospital *sb* hospital. Se også *sykehus.*

hoste 1 *sb* cough, coughing; **2** *vb* cough; *hun ~r stygt* she has a bad cough. **hoste|anfall, ~kule** *sb* fit of coughing. **~mikstur** se *~saft.* **~pastill** *sb* cough lozenge. **~saft** cough mixture; cough syrup.

hotell *sb* hotel; *de bodde på* ~ *Carlton* they stayed at the Carlton (Hotel); *vi tok inn på et* ~ we put up at a hotel.

hov *sb* hoof.

hoved|bygning *sb* main building. **~dør** *sb* front door. **~gate** *sb* main street. **~inngang** *sb* main entrance. **~innhold** *sb* principal contents; *(resymé)* summary. **~kvarter** *sb* headquarters. **~mann** *sb* head; chief, leader. **~nøkkel** *sb* master key. **~person** *sb (i bok etc)* main/principal character; hero, protagonist. **~punkt** *sb* main point. **~reparasjon** *sb* complete overhaul. **~rett** *sb* main course. **~rolle** *sb* principal part. **~rørledning** *sb* **1** main conduit/pipeline; *også* main(s); *petro* trunk line. **~sak** *sb* main thing. **~saklig** *adv* mainly, chiefly. **~setning** *sb* main clause. **~stad** *sb* capital. **~trekk** *sb fl* main features; outlines. **~vei** *sb* main road. **~vekt** *sb* main stress; emphasis. **~verk** *sb* chief/principal work. **~årsak** *sb* principal cause.

hoven *adj (oppsvulmet)* swollen; *(viktig)* arrogant.

hovere *vb* exult, triumph.

hovmester *sb (i et hus)* butler; *(på restaurant)* head waiter.

hovmod *sb* arrogance, pride; ~ *står for fall* pride goes before a fall. **hovmodig** *adj* haughty; arrogant, proud.

hovne *vb:* ~ *(opp)* swell.

hu se *hug.*

hud *sb* skin; *(tykk, håret* ~*)* hide. **hud|farge** *sb* colour (of the skin). **~flette** *vb* flay, flog. **~lege** *sb* skin specialist; dermatologist.

hug *sb (sinn)* mind; *komme i* ~ remember; call to mind.

hugenott *sb* Huguenot.

hugg *sb* cut, slash; blow. **hugge** *vb* **1** cut, hew; ~ *ved* chop wood; **2** *med adv/prep* ~ **av** cut off; *hun hugde av seg fingeren* she cut off her finger; ~ **i:** *han hugde seg i beinet* he cut his leg; *jeg hugg (el hugde) bremsene i* I jammed/slammed on the brakes; ~ **ned** fell; cut down; *vi hugde ned alle trærne* we cut down/felled all the trees; ~ **opp** *(biler, skip etc)* break up. **huggestabbe** *sb* chopping block. **hugg|jern** *sb* chisel. **~orm** *sb* viper. **~tann** *sb (på pattedyr)* tusk; *(på orm)* fang. **hugst** *sb* cutting, felling.

hui *sb: i* ~ *og hast* in great hurry; in hot haste. **huie** *vb* hoot, yell.

huk *sb: sitte på* ~ squat. **huke** *vb* **1** ~ *seg ned* squat (down); crouch; **2** *(fakke)* arrest, cop, pinch; ~ *seg fast i* grapple; hang on to.

hukommelse *sb* memory; *etter ~n* from memory.

hul *adj* hollow; *en* ~ *tann* a hollow tooth; *den ~e hånd* the hollow of the hand. **hule 1** *sb* cave; *(stor* ~*)* cavern; *(malerisk* ~*)* grotto; *(vilt dyrs* ~*)* den; the lion's den; **2** *vb:* ~ *ut* hollow (out). **huleboer** *sb* cave-dweller. **hulhet** *sb* hollowness.

hulke *vb* sob. **hulking** *sb* sobbing, sobs.

hull *sb* hole; *(gap, mellomrom)* gap; *et* ~ *i hekken* a gap in the hedge; *(som man kan smutte igjennom)* loop-hole; *han tok* ~ *på en eske sjokolade* he opened a box of chocolates; *jeg boret* ~ *i veggen* I bored a hole in the wall. **hullet(e)** *adj* full of holes; *(utett)* leaky; *strømpene hans var fulle av* ~ his stockings were full of holes. **hull|fall** *sb* hemstitch. **~kort** *sb data* data card; punch(ed) card. **~sleiv** *sb* perforated ladle. **~tang** *sb* punching tongs.

hul|mål *sb* measure of capacity. **~speil** *sb* concave mirror.

hulter *adv:* ~ *til bulter* in a mess.

human *adj* humane.

humanisme *sb* humanism. **humanistisk** *adj* humanistic; *de humanistiske fag* the arts. **humanitær** *adj* humanitarian.

humbug *sb* humbug; *det er det rene* ~ it is all humbug. **humbugmaker** *sb* humbug, swindler; charlatan.

humle *sb* **A** *(plante)* hop; *(brukt til brygging)* hops; **B** *(insekt)* bumble-bee; *la humla suse* be a happy-go-lucky sort of person. **humlebol** *sb* bumble-bee's nest.

hummer *sb* lobster. **hummer|klo** *sb* lobster's claw. **~teine** *sb* lobster pot.

humor *sb* humour. **humorist** *sb* humorist. **humoristisk** *adj* humoristic; *~ sans* sense of humour.

hump *sb* bump. **humpe** *vb* **1** *(gå haltende)* hobble, limp; **2** *(under kjøring)* bump. **humpet(e)** *adj* bumpy.

humre *vb* **1** *(om hest)* whinny; **2** *(le)* chuckle.

humør *sb* **1** *(sinnsstemning)* mood, temper; spirits *(fl)*; *i godt ~* in high spirits; in a cheerful mood; *i dårlig ~* in low spirits; in a bad temper; *være i ~ til* be in the mood for/to; *jeg er ikke i ~ til å gå på kino* I am not in the mood to go to the cinema; **2** *(varig ~)* disposition; *hun har godt ~* she is of a cheerful/sunny disposition.

hun *sb (bakhun)* slab.

hund *sb* dog; *(jakt~ også)* hound; gå i *~ene* go to the dogs; *leve som ~ og katt* lead a cat-and-dog life; *en skal ikke skue hunden på hårene* judge not the dog by its coat; appearances are deceptive. **hunde|dagene** *sb* the dog days. **~galskap** *sb* rabies. **~hus** *sb* kennel. **~leven** *sb* racket, uproar. **~liv** *sb: leve et ~liv* lead a dog's life. **~vakt** *sb* middle watch. **~valp** *sb* pup, puppy. **~veddeløp** *sb (et enkelt)* dog race; *(sporten)* dog racing; the dogs.

hundre hundred; *én av ~* one in a hundred. **hundre|vis** *adv: bøker i ~vis* books by the hundred/hundreds of books. **~år** *sb* century. **~årsjubileum** *sb* centenary.

hundse *sb* bully.

hunger *sb* hunger; *(hungersnød)* famine. **hungre** *vb* be hungry/starving; *(lide sult)* starve; *han ~t etter vennlighet* he was starving for/after kindness.

hunkjønn *sb (i grammatikk)* the feminine (gender). Se også *hunnkjønn*. **hunkjønnsord** *sb* feminine (noun). **hunn** *sb* she, female; *en ~ og tre hanner* a she and three hes; *(om enkelte fugler)* hen; *(om enkelte store dyr)* cow. **hunn|dyr** *sb* female. **~katt** *sb* she-cat, tabby-cat. **~kjønn** *sb* female sex. Se også *hunkjønn*. **~løve** *sb* lioness. **~plante** *sb* female plant. **~rev** *sb* she-fox, vixen.

hurlumhei *sb* hubbub, hullabaloo.

hurra *interj, sb* hurra(h); *rope ~* cheer; give a cheer; *de ropte tre ganger ~ for ham* they gave him three cheers. **hurrarop** *sb* cheer.

hurtig *adj* quick, rapid, swift; *(om konstant, stor fart)* fast; *(adv)* quickly; *(med stor hastighet)* fast. Se også *fort* og *rask*. **hurtig|het** *sb* quickness, speed. **~løp** *sb (på skøyter)* speed skating. **~tog** *sb* fast train.

hus *sb (beboelseshus)* house; *(bygning)* building; *~et ved siden av* the house next door; *de bor i ~et ved siden av* they live next door; *her i ~et* in this house; *hjelpe til i ~et* help in/about the house. **hus|arbeid** *sb* house-work, domestic work. **~dyr** *sb* domestic animal; *hesten er et ~* horses are domestic animals. **huse** *vb (gi husly)* house; *kan du ~ meg en dag eller to?* can you put me up (for) a day or two? **hus|eier** *sb* house-owner; *(husvert)* landlord. **~far** *sb* head of the family; *(på institusjon)* pater. **~flid** *sb* domestic/home industry. **~flue** *sb* house-fly. **~fred** *sb* domestic peace. **~hjelp** *sb* domestic help. **~holderske** *sb* housekeeper.

husere *vb (bråke, herje)* make/play havoc.

hus|holdning *sb* housekeeping. **~holdningspenger** *sb* housekeeping money/allowance.

huske A 1 *sb (lekeapparat)* swing; *(dump~, vippe~)* see-saw; **2** *vb (i lekeapparat)* swing, *(i vippehuske)* see-saw, *(~ et barn opp og ned)* dandle; **B** *vb (minnes)* remember; *(gjenkalle i erindringen)* recall, recollect; *~ dårlig/godt* have a poor/good memory; *~r du hva jeg fortalte deg?* do you remember what I told you? *du ~r feil* you are mistaken; *han forsøkte å ~ navnet hennes* he tried to recall her name; *jeg ~r ikke det nøyaktig beløpet* I cannot recollect the exact amount; *(også)* I forget the exact amount; *om jeg ikke ~r feil* if I am not mistaken; if my memory serves me right; *så vidt jeg ~r* as far as I remember; to the best of my recollection. **huske|stue** *sb* row. **~lapp** *sb (handleliste)* shopping list; *(for ølvrig)* mermo(randum).

hus|klynge *sb* hamlet. **~leie** *sb* rent. **~lege** *sb* family doctor. **~lig** *adj* domestic. **~ly** *sb* shelter; *gi ~ly* house; put up. **~lærer** *sb* private tutor. **~mor** *sb* housewife; *(ved institusjon)* mater. **~morskole** *sb* domestic science school. **~morvikar** *sb* home help.

hustru wife.

hus|vert *sb* landlord. **~vill** *adj* homeless.

hutre *vb* shiver, shudder.

hva *pron* what; *~? ~behager? ~ sa De/du?* I beg your pardon? what (did you say)? *~ for en/et, ~ for noe/noen* what; *~ koster det?* how much does it cost? how much is it? *~ som enn* no matter what; whatever; *~ som enn skjer* whatever happens; *~ som helst* anything; *jeg er villig til å gjøre ~ som helst for deg* I would do anything for you; *~ så?* så what? (well) what of it? *vet du ~?* I'll tell you what/I say! Se også *hvilken* og *hvor (mange, mye)*.

hval *sb* whale. **hval|fanger** *sb* whaler. **~fangst** *sb* whaling. **~ross** *sb* walrus.

hvelv *sb (hvelving)* arch, vault; *(i bank etc)* strong-room, vault; *(båt~)* overturned (boat) bottom. **hvelve** *vb* **1** *~ seg* arch, vault; **2** = *velte*. **hvelving** *sb* arch, vault.

hvem *pron* who; *(etter prep)* whom; *(som avhengighetsform ellers)* whom (*skjønt i dagligtale* who); *(~ av et visst antall, særlig foran* of) which; *~ av guttene kom først?* which of the boys came first? *~ andre?* who else? *~ fortalte du det til?* to whom did you tell it? who(m) did you tell it to? *~ så deg?* who saw you? *~ så du?* who(m) did you see? *~ hun enn er, ~ hun så er* whoever she is; whoever she may be; *~ som helst* anybody; *~ som helst kan gjøre det* anybody can do that. Se også *hvilken*.

hver *pron* every; *(foran* of) each; every one; *~ av dem* each of them; *(~ av et bestemt antall)* each; *det er 200 hager, ~ med sin flaggstang* there are 200 gardens, each with a flagstaff of its own; *~ annen* se *annenhver*; *de har ~ sin sykkel* they have got a bicycle each; *de kan være her ~t øyeblikk* they may be here any moment; *en* *gang* ~ *uke* once a week; once every week; *etter* ~*t* by and by; little by little; *etter* ~*t som* as; *etter* ~*t som vi blir gamle* as we grow old; *i* ~*t fall* at any rate; *litt av* ~*t* a little of everything.

hverandre *pron (især når det dreier seg om to)* each other; *(især når det dreier seg om flere enn to)* one another; *etter* ~ one after another; *hvor har dere truffet* ~? where did you meet? *skjelne fra* ~ tell apart; *ta fra* ~ take apart; *(demontere)* dismantle; *ved siden av* ~ side by side.

hverdag *sb* week-dag. **hverdags|bruk** *sb: til* ~*bruk* for everyday use. ~**klær** *sb fl* everyday clothes. ~**kost** *sb* daily/homely fare. **hverdagslig** *adj (kjedelig)* humdrum, monotonous.

hvese *vb (om gås, slange)* hiss; *(om katt)* spit.

hvete *sb* wheat; *(i land/landsdeler hvor* ~ *er eneste/viktigste kornslag ofte)* corn. Jf *mais*. **hvete|brødsdager** *sb* honeymoon. ~**mel** *sb* wheat flour.

hvil *sb (hvilepause, rast)* rest; *vi tok (oss) en* ~ we rested/took a rest. **hvile 1** *sb (det å* ~*)* rest; *trenge* ~ need rest; **2** *vb* rest; *de hvilte en time* they rested (for) an hour; *taket* ~*r på åtte søyler* the roof rests on eight columns. **hvile|dag** *sb* day of rest. ~**hjem** *sb* rest home/house. ~**løs** *adj* restless. ~**sted** *sb* place of rest.

hvilke(n) *pron* what; *(av et begrenset antall, især foran* of*)* which; *hvilke bøker har du lest* what books have you read? ~ *av disse bøkene har du lest?* which of these books have you read? *hvilken ... enn/så* whatever; *(om begrenset antall og foran* of*)* whichever; *hvilke ordrer han enn gir deg* whatever orders he gives you; ~ *av bøkene mine han så ber om* whichever of my books he asks for; ~ *som helst* any. **hvilket** *(bokl rel pron = noe som)* which; *han bad meg komme inn,* ~ *jeg gjorde* he asked me to enter, which I did.

hvin *sb* shriek; screech, squeal. **hvine** *vb (om personer)* squeal, shriek; *(om geværkuler)* whistle.

hvis I *konj (dersom)* if; ~ *bare* ... if only ...; **II** *pron* **1** *(genitiv av hvem)* whose; ~ *bok er det?* whose book is that? **2** *(gen av som)* whose; *(om ting etc også)* of which; *et fly* ~ *fører ble drept* an aeroplane the pilot of which/whose pilot was killed.

hviske *vb* whisper. **hvisking** *sb* whisper(ing).

hvit *adj, sb* white; *(US om rase også)* Caucasian. **hvite** *sb (egge*~*)* white. **hvit|kalket** *adj* whitewashed. ~**lig** *adj* whitish. ~**løk** *sb* garlic. **hvitne** *vb* whiten. **hvitte** *vb (hvitkalke)* whitewash.

hvitting *sb* whiting.

hvit|veis *sb* wood anemone. ~**vin** *sb* white wine.

hvor *adv* **1** *(om stedet)* where; ~ *bor du?* where do you live? ~ *skal du hen?* where are you going? *der* ~ *jeg kommer fra* where I come from; *det stedet* ~ *han bodde* the place where he lived; ~ ... *(enn/så)* wherever; ~ *hun enn/så kom* wherever she came; ~ *som helst* anywhere; **2** *(foran adj etc)* how; ~ *gammel er du?* how old are you? ~ *mange* how many; ~ *mye* how much; *jeg lurer på* ~ *mye de tjener* I wonder how much they earn; ~ ... *enn* ~ ... *så* however; ~ *rik han enn er* however rich he is; *vi greier det aldri,* ~ *mye vi så prøver* we shall never succeed, however much we try.

hvorav *adv, prep (om personer)* of whom; *passasjerene,* ~ *flere var engelskmenn* the passengers several of whom were English; *(om ting etc)* of which; *40 hus* ~ *mange er nye* 40 houses many of which are new.

hvordan *adv* how; ~ *det?* how is that? ~ ... *enn (*el *nå* el *så)* however; no matter how; ~ *det nå har seg med det* however that may be; ~ *vi enn ser på det* no matter how we look at it; ~ *har du det?* how are you? ~ *kan det ha seg/henge sammen at* how can it be that; ~ *kom du inn?* how did you get in? ~ *ser han ut?* what does he look like?

hvoretter *adv* after which; when; *han ble til klokken 8* ~ *han gikk hjem* he stayed till 8 o'clock when he went home.

hvorfor *adv* why; ~ *det?* why so? ~ *gjorde du det?* why did you do it? ~ *i all verden?* why on earth?

hvorhen *adv* where. Se også *hvor 1*.

hvorledes se *hvordan*.

hybel *sb* lodgings, rooms *(fl)*; *(student*~ *etc)* digs *(fl)*. **hybel|leilighet** bed-sitter; bed-sitting-room; flatlet. ~**vertinne** *sb* landlady.

hydrofoilbåt *sb* hydrofoil boat; hydroplane. **hydrogen** *sb* hydrogen. **hydrogenbombe** *sb* hydrogen bomb. **hydroplan** *sb (hydrofoilbåt, sjøfly)* hydroplane.

hygge 1 *sb* comfort; *hjemlig* ~ home comfort; *(hyggelig stemning)* cheerfulness; friendly atmosphere; **2** *vb:* ~ *seg* make oneself comfortable, pass the time in a pleasant way; *hun prøvde å* ~ *for oss på alle måter* she tried in every way to make us comfortable/make us feel at home. **hyggelig** *adj* cosy, snug; comfortable; cheerful; *(snill, vennlig)* nice, pleasant; *en* ~ *gammel mann* a nice old man; *en* ~ *prat* a cosy chat; *en* ~ *varme på peisen* a cheerful fire; *den gamle byen med de* ~*e gatene* the old town with its friendly streets; *gjøre det* ~ *for* se *hygge for; ha det* ~ enjoy oneself; have a nice time; *(nei,) så* ~*!* how nice!

hygiene *sb* hygiene. **hygienisk** *adj* hygienic.

hykkelsk *adj* hypocritical. **hykle** *vb* feign, simulate; dissemble. **hykler** *sb* hypocrite. **hykleri** *sb* hypocricy. **hyklersk** *adj* hypocritical.

hyl *sb* howl, yell; *et* ~ *av smerte/redsel* a howl of pain/of terror. **hyle** *vb* howl, yell.

hylle *sb* shelf; *(bagasje*~*)* rack; *(*~ *i fjellvegg)* ledge, shelf; *hun er kommet på sin rette* ~ she has found the right niche for herself; she is the right person/woman in the right place; *han er kommet på feil* ~ he is a square peg in a round hole; *legge på* ~*n (dvs legge til side, utsette)* put on the shelf; shelve; *planene hans ble lagt på* ~*n* his plans were shelved/put on the shelf.

hylle *vb:* ~ *inn* wrap up.

hylle *vb (*~ *konge etc)* pay homage to; *(vise anerkjennelse)* praise; *(applaudere)* acclaim, applaud; *(med festligheter)* fête; *(med hurrarop)* cheer; *de ble* ~*t av mengden* they were cheered by the crowd. **hyllest** *sb* homage, ovation; *(bifall)* applause.

hylse *sb (patron*~*)* case, shell; *(kapsel)* case, capsule; *(holk)* ferrule. **hylster** *sb* case; *(pistol~)* holster.

hymne *sb* ode; song of praise; *(særlig religiøs ~)* hymn; *en ~ til friheten* an ode to liberty.

hyperbel *sb (mat)* hyperbola.

hypermoderne *adj* ultra-fashionable, ultra--modern.

hypnose *sb* hypnosis. **hypnotisere** *vb* hypnotize. **hypnotisk** *adj* hypnotic. **hypnotisme** *sb* hypnotism.

hypo|konder *adj, sb* hypochondriac. **~kondri** *sb* hypochondria. **~kondriker** se *hypokonder.* **~tenus** *sb* hypotenuse. **~tese** *sb* hypothesis. **~tetisk** *adj* hypothetical.

hyppe *vb (~ poteter etc)* earth up; *US* hill.

hyppig *adj* frequent; *adv* frequently; *en ~ gjest* a frequent guest.

hyre I *sb* **1** *(arbeid om bord)* berth; employment, job; *ta ~ (på en båt)* sign on (board a ship); *ta ~ som fyrbøter* ship/sign on as a stoker; **2** *(sjømannslønn)* pay, wages; **3** *fig: ha sin fulle ~* be hard put to it; have no end of a job; **II** *vb (leie)* hire; *~ (et) mannskap* sign on a crew.

hysj, hyss *interj* hush. **hysje, hysse** *vb* hush; *~ på* ask to be quiet; cry hush to.

hyssing *sb* string.

hysteri *sb* hysterics. **hysterisk** *adj* hysteric(al); *få et ~ anfall* go into hysterics.

hytt *sb: i ~ og vær* at random.

hytte A *sb (lite landsens hus)* cottage; *(ferie~ etc)* cabin, chalet; *(liten, primitiv ~)* hut, shack; **B** *vb: ~ til* shake one's fist at.

hæl *sb* heel; *de var like i ~ene på meg* they were close upon my heels.

hær *sb* army. **hærfører** *sb* commander. **hærverk** *sb* malicious damage; wanton destruction (of property).

høflig *adj (meget ~)* polite; *(med korrekt ~het)* civil; *(med utsøkt ~het)* courteous. **høflighet** *sb* politeness; civility; courtesy.

høl *sb (kulp)* pool.

hølje *vb* pour; *det ~t ned* it rained cats and dogs; *regnet ~t ned* the rain came down in sheets. **høljregne** = *hølje.*

høne *sb* hen; *det går den veien høna sparker* it goes to rack and ruin; *ha en ~ å plukke med* have a bone to pick with. **høns** *sb koll* chickens, fowls; *de holdt ~* they kept poultry. **hønse|gård** *sb* fowl-run, poultry--yard. **~hauk** *sb* goshawk. **~hjerne** *sb* bird brain. **~netting** *sb* chicken wire.

hørbar *adj* audible. **høre** *vb* **1** *(oppfatte med ørene)* hear; *jeg ~r ikke/kan ikke ~ (noe) på grunn av bråket* I cannot hear for the noise; *vi hørte (at) han kom* we heard him come/coming; **2** *(få vite)* hear; *jeg ~r at faren din er syk* I hear that your father is ill; **3** *(~ etter, lytte)* listen; *hør her!* listen! *Hør! Hører du ikke musikkorpset?* Listen! Don't you hear the band? **4** *(uttrykk) ~* **av** hear from/through; *jeg hørte det av søsteren din* I heard it from your sister; *~* **etter** listen; *han ~r bare etter med det ene øret* he is only listening with one ear; *~* **fra** hear from; *har du hørt fra datteren din?* have you heard from your daughter? *~* **hjemme** belong; *~r de hjemme her?* do they belong here? *~* **om** hear about/of; *har du hørt om ulykken?* have you heard of the accident? *jeg vil ikke ~ tale om det* I won't hear of it; *~* **på** listen to; *vi hørte på musikken* we listened to the music; *~ på radio* listen in (to); *~* **sammen** belong together; *~* **til** belong to; jf *til~*; se også *~ hjemme.* **høre|apparat** *sb* hearing aid. **~sans** *sb* sense of hearing. **~spill** *sb* radio play. **~vidde** *sb: innen ~vidde* within earshot. **hørlig** *adj* audible. **hørsel** *sb* hearing.

høst *sb* **1** *(årstiden)* autumn; *US* fall; *~en 1990* (in) the autumn of 1990; *en mild ~* a mild autumn; *(nå) i ~* this autumn; *i fjor ~, sist ~* last autumn; *neste ~, til ~en* next autumn; *om ~en* during/in (the) autumn; **2** *(avling)* crop, harvest. **høst|aktig** *adj* autumnal. **~arbeid** *sb (på gård)* harvesting. **høste** *vb (få i hus)* harvest, reap; *(få utbytte)* gain, win; reap; *~ erfaring* gain experience; *~ fordel av* benefit/profit by; *~ fruktene av* reap the fruits of; *~ ære* win glory. **høst|lig** *adj* autumnal. **~jevndøgn** *sb* autumnal equinox.

høvding *sb* chief.

høve 1 *sb* occasion; *nytte ~t* avail oneself of the opportunity; *ved det ~t* on that occasion; **2** *vb* be convenient; suit

høvel *sb* plane. **høvel|benk** *sb* carpenter's bench. **~flis** *sb* shavings.

høvelig *adj* convenient, suitable.

høvle *vb* plane. **høvleri** *sb* planing mill.

høy *adj* **1** high; *(om mennesker og ting som er høyere enn de er brede)* tall; *~e priser* high prices; *~ snø* deep snow; *en meget ~ kvinne* a very tall woman; *en ~ mur/vegg* a high wall; *(opp)nå (en) ~ alder* reach a great age; *seks fot ~* six feet high/tall; **2** *(om lyd)* loud; *et ~t skrik* a loud cry; *med ~ stemme* in a loud voice; **3** *(om tonehøyde)* high; *en ~ tone* a high note. Se også *høyt.*

høy *sb* hay.

høyde *sb* **1** height; *i fem meters ~* at a height of five metres; **2** *(~ i terrenget)* hill; **3** *(nivå)* level; **4** *(om skipsposisjon) på ~ med Kapp Horn* off Cape Horn. **høyde|hopp** *sb* high jump. **~punkt** *sb* height; climax, culmination, zenith. **~sprang** = *~hopp.*

høyesterett *sb* ≈ the Supreme Court (of Justice); *US* the Supreme Court.

høyfeber *sb* hay fever.

høy|fjell *sb* mountain plateau. **~forræderi** *sb* high treason.

høygaffel *sb* hayfork, pitchfork.

høy|het *sb: Deres/Hans/Hennes kongelige ~* Your/His/Her Royal Highness. **~kant** *sb: på ~* on (its) end. **~land** *sb* highland. **~lig** *adv* greatly, highly. **~loftet** *adj* lofty. **~lys** *adj: ved ~lys dag* in broad daylight. **~lytt** *adj* loud; *adv* loudly. **~messe** *sb* morning service; *(katolsk ~messe)* High Mass. **~mælt** *adj* loud--spoken.1 **høyonn** *sb* hay-making; *drive med høyonna* make hay.

høyre *adj, sb* right, right-hand; *gå/kjøre på ~ side*

keep to the right; *hans ~ lomme* his right-hand pocket; *på ~ hånd* on the right; *på ~ side* on the right-hand side; on the right; *til ~* to the right; *til ~ for meg* to the right of me. **høyre|kjøring** *sb* right-hand traffic. **~stille** *vb data* right-justify. **~tast** *sb data* right arrow key.

høy|rød *adj* bright red; scarlet. **~røstet** *adj* loud. **~sesong** *sb* the height of the season. **~skole** *sb* college. **~slette** *sb* highland, plateau. **~spenning** *sb* high tension/voltage.

høyst *adv (svært)* highly; extremely, most; *(i det høyeste)* at most; not more than; *~ ubehagelig* most unpleasant; *han er ~ 20 år* he is not more than 20 years; *ett eller ~ to år* one or, at most, two years.

høy|stakk *sb* hayrick, haystack. **~såte** *sb* haycock.

høyt *adv* **1** high; *(i høy grad)* highly; *~ begavet* highly gifted; *elske ~* love dearly; **2** *(om lyd)* aloud, loud(ly); *lese ~ a) (dvs lese opp)* he read aloud; *b) (dvs lese med høy stemme)* read loud; *snakke/synge ~* speak/sing loud(ly); *tenke ~* think aloud.

høy|tid *sb* festival, feast; *bevegelige ~er* movable feasts; *de store høytider* the high festivals. **~tidelig** *adj* solemn.

høytrykk *sb* high pressure. **høytrykks|område** *sb* high pressure area. **~rygg** *sb* high pressure ridge.

høytstående *adj* high, high-ranking; important, prominent; *en ~ offiser* a high(-ranking) officer; *en ~ person* an important person.

høyt|taler *sb* loud-speaker. **~travende** *adj* high-flown, lofty; bombastic.

høyvann *sb* high water/tide; *ved ~* at high water.

hå *sb (etterslått)* aftermath.

hål *adj (glatt)* slippery. **hålke** *sb* icy, slippery surface. **hålkeføre** *sb* icy roads.

hån *sb* scorn.

hånd *sb* **1** hand; *~ i ~* hand in hand; *gi hverandre ~en (på det)* shake hands (on it); *han gav henne ~en* he shook hands with her; *holde hverandre i ~en/i hendene* hold hands; *klappe i hendene* clap one's hands; **2** *(uttrykk) ha* **frie hender** have a free hand; have free play; **for ~en** at hand; *få arbeidet* **fra ~en** get the work done; *leve* **fra ~ til munn** live from hand to mouth; **i gode hender** in good hands; **i hende** to hand; in one's possession; *ha* **på ~en** have an option on; *jeg har huset på ~en* I have an option on the house; **på egen ~** on one's own; *hun ville begynne på egen ~ (dvs for seg selv)* she wanted to begin on her own. **hånd|arbeid** *sb* **1** *(sytøy etc)* needlework; *et ~* a piece of needlework; **2** *(motsatt maskinarbeid)* handwork. **~bevegelse** *sb* gesture. **~bok** *sb* handbook, manual. **~brems** *sb* hand-brake. **~flate** *sb* palm (of the hand). **~full** *sb* handful. **~grep** *sb* movement/turn of the hand. **~gripelig** *adj* palpable, tangible. **~heve** *vb* enforce, maintain; *~heve lov og orden* maintain law and order. **~hilse** *vb* shake hands. **~kjerre** *sb* hand--barrow. **~kle** *sb* towel. **~koffert** *sb* suitcase. **~kraft** *sb* hand-power; manual power; *drive med ~kraft* work by hand. **~lag** *sb* dexterity, handiness. **~laget** *adj* hand-made. **~ledd** *sb* wrist. **~skrevet** *adj* hand-written. **~skrift** *sb* hand-writing.

håndsrekning *sb* a (helping) hand; *hun gav dem en ~* she lent them a hand. **håndtak** *sb* handle.

håndtere *vb* handle, manage.

hånd|trykk *sb* handshake. **~verk** *sb* trade; craft, handicraft; *~verk og industri* trade and industry. **~verker** *sb* artisan; *fl ofte* workmen; *(især kunsthåndverker)* craftsman. **~verksmessig** *adj* craftsmanlike. **~verksmester** *sb* master artisan. **~veske** *sb* handbag.

håne *vb* mock; scoff at. **hån|flir** *sb* sneer. **~latter** *sb* scornful laughter. **~lig** *adj* contemptuous, scornful.

håp *sb* hope; *alt ~ er ute* there is no longer any hope; *de oppgav alt ~* they gave up (all) hope; *leve i ~et* live in hope; *leve i ~et om* live in the hope of. **håpe** *vb* hope (*på* for); *jeg ~r det* I hope so; *jeg ~r ikke det* I hope not; *vi ~r hun kommer* we hope she will come; *vi ~r det beste* we hope for the best. **håpefull** *adj* hopeful, promising. **håpløs** *adj* hopeless; *(fortvilet også)* desperate; *en ~ stilling* a hopeless/desperate position.

hår *sb* hair; *det fikk ~ene til å reise seg på hodet hans* it made his hair stand on end; *det var på et hengende ~ at de hadde druknet* they had a narrow escape/a hairbreath escape from drowning; *ikke et ~ bedre* not a bit/scrap better. **hår|avfall** *sb* loss of hair. **~børste** *sb* hairbrush.

hård|hjertet *adj* hard-hearted. **~nakket** *adj* stiff--necked, obstinate.

håret(e) *adj* hairy, hirsute. **hår|fasong** *sb* hair-do. **~feste** *sb* hairline. **~fin** *adj* subtle, minute; *beregne det (tiden etc) ~fint* cut it fine. **~kløyveri** *sb* hairsplitting. **~reisende** *adj* hair-rising. **~spenne** *sb* hair grip; *især US* bobby pin. **~tørrer** *sb* hair drier. **~vekst** *sb: en frodig ~vekst* an abundant crop of hair; *sjenerende ~vekst* superfluous hair.

I

i *(bokstaven)* i.

i I *adv* in; *(oversettes ofte ikke) en sokk med hull i* a sock with a hole; **II** *prep* **1** *(om sted) i huset* in the house; *(om store byer) i London* in London; *men: jeg har aldri vært i London* I have never been to London; *et besøk i London* a visit to London*)*; *(om mindre byer og om adresse)* at; *de bor i Mill Street 8* they live at No. 8 Mill Street; **2** *(i = inn/ned/opp/ut etc i)* into; *de gikk inn i huset* they went into the house; *han brast (ut) i gråt* he burst into tears; *jeg falt (ut) i vannet* I fell into the water; *vi kom (opp) i vanskeligheter* we got into difficulties; *(etter* put, place, lay *likevel som oftest)* in; *han stakk hånden i lommen* he put his hand in his pocket; **3** *(om tidsrom)* in; *i 1905* in (the year) 1905; **4** *(om tidspunkt)* at; *i dette øyeblikk* at this moment; **5** *(om varighet)* for; *i fem dager/to måneder/tre år* for five days/two months/three years; **6** *(uttrykk) kongen i landet* the king of the country; *lærer i engelsk* teacher of English; *60 miles i timen* sixty miles an hour/per hour.

i aften *adv* tonight; this evening. Se også *aften.*

iaktta *vb (se på)* watch; *(legge merke til)* notice, observe. **iakttakelse** *sb* observation. **iakttaker** *sb* observer.

iallfall *adv (i hvert fall)* at any rate; in any case; *(i det minste)* at least.

i alt *adv* in all; *~ ~ femti* fifty in all.

ibenholt *sb* ebony.

iberegnet *perf part* included; *alt ~* everything included.

iblant *adv* now and then; *en gang ~* once in a while. Se ellers *blant.*

i dag *adv* today. Se også *dag.*

idé *sb* idea, notion; *en god ~* a good idea; a happy thought; *han fikk en god ~* a good idea struck him. **ideal** *sb* ideal; *hun er mitt ~ som lærer* she is my ideal of a teacher. **idealisme** *sb* idealism. **idealist** *sb* idealist. **idealistisk** *adj* idealistic. **ideell** *adj* ideal; *et ideelt feriested* an ideal place for a holiday.

identifikasjon *sb* identification. **identifisere** *vb* identify; *~ seg med* identify oneself with. **identisk** *adj* identical. **identitet** *sb* identity. **identitetskort** *sb* identity card.

ideologi *sb* ideology. **ideologisk** *adj* ideological.

idet *konj* as; *de kom akkurat ~ jeg åpnet døren* they arrived just as I was opening the door; *~ han kom inn, så han henne* as he entered, he saw her; *(omskrevet med* -ing-*form)* on entering he saw her.

idiot *sb* idiot; *(som skjellsord også)* fool. **idiotisk** *adj* idiotic. **idiotsikker** *adj* fool-proof.

idrett *sb* (athletic) sports; *(især fri~)* athletics; *drive ~* engage in/go in for athletics/athletic activities. **idretts|kvinne** *sb* athlete, sportswoman. **~lag** *sb* athletic club. **~mann** *sb* athlete, sportsman. **~plass** *sb* playing-field; sports ground. **~stevne** *sb* sports meeting.

idyll *sb* idyl(l); *den rene ~* a perfect idyll. **idyllisk** *adj* idyllic.

idømme *vb* condemn, sentence; *(om bøter)* fine. Jf *ilegge.* Se ellers *dømme.*

i fall *konj (hvis)* if; in case.

i fjor *adv* last year. **i forfjor** *adv* the year before last; *dgl, hum* yesteryear.

i forgårs *adv* the day before yesterday.

ifølge *prep* according to; in accordance with/*US* to; *~ avisene* according to the papers; *~ bestemmelsene* in accordance with the regulations.

igjen *adv* **1** *(atter)* again; *om ~* again; once more; over again; *prøv ~!* try again! *(ved verb ofte)* re-; *hun leste boken (om) ~* she reread the book; **2** *(tilbake)* back; *jeg har fått ~ appetitten* I have got my appetite back; **3** *(til overs)* left; *det er bare fem ~* there are only five left.

igjennom 1 *adv* through; *boken er vanskelig å komme ~* the book is hard to get through; *hele året ~* all the year round; all through the year; throughout the year; **2** *prep* se *gjennom.*

igle *sb* leech.

ignorere *vb* ignore: take no notice of; *vi ignorerte truslene deres* we ignored/took no notice of their threats.

i går *adv* yesterday; *~ ~ aftes/kveld* last evening/ night; yesterday evening/night; *~ ~ morges* yesterday morning.

i hende *adv* in one's possession; to hand. **ihendehaver** *sb* bearer, holder.

iherdig *adj* energetic, persistant. **iherdighet** *sb* persistence.

i hjel *adv* to death; *fryse ~ ~* freeze to death; *slå ~ ~* kill.

i hvert fall *adv* at any rate; in any case.

ikke *adv* **1** not; *de nådde ~ bussen* they missed the bus; *han er rik, ~ sant?* he is rich, isn't he? **2** *(foran komparativ)* no, not; *~ lenger/mer* no longer/more; *~ noe* se *ingenting*; *~ noen* se *ingen*; jf *noe, noen*; *hun er ~ større enn jeg* she is no bigger than I. **ikke|angrepspakt** *sb* non-aggression pact. **~-røyker** *sb* non-smoker. **~vold** *sb* non-violence.

i kveld *adv* tonight; this evening.

ilandføre *vb* bring ashore. **ilandføringsrør** *sb petro* trunk line.

il|brev *sb* express letter; *US* special delivery letter. **~bud** *sb (om meldingen)* express message; *(om budbringeren)* express messenger.

ild *sb* fire; *bli herre over ~en* bring the fire under control; *brent barn skyr ~en* a burnt child dreads the fire; *gå gjennom ~ og vann for* go through fire and water for; *gå/spre seg som ~ i tørt gress* run like wildfire; *leke med ~en* play with fire; *ha mange jern i ~en* have many irons in the fire; *mellom dobbelt ~* between two fires. **ildebrann** se *brann 1*. **ild|fast** *adj* fire-proof; *~fast form* casserole; *~fast stein* fire-brick. **~linje** *sb* firing line. **~prøve** *sb* ordeal. **~rake(r)** *sb* poker. **~rød** *adj* fiery red. **ilds|farlig** *adj* combustible, inflammable. **~påsettelse** *sb* arson, fire-raising. **ild|sted** *sb* fire-place, hearth, **~vann** *sb (brennevin)* fire-water. **~våpen** *sb fl* fire-arms.

ile *vb (skynde seg)* hasten, hurry; make haste; *hun ilte ham i møte* she hurried to meet him.

ilegge *vb: ~ en bot* fine. Jf *dømme*.

ilgods *sb* express goods.

iligne *vb* tax; *jeg ble ~t kr 120 000 (i skatt)* I was taxed kr 120,000.

ille 1 *adj* bad; *det er slett ikke så ~ (dvs det er ganske bra)* it is not half bad; *ta ~ opp* take amiss; mind; *jeg håper De ikke tar det ~ opp at jeg sier det* I hope you won't mind my saying so; **2** *adv* badly, ill. **illebefinnende** *sb* indisposition; *han har fått et ~* he does not feel quite well.

illegal *adj* illegal.

ille|luktende *adj* evil-smelling, stinking. **~varslende** *adj* ominous.

illojal *adj* disloyal. **illojalitet** *sb* disloyalty.

illumination *sb* illumination. **illuminere** *vb* illuminate.

illusjon *sb* illusion; *jeg har/nærer ingen ~er* I have no illusions. **illusjonist** *sb (tryllekunstner)* conjurer. **illusorisk** *adj* illusory.

illustrasjon *sb* illustration, picture. **illustratør** *sb* illustrator. **illustrere** *vb* illustrate.

il|marsj *sb* forced march. **~pakke** *sb* express parcel. **~telegram** *sb* express telegram.

ilter *adj* hot-headed, irascible.

iltog *sb* express (train); fast train.

imaginær *adj* imaginary.

imbesill *adj* imbecile. **imbesillitet** *sb* imbecility.

imellom *adv: en gang ~* now and then; once in a while; *komme ~* intervene; *hvis ikke noe kommer ~* should nothing intervene; *legge seg ~* interpose, intervene; *venner ~* among friends. Jf *mellom*.

imens 1 *adv* in the meantime; *du kan se litt på avisen ~* in the meantime, you can have a look the newspaper; **2** *konj* se *mens*.

imidlertid *adv* **1** *(likevel, men)* however; *jeg tok ~ feil* I was mistaken, however; *senere bestemte han seg ~ for å gå* later, however, he decided to go; **2** *(i mellomtiden)* meanwhile; in the meantime; *~ gjorde han seg ferdig med arbeidet (sitt)* meanwhile/in the meantime, he finished his work.

imitasjon *sb* imitation. **imitere** *vb* imitate; *(især parodisk)* impersonate.

immatrikulering *sb* matriculation. **immatrikulere** *vb* matriculate; *bli immatrikulert ved et universitet* matriculate at a university.

immigrant *sb* immigrant. **immigrasjon** *sb* immigration.

immun *adj* immune (*mot* against, from, to). **immunitet** *sb* immunity.

i morgen *adv* tomorrow. **i morges** *adv* this morning.

imot *adv: det er ikke meg ~, jeg har ikke noe ~ det* I don't mind (it); *for og ~* for and against; pro and con; *få ~ noen* take a dislike to somebody; *ha ~ noen* dislike somebody; *har De noe ~ at jeg røyker?* do you mind my smoking? *midt ~* (just) opposite; *si ~* oppose, protest; *stikk ~* dead against; *tvert ~* on the contrary. Jf *mot*.

imperativ *sb (gram)* the imperative. **imperfektum** *sb (gram)* the past tense; the preterite.

imperialisme *sb* imperialism. **imperialist** *sb* imperialist. **imperialistisk** *adj* imperialist(ic). **imperium** *sb* empire.

imponere *vb* impress; *han ble imponert av ordene hennes* he was impressed by her words. **imponerende** *adj* impressive; *(sterkere)* imposing.

import *sb* import, importation; *(om varene)* imports; *~ av tobakk er forbudt* importation of tobacco is prohibited; *~en oversteg eksporten i verdi* imports exceeded exports in value. **importere** *vb* import. **import|forbud** *sb* embargo. **~overskudd** *sb* excess of imports.

impregnert *adj (om trematerialer)* impregnated; *(om stoffer)* (made) waterproof.

impresjonisme *sb* impressionism. **impresjonist** *sb* impressionist. **impresjonistisk** *adj* impressionist(ic).

improvisasjon *sb* improvisation. **improvisere** *vb* improvise.

impuls *sb* impulse. **impulsiv** *adj* impulsive; *en ~ mann* an impulsive man/a man of impulse.

imøte *adv: hun kom ham ~* she came towards him. Se ellers *møte II*. **imøte|gå** *vb (opponere mot)* oppose; *(motbevise)* refute. **~kommende** *adj* obliging; kind. **~kommenhet** *sb* courtesy, kindness. **~se** *vb* await, expect; anticipate; *(med glede)* look forward to.

i natt *adv (kommende el nærværende natt)* tonight; this night; *(forrige natt)* last night.

inderlig *adj* heartfelt, sincere; *adv* fervently, intensely; *han elsket henne ~* he loved her dearly; *jeg ønsker ~ at* I wish with all my heart that.

indianer *sb* (Red) Indian; American Indian. **indiansk** *adj* (American) Indian.

indignasjon *sb* indignation. **indignert** *adj* indignant; *~ over* indignant at.

indikativ *sb (gram)* the indicative (mood).

indirekte *adj* indirect; *~ tale* indirect speech.

indisium *sb* (piece of) circumstantial evidence; *de ble dømt på indisier* they were convicted on circumstantial evidence.

in|diskresjon *sb* indiscretion; breach of confidence. **~diskret** *adj* indiscreet.

individ *sb* individual. **individuell** *adj* individual.

indo|europeer *sb* Indo-European. **~europeisk** *adj* Indo-European.

indre I *adj* **1** inner, interior; ~ *høyre/venstre (i fotball)* inside right/left; *det* ~ *Afrika* Central Africa; det ~ menneske the inner man; *det* ~ *øre* the inner ear; **2** *(innenriksk)* internal; *landets* ~ *forhold* the internal affairs of the country; **II** *sb* interior; *det* ~ *av landet* the interior of the country. **indre|løper** *sb (i fotball)* inner forward. **~medisin** *sb* internal medicine. **~medisiner** *sb* internist. **~medisinsk** *adj:* ~ *avdeling (på sykehus)* medical ward. **~misjon** *sb* home mission.

induksjon *sb* induction. **indusere** *vb* induce.

industri *sb* industry. **industri|arbeider** *sb* industrial worker. **~bedrift** *sb* industrial concern. **industriell** *adj* industrial. **industrivarer** *sb fl* industrial articles/products.

infam *adj* infamous.

infanteri *sb* infantry; foot (soldiers). **infanteri|-mann, soldat, infanterist** *sb* infantryman.

infantil *adj* infantile.

infernalsk *adj* infernal.

infeksjon *sb* infection. **infeksjonssykdom** *sb* infectious disease; infection.

infiltrasjon *sb* infiltration. **infiltrere** *vb* infiltrate.

infinitiv *sb (gram)* the infinitive.

infisere *vb* infect.

inflasjon *sb* inflation.

influensa *sb* influenza; *dgl* (the) flu. **influere på** *vb* influence.

informasjon *sb* information. **informatikk** *sb data* computer science. **informere** *vb* inform.

ingefær *sb* ginger.

ingen *pron* **1** nobody; no one; ~ *andre (om personer)* nobody else; *(om ting)* no other; ~ *andre enn du* no one but you; ~ *vet at jeg er her* nobody knows I am here; **2** *(foran sb)* no; ~ *bøker* no books; ~ *penger i det hele tatt* no money at all; *det er* ~ *som helst tvil* there is no doubt whatever; **3** *(skilt fra sb og især foran* of) none; ~ *av guttene* none of the boys; **4** *(~ av to)* neither; ~ *av tvillingene* neither of the twins.

ingeniør *sb* engineer. **ingeniør|soldat** *sb* engineer, sapper. **~vesen** *sb* engineering. **~våpenet** *sb (GB mil)* the Royal Engineers.

ingenlunde *adv* by no means; not at all. **ingensteds** *adv* nowhere. **ingenting** *pron* nothing.

ingrediens *sb* ingredient.

inhabil *adj* disqualified.

inhalere *vb* inhale. **inhalering** *sb* inhalation.

initialer *sb fl* initials.

initiativ *sb* initiative; *de tok ~et til å gjøre det* they took the initiative in doing it; *på hennes* ~ on her initiative; *privat* ~ private enterprise.

injeksjon *sb* injection.

injurie *sb (muntlig)* slander; *(skriftlig)* libel; *avisen ble saksøkt for ~r* the paper was sued for libel. **injurierende** *adj* slanderous, libellous.

inkludere *vb* include. **inklusiv(e)** *adv, prep (foran sb)* including; *et selskap på 10,* ~ *verten* a party of ten, including the host; *(etter sb)* included; *alle damene* ~ all the ladies included.

inkognito *adv* incognito.

inkompetent *adj* incompetent.

inkonsekvens *sb* inconsistency. **inkonsekvent** *adj* inconsistent.

Inkvisisjonen *sb* the Inquisition.

inn *adv* in; ~ *i* into; ~ *til byen/til Oslo* up to town/to Oslo; *han gikk* ~ *i en kirke* he went into a church.

inn|beretning *sb* report. **~berette** *vb* report. **~bille** *vb:* *~bille en noe* make somebody believe something; *~bille seg at* fancy/imagine that. **~bilning** *sb* fancy, imagination. **~bilsk** *adj* conceited. **~bilt** *adj* imaginary; *en* ~ *sykdom* an imaginary illness. **~binde** *(~ bøker)* se *binde 3.* **~binding** *sb* binding. **~blanding** *sb* intervention; *(påtrengende, uvelkommen ~)* meddling; interference. **~blikk (i)** *sb* glimpse (of); insight (into). **~bo** *sb* furniture, movables. **~bringende** *adj* lucrative, profitable. **~brudd** *sb (om dagen)* housebreaking; *(om natten)* burglary; *han gjorde* ~ *i et hus* he broke into a house. **~bruddstyv** *sb* housebreaker; burglar. **~by** *vb* invite; *vi ble ~budt til bryllupet deres* we were invited to their wedding reception. **~bydelse** *sb* invitation; *jeg fikk en* ~ *til middag* I received an invitation to dinner. **~bygger** *sb* inhabitant. **~byrdes** *adj* mutual; *de sloss* ~ they fought among themselves. **~dele** *vb* divide; *landet var ~delt i distrikter* the country was divided into districts. **~deling** *sb* division. **~dra** *vb (konfiskere)* confiscate, seize. **~drive** *vb (innkassere)* collect.

inne *adv* **1** in; ~ *i bilen* in/inside the car; ~ *i byen* in/within the town; ~ *mellom trærne* in among the trees; *er faren din ~?* is your father in? *langt* ~ *i landet* far inland; *langt* ~ *i salen* at the far end of the hall; *når er båten ~?* when will the boat be in? **2** *(innendørs)* indoors; *det er kaldere* ~ *enn ute* it is colder indoors than out (of doors); ~ *i* in, within, inside; **3** *(uttrykk) holde seg/være* ~ *med (dvs stå på god fot med)* be in with; *tiden er* ~ the time has come; *være* ~ *på en tanke* entertain an idea.

innefra *adv* from within.

inne|ha *vb* own; hold; occupy. **~haver** *sb* owner; bearer, holder; occupier; *~en av butikken* the owner of the shop; *~en av leiligheten* the occupier of the flat. **~holde** *vb* contain; *hva ~r den kassen?* what does that crate contain?

innen I *prep* **1** *(innenfor et tidsrom)* within; *vi måtte forlate landet* ~ *tre dager* we had to leave the country within three days; **2** *(ikke senere ern)* by; *jeg må ha pengene* ~ *mandag* I must have the money by Monday; **II** *konj* before; *dagen gikk* ~ *de kom frem* the day passed before they arrived. **innen|dørs 1** *adj* indoor; ~ *leker* indoor games; **2** *adv* indoors; *han holdt seg* ~ he kept indoors. **~for** *adv, prep* inside; *hun stod like* ~ *døren* she was standing just inside the door; *ingen fikk lov til å komme* ~ no one were allowed inside. **~fra, ~ifra** *adv* from within. **~landsk** *adj* domestic, home.

innenriks|departement *sb* Ministry/*US* Department of the Interior; *GB* Home Office. **~fart** *sb* domestic shipping/trade. **~handel** *sb* domestic/home trade. **~minister** *sb* Minister of the Interior; *GB* Home Secretary; *US* Secretary of the Interior. **~politikk** domestic policy/politics. Se også *politikk).*

innerlomme *sb* inside pocket.

innerst *adj, adv* inmost; *~ inne* at the (very) centre of; in the middle of; *hennes ~e tanker* her inmost thoughts.

innesluttet *adj* reserved, retiring.

innesperre *vb* lock/shut up; *(i fengsel)* imprison. Jf *sperre 3.*

inn|fall *sb* idea, thought; caprice, whim. **~finne seg** *vb* appear, arrive, come. **~flytelse** *sb* influence; *ha ~ på* influence. **~født** *adj, sb* native. **~føre** *vb (importere varer)* import; *(~føre noe nytt)* introduce. **~førsel** *sb (import)* import, importation, *(innførte varer)* import. Se også *import.*

inngang *sb* entrance. **inngangs|billett** *sb* admission ticket. **~penger** *sb* admission fee.

inn|grep *sb* **1** *(innblanding)* interference, intervention; **2** *(overgrep)* encroachment (*i* on); **3** *(operativt ~)* operation. **~grodd** *adj* deep-rooted. **~hegning** *sb* enclosure. **~hente** *vb* **1** *(ta igjen)* catch up with; overtake; *~ det forsømte* make up for lost time/for the time lost; **2** *~ anbud* invite tenders; *~ opplysninger* obtain information; *~ samtykke/tillatelse* obtain consent/permission. **~hold** *sb* **1** contents *fl*; *~et i kassen ble skadet* the contents of the box were damaged; **2** = **innholds|fortegnelse, ~liste** *sb* table of contents. **~hylle** *vb* envelop; wrap up. **~høst(n)ing** *sb* harvest (ing).

inniblant 1 *adv* here and there; *(om tid)* now and then; once in a while; occasionally; **2** *prep* among.

inni *adv* inside, within. **innimellom 1** *adv* se *inniblant 1*; **2** *prep* in between.

inn|kalle *vb (til møte etc)* summon; *(til militærtjeneste)* call up; *US* draft. **~kalling** *sb (til møte etc)* summons; *(til militærtjeneste)* calling up; *US* draft. **~kassere** *vb* collect. **~kast** *sb (i fotball)* throw-in. **~kjøp** *sb* purchase; *gjøre ~* go shopping; *jeg har et par ~kjøp å gjøre* I have a few purchases to make. **~kjøpspris** purchase price; buying/cost price. **~kjørsel** *sb (til hus etc)* drive; *(innkjøring)* entry; *ingen ~! ~ forbudt!* no entry! **~kreve** *vb* collect; demand payment of. **~kvartere** *vb* lodge; *(~ soldater)* billet, quarter. **~kvartering** *sb* lodging; *(militær ~)* billeting, quartering. **~land** *sb: i ~ og utland* at home and abroad. **~landsklima** *sb* continental climate.

inn|lede *vb* begin, open; *han ~t med å si* he began by saying; *hun ~t møtet* she opened the meeting. **~ledning** *sb (begynnelse)* beginning, opening; introduction, preface. **~legg** *sb (i debatt)* contribution; *(muntlig også)* speech; *(av sakfører i retten)* plea. **~legge** *vb (på sykehus)* se *legge 3.* **~levere** *vb* hand/send in. **~losjere** *vb* lodge. **~mari** *adj (ondskapsfull)* spiteful, venomous; *(som forsterkende adv)* awfully, dreadfully, terribly. **~mark** *sb* home fields. **~marsj** *sb* entry. **~melding** *sb* enrolment, entry; registration; *(søknad om ~)* application (for membership). **~meldingsblankett, ~meldingsskjema** *sb* application/entry form.

inn|om *adv: stikke ~* drop/pop in. **~over** *adv* in, inward(s); *døren går/åpner ~* the door opens inward(s).

inn|pakning *sb* packing, wrapping. **~paknings-papir** *sb* wrapping paper. **~pode** *vb (meninger)* indoctrinate. Se også *pode 3.* **~prente** *vb* drive home; impress upon; *~prente i hukommelsen* fix in one's mind.

inn|på *adv: hale ~* gain on; *vi halte ~ dem* we gained on them. **~påsliten** *adj* importunate, obtrusive, troublesome.

inn|rede *vb* fit out/up. **~redning** *sb (det å innrede)* fitting out/up; *(~redningsutstyr)* fittings. **~reise** *sb* arrival, entry. **~reisetillatelse** *sb* entry permit. **~retning** *sb (apparat etc)* appliance, contrivance. **~rette** *vb (arrangere, ordne)* arrange, organize; *~ seg etter* adapt oneself to; *vi hadde ~t oss på å tilbringe ferien sammen* we had arranged to spend our holiday together. **~rykk** *sb: ~rykk av gjester* influx of guests. **~rykning** *sb* **1** *(av annonse)* insertion; **2** *(av linje)* indentation, indention. **~rømme** *vb (vedgå)* acknowledge, admit. **~rømmelse** *sb* admission; *(det å gi etter)* concession; *de gjorde/kom med ~r* they made concessions. **~samling** *sb* collection. **~sats** *sb* **1** *(anstrengelse)* effort; *du må gjøre en ~sats* you must make an effort; **2** *(~sats i spill)* stake(s); *(samtlige spilleres ~)* pool. **~se** *vb* realize, see, understand; *han innså sine feil* he realized/saw his error; *jeg kan ikke ~ at/jeg innser ikke at ...* I do not see that ... **~sikt** *sb* insight. **~side** *sb* inside; *på ~siden* on the inside. **~sigelse** *sb* objection, protest. **~sjø** *sb* lake, water. **~skipe** *vb: ~ seg* embark; go on board. **~skjerpe** *vb* enjoin. **~skrenke** *vb* reduce, restrict; confine, limit; *~skrenke seg til* confine oneself to. **~skrenket** *adj* **1** *(begrenset)* limited; *på en ~ plass* within a limited space; **2** *(dum)* dull, unintelligent. **~skrenkning** *sb* reduction, restriction. **~skrift** *sb* inscription, legend. **~skudd** *sb (i bank)* deposit; *(i setning)* parenthesis. **~skyte** *vb (tilføye)* add. **~stendig** *adj* pressing, urgent; *adv* urgently. **~stille** *vb* **1** *(slutte med)* discontinue; leave off; stop; *(for en tid)* suspend; *de ~stilte arbeidet* they stopped work; *(midlertidig)* they suspended work; **2** *(foreslå som kandidat etc)* nominate, propose, recommend; **3** se *justere, regulere*; jf *stille II 2.* **~stilling** *sb* **1** *(justering, regulering)* adjustment, setting; **2** *(slutt, stans)* stoppage; suspension; **3** *(nominering)* nomination, recommendation; **4** *(rapport)* report; *med (rosende) ~stilling* with special mention; **5** attitude, mentality. **~ta** *vb (erobre)* capture, take; *de ~tok byen* they captured/took the town. **~tagende** *adj* attractive, charming. **~tekt** *sb* income; *en årlig ~tekt på 8000 pund* a yearly income of £8000.

inntil *adv, konj, prep* till, until; up to; *~ da* till then; *~ videre* till/until further notice; *~ år 1814* up to the year 1814.

inn|tre *vb* **1** *(begynne)* set in; *(inntreffe, oppstå også)* happen; take place; *det ~trådte en forandring* a change set in. **~treffe** *vb* happen; take place. **~trengende** *adj* earnest, urgent; *en ~trengende anmodning* an urgent request. **~trykk** *sb* impression; *han gir ~trykk av å være en hyggelig fyr* he seems/appears to be a nice fellow; *hun gjorde et godt ~trykk på meg* she made a good impression on me. **~under** *prep: ~under jul* just before Christmas. **~vandre** *vb* immigrate. **~vandrer** *sb* immigrant. **~vandring** *sb* immigration. **~vende** *vb* object; *har De noe å ~vende?* have you any objection(s)? *jeg ~vendte at hun var altfor ung* I objected that the she was far too young. **~vendig** *adj* inside, internal. **~vending** *sb* objection; *vår ~vending mot forslaget* our objection against/to the proposal. **~vie** *vb* **1** consecrate; *(mindre høytidelig)* dedicate; *~viet jord* consecrated ground; **2** *~vie i* initiate/let into; *jeg ble ~viet i hemmeligheten deres* I was let into their secret. **~viklet** *adj* complicated. **~virke på** *vb* influence. **~virkning** *sb* influence; *(virkning)* effect. **~voller** *sb* bowels, guts; *(dyrs ~)* entrails; *(fisks ~)* guts. **~vortes** *adj* internal; *til ~vortes bruk* for internal use. **~øve** *vb* practice; *(~øve en rolle)* rehearse.

insekt *sb* insect.

insinuasjon *sb* insinuation. **insinuere** *vb* insinuate.

insistere *vb* insist; *de insisterte på å gjøre det* they insisted on doing it.

inskripsjon *sb* inscription.

inspeksjon *sb* inspection. **inspektør** *sb (især offisielt utnevnt ~)* inspector; *(på skole)* assistant headmaster; *US* assistant principal; *(i stormagasin)* shopwalker; *US* floor-walker.

inspirasjon *sb* inspiration. **inspirere** *vb* inspire.

inspisere *vb* inspect.

installasjon *sb* installation. **installatør** *sb* electrician. **installere** *vb* install; put in; *vi har fått installert elektrisk lys* we have had electric light put in.

instinkt *sb* instinct. **instinktiv** *adj* instinctive. **instinktivt** *(adv)* instinctively.

institusjon *sb* institution. **institutt** *sb* institute, institution.

instruere *vb* direct, instruct. **instruks** *sb* instructions *fl*; directive. **instruksjon** *sb* direction, instruction. **instruktør** *sb* instructor; *(teater~)* producer; *(film~)* director.

instrument *sb* instrument.

integrerende *adj: en ~ del av* an integral part of.

intellektuell *adj, sb* intellectual. **intelligens** *sb* intelligence. **intelligens|alder** *sb* mental age. **~kvotient** *sb* intelligence quotient; IQ. **~prøve** *sb* intelligence/mental test. **intelligent** *adj* intelligent.

intens *adj* intense, intensive. **intensitet** *sb* intensity.

intensjon *sb* intention.

interessant *adj* interesting. **interesse** *sb* interest; *få ~ for* begin to take an interest in; become interested in; *ha ~ for* take an interest in; *være av ~* be of interest. **interessere** *vb* interest; *jeg ~r meg for saken* I am interested in the matter; I take an interest in the matter. **interessert** *adj* interested.

interiør *sb* interior. **interiørarkitekt** *sb* interior decorator/architect.

interjeksjon *sb (gram)* interjection.

internasjonal *adj* international.

internatskole *sb* boarding-school.

internere *vb* intern. **internering** *sb* internment.

internhukommelse *sb data* random access memory (RAM).

inter|venere *vb* intervene. **~vensjon** *sb* intervention.

inter|vju *sb* interview. **~vjue** *vb* interview. **~vjuer** *sb* interviewer.

intet se *ingen, ingenting, (ikke) noe.*

intetkjønn *sb (gram)* the neuter (gender).

intim *adj* intimate.

intoleranse *sb* intolerance. **intolerant** *adj* intolerant.

intransitiv *adj (gram)* intransitive.

intrige *sb* intrigue, plot.

intro|duksjon *sb* introduction. **~dusere** *vb* introduce.

intuisjon *sb* intuition. **intuitiv** *adj* intuitive.

invalid *sb* disabled person. **invalidepensjon** *sb* disablement pension. **invalidisere** *vb* cripple, disable. **invaliditet** *sb* disablement. Se også *ufør, uførhet.*

invasjon *sb* invasion.

inventar *sb* furniture; *fast ~* fixtures.

investere *vb* invest. **investering** *sb* investment.

invitasjon *sb* invitation. **invitere** *vb* invite, ask.

i overmorgen *adv* the day after tomorrow.

ire Irishman; *(kvinne)* Irishwoman; *~ne* the Irish.

irettesette *vb* reprimand, reprove; take to task. **irettesettelse** *sb* reprimand, reproof.

Irland Ireland; *(staten)* Eire, the Republic of Ireland. **irlending** se *ire.*

ironi *sb* irony. **ironisk** *adj* ironical.

irr *sb* verdigris; copper rust; green rust.

irritabel *adj* irritable. **irritasjon** *sb* irritation. **irritere** *vb* annoy, irritate.

irsk *adj* Irish; *(om språket også)* Erse.

is *sb* ice; *(iskrem)* ice, ice-cream. **is|bjørn** *sb* polar bear. **~bre** *sb* glacier. **~bryter** *sb* ice-breaker.

iscene|sette *vb* produce, stage; *(film)* direct. **~settelse** *sb* production, staging; *(av film)* direction. **~setter** *sb* producer; *(av film)* director.

isenkram *sb* hardware, ironmongery. **isenkramforretning** *sb* hardware shop/*US* store; ironmonger's (shop). **isenkramhandler** *sb* hardware dealer; ironmonger.

is|fjell *sb* iceberg. **~flak** *sb* ice floe. **~fri** *adj* ice-free. **~hav** *sb* arctic/polar sea. **~hockey** *sb* ice-hockey.

isjias *sb* sciatica.

is|kald *adj* ice-cold, icy. **~krem** *sb* ice-cream.

islett *sb* weft, woof.

isolasjon *sb* **1** *(teknisk ~)* insulation; *(mot varmetap)* lagging; **2** *(avsondring)* isolation. **isolere** *vb* **1** *(teknisk)* insulate; *(mot varmetap)* lag; **2** *(avsondre)* isolate.

ispinne *sb* ice lolly.

isse *sb* crown; top (of the head).

i stand se *stand.*

istapp *sb* icicle.

isteden *adv* instead; *~for* instead of.

istid *sb* Ice/Glacial Age.

i stykker se *stykke.*

i stå se *stå.*

især *adv* especially, particularly; *~ interessert i kunst* especially interested in art; *hva jeg ~ ønsker å vite* what I particularly want to know.

ivareta *vb* attend to; look after; take care of; *~ sine interesser* look after one's interests.

iver *sb* eagerness.

iverksette *vb* carry into effect; carry out; effect.

ivrig *adj* **1** eager; *~ etter å begynne* eager to begin; *(oppsatt på)* anxious; *han er ~ etter å gjøre meg til lags* he is anxious to please me; **2** *(~ interessert)* keen; *en ~ jeger* a keen sportsman; *han er ~ etter å spille tennis* he is keen on (playing) tennis; **3** *(uttrykk) han ble ~* he got excited.

iøynefallende *adj* conspicuous.

J

j *(bokstaven)* j.

ja 1 *svarord (bekreftende)* yes; *(~, gjerne, ~ visst)* certainly; **2** *(som innledning)* well; *blir De med? Ja, jeg vet ikke* are you coming? Well, I don't know; *~ vel* all right; **3** *(som forsterkning)* in fact; indeed; *(boklig, i skrift også)* nay; *det var en stor fisk, ~, det var den største jeg har sett* it was a big fish, in fact/indeed it was the biggest I have seen; *jeg har en mistanke om, ~, jeg er sikker på at han tar feil* I suspect, nay, I am certain, that he is wrong.

jafs *sb: i en ~* at one gulp; in one mouthful.

jag *sb (voldsom bevegelse)* rush; *(hastverk)* haste, hurry. **jage** *vb* **1** *(drive vekk)* chase, drive, hunt (away, out *etc*); *jeg ble ~t ut av huset* I was driven out of the house; *jag vekk den katten!* hunt that cat away! **2** *(forfølge)* chase, hunt; *forbryteren ble ~t fra by til by* the criminal was chased/hunted from town to town; **3** *(skynde seg)* rush; tear along; hurry; **4** *(drive jakt)* hunt. **jager** *sb (torpedo~)* destroyer. **jager(fly)** *sb* fighter (plane).

jakke *sb* coat, jacket.

jakt *sb* **A 1** *(med børse)* shooting; *(til hest og som yrke)* hunting; *de gikk på ~* they went (out) hunting/shooting; **2** *(forfølgelse)* chase, pursuit; hunt; **B** *(fartøy)* sloop. **jakt|bytte** *sb* kill. **~hund** *sb* hunting/sporting dog; *(især til revejakt)* hound. **~tid** *sb* hunting/shooting season.

jambe *sb* iamb. **jambisk** *adj* iambic.

jammen *adv (sannelig)* indeed, certainly.

jammer *sb* lamentation. **jammerlig** *adj* miserable, wretched. **jamring** = *jammer.*

jamre *vb* lament, wail; moan.

januar January; *første ~* the first of January; January 1st.

jare, jarekant *sb* selvage, selvedge.

jarl *sb* earl.

jaså *adv: ~?* really? is that so? *nei ~!* indeed!

jatte *vb: ~ med* be a yes-man.

jeg *pron* I; *~ selv* I myself; *(som sb)* ego, self; *hennes annet ~* her other self; her alter ego.

jeger *sb* hunter; *(pels~)* trapper; *(sports~ ofte)* sportsman.

jekk *sb* jack. **jekke opp** *vb* jack (up).

jeksel *sb* molar.

jenke *vb* put/set to rights; *~ seg (gi etter)* comply; *~ seg etter* adapt oneself to; comply with; *det ~r seg nok* it will be all right; it will work itself out.

jente *sb* girl. **jente|aktig** *adj* girlish; *(om gutt)* feminine, sissy. **~dager** *sb* girlhood (days). **~fut** *sb* girl chaser; skirt chaser. **~navn** *sb* girl's name; *(pikenavn)* maiden name; *ta igjen ~navnet sitt* resume one's maiden name. **~skole** *sb* girls' school. **~speider** *sb* girl guide. **jentunge** *sb* little girl; slip of a girl.

jern *sb* iron; *ha mange ~ i ilden* have many irons in the fire; *han er et ~ til å arbeide* he is an indefatigable/untiring worker; *smi mens ~et er varmt* strike while the iron is hot. **jernalder** *sb* iron age. **jernbane** *sb* railway; *US* railroad; *reise med ~n* go by rail. **jernbane|-forbindelse** *sb* rail/train service; railway connection. **~kupé** *sb* (railway) compartment. **~overgang** *sb* level crossing. **~reise** *sb* railway journey. **~skinne** *sb* rail. **~stasjon** *sb* railway station. **~vogn** *sb* railway carriage; *US* railroad car; railcar. Se også *godsvogn.* **jern|disiplin** *sb* iron dicipline. **~industri** *sb* iron industry. **~malm** *sb* iron ore. **~mangel** *sb* iron deficiency. **~stang** *sb* iron bar. **~støperi** *sb* iron-foundry. **~teppe** *sb* iron curtain; *fig* blackout; *få/ha ~teppe* have (got) a blackout. **~vareforretning, ~va-**

rehandel *sb* hardware shop/*US* store; ironmonger's (shop). **~varehandler** *sb* hardware dealer; ironmonger. **~varer** *sb* hardware.

jesuitt *sb* Jesuit.

jet|fly *sb* jet plane. **~jager** *sb* jet fighter. **~motor** *sb* jet engine.

jevn *adj* **1** *(flat, glatt)* even, smooth; *en ~ (gress)plen* a smooth lawn; **2** *(regelmessig)* even, uniform; steady; *~ fart* even/steady/uniform speed; **3** *(likelig)* even; *~ fordeling* even distribution; **4** *(dagligdags)* common, everyday; plain; **5** *som adv: ~t bra* moderately well; acceptable, passable. **jevn|aldrende** *adj* of the same age; *han har ingen ~aldrende venner* he has no friends of his own age. **~byrdig** *adj: være ~byrdig med* be a match for; be equal to. **~døgn** *sb* equinox. **jevne** *vb* **1** *(gjøre flat)* level, smooth; *~ med jorden* level with the ground; **2** *(om saus etc)* thicken. **jevnføre** *vb* compare. Se *sammenligne.* **jevnhet** *sb* evenness, smoothness. **jevning** *sb (i saus etc)* thickening.

jo *svarord* **1** yes; *så du ham ikke? Jo, det gjorde jeg* didn't you see him? Yes I did; **2** *(forklarende)* you know; *han er ~ offiser* he is an officer, you know; **3** *(bebreidende, overrasket)* why; *(men) det er ~ John!* why, it's John! **4** *(innrømmende)* of course; *han er ~ ikke et geni* of course, he is no genius; *han er ~ ikke rik* he isn't rich, is he? **5** *jo ... jo* the ... the; *~ mer han får, ~ mer vil han ha* the more he gets, the more he wants; *~ før ~ heller* the sooner the better.

jobb *sb* job; piece of work. **jobbe** *vb* **1** work; **2** *(spekulere i aksjer)* speculate. **jobber** *sb* speculator. **jobbetid** *sb* boom period.

jod *sb* iodine.

jogge *vb* jog. **joggesko** *sb* running shoes.

joker *sb* **1** *(i kortspill)* joker; **2** *data* wild card.

jolle *sb* dingey, dinghy; jolly-boat.

jomfru *sb* virgin; *~ Maria* the Holy Virgin; the Virgin Mary; *gammel ~* old maid. **jomfruelig** *adj* virgin, virginal; *~ jord/mark* virgin soil. **jomfrunalsk** *adj* old-maidish, spinsterish. **jomfrutale** *sb* maiden speech.

jord *sb* **1** *~en (vår klode)* the earth; *~en er rund* the earth is round; *reise rundt ~en* travel round the world; **2** *(muld~)* earth; *(US også)* dirt; *en neve (med) ~* a handful of earth; **3** *(~overflate)* ground; *falle til ~en* fall on the ground; *under ~en* underground; **4** *(dyrknings~)* land; *den amerikanske stat gav fri ~ til nybyggere* the American State gave free land to settlers; **5** *(jordsmonn)* soil; *sandholdig/fruktbar ~* sandy/fertile soil. **jord|bruk** *sb* agriculture, farming. **~bruker** *sb* farmer. **~bruksprodukt** *sb* agricultural product. **~bunn** *sb* soil. **~bær** *sb* strawberry. **~dyrker** *sb* farmer. **jorde** **1** *sb* hayfield; *være helt på ~t* be all abroad/all at sea; **2** *vb elek (forbinde til jord)* earth; *US* ground. **jord|eiendom** *sb* landed property; lands. **jordisk** *adj* earthly. **jord|kabel** *sb* underground cable. **~kloden** *sb* the globe. **~ledning** *sb* earth; *US* ground. **~mor** *sb* midwife. **~overflaten** *sb* the surface of the earth. **~skjelv** *sb* earthquake. **~skorpen** *sb* the crust of the earth. **~skred** *sb* landslide. **jordsmonn** *sb* soil.

jort *sb* cud. **jorte** *vb (tygge drøv)* chew the cud, ruminate. Jf *drøvtygge.*

journal *sb* journal; *(sykehus~)* case record; *(for den enkelte pasient)* case sheet. **journalist** *sb* journalist.

jovial *adj* genial, jovial.

jubel *sb* shouts of joy; *(sterk fryd)* exultation, rejoicing(s). **jubileum** *sb* jubilee. **juble** *vb* rejoice; shout with joy.

jugl *sb* gimcrack, rubbish.

juks *sb* **1** *(fusk)* cheating; foul play; **2** *(fanteri, tral)* rubbish, trash. **jukse** *vb* cheat.

jul *sb* Christmas; *gledelig ~* (a) merry Christmas; *i ~en* at/during Christmas. **julaften** *sb* Christmas Eve.

jule (opp) *vb (denge)* beat (up); thrash; lick.

jule|bukk *sb* ≈ carol singer. **~dag** *sb (første ~dag)* Christmas Day; *annen ~dag* Boxing Day. **~ferie** *sb* Christmas holidays. **~gave** *sb* Christmas gift/present. **~helg** *sb* Christmas season. **~hilsen** *sb* Christmas greeting. **~kort** *sb* Christmas card. **~kveld** *sb* Christmas Eve. **~lys** *sb* Christmas candle. **~nisse** *sb* Father Christmas; Santa Claus. **~sang** *sb* ≈ Christmas carol. II *vb* 1 **tid** *sb* Christmas time. **~tre** *sb* Christmas tree. **~utstilling** *sb* Christmas display.

juli July; *annen ~* the second of July; July 2nd.

juling *sb* beating, thrashing; *få/gi kraftig ~* get/give a good beating.

jungel *sb* jungle.

juni June; *tredje ~* the third of June; June 3rd.

jur *sb* udder.

juridisk *adj* juridical, legal; *~ kandidat* graduate in law; *~ rådgiver* legal adviser; *~ student* law student; *et ~ spørsmål* a legal matter; a matter of law. **jurist** *sb (praktiserende ~)* lawyer. **jury** *sb* jury. **jus** *sb* law; *studere ~* study law.

just *adv* exactly, just. Se ellers *akkurat, nettopp; nylig.*

justere *vb* adjust, regulate, tune. **justering** *sb* adjustment, tuning.

justis|minister *sb* ≈ Minister of Justice. **~mord** *sb* miscarriage of justice. **justitiarius** *sb* ≈ Lord Chief Justice.

juv *sb* canyon, gorge.

juvel *sb* gem, jewel. **juveler** *sb* jeweller.

jypling *sb* whipper-snapper.

jævlig *adv dgl* damn; *~ god* damn good. Jf *djevelsk.*

jøde *sb* Jew. **jødehat** *sb* anti-Semitism. **jødinne** *sb* Jewess. **jødisk** *adj* Jewish.

jøkel *sb (bre)* glacier.

jøss, jøssenavn, jøsses *interj* gosh; good grief; good Lord.

jåle *sb* la-di-da, prude; silly woman. **jåleri** *sb* affectation. **jålet(e)** *adj* affected, la-di-da, niminy-piminy.

K

k *(bokstaven)* k.

kabal *sb: legge* ~ play patience; *US* play solitaire.

kabaret *sb (~forestilling)* cabaret (show).

kabel *sb* cable. **kabel|bane** *sb* cable railway. **~lengde** *sb* cable length. Jf midtsidene.

kabin *sb (i fly etc)* cabin. **kabinett** *sb* cabinet. **kabinettspørsmål** *sb: stille* ~ demand a vote of confidence.

kadaver *sb* carcase, carcass.

kadett *sb (offiserselev)* cadet; *(i marinen)* midshipman.

kafé *sb* restaurant; *(uten rettigheter og med bare lett servering)* café. **kafeteria** *sb* cafeteria.

kaffe *sb* coffee. **kaffe|bønne** *sb* coffee bean. **~grut** *sb* coffee-grounds. **~kanne, ~kjele** *sb* coffee-pot. **~kopp** *sb* coffee cup; *(kopp ~)* cup of coffee. **~kvern** *sb* coffee-mill. **~maskin** *sb* coffee machine/maker. **~pause** *sb* coffe break. **~service** *sb* coffee service/set. **~trakter** *sb* percolator.

kagge *sb* keg.

kahytt *sb* cabin. Se også *lugar.*

kai *sb* quay; *(bare for gods)* wharf.

kajakk *sb* kayak.

kakao *sb* cocoa.

kake *sb* cake; *(konditor~)* pastry; *en (konditor)~* a piece of pastry; *småkaker* biscuits; tea cakes; *US* cookies; *te og ~r* tea and cake. **kake|bu** *sb* glasshouse; *US* guardhouse. **~deig** *sb* paste, pastry. **~fat** *sb* cake dish. **~form** *sb* baking/cake tin. **~pynt** *sb* hundreds and thousands.

kakerlakk *sb* cockroach.

kakespade *sb* cake server.

kaki *sb* khaki.

kakke *vb (banke lett)* tap; knock, rap.

kakkelovn *sb* ≈ stove; fireplace.

kakle *vb* cackle. **kakling** *sb* cackle.

kaktus *sb* cactus.

kalas *sb* big feast/party.

kald *adj* cold; *(også fig)* frigid; *(ubehagelig ~)* chilly; *det er ~t i dag* it is cold today; *med ~t blod* in cold blood. **kald|blodig** *adj* cold-blooded; *(fig også)* cool, calm. **~flir** *sb* sneer. **~flire** *vb* sneer. **~start** *sb* cold starting. **~svette 1** *sb* cold sweat; **2** *vb* be in a cold sweat. Se også *kold etc.*

kalender *sb* calender.

kalesje *sb (på barnevogn, bil)* hood; *US* folding top.

kaliber *sb* bore; *(også fig)* calibre.

kalif *sb* caliph, calif). **kalifat** *sb* caliphate.

kalk *sb* **A** *(~stein)* lime; *(hvitte~)* whitewash; *(mure~)* mortar; *(pusse~)* plaster; **B** *(alter~)* chalice. **kalke** *vb (hvitte)* whitewash. **kalk|maleri** *sb* fresco. **~stein** *sb* limestone.

kalkulasjon *sb* calculation. **kalkulere** *sb* calculate.

kalkun *sb* turkey.

kalkyle *sb* calculation, estimate.

kall *sb* **A 1** *(livsoppgave)* vocation; *preste~* living; **2** *data* cure; **B** *(gamling)* gaffer; old mann. **kalle** *vb* call; *(bruke økenavn på)* call names; *~ opp etter* call/name after; *~ sammen* call together; summon. **kallesignal** *sb data* selection signal.

kalori *sb* calorie. **kaloriinnhold** *sb* calorific value.

kalosje *sb* galosh, golosh; *US* overshoe.

kalv *sb* calf. **kalvbeint** *adj* knock-kneed. **kalve** *vb* calve. **kalve|kjøtt** *sb* veal. **~stek** *sb* roast veal.

kam *sb (hår~, hane~)* comb; *(på slakt)* back, loin; *skjære alle over en ~* apply the same yardstick to everybody. **kamaksel** *sb* camshaft.

kamel *sb* camel. **kameldriver** *sb* camel driver.

kameleon *sb* chameleon. **kameleonaktig** *adj* chameleonic.

kamera *sb* camera. **kameramann** *sb* cameraman; camera operator.

kamerat *sb* companion; *ofte* friend; *dgl* buddy, pal; *(i tiltale)* old fellow; *(høytidelig og blant kommunister)* comrade; *(blant arbeidere og soldater)* mate; *dårlig ~* bad sport. **kameratekteskap** *sb* companionate marriage. **kameratskap** *sb* companionship; (good) fellowship. **kameratslig** *adj* chummy, friendly; *(uformell)* informal.

kamfer *sb* camphor. **kamferdråper** *sb* camphorated spirits.

kamgarn *sb* worsted.

kamin *sb* fireplace. **kaminhylle** mantelpiece.

kammer sb *(i nasjonalforsamling)* chamber, house. Se ellers *kammers.* **kammer|herre** *sb* chamberlain. **~musikk** *sb* chamber music. **~pike** *sb* lady's maid. **kammers** *sb* (small) room; *på ~et (fig)* in privacy; on one's own. **kammertjener** *sb* valet; gentleman's gentleman.

kamp *sb* fight, struggle; *(især i krig)* battle, combat; action; *(idretts~)* match; *også* event, game; *en avgjørende ~* a decisive battle/fight; *en fortvilet ~* a desperate struggle; *en hard ~* a hard struggle; *harde ~er (mil)* heavy fighting; *en ~ på liv og død* a fight to the death; *~en for tilværelsen* the struggle for existence/for life; *~en mot sykdom* the battle/fight against disease; *i ~ens hete* in the heat of battle; *kjempe en håpløs ~* fight a loosing battle; *spille en god ~* play a good game; *ta opp ~en* give battle; go into battle.

kampanje *sb* campaign.

kampere *sb* camp.

kampestein *sb* boulder.

kamp|felle *sb* comrade-in-arms. **~plass** *sb (slag-*

mark) battle-field; *(turneringsplass)* arena. **~rop** battle-cry, war-cry; *(fig)* slogan. **~tummel** *sb* tumult of battle. **~ånd** *sb* fighting spirit.

kamuflasje *sb* camouflage. **kamuflere** *vb* camouflage.

kanal *sb* **1** *(kunstig ~)* canal; **2** *(naturlig ~)* channel; *Kanalen (mellom England og Frankrike)* the Channel; **3** *fig* channel.

kanarifugl *sb* canary.

kandidat *sb* candidate; *(uteksaminert ~)* graduate; *(på sykehus)* house physician/surgeon; *US* intern.

kanel *sb* cinnamon.

kanin *sb* rabbit.

kanne *sb (til kaffe, te etc)* pot; *(metall~)* can.

kannibal *sb* cannibal. **kannibalisme** *sb* cannibalism.

kano *sb* canoe.

kanon *sb* **A** *(krigsvåpen)* gun; *(gammeldags ~)* cannon; **B 1** *(regel, rettesnor)* canon; **2** *(kjedesang)* canon. **kanonade** *sb* cannonade. **kanonbåt** *sb* gunboat. **kanonér** *sb* gunner. **kanon|kule** *sb* cannon-ball. **~skudd** *sb* gunshot.

kanskje *adv* perhaps, may-be.

kansler *sb* chancellor.

kant *sb* **1** *(ytterrand)* edge; *(nær ytterenden også)* border; *(rund ~)* rim; *på ~ med* at loggerheads/odds with; **2** *(~ av et stup)* brink; **3** *(distrikt, strøk)* parts, region; *de er ikke fra disse ~er* they are not from these parts; **4** *(retning)* direction, quarter; *fra alle ~er* from all quarters/directions. **kante** *vb* edge; *(kantsy)* hem. **kantet(e)** *adj* angular.

kantine *sb* canteen.

kantre *vb* capsize; turn over.

kantstein *sb* curb-stone, kerb-stone.

kaos *sb* chaos. **kaotisk** *adj* chaotic.

kapasitet *sb* capacity; *(ekspert)* adept, expert.

kapell *sb* chapel. **kapellan** *sb* curate. **kapellmester** *sb* orchestra conductor.

kaper(skip) *sb* privateer.

kapital *sb* capital. **kapitalisme** *sb* capitalism. **kapitalist** *sb* capitalist. **kapitalistisk** *adj* capitalistic. **kapital|krevende** *adj* capital-demanding. **~mangel** *sb* lack of capital. **~sterk** *adj* financially strong.

kapittel *sb* chapter. **kapittleoverskrift** *sb* chapter heading.

kapitulasjon *sb* capitulation; *betingelsesløs ~* unconditional surrender. **kapitulere** *vb* capitulate, surrender.

kapp *sb* **A:** *løpe om ~* race; *løpe om ~ med noen* race somebody; *skal vi løpe om ~ til porten?* I'll race you to the gate. **B** *(bergodde)* cape.

kappe I *sb* **1** *(yttertøy)* cloak, mantle; **2** *(advokat~, dommer~)* gown; **3** *(hodeplagg)* cap; **II** *vb (hugge/sage av)* cut. **kappelyst** *sb* competitive spirit.

kappes *vb* compete; *~ om førsteplassen* compete for the first place. **kappestrid** *sb* competition, rivalry. **kapp|kjøre** *vb* race. **~kjøring** *sb* (motor etc) race. **~løpe** *vb* race one another. Se også *kapp A*. **~løp(ing)** *sb* running race. **~ritt** *sb* horse race. **~roing** *sb* boat-race. **~ruste** *vb* compete in armament. **~rustning** *sb* armaments race.

kappsag *sb* cross-cut saw.

kapp|seilas *sb* regatta; sailing race. **~skyting** *sb* shooting match. **~svømming** *sb* swimming match.

kapre *vb* capture, seize; *(især ~ fly)* high-jack. **kaprer** *sb (fly~)* hijacker.

kapsel *sb* capsule; *(på melkeflaske)* cap; *(på brusflaske etc)* crown cork; top.

kaptein *sb* captain.

kar *sb* **A** *(beholder)* vessel; *(stort ~)* vat; **B** *(mannfolk)* man; *(fyr)* chap, fellow; *US også* guy; *en kjekk ~* a fine fellow; a decent sort.

karaffel *sb (til vin)* decanter; *(til vann)* water-bottle.

karakter *sb* **1** *(beskaffenhet)* character; *en kvinne/mann med svak ~* a woman/man of weak character; **2** *(~ på skolen)* mark; *US* grade; *jeg fikk bestandig dårlig ~ i geografi* I always got a bad mark for geography. **karakter|bok** *sb* mark book. **~fast** *adj* firm, strong; principled. **~giving** *sb* marking, rating; *US* grading. **karakterisere** *vb* characterize. **karakteristikk** *sb* characterization; *(av en person også)* character sketch. **karakteristisk** *adj* characteristic; *det er ~ for ham* it is characteristic of him. **karakterkort** *sb US* report card. **karakteroppgjør** *sb (på skole)* quarterly report.

karamell *sb* caramel, toffee.

karantene *sb* quarantine.

karat *sb* carat.

karavane *sb* caravan.

karbad *sb* tub bath.

karbid *sb* carbide.

karbonade *sb* ≈ beefburger, hamburger. **karbonpapir** *sb* carbon paper.

karde *sb/vb* card.

kardemomme *sb* cardamom.

kardialgi *sb* cardialgia, heartburn.

kardinal *sb* cardinal.

kardiogram *sb* cardiogram.

kare *vb* poke; rake, scrape; dig; *~ sammen penger* scrape together/up money; *~ seg (slepe seg)* drag oneself; *han ~t seg ut av sengen* he dragged himself out of bed.

karikatur *sb* caricature. **karikaturtegner** *sb* caricaturist, cartoonist. **karikere** *vb* caricature.

Karlsvognen the Great Bear; *US* the Big Dipper.

karm *sb (dør~)* door-case; *(vindus~)* window--frame.

karnapp *sb* bay. **karnappvindu** *sb* bay/bow window.

karneval *sb (karnevals|fest, -tid)* carnival; *(maskeball)* fancy-dress ball. **karnevalsdrakt** *sb* fancy dress.

karosseri *sb* body (of a motor vehicle).

karri *sb* curry.

karriere *sb* career. **karriere|diplomat** *sb* career

diplomat. **~kvinne** *sb* career woman.

karrig *adj (mager, skrinn)* meagre, scanty; *(om jord)* barren.

karslig *adj* masculine, manly; *(bråkjekk)* swaggering.

kart *sb* **A** *(umoden frukt)* unripe fruit/berry; **B** *(geografisk ~)* map; *et ~ over England* a map of England; *(sjø~, vær~)* chart.

kartell *sb* cartel.

kartlegge *vb (~ landområde)* map; *(~ sjøområde)* chart.

kartong *sb (papp)* cardboard, pasteboard; *(pappeske)* carton.

kartotek *sb* card file/index; *føre ~ over* keep a file of. **kartotek|føre** *vb* file. **~kort** *sb* index card. **~skap** *sb* filing cabinet. **~skuff** *sb* card-index box/drawer.

karusell *sb* merry-go-round, roundabout.

karve A *sb* caraway, cumin; **B** *vb (skjære) ~ up* cut up.

kaserne *sb* barracks; *(leie~)* tenement house.

kaskoforsikring *(for bil)* comprehensive (motor) insurance; *(for skip)* hull insurance.

kassa|apparat *sb* cash register. **~beholdning** *sb* cash balance; cash in hand. **~bok** *sb* cash book. **~kreditt** *sb* cash credit. **kasse** *sb* **1** box, case; *en ~ sigarer* a box of cigars; *en ~ øl* a case of beer; **2** *(i turnapparat)* box (horse); **3** *(i bank etc)* (cash) desk; pay desk. **kassere** *vb* discard, scrap; *en gammel, kassert jakke* an old discarded jacket; *jeg har kassert den gamle sykkelen min* I have scrapped my old bike; *~ inn* se *innkassere*. **kasserer** *sb* cashier; *(i forening, selskap)* treasurer.

kasserolle *sb* saucepan.

kassett *sb* cassette; *også data* cartridge. **kassettspiller** *sb* cassette (tape) player/recorder.

kast *sb* throw, toss; *et godt ~* a good throw; *et ~ med hodet* a toss of the head; *gi seg i ~ med* tackle.

kastanje *sb* chestnut.

kaste *sb (i India)* caste.

kaste *vb* **1** throw; *(især fig)* cast; *~ anker* cast anchor; *han ~t stein* he threw stones; *hun ~t et blikk på oss* she cast a glance at us; **2** *(kyle, slenge)* fling; *jeg ~t meg ned i en stol* I flung myself into a chair; **3** *(~ opp i luften, ~ (seg) hit og dit)* toss; *han ~t seg rundt i sengen* he tossed around on his bed; **4** *(uttrykk)* **~ bort** *(forlegge, miste)* mislay; throw away; *(somle etc bort)* waste; dally/fool away; **~ opp** *(spy)* be sick; throw up; vomit; **~ seg over** *en fiende* fall upon an enemy. **kaste|not** *sb* casting net. **~pil** *sb* dart. **~sluk** *sb* spoon-bait; *US* casting plug. **~vind** *sb* sudden gust of wind. **~våpen** *sb* missile.

kastrere *vb* castrate.

kasus *sb* case.

katakombe *sb* catacomb.

katalog *sb* catalogue; *data (fil~)* directory.

katarr *sb* catarrh.

katastrofal *adj* disastrous. **katastrofe** *sb* catastrophe, disaster.

katedral *sb* cathedral.

kategori *sb* category. **kategorisk** *adj* categorical.

katekisme *sb* catechism.

kateter *sb* **1** *(på skole)* (master's) desk; *(på universitet)* chair, lectern; **3** *(medisinsk ~)* catheter.

katolikk *sb* (Roman) Catholic. **katolisisme** *sb* (Roman) Catholicism. **katolsk** *adj* Catholic.

katt *sb* cat; *gå som ~en om den varme grøten* beat about the bush; *han gjør ikke en ~ fortred* he wouldn't hurt a fly; *henge bjella på ~en* bell the cat; *hun er ikke for ~en* she is not to be sneezed at; *i mørke er alle ~er grå* in the night all cats are grey; *kjøpe ~a i sekken* buy a pig in a poke; *når ~en er borte, danser musene på bordet* when the cat is away, the mice will play. **katte|pine** *sb: være i ~* be in a dilemma/a tight place. **~vask** *sb* a lick and a promise. **katt|ugle** *sb* brown/tawny owl. **~unge** *sb* kitten. **~øye** *sb* cat's eye; *(på sykkel etc også)* rear reflector.

kausjon *sb* security, surety; *(for løslatelse)* bail; *låne ut penger mot ~* lend money on security; *stille ~* give security; find bail; *bli løslatt mot ~* be bailed out; be released on bail. **kausjonere (for)** *vb* stand security/surety (for); *(for løslatelse)* go bail (for). **kausjonist** *sb* surety, bail.

kav *sb (jag, mas)* hustle and bustle.

kavaler *sb (herre)* gentleman; *(en dames ~)* partner. **kavaleri** *sb* cavalry, horse; *500 mann ~* 500 horse. **kavaleriregiment** *sb* regiment of horse. **kavalerist** *sb* cavalryman, trooper.

kave *vb* flail one's arms; strike the air/water; *(mase, streve)* bustle/fuss about.

kaviar *sb* caviar(e).

kavring *sb* rusk.

kei se *kjed*.

keiser *sb* emperor; *~ Vilhelm* the Emperor William. **keiser|dømme** *sb* empire. **~inne** *sb* empress; *~inne Eugenie* the Empress Eugenie. **~rike** *sb* empire. **~snitt** *sb* Caesarian operation/section.

keitet(e) *adj* awkward, clumsy.

keivhendt *adj* left-handed.

kelner *sb* waiter. Jf *servitør*.

kelter *sb* Celt. **keltisk** *adj* Celtic.

kemner *sb* city treasurer.

kenguru *sb* kangaroo.

kennel *sb* kennels *fl*.

keramiker *sb* ceramist, potter. **keramikk** *sb* ceramics *fl*; pottery.

kidnappe *vb* kidnap. **kidnapper** *sb* kidnapper.

kike *vb (ved kikhoste)* whoop. **kikhoste** *sb* whooping-cough.

kikk *sb: ta en ~ på* have a look at. **kikke** *vb* peep. **kikkert** *sb* (a pair of) binoculars/field glasses; *(stjerne~ etc)* telescope; *(teater~)* (a pair of) opera-glasses.

kilde *sb* **1** *(oppkomme)* spring; **2** *(opphav, årsak)* source; *en ~ til glede* a source of joy; *fra pålitelig ~* on good authority. **kilde|kode** *sb data* source code. **~skrift** *sb* primary source. **~språk** *sb* source language. **~vann** *sb* spring water.

kildre = *kile B.* **kile A I 1** *sb (blei)* wedge; **2** *(i plagg)* gusset; **II** *vb (bruke kile)* wedge; **B** *vb (irritere, kildre)* tickle; *det ~r i halsen* my throat tickles. **kilen** *adj* ticklish.

kilevink *sb* box on the ear.

killing *sb* kid.

kilo|(gram) *sb* kilogram(me). **~meter** *sb* kilometre.

kim(e) *sb* germ; embryo.

kime *vb* chime; peal, ring.

kim(m)ing *sb (synsrand)* (visible) horizon.

kimono *sb* kimono.

kinaputt *sb* Chinese cracker; firecracker.

kingel *sb* spider. **kingelvev** *sb* cobweb, spider web.

kinin *sb* quinine.

kink *sb: ~ i ryggen* a crick in one's back.

kinkig *adj* delicate, ticklish; awkward.

kinn *sb* cheek.

kino *sb* cinema; picture palace, *US også* movies; movie theater; *gå på ~* go to the movies/the pictures.

kiosk *sb* kiosk; *avis~* news-stand; *telefon~* call box; *US* booth.

kippe *vb (rykke)* flip, jerk; *skoen ~r* the shoe slips off at the heel.

kippers *sb* kipper.

kirke *sb* **1** church; *i ~n (om selve bygningen)* in the church; *(om gudstjenesten)* in church; *de gikk i ~n hver søndag* they went to church every Sunday; **2** *(dissenter~)* chapel. **kirke|gård** *sb* churchyard; *(om gravlund uten kirke)* cemetery. **~klokke** *sb* church bell. Jf *~ur.* **~samfunn** *sb* religious community. **~sogn** *sb* parish. **~stol** *sb* pew. **~tjener** *sb* verger; *(~tjener og graver)* sexton. **~tårn** *sb* church tower. **~ur** church clock. **~verge** *sb* church-warden. **~år** *sb* church year; ecclesiastical year.

kirsebær *sb* cherry.

kirurg *sb* surgeon.

kiste *sb* chest; *(lik~)* coffin; *US* casket.

kitt *sb* putty. **kitte** *vb* putty.

kittel *sb (dame~, kunstners ~)* smock; *(stundom)* overall; *(leges hvite ~)* (white) coat.

kiv *sb* quarrel. **kives** *vb* quarrel.

kjake *sb* jaw, jowl.

kjapp *adj* fast, quick.

kjas *sb* bustle, fuss; *~ og mas* toil and moil.

kje *sb* kid.

kjede A 1 *sb* chain; **2** *vb: ~ sammen* link up; **B** *vb (virke ~lig)* bore; *~ seg* be bored; *de ~t seg* they were bored; *du ~r meg* you are boring me; *han så ut til å ~ seg* he looked bored; *vi holdt på å ~ oss i hjel* we were bored to death. **kjedelig** *adj* **1** *(lite morsom)* boring, dull; *en ~ bok* a dull book; **2** *(besværlig)* tiresome; *en ~ jobb* a tiresome job; **3** *(pinlig, uheldig)* awkward; *en ~ situasjon* an awkward/unpleasant situation. **kjede|røyke** *vb* chain-smoke. **~røyker** *sb* chain smoker. **kjedsommelig** *adj* boring, dull. **kjedsommelighet** *sb* boredom; tediousness, tedium.

kjeft *sb: bruke ~* scold; jaw, nag; *få ~* get a scolding; *hold ~!* shut up! hold your tongue! *ikke en ~* not a living soul; *være stor i kjeften* talk big. **kjefte** *vb* scold; jaw, nag.

kjegle *sb* cone. **kjegle|formet** *adj* conical. **~snitt** *sb* conic section.

kjekk *adj* **1** *(freidig, frimodig)* cheerful; free and easy; **2** *(dristig)* brave, plucky; **3** *(pen, tiltalende)* handsome; likable, nice; *en ~ kar* a fine fellow; a good sort; **4** *(i vigør)* fit, healthy. **kjekke seg** *vb* swagger, swank; ride the high horse.

kjekle *vb* quarrel, wrangle; argue.

kjeks *sb* biscuit, cracker.

kjel(e) sb *(te~, vann~ etc)* kettle; *(damp~, sentralfyr~ etc)* boiler. **kjeledress** *sb* boiler suit; *(for barn)* combination suit; storm suit.

kjelke *sb* sledge; *US* sled, toboggan; *ake på ~* sledge, toboggan.

kjeller *sb (~etasje)* basement; *(~rom)* cellar; *i ~en* in the basement. **kjeller|bod, ~bu** *sb* cellar. **~dekk** *sb petro* cellar deck.

kjeltring *sb* scoundrel. **kjeltring|aktig** *adj* scoundrelly. **~pakk** *sb* pack of scoundrels. **~strek** *sb* scoundrelly/vile trick.

kjemi *sb* chemistry. **kjemikalier** *sb fl* chemicals. **kjemiker** *sb* (pure) chemist. Jf *apoteker).* **kjemisk** *adj* chemical.

kjemme *vb* comb.

kjempe 1 *sb* giant; *(sagnhelt)* hero; **2** *vb (slåss)* fight; *(~ seigt, stritte imot)* struggle; *(konkurrere)* compete; *de ~t for sitt land* they fought for their country; *hun måtte ~ mot store vanskeligheter* she struggled/had to struggle with serious difficulties. **kjempe|arbeid** *sb* Herculean task. **~messig** *adj* gigantic, huge.

kjenne *vb* **1** *(ha kjennskap til)* know; *jeg ~r dem godt* I know them well; **2** *(føle)* feel; *hun kjente at hjertet banket* she felt her heart beating; **3** *(uttrykk)* **~ av navn/utseende** know by name/sight; **~ fra hverandre** know one from the other; tell apart; **~ igjen** recognize; *~r du deg igjen her?* do you recognize the place? *jeg kjente henne nesten ikke igjen* I hardly recognized her; **lære å ~** come/get to know; become/get acquainted with; *hvordan lærte dere å ~ hverandre?* how did you come to know each other? **~ på** *(dvs ta på)* feel; *kjenn på dette stoffet* feel this material; *~ noen på ...* know somebody by ...; *jeg ~r ham på stemmen* I know him by his voice; **~ på seg** feel; have a feeling; *jeg ~r på meg at noe kommer til å hende* I have a feeling that something is going to happen; **~ seg** feel; *hun kjente seg bedre* she felt better; **~ skyldig** find guilty; **~ til** know about; *jeg ~r til den historien* I know about that affair. **kjennelig** *adj* recognizable (*på* by). **kjennelse** *sb* decision; *(jurys ~)* verdict. **kjennemerke** *sb* mark, sign. **kjenner** *sb* judge, connoisseur. **kjennetegn** *sb* mark, sign; characteristic. **kjenning** *sb* acquaintance. **kjennskap** *sb* knowledge. **kjensel** *sb: dra ~ på* recognize. **kjensgjerning** *sb* fact.

kjensle *sb* feeling. Se for øvrig *følelse.*

kjent *adj* well-known, famous; *(vel~)* familiar; *han er ~ for sin lærdom/som sanger* he is known for his learning/as a singer; *jeg er godt ~ i byen* I know the town well; *jeg er ikke ~ her* I am a stranger here. **kjentmann** *sb* guide, pilot.

kjepp *sb* rod, stick, switch. **kjepphest** *sb* hobbyhorse; *(fig også)* hobby; *det er ~en hans ~* that is his favourite subject.

kjerne A *sb* **1** *a) (i nøtter)* kernel; *b) (i epler, pærer, appelsiner)* pip, seed; *c) (i druer)* stone; **2** *fig* core, heart; essence; **B 1** *sb (til å lage smør i)* churn; **2** *vb (lage smør)* churn. **kjerne|boring** *sb* core drilling. **~fysiker** *sb* nuclear physicist. **~fysikk** *sb* nuclear physics. **~hus** *sb* core. **~kar** *sb* splendid fellow. **~prøve** *sb (ved boring)* core sample. **~punkt** *sb* essential point; crux of the matter; core. **~sunn** *adj* thoroughly healthy. **~tropper** *sb fl* picked/choice troops.

kjerre *sb* cart.

kjerring *sb* old woman.

kjertel *sb* gland.

kjette she-cat, tabby, tabby-cat.

kjetter *sb* heretic. **kjetteri** *sb* heresy. **kjettersk** *adj* heretical.

kjetting *sb* chain.

kjeve *adj* jaw.

kjevle 1 *sb (til bakst)* rolling-pin; **2** *vb* roll out.

kjole *sb (dame~)* dress, frock; *(selskaps~)* gown; *(herre~)* dress coat; tailcoat; *~ og hvitt* (full) evening dress; white tie; tails.

kjæle *vb* caress, fondle, pet; cuddle, hug. **kjæle|degge** *sb* pet, darling. **~dyr** *sb* pet. **kjælen** *adj* cuddlesome; affectionate, loving. **kjælenavn** *sb* pet name. **kjæling** *sb* caressing, petting.

kjær *adj* beloved, dear; *en ~ venn* a dear friend; *hennes ~e mann* her beloved husband; *få ~* get fond of; *(bli forelsket i)* fall in love with; *ha ~* be fond of; love.

kjæremål *sb (jur)* appeal.

kjæreste *sb* sweetheart; *(gutts ~)* girl friend; *(pikes ~)* boy friend. Se også *forlovede*.

kjærkommen *adj* welcome; *en ~ gjest* a welcome guest.

kjærlig *adj* affectionate, loving; fond; *~ hilsen* se hilsen.

kjærlighet *sb* love, affection; *(neste~)* charity; *~ ved første blikk* love at first sight; *~en er blind* love is blind; *tro, håp og ~* faith, hope and charity; *~ til a) (om personer)* love for; *en mors ~ til sine barn* a mother's love for her children; *b) (for øvrig)* love of; *~ til sitt land* love of one's country. **kjærlighet på pinne** *sb* lollipop; *US* (candy) sucker. **kjærlighets|affære** *sb* love-affair. **~brev** *sb* love-letter. **~forhold** *sb* love--affair. **~historie** *sb* love-affair; *(~fortelling)* love story. **~sorg** *sb: dø av ~sorg* die of a broken heart. **kjær|tegn** *sb* caress. **~tegne** *vb* caress, fondle, pet.

kjøkken *sb* kitchen. **kjøkken|benk** *sb* kitchen unit/workbench. **~hage** *sb* kitchen/vegetable garden. **~redskaper** *sb fl* kitchen utensils. II *vb* 1 **sjef** *sb* chef. **~skriver** *sb* kitchen snooper. **~tjeneste** *sb (mil)* kitchen fatigues. **~trapp** *sb* backstairs.

kjøl *sb* keel; *på rett ~* on an even keel; *få på rett ~ (fig)* help to get straight; *komme på rett ~* right oneself.

kjøle|skap *sb* refrigerator; *dgl* fridge. **~væske** *sb* coolant. **kjølig** *adj (behagelig ~)* cool; *(ubehagelig ~)* chilly. **kjølighet** *sb* coolness, chill. **kjølne** *vb* cool (down).

kjønn *sb* sex; *(gram)* gender; *det svake ~* the weaker sex. **kjønns|deler** = *~organer*. **~diskriminering** *sb* sex discrimination; sexism. **~drift** *sb* sex(ual) instinct/urge. **~liv** *sb* sex(ual) life. **~løs** *adj* sexless. **~moden** *adj* sexually mature. **~moral** *sb* sexual morality. **~organer** *sb fl* genitals. **~roller** *sb fl* sex roles. **~sykdom** *sb* venereal disease.

kjøp *sb* **1** *(innkjøp)* buying, purchase; *~-og-kast* buy-and-scrap; *~ og salg* purchase and sale; *ved ~et av bilen* at the purchase of the car; **2** *(handel)* bargain, deal; *det var godt ~* it was a good bargain; *på ~et* into the bargain. **kjøpe** *vb* buy; *~ billig/dyrt* buy cheap/dear; *han kjøpte kniven av meg for tre pund* he bought the knife from me for £3; *jeg hadde kjøpt den til nedsatt pris* I had bought it at a reduced price. **kjøpe|kontrakt** *sb* sales contract. **~kraft** *sb* purchasing/spending power. **kjøper** *sb* buyer. **kjøpe|senter** *sb* shopping centre. **~sum** *sb* purchase price. **kjøpmann** *sb* shopkeeper; *US* storekeeper; *(dagligvare~)* grocer; *(engros~)* merchant.

kjør *sb: i ett ~* at a stretch; without a break. **kjøre** *vb* **1** *(føre ~tøy)* drive; *~ bil* drive a car; *hun ~r godt* she drives well; **2** *(~ med kjøretøy)* ride; *~ med buss/karusell* ride in a bus/on a merry-go-round; *~ (på) sykkel* ride (on) a bicycle; **3** *(~ personer)* drive, take; *jeg kjørte dem til stasjonen* I drove them to the station; *kan du ~ meg til Hamar?* can you drive/take me to Hamar? **4** *(om ~tøyet)* run; *bilen kjørte mot et tre* the car ran against a tree; *toget kjørte fort* the train ran/travelled fast; **5** *(betjene maskiner etc)* operate; *(om dataprogram også)* run; **6** *(uttrykk) ~ en film* run a film; *~ en tur* go for a ride; *~ over* run over; *~ på en* run into somebody; *~ utfor* run off the road. **kjøre|bane** *sb* roadway. **~felt** *sb* lane. **~kort** *sb* driver's license. **~prøve** *sb* driving/*US* driver's test. **~tur** *sb* ride. **~tøy** *sb* carriage, vehicle. **kjøring** *sb* driving, motoring; operation, run(ning).

kjøter *sb* cur, mongrel.

kjøtt *sb (på levende vesener)* flesh; *~ og blod* flesh and blood; *(~ som mat)* meat; *fersk/frosset ~* fresh/frozen meat. **kjøtt|bein** *sb* bone. **~bolle** *sb* meat-ball. **~deig** *sb* minced/*US* ground meat. **~forretning** *sb* butcher's shop. **~kake** *sb* rissole. **~kraft** *sb* meat juice; gravy. **~kvern** *sb* meat-mincer; mincing machine; *US* meat grinder. **kjøttmeis** *sb* titmouse.

kl. *(fork* for *klokken)* o'clock; *~ 5* at 5 o'clock.

klabb *sb: ~ og babb* a big mess.

kladd *sb* rough draft. **kladde** *vb* **1** *(skrive kladd)* draft; make a rough draft (of); **2** *(om skiføre) det ~r, skiene ~r* the snow is sticking to the skis. **kladde|bok** *sb* rough book. **~føre** *sb* sticking skiing conditions.

~papir rough paper; draft paper.

klaff *sb* flap; *(bordklaff også)* leaf; *(på musikkinstrument)* key; *få full ~* carry all before one; click good and proper. **klaffe** *(passe, stemme)* fit; *det ~r* it fits (properly); it tallies; *alt ~t* everything came off well.

klage I *sb* **1** *(klagemål)* complaint; *det er ingen grunn til ~* there is no cause for complaint; **2** *(uttrykk for sorg)* lament; *(jamring)* wailing; **II** *vb (beklage seg)* complain; *han ~t over smerter* he complained of a pain; *har De noe å ~ over?* have you any complaints? **klage|mål, ~punkt** *sb* complaint, grievance. **~sang** *sb* dirge, elegy.

klam *adj* clammy, damp.

klamme *(sb* bracket; *sette i ~r* put in brackets. **klammeri** *sb* quarrel; brawl, row.

klamp *sb* block; *en ~ om foten* a clog on one's movements.

klamre *vb: ~ seg til* cling to.

klan *sb* clan.

klander *sb* blame. **klandre** *vb* blame.

klang *sb* ring, sound; *(tonefall også)* tone; *klokke~* ringing; *det var en vennlig ~ i stemmen hennes* there was a friendly ring in her voice.

klapp *sb (lett slag)* pat, tap, rap; *(raskere)* slap; *(som kjærtegn)* pat; *(som bifall)* applause; clapping (of hands). **klappe** *vb* **1** *(kjærtegnende)* pat; *(med strykende bevegelse)* stroke; **2** *(~ i hendene)* clap; applaud; *de ~t for ham* they applauded him.

klapperslange *sb* rattlesnake. **klapre** *vb* rattle; *(om tenner)* chatter.

klaps *sb* slap. **klapse** *vb* slap.

klar *adj* **1** clear; *~ himmel* a clear sky; *~t vann* clear water; *en ~ stemme* a clear voice; *meningen er ganske klar* the meaning is quite clear; **2** *(lysende)* bright; *~t solskinn* bright sunshine; **3** *(parat)* ready; *~ til bruk* ready for use; *er du ~* are you ready? **4** *(ved bevissthet)* conscious; **5** *(uttrykk)* **gå ~ av** clear; *bilen gikk så vidt ~ av portstolpen* the car just cleared the gate-post; **~t som dagen** clear as daylight; *være/bli ~* **over** *(også)* realize; *da han ble ~ over hva som var hendt* when he realized what had happened; *er du ~ over det?* do you realize that? **klare** *vb (greie)* manage; *han klarte seg bra* he did well/splendidly; *jeg ~r meg ikke uten din hjelp* I cannot do without your help; *~r du deg med hundre pund i måneden?* can you manage on £100 a month? **klargjøre** *vb* **1** *(gjøre klar)* get/make ready; **2** *(forklare)* make clear; elucidate, explain.

klarhet *sb* clearness.

klarinett *sb* clarinet.

klarsynt *adj* clear-sighted.

klase *sb* bunch, cluster.

klask *sb* slap, smack. **klaske** *vb* slap, smack.

klasse *sb* class; *(i videregående skole)* form; *(~værelse)* class-room, form-room. **klasse|bevisst** *adj* class-conscious. **~forskjell** *sb* class distinction. **~forstander** *sb* formmaster. **~kamerat** *sb* class-mate, formmate. **~kamp** *sb* class struggle. **~lærer** *sb* formmaster. **~værelse** *sb* class-room, form-room.

klassiker *sb* classic. **klassisk** *adj* classic; *(især om gresk og romersk oldtid)* classical; *~ musikk* classical music; *~ mytologi* classical mythology.

klatre *vb* climb; *vi ~t opp i treet* we climbed the tree.

klatt *sb* **1** *(klump)* small lump; *en smør~* a lump of butter; **2** *(flekk)* blot.

klave *sb* collar.

klaver *sb* piano; *han spilte ~* he played the piano.

kle *vb* **1** *(iføre klær)* dress; *~ seg stygt* dress badly; **2** *(holde med klær)* clothe; *fø og ~ barna* feed and clothe the children; **3** *(være kledelig)* become; *den kjolen ~r deg* that dress becomes you; **4** *(dekke)* coat, cover; *(~ innvendig)* line; **5** *(uttrykk)* **~ av** undress; **~ på** dress; **~ seg** dress; **~ seg om** change; *(skifte til finklær også)* dress; **~ seg ut** *som* dress up as.

klebe *vb* stick; *(med lim)* glue; *(med klister)* paste; *(henge fast)* stick. **klebrig** *adj* sticky.

klede *sb (stoff)* cloth. Se også *klær*. **kledelig** *adj* becoming. **kledning** *sb (ytre lag)* covering; *(klær)* dress.

klegg *sb* gadfly, horsefly.

klein *(dårlig)* bad, poor; *(syk)* ill. Se for øvrig *dårlig, syk*.

kleiv *sb* steep rocky path.

klekke ut *vb* hatch (out); *~ ut kyllinger/en plan* hatch chickens/hatch out a plan. **klekkelig** *adj: en ~ sum* substantial sum of money; *et ~ honorar* a handsome fee.

klem *sb (kjærtegn)* hug, squeeze; *med fynd og ~* forcibly; *på ~* ajar. **klemme** *vb (presse)* press, squeeze; *(om sko)* pinch; *(som kjærtegn)* hug, squeeze; *klem i vei! klem på!* fire away! go ahead!

klemt *sb* toll; *(av trikk)* clang. **klemte** *vb* toll; clang.

klenge *vb* cling; *~ seg inn på* force one's company on. **klengenavn** *sb* nickname. **klengete** *adj* clinging, importunate.

klenodie, klenodium *sb* gem, jewel, treasure.

kles|børste *sb* clothes-brush. **~henger** *sb* clothes-hanger. **~klype** *sb* clothes-peg; *US* clothes-pin. **~plagg** *sb* garment; piece of clothing; *fl* clothes. **~skap** *sb* wardrobe. **~snor** *sb* clothes-line. **~vask** *sb* washing; *(vasketøy også)* wash.

kli *sb* bran.

klient *sb* client. **klientell** *sb* clientèle.

klikk *sb* **1** *(gruppe)* clique, set; **2** *(lyd)* click, snap; *slå ~* fail. **klikke** *vb (om skytevåpen)* misfire; *(mislykkes)* fail; *(om lyd)* click, snap.

klima *sb* climate.

klimaks *sb* climax.

klimpre *vb* strum, thrum.

kline *vb* **1** *(smøre)* smear; **2** *(kjæle)* neck, pet.

klinge *vb* ring, sound.

klinikk *sb* hospital; *fødsels~* lying-in/maternity hospital.

klining *sb (kjæling)* necking, petting.

klinke A *sb (dør~)* door handle; latch; **B** *vb* **1** *(med nagler)* rivet; **2** *(med glass: skåle)* touch glasses.

klipp *sb* cut; *(hår~)* hair-cut.

klippe A *sb (berg)* rock; *(bratt ~ ved havet)* cliff; **B** *vb (med saks etc)* cut, clip; *(stusse)* trim; *(~ sauer)* shear; *~ hull* punch; *han klipte gutten* he cut the boy's hair; *hekken ble klipt* the hedge was trimmed; *konduktøren klipte billetten* the guard punched the ticket. **klippfisk** *sb* dried cod.

klips *sb (til øret)* ear clips.

klirre *vb* rattle; *det ~t i vindusrutene* the window--panes rattled.

klisjé *sb* (printing) block; *fig* cliché.

kliss *sb* sticky mass. **klisset(e)** *adj* sticky, smeary; *fig* sentimental.

klister *sb* paste. **klistre** *vb* paste.

klo *sb* claw.

kloakk *sb* sewer.

klode *sb* globe.

klok *adj* **1** *(erfaren, vis)* wise; *det var ~t av deg* it was wise of you; *en ~ gammel mann* a wise old man; **2** *(fornuftig)* sensible; *det ~este du kan gjøre* the most sensible thing you can do; *en ~ plan* a sensible plan; *så ~t av deg* how sensible of you; **3** *(intelligent, også om dyr)* clever, intelligent.

klokke *sb* **1** *(til å ringe med)* bell; *ringe med/på ~n* ring the bell; **2** *(armbåndsur, lommeur)* watch; *(større ur)* clock; *~n er mange* it is late; *~n er tolv* it is 12 o'clock; *de kom ~n tre* they came at 3 o'clock. **klokke|slag** *sb* stroke of a bell/clock. **~slett** *sb* hour.

klokskap *sb (visdom)* wisdom; *(intelligens)* intelligence.

klor *sb (risp)* scratch. **klore** claw, scratch; *~ ned* scrawl.

kloroform *sb* chloroform. **kloroformere** *vb* chloroform.

klosett *sb* lavatory, toilet.

kloss A *adj, adv: ~ inntil* close to; *på ~ hold* at a close range; **B** *sb* block; *bygge~ (som leketøy)* brick; *en tre~* a block of wood. **klosset(e)** *adj* clumsy, awkward; *~ oppførsel* clumsy behaviour; *en ~ opptreden* awkward manners.

kloster *sb(munke~)* monastery; *(nonne~)* convent.

klov *sb* hoof.

klovn *sb* clown; *(nedsettende)* buffoon; *(kløne)* clumsy fool.

klubb *sb* club; *i klubben* at the club. **klubbe 1** *sb* mallet; *(formanns~)* gavel; **2** *~ ned* bang, gavel; *(på møte etc også)* call to order.

klukke *vb (om høne)* cluck; *(i flaske)* gurgle; *(le)* chuckle.

klump *sb* lump. **klumpe** *vb: ~ seg sammen* crowd/huddle together. **klumpfot** *sb* clubfoot.

klunke *vb (på instrument)* strum.

klusse *vb (i skrivebok)* blot; *(arbeide klosset)* bungle (up); mess about.

klut *sb* cloth.

klynge 1 *sb* cluster, group; **2** *vb: ~ seg sammen* cluster; crowd (together); *~ seg til* cling to; *de ~t seg til hverandre* they clung together/to one another.

klynke *vb* whimper. **klynking** *sb* whimpering.

klype *sb* pinch; *en ~ salt* a pinch of salt. **klype** *vb* pinch; *han kløp meg i armen* he pinched my arm.

klyse *sb* clot, gob.

klystér *sb* enema.

klyve *vb* climb; *hun kløv opp i et tre* she climbed a tree.

klær *sb koll* clothes.

klø *vb* **1** *(med neglene etc)* scratch; *jeg ~dde henne på ryggen* I scratched her back; **2** *(føle kløe)* itch, tickle; *~ deg hvis det ~r* scratch yourself if you itch; *jeg ~r i nesen* my nose tickles; *jeg ~r i fingrene etter å* my fingers itch to. **kløe** *sb* itch(ing).

kløft *sb* cleft; *(i jordoverflaten)* gap, ravine; *(bred, dyp avgrunn)* chasm; *(mellom bratte fjell)* gorge.

kløkt *sb* sagacity, shrewdness.

kløne *sb* bungler; clumsy person. **kløenet(e)** *adj* awkward, clumsy.

kløpper *sb: en ~ til* a dab hand/a masterhand at.

kløtsj *sb (på bil)* clutch.

kløver *sb* **1** *(planten)* clover; **2** *(i kort)* clubs; *~ess* ace of clubs.

kløv|hest *sb* packhorse. **~sal** *sb* pack-saddle.

kløyve cleave, split.

kna *vb* knead.

knabbe *vb* pinch.

knagg *sb* peg.

knake *vb* crackle, creak, groan; *det ~r i isen* the ice is creaking.

knakke *vb* knock.

knall *sb* bang, crack, pop; report. **knalle** *vb* bang, crack, pop. **knall|hette, ~perle** *sb* percussion cap.

knapp *adj (snau)* scarce; *det er knapt med tobakk* tobacco is scarce; *tiden er ~* time is short. Se også *knapt.*

knapp *sb* button. **knappe** *sb* button; *~ igjen* button down/up; *~ opp* unbutton. **knappenål** *sb* pin.

knapphet *sb* **1** *(mangel)* scarcity, shortage; **2** *(korthet)* brevity, conciseness.

knapt *adv* hardly, scarcely; *~ ... før* hardly/scarcely ... when; *han hadde ~ begynt å tale før ...* he had hardly/scarcely begun to speak when ...

knas *sb: gå i ~* be smashed. **knase** *vb* **1** *(om lyd)* crunch, crackle; **2** *(knuse)* crush, crunch.

knask *sb koll* sweets; *US* candy. **knaske** *vb* crunch.

knatt, knaus *sb* crag, rock.

kne *sb* knee; *de falt på ~* they went down on their knees.

knebel *sb* gag. **kneble** *sb* gag.

knebukser *sb (korte)* shorts; *(trange)* breeches; *(nikkers)* plus-fours.

knegge *vb* **1** *(om hest)* neigh, whinny; **2** *(le)* chuckle.

kneise *vb* **1** *(løfte hodet)* hold one's head high; **2** *(om ting)* tower; *kirketårnet ~r over landsbyen* the church towers above the village.

knekk *sb* **1** *(lyd, sprekk)* crack; **2** *(bøy, vinkel)* bend; **3** *fig: han har fått en ~ (fysisk)* his health is broken;

(mentalt) he has been a broken man ever since.

knekke *vb* break, crack, snap; ~ *nakken* break one's neck; ~ *nøtter* crack nuts.

knekt *sb* boy, lad; fellow; *(nedsettende)* rascal; *(i kortspill)* Jack, knave.

knele *vb* kneel; *han knelte for henne* he knelt before/to her.

knep *sb* trick; *han kan/kjenner alle ~ene* he knows all the tricks.

knepen *adj: en ~ seier* a narrow victory; *knepent flertall* a narrow majority.

knepp *sb* click. **kneppe** *vb* click. Jf *knappe*.

knipe 1 *sb (vanskelighet)* fix, pinch; difficulty, difficulties; *jeg kom i ~* I got (myself) into a fix/difficulties; **2** *vb* pinch; ~ *(inn) på* be niggardly with/sparing of; *morderen ble ~t* the murderer was caught; *om det ~r* at a pinch. **knipe|tak** *sb: i et ~* at a pinch. **~tang** *sb: en ~* (a pair of) pincers.

kniple *vb* make lace. **kniplinger** *sb* lace.

knippe *sb* bunch, bundle.

knips *sb* rap, snap. **knipse** *vb* fillip; *(med smell)* snap; ~ *med fingrene* snap one's fingers.

knirke *vb* creak; ~ *og knake* creak and groan; *det gikk ~fritt* it went off smoothly.

knis *sb* giggle, snigger, titter. **knise** *vb* giggle, snigger, titter.

knitre *vb* crackle.

kniv *sb* knife; *krig på ~en* war to the knife; *sette en ~en på strupen* present somebody with an ultimatum.

knoke *sb* knuckle. **knokkel** *sb* bone. **knoklet(e)** *adj* bony, angular.

knoll *sb (på rot)* tuber; *(slang: hode)* nut.

knop *sb* knot.

knopp *sb* bud; *i ~* in bud; *skyte ~* be in bud. **knoppe seg** *vb* bud. **knoppskyting** *sb* budding.

knott *sb* **1** button, knob; **2** *(mygg)* gnat, midge.

knudret(e) *adj* rough, rugged; *(om tre)* gnarled, knotty.

knuge *vb (klemme)* press, squeeze; *(tynge)* depress, oppress; *(omfavne hardt)* hug.

knupp *sb: du er en ~* you are a brick/peach. Se for øvrig *knopp*.

knurre *vb (om dyr)* growl; snarl; *(mukke)* grumble.

knuse *vb* **1** *(slå i stykker)* break, smash; *(finknuse)* crush; ~ *til fint pulver* crush into fine powder; *glasset ble knust* the glass was broken; **2** *(klemme i stykker)* crush; ~ *bær (for safting etc)* crush berries; **3** *(tilintetgjøre)* break, crush.

knute *sb* knot; *en ~ på tråden* a disagreement; a tiff; *knyte en ~* tie a knot. **knutepunkt** *sb (for jernbane etc)* junction.

kny *vb: uten å ~* without a murmur.

knytte I *sb (bunt)* bundle; **II** *vb* **1** *(binde sammen, lage knute)* tie; **2** *(uttrykk)* ~ *neven* clench one's fist; ~ *sammen (forene)* unite; *de to familiene er ~t sammen ved ekteskap* the two families are united by marriage; ~ *til* attach to; *hun var sterkt ~t til broren (sin)* she was strongly attached to her brother; ~ *betingelser til* attach conditions to; ~ *noen bemerkninger til* say a few words about. **knyttneve** *sb* (clenched) fist.

koagulere *vb* coagulate.

koalisjon *sb* coalition.

kobbe *sb* seal.

kobbel *sb (på to hunder)* couple; *(på tre)* leash; *(på flere)* pack.

kobber *sb* copper. **~kobbermynt** *sb* copper.

koble *vb* couple; ~ *av (slappe av)* relax; ~ *fra* disconnect, uncouple; unplug; ~ *til* attach/connect/couple (to); plug in; ~ *ut (kløtsjen)* disengage the clutch.

kode *sb* code. **kodeomformer** *sb data* code converter.

koeffisient *sb* coefficient.

koffein *sb* caffeine.

koffert *sb* suitcase; *(stor ~)* trunk.

kofte *sb* ≈ (Norwegian) sweater.

kokain *sb* cocaine.

koke 1 *vb* boil; *jeg kokte (meg) et egg* I boiled (myself) an egg; *vannet ~r* the water is boiling; **2** *(lage mat)* cook. **koke|apparat** *sb* cooker. **~bok** *sb* cookery book. **~plate** *sb* hot plate. **~punkt** *sb* boiling-point.

kokett *adj* coquettish.

kokhet *adj* boiling hot.

kokk, kokke *sb* cook.

kokosnøtt *sb* coconut.

koks *sb* coke. **koks|gass** *sb* coker gas. **~verk** *sb* coker.

kolbe *sb* **1** *(gevær~)* butt; **2** *(beholder)* flask.

koldbrann *sb* gangrene.

koldkrem *sb* cold cream.

kolera *sb* cholera.

kolje *sb* haddock.

kollbøtte *sb* somersault; *slå ~* turn/throw a somersault.

kollega *sb* colleague, fellow.

kollektiv *adj, sb* collective.

kolli *sb* package; piece of luggage.

kollidere *vb* collide. **kollisjon** *sb* collision.

kolon *sb* colon.

koloni *sb* colony.

kolonial|forretning, ~handel *sb* grocer's (shop). **~varer** *sb koll* groceries. Jf *dagligvarer etc*.

kolonisasjon *sb* colonization. **kolonisere** *vb* colonize. **kolonist** *sb* colonist.

kolonne *sb* column; *petro også* tower.

koloss *sb* colossus. **kolossal** *adj* colossal, enormous.

kombinasjon *sb* combination. **kombinere** *vb* combine.

komedie *sb* comedy.

komet *sb* comet.

komfort *sb* comfort. **komfortabel** *adj* comfortable.

komfyr *sb* kitchen range; *(gass~, elektrisk ~) sb* cooker.

komisk *adj (bevisst, som kunst)* comic; *(ufrivillig ~,* *latterlig)* comical, funny; *det komiske ved saken* the funny part of it.

komité *sb* committee; *hun satt i flere ~er* she was on several committees.

komma *sb* comma.

kommandere *vb* command, order; *han kommanderte meg til å gjøre det* he commanded/ordered me to do it. **kommando** *sb* **1** *(herredømme, ordre)* command; *ha ~en (over)* be in command (of). **kommando|bro** *sb* bridge. **~kode** *sb data* command code. **~meny** *sb data* command menu.

komme *vb* **1** *(~ til stede)* come; *jeg ventet dem, men de kom ikke* I expected them, but they never came; **2** *(ankomme)* arrive, come; *gjestene kom* the guests arrived; **3** *(greie å ~, nå)* get; *hvordan ~r man herfra til London?* how does one get from here to London? *pakken kom aldri hit* the parcel never got here; *vi kunne ikke ~ inn* we couldn't get in; **4** *(utrykk)* **~ an:** *kom an!* come along! *~ an på* depend on; *det ~r an på været* it depends on the weather; **~ av:** *det ~r av* it is due to; it is because; *det ~r av at de er gamle* it is because they are old; *hva ~r jordskjelv av?* what are earthquakes due to? **~ bort** *(forsvinne)* disappear; get lost; **~ etter** *(for å hente)* come to fetch; *hun kom for å hente boken* she came to fetch the book; **~ fra det:** *han kom fra det med livet* he escaped alive/with his life; **~ frem** arrive; *de kom frem klokken seks* they arrived at six o'clock; *~ frem i livet/i verden* get on; **~ igjen** come back; return; **~ med** *(ha med seg)* bring; *~ godt med* come in handy/useful; **~ opp** *(bli kjent)* be discovered; be known; come to light; **~ over** *(støte på tilfeldig)* come across; *jeg kom over en interessant bok her forleden* I came across an interesting book the other day; **~ på** *(huske)* remember; think of; *jeg kan ikke ~ på hva han heter* I can't think of his name; **~ sammen** gather, meet; **~ seg** *(bli frisk)* recover; *(bli dyktigere)* improve; *~ seg opp/inn/ut etc* get up/in/out etc; **~ til:** *~ til å (gjøre noe tilfeldigvis)* happen to; *jeg kom til å se bak meg* I happened to look behind me; *(om noe fremtidig)* shall, will; *jeg tror det ~r til å bli regn i morgen* I think it will rain tomorrow; *det kom til slag* a battle was fought; **~ ut** *(om hemmelighet etc)* be known; get about/abroad; **~ ut for:** *han kom ut for en ulykke* he met with an accident.

kommentar *sb* **1** *(bemerkning)* comment; *har De noen ~er?* have you any comments? **2** *(forklaring til vanskelig tekst etc)* commentary. **kommentere** *vb* comment on.

kommisjon *sb* commission.

kommode *sb* chest of drawers.

kommunal *adj* municipal. **kommune** *sb (i by)* municipality; *(på landet)* rural district. **kommuneskatt** *sb* rate.

kommunikasjon *sb* communication. **kommunikasjonsmiddel** *sb* means of communication. **kommuniké** *sb* communiqué.

kommunisme *sb* communism. **kommunist** *sb* communist. **kommunistisk** *adj* communist(ic).

kompani *sb* company. **kompaniskap** *sb* partnership; *hun gikk i ~ med sine to kusiner* she entered into partnership with her two cousins. **kompanjong** *sb* partner.

komparasjon *sb* comparison. **komparativ** *sb (gram)* the comparative.

kompass *sb* compass.

kompensasjon *sb* compensation.

kompetent *adj* competent.

kompilator *sb data* compiler. **kompilere** *vb data* compile.

kompleks **1** *adj* complex; **2** *sb (bygnings~)* block.

komplement *sb (gram)* prepositional phrase.

komplett *adj* complete; *adv* completely.

kompliment *sb* compliment; *gi ~ for* compliment on.

komplisere *vb* complicate. **komplisert** *adj* complicated, complex.

komplott *sb* conspiracy, plot.

komponere *vb* compose. **komponist** *sb* composer. **komposisjon** *sb* composition.

kompott *sb* stewed fruit.

kompromiss *sb* compromise; *inngå ~* compromise.

kompromittere (seg) *vb* compromise (oneself).

kondensator *sb* capacitor, condenser; *også petro* cooler. **kondensatorolje** *sb* condenser oil. **kondensere** *vb* condense.

kondisjon *sb* condition; *i god/dårlig ~* in/out of condition.

konditor *sb* confectioner. **konditori** *sb* confectioner's shop; *(om lokalet)* café, tea-rooms.

kondolanse *sb* condolence. **kondolansevisitt** *sb* visit of condolence. **kondolere** *vb* offer one's condolences.

konduktør *sb (på buss, trikk)* conductor; *(om kvinne også)* conductress; *(på tog)* guard; ticket collector; *US* conductor.

kone *sb* **1** *(kvinne)* woman; **2** *(hustru)* wife; *han hadde ~ og barn* he had a wife and family; **3** *(husmor)* housewife; mistress of the house.

konfeksjon *sb* ready-made clothing. **konfeksjonssydd** *adj: dressen er ~* the suit is ready-made.

konfekt *sb* chocolates *fl.*

konferanse *sb* conference; *(om stilling en har søkt)* interview. **konferere med** *vb* confer with; *(sammenligne)* check, compare.

konfigurasjon *sb data* configuration.

konfirmasjon *sb* confirmation. **konfirmere** *vb* confirm.

konfiskasjon *sb* confiscation, seizure. **konfiskere** *vb* confiscate, seize.

konflikt *sb* conflict.

konge *sb* king. **konge|dømme** *sb (monarki)* monarchy; *(kongerike)* kingdom. **~familie** *sb* royal family. **~krone** *sb* royal crown. **kongelig** *adj* royal; *de kongelige* the Royal Family. **konge|par** *sb* King and Queen. **~rike** *sb* kingdom. **~slott** *sb* royal palace.

kongle *sb* cone.

kongress *sb* congress, conference; *Kongressen (i US)* (the) Congress.

kongruent *adj* congruent.

konjakk *sb* brandy, cognac.

konjunksjon *sb* conjunction.

konjunktiv *sb (gram)* the subjunctive.

konjunkturer *sb fl* business/trade cycles; trade outlook; trading conditions; *dårlige* ~ depression, slump; *gode* ~ boom, prosperity.

konklusjon *sb* conclusion.

konkret *adj* concrete.

konkurranse *sb* competition; ~ *om* competition for. **konkurrent** *sb* competitor, rival. **konkurrere** *vb* compete.

konkurs *sb* bankrupcy, failure; *gå* ~ go bankrupt.

konsekvens *sb* consequence. **konsekvent** *adj* consistent.

konsentrasjon *sb* concentration. **konsentrere** *vb* concentrate; ~ *seg om* concentrate on.

konsert *sb (om fremføring)* concert; *(om den enkelte kunstners* ~ *også)* recital; *(om komposisjonen)* concerto.

konservativ *adj, sb* conservative. **konservere** *vb* preserve.

konsis *adj* consise.

konsolidere *vb* consolidate.

konsoll *sb data etc* console.

konsonant *sb* consonant.

konstabel *sb* constable.

konstant *adj* constant.

konstatere *vb* **1** *(finne ut av)* ascertain; *det er vanskelig å* ~ *hva som egentlig hendte* it is difficult to ascertain what really happened; *(påvise)* **2** demonstrate.

konstitusjon *sb* constitution.

konstruere *vb* construct. **konstruksjon** *sb* construction.

konsul *sb* consul. **konsulat** *sb* consulate. **konsultasjon** *sb* consultation. **konsultere** *vb* consult; ~ *en lege* consult/see a doctor.

kontakt *sb* **1** *(forbindelse)* contact, touch; *jeg mistet* ~*en med dem* I lost contact with them; *komme i* ~ *med* get into touch with; **2** *(bryter)* switch.

kontant *adj, adv* cash; *et* ~ *svar* a prompt/ready answer; *han betalte* ~ he paid (in) cash. **kontanter** *sb (rede penger)* cash.

kontinent *sb* continent.

kontingent *sb (medlems~ etc)* subscription.

konto *sb* account; *ha* ~ *i banken/i et firma* have/keep an account in/with a bank/with a firm.

kontor *sb* office; *på kontoret* at/in the office. **kontor|arbeid** *sb* office work; paper work. **~bygning** *sb* office block/building. **~dame, ~ist, ~mann** *sb* clerk, typist. **~personale** *sb koll* (clerical/office) staff. **~rekvisita** *sb koll* office accessories (appliances, supplies). **~sjef** *sb* head clerk. **~søster** *sb* receptionist. **~tid** *sb* (office) hours.

kontrakt *sb* contract.

kontrast *sb* contrast.

kontroll *sb* **1** *(herredømme)* control; *brannen er under* ~ the fire is under control; **2** *(oppsikt)* inspection, supervision; *~en med meieriene* the supervision of dairies. **kontrollere** *vb* **1** *(beherske)* control; *USA ~r halvparten av verdens olje* the U.S.A. controls half the world's oil supplies; **2** *(inspisere, holde oppsyn med)* inspect, supervise; **3** *(undersøke om noe er som det skal være)* check; ~ *regnskapene* check the accounts. **kontrollkort** *sb data* check card. **kontrollør** *sb* controller; inspector, supervisor; *(billett~)* ticket-collector; *(ved inngangen til idrettsplass etc)* gate-keeper.

kontur *sb* outline.

konvall *sb* lily of the valley.

konvensjonell *adj* conventional.

konversasjon *sb* conversation. **konversasjonsleksikon** *sb* encyclopedia. **konversere** *vb* make conversation; talk; *vt* entertain.

konvolutt *sb* envelope.

kopi *sb* copy. **kopiere** *vb* copy.

kopp *sb* cup.

kor **1** chorus; *lese i* ~ read in chorus; **2** *(sang~)* choir; **3** *(del av kirkebygning)* chancel, choir.

korall *sb* coral. **korall|rev** *sb* coral reef. **~øy** *sb* coral island.

korde *sb* chord.

kordfløyel *sb* corduroy. **kordfløyelsbukser** *sb* corduroys.

korint *sb* currant.

kork *sb* cork. **korketrekker** *sb* cork-screw.

korn **1** *(matkorn)* corn, grain; *US (oftest)* grain; jf *hvete* og *mais*; **2** *(partikkel)* grain; **3** *(siktemiddel)* foresight, bead. **kornet(e)** *adj* grainy, granular.

korporal *sb* corporal. **korps** *sb* corps. **korpulent** *adj* corpulent, stout.

korrekt *adj* **1** *(etter reglene)* correct; **2** *(nøyaktig)* accurate. **korrektur** *sb* proof; *lese* ~ proofread. **korrekturleser** *sb* proofreader.

korrespondanse *sb* **1** *(brevskriving etc)* correspondence; **2** *(forbindelse)* connection. **korrespondanse|-kurs** *sb* correspondence course. **~skole** *sb* correspondence school. **korrespondent** *sb* correspondent; *(journalist)* reporter. **korrespondere** *vb* correspond.

korridor *sb* corridor, passage.

korrodere *vb* corrode. **korrosjon** *sb* corrosion.

korrupsjon *sb* corruptioon. **corrupt** *vb* corrupt.

kors *sb* cross; *Røde Kors* the Red Cross.

korsang *sb (det å synge)* choral singing; choir-singing; *(selve sangen)* part-song. **korse seg** *vb* cross oneself; make the sign of the cross. **kors|farer** *sb* crusader. **~feste** *vb* crucify. **~festelse** *sb* crucifixion. **~lagt** *adj* crossed. **~rygg** *sb* small of the back. **~tegn** *sb* sign of the cross. **~tog** *sb* crusade.

kort **A** *adj* **1** short; ~ *etter* shortly/soon after; ~ *før* shortly before; ~ *sagt* in short; *en* ~ *avstand;* a short distance; *om* ~ *tid* shortly, soon; **2** *(~fattet, ~varig)* brief; *et* ~ *opphold* a brief/short stay; ~ *og godt* in so many words; *dgl* short and sweet; **B** *sb* card; *(post~)* postcard; *(med bilde)* picture postcard; *et slag* ~ a game of cards. **kortfattet** *adj* brief, concise. **korthet** *sb: fatte seg i* ~ be brief. **kort|huller** *sb data* card punch. **~klipt** *adj* close-cropped. **~kode** *sb data* card code. **~leik** = *~stokk.* **~mater** *sb data* card feed. **~slutning** *sb* short circuit. **~slutte** *vb* short-circuit. **~stokk** *sb* pack/*US* deck of cards. **~varig** *adj* brief.

kos *sb* **A:** *dra sin* ~ leave; **B** *(hygge)* ≈ cosiness; a good time. **kose seg** *vb* ≈ have a good time. **koselig** *adj* ≈ comfortable, cosy, snug.

kosmonaut *sb* cosmonaut. **kosmopolitisk** *adj* cosmopolitan. **kosmopolitt** *sb* cosmopolitan.

kost *sb* **A** *(feie~ med langt skaft)* broom; *(med kort skaft)* brush; *(barber~, maler~ etc)* brush; **B** *(mat)* food; *god/nærende* ~ wholesome food; *(kosthold)* board; ~ *og losji* board and lodging; *holde seg selv med ~en* find one's own food; get one's own meals . **kostbar** *adj* **1** *(dyr)* costly, expensive; *en ~ utdannelse/reise* an expensive education/journey; **2** *(verdifull)* precious, valuable; *en ~ samling* a valuable collection; **3** *gjøre seg* ~ play hard to get (please, satisfy etc). **koste** *vb* cost; *(dgl brukes især)* be; ~ *på* spend on; *det ~r for mye* it costs too much; *det kommer til ~ ham livet* it will cost him his life; *hvor mye koster det?* how much is it? *vi har ~t en god del på huset vårt* we have spent a lot on our house.

kosteskaft *sb* broomstick.

kostyme *sb* costume. **kostymeball** *sb* fancy-dress ball.

kotelett *sb* chop; *(liten kalve- el. lamme~)* cutlet.

kott *sb* closet, cubby-hole; *(kles~)* wardrobe; (hanging) cupboard; *US* closet.

krabbe 1 *sb* crab; **2** *vb (krype)* crawl. **krabbefelt** *sb* crawler lane.

kraft *sb* **1** *(styrke)* strength; *med full* ~ with all her/his etc strength; **2** *(drivkraft, mekanisk energi)* power; *elektrisk* ~ electric power; **3** *(natur~)* force; *naturkreftene* the forces of nature; **4** *(uttrykk)* **av all ~,** *av alle krefter* with all one's might; *sette* **i** ~ put into force; *tre i* ~ come into force; *komme* **til krefter** recover (one's strength); *sette* **ut av** ~ annul, cancel; *(midlertidig)* suspend. **kraft|anlegg** *sb* power plant. **~anstrengelse** *sb* effort. **kraftig** *adj* powerful, strong, vigorous; ~ *bygd* strongly built; *en ~ stemme* a powerful/strong voice. **kraft|kilde** *sb* source of energy. **~ledning** *sb* power line. **~ledningsmast** *sb* pylon. **~patriot** *sb* chauvinist, jingo. **~patriotisme** *sb* chauvinism, jingoism.**~stasjon** *sb* power house/station. **~tak** *sb* great effort.

krakk *sb* **1** *(benk)* bench, stool, bench; **2** *(økonomisk ~)* collapse, crash. **krakke** *vb petro (spalte)* crack. **krakker** *sb petro* cracking plant.

kram|bu *sb* store. **~kar** *sb* huckster; peddler, pedlar.

krampaktig *adj* convulsive. **krampe** *sb* **1** convulsion; *(ved f.eks. bading)* cramp; *han fikk* ~ he had convulsions; *jeg har ~ i beina* I have got cramp in my legs; **2** *(krok)* cramp.

kran *sb* **1** *(heise~)* crane; **2** *(vann~)* cock, tap; *(især US)* faucet.

krangel *sb* quarrel. **krangle** *vb* quarrel. **kranglet(e)** *adj* quarrelsome.

kraniebrudd *sb* fracture of the skull. **kranium** *sb* cranium, skull.

krans *sb* wreath; *de bandt en* ~ they made a wreath.

krapp *adj (om bølger)* short; *(om sjø)* choppy; *(om sving)* sharp, sudden; *en ~ sving* a sharp turn.

krass *adj* crass, gross.

krater *sb* crater.

kratt *sb* scrub, thicket; underbush, underbrush.

krav *sb* **1** *(forlangende)* demand; ~ *om høyere lønn* demand for higher wages; **2** *(noe man hevder rett til)* claim; *(noe som kreves av en)* requirement; *lovens* ~ the requirements of the law.

krave *sb* collar.

kreditor *sb* creditor. **kreditt** *sb* credit; *vi kjøper aldri på* ~ we never buy/take on credit.

kreft *sb* cancer. **kreft|fremkallende** *adj* carcinogenic. **~svulst** *sb* cancerous tumour.

kreke *vb* crawl, creep.

krem *sb (hud~)* cream; *(pisket ~)* whipped cream. **kremfløte** *sb* full cream.

kremmer *sb* shopkeeper; *(kramkar)* huckster; peddler, pedlar.

kremte *vb* clear one's throat.

krenge *vb* **1** *(helle)* careen, heel, lurch; *(om fly)* bank; **2** *(vrenge)* turn inside out.

krenke *vb (fornærme)* offend; *(gi anledning til forargelse)* offend against; *hun ~t skikk og bruk/loven* she offended against custom/the law. **krenkelse** *sb* **1** *(fornærmelse)* offence; **2** *(overtredelse)* violation. **krenkende** *adj* insulting, offensive.

krepere *vb* die; pop off.

kreps *sb* crayfish.

kresen *adj (fordringsfull)* particular; *han er* ~ he is hard to please; *hun er ~ på maten* she is particular about her food.

krets *sb* circle, ring. **kretse** *vb* circle; *flyet ~t over hodene på oss* the plane kept circling overhead.

kreve *vb* **1** *(forlange)* ask for; demand; ~ *inn/opp (penger)* collect; *vi krever omgående betaling* we demand immediate payment; **2** *(gjøre krav på)* claim; ~ *belønning* claimed one's reward; **3** *(nødvendiggjøre)* require; *dette ~r omhyggelig overveielse* this requires careful consideration.

krible *vb* prickle, tingle; *det kribler i huden* my skin prickles.

krig *sb* war; *(krigføring)* warfare; *erklære* ~ declare war; *føre* ~ make/wage war; *kjemisk* ~ chemical warfare. **kriger** *sb* warrior. *adj* **krigersk** *adj* aggressive, belligerent; martial, warlike. **krig|førende** *adj, sb: de* ~ the belligerent powers. **~føring** *sb* warfare. **krigs|bytte** *sb* booty, spoils (of war). **~erklæring** *sb* declaration of war. **~fange** *sb* prisoner of war. **~fare** *sb* danger of war. **~flåte** *sb* battle fleet; *(hele flåten)* navy. **~forbryter** *sb* war criminal. **~hisser** *sb* warmonger. **~humør** *sb: være i ~humør* be on the warpath. **~in-**

valid *sb* war cripple. **~list** *sb* stratagem. **~lykke** *sb* fortunes of war. **~materiell** *sb* war material; munitions. **~rett** *sb* court-martial; *stille for ~* court-martial. **~rop** *sb* war cry. **~råd** *sb* council of war. **~skip** *sb* warship. **~skueplass** *sb* combat area; *(større)* theatre of war. **~tid** *sb* wartime. **~tjeneste** *sb* active service. **~trussel** *sb* threat of war. **~utbrudd** *sb* outbreak of war. **~viktig** *adj* of military importance.

kriminal|film *sb* detective film. **~fortelling, ~historie** *sb* crime story. **~itet** *sb* crime, criminality; *økende ~itet* increasing/rising criminality. **~roman** *sb* crime/detective novel. **kriminell** *adj* criminal.

kring|kaste *vb* broadcast. **~kasting** *sb* broadcasting.

krise *sb* crisis.

kristelig *adj* Christian. **kristen** *adj, sb* Christian; *de kristne* the Christians. **kristendom** *sb* Christianity. **kristenhet** *sb (alle kristne)* Christendom. **kristtorn** *sb* holly. **Kristus** Christ; *Kristi* Christ's; of Christ; *etter Kristi fødsel* A.D. (*fork for* Anno Domini); *før Kristi fødsel* B.C. (*fork for* before Christ).

kritiker *sb* critic; *(anmelder også)* reviewer. **kritikk** *sb* criticism; *(anmeldelse)* review; *hard ~* severe criticism; *hun rettet ~ mot ham* she criticized him. **kritikkløs** *adj* uncritical. **kritisere** *vb* criticize; *vi ble sterkt kritisert* we were criticized severely. **kritisk** *adj* critical; *en ~ situasjon* a critical situation.

kritt *sb* chalk; *farge~* crayon; *et stykke ~* a piece of chalk/crayon.

kro *sb* pub; public house; *(~ med nattelosji)* inn.

krok *sb* **1** *(hjørne)* corner, nook; **2** *(av metall etc)* hook. **kroket(e)** *adj* crooked, winding; *en ~ gate* a winding street.

krokodille *sb* crocodile.

krokus *sb* crocus.

krone 1 *sb* crown; **2** *vb* crown; *han ble ~t til konge* he was crowned king.

kronglet(e) *adj* **1** *(om trær)* crooked, twisted; gnarled; **2** *(om sti, terreng)* rough, rugged; uneven; **3** *(innviklet, vanskelig)* difficult, intricate.

kronikk *sb (i avis etc)* feature article.

kroning *sb* coronation.

kronisk *adj* chronic. **kronometer** *adv* chronometer. **kronologi** *sb* chronology. **kronologisk** *adj* chronological.

kron|prins *sb* crown prince. **~prinsesse** *sb* crown princess.

kropp *sb* body; *(torso)* trunk; *han skalv over hele ~en* he was trembling all over. **kropps|arbeid** *sb* manual work/labour. **~arbeider** *sb* manual worker. **kroppslig** *adj* bodily. **kroppsøving** *sb* physical exercise/training; gymnastics.

krukke *sb* pot; jar; pitcher.

krum *adj* curved, crooked; *en~ linje* a curved line. **krumme** *vb* bend, bow, curve.

krus *sb* **A** mug, tankard; **B** *gjøre ~ på* make a great fuss about/of. **kruset(e)** *adj* curly; *(om sterkt ~ hår)* woolly; *(om vann)* rippled.

krusifiks *sb* crucifix.

krusning *sb (på vann)* ripple.

krutt *sb* (gun)powder.

kry *adj* **1** *(stolt)* proud; **2** *(hoven, overlegen)* cocky, stuck-up.

kry *vb (myldre)* swarm; *det ~dde av folk i gatene* the streets swarmed with people.

krybbe *sb* crib, manger.

krydder, krydderi *sb* seasoning, spice. **krydre** *vb* season, spice.

krykke *sb* crutch.

krympe *vb* **1** *~ seg* flinch, shrink, wince; **2** = *krype 2.*

krypdyr *sb* reptile. **krype 1** *(kravle)* crawl; *(~ lydløst)* creep; *tyven krøp inn gjennom vinduet* the thief crept in through the window; **2** *(~ i vask)* shrink; **3** *(uttrykk)* **~ for** cringe before/to; fawn on; **~ sammen** crouch; *(av frykt, kulde etc)* cower; *(i velvære)* nestle. **krypende** *adj (underdanig)* cringing, fawning, servile. **krypskytter** *sb* poacher.

kryss *sb* cross; *(gate~, vei~)* crossing, cross-roads; *han satte et ~ ved navnet mitt* he put a cross against my name; *på ~ og tvers* in all directions. **krysse** *vb* cross; *(mot vinden)* tack; *~ ens planer* cross/thwart somebody's plans. **krysser** *sb* cruiser. **kryssfinér** *sb* plywood. **kryss|forhør** *sb* cross questioning; *(av motpartens vitne)* cross-examination. **~forhøre** *vb* cross-question; cross-examine. **kryssord(oppgave)** *sb* crossword puzzle.

krystall *sb* crystal.

kryste *vb* press, squeeze.

krøke *vb* bend, crook.

krøll *sb* curl; *slå ~ på seg* kink. **krølle 1** *sb* curl; **2** *vb* curl; *(~ sammen)* crumple, crease. **krøllet(e)** *adj* curly; crumpled, creased; *~ hår* curly hair; *en ~ kjole* a crumpled/creased dress.

krønike *sb* chronicle.

krøpling *sb* cripple; *han ble ~* he was crippled.

krøtter *sb koll* cattle.

kråke *sb* crow.

ku *sb* cow.

kubbe *sb* log.

kube *sb (bi~)* hive.

kubikk|innhold *sb* cubic content; volume. **~meter** *sb* cubic metre.

kue *vb* cow, subdue; *hun lot seg ikke ~* she was not cowed.

kujon *sb* coward.

kul *sb* bump.

kulde *sb* cold, frost; coldness; *de døde av ~* they died from cold. **kulde|grad** *sb* degree of cold/frost. **~gysning** *sb* chill; cold shiver.

kule *sb* **1** ball; **2** *a) (gevær~, pistol~)* bullet; *b) (kanon~)* ball; **3** *(til ~støt)* shot, weight; *støte ~* put the shot/weight; **4** *petro* = *~tank.* **kule|lager** *sb* ball bearings. **~lyn** *sb* ball lightning. **~penn** *sb* ball-pen, ballpoint-pen. **~ramme** *sb* abacus. **~støt** *sb (idrettsgrenen)* putting the shot/weight; *(et enkelt støt)* put.

~tank *sb petro* sphere; spherical tank.

kuling *sb* breeze, wind; *liten ~* strong breeze; *stiv ~* high wind; moderate gale; *sterk ~* fresh gale. **kulingvarsel** *sb* gale warning.

kulisse *sb* setpiece; flat, scene; *(især side~)* wind; *bak ~ne* behind the scenes.

kull *sb* **A 1** *(ungeflokk) (av fugler)* brood; *(av pattedyr)* litter; **2** *(årsklasse)* age group; class; **B** coal; *tre~* charcoal. **kull|felt** *sb* coal-field. **~gruve** *sb* coal-mine; (coal-)pit. **~gruvearbeider** *sb* collier. **~hydrater** *sb fl* carbohydrates.

kullkaste *vb* upset; *planene våre ble ~t* our plans were upset.

kull|kjeller *sb* coal cellar. **~oksyd, ~os** *sb* carbon monoxide. **~syre** *sb* carbonic acid.

kullseile *vb* kapsize.

kull|støv *sb* coal dust. **~sviertro** *sb* blind faith. **~tegning** *sb* charcoal drawing.

kulminasjon *sb* culmination. **kulminere** *vb* culminate.

kulse *vb* shudder with cold.

kulten *adj (vemmelig)* mean.

kultivere *vb* cultivate; *en kultivert mann* a man of culture. **kultivert** *adj* **1** *(oppdyrket)* cultivated; **2** *(dannet)* cultured. **kultur** *sb* **1** *(især om åndelig)* culture; *gresk ~* Greek culture; *(materiell ~, sivilisasjon)* civilization; *(ofte)* way of life; *amerikansk ~* the American way of life; **2** *(jorddyrking)* cultivation. **kultur|arv** *sb* cultural heritage. **~beite** *sb* cultivated pasture. **kulturell** *adj* cultural.

kultur|fattig *adj* culturally deprived. **~film** *sb* documentary (film). **~folk** *sb* civilized people. **~fiendtlig** *adj* anti-cultural. **~formidling** *sb* dissemination/spreading of culture. **~gjenstand** *sb* artifact. **~perle** *sb* cultured pearl. **~personlighet** *sb* intellectual leader. **~plante** cultivated plant. **~radikaler** *sb* radical intellectual. **~senter** *sb* cultural centre; *(om bygning, institusjon etc)* community centre. **~stat** *sb* civilized country.

kulør *sb* colour. **kulørt** *adj* coloured.

kum *sb (stort kar)* vat, tank.

kun = *bare.*

kunde *sb* customer; *fast ~* regular customer.

kunne *vb pres* can, may; *pret* could, might: **1** *(greie, makte)* be able to; can; *de ~ ikke se forskjell* they were unable to see the difference; *han ~ ikke løfte steinen* he could not lift the stone; *han ~ ikke noe for det* he couldn't help it; *jeg kan ikke noe med ham* I do not like him/I can't get on with him; **2** *(ha lært) a) (med sb)* know; *hun kan fransk* she knows French; *kan du melodien til den sangen?* do you know the tune of that song? *b) (med infinitiv)* can; know how to; *han kan snakke russisk* he can speak Russian; **3** *(få lov)* can, may; *kan vi (få lov til å) gå nå?* can/may we leave now? **4** *(kanskje ~)* may; *de kan være her hvert øyeblikk* they may be here any moment; *det falt meg aldri inn at han kunne være en tyv* it never occured to me that he might be a thief; **5** *(om det som hender av og til)* can; *hun kan være ganske sjarmerende* she can be quite charming; **7** *(om regelmessighet og vane)* will, would; *slik kan de sitte i timevis* they will sit like this for hours.

kunngjøre *vb* announce; make known. **kunngjøring** *sb* announcement. **kunnskap(er)** *sb (fl)* knowledge, information; *~ er makt* knowledge is power; *gode ~er i historie* a sound knowledge of history. **kunnskapsrik** *adj* well-informed, well-read; learned.

kunst *sb* **1** art; *fransk ~* French art; **2** *(~stykke)* trick; *jeg lærte hunden vår en ny ~* I taught our dog a new trick. **kunstgjødsel** *sb* fertilizer. **kunstig** *adj* **1** *(uekte)* artificial; *~e blomster* artificial flowers; **2** *(nedsettende)* false, imitation; *~e tenner* artificial/false teeth; *~ edelstein* imitation gem. **kunstløp** *sb* figure skating. **kunstner** *sb* artist. **kunstnerisk** *adj* artistic. **kunst|silke** *sb* artificial silk; rayon. **~stykke** *sb* trick. **~utstilling** *sb* art exhibition. **~verk** *sb* work of art.

kupé *sb* **1** *(på tog)* compartment; **2** *(om bil)* coupé.

kupert *adj (om terreng)* hilly; rough, rugged.

kupong *sb* coupon.

kupp *sb* **1** *(plutselig aksjon)* coup; *stats~* coup d'état; **2** *(overrumpling)* surprise; *byen ble tatt ved et ~* the town was taken by surprise; **3** *(journalistisk ~)* scoop; **4** *(fangst, utbytte)* haul

kuppel *sb (på bygning)* dome; *lampe~* globe.

kur *sb* cure, treatment; *hard ~* severe cure.

kurant *adj* **1** *(salgbar)* marketable, saleable; **2** *en ~ sak* a matter of routine; an easy process (proposition, thing etc).

kurere *vb* cure; *jeg ble kurert for astmaen min* I was cured of my asthma.

kur|fyrste *sb* elector. **~fyrstedømme** *sb* electorate. **~fyrstinne** *sb* electress.

kuriositet *sb (sjeldenhet)* curiosity; *(raritet også)* curio; *for ~ens skyld* for the sake of curiosity.

kurre *vb* coo.

kurs *sb* **1** *(retning)* course; *han endret ~* he altered/changed his course; **2** *(valuta~)* (rate of) exchange; **3** *(kursus)* course, class(es); *hun tok et ~ i (electronic) tekstbehandling* she took a course in (electronic) word processing.

kursiv *sb (~skrift)* italics; *i ~* in italics. **kursivere** *vb* italicize. **kursivskrift** *sb* italics.

kurtise *sb* flirtation. **kurtisere** *vb* flirt with.

kurv *sb* basket; *en ~ med egg* a basket of eggs.

kurvball *sb* basketball.

kurve *sb* curve; *en skarp ~ på veien* a sharp curve in the road.

kurv|fletning *sb* basketwork, wickerwork. **~stol** *sb* wicker chair.

kusine *sb* cousin.

kusk *sb* driver.

kusma *sb* the mumps.

kutt *sb* cut. **kutte** *vb* cut.

kutter *sb* cutter.

kuvert *sb* cover.

kuøye *sb (på skip)* porthole.

kvad *sb* lay, song.

kvadrat *sb* square. **kvadratinnhold** *sb* area. **kvadratisk** *adj* square. **kvadrat|meter** *sb* square metre. **~rot** *sb* square root. **~tall** *sb* square number.

kvae *sb* resin.

kvakksalver *sb* quack.

kval *sb (pine)* agony; *(også sjele~)* anguish.

kvalifikasjon *sb* qualification; *han har ingen~er for jobben* he has no qualifications for the job. **kvalifisere (seg)** *vb* qualify. **kvalifisert** *adj* qualified. **kvalitet** *sb* quality; *beste ~* best quality; *dårlig ~* poor quality.

kvalm *adj (uvel)* sick. **kvalme** *sb* sickness; *han fikk/hadde ~* he felt sick.

kvantitet, kvantum *sb* quantity.

kvart *sb* quarter; *en ~ ost* a quarter of a cheese. **kvartal** *sb* **1** *(1/4 år)* quarter; **2** *(by~)* block. **kvarter** *sb* **1** *(1/4 time)* a quarter of an hour; *et ~ over seks* a quarter past six; **2** *(distrikt, strøk)* quarter.

kvartett *sb* quartet.

kvarts *sb* quarts.

kvass *adj* sharp, keen; *(om ytring)* caustic; *en ~ tunge* a sharp tongue.

kvast *sb* **1** *(dusk)* tassel, tuft; **2** *(blomsterstand)* cyme.

kve *sb* fold, pen.

kveg *sb* cattle.

kveik *sb (stimulans)* stimulation. **kveike** *vb* **1** *(stimulere)* refresh, encourage; **2** *(tenne)* kindle.

kveil *sb* coil. **kveile** *vb* coil (up).

kveite *sb (fisk)* halibut.

kveker *sb* Quaker.

kvekk *sb: ikke et ~* not a single word.

kveld *sb* evening, night; *i ~* this evening; tonight; *om ~en* in the evening. **kveldskole** *sb* evening/night school; evening classes.

kvele *vb* **1** *(ved tilstopping av luftrøret)* choke; *han svelget en plommestein og holdt på å bli kvalt* he swallowed a plumstone and was nearly choked; **2** *(ved å snøre sammen halsen)* strangle; *kvalt med et reip* strangled with a rope; **3** *(ved tilstopping av munn og nese)* smother; *hun ble kvalt med en pute* she was smothered with a pillow; **4** *(ved mangel på luft)* suffocate; *kvalt av røyk* suffocated with smoke; **5** *(undertrykke)* stifle, suppress; quell; *~ i fødselen* nip in the bud; *han kvalte en gjesp* he stifled/suppressed a yawn. **kvelerslange** *sb* python, boa(constrictor).

kvern *sb* mill. **kvernstein** *sb* millstone.

kvesse *vb* sharpen, whet.

kveste *vb* injure, hurt; *han ble ~t ved en bilulykke* he was injured in a motor accident; *hånden hennes ble kvestet* her hand was injured/hurt. **kvestelse** *sb* injury.

kvi(e) seg for *vb* shrink from.

kvige *sb* heifer.

kvikk *adj* alert; bright, quickwitted; clever, smart. **kvikke** *vb: ~ opp* refresh, stimulate. **kvikk|sand** *sb* quicksand. **~sølv** *sb* mercury, quicksilver. **kvikne til** *vb* rally, recover, revive.

kvinne *sb* woman. **kvinne|bevegelse** *sb* woman movement; jf *~sak*. **~blad** *sb* women's mag(azine). **~forening** *sb* women's club. **~frigjøring** *sb* women's liberation. **~hater** *sb* woman-hater. **~jeger** *sb* woman|-chaser, -hunter; *dgl* skirt-chaser, womanizer. **~klinikk** *sb (fødselsklinikk)* maternity hospital. **~klær** *sb koll* women's wear. **~lege** gynaecologist. **kvinnelig** *adj* **1** *(motsatt mannlig)* female; woman, women; *~ arving* female heir; *~ politi* women police; *~ stemmerett* female suffrage; woman/women's suffrage; *~ tannlege* woman dentist; *~e tannleger* women dentists; **2** *(typisk for kvinner)* feminine; *(rosende)* womanly; *~ beskjedenhet* womanly modesty; *~e dyder* womanly virtues; *~e følelser* feminine emotions. **kvinnelighet** *sb* femininity, womanliness. **kvinne|list** *sb* female cunning. **~logikk** *sb* female logic. **~sak, ~saksbevegelse** *sb* feminism. **~saksforkjemper, ~sakskvinne** *sb* feminist; women's liberationist; *dgl* women's libber. **~skikkelse** *sb (i roman etc)* woman character. **~sykdom** *sb* women's disease. **kvinnfolk** *sb* woman.

kvise *sb* pimple; acne, blackhead.

kvist *sb* **1** *(på tre)* twig; **2** *(i trevirke)* knot; **3** *(på hus)* attic, garret; *de bodde på ~en* they lived in the attic/garret.

kvitre *vb* chirp, chirrup; twitter. **kvitring** se *kvitter.*

kvitt *adj: deilig å bli ~ ham (etc)!* good riddance! *jeg ble ~ dem til slutt* I got rid of them at last; *vi er ~* we are quits. **kvitte seg med** *vb* get rid of; rid oneself of.

kvitter *sb* chirp, chirrup; twitter.

kvittere *vb* receipt; give a receipt; *jeg gav henne kvittering for pengene* I gave her a receipt for the money. **kvittering** *sb* receipt; *mot ~* against receipt.

kvote *sb* quota.

kvotient *sb* quotient,

kykeliky *interj* cock-a-doodle-doo.

kyle *vb* fling, hurl.

kylling *sb* chicken.

kyndig *adj* competent, skilled; expert; *~ assistanse/hjelp* expert assistance; *~ veiledning* expert guidance. **kyndighet** *sb* skill; knowledge; expertise.

kyniker *sb* cynic. **kynisk** *adj* cynical. **kynisme** *sb* cynicism.

kyse *sb* bonnet.

kysk *adj* chaste. **kyskhet** *sb* chastity.

kyss *sb* kiss. **kysse** *vb* kiss; *~ hverandre* kiss; *~ på hånden* kiss hands; *he ~et henne på pannen* he kissed her forehead.

kyst *sb* coast; *(strandbredd)* beach; *(som feriested)* seaside; *byene ved ~en* the towns on the coast; *en farlig ~* a dangerous coast; *vi drar (ut) til ~en i ferien* we are going to the seaside for the holidays. **kyst|fart** *sb* coastal traffic. **~fiske** *sb* inshore fishing/fisheries. **~linje** *sb* coastline, shoreline. **~stripe** *sb* coast strip. **~vakt** *sb* coastguard.

kø *sb* line, queue; *de stilte seg i ~* they queued up.

kølle *sb* club, cudgel; bludgeon; *(golf~)* club; *(politi~)* baton.

køy(e) *sb (på skip)* berth; *(i hytte etc)* bunk; *(henge~)* hammock; *de gikk til køys* they turned in/ went to bed. **køye** *vb* go to bed; turn in. **køyeseng** *sb* bunk.

kål *sb (hodekål)* cabbage. **kål|mark** *sb* caterpillar. **~rabi** *sb* swede; *US* rutabaga.

kåpe *sb* coat.

kår *sb (forhold)* circumstances, conditions; *i slike ~* in such circumstances; *arbeidernes ~* the conditions of the working classes; *de satt i gode ~* they were well off.

kårde *sb* rapier.

kåre *vb (velge)* choose, elect.

kåt *adj* **1** *(lystig)* playful; **2** *(løssluppen)* wanton; **3** *(seksuelt tent)* randy; *(især om mann)* horny.

L

l *(bokstaven)* l.

la *vb* **A 1** let; *~ dem bare prøve (seg)!* just let them try! *~ oss be!* let us pray! *~ oss gå/ta en tur* let us go for a walk; *bonden lot oss plukke noen av eplene* the farmer let us pick some of the apples; *faren (hennes) ville ikke ~ henne gå* her father would not let her go; **2** *(~ bli liggende, stående etc)* leave; *du kan ~ døren stå åpen* you can leave the door open; *hun lot boken bli liggende på bordet* she left the book on the table; **3** *(sette til å)* make; *han lot gutten bære vesken* he made the boy carry the bag; **4** *(uttrykk)* *~* **gå!** all right! *~* **være** *(i fred)* let be; let/ leave alone; *~ være (å gjøre); hun lot være å lese leksene* she did not do her homework; *~ være (med det der)!* don't do that! stop that! *jeg kunne ikke ~ være* I could not help it; **B** *(om skytevåpen)* se *lade.* Se også *late.*

laban *sb* lout, rascal, scamp.

labb *sb* paw.

labbe *vb* pad.

laber *adj: ~ bris* moderate/slight breeze.

labil *adj* labile, unstable.

laboratorium *sb* laboratory; *dgl* lab.

labyrint *sb* labyrinth, maze.

la(de) *vb (skytevåpen)* load.

ladning *sb* **1** *(lass)* load; *(skips~)* cargo; **2** *(i skytevåpen)* charge.

lag *sb* **1** layer, stratum; *et ~ av leire* a layer of clay; **2** *(overtrekk)* coat(ing); *et ~ maling* a coat of paint; **3** *(sosialt ~)* class; social stratum; **4** *(forening)* association, society; club; **5** *(selskap)* company, party; *i lystig ~* in merry company; **6** *(arbeids~)* gang; **7** *(idretts~ etc)* team; *klubben har et meget godt lag denne sesongen* the club has a very good team this season; **8** *(uttrykk) gi ham det* **glatte** *~* give him a broadside; let him have it; **i** *~ med* in the company of; together with; *gi seg i ~ med* join; *i korteste/lengste/tidligste etc ~et* pretty/rather short/long/early etc; *holde* **ved** *~* keep up; *stå ved ~* remain in force.

lage *vb* **1** make; *jeg lagde syltetøy av bærene* I made jam of the berries; **2** *(uttrykk) ~* **av** make of/*om råmaterialer ofte* from; *en kjole lagd av silke* a dress made of silk; *vin er lagd av/på druer* wine is made from grapes; *~* **bråk** kick up/make a row; *~* **seg:** *det ~r seg nok* it will come right; it will be all right; *~ seg til å (gjøre seg i stand)* prepare oneself to; make arrangements to.

lager *sb (beholdning)* stock, store; *(opplagssted)* store/storage room; *(pakkhus)* warehouse; *ha på ~* have/keep in stock. **lager|blokk** *sb data* storage block. **~bygning** *sb* storehouse; *(pakkhus)* warehouse. **~kapasitet** *sb* storage capacity/*data* size. **~liste** *sb* stock record(s); *data* storage map. **~plass** *sb* storage capacity/room/space. **~tomt** *sb* yard. **~varer** *sb koll* stock gods. **~veksling** *sb data* swapping.

lagnad *sb* destiny, fate.

lagre *vb* **1** *(oppbevare)* store; **2** *(forbedre, modne)* mature, season; *vellagret ost* well-seasoned cheese; **3** *data* save.

lagrett(e) *sb* jury. **lagrettemann** *sb* juror.

lagring *sb* **1** *(oppbevaring)* storage, storing; **2** *(modning)* maturing, seasoning; **3** *data* storage. **lagringsfast** *adj data* resident.

lags: *gjøre til ~* please/satisfy somebody.

lagune *sb* lagoon.

lake *sb* brine, pickle.

lakei *sb* footman, lackey.

laken *sb* sheet; *hvit som et ~* white as a sheet.

lakk *sb* lacquer, varnish; *(emalje~)* enamel.

lakke *vb: det ~r mot sommer* summer is drawing near.

lakkere *vb (med ferniss)* varnish; *(med emaljelakk)* enamel; *(sprøyte~)* spray. **lakksko** *sb* patent leather shoes.

lakonisk *adj* laconic.

lakris *sb* liquorice.

laks *sb* salmon.

lam A *adj (lammet)* paralysed; *han er ~ i venstre bein* his left leg is paralysed; **B** *sb (av sau)* lamb. **lamme** *vb* **A** *(gjøre lam)* paralyse; *jeg var lammet av frykt* I was paralysed with fear; **B** *(få lam)* lamb. **lammekjøtt** *sb* lamb. **lammelse** *sb* palsy, paralysis.

lampe *sb* lamp; *(elektrisk pære)* bulb. **lampe|feber** *sb* stage fright. **~holder** *sb* lamp socket. **~kuppel** *sb* lamp globe. **~lys** *sb* lamplight. **~skjerm** *sb* lamp--shade. **lampett** *sb* bracket lamp.

land *sb* **1** *(rike)* country; *(poetisk)* land; *Det hellige land* the Holy Land; *Midnattssolens land* the Land of the Midnight Sun; **2** *(det motsatte av by)* country; *by og land* town and country; **3** *(det motsatte av sjø, vann)* land; *de så ikke ~* they could/did not see land; **4** *(dyrkningsjord)* land; **5** *(uttrykk)* **i ~** ashore; *drive i ~* be washed ashore; *sette i ~* put ashore; **inne i ~et** inland; *en by inne i ~et* an inland town; *lenger inne i ~et* further inland; **over ~:** *reise over ~* go by land; *over hele ~et* all over the country; **på ~et** in the country; *hun hadde bodd på ~et hele sitt liv* she had lived in the country all her life; *dra på landet* go into the country; **til ~s** by land; *her til ~s* in this country; *til ~s og til vanns* by land and sea. **land|befolkning** *sb* rural population. **~bruk** *sb* agriculture, farming. **land-bruks|skole** *sb* agricultural college/school. **~varer** *sb koll* agricultural products; farm produce.

lande *vb* land; *(om fly også)* come down. **lande|-plage** *sb* pest, scourge, pest. **~vei** *sb* highway.

land|flyktig *adj* exiled, in exile; *en ~* an exile. **~flyktighet** *sb* exile. **~gang** *sb* landing. **~gangsbro** *sb* gangway. **~gangsfartøy** *sb* landing craft. **~han-del** general store; village store. **~handler** *sb* village shopkeeper. **~jord** *sb: på landjorden* on dry land. **~kjenning** *sb* landfall; *få ~kjenning* make a landfall. **~krabbe** *sb* landlubber.

landlig *adj* rural, rustic.

land|lov *sb* shore leave. **~måler** *sb* surveyor. **~område** *sb* area, territory.

lands|by *sb* village; *(liten ~by)* hamlet. **~bygd** *sb* country district; countryside; *flukten fra ~bygden* the flight from the land; the rural exodus. **~del** *sb* part of the country.

landsens *adj* rural, provincial.

landsetning *sb* disembarkation, landing. **land-sette** *vb* disembark, land.

lands|forræder *sb* traitor. **~forræderi** *sb* treason. **~forvise** *vb* exile, banish. **~forvisning** *sb* exile, banishment. **~kamp** *sb* international match.

landskap *sb* scenery; *(især om maleri)* landscape.

lands|lag *sb* national team. **~mann** *sb* (fellow-)-countryman. **~omfattende** *adj* nation-wide. **~svik** *sb* treason. **~sviker** *sb* traitor.

land|sted *sb* country-house. **~stryker** *sb* tramp, vagabond. **~tunge** *sb* isthmus; neck of land. **~tur** *sb* outing, picnic. **~vind** *sb* off-shore wind. **~vinning** *sb* *(erobring)* conquest.

lang *adj* **1** long; *dagen ~* all day long; *fem fot ~* five feet long; *hvor ~ tid tar det?* how long does it take? *i ~ tid* for a long time; **2** *(høy)* tall; *en ~ fyr* a tall fellow. Se også *langt*. **langdrag** *sb: trekke i ~* delay, retard; *det trakk i ~* it took a long time.

lange A *sb (om fisken)* ling; **B** *vb: ~ til en* fetch/land someone a blow; *(gå etc fort)* step out; *~ ut etter* stretch out (one's arm) (for).

lang|finger *sb* middle finger. **~fingret** *adj* light--fingered. **~fredag** *sb* Good Friday. **~kost** *sb* long--handed scrubbing-brush. **~modig** *adj* long-suffering. **~renn** *sb* cross-country (skiing race). **~renns-ski** *sb koll* racing skis.

langs *adv, prep* along; *~ kysten* along the coast; *på ~* lengthwise. **langsmed** *prep* along.

langsom *adj* slow. **langsomt** *adv* slowly; *han kjørte ~* he drove slowly.

langt *adv* **1** *(om avstand i spørrende og nektende setninger)* far; *~ borte* far away; *er det ~ til Oxford?* is it far to Oxford? *vi gikk ikke ~* we did not walk far; **2** *(i andre tilfeller)* a long way; *vi har ~ å gå* we have a long way to walk; **3** *(som gradsadv)* far; by far; very much; *~ bedre* far better; better by far; *~ verre* very much worse; **4** *(uttrykk)* **~ (i)fra** far from; not nearly; **~ mindre** *(mye mindre)* far less; *(slett ikke)* let alone; *jeg har ikke tid, ~ mindre penger* I haven't the time, let alone the money; **~ på** *natt* late in the night; *til ~ på natt* till far into the night; **på ~ nær** not nearly; not by a long chalk; *han er på ~ nær så høy som broren (sin)* he is not nearly so tall as his brother; **~ om lenge** at length; at long last.

lang|varig *adj* long. **~veisfra** *adj* from far away. **~viser** *sb* minute hand.

lanse *sb* lance.

lansere *vb* launch.

lanterne *sb* lantern.

lapp *sb* **1** *(papir~)* scrap of paper; **2** *(bot)* patch. **lappe** *vb* patch, mend; *han ~t buksen sin* he patched his trousers. **lappe|saker** *sb* repair outfit/set. **~sko-maker** *sb* cobbler. **~teppe** *sb* patchwork quilt.

laps *sb* dandy.

larm *sb* noise. **larme** *vb* make a noise. **larmende** *adj* noisy. Jf *bråk(e)* etc.

larve *sb* larva, grub; *(av f.eks. sommerfugl også)* caterpillar.

lasarett *sb* (field) hospital.

lasaron *sb* tramp.

lass *sb* load; *(vogn~)* cart-load; *et tungt ~* a heavy load.

lasso *sb* lasso; *fange med ~* lasso.

last *sb* **1** *(synd, uvane)* vice; *drukkenskap er en ~* drinking is a vice; **2** *(bør, ladning)* burden, load; *(skips~)* cargo; **3** = *lasterom*. **laste** *vb* **1** *(klandre)* blame; **2** *(fylle på/ta inn last)* load; **3** *(romme)* carry. **laste|bil** *sb* lorry; *US* truck. **~båt, ~damper** *sb* cargo boat/steamer. **~dyr** *sb* beast of burden. **~full** *adj* *(umoralsk)* depraved. **~lastefullhet** *sb* depravity. **~plan** *sb* truck body. **~pram** *sb* lighter. **~rampe** *sb* loading platform. **~rom** *sb (i båt)* hold. **~skip** *sb* cargo ship; freighter.

lastverk *sb: hastverk er ~* haste is waste.

lat *adj* lazy.

late *vb* **1** *~ som (om)* pretend to; *~ som ingenting* behave as if nothing had happened; *han lot som om han arbeidet/sov* he pretended to work/be asleep; *hun lot som hun ikke så meg* she pretended not to see me; **2** *~ til* appear, seem; *de ~r til å være lykkelige* they appear/seem to be happy; *ja, det ~r til det* yes, so it appears/seems; *ingen lot til å kjenne noe til saken* nobody seemed to know anything of the matter; **3** *(uttrykk)* **~ i stikken** let down; **~ livet** lose one's life; **~ vannet** make water; urinate.

latent *adj* latent.

lathans *sb* lazy-bones.

latin *sb* Latin. **latinsk** *adj* Latin.

latter *sb* laughter; *(enkelt ~utbrudd, måte å le på)* laugh; *han brast i ~* he burst into laughter; he burst out laughing; *vi fikk oss en god ~ av det* we had a good laugh over it; *være til ~ for hele byen* be the laughing--stock of the whole town. **latteranfall** *sb* fit of laughter. **latterlig** *adj* ridiculous, ludicrous; *~ billig* ridiculously cheap; *et ~ beløp* a ridiculous sum.

laug *sb* guild.

laurbær *sb* bayberry; *(fig: ære)* laurels; *hvile på sine ~* rest on one's laurels. **laurbær|blad** *sb* bay-leaf. **~krans** *sb* laurel wreath.

lauv Se *løv*.

lav 1 *adj* low; *(ussel også)* mean; *av ~ ætt* of low birth; *en ~ pris/stemme/temperatur* a low price/voice/temperature; *lete høyt og ~t etter* look high and low for. Se også *lavt*. **2** *sb (mose)* lichen.

lava *sb* lava.

lave *vb (være mye av)* abound; *(drysse tett)* fall heavily; *snøen ~t ned* the snow was falling heavily. **laverestående** *adj* inferior, lower.

lav|konjunktur *sb* depression, slump. **~land** *sb* lowland(s); low-lying country. **~mælt** *adj* low--voiced. **~slette** *sb* lowland plain. **~spent** *adj* low--tension. **lavt** *adv* low; *snakke ~* speak low; *svalene flyr ~* the swallows fly low. **lavtliggende** low-lying. **lavtrykk** *sb* low pressure; *(i værvarsling også)* depression. **lavtstående** *adj* inferior, low; *(om kultur)* primitive. **lavvann** *sb* low water; *(ebbe)* ebb; low tide; *ved ~* at low water.

le A *sb* **1** *(ly)* shelter; **2** *(til sjøs)* lee, leeward; *i ~* to leeward; **B** *vb* laugh; *det er ikke noe å ~ av* it is noe laughing matter; *hva ~r du av?* what are you laughing at? *hun lo av glede* she laughed with joy.

led *sb (grind)* gate.

ledd *sb* joint; *(~ i en kjede)* link; *(ut, ute) av ~* dislocated; out of joint; *få ut av ~* dislocate; put out of joint; *få/sette i ~* reduce a dislocation. **leddbuss** *sb* articulated bus. **leddelt, leddet** *adj* articulated. **ledd|gikt** *sb* arthritis. **~setning** *sb* (subordinate) clause.

lede *vb* **1** *(styre, stå i spissen for)* lead; conduct, manage; *(~ møte)* be in the chair; preside (at, over): *~ en ekspedisjon* lead an expedition; *~ en forretning* conduct/manage a business; **2** *(~ gjennom rør)* conduct, lead, pipe; **3** *(~ elektrisitet, varme)* conduct; *metall ~r varme bedre enn tre* metal conducts heat better than wood; **4** *(i en konkurranse)* lead; *hvilket lag ~r?* which team is leading? **5** *(påvirke)* lead; *han kan ~s, men lar seg ikke tvinge* he may be led, but (he) won't be coerced. **ledelse** *sb* leadership; direction, management; *ha ~n (av) (også)* be in charge (of). **ledende** *adj* leading; *en ~ stilling* a leading position. **leder** *sb* **1** leader; **2** *(av elektrisitet, varme)* conductor; **3** *(~artikkel)* editorial.

ledig *adj* **1** *(ubeskjeftiget)* idle, unoccupied; *~e hender/timer* idle hands/hours; **2** *(arbeids~)* unemployed; out of work; **3** *(om plass, leilighet)* vacant; *~ leilighet/plass* vacant flat/seat; **4** *(ubundet)* disengaged, free; *er du ~ i aften?* are you free tonight? **5** *(om tid)* spare, leisure. **lediggang** *sb* idleness.

ledning *sb* cable, wire; *(elektrisk ~ også)* cord, flex; *(især telefon~)* line; *(rør~)* pipe, pipeline. **lednings|evne** *sb (elek)* conductance, conductivity. **~mast** *sb* pylon. **~nett** *sb* mains system; wiring.

ledsage *vb* accompany. **ledsagelse** *sb* accompaniment. **ledsager** *sb* companion, escort. Se også *følge*.

lee *vb (bevege)* move.

leg *adj (ulært)* lay.

legal *adj* legal.

legasjon *sb* legation.

legat *sb* endowment, foundation.

leg|bror *sb* lay brother. **~dommer** *sb* juryman, juror.

lege 1 *sb* doctor, physician; *(kirurg)* surgeon; *du burde gå til ~ med den hosten (din)* you ought to see a doctor about that cough of yours; *sende bud etter ~n* send for the doctor; **2** *vb (helbrede)* cure, heal. **lege|attest** *sb* medical certificate. **~behandling** *sb* medical treatment. **~besøk** *sb* doctor's call. **~hjelp** *sb* medical assistance/treatment. **~honorar** *sb* doctor's fee. **~kunst** *sb* medicine.

legeme *sb* body.

legemiddel *sb* remedy.

legemlig *adj* bodily; corporal, corporeal.

legendarisk *adj* legendary. **legende** *sb* legend.

legering *sb* alloy.

lege|standen *sb* the medical profession. **~tilsyn** *sb* medical attendance. **~undersøkelse** *sb* medical examination. **~vakt** *sb* first-aid station; *(især US)* emergency ward.

legfolk laymen; lay people; *(som gruppe)* the laity.

legg *sb* **1** *(del av beinet)* calf; **2** *(fold)* pleat. **legge** *vb* **1** lay; place, put; *hun la boken på bordet* she laid/placed/put the book on the table; **2** *~ seg* lie down; *(gå til sengs)* go to bed; *de ~r seg vanligvis klokken elleve* they usually go to bed at eleven; *han la seg på sofaen* he lay down on the sofa; **3** *(uttrykk)* **~ an på å** aim at; try hard to; **~ for dagen** display, show; reveal; **~ frem:** *~ frem et forslag* put forward a proposal; **~ i vei** start; *(sette opp farten)* hurry along; **~ inn** *(om elektrisitet)* wire (a house for electricity); *(om gass, sentralfyring, vann etc)* install; lay on; put in; *~ inn på sykehus* hospitalize; send to hospital; *(på mentalsykehus også)* certify; **~ merke til** notice; **~ ned** lay/put down; *(om frukt/grønnsaker etc)* preserve; *(om klesplagg)* let down; *~ned arbeidet* cease/stop; go on strike; *~ ned våpnene* lay down arms; **~ på:** *~ på prisen* raise the price; *~ på røret (etter telefonsamtale)* hang up; **~ på seg**

put on weight; ~ **seg** *(om vind)* drop; ~ *seg bakover* lean back; ~ **seg etter** *(prøve å lære)* take up; ~ **seg imellom** *(for å megle)* intervene; ~ **seg opp** *(spare)* put by; save; ~ **seg opp i** interfere in/with; meddle in/with; ~ **seg til** *vaner/uvaner* contract habits/bad habits; ~ **seg ut med** fall out with; quarrel with; ~ **sammen** *(addere)* add; *(brette sammen)* fold up; ~ **til** *(tilføye)* add; ~ **til side** *(for senere bruk)* lay aside; put by; ~ **under seg** *(erobre)* conquer. **legge|tid** *sb (sengetid)* bedtime. **~vann** *sb* setting lotion.

legitim *adj* lawful, legitimate.

legitimasjon *sb* identification (papers); *har De (noen) ~?* can you prove your identity? **legitimasjonskort** *sb* identity card. **legitimere seg** *vb* establish one's identity.

leg|mann *sb* layman. **~predikant** *sb* lay preacher.

lei A *adj* **1** *(kjedelig, ubehagelig)* awkward, disagreeable, unpleasant; *(pinlig)* embarrassing, painful; *det var da leit!* that's too bad! **2** *(lei seg)* sorry; *være ~ seg* feel sorry; *være ~ for* be sorry for; **3** *(trett av)* tired (of); *jeg er luta ~ det* I am fed up with it; **B** *sb* **1** *(retning)* direction, side; **2** *(farvann)* channel, fairway; *langt av ~* far away; *på lang ~* from far off.

leie A *sb (liggeplass)* bed, couch; *(vilt dyrs ~)* den, lair; **B I** *sb* **1** *(om ~forhold)* hire, rent; *(for lengre tid)* lease; *til ~* for hire; *(om husrom)* to let; *sykler til ~* bicycles for hire; *hus til ~* house to let; **2** *(betaling for ~)* rent; *vi betaler 250 pund i ~* we pay a rent of £250; **II** *vb* **1** hire; *(om hus etc)* rent; *hun leide huset av Mr Brown* she rented the house from Mr Brown; *vi leide en mann til å male huset* we hired a man to paint our house; **2** *(leie ut)* hire out; let; *vi skal ~ ut huset vårt i vinter* we shall let our house for the winter; **C** *vb (~ i hånden)* lead; take by the hand. **leie|boer** *sb* tenant; *(av hybel)* lodger. **~gård** *sb* block of flats; *US* tenement house. **leier** *sb (av bolig)* tenant; *(av værelse)* lodger; *(av ting)* hirer. **leie|soldat** *sb* mercenary. **~trooper** *sb koll* mercenaries.

leik etc se *lek etc.*

leilending *sb* tenant farmer; leaseholder.

leilighet *sb* **1** *(bolig)* flat; *US* apartment; *en treværelses ~* a three-rom flat/apartment; *vi leide oss en ~* we took a flat; **2** *(anledning, situasjon)* opportunity; occasion; *~ gjør tyv* opportunity makes thief.

leir *sb* camp; *ligge i ~* camp; *slå ~* camp; pitch camp; *hvor skal vi slå ~ i kveld?* where shall we camp tonight? **leirbål** *sb* campfire. **leir(e)** *sb* clay. **leire** *vb: ~ seg (slå leir, slå seg ned)* camp; *de ~t seg i gresset* they lay down on the grass. **leiret(e)** *adj* clayey. **leir|jord** *sb* clay/clayey soil. **~krukke** *sb* earthen jar; earthenware pot. **leir|liv** *sb* camping. **~plass** *sb* camping ground/site. **~skole** *sb* camp school. **~sport** *sb* camping.

leite 1 *sb: ved det ~* about that time; **2** *vb: det ~r på* it is tiring; it is a great strain.

lek *sb* **1** *(det å leke)* play; *det gikk som en ~* it was a child's play; *holde opp mens ~en er god* stop while the going is good; **2** *(~, spill)* game; *gjemsel er en ~ for barn* hide-and-seek is a game for children. **leke I** *sb* plaything, toy; **II** *vb* **1** play; *barn liker å ~* children are fond of playing; **2** *(~ å være eller utføre noe)* play at; *~ indianere* play at Indians; *vi lekte vi var sigøynere* we pretended we were gipsies. **leke|grind** *sb* playpen. **~kamerat** *sb* playfellow, playmate. **leken** *adj* playful. **leke|pistol** *sb* toy pistol. **~plass** *sb* playground. **~saker** *sb fl* playthings, toys. **~tøy** *sb koll* toys.

lekk 1 *adj* leaking, leaky; *springe ~* spring a leak; **2** *sb* = **lekkasje** *sb* **1** *(lekking)* leakage; **2** *(utett sted)* leak; *det er en ~ i taket* there is a leak in the roof. **lekke** *vb* leak; *kjelen ~r* the kettle is leaking; *nyheten har ~t ut* the news has leaked out.

lekker *adj* **1** *(delikat)* appetizing, delicious; dainty; *en ~ kake* a delicious cake; **2** *(deilig)* lovely, nice; *en ~ kjole* a lovely/nice frock. **lekkerbisken** *sb* dainty, titbit.

lekse *sb* lesson, task; *(ofte)* homework; *han leste alltid på ~ne (sine)* he always did/prepared his homework; *hun kunne ~ne (sine)* she knew her lessons. **lekse opp** *vb* jaw; *læreren ~t opp for de dovne elevene* the teacher jawed the lazy pupils. **lekselesing** *sb* doing one's homework.

leksikon *sb* **1** *(konversasjons~)* encyclopaedia; **2** *(ordbok)* dictionary.

leksjon *sb* lesson.

lekte *sb* lath.

lekter *sb* barge, lighter.

lektor *(ved videregående skole)* ≈ grammar school teacher; *(ved universitet)* ≈ lecturer. **lektyre** *sb* reading matter.

lell *adv (likevel)* after all; all the same.

lem *sb* **A** *(legemsdel)* limb; **B** *(for vindu)* shutter; *(i gulv)* trapdoor; *(på lasteplan)* side.

lemen *sb* lemming.

lemfeldig *adj* indulgent, lenient.

lemleste *sb* maim, mutilate; cripple, disable. **lemlestelse** *sb* mutilation.

lempe I *sb: med ~* gently; **II** *vb* **1** *(flytte, slenge)* heave; *~ kull* heave coal; *~ noe over bord* heave something overboard; **2** *~ på* modify, relax; *~ på disiplinen* relax discipline; *~ på kravene* modify one's demands. **lempelig** *adj* gentle; *(adv)* gently.

lemster *adj* stiff.

lend *sb* loin.

lende *sb (terreng)* terrain.

lendmann *sb* vassal, tenant.

lene *vb: ~ seg* lean; *~ seg frem/tilbake* lean forward/back; *~ seg mot noe* lean against something. **lenestol** *sb* armchair, easy-chair.

lengde *sb* length; *(geografisk ~)* longitude; *i ~n er det ikke så lett å finne seg i det* in the long run it is not so easy to put up with it; *vestlig/østlig ~* west/east longitude. **lengde|grad** *sb* degree of longitude. **~hopp, ~sprang** *sb* long jump; *US* broad jump.

lenge *adv* **1** *(mest i spørrende og nektende setninger)* long; *hvor ~ er det til jul?* how long is it to Christmas? *vi hadde ikke vært ~ borte* we had not been away long; **2**

(i andre tilfeller) (for) a long time; *det er ~ til jul* it is a long time to Christmas; *det er ~ siden sist* it is a long time ago; **3** *(uttrykk)* **for ~ siden** long ago; a long time ago; **langt om ~** at length; at long last; **om ikke så ~** before long; **så ~** as long; so long; *adjø så ~!* so long! *du kan bli/være så ~ du vil* you may stay as long as you want; *jeg går en tur så ~* in the meantime I'll go for a walk; *sitt ned så ~* sit down while you wait; **så ~ som** as/so long as; *det spiller ingen rolle, så ~ vi ikke blir oppdaget* it does not matter, so long as we are not found out.

lenger *adv* **1** *(av lenge)* longer; *det varer ikke stort ~* it won't last much longer; *ikke ~* no longer; not any longer; no more; *jeg kan ikke bli ~* I can't stay any longer; *det er ikke ~ siden enn i går at jeg snakket med ham* I talked to him only yesterday; **2** *(av langt)* farther, further; *~ borte* farther off; *litt ~ fremme* a little farther on; *Manchester er ~ fra London enn Oxford* Manchester is farther from London than Oxford is.

lengsel *sb* longing; *~ etter* longing for.

lengst I *adj (av lang)* **1** longest; *den ~e dagen i mitt liv* the longest day of my life; **2** *(om avstand)* farthest; *~ borte* farthest away; **II** *adv (av lenge)* the longest time; *for ~* long ago/since.

lengte *vb* long; *hun ~t etter å se igjen moren sin* she longed to see her mother again; *hun lengter etter moren sin* she misses her mother; *(sterkere)* she is longing for her mother; *~ hjem* be homesick.

lenke *sb* chain; *(fangelenker)* irons. **lenke** *vb* chain; *han var ~t til veggen* he was chained to the wall.

lens *adv* clear, empty; *(penge~)* broke; *øse ~* bail.

lens|adel *sb* feudal nobility. **~avgift** *sb* fee.

lense I *sb (tømmer~)* (timber) boom; **II** *vb* **1** *(tømme)* bail, empty; *~ en båt* bail (out) a boat; **2** *(seile unna vinden)* run before the wind.

lens|ed *sb* oath of fealty. **~herre** *sb* feudal overlord.

leopard *sb* leopard.

lepe *vb: kjolen din ~r* your dress dips.

lepje *vb* lap; *katten ~t i seg melken* the cat lapped up the milk.

leppe *sb* lip; *hun bet seg i ~n* she bit her lip. **leppestoft** *sb* lipstick.

lerk *sb (lerketre)* larch.

lerke *sb* lark.

lerret *sb* linen; *(grovt ~, maler~)* canvas; *det hvite ~ (dvs kino)* the screen.

lese *vb* read; *han leste for dem* he read to them; *jeg ~r i Bibelen hver dag* I read the Bible every day; *vi leste (på) leksene om ettermiddagen* we did our homework in the afternoon. **lese|bok** *sb* reader. **~briller** *sb* reading glasses. **~hode** *sb data* read head. **~krets** *sb* (circle of) readers. **~lager** *sb data* read-only memory (ROM). **leselig** *adj* legible, readable. **leser** *sb* reader; *ivrig ~* great reader. **lese|sal** *sb* reading-room. **~stasjon** *sb data* sensing station. **~stoff** *sb* reading; reading matter/material. **~verdig** *adj* readable.

lesjon *sb* injury.

leske *vb* quench, slake; *~ kalk* slaked lime. **leskedrikk** *sb* refreshing/soft drink.

lesning *sb* reading.

lespe *vb* lisp. **lesping** *sb* lisp.

lesse load; *~ av* unload.

lest *sb* last; *bli ved sin ~* stick to one's last.

lete *vb* look for; search; *de lette etter henne overalt* they looked for her everywhere; *han lette i lommene (sine)* he searched his pockets; *hun lette etter brillene sine* she was looking for her spectacles. **leteskip** *sb petro* survey ship.

letne *vb* lighten; *(klarne opp)* clear away/up.

lett *sb (farge)* colour.

lett *adj* **1** light; *(om øl og tobakk)* mild; *(om vind)* gentle; *en ~ bris* a gentle breeze; *et ~ måltid* a light meal; **2** *(ikke vanskelig)* easy; *adv* easily; *~ arbeid* easy work; *det er ~ gjort* that is easily done; **3** *(uttrykk)* **ha ~ for** *a) (være tilbøyelig til)* be apt to; *støpejern har ~ for å briste* cast iron is apt to break; *b) (ha ~ for å lære): han har ~ for regning* arithmetic comes easily to him; *hun har ~ for å bli fornærmet* she is easily hurt; *være ~* **på tråden** have loose morals; **~ til beins** light-footed. **lette** *vb* **1** *(gjøre lettere)* lighten; relieve; **2** *(fly opp, om fugler)* rise; *(om fly)* take off; **3** *(om tåke)* lift; *tåken ~t* the fog lifted. **lettelse** *sb* relief. **lettfattelig** *adj* easily understood; plain. **letthet** *sb (om vekt)* lightness; *(motsatt vanskelighet)* ease; *med ~* easily/with ease. **lett|kjøpt** *adj* cheap, easy; *en ~kjøpt seier* an easy victory. **~lest** *adj* easily read. **~sindig** *adj (ubesindig)* improvident; *(ansvarsløs)* rash, reckless; irresponsible; *(lettlivet)* frivolous. **~sindighet** *sb* rashness, recklessness; irresponsibility; frivolity. **~skyet** *adj* lightly overcast. **~-tjent** *adj: ~-tjente penger* easy money. **~-troende** *adj* credulous, gullible. **~-troenhet** *sb* credulity, gullibility. **~vekt** *sb* lightweight. **~vint** *adj* **1** *(lett)* easy; *en ~vint jobb* an easy job; **2** *(praktisk)* ready; *en ~vint fremgangsmåte/metode* a ready method; **3** *(overflatisk)* careless, heedless; irresponsible; *han tok det ~vint* he made light of it; he did not care much about it; **4** *(rask, smidig)* agile, nimble. **~vinthet** *sb: for ~vinthets skyld* for (the sake of) convenience.

leve I *sb* cheer; *han utbrakte et ~ for kongen* he called for three cheers for the King; **II** *vb* **1** live; be alive/living; *~ et lykkelig liv* lead a happy life; *~r foreldrene dine ennå?* are your parents still living? *hun levde til hun ble nitti* she lived to the age of 90; *mens han levde* during his lifetime; *så sant jeg lever!* upon my life! **2** *(uttrykk)* **~ av** live on; *de ~r av frukt* they live on fruit; *han ~r av pensjonen sin* he lives on his pension; *(om levebrød)* live by; *det var umulig for ham å ~ av sin penn (dvs av å skrive)* it was impossible for him to live by his pen; *hva ~r hun av?* what does she do for a living? **~ for** live for; *hun ~r for sitt arbeid* she lives for her work; **~ på** live on; *er det mulig å ~ på 2000 pund om året?* is it possible to live on £2000 a year? **leve|alder** *sb* age; duration of life. **~brød** *sb* means of livelihood; living.

~dyktig *adj* viable; *(kraftig)* vigorous; *et ~dyktig foretagende* a viable undertaking. **~kostnader** *sb fl* cost of living. **~lig** *adj* endurable, livable.

leven *sb* noise, uproar; *(moro)* fun, merriment; *(støyende moro)* horseplay; *for/på ~* for fun; for the fun of it.

levende *adj* **1** *(som predikatsord)* alive, living; *fisken var ~* the fish were alive; **2** *(foranstilt)* living, live; *en ~ fisk* a live fish; **3** *(livlig)* lively, vivid.

leveomkostninger *sb fl* cost of living.

lever *sb* liver.

leverandør *sb* supplier; *(stor~ også)* contractor; *(av matvarer)* purveyor. **leveranse** *sb* order, supply; *(levering)* delivery; *(kontraktsmessig ~)* contract. **levere** *vb* **1** *(overrekke)* deliver; *(gi fra seg)* give up; hand over; *~ tilbake* return; *når kan De ~ varene?* when can you deliver the goods; **2** *(forsyne med)* furnish, supply; **3** *(frembringe)* produce.

leveregel *sb* maxim; rule (of conduct).

levering *sb* **1** delivery; *ved ~* on delivery; **2** *(leveranse)* order, supply.

leverpostei *sb* liver paste.

leve|sett *sb* mode of living; way of life. **~standard** *sb* standard of living. **~tid** *sb* lifetime. **~vei** *sb* career, vocation. **~vilkår** *sb* conditions of life. **~vis** *sb* mode/way of life.

levne *vb* leave (over).

levnet *sb* life. **levnets|beskrivelse** *sb* biography, life. **~løp** *sb* career, life. **~midler** *sb koll* foodstuffs, provisions; victuals.

levning *sb* remain, remnant; *~er (fra måltid)* left-overs; *fortids~* relic.

li A *sb* hillside, mountainside; **B** *vb (om tid)* pass; wear on; *det led på dagen* the day was wearing on; *det lir mot høst/slutten* autumn/the end is drawing near; **C** *vb* se *lide.*

liberal *adj* liberal; *det liberale parti/de liberale* the Liberals. **liberalisme** *sb* liberalism. **liberalitet** *sb* liberality.

lide *vb* suffer; *~ av* suffer from; *de led tørst* they suffered from thirst; *hun led meget før hun døde* she suffered much before she died; *pasienten ~r meget* the patient is in great pain. **lidelse** *sb* suffering; *(fysisk også)* pain; *de døde under store lidelser* they died in great pain. **lidelsesfelle** *sb* fellow-sufferer.

lidenskap *sb* passion. **lidenskapelig** *adj* passionate. **lidenskapelighet** *sb* passion.

liga *sb* league. **liga|kamp** *sb* league match. **~mester** *sb* league champion. **~mesterskap** *sb* league championship.

ligge *vb* **1** lie; *(om ting ofte)* be; *(om bygninger)* be situated; stand; *ligg ikke (bare) der!~* don't just lie there! *~ til sengs* be/lie in bed; *~ syk* be ill in bed; *~ på sykehus* be in hospital; *byen ~r mellom fjell/ved en elv* the town is situated among hills/stands on a river; *kirken ~r høyt over landsbyen* the church stands high above the village; **2** *(uttrykk)* *~* **for:** *det ~r for henne* she has a natural gift/a talent for it; se også *lett: ha lett for*; *~* **i** *(være underforstått)* imply; be implied by; *jeg forstår ikke hva som ~r i det ordet* I don't see what is implied by that word/what that word implies; *~* **i:** *de ~r i influensa, alle sammen* they are laid up/are down with influenza, all of them; *~* **på:** *hønen ~r på eggene sine* the hen sits on her eggs; *~* **under:** *her ~r det noe under* there is more here than meets the eye; *~* **under for** *(en last)* be addicted to; *(en fristelse)* succumb to.

ligne 1 *vb* be like; resemble; *de ~r mye på hverandre* they are very much alike/they resemble each other closely; *det ~r ikke deg å si noe slikt* it is not like you to say such a thing; *han ~r mye på meg* he is very like me; **2** *(bare om ytre likhet)* look alike; *han ~r en ugle* he looks like an owl. **lignelse** *sb (i Bibelen)* parable. **lignende** *adj* like, similar; *noe ~* something like that; *på ~ måte* in a similar way. **ligning** *sb* **1** *(mat)* equation; **2** *(skatte~)* assessment.

lik *adj* like; similar to; *(~ med)* equal to; *~ lønn for ~t arbeid* equal pay for equal work; *alle mennesker er ~e* all men are equal; *hun er ~ sin far* she is like her father; *under ~e vilkår* under equal conditions. Se også *like, likere, likt.*

lik *sb (dødt menneske)* body, corpse. **likblek** *adj* deathly pale; pale as a sheet.

like A *adv* **1** *(direkte)* straight; *jeg gikk ~ bort til dem* I went straight up to them; **2** *(i samme grad)* equally; *~ tykk over det hele* equally thick all over; **3** *(tett, umiddelbart)* just; *~ bak/foran/* just behind/in front of; **4** *(uttrykk)* *~* **for** *øynene på deg* under your very eyes; *~* **fra** ever since; *~ fra reformasjonen* ever since the Reformation; *jeg sa det ~* **opp i** *ansiktet på ham* I told him so to his face; *~* **overfor** (just) opposite; *~* **siden** *krigen* ever since the war; *~* **til** *i dag* until today; **B** *sb: ~* **for** *~* tit for tat; **uten** *~ (rosende)* matchless, unequalled; peerless; *(nedsettende)* unexampled, unparalleled; *holde* **ved** *~* keep in repair; maintain; **C** *vb (synes godt om)* like; *jeg ~r å danse* I like dancing; *jeg ~r å se dem danse* I like to see them dance; *jeg ~r kaffe bedre enn te* I like coffee better than tea; *jeg ~r pærer best* I like pears best.

like|artet *adj* homogeneous. **~berettiget** *adj: være ~ til* have an equal right to. **~dan** *adv* in the same manner/way. **~frem 1** *adj = ~til 1*; **2** *adv* just, simply; plainly; *det er ~frem grusomt* it is simply awful. **~glad** *adj (skjødesløs)* careless; *(uinteressert)* indifferent; *jeg er ~glad* I don't care. **~gyldig** *adj (uten betydning)* unimportant; *(uinteressert)* indifferent; *(skjødesløs)* careless. **~ledes** *adv* also, likewise. **~lig** *adv: ~ fordelt* evenly distributed. **~mann** *sb* equal, match; *mine ~menn* my equals.

likere *adj (bedre)* better.

likesinnet *adj* like-minded.

likesom *adj, konj* **1** *(slik som)* (just) as; like; *han er offiser ~ sin far* he is an officer like his father; **2** *(på en måte)* somehow; as if; as it were; in a way; *(også omskriving med* seem*)*; *det er ~ jeg hører underlige stemmer* I seem to hear strange voices; *han var ~ litt sjenert* he was a little shy, as it were; *hun åpnet munnen ~ for å* *si noe* she opened her mouth as if to say something; *jeg har ~ ikke tiltro til ham* somehow I do not trust him. Jf *liksom.*

like|stilling *sb* equality of status. **~stilt** *adj* equal. **~så** *adv* also, likewise. Se også *likså.* **~til** *adj* **1** *(omgjengelig og grei)* simple, unpretending; *(enkel)* artless, informal; plain, simple; *(oppriktig)* frank, candid; **2** *(lett)* easy, simple; *ikke så ~* not so easy/simple. **~vekt** *sb* balance. **~likevektig** *adj* balanced; *(rolig også)* composed, event-empered.

likevel *adv* still, yet; after all; all the same; *det er merkelig, men ~ sant* it is strange yet true; *du burde ~ hjelpe dem* still, you ought to help them; *jeg hadde ~ rett* I was right after all.

likeverdig *adj* equivalent.

likhet *sb* likeness, resemblance, similarity; *(om rang og rettigheter)* equality; *~ for loven* equality before the law; *sosial ~* social equality; *sterk/svak ~* strong/faint resemblance; *er det noen ~ mellom Shaw og Ibsen?* are there any similarities between Shaw and Ibsen? *i ~ med England har Norge en flåte* like England Norway has a navy; *jeg kan ikke se noen ~ mellom dem* I can see no likeness between them. **likhets|punkt** *sb* point of resemblance. **~tegn** *sb* equation mark; sign of equation.

likkiste *sb* coffin.

likne etc se *ligne etc.*

liksom *adv* kind of; sort of; *det er bare på ~* it is only make-believe; *gjøre noe på ~* make believe to do something; *jeg hadde ~ på følelsen at* I kind of/sort of felt that. Se for øvrig *likesom.*

likså *adv* (just) as; *han er ~ stor* he is as big; *han er ~ stor som sin bror* he is as big as his brother; *jeg har ~ mange penger som han* I have as much money as he. Jf *likeså.*

liktorn *sb* corn.

likør *sb* liqueur.

lilje *sb* lily. **liljekonvall** *sb* lily of the valley.

lilla *adj, sb* lilac, mauve.

lille se *liten.* **lille|finger** *sb* little finger. **~slem** *sb* little slam. **~tå** *sb* little toe. **~viser** *sb* hour hand.

lim *sb* glue. **limbånd** *sb* adhesive tape. **lime** *sb* glue.

lime *sb (sope~)* broom.

limonade *sb* lemonade.

limpinne *sb: gå på ~n* be led up the garden path; swallow the bait.

lin *sb* flax.

lind *sb* lime, lime-tree.

lindre *vb* relieve; *denne medisinen vil ~ smertene dine* this medicine will relieve you pain. **lindring** *sb* relief.

line *sb* line; *danse på ~* walk on a tight-rope; walk the rope. **line|dans** *sb* tight-rope walking. **~danser** *sb* tight-rope walker. **~fiske** line-fishing.

linerle *sb* wagtail.

lin|gul, ~håret *adj* flaxen.

linjal *sb* ruler.

linje *sb* line; *en rett ~* a straight line; *(i ~delt skole)* side. **linje|avstand** *sb data* array pitch. **~brudd** *sb* disconnection; line break. **~båt** *sb* liner. **~mann** *sb (i sport)* linesman. **linjere** *vb* line, rule.

linn *adj* gentle, mild, soft.

linnea *sb* twinflower.

linning *sb* band.

linoleum *sb* linoleum, lino. **linolje** *sb* linseed oil.

linse *sb* **1** *(optisk ~)* lens; *konkave og konvekse ~r* concave and convex lenses; **2** *(om belgfrukten)* lentil.

lintøy *sb* linen.

lire *vb: ~ av seg* reel off. **lire|kasse** *sb* barrel-organ; *spille på ~* grind an organ. **~kassemann** *sb* organ grinder.

lirke *vb: han ~t nøkkelen inn i låsen* he coaxed the key into the lock; *hun ~t hemmeligheten ut av ham* she wormed the secret out of him.

lise *sb* alleviation, relief; *det var en ~ for nervene (mine)* it was a balm to my nerves.

lisens *sb* licence; *(~avgift)* licence fee.

lisse *sb* lace.

lissom se *liksom.*

list A *sb* **1** *(lurhet)* cunning; *sette ~ mot ~* meet cunning by cunning; **2** *(listig påfunn)* stratagem, trick; *bruke ~* employ a stratagem; use tricks/trickery; **B** *(av tre, på tøy etc)* list.

liste *sb (fortegnelse)* list; *stå på ~n* be on the list; *vi ble ført opp på ~n* we were entered on the list/roll. **listepapir** *sb data* fanfold paper; Z-fold paper.

liste seg walk softly; creep, steal; *hun ~t seg vekk* she stole away; *jeg ~t meg opp trappen* I crept upstairs.

listig *adj* cunning, sly.

lit *sb (tiltro)* confidence, trust; *feste ~ til* trust; place confidence in.

lite *adj* little; not much; *det er ~ håp* there is little hope; *hun spiser og sover ~* she eats and sleeps little; *jeg ser svært ~ til dem* I see very little of them; *vi har ~ mat* we have little food.

lite på *vb* trust; depend/rely on.

liten *adj* **1** *(om antall, betydning, størrelse)* small; *hun er ~ for alderen/for sin alder* she is small for her age; **2** *(mer følelsesbetont: ~ og nett/søt etc)* little; *en pen ~ hund* a nice little dog; **3** *(om avstand, tid og vekst)* short; *Napoleon var en ~ mann* Napoleon was a short man. **litenhet** *sb* littleness, smallness.

liter *sb* litre.

litt *adv* a little; somewhat; *~ etter* after a while; a little later; *~ etter ~* gradually; by degrees; *~ etter middag* soon/a little after dinner; *~ vin* a little wine; *jeg var ~ forbauset* I was a little surprised; *om ~* in a moment; presently; *vent ~!* wait a moment!

litteratur *sb* literature. **litteraturhistorie** *sb* literary history; history of literature. **litterær** *adj* literary.

liv *sb* **1** life; *de mistet ~et* they lost their lives; *han mistet ~et* he lost his life; **2** *(midje)* waist; *rundt ~et* round the waist; **3** *(kjole~ etc)* bodice; **4** *(uttrykk)* **aldri i ~et:** *jeg har aldri i ~et sett på maken* I have never in my life seen anything like it; *aldri i ~et!* not on your life! *for mitt* **bare ~** for the life of me; *jeg kan ikke* *for mitt bare ~ forstå hvorfor de gjorde det* I cannot for the life of me understand why they did it; *kjempe* **for ~et** fight for life; *løpe for ~et* run for (dear) life; *hun ble krøpling for ~et* she was crippled for life; **gjelde ~et:** *det gjelder ~et* it is a matter of life and death; **i ~e** alive; *de er fremdeles i ~e* they are still alive; *de holdt henne i ~e* they kept her alive; *det gikk på* **~et løs** it was a matter of life and death; **med ~** *og sjel* with heart and soul; *sveve* **mellom ~ og død** hover between life and death; *skyte hjertet* **opp i ~et** pluck up courage; *en kamp* **på ~ og død** a life-and-death struggle; a mortal fight; *få en* **skrekk i ~et** get a fright/a scare; **ta ~et av** kill; do away with; *ta ~et av seg* kill oneself; commit suicide; take one's own life; *sette* **ut i livet** carry into effect; carry out; realize. **livaktig** *adj* lifelike, vivid. **livat** *adj* lively, gay.

liv|belte *sb* life-belt. **~berge seg** *vb* keep body and soul together; support oneself. **~båt** *sb* life-boat.

live *vb: ~ opp* cheer (opp); refresh; brighten; liven up; *det ~t dem opp* it cheered them up; *disse blomstene ~r opp i rommet* these flowers brighten/liven up the room.

livegen *sb* serf. **livegenskap** *sb* serfdom.

livende redd = *livredd.*

liv|full *adj* lively, vivid; animated. **~garde** *sb* life guard; *(~vakt)* bodyguard. **~kjole** *sb* dress coat; tails. **~lig** *adj* lively, vivid; animated; *en ~ fantasi* a lively/vivid imagination; *et ~ selskap* an animated party. **~løs** *adj* lifeless; inanimate. **~mor** *sb* uterus, womb.

livne *vb: ~ til* revive.

livnære seg *vb* support oneself; keep body and soul together.

livré *sb* livery.

liv|redd *adj* scared to death. **~redning** *sb* life-saving. **~reim** *sb* belt. **~rente** *sb* (life) annuity. **~rett** *sb* favourite dish.

livs|anskuelse *sb* philosophy; view of life. **~betingelse** *sb* vital necessity. **~fare** *sb* mortal danger; peril; *vi var i ~fare* our lives were in danger. **~farlig** *adj* perilous. **~forsikring** *sb* life assurance/insurance. **~oppgave** mission in life. **~polise** *sb* life (assurance) policy. **~syn** *sb* philosophy; view of life. **~trett** *adj* weary of life. **~verk** *sb* life-work. **~viktig** *adj* vital; of vital importance. **~vilkår** *sb fl* conditions of life.

liv|vakt *sb* bodyguard. **~vidde** *sb* girth; waist measurement.

ljom *sb* echo. **ljome** *vb* resound, ring; echo.

ljuge se *lyve.*

ljå *sb* scythe.

lo *sb (på tøy)* nap, pile.

lodd *sb* **1** *(vekt)* weight; **2** *(skjebne)* lot; destiny, fate; **3** *(ved ~trekning)* lot; *(i lotteri)* lottery ticket; *trekke ~* draw lots; *~et er kastet* the die is cast.

lodde A *sb (om fisken)* capelin; **B** *vb* **I** *(måle dybde)* sound; **II** *~ ut* raffle; **III** *vb (med ~bolt)* solder. **lodde|bolt** *sb* soldering iron. **~lampe** *sb* soldering lamp.

lodden *adj* shaggy; hairy, woolly.

lodd|rett *adj* perpendicular; *(i kryssord)* down. **~trekning** *sb* drawing lots; *avgjøre ved ~* decide by lot.

loe *vb* get nappy/pily. **loet(e)** *adj* nappy, pily.

loff *sb* **A** white bread; *en ~* a loaf of white bread; **B:** *gå på ~en* bum/loaf around. **loffe** *vb (gå på loffen)* bum/loaf around. **loffer** *sb* bum, loafer.

loft *sb* loft; attic; *på loftet* in the attic. **lofts|bod, ~bu** *sb* attic storeroom. **~etasje** *sb* attic storey. **~vindu** *sb* skylight. **~værelse** *sb* attic, garret.

logaritme *sb* logarithm. **logaritmetabell** *sb* table of logarithms.

loggbok *sb* logbook.

logiker *sb* logician. **logikk** *sb* logic. **logisk** *adj* logical.

logn se *lun.*

logre *vb: hunden ~r med halen* the dog wags his tail.

lojal *adj* loyal. **lojalitet** *sb* loyalty.

lokal *adj* local; *~e forhold* local conditions. **lokale** *sb* hall, room; *fl også* premises; *(kontor~)* office; business premises. **lokalbedøvelse** *sb* local anaesthetic. **lokalisere** *vb* localize. **lokalitet** *sb* locality. **lokal|kjent** *adj* acquainted with the locality. **~patriot** *sb* local patriot. **~patriotisk** *adj* localistic. **~patriotisme** *sb* local patriotism; regionalism, *(nedsettende)* parochialism. **~samtale** *sb* local call. **~tok** *sb* local train. **~trafikk** *sb* local traffic.

lokk *sb* **A** *(på kiste, spann etc)* lid, cover; **B** *(av hår)* lock; curl, ringlet.

lokke *vb* entice, lure, tempt; *de ~t ham frem* they tempted him to come out. **lokkemat** *sb* bait.

lokomotiv *sb* (railway) engine; locomotive. **lokomotivfører** *sb* engine driver; *US* (locomotive) engineer.

lomme *sb* pocket. **lomme|bok** *sb* wallet. **~kniv** *sb* pocket-knife. **~lerke** *sb* flask, hip-flask. **~lykt** *sb* electric torch; flashlight. **~penger** *sb* pocket-money. **~regner** *sb* calculator. **~rusk** *sb* pocket fluff. **~tyv** *sb* pickpocket. **~tørkle** *sb* (pocket-)handkerchief. **~ur** *sb* watch.

loppe *sb* flea. **loppe|marked** *sb* jumble/rummage sale. **~stikk** *sb* flea-bite.

lort *sb (skitt)* dirt, filth; *(~klump)* turd; *(om avføring også)* excrement.

los *sb* **1** *(fører)* pilot; **2** *(om hund under jakt)* baying; *ha ~* give tongue. **lose** *vb* pilot.

losje *sb* **1** *(i teater)* box; **2** *(frimurer~)* lodge. **losjerad** *sb: første/annen ~* dress/upper circle. **losjere** *vb* lodge. **losjerende** *sb* lodger. **losji** *sb* lodging(s); *kost og ~* board and lodging.

loslitt *adj* threadbare.

loss *sb: kaste ~* cast off. **losse** *vb* unload. **lossing** *sb* unloading.

lott *sb (andel)* share.

lotte *sb* ≈ W.R.A.C. (Women's Royal Army Corps).

lotteri *sb* lottery. **lotterigevinst** *sb* lottery prize.

lov *sb* **1** *(tillatelse)* leave, permission; *han bad om ~ til å dra til London* he asked permission to go to London; *hun fikk ~ til å gå hjem* she was allowed/permitted to go home; **2** *(juridisk)* law; *(en enkelt ~)* Act of Parliament/*US* Congress; statute (law); *(foreningslover etc)* rules, statutes; *~ og orden/rett* law and order; *etter/ifølge ~en* according to law; *likhet for ~en* equality before the law; *mot ~en* against the law; *uten ~ og dom* without charge or trial; **3** *(pris, ros)* praise; *Gud skje ~!* thank God! **lov|bestemmelse** *sb* legal/statutory provision. **~bestemt** *adj* fixed by law; legal. **~brudd** *sb* violation of the law.

love *vb* **A** *(gi løfte)* promise; *hun lovte å være der* she promised to be there; **B** *(prise, rose)* praise; *Gud være ~et!* God be praised! thank God!

lovende *adj* promising.

lov|endring *sb* amendment (to an Act). **~feste** *vb* establish by law; legalize. **~formelig** *adj* legal. **~forslag** *sb* bill. **~givende** *adj* legislative; *~givende forsamling* legislative assembly; *~givende makt* legislative power. **~giver** *sb* legislator. **~givning** *sb* legislation. **~hjemlet** *adj* authorized/warranted by law. **~hjemmel** *sb* legal authority. **~kyndig** *adj* legally trained.

lovlig *adj* **1** *(~festet)* lawful, legal; *~ forfall* lawful absence; **2** *(tillatt)* permitted; **3** *(adv)* *(litt for)* rather (too); *~ varmt* rather too warm. **lovlighet** *sb* lawfulness, legality.

lov|lydig *adj* law-abiding. **~lydighet** *sb* law-abidingness. **~løs** *adj* lawless. **~løshet** *sb* lawlessness. **~messig** *adj* **1** *(ifølge loven)* lawful, legal; **2** *(regelmessig)* regular. **~messighet** *sb* **1** lawfulness, legality; **2** regularity.

lovord *sb (fl)* word/words of praise.

lovovertredelse *sb* breach of the law; offence.

lov|prise *vb* praise. **~prisning** *sb* praise.

lov|stridig *adj* contrary to the law; illegal. **~stridighet** *sb* illegality.

lovtale *sb* eulogy, praise.

lubben *adj* chubby, plump.

ludder *sb* whore.

lue A *sb (hodeplagg)* cap, hat; **B 1** *sb (flamme)* blaze, flame; *bryte ut i lys ~* burst into flames; *stå i lys ~* be in flames. **2** *vb: ~ opp* blaze up; burst into flames.

luft *sb* air; *de sprengte huset i ~en* they blew up the house; *han gav sin vrede ~* he gave vent to his anger; *i fri ~* in the open (air). **luft|ballong** *sb* balloon. **~bro** *sb* air lift. **~drag** *sb (luftning)* breeze; puff of air; *(trekk)* draught.

lufte *vb* air; *~ bremsene* bleed the brakes; *~ hunden* take out the dog; *~ sine meninger* air one's opinions. **luftetur** *sb* airing, walk.

luft|fart *sb (flyging)* aviation; *(flytrafikk)* air traffic. **~fartsselskap** *sb* airline company. **~forandring** *sb* change of air. **~forsvar** *sb* air defence. **~forurensing** *sb* air pollution. **~fotografering** *sb* aerial photography. **~frakt** *sb* air freight. **~gevær** *sb* air gun. **~havn** *sb* airport.

luftig *adj* airy. **lufting** *sb* airing; *(~ av rom også)* ventilation.

luft|kjølt *adv* air-cooled. **~lag** *sb* stratum of air. **~ledning** *sb* aerial/overhead conductor. **~linje** *sb: i ~linje* as the crow flies. **~motstand** *sb* air resistance.

luftning breeze; puff of air.

luft|putefartøy *sb* hovercraft. **~rom** *sb* airspace. **~rør** *sb* windpipe. **~skip** *sb* airship. **~slott** *sb* castle in Spain. **~speiling** *sb* mirage. **~syk** *adj* airsick. **~tett** *adj* airtight. **~tom** *adj* void of air; *~tomt rom* vacuum. **~trafikk** *sb* air traffic. **~trykk** *sb* atmospheric air pressure. **~ventil** *sb* air valve. **~vern** *sb* air defence; anti-aircraft defence. **~vernkanon** *sb* anti-aircraft gun; *dgl* ack-ack gun.

lugar *sb* cabin. **lugar|pike** *sb* stewardess. **~tjener** *sb* steward. **~trapp** *sb* companionway.

lugg *sb* forelock. **lugge** *vb* pull (by) the hair; *hun ~t meg* she pulled my hair.

luke A *sb* trapdoor; *(på skip)* hatch; *(om åpningen)* hatchway; **B** *vb (~ bort ugress)* weed.

lukke *vb* shut; *(især ved stengetid også)* close; *lukk døren!* shut the door! *~ igjen* close, shut; *~ inne* shut up; *~ opp* open; *(~ opp når det ringer)* answer the door/the bell; *~ ut* let out; *~ ute* shut out. Se også *stenge.* **lukket** *adj* closed; *en ~ bok* a closed book.

Lukkøye: *Ole ~* the Sandman.

luksuriøs *adj* luxurious. **luksus** *sb* luxury.

lukt *sb* smell, odour. **lukte** *vb* smell; *det ~r godt/vondt* it smells good/bad; *hun ~t på blomsten* she smelt the flower. **lukte|salt** *sb* smelling salt. **~sans** *sb* sense of smell. **luktfri** *adj* odourless.

lumbago *sb* lumbago.

lummer *adj* sultry.

lumpen *adj* mean. **lumpenhet** *sb* meanness.

lumsk *adj* insidious; *et ~t angrep* an insidious attack.

lun *adj* **1** *(varm)* warm, mild; **2** *(hyggelig)* cosy; *(om person)* good-natured; **3** *(i le)* sheltered;

lund *sb* grove.

lune *sb* **1** *(sinnsstemning)* humour; *i dårlig ~* in a bad humour; **2** *(innfall, nykke)* caprice, whim; *motens ~r* the whims of fashion. **lunefull, lunet(e)** *adj* capricious.

lunge *sb* lung. **lungebetennelse** *sb* pneumonia.

lunhet *sb (hygge)* coziness; *(varme)* warmth; *(om person)* geniality.

lunken *adj* lukewarm, tepid.

lunsj *sb* lunch; *(mer formelt)* luncheon.

lunte *sb* fuse; *lukte ~n* smell a rat.

lunte *vb (småtrave)* trot.

lupe *sb* magnifying glass.

lur A 1 *adj* cunning; *en ~ idé* a clever idea; **2** *sb: ligge på ~ etter* lie in ambush for; lie in wait for; **B** *sb (søvn)* nap; *hun fikk/tok seg en ~* she took a nap. **lure** *vb* **1** *(narre)* fool, trick; take in; *du ~r ikke meg!* you can't fool me! *han ble lurt til å* he was tricked into; *hun er lett å ~* she is easily taken in; **2** *(~ på: lytte)* eavesdrop; *(speide)* spy, watch; **3** *~ seg* sneak, steal; *de lurte* *seg unna* they sneaked/stole away; **4** *(undres)* speculate; ~ *på* wonder; *jeg ~r på om* I wonder if. **lurendreier** *sb* slyboots. **lureri** *sb* trickery, hoax. **lurifas, luring** *sb* slyboots.

lurveleven *sb* hubbub, uproar. **lurvet(e)** *adj* shabby.

lus *sb* louse. **lusekjører** *sb* crawler. **lusen** *adj* *(gjerrig, smålig)* mean, niggardly. **luset(e)** *adj* lousy.

lusing *sb (ørefik)* box on the ear.

luske *vb* prowl, slink; *en rev kom ~nde* a fox came prowling.

lut A *adj (bøyd)* bent, stooping; **B** *adv:* ~ *lei av* fed up with; **C** *sb* lye; *gå for ~ og kaldt vann* be left out in the cold. **luta** *adv = lut B.* **lute** *vb (være bøyd)* stoop; hang down.

lutheraner *sb* Lutheran. **luthersk** *adj* Lutheran.

lutre *vb* purify.

lutt *sb* lute.

lutter *adj, adv* all, pure; nothing but; *av ~ vennlighet* out of pure kindness; *hun er ~ smil* she is all smiles.

ly *sb* cover, shelter; *hvor kan vi finne ~?* where can we find shelter? *i ~ av* under shelter of; *søke ~ for/mot* seek/take shelter from.

lyd *sb* sound; *vi hørte ~(en) av stemmer* we heard the sound of voices. **lyd|bølge** *sb* sound wave. **~bånd** *sb* recording tape; *ta opp på ~bånd* tape-record. **~båndopptak** *sb* tape recording. **~båndopptaker** *sb* tape recorder. **~demper** *sb* silencer.

lyde *vb* **A** sound; *brevet ~r som følger* the letter reads/runs as follows; *det ~r utrolig* it sounds incredible; *sjekken ~r på 200 pund* the cheque is for £200; **B** *(lystre)* obey. **lydig** *adj* obedient; ~ *mot* obedient to. **lydighet** *sb* obedience.

lyd|løs *adj* noiseless, silent. **~mur** *sb* sound barrier. **~potte** *sb* exhaust box; silencer. **~skrift** *sb* phonetic script. **~styrke** *sb* sound intensity; *(i høyttaler)* volume.

lye *vb (lytte)* listen. Se også *lytte.*

lykke 1 *(~følelse)* happiness; *det brakte ~* it brought happiness; **2** *(fremgang)* (good) fortune/luck; success; *han ville gjerne prøve ~n* he would like to try his luck; *hun gjorde ~ som taler* she was a success as a speaker; **til** ~ congratulations; I congratulate you; *jeg ønsket ham* **til ~ med** *fødselsdagen* I congratulated him on his birthday; *til ~ med fødselsdagen!* many happy returns (of the day)! **3** *(gode, hell)* blessing; a piece of good luck; *det var en ~ at du kom* it was a piece of good luck that you came. **lykkelig** *adj* **1** *(til sinns)* happy; *hun var ~ over resultatet* she was happy about the result; *jeg er ~ over å kunne hjelpe deg* I am happy to be able to help you; **2** *(heldig)* fortunate, lucky. **lykkeligvis** *adv* fortunately, happily, luckily. **lykkes** *vb* succeed; *det lyktes oss å finne dem* we succeeded in finding them; *planen lyktes* the plan succeeded; *planen lyktes for dem* they succeeded in their plan. **lykketreff** *sb* stroke of good fortune. **lykksalig** *adj* blissful. **lykkønske** *vb* congratulate; *jeg ~r deg med din forlovelse* I congratulate you on your engagement. **lykkønsking** *sb* congratulation.

lykt *sb* lantern; *(bil~, sykkel~)* lamp; *(lomme~)* flashlight, torch. **lyktestolpe** *sb* lamp-post.

lyn *sb* lightning; *(lynglimt)* flash of lightning; *~et slo ned i huset* the house was struck by lightning; *med lynets fart* with lightning speed; *som ~ fra klar himmel* like a bolt from the blue. **lyn|avleder** *sb* lightning conductor/rod. **~blink, ~glimt** *sb* flash of lightning. **lyne** *vb* lighten; flash; *det ~r* it is lightening; *med ~nde fart* with lightning speed; *øynene hans lynte* his eyes flashed.

lyng *sb* heather.

lynglimt *sb* flash of lightning.

lyngmo *sb* moor, heath.

lynne *sb* disposition; temper, temperament.

lyn|nedslag *sb* (stroke of) lightning. **~snar** *adj* quick as lightning. **~tog** *sb* express train.

lyriker *sb* (lyric) poet. **lyrikk** *sb* (lyric) poetry. **lyrisk** lyric(al).

lys I *adj* light; *(også fig)* bright, brilliant; *(om hudfarge og hår)* blond(e), fair; *~e farger* bright colours; *~t hår* fair hair; *en ~ idé* a bright idea; *mens det ennå er ~t* while it is still (day)light; **II** *adv:* ~ *levende* as large as life; ~ *våken* broad/wide awake; **III** *sb* **1** light; *(talg~)* candle; *~et gikk* the light went out; *han tente/slokket ~et (om talg~)* he lighted/put out the candle; *(om elektrisk ~)* he switched on/off the light; **2** *(uttrykk) se* **dagens** ~ be born; come into the world; **føre bak ~et** deceive; take in; *se saken* **i et nytt** ~ see the matter in another light; *lete med* ~ **og lykte** *etter* hunt high and low for; *det gikk et* ~ **opp for** *meg* it dawned upon me.

lysbølge *sb* light wave. **lyse** *vb* **1** give out light; shine; ~ *opp* brighten, illuminate; *denne lampen ~r godt* this lamp gives a good light; *lampen lyste klart* the lamp shone broghtly; **2** ~ *til eksteskap* publish the banns.

lyse|blå, ~grå etc *adj* light blue/grey etc; *(stundom)* pale blue/grey etc. **~krone** *sb* chandelier. **~rød** *adj* pink. **~slokker** *sb (glededreper)* killjoy, spoilsport; wet blanket. **~stake** *sb* candlestick. **~stump** *sb* candle end.

lys|horn *sb (på bil)* light hooter. **~håret** *adj* blond(e), fair-haired.

lysing *sb (kunngjøring)* announcement; *(ekteskaps~)* banns.

lys|kaster *sb (søkelys)* searchlight; *(til flombelysning)* floodlights; *(på bil)* headlights.

lyske *sb* groin.

lys|kjegle *sb* beam of light. **~kopi** *sb* photocopy; *(blåkopi)* blueprint. **~kryss** *sb* traffic lights. **~ledning** *sb* light(ing) cable/wire. **~løype** *sb* flood-lit track. **~mast** *sb* pylon. **~måler** *sb (foto)* exposure meter.

lysne *vb* brighten; grow light; *(om været)* clear up; *det ~r* it is getting light; *(om været)* it is clearing up.

lysnett *sb* (electric) mains; light circuit; *(for større område)* grid.

lysning *sb (lysskjær)* glimmer; *(~ i været)* clearing up; let-up; *(bedre utsikter)* improvement; brighter prospects; *(~ i skogen)* clearing, glade.

lys|penn *sb data etc* selector pen. **~punkt** *sb (især fig)* bright spot. **~pære** *sb* bulb. **~reklame** *sb (skilt)* electric sign; *(på tak)* sky sign. **~signal** *sb* light signal. **~skjær** *sb* glimmer; gleam of light. **~sky** *adj* fishy, shady. **~stolpe** *sb* light pole. **~strime, ~stripe** *sb* streak of light. **~stråle** *sb* beam; ray of light. **~styrke** *sb* brightness; candle power.

lyst *sb* **1** *(ønske)* desire, wish; inclination; **2** *(lystfølelse)* delight, pleasure; **3** *(uttrykk)* **av hjertens ~** to one's heart's content; **få ~ på** take a fancy to; **ha ~** like, want; have a mind to; *bli så lenge du har ~* stay as long as you like/want; **ha ~ på** want; feel like; *jeg har ~ på en kopp kaffe* I'd like/I feel like a cup of coffee; *jeg har ikke ~ på frokost i dag* I don't feel like breakfast today; **ha ~ til:** *jeg kunne ha ~ til å treffe henne* I should like to meet her; **hver sin ~** everyone to his taste; **med ~:** *arbeide med ~* be keen on one's work; work with a will. **lyst|betont** *adj* pleasureable, pleasant. **~hus** *sb* arbour. **lystig** *adj* merry; gay, jolly. **lystighet** merriment, mirth; gaiety.

lystre *vb* obey; *soldater må ~ ordre* soldiers must obey orders.

lystspill *sb* comedy.

lysvåken *adj* broad/wide awake.

lyte *sb* defect, flaw; blemish; fault; *(kropps~)* handicap.

lytte *vb* listen; *de ~t til hvert ord hun sa* they listened to every word she said; *jeg ~t (ventende) etter fottrinnene hans* I listened for his footsteps. **lytter** *sb (også radio~)* listener.

lyve *vb* lie; tell a lie; *du ~r!* you are lying! *han løy for meg* he told me a lie.

lær *sb* leather. **læraktig** *adj* leathery.

lærd *adj* learned; *en ~* a learned man/woman/person; a scholar; *de ~e strides* doctors disagree. **lærdom** *sb* learning.

lære I *sb* **1** *(håndverks~ etc)* apprenticeship; *han kom i ~ hos en skredder* he was apprenticed to/with a tailor; *hun gikk i ~ hos en gullsmed* she served her apprenticeship with a goldsmith; **2** *(forkynnelse, undervisning)* teaching; *Luthers ~* the teaching of Luther; **II** *vb* **1** learn; *~ å kjenne* become acquainted with; get to know; *han ville gjerne ~ henne bedre å kjenne* he would like to know her better; *jeg lærte dem å kjenne ganske godt* I got to know them rather well; *vi lærte å danse* we learned to dance/dancing; **2** *(undervise)* teach; *hvem har lært dere tysk* who taught you German? **lære|bok** *sb* textbook. **~gutt** se *lærling*. **~nem** *adj* quick to learn. **~penge** *sb* lesson; *la dette være en ~!* let this be a lesson to you! **lærer** *sb (i grunnskolen oftest)* teacher; *(i videregående skole især)* master; *(for øvrig ofte)* schoolmaster; *~ i historie* teacher of history; history master. **lærerik** *adj* instructive. **lærer|inne** *sb* teacher; *(også)* schoolmistress. Se for øvrig *lærer*. **~skole** *sb* training college; *US* teacher's college. **~personale** *sb* (teaching) staff. **~værelse** *sb* staff room. **lære|setning** *sb* doctrine, dogma. **~tid** *sb* apprenticeship. **lær(e)villig** *adj* eager/willing to learn; docile. **lærling** *sb* apprentice.

lødig *adj* pure, sterling.

løe *sb* barn.

løft *sb* lift. **løfte 1** *sb* promise; *et ~ om hjelp* a promise of assistance; *et ~ om å hjelpe* a promise to assist; *han brøt/holdt sitt ~* he broke/kept his promise; **2** *vb* lift, raise; *hun ~t armen* she raised her arm; *kan du ~ denne kassen?* can you lift this crate? **løftebrudd** *sb* breach of promise.

løgn *sb* lie; *det er ~* it is a lie. **løgner, løgnhals** *sb* liar; *du er en ~!* you are a liar!.

løk *sb* onion.

løkke *sb (på tau etc)* loop, noose.

lømmel *sb* lout, scamp.

lønn *sb* **A 1** *(for kroppsarbeid)* pay; wages *(oftest i fl)*; *(gasje)* salary; *høy/lav ~* high/low wages; *en ~ som en kan leve av* a living wage; *~en hans er 95 pund om uken* his wages are £95 a week; *på full ~* at full pay; **2** *(belønning)* reward; *seierens ~* the reward of victory; **B** *(lønnetre)* maple; **C** *(skjul) i ~* in secret; secretly. **lønne** *vb* **1** pay; *det ~r seg ikke* it does not pay; **2** *(belønne)* reward. **lønning** pay, wages. Se også *lønn*. **lønnings|dag** *sb* pay-day. **~liste** *sb* pay-roll. **~pose** *sb* pay-packet. **lønnkammer** *sb* private closet/room. **lønnlig** *adj* secret.

lønns|avtale *sb* wage agreement. **~forhandlinger** *sb* wage negotiations. **~forhøyelse** *sb* wage increase. **~glidning** *sb* wage drift. **~inntekt** *sb* earned income. **~kamp** *sb* wage conflict/war. **~klasse** *sb* salary class/group; *(stundom)* income bracket. **~konto** *sb* salary account. **~krav** *sb* wage demand. **~mottaker** *sb* wage-earner.

lønnsom *adj* profitable.

lønns|oppgjør *sb* wages settlement. **~pålegg** *sb* wage increase. **~skala** *sb* salary scale. **~sjekk** *sb* pay cheque/*US* check. **~slipp** *sb* pay slip. **~stopp** *sb* wage freeze.

løp *sb* **1** *(det å løpe)* running; **2** *(et enkelt ~)* run; **3** *(kapp~, vedde~)* race; *hun vant ~et* she won the race; **4** *(tidens ~)* course; *i ~et av året, i årets ~* in the course of a year; **5** *(børsepipe)* barrel; **6** (uttrykk) *gi* **fritt ~** give vent/(a) free rein to; *han gav sinnet (sitt) fritt ~* he gave vent/(a) free rein to his anger; *i det* **lange ~** in the long run; **i ~et av** *kort tid* in a short time; *i ~et av sommeren* during the summer. **løpe** *vb* run; *~ (bak)etter* run after; *~ etter (for å hente etc)* run for; *~ etter guttene/jentene* chase the boys/girls; *~ om kapp* (run a) race; *~ ut i sanden* come to nothing; *de løp sin vei* they ran away/off. **løpebane** *sb* **1** *(på idrettsplass)* track; **2** *(livsløp)* career. **løper** *sb* **1** *(en som ~)* runner; **2** *(bord~)* runner; *(trappe~)* carpet; **3** *(i sjakk)* bishop. **løperekke** *sb* forwards. **løpsk** *adj: hesten løp ~* the horse bolted.

lørdag *sb* Saturday; *forrige ~* last Saturday; *til ~* next Saturday.

løs *adj* loose; *en ~ tann* a loose tooth; *ha en skrue ~* have a screw loose; *han slapp ~* he was set free; *hesten ble sluppet ~* the horse was let loose; *hunden for ~ på ham* the dog rushed at him. **løse** *vb* **1** *(gjøre løsere)* loosen; **2** *(sette fri)* let loose; *hun løste hunden* she let loose the dog; **3** *~ billett* buy a ticket; *~ en oppgave* make out/solve a problem. **løsepenger** *sb* ransom; *bandittene krevde 50.000 pund i ~ for ham* the bandits demanded £50 000 in ransom for him. **løs|gjenger** *sb* tramp, vagrant. **~late** *vb* release; set free. **løsne** *vb* **1** loosen; come/work loose; *skruen har ~t* the screw has loosened; **2** *(~ skudd)* fire; *uten å ~ et skudd* without firing a shot. **løsning** *sb* solution; *en ~ av/på problemet* a solution of/to the problem. **løsningsmiddel** *sb* solvent. **løs|sluppen** *adj* abandoned; riotous, wild. **~øre** *sb koll* chattels, movables.

løv *sb* leaves *(fl)*; *vissent ~* dead leaves.

løve *sb* lion. **løvetann** *sb* dandelion. **løvinne** *sb* lioness.

løvsag *sb* fretsaw.

løye *vb: vinden ~r* the wind drops/lulls.

løyer *sb* fun, joke. **løyerlig** *adj* comical, droll.

løype *sb (ski~)* ski track.

løytnant lieutenant. Se også midtsidene.

løyve *sb* permission, permit. **løyve** *vb (bevilge)* grant, vote. **løyving** *sb* grant.

lån *sb* loan; *et ~ på 500 pund* a loan of £500; *jeg fikk boken til ~s* I borrowed the book; *takk for ~et* thank you (for lending it me); *takk for ~et av boken* thank you for the loan of/for lending me the book. **låne** *vb* **1** *(motta som lån)* borrow; *jeg lånte boken av/hos ham* I borrowed the book from him; *kan jeg få ~ bilen din?* can I have the loan of your car? *kan jeg få ~ telefonen?* may I use your telephone? **2** *(~ bort)* lend; *kan du ~ meg 5 pund til i morgen?* can you lend me/let me have £5 till tomorrow? **lån|giver** *sb* lender. **~taker** *sb* borrower.

lår *sb* thigh; *(på slakt)* leg. **lår|hals** *sb* neck of the femur. **~kort** *adj: ~ skjørt* miniskirt.

lås *sb* lock; *(henge~)* padlock; *(~ på veske, smykke etc)* fastener; catch, snap; *bak ~ og slå* behind bars. **låse** *vb* lock; *(med hengelås)* padlock; *hun låste porten* she locked the gate; *han låste henne inne på værelset* he locked her (up) in her room; *jeg låste opp kofferten* I unlocked the trunk; *de låste meg ut* they let me out. **låsesmed** *sb* locksmith. **låst** *adj* locked (up).

låt *sb* sound, ring. **låte** *vb* sound, ring.

låve *sb (~bygning)* barn; *(~gulv)* threshing-floor. **låve|bro** *sb* barn bridge. **~dør** *sb* barn door.

M

m *(bokstaven)* m.

madonna *sb* (the) Madonna.

madrass *sb* mattress.

magasin *sb* **1** *(lagerbygning)* storehouse, warehouse; **2** *(stor~)* department store; **3** *(blad)* magazine; **4** *(i skytevåpen)* magazine.

mager *adj* **1** *(om personer og levende dyr)* thin; lean, spare; *et ~t ansikt* a lean face; *en ~ mann* a thin man; **2** *(om kjøtt)* lean; *~t bacon* lean bacon; **3** *(skral, skrinn)* meagre; poor, thin; *~ jord* poor/thin soil; *et ~t resultat* a meagre/poor result.

magi *sb* magic. **magiker** *sb* magician. **magisk** *adj* magic.

magnat *sb* magnate, tycoon.

magnet *sb* magnet; *(i dynamo etc)* magneto. **magnetbånd** *sb* (magnetic) tape. **magnetbånddrev** *sb data* tape drive. **magnetisk** *adj* magnetic. **magnetisere** *vb* magnetize. **magnetisme** *sb* magnetism. **magnet|nål** *sb* magnetic needle. **~plate** *sb data* disk.

mahogny *sb* mahogany.

mai May; *~ måned* the month of May.

mais *sb* maize; Indian corn; *(US ofte bare)* corn. Jf *hvete* og *korn 1.* **maiskolbe** *sb* corncob.

majestet *sb* majesty; *Deres ~ har rett* Your Majesty is right. **majestetisk** *adj* majestic. **majestetsforbrytelse** *sb* lese-majesty.

majones *sb* mayonnaise.

major *sb* major. Se midtsidene. **majoritet** *sb* majority; *med en ~ på 25* by a majority of 25; *være i ~* be in (the) majority.

mak *sb: i ro og ~* at one's leisure.

makaber *adj* macabre.

makaroni *sb* macaroni.

make I *sb* **1** *(likemann)* equal, like; *~n til frekkhet!* what cheek! *det finns ikke hennes ~* she hasn't an equal; there is nobody to touch her; *jeg har aldri hørt/sett ~n!* well, I never! *kan De skaffe meg ~n til dette stoffet?* can you match this material for me? **2** *(ektefelle)* spouse; **3** *(dyrs ~)* mate; **II** *vb: ~ det slik at* arrange matters so as to. **makelig** *adj* comfortable, easy; *(~ anlagt)* indolent; *en ~ stol* a comfortable chair; *et ~ liv* an easy life; *jeg kan ~ gjøre det* I can easily do it. **makelighet** *sb* ease, comfort; *(dovenskap)* indolence. **makeløs** *adj* exceptional, unrivalled; unique; *(vidunderlig)* wonderful; *makeløst billig* exceptionally cheap.

makk *sb* maggot, worm.

makker *sb* partner.

makkverk *sb* botchwork; piece of botching.

makrell *sb* mackerel. **makrellstørje** *sb* tunny; *US også* tuna.

makron *sb* macaroon.

maksimal *adj* maximum. **maksimalpris** *sb* maximum price. **maksimum** *sb* maximum.

makt *sb* **1** *(herredømme, stat)* power; *kampen om ~en* the struggle for power; *stormaktene* the Big/Great Powers; **2** *(styrke, vold)* force; *bruke ~* employ force; *væpnet ~* armed force; **3** *(uttrykk)* **få ~ over** obtain power over; **med ~** by (main) force; **stå ved ~** be in force. **makte** *vb* be able to; manage; *jeg ~r ikke å gjøre det* I am unable to do it. **makteslos** *adj* powerless; *politiet stod ~* the police could do nothing. **maktpåliggende** *adj* imperative; essential, important; urgent.

male *vb* **1** *(påføre maling)* paint; *~ med vannfarger* paint in water colour; *vi malte huset grønt* we painted the house green; **2** *(~ kaffe, korn etc)* grind; *~ til mel* grind into flour; **3** *(om katt)* purr. **malende** *adj* graphic, vivid; *en ~ beskrivelse* a graphic/vivid description. **maler** *sb* painter; *(om håndverker især)* house-painter; *(om kunst~ også)* artist. **maleri** *sb* painting, picture. **malerisamling** *sb* collection of paintings/pictures; *(stor ~)* (picture) gallery. **malerisk** *adj* picturesque; *(kunstnerisk også)* artistic, pictorial; *en ~ landsby* a picturesque village. **maleriutstilling** *sb* picture exhibition. **maler|kost, ~pensel** *sb* paint-brush. **~skrin** *sb* paintbox. **maling** *sb* *(det å male)* painting; *(malerfarge)* paint.

malje *sb* eye; *hekte og ~* hook and eye.

malm *sb* ore. **malm|felt** *sb* ore deposit. **~full** *adj* sonorous. **~leie** *sb* ore deposit. **~åre** *sb* lode; vein of ore.

malplassert *adj* ill-placed, ill-timed; untimely.

malstrøm *sb* maelstrom.

malt *sb* malt. **maltekstrakt** *sb* malt extract.

maltraktere *vb* maltreat, ill-treat.

malurt *sb* wormwood; *blande ~ i ens beger* embitter somebody's joy.

mamma *sb* mamma; ma, mummy.

man *ubest pron* **1** *(omskrives ofte med passiv) ~ lo av ham* he was laughed at; *~ lovte meg en belønning* I was promised a reward; *~ sendte bud etter legen* the doctor was sent for; **2** *(når den talende innbefattes)* one; *~ bryr seg ikke om å fornærme sine venner* one does not like to offend one's friends; **3** *(når den tiltalte innbefattes)* you, we; *~ kan aldri vite* you can never tell; *~ kommer inn i slottet gjennom hovedporten* you/we enter the palace by the main gate; **4** *(når verken den talende eller den tiltalte innbefattes)* people, they; *i Tyskland drikker ~ mye øl* in Germany they drink much beer; *~ begynte å snakke om det* people began to talk about it.

man *sb (på hest etc)* mane.

mandag *sb* Monday; *forrige ~* last Monday; *om ~en (hver ~)* on Mondays.

mandarin *sb* **1** *(kinesisk embetsmann)* mandarin; **2** *(om frukten)* tangerine.

mandat *sb* **1** *(fullmakt)* authority, authorization; **2** *(stortings~)* seat; *de liberale erobret to ~er* the Liberals won two seats; **3** *(~område, ~styre)* mandate; *Palestina ble britisk ~ i 1920* Palestine became a British mandate in 1920. **mandatområde** *sb* mandate.

mandel *sb* **1** *(frukten)* almond; **2** *(i halsen)* tonsil.

mandig *adj* manly, manful; virile. **mandighet** manliness, manfullness; virility.

mandolin *sb* mandolin.

mane *vb* conjure; *~ frem* conjure up; *dette ~r til ettertanke* this gives food for thought; this invites reflection.

manerer *sb fl* manners; *han eier ikke ~* he has no manners.

manesje *sb* ring.

manet *sb* jellyfish.

mang *pron: ~ en* many a; *~ en gang* many a time.

mange *pron* many; *(ofte, især i bekreftende svar)* a lot of; a great many; a great number of; *(foran engelske entallsord)* much; a lot of; a great deal of; *~ penger* much money; *~ takk* thank you very much; *(især skriftlig)* many thanks; *klokken er ~* it is late. **mange|artet** *adj* multifarious; of many different kinds. **~doble** *vb* multiply. **~farget** *adj* multi-coloured. **~kant** *sb* polygon.

mangel *sb* **1** want; lack, shortage; scarcity; *~ på erfaring* inexperience; lack of experience; *~ på mat* lack/shortage of food; *av ~ på, i ~ av* for want of; *de døde av ~ på frisk luft* they died from want of fresh air; **2** *(lyte)* flaw, handicap; **3** *(ufullkommenhet)* defect; *fordeler og mangler* advantages and disadvantages; **4** *(ulempe)* drawback. **mangel|full** *adj* defective, faulty. **~sykdom** *sb* deficiency disease.

mang en se *mang*.

mange|millionær *sb* multi-millionaire. **~sidig** *adj* many-sided; *(om personer også)* versatile. **~sidighet** *sb* many-sidedness; *(om personer)* versatility. **~årig** *adj: en ~årig venn* a very old friend; a friend of very long standing. **mangfoldig** *adj* complex; resourceful, versatile. **mangfoldige** *adj (svært mange)* numerous; ever so many; very many. **mangfoldiggjøre** *vb* multiply; *(kopiere)* duplicate.

mangle *vb* **1** *(ikke ha)* lack; be short of; have no ...; *de ~r penger* they have no money; *hun ~r erfaring* she lacks experience; *vi ~t mat og vann* we were short of food and water; **2** *(trenge til)* need; *jeg ~r øvelse* I need practice; **3** *(ikke være til stede)* be missing; *to av guttene ~t* two of the boys were missing/were not there; **4** *det skulle bare ~!* certainly not! I should think not! **manglende** *adj* lacking, missing; absent; *det ~ mellomledd* the missing link.

mangt *pron* many things; *~ og mye* a great many things; *~ et* se *mang*.

mani *sb* craze, mania; *ha ~ for* have a craze/a mania for.

manifest *sb* manifesto.

manikyr(e) *sb* manicure. **manikyrere** *sb* manicure. **manikyrist** *sb* manicurist.

manipulasjon *sb* manipulation. **manipulere** *vb* manipulate.

manke *sb (på hest etc)* mane; *(tykt hår for øvrig)* shock of hair.

manko *sb* deficit, deficiency.

mann *sb* man; *femti* ~ fifty men; *(ektemann)* husband; ~ *og kone* husband and wife; *han er* ~ *for å* he is the sort of fellow who can; *i manns minne* within living memory; *som én* ~ to a man; *være* ~ *for sin hatt* be equal to the occasion.

manna *sb* manna.

mann|dom *sb* **1** *(manndomsalder)* manhood; **2** *(mandighet)* manliness. **~drap** *sb* homicide. **manne** *vb:* ~ *seg opp* pull oneself together. **mannefall** *sb* loss of life.

mannekeng, mannequin *sb* mannequin, model.

mann|folk *sb* man. **~gard** *sb: gå ~gard* raise a posse. **~haftig** *adj* mannish. **mannlig** *adj* **1** *(av hannkjønn)* male; ~ *hushjelp* male servant; **2** *(typisk for menn)* male, masculine. **mannsalder** *sb* generation. **mannskap** *sb* men, personnel; *(besetning)* crew; *marinens* ~ the personnel of the navy; *offiserer og* ~ officers and men. **manns|klær** *sb koll* men's clothes. **~kor** *sb* male choir. **mannsling** *sb* manikin. **mannsmot** *sb* manly courage. **mannsterk** *adj: de var ~e* there were many of them; they were strong in number. **mann|-tall** *sb* census; *holde ~tall* take a census. **~vond** adj *(om dyr)* fierce; *(om hest også)* vicious.

mansjett *sb* cuff. **mansjettknapp** *sb* cuff-link.

manual *sb (til styrketrening)* dumb-bell.

manuell *sb* manual.

manufaktur|forretning *sb* draper's shop; *US* dry goods store. **~handler** *sb* draper; *US* dry-goods dealer. **~varer** *sb* drapery goods; *US* dry goods.

manuskript *sb* manuscript.

manøver *sb* manoeuvre. **manøvrere** *vb* manoeuvre.

mappe *sb (lær~)* attaché case; brief-case; *(stor)* portfolio; *(av papp etc)* folder.

mareritt *sb* nightmare.

marg *sb* **1** *(bein~)* marrow; *gjennom* ~ *og bein* to the marrow/bone; **2** *(i bok)* margin.

margarin *sb* margarine; *dgl* marge.

margin *sb* margin.

Maria Mary; *jomfru* ~ the Virgin Mary; the Holy Virgin.

marihuana *sb* marihuana, marijuana.

marihøne *sb* ladybird.

marine *sb* navy; *GB mil også* the Senior Service. **marine|infanteriet** the Royal Marines; *US* the United States Marine Corps. **~infanterist, ~soldat** *sb* marine.

marinøkleband *sb* primrose.

marionett *sb* puppet. Jf *dukke A 2.* **marionetteater** = *dukketeater.*

maritim *adj* maritime, marine.

mark *(mynt)* mark; *30* ~ thirty marks.

mark *sb* **A** *(makk)* maggot, worm; **B 1** *(åker og eng)* field; **2** *(bakke, jord)* ground; *på ~en* on the ground. **markblomst** *sb* field flower; meadow flower.

marked *sb* market; *(~ med underholdning)* fair; *komme på ~et* come on the market; *sende ut på ~et* put on the market; market; *være på ~et* be on the market; **markeds|bod, ~bu** *sb* market stall. **~føre** *vb* market. **~pris** *sb* market price; *petro også* arm's length price. **~verdi** *sb* market value.

markere *vb* indicate, mark.

markise *sb (solseil)* awning.

markør *sb data* cursor.

marmelade *sb (appelsin~)* marmalade.

marmor *sb* marble.

mars March; *i* ~ *måned* in the month of March.

marsipan *sb* marzipan.

marsj *sb* march; *på* ~ on the march. **marsjere** *vb* march; *de marsjerte mot Paris* they marched on Paris. **marsjfart** *sb* cruising speed.

marskalk *sb* marshal; *(ved begravelse)* pall-bearer.

marsvin *sb* guinea pig.

martyr *sb* martyr; *han døde som* ~ he died a martyr. **martyrdød, martyrium** *sb* martyrdom.

mas *sb* **1** *(gnål)* importunities *(fl)*; **2** *(strev)* trouble; bother; bustle. **mase** *vb* **1** *(gnåle)* importune; *han maste på moren om flere penger* he importuned his mother for more money; **2** *(kave)* bustle about; fuss; **3** *(streve)* slave, toil. **maset(e)** *adj (gnålete)* importunate; *(vimsete)* fussy.

maske *sb* **1** *(garnløkke)* stitch; *hun slapp en* ~ she dropped a stitch; **2** *(for ansiktet)* mask; *hun hadde tatt på seg en* ~ she had put on a mask. **maskeball, maskerade** *sb* fancy-dress ball. **maskere** *vb* mask; *en maskert kvinne* a masked woman.

maskin *sb* **1** *(arbeids~)* machine; *fl ofte* machinery; **2** *(kraft~)* engine; *damp~* steam engine; **3** *skrive på* ~ type; *brevet var ~skrevet* the letter was typed. **maskinarbeider** *sb* mechanic. **maskineri** *sb* machinery. **maskin|gevær** *sb* machine gun. **~ingeniør** *sb* mechanical engineer. **maskinist, maskinmester** *sb* engineer. **maskin|messig** *adj* mechanical; *(automatisk)* automatic. **~park** *sb* machinery. **~pistol** *sb* machine pistol. **~skrive** *vb* type. **~skriver** *sb* typist. **~språk** *sb data* computer language. **~vare** *sb data* hardware.

maskot *sb* mascot.

maskulin *adj* masculine.

masovn *sb (smelteovn)* blast furnace.

massakre *sb* massacre. **massakrere** *vb* massacre.

massasje *sb* massage.

masse *sb* **1** mass; *en seig* ~ a tough mass; *den store* ~ *(dvs folk flest)* the masses; *en bok for den store* ~ a book for the masses; **2** *(stor mengde)* heaps; lots, masses; a lot; *en* ~ *bry* a lot of trouble; *en* ~ *mennesker* a lot/lots/crowds of people; *en* ~ *penger* heaps of money; *en* ~ *snø* masses of snow. **masse|grav** *sb* common grave; mass grave. **~lager** *sb data* bulk storage. **~medium** *sb* mass medium. **~morder** *sb* mass murderer. **~møte** *sb* mass meeting. **~produksjon** *sb* mass production.

massere *vb* massage.

massevis *adv: ~ av penger/penger i ~* a lot of/heaps of/lots of money. **massiv** *adj* **1** *(ikke hul)* solid; *~t gull* solid gold; **2** *(svær)* heavy, massive; solid; *en ~ bygning* a massive building.

massør *sb* masseur. **massøse** *sb* masseuse.

mast *sb (skip~ etc)* mast; *(kraft~)* pylon.

mat *sb* food; *(måltid)* meal; *~ og drikke* food and drink; *~en er ferdig* dinner (etc) is ready; *~en er ikke videre god her* the cooking is not very good here; *varm ~* a hot meal; hot meals; *hun kan ikke lage ~* she cannot cook; *jeg laget ~en selv* I cooked my own meals. **matbit(e)** *sb* bite, morsel (of food); *jeg har ikke smakt en ~ siden frokost* I haven't had a bite/a morsel of food since breakfast; *ta seg en ~* have a snack. **mate** *vb* feed.

matematiker *sb* mathematician. **matematikk** *sb* mathematics. **matematisk** *adj* mathematical.

material(e) *sb* material. **materialisme** *sb* materialism. **materialist** *sb* materialist. **materialistisk** *adj* materialistic. **materie** *sb (stoff)* matter, substance; *(i sår)* matter, pus. **materiell** **1** *adj* material; **2** *sb* equipment; *rullende ~ (på jernbane)* rolling stock.

mat|fett *sb* edible fat; lard. **~forgiftning** *sb* food poisoning. **mating** *sb* feeding. **mat|jord** *sb* humus, topsoil. **~laging** *sb* cooking, cookery. **~lyst** *sb* appetite. **~mor** *sb* mistress of the house. **~olje** *sb* cooking oil. **~pakke** *sb* (packed) lunch; lunch packet. **~papir** *sb* sandwich paper. **~rester** *sb fl* left-overs.

matriseskriver *sb data* dot/matrix writer.

matros *sb* able seaman.

mat|skap *sb* food cupboard. **~smule** *sb* crumb; *(matbit)* morsel (of food). **~stell** *sb* cooking.

matt *adj* **1** *(uten kraft)* faint, weak; *hun følte seg ~* she felt faint; **2** *(uten glans, klang)* dull, mat (matt, matte); dead; *~ farge/lys* dull colour/light; **3** *(i sjakk)* (check)mate.

matte *sb* mat.

matthet *sb* faintness, weakness; dullness.

matvarer *sb fl* food, victuals; provisions.

maur *sb* ant. **maurtue** *sb* anthill.

mave *sb* stomach; *(stor ~)* paunch, pot-belly; *dårlig ~* indigestion; *løs ~* loose bowels; *jeg har vondt i ~n* I have a pain in my stomach. **maveknip** *sb* stomach-ache. **maveplask** *sb* belly flop; flatter.

med I *adv* **1** *(uten pron, sb)* with me, us etc; *har du boken ~?* have you brought the book? *hun ble ~* she went with us; **2** *(også)* too; *det synes jeg ~!* I think so too! *han ble ~ inn* he went in too; **II** *prep* **1** with; *~ ett unntak* with one exception; *~ glede!* with pleasure! *de spilte cricket ~ oss* they played cricket with us; *hun vendte seg bort ~ et sukk* she turned away with a sigh; *hva gjør du ~ all frukten du dyrker?* what do you do with all the fruit you grow? *~ med tyrannen!* down with the tyrant! **2** *(om reisemåte)* by; *reise ~ bil/buss/tog etc* go by car/bus/train etc; **3** *(om innhold etc)* of; *en kasse ~ appelsiner* a box of oranges; *en mann ~ ideer* a man of ideas; **III** *sb (landemerke)* landmark; *uten mål og ~* aimlessly.

medalje *sb* medal. **medaljong** *sb (stor medalje, ornament)* medallion; *(smykke)* locket.

med|arbeider *sb* colleague, collaborator. **~borger** *sb* fellow-citizen. **~bør** *sb* fair wind; *fig* success.

meddele *vb* **1** *(la vite)* inform, tell; *han meddelte oss nyheten* he told us the news; **2** *(om avis)* announce, report, state. **meddelelse** *sb* message, notice; (piece of) information; *~r (etterretninger)* information, news; *telefonisk ~* a telephone message. **meddelsom** *adj* communicative.

med|fange *sb* fellow-prisoner. **~fart** *sb* treatment. **~født** *adj* congenital; natural; native; *~ døvhet* congenital deafness; *~ sjarm* natural charm; *~ takt* native tact; *det er ~* he/she was born with it. **~følelse** *sb* compassion, pity; sympathy. **~følende** *adj* sympathetic. Jf *medlidenhet, medlidende.* **~gang** *sb* good fortune; luck, success; *ha ~* be in luck. **~gift** *sb* dowry; marriage portion. **~gjørlig** *adj* amenable, manageable, tractable. **~gjørlighet** *sb* amenability, manageability, tractability. **~hjelper** *sb* assistant. **~hold** *sb: han fikk ~ hos alle/alle gav ham ~* everybody agreed with him.

medikament *sb* drug, medicine.

medinnehaver *sb* joint owner; partner.

medisin *sb* medicine; *studere ~* study medicine. **medisinalvesen** *sb* public health administration. **medisiner** *sb (lege)* doctor; *(indre~)* physician; *(student)* medical student. **medisin|flaske** *sb* medicine bottle; phial. **~mann** *sb* medicine man. **medisinsk** *adj* medical; *(helbredende)* medicinal; *~ avdeling* medical ward; *~e preparater* medicinal preparations. **medisin|skap** *sb* medicine cupboard. **~tran** *sb* cod-liver oil.

meditasjon *sb* meditation. **meditere** *vb* meditate.

medium *sb* medium.

medlem *sb* member; *~mene av klubben* the members of the club. **medlemskap** *sb* membership.

med|lidende *adj* compassionate, pitying; sympathetic; *et ~ blikk* a pitying look; *hun så ~ på ham* she looked compassionately at him. **~lidenhet** *sb* compassion, pity; *(medfølelse)* sympathy; *han gjorde det av ~ med henne* he did it out of compassion/pity for her; *jeg følte/hadde ~ med dem* I felt pity for them. Jf *medfølende, medfølelse.* **~løper** *sb (sympatisør)* fellow traveller. **~menneske** *sb* fellow; fellow creature; fellow human being. **~menneskelig** *adj* humane.

med mindre *konj* unless; *jeg går ikke ~ ~ det blir fint vær* I shall not go unless the weather is fine.

med|regnet *adj* included; inclusive of. **~reisende** *sb* **1** *(reisefelle)* fellow-traveller. Jf *medløper.* **~skapning** *sb* fellow-creature. **~skyldig 1** *adj: ~skyldig i en forbrytelse* accessory to a crime; **2** *sb* accessory, accomplice. **~spiller** *sb (i kortspill, tennis etc)* partner; *(når det er mange deltakere)* fellow-player; *(om skuespillere)* fellow actor/actress. **~tatt** *adj (skadet)* damaged; *(ramponert)* battered; *(slitt)* worn; *(avkreftet)* weak; worn out; *(utkjørt)* exhausted. **~vind** *sb* fair wind; following wind; *vi hadde ~vind* we had the wind behind us. **~virke** *vb* co-operate; assist; contribute. **~virkende** *adj* contributing, co-operating; *de ~virkende* those taking part; the actors/performers; *en ~virkende årsak* a contributory cause. **~viter** *sb: være ~viter i en hemmelighet* be privy to a secret. **~ynk** *sb* compassion, pity.

meget *adj, adv* much, very; *~ bedre* much better; *~ forbausende* very surprising; *~ glad* very pleased; *~ verre* much worse; *det er ennå ~ å gjøre* there is still much to be done; *det er virkelig altfor ~* it is really far to much; *jeg er ~ glad i dem* I am very fond of them. Se også *mye* og *svært*.

megle *sb* mediate. **megler** *sb* mediator; *(aksje~)* broker, stockbroker. **megling** mediation; *(i arbeidskonflikt)* conciliation.

mei *sb (på kjelke etc)* runner; *(på gyngestol)* rocker.

meie *vb* mow.

meieri *sb* dairy.

meis *sb (på ryggsekk)* rucksack frame.

meis(e) *sb* titmouse, tit.

meisel *sb* chisel. **meisle** *vb* chisel.

meitemark *sb* earthworm.

mekaniker *sb* mechanic. **mekanikk** *sb* mechanics. **mekanisme** *sb* mechanism; *(innretning)* contrivance.

mekle etc se *megle etc*.

mekre *vb* bleat, baa.

mektig *adj* **1** *(sterk)* powerful, strong; **2** *(stor)* gigantic, huge; vast..

mel *sb* meal; *(hvete~)* flour.

melankoli *sb* melancholy. **melankoliker** *sb* melancholi(a)c. **melankolsk** *adj* melancholy.

melasse *sb* molasses.

melde *vb* report; *(i kortspill)* bid; *~ seg inn i en klubb* join a club; *~ seg til tjeneste* report for duty; *det meldte seg mange problemer* many problems arose; *hun ble meldt til politiet* she was reported to the police; *vær så vennlig å ~ Dem på kontoret* please, report at the office. **melding** *sb* report; *(i kortspill)* bid. **meldingsbok** *sb* report book.

melis *sb* icing sugar.

melk *sb* milk. **melke A** *sb (i fisk)* milt; **B** vb milk; *kuene blir ~t hver morgen* the cows are milked every morning. **melke|kyr** *sb koll* dairy cattle. **~maskin** *sb* milking machine. **~tann** *sb* milk-tooth. **~utsalg** *sb* dairy. **Melkeveien** the Milky Way; the Galaxy.

mellom *prep* **1** *(særlig ~ to)* between; *~ oss sagt* between you and me; between ourselves; *avstanden ~ London og Oxford* the distance between London and Oxford; **2** *(blant)* among; *~ passasjerene* among the passengers; *en landsby ~ åsene (dvs med åser på alle kanter)* a village among the hills. Se også *imellom*. **mellomalderen** *sb* the Middle Ages *fl*. **Mellom|Amerika** Central America. **~Europa** Central Europe. **mellom|folkelig** *adj* international. **~fornøyd** *adj* disgruntled; not very pleased. **~gulv** *sb* diaphragm, midriff. **~lande** *vb* touch down. **~landing** *sb* intermediate landing/stop. **~ledd** *sb* connecting link; *(om person)* intermediary. **~mann** *sb* intermediary; *(megler)* mediator.

mellomrom *sb* space, interval; *med ~* at intervals; *med ca. en meters ~* at intervals of about one metre. **mellomroms|tast** *sb data etc* space bar/key. **~tegn** *sb data* space character.

mellomste *adj: den/det ~* the middlemost; the midmost.

mellom|stadium *sb* intermediate stage. **~standpunkt** *sb* intermediate position/attitude. **~stor** *adj* medium-sized. **~størrelse** *sb* medium size. **~tid** *sb* interval; *i ~tiden* in the meantime; meanwhile. **~ting** *sb* something between. **~vegg** *sb* partition (wall). **~vekt** *sb* middle weight. **~værende** *sb (regnskap)* account; *(tvist)* difference; *gjøre opp et ~* settle an account/a difference.

melodi *sb* tune; *sangen synges på denne ~en* the song is sung to this tune. **melodisk** *adj* melodic. **melodiøs** *adj* melodious.

melon *sb* melon.

memoarer *sb fl* memoirs.

men *konj* but; **2** *sb (skade)* harm, injury (of a permanent character).

menasjeri *sb* menagerie.

mene *vb* **1** *(synes, tenke, tro)* believe, think; be of the opionion that; *jeg/han etc ~r (også)* in my/his etc opinion; *jeg ~r skattene er for høye, hva ~r du?* in my opinion the taxes are too heavy, what do you think? **2** *(ha til hensikt, sikte til, tenke på)* mean; *hvem av oss ~r du?* which of us do you mean? *~r du meg?* do you mean me? **3** *(uttrykk)* *~* **det godt** mean well; *~* **med** mean by; *jeg mente ikke noe vondt med det!* I meant no harm! no offence (meant)! *~* **om** think of; *hva ~r du om denne boken?* what do you think of this book? *jeg mener nei!* I think not!

mened *sb* perjury; *gjøre seg skyldig i ~* commit perjury.

mengde *sb* **1** *(av noe som kan telles)* number; a great many; lots of; *en ~ mennesker* lots of people; a great number of people; **2** *(av noe som ikke kan telles)* quantity; a lot of; *en stor ~ smør* a large quantity of butter; a lot of butter; **3** *(menneske~)* crowd. **mengdevis** *adv: ~ av, i ~* a great many; lots of; *~ av bøker* lots of books; a great many books.

menig *sb* common, private; *~ soldat* private (soldier).

menighet *sb* parish; *(om forsamlingen)* congregation; *(om medlemmene, sognefolket)* parishioners; *(om trossamfunn)* Church.

menigmann *sb* the man in the street.

mening *sb* **1** *(oppfatning)* opinion; *(fornuftig ~)* sense; *det er ingen ~ i å gjøre det* there is no sense in doing it; *jeg er av den ~* I am of (the) opinion; **2** *(betydning, innhold)* meaning; *hva er ~en med alt dette?* what is the meaning of all this? **3** *(hensikt)* intention; *det var ~en/min ~ å ...* it was my intention to ... *si sin ~* speak one's mind. **menings|løs** *adj* senseless, absurd. **~løshet** *sb* absurdity. **~måling** *sb* public opinion poll; Gallup poll.

menneske *sb* man, person; human being; *~t spår, Gud rår* man proposes, God disposes; *alle ~r* everybody; *en dommer er også et ~* even a judge is a human being; *hun er et meget godt ~* she is a very kind person; *ikke et/noe ~* nobody; *intet ~ kan gjøre det* no man can do it. **menneske|alder** *sb* generation. **~eter** *sb* cannibal. **~fiende** *sb* misanthrope. **~fiendtlig** *adj* misanthropic. **~hater** *sb* misanthrope. **~heten** *sb* mankind. **~kjærlig** *adj* philanthropic; charitable, humane. **menneskelig** *adj* **1** human; *~ svakhet* human weakness; **2** *(human, menneskekjærlig)* humane. **menneskelighet** *sb* humanity. **menneske|liv** *sb* human life; *tap av ~* loss of (human) life. **~mengde** *sb* crowd (of people). **~rett** *sb* human right. **~venn** *sb* philanthropist.

mens *konj* **1** *(om tid)* while; *han skadet seg ~ han sparket fotball* he hurt himself while he was playing football; **2** *(om motsetning)* while, whereas; *noen mennesker er rike ~ andre er fattige* some men are rich while/whereas others are poor.

menstruasjon *sb* menses, menstruation. **menstruere** *vb* menstruate.

mental *adj* mental. **mentalhygiene** *sb* mental hygiene. **mentalitet** *sb* mentality. **mentalundersøkelse** *sb* mental examination.

mentol *sb* menthol.

menuett *sb* minuet.

meny *sb* bill of fare; menu.

mer *adj, adv* more; *(ved spørsmål og nektelse)* any more; *aldri ~* never again; *~ eller mindre* more or less; *det var ikke ~ å si* there was nothing more to say/nothing more to be said; *er det (noe) ~ kaffe igjen?* is there any more coffee left? *ikke ~* no more; not any more; *ikke ~ enn a) (dvs bare)* no more than; *b) (ikke over)* not more than; *jeg vil ikke/ønsker ikke å si noe ~* I do not want to say any more.

meridian *sb* meridian.

meritter *sb fl* **1** *(bedrifter)* achievments, exploits; **2** *(gale streker)* escapades.

merkantil *adj* mercantile, commercial. **merkantilisme** *sb* mercantilism; mercantile system. **merkantilistisk** *adj* mercantilistic.

merkbar *adj* perceptible, noticeable; appreciable.

merke I *sb* **1** *(avtrykk, spor)* mark; *~r etter skitne fingrer* marks of dirty fingers; **2** *(emblem)* badge; **3** *(etikett)* label; *(fabrikat)* brand, make; *en sykkel av beste ~* a bicycle of the best make; **4** (uttrykk) **bite ~ i** mark, note; *jeg bet ~ i hva han sa* I noted what he said; **legge ~ til** notice; *jeg la ikke ~ til at du gikk tidlig* I did not notice that you left early; *legg godt ~ til hva jeg sier* mark my words; **II** *vb* **1** *(sette merke/spor)* mark; *hun hadde ~t alle blyantene med initialene sine* she had marked all the pencils with her initials; **2** *(føle, legge ~ til)* feel; notice, realize; *(ofte)* hear, see, smell, taste; *en ~r ikke kulden her inne* one does not feel the cold in here; *jeg kunne ~ at han var lei seg* I could hear that he was sorry; **3** *~ seg* mark, note; *merk mine ord!* mark my words! **merke|dag** *sb* red-letter day. **~lapp** *sb* label.

merkelig *adj* **1** *(besynderlig)* odd, queer; funny; *~ nok* strange to say; *~ oppførsel* queer behaviour; *det var noe ~ ved ham* there was something funny about him; **2** *(merkverdig)* extraordinary, strange; curious; *et ~ syn* an extraordinary/a strange sight; *det er ikke noe ~ ved det* there is nothing extraordinary about that; **3** *(bemerkelsesverdig)* remarkable, striking. **merknad** *sb* *(anmerkning, kommentar)* comment, note. **merkverdig** *adj* *(påfallende)* strange; *(bemerkelsesverdig)* curious; remarkable, striking.

merr *sb* mare.

merskum *sb* meerschaum.

mersmak *sb: det gir ~* it whets the appetite.

mesen *sb* patron of the arts/of literature.

meslinger *sb* measles.

messe I *sb* **1** *(gudstjeneste)* service; *(katolsk ~)* mass, the Mass; **2** *(marked)* fair; **3** *(kantine)* mess, messroom; **II** *vb* *(synge)* chant.

Messias the Messiah.

messing *sb* brass.

mest *adj, adv* most; *(for størstedelen, som regel)* mostly; *det ~e av lasten* most of the cargo; *for det ~e* mostly; for the most part; generally, mainly; *han er ~ kjent* he is best known; *jeg fikk ~* I got most; *medlemmene er ~ bønder* the members are mostly farmers; *vi hørte det ~e* we heard most of it. **mesteparten** *sb* most; the greater/greatest part; *~ av innboet* most of/the greater part of the furniture; *~ av året* the greater part of the year.

mester *sb* **1** master; *ingen er født som ~* no man is born a master; *de store malerne fra det 13. til det syttende hundreåret kalles ofte for de gamle ~e* the great painters of the 13th to 17th centuries are often called the old masters; **2** *(i idrett)* champion. **mesterlig** *adj* masterly. **mester|skap** *sb* **1** mastership; **2** *(i idrett)* championship. **~stykke, ~verk** *sb* masterpiece. **mestre** *vb* master.

metafor *sb* metaphor.

metafysikk *sb* metaphysics.

metall *sb* metal. **metall|sløyd** *sb* metalwork. **~tråd** *sb* wire.

metamorfose *sb* metamorphosis.

meteor *sb* meteor. **meteorolog** *sb* meteorologist. **meteorologi** *sb* meteorology. **meteorologisk** *adj* meteorological; *~ institutt (GB)* the Meteorological Office; *(US)* the Weather Bureau.

meter *sb* metre; *5 ~* 5 metres.

metode *sb* method. **metodisk** *adj* methodical; *gå ~ til verks* proceed methodically. **metodisme** *sb* Methodism. **metodist** *sb* Methodist. **metodistisk** *adj* Methodist.

metropol *sb* metropolis.

mett *adj, adv* satisfied; *han spiste seg ~* he got enough to eat. **mette** *vb* satisfy; *(skaffe mat)* feed; *mange munner å ~* many mouths to feed.

midd *sb* mite.

middag *sb* **1** *(tidspunkt)* midday, noon; *i går ~* yesterday (at) noon; *lørdag ~* at noon on Saturday; **2**

(måltid) dinner; *de spiste ~ kl. 7* they had dinner at 7; *(høytidligere)* they dined at 7; *hva fikk dere til ~?* what did you have for dinner? *sove ~* take an after-dinner nap. **middags|bord** *sb* dinner-table; *ved ~bordet* at dinner. **~hvil** *sb* after-dinner nap. **~høyde** *sb* meridian altitude. **~mat, ~måltid** *sb* dinner. **~selskap** *sb* dinner-party. **~tid** *sb* noon.

middel *sb* **1** means; *med alle mulige midler* by fair means and foul; *ved dette ~* by this means; **2** *(lege~)* remedy; *et godt ~ mot forkjølelse* a good remedy for a cold; *et ~ mot malaria* a remedy against malaria; **3** *(midler, penger)* means, resources; money. **middel|alderen** the Middle Ages *fl.* **~aldersk** *adj* medieval.

Middelhavet the Mediterranean.

middel|klassen *sb* the middle classes. **~måtig** *adj* indifferent, mediocre. **~måtighet** *sb* mediocrity. **middels** *adj* average, medium, middling; *~ størrelse* medium/middling size; *over/under ~* above/below the average. **middel|standen** *sb* the middle classes *(fl)*. **~stor** *adj* of average size. **~temperatur** *sb* mean temperature. **~vei** middle course; *den gylne ~* the golden mean.

midje *sb* waist.

midlertidig *adj* temporary; *(adv også)* for the time being; *hun er ~ bortreist* she is away for the time being.

midnatt *sb* midnight; *ved ~* at midnight. **midnattssol** *sb* midnight sun.

midt *adv* **1** *~ i* in the middle of; *~ i byen* in the middle/centre of the town; **2** *(omgitt, truet av)* in the midst of; *~ i vanskelighetene hans* in the midst of his troubles; **3** *(uttrykk)* *~* **imot** (just) opposite; *~* **mellom** *Oslo og Bergen* halfway between Oslo and Bergen; *~* **på** *sommeren* in the middle of the summer. **midte** *sb: i vår ~* in our midst; among us. **midten** *sb* the middle; *(om sted også)* the centre; *i/på ~* in/at the centre; in the middle. **midterst** *adj* central, middle; *den/det ~e* the middle one. **midtpunkt** *sb* centre. **midtre** *adj* middle. **midt|sommer** *sb* midsummer. **~sommers** *adv* in the middle of summer. **~veis** *adv* halfway, midway. **~vinters** *adv* in the middle of winter.

migrene *sb* migraine.

mikrobe *sb* microbe.

mikro|fon *sb* microphone. **~skop** *sb* microscope. **~skopisk** *adj* microscopic(al).

mikstur *sb* mixture.

mil *sb (10 km)* ten kilometres. (En engelsk *mile* er 1609 m).

mild *adj* mild; gentle, soft; *~t regn* gentle rain; *en ~ bris* a soft breeze; *en ~ vinter* a mild winter. **mildhet** *sb* mildness; gentlemess, softness. **mildvær** *sb* mild weather; thaw.

milepæl *sb* milestone.

militarisme *sb* militarism. **militaristisk** *adj* militarist. **militær** *adj* military; *~ ledere* military leaders; *en ~* a military man; a soldier; *det ~e* the military; *han er i ~et* he is in the military. **militær|diktatur** *sb* military dictatorship. **~kupp** *sb* military coup. **~nekter** *sb* conscientious objector. **~styre** *sb* military rule. **~tjeneste** *sb* military service. **~utdannelse** *sb* military training.

miljø *sb* environment, surroundings; background; milieu. **miljø|bestemt** *adj* determined by environment; environmental. **~skade** *sb* maladjustment. **~skadet** *adj* maladjusted. **~skildring** *sb* description of (social) background. **~vern** *sb* environmental protection; conservation/protection of environment. **~vernarbeid** *sb* environmental work.

milliard *sb* milliard; *US* billion. **milli|bar** *sb* millibar. **~gram** *sb* milligramme. **~meter** *sb* millimetre. **million** *sb* million. **millionær** *sb* millionaire.

milt *sb* spleen.

mimikk *sb* facial expression(s).

min, mitt, mine *eiend pron* my; *(stående alene)* mine; *den hatten er ~* that hat is mine; *det er ~ hatt* it is my hat.

mindre *adj, adv* **1** *(om størrelse)* smaller; *hun er ~ enn søsteren sin* she is smaller than her sister; **2** *(om grad, mengde)* less; *~ smør* less butter; *fem er ~ enn åtte* five is less than eight; *på ~ enn ett minutt* in less than one minute; **3** *(ikke noe større/særlig)* slight; not very; *~ behagelig* not very pleasant; **5** *(uttrykk) ikke* **desto ~** nevertheless; **ikke ~ enn** not less than; *(ikke færre enn)* no less than; **med ~** unless. **mindre|tall** *sb* minority. **~verdig** *adj* inferior. **~verd** *sb* inferiority. **~verdskompleks** *sb* inferiority complex.

mine *sb* **A** *(ansiktsuttrykk)* air, look; *gjøre gode ~r til slett spill* put the best face on the matter; *gjøre ~ til å* make as if to; *han gjorde ~ til å gå* he made as if to go; **B 1** *(gruve)* mine, pit; **2** *(som kan eksplodere)* mine; *drivende ~* drifting mine. **mine|legge** *vb* mine. **~legger** *sb* minelayer. **~legging** *sb* minelaying.

mineral *sb* mineral.

mineral|olje *sb* mineral oil; petroleum. **~vann** *sb* mineral water.

minere *vb* blast, mine. **mineskudd** *sb* blast; blasting shot.

minespill *sb* shifting facial expression.

minesveiper *sb* mine-sweeper.

miniatyr miniature; *i ~* in miniature.

minimal *adj (av minste størrelse)* minimal, minimum; *(svært lite)* diminutive. **minimum** *sb* minimum. **minimumstemperatur** *sb* minimum temperature. **miniskjørt** *sb* mini-skirt.

minister *sb* minister; *(GB stundom også)* Secretary of State. Jf *statsråd.* **ministerium** *sb* ministry; *(regjering)* Cabinet.

mink *sb* mink.

minke *vb* decrease, shrink; abate, ebb.

minne I *sb* **1** *(erindring)* memory, recollection, remembrance; *til ~ om hennes far* in memory of her fathers; **2** *(ting til ~)* keepsake, remembrance, souvenir; *hun gav meg ringen til ~* she gave me the ring as a remembrance/keepsake; **3** *(ettermæle)* memory; **4** *(hukommelse)* memory; *i manns ~* within living memory; **II** *vb* remind; *minn meg på at jeg skal skrive i morgen* remind me to write tomorrow; *du ~r meg om* *min mor* you remind me of my mother; *jeg ~t ham på hans løfte* I reminded him of his promise. **minnelig** *adj: ~ ordning* amicable settlement. **minnelighet** *sb: det ble ordnet i ~* it was settled out of court. **minnes** *vb* **1** *(huske)* remember, recollect; **2** *(feire minnet om)* commemorate; *de mintes de døde* they commemorated the dead. **minnesmerke** *sb* memorial, monument. **minneverdig** *adj* memorable.

minoritet *sb* minority; *være i ~* be in the/a minority.

min santen *adv, interj* really, why; *det er ~ ekte gull!* why, it is real gold!

minske *vb* **1** *(gjøre mindre)* reduce; diminish, lessen; **2** *(bli mindre)* decrease, diminish.

minst *adj, adv* **1** *(~ i størrelse)* smallest; *(av to)* smaller; *han er den ~e av de to)* he is the smaller of the two; *jeg fikk det ~e stykket* I got the smallest piece; **2** *(~ i mengde)* least; *jeg fikk ~ hjelp* I received least assistance; **3** *(ubetydeligst)* least, slightest; *ved den ~e berøring* at the slightest touch; **4** *(yngst)* youngest; **5** least, *når de ~ ventet det* when they least expected it; **6** *(ikke under, i hvert fall)* at least; not less than; *det kommer til å koste/vil koste ~ femti pund* it will cost at least £50; **7** *i det ~e* at least; at any rate; *ikke det ~e* not in the least. **minstelønn** *sb* minimum wage.

minus *adv, sb* minus; *seks ~ fire er to* six minus four is two.

minutt *sb* minute. **minuttviser** *sb* minute hand.

mirakel *sb* miracle. **mirakuløs** *adj* miraculous.

misantrop *sb* misanthrope.

mis|billige *vb* disapprove (of). **~billigelse** *sb* disapproval.

mis|bruk *sb* abuse; *makt~* abuse of power. **~bruke** *vb* abuse; *han misbrukte makten sin* he abused his power.

mis|dannelse *sb* deformity. **~dannet** *adj* deformed.

miserabel *adj* miserable.

misforhold *sb (uheldig forskjell)* disproportion, disparity; *(uheldig forhold)* abuse; *rette på et ~* remedy an abuse; *stå i (skjærende) ~ til* be out of (all) proportion to.

mis|fornøyd *adj* dissatisfied, displeased, discontented. **~fornøyelse** *sb* dissatisfaction, discontent.

mis|forstå *vb* misunderstand, mistake; *~ meg ikke!* don't misunderstand me! *det er ikke til å ~* there is no mistaking it. **~forståelse** *sb* misunderstanding, mistake; *det var en stor ~* it was a complete mistake.

misgjerning *sb* misdeed; ill/evil deed.

misgrep *sb* mistake, error.

mis|hag *sb* dislike, displeasure. **~hage** *vb* displease.

mis|handle *vb* ill-treat. **~handling** *vb* ill-treatment, cruelty.

misjon *sb* mission. **misjonere** *vb* do missionary work; do propaganda. **misjonær** *sb* missionary.

miskreditt *sb* discredit; *komme i ~* fall into discredit.

miskunn *sb* mercy. **miskunne** *vb: ~ seg over* have mercy on.

mislike *vb* dislike.

mislyd *sb* dissonance.

mislykkes *vb* fail; be unsuccessful; *det mislyktes for ham, han mislyktes* he failed; he did not succeed; *et mislykket tiltak* a failure.

mis|modig *adj* despondent, discouraged, disheartened. **~nøyd** *adj* discontented. **~nøye** *sb* discontent.

misse *vb (bomme)* miss.

mis|stemning *sb (uvilje)* bad feeling; ill-feeling; *(nedtrykt stemning)* despondency, gloom. **~tak** *sb* mistake, error. **~tanke** *sb* suspicion; *~tanken falt på meg* I was suspected; suspicion fell on me; *jeg fikk/fattet ~tanke til dem* I began to suspect them.

mistbenk *sb* hotbed.

miste *vb* lose; *han ~t livet* he lost his life.

misteltein *sb* mistletoe.

mis|tenke *vb* suspect; *han er ~tenkt for mord* he is suspected of murder; *hun er ~tenkt for å ha drept sin mann* she is suspected of having killed her husband; *jeg ~tenker henne for å lyve* I suspect her to be a liar/ that she is a liar. **~tenkelig** suspicious *adj: det er noe ~tenkelig ved det* there is something suspicious about it. **~tenksom** *adj* suspicious, distrustful. **~tenksomhet** *sb* suspiciousness, suspicion.

mistillit *sb* distrust, mistrust. **mistillitsvotum** *sb* vote of no confidence/of censure.

mis|tro *sb, vb* distrust, mistrust. **~troisk** *adj* distrustful, suspicious.

mis|unne *vb* envy; *jeg ~r deg hellet ditt* I envy you your luck. **~unnelig** *adj* envious, jealous; *~ på* envious/jealous of; *han er ~ på søsteren sin* he is envious/jealous of his sister. **~unnelse** *sb* envy, jealousy; *grønn av ~* green with envy. **~unnelsesverdig** *adj* enviable.

misvisende *adj* misleading.

mitraljøse *sb* mitrailleuse; machine gun.

mitt, se *min.*

mixmaster *sb* food processor.

mjaue *vb* miaow.

mjød *sb* mead.

mo *sb* **1** *(lyngslette)* heath, moor; **2** *(ekserserplass)* drill ground.

mobb *sb* crowd, mob. **mobbe** *vb* mob, crowd; persecute.

mobil *adj* mobile.

mobilisere *vb* mobilize. **mobilisering** *sb* mobilization.

modell *sb* model; *(fabrikat, type)* design; *en bil av siste ~* a car of the latest design. **modellere** *vb* model. **modellfly** *sb* model airplane/plane.

moden *adj* **1** ripe; *en ~ pære* a ripe pear; *eplene ble modne* the apples ripened/grew ripe; **2** *(om alder, utvikling)* mature; *~ alder* mature years. **modenhet** *sb* ripeness; maturity.

moderasjon *sb (måtehold)* moderation; *(avslag i*

pris) price reduction; discount. **moderat** *adj* moderate, reasonable. **moderere** *vb* moderate, modify.

moder|land *sb* mother country. **~lig** *adj* maternal, motherly. **~skip** *sb* support vessel.

moderne *adj* **1** *(moteriktig)* fashionable; in fashion; *~ hatter* fashionable hats; *de er ikke ~ lenger* they are out of fashion; *disse hattene er ~ nå* these hats are in (fashion) now; **2** *(tidsmessig)* contemporary, modern; *~ historie* contemporary/modern history; *et hus med alt ~ utstyr* a house with all modern conveniences. **modernisere** *vb* modernize.

modifikasjon *sb* modification, qualification; *en sannhet med ~er* a qualified truth. **modifisere** *vb* modify, qualify.

modig *adj* brave, courageous.

modne(s) *vb* ripen; *fig* mature.

modus *sb (gram)* mood.

mokasin *sb* moccasin.

mokka(-kaffe) *sb* mocha.

mold etc se *muld etc.*

molekyl *sb* molecule.

moll *sb (mus)* minor; *i ~* in the minor key.

molo *sb* breakwater, mole.

molte *sb* cloudberry.

moment *sb (hovedpunkt)* point; *(faktor som spiller inn)* element, factor. **momentan** *adj, adv (plutselig)* sudden; *(forbigående)* momentary; *han døde ~t* he died instantly.

mon *spørreord (gadd vite om)* I wonder.

monark *sb* monarch. **monarki** *sb* monarchy.

monetær *adj* monetary.

monn *sb* **1** *(forøkelse, tilvekst)* addition, increase; **2** *(noe som er virkningsfullt)* advantage, help; **3** *(grad, utstrekning)* degree; **4** *(uttrykk) alle ~er drar* every little helps; *i noen ~* to some degree; somewhat; *i stor ~* largely; to a great degree; *det gjør god ~* it is a great help; *ta sin ~ igjen* even things up. **monne** *vb* **1** *(øke)* grow, increase; **2** *(gjøre virkning)* avail, help; *alt det hun strevde, så monnet det lite* her efforts were of little avail.

monogam *adj* monogamous. **monogami** *sb* monogamy.

monogram *sb* monogram.

monolog *sb* monologue.

monoman *adj* monomaniac. **monomani** *sb* monomania.

monopol *sb* monopoly; *ha ~ på* have the monopoly of.

monoteisme *sb* monotheism. **monoteistisk** *adj* monotheistic.

monoton *adj* monotonous. **monotoni** *sb* monotony.

monstrum *sb* monster.

monsun *sb* monsoon.

montere *vb* **1** *(sette sammen)* assemble; **2** *(sette på plass)* erect, mount; **3** *(installere)* install. **monteringsplattform** *sb petro* stabbing board.

montre *sb* show-case; exhibition case.

monument *sb* monument.

mops *sb* pug, pug-dog.

mor *sb* mother; *dgl* ma, mummy; *hun er ~ til tre barn* she is the mother of three children.

moral *sb* **1** *(om livsførelse)* morals; *hun her ingen ~* she has no morals; **2** *(~ i en historie etc)* moral; *~en i fortellingen* the moral of the story; **3** *(disiplin, kampånd)* morale; *soldatenes ~ er utmerket* the morale of the soldiers is excellent. **moralisere** *vb* moralize. **moral|lære** *sb* ethics. **~preken** *sb* lecture. **moralsk** *adj* moral; *~ plikt* moral duty.

morbror *sb* (maternal) uncle.

morbærtre *sb* mulberry.

mord *sb* murder; *(drap)* homicide, manslaughter. **morder** *sb* murderer. **morderisk** *adj* murderous. **mord|forsøk** *sb* attempted murder. **~våpen** *sb* murder weapon.

more *vb* amuse; divert, entertain; *~ seg* enjoy oneself; have a good time; *de ~t seg med å skyte spurver* they amused themselves by shooting sparrows; *de ~t seg over kunststykkene hans* they were amused at his tricks; *det ~t meg å gjøre det* it amused me to do it; *vi ~t oss over stykket* we enjoyed the play.

morell *sb* morello (cherry).

morene *sb* moraine.

morfar *sb* (maternal) grandfather.

morfin *sb* morphia, morphine.

morgen *sb* morning; *god ~!* good morning! *i ~* tomorrow; *i ~ tidlig* tomorrow morning; *i morges* this morning; *om ~en* in the morning; *søndag ~ den 6. november* on the morning of Sunday, November 6th. **morgen|avis** *sb* morning paper. **~demring** *sb* dawn, daybreak. **~fugl** *sb* early riser. **~kvist** *sb: på ~kvisten* in the early morning. **~side** *sb: på ~siden* in the early morning. **~stund** *sb: ~stund har gull i munnen* it is the early bird that catches the worm.

morild *sb* phosphorescence.

morken *adj* decaying, rotting.

morløs *sb* motherless.

mormor *sb* (maternal) grandmother.

moro *sb* fun, amusement; *for ~ skyld* for fun; for the fun of it; *vi hadde det veldig ~* we had a great time/a lot of fun; *det er ~ å seile* sailing a is (great) fun.

morsarv *sb* maternal inheritance. **morsdag** *sb* Mother's Day.

morse *vb* morse. **morsealfabet** *sb* Morse code.

morsk *adj* fierce, grim; *han så ~ ut* he had a fierce look on his face.

morskap *sb* amusement, entertainment.

morske *vb: ~ seg* look fierce; frown.

morsmål *sb* mother tongue.

morsom *adj* **1** *(som morer eller underholder)* amusing, entertaining; *en ~ fortelling/historie* an amusing story; **2** *(lattervekkende)* funny; *et ~t syn* a funny sight; **3** *(hyggelig)* nice, pleasant; *det er ~t å treffe gamle venner* it is pleasant to see old friends; **4** *(interessant)* interesting; *det er ~t å se at* it is interesting to notice that. **morsomhet** *sb* joke.

morter *sb* mortar.

mosaikk *sb* mosaic.

mose *sb* moss.

mosjon *sb* exercise. **mosjonere** *vb* take exercise.

moské *sb* mosque.

moskito *sb* mosquito.

moskus *sb* musk. **moskusokse** *sb* musk deer.

most *sb (drue~)* must; *(eple~)* cider.

mot I *prep* **1** *(i retning av)* towards; *det går ~ jul* it is getting on towards Christmas; *en mann kom ~ oss* a man came towards us; **2** *(i forbindelse med gå, kjempe etc)* against; *han stod med ryggen ~ veggen* he stood with his back against the wall; *hun løp ~ et tre* she ran against a tree; *jeg har ingenting ~ dem* I have nothing against them; *kjempe ~ en fiende/en sykdom* fight against an enemy/a disease; *lene/støtte seg ~* lean against; **3** *(opp etc ~)* against; *holde noe opp ~ lyset* hold something against the light; **4** *(om forholdsregler) forsikre seg ~ ulykker* insure against accidents; *advare ~ lommetyver* warn against pickpockets; **5** *(om oppførsel, sammenligning etc)* to; *dette er ingenting ~ hva jeg så* this is nothing to what I saw; *du er bare barnet ~ ham* you are but a child to him; *hans plikt ~ foreldrene* his duty to his parents; *være høflig (snill, takknemlig etc) ~* be civil (kind, grateful etc) to; **6** *(om konkurranser, rettssaker etc)* versus *(fork)* v; *Arsenal ~ Leeds* Arsenal v. Leeds; *Jones ~ Smith* Jones versus Smith. Se også *imot*. **mot II** *sb (tapperhet)* courage, heart; *~et sviktet meg* my courage failed me; *han var ille til ~e* he was ill at ease; *hun mistet ~et* she lost heart/courage.

mot|arbeide *vb* counteract, oppose; *(bekjempe)* combat. **~bakke** *sb* climb, uphill. **~bevise** *vb* disprove, refute. **~bydelig** *adj* abominable, disgusting. **~bør** *sb* contrary wind; *(motstand)* opposition; *møte ~bør* be opposed.

mote *sb* fashon; *det er (på) ~* it is in fashion; *det gikk av ~* it went out of fashion; *det kom på ~* it came into fashion; it became the fashion; *siste ~* the latest fashion.

motell *sb* motel.

motejournal *sb* fashion paper/magazine. **~sak** *sb* matter of fashion.

motfallen *adj* depressed, dejected; crestfallen.

mot|gang *sb* adversity; bad luck. **~gift** *sb* antidote. **~hake** *sb* barb.

motiv *sb* motive; *(emne)* subject; *et ~ for en roman* a subject for a novel; *hva er ~et hans for å gjøre det?* what is his motive in doing that? **motivere** *vb (begrunne)* give the grounds for; state the reason of; justify; *(psykologisk, pedagogisk)* motivate. **motivering** *sb* statement of reasons; justification; motivation.

motkandidat *sb* opponent; rival candidate.

motløs *adj* disheartened; *gjøre ~* discourage.

motmæle *sb: ta til ~* retort, reply.

motor *sb (især om elektrisk ~)* motor; *(især om forbrennings~)* engine. **motorbåt** *sb* motor-boat; *(større)* motorlaunch. **motorisere** *vb* motorize. **motor|kjøretøy** *sb* motor vehicle. **~skip** *sb* motor ship. **~sport** *sb* motoring. **~stans, ~stopp** *sb* engine failure/breakdown. **~sykkel** *sb* motor cycle; *dgl* motor-bike. **~vei** *sb* motorway.

mot|part *sb* adversary, opponent. **~revolusjon** *sb* counter-revolution. **~satt** *adj* opposite; *han gjorde det ~satte* he did the opposite. **~setning** *sb* contrast; *i ~setning til det man hadde ventet* contrary to what was expected. **~sette seg** *vb* oppose; set one's face against. **~si** *vb* contradict; *de ~sa hverandre* they contradicted each other. **~sigelse** *sb* contradiction. **~stand** *sb* opposition, resistance; *de møtte ~stand* they met with opposition/resistance; *gjøre ~stand mot* resist; offer resistance to. **~stander** *sb* adversary, opponent, rival. **~standsdyktig** *adj* resistant. **~strebende** *adj* reluctant. **~strid** *sb: i ~strid med* contrary to. **~stridende** *adj* conflicting. **~stykke** *sb* counterpart. **~stå** *vb* resist, withstand.

motta *vb* **1** *(få)* receive; *jeg mottok et brev fra dem i går* I received a letter from them yesterday; *stykket ble godt ~tt (dvs fikk god kritikk)* the play was favourably received; **2** *(akseptere)* accept. Se for øvrig *ta imot; akseptere, godta*. **mottakelig** *adj* susceptible (amenable, responsive) *(for* to). **mottakelse** *sb* **1** *(~ av brev, penger, varer etc)* receipt; **2** *(~ av gjester etc)* reception; *vi fikk en hjertelig ~* we received a hearty welcome. **mottaker** *sb (person)* recipient; *(radio~)* receiver; *(om apparat)* receiving set. **mottakerstasjon** *sb* terminal.

motto *sb* motto.

mot|trekk *sb* counter-move. **~vekt** *sb* counterweight. **~verge** *sb: sette seg til ~* offer resistance; put up a fight. **~vilje** *sb* dislike, aversion; *få ~ mot* take a dislike to. **~villig** *adj* reluctant. **~vind** *sb* contrary wind; head wind. **~virke** *vb* counteract. **~ytelse** *sb* return.

mudder *sb (gjørme)* mud; *gjøre ~ (dvs oppheveIser)* cavil. **muddermaskin** *sb* dredge. **mudre** *vb* dredge.

mudret(e) *adj* muddy.

muffe *sb* muff.

mugg *sb* mildew, mold.

mugge jug; *(stor ~)* pitcher.

muggen *adj* mouldy, musty; *(gretten)* sulky, moody. **mugne** *vb* mould.

mukk *sb: han sa ikke et ~* he never uttered a syllable; *jeg skjønner ikke et ~ av det han sier* I don't understand a syllable of what he says. **mukke** *vb* grumble.

mulatt *sb* mulatto.

muld, muldjord *sb* mould. **muldvarp** *sb* mole.

muldyr *sb* mule.

mule *sb* muzzle.

mulig *adj* possible; *flest ~* as many as possible; *mest ~* as much as possible; *på alle ~e måter* in every possible way; *om (det er) ~* if (it is) possible; *så vidt ~* as far as possible; *snarest ~* as soon as possible. **muligens** *adv* possibly; perhaps; *det er ~ galt* it may possibly be wrong. **mulighet** *sb* possibility: chance; *ikke den ringeste ~* not he least chance/possibility.

mulkt *sb* fine; *få* ~ be fined; *ilegge* ~ fine. **mulktere** *vb* fine.

mulm *sb: i nattens* ~ *og mørke* at dead of/in the dead of night; in pitch darkness.

multe *sb* cloudberry.

multiplikasjon *sb* multiplication. **multiplisere** *vb* multiply.

mumie *sb* mummy.

mumle *vb (snakke lavt med seg selv)* mutter; *(snakke utydelig)* mumble; *(snakke dempet, enstonig)* murmur.

munk *sb* monk. **munke|kloster** *sb* monastery. **~orden** *sb* monastic order.

munn *sb* mouth; *bruke* ~ jaw, scold; *bruke* ~ *på* scold; *fra hånd til* ~ from hand to mouth; *gå fra* ~ *til* ~ pass from mouth to mouth; *holde* ~ hold one's tongue; *hold* ~*!* shut up! *legge ordene i* ~*en på noen* put the words into somebody's mouth; *mange* ~*er å mette* many mouths to feed; *snakke i* ~*en på hverandre* speak all at once; *snakke noen etter* ~*en* play up to somebody; *stoppe* ~*en på* gag, silence; *ta ordet ut av* ~*en på noen* take the word(s) out of somebody's mouth. **munne ut** *vb (om elv)* flow into; *(om gate etc)* lead to; run into; *(fig: ende med)* conclude/end in. **munn|full** *sb* mouthful. **~huggeri** *sb* quarrelling; bickering, wrangle, wrangling. **~hugges** *vb* quarrel; bicker, wrangle. **munning** *sb* **1** *(elve~)* mouth; *(vid elve~)* estuary; **2** *(av rør etc)* nose; *(på geværløp etc)* mouth, muzzle. **munn|kurv** *sb* muzzle; *sette* ~ *på* muzzle. **~-mot~metoden** *sb* the mouth-to-mouth method; *dgl* the kiss of life. **~-og-klovsyke** *sb* foot-and-mouth disease. **~rapp** *adj* voluble. **~spill** *sb* mouth-organ. **~stykke** *sb (på pipe, fløyte etc)* mouth-piece; *(på rør etc)* nozzle. **~vik** *sb* corner of the mouth.

munter *adj* gay, jolly, merry; cheerful; ~ *stemning* high spirits. **munterhet** *sb* gaiety, liveliness; merriment, mirth; cheerfulness; *overstadig* ~ boisterous gaiety.

muntlig 1 *adj* oral, verbal; ~ *eksamen* oral examination; *engelsk* ~ oral English. **2** *(adv)* by word of mouth; *budskapet ble avlevert* ~ the message was delivered by word of mouth.

mur *sb* wall. **mure** *vb* build; do brickwork/masonry work. **murer** *sb* bricklayer; *(gråsteins~)* mason. **murerlærling** *sb* bricklayer's apprentice.

murmeldyr *sb* marmot.

murpuss *sb* plaster.

murre *vb* murmur; *(misnøyd)* grumble.

murstein *sb* brick.

mus *sb* mouse. **muse|bol, ~rede** *sb* mouse nest. **~felle** *sb* mousetrap. **~hull** *sb* mouse-hole. **~lort** *sb* mouse dirt.

museum *sb* museum.

musikalsk *adj* musical; *hun er* ~ she has an ear for music. **musiker** *sb* musician. **musikk** *sb* music. **musikk|handel** *sb* music shop. **~handler** *sb* music-dealer. **~instrument** *sb* musical instrument. **~-korps** *sb* (brass) band. **~lærer** *sb* music teacher. **~stykke** *sb* piece of music. **~time** *sb* music lesson. **~undervisning** *sb* teaching of music.

muskel *sb* muscle. **muskulatur** *sb* musculature, muscles. **muskuløs** *adj* brawny, muscular.

musling *sb* bivalve; *(blåskjell)* mussel.

musselin *sb* muslin.

mussere *vb* effervesce, sparkle; fizz. **musserende** *adj* effervescent; sparkling; fizzy.

mustasje *sb* moustache.

mutasjon *sb* mutation.

mutt *adj* moody, sulky.

mutter *sb* **1** *(til skrue)* nut; **2** *dgl (mor)* mummy.

mutters alene *adv* all alone.

mye *adj, adv (i nektende og spørrende setninger især)* much; *(i andre tilfeller ofte)* a good/great deal; *(foran komparativ)* much; a lot; *(ved verb)* (very) much; a good/great deal; a lot; ~ *bedre/større etc* much better/bigger etc; ~ *bryderi* a great deal of trouble; *dobbelt så* ~ twice as much; *han pratet mye, men gjorde ikke stort* he talked a lot, but did not do much; *hun har studert* ~ she has studied a lot; *jeg har reist* ~ I have travelled a good deal; *rir du* ~*?* do you ride much? *så* ~ *som mulig* as much as possible. Se også *meget* og *svært.*

mygg *sb* gnat, mosquito; *gjøre en* ~ *til en elefant* make a mountain out of a molehill. **mygg|nett** *sb* mosquito net. **~stikk** *sb* mosquito bite.

myk *adj* **1** *(motsatt stiv)* flexible, pliable; **2** *(motsatt hard)* soft; **3** *(smidig)* supple; **4** *(føyelig)* meek, submissive. **mykdata** *sb data* soft data. **myke opp** *vb* **1** *gjøre bløt)* soften; **2** *(gjøre bøyelig)* make pliable; **3** ~ *seg opp* limber (oneself) up. **mykfeil** *sb data* soft error. **mykne** *vb* soften; become pliable.

mylder *sb* swarm, crowd. **myldre** *vb* **1** *(opptre i massevis)* swarm, teem; *det* ~*r av fisk i elven* the river is teeming with fish; **2** *(bevege seg i massevis)* swarm, crowd; *barna* ~*t inn i jernbanekupeen* the children crowded into the railway carriage.

mynde *sb* greyhound.

myndig *adj* **1** authoritative, masterful; *en* ~ *stemme/tone* a masterful tone of voice; *(også)* a tone of authority; **2** *(om skjells år og alder)* of age; *han ble* ~ he came of age. **myndighet** *sb* authority; ~*ene* the authorities; *de har ingen* ~ *til å gjøre det* they have no authority to do that. **myndighetsalder** *sb* (age of) majority; full age.

mynt *sb* **1** *(pengestykke)* coin; *falsk* ~ bad/false coin; *slå* ~ *på* cash in on; *svare (en) med samme* ~ pay (somebody) back in his (her etc) own coin; give tit for tat; repay in kind; **2** *(~side på pengestykke)* tail; ~ *eller krone?* head or tails? *kaste* ~ *og krone om* toss for; **3** *(landets mynt, valuta)* currency; *utenlandsk* ~ foreign currency. **mynte på** *vb* aim at; *det var* ~*t på deg* that was a dig at you. **myntenhet** *sb* monetary unit.

myr *sb* bog.

myrde *vb* murder; *den* ~*de* the murdered man/woman. **myrderi** *sb* massacre, slaughter.

myriade *sb* myriad.

myrlendt *adj* boggy.

myrt *sb* myrtle.

myrull *sb* bog cotton; cotton grass.

myse A *sb (av melk)* whey; **B** *vb (se med sammenknepne øyne)* squint.

mysterium *sb* mystery. **mystikk** *sb* mysteriousness. **mystisk** *adj (gåtefull)* mysterious; *(mistenkelig)* suspicious.

myte A *sb (overlevering, sagn)* myth; **B** *vb (felle fjær)* moult. **mytisk** *adj* mythical. **mytologi** *sb* mythology. **mytologisk** *adj* mythological.

mytteri *sb* mutiny; *begå/gjøre ~* mutiny. **mytterist** *sb (deltaker i mytteri)* mutineer.

mæle *sb: miste munn og ~* become speechless.

møbel *sb* piece of furniture; *møbler* furniture; *mange møbler* much furniture; *møblene er gode* the furniture is good. **møbel|handler** *sb* furniture dealer. **~plate** *sb* laminated wood. **~snekker** *sb* cabinet--maker. **~stoff** *sb* upholstery. **møblement** *sb* set of furniture; suite; furniture; *~ til en spisestue* dining--room set/suite. **møblere** *vb* furnish; *en møblert leilighet* a furnished flat.

møkk *sb* dung, muck. **møkket(e)** *adj* dirty, filthy. **møkk|greip** *sb* dung-fork. **~haug** *sb* dung-hill. **~kjerre** *sb* dung-cart.

mølje *sb (masse)* jam.

møll *sb* moth; *det er gått ~ i frakken* the moths have got at/into the coat.

mølle *sb* mill. **møller** *sb* miller. Se også *kvern.*

møll|kule *sb* moth-ball. **~pose** *sb* moth-proof bag. **~sikker** *adj* moth-proof; moth resistant. **~spist** *adj* moth-eaten.

møne *sb* ridge of a roof.

mønje *adj* minium; red lead.

mønster *sb* pattern; *~et i teppet* the pattern of the carpet; *et ~ på flid* a pattern of industry. **mønster|-beskyttet** *adj* (of) registered design; patented. **~bruk** *sb* model farm. **~gyldig** *adj* model; exemplary, ideal. **~strikking** *sb* pattern knitting. **mønstre** *vb (betrakte kritisk)* examine, scrutinize; *(inspisere)* inspect, muster; *(om mannskaper)* assemble, muster; *(stille opp med)* bring together; collect, muster; **~ av** sign off; **~ på** sign on. **mønstret** *adj* figured; *~ silke* figured silk. **mønstring** *sb* review; inspection, muster.

mør *adj* tender. **mørbanke** *vb* beat black and blue.

mørk *adj* dark; *~e skyer* dark clouds; *det begynner å bli ~t* it is getting dark. **mørke** *sb* dark, darkness; *~t faller på* darkness/night falls; *i nattens ~* in the dark of night; *katter kan se i ~* cats can see in the dark. **mørke|blå, ~brun etc** *adj* dark blue/brown etc. **~rom** *sb* darkroom. **~tid** *sb* polar night. **mørklegge** *vb* black out; *byen var mørklagt* the town was blacked out. **mørkne** *vb* darken; *det var begynt å ~* it was getting dark. **mørkning** *sb* dusk, twilight; nightfall; *i ~en* at dusk. **mørkredd** *adj* afraid of the dark.

mørtel *sb* mortar.

møte I *sb* meeting; *(avtalt ~)* appointment; *(tilfeldig ~)* encounter; *(samtale)* interview; *de holdt ~* they held a meeting; *et ~ med en ukjent kvinne* an encounter with an unknown woman; *et ~ mellom utenriksministrene* a meeting of the Foreign Ministers; *innkalle til ~* call a meeting; *jeg har et ~ med dem klokken 4* I have an appointment with dem at 4 o'clock; *komme/gå/løpe etc noen i ~* come/go/run etc to meet somebody; **II** *vb* **1** *(især etter avtale)* meet; *(~ tilfeldig, støte på)* come across; meet with; run into; *jeg møtte ham på en restaurant* I met him at a restaurant; **2** *(innfinne seg)* appear, be; *~ frem/opp* appear; make/put in an appearance; *hun møtte (frem) i retten* she appeared in court; **3** *(bli gjenstand for, komme ut for)* meet with; *vi møtte stor vennlighet* we met with much kindness. **møtes** *vb* meet; *de møttes* they met.

møy *sb* maid, virgin.

møye *sb* trouble; *med ~* with difficulty. **møysommelig** *adj* difficult, laborious, toilsome; *(adv)* laboriously; with difficulty.

måfå: *på ~* aimlessly; at random; in a haphazard way.

måke A *sb (måse)* gull, sea-gull; mew; **B** *vb (skyfle)* shovel; clear away.

mål *sb* **A 1** *(stemme)* voice; **2** *(språk)* language, tongue; **B 1** *(måleenhet etc)* measure; *(især om lengdemål)* measurement; *gi godt/knapt ~* give full/short measure; *ta ~ av* measure; take the measurements of; *(fig)* size up; *de tok ~ av hverandre* they sized each other up; *lagd/sydd etter ~* made to measure; *skredderen tok ~ av meg til en dress* the tailor took my measurements for a suit; **2** *(~ for reise etc)* destination, goal; **3** *(~ for strev, ønsker etc)* aim, end, goal, object; *hans ~ i livet var å bli rik* his aim in life was to get rich; *mine ønskers ~* the goal of my desires; *nå sitt ~* attain one's end/object; **4** *(~ i fotball etc)* goal; *lage ~* score a goal; **5** *(~ en prøver å treffe)* mark, target; *~et for bombetoktet* the target for the bombing raid; **6** *(dekar)* ≈ a quarter of an acre (se midtsidene); **7** *(~tid)* meal.

mål|bar *adj* measureable. **~bevisst** *adj* determined, purposeful. **~binde** *vb* nonplus, silence.

måle *vb* measure; *(om rominnhold især)* gauge; *han kan ikke ~ seg med deg* he cannot compare with you; *hun målte ham fra topp til tå* she looked him up and down. **måle|bånd** *sb* tape measure. **~enhet** *sb* unit of measurement. **måler** *sb (elektrisitets~ etc)* meter; *lese av ~en* read the meter. **målestokk** *sb* **1** *(på kart etc)* scale; *i forminsket ~* on reduced scale; **2** *(omfang)* measure, scale; *i stor ~* on a large scale; in a large measure; **3** *(vurderingsgrunnlag)* standard, yardstick; *hun måler alt ut fra sin egen ~* she measures everything by her own standards.

mål|føre *sb* dialect. **~løs** *adj* speechless.

mål|mann *sb (i fotball)* goalkeeper. **~setting** *sb* aim, purpose, goal. **~snor** *sb* tape. **~språk** *sb* target language. **~stang** *sb* goal-post. **~studie** *sb data etc* target study.

måltid *sb* meal.

måltrost *sb* song thrush.

måne *sb* **1** moon; **2** *(skallet flekk)* bald spot.

måned *sb* month; *august ~* the month of August; *i dag om en ~* this day a month; in a month from today;

i denne ~ (during) this month; *om en* ~ in a month. **månedlig** *adj* monthly.

måne|fase *sb* phase of the moon. **~ferd** *sb* lunar flight. **~formørkelse** *sb* eclipse of the moon. **~landing** *sb* landing/touchdown on the moon. **~landingsfartøy** *sb* lunar module. **~rakett** *sb* lunar rocket. **~sigd** *sb* crescent. **~skinn** *sb* moonlight; *det var* ~ it was a moonlight night; *i* ~ by moonlight.

måpe *vb* gape. **måpende** *adj* gaping.

mår *sb* marten.

måte *sb* manner, way; *(henseende)* respect; *holde* ~ be moderate; *ikke holde* ~ *(også)* not know when to say stop; *ikke på noen* ~ by no means, not at all; *i like* ~*!* the same to you! *med* ~ moderately; in moderation; *alt med* ~ moderation in all things; *på alle* ~*r* in every respect/way; *på en eller annen* ~ somehow (or other). **måte|hold** *sb* moderation. **~holden(de)** *adj* moderate. **måtelig** *adj* indifferent, second-rate.

måtte *vb* **1** *(være nødt til)* have (got) to; *(bare i presens, og i imperfektum i indirekte tale)* must; *du må gjøre det med en gang* you must do it at once; *hun sa hun* ~ *gå* she said (that) she must go; *jeg må dra til London* I have to go to London; *jeg må hjem/inn* I must go home/in; *jeg må gå nå* I must go now; *vi* ~ *gjøre det før eller senere* we had to do it sooner or later; **2** *(om logisk nødvendighet eller stor sannsynlighet)* must; *han må jo være gal!* why, he must be mad! *klokken må ha vært ni da jeg kom hjem* it must have been nine o'clock when I got home; **3** *(gid)* ~ *de bare greie det!* may they succeed! I wish they may succeed!

N

n *(bokstaven)* n.

nabo *sb* neighbour. **nabo|by** *sb* neighbouring town. **~hus** *sb* house next door. **~lag** *sb* neighbourhood, vicinity. **~skap** *sb* neighbourhood.

nafta *sb* naphtha. **naftalin** *sb* naphthalene.

nag *sb: hun bærer* ~ *til meg* she bears me a grudge; she has a grudge against me. **nage** *vb* gnaw at; rankle; *~nde misunnelse* rankling envy.

nagle 1 *sb* peg; *(klinke~)* rivet; **2** *vb* rivet. **naglefast** *adj:* ~ *innredning/inventar* fixtures.

naiv *adj* naïve, simple(-minded); *en* ~ *bemerkning* a naïve remark. **naivitet** *sb* naïveté, simple-mindedness.

naken *adj* **1** naked; *en* ~ *gren* a naked branch; **2** *(bar)* bare; *en* ~ *åsside* a bare hillside.

nakke *sb* back of the head; nape of the neck; *ha øyne i ~n* have eyes at the back of one's head; *kaste på ~n, kneise med ~n* toss one's head; *ta beina på ~n* take to one's heels; *ta ham i ~n* take him by the scruff of his neck; *ta seg selv i ~n* pull oneself together. **nakke|drag** *sb* clout on the head, **~grop** *sb* hollow of the neck. **~kast** *sb* toss of the head.

napp *sb* pluck; *(av fisk)* bite; *(på flue eller sluk)* rise; *(lett ~)* nibble; *i rykk og* ~ by fits and starts; *jeg fikk* ~ I had a bite/got a nibble/rise. **nappe** *vb* snatch; *(om fisk)* bite, rise. **nappetak** *sb* fight, tussle.

narkoman *sb* drug addict; *US også* dope addict. **narkomani** *sb* drug addiction. **narkose** *sb* narcosis; general anaesthesia. **narkotika** *sb fl* drugs, narcotics; *US også* dope. **narkotiker** *sb* drug addict; *US* dope addict. **narkotikum** *sb* drug, narcotic; *US også* dope. **narkotisk** *adj* narcotic.

narr *sb* fool; *de gjør* ~ *av ham, de holder ham for* ~ they make a fool of him; *hun gjør seg til* ~ she makes a fool of herself. **narraktig** *adj* foolish. **narraktighet** *sb* foolishness. **narre** *vb* **1** deceive, fool, trick; take in; *forsøk bare ikke å* ~ *meg!* just don't try to deceive me! **2** *(skuffe ved ikke å holde ord)* let down; *skredderen lovte meg frakken min i dag, men han ~t meg* my tailor promised me the coat today, but he has let me down. **narre|smokk** *sb* comforter; dummy teat. **~streker** *sb fl* pranks; buffoonery, tomfoolery..

nasjon *sb* nation, people; *De forente ~er* the United Nations; *folk av alle ~er* people of all nations. **nasjonal** *adj* national. **nasjonal|dag** *sb* national day. **~drakt** *sb* national costume. **~forsamling** *sb* national assembly; parliament. **~følelse** *sb* national feeling; patriotism. **nasjonalisere** *vb* nationalize. **nasjonalisering** *sb* nationalization. **nasjonalisme** *sb* nationalism. **nasjonalist** *sb* nationalist. **nasjonalitet** *sb* nationality. **nasjonal|karakter** *sb* national character. **~sang** *sb* national anthem.

naske *vb* filch, pilfer. **naskeri** filching; petty larceny.

natron *sb* (baking) soda.

natt *sb* night; *god* ~*!* good night! *hele ~en* all night; *i* ~ *(om foregående)* last night; *(om inneværende el kommende* ~*)* tonight; *~en faller på* night is falling; *~en igjennom* throughout the night; *om ~en* at night; in the night; *arbeide om ~en* work at/by night. **natt|bord** *sb* bedside table. **~vakt** se *nattevakt.* **natte|gjest** *sb* over--night guest. **~losji** *sb* night's lodging; accomodation for the night. **~rangel** *sb* night revels. **~rangler** *sb* night reveller.

nattergal *sb* nightingale.

natte|ro *sb* night's rest. **~søvn** *sb* night's sleep.

~vakt *sb* night watch(man); *(om sykepleier)* night nurse; *ha ~* be on night duty. **natt|herberge** *sb* doss-house. **~kjole** *sb* nightgown; nightie, nighty. **~lampe** *sb* bedside lamp. **~linnet** *sb* nightgown; nightie, nighty. **~-tog** *sb* night train. **~-tøy** *sb* night wear; night things; nighties. **~verd** *sb* supper; *~verden* the Lord's Supper; the Holy Communion.

natur *sb* **1** *(landskap)* scenery; **2** *(for øvrig)* nature; *(om et menneskes ~ også)* character, disposition; *den menneskelige ~* human nature; *det er ikke hans ~* it is not in his nature; *en freidig ~* a cheerful character/disposition/nature; *kjærlighet til ~en* love of nature; *studiet av ~en* the study of nature; **3** *(uttrykk)* **av ~** by nature; *tigere er grusomme av ~* tigers are cruel by nature; **i sakens ~** in the nature of things that; **ute i ~en** in the open; out of doors. **naturalhusholdning** *sb* barter economy; subsistence economy. **naturalier** *sb fl: betale i ~* pay in kind. **naturalisere** *vb* naturalize. **naturalisering** *sb* naturalizing. **naturalisme** *sb* naturalism. **naturalistisk** *adj* naturalistic. **natur|fag** *sb* (natural) science. **~fenomen** *sb* natural phenomenon. **~folk** *sb koll* primitive people. **~forhold** *sb fl* nature; natural conditions. **~forsker** *sb* naturalist. **~gass** *sb* natural gas. **~historie** *sb* natural history. **~katastrofe** *sb* natural disaster. **~kraft** *sb* natural force.

naturlig *adj* natural; *det faller ~ for henne* it comes natural(ly) to her; *en ~ forklaring* a natural explanation. **naturligvis** *adv* naturally; of course.

natur|lov *sb* law of nature; natural law. **~nødvendig** *adj* inevitable. **~sans** *sb* feeling for nature. **~silke** *sb* real silk. **~skildring** *sb* description of nature/scenery. **~svin** *sb* litter bug/lout. **~tilstand** *sb* natural state; state of nature. **~vern** *sb* conservation of nature. **~vitenskap** *sb* (natural) science. **~vitenskaplig** *adj* scientific. **~vitenskapskvinne, ~vitenskapsmann** *sb* scientist.

naust *sb* boat-house.

naut *sb* **1** *(storfe)* (head of) cattle; ox; **2** *(tosk)* fool.

nautisk *adj: en ~ mil* a nautical mile.

nav *sb(på hjul)* hub.

navar *sb* auger.

navigasjon *sb* navigation. **navigere** *vb* navigate.

navle *sb* navel. **navle|bind** *sb* umbilical bandage. **~brokk** *sb* umbilical hernia. **~streng** *sb* umbilical cord.

navn *sb* name; *en gutt ved ~ Tom* a boy by name Tom/called Tom; *hun fikk ~et June* she was called June; *June er et vanlig ~ i England* June is a common name in England; *konge i ~et* a king in name only; *vi kjenner dem av ~* we know them by name. **navne 1** *sb* namesake; **2** *vb (merke med navn)* mark (with name). **navne|blekk** *sb* marking-ink. **~bror, ~fetter** *sb* namesake. **~liste** *sb* list of names. **~opprop** *sb* call-over; roll-call; *foreta ~opprop* call the roll. **~skilt** *sb* name plate. **~stempel** *sb* signature stamp. **~trekk** *sb* signature; *(monogram)* monogram. **navn|gi** *vb* name; mention by name. **~gjeten** *adj* renowned; celebrated, famous. **~løs** *adj* nameless.

nazisme *sb* Nazism. **nazist** *sb* Nazi. **nazistisk** *adj* Nazi.

ne *sb* wane (of the moon); *månen er i ~* the moon is on the wane; *i ny og ~* now and then; on and off; once in a while.

nebb *sb* beak, bill; *blek om ~et* green about the gills; *forsvare seg med ~ og klør* defend oneself tooth and nail. **nebbet(e)** *adj* pert, saucy.

ned *adv* down; *jeg vil ~* I want to get down; *solen gikk ~* the sun went down/set. **ned|brutt** *adj* broken down; *dypt ~* broken-hearted. **~bør** *sb* precipitation; fall of rain/snow. **nede** *adv* down; *der ~* down there; *her ~* down here; *(her ~ på jorden)* here below; *langt ~* low down; *lenger ~* further down. **neden|for** *prep* below; *bussholdeplassen ligger like ~for posthuset* the bus stop is a few yards below the post office. **~fra** *adv* from below; from the bottom; *fem linjer ~fra* five lines from the bottom of the page. **~under** *adv* beneath, underneath; *(i etasjen under)* downstairs.

neder|drektig *adj (sjofel)* infamous; *(vemmelig)* beastly, nasty. **~lag** *sb* defeat; *de led ~* they suffered defeat; they were defeated.

nederst *adj* bottom, lowest; *(adv)* at the bottom; *~ på siden* at the bottom of the page; *den ~e delen* the lowest part; *den ~e skuffen* the bottom drawer.

ned|etter *adv* down, downwards. **~fall** *sb: radioaktivt ~* (radioactive) fallout. **~fallseple, ~fallsfrukt** *sb* windfall. **~for** *adj (nedslått)* dejected, despondent. **~gang** *sb* **1** *(det å gå ned)* going down; **2** *(trapp, vei etc ned)* descent; way down; **3** *(reduksjon, tilbakegang)* decline, decrease, fall; *~gang i prisene* decline/fall of the prices. **~gangstid** *sb* **1** *(økonomisk)* depression, slump; **2** *(kulturelt)* period of decline. **~komme** *vb (føde)* be delivered; *hun ~kom med en pike* she was delivered of/gave birth to a girl. **~late** *vb: ~late seg til* condescend to. **~latende** *adj* condescending.

nedlegge *vb (avvikle)* close/shut down; *fabrikken/skolen ble nedlagt* the factory/the school was closed/shut down; **2** *(oppgi, si fra seg)* lay down; *~ vervet som ordstyrer* retire from the chair; **3** *(drepe under jakt)* kill; **4** *~ protest* make a protest. Se for øvrig *legge ned.*

ned|over 1 *prep* down; *båten drev ~ elven* the boat drifted down the river; *de gikk ~ gaten* they walked down the street; **2** *(adv)* downwards. **~overbakke** *adv* downhill; *sb* downhill slope; *det går ~ med dem* they are going downhill. **~rakking** *sb* abuse.

nedre *adj* lower; *Donaus ~ løp* Lower Danube.

ned|ringet *adj (om kjole)* low(-necked); *(også om person)* décolletée. **~riving** *sb* demolition. **~ruste** *vb* disarm. **~rustning** *sb* disarmament. **~satt** *adj: ~ pris* reduced price. **~senkbar** *adj* submersible. **~sette** *vb (oppnevne)* appoint; *~sette en komité* appoint a committee. Se for øvrig *sette ned.* **~settelse** *sb* **1** *(av priser etc)* reduction; **2** *(av komité etc)* appointment. Jf *~satt.* **~settende** *adj: en ~ bemerkning* a depreciatory remark; *snakke ~ om* disparage; speak with disparagement of. **~slag** *sb* **1** *(om bombe etc)* impact; **2** *(om* *skihopper)* landing; **3** *(om priser)* discount, reduction. **~slående** *adj* discouraging, disheartening. **~slått** *adj* **1** *med ~slått blikk* with downcast eyes; **2** *(om paraply etc)* closed; **3** *(nedtrykt)* dejected, depressed; in low spirits. **~stamme** *vb: ~ fra* descend from. **~stemt** *adj* **1** *(ved votering)* outvoted; *forslaget ble ~stemt* the motion was defeated/not carried; **2** *(nedtrykt)* dejected, depressed; downcast. **~stigning** *sb* descent. **~tegne** *vb* put down in writing; take/write down. Se for øvrig *skrive ned.* **~trykt** *adj* depressed; in low spirits. **~trykthet** *sb* depression. **~verdige** *vb* degrade, disgrace; *~ seg til å* stoop to; demean oneself to. **~verdigelse** *sb* degradation, debasement. **~verdigende** *adj* degrading. **~vurdere** *vb* depreciate, disparage; belittle.

negativ *adj, sb* negative. **negativ skrift** *sb data* reverse print. **negativt bilde** *sb data* reverse video.

neger *sb* negro.

negl *sb* nail. **negle|børste** *sb* nail-brush. **~fil** *sb* nail file. **~lakk** nail-varnish. **~saks** *sb* nail scissors.

neglisjere *vb* neglect; ignore, overlook.

negresse *sb* negress.

nei *adv* **1** no; *~, takk* no, thank you; no, thanks; *si ~ til (også)* decline, refuse; **2** *(som interj)* oh, why; *~, for en overraskelse!* oh, what a surprise; **3** *(forsterkende)* indeed; *jeg tror, ~, jeg er sikker på, at jeg har sett ham før* I think, indeed, I'm sure I have seen him before.

neie *vb* curts(e)y; drop/make a curts(e)y.

neimen *adv: ~ om jeg gjør!* catch me doing that! *det vet jeg ~ ikke* I am sure I do not know.

nek *sb* sheaf.

nekrolog *sb* obituary.

nekte 1 *(~ for, si nei)* deny; *det kan ikke ~s* it cannot be denied; there is no denying it; *han ~t (for) at han hadde gjort det* he denied that he had done it; he denied having done it; *hun kan ikke ~ sønnen sin noen ting* she can deny her son nothing; **2** *(avslå)* refuse; *(høfligere)* decline. **nektelse** *sb (gram)* negation, negative.

nellik *sb* **1** *(om blomsten)* carnation; **2** *(krydder~)* clove.

nemesis *sb* Nemesis.

nemlig *adv* **1** as, because, for; you see; *hun kom ikke, hun var ~ syk* she did not come, as/because/for she was ill; ...she was ill, you see; *jeg var tørst, det var ~ svært varmt* I was thirsty, for it was a very hot day; **2** *(ved nærmere forklaring etc)* namely; *to av jentene var søstre, ~ Ingrid og Karen* two of the girls were sisters, namely Ingrid and Karen.

nemnd *sb* committee.

nennsom *adj* gentle, light-handed.

nepe *sb* garden turnip.

neppe *adv* hardly; *(trolig ikke)* hardly, scarcely; *med nød og ~* only just; *vi blir ~ ferdige med dette i dag* we shall hardly/scarcely get this finished today.

nerve *sb* nerve; *dårlige ~r* bad nerves; *han går meg på ~ne* he gets on my nerves. **nerve|celle** *sb* nerve cell. **~feber** *sb* typhoid (fever). **~lege** *sb* neurologist. **~påkjenning** *sb* strain of the nerves. **~system** *sb* nervous system. **nervøs** *adj* nervous; *han ble ~ (dvs urolig)* he got nervous; *(men om sykdom)* he became nervous. **nervøsitet** *sb* nervousness.

nes *sb* headland, promontory; cape.

nese *sb* nose; *få lang ~* be disappointed; *han holdt seg for ~n* he held his nose; *hun rynket på ~n av det* she turned up her nose at it; *jeg pusset ~n* I blowed my nose; *like for ~n på ham* under his very nose; *like opp i ~n på henne* to her very face. **nese|blod** *sb: jeg blør ~* my nose is bleeding. **~bor** *sb* nostril. **~grus** *adj, adv* prone, prostrate; flat on one's face. **~ring** *sb* nose-ring. **~tipp** *sb* tip of the nose. **~vis** *adj* impertinent, impudent; saucy. **~vishet** *sb* impertinence, impudence; sauciness.

neshorn *sb* rhinoceros; *dgl* rhino.

nesle *sb* (stinging) nettle.

nest *sb (sting)* tack.

nest *adv* next; *~ etter* next to; *(foran superlativ også)* second; but one. **~ best** *adj* next/second best. **~ eldst** *adj* oldest but one; *den ~ eldste datteren* the second daughter. **~ sist** *adj* last but one; penultimate; *den ~ siste stavelsen* the penultimate syllable; *den ~ viktigste byen* the second most important town. **neste 1** *adj* next; the following; *~ søndag (dvs førstkommende)* next Sunday; on Sunday (next); *ikke førstkommende søndag, men neste* not on Sunday next, but Sunday week; *~ år* (the) next year; *den ~ jeg møter* the next person I meet; **2** *sb* neighbour; *elsk din ~* love thy neighbour; **3** *vb (tråkle)* baste, tack. **neste|mann** *sb* next man; *hvem er ~?* who comes next? **~kjærlig** *adj* charitable. **~kjærlighet** *sb* charity.

nesten *adv* nearly, almost; *(~ + nektelse)* hardly; *~ en halvtime* nearly half an hour; *~ ingen* hardly anyone; *~ ingenting* hardly anything; *~ umulig* hardly possible; *det er ~ for mye* it is almost too much; *jeg kan ~ ikke tro det* I can hardly believe it; *jeg kjenner ~ ingen her* I hardly know anybody here; *jeg skulle ~ ønske* I almost wish; *klokken er ~ tre* it is nearly/almost three o'clock.

nest|formann *sb* deputy chairman; vice-president. **~kommanderende** *adj, sb* second in command. **~leder** *sb* deputy chairperson; vice president.

nett A *adj* neat, pretty; *hun er liten og ~* she is small and pretty; **B** *sb* net; *(bære~)* string bag. **nette** *vb (lage mål i fotball etc)* net. **nett|hendt** *adj* deft, dexterous; handy. **~hinne** *sb* retina. **netting** *sb* netting.

netto *adj, adv* net; *ti pund ~* ten pounds net; *jeg tjente fem hundre pund ~* I netted £500. **netto|fortjeneste** *sb* net profit. **~inntekt** *sb* net income.

nettopp *adj* just, exactly; *(ofte)* very; *(om tid især)* just; *~!* exactly! *~ den dagen det skjedde* the very day it happened; *~ hva jeg sa* just what I said; *han er ikke ~ elskverdig* he is not exactly amiable; *jeg har ~ hørte om det* I have just heard about it. Jf *akkurat* og *nylig.*

nettverk *sb* network.

neuralgi etc se *nevralgi etc.*

neve *sb* fist; *fra han var en ~ stor* since he was a tiny boy; *jeg knyttet ~ne* I clenched my fists. **neve|kamp**

sb boxing match; fisticuffs. **~nyttig** *adj* handy.

never *sb* birch bark.

neverett *sb* club-law, jungle law.

nevne *vb* mention; *uten å ~ navn* without giving any name(s). **nevner** *sb* denominator. **nevneverdig** *adj* worth mentioning.

nevralgi *sb* neuralgia. **nevrolog** *sb* neurologist. **nevrose** *sb* neurosis. **nevrotiker** *sb* neurotic. **nevrotisk** *adj* neurotic.

nevø *sb* nephew.

nidkjær *adj* zealous. **nidkjærhet** *sb* zeal.

niese *sb* niece.

nifs *adj* creepy, eerie, uncanny.

nihilisme *sb* nihilism. **nihilist** *sb* nihilist. **nihilistisk** *adj* nihilistic.

nikk *sb* nod. **nikke** *vb* nod; *hun nikket* she nodded her head.

nikkel *sb* nickel.

nikkers *sb* plus-fours, knicker-bockers.

nikotin *sb* nicotine. **nikotinforgiftning** *sb* nicotine poisoning.

nippe *vb* sip; *~ til vinen* sip the wine.

nippet *sb: være på ~ til* be on the point of; *det var på ~* it was a close shave/a near thing.

nips *sb koll* knick-knacks.

nise *sb* porpoise.

nisje *sb* niche.

nisse A *sb* ≈ goblin, pixy; **B** *vb (tisse)* pee, piddle.

niste *sb: de hadde med seg ~* they brought their lunch along. **nistepakke** *sb* packed lunch.

nitid *adj* painstaking; very thorough.

nivellere *vb* level (out). **nivå** *sb* level; *(fig også)* standard; *senke ~et* lower the standard.

nobel *adj (om handling)* generous, noble; *(om person også)* noble-minded.

noe A *pron* **I** *(foran sb) for ~ tull!* what nonsense! Se for øvrig *noen*; **II** *(for øvrig)* **1** *(et eller annet)* something; *~ må ha hendt* something must have happened; *du må få deg ~ å spise* you must get something to eat; **2** *(noe i det hele tatt)* anything, something; *har det hendt ~? (når en venter ja som svar)* has something happened? *(uten tanke på svaret)* has anything happened? **3** *ikke ~* not anything; none; *(ingenting)* nothing; *de hadde ikke ~ å spise* they had nothing to eat; *er det ~ brød igjen? Nei, det er ikke ~ igjen i det hele tatt* is there any bread left? No, none at all; **B** *adv (en del, litt)* a little; somewhat; *~ overrasket* somewhat surprised.

noen *pron* **I** *(foran sb og når sb er underforstått)* **1** *a)* some; *jeg gav ham ~ penger* I gave him some money; *jeg må få meg ~ nye klær* I must get some new clothes; *b) for ~ idioter!* what idiots! *~ og femti år* fifty odd years; **2** *(ved nektelse, og når en venter nei som svar)* any; *er det ~ brev til meg?* is there any letters for me? *(men dersom en venter brev)* are there some letters for me? **3** *ikke ~* no; *det var ikke ~ kvinner til stede* there were no women present; *om du ikke har ~ penger, skal jeg låne deg ~* if you have noe moeny, I'll lend you some; **II** *(for øvrig)* **1** *(somme)* some; *~ liker kaffe, og ~ liker te* some like coffee, and some like tea; **2** *(en eller annen)* somebody; some one; *det er ~ i rommet ved siden av* there is somebody/some one in the next room; **3** *(~ i det hele tatt)* anybody; any one; *kan dere se ~ der borte?* can you see anybody over there? *vi kunne ikke ha sett ~ på den avstanden* we could not have seen anybody at that distance; **4** *ikke ~* nobody; no one; *det var ikke ~ til stede* there was nobody present; *hun sa det ikke til ~* she told no one; *ikke ~ av dem var til stede* none/ *(om to)* neither of them was/were present; *kan du låne meg ~ penger? Jeg har ikke ~* can you lend me some money? I have none.

noen|lunde I *(adj)* fairly good; *været er (sånn) ~* the weather is fairly good; **II** *adv* **1** *(nokså)* fairly/tolerably; *jeg kan høre deg ~ bra* I can hear you fairly well; **2** *(omtrent)* about; more or less; *de er av ~ samme størrelse* they are about the same height. **~sinne** *adv* ever; *har du ~ hørt på maken?* did you ever hear anything like that? **~steds** *adv* anywhere.

nok *adj, adv* **1** *(tilstrekkelig)* enough, sufficient; *ha ~ å gjøre* have one's hands full; *ha ~ penger ~, ha penger ~* have enough money/money enough; *hun er gammel ~* she is old enough; *merkelig ~* oddly enough; *ofte ~* often enough; sufficiently often; *~* **av** plenty of; *det er ~ av mat her* there is plenty of food here; *~* **om** *det* enough of that; **ikke ~ med det** not only that; **2** *(trolig)* probably; I dare say; I suppose; *det kan ~ være* it may be; *de kommer ~ til å si nei* they will probably refuse; *han kjøper den ~* I dare say he will buy it; *jeg må ~ gå nå* I suppose I had better go now; *hun kommer ~* she is sure to come.

nokså *adv* fairly, rather; tolerably; *jeg ser/kan se ~ godt herfra* I can see fairly/tolerably well from here; *vi var ~ slitne* we were rather tired.

nomade *sb* nomad. **nomade|folk** *sb* nomadic people. **~liv** *sb* nomadic life.

nominasjon *sb* nomination.

nominativ *sb (gram)* the nominative.

nominere *vb* nominate.

nonchalance *sb* nonchalance; off-hand manner. **nonchalant** *adj* casual, nonchalant; off-hand; *adv* casually, nonchalantly.

nonne nun. **nonnekloster** *sb* convent, nunnery.

nonsens *sb* nonsense.

nord *adj, sb* north; *~ for byen* (to the) north of the town; *fra ~* from the north; *i ~* in the north; *mot ~* north, northward; *vende mot ~* face north. **norda|for** *prep* northward of; (to the) north of. **~fra** *adv* from the north. **~vind** *sb* north/northerly wind. **Norden** the North, Scandinavia. **nordenom** *prep* (to the) north of. **nord|fra** *adv* from the north. **~gående** *adj* northbound. **nordisk** *adj* northern. **nordkyst** *sb* north(ern) coast. **nordlig** *adj* northern; *(om vind også)* northerly. **nordligst** *adj* northernmost. **nord|lys** *sb* northern lights. **~over** *adv* north, northward(s); towards the north. **Nordpolen** the North Pole. **nordpå** *adv* in the north; up north. **nordre** *adj* northern. **nordside** *sb* north(ern) side. **Nord|sjøen**

the North Sea. **~statene** *(i USA)* the Northern States; the North. **nord|vest** *adj, sb* north-west. **~øst** *adj, sb* north-east.

norm *sb* norm, standard.

normal *adj* **1** *(vanlig)* normal; *over/under ~en* above/below normal; **2** *(data) normal-* default; **3** *(tilregnelig)* sane; right in one's head; *han er ikke helt ~* he is not quite right in his head. **normal|betingelse** *sb (data)* default option. **~lys** candle-power. **~verdi** *sb (data)* default value.

normanner *sb* Norman. **normannisk** *adj* Norman.

norne *sb* Norn.

norrøn *adj* Norse.

norsk *adj, sb* Norwegian. **norsk-|amerikaner** *sb* Norwegian-American. **~amerikansk** *adj* Norwegian-American.

not *sb* **A** *(fiske~)* seine; **B** *(i bord)* groove, rabbet.

nota *sb* account, bill.

notat *sb* note; *hun gjorde ~er* she took notes.

note *sb (~tegn)* note; *(~r til musikkstykke)* music; *tekst og ~r* words and music. **note|hefte** *sb* music book. **~stativ** *sb* music-stand. **~tegn** *sb* note. **notere** *vb* note; take down; take notes; *~ seg* make a note of. **notis** *sb* **1** note, notice; *jeg tok ingen ~ av dem* I took no notice of them; **2** *(avis~)* paragraph. **notis|blokk** *sb* note-pad, scratch-pad. **~bok** *sb* notebook.

novelle *sb* short story. **novelleforfatter** *sb* short--story writer.

november November; *første ~* the first of November/Nov. 1st.

nudisme *sb* naturism, nudism. **nudist** *sb* naturist, nudist.

null nought, zero; *(i telefonen etc)* o; *temperaturen falt under ~* the temperature fell below zero. Se for øvrig midtsidene. **null|meridian** *sb* prime meridian. **~punkt** *sb* zero.

nummen *adj* numb.

nummer *sb* **1** number; *(i katalog, på liste etc)* item; **2** *(om størrelse i klær)* size; *hvilket ~ bruker du i sko?* what size do you take in shoes? **3** *(~ av blad)* copy; **4** *(på basar)* raffle ticket; **5** *gjøre et (stort) ~ av* make a fuss about/great play with. **nummerere** *vb* number; *nummererte plasser* numbered/reserved seats. **nummerskilt** *sb (på bil)* licence plate.

nupereller *sb* tatting; *slå ~* tat.

nut *sb* mountain.

ny I *adj* **1** *(motsatt gammel)* new; *en ~ bok* a new book; **2** *(~laget)* fresh; *hun traktet en ~ kanne te* she made a fresh pot of tea; **3** *(~oppdukket etc)* novel; *en ~ måte å skrive på* a novel style of writing; **4** *(en annen, en til)* another; *gi meg et ~tt håndkle* give me another towel; **5** *(annerledes)* different; *han har ~ jakke hver dag* he wears a different jacket every day; **II** *sb (om månen)* new moon; *i ~ og ne* now and then; on and off; once in a while.

nyanse *sb* nuance, shade.

ny|anskaffelse *sb* new acquisition. **~bakt** *adj: ~bakt brød* fresh bread. **~begynner** *sb* beginner, novice. **~brott** *sb* newly cleared ground; new farm. **~brottsarbeid** *sb* pioneer work. **~bygd** *sb* settlement, colony. **~bygg** *sb* building under construction; new building/house. **~bygger** *sb* settler, colonist.

nydelig *adj* pretty, nice; *en ~ kjole* a pretty dress.

nyere *adj* newer; *(fra ~ tid)* modern; *~ historie* modern history. **ny|fiken** *adj* curious. **~født** *adj* new--born. **~gift** *adj* newly married; *de ~gifte* the newly--weds.

nyhet *sb* **1** (piece of) news; *~er* news; *en god ~* a piece of good news; *foruroligende ~er* alarming news; **2** *(ny ting, type etc)* novelty; *det var mange ~er på utstillingen* there were many novelties of the exhibition.

nying *sb* fire, bonfire,

nykk *sb (rykk)* jerk, tug. **nykke A** *sb (lune, påfunn)* whim, caprice; *få ~r* get ideas into one's head; **B** *vb (rykke)* jerk, pull.

ny|komling, ~kommer *sb* newcomer; new arrival. **~lagte egg** *sb fl* newlaid eggs.

nylig *adv* just; lately, recently.

nylon *sb* nylon. **nylonstrømper** *sb* nylons.

nymalt *adj* freshly painted; *~!* fresh/wet paint!

nymfe *sb* nymph.

nymotens *adj* new-fangled.

nynne *vb* hum.

nyordning *sb* reform.

nype A *sb* (rose)hip; **B** *vb (klype)* pinch. **nype|-rose** *sb* dog rose. **~tornbusk** *sb* (sweet)briar.

nyre *sb* kidney. **nyrestein** *sb* kidney stone.

nyse *vb* sneeze.

nysgjerrig *adj* curious; *jeg er ~ etter å vite hva hun sa* I am curious to know what she said. **nysgjerrighet** *sb* curiosity; *av ~* from/out of curiosity.

nyss A *adv (nylig)* lately, recently; **B** *sb: få ~ om* get wind of.

nysølv *sb* German silver.

nyte *vb* enjoy; *~ godt av* benefit by/from; profit by/from; *jeg ~r å lytte til god musikk* I enjoy listening to good music; *vi nøt den gode middagen* we enjoyed the good dinner. **nytelse** *sb* enjoyment, pleasure.

nytt *sb (nyheter)* news; *hva ~?* what is the news? *på ~* afresh, anew; again; *siste ~* the latest news.

nytte I *sb* use; *(fordel)* advantage; *det er til ingen ~* it is noe good/use; *hva ~ gjør han?* what use is he? *jeg har hatt mye ~ av det* it has been very useful to me; *komme til ~* come in handy/useful; **II** *vb* **1** *(gagne, hjelpe)* be of use; help; *det ~r ikke (å gråte etc)* it is no use (crying etc); *hva nytter (vel) det/hva kan (vel)det ~?* what is the use (of that)? **2** *(bruke)* use; make use of; avail oneself of; *~ høvet* take/seize the opportunity; *~ tiden* make the most of one's time. Se også *benytte, bruke* og *utnytte*. **nytteløs** *adj* useless. **nyttig** *adj* useful, profitable.

nyttår New Year; *godt ~* (a) Happy New Year; *med ønske om et godt ~* with best wishes for the New Year. **nyttårs|aften** *sb* New Year's eve. **~dag** *sb* New Year's day.

nyve *sb: sette ~r* frown.

nær 1 *adj* near; *(tett ved)* close; *en ~ slektning* a near relation; *i ~ fremtid* in the near future; **2** *(adv også)* closely; *~ beslektet* closely related; *for ~* too near; *han stod ~ ved* he stood close by; *jeg var ~ ved å falle* I was on the point of falling; I very nearly fell; **3** *prep* near; close to; *det huset står altfor ~ veien* that house is too close to the road; **4** *(uttrykk) jeg hadde ~* **sagt** I almost said; I was close to saying; **komme ~** *(røre ved)* (happen to) touch; *(ikke)* **på langt ~** not nearly; *det er på langt ~ så alvorlig som du tror* it is not nearly so serious as you think; *det var* **på ~e nippet** it was a close shave; **stå** *(en)* **~** be close to/intimate with; **så ~ som** but; *alle så ~ som du later til å vite det* everybody but you seems to know it; **ta seg ~ av** be hurt by; take to heart; *hun tok seg ~ av ordene hans* she was hurt by his words.

nære *vb (om følelser)* have; *~ mistanke om* have a suspicion that/suspect that; *~ ønske om* have a desire to. **nærende** *adj* nourishing.

nærgående *adj (påtrengende)* aggressive.

nærhet *sb (nabolag)* neighbourhood, vicinity; *de bor i ~en* they live near by; *en landsby i ~ av Cambridge* a village in the neighbourhood/vicinity of Cambridge; *et hus i ~en av stasjonen* a house near the station; *i ~en* near by; in the vicinity.

næring *sb* **1** *(føde)* food, nourishment; nutriment; **2** *(virksomhet, yrke)* business, trade. **nærings|drivende** *sb* tradesman. **~frihet** *sb* freedom of trade. **~liv** *sb* economic life; trade. **~middel** *sb* food(-stuff), nutrient. **~midler** *sb koll* provisions, supplies. **~vei** *sb* industry, trade; occupation; *Islands viktigste ~ er fiske* the principal industry of Iceland is fishing. **~verdi** *sb* nutritional value.

nær|kamp *sb* hand-to-hand fighting. **~liggende** *adj* adjacent, neighbouring; *et ~ spørsmål* a natural/an obvious question. **nærme seg** *vb* approach; come nearer; draw near, come nearer. **nærmere 1** *adj (om avstand)* nearer, closer; *(ytterligere)* further; *~ opplysninger* further information; **2** *adv* nearer, closer; more closely; *de kunne ikke komme sannheten ~* they could not get closer to the truth; *se ~ på* look closer at; *undersøke ~* examine more closely. **nærmest** *adj* **1** nearest; *(neste)* next; *de ~e dager* the next few days; *en av de ~e dager* one of these days; *i (den) ~e fremtid* in the near/immediate future; **2** *adv* nearest; *(nesten)* almost, nearly; *han er ~ idiot* he is almost idiot. **nær|synt** *adj* near-sighted, short-sighted. **~synthet** *sb* near-sightedness, short-sightedness. **~tagende** *adj* touchy, sensitive. **~tagenhet** *sb* touchiness, sensitiveness. **~trafikk** *sb* local traffic. **~vær** *sb* presence; *i ~ av mange mennesker* in the presence of a large number of people.

nød *sb* distress; *(fattigdom også)* need, want; necessity; *de led ~* they suffered distress; *det hersket stor ~* there was great distress; *i ~ens stund* in the (his, their etc) hour of need; *med ~ og neppe* with difficulty; only just. **nød|anker** *sb* sheet anchor. **~bluss** *sb* signal flare. **~brems** *sb* emergency brake.

nøde *vb (overtale)* press, urge; *(tvinge)* compel, force.

nød|havn *sb* port of refuge. **~hjelp** *sb* make-shift; temporary expedient.

nødig *adv: jeg gjør det ~* I am not much for doing it; I don't like to do it; *jeg vil ~ gjøre det* I don't like to do it.

nød|lande *vb* make a forced landing. **~landing** *sb* forced landing. **~lidende** *adj* destitute, needy. **~løgn** *sb* white lie. **~rop** *sb* cry for help/of distress. **nødsfall** *sb: i ~* in an emergency. **nødsignal** *sb* distress signal; S.O.S. **nødssituasjon** *sb* emergency.

nødt *adj: bli/være ~ til* be compelled/obliged to; have to.

nød|utgang *sb* emergency exit. **~vendig** *adj* necessary. **~vendighet** *sb* necessity. **~vendigvis** *adv* necessarily. **~verge** *sb* self-defence.

nøff *interj, sb* oink!

nøkk *sb* nix.

nøkkel *sb* **1** *(til lås)* key; *~en til døren* the key for/to the door; **2** *(hjelp til løsning)* clue. **nøkkel|barn** *sb* latchkey child. **~hull** *sb* keyhole. **~industri** *sb* key industry. **~knippe** *sb* bunch of keys. **~posisjon** *sb* key position. **~skilt** *sb* key tag.

nøktern *adj* sober.

nøle *vb* hesitate; *hva ~r dere etter?* what are you hesitating for? *uten å ~* without hesitating. **nølende** *adj* hesitating. **nøling** *sb* hesitation; *uten ~* without hesitating.

nøre *vb* kindle; *~ opp* light a fire.

nøste 1 *sb* ball (of thread, wool); **2** *vb: ~ opp* wind up (into a ball).

nøtt *sb* nut; *en hard ~ å knekke* a hard nut to crack. **nøtte|kjerne** *sb* kernel of a nut. **~knekker** *sb* nut-crackers *fl*; *en ~knekker* a pair of nut-crackers. **~skall** *sb* nutshell.

nøyaktig *adj* exact, precise; accurate; *~ på tiden* exactly on time; *fortell meg ~ hva du så* tell me exactly what you saw. **nøyaktighet** *sb* exactness, precision; accuracy. **nøye A** *adj* careful, close; intimate; *~ overveielse* close consideration; *han overveiet det ~* he considered it carefully; *passe ~ på* take great care of; *stå i ~ sammenheng med* be closely/intimately connected with; **B** *vb: ~ seg med* be content/satisfied with; *det kan jeg ikke ~ meg med* that is not enough for me; *hun ~r seg med lite* she is content with very little. **nøyeregnende** *adj* particular (*med* about). **nøysom** *adj* content with little; easily satisfied; *også* modest; *(i matveien)* frugal. **nøysomhet** *sb* contentment; *(i matveien)* frugality.

nøytral *adj* neutral; *~ holdning* neutral attitude; *de nøytrale* the neutrals. **nøytralisere** *vb* neutralize. **nøytralitet** *sb* neutrality.

nå A *adv* now; at this moment; *(senest på dette tidspunkt)* by now; *~ da de er vekk* now that they are gone; *~ må de være fremme i London* by now they must have arrived in London; *~ og da* now and then; *~ til dags* nowadays; *fra ~ av* from now (on); **2** *(trykkløst ~ kan ofte oversettes med)* well; *det var ~ det* well, that was that; **B** *vb (rekke)* reach; *~r du/kan du ~ den grenen?* can you reach that branch? *da skipet ~dde Newcastle* when the ship reached Newcastle; *vannet ~dde henne til livet* the water reached to her waist. Se også *rekke*. **nåda** *interj* well! *(beroligende)* there! *(forundret)* oh! why! indeed! I say! *(protesterende)* come, come! *(advarende, truende)* there! why! come! now, now! now then!

nåde I *sb* **1** *(barmhjertighet)* mercy; *be om ~* ask for mercy; *uten ~* without mercy; **2** *(gunst)* grace; *kongens ~* the grace of the king; **II** *vb: Gud ~ deg dersom ...* God help you if ... **nåde|full** *adj* = *~rik*. **~løs** *adj* merciless, ruthless. **~rik** *sb* gracious. **~støt** *sb* death-blow; coup de grâce. **nådig** *adj* gracious.

någjeldende *adj* present; now in force; *de ~ regler* the regulations now in force.

nådig *adj* merciful; *en ~ skjebne, et ~ forsyn* a merciful fate.

nål *sb (bar~, sy~)* needle; *(knappe~, pynte~)* pin. **nåle|pute** *sb* pin cushion. **~skog** *sb* coniferous forest. **~stikk** *sb* pinprick. **~tre** *sb* conifer.

nålevende *adj* (now) living.

når *adv, konj* **1** when; *la oss gå ~ dette er over* let us leave when this is over; **2** *~ ... engang/først* once; *~ veien først er bygd* once the road is built; **3** *(~ som helst)* whenever; at any time; *du kan komme ~ du vil* you may come whenever you like; *du kan komme ~ som helst mellom to og fire* you may come at any time between two and four.

nå|tid *sb* **1** present (time); *~ens mennesker* people of today; **2** *(gram: presens)* the present (tense). **~ til dags** *adv* nowadays. **~vel** *adv* well (then). **~værende** *adj* present, existing; *den ~værende regjering* the present government.

O

o *(bokstaven)* o.

oase *sb* oasis.

obduksjon *sb* post-mortem (examination). **obdusere** *vb* perform a post-morten on.

oberst *sb* colonel. **oberstløytnant** *sb* lieutenant-colonel.

objekt *sb* object. **objektiv 1** *adj* objective; **2** *sb (på fotoapparat etc)* lens. **objektivitet** *sb* objectivity.

obligasjon *sb* bond.

obligatorisk *adj* compulsory; *et ~ emne/fag* a compulsory subject.

obo *sb* oboe. **oboist** *sb* oboist.

observant *adj* observant. **observasjon** *sb* observation. **observatorium** *sb* observatory. **observere** *vb* observe.

obskøn *adj* obscene. **obskønitet** *sb* obscenity.

odd *sb* point.

odde A *adj (om tall)* odd, uneven; **B** *sb (nes)* headland, point. **oddetall** *sb* odd/uneven number.

ode *sb* ode.

odelsbonde *sb* freeholder.

offensiv *adj, sb* offensive; *~ våpen* offensive weapons; *ta ~en* take the offensive.

offentlig *adj* public; *~ bygning* public building; *~ tilgjengelig* open to the public. **offentlig|gjøre** *vb* publish. **~gjøring** *sb* publication. **~het** *sb* **2** publicity; **2** *~en* people (at large); the (general) public; the people.

offer *sb* **1** victim; *ulykken krevde mange ofre* the accident claimed many victims; **2** *(~ til guddom)* offering, sacrifice; **3** *(oppofrelse)* sacrifice; *foreldre bringer ofte ofre for å gi barna sine en god utdannelse* parents often make sacrifices to give their children a good education. **offervillig** *adj* self sacrificing; generous.

offiser *sb* officer.

offisiell *adj* official; *et offisielt besøk* an official visit.

ofre *vb* **1** sacrifice; *hun ~t livet for å redde et druknende barn* she sacrificed her life to save a drowning child; **2** *(gi, vie)* give, spend; devote; *~ tid på* spend the time on; *de ~r oss ikke en tanke* they do not give a thought to us; *han ~t seg for musikken* he devoted himself to music.

ofte *adv* often. **oftere** *adv* more often; *han var ~ hos oss enn hjemme hos seg selv* he was at our house more often than at home.

og *konj* and; *de gikk to ~ to* they walked two by two; *hun satt ~ spiste eplet sitt* she sat/she was eating her apple.

også *adv* **1** also, too; as well; *det var ~ noen tyskere til stede* there were also some Germans present; *han er dikter, og ~ kritiker* he is a poet, and a critic as well; *hun snakker fransk ~* she speaks French too; **2** *(uttrykk) de hadde lovet å sende pengene, og det gjorde de ~* they had promised to send the money, and so they did; *det er jeg ~* (and) so am I; *det gjør vi ~* (and) so do we; *det var da ~ et spørsmål* what a question!

ohoi! *interj* ahoy!

oker *sb* ochre.

okkupant *sb* occupier. **okkupasjon** *sb* occupation. **okkupere** *vb* occupy.

okse *sb* bull; *(kastrert ~, trekk~)* ox; *(ung~)* steer. **okse|kjøtt** *sb* beef. **~stek** *sb* roast beef; *(om hele steken)* joint of beef.

oksid *sb* oxide. **oksidere** *vb* oxidize.

oksygen *sb* oxygen.

oktav 1 *mus* octave; **2** *(bokformat)* octavo.

oktober October; *første ~* the first of October/Oct. 1st.

olabukser *sb* jeans.

olde|far *sb* great-grandfather. **~foreldre** *sb* great-grandparents. **~mor** *sb* great-grandmother.

oldfrue *sb* matron, housekeeper.

olding *sb* (very) old man. **oldingaktig** *adj* senile. **old|saker** *sb fl* antiquities. **~tid** *sb* antiquity.

oliven *sb* olive.

olje 1 *sb* oil; **2** *vb (smøre)* oil, lubricate. **olje|aktig** *adj* oily. **~anlegg** *sb petro* oil plant; oil refinery. **~arbeider** *sb* oil worker; *petro dgl* roughneck, roustabout. **~boring** *sb* oil drilling; *(til havs)* offshore drilling. **~brønn** *sb petro* oil well. **~farge** *sb* oil-colour. **~fat** *sb* oil drum. **~felt** *sb* oil discovery; oil field. **~filter** *sb* oil filter. **~flak** *sb* oil slick. **~forekomst** *sb* oil deposit. **~funn** *sb* oil find; oil strike. **~fyring** *sb* oil heating. **~førende, ~holdig** *adj* oil bearing. **~hyre** *sb* oilskins *fl*. **~inntekter** *sb fl* oil revenues. **~kilde** *sb* oil well. **~lampe** *sb* oil lamp. **~ledning** *sb* oil pipe(line). **~lense** *sb* oil boom. **~lerret** *sb* oilcloth, oilskin. **~leting** *sb* oil exploration; *(leteboring)* exploration drilling. **~maleri** *sb* oil painting. **~maling** *sb* oil paint. **~opptaker** *sb = ~skummer*. **~opptak(ing)** *sb = ~ skumming*. **~plattform** *sb petro* oil platform; oil rig. **~raffineri** *sb* oil plant; oil refinery. **~rigg** *petro* oil rig. **~riggarbeider** *sb petro* roughneck, roustabout. **~skifer** *sb* oil shale. **~skift** *sb* oil change; *smøring og ~skift* grease-up and oil change. **~skummer** *sb petro* skimmer. **~skumming** *sb petro* skimming. **~tanker, ~tankskip** *sb* oil tanker. **~terminal** *sb petro* oil(-loading) terminal. **~tårn** *sb petro* oil derrick. **~utvinning** *sb* oil extraction; oil drilling. **~vern** *sb* oil protection. **~virksomhet** *sb* oil activity.

olm *adj* mad, angry; nasty; *(om okse især)* fierce.

olympiade *sb* Olympiad; Olympic Games. **olympisk** *adj* Olympian, Olympic; *~ ro* Olympian calm; *~ mester* Olympic champion.

om I *adv* **1** *(omkring)* about, around; round; *han så seg ~* he looked round; he looked about him; **2** *(~ igjen)* again; once more; *~ og ~ igjen* over and over (again); *vi har bygd ~ huset vårt* we have rebuilt our house/had our house rebuilt; **II** *konj* if, whether; *gjør det ~ du tør!* do it if you dare! *han spurte ~ de var hjemme* he asked if/whether they were at home; *jeg vet ikke ~ hun er lykkelig eller ikke* I don't know whether she is happy or not; *~ så, selv ~* even if; *som ~* as if; *du ser ut som ~ du skulle ha sett et spøkelse* you look as you he have seen a ghost; *~ jeg gjør!* rather! you bet I do! **III** *prep* **1** *(rundt ~)* about, round; se for øvrig *omkring*; **2** *(angående)* about; *(~ bestemt, enkelt ting)* of; *de snakket ~ været* they talked about the weather; *en bok ~ hagestell* a book about gardening; *har du hørt ~ hennes brors død?* have you heard of her brother's death? **3** *(ved anmodning, konkurranse etc)* for; *de kjempet ~ prisen* they fought for the prize; *hun bad ~ en kake* she asked for a cake; **4** *(ved tidsangivelse)* in, by, on; *~ aftenen/kvelden* in the evening; *~ dagen* by day; in the daytime; *~ natten* at/by night; *~ sommeren* in (the) summer; *~ søndagen (hver søndag)* on Sundays; *~ tre dager* in three days; **5** *(per)* a; *én gang ~ uken* once a week; **6** *(uttrykk) ~ bord* on board; *~ bord på et skip* on board a ship; *det var flere ~ det* it was the work of several persons; *være ~ seg* look after/take care of number one; *det er ~ å gjøre/det er mye ~ å gjøre for meg at du kommer* I am very anxious that you should come; *nå er det ~ å gjøre å finne dem* now the great thing is to find them.

om|adressere *vb* forward. **~arbeide** *vb* revise. **~bestemme seg** *vb* change one's mind. **~budsmann** *sb* ombudsman; *(offisielt, i GB)* Parliamentary Commissioner. **~danne** *vb* convert, transform. **~debattert** *adj* debated; under discussion. **~dreining** *sb* rotation, revolution; the revolution of the earth.

omegn *sb* neighbourhood; surrounding country; *i ~en av Oslo* in the neighbourhood of Oslo.

omelett *sb* omelet(te).

om|fang *sb* extent, size; *bokens ~* the size of the book; *ulykkens ~* the extent of the accident; *i lite/stort ~* to a small/great extent. **~fangsrik** *adj* extensive. **~fatte** *vb* **1** *(innbefatte)* include, cover; *hvert distrikt ~r flere (kirke)sogn* each district includes several parishes; **2** *(angå, berøre)* affect; *streiken ~r bare gruveindustrien* the strike only affects the mining industry; **3** *(bestå av)* consist of; *leiren ~r 50 telt* the camp consists of 50 tents. **~fattende** *adj* comprehensive, extensive. **~favne** *vb* embrace, hug. **~favnelse** *sb* embrace, hug. **~flakkende** *adj* roaming, roving, vagrant. **~forme** *vb* convert, transform.

omgang *sb* **1** *(runde, tur)* round, turn; *det går på ~ mellom dem* they do it by turns; *hun vant første ~* she won the first round; **2** *(i fotball)* half-time; **3** *(på strikketøy)* row; **4** *(samkvem)* company, intercourse; se også *omgangskrets;* **5** *(behandling)* handling, treatment; *uforsiktig ~ med dynamitt* recklessness in handling dynamite. **omgangs|krets** *sb* associates *fl*; circle of acquaintances. **~syke** *sb* epidemic. **~venn** *sb* associate, friend.

om|gi *vb* surround; *~tt av venner* surrounded by friends. **~givelser** *sb fl* surroundings; environs, neighbourhood; *(miljø)* environment.

om|gjengelig *adj* companionable, sociable. **~gjengelighet** *sb* sociability.

om|gå *vb: ~gå loven* evade/get round the law. **~gåelse** *sb* evasion; getting round. **~gående** *adj* immediate; *adv* immediately; at once; *svare ~* answer by return (of post). **~gås** *vb (vanke sammen med)* associate with; *~ barn* handle children *de er lett å ~* they are easy to get on with.

om|hu *sb* care; *med* ~ with care; *uten* ~ carelessly. **~hyggelig** *adj* careful; *adv* carefully; *han var* ~ *med å lukke dørene* he was careful about closing the doors; *maten ble* ~ *tilberedt* the food was carefully prepared.

om|kalfatre *vb* turn upside down. **~kamp** *sb* play-off. **~kjøring** *sb* diversion; *US* detour. **~komme** *vb* be killed; be lost; *hun omkom ved en ulykke* she was killed in an accident. **~kostninger** *sb fl* expense(s); *store* ~ heavy expenses; *med små/store* ~ at small/great expense.

om|krets *sb* circumference; *i vid* ~ for many miles round. **~kring** *adv, prep* **1** about, round; *en mur* ~ *byen* a wall round the town; *en park med en mur* ~ a park with a wall round it; *han gikk* ~ he walked about; **2** *(cirka)* about; ~ *(klokken) seks* about six o'clock. **~kved** *sb* refrain. **~liggende** *adj* surrounding. **~lyd** *sb* mutation. **~løp** *sb* **1** circulation; *det er falske sedler i* ~ forged banknotes are in circulation; *hun har* ~ *i hodet* she has presence of mind; she is clever; **2** *(i sport)* new race.

omme *(slutt)* over, up; at an end; *tiden er* ~ time is up.

om|organisere *vb* reorganize. **~plante** *vb* replant, transplant. **~reisende** *adj* travelling; *et* ~ *sirkus* a travelling circus. **~ringe** *vb* surround, encircle. **~riss** *sb* outline; *i* ~ in outline.

områ seg *vb* consider; think (it over); *jeg må ha tid til å* ~ *meg* I must have time to think (it over).

område *sb* area, field, territory; *store* ~*r i Australia* large areas of Australia; **2** *på alle områder* in all fields/respects; *utenfor mitt* ~ *(om kunnskaper)* outside my field.

om|setning *sb* sale(s), turnover; business, trade; *livlig* ~ brisk trade/turnover; *en* ~ *på* a turnover of; *årlig* ~ annual turnover. **~setningsavgift** *sb* purchase tax. **~sette** *vb* **1** *(selge)* sell; **2** *(oversette)* translate; ~ *til engelsk* translate into English.

omsider *adv* at length.

om|skiftelig *adj* changeable; *(om været også)* unsettled. **~skolere** *vb* re-educate, retrain. **~skolering** *sb* re-education, retraining.

omslag 1 *(bind, perm etc)* cover; *boken trenger nytt* ~ the book needs a new cover; **2** *(forandring)* change; *vær*~ change of/in the weather; **3** *(forbinding)* compress.

omsorg *sb* care; *eldre*~ care of the old; *dra/ha* ~ *for* look after; take care of; *under deres* ~ under their care. **omsorgsfull** *adj (omhyggelig)* careful; *(beskyttende)* considerate.

omstart *sb data* rerun. **omstarte** *vb data* rerun.

omstendelig *adj* **1** *(pirkete)* fussy, over-careful; **2** *(detaljert)* detailed; *(innviklet)* laborious; troublesome. **omstendighet** *sb* circumstance, fact; *under disse* ~*er* under these circumstances; *under ingen* ~ in no circumstances; on no account; *være i (lykkelige)* ~*er* be pregnant. **omstendighetskjole** *sb* maternity frock/dress.

omstreifer *sb* **1** *(landstryker)* vagabond, tramp; **2** *(tater)* gipsy, gypsy.

om|stridd *adj* disputed. **~styrte** *vb* overthrow. Jf *styrte*. **~støte** *vb* annul. **~svermet** *adj* fêted; much courted. **~svøp** *sb: uten* ~*svøp* plainly; to the point; in so many words. **~sydd** *adj* altered. **~syn** *sb* consideration, regard. Se også *hensyn*. **~synsledd** *sb* indirect object. **~tale 1** *sb* mention; *de fortjener spesiell* ~ they deserve special mention; *jeg kjenner henne av* ~ I know her by repute; **2** *vb* mention; refer to. Se for øvrig *snakke, tale*. **~tanke** *sb* consideration; care, thought. **~tenksom** *adj* considerate, thoughtful.

omtrent *adv* **1** about; ~ *på min alder* about my age; **2** *(nesten, litt mindre enn)* almost, nearly; ~ *så stor som* about/nearly as big as.

om|tumlet *adj: han har hatt en* ~ *tilværelse* he has had a chequered (stormy, unsettled etc) life; he has knocked about a good deal. **~tvistet** *adj* controversial, disputed. **~tåket** *adj* fuddled, muzzy. **~valg** *sb* second ballot. **~vei** *sb* detour; *gjøre/ta en* ~ make a detour. **~veltning** *sb* revolution. **~vende** *vb* convert; ~ *seg* be converted; *en omvendt* a convert; *de omvendte* the converts. **~vendelse** *sb* conversion. **~vendt** *adj* **1** *(motsatt)* opposite, reverse; ~ *rekkefølge* reverse order; *det er akkurat* ~ it is the other way round; *det* ~*e av* the opposite/reverse of; *og* ~ and vice versa; **2** *(i religiøs forstand)* converted. Se også ~*vende*. **~verden** *sb* surroundings; outside world. **~viser** *sb* guide. **~vising** *sb* conducted tour.

onanere *vb* masturbate. **onani** *sb* masturbation.

ond *adj* evil, wicked; bad; ~*e tanker* evil thoughts. **ondartet** *adj (om sykdom)* malignant. **onde** *sb* evil; *et nødvendig* ~ a necessary evil. **ond|sinnet** *adj* evil; ill-natured, spiteful. **~sinnethet** *sb* ill-nature. **ondskap** *sb* wickedness, malice. **ondskapsfull** *adj* malicious, spiteful; *en* ~ *strek* a dirty trick.

onkel *sb* uncle.

onsdag *sb* Wednesday.

opera *sb* opera. **operasanger(inne)** *sb* opera singer.

operasjon *sb* operation, surgery; *de foretok en* ~ they undertook/performed an operation; *han underkastet seg en* ~ he underwent an operation. **operere** *vb* operate; *(med: foreta en operasjon på)* operate on; *de opererte pasienten* they operated on the patient; *han ble operert* he was operated on.

operette *sb* musical (comedy).

opinion *sb* public opinion. **opinionsundersøkelse** *sb* (public) opinion poll.

opium *sb* opium. **opiumsdråper** *sb* laudanum.

opp *adv* **1** up; ~ *og ned* up and down; *bakke* ~ *og bakke ned* up hill and down dale; *de gikk* ~ *bakken* they walked up the hill; *katten klatret* ~ *i et tre* the cat climbed up a tree; *brenne (drikke, spise etc)* ~ burn (drink, eat etc) up; **2** *(så det blir åpning)* open; *vinduet fløy* ~ the window flew open; *vi brøt* ~ *kassen* we broke the crate open; **3** *(~ av lommen, sengen, vannet etc)* out; *hun kom* ~ *av vannet* she came out of the water; **4** *(fra* *hverandre etc, især)* un-; *knappe* ~ unbutton; *låse* ~ unlock; *pakke* ~ unpack; **5** (uttrykk) **lukke** ~ open; *han lukket* ~ *døren* he opened the door; ~ **med** *humøret!* cheer up! *han stilte sykkelen* ~ **mot** *veggen* he propped his bicycle against the wall; *snu* ~ **ned** turn upside down; *jeg skal* ~ **til** *eksamen til våren* I am taking/sitting for his examination next spring.

opp|bakking *sb* **1** support; **2** *data (sikkerhetskopiering)* backup. **~bevare** *vb* keep, save; *det må ~bevares tørt* it must be kept dry. **~bevaring** *sb* keeping, storage. **~bevaringen** *sb (på jernbanestasjon etc)* left-luggage office; *US* checkroom. **~blåst** *adj* **1** swollen, puffy; **2** *(blærete, viktig)* conceited; puffed up. **~blomstring** *sb* flourishing. **~brakt** *adj (ergerlig)* indignant. **~brudd** *sb* departure. **~by** *vb: ~by alle sine krefter* summon all one's strength. **~byggelig** *adj* edifying. **~byggelse** *sb (andakt etc)* prayer meeting.

oppdage *vb* **1** *(finne noe nytt)* discover; *Amerika ble ~t av Columbus* America was discovered by Columbus; **2** *(finne ut av noe ukjent)* find out; *jeg ~t hvem hun var* I found out who she was; **3** *(oppspore)* detect; *jeg kunne ikke ~ noe tegn til sykdom* I could detect no sign of disease; **4** *(bli klar over)* discover, find; realize; *han ~t at sykkelen hans var stjålet* he discovered/found that his bicycle was stolen. **oppdagelse** *sb* discovery; *de gjorde en viktig ~* they made an important discovery. **oppdagelses|reise** *sb* expedition. **~reisende** *sb* explorer.

oppdiktet *adj* ficticious; *et ~ navn* a ficticious name.

oppdra *vb* bring up, educate.

opp|drag *sb* task, commission; *få i ~ å gjøre noe* be commissioned to do something. **~dragelse** *sb* **1** upbringing; **2** *(skolegang, utdannelse)* education; **3** *(om oppførsel)* manners; *han eier ikke ~* he has no manners. **~drett** *sb* breeding, rearing. **~drift** *sb* **1** *(fysikk)* buoyancy; **2** *(ærgjerrighet etc)* ambition. **~drive** *vb: det er ikke til å ~drive* it is not to be had for love or money. **~dyrket** *adj* cultivated. **~dyrking** *sb* cultivation.

oppe *adv* **1** up; ~ *i fjellene* up in the mountains; **2** *(åpen)* open; *alle vinduene stod ~* all the windows were open; **3 være ~:** *a) (ha stått opp)* be up; be out of bed; *han er ikke ~ ennå* he is not up yet; *b) (ikke ha lagt seg)* stay up; *han var ~ hele natten* he stayed up all night; *ungene fikk lov til å være ~* the kids were allowed to stay up; *c) saken er ~ for høyesterett* the case is up before the High Court; *d) være ~ til eksamen* sit for an exam. **oppegående** *adj: han er ~* he is up and about.

opp|fatte *vb* **1** perceive; *det kan ikke ~s med sansene* it cannot be perceived by our senses; **2** *(forstå)* understand; make out; *(få tak i meningen med også)* catch; *jeg ~t ikke hva han mente* I could not make out what he meant; *jeg ~t ikke hva han sa* I did not catch what he said. **~fatning** *sb* **1** *(forståelse)* understanding; **2** *(mening)* opinion, view; *etter min ~* in my opinion; *jeg er av den ~ at* my opinion is that; I am of the opinion that.

opp|finne *vb* invent. **~finnelse** *sb* invention. **~finner** *sb* inventor. **~finnsom** *adj* inventive. **~finnsomhet** *sb* ingenuity, inventiveness. **~fordre** *vb* ask; call on; invite; *de ~fordret dem til å overgi seg* they called on them to surrender; *jeg er blitt ~fordret til å* I have been asked to. **~fordring** *sb* request; invitation; *etter/på ~fordring* by request. **~fostre** *vb* bring up; rear. **~fylle** *vb* fulfill; *deres håp ble ~fylt* their hopes were fulfilled; *han oppfylte mitt ønske* he complied with my wish. **~fyllelse** *sb* fulfilment; *det gikk i ~* it came true.

opp|føre **1** *(bygge)* build, erect; *huset ble ~ført i 1960* the house was built in 1960; **2** *(fremføre)* act, perform; *de ~førte et stykke av Shaw* they performed a play by Shaw; **3** *(føre/skrive opp)* enter; se for øvrig *føre inn*; **4** *~føre seg* behave; *(føre seg)* conduct oneself; *~før deg ordentlig!* behave yourself! *de ~førte seg dårlig* they behaved badly. **~førelse** *sb* **1** *(bygging)* building, erection; *huset er under ~førelse* the house is being built; **2** *(fremføring)* performance; *første ~førelse* first performance/night. **~førsel** *sb* **1** *(ytre opptreden)* behaviour; *(handlemåte)* conduct; *(manerer, vesen)* manners.

oppgang *sb* **1** *(trappe~)* staircase; *leilighetene har felles ~* the flats open to one staircase; **2** *(stigning)* rise.

oppgave *sb* **1** *(arbeid, oppdrag)* duty, task; business; *en vanskelig ~* a difficult task; *vokse med ~n* rise to the occasion; **2** *(formål)* purpose; *med den ~ å finne* with the purpose of finding; **3** *(skole~)* exercise; *(eksamens~)* paper; *(matematikk~)* problem; *(stil~)* subject; **4** *(gåte)* puzzle; *løse en ~* solve a problem/puzzle.

opp|gi *vb* **1** give up; *de ~gav tanken på å...* they gave up the idea of...; *han er ~gitt av legene* he is given up by the doctors; se for øvrig *gi opp*; **2** *(meddele)* give, state; *han ~gav navn og adresse* he stated his name and address. **~gitt** *adj* **1** *(meddelt, opplyst)* given, provided; **2** *(fortvilet)* in despair; *hun var helt ~gitt* she was in despair.

opp|gjort *adj* settled. **~gjør** *sb* **1** *(av regnskap etc)* settlement; **2** *(strid)* scene; argument, quarrel; *de hadde et ~* they had a scene.

opp|glødd *adj* enthusiastic. **~hav** *sb* origin, source. **~havsmann** *sb* author, source. **~heve** *vb* *(avskaffe)* abolish; *(om beleiring, forbud)* raise; *(om kontrakt)* cancel; *(om lov)* repeal. **~hevelse** *sb* abolition; raising; cancellation. **~hisselse** *sb* agitation, exitement; *(sinne)* exasperation. **~hisset** *adj* agitated, excited; *(nervøst ~)* excited; *(rasende)* furious.

opp|hold *sb* **1** *(midlertidig, på et sted)* stay; *to ukers ~hold* a fortnight's stay; **2** *(for lengre tid)* residence; *etter fem års ~hold i landet* after five years' residence in the country; **2** *(stans)* stop; *(pause)* let-up, pause; *det var et ~hold i regnet* there was a let-up in the rain; **3** *tjene til livets ~hold* earn one's living. **~holde** *vb* **1** *(forsinke, hefte)* delay, keep; *jeg ble ~holdt en time* I was kept for an hour; **2** *~holde seg* live; *(midlertidig)* stay;

~holde seg hos venner stay with friends. **~holdssted** *sb* (place of) residence. **~holdstillatelse** *sb* residence permit. **~hoping** *sb* accumulation. **~hovnet** *adj* swollen. **~hør** *sb (slutt)* close, end; *uten ~hør* continually, unceasingly. **~høre** *vb* cease, end, stop. Se for øvrig *slutte, stanse.* **~hørssalg** *sb* closing-down sale. **~ildne** *vb* incite, inflame.

oppi *prep* in; in the midst of.

opp|irre *vb* exasperate, irritate, provoke. **~kalle** *vb: ~kalle etter* name after. Se for øvrig *kalle.* **~kjøp** *sb* buying up. **~kjøper** *sb* buyer. **~klare** *vb* clear up; solve; *mysteriet ble ~klart* the mystery was cleared up/ solved. **~komling** *sb* parvenu; *(en som plutselig er kommet seg opp)* upstart. **~komme** *sb* spring. **~komst** *sb* origin, rise. **~krav** *sb: sende mot ~krav* send C.O.D. (= cash on delivery). **~kreve** *vb* collect. Se også *innkreve, kreve.* **~kvikke** *vb* refresh, stimulate.

opp|lag 1 *(av varer)* stock; **2** *(av bøker etc)* impression, run; *(utgave)* edition; **3** *(om skip) i ~* laid up. **~lagt** *adj* **1** *(innlysende)* evident, obvious; *en ~ sak (også)* a matter of course; **2** *(i stemning)* in a good mood/fine fettle; *jeg er ikke ~ til det* I am not in the mood for it; I do not feel like it. **~legg** *sb (plan)* plan; *(i fotball)* pass. **~lesning** *sb* reading (aloud).

opp|leve *vb* **1** *(erfare)* experience; meet with; *~leve fattigdom* experience poverty; *~leve mange eventyr* meet with many adventures; **2** *(overvære)* see, witness; *hun har ~levd en god del* she has seen a good deal; **3** *(leve lenge nok til å se)* live to see; *jeg håper jeg får ~leve det* I hope I shall live to see it; **4** *(gjennomgå)* go/live through. **~levelse** *sb* **1** *(erfaring)* experience; *det var en stor ~levelse for meg* it was a great experience for me; **2** *(eventyrlig ~levelse)* adventure; *våre ~levelser i Afrika* our adventures in Africa. **~live** *vb* 1 *(bringe liv i, stimulere)* stimulate; **2** *(oppmuntre)* cheer, encourage. **~livende** *adj (stimulerende)* stimulating; *(morsom)* amusing. **~livningsforsøk** *sb* attempt at resuscitation. **~lyse** *vb* **1** *(lyse opp)* light (up); *(især festlig)* illuminate; **2** *(belyse)* throw light on; **3** *(meddele)* explain, state. **~lysende** *adj* instructive. **~lysning** *sb* **1** *(meddelelse)* information; *(i enkeltheter)* particulars; *en ~lysning* a piece of information; *mange ~lysninger* much information; *nærmere ~lysning(er)* (further) particulars; **2** *(folke~, kunnskaper)* education, knowledge; **3** *(belysning)* lighting; *(især festlig)* illumination. **~lyst** *adj* **1** *(om belysning)* illuminated; lit (up); **2** *(om kunnskaper)* educated, enlightened. **~løp** *sb* **1** *(uroligheter)* disturbance, riot; **2** *(i fotball)* run. **~løpen** *adj* lanky. **~løpsside** *sb* straight. **~løse** *vb* dissolve; *hun var ~løst i tårer* she was dissolved in tears; *parlamentet ble ~løst* Parliament was dissolved; *sukker ~løses i vann* sugar dissolves in water. **~løsning** *sb* **1** *(det å ~løse)* dissolution; *gå i ~løsning* disintegrate; **2** *(resultatet av ~løsningen)* solution; **3** *data, foto, TV etc* resolution.

oppmann *sb* arbitrator, umpire.

opp|merksom *adj* **1** *(aktpågivende)* attentive; *adv* attentively; *han lyttet ~merksomt* he listened attentively; *hun gjorde meg ~merksom på hva som var hendt* she called my attention to what had happened; **2** *(hensynsfull)* considerate; *~merksom mot* considerate to/ towards. **~merksomhet** *sb* **1** attention; *de viste den gamle damen tallrike små ~merksomheter* they showed the old lady numerous little attentions; *hun ropte for å påkalle ~merksomhet* she shouted to attract attention; **2** *(gave)* present.

opp|muntre *vb* **1** *(gjøre gladere)* cheer up; **2** *(trøste)* comfort; **3** *(tilskynde)* encourage; *de ~muntret oss til å gjøre det* they encouraged us to do it. **~muntrende** *adj* cheering, encouraging. **~muntring** *sb* encouragement. **~navn** *sb* nickname. **~nevne** *sb* appoint. **~nå** *vb* obtain, get; *(vinne)* gain; *vi ~når ingenting ved det* we shall gain nothing by that. **~nåelig** *adj* obtainable, attainable. **~ofrelse** *sb* sacrifice. **~ofrende** *adj* selfsacrificing, devoted.

opponent *sb* opponent. **opponere** *vb* object; raise objections; *~ mot* oppose; raise objections to.

opportunisme *sb* opportunism. **opportunist** *sb* opportunist. **opportunistisk** *adj* opportunist.

opposisjon *sb* opposition.

oppover *adv, prep* up, upwards; *de drog ~* they travelled/went upwards; *de rodde ~ elven* they rowed upstream; *han gikk ~ gaten* he walked up the street.

opp|-pakning *sb* pack. **~-pussing** *sb* redecoration, renovation; smartening up. **~ramsing** *sb* reeling off. **~regning** *sb* enumeration. **~reisning** *sb* reparation, satisfaction; redress. **~reist** *adj* erect, upright. **~reklamere** *vb* advertise, boost. **~rette** *vb* **1** *(grunnlegge)* establish, found; *firmaet ble ~rettet i 1890* the firm was established in 1890; **2** *data etc* create. **~rettelse** *sb* establishment, foundation. **~rettholde** *vb* maintain; *~ ro og orden* maintain order. **~holdelse** *sb* maintenance. **~riktig 1** *adj* sincere, frank; *en ~riktig venn* a sincere friend; **2** *adv* sincerely, frankly; *jeg håper ~riktig* I hope sincerely. **~riktighet** *sb* sincerity, frankness. **~ringning** *sb (i telefon)* call. **~rinnelig** *adj* original; *adv* originally; *~rinnelig kom de fra Russland* originally they came from Russia. **~rinnelse** *sb* origin. **~rivende** *adj* harrowing; *en ~rivende scene* a harrowing scene. **~rop** *sb* proclamation; *(~rop av navn)* call-over, roll-call. **~ruste** *vb* arm, rearm. **~rusting** *sb* armament, rearmament. **~rømt** *adj* elated; in high spirits. **~rydningssalg** *sb* clearance sale.

opp|rør *sb* **1** *(mot regjering)* rebellion, revolt; *(især mindre)* rising; *folket gjorde ~ mot sine herskere* the people revolted against their rulers; **2** *(bevegelse)* commotion, excitement; *havet var i ~* the sea was agitated/rough; *huset var i ~* the house was in (a) commotion. **~røre** *vb* revolt, shock; *scenen ~rørte ham* the scene revolted him. **~rørende** *adj* revolting, shocking. **~rører** *sb* rebel. **~rørsk** *adj* rebellious. **~rørt** *adj* **1** *(forferdet, indignert)* indignant, shocked; **2** *(om havet)* rough, troubled. **~rådd** *adj* at a loss; *hun er aldri ~rådd for ord* she is never at a loss for words.

opp|sagt *adj: bli ~* get/be given notice; *(fra stilling også)* be dismissed. **~satt** *adj: ~ på* anxious/eager to;

keen on; *de var ~satt på å begynne straks* they were anxious/eager to begin at once. **~seiling** *sb: være under ~* be in the offing/under way. **~setsig** *adj* disobedient, insubordinate. **~setsighet** *sb* disobedience, insubordination. **~sette, ~settelse** se *utsette, utsettelse.* **~setting** *sb data etc* setup. **~si** se *si opp.* **~sigelse** *sb* notice. **~sikt** *sb* **1** *(oppmerksomhet)* attention, sensation, stir; *det vakte stor ~* it attracted great attention; *(sterkere)* it made a sensation; **2** *(oppsyn)* supervision. **~siktvekkende** *adj* sensational. **~skaket** *adj* upset. **~skjørtet** *adj* flustered, bustling; excited. **~skrift** *sb* recipe. **~slag** *sb* **1** *(plakat)* bill, poster; **2** *(på erme)* cuff; **3** *(på bukser)* turn-up. **~slagsbok** *sb* reference book. **~slagstavle** *sb* notice board. **~slitende** *adj* fatiguing. **~slukt** *adj: ~ av* absorbed in.

opp|snappe se *snappe opp.* **~snuse** se *snuse opp.* **~sparing** *sb* saving. **~spilt** *adj* keyed up. **~spinn** *sb* fabrication, lie. **~spore** *vb (ved å forfølge)* track dowm; *(ved leting)* discover, trace. **~stand** *sb* rising, revolt; *(større)* rebellion; *gjøre ~stand* rise in rebellion; revolt. **~standelse** *sb* **1** *(fra de døde)* resurrection; **2** *(ståhei)* excitement, stir. **~starting** *sb* start-up. **~startings|diskett** *sb data* boot diskette. **~startingstast** *sb data* boot button. **~stemt** *adj (munter)* in high spirits. **~stigning** *sb* ascent. **~stiver** *sb* tonic, pick-me-up. **~stoppernese** *sb* retroussé/turned-up nose; stub-nose. **~strammer** *sb* talking-to; ticking-off. **~stuss** *sb* commotion, stir. **~stykke** se *stykke opp.* **~stykket** *adj* fragmentary. **~styltet** *adj* stilted. **~styr** *sb* fuss; agitation, commotion, stir. **~støt** *sb (fra maven)* belch. **~stå** *vb* **1** *(inntreffe)* arise; break out; *det ~stod uenighet* differences arose; **2** *(~stå fra de døde)* rise. **~summere** *vb* sum up. **~sving** *sb (i næringslivet)* boom. **~syn** *sb* **1** *(tilsyn)* supervision; care, charge; custody; *de stod/var under ~syn av en fengselsbetjent* they were in the custody/under the care of a prison officer; *ha ~syn med* superintend; be in charge of; look after; **2** *(ansikt, utseende)* face, look. **~synsmann** inspector, superintendent; attendant; keeper. **~søke** *vb* go to see; *(gå for å finne)* seek out.

opp|ta *vb* **1** *(legge beslag på)* take up; occupy; *~ta plass* take up room; *det ~tok tankene våre* it occupied our thoughts; **2** *(ta opp som elev, medlem etc)* admit. **~tak** *sb* **1** *a) (bånd~, plate~)* recording; *b) (film~)* shot; *(om fotograferingen)* shooting; *c) (radio~)* broadcast commentary; **2** *(også ~takelse, ~taking, f.eks som elev)* admission. **~takprøve** *sb* entrance examination. **~takt** *sb (musikk)* upbeat; *fig* prelude. **~tatt** *adj* **1** *(om person)* busy, engaged; **2** *(om ting)* engaged, occupied; *denne plassen er ~* this seat is taken. **~tegnelse** *sb* note, record; *jeg gjorde mange ~tegnelser* I took many notes. **~telling** *sb* counting.

opptil *prep* up to.

opp|tog *sb* procession. **~trapping** *sb* escalation, stepping-up. **~tre** **1** *(på scene etc)* appear, act; *hun ~trer i siste akt* she appears in the last act; **2** *(oppføre seg)* behave, act; *han ~trådte uforskammet* he behaved insolently; **3** *(finnes)* occur; be found; *denne sykdommen ~trer meget sjelden* this disease occurs very rarely. **~treden** *sb* **1** *(det å opptre, vise seg)* appearance; **2** *(a) handlemåte)* conduct; *b) (oppførsel)* behaviour. **~tredende** *sb: de ~* the actors: those taking part. **~trekker** *(flaskeåpner)* bottle opener. **~trekkeri** *sb* extortion, swindling; *slike priser er det rene ~* such prices are highway robbery. **~trinn** scene, episode, incident. **~trykk** impression, reprint. **~tråkket** *adj* trodden. **~tøyer** *sb* riots; a riot.

opp|vakt *adj* bright, intelligent. **~varme** *vb* heat; *(mindre sterkt)* warm; *~varmet mat* warmed-up food. **~varming** *sb* heating. **~varte** *vb* attend/wait on; serve. Se for øvrig *varte opp.* **~vask** *sb* washing-up; *(det som vaskes opp)* the dishes; *hjelpe til med ~vasken* lend a hand with the dishes. **~vaskklut** *sb* dish-cloth. **~vaskmaskin** *sb* (automatic) dishwasher; dishwashing machine. **~vaskvann** *sb* dish-water. **~veie** *vb* counterbalance; *(fig også)* compensate/make up for; offset. **~vekke** *vb: ~vekke fra de døde* raise from the dead: **~vekst** *sb* adolescence. **~vigle** *vb* stir up. **~vigler** *sb* firebrand, incendiary. **~vigleri** *sb* agitation, subversive activities. **~vise** *vb* exhibit, show. **~visning** *sb* display, show. **~våkning** *sb* awakening. **~øve** *vb* develop, train. **~øving** *sb* training.

optiker *sb* optician.

opti|misme *sb* optimism. **~mist** *sb* optimist. **~mistisk** *adj* optimistic.

optisk *adj* optical.

or *sb* alder.

orakel *sb* oracle. **orakelsvar** *sb* oracle; oracular reply.

orangutang *sb* orang-outan.

oransje *adj, sb* orange.

ord *sb* **1** word; *~et hest* the word horse; *ikke et engelsk ~* not a word of English; **2** *(løfte)* word, promise; *bryte/holde sitt ~* break/keep one's word; *en mann er en mann og ~ er et ~* a bargain is a bargain; a promise is a promise. **3** *(uttrykk)* **~ for ~** word for word; *ha ~* **på seg** *for* have a reputation for; *før jeg visste* **~et av** before I could say Jack Robinson; **be om ~et** request leave to speak; catch the chairman's/*(i parlamentet)* the Speaker's eye; **føre ~et** act as spokesman; **få ~et** be called upon (to speak); be given the floor; *for et* **godt ~** on the slightest provocation; on the least excuse; **ha ~et** have/hold the floor; *ha ~et i sin makt* be a fluent speaker; *dgl* have the gift of the gab; *ha et ~ med i laget* have a voice in the matter; **med andre ~** in other words; **med disse ~** with these words; so saying; **med ett ~** in a word; **med rene ~**: *jeg sa ham det med rene ~* I told him in so many words; *det var rene ~ for pengene* that was plain speaking; *ta ham* **på ~et** take him at his word; *tro meg* **på mitt ~** take my word for it; *ta* **til ~e** begin to speak. **ord|blind** *adj* word-blind. **~blindhet** *sb* word-blindness. **~bok** *sb* dictionary.

orden *sb* order; *alt er i ~* everything is in order;

holde ~ keep order; *ikke i* ~ out of order; not working; *saken gikk i* ~ the matter was settled. **ordens|menneske** *sb* methodical person. **~politiet** *sb* the uniformed police. **~tall** *sb* ordinal (number). **ordentlig** *adj* **1** *(ryddig)* neat, tidy; **2** *(nøyaktig, punktlig)* accurate, careful; *hun er meget* ~ *i arbeidet sitt* she is very careful with her work; **3** *(riktig, skikkelig)* proper; *det er ikke noe* ~ *svar på spørsmålet mitt* it is no proper answer to my question; ~ *gift* properly married; **4** *(anstendig, skikkelig)* decent; **5** *(veldig)* big, colossal; *en* ~ *dumhet* a colossal blunder; *en* ~ *overraskelse* a big surprise.

ord|fattig *adj* having a limited vocabulary. **~forklaring** *sb* explanation of a word/of words. **~forråd** *sb* vocabulary; *hun har et rikt ~forråd* she has a rich vocabulary. **~følge** *sb* word order. **~holden** *adj* honest, reliable; *han er* ~ his word is as good as his bond. **~holdenhet** *sb* honesty.

ordinasjon *sb* ordination. **ordinere** *vb* **1** *(prestevie)* ordain; *bli ordinert (også)* take holy orders; **2** *(skrive ut medisin)* prescribe.

ordinær *adj* **1** *(vanlig)* ordinary; **2** *(simpel)* common.

ord|klasse *sb* part of speech. **~kløyveri** *sb* hair-splitting. **~knapp** *adj* sparing of words; reticent, taciturn. **~knapphet** *sb* reticence, taciturnity. **~liste** *sb* list of words.

ordne *vb* **1** *(arrangere)* arrange; *han ~t blomstene* he arranged the flowers; **2** *(rydde)* put in order; tidy; *~de forhold* orderly conditions; **3** *(greie opp i)* put right; manage; ~ *seg* turn out all right; *det skal vi snart* ~ we'll soon put that right. **ordning** *sb* **1** *(arrangement)* arrangement; **2** *(overenskomst)* agreement; *vi kom frem til en* ~ we reached an agreement; **3** *(system)* system; *den nåværende ~en kan ikke fortsette* the present system cannot go on.

ordre *sb* **1** *(befaling)* command, order; *de handlet etter* ~ they acted by order; *jeg utførte ~n* jeg carried out the order; *vi fikk* ~ *om å reise neste dag* we were ordered to leave next day; **2** *(bestilling)* order.

ord|rett *adj* word-for-word. **~rik** *adj* rich in words; *(nedsettende)* wordy, verbose. **~skifte** *sb* debate, discussion. Se også *diskusjon*. **~spill** *sb* pun. **~språk** *sb* proverb. **~stamme** *sb* root, stem. **~stilling** *sb* word order. **~styrer** *sb* chair|man, person, -woman. **~tak** *sb (ordspråk)* proverb; *(uttrykk)* saying. **~valg** *sb* choice of words. **~veksling** *sb* exchange of words.

organ *sb* organ; *(stemme)* organ of speech. **organisasjon** *sb* organization. **organisator** *sb* organizer. **organisere** *vb* organize. **organisk** *sb* organic. **organisme** *sb* organism.

organist *sb* organist. **orgel** *sb* organ; *han spilte (på)* ~ he played the organ.

orgie *sb* orgy.

Orienten *sb* the East, the Orient. **orientaler** *sb* Oriental. **orientalsk** *adj* Oriental.

orientere *vb* brief, inform; supply with information; ~ *seg* find one's bearings; *godt orientert* well informed; *være orientert* be informed. **orientering** *sb* briefing, information; guidance; *(retningsbestemmelse)* orientation.

original I *adj* original; *(sær)* eccentric; **II** *sb* **1** original; *dette er ikke ~en, det er bare en kopi* this is not the original, it is only a copy; **2** *(særling)* character; *han er litt av en* ~ he is quite a character.

ork *sb* effort.

orkan *sb* hurricane.

orke *vb* **1** *(klare, makte)* be able to; manage; **2** *(tåle, utstå) jeg ~r ikke synet av...* I cannot bear the sight of...

orkester *sb* orchestra; *(især mindre)* band.

orkidé *sb* orchid.

orm *sb* snake, serpent.

ornament *sb* ornament. **ornamentikk** *sb* ornamentation, decoration. **ornat** *sb* vestments.

orre, orr|fugl *sb* black grouse. **~hane** *sb* blackcock. **~høne** *sb* grey hen.

ortodoks *adj* orthodox. **ortodoksi** *sb* orthodoxy.

ortografi orthography. **ortografisk** orthographic.

ortoped *sb* orthopaedist. **ortopedisk** *adj* orthopaedic.

orv *sb* snaithe.

os *sb* **1** *(elveutløp)* mouth of a river, outlet; **2** *(røyk)* smoke. **ose** *vb* **1** *(ryke)* smoke; **2** *(lukte)* reek.

osean *sb* ocean.

oson *sb* ozone.

osp se *asp*.

oss *pron* us; *(refleksivt)* ourselves; *en venn av* ~ a friend of ours; *han forsvarte* ~ he defended us; *vi forsvarte* ~ we defended ourselves; *mellom* ~ *sagt* between ourselves.

ost A se *øst*; **B** *sb* cheese.

oter *sb* otter.

otium *sb* leisure, retirement.

otte *sb* **1** *(morgengry)* early morning; *stå opp i otta* get up at the crack of dawn; **2** *(engstelse)* anxiety, fear.

outrert *adj* exaggerated, outré.

ouverture *sb* overture.

oval *adj, sb* oval.

ovasjon *sb* ovation.

oven|for *adv, prep* above; higher up. **~fra** *adv* from above; from the top. **~på** *adv, prep* on, upon; on top of; *(i etasjen over)* upstairs. **~til** *adv* from above, at the top.

over *prep* **1** *(ovenpå, som ligger etc oppå)* over; *han er svart* ~ *det hele* he is black all over; **2** *(høyere oppe)* above; ~ *havet/havflaten* above sea-level; *stjernene* ~ *oss* the stars above us; **3** *(tvers* ~*)* across, over; *hoppe* ~ *bekken* jump over the brook; *løpe* ~ *gaten* run across the street; **4** *(mer enn)* above, over; ~ *en time* over an hour; ~ *hundre mennesker* above/over a hundred people; **5** *(om klokkeslett)* past; *den er* ~ *åtte* it is past eight o'clock.

overalt *adv* everywhere; ~ *hvor* wherever; ~ *hvor det snakkes engelsk* wherever English is spoken; ~ *i byen* all over the town.

over|anstrenge seg *vb* over-exert/overstrain oneself. **~anstrengelse** *sb* overexertion, overstrain. **~anstrengt** *adj* overworked. **~arm** *sb* upper arm. **~balanse** *sb: ta ~balanse* lose one's balance. **~befolket** *adj* over-populated. **~befolkning** *sb* overpopulation. **~bevise** *vb* convince; *jeg klarte ikke å ~bevise ham om at han tok feil* I could not convince him of his mistake/that he was mistaken. **~bevisende** *adj* convincing. **~bevisning** *sb* conviction. **~bevist** *adj* convinced; *jeg er fast ~bevist om at hun har rett* I am firmly convinced that she is right. **~blikk** *sb* general view; *(de viktigste fakta)* survey; *vi tok et ~blikk over stillingen* he surveyed the position.

over bord *adv* overboard.

over|bringe *vb* bring, deliver. **~bringelse** *sb* delivery. **~bringer** *sb* bearer. **~bærende** *adj* indulgent, tolerant; *et ~bærende smil* an indulgent smile. **~bærenhet** *sb* indulgence, tolerance. **~dra** *vb* hand/make over; transfer; *(~ ansvar, myndighet)* delegate. **~dragelse** *sb* transfer, transference. **~dreven** *adj* exaggerated. **~drive** *vb (i ord)* exaggerate; *(i handling)* overdo. **~drivelse** *sb* exaggeration. **~døve** *vb* drown; *stemmene våre ble ~døvet av bråket fra maskinene* our voices were drowned by the noise of the machinery. **~dådig** *adj* sumptuous, luxurious; *(rikelig)* lavish. **~dådighet** *sb* luxuriousness, sumptuousness; *(rikelighet)* abundance, profusion.

over ende *adv* down, over; *falle ~ ~* fall down; *kaste ~ ~* throw over.

overens *adv: komme/stemme ~* agree. **overens|komst** *sb* agreement, arrangement. **~stemmelse** *sb: i ~stemmelse med* in accordance/agreement with.

over|fall *sb* assault. **~falle** *vb* assault. **~fallsmann** *sb* assailant, assaulter. **~fart** *sb* crossing, passage. **~fladisk** *adj* superficial, shallow; *~fladisk kjennskap, ~fladiske kunnskaper* superficial knowledge. **~flate** *sb* surface. **~flod** *sb* abundance, plenty. **~flytte** *vb* transfer. **~flytning** *sb* transfer. **~flødig** *adj* superfluous. **~flødighet** *sb* superfluity.

overfor *adv* opposite; *huset like ~* the house opposite; the house across the road.

over|forbruk *sb* excess consumption. **~fuse** *vb* abuse; heap abuse upon. **~følsom** *adj* hypersensitive. **~føre** *vb* **1** *(flytte)* transport; convey, transfer; **2** *(~føre elektrisitet, smitte etc)* transmit. **~føring** *sb* transmission. **~føringslinje** *sb* transmission line. **~ført** *adj: ~ført betydning* figurative sense; *i ~ført betydning (også)* figuratively.

overgang *sb* **1** *(konkret)* crossing, passage; **2** *(skifte)* change, transition; *~en fra natt til dag* the change from night to day; *uten ~* without transition; *det er bare en ~* it won't last; it is only a passing phase. **overgangs|alder** *sb* **1** *(hos barn)* years of puberty; **2** *(hos kvinne)* climacteric. **~billett** *sb* transfer (ticket). **~tid** *sb* period of transition; transitional period.

over|gi *vb* **1** *(overrekke)* deliver; hand (over); **2** *(oppgi, utlevere)* surrender; *~ seg* surrender. **~givelse** *sb* surrender. **~grep** *sb* encroachment, infringement. **~gå** *vb (være overlegen)* surpass, exceed. **~hale** *vb (etterse)* overhaul. **~haling** *sb* **1** *(ettersyn)* overhaul; **2** *(nesten velt)* lurch; *ta en ~haling* lurch; **3** *(irettesettelse)* dressing down; *gi ham en kraftig ~haling* give him a good dressing down. **~hendig** *adj* tremendous, violent. **~hengende** *adj: ~hengende fare* imminent danger. **~herre** *sb* overlord. **~herredømme** *sb* supremacy. **~hode** *sb* head; *(~ for stamme)* chief.

overhodet *adv* at all; *om han ~ kommer* if he comes at all.

overholde *vb* keep, observe; *vi overholdt alle reglene* we observed all the rules.

Overhuset *sb GB* the House of Lords.

over|høre *vb* **1** *(ikke høre)* miss; *(ikke ville høre)* ignore; *jeg ~hørte bemerkningene hans* I ignored his remarks; **2** *(få høre ved et tilfelle)* overhear; **3** *(eksaminere)* examine. **~høvle** *vb* dress down; scold. **~hånd** *sb: ta ~hånd* get out of control/out of hand; get the upper hand; *(bli utbredt)* become rampant. **~håndtagende** *adj* rampant; growing, spreading. **~ilet** *adj* rash; without thinking. **~kant** *sb* top; upper edge; *i ~kant av* on the extreme border of. **~kjørt** *adj: bli ~kjørt* get run over. **~klassen** *sb* the upper classes *fl.* **~kommando** *sb* supreme command. **~komme** *vb (greie)* manage; cope with. **~kommelig** *adj: prisen var ~kommelig* the price was reasonable. **~kropp** *sb* upper part of the body. **~lagt** *adj* premeditated, wilful. **~last** *sb: lide ~last* suffer harm/injury; be wronged. **~late** *vb* **1** *(overgi)* hand over; *han ~lot alle pengene til meg* he handed over all the money to me; **2** *(la få)* let have; **3** *(betro)* entrust, leave; *~lat det til meg* leave that to me; *~latt til seg selv* left alone; *de ~lot ham til sin skjebne* they left him to his fate; *jeg ~later det til andre* I leave that to others. **~ledning** *sb* current leakage. **~lege** *sb* chief physician/surgeon. **~legen** *adj* **1** *(meget dyktig)* brilliant, masterly; **2** *(som har overtaket)* superior; **3** *(viktig)* haughty. **~legenhet** *sb* superiority; *(viktighet)* haughtiness. **~legent** *adv* easily; *de vant ~legent* they won easily. **~legg** *sb* premeditation; *med ~legg* on purpose; premeditated; wilfully. **~leppe** *sb* upper lip. **~lesset** *adj* overburdened; *~lesset stil* ornate style. **~leve** *vb* survive. **~levende** *adj* surviving; *de ~levende* the survivors. **~levere** *vb* deliver; hand over. **~levering** *sb* **1** *(avlevering)* delivery; **2** *(tradisjon)* tradition. **~liste** *vb* outwit. **~løper** *sb* renegade. **~makt** *sb* superiority; superior force; *kjempe mot stor ~makt* fight against heavy odds. **~mann** *sb* superior. **~manne** *vb* overpower. **~menneske** *sb* superman. **~moden** *adj* overripe. **~modig** *adj* arrogant. **~morgen** *sb: i ~morgen* the day after tomorrow. **~mot** *sb* arrogance.

overmåte *adv* extremely.

over|natte *vb* spend the night. **~naturlig** supernatural. **~nervøs** *adj* overstrung. **~ordnet** *adj, sb* superior; *en ~ stilling* a responsible post; *hans nærmeste overordnede (entall)* his next superior; *hans overordnede (fl)* his superiors. **~pris** *sb* overcharge. **~produksjon** *sb* over-production. **~raske** *vb* surprise; *(komme*

~raskende på) take by surprise; *(forbløffe)* amaze, astonish; *det ~rasker meg å se deg her* I am surprised to see you here; *vi ble ~rasket av regnet* we caught in the rain. **~raskelse** *sb* surprise; *en behagelig/ubehagelig ~raskelse* a pleasant/unpleasant surprise; *til min store ~raskelse* to my great surprise. **~raskende** *adj* surprising; *adv* surprisingly; *~raskende få* surprisingly few. **~rekke** *vb: ~rekke en noe* present somebody with something.

overrettsakfører *sb* ≈ barrister.

overrumple *vb* take by surprise.

overs *sb: til ~* left, remaining; *(tilsidesatt)* not wanted; *føle seg til ~* feel unwanted.

over|se *vb (ikke se)* overlook, miss; fail to see; *(ikke ville se)* disregard, ignore; *(~ en person)* slight; look down on. **~sende** *vb* send. **~sette** *vb* translate; *hun ~satte fra norsk til engelsk* she translated from Norwegian into English. **~settelse** *sb* translation. **~setter** *sb* translator. **~sikt** *sb* survey; *(resymé)* outline, summary. **~siktlig** *adj* well arranged; easy to grasp. **~sjøisk** *adj* oversea(s). **~skride** *vb* exceed, overstep. **~skridelse** *sb* excess. **~skrift** *sb* heading; *(i avis etc)* headline. **~skudd** *sb* surplus, excess; *(økonomisk ~)* profit. **~skuelig** *sb: i ~skuelig fremtid* in the forseeable future. **~skyet** *adj (om himmelen)* overcast; *(om været også)* cloudy. **~skygge** *vb* overshadow. **~skytende** *adj* surplus, excess. **~slag** *sb* estimate; *gjøre et ~slag* make an estimate. **~spent** *adj* highly strung; overwrought; *(om idéer)* high-flown. **~stige** *vb* exceed, surpass. **~strykning** *sb (i skrift)* crossing out; deletion. **~strømmende** *adj* exceeding, unrestrained; *(~strømmende vennlig)* effusive; *han takket meg ~* he thanked me effusively.

over styr *adv: gå ~ ~* come to nothing, fail; *sette ~ ~* squander.

overstyrmann *sb* chief officer; first officer.

overstått *adv* over; *få det ~* get it over.

over|svømme *vb* flood. **~svømmelse** *sb* flood(s). **~søster** *sb* head nurse. **~ta** *vb* take over. **~tak** *sb: få/ha ~taket* get/have the upper hand. **~takelse** *sb* taking over; *~takelse av makt* assumption of power. **~tale** *vb* persuade; *hun ~talte meg til å komme* she persuaded me to come; *de ~talte meg til ikke å reise* they persuaded me not to leave. **~talelse** *sb* persuasion; *etter mange ~talelser* after much persuasion. **~tallig** *adj* supernumerary. **~tann** *sb* upper tooth. **~tid** *sb: arbeide ~tid* work overtime. **~tidsarbeid** *sb* overtime work. **~tre** *vb* break; *~tre loven* break the law. **~tredelse** *sb* breach, violation; offence. **~treffe** *vb* exceed, surpass; *det ~traff våre forventninger* it surpassed our expectations. **~trekk** *sb* **1** *(beskyttende trekk)* casing; **2** *(beskyttende lag)* coat; **3** *(~trekk av konto)* overdraft. **~trekke** *vb (~ konto)* overdraw. **~tro** *sb* superstition. **~troisk** *adj* superstitious.

over tvert *adv: bryte ~ ~* cut short.

over|veie *vb* consider; think over; *vi må ~veie om det er umaken verd* we must consider whether it will be worth while. **~veielse** *sb* consideration, reflection; thought. **~veiende** *adj: det ~veiende antall* by far the greater number; *det er ~veiende sannsynlig at* there is every probability that. **~vekt** *sb* **1** *(for høy vekt)* overweight; **2** *(majoritet)* majority; *med ti stemmers ~vekt* with a majority of ten; **3** *(overlegenhet) få ~vekt* get the upper hand. **~vektig** *adj* overweight. **~velde** *vb* overwhelm, overcome; *~veldet av arbeid* overwhelmed by work; *smertene ~veldet ham* he was overcome by pain. **~vettes** *adv* extraordinarily, inordinately. **~vinne** *vb* **1** *(om fiende)* defeat, conquer; **2** *(om vanskeligheter)* overcome; overcome an obstacle; **3** *(om følelser)* master. **~vinnelse** *sb: det koster meg ~vinnelse å gjøre det* it costs me a great effort to do it; I have to force myself to do it. **~vintre** *vb* winter; spend the winter. **~vintring** *sb* wintering. **~vurdere** *vb* overestimate, overrate. **~være** *vb* attend; be present; watch; *de ~var gudstjenesten* they attended the service. **~våke** *vb* watch (over); look after; supervise; *~våke at* see to it that; take care that. **~ømfintlig** *adj* oversensitive. **~øse** *vb: ~øse en med noe* shower something on somebody.

ovn *sb* stove; *elektrisk ~* electric heater/stove.

P

p *(bokstaven)* p.

padde *sb* toad.

padle *vb* paddle. **paddleåre** *sb* paddle.

paff *adj* dumbfounded, staggered.

paginere *vb* paginate. **paginering** *sb* pagination.

pai *sb* pie.

pakk *sb* mob, rabble, riff-raff, scum.

pakke I *sb* **1** *(laget for anledningen)* parcel; **2** *(liten, fabrikkfremstilt)* packet; *en ~ sigaretter, en sigarett~* a packet of cigarettes; **3** *(stor ~)* package; **II** *vb* pack; *~ inn* wrap up; *~ sammen* pack up *(især fig)*; *~ opp (el. ut)* unpack. **pakke|post** *sb* parcel post. **~strikk** *sb* rubber band. **pakk|hus** *sb* warehouse. **~is** *sb* pack-ice. **~-kasse** *sb* box, crate; (packing-)case. **pakning** *sb* **1** *(emballasje)* package, packing; **2** *(oppakning)* kit, pack; **3** *(i kran, stempel etc)* gasket.

pakt *sb* pact; *være i ~ med* be in harmony with.

palass *sb* palace.

palett *sb* palette.

palisade *sb* palisade, stockade.

palme *sb* palm. **palmesøndag** *sb* Palm Sunday.

panel *sb* **1** *(paneling)* boarding; **2** *(brystpanel)* wainscot, wainscoting. **panele** *vb* board.

pang *interj* bang.

panikk *sb* panic; *(om dyr også)* stampede; *det oppstod ~* there was a panic; *få (el. bli grepet av) ~* panic, get panicky; *(om dyr også)* stampede. **panisk** *adj* panic; *~ redsel/skrekk)* panic fear.

panne *sb* **A** *(del av ansiktet)* brow, forehead; **B** *(til steking)* frying-pan. **pannekake** *sb* pancake.

panser *sb* **1** *(pansring)* armour; **2** *(stridsvogner)* tanks; **3** *(på bil)* bonnet; *US* hood. **panser|bil** *sb* armoured car. **~hvelv** *sb* strongroom; *US* walk-in--safe.

pant *sb* **1** security; *(i fast eiendom)* mortgage; **2** *(depositum)* deposit; *han betalte ~ for flasken* he paid a deposit for the bottle; **3** *(i pantelek)* forfeit. **pante|-gjeld** *sb* mortgage debt. **~heftelse** *sb* mortgage.

pan|teisme *sb* pantheism. **~teist** *sb* pantheist. **~teistisk** *adj* pantheistic(al).

pante|lek *sb* (game of) forfeits. **~lån** *sb* mortgage loan. **~låner** *sb* pawnbroker. **~lånerforretning** *sb* pawnshop. **pant|haver** *sb* mortgagee. **~obligasjon** *sb* mortgage bond/deed. **~sette** *vb* **1** pawn; *jeg ~satte klokken min* I pawned my watch; *klokken er ~satt* the watch is in the pawn; **2** *(om fast eiendom)* mortgage.

papegøye *sb* parrot.

papir *sb* paper; *(skrive~ som handelsvare)* stationery. **papir|ark** *sb* sheet of paper. **~fabrikk** *sb* paper mill. **~handel** *sb* stationer's shop. **~handler** *sb* stationer. **~kurv** *sb* waste-paper basket, *US* waste-basket. **~lapp** *sb* bit/piece of paper. **~lommetørkle** *sb* tissue. **~masse** *sb* (paper) pulp. **~mølle** *sb fig* red tape. **~penger** *sb* paper money; notes. **~pose** *sb* paper bag. **~serviett** *sb* paper napkin. **~varer** *sb* stationery. **papp** *sb* cardboard.

pappa *sb* papa; *dgl* dad, daddy.

pappeske *sb* cardboard box; carton.

par *sb* **1** *(to som hører naturlig sammen)* pair; *et ~ støvler* a pair of boots; *to ~ sko* two pair(s) of shoes; **2** *(to tilfeldig sammenstilte)* couple; *~ om ~* in pairs; *et ekte~* a married couple; **3** *(noen få)* a couple; a few; one or two; two or three; *et ~ ganger* once or twice; *et ~ måneder* a few months; *et ~ og førti* forty-odd; *om et ~ dager* in a few days; in a day or two.

parade *sb* parade. **paradere** *vb* parade.

paradis *sb* paradise; *hoppe ~* play hopscotch.

paradoks *sb* paradox. **paradoksal** *adj* paradoxical.

parafin *sb* paraffin, kerosene; *(fast ~)* paraffin(wax); *renset ~* (liquid) paraffin. **parafinlampe** *sb* kerosene/oil lamp.

paragraf *sb* section. **paragraftegn** *sb* section mark.

parallell *sb* parallel; *trekke en ~* draw a parallel; *~e linjer* parallel lines; parallels; *gaten går parallelt med elven* the street runs parallel to/with the river. **parallellklasse** *sb* parallel class. **parallellogram** *sb* parallelogram.

paraply *sb* umbrella; *gå med ~* wear an umbrella; *slå ned ~en* close one's umbrella; *slå opp ~en* put up one's umbrella.

parasitt *sb* parasite.

parasoll *sb* parasol, sunshade.

parat *adj* prepared, ready; *~ til å reise* ready to leave.

pardong *sb* quarter; *det ble ikke gitt ~* quarter was not given.

pare *vb (ordne parvis)* pair, match; *(om dyr) ~ seg* copulate, mate; pair.

parentes *sb* parenthesis, brackets; *i ~* in brackets/parentheses. **parentetisk** *adj* parenthetic(al).

parere *vb* parry; ward off; *~ ordre* obey orders.

parfyme *sb* perfume, scent. **parfymere** *vb* perfume, scent. **parfymeri** *sb* perfumer's (shop).

pari *sb* par; *i/over/under ~* at/above/under par.

paria *sb* pariah.

paringstid *sb* mating season.

park *sb* park. **parkere** *vb* park. **parkering** *sb* parking; *(for av- og pålessing)* waiting; *~ forbudt* no parking/waiting (here). **parkerings|hus** *sb* parking house. **~plass** *sb* parking place/*US* lot; *(større)* car--park.

parkett *sb* **1** *(på gulv)* parquet; **2** *(i teater)* stalls.

parlament *sb* parliament. **parlamentarisk** *adj* parliamentary. **parlamentarisme** *sb* cabinet responsibility. **parlaments|bygning** *sb* House of Parliament. **~medlem** *sb* member of Parliament (*fork* M.P.). **~valg** *sb* (Parliamentary) election.

parlør *sb* phrase book.

parodi *sb* parody. **parodiere** *vb* parody. **parodisk** *adj* parodic.

parole *sb (ordre)* order; *(slagord)* slogan, watchword.

parsell *sb* lot; plot (of land). **parsellere** *vb: ~ ut* parcel out. **part** *sb* **1** *(andel)* share; **2** *(~ i en sak)* party; *alle ~er* all parties; *jeg for min ~* as for me; I for my part. **partere** *vb* cut up; cut into pieces.

parterr(e) *sb (i teater)* pit.

parti *sb* **1** *(gruppe, politisk etc ~)* party; *hun stod utenfor ~ene* she was outside the parties; *ta ~* take sides; *ta ~ for* side with; take the side of; *ta ~ mot* side against; take sides against; **2** *(vare~)* lot; **3** *(kort~, sjakk~ etc)* game; *et ~ sjakk* a game of chess; **4** *(i sport)* side, team. **partiell** *adj* partial. **partikkel** *sb* particle. **partisan** *sb* partisan.

partisipp *sb* participle; *perfektum ~* the past participle; *presens ~* the present participle.

partisk *adj* biassed, one-sided, partial. **partiskhet** *sb* partiality, bias.

partner *sb* partner.

partout *adv: ville ~* insist on. **partoutkort** *sb* permanent pass.

parveny *sb* parvenu, upstart.

parvis *adv* in couples/pairs; *ordne ~* pair (off).

parykk *sb* wig.

pasient *sb* patient.

pasifisere *vb* pacify. **pasifisme** *sb* pacifism. **pasifist** *sb* pacifist. **pasifistisk** *adj* pacifist.

pasje *sb* page.

pasjon *sb* passion. **pasjonert** *adj* ardent, keen.

pasning *sb (i fotball)* pass.

pass *sb* **A 1** *(til utenlandsreise)* passport; **2** *(fjell~)* pass; **3** *(i kortspill)* pass; **B** *(pleie, stell)* care, tending; *~ av barn* care of the children; *~ av maskineri* tending of machinery.

passasje *sb* passage. **passasjer** *sb* passenger.

passasjer|befordring *sb* passenger transport/service. **~damper** *sb* passenger steamer. **~fly** *sb* passenger plane. **~trafikk** *sb* passenger traffic.

passat *sb* trade wind.

passe I *adj: jakken er akkurat ~* the jacket is just the right size; *sånn ~* middling, so-so; **II** *vb* **1** *(ha rett form, størrelse etc)* fit; *nøkkelen ~r til låsen* the key fits the lock; **2** *(~ for)* suit; *når ~r det Dem å begynne?* when will it suit you to begin? **3** *(pleie, ta seg av)* look after; take care of; *(~ syke)* nurse; *(~ maskiner)* operate; look after; tend; **4** *(uttrykk)* *~* **på** *(være forsiktig)* be careful; look out; take care; *(ta seg av)* look after; take care of; *(gjelde for)* fit; apply to; *beskrivelsen ~r på henne* the description fits her; *det ~r ikke på ham* it does not apply to him; *~* **seg** be careful; look out; take care; *pass Dem for hunden!* beware of the dog! *~ deg selv!* mind your own business! *pass* **opp for** *døren!* stand clear of the door! *~* **sammen** *(om mennesker)* be well matched; *(om ting)* go well together; *det ~r seg ikke* it is not proper; *det ~r seg ikke for meg å* it is not for me to; *~* **til** go well with; *gardinene ~r bra til møblene* the curtains go well with the furniture. **passelig** *adj* fitting, suitable; of the right size. **passende** *adj* **1** suitable; *en ~ erstatning* a suitable compensation; **2** *(sømmelig)* decent, proper; correct; *~ oppførsel* correct/proper behaviour.

passer *sb: en ~* a pair of compasses.

passere *vb (dra forbi)* go past; pass (by); *hun lot det ~* she let it pass; *la ~ revy* review; pass in review.

passiar *sb* chat, talk. **passiare** *vb* chat, talk; have a chat/talk.

passiv 1 *adj* passive; *~ motstand* passive resistance; *jeg forholdt meg ~* I remained passive; **2** *sb (gram)* the passive (voice). **passiva** *sb fl* liabilities. **passivitet** *sb* passivity, passiveness.

pass|kontroll *sb* examination of passports; passport check; *(om kontrollørene)* passport officials. **~tvang** *sb: det er ~ tvang* passports are compulsory.

passus *sb* passage.

pasta *sb* paste.

pasteurisere *vb* pasteurize.

pastill *sb* lozenge, pastille.

patent 1 *adj* first-class, topping; **2** *sb* patent; *ha ~ på* hold a patent for; *ta ~ på* take out a patent for.

patina *sb* patina.

patetisk *adj* high-flown.

patolog *sb* pathologist. **patologisk** *adj* pathological.

patos *sb* passion; *(affektert ~)* bombast.

patriark *sb* patriarch. **patriarkalsk** *adj* patriarchal. **patriot** *sb* patriot. **patriotisk** *adj* patriotic. **patriotisme** *sb* patriotism.

patron *sb* cartridge.

patrulje *sb* patrol; *en ~ på seks mann* a patrol of six men. **patruljere** *vb* patrol.

patte 1 *sb (spene)* teat; 2 *vb* suck; *~ på* suck. **patte|barn** *sb* baby. **~dyr** *sb* mammal.

pauke *sb* kettledrum.

paulun *sb: slå opp sitt ~* pitch one's tent.

pause *sb* **1** pause; *det oppstod en ~ i samtalen* there was a pause in the conversation; **2** *(i forestilling, konsert etc)* interval. **pausesignal** *sb* interval signal.

pave *sb* pope. **pavelig** *adj* papal.

paviljong *sb* pavilion.

peanøtt *sb* peanut, groundnut.

pedagog *sb* educationalist; *(nedsettende)* pedagogue. **pedagogikk** *sb* pedagogy; *(som fag)* education. **pedagogisk** pedagogic(al), educational.

pedal *sb* pedal.

pedant *sb* pedant. **pedanteri** *sb* pedantry. **pedantisk** *adj* pedantic.

peile *vb* take a bearing; take bearings. **peile|pinne, ~stav** *sb* dipstick. **peiling** *sb* bearing(s); *jeg har ikke ~* I have not the foggiest (idea); *ta ~ på* aim at; head for.

peis *sb* (open) fire-place. **peis|hylle** *sb* mantelpiece. **~krok** *sb* chimney corner; ingle-nook. **~puster** *sb: en ~* a pair of bellows.

pek *sb: gjøre en et ~* do somebody a dirty trick/an ill office.

peke *vb* point; *~ på* point at; *fig* call attention to; point out. **peke|finger** *sb* forefinger, index finger. **~stokk** *sb* pointer.

pekuniær *adj* pecuniary.

pels *sb* **1** *(på dyr)* fur; *en bjørne~ er svært tykk* the fur of a bear is very thick; **2** *(~plagg)* fur coat; *hun hadde på seg en ~* she wore/was wearing a fur coat; **3** *få/gi på ~en* give/get a good hiding. **pels|dyr** *sb* fur-bearing animal. **~dyravl** *sb* fur-farming. **~fôret** *adj* fur-lined. **~handler** *sb* furrier. **~jeger** *sb* trapper. **~kledd** *adj* fur-clad. **~krave** *sb* fur collar. **~lue** *sb* fur cap. **~verk** *sb* furs.

pen *adj* nice; *(vakker, om personer også)* good-looking; *~e manerer* nice manners; *det var ~t av deg å hjelpe meg* it was kind of you to help me; *et ~t hus* a nice house; *så pent av Dem å si det* how nice of you to say so.

pendel *sb* pendulum. **pendel|trafikk** *sb* shuttle service. **~ur** *sb* pendulum clock. **pendle** *vb* **1** oscillate; **2** *(reise til og fra arbeidssted)* commute. **pendler** *sb* commuter.

penge|anbringelse *sb* investment. **~beløp** *sb* amount/sum (of money). **~folk** *sb* moneyed people. **~forlegenhet** *sb* pecuniary difficulty. **~hjelp** *sb* pecuniary assistance. **~knipe** *sb* pecuniary difficulty; *være i ~knipe* be hard up. **~lens** *adj* broke, penniless. **~mangel** *sb* lack of money. **~nød** *sb* pecuniary distress. **~pung** *sb* purse. **penger** *sb koll* money; *hvor er pengene?* where is the money? *kontante ~* cash; ready money; *mange ~* much money. **penge|seddel** *sb* banknote. **~skap** *sb* safe. **~skrin** *sb* money box. **~sorger** *sb fl* pecuniary worries. **~stykke** *sb* coin. **~sum** *sb* amount/sum (of money). **~vanskeligheter** *sb fl* pecuniary difficulty. **~verdi** *sb* money/monetary value. **~vesen** *sb* monetary matters; finances.

penibel *adj* painful.

penicillin *sb* penicillin.

penn *sb* pen; *(om pennesplitten, uten skaft)* nib. **pennal** *sb* pencil case. **penne|kniv** *sb* pen-knife, pocket-knife. **~skaft** *sb* pen-holder. **~splitt** *sb* nib. **~strøk** *sb* stroke of the pen. **~tegning** *sb* pen(-and--ink) drawing. **~venn** *sb* pen-friend, pen pal.

penny *sb* penny (*fl om beløpet* pence; *om myntene* pennies). Se for øvrig midtsidene.

pens *sb* points; *(penseapparat)* switch. **pense** *vb* shunt; *US* switch.

pensel *sb* brush.

pensjon *sb* **1** *(pensjoniststatus)* retirement; **2** *(pensjonsbeløp)* pension; *gå av med ~* retire on a pension; **3** *(kost)* board; *full ~* full board and lodging; **4** *(pensjonat)* boarding-house; *bo i ~ hos* board with. **pensjonat** *sb* boardinghouse. **pensjonat|skole** *sb* boarding school. **~vert** *sb* landlord. **~vertinne** *sb* landlady. **pensjonere** *vb* pension (off); *pensjonert* retired. **pensjonist** *sb* pensioner. **pensjons|alder** *sb* pensionable age; retirement age. **~berettiget** *adj* pensionable; entitled to a pension. **~innskudd** *sb* contribution to a pension fund. **pensjonær** *sb* boarder; *(finere)* paying guest.

pensle *vb (et sår etc)* swab.

pensum *sb* curriculum, syllabus; *eksamens~* examination requirements. **pensumbøker** *sb fl* set books.

pepper *sb* pepper; *støtt ~* ground pepper; *ønske en dit pepperen gror* wish somebody further. **pepper|-bøsse** *sb* pepperbox. **~korn** *sb* peppercorn. **~kvern** *sb* pepper mill. **~mynte** *sb* peppermint. **~møy** *sb* spinster. **~svenn** *sb* bachelor. **pepre** *vb* pepper.

per, pr. *adj* **1** *(med, ved hjelp av)* by; *~ brev* by letter; *~ omgående* by return of post; **2** *(om fordeling)* per, a; *~ innbygger* per inhabitant; *15 pund ~ dag* £15 a day; **3** *~ måned* monthly; ... a month; *~ år* yearly; ... a year; per annum.

perfeksjonere *vb: ~ seg i* improve one's knowledge of.

perfekt *adj: ~ i* perfect in.

perfektum *sb (gram)* the perfect (tense); *~ partisipp* the past particle.

perfid *adj (svikefull)* perfidious.

perforere *vb* perforate. **perforering** *sb* perforation.

pergament *sb* parchment.

periferi *sb* circumference, periphery. **periferisk** *adj* peripheral.

periode *sb* period. **periode|dranker** *sb* dipsomaniac. **~vis** *adj* periodic(al); *adv* periodically. **periodisk** *adj* periodic.

periskop *sb* periscope.

perle I *sb* **1** *(ekte eller imitert)* pearl; *ekte ~* real/genuine pearl; **2** *(av glass, tre etc)* bead; **3** *(dråpe)* drop; *~r av dugg/svette* drops of dew/sweat; **4** *(uttrykk) du er en ~!* you are a brick! *kaste ~r for svin* cast pearls before swine; **II** *vb* **1** bead; form beads; **2** *(bruse, skumme)* effervesce. **perle|fiske** *sb* pearl fishing; pearling. **~fisker** *sb* pearl diver/fisher. **~garn** *sb* pearl cotton. **~humør** *sb* excellent spirits. **~kjede** *sb* string of pearls; *(stort)* rope of pearls. **~mor** *sb* mother-of-pearl. **~venn** *sb: de er ~venner* they are great friends.

perlon *sb* perlon.

perm *sb* **A** cover; *fra ~ til ~* from cover to cover; **B** *(fork for permisjon)* leave; *han har ~* he is on leave.

permanent 1 *adj* permanent; **2** *sb (frisyre)* permanent wave; *ta ~* have a perm.

permisjon *sb* leave of absence; *få ~* be granted leave; *søke om ~* apply for a leave. **permittere** *vb* **1** *(gi permisjon)* grant leave; **2** *(sende hjem)* send home; **3** *(sende bort)* dismiss; send away.

perpendikulær *adj, sb* perpendicular.

perpetuum mobile *sb* perpetual motion machine; perpetuum mobile.

perpleks *adj* bewildered.

perrong *sb* platform.

pers *sb: de måtte til ~* they were in for it.

persianer *sb* Persian lamb, Astrakhan.

persienne *sb* Venetian blind.

persille *sb* parsley.

person *sb* person; *(i bok, skuespill)* character; *per ~* each; per person. **personale** *sb* personnel, staff. **personalia** *sb* biographical data. **personell** *sb* personnel. **personifikasjon** *sb* personification. **personifisere** *vb* personify. **person|lig** *adj* personal; *adv* personally; *hun kom ~lig* she came in person; *jeg kjenner ham ~lig.* I know him personally. **~lighet** *sb* character, personality; *han er en ~lighet* he has personality; *historisk ~lighet* historic personality; *en sterk ~* a man/woman of character. **~skildring** *sb* delineation of character. **~tog** *sb* passenger train. **~vekt** *sb* weighing-machine. **~vern** *sb data* data security. **~vogn** *sb (på tog)* passenger coach/carriage.

perspektiv *sb* perspective,

pertentlig *adj* meticulous, punctilious; prim. **pertentlighet** *sb* meticulousness, punctiliousness, primness.

pervers *adj* perverted. **perversitet** *sb* pervertedness; sexual perversion.

pese *vb* pant, puff; *puste og ~* puff and blow.

pessimisme *sb* pessimism. **pessimist** *sb* pessimist. **pessimistisk** *adj* pessimistic.

pest *sb* plague; *(også fig)* pestilence. **pest|aktig** *adj* pestilential. **~befengt** *adj (pestsyk)* plague-stricken; *(full av ~basiller)* pestiferous. **~byll** *sb* bubo. **~epidemi** *sb* plague epidemic.

petit|artikkel *sb* paragraph, par. **~journalist** *sb* columnist; paragraphist, par-writer.

petroleum *sb (parafin)* kerosene; *(GB som oftest)* paraffin oil; oil.

pianist *sb* pianist. **piano** *sb* (upright) piano; *hun spilte (på) ~* she played the piano. **pianokrakk** *sb* music-stool.

pickles *sb* pickles.

pidestall *sb* pedestal; *sette en på en ~* place somebody on a pedestal; *rive ned fra ~en* debunk.

pietet *sb* reverence, veneration. **pietets|full** *adj* reverent. **~hensyn** *sb: av ~hensyn* out of reverence/respect. **~løs** *adj* irreverent. **pietisme** *sb* pietism. **pietist** *sb* pietist. **pietistisk** *adj* pietistic.

pigg *sb* **1** *(av metall)* spike; *(på piggtråd)* barb; **2** *(på pinnsvin)* quill, spine; **3** *(på planter)* spine, prickle. **piggdekk** *sb* (steel-)studded tyre. **pigge** *vb* prod, spike; *~ av (gårde/sted)* hurry off; *~ opp* prod, stimulate. **pigg|sko** *sb* spiked shoe. **~stav** *sb* spike-staff. **~tråd** *sb* barbed wire. **~trådgjerde** *sb* barbed-wire fence. **~trådsperring** *sb* barbed-wire entanglement; wire.

pigment *sb* pigment.

pikant *adj* piquant.

pike 1 *(jente)* girl; **2** *(hushjelp)* maid(-servant); servantgirl. **pike|barn** *sb* girl. **~klasse** *sb* girls' class. **~navn** *sb* **1** *(pikes fornavn)* girl's name; **2** *(etternavn før ekteskap)* maiden name. **~skole** *sb* girls' school. **~speider** *sb* girl guide. **~værelse** *sb* maid's room.

pikke *vb* knock, tap.

pikkolo *sb (på hotell)* page boy; buttons; *US* bellboy, bellhop. **pikkolofløyte** *sb* piccolo.

pil *sb* **1** *(treet)* willow; **2** *(til bue)* arrow; **3** *(kaste~ og ~ til luftgevær)* dart.

pilar *sb* column, pillar; *(bro~)* pier.

pile *vb* hurry, run, scurry.

pilegrim *sb* pilgrim. **pilegrimsferd** *sb* pilgrimage.

piletre *sb* willow (tree).

pilk *sb* jig. **pilke** *vb* jig.

pille 1 *sb* pill; **2** *vb (plukke)* pick; *~ seg i nesen* pick one's nose.

pillråtten *adj* crumbling.

pilot *sb (flyger)* pilot.

pilsnar *adj* swift as an arrow.

pils *sb* lager.

pilt *sb* boy, lad.

piltast *sb data* arrow key.

pimpe *vb* booze, tipple; bib.

pimpernell *sb* pimpernel.

pinaktig *adj* painful.

pine 1 *sb* pain; suffering, torment(s); **2** *vb (fremkalle smerte hos)* pain; torture; *det ~r meg å se henne så nedtrykt* it pains me to see her so depressed. **pine|benk** *sb* rack; *ha ble lagt på ~benken* he was racked/put on the rack. **~full** *adj* painful.

pingpong *sb* ping-pong.

pingvin *sb* penguin.

pinje *sb* stone pine.

pinlig *adj* **1** *(ubehagelig)* painful; awkward; embarrassing; *en ~ pause* an awkward pause; *en ~ situasjon* an embarrassing situation; **2** *(meget omhyggelig)* scrupulous.

pinne *sb* **1** stick; **2** *(vagle etc)* perch; **3** *(rekke masker i strikketøy)* row; **4** *(uttrykk) ikke legge to ~r i kors* not lift a finger; *stiv som en ~* stiff as a poker; *stå på ~ for en* be at somebody's beck and call; dance attendance for somebody; *vippe en av ~n* knock him off his perch. **pinne|stol** *sb* spindleback chair. **~ved** *sb: bli knust til ~ved* be smatched to matchwood.

pinnsvin *sb* hedgehog.

pinse *sb* Whitsun(tide). **pinse|aften** *sb* Whit Sunday. **~dag** *sb: første ~dag* Whit Sunday; *annen ~dag* Whit Monday. **~ferie** *sb* Whitsun holidays.

pinsel *sb* torment, torture.

pinse|bevegelsen *sb* the Pentecostal movement. **~lilje** *sb* white narcissus.

pinsett *sb: en ~* a pair of tweezers.

pinsevenn *sb* Pentecostalist.

pioner *sb* pioneer.

pip *sb* chirp; cheep, peep.

pipe I *sb* **1** *(tobakks~, fløyte etc)* pipe; *da fikk ~n en annen lyd* that made him change his tune; *stikke ~n i sekk* change one's tune; *han røykte ~* he smoked a pipe; **2** *(skorsteins~)* chimney; **3** *(børse~)* barrel; **II** *vb* **1** *(om fugler)* cheep; **2** *(om smådyr etc)* squeak; **3** *(om større dyr etc)* whimper; **4** *(om dampfløyte, kuler, vind etc)* whistle; **5** *(under ~konsert)* boo, hiss; *han ble pepet ut* he was hissed. **pipe|hode** *sb* (pipe) bowl. **~konsert** *sb* catcalls *fl*, hissing. **~renser** *sb* pipe cleaner. **~stilk** *sb* pipestem.

pipette *sb* pipette.

piple *vb* tricle, ooze.

pipp sb chirp, cheep, peep; *ta ~en fra noen* deflate/overwhelm somebody.

pir *sb* **A** *(utstikkerbrygge)* pier; **B** *(småmakrell)* young mackerel.

pirat *sb* pirate.

pirk *sb* **1** *(pirkearbeid)* niggling work; precision work; **2** *(smålig kritikk)* petty criticism; **3** *(ordkløyveri)* hair-splitting. **pirke** *vb* **1** *(grave forsiktig)* pick; *~ på et sår* pick at a sore; *~ seg i tennene* pick one's teeth; **2** *(være overdrevent nøye)* niggle; **3** *(kritisere smålig)* pick at; find fault with. **pirkearbeid** *sb* niggling work; precision work. **pirket(e)** *adj* pedantic, meticulous; punctilious.

pirre *vb* excite, tickle; stimulate; *~ noens nysgjerrighet* rouse somebody's curiosity.

pirrelig *adj* irritable. **pirrelighet** *sb* irritability.

pisk *sb* **1** whip; *ha ham under ~en* have the whip-hand of him; *være under ~en* be led by the nose; **2** *(hår~)* pigtail; **3** *(~ing)* whipping. **piske 1** whip; *(som straff)* flog; *han ~t på hesten* he whipped the horse; **2** *(~ fløte, egg etc)* beat, whip; **3** *(om hagl, regn etc)* beat, pelt. **piske|smell** *sb* crack of a whip. **~snert** *sb* whiplash.

piss *sb* piss. **pisse** *vb* piss. **pissoar** *sb* urinal.

pistol *sb* pistol.

pistre *vb* **1** *(klynke)* whimper; **2** *(hvine)* whine.

pjatt *sb* empty chatter; nonsense, twaddle. **pjatte** *vb* chatter idly.

pjekkert *sb* pee jacket; reefer.

pjokk *sb* little fellow.

pjolter *sb* whisky and soda; *US* highball.

pjusket(e) *adj* dishevelled, rumpled, tousled.

pladask *adv: han falt ~* down he went with a wallop.

plaffe *vb* pop; fire, shoot; *~ ned* pick off.

plage I *sb* **1** *(besvær)* bother, nuisance, worry; *for en ~ den ungen er!* what a nuisance that child is! **2** *(lande~)* pest, curse; **II** *vb* **1** *(pine)* torment; *(sterkere)* torture; **2** *(bry)* pester; trouble, worry; *han ~t meg med spørsmål* he pestered me with questions; *hun ~t nesten livet av him* she worried him to death. **plageånd** *sb* nuisance, pest; *(sterkere)* tormentor.

plagg *sb* garment; article/piece of clothing.

plagiat *sb* plagiarism. **plagiator** *sb* plagiarist. **plagiere** *vb* plagiarize.

plagsom *adj* troublesome; annoying; *en ~ person* a nuisance.

plakat *sb* **1** bill, placard; *(især med bilde)* poster; **2** *(kunngjøring, oppslag)* public notice.

plan A 1 *adj* plane; flat, level; *en ~ (over)flate* a plane surface; **2** *sb (nivå etc)* level; plane; *en debatt på et høyere ~* a debate on a higher plane; *i ~ med* on level with; *på høyeste ~* at the highest level/plane; **B** *sb* **1** *(prosjekt)* plan, project, scheme; *(program)* programme; *de la en ~* they made a plan/scheme; *det gikk etter ~en* it went according to the plan/programme; *omgås med ~er om* entertain schemes of; *utføre en ~* carry out a plan/scheme; **2** *(riss)* plan, map. **planere** *vb (~ ut)* level.

planet *sb* planet. **planetsystem** *sb* planetary system.

plangeometri *sb* plane geometry.

planke *sb* plank. **planke|gjerde** *sb* hoarding. **~kjøring** *sb: det er ren ~* it is plain sailing (a holiday task, child's play).

plankton *sb* plankton.

plan|legge *vb* plan; make plans (for). **~legging** *sb* planning. **~løs** *adj* planless. **~messig** *adj* methodical, systematic; *(adv)* methodically, systematically. **planovergang** *sb* level crossing; *US* grade crossing.

plansje *sb (i bok)* plate; *(vegg~)* wall chart.

plantasje *sb* plantation; *(frukt~)* orchard. **plantasjeeier** *sb* planter. **plante 1** *sb* plant; *en fin/nydelig ~* a nice specimen; **2** *vb* plant; *~ om* replant, transplant; *~ ut* plant out; bed out. **plante|etende** *adj* herbivorous; *~etende dyr* herbivore. **~farge** *sb* vegetable dye. **~felt** *sb* plantation. **~fett** *sb* vegetable fat. **~føde** *sb* vegetable food. **~liv** *sb* plant life, vegetation; flora. **~lære** *sb* botany. **~rikdom** *sb* rich flora. **~riket** *sb* the vegetable kingdom. **~skole** *sb* nursery. **~vekst** *sb* vegetation.

planøkonomi *sb* planned economy.

plapre *vb* blab, gabble, jabber; *~ ut med* blurt out; *~ ut med alt sammen* give the whole show away; let the cat out of the bag.

plask *sb* splash. **plaske** *vb* splash.

plask|regn *sb* downpour. **~regne** *vb: det ~regner* it is raining cats and dogs; it is coming down in buckets. **~våt** *adj* drenched, soaked; sopping wet.

plasma *sb* plasma.

plass 1 *(sted beregnet til noe)* place; *legge noe (tilbake) på ~* put something (back) in its right place; **2** *(rom, ~ nok)* room; *det er ikke ~ til det* there is noe room for it; *det tar for stor ~* it takes up too much room; *gjøre ~ til det* make room for it; **3** *(sitte~)* seat; *det var ikke flere ~er igjen* there were no more seats left; *ta ~!* take a seat! **4** *(åpent areal)* space; *en åpen ~ mellom trærne* an open space among the trees; **5** *(~ i en by) (firkantet)* square; *(rund)* circus; **6** *(post stilling)* job, post; *(huspost)* place, situation: **7** *(uttrykk)* **bestille ~** *(på hotell)* book a room; *(i teater, på tog etc)* book a seat; **bytte ~** *med* change places with; **innta** *~ene!* on your marks! **på** *sin ~ (passende)* appropriate, suitable; *ikke på sin ~* out of place; inappropriate; **sette på ~** put where it belongs; *sette en på ~ (irettesette)* put somebody in his/her place. **plassbillett** *sb* reserved ticket; seat reservation. **plassere** *vb* place, put; *(~ penger også)* invest; *bøkene ble plassert i riktig rekkefølge* the books were placed in the right order. **plassering** *sb* placing. **plass|hensyn** *sb: av ~hensyn* to save space. **~mangel** *sb* lack of room/space; *på grunn av ~mangel* owing to overcrowding.

plast *sb* plastic.

plaster *sb* plaster; *jeg la (et) ~ på såret* I applied/put a plaster to/on the wound.

plastisk *adj* plastic; *~ kirurgi* plastic surgery.

plastre *vb* plaster.

plate *sb* **1** plate; *(glass~ etc)* sheet; *(grammofon~)* record, disk; *(koke~)* boiling/hot plate; *(rund ~)* disc, disk; *(stein~)* slab; **2** *data* disk; **3** *(løgn)* fib; *slå en ~* tell a fib. **plate|bar** *sb* melody-bar. **~drev** *sb data* disk drive. **~prater** *sb* disk jockey. **~samling** *sb* record collection. **~skifter** *sb* record changer. **~spiller** *sb* (automatic) record-player.

platina *sb* platinum. **platinarev** *sb* platinum fox.

platonisk *adj* platonic.

platt *adj* coarse; low, vulgar; *~ umulig* absolutely impossible. **plattenslager** *sb* swindler, cheat. **plattform** *sb* platform. **platt|fot** *sb* flatfoot; *være/ha ~fot* be flatfooted; have flatfoot. **~fotet** *adj* flatfooted. **platthet** *sb* coarseness, platitude; vulgarity.

platå *sb* plateau.

plausibel *adj* plausible.

pledd *sb* (travelling) rug.

pleie A I *sb* nursing, care; *hud~* care of the skin; **II** *vb* **1** *(passe, stelle)* nurse; care for; **2** *(dyrke)* cultivate; *vi ~r våre interesser* we cultivate our interests; **B** *vb (være vant til)* **1** *(i presens kan ~ uttrykkes ved adv* usually*)*; *jeg ~r å stå tidlig opp* I usually get up early; I am in the habit of getting up early; **2** *(bare i imperfektum, især om det som til stadighet fant sted, men ikke finner sted nå)* used to; *hun pleide å reise utenlands hvert år* she used to go abroad every year; **3** *(om det som vanligvis finner sted)* would; *han pleide si* he would say. **pleie|barn** *sb* foster-child; *(adoptert)* adopted child. **~bror** *sb* foster-brother. **~datter** *sb* foster-daughter; *(adoptert)* adopted daughter. **~foreldre** *sb* foster-parents. **~hjem** *sb* nursing home. **~mor** *sb* foster-mother.

pleier *sb (om kvinne)* (female) nurse; *(om mann)* (male) nurse; *(også)* sick nurse. **pleierske** *sb* (female) nurse.

pleie|sønn *sb* foster-son; *(adoptert)* adopted son. **~søster** *sb* foster-sister.

plen *sb* lawn. **plenklipper** *sb* lawn-mower.

plent *adv* absolutely.

plenum *sb: i ~* in plenary assembly/session. **plenumsmøte** *sb* plenary session.

plett *sb* **A** *(avgrenset sted)* spot; *på ~en* on the spot; *sette en ~ på sitt gode navn* stain one's reputation; *uten ~ og lyte* without blemish, flawless; **B** *(sølv~)* plateware. **plettfri** *adj* spotless, blameless.

pleuritt, plevritt *sb* pleurisy.

plikt *sb* duty; *din ~ mot dem* your duty to them; *jeg gjorde min~* I did my duty. **plikte** *sb: de ~r å* ... it is their duty to ... **plikt|forsømmelse** *sb* neglect of duty. **~følelse** *sb* sense of duty. **pliktig** *adj* (in duty) bound; under an obligation to. **plikt|messig** *adj* compulsory, due. **~oppfyllende** *adj* conscientious, dutiful. **~tro** *adj* conscientious, faithful. **~troskap** *sb* conscientiousness, faithfulness.

plir *sb* blink, squint. **plire** *vb* blink, squint.

plissé *sb* pleat, pleating. **plissering** *sb* pleat.

plog *sb* plough. **plog|får** *sb* furrow. **~skjær** *sb* ploughshare.

plombe *sb* **1** *(i tann)* filling, stopping; **2** *(blysegl)* (lead) seal. **plombere** *vb* **1** *(tann)* fill, stop; **2** *(forsegle)* seal. **plombering** *sb* stopping; *(forsegling)* sealing.

plomme *sb* 1 (i egg) yolk; *vi har det som ~n i egget* we are in clover; **2** *(frukt)* plum. **plommetre** *sb* plum tree.

pludder *sb* babble, prattle. **pludre** *vb* babble, prattle.

plugg *sb* **1** *(nagle etc)* peg, plug; tack; **2** *(tettbygd gutt eller mann)* stocky/sturdy fellow. **plugge** *vb* fasten with a peg/pegs; *~ igjen* plug; stop up.

plukk *sb: ikke det ~* not a bit.

plukke *vb* **1** *(~ blomster og bær)* pick, gather; *(~ frukt)* pick; *frukten bør ~s når den er moden* the fruit should be picked when it is ripe; **2** *(~ fjærkre)* pluck; **3** *(uttrykk) ~ ut* pick out; *ha ei høne å ~ med* have a bone to pick with somebody. **plukkfisk** *sb* stewed codfish.

plump *adj* **1** *(grovbygd)* large and awkward; **2** *(klossete)* clumsy; **2** *(taktløs, ubehøvlet)* coarse, low, vulgar. **plumpe** *vb* flop, plump; *~ ut med* blurt/let out; *han ~t ut med hele greia* he gave the whole show away; he let the cat out of the bag. **plumphet** *sb* coarseness, vulgarity; *(klossethet)* awkwardness.

plunder *sb* bother; tiresome work. **plundre** *vb* struggle, toil.

pluskvamperfektum *sb (gram)* the pluperfect.

pluss *adv, sb* plus; *det er et ~* it is an advantage.

plusse *vb: ~ på* add.

plutselig 1 *adj* sudden; *et ~ angrep* a sudden death; **2** *adv* suddenly; all at once; *han døde ~* he died suddenly; *hun stanset ~* she stopped short.

plyndre *vb* **1** *(især om soldater)* plunder; *soldatene ~t byen* the soldiers plundered the town; **2** *(rane røve)* rob; *de ~t ham for pengene hans* they robbed him of his money. **plyndring** *sb* plunder, plundering.

plysj *sb* plush.

plystre *vb* whistle. **plystring** *sb* whistling; *(plystretone)* whistle.

pløse *sb (i sko)* tongue.

pløset(e) *adj* bloated, swollen; baggy.

pløye *sb* plough; *US* plow; *~ (seg) igjennom* plough one's way through; wade through.

podagra *sb* gout.

pode 1 *sb (liten gutt)* lad; little boy; offspring, scion; **2** *vb (~ trær)* graft. Se også *innpode*. **pode|kvist** *sb* scion. **~voks** *sb* grafting wax.

podium *sb* dais, platform.

poeng *sb* point; *han fikk ikke tak i ~et* he missed the point; *hun fikk/skåret 30 ~* she got/scored 30 points.

poengtere *vb* emphasize, stress.

poesi *sb* poetry. **poet** *sb* poet. **poetisk** *adj* poetic(al).

pokal *sb* cup. **pokalkamp** *sb* cup tie.

poker *sb* poker.

pokker *interj, sb* the devil/deuce; *~ (også)!* damn! oh, bother! oh, hang it! *hva/hvem ~?* what/who the deuce?

pol *sb (geografisk, elektrisk)* pole. **polar|luft** *sb* polar air. **~sirkel** *sb* polar circle. **~stjerne** *sb* Polar Star.

polemikk *sb* controversy, polemic. **polemisere** *vb* polemize. **polemisk** *adj* polemic(al).

polere *vb* polish; *(~ metall)* burnish.

pol|farer *sb* polar explorer. **~ferd** *sb* polar expedition. **~høyde** *sb* polar altitude.

poliklinikk *sb* policlinic; out-patients' department.

polio *sb* polio. **poliomyelitt** *sb* poliomyelitis.

polise *sb* policy; *vi tegnet en ~* we took out a policy.

politi *sb* police; *ridende ~* mounted police; *ettersøkt av ~et* wanted by the police; *~et er etter dem* the police are after them. **politi|hund** *sb* police dog. **~kammer**

sb police station. **politiker** *sb* politician. **politikk** *sb* **1** *(politisk virksomhet)* politics; *alle burde være interessert i ~* everybody should be interested in politics; **2** *(fremgangsmåte, plan)* policy; *han kritiserte selskapets ~* he criticized the company's policy. **politi|konstabel** *sb* (police) constable. **~mann** *sb* policeman; police officer; *(i tiltale sies ofte)* officer. **~mester** *sb* Chief Constable; Police Commissioner. **~rassia, ~razzia** *sb* (police) raid. **politisk** *adj* political. **politistasjon** *sb* police-station.

politur *sb* polish, varnish.

polonese *sb* polonaise.

polstre *vb* pad, stuff, upholster; *polstrede møbler* upholstered furniture.

poly|andri *sb* polyandry. **~gam** *adj* polygamous. **~gami** *sb* polygamy. **~gon** *sb* polygon.

polypp *sb* **1** *(dyr)* polyp; **2** *(på slimhinne)* polyp(us).

poly|teisme *sb* polytheism. **~teistisk** *adj* polytheistic(al).

pomade *sb* pomade.

pomp *sb* pomp; *~ og prakt* pomp and circumstance.

pompong *sb* pompon.

pompøs *adj* stately. **pompøst** *adv* in a stately manner.

pondus *sb* gravity, weight; authority.

pongtong *sb* pontoon. **pongtongbro** *sb* pontoon bridge.

ponni *sb* pony.

poplin *sb* poplin.

poppel *sb* poplar.

popularisere *vb* popularize. **popularisering** *sb* popularization. **popularitet** *sb* popularity. **populær** *adj* popular. **populær|vitenskap** *sb* popular science; *et ~vitenskapelig tidsskrift* a popular science journal/magazine.

pore *sb* pore.

pornografi *sb* pornography. **pornografisk** *adj* pornographic.

porselen *sb* **1** *(stoffet, om kunstgjenstander og til teknisk bruk)* porcelain; **2** *(til servise etc)* china.

porsjon *sb* **1** portion; *(det en forsyner seg/blir forsynt med av mat)* helping; *vil De ha en ~ til?* do you want another helping? **2** *(part)* portion; part, share; *små ~er* small doses. **porsjonere ut** *vb* parcel/portion out. **porsjonsvis** *adj* in portions.

port *sb* gate; *(~åpning, ~rom)* gateway. **portal** *sb* portal.

portefølje *sb* portfolio; *minister uten ~* minister without portfolio.

portforbud *sb* **1** *(under unntakstilstand etc)* curfew; *innføre ~ i en by* impose a curfew on a town; *oppheve ~et* end/lift the curfew; **2** *(for militære)* confinement to barracks. **portier** *sb* hall porter; chief receptionist. **portière** *sb* door curtain, portière. **portner** *sb* doorman, janitor.

porto *sb* postage. **portotakst** *sb* postal rate.

portrett *sb* portrait.

portstolpe *sb* gatepost.

portvin *sb* port.

portør *sb* hospital porter/orderly.

porøs *adj* porous. **porøsitet** *sb* porosity.

pose *sb* bag; *en kan ikke få både i ~ og sekk* you cannot eat your cake and have it; *ha rent mel i ~n* have a clear conscience.

posere *sb* pose. **posisjon** *sb* position.

positiv *sb* positive; *(gram)* the positive (degree); *~ reaksjon* positive reaction; *reagere ~t* react positively; *~t svar* affirmative reply.

positur *sb* pose, posture; *stille seg i ~* strike an attitude, pose.

post *sb* **1** *(sted for utkikk, vakttjeneste etc)* post; *bli på sin ~* remain at one's post; *forlate sin ~* leave one's post; *stå på ~* stand guard; stand sentry; *være på ~ mot* be on one's guard against; **2** *(vakt~)* sentry; **3** *(stilling)* appointment, post; *hun overtok en ny ~* she took over a new appointment/post; **4** *(~vesen, ~saker)* post; *(postsaker også)* mail; *med ~(en)* by post/mail; *sende med ~en* send by post/mail; **5** *(~ i protokoll, regnskap etc)* entry; *(enkelt punkt i oppregning)* item; **6** *data* record. **post|adresse** *sb* postal address. **~anvisning** *sb* postal order. **~boks** *sb* post-office box; P.O.box. **~bud** *sb* postman. **~distrikt** *sb* postal district. **poste** *vb* post, mail.

postei *sb* pie.

postekspeditør *sb* postal officer. **postere** *sb* *(i regnskap)* post, enter. **poste restante** to be called for; poste restante. **post|forbindelse** *sb* postal communication. **~forsendelse** se ~sending. **~førende** *adj* mail-carrying; *~ båt/tog* mail boat/train. **~gang** *sb* postal service. **~giro** *sb* post giro. **~girokonto** *sb* Giro account. **~girokontoret** *sb* *GB* ≈ Post Office National Giro. **~hus** *sb* post-office. **~kasse** *sb* letter-box; *(frittstående)* pillar-box. **~kontor** *sb* post-office. **~kort** *sb* postcard; *(prospektkort)* picture postcard. **~legge** *vb* post. **~mann** *sb* postman. **~minister** *sb* *GB* Postmaster General. **~nummer** *sb* postal code; post-code; *US* zip code. **~oppkrav** *sb* cash on delivery, C.O.D.; *sende mot ~* send C.O.D. **~ordre** *sb* mail order. **~ordreforretning** *sb* mail order business. **~pakke** *sb* (postal) parcel. **~ran** *sb* mail robbery. **~sekk** *sb* mail bag. **~sending** *sb* postal item/packet. **~sparebank** postoffice savings bank. **~stempel** *sb* postmark.

postsøster *sb* head nurse.

postulat *sb* postulate.

post|verk *sb* Post Office. **~åpner** *sb* sub-postmaster.

posør *sb* poseur.

pote *sb* paw.

potens *sb* **1** *(mat)* power; *annen ~ av tall* the square of a number; *x i annen ~* x squared; *tredje ~ av et tall* the cube of a number; *tredje ~ av x* x cubed; the cube of x; *fjerde ~ av et tall* the fourth power of a number; *opphøye i fjerde ~* raise to the fourth power; **2** *(kjønns-*

kraft) potency; sexual power.

potet *sb* potato; *sette ~er* plant potatoes; *ta opp ~er* dig up/lift potatoes. **potet|mel** *sb* potato flour. **~opptaker** *sb* potato-spinner. **~puré** *sb* mashed potatoes. **~ris** *sb* potato plants/tops. **~setter** *sb* potato planter. **~skrell** *sb* potato peel. **~skreller** *sb* potato peeler. **~stappe** *sb* mashed potatoes.

potpurri potpourri.

potte *sb* **1** *(blomster~)* (flower-)pot; **2** *(natt~)* chamber pot. **potte|blomst** *sb* pot plant; potted plant. **~maker** *sb* potter. **~makerarbeid** *sb* pottery. **~plante** *sb* pot plant; potted plant. **~skår** *sb* potsherd.

p-pille *sb* birth pill; *p-pillen* the pill.

pragmatiker *sb* pragmatist. **pragmatisk** *sb* pragmatic.

praie *vb* hail; *(om drosje også)* flag down; *vi ~t en båt* we hailed a boat.

prakke *vb: ~ noe på en* foist something (off) on somebody; palm something off on somebody.

praksis *sb* practice; *la oss se hvordan det virker i ~* let us see how it works out in practice; *legen hadde (en) stor ~* the doctor had a large practice; *sette om i ~* put into practice; *ugjennomførlig i ~* impracticable.

prakt *sb* splendour, magnificence; *(prektige omgivelser)* pomp, state; *fordums ~* past splendours; *i all sin ~* in all its (her, his etc) glory. **prakt|eksemplar** *sb* magnificent specimen; *(om personer ofte)* beauty, jewel. **~full** magnificent, spendid; glorious.

praktikant *sb* probationer, trainee. **praktisere** *vb* practise; *(bruke i praksis også)* put into practice. **praktisk** *adj (dyktig)* practical; *(hensiktsmessig også)* useful; *~ talt* practically; *hun er ~ (anlagt)* she is practical.

prakt|kar *sb* brick; first-rate fellow. **~syk** *adj* splendour-loving. **~utfoldelse** *sb* display. **~utgave** *sb* de luxe edition.

pram *sb* rowing-boat; *(flatbunnet)* barge, lighter.

prange *vb* be resplendent.

prat *sb* talk. **prate** *vb* talk, chat.

prat|maker *sb* windbag. **~som** *adj* talkative; *i det ~somme hjørnet* in the talkative mood.

pre *sb (fortrinn)* advantage.

predikant *sb* preacher.

predikat *sb* predicate. **predikatsord** *sb* complement; *brukt som ~* used predicatively.

pre|fabrikasjon *sb* prefabrication. **~fabrikkere** *vb* prefabricate, prefab.

preferanse *sb* preference. **preferanseaksje** *sb* preference share. **prefiks** *sb* prefix.

preg *sb* impression, stamp; *bære ~ av* bear the stamp of; *yrket (hans) har satt sitt ~ på ham* his trade has left its stamp on him. **prege** *vb* stamp; mark; characterize.

pregnans *sb* pregnancy, pithiness. **pregnant** *adj* pregnant, pithy; concise.

prek *sb* talk. **preke** *vb* preach. **preken** *sb* sermon; *holde en ~* deliver a sermon. **prekestol** *sb* pulpit; *på ~en* in the pulpit.

prektig *adj* magnificent, splendid.

prekær *adj* precarious.

prelat *sb* prelate.

prelle *vb: ~ av på* glance off (from); *(fig)* be lost on; *bebreidelser ~r av på ham* reproaches are lost on him.

preludium *sb* prelude.

premie *sb* **1** *(gevinst, prisbelønning)* prize; *dele ut ~ne* give away the prizes; **2** *(belønning)* reward; **3** *(forsikrings~ etc)* premium. **premie|konkurranse** *sb* prize competition; *delta i en ~* compete for a prize. **~liste** *sb* prize list. **~obligasjon** *sb* premium bond. **premiere** *vb* give a prize to.

première *sb* first night; *(av film)* first performance. **premièrepublikum** *sb* first-night audience.

premiert *adj* prized.

premiss *sb* premise; *på falske ~er* on false premises.

prent *sb: på ~* in print. **prente** *vb* stamp.

preparat *sb* preparation. **preparere** *vb* prepare.

preposisjon *sb (gram)* preposition.

presang *sb* gift, present. **~kort** *sb* gift token.

presedens *sb* precedent.

presenning *sb* tarpaulin.

presens *sb (gram)* the present (tense); *~ partisipp* the present participle.

presentabel *adj* presentable.

presentasjon *sb* introduction.

presentere *vb* **1** *(forestille)* introduce; *la meg ~ herr B (for Dem)* allow/let me to introduce Mr B to you; *(også)* this is Mr B; **2** *(forelegge)* present; *han presenterte regningen* he presented the bill; **3** *~ gevær* present arms.

preservere *vb (hermetisere, ta vare på)* preserve.

president *sb* president. **presidentvalg** *sb* presidential election. **presidere** *vb* preside; *~ ved et møte* preside at a meeting. **presidium** *sb* chairmanship.

presisere *vb* stress, emphasize.

presis *adj* **1** *(nøyaktig)* exact, precise; *~e mål* precise measurements; **2** *(om klokkeslett)* sharp; *klokken åtte ~* at eight o'clock sharp; **3** *(om tid for øvrig)* punctual. **presisjon** *sb* **1** *(nøyaktighet)* precision; **2** *(om tid)* punctuality. **presisjons|arbeid** *sb* precision work. **~våpen** *sb* weapon of precision.

press *sb* pressure; strain, stress; *(især jur)* duress; *gjøre noe under ~* do something under duress/pressure.

presse *sb* press; *~n* the Press.

presse *vb* press, squeeze; they pressed him to do it; *~ sitroner* squeeze lemons; *(med pressejern)* iron; *(~ bukser)* press, crease.

presse|attaché *sb* press attaché. **~byrå** *sb* news agency. **~konferanse** *sb* press conference. **~kort** *sb* press card/pass; reporter's pass.

presserende *adj* urgent, pressing.

pressgruppe *sb* pressure group.

prest *sb* **1** *(engelsk statskirke~)* clergyman; *bli ~*

enter the church; *min far er ~* my father is a clergyman; **2** *(sogne~)* rector, vicar; *(dgl ord for stedets ~)* parson; **3** *(fengsels~, skips~, sykehus~ etc)* chaplain; **4** *(frikirke~, skotsk ~)* minister; **5** *(katolsk ~, hedensk prest etc)* priest.

prestasjon *sb* **1** *(arbeidsytelse)* piece of work; achievement; **2** *(bragd)* achievement, feat.

preste|gjeld *sb* parish. **~gård** *sb* rectory, vicarage. **~kall** *sb* living. **~krave 1** *sb* clergyman's ruff; **2** *(blomsten)* marguerite, oxeye daisy.

prestere *vb (utføre)* do, perform; achieve.

preste|skap *sb* clergy. **~velde** *sb* theocracy. **~vie** *vb* ordain.

prestisje *sb* prestige. **prestisje|hensyn** *sb* considerations of prestige. **~sak** *sb* matter of prestige, **~tap** *sb* loss of prestige.

pretendent *sb* pretender. **pretensiøs** *adj* pretentious. **pretensjon** *sb* pretension.

prevensjon *sb* birth control; contraception.

preventiv *adj* preventive; *~e midler* contraceptives.

prikk *sb* dot, point; *(liten flekk)* spot; *på en ~* to a T; exactly, precisely; *til punkt og ~e* to the letter. **prikke** *vb (sette prikker)* dot; *en ~t linje* a dotted line. **prikkfri** *adj* perfect, excellent.

prima *adj* first-class, first-rate; *~ kvalitet* top quality. **primadonna** *sb* prima-donna.

primitiv *adj* primitive.

primtall *sb* prime number.

primus *sb (kokeapparat)* primus. **primus motor** *sb* prime mover.

primær *adj* primary. **primærlaster** *sb data* bootstrap.

prins *sb* prince. **prinselig** *adj* princely. **prinsesse** *sb* princess. **prinsgemal** *sb* Prince Consort.

prinsipal 1 *adj* principal; chief, primary; *vårt ~e forslag* our primary proposal; **2** *sb (arbeidsgiver)* enployer; *(sjef for et firma)* chief, head. **prinsipiell** *adj* fundamental; in principle; *~ enighet* agreement in principle; *av ~e grunner* on grounds of principle. **prinsipp** *sb* principle; *av ~* on principle; *i ~et* in principle. **prinsipp|fast** *adj: en ~ kvinne* a woman of principle; a high-principled woman. **~fasthet** *sb* firmness of principle. **~løs** *adj* unprincipled. **~rytter** *sb* doctrinaire. **~rytteri** *sb* doctrinairianism. **~spørsmål** *sb* question/matter of principle.

prinsregent *sb* Prince Regent.

prioritere *vb* give preference to. **prioritert** *adj* preferential, secured; *~ fordringer/krav* preferential claims; *være ~* have/take priority. **prioritet** *sb* **1** priority; **2** *(panterett)* mortgage; *ha første ~* have a first mortgage on.

prippen *adj* testy, touchy.

pris *sb* **1** price; *~en for/på varene* the price of the goods; *for enhver ~* at any price; *(fig også)* at all costs; *ikke for noen ~* not at any price; *(fig også)* on no account; *sette ~ på* value; *(især fig)* appreciate; *jeg setter ~ på ham* I appreciate him; *til en ~ av* at a price of; **2** *(belønning, premie)* prize; *ingen vant ~en* nobody won the prize. **prisbelønne** *vb* award a prize; *en ~t roman* a prize novel. **prise A** *sb (oppbrakt skip)* prize; **B** *vb (rose)* praise. **pris|fall** *sb* fall in prices. **~forhøyelse** *sb* rise in/of price(s). **~forskjell** *sb* difference in price. **prisgi** *vb* give up, abandon; *være ~tt* be at the mercy of. **pris|indeks** *sb* price index. **~klasse** *sb* price bracket/range. **~kontroll** *sb* price control/regulation(s). **~lapp** *sb* price label/tag. **~liste** *sb* price list.

prisme *sb* prism. **prismekikkert** *sb* prismatic/prism binoculars.

pris|nedsettelse *sb* reduction in prices. **~nivå** *sb* price level. **~regulering** *sb* price regulation(s). **~stopp** *sb* price freeze; *innføre ~stopp* freeze prices.

privat *adj* private; *han selger ikke til ~e* he does not sell to private people; *jeg kjenner ham ~* I know him in private. **privat|bil** *sb* private car. **~brev** *sb* personal letter. **~detektiv** *sb* private detective; *dgl* private eye. **~eiendom** *sb* private property. **~elev** *sb* private pupil. **~klinikk** *sb* nursing-home. **~liv** *sb* private life; privacy. **~lærer** *sb* private teacher; coach, crammer. **~person** *sb* private individual. **~sak** *sb* private affair. **~undervisning** *sb* private lessons.

privilegert *adj* privileged. **privilegium** *sb* privilege.

pro *prep: ~ anno* per annum; *~ persona* per head; per person.

pro! *interj* wo, whoa.

probat *adj* effective; *et ~ middel* an effective remedy.

problem *sb* problem. **problematisk** *adj* problematic. **problem|barn** *sb* problem child. **~stilling** *sb* way of presenting the problem(s).

produksjon *sb* **1** production; *(mengden av produserte varer også)* output; *~en er større i år enn i fjor* the output is larger this year than (it was) last year; **2** *(kunstners ~)* works. **produksjons|evne** *sb* productive capacity. **~middel** *sb* means of production. **~omkostninger** *sb fl* cost(s) of production. **produkt** *sb* product; *(fabrikat også)* make, manufacture; *(især om landbruks~ og natur~ også)* produce; *landets ~er* the produce of the country. **produktiv** *adj* productive. **produktivitet** *sb* productivity. **produktledning** *sb petro* run down line. **produsent** *sb* producer. **produsere** *vb* produce.

profan *adj* profane.

profesjon *sb* **1** *(beskjeftigelse)* occupation; *(håndverk, yrke)* trade; *(~ som krever større, især boklig, utdannelse)* profession; *av ~* by trade; *lege/lærer av ~* a doctor/teacher by profession. **profesjonell** *adj* professional; *(dgl, også sb)* pro; *en ~ fotballspiller* a football professional/pro; *~ bokser (også)* prize-fighter. **profesjonisme** *sb* professionalism. **profesjonist** *sb* professional. **professor** *sb* professor; *hun er ~ i engelsk* she is a professor of English. **professorat** *sb* chair, professorship; *et ~ i historie* a chair/professorship of history.

profet *sb* prophet. **profetere** *vb* prophesy. **profeti** *sb* prophecy. **profetisk** *adj* prophetic.

profil *sb* profile; *i ~* in profile.

profitt *sb* profit, gain; *med ~* at a profit. **profittere** *vb* profit; *han ~erte på det* he profited by it. **profittjeger** *sb* profit-monger. **profitør** *sb* profiteer.

proforma *adj, adv* pro forma; as a matter of form.

prognose *sb* prognosis.

program *sb* programme; *US (og som regel data)* program; *det står ikke på ~met* it is not in/on the programme. **program|brudd** *sb data* abort. **~erklæring** *sb* manifesto. **~feil** *sb data* bug. **~kompatibel** *adj data* software compatible. **programmerbar** *adj data* programmable. **programmerbar tast** *sb data* soft key. **program|messig** *adj* according to programme. **~pakke** *sb data* software package. **~vare** *sb data* software.

progresjon *sb* progression.

progressiv *adj* progressive; *~ beskatning* graduated system of taxation.

projeksjon *sb* projection. **projeksjonstegning** *sb* descriptive geometry.

projektør se *prosjektør*.

projisere *vb* project.

proklamasjon *sb* proclamation. **proklamere** *vb* proclaim.

prokura *sb: ha ~ i firmaet* be authorized to sign for the firm. **prokurist** *sb* confidential clerk.

proletar *sb* proletarian. **proletariat** *sb* proletariat; *~ets diktatur* the dictatorship of the proletariat.

prolog *sb* prologue.

prolongere *vb* prolong, renew. **prolongering** *sb* prolongation.

promenade *sb* promenade. **promenadedekk** *sb* promenade deck.

promille *sb* per thousand.

prominent *adj* prominent.

prompt(e) *adj* prompt, punctual; *(adv)* promptly; *han svarte ~* he replied promptly.

pronomen *sb (gram)* pronoun.

propaganda *sb* propaganda; *(reklame)* advertising.

propell *sb* propeller. **propell|akse** *sb* propeller shaft. **~blad** *sb* propeller blade.

proper *adj* neat, tidy.

proporsjon *sb* proportion. **proporsjonal** *adj* proportional; *~ med* proportional to; *omvendt ~* inversely proportional.

proposisjon *sb: kongelig ~* government bill.

propp *sb* stopper; peg; *(i badekar, kum)* plug. **proppe** *vb* cram, stuff; *(sette propp i)* plug. **proppfull** *adj* brimful, crammed.

props *sb* pitprops.

prosa *sb* prose; *på ~* in prose. **prosaisk** *adj* prosaic.

prosedere *vb* plead.

prosedyre *sb* procedure; *(sakførernes innlegg i en rettssak)* the (final) addresses of counsel.

prosent *sb* **1** per cent; *fem ~* five per cent; *hvor mange ~?* how much per cent? *6 ~ i rente* six per cent interest; **2** *(~andel)* percentage; *en høy/lav ~* a high/low percentage; *jeg får ~er* I get a percentage.

prosesjon *sb* procession.

prosess *sb* process; *(rettsak)* lawsuit. **prosessor|(enhet)** *sb data* (central) processing unit (CPU). **~tid** *sb data* CPU-time.

prosjekt *sb* project; plan, scheme.

prosjektil *sb* projectile.

prosjektør *(lyskaster, søkelys)* searchlight; *(film~)* projector. *(flomlys~)* flood-light projector; *(teater~)* spotlight.

prospekt *sb* prospectus. **prospektkort** *sb* picture postcard.

prostata *sb* the prostate.

prostituere *vb* prostitute. **prostituert** *sb* prostitute. **prostitusjon** *sb* prostitution.

protein *sb* protein.

proteksjon *sb* patronage. **proteksjonisme** *sb* protectionism. **proteksjonist** *sb* protectionist. **proteksjonistisk** *adj* protectionist.

protese *sb* artificial limb; *(tann~)* denture.

protest *sb* protest; *vi nedla ~* we protested. **protestant** *sb* Protestant. **protestantisk** *adj* Protestant. **protestantisme** *sb* Protestantism. **protestere** *sb* protest; *dette ~r jeg mot* I protest against this.

protokoll *sb* **1** *(regnskaps~)* ledger; **2** *(forhandlings~)* minute book; **3** *(navneliste)* register; **4** *(klasse~)* school register. **protokollere** *vb* enter; record, register.

protoplasma *sb* protoplasm.

proviant *sb* provisions; *(ofte)* supplies *fl.* **proviantere** *vb* take in supplies.

provins *sb* province; *~en (i motsetning til hovedstaden)* the provinces. **provinsiell** *adj* provincial; *(bornert, transynt også)* parochial.

provisjon *sb* commission. **provisjonsbasis** *sb: på ~* on a commission basis.

provisor *sb* head dispenser.

provisorisk *adj* provisional, temporary; makeshift.

provokasjon *sb* provocation. **provokatorisk** *adj* provocative. **provokatør** *sb* provocateur.

provosere provoke.

pruste *vb* snort.

prute *vb* haggle, bargain; *~ på noe* haggle over (the price of) something. **prutningsmonn** *sb* margin.

pryd *sb* ornament; *til ~* for ornament; ornamental. **prydbusk** *sb* ornamental shrub. **pryde** *vb* decorate; adorn, ornament. **prydelse** *sb* decoration, ornamentation. **pryd|plante** *sb* ornamental plant. **~søm** *sb* embroidery.

pryl *sb* a beating, thrashing. **pryle** *vb* beat, thrash, whip. **prylestraff** *sb* corporal punishment; *(pisking)* flogging.

prærie *sb* prairie. **prærie|brann** *sb* prairie fire. **~ulv** *sb* coyote.

prøve I *sb* **1** *(forsøk)* test, trial; **2** *(undersøkelse)* examination; test, trial; *vi tok maskinen på ~* we took the machine on trial; **3** *(eksamens~ etc)* examination, test; *hun greide ~n* she passed the test; *muntlig/skriftlig ~* oral/written examination/test; **4** *(teater~)* rehearsel; **5** *(vare~)* sample; *(stoff~, tapet~)* pattern, cutting; **6** *(bevis)* proof, sample; *gi en ~ på sin dyktighet* give a proof/sample of one's skill; **7** *bli løslatt på ~* be released on probation/*US* on parole; *bli oppflyttet på ~* get a conditional remove; **II** *vb* **1** *(forsøke)* attempt, try; *~ seg frem* feel one's way; *han prøvde å flykte* he attempted/tried to escape; **2** *(undersøke)* examine, test; *vi prøvde maskinen* we tested the machine; **3** *(~ klær)* try on; *hun prøvde kåpen (på)* she tried the coat on. **prøve|ballong** *sb: sende opp en ~ballong* put out a feeler. **~bilde** *sb TV* resolution chart; test pattern. **~eksemplar** *sb* sample, specimen; *(av bok)* specimen copy. **~kjøre** *vb* test-drive, test. **~klut** *sb* guinea-pig. **prøvelse** *sb* ordeal, trial. **prøve|måltid** *sb* test meal. **~rør** *sb* test tube. **~rørsbarn** *sb* test tube baby. **~stav** *sb petro* test probe. **~tid** *sb* (period of) probation. **~tur** *sb* trial cruise/trip. **~ventil** *sb petro* check valve.

prøysser *sb* Prussian. **prøyssisk** *adj* Prussian.

psevdonym *sb* pseudonym; pen name.

pst! hist!

psyke *sb* psyche; mentality, mind. **psykiater** *sb* psychiatrist. **psykiatri** *sb* psychiatry. **psykiatrisk** *adj* psychiatric(al). **psykisk** *adj* psychich(al). **psyko|analyse** *sb* psychoanalysis. **~analytiker** *sb* psychoanalyst. **~analytisk** *adj* psychoanalytic. **psykolog** *sb* psychologist. **psykologi** *sb* psychology. **psykologisk** *adj* psychologic(al). **psyko|pat** *sb* psychopath. **~patisk** *adj* psychopathic. **psykose** *sb* psychosis. **psykosomatisk** *adj* psychosomatic.

ptro! wo, whoa!

pubertet *sb* puberty. **pubertetsalder** *sb* age of puberty.

publikasjon *sb* publication. **publikum** *sb* **1** *(offentligheten)* the public; *~ anmodes om ikke å plukke blomstene* the public are requested not to pick the flowers; **2** *(tilskuere)* spectators; *(tilhørere)* audience; *det var mange utlendinger blant ~* there were many foreigners among the audience; **3** *(interessenter, kjøpere etc)* public; *bøker av den typen har ikke noe ~* books of that kind have no public. **publisere** *vb* publish. **publisitet** *sb* publicity.

puddel(hund) *sb* poodle.

pudder *sb* powder. **pudder|dåse** *sb* compact; *(større)* powder box. **~kvast** *sb* powder puff.

pudding *sb* pudding.

pudre *vb* powder; *~ seg* powder (oneself).

puff *sb* **A** *(dytt, skubb)* push; *hun gav ham et ~* she pushed him; **B** *(møbel)* pouf(fe); *(lang)* (box) ottoman. **puffe** *vb* push. **pufferme** *sb* puff sleeve.

pugg *sb* **1** *(utenatlæring)* learning by rote; **2** *(flittig lesing)* cramming, swotting. **pugge** *vb* **1** *(lære på rams)* learn by rote; **2** *(lese ivrig)* cram, swot. **pugghest** *sb* swot.

puh *interj* ugh.

pukk *sb* ballast. **pukka nødt** *adj* forced (*til* to).

pukke *vb* **A** *~ stein* crush; **B** *~ på* insist on; stand on.

pukkel *sb* hump, hunch. **pukkelrygget** *adj* hunchbacked, humpbacked; *en ~ person* a humpback/hunchback.

pukk|stein *sb koll* broken stones; road metal. **~verk** *sb* crushing plant.

pulje *sb* group, heat. **~vis** *adj, adv* by groups.

pull *sb (på hatt)* crown.

pullover *sb* pull-over.

puls *sb* pulse. **pulsere** *vb* pulsate; beat, throb; *det ~nde liv* the throbbing life. **puls|slag** *sb* pulsation. **~åre** *sb* artery.

pult *sb* desk.

pulterkammer *sb* box-room, lumber-room.

pulver *sb* powder. **pulverisere** *vb* pulverize, smash.

pumpe I *sb* pump; **II** *vb* **1** pump; *~ opp* blow/pump up; **2** *(lense, tømme)* empty.

pumps *sb fl* court shoes; pumps.

pund *sb* pound (mynt- og vektenhet); *det koster fem ~* it costs five pounds; *et halvt ~* half a pound; *to ~ sukker* two pounds of sugar. Se for øvrig midtsidene.

pung *sb (penge~)* purse; *(tobakks~)* pouch. **pungdyr** *sb* marsupial. **punge ut med** *vb* cough up; fork out.

punkt *sb* **1** point; *(prikk også)* dot; *~ for ~* point by point; **2** *(~ på dagsorden, program etc)* item; **3** *(henseende)* respect; *på dette ~et er de forskjellige* in this respect they are different. **punktere** *vb (om dekk, slange)* be punctured; *(om bilist, syklist)* have a puncture; *jeg/sykkelen min har punktert* I have (had) a puncture/*dgl* a flat. **punktering** *sb* puncture; *dgl* flat. **punktlig** *adj* punctual; *adv* punctually. **punktlighet** *sb* punctuality. **punktum** *sb* (full) stop; *sette ~* put a full stop. **punktvis** *adv* point by point.

punsj *sb* punch.

pupill *sb* pupil.

puppe *sb* chrysalis, pupa. **puppe|hylster** *sb* cocoon. **~stadium** *sb* pupal stage.

pur *adj* **1** *(ren, skjær)* pure, sheer; *den ~e sannhet* the pure truth; **2** *(ganske) ~ ung* very young.

puré *sb* purée.

purisme *sb* purism. **purist** *sb* purist.

puritaner *sb* Puritan. **puritanisme** *sb* Puritanism. **puritansk** *adj* Puritan; *(nedsettende)* puritanical.

purke *sb* sow.

purpur(farget) *adj* purple; *(høyrød)* crimson, scarlet.

purre A *sb (planten)* leek; **B** *vb* **1** *(vekke)* call, rouse; **2** *(påminne, varsle)* press, remind; *~ noen for betaling* press somebody for payment.

pus *sb* pussy.

pusle *vb* **1** *(små~)* fiddle, finger, potter; **2** *(tusle)* move softly; shuffle about; **3** *(leke med puslespill)* do a jig-saw puzzle. **pusle|arbeid** *sb* petty/pottering/fiddling work. **~spill** *sb* jig-saw puzzle. **pusling** *sb (liten fyr)* manikin, midget.

puss I *interj: ~ ta 'n!* at her/him! **II** *sb* **A 1** *(mur~)* plaster; **2** *(pynt, stas)* finery; *i full ~* in one's (her, his etc) Sunday best; **B** *(skøyerstrek)* trick; *han spilte meg et ~* he played a trick on me; he played me a trick; **C** *(i materie, verk)* pus. **pussa** *adj dgl* tipsy, tight. **pusse** *vb* **A** *(gjøre blankt, rent etc)* clean, polish; *~ opp (hus, leilighet)* redecorate, redo; *han ~t vinduene* he cleaned the windows; *hun ~t skoene sine* she polished her shoes; *jeg ~t nesen* I blew my nose; **B:** *~ hunden på noen* set the dog on somebody. **pusse|middel** *sb* polish. **~skinn** *sb* chamois/*dgl* shammy leather; wash leather.

pussig *adj* droll, funny; *~ nok* curiously enough; funny thing, you know.

pust *sb* **1** *(ånde)* breath; *han mistet ~en* he got out of breath; *ta ~en fra noen* take somebody's breath away; **2** *(vind~)* breath of air; puff (of wind); *(sterkere)* gust of wind. **puste** *vb* **1** *(ånde)* breathe; *~ inn* inhale; *~ ut* exhale; *(slappe av)* relax; **2** *(blåse)* blow; *han ~t til ilden (fig)* he added fuel to the fire. **puste|hull** *sb* breathing-hole. **~rom** *sb* breathing-space. **~rør** *sb* *(våpen)* blowgun.

pute *sb (hode~)* pillow; *(sofa~)* cushion; *sy ~r under armene på dem* make things too easy for them. **pute|krig** *sb* pillow fight. **~trekk, ~var** *sb* pillow case/slip.

putre *vb* bubble; frizzle, sputter; *(om motor)* chug.

putte *vb* put.

pyjamas *sb* pyjamas *fl*; *~en hans er blå* his pyjamas are blue.

pynt *sb* **1** ornament; *det er bare til ~* it is purely ornamental; **2** *(besetning på tøy)* trimmings: **3** *(odde)* point; *(kant av stup)* brink. **pynte** *vb* decorate; *~ seg* dress (up); smarten oneself; *bordet var ~t med blomster* the table was decorated with flowers. **pynte|dukke** *sb* doll. **~forkle** *sb* fancy apron. **~håndkle** *sb* ornamental towel. **~syk** *adj* dressy; too fond of finery.

pyramide *sb* pyramid. **pyramideformet** *adj* pyramidal.

pyroman *sb* pyromaniac. **pyromani** *sb* pyromania.

pyse *sb* milksop, sissy. **pyset(e)** *adj* sissified.

pytagoreisk *adj: den ~e læresetning* the theorem of Pythagoras.

pytt 1 *interj* pooh; *~ sann!* never mind! **2** *sb* *(vann~)* puddle.

pæl *sb* pole, post, stake. **pæleverk** *sb* palisade.

pære *sb* **1** *(frukt)* pear; **2** *(lys~)* bulb. **pæretre** *sb* pear tree.

pøbel *sb* mob, rabble. **pøbel|aktig** *adj* caddish, curlish; vulgar. **~herredømme, ~velde** *sb* mob rule.

pøl *sb* mud, puddle.

pølle *sb* (cylindrical) cushion.

pølse *sb* sausage; *varme ~r (også)* hot dogs. **pølse|-bod, ~bu** *sb* hot-dog stand. **~maker** *sb* sausage maker. **~snakk, ~vev** *sb* nonsense; *US* baloney, boloney.

pøns(k)e *vb* meditate, ponder; muse; *~ på hevn* plan revenge; *~ ut* hatch/think out; devise.

pøs *sb* bucket, pail. **pøse** *vb* sluice; *(~regne)* pour down. **pøs|regn** *sb* downpour. **~regne** *vb: det ~regner* it is pouring down; it is raining cats and dogs.

på I *adv* on; *lokket er ~* the lid is on; *hun hadde hatt ~* she was wearing a hat; **II** *prep* **1** *(oppå)* on; *(mest bokl)* upon; *~ bakken* on the ground; *~ veggen* on the wall; **2** *(ved)* at; *~ hjørnet* at the corner; *~ kontoret* at the office; *~ stasjonen* at the station; **3** *(innenfor et bestemt område i tid eller rom)* in; *~ bildet* in the picture; *~ gaten* in the street; *jorden rundt ~ 24 timer* around the world in 24 hours; **4** *(om dag, dato etc)* at, on; *~ den tiden* at that time; *~ mandag* on Monday; **5** *(om klokkeslett)* to; *ti (minutter) ~ ni* ten minutes to nine; **6** *(om måte, språk)* in; *~ denne måten* in this way; *~ engelsk* in English; **7** *(om samhørighet etc)* of; *bladene ~ trærne* the leaves of the trees; *en gutt på ti* a boy of ten; *en bok ~ 300 sider* a book of 300 pages. **på|berope seg** *vb: de ~beropte seg at de ikke visste det* they pleaded ignorance. **~bud** *sb* command, order. **~by** *vb* command, order. **~dra seg** *vb* incur, *(om sykdom)* catch, contract; *han ~drog seg gjeld/utgifter* he incurred debts/expenses; **~fallende** *adj* striking; *(underlig)* strange. *~fallende likhet* striking likeness.

påfugl *sb* peacock; *(om hunnfuglen)* peahen.

på|funn *sb (innfall)* idea; *(lune)* caprice. **~føre** *vb: ~føre noen utgifter* put somebody to expense. **~gang** *sb: det er sterk ~gang av kreditorer* creditors are pressing hard for payment. **~gangsmot** *sb* go-ahead spirit; push. **~gripe** *vb* arrest, seize. **~gå** *vb* be in progress; go on. **~gående** *adj* aggressive, pressing. **~heng** *sb* hanger(s)-on. **~hengsmotor** *sb* outboard motor. **~hitt** *sb* idea. **~holden, ~holdende** *adj* close-fisted. **~hør** *sb: i hans ~hør* in front of him/in his presence.

påk *sb* rod, stick.

på|kalle *vb* invoke; call upon; *~kalle oppmerksomhet* attract attention. **~kjenning** *sb* strain, stress. **~kjørt** *adj: jeg ble ~kjørt* I was run into/run over/knocked down. **~kledd** *adj* dressed; fully clothed. **~krevd** *adj* called for; necessary. **~landsvind** *sb* onshore wind.

påle *sb* pole, stake.

på|legg *sb* **1** *(på smørbrød)* slices of meat, sausage etc laid on an open sandwich; **2** *(forskrift, formaning)* order; *jeg fikk ~ om å gjøre det* I was ordered to do it; **3** *(forhøyelse)* increase, rise; *~ på lønnen* rise in the wages/salary; *et ~ på femti pund* a rise of £50. **~legge** *vb* **1** *(befale)* order; *de ble ~lagt å gjøre det* they were ordered to do it; **2** *husleien ble ~lagt* the rent was raised. **~litelig** *adj* reliable. **~litelighet** *sb* reliability. **~lydende** *sb* face value. **~minnelse** *sb* reminder, warning; admonition. **~mønstre** *vb* sign on. **~mønstring** *sb* signing on. **~pakning** *sb* dressing--down; reprimand. **~passelig** *adj* careful; *han er ~passelig med leksene* he is careful about his homework; *hun er meget ~passelig med å gjøre det* she is very careful about doing it. **~peke** *vb* point out; *~pekende pronomen* demonstrative pronoun. **~rørende** *sb* relation, relative; *de ~rørende* the next of kin. **~se at** *vb* see to it that, take care that.

påske *sb* Easter. **påske|aften** *sb* Easter Eve. **~dag** *sb* Easter Day; Easter Sunday; *2. ~dag* Easter Monday. **~egg** *sb* Easter egg. **~ferie** *sb* Easter holidays; *(ved universitetet)* Easter vacation.

påskelilje *sb* daffodil.

på skjeve *adv* aslant, askew.

på|skjønne *vb* **1** *(sette pris på)* appreciate; **2** *(belønne)* reward. **~skjønnelse** *sb* **1** appreciation; **2** *(belønning)* reward. **~skrift** *sb* inscription; *(underskrift)* signature.

på skrå *adv* aslant, slantingly; diagonally.

på|skudd *sb* pretext, pretence; excuse; *komme med ~skudd (for å unngå å gjøre noe)* make excuses; *under ~skudd av å hjelpe* under (the) pretext of helping. **~skynde** *vb* hasten, quicken; accelerate.

på snei *adv* askew, aslant.

på|stand *sb* **1** *(det å hevde noe)* assertion; *en løs ~stand* an ill-founded assertion; **2** *(erklæring)* declaration; **3** *(krav)* claim. **~stå** *vb* **1** *(hevde)* assert; *hun ~stod at hun hadde sett meg* she asserted that she had seen me; **2** *(fastholde)* insist, maintain; *han ~står at historien er sann* he insists that the story is true. **~ståelig** *adj* obstinate, stubborn; pig-headed. **~ståelighet** *sb* obstinacy, stubbornness. **~syn** *sb: i deres ~syn* in their presence; before them; *i alles ~syn* in public; publicly. **~ta** *vb: ~ta seg* undertake; take upon oneself; *hun ~tok seg å få ham til fornuft* she took upon herself to bring him to reason. **~takelig** *adj (åpenbar)* obvious.

påtale I *sb* **1** *(irettesettelse)* reprimand, reproof; **2** *(rettslig anklage)* charge, indictment; *reise ~ mot noen for noe* bring in an indictment against somebody for something; lay something to somebody's charge; **II** *vb* **1** *(klage over)* complain of; **2** *(kritisere)* criticize. **påtale|myndighet** *sb* prosecuting authority; *GB* the Crown; *US* the People. **~unnlatelse** *sb* dropping of charges.

på|tatt *adj: under (et) ~ navn* under an assumed name. **~tegning** *sb* **1** *(underskrift)* signature; **2** *(attestasjon, kausjon, kvittering)* endorsement. **~trengende** *adj* **1** *(om person)* importunate, insistent; **2** *(uavviselig)* pressing, urgent. **~trykk** *sb* pressure; *etter ~trykk av* under pressure from. **~tvinge** *vb: ~tvinge en noe* force something on somebody. **~vente** *sb: i ~vente av* in anticipation/expectation of. **~virke** *vb* affect, influence; *klimaet ~virker helsen deres* the climate affects their health. **~virkelig** *adj* impressionable; susceptible to influence. **~virket** *adj* affected, influenced; *(av alkohol)* under the influence (of drink). **~virkning** *sb* influence; *under ~virkning av* influenced by; under the influence of. **~vise** *vb* **1** *(peke på)* point out; **2** *(bevise)* prove. **~viselig** *adj: uten ~viselig grunn* for no apparent reason. **~visning** demonstration, proof; pointing out.

R

r *(bokstaven)* r.

rabalder *sb* **1** *(bråk)* noise; **2** *(oppstyr)* row. **rabaldermøte** *sb* tumultuous/disorderly meeting.

rabarbra *sb* rhubarb.

rabatt A *sb (prisreduksjon)* discount; *en ~ på 2 prosent* a discount of two per cent; *vi gir ti prosent kontant~* we give ten per cent discount for cash; **B 1** *(blomster~)* border of flowers; **2** *(midt~ på vei)* centre strip; central reserve/reservation.

rabb(e) *sb* ridge.

rabbel *sb* scribbling.

rabbi, rabbiner *sb* rabbi.

rabiat *adj* rabid, raving.

rable *vb* scribble; *~ ned* jot down; *det ~r for ham* he is going off his head.

racer|bil *sb* racing car. **~båt** *sb* racing boat. **~sykkel** *sb* racing bicycle.

racket *sb* racket.

rad *sb (rekke)* row, line; *på ~* in a row/line; *tre dager på ~* three days on end; three days running.

radar *sb* radar. **radarskjerm** *sb* radar screen.

radbrekke *vb: ~ et navn* mangle a name; *~ språket* murder the language.

radere *vb* **1** *(viske ut)* erase; **2** *(om grafisk kunst)* etch. **radering** *sb* **1** *(visking)* erasure; **2** *(grafisk kunstverk)* etching.

radiator *sb* radiator.

radikal *adj* radical; *(adv)* radically. **radikaler** *sb* radical. **radikalisme** *sb* radicalism.

radio *sb* radio, wireless; *(radioapparat)* radio/wireless set; *de hørte ~* they listened to the radio, they listened in; *hun talte i ~(en)* she spoke over the radio; *i radio(en)* on the wireless/radio; *slå av/på radioen* turn off/on the radio/wireless; *talen ble sendt over ~* the speech was broadcast. **radio|aktiv** *adj* radioactive. **~antenne** *sb* aerial. **~apparat** *sb* radio/wireless set; (radio) receiver. **~foredrag** *sb* radio talk. **~forhandler** *sb* radio dealer. **~grammofon** *sb* radiogramophone. **~lisens** *sb* wireless licence. **~lytter** *sb* listener. **~mast** *sb* radio mast/*US* tower. **~mottaker**

sb radio receiver. **~peiling** *sb* radio direction finding. **~program** *sb* broadcast/radio programme. **~reportasje** *sb* running commentary. **~sender** *sb* radio transmitter. **~sending** *sb* broadcast. **~stasjon** *sb* radio station. **~telegraf** *sb* radio telegraph. **~telegrafist** *sb* radio operator. **~telegram** *sb* radio telegram; wireless (message).

radium *sb* radium. **radiumbehandling** *sb* radium treatment.

radius *sb* radius.

radmager *adj* bony, skinny.

radvis *adv* in rows.

raffinement *sb* refinement, sophistication; subtlety. **raffinert** *adj* refined, subtle; sophisticated. **raffineri** *sb* refinery.

rage *vb* **1** *~ frem* project; stick out; **2** *~ opp* project, rise; stand out; *~ opp over* tower over; *(fig)* be head and shoulders above; tower above; *skyskraperne som ~r opp over New York* the skyscrapers that tower over New York; *en mann som ~t opp over sine samtidige* a man who towered above his contemporaries.

ragg *sb* thick, shaggy hair. **ragget(e)** *adj* shaggy.

ragu *sb* ragout.

rak *adj (rett)* straight; *(rank)* erect.

raka *adj: ~ fant* dead broke. **rake I** *sb: rubb og ~* every bit/scrap; **II** *vb* **1** poke, rake; stir (up); *~ i varmen* poke the fire; *~ sammen* rake together; **2** *(barbere)* shave; **3** *(angå)* concern; *det ~r deg ikke* that's none of your business.

rakett *sb* rocket. **rakett|utskyting** *sb* rocket launching. **~utskytingsplattform** *sb* launching pad.

rakke *vb: ~ ned på* abuse, revile; throw dirt on; *~ til* dirty, soil.

rakker *sb (kjeltring)* rascal, scoundrel, villain; **rakkerpakk** *sb* rabble, riff-raff.

rakle *sb (på tre)* catkin.

rakne *vb* come unsewn/unstitched; *(om strømper)* ladder, run. **raknefri** *adj* ladder-proof, run-proof.

rak|rygget *adj* erect; *(også fig)* upright.

rallar *sb* navvy.

ralle *vb (i dødskamp)* rattle (in one's throat).

ram I *adj* **1** *(om lukt, smak)* pungent, rank; acrid; **2** *for ~me alvor* in dead earnest; **II** *sb: få ~ på* get at.

ramaskrik *sb* outcry.

rambukk *sb* pile driver.

ramle *vb* **1** *(bråke)* clatter, rattle, rumble; **2** *(falle)* tumble; *ungen ~t ned trappen* the child tumbled down the stairs.

ramme A 1 *sb (om bilde, dør, vindu)* frame; **2** *(grenser, omfang)* scope; *det faller utenfor ~n av denne boken* it falls outside the scope of this book; **2** *vb: ~ inn* frame; **B** *vb* **1** *(råke, treffe)* hit; *(fig)* overtake; *de ble ~t av en ulykke* they were overtaken by a disaster; *~et av (fig også)* stricken with; *~t av pest* stricken with pestilence; *som ~t av lynet* thunderstruck; **2** *(drive/slå ned)* drive, ram; *~ ned* drive in.

rammel *sb* clatter, noise; din.

rammende *adj: en ~ bemerkning* a remark very much to the point.

ramp *sb (pøbelaktig person)* hooligan, ruffian, roughneck; *(koll)* mob, rabble, riff-raff.

rampe *sb* **1** *(laste~ etc)* ramp; *petro* stinger; **2** *teater* apron. **rampelys** *sb* footlights; *fig* limelight.

rampe|gjeng *sb* gang of hooligans. **~streker** *sb fl* dirty tricks; vandalism. **rampet(e)** *adj* boorish; ill-bred, ill-mannered. **ramponere** *vb* damage.

rams *sb: på ~* by rote.

ramse 1 *sb* jingle, nursery rhyme; **2** *vb: ~ opp* reel/rattle off.

ramsvart *adj* coal-black.

ran *sb* robbery; hold-up, stick-up.

rand *sb* **1** *(kant)* edge; *(langs rund gjenstand)* rim; *(på glass etc)* brim; *fylt til ~en* filled to the brim; **2** *(brem)* border; **3** *(stripe)* stripe; **4** *(fig)* brink, verge; *på ~en av ruin* on the brink/verge of ruin; *være på gravens ~* have one foot in the grave. **randbemerkning** *sb* marginal note. **randet(e)** *adj* striped. **randfjell** *sb* border mountains.

rane *vb* rob.

rang *sb* rank; *av første ~* first-rate, first-class; *etter ~* according to rank; *han har oberstss ~/~ som oberst* he holds the rank of a colonel.

rangel *sb* booze, spree; *gå på ~* go on the booze/spree.

rangere *vb* rank.

rangle 1 *sb, vb (skrangle)* rattle; **2** *vb (gå på rangel)* go on the booze/spree. **ranglefant** *sb* boozer.

rangorden *sb* order of precedence; ranking. **rangsperson** *sb* person of rank. **rangstige** *sb* social ladder; hierarchy.

rank *adj* erect, straight; *en ~ rygg* a straight back; *hun holdt seg ~* she held herself erect.

ranke *sb* **A** *(vin~)* vine; **B:** *ride ~* be dandled on the knees; *ride ~ med* dandle.

ransake *vb* ransack, search.

ransel *sb* knapsack; *mil* haversack.

ransmann *sb* robber.

rap *sb* belch. **rape** *vb* belch.

rapp A *adj (snar)* quick, swift; **B** *sb: på røde rappen/rappet* at once; this minute; immediately, instantly; **C** *(slag)* blow, rap.

rappe *vb* **1** *(stjele)* pilfer, pinch; filch.

rappe seg *vb* hurry; be quick.

rapp|fotet *adj* light-footed, swift-footed. **~kjeftet** *adj* glib; *være ~* have a glib tongue.

rapport *sb* report; *han avla ~ om reisen* he made a report on the journey. **rapportere** *vb* report; *hun rapporterte hva hun hadde sett* she reported what she had seen.

raptus *sb* craze, fit.

rar *adj* strange; curious, odd, peculiar; queer. **raring** *sb* eccentric; queer fellow. **raritet** *sb* curiosity, curio.

ras *sb (av jord, stein)* landslide, landslip; *(av snø)* avalanche.

rase A *sb (menneske~)* race; *(husdyr~)* breed; **B** *vb*

1 *(gli, skli ut)* slide; ~ *sammen* collapse; cave in; *det raste fra taket* snow was sliding off the roof; **2** *(fare av gårde)* tear along; **3** *(skjelle og smelle)* fume, rage; be in a rage; ~ *over* rage against/at. **rase|blanding** *sb* mixture of races. **~diskriminering** *sb* racial discrimination. **~fanatiker** *sb* racist. **~fanatisme** *sb* racism. **~fordom** *sb* racial prejudice. **~frende** *sb* memeber of the same race. **~hat** *sb* racial hatred. **~hest** *sb* blood horse, thoroughbred. **~kamp** racial struggle, race conflict.

rasende *adj* furious, mad; ~ *over at* furious that; *bli* ~ fly into a rage; *han var ~ over det han hadde gjort* he was furious at what he had done; *han oppførte seg som en* ~ he behaved like a madman; *hun var ~ på sin bror* she was furious with her brother;

rasere *vb* raze to the ground.

raseri *sb* fury, rage; *hun ble grepet av* ~ she flew into a rage. **raserianfall** *sb* fit of rage; *få (et) ~anfall* fly into a passion/rage.

rase|skille *sb* colour-bar; *(i Sør-Afrika)* apartheid. **~strid** *sb* racial conflict; race struggle. **rasisme** *sb* racialism, racism. **rasist** *sb* racist. **rasistisk** *adj* racialist, racist.

rasjon *sb* ration; *de ble satt på halv* ~ they were put on half rations. **rasjonalisere** *vb* rationalize. **rasjonalisering** *vb* rationalization. **rasjonalisme** *sb* rationalism. **rasjonalist** *sb* rationalist. **rasjonalistisk** *adj* rationalistic, rationalist. **rasjonell** *adj* rational. **rasjonere** *vb* ration. **rasjonering** *sb* rationing. **rasjonerings|kort** *sb* ration card. **~merke** *sb* coupon.

rask A *adj (hurtig, snar)* fast, quick, swift; ~ *biler* fast cars; ~ *og rørig (om eldre mennesker)* strong and hale; hale and hearty; **B** *sb (skrot)* rubbish, trash. **raske** *vb:* ~ *sammen* scrape together; ~ *til seg* grab, snatch.

rasle *vb* rattle; *(om papir, løv etc)* rustle; *vinden ~r i bladene* the wind rustles in the leaves.

rasp *sb (fil)* rasp; *(rivjern)* grater. **raspe** *vb (file)* rasp; *(på rivjern)* grate.

rassia *sb* raid; *foreta en ~ i* raid.

rast *sb* halt, rest; *de holdt* ~ they made a halt. **raste** *vb* rest; make a halt.

rastløs *adj* restless. **rastløshet** *sb* restlessness.

ratifikasjon *sb* ratification. **ratifisere** *vb* ratify.

rate *sb* instalment.

ratt *sb* (steering-)wheel; *(i fly)* control wheel.

raut *sb* low. **raute** *vb* low, bellow.

rauv arse; *US* ass.

rav *sb* amber.

rave *vb* stagger; lurch, reel.

ravn *sb* raven.

razzia se *rassia*.

re *vb:* ~ *en seng* make a bed.

reagens|glass, ~rør *sb* test tube. **reagere** *vb* react; ~ *mot* react against; *på* react to.

reaksjon *sb* reaction; *min ~ på dette forslaget* my reaction to this proposal. **reaksjonær** *adj* reactionary. **reaktor** *sb* reactor.

real *adj* **1** *(grei, ærlig)* fair, honest; ~ *behandling* fair treatment; *en ~ kar* an honest fellow; **2** *(dugelig)* proper, thorough; *en ~ omgang med juling* a proper hiding. **realfag** *sb* science (and mathematics); *et* ~ a science subject. **realisasjon** *sb* realization. **realisasjonssalg** *sb* clearance sale. **realisere** *vb* **1** *(gjennomføre)* realize; carry out; *planen ble realisert* the plan was carried out; **2** *(selge)* realize. **realisme** *sb* realism. **realist** *sb* **1** *(motsatt f.eks drømmer, romantiker)* realist; **2** *(realfaglærer)* science teacher; **3** *(realfagstudent)* science student. **realistisk** *adj* realistic. **realitet** *sb* reality; *~er* facts, realities; *i ~en* really; in reality. **reallønn** *sb* real wages.

rebelsk *adj* **1** *(oppsetsig)* refractory; **2** *(ustyrlig)* unruly.

rebus *sb* picture puzzle; rebus.

red *sb (havn, kai)* roads *fl*; roadstead; *på ~en* in the roads.

redaksjon sb 1 *(kontoret)* editorial office; **2** *(personalet)* editorial staff; **3** *(redaktørstab)* editors; **4** *(redigering, utforming)* framing, wording. **redaksjonell** *adj* editorial. **redaksjons|artikkel** *sb* editorial. **~sekretær** *sb* assistant editor. **redaktør** *sb* editor.

redd *adj* frightened, scared; *(bare som predikatsord)* afraid; *(engstelig, ~ av seg)* timid; ~ *for (noe farlig)* afraid of; *han er ~ for hunden* he is afraid of the dog; *(bekymret for)* afraid for; anxious about; *bli* ~ get frightened/scared; take fright; *hun var ~ for barnet* she was afraid for/anxious about the child. **redde** *vb (berge)* save; *han ~t livet* he saved his life; *hun ~t barnet fra å drukne* she saved the child from drowning; *(~ fra fare, nød)* rescue; *passasjerene fra det synkende skipet ble ~t* the passengers from the sinking ship were rescued. **reddhare** *sb* coward, funk.

reddik *sb* radish.

reddsom *adj* dreadful, horrible.

rede A *adj* **1** *(parat)* ready; *han gjorde seg ~ til å starte* he made (himself) ready to start; **2** *(greie, klarhet) få ~ på* get to know; *gjøre ~ for* account for; give an account of; *ha ~ på* know about; *holde ~ på* keep in order; *(fig)* tell one thing from another; **B** *sb (fugle~ etc)* nest. **rede|gjøre (for)** *vb* account for; give an account of. **~gjørelse** *sb* account, explanation; *hun gav en ~ for begivenheten* she gave an account of the event. **redelig** *adj* honest, upright. **redelighet** *sb* honesty.

reder *sb* shipowner, owner. **rederi** *sb* shipping company.

redigere *vb* edit; *(formulere)* draft, formulate.

redning *sb* **1** rescue, rescuing; *~en av de overlevende var vanskelig* the rescuing of the survivors was difficult; **2** *(utvei)* hope, resort; *det er ingen* ~ there is no hope. **rednings|anker** *sb (fig)* sheet anchor. **~klokke** *sb petro etc* survival capsule. **~løst** *adv: ~løst fortapt* irretrievably lost. **~mannskap** *sb* rescue party. **~planke** *sb* last hope/resort. **~skøyte** *sb* rescue boat. **~utstyr** *sb* rescue equipment. **~vest** *sb* life jacket.

redsel *sb* fear, horror, terror; *krigens redsler* the

horrors of war. **redsels|full** *adj* dreadful, horrible; awful; *han sier de mest ~fulle ting* he says the most awful things. **~slagen** *adj* horror-struck/-stricken.

redskap *sb* tool; *(instrument)* instrument; *(især kjøkken~)* utensil.

reduksjon *sb* reduction. **redusere** *vb* reduce.

reell *adj* **1** *(virkelig)* real; **2** *(redelig)* fair; *~ behandling* fair treatment.

referanse *sb* reference; *oppgi som ~* give as (a) reference.

referat *sb* account, report. **referent** *sb* reporter. **referere** *vb* report; give an account of.

refleks *sb* reflex. **refleksbevegelse** *sb* reflex movement. **refleksiv** reflexive. **refleksjon** *sb* reflection. **reflektere** *vb* reflect; *~ over* reflect (up)on; *~ på (annonse)* reply to; *(på tilbud)* consider, entertain; *~ på tilbudet* consider the offer.

reform *sb* reform. **reformasjonen** *sb* reformation. **reformator** *sb* reformer. **reformere** *vb* reform; *den reformerte kirke* the Reformed Church. **reform|iver** *sb* reformatory zeal. **~venn** *sb* reformist. **~vennlig** *adj* reformist.

refreng *adj* chorus, refrain; *de sang med i ~et* they joined in the chorus.

refse *vb* **1** *(straffe)* chastise, punish; **2** *(irettesette)* reprimand. **refselse** *sb* **1** *(straff)* chastisement, punishment; **2** *(irettesettelse)* reprimand.

refundere *vb* refund, reimburse.

refusere *vb* refuse, reject. **refusjon** *sb* **1** *(tilbakebetaling)* repayment, reimbursement; **2** *(avslag)* refusal, rejection.

regatta *sb* regatta.

regel *sb* **1** rule; *en fast ~* a fixed rule; *etter faste regler* according to fixed rules; *et unntak fra ~en* an exception to the rule; *i ~en, som ~* as a rule; generally, usually; *vi rettet oss etter reglene* we followed/obeyed the rules; **2** *(forskrift)* regulation; *de holdt seg til reglene* they kept to the regulations. **regel|bunden**, **~messig** **1** *adj* regular; *~messige mellomrom* regular intervals; **2** *adv* regularly; *han går ~messig i kirken* he goes to church regularly. **~messighet** *sb* regularity. **~rett** *adj* regular.

regent *sb* **1** *(monark)* sovereign, ruler; **2** *(midlertidig ~)* regent. **regentskap** *sb* regency. **regi** *sb* stage management; *(iscenesettelse)* direction; production, staging. **regime** *sb* regime, rule; government. **regiment** *sb* regiment.

region *sb* region; *i de øvre ~er* in the upper regions. **regional** *adj* regional. **regionalplanlegging** *sb* regional planning.

regissør stage manager; producer; *(film~)* film director.

register *sb* **1** *(alfabetisk innholdsliste)* index; **2** *(toneleie)* register. **registrere** *vb* register, record.

regjere *vb* **1** *(styre)* govern, rule; *landet ~s av ansvarlige ministere* the country is governed by responsible ministers; **2** *(herske, være konge)* reign. **regjerende** *adj* governing, reigning. **regjering** *sb* **1** government, ministry; **2** *(statsrådene som gruppe)* (the) cabinet; **3** *(regjeringstid)* reign; *under Georg 3s ~* during the reign of George III. **regjerings|dyktig** *adj: ~dyktig flertall* working majority. **~krise** *sb* cabinet crisis. **~makt** *sb: ha ~makten* be in office. **~parti** *sb* the Government Party; the party in power. **~sjef** *sb* premier; prime minister. **~skifte** *sb* change of government. **~tid** *sb* reign. **~tilhenger** *sb* supporter of the government.

regle *sb (barne~)* jingle; nursery rhyme.

reglement *sb* regulations *fl*; *etter ~et* according to regulations. **reglementert** *adj* prescribed, regular.

regn *sb* rain; *det ser ut til å bli ~* it looks like rain; *kraftig ~* heavy rain; *lett ~* fine rain; *øsende ~* pouring rain. **regnbue** *sb* rainbow. **regnbue|ørret** *sb* rainbow trout. **~hinne** *sb* iris. **regn|byge** *sb* shower. **~dråpe** *sb* raindrop.

regne *vb* **A** *(om regn)* rain; *det ~r voldsomt* it is pouring down/raining hard; **B 1** *(foreta utregninger)* figure, reckon; do sums/arithmetic; *lese, skrive og ~* read, write, and reckon; **2** *(løse regneoppgaver)* work out; *~ et regnestykke* work out a problem in arithmetic; **3** *(uttrykk)* **~ (med) blant** consider (count, number, reckon) among; *jeg ~r ham blant mine venner* I count (include, number) him among my friends; **~ for** consider; regard as; *jeg ~r det for en stor ulykke* I regard that as a great disaster; **~ med** 1 *(inkludere)* include; 2 *(forutsette, gå ut fra)* take for granted; 3 *(stole på)* count (depend, rely) on; **~ opp** enumerate; **~ over** *(kontrollere)* check; *(gjøre et overslag)* calculate. **regne|ark** *sb data* spreadsheet. **~bok** *sb* arithmetic book. **~feil** *sb* miscalculation. **~lærer** *sb* teacher of arithmetic; arithmetic master/teacher. **~maskin** *sb* calculator; calculating machine. **~stav** *sb* slide rule. **~stykke** *sb* arithmetical problem; sum.

regn|frakk *sb* raincoat; mackintosh; *dgl* mac. **~full** *adj* rainy, wet.

regning *sb* **1** *(nota)* bill; *en stor ~* a heavy bill; *hun betalte ~en for de nye klærne* she paid the bill for the new clothes; **2** *(faget ~)* arithmetic; *han er flink i ~* he is good at arithmetic; **3** *(uttrykk)* **for** *egen ~* at one's own expense; on one's own account; **gjøre ~ med** count/reckon on; *gjøre ~ uten vert* reckon without one's host; **holde ~ med** keep count of; *en* **strek i ~en** an unforeseen obstacle; *sette* **på ~en** put down/charge in the bill; *skriv det på min ~* charge it to my account. **regningsbud** *sb* bill collector.

regn|kappe *sb* raincoat; mackintosh; *dgl* mac. **~mengde** *sb* rainfall.

regnskap *sb* account(s); *de må gjøre ~ for hver penny de har brukt* they will have to account for every penny they have spent; *vi førte alltid ~* we always kept accounts. **regnskaps|bok** *sb* account book. **~fører** *sb* accountant. **~føring, ~førsel** *sb* accounting, accountancy; keeping of accounts,.

regn|skur *sb* shower. **~sky** *sb* rain cloud. **~skyll** *sb* downpour. **~slag** *sb* rain-cape. **~tid** *sb* rainy season. **~vær** *sb* rainy weather; *det er ~vær* it is raining/rainy. **~værsdag** *sb* rainy/wet day.

regulativ *sb (lønns~)* scale of wages. **regulator** *sb* regulator. **regulerbar** *adj* adjustable. **regulere** *vb* adjust, regulate. **regulering** *sb* adjustment, regulation. **regulær** *adj* regular.

rehabilitering *sb* rehabilitation. **rehabilitere** *vb* rehabilitate.

reim *sb* strap.

rein *sb (reinsdyr)* reindeer.

reinkarnasjon *sb* reincarnation.

reip *sb* rope.

reir se *rede B*.

reise A I *sb* **1** *(især lengre ~)* journey; *de er på ~* they are on a journey; *god ~!* a pleasant journey! *hun la ut på en ~* she went out on a journey; **2** *(lengre sjø~)* voyage; *en ~ rundt jorden* a journey/voyage round the world; *en ~ til Det fjerne østen* a voyage to the Far East; **3** *(især kortere tur)* trip; **4** *(kortere overfart)* passage; **5** *(vidstrakte ~r)* travels; *på mine ~r* during my travels; **6** *(turist~, rund~)* tour; **II** *vb* **1** *(~ til et bestemt sted, ~ på en bestemt måte)* go; *han reiste til Italia* he went to Italy; *vi ~r alltid med tog* we always go by train; **2** *(dra av gårde)* leave, start; set out; *når ~r du?* when are you leaving? **3** *(være på ~)* travel; *hun ~r mye* she travels a lot; **B** *vb* **1** *(heve, løfte)* raise; *han reiste hodet* he raised his head; **2** *(føre/sette opp)* erect; put/set up; *stigen ble reist* the ladder was put up; **3** *~ seg* get up; rise (to one's feet); stand up; *alle reiste seg da kongen kom inn* everybody got up when the King entered; *håret reiste seg på hans hode* his hears stood on end. **reise|byrå** *sb* travel/tourist agency. **~ferdig** *adj* ready to start. **~følge** *sb* **1** *(medreisende)* travelling companions; **2** *(gruppe av turister)* party of tourists. **~fører** *sb* guide; *(om bok)* guide (book). **~gods** *sb (bagasje)* luggage; *(ekspedert bagasje)* registered luggage; *~godsekspedisjon* luggage room/office. **~håndbok** *sb* guide (book).

~kamerat *sb* travelling companion. **~kledd** *adj* dressed for the journey. **~leder** *sb* conductor (of a party of travellers); guide. **reisende** *sb* traveller; *de ~* the travellers. **reise|pass** *sb: gi noen ~* send somebody packing. **~penger** *sb* travelling funds. **~pledd** *sb* travelling rug. **~radio** *sb* portable radio. **~rute** *sb* itinerary; (travelling) route. **~selskap** *sb* party of tourists. **~sjekk** *sb* traveller's cheque. **~skrivemaskin** *sb* portable typewriter. **~tid** *sb* travelling time. **~vekkerur** *sb* travelling alarm clock.

reisning *sb* **1** *(opprør)* rebellion, rising; **2** *(holdning)* carriage.

reisverk *sb* timber-frame.

rekapitulere *vb* recapitulate, sum up. **rekapitulering** *sb* recapitulation; summing up.

reke A *sb (skalldyr)* shrimp; **B** *vb (drive)* ramble, roam; knock about.

rekke A I *sb* **1** *(rad)* row; *en hus~* a row of houses; **2** *(antall)* number; *en år~* a number of years; **3** *(sammenhørende ~, serie)* series; *en forelesnings~* a series of lectures; **4** *(mat)* progression; *aritmetisk/geometrisk ~* arithmetical/geometrical progression; **5** *(reling)* rail; **6** *(uttrykk)* **i første ~** in the first row; *(først og fremst)* above all; first and foremost; first of all; *(blant de beste)* in the front rank; **II** *vb* **1** *(levere)* hand, pass; *han rakte meg kniven* he handed me the knife; *hun rakte meg saltet* she passed me the salt; **2** *(nå)* reach; *jeg ~r ikke opp til den øverste hyllen* I cannot reach up to the top shelf; **3** *(komme tidsnok til)* catch; *US* reach; *rakk de toget?* did they catch the train? **4** *(ha tid til)* find/have time to; **5** (uttrykk) **~ en hånden** offer somebody the hand; **~ opp hånden** put up one's hand; **~ tunge til** put out one's tongue to; **C** *vb: ~ opp (strikketøy etc)* unravel. **rekke|følge** *sb* order; *også data* sequence; *i ~følge* in succession; *(etter tur)* by/in turns; *i alfabetisk rekke~* in alphabetical order. **~hus** *sb* terrace house; *US* row house; *ofte* semidetached/undetached house. **~vidde** *sb* reach; *innen(for) ~vidde* within reach; *utenfor min ~vidde* beyond my reach. **rekkverk** *(på bro, skip etc)* rail; *(trappegelender)* banisters *fl*.

reklamasjon *sb (klage)* complaint. **reklame** *sb* advertising; *(~annonse)* advertisement; *gjøre ~ for* advertise. **reklame|byrå** *sb* advertising agency. **~film** *sb* screen advertisement; publicity film. **~kampanje** *sb* publicity campaign. **reklamere** *vb* **1** *(gjøre reklame (for))* advertise; **2** *(klage)* complain; make a claim/complaint.

rekognosere *vb* reconnoitre. **rekognosering** *sb* reconnaissance.

rekommandere *vb* register; *et rekommandert brev* a registered letter.

rekonstruere *vb* reconstruct. **rekonstruksjon** *sb* reconstruction.

rekonvalesens *sb* concalescence. **rekonvalesent** *sb* convalescent.

rekord *sb* record; *det slår alle ~er* it beats all records; *hun har ~en* she holds the record. **rekordjag** *sb* craze for record-breaking.

rekreasjon *sb* **1** *(hvileferie)* convalescene; ≈ holiday; *dra til Spania på ~* go to Spain for a holiday; **2** *(atspredelse, fornøyelse)* recreation. **rekreasjonshjem** *sb* convalescent/rest home. **rekreasjonssted** *sb* health resort.

rekrutt *sb* recruit. **rekruttere** *vb* recruit.

rektangel *sb* rectangle. **rektangulær** *adj* rectangular.

rektor *sb* head (og head|master, -mistress, -teacher); *US* principal.

rekved *sb* driftwood.

rekvirere *vb* order; *(mil)* requisition. **rekvisisjon** *sb* requisition. **rekvisitt** *sb* requisite; *~er, rekvisita* accessories; *(teater~)* properties, props.

relasjon *sb* relation. **relativ** *adj* relative; *~t pronomen* relative pronoun. **relativitet** *sb* relativity.

relé *sb* relay.

relevans *sb* relevance. **relevant** *adj* relevant.

relieff *sb* relief; *sette i ~* throw in relief.

religion *sb* religion; *(tro)* faith; *(fag i skolen)* scripture; religious instruction. **religions|frihet** *sb* freedom of religion; religious liberty. **~krig** *sb* religious war. **~undervisning** *sb* religious instruction. **religiøs** *adj* religious. **religiøsitet** *sb* religiousness; *(fromhet)* piety.

relikvie *sb* relic.

reling *sb (båtripe)* gunwale, rail; *lene seg over ~en* lean over the rail.

remedier *sb fl* things, paraphernalia.

reminisens *sb* reminiscence.

remis *sb* draw; drawn game.

remplasere *vb* replace.

remse *sb* strip.

ren *adj* **1** *(ikke skitten)* clean; *en ~ skjorte* a clean shirt; **2** *(ublandet)* pure, unadulterated; *~t vann* pure water; **3** *(fig: ~ og skjær)* pure, sheer; *~t tøv* pure nonsense; *~ uvitenhet* sheer ignorance; *ved et ~t tilfelle* by sheer accident; **4** *(fig: blott og bar)* mere; *hun er ~e barnet* she is a mere child; **5** *(uttrykk) ~ fortjeneste* clear profit; *~ sannhet* plain truth; *~t trav* regular trot; *bringe på det ~e* ascertain; clear up; *gjøre ~t* clean, wash; *gjøre ~t bord* make a clean sweep of it; *med ~e ord* in so many words; bluntly, plainly; *det var ~e ord for pengene* that was plain speaking; *være på det ~e med at* be aware that; realize that; *det er på det ~e at* it is a fact that. **rendyrke** *vb* cultivate.

renessanse *sb* renaissance; *under ~n* at/during the Renaissance.

ren|gjøre *vb* clean. **~gjøring** *sb* (house-)cleaning. **~gjøringskone** *sb* charwoman. **~het** *sb* cleanness, purity. **~hold** *sb* cleaning. **~holdsverk** *sb* sanitation/scavenging department.

renke *sb* intrigue, plot, wiles. **renke|full** *adj* crafty, wily. **~smed** *sb* intriguer, schemer.

renn *sb* run; *(kappløping etc også)* race.

renne 1 *sb* race, sluice; flume, lead; *(især transport~ etc)* chute, shoot; **2** *vb (fare, løpe)* run; *(flyte)* flow, run; *~ hodet mot veggen* run one's head against a (brick) wall; *~ over* overflow; flow/run over. **renne|løkke** *sb* noose. **~stein** *sb* gutter.

renning *sb (i vev)* warp.

renommé *sb* reputation.

renons *sb (i kortspill)* void; *gjøre seg ~ i spar* void one's hand of spades. **renonsere** *vb: ~ på* do without; give up; renounce.

renovasjon *sb* scavenging. **renovasjons|arbeider** *sb* dustman, scavenger. **~vesen** *sb* sanitation/scavenger department. **~vogn** *sb* dustcart.

rense *vb* clean; *(~ svært grundig)* cleanse; *(~ luft, væske etc)* purify; *legen ~t såret* the doctor cleansed the wound; *han ~t seg for mistanken* he cleared himself of the suspicion. **renselse** *sb* cleaning, purification. **renseri** *sb: han sendte tøyet til ~et* he sent his clothes to the (dry-)cleaner's.

renske *vb* clean, cleanse. Se også *rense.*

renslig *adj* cleanly. **renslighet** *sb* cleanliness; *~ er en dyd* ≈ cleanliness is next to godliness.

rente *sb* interest; *~r* interest; *de tok 4 % ~* they charged four per cent interest; *han betalte 6 % ~ av lånet* he paid six per cent interest on the loan; *årlig ~* annual interest. **rente|fot** *adj* rate of interest. **~fri** *adj* free of interest. **rentesrente** *sb* compound interest; *med renter og ~* at compound interest.

reol *sb* shelves *fl*; *(bok~)* bookcase; bookshelves *fl*; *i ~en* on the shelves.

reorganisere *vb* reorganize. **reorganisering** *sb* reorganization.

reparasjon *sb* **1** repair(s); *skipet er gått i dokk for ~* the ship has docked for repairs; *taket trenger ~* the roof is in need of repair; *være til/under ~* be under repairs; **2** *(mindre ~ av sykkel, tøy etc; lapping, stopping)* mending. **reparasjonsverksted** *sb* repair shop; *(for biler)* garage. **reparatør** *sb* repairer. **reparere** *vb* repair; *(~ sykkel, tøy etc; lappe, stoppe)* mend.

repertoar *sb* repertory, repertoire.

repetere *vb* **1** *(gjenta)* repeat; **2** *(~ pensum)* revise; *(intransitivt)* do revision; **3** *(prøve teaterrolle etc)* rehearse. **repetisjon** *sb* **1** repetition; **2** revision; **3** *(rolleprøve)* rehearsal.

replikk *sb* **1** *(svar)* reply, retort; **2** *(i skuespill)* lines *fl*; speech.

reportasje *sb* report; *(i radio)* running commentary. **reporter** *sb* reporter.

represalier *sb fl: ta ~ mot* make/resort to reprisals against.

representant *sb* representative. **representasjon** *sb* representation. **representativ** *adj: ~ for* representative of. **representere** *vb* represent.

reprimande *sb* reprimand; *gi en en ~* reprimand him/her.

reprise *sb (av film, teaterstykke)* revival; *(i radio)* repeat.

reproduksjon *sb* reproduction. **reprodusere** *vb* reproduce.

republikaner *sb* Republican. **republikansk** *adj* Republican. **republikk** *sb* republic.

resepsjon *sb (på hotell)* reception desk.

resept *sb* prescription; *det fås bare på ~* you cannot get it without a prescription.

reservasjon *sb* reservation, reserve. **reservat** *sb* reserve; *(særlig US)* reservation; *indiansk ~, indianer~* Indian reservation. **reserve** *vb* reserve; *bankens ~r* the bank's reserves; *ha i ~* have in reserve. **reserve|dekk** *sb* spare tyre/*US* tire. **~del** *sb* spare part. **~hjul** *sb* spare wheel. **~lege** *sb* assistant physician/surgeon. **reservere** *vb* **1** reserve; set aside; *data* dedicate; *jeg reserverte (en) plass for henne* I reserved a seat for her; **2** *(forutbestille) (i teater)* book; *(på hotell)* **3** *~ seg mot* guard against. **reservert** *adj* reserved; *(forsiktig)* cautious. **reservoar** *sb* reservoir.

residens *sb* residence. **residere** *vb* reside.

resignasjon *sb* resignation. **resignere** *vb* resign oneself to one's fate.

resiprok *adj* reciprocal.

resirkulere *vb* recycle. **resirkulering** *sb* recycling.

resolusjon *sb* resolution.

resolutt *adj (besluttsom)* determined, resolute; *(uten å nøle)* prompt, quick.

resonans *sb* resonance.

resong *sb (fornuft)* reason, sense; *det er det ingen ~ i* there is no sense in that; *han ville ikke ta mot ~* he would not listen to reason. **resonnement** *sb* argumentation, reasoning. **resonnere** *vb* argue, reason.

respekt *sb* respect. **respektabel** *adj* respectable. **respektere** *vb* respect. **respektinngytende** *adj* awe-inspiring. **respektiv** *adj* respective. **respektive** *adv* respectively. **respektløs** *adj* disrespectful.

respitt *sb* respite.

ressurser *sb fl* resources.

rest *sb* **1** *(de/det øvrige)* the rest; *noen var utlendinger, ~en var britiske* some were foreigners, the rest were British; **2** *(de/det som er igjen)* the rest; the remainder; *han tilbrakte ~en av livet i (et) kloster* he spent the rest/the remainder of his life in a monastery; **3** *(levning)* remains, remnant; *~ene etter et måltid* the remains/remnants of a meal.

restanse *sb* arrears.

restaurant *sb* **1** restaurant; *på en ~* at/in a restaurant; **2** *(spisesal på hotell)* dining-room; **3** *(jernbane~)* refreshment room. **restauratør** *sb* restaurant-keeper.

restaurere *vb* restore. **restaurering** *sb* restoration.

resterende *adj* left over; remaining.

restituere *vb* restore (to health).

restriksjon *sb* restriction. **restriktiv** *adj* restrictive.

resultat *sb* **1** result; *~et var over forventning* the result was beyond expectation; *med godt ~* with good results; **2** *(virkning)* effect; *ett ~ av krigen var at...* one effect of the war was that... **resultere** *vb* result; *~ i* result in.

resymé *sb* summary. **resymere** *vb* summarize; sum up.

retning *sb* **1** direction; *i alle ~er* in all directions; **2** *(henseende)* respect, way; *noe i den ~* something of that kind.

retningsviser *sb (på bil)* direction indicator; trafficator.

retorikk *sb* rhetoric. **retorisk** *adj* rhetorical.

retrett *sb* retreat.

rett I *adj* **1** *(ikke bøyd/kroket)* straight; *en ~ linje/rygg* a straight line/back; **2** *(passende, riktig)* proper, right; *alt er på sin ~e plass* everything is in its proper place; *den ~e* the right person; *det ~e* the right thing; *rettere sagt* or rather; **3** *(rettmessig)* rightful; *den ~e eier* the rightful owner; **II** *adv* **1** *(direkte)* straight; *~ vest* due west; *gå ~ frem* walk straight on; *jeg sa det ~ opp i ansiktet på ham* I told him so to his face; *det er ~ og slett løgn* it is a downright lie; **2** *(riktig)* properly, rightly; *det gjorde du ~* **i** you were quite right; *om jeg husker ~* if I remember rightly; **3** *(like)* just; *~ før jul* just before Christmas; *~ utenfor huset* just outside the house; **4** *~ som det er/var (plutselig)* all at once; all of a sudden; *(alt i ett)* every now and again.

rett *sb* **A 1** *(del av et måltid)* course; *en middag med tre ~er* a three-course dinner; **2** *(mat~)* dish; **B 1** *(rettighet)* right; *~en til tronen* the right to the throne; **2** *(domstol)* court (of justice); law-court; *i ~en* in court; *(i rettslokalet)* in the court; **3** *(uttrykk) de fikk ~* they proved right; *du har ~* you are right; *hun skulle med ~e vært dronning* by right(s) she should have been queen; *jeg har ~* I am right; *jeg må gi dem ~* I must admit that they are right; *lov og ~* law and order; *med ~e* by right(s); justly, rightly; *med hvilken ~* by what right.

rette I *sb (rettside)* right side; **II** *vb* **1** *(~ ut)* straighten; *hun ~t ryggen* she straightened her back; **2** *(gi bestemt retning)* direct turn; aim; *han ~t geværet mot tyven* he aimed his gun at the thief; *hun ~t blikket mot den fremmede* she directed/turned her eyes to the stranger; **3** *(korrigere)* correct; *(~ oppgaver)* mark; **4** *(uttrykk) han ~t seg etter reglene* he followed the rules; *hun ~t et spørsmål til meg* she put a question to me; *jeg ~t meg etter deres ønske* I complied with their wish. **rettelse** *sb* correcting, correction; *jeg foretok/gjorde en ~* I made a correction.

retter|gang *sb* legal procedure. **~sted** *sb* place of execution. **rettesnor** *sb* example, guide, rule.

rett|ferdig *adj* just; *en ~ sak* a just cause. **~ferdighet** *sb* justice. **~ferdighetssans** *sb* sense of justice.

rettighet *sb* right; *(særrett)* privilege. **rettighetshaver** *sb* possessor of a right; rightful claimant/owner; *petro etc* concessionary.

rett|lede *vb* direct, guide. **~ledning** *sb* guidance. **~linjet** *adj* rectilineal; *(fig)* honest, straightforward, upright. **~messig** *adj* lawful; *en ~ arving* a lawful/rightful heir.

retts|avgjørelse *sb* court decision. **~belæring** *sb* direction to the jury. **~beskyttelse** *sb* legal protection. **~bevissthet** *sb* sense of justice. **~gyldig** *adj* valid, legal.

rettside *sb* right side.

rett|sindig, ~skaffen *adj* upright, honourable.

rettskjennelse *sb* dicision/finding by the court.

rett|skrivning *sb* orthography, spelling. **~skrivningsfeil** *sb* spelling mistake. **~skrivningsreform** *sb* spelling reform. **~skrivningregel** *sb* spelling rule.

rettslig *adj* judicial, legal.

retts|lærd *sb* jurist. **~medisin** *sb* forensic medicine. **~medisinsk** *adj* medico-legal. **~sak** *sb* case. **~sal** *sb* court(-room). **~sikkerhet** *sb* law and order. **~stridig** *adj* illegal, unlawful. **~vesen** *sb* administration of justice.

rettroende *adj* orthodox. **rettvinklet** *adj* rectangular, right-angled.

retur *sb* return; *varene kom i ~* the goods were returned; *vi sendte varene i ~* we returned the goods. **returbillett** *sb* return ticket. **returnere** *vb* return.

retusjere *vb* retouch.

reumatiker, reumatisk, reumatisme se *revmatiker etc.*

rev *sb* **A** *(dyr)* fox; **B** *(skjær)* reef; **C** *(i seil)* reef; *ta ~ i seilene (også fig)* take in a reef.

revaksinere *vb* revaccinate. **revaksinering** *sb* revaccination.

revansje *sb* revenge. **revansjekamp** *sb* return match.

reve *sb (seil)* reef.

revelje *sb* reveille.

reve|avl *sb* fox farming. **~gård** *sb* fox farm. **~saks** *sb* fox trap. **~strek** *sb* hanky-panky; sharp practice/trick.

revidere *vb* **1** *(endre)* revise; *han reviderte sin oppfatning* he revised his opinion; **2** *(~ regnskap)* audit, check. **revisjon** *sb* revision; *(regnskaps~)* audit(ing). **revisor** *sb* auditor, accountant; *statsautorisert ~* chartered/*US* certified accountant.

revmatiker *sb* rheumatic. **revmatisk** *adj* rheumatic. **revmatisme** *sb* rheumatism.

revne 1 *sb* crack; *en ~ i fjellet* a crevice in the rock; **2** *vb* burst, crack, split, tear; *hansker ~r ofte* gloves often split; *det er (meg) revnende likegyldig* I couldn't care less; I don't care a damn.

revolusjon *sb* revolution. **revolusjonere** *vb* revolutionize. **revolusjonær** *sb* revolutionary.

revolver *sb* revolver; *han går alltid med ~* he always carries a revolver.

revy *sb* **1** *(teater~)* revue; **2** *(troppe~)* review; *la passere ~ (fig)* pass in review.

ri A *sb (anfall, tokt)* attack, fit, spell; **B** *vb (~ på hest etc)* ride (on horseback); go on horseback; *de red en tur* they went for a ride; *hun red på en gammel hest* she rode (on) an old horse.

ribbe A *sb* **1** *(på slakt)* rib; **2** *(~vegg)* wall-bar; **B** *vb* **1** *(~ fugl)* pluck; **2** *(plyndre)* rob, strip. **ribbein** *sb* rib. **ribbevegg** *sb* wall-bars, ribstalls.

ridder *sb* knight. **ridderlig** *adj* chivalrous. **ridderlighet** *sb* chivalry. **riddervesen** *sb* chivalry.

ride|bukser *sb* riding-breeches. **~hest** *sb* saddle-horse. **ridende** *adj* mounted; *~ politi* mounted police; *de kom ~* the came riding/on horseback.

rifle *sb (gevær)* rifle. **riflet(e)** *adj* fluted, grooved.

rift *sb* **1** *(i tøy)* rent, tear; **2** *(i huden)* scratch; **3** *(etterspørsel)* demand; *det er stor ~ om boken* the book is in great demand; there is a great demand for the book.

rigg *sb* rig, rigging; *(olje~)* rig; *bore~* drilling rig.

rigorøs *adj* rigorous, severe, strict.

rik *adj* rich, wealthy; *de rike* the rich; *den rike* the rich man/woman; *en ~* a rich person; *en ~ familie* a wealthy family; *han ble ~* he got rich; *England er ~t på kull* England is rich in coal. **rikdom** *sb* **1** riches *(fl)*; **2** *(velstand)* affluence, wealth; **3** *(formue)* fortune; **4** *(overflod)* plenty, wealth; affluence. **rikdomskilde** *sb* source of wealth.

rike *sb* **1** *(keiser~, verdens~)* empire; *Romerriket* the Roman Empire; **2** *(konge~)* kingdom; *Guds ~* the Kingdom of God.

rikelig *adj* **1** *(mer enn nok)* abundant, plentiful; **2** *(raus)* liberal; a liberal portion/reward. **rikfolk** *sb koll* rich people; the rich. **rikholdig** *adj* rich, abundant, copious.

rikke *vb* move.

riks|advokat *sb* Attorney General. **~arkiv** *sb* Public Record Office. **~dag** *sb* parliament. **~rett** *sb: stille for ~* impeach. **~rettsanklage** impeachment. **~telefon** *sb* trunk/long distance call. **~trygdeverk** *sb* national insurance system.

riktig I *adj* **1** right; *gjøre det riktige* do the right thing; **2** *(feilfri)* correct; *svaret ditt er ikke ~* your answer is not correct; **3** *(korrekt, passende)* correct, proper; *~ antrekk* proper dress; **4** *(sann)* true; *det er ~ at han er død* it is true that he is dead; **5** *(virkelig, ekte)* real; **II** *adv* **1** correctly, right; (in) the right way; *du gjettet ~* you guessed right; *han gjorde det på den ~e måten* he did it the right way; *vi har alltid regnet ~* we have always calculated correctly; **2** quite, very: *det er ~ kaldt i dag* it is very cold today; *jeg forstår ikke ~* I do not quite understand; *jeg liker dem ~ godt* I like them very well. **riktighet** *sb* correctness; *(sannhet)* truth; *det har sin ~* it is quite correct; it is true/a fact. **riktignok** *adv* to be sure; *~ er han dum, men...* to be sure he is stupid, but ...

rim *sb* **A** *(rimfrost)* hoar-frost, rime; **B** *(av ord)* rhyme. **rime** *vb* **A** *(bli rimfrosset)* rime; **B 1** rhyme; *~ på* rhyme with; **2** *(passe, stemme)* agree.

rimelig *adj* fair, reasonable; *det er bare ~ at...* it is only fair/reasonable that...; *en ~ pris* a fair price. **rimelighet** *sb: innenfor ~ens grenser* within the limits of reason; *etter all ~* in all probability. **rimeligvis** *adv* probably.

rimfrost *sb* hoar-frost, rime.

ring *sb* **1** ring; *han går med ~* he wears a ring; **2** *(sirkel)* circle; *de stod i ring* they stood in a circle; **3** *(bil~)* tyre; *US* tire. **ringbrynje** *sb* shirt of (chain) mail.

ringe A *adj (ubetydelig)* slight, small; *ingen ~ere enn* no less a person than; *uten ~ste vanskelighet* without the slightest difficulty; **B** *vb* **1** *(om lyd)* ring; *det ~r* the bell rings; *han ringte på* he rang the bell; *hun ringte til meg* she rang me up; *telefonen ringte* the telephone rang; **2** *(danne ring)* form a ring; *~ inn* encircle, surround. **ringe|akt** *sb* contempt; *føle ~ for* feel contempt for. **~akte** *vb* despise; *tale ~aktende om* disparage; speak contemptuously of. **~apparat** *sb* (electric) bell. **~knapp** *sb* bellpush. **~ledning** *sb* bell wire. **ringfinger** *sb* ring-finger, third finger. **ringing** *sb* ringing; *(et enkelt ringesignal)* ring.

ring|perm *sb* ring leaf book; *US* loose-leaf binder. **~rev** *sb* **A** *(atoll)* atoll; **B** *(luring)* sly fox. **~spill** *sb* quoits *fl.*

rip(e) *sb (båt~)* gunwale.

ripe *sb/vb* scratch.

rippe *vb: ~ opp i gamle skandaler* rake up old scandals; *la oss ikke ~ opp i det* let bygones be bygones.

rips *sb* red currant. **ripsbusk** *sb* red currant bush.

ris *sb* **A** *(kornslaget)* rice; *japansk ~* puffed rice; **B 1** *(småkvist)* twigs; **2** *(bjerke~, som strafferedskap)* birch (rod); *få ~* get a birching; **3** *(potet~)* (potato) foliage.

rise A *sb (kjempe)* giant; **B** *vb (gi ris)* birch. **risengryn** *sb* rice. **risengrynsgrøt, risgrøt** *sb* rice pudding.

risikabel *adj* hazardous, risky. **risikere** *vb* **1** *(sette på spill)* risk; *han risikerte livet* he risked his life; **2** *(utsette seg for)* risk; run the risk of; *vi kan ikke ~ det* we cannot risk that; *vi ~r å bli oppdaget* we risk being discovered; we run the risk of being discovered. **risiko** *sb* risk; *hun tok/løp en stor ~* she took/ran a big risk; *på egen ~* at one's own risk.

risle *vb* run; *(om lyden)* murmur.

risp *sb* slash, slit, tear. **rispe** *vb* slash, slit, tear.

riss *sb (skisse)* sketch. **risse** *vb (~ opp)* outline, sketch; *(~ inn med fint redskap)* carve, cut. **rissefjær** *sb* drawing-pen.

rist *sb* **A 1** grating, grid; **2** *(steke~)* gridiron, grill; *kjøtt stekt på ~* grilled meat; **3** *(fotskraper)* scraper; **B** *verken ~ eller ro* no rest; **C** se *vrist.*

riste *vb* **A** *(steke)* grill; *US* broil; *(~ i ovn/panne)* roast; *(om brød)* toast; *~t brød* (a piece of) toast; **B 1** *(bevege frem og tilbake)* shake; *han ~t treet* he shook the tree; *hun ~t på hodet* she shook her head; **2** *(dirre, skake)* shiver, tremble. Se også *ryste.*

ritt *sb* ride; *et tre dagers ~* a three day's ride.

ritual *sb* ritual. **rituell** *adj* ritual.

riv *adv: ~ ruskende gal* stark staring mad.

rival, rivalinne *sb* rival.

rive *sb* rake.

rive *vb* **1** *(flenge)* rip, tear; *~ i stykker* tear to pieces; tear up; *jeg rev hull i buksen min* I tore a hole in my trousers; **2** *(rykke)* tear; *blomstene var revet opp med roten* the flowers had been torn up by the roots; **3** *(snappe)* snatch; *hun rev til seg lommeboken min* she snatched my wallet; **4** *(~ på rivjern)* grate, rasp; **5** *(uttrykk)* **~ av** *seg vitser* crack jokes; **~ i** *nesen* tickle the nose; **~ i** *på (spandere)* stand; **~ i** *på seg selv* treat oneself to; *han rev i middag på meg* he stood me a dinner; **~ med** carry away; sweep along; *hun ble revet med av mengden* she was swept along by the crowd; *jeg ble revet med av følelsene mine* I was carried away by my feelings; **~ ned** pull down; **~ over ende** knock down/over; **~ seg løs** *(fra)* break away (from); **~ til seg** seize; possess oneself of; *~ til seg makten* usurp the power *bli* **revet bort** *(om varer)* be snatched off; sell like hot cakes; *(dø brått)* be carried/snatched off. **rivende** *adj (om fart)* tearing; *(om strøm etc)* rapid; *~ avsetning* rapid sale; *~ galt* completely wrong; *~ utvikling* rapid development/progress. **rivjern** *sb* grater. **rivninger** *sb fl (strid, uro)* friction.

ro A *sb* **1** *(hvile)* rest; *pasienten trenger ~* the patient needs rest; **2** *(fred, uforstyrrethet)* peace; *få arbeids~* get peace to work; **3** *(stillhet)* quiet, stillness; *de levde i fred og ~* they lived in peace and quiet; **4** *(uttrykk)* **falle til ~** calm down; **gå til ~** *(legge seg)* go to bed; **i ~ og mak** at one's leisure; **slå seg til ~** settle down; *slå seg til ~ med* resign oneself to, rest content with; **ta det med ~** take it easy; **B** *vb* **1** row, pull; *~ en boat* row a boat; *~ kraftig* pull hard; **2** *fig: ~ seg i land* try to back out; crawfish; *~ seg for langt ut* get/go out of one's depth.

robber *sb (i spill)* rubber.

robot *sb* robot.

robust *adj* hardy, robust.

robåt *sb* rowboat, rowing-boat.

roe A *sb* beet, turnip; *sukker~* sugar-beet; **B** *vb: ~ seg (ned)* calm down; settle down; become quiet.

roer *sb* oarsman, rower.

roesukker *sb* beet sugar.

rogaffel *sb* rowlock.

rogn *sb* **A** *(tre)* rowan; **B** *(fiske~)* roe; *gytt ~* spawn; *torske~* cod's roe. **rognebær** rowan(-berry).

rojalisme *sb* royalism. **rojalist** *sb* royalist. **rojalistisk** *adj* royalist.

rokk *sb* **A** *(spinne~)* spinning-wheel; **B** *(sjø~)* sea spray.

rokke A *sb (fisk)* skate; **B** *vb* **1** *(flytte, rikke)* budge; **2** *(svekke)* shake; *de kunne ikke ~ ved hennes tro* they could not shake her faith.

roklubb *sb* boat club; rowing club.

rolig *adj, adv* **1** *(uten bevegelse)* quiet, still; *~ sjø* a quiet sea; *han holdt seg ~* he kept quiet; *stå rolig* stand still; **2** *(stille, uten støy)* quiet; *en ~ gate* a quiet street; **3** *(fredelig)* quiet, peaceful; **4** *(om ansikt, sinn, vær)* calm, quiet; *føle seg ~* feel at ease; *ta det ~* take it easy; **5** *(jevn, regelmessig)* steady; *en ~ flamme* a steady flame.

rolle *sb* part, role; *det spiller ingen ~* it does not matter; *hun spilte ~n som Ophelia* she played/took the part of Ophelia; *ledende ~* leading part; *viktig ~* important part. **rolle|besetning** *sb* cast. **~bytte** *sb* exchange of parts.

rolling *sb* toddler; tiny tot.

rom A *adj: ~ sjø* in the open sea; **B** *sb* **1** *(plass)* room, space; **2** *(værelse)* room; *hvor mange ~ er det i dette huset?* how many rooms are there in this house? **3** *(del av noe)* compartment, partition; *en pung med mange ~* a purse with many compartments; **4** *(verdensrom)* space; *tid og ~* time and space; **C** *sb (drikk)* rum.

roman *sb* novel. **roman|figur** *sb* character in a novel. **~forfatter** *sb* novelist. **romanse** *sb* **1** *(dikt)* ballad, romance; **2** *(musikkstykke)* romance; **3** *(kjærlighetshistorie)* love affair. **romanserie** *sb* cycle/sequence of novels. **romansk** *adj* Romance; *(om arkitektur)* Norman, Romanesque; *~e språk* Romance languages. **romantiker** *sb* romantic, romanticist. **romantikk** *sb (stemning)* romance; *(åndsretning i kunst)* romanticism. **romantisk** *adj* romantic. **romersk** *adj* Roman. **romersk-katolsk** *adj* Roman Catholic. **romertall** *sb* Roman numeral.

romfang *sb* volume, cubic content.

rom|farer *sb* astronaut. **~fart** *sb* space travelling. **~innhold** *sb* cubic content.

romme *vb (kunne) inneholde)* contain; (can/will) hold; *hver kasse ~r 100 bokser* each box will contain 100 tins; *hallen ~t 3000 mennesker* the hall could hold

3000 people. **rommelig** *adj* roomy, spacious; ~ *tid* ample time. **romskip** *sb* space craft/ship. **romslig** *adj (fordomsfri)* liberal, tolerant.

romstere *vb* rummage.

rop *sb* call, cry, shout; *et ~ om hjelp* a call/cry for help. **rope** *vb* call (out); cry, shout; ~ **opp:** *læreren ropte opp elevene* the teacher made a roll-call; *navnet mitt ble ropt opp* my name was called; ~ **om** *hjelp* call for help; cry help; ~ **på** call; ~ **til** call to. **ropert** *sb* megaphone; speaking-trumpet.

ror *sb (selve rorbladet)* rudder; *(hele styreapparatet)* helm; *stå til ~s, stå ved ~et* be at the helm. **ror|kult** *sb* tiller. **~mann** *sb* helmsman, steersman. **~pinne** *sb* tiller.

ros *sb* praise; *den høyeste ~ vi kan gi dem* the highest praise we can give them; *hun fikk ~* she was praised. **rosa** *adj* pink, rose-coloured. **rose A** sb rose; *ingen ~r uten torner* no rose without a thorn; every rose has its thorn; *livet er ingen dans på ~r* life is no bed of roses; **B** *vb (gi ros)* praise; ~ *seg av* pride oneself on; *han roste dem* he praised them. **rosebusk** *sb* rose-bush. **rosende** *adj* complimentary. **rosen|krans** *sb* rosary. **~kål** *sb* Brussels sprouts. **~olje** *sb* rose oil; attar. **rosett** *sb* rosette.

rosignal *sb* taps, tattoo.

rosin *sb* raisin; *~en i pølsen* the culminating treat; *steinfrie ~er* seedless raisins.

rosverdig *adj* laudable, praiseworthy.

rot *sb* **A** *(plante~)* root; *planten slo røtter* the plant struck/took root; **B** *(uorden)* mess, disorder; *for et ~!* what a mess!

rotasjon *sb* rotation. **rotasjonspresse** *sb* rotatory press.

rot|behandling *sb* root treatment. **~bløyte** *sb* soaker.

rote *vb* **1** *(urydde)* make a mess; **2** *(~ i jorden)* root; **3** *(~ under leting)* rummage, search. **rotekopp** *sb* bungler, muddler.

rotekte *adj (om plante)* ungrafted; *fig* genuine.

rotere *vb* rotate. **roterende** *adj* rotary, rotatory, revolving.

rotet(e) *adj* messy, untidy.

rot|fast, ~festet *adj* well-rooted. **~frukter** *sb fl* roots; root crops/vegetables. **~fylling** *sb* root filling. **~løs** *adj* rootless. **~skudd** *sb* sucker. **~stavelse** *sb* root syllable. **~stokk** *sb* rhizone; root stock.

rotte A *sb* rat; **B** *vb:* ~ *seg sammen mot* conspire against; gang up against. **rotte|felle** *sb* rat trap. **~gift** *sb* rat poison; ratsbane.

rottegn *sb* radical (sign).

rotur *sb* row; *de drog på ~* they went for a row; they went rowing.

rot|vekst *sb* root crop. **~velte** *sb* uprooted tree; *US* windfall.

rouge *sb (sminke)* rouge.

rov *sb* **1** *(jakt)* prey; *tigeren gikk på ~* the tiger went in search of prey; **2** *(bytte)* booty; loot, plunder, spoils. **rov|drift** *sb* ruthless exploitation. **~dyr** *sb* beast of prey. **~fisk** *sb* fish of prey. **~fugl** *sb* bird of prey. **~hugst** *sb* overcutting. **~lyst** *sb* rapacity. **~tann** *sb* sectorial tooth.

ru *adj* **1** *(ujevn)* rough; **2** *(hes)* hoarse.

rubb *sb:* ~ *og stubb* lock, stock and barrel.

rubin *sb* ruby.

rubrikk *sb* **1** *(plass til utfylling)* blank, space; *i ~en til høyre* in the space to the right; **2** *(spalte)* column.

ruff *sb* deck-house; forecastle, poop.

rug *sb* rye. **rug|aks** *sb* ear of rye. **~brød** *sb* rye--bread; *et ~* a rye loaf.

ruge *vb* **1** *(om fugler)* brood, sit; ~ *ut* hatch (out); **2** *(spekulere)* brood about/over. **ruge|høne** *sb* sitter; sitting hen. **~kasse** *sb* sitting box/nest. **~maskin** *sb* incubator.

rugg *sb* large, heavy person (animal, object etc).

rugge *vb* **1** *(gynge, vugge)* rock; **2** *(rikke)* move, stir; **3** *(stabbe)* plod one's way; trudge.

ruglet(e) *adj* **1** *(ustø)* tottering, unsteady; **2** *(ujevn)* rough.

ruhåret *adj* wire-haired; ~ *terrier* wire-haired terrier.

ruin *sb* ruin; *bombeangrepet la byen i ~er* the bombardment laid the town in ruins; *det blir deres ~* it will be their ruin; *ligge i ~er* be in ruins. **ruinere** *vb* ruin; *de ble ruinert* they were ruined. **ruinerende** *adj* ruinous. **ruinhaug** *sb* heap of ruins.

rujern *sb* pig iron.

rulett *sb* roulette.

rull *sb* **1** *(noe sammenrullet)* roll; **2** *(valse)* roller. **rulle I** *sb (til rulling av tøy)* mangle; **II** *vb* **1** roll; ~ *ned rullegardinen* draw the blind; ~ *opp (noe sammenrullet)* unroll; ~ *opp rullegardinen* pull up the blind; ~ *sammen* roll up; *han ~t med øynene* he rolled his eyes; *skipet ~t sterkt* the ship rolled badly; *steinene ~t nedover åssiden* the stones rolled down the hillside; *han rullet med øynene* he rolled his eyes; **2** *(~ tøy)* mangle. **rulle|bane** *sb* runway. **~blad** *sb* record. **~gardin** *sb* blind; *(US også)* shade. **~krone** *sb petro* rick bit. **~skøyter** *sb fl* roller skates. **~stein** *sb (rund småstein)* pebble; *(rund kampestein)* boulder. **~stol** *sb* wheelchair. **~trapp** *sb* escalator.

rumle *vb* rumble. **rumling** *sb* rumble.

rumpe *sb* **1** *(bakende)* behind, buttocks, rump; **2** *(hale)* tail. **rumpetroll** *sb* tadpole.

rund *adj* round. Se også *rundt*. **rund|aktig** *adj* roundish. **runde I** *sb* **1** beat, round; *politikonstabels ~* policeman's beat; *postbuds ~* postman's round; **2** *(tur)* stroll, turn; *en ~ i parken* a stroll in the park; **3** *(i baneløp etc)* lap; **II** *vb* **1** *(gjøre rund)* round; make round; ~ *leppene* round the lips; *av~, ~ av* round off; **2** *(gå/reise etc rundt)* round; ~ *Kapp Horn* round the Horn. **rundelig** *adj* abundant, ample. **rundgang** *sb* round(s), tour; circuit, turn. **rundhet** *sb* roundness. **rundhåndet** *adj* generous, liberal; *(~ med penger)* free with one's money. **runding** *sb* **1** *(rundhet)* roundness; **2** *(det å runde)* rounding; **3** *(ring, sirkel)* circle, ring.

rund|jule *vb* give a good beating. **~kjøring** *sb* roundabout; *US* traffic circle. **~reise** *sb* circular tour. **~rygget** *adj* roundshouldered, stooping. **~skriv** *sb* circular. **~spørring** *sb* poll. **~stykke** *sb* roll. **rundt** *adv/prep* round; about, around; *de reiste ~* they travelled about; *det er trær ~ huset* there are trees on all sides of the house; *det er trær ~ omkring* there are trees on all sides; *han gikk ~ i rommet* he walked about the room; *hele året ~* all the year round; *vi gikk ~ huset* we walked round the house. **rundtur** se *rundreise*.

rune *sb* rune. **rune|alfabet** *sb* runic alphabet. **~tegn** *sb* runic letter.

runge *vb* resound, ring; *rop og latter ~t i salen* the hall rang with shouts and laughter.

rus *sb (beruselse)* intoxication. **rusdrikk** *sb* intoxicant.

ruse *sb (fiske~)* fish-trap.

ruse *vb* **1** *(fare, styrte)* rush; **2** *~ motoren* race the engine; **3** *(beruse)* intoxicate. **rusende** *adj (berusende)* intoxicating. **rusgift** *sb* drug.

rushtid *sb* rush hours *fl*.

rusk A *adj: er du ~?* are you out of your mind? **B** *sb (svær fyr)* hulk, giant; **C** *sb (støvgrann)* mote, particle; *(støv)* fluff; *(skrap)* trash. **ruske** *vb* shake; jerk, pull; *~ opp i* shake up; give a shaking to; *han ~t gutten i håret* he pulled the boy's hair. **ruskevær** *sb* drizzly weather.

rusle *vb* amble, loiter, potter.

rust *sb* rust; *tæret av ~* eaten away by rust. **ruste** *vb* **A** *(bli rusten)* rust; become rusty; **B** *(~ til krig)* arm; prepare for war; *~ seg til* prepare for; get ready for; *~ ut* equip. **rusten** *adj* rusty; a rusty needle; *en ~ stemme* a hoarse voice. **rustfri** *adj* stainless.

rustning *sb* **1** armour; *i full ~* in complete armour; **2** se *opprusting*. **rustnings|begrensning** *sb* limitation/reduction of armaments. **~industri** *sb* armament industry. **~kappløp** *sb* armament(s) race.

rute *sb* **A 1** *(firkant)* square; **2** *(vindus~)* pane; *matt ~* frosted pane; **B 1** *(fastsatt vei)* route; **2** *(trafikkforbindelse)* service; *fast ~* regular service; *gå i ~ mellom* ply/run between; *holde ~n* keep schedule time; *være i ~* be on time. **rute|bil** *sb* (motor)coach, bus. **~bok** *sb (for jernbaner)* railway guide. **~båt** *sb* liner; *(kystrutebåt)* coasting steamer. **~fart** *sb* regular service. **~fly** *sb* airliner. **~flyging** *sb* air service(s). **rutepapir** *sb* squared (cross-ruled or square-ruled) paper. **ruter** *sb koll (i kortspill)* diamonds; *~ ess/konge/ti* the ace/king/ten of diamonds. **rutet(e)** *adj* check, checked, chequered.

rutine *sb* **1** *(erfaring, øvelse)* experience, practice; **2** *(vanlig fremgangsmåte)* routine. **rutine|arbeid** *sb* routine work. **~menneske** *sb* routinist. **~messig** *adj* routine. **rutinert** *adj* experienced, skilled.

rutsje *vb* glide, slide; *han ~t ned på gelenderet* he slid down the banisters. **rutsjebane** *sb* chute, slide; *(berg- og dalbane)* scenic railway; *US* roller coaster.

ruve *vb* bulk large. **ruvende** *adj* bulky.

ry *sb* fame, renown.

rydde *vb* clear; *~ opp* tidy up; *~ veien for snø* clear the road of snow. **ryddig** *adj* tidy, neat, orderly. **rydning** *sb* clearing. **rydnings|arbeid** *sb* pioneer work. **~mann** *sb* pioneer.

rygg *sb* back; *bak hans ~* behind his back; *han snudde ~en til meg* he turned his back on me; *hun stod med hendene på ~en* she stood with her hands behind her/behind her back. **rygge** *vb* back, reverse; *(gå bakover)* step back; *hun ~t bilen inn i garasjen* she backed/reversed the car into the garage. **ryggesløs** *adj* depraved, dissolute, god-forsaken, profligate. **ryggesløshet** *sb* depravity, dissoluteness, profligacy. **rygg|marg** *sb* spinal marrow/cord. **~rad** *sb* spine; spinal column. **~sekk** *sb* rucksack. **~stø** *sb* back. **~svømming** *sb* backstroke (swimming). **~virvel** *sb* vertebra.

ryke A *vb* **1** *(sende ut røyk)* smoke; **B** *(gå tvert av)* break, snap; *tauet røk* the rope broke/snapped; **C** *(uttrykk) ~ i tottene på hverandre* fall to loggerheads; come to blows; *~ løs på* fly/rush at; *~ over ende* tumble over; *~ uklar* fall out; *ryk og reis!* get/go away! *sjansen røk* the chance went to pot. **rykende** *adj: ~ varm* piping/steaming hot; *i ~ fart* at a furious speed; at a tearing pace.

rykk *sb* **1** tug; *(kort og hurtig)* jerk; *i ~ og napp* by fits and starts; *jeg gav et ~ i tauet* I gave the rope a tug; **2** *(plutselig, uvilkårlig bevegelse)* start; *det gav et ~ i henne da hun hørte det* she started/gave a start when she heard it. **rykke** *vb* **1** *(trekke)* pull, tug; *hun ~t ham i ermet/i håret* she pulled his sleeve/hair; **2** *(flytte)* move; *de ~t tett sammen* they moved close together; **3** *(uttrykk) ~ inn (om tropper)* enter, invade; *~ inn en annonse i en avis* insert an advertisement in a newspaper; *~ nærmere* approach; advance; *~ opp (om fotballklubb)* move up; *(bli forfremmet)* be promoted; *~ ut* turn out; *brannvesenet ~t ut* the fire-brigade turned out; *(dra i felten)* march off. **rykkerbrev** *sb* dunning letter. **rykkevis** *adv* by fits and starts. **rykning** *sb* twitch; *en ~ i en muskel* a twitch of a muscle; *han har rykninger i ansiktet* his face twitches.

rykte *sb* **1** *(forlydende)* rumour; *jeg hørte (et) ~ om at kongen er/skulle være død* I heard a rumour that the king is dead; *~t forteller/sier at han er død* rumour has it that he is dead; **2** *(omdømme)* reputation; *ens gode navn og ~* one's good name; one's character/reputation; *han er bedre enn sitt ~* he is not so black as he is painted; *hun har dårlig ~* she has a bad reputation. **ryktes** *vb* be rumoured; get about; *det ~ at han hadde vært i fengsel* it got about that he had been in gaol. **ryktesmed** *sb* rumour-monger.

rynke I *sb* **1** wrinkle, line; *(dyp ~)* furrow; *han fikk ~r* he became/grew wrinkled/lined/furrowed; **2** *(~r på tøy)* gathers; **II** *vb* wrinkle; *~ brynene/pannen* wrinkle one's brows; *(ettertenksomt)* knit one's brows; *(i sinne)* frown; *~ på nesen* turn up one's nose; *~ tøy* gather; *med rynkede bryn/rynket panne* with knitted/wrinkled brows; *(av sinne)* frowning.

rype *sb* mountain grouse, ptarmigan.

ryste *vb* shake; *(skjelve også)* tremble, shiver; *han skalv av frykt* he trembled with fear; *jeg skalv av feber/kulde* I shivered with fever/cold; se også *riste, rystende, rystet.* **rystelse** *sb* **1** shake, shaking; *(svakere)* tremor; **2** *(forferdelse)* shock. **rystende** *adj* appalling, shocking. **rystet** *adj* shaken, shocked; *han ble ~ over nyheten* he was shocked at the news.

rytme *sb* rhythm. **rytmisk** *adj* rhythmical.

rytter *sb* rider; *(om mann ofte)* horseman; *(om kvinne)* horsewoman. **rytteri** *sb* cavalry, horse. **rytterstatue** *sb* equestrian statue.

ræv se *rauv.*

rød *adj* red; *(høyrød)* crimson; *(sterkt ~)* scarlet; *de stanset for ~ lys* they stopped at the red light; *han ble ~* he turned (became, went) red; *(av sjenerthet)* he blushed; *(av sinne)* he flushed. **rød|bete** *sb* beetroot. **~blond** *adj* sandy. **~blå** *adj* reddish blue. **~brun** *adj* reddish brown. **røde hunder** *sb fl* German measles. **Røde Kors** the Red Cross. **rød|glødende** *adj* red-hot. **~gul** *adj* reddish yellow. **Rødhette** Little Red Ridinghood. **rød|hud** *sb* Redskin. **~kløver** *sb* red clover. **~kål** *sb* red cabbage. **rødlig** *adj* reddish. **rødme 1** *sb* blush, flush; **2** *vb (av sjenerthet)* blush; *(av sinne)* flush; *han ~t av skam* he blushed with shame; *hun ~t ved å tenke på det* she blushed to think of it. **rød|musset** *adj* red-cheeked, ruddy. **~rev** *sb* red fox. **~sprengt** *adj(om ansikt)* red-veined, weather-beaten; *(om øyne)* bloodshot. **~strupe** *sb* robin. **rødt** *sb (rødfarge)* red. **rødvin** *sb* red wine; *(bordeaux)* claret.

røffel *sb* rebuke, reprimand; *få en ~* be reprimanded.

røkelse *sb* incense.

røkt *sb (pass, stell)* care, tending. **røkte** *vb* tend; look after. **røkter** *sb* cattleman, cowman.

rømling *sb* fugitive, runaway.

rømme A *sb* (heavy) cream; ≈ crème fraîche; **B** *vb (flykte)* run away; *(desertere)* desert, leave; *(om fange)* escape; *(evakuere, tømme for folk ved truende ulykke etc)* evacuate. **rømning** *sb* escape, flight. **rømningsforsøk** *sb* attempted escape.

rønne *sb* hovel, shack.

røntgen *sb (~stråler)* X-rays. **røntgen|behandle** *vb* X-ray; treat with X-rays. **~behandling** *sb* X-ray treatment. **~bilde** *sb* X-ray (picture); radiograph; *ta ~bilde* X-ray. **~fotografere** *vb* X-ray. **~undersøkelse** *sb* X-ray examination.

røpe *vb* **1** *(avsløre)* betray; give away; *hun ~t hemmeligheten* she betrayed the secret; *han ~t seg* he gave himself away; *stemmen ~r deg* your voice gives you away; **2** *(vise)* show.

rør *sb* **A** *(tøys)* nonsense; **B 1** *(vann~ etc av metall)* pipe; *(av andre materialer ofte)* tube; *glass~* glass tube; **2** *bambus~* cane; *sukker~* (sugar) cane; **3** *hun la på (telefon)røret* she put down the receiver. **rørbro** *sb petro etc* cat-walk.

røre I *sb (oppstyr)* commotion, stir; *liv og ~* hustle and bustle; *meldingen vakte ~* the report caused/made a great commotion/stir; **II** *vb* **1** *(~ ved, ta på)* touch; **2** *(~ (på) seg)* move, stir; *hun rørte på seg i søvne* she moved/stirred in her sleep; *jeg våget ikke ~ meg* I dared not stir; **3** *(sette i bevegelse)* move, stir; *hun kunne ikke ~ en finger* she could not move/stir a finger; **4** *(røre rundt i)* stir; *~ i (havre)grøten* stir the porridge. **rørelse** *sb (sinnsbevegelse)* emotion. **rørende** *adj* **1** moving, touching; *et ~ syn* a moving/touching sight; **2** *(litt ynkelig)* pathetic; *en ~, liten fyr* a pathetic little fellow. **røret(e)** *adj* confused, twaddling.

rørgate *sb (til kraftverk)* penstock.

rørig *adj: rask og ~* hale (and hearty); still going strong.

rør|kobling *sb petro* tool joint. **~ledning** *sb* pipeline. **rørlegger** *sb* plumber. **rørlegger|arbeid** *sb* plumbing. **~tang** *sb* pipe wrench.

rørlig *adj* movable.

rør|oppheng *sb petro* casing/tubing hanger. **~passtykke** *sb petro* spool piece. **~sats** *sb petro* tube bundle. **~skrape** *sb petro* scraper. **~sukker** *sb* cane sugar. **~sville** *sb petro* sleeper.

rørt *adj* moved, touched; *dypt ~* deeply moved; *fiske i ~ vann* fish in troubled waters.

røslig *adj* husky, sturdy; big and strong.

røsslyng *sb* heather.

røst *sb (stemme)* voice; *han talte med høy ~* he spoke in a loud voice.

røve *vb* rob; *de ~t pengene fra meg* they robbed me of my money. **røver** *sb* bandit, highwayman, robber. **røver|bande, ~gjeng** *sb* gang of robbers. **~historie** *sb* cock-and-bull story. **~høvding** *sb* robber chief. **røveri** *sb* robbery. **røver|kjøp** *sb: det er ~* it is dirt cheap. **~pakk** *sb* robbery. **~unge** *sb* urchin.

røyk *sb* smoke. **røykbombe** *sb* smoke bomb. **røyke** *vb* smoke; *~r De?* do you smoke? **røyke|kupé** *sb* smoker, smoking-compartment. **~laks** *sb* smoked salmon. **røykelse** se *røkelse.* **røykeri** *sb* smokehouse. **røyke|salong** *sb* smoking-room. **~tobakk** *sb* smoking tobacco. **~værelse** *sb* smoking room. **røyking** *sb (tobakks~)* smoking. **røyk|legge** *vb* cover with a smoke screen. **~punkt** *sb petro etc* smoke point. **røykt** *adj* smoked, smoke-cured; *~ fisk* smoked fish; *~ skinke* smoke-cured ham. **røykteppe** *sb* smoke-screen.

røys *sb* heap of stones.

røyskatt *sb* stoat; *(i vinterdrakt)* ermine.

røyte *vb (felle hår)* shed.

rå A *adj* **1** *(ikke bearbeidet eller tilberedt)* raw; *~ grønnsaker* raw vegetables; **2** *(fuktig)* damp, dank; *~ tåke* dank fog; *~tt vær* damp/raw weather; **3** *(brutal, grov)* brutal, coarse; **4** *(uanstendig)* obscene, salacious; dirty, smutty; **B** *sb (på mast)* yard; **C** *vb* se *råde.*

rå|aluminium *sb* crude aluminium. **~barket** *adj* coarse, rough.

råd *sb* **1** *(rådsforsamling)* board, council; *de holdt ~* they held a council; **2** *(veiledning)* advice; *et (godt) ~* a piece of (good) advice; *han fulgte deres ~* he took their advice; *jeg spurte henne om ~* I asked her advice; *mange gode ~* much good advice; **3** *(legemiddel)* remedy; *et godt ~ for/mot forkjølelse* a good remedy for a cold; **4** *(utvei)* way out; **5** *(uttrykk) det er ingen ~ med det* it cannot be helped; *ha ~ til* can afford; *jeg har ikke ~ til det* I cannot afford it; *jeg har ikke hatt ~ til det* I have not been able to afford it; *jeg visste ingen annen ~ enn å* I had no choice but to; *så snart (som) ~ (er)* as soon as possible.

rå(de), *vb (gi råd)* **1** advise; *det var ingen som kunne ~ henne* there was no one to advise her; *jeg ville ~ deg til ikke å gå dit* I should advise you not to go there; **2** *(bestemme, herske)* command, rule; be master/mistress; *mennesket spår, Gud rår* man proposes, God disposes.

rådelig *adj* advisable. **råd|føre** *vb: ~ seg med* consult; *han ~førte seg med legen sin* he consulted his doctor. **~givende** *adj* advisory, consultative. **~giver** *sb* adviser. **rådhus** *sb* town hall; (i *cities* og *USA*) city hall. **rådighet** *sb* command, disposal; *pengene står til Deres ~* the money is at your disposal. **råd|legge** *vb* consult, deliberate; make plans. **~løs** *adj* bewildered; at a loss (what to do); perplexed. **~løshet** *sb* perplexity; helplessness; irresolution. **~slagning** *sb* consultation. **~slå** *vb* consult, deliberate. **~snar** *adj* resourceful. **~snarhet** *sb* resourcefulness. **~vill** se *rådløs.*

rådyr *sb* roe(-deer).

rå|emne *sb* raw material. **~flott** *adj* lavish, prodigal; extravagant. **~gass** *sb petro* charge/crude gas. **~gjenger** *sb* jaywalker. **~gummi** *sb* crepe rubber.

råhet *sb (brutalitet, ukultur)* coarseness, brutality.

råk *sb* lane.

råkald *adj* raw.

råke *sb (toppmål)* heaped measure.

råke *vb* hit, meet. Se også *treffe.*

rå|kjøre *vb* drive recklessly; scorch. **~kjører** *sb* roadhog; speeder, speedhog. **~kost** *sb* raw/uncooked vegetables and fruit. **~materiale** *sb* raw material. **~olje** *petro* crude (oil). **~prat** *sb* dirty language. **~produkt** *sb* raw product. **~seil** *sb* square sail. **~silke** *sb* raw silk. **~skap** *sb* coarseness, vulgarity; brutality. **~skinn** *sb* brutal/vulgar person. **~skodde** *sb* dank fog. **~stoff** *sb* raw material; *petro* charge stock. **~tamp** se *råskinn.* **~tjære** *sb petro* crude tar.

råte *sb* rotting; decay, rottenness; *(især i tømmer)* rot. **råtne** *vb* rot; decay, putrefy; go bad; *~nde grønnsaker* decaying vegetables. **råtten** *adj* rotten, decayed; bad; *~ frukt* rotten/decayed fruit; *råtne egg* bad eggs. **råttenskap** *sb* rottenness, decay; *(fig)* corruption.

råvare *sb* raw material.

S

s *(bokstaven)* s.

sabbat *sb* Sabbath.

sabel *sb* sabre. **sable ned** *vb (fig)* slate.

sabotasje *sb* sabotage. **sabotere** *vb* sabotage. **sabotør** *sb* saboteur.

sadel se *sal B.*

sadisme *sb* sadism. **sadist** *sb* sadist. **sadistisk** *adj* sadistic.

sadle se *sale.*

safir *sb* sapphire.

saft *sb* **1** *(frukt~ etc)* juice; *(~ med sukker)* syrup; *sitron~* lemon juice; **2** *(sevje)* sap. **saftig** *adj* juicy.

sag *sb* saw; *(sagbruk)* mill.

saga *sb* saga; *sagaen om X* the saga of X.

sag|blad *sb* saw blade. **~bruk** *sb* sawmill, lumbermill. **sage** *vb* saw; *jeg ~t av grenen* I sawed the branch off. **sag|flis** *sb* sawdust. **~krakk** *sb* sawhorse; *US* (saw-)buck. **~mugg** *sb* sawdust.

sagn *sb* legend, tradition; *etter ~et* according to the legend/to tradition. **sagn|figur** *sb* legendary character. **~krets** *sb* cycle of legends.

sago *sb* sago.

sagt *pp* av *si: (uttrykk) det er ikke ~ at* it doesn't follow/isn't certain that; that doesn't mean that; *det er lettere ~ enn gjort* it is easier said than done; *kort ~* briefly; in few words; *mellom oss ~* between you and me; just between us; *rent ut ~* actually; to tell the truth; *som ~* as already mentioned; as I told you; as mentioned/said before; *som ~, så gjort* no sooner said than done. Se for øvrig *si.*

sak *sb* **1** *(anliggende)* matter; *det er ingen ~* it is an easy matter; *enden på ~en ble at* the end of the matter was that; *for den ~s skyld* for that matter; **2** *(~ man kjemper for)* cause; *en god ~* a good cause; **3** *(sakens kjerne, poeng)* point; *~en er (den) at* the fact is that; *det vedkommer ikke ~en* that is beside the point/irrelevant; *han er sikker i sin ~* he is convinced that he is right; *holde seg til ~en* keep/stick to the point; *komme til ~en* come to the point; **4** *(affære)* affair; *det er hans ~* it/that is his affair/business; **5** *(oppgave)* business, concern; **6** *(retts~)* case; (law)suit; *hun vant/tapte ~en* she won/lost her case; *ligge i ~ med* carry on a lawsuit against; **7** *(søksmål)* action, suit; *anlegge/gå til ~ mot* bring an action/a suit against; **8** *(fl: saker, ting)* things; *jeg pakket ~ene mine* I packed up my things. **sakfører** *sb (fellesbetegnelse)* lawyer; *(~ ved lavere domstoler)* solicitor; *(advokat)* barrister; *(tiltaleform i retten)* counsel.

sakke *vb:* ~ *akterut* fall/lag behind; ~ *av* slow down.

sak|kunnskap *sb* expert knowledge; know-how. **~kyndig** *adj, sb* expert. **saklig** *adj* objective, impartial; matter-of-fact. **saklighet** *sb* objectivity, impartiality. **sakliste** *sb* agenda; *neste punkt på ~listen* the next item on the agenda.

sakn(e) se *savn(e).*

sakrament *sb* sacrament.

sakristi *sb* vestry, sacristy.

saks *sb* **1** scissors *fl*; *(større ~, hage~, saue~ etc)* shears *fl*; *en ~* a pair of scissors/shears; **2** *(til fangst)* trap.

saksanlegg *sb* action; legal proceedings; *true med ~* threaten proceedings.

sakser *sb* Saxon. **saksisk** *adj* Saxon.

saksofon *sb* saxophone.

saksomkostninger *sb fl* costs; *vi ble idømt/tilkjent ~* we were ordered to pay/awarded costs. **sak|søke** *vb* sue; bring an action/a suit against; take to court. **~søker** *sb* plaintiff; *ta ~søkerens påstand til følge* find for the plaintiff. **~søkte** *sb* the defendant; *ta ~søktes påstand til følge* find for the defendant.

sakte *adj (langsom)* slow; *med ~ fart* at slow speed; *klokken min går ti minutter for ~* my watch is ten minutes slow.

saktens *adv* no doubt; undoubtedly; *(også)* I suppose/dare say (that)...; *du er ~ trett* I dare say you are tired; *du kan ~ le* it's all very well for you to laugh; *han kommer ~ senere* no doubt he will come later.

saktmodig *adj* meek; gentle, mild.

saktne *vb* slacken; slow down; *(om klokke)* lose; *~ farten* slacken speed; slow down; *klokken min ~r tre minutter om dagen* my watch loses three minutes a day.

sal *sb* **A** *(stort lokale)* hall; **B** *(sadel)* saddle; *sitte fast/trygt i ~en (fig)* be firmly in the saddle; be secure.

salat *sb* **1** *(planten, blad~)* lettuce; **2** *(matrett)* salad.

saldere *vb* balance. **saldo** *sb* balance.

sale *vb* saddle; *hun ~t hesten (sin)* she saddled her horse.

salg *sb* sale; *kjøp og ~* buying and selling; purchase and sale; *på ~* on sale; *til ~s* for sale. **salgbar** *adj* saleable. **salgs|avdeling** *sb* sales department. **~pris** *sb* selling price. **~verdi** *sb* sales value. **~vilkår** *sb* terms of sale.

salig *adj* **1** *(frelst)* saved; *(velsignet)* blessed; *~e er de rene av hjertet* blessed are the pure in heart; **2** *(lykkelig)* blissful. **salighet** *sb* salvation; blessedness.

sal|maker *sb* saddler; *(møbelstopper)* upholsterer. **~makerarbeid** *sb* saddlery; upholstery.

salme *sb* hymn; *(om Davids ~r)* psalm. **salmebok** *sb* hymn-book.

salmiakk *sb* sal ammoniac.

Salomo(n) Solomon; *Salomos ordspråk* the Book of Proverbs. **salomonisk** *adj* Solomonic.

salong *sb* **1** *(i privathus)* drawing-room; **2** *(på hotell)* lounge, salon; **3** *(på skip)* saloon. **salong|møblement** *sb* drawingroom suite. **~radikaler** *sb* parlour pink. **~rifle** *sb* saloon/gallery rifle.

salpeter *sb* saltpetre, nitre. **salpetersyre** *sb* nitric acid.

salrygget *adj* sway-backed.

salt *adj, sb* salt; *ta det med en klype ~* take it with a grain of salt. **saltbøsse** *sb* salt castor/shaker/sprinkler. **salte** *vb* **1** *(strø salt på)* salt; sprinkle with salt; **2** *(ned~)* salt down; *(~ i lake)* pickle. **salt|kar** *sb* saltcellar. **~lake** *sb* brine.

saltomortale *sb* somersault; *gjøre/slå (en) ~* somersault; make a somersault.

salt|syre *sb* hydrochloric acid. **~vann** *sb* salt water.

salutt *sb* salute. **saluttere** *vb* salute; give a salute.

salve I *sb* **A** *(skudd~)* volley; **B 1** *sb (til å smøre inn)* ointment; **2** *vb (smøre inn med ~)* anoint. **salvelse** *sb* unction. **salvelsesfull** *adj* unctuous.

sam|arbeid *sb* co-operation, team-work; collaboration. **~arbeide** *vb* co-operate, collaborate. **~arbeidsvillig** *adj* cooperative.

samaritan *sb* Samaritan; *den barmhjertige ~* the good Samaritan.

samboer *sb* cohabitant. **samboerskap** *sb* cohabitation.

same *sb* Lapp.

sam|eie *sb (felles eiendomsrett)* joint ownership; *(felles eiendom)* joint property. **~eksistens** *sb* coexistence.

sam|ferdsel *sb* communication(s), traffic. **~ferdselsmidler** *sb fl* means of communication (kan også brukes i entall).

samfunn *sb* **1** *(et enkelt konkret ~)* community; *~et vi lever i* the community in which we live; **2** *(~ som begrep)* society; **3** *(forening)* society. **samfunns|forhold** *sb* social conditions. **~form** *sb* social system. **~hus** *sb* community centre. **~lære** *sb* civics. **~ånd** *sb* public spirit.

sam|følelse *sb* fellow-feeling, solidarity. **~handel** *sb* mutual trade. **~hold** *sb* solidarity, concord. **~hørighet** *sb* belonging (together); interdependence, solidarity.

samisk *adj* Lappish.

sam|klang *sb* harmony. **~kvem** *sb* communication, intercourse.

samle *vb* **1** *(~ opp/sammen)* gather; pick up; *han ~t (sammen) tingene sine og gikk* he picked up his things and left; **2** *(~ inn)* collect; *hun ~t inn penger til de fattige* she collected money for the poor; **3** *(~ på)* collect; *~r du på frimerker?* do you collect stamps? **4** *(for~)* assemble; *vi ~t elevene i hallen* we assembled the pupils in the hall; **5** *(~ seg)* collect, gather; *(fig)* concentrate; *det hadde ~t seg støv på bøkene* dust had collected on the books; *vi ~t oss rundt bålet* we gathered round the fire. Jf *samlet.* **samlebånd** *sb* assembly belt/line; conveyor belt.

samleie *sb* (sexual) intercourse.

samler *sb* collector. **samlet** *adj, pp: det samlede* *beløp* the sum total; the total amount; *i ~ flokk* in a body; *opptre ~* act in concert; *samlede verker* collected/complete works. **samling** *sb* **1** *(det å samle)* gathering, collection; **2** *(det som samles)* collection; *hennes ~ av sjeldne bøker* her collection of rare books; **3** *er du fra sans og ~?* are you out of your senses? *gå fra sans og ~* lose one's senses. **samlings|merke** *sb* symbol of unity. **~regjering** *sb* coalition government. **~sted** *sb* place of meeting.

samliv *sb* life together; *(ekteskapelig ~)* married life; *(samboerskap)* cohabitation.

samme *adj, sb* **1** the same; *~ år* the same year; *de er på ~ alder* they are of an age; they are the same age; **2** *(ens, lik)* equal; **3** *(uttrykk) det er* **det** *~ for meg* it is all the same to me; *det er det ~ som avslag* it amounts to a refusal; *det er det ~ som å si* it is as much as to say; *det* **går for det** *~* it makes no difference; **i det** *~* at that very moment; just then; *i det ~ de kom* the moment they came; **med det** *~* at once; at the same time; *det kan* **være det** *~* never mind.

sammen *adv* **1** together; *de bor ~* they live together; *han tok seg ~* he pulled himself together; *~ med* with; *(også)* along with; together with; *hun kom ~ med foreldrene sine* she arrived with her parents; *jeg sender deg noen egg ~ med litt smør* I send you a few eggs along/together with a little butter; **2** *alle ~* all (of them/you/us); *alt ~* all (of it).

sammen|bitt *adj: ~bitte tenner* clenched teeth; *~bitt energi* dogged energy. **~blande** *vb (forveksle)* mix up; confuse. **~blanding** *sb* mixture; confusion. **~brudd** *sb* break-down, collapse. **~drag** *sb* summary; digest, précis. **~fall** *sb (sammentreff)* coincidence; *(sammensmelting)* merging. **~filtret** *adj* tangled. **~føyning** *sb (det å føye sammen)* joining; *(det ~føyde stedet)* joint. **~heng** sb 1 *(innbyrdes forbindelse)* connection; *i denne ~heng* in this connection; **2** *(omstendigheter)* facts; the truth; *da jeg fikk greie på ~hengen* when I learned the truth; *sakens rette ~heng* the facts of the case; **3** *(logisk ~)* coherence; **4** *(tekst~)* context; *kan du ikke gjette hva ordet betyr ut fra ~hengen?* can't you guess the meaning of the word from the context? **~hengende** *adj (uavbrutt)* continuous; *(logisk ~)* coherent. **~kalle** *vb* call (together); summon. **~komst** *sb* gathering, meeting. **~krøpet** *adj* crouching, huddled (up). **~lagt** *adj* combined; put together. **~leggbar** *adj* collapsible, folding.

sammen|ligne *vb* compare; *~ligne med* compare with; *~lign denne kopien med originalen* compare this copy with the original; *(finne likhetspunkter)* compare to; *man kan ~ligne hjertet med en pumpe* you can compare the heart to a pump. **~ligning** *sb* comparison; *i ~ligning med* in comparison with/compared with.

sammen|satt *adj* compound; *(innviklet)* complex; *~satt av* composed/made of; *en ~satt karakter* a complex character; *et ~satt ord* a compound word. **~setning** *sb* composition; *(sammensatt ord)* compound. **~skrumpet** *adj* shrivelled, shrunk(en). **~slutning** *sb* union, combination; *merk* merger; *(forening)* association, union. **~smeltet** *adj, pp* fused/melted together; *(fig)* amalgamated, merged. **~smelting** *sb* melting together; fusion; *fig* amalgamation, merger. **~stimling** *sb* crowd. **~støt** *sb* **1** collision; *~et støt mellom en buss og en lastebil* a collision between a bus and a lorry; **2** *(trette)* quarrel; *(strid)* controversy, dispute. **~sunket** *adj* collapsed; *sitte ~sunket* sit hunched up. **~surium** *sb* hotchpotch, jumble. **~sverge seg** *vb* conspire. **~svergelse** *sb* conspiracy, plot. **~svoren** *adj: de ~svorne* the conspirators. **~treff** *sb* coincidence. **~trengt** *adj* compressed, condensed. **~vokst** *adj* grown together.

sam|ordne *vb* coordinate. **~råd** *sb* consultation; *i ~råd med* after consultation with; in agreement with.

sams *adj (felles)* common, joint. Se for øvrig *felles*.

sam|skipnad *sb* association, organization. **~spill** *sb* teamwork; *et ~spill av mange faktorer* an interplay of many factors. **~stemme (med)** *vb (stemme overens med)* agree/tally with. **~stemmig** *adj* unanimous. **~svar** *adj* accordance, agreement; *i ~svar med* in accordance/agreement with; in keeping with. **~svare** *vb* agree/tally with.

samt *konj* and; and also; plus.

samtale 1 *sb* conversation, talk; *(telefon~)* call; *jeg hadde en lang ~ i telefonen* I had a long talk over the telephone; *kan du føre en ~ på engelsk?* can you carry on a conversation in English? *vi tok alle del i ~n* we all joined in the conversation; **2** *vb* converse, talk. **samtaleemne** *sb* topic; subject of conversation.

samtid *sb* **1** *(om nåtiden)* our age/days/time; **2** *(om fortiden)* that age/time; those days; his/her time(s); *Milton og hans ~* Milton and his times. **samtidig 1** *adj a) (som inntreffer etc ~)* contemporaneous; simultaneous; *(også som sb)* contemporary; *Bacon og hans ~e* Bacon and his contemporaries; **2** *adv* at the same time; contemporaneously, simultaneously; *inntreffe ~ med* coincide with.

samtlige *pron* all.

samtykke 1 *sb* consent; *gi sitt ~ til* consent to; give one's consent to; **2** *vb* agree, consent; *~ i* agree/consent to; *~ med* agree with; *de nikket ~nde* they nodded their assent; *den som tier, ~r* silence gives consent.

sam|velde *sb: Det britiske ~velde* the British Commonwealth. **~virkelag** *sb* co-operative society; *(om butikken)* co-op.

samvittighet *sb* conscience; *en dårlig/vond ~* a bad conscience; *en god/ren ~* a clear conscience; *ha noe på ~en* have something on one's conscience; *lette sin ~* clear one's conscience. **samvittighets|full** *adj* conscientious; *(omhyggelig også)* careful, painstaking. **~fullhet** *sb* conscientiousness. **~løs** *adj* unscrupulous. **~nag** *sb* pangs of conscience; remorse, self-reproach. **~sak** *sb* matter/point of conscience. **~spørsmål** *sb* matter/question of conscience.

samvær *sb* being together; company; *deres ~ i England* the time they spent together in England.

sanatorium *sb* sanatorium.

sand *sb* sand; *løpe ut i ~en* be abortive; come to

nothing; peter out; *strø ~ på* sand; sprinkle with sand; *fig* blindly endorse; rubber-stamp; *bygge sitt hus på ~* build on sand.

sandal *sb* sandal.

sand|banke *sb (i havet)* sandbank; *(på land)* sandhill. **~bunn** *sb* sand(y) bottom. **sandet(e)** *adj* sandy. **sand|kasse** *sb* sandpit. **~korn** *sb* grain of sand. **~papir** *sb* sandpaper; *pusse med ~papir* sandpaper. **~sekk** *sb* sandbag. **~stein** *sb* sandstone. **~strø** *vb* sand; sprinkle with sand. **~tak** *sb* sand-pit.

sanere *vb (~ bydeler)* effect slum clearance; *(~ et foretagende)* reconstruct, reorganize.

sang *sb* song; *(det å synge også)* singing. **sangbok** *sb* songbook. **sanger, sangerinne** *sb* singer. **sang|fugl** *sb* song-bird. **~kor** *sb* choir. **~lærer** *sb* singing-master; *(om kvinne også)* singing-mistress. **~lerke** *sb* skylark. **~stemme** *sb* singing voice. **~time** *sb* singing lesson. **~undervisning** *sb* singing lessons.

sangviniker *sb* sanguine person. **sangvinsk** *adj* sanguine.

sanitet *sb mil* medical service/corps. **Saniteten** *sb GB* the Royal Army Medical Corps (R.A.M.C); *US* the Medical Corps. **sanitets|bind** *sb* sanitary napkin. **~lege** *sb* medico. **~offiser** *sb* medical officer. **~soldat** *sb* medic; *US* corpsman. **~tjeneste** *sb* medical service.

sanitæranlegg *sb* plumbing; sanitary installation.

sanke *vb* collect, gather.

sanksjon *sb* sanction; *kongelig ~* Royal Assent. **sanksjonere** *vb* sanction; *(~ en lov) GB* give the Royal Assent.

sanktbernhardshund *sb* St. Bernhard dog. **sankthans** *sb* Midsummer. **~orm** *sb* glow-worm.

sann *adj, adv* true; *det er ikke et sant ord i det* there is not a word of truth in it; *det er sant (riktig)* it is true; *(forresten)* by the way; *det var et sant ord* you never spoke a truer word; *en ~ historie* a true story; *han talte sant* he spoke/told the truth; *sant å si* to tell the truth; **ikke sant:** *du kommer, ikke sant?* you are coming, aren't you? *han så det, ikke sant?* he saw it, didn't he? **så sant:** *~ ~ jeg lever* as I live *jeg kommer ~ ~ det ikke regner* I'll come provided/providing it doesn't rain. **sannelig** *adv, interj* indeed. **sann|ferdig** *adj* truthful; *(også)* true; *en ~ferdig historie* a true story. **~ferdighet** truthfulness, veracity.

sann|het *sb* truth; *i ~het* indeed. **~hetskjærlig** *adj* truth-loving, veracious.

sannspådd *adj: han var ~* what he predicted came true.

sann|synlig *adj* likely, probable; *det er mulig, men ikke ~synlig* it is possible, but not probable; *det er ikke særlig ~synlig at de kommer* it is not very likely that they will come; *høyst ~synlig* as likely as not. **~synlighet** *sb* likelihood, probability; *etter all ~synlighet* in all likelihood/probability. **~synligvis** *adv* probably; *hun kommer ~synligvis* she is likely to come.

sans *sb* sense; *de fem ~er* the five senses; *er du fra ~ og samling?* are you out of your senses? *humoristisk ~* sense of humour; *hun har ~ for rytme* she has a sense of rhythm; *sunn ~* common sense. **sanse** *vb* perceive, notice. **sanse|bedrag** *sb* illusion, hallucination. **~lig** *adj* sensual, carnal. **~lighet** *sb* sensuality. **~løs** *adj* distracted, frantic; *~løs av skrekk* frantic with terror. **~organ** *sb* sense organ.

sant se *sann.*

sardin *sb* sardine.

sarkasme *sb* sarcasm. **sarkastisk** *adj* sarcastic. **sarkofag** *sb* sarcophagus.

sart *adj* delicate.

satelitt *sb* satellite.

sateng *sb* sateen.

satire *sb* satire. **satiriker** *sb* satirist. **satirisk** *adj* satiric, satirical.

sats *sb* **1** *(ved hopp)* takeoff; **2** *(takst)* rate; **3** *(mus)* movement; **4** *(ferdigsatt trykksak)* matter. **satse** *vb* **1** *(ved hopp)* take off; **2** *(i spill, veddeløp etc) ~ på* bet/stake on; put one's money on; *~ alt på ett kort* put all one's money in one basket; *~ på en hest (også)* back a horse; **3** *(ta sikte på)* aim at; have in view.

satt *adj: i ~ alder* of mature years.

sau *sb* sheep; *(søye)* ewe. **saubukk** *sb* ram. **saue|flokk** *sb* flock of sheep. **~gjeter** *sb* shepherd. **~kjøtt** *sb* mutton. **~saks** *sb* shears *fl.*

saus *sb* sauce; *brun ~* gravy; *vanilje~* custard. **saus|e|kopp, ~nebbe** *sb* gravy/sauce boat. **~skje** *sb* sauce ladle.

savne 1 *vb* miss; *hun vil ikke bli ~t* she won't be missed; *jeg kommer til å ~ deg* I shall miss you; *vi ~r ham sterkt* we miss him badly; **2** *(mangle)* want; *er det noe du ~r?* is there anything you want? **3** *(være ~t)* be missing; *én mann er ~t* one man is missing.

scene *sb* scene; *(teater~)* stage; *for åpen ~ (fig)* in public. **scene|anvisning** *sb* stage direction. **~forandring** *sb* change of scene.

score *vb (i fotball etc)* score. Jf *skåre.*

se *vb* **1** *(om synsevnen og for øvrig i de fleste tilfeller)* see; *~ godt/dårlig* have a good/bad eyesight; *han har sett bedre dager* he has seen better days; *ikke ~ skogen for bare trær* not see the wood for trees; *jeg ~r av Deres brev at...* I see from your letter that...; *jeg så (at) hun kom/jeg så henne komme* I saw her come/coming; *vi så en god film i går* we saw a good film yesterday; *ugler ~r best om natten* owls see best at night; **2** *(betrakte, ~ på)* look; *vi så (etter), men så ingenting/kunne ikke ~ noe* we looked, but (we) saw nothing/couldn't se anything; **3** *(med adv og prep)* **~ bort** look the other way; *~ bort fra* ignore; leave out of/not take into account; **~ etter** *a) (følge med øynene)* look after; *b) (lete etter)* look for; *hva ~r dere etter?* what are you looking for? *c) (passe, pleie)* look after; *han så etter barna mens hun var i byen* he looked after the children while she was in town; *d) (forvisse seg om)* make sure (that); *jeg så etter at døren var låst* I made sure that the door was locked; **~ seg for:** *~ deg for!* look out! look where you are going! **~ i:** *~ seg i speilet* look at oneself in the mirror; look into the mirror; **~ i øynene:** *~ faren/virkeligheten i øynene* face the danger/the facts; *hun så meg (inn) i øynene* she looked me full in the face; ~ **(i)gjennom** look over/through; *jeg har sett (i)gjennom stilen* I have looked through the essay; ~ *gjennom fingrene med* overlook; connive/wink at; shut one's eyes to; ~ **innom** look/pop in; look up; ~ **ned** look down; ~ *ned på (forakte)* look down on; despise; ~ **om** look if; ~ *om hun er hjemme* look if she is at home; ~ *seg om* look about (one); *jeg så meg om i rommet* I looked about in the room; ~ **opp!** look out! ~ *opp til (beundre)* look up to; admire; ~ **over** look over/through; *han så over regnskapet (sitt)* he looked over his accounts; ~ **på** *a) (betrakte)* look at; *hva ~r du på?* what are you looking at? *b) (oppfatte, vurdere)* look at/on; regard; *jeg ~r det ikke slik* I don't look at/on it in that light; *han ~r visst på meg med mistillit* he seems to look on me with distrust; *man kan ikke ~ det på ham* you would not think so to look at him; *man kan ikke ~ på henne at hun er så gammel* she does not look her age; *en kan ~ på ansiktet hans at...* you can tell by/read in his face that ...; *c) (overveie)* see about it; *hun sa hun skulle/ville ~ på det* she said she would see about it; *d) (ta hensyn til)* mind; *han så ikke på utgiftene* he did not mind the expenses; ~ **til** *a) (besøke)* go and see; visit; *b) (få besøk av, treffe) vi ~r ikke stort til ham* we do not see much of him; *c) (påse, sørge for)* see (to it) that; take care that; ~ *til at billettene blir bestilt i god tid* see that the tickets are booked in good time; ~ **ut** *(rette blikket utover)* look out; *han stod ved vinduet og så ut* he stood at the window looking out; *b) (ha et visst utseende)* look; *det ~r galt ut* things are looking bad; *det ~r ut til (å bli) regn* it looks like rain; *du ~r lykkelig ut* you look happy; *hvordan ~r han ut?* what does he look like?

sed *sb (skikk)* custom; ~ *og skikk* manners and customs.

seddel *sb* **1** *(papirlapp)* slip (of paper); *(lite brev)* note; **2** *(penge~)* note; *US* bill.

sedelig *adj* moral; of good morals. **sedelighet** *sb* morality. **sedelighets|forbrytelse** *sb* sexual crime. **~forbryter** *sb* sexual criminal; *dgl* sex maniac.

sedvane *sb* custom; *(persons ~)* habit; *mot ~* contrary to custom. **sedvanemessig** *adj* customary. **sedvanerett** *sb* common law. **sedvanlig** *adj* usual; *som ~* as usual. **sedvanligvis** *adv* usually; as a rule.

seer *sb* seer.

sees *vr* see one another; meet; *vi ~ på torsdag* see you on Thursday.

seg 1 *(etter vb)* oneself, himself, herself, itself, themselves; *hun forsvarte ~ energisk* she defended herself vigorously; **2** *(ofte oversettes ~ ikke)*; *barbere ~* shave; *gifte ~* marry; *vaske ~* wash; **3** *(etter prep)* him, her, it; *han lukket døren bak ~* he shut the door behind him; *hun så ~ omkring* she looked about her; **4** *(uttrykk) han er redd* **av** ~ he is naturally timid; *det er i en klasse* **for** ~ it forms a class by itself; *det er en sak for ~* that is another matter; **i og for** ~ in itself; *(i virkeligheten)* actually; **hver for** ~ separately.

segl *sb* seal.

segne *vb* **1** drop, sink; *hun ~t under byrden* she sank under the burden; **2** *(falle død om)* die, drop. **segneferdig** *adj* ready to drop.

sei *sb* coalfish.

seidel *sb* mug, tankard.

seier *sb* victory; *de vant en stor ~* they gained/won a great victory; *det var en stor ~ for dem* it was a great triumph/success for them. **seier|herre** *sb (i krig)* conqueror, victor; *(i idrett)* winner, victor. **~rik** *adj* victorious. **~sikker** *adj* confident of victory/success.

seig *adj* tough; *(hårdnakket)* dogged; ~ *motstand* dogged resistance. **seig|het** *sb* toughness. **~livet** *adj* tough; tenacious of life; *gammel overtro er ~livet* old superstitions die hard. **~pine** *vb* torment.

seil *sb* sail; *for fulle ~* at/under full sail. **seilas** *sb (seiling)* sailing; *(seiltur)* sail; *(sjøreise)* voyage. **seil|bar** *adj (farbar)* navigable. **~båt** *sb* sailing-boat. **~duk** *sb* canvas. **seile** *vb* sail; *la ham ~ sin egen sjø* let him shift for himself; ~ *under falskt flagg* sail under false colours. **seiler** *sb* yachtsman. **seiling** *sb (seilsport)* yachting. **seil|maker** *sb* sailmaker. **~skip, ~skute** *sb* sailing-ship. **~sport** *sb* yachting.

seire *vb* **1** *(i krig)* conquer; win/gain a victory; *han ~t over fienden* he conquered the enemy; **2** *(i sport)* win; *hun ~t i Oslo Maraton* she won the Oslo Marathon. **seirende** *adj* victorious.

sekel *sb* century. **sekelskifte** *sb: ved ~t* at the turn of the century.

sekk *sb* sack; *(mindre ~)* bag; *en kan ikke få både i pose og ~* you cannot eat your cake and have it; *kjøpe katta i ~en* buy a pig in a poke. **sekkepipe** *sb* bagpipe.

sekretariat *sb* secretariat. **sekretær** *sb* secretary.

seksjon *sb* section.

sekskant *sb* hexagon.

sekstant *sb* sextant.

seksual|drift *sb* sexual urge/instinct. **seksualitet** *sb* sexuality. **seksual|liv** *sb* sex/sexual life. **~opplysning** *sb* sex guidance. **~undervisning** *sb* sex instruction. **seksuell** *adj* sexual.

sekt *sb* sect. **sekterisk** *adj* sectarian.

sektor *sb* sector.

sekularisere *vb* secularize. **sekularisering** *sb* secularization.

sekund *sb* second. **sekunda** *adj* second-rate. **sekundant** *sb* second; *være ~ for* second. **sekundere** *vb* second. **sekundviser** *sb* second-hand. **sekundær** *adj* secondary.

sel *sb* seal.

sele *sb* **1** *(seletøy)* harness; **2** *(bukse~)* braces; *US* suspenders *(fl)*; *et par ~r* (a pair of) braces/suspenders; *legge seg i ~n* put one's back into it; put one's shoulder to the wheel. **sele** *vb: ~ av* unharness; *~ på* harness.

sel|fanger *sb* sealer. **~fangst** *sb* sealing.

selge *vb* sell; ~ *billig/dyrt* sell cheap/dear; ~ *ut* sell out; ~ *skinnet før bjørnen er skutt* count one's chickens before they are hatched. **selger** *sb* seller; *(av profe-*

sjon) sales|man, -person, -woman.

selje *sb* sallow; goat willow.

selleri *sb* celery.

selskap *sb* **1** *(gruppe mennesker, selskapelig sammenkomst)* party; *et turist~* a party of tourists; *vi hadde/holdt ~ i går* we gave a party yesterday; **2** *(gjester, samvær)* company; *han kom i dårlig ~* he got into bad company; *hun holdt ham med ~* she kept him company; **3** *(handels~)* company; *et forsikrings~ an* insurance company; **4** *(forening)* association, society. **selskapelig** *adj* **1** social; *~ sammenkomst* social gathering; **2** *(som liker selskap)* sociable, companionable. **selskapelighet** *sb* sociability; entertainment, parties. **selskaps|antrekk** *sb (for menn)* evening dress; *(for damer)* evening gown. **~lek** *sb* parlour game. **~livet** *sb* social life. **~reise** *sb* conducted tour. **~syk** *adj* fond of society; longing for society.

selskinn *sb* sealskin.

selsom *adj* odd, strange; mysterious.

selters *sb* seltzer water.

selv I *pron* **1** *a)* myself, yourself, himself etc; *du så det ~* you saw it yourselves; *gjør det ~!* do it yourself! *jeg er ikke helt meg ~ i dag* I am not quite myself today; *b) (ofte sies)* own; *han bar sin bagasje ~* he carried his own luggage; **2** *(uttrykk) koppen gikk i stykker* **av seg** *~* the cup came to pieces of itself; *han arbeidet* **for seg** *~* he worked for himself; *(alene)* he worked alone/by himself; *han hadde en kupé for seg ~* he had a compartment to himself; *det* **sier seg** *~* that goes without saying; *han* **kom til seg** *~* he came to; **II** *(adv)* even; *~ du må innrømme at hun har rett* even you must admit that she is right; *~* **om** even if/though; *~ om han hadde penger* even if he had money. **selv|aktelse** *sb* self-respect. **~angivelse** *sb* income tax return. **~bebreidelse** *sb* self-reproach. **~bedrag** *sb* self-deception; self-delusion. **~beherskelse** *sb* self-control. **~berget** *adj* self-supporting. **~bestemmelse** *sb* self-determination. **~betjening** *sb* self-service. **~bevisst** *adj* arrogant. **~binder** *sb* reaper-binder. **~biografi** *sb* autobiography. **~biografisk** *adj* autobiographical.

selve *adj* himself, herself, itself; *(ofte sies)* very; *~ kongen* the King himself; *~ stedet der jeg fant det* the very spot where I found it; *på ~ dagen* on the very day.

selv|eier *sb* freeholder; owner-occupier. **~eiertomt** *sb* freehold site. **~erkjennelse** *sb* self-knowledge. **~fornektelse** *sb* self-denial. **~forsvar** *sb* self-defence. **~følelse** *sb* self-respect.

selv|følge *sb* matter of course. **~følgelig 1** *adj* natural; *det ~e resultat* the natural result; **2** *adv* naturally; of course. **~følgelighet** *sb* matter of course; *(naturlighet)* naturalness.

selv|gjort *adj* self-made. **~god** *adj* conceited, priggish; self-righteous; *en ~god person* a prig. **~hevdelse** *sb* self-assertion. **~hjelp** *sb* self-help. **~hjulpen** *adj* self-supporting, self-sufficient. **~innlysende** *adj* obvious, self-evident. **~ironi** *sb* self-irony.

selvisk *adj* selfish. **selviskhet** *sb* selfishness.

selv|kontroll *sb* self-control. **~kritikk** *sb* self-criticism. **~lysende** *adj* luminous. **~lært** *adj* self-taught. **~medlidenhet** *sb* self-pity. **~mord** *sb* suicide; *begå ~mord* commit suicide. **~morder** *adj* suicide. **~mordsforsøk** *sb* attempted suicide. **~motsigelse** *sb* contradiction (in terms). **~motsigende** *adj* (self)-contradictory. **~oppholdelsesdrift** *sb* instinct of self-preservation. **~oppofrelse** *sb* self-sacrifice. **~oppofrende** *adj* self-sacrificing. **~opptatt** *adj* self-centred. **~opptatthet** *sb* self-centredness. **~overvinnelse** *sb* self-conquest, resignation. **~portrett** *sb* self-portrait. **~respekt** *sb* self-respect. **~rådig** *adj* self-willed, wilful. **~rådighet** *sb* wilfulness.

selv|sagt se *selvfølgelig*. **~sikker** *adj* self-confident. **~sikkerhet** *sb* self-confidence. **~stendig** *adj* independent. **~stendighet** *sb* independence. **~studium** *sb* private study. **~styre** *sb* autonomy, self-government; *(især for Irland)* Home Rule. **~suggestion** *sb* auto-suggestion. **~syn** *sb: av ~syn* from personal experience. **~tekt** *sb* taking the law into one's own hands. **~tilfreds** *adj* self-satisfied. **~tillit** *sb* self-confidence.

sement *sb* cement. **sementere** *vb* cement.

semester *sb* term.

semikolon *sb* semicolon.

semsket *adj: ~ skinn* chamois-leather; *semskede sko* suède shoes.

sen *adj* **1** *(motsatt tidlig)* late; *en ~ høst* a late harvest; **2** *(som tar lang tid)* slow; *han har alltid vært ~ i arbeidet* he has always been a slow worker; *~ i vendingen* slow to move; lumbering, slow-moving. Se også *senere, senest* og *sent*.

senat *sb* senate. **senator** *sb* senator.

sende *vb* **1** send; *hun sendte gutten etter en flaske melk* she sent the boy for a bottle of milk; *jeg sendte boken tilbake* I returned the book; **2** *(ved bordet)* pass; *send saltet, er du snill* pass (me) the salt, please; **3** *(om radio)* transmit; **4** *(uttrykk) ~* **bud etter** send for; *det ble sendt bud etter doktoren* the doctor was sent for; *~* **bud til** send word to. **sende|bud** *sb* messenger. **~mann** *sb* ambassador. **sender** *sb* **1** *(avsender)* sender; **2** *(radio~)* transmitter. **senderstasjon** *sb* transmitting station. **sendetid** *sb* broadcasting time. **sending** *sb* **1** *(vareparti)* consignment; **2** *(i radio)* transmission.

sene *sb* sinew. **seneknute** *sb* ganglion.

senere *adj* later; *før eller ~* sooner or later; *i den ~ tid* lately; *i de ~ år* in recent years; in the last few years; *tre år ~* three years later. **senest** *adj* slowest; *(adv)* at the latest; by; *jeg må ha Deres svar ~ 1. mai* I must have your reply by may 1st; *vi må være hjemme ~ ti* we must be home at ten at the latest.

senete *adj* sinewy.

seng *sb* bed; *han fikk barna i ~* he put the children to bed; *holde ~en* be confined to bed; keep one's bed; *dgl* be laid up; *hun lå til ~s* she was (ill) in bed; *jeg gikk til ~s* I went to bed. **senge|forlegger** *sb* (bedside) rug. **~kant** *sb* bedside; edge of the bed. **~liggende** *adj* confined to bed; *(for lengre tid)* bed ridden. **~plass** *sb* sleeping accomodation. **~teppe** *sb (ullteppe)* blanket; *(vatteppe)* quilt; *(til pynt)* bedspread, counterpane. **~tid** *sb* bedtime. **sengklær** *sb* bed--clothes, bedding.

senil *adj* senile. **senilitet** *sb* senility.

senior *adj, sb* senior.

senit *sb* zenith.

senk *sb: bære/renne/skyte i ~* sink. **senke** *vb* lower, sink; *~ priser* lower/reduce prices; *han ~t armene/blikket/stemmen* he lowered his arms/his eyes/his voice; *skipet ble ~et* the ship was sunk. **senkning** *sb (med)* sedimentation rate/reaction; *måle/ta ~en* have one's sedimentation checked; *senkningen (hennes) er 6* her sedimentation is 6.

senn *sb: smått om ~* little by little; gradually.

sennep *sb* mustard.

sensasjon *sb* sensation; *nyheten om seieren vakte ~* the news of the victory caused/made a sensation. **sensasjonell** *adj* sensational.

sensibel *adj* sensitive.

sensor *sb* **1** *(film~ etc)* censor; **2** *(ved eksamen)* (external) examiner. **sensur** *sb* **1** *(presse~ etc)* censorship; **2** *(eksamens~)* evaluation, marking; *US* grading; *~en faller i morgen* the examination results will be announced tomorrow.

sent *adv* (too) late; *~ på kvelden* late at night; *han kom for ~ på skolen* he was late for school; *jeg kom (to minutter) for ~ til toget* I missed the train (by two minutes); *så ~ som i går* only yesterday.

sentens *sb* maxim.

senter *sb* centre; *US* center.

sentimental *adj* sentimental. **sentimentalitet** *sb* sentimentality.

sentral I *adj* central; *~ beliggenhet* central position; *~t beliggende* central; **II** *sb* **1** central agency; **2** *(telefon~)* (telephone) exchange; *(US også)* (telephone) central. **sentral|bord** *sb* switchboard. **~borddame, ~bordmann** *sb* switchboard operator. **~fyring** *sb* central heating. **sentralisere** *vb* centralize. **sentralisering** *sb* centralization. **sentral|oppvarming, ~varme** *sb* central heating. **sentre** *vb (i fotball)* pass (the ball).

sentrifuge *sb (tørketrommel)* spin-drier. **sentrifugere** *vb* spin-dry.

sentrum *sb* centre; *US* center.

separasjon *sb* separation. **separat** *adj* separate. **separator** *sb* cream separator. **separere** *vb* separate. **separering** *sb* separating, separation.

september September; *~ måned* the month of September.

septer *sb* scepter.

septiktank *sb* septic tank.

seremoni *sb* ceremony. **seremoniell 1** *adj* ceremonial, ceremonious; **2** *sb* ceremonial.

serenade *sb* serenade.

serie *sb* series; *en ~ mynter* a series of coins. **serie|fabrikasjon, ~fremstilling** *sb* mass production; *(av hus)* prefabrication. **~kamp** *sb (i fotball)* league match. **~mester** *sb* league champion. **~mesterskap** *sb* league championship.

seriøs *adj* serious.

sersjant *sb* sergeant.

sertifikat *sb (kjørekort)* driving licence; *(for øvrig)* certificate; *ta ~* take the driving test.

serum *sb* serum.

servere *vb (sette på bordet)* serve; *(varte opp)* wait on; *middagen er servert* dinner is served. **servering** *sb* service; *~en gikk for langsomt* the service was too slow. **serveringsdame** se *servitør*. **service** *sb (tjeneste)* service. **service|bil** *sb* breakdown lorry; *US* wrecker; wrecking car. **~stasjon** *sb (for motorkjørende)* service station. **serviett** *sb* (table) napkin; serviette. **serviettring** *sb* napkin/serviette ring. **servil** *adj* servile. **servilitet** *sb* servility. **servise** *sb (bord~)* service, set; *et te~* a tea set. **servitør** *sb* waiter; *(om kvinne også)* waitress.

sesam *interj, sb* sesame; *~ lukk deg opp!* open sesame!

sesjon *sb* **1** *(tid da nasjonalforsamling etc sitter sammen)* session; **2** *(mil) bli innkalt/møte til ~* be called up for registration and medical examination; *US* come up before the draft board.

sesong *sb* season. **sesong|arbeid** *sb* seasonal work; **~billett, ~kort** *sb* season ticket. **~salg** *sb* end--of-season sale.

sete *sb* **1** *(stol~ etc)* seat; **2** *(bak)* buttocks *fl.*

seter *sb* mountain farm; summer dairy; summer mountain pasture.

setning *sb* **1** *(gram)* sentence; *(ledd~)* clause; **2** *(logikk, matematikk etc)* theorem; *(påstand)* thesis. **setnings|bygning** *sb* sentence structure. **~ledd** *sb* member of a sentence. **~lære** *sb* syntax. **~melodi** *sb* intonation.

sett A *sb (av sammenhørende deler)* set; *undertøys~* set of underwear; **B** *sb* **1** *(byks)* jump; *(rykk)* start; *det gav et ~ i ham* he started; **3** *(måte) på ~ og vis* in a way; somehow (or other); **C** *vb* **1** *(pp av se) politisk ~* from a political point of view; *stort ~* broadly speaking; by and large; **2** *vb (pr av sette) ~ at* suppose (that); *~ at han er skyldig* suppose he is guilty.

settbord *sb* nest of tables.

sette *vb* **1** *(anbringe)* put, place, set; *hun satte koppen på bordet* she put/placed/set the cup on the table; **2** *~ seg* se eget oppslag nedenfor; **3** *(forutsette)* suppose; se også *sett C 2*; **4** *(~ tekst for trykning)* compose, set; **5** *(~ poteter etc)* plant, sow; **6** *(~ fiskegarn)* cast, shoot, throw; **7** *(uttrykk)* **~ av** *a) (~ av passasjerer)* drop; set down; *jeg kan ~ deg av ved stasjonen* I can drop you at the station; *b) (~ av penger)* earmark; *c) ~ av gårde* rush away; set off (in a hurry); **~ etter** start out after/in pursuit of; **~ fast** *(feste)* fix; make fast; *(arrestere)* arrest; **~ for:** *hun satte glasset for munnen* she put the glass to her lips; **~ fra seg** put down; **~ frem** *(om ting)* display; *(om forslag, teori etc)* put forward; ~ **høyt** have a high opinion of; value highly; ~ **i:** ~ *i arbeid* set to work; ~ *(penger) i banken* deposit money in a bank; ~ *i fengsel* put in/send to prison; ~ *i gang* start; ~ *i stand* fix, mend, repair; ~ *i å le* burst out laughing; ~ **igjennom:** ~ *igjennom viljen sin* carry one's point; have one's way; *(få vedtatt)* carry; *(realisere)* carry through; ~ **inn:** *vinteren satte inn tidlig* the winter set in early; *(~ i fengsel)* put in jail; ~ *alt inn på å* do everything in one's power to; ~ *en inn i noe* inform somebody of something; ~ *livet inn* risk/stake one's life; ~ **ned** *(minske)* lower, reduce; ~ *ned farten* reduce the speed; slow down; ~ *ned en komité* appoint a committee; ~ **opp:** *(forhøye, øke)* raise; ~ *opp farten* speed up; ~ *opp en alvorlig mine* put on a grave face; *hun satte dem opp mot sjefen* she turned/set them against the chief; ~ **over:** ~ *over en elv (vi)* cross a river; *(vt)* ferry across a river; ~ *over kaffen* put the kettle on; ~ **på:** ~ *fingeren på* put one's finger on; ~ *alt på ett kort* put all one's eggs in one basket; stake everything on one card; ~ *sitt preg på* leave one's mark/impression on; ~ *på spill* risk; ~ *på spissen* exaggerate; ~ *på sporet* put on the right track; ~ *på sprang* start running; ~ *en på noe* give somebody an idea; ~ **til** *(tilsette)* add; ~ *livet til* lose one's life; ~ *til livs* consume, eat; ~ *en til å gjøre noe* set somebody to do something; ~ **tilbake** put back; *(fig)* handicap, retard; ~ **ut:** ~ *ut av kraft* declare null and void; ~ *ut i livet* execute; carry into effect; realize; ~ **utenfor** exclude.

settepoteter *sb fl* seed potatoes.

setter *sb* **A** *(hund)* setter; **B** *(i trykkeri)* compositor. **setteri** *sb* composing room.

sette seg *vr* sit down; seat oneself; take a seat; ~ ~ *fast* jam, stick; become fixed; ~ ~ *i bevegelse* start moving; ~ ~ *i hodet* take it into one's head; ~ ~ *imot* oppose; ~ ~ *opp imot* oppose; revolt against; ~ ~ *til bords* sit down at the table; ~ ~ *til å gjøre noe* set about doing; *hun satte seg til å skrive brev* she set about writing some letters.

severdig *adj* worth seeing. **severdighet** *sb* sight; *byens ~er* the sights of the town.

sevje *sb* sap.

sfinks *sb* sphinx.

sfære *sb* sphere. **sfærisk** *adj* spherical.

shipping *sb* shipping.

si *vb* **1** say; *det ~es at han er syk* he is said to be ill; *hva ~er du?* what do you say? **2** *(fortelle, meddele)* tell; ~ *sannheten* tell the truth; *han sa til meg at han kom/ville komme* he told me that he was coming; *hun sa til ham at han skulle gå* she told him to go; *jeg skal ~ deg hva som hendte* I will tell you what happened; *kan du ~ meg hva du heter?* can you tell me your name? *var det ikke det jeg sa?* didn't I tell you? what did I tell you? **3** *(uttrykk)* **enn** ~ let alone; still less; *jeg har ikke tid, enn ~ penger* I haven't the time, let alone the money; **ha å si:** ~ *det en har å ~* speak one's piece; *det har ikke noe å ~* it does not matter; *det har mye å ~* it is very important; *hun har mye å ~* she has great influence; ~ **(i)fra** *(gi beskjed)* inform, tell; let him/her etc know; say so; *(synge ut)* speak out/up; ~ *fra når det er nok!* say when! ~ *bare (i)fra om du trenger penger* just let me know if you need some money; *hun drog hjemmefra uten å ~ fra til noen* she left home without telling anybody; ~ **imot** contradict, gainsay; *du* **kan så** ~ you can say that again; you may well say so; *det* **må jeg ~!** well, I never! ~ **opp** give notice; *(ta avskjed)* resign; ~ *opp en avis* cancel a paper; ~ **på** find fault with; criticize; *det er ikke noe å ~ på det* there's nothing wrong with that; *det* **~er seg selv** that goes without saying; ~ **sin mening** speak one's mind; **skulle ~:** *det skal jeg ikke kunne ~ for sikkert* I wouldn't know; *jeg skal ~ deg noe* I'll tell you what; *jeg skal ~ han er freidig!* he is cheeky indeed! *om jeg så skal ~ det selv* though I say it myself; *det* **vil** ~ that is (to say); **så å** ~ so to speak; as it were.

sid *adj* long; *et ~t skjørt* a long skirt. **sidde** *sb* length.

side *sb* **1** side; *(også mil)* flank; *angripe fra ~n* attack in the flank; *enhver sak har to ~r* there are two sides to every question; *han ble såret i ~n* he was wounded in the side; *på den andre ~n av huset* on the other side of the house; **2** *(bok~ etc)* page; **3** *(uttrykk)* ~ **om** ~ side by side; ~ **opp og** ~ **ned** page after page; pages and pages; *med hendene* **i ~n** arms akimbo; **på den annen** ~ on the other hand; *han er dårlig i grammatikk, men på den annen ~ er han god i regning* he is weak in grammar, but on the other hand he is good at arithmetic; *ingen kommer* **opp på ~n av** *henne* no one can match her; **til** ~ aside; *han gikk/trådte til ~* he stepped aside; *legge til ~ (spare)* put aside; put/lay by; *spøk til ~!* joking apart! **ved ~n av** beside; next to; *(fig)* on the side; *han satt ved ~n av meg* he was sitting beside me; *rommet hennes ligger ved ~n av mitt* her room is next to mine; *vi bor like ved ~n av* we live next door; *(som bibeskjeftigelse)* on the side. **side|bein** *sb* rib. **~blikk** *sb* side glance. **~dør** *sb* side door. **~gate** *sb* side street. **~hensyn** *sb* ulterior motive. **~linje** *sb* **1** *(på jernbane)* branch line; **2** *(på fotballbane)* touchline; **3** *(av slekt)* collateral branch.

siden 1 *adv a)* since; *jeg har ikke sett dem ~* I have not seen them since; *b) (senere)* afterwards, later; *vi ses/treffes ~* see you later; *c) for lenge ~* long ago; *for mange år ~* many years ago; **2** *konj (ettersom)* since; ~ *det er fødselsdagen din i dag, har jeg bakt en kake* since it is your birthday to day I have baked a cake; **3** *prep* since; ~ *jul* since Christmas.

side|ordne *vb* co-ordinate. **~ordnende** *adj: ~ordnende konkunksjon* co-ordinating conjunction.

sider *sb (eplevin)* cider.

side|spor *sb* side track; *føre samtalen inn på et ~spor* sidetrack the conversation. **~stykke** *sb: uten ~stykke* without parallel; unparalleled. **~tall** *sb (antall sider)* number of pages; *(~nummer)* page number. **~vei** *sb* side road. **~vind** *sb* side wind. **~værelse** *sb* adjoining room; *i ~værelset* in the next room.

siffer *sb (talltegn)* figure. **sifferskrift** *sb* cipher.

sig *sb (av væske)* trickle; *komme i ~* gain momentum; *være i ~(et)* be in motion.

sigar *sb* cigar. **sigarett** *sb* cigarette.

sigd *sb* sickle.

sige *vb* **1** *(gli)* glide; *(drive)* drift; *(om væske)* trickle; *(gi etter)* sag; *~ sammen* collapse; *taket har seget* the roof has sagged; **2** *(fig)* steal; *mørket seg på* darkness gathered; darkness stole upon them (us etc).

sigende *(pres part* av *si) etter ~* from what I/we etc hear.

signal *sb* signal. **signalement** *sb* description. **signalisere** *vb* signal. **signatur** *sb* signature.

signe *vb (velsigne)* bless.

signere *vb* sign. **signet** *sb* seal, signet. **signetring** *sb* signet ring.

sigøyner *sb* gipsy.

sikkel se *sikl.*

sikker *adj* **1** *(pålitelig)* sure; *et ~t blikk/øye* a sure eye; *jeg er ~ på det* I am sure of it; **2** *(overbevist)* certain; *jeg er ganske ~ på det* I am quite certain of it; **3** *(viss)* certain; *seieren syntes ~* the victory seemed certain; **4** *(utenfor fare)* safe; *et ~t sted* a safe place; *isen er ~* the ice is safe; **5** *(trygg)* secure; *her er vi sikre mot angrep* here we are secure against/from attack. Se også *sikkert.* **sikkerhet** *sb* **1** *(visshet)* certainty; *få ~ for* get proof that; *jeg kan si med absolutt ~ at* I can say with absolute certainty that; **2** *(~ i opptreden)* (self)assurance; **3** *(trygghet)* safety, security; *for ~s skyld* for safety's sake; to be on the safe side; *vi er i ~ nå* we are in safety now; **4** *(mil)* security. **sikkerhets|belte** *sb* safety/seat belt. **~foranstaltning** se *~tiltak.* **~lenke** *sb* safety chain. **~lås** *sb* safety lock. **~nål** *sb* safety pin. **Sikkerhetsrådet** the Security Council. **sikkerhets|tiltak** *sb* precaution; precautionary measure. **~ventil** *sb* safety valve.

sikkert *adv* **1** *(uten fare eller risiko)* safely; **2** *(utvilsomt)* (for) certain; *han kommer ~* he is certain/sure to come; *jeg vet det ~* I know it for certain; **3** *(formodentlig)* probably; *han gjør det ~* he will probably do it; *(ofte sies)* be likely; *hun vinner ~* she is likely to win.

sikksakk *adv* zigzag; *gå i ~* zigzag.

sikl *sb* slaver, slobber. **sikle** *vb* slaver, slobber.

sikre *vb* **1** *(beskytte)* secure; make safe/secure; *de ville ~ byen mot angrep* they wanted to secure the town against attack; **2** *(gjøre fast)* secure; *vi ~t dørene og vinduene* we secured doors and windows; **3** *~ seg* secure; *hun sikret seg en god plass* she secured a good seat. **sikring** *sb* **1** *(elektrisk ~)* fuse; *~en er gått* the fuse has blown; **2** *(på skytevåpen)* safety catch; **3** *(~ av kriminelle etc)* preventive detention.

sikt *sb* **1** *(siktbarhet)* visibility; **2** *arbeide på lang ~* plan far ahead. **siktbar** *adj* clear. **siktbarhet** *sb* visibility.

sikte I *sb* **1** *(synlighet)* sight; *tape noe av ~* lose sight of something; *ute av ~* out of sight; **2** *(på skytevåpen)* sight; **3** *(det å ~)* aim; *bystyret tar ~ på å sanere alle slumstrøkene* the city council aims at demolishing all the slum areas; *han tok omhyggelig ~* he took careful aim; **II** *vb* **1** *(ta sikte)* aim; *~ på* aim (one's gun etc) at; *~ til* aim at; allude to; drive at; *han ~t til sin bror* he was alluding to his brother; *jeg skjønner ikke hva du ~r til* I do not understand what you are driving at; **2** *(jur) ~ for* charge with; *hun er ~t for mord* she is charged with murder. **siktelse** *sb* charge, indictment.

sil *sb (gjennom sil)* strainer; *en te~* a tea strainer.

sild *sb* herring; *som ~ i tønne* like sardines (in a tin).

sildre *vb* trickle.

sile *vb (gjennom sil)* strain.

silhuett *sb* silhouette.

silke *sb* silk. **silke|bånd** *sb* silk ribbon. **~hansker** *sb: ta på med ~hansker* handle with kid gloves. **~kjole** *sb* silk dress. **~orm** *sb* silk worm. **~papir** *sb* tissue paper. **~strømpe** *sb* silk stocking.

silo *sb* silo; *(korn~ også)* elevator.

sil|regn *sb* pouring rain. **~regne** *vb* pour down; rain heavily.

simpel *adj* **1** *(tarvelig)* bad, poor; **2** *(udannet)* common, vulgar; low; *(sterkt nedsettende)* mean; *en ~ bemerkning* a mean remark; *~t språk* vulgar language; *simple manerer* common manners; **3** (uttrykk) *det er din simple plikt* it is no more than your duty; it is your bounden duty; *~t flertall* simple majority. **simpelhet** *sb* commonness, meanness. **simpelthen** *adv* simply; *det er ~ forferdelig* it is simply terrible.

simulere *vb* feign; pretend to be; *han simulerte sykdom* he feigned illness; he pretended to be ill.

sin, sitt, sine *pron* **1** his, her(s), its, one's, their(s); *de har solgt sitt gamle hus* they have sold their old house; *en må gjøre sin plikt* one must do one's duty; *han tok boken sin/klærne sine* he took his book/clothes; *jeg tok min paraply, hun tok sin* I took my umbrella, she took hers; **2** *(uttrykk) de har gjort sitt* they have done their share; they have done what was in their power; *det har sine fordeler* there are certain advantages in it; *ha sitt på det tørre* be on the safe side; *han kunne ikke underholde seg og sine* he was not able to support himself and his family; *holde på sitt* stick to one's point; *hun har sine grunner* she knows what she is doing; *i sin alminnelighet* generally.

sindig *adj (likevektig)* sober-minded; *(rolig)* calm, steady; *(langsom)* slow. **sindighet** *sb* sobriety; calmness, steadiness; slowness.

singel *sb (grus)* gravel.

single *vb (klirre)* jingle, tinkle.

sink *sb* zinc.

sinke 1 *sb (tilbakestående person)* backward/retarded person; **2** *vb (hefte, forsinke)* delay, detain.

sinn *sb* **1** mind; *et åpent ~* an open mind; *ute av syne, ute av ~* out of sight, out of mind; **2** *(temperament)* temper, teperament; **3** *(uttrykk) ha i ~e* intend, mean; *i sitt stille ~* in one's (secret) heart; secretly.

sinna se *sint.* **sinnatagg** *sb* spitfire. **sinne** *sb* anger, temper; *fare opp i ~* fly into a passion. **sinnelag** *sb* disposition; temper, temperament.

sinnrik *adj* clever, ingenious.

sinns|bevegelse *sb* agitation, emotion. **~forvirret** *adj* distracted, insane. **~forvirring** *sb* distraction, insanity. **~lidelse** *sb* mental disorder. **~opprør** *sb* agitation (of mind). **~ro** *sb* peace of mind; *(uanfektethet)* composure, coolness; *bevare ~roen* remain calm. **~svak** *adj* crazy, mad; *en ~svak idé* a mad/crazy idea. **~syk** insane; mentally deranged; *dgl* crazy, mad; *en ~syk* an insane person; a lunatic. **~sykdom** *sb* mental disease. **~sykehus** *sb* mental hospital. **~tilstand** *sb* state of mind.

sint *adj* angry; *US* mad; *være/bli ~ for* be/get angry about (at, over, with); *være/bli ~ på* be/get angry with.

sippe 1 *sb* sniveller, whiner; **2** *vb (smågråte, sutre)* snivel. **sippet(e)** *adj* snivelling.

sirene *sb* siren; *(fabrikk~)* hooter.

sirkel *sb* circle; *slå en ~* draw a circle. **sirkel|rund** *adj* circular. **~sag** *sb* circular saw. **sirkle** *vb* circle; *~ inn* encircle. **sirkulasjon** *sb* circulation. **sirkulere** *vb* circulate. **sirkulære** *sb* circular.

sirkus *sb* circus. **sirkusartist** *sb* circus performer.

sirlig *adj* neat, trim; *en ~ håndskrift* a neat hand-writing. **sirlighet** *sb* neatness.

sirup *sb (lys ~)* syrup; *(mørk ~)* treacle.

sisik *sb* siskin.

sist *adj, adv* **1** *a)* last; *de ~e dagene i januar* the last days of January; *hennes ~e år* her last years; *nest ~* last but one; *b) de ~e (dvs de som en nylig er ferdig med etc)* the last few; *de ~e dagene/ukene/årene* the last few days/weeks/years; **2** *(~ av to)* latter; *(den) ~ halvpart av juni* the latter half of June; **3** *(nyeste, seneste)* latest; *~e mote* the latest fashion; *~e nytt* the latest news; **4** *som konj* when ... last; *~ jeg så dem* when I saw them last; **5** *(uttrykk) ~ i juli* late in July; *~, men ikke minst* last but not least; *den som ler ~, ler best* he laughs best who laughs last; *i det ~e/i den ~e tiden* lately; *ligge på det/på sitt ~e* be near death; *til det ~e* to the last; *til ~ (etter ventetid)* at last; *(som siste punkt)* finally, lastly. **sistemann** *sb* the last one. **sisten** *sb: leke ~* play tag. **sistnevnte** *adj, sb* last-mentioned; *den ~ (om én av to)* the latter.

sitat *sb* quotation. **sitere** *vb* quote.

sitre *vb* quiver, tremble. **sitring** *sb* trembling.

sitron *sb* lemon. **sitron|brus** *sb* ≈ lemonade. **~saft** *sb* lemon juice. **~frukt** *sb* citrus fruit.

sitt se *sin*.

sitte *vb* **1** sit; *han satt på en stol* he was sitting on a chair; **2** *(være anbrakt)* be; *han ~r i fengsel* he is in prison; *hun satt og leste* she was reading; *nøkkelen ~r i døren* the key is in the door; **3** *(uttrykk) ~ dårlig/godt i det* be badly/well off; *~ fast* stick; be stuck; *bilen satt fast i søla* the car stuck in the mud; *~ i hell/uhell* be in luck/bad luck; *~ i en komité* be on a committee; *~ igjen (på skolen)* not go up; *(bli etterlatt)* be left; *hun satt igjen som enke* she was left a widow; *~ oppe* sit up; *~ på (med kjøretøy)* get a lift; *jeg fikk ~ på ham* he gave me a lift; *~ til bords* be at the table. **sittende** *adj* seated, sitting; *bli endelig ~!* don't get up! *de ble ~* they remained sitting/seated. **sitteplass** *sb* seat; *antall sitteplasser* seating capacity; *bestille ~* reserve a seat; *salen har ~ til fem hundre* the hall can seat five hundred.

situasjon *sb* situation. **situert** *adj: godt ~* well off.

siv *sb* reed, rush. **sivmatte** *sb* rush mat.

sive *vb* ooze, filter; *(om væske også)* seep; *(om lys)* filter; *~ ut (fig)* leak out.

sivil *adj* **1** *(motsatt militær)* civilian; **2** *(ikke-militær)* civil; *hva er du i det ~e liv?* what are you in civil life? *i ~ (om politikonstabel)* in plain clothes; *(om militære)* in civilian clothes/mufti. **sivil|befolkning** *sb* civilian population. **~ingeniør** *sb* chartered/graduate engineer; engineer (with an academic degree). **sivilisasjon** *sb* civilization; *(ofte)* culture. **sivilisere** *vb* civilize. **sivilisert** *adj* civilized. **sivilkledd** se *sivil.*

sjaber *adj* out of sorts; poorly.

sjablon *sb* pattern, template. **sjablonmessig** *adj* stereotyped; according to a set pattern.

sjah *sb* shah.

sjakett *sb* morning coat.

sjakk *sb* chess; *~!* check! *holde i ~* keep in check; *sette ~* give check; *spille ~* play chess. **sjakk|brett** *sb* chessboard. **~brikke** *sb* chessman. **~matt** *sb* checkmate; *sette ~matt* checkmate; *være ~matt (fig)* be dead/beat/fagged out. **~trekk** *sb* move.

sjakt *sb* shaft, pit.

sjal *sb* shawl.

sjalte *vb* switch; *~ inn* switch/turn on; *~ ut* switch/turn off; *fig* cut out; eliminate; leave out of account.

sjalu *adj* jealous; *~ på* jealous of. **sjalusi** *sb* **1** *(skinnsyke)* jealousy; **2** *(persienne)* Venetian blind.

sjampinjong *sb* mushroom.

sjampo *sb* shampoo. **sjamponere** *vb* shampoo.

sjangle *vb* reel, stagger.

sjanse *sb* chance; *ta ~r* take risks. **sjanse|seilas, ~spill** *sb* gamble.

sjapp(e) *sb* shop.

sjargong *sb* jargon.

sjarlatan *sb* charlatan, quack.

sjarm *sb* charm. **sjarmere** *vb* charm. **sjarmerende** *adj* charming. **sjarmør** *sb* charmer, enchanter.

sjasket(e) *adj (om stoff)* limp, shabby; *(sjuskete)* slovenly, untidy.

sjattere *vb* shade. **sjattering** *sb* shade.

sjau *sb (mas)* bustle, hustle; *(larm, spetakkel)* racket. **sjaue** *vb* **1** *(gjøre sjauerarbeid)* work on the quays/in the docks; **2** *(streve)* bustle, hustle; **3** *(holde leven)* romp. **sjauer** *sb* docker, stevedore.

sjef *sb* chief, head, principal.

sjeik *sb* sheik.

sjekk *sb* cheque; *US* check; *en ~ på 50 pund* a cheque for £50; *heve en ~* cash a cheque; *skrive ut en ~* write out a cheque. **sjekke** *vb* check. **sjekk|hefte** *sb* cheque-book. **~konto** *sb* cheque account.

sjel *sb* soul; *av hele sin ~* with all her (his, one's) soul; *hun la hele sin ~ i arbeidet* she put her heart and soul into the work; *på legeme og ~* in mind and body.

sjelden 1 *adj* rare; *en ~ gang* at rare intervals; *dgl* once in a blue moon; *ved sjeldne anledninger* on rare occasions; **2** *adv* seldom, rarely; *(usedvanlig)* exceptionally; ~ *eller aldri* seldom or never; *jeg ser ham* ~ I seldom see him. **sjeldenhet** *sb* rarity; rare thing; *det hører til ~ene at de går ut* it is a rare thing for them to go out.

sjele|fred *sb* peace of mind. **~glad** *adj* delighted. **~kval** *sb* agony. **sjelelig** *adj* mental. **sjele|liv** *sb* mental life. **~messe** *sb* requiem. **~sorg** *sb* spiritual guidance. **~sørger** *sb* clergyman, pastor; spiritual adviser. **~vandring** *sb* transmigration of souls; reincarnation. **sjel|full** *adj* soulful, expressive. **~løs** *adj* soulless. **sjels|styrke** *sb* strength of mind. **~tilstand** *sb* mental state, state of mind.

sjenanse *sb* shyness, self-consciousness; bashfulness. **sjenere** *vb* **1** *(hemme)* hamper, handicap; bother; *varmen ~r meg* the heat bothers me; **2** *(forstyrre)* disturb; *du kommer ikke til å bli sjenert her* you won't be disturbed here; **3** *(irritere)* annoy. **sjenerende** *adj* inconvenient; troublesome; annoying. **sjenert** *adj* shy, self-conscious; bashful; embarrassed; *en ~ ung mann* a shy young man. **sjenerthet** *sb* shyness, self-consciousness; bashfulness.

sjenerøs *adj* generous, liberal. **sjenerøsitet** *sb* generosity, liberality.

sjeviot *sb* cheviot.

sjikane *sb* spite, malice. **sjikanere** *vb* spite. **sjikanøs** *adj* spiteful.

sjikt *sb* layer, stratum.

sjimpanse *sb* chimpanzee.

sjiraff *sb* giraffe.

sjirting *sb: innbundet i ~* clothbound; in cloth. **sjirtingbind** *sb* cloth binding.

sjofel *adj* mean, dirty; *en ~ fyr* a mean fellow; *en ~ strek* a dirty trick. **sjofelhet** *sb* meanness.

sjokk *sb* shock. **sjokkbehandling** *sb* shock treatment.

sjokke *vb* shuffle.

sjokkere *vb* shock; *sjokkert over* shocked at.

sjokolade *sb* chocolate. **sjokoladeplate** *sb* chocolate bar.

sjonglere *vb* juggle. **sjonglør** *sb* juggler.

sjuende: *i den ~ himmel* in the seventh heaven; *til ~ og sist* at long last; *(når alt kommer til alt)* when all is said and done.

sjuk etc se *syk etc.* **sjukling** *sb* sickly person.

sjuske 1 *sb* slattern, slut; **2** *vb (slurve)* scamp one's work. **sjusket(e)** *adj* slovenly.

sjusover *sb* lie-abed; *dgl* stay-abed.

sjy *sb* gravy.

sjø *sb* **1** *(hav)* sea, ocean; *dra til ~s* go to sea; *i rom ~* on the open sea; *la dem seile sin egen ~* let them shift for themselves; *ved ~en* at/by the seaside; *være til ~s* be at sea; be a sailor; **2** *(sjøgang)* sea; *det var høy ~* there was a heavy sea; *han tåler ikke ~en* he is a bad sailor; **3** *(stor bølge)* sea. **sjø|assuranse** se *~forsikring.* **~by** *sb* seaside town. **~dyktig** *adj* seaworthy. **~dyktighet** *sb* seaworthiness. **~dyr** *sb* marine animal. **~farende** *adj* sea-faring. **~farer** *sb* seafarer. **~fart** *sb* navigation, shipping. **~fartsby** *sb* shipping town. **~fartsnasjon** *sb* seafaring nation. **~fly** *sb* hydroplane, seaplane. **~folk** *sb koll* sailors. **~forklaring** *sb* maritime declaration. **~forsikring** *sb* marine insurance. **~fugl** *sb* sea bird. **~gang** *sb* sea; *det var høy ~gang* there was a heavy sea. **~helt** *sb* naval hero. **~hyre** *sb* sea-going kit. **~kart** *sb* chart. **~krig** *sb* naval war.

sjøl se *selv.*

sjø|liv *sb* life at sea. **~makt** *sb* naval power. **~mann** *sb* sailor, seaman. **~mil** *sb* nautical mile. **~orm** *sb* sea serpent. **~pølse** *sb* sea cucumber. **~reise** *sb* voyage; *(lysttur)* cruise. **~rokk** *sb* sea spray. **~røver** *sb* pirate. **~røveri** *sb* piracy. **~sette** *vb* launch. **~slag** *sb* sea/naval battle. **~sterk** *adj: være ~sterk* be a good sailor. **~stridskrefter** *sb koll* naval forces. **~støvler** *sb fl* high boots; *(gummistøvler)* rubber boots. **~syk** *adj* seasick. **~syke** *sb* seasickness. **~territorium** *sb* territorial waters/sea. **~transport** *sb* carriage by sea. **~uhyre** *sb* sea monster. **~ulk** *sb* old salt; (jack) tar. **~vann** *sb* sea water. **~vant** *adj* accustomed/used to the sea. **~vei** *sb* sea route; *reise ~veien* go by sea. **~ørret** *sb* sea trout.

sjåfør *sb* driver; *(privat~)* chauffeur. **sjåfør|lærer** *sb* driving instructor. **~skole** *sb* driving school.

sjåvinisme *sb* chauvinism, jingoism. **sjåvinist** *sb* chauvinist, jingo. **sjåvinistisk** *adj* chauvinistic, jingoist(ic).

ska se *skade II.*

skade I *sb* **1** *(~ på ting)* damage; *~ på motoren* damage to the engine; *lide/ta ~* suffer damage; be damaged; **2** *(~ på person)* injury; *av ~ blir man klok* once bit twice shy; *ingen mennesker kom til ~* nobody was injured; *(om mindre ~)* nobody got/was hurt; **3** *(mindre ~, svakere enn* damage *og* injury*)* harm; *det gjorde mer ~ en gagn* it did more harm than good; *ingen ~ skjedd* no harm done; **II** *vb* **1** *(om ~ på ting)* damage; *bygningen ble sterkt ~t av en bombe* the building was badly damaged by a bomb; **2** *(om ~ på person)* injure; *hånden hans ble ~t i ulykken* his hand was injured in the accident; **3** *(uttrykk) ~ sin sak* damage/harm one's case; *det kan ikke ~ å* it will do no harm to; *det ~r ikke å prøve* there is no harm in trying. **skade|dyr** *sb* vermin. **~forsikring** *sb* general insurance. **~fro** *adj* malicious; *være ~fro over* gloat over. **~fryd** *sb* malicious pleasure. **skadelig** *adj* harmful, injurious; bad; *~ for helsen* injurious to health; *~ for øynene* bad for the eyes; harmful to the eyes. **skadeserstatning** *sb* compensation; damages *fl.* **skadeskyte** *vb* wound. **skadesløs** *adj: holde ~* indemnify. **skadevirkning** *sb* damage; bad consequence.

skaffe *vb* **1** get; procure, secure; provide; *~ hjelp* get help; *vanskelig å ~* difficult to procure; *han forsøkte å ~ billetter* he tried to secure tickets; **2** *~ seg* get, secure; *han ~t seg ny bil* he got a new car; *han ~t seg et værelse* he secured a room; **3** *(volde)* cause; *det ~t ham en masse bryderi* it caused him lots of trouble/worry.

skafott *sb* scaffold.

skaft *sb* handle; *(især på øks)* haft.

skake *vb* shake, jolt.

skakk *adj* crooked, lopsided; *(adv)* askew. **skakke** *adv: på ~* aslant, askew.

skakkjørt *adj (fordervet)* perverse.

skal se *skulle.*

skala *sb* scale; *i stor ~* on a large scale.

skalk *sb* **A** *(brød~)* first cut; *US* heel; **B** *(stiv hatt)* bowler (hat). **skalke** *vb: ~ lukene* batten down the hatches. **skalkeskjul** *sb: bare et ~* just a blind.

skall *sb* shell; *(banan~)* skin; *(appelsin~, sitron~)* peel. **skalldyr** *sb* shellfish.

skalle A *sb (hode~)* skull; **B** *vb: ~ av* peel (off); *(om maling, murpuss etc også)* scale off; *(mur)pussen begynte å ~ av (veggen)* the plaster began scaling off the wall. **skallet(e)** *adj* bald, bald-headed. **skallethet** *sb* baldness.

skalp *sb* scalp. **skalpere** *vb* scalp.

skalte *vb: ~ og valte som en selv vil* have one's own way; do as one likes.

skam *sb* **1** *(vanære)* shame, disgrace; *han brakte ~ over familien* he brought shame on his family; *hun sa jeg var en ~ for familien* she said I was a disgrace to my family; **2** *(skamfølelse)* shame; *jeg rødmet av ~* I flushed with shame; **3** *(uttrykk) det er en ~* it is a shame; *for ~s skyld* out of common decency.

skamfere *vb* **1** *(vansire)* disfigure; *ansiktet hans ble skamfert* his face was disfigured; **2** *(tilføye skade)* damage, maim, mangle, mutilate; **3** *(ødelegge)* ruin.

skam|full *adj* **1** *(som føler skam)* ashamed; *jeg er ~full over å fortelle deg det* I am/feel ashamed to tell you; **2** *(flau)* shamefaced. **~følelse** *sb* (sense of) shame. **~løs** *adj* shameless.

skamme *vb: ~ seg* be/feel ashamed of oneself; *du burde/skulle ~ deg* you ought to be ashamed of yourself; *hun ~t seg over å si det* she was ashamed to tell us.

skammel *sb* stool.

skammelig *adj* **1** *(vanærende)* disgraceful, shameful; *~ oppførsel* disgraceful/shameful behaviour; **2** *(skjendig)* infamous, scandalous. **skam|plett** *sb* stain, stigma; *sette en ~plett på* cast a stain on; stigmatize; *være en ~plett på* be a disgrace to. **~rose** *vb* praise fulsomely. **~slå** *vb* cripple, lame.

skandale *sb* scandal. **skandale|avis** *sb* mud-raking paper. **~historie** *sb* (piece of) scandal. **~journalist** *sb* muck-rake. **skandalisere** *vb* disgrace. **skandaløs** *adj* scandalous, disgraceful.

skanse *sb* **1** *(jordvoll)* earthwork; **2** *sjø (akterdekk)* quarterdeck. **skansekledning** *sb* bulwark.

skap *sb* **1** cupboard; *(finere)* cabinet; *et ~ med glassdører* a cabinet with glass doors; **2** *(kles~)* wardrobe; *(~ i gymnastikksal, på bad etc)* locker.

skape *vb* **1** create, make; *Gud skapte verden* God created the world; *hun skapte seg et navn* she made a name for herself; *klær ~r folk* fine feathers make fine birds; *være som skapt til* be cut out for; **2** *~ seg (dvs gjøre seg til)* playact; *ikke skap deg!* stop playacting! **3** *(forårsake)* cause; *det skapte utilfredshet/uro* it caused dissatisfaction/unrest. **skapelse** *sb* creation. **skapende** *adj* creative. **skaper** *sb* creator, maker; *Skaperen (Gud)* the Creator. **skaperi** *sb* affectation. **skapning** *sb* **1** *(levende vesen)* creature; **2** *(frembringelse)* creation; *~ens herre (dvs mennesket)* the lord of creation.

skar *sb (fjell~)* pass; gorge, ravine.

skare *sb* **A** *(flokk)* band, troop; *en pilegrims~* a band of pilgrims; **B** *(på snø)* crust.

skarlagen *sb* scarlet. **skarlagens|feber** *sb* scarlet fever. **~rød** *adj* scarlet.

skarntyde *sb* hemlock.

skarp *adj* **1** sharp; *fig også* keen; *en ~ kniv (kontrast, tunge etc)* a sharp knife (contrast, tongue etc); *en ~ iakttaker (intelligens, konkurranse etc)* a keen observer (intelligence, competition etc); *ha et ~t øye for* have a keen eye for; *~e konturer (også)* distinct outlines; **2** *(skjærende, streng etc)* severe; *~ kritikk* severe criticism; *~t lys* blinding/glaring light; **3** *adv* sharply; *se ~t på* look keenly at; *skjelne ~t mellom* make a clear distinction between; **4** *(som sb) skyte med ~t* fire live cartridges. **skarphet** *sb* sharpness; *fig også* keenness. **skarp|ladd** *adj* loaded with live cartridges. **~retter** *sb* executioner, hangman. **~sindig** *adj* penetrating; acute, keen, shrewd. **~sindighet** *sb* penetration; acuteness, shrewdness. **~skytter** *sb* sharpshooter. **~synt** *adj* skarp-sighted; *fig* penetrating; acute.

skarre *vb* use a uvular r.

skarv *sb (om fuglen)* cormorant; **2** *(kjeltring)* rogue, scoundrel.

skarve *adj* miserable, wretched.

skatoll *sb* secretaire, secretary.

skatt 1 *(stats~)* tax; *~ av årets inntekt* the Pay-As-You-Earn system; P.A.Y.E.; *hun betalte nesten to tusen pund i ~* she paid nearly £2000 in taxes; *høye ~er* high/heavy taxes; *legge ~ på* tax; put (impose, levy) a tax on; **2** *(kommune~, i GB bare på fast eiendom)* rate(s); *(i andre land)* local taxes; **3** *(avgift, toll)* duty; **4** *(~ på alkohol og tobakk)* duty, excise; **5** *(kostbarhet)* treasure; *den skjulte ~* the hidden treasure; *museets ~er* the treasures of the museum. **skattbar** *adj* taxable; rateable; assessable. **skatte** *vb* **1** *(betale skatt)* pay taxes; **2** *(sette høyt)* value (appreciate, esteem) highly. **skatte|betaler** *sb* taxpayer; ratepayer. **~byrde** *sb* burden of taxation. **~fri** *adj* tax-free. **~frihet** *sb* exemption from taxation. **~graver** *sb* treasure hunter. **~lettelse** *sb* tax relief. **~ligning** *sb* assessment (of taxes). **~plikt** *sb* tax liability. **~pliktig** *adj (om person)* liable to pay taxes; *(om skatteobjekt)* taxable. **~prosent** *sb* rate of taxation. **~seddel** *sb* demand note; *US* tax bill. **~snyter** *sb* tax evader. **~snyteri** *sb* tax evasion. **~ takst** *sb (taksering)* valuation (of property for rating purposes); *(summen)* rateable value. **~trekk** *sb* deduction of tax. **~trykk** *sb* burden of taxation. **~vesen** *sb* taxation authorities. **skatt|kammer** *sb* treasury. **~kiste** *sb* treasure chest. **~legge** *vb* tax. **~yter** *sb* taxpayer; ratepayer.

skaut *sb* headscarf.

skavank *sb* defect, fault, shortcoming; *(mindre ~)* flaw.

skave *vb* scrape, whittle.

skavl *sb* snowdrift.

skeie *vb:* ~ *ut* go astray; kick over the traces.

skeis *adv: gå* ~ be a failure; go to pot.

skeiv(t) se *skjev(t)*.

skepsis *sb* scepticism; *(tvil)* doubt. **skeptiker** *sb* sceptic. **skeptisk** *adj* sceptical.

sketsj *sb* sketch.

ski *sb* ski; *gå/stå på* ~ ski; *de drog/gikk på* ~ they went skiing. **skibakke** *sb* ski hill; ski-jumping hill.

skibbrudd *sb* shipwreck; *de led* ~ they were shipwrecked, **skibbrudden** *adj* shipwrecked.

skifer *sb* slate. **~brudd** *sb* slate quarry.

skift *sb* **1** *(alternerende arbeidslag)* relay, shift; *arbeide i/på* ~ work by/in relays/shift; **2** *(tid som et skiftlag arbeider)* shift; *et åttetimers~* an eight-hour shift; *på dag~* on the day shift. **skifte I** *sb (forandring)* **1** change; **2** *(~ av arv)* division of an inheritance; **II** *vb* **1** change; *hun har ~t adresse* she has changed her address; **2** *(variere)* vary; *temperaturen ~r fra time til time* the temperature varies from hour to hour; **3** *(uttrykk)* ~ *om (å arbeide etc)* take turns (to work etc); ~ *ut* replace. **skifte|nøkkel** *sb* (adjustable) spanner, wrench; *US også* monkey-wrench. **~spor** *sb* siding; shunting track. **~vis** *adv* alternately; by turns.

skikk *sb* custom; ~ *og bruk* custom; *en får følge/ta ~en der en kommer* when in Rome do as the Romans do; *få* ~ *på* get/lick into shape; put right/straight. **skikke** *vb* **A** ~ *seg bra/vel* behave properly; **B** *(sende)* send. **skikkelig** *adj* decent, proper; respectable; ~ *oppførsel* decent/proper behaviour; *en* ~ *pike* a respectable girl; *et* ~ *måltid* a decent/square meal; *oppføre seg* ~ behave properly. **skikkelse** *sb* figure; *(form)* form, shape; *(i roman)* character; *djevelen viste seg i en hunds* ~ the devil appeared in the shape of a dog. **skikket** *adj* fit, fitted; suitable.

skildre *vb* describe, portray; depict. **skildring** *sb* description.

skill *sb (i håret)* parting; *US* part.

skille *sb* dividing line; division; distinction.

skille *vb* **1** part, separate; *ingenting skal (få)* ~ *oss* nothing shall separate us; *Kanalen ~r England fra Frankrike* the Channel separates England from France; *til døden ~r oss at* till death us do part; *vi forsøkte å* ~ *de to kjempende* we tried to part/separate the two fighters; **2** ~ *seg fra (ektefelle)* divorce; *han skilte seg fra sin fjerde kone* he divorced his fourth wife; **3** *(uttrykk)* ~ **lag** part company; ~ **seg av med** part with; *vi måtte* ~ *oss av med bilen (vår)* we had to part with our car; ~ **seg ut** stand out; *hennes arbeid* ~ *seg ut fra alle de andre elevenes* her work stands out from that of all the other pupils. Se også *skilles*. **skille|linje** *sb* dividing line. **~mur** *sb* partition wall. **~mynt** *sb* change. **skilles** *vb* **1** *(gå fra hverandre)* part; *deres veier skiltes* their ways parted; *de skiltes i sinne* they parted in anger; *la oss* ~ *som venner* let us part friends; **2** *(om ektepar)* be divorced. **skille|tegn** *sb* punctuation mark. **~vegg** *sb* partition. **~vei** *sb* crossroads; *vi var kommet til en ~vei* we had come to a crossroads.

skillinge *vb:* ~ *sammen* club together; get up a subscription.

skilpadde *sb (især land~)* tortoise; *(hav~)* turtle; *forloren* ~ mock-turtle.

skilsmisse *sb* **1** *(avskjed)* parting; **2** *(oppløsning av ekteskap)* divorce. **skilsmissesak** *sb* divorce case.

skilt *sb* **1** *(butikk~)* sign, signboard; **2** *(gate~, trafikk~)* sign; **3** *(reklame~)* advertisement board; **4** *(navneplate, lege~)* plate. **skiltvakt** *sb* sentry; *stå ~vakt* stand sentry.

ski|løper *sb* skier. **~løype** *sb* ski track.

skimt *sb: få/se ~(en) av* get/catch a glimpse of. **skimte** *vb (så vidt se)* see dimly.

skingre *vb* shrill; *med ~nde stemme* in a shrill voice.

skinke *sb* ham.

skinn *sb* **A 1** *(lys)* light; *(blendende ~)* glare; **2** *(utseende som ikke svarer til virkeligheten)* appearance; *~et bedrar* appearances are deceptive; *han har ~et mot seg* appearances are against him; *under* ~ *av vennskap* under the show of friendship; **B 1** *(hud)* skin; *han er bare* ~ *og bein* he is only skin and bones; *hun reddet ~et* she saved her skin; *våt til ~et* wet to the skin; **2** *(hud av større dyr)* hide; **3** *(pelsverk)* fur; **4** *(lær)* leather; **5** *(uttrykk) gå ut av sitt gode* ~ jump out of one's skin; *holde seg i ~et* toe the line; *selge ~et før bjørnen er skutt* count one's chickens before they are hatched; *våge ~et* risk one's life.

skinn|angrep *sb* feint; mock attack. **~bind** *sb* leather cover. **~død** *adj* apparently dead; asphyxiated.

skinne A *sb (jernbane~ etc)* rail; *toget gikk av ~ene* the train ran off the rails/was derailed; **B** *vb* **1** *(lyse, stråle)* shine; *(sterkere)* blaze; *månen skinte inn i rommet* the moon shone into the room; **2** *(glitre)* sparkle; *øynene hans skinte av glede* his eyes sparkled with joy. **skinne|bein** *sb* shin(bone), tibia. **~buss** *sb* railbus. **~gang** *sb* rails, track.

skinnende *adj* shining; bright.

skinn|fell *sb* fur rug. **~hanske** *sb* leather glove.

skinnhellig *adj* hypocritical.

skinn|kåpe *sb* fur cloak. **~lue** *sb* fur cap. **~mager** *adj* skinny.

skinnmanøvre *sb* feint.

skinnpose *sb* leather bag; *(til baby)* fur bag.

skinnsyk *adj* jealous; *han var* ~ *på sin venn* he was jealous of his friend. **skinnsyke** *sb* jealousy.

skip *sb* ship; *(fartøy)* vessel; *ombord på et* ~ on board a ship. **skipe** *vb (sende med skip)* ship. **skipper** *sb* shipmaster, skipper. **skipper|skjønn** *sb* rough estimate; *etter ~skjønn* by rule of thumb. **~skrøne** *sb* tall story; cock-and-bull story. **~tak** *sb: ta arbeidet i ~tak* work by fits and starts; *ta et* ~ make an all-out effort.

skips|aksje *sb* shipping share. **~besetning** *sb* crew. **~byggeri** *sb (verft)* shipyard; shipbuilding yard. **~bygging** *sb* shipbuilding. **~dekk** *sb* deck (of a ship). **~fart** *sb* **1** *(seilas)* navigation; *farlig for ~farten* dangerous to navigation; *isen har stanset all ~fart* the ice has stopped all navigation; **2** *(~fart som næringsvei)* shipping. **~fører** *sb* captain; master mariner. **~journal** *sb* log (book). **~kaptein** *sb* sea captain. **~kiste** *sb* sea chest. **~lege** *sb* ship's doctor. **~leilighet** *sb: få ~leilighet til* obtain a passage to. **~mannskap** *sb* crew. **~megler** *sb* shipbroker. **~offiser** *sb* ship officer. **~reder** *sb* shipowner. **~rederi** *sb* shipping company. **~verft** *sb* shipyard; shipbuilding yard.

ski|renn *sb* skiing competition. **~sport** *sb* skiing.

skisse *sb* **1** *(utkast)* outline, sketch; **2** *(tegnet ~)* sketch. **skissebok** *sb* sketch-book. **skissere** *vb* sketch.

skistav *sb* ski stick.

skitne *vb: ~ til* dirty, soil. **skitt 1** *sb* dirt; *(sterkere)* filth; **2** *som adv: det går ~* things are going badly. **skitten** *adj* dirty, soiled. **skitten|grå** *adj* dirty grey. **~tøy** *sb* soiled linen. **skitt|viktig** *adj* stuck up. **~vær** *sb* nasty weather.

skitur *sb: dra på ~* go skiing.

skive *sb* **1** *(rund plate)* disc, disk; **2** *(brød~ etc)* slice; *(tykk ~)* chunk; *jeg skar brødet opp i ~r* I cut the loaf into slices; **3** *(skyte~)* target.

skje A *sb* spoon; *få det inn med ~er* be spoon-fed; *ta ~en i en annen hånd* turn over a new leaf; **B** *vb* **1** *(hende, især tilfeldig)* happen; *det har ikke ~dd noenting* nothing has happened; **2** *(finne sted)* occur; take place; (ofte brukes former av *to be*) be; *det har ~dd en ulykke* there has been an accident.

skjebne *sb* **1** *(blind ~)* fate; *~n har bestemt det* fate has decided it; *en tung ~* a hard fate; **2** *(forsynet)* destiny; *(ofte)* fortune; *(tilfeldig ~)* chance; *~n har brakt dem sammen* chance has brought them together; *begunstiget av ~n* favoured by fortune; *ingen kan kjempe mot (sin) ~* no one can fight against destiny; *ved (en) ~ns gunst* by good fortune; **4** *(lodd i livet)* lot; *hans ~ har vært hard* his lot has been a hard one. **skjebne|bestemt** *adj* destined, fated. **~svanger** *adj* **1** *(ødeleggende)* fatal; *et ~svangert slag* a fatal blow; **2** *(ulykkelig)* disastrous; *en ~svanger plan* a disastrous scheme; **3** *(avgjørende)* fateful; *et ~svangert øyeblikk* a fateful moment. **~tro** *sb* fatalism.

skjede *sb* **1** *(slire)* sheath; **2** *(vagina)* vagina.

skjefull *sb* spoonful.

skjegg *sb* beard; *en mann med ~* a bearded man; *han har ~* he grows/has a beard; *le i ~et* laugh in/up one's sleeve. **skjegget(e)** *adj* **1** *(ubarbert)* unshaved; **2** *(med skjegg)* bearded. **skjeggstubb** *sb* stubble.

skjele *vb* squint; *~ til noe* squint at something; *han ~r på venstre øye* he has a squint in his left eye.

skjelett *sb* skeleton; *(om reisverk etc også)* framework.

skjell *sb* **A** scale; **B** *gjøre rett og ~ (for seg)* do the right thing; give everyone his due; *gjøre rett og ~ mot* do the right thing by; *~s år og alder* age/years of discretion.

skjelle *vb* **A** *~ og smelle* fume and rage; *~ på* scold; *~ ut* abuse; *~ ut for* call; *hun skjelte på ham fordi han var lat* she scolded him for being lazy; **B** *det ~r deg ikke* it is none of your business.

skjellig *adj: ~ grunn* good reason; sufficient cause.

skjellsord *sb* term of abuse; *koll* abuse.

skjelm *sb (skøyer)* rogue; *en kan gjøre en ~ urett* ≈ one must give the devil his due. **skjelmsk** *adj* roguish.

skjelne *vb* distinguish; make out; *han hørte stemmer, men kunne ikke ~ ordene* he heard voices, but could not distinguish the words; *jeg kunne så vidt ~ fjellene i det fjerne* I could just discern/make out the mountains far off; *kan du ~ mellom de to tvillingene?* can you distinguish/tell the two twins apart?

skjelv *sb* shaking, trembling; *få den store ~en* get the jitters. **skjelve** *vb* tremble; *hun skalv av kulde/sinne* she trembled with cold/anger; *stemmen hans skalv* his voice trembled. **skjelven** *adj* shaky; *den gamle mannen var svak og ~* the old man was weak and shaky. **skjelvhendt** *adj: han var ~* his hands were shaky. **skjelving** *sb* tremble, trembling; shake, shaking.

skjeløyd *adj* squinting; cross-eyed, squint-eyed.

skjema *sb* form; *fylle ut et ~* fill in a form. **skjematisere** *vb* schematize. **skjematisk** *adj* schematic.

skjemme *vb* **1** *(vansire)* disfigure; *arrene ~r ansiktet hans* the scars disfigure his face; **2** *(forderve)* spoil; *grønnsakene blir skjemt om du koker dem for lenge* the vegetables will be spoilt if you let them boil too long; **3** *~ bort* spoil; *de skjemte bort barna sine* they spoilt their children; **4** *~ en kniv* dull a knife.

skjemmes *vb* be ashamed of oneself.

skjemt *sb* jest, joke; *på ~* in jest. **skjemte** *vb* banter; jest, joke.

skjendig *adj* **1** *(skammelig)* outrageous; *en ~ urett* an outrageous injustice/wrong; **2** *(vanærende)* disgraceful, shameful; *~ oppførsel* disgraceful/shameful conduct. **skjendighet** *sb (skjendig handling)* outrage.

skjene *vb: ~ ut/til siden* swerve, side-slip; fly off at a tangent.

skjenk *sb* **1** *(drink)* drink; *de fikk ~* they were served a drink; **2** *(gave)* gift, present; **3** *(møbel)* sideboard. **skjenke** *vb* **1** *(helle opp)* pour out; *~ te* pour out the tea; **2** *(beverte med drikkevarer)* serve drinks/a drink; *jeg ble ~t full* I was made drunk; **3** *(gi)* bestow, give; present with; *~ dem det* bestow it on them; *hun ~t ham fem tusen pund* she presented him with five thousand pounds. **skjenkerett** *sb* licence; *ha ~* be licenced; *hotellet har ~* the hotel is licenced.

skjenn *sb* scolding; *få ~* get a scolding. **skjenne** *vb* scold; *de skjente på ham fordi han var doven* they scolded him for being lazy. **skjennepreken** *sb* scolding, lecture.

skjensel *sb* disgrace, dishonour.

skjeppe *sb* bushel; *stille sitt lys under en ~* hide one's light under a bushel.

skjerf *sb* muffler, scarf; comforter.

skjerm *sb* **1** screen; **2** *(skvett~ på bil etc)* mudguard; **3** *(lampe~)* shade; **4** *(beskyttelses~)* shield. **skjerm|bilde** *sb* X-ray. **~bildefotografere** *vb: bli skjermbildefotografert* have an X-ray examination. **~brett** *sb* screen. **skjerme** *vb* protect, shield.

skjerpe *vb* **1** *(gjøre skarp)* sharpen; **2** *(gjøre strengere)* make more rigorous/stringent; intensify, tighten up; *kontrollen ble ~t* the control was intensified/was made more stringent. **skjerpende** *adj: ~ omstendigheter* aggravating circumstances.

skjerv *sb: enkens ~* the widow's mite; *yte sin ~* offer one's mite.

skjev *adj* **1** wry; crooked, lopsided; *med et ~t smil* with a wry smile. **skjevt** *adv* askew; awry, wryly; *han smilte ~* he smiled wryly; *gardinene hang ~* the curtains hung askew; *slipset ditt sitter ~* your tie is awry/not straight. **skjevhet** *sb* wryness; crookedness, lopsidedness.

skjold *sb* **1** *(dekkvåpen)* shield; **2** *(på skilpadder etc)* carapace. **skjoldbruskkjertel** *sb* thyriod gland. **skjoldet(e)** *adj* blotched, blotchy.

skjorte *sb* shirt. **skjorte|bryst** *sb* shirt front. **~erme** *sb* shirt-sleeve; *i ~ermene* in one's shirt--sleeves. **~flak** *sb* shirt tail. **~knapp** *sb* shirt button; *(kraveknapp)* (collar-)stud. **~krave** *sb* shirt collar. **~stoff** *sb* shirting.

skjul *sb* **1** *(skjulested)* hiding-place; *legge ~ på* make a secret of; **2** *(ly)* cover, shelter; **3** *(uthus)* shed. **skjule** *vb* conceal, hide; *~ sine følelser* hide/conceal one's feelings; *han skjulte ansiktet i hendene* he hid his face in his hands. **skjulested** *sb* hiding-place. **skjult** *adj* concealed, hidden; *en ~ mening* a hidden meaning; *holde seg ~* be (in) hiding; *i det ~e* secretly; in secret.

skjær A *adj (om åker)* ripe; **B** *sb (i sjøen)* rock, skerry; *de støtte på et ~* they struck a rock; **C** *sb (lys~)* gleam, glow; light; *(sterkere)* flare, glare; *~et fra ilden* the glow of the fire; **C** *sb (på plog etc)* (plough)share.

skjære A *sb (fugl)* magpie; **B** *vb (med kniv etc)* cut; *~ brød* cut bread; *hun skar seg* she cut herself; *hun skar seg i fingeren* she cut her finger; **2** *(~ ut)* carve; *de skar (ut) navnene sine i et tre* they carved their names in a tree; **3** *(uttrykk) ~ ansikter* make faces; *~ ned (på) utgiftene* cut down/reduce the expenses; *(om offentlige utgifter også)* apply the axe; *~ tenner* grind one's teeth; *det skar dem i øynene* the light hurt their eyes; *det skar meg i hjertet* it wrung my heart. **skjærende** *adj (om lyd)* piercing, shrill; *~ ironi* scathing irony; *~ motsetning* glaring contrast. **skjæring** *sb (jernbane~, vei~)* cutting. **skjæringspunkt** *sb* (point of) intersection.

skjærsild *sb* purgatory.

skjærtorsdag *sb* Maunday Thursday.

skjød *sb (fang)* lap, knee. **skjødehund** *sb* lap-dog. **skjødesløs** *adj* careless; *~ med sin person* careless of one's person; *han er ~ med sitt arbeid* he is careless in his work. **skjødesløshet** *sb* carelessness.

skjønn I *adj (vakker)* beautiful, lovely; *i (sin) ~este orden* in apple-pie order; **II** *sb* **1** *(dømmekraft)* judg(e)ment; *en kvinne med (et) godt ~* a woman of sound judgement; **2** *(bedømmelse)* estimate, judg(e)ment; opinion; *etter beste ~* to the best of one's judgement; *etter mitt ~* in my opinion; *handle etter ~* use one's discretion; **3** *(takst)* valuation.

skjønne *vb* understand; *~ seg på* be a judge of; understand/know about; *de er forlovet, ~r du* they are engaged, you see; *så vidt jeg ~r* as far as I can make out. **skjønner** *sb* connoisseur; a good judge.

skjønnhet *sb* beauty. **skjønnhets|konkurranse** *sb* beauty contest. **~middel** *sb* cosmetic. **~plett** *sb* beauty spot. **~salong** *sb* beauty parlour. **~sans** *sb* sense of beauty.

skjønn|litteratur *sb* belles lettres; *(om romaner og noveller)* fiction. **~litterær** *adj: en ~litterær forfatter* a writer of fiction.

skjønns|mann *sb* appraiser, valuer. **~messig** *adj* rough; *et ~messig overslag* a rough estimate.

skjønt *konj* although, though; *jeg skal komme ~ jeg er svært opptatt* I'll come though I am rather busy.

skjør *adj* **1** *(som går lett i stykker)* fragile; *disse glassene er nokså ~e* these glasses are rather fragile; **2** *(forrykt)* crazy. **skjørbuk** *sb* scurvy.

skjørt *sb* skirt; *(skotte~)* kilt. **skjørtejeger** *sb* skirt chaser; womanizer.

skjøt *sb (sammenføyning)* joint. **skjøte A** *sb (dokument)* deed; **B** *vb* **1** *(føye sammen)* join; **2** *(forlenge)* lengthen. **skjøteledning** *sb* extension cord.

skjøtsel *sb* care, management.

skjøtte *vb* look after; take care of.

skli *vb* slide; *(skrense)* skid. **sklie** *sb* slide.

sko 1 *sb* shoe; *den vet best hvor ~en trykker som har den på* everyone knows best where his own shoe pinches; *over en lav ~* indiscriminately; **2** *vb* shoe; *~ en hest* shoe a horse. **skobørste** *sb* shoe brush. **skodd** *adj, pp* shod.

skodde *sb* **A** *(tåke)* fog, mist; **B** *(vinduslem)* (window) shutter.

skoft *sb* absenteeism. **skofte** *vb* cut work; shirk.

skog *sb* wood; *(større ~)* forest; *vi gikk en tur i ~en* we went for a walk in the woods. **skog|belte** *sb* forest belt. **~bevokst** *adj* wooded; well-timbered; well--wooded. **~brann** *sb* forest fire. **~bruk** *sb* forestry. **~bruker** *sb* forest owner. **~bryn** *sb* edge of a forest. **~bunn** *sb* forest floor. **~bygd, ~distrikt** *sb* wooded district. **~eiendom** *sb* forest property. **~eier** *sb* forest owner. **~fattig** *adj* poorly/sparsely wooded.

skogger|latter *sb* roar of laughter; *(neds)* guffaw, horselaugh. **~le** *vb* roar with laughter; guffaw.

skog|grense *sb* timber line. **~holt** *sb* grove, spinney. **~kant** *sb* edge of a wood. **~kledd** *adj* forest-clad, wooded. **~lendt** *adj* wooded. **~løs** *adj* treeless. **~planting** *sb* (af)forestation. **~rik** *adj* wooded; well--timbered, well-wooded. **skogs|arbeid** *sb* forest labour; *US* lumbering. **~arbeider** woodman; *US* lumberjack.

sko|horn shoehorn, shoeing-horn. **~hæl** heel (of a shoe).

skokk *sb* crowd.

skokrem *sb* shoe polish.

skole *sb* school; *av den gamle ~* of the old school; *begynne på ~en* be sent to school; enter school; *foreldrene deres er borte på ~en* their parents are at the school; *gå på ~en* go to school; *gå ut av ~en* leave school; *hvilken ~ går de på?* what school are they at? *ta i ~* take to task; *vi gikk sammen på ~en* we were at school together. **skole|alder** *sb* school age. **~arbeid** *sb* school work. **~attest** *sb* school certificate. **~ball** *sb* school dance. **~barn** *sb fl* school children. **~benk** *sb* form; *rett fra ~benken* fresh from school. **~bok** *sb* schoolbook, textbook. **~bygning** *sb* school house. **~dag** *sb* school-day; *i mine ~dager* in my school-days. **~eksempel** *sb* textbook example. **~elev** *sb* pupil; schoolboy, schoolgirl. **~fag** *sb* school subject. **~ferie** *sb* school holidays; vacation. **~film** *sb* educational film. **~fri** *sb: ha ~fri* have a day off from school. **~gang** *sb* school attendance; schooling. **~gutt** *sb* schoolboy. **~gård** *sb* schoolyard. **~hjem** *sb (for vanskelige barn)* approved school; reform school; reformatory. **~kamerat** school fellow; schoolmate. **~kjøkken** *sb* school kitchen. **~korps** *sb* school band. **~kringkasting** *sb* school broadcast; school radio. **~lege** *sb* school doctor. **~lærer** *sb* schoolmaster, teacher. **~mat** *sb* lunch packet. **~mester** *sb* teacher. **~modenhet** *sb* school readiness. **~penger** *sb* school fees. **~pike** *sb* schoolgirl. **~plan** *sb (fastsatt pensum)* curriculum, syllabus. **~plikt** *sb* compulsory school attendance. **~pliktig** *adj* of school age.

skolere *vb* school, train.

skole|stil *sb* essay, composition. **~styrer** *sb* headmaster; *US* principal. **~styre** *sb* Local Education Authority; the L.E.A. **~styrer** *sb* headmaster, headteacher. **~tid** *sb* **1** *(skoledag)* school hours; *etter/før ~tid* after/before school hours; *i ~tiden* during school hours; *utenfor ~tiden* out of school hours; **2** *(den tid da man gikk på skolen)* school-days; *i min ~* in my school-days. **~time** *sb* lesson. **~tur** *sb* school excursion/outing. **~utdannelse** *sb* schooling. **~veske** *sb* school bag.

sko|lisse *sb* shoe-lace, shoe-string. **~maker** *sb* shoemaker, bootmaker; *(lappe~ også)* cobbler.

skonnert *sb* schooner.

sko|puss *sb* shoe polishing. **~pusser** *sb* shoeblack; *US* shoeshine.

skorpe *sb* crust; *(på sår også)* scab; *(på ost)* rind.

skorstein *sb* **1** *(grue)* fireplace; **2** *(pipe)* chimney; *(på skip)* funnel. **skorsteins|feier** *sb* chimney-sweep(er). **~pipe** chimney-pot.

skort *sb (mangel)* lack, shortage. **skorte** *vb: det ~r på* there is a lack/shortage of.

skosverte *sb* shoe polish.

skotsk *adj* Scottish; *(især brukt av skotter)* Scots; *(om whisky, terrier og språket)* Scotch. **skotskrutet** *adj* tartan.

skott *sb* bulkhead.

skotte *sb (person fra Skottland)* Scot, Scotchman, Scotsman; *(om kvinne)* Scotchwoman, Scotswoman; *~ne (som nasjon)* the Scotch; the Scots.

skotte *vb (gløtte, kikke) ~ på* steal a glance at.

skottelue *sb* tam-o-shanter.

skotøy *sb* foot-wear. **skotøybutikk** *sb* shoe shop.

skovl *sb* **1** *(skuffe)* shovel; **2** *(på hjulbåt)* paddle; **3** *(på turbin)* blade, vane; **4** *(på gravemaskin)* bucket; **5** *(på vaskemaskin)* spinner. **skovlhjul** *sb* **1** *(i kvern etc)* mill-wheel; **2** *(på hjulbåt)* paddle-wheel.

skral *adj* **1** *(om helsetilstand)* frail, poorly; **2** *(avfeldig)* decrepit; **3** *(falleferdig)* ramshackle, cranky.

skrall *sb (brak, knall)* crack, crash; *(om torden~ også)* clap, peal.

skralle I *sb (på verktøy)* ratchet; **II** *vb* **1** *(runge)* peal; ring out; **2** *(om blåseinstrument)* blare; **3** *(skramle)* clatter, rattle. **skrallende** *adj: ~ latter* roar of laughter; *(neds)* guffaw.

skramle *vb* rattle.

skramme *sb* scratch; *uten en ~* without a scratch.

skrammel *sb* **1** *(skramling)* clatter, rattle; **2** *(skrap)* rubbish, junk, lumber.

skrangle 1 *sb (rangle)* rattle; **2** *vb (skramle)* rattle; *~ av sted* rattle along. **skrangle|kasse, ~kjerre** *sb* crock, rattletrap. **skranglet(e)** *adj (skrøpelig)* rattling, rickety; *(ulenkelig)* lanky. **skranglevei** *sb* bumpy road.

skranke *sb* bar, barrier; *(disk)* counter; *(i turn)* parallel bars; *sette ~ for* set bounds to; *tre i ~n for* champion; take up the cudgels for.

skrante *vb* be ailing; be in bad health; *et ~nde barn* a sickly child. **skranten** *adj* ailing, sickly.

skrap *sb* junk, rubbish, trash.

skrape I *sb* **1** *(redskap)* scraper; **2** *(irettesettelse)* reprimand; *få en ~* be reprimanded; **II** *vb* scrape; *~ sammen* scrape together; *bukke og ~* bow and scrape; *han skrapte av all malingen* he scraped all the paint off. **skrap|handel** *sb* junk-shop; second-hand shop. **~handler** *sb* junkman. **~handlertomt** *sb* junkyard. **~haug** *sb* junk heap. **~jern** *sb* scrap iron. **~kake** *sb (attpåklatt)* afterthought.

skratt *sb (latter)* cackle. **skratte** *vb* **1** *(le)* cackle; **2** *(om fugler)* chatter.

skravl *sb* chatter, jabbering; babble. **skravle** *vb* chatter, jabber; *(sladre)* gossip. **skravlebøtte** *sb* chatterbox, gossip. **skravlet(e)** *adj* talkative.

skred *sb (snø~)* avalanche; *(jord~, og fig)* landslide.

skredder *sb* tailor.

skredder|forretning *sb* tailor's shop. **~sydd** *adj* tailored, tailor-made.

skrei *sb (torsk)* cod.

skrekk *sb* terror; alarm, fear; fright; *de skalv av ~* they shook/trembled with fear; *få en ~ i livet* get a fright; get frightened; *til ~ og advarsel* as a deterrent; *slippe med ~en* be more frightened than hurt. **skrekkelig** *adj* **1** horrible, terrible; dreadful, frightful; **2** *(svært dårlig)* awful; *en ~ bok* an awful book; **3** *dgl (veldig)* awful; *~ mange penger* an awful lot of money. **skrekk|innjagende** *adj* terrifying. **~slagen** *adj* terrified; terror-stricken, terror-struck.

skrell *sb* peel; *eple~* the peel of an apple. **skrelle** *vb* peel.

skremme *vb* frighten, scare; *(~ plutselig)* startle; *hun ble skremt* she got/was frightened/scared. **skremmebilde** *sb* bog(e)y.

skremsel *sb (trusel)* threat.

skrense *vb* swerve, skid.

skrent *sb* steep slope.

skreppe *sb* knapsack. **skreppekar** *sb* pedlar.

skrev *sb* crotch, crutch; fork. **skreve** *vb (sprike med beina)* spread the legs; *(ta lange skritt)* stride; *~ over (stige over)* stride over; *(stå skrevs over)* straddle. **skrevs** *adv: ~ over* astride; *sitte ~ over en stol* sit astride a chair; straddle a chair.

skribent *sb* writer, author.

skri(de) *vb (gå langsomt og verdig)* stalk, stride; *~ frem (gjøre fremgang)* progress; *~ inn* step in; take measures; *~ til handling* take action; *arbeidet ~r jevnt frem(over)* the work is progressing steadily.

skrift *sb* **1** *a) (skrivemåte)* hand; *b) (hånd~)* (hand)writing; *med hennes ~* in her handwriting; **2** *(motsatt tale)* writing; *i ~ og tale* in writing and speeches; **3** *(trykksak)* publication; *(hefte)* pamphlet; *Wergelands samlede ~er* the complete works of Wergeland; *Skriften (Bibelen)* (the) Scripture(s). **skrifte 1** *sb (bekjennelse av synd)* confession; *gå til ~* go to confession; **2** *vb (bekjenne)* confess. **skrifte|far** *sb* (father) confessor. **~mål** *sb* confession. **~stol** *sb* confessional. **skriftlig 1** *adj* written; in writing; *et ~ svar* a written answer; an answer in writing; **2** *(adv)* by writing; by letter; *han svarte ~* he answered by letter. **skriftspråk** *sb* written language.

skrik *sb* **1** cry; *han utstøtte et ~ om hjelp* he gave/uttered a cry for help; *siste ~ i hatter* the last word in hats; **2** *(sterkere, uartikulert ~)* scream, shriek; *smerte~* scream of pain; *angst~* shriek of anguish; *hun utstøtte et ~ av redsel* she screamed/shrieked with horror; **3** *(hyl)* yell.

skrike *vb* **1** *(rope)* cry (out); call; *han skrek av smerte* he cried out with pain; *hun skrek om hjelp* she cried/called for help; **2** *(~ sterkere, uartikulert)* scream, shriek; *han skrek av redsel* he shrieked with horror; *(sped)barnet skrek hele natten* the baby screamed all night; **3** *(brøle)* bawl, bellow; **4** *(skråle)* yell; **5** *(uttrykk) ~nde farger* glaring/gaudy colours; *~nde urett* crying/flagrant injustice; *stå i ~nde misforhold til* be out of all proportion to. **skrikerunge** *sb* cry-baby.

skrin *sb* box, case; chest. **skrinlegge** *vb: ~ en plan* abandon/pigeon-hole/shelve a plan.

skrinn *adj (om mennesker og dyr)* lean, scraggy; *(om jord)* barren, poor.

skritt *sb* **1** *(steg)* step, pace; *~ for ~* step by step; *han gikk med tunge ~* he walked heavily; *hun tok et ~ mot meg* she took a step towards me; **2** *(skrev)* crotch, crutch; fork. **skritte** *vb: ~ opp* pace out; *~ ut* step out briskly. **skritt|gang** *sb: i ~* at a walking pace. **~lengde** *sb* (length of) pace.

skriv *sb* letter. **skrive** *vb* **1** write; *(~ på maskin)* type(write); *brevet var maskinskrevet* the letter was typewritten; **2** *(stave)* write, spell; *hvordan ~r du navnet ditt?* how do you spell your name? *ordet ~s med p* the word is written/spelt with a p; **3** *(uttrykk)* **~ av** *(kopiere)* copy; *(fuske)* crib off; **~ seg fra** date back to; date from; *min interesse for sjeldne mynter ~r seg fra skoledagene* my interest in rare coins dates back to my schooldays; **~ inn** *(i protokoll etc)* enter; *hun skrev summen inn i protokollen* she entered the sum in the ledger; **~ med:** *skrevet med blyant* written in pencil; *skrevet med stor bokstav* write with a capital letter; **~ ned** put/write down; record; *alt han sa ble skrevet ned* everything he said was put down; **~ opp** write down (jf *~ ned*); **~ under** sign. **skrive|blokk** *sb* writing pad. **~bok** *sb* exercise book. **~bord** *sb* (writing-)-desk; *(større)* writing-table. **~feil** *sb* slip of the pen; *(på skrivemaskin)* typing error. **~krampe** *sb* writer's cramp. **skrivelse** *sb* letter. **skrive|maskin** *sb* typewriter. **~maskinoperatør** *sb* typist. **~papir** *sb* writing-paper; notepaper. **~pult** *sb* (writing-)desk. **~redskap** *sb* writing utensil. **~saker** *sb* writing materials. **~underlag** blotting-pad. **skrivning** *sb* writing.

skrog *sb* **1** *(om skip)* hull; **2** *(om fly)* fuselage; **3** *(om biler)* chassis.

skrot *sb* rubbish, trash; junk. **skrothaug** *sb* junk heap.

skrott *sb* **1** *(kropp)* body; **2** *(dødt dyr, slakt)* carcass, carcase; **3** *(kjernehus)* core; *eple~* the core of an apple.

skru *vb* screw; **~ av** unscrew; screw off; *~ av vannet* turn off the water; *~ av lyset* switch off the light; **~ fast** screw on; fasten with screws; **~ på** *vannet* turn on the water; *~ på lyset* switch on the light.

skrubb *sb* scrubbing brush. **skrubbe** *vb* scrub. **skrubbsulten** *adj* ravenous. **skrubbsår** *sb* graze.

skrublyant *sb* propelling pencil; *US* automatic pencil. **skrue** *sb* screw; *en underlig ~ (fig)* a character; an eccentric; *ha en ~ løs* have a screw loose. **skrue|gang, ~gjenge** *sb* screw thread. **~stikke** *sb* se *skrustikke.* **skru|is** *sb* pack-ice. **~jern** *sb* screwdriver.

skrukk(e) *sb* wrinkle. **skrukke** *vb* wrinkle. **skrukket(e)** *adj* wrinkled.

skrukork *sb* screw-cap.

skrullet(e) *adj* crazy, barmy. **skrulling** *sb* crackpot.

skrulokk *sb* screw-cap.

skrumpe *vb: ~ inn/sammen* shrink; shrivel up.

skrunøkkel *sb* spanner, wrench.

skruppel *sb* scruple; *uten skrupler* without scruple; *vi fikk skrupler* we had scruples. **skruppelløs** *adj* unscrupulous.

skrupuløs *adj* scrupulous.

skru|stikke *sb* vice. **~trekker** *sb* screwdriver.

skryt *sb* boasting, bragging. **skryte** *vb* boast, brag; *han ~r av at han er den beste fotballspilleren på laget* he boasts that he is the best footballer of the team. **skrythals** *sb* boaster, braggart.

skrøne 1 *sb (liten løgn)* fib; *(historie)* cock-and-bull story; **2** *vb (smålyve)* tell a fib/fibs. **skrønemaker** *sb* fibber, storyteller.

skrøpelig *adj* **1** *(om helsesvak)* frail, weak; *~ helse* weak health; *en ~ gammel dame* a frail old woman; **2** *(som lett går i stykker)* fragile; **3** *(falleferdig, skral)* ramshackle, cranky. **skrøpelighet** *sb* frailty, weakness.

skrå A 1 *adj* slanting, sloping; *et ~tak* a slanting/sloping roof; *på ~* se *skrått*; **2** *vb (gå på skrå) ~ over gaten* cross the street (diagonally); **B 1** *sb (~tobakk)* chewing tobacco; *(om bussen)* quid, plug; **2** *vb (tygge ~tobakk)* chew tobacco.

skrål *sb* bawl(ing), howl(ing), shout(ing), yell(ing). **skråle** *vb* bawl, howl, shout, yell. **skrålhals** *sb* bawler.

skråne *vb* slant, slope; *gaten ~t svakt nedover* the road sloped down gently/gradually. **skråning** *sb* **1** *(bakke~)* slope; **2** *(fjell~)* hillside; mountain side. **skrå|plan** *sb* **1** inclined plane; **2** *fig* downward path, slippery slope. **~sikker** *adj (om person)* cocksure; *det er ~sikkert* it is quite certain. **~sikkerhet** *sb* cocksureness. **skrå|strek** *sb* diagonal; slash. **~tak** *sb* slanting/sloped roof. **~tobakk** *sb* chewing tobacco. **skrått** *adv: sollyset falt ~ ned over huset* the sunlight slanted over the house; *stolpen stod ~/på skrå* the pole slanted/sloped.

skubb *sb* push; *(støt)* thrust. **skubbe** *vb* push; *(~ kraftig)* shove.

skudd *sb* **1** *(~ med våpen etc)* shot; *det falt et ~* a shot was fired; there was a shot; *~et gikk av* the gun/rifle etc went off; *som et ~* like a shot; *være i ~et* be popular **2** *(plante~)* shoot. **skudd|fri** *adj: gå ~fri* get off scot-free. **~hold** *sb* range; *komme på ~hold* get within range. **~linje** *sb* line of fire. **~sikker** *adj* bullet-proof. **~sår** *sb* bullet wound. **~veksling** *sb* exchange of fire. **~vidde** se *~hold*. **~år** *sb* leap-year.

skue 1 *sb* sight, spectacle; *bære til ~* display; *det var et storslått ~* it was a magnificent spectacle/sight; **2** *vb (se)* see; *en skal ikke ~ hunden på hårene* appearances are deceptive. **skueplass** *sb* scene. **skuespill** *sb* play. **skuespiller** *sb* actor. **skuespillerinne** *sb* actress. **skuespillforfatter** *sb* playwright.

skuff *sb (i kommode, skap)* drawer.

skuffe A 1 *sb (sne~ etc)* shovel; **2** *vb (måke)* shovel; *~ snø* shovel the snow away; **B** *vb (ikke oppfylle forventninger)* disappoint; *~t over* disappointed at/in; *han ~t meg* I was disappointed in him. **skuffelse** *sb* disappointment; *(sterk ~ stundom)* frustration; *~ over* disappointment at; *vi fikk en stor ~* we met with/suffered a great disappointment. **skuffende** *adj* **1** disappointing; **2** *(illuderende)* striking; *en ~ likhet* a striking likeness.

skulder *sb* shoulder; *han trakk på skuldrene* he shrugged (his shoulders). **skulder|blad** *sb* shoulder-blade. **~bredde** *sb* width across the shoulders. **~trekning** *sb* shrug. **~veske** *sb* shoulder-bag.

skule *vb* scowl; *han skulte på meg* he scowled at me. **skuling** *sb* scowl.

skulke *vb (~ skolen)* play truant; shirk school; *~ unna* shirk. **skulker** *sb (på skolen)* truant boy/girl. **skulk(ing)** *sb (på skolen)* truancy.

skulle *vb* (har på engelsk ingen infinitiv- eller partisippformer; de bøyde formene *shall, should* og *will, would* brukes som det fremgår av det følgende; se også *ville*) **1** *(ved befaling, påbud)* shall, should; be to; *han sier han ikke vil gå, men jeg sier han skal* he says he won't go, but I say he shall; *det der skal du gi (til) moren din* you are to give that to your mother; **2** *(ved løfte, trusel)* will, would *(især i 1. person)*; shall, should *(især i 2. og 3. person)*; *dette skal han få svi for!* he shall pay for this! *jeg skal vise ham hvem som er herre!* I will show him who is the master! *vi skal møte dem utenfor teatret* we will meet them outside the theatre; **3** *(om det som er avtalt eller uavvendelig)* be (going) to; *han skulle møte sin kone i Paris* he was to meet his wife in Paris; *jeg skulle aldri se ham igjen* I was never to see him again; *når skal du være der?* at what time are you to be there? *vi skal alle dø en gang* we are all going to die one day; **4** *(bør, burde)* ought to; should; *du skulle ha sagt det til meg i går* you ought to have told me yesterday; *toget skulle ha vært her nå* the train ought to be here by now; **5** *(om folkesnakk og rykter) han skal være rik* he is said to be/he is supposed to be rich; *hun skal ha vært i fengsel* they say she has been in prison; **6** *(i forbindelse med spørsmål og tvil)* shall, should; *de visste ikke hva de skulle gjøre* they did not know what to do; *han spurte om han skulle få tak i en drosje til henne* he asked whether he should get her a taxi; *hva skal vi gjøre?* what shall we/are we to do? *skal jeg fortelle ham det/si det til ham?* shall I tell him? *skal vi gå på kino?* shall we go to the cinema? **7** *(om eventualitet)* should; *om du skulle finne pengene, så si det ikke til noen* if you should find the money, don't tell anybody; **8** *(om hensikt)* be going to; *hun skal kjøpe ny bil* she is going to buy a new car; *(i hensiktssetninger)* might, should; *vi holdt oss stille så han ikke skulle bli forstyrret* we kept quiet that he might/should not be disturbed; **9** *(om nær fremtid) a)* be going to; be + *ing-*form; *jeg trodde hun skulle komme hjem snart* I thought she was coming home soon; *vi skal i teateret i aften* we are going to the theatre tonight; *b) (om noe nærmest sikkert)* be going to; *min kone skal ha en liten (en)* my wife is going to have a baby; **10** *(i at-setninger)* should; *det er da merkelig at du skulle tro det* it is strange that you should think so; *det er synd han skal være så gammel* it is a pity he should be so old; **11** *(uttrykk) jeg skal* **av** *her (sagt til konduktør, sjåfør etc)* I want to get off here; *(sagt til reisefølge)* this is where I get off; *hvor skal du* **hen?** where are you going? *jeg skal hjem* I am going home; *han skal til London, og jeg skal være med* he is going to London, and I am going with him; **~ til** *(behøves)* be necessary; take; *alt som skal til* everything necessary; *det skal to mann til for å holde ham* it takes two men to hold him; **~ til å** be going to; be about to; be on the point of; *jeg skulle akkurat til å* *ringe deg da du kom* I was on the point of ringing you up when you came; *jeg vet hva du skal til å si* I know what you are going to say; **si at** *de (han, hun etc) skal* tell them (him, her etc) to; *jeg sa hun skulle være hjemme innen klokken ti* I told her to be home by ten o'clock; *si at han skal vente* tell him to wait.

skulptur(arbeid) *sb* sculpture.

skuls *adj: bli* ~ get even; *være* ~ be quits.

skum *sb* **1** foam; *(~ på øl også)* froth; **2** *(såpe~)* lather; **3** *(~sprøyt)* spray. **skum|gummi** *sb* foam-rubber.

skumle *vb* insinuate; *det skumles om at det er begått underslag* it is insinuated that here has been an embezzlement. **skumlerier** *sb fl* insinuations.

skumme *vb* **1** *(danne skum)* foam; **2** *(skumme vekk)* skim; *~t melk* skimmed milk.

skummel *adj* **1** *(lumsk)* sinister; *skumle planer* sinister designs; **2** *(mørk og trist)* gloomy, sombre; dismal.

skumpe *vb* bomp, jolt.

skumre *vb: det ~r* it is getting dark. **skumring** *sb* dusk, twilight.

skur *sb* **A** shed; *(uværsskur)* shelter; *(liten hytte)* shanty hut; **B** *(regn~)* shower.

skur(d) *sb (skuronn)* harvesting/reaping season.

skure *vb* **1** scour; *(med børste og såpe)* scrub; *han skurte gulvet* he scrubbed the floor; **2** *la det* ~ let things slide. **skure|børste** *sb* scrubbing-brush. **~fille, ~klut** *sb* floor cloth. **~kone** *sb* charwoman. **~pulver** *sb* scouring powder.

skurfolk *sb* harvesters, reapers.

skuring *sb: det er grei* ~ that stands to reason.

skurk *sb* scoundrel, villain; *(hum)* rascal, rogue. **skurk|aktig** *adj* villainous. **~aktighet** *sb* villainy. **skurkestrek** *sb* dirty/vile trick.

skuronn *sb* harvesting/reaping season.

skurre *vb* grate, jar; *~ i ørene* grate/jar on the ears; *en ~nde lyd* a grating/jarring sound.

skurtresker *sb* combine; combine-harvester.

skusle *vb: ~ bort* waste.

skussmål *sb* character; *arbeidsgiveren (hans) gav ham (et) godt* ~ his employer gave him a good character.

skute *sb* ship, vessel; craft.

skutrygget *adj* round-shouldered.

skvalder *sb* babble, chatter. **skvaldre** *vb* babble, chatter. **skvaldrebøtte** *sb* chatterbox.

skvalpe *vb* lap, splash. **skvalp(ing)** *sb* lap(ping), splash(ing).

skvett *sb* **1** splash; *det er søleskvetter på frakken din* there are splashes of mud on your coat; **2** *(liten dråpe/slant)* dash, drop. **skvette** *vb* **1** splash; *som å ~ vann på gåsa* like water off a duck's back; **2** *(fare sammen)* start. **skvetten** *adj* jumpy.

skvett|lapp *sb* mudflap. **~skjerm** *sb* mudguard; *US* fender.

skvip *sb* dishwater; cat-lap, hogwash.

skvulp *sb (om lyd)en* lap(ping), splash(ing); *(om bevegelsen)* lap, ripple. **skvulpe** *vb* lap, splash; ripple.

skvær *adj* honest, square; *være* ~ play the game. **skvære** *vb: ~ opp* square up; settle.

sky A 1 *adj (fryktsom)* timid; *(om dyr)* shy; **2** *vb (holde seg unna)* avoid, shun; *alle ~r ham* everybody avoids him; *brent barn ~r ilden* once bitten twice shy; *hun ~r dårlig selskap* she shuns evil company; *ikke ~ noen anstrengelse/utgift* spare no effort/expense; **B** *sb (~ av damp, røyk etc)* cloud; *bakom ~ene er himmelen alltid blå* ≈ every cloud has a silver lining; *over ~ene* above the clouds. **sky|banke** *sb* bank of clouds. **~brudd** *sb* cloudburst. **~dekke** *sb: skiftende ~dekke* variable cloud (cover). **~dott** *sb* cloudlet. **skyet(e)** *adj* cloudy, clouded; *(overskyet)* overcast. **skyfri** *adj* cloudless, unclouded.

skygge I *sb* **1** *(motsatt lys)* shade; *ligge i ~n* lie in the shade; *tretti grader i ~n* thirty degrees in the shade; **2** *(egen~, slag~)* shadow; *~n av jorden faller av og til på månen* the shadow of the earth sometimes fall on the moon; **3** *(lue~ etc)* peak; *US* visor; **4** *(hemmelig forfølger)* shadow; *slang* tail; **5** *(uttrykk) han er bare en ~ av seg selv* he is a mere shadow/only a shadow of his former self; *ikke ~ av tvil* not a shade/shadow of doubt; *stille i ~n (fig)* overshadow, outshine; *hun stilte alle rivalene i ~n* she outshone all her rivals; **II** *vb* **1** *(gi skygge)* shade; give shade; *~ for øynene* shade one's eyes; *du ~ for meg* you are standing in my light; **2** *(følge etter i hemmelighet)* shadow; *jeg tror jeg ble ~t* I believe I was shadowed. **skygge|bokse** *vb* shadow-box. **~full** *adj* shady, shadowy. **~kabinett** *sb* shadow cabinet. **~lue** *sb* peaked cap. **~side** *sb* shady side; *(fig: mangel)* drawback.

skyhet *sb* timidity; *(om dyr)* shyness.

sky|høy *adj* skyhigh. **~lag** *sb* layer of cloud. **~lapper** *sb fl* blinkers.

skyld *sb* **1** *(juridisk/moralsk etc ~)* guilt; *den anklagedes ~ ble bevist* the guilt of the accused was proved; **2** *(~ som blir tillagt en)* blame; *det er alltid jeg som får ~en* it is always me who gets the blame; *hun gav meg ~en* she blamed me for it; she put the blame on me; **3** *(feil)* fault; *det er min* ~ it is my fault; *hvem har ~en?* whose fault is it? who is to blame? *være ~ i* be the cause of; be to blame for; **4** *for ... ~* for ... sake; *for den saks ~* for that matter; *for familiens ~* for the sake of my family/of the family; *for min ~ kan De godt røyke* I don't mind if you smoke; *jeg gjorde det for din ~* I did it for your sake. **skyldbevisst** *adj* conscious of guilt; guilty. **skylde** *vb* **1** owe; *~ en noe* owe somebody something; owe something to somebody; *jeg ~r deg fremdeles ti pund* I still owe you £10; *jeg ~r foreldrene mine alt* I owe everything to my parents; **2** *(gi skylden for)* blame; put the blame on; *han ~r alltid på søsteren sin* he always puts the blame on his sister; **3** *~ på (dvs unnskylde seg med)* plead; *han skyldte på at han ikke visste bedre* he pleaded ignorance. **skyldes** *vb* be due to; be owing to; *disse høye prisene ~ krigen* these high prices are due to the war; *hans død skyldtes en ulykke* his death was owing to an accident. **skyldfri** *adj* **1**

(uten skyld) blameless, guiltless; innocent; **2** *(gjeldfri)* free from debt. **skyldfølelse** *sb* sense of guilt. **skyldig** *adj* **1** *(som har skylden)* guilty; *den skyldige* the culprit; the offender; *du har gjort deg ~ i en alvorlig bommert* you are guilty of a serious blunder; *nekte seg ~ (i retten)* plead not guilty; **2** *(som en skylder) bli svar ~* be at a loss for an answer; *det ~e beløp* the amount owed. **skyldighet** *sb* duty. **skyldløs** se *skyldfri*. **skyldner** *sb* debtor. **skyldspørsmål** *sb* question of guilt; *det er juryen som avgjør ~et* it is the jury that decide the verdict.

skylle *vb* **1** *(rense)* rinse; *~ munnen* rinse one's mouth; **2** *(~ vekk)* wash (away etc); *tre menn ble skylt over bord* three men were washed overboard; **3** *(om regn)* pour; *regnet skylte ned* it was pouring (down); the rain came pouring down. **skylle|bøtte** *sb* **1** = *skylledunk;* **2** *(utskjelling)* flood of abuse. **~dunk** *sb* garbage pail. **skyller** *sb koll* garbage. **skyllevann** *sb* rinsing water.

skynde *vb* **1** *~ seg* hurry (up); make haste; *han skyndte seg å fortelle meg nyhetene* he hastened to tell me the news; *jeg må ~ meg* I am in a hurry; *vi skyndte oss hjem* we hurried home; **2** *~ på noen* hurry, hustle somebody. **skynding** *sb: i skyndingen* in one's hurry.

sky|pumpe *sb* waterspout. **~skraper** *sb* skyscraper.

skyss *sb: få ~* get a lift.

skyte *vb* **1** shoot; *han ble skutt i foten* he was shot in the foot; **2** *(uttrykk)* **~ bom** miss (the mark); **~ i** *været* shoot up; *gutten har skutt i været det siste året* the boy has shot up during the last year; **~ inn** *(innskyte)* throw in; *Jane skjøt inn et par ord nå og da* Jane threw in a word or two now and again; *øynene hans skjøt* **lyn** his eyes flashed; **~ mot** = *~ på*; **~ mål** score/shoot a goal; **~ ned** shoot down; **~ på** shoot at; **~ rygg:** *katten skjøt rygg* the cat arched her back; **~ utenfor** *(i fotball)* miss the goal; **~ vekst** grow apace; *fig* make rapid progress. **skyte|bane** *sb* rifle/shooting range; *(innendørs)* shooting gallery. **~skive** *sb* target; *fig* butt. **~våpen** *sb koll* fire-arms. **skyting** *sb* fire, firing; shooting; *de begynte/sluttet med ~en* they opened/ceased fire. **skyts** *sb koll* artillery, guns; ordnance.

skytsengel *sb* guardian angel.

skyttel *sb* shuttle.

skytter *sb* marksman; good shot; *han er en dårlig ~* he is a bad shot/a poor marksman. **skytter|grav** *sb* trench. **~lag** *sb* rifle club.

skyve *vb* push, shove. **skyve|dør** *sb* sliding door. **~tak** *(på bil)* slide-back top. **~vindu** *sb* sash window.

skøy *sb* fun. **skøyer** *sb* wag, rogue. **skøyer|aktig** *adj* waggish, roguish. **~strek** *sb* prank; practical joke.

skøyte A *sb (båt)* smack; **B 1** *sb (til ~løp)* skate; *et par ~r* a pair of skates; *gå på ~r* skate; **2** *vb (gå på skøyter; ta ~tak)* skate. **skøyte|bane** *sb* skating-rink. **~løp** *sb* skating; *(hurtigløp)* speed skating. **~løper** *sb* skater.

skål *sb* **1** saucer; *kopp og ~* a cup and saucer; **2** *(~ som utbringes)* toast; *utbringe en ~* propose a toast; *skål!* your health! *(mindre formelt)* cheerio!

skålde *vb* scald.

skåle *vb* drink, toast; *~ for (om personer)* drink the health of; *(især om ting)* drink to; *la oss ~ for det* let's drink to that; we'll drink to that.

skålvekt *sb* balance; (pair of) scales.

skåne *vb* be careful about/of; take care of; *han måtte ~ helsen sin* he had to take care of his health. **skånsel** *sb* mercy; *uten ~* they were treated without mercy. **skånselløs** *adj* merciless. **skånsom** *adj* gentle; *(varsom)* careful; *hun behandlet dem meget ~t* she was very gentle with them.

skår *sb* **1** *(glasskår etc)* shard; broken piece(s) (of a plate, vase etc); **2** *(hakk)* cut, incision; chip; *en kopp med ~* a chipped cup; *et ~ i gleden* a fly in the ointment.

skåre *vb (oppnå poeng)* score.

skåte A *sb (for dør etc)* bolt, latch; *skyve ~n for døren* bolt/latch the door; *skyve ~n fra* unbolt, unlatch; **B** *vb (med årer)* back the oars/water.

slabbedask *sb* scamp.

sladder *sb* gossip; *ikke tro på all ~en du hører* don't believe all the gossip you hear. **sladder|aktig** *adj* gossipy. **~hank** *sb* telltale. **~historie** *sb* piece of gossip. **sladre** *vb* **1** *(fare med sladder)* gossip; **2** *(være angiver)* peach; tell (tales); *John ~t på broren sin* John peached against/on/told on his brother. **sladrekjerring** *sb* gossip.

slag *sb* **A** kind, sort; se også *slags*; **B** *sb* **1** *a) (enkelt, hardt ~, også fig)* blow; *han gav meg et ~ i hodet* he struck/gave me a blow on the head; *hennes manns død var et hardt ~ for henne* her husband's death was a great blow to her; *b) (om ~ som kanskje gjentas)* stroke; *gutten fikk fem ~* the boy got five strokes; **2** *(om maskiner etc og i sport)* stroke; **3** *(hjerte~, takt~, tromme~ etc)* beat; *(om bølge~)* beating; **4** *(i krig)* battle; *~et ved Stiklestad* the battle of Stiklestad; *det stod et ~* a battle was fought; **5** *(hjerne~)* stroke, apoplexy; *(hjerte~)* heart failure; **6** *(jakke~ etc)* lapel; **7** *et ~ kort* a game of cards; **9** *(uttrykk) et ~ i luften* a flash in the pan; *slå et ~ for* take up the cudgels for. **slager** *sb* hit (song/tune); *(populær gammel ~)* evergreen. **slagferdig** *adj* quick-witted. **slagferdighet** *sb* ready wit.

slagg *sb (på smeltemasse)* dross, slag; *(av koks)* cinders; *fig* dross.

slag|kraft *sb* striking power; effectiveness. **~kraftig** *adj* effective. **~krysser** *sb* battle cruiser. **~linje** *sb* line of battle. **~mark** *sb* battle-field. **~ord** *sb* slogan, watchword. **~orden** *sb* battle order. **~plan** *sb* plan of action.

slags kind, sort; *(kvalitet)* quality; *all(e) ~* all sorts/kinds of; *den ~ bøker* that sort of books; *hva ~ tre er det der?* what kind of tree is that?

slagsbror *sb* brawler.

slagside *sb* **1** *(på grunn av lasten)* list; **2** *(på grunn av konstruksjonsfeil)* lopsidedness; **3** *fig* bias, lopsidedness.

slag|skip *sb* battleship. **~skygge** *sb* shadow.

slagsmål *sb* fight; *komme i ~* get into a fight.

slagtilfelle se *slag 5*.

slak *adj (svakt buet/skrånende)* gentle, slight; *en ~ skråning* a gentle slope.

slakk *adj, sb* slack. **slakke** *vb (~ på)* slacken. **slakne** *vb* become slack; slacken.

slakt *sb (slaktet dyr)* carcass, carcase; *ale opp fe til ~* raise beef cattle. **slakte** *vb* kill, slaughter; *~ gjøkalven* kill the fatted calf. **slakte|fe** *sb* beef cattle. **~hus** slaughter-house, abattoir. **slakter** *sb* butcher. **slakterbutikk** *sb* butcher's (shop). **slakteri** = *slaktehus*.

slalåm *sb* slalom.

slam *sb* mud, ooze.

slamp *sb (slubbert)* scamp, scallywag.

slang *sb* slang; *bruke ~* talk slang.

slange *sb* **1** *(orm)* snake; *en gift~* a poisonous snake; **2** *(gummi~)* tube; **3** *(hage~ etc)* hose. **slange|agurk** *sb* (snake) cucumber. **~klemme** *sb* hose clamp/clip. **~løs** *adj* tubeless. **~menneske** *sb* contortionist.

slank *adj* slender, slim. **slanke** *vb: ~ seg* slim, reduce; *dgl ofte* diet. **slankhet** *sb* slimness, slenderness.

slant *sb* **1** *(mynt)* copper, smallcoin; **2** *(bunnskvett)* heeltap.

slapp *adj* **1** *(motsatt av stram)* slack; **2** *(nedfor, uopplagt)* limp, listless; *(giddeløs)* slack; **3** *(om disiplin, moral etc)* lax. **slappe** *vb: ~ av* relax; *du må lære å ~ av* you must learn to relax. **slappfisk** *sb* spineless fellow; cissy, sissy. **slapphet** *sb* looseness, slackness; weakness.

slaps *sb* slush. **slapseføre** *sb (på vei)* slushy roads; *(i skiløype)* slushy snow. **slapset(e)** *adj* slushy.

slaraffen|land *sb* land of milk and honey. **~liv** *sb: leve et ~* lead a life in idleness and luxury.

slarke *vb* wobble.

slarve *vb* gossip, tattle.

slask *sb* scamp, scallywag.

slasket(e) *adj* **1** *(slapp)* flabby, limp; **2** *(slapsete)* slushy.

slave *sb* slave; *romerne holdt ~r* the Romans kept slaves. **slave|arbeid** *sb* slave work. **~binde** *vb* enslave. **~handel** *sb* slavetrade. **~handler** *sb* slave-dealer. **slaver** *sb (folkeslag)* Slav. **slaveri** *sb* slavery. **slavinne** *sb* (female) slave; slave-girl, slave-woman. **slavisk** *adj* **A** *(nøye)* slavish; *~ etterligning* slavish imitation; **B** *(om folk og språk)* Slavonic, Slavic.

slede *sb* sledge; *US* sled, sleigh; *kjøre med ~* go sledging/sleighing.

slegge *sb* sledge, sledge-hammer; *(til sleggekast)* hammer. **slegge|kast** *sb* throwing the hammer. **~kaster** *sb* hammer-thrower. **sleid** slide.

sleip *adj* slippery; *fig* oily, shifty, sly.

sleiv *sb* ladle; *hun øste opp suppen med ~* she ladled out the soup.

slekt *sb* **1** family; *~ og venner* friends and relatives; *hvordan er han i ~ med deg?* how is he related to you? **2** *(generasjon)* age, generation; *kommende ~er* coming generations. **slekte** *vb: han ~r på moren* he takes after his mother. **slektledd** *sb* generation. **slektning** *sb* relation, relative; *er hun en ~ av deg?* is she a relative of yours? *fjern ~* distant relation; *nære ~er* near relations. **slektskap** *sb* relationship. **slektstavle** *sb* genealogical table.

slem I *adj* **1** *(uoppdragen)* naughty; *(grusom, ond)* bad, cruel; *være ~ mot* be cruel to; treat badly; **2** *(ille, ubehagelig)* bad; *en ~ hoste* a bad cough; *han er ~ til å overdrive* he is given to exaggerating; **II** *sb (i kortspill)* slam.

slendrian *sb* carelessness, nonchalance; *gammel ~* old jogtrot.

slenge *vb* **1** *(hive)* fling, hurl; *han slengte jakken sin over en stol* he flung his coat upon a chair; *hun slengte seg (ned) på sofaen* she flung herself on the sofa; **2** *(henge og dingle)* dangle, swing; flop; **3** *(slentre, gå og ~)* idle, loaf; *han går bare her og ~r hele dagen* he is idling about all day; **4** *(uttrykk) ligge og ~* lie about; *~ en noe i ansiktet* fling something in someone's teeth. **slengkyss** *sb: slenge en et ~* blow someone a kiss.

slentre *vb* saunter, stroll.

slep *sb* **1** *(på kjole)* train; **2** *(slit og strev)* drudgery; **3** *ha/ta på ~* have/take in tow. **slepe** *vb* **1** *(hale, trekke)* drag; *han kunne knapt ~ seg av sted* he could hardly drag himself along; **2** *(buksere)* tow, tug; *skipet ble slept inn* the ship was towed in. **slepe|båt, ~damper** *sb* tug. **slepende** *adj* **1** *(om gange)* shuffling; **2** *(om stemme)* drawling. **slepe|not** *sb* drag-net. **~tau** tow-line.

sleppe se *slippe*. **slepphendt** *adj* butter-fingered.

slesk *adj* fawning, oily. **sleske** *vb: ~ for* fawn on.

slett I *adj* **1** *(flat, plan)* even, level; *(glatt)* smooth; **2** *(dårlig)* bad; *~ selskap* bad company; *du slette tid!* oh, my! my goodness! **II** *adv* **1** *(forsterkende ved nektelse)* at all; whatever; *~ ikke* not at all; *~ ikke forbauset* not at all surprised; *~ ikke noe* nothing at all/whatever; *~ ingen* none at all/whatever; **2** *rett og ~* downright; *det er rett og ~ løgn* it is a downright lie; *han var rett og ~ uforskammet* he was downright rude.

slette I *sb (flatt land)* plain; *på ~en* in the plain; **II** *vb* **1** *(glatte, jevne)* level (out); smooth; **2** *(annullere, stryke)* erase; wipe out; *data især* delete. **sletteland** *sb* level country; plains.

slibrig *adj (uanstendig)* obscene, smutty; indecent. **slibrighet** *sb* obscenity.

slik *adj, adv, pron* **1** such; like this/that; *~ er det* that is the way it is; that is the way things are; *det er ikke ~ å forstå at* I do not mean to say that; *du må gjøre det ~* you must do it like this; *enten resultatet blir ~ eller ~* no matter what the result may be; *er det ~ slik å forstå at...?* do you mean (to say) that...? *noe ~t som 500 pund* a matter of five hundred pounds; *snakk ikke ~!* don't speak like that! *skulle du ha sett ~t!* did you ever! *(skulle du ha sett) ~t tøys!* what nonsense! *ved en ~ anledning* on such an occasion; **2 ~ at** in such a way that; so that; *du må ordne det ~ at jeg kan reise i dag* you must arrange matters in such a way that I can leave today; **3 ~ som** as, like; *det kan ikke gjøres ~ som du tror* it can't be done the way you think; *hun ønsket ikke å være ~ som moren* she did not want to be like her mother; *jeg vil gjøre det ~ du har gjort det* I want to do it as you did it.

slikk *sb* lick; *en ~ og (en) ingenting* next to nothing; *hun kjøpte det for en ~ og en ingenting* she bought it for a song. **slikke** *vb* lick; *hunden ~t hånden min* the dog licked my hand. **slikkepott** *sb* **1** *(pekefinger)* forefinger; **2** *(kjøkkenredskap)* dough-scraper; baker's scraper. **slikkeri(er)** *sb koll* sweets; *US* candy.

slim *sb* slime; *(fra slimhinner især)* mucus; *(i nese og hals)* phlegm. **slimaktig** *adj* mucous, slimy. **slimet(e)** *adj* slimy. **slimhinne** *sb* mucous membrane.

slinger *sb: ikke noe ~ i valsen* no nonsense. **slingre** *vb (om hjul etc)* wobble; *(om skip)* roll; *(om kjøretøy)* rock, sway; *(rave, sjangle)* lurch, reel. **slingring** *sb* wobble, wobbling; rolling; rocking, swaying; reel, reeling; lurch, lurching. **slingringsmonn** *sb* margin (for variations).

slintre *sb* shred (of meat).

slipe *vb* **1** *(gjøre skarp)* grind, sharpen; *han slipte kniven* he ground/sharpened the knife; **2** *(~ til)* grind; *~ en linse* grind a lens; **3** *(polere, pusse)* polish; *~ marmor* polish marble; **4** *~ edelsteiner, glass etc)* cut; *slepet krystall* cut glass. **sliperi** *sb (tre~)* pulp mill. **slipestein** *sb* grindstone.

slipp *sb* **A** *(båt~)* slipway, slip; **B** *(seddel, talong)* slip (of paper); check; **C:** *gi ~ på* give up; let go. **slippe** *vb* **1** *(la falle, ~ ned)* drop; *forsyninger ble sluppet ned med fallskjerm* supplies were dropped by parachute; *hauken slapp byttet (sitt)* the hawk dropped its prey; **2** *(~ taket)* let go (one's hold); *slipp meg!* let me go! *han slapp tauet* he let go (his hold of) the rope; **3** *(~ unna)* be let off; escape; *de slapp straff* they escaped punishment; *guttene slapp lekse* the boys were let off their homework; **4** *(uttrykk)* **~ av syne:** *hun ~r ham aldri av syne* she never lets him out of her sight; **~ forbi** *a) (la passere)* let by; let pass; *vaktposten slapp ikke noen forbi* the sentry let no one pass; *b) (komme seg forbi)* get by; get past; **~ fra:** *~ fra det med livet* escape with one's life; survive; *~ uskadd fra det* escape unhurt; **~ fri** *a) (løslate)* let go; release; set free; *b) (bli løslatt)* be let off; *c) (komme seg unna)* escape; **~ inn** *a) (gi adgang)* admit; let in; *de ville ikke slippe meg inn* they would not let me in; *b) (få adgang)* be admitted; get in; *bare medlemmer ble sluppet inn* only members were admitted; **~ løs** se *~ fri;* **~ opp** *(ta slutt)* give/run out; *~ opp for* run out/short of; *vi slapp opp for bensin* we ran out of petrol; **~ unna** escape; get away/off; *~ unna med nød og neppe* have a narrow escape; **~ ut** *a) (sette fri etc)* let out; release; *b) (komme seg løs etc)* be released; get out; *~ katten ut av sekken* let the cat out of the bag.

slips *sb* (neck)tie.

slire *sb* scabbard, sheath; *stikke kniven i ~en* sheathe the knife. **slirekniv** *sb* sheath-knife.

slit *sb* **1** *(hardt arbeid)* drudgery, grind; *det daglige ~et* the daily grind; **2** = **slitasje** *sb* wear; *teppet viser tegn på ~* the carpet shows signs of wear. **slite** *vb* **1** *(hale, rive)* pull, tear; *~ i* pull at; **2** *(~ ned/ut)* wear; *~ ut* wear out; *jeg har slitt hull i/på sokkene mine* I have worn my socks into holes; **3** *(arbeide hardt)* toil; work hard; drudge; *han slet seg i hjel* he worked himself to death. **sliten** *adj* tired, weary; exhausted. **sliter** *sb* drudge; hard worker. **slitesterk** *adj* durable. **slitsom** *adj* tiring; hard, strenuous.

slokke *vb* **1** *(om levende ild/lys)* put out; *brannen ble raskt slokt* the fire was quickly put out; *hun slokte lyset* she put out the candle; **2** *(om elektrisk lys)* switch off; *han slokte lyset i spisestuen* he switched off the light in the dining-room; **3** *~ tørsten* quench the thirst. **slokne** *vb* go out; *ilden/lyset ~t* the fire/light went out.

slott *sb* palace; *(opprinnelig befestet ~)* castle.

slu *adj (listig)* cunning, sly; crafty.

slubbert *sb* scamp.

sludd *sb* sleet. **sludde** *vb* sleet.

sludder *sb (vrøvl)* nonsense; *de snakket en masse ~* they talked a lot of nonsense. **sludre** *vb* **1** *(vrøvle)* talk nonsense; **2** *(skravle)* chat; have a chat.

sluffe *sb* sledge; *US* sled, sleigh.

sluk *sb* **1** *(avgrunn)* abyss; **2** *(kloakk~)* drain, gully; **3** *(fiske~)* spoon (bait); spinner. **sluke** *vb* swallow; *(fortære)* devour, gobble; *hun slukte ham med øynene* she devoured him with her eyes. **slukhals** *sb* glutton.

slukkøret *adj* crestfallen.

slukt *sb* gorge, ravine; *US* canyon.

slukvoren *adj* gluttonous.

slum *sb* slum. **slum|distrikt, -kvarter** *sb* slum area/district.

slummer *sb* slumber; *(lur)* nap.

slump *sb* **1** *(tilfeldighet)* accident, chance; *(sammentreff)* coincidence; *det var en ren ~ at vi møttes* our meeting was quite accidental; *det er rene ~en om det går godt for oss eller ikke* it is a toss-up whether we succeed or not; **2** *(ganske stor mengde)* a nice lot; quite a lot; *en god ~ penger* a handsome sum of money; **3** *(siste rest)* remainder, rest; **4** *(uttrykk) på ~* at random; *han gjør alt arbeidet på ~* he does all his work by rule of thumb; *jeg fyrte av et skudd på ~* I fired a shot at random; *la slumpen rå* leave it to chance; let chance decide. **slumpe** *vb* **1** *(gjøre på slump)* do at random; **2** *(hende tilfeldig)* happen (by chance); *~ til å* happen to; *de ~t til å møtes i Bergen* they happened to meet in Bergen; *det kan jo ~ (til) at vi møtes igjen* it may happen that we meet again. **slumpe|hell** *sb* stroke of luck. **~treff** *sb* chance; *(sammentreff)* coincidence.

slunken *adj (mager)* lean; *en ~ mave* an empty stomach.

slunt(r)e *vb: ~ unna* shirk one's duty.

slurk *sb* gulp; *en ~ konjakk* a drop of brandy; *han svelget det i én ~* he swallowed it at one gulp.

slurpe *vb* slurp.

slurv *sb* carelessness, negligence. **slurve** *vb* scamp one's work. **slurvefeil** *sb* slip; *(skrivefeil)* slip of the pen. **slurvet(e)** *adj* careless, negligent.

sluse *sb* **1** *(for skip)* lock; **2** *(til vannstandregulering)* sluice.

slusk *sb* **1** *(anleggsarbeider)* navvy; **2** *(lasaron)* bum, tramp.

slutning *sb* **1** *(av~)* end(ing), finish; **2** *(konklusjon)* conclusion; *komme til en ~* arrive at (come to, reach) a conclusion; *trekke en ~* draw a conclusion; conclude; *trekke forhastede ~er* jump to conclusions. **slutt** *sb* **1** *(ende)* end, finish; *(bokl)* close; *en verdig ~ på et strevsomt liv* a fitting close of a strenuous life; *etter møtets ~* after/when the meeting was over; **2** *(måte noe slutter på)* ending; *lykkelig ~* happy ending; **3** *(uttrykk)* **bli ~ på** come to an end; *det ble ~ på ferien* the holidays came to an end; **få ~ på** put an end to; *vi må få ~ på denne tåpelige oppførselen* we must put an end to this foolish behaviour; **i ~en** at the end; *i ~en av måneden/året* at the end of the month/the year; **mot ~en** toward the end; *mot ~en av kampen* toward the end of the match; **på ~en** at the end; *på ~en av brevet* at the end of the letter; **ta ~** end; come to an end; **til ~** finally; at last; in the end; *(som avslutning)* in conclusion; **være ~** be at an end; *vi kom ikke før møtet var ~* we did not arrive till the meeting was at an end. **slutte** *vb* **1** *(avslutte)* end, finish; close; *~ skolen* leave school; *møtet ~t klokken åtte* the meeting ended at eight o'clock; **2** *(dra slutning)* conclude; *jeg ~r av det du sier at...* I conclude from what you say that...; **3** *(inngå)* conclude; *~ en avtale* conclude an agreement; *~ fred* make peace; *de ~t vennskap* they made friends. **4** *(uttrykk)* **~ med** conclude (end, finish) by (with, in); *de ~t (= avsluttet) med å synge nasjonalsangen* they finished by singing the National Anthem; *de ~t med nasjonalsangen* they finished with the National Anthem; *han ~t med å si at...* he ended/concluded by saying that ...; **~ opp om** rally round; *alle medlemmene ~t opp om partilederen* all the members rallied round the party leader; *ringen er ~t* the ring is closed; **~ seg sammen** unite; **~ seg til** *a) (bli medlem av etc)* join; *hun ~t seg til de liberale* she joined the Librals; *b) (si seg enig)* agree; *jeg ~r meg helt til dette* I entirely agree in this; *c) (dra en slutning)* conclude; **~ som** end as; *hun sluttet som forkvinne* she finished her chairwomanship. **slutt|kamp** *sb (i sport)* final. **~resultat** *sb* final result. **~spurt** *sb* final spurt.

slyng *sb* loop, winding; *~ på linjen* crossed wires.

slynge I *sb* sling; **II** *vb* **1** *(kaste)* fling, hurl, throw; **2** *~ seg* twine, wind; *eføyen ~t seg om treet* the ivy twined round the tree; *veien ~r seg nedover bakken* the road winds down the hill.

slyngel *sb* scoundrel.

slyngel|aktig *adj* rascally. **~alder** *sb* the teens. **~strek** *sb* dirty trick.

slyngning *sb* winding.

slyng|plante *sb* climber, twiner. **~rose** *sb* climbing rose; rambler.

slør *sb* veil. **sløret** *adj (om stemme)* husky.

sløse *vb: ~ bort, ~ med* squander, waste. **sløseri** *sb* waste.

sløv *adj* **1** *(ikke skarp)* blunt; *(især fig)* dull; *en ~ kniv* a blunt knife; *et ~t blikk* a dull glance; **2** *(alders~, apatisk)* apathetic, gaga. **sløv|het** *sb* bluntness; *fig* apathy, stupor. **~sinn** *sb* stupor.

sløyd *sb* woodwork; *især US* carpentry; *(metall~)* metal-work. **~lærer** *sb* woodwork master/teacher.

sløyfe I *sb* **1** *(bundet ~)* bow; *han knyttet/knyttet opp en ~* he tied/untied a bow; **2** *(buktet linje)* loop; **II** *vb* **1** *(utelate)* leave out; **2** *(avskaffe)* discontinue; *sporvognslinjen ble ~t* the tramline was discontinued.

slå *sb* bolt, latch; *han slo ~en for døren* he bolted/latched the door; *han slo ~en fra døran* he unbolted/unlatched the door.

slå *vb* **1** *(~ hardt)* knock; *han slo hodet i/mot veggen* he knocked his head against the wall; **2** *(især om enkelt slag)* hit, strike; *hun slo ham i hodet* she hit/struck him on the head; *hvem slo det første slag?* who struck the first blow? *klokken slo to* the clock struck two; **3** *(især om gjentatte slag)* beat; *~ takten* beat time; *hjertet ~r* the heart beats; *hun slo gutten* she beat the boy; **3** *(beseire)* beat, defeat; *ingen ~r henne i svømming* noone beats her at swimming; *vår hær er aldri blitt slått* our army has never been defeated; **4** *(gjøre inntrykk på)* strike; *det slo meg at* it struck me that; **5** *(meie)* mow; *de slo gresset* they mowed the lawn; **6** *(helle)* pour; *han slo vann i fatet* he poured water into the basin; **7** *(uttrykk)* **~ an** *(bli populær)* become popular; be a hit/a success; get across; *~ an med/på* pick up with; *~ an tonen* strike the keynote; **~ av** *(skru av)* switch/turn off; *(om lys også)* put out; *(om pris)* reduce; knock off; *(om fart)* reduce, slacken, *~ av farten (også)* slow down; *~ av en handel* strike a bargain; *~ av en prat* have a chat; **~ feil** fail; be a failure; go wrong; come to little/nothing; **~ fra seg** defend oneself; put up a fight; *~ fra seg tanken på* dismiss the thought of; **~ frempå** hint, suggest; drop/give a hint; she hinted/suggested that I should go and see her father; **~ i:** *~ i en spiker* drive/hammer in a nail/a nail in; *~ i hjel* kill; *~ i stykker* break, smash; **~ igjennom** *(om person)* be successful; make a name for oneself; *(om bok, melodi etc)* catch on; make a hit; *(om idé)* prevail; **~ inn på** go in for; take up; **~ ned** knock down; *(om lyn)* strike; *~ ned et opprør* beat/put down a revolt; *~ ned prisene* cut down/reduce the prices; *~ ned på* pounce on; crack/swoop down on; *politiet slo ned på smuglerne* the police cracked down the smugglers; **~ om** *(forandre seg)* change; *været har slått om* the weather has changed; **~ om seg** lay about one; *~ om seg med penger* spend lavishly; **~ opp** *(plakat etc)* post (put, stick) up; *(bryte forlovelse)* break off an engagement; *hun slo opp med ham (også)* she jilted him; *~ opp et ord (i ordboken)* look up a word (in the dictionary); *~ opp i en ordbok* consult a dictionary; *~ opp på side 72* open the book at page 72; **~ en plate** tell a fib; fib; **~ på** *(lys, radio, vann)* turn/switch on; *(antyde)* se *~ frempå;* *~ på flukt* put to flight; rout; *~ stort på* live on a grand scale; live in style; ~ **sammen** *(noe sammenleggbart)* fold up; *(forene)* combine, unite; ~ **til** hit; *(akseptere) han slo til med en gang* he accepted like a shot; he jumped at the chance at once; *(om spådom)* come true; ~ *til ridder* knight; ~ **tilbake** *(drive tilbake)* drive back; fight off; repel, repulse; ~ **ut** *(tømme ut)* tip/pour out; *(i boksing)* knock out; ~ *ut av tankene* put out of one's head; **8** *(refleksive uttrykk)* ~ **seg** be hurt; hurt oneself; *(om trematerialer etc)* warp; *bordplaten har slått seg* the table-top has warped; ~ **seg frem** fight one's way; rise in the world; ~ **seg igjennom** make ends meet; pull through; *(mil også)* cut through; ~ **seg i hjel** be killed; ~ **seg ned** settle; *de slo seg ned i Hamar* they settled in Hamar; ~ **seg opp** se ~ *seg frem*; ~ **seg på** take to; *han slo seg på flasken* he hit the bottle/took to drink(ing); se ellers ~ *inn på*; ~ **seg sammen** combine, unite; merge; *de slo seg sammen for å danne et nytt selskap* they united to form a new company.

slåbrok *sb* dressing-gown.

slående *adj: en ~ likhet* a striking likeness; *et ~ bevis* a convincing proof. **slåmaskin** *sb* mower; mowing-machine.

slåss fight; *de begynte å ~* they started a fight; *hundene sloss om et bein* the dogs fought over a bone. **slåsskjempe** *sb* rowdy.

slått *sb* **A** *(melodi)* air, melody; **B** = **slottonn** *sb* haymaking.

smadre *vb* bust, smash (up).

smak *sb* taste; *dårlig ~* bad taste; *vond ~* unpleasant taste; *det falt ikke i hennes ~* it was not to her taste; *etter min ~* to my taste. **smake** *vb* taste; ~ *på* taste; sample, try; *det ~r surt* it tastes sour; it has a sour taste. **smakebit** *sb* sample, taste. **smak|full** *adj* tasteful; in good taste. **~løs** *adj* tasteless; in bad taste. **~løshet** *sb* bad taste; tastelessness. **smakssak** *sb* matter of taste.

smal *adj* narrow; *en ~ gate* a narrow street; *en ~ sak* an easy matter. **smal|hans** *sb* poverty, want. **~skuldret** *adj* narrow-houldered. **~sporet** *adj* narrow-gauge; *fig* narrow-minded.

smaragd *sb* emerald.

smart *adj* **1** *(fiks)* smart; *en ~ hatt* a smart hat; **2** *(lur, slu også)* clever. **smarthet** *sb* smartness.

smaske *vb* smack (one's lips).

smatte *vb* smack (one's lips).

smed *sb* smith; *(grov~)* blacksmith; *passe på som en ~* keep a sharp look-out.

smede|dikt, ~skrift *sb* lampoon, libel.

smekk *sb* **A** *(bukse~)* fly; **B** *(lite smell)* click, smack, snap; *slå to fluer i én/ett ~* kill two birds with one stone. **smekke A** *sb* bib; **B** *vb* click; *han ~t med tungen* he clicked his tongue; *jeg ~t igjen døren* I clicked the door (to); *låsen ~t igjen* the lock clicked shut.

smekker *adj* slender, slim.

smekkfull *adj* chock-full.

smekklås latch, spring-lock.

smell *sb* crack; *piske~* crack of a whip. **smelle** *vb* crack; ~ *igjen døren* bang/slam the door; *han smelte med svepen* he cracked his whip; *skjelle og ~* storm and rage.

smell|feit *adj* obese; very fat. **~kyss** *sb* smack; smacking kiss.

smelte *vb* **1** melt; ~ *om* melt down; *~t smør* melted butter; **2** *(om metaller) ~t jern* molten iron; ~ *sammen* **3** *fig* fuse; ~ *sammen med* merge into; be merged with. **smelte|ovn** *sb* melting furnace. **~punkt** *sb* melting-point. **~varme** *sb* melting heat.

smergel *sb* emery. **smergel|papir** *sb* emery-paper. **~skive** *sb* emery-wheel.

smerte I *sb* **1** *(fysisk ~)* pain; bodily pain; *har han ~r?* is he in pain? *jeg hadde ikke store ~r* I did not feel much pain; **2** *(lidelse)* suffering; **3** *(sorg)* grief, sorrow; **II** *vb* **1** *(gjøre fysisk vondt)* ache; be painful; **2** *(bedrøve)* grieve, pain; *det ~t meg å høre henne si det* it grieved me to hear her say that. **smerte|fri** *adj* painless. **~full** *adj* painful. **smertelig** *adj* painful, sad; *et ~ tap* a painful loss. **smertestillende** *adj: ~ middel* pain-killer; analgesic, anodyne.

smette *vb* slip; *hun smatt unna* she slipped away.

smi *vb* forge; ~ *mens jernet er varmt* strike while the iron is hot; make hay while the sun shines.

smidig *adj* **1** *(bøyelig)* supple; **2** *(ikke stiv eller striks)* elastic; ~ *regler* elastic rules.

smie *sb* forge, smithy. **smie|avl** *sb* forge hearth. **~belg** *sb* forge bellows.

smiger *sb* flattery. **smigre** *vb* flatter; *han følte seg ~t ved inbydelsen hennes* he felt flattered by her invitation.

smijern *sb* wrought iron.

smil *sb* smile; *et bredt ~* a broad smile. **smile** *vb* smile; *han smilte over hele ansiktet* he was all smiles *hun smilte til gutten* she smiled at the boy; *lykken smilte til ham* fortune smiled on him. **smile|bånd** *sb: trekke på ~båndet* smile. **~hull** *sb* dimple.

sminke *sb* make-up. **sminke** *vb* make up; paint; *hun ~t seg* she rouged/made up her face; *sterkt ~t* heavily made up.

smiske *vb: ~ for* fawn on. **smisket(e)** *adj* fawning.

smitt *sb: hver ~ og smule* every particle.

smitte I *sb* infection; *~n har spredd seg* the infection has spread; **II** *vb* **1** *vt* infect; *søsteren ~t ham med meslingene* his sister infected him with the measles; **2** *vi (via luftveiene)* be infectious; *(ved berøring og ofte dgl)* be contagious; *(især fig)* be catching; **3** *malingen ~r av* the paint comes off. **smitte|bærer** *sb* carrier (of infection). **~fare** *sb* danger of infection. **~fri** *adj* non-infectious. **~kilde** *sb* source of infection. **smittende** *adj fig* catching. **smitte|spreder** se *~bærer*. **~stoff** *sb* infectious matter; virus. **smittsom** *adj (via luftveiene)* infectious; *(ved berøring og ofte dgl)* contagious, catching; *(især fig)* catching.

smoking *sb* dinner-jacket; *US* tuxedo; *dgl* tux.

smokk *sb (på tåteflaske)* nipple; *(finger~)* finger-stall.

smug *sb* alley, lane; *i ~* secretly.

18. Svenkerud: Ordbok.

smugle *vb* smuggle; *hun ~t ut et brev* she smuggled a letter out. **smugler** *sb* smuggler. **smugler|bande** *sb* gang of smugglers. **~båt** *sb* smuggling boat. **~gods** *sb koll* smuggled goods; contraband. **smugling** *sb* smuggling.

smukk *adj: det ~e kjønn* the fair sex.

smul *adj* calm; *i ~t farvann* in calm waters.

smuldre *vb* crumble; *~nde steiner* crumbling stones.

smule *sb* bit; *(brød~)* crumb.

smult *sb* lard.

smurning *sb* grease, lubricant.

smuss *sb* dirt; *(sterkere)* filth. **smuss|avis, ~blad** *sb* gutter/mudraking paper. **~litteratur** *sb* pornography.

smutt *sb: kaste ~* play at ducks and drakes. **smutte** se *smette*. **smutthull** *sb* hideout, hiding-place; *fig* loophole.

smyge *vb* **1** *(krype, sno seg)* crawl, slip; **2** *(liste seg)* steal; *de smøg (seg) unna* they stole away.

smykke 1 *sb* piece of jewellery; *~r* jewellery, jewels; **2** *vb* decorate; *salen var ~t med flagg* the hall was decorated with flags. **smykkeskrin** *sb* jewel box/case.

smør *sb* butter; *jammen sa jeg ~!* my foot! **smør|blid** *adj* smirking. **~blomst** *sb* buttercup. **~brød** *sb* ≈ open sandwich (NB: *sandwich* er i engelsktalende land oftest brødskiver, halve rundstykker etc lagt mot hverandre med pålegg imellom. *Bread and butter* = brød og smør). **smøre** *vb* **1** *(med olje)* oil; *hun smurte sykkelen sin* she oiled her bicycle; **2** *(med fett, og fig: bestikke)* grease; **3** *(overstryke)* smear; **4** *(~ smør på)* butter; *~ smør på brødet* butter the bread; *~ smørbrød* make sandwiches. **smøre|kanne** *sb* oil can. **~kopp** *sb* oil cup. **~olje** *sb* lubricating oil. **smøreri** *sb (med maling)* daub; *(i skrift)* scribbling. **smøring** *sb* lubrication, oiling; *(også fig)* greasing.

små *adj, sb* (jf *liten, smått*) *begynne i det ~* start in a small way; *de ~* the little ones; *for ~ sko* tight shoes. **små|barn** *sb koll (spedbarn)* babies; *(dgl: ~unger)* kids. **~borger** *sb* lower middle class person; petit bourgeois. **~borgerlig** *adj* (petit) bourgeois. **~bruk** *sb* small farm. **~bruker** *sb* small-holder. **~by** *sb* small town. **~fe** *sb* sheep and goats. **~folk** *sb* **1** *(barn)* little ones; **2** = *~kårsfolk*. **~fryse** *vb* shiver. **~gutt** *sb* little/small boy; lad, laddie. **~jobber** *sb fl* odd jobs. **~kjekle** *vb* bicker. **~koke** *vb* simmer. **~kryp** *sb* small fry. **~kupert** *adj: ~kupert landskap* undulating country. **~kårsfolk** people of humble means. **~le** *vb* chuckle.

smålig *adj* **1** *(gjerrig)* mean, stingy; **2** *(småskåren)* narrow-minded; **3** *(altfor nøyeregnende)* fussy, pettifogging. **smålighet** *sb* meanness, stingyness; narrow-mindedness; pettifogging.

små|løpe *vb* trot. **~nøyd** *adj* modest. **~penger** *sb koll* (small) change. **~pike** *sb* little/small girl; lass. lassie. **~plukk** *sb koll* trifles. **~prate** *vb* chat. **~prat(ing)** *sb* small talk. **~pussig** *adj* droll. **~putre** *sb* simmer. **~regn(e)** *sb, vb* drizzle. **~rolling** *sb* toddler. **~rutet(e)** *adj (om stoff)* pin-checked. **~skjenne** *vb* grumble. **~skåren** *adj* narrow-minded. **~snakke** *vb* chat. **~spise** *vb* nibble. **~stein** *sb* pebble. **~sutre** *vb* whimper. **~ting** *sb* trifle.

smått *adv, sb: ~ om senn* little by little; gradually; *~ stell* poor conditions; *begynne ~* start on a small scale; *det begynte så ~ å regne* it began raining a little; *det går ~ med arbeidet* the work is making slow headway; *det ser ~ ut* prospects are poor; *det var ~ med/om mat* food was scarce; *med stort og ~* including everything; *selge i ~* sell (by) retail; *så ~* a little; little by little. **småtteri** *sb* small matter, trifle.

småvilt *sb koll* small game.

snabel *sb* trunk.

snadde *sb* pipe.

snadre *vb (som and)* quack; *(skravle)* chatter, jabber.

snakk *sb* **1** *(prat)* chat, talk; *jeg kom i ~ med dem* I got into talk with them; **2** *(vrøvl)* nonsense; *det er noe ~!* it is all nonsense! **3** *(folke~, sladder)* gossip; *løst ~* gossip. **snakke** *vb* **1** chat, talk; *~ (om) forretninger (etc)* talk business (etc); *du ~r for mye* you talk too much; *han ~r alltid om været* he always talks about/of the weather; *ikke gå før jeg får ~t med deg!* don't go before I have had a talk with you! **2** *(uttrykk) for ikke å ~ om* let alone; *~ over seg* rave; be delirious. **snakke|salig** *adj* talkative, garrulous. **~tøy** *sb: ha ~tøyet i orden* have the gift of the gab.

snappe *vb* **1** snatch; *hun ~t etter været* she gasped for breath; *tyven ~t vesken hennes* the thief snatched her bag; **2** *~ opp (f.eks. meddelelse)* intercept; *(få fatt i)* get hold of.

snar *adj* quick, swift.

snare *sb* snare.

snarere *adv* **1** *(fortere)* sooner; **2** *(i høyere grad)* rather; *den er ~ grønn enn blå* it is green rather than blue. **snarest** *adv (så snart som mulig)* as soon as possible; *send brevet ~ mulig!* send the letter as soon as possible! *som ~* just for a moment. **snar|rådig** *adj* resourceful. **~rådighet** *sb* resourcefulness. **~sint** *adj* quick-tempered.

snart *adv* **1** *(om kort tid)* soon, shortly; presently; *det er ~ over* it will soon be over; *så ~ som mulig* as soon as possible; **2** *(kort etter)* soon (after); shortly after; presently; **3** *(nesten)* almost, nearly; *for ~ ti år siden* nearly ten years ago; **4** *aldri så ~ hadde hun sagt det, før hun angret på det* no sooner had she said it/she had no sooner said it than she regretted it. **snar|tur** *sb* short-flying visit; trip. **~vei** *sb* short cut. **~vending** *sb: i en ~vending* in a jiffy.

snau *adj* **1** *(knapp)* scant, scanty; *~ vekt* scant weight; *~ kost* scanty fare; *en ~ måned* less than a month; **2** *(bar)* bare; **3** *(skallet)* bald. **snau|hugge** *vb* clear-cut; clear-fell. **~hugst** *sb* clearing. **~klippe** *vb* crop. **~klippet** *adj* close-cropped.

snavl *sb: hold snavla!* hold your tongue!

snegl *sb* snail, slug. **snegle|fart** *sb* a snail's pace.

~hus *sb* snail shell. **snegle seg** *vr* crawl, creep; move at a snail's pace.

snei *sb: på ~* aslant, askew.

snekker *sb* **1** *(møbel~)* cabinet-maker, furniture-maker; **2** *(bygnings~)* joiner; *(ofte)* carpenter. **snekre** *vb* do carpentering; do joiner's work.

snelle *sb* reel.

snerk *sb* skin.

snerpe *sb* prude. **snerperi** *sb* prudery, prudishness. **snerpet(e)** *adj* prim, prudish.

snerre *vb* growl, snarl.

snert *sb* flick, flip; lash; *fig* sarcasm. **snerte** *vb* flick, flip.

snes *sb* score; *et halvt ~ mennesker* about a dozen people. **snesevis** *adv* by the score; (in) scores; *~ av gangen* scores of times.

snev *sb* **1** *(antydning)* touch; *det var en ~ av ironi i stemmen hans* there was a touch of irony in his words; **2** *(lukt)* odour.

snever *adj (trang)* narrow; *i en ~ vending* at a pinch. **sneverhet** *sb* narrowness; *(trangsynthet)* narrow-mindedness. **sneversynt** *adj* narrow-minded.

snik *sb* sneak. **snike** *vb* steal; *(lumskt)* sneak; *han snek seg opp trappen* he stole upstairs; *jeg snek meg vekk* I sneaked away.

snikksnakk *sb* nonsense.

snik|mord *sb* assassination. **~morder** *sb* assassin. **~myrde** *vb* assassinate. **~skytter** *sb* sniper.

snill *adj* kind, good; *~ mot* kind to; *vær så ~* please.

snipp *sb* **1** *(til skjorte)* collar; **2** *(flik)* corner, end. **snippkjole** *sb* dress coat.

snirkel *sb* flourish. **snirklet(e)** *adj* flourishy.

snitt *sb* **1** *(kutt)* cut; *et ~ i fingeren* a cut in the finger; *et raskt ~ med kniven* a quick cut of the knife; **2** *(tilskjæring)* cut; *siste ~* latest cut; **3** *(hakk)* notch; **4** *han så sitt ~ til å slippe vekk* he saw his chance to get away. **snitte** *vb* cut.

snittebønne *sb* French bean; haricot bean; kidney bean. **snitter** se *smørbrød*. **snittflate** *sb* cut.

sno A 1 *sb* biting wind; **2** *vb* blow cold; **B** *vb* **1** *(tvinne)* twine, twist; *eføyen ~dde seg om treet* the ivy twined round the tree; *slangen ~dde seg om beinet mitt* the snake twisted round my leg; **2** *(bukte seg)* wind; *veien ~r seg oppover bakken* the road winds up the hill.

snobb *sb* snob; *(laps)* dandy, fop; *US* dude. **snobbe** *vb: ~ seg* show off. **snobberi** *sb* snobbery, dandyism. **snobbet(e)** *adj* snobbish; dandified, foppish.

snodig *adj* old, queer; droll; funny.

snok *sb* grass snake.

snop *sb koll* sweets.

snor *sb (tynn ~)* string; *(tykkere ~, gardin~)* cord; *trekke i ~en (på W.C.)* pull the chain.

snorke *vb* snore. **snorking** *sb* snoring, snore.

snorrett *adj* straight as an arrow.

snu *vb* turn; *~ opp ned på* turn upside down; *~ seg* turn; *de ~dde seg mot/til venstre* they turned to the left *han ~dde ryggen til meg* he turned his back on me; *hun ~dde hodet og så på meg* she turned her head and looked at me; *vi ~dde (og gikk tilbake)* we turned (and went back).

snuble *vb* stumble, trip; *jeg ~t over en stein* I stumbled/tripped over a stone.

snue *sb* cold (in the head); *han fikk ~* he caught a cold in the head.

snufs *sb* sniff, sniffle. **snufse** sniff, snuffle.

snurpe *vb: ~ (= sy) sammen* sew up; *~ sammen munnen* purse the lips. **snurpenot** *sb* (purse) seine; seine net.

snurre *vb* spin, whirl. **snurrebass** *sb* top.

snurrig *adj* droll, odd, queer.

snurt A *adj* nettled, offended; **B** *sb: ikke se ~en av* not get a glimpse of.

snus *sb* snuff; *få ~en i* get wind of. **snuse** *vb* **1** *(lukte, sniffe)* sniff; *hunden ~te på klærne hennes* the dog sniffed at her clothes; **2** *(lete, spionere)* nose about/around; *~ opp* ferret out; hunt out/up; *han liker å ~ i andre folks saker* he likes to nose into other people's affairs; **3** *(ta snus)* snuff. **snus|fornuft** *sb* matter-of-factness, stolidity. **~fornuftig** *adj* prosy, matter-of-fact. **~hane** *sb* snooper.

snusket(e) *adj* shabby; dingy, drab; *(om person)* mean.

snute *sb* muzzle, nose.

snylte *vb: ~ på* be a parasite on; *(om mennesker også)* sponge on. **snylte|dyr** *sb* parasite. **~gjest** *sb* parasite. **~plante** *sb* parasite. **snylter** *sb* parasite.

snyta *adv: ~ full* drunk/tight as a lord.

snyte *vb* **1** *(bedra)* cheat; take in; *han snøt i kortspill* he cheated at cards; *hun snøt meg for pengene mine* she cheated me out of my money; **2** *~ seg (pusse nesen)* blow one's nose. **snyteri** *sb* cheating, swindle; *det er noe ~* it is a swindle.

snø 1 *sb* snow; **2** *vb* snow. **snø|ball** *sb* snowball; *de kastet ~* they threw snowballs. **~blind** *adj* snow-blind. **~blindhet** *sb* snowblindness. **~bre** *sb* glacier. **~briller** *sb* snow goggles. **~drev** *sb* drifting snow. **~drive** *sb* snow-drift. **~fall** *sb* snow-fall. **~fille, ~fnugg** *sb* snow-flake. **~fokk** *sb* drifting snow. **~fonn** *sb* snowdrift. **~freser** *sb* rotary snow cutter.

snøfte *vb* snort.

snø|føyke *sb* drifting snow. **~grense** *sb* snow line. **~hvit** *adj* snow-white. **~kjettinger** *sb fl* snow/non-skid chains. **~måking** *sb* snow-clearing, snow-shovelling. **~plog** *sb* snow-plough.

snøre 1 *sb* cord, string; *(fiske~)* line; **2** *vb* lace (up); *han snørte/snørte opp skoene sine* he laced (up)/unlaced his shoes.

snørr *sb* snot. **snørret(e)** *adj* snotty.

snø|skred *sb* snow-slide, avalanche. **~skuffe** *sb* snow-shovel. **~slaps** *sb* slush. **~storm** *sb* snow-storm; blizzard.

snøvle *vb* speak through one's nose.

snøvær *sb* snow, snowfall; snowy weather.

snål *adj (rar)* droll, odd, queer. **snåling** *sb* character.

sober *adj* sober; *(om person også)* sober-minded.

soda *sb* **1** (washing) soda; **2** *(~vann)* soda-water.

sodd *sb (suppe)* broth.

sofa *sb* sofa. **sofapute** *sb* sofa cushion.

sogn *sb* parish. **sogneprest** *sb* rector, vicar; *dgl* parson; *(katolsk)* parish priest; *(i Skottland)* minister.

soignert *adj* neat, trim; well-groomed.

sokk *sb* sock. **sokkeholder** *sb* suspender; *US* garter.

sokkel *sb* pedestal, plinth; base.

sokkelest *sb: på ~en* in one's stocking(ed) feet.

sokne *vb: ~ etter* drag/sweep for.

sol *sb* sun. **sol|bad** *sb* sun-bath. **~badolje** *sb* suntan oil. **~brent** *adj* sunburnt. **~briller** *sb* sun-glasses. **~brun** *adj* tanned.

solbær *sb* black currant.

sold *sb (lønning)* pay.

soldat *sb* soldier; *menig ~* private (soldier); *da jeg var ~* when I was in the army; *de lekte ~er* they played at soldiers.

sole *vb: ~ seg* sun oneself; bask in the sun. **sole-glad** *sb* sunset. **soleie** *sb* buttercup. **soleklar** *adj* obvious; as clear as daylight; *vår ~e rett* our unquestionable right. **sol|formørkelse** *sb* solar eclipse; eclipse of the sun.

solid *adj* **1** *(sikker, økonomisk pålitelig)* solid; *en ~ bygning* a solid building; *et ~ firma* a solid firm; **2** *(pålitelig)* reliable, steady; **3** *(forstandig)* sound; *han har ~e grunner for å gjøre det* he has sound reasons for doing so. **solidarisk** *adj, adv: opptre ~ med* make common cause with. **solidaritet** *sb* solidarity.

solist *sb* soloist.

sol|liv *sb* sun top. **~lys 1** *adj* sunny; **2** *sb* sunlight. **~nedgang** *sb* sunset.

solo 1 *adv* alone; by oneself; **2** *sb* solo.

sol|oppgang *sb* sunrise. **~rik** *adj* sunny. **~sikke** *sb* sunflower. **~skinn** *sb* sunshine. **~skinnsdag** *sb* sunny day. **~stikk** *sb* sunstroke. **~stråle** *sb* sunbeam. **~ur** *sb* sundial.

solvent *adj* solvent.

solverv *sb* solstice.

som A *konj* **1** *(når ~ innleder bisetning)* as; *hun ble snillere etter (hvert) ~ hun ble eldre* she became kinder as she grew older; **2** *(når ~ ikke innleder bisetning) a) (slik ~)* like; *du oppfører deg ~ en tosk* you behave like a fool; *b) (i egenskap av)* as; *han kom ~ en venn av familien* he came as a friend of the family; *c) (stundom oversettes ~ ikke) han døde ~ tigger* he died a beggar; **3** *(uttrykk)* **~ oftest** generally, usually; **~ om** as if; *de behandlet henne ~ om hun skulle vært deres egen datter* they treated her as if she was their own daughter; **B** *rel pron* **I** *(i unødv relativsetninger)* **1** *(om personer) a) (som subjekt)* who; *Martin, ~ kom i går, har...* Martin, who came yesterday, has...; *b) (som objekt og omsynsledd)* who(m); *Jenny, ~ jeg bad om hjelp, sier...* Jenny, who(m) I asked for help, says ...; *c) (etter preposisjon)* whom; *broren hennes, ~ jeg snakket om i går, er nettopp kommet* her brother, about whom I spoke yesterday, has just arrived; **2** *(om ting)* which; *dette huset, ~ er over hundre år gammelt, er...* this house, which is over a hundred years old, is ...; **II** *(i nødv relativsetninger)* **1** that; *(om personer, især som subjekt også)* who; *den eneste mannen ~ kan gjøre det* the only man that/who can do it; *brevet som kom i går* the letter that came yesterday; **2** *(når ~ ikke er subjekt, kan det, som på norsk, sløyfes) den mannen (~) hun snakket om* the man she was talking about; *de bøkene (~) hun har lest* the books she has read; *(MEN) de samme bøkene ~ jeg har lest* the same books that I have read; **3** *(uttrykk)* **den ~** *(om personer)* he/she who; *(ubestemt)* whoever; **de ~** those who/that; **det ~** that which; what; *det (~) han sa* what he said.

somle *vb* dawdle; **~ bort** *a) (ødsle)* dawdle away; waste; *han ~t bort alle pengene sine* he wasted all his money; *b) (forlegge)* mislay; *jeg har ~t bort brillene mine igjen* I have mislaid my spectacles again; *c) (miste)* manage to lose; *hun ~t bort den nye paraplyen sin* she managed to lose her new umbrella. **somle|bøtte, ~kopp** *sb* dawdler, slowcoach. **somlete** *adj* dawdling, slow.

somme *pron* some; *~ tider* sometimes.

sommel *sb* dawdling.

sommer *sb* summer; *~en 1990* (in) the summer of 1990; *en fin ~* a fine summer; *(nå) i ~* this summer; *i fjor ~, sist ~* last summer; *neste ~, til ~en* next summer; *om ~en* during/in (the) summer. **sommer|dag** *sb* summer/summer's day. **~ferie** *sb* summer holidays. **~fugl** *sb* butterfly. **~solverv** *sb* summer solstice. **~tid** *sb (om årstiden)* summertime; summer-time; *(om forskjøvet ~tid)* summer time.

sondere *vb: ~ terrenget* reconnoitre; *fig* see how the land lies.

sondre *vb* distinguish.

sone A *sb (distrikt, område)* zone; **B** *vb (bøte for)* atone (for); expiate; *~ en straff* serve a sentence.

sonett *sb* sonnet.

soning *sb* **1** *(~ av synd)* atonement, expiation; **2** *(~ av straff)* serving (of a sentence).

sope *vb* sweep. **sopelime** *sb* besom, broom.

sopp *sb* **1** fungus; **2** *a) (om spiselig ~ især)* mushroom; *b) (om giftig ~)* toadstool; **3** *(hus~)* dry rot.

sopran *sb (stemme)* soprano.

sorg *sb* **1** grief, sorrow; *~ over farens død* grief for her/his father's death; *til min store ~* to my great sorrow; **2** *(beklagelse/sorg over noe mistet også)* regret; *hun følte stor ~ over å ha mistet sin venn* she felt great regret at having lost her friend; *med ~* with great regret; **3** *(sørgedrakt)* mourning; *de bar ~* they were in/wore mourning. **sorg|fri** *adj* carefree; *(økonomisk ~fri)* comfortable. **~full** *adj* sorrowful. **~løs** *adj* carefree.

sort A *adj* se *svart*; **B** *sb (art, slag)* kind, sort; *alle ~er frukt* all sorts of fruits. **sortere** *vb* sort; *den saken ~r under en annen avdeling* that matter belongs under another department; *han sorterte fra de dårlige* he sorted out the bad ones.

sorti *sb* exit; *gjøre (sin) ~* make one's exit.

sosial *adj* social. **sosial|demokrat** *sb* social democrat. **~demokrati** *sb* social democracy. **~demokratisk** *adj* social democratic. **~isere** *vb* nationalize, socialize. **~isering** *sb* nationalization, socialization. **~isme** *sb* Socialism. **~ist** *sb* Socialist. **~istisk** *adj* Socialistic. **~kurator** *sb* social worker; welfare officer. **~omsorg** *sb* social services. **~trygd** *sb* social security. **~økonom** *sb* economist. **~økonomi** *sb* economics; political economy. **sosietet** *sb* society. **sosio|log** *sb* sociologist. **~logi** *sb* sociology. **~logisk** *adj* sociological.

sot *sb* soot. **sote** *vb* soot. **sotet(e)** *adj* sooty.

sove *vb* sleep; be asleep; *de sov lenge* they slept late; *han la seg til å ~* he went to sleep; *hun sov tungt* she was fast asleep; *jeg sov dårlig i natt* I slept badly last night; *jeg ~r dårlig (til stadighet)* I am a bad sleeper; *sov godt!* sleep well! **sove|hjerte** *sb: ha et godt ~* be a sound sleeper. **~middel** *sb* sleeping medicine; soporific. **~pille** *sb* sleeping pill. **~plass** *sb* sleeping accomodation; berth. **~pose** *sb* sleeping-bag. **~sal** *sb* dormitory. **~sofa** *sb* sofa-bed, studio couch. **~syke** *sb* sleeping sickness. **~tablett** *sb* sleeping pill. **~vogn** *sb* sleeping car; sleeper. **~værelse** *sb* bedroom.

sovne *vb* fall asleep.

soya *sb* soya. **soya|bønne** *sb* soya bean; *US* soybean. **~olje** *sb* soya oil; *US* soybean oil.

spa *vb* spade. **spade** *sb* spade.

spagat *sb: gå ned i ~en* do the splits.

spagetti *sb* spagetti.

spak A *adj* meek, submissive; mild; **B** *sb (håndtak etc)* lever; *(gir~)* gear lever; *(i fly)* control column; *dgl* stick. **spakne** *vb* become more amenable; calm/*dgl* pipe down; *(om vind etc)* drop, subside.

spalte I *sb* **1** *(sprekk)* cleft, crack; **2** *(i avis etc)* column. **spalte** *vb* cleave. **spaltist** *sb* columnist.

spandabel *adj* generous, open-handed.

spandere *vb (bruke, rive i)* spend; *~ (noe) på (en)* stand (somebody something); treat (somebody to something); *nykommeren tilbød å ~ en drink på oss* the newcomer offered to stand us a drink; *han spanderte en god middag på seg selv* he treated himself to a good dinner.

spankulere *sb* strut.

spann *sb* **A** *(bøtte etc)* bucket; **B** *(av trekkdyr)* team; *(om to også)* pair; *et hunde~* a dog team; **C** *(tidsrom)* span.

spanskrør *sb* cane.

spant *sb* rib.

spar *sb (i kortspill)* spade; *~dame* queen of spades; *~ess* ace of spades.

spare *vb* **1** *(legge til side)* save; *~ (sammen) for å kjøpe noe* save up to buy something; *vi sparte 500 pund til sommerferien* we saved £500 for our summer holidays; **2** *(være sparsommelig med)* economize; *vi må ~ på brenselet* we must economize on the fuel; **3** *(skåne)* spare; *~ meg! ~ livet mitt!* spare me! spare my life! *de ~r seg ikke* they don't spare themselves; *det ~r oss for en masse bryderi* it will save us a lot of trouble. **spare|bank** *sb* savings bank. **~bøsse** *sb* savings-box, money-box. **~gris** *sb* piggy bank. **~kniv** *sb: bruke ~kniven* apply the axe. **~penger** *sb koll* savings.

spark *sb* **1** *(spenn)* kick; *han fikk et ~* he got kicked; *jeg gav ham et ~* I kicked him; **2** *(fig) få ~en* be fired/sacked; get the sack; **3** se *~støtting*. **sparke** *vb* kick; *jeg ~t etter ballen* I kicked at the ball; *jeg ~t til ballen* I kicked the ball. **sparkebukse** *sb* rompers.

sparkel *sb* **1** *(om stoffet)* stopper, surfacer; **2** *(om redskapet)* palette-knife, putty-knife. **sparkle** *vb* stop (up).

sparkstøtting *sb* ≈ kick (push, tread) sledge.

sparsom *adj, adv: ~ plantevekst* a spare vegetation; *det er ~t med frukt i år* fruit is scarce this year; *han er ~ med ros* he is sparing of praise. **sparsomhet** se *sparsommelighet*. **sparsommelig** *adj* economical, thrifty; *han er ~ med brenselet* he economizes on the fuel. **sparsommelighet** *sb* economy, thrift.

spartaner *sb* Spartan. **spartansk** *adj* Spartan.

spasere *vb* walk; *de gikk ut for å ~* they went out for a walk; *de var ute og spaserte* they were out walking; they were out for a walk. **spaser|sko** *sb* walking-shoes. **~stokk** *sb* walking-stick. **~tur** *sb* walk; *de gikk/tok (seg) en lang ~tur* they went for/took a long walk.

spe A *sb: være til spott og ~ for* be the laughing-stock of; **B** *vb (tynne ut)* dilute, thin.

sped *adj* delicate, tender; slender; *fra hans/hennes ~este barndom* from his/her early childhood; from his/her infancy.

spedalsk 1 *adj* leprous; **2** *sb* leper. **spedalskhet** *sb* leprosy.

spedbarn *sb* baby, infant.

spedisjon *sb* forwarding (of goods). **speditør** *sb* forwarding agent.

speedometer *sb* speedometer.

speide *vb* **1** *(holde utkikk)* watch; be on the look-out; *de ~t etter fienden* they were on the look-out for the enemy; *vi ~t etter et tegn* we watched for a sign; **2** *(være på speiding)* scout, reconnoitre. **speider** *sb* scout; *(~gutt)* boy scout; *(~pike)* girl guide. **speiderleir** *sb* scout camp; jamboree.

speil *sb* looking-glass, mirror; glass; *hun så seg i ~et* she looked at herself in the glass/mirror. **speil|bilde** *sb* reflection; image. **~blank** *adj* glassy, shiny; bright. **speile** *vb* mirror, reflect; *~ egg* fry eggs; *~ seg* look (at oneself) in the mirror; *trærne speilte seg i vannet* the trees were reflected in the water. **speil|egg** *sb* fried egg. **~glass** *sb* plate-glass. **~glassrute** *sb* plate-glass window. **~glatt** *adj* slippery.

speke|sild *sb* salt herring. **~skinke** *sb* cured ham.

spekk *sb* blubber, lard. **spekke** *vb* lard; *fig også* interlard; *~t kjøtt* larded meat; *en ~t lommebok* a well-lined wallet; *talen hans var ~t med fremmedord (utenlandske ord)* his speech was (inter)larded with foreign words.

spektrum *sb* spectrum.

spekulant *sb* speculator. **spekulasjon** *sb* speculation, **spekulativ** *adj* speculative. **spekulere** *vb* **1** *(især om forretninger)* speculate; **2** *(grunne, overveie)* meditate; think of; ~ *på* wonder; *jeg ~r på hvem som gjorde det* I wonder who did it; *jeg ~r på å kjøpe bil* I am thinking of buying a car.

spene *sb* teat.

spenn *sb* **1** *(spark)* kick; **2** *(på bro etc)* span; **3** *stå i ~ (være stram)* be strained; be under tension; *(om skytevåpen)* be cocked; be at full cock. **spenne I** *sb (belte~ etc)* buckle; **II** *vb* **1** *(sparke)* kick; **2** *(stramme, spile ut)* stretch; *de spente (opp) et tau mellom to stolper* they stretched a rope between two posts; **3** (uttrykk) ~ *en bue* bend/draw a bow; ~ *buen for høyt* aim too high; overreach oneself; ~ *en hest for en vogn* harness/hitch a horse to a carriage/waggon; ~ *hanen (på skytevåpen)* cock; ~ *musklene* contract/tense the muscles; ~ *ens nysgjerrighet* raise somebody's curiosity; ~ *ens oppmerksomhet* engross somebody's attention; ~ *over* span; *fig* cover; ~ *over et vidt område* cover a wide field; ~ *på (seg)* buckle/strap on; ~ *på pinebenken* put on the rack. **spennende** *adj* **1** exciting; *en ~ bok/film* an exciting book/film; *et ~ (= eventyrlig) liv* an adventurous/exciting life; **2** *(grøssende ~)* thrilling; *en ~ historie* a thriller; **3** *(full av spenning og engstelse)* anxious; *en ~ tid* an anxious time. **spenning** *sb* **1** tension; *~en i en fjær* the tension of a spring; *~en mellom de to landene* the tension between the two countries; *øke ~en* increase the tension; **2** *(spent interesse, usikkerhet)* suspense; *de ventet i stor ~ på legens uttalelse* they waited in great suspense for the doctor's opinion; **3** *(engstelse)* anxiety; **4** *(~ og opphisselse)* excitement; **5** *(elektrisk ~)* voltage. **spenn|kraft** *sb* elasticity. **~tak** *sb: ta ~tak* dig one's heels in. **~vidde** *sb* span; *fig* range, scope.

spenstig *adj* elastic, springy; *en ~ gange* a springy step. **spenstighet** *sb* elasticity, springiness.

spent *adj* **1** *(strammet)* tense, tight; stretched; **2** *(anstrengt)* tense; *en ~ situasjon* a tense situation; *hun lyttet ~* she listened intently; **3** *(ivrig, nysgjerrig)* anxious, curious; *han er ~ på resultatet* he is anxious to know the result.

sperre *vb* **1** *(blokkere)* block (up); *bilene ~t veien* the cars blocked the road; *døren var ~t* the door was blocked up; **2** *(stenge)* close; *veien er ~t for trafikk* the road is closed to traffic; **3** *~ inne* lock/shut up; *(i fengsel)* imprison; *fangen ble ~t inne* the prisoner was locked up; *han ~t øynene opp* he opened his eyes wide. **sperre|ballong** *sb* barrage balloon. **~ild** *sb* barrage. **sperring** *sb* obstruction; *(vei~)* road block.

spesialisere *vb* specialize. **spesialisering** *sb* specializing. **spesialist** *sb* specialist. **spesialitet** *sb* speciality, specialty. **spesial|kunnskap** *sb* specialist knowledge. **~område** *sb* special field. **~utdannelse** *sb* special training. **spesiell** *adj* special; *en ~ gunst/tjeneste* a special favour. **spesielt** *adv* **1** specially; *jeg gikk dit ~ for å treffe ham* I went there specially to see him; **2** *(især)* especially; *dette er et vanlig ord, ~ i engelsk dagligtale* this is a very common word, especially in colloquial English. **spesifikk** *adj* specific; *~ vekt* specific gravity. **spesifikasjon** *sb* specification. **spesifisere** *vb* specify. **spesifisert** *adj* specified.

spetakkel *sb* **1** *(bråk)* noise; *ungene holdt et svare ~* the children/kids made a great noise; **2** *(slagsmål)* riot, row; *de laget ~* they kicked up a row.

spett *sb* bar, crowbar.

spidd *sb* spit. **spidde** *vb* spit.

spiker *sb* nail; *hun traff ~en på hodet* she hit the nail on the head; *slå i en ~* drive/hammer in a nail. **spiker|hode** *sb* nail head. **~slag** *sb* nailing strip.

spikk *sb* prank, trick; *gjøre en et ~* play a trick on somebody.

spikke *vb* whittle.

spikre *vb* nail; *~ fast* nail down.

spile 1 *sb (tre~)* lath; *(paraply~)* rib; **2** *vb: ~ ut* stretch, distend; *~ opp øynene* open one's eyes wide.

spill *sb* **A** *(ødsling)* loss, waste; *~ av tid* loss/waste of time; *gå til ~e* go/run to waste; **B 1** *(det å spille)* play; **2** *(det som spilles)* game; *~ets regler* the rules of the game; *hun vant spillet* she won the game; **3** *(uttrykk) de hadde en finger med i ~et* they had something to do with it; *han satte livet på ~* he risked his life; *hun er ute av ~et* he is out of the running; *stå på ~* be at stake. **spille** *vb* **A 1** *(miste, søle)* lose, spill; *spilt møye* lost/wasted effort(s); *han spilte suppe på klærne sine* he spilt/spilled soup on his clothes; **2** *(ødsle bort)* waste; *det er ingen tid å ~* there is noe time to be lost/to lose; *han spilte både tid og penger på det* he wasted both his time and his money on it; **B 1** *(om lek og musikk)* play; *~ om penger* play for money; *~ på (et bestemt instrument)* play on; *~ ut (i kort)* lead; *han spilte en sonate* he played a sonata; *hun ~r fiolin* she plays the violin; *jeg kommer aldri til å ~ Peer Gynt* I shall never play Peer Gynt; *vi spilte kort* we played cards; **2** *(~ hasard)* gamble; *han spilte bort alle pengene sine* he gambled away all his money; **3** *(late som)* pretend to be; *han spilte dum* he pretended to be stupid. **spille|lærer, ~lærerinne** *sb* music teacher. **~mann** *sb* fiddler, musician. **spiller** *sb* player; *(hasard~)* gambler. **spille|rom** *sb: de hadde fritt ~rom* they had a free hand; *vi gav dem fritt ~rom* we gave them a free hand. **~time** *sb* music lesson.

spillfekteri *sb* make-believe; humbug, pretence.

spillopper *sb fl* fun, mischief, pranks; *lage ~* make fun; play pranks/tricks. **spilloppmaker** *sb* mischief; *den gutten er en ordentlig ~* that boy is a regular mischief.

spiltau *sb* stall.

spinat *sb* spinach.

spindel *sb* spindle. **spindelvev** *sb* cobweb; spider's web.

spinke *vb: ~ og spare* pinch and scrape/screw.

spinkel *adj* slight, thin; *en ~ skikkelse* a slight figure.

spinn *sb* **1** web; *edderkopp~* spider's web; *et ~ av løgner* a web of lies; **2** *gå i ~* get into a spin; *flyet gikk i ~* the plane got into a spin. **spinne** *vb* spin; *~ silke* spin silk. **spinnemaskin** *sb* spinning machine. **spin-**

neri *sb* spinning mill. **spinning** *sb: vinningen går opp i ~en* the expenses absorb the profits.

spion *sb* spy; *også* agent. **spionasje** *sb* espionage. **spionere** *sb* spy.

spir *sb* spire; *~et på kirken* the spire of the church.

spiral *sb* spiral.

spire *sb* shoot, sprout; *fig* germ; *~en til en plan* the germ of a plan. **spire** *vb* sprout.

spiritisme *sb* spiritualism. **spiritist** *sb* spiritualist. **spiritistisk** *adj* spiritualistic. **spirituell** *adj* brilliant, witty. **spirituosa** *sb fl* spirits; liquor. **spiritus** *sb* alcohol, spirits.

spirrevipp *sb* **1** *(liten fyr)* manikin; **2** *(spradebasse)* dude, fop.

spise eat; *(ofte)* have (a meal etc); *~ aftens/kveldsmat* have supper; *~ frokost* breakfast; have breakfast; *~ lunch* lunch; have lunch(eon); *~ middag* dine; have dinner; *de spiste kylling til middag* they had chicken for dinner; *jeg spiste et egg til frokost* I had an egg with my breakfast; *vi ~r alltid hjemme* we always have our meals at home. **spise|bestikk** *sb koll* cutlery. **~bord** *sb* dining-table. **~frikvarter** *sb* lunch interval. **~kjøkken** *sb* kitchen-dining-room. **spiselig** *adj* **1** *(ikke giftig)* edible; *en ~ sopp* an edible mushroom; **2** *(som det går an å spise)* eatable; *denne maten er knapt ~* this food is hardly eatable. **spise|rør** *sb* gullet, (o)esophagus. **~sal** *sb* dining-hall. **~seddel** *sb* menu. **~skje** *sb* table-spoon. **~stue** *sb* dining-room. **~tid** *sb* mealtime. **~vogn** *sb* diner, dining-car; buffet-/restaurant car. **spiskammer** *sb* larder; *(også til servise)* pantry.

spiss I *adj* **1** pointed, sharp; *en ~ blyant* a sharp pencil; *en ~ nese* a pointed nose; **2** *(om vinkel)* acute; **II** *sb (ytterste ende)* point, tip; end; *sette (en) ~ på* add relish to; *sette på ~en* push to extremes; *stå/være i ~en for noe* be at the head of something. **spiss|borger** *sb* philistine. **~borgerlig** *adj* philistine. **~bue** *sb* Gothic/pointed arch. **spisse** *vb* point, sharpen; *han ~t ører* he pricked up his ears. **spissfindig** *adj* hair-splitting, quibbling; nice, subtle. **spissfindighet** *sb* quibble; nicety, subtlety. **spiss|mus** *sb* shrew, shrew-mouse. **~rot** *sb: løpe ~rot* run the gauntlet.

spjeld *sb* damper, register.

spjelke *vb* put in splints; *den brukne armen ble ~t* the broken arm was put in splints.

spjære *vb* rend, rip, tear.

spjåke *vb: ~ seg ut* rig oneself out; *utspjåket* (all) dolled up.

spleis *sb (~ av tauverk)* splice. **spleise 1** *(skjøte tauverk)* splice; **2** *(dele utgifter etc)* pool; go Dutch; **3** *(dgl: gifte)* match, marry. **spleise|fest, ~lag** *sb* Dutch treat.

splid *sb* discord, dissension, quarrel; *han skapte ~ i familien* he caused discord in the family.

splint *sb* **1** *(flis etc)* chip, splinter; **2** *(granat~)* fragment/splinter (of a shell).

splinter *adv: ~ ny* brand new.

splintre *vb* shatter, smash.

splitt *sb* slit. **splitte** *vb* **1** *(spre)* disperse, scatter; *folkemassen ble ~t av politiet* the crowd was dispersed/scattered by the police; **2** *(kløyve)* split; *partiet ble ~t i grupper* the party split up into groups. **splittelse** *sb* **1** *(oppdeling)* disruption, split-up; **2** *(uenighet)* discord; disunion, division.

splitter *adv: ~ gal* stark, staring mad; *~ naken* stark naked.

splittet *adj* divided; *(delt)* split up. **splittflagg** *sb* swallow-tailed flag. **splittnagle** *sb* split pin/rivet.

spole *sb (til film, garn etc)* spool; *(garn~ også)* bobbin; *(smalfilmrull især)* reel. **spole** *vb* spool, wind; reel.

spolere *vb* ruin, spoil.

spolorm *sb* roundworm.

spon chip; *(høvel~)* shavings; *(fil~)* filings.

spontan *adj* spontaneous. **spontant** *adv* spontaneously; *han gjorde det ~* he did it spontaneously. **spontanitet** *sb* spontaneity.

spor *sb* **1** *(fotspor)* footprint(s), track(s); *hun fulgte i morens (i sin mors) ~* she followed in her mother's footprints; *~et var lett å følge* the track was easy to follow; **2** *(hjul~)* rut, wheel-track; **3** *(jernbane~)* track; *det toget går på et annet ~* that train runs on the other track; **4** *(merker etter noe)* mark, trace; *ansiktet hennes bar ~ av lidelser* her face bore/showed marks/traces of sufferings; *ethvert ~ av forbrytelsen var fjernet* every trace of the crime had been removed; **5** *(nøkkel til mysterium etc)* clue; *politiet er/står uten ~* the police are without a clue; **6** *ikke ~ (ingenting)* nothing at all; *(slett ikke)* not a bit; not at all; *han er ikke det ~ intelligent* he is not at all intelligent; *ikke det ~ overrasket* not a bit surprised.

sporadisk *adj* sporadic.

spore I *sb* spur; *(på bregne)* spore; *(fig: ansporing)* incentive, stimulus; *en ~ til arbeid* an incentive/a stimulus to work; **II** *vb* **1** *(føle, merke)* feel, notice; detect; **2** *(~ en hest)* spur; *(fig: anspore)* spur on. **sporenstreks** *adv* **1** *(straks)* at once; immediately; **2** *(med stor hast)* post-haste. **spor|hund** *sb* **1** tracker dog; **2** *(også fig)* sleuth(-hound). **~løst** *adv* without leaving a trace; *de forsvant ~løst* they disappeared completely.

sport *sb* sport(s). Se også *idrett.* **sports|fiske** *sb* angling. **~fisker** *sb* angler. **~forretning** *sb* sports shop. **~journalist** *sb* sporting journalist; sports reporter. **~vogn** *sb (bil)* roadster; *(barnevogn)* push-chair.

sporvidde *sb (på jernbane)* gauge.

sporvogn se *trikk.*

spotsk *adj (spottende)* derisive; *(ertende)* mocking; *(hånlig)* scoffing, sneering. **spott** *sb* mockery, ridicule; derision; *(spottende bemerkning)* sarcastic remark. **spotte** *vb* mock; *~ over* jeer/mock at; deride. **spottefugl** *sb* mocker, scoffer. **spottende** *adj* mocking, derisive. **spotter** *sb* mocker, scoffer.

sprade 1 *sb* dandy, fop; **2** *vb* show off; strut, swagger. **spradebasse** *sb* dandy, fop.

spraglet(e) *adj* motley, mottled; gaudy.

sprake *vb* crackle.

sprang *sb* **1** *(hopp)* jump, leap; bound; *fig* jump; *(tanke~ etc)* sudden transition; **2** *(løp)* run; *sette på ~* start running.

sprayflaske *sb* atomizer; spray bottle.

spre *vb* **1** *(fordele jevnt)* spread; **2** *(fordele ujevnt, drive bort)* scatter; *~ seg* scatter, spread; *de ble spredt for alle vinder* they were scattered to the four winds; *vinden spredte skyene* the wind scattered the clouds. **spredning** *sb* scattering, spreading; *(i statistikk)* dispersion. **spredt** *adj, adv* **1** scattered; *(~ og fåtallig)* sparse; *~ befolket* sparsely populated; *~e byger* scattered showers.

sprek *adj* fit, vigorous; brisk.

sprekk *sb* **1** *(brist)* crack; *det var en ~ i koppen* there was alcrack in the cup; **2** *(revne)* fissure; *(i fjell, mur)* crevice; *(i isbre)* crevasse; **3** *(smal åpning)* chink; *vinden blåste inn gjennom ~ene i veggen* the wind blew through the chinks in the wall. **sprekke** *vb* **1** *(slå sprekker)* crack; **2** *(sprenges)* burst. **sprekkeferdig** *adj: ~ av* bursting with.

sprelle *vb* **1** *(med armer og bein)* kick about; fling one's arms and legs about; *(også)* kick and struggle; **2** *(i vannet)* splash; **3** *(om fisk)* flop. **sprellemann** *sb* jumping jack. **sprelsk** *adj* **1** *(livlig)* frisky, lively; **2** *(vilter)* unruly.

spreng *sb: arbeide på ~* work feverishly/furiously/at high pressure; *lese på ~* cram. **sprenge** *vb* **1** *(få til å briste/sprekke)* burst; *~ lenkene sine* burst one's bonds; **2** *(åpne med makt)* break (burst, bust) open; *politiet sprengte døren* the police broke the door; **3** *(~ i luften)* blow up; *de sprengte broen (i luften)* they blew up the bridge; **4** *(~ fjell etc)* blast; *det ble sprengt en tunnel gjennom fjellet* a tunnel was blasted through the mountain; **5** *(overanstrenge)* overstrain; **6** *(overbefolke etc)* overcrowd; *universitetene er sprengt* the universities are overcrowded. **sprengstoff** *sb koll* explosives.

sprett *sb (hopp)* jump; bound, start; *(om ball)* bounce. **sprette** *vb* **1** *(hoppe)* jump, leap; *(om ball)* bounce, bound; **2** *(om trær)* come into leaf; **3** *~ opp* rip/slit open; *(~ opp sømmer)* unstitch. **spretten** *adj* frisky. **sprettert** *sb* slingshot, catapult.

sprike *vb (stå ut)* stand out; *~ med* spread.

springbrett *sb* spring-board; *fig* stepping-stone; *et ~ til suksess* a stepping-stone to success. **springe** *vb* **1** *(hoppe)* jump, leap; spring; *hun sprang i vannet* she jumped into the water; *jeg sprang opp fra plassen/stolen min* I sprang (up) from my seat; **2** *a) (fare)* jump; *b) (løpe)* run; **3** *(revne, sprekke)* burst; *(gå i stykker)* break; *kjelen/vannrøret sprang* the boiler/waterpipe burst; **4** *(uttrykk) ~ (= stikke)* **frem** jut out; project; **~ i luften** blow up; *skipet sprang i luften* the ship blew up; **~ i øynene:** *det ~r en i øynene* it hits you in the eye; **~ ut** *(om trær)* burst/come into leaf; *(om blomster)* open; come out; *(om knopper)* burst, open. **springende** *adj (usammenhengende)* disconnected, desultory, rambling; *det ~ punkt* the salient point. **springer** *sb (i sjakk)* knight. **spring|flo** *sb* spring tide. **~madrass** *sb* spring mattress. **~marsj** *sb* run; *i ~* at the double. **~vann** *sb* **1** *(fontene)* fountain; **2** *(innlagt vann)* running water.

sprinkel|kasse *sb* crate. **~verk** *sb* lattice, trellis. **sprinkler** *sb fl* **1** *(gitter)* bars; **2** *(~anlegg)* sprinkler.

sprit *sb* spirit, alcohol; *(om brennevin især)* liquor. **sprit|apparat** *sb* spirit-heater/-stove. **~lampe** *sb* spirit-lamp.

sprosse *sb* **1** *(vannrett list)* crossbar; **2** *(stigetrinn)* rung.

sprudle *vb* bubble; gush, well; *~ av godt humør* bubble over with high spirits; *~nde vidd* sparkling wit.

sprut *sb* gush, spurt; *(tynn stråle)* squirt. **sprute** *vb (stråle frem)* gush, spurt; *(i tynn stråle)* squirt; *(skvette)* splash.

sprø *adj (skjør)* brittle; *(om mat)* crisp; *(gal)* crazy.

sprøyt *sb* **1** *(sprut)* splash; *(sjø~)* spray; **2** *(vrøvl)* nonsense, rubbish. **sprøyte I** *sb* **1** *(injeksjons~ etc)* syringe; **2** *(innsprøytning, ~stikk)* hypodermic, injection; *(især dgl)* shot; *få en ~* get a shot/an injection; **3** *(brann~)* fire-engine; **II** *vb* spray, sprinkle; *~ plenen med ugressmiddel* sprinkle the lawn with weed killer; *frukttrærne ble ~t* the fruit-trees were sprayed. **sprøyte|lakkere** *vb* spray, spray-paint. **~narkoman** *sb* needleman. **~pistol** *sb* spray gun.

språk *sb* language. **språk|bruk** *sb* usage. **~feil** *sb* grammatical error. **~kunnskaper** *sb fl* knowledge of (foreign) languages. **språklig** *adj* linguistic. **språk|melodi** *sb* intonation. **~vitenskap** *sb* linguistics.

spurv *sb* sparrow. **spurvehauk** *sb* sparrowhawk.

spy *vb* vomit; *~ ut røyk* belch forth smoke.

spyd *sb* spear; *(til spydkast)* javelin.

spydig *adj* sarcastic. **spydighet** *sb* sarcasm.

spyd|kast *sb* throwing the javelin. **~kaster** *sb* javelin thrower.

spyflue *sb* bluebottle.

spyle *vb* flush; *(~ med slange)* hose.

spytt *sb* saliva, spittle. **spytte** *vb* spit. **spytteklyse** *sb* clot of spittle. **spytt|kjertel** *sb* salivary gland. **~slikker** *sb* bootlicker, lickspittle; toady. **~slikkeri** *sb* toadyism.

spøk *sb* joke, jest; *(i handling ofte)* practical joke; *det er ikke/ingen ~* it is no joke; it is no joking matter; *du forstår ikke ~* you can't take a joke; *hun sa det for/på ~* she said it for a joke. **spøke** *vb* **A** *(drive spøk)* joke, jest; *de spøkte med henne* they joked with her; *han spøkte med saken* he joked about the matter; he made a joke of the matter; *hun er ikke å ~ med* she is not to be trifled with; **B** *vb (gå igjen) ~ på et sted* haunt a place; *det ~r på slottet* the castle is haunted; *et hus der det ~r* a haunted house. **spøkefugl** *sb* wag. **spøke|full** *adj* jocular, playful. **~fullhet** *sb* jocularity. **spøkelse** *sb* **1** *(gjenferd)* ghost; *tror du på ~r?* do you believe in ghosts? **2** *(noe nifst/skremmende)* spectre; *krigens ~* the spectre of war. **spøkelses|aktig** *adj* spooky, weird. **~historie** *sb* ghost story. **~hus** *sb* haunted house. **spøkeri** *sb* ghosts.

spørre *vb* ask, inquire; *(stille spørsmål)* ask questions; *(stille spørsmål til også)* put questions to; *(~ ut)* interrogate, question; *ingen spør ham/om hans mening* nobody asks him/his opinion; ~ **etter:** *hun spurte etter Mr S.* she asked for Mr S; *jeg spurte etter boken hos bokhandleren* I inquired for the book at the bookseller's; ~ **om:** *de spurte om vi hadde sett filmen* they asked if/whether we had seen the film; *han spurte meg om prisen* he asked me the price; *spør du meg* **om** *min mening?* do you ask my opinion? **spørre|konkurranse** *sb* quiz. **~lyst** *sb* curiosity, inquisitiveness. **~lysten** *adj* curious, inquisitive. **~pronomen** *sb* interrogative pronoun. **~setning** *sb* interrogative sentence. **~skjema** *sb* questionnaire. **~time** *sb (i parlamentet)* Question Time. **spørsmål** *sb* question; *et ~ om liv eller død* a matter of life or death; *et ~ om penger* a question of money; *et ledende ~* a leading question; *hun stilte meg et ~* she asked me a question; she put a question to me. **spørsmålstegn** *sb* question mark.

spøtt *sb: ikke det ~* not a bit; not the slightest.

spå *vb* predict (the future); prophesy; *hun ~dde ham* she told him his fortune; *hun ~dde ham en strålende fremtid* she predicted him a glorious future; *mennesket ~r, Gud rår* man proposes, God disposes. **spå|dom** *sb* prophesy. **~kone, ~mann** *sb* fortune-teller.

sta *adj* obstinate, stubborn; *(om hest)* restive; *fig* restive.

stab *sb* staff; *hun hører (med) til ~en* she is one of the staff.

stabbe *vb* trudge, toddle. **stabbur** *sb* ≈ storehouse.

stabeis *sb: en gammel ~* an old fogey.

stabel *sb* **1** pile, stack; *en ~ (med) mynter/bøker* a pile of coins/books; **2** *skipet gikk av ~en* the ship was launched. **stabelavløpning** *sb* launching, launch.

stabil *adj* stable, constant; *(om person)* steady; *~e priser* stable prices; *~ temperatur* constant temperature. **stabilisere** *vb* stabilize. **stabilitet** *sb* stability.

stable *vb: ~ opp* pile (up); stack; *jeg ~t opp veden* I stacked the wood.

stadfeste *vb* confirm, affirm. **stadfestelse** *sb* confirmation.

stadig *adj* **1** *(uforanderlig)* constant; *adv* constantly; **2** *(uavbrutt, vedvarende)* continuous, steady; *adv* continually; *~ bedre/verre* better and better/worse and worse; *det blir ~ vanskeligere* it is becoming increasingly difficult; **3** *(hyppig gjentatt)* continual, repeated; *adv* continually; *det hender ~ (vekk)* it continually happens; **4** *(ennå)* still; *han er ~ sykmeldt* he is still reported sick. **stadighet** *sb* steadiness; *til ~* constantly.

stadion *sb* stadium.

stadium *sb* stage; *på et tidlig ~* at an early stage.

stafett|løp *sb* relay race. **~pinne** *sb* baton.

staffasje *sb* decor, ornaments *fl.*

staffeli *sb* easel.

stagge *vb* **1** *(berolige)* soothe; **2** *(legge demper på)* check, curb.

stagnasjon *sb* stagnation. **stagnere** *vb* stagnate; be stagnant.

stahet *adj* obstinact, stubbornness; restiveness.

stake A *sb (stang)* pole; *(pæl)* stake; *(lyse~)* candlestick; **B** *vb (~ en båt frem)* pole, punt.

stakitt *sb* paling; *(jern~)* railing.

stakk *sb* **1** *(skjørt)* skirt; **2** *(høy~ etc)* rick, stack; *de satte høyet i ~* they stacked the hay.

stakkar *sb* poor creature (fellow, man, woman etc); *en ynkelig (elendig, ussel etc) ~* a wretch. **stakkars** *adj* poor, wretched; *~ deg* poor you; *den ~ gutten* the wretched boy.

stakkato *sb* staccato.

stakkåndet *adj* breathless; out of breath.

stall *sb* stable.

stam *adj være ~* be a stammerer.

stamfar *sb* ancestor, progenitor.

stamgjest *sb* regular (customer).

stamme A *sb* **1** *(tre~)* stem, trunk; **2** *(folke~)* tribe; *Juda ~* the tribe of Judah; **3** *(ord~)* root, stem; **B** *vb (ned~ fra)* be descended from; *~r menneskene fra apene?* are men descended from apes? **C** *vb (tale hakkete)* stammer, stutter; *han ~r* he is a stammerer.

stamp *sb* **A** *(balje, kar)* tub; **B** *(pantelånerforretning)* pawn shop. **stampe A** *sb: stå i ~* be at a deadlock/a standstill; **B 1** *vb (gå tungt, tråkke)* stamp, tramp; *~ med foten* stamp one's foot; *de kom ~nde* they came tramping; **2** *(om skip)* pitch; **C** *vb (pantsette)* pawn.

stamtavle *sb* **1** *(ætt)* pedigree; **2** *(skrevet)* genealogical table. **stamtre** *sb* pedigree; genealogical tree.

stand *sb* **1** *(samfunnsklasse)* class, rank; *hist* estate; *han giftet seg med en pike fra sin egen ~* he married a girl of his own class; *rikets stender* the estates of the realm; **2** *(tilstand)* condition, state; *i brukbar ~* in working order; *i god ~* in good condition; **3** *(uttrykk)* **holde ~** stand firm; stand one's ground; *få* **i** *~* arrange; bring about; *sette i ~ (reparere)* mend, repair; *sette* **i ~ til** enable to; *pengene satte ham i ~ til å reise utenlands* the money enabled him to go abroad; *stelle i ~* arrange; *være i ~* be in order/in good repair; *ute av ~ til* incapable of; unable to.

standard *sb* standard. **standardisere** *vb* standardize.

standhaftig *adj* firm, steadfast. **standhaftighet** *sb* firmness, steadfastness.

standpunkt *sb* **1** *(synsmåte)* standpoint; point of view; **2** *(nivå)* level; *(kunnskapsnivå)* standard; **3** *(holdning)* attitude; *ta ~ til* make up one's mind about.

standrett *sb* court-martial.

standsforskjell *sb* difference of station/rank.

stang *sb* **1** *(stake)* pole; *(metall~ især)* bar; *(fiske~)* rod; *(flagg~)* staff; *(~ på herresykkel)* top tube; *på halv ~* at halfmast.

stange *vb* butt; *(spidde, ~ til blods)* gore.

stang|fiske *sb* angling. **~fisker** *sb* angler.

stank *sb* stench.

stankelbein *sb* cranefly; daddy-long-legs.

stans *sb (avbrytelse, opphold)* break, pause; halt; *(stopp)* stop, cessation. **stanse** *vb* stop; *vognen ~t* the carriage stopped. **stanse** *vb (presse ut)* punch, stamp. **stansemaskin** *sb* punching/stamping machine.

stappe I *sb (puré)* mash; **II** *vb* cram, stuff. **stappfull** *adj* chock-full; crammed full.

start *sb* start; *en god ~ i livet* a good start in life. **startbane** *sb (på flyplass)* runway. **starte** *vb* start; *motoren ~r ikke/vil ikke ~* the engine won't start. **start|grop** *sb* starting hole. **~klar** *sb* ready to start. **~skudd** *sb* starting shot. **~strek** *sb* starting line/mark.

stas *sb (pynt)* finery; *(prakt)* pomp; *det er bare til ~* that is only for show; *han gjorde ~ på henne* he made much of her; *hele ~en* the whole lot. **stase** *vb: ~ opp* dress up; rig out. **staselig** *adj* stately; fine, handsome.

stasjon *sb* station; *jernbane~* railway station; *over alle ~er (radio)* from all stations. **stasjonere** *sb* station. **stasjonsmester** *sb* station-master. **stasjonsvogn** *sb* estate car; *US* station wagon. **stasjonær** *adj* stationary.

stat *sb* state.

statelig *adj* stately, portly.

statisk *adj* static.

statist *sb (i film)* extra; *(teater)* walker-on, supernumerary.

statistiker *sb* statistician. **statistikk** *sb* statistics; *~ over dødsfall* statistics of deaths. **statistisk** *adj* statistical.

stativ *sb* stand, rack; *(foto~ etc)* tripod.

stats|advokat *sb* public prosecutor; *US* district attorney. **~autorisert** *adj* chartered; *US* certified; *~autorisert revisor* chartered accountant; *US* certified public accountant. **~baner** *sb koll* national railways; State railways. **~bidrag** *sb* government grant. **~borger** *sb* citizen. **~borgerlig** *adj* civic, civil. **~borgerskap** *sb* citizenship. **~forfatning** *sb* constitution. **~funksjonær** *sb* civil servant. **~gjeld** *sb* national debt. **~kapitalisme** *sb* state capitalism. **~kassen** *sb* the public purse. **~kirke** *sb* established (national, State) church. **~kupp** *sb* coup d'état. **~løs** *adj* stateless. **~lån** *sb* government loan. **~mann** *sb* statesman. **~minister** *sb* prime minister; premier. **~obligasjon** *sb* government bond. **~overhode** *sb* head of State. **~rett** *sb* constitutional law. **~rettslig** *adj* constitutional. **~råd** *sb* **1** *(regjeringsmedlem)* Cabinet minister; *(...minister)* Secretary of State for... **2** *(regjeringsmøte)* Cabinet meeting. **~sekretær** *sb* ≈ Parliamentary Under-Secretary (of State); Permanent Secretary. **~sjef** head of State. **~skatt** *sb* tax. **~støtte** *sb* State aid. **~tjenestemann** Government official; *(i administrasjonen)* civil servant.

statholder *sb* governor.

statue *sb* monument, statue.

statuere *vb: ~ et eksempel* set a warning example.

statuett *sb* statuette.

status *sb* **1** *(tilstand)* state of affairs; **2** *(i regnskap)* balance-sheet; *gjøre opp ~* make out/draw up the balance-sheet. **statussymbol** *sb* status symbol.

statutt *sb* regulation, statute; *(foreningsstatutter også)* rules. **statuttmessig** *adj* statutory.

staude *sb* perennial.

staur *sb* pole.

staut *adj* burly, strapping; stalwart.

stav *sb (stokk)* stick; *(ski~)* stick; *US* pole; *(stang, ~ til stavsprang)* pole; *falle i ~er* be lost in thought. **stave** *vb* spell; *hvordan ~s dette ordet?* how do you spell this word? *det ~s med to e-er* it is spelled with to e's; *han har ~t det galt* he has misspelt it; *jeg har ~t det riktig* I have spelled it correctly. **stavefeil** *sb* mistake in spelling. **stavelse** *sb* syllable; *et ord med/på to stavelser* a word of two syllables.

stav|hopp se *~sprang.*

stavn *sb (for~)* stem; *(bak~)* stern.

stavns|bundet *adj* adscript; bound to the soil. **~bånd** *sb* adscription.

stavre *vb* dodder.

stavsprang *sb* pole-vault, pole-jump..

stebarn *sb* stepchild.

sted 1 place, spot; *alle ~er* everywhere; *alle andre ~er* (in) all other places; *et annet ~* another place; *ingen ~er* nowhere; *ingen andre ~er* nowhere else; **2** *(uttrykk)* **av ~:** *de drog av ~* they set off (left, started etc); *jeg må av ~* I must be off; **finne ~** take place; *bryllupet fant sted i kirken* the wedding took place in the church; **i ~et for** instead of; *jeg kommer i ~et for ham* I come instead of him; **på ~et** on the spot; *på det ~et* in that place; **til ~e** present.

stedatter *sb* stepdaughter.

sted|bunden *adj* attached to a locality. **~egen** *adj* local; *(om sykdom)* endemic. **~feste** *vb* localize. **~fortreder** *sb* deputy, substitute.

stedig *adj, adv* obstinate(ly), stubborn(ly); *(neds)* pigheaded. **stedighet** *sb* obstinacy, stubbornness.

stedlig *adj* local.

stedsadverb *sb* adverb of place.

stedsans *sb* sense (*dgl* bump) of locality.

stedsnavn *sb* place-name.

stedt *adj, pp: ille ~* in a bad way; in great trouble.

stefar *sb* stepfather.

steil *adj (bratt)* steep, abrupt; *(fig: sta, stivnakket)* obstinate, stubborn.

steile *vb* **1** *(om hest)* rear; **2** *(fig: bli forbløffet)* be staggered; *han ~t da han hørte prisen* he was staggered to hear what it cost; **3** *(fig: bli forarget)* bridle (up); *hun ~t over/ved bemerkningen hans* she bridled at his remark.

stein *sb* stone; *(kampe~)* boulder rock; *(liten, rund ~)* pebble; *de kastet (med) ~ etter hunden* they threw stones at the dog. **stein|alder** *vb* Stone Age; *eldre ~* the Paleolithic age; *yngre ~* the Neolithic age. **~bed** *sb* rockery; rock garden. **~brudd** *sb* (stone) quarry. **steine** *vb* stone. **steinet(e)** *adj* stony. **stein|frukt** *sb* stone fruit. **~gjerde** *sb* stone fence/wall. **~helle** *sb* flat stone; *(til hellelegging)* flag, flagstone. **~hugger** *sb* stone cutter. **~kast** *sb* stone's throw. **~kull** *sb* coal. **~ras** *sb* rockslide. **~røys** *sb* heap of stones. **~skred** *sb* rockslide. **~tøy** *sb* crockery, pottery; earthenware; stoneware. **~ull** *sb* rock wool. **~ur** *sb (ved foten av fjell)* scree.

stek *sb (stekt kjøtt)* roast; *(om en hel stek)* joint. **steke** *vb* **1** *(i ovn)* bake; *(om kjøtt)* roast; *stekt kylling* roasted chicken; **2** *(~ i panne)* fry; *stekt fisk* fried fish; **3** *(grill~)* grill; **4** *(om solen)* beat down; *~nde sol* scorching sun; *~nde varmt* baking hot. **steke|ovn** *sb* oven. **~panne** *sb* frying-pan. **~rist** *sb* gridiron, grill.

stell *sb* **1** *(det å stelle)* chores, work; *det daglige ~ i huset og på gården* the daily housework and the chores on the farm; **2** *(pleie)* care, nursing; **3** *(ettersyn)* care, maintenance; **4** *(redskaper, utstyr)* gear, things; **5** *(skjelett, skrog)* framework. **stelle** *vb (pleie)* nurse; *(røkte)* tend; *~ i hagen* work/potter about in the garden; *~ i huset* keep house; work in the house; *~ (i huset) for* do for; *han ~r seg selv* he does his own housework; *hun holder på å ~ seg* she is making herself ready. **stellebord** *sb* dressing table; *(for spedbarn, kombinert med badekar)* bathinette.

stemme I *sb* **1** *(røst)* voice; *med høy ~* in a loud voice; **2** *(~ i musikk)* part; *hvilken ~ synger du?* what part do you take? **3** *(ved avstemning)* vote; **II** *vb* **1** *(~ overens)* agree; *regnskapet ~r* the accounts agree/tally; **2** *(~ et instrument)* tune; *~ et piano* tune a piano; **3** *(~ ved valg)* vote; **4** *(uttrykk)* *~* **for** vote for; *de som ~r for, rekker hånden i været* those in favour will raise their hands; *~* **imot** vote against; *de som ~r imot* those against; *~* **med** agree/tally with; *~r din liste med min?* does your list tally with mine? *det ~r med hva hun har sagt* it agrees with what she has said; *~* **over** vote on; *~* **på** vote for; *vi har alltid stemt på Arbeiderpartiet* we have always voted Labour. **stemmeberettiget** *adj* qualified to vote. **stemme|bånd** *sb* vocal chord. **~gaffel** *sb* tuning fork. **~rett** *sb* franchise, suffrage; vote; right of voting; *alminnelig ~rett* universal suffrage. **~rettsalder** *sb* voting age. **~seddel** *sb* voting slip; ballot paper. **~tall** *sb* number of votes. **~urne** *sb (valgurne)* ballot box.

stemning *sb* **1** *(sinnstilstand)* mood, temper; *han er i (en) munter/bedrøvet ~* he is in a gay/sad mood/temper; **2** *(~ blant folk, i en situasjon etc)* atmosphere; *~en er rolig og fredfylt* the atmosphere is calm and peaceful; *høy ~* high spirits. **stemnings|betont** *adj* emotional, sentimental. **~full** *adj* lyrical, poetic. **~menneske** *sb* impulsive/temperamental person.

ste|moderlig *adj, adv: bli ~ behandlet* be left out in the cold; not get a fair deal. **~mor** *sb* stepmother. **~morsblomst** *sb* pansy.

stempel *sb* **1** *(til å stemple med)* stamp; **2** *(~avtrykk)* mark, stamp; *(post~)* postmark; *sette sitt ~ på* leave one's mark on; **3** *(~ i dampmaskin etc)* piston. **stempel|avgift** *sb* stamp duty. **~merke** *sb* stamp. **~slag** *sb* piston stroke. **~stang** *sb* piston rod. **stemple** *vb* stamp; *(~ med poststempel)* postmark; *brevet var (post)stemplet London* the letter was postmarked London; *hans oppførsel ~r ham som en tarvelig fyr* his manners stamp him as a cad.

stemt *adj: være ~ for* be/feel inclined to; be in favour of; *være vennlig ~* be in a friendly mood.

steng *sb (av fisk)* catch, seineful.

stenge *vb* **1** *(låse)* lock; *~ (med slå)* bolt; *(med tverrstang)* bar; *~ inne* lock up; *~ ute* shut out; **2** *(lukke)* close; *butikkene er stengt søndag* the shops are closed on Sundays; *denne veien er stengt for tungtrafikk* this road is closed to heavy motor traffic.

stengel *sb* stem; *(stilk)* stalk.

stengetid *sb* closing time; *etter ~* after hours. **stengsel** *sb* bar, barrier.

stenk *sb (antydning)* dash, touch.

stenograf *sb* shorthand writer. **stenografere** *vb* take down in shorthand. **stenografi** *sb* shorthand. **stenogram** *sb* shorthand note.

stensil *sb* stencil. **stensilere** *vb* stencil, duplicate.

steppe A *sb (gresslette)* steppe; **B** *vb (danse step)* do tapdancing. **stepping** *sb* tap-dancing.

stereo *adj, sb* stereo. **stereo|anlegg** *sb* stereo (outfit, radio). **~fonisk** *adj* stereo(phonic). **~metri** *sb* stereometry. **~skop** *sb* stereoscope. **~typ** *adj* stereotyped.

steril *adj* sterile. **sterilisering** *sb* sterilization. **sterilisere** *vb* sterilize. **sterilitet** *sb* sterility.

sterk *adj* strong; *(om lyd)* loud; *(holdbar)* solid; durable, lasting; *~ fart* high speed; *~ frost* heavy frost; *~ kulde* severe cold. **sterkstrøm** *sb* power current. **sterkt** *adv (kraftig)* strongly; *(som lyder høyt)* loudly; *(i svært høy grad)* greatly, hard, heavily, highly; (very) much; *~ interessert* greatly interested; *jeg er ~ i tvil om det* I am very much in doubt about it.

ste|sønn *sb* stepson. **~søster** *sb* stepsister.

stetoskop *sb* stethoscope.

stett *sb* stem.

stevn se *stavn.*

stevne I *sb (sammenkomst)* rally; *(idretts~)* meeting; sports festival; *et politisk ~* a political rally; **II** *vb* **1** *(innkalle)* summon; *~ for retten* take to court; sue; **2** *~ mot* head for. **stevnemøte** *sb* rendezvouz, date.

stewardess *sb (på fly)* (air) hostess.

sti *sb (gang~)* path, foot-path; *(i ubebodd terreng)* track.

stift *sb (liten spiker)* brad, nail; *(med flatt hode)* tack; *(tegne~)* (drawing-)pin; *(grammofon~)* needle; *(til blyant)* lead. **stifte** *vb* **A** *(feste med stift)* nail, pin, tack; *(med stiftemaskin)* staple; **B** *(grunnlegge, opprette)* establish, found; *~ gjeld* contract/incur a debt (debts); *det ble stiftet fred* peace was made; *firmaet ble ~t i 1906* the firm was established in 1906; *han ~t familie* he married and had a family. **stiftemaskin** *sb* stapler, stapling-machine. **stifter** *sb (grunnlegger)* founder.

stig|brett *sb* running board. **~bøyle** *sb* stirrup.

stige I *sb* ladder; **II** *vb* **1** *(bevege seg oppover)* rise; go up; *røyken steg rett opp/til værs* the smoke rose/went straight up; **2** *(tilta, vokse)* rise, grow; *elven har steget* the river has risen; *lønningene steg med ti prosent* wages rose by ten per cent; **3** *(bli dyrere)* go up; rise; **4** *(uttrykk)* ~ *av* get off. **stigning** *sb* **1** *(bevegelse oppover)* rising, rise; **2** *(i pris)* rise; *en* ~ *i hveteprisen* a rise in/of the price of wheat; **3** *(på vei)* gradient, rise; climb.

stikk I *adv* dead, directly; ~ *imot* directly against; **II** *sb* **1** *(med ~ende redskap etc) (lite ~)* prick; *et nåle~* a pinprick; *(av dolk eller kniv)* stab, thrust; *(insekt~)* bite, sting; *(~ende smerte)* stab of pain; **2** *(i kortspill)* trick; **3** *holde* ~ hold good. **stikke I** *sb (flis)* splinter; *(pinne)* stick; *kaste på stikka* pitch and toss; **II** *vb* **1** *(~ med kniv, nål etc)* stick; **2** *(støte med kniv)* stab, thrust; **3** *(om lopper, mygg)* bite; **4** *(om bie, veps)* sting; **5** *(~ med ball i ballek)* hit; **6** *(putte)* put; *han stakk hånden i lommen* he put his hand in his pocket; **7** *(uttrykk)* ~ **av** run away; make off; ~ **dypt** *(om skip)* draw much water; *fig* be deep-seated; ~ **frem** project; jut out; ~ *seg frem* make oneself conspicuous; push oneself forward; ~ **i**: *det stikker i at ...* it is because; *jeg vet ikke hva det stikker i* I don't know why; ~ **innom** drop/pop in; ~ **opp** project; stick out/up; *en gren stakk opp av vannet* a branch stuck up out of the water; ~ **ut:** ~ *ut en jernbane* peg out/stake a railway line.

stikkelsbær *sb* gooseberry.

stikken *sb: la noen i* ~ leave somebody in the lurch.

stikkhevert *sb* pipette. **stikkontakt** *sb* socket; *(i veggen)* wall socket; *det er ~er i alle rommene* there are points in all the rooms. **stikk|ord** *sb* **1** *(på teater)* cue; **2** *(oppslagsord etc)* entry, headword. **~pille** *sb* suppository; *(fig: spydighet)* sneer, taunt. **~prøve** *sb* random sampling; spot check/test. **~renne** *sb* subdrain. **~sag** *sb* hand-saw. **~våpen** *sb* pointed weapon.

stikling *sb* cutting.

stil *sb* **1** *(stiloppgave)* paper; *(med oppgitt emne især)* essay; *(med selvvalgt emne)* free composition; *(norsk ~ som fag)* Norwegian composition; *(om enkelt ~oppgave)* Norwegian essay; *læreren gav oss en lett* ~ the teacher set us an easy paper; **2** *(kunstnerisk etc ~)* style; *gotisk* ~ Gothic style; **3** *(uttrykk) noe* **i den** ~ something on those lines; *i* **stor** ~ on a large scale. **stilart** *sb* style. **stile** *vb (henvende)* address; *hun ~t brevet til meg* she addressed the letter to me. **stilebok** *sb* exercise book.

stilett *sb* stiletto.

stilfull *adj* stylish; elegant; in good taste. **stilig** *adj* elegant, smart, stylish. **stilisere** *vb* stylize. **stilist** *sb* stylist. **stilistikk** *sb* stylistics.

stilk *sb (på blomst, plante)* stalk, stem.

still se *stille, adj.*

stillas *sb* scaffold(ing); *de satte opp et* ~ they put up a scaffold.

stille I *adj* **1** *(uten bevegelse)* quiet; calm, still; *de lå/stod* ~ they lay/stood still; ~ *vann har dypest grunn* still waters run deep; **2** *(uten støy)* quiet, silent; *alt er* ~ *nå* everything is quiet now; *de tidde* ~ they were silent; **3** *(uten uro/opphisselse)* peaceful, quiet; **II** *vb* **1** *a) (plassere)* place, put, set; *de stilte bordet ved vinduet* they placed the table near the window; *han stilte vasen på bordet* he set the vase on the table; *hun stilte meg et spørsmål* she put a question to me; *b)* ~ **seg:** *hvordan ~r de seg til dette?* what is their attitude to this? ~ **(seg) opp** line up; *soldatene stilte (seg) opp* the soldiers lined up; ~ **ut** display, exhibit; **2** *(~ inn)* adjust, set; *(om radio)* tune in; ~ *inn tenningen* set/time the ignition; *hun stilte klokken sin etter tidssignalet* she set her watch by the time-signal; *jeg stilte inn radioen på England* I tuned in (the radio) on England; **3** *(tilfreds~)* satisfy; ~ *sulten* satisfy one's hunger; **4** *(lindre)* relieve, soothe. **stilleben** *sb* still life. **Stillehavet** the Pacific (Ocean). **stille|sittende** *adj* sedentary. **~stående** *adj* stationary; *(fig og om vann etc)* stagnant. **stillferdig** *adj* quiet, gentle; *på sin ~e måte* in his/her etc quiet/gentle way. **stillhet** *sb* **1** quiet, stillness; calm; *nattens* ~ the quiet of the night; **2** *(taushet)* silence; *åndeløs* ~ breathless silence; **3 i** ~ quietly, privately; *(i taushet)* silently; *(i hemmelighet)* secretly.

stilling 1 *(måte noe er anbrakt på)* position; *sitte i en ubekvem* ~ sit in an uncomfortable position; **2** *(yrke)* occupation; *(om høyere ~, embete)* post, position; *(især om beskjednere ~)* place, situation; job; *(ledig ~)* vacancy; *en kvinne i ledende* ~ a woman in a leading/prominent position; *jeg søker* ~ I am looking for a job; *oppgi navn, adresse og* ~ give one's name, address and occupation; *overordnet/selvstendig* ~ responsible post; **3** *(situasjon)* position, situation; *~en var håpløs* the situation was hopeless; *hun befant seg i en vanskelig* ~ she was in a difficult position; **4** *(holdning)* attitude; *hans* ~ *til kunsten* his attitude to art. **stillingskrig** *sb* trench warfare.

still|stand *sb* standstill, stagnation. **~tiende** *adj* implied, tacit; ~ *overenskomst* implied/tacit agreement. **stilne** *vb* abate; calm/die down.

stil|oppgave *sb* subject for composition. **~sans** *sb* sense of style.

stilt *adj, pp: dårlig/godt* ~ badly/well off; *hun er bedre* ~ *enn de andre* she is better off than the others.

stiltre *vb:* ~ *seg* steal; tip-toe.

stim *sb (av fisk)* shoal; *(folkestimmel)* crowd, throng. **stime** *vb* crowd, flock. **stimle** *vb (~ sammen)* crowd, flock, throng. **stimmel** *sb* crowd, throng.

stimulans *sb* stimulant. **stimulere** *vb* stimulate.

sting *sb* stitch; *(om smerte~ også)* stabbing pain.

stink|bombe *sb* stink bomb. **~dyr** *sb* skunk. **stinke** *vb* stink.

stinn *adj* **1** *(fullstappet)* replete; *dgl* lousy; *han er* ~ *av penger* he is lousy with money; **2** *(tykk)* hulking, obese.

stipend *sb* grant, scholarship. **stipendiat** *sb* **1** scholarship holder/recipient; **2** *(universitets~)* fellow. **stipendium** = *stipend.*

stiple *vb* stipple.

stipulere *vb:* ~ *prisen* fix the price.

stirre *vb* stare; *(også poet)* gaze; *han ~t rett fremfor seg* he stared straight in front of him; *hun ~t på meg* she stared at me.

stiv *adj* **1** *(ubøyelig)* rigid, stiff; ~ *av kulde* stiff/numb with cold; ~ *snipp* stiff/starched collar; *et ~t bein* a stiff leg; **2** *(formell, reservert)* formal, stiff; **3** *(streng, uelastisk)* rigid, strict; ~ *pris* stiff price; *~e regler* rigid/strict rules; **4** *(uttrykk)* ~ *av skrekk* paralysed with terror; ~ *kuling* high wind; *en ~ klokketime* a full hour by the clock. **stivbeint** *adj fig* inelastic, rigid. **stive** *vb (~ skjorter etc)* starch; ~ *seg opp* brace oneself. **stivelse** *sb* **1** *(til stiving)* starch; **2** *(i kjemi)* amyl. **stiveskjorte** *sb* dress shirt, boiled shirt. **stiv|frossen** *adj* frozen stiff. **~het** *sb* **1** rigidity, stiffness; **2** *(formellhet, reserverthet)* formality, stiffness; reserve. **~krampe** *sb* tetanus. **~nakket** *adj* stiff-necked. **stivne** *vb* **1** stiffen; get stiff; *(om gelé, sement etc)* set. **stiv|sinn** *sb* obstinacy, stubbornness. **~sinnet** *adj* obstinate, stubborn.

stjele *vb* steal; *noen har stjålet pengene mine* somebody has stolen my money.

stjerne *sb* star. **stjerne|banneret** *sb (USAs nasjonalflagg)* the Star-Spangled Banner. **~bilde** *sb* constellation. **~himmel** *sb* starry sky. **~klar** *adj* starry. **~skudd** *sb* shooting star.

stjert *sb* (bird's) tail.

stjålen *adj, pp: et stjålent øyekast* a stealthy/covert glance.

stoff *sb* **1** *(fys)* matter, substance; *et hardt ~* a hard substance; **2** *(tøy)* cloth, fabric; (woven) material; stuff; *~et (som) kjolen hennes var laget/sydd av* the stuff her dress was made of; *ullstoffer* woollen fabrics; **3** *(materiale)* material; ~ *til en bok* material for a book; ~ *til ettertanke* food for thought; *han har godt ~ i seg* he has got the right stuff in him; **4** *(narkotika)* dope, junk. **stoffskifte** *sb* metabolism. **stoffskiftesykdom** *sb* metabolic disorder.

stoiker *sb* stoic. **stoisisme** *sb* stoicism. **stoisk** *adj* stoic.

stokk A *adv:* ~ *blind* totally blind; ~ *døv* deaf as a post; ~ *konservativ* die-hard, true-blue; **B** *sb* **1** *(tømmer~)* log; **2** *(spaser~)* cane, stick; *han går med (dvs støtter seg til en)* ~ he walks with a stick.

stokke *vb (kortstokk)* shuffle.

stol *sb* chair; *falle mellom to ~er* fall between two stools; *stikke under ~* conceal; hold back.

stola *sb* stole.

stole *vb:* ~ *på* trust; depend/rely on; *(regne med)* count on; *de er ikke til å ~ på* they are not to be trusted; *du kan ikke ~ på at de er presise* you cannot rely on their being punctual; *hun stolte på ham* she relied on him; she trusted him; *jeg ~r på din hjelp* I count on your help; *kan jeg ~ på det?* can I depend/rely on that? *man kan ~ på hva han sier* one/you can depend on what he says.

stolpe *sb* post.

stolpre *vb* hobble along; plod one's way.

stolt *adj* **1** proud; ~ *av/over* proud of; *jeg er ~ over å kalle deg min venn* I am proud to call you my friend; **2** *(forfengelig, hoven)* arrogant, haughty; proud; **3** *(prektig)* grand, proud; *den ~este dagen i mitt liv* the proudest day of my life; *et ~ syn* a grand spectacle. **stolthet** *sb* pride; *(forfengelighet)* arrogance, haughtiness.

stopp *sb* **A** *(stans)* stop, stoppage; *si ~* call a halt; **B** *(i pute etc)* padding, stuffing. **stoppe** *vb* **A** *(holde opp, stanse)* leave off; stop; *han ~t plutselig/bråstoppet* he stopped short; *jeg ~t motoren* I stopped the engine; **B** **1** *(fylle, stappe)* fill; *(~ møbler)* upholster; ~ *ut* stuff; *han ~t pipen (sin)* he filled his pipe; **2** *(lukke, tette igjen)* fill up; stop; **3** *(~ strømpe etc)* darn, mend. **stoppeklokke** *sb* stop watch. **stoppe|garn** *sb (ullgarn)* mending wool; *(bomullsgarn)* mending cotton. **~nål** *sb* darning-needle. **stoppeplikt** *sb* obligation to stop. **stopper** *sb: sette en ~ for* put an end/a stop to. **stoppe|signal** *sb* halt/stop signal. **~sted** *sb* stop. **stopping** *sb (av strømper)* darning, mending.

stor *adj* **1** *(om størrelse, især om noe som forundrer og imponerer)* big; *et ~t hus* a big house; *(nei,) for en ~ hund* what a big dog; **2** *(om størrelse, mer nøkternt)* large; *en ~ bil/hage* a large car/garden; **3** *(om ikke-romlig størrelse, nøkternt)* great, large; *en ~ forskjell* a great difference; *et ~t antall* a large number; *med ~ glede/tålmodighet* with great pleasure/patience; **4** *(om egenskaper, og beundrende om åndelig storhet etc)* great; *en ~ forfatter* a great author; *jeg er en ~ beundrer av hennes dikt* I am a great admirer of her poems; **5** *(høy)* tall, high; *bli ~ (dvs bli voksen)* grow up; *han har vokst seg ~* he has grown tall; **6** *(uttrykk) ~t sett* generally speaking; on the whole; *du ~e verden!* good gracious! *med ~e bokstaver* with capital letters; *(med ~ skrift)* with big letters; *føre det ~e ord* lay down the law; *i det ~e og hele* in general; on the whole; *ikke ~t annet/bedre enn* little more/little better than; *være ~ på det* be stuck-up; put on airs. **stor|aktig** *adj* haughty, proud; overbearing. **~artet** *adj* grand; excellent, splendid; *han er en ~artet fyr* he is a grand fellow. **~bonde** *sb* large farmer. **~dåd** *sb* feat (of valour etc); glorious deed; great achievement.

stores *sb* net curtain.

stor|eter *sb* glutton. **~fe** *sb* cattle. **~folk** *sb* great people; *dgl* bigwigs. **storhet** *sb* greatness. **storhetstid** *sb* heyday; days of glory. **storindustri** *sb* large--scale industry.

stork *sb* stork.

storm *sb* **1** *(sterk vind)* gale; *det brøt ut ~/en ~ brøt ut* a gale set in; *liten ~* strong gale; *full ~* whole gale; **2** *(uvær, med regn, snø, torden etc)* storm; **3** *fig* storm; ~ **i** *et vannglass* a storm in a tea-cup; *en ~* **av** *bifall* a storm of applause; *ta* **med** ~ take/carry by storm; *~en* **på** *byen* the storming of the town.

stor|magasin *sb* (department) store(s). **~makt** *sb* Great Power.

stormangrep *sb* assault, storm.

stor|mann *sb* magnate; *US* tycoon. **~mannsgal** *adj* megalomaniac. **~mannsgalskap** *sb* megalomania. **~masket** *adj* wide-meshed.

storme *vb* **1** *(blåse sterkt)* blow heavily; storm; **2** *(fare, styrte)* dash, rush; *de ~t ut* they dashed/rushed out; **3** *(ta med storm)* storm; *de besluttet å ~ fortet* they decided to storm the fort; **4** *(forsere)* rush; *folkemengden ~t sperringen* the crowd rushed the barrier. **stormende** *adj* **1** *(om havet, været)* stormy; *et ~ hav* a stormy sea; **2** *(fig også)* tumultuous; *~ bifall* tumultuous applause; a storm of applause; *det gjorde ~ lykke* it was a tremendous success; *(om teaterstykke)* it brought down the house; *et ~ møte* a stormy/tumultuous meeting. **storm|full** *adj* stormy. **~kast** *sb* violent gust of wind. **~lykt** *sb* hurricane-lamp, hurricane-lantern. **~skritt** *sb: med ~* by leaps and bounds. **~varsel** *sb* gale warning. **~vær** *sb* stormy weather.

stor|parten *sb* the greater/main part; the majority. **~politikk** *sb* high/international politics. **~rengjøring** *sb* house cleaning. **~rutet(e)** *adj* large-chequered. **~sinn** *sb* generosity, magnanimity. **~sinnet** *adj* generous, magnanimous; large-minded. **~slått** *adj* grand, magnificent. **~snutet** *adj* arrogant, haughty. **~stilt** *adj* large-scale; se også *~slått*. **~trives** *vb* enjoy oneself tremendously/very much. **~tromme** *sb: slå på ~trommen* bang the big drum. **~vask** *sb* wash, washing; *de hadde ~vask* they had their wash(ing)-day. **~verk** *sb* great achievement. **~vilt** *sb* big game. **~øyd** *adj* wide-eyed.

stotre *vb* stammer, stutter.

strabaser *sb fl* hardships; *de greide strabasene uten klage* they bore the hardships without complaint. **strabasiøs** *adj* fatiguing.

straff *sb* **1** punishment; *de fikk sin ~* they were punished; *han slapp ~* he escaped punishment; he was let off; *til ~* as a punishment; **2** *(dom)* sentence; *en streng ~* a severe sentence; *han sonet en ~* he served a sentence. **straff|ansvar** *sb: det medfører ~ansvar* it is an offence. **~arbeid** *sb* penal servitude. **~bar** *adj* punishable. **straffe** *vb* punish. **straffe|anstalt** *sb* penitentiary, prison. **~avskrift** *sb* lines. **~kast** *sb* penalty throw. **~lov** *sb* penal code. **~porto** *sb* surcharge. **~preken** *sb* lecture. **~sak** *sb* criminal case. **~spark** *sb* penalty kick. **~(spark)felt** *sb* penalty area. **~trusel** *sb* threat of punishment. **straff|fange** *sb* convict. **~skyldig** *adj* culpable, guilty. **~utmålingen** *sb* (the fixing of) the sentence.

strak *adj* straight.

straks *adv* **1** *(omgående, øyeblikkelig)* at once; immediately, straight away; directly; *~ etter* immediately after; *han gjorde det ~* he did it at once/immediately; *jeg gjettet det ~* I guessed it straight away; **2** *(snart)* presently.

stram *adj* **1** *(stramt utspent)* tight; *hyssingen er for ~* the string is too tight; **2** *(med ~ holdning)* erect, upright; *en ~ holdning* an upright/erect carriage; **3** *(streng)* severe, strict; **4** *(om lukt, smak)* acrid, rank. **stramme** *vb (gjøre stram)* tighten; *~ seg opp (gjøre seg stram)* square one's shoulders; *(ta seg sammen)* pull oneself together; *han ~t beltet* he tightened his belt. **stramtsittende** *adj* tight; tight-fitting.

strand *sb* beach; *(sand~)* (sea)shore; *barna lekte på ~en* the children played on the beach. **strand|bredd** *sb* beach. **~drakt** *sb* beach costume. **strande** *vb* **1** *(om skip)* be stranded; **2** *(om person)* be shipwrecked; **3** *fig* fail, miscarry; *det ~t på hennes motstand* it failed owing to her opposition; *foretaket ~t* the enterprise failed; *planen ~t* the scheme miscarried. **strandhugg** *sb* raid. **stranding** *sb (med forlis)* wreck; *(ofte)* loss. **strand|kant** *sb* beach; water's edge. **~linje** *sb* seaboard, shoreline.

strantet(e) *adj* spindly.

strateg *sb* strategist. **strategi** *sb* strategy. **strategisk** *adj* strategic.

stratosfære *sb* stratosphere.

strebe *vb* strive; *~ etter ære* strive after honour. **streber** *sb* climber, careerist.

strede *sb* **1** *(sund)* strait(s); *~t ved Dover* the Straits of Dover; **2** *(smal gate)* lane; narrow street; *gater og ~r* highways and byways.

streif *sb* **1** *(glimt)* gleam, ray; *et ~ av sol(skinn)* a gleam/ray of sunshine; **2** *(lett berøring)* brush, graze. **streife** *vb* **1** *(berøre lett)* touch lightly; just touch; *tanken ~t meg* the idea just crossed my mind; **2** *(omtale flyktig)* touch (lightly) on; **3** *(~ med blikket)* glance at; **4** *~ om(kring)* roam; *(planløst)* wander; *~ gatelangs* roamed/wander about in the streets. **streif|skudd** *sb* grazing shot. **~sår** *sb* graze. **~tog** *sb* raid.

streik *sb* strike; *ulovlig ~* unofficial strike. **streike** *vb* **1** *(nedlegge arbeidet)* go on strike; **2** *(ha nedlagt arbeidet)* be on strike. **streike|bryter** *sb* blackleg, strike-breaker. **~kasse** *sb* strike fund. **~trusel** *sb* strike threat. **~vakt** *sb* picket. **~varsel** *sb* strike notice.

strek *sb* **1** line; *(især i skrift)* stroke; *fin ~* thin line; *han trakk en ~* he drew a line; *sette ~ over et ord* cross out a word; **2** *(stripe)* streak; **3** *(pek, påfunn)* trick; *det var en stygg ~* it was a nasty/dirty trick; **4** *(uttrykk) gå over ~en* go too far; overstep the mark; *en ~ i regningen* a fly in the ointment; *sette ~ (i debatt)* close the debate. **streke** *vb (sette streker)* draw lines; *(linjere)* rule; *~ under* underline.

strekk *sb: i ett ~* at a stretch. **strekke** *vb* **1** stretch; *~ på beina* stretch one's legs; **2** *(uttrykk) ~ seg (= bre seg, nå/rekke utover)* stretch; *~ seg langt* go to a great length; *~ seg over (om område og tid)* cover; spread over; *denne perioden strakte seg over flere hundre år* this period covered several hundred years; *ørkenen ~r seg så langt øyet kan se* the desert stretches as far as the eye can see; *~* **til** be enough; *brødet strakk ikke til* there was not enough bread. **strekning** *sb* **1** *(stykke vei)* stretch; *en ~ på ti kilometer* a stretch of ten kilometres; **2** *(distanse)* distance, way.

streng *adj* **1** *(bestemt, strikt)* strict; *~e lærere* strict teachers; **2** *(hard)* hard, severe; *~ kulde* hard frost; *~ straff* severe punishment. Se også *strengt*.

streng *sb (bue~, fiolin~)* string. **strengeinstrument** *sb* stringed instrument.

strenghet *sb* strictness; hardness, severity. **strengt** *adv* strictly, hard, severely; *~ forbudt* strictly forbidden/prohibited; *~ nødvendig* absolutely necessary; ~

tatt strictly speaking; *straffe* ~ punish severely.

strev *sb* **1** *(slit)* labour, toil; **2** *(bry)* trouble; *han hadde mye* ~ *med å ...* he had a lot of trouble to ... **streve** *vb (slite)* drudge, toil; work hard. **strevsom** *adj (arbeidsom)* industrious. **strevsomhet** *sb* industry.

stri *vb (bale, slite)* struggle, toil; work hard; ~ *mot* be contrary to; be against; *det* ~*r mot fornuften* it is against reason; *det* ~*r mot loven/mine interesser* it is contrary to the law/my interests; *det* ~*r mot reglene* it is against the rules. Se også *strides*. **stri(d)** *adj* **1** *(hard, ubøyelig)* obstinate, stubborn; **2** *a) (om strøm)* swift; *b) (om vind)* stiff; **3** *(slitsom)* hard, strenuous; *en* ~ *dag* a strenuous day; *en* ~ *jobb* a hard job; **4** *(strittende)* bristly, hard, rough; ~*t hår* bristly hair. **strid** *sb (kamp, splid)* dispute, quarrel; conflict; *(uenighet)* controversy; *en* ~ *om lønninger* a dispute about wages; *et* ~*ens eple* an apple of discord; a bone of contention; *handle i* ~ *med loven* act in defiance of the law; *han kom i* ~ *med sin bror* he quarrelled with his brother; *vi lå i* ~ *med dem* we had a dispute/quarrel with them. **stridbar** *(trettekjær)* aggressive, quarrelsome; *(krigersk)* combative. **stride** = *stri*. **stridende**, *de* ~ *parter* the contending parties. **strides** *vb (trette)* quarrel; *(disputere)* argue, dispute. **stridig** *adj* headstrong, obstinate. **stridighet** *sb* conflict, controversy; dispute. **stri(d)|regn** *sb* heavy rain. ~**regne** *vb* rain heavily, pour down. **strids|dyktig** *adj* fit for military service. ~**hanske** *sb* gauntlet. ~**krefter** *sb fl* (armed/military) forces. ~**lysten** *adj* eager to fight. ~**mann** *sb* warrior. ~**punkt** *sb* point in dispute; (point of) issue. ~**spørsmål** *sb* controversial question; (matter at) issue. ~**vant** *adj* seasoned, veteran; ~*vante soldater* seasoned soldiers. ~**vogn** *sb* tank; *hist* chariot. ~**øks** *sb* battle axe; *begrave* ~*øksen* bury the hatchet.

strie *sb* sacking.

strikk *sb (gummi~)* rubber band; elastic (band).

strikke A *sb (galgereip)* halter, rope; **B** *vb (~ f.eks. strømper)* knit; *jeg har begynt å* ~ I have taken up knitting. **strikke|garn** *sb* knitting-wool/yarn. ~**jakke** *sb* cardigan. ~**pinne** *sb* knitting-needle. ~**tøy** *sb* knitting.

striks *adj* strict.

strime *sb* stripe. **strimet(e)** *adj* striped.

strimmel *sb* ribbon, strip; slip.

stringent *adj* stringent, cogent.

stripe *sb (regelmessig)* stripe; *(mer tilfeldig)* streak; *(strimmel)* strip; *en* ~ *land* a strip of land. **stripet(e)** *adj* striped; streaked, streaky.

stritte *vb (om bust, hår)* bristle; ~ *imot* resist; *håret* ~*t på hodet hans* the hair bristled on his head. **strittende** *adj* bristly, erect.

strofe *sb (vers)* stanza.

stropp *sb* strap.

struktur *sb* structure.

struma *sb* goitre, struma.

strunk *adj* erect, upright.

strupe *sb* throat; *hun grep ham i* ~*n* she seized/took him by the throat; *sette en kniven på* ~*n* give somebody an ultimatum. **strupe|hode** *sb* larynx. ~**hoste** *sb* croup. ~**tak** *sb* stranglehold; *ta* ~*tak på* seize by the throat.

struts *sb* ostrich.

strutte *vb* bristle; burst; be nearly bursting; bulge; ~ *av sunnhet* be bursting with health. **struttende** *adj* buxom, healthy.

stry *sb* tow; *narre (en) opp i* ~ pull somebody's leg; take somebody in.

stryk *sb* **1** *(ved eksamen etc)* failure; **2** *(i elv)* rapid; chute, race; **3** *(juling)* beating, thrashing. **stryke** *vb* **1** *(~ med hånden etc)* stroke; *han strøk seg over skjegget* he stroked his beard; **2** *(med ~jern)* iron; *vil du jeg skal ~ skjorten din?* do you want me to iron your shirt? **3** *(slette, ~ ut)* cross/cut out; strike off; cancel; ~ *over* delete; cross out; ~ *ut (med svamp etc)* wipe out; *gjelden vår ble strøket* our debt was cancelled; *hun strøk en setning* she crossed/cut out a sentence; *navnet hans ble strøket av listen* his name was struck off the list; **4** *(fare, styrte)* rush; ~ *av gårde* dash off; ~ *sin vei* beat it; disappear; *han strøk på dør* he rushed out of the room; **5** *(~ til eksamen)* fail; *US* flunk; *hun strøk til eksamen* she failed/flunked in the examination; *læreren strøk henne* the teacher failed/flunked her; **6** *(uttrykk)* ~ **med** *(dø)* die; lose one's life; *ti personer strøk med i ulykken* ten persons lost their lives in the accident; *(bli totalskadd)* be destroyed/lost; *alle bøkene mine strøk med i brannen* all my books were destroyed in the fire; *alle pengene strøk med* all the money was lost; ~ **med/mot hårene** rub the right/wrong way. **stryke|brett** *sb* ironing-board. ~**instrument** *sb* string instrument. ~**jern** *sb* iron. ~**kvartett** *sb* string quartet. **strykende** *adj:* ~ *avsetning* rapid sale; *det går* ~ it goes swimmingly; *i* ~ *fart* at a flashing speed. **strykeorkester** *sb adv* string band. **stryker** *sb (i orkester)* string player; ~*ne* the strings. **strykkarakter** *sb* fail mark.

stryknin *sb* strychnine.

strø *vb* sprinkle, strew; ~ *sand på (fig)* rubber-stamp; *han* ~*dde sand på gulvet* he sprinkled/strewed sand on the floor; he sprinkled/strewed the floor with sand.

strøk *sb* **1** *(~ med bue, penn, pensel)* stroke; **2** *(lag, sjikt) et* ~ *maling* a coat of paint; **3** *(egn, område)* part, neighbourhood.

strøken *adj: en* ~ *spiseskje* a level spoonful.

strøm *sb* **1** current; *hun svømte mot* ~*men* she swam against the current; *skru/slå av* ~*men* switch off the current; *skru/slå på* ~*men* switch on the current; **2** *(noe som strømmer)* stream; *en* ~ *av blod, en blod~* a stream of blood; *en* ~ *av mennesker og biler* a stream of people and motor-cars; *regnet falt i* ~*mer* the rain poured down; *regnet falt i stride* ~*mer* the rain fell in torrents. **strømlinjet** *adj* streamlined. **strømme** *vb* flow, run, stream; pour; *(komme i stort antall)* crowd, flock; *folk* ~*t til landsbyen* people flocked to the village; *lyset* ~*met inn* the light was streaming in; *regnet* ~*r ned* the rain is pouring down; *turister ~r inn/til fra alle kanter* tourists pour in from all quarters. **strømning** *sb* tendency, trend; *en ~ i tiden* a tendency of the period; *litterære ~er* literary trends.

strømpe *sb* stocking. **strømpe|bukse(r)** *sb* tights. **~bånd** *sb* garter. **~holder** *sb* suspender belt; *US* garter belt. **~lest** *sb: på ~lesten* in one's stockings; in one's stocking(ed) feet.

strøm|styrke *sb* amperage. **~hvirvel** *sb* eddy, whirlpool.

strå *sb* straw; *(om gresstrå etc også)* blade (of grass, wheat etc); *komme høyt på ~* rise in the world; *trekke ~* draw lots; *trekke det korteste ~* get the worst of it; *trekke det lengste ~* have the best of it.

stråle I *sb* **1** *(lys~)* beam; ray (of light); *en lyskaster~* a searchlight beam; **2** *(vann~)* jet; *(tynn ~)* squirt; **II** *vb* **1** *(skinne)* beam, shine; *ansiktet hennes strålte av tilfredshet* her face shone with happiness; *hun strålte av tilfredshet* she beamed with satisfaction; **2** *(glitre)* sparkle. **stråleglans** *sb* radiance. **strålende** *adj* **1** beaming, radiant; **2** *(glitrende)* sparkling; **3** *(herlig, storartet)* brilliant; glorious, splendid. **stråle|skade** sb radiation damage. **~varme** *sb* radiant heat. **stråling** *sb* radiation. **strålingsfare** *sb* danger of radio-activity.

strå|mann *sb fig* dummy, puppet; *US* stooge. **~tak** *sb* thatched roof.

stubb *sb (stump)* stub. **stubbe** *sb* stump.

student *sb* (university) student; undergraduate. **studere** *vb* **1** study; *~ til lege* study medicine; **2** *(gruble, spekulere) ~ på* puzzle over; speculate about. **studer|kammer, ~værelse** *sb* study. **studie** *sb* **1** *(utkast)* study; **2** *(kort avhandling)* essay. Se også *studium*. **studie|plan** *sb* syllabus. **~sirkel** *sb* study circle. **studio** *sb* studio. **studium** *sb* study.

stue *sb* **1** *(rom)* room, sitting-room; **2** *(lite hus)* cabin, cottage. **stue|arrest** *sb* house arrest. **~gris** *sb* stay-at-home. **~lærd** *sb: en ~lærd* a bookish person. **~pike** *sb* housemaid, parlourmaid. **~plante** *sb* indoor plant.

stuert *sb* steward.

stuing *sb* **1** *(~ med kjøtt, poteter etc)* stew; **2** *(grønnsak~)* creamed vegetables.

stum *adj* **1** *(som ikke kan snakke)* mute, dumb; **2** *(målløs, ordløs av overraskelse etc)* mute, speechless; *~ beundring* mute admiration; *~ forbløffelse* speechless amazement; **3** *(om bokstaver som ikke uttales)* mute, silent. **stumfilm** *sb* silent film. **stumhet** dumbness, mutness. **stummende** *adj: ~ mørke* utter darkness.

stump A *adj* **1** *(butt, uskarp)* blun, dull; **2** *en ~ vinkel* an obtuse angle; **B** *sb (stubb)* stub, stump; bit; *redde ~ene* save something out of the wreck; *slå i ~er og stykker* smash to pieces. **stumpe** *vb (~ f.eks sigarett)* crush out. **stumpnese** *sb* stub nose.

stund *sb* **1** *(tidspunkt)* hour, moment; *en lykkelig ~* a happy hour/moment; **2** *(tidsrom)* while; *i en kort ~* for a short while. **stunde** *vb* **1** *(lengte) ~ etter* long/yearn for; **2** *(li) det ~r til jul* Christmas is drawing near. **stundimellom** *adv* now and then; occasionally. **stundom** *adv* at times; now and then; sometimes.

stup *sb* **1** *(det å stupe under bading)* dive; **2** *(bratt bergvegg)* precipice. **stup|bomber** *sb* dive bomber. **~bratt** *adj* precipitous. **stupe** *vb* **1** *(falle forover)* fall headlong; pitch; **2** *(~ under bading)* dive; **3** *~ kråke* turn a somersault. **stupebrett** *sb* diving board.

stupid *adj* stupid. **stupiditet** *sb* stupidity.

stur *adj* depressed, downcast; out of sorts. **sture** *vb* **1** *(om mennesker)* be dejected (depressed, out of sorts); **2** *(om dyr og planter)* droop; not thrive. **sturen** = *stur*.

stusse *vb* **A** *(klippe)* trim; *jeg fikk ~t håret* I had my hair trimmed; **B** *(undres)* be astonished/startled; wonder; *~ over/ved* be astonished/startled at; wonder at.

stusslig *adj* cheerless, lonesome.

stut *sb* bull.

stutt *adj* short. **stuttvoksen** *adj* undersized.

stygg *adj* **1** *(om utseende)* ugly; *et stygt dyr* an ugly animal/beast; **2** *(lei, ubehagelig)* bad, nasty, ugly; *stygt vær* nasty/ugly weather; *det ser stygt ut* it looks bad; *en ~ ulykke* a bad accident; *en ~ (u)vane* a bad habit; **3** *(slem)* mean, naughty; *det var stygt av ham* it was mean of him. **styggvær** *sb* foul weather.

stykk: *pr ~* se *stykke I 3*. **stykke I** *sb* **1** *(bite, del)* piece; bit, part; *~ for ~* bit by bit; piece by piece; *et ~ kake, et kake~* a piece of cake; *han gikk et ~ (av veien) til fots* he went part of the way by foot; **2** *(skive)* slice; *et ~ brød, et brød~* a slice of bread; **3** *(om antall) noen ~r* some; a few; *et par ~r* one or two; a couple; *de koster to pund (for) ~t* they cost two pound apiece/two pound each; **4** *(~ i avis)* piece; (short) article; **5** *(skuespill)* play; **6** *(regne~)* problem, sum; **7** *(avstand)* distance; *et godt ~* a considerable distance; *han bor et lite ~ herfra* he lives a short distance from here; **8** *(uttrykk)* **gå i ~r** go to pieces; break; *vasen gikk i ~r* the vase went to pieces; **komme til ~t:** *da det kom til ~t* when it came to the point; *når det kommer til ~t* when all is said and done; **rive i ~r** tear (to pieces); *hun rev brevet i ~r* she tore the letter to pieces; *jeg har revet i ~r jakken min* I have torn my coat; **slå i ~r** break, smash; *han slo i ~r glasset* he broke/smashed the glass; **være i ~r** be broken/out of order; *leken er i ~r* the toy is broken; *maskinen er i ~r* the machine is out of order; **II** *vb: ~ opp* divide; split up; *~ ut* parcel out. **stykkevis** *adv* **1** by the piece; piece by piece; **2** *(etappevis) ~ måtte vi gå til fots* parts of the way we had to walk. **stykkgods** *sb* parcels; *(på båt)* general cargo.

stylte *sb* stilt; *gå på ~r* walk on stilts.

stymper *sb (stakkar)* poor devil.

styr *sb:* **gå over ~** fail; come to nothing; *forlovelsen gikk over ~* the engagement was broken; **holde ~ på** *(holde i tømme)* keep in check; control; *(mestre)* master, manage; *lett å holde ~ på* easy to manage; *moren (hans) kan ikke holde ~ på ham* his mother cannot manage him; **sette over ~** squander. **styrbar** *adj* dirigible. **styrbord** *sb* starboard. **styre I** *sb* **1** *(ledelse)* government, rule; ~ *og stell* affairs, management; *demokratisk* ~ *(sett)* democratic government; *stå for* ~ *og stell* be at the head of affairs; *under norsk* ~ under Norwegian rule; **2** *(i aksjeselskap, forening etc)* board, committee; *de er begge med/sitter begge i* ~*t* they are both on the board/on the committee; **3** *(på sykkel etc)* handlebars; **II** *vb* **1** *(dirigere i bestemt retning)* steer; ~ *mot* head for; *skipet styrte mot kysten* the ship was heading for the coast; **2** *(regjere, stå i spissen for)* govern, rule; be at the head of; *kongen styrte landet* the king governed/ruled the country; **3** *(administrere)* administer, manage; ~ *huset* manage the household; **4** ~ *seg* restrain oneself. **styre|form** *sb* system of government. **~formann** *sb* chairman, leader. Se også *forkvinne, formann*. **styrelse** *sb* **1** *en Guds* ~ an act of Providence; **2** *gram* prepositional. **styremedlem** *sb* committee member; executive member. **styrer** *sb* governor, leader, master; *(skole~)* headmaster, headteacher; *US* principal. **styresett** = *~form*. **styre(s)-maktene** *sb fl* the authorities. **styring** *sb* control, leadership; *miste* ~*en* lose control. **styringsverk** *sb* administration, government.

styrke I *sb* **1** strength; force, power; *(hær~, militær ~)* force; *de allierte* ~*r* the allied forces; **2** *(om optiske linser)* power; **II** *vb* **1** *(gi kraft og mot)* fortify, refresh; *hun følte seg* ~*t* she felt refreshed; **2** *(forsterke)* fortify, strengthen; *det* ~*t deres stilling* it strengthened their position. **styrke|grad** *sb* strength. **~middel** *sb* tonic. **~prøve** *sb* trial of strength.

styrmann *sb* mate, officer; *(i robåt)* coxswain.

styrte *vb* **1** *(falle ned)* fall/tumble down; fall to the ground; *(om fly)* crash; *flyet* ~*t brennende ned* the plane crashed in flames; **2** *(fare, ruse)* dash, rush, tear; hurry; *hunden* ~*t løs på dem* the dog rushed at them; **3** *(berøve makten)* overthrow; *regjeringen ble* ~*t* the government was overthrown. **styrt|hjelm** *sb* crash-helmet. **~regn** *sb* heavy downpour. **~regne** *vb* come down in buckets; pour down.

stær *sb* **A** *(fugl)* starling; **B** *(øyesykdom) grønn* ~ glaucoma; *grå* ~ cataract.

stø A *adj (fast, pålitelig)* steady; **B** *sb (båt~)* landing-place. **støhet** *sb* steadiness.

støkk *sb* shock; *jeg fikk en* ~ I got a shock; I was startled. **støkke** *vb (skremme)* startle; *(bli skremt)* be startled; give a start.

støl A *adj* sore and stiff; *jeg er* ~ *i beina* my legs ache; **B** *sb (seter)* summer dairy; summer mountain pasture.

stønad *sb* aid, relief.

stønn *sb* groan. **stønne** *vb* groan; *(~ svakt)* moan; *han* ~*t av smerte* he groaned in/with pain.

støpe *vb* **1** *(i metall)* cast, found; *(~ i form også)* mould; *de støpte en bronsestatue* they cast a bronze statue; *sitte som støpt* fit like a glove; **2** *(i betong)* concrete. **støpe|gods** *sb koll* castings; cast-iron goods. **~jern** *sb* cast iron. **~masse** *sb (av metall)* molten metal. **støperi** *sb* foundry. **støpe|sand** *sb* moulding sand. **~skje** *sb: i ~skjeen (fig)* in the melting pot.

støpning *sb: en mann av hans* ~ a man of his cast of character.

støpsel *sb* plug.

størje *sb* tunny.

størkne *vb* harden; *(om blod)* clot, coagulate; *(om gelé og sement)* set.

større *adj (komp av stor)* bigger, larger; greater; *(om høyde)* taller; *(temmelig stor)* big, large; *de* ~ *barna* the older children; *ikke noe* ~ not much; nothing much; *uten* ~ *vanskelighet* without much difficulty. **størrelse** *sb* size; *(omfang)* extent; *hvilken* ~ *er det?* what size is it? *parkens* ~ the extent of the park; *steinen var på* ~ *med et egg* the stone was the size of an egg. **størrelsesorden** *sb* magnitude, size. **største|delen, ~parten** *sb* the greater part.

støt *sb* **1** *(dytt)* push; *(med stikkvåpen)* thrust; *(med kniv især)* stab; *(i biljard)* stroke; *gi* ~*et til* be the cause of; give rise to; *rette et* ~ *mot* make a thrust at; **2** *elektrisk* ~ electric shock; **3** *(vind~)* gust, puff; *(~ i fløyte/trompet etc)* blast; **4** *(om de* ~ *livet gir)* blow, shock. **støte** *vb* **1** *(dytte, puffe)* push, shove; *(med stikkvåpen)* thrust; ~ *kule* put the shot; ~ **mot** hit; *(sterkere)* crash against; ~ **på** *(dvs finne, møte, se tilfeldig)* come across; *jeg har aldri støtt på det ordet* I have never come across that word; ~ **sammen** collide; run into each other; *der stien* ~*r sammen med veien* where the foot-path joins the road; **2** *(fornærme)* offend. **støtende** *adj* offensive; *en* ~ *bemerkning* an offensive remark; *meget* ~ shocking. **støt|fanger** *sb* bumper. **~pute** *sb* buffer. **støtt A** *adj, pp (av støte)* **1** *(knust)* ground, powdered; ~ *pepper* ground pepper; **2** *(fornærmet, krenket)* offended; *(meget ~)* shocked; *bli* ~ *over noe* be offended/shocked at something; *han blir lett* ~ he is easily offended; **B** *adv (stadig)* always, constantly. **støttann** *sb* tusk.

støtte I *sb* **1** *(noe som støtter)* support; **2** *(frittstående søyle)* pillar; **3** *(hjelp)* support; *jeg må ha din* ~ I must have your support; *til* ~ *for* in support of; **II** *vb* **1** support; *partiet ble* ~*t av presteskapet* the party was supported by the clergy; **2** ~ *seg* lean; ~ *seg mot* lean against; ~ *seg på* lean on. **støtte|aksjon** *sb* relief action. **~bandasje** *sb* supporting bandage. **~punkt** *sb* point of support; *(mil etc)* stronghold.

støtvis *adj* by fits and starts; jerkily, spasmodically; *(om vind)* in gusts.

støv *sb* dust; *tørke* ~ *av møblene* dust the furniture. **støve** *vb: det* ~*r* dust is blowing; it is dusty. **støve|klut** *sb* duster. **~kost** *sb* duster; dusting brush.

støvel *sb* boot; *et par støvler* a pair of boots.

støvet(e) *adj* dusty. **støv|fnugg, ~grann** *sb* speck of dust. **~plage** *sb* dust nuisance. **~sky** *sb* cloud of dust. **~suge** *vb* vacuum-clean. **~suger** *sb* vacuum cleaner.

støy *sb* noise. **støye** *vb* make a noise. **støyende** *adj* noisy. **støy|filter** *sb (i radio etc)* noise filter; static filter. **~fri** *adj* noiseless. **~plage** *sb* noise nuisance. **~skjerm** *sb* noise baffle. **~svak** *adj* muffled.

støyt *sb: ta* ~*en* bear the brunt; take the blow; *ta* *seg en* ~ *(dvs en drink)* take a drink/a swig. Se ellers *støt*.

stå I *sb: gå i* ~ come/grind to a standstill; stop (short); **II** *vb* **1** stand; *hun kunne knapt* ~ *(på beina)* she could hardly stand (on her two legs); *jeg har* ~*tt her i hele dag* I have been standing here all day; **2** *(befinne seg, være)* be, stand; *det stod et stort tre foran huset* a big tree stood in front of the house; there was a big tree in front of the house; *han* ~*r ikke på listen* he is not on the list; **3** *(*~ *og ... + et annet vb)* be + -ing; *jeg stod og så på barnetoget* I was looking at the children's parade; **4** *(*~ *skrevet) det* ~*r i avisen* it says in the paper; *hva* ~*r det på det skiltet?* what does it say on that signboard? **5** *(være stanset, uvirksom etc) klokken min* ~*r* my watch has stopped; *maskinene* ~*r om søndagene* the machines are idle on Sundays; **6** *(om slag)* be fought; *det stod et slag* a battle was fought; **7** *(til eksamen)* pass; **8** *(uttrykk)* ~ **frem** *(stikke frem)* jut/stick out; project, protrude; *(berette/tilstå etc åpent)* come forward; ~ **i:** *hun har mye å* ~ *i (med)* she is very busy; ~ **igjen** be left; remain; *bli* ~*ende igjen* be left (behind); ~ **og falle med:** *det* ~*r og faller med deg* it all depends on you; *det* ~*r og faller med været* it turns on the weather; ~ **opp** *(reise seg)* get/stand up; rise; *(*~ *opp av sengen)* get up; rise; *(som regel) stå sent/tidlig opp* be a late/early riser; ~ *opp fra de døde* rise from the dead; ~ **på:** *radioen* ~*r på* the radio is on; *er det noe som* ~*r på?* is anything the matter? ~ *på egne bein* stand on one's own feet; ~ **til:** *hvordan* ~*r det til?* how are you? *la det* ~ *til* chance it; *det slipset* ~*r ikke til skjorten din* that tie does not go (very well) with/does not match your shirt. **stående** *adj: et* ~ *uttrykk* a set/stock phrase; *på* ~ *fot* offhand; on the spur of the moment.

ståhei *sb* ado, fuss.

ståk *sb (bråk)* noise, din.

ståkarakter *sb* pass.

ståke *vb (bråke)* make noise.

stål *sb* steel; *rustfritt* ~ stainless steel.

stålampe *sb* standard lamp.

stål|fjær *sb* steel spring. ~**orm** *sb* slow-worm; *US* blind-worm. ~**sette** *vb:* ~ *seg* steel oneself. ~**tråd** *sb* (steel) wire. ~**trådgjerde** *sb* wire fence. ~**ull** *sb* steel wool. ~**vaier** *sb* steel wire. ~**verk** *sb* steel mill.

ståplass *sb* standing place/room; *det er fem* ~*er* there is standing room for five; *du kan få (en)* ~ *her* you can stand here.

subb *sb (rusk og rask)* refuse, waste. **subbe** *vb (gå slepende)* shuffle.

subjekt *sb* subject. **subjektiv** *adj* subjective. **subjektivitet** *sb* subjectivity.

sublim *sb* sublime. **sublimere** *vb* sublimate.

subsidier *sb fl* subsidies. **subsidiere** *vb* subsidize. **subsidiær** *adj* subsidiary. **subsidiært** *adv* alternatively.

subskribent *sb* subscriber. **subskribere** *vb* subscribe; ~ *på* subscribe for. **subskripsjon** *sb* subscription.

substantiv *sb* noun, substantive. **substantivisk** *adj* substantival.

subtil *adj* subtle. **subtilitet** *sb* subtlety.

subtrahere *vb* subtract. **subtraksjon** *sb* subtraction.

subtropisk *adj* subtropical.

suffiks *sb* suffix.

sufflere *vb* prompt. **sufflør, suffløse** *sb* prompter.

sug *sb* suction; *et* ~ *av smerte* a gnawing pain. **suge** *vb* suck; *han sugde saften av en appelsin* he sucked an orange. **sugen** *adj:* ~ *på en røyk* dying/pining for a smoke. **suge|pumpe** *sb* suction pump. ~**rør** *sb (drikkestrå)* straw.

suggerere *vb* hypnotize. **suggestibel** *adj* suggestible. **suggestion** *sb* hypnotic suggestion.

suite *sb* suite.

sujett *sb* subject, theme.

sukat *sb* candied peel.

sukk *sb* sigh; *før han fikk* ~ *for seg* before he could say Jack Robinson; *han trakk et lettelsens* ~ he breathed a sigh of relief. **sukke** *vb* sigh.

sukker *sb* sugar. **sukker|bete** se ~*roe*. ~**bit** *sb* lump of sugar; ~*biter (også)* cube/lump sugar. ~**bøsse** *sb* sugar castor. ~**ert** *sb* sugar pea. ~**klype** *sb* sugar tongs *(fl)*; *en* ~*klype* a pair of sugar tongs. ~**lake** *sb* syrup. ~**roe** *sb* sugar-beet. ~**rør** *sb* sugar-cane. ~**skål** *sb* sugar-basin. ~**syk** *adj* diabetic. ~**syke** *sb* diabetes. ~**tang** se ~*klype*. ~**tøy** *sb koll* sweets; *US* candy. **sukre** *vb* sugar, sweeten.

suksess *sb* success. **suksessiv** *adj* successive.

sulamitt *sb: hele* ~*en* the whole lot.

sulfapreparat *sb* sulpha/*US* sulfa drug.

sull *sb (vuggesang etc)* lullaby. **sulle** *vb* croon, hum.

sult *sb* hunger; *de var medtatt av* ~ they were weak with hunger.

sultan *sb* sultan.

sulte *vb* starve; be starving; ~ *i hjel* starve to death; die of starvation; ~ *ut* starve out. **sulte|fore** *vb* underfeed. ~**grense** *sb* starvation line. ~**kost** *sb* starvation diet. ~**lønn** *sb* starvation wages. **sulten** *adj* hungry. **sulte|streik** *sb* hunger-strike. ~**streike** *vb* go on a hunger strike.

sum *sb* sum; *en stor* ~ a large sum. **summarisk** *adj* summary.

summe *vb* buzz, hum. **summe seg** *vb* collect oneself.

summere *vb:* ~ *opp/sammen* sum up.

summetone *sb* dialling tone.

sump *sb* swamp. **sumpaktig** *adj* swampy.

sund *sb (strede)* sound, strait(s).

sunn *adj* **1** *(ikke syk)* healthy; *barna ser* ~*e ut* the children look healthy; **2** *(sunnhetsgagnlig)* healthy, wholesome; ~ *mat* wholesome food; *et sunt klima* a healthy climate; *melk hevdes å være sunt for barn* milk is said to be good for children; **3** *(som tyder på sunnhet)* healthy; *en* ~ *appetitt* a healthy appetite; **4** *(fornuftig, riktig)* sound; ~ *fornuft* common sense; *et sunt prinsipp* a sound principle. **sunnhet** *sb* health. **sunn-**

hets|farlig, ~skadelig unhealthy. **~pleie** *sb* hygiene.

sup *sb (slurk)* swig; *(liten ~)* nip, sip. **supe** *vb* imbibe, suck.

supé *sb (festmåltid)* banquet.

super *adj* grand, rattling.

supere *vb* dine out.

superlativ *sb* the superlative.

supermarked *sb* supermarket.

supersonisk *adj* supersonic.

suppe *sb* soup; *(kjøtt~ også)* broth; *koke ~ på noe* make soup from something.

suppedas *sb: hele ~en* the whole caboodle.

suppleant *sb* deputy, substitute. **supplement** *sb* supplement. **supplere** *vb* supplement; *~ hverandre* complement each other. **suppleringsvalg** *sb* by-election.

sur *adj* **1** acid, sour; *~ lukt/smak* sour smell/taste; *et ~t eple* a sour apple; *melken ble ~* the milk turned/became sour; **2** *(gretten)* sour, surly; *et ~t ansikt* a sour face; *sette opp et ~t ansikt* look sour; **3** *(uttrykk) ~t vær* cold and wet weather; *bite i det ~e eple* swallow a bitter pill; *han gjorde livet ~t for henne* he led her a dog's life. **surhet** *sb* acidity, sourness.

surkle *vb* gurgle.

sur|melk *sb* curdled milk. **~mule** *vb* mope, sulk. **surne** *vb* turn/become sour.

surr *sb* **1** *(~ende lyd)* buzz, hum; *et ~ av stemmer* a buzz of voices; **2** *(ugreie) jeg går helt ~ i det* I get it all mixed up. **surre** *vb* **A** *(om lyd)* **1** buzz, drone; hum; **2** *(tulle, tøyse)* talk nonsense; **B** *(binde/vikle med tau etc)* lash, wind.

surrealisme *sb* surrealism. **surrealist** *sb* surrealist. **surrealistisk** *adj* surrealistic.

surret(e) *adj* muddleheaded.

surring *sb (med tau etc)* lashing, roping.

surrogat *sb* substitute.

sursøt *adj fig* subacid; *et ~t smil* a subacid smile.

sus *sb (~ende lyd)* whisper, whistling; *~ for ørene* buzzing (in one's ears); *~ i bladverk/grener* rustling (in the leaves). **suse** *vb* **1** *(om lyd)* whistle; *(mer dempet)* whisper, sigh; *kulene suste om ørene på oss* the bullets whistled about our ears; *la humla ~* let things drift/slide; **2** *(fare av sted)* rush; *i ~ende fart* at full/top speed. **suset(e)** *adj (omtåket)* confused, muddled.

suspekt *adj (mistenkelig)* suspicious.

suspendere *vb* suspend. **suspensjon** *sb* suspension.

sutre *vb* whimper, whine.

sutte *vb* suck; *~ på fingrene* suck one's fingers.

suvenir *sb* souvenir.

suveren *adj* sovereign; *en ~ stat* a sovereign state. **suverenitet** *sb* sovereignty.

svaber *sb* mop, swab.

svada *sb* claptrap; hot air.

svai *adj (smekker og smidig)* lissom, willowy; *~ i ryggen* sway-backed. **svaie** *vb* sway, swing; *trærne ~t i vinden* the trees swayed in the wind.

svak *adj* **1** weak; *(svært ~ og ynkelig)* feeble; *~ puls* feeble pulse; *et ~t forsøk* a feeble attempt; **2** *(knapt merkbar)* faint; *en ~ lyd* a faint noise; *et ~t håp* a faint hope. **svakelig** *adv* delicate, weak; *(kronisk syk)* invalid; *han har alltid vært ~* his health has always been delicate. **svakhet** *sb* feebleness, weakness; *(svakt punkt)* weakness; weak point; *ha en ~ for* have a weakness for. **svak|strøm** *sb* low-power current. **~synt** *adj* weak-sighted, purblind.

sval *adj* cool; *en ~ vind* a cool wind.

svale *sb* swallow. **svalestup** *sb* swallow dive.

svalhet *sb* coolness.

svamp *sb* sponge; *drikke som en ~* drink like a fish. **svampet(e)** *adj* spongy.

svane *sb* swan. **svane|hals** *sb* swan's neck. **~sang** *sb* swan song.

svanger *adj* pregnant. **svangerskap** *sb* pregnancy.

svans *sb* tail.

svar *sb* answer, reply; *gi/komme med et ~* give an answer; make a reply; *ha ~ på rede hånd* never be at a loss for an answer; *som ~ på ditt brev* in reply to your letter; *til ~* in reply; *vi imøteser Deres ~* we are looking forward to hearing from you/to receiving your answer. **svare A** *adj: et ~ strev* a tough job; **B** *vb* **1** answer, reply; *han svarte at han ikke visste noe om det* he answered/replied that he did not know anything about it; *hun svarte ikke på brevet mitt* she did not ansver my letter/did not reply to my letter; *hva svarte du til det?* what did you reply to that? **2 ~ til** *(være tilsvarende)* correspond to; *~ til en beskrivelse* answer to a description; *~ til hensikten* answer the purpose.

svart *adj* black; *~ kaffe* black coffee; *~ på hvitt* in black and white; *gaten var ~ av mennesker* the street was black with people. **svarte|børs** *sb* black market. **~dauden** *sb* the Black Death. **~liste** *vb* blacklist. **~håret** *adj* black-haired. **~kledd** *adj* (dressed) in black. **~male** *vb (også fig)* paint in black. **~seer** *sb* pessimist. **~smusket** *adj* swarthy. **~syn** *sb* pessimism. **~trost** *sb* blackbird.

sveis *sb* hair fashion; *få ~ på* fix up.

sveise *vb* weld. **sveiseapparat** *sb* welder; welding apparatus.

sveisen *adj* smart, stylish.

sveiser *sb* **A** *(fjøskar)* dairyman; **B** *(metall~)* welder.

sveiv *sb* crank. **sveive** *sb* crank (up); turn.

svekke *vb* impair, weaken; *helsen hans er ~t* his health has been impaired; *sykdommen har ~t ham* his/the illness has weakened him. **svekkelse** *sb* impairment, weakening. **svekling** *sb* weakling.

svelg *sb (del av halsen)* throat; *(avgrunn)* gulf. **svelge** *sb* swallow; *~ gråten* choke back one's tears.

svelle *vb* swell.

svelte *vb* starve. Se for øvrig *sulte, sulte-*.

svenn *sb (håndverks~)* journeyman.

svepe *sb* whip. Se også *svøpe*.

sverd *sb* sword.

sverge *vb* **1** swear; *jeg ~r (på) at jeg vil gjøre det* I swear to do it/that I will do it; *jeg kan ikke ~ på det* I cannot swear to it; **2** *(banne)* curse, swear; *banne og ~* curse and swear.

sverm *sb* swarm; *(om mennesker også)* crowd; *en mygg~* a swarm of gnats. **sverme** *vb* **1** swarm; *(om mennesker også)* crowd; *folk ~t om stedet* people swarmed/crowded about the place; **2** *~ for* have a passion for; *(dgl)* have a crush on; *alle pikene ~t for den nye læreren* all the girls had a crush on the new teacher. **svermeri** *sb (forelskelse)* passion; *(gjenstand for ~)* flame; *(religiøst ~)* fanaticism. **svermerisk** *adj* romantic; *(fanatisk)* fanatical.

sverte 1 *sb* blacking; **2** *vb* blacken.

svett *adj* perspiring, sweaty. **svette 1** *sb* perspiration; *dgl* sweat; *han var badet i ~* he was bathed in perspiration; he was in a sweat; **2** *vb* perspire; *dgl* sweat; *han begynte å ~* he got into a sweat; *jeg ~r på hendene* my hands are sweaty.

sveve *vb* **1** float, hang, hover; *(~ høyt oppe)* soar; *(om glidefly)* glide; *en måke svevde over båten* a gull hung/hovered over the boat; **2** *(være, befinne seg)* be; *~ i fare (for sitt liv)* be in danger (of one's life). **sveve|fly etc** se *glidefly etc.* **svevende** *adj* **1** floating, hovering; **2** *(usikker)* uncertain, vague.

svi *vb* **1** *(brenne)* singe, scorch; *(især om mat)* burn; **2** *(smerte)* smart, sting; *røyken sved (meg) i øynene* the smoke made my eyes smart; **3** *de fikk ~ for det* they had to pay for it. **svidd** *adj (om mat, smak, lukt)* burnt; *(om hår, klær)* singed; *~ (havre)grøt* burnt porridge. **svie** *sb* pain, sting; *tort og ~* pain and suffering.

sviger|datter *sb* daughter-in-law. **~far** *sb* father-in-law. **~foreldre** *sb fl* parents-in-law. **svigerinne** *sb* sister-in-law. **~mor** *sb* mother-in-law. **~sønn** *sb* son-in-law.

svik *sb* deceit, treachery; fraud. **svike** *vb* betray, deceive. **svikefull** *adj* fraudulent, trecherous; *(bokl)* perfidious.

svikt *sb* **1** *(fjærende motstand)* elasticity, resilience; **2** *(brist)* flaw, weakness; *en ~ i hans karakter* a flaw in his character; **3** *(mangel, uteblivelse)* failure; *en ~ i tilførslene* a failure of supplies. **svikte** *vb* **1** *(la i stikken)* betray; desert, fail; *hun ~t meg i nødens stund* she failed me in the hour of need; *om alt annet skulle ~* if everything else should fail; **2** *(om evner, organer etc)* fail; *motet/stemmen hans ~t* his courage/voice failed him; **3** *(skuffe)* be a disappointment; fail. **sviktende** *adj* failing; *~ helse* failing health; *med aldri ~ iver* with unfailing zeal; *på ~ grunnlag* on an unsound basis.

sville *sb (jernbane~)* sleeper.

svime 1 *sb: slå i ~* knock out; **2** *vb: ~ av* faint. **svimeslå** *vb* knock out. **svimle** *vb: det ~r for meg* I feel dizzy; *~nde høyde* dizzy height; *~nde priser* enormous prices. **svimmel** *adj* dizzy, giddy. **svimmelhet** *sb* dizziness, giddiness.

svin *sb fig* swine; *kaste perler for ~* throw pearls before swine. Se for øvrig *gris.* **svinaktig** *adj (skrekkelig)* awfully; *det gjør ~ vondt* it hurts awfully.

svindel *sb* humbug, swindle. **svindle** *vb* swindle. **svindler** *sb* swindler.

svine *vb: ~ til* dirty, soil; make dirty. **svine|heldig** *adj* (very) lucky; *du er ~heldig* you are a lucky devil. **~kjøtt** *sb* pork. **~kotelett** *sb* pork chop. **~lær** *sb* pigskin. **svineri** *sb* filth, filthiness; *det er noe ~* it is a nuisance. **svinestek** *sb* roast pork.

sving *sb* **1** *(dreining, forandring av retning)* turn; *en skarp ~ til venstre* a sharp turn to the left; **2** *(på vei)* bend, curve; turning; **3** *(uttrykk) få ~ på* put snap into; ginger up; *i full ~* in full swing; *komme i ~* get started; get into one's stride; *sette i ~* start. **svinge** *vb* **1** *(dreie, forandre retning)* swing; *(om kjøretøy etc og vei især)* turn; *hun svingte om hjørnet* she turned the corner; *veien svingte til høyre* the road turned to the right; **2** *(veive, vinke)* swing, wave; *han svingte med hatten* he swung his hat; *apekatten svingte seg fra gren til gren* the monkey swung from branch to branch; **3** *(variere)* fluctuate; *~ mellom håp og fortvilelse* fluctuate between hope and despair. **svinget(e)** *adj* winding; full of curves. **svingning** *sb* **1** oscilliation, swing; **2** *(dreining, sving)* turn; *en ~ til venstre* a turn to the left; **3** *(variasjon)* fluctuation; *~er i temperaturen* fluctuations of temperature. **svingom** *sb dgl* hop; *ta seg en ~* shake a leg; foot it. **sving|stang** *sb* (horizontal) bar. **~stol** *sb* swivel chair.

svinn *sb* loss, waste; *~ i vekt* loss of weight. **svinne** *vb* dwindle (away); vanish; *vårt håp svant (hen)* our hope dwindled away.

svinse *vb: ~ omkring* bustle about.

svinsk *adj* filthy; *(uanstendig)* smutty.

svint *adj* quick, swift.

svipptur *sb* flying trip/visit.

svir *sb* carousing; *drikk og ~* drinking and carousing. **svire** *vb* booze, carouse. **svirebror** *sb* drinking companion. **svirelag** *sb* drinking bout.

svirre *vb* whirr; *(også fig)* buzz; *ryktene ~t* rumours buzzed.

sviske *sb* prune.

svive *vb (gå rundt)* revolve, rotate, turn.

svoger *sb* brother-in-law. **svogerskap** *sb* relationship by marriage.

svolk *sb* switch, stick.

svor *sb (fleske~)* rind.

svovel *sb* sulphur. **svovelsyre** *sb* sulphuric acid.

svulme *vb* swell; *hjertet hans ~t av stolthet* his heart swelled with pride.

svulst *sb* tumour. **svulstig** *adj* bombastic. **svulstighet** *sb* bombast.

svunnen *adj: i en ~ tid/i svunne tider* in times past.

svær *adj* **1** big, huge; *en ~ ørret* a big trout; *en ~ lastebil* a huge lorry; **2** *(fig: vanskelig)* hard, severe, great. **svært** *adv* **1** extremely, very; *~ mye* very much; *~ rik* extremely rich; **2** *(stundom)* greatly, highly, much; *~ overrasket* greatly/highly/much astonished; *de er ~ like* they are much alike. **svær|vekt** *sb* heavyweight. **~vekter** *sb (sværing)* giant.

svøm *sb: (legge) på ~* (start) swimming. **svømme**

vb swim; *vi svømte over elven* we swam across the river. **svømme|basseng** *sb* swimming-pool. **~belte** *sb* swimming-belt. **~blære** *sb* swimming bladder. **~dyktig** *adj* able to swim. **~fot** *sb (på fugl)* webbed foot; web-foot; *(på froskemanndrakt)* flipper; frogman's foot. **~fugl** web-footed bird. **~hall** *sb* swimming-bath. **~hud** *sb* web; *med ~hud* webbed. **svømmer** *sb* swimmer. **svømme|stadion** *sb* swimming stadium. **~tak** *sb* (swimming) stroke. **~tur** *sb* swim. **~undervisning** *sb* swimming instruction; swimming-lesson.

svøpe *sb (forbannelse, plage)* scourge; *krig er en ~ for menneskeheten* war is a scourge for mankind. Jf *svepe.*

sy *vb* sew; *~ en kjole (især)* make a dress; *~ i en knapp* sew on a button; *~ igjen* sew up. **sydame** *sb* dressmaker.

syd *adj, sb* south; *~ for byen* (to the) south of the town; *fra ~* from the south; *i ~* in the south; *mot ~* south, southward; *vende mot ~* face south. **Syden** the South; *(i Europa)* the Mediterranean countries. **syd|fra** *adv* from the south. **~frukter** *sb fl* tropical fruits; *(sitrusfrukter)* citrus fruits. **~gående** *adj* southbound. **~kyst** *sb* south(ern) coast. **~landsk** *adj* southern. **~lending** *sb* southerner. **sydlig** *adj* southern; *(om vind også)* southerly. **sydligst** *adj* southernmost. **sydover** *adv* south, southward(s); towards the south. **Sydpolen** the South Pole. **syd|på** *adv* in the south; down south. **~side** *sb* south(ern) side. **Sydstatene** *(i USA)* the Southern States; the South. **syd|vest** *adj, sb* south-west; *(hodeplagg)* sou'wester. **~øst** *adj, sb* south-east.

syerske *sb* seamstress, sempstress; *(kjole~)* dressmaker.

syfilis *adj* syphilis.

syk *adj* **1** *(som predikatsord)* ill; *(US også)* sick; *bli ~* become/get ill; be taken/fall ill; *ligge ~* be ill in bed; *være alvorlig ~* be seriously/very ill; **2** *(foran sb)* sick; *~e mennesker* sick people; *den ~e* the sick person; **3** *(om legemsdeler og organer)* diseased, disordered. **sykdom** *sb* **1** *(det å være syk)* illness; *det har vært en god del ~ i vinter* there has been a good deal of illness this winter; **2** *(om bestemt, især alvorlig ~)* disease; *en alvorlig ~* a serious disease; **3** *(om lettere ~)* complaint; *forkjølelse er en vanlig ~* a cold is a common complaint. **syke|bil** *sb* ambulance. **~hus** *sb* hospital. **~leie** *sb* sickbed. **sykelig** *adj* **1** *(tilbøyelig til sykdom)* sickly; *et ~ barn* a sickly child; **2** *(abnorm, overdreven)* morbid; *~ nysgjerrighet* morbid curiosity. **syke|penger** *sb* sickness benefit. **~permisjon** *sb* sick leave. **~pleie** *sb* nursing. **~pleier** *sb* nurse; *(om mann)* male nurse. **~pleierske** *sb (utdannet ~)* trained nurse; *(på sykehus)* hospital nurse. Jf *~pleier.* **~sal** *sb* ward. **~søster** se *~pleier.* **~trygd** *sb* health insurance.

sykkel *sb* bicycle; *dgl* bike. **sykkel|dekk** *sb* bicycle tyre. **~lykt** *sb* bicycle lamp. **~løp** *sb* bicycle race. **~pumpe** *sb* bicycle pump. **~slange** *sb* bicycle (inner) tube. **~styre** *sb* handlebars *(fl).* **~tur** *sb* (bicycle) ride; *(kort tur)* spin; *(lengre tur)* bicycle tour. **~veske** *sb* pannier. **sykle** *vb* cycle; ride a bicycle; *dgl* bike. **syklist** *sb* cyclist.

syklon *sb* cyclone.

syklubb *sb* sewing circle.

sykmelde *vb* report sick; *~ seg* report oneself sick.

sykne *vb: ~ hen* waste away.

syl *sb* awl.

sylinder *sb* cylinder. **sylindrisk** *adj* cylindrical.

sylte 1 *sb (grise~, hode~)* head cheese; **2** *vb* **1** *(~ bær, frukt)* preserve; *(lage ~tøy)* make jam; **2** *(~ i eddik)* pickle; *~de agurker* pickled cucumber. **sylte|labber** *sb fl* (boiled) pig trotters. **~tøy** *sb* jam. **~tøyglass, ~tøykrukke** *sb* jam jar.

symaskin *sb* sewing-machine.

symbol *sb* symbol. **symbolikk** *sb* symbolism. **symbolisere** *vb* symbolize. **symbolsk** *adj* symbolic.

symfoni *sb* symphony. **symfoniorkester** *sb* symphony orchestra.

symmetri *sb* symmetry. **symmetrisk** *adj* symmetrical.

sympati *sb* sympathy; *føle ~ for (ha medfølelse med)* feel sympathy for; *(like, være stemt for)* feel attracted by; like; *~er og antipatier* likes and dislikes; *du har min ~* you have my sympathies. **sympatisere** *vb: ~ med (ha medfølelse med)* sympathize with. **sympatisk** *adj* lik(e)able, pleasant. **sympatistreik** *sb* sympathy strike.

symptom *sb* symptom. **symptomatisk** *adj* symptomatic.

syn *sb* **1** *(synsevne, -sans)* (eye)sight; *hun mistet ~et* she lost her (eye)sight; **2** *(noe en ser)* sight; *(bare) ~et av det gjør meg syk* the mere sight of it makes me sick; *et sørgelig ~* a sad sight; **3** *(indre ~)* vision; **4** *(ånde~, spøkelse)* apparition; **5** *(mening)* view(s); *hva er Deres ~ på saken?* what are your views on the matter? **6** *(uttrykk) vi mistet dem* **av ~e** we lost sight of them; **for ~s skyld** for the sake of appearance; *jeg sa det rett* **opp i ~et på** *ham* I told him so in/to his face; *komme* **til ~e** appear; come in sight/in(to) view; **ute av ~e** out of sight; **ved ~et av** at the sight of.

synagoge *sb* synagogue.

synd *sb* **1** sin; *begå en ~* commit a sin; *de skal ikke få dø i ~en* they won't get away with it; **2** *(uttrykk) det er ~ (dvs ergerlig) at* it is a pity that; *det er ~ på dem* I am sorry for them; *det er ~ å si at...* it would be wrong to say that... **synde** *vb* sin; commit a sin. **synde|bukk** *sb* scapegoat. **~fallet** *sb* the fall of man. **~full** *adj* sinful. **synder** *sb* **1** *(~ mot Gud)* sinner; **2** *(en som har gjort noe galt)* culprit, offender; *hvem er ~en?* who is the culprit? **synderegister** *sb* list of one's sins.

synderlig *adj: ikke ~* not (very) much; very little; *uten ~ vanskelighet* without much difficulty.

syndflod *sb* flood; *(Syndfloden i Bibelen)* the Flood. **syndig** *adj* sinful. **synds|bekjennelse** *sb* confession (of sins). **~forlatelse** *sb* absolution; remission of sins.

syne: *av ~, til ~* se *syn 6.*

synes *vb* **1** *(mene)* think; *~ synd på* pity; *hva ~ du?*

what do you think? *hva ~ du om talen hans?* what do you think of his speech? **2** *(forekomme, se ut/virke som)* appear, seem; *det som ~ lett for deg, er vanskelig for meg* what seems easy to you is difficult for me; *jeg syntes jeg hørte noe* I seemed to hear something; **3** *(like)* like; *jeg ~ ikke noe om det* I do not like it.

synge *vb* sing; *~ ut* speak out/up.

synke *vb* sink; *bygningen sank sammen* the building fell in; *han sank om/sammen* he collapsed; *skipet sank* the ship sank/went down.

synlig *adj* visible; *~ for alle* visible to everybody; *huset ble ~* the house became visible/came in sight/ into view.

synonym *adj* synonymous. **synonym** *sb* synonym.

syns|bedrag *sb* optical delusion. **~felt** *sb* field of vision. **synsk** *adj* clairvoyant, secondsighted. **syns|-krets** *sb* horizon. **~linje** *sb* line of vision. **~måte** *sb* view. **~organ** *sb* organ of sight/vision. **~punkt** *sb* point of view. **~rand** *sb* horizon. **~sans** *sb* sight. **~vidde** *sb: utenfor ~vidde* out of sight. **~vinkel** *sb fig* angle, aspect; point of view; *se det under alle ~vinkler* consider it from every angle/from all sides/from all points of view.

syntaks *sb* syntax.

syntese *sb* synthesis. **syntetisk** *adj* synthetic.

synål *sb* sewing-needle.

sypress *sb* cypress.

syre *sb (kjemisk væske)* acid.

syrin *sb* lilac.

syrlig *adj* acidulous, sourish; *(også fig)* subacid; *et ~ smil* a subacid smile.

sy|saker *sb fl* sewing things. **~skrin** *sb* workbox.

sysle *vb: ~ med* be busy with; be doing. **syssel** *sb* occupation. **syssel|sette** *vb* employ; *være ~satt med* be occupied with. **~setting** *sb* employment.

system *sb* system. **systematisk** *adj* systematic.

syte *(klage)* complain; *(klynke)* whimper, whine.

sytråd *sb* sewing cotton/thread. **sytøy** *sb* needlework.

sæd *sb* **1** *(såkorn)* seed; **2** *(sædvæske)* semen, sperm.

sær *adj* eccentric, odd; *(underlig)* peculiar, queer; *(gretten)* cross; *(umedgjørlig)* difficult. **særdeles** *adv* most, very; highly; *~ tilfredsstillende* highly satisfactory. **særdeleshet** *sb: i ~* in particular. **sær|drag** *sb* individuality. **~egen** *adj* peculiar; *(underlig også)* odd, strange. **sær|eie** *sb* separate estate. **~interesse** *sb* special interest; *(gruppes ~)* sectional interest. **~kjenne** = *~merke 1.* **~klasse** *sb* **1** *(hjelpeklasse på skole)* special class; **2** *(klasse for seg) hun står i en ~klasse* she is in a class by herself. **særlig** *adj* **1** particular, special; *av ~ interesse* of particular interest; **2** *(særegen)* peculiar; **3** *adv* particularly, specially; *(først og fremst)* especially; *et ~ vanskelig problem* a particularly difficult problem; *hun liker landet, ~ om våren* she likes the country, especially in spring; **4** *(uttrykk) i ~ grad* particularly; *ikke ~* not particularly; not very; *han danser ikke ~ godt* he does not dance very well. Jf *spesielt.* **særling** *sb* eccentric; *(person med underlige idéer)* crank. **sær|merke 1** *sb* characteristic; distinctive feature; **2** *vb* characterize; be characteristic of. **~preg** *sb* distinctive stamp. **~preget** *adj* distinctive. **~rett** *sb* privilege. **særs** *adv* particularly, specially. Jf *særlig 3.* **særskilt 1** *adj* individual, separate; **2** *adv* individually, separately; *han nevnte henne ~* he mentioned her separately. **sær|stilling** *sb: stå i en ~* be a special case; stand in a class by oneself. **~syn** *sb* rare thing.

sødme *sb* sweetness.

søke vb **1** *(lete, se seg om)* look for; *~ arbeid* look for a job; *hvem søker De?* who(m) do you want to see? **2** *(forsøke å oppnå etc)* endeavour, try; *han søkte å hjelpe oss* he tried to help us; **3** *(sende søknad)* apply for; *hun søkte stillingen* she applied for the post; **4** *(uttrykk) ~ hjelp* apply for assistance; *~ lege* consult a doctor; *~ opplysninger* make inquiries; *~ råd* seek advice. **søke-lys** *sb (lyskaster)* searchlight; *han er i politiets ~lys* the police are keeping an eye on him. **søker** *sb* **1** *(ansøker)* applicant; **2** *(på kamera etc)* viewfinder.

søkk A *adv: bli ~ borte* disappear without leaving a trace; vanish into the air; **B** *sb* **1** *(fordypning)* hollow, depression; **2** *(rykk)* start; *det gav et ~ i henne* she gave a start. **søkke 1** *sb* sinker; **2** *vb (senke, synke)* sink. **søkk|full** *adj* brimfull, chockfull, crammed. **~laste** *vb* load to sinking-point. **~rik** *adj* rolling in money. **~våt** *adj* drenched, soaked.

søknad *sb* application. **søknads|frist** *sb* closing date for applications. **~skjema** *sb* application form.

søknedag *sb* weekday.

søkning *sb* **1** *(av kunder etc)* custom, patronage; **2** *(søkere)* applicants. **søksmål** *sb* action, suit. **søkt** *adj (unaturlig)* far-fetched; out-of-the-way.

søl *sb* mess, dirt; *jo flere kokker, jo mer ~* too many cooks spoil the broth. **søle 1** *sb* mud, slush; **2** *vb (spille væske)* slop, spill; *han sølte saus på duken* he spilt gravy on the tablecloth; *jeg sølte maling utover hele gulvet* I slopped paint all over the floor; *~ til, ~ ut* soil, dirty; *~ bort, ~ vekk* waste, squander; *~ ikke bort tiden din!* do not waste your time! *hun sølte vekk pengene sine* she squandered her money. **søle|gris** *sb* mudlark. **~kake** *sb* mud-pie. **~pytt** *sb* puddle. **~skvett** *sb* splash of mud. **sølet(e)** *adj* muddy, dirty.

sølibat *sb* celibacy.

sølje *sb* brooch.

sølv *sb* silver. **sølv|bryllup** *sb* silver wedding. **~beger** *sb* silver cup. **~mynt** *sb* silver coin. **~papir** *sb* tinfoil; silver paper. **~penger** *sb fl* silver (money). **~rev** *sb* silver fox. **~smed** *sb* silversmith. **~tøy** *sb koll* silver.

søm *sb* sewing; *(sammensying)* seam.

sømmelig *adj (anstendig)* decent; proper, seemly. **sømmelighet** *sb* decency, propriety. **sømme seg** *vb* be becoming/proper/seemly; *det ~r seg ikke for en dame* it is unbecoming in a lady; *det ~r seg ikke for oss* it is not proper/seemly for us.

søndag *sb* Sunday; *forrige ~* last Sunday; *om ~en*

(hver ~) om Sundays. **søndags|avis** *sb* Sunday paper. **~skole** *sb* Sunday school.

sønder *adv: ~ og sammen* to bits (pieces, atoms). **sønderknust** *adj fig* broken-hearted.

søndre *adj* southern.

sønn *sb* son.

sønna|for *prep* southward of; (to the) south of. **~fra** *adv* from the south. **~vind** *sb* south/southerly wind.

sønnedatter *sb* granddaughter.

sønnenom *prep* (to the) south of.

sønnesønn *sb* grandson.

søppel *sb* refuse, rubbish; junk; *US* garbage, junk. **søppel|bil** *sb* dustcart; *US* garbage truck. **~brett** *sb* dustpan. **~bøtte, ~dunk** *sb* dustbin; refuse bin. **~dynge** *sb* junk/refuse (*US* garbage) heap. **~kasse** *sb* dustbin; *US* garbage can. **~kjører** *sb* dustman. **~kurv** *sb* litter bin. **~sjakt** *sb* rubbish chute. **~tømming** *sb* refuse collection and disposal.

sør etc se *syd etc.*

sørge 1 *(føle sorg)* grieve; *de ~t over sin fars død* the grieved at (for, over) the death of their father; *han ~t dypt* he grieved deeply; **2** *(føle eller vise sorg ved dødsfall)* mourn; *de ~t over tapet av vennen* they mourned the loss of their friend; *hun ~t over sin manns død* she mourned over the death of her husband; **3** *~ for (skaffe)* provide; *(ta seg av)* provide for; take care of; *~ for barna* provide for/look after the children; *vi kan ~ for oss selv* we can look after/take care of ourselves; *~ for at det blir gjort* see that it is done. **sørgekledd** *adj* (dressed) in mourning. **sørgelig** *adj* **1** *(bedrøvelig, beklagelig)* sad; *~e nyheter* sad news; *et ~ tap* a sad loss; **2** *(ynkelig)* poor, wretched. **sørgemarsj** *sb* funeral march. **sørgmodig** *adj* sad, melancholy.

sørpe *sb* slush, sludge.

søsken *sb koll* brothers and sisters; *(i lovspråk etc)* siblings. **søsken|barn** *sb* cousin. **~flokk** *sb* family (of brothers and sisters).

søster *sb* sister. **søster|datter** *sb* niece; sister's daughter. **~sønn** *sb* nephew; sister's son.

søt *adj* sweet; *~saker, ~e saker* sweets; *(adv) blomstene duftet søtt* the flowers smelt sweet; *hun smilte søtt* she smiled sweetly. **søtlig** *adj* sweetish.

søvn *sb* sleep; *han gråt seg i ~* he cried himself to sleep; *hun gikk i ~e* she walked in her sleep; *jeg falt i ~* I fell asleep. **søvn|drukken** *adj* drowsy; heavy with sleep. **~dyssende** *adj* soporific. **~gjenger** *sb* sleepwalker, somnambulist. **~gjengeraktig** *adj* somnambulistic. **søvnig** *adj* sleepy. **søvnighet** *sb* sleepiness. **søvn|løs** *adj* sleepless. **~løshet** *sb* sleeplessness, insomnia.

søyle *sb* column, pillar.

så I *adv* **1** *(svært)* so; *(især i nektende uttrykk)* very; *de var ~ trette* they were so tired; *jeg synger ikke ~ godt* I do not sing very well; **2** *(foran følgesetning eller adj + infinitiv)* so; *hun var ~ trett at hun måtte legge seg* she was so tired that she had to lie down; *vil De være ~ vennlig å hjelpe meg* will you be so kind as to help me; **3** *(ved sammenligning) ~ ... som* as ... as; *han gjorde det ~ godt (som) han kunne* he did it as well as he could; *ikke ~ ... som* not so/as ... as; *hun er ikke ~ gammel som bestemoren din* she is not as old as your grandmother; **4** *(om tid: da, deretter)* then; *drikk et glass varm melk og gå ~ til sengs* drink a glass of warm milk and then go to bed; **5** *(derfor)* so; *det var sent, ~ vi gikk hjem* it was late, so we went home; **6** *(etter imperativ + løfte)* and; *hent boken, ~ skal jeg lese en historie for deg!* fetch me the book and I will read you a story! **7** *(imperativ + ros)* that's, there's; *hent boken, ~ er du snill gutt/pike* fetch me the book that's/there's a good boy/girl! **8** *(uttrykk)* **~ godt som:** *~ godt som alle* practically everybody; *~ godt som avgjort* as good as settled; **~ nær som** except; with the exception of; **~ som ~** so - so; **~ vel som** as well as; both - and; **og ~ videre** and so on; **så vidt:** *~ vidt jeg vet* as far as I know; *det var ~ vidt jeg kjente henne igjen* I only just recognized her; **~ å si** as it were; so to speak; **II** *konj* so that; in order that; *gå tidlig, ~ du får god plass* go early so that/in order that you will get a good seat; *han tok av seg skoene, ~ jeg ikke skulle høre ham* he took off his shoes, so that I shouldn't hear him; *hun arbeidet hardt ~ hun skulle vinne prisen* she worked hard so that she might win the prize.

så *vb (~ korn etc)* sow.

sådan se *slik*.

såfremt *konj* provided that; providing.

sågar *adv (til og med)* even; in fact.

såkalt *adj* so-called.

såkorn *sb* seed-corn.

såld *sb* riddle.

såle 1 *sb (fot~, ~ på sko)* sole; **2** *vb* sole.

således *adv* thus; like that/this; (in) that/this way. Se for øvrig *slik*.

såmaskin *sb* sowing-machine.

så menn *adv (sannelig)* indeed; *det er ~ ~ helt sant* that is quite true, indeed.

sånn se *slik*.

såpass *adv: ~ som femten år* about fifteen years; *~ gammel at...* so old that...

såpe 1 *sb* soap; **2** *vb: ~ inn* lather. **såpe|boble** *sb* soap-bubble. **~kopp** *sb* soap dish. **~pulver** *sb* soap powder. **~skum** *sb* lather. **~stykke** *sb* cake of soap. **~vann** *sb* soapy water.

sår 1 *adj* sore; *jeg er ~ i halsen* I have a sore throat; **2** *sb* wound; *(flenge, kutt)* cut; *(brann~)* burn; *(skrubb~)* graze; *(stikk~)* stab (wound); *(betent ~, kronisk ~)* sore; *et åpent ~* an open wound. **sår|bar** *adj* vulnerable. **~barhet** *sb* vulnerability. **~beint** *adj* footsore. **såre** *vb* **1** *(tilføye sår)* wound; *soldaten ble ~t* the soldier was wounded; **2** *(krenke)* hurt, wound; *det ~t meg dypt* it hurt me deeply. **sårende** *adj* hurting, wounding.

såte *sb* haycock.

så vidt *adv* barely; only just. Se også *vidt*.

T

t *(bokstaven)* t.

ta *vb* **1** take; ~ *det med ro,* ~ *det rolig* take it easy; ~ *(en) drosje/toget* take a taxi/the train; ~ *en (spaser)tur* take a walk; ~ *(seg) ferie* take a holiday; *det* ~*r fem minutter* it takes five minutes; *hvem har* ~*tt pennen min?* who has taken my pen? *legen tok temperaturen min* the doctor took my temperature; **2** *(uttrykk)* ~ **av** *(om fly)* take off; *(gå ned i vekt)* lose weight; reduce; *jeg har* ~*tt av fem kilo* I have reduced five kilos; ~ **av seg** take off; *hun tok av seg hanskene (sine)* she took off her gloves; ~ **avskjed** *(si farvel)* take leave; *han tok avskjed med sine venner* he took leave of his friends; *(trekke seg tilbake fra stilling)* retire; *hun tok avskjed da hun var 65* she retired when she was 65; ~ **eksamen** pass an examination; ~ **etter** *(rekke hånden etter)* reach for; *(etterligne)* imitate, mimic; copy; ~ **fatt** set to work; ~ **feil** be mistaken; make a mistake; *(ha urett)* be wrong; *du* ~*r feil* you are wrong; ~ **for** *(forlange for)* charge for; *hvor meget* ~*r De for denne hatten?* how much do you charge for this hat? *(mista for)* take for; *hva* ~*r De meg for?* what do you take me for? *jeg tok henne for hennes søster* I took her for her sister; ~ **for gitt** take for granted; ~ **for seg** *av maten* do justice to the food; ~ **fra** *hverandre* take to pieces; *(demontere)* dismantle; ~ **frem** take out; ~ **i** *(anstrenge seg)* exert oneself; make an effort; ~ **igjen** *(sette seg til motverge)* fight back; *(svare igjen)* answer back; *(innhente)* catch up with; *(innhente og kjøre forbi)* overtake; ~ *igjen det forsømte* make up for lost time; ~ **imot** *(om gjester)* receive, welcome; *de tok imot oss med åpne armer* they received us with open arms; *(om innbydelse, tilbud)* accept; *vi* ~*r imot innbydelsen/tilbudet* we accept the invitation/the offer; ~ **inn** *(~ inn arbeidskraft)* take on; *formannen tok inn fem arbeidere til* the foreman took on five more workers; *(~ inn på hotell)* put up; *vi tok inn på det nye hotellet* we put up at the new hotel; ~ **innpå** gain upon; ~ **med** *(dit en kommer)* bring; *hvorfor tok du ikke med din venn?* why did you not bring your friend? *(dit en drar)* take with one; *jeg tok dem med til Paris* I took them with me to Paris; ~ **opp:** ~ *opp en sak* take up a matter; ~ *ille opp* resent; take amiss; *hun tok hans bemerkning ille* ~ she resented his remark; ~ **på** *(røre ved)* touch; ~ *på (kreftene)* tell on; *anstrengelsen tok på* the strain was telling on her/him etc; ~ **på ordet:** ~ *henne på ordet* take her at her word; ~ **på seg** put on; *han tok på seg jakken* he put on his coat; ~ **på vei** carry on; *hun tok skrekkelig på vei* she carried on terribly; ~ **seg av** take care of; look after; see to; *hvem skal* ~ *seg av barna mens jeg borte?* who will look after the children while I am away? *jeg skal* ~ *meg av det* I shall take care of it/see to it; *(~ seg av en sak)* attend to; deal with; *hun tok seg av saken selv* she attended to/dealt with the matter herself; ~ **seg sammen** pull oneself together; ~ **telefonen** answer the (tele)-phone; ~ **til** *(begynne)* begin, start; ~ **seg til:** *hva* ~*r du deg til for tiden?* what are you doing with yourself these days? ~ **seg ut:** *(~ seg godt ut)* look fine; make a good show; *(~ seg helt ut i konkurranse)* go all out. ~ **til seg** *(adoptere)* adopt.

tabbe *sb* blunder.

tabell *sb* table.

tablett *sb* tablet.

tablå *sb* tableau.

tabu *sb* taboo.

tabulator *sb* tab, tabulator.

taburett *sb* stool.

tafatt *adj* perplexed, puzzled.

taffel *sb* table; *heve* ~*et* end the meal.

tafs *sb* tuft, wisp. **tafset(e)** *adj (om hår)* dishevelled.

tagg *sb* spike, point. **tagget(e)** *adj* spiked, thorny.

tagl *sb* horsehair.

tak A *sb* **1** *(grep)* hold; grasp, grip; *få* ~ *i* get hold of; *(fig: begripe)* grasp, understand; *slippe* ~*et i* let go one's hold of; **2** *(åre~, svømme~)* stroke; *de rodde med lange* ~ they pulled long strokes; **B** *(på hus: utvendig)* roof; *(innvendig)* ceiling.

takk *sb* **A** *(spiss)* point, tooth; *takker (på gevir)* antlers; **B** *sb* thanks *fl*; ~, *det samme!* thank you, the same to you! *ja* ~*! (som svar på forespørsel)* yes, thanks/thank you; *(som svar på tilbud)* yes, please! *vil De ha te? ja* ~*!* do you want some tea? yes, please! *har De fått te? ja* ~*!* have you had your tea? yes, thanks/thank you! *mange* ~*!* (many) thanks! thank you (very much)! *nei* ~ no, thanks/thank you! *på forhånd* ~ thanking you in advance.

takkammer *sb* attic, garret.

takke *vb* thank; *du har bare deg selv å* ~ *for det* you have only yourself to thank for that; *han* ~*t henne for hjelpen* he thanked her for her help; *ha å* ~ *for* be indebted to; owe; *ikke noe å* ~ *for* don't mention it; not at all; *vi ble reddet* ~*t være hennes mot* we were saved thanks to her courage. **takke|brev** *sb* letter of thanks. ~**kort** *sb* printed/written acknowledgement. ~**skriv** *sb* letter of thanks. ~**tale** *sb* speech of thanks.

takket(e) *adj* indented, jagged, notched; *(om horn)* branched.

takknemlig *adj* grateful; *(mot Gud, skjebnen etc)* thankful; ~ *mot Gud* thankful to God; *hun var* ~ *over at det ikke var verre* she was thankful that it was not worse; *jeg er (ham)* ~ *fordi han hjalp meg* I am grateful to him for having helped me/for his help. **takknemlighet** *sb* **1** gratitude; *han viste sin* ~ he showed his gratitude; **2** *(mot Gud, skjebnen etc)* thankfulness; *de-*

res ~ *fordi de var reddet* their thankfulness for safety. **takksigelse** *sb* thanksgiving.

takle *vb* tackle.

takrenne *sb* gutter.

taksameter *sb* taximeter. **taksere** *vb* appraise, estimate, value. **taksering** appraisal, assessment, valuation.

tak|skjegg *sb* eaves *fl*. **~sperre** *sb* rafter.

takst *sb* rate; *(på buss, trikk etc)* fare; *full/halv* ~ full/half rate; *til fast* ~ at fixed rate.

takstein *sb* tile.

takt *sb* **1** time; *holde ~en* keep time; *(under marsj etc)* keep step; *i* ~ in time; *ro i* ~ keep stroke; *valse~* waltz time; **2** *(mellom to taktstreker)* bar; *en pause på to ~er* a rest of two bars; *spille noen (få) ~er av nasjonalsangen* play a few bars of the national anthem; **3** *(finfølelse)* tact, tactfulness; *mangel på* ~ want of tact; *med* ~ tactfully. **takt|fast** *adj* rhytmic(al), measured. **~full** *adj* tactful, discreet.

taktiker *sb* tactician. **taktikk** *sb* tactics. **taktisk** *adj* tactical.

takt|løs *adj* tactless. **~løshet** *sb* tactlessness; want of tact; *en* ~ a piece of tactlessness. **~slag** *sb* beat. **~stokk** *sb* baton.

tak|vindu *sb* skylight. **~værelse** *sb* attic, garret.

tale 1 *sb* speech; *den mannen det er* ~ *om* the man in question; *det kan det ikke være* ~ *om* that is out of the question; *hun holdt en stor(artet)* ~ she made a great speech; **2** *vb (holde tale)* speak; make a speech; *han talte i en time, og han talte godt* he spoke for an hour, and he spoke well. Jf *snakke*. **tale|feil** *sb* impediment of speech; speech defect. **~ferdighet 1** *(veltalenhet)* eloquence; **2** *(i språk)* fluency. **~film** *sb* soundfilm. **~fot** *sb: komme/være på ~fot med* get/be on speaking terms with. **~frihet** *sb* freedom of speech. **~gaver** *sb fl: ha gode ~gaver* be a fluent speaker; have the gift of the gab. **~måte** *sb (tomme ord)* empty phrases; mere words. **talende** *sb: den* ~ the speaker; *de* ~ the speakers.

talent *sb* talent, gift; *hun har* ~ *for maling* she has a talent for painting. **talent|full** *adj* talented, gifted. **~løs** *adj* untalented. **~løshet** *sb* want of talent.

taleorgan *sb* speech organ. **taler** *sb* **1** speaker; *jeg er ingen* ~ I am not much of a speaker; **2** *(talerbegavelse)* orator; *Churchill var en stor* ~ Churchill was a great orator. **talerstol** *sb* platform, rostrum. **tale|rør** *sb* speaking-tube; *fig* mouthpiece; *den avisen er Arbeiderpartiets ~rør* that paper is the mouthpiece of the Labour Party. **~språk** *sb* spoken language; *det engelske* ~ spoken English. **~trengt** *adj* garrulous, talkative.

talg *sb* tallow; *(nyre~)* suet.

talje *sb* (block and) tackle.

talkum *sb* talc(um) powder.

tall *sb* number; *(talltegn)* figure; *~ene taler for seg selv* the figures speak for themselves.

tallerken *sb* plate; *dyp* ~ soup-plate; *en* ~ *suppe* a plateful of soup; *flygende* ~ flying saucer.

talløs *adj* countless, innumerable. **tall|messig** *adj* numerical. **~ord** *sb* numeral. **~rik** *adj* numerous. **~skive** *sb* dial. **~verdi** *sb* numerical value.

talong *sb (i sjekkhefte etc)* counterfoil; *US* stub.

talsmann *sb* advocate, spokesman; *gjøre seg til* ~ *for* advocate.

tam *adj* **1** *(ikke vill)* tame; **2** *(temmet)* domestic; *~duer* domestic pigeons.

tamp *sb (tauende)* rope end; *~en brenner! (lek)* you are getting warm!

tampong *sb* plug, tampon.

tandem *sb* tandem (bicycle).

tander *adj* delicate, frail.

tang *sb* **A** *(knipe~)* pincers *fl*; *(ild~, rørlegger~ etc)* tongs *fl*; *en* ~ a pair of pincers/tongs; **B** *(sjøgress)* seaweed.

tange *sb (land~)* tongue (of land).

tangent *sb* **1** *(i matematikk)* tangent; **2** *(på piano etc)* key; *hvite og svarte ~er* white and black keys. **tangent|bord** *sb* keyboard. **~instrument** *sb* keyboard instrument. **tangere** *vb* touch; be tangent to; ~ *en rekord* touch a record.

tango *sb* tango.

tank *sb (beholder, stridsvogn)* tank. **tank|bil** *sb* tanker; tank lorry. **~båt** *sb* tanker.

tanke *sb* **1** thought; *ha høye ~r om* think much of; *hun satt i dype ~r* she was sitting deep in thought; *jeg falt i ~r* I became lost in thought; **2** *(idé, innfall)* idea; *~n er/var å...* the idea is/was to...; *den ~n falt meg inn/streifet meg, jeg kom på den ~n* it struck me/occurred to me; *jeg har mine egne ~r om det* I have my own ideas about that. **tanke|eksperiment** *sb: som et ~eksperiment* for the sake of argument. **~full** *adj* thoughtful. **~gang** *sb (tenkemåte)* way of thinking. **~leser** *sb* mind/thought reader. **~lesning** *sb* mind/thought reading. **~løs** *adj* thoughtless. **~løshet** *sb* thoughtlessness. **~overføring** *sb* telepathy. **~strek** *sb* dash. **~vekkende** *adj* thought-provoking; suggestive.

tank|fart *sb* tanker shipping. **~skip** *sb* tanker. **~vogn** *sb* tanker; tank lorry.

tann *sb* tooth; *bite tennene sammen* clench one's teeth; *felle tenner* shed one's (milk) teeth; *føle en på tennene* sound somebody; *få blod på* ~ taste blood; *få tenner* cut one's teeth; *hun hakket tenner* her teeth were chattering; *skjære tenner* gnash/grind one's teeth; *tennene mine løp i vann* my mouth watered. **tann|behandling** *sb* dental treatment. **~byll** *sb* gumboil. **~børste** *sb* tooth-brush. **~felling** *sb* shedding of (milk) teeth. **~gard** *sb* row of teeth. **~hjul** *sb* cogwheel, gear. **~kjøtt** *sb* gum. **~krem** *sb* tooth-paste. **~lege** *sb* dentist. **~pasta** = *~krem*. **~pine** *sb* toothache. **~regulering** *sb* orthodontics. **~råte** *sb* tooth decay; (dental) caries. **~verk** *sb* toothache.

tante *sb* aunt.

tap *sb* loss; *lide svære/tunge* ~ suffer heavy losses; *selge med* ~ sell at a loss. **tape** *vb* lose; *de tapte slaget* they lost the battle; *han tapte pengene sine* he lost his money; *brevene gikk tapt* the letters were lost. **taper** *sb* loser.

tapet *sb* wallpaper; *bringe på ~et* bring up; introduce; *være på tapetet* be under discussion. **tapetsere** *vb* paper. **tapetserer** *sb* paperhanger.

tapp *sb* **1** *(plugg, tre~)* tenon; **2** *(spuns)* bung. **tappe** *vb (~ ut)* draw, tap; *(~ i)* run; *~ vann i et spann* run water into a pail.

tapper *adj* brave. **tapperhet** *sb* bravery, valour.

tare *sb* sea tangle.

tariff *sb* tariff. **tariffavtale** *sb* wage agreement.

tarm *sb (mennesketarmer)* intestines; *dgl* bowels; *(dgl og især om dyretarmer)* guts.

tarvelig *adj* **1** *(enkel, nøysom)* modest, plain, simple; **2** *(dårlig, ringe)* cheap, poor; **3** *(simpel)* common, low, mean; *det var ~ av ham* it was mean of him.

taske *sb (veske)* bag. **taskenspiller** *sb* conjurer, illusionist.

tasle, tasse *vb* shuffle; *(rasle)* rustle.

tast *sb* key. **tastatur** *sb* keyboard.

tater *sb* gipsy.

tatovere *vb* tattoo. **tatovering** *sb* tattoo.

tau *sb* rope. **tau|bane** *sb* aerial cableway. **~båt** *sb* tug, tugboat; towboat. **taue** *vb* tow.

taus *sb* silent. **taushet** *sb* **1** silence; *de lyttet i dyp ~* they listened in deep silence; **2** *(hemmeligholdelse)* secrecy, silence. **taushets|løfte** *sb* promise of secrecy. **~plikt** *sb* professional secrecy.

tau|stige *sb* rope-ladder. **~trekking** *sb* tug of war. **~verk** *sb koll* cordage, ropes.

tavle *sb* **1** *(skole~)* black-board; **2** *(sikrings~)* fuse box.

taxi *sb* cab, taxi.

te *sb* tea; *en kopp ~* a cup of tea; *dgl* a cuppa.

teater *sb* **1** *(om bygningen, institusjonen)* theatre; *US* theater; *vi var ofte i ~et* we often went to a theatre; **2** *(om scenen, dvs scenekunsten)* stage; *hun gikk til ~et (dvs til scenen)* she went on the stage. **teater|billett** *sb* theatre ticket. **~direktør** *sb* theatre manager. **~forestilling** *sb* theatrical performance. **~gal** *adj* stage-struck. **~gjenger** *sb* play-goer, theatre-goer. **~kikkert** *sb* opera-glasses *fl*. **~kritiker** *sb* dramatic critic. **~maler** *sb* scene painter. **~plakat** *sb* playbill. **~publikum** *sb koll* play-goers. **~sal, ~salong** *sb* auditorium. **~stykke** *sb* play. **teatralsk** *adj* theatrical.

te|blad *sb* tea leaf. **~boks** *sb* tea caddy.

teddybjørn *sb* teddy bear.

teft *sb* scent; *få ~en av* get wind of; *ha fin ~* have a good nose.

tegl|stein *sb* tile. **~verk** *sb* brick-field.

tegn *sb* **1** sign; *et godt ~* a good sign; *gjøre ~ til (noen)* make a sign to (somebody); *på et gitt ~* at/on a given sign; *som ~ på* in token of; **2** *(skille~)* (punctuation) mark; *sette ~* punctuate. **tegne** *vb* **1** draw; *hun ~t et portrett av ham* she drew a portrait of him; **2** *~ seg (for et bestemt beløp etc)* put down one's name (for a certain amount of money etc); **3** *det ~r til å bli varmt/en varm dag* it promises to be a hot day. **tegne|-bestikk** *sb* drawing-set. **~blokk** *sb* drawing-pad. **~blyant** *sb* drawing-pencil. **~blokk, ~bok** *sb* sketch-book. **~brett** *sb* drawing-board. **~film** *sb* (animated) cartoon. **~lærer** *sb* drawing/art master. **tegner** *sb* **1** *(på arkitekt- eller ingeniørkontor)* draughtsman; **2** *(kunstner)* black-and-white artist; **3** *(vittighetstegner)* cartoonist. **tegne|sal** *sb* classroom for drawing. **~serie** *sb* comic strip; strip cartoon. **~stift** *sb* drawing-pin. **~time** *sb* drawing lesson. **tegning** *sb* drawing; *(arbeids~ også)* plan; *en ~ av et tre* a drawing of a tree; *en ~ til en bygning* a plan of a building. **tegnsetning** *sb* punctuation.

teig *sb* strip of field.

teine *sb* fish pot; *(hummer~)* lobster pot.

teint *sb* complexion, colour.

te|kanne *sb* tea-pot. **~kjele** *sb* tea-kettle. **~kjøkken** *sb* kitchenette.

tekke *vb (legge tak på)* roof; *(~ med strå)* thatch; *et stråtekt hus* a thatched house.

tekkelig *adj* decent, nice, proper.

tekniker *sb* technician. **teknikk** *sb* **1** *(fremgangsmåte)* technique; method; *vi måtte lære en ny ~* we had to learn a new technique; **2** *(praktisk dyktighet)* skill, technique; **3** *(~ som fag)* engineering. **teknisk** *adj* technical. **teknologi** *sb* technology. **teknologisk** *adj* technological.

tekst *sb* text; *(billed~)* caption; *(film~)* subtitles; *(sang~, vise~)*. **tekste** write a text for; *(film)* subtitle.

tekstil *sb* textile. **tekstil|arbeider** *sb* textile worker. **~fabrikk** *sb* textile factory, mill. **~industri** *sb* textile industry.

teksting *sb (av film etc)* subtitles; subtitling.

tekst-tv *sb* teletext.

tele *sb: det er ~ i jorden* the ground is frozen/frostbound.

telefaks *sb* telefax.

telefon *sb* telephone; *dgl* phone; *det er ~ til deg* you are wanted on the phone; *jeg fortalte ham det i ~en* I told him over/on the telephone. **telefonere** *vb* telephone; *dgl* phone; *jeg telefonerte (til) henne* I (tele)-phoned her/rang her up. **telefon|apparat** *sb* telephone (apparatus). **~automat** *sb* coin-operated telephone; (public) call box; *US* pay phone. **~beskjed** *sb* telephone message. **~forbindelse** *sb* telephone connection. **~katalog** *sb* telephone directory. **~kiosk** *sb* (public) call box. **~nummer** *sb* (tele)phone number. **~oppringing** *sb* telephone) call. **~samtale** *sb* call; telephone conversation. **~sentral** *sb* (telephone) exchange. **~stolpe** *sb* telephone pole. **~svarer** *sb* answering machine.

telegraf *sb* telegraph. **telegrafere** *vb* telegraph, wire; *(over hav)* cable. **telegrafisk** *adj* telegraphic; *~ svar* reply by cable/wire; telegraphic reply. **telegrafist** *sb* telegraphist; telegraph/wireless operator. **telegraf|stasjon** *sb* telegraph station. **~stolpe** *sb* telegraph pole. **telegram** *sb* telegram, wire; *(over hav)* cable; *(radio~)* radiogram; wireless message. **telegram|adresse** *sb* telegraphic address. **~blankett** *sb* telegram form. **~byrå** *sb* news agency.

telehiv(ning) *sb* frost heaving.

telekommunikasjon *sb* telecommunication.

teleks *sb* telex.

tele|linse, ~objektiv *sb* telephoto lens; teleobjective. **~pati** *sb* telepathy. **~patisk** *adj* telepathic. **~skop** *sb* telescope. **~skopisk** *adj* telescopic. **~visjon** *sb* television.

telle *vb* count; *~ penger* count one's money; *~ til ti* count (up) to ten. **telleapparat** *sb* turnstile counter. **teller** *sb (i brøk)* numerator.

telt *sb* tent; *reise/slå opp et ~* pitch/put up a tent; *ta ned ~et* strike the tent. **teltduk** *sb* tent canvas. **telte** *vb* **1** *(slå opp telt)* pitch/set up a tent; **2** *(bo i telt)* camp. **telt|leir** *sb* camp of tents. **~plass** *sb* camping-ground. **~plugg** *sb* tent peg. **~stang** *sb* tent pole. **~tur** *sb: dra på ~tur* go camping.

tema *sb* theme. **tematisk** *adj* thematic.

temme *vb* tame; *(gjøre til husdyr)* domesticate.

temmelig *adv (især om noe negativt)* rather; *(især om noe positivt)* fairly, somewhat; quite; *dgl* pretty; *~ dum* rather stupid; *~ oppvakt* fairly bright.

tempel *sb* temple.

temperament *sb* temperament; *en kvinne med ~* a woman of temperament. **temperamentsfull** *adj* spirited, temperamental.

temperatur *sb* temperature. **temperere** *vb* temper; *den tempererte sone* the temperate zone.

tempo *sb* speed; pace, rate; *i (et) rolig ~* at a quiet pace.

tendens *sb* tendency, trend; *han har en ~ til tungsinn* he has a tendency to melancholy; *prisene har fremdeles (en) stigende ~* the trend of prices is still upwards. **tendensiøs** *adj* tendentious, bias(s)ed. **tendere** *vb* tend; *~ mot* tend towards.

tenke *vb* **1** think; *~ (deg om) før du svarer* think before you answer; *er dyr i stand til å ~* are animals able to think? **2** *(ha til hensikt)* mean; intend, plan; think of; *jeg har tenkt å skrive en bok om det* I intend/mean to write/have been thinking of writing a book about it; **3** *(forestille seg)* fancy, imagine, think; *tenk bare!* imagine! just fancy/think! *tenk hva som kunne ha hendt* just imagine/think what might have happened; **4** *(uttrykk)* *~* **etter** consider; *la meg ~ etter* let me consider; *~* **over** think over; *jeg skal ~ over det* I'll consider it/think it over; *~* **på** think about/of; *hva ~r du på?* what are you thinking about/of? *~* **seg** *(anta)* suppose; *la oss ~ oss at han har rett* let us suppose he is right; *~* **seg om** consider, reflect, think; *hun tenkte seg om et øyeblikk* she considered for a moment; *jeg må ha tid til å ~ meg om* I must have time to think; *uten å ~ seg om* without thinking; *~* **seg til** imagine, guess; *det er lett å ~ seg til virkningen* it is easy to imagine the effect; *~* **ut** think out; design, devise; invent; *hun tenkte ut en ny metode* she devised a new method; *~* **ved** *seg selv* think to oneself. **tenkelig** *adj* imaginable, conceivable. **tenkemåte** *sb* way of thinking. **tenker** *sb* thinker. **tenkesett** = *tenkemåte*. **tenkning** *sb* thinking, thought. **tenksom** *adj* thoughtful. **tenkt** *adj, pp* imaginary; *en ~ linje* an imaginary line; *boken er ~ som en gave* the book is intended as a present.

tenne 1 light; *de tente opp (i ovnen)* they lighted/lit a fire; *han tente fyr på huset* he set fire to the house; *jeg tente en fyrstikk* I struck a match; **2** *(elektrisk lys)* switch/turn on. **tenner** *sb (sigarett~)* lighter. **tennhette** *sb* percussion cap. **tenning** *sb* ignition.

tennis *sb* tennis. **tennisbane** *sb* tennis-court.

tenn|plugg *sb* spark(ing) plug. **~sats** *sb* **1** percussion cap; **2** *(på fyrstikk)* matchhead.

tenor *sb (stemme)* tenor. **tenorstemme** *sb* tenor voice.

tentamen *sb* rehearsal examination.

tenåring *sb* teenager.

teolog *sb* theologian. **teologi** *sb* theology. **teologisk** *adj* theological.

teoretisk *adj* theoretic(al). **teori** *sb* theory; *i ~en* in theory; theoretically.

teppe *sb* **1** *(gulv~)* carpet; *(mindre ~)* rug; **2** *(ull~, især til seng)* blanket; **3** *(vegg~)* (piece of) tapestry; **4** *(scene~)* curtain; *~t går opp* the curtain rises. **teppebanker** *sb* carpet beater.

terapeut *sb* therapist. **terapeutisk** *adj* therapeutic. **terapi** *sb* therapeutics.

terge *vb* tease, provoke.

termin *sb* term. **terminologi** *sb* terminology.

termometer *sb* thermometer. **termos, termosflaske** *sb* thermos flask. **termostat** *sb* thermostat.

ternet(e) *adj* chequered, check. **terning** *sb* cube; *(til spill)* die; *de spilte ~* they threw dice. **terning|kast** *sb* throw of the dice. **~spill** *sb* game of dice.

terpe *vb* cram, grind.

terpentin *sb* turpentine.

terrasse *sb* terrace.

terreng *sb* country, ground; *bakkete/flatt ~* hilly/flat ground; *tape/vinne ~* lose/gain ground. **terreng|løp** *sb* cross-country race. **~løper** *sb* cross-country runner.

terrier *sb* terrier.

terrin *sb* tureen.

territorial|farvann *sb* territorial waters. **~grense** *sb* limit of territorial waters. **territorium** *sb* territory; *på norsk ~* in Norwegian territory.

terror *sb* terror. **terrorisere** *vb* terrorize. **terrorisme** *sb* terrorism. **terrorist** *sb* terrorist. **terroristisk** *adj: ~ virksomhet* terrorist activities; *en ~ handling* an act of terrorism.

terskel *sb* threshold.

terte *sb* tart.

terylene *sb* terylene.

te|servise *sb* tea-set, tea-service. **~sil** *sb* tea-strainer. **~skje** *sb* tea-spoon; *en ~skje sukker* a tea-spoonful of sugar.

tess *adj: ikke noe ~* no good; *ikke stort ~* not much good.

testament(e) *sb* **1** will, testament; *han opprettet ~* he made his/a will; *ved ~* by will; **2** *(i Bibelen) Det gamle/nye ~* the Old/New Testament. **testamentarisk** *adj* testamentary; *~ gave* legacy. **testamentere**

vb bequeath; leave (by will); *hun testamenterte meg 5000 pund* she bequeathed/left me £5000. **testator** *sb* testator. **testimonium** *sb* testimonial.

tet *sb: gå i ~en* lead the way; *ta ~en* take the lead.

tett *adj, adv* **1** *(nær)* close; *~ bak* close behind; *~ sammen* close together; *~ ved* close by; *rykk ~ere sammen!* come closer together! **2** *(motsatt lett eller spredt)* dense, thick; *~ befolket* densely populated; *~ tåke* heavy (dense, thick) fog; *en ~ skog* a dense wood; **3** *(motsatt utett)* tight; *taket er ikke ~* the roof is not watertight; **4** *holde ~* keep one's tongue; keep a secret; keep mum. **tette** *vb* make tight; tighten; *(~ igjen)* clog; *(~ igjen en lekkasje)* stop. **tetthet** *sb* density, tightness; closeness. **tett|pakket** *adj* tightly packed; *(av mennesker)* crowded. **~sittende** *adj* tight-fitting. **~skrevet** *adj* closely written. **~vokst** *adj* squarely built; stocky.

tev *sb (stank)* stench, stink.

tevarmer *sb* (tea) cosy.

tevle *vb* compete. **tevling** *sb* competition.

tevogn *sb* tea trolly/wagon.

tid *sb* **1** time; *(tidspunkt også)* moment, hour; *(tidsalder også)* age; *(i grammatikk)* tense; *~en er kort* time is short; *~ er penger* time is money; *den ~, den sorg* it is no good looking ahead for trouble; *dårlige ~er* hard/bad times; *en times ~* an hour's time; an hour or so; *fra ~ til annen* from time to time; *fra uminnelige ~er* from time immemorial; *følge med ~en* keep up/move with the times; keep abreast of the times; *har du ~ et øyeblikk?* can you spare me a moment? *håpe på bedre ~er* hope for better times; *i ~er som disse* in times like the present; *i lang ~* for a long time; for long; *i rett(e) ~* in time; *i den senere ~* of late; *jeg har ikke ~ (til det)* I have no time for that; I can't spare the time; *neste år på denne ~en* this time next year; *om et års ~* in a year or so; *på den ~en* at that time; *på samme ~* at the same time; *på ubestemt ~* for an indefinite/unspecified period; *siden den ~* since then; *ta ~en (ved konkurranser)* time; **2** *(andre uttrykk)* **alle ~ers** *sjanse* the chance of a lifetime; *det var alle ~ers!* we had a topping time! it was smashing/splendid! **(be)nytte ~en** make the most of/make good use of one's time; **for ~en** at present; for the time being; **forut** *for sin ~* ahead/in advance of one's time/age; **fordrive ~en** pass the time; **før i ~en** formerly; *når jeg* **får** *~* when I get the time/can spare the time; **gi seg** *(god) ~* take one's time; **god** *~* plenty of time; *gode ~er* times of prosperity; **i ~e** in time; **med ~en** in time; **om kort ~** shortly, soon; *det er* **på ~e** it is about time; it is high time; **somme ~er** sometimes; **til alle ~er** at all times; *til alle døgnets ~er* at all hours; *alt* **til sin ~** all in good time! one thing at a time! *til sine ~er* at times; sometimes; **vinne ~** gain time; *prøve å vinne ~* play for time.

tidende *sb* news, tidings.

tidevann *sb* tide.

tid|feste *vb* date. **~kort** se *tidsfordriv*. **~krevende** *adj* time-consuming.

tidlig *adj, adv* early; *i morgen ~* tomorrow morning. **tidligere** *adj, adv* **1** *(motsatt senere)* earlier; *påsken faller ~ i år* Easter is earlier this year; *~ bodde vi i London* we used to live in London; **2** *(forutgående)* previous; *ved en ~ anledning* on a previous occasion; **3** *(forhenværende)* former; *vår ~ direktør* our former manager. **tidligst** *adj, adv* earliest; *~ kl. 8* at 8 o'clock at the earliest; *hennes ~e barndom* her earliest childhood.

tids|adverb *sb* adverb of time. **~alder** *sb* age. **~avsnitt** *sb* period. **~begrenset** *adj* limited (in time). **~bisetning** *sb* temporal clause. **~fordriv** *sb* pastime; *som ~fordriv* to pass the time. **~frist** *sb* time limit. **~innstilt** *adj: ~innstilt bombe* time bomb. **~konjunksjon** *sb* conjunction of time. **~messig** *adj* modern; up to date. **~nok** *adv* in time; *det er ~nok i overmorgen* the day after tomorrow will be all right. **~nød** *sb: være i ~nød* be pressed for time. **~punkt** *sb* moment, time. **~regning** *sb* chronology. **~rom** *sb* period. **~skrift** *sb* periodical.

tidtaker *sb* timekeeper.

tie *vb* be/keep silent; be quiet; *(slutte å snakke)* become silent; stop talking; *ti stille!* be silent!

tiende *sb (avgift)* tithe.

tiger *sb* tiger. **tiger|sprang** *sb* tiger leap. **~unge** *sb* tiger cub.

tigge *vb* beg; *~ fra dør til dør, gå fra dør til dør og ~* beg from door to door; *~ om mat* beg for food; *~ penger av* begged money from. **tigger** *sb* beggar. **tiggeri** *sb* begging. **tiggermunk** *sb* mendicant friar.

tikamp *sb* decathlon.

tikke *vb* tick; *klokken ~r* the clock ticks.

til I *adv* **1** *(ytterligere)* another, more; *en gang ~* once more; *han fikk en kopp te ~* he had another cup of tea; *hun gav meg ti pund ~* she gave me another ten pounds; **2** *(uttrykk)* **av og ~** now and then; sometimes; **~ og med** *(endog)* even, too; *jeg lånte ham ~ og med mine egne bøker* I even lent him my own books; *(medregnet) ~ og med torsdag* till Thursday inclusive; *fra mandag ~ og med torsdag (også)* from Monday through Thursday; **II** *konj* till, until; *vent her ~ jeg kommer* wait here until I come; **III** *prep* **1** *(om retning)* to; *dra/reise ~ London* go to London; *fra Oslo til Lillehammer* from Oslo to Lillehammer; *holde til høyre* keep to the right; **2** (om bestemmelsested ved vb som *depart, leave, start* osv) for; *han reiste ~ India* he left for India; **3** *(om ankomst)* at; *(til land og store byer)* in; *hun kom ~ Dover/~ stasjonen* she arrived at Dover/at the station; *jeg kom ~ Paris/~ Frankrike* I arrived in France/in London; *ved sin ankomst ~ byen/~ London* on her (his etc) arrival at the town/in London; **4** *(om tid: inntil)* till, until; *vent ~ neste sommer!* wait till next summer! **5** (etter *from*) till, to; *fra tirsdag ~ fredag* from Tuesday to Friday; *fra morgen ~ kveld* from morning till night; **6** *(om tidspunkt)* at; next; for; *de kommer ~ påske* they will arrive at Easter; *han kommer ~ sommeren* he will arrive next summer; *møtet ble arrangert ~ klokken to* the meeting was arranged for 2 o'clock; **7** *(bestemt ~)* for; *~ bruk i kjøkkenet* for use in the kitchen; *her er et brev ~ deg* here is a letter for you; **8** *(ved tilhørighet)* of; *faren ~ guttene* the father of the boys; *nøkkelen ~ rommet* the key of the door.

tilbake *adv* **1** back, behind; *jeg fikk ~ boken min* I got my book back; **2** *(til overs)* left; *hun hadde fem pund ~* she had £5 left. **tilbake|betale** *vb* pay back. **~betaling** *sb* repayment. **~blikk** *sb* retrospect, review. **~fall** *sb* relapse. **~gang** *sb* decline. **~holden** *adj* reserved; *(beskjeden)* modest. **~kalle** *vb* call back; recall; *(ta tilbake)* take back; withdraw. **~komst** *sb* return; *ved hans ~komst* at his return; *etter hans ~komst* on his return. **~legge** *vb* cover; *et ~lagt stadium* a thing of the past. **~reise** *sb* return journey. **~skritt** *sb* step backward(s). **~slag** *sb* reaction, setback. **~stående** *adj* backward. **~tog** *sb* retreat. **~trekning** *sb* withdrawal, retreat. **~trukket** *adj* retired. **~tur** *sb* return trip; way back. **~vei** *sb* way back.

tilbe *vb* adore; *(også religiøst: dyrke)* worship; *de tilbad solen* they worshipped the sun; *han tilbad sin mor* he adored/worshipped his mother. **tilbedelse** *sb* adoration, worship. **tilbeder** *sb* admirer; *(religiøst)* worshipper.

tilbehør *sb koll* accessories.

til|berede *vb* prepare, make; *(om mat også)* cook. **~beredelse** *sb* preparation.

tilblivelse *sb* coming into existence; making, origin.

tilbringe *vb* spend, pass; *hun tilbrakte natten med å lese* she spent the night reading.

tilbud *sb* offer; *han aksepterte ~et* he accepted the offer; *hun fikk ~ om en stilling* she was offered a job/post. **tilby** *vb* offer; *de tilbød meg skyss* they offered me a lift; *hun tilbød seg å gjøre det* she offered to do it; *vi tilbød vår hjelp* we offered our help.

tilbygg *sb* extension.

tilbørlig *adj* due, proper; *~ aktelse* due respect; *ta ~ hensyn til* pay due regard to.

tilbøyelig *adj* disposed, inclined; *~ til (også)* given/liable to; *jeg er ~ til å tro det* I am inclined to believe it. **tilbøyelighet** *sb* disposition, inclination; tendency; *han fulgte sine ~er* he followed his inclinations.

tildele *vb* allot, award. **tildeling** *sb* allotment, award.

tilegne *vb: ~ seg* possess oneself of; take possession of; *(især om kunnskaper etc)* acquire.

tilfalle *vb: ~ noen* fall on somebody's lot.

tilfeldig *adj* **1** chance, fortuitous; accidental, casual; *et ~ møte* a chance/fortuitous meeting; *rent ~ (adv)* (quite) accidentally; **2** *(leilighetsvis)* occasional. **tilfeldighet** *sb* chance, fortuity; accident; *det var en ren ~* it was a mere chance; *ved en ~* by a mere chance; quite accidentally. **tilfeldigvis** *adv* accidentally; by accident/chance; *(ofte omskrives med)* happen to; *jeg så ham ~* I happened to see him. **tilfelle** *sb* **1** case, instance; *i de fleste ~r* in most cases; *i ~ de skulle komme* in case (that) they should come; **2** *(skjebne)* chance; *la ~t råde* let chance decide; *overlate til ~t* leave it to chance; *ved et ~* by chance; *vi fikk se det ved et ~* we happened to be there.

tilflukt *sb* refuge; *han søkte ~ i kjelleren* he took refuge in the cellar. **tilflukts|rom** *sb* air-raid shelter. **~sted** *sb* refuge, retreat.

tilfreds *adj* satisfied; *(fornøyd)* contented; *(bare som predikatsord)* content; *de var ~ med arbeidet mitt* they were satisfied with my work; *et ~ smil* a contented smile; *jeg er ~ med dette* I am content with this. **tilfredshet** *sb* satisfaction; *(følelse av ~)* content(ment); *det vakte ~* it gave satisfaction. **tilfredsstille** *vb* satisfy; *ingenting ~r ham* nothing satisfies him. **tilfredsstillende** *adj* satisfactory. **tilfredsstillelse** *sb* satisfaction.

tilførsel *sb (forsyning)* supply.

tilføye *vb* **1** *(føye til)* add; *hun tilføyde at...* she added that ...; **2** *(volde)* cause; *han tilføyde meg stor skade* he caused me great damage. **tilføyelse** *sb* addition.

tilgi forgive, pardon; *han tilgav sine fiender* he forgave his enemies. **tilgivelig** *adj* pardonable. **tilgivelse** *sb* forgiveness, pardon; *han bad henne om ~* he asked her forgiveness/pardon; *han fikk ~* he was pardoned.

tilgjengelig *adj* accessible; *~ for publikum* open to the public.

tilgjort *adj* affected.

tilgodehavende *sb* outstanding account/debt(s); amount due to one; *mitt ~* the amount due to me; the balance in my favour.

tilhenger *sb* **1** *(~ av person)* follower; *(~ av sak)* supporter; *være (en) ~ av* believe in; **2** *(tilhengervogn)* trailer.

tilhold, tilholdssted *sb* haunt, resort.

tilhøre *vb* belong to; *huset ~r min gamle tante* the house belongs to my old aunt. **tilhører** *sb* listener, hearer; *~ne (også)* the audience; *blant ~ne* among the audience.

tilintet|gjøre *vb* annihilate, destroy; *alt ble ~gjort* everything was destroyed. **~gjørelse** *sb* destruction.

tilje *sb* floorboard.

tiljuble *vb* cheer.

tilkalle *vb* send for; *~ hjelp* call in assistance/help; *(en) lege/politiet ble tilkalt* a doctor was/the police were sent for.

tilkjempe seg *vb* win; *~ ~ seieren* carry off the victory.

tilkjenne *vb* award; *hun ble tilkjent erstatning* she was awarded damages.

tilkjennegi *vb (gi uttrykk for)* make known; declare.

tilknytning *sb* connection; *i ~ til* in connection with.

tilkomme *vb: det ~r ikke oss å dømme* it is not for us to judge; *han fikk det som tilkom ham* he got what he was entitled to/had a right to. **tilkommende** *adj: hans/hennes ~* his/her future wife/husband.

tillate *vb* allow, permit; let; *røyking er ikke tillatt her* smoking is not allowed/permitted here; *~r De at jeg røyker?* do you mind if I smoke? *tillat meg å hjelpe Dem (meget høflig)* please, allow/will you allow me to help you; *vi ~r oss å meddele (meget stivt i forretningsbrev)* we beg to inform. **tillatelse** *sb* permission; *hun bad om ~ til å gå* she asked permission to go/to leave; *med Deres ~* with your permission; *vi fikk ~ til å gå* we were allowed/permitted to go/leave.

tillegg *sb* addition; *(supplement)* supplement; *(lønnstillegg)* rise; increase of salary; *US* raise; *i ~ til* in addition to. **tillegge** *vb: ~ stor betydning* attach great importance to. **tilleggs|bevilgning** *sb* additional grant. **~porto** *sb* surcharge.

tillempe *vb: ~ etter/til* adapt to. **tillemp(n)ing** *sb* adaptation.

tillike *adv* also, too; besides; as well; *~ med* together with.

tillit *sb* confidence, trust; faith; *jeg har/nærer ingen ~ til dem* I have no confidence/faith in them; *jeg har ~ til ham* I have faith in him; I trust him; *jeg har mistet ~en til henne* I have lost confidence/faith in her. **tillits|full** *adj* **1** *(mot mennesker)* trusting, trustful; **2** *(med hensyn til fremtiden)* confident; full of confidence; **~kvinne, ~mann, ~person** *sb* representative; *(i fagforening: klubbleder)* shop steward. **~verv** *sb* honorary office. **~votum** *sb* vote of confidence. **tillitvekkende** *adj: være ~* inspire confidence.

tillokkende *adj* attractive.

tillyse *vb: ~ et møte* announce a meeting.

tillært *adj* acquired; *(stundom)* artificial.

tilløp *sb* **1** *(usikker begynnelse) ~ til uro* signs of unrest; *et ~ til smil* the ghost of a smile; **2** *(til hopp)* starting run; **3** *(bielv)* tributary.

tilmålt *adj* allotted.

tilnavn *sb* epithet; *(oppnavn)* nickname.

tilnærmelser *sb fl* approaches, overtures; *gjøre ~ til (en dame)* make advances to; make passes at. **tilnærmelsesvis** *adv: ikke ~* not nearly; far from. **tilnærmet** *adj* approximate; *~ riktig* approximately correct.

til overs se *overs.*

tilpasning *sb* adaptation, adjustment.

til pass *adv: det er ~ ~ til deg!* serves you right!

tilpasse *vb: ~ seg nye forhold* adapt/adjust (oneself) to new conditions.

til|regnelig *adj* sane. **~regnelighet** *sb* sanity.

tilreisende *sb* visitor.

tilrette|legge *vb* arrange, prepare. **~vise** *vb* reprimand, rebuke. **~visning** *sb* reprimand.

tilrop *sb* cry, shout; *(bifalls~)* cheering; *(hånlig ~)* jeer, taunt.

tilrå(de) *vb* advise, recommend. **tilrådelig** *adj* advisable; *ikke ~* inadvisable. **tilråding** *sb* recommendation; *(innstilling også)* proposal.

tilse *vb (ha tilsyn med)* look after; inspect.

tilsetning *sb* admixture; *(~ av krydder etc)* seasoning. **tilsette** *vb* **1** *(sette til)* add; **2** *(ansette)* appoint.

tilside|sette *vb (ikke ense)* disregard, ignore; take no notice of; *(på krenkende måte)* slight; *hun følte seg ~satt* she felt slighted. **~settelse** *sb* disregard, neglect.

tilsig *sb* inflow, influx.

tilsiktet *adj* deliberate, intended, intentional; *det var ikke ~* it was unintentional.

tilskadekommen *adj: de tilskadekomne* the injured persons.

tilskudd *sb* contribution, grant, subsidy.

tilskuer *sb* onlooker, spectator; *(tilfeldig ~)* bystander; *~ne (i teater etc)* the audience; *(på idrettsstevne)* the crowd.

tilskynde *vb* prompt, urge. **tilskyndelse** *sb* incitement, instigation.

tilslutning *sb* **1** *(forbindelse)* connection; *i ~ til* in connection with; **2** *(samtykke)* consent; *de gav sin ~* they gave their consent; **3** *(bifall)* approval, response; *din plan har min ~* your plan has my approval; *appellen fikk stor ~* the appeal met with great response; **4** *(fremmøte)* attendance.

tilsløre *vb* **1** *(dekke med slør)* veil; *orientalske kvinner ~r ofte ansiktet* Oriental women often veil their faces; **2** *(forsøke å skjule)* conceal, hide, veil.

tilsnikelse *sb* deliberate misrepresentation.

tilspisset *adj: en ~ situasjon* a critical/tense situation.

tilstand *sb* condition; state (of things).

tilstede|værelse *sb* presence; *din ~værelse er nødvendig* your presence is requested. **~værende** *adj* present; *de ~* those present; *en ~* a person (who is/was) present.

tilstelning *sb* arrangement; *(festlig ~)* entertainment.

tilstoppe se *tette (igjen).*

tilstrebe *vb* aim at; strive for.

tilstrekkelig *adj* enough, sufficient; *det er ~ (med) mat* there is food enough; *(som adv) ~ stor* large sufficiently large;

tilstrømning *sb* influx; *det var stor ~ av skuelystne* there was a great influx of sightseers; *det var stor ~ til forestillingen* the play drew crowded audiences.

til|støte *vb* happen to; *jeg håper det ikke har ~støtt ham noe* I hope nothing has happened to him. **~støtende** *adj* adjacent, adjoining; *~støtende rom* adjoining room(s).

til|stå *vb (bekjenne)* confess; *han ~stod for meg at han ...* he confessed to me that he ... **~ståelse** *sb* confession.

tilsvarende *adj* corresponding.

til|syn *sb* supervision; *føre/ha ~syn med* look after; be in charge of; *under ~syn av* under the supervision of. **~synekomst** *sb* appearance. **~synelatende** *adj* seeming; *(adv)* apparently, seemingly; *han var ~synelatende ærlig* he was seemingly loyal; he seemed to be loyal.

til|ta *vb* increase; grow larger (better, worse etc). **~tagende** increasing. **~tak** *sb* **1** *(foretagende)* enterprise, undertaking; *treffe ~tak* take steps/measures; **2**

(anstrengelse, initiativ) effort; *det er sånt ~tak å begynne med leksene* it is such an effort to set about the homework. **~takslyst** *sb* drive, initiative; enterprise.

til|tale I *sb* **1** *(henvendelse, ord som rettes til en)* address; *gi svar på ~tale* give tit for tat; **2** *(jur: anklage)* charge, prosecution; *reise ~tale mot* bring a charge against; indict; **II** *vb* **1** *(henvende seg til)* address; speak to; *du må aldri glemme å ~tale ham (som) doktor* you must never forget to address him Doctor; *han kom bort og ~talte meg på gaten* he came up and spoke to me in the street; **2** *(jur: anklage)* charge, prosecute; *den ~talte* the accused; *hun ble ~talt for mord* she was charged with murder; **3** *(behage)* be attractive to; please; *det ~taler meg* I like it. **~talebenk** *sb* dock; *sitte på ~talebenken* stand trial. **~talebeslutning** *sb* indictment. **~talende** *adj* attractive, engaging, lik(e)able. **~talepunkt** *sb* count (of indictment).

tiltenke *vb* intend/mean for.

til|tre *vb: ~tre et embete* take up an appointment/a post; *(om statsråd etc)* take office; *(om president også)* be inaugurated. **~tredelse** *sb: ~tredelse av et embete* accession to an office; *presidentens ~tredelse* the inauguration of the President.

til|trekke *vb* attract; *~trekke seg oppmerksomheten* attract attention. **~trekkende** *adj* attractive; *hun har et ~trekkende vesen* she has attractive manners. **~trekning** *sb* attraction; *øve ~trekning på noen* attract somebody; have an attraction on somebody. **~trekningskraft** *sb* attractive force, power of attraction.

tiltro 1 *sb* confidence, faith, trust; *ha ~ til* have confidence/faith in; trust; **2** *vb: det ~r jeg dem så gjerne* I would not put it past them.

tiltvinge *vb: ~ seg adgang til et hus* force an entrance/one's way into a house.

til|vant *adj: ~vante forestillinger* conventional ideas.

tilveiebringe *vb* provide, procure.

tilvekst *sb* increase, growth.

tilvenning *sb* habituation; *(til narkotika)* addiction.

tilvirke *vb* make, manufacture, produce. **tilvirkning** *sb* making, manufacture, production.

tilværelse *sb* existence, life; *kampen for ~n* the struggle for life/existence.

time *sb* **1** hour; *en ~s tid* an hour or so; *for en ~ siden* an hour ago; *i en hel ~* for a full hour; *om en ~* in an hour; **2** *(undervisnings~)* lesson; *hun tok timer i russisk* she took lessons in Russian; *i ~n* during the lesson; **3** *(avtalt ~)* appointment; *tannlegen gav meg ~ klokken ti* the dentist gave me an appointment for 10 o'clock. **time|betaling** *sb* payment by the hour. **~betalt** *adj* paid by the hour. **~glass** *sb* hourglass. **~plan, ~tabell** *sb* timetable. **~seddel** *sb* time sheet. **~skriver** *sb* timekeeper.

tind *sb* **1** *(fjell~)* peak, summit; **2** *(~ på redskap)* tine; *(på gaffel)* prong. **tindebestiger** *sb* mountaineer.

tindre *sb* sparkle; *~nde stjerner* sparkling/twinkling stars; *øynene hans ~t av fryd* his eyes sparkled with joy.

tine *vb* thaw, melt.

ting *sb* **A** *(gjenstand etc)* thing; *(også)* object; *ingen~ (intet)* nothing; *kopper, skåler og andre ~* cups, saucers and other things/objects; *vi har andre ~ (annet) å gjøre* we have other things to do; **B 1** *forsamling, møte* ≈ parliament; *hist* moot; **2** *jur* assizes.

tinge *vb (bestille)* book, order.

tingest *sb* little thing; small object.

tingreise *sb* circuit.

tinn *sb (om metallet)* tin; *(om ting av tinn)* pewter.

tinnfolie *sb* tinfoil.

tinning *sb* temple.

tipp *sb* **A** *(på lastebil etc)* tipping/*US* dumping gear; *lastebil med ~* tipper; tip(ping) lorry; *US* dump(ing) truck; **B** *~ topp* first-rate; tiptop. **tippe** *vb* **A 1** *(~ over, velte)* topple; **2** *(tømme)* tip; **B 1** *(gjette)* tip; *~ vinneren* tip the winner; **2** *(~ i tippeselskap)* do the pools. **tippe|kupong** *sb* pools coupon. **~premie** *sb* pools prize. **tipper** *sb* pools punter. **tippeselskap** *sb* betting-pool. **tipping** *sb* doing the pools; *vinne i ~* win the pools; *vinne femti pund i ~* win £50 on the pools.

tippolde|far *sb* great-great-grandfather. **~foreldre** *sb* great-great-grandparents. **~mor** *sb* great-great-grandmother.

tippvogn *sb* tipcart.

tips *sb* tip, tip-off; *(drikkepenger)* tip.

tirre *vb* irritate, provoke, tease.

tirsdag *sb* Tuesday; *forrige ~* last Tuesday; *om ~en (hver ~)* on Tuesdays.

tiske *vb* whisper.

tispe *sb* bitch.

tiss *sb* pee, wee-wee. **tisse** *vb* pee, wee-wee.

tistel *sb* thistle.

titt A *adv* often; **B** *sb: ta en ~ på* take a look at. **titte** *vb* peep; *~ frem* peep out.

tittel *sb* title; *~en på en bok* the title of a book; *en bok med ~en «Teater»* a book entitled «Teater». **tittel|blad** *sb* title page. **~innehaver** *sb* title holder. **~kamp** *sb* championship/title match. **~rolle** *sb* title part/role.

titulere *vb: ~ (som)* address as.

tivoli *sb* amusement park; fun fair.

ti|år *sb* decade. **~årig, ~års** *adj* **1** *(om alder)* ten-year-old; of ten (years); *~års fødselsdag* tenth birthday; *en ~års pike* a girl of ten; **2** *(om varighet)* of ten years.

tja *adv* hm, well; weel, yes.

tjafs *sb* tuft, wisp; tangle. **tafset(e)** *adj* dishevelled, tangled.

tjene *vb* **1** *(gjøre tjeneste)* serve; *en kasse tjente som bord* a box served as a table; *han tjente hos en kjøpmann* he was in the service of a grocer; *jeg hadde tjent dem vel i over tretti år* I had served them well for over thirty years; **2** *~ penger* earn/make money; *hun tjente en formue/mange penger* she made a fortune/a lot of money; **3** *(uttrykk)* **~ på** profit by; make a profit by/on; **~ til**; *hva skal det ~ til* what is the good of that? *det ~r ikke til noe* it is of no use. **tjener** *sb* servant. **tjeneste** *sb* **1**

service; *han var i vår ~ i fem år* he was in our service for five years; *kan jeg være til ~?* can I be of service to you? **2** *(post)* duty; *politimannen hadde ~ fra kl. 8 til kl. 16* the policeman was on duty from 8 a.m. to 4 p.m.; **3** *(uttrykk) den ene ~n er den annen verd* one good turn deserves another; *gjøre noen en ~* do somebody a favour; *vil du gjøre meg den ~ å hente boken?* will you be so kind as to fetch me the book? **tjeneste|folk** *sb koll* servants. **~gjøre** *vb* serve. **~gutt** *sb* farm-hand. **~iver** *sb* zeal. **~jente** *sb* maid(servant). **~villig** *adj* helpful, obliging. **~villighet** *sb* helpfulness, obligingness.

tjenlig *adj* serviceable, useful.

tjern *sb* tarn; small lake.

tjor *sb* tether. **tjore** *vb* tether.

tjukka *sb* fatty. **tjukken** *sb* fatty; *(især US)* fatso. Se for øvrig *tykk*.

tjuv|perm *sb* absence without (official) leave. **~start** *sb* false start. **~starte** *vb* beat/jump the gun; make a false start. **~trene** *vb* train in secret. Se for øvrig *tyv etc*.

tjære *sb* tar. **tjære|bre** *vb* tar. **~brenner** *sb* tar maker. **~papp** *sb* tarred roofing felt.

to 1 *sb: det er godt ~ i dem* there is good stuff in them; **2** *tallord* two; *~ ganger* twice; *~ eller tre ganger* a couple of times; two or three times; *~-tre dager* a couple of days; two or three days; *begge ~* both (of them); *de ~* the two of them; *dere ~* you two; the two of you.

toalett *sb* toilet, lavatory; *offentlig ~* public convenience; *(US især)* rest room(s). **toalett|bord** *sb* toilet-table. **~etui** *sb* toilet-case. **~kommode** *sb* dressing-table. **~papir** *sb* toilet paper. **~saker** *sb* toilet requisites. **~speil** *sb* toilet mirror. **~såpe** *sb* toilet soap.

tobakk *sb* tobacco. **tobakks|forretning** *sb* tobacconist's (shop). **~handler** *sb* tobacconist. **~pipe** *sb* (tobacco) pipe. **~røyk** *sb* tobacco smoke.

toddi *sb* toddy.

toer *sb* two; *(i kortstokk, på terning)* deuce. **toetasjes** *adj* two-storeyed; *~ buss* double-decker.

tofte *sb* thwart.

tog *sb* **1** *(jernbane~)* train; *~ til Bergen* trains for Bergen; *han reiste med/tok ~et* he went by train/took the train; *på ~et* in/on the train; **2** *(opp~)* parade, procession; *gå i ~* parade; join a march; **3** *(felt~)* campaign; *Napoleons ~ til Russland* Napoleon's Russian campaign. **tog|bytte** *sb* change of trains. **~forbindelse** *sb* train service. **~reise** *sb* journey by train. **~rute** *sb* railway timetable.

tokt *sb* **1** *(mil)* mission; **2** *(sjø~)* cruise.

toleranse *sb* tolerance, permissiveness. **tolerant** *adj* tolerant, permissive. **tolerere** *vb* tolerate.

tolk *sb* interpreter; *han var ~ for meg* he was interpreter to me. **tolke** *vb* interpret, translate; explain. **tolkning** *sb* interpretation.

toll *sb* **1** *(avgift)* duty; **2** *(import~)* customs; *(~avgift)* customs duty; *de la ~ på varene* they put a duty on the goods; *høy/lav ~* heavy/low duty; *vi måtte betale ~ på vinen* we had to pay duty on the wine. **toll|avgift** *sb* customs duty. **~beskyttelse** *sb* protective duties. **~betjent** *sb* customs officer. **~bod** *sb* custom-house.

tolle|gang *sb* oarlock, rowlock. **~kniv** *sb* sheath knife. **~pinne** *sb* thole, thole-pin.

toller *sb* customs officer; *(i Bibelen)* publican. **toll|fri** *adj* duty-free; *(som predikatsord også)* exempt from/free of duty. **~grense** *sb* customs frontier. **~krig** *sb* tariff wall/barrier. **~pliktig** *adj* dutiable. **~sats** *sb* rate of duty; tariff rate. **~union** *sb* customs union. **~vesenet** *sb* the Customs. **~visitasjon** *sb* customs examination.

tom *adj* empty; *~e løfter* empty promises; *leiligheten står ~* the flat is empty/vacant.

tomat *sb* tomato.

tom|flaske *sb* empty bottle; *fl også* empties. **~gang** *sb* idling; idle running; *gå på ~* idle; run idle; be ticking over. **~gods** *sb koll* empties. **~hendt** *adj* empty-handed. **~het** *sb* emptiness.

tomme *sb* inch. Se for øvrig midtsidene.

tommelfinger *sb* thumb. **Tommeliten** Tom Thumb. **tommeltott** *sb* thumb.

tommestokk *sb* folding rule.

romrom *sb* gap, void.

tomset(e) *adj* half-witted. **tomsing** *sb* half-wit.

tomt *sb* site; *US* lot.

tone I *sb* **1** *(enkelt ~, note)* note; *en falsk ~* a false note; **2** *(melodi)* melody, tune; **2** *(~fall)* tone (of voice); intonation; *(om ~høyde)* pitch; *~n i brevet var dyster* the tone of the letter was gloomy; **4** *(oppførsel) det er ikke god ~* it is not good form; **II** *vb* **1** *(klinge)* sound; **2** *(vise) ~ flagg* show one's (true) colours; **3** *(farge~)* tone. **toneangivende** *adj* leading; setting the fashion; *de ~angivende* the leading people. **tone|art** *sb* key. **~fall** *sb* tone (of voice); intonation; *(aksent)* accent. **tonløs** *adj* toneless.

tonn *sb* ton; *et ~ kull* a ton of coal; *et skip på 5000 ~* a ship of 5,000 tons. Se for øvrig om mål og vekt på midtsidene. **tonnasje** *sb* tonnage.

tonsur *sb* tonsure.

topografi *sb* topography. **topografisk** *adj* topographic.

topp *sb* **1** top; *(fig og fjell~ også)* summit; *fra ~ til tå* from top to toe; *på ~en av sin karriere* at the summit of one's fame; **2** *fig: det er ~en!* that's the limit! **toppe** *vb* top; *~ listen* top the list; *~ seg (kulminere)* culminate; reach its summit; *(om bølger)* comb, crest. **topp|fart** *sb* maximum/top speed. **~figur** *sb* figurehead. **~form** *sb* top form. **~gasje** *sb* maximum salary. **~klasse** *sb* top class; *(om varer)* top grade. **~kvalitet** *sb* top quality. **~lønn** se *~gasje*. **~møte** *sb* summit meeting. **~målt** *adj: (en) ~målt frekkhet* the height of impudence. **~prestasjon** *sb* top performance. **~pris** *sb* top price. **~punkt** *sb* summit; *(i geometri)* vertex. **~vinkel** *sb* vertical angle.

torden *sb* thunder; *(tordenvær)* thunderstorm; *(buldring)* thunder, roar. **torden|brak** *sb* clap/peal of thunder. **~røst** *sb* thunderous voice. **~skrall** se *~brak.* **~sky** *sb* thundercloud. **~tale** *sb* thundering speech. **~vær** *sb* thunderstorm; *det ble/var ~* there was a thunderstorm.

tordivel *sb* dung beetle.

tordne *vb* thunder; *det ~r og lyner* it is thundering and lightening; *kanonene begynte å ~* the guns began to thunder/roar.

tore *vb* dare; *(våge også)* venture; *de tør ikke gjøre det* they dare not do it; *han tør ikke komme* he dare not come/does not dare to come; *hun torde ikke svare* she dared not answer/did not dare (to) answer; *jeg har aldri tort forstyrre henne* I (have) never dared (to) disturb her; *jeg tør påstå* I venture to say; *tør jeg spørre?* may I ask?

torg *sb* **1** *(firkantet)* square; *(rundt ofte)* circus; **2** *(salgs~)* market(place); *på ~et* in the market(place). **torg|bod** *sb* market stall. **~dag** *sb* market day. **~hall** *sb* market hall. **~kone** *sb* market woman. **~pris** *sb* market price.

torn *sb* thorn; *ingen roser uten ~er* no roses without a thorn. **torne|busk** *sb* wild rose bush. **~full** *adj* thorny. **~krone** *sb* crown of thorns. **Tornerose** the Sleeping Beauty. **tornet(e)** *adj* thorny.

torpedere *vb* torpedo. **torpedo** *sb* torpedo. **torpedo|båt** *sb* torpedo boat. **~jager** *sb* destroyer.

torsdag *sb* Thursday; *forrige ~* last Thursday; *om ~en (hver ~)* on Thursdays.

torsk *sb* cod, cod-fish. **torske|fiske** *sb* cod fishing. **~lever** *sb* cod liver. **~levertran** *sb* cod-liver oil. **~rogn** *sb* cod roe.

tort *sb: erstatning for ~ og svie* damages in tort. **tortur** *sb* torture; *han ble underkastet ~* he was put to the torture. **torturere** *vb* torture. **torturist** *sb* torturer. **tortur|kammer** *sb* torture chamber. **~redskap** *sb* instrument of torture.

torv *sb (myr~)* peat; *(gress~)* turf. **torve** *sb* piece of turf.

toseter *sb* two-seater; *liten ~* roadster.

tosk *sb* fool. **tosket(e)** *adj* foolish, silly.

totakts *adj: ~ motor* two-stroke engine.

total *adj* total; *(adv)* totally, completely; *det var ~t mislykket* it was a complete failure; it failed completely. **total|avhold** *sb* teetotalism; total abstinence. **~avholdsmann** *sb* teetotaller; total abstainer. **~forbud** *sb* total prohibition. **~forlis** *sb* total loss. **~inntrykk** *sb* general impression. **totalisator** *sb* totalizator. **totalitær** *adj* totalitarian. **~omkostninger** *sb fl* total cost(s). **~skade 1** *sb* total loss; **2** *vb* damage irreparably; destroy (totally). **~verdi** *sb* aggregate value. **~ødeleggelse** *sb* total/utter destruction; ruin.

tott *sb* tuft; *fare/ryke i ~ene på hverandre* come to blows; *være i ~ene på hverandre* be at loggerheads.

to|årig, ~års *adj (to år gammel)* two-year-old; *(som varer to år)* two-year; *toårig plante* biennial.

tradisjon *sb* tradition. **tradisjonell** *adj* traditional.

trafikant *sb* road-user, driver. **trafikk** *sb* traffic; *sterk ~* heavy traffic. **trafikkere** *vb* traffick; *en sterkt trafikkert jernbanelinje* a heavily trafficked line; *sterkt trafikkert* busy; carrying a great deal of traffic; *(om gate også)* crowded. **trafikk|flyger** *sb* airline pilot. **~fyr** *sb* traffic light. **~knutepunkt** *sb* traffic centre. **~-konstabel** *sb* traffic policeman. **~-kork** *sb* traffic jam (block, hold-up). **~-kultur** *sb* road manners/sense. **~lys** *sb* traffic light. **~politi** *sb* traffic police. **~regler** *sb fl* traffic regulations; *trafikkreglene* ≈ the Highway Code. **~regulering** *sb* regulation of traffic. **~sammenbrudd** *sb* traffic breakdown. **~signal** *sb* traffic signal. **~sikkerhet** *sb* road safety. **~skilt** *sb* road sign. **~stans** se *~kork, ~sammenbrudd.* **~tetthet** *sb* traffic density. **~uhell** *sb* traffic/road accident. **~ulykke** *sb* road/traffic accident. **~vett** *sb* road sense. **~øy** *sb* traffic island; street refuge. **~åre** *sb* artery; arterial road.

tragedie *sb* tragedy. **tragi|komedie** *sb* tragi-comedy. **~komisk** *adj* tragi-comic. **tragisk** *adj* tragic.

trailer se *vogntog 2.* **trailersjåfør** *sb* (long distance) lorry driver.

trakt *sb* **1** *(egn, strøk)* region, tract; **2** *(til væsker)* funnel.

traktat *sb (overenskomst)* treaty; *de sluttet en ~* they entered into/made a treaty. **traktat|brudd** *sb* breach of a/the treaty. **~messig** *adj* according to a/the treaty; *~ forpliktelse* treaty obligation. **~stridig** *adj* contrary to the terms of a/the treaty.

trakte *vb* **A** *(filtrere)* filter, percolate; *~ kaffe* percolate coffee; **B:** *~ etter* aspire to. **traktekaffe** *sb* percolator coffee. **traktement** *sb* entertainment; *et godt ~* a good entertainment. **traktepose** *sb* filtering bag. **traktere** *vb: ~ noen med en god middag* treat somebody to a good dinner.

traktor *sb* tractor. **traktorfører** *sb* tractor driver.

trall *sb* melody, tune. **tralle** *vb* hum, sing.

tralle *sb* trolley; *(bagasje~)* (platform) truck.

tralt *sb: gå i (den) samme ~en* run in a groove/rut.

tram *sb* steps.

tramp *sb* stamp, tramp. **trampe** *vb* stamp, tramp; *~ ned* trample; *bli ~t ned* be trampled to death; *han ~t med føttene* he stamped his feet; *~ opp trappen* stamp upstairs.

trampfart *sb* tramp trade.

tran *sb (medisin~)* cod-liver oil.

trance *sb* trance.

trane *sb* crane. **tranedans** *sb: en spurv i ~* a sparrow among hawks; a dwarf among giants.

trang A *adj* **1** *(snever)* narrow; *en ~ gate* a narrow street; **2** *(stram)* tight; **3** *(om levekår)* difficult, hard; *~e tider* hard times; **A 1** *(lyst)* desire; *jeg føler ingen ~ til å si noe* I feel no desire/I do not want to say anything; *jeg føler ~ til å si* I want to say; **2** *(behov)* need; **3** *(nød)* want, need. **trangsyn** *sb* narrow-mindedness, narrowness. **trangsynt** *adj* narrow-minded.

transaksjon *sb* transaction.

transformator *sb* transformer.

transistor *sb* transistor.

transitiv *adj* transitive.

transitt *sb* transit. **transitt|gods** *sb* transit goods. **~handel** *sb* transit trade.

transkribere *vb* transcribe. **transkripsjon** *sb* transcription.

translatør *sb* translator.

transparent 1 *adj* transparent; **2** *sb* (transparent) banner.

transplantasjon *sb* transplantation.

transport *sb* transport. **transportabel** *adj* **1** *(bærbar)* portable; **2** *(flyttbar)* movable. **transport|arbeider** *sb* transport worker. **~byrå** *sb* transport agency. **~bånd** *sb* belt conveyer; conveyer belt. **transportere** *vb* transport, carry. **transport|fly** *sb* transport plane; freighter. **~formidling** *sb* forwarding of goods. **~forsikring** *sb* transport insurance. **~middel** *sb* means of transport.

trapes *sb* **1** *(geometrisk figur)* trapezium; **2** *(i turn)* trapeze.

trapp *sb* **1** staircase, stairs; *ned ~en* downstairs; *opp ~en* upstairs; *ved foten av ~en* at the foot of the stairs; *vi møtte dem i ~en* we met them on the stairs; **2** *(især utvendig ~)* steps; *(utenfor gatedør)* doorstep(s); *han stod på ~en til huset sitt* he stood on the steps of his house. **trappe|avsats** *sb* landing. **~gang** *sb* staircase. **~gelender** *sb* banisters. **~oppgang** *sb* staircase. **~trinn** *sb* step.

trase *sb (fille)* rag, shred.

trasé *sb* track.

traske *vb* plod, trudge.

trass 1 *prep (jf trass 1)* in spite of; though; *~ alt* in spite of all/everything; **2** *sb (jf tross 2)* defiance, spite; obstinacy, stubbornness; *~ i* in spite of; *~ i alt* in spite of everything; *~ i at hun sa det* in spite of the fact that she said so; though she said so; *~ i hva de sier* in spite of what they say; *på ~* in defiance/spite. **trassalder** *sb* difficult/obstinate age. **trasse** *vb (jf trosse)* defy; bid defiance to; *~ foreldrene sine* defy one's parents. **trassig** *adj* defiant; obstinate, stubborn. **trassighet** *sb* defiance, obstinacy, stubbornness.

trau *sb* trough.

traust *adj* steady; solid; sturdy.

trav *sb* trot; *(travsport)* trotting; *i ~* at a trot; *i raskt ~* at a brisk trot; *rent/urent ~* regular/irregular trot. **travbane** *sb* trotting track. **trave** *vb* trot; *~ av sted* trot along.

travel *adj, adv* busy; *en ~ dag* a busy day; *få/ha det ~t med å arbeide (etc)* get/be busy with working (etc); *han hadde det svært ~t (dvs hadde mye å gjøre)* he was very busy; *hun hadde det svært ~t (dvs hadde liten tid)* she was in a hurry. **travelhet** *sb* busyness, bustle; *(rastløs ~)* hurry.

traver *sb (hest)* trotter. **travløp** *sb* trotting race.

tre A *sb* **1** tree; *trærne i skogen* the trees in the wood; **2** *(~virke, ved)* wood; *huset er av ~* the house is made of wood; **B** *vb (jf trå)* step, tread; *~ frem/tilbake* step forward/backward; *de trådte inn i værelset* they entered the room; *hun trådte ut av regjeringen* she resigned from the Cabinet; *parlamentet ~r sammen i morgen* Parliament meets tomorrow.

tre|bein *sb* wooden leg. **~bevokst** *adj* wooded.

tredemølle *sb* treadmill.

tredje third; *den ~ mai* the third of May; May the third; *den ~ største byen* the third largest town; *for det ~* third(ly); in the third place. **tre(dje)del** *sb* third; *to ~er* two thirds. **tredje|gradsforhør** *sb* the third degree. **~standen** *sb* the third estate. **tredobbelt** *adj* threefold. **treenighet** *sb* Trinity. **treer** *sb* three.

treff *sb* **1** *(møte)* meeting; **2** *(slumpe~)* accident, chance; *ved et ~* by accident/chance. **treffe** *vb* **1** *(ramme)* hit; *kulen traff ham i beinet* the bullet hit him in the leg; **2** *(møte)* meet; *(~ ved et tilfelle også)* come across; *de traff hverandre i Paris* they met in Paris; *jeg har aldri truffet dem* I have never met them; **3** *(finne)* find; *vi traff ingen hjemme* we found nobody at home; **4** *(foreta)* make; *det er vanskelig å ~ et valg* it is difficult to make a choice; *han traff sine siste forberedelser* he made his last preparations; **5** *~ seg* happen; *det traff seg så at han kom til London* it so happened that he came to London. **treffende** *adj* **1** *(om bemerkning)* apt; *en ~bemerkning* an apt remark; **2** *(om likhet)* striking. **treffetid** *sb* office hours. **treffsikker** *adj* accurate. **treffsikkerhet** *sb* accuracy. **trefning** *sb* skirmish, engagement.

treforedlingsindustri *sb* wood-processing industry; wood products industry.

treg *adj* slack, slow; indolent, sluggish; *(især fys)* inert. **treghet** *sb* slowness, sluggishness; indolence, sluggishness; *(især fys)* inertia.

tre|gulv *sb* wooden floor. **~grense** *sb* timber line.

trehjulssykkel *sb* tricycle.

trehus *sb* wooden house.

tre|kant *sb* triangle. **~kantet** *adj* triangular.

tre|kasse *sb* wooden box. **~kirke** *sb* wooden church.

trekk *sb* **1** *(rykk)* pull; *et ~ i snoren* a pull at the cord; **2** *(ansikts~)* feature; *rene ~* clear-cut features; **3** *(karakter~)* trait; *de viktigste ~ene i karakteren hans* the chief traits in his character; **4** *(episode, hendelse)* episode; *~ fra barndommen hennes* episodes from her childhood; **5** *(i sjakk)* move; **6** *(møbel~ etc)* cover; **7** *(luftdrag)* draught; *sitt ikke i ~en!* do not sit in the draught! **8** *(uttrykk) i ett ~* without a stop; without stopping; *i store ~* in broad outline; *to uker i ~* two weeks on end; *tre ganger i ~* three times running. **trekkdyr** *sb* beast of draught. **trekke** *vb* **1** draw, pull; *~ seg tilbake* retire; *han trakk henne i håret* he pulled her hair; *hun lot teen ~ i fem minutter* she let the tea draw for five minutes; **2** *(uttrykk) det ~r* there is a draught; *det ~r opp til regn* it looks like rain; *han trakk klokken* he wound up the watch; *hun trakk på skuldrene* she shrugged (her shoulders). **trekk|fugl** *sb* bird of passage; migratory bird. **~full** *adj* draughty. **~hund** *sb* sledge/*US* sled dog. **~kraft** *sb* pulling power; tractive force. **~papir** *sb* blotting paper. **~plaster** *sb* plaster; *fig* attraction, draw. **~spill** *sb* accordion.

treklang *sb* triad. **trekløver** *sb* trefoil; *fig* trio, triumvirate.

trekning *sb* **1** drawing; **2** *(i kroppen)* spasm, twitch(ing); *(i ansiktet også)* tic; **3** *(i lotteri)* draw; *når finner ~en sted?* when does the draw take place? **trekningsliste** *sb* list of prizes.

trekull *sb* charcoal.

trelast *sb* timber; *US* lumber.

trell *sb* slave. **trell|binde** *vb* enslave. **~dom** *sb* slavery, bondage. **~trelle** *vb* slave.

tremasse *sb* wood pulp.

tremenning *sb* second cousin.

tremme *sb* bar. **tremmeverk** *sb* trellis.

trene *vb* practise, train; *~ til en kamp* train for a match; *jeg ~r i løp* I practise running. **trener** *sb* trainer; *(idretts~)* coach. **trenere** *vb* delay, retard.

trenge *vb* **A** *(presse, trykke)* press, push; drive; force; **~ (seg) frem** advance; push forward; **~ igjennom** push one's way through; penetrate; *(bli godtatt)* prevail; be accepted; **~ (seg) inn (i)** force one's way in(to); *(invadere)* invade; **~ opp:** *~ opp i et hjørne* drive into a corner; **~ (seg) på** push forward; **~ sammen** compress; *~ seg sammen* crowd/press together; **~ tilbake** drive back; **B** *(behøve, ~ til)* need; require, want; *~ hardt/sårt (til)* need/want badly; *barn ~r mye søvn* children want plenty of sleep; *jeg ~r et par nye sko* I need a pair of new shoes; *maskinen ~r smøring* the machine requires oiling. **trengende** *adj* needy, poor. **trengsel** *sb* **1** *(av folk)* crowd, throng; *det var ~ om ham* people crowded round him; **2** *(motgang)* adversity; hardships, troubles.

trening *sb* training; *(trenervirksomhet)* coaching. **treningsdrakt** *sb* track/training suit.

treske *sb* thresh.

treskel *sb* treshold.

treskeverk *sb* threshing machine.

tre|skjærer *sb* wood carver. **~sko** *sb* wooden shoe; clog. **~sliperi** *sb* pulp mill. **~sløyd** *sb* woodwork. **~snitt** *sb* woodcut. **~sprit** *sb* wood alcohol.

tresse *sb* braid.

trestamme *sb* trunk (of a tree); bole.

tresteg *sb* hop, step, and jump; triple jump.

trestjerners *adj: ~ konjakk* three-star brandy.

trestubbe *sb* stump (of a tree).

tretne *vb* become (get, grow) tired. **trett** *adj* tired, weary; *(utmattet av)* tired from/with; *et ~ smil* a tired smile; *han ble fort ~* he soon got tired; *hun var ~ etter reisen* she was tired from the journey; *jeg er ~ av historiene hans* I am tired of his stories.

trette A *sb* **1** *sb (krangel)* quarrel; argument, dispute; *avgjøre/bilegge en ~* settle a dispute; **2** *vb (krangle)* quarrel; *de ~t om ingenting* they quarrelled over trifles; **B** *vb (gjøre trett)* tire; *det lange foredraget ~t forsamlingen* the long lecture tired the audience. **trettende** *adj* **1** tiring, wearisome; *(kjedelig)* boring. **tretthet** *sb* fatigue, tiredness; *(høytideligere)* weariness.

trettekjær *adj* quarrelsome.

treull *sb* wood wool; *US også* excelsior.

trev *sb* loft.

trevarefabrikk *sb* woodworking factory. **trevarer** *sb koll* woodware; articles of wood; wooden articles. **tre|verk** *sb* woodwork. **~virke** *sb* wood.

trevl *sb* **1** *(i plante, muskel)* fibre; **2** *(av tøy)* thread; **3** *(fille)* rag. **trevle** *vb: ~ opp* shred, (un)ravel; *trevles/trevle seg opp* fray, (un)ravel.

triangel *sb* triangle.

tribune *sb* stand; *(med tak og sitteplasser)* grandstand.

tributt *sb* tribute.

trigonometri *sb* trigonometry. **trigonometrisk** *adj* trigonometric(al).

trikk *sb (knep)* trick.

trikk *sb (sporvogn)* tram(car); *US* streetcar. **trikke** *vb* go by tram; take the tram.

trikot *sb* tights; *(også, især US)* bodystocking, pantihose. **trikotasje** *sb* knitwear. **trikotasjeforretning** *sb* hosier's; knitwear shop.

trill *adv: det gikk ~ rundt for meg* I was all at sea.

trille A *sb (i musikk, sang)* trill; *(om fugletriller)* warble; *slå ~r* trill, warble; **B** *vb* **1** *(rulle)* roll; *~ ball* roll a ball (along the ground); **2** *(kjøre)* wheel. **trille|bår** *sb* wheelbarrow. **~pike** *sb* pram pusher.

trilling *sb* triplet.

trillrund *adj* round as a ball.

trilogi *sb* trilogy.

trim *sb* trim; *være i ~* be in trim. **trimme** *vb* trim.

trine *vb* step, tread.

trinn *sb* **1** *(fot~, skritt)* step; *vi hørte ~ utenfor* we heard steps outside; **2** *(trappe~)* step; *en trapp med tolv ~* a staircase of twelve steps; **3** *(stige~)* rung; *det nederste ~et på stigen* the lowest rung of the ladder; **4** *(fig: stadium)* stage. **trinnvis** *adj* step by step; gradual, successive.

trinse *sb* **1** *(lite hjul)* castor; **2** *(til heising)* pulley; **3** *(på skistav)* stick disc/disk.

trio *sb* trio.

tripp *sb* trip. **trippe** *vb* trip; *~ av utålmodighet* fidget with impatience.

trise *sb* waitress.

trist *adj* **1** *(bedrøvet, sørgelig)* sad; *en ~ historie* a sad affair; *nei, så ~!* what a pity! **2** *(dyster, forstemmende)* dismal, dreary, gloomy; *~e utsikter* dismal/gloomy prospects. **tristhet** *sb* sadness; dreariness, gloom.

tritt *sb: holde ~ med* keep pace with; keep up with.

triumf *sb* triumph. **triumfator** *sb* triumphator. **triumfere** *vb* triumph. **triumferende** *adj* triumphant.

triumvirat *sb* triumvirate.

trive *vb* grasp, seize, snatch.

trivelig *adj* **1** *(frodig, rund)* plump, round; well-fed, *(bare om kvinner)* buxom; **2** *(hyggelig)* pleasant; cosy; inviting. **trives** *vb* **1** *(befinne seg vel)* be/feel happy; **2** *(utvikle seg, vokse)* thrive; *barn ~ med god mat og frisk luft* children thrive on good food and fresh air.

triviell *adj (kjedelig)* boring, dull; *(fortersket)* commonplace.

trivsel *sb* prosperity; *(velvære)* well-being.

tro A *adj* se *trofast*; **B** *sb (kar, trau)* trough; **C I** *sb* **1** *(religiøs ~)* belief, faith; *~ på Gud* belief in God; *den kristne ~* the Christian faith; **2** *(tillit)* faith, trust; *i god ~* in good faith; **3** *(overbevisning, antakelse)* belief; *jeg var i den ~ at du var reist* I thought you had left; **II** *vb* **1** *(~ i religiøs forstand)* believe; *~r du på Gud?* do you believe in God? **2** *(ha tillit til)* believe, trust; *jeg ~r på den mannen* I believe in/trust that man. **3** *(anta, mene)* think; *jeg ~dde hun var død* I thought she was dead; **4** *(føle seg sikker på)* believe; *jeg ~r hva han sier* I believe what he says. **trofast** *adj* faithful, loyal; *en ~ venn* a faithful friend. **trolig** *adj* **1** *(sannsynlig)* likely; *det er ~ nok* it is very likely; **2** *(til å tro)* credible.

troll *sb (i eventyr)* ogre, monster. **troll|binde** *vb* cast a spell (up)on; spellbind. **~dom** *sb* witchcraft, sorcery; magic. **~kjerring** *sb* sorceress, witch. **~mann** *sb* sorcerer.

trolleybuss *sb* trolley bus.

troløs *adj* faithless; *(forrædersk)* treacherous. **troløshet** *sb* faithlessness, treachery.

tromle *vb* roll.

tromme *sb* drum; *han slo på ~* he beat/played the drum. **tromme** *vb* drum; beat/play the drum; *han ~t på bordet med fingrene* he drummed on the table with his fingers. **trommehinne** *sb* eardrum.

trommel *sb* **1** *(hage~, vei~ etc)* roller; **2** *(hjul, sylinder)* drum; **3** *(tørke~)* spin dryer. **trommelbrems** *sb* drum brake; expanding brake.

tromme|slager *sb* drummer. **~stikke** *sb* drumstick.

trompet *sb* trumpet; *han spilte ~* he played the trumpet. **trompeter** se *trompetist*. **trompetfanfare** *sb* flourish of trumpets. **trompetist** *sb* trumpeter. **trompetstøt** *sb* trumpet blast.

tron|arving *sb* heir to the throne. **~bestigelse** *sb* accession (to the throne). **trone** *sb* throne; *hun besteg/kom på tronen i 1962* she came to the Throne in 1962. **trone** *vb* sit enthroned; sit in state; throne. **tron|frasigelse** *sb* abdication. **~følge** *sb* (order of) succession. **~følger** *sb* successor (to the Throne). **~himmel** *sb* canopy. **~kandidat, ~pretendent** *sb* pretender (to the Throne). **~raner, ~røver** *sb* usurper. **~stol** *sb* throne. **~tale** *sb* speech from the Throne.

trope|hjelm *sb* sun-helmet. **~klima** *sb* tropical climate. **~luft** *sb* tropical air. **tropene** *sb fl* the tropics. **trope|regn** *sb* tropical rain. **~sykdom** *sb* tropical disease. **tropisk** *adj* tropical.

tropp *sb* troop; *(bare om soldater)* detachment; *i sluttet ~* in a body. **troppe** *vb: ~ opp* show/turn up. **troppe|revy** *sb* parade, review. **~styrker** *sb fl* (military) forces; troops. **troppsfører** *sb (for guttespeidere)* scoutmaster; *(for jentespeidere)* captain.

tros|artikkel *sb* article of faith. **~bekjennelse** *sb* creed. **~felle** *sb* co-religionist; *politisk ~felle* fellow partisan. **~fellesskap** *sb* community of religion. **~frihet** *sb* religious liberty/freedom.

troskap *sb* faithfulness, fidelity; loyalty; *hans ~ mot sine overordnede* his loyalty to his superiors; *hennes ~ mot sine venner* her faithfulness/fidelity to her friends. **troskaps|ed** *sb* oath of allegiance. **~løfte** *sb* vow of fidelity.

troskyldig *adj* simple-minded; artless, ingenuous; *(tillitsfull)* unsuspicious. **troskyldighet** *sb* simple-mindedness, artlessness; unsuspiciousness.

tross 1 *prep (jf trass i)* in spite of; though; *~ alt* in spite of all/everything; **2** *sb (jf trass)* defiance, spite; obstinacy, stubbornness; *i ~* in defiance/spite; *på ~ av, til ~ for* in spite of; *til ~ for at hun sa det* in spite of the fact that she said so; though she said so; *til ~ for hva de sier* in spite of what they say.

tros|sak *sb* matter of faith. **~samfunn** *sb* religious community; *(stundom)* denomination.

trosse A *vb (jf trasse)* defy; bid defiance to; *~ fare(r)* defy danger; *~ sine foreldre* defy one's parents; *døren ~t alle forsøk på å åpne den* the door defied all attempts to open it. **trossig** *adj (jf trassig)* defiant; obstinate, stubborn; **B** *sb (grovt tau)* hawser. **trossighet** *sb (jf trassighet)* defiance; obstinacy, stubbornness.

trost *sb* thrush.

troverdig *adj* **1** *(trolig)* credible; **2** *(sannsynlig)* credible, likely; *en ~ historie* a credible/likely story; **3** *(til å stole på)* reliable, trustworthy; *en ~ person* a trustworthy person; *et ~ vitne* a reliable witness; **4** *(sannferdig)* truthful. **troverdighet** *sb* credibility, reliability.

trubadur *sb* minstrel, troubadour.

true *vb* threaten; *han ~t med å drepe meg* he threatened to kill me. **truende** *adj* **1** threatening, menacing; *~ utsikter* menacing prospects; **2** *(overhengende)* imminent; *~ fare* imminent danger; **3** *(illevarslende)* ominous.

truffet *adj, pp: føle seg ~* find that the cap fits; stand abashed.

trumf *sb* trump; *spar er ~* spades are trumps. **trumfe** *vb* trump; play trump; *~ igjennom* force through. **trumf|ess** *sb* ace of trumps. **~kort** *sb* trump card.

trupp *sb* company, troupe; *en skuespiller~* a troupe/company of actors.

truser *sb* briefs.

trussel *sb* threat, menace; *en ~ mot freden i Europa* a menace to the peace of Europe; *hans ~ om å gjøre det* his threat to do it. **trusselbrev** *sb* threatening letter.

trust *sb* trust. **trust|dannelse** *sb* trust formation. **~kontroll** *sb* regulation of trusts.

trut *sb: sette ~* pout.

truten *adj* swollen. **trutne** *vb* swell.

trutt *adv: arbeide ~* work persistently/assiduously.

trygd *sb* insurance. **trygde** *vb* insure. **trygde|avgift** *sb* (insurance) contribution. **~kasse** *sb* Health Insurance Office. **~premie**, *se ~avgift.*

trygg *adj* **1** *(om følelsen av trygghet)* secure; *føle seg*

~ feel secure; **2** *(sikker mot fare)* safe; *være* ~ be safe; **3** *(rolig)* easy; ~ *til sinns* easy in one's mind; *en* ~ *søvn* a sound sleep. **trygge** *vb* make safe; secure. **trygghet** *sb* **1** safety, security; **2** *(tillit)* confidence. **trygghetsfølelse** *sb* feeling of security.

trygle *vb* beg, entreat, implore; *de* ~*t oss om ikke å straffe dem* they begged/entreated/implored us not to punish them.

trykk A *sb* **1** *(press)* pressure; *handle under* ~ act under pressure; **2** *(vekt)* stress; *dette ordet har* ~*et på siste stavelse* in this word the stress falls/is on the last syllable; **B** *(om boktrykk)* print; *på* ~ in print. **trykke** *vb* **A 1** *(presse) a)* press; *han trykte på knappen* he pressed a button; *b)* ~ *noen i hånden* shake hands with somebody; *(hjerteligere)* press somebody's hand; **2** *(dytte, skyve)* push; *hun ble trykt opp mot veggen* she was pushed up against the wall; **3** *(klemme)* pinch; *skoen* ~*r* the shoe pinches; **4** *(plage, tynge)* lie heavy on; **B** *(~ bøker etc)* print.

trykkefrihet *adj* freedom of the press. **trykkende** *adj* **1** *(om været)* oppressive, close; ~ *varme* oppressive heat; **2** *(pinlig)* awkward, uneasy; ~ *taushet* awkward/uneasy silence. **trykkeri** *sb* printing-house; printing-office. **trykket** *adj* depressed, oppressed; ~ *av situasjonen* he was ill at ease; ~ *stemning* gloomy atmosphere. **trykkfeil** *sb* misprint. **trykknapp** *sb* **1** *(til å knappe med)* snap, snap-fastener; **2** *(til å trykke på)* push-button. **trykkoker** *sb* pressure cooker. **trykk|saker** *sb koll* printed matter. **~sverte** *sb* printer's ink. **trykning** *sb* printing; *boken er under* ~ the book is being printed/is in the press.

trylle *vb* conjure. **trylle|kraft** *sb* magic power. **~kunst** *sb* conjuring trick. **~kunstner** *sb* conjurer. **trylleri** *sb* magic, witchcraft. **trylle|slag** *sb: som ved et* ~ as if by magic. **~stav** *sb* magic wand.

tryne *sb* snout; ~*t på en gris* the snout of a pig.

træ *vb:* ~ *en nål* thread a needle.

træl *sb (fortykket hud)* callus.

trø *vb* step, tread. Se for øvrig *tre* og *trå*.

trøst *sb* comfort, consolation; *en dårlig* ~ a poor consolation; *til* ~ *gav jeg ham en liten gave* as a consolation I gave him a small present. **trøste** *vb* comfort; *jeg* ~*t det hulkende barnet* I comforted the sobbing child. **trøstesløs** *adj* **1** *(utrøstelig)* disconsolate, inconsolable; **2** *(trist)* bleak, dreary; *et* ~ *landskap* a bleak/dreary countryside; **3** *(håpløs)* hopeless; *en* ~ *situasjon* a hopeless situation.

trøtne, trøtt etc se *tretne, trett etc*.

trøye *sb (under~)* vest; *ull~* woolen vest.

trå A *adj (harsk)* rancid; **B** *vb (jf tre B og tråkke)* step, tread; ~ *noen på tærne* step/tread on somebody's corns; *han tro/trådde på en stein* he stepped/trod on a stone; *hun tro/trådde feil* she stumbled/took a false step. **tråbil** *sb* pedal car.

tråd *sb* thread; *(metall~)* wire; *en tykk/tynn* ~ a thick/thin thread; *han mistet* ~*en i talen sin* he lost the thread of his speech; *trekke i* ~*ene* pull (the) wires. **tråd|løs** *adj* wireless. **~snelle** *sb* (cotton) reel; *US* spool (of thread).

tråkk *sb (~ing)* trampling; *et stadig* ~ a continuous coming and going. **tråkke** *vb (trampe)* trample; ~ *en på tærne* tread/step on his/her corns; *jeg har* ~*t omkring i hele dag* I have been on my feet all day.

tråkle *vb* baste, tack. **tråkletråd** *sb* tacking thread.

trål *sb* trawl. **tråle** *vb* trawl. **tråler** *sb* trawler.

trått *adv: det går* ~ it is slow going.

tsar *sb* czar.

tube *sb* tube; *en* ~ *(med) tannkrem* a tube of toothpaste.

tuberkulose *sb* tuberculosis. **tuberkuløs** *adj* tuberculous.

tue *sb* hillock, mound; *(maur~)* ant-hill; *liten* ~ *kan velte stort lass* little strokes fell great oaks.

tufs I *adj: jeg er/føler meg (så)* ~ I am out of sorts; **II** *sb* **1** *(hår~)* tuft; **2** *(pusling)* manikin; **3** *(dott, godfjott)* fool, weakling. **tufset(e)** *adj* dishevelled.

tuft *sb* site.

tukle *vb:* ~ *med* fumble with.

tukt *sb* **1** discipline; **2** *(straff)* chastisement, punishment. **tukte** *vb* chastise; punish (severely); *(~ med slag)* castigate. **tukthus** *sb* prison; gaol, jail; *(om straffen)* imprisonment with hard labour. **tukthusfange** *sb* convict.

tulipan *sb* tulip.

tull *sb* **1** *(noe sammentullet)* bundle; **2** *(tøys)* nonsense. **tulle A** *sb* baby(girl); **B** *vb* **1** ~ *inn/sammen* wrap up; **2** *(tøyse)* talk nonsense; **3** ~ *seg bort* get lost. **tulle|bukk, ~kopp** *sb* fool, twaddler. **tullet(e)** *adj* crazy. **tulling** *sb* fool, half-wit. **tullprat** *sb* nonsense.

tumle *vb* **1** *(sjangle, vakle)* tumble; *han* ~*t inn* he tumbled/came tumbling in; **2** *(boltre seg)* gambol; *de* ~*t omkring på plenen* they gambolled on the lawn; **3** ~ *med* struggle with. **tumleplass** *sb* playground.

tummel *sb* **1** *(bråk, oppstyr)* bustle; **2** *(forvirring)* turmoil.

tumult *sb* **1** *(larm, tummel)* tumult; confused noise; uproar; **2** *(oppstand)* riot; **3** *(slagsmål)* scuffle.

tun *sb* yard.

tundra *sb* tundra.

tung *adj* **1** heavy; *en tung byrde/plikt/søvn* a heavy burden/duty/sleep; **2** *(besværlig)* difficult, hard; ~*t arbeid* hard work; *det har vært en* ~ *tid for dem* it has been a difficult time for them; **3** *(sørgelig)* hard, sad; *en* ~ *skjebne* a hard fate.

tunge *sb* tongue; *han rakte* ~ *til henne* he put out his tongue at her. **tunge|bånd** *sb* fraenum, frenum; *være godt skåret for* ~*et* have the gift of the gab. **~ferdighet** *sb* glibness, volubility. **~mål** *sb* language. **~spiss** *sb* tip of the tongue. **~tale** *sb* gift of the tongues.

tung|hørt *adj* hard of hearing. **~hørthet** *sb* hardness of hearing. **~industri** *sb* heavy industry. **~lynt** *adj* melancholy. **~nem** *adj* dull, slow. **~pustet** *adj* short-winded. **~sindig** *adj* melancholy. **~sinn** *sb* melancholy, sadness. **tungtveiende** *adj* weighty; ~ *grunner* weighty reasons. **tung|vekt** *sb* heavyweight. **~vinn, ~vint** *adj* cumbersome, clumsy.

tunnel *sb* tunnel. **tunnelbane** *sb* tube; underground (railway); tube; *US* subway.

tupere *vb* backcomb.

tupp *sb* tip.

tur *sb* **1** *(spaser~)* walk; *de gikk en ~* they went for a walk; **2** *(utflukt)* excursion; *(~ med niste)* picnic; **3** *(reise)* journey, trip; *(til sjøs)* voyage; **4** *(bil~)* drive; *(lengre ~)* tour, trip; *vi kjørte en ~* we went for a drive; **5** *(sykkel~)* ride; *(lengre ~)* cycling tour; *jeg syklet en ~* I went for a (bicycle) ride; **6** *(~ til å gjøre noe)* turn; *etter ~* by turns; in turn; *vente på ~* wait one's turn.

turban *sb* turban.

turbin *sb* turbine.

ture *vb* booze.

turgjenger *sb* hiker.

turisme *sb* tourism. **turist** *sb* tourist. **turist|byrå** *sb* travel/tourist agency. **~sesong** *sb* tourist season. **~trafikk** *sb* tourism; tourist trade/traffic.

turkis *adj, sb* turquoise.

turn *sb* gymnastics. **turnapparat** *sb* gym apparatus. **turne** *vb* do gymnastics.

turné *sb* tour; *på ~* on tour; *truppen er på ~ i provinsen* the company is touring the provinces.

turner *sb* gymnast.

turnere *vb (dra på ~)* tour. **turnering** *sb* tournament. **turn|forening** *sb* gymnastics club. **~hall** *sb* gymnasium.

turnips *sb* turnip.

turnsko *sb* gym shoe.

tur-retur-billett *sb* return ticket.

turteldue *sb* turtle-dove.

tusen *tallord* a thousand; *mange ~ mennesker* many thousand people; thousands of people; *Tusen og en natt* Arabian Nights. **tusen|fryd** *sb* daisy. **~kunstner** *sb* **1** *(altmuligmann)* Jack of all trades; **2** *(tryllekunstner)* conjurer. **~vis** *adv* in thousands; by the thousand. **tusen|år** *sb* millenium. **~årig** *adj* a thousand years old. **~årsrike** *sb* millenium.

tusj *sb* Indian ink.

tusle *vb (pusle)* potter; *(om lyd)* rustle. **tuslet(e)** *adj* small and weak. **tusling** *sb* weakling.

tusmørk *adj* dim, dusky. **tusmørke** *sb* dusk, twilight.

tusset(e) *adj* crazy.

tust *sb (hår~)* wisp (of hair). **tuste** *vb (floke)* tangle. **tustet(e)** *adj* dishevelled.

tut *sb* **A** *(på kanne etc)* spout; **B** *(ul)* howl; *(av dampfløyte etc)* hoot. **tute** *vb* **1** *(ule)* howl; **2** *(om bilhorn, sirene, ugle etc)* hoot; *han ~t med hornet* he hooted; **3** *(gråte)* cry.

tutt *sb (kremmerhus)* cornet.

tvang *sb* compulsion; *han brukte/øvde ~ mot dem* he used force/compulsion against them; *under ~* under compulsion. **tvangfri** *adj (uformell)* informal. **tvangs|arbeid** *sb* hard labour. **~auksjon** *sb* forced sale. **~forestilling** se *~tanke*. **~situasjon** *sb* situation that leaves no choice; *(ofte)* emergency. **~tanke** *sb* obsession. **~trøye** *sb* strait-jacket.

tve|egget *adj* double-edged. **~kamp** *sb* duel; single combat.

tverke *sb: komme på ~ for* be inconvenient to.

tverr *adj* **1** *(gretten)* cross, sullen; **2** *(vrang)* stubborn, unwilling. **tverrhet** *sb* sulkiness, surliness; *(vranghet)* contrariness. **tverr|ligger** *sb (i fotballmål)* crossbar. **~snitt** *sb* cross-section; *i ~snitt* in section. **~stanse** *vb* stop dead/short. **~sum** *sb* sum of the digits. **tvers** *adv: ~ igjennom* straight/right through; *~ over* right/straight across; *på ~* crosswise; *på kryss og ~* in all directions. **tvert 1** *adv: ~ imot/om* on the contrary; **2** *(prep)* contrary to; contrary to my expectations.

tvetydig *adj* **1** *(dobbelttydig)* ambiguous; **2** *(uanstendig)* suggestive. **tvetydighet** *sb* ambiguity; *(uanstendighet)* double entendre.

tvi! *interj* phew!

tvil *sb* doubt; *det er ingen ~ om at de er reist* there is no doubt that they have left; *ingen ~ om det* no doubt about it; *i ~* in doubt; *uten ~* without doubt. **tvile** *vb* doubt; *jeg ~r på hennes ærlighet* I doubt her honesty; *jeg ~r på om han er sterk nok* I doubt if he is strong enough. **tvilende** *adj* **1** *(som føler tvil)* doubting; *(som rommer eller gir uttrykk for tvil)* doubtful; *et ~ tonefall* a doubtful tone. **tviler** *sb* doubter.

tvilling *sb* twin. **tvilling|bror** *sb* twin brother. **~par** *sb* pair of twins. **~vogn** *sb* twin pram.

tvil|rådig *adj* in doubt; in two minds. **~som** *adj* doubtful; *ytterst ~som* very doubtful. **tvilstilfelle** *sb: i ~* in case of doubt.

tvinge *vb* force, compel; *han tvang seg til å smile* he forced himself to smile; *ingen kan ~ meg til å gjøre det* no one can compel me to do it. Se også *tvungen*. **tvingende** *adj* compelling; *~ nødvendig* urgent.

tvinne *vb* twine, twist, wind.

tvist *sb* **A** *(bomulls~)* cotton waste; **B** *(strid)* conflict, dispute. **tviste|mål** *sb* dispute. **~punkt** *sb* point at issue; point in dispute. **tvistighet** *sb* dispute.

tvungen *adj* **1** *(pliktig, påbudt)* compulsory; *~ verneplikt* compulsory military service; *(også)* conscription; national service; **2** *(påtvunget)* enforced; **3** *(unaturlig)* forced; *en ~ latter* a forced laugh.

tvære ut *vb* drag out.

ty til *vb* **1** *(gripe til)* fall back on; resort to; have recourse to; **2** *(søke tilflukt hos)* take refuge with.

tyde *vb (tolke)* interpret; *~ på* indicate, suggest. **tydelig 1** *adj* clear, distinct; evident; *det er ~ nok* that is clear enough; *en ~ forestilling om* a clear idea of; **2** *adv* clearly, distinctly; *høre/snakke ~* hear/speak distinctly; *jeg husker ~ at* I distinctly remember that; *skrive ~* write clearly. **tydelighet** *med all (ønskelig) ~* so as to leave no room for doubt. **tydeligvis** *adv* clearly, evidently, obviously, evidently.

tyfus *sb* typhoid fever.

tygge *vb* chew; *~ maten godt* chew one's food well; *~ på* chew at. **tyggegummi** *sb* chewing-gum.

tykk *adj* thick; *(om person også)* fat, stout; plump; *en ~ bok/vegg* a thick book/wall; *han ble ~* he got fat;

he grew stout. **tykkelse** *sb* thickness. **tykkfallen** *adj* plump. **tykksak** *sb* fatty, tub. **tykktarm** *sb* large intestine; colon. **tykne** *vb* thicken. **tykning** *sb* thicket.

tylft *sb* dozen.

tyll *sb* tulle.

tylle *vb (helle)* pour; ~ *i seg* gulp/pour down.

tyne *vb* **1** *(plage)* torment; **2** *(drepe)* kill.

tyngd(e) *sb* **1** *(tunghet)* heaviness; **2** *(vekt)* weight. **tyngde|kraft** *sb* (force of) gravity; gravitation. **~punkt** *sb* centre of gravity. **tynge** *vb* be heavy; weigh down; weigh heavy/heavily; *(fig også)* oppress; *~t av sorg* weighed down with sorrow. **tyngsel** *sb* **1** *(byrde)* burden; **2** *(nedstemthet)* dejection, depression.

tynn *adj* **1** thin; *(slank)* slender, slim; *en ~ gren* a thin branch; **2** *(om drikk etc: motsatt sterk)* weak; *~ kaffe* weak coffee. **tynne** *vb* thin; *~ ut* thin out. **tynn|kledd** *adj* lightly/thinly dressed. **~slitt** *adj* worn thin. **~tarm** *sb* small intestine.

type *sb* type; *menn av hans ~* men of his type. **typisk** *adj* typical; *det er ~ for henne* it it typical of her; *en ~ engelskmann* a typical Englishman.

typograf *sb* typographer, printer. **typografisk** *adj* typographic(al).

tyrann *sb* tyrant; *(i det små især)* bully. **tyranni** *sb* tyranny. **tyrannisere** *vb* tyrannize; *(i det små især)* bully. **tyrannisk** *adj* tyrannical.

tyre|fekter *sb* bullfighter. **~fekting** *sb* bullfighting.

tyss! *interj* hush! **tysse** *vb* hush; *~ på* ask to be quiet; cry hush to. **tyst** *adj* hushed, silent. **tyste** *vb* inform, squeal. **tyster** *sb* informer, squealer.

tyte *vb (sive)* ooze, seep.

tyttebær *sb* mountain cranberry.

tyv *sb* thief; *(innbrudds~)* burglar. **tyvaktig** *adj* thievish. **tyve|bande** *sb* gang of thieves. **~gods** *sb koll* stolen goods. **tyveri** *sb* theft. **tyv|perm, ~start(e), ~trene** se *tjuv-*.

tære *vb* **1** *(om rust etc)* corrode; **2** *(uttrykk) ~ på kapitalen* eat into one's capital; *~ på kreftene* sap/tax one's strength; *~s hen* waste away. **tæring** *sb (tuberkulose)* consumption.

tø *vb* thaw; *~ opp* thaw.

tøddel *sb: ikke en ~* not a jot or tittle.

tøffe *vb (om motor)* chug; *båten ~t av sted* the boat chugged along.

tøffel *sb* slipper; *være under ~en* be henpecked. **tøffelhelt** *sb* henpecked husband.

tølper *sb* boor. **tølperaktig** *adj* boorish.

tømme A *sb (styrereim)* rein; *holde i ~* keep in check; **B** *vb (motsatt av fylle)* empty; *han tømte flasken* he emptied the bottle; *salen tømtes* the hall emptied.

tømmer *sb* timber. **tømmer|fløter** *sb* floater, raftsman. **fløting** *sb* floating, rafting. **~flåte** *sb* raft. **~hugger** *sb* lumberjack, woodcutter. **~hugst** *sb* felling, woodcutting. **~hytte** *sb* log cabin. **~lunne** *sb* pile of timber. **~mann** *sb* carpenter. **~menn** *sb: ha ~menn* be hungover; have a hangover. **~stabel** se *~lunne*. **~stokk** *sb* log. **~velte** se *~lunne*. **tømre** *vb* put up; make.

tønne *sb* barrel, cask. **tønne|bånd** *sb* hoop. **~stav** *sb* barrel stave.

tørk *sb* drying; *henge opp til ~* hang up to dry. **tørke I** *sb* drought; **II** *vb* **1** *(bli/gjøre tørr)* dry; *~ seg* dry oneself; *hun ~t de våte klærne (sine) ved varmen* she dried her wet clothes before the fire; **2** *(tørke av)* wipe; *han ~t blodet av ansiktet* he wiped the blood off his face; *hun ~t seg om/under nesen* she wiped her nose; *jeg ~t (av) føttene på matten* I wiped my feet on the mat; **3** *~ opp* wipe/mop up. **tørke|plass** *sb* drying place/yard. **~stativ** *sb* drying stand.

tørkle *sb (hals~)* scarf; *(hode~)* headscarf.

tørn *sb* turn; *en hard ~* a tough job; *han tok sin ~* he took his turn. **tørne** *vb: ~ inn (gå til køys)* turn in; *~ sammen* collide; *~ ut* turn out.

tørr 1 *adj* dry; *(regnfattig)* arid; *~ ved* dry wood; *tørt klima* dry/arid climate; *tørt vær* dry weather; *ha sitt på det ~e* be on the safe side; **2** *adv (tørt)* dryly; *svare tørt* answer dryly. **tørr|dokk** *sb* dry dock. **~fisk** *sb* stockfish. **~is** *sb* dry ice. **~legge** *vb* drain; *fig* make dry. **~lendt** *adj* dry. **~melk** *sb* dried milk; milk powder. **~skodd** *adj* dry-shod. **tørrvittig** *adj: være ~* have a dry sense of humour.

tørst 1 *adj* thirsty; *man blir ~ av det* it makes one thirsty; **2** *sb* thirst; *han slokket ~en* he quenched/satisfied his thirst; *vi led alle av ~* we all suffered from thirst. **tørste 1** *sb = tørst 2*; **2** *vb (være tørst)* be thirsty; thirst; *de ~t etter øl* they were thirsting for beer.

tøs *sb (løsaktig kvinne)* tart, hussy.

tøv *sb* nonsense. **tøve** *vb* talk nonsense. **tøvekopp** *sb* twaddler. **tøvet(e)** *adj* silly, nonsensical.

tøvær *sb* thaw.

tøy *sb* **1** *(klær)* clothes; **2** *(stoff)* cloth, fabric; (woven) material; stuff; *en ~bit* a piece of material/fabric/cloth.

tøye *vb* stretch; draw out; *~ seg* stretch. **tøyelig** *adj* elastic; *fig* flexible.

tøyle 1 *sb (tømme)* rein; *gi frie ~r* give the rein(s) to; *han slapp ~ne* he dropped/let go the rein(s); *holde i stramme tøyler* keep a tight rein on; **2** *vb* bridle, curb. **tøyleløs** *adj (ubehersket)* unrestrained; *(utsvevende)* dissolute; *~ lidenskap* unrestrained passion; *de levde et ~t liv* they led a dissolute life. **tøylesløshet** *sb* lack of restraint; dissoluteness.

tøys *sb* nonsense. **tøyse** *vb* talk nonsense. **tøyse|bøtte, ~kopp** *sb* twaddler. **tøyset(e)** *adj* silly, nonsensical.

tøyte *sb* tart, hussy.

tå *sb* toe; *de gikk/listet seg på ~* they walked on tiptoe; *han trådte henne på tærne* he trod on her toes/*fig* corns (jf *trå B*); *lett på ~* light-footed.

tåke *sb* fog; *(tåkedis)* mist, haze. **tåke|banke** *sb* fog bank. **~legge** *vb fig* obscure; *~legge fakta/kjensgjerningene* obscure the facts. **~lur** *sb* fog-horn. **tåket(e)** *adj* foggy; *(lettere)* misty; *(diset)* hazy; *fig* hazy; *~ vær* foggy/misty weather.

tål *sb: gi* ~ be patient; *slå seg til* ~*s (med)* resign oneself (to); be content with. **tåle** *sb* **1** *(holde ut)* bear, suffer; endure; he suffered hardships without complaining; *jeg* ~*r ikke (kan ikke* ~*) den fyren* I cannot bear that fellow; *smerten var nesten mer enn hun kunne* ~ the pain was almost more than she could bear/ endure; **2** *(ikke ta skade av)* stand; ~*r du denne kulden?* can you stand this cold? **3** *(finne seg i)* put up with; *vi måtte* ~ *mye* we had to put up with a good deal; **4** *(om mat etc) jeg* ~*r ikke kaffe* coffee does not agree with me.

tålelig, tålig *adj (ikke verst)* passable; so-so.

tålmod se *tålmodighet.* **tålmodig** *adj, adv* patient; *en* ~ *sykepleier* a patient nurse; *han bar sin sykdom* ~ he bore his illness patiently. **tålmodighet** *sb* patience; *hun mistet* ~*en med barnet* she lost patience with the child; *min* ~ *er forbi* my patience is at an end. **tålmodighetsprøve** *sb* trial of one's patience. **tålsom** *adj* tolerant. **tålsomhet** *sb* tolerance.

tåpe *sb* fool. **tåpelig** *adj* **1** *a) (dum)* foolish, silly; stupid; *han var så* ~ *at han løp sin vei* he was foolish enough to run away; *b) (som adv)* foolishly, stupidly; *han oppførte seg* ~ *(også)* he made a fool of himself; **2** *(meningsløs)* absurd. **tåpelighet** *sb* foolishness, silliness; stupidity.

tår *sb* drop; *ta (seg) en* ~ *over tørsten* have a drop too much. **tåre** *sb* tear; *jeg fikk* ~*r i øynene* my eyes filled with tears.

tårn *sb* tower; *(mindre* ~*)* turret; *(kirke*~*, spir)* steeple; *(*~ *i sjakk)* rook, castle.

tårne *vb:* ~ *seg opp* rise, tower.

tåspiss *sb* tip of the toe; *på* ~*ene* on tiptoe.

tåte|flaske *sb* feeding bottle. ~**smokk** *sb* (rubber) nipple; *(narresmokk)* comforter.

U

u *(bokstaven)* u.

uaktet **1** *konj* (al)though; **2** *prep* in spite of. **uaktsom** *adj* negligent; ~*t drap* negligent homicide. **uaktsomhet** *sb* negligence; *grov* ~ gross negligence.

ualminnelig *adj* uncommon, unusual; exceptional.

uanfektet *adj* unmoved, unconcerned. **uangripelig** *adj* **1** *(ugjendrivelig)* irrefutable; **2** *(ulastelig)* irreproachable. **uanmeldt** *adj* unannounced. **uanselig** *adj (ubetydelig)* insignificant. **uansett** *adv, prep* irrespective of; without regard to; ~ *hva som hender* no matter what may happen. **uanstendig** *adj* **1** *(upassende)* improper; **2** *(usømmelig)* indecent. **uanstendighet** *sb* impropriety; indecency; *(slibrighet)* obscenity. **uanstrengt** *adj* effortless. **uansvarlig** *adj* irresponsible. **uansvarlighet** *sb* irresponsibility. **uantakelig** *adj* unacceptable.

uappetittelig *adj* unappetizing; *(motbydelig)* disgusting, repulsive.

uatskillelig *adj* inseparable; ~*e venner* inseparable friends.

uavbrutt *adj* **1** *(uten avbrytelse)* continuous; *(uopphørlig)* incessant; *(som adv)* incessantly; *han snakker* ~ *om seg selv* he speaks incessantly about himself; *vi arbeidet* ~ *i 6 timer* we worked for six hours without a break; **2** *(stadig gjentatt)* continual. **uavgjort** *adj* undecided, unsettled; ~ *kamp* draw, tie; *de spilte* ~ *2-2* they drew 2-2; *kampen endte* ~ the game ended in a draw. **uavhengig** *adj* independent; ~ *av* independent of; *en* ~ *stat* an independent state. **uavhengighet** *sb* independence; *(stundom)* autonomy. **uavhengighetserklæring** *sb* declaration of independence. **uavhentet** *adj (om postsending etc)* unclaimed. **uavkortet** *adj* unabridged. **uavlatelig** *adj (stadig)* constant, continual. **uavsettelig** *adj* irremovable. **uavvendelig** *adj* inescapable, inevitable.

ubalanse *sb* imbalance. **ubarbert** *adj* unshaved, unshaven. **ubarmhjertig** *adj* merciless, pitiless; cruel. **ubarmhertighet** mercilessness, pitilessness; cruelty.

ubearbeidet *adj* raw, crude. **ubebodd** *adj* uninhabited; *(om hus også)* unoccupied. **ubeboelig** *adj* uninhabitable. **ubedt** *adj* unbidden, uninvited; *han kom* ~ he came uninvited. **ubegavet** *adj* unintelligent. **ubegrenset** *adj* boundless, unlimited, infinite. **ubegripelig** *adj* incomprehensible. **ubehag** *sb* dislike, distaste. **ubehagelig** *adj* **1** *(utiltalende, uvennlig)* disagreeable, unpleasant; *de var* ~*e mot meg* they were unpleasant to me; **2** *(ubekvem)* uncomfortable. **ubehagelighet** *sb* unpleasantness; ~*er* trouble; *jeg fikk* ~*er for det* I got into trouble over it. **ubehersket** *adj: bli* ~ lose one's self-control; *han er så* ~ he has no self--control. **ubehjelpelig** *adj* awkward, clumsy. **ubehjelpelighet** *sb* awkwardness, clumsiness. **ubehøvlet** *adj* boorish, rude, unmannered. **ubekvem** *adj* uncomfortable. **ubekymret** *adj* unconcerned; *han er* ~ *for fremtiden* he is unconcerned about/for the future; he does not worry about the future. **ubeleilig** *adj* inconvenient. **ubemerket** *adj* unnoticed, unobserved; *føre en* ~ *tilværelse* live in obscurity. **ubemerkethet** *sb* obscurity. **ubendig** *adj* indomitable, uncontrollable. **uberegnelig** *adj* unpredictable; *en* ~

faktor (også) a dark horse. **uberegnelighet** *sb* capriciousness. **uberettiget** *adj* unjustified, unwarranted. **uberørt** *adj* **1** untouched, virgin.

ubeseiret *adj* unconquered, undefeated. **ubesindig** *adj* hasty, rash. **ubesindighet** *sb* rashness. **ubeskjeden** *adj* immoderate; *(frekk især)* immodest. **ubeskrivelig** *adj* indescribable; *adv* indescribably; ~ *komisk* indescribably comic. **ubeskyttet** *adj* unprotected, unsheltered. **ubeslektet** *adj* unrelated. **ubesluttsom** *adj* irresolute. **ubestemmelig** *adj:* ~ *alder* uncertain/indeterminate age; *en* ~ *følelse* a vague/undefinable feeling. **ubestemt** *adj* **1** indefinite; ~ *artikkel/pronomen* indefinite article/pronoun; *på* ~ *tid* indefinitely; **2** *(ubesluttsom)* undecided, irresolute. **ubestikkelig** *adj* incorruptible. **ubestikkelighet** *sb* incorruptibility. **ubestridelig** *adj* incontestable, unquestionable. **ubestridt** *adj* unchallenged. **ubesvart** *adj* unanswered. **ubesørgelig** adj (om postsending etc) undeliverable. **ubesørget** *adj* undelivered. **ubetalelig** *adj* invaluable; *(også fig)* priceless. **ubetenksom** *adj* **1** *(uten omtanke)* thoughtless; **2** *(hensynsløs)* inconsiderate; **3** *(overilt)* rash. **ubetenksomhet** *sb* thoughtlessness; rashness. **ubetinget** *adj* **1** *(uforbeholden)* unqualified, implicit; ~ *lydighet* implicit obedience; ~ *ros* unqualified praise; **2** *(absolutt)* absolute; *en* ~ *nødvendighet* an absolute necessity. **ubetydelig** *adj* insignificant, inconsiderable; unimportant; *en* ~ *by* an insignificant town; *et* ~ *antall* an inconsiderable number. **ubetydelighet** *sb* trifle. **ubevegelig** *adj* **1** *(om ting som ikke kan røre seg eller flyttes)* immovable; **2** *(om ting som i øyeblikket ikke beveger seg)* motionless, immovable. **ubevisst** *adj* unconscious. **ubevoktet** *adj* unguarded; *i et* ~ *øyeblikk* in an unguarded moment.

ublid *adj* harsh, rough; unkind; *en* ~ *skjebne* a hard/unkind fate. **ublodig** *adj* bloodless. **ublu** *adj:* ~ *pris* exorbitant price. **ubotelig** *adj:* ~ *skade* irreparable damage. **ubrukbar, ubrukelig** *adj* useless; unfit for use; unserviceable; *gjøre* ~ render useless. **ubrutt** *adj* unbroken, intact. **ubuden** *adj: en* ~ *gjest* an uninvited guest; an intruder. **ubønnhørlig** *adj* implacable, inexorable. **ubåt** *sb* submarine.

udannet *adj* **1** *(kunnskapsløs)* uneducated; **2** *(uoppdragen)* rude; ill-bred, ill-mannered. **udefinerbar** *adj* indefinable. **udekket** *adj* **1** uncovered; *(i fotball etc)* unmarked; **2** *(ubetalt)* unpaid. **udelelig** *adj* indivisible. **udelt** *adj* undivided; *(hel)* entire. **udemokratisk** *adj* undemocratic. **udiplomatisk** *adj* undiplomatic. **udisiplinert** *adj* undisciplined. **udiskutabel** *adj* indisputable. **udramatisk** *adj* undramatic. **udrøy** *adj* uneconomical. **udugelig** *adj* incapable, incompetent; ~ *til* unfit for. **udugelighet** *sb* incapability, incompetence. **udyktig** *adj* incompetent. **udyktighet** *sb* incompetence. **udyr** *sb (om menneske)* brute, monster. **udyrkbar** *adj* uncultivable. **udyrket** *adj* uncultivated. **udødelig** *adj* immortal, undying; ~ *ry* immortal/undying fame. **udødelighet** *sb* immortality. **udåd** *sb* atrocity, misdeed.

ueffent *adj: ikke så* ~ not (half) bad. **uegennytte** *sb* disinterestedness, unselfishness. **uegennyttig** *adj* disinterested, unselfish. **uegnet** *adj* unsuited; ~ *til* unfit for. **uekte** *adj* **1** *(kunstig)* artificial; imitation, sham; **2** *(om falsum)* false, spurious; **3** *(unaturlig)* affected, artificial; **4** ~ *barn* illegitimate child. **uendelig** *adj, adv* **1** infinite; ~ *liten* infinitely small; **2** *(overordentlig stor også)* immense; **3** *(endeløs)* endless, unending; **4** *i det uendelige* indefinitely, for ever; endlessly. **uendelighet** *sb* infinity, endlessness. **uendret** *adj* unchanged, unaltered. **uengasjert** *adj* uncommitted, uninvolved; disinterested. **uenig** *adj: bli/være* ~ disagree; *det er jeg* ~ *med deg i* I disagree with you on that point; *selv gode venner blir/er av og til* ~*e* even good friends sometimes disagree; *to* ~*e brødre* two brothers who cannot agree. **uenighet** *sb* disagreement; *(strid også)* quarrel. **uensartet** *adj* heterogeneous. **uensartethet** *sb* heterogeneity. **uerfaren** *adj* inexperienced. **uerfarenhet** *sb* inexperience. **uerstattelig** *adj* irreplaceable, irretrievable; *(fig også)* irreparable.

ufaglært *adj* unskilled; ~ *arbeidskraft* unskilled labour. **ufarbar** *adj* impassable. **ufarlig** *adj* harmless; safe. **ufattelig** *adj* incomprehensible, inconceivable. **ufeilbar(lig)** *adj* infallible; *(om middel også)* unfailing. **uferdig** *adj* unfinished; *fig* incomplete; crude, rough. **uff!** *interj* oh! ugh! **uffe seg** *vb* complain, groan. **ufin** *adj* tactless; coarse, rude; vulgar. **ufinhet** *sb* tactlessness; coarseness, rudeness; bad taste. **uflaks** *sb* bad/rotten luck. **uflidd** *adj* messy, unkempt.

uforanderlig *adj* unchangeable; unalterable; constant, invariable. **uforanderlighet** *sb* unalterableness; invariability. **uforandret** *adj* unchanged, unaltered. **uforbederlig** *adj* incorrigible. **uforbeholden** *adj* unqualified, unreserved. **uforberedt** *adj* unprepared. **ufordelaktig** *adj* disadvantageous, unfavourable; *(om handel)* unprofitable; *en* ~ *stilling* an unfavourable position; *gjøre seg* ~ *bemerket* attract (unfavourable) attention. **ufordervet** *adj* uncorrupted, unspoiled. **ufordragelig** *adj* intolerable, unbearable. **ufordragelighet** *sb* intolerableness. **ufordøyd** *adj* undigested. **ufordøyelig** *adj* indigestible. **uforen(e)lig** *adj* incompatible, inconsistent; irreconcilable. **uforfalsket** *adj* unadulterated; genuine, pure. **uforferdet** *adj* fearless, intrepid. **uforferdethet** *sb* fearlessness, intrepidity. **uforgjengelig** *adj* imperishable; everlasting; *(udødelig)* immortal, undying. **uforgjengelighet** *sb* imperishableness; *(udødelighet)* immortality. **uforglemmelig** *adj* unforgettable. **uforholdsmessig** *adj, adv* disproportionate(ly). **uforklarlig** *adj* inexplicable. **uforkortet** *adj* unabridged. **uforlikt** *adj: være* ~ disagree, differ.

uformelig *adj* formless, shapeless. **uformelighet** *sb* shapelessness. **uformell** *adj* informal. **uforminsket** *adj* undiminished; *(usvekket)* unabated. **ufornuft** *sb* foolishness, folly; unreasonableness. **ufornuftig** *adj* foolish; unreasonable, unwise. **uforpliktende** *adj* non-committal. **uforrettet** *adj: med ~ sak* without having accomplished one's object; without success. **uforsiktig** *adj (som ikke passer seg, ser seg for etc)* incautious; *(skjødesløs)* careless; *(ubetenksom)* rash; *(også)* indiscreet. **uforsiktighet** *sb* incautiousness; carelessness. **uforskammet** *adj* impudent, insolent, rude. **uforskammethet** *sb* impudence, insolence. **uforskyldt** *adj* undeserved. **uforsonlig** *adj* inplacable. **uforsonlighet** *sb* implacability. **uforstand** *sb* foolishness. **uforstandig** *adj* unwise, foolish. **uforstyrrelig** *adj* imperturbable, unruffled. **uforstyrret** *adj* undisturbed. **uforståelig** *adj* unintelligible. **uforstående** *adj* uncomprehending; puzzled; *(udeltagende)* unappreciative, unsympathetic. **uforsvarlig** *adj* indefensible, inexcusable. **uforsøkt** *adj* untried. **ufortjent** *adj* undeserved, unmerited. **uforutsett** *adj* unforeseen; *~e omstendigheter/utgifter* unforeseen circumstances/expenses. **uforvarende** *adv (uventet)* unexpectedly; *(ufrivillig)* unintentionally.

ufravendt *adv: stirre ~ på* stare fixedly at. **ufravikelig** *adj: en ~ betingelse* an absolute condition; *en ~ regel* an invariable rule. **ufred** *sb (krig)* war; *(strid)* quarrel, strife. **ufremkommelig** *adj* impassable. **ufri** *adj* unfree; *(hemmet)* inhibited. **ufrihet** *sb* lack of freedom; *(slaveri)* bondage. **ufrivillig** *adj* involuntary; unintentional. **ufruktbar** *adj* barren, infertile, sterile. **ufruktbarhet** *sb* barrenness, infertility; sterility.

ufullendt *adj* unfinished. **ufullkommen** *adj* imperfect. **ufullkommenhet** *sb* imperfection. **ufullstendig** *adj* incomplete. **ufullstendighet** *sb* incompleteness. **ufyselig** *adj* disgusting, unappetizing. **ufødt** *adj* unborn. **ufølsom** *adj* insensitive, unfeeling; callous. **ufølsomhet** *sb* insensitiveness, unfeelingness; callousness. **ufør** *adj* disabled, invalid; *han er ~* he is an invalid. **uføretrygd** *sb* disablement benefit. **uførhet** *sb* disability, disablement.

ugagn *sb* mischief. **ugagnskråke** *sb* mischief--maker. **ugiddelig** *adj* feckless, indolent; lazy. **ugift** *adj* unmarried, single; *~ mann (også)* bachelor; *han er ~* he is unmarried/single/a bachelor.

ugjendrivelig *adj* irrefutable. **ugjenkallelig** *adj* irrevocable. **ugjenkjennelig** *adj* irrecognizable. **ugjennomførlig** *adj* impracticable, unworkable. **ugjennomførlighet** *sb* impracticableness. **ugjennomsiktig** *adj* opaque. **ugjennomsiktighet** *sb* opacity. **ugjennomtrengelig** *adj* impenetrable, impervious.

ugjerne *adj* unwillingly, reluctantly. **ugjerning** *sb* misdeed, outrage; crime. **ugjerningsmann** *sb* evil--doer, malefactor, miscreant. **ugjestfri** *adj* inhospitable. **ugjørlig** *adj* impossible, impracticable.

ugle *sb* owl; *det er ugler i mosen* there is some mischief brewing. **uglesett** *adj* frowned upon; disliked.

ugress *sb* weed. **ugress|dreper, ~middel** *sb* herbicide, weedkiller. **ugrunnet** *adj* groundless; baseless, unfounded. **ugudelig** *adj* impious, ungodly. **ugudelighet** *sb* impiety, ungodliness. **ugunst** *sb* **1** disfavour, displeasure; *han var i ~ hos generalen* he was in disfavour with the general; **2** *(skade)* prejudice; *til ~ for søsteren* to the prejudice of the (her, his, their etc) sister. **ugunstig** *adj* unfavourable. **ugyldig** *adj* invalid, void; *erklære ~* declare invalid/null and void. **ugyldighet** *sb* invalidity

uhederlig *adj* dishonest. **uhederlighet** *sb* dishonesty. **uhelbredelig** *adj* incurable. **uheldig** *adj* **1** *(som ikke har hell med seg)* unlucky, unsuccessful; **2** *(ikke vellykket)* bad; *en ~ begynnelse* a bad beginning; **3** *(beklagelig)* unfortunate. **uheldigvis** *adv* unfortunately. **uhell** *sb* **1** bad luck; *et ~* a piece of bad luck; **2** *(ulykke)* accident; *han var ute for et ~* he met with/had an accident. **uhemmet** *adj* unhampered, unrestrained; *(sjelelig)* uninhibited. **uhensiktsmessig** *adj* unsuitable, inexpedient. **uhildet** *adj* impartial, unbiassed. **uhindret** *adj* unchecked, unimpeded; unobstructed. **u-hjelp** se *utviklingshjelp*. **uhjemlet** *adj* unauthorized, unwarranted. **uholdbar** *adj* untenable. **uhumsk** *adj* filthy. **uhumskhet** *sb* filthiness, filth. **uhygge** *sb* **1** *(gru, redsel)* horror; **2** *(trist stemning)* dismal atmosphere; **3** *(ubehag)* discomfort. **uhyggelig** *adj* **1** *(nifs)* ghastly, grim, horrifying, uncanny, weird; **2** *(illevarslende)* ominous, sinister; **3** *(ubehagelig)* uncomfortable. **uhygienisk** *adj* unhygienic, insanitary. **uhyre** **1** *adj* huge, enormous, immense, vast; **2** *sb* monster. **uhyrlig** *adj* monstrous. **uhyrlighet** *sb* monstrosity. **uhøflig** *adj* impolite, rude; discourteous. **uhøflighet** *sb* impoliteness, rudenss; discourtesy. **uhørlig** *adj* inaudible. **uhørt** *adj* **1** *(enestående)* unheard of; *det er ~ at* ... it is unheard of that ...; **2** *(som ikke får uttale seg)* unheard; *de dømte dem ~* they condemned them unheard. **uhøytidelig** *adj* unceremonious. **uhåndgripelig** *adj* impalpable, intangible. **uhåndterlig** *adj* unwieldy, cumbersome, unhandy. **uhåndterlighet** *sb* unwieldiness.

uidentifisert *adj* unidentified. **uimotsagt** *adj* unchallenged, uncontradicted. **uimotsigelig** *adj* incontestable, indisputable; unquestionable. **uimotståelig** *adj* irresistible. **uimottakelig** *adj* **1** impervious, insusceptible, proof; *~ for fornuft* impervious to reason; *~ for ros* insusceptible to flattery; **2** *(immun)* immune. **uimottakelighet** *sb* imperviousness, insusceptibility; immunity. **uinnskrenket** *adj* unrestricted, absolute; *~ frihet* unrestricted liberty; *~ makt* absolute/unrestricted power. **uinntakelig** *adj* impregnable. **uinntakelighet** *sb* impregnability. **uinteressant** *adj* uninteresting. **uinteressert** *adj* uninterested. **uisolert** *adj* uninsulated; *(elek også)* uncovered.

ujevn *adj* **1** uneven; rough; **2** *(ulik)* unequal; *~ fordeling* unequal distribution. **ujevnhet** *sb* **1** unevenness; roughness, **2** inequality. **ujordet** *adj elek* unearthed.

uke *sb* week; *om en ~s tid* in a week or so. **uke|blad** *sb* weekly (magazine). **~dag** *sb* day of the week; *(hverdag)* weekday. **~lønn** *sb* (weekly) wages. **ukentlig** *adj, adv* weekly. **uke|penger** *sb* weekly allowance. **~vis** *adv: i ~vis* for weeks.

ukjennelig *adj* unrecognizable; *gjøre ~* disguise. **ukjennelighet** *sb: forandret til ~* changed beyond/ out of all recognition. **ukjent** *adj* unknown, unfamiliar; *~e omgivelser* unfamiliar surroundings; *et bilde av en ~ mester* a picture by an unknown master. **uklanderlig** *adj* blameless, irreproachable

uklar *adj* **1** *(disig)* hazy; **2** *(om væske)* cloudy, muddy, turbid; **3** *(utydelig)* blurred, indistinct; **4** *(vag)* hazy, vague; **5** *(vanskelig å forstå)* obscure; **6** *(forvirret)* confused; *(om pasient)* delirious, light-headed; **7** *ryke ~ med* fall out with. **uklarhet** *sb* dimness, haziness; indistinctness; obscurity; vagueness; confusion.

ukledelig *adj* unbecoming. **uklok** *adj* imprudent, unwise. **uklokskap** *sb* imprudence. **uknuselig** *adj* unbreakable. **ukomplett** *adj* incomplete. **ukontrollert** *adj* uncontrolled, unchecked. **ukorrekt** *adj* incorrect, wrong. **ukrenkelig** *adj* inviolable. **ukrenkelighet** *sb* inviolability. **ukritisk** *adj* uncritical. **ukrutt** *sb: ~ forgår ikke så lett* ill weeds grow apace. **ukuelig** *adj* indomitable. **ukurant** *adj: ~e varer* unsalable goods; dead stock. **ukultivert** *adj* uncultured. **ukvalifisert** *adj* unqualified. **ukvinnelig** *adj* unwomanly. **ukyndig** *adj* unskilled; ignorant. **ukyndighet** *sb* lack of skill; ignorance.

ul *sb* howl, howling.

ulag(e) *sb* **1** *bringe i ~* put out of order; upset; *være i ~* be in disorder/out of order; **2** *(ute av humør)* out of sorts. **u-land** se *utviklingsland.* **ulastelig** *adj* blameless, irreproachable; *(som adv) ~ antrukket/kledd* immaculately dressed.

ule *vb* hoot, howl.

uleilige *vb* inconvenience, trouble. **uleilighet** *sb* inconvenience, trouble; *jeg håper jeg ikke kommer til ~* I hope I am not intruding; *være til ~* give trouble. **ulempe** *sb* drawback, disadvantage, inconvenience. **ulendt** *adj* rugged, rough. **ulenkelig** *adj* lanky, ungainly. **uleselig** *adj* **1** *(vanskelig å lese)* illegible, unreadable; *en ~ håndskrift* an illegible/unreadable handwriting; **2** *(ikke verd å lese)* unreadable. **uleselighet** *sb* illegibility; unreadableness. **ulidelig** *adj* insufferable, intolerable.

ulik *adj* unlike, different. **ulike** *adj* unequal, uneven; *~ tall* odd/uneven numbers; *en ~ kamp* an unequal struggle. **ulike|artet** *adj* heterogeneous. **~vektig** *adj* unbalanced. **ulikhet** *sb* dissimilarity, difference; *(mangel på likestilling)* inequality; *sosial ~* social inequality.

ull *sb* wool. **ullen** *adj* woollen. **ull|garn** *sb* wool; woollen yarn. **~skjerf** *sb* woolen scarf; *(især US)* muffler. **~strømpe** *sb* woolen stocking. **~teppe** *sb* blanket. **~trøye** *sb* woollen vest.

ulme *vb* smoulder.

ulogisk *adj* illogical.

ulovlig *adj* illegal, unlawful. **ulovlighet** *sb* illegality, unlawfulness.

ultimatum *sb* ultimatum; *stille et ~* give an ultimatum.

ultra|fiolett *adj, sb* ultraviolet. **~lyd** *sb* ultrasound. **~marin** *adj* ultramarine.

ulv *sb* wolf. **ulve|flokk** *sb* pack of wolves. **~hi** *sb* wolf's lair. **~unge** *sb* wolf cub.

ulyd *sb* discord, dissonance. **ulydig** *adj* disobedient; *være ~ mot* disobey. **ulydighet** *sb* disobedience.

ulykke *sb* **1** accident; *det er hendt en ~* there has been an accident; *han omkom ved en ~* he was killed in an accident; **2** *(mer omfattende ~)* disaster; **3** *(uhell)* bad luck; misfortune; *det har vært hennes ~* that has been her misfortune; **4** *(motgang)* adversity, trouble. **ulykkelig** *adj* **1** unhappy; *et ~ liv* an unhappy life; *jeg var ~ over det* I was unhappy about it; **2** *(meget ~)* miserable, wretched; **3** *(uheldig)* unfortunate, unhappy. **ulykkeligvis** *adv* unfortunately, unhappily. **ulykkes|budskap** *sb* sad/tragic news. **~forsikre** *vb* insure against accidents. **~forsikring** *sb* accident insurance. **~fugl** *sb (en som stadig er utsatt for ulykker)* accident-prone person. **~profet** *sb* alarmist; *US* calamity howler. **~tilfelle** *sb* accident. **ulykksalig** *adj* disastrous, fatal; unhappy.

ulyst *sb* reluctance; *de gjorde det med ~* they did it reluctantly; they hated to do it. **ulystbetont** *adj* unpleasant. **ulærd** *adj* unlettered, unlearned. **ulønnet** *adj* unpaid. **ulønnsom** *adj* unprofitable. **uløselig** *adj* insoluble. **uløst** *adj* unsolved.

umak se *umake 2.* **umake 1** *adj* odd; *en ~ hanske* an odd glove; **2** *sb (uleilighet, umak)* pains, trouble; *er det ~n verdt?* is it worth while? *han gjorde seg ~ med arbeidet* he took pains/trouble over his work; *hun gjorde seg stor ~* she took great pains; **3** *vb: ~ seg* take pains.

umalt *adj* unpainted. **umandig** *adj* unmanly, effeminate. **umeddelsom** *adj* uncommunicative. **umedgjørlig** *adj* intractable, unmanageable; stubborn. **umenneske** *sb* brute, monster. **umenneskelig** *adj* **1** *(grusom)* inhuman; *~ grusomhet* inhuman cruelty; **2** *(overmenneskelig)* superhuman; *~e anstrengelser* superhuman efforts. **umerkelig** *adj* imperceptible, unnoticeable. **umettelig** *adj* insatiable. **umettelighet** *sb* insatiability. **umettet** *adj* unsaturated; *umettede fettsyrer* unsaturated fatty acids.

umiddelbar *adj* **1** immediate; *i ~ nærhet av skogen* in the immediate vicinity of the wood; **2** *(impulsiv)* impulsive, spontaneous. **umiddelbarhet** *sb* impulsiveness, spontaneity. **umiddelbart** *adv: umiddelbart etter/før* immediately after/before. **uminnelig** *adj: fra ~e tider* from time immemorial/out of mind. **umiskjennelig** *adj* unmistakable. **umistelig** *adj: ~e rettigheter* inalienable rights. **umoden** *adj* unripe; *(fig)* immature. **umodenhet** *adj* unripeness; *(fig)* immaturity. **umoderne** *adj* out of fashion; *(gammeldags)* old-fashioned; *bli ~* get out of fashion. **umoral** *sb* immorality. **umoralsk** *adj* immoral. **umotivert** *adj* unmotivated; *helt ~* for no reason whatever. **umulig** *adj* impossible; *ingenting er ~ for henne* nothing is impossible to her. **umulighet** *sb* impossibility. **umyndig** *adj* minor; under age. **umælende** *adj* dumb. **umøblert** *adj* unfurnished. **umåtelig 1** *adj* immense; enormous, huge; tremendous; **2** *adv* immensely; enormously; tremendously; ~ *rik* tremendously rich.

unatur *sb* unnaturalness. **unaturlig** *adj* **1** *(stridende mot naturen)* unnatural; *det er ~ ikke å være glad i barna sine* it is unnatural not to love one's children; **2** *(affektert, kunstig)* affected; **3** *(tvungen)* forced. **unaturlighet** se *unatur.*

under A *prep* **1** under; *~ sengen* under the bed; *barn ~ fem år* children under five years of age; *han har femti menn ~ seg* he has fifty men under him; **2** *(lavere enn etc)* below; *~ overflaten* below the surface; *det er ~ min verdighet* it is below my dignity; *en kaptein er/står ~ en general i rang* a captain is below a genral in rank; *temperaturer ~ null* temperatures below zero; **3** *(om tid)* during; *~ sitt opphold i Bergen* during her (his, their) stay in Bergen; **B** *sb (mirakel)* wonder, miracle; *det er et ~* it is a wonder; *hun tror på ~* she believes in miracles.

under|agent *sb* sub-agent. **~ansikt** *sb* lower part of the face. **~arm** *sb* forearm. **~avdeling** *sb* subdivision. **~balanse** *sb* deficit. **~betale** *vb* underpay. **~betaling** *sb* underpayment. **~bevisst** *adj* subconscious. **~bevissthet** *sb* subconsciousness; the subconscious. **~bitt** *sb* underhung/*US* undershot jaw. **~bukser** *sb* pants, underpants; underwear; *(korte ~bukser)* trunks; short underpants/underwear; *(især US)* (under)shorts; *(lange ~bukser)* long underpants/underwear; *(dame~ også)* knickers; *(truser)* briefs; *(især US)* panties. **~by** *vb* underbid, undercut; undersell. **~bygge** *vb* substantiate, support. **~danig** *adj* submissive, subservient; *(ydmyk)* humble. **~danighet** *sb* submissiveness, subservience. **~direktør** *sb* ≈ assistant/deputy director. **~entreprenør** *sb* sub-contractor. **~ernæring** *sb* undernourishment; *(pga feilaktig kosthold)* malnutrition. **~ernært** *adj* undernourished. **~etasje** *sb* basement. **~forstå** *vb* imply. **~fundig** *adj* **1** *(skjelmsk)* roguish; **2** *(spissfindig)* subtle. **~gang** *sb* **1** *(under gate etc)* subway; **2** *(ødeleggelse)* destruction, ruin, fall; *Romerrikets ~* the fall of the Roman Empire; **3** *(forlis)* loss. **~grave** *vb* undermine. **~gravningsvirksomhet** *sb* subversive activity. **~grunnsbane** *sb* underground (railway); tube; *US* subway. **~handle** *vb (forhandle)* negotiate. **~handling** *sb* negotiation; *de innledet ~er med fienden* they entered into negotiations with the enemy. **~hold** *sb* maintenance, support. **~holde** *vb* **1** *(forsørge)* support; *hun må ~holde sine gamle foreldre* she has to support her old parents; **2** *(more)* entertain, amuse; *tryllekunstneren ~holdt selskapet* the conjurer entertained the company. **~holdende** *adj* entertaining, amusing. **~holdning** *sb* entertainment. **~holdningsmusikk** *sb* light music. **~holdsbidrag** *sb* alimony, maintenance.

Underhuset the House of Commons.

under|hånden *adj* privately. **~jordisk** *adj* underground. **~kant** *sb: i ~kant av hva jeg hadde ventet* rather less than I had expected. **~kaste** *vb: ~ seg (gi etter)* submit; give in; *de nektet å ~kaste seg* they refused to submit. **~kastelse** *sb* subjection, submission. **~kjenne** *vb* reject; not approve; *jur* overrule. **~kjennelse** *sb* non-approval; *jur* overruling. **~kjeve** *sb* lower jaw. **~kjole** *sb* petticoat, slip. **~klassen** *sb* the lower classes *fl.* **~kropp** *sb* lower part of the body. **~kue** *vb* subdue, subjugate, suppress. **~kuelse** *sb* subjugation, suppression. **~køy(e)** *sb* lower berth. **~lag** *sb* support; base, foundation; bed(ding); *(skriveunderlag)* blotting pad; *(teltunderlag)* ground sheet. **~laken** *sb* bottom sheet. **~legen** *adj* inferior; *han er henne ~legen* he is inferior to her. **~legenhet** *sb* inferiority. **~legge** *vb: ~legge seg* subdue, subjugate; conquer. **~leppe** *sb* lower lip.

underlig *adj (merkelig, rar)* curious, odd, strange; *(oftest med kritiserende undertone)* peculiar; *for en ~ ting å gjøre!* what a peculiar thing to do!

under|liggende *adj: ~liggende motiver* underlying motives. **~liv** *sb* abdomen. **~livssykdom** *sb* abdominal disease. **~minere** *vb* undermine. **~munn** *sb* lower part of the mouth. **~måler** *sb* dunce, numskull. **~måls** *adj* below standard. **~offiser** *sb* non-commissioned officer. **~ordne** *vb: ~ordne seg* subordinate oneself to. **~ordnet** *adj* subordinate; *(uviktig)* minor, secondary; *av ~ betydning* of secondary importance. **~representert** *adj* underrepresented. **~retning** *sb* information; *de fikk ~retning om farens død* they were informed of their father's death; they learned/received information about their father's death; *få ~retning om at...* be informed that... **~rett** *sb* ≈ lower court. **~rette** *vb* inform; *de er godt ~rettet* they are well informed; *vi ble ~rettet om at fangen var unnsluppet* we were informed that the prisoner had escaped. **~setsig** *adj* squat, stocky, thickset. **~side** *sb* underside. **~sjøisk** *adj* submarine. **~skjorte** *sb* vest; *US* undershirt. **~skjørt** *sb* petticoat, slip; underskirt. **~skrift** *sb* signature. **~skrive** *vb* sign. **~skudd** *sb* deficit; *gå med ~skudd* show a deficit. **~slag** *sb* embezzlement; *begå ~slag* embezzle. **~slå** *vb* **1** *(begå underslag)* embezzle; **2** *(holde tilbake opplysninger etc)* suppress, intercept.

underst *adj* lowest, bottom; *han la bøkene mine ~* he placed my books at the bottom.

under|stell *sb* chassis. **~stellsbehandling** *sb (av bil)* undersealing. **~streke** *vb* underline, (under)score; emphasize. **~strekning** *sb* underlining, (under)scoring; emphasizing. **~støtte** *vb* support. **~støttelse** *sb* support; *(til særlig trengende)* relief. **~søke** *vb* examine; *(forske, granske)* explore, research; *jeg ~søkte bildet* I examined the picture; *legen ~søkte pasienten* the doctor examined the patient. **~søkelse** *sb* examination; *(gransking, utforskning)* exploration; *(vitenskapelig ~søkelse)* research; *en nærmere ~søkelse av papirene* a closer examination of the papers. **~søkelseskommisjon** *sb* fact-finding committee. **~sått** *sb* subject. **~tegne** *vb* sign. **~tegnede** *sb* the undersigned. **~tiden** *adv* sometimes; now and then. **~tittel** *sb* subheading, subtitle. **~trykke** *vb* **1**

(hindre, holde tilbake) suppress; *de ~trykker sannheten* they suppress the truth; **2** *(underkue)* oppress. **~trykkelse** suppression; oppression; *~trykkelsen av de fattige* the oppression of the poor. **~trykker** *sb (tyrann)* oppressor, tyrant. **~trøye** *sb* vest; *US* undershirt. **~tvinge** *vb* subdue, subjugate. **~tvingelse** *sb* subjection, subjugation. **~tøy** *sb* underwear. **~utviklet** *adj* underdeveloped. **~vannsbåt** *sb* submarine; *(også)* U-boat. **~veis** *adv: han er ~* he is on the way. **~vekt** *sb* underweight. **~vektig** *adj* underweight; *(om varer)* deficient/short in weight. **~verden** *sb* underworld. **~verk** *sb* wonder, miracle; *Verdens syv ~verk* the Seven Wonders of the World.

under|vise *vb* teach; *han ~viser klassen i spansk* he takes the class in Spanish; *hun ~viser i russisk* she teaches Russian. **~visning** instruction, tuition; lessons; *(om ~ man gir også)* teaching; *(~ man får også)* education, training; *hun fikk/tok ~visning i norsk* she took lessons in Norwegian; *jeg gir ~visning i engelsk* I teach English; *(privat)* I give lessons in English; *språkundervisning* language teaching; *svømmeundervisning* instruction in swimming. **undervisnings|departement** *sb GB* Department of Education and Science. **~film** *sb* educational film. **~kompetanse** *sb* teaching qualifications. **~materiell** *sb* educational/teaching material. **~metode** *sb* teaching method. **~minister** *sb GB* Secretary of State for Education and Science. **~time** *sb* lesson.

under|vurdere *vb* underestimate, underrate, undervalue. **~vurdering** *sb* underestimation, underestimate, undervaluation.

undre *vb* astonish, surprise, wonder; *det ~r meg å se deg her* I am astonished/surprised to see you here; *jeg ~r meg over hans engstelse* I wonder/am astonished/surprised at his anxiety. **undres** *vb* wonder; *jeg ~ på om* I wonder if. **undring** *sb* astonishment, surprise, wonder.

undulat *sb* budgerigar.

unektelig *adv* without a doubt; certainly; *det er ~ en stor risiko, men...* it is certainly a great risk, but...

ung *adj* young; *en ~ mann* a young man; *en ~ pike* a girl; *(en ganske ~ pike)* a young girl; *som ~* as a young girl/man. **ungdom** *sb* **1** *(ungdomsalder, -tid)* youth; *(tidlig ~ også)* adolescence; *i hennes (sin) første ~* in her early youth; in her adolescence; **2** *(ungt menneske)* youth; *en ~ på atten år,* a youth of eighteen; *et halvt dusin ~mer* half a dozen youths; *landsbyens ~* the youth/the young people of the village. **ungdommelig** *adj* youthful; *se ~ ut* look young. **ungdommelighet** *sb* youthfulness. **ungdoms|forbryter** *sb* juvenile delinquent; young offender. **~herberge** *sb* youth hostel. **~kriminalitet** *sb* juvenile delinquency. **~skole** *sb* ≈ secondary school; *US* ≈ junior high school.

unge *sb* **1** *(barn)* child; *(især US)* kid; *(neds)* brat; *(fl også)* young ones; **2** *(dyre~)* young one; *(~ av bjørn, rev, ulv)* cub; *et dyr med (sine) unger* an animal with its young (ones).

ungkar *sb* bachelor.

uniform *sb* uniform. **uniformere** *vb fig* standardize. **uniformitet** *sb* uniformity. **unikum** *sb: være et ~* be unique. **union** *sb* union. **unisont** *adv: ynge ~* sing in unison. **univers** *sb* universe. **universal|arving** *sb* residuary legatee. **~geni** *sb* universal genius. **~middel** *sb* panacea. **universell** *adj* universal. **universitet** *sb* university; *hun studerte ved ~et* she studied at the university.

unna *adv* **1** away, off; *langt ~* far away/off; **2** *(av veien)* out of the way; *få ~* get out of the way; clear away; *(om arbeid etc)* get done; finish; *gjemme/stikke ~* hide/put away; *gå ~* get out of the way; *(om varer)* be sold; sell; *komme (seg)/slippe ~* escape/get away (from). **unna|bakke** *sb* downhill slope. **~gjort** *adj, pp: arbeidet er ~gjort* the work is finished.

unndra *vb* **1** deprive of; withhold from; **2** *~ seg* evade, shirk; *~ seg oppmerksomheten* escape notice.

unne *vb: det er deg vel unt* you are welcome (to it); *jeg ~r ham hans hell* I am glad for his success.

unn|gjelde *vb* pay; *~ for* pay/suffer for; *jeg fikk ~ for min nysgjerrighet* I had to pay/was made to suffer for my prying. **~gå** *vb* **1** *(med vilje)* avoid; *han ~r meg* he avoids me; *hun unngikk å bli sett* she avoided being seen; *jeg kan ikke ~ å gjøre det* I cannot avoid/help doing it; **2** *(slippe fra)* escape; *du var heldig som unngikk faren* you were lucky to escape the danger; **3** *(~ på en smart måte)* evade; *han unngikk spørsmålet* he evaded the question. **~komme** *vb* escape. **~late** *vb* fail, omit; *~ å stemme* abstain; *han unnlot å gjøre det* he failed/omitted to do it. **~seelse** *sb* bashfulness. **~selig** *adj* bashful, shy. **~selighet** *sb* bashfulness, shyness. **~setning** *sb* relief, rescue; *komme til ~* come to the rescue. **~sette** *vb* relieve, rescue.

unn|skylde *vb* excuse; *unnskyld! (når man har gjort noe galt etc)* I am sorry! so sorry! *(når man står i begrep med å gjøre noe)* excuse me! *(fornærmet)* pardon me! *jeg finner det vanskelig å ~ oppførselen hans* I find it hard to excuse his conduct; *unnskyld at jeg kommer for sent!* excuse me for coming late! excuse my being late! **~skyldning** *sb* **1** *(det å be om forlatelse)* apology; *hun bad om ~skyldning* she made an apology; she apologized; *jeg bad om ~skyldning fordi jeg kom for sent* I apologized for being late; **2** *(påskudd)* excuse, pretext; *en dårlig ~* a poor excuse.

unn|slippe *vb* escape. **~slå** *vb: ~slå seg* decline, refuse; excuse oneself.

unn|ta *vb* except; make an exception of; *jeg ~r din mor* I except/make an exception of your mother; *når en ~r, når ~s* except for. **~tagen** se *unntatt.* **~tak** *sb* exception; *et ~ fra regelen* an exception to the rule; *jeg kan ikke gjøre noe ~ for deg* I can make no exception for you; *med ~ av* with the exception of; *uten ~* without exception. **~takelse** se *unntak.* **~takstilstand** *sb* state of emergency. **~tatt** *prep* except; *(etter ubestemt pron)* but; *~ hvis/om* unless.

unn|vikende *adj* evasive; *adv* evasively; *han svarte ~* he answered evasively. **~være** *vb* **1** do/go without; *jeg kan ikke ~ ham* I cannot do without him; **2** *(avse,* *ikke bruke)* spare; *jeg har ingen tid å ~* I have no time to spare. **~værlig** adj dispensable.

unormal *adj* abnormal. **unote** *sb* bad habit. **unyansert** *adj* indiscriminate, over-simplified. **unytte** *sb: til ~* useless(ly); of no purpose; *(fåfengt)* in vain. **unyttig** *adj* useless. **unødig 1** *adj* needless; *~ sløsing* needless waste; **2** *adv* needlessly; *ikke plag ham ~* do not trouble him needlessly. **unødvendig** *adj* unnecessary, needless. **unødvendighet** *sb* needlessness. **unøyaktig** *adj* inaccurate. **unøyaktighet** *sb* inaccuracy. **unåde** *sb* disgrace; *falle i ~* fall into disgrace. **unådig** *adj* ungracious; *som adv: han tok det ~ opp* he took it ill.

uoffisiell *adj* inofficial; informal.

uomgjengelig *adv: ~ nødvendig* absolutely necessary. **uomtvistelig** *adv* incontestable, indisputable.

uoppdragen *adj* ill-mannered, rude. **uoppdragenhet** *sb* bad manners. **uoppdyrket** *adj* uncultivated, untilled. **uoppgjort** *adj* unsettled. **uoppholdelig** *adv* without delay. **upphørlig** *adj* incessant; *adv* incessantly; *det regnet ~* it rained incessantly. **uoppklart** *adj* unsolved, unexplained. **uopplagt** *adj* indisposed; not in form. **uoppmerksom** *adj* inattentive. **uoppmerksomhet** *sb* inattention. **uoppnåelig** *adj* unattainable. **uopprettelig** *adj* irreparable. **uoppriktig** *adj* insincere. **uoppriktighet** *sb* insincerity. **uoppsigelig** *adj* **1** *(om person i arbeidsforhold)* irremovable; **2** *(om lån etc)* irredeemable; **3** *(om kontrakt etc)* non-terminable. **uoppslitelig** *adj* inexhaustible; *~ energi* inexhaustible/untiring energy; *~ godt humør* unfailing good humour.

uorden *sb* disorder. **uordentlig** *adj* disorderly; *(uryddig)* untidy; *(sjusket)* slovenly. **uordentlighet** *sb* disorderliness, untidiness. **uorganisert** *adj* unorganized; *(om ~ arbeider også)* non-union. **uorganisk** *adj* inorganic. **uortodoks** *adj* unorthodox.

uoverensstemmelse *sb* **1** *(uenighet)* disagreement; **2** *(avvik)* discrepancy. **uoverkommelig** *adj* insurmountable; impossible, impracticable. **uoverkommelighet** *sb* impossibility. **uoverlagt** *adj* umpremeditated; rash. **uoversettelig** *adj* untranslatable. **uoversiktlig** *adj: en ~ sving* a blind curve. **uoverskuelig** *adj: ~e følger* incalculable consequences; *i ~ fremtid* for an indefinite period. **uoverstigelig** *adj* insurmountable **uovertruffet** *adj* unrivalled, unsurpassed. **uoverveid** *adj* ill-considered, rash. **uovervinnelig** *adj* invincible. **uovervinnelighet** *sb* invincibility.

uparlamentarisk *adj* unparliamentary. **upartisk** *adj* impartial. **upartiskhet** *sb* impartiality. **upassende** *adj* improper, unbecoming, unseemly. **upatriotisk** *adj* unpatriotic. **upersonlig** *adj* impersonal. **upolitisk** *adj* unpolitical. **upopulær** *adj* unpopular. **upraktisk** *adj* **1** unpractical; *en ~ metode/person* an unpractical method/person; **2** *(om ting)* awkward; *~ redskap* awkward tools. **uprioritert** *adj* unsecured. **uprivilegert** *adj* unprivileged. **uproduktiv** *adj* unproductive. **uprøvd** *adj* untried. **upåaktet** *adj* unheeded, unnoticed; disregarded. **upåklagelig** *adj* irreproachable; (entirely) satisfactory; *(som adv) arbeidet var ~ utført* the work was satisfactorily done. **upålitelig** *adj* unreliable. **upålitelighet** *sb* unreliability. **upåtalt** *adj* unchallenged; *la noe gå ~ (også)* overlook something. **upåvirkelig** *adj* **1** *(ufølsom)* insensitive; **2** *(uaffisert, urokkelig)* impassive, stolid. **upåvirket** *adj* unaffected, unmoved.

ur *sb* **A** *(stein~)* scree; **B** *(klokke)* watch; *(større ~)* clock.

uran *sb* uranium. **uranmile** *sb* uranium pile.

uransakelig *adj* inscrutable.

uravstemning *sb* ballot; *foreta ~ blant medlemmene* ballot the members.

urealistisk *adj* unrealistic. **uredd** *adj* fearless, intrepid, undaunted. **uredelig** *adj* dishonest, unfair. **uredelighet** *sb* dishonesty, unfairness. **uregelmessig** *adj* irregular; *~ puls* irregular pulse; *han levde ~* he led an irregular life. **uregelmessighet** *sb* irregularity. **uregjerlig** *adj* unruly; intractable, unmanageable; *bli ~* get out of hand. **ureglementert** *adj* non-regulation; *(dgl også)* not according to the book.

uren *adj* dirty, unclean; *(også fig)* impure. **urenhet** *sb* impurity. **urenslig** *adj* uncleanly. **urenslighet** *sb* uncleanliness.

urett *sb* wrong, injustice; *~ mot noen* injustice to somebody; *den ~ jeg har lidd* the wrongs I have suffered; *du gjør ~ i å sende dem bort* you are wrong in sending them away; *han hadde ~* he was wrong; *hun gjorde sin bror ~* she did her brother an injustice; *jeg handlet ~* I did wrong. **urettferdig** *adj* unfair, unjust; *han var ~ mot meg* he was unfair/unjust to me. **urettferdighet** *sb* injustice; *hun begikk en ~ mot meg* she did me an injustice. **urettmessig** *adj* anlawful. **urettmessighet** *sb* unlawfulness.

uriaspost *sb* post of danger.

uridderlig *adj* unchivalrous. **uriktig** *adj (gal)* incorrect, wrong. **uriktighet** *sb* incorrectness, wrong. **urimelig** *adj* **1** *(meningsløs)* absurd; **2** *(vanskelig å omgås etc)* unreasonable; *en ~ person* an unreasonable person; *et ~ krav* an unreasonable claim. **urimelighet** *sb* absurdity, unreasonableness.

urin *sb* urine. **urinere** *vb* urinate.

urinnbyggere *sb fl* aborigines.

urinprøve *sb* urine specimen.

ur|kasse *sb* clock case. **~kjede** *sb* watch chain. **~maker** *sb* watch-maker, clock-maker.

urne *sb* urn; *(valg~)* ballot box.

uro *sb* **1** unrest; *(engstelse)* anxiety, uneasiness; alarm; *(opphisselse)* excitement; *det vakte stor ~* it caused great anxiety; *hun følte ~ for det* she was alarmed/anxious about it; *min ~ for ham* my anxiety for him; **2** se *uroligheter*. **uroe** *vb* disturb, trouble. **uroelement** *sb* disturbing element/factor.

urokkelig *adj* firm, steadfast; inflexible. **urokket** *adj* unmoved, unshaken; firm.

urolig *adj* **1** *(hvileløs)* restless; *en ~ natt* a restless night; **2** *(vimsete)* fidgety; *et ~ barn* a fidgety child; **3**

(engstelig) troubled; *hun var ~ fordi han ble/var så lenge borte* she was troubled about his long absence; **4** *(bekymringsfull, vanskelig)* troubled: *~e tider* troubled times; **5** *(bråkete)* noisy; **6** *(uttrykk) ~ hav* rough sea; *være ~ (i kroppen)* fidget; *(i sinnet)* worry; be uneasy; *jeg er ~ for fremtiden* I am uneasy about the future. **uroligheter** *sb fl* disturbances, tumults; troubles; unrest; *~ blant arbeiderne* labour troubles; *indre ~* domestic unrest. **urostifter** *sb* rioter, trouble-maker; *(politisk)* (political) firebrand. **urovekkende** *adj* disquieting.

urpremiere *sb* first performance; *(om film)* first showing.

urskive *sb* dial; face of a clock/watch.

urskog *sb* virgin/primeval forest.

urt *sb* herb. **urtete** *sb* herb-tea.

urtid *sb* prehistoric times.

ur|verk *sb* works of a clock/watch; *(fjærmotor)* clock-work; *som et ~verk* like clock-work. **~viser** *sb* hand of clock/watch.

uryddig *adj* untidy, messy; *fig* confused. **urørlig** *adj* motionless; *han lå (satt, stod) ~* he did not stir. **urørt** *adj* untouched; *(især fig: uberørt)* intact. **uråd** *sb* **1** *ane ~* smell a rat; suspect mischief; **2** *det er ~* it is impossible.

usagt *pp: det skal være ~* I cannot say/tell; it/that is an open question. **usaklig** *sb* biassed; not objective. **usammenhengende** *adj* disconnected, incoherent. **usammensatt** *adj* simple, uncompounded. **usann** *adj* untrue. **usannferdig** *adj* untruthful. **usannhet** *adj* untruth; falsehood, lie. **usannsynlig** *adj, adv* improbable, unlikely; *det er slett ikke ~ at han kommer* it is not at all unlikely that he will come; *en ~ historie* an improbable story; *høyst ~* most unlikely. **usannsynlighet** *sb* improbability, unlikelihood.

usedelig *adj* immoral. **usedelighet** *sb* immorality. **usedvanlig 1** *adj (uvanlig)* extraordinary; uncommon, unusual; *intet ~* nothing unusual; **2** *adv* extraordinarily; uncommonly, unusually. **uselgelig** *adj* unmarketable, unsaleable. **uselskapelig** *adj* unsociable. **uselskapelighet** *sb* unsociability. **uselvisk** *adj* unselfish. **uselviskhet** *sb* unselfishness. **uselvstendig** *adj* **1** *(om person)* dependent (on others); weak; **2** *(om arbeid)* unoriginal. **uselvstendighet** *sb* dependence (on others); weakness. **usett** *adj* unseen.

usigelig *adj* unspeakable, unutterable; *adv især* unspeakably. **usikker** *adj* **1** *(forbundet med fare)* insecure, unsafe; *en ~ stilling* an unsafe position; **2** *(ikke til å stole på)* uncertain, unreliable; *en ~ hukommelse* an uncertain/unreliable memory; **3** *(tvilende, tvilsom)* doubtful; *jeg var ~ på resultatet* I was doubtful about/of the outcome; *resultatet er ~t* the result is doubtful; **4** *(ustø)* unsteady. **usikkerhet** *sb* insecurity, uncertainty; doubt; unsteadiness. **usikkerhetsmoment** *sb* uncertain factor. **usivilisert** *sb* uncivilized, savage. **usjenert** *adj (uforstyrret)* undisturbed.

uskadd *adj* unharmed, unhurt; uninjured; safe; *(om person ofte)* safe and sound; *(om ting også)* undamaged. **uskadelig** *adj* harmless, innocuous. **uskadelig|gjøre** *vb* render harmless; *bomben ble ~gjort* the bomb was rendered harmless. **uskikk** *sb* bad habit/custom. **uskikkelig** *adj* naughty. **uskikkelighet** *sb* naughtiness. **uskikket** *adj* unfit, unsuited; unqualified. **uskyld** *sb* innocence. **uskyldig** *adj* innocent; *~e fornøyelser* innocent amusements; *et ~ barn* an innocent child; *han er ~ i forbrytelsen* he is innocent of the crime. **uskyldighet** se *uskyld*. **uskylds|hvit, ~ren** *adj* lily-white; pure and innocent.

usling *sb* scoundrel, wretch; cad, heel. **uslitelig** *adj* everlasting, indestructible; longwearing. **usmak** *sb* disagreeable taste. **usmakelig** *adj* unsavoury. **usminket** *adj* without make-up; unpainted; *den usminkede sannhet* the plain (naked, unvarnished) truth. **uspesifisert** *adj* unspecified. **uspiselig** *adj* **1** *(som kan ikke spises)* inedible; **2** *(som er dårlig tillaget)* uneatable, inedible. **uspurt** *adj* unasked. **ussel** *adj* **1** *(elendig)* miserable, wretched; *(som adv: ~t)* miserably, wretchedly; **2** *(sjofel)* low, mean; base; *en ~ handling* a low/base/mean action. **usselhet** *sb* misery, wretchedness, meanness.

ustabil *adj* unstable. **ustadig** *adj* changeable, inconstant; unstable, unsteady; *~ vær* changeable weather; *en ~ karakter* an unstable character. **ustadighet** *sb* inconstancy, instability. **ustand** *sb: i ~* out of order. **ustanselig** *adj (stadig gjentatt)* continual; *(uavbrutt)* ceaseless, continuous; *(uopphørlig)* constant, incessant, continual, steady. Jf *uavbrutt*. **ustelt** *adj* unkempt, untidy. **ustemt** *adj* **1** *(om språklyd)* unvoiced, voiceless; **2** *(om musikkinstrument)* untuned. **ustraffet** *adj* unpunished; *gjøre noe ~* do something with impunity; *hun var tidligere ~* she was a first offender. **ustyrlig** *adj* unruly, intractable. **ustyrlighet** *sb* unruliness, intractability. **ustyrtelig 1** *adj: en ~ mengde* a prodigious amount/number; **2** *adv* enormously, incredibly. **ustø** *adj* unstable, unsteady. **ustøhet** *sb* instability, unsteadiness.

usukret *adj* unsweetened. **usunn** *adj* unhealthy, unwholesome; *~ mat* unwholesome food; *et ~ arbeid* an unhealthy occupation. **usurpator** *sb* usurper. **usurpere** *vb* usurp. **usvekket** *adj* unimpaired; unabated, unflagging; undiminished; *~ energi* undiminshed energy; *~ interesse* unabated/unflagging interest; *~ syn* unimpaired vision. **usvikelig** *adj* unfailing, unfaltering. **usympatisk** *adj* not lik(e)able; unpleasant, unattractive; *jeg synes de er ~e* I do not like them. **usynlig** *adj* invisible. **usynlighet** *sb* invisibility. **usømmelig** *adj* improper, indecent. **usømmelighet** *sb* impropriety, indecency. **usårlig** *adj* invulnerable. **usårlighet** *sb* invulnerability.

ut *adv* out; *han løp ~* he ran out; *hun leste ~ boken* she read the book through; *jeg vil ~* I want to go/get out; *in av det ene øret og ~* **av** *det andre* in at one ear out at the other; *~* **fra** *ditt synspunkt* from your point of view; *kjenne ~* **og inn** know inside out; know the ins and outs (of); *jeg vet verken ~* **eller inn** I am at a loss what to do; I am quite at sea; *~* **med** *det!* out with it!

han måtte ~ *med 20 pund* he had to pay £20; ~ **på** *natten/vinteren* late at night/in the winter. **utad** *adv* outwards; *situasjonen* ~ the external situation. **utadvendt** *adj fig* extrovert.

utakk *sb* ingratitude; ~ *er verdens lønn* ingratitude is the way of the world. **utakknemlig** *adj* ungrateful; *en* ~ *jobb* an ungrateful job. **utakknemlighet** *sb* ingratitude; *hun viste ham* ~ she showed ingratitude to him. **utakt** *sb: i* ~ out of time; *(under marsj)* out of step. **utall** *sb* countless number. **utallig** *adj* countless, innumerable.

ut|arbeide *vb* draw up; prepare; ~*arbeide en tale (også)* compose a speech; *de* ~*arbeidet en rapport* they drew up/prepared a report. ~**arbeidelse** *sb: under* ~*arbeidelse* in course of preparation. ~**armet** *adj* impoverished. ~**arte** *vb* degenerate; ~*arte til* develop into. ~**arting** *sb* degeneration.

ut|basunere *vb* blazon/trumpet abroad; shout from the housetops. ~**be** *vb:* ~*be seg* ask for; request. ~**bedre** *vb* mend, repair. ~**bedring** *sb* repair. ~**betale** *vb* pay. ~**betaling** *sb* payment; *kontant* ~*betaling* cash payment. ~**blåsing** *sb petro* blowout. ~**bre** *vb* circulate, distribute, spread. ~**bredelse** *sb* distribution; *(om aviser etc)* circulation; *avisen har stor* ~*bredelse* the paper has a wide circulation; *denne planten har stor* ~*bredelse* this plant has a wide distribution. ~**bredt** *adj* widespread, common; *en* ~*bredt tro* a widespread/common belief. ~**brent** *adj* burnt-out. ~**bringe** *vb:* ~*bringe en skål for* propose a toast of. ~**brodere** *vb fig* embroider upon. ~**brudd** *sb* **1** *(begynnelse)* outbreak; *ved krigsutbruddet* at the outbreak of the war; **2** *(anfall)* outburst; **3** *(rop)* burst out; cry, exclamation; *et* ~*brudd av overraskelse* a cry of surprise; **4** *(vulkanutbrudd)* eruption. ~**brukt** *adj* worn out. ~**bryte** *vb* burst out; cry, exclaim. ~**bygge** *vb* develop. ~**bygging** *sb* developing, development. ~**bytte I** *sb* **1** *(fortjeneste)* profit(s), return(s); *få stort* ~*bytte* make a large profit/large profits; *selge med* ~*bytte* sell at a profit; **2** *(fordel)* benefit, profit; *han fikk* ~*bytte av sitt opphold i London* he profited by his stay in London; **II** *vb (utnytte grovt)* exploit. ~**bytterik** *adj* profitable. ~**bytting** *sb* exploitation.

ut|danne *vb* educate; *(især om praktisk eller lavere* ~*dannelse)* train; ~*dannet ved Eton og Oxford* educated at Eton and Oxford; *fullt* ~*dannet* fully trained/qualified; *han* ~*dannet seg i tysk* he studied German; *hun* ~*dannet seg som lærer/til en stilling* she qualified as a teacher/for a post. ~**dannelse** *sb* education; *(især om praktisk eller lavere* ~*dannelse)* training. ~**debattere** *vb: emnet er* ~*debattert* the subject is exhausted. ~**dele** *vb* distribute. Se for øvrig *dele*. ~**deling** *sb* distribution. ~**drag** *sb* extract, summary. ~**dype** *vb fig* amplify; *kan De* ~*dype den uttalelsen?* can you amplify that statement? ~**dypning** *sb* amplification. ~**dødd** *adj* extinct; *en* ~*dødd rase* an extinct race.

ute *adv* **1** out; outside; out of doors; ~ *på havet* (out) at sea; ~ *på landet* (out) in the country; *der/her* ~ out there/here; *han var* ~ *en tur* he was out for a walk; *hun er* ~ *med noen venner* she is out with some friends; *vi lar bilen stå* ~ *hele natten* we leave our car out all night; **2** *(over, slutt)* at an end; up; *alt håp er* ~ all hope is at an end; *tiden er* ~ time is up; **3** *(uttrykk)* ~ **av seg** beside oneself; ~ **av syne** out of sight; *jeg er* ~ **av stand til** *å gjøre det* I am unable to do it.

ute|arbeid *sb* outdoor work. ~**bli** *vb* fail to appear/come; stay away; *resultatet* ~*ble ikke* the result was what might have been expected. ~**blivelse** *sb* non-attendance; *jur* default. ~**fra** se *utenfra*. ~**glemt** *adj, pp* left out by mistake.

utekkelig *adj:* ~ *oppførsel* offensive/odious behaviour.

uteksaminert *adj, pp: hun er* ~ *fra Tromsø* she graduated from Tromsø.

ute|late *vb* leave out; omit; *han* ~*lot et ord* he left out a word. ~**latelse** *sb* omission. ~**liv** *sb* outdoor life. ~**lukke** *vb* exclude; *de er* ~*lukket fra det gode selskap* they are excluded from respectable society; *det er* ~*lukket at hun gjør det* it is impossible/out of the question that she should do it. ~**lukkelse** *sb* exclusion. ~**lukkende** *adv* exclusively.

uten *prep* **1** without; ~ *at de visste det* without their knowing it; ~ *penger* without money; with no money; ~ *tvil* without doubt; ~ *å snakke* without speaking; *gå ut* ~ *hatt* go out with no hat on; **2** *(unntatt)* except, but; *alle* ~ *du* everybody except you; *ingen* ~ *ham* no one but he/him.

uten|at *adv* by heart; *jeg kan det* ~*at* I know it by heart; *lære* ~*at* learn by heart. ~**bords** *adj, adv* outboard. ~**bys** *adj, adv* outside the town; ~*bys slektninger* relatives in/from the provinces. ~**dørs** *adj* outdoor; *adv* outdoors; ~*dørs aktiviteter* outdoor activities; *barna leker* ~*dørs hele dagen* the children play outdoors all day.

uten|for *adv, prep* outside; *jeg lot kofferten stå igjen* ~*for* I left the trunk outside/outside the house; *vi holdt oss* ~*for (dvs vi blandet oss ikke inn)* we kept out of it. ~**forstående** *sb: en* ~*forstående* an outsider. ~**fra** *adv* from (the) outside; *intet lys kunne ses* ~*fra* no light could be seen from the outside; *jeg åpnet døren* ~*fra* I opened the door from the outside.

utenkelig *adj: det er* ~ *at* ... it is out of the question that ...

uten|lands *adv* abroad; *vi reiste* ~*lands* we went abroad. ~**landsk** *adj* foreign; from abroad; *våre* ~*landske gjester* our guests/visitors from abroad. ~**landsreise** *sb* journey abroad.

utenom *adv:* ~ *det vanlige* out of the ordinary; *gå* ~ *saken* evade the issue; *han gikk* ~ he went round it. **utenom|ekteskapelig** *adj* extra-marital. ~**snakk** *sb* irrelevant talk; *komme med* ~ beat about the bush.

uten|på *adv* outside; on the outside. ~**påskrift** *sb* outside address.

utenriks|departementet *sb GB* Ministry of Foreign Affairs; *dgl* Foreign Office; *US* Department of State; *dgl* State Department. ~**fart** *sb* foreign trade. ~**handel** *sb* foreign trade. ~**minister** *sb* Minister for/of Foreign Affairs; *GB* Foreign Secretary; *US* Secretary of State. **~politikk** *sb* foreign affairs/politics; *(om en bestemt politikk)* foreign policy; *Napoleons ~politikk* Napoleon's foreign policy.

utenverdenen *sb* the outside world.

ute|stenge *vb* exclude. Se også *utelukke*. **~stående** *adj: ~ fordringer* outstanding claims.

utett *adj* **1** *(ikke tettsluttende)* not tight; **2** *(som lekker)* leaking, leaky.

ut|fall *sb* **1** *(resultat)* result; *~fallet av fotballkampen* the result of the football match; **2** *(angrep)* attack; *et ~fall mot statsråden* an attack on the minister. **~fart** *sb* exodus; *~farten fra byene* the exodus from the towns. **~fartssted** *sb* excursion spot; resort. **~ferdige** *vb* draw up; make/write out; prepare. **~flod** *sb* discarge. **~flukt** *sb* **1** *(tur)* excursion; *(med niste)* picnic; *de foretok en ~flukt til Cambridge* they went on/made an excursion to Cambridge; **2** *(dårlig unnskyldning)* excuse; evasion; *(også)* evasive answer; *komme med ~flukter* prevaricate, quibble; beat about the bush. **~fluktssted** resort. **~flytende** *adj* diffuse. **~flytning** *sb* emigration. **~flytter** *sb* emigrant. **~folde** *vb* **1** *(folde ut)* unfold; *~folde seg (fig)* expand; blossom out; **2** *(legge for dagen)* display; *de ~foldet stor energi* they displayed great energy. **~foldelse** *sb* development, display.

utfor *adv* downhill. **utfor|bakke** *sb* downhill slope; descent. **~renn** *sb* downhill race.

ut|fordre *vb* challenge, dare, defy. **~fordrende** *adj* challenging. **~fordring** *sb* challenge. **~forme** *vb* model, shape; frame. **~forming** *sb* modelling, shaping; framing. **~forske** *vb* explore. **~forsking** *sb* exploration. **~fylle** *vb* **1** *(fylle ut)* fill in; *~fylle en blankett* fill in a form; **2** *(supplere)* complement, supplement. **~fylling** *sb* filling in; complementing, supplementing. **~føre** *vb* **1** *(besørge, sette i verk)* carry out; do; *~føre et eksperiment* carry out an experiment; **2** *(eksportere)* export. **~førelse** *sb: fagmessig ~førelse* fine workmanship; *planen kom aldri til ~førelse* the plan never materialized/was never carried out. **~førlig 1** *adj* detailed, elaborate, full; *en ~førlig utgreiing* a detailed/elaborate/full account; **2** *adv* fully; in detail; *beskrive ~førlig* describe in detail. **~førsel** *sb* export; *vår ~ overgikk vår innførsel i verdi* our exports exceeded our imports in value. **~førselsforbud** *sb* embargo; export ban/prohibition.

ut|gang *sb* **1** *(dør etc)* exit; way out; *hvor er ~gangen?* where is the exit/the way out? **2** *(avslutning, ende)* end; *ved ~gangen av måneden* at the end of the month; **3** *(utfall)* outcome, result; issue. **~gangspunkt** *sb* starting point; point of departure; *(fig også)* basis. **~gave** *sb* edition; *en ny ~gave av boken* a new edition of the book. **~gi** *vb* publish; *denne boken ble ~gitt i fjor* this book was published last year. **~gift** *sb* expense; *løpende ~gifter* current expenses; *samlede ~gifter* total expenditure; *tilfeldige ~gifter* incidentals; *uforutsette ~gifter* unforeseen expenditure. **~givelse** *sb* publication; *under ~givelse* in course of publication. **~giver** *sb* publisher. **~gjøre** *vb* **1** *(danne)* constitute; make up; **2** *(beløpe seg til)* amount to; be; *inntekten hennes ~gjør 18.000 pund* her income amounts to £18 000. **~glidning** *sb: moralsk ~glidning* moral deterioration. **~grave** *vb* dig out; excavate. **~gravning** *sb* excavation. **~greiing** *sb* account. **~gyte** *vb* pour out. **~gytelse** *sb* outpouring. **~gå** *vb (utelates)* be left out; *et ord ~gikk* one word was left out. **~gående** *adj* out-going. **~gått** *adj (om sko)* worn out.

ut|heve *vb* emphasize, stress; *(med kursiv)* italicize. **~hevelse** *sb* emphasizing, stressing; *(kursivering)* italics; *~hevelsene er mine/er foretatt av meg* the italics are mine. **~holdende** *adj* persevering; *være ~holdende* have staying power. **~holdenhet** *sb* endurance, perseverance; staying power. **~hungret** *adj* starved. **~hus** *sb* outhouse. **~hvilt** *adj* rested, refreshed.

utide *sb: i ~* out of season; at the wrong moment; *i tide og ~* in season and out of season. **utidig** *adj (urimelig)* unreasonable. **utidighet** *sb* unreasonableness. **utidsmessig** *adj* out of date; oldfashioned.

utilbørlig *adj* improper, undue; *~ press* undue pressure. **utilbørlighet** *sb* impropriety. **utilbøyelig** *adj* disinclined. **utilfreds** *adj* discontented, dissatisfied; *(skuffet)* disappointed. **utilfredshet** *sb* discontent, dissatisfaction; *læreren uttrykte stor ~ med elevenes arbeid* the teacher expressed great dissatisfaction with the work of his pupils. **utilfredsstillende** *adj* unsatisfactory. **utilfredsstilt** *adj* unsatisfied; *(stundom)* unappeased. **utilgivelig** *adj* unforgivable, unpardonable, inexcusable. **utilgjengelig** *adj* inaccessible, unapproachable. **utillatelig** *adj* inadmissable, unforgivable. **utilnærmelig** *adj* unapproachable, reserved, standoffish. **utilpass** *adj* indisposed; not very well. **utilregnelig** *adj* insane; not accountable for one's actions. **utilregnelighet** *sb* insanity. **utilslørt** *adj* unveiled; *(fig også)* undisguised. **utilstrekkelig** *adj* insufficient. **utiltalende** *adj* unattractive, unpleasant.

uting *sb: en ~* a nuisance; *lange taler er en ~* long speeches are a nuisance.

utjenlig *adj* unserviceable, useless.

ut|jevne *vb* even up; smoothe out; level. **~jevning** *sb* smoothing out; levelling. **~kant** *sb* outskirts, border; *i ~kanten av byen* on the outskirts of the town. **~kast** *sb* (rough) draft; sketch. **~kastelse** *sb (av leieboer etc)* eviction. **~kikk** *sb* lookout, watch; *holde god ~kikk* keep/maintain a good look-ou; *være på ~kikk etter* be on the look-out for. **~kjempe** *vb* fight out. **~kjørsel** *sb* exit; exit gateway. **~kjørt** *adj* exhausted.

ut|kledd *adj* dressed up; rigged out; *(forkledd)* disguised. **~klekke** *vb* hatch. **~klekning** *sb* hatching. **~klekningsanstalt** *sb fig* nursery. **~kobling** *sb* cutting off/out; disconnecting. **~klipp** *sb (fra avis etc)* cutting. **~kommandere** *vb* call out. **~komme A** *sb: ha sitt ~komme* make a living; *tjene til ~kommet* earn a living; **B** *vb (om bok)* appear; come out. **~konkurrere** *vb* throw out of competition; *(fortrenge)* oust. **~kåre** *vb* choose, elect.

ut|ladet *adj, pp* discharged, flat. **~ladning** *sb* discharge. **~landet** *sb* foreign countries; *(i GB om resten av Europa)* the Continent; *fra ~landet* from abroad; *i ~landet* abroad; *han bor i ~landet* he lives abroad; *vi reiste til ~landet* we went abroad. **~lede** *vb* deduce. **~legg** *sb (utgift)* expense, outlay; disbursement. **~leie** *sb* hiring out; letting (out on hire). **~leier** *sb* letter, owner; lessor. **~lendighet** *sb* staying abroad; *(især påtvunget)* exile. **~lending** *sb* foreigner. **~levere** *vb* **1** *(gi, overlate)* deliver; hand over; **2** *(dele ut)* distribute; *program ble ~levert til alle besøkende* programmes were distributed to all visitors. **~levering** *sb* **1** delivery; **2** distribution; **3** *(~levering av forbryter over landegrense)* extradition. **~ligne** *vb* **1** *(balansere, motvirke)* (counter)balance; offset; **2** *(i fotball etc)* equalize; quit scores; **3** *(om avgift, skatt etc)* assess. **~ligning** *sb* **1** *(balansering, motvirkning)* (counter)balancing; **2** *(i fotball etc)* equalization; **3** *(om avgift, skatt etc)* assessment. **~lodning** *sb* raffle. **~love** *vb* offer, promise. **~lært** *adj* (fully) qualified. **~løp** *sb* **1** *(os)* mouth, outlet; **2** *(av tidsfrist)* expiration; *~løpet av leiekontrakten* the expiration of the lease. **utløpe** *vb* expire. **~løse** *vb* **1** *(frigjøre)* release; **2** *(fremkalle)* provoke; *~løsende faktor* provoking factor; **3** *(sette i gang)* trigger off. **~løsning** *sb* releasing; *seksuell ~løsning* orgasm; sexual satisfaction. **~lån** *sb* loan. **~lånsbibliotek** *sb* lending library. **~lånsrente** *sb* interest of loans.

ut|magret *adj* emaciated. **~male** *vb* depict. **~matte** *vb* exhaust, fatigue; *han følte seg ~mattet etter (spaser)turen* he felt exhausted/fatigued after the walk. **~mattelse** *sb* exhaustion, fatigue. **~mattet** *adj* exhausted. **~melding** *sb* resignation, withdrawal. **~merke** *vb: ~merke seg* distinguish oneself; *~merke seg i/som* excel at/in/as; *hun ~merket seg i idrett/som politiker* she excelled in/at sport/as a politician. **~merkelse** *sb* distinction, honour. **~merket** *adj* excellent; *(som adv) det passer meg ~merket* it suits me excellently. **~nevne** *vb* **1** *(til stilling etc)* appoint; *han ble ~nevnt til borgermester/ordfører i byen* he was appointed mayor of the town; **2** *(forfremme)* promote; *han ble ~nevnt til oberst* he was promoted colonel. **~nevnelse, ~nevning** *sb* **1** appointment; **2** *(forfremmelse)* promotion. **~nytte** *vb* **1** make use of; make the most of; exploit; *vi ~nytter vannkraften* we exploit the water-power; **2** *(utbytte)* exploit; *de ~nyttet de innfødte* they exploited the natives. **~nyttelse, ~nytting** *sb* utilization; exploitation.

utopi *sb: en ~* a Utopian idea. **utopisk** *adj* Utopian.

utover *adv* **1** out, outwards; *hun rodde ~* she rowed out; **2** *(mer enn)* beyond; *vi kan ikke gjøre noe ~ hva vi allerede har gjort* we can do nothing beyond what we have done already.

ut|parsellere *vb* parcel out. **~peke** *vb* point out. Jf *utnevne.* **~pint** *adj (om jord)* exhausted; *(utsuget)* exploited; bled white. **~plyndre** *sb (~plyndre en person)* rob, fleece; *(~plyndre et land)* plunder; *vi ble ~plyndret* we were robbed/fleeced. **~plyndring** *sb* robbing, fleecing; plunder, plundering. **~post** *sb* outpost. **~preget** *adj* marked, pronounced; *(typisk)* typical; *en ~preget forskjell* a marked difference; *en ~preget snobb* a typical snob. **~pressing** *sb (pengeutpressing)* blackmail.

ut|rangere *vb* discard, scrap. **~rede** *vb* **1** *(forklare, redegjøre)* clear up; elucidate; *~rede et problem* elucidate a problem; **2** *(bestride, betale)* defray, meet; pay. **utredning** *sb* elucidation; *(beretning)* account, report. **~regning** *sb* calculation, computation. **~reise** *sb* outward journey; *(fra et land)* departure.

utrengsmål *sb: i ~* needlessly.

ut|rensking *sb (av politiske motstandere)* purge. **~rette** *vb (prestere)* achieve; *(gjøre)* do; *han har ikke ~rettet noen ting* he has achieved/done nothing.

utrettelig *adj* indefatigable, untiring.

utringet *adj* low-necked, low-cut.

utrivelig *adj* unpleasant, disagreeable. **utro** *adj* unfaithful, false. **utrolig** *adj* incredible; *(forbløffende)* amazing; *det høres/lyder utrolig* it sounds incredible.

ut|rop *sb* exclamation. **~ropstegn** *sb* exclamation mark.

utroskap *sb* unfaithfulness, infidelity.

ut|ruste *vb* equip; fit out. **~rustning** *sb* equipment, outfit. **~rydde** *vb* eradicate, exterminate. **~ryddelse, ~rydding** *sb* extermination, eradication.

utrygg *adj* insecure, unsafe. **utrygghet** *sb* insecurity. **utrøstelig** *adj* disconsolate, inconsolable. **utrøstelighet** *sb* disconsolateness.

ut|sagn *sb* statement; *(påstand)* assertion. **~salg** *sb* **1** *(utsalgssted)* shop; **2** *(realisasjon)* sale; *jeg kjøpte hatten på ~salg* I bought the hat at the sales. **~satt** *adj (ubeskyttet)* exposed; *~satt for fare* exposed to danger; *en ~satt stilling* an exposed position. **~se** *vb: ~se seg* pick out; select. **~seende** *sb* **1** *(ytre)* appearance, look; *jeg kjenner henne av ~seende* I know her by appearance/sight; **2** *(om person ~seende)* looks; *han var kry av sitt gode ~seende* he was proud of his good looks; **3** *(skinn) gi det ~seende av* make a pretence of; make it appear that. **~sendelse** *sb* sending (out); *(radiosending)* broadcast; *(fjernsynssending)* telecast. **~sending** *sb* **1** *(sendebud)* messenger, delegate; **2** *(diplomat)* envoy, minister; **3** se *~sendelse.* **~sette** *vb* **1** *(oppsette)* postpone; put off; delay; *møtet ble ~satt* the meeting was postponed; *vi ~satte det til dagen etter* we put it off to the next day; **2** *(~sette for virkningen av)* expose; *han ~satte dem for fare* he exposed them to danger; **3** *(kritisere) har du noe å ~sette?* have you any objections. **~settelse** *sb* postponement, delay; *uten ~settelse* without delay. **~sikt** *sb* **1** *(utsyn)* view; *det er flott ~sikt fra vinduene mine* there is an excellent view from my windows; *med ~sikt til* with a view to; **2** *(mulighet)* prospect, chance; *dårlige ~sikter* poor prospects; *de har ingen ~sikter til å vinne* they have no chance of winning. **~skeielser** *sb fl* excesses. **~skipe** *vb* export, ship. **~skjemt** *adj* spoiled, spoilt. **~skjæ-**

ring *sb* carving. **~skudd** *sb* outcast, pariah; *samfunnets ~skudd* the dregs/scum of society.

utskytning *sb (av rakett)* launching. **utskytnings|plattform, ~rampe** *sb* launching pad.

ut|skåret *adj* carved. **~slag** *sb (av viser)* deflection; *et ~slag av* an outcome/a result of; *gi seg ~slag i* be reflected/show itself in; manifest itself in; *(resultere i)* result in; *gjøre ~slaget* be the decisive factor; decide the matter; turn/tip the scales. **~slagsgivende** *adj* decisive. **~slett** *sb* rash; skin eruption. **~slette** *vb* **1** wipe out; efface, obliterate; **2** *(tilintetgjøre også)* annihilate, destroy. **~slettelse** *sb* obliteration; wiping out; annihilation, destruction. **~slitt** *adj* worn out. **~smykke** *vb* decorate; *(~ kunstnerisk, rikt)* ornament. **~smykning** *sb* decoration. **~solgt** *adj, pp* sold out; *boken er ~solgt fra forlaget* the book is out of print. **~spark** *sb (fra mål)* goal kick; kick-out. **~spekulert** *adj* artful, cunning, sly. **~spionere** *vb* spy on. **~spring** *sb* source. **~sprunget** *adj* full-blown; out; *en ~sprunget rose* a full-blown rose; *prestekravene er ~sprunget* the daisies are out. **~spørre** *vb* interrogate, question. **~stikker** *sb (brygge)* pier.

utstilling *sb* exhibition, show. **utstillings|gjenstand** *sb* exhibit. **~kasse, ~monter** *sb* showcase. **~vindu** *sb* show-window.

ut|stoppe *vb* stuff; *et ~stoppet dyr* a stuffed animal. **~strakt** *adj* **1** outstretched; *en ~strakt hånd* an outstretched hand; **2** *(stor)* extensive; *~strakte marker* extensive fields; *gjøre ~strakt bruk av* make extensive use of. **~strekning** *sb* extent; *av stor ~strekning* of a great size; *i stor ~strekning* to a great/large extent. **~strykning** *sb* deletion; crossing out. **~stråle** *vb* radiate. **~stråling** *sb* radiation. **~styr** *sb* equipment; *(personlig ~)* outfit; *(brudeutstyr)* trousseau. **~styre** *vb* **1** equip; *skipet ble ~styrt for en reise* the ship was equipped for a voyage; **2** *(forsyne)* furnish, provide, supply; *bilen er ~styrt med radio* the car is supplied with a radio set; *han ~styrte seg med paraply* he provided himself with an umbrella. **~støte** *vb* **1** *(~støte skrik)* give, utter; *hun ~støtte et skrik* she uttered a cry; **2** *(fjerne, utvise)* expel; *han ble ~støtt fra hæren* he was expelled from the army. **~stå** *vb* **1** *(fordra) jeg kan ikke ~stå dem* I cannot stand them; **2** *(bli utsatt) det får ~stå* we must let it stand over. **~stående** *adj* projecting, protruding. **~suge** *vb* bleed white; fleece. **~sultet** *adj* famished, starved. **~svevelser** *sb fl* excesses; debauchery, dissipation. **~syn** *sb* **1** *(oversikt)* review: **2** *(utsikt)* view. **~sæd** *sb* seed. **~søkt** *adj* choice, select; exquisite.

ut|tak *sb (i bank)* withdrawal. **~taking** *sb (i idrett)* selection.

uttale I *sb* pronunciation; **II** *vb* **1** pronounce; *hvordan ~r en/hvordan ~s dette ordet?* how do you pronounce this word? **2** *(erklære, si)* declare, say; *statsråden uttalte at...* the Minister declared/said that...; **3** *(uttrykke)* express; *~ håp om* express the hope that; *~ seg* make a statement; *~ seg om* give an opinion on; speak about; *hun ville ikke ~ seg til pressen* she would make no statement to the press. **uttalelse** *sb* statement; *komme med en ~* make a statement; give an opinion.

uttrykk *sb* **1** expression; *et bedrøvet ~* a sad expression; **2** *(språkvending)* phrase, term; idiom; *et engelsk ~* an English idiom; *et teknisk ~* a technical term; **3** *(uttrykk) gi ~ for* give expression to; voice; *gi seg ~ i* find expression in; show itself in; *komme til ~* find expression; express itself; *være et ~ for* be expressive of; express. **uttrykke** *vb* express, put; *~ seg* express oneself; *hun ~r seg meget tydelig* she expresses herself very clearly. **uttrykkelig** *adj* express; *hans ~e ordre* his express command. **uttrykks|full** *adj* expressive. **~løs** *adj* expressionless. **~middel** *sb* means of expression. **~måte** *sb* mode of expression.

ut|tur *sb* outward yourney. **~tært** *adj* emaciated, haggard. **~tømmende** *adj* exhaustive, full.

utukt *sb* fornication; *(ervervsmessig)* prostitution. **utuktig** *adj (om personer)* immoral, lewd; *(om bøker etc)* obscene; *~ omgang med mindreårige* sexual abuse of minors. **utur** *sb* bad luck.

ut|valg *sb* **1** *(av ting)* selection; *vi har (et) stort ~valg* we have a large selection; **2** *(komité)* committee. **~valgt** *adj (utsøkt)* choice, select. **~vandre** *vb* emigrate. **~vandrer** *sb* emigrant. **~vandring** *sb* emigration. **~vanne** *vb* water down; *(fortynne)* dilute. **~vannet** *adj fig* insipid. **~vei** *sb (middel)* means; way out; *de fant en ~vei til å gjøre det* they found (a) means to do it. **~veksle** *vb* exchange; *~veksle ideer* exchange ideas. **~veksling** *sb* **1** *(bytte)* exchange; **2** *(i maskin etc)* gear. **~vekst** *sb* excrescence; *(om svulst også)* growth. **~velge** *sb* choose, pick, select. **~velgelse** *sb* choice, selection. **~vendig** *adj* external, outside.

utvetydig *adj* unambiguous, unequivocal.

ut|vide *vb* enlarge, extend; *~vide seg* expand. **~videlse** *sb* enlargement, extension; expansion.

ut|vikle *vb* develop; *landsbyen ~viklet seg til en by* the village developed into a town; *mosjon ~vikler musklene* exercise develops the muscles; *planter ~vikler seg av frø* plants develop from seeds. **~viklet** *adj* developed, matured; advanced. **~vikling** *sb* **1** development, growth; **2** *(fremgang)* advance, progress. **utviklings|hemmet** *adj* (mentally) retarded. **~hjelp** *sb* development aid. **~land** *sb* developing country. **~lære** *sb* evolutionism. **~trinn** *sb* stage of development.

utvilsom *adj* undoubted; *en ~ fordel* an undoubted advantage. **utvilsomt** *adv* undoubtedly; no doubt; *han har ~ rett* he is undoubtedly right.

ut|vinne *vb* extract, win. **~virke** bring about; effect. **~vise** *vb* **1** *(legge for dagen, vise)* exercise, show; **2** *(forvise etc, som straff)* expel; send out; *(i fotball etc)* send off; *(fra skole også)* kick out of. **~viske** *vb* efface, obliterate. **~visket** *adj* blurred, dim, indistinct. **~visning** *sb* expulsion; *(i ishockey)* penalty. **~vokst** *adj* full-grown. **~vortes** *adj: til ~ bruk* for external use.

utvungen *adj (freidig, usjenert)* free and easy; unconstrained. **utydelig 1** *adj* indistinct, dim; *~ omriss* indistinct/dim outline; **2** *adv* indistinctly; *hun* *snakket* ~ she spoke indistinctly. **utyske** *sb* monster.

ut|øse *vb:* *~øse sin vrede* vent one's anger; *~øse sitt hjerte for* unbosom oneself to. **~øve** *vb* exercise, practise. **~øvelse** *sb* discharge, exercise. **~øvende** *adj* executive; *den ~øvende makt* the Executive.

utøy *sb koll* vermin. **utøylet** *adj* unbridled. **utålelig** *adj* intolerable, unbearable. **utålmodig** *adj* impatient; *han ble* ~ he got impatient/he lost patience; *hun er ~ etter å begynne* she is impatient to begin; *jeg var ~ over forsinkelsen* I was impatient at the delay. **utålmodighet** *sb* impatience.

utånde *vb (dø)* breathe one's last; expire.

uunn|gåelig *adj* inevitable; *adv* inevitably. **~værlig** *adj* indispensable.

uut|holdelig *adj* intolerable, unbearable, unendurable. **~sigelig** *adj* unspeakable, unutterable. **~slettelig** *adj: et ~slettelig inntrykk* an indelible impression. **~tømmelig** *adj* inexhaustible. **~viklet** *adv* underdeveloped; *(også)* backward.

uvane *sb* bad habit. **uvanlig** *adj* uncommon, unusual; extraordinary. **uvant** *adj* unaccustomed; *en ~ jobb* an unaccustomed job; *han er ~ med arbeidet/med å gjøre det* he is unaccustomed to the work/to doing it. **uvederheftig** *adj* unreliable, untrustworthy. **uvedkommende** *adj* irrelevant; *det er meg ~* it is no business of mine; *en ~ (dvs en som trenger seg inn etc)* an intruder; *(på privat område)* a trespasser. **uvel** *adj* unwell; *føle seg ~* feel unwell. **uvelkommen** *adj* unwelcome. **uvenn** *sb* enemy; *de ble ~er* they fell out; *de var ~er* they were on bad terms. **uvennlig** *adj, adv* unfriendly, unkind; *han var ~ mot meg* he was unkind to me; *hun så ~ på meg* she looked unfriendly at me. **uvennskap** *sb* enmity, hostility. **uventet** **1** *adj* unexpected; *et ~ møte* an unexpected meeting; **2** *adv* unexpectedly; *de kom ~* they arrived unexpectedly. **uverdig** *adj* unworthy; *jeg er ~ til denne ære* I am unworthy of this honour. **uvesen** *sb* nuisance; odious practice. **uvesentlig** *adj* immaterial, unessential. **uvettig** *adj* foolish, senseless.

uviktig *adj* unimportant. **uvilje** *sb* **1** *(fiendskap)* displeasure; ill-will; **2** *(motvilje)* dislike; **3** *(ulyst)* reluctance. **uvilkårlig** *adj* involuntary. **uvillig** *adj* unwilling. **uvirksom** *adj* **1** *(ubeskjeftiget)* idle; *de stod ~e* they stood idle; **2** *(virkningsløs)* ineffective. **uvirkelig** *adj* unreal. **uvirksom** *adj* idle, inactive. **uvirksomhet** *sb* idleness, inactivity. **uviss** *adj* uncertain. **uvisnelig** *adj* imperishable, unfading. **uviss** *adj* doubtfull, uncertain. **uvisshet** *sb* uncertainty. **uvitende** *adj* ignorant; *han er ~ om det som har hendt* he is ignorant of what has happened. **uvitenhet** *sb* ignorance; *av ~* from/through ignorance. **uvurderlig** *adj* invaluable. **uvæpnet** *sb* unarmed. **uvær** *sb* storm; *det ble ~* a storm arose/came up; *det er ~* it is stormy. **uvøren** *adj* daring, reckless; careless. **uvørenhet** *sb* daring, recklessness; carelessness.

uærbødig *adj* disrespectful, irreverent. **uærbødighet** *sb* disrespect, irreverence. **uærlig** *adj* dishonest; *på ~ vis* dishonestly. **uærlighet** *sb* dishonesty.

uøkonomisk *adj* **1** uneconomical; *(som sløser)* wasteful; **2** *(som ikke lønner seg)* unprofitable. **uønsket** *adj* unwanted. **uønskverdig** *adj* undesirable.

uår *sb* bad year; crop failure.

v *(bokstaven)* v.

va *vb (vasse)* wade.

vable *sb* blister.

vade *vb* wade. **vade|fugl** *sb* wading bird. **~sted** *sb* ford.

vaffel *sb* waffle. **vaffeljern** *adj* waffle-iron.

vag *adj* dim, vague; *en ~ forestilling* a vague idea.

vagabond *sb* tramp, vagabond.

vagge *vb* rock, sway; *(gå vaggende)* walk with a rolling gait.

vagle *sb* perch, roost. **vagle** *vb: ~ seg* perch, roost.

vaie *vb* fly, wave; *flagg ~t fra alle master* flags flew from all masts.

vaier *sb* wire.

vaisenhus *sb* orphanage.

vake *vb* **1** *(om fisk)* rise, surface; *(hoppe også)* jump, leap; **2** se *våke*.

vakker *adj (især om kvinne)* beautiful; *(pen, søt)* pretty, nice; *(om menn)* good-looking, handsome.

vakle *vb* **1** reel, stagger; *han ~t under slaget* he was reeling under the blow; **2** *(være i tvil)* falter, hesitate; vacillate. **vaklevoren** *adj* rickety.

vaksinasjon *sb* vaccination. **vaksine** *sb* vaccine. **vaksinere** *vb* vaccinate; *hun ble vaksinert/lot seg ~* she got/was vaccinated.

vakt *sb* **1** *(~tjeneste etc)* guard, watch; *holde ~* keep guard/watch; *på ~ ved døren* on guard at the door; *være på ~ mot* be on one's guard against; **2** *(~person)* guard; *(især natt~ etc)* watchman; **3** *(skilt~)* sentry; **4** *(~mannskap)* guard; **5** *(~tjeneste)* duty; *hun hadde ~* she was on duty. **vakt|havende** *adj* on duty; *~havende lege* the doctor on duty. **~hold** *sb* guard, watch. **~hund** *sb* watchdog. **~mester** *sb (ved institusjon etc)* caretaker; *(i leiegård)* (house)porter; *(især US)* janitor. **~post** *sb* guard; *(skilt~)* sentry. **~skifte** *sb* changing of the guard. **~tjeneste** *sb* guard duty.

vakuum *sb* vacuum.

valen *adj* numb. **valenhet** *sb* numbness.

valfart *sb* pilgrimage. **valfarte** *vb* make a pilgrimage.

valg *sb* **1** *(det å velge)* choice; *jeg gjorde/traff mitt ~* I made my choice; *~et falt på henne* the choice fell on her; **2** *(politisk ~)* election; *de konservative tapte/vant ~et* the Conservatives lost/won the election; **3** *(valghandling)* poll. **valg|agitasjon** *sb* electioneering; *(fra dør til dør)* canvassing. **~bar** *adj* eligible. **~barhet** *sb* eligibility. **~dag** *sb* election/polling day. **~deltakelse** *sb: liten/stor ~* a light/heavy poll. **~fri** *adj* optional; *~frie fag* optional subjects. **~frihet** *sb* freedom of choice. **~kamp** *sb* election/electioneering campaign. **~krets** *sb* constituency. **~lokale** *sb* polling station. **~løfte** *sb* electoral pledge/promise. **~møte** *sb* election/electioneering meeting. **~seier** *sb* election victory. **~skred** *sb* landslide. **~språk** *sb* motto. **~urne** *sb* ballot box.

valk *sb* **1** *(hår~)* hair pad; **2** *(fett~)* roll of fat.

valmue *sb* poppy.

valnøtt *sb* walnut.

valp *sb* pup, puppy; whelp. **valpe** *vb* whelp. **valpesyke** *sb* distemper.

valplass *sb* battlefield; field of battle.

vals *sb* waltz. **vals(e)** *sb (trommel etc)* roller, cylinder; *(på skrivemaskin)* platen. **valse** *vb* **A** *(danse vals)* waltz; **B** *(~ ut)* roll.

valuta *sb* **1** *(verdi)* value; *vi fikk ~ for pengene våre* we got value for our money; **2** *(pengesort)* currency, money; *de fikk betaling i britisk ~* they were paid in British currency/money. **valutakurs** *sb* (rate of) exchange.

valør *sb* **1** *(verdi)* value; **2** *(nyanse)* shade, nuance.

vammel *adj* sickly, nauseous. **vammelhet** *sb* sickliness, nauseousness.

vamp *sb* vamp. **vampyr** *sb* vampire.

vandal *sb* vandal. **vandalisme** *sb* vandalism.

vandel *sb* conduct; *ha en plettfri ~* have a spotless reputation; *i handel og ~* in all one's dealings. **vandelsattest** *sb* certificate of good conduct.

vandre *vb* walk; *(~ uten mål og med)* wander; *(om blikk og tanker)* travel; *håndverkere pleide å ~ fra by til by* artisans used to walk from one town to another; *jeg ~t omkring* I was wandering about; *tankene deres ~t vidt og bredt* their thoughts travelled far and wide. **vandre|bibliotek** *sb* travelling library. **~pokal** *sb* challenge cup. **~utstilling** *sb* travelling exhibition.

vane *sb* custom, habit; *det var blitt en ~* it had grown into a habit; *en dårlig/god ~* a bad/good habit; *jeg har for ~ å stå tidlig opp* I am in the habit of rising early. **vane|dranker** *sb* habitual drunkard. **~dyr** *sb* slave of routine. **~forbryter** *sb* habitual criminal. **~gjenger, ~menneske** *sb* person of fixed habits. Se også *~dyr*. **~messig** *adj* habitual. **~sak** *sb* matter of habit.

vanfør *adj* crippled, disabled; *en ~* a cripple; a disabled person. **vanførhet** *sb* disablement.

van|hellig *adj* profane. **~hellige** *vb* profane, desecrate. **~hjulpen** *adj* badly served.

vanilje *sb* vanilla.

vanke *vb* **1** *(ha sin gang)* frequent; visit often; *han ~r ikke lenger på puben* he no longer frequents the pub; *jeg ~r der i huset* I often visit/comes to see the family; **2** *(få servert etc) det ~r kaker og sjokolade* there will be cakes and chocolate.

vanlig *adj* common, usual; *som ~* as usual. **vanligvis** *adv* usually; generally.

vann *sb* **1** water; *et glass ~* a glass of water; *fiske i rørt ~* fish in troubled waters; *gå i ~et (dvs gjøre en dumhet, bli narret etc)* be led up the garden path; be taken in; put one's foot in it; *ta seg ~ over hodet* bite off more than one can chew; *til lands og til ~s og i luften* by sea and land and in the air; **2** *(innsjø, tjern)* lake, water. **vanne** *vb* water; *~ blomstene* water the flowers. **vannforsyning** *sb* water supply. **vanning** *sb* watering; *(av jord)* irrigation. **vann|kant** *sb* the water's edge. **~kopper** *sb* chickenpox. **~kraft** water power. **~kran** *sb* faucet; water tap. **~ledning** *sb* water pipe; *(større ~rør)* conduit. **~melon** *sb* watermelon. **~mølle** *sb* water mill. **~pytt** *sb* pool of water; puddle. **~rett** *adj (horisontal)* horizontal; *(i kryssord)* across. **~rør** se *~ledning*. **~skade** *sb* damage by water; water damage. **~skille** *sb* watershed. **~slange** *sb (hage~ etc)* water/garden hose. **~stand** *sb* height of the water. **~tett** *adj (om beholder)* watertight; *(om stoff)* waterproof. **~verk** *sb* waterworks.

van|ry *sb: komme i ~* get into bad repute. **~røkt** *sb* mismanagement, neglect. **~røkte** *vb* mismanage, neglect. **~sire** *vb* disfigure. **~skapning** *sb* deformed person/animal; freak. **~skapt** *adj* deformed; *en ~skapt fot* a deformed foot.

vanske *sb* difficulty. **vanskelig** *adj* difficult, hard; *~ arbeid* difficult work; *~e tider* hard times; *det er ~ for meg å tro det* I find it difficult to believe it. **vanskeliggjøre** *vb* render difficult; complicate. **vanskelighet** *sb* difficulty; *vi var i ~er* we were in difficulties/trouble.

van|skjebne *sb* misfortune. **~skjøtte** *vb* neglect, mismanage. **~stell** *sb* mismanagement; bad management. **~styre** *sb* bad rule.

vant *adj* accustomed, used; *~ til* accustomed to; *jeg ble ~ til å vente* I got used to waiting.

vante *sb* wollen glove.

vantrives *vb* feel uncomfortable/ill at ease; not feel at home; get on badly; *(især om dyr og planter)* not thrive; thrive badly. **vantrivsel** *sb* discomfort, unhappiness; *(om dyr og planter)* failure to thrive.

vantro *adj* incredulous; *rel* unbelieving, infidel; *en ~ Tomas* a doubting Thomas. **vantro** *sb* disbelief; *rel* unbelief.

vanvare *sb: av ~* by accident; by mistake; inadvertently.

vanvidd *sb* madness; *(sinnsykdom)* insanity. **van-**

vittig *adj* **1** crazy, mad; ~ *av smerte* mad with pain; *han ble* ~ he went mad; *jeg er* ~ *forelsket i henne* I am madly in love with her; **2** *(sinnsyk)* insane.

vanvøre *vb* despise, disdain; hold in contempt.

vanære *sb* disgrace, dishonour. **vanære** *vb* disgrace, dishonour. **vanærende** *adj* disgraceful; ~ *oppførsel* disgraceful behaviour.

var A *adj* **1** *(forsiktig)* cautious, wary; **2** *(sky)* shy; **3** *(årvåken)* vigilant; *bedre føre* ~ *enn etter snar* better safe than sorry; *være* ~ *for* be sensitive to; **B** *sb (overtrekk)* case.

vara|formann *sb* deputy chairman. **~mann** *sb* deputy, substitute. **~person** *sb* deputy (person).

vare A *sb: ta* ~ *på* take care of; look after; *ta seg i* ~ be on one's guard; take care; **B** *sb (handels~)* article; *~r* goods, products; *(stundom)* wares; *jeg kjøpte alle disse ~ne i den samme butikken* I bought all these articles in the same shop; **C** *vb* **1** *(holde på lenge, holde seg etc)* last; *disse støvlene ~r ikke lenge* these boots will not last long; *filmen ~r i to timer* the film lasts two hours; **2** *(om tid som går før noe skjer)* be; *det varte lenge før vi møttes igjen* it was long before we met again; **3** *(bli ved)* continue. **vare|beholdning** *sb* stock (of goods). **~bil** *sb* (delivery) van. **~bind** *sb* book jacket; dust cover. **~bytte** *sb* exchange of goods. **~heis** *sb* goods lift. **~lager** se *~beholdning*. **~merke** *sb* trade mark. **~messe** *sb* industrial fair. **~prøve** *sb* sample. **~sykkel** *sb* carrier bicycle/bike.

vare|ta *vb* attend to; look after; take care of. **~tekt** *sb* custody; *bli dømt til to ukers ~tekt* be remanded in custody for two weeks; *hun ble satt i ~tekt* she was taken in custody. **~tektsarrest** *sb* custody. **~tektsfange** *sb* prisoner in custody; *(etter kjennelsen)* remanded prisoner.

varetrekk *sb* cover.

varevogn *sb* (delivery) van.

variabel *adj* changeable, variable. **variant** *sb* variant. **variasjon** *sb* variation. **variere** *vb* vary.

varieté *sb* music-hall; *(US også)* burlesque.

varig *adj* lasting, permanent; ~ *berømmelse* lasting fame. **varighet** *sb* duration; *av kort* ~ of short duration.

varlig *adj* careful, cautious.

varm *adj* warm; *(svært ~)* hot; *~e klær* warm clothes; *~t klima* warm climate; *et ~t bad* a hot bath. **varmblodig** *adj* **1** *biol* warmblooded; **2** *(temperamentsfull)* warm-blooded, hot-blooded. **varme I** *sb* **1** heat, warmth; *10 graders* ~ ten degrees above the freezing point; *sterk* ~ great heat; **2** *(bål, ild)* fire; *ha* ~ *på peisen* have a fire; *vi gjorde opp* ~ we made a fire; **II** *vb* *(~ opp)* heat, warm; *hun ~t hendene (sine) ved bålet/varmen* she warmed her hands at the fire; *jeg ~t litt vann* I heated some water. **varme|bølge** *sb* heat wave. **~flaske** *sb* hot-water bottle. **~grad** *sb* degree of heat. **~leder** *sb* heat conductor. **~ovn** *sb* electric heater. **varmhjertet** *adj* warm-hearted. **varmstart** *sb data* quick start; system restart. **varmtvanns|beholder** *sb* hot-water tank. **~bereder** *sb* geyser; hotwater heater.

varp *sb* **1** *sjø* warp; **2** *fig* coup, scoop; *gjøre et godt* ~ make/pull a great coup. **varpe** *vb sjø* warp.

varsel *sb* **1** *(underretning)* notice; *på kort* ~ at short notice; *skriftlig* ~ written notice; *uten* ~ without notice/warning; **2** *(forvarsel, tegn)* omen, sign; *jeg tar det som et* ~ I take it as a sign. **varsels|skilt** *sb* danger/warning sign. **~skudd** *sb* warning shot. **varsku** **1** *sb: rope et* ~ sound a warning; **2** *vb* warn. **varsle** *vb* **1** *(gi melding)* give notice; notify; **2** *(advare, varsku)* warn; **3** *(være varsel om)* (fore)bode, portend.

varsom *adj* careful, cautious. **varsomhet** *sb* care, caution, cautionness.

varte opp *vb* wait; *han* ~ ~ *ved bordet* he waited at table.

vas *sb* nonsense, rubbish, twaddle

vasall *sb* vasall. **vasallstat** *sb* vassal/satellite state.

vase A *sb (til blomster etc)* vase; **B** *sb (floke)* tangle; tangled mass; **C** *vb (tøyse)* talk nonsense; twaddle. **vasekopp** *sb* twaddler.

vaselin *sb* vaseline.

vask *sb* **1** wash, washing; *(vasketøy)* laundry; ~ *og stryking* washing and ironing; *jeg hengte ut ~en* I hung out the washing; **2** *(utslags~)* sink; *gå i ~en* go by the board; come to nothing; *hun helte det i ~en* she poured it down the sink. **vaske** *vb* wash; ~ *opp* do the dishes; wash up; *han ~t seg i ansiktet* he washed his face; *vi ~r i dag* we are washing today. **vaske|balje** *sb* wash-tub. **~brett** *sb* wash(ing)-board. **~dag** *sb* wash(ing)-day. **~ekte** *adj* washproof, washable. **~hjelp** *sb* cleaner. Jf *~kone*. **~klut** *sb* dish-cloth, dishrag. **~kone** *sb* charlady, charwoman; cleaner. **~maskin** *sb* washing--machine. **~middel** *sb* detergent. **~pulver** *sb* washing-powder. **vaskeri** *sb* laundry. **vaske|servant** *sb* wash-stand. **~tapet** *sb* washable wallpaper. **~tøy** *sb* laundry, washing. **~vann** *sb* **1** *(til å vaske i)* wash--water; **2** *(som noe er vasket i)* slops.

vassdrag *sb* watercourse. **vasse** *vb* wade. **vassen** *adj* watery. **vasstrukken** *adj* soaked, water-logged.

vater *sb: i* ~ level. **vaterpass** *sb* spirit-level.

Vatikanet the Vatican.

vatn *sb (sjø, tjern)* lake. Se for øvrig *vann*.

vatt *sb* cotton (wool); *(plate~)* padding. **vattdot** *sb* swab/wad of cotton. **vatteppe** *sb* quilt. **vattere** *vb* pad, wad; *vatterte skuldre* padded shoulders.

ve *sb* **A** pain, woe; *(om fødende) ha ~er* be in labour; **B** *(velferd) deres* ~ *og vel* their welfare.

ved *prep* **1** *(om bestemt sted) a)* at; ~ *døren/vinduet* at the door/window; *b) (i nærheten/~ siden av)* by; ~ *peisen/varmen* by the fire; *c) (~ grense, linje etc)* at, by, on; ~ *grensen/kysten* on the frontier/the coast; *en pub* ~ *elven* a pub on the river; **2** *(om tidspunkt)* at, by, on; *(omtrent ~)* about; ~ *dag/natt* by day/night; ~ *denne tiden i morgen* about this time tomorrow; ~ *farens død ble han konge* on the death of his father he became king; ~ *solnedgang* at sunset; ~ *utbruddet av krigen* at the outbreak of the war; **3** *(om middel, årsak)* by; *hun reddet livet* ~ *å svømme* she saved her life by swimming; **4** *(om arbeid, yrke)* at, on; *en jobb* ~ *jernbanen* a job on the railway; *han er (ansatt)* ~ *Nationaltheatret* ≈ he is at the National Theatre; **5** *(om forskjellige forhold)* about, at, of, over; ~ *en kopp te* over a cup of tea; *det er noe galt* ~ *det* there is something wrong about it; *han rørte* ~ *bordet* he touched the table; *hun satt* ~ *siden av meg* she sat beside me/at my side; *slaget* ~ *Stiklestad* the battle of Stiklestad.

ved *sb (tre)* wood; *(til brensel også)* firewood.

ved|bli *vb* continue; go on; keep; *han* ~*ble å snakke* he continued speaking/to speak; he went on/kept talking; *de* ~*ble å være venner* they remained friends.

vedde *vb* bet; *jeg skal* ~ *femti dollar (med deg) på at han vinner* I bet you fifty dollars that he will win. **vedde|løp** *sb* race; *(bil~)* motor-race; *(heste~)* horse-race. ~**løpsbane** *sb* racecourse. ~**mål** *sb* bet; *jeg inngikk et* ~*mål om hvor lenge det ville vare* I took a bet on how long it would take.

veder|heftig *adj* reliable, trustworthy. ~**heftighet** *sb* reliability, trustworthiness. ~**lag** *sb* compensation, recompense.

ved|fang(e) *sb* armful of firewood. ~**fyring** *sb* wood-burning.

ved|gå *vb (innrømme)* admit, own. ~**holdende** *adj* continuous, persevering. ~**kjenne** *vb:* ~*kjenne seg* acknowledge, recognize; own. ~**komme** *vb* concern; *det* ~*kommer deg ikke* it/that does not concern you; it/that is none of your business. ~**kommende** *adj* the person concerned/in question; ~*kommende avis* the paper in question; *jeg for mitt* ~*kommende* I for my part; *rette* ~*kommende* the person concerned.

ved|legg *sb* enclosure. ~**legge** *vb* enclose; *en sjekk på beløpet følger* ~*lagt* a cheque for the amount is enclosed; *jeg* ~*legger kopier av attestene mine* I enclose copies of my testimonials.

vedlike|hold *sb* maintenance, upkeep. ~**holde** *vb* maintain; keep in repair; *godt* ~*holdt* in good repair; well preserved.

vedrøre *vb (angå)* affect, concern; *de opplysningene som* ~*r saken* the relevant information.

vedskjul *sb* wood-shed.

vedstå *vb (innrømme)* admit, own.

ved|ta *vb* **1** *(beslutte)* decide on; *de* ~*tok en ny fremgangsmåte* they decided on a new course of action; **2** *(bli enige om)* agree; *de* ~*tatte betingelser* the conditions agreed upon; **3** *(godta)* adopt; *de* ~*tok forslaget* they adopted the proposal; **4** *(*~*ta lov)* carry, pass; *loven ble* ~*tatt* the act was carried/passed. ~**tak** *sb* decision, resolution; *fatte/gjøre et* ~*tak* pass a resolution. ~**takelse** *sb* adoption, approval; carrying, passing. ~**tekter** *sb fl* regulations, rules. **vedtektsmessig** *adj, adv* in accordance with the regulations.

ved|vare *vb* continue, last. ~**varende** *adj* constant, continued, continuous; ~*varende regn* constant rain.

veg etc se *vei etc.*

vegetarianer *sb* vegetarian. **vegetariansk** *adj* vegetarian. **vegetasjon** *sb* vegetation.

vegg *sb* wall. **vegge|dyr,** ~**lus** *sb* bedbug. **vegg|-fast** *adj:* ~ *inventar* fixtures. ~**maleri** *sb* mural. ~**tavle** *sb* blackboard. ~**teppe** *sb* tapestry. ~**-til-**~**-teppe** *sb* wall-to-wall carpet.

vegne *sb: alle* ~ everywhere; *på* ~ *av min venn* on behalf of my friend; *på mine* ~ on my behalf.

vegre *vb:* ~ *seg* decline, refuse.

vei *sb* **1** *(anlagt* ~*)* road; *fører/går denne* ~*en til stasjonen?* does this road lead to the station? **2** *(retning, rute etc)* way; *kjenner/vet du* ~*en?* do you know the way? **3** *(avstand)* distance; *det er lang* ~ *til byen* it is a long way to the town; **4** *(uttrykk)* **av** ~**en!** stand back! stand off! *det ville ikke være* **av** ~**en** it would not be amiss; *gå* **av** ~**en for** *noen* go out of somebody's way; *gå/legge* **i** ~ start; *det kom noe i* ~*en* something happened to prevent me (etc); *er det noe i* ~*en?* is anything the matter? *hva er i* ~*en med deg?* what is the matter with you? *spørre* **om** ~**en** ask one's/the way; *ta* **på** ~ *(i sinne)* carry on; make a fuss; *gå* **sin** ~ go away; leave; *skaffe* **til** ~**e** get; procure, provide. **vei-bygging** *sb* road construction/making.

veide *vb* hunt. **veidefolk** *sb koll* hunters.

veidekke *sb* road surface.

veie *sb* weigh; *hvor mye* ~*r du?* how much do you weigh? *jeg er redd jeg* ~*r altfor mye* I'm afraid I weigh far too much.

vei|dele *sb* road fork. ~**farende** *sb* wayfarer, traveller. ~**forbindelse** *sb* road connection. ~**grep** *sb* grip. ~**grøft** *sb* (roadside) ditch.

veik *sb* weak. Jf *svak.*

vei|kant *sb* roadside; *ved* ~*kanten* at the roadside. ~**kryss** *sb* cross-roads; *et* ~*kryss* a cross-roads.

vei|lede *vb* guide; *(undervise)* instruct. ~**ledende** *adj* guiding; instructive; ~*ledende pris* suggested price. **veileder** *sb* guide; instructor. **veiledning** *sb* guidance; instruction.

vei|legeme *sb* road-bed. ~**lengde** *sb* distance. ~**nett** *sb* network of roads. ~**skille** *sb* road fork. ~**skilt** *sb* signpost. ~**skrape** *sb* road grader. ~**sperring** *sb* road block.

veit *sb (grøft)* ditch.

veiv *sb* crank. **veivaksel** *sb* crankshaft.

veivals(e) *sb* road roller.

veive *vb* **1** *(svinge)* swing, wave; **2** *(sveive)* turn; *(med sveiv)* crank.

vekk *adv* **1** *(forsvunnet)* gone; *pengene er* ~ the money is gone; **2** *(fraværende)* away; *langt* ~ far away; **3** *(som mangler)* missing; *paraplyen min er (blitt)* ~ my umbrella is missing.

vekke *vb* **1** *(av søvn)* awake; wake (up); *bråket* ~*t meg* the noise (a)woke me; **2** *(*~ *etter avtale, purre)* call; ~ *vekk meg klokken seks!* call me at six o'clock! **3** *(*~ *følelser etc)* awake, awaken; arouse, excite; *det vakte min mistanke* it aroused/excited my suspicion; *ingenting kan* ~ *interessen deres* nothing can arouse/awake their interest. **vekkelse** *sb rel* revival. **vekkelsespredikant** *sb* revivalist. **vekker** *sb (oppstrammer)* eye-opener. **vekke(r)|klokke** *sb* alarm-clock; *han stilte* ~*klokken på 7 (til å ringe kl. 7)* he set the alarm for 7 (o'clock).

veksel *sb* bill (of exchange); *akseptere en ~* accept a bill; *diskontere en ~* discount a bill; *trekke veksler på (fig)* draw heavily on; make great demands on. **veksel|strøm** *sb* alternating current; AC. **~virkning** *sb* interaction. **~vis 1** *adj* alternate, alternating; **2** *(adv)* alternately; in turns. **veksle** *vb* **1** *(ombytte)* change; *hun ~t en pundseddel i småpenger* she changed a pound note into small change; **2** *(ut~, ~ valuta)* exchange; *de brevvekslet* they exchanged letters; *han ~t de engelske pengene sine i franske* he exchanged his English money into French. **vekslepenger** *sb koll* change.

vekst *sb* growth; *(høyde)* stature; *liten av ~* short of stature. **vekst|hus** *sb* greenhouse. **~liv** *sb* flora, vegetation.

vekt *sb* **1** *(lodd, tyngde)* weight; *jeg gikk ned/opp i ~* I lost/put on weight; **2** *(veieinnretning)* balance; *(skål~)* pair of scales; *han veide det på en ~* he weighed it in a balance/in a pair of scales; **3** *(uttrykk) legge ~ på* stress; attach importance to; *selge etter ~* sell by weight. **vektenhet** *sb* unit of weight. **vektig** *adj* weighty. **vekt|løfting** *sb* weight-lifting. **~løfter** *sb* weight-lifter. **~løs** *adj* weightless. **~løshet** *sb* weightlessness. **~skål** *sb* pan, scale. **~stang** *sb* lever; *(på vekt)* beam. **~tap** *sb* loss of weight.

vel I *adj* well; *alt ~* all's well; *jeg føler seg ikke riktig ~* I am not feeling very well; **II** *adv* **1** *(godt)* well; *vi ble ~ mottatt* we were well received; **2** *(formodentlig)* I (etc) may suppose, think); *han kan ~ være 40* he may be 40; he is 40, I think; *jeg skal ~ gjøre det?* I suppose I am to do it? **3** *(forhåpentlig)* I hope; *du har ~ fått brevet mitt?* you have received my letter, I hope? **4** *(etter nektende spørsmål) du er ~ ikke sint på meg?* you are not angry with me, are you? *du så ham ~ ikke?* you did not see him, did you? **5** *(litt for)* a little too; rather; *det blir/er ~ dyrt for meg* it is rather too expensive for me; *det er ~ sent for det nå* it is a little too late for that now; **6** *(litt mer enn) de var (godt og) ~ 100* they were rather over a hundred; *(godt og) ~ to år* a good two years; *hun er ~ 40 år* she is past 40; **III** *sb (beste, velferd)* good, welfare; *arbeide for byens ~* work for the welfare of the town. **vel|assortert** *adj* well assorted. **~befinnende** *sb* well-being. **~behag** *sb* delight, enjoyment. **~berget** *adj* **1** *(i god behold)* safe; **2** *(vel forsynt)* well supplied. **~brukt** *adj* well-worn. **~bygd** *adj* well--built.

velde *sb* might, power; majesty.

veldedig *adj* charitable. **veldedighet** *sb* charity.

veldekket *adj: et ~ bord* a well-provided table.

veldig 1 *adj (stor)* enormous, huge; tremendous; **2** *(adv) (svært)* awfully, enormously, tremendously; very; *det er ~ snilt av deg* it/that's awfully kind of you.

vel|disponert *adj* well-arranged, well-organized. **~egnet** *adj* (well) suited. **~ferd** *sb* welfare; *nasjonens ~ferd* the welfare of the people. **~ferdsstat** *sb* welfare state.

velge *vb* **1** choose; **2** *(~ ut)* pick (out); select; *jeg valgte ut de bøkene jeg ville ha* I selected the books I wanted; *vi kan ikke ~ og vrake* we cannot pick and choose; **3** *(ved avstemning)* elect; *hun ble valgt til president* she was elected president. **velger** *sb* elector.

vel|gjerning *sb* good deed; kindness. **~gjort** *adj* well done. **~gjørende** *adj* **1** *(godgjørende)* benevolent, charitable; *en ~gjørende institusjon* a charitable institution; **2** *(hyggelig)* nice, pleasant; *det er ~gjørende å møte en person som Dem* it is pleasant/nice to meet a person like you. **~gjørenhet** *sb* charity. **~gjører** *sb* benefactor; *(om kvinne)* benefactress. **~gående** *sb* health; *de lever i beste ~* they are in perfect health. **~havende** *adj* well-to-do; prosperous; well off; *svært ~havende* wealthy. **~kjent** *adj* well-known; familiar. **~klang** *sb* euphony, harmony. **~kledd** *adj* well-dressed. **~klingende** *adj* euphonious, harmonious; melodious. **~kommen** *adj* welcome; *ønske ~kommen* welcome; bid/wish welcome. **~komst** *sb* welcome.

vell *sb (flom)* flood, wealth. **velle** *vb: ~ frem* gush (well, spring) forth.

vellevnet *sb* luxurious living; luxury.

velling *sb* gruel.

vel|lukt *sb* fragrance, scent. **~luktende** *adj* fragrant, sweet-smelling. **~lyd** *sb* euphony. **~lykket** *adj* successful; *det var ~lykket* it was a success. **~lyst** *sb* lust; sensual pleasure. **~maktsdager** *sb fl: i sine ~maktsdager* in her (his, their) days of prosperity; in her (his, their) prime. **~menende** *adj* well-meaning. **~ment** *adj* well-meant. **~nøyd** *adj* well contented/satisfied; *(bare som predikatsord)* well content. **~oppdragen** *adj* well-behaved, well-mannered. **~rettet** *adj* well-directed; *et ~rettet slag* a well-directed blow. **~sett** *adj* welcome; *en ~sett gjest* a welcome guest.

velsigne *vb* bless; *Gud ~ deg!* God bless you! **velsignelse** *sb* blessing.

vel|sittende *adj* well-fitting. **~skapt** *adj* shapely, well-shaped; well-made. **~skikket** *adj* well qualified. **~smak** *sb* agreeable taste; tastiness; savour. **~smakende** *adj* tasty, savoury. **~stand** *sb* prosperity. **~standssamfunnet** the Affluent Society. **~stelt** *adj* neat, trim; well-groomed. **~stående** *adj* well-to-do; prosperous; well-off. **~talende** *adj* eloquent. **~talenhet** *sb* eloquence.

velte *vb* **1** overturn, upset; *(vi også)* be upset; *(vt også)* knock down/over; *glasset ~t* the glass upset; *katten ~t glasset* the cat upset the glass; *kvinnen ble ~t over ende av en bil* the woman was knocked down by a car; **2** *(kantre)* capsize; *båten ~t* the boat capsized; **3** *(rulle)* roll; *de ~t steinen unna* they rolled the stone away; **4** *~ ansvaret over på* shift the responsibility on to.

vel|tilfreds *adj* contented. **~tillaget** *adj* well cooked. **~trent** *adj* well-trained. **~underrettet** *adj* well-informed. **~valgt** *adj* well-chosen. **~vilje** *sb* benevolence, goodwill; kindness. **~villig** *adj* benevolent, friendly, kind. **~være** *sb* well-being; comfort. **~ynder** *sb* patron.

vemmelig *adj* disgusting, nasty; beastly; *en ~ lukt* a beastly/nasty smell. **vemmelse** *sb* disgust. **vemmes** *vb* be disgusted; *jeg ~ ved det* it disgusts me.

vemod *sb* sadness. **vemodig** *adj* sad.

vende *vb* turn, turn over; ~ *om* turn back; ~ *seg mot (snu seg mot)* turn towards; *(henvende seg til)* turn to; *(angripe)* turn on; *(gjøre motstand mot)* turn against; *folket vendte seg mot kongen* the people turned against the king; *han vendte seg bort* he turned away; *hun vendte meg ryggen* she turned her back on me; *vi vendte tilbake dagen etter* we returned/came back the next day; *værelset ~r ut mot hagen* the room faces/overlooks the garden. **vendepunkt** *sb* turning-point. **vending** *sb* **1** *(dreining)* turn, turning; **2** *(forandring)* turn; *sykdommen tok en gunstig ~* the illness took a favourable turn; **3** *(talemåte)* phrase; **4** *(uttrykk) en ~ til det bedre* a turn for the better; *i en snever ~* at a pinch; in an emergency; *være sen/snar i ~en* be slow/quick.

venerisk *adj* venereal; ~ *sykdom* venereal disease.

venn *sb* friend; *de er fine/gode ~er* they are great friends; *en ~ av meg* a friend of mine; *en ~ av min far* a friend of my father's; *han ble ~er med min fetter* he made friends with my cousin.

venne *vb:* ~ *(seg) til* accustom (oneself) to; *hun må ~ seg til hardt arbeid* she will have to accustom herself to hard work; *jeg har vent meg av med å røyke* I have broken myself of the habit of smoking.

vennesæl *adj* popular; well liked. **venninne** *sb* friend; girl friend. **vennlig** *adj* **1** *(imøtekommende, snill)* kind; *det er meget ~ av Dem* it is very kind of you; *han var ~ mot meg* he was kind to me; **2** *(vennskapelig)* friendly; *på en ~ måte* in a friendly way; *vil De være så ~ å hjelpe meg* will you be kind enough to help me? *vil De være så ~ å lukke døren! (bestemt)* will you please shut door! *(strengt)* will you be good enough to shut the that door, please! **vennlighet** *sb* kindness, friendliness; *takk for din ~ mot min datter* thank you for your kindness to my daughter! **vennligsinnet** *adj* friendly (disposed). **vennskap** *sb* friendship. **vennskapelig** *adj* amicable, friendly; *på en ~ måte* in an amicable/a friendly way. **vennskapelighet** *sb: i all ~* amicably; in a friendly spirit.

venstre *adj, sb* left, left-hand; *gå/kjøre på ~ side* keep to the left; *hennes ~ lomme* her left-hand pocket; *på ~ hånd* on the left; *på ~ side* on the left-hand side; on the left; *til ~* to the left; *til ~ for meg* to the left of me. **venstrekjøring** *sb* lefthand traffic.

vente I *sb: han har skuffelser i ~* there are disappointments in store for him; **II** *vb* **1** wait; *hun lot oss ~* she kept us waiting; she let us wait; *jeg ~r til de er ferdige* I shall wait till they are ready; *vi ~r på ham* we are waiting for him; **2** *(for~, regne med)* expect; *det er bare hva jeg ~t meg av dem* it is only what I expected from/of them; *jeg ~r at han gjør det* I expect him to do it/that he will do it; **3** *(vente på)* await; *de ~t på kongens ankomst* they awaited the arrival of the king; *den skjebnen som ~r ham* the fate that awaits him. **ventelig** *adj* probably: to be expected. **vente|liste** *sb* waiting-list. **~værelse** *sb* waiting-room.

ventil *sb* valve. **ventilasjon** *sb* ventilation. **ventilere** *vb* ventilate. **ventilgummi** *sb* valve rubber.

veps *sb* wasp. **vepsebol** *sb* wasp's nest.

veranda *sb* veranda; *US* porch.

verb *vb* verb. **verbal** *adj* verbal. **verbalbøyning** *sb* verbal inflection; conjugation. **verbum** *sb* verb.

verd 1 *adj* worth. Se også *verdt;* **2** *sb (verdi)* value, worth.

verden *sb* world; *hele ~* the whole world; all the world; **all ~:** *all ~s rikdom* all the riches in the world; *hvem i all ~* who ever; whoever; *hvordan i all ~* how on earth; *ikke for* **alt i** ~ not for (anything in) the world; *den letteste ting* **av** ~ the easiest thing in the world; *ingenting* **i** ~ nothing in the world; **ingen ~s:** *ingen ~s nytte* no earthly use; *ingen ~s ting* no earthly thing; *komme* **til** ~ be born. **verdens|altet** *sb* the universe. **~berømmelse** *sb* world-wide fame. **~berømt** *adj* world-famous. **~berømthet** *sb* world-famous person. **~bilde** *sb* picture of the world. **~borger** *sb* citizen of the world; cosmopolitan. **~del** *sb* continent; part of the world. **~hav** *sb* ocean. **~herredømme** *sb* world dominion (hegemony, supremacy). **~historie** *sb* world history. **~historisk** *adj: en ~historisk begivenhet* a historic event. **~hjørne** *sb: de fire ~hjørner* the four points of the compass; *fra alle ~hjørner* from the four quarters of the globe. **~kart** map of the world. **~kjent** *adj* world-famed, world-famous. **~krig** *sb* world war. **~krise** *sb* world crisis. **~mester** *sb* world champion. **~mesterskap** *sb* world championship. **~omseiling** *sb* circumnavigation of the world. **~rekord** *sb* world record. **~rike** *sb* empire. **~rommet** *sb* space. **~språk** *sb* world language. **~utstilling** *sb* world exhibition.

verdi *sb* value; *til en ~ av 10 pund* to the value of £10. **verdifull** *adj* valuable; *en samling ~fulle bilder* a collection of valuable pictures.

verdig *adj* **1** *(om ytre opptreden)* dignified; *med en ~ mine* with a dignified air; **2** *(fortjent)* worthy; ~ *til* worthy of; deserving; *han er ikke ~ din tillit* he is not worthy of your confidence. **verdige** *vb* deign; *han ~t meg ikke et svar* he did not deign to answer me. **verdighet** *sb* dignity; *under hans ~* below/beneath his dignity.

verdigjenstand *sb* article of value; *(fl også)* valuables. **verdi|løs** *adj* worthless; of no value. **~mål** *sb* standard of value. **~papirer** *sb fl* securities. **~saker** *sb fl* valuables. **~stigning** *sb* increase in value; increment. **verd|sette** *vb* **1** *(taksere)* estimate; evaluate, value; **2** *(sette pris på)* appreciate. **~settelse** *sb* valuation.

verdslig *adj* **1** *(motsatt kirkelig)* secular, temporal; **2** *(verdensbundet)* worldly. **verdslighet** *sb* worldliness.

verdt *adj* **1** worth; *det er ~ 10 pund* it is worth £10; *det er ikke noe ~* it is worth nothing; *stykket er vel ~ å se* the play is well worth seeing; **2** *det er ikke ~ du gjør det* you had better not do it.

verft *sb* shipyard; shipbuilding yard.

verge I *sb* **1** *(formynder)* guardian; **2** *(våpen)* sword, weapon; **II** *vb (forsvare)* defend, protect. **vergeløs** *adj* defenceless. **vergemål** *sb* guardianship.

verifisere *vb* verify. **verifisering** *sb* verification.

veritabel *adj* regular, veritable.

verk *sb* **A 1** *(~ing)* ache, pain; **2** *(betennelse)* inflammation; *det hadde satt seg ~ i såret* the wound festered/became infected; **3** *(betent byll)* abscess, boil; **B 1** *(arbeid)* work; *et øyeblikks ~* the work of a moment; *Hamsun's ~er* Hamsun's works; the works of Hamsun; **2** *(fabrikk)* works; **3** *sette i ~ (starte)* organize, start; *(realisere)* carry/put into effect. **verke** *vb* **1** *(gjøre vondt)* ache; *det ~r i hodet mitt* my head is aching; **2** *~ etter* be itching for; *gå og ~ med noe* have something on one's mind. **verkefinger** *sb* swollen finger.

verken *konj: ~ ... eller* neither ... nor; *~ det ene eller det andre* neither one thing nor the other.

verk|sted *sb* workshop; *på et ~sted* in a workshop. **~tøy** *sb koll* tools; *et stykke ~tøy* a tool.

vern *sb* defence, protection; *(fig)* bulwark. **verne** *vb* defend, protect. **verne|plikt** *sb* compulsory military service; *(også)* conscription. **~pliktig** *adj* liable for military service; *en ~pliktig* a conscript; a (national) serviceman. **~skog** *sb* protection forest.

verpe *vb* lay (eggs). **verpehøne** *sb* laying hen.

verre *adj (komp av dårlig, vond etc)* worse; *~ enn noen gang* worse than ever; *~ og ~* worse and worse; *det var ~!* that's more serious!

vers *sb* stanza, verse; *(i Bibelen)* verse; *la oss synge første ~* let us sing the first verse; *på ~* in verse; *skrive ~* write poetry.

versjon *sb* version.

verse|linje *sb* verse. **~skjema** *sb* metrical pattern.

verst *adj (sup av dårlig, vond etc)* worst; *hans ~e fiende* his worst enemy; *i ~e fall* at (the) worst; *ikke (så) ~* not at all bad; not half bad.

vert *sb* **1** *(privat)* host; **2** *(på hotell etc)* landlord.

vertikal *adj, sb* vertical; *~delt hus* semi-detached house.

vertinne 1 *(privat)* hostess; **2** *(på hotell etc)* landlady. **verts|folk** *sb koll* host and hostess. **~hus** *sb* public house; pub; inn.

vertskap se *vertsfolk.*

verv *sb* commission, task. **verve** *vb* enlist, recruit; *la seg ~* enlist.

vesen *sb* **1** *(opptreden)* manners *(fl)*; *ha et elskverdig ~* have pleasant manners; **2** *(beskaffenhet, natur)* nature; *hun er beskjeden av ~* she is modest by nature; **3** *(skapning)* being, person; thing; *et levende ~* a living being; *et stakkars lite ~* a poor little thing; **4** *(oppstyr)* fuss; *gjøre ~ av noe* make a fuss about/of something. **vesens|forskjell** *sb* basic/essential difference. **~forskjellig** *adj* essentially different. **vesentlig** *adj* essential; *(betydelig også)* considerable; *(som adv)* essentially, considerably; *av ~ betydning* essential; *en ~ del* a considerable/an essential part; *i alt ~* in all essentials; *i det ~e* essentially; *i ~ grad* essentially, materially; *skjelne mellom ~ og u~* distinguish between essentials and inessentials.

veske *sb* bag, handbag; *(dokumentmappe)* briefcase, portfolio; *(skole~ også)* satchel. **veskenapper** *sb* bag-snatcher.

vesle *adj* little. Se *liten.* **veslevoksen** *adj* precocious.

vest *adj, sb* west; *~ for byen* (to the) west of the town; *fra ~* from the west; *i ~* in the west; *mot ~* west, westward; *vende mot ~* face west. **vesta|for** *prep* (to the) west of; westward of. **~fra** *adv* from the west. **~vind** *sb* west/westerly wind. **Vesten** *sb* the West; the Western World. Se også *vestmaktene.* **vestenom** *prep* (to the) west of. **vesterlandsk** *adj* Western; Occidental. **vestgående** *adj* westbound.

vest *sb (plagg)* waistcoat; *US* vest.

vestibyle *sb* (entrance) hall; lobby; vestibule.

vest|kant *sb* west side; *(i by)* West-End. **~kyst** *sb* west(ern) coast. **vestlig** *adj* western; *(om vind også)* westerly. **vestligst** *adj* westernmost. **vest|maktene** *sb fl* the Western Powers. **~over** *adv* west, westward(s); towards the west. **~på** *adv* in the west; out west. **vestre** *adj* western. **vestside** *sb* west(ern) side.

veteran *sb* veteran; old hand; old-timer.

veterinær *sb* veterinary (surgeon); *dgl* vet. **veterinærhøyskole** *sb* veterinary college.

veto *sb* veto; *nedlegge ~ mot* veto. **vetorett** *sb* right of veto.

vett *sb* brains, sense; intelligence; *er du fra ~et?* have you taken leave of your senses? *gå fra ~et* lose/take leave of one's senses; *han har godt ~* he has good sense; *skremme ~et av* frighten out of her (his etc) wits; *være fra ~et* have lost one's wits/senses; be out of one's wits. **vettig** *adj* sensible. **vett|løs** *adj* foolish, stupid. **~skremme** *sb* frighten/scare out of her (his etc) wits; *han ble ~skremt* he was scared stiff.

vev *sb* **1** *(celle~ etc)* (organic) tissue; **2** *(vevd stoff)* woven fabric; **3** *(fig: spinn)* web; *et ~ av løgn(er)* a web of lies; **4** *(tøys)* nonsense, twaddle; **5** *(vevstol)* loom. **veve** *vb* weave.

vever *adj* agile; active, quick; nimble.

veveri *sb* weaving mill.

via *prep* by way of; via. **viadukt** *sb* viaduct.

vibrasjon *sb* vibration. **vibrere** *vb* vibrate. **vibrerende** *adj* vibratory.

vid *adj* wide; *(om klær også)* loose; *~e benklær/bukser* loose/wide trousers; *den ~ verden* the wide world; *på ~ vegg* wide open. Se også *vidt.*

vidd *sb (åndrikhet)* wit.

vidde *sb* **1** *(omfang)* width; *av forskjellig ~* of different widths; **2** *(vidt område)* plain; wide expanse; *(fjell~)* mountain plateau; *komme ut på ~ne (fig)* stray from one's subject.

vide *vb: ~ seg ut* expand; enlarge, widen.

videre *adj, adv* **1** *(ytterligere)* further; *~ opplysninger* further information; **2** *(lenger frem)* farther, further; *de kom ikke/kunne ikke komme ~* they could come (go, walk etc) no farther; **3** *(for å uttrykke fortsettelse)* on; go on ...ing; *de marsjerte ~* they marched on; *jeg arbeidet ~* I went on working; *vi må ~* we must be getting along; **4** *(særlig)* very; *det er ikke ~ morsomt* it is not very funny; *jeg bryr meg ikke noe ~ om* I do not care very much for; **5** *(mye)* much; *ser du noe ~ til dem?* do you see much of them? **6** *(uttrykk) i ~ forstand* in a wider sense; *inntil ~* for the time being; *legg bøkene i kroken inntil ~* put the books in the corner for the time being; *la det ikke komme ~!* don't let it go any further! *og så ~* and so on; *uten ~* straight away; without any ado/ceremony. **videre|gående** *adj* advanced; *~ skole* ≈ secondary school; *(ofte, især US)* (junior) college; *~ studium* advanced studies; *~ utdannelse* advanced/further education. **~kommen** *adj* advanced.

vid|løftig *adj* circumstantial, long-winded. **~strakt** *adj* extensive, wide. **~synt** *adj* broadminded, liberal.

vidt *adv* far; wide, widely; *du går for ~* you are going too far; *på ~ gap* wide open; *~ og bredt* far and wide; *~ forskjellig* widely different; *drive det ~* be successful; go far; *så ~* barely; only just; *det var så ~ hun kom fra det (med livet)* she had a narrow escape; *det var så ~ jeg greide å krabbe opp trappen* I barely managed to crawl upstairs; *ikke så ~ jeg vet* not that I know of; *så ~ jeg husker/vet* as far as I remember/know; *vi nådde så ~ toget* we only just caught the train; *for så ~* in a sense/way; *for så ~ har han helt rett* in a sense he is quite right; *for så ~ som* in so far as; *for så ~ som det er nødvendig* in so far as it is necessary.

vidunder *sb* wonder; *(under)* miracle. **vidunderbarn** *sb* (child) prodigy. **vidunderlig** *adj* wonderful, marvellous; *et ~ syn* a wonderful sight.

vidåpen *adj* wide open.

vie *vb* **1** *(ektevie)* marry; *de ble ~t av sognepresten* they were married by the vicar; **2** *(innvie, ofre)* consecrate, dedicate, devote; *~ sitt liv til Gud* dedicate one's life to God. **vielse** *sb* marriage, wedding; *borgerlig ~* civil marriage; *kirkelig ~* church wedding. **vielsesattest** *sb* marriage certificate/lines.

vifte *sb* fan. **vifte** *vb* wave; *(bruke ~)* fan; *han ~t med hatten* he waved his hat.

vigør *sb: i ~* in good form; *ikke i ~* out of/not in form; off colour.

vik *sb* cove, inlet; creek.

vikar *sb* deputy, substitute. **vikariat** *sb* deputyship; *jeg fikk et ~* I got a job as a substitute. **vikariere** *vb* act as a substitute.

vike *vb* **1** *(trekke seg tilbake)* give way; retreat; *han vek tre skritt tilbake* he retreated three steps; *hun vek tilbake for å gjøre det* she shrank from doing it; **2** *(gi etter)* give way; *du må ikke ~* don't give way; **3** *(tre til side)* step aside; *han vek til side for en bil* he gave way to a car. **vikeplass** *sb* lay-by. **vikeplikt** *sb: du hadde ~ for meg* I had the right of way over you.

viking *sb* viking. **vikingtog** *sb* viking raid.

vikle *vb* wind, wrap; twist; *~ en bandasje om fingeren* wind a bandage round one's finger.

viktig *adj* **1** *(betydningsfull)* important; *~e begivenheter* important events; *det er ~ for deg å vite det* it is important for you to know it; **2** *(innbilsk)* conceited; *(hoven)* stuck-up; *han er så ~ at han holder på å sprekke* he is bursting with conceit; *hva har du å være så ~ av?* what have you to be so conceited about? **viktighet** *sb* **1** *(betydning)* importance; *det var av stor ~ for dem* it was of great importance to them; **2** *(innbilskhet)* conceit.

viktoriansk *adj* Victorian.

vil se *ville.*

vilje *sb* will; *en sterk ~* a strong will; *han gjorde det med ~* he did it deliberately/on purpose; *hun fikk ~n sin* she had her way; *mot sin ~* against one's will. **vilje|anstrengelse** *sb* effort of will. **~fast** *adj* determined, firm; strong-willed. **~kraft** *sb* willpower. **~kraftig** *adj* strong-willed. **~løs** *adj* weak-willed; passive; *et ~løst redskap for* a passive tool in the hands of. **~sak** *sb: det er en ~sak* it is a matter of will. **~sterk** *adj* strong-willed. **~styrke** *sb* willpower.

vilkår *sb* condition; *(fl også)* terms; *på det ~ at* on condition that; *under gunstige ~* under favourable conditions; *vi gikk inn på disse ~ene* we accepted these terms. **vilkårlig** *adj* arbitrary; *et ~ valg* an arbitrary choice. **vilkårlighet** *sb* arbitrariness.

vill *adj* **1** wild; *~e dyr* wild animals/beasts; *i ~ fart* at a furious rate; *være ~ etter* be crazy/mad about. **2** *(usivilisert)* savage; *~e stammer* savage tribes; **3** *han gikk seg ~* he lost his way.

villa *sb* detached house; *(om liten ~ ofte)* cottage; *(bare om stor, flott ~)* villa.

villdyr *sb* wild beast.

ville *vb* (har på engelsk ingen infinitiv- eller partisippformer; de bøyde formene *will, would* og *shall, should* brukes som det fremgår av det følgende; se også *skulle*) **1** *(om vilje, hensikt, ønske)* want; *(især i nektende setninger)* will; *hva vil hun?* what does she want? *hun vil ha pengene dine* she wants your money; *jeg vil at du skal hjelpe meg* I want you to help me; *jeg vil ikke gjøre det* i will not do it; *man kan hva man vil* where there's a will there's a way; *som du vil* as you like/please; *uten å ~ det* unintentionally. **2** *(i futurum) (i 1. person)* shall, *(i 2. og 3. person)* will; *det vil ta lang tid* it will take long; *du vil bli overrasket* you'll be surprised; *han vil være fremme i god tid* he will be there in good time; *vi vil være tilbake om en halv time* we shall be back in half an hour; **3** *(om tenkte tilfeller) (i 1. person)* should *(i 2. og 3. person)* would; *om han hadde vært skyldig, ville han ha tilstått* if he had been guilty, he would have confessed; **4** *(om mål, retning)* be going (to); want to go (to); *han vil hjem* he wants to go home; *hvor vil du hen?* where are you going? *jeg skjønner ikke hvor du vil hen (fig: dvs hva du sikter til etc)* I do not understand what you are driving at.

villede *vb* lead astray; mislead. **villedende** *adj* misleading. **villelse** *sb: han snakker i ~* he is delirious; his mind is wandering. **vill|farelse** *sb* error, mistake. **~het** wildness, fierceness, savageness.

villig *adj* willing, ready; *hun var ~ til å gjøre det* she was willing/ready to do it. **villighet** *sb* willingness.

vill|mann *sb* savage. **~mark** *sb* wilderness, wilds.

~nis *sb* tangle, wilderness; jungle. **~rede** *sb: i ~rede* perplexed, puzzled; at a loss. **~skap** *sb* wildness; savageness, savagery. **~spor** *sb: på ~spor* on the wrong track. **~strå** *sb: på ~strå* lost. **~styring** *sb* madcap. **~vin** *sb* Virginia creeper.

vilt *sb (jakt~)* game.

vilter *adj* frisky, wild; *(livlig)* lively; *(overstadig)* abandoned. **vilterhet** *sb* friskiness, wildness; abandon.

vilt|handel *sb* poulterer's (shop). **~handler** *sb* poulterer. **~pleie** *sb* game preservation.

vimpel *sb* pennant, streamer.

vims *sb* restless person; fussbox, fusspot; *US* fussbudget. **vimse** *vb* fuss; bustle. **vimsete** *adj* fussy, restless.

vin *sb* wine.

vind *sb* wind; *vi hadde ~en med oss* we had the wind behind us; *være i ~en* be popular/much sought after.

vinde 1 *sb (heisverk)* windlass; *(garn~)* (yarn) reel; **2** *vb* wind. **vindebro** *sb* drawbridge. **vindeltrapp** *sb* spiral/winding staircase. **vinding** *sb* winding; *(av spiral, tråd etc)* turn.

vind|jakke *sb* wind(proof) jacket; *(især US)* windbreaker. **~kast** *sb* gust of wind. **~mølle** *sb* windmill. **~pust** *sb* breath of wind. **~skjev** *adj* warped. **~stille** *adj* calm; *ligge i ~stilla* be becalmed. **~styrke** *sb* wind force. **~støt** *sb* gust of wind. **~tørket** *sb* air-dried.

vindu *sb* window. **vindus|karm** *sb* window frame. **~plass** *sb* window seat. **~post** *sb* window sill. **~pusser** *sb* **1** *(person)* window cleaner; **2** *(i bil)* se *~visker*. **~rute** *sb* window-pane. **~utstilling** *sb* window display. **~visker** *sb* windscreen wiper.

ving *sb (i flyvåpenet og i fotball etc)* wing. **vinge** *sb (fugle~, fly~ etc)* wing; *slå med ~ne* flap one's wings. **vinge|fang** se *~spenn*. **~slag** *sb* flap/stroke of the wings. **~spenn** *sb* wing span.

vingle *vb* stagger; *(især fig)* vacillate. **vinglete** *adj* fickle; double-minded, inconstant; vacillating; *han er veldig ~* he's always chopping and changing.

vin|gård, ~hage *sb* vineyard. **~handel** *sb (butikk)* wine-shop. **~handler** *sb* wine-merchant, vintner.

vink *sb* **1** *(tegn, f.eks. med hånden)* sign; *hun gav meg et ~ om å komme nærmere* she gave me a sign to come nearer; **2** *(råd)* advice; hint, suggestion; *han forstod/fulgte ~et* he took the hint; *praktiske ~* practical advice. **vinke** *vb* **1** *(~ til seg)* beckon; *han ~t til meg at jeg skulle komme nærmere* he beckoned me to come nearer; **2** *(som hilsen)* wave; *de ~t farvel* they waved good-bye; *han ~t med hatten/hånden* he waved his hat/his hand.

vinkel *sb* **1** angle; *rett ~* right angle; **2** *(~hake)* square.

vinkjenner *sb* connoisseur of wine.

vinn *sb: legge ~ på (gjøre seg umak med)* endeavour to; *(legge vekt på)* attach great importance to.

vinne *vb* **1** *(især i kamp, spill)* win; *de vant slaget* they won the battle; **2** *(oppnå, især ved personlig anstrengelse)* gain; *jeg vant hennes vennskap* I gained her friendship; *vi vant tid* we gained time; **3** *(uttrykk) det er ikke noe vunnet med å* ... there is nothing to be gained by ...; *den som intet våger, han intet vinner* nothing venture, nothing win. **vinnende** *adj* winning; attractive, engaging. **vinner** *sb* winner; *du er en sikker ~* you are a sure winner. **vinning** *sb (inntekt)* gain, profit; *vinningen går opp i spinningen* the expenses absorb the profit. **vinningsforbrytelse** *sb* crime for profit.

vinranke *sb* vine.

vinsj *sb* winch.

vin|skjønner se *~kjenner*. **~stokk** *sb* vine.

vinter *sb* winter; *~en 1990* (in) the winter of 1990; *en streng ~* a hard winter; *(nå) i ~* this winter; *i fjor ~, sist ~* last winter; *neste ~, til ~en* next winter; *om ~en* in/during (the) winter. **vinter|dag** *sb* winter/winter's day. **~dekk** *sb* snow tire. **~dvale** *sb* hibernation; *ligge i ~* hibernate. **~ferie** *sb* winter sports holiday. **~frakk** *sb* greatcoat. **~hi** *sb* winter lair. **vinterlig** *adj* wintry.

vinter|solverv *sb* winter solstice. **~sportssted** *sb* winter resort.

vippe I *sb* **1** *(~huske)* seesaw; **2** *(elektrisk ~)* current limiter; *(i bil)* constant voltage control; **II** *vb* **1** *(~ på huske)* seesaw; play at seesaw; **2** *(bevege seg opp og ned)* rock; *båten ~t* the boat rocked; **3** *(duppe, nikke)* bob, nod; **4** *(ta/få til å ta overhaling)* tilt, tip; *bordet ~t over ende* the table tilted over/tipped up; *han ~t bordet over ende* he tipped the table up; *ikke sitt og vipp på stolen!* don't tilt your chair! **5** *det står og ~r (dvs er uvisst)* it hangs/is in the balance; it is touch and go. **vippen** *sb: stå/være på ~* be/hang in the balance; *det står på ~* it's touch and go. **vippe|brett, ~huske** *sb* seesaw.

vips! *interj* flip! pop!

virak *sb* homage, praise; incense.

viril *adj* virile. **virilitet** *sb* virility.

virke I *sb* **1** *(arbeid)* activity, work; **2** *(materiale)* material; **II** *vb* **1** *(arbeide, funksjonere)* act, work; *giften ~r langsomt* the poison acts slowly; *hun ~r som lege* she acts/works as a doctor; *ringeklokken ~r ikke* the electic bell is not working; **2** *(gi inntrykk av å være)* look, seem; *han ~t noe nervøs* he seemed a little nervous. **virke|dag** *sb* week-day, workday. **~felt** *sb* field of activity; sphere of operation.

virkelig I *adj* **1** real; *landets ~e hersker* the real ruler of the country; **2** *(sann)* true; *en ~ venn* a true friend; **II** *(adv)* really; indeed; *du talte ~ meget godt* you spoke very well indeed; *er det ~ deg?* is it really you? *jeg håper ~ at han kommer* I do hope he will come; *jeg vet ~ ikke* I am sure I don't know. **virkeliggjøre** *vb* realize; carry into effect. **virkelighet** *sb* **1** reality; *bli til ~* be realized; materialize; *(gå i oppfyllelse)* come true; *gjøre til ~* realize; *i ~en (dvs i det virkelige liv)* in real life; *slike dyr finnes ikke i ~en* such animals are not found in real life; **2** *(motsatt tilsynelatende)* in reality; *han ser sterk ut, men i ~en er han svak* he looks strong, but in reality he is weak; *hun er i ~en ikke noe* *større syk* she is not very ill, really. **virkelighets|fjern** *adj* unrealistic. **~flukt** *sb* escape from reality. **~sans** *sb* realism. **~tro** *adj* realistic. **virke|lyst** *sb* energy, enterprise. **~lysten** *adj* energetic, enterprising. **~middel** *sb* agent, means; *kunstneriske ~midler* artistic effects. **~trang** *sb* urge for action.

virkning *sb* effect; *det gjorde sin ~* it had its effect; *det var uten ~* it had no effect. **virknings|full** *adj* effective. **~løs** *adj* ineffective.

virksom *adj* active; *(om legemiddel)* effective. **virksomhet** *sb* **1** *(aktivitet)* activity, activities; work; *i ~* at work; *i full ~* in full activity; **2** *(forretning, verkested etc)* business, shop.

virtuos *sb* master, vituoso. **virtuositet** *sb* eminent skill; virtuosity. **virtuosmessig** *adj* brilliant; with virtuosity.

virus *sb* virus. **virussykdom** *sb* virus disease.

virvar *sb* confusion; *det var et eneste ~* everything was in confusion.

virvel *sb* **1** *(ringbevegelse)* whirl; **2** *(i vann)* eddy, whirl; **3** *fig* whirl, vortex; **4** *(rygg~)* vertebra.

virvel|dyr *sb* vertebrate (animal). **~løs** *adj* invertebrate. **~vind** *sb* whirlwind. **virvle** *vb* whirl; *de visne bladene/det visne løvet ~t i vinden* the dead leaves whirled in the wind.

vis A *adj (klok)* wise; *en ~ kvinne* a wise woman; **B** *sb (måte)* way, manner; *på sitt ~ var det vakkert* in its way it was beautiful; *på ærlig ~* honestly.

vis-à-vis *adv, prep* (right) opposite.

visdom *sb* wisdom.

vise A *sb (sang)* song, tune; *(folke~, gate~)* ballad; **B** *vb* **1** *(syne frem)* show; *jeg viste dem at jeg ikke var ergerlig/sint* I showed them that I was not annoyed; *tiden vil ~ det* time will show; **2** *(komme til syne)* appear; *han viste seg i vinduet* he appeared at the window; *et lys viste seg i kjøkkenet* a light showed in the kitchen; **3 ~ seg** *a) (la seg se)* show oneself; *de våget ikke ~ seg på gaten* they dared not show themselves in the street; *sjalusien hans viste seg i et raserianfall* his jealousy showed itself in a fit of rage; *b) (innfinne seg)* turn up; *han viste seg uventet* he turned up unexpectedly; *c) ~ seg å være* prove; turn out; *det viste seg å være nyttig* it proved useful; *hun viste seg å være en svindler* she turned out (to be) a swindler; *d) ~ seg (kjekke seg)* show off; *han skal alltid ~ seg* he is showing off.

vise|formann *sb* vice-chairman, vice-president. **~konge** *sb* viceroy.

viser *sb (på klokke)* hand; *(på instrument)* needle, pointer.

visergutt *sb* errand-boy.

visestubb *sb* ditty.

visitas *sb* visitation. **visitere** *vb* search, examine. **visitt** *sb* call, visit; *(lege~ på sykehus)* round(s); *de kom på ~* they called; *vi avla henne en ~* we called on her; we paid her a call/visit. **visitt|kort** *sb* visiting card. **~tid** *sb (på sykehus)* visiting hours.

visjon *sb* vision. **visjonær** *adj* visionary.

viske *vb (~ ut)* rub (out); *jeg ~t ut et ord* I rubbed out a word. **viskelær** *sb* eraser.

visle *vb (om dyr)* hiss; *(om kuler og vind)* whistle. **vislelyd** *sb* hissing sound.

vismann *sb* wise man; sage; *hum* pundit.

visne *vb* wither, fade; *~ bort/hen* die, dwindle; wither away; *blomstene ~t* the flowers withered; *blomstene er ~t* the flowers have faded.

visp *sb* whisk. **vispe** *vb* whip, beat.

viss 1 *adj* certain, some; sure; *det er ~e folk som tror at* ... there are some people who think that...; *en viss frøken Jones* a certain Miss Jones; **2** *adv* certain, sure; *jeg er ~ på at jeg kan gjøre det* I am certain I can do it. **visselig** *adv* certainly, surely; to be sure.

vissen *adj* withered, faded, dead; *~t løv* dead leaves.

visshet *sb* certainty; *jeg kan ikke si med ~ hvor de er* I cannot say with certainty where they are.

visst *adv* **1** *(visstnok)* probably; I think; *han kommer ~ ikke* he propably won't come; *hun er ~ syk* I think she is ill; **2** *(riktignok)* to be sure; indeed; *~ er han sterk, men* ... to be sure he is strong but ...; **3** *(ja ~)* certainly; of course; *Kommer du? Ja, ~!* Are you coming? Certainly! **visstnok** se *visst 1* og *2*.

visuell *adj* visual; *~e hjelpemidler* visual aids.

visum *sb* visa.

vita *sb* life story. **vital** *adj* vital. **vitalitet** *sb* vitality. **vitamin** *sb* vitamin; *A ~* vitamin A. **vitaminfattig** *sb* vitamin-deficient. **vitaminisere** *vb* vitaminize. **vitamin|mangel** *sb* vitamin deficiency. **~rik** *adj* rich in vitamins.

vite *vb* **1** know; *~ av erfaring* know from experience; *jeg vet ikke* I don't know; *jeg visste ikke noe om det* I knew nothing about it; *som alle vet* as everybody knows; **2** *(uttrykk) en kan* **aldri** *~* you never can tell; **~ av:** *jeg vil ikke ~ (noe) av det* I will have none of it! *før jeg visste ordet av det* before I could say Jack Robinson; **få** *~* learn; get to know; hear; be told; *jeg fikk ~ det i går* I heard of it yesterday; *jeg fikk ikke ~ noen ting* I was told nothing; **gadd** *~* I wonder; I should like to know; *det er* **ikke godt å** *~* there is no knowing; one never knows; **vet du hva** I say; I'll tell you what; *nei, vet De hva!* really now! that's a bit thick! **så vidt en (etc) vet** as far as one (etc) knows; *ikke så vidt jeg vet* not that I know (of); *så vidt du vet det!* I tell you! *jeg gjør det ikke, så vidt du vet det!* I tell you I won't do it! **~ verken** *ut eller inn* be at one's wits' end; be quite at sea.

vite|begjærlig *adj* eager to know/learn; curious, inquiring. **~begjær(lighet)** *sb* eagerness to learn; inquisitiveness.

viten *sb* knowledge.

vitende *sb: handle mot bedre ~* act in bad faith; *med ~ og vilje* deliberately; *uten foreldrenes ~* without the knowledge of his/her parents. **vitenskap** *sb (natur~)* science; *(især om andre ~er)* branch of knowledge. **vitenskapelig** *adj (natur~)* scientific; *(især ånds~)* scholarly. **vitenskaps|kvinne, -mann** *sb (natur~)* scientist; *(især om andre lærde)* scholar.

vitne I *sb* witness; *~ne ble avhørt* the witnesses were examined; *~ne til ulykken* the witnesses of the accident; *vi var begge ~ til ulykken* we both witnessed the accident; **II** *vb* **1** *(i retten)* give evidence; *hun vitnet for broren/mot svogeren* she gave evidence in favour of her brother/against her brother-in-law; **2** *~ om (dvs være bevis/tegn på)* bear witness of/to; show; testify to. **vitne|mål** *sb (f.eks. fra skole)* certificate. **~prov** *sb* evidence, testimony. **vitnesbyrd** *sb* **1** *(i retten)* evidence; **2** *(fra skole etc)* certificate.

vits *sb* joke, witticism; *hva er ~en ved det?* what's the idea? *slå ~er* crack jokes. **vitse** *vb* crack/tell jokes.

vitterlig *adj: det er ~ for alle at ...* it is notorious that ...; *det er ~ ikke sant* it is patently untrue.

vittig *adj* witty; *en ~ bemerkning* a witty remark. **vittighet** se *vits.* **vittighets|avis, ~blad** *sb* comic paper.

viviseksjon *sb* vivisection.

vogge etc se *vugge etc.*

vogn *sb* **1** carriage, waggon; **2** *(kjerre)* cart; **3** *(jernbane~, passasjer~)* carriage, coach. **vogn|fører** *sb* driver. **~kort** *sb* (motor vehicle) registration book; *(også)* log book. **~lass** *sb* cartload. **~tog** *sb* **1** wagon train; **2** *(trekkvogn med tilhenger)* articulated/long haul lorry; *US* trailer truck.

vokabular *sb* vocabulary.

vokal *sb* vowel.

voks *sb* wax. **voks|bønne** *sb* wax bean. **~duk** *sb* oilcloth.

vokse A *vb* **1** grow; *barna har vokst* the children have grown; *det vil ikke ~ noen ting her* nothing will grow here; *hun har vokst seg pen* she has grown into a pretty girl; *plantene vokste vilt* the plants grew wild; *~ seg stor* grow big; **2** *(uttrykk)* **~ fra** grow out of; *(fig)* outgrow; grow too old for; **~ frem** grow/spring up; **~ med:** *han vokste med oppgaven* he rose to the occasion; **~ opp** grow up; *ikke ~* **på trærne** be few and far between; not grow on every bush; **~ over hodet på** outgrow; *(om arbeid etc)* become too much for one; get beyond one's control; **~ til** *(~ opp)* grow up; *(bli tilvokst)* become overgrown; **B** *vb (voksbehandle)* wax. **voksen** *adj* grown-up, adult; *bli ~* grow up; *de har voksne barn* they have grown-up children; *de voksne* the grown-ups; the adults; *en ~ mann* a grown man; *takst for voksne* adult fare; *være oppgaven ~* be equal to the task. **voksenopplæring** *sb* adult education. **voksested** *sb* habitat.

voks|figur *sb* wax figure. **~kabinett** *sb* waxworks; waxwork show. **~kake** *sb* honeycomb. **~lys** *sb* wax candle.

vokte *vb* guard, watch; *~ seg for å* take care not to. **vokter** *sb* guard, keeper; watcher.

vold *sb* **1** violence, force; *de holdt ham (godt) fast, men brukte ikke ~* they held him firmly, but used no force; **2** *(makt)* power; *han var i hennes ~* he was in her power. **volde** *vb (forårsake)* cause.

voldgift *sb* arbitration; *avgjøre ved ~* settle by arbitration; *la avgjøre ved ~* refer/submit to arbitration. **voldgifts|dommer** *sb* arbitrator. **~domstol** *sb* court of arbitration. **~kjennelse** *sb* (arbitration) award. **~mann** *sb* arbitrator. **~rett** se *~domstol.*

volds|dåd se *~handling.* **~forbrytelse** *sb* crime of violence. **~forbryter** *sb* violent criminal. **~handling** *sb* act of violence; outrage. **~herredømme** *sb* despotism, tyrrany. **voldsom** *adj* **1** violent; *en ~ anstrengelse/død* a violent effort/death; **2** *(stor, sterk)* terrible, tremendous; *~ applaus* tremendous applause. **voldsomhet** violence.

voldta *vb* rape, ravish. **voldtekt** *sb* rape. **voldtekts|forbryter** *sb* rapist. **~forsøk** *sb* attempted rape.

voll *sb* **1** *(eng)* meadow; **2** *(jord~)* bank, dike; *(festnings~)* rampart. **vollgrav** *sb* moat.

volontør *sb* (unpaid) apprentice; junior clerk.

volt *sb* volt.

volum *sb* volume. **voluminøs** *adj* bulky, voluminous.

vom *sb (om mennesker)* paunch, pot-belly; *(om drøvtyggere)* maw.

von *sb* hope.

vond *adj* **1** *(smertefull)* painful, sore; aching; *en ~ tann* an aching tooth; *en ~ tå* a sore toe; **2** *(dårlig, slett)* bad; *~ samvittighet* bad conscience; *~ smak* bad taste; **3** *(uttrykk)* **få ~t:** *jeg får ~t av å se det* it makes me sick to see it; *jeg fikk ~t i armene* my arms began to ache; **gjøre ~t** hurt; *det gjør ~t* it hurts; *det gjør meg ~t å høre det* I am sorry to hear that; *det gjør ~t i fingeren* my finger hurts; *gjøre ~t verre* make bad worse; **ha (det) ~t:** *de har det ~t* they are unhappy; *har du ~t?* does it hurt? *har hun ~t?* is she in pain? **ha ~t av** *(ta skade av) det har du ikke ~t av* that won't do you any harm; *(synes synd på)* be/feel sorry for; *jeg har ~t av dem* I feel sorry for them; **ha ~t for** find it difficult; *jeg har ~t for å tro det* I find it difficult to believe it; *jeg har* **~t i** *fingeren* my finger hurts; *jeg har ~t i halsen* I have a sore throat; *jeg har ~t i ryggen* I have a pain in my back; **mene ~t:** *det var ikke ~t ment* no harm was meant. **vondord** *sb koll* angry words.

vorden *sb: i sin ~* in the making. **vordende** *adj* future; to be; *min ~ svigerdatter* my daughter-in-law to be.

vorte *sb* wart.

votere *vb* vote. **votering** *sb* voting.

vott *sb* mitten.

votum *sb* vote.

vrak *sb* wreck; *kaste ~ på* reject. **vrake** *vb* reject; *velge og ~* pick and choose. **vrakgods** *sb* wreckage.

vralte *vb* waddle.

vrang *adj* **1** *(med vrangen ut)* (turned) inside out; **2** *(vanskelig)* difficult, troublesome; awkward; **3** *(sur, vrien)* surly, unfriendly; *(sta)* obstinate, pig-headed, stubborn; *slå seg ~* become restive; jib; *gutten slo seg ~* the boy became restive; *motoren slo seg ~* the motor jibbed. **vrange** *sb* **1** *(~side)* the wrong side; *på ~n* on the wrong side; **2** *(~strupe); få/sette i ~n* swallow the wrong way. **vrang|forestilling** *sb* delusion. **~lære** *sb* false doctrine; heresy. **~lærer** *sb* false teacher. **~lås** *sb: døren gikk i ~lås* the lock caught. **~strupe** se *vrange.* **~vilje** *sb* contrariness; ill-will, unwillingness; obstinacy. **~villig** *adj* contrary, disobliging; obstinate. **vranten** *adj* sulky, surly; *(innesluttet og ~)* sullen.

vred *adj* wroth. **vrede** *sb* wrath.

vrenge *vb* turn inside out. **vrengebilde** *sb* distorted picture; caricature.

vri 1 *sb* twist; **2** *vb* twist, wring; *~ hendene* wring one's hands; *~ (opp) vasketøyet* wring the washing; *~ seg* writhe; *~ seg av/i smerte* writhe with/in agony. **vrien** *adj* **1** *(ikke enkel)* difficult, intricate; **2** *(vrang)* contrary; obstinate, pig-headed.

vrikke *vb* **1** *(bevege seg fra side til side)* wriggle; **2** *(forvri)* sprain; *han ~t ankelen* he sprained his ankle.

vrimle *vb* swarm, teem; *det ~t med barn på gatene* children swarmed in the streets; the streets swarmed with children. **vrimmel** *sb* swarm.

vrinsk *sb* neigh, neighing. **vrinske** *vb* neigh.

vriompeis *sb* mule, pighead.

vrist *sb* instep.

vriste *vb* wring; *(plutselig og voldsomt)* wrench; *de ~t geværet ut av hendene hans* they wrenched the gun out of his hands.

vræl *sb* roar, yell. **vræle** *vb* roar, yell.

vrøvl *sb* **1** *(sludder)* nonsense; *hun snakket en masse ~* she talked a lot of nonsense; **2** *(innvendinger)* fuss; *de gjorde ~ om det* they made fuss about it; **3** *(ubehageligheter)* trouble. **vrøvle** *vb* talk nonsense; twaddle. **vrøvlebøtte** *sb* twaddler.

vugge 1 *sb* cradle; *fra ~n til graven* from the cradle to the grave; **2** *vb* rock; *båten ~t på bølgene* the boat was rocking on the waves; *han ~t barnet i søvn* he rocked the child to sleep. **vugge|vise, ~sang** *sb* lullaby.

vulgær *adj* vulgar; *~ oppførsel* vulgar behaviour.

vulkan *sb* volcano. **vulkanisere** *sb* vulcanize. **vulkansk** *adj* volcanic. **vulkanutbrudd** *sb* volcanic eruption.

vurdere *vb* **1** *(taksere)* estimate; *skaden ble vurdert til 50.000 pund* the damage was estimated at £50 000; **2** *(verdsette)* appreciate; *han ble ikke vurdert etter fortjeneste* he was not appreciated at his true value. **vurdering** *sb* estimate, valuation; *(især fig)* evaluation.

væpne *vb* arm; *~t motstand* armed resistance.

vær A *sb* **1** weather; *(ofte)* day, morning (etc); *det var fint ~* the day (etc) was fine; *det var varmt i ~et* the weather was hot; it was a hot day; *dårlig ~* bad weather; **2** *(pust)* breath; *snappe etter ~et* gasp for breath; **3** *(uttrykk) med bunnen i ~et* upside down; *prisene gikk i ~et* prices rose/went up; **B** *(fiske~)* fishing station; **C** *(saubukk)* ram.

være *vb* **1** be; *de kan da ikke ~ så dumme* they can't be that stupid; **2** *(som hjelpeverb)* have; *hun er nettopp kommet* she has just arrived; *hva er det blitt av ham?* what has become of him? **3** *(uttrykk) ~* **for** be for/in favour of; *~* **imot** be against; be opposed to; **kan ~** may be; *det kan godt ~ (at) han kommer* he may come; *jeg kunne ikke* **la** *~ å smile* I could not help smiling; *~* **med** accompany; come along; *~* **med på** take part in; *det er en lek/et spill (som) alle kan ~ med på* that is a game everybody can take part in; *~* **til** exist; *~* **ved** admit; *de ville ikke ~ ved at de hadde vært redde* they would not admit that they had been afraid.

værelse *sb* room; *~ til gaten* front room; *~ til gården* back room. **værelseskamerat** *sb* room-mate.

vær|fast *adj* weather-bound. **~forandring** *sb* weather change. **~forhold** *sb* weather conditions. **~hane** *sb* weathercock.

værhår *sb* whisker.

vær|kart *sb* weather chart. **~lag** *sb* climate. **~melding, ~varsel** *sb* weather forecast/report.

væske 1 *sb* liquid; **2** *vb (utsondre ~)* run; *med* suppurate. **væte** *sb* moisture; dampness, humidity. **væte** *vb* moisten, wet.

vøle *vb* mend, repair.

vøre *vb (akte)* esteem, respect; *(ta hensyn til)* heed; pay heed to; take heed of; *de ble advart, men vørte det ikke* they were warned, but did not heed; *de vørte ikke faren* they took no heed of danger. **vørnad** *sb* esteem, respect.

våde|skudd *sb* accidental shot.

våg *sb (bukt)* bay.

vågal *adj* daring, foolhardy; reckless. **våge** *vb* **1** *(utsette for fare)* risk, venture; *den som intet ~r, intet vinner* nothing venture, nothing win; *han ~t livet for å redde hunden hennes* he risked/ventured his life to save her dog; *jeg ~t meg ut på isen* I ventured out on the ice; *vi ~t oss inn i skogen* we ventured into the wood; **2** *(tore)* dare; *hun ~t ikke komme* she dared not come; *hvordan ~r du å gjøre det* how dare you do it? **våge|hals** *sb* daredevil. **~mot** *sb* daring. **~spill, ~stykke** *sb* (daring) venture.

våke *vb* **1** *(være våken)* be awake; **2** *(sitte oppe)* watch; sit up; *(om sykepleier)* be on night duty; *~ ved en sykeseng* watch beside a sick-bed; **3** *(holde våkenatt)* keep vigil. **våken** *adj* **1** *(ikke sovende)* awake, waking; *han holdt meg ~* he kept me awake; *hun holdt seg ~* she kept awake; **2** *(påpasselig, årvåken)* watchful, wakeful; **3** *(oppvakt)* bright; *en ~ jentunge* a bright girl/lass. **våkenatt** *sb* **1** vigil; **2** *(søvnløs natt)* sleepless night. **våkne** *vb* **1** *(~ etter søvn)* wake (up); *(bokl)* awake, awaken, waken; *jeg ~t tidlig* I woke (up) early; **2** *(etter besvimelse etc)* come round; come to.

våningshus *sb* farmhouse.

våpen *sb* **1** *(kampmiddel)* weapon; *et hemmelig ~* a secret weapon; **2** *(især om håndvåpen)* arms *fl*; *gripe til ~* take up arms; **3** *(våpenskjold)* coat of arms. **våpen|før** *adj* fit for military service. **~hvile** *sb* armistice, truce. **~makt** *sb* military power/force; *med ~makt* by force of arms. **~merke** *sb* device. **~skjold** *sb* coat of arms; escutcheon. **~stillstand** *sb* armistice, truce. **~øvelse** *sb* military drill/training.

vår A *eiend pron* our; *(stående alene)* ours; *det er ~t hus* it is our house; *huset er ~t* the house is ours; **B** *sb* *(forår)* spring; *~en 1990* (in) the spring of 1990; *~en er en deilig tid* spring is a lovely season; *(nå) i ~, i ~es* this spring; *i fjor ~, sist ~* last spring; *neste ~, til ~en* next spring; *om ~en* during/in (the) spring).

Vårherre Our Lord; the Lord; God; *~ bevares!* Good Lord! Good gracious!

vårjevndøgn *sb* spring equinox. **vårlig** *adj* vernal.

vår|løsning *sb* spring thaw. **~onn** *sb* spring farming. **~rengjøring** *sb* spring cleaning. **~slapphet** *sb* spring lassitude.

vås *sb* nonsense, rubbish, twaddle. **våse** *vb* talk nonsense; twaddle. **våsekopp** *sb* twaddler. **våsete** *adj* nonsensical, silly.

våt *adj adj* wet; *jeg ble ~ på beina* I got wet feet.

W

w *(bokstaven)* w.

Wales Wales. **waliser** *sb* Welshman; *waliserne* the Welsh. **walisisk** *adj* Welsh.

watt *sb* watt; *100 ~* 100 watts.

WC *sb* lavatory; *US* bathroom, washroom; *(især på hotell)* toilet; *(om offentlig toalett)* public convenience; *US* restroom.

whisky *sb* whisky; *(især om irsk ~)* whiskey.

wiener|brød *sb* Danish (pastry). **~pølse** *sb* frankfurter. **~vals** Viennese waltz.

X-Y-Z

x *(bokstaven)* x.

Xanthippe *(personen)* Xanthippe; *(hissig kone)* shrew, vixen; termagant.

X-krok *sb* picture hook.

xylofon *sb* xylophone.

y *(bokstaven)* y.

yacht *sb* yacht.

ydmyk *adj* humble; *en ~ anmodning* a humble request. **ydmyke** *vb* humiliate, humble; *~ seg for* humble oneself before. **ydmykelse** *sb* humiliation; *han måtte tåle mange ~r* he suffered many humiliations. **ydmykhet** *sb* humility.

ymse se *forskjellig, ulik*.

ymt *sb* hint, inkling. **ymte** *vb* hint; *det ~es om at...* it is rumoured that...

ynde 1 *sb* charm, grace; **2** *vb* like, love; be fond of. **yndefull** *adj* graceful. **yndest** *sb* favour; *han var/stod i stor ~ hos kongen* he was in great favour with the King. **ynder** *sb: jeg er ingen ~ av henne* I am no admirer of hers. **yndet** *adj* popular; in favour. **yndig** *adj* lovely, charming; *et ~ lite hus* a charming little house. **yndling** *sb* favourite; *alles ~* everybody's favourite. **yndlings-** *forst* favourite. **yndlings|beskjeftigelse** *sb* favourite occupation. **~tema** *sb* favourite/pet subject.

yngel *sb* brood; *(fiske~)* fry, spawn. **yngle** *vb* breed, multiply. **yngleplass** *sb (for fisk)* spawning ground; *(for fugler etc)* rookery. **yngling** *sb* **1** *(det å yngle)* breeding, multiplying; **2** *(ung mann)* young man; youth; *(også)* youngster. **ynglingalder** *sb* youth, adolescence.

yngre *adj* **1** *(om alder)* younger, junior; *han er ti år ~ enn hun* he is ten years younger than she; *hun er to år ~ enn jeg* she is two years my junior; **2** *(om tidsalder)* later; *den ~ steinalder* the later Stone Age. **yngst** *adj* youngest; *den ~ av de to* the younger. **yngstemann** *sb* junior.

ynk *sb: det var en ~ å se* it was a pitiful sight. **ynke** *vb* **1** *~ seg* moan, whimper; **2** *~s over* pity; feel sorry for. **ynkelig** *adj* pitiful; *(dårlig, elendig)* miserable, wretched; *en ~ forfatning* a pitiful state; *et ~ resultat* a miserable result; *han så ~ ut* he looked miserable/wretched. **ynkelighet** *sb* wretchedness. **ynkes** se *ynke*. **ynkverdig** *adj* pitiable, pitiful.

yppal *adj* aggressive, quarrelsome. **yppe** *vb* incite, instigate; stir up; *~ seg (kjekke seg)* show off; *(opptre utfordrende)* be quarrelsome/aggressive; *~ strid* pick a quarrel;

ypperlig *adj* excellent, superb; *dgl* capital. **ypperst** *adj* most outstanding; best, first. **yppersteprest** *sb* high priest.

yppig *adj* **1** *(frodig)* exuberant, luxuriant; *~ vegeta-*

sjon exuberant/luxuriant growth/vegetation; **2** *(om kvinnekropp)* ample, voluptuous; *~e former/kurver* voluptuous curves; *en ~ barm* an ample bosom. **yppighet** *sb* exuberance; luxuriance, luxury.

yr A *adj (vilter)* giddy; **B** *sb (duskregn)* drizzle. **yre** *vb* **A** *(kry)* swarm, teem; **B** *(duskregne)* drizzle. **yrhet** *sb* giddiness.

yrke *sb* occupation; *(håndverks~)* craft, trade; *(akademisk ~)* profession; *lærer av ~* a teacher by profession; *møbelsnekker av ~* a cabinet-maker by trade. **yrkedag** *sb* workday, weekday.

yrkes- *forst* professional, vocational. **yrkes|aktiv** *adj* working. **~befolkning** *sb* working population. **~betont** *adj* vocationally oriented. **~ektepar** *sb* professional/working couple. **~erfaring** *sb* professional experience. II *vb* 1 **etikk** *sb* professional code. **~faglig** *adj* vocational. **~forbryter** *sb* professional criminal. **~gruppe** *sb* occupational group. **~hygiene** *sb* industrial/occupational hygiene. **~karriere** *sb* professional/working career. **~kvinne** career (business, professional, working) woman. **~messig** occupational, professional. **~muligheter** *sb fl* career opportunities. **~nevrose** *sb* occupational neurosis. **~opplæring** *sb* vocational trading. **~organisasjon** *sb* professional body; trade organization. **~orientert** *adj* professional, vocational. **~praksis** se *~erfaring*. **~skole** *sb* vocational school. **~sykdom** *sb* occupational disease. **~utdanning** se *~opplæring*. **~utøvelse** *sb: fri ~utøvelse* free trade. **~veileder** *sb* (youth) employment officer. **~veiledning** *sb* vocational guidance.

yste *vb* make cheese. **ysteri** *sb* cheese factory.

yte *vb* **1** *(gi, skjenke)* give, grant; *~ beskyttelse* give protection; *~ erstatning* pay compensation; *~ kreditt* grant a credit; *~ motstand* offer resistance; *~ noen rettferdighet* do somebody justice; *~ sitt bidrag* contribute one's share; *de ~t oss hjelp* they helped us; **2** *(prestere)* do; *hun ~t godt arbeid* she did good work. **yte|dyktig** *adj* productive. **~dyktighet** *sb* productivity. **~evne** *sb* capacity, efficiency; *(produktivitet)* productivity. **ytelse** *sb* **1** *(prestasjon)* performance; **2** *(betaling)* payment; **3** *(bidrag)* contribution; *sosiale ~r* social benefits.

ytre 1 *adj* outer, external; *~ fiender* external enemies; *den ~ havnen* the outer harbour; **2** *sb (eksteriør, utseende)* appearance; exterior, outside; *av ~* in appearance; **3** *vb (si, uttale)* express, utter; *han ~t et ønske* he expressed a desire; *uten å ~ et ord* without uttering a word. **ytring** *sb* expression, remark. **ytringsfrihet** *sb* freedom of speech.

ytter|dør *sb* front door; outer door. **~grense** *sb* extreme limit. **~kant** *sb* (extreme) border/edge. **~klær** *sb koll* outer garments; wraps.

ytterligere *adj* further; *~ detaljer/opplysninger* further particulars/information. **ytterliggående** *adj* extreme, radical; *~ meninger/synspunkter* extreme views. **ytterlighet** *sb* extreme; *fra den ene ~ til den andre* from one extreme to the other.

ytter|lomme *sb* outside pocket. **~mur** *sb* outer wall. **~plagg** *sb* outer garment. **~punkt** *sb* extreme point. **~side** *sb* outside; outer side.

ytterst *adj, adv* **1** *(lengst ute)* ut(ter)most; farthest away/out; *~ til venstre* farthest to the left; *vi stod ~* we stood farthest out; **2** *(den høyeste grad av)* utmost; *hun gjorde sitt ~e* she did her utmost; *i den ~e fare* in the greatest/utmost danger; *til det ~e* to the utmost; **3** *(i høyeste grad)* extremely, highly; *~ farlig* extremely dangerous.

ytter|tøy *sb* outer clothing/wear. **~vegg** *sb* outer wall.

z *(bokstaven)* z.

zeppeliner *sb* zeppelin.

zoolog *sb* zoologist. **zoologi** *sb* zoology. **zoologisk** *adj* zoological; *~ hage* zoological garden(s); *dgl* zoo; *gå i ~ hage* go to the Zoo.

zoomlinse *sb* zoom lens.

æra *sb* era.

ærbar *adj* chaste, decent; modest. **ærbarhet** *sb* chastity, decency; modesty.

ærbødig *adj* respectful; *Deres ærbødige (i brev)* Yours faithfully/sincerely. **ærbødighet** *sb* respect, deference; *behandle med ~* treat with deference. **ærbødigst** *adv (i brev etc)* Yours faithfully/sincerely.

ære 1 *sb* honour, credit; *dere gjør skolen vår ~* you are a credit to our school; *det gjør deg ~* it does you credit; *en mann av ~* a man of honour; *til ~ for kongen* in honour of the King; *til hennes ~* in her honour; **2** *vb* honour. **ære|frykt** *sb* veneration; awe; *grepet av ~frykt* awe-stricken, awe-struck: *fylle med ~frykt* awe; *ha ~frykt for* venerate, revere. **~fryktinngytende** *adj* awe-inspiring. **~full** *adj* honourable, glorious. **~kjær** *adj* proud; high-spirited; jealous of one's honour. **~krenkelse** *sb* defamation, slander. **~krenkende** *adj* defamatory. **~løs** *adj* dishonourable; ignominious, infamous. **~løshet** *sb* dishonour; ignominy, infamy.

ærend *sb* errand; *i et ~* on an errand; *jeg gikk/løp ~ for moren min* I ran errands for my mother.

æres|begreper *sb koll* code of honour. **~bevisning** *sb* mark of honour/respect. **~bolig** *sb* honorary residence. **~borger** *sb* honorary citizen; *gjøre noen til ~borger* give somebody the freedom of the city. **~doktor** *sb* honorary doctor. **~følelse** *sb* sense of honour. **~gjeld** *sb* debt of honour. **~gjest** *sb* guest of honour.

æreskjelle *vb* abuse, defame.

æres|kompani se *~vakt.* **~legion** *sb* legion of honour. **medlem** *sb* honorary member. **~oppdrag** *sb* honorary task; post of honour. **~oppreisning** *sb* satisfaction. **~ord** *sb* word of honour; *(især mil)* parole. **~runde** *sb* triumphal progress. **~sak** *sb* matter/point of honour. **~tittel** *sb* honorary title. **~vakt** *sb* guard of honour. **~verv** se *~oppdrag.*

ærfugl *sb* eider duck.

ærgjerrig *adj* ambitious. **ærgjerrighet** *sb* ambition.

ærlig *adj* honest; *~ spill* fair play; *(som adv) ~ talt* honestly. **ærlighet** *sb* honesty; *~ varer lengst* honesty is the best policy.

ærverdig *adj* venerable.

æsj! *interj* ugh!

ætling *sb* descendant. **ætt** *sb (slekt)* family; *av høy ~* highborn. **ætte** *vb: ~ fra* be descended from. **ætte|følelse** *sb* family feeling/pride. **~saga** *sb* family saga. **~tavle** *sb* genealogical table; family tree. **ættledd** *sb* generation.

øde *adj* **1** desert, desolate; waste; *~ land* waste land; *en ~ øy* a desert island; *landet lå ~* the country lay waste; **2** *(mennesketom)* deserted; *en ~ gate* a deserted/empty street. **ødeland** *sb* spendthrift.

øde|legge *vb* **1** destroy, ruin; *han ~la helsen sin* he ruined his health; *huset ble ~lagt av brannen* the house was destroyed by fire; **2** *(skade)* damage; *regnet ~la veiene* the rain has damaged the roads; **3** *(gjøre ubrukelig)* spoil. **~leggelse** *sb* destruction, ruin; *ildens ~leggelser* the destruction caused by the fire. **~leggelseslyst** *sb* destructive urge. **~leggende** *adj* destructive, ruinous; devastating; *~leggende kriger/våpen* destructive wars/weapons.

ødemark *sb* wilderness, waste.

ødipuskompleks *sb* Oedipus complex.

ødsel *adj* **1** wasteful, extravagant; *~ vaner* extravagant habits; *en ~ person* a wasteful/extravagant person; **2** *(gavmild)* lavish; *han er ~ med penger/ros* he is lavish of money/praise. **ødselhet** *sb* wastefulness, extravagance. **ødsle** *vb: ~ bort* waste; *hun ~r bort tiden sin* she wastes her time.

ødslig *adj* bleak, desolate, dreary. **ødslighet** *sb* desolation, dreariness.

øgle *sb* lizard.

øk *sb* jade.

øke *vb* increase; *(vt også)* add to.

økenavn *sb* nickname; *hun fikk ~et Rødtopp* she was nicknamed Carrots.

økende *adj* growing, increasing. **økning** *sb* increase.

økologi *sb* ecology. **økologisk** *adj* ecological.

økonom *sb* economist. **økonomi** *sb* **1** economy; *(om vitenskapen)* economics; *landets ~* the economy of the country. **økonomisere** *vb* economize. **økonomisk** *adj* **1** *(besparende, sparsommelig)* economical; *en ~ metode/person* an economical method/person; **2** *(som angår økonomi)* economic; *~e vanskeligheter* financial difficulties; *et ~ problem* an economic problem.

økosystem *sb* eco-system.

øks *sb* axe. **økse|hode** *sb* axe head. **~skaft** *sb* axe handle.

økt *sb* working spell.

økumenisk *adj* ecumenical.

øl *sb* beer, ale. **øl|brygger** *sb* brewer. **~bryggeri** *sb* brewery. **~fat** *sb* beer cask. **~flaske** *sb* beer bottle. **~gjær** *sb* brewer's yeast. **~krus** *sb* tankard. **~tønne** *sb* beer barrel.

øm *adj* **1** *(som gjør vondt)* tender, sore; *~me føtter* tender/sore feet; *jeg er ~ over hele kroppen* I am sore all over; **2** *(kjærlig)* tender; affectionate, loving; *~me følelser/ord* tender feelings/words; *(som adv) hun så ~t på ham* she looked tenderly at him. **ømfintlig** *adj* sensitive. **ømfintlighet** *sb* sensitiveness. **ømhet** *sb* **1** *(sårhet etc)* soreness; **2** *(ømme følelser)* tenderness; affection. **øm|hjertet** *adj* tender-hearted. **~skinnet** *adj* sensitive, thin-skinned. **~tålig** *adj* delicate.

ønske I *sb* desire, wish; *de beste ~r!* best wishes! *det skjedde mot mitt ~* it was done against my wishes; *et ~ om noe* a wish for something; *han yttrykte et sterkt ~ om å gå* he expressed a strong desire to go; *hun fikk sitt ~ oppfylt* she got what she wanted; **II** *vb* **1** *(gjerne ville, ville ha)* want; *de ~t å treffe meg* they wanted to see me; *hva ~r du deg til jul?* what do you want for Christmas? **2** *(om høflig, inderlig etc ~)* wish; *alt (det) jeg kunne ~ meg* all I could wish for; *jeg skulle ~ jeg kunne se ham nå* I wish I could see him now; *vi ~r (oss) regn* we wish for rain. **ønske|drøm** *sb* pipedream; wishful dream. **~konsert** *sb* request programme. **~kvist** *sb* divining/dowsing rod; *gå med ~* divine, dowse. **ønskelig** *adj* desirable. **ønskelighet** *sb* desirability. **ønske|-jobb** *sb* ideal job/post. **~liste** *sb* want list. **~mål** *sb* goal, hope; desired end. **~plate** *sb* request record. **~stilling** se *~jobb*. **~tenkning** *sb* wishful thinking. **ønskverdig** se *ønskelig*.

ør A *adj* confused, giddy; *hun ble ~ i hodet av det* it made her head swim; **B** *sb* delta, sandbank.

øre *sb* **1** ear; *han er døv på høyre ~* he is deaf in the right ear; *små gryter har også ~r* little pitchers have big ears; **2** *(uttrykk)* **bak ~t:** *ha en rev bak ~t* have something up one's sleeve; *skrive seg noe bak ~t* make a mental note of something; *komme en* **for ~** come to/reach one's ears; *hun har ~* **for** *musikk* she has an ear for music; *holde noen* **i ~ne** keep somebody in line; make somebody toe the mark; **inn av** *det ene ~t og ut av det andre* in at one ear and out at the other; *jeg er* **lutter ~** I am all ears! *han er forelsket i henne til* **opp over** *(begge)* **~ne** he is head over ears in love with her; **spisse ~r** prick up one's ears. **øre|betennelse** *sb* inflammation of the ear. **~dobb** *sb* eardrop. **~døvende** *adj* deafening. **~fik** *sb* box on the ear. **~flipp** *sb* ear lobe. **~lappstol** *sb* wing chair. **~lege** *sb* ear specialist. **~merke** *vb* earmark; *pengene var ~merket til stipendier* the money was earmarked for scholarships.

ørende *adv: ~ liten* tiny.

ørenslyd *sb: det er ikke ~ å få her* one can't make oneself heard above the din. **øre|ring** *sb* earring. **~sus** *sb* buzzing in the ears. **~telefon** *sb* earpiece; *fl* headphones, headset. **~verk** *sb* earache. **~voks** *sb* earwax.

ørken *sb* desert.

ørkesløs *adj* idle. **ørkesløshet** *sb* idleness.

ørliten *adj* tiny.

ørn *sb* eagle. **ørne|nese** *sb* aquiline nose. **~rede** *sb* eagle's nest. **~unge** *sb* young eagle; eaglet.

ørret *sb* trout.

ørsk *adj* confused, dazed, giddy. **ørske** *sb* confusion, daze, giddiness; *gå i ørska* be half asleep.

øse 1 *sb* ladle; **2** *vb* bail, bale; scoop; *(med øse)* ladle; *~ en båt* bail/bale a boat; *~ opp suppe* ladle out soup; *regnet ~r ned* the rain is pouring down; it is raining cats and dogs; *~nde regn* pouring rain. **øsekar** *sb* baler, scoop. **øs|regn** *sb* pouring rain; downpour. **~regne** *vb: det ~regner* it is pouring down; it is raining cats and dogs.

øst *adj, sb* east; *~ for byen* (to the) east of the town; *fra ~* from the east; *i ~* in the east; *mot ~* east, eastward; *vende mot ~* face east. **østa|for** *prep* eastward of; (to the) east of. **~fra** *adv* from the east. **~vind** *sb* east/easterly wind. **Østen** the East; *Det fjerne ~* the Far East. **østenom** *prep* (to the) east of. **østerlandsk** *adj* Eastern, Oriental.

østers *sb* oyster.

øst|fra *adv* from the east. **~gående** *adj* eastbound. **~kant** *sb* east(ern) side; *(i by)* East-End. **~kyst** *sb* east(ern) coast. **østlig** *adj* eastern; *(om vind også)* easterly. **østligst** *adj* easternmost. **øst|over** *adv* east, eastward(s); towards the east. **~på** *adv* in the east; out east. **østre** *adj* eastern. **østside** *sb* east(ern) side.

øvd se *øvet*. **øve** *vb* **1** *(øve seg)* practice, train; *han ~r seg i å danse* he practices dancing; *jeg ~r (meg) på pianoet hver dag* I practice (on) the piano every day; **2** *(utøve)* exercise; *hun ~r stor innflytelse på sin mann* she exercises great influence on her husband. **øvelse** *sb* **1** *(det å øve)* practice, training; *~ gjør mester* practice makes perfect; *daglig ~* daily practice; *det krever mye ~* it takes a lot of practice; **2** *(om den enkelte ~)* exercise; *denne ~n er god for ryggen* this exercise is good for the/your back.

øverst *adj* top, upper; *adv* at the top; on top; *~ oppe* at the top; *~ på siden* at the top of the page; *~ ved bordet* at the head of the table; *de la de beste eplene ~* they put the best apples on top; *den ~e etasjen* the upper storey; *den ~e hyllen* the top shelf; *fra ~ til nederst* from top to bottom; *(om person)* from top to toe. **øverst|befalende, ~kommanderende** *sb* commander-in--chief.

øvet *adj* experienced, skilled. **øving** se *øvelse*.

øvre *adj* upper.

øvrig *adj: de ~e* the others; the rest; *det ~e* the rest; *for ~ (hva resten angår)* for the rest; *(ellers)* else, otherwise; in other respects.

øvrigheten *sb* the authorities *fl.*

øy *sb* island; *(i egennavn ofte)* isle; *på en ~* in an island; *(om mindre ~er ofte)* on an island; *De britiske ~er* the British Isles; *øya Man* the Isle of man. **øyboer** *sb* islander.

øye *sb* **1** eye; *blind på det ene ~t* blind in/of one eye; *det blotte ~* the naked eye; **2** *(uttrykk)* **~ for ~** an eye for an eye; **for ~, for øynene:** *ha noe for øye* have something in mind/in view; *jeg vil ikke se henne for mine øyne mer* I never want to set eyes on her again; *like/rett for øynene på meg* before my very eyes; *en* **fryd for øyet** easy on the eye; **få ~ på** catch sight of; **ha ~ for** *noe* have an eye for something; **ha øynene med seg** keep one's eyes open; *med et* **halvt ~** with half an eye; **holde ~ med** keep an eye on; **i øynene:** *se døden/kjensgjerningene etc) i øynene* face death/the facts; *se noen like/rett i øynene* look somebody straight in the eye; *jeg sa det* **like/rett opp i øynene** *på ham* I told him to his face; *gjøre* **store øyne** stare; open one's eyes wide; **under fire øyne** in private; privately; *en samtale under fire øyne* a private interview; **ute av ~**, *ute av sinn* out of sight, out of mind.

øyeblikk *sb* instant, moment; *et ~ trodde jeg alt var tapt* for a moment I thought all was lost; *for/i ~et* at the moment; *(for tiden)* for the moment; *fra det ~ da han kom* from the moment (that/when) he came; *i første (rette, siste etc) ~* at the first (right, last etc) moment; *i løpet av et ~* in a moment; *i neste ~* the next moment; *i samme ~ som* the very moment that; *om/på et ~* in a moment. **øyeblikkelig** *adj* **1** *a) (som inntref-*

fer straks) immediate; ~ *hjelp* immediate help; *b) (som adv)* immediately; *de kom* ~ they came immediately/at once; **2** *(nåværende)* present; *den ~e situasjon* the present situation; **3** *(kortvarig)* momentary. **øyeblikksbilde** *sb* snapshot.

øye|bryn *sb* eyebrow, brow. **~eple** *sb* eyeball. **~kast** *sb* glance. **~lege** *sb* oculist, ophthalmologist; eye specialist. **~lokk** *sb* eyelid. **~med** *sb* aim, purpose; object. **~mål** *sb: etter ~mål* judged by the eye.

øyen|stikker *sb* dragonfly. **~synlig 1** *adj (innlysende)* obvious; *(åpenbar)* evident; **2** *(adv)* obviously; evidently; *han var ~synlig redd* he was evidently afraid; *hun hadde ~ vært der* she had obviously/evidently been there. **~tjener** *sb* timeserver.

øye|skrue *sb* eyelet screw. **~skygge** *sb* eye shadow. **~sverte** *sb* mascara. **~syn** *sb* eyesight; *ta i ~* inspect; take a view of. **~vipper** *sb fl* eyelashes. **~vitne** *sb* eye-witness.

øygruppe *sb* archipelago; group of islands.

øyne *vb* discern, see.

å 1 *(infinitivsmerke)* to; **2** *interj* oh! well! *~, gi meg boken!* give me the book, please! *~, hør her!* look here!

åger *sb* usury; *drive ~* practise usury. **åger|kar** *sb* usurer. **~pris** *sb* exorbitant price. **~rente** *sb* usury; exorbitant interest. **ågre** *vb: ~ med sitt pund* make the most of one's talents.

åk *sb* yoke; *under ~et* under the yoke.

åker *sb* field. **åker|land** *sb* arable land. **~sennep** *sb* wild mustard; charlock.

åkle *sb* **1** *(på seng)* coverlet; **2** *(veggteppe)* tapestry.

ål *sb* eel. **åle** *vb: ~ seg* wriggle along; snake one's way. **åleslank** *adj* slinky.

åme *sb* maggot.

ånd *sb* **1** mind; *en stor ~* a great mind; **2** *(spøkelse)* ghost, spirit; *en ond ~* an evil spirit; **3** *Den hellige ånd* the Holy Ghost. **ånde 1** *sb (pust)* breath; *~n hans stinker av whisky* his breath reeks of whisky; *holde tilhørerne i ~* hold the attention of one's audience; **2** *vb (puste)* breathe. **ånde|drag** *sb* breath; *til mitt siste ~drag* till my last breath. **~drett** *sb* breathing, respiration; *gi noen kunstig ~drett* administer artificial respiration to somebody; *i samme ~drett* in the same breath. **åndedrettsorgan** *sb* respiratory organ.

åndelig *adj* **1** spiritual; *~ liv/vekst* spiritual life/growth; **2** *(intellektuell, ånds-)* mental, intellectual. **åndelighet** *sb* spirituality. **ånde|løs** *adj* breathless; *~ stillhet* breathless silence. **~maner** *sb* exorcist, necromancer. **~nød** *sb* difficulty in breathing.

ånd|full, ~rik *adj* brilliant, witty. **~fullhet, ~rikhet** *sb* witty remark. **~løs** *adj* dull, uninspired; insipid.

ånds|arbeid *sb* brain work; intellectual work. **~arbeider** *sb* intellectual worker. **~aristokrat** *sb* intellectual aristocrat. **~beslektet** *adj* congenial. **~evner** *sb fl* intellectual talents; mental ability/faculties. **~forlatt** *adj* dull, insipid; boring. **~fraværende** *adj* absent-minded. **~fraværenhet** *sb* absence of mind. **~frihet** *sb* intellectual freedom/liberty. **~frisk** *adj* of unimpaired mental faculties; of sound mind. **~høvding** *sb* spiritual leader. **~kraft** *sb* mental power; strength of mind. **~liv** *sb* cultural/intellectual life; culture. **~nærværelse** *sb* presence of mind. **~produkt** *sb* intellectual product. **~retning** *sb* mentality, outlook; school of thought. **~snobb** *sb* intellectual snob. **~svak** *adj* feeble-minded; mentally deficient. **~verk** *sb* creative work; intellectual achievement. **~verklov** *sb* copyright act. **~virksomhet** *sb* mental activity. **~vitenskapene** *sb koll* the humanities.

åpen *adj* open; *~ for (publikum etc)* open to (the public etc); *døren var ~* the door was open; *en ~ båt* an open boat; *han lå med øynene åpne* he was lying with his eyes open; *sove for ~t vindu* sleep with one's window open; *under ~ himmel* in the open (air). **åpenbar** *adj* evident, obvious; clear. **åpen|bare** *vb* **1** reveal; make known; *Jesus ~barte seg for disiplene (sine)* Jesus revealed himself to his disciples; **2** *(røpe)* betray, reveal; *hun ~barte hemmeligheten for ham* she revealed the secret to him. **~barelse, ~baring** *sb* revelation; *Johannes ~baring* the Revelation of St. John; Revelations. **åpen|het** *sb* openness, frankness; candour. **~hjertig** *adj* open, frank; candid. **~hjertighet** *sb* openness, frankness; candour. **~lys** *adj* open, plain, undisguised. **~munnet** *adj* indiscreet. **~munnethet** *sb* indiscretion. **åpne** *vb* open; *(låse opp)* unlock; *hun ~t brevet/døren* she opened the letter/the door. **åpning** *sb* opening; *~en av utstillingen* the opening of the exhibition; *en ~ i veggen* an opening in a wall. **åpningstid** *sb* opening hours; business/office hours.

år *sb* **1** year; *~ etter ~* year after year; *~ for ~* year by year; *(også)* annually, yearly; *et halvt ~* half a year; six months; *for fem (etc) ~ siden* five (etc) years ago; *halvannet ~* a year and a half; eighteen months; *hele ~et* all the year round; *i ~* this year; *i de siste ~ene* during recent years; *i mange ~* for many years; *i ~et 1814* in (the year) 1814; *om fem (etc) ~* in five (etc) years; *tidlig på ~et* early in the year; **2** *(årsvekst)* year;

crop, harvest; *et dårlig/godt år* a bad/good year; a bad/good crop/harvest; **3** *(uttrykk) i sine* **beste ~** in the prime of life; **bli/fylle år:** *hun er akkurat fylt 20 ~* she has just (only) completed her twentieth year; *jeg blir/fyller 20 ~ på onsdag* I shall be 20 next Wednesday; **fra ~ til ~** from year to year; *han* **går i sitt** *femtiende (etc) ~* he is in his fiftieth (etc) year; **i/om året** a year; *han har en inntekt på 25.000 pund i ~et* he has an income of £25 000 a year/an annual income of £25 000; **med ~ene** with the years; **opp i ~ene:** *når en kommer opp i ~ene* when you are getting on in years; *være opp i ~ene* be advanced/well on in years; *opp* **gjennom ~ene** through the years; *et barn* **på** *fire (etc) ~* a child of four (etc); a four-year-old (etc) child; **trekke på ~ene** be getting on in years.

årbok *sb* yearbook.

åre *sb* **A** *(til å ro med)* oar; **B** *(blod~, vene)* vein; *(puls~)* artery; *~ne i pannen hans* the veins on his forehead. **åre|betennelse** *sb* phlebitis. **~forkalket** *adj* suffering from arteriosclerosis; *(senil)* senile; *dgl* mental. **~forkalkning** *sb* arteriosclerosis. **~knute** *sb* varicosity; varicose vein.

årelang *adj* yearlong.

åre|late *vb* bleed. **~lating** *sb* bleeding, blood-letting.

åremål *sb: på ~* for a term of years.

åretak *sb* stroke.

årevis *adv: i ~* for years (and years).

år|gang *sb (av tidsskrift etc)* (annual) volume; *(av vin)* vintage; *~gangsvin* vintage wine. **~hundre** *sb* century; *i ~hundrer* for centuries; *det 19. og 20. ~* the 19th and 20th centuries. **~hundreskifte** *sb* turn of the century. **~lig** *adj, adv* annual, yearly; *hennes ~lige inntekt* her annual income; *tre ganger ~lig* three times a year. **~rekke** *sb: i en lang ~rekke* for many years. **~ring** *sb* annual ring.

årsak *sb* cause; *~en til sykdommen* the cause of the disease; *ingen ~!* don't mention it! not at all! **årsaks|forhold** *sb* causality; causal relation. **~konjunksjon** *sb* causal conjunction. **~loven** *sb* the law of causation. **~sammenheng** *sb* causality; causal relation.

års|avslutning *sb (på skole)* end-of-term celebration. **~beretning** *sb* annual report. **~dag** *sb* anniversary. **~fest** *sb* annual celebration/festival; anniversary. **~forbruk** *sb* annual consumption. **~inntekt** *sb* annual income. **~klasse** *sb* age group; class. **~kull** *sb* class, set. **~lønn** *sb* yearly salary. **~melding** *sb* annual report. **~møte** *sb* annual meeting. **~oppgjør** *sb* annual/yearly settlement. **~oversikt** *sb* annual survey. **~regnskap** *sb* annual accounts. **~skifte** *sb* turn of the year. **~tall** *sb* year, date. **~tid** *sb* season; time of the year. **~vekst** *sb* the year's crop. **~verk** *sb* man-labour year.

år|tier *sb fl* decades. **~tusen** *sb* millennium. **~viss** *adj* annual, yearly.

årvåken *adj* alert, watchful; vigilant. **årvåkenhet** *sb* alertness, watchfulness; vigilance.

ås *sb* hill, ridge. **ås|rygg** *sb* ridge (of a hill). **~side** *sb* hillside.

åsted *sb* scene (of the crime); *på ~et* on the spot. **åstedsbefaring** *sb: det ble holdt ~* an on-the-spot inquiry was held.

åsyn *sb (bokl: ansikt)* countenance; *for Guds ~* in the sight of God; before God.

åte *sb* bait.

åtsel *sb* carcass, carrion. **åtseldyr** *sb* scavenger.

åtte *tallord* eight; *~ dager* a week; *~ dager i dag* this day week; today week; *lørdag (om) ~ dager* Saturday week. **åttende** *adj, ordenstall* eighth; *hver ~ dag* once a week. **åtter** *sb* **1** *(båt)* eight-oared boat; **2** *(i kortstokk etc)* eight.

A KEY TO THE PRONUNCIATION OF NORWEGIAN

STRESS AND LENGTH

Most Norwegian words have stress on the first syllable. In words of foreign origin the stress can be on the last or the second-to-last syllable.

In a stressed syllable either the vowel or the consonant will be long. A long vowel can be followed by a short, single consonant, while a short vowel is followed by a long consonant, either as a combination (e.g. **-ng**: **sang**) or as a single, long consonant which is usually written as a double consonant (e.g. **søtt**):

Long vowel	*Long consonant*
søt	søtt
gul	gull
sa	sang

In unstressed syllables both the vowel and the consonants are short.

VOWELS

Letter	*Imitated pronunciation*	*Comments*	*Examples*
a	/a:/	as in ‘car’	**dag, lage**
	/a/	more open than the long ‘a’	**hatt, land**
e	/e:/	similar to the ‘ai’ in ‘hair’; it is a single vowel, not a diphthong	**lese, pen**
	/e/	as in ‘bet’	**penn, sitte**
	/æ:/	before an ‘r’; as in ‘glad’	**er, verden**
	/i:/	as in ‘see’	**de, De**
i	/i:/	as in ‘see’	**mil, bil**
	/i/	more relaxed than the long ‘i’; as in ‘bit’	**sitte, min**
o	/ω:/	resembles the ‘oo’ in ‘fool’, but with far more rounded lips and further back in the mouth	**bok, mor**
	/ω/	less close than the long ‘o’	**rom, ropte**
	/ɔ:/	before a ‘v’; like the ‘aw’ in ‘saw’	**lov, sove**
	/ɔ/		**holde, opp**

u	/u:/	similar to the 'ue' in 'true' but has a closer and more frontal pronunciation	**full, gull**
	/u/	before 'kk', 'ks', 'kt', 'nk' and 'ng'	**bukke, ung**
y	/y:/	like the long 'i', pronounced with rounded lips	**lys, syk**
	/y/	more relaxed than the long 'y'	**hytte, sykle**
æ	/æ:/	like the 'a' in 'glad'	**være, nær**
	/æ/		**vært, færre**
ø	/ø:/	similar to the 'i' in 'sir', but more rounded	**søt, møte**
	/ø/	like the long 'ø', but shorter and more open	**søtt, møtte**
å	/ɔ:/	similar to the 'a' in 'call', but more rounded	**båt, språk**
	/ɔ/	like the long 'å', but shorter and more relaxed	**fått, gått**

DIPHTHONGS

ai	/ai/	as in 'I', 'by'	**kai, mai**
au	/æu/	similar to 'ow' in 'how'	**sau, maur**
ei	/æi/	similar to the 'ay' in 'day'	**reise, nei**
eg			**regn, deg**
øy	/øy/		**øy, høy**
øg			**døgn, gøy**

CONSONANTS

The pronunciation of Norwegian consonants is very similar to English ones, with some exceptions:

c		occurs only in foreign words	
	/k/	in most cases as in 'car'	camping
	/s/	before 'e', 'i' and 'y'	scene, cirka
	/ /	as in 'she'; spelt 'ch'	champagne
d	/d/	in most cases as in 'day'	**dag, lide**
	silent	at the ends of words, after a vowel and usually after 'r', 'l' and 'n'	**god, bord, kald, land**

g	/g/	in most cases as in 'good'	**gul, gnage**
	/j/	like the 'y' in 'yes'; before 'ei', 'i' and 'y'	**gift, geit**
	silent	– before 'j' and in words ending in '-ig'	**gjøre, veldig**
		– in certain other words	**morgen**
		– 'lg' becomes 'll' in certain words	**selge, følge**
	/ʒ/	– 'ng', at the end of words; the same pronunciation as in English. If an 'e' is added in Norwegian the 'ng' is still pronounced /ʒ/	**lang, lenge**
h	silent	before 'j' and 'v'	**hjelp, hvit**
j	/j/	like the 'y' in 'yes'	**jern, jente**
k	/k/	in most cases as in 'cat'	**kone, nikker**
	/ç/	resembles a strongly aspirated 'h', as in 'huge'; spelt 'kj', 'ki', 'ky', 'kei'	**kjenne, kino, kylling**
	/æi/	spelt 'ks'	**seksten**
n	/n/	in most cases as in 'nine'	**ni, noe**
	/ʒ/	*see under* 'g'	
r		pronounced differently in various parts of Norway. Most common is a rolled 'r', similar to the Scottish rolled 'r'; it must always be pronounced	**rød, for, doktor**
s	/s/	in most cases as in 'sleep'	**sove, slå**
	/ʃ/	as in 'she'; spelt 'sj', 'skj' and 'sk + i, y, ei, øy'	**sjø, skjorte, ski, sky, skei, skøyte**
t	/t/	in most cases as in 'take'	**takk, late**
	/ç/	resembles a strongly aspirated 'h', as in 'huge'; spelt 'tj'	**tjern**
	silent	in the pronoun **det** and in the definite form singular of neuter nouns (but pronounced before a genitive: **landets**)	**huset, det**

v	/v/	in most cases as in 'village'	**vår, vinter**
	silent	in most cases at the ends of words, after 'l'	**sølv, tolv**
w	/v/	occurs only in foreign words	whisky
x		occurs only in foreign words	
	/s/	in front position	**xylofon**
	/ks/	in other positions	
z	/s/	occurs only in foreign words	**zoologi**

NOTES ON NORWEGIAN GRAMMAR

NOUNS AND ARTICLES

GENDER

There are three genders in Norwegian: masculine, feminine and neuter.

The indefinite articles, which exist only in the singular, *precede* the nouns and are: **en** (masc.), **en/ei** (fem.) and **et** (neu.).

The definite articles are attached to the *ends* of the nouns. In the singular they are: **-en** (masc.), **-en/-a** (fem.) and **-et** (neu.); in the plural they are: **-ene** (masc. and fem.) and **-ene/-a** (neu.).

For example:

	Indefinite singular	*Definite singular*	*Indefinite plural*	*Definite plural*
Masc.	en gutt	gutten	gutter	guttene
Fem.	en/ei veske	vesken/veska	vesker	veskene
Neu.	et hus	huset	hus	husene/husa

Note on feminine nouns: in most cases there is a choice between the specific feminine forms (with **ei** in the indefinite form singular and **-a** in the definite form singular) and the'common gender', which is identical to the masculine gender. However, a few feminine nouns would almost always have the specific feminine forms: **jente**, **kjerring**, **hytte**, **bikkje**, **geit**, **ku**, **høne**, **gate**, **bygd**, **li**, **myr**, **mark**, **øy**. In general the specific feminine forms are more informal and used mostly in spoken Norwegian, while the 'common gender' forms are more formal and used in writing.

Note on neuter nouns: almost all neuter nouns have a choice between **-ene** and **-a** in the definite form plural. In general the **-a** form is more informal and used mostly in spoken Norwegian, while the **-ene** form is more formal and used in writing. Only a very few nouns will almost always take the **-a** form: **barn**, **bein/ben**, **dyr**, **krøtter**.

HOW TO TELL WHICH GENDER A NOUN BELONGS TO

Masculine nouns

1 Biological gender: **mann**, **gutt**, **far**, **sønn**, **bror**, **okse**, **hane**, etc.
2 Nouns denoting:

- stones: **stein**, **malm**, **granitt**, etc.

- division of time: **vinter**, **sommer**, **vår**, **høst**, **dag**, **måned**, **time**, but **et år**, **et døgn**, **et minutt**, **et sekund**
- sciences and subjects: **vitenskap**, **matematikk**, **fysikk**, **teologi**, etc.

3 Nouns ending in:

-er: **lærer**, **tysker**, **keiser**, **hammer**, **sommer**, but **et mønster**, **et filter**, etc.
-nad: **søknad**, **bunad**, etc.
-else: **følelse**, **utdannelse**, etc., but **et værelse**, **et spøkelse**
-ning: **bygning**, **redning**, etc.
-het: **kjærlighet**, **virkelighet**, etc.
-dom: **barndom**, **ungdom**, **eiendom**, etc.
-sel: **redsel**, **trengsel**, etc., but **et fengsel**

Feminine nouns

1 Biological gender: **kvinne**, **jente**, **mor**, **søster**, **tante**, **ku**, **høne**.
2 Nouns denoting:

- species of trees: **furu**, **gran**, **bjørk**, etc., but **et tre**
- fruits: **pære**, **plomme**, **drue**, etc., but **et eple**
- parts of the body: **panne**, **hake**, **lunge**, **leppe**, etc., but **en rygg**, **en arm**, **en fot**, **et øye**, **et hjerte**, etc.

3 Nouns ending in:

-inne: **lærerinne**, **prostinne**, etc.
-ing (verbal nouns): **ettersøking**, **lesing**, etc.

Neuter nouns

1 Biological gender (offspring and 'people'): **barn**, **føll**, **kje**, **lam**, **menneske**, **folk**.
2 Nouns denoting:

- metals: **gull**, **sølv**, etc., but **en messing**, **en malm**
- substances: **papir**, **lær**, **vann**, **salt**, **sukker**, **øl**, **kjøtt**, **flesk**, **smør**, **brød**, **gras**, **høy**, etc., but **en melk**, **en fløte**, **en te**, **en kaffe**, **en olje**

3 Nouns having the same form as the verbal stem (infinitive minus the **-e**):

rop, **svar**, **arbeid**, etc.

4 Nouns ending in:

-eri: **maleri**, **vaskeri**, etc.
-skap: **selskap**, **vennskap**, etc., but **en vitenskap**, **en kunnskap**, **en lidenskap**
-dømme: **kongedømme**, **bispedømme**
-mål: **slagsmål**

DECLENSIONS

Masculine nouns

1 Main pattern:

en gutt	**gutten**	**gutter**	**guttene**

2 Nouns with more than one syllable ending in an unstressed **-e** have only **-r** in the indefinite form plural and **-ne** in the definite form plural:

en hane	**hanen**	**haner**	**hanene**

3 Nouns ending in **-el** and a few ending in **-er** are contracted in the plural and lose the **-e**. A double consonant is reduced to a single one:

en nøkkel	**nøkkelen**	**nøkler**	**nøklene**
en sommer	**sommeren**	**somrer**	**somrene**

4 Most nouns ending in **-er** lose the final **-r** in the indefinite form plural and the initial **-e-** of the ending in the definite form plural:

en lærer	**læreren**	**lærere**	**lærerne**

5 (a) Some nouns change their stem vowel and have irregular endings in the indefinite form plural:

en mann	**mannen**	**menn**	**mennene**
en far	**faren**	**fedre**	**fedrene**
en bror	**broren**	**brødre**	**brødrene**

(b) Some have a change of vowel, but **-er** and **-ene** in the plural:

en bonde	**bonden**	**bønder**	**bøndene**
en fot	**foten**	**føtter**	**føttene**

6 Some nouns have no ending in the indefinite form plural:

en feil	**feilen**	**feil**	**feilene**

liter, meter, dollar, løk, kjeks, laks, torsk, maur, mygg, sko, ting are the most common

7 Some foreign words have irregular forms in the plural:

en konto	**kontoen**	**konti**	**kontiene**

Feminine nouns

1 Main pattern:

ei seng	**senga**	**senger**	**sengene**

2 Most nouns with more than one syllable ending in an unstressed **-e** have only **-r** in the indefinite form and **-ne** in the definite form plural:

ei veske	**veska**	**vesker**	**veskene**

3 (a) Some nouns have a vowel change in the plural:

ei tann	**tanna**	**tenner**	**tennene**

and, strand, natt, stang, kraft are the most common

ei bok	**boka**	**bøker**	**bøkene**

bot, rot are the most common

ei hånd/hand	**handa**	**hender**	**hendene**

(b) Some one-syllable nouns ending in a vowel have a vowel change and contracted forms in the plural:

ei tå	**tåa**	**tær**	**tærne**
ei klo	**kloa**	**klør**	**klørne**

4 (a) Nouns ending in **-el**, **-er** and **-en** have contracted forms:

ei aksel	**aksla**	**aksler**	**akslene**
ei søster	**søstera**	**søstre**	**søstrene**
ei frøken	**frøkna**	**frøkner**	**frøknene**

(b) Some nouns ending in **-er** have a vowel change and contracted forms in the plural:

ei mor	**mora**	**mødrer**	**mødrene**

Others: **datter**

5 Some nouns have no ending in the indefinite form plural:

ei mil	**mila**	**mil**	**milene**

lus, sild, ki, mus are the most common

Neuter nouns

1 Main pattern, one-syllable nouns:

et hus	**huset**	**hus**	**husene**
Exception: **et sted**	**stedet**	**steder**	**stedene**

2 Main pattern, nouns with more than one syllable:

et vindu	**vinduet**	**vinduer**	**vinduene**

3 Main pattern, nouns with more than one syllable ending in an unstressed **-e** have only **-r** in the indefinite form and **-ne** in the definite form plural:

et eple	**epler**	**epler**	**eplene**

4 Some nouns ending in **-el**, **-er** or **-en** have contracted forms:

et fengsel	**fengs(e)let**	**fengsler/fengsel**	**fengslene**
et teater	**teat(e)ret**	**teatre/teater**	**teatrene**
et kjøkken	**kjøkkenet**	**kjøkkener/kjøkken**	**kjøkkenene**

5 Vowel change in the plural:

et tre	**treet**	**trær**	**trærne**

6 Some words ending in **-um** have irregular forms:

(a) **et faktum** **faktumet** **fakta** **faktaene**
antibiotikum, **kvantum**, **narkotikum**, **plenum**, **visum** are the most common

(b) **forum** **forumet** **fora/forumer** **foraene/forumene**

7 Most words ending in **-ium** and **-eum**:

museum	**museet**	**museer**	**museene**

studium, **medium** are the most common

PRONOUNS

PERSONAL PRONOUNS

	Subject form		*Object form*	
	Singular	*Plural*	*Singular*	*Plural*
1st person	jeg	vi	meg	oss
2nd person	du	dere	deg	dere
	De	De	Dem	Dem
3rd person	han	de	ham	dem
	hun		henne	
	den		den	
	det		det	

REFLEXIVE PRONOUNS

	Singular	*Plural*		*Singular*	*Plural*
1st person	meg	oss	3rd person	seg	seg
2nd person	deg	dere			
	Dem	Dem			

De and **Dem** are the polite forms.

POSSESSIVE PRONOUNS

The possessive pronouns are declined according to the gender and number of the nouns referred to: in the following table, the pronouns in the first three columns are used when one noun is referred to, while the pronouns in the last column are used for more than one noun.

	Masculine	*Feminine*	*Neuter*	*Plural*
Singular				
1st person	min	mi	mitt	mine
2nd person	din	di	ditt	dine
	Deres	Deres	Deres	Deres
3rd person	hans	hans	hans	hans
	hennes/sin	hennes/si	hennes/sitt	hennes/sine
	dens	dens	dens	dens
	dets	dets	dets	dets
Plural				
1st person	vår	vår	vårt	våre
2nd person	deres	deres	deres	deres
	Deres	Deres	Deres	Deres
3rd person	deres/sin	deres/si	deres/sitt	deres/sine

Deres is the polite form.

REFLEXIVE POSSESSIVE PRONOUNS

Sin/si/sitt/sine are used if the subject is the third person singular or plural, and the subject and the owner is the same person:

Han malte huset sitt. He painted his (own) house.

In comparison, if he painted someone else's house, the form would be:

Han malte huset hans/hennes/deres. He painted his/her/their house.

VERBS

The **infinitive** is the form found in the dictionary: **kaste, lese, leve, bo, be.**

The **present tense** is formed by adding **-r** to the infinitive: **kaster, leser, lever, bor, ber.**

The **past tense** and the **past participle** are formed from regular verbs by adding certain endings, and from irregular verbs by changing vowels (see the examples below).

The **present participle** is formed by adding **-ende** to the stem of the verb. The stem of the verb is the infinitive form minus the final **-e** if appropriate:

Infinitive	*Stem*	*Present participle*
kaste	kast	kastende
lese	les	lesende
leve	lev	levende
bo	bo	boende
be	be	beende

The **imperative** is identical to the stem of the verb: **kast, les, lev, bo, be.**

REGULAR VERBS

Regular verbs are divided into four groups according to which ending is added to the stem of the verb in the past tense and the past participle:

	Past tense	*Past participle*
Group 1	-et	-et
Group 2	-te	-t
Group 3	-de	-d
Group 4	-dde	-dd

For example:

	Infinitive	*Present tense*	*Past tense*	*Past participle*
Group 1	å kaste	kaster (kaste+r)	kastet (kast+et)	kastet (kast+et)
Group 2	å lese	leser (lese+r)	leste (les+te)	lest (les+t)
Group 3	å prøve	prøver (prøve+r)	prøvde (prøv+de)	prøvd (prøv+d)
Group 4	å bo	bor (bo+r)	bodde (bo+dde)	bodd (bo+dd)

IRREGULAR VERBS

The most common irregular verbs are listed below. The present tense is included only when it is irregular. An asterix indicates that the verb also has a regular form.

Infinitive	*Present tense*	*Past tense*	*Past participle*
be		bad	bedt
binde		bandt	bundet
bite		bet	bitt
bli		ble	blitt
brekke		brakk	brukket
brenne*		brant	brent
bringe		brakte	brakt
briste		brast	bristet/brustet

bryte		brøt	brutt
by		bød	budt
bære		bar	båret
dette		datt	dettet
dra		drog	dratt
drikke		drakk	drukket
drive		drev	drevet
ete		åt	ett
falle		falt	falt
fare		for	far(e)t
finne		fant	funnet
fly		fløy	fløyet
flyte		fløt	flytt
forby		forbød	forbudt
forlate		forlot	forlatt
forstå		forstod	forstått
forsvinne		forsvant	forsvunnet
fortelle		fortalte	fortalt
fryse		frøs	frosset
fyke		føk	føket
følge		fulgte	fulgt
få		fikk	fått
gale		gol	galt
gi		gav	gitt
gidde		gadd	giddet
gjelde		gjaldt	gjeldt
gjøre	gjør	gjorde	gjordt
gli		gled	glidd
glippe		glapp	glippet
gni		gned	gnidd
grine		grein	grint
gripe		grep	grepet
gråte		gråt	grått
gå		gikk	gått
ha		hadde	hatt
henge*		hang	hengt
hete		het	hett
hive		hev	hivd
hjelpe		hjalp	hjulpet
holde		holdt	holdt
klinge		klang	kling(e)t

klype		kløp	kløpet
klyve		kløv	kløvet
knekke		knakk	knekket
knipe		knepæ	knepet
komme		kom	kommet
krype		krøp	krøpet
kunne	kan	kan	kunnet
kvekke		kvakk	kvekket
la		lot	latt
late		lot	latt
le		lo	ledd
legge		la	lagt
lide		led	lidd
ligge		lå	ligget
lyde*		lød	lydt
lyve		løy	løyet
løpe		løp	løpt/løpet
måtte	må	måtte	måttet
nyse		nøs	nyst
nyte		nøt	nytt
pipe		pep	pepet
rekke		rakk	rukket
renne		rant	runnet
ri		red	ridd
rive		rev	revet
ryke		røk	røket
se		så	sett
selge		solgte	solgt
sette		satte	satt
si	sier	sa	sagt
sige		seg	seget
sitte		satt	sittet
skjelve		skalv	skjelvet
skjære		skar	skåret
skli		skled	sklidd
skride		skred	skredet/skridd
skrike		skrek	skreket
skrive		skrev	skrevet
skryte		skrøt	skrytt
skvette		skvatt	skvettet
skulle	skal	skulle	skullet

skyte		skjøt	skutt
skyve		skjøv	skjøvet
slenge*		slang	slengt
slippe		slapp	sluppet
slite		slet	slitt
slå		slo	slått
smelle*		smalt	smelt
smette		smatt	smettet
smyge		smøg	smøget
smøre		smurte	smurt
snike		snek	sneket
sove		sov	sovet
spinne		spant	spunnet
sprekke		sprakk	sprukket
sprette		spratt	sprettet
springe		sprang	sprunget
spørre	spør	spurte	spurt
stige		steg	steget
stikke		stakk	stukket
stjele		stjal	stjålet
strekke		strakk	strukket
stryke		strøk	strøket
stå		stod	stått
svi		sved	svidd
svike		svek	sveket
synge		sang	sunget
synke		sank	sunket
ta		tok	tatt
tigge		tagg	tigget
tore	tør	torde	tort
treffe		traff	truffet
trekke		trakk	trukket
tvinge		tvang	tvunget
velge		valgte	valgt
ville	vil	ville	villet
vinne		vant	vunnet
vite	vet	visste	visst
være	er	var	vært

ADJECTIVES

The adjective can appear in three different forms:

Basic form:	**stor**	**gul**	**pen**
-t form:	**stort**	**gult**	**pent**
-e form:	**store**	**gule**	**pene**

The basic form is used with masculine and feminine nouns in the indefinite form singular, the **-t** form with a neuter noun in the indefinite form singular, and the **-e** form with nouns in the plural indefinite forms and all nouns in the definite forms, as shown below.

Indefinite forms

The adjective agrees in gender and number with the noun it refers to:

	Singular	*Plural*
Masc.	en stor hage	store hager
Fem.	ei gul plomme	gule plommer
Neu.	et pent hus	pene hus

Definite forms

The adjective always ends in **-e**:

	Singular	*Plural*
Masc.	Den store hagen	De store hagene
Fem.	Den gule plomma	De gule plommene
Neu.	Det pene huset	De pene husene

Exceptions:

1 Some adjectives do not add **-t** in the **-t** form:

(a) adjectives ending in **-sk**: those with more than one syllable; those denoting nationality; some ending in a consonant + **-sk**: **synsk, trolsk, glemsk**

viktoriansk	**viktoriansk**	**viktorianske**

(b) adjectives ending in **-ig**:

nydelig	**nydelig**	**nydelige**

(c) adjectives ending in a consonant or an unstressed vowel + **-t**:

interessant	**interessant**	**interessante**

(d) some adjectives ending in **-d**, of which **glad, redd, solid, fremmed, lærd** are the most common:

glad	**glad**	**glade**

2 Adjectives ending in a double consonant lose one of the consonants in front of the **-t** in the **-t** form:

grønn	**grønt**	**grønne**

3 Adjectives ending in a stressed vowel add an extra **-t** in the **-t** form:

ny	**nytt**	**nye**

Note that with the adjectives **blå**, **grå**, **rå**, **skrå**, the final **-e** in the **-e** form is omitted.

4 For adjectives ending in **-el**, **-en** or **-er**, in the **-e** form the **-e-** from the second syllable disappears and double consonants are simplified:

gammel	**gammelt**	**gamle**

5 Some adjectives do not change at all:

(a) those ending in an unstressed **-e**:

moderne	**moderne**	**moderne**

(b) some ending in **-s**, of which the most common are: **felles**, **stakkars**, **middels**, **gammeldags**, **nymotens**, **gratis**, **forgjeves**, **innvortes**

(c) some ending in a stressed vowel; most are monosyllables, and the most common are: **bra**, **tro**, **sta**, **sjalu**, **slu**, **edru**, **sky**, **kry**

6 The only really irregular adjective is **liten**, which has five forms:

	Indefinite forms		*Definite forms*	
	Singular	*Plural*	*Singular*	*Plural*
Masc.	**liten**			
Fem.	**lita**	**små**	**lille**	**små**
Neu.	**lite**			

COMPARISON

Most adjectives are compared by adding **-ere** in the comparative and **-est** in the superlative:

Positive	*Comparative*	*Superlative*
pen	**penere**	**penest**

Exceptions:

1 Adjectives ending in an unstressed **-e** end in **-re** and **-st**:

stille	**stillere**	**stillest**

2 Adjectives ending in **-er**, **-el** and **-en** are contracted:

vakker	**vakrere**	**vakrest**

3 Adjectives ending in **-ig** end in **-st** in the superlative:

modig	**modigere**	**modigst**

4 Some adjectives are compared with **mer** and **mest**:
(a) polysyllabic adjectives:

interessantmer	**interessantmest**	**interessant**

(b) participles:

kritisertmer	**kritisertmest**	**kritisert**

(c) many adjectives ending in **-sk**:

glemskmer	**glemskmest**	**glemsk**

(d) adjectives ending in **-et** and **-ed**:

fremmedmer	**fremmedmest**	**fremmed**

5 Irregular forms:

liten	**mindre**	**minst**
stor	**større**	**størst**
lang	**lengre**	**lengst**
tung	**tyngre**	**tyngst**
mange	**flere**	**flest**
mye	**mer**	**mest**
få	**færre**	**færest**
god/bra	**bedre**	**best**
dårlig/ille	**verre**	**verst**
gammel	**eldre**	**eldst**
ung	**yngre**	**yngst**
nær	**nærmere**	**nærmest**

NUMERALS

	Cardinals	*Ordinals*
0	null	nulte
1	en/ei/ett	første
2	to	annen/annet/andre
3	tre	tredje
4	fire	fjerde
5	fem	femte
6	seks	sjette
7	sju/syv	sjuende/syvende
8	åtte	åttende
9	ni	niende

10	ti	tiende
11	elleve	ellevte
12	tolv	tolvte
13	tretten	trettende
14	fjorten	fjortende
15	femten	femtende
16	seksten	sekstende
17	sytten	syttende
18	atten	attende
19	nitten	nittende
20	tjue/tyve	tjuende/tyvende
21	tjueen/enogtyve	tjueførste/enogtyvende
30	tretti/tredve	trettiende/tredevte
40	førti	førtiende
50	femti	femtiende
60	seksti	sekstiende
70	sytti	syttiende
80	åtti	åttiende
90	nitti	nittiende
100	hundre	hundrede
101	hundreogen	hundreogførste
110	hundreogti	hundreogtiende
200	to hundre	to hundrede
1000	(ett)tusen	tusende
1001	ett tusenogen	tusenogførste
2000	to tusen	to tusende
1,000,000	en million	millionte
2,000,000	to millioner	
1,000,000,000	en milliard	
2,000,000,000	to milliarder	

CARDINALS

En/ei/ett

The number one has a masculine form (**en**), a feminine form (**ei**) and a neuter form (**ett**):

> **Det er en uke igjen.**
> **Vi måtte vente ett år.**

En is not inflected when it forms part of a compound or is part of a decimal figure:

21 år	**tjueen år**
2.1 kg	**to komma en kilo**

Note: **En** is sometimes written **én** to distinguish it from the article **en**.

ORDINALS

Annen/annet/andre

Andre and **annen/annet** are interchangeable in certain cases:

2. januar: andre/annen januar

Andre is used in the definite form:

Det andre huset til venstre.

When the ordinals are written as a figure, a full stop follows:

17. mai, 1. premie

FRACTIONS

1/2	en halv
1/3	en tredel/tredjedel
2/3	to tredeler/tredjedeler
1/4	en firedel/fjerdedel, en kvart
1/5	en femdel/femtedel
1/12	en tolvdel/tolvtedel
1/15	en femtendel
1 1/2	en og en halv/halvannen
2 1/2	to og en halv

A noun is always in the singular after a fraction:

2 1/2 måned

A

aback [ə'bæk] *adv* **1** *sjø* bakk; **2** bakover; *taken ~* forfjamset; over|rasket, -rumplet.

abandon [ə'bændən] **I** *sb* **1** løssluppenhet; **2** løsaktighet; **II** *vt* **1** forlate; svikte; **2** oppgi; overgi. **abandoned** [ə'bændənd] *adj* **1** forlatt; sviktet; oppgitt; **2** løsaktig; fordervet, skamløs.

abase [ə'beɪs] *vt* fornedre.

abashed [ə'bæʃt] *adj* flau, forlegen.

abate [ə'beɪt] *vb* **1** minke; avta, løye; **2** dempe, redusere; *ofte* bekjempe; **3** få/gjøre (en) slutt på.

abbess ['æbɪs] *sb* abbedisse. **abbey** ['æbɪ] *sb* abbedi. **abbot** ['æbət] *sb* abbed.

abbreviate [ə'bri:vɪeɪt] *vt* forkorte (især ord). **abbreviation** [ə,bri:vɪ'eɪʃn] *sb* forkortelse.

abdicate ['æbdɪkeɪt] *vi* abdisere, si fra seg tronen. **abdication** [,æbdɪ'keɪʃn] *sb* abdikasjon, tronfrasigelse.

abdomen ['æbdəmən] *sb* buk, underliv; mave. **abdominal** [æb'dɒmɪnl] *adj* buk-, underlivs-; mave-.

abduct [æb'dʌkt] *vt* bortføre (især kvinner).

aberation [,æbə'reɪʃn] *sb* avvik(else); *mental ~* sinnsforvirring.

abet [ə'bet] *vt* oppmuntre til forbrytelse.

abeyance [ə'beɪəns] *sb*: *in ~* i bero.

abhor [əb'hɔ:] *vt* avsky. **abhorrence** [əb'hɒrəns] *sb* avsky. **abhorrent** [əb'hɒrənt] *adj* avskyelig.

abide [ə'baɪd] *vb* **A 1** *~ with* overholde; stå ved; **2** fordra, utstå; **B** *bokl* **1** forbli; *~ with me* bli hos meg; *abiding* varig; **2** oppholde seg; **3** avvente, vente på.

ability [ə'bɪlətɪ] *sb* dyktighet, evne; *fl også* åndsevner.

abject ['æbdʒekt] *adj* foraktelig, ynkelig; krypende, underdanig.

abjure [əb'dʒʊə] *vt* avsverge, fornekte.

ablaze [ə'bleɪz] *adj, adv* **1** i lys lue; **2** strålende (opplyst); **3** *fig* glødende (*with* av).

able ['eɪbl] *adj* **1** dyktig, flink; kvalifisert; *~ to* i stand til; **2** rask og rørig.

ablutions [ə'blu:ʃnz] *sb fl* renselse; tvetting; *især hum* vask(ing).

abnormal [æb'nɔ:ml] *adj* abnorm, unormal.

aboard [ə'bɔ:d] *adv, prep* om bord (i/på).

abode [ə'bəʊd] *sb bokl* **1** opphold; **2** oppholdssted; *især hum* bolig.

abolish [ə'bɒlɪʃ] *vt* avskaffe, oppheve. **abolition** [,æbəʊ'lɪʃn] *sb* avskaffelse, opphevelse.

abominable [ə'bɒmɪnəbl] *adj* avskyelig, fæl. **abominate** [ə'bɒmɪneɪt] *vt* avsky. **abomination** [ə,bɒmɪ'neɪʃn] *sb* **1** plage; *fig* pest, styggedom; **2** avsky.

aboriginal [,æbə'rɪdʒənl] **1** *adj* opprinnelig, ur-; **2** *sb* urinnbygger; innfødt. **aborigines** [,æbə'rɪdʒəni:z] *sb fl* urinnbyggere (især om urinnbyggerne i Australia).

abort [ə'bɔ:t] **I** *sb* **1** *især mil* avbrutt/ikke fullført oppdrag *etc*; **2** *data* programbrudd; **II** *vb* **1** abortere; **2** *også mil* mislykkes, ikke bli noe av; *dgl* gå i vasken; **3** *data* avbryte (program). **abortion** [ə'bɔ:ʃn] *sb* **1** abort(ering); *fig* bomskudd; **2** misfoster. **abortive** [ə'bɔ:tɪv] *adj* **1** abortiv; **2** mislykket; *fig* dødfødt.

abound [ə'baʊnd] *vi* kry, myldre, vrimle, yre (*in/with* av).

about [ə'baʊt] **I** *adj* **1** (rundt) omkring; **2** i nærheten; **3** på farten; i omløp, ute (blant folk); **4** om lag, omtrent; **II** *prep* **1** omkring (i); rundt (omkring); *have money (etc) ~ one* ha (penger etc) på seg; **2** angående, om; *be ~ to* skulle til å.

above [ə'bʌv] **I** *adv* **1** over, ovenpå; **2** ovenfor; lenger oppe; **3** foran, tidligere; **4** derover; **II** *prep* **1** over; høyere enn; *~ board* likefrem, åpen(t); *~ criticism* hevet over kritikk; **2** mer enn; *~ all* fremfor alt.

abrasion [ə'breɪʒn] *sb* **1** avskrapning; skrubbsår; **2** (av)sliping. **abrasive** [ə'breɪsɪv] *sb* slipemiddel. **abrasive paper** *sb* sandpapir.

abreast [ə'brest] *adv* side om side; *~ of* på høyde/linje med.

abridge [ə'brɪdʒ] *vt* forkorte (især tekst). **abridgement** [ə'brɪdʒmənt] *sb* sammendrag; forkortet versjon/utgave *etc*; forkortelse.

abroad [ə'brɔ:d] *adv* **1** utenlands; **2** oppe/ute (etter sykdom etc); **3** i omløp; **4** *slang: all ~* helt på jordet (dvs i villrede).

abrupt [ə'brʌpt] *adj* **1** plutselig, uventet; **2** barsk, brysk; brå, kort; **3** bratt, steil.

abscess ['æbsɪs] *sb* (verke)byll.

abscond [əb'skɒnd] *vi* stikke av.

absence ['æbsəns] *sb* fravær (*from* fra); mangel (*of* av, på); *~ (of mind)* (ånds)fraværenhet. **absent 1**

['æbsənt] *adj* fraværende; manglende; **2** [æb'sent] *vt:* ~ *oneself* fjerne seg. **absentee** [ˌæbsən'ti:] *sb* fraværende (person).

absolute ['æbsəlu:t] *adj* **1** absolutt (også *data*); fullstendig; **2** eneveldig, uinnskrenket.

absolution [ˌæbsə'lu:ʃn] *sb* absolusjon, syndsforlatelse. **absolve** [əb'zɒlv] *vt* **1** gi syndsforlatelse, tilgi; **2** frifinne.

absorb [əb'sɔ:b] *vt* **1** absorbere, suge opp; **2** *~ed in* fordypet i. **absorbent** [əb'sɔ:bənt] *adj* absorberende. **absorbing** [əb'sɔ:bɪŋ] *adj fig* fengslende, spennende. **absorption** [əb'sɔ:pʃn] *sb* absorpsjon.

abstain [əb'steɪn] *vi* **1** avstå/avholde seg (*from* fra); **2** unnlate å stemme (ved valg). **abstainer** [əb'steɪnə] *sb* avholds|kvinne, -mann. **abstemious** [əb'sti:mɪəs] *adj* måteholden, nøysom. **abstention** [əb'stenʃn] *sb* **1** avhold; **2** stemmeunnnlatelse. **abstinence** ['æbstɪnəns] *sb* avhold. **abstinent** ['æbstɪnənt] *adj* avholdende.

abstract I ['æbstrækt] **1** *adj* abstrakt; **2** *sb* sammendrag, utdrag; **II** [æb'strækt] *vt* **1** abstrahere; skille (el. ta) ut; **2** *slang* kvarte, rappe. **abstraction** [æb'strækʃn] *sb* abstraksjon.

abstruse [æb'stru:s] *adj* dunkel, dyp (dvs vanskelig å forstå).

abundance [ə'bʌndəns] *sb* mengde, overflod (jf *abound*). **abundant** [ə'bʌndənt] *adj* rikelig; ~ *in* rik på.

abuse I [ə'bju:s] *sb* **1** misbruk; **2** mishandling; **3** overhøvling, skjellsord; **II** [ə'bju:z] *vt* **1** misbruke; **2** mishandle; **3** rakke ned på; skjelle ut. **abusive** [ə'bju:siv] *adj* fornærmelig, grov.

abysmal [ə'bɪzməl] *adj* avgrunnsdyp, bunnløs. **abyss** [ə'bis] *sb* avgrunn.

academic [ˌækə'demɪk] **1** *adj* akademisk [især i betydningen teoretisk]; **2** *sb* akademiker. **academical** [ˌækə'demɪkl] *adj* akademisk (dvs som angår et akademi). **academician** [əˌkædə'mɪʃn] *sb* akademimedlem. **academy** [ə'kædəmɪ] *sb* akademi.

accede [æk'si:d] *vi:* ~ *to* tiltre (dvs gå med på, slutte seg til); ~ *to an office* tiltre et embete; ~ *to the throne* bestige tronen.

accelerate [ək'seləreɪt] *vb* akselerere, øke (el. sette opp) farten. **acceleration** [ækˌselə'reɪʃn] *sb* akselerasjon. **accelerator** [ək'seləreɪtə] *sb* gasspedal (på bil).

accent I ['æksənt] *sb* **1** tyngde, vekt (*fig*); **2** aksent; tonelag, trykk; **3** aksent(tegn); **II** [æk'sent] *vt* **1** legge trykket på; **2** aksentuere, betone, legge vekt på. **accent mark** *sb* aksenttegn (også *data*). **accentuate** [æk'sentjʊeɪt] *vt* aksentuere, fremheve, understreke. **accentuation** [ækˌsentjʊ'eɪʃn] *sb* aksentuering *etc.*

accept [ək'sept] *vt* akseptere, godta; motta. **acceptable** [ək'septəbl] *adj* akseptabel. **acceptance** [ək'septəns] *sb* godtakelse, godkjenning; *merk* aksept.

access ['æksəs] **I** *sb* **1** adgang; innkjørsel, oppkjørsel; **2** adgang; *også data* tilgang; **3** anfall; **II** *vb data* aksessere. **access arm** *sb data* søkearm. **accessary** [ək'sesərɪ] *adj, sb* medskyldig (person). **accessible** [ək'sesəbl] *adj* tilgjengelig. **accession** [ək'seʃn] *sb* tiltredelse (etc, jf *accede*); **2** tilvekst. **access mechanism** *sb data* søkearmsett. **accessory** [ək'sesərɪ] **I** *adj* hjelpe-, tilleggs-; **2** *sb* rekvisitt; *fl især* tilbehør, utstyr; **II** = *accessary*.

accident ['æksɪdənt] *sb* **1** slump, tilfelle; *by* ~ tilfeldigvis; **2** uhell, ulykkestilfelle. **accidental** [ˌæksɪ'dentl] *adj* tilfeldig; uvesentlig.

acclaim [ə'kleɪm] **1** *sb* bifall; bifalls|rop, -ytring; **2** *vt* hylle; utrope [f.eks. til konge]. **acclamation** [ˌæklə'meɪʃn] *sb* bifall; akklamasjon.

acclimatization [əˌklaɪmətaɪ'zeɪʃn] *sb* akklimatisering. **acclimatize** [ə'klaɪmətaɪz] *vb* akklimatisere(s); tilpasse (seg); venne (seg) til.

accommodate [ə'kɒmədeɪt] *vt* **1** huse, romme; **2** forstrekke/hjelpe (*with* med); **3** til|lempe, -passe. **accommodation** [əˌkɒmə'deɪʃn] *sb* **1** innlosjering; husrom, losji; **2** tilpasning. **accommodation | barge** *sb petro* boliglekter. ~ **deck** *sb petro* boligdekk. ~ **platform** *sb petro* boligplattform.

accompaniment [ə'kʌmpənɪmənt] *sb* akkompagnement, tonefølge; følge. **accompany** [ə'kʌmpənɪ] *vt* akkompagnere; følge, ledsage.

accomplice [ə'kʌmplɪs] *sb* medskyldig (person).

accomplish [ə'kʌmplɪʃ] *vt* **1** fullføre; **2** oppnå. **accomplished** [ə'kʌmplɪʃt] *adj* **1** fullført; **2** oppnådd; **3** dyktig, flink; (fullt) utlært; **4** dannet. **accomplishment** [ə'kʌmplɪʃmənt] *sb* **1** fullføring; **2** prestasjon; **3** dyktighet, ferdighet.

accord [ə'kɔ:d] **I** *sb* **1** enighet, samstemmighet; *of one's own* ~ av egen fri vilje; **2** pakt; **II** *vb* **1** bevilge; gi, tildele; **2** stemme (overens); *~ing to* ifølge, i samsvar med. **accordance** [ə'kɔ:dəns] *sb* samsvar(ighet). **accordingly** [ə'kɔ:dɪŋlɪ] *adv* altså, følgelig; deretter.

accordion [ə'kɔ:dɪən] *sb* trekkspill.

accost [ə'kɒst] *vt* henvende seg/snakke til (fremmed på gaten etc); antaste.

account [ə'kaʊnt] **I** *sb* **1** konto; **2** avregning; regnskap; *fig* mellomværende; *call to* ~ kreve til regnskap; **3** beregning, utregning; *take* ~ *of, take into* ~ regne med, ta i betraktning; **4** beretning, utredning; *by all ~s* etter alt å dømme; **5** hensyn; betydning, nytte; **6** *on* ~ *of* på grunn av; *on my* ~ for min skyld; *on no* ~ langt ifra, på ingen måte; **II** *vb* **1** betrakte som; **2** ~ *for* svare/gjøre rede for. **accountable** [ə'kaʊntəbl] *adj* ansvarlig. **accountancy** [ə'kaʊntənsɪ] *sb* **1** regnskapsførsel; bok|føring, holderi; **2** revisjon. **accountant** [ə'kaʊntənt] *sb* **1** regnskapsfører, bokholder; **2** revisor.

accredit [ə'kredɪt] *vt* akkreditere, utstyre (især diplomat) med fullmakter.

accrue [ə'kru:] *vi* vokse (gradvis); ~ *from* skrive seg fra; ~ *to* tilfalle.

accumulate [ə'kju:mjʊleɪt] *vb* akkumulere(s), hope (seg) opp. **accumulation** [əˌkju:mjʊ'leiʃn] *sb* **1** akkumulering, opphoping; **2** ansamling, opphopning. **accumulator** [ə'kju:mjuleɪtə] *sb* akkumulator, batteri.

accuracy ['ækjurəsɪ] *sb* nøyaktighet. **accurate** ['ækjurət] *adj* nøyaktig.

accursed [ə'kɜ:sɪd], **accurst** [ə'kɜ:st] *adj* forbannet, fordømt.

accusation [ˌækju'zeɪʃn] *sb* anklage, beskyldning. **accuse** [ə'kju:z] *vt* anklage/beskylde (*of* for).

accustom [ə'kʌstəm] *vt* venne (*to* til); *~ed to* vant til.

ace [eɪs] *sb* **1** ess (i kortspill); **2** ener (i terningkast); *within an ~ of* på nippet til; **3** ener, stjerne (i idrett etc).

ache [eɪk] **1** *sb* smerte, (-)verk; -pine; **2** *vi* gjøre vondt, verke; *~ for* lengte etter.

achieve [ə'tʃi:v] *vt* **1** fullføre; **2** oppnå, vinne. **achievement** [ə'tʃi:vmənt] *sb* **1** fullføring; **2** prestasjon.

acid ['æsɪd] **1** *adj* sur; **2** *sb* syre. **acid | gas** *sb petro* syregass. **acidity** [ə'sɪdətɪ] *sb* syrlighet. **acid | number** *sb petro* syretall. **~ oil** *sb petro* sur olje. **~ sludge** *sb petro* syreslam.

ack-ack ['æk'æk] *adj, sb* luftvern(-).

acknowledge [ək'nɒlɪdʒ] *vt* **1** erkjenne, innrømme; **2** kjennes ved; **3** bekrefte; **4** påskjønne. **acknowledgement** [ək'nɒlɪdʒmənt] *sb* **1** (an)erkjennelse *etc*; **2** bekreftelse; kvittering.

acme ['ækmɪ] *sb* høydepunkt.

acorn ['eɪkɔ:n] *sb* eikenøtt.

acoustic [ə'ku:stɪk] *adj* akustisk. **acoustic | log** *sb petro* akustisk logg. **~ pig** *sb petro* akustisk pigg. **~ storage** *sb data* akustisk lager. **acoustics** [ə'ku:stɪks] *sb fl* akustikk.

acquaint [ə'kweɪnt] *vt* gjøre kjent; *~ed with* kjent med. **acquaintance** [ə'kweɪntəns] *sb* **1** kjennskap (*with* til); **2** bekjentskap; **3** bekjent, kjenning.

acquiesce [ˌækwɪ'es] *vi* føye seg; *~ in* gå med på, samtykke i; finne seg i. **acquiescence** [ˌækwɪ'esns] *sb* føyelighet *etc*. **acquiescent** [ˌækwɪ'esnt] *adj* føyelig, medgjørlig.

acquire [ə'kwaɪə] *vt* skaffe (seg). **acquirement** [ə'kwaɪəmənt] *sb* ferdighet; *fl også* kunnskaper, talenter. **acquisition** [ˌækwɪ'zɪʃn] *sb* **1** ervervelse; *merk* akkvisisjon; **2** tilvekst.

acquit [ə'kwɪt] *vt* **1** fri|finne, -kjenne (*of* for); **2** betale (gjeld); **3** *~ oneself well of* klare bra. **acquittal** [ə'kwɪtl] *sb* frifinnelse *etc*.

acre [eɪkə] *sb* **1** flatemål, se midtsidene; **2** *især fl* jorde(r); *God's ~* kirkegård. **acreage** ['eɪkərɪdʒ] *sb* **1** areal (målt i *acres*); **2** land(område).

acrid ['ækrɪd] *adj* bitter, skarp. **acrimonious** [ˌækrɪ'məunɪəs] *adj* bitende, skarp.

across [ə'krɒs] **1** *adv, prep* (tvers) over; **2** *sb* vannrett [i kryssord].

act [ækt] **I** *sb* **1** gjerning; *~ of God* naturkatastrofe; *også* force majeure; **2** handling; *in the ~ of* i ferd med å; **3** lov; **4** akt [i skuespill]; opptreden; *put on an ~* spille (komedie); **II** *vb* **1** handle; foreta (seg)/gjøre noe; **2** arbeide; funksjonere, virke; fungere; **3** oppføre seg; *~ up to* leve opp til; **4** utføre; oppføre, spille; opptre; **5** late som, spille (komedie). **acting** ['æktɪŋ] **I** *adj* **1** handlende *etc*; **2** fungerende, konstituert; **II** *sb* opptreden. **action** ['ækʃn] *sb* **1** gjerning; aksjon, handling; **2** arbeid; funksjon; virksomhet; **3** oppførsel; **4** (inn)virkning; **5** kamp(handling); **6** *jur* sak, saksanlegg.

activate ['æktɪveɪt] *vt* **1** aktivisere, sette i gang; **2** aktivere. **activated | carbon, ~ charcoal** *sb* aktivert kull, aktivkull. **~ sludge** *sb petro* aktivert slam, aktivslam.

activation [ˌæktɪ'veɪʃn] *sb* aktivisering *etc*.

active ['æktɪv] *adj* aktiv, virksom. **activity** [æk'tɪvətɪ] *sb* **1** aktivitet, virksomhet; **2** beskjeftigelse. **activity | network** *sb data* aktivitetsnett. **~ ratio** *sb data* aktivitetsgrad.

actor ['æktə] *sb* skuespiller [om mann]. **actress** ['æktrɪs] *sb* skuespiller [om kvinne]; skuespillerinne.

actual ['æktʃuəl] *adj* **1** faktisk; reell, virkelig; egentlig; **2** nåværende. **actual | address** *sb data* absolutt adresse. **~ instruction** *sb data* effektiv instruksjon.

actually ['æktʃuəlɪ] *adv* **1** egentlig, i virkeligheten; **2** for tiden/øyeblikket.

actuate ['æktjueɪt] *vt fig* bevege, drive.

acumen ['ækjumən] *sb* skarpsindighet, teft. **acute** [ə'kju:t] *adj* **1** fin, skarp: **2** spiss; **3** høy, skingrende; **4** akutt, heftig.

adage ['ædɪdʒ] *sb* fyndord, ordtak.

adamant ['ædəmənt] *adj* hard, ubøyelig.

adapt [ə'dæpt] *vt* tilpasse (*to* til); bearbeide (*for* for). **adaptable** [ə'dæptəbl] *adj* tilpasningsdyktig; smidig. **adaptation** [ˌædæp'teɪʃn] *sb* tilpasning; bearbeidelse; *screen ~* filmversjon.

add [æd] *vb* addere, legge sammen; tilføye; *~ in* regne med; *it ~s up* det stemmer; *it ~s up to* det blir/utgjør (til sammen); *fig* det betyr (så mye som). **adder** ['ædə] *sb* **A** huggorm; **B** *data* adderer.

addict 1 ['ædɪkt] *sb fig* slave; *drug ~* narkotiker; **2** [ə'dɪkt] *vt: ~ed to* avhengig av, henfallen til. **addiction** [ə'dɪkʃn] *sb* avhengighet. **addictive** [ə'dɪktɪv] *adj* vanedannende.

addition [ə'dɪʃn] *sb* **1** addisjon, summering; **2** tilføyelse, tillegg. **additional** [ə'dɪʃənl] *adj* till|føyd, -lagt; ytterligere. **additive** ['ædɪtɪv] *sb* tilsetning, tilsetningsstoff.

addle ['ædl] **I** *adj: ~-brained, ~-pated* bløt (dvs forvirret, røret etc); **II** *vb* **1** råtne (om egg); **2** gjøre forvirret *etc*.

add-on 1 *adj* tilleggs-, **2** *sb (~ equipment)* tillegg, tilleggsutstyr.

address [ə'dres] **I** *sb* **1** adresse (også *data*); **2** henvendelse; tale; **3** bønnskrift; **4** opptreden; **5** *pay one's ~es to* gjøre kur til; **II** *vt* **1** adressere (også *data*); **2** henvende seg (til); snakke/tale (til); rette (*to* til); *~ oneself to* gi seg i kast med. **addressable** [ə'dresəbl] *adj data* adresserbar. **address bus** *sb data* adresse-buss. **addressee** [ˌædrə'siː] *sb* adressat. **address | reference** *sb data* adresse. ~ **space** *sb data* adresseområde.

adept ['ædept] **1** *adj* dyktig, flink (*at* til); **2** *sb* ekspert (*in* på).

adequacy ['ædɪkwəsɪ] *sb* tilstrekkelig mengde *etc*. **adequate** ['ædɪkwət] *adj* **1** nok, tilstrekkelig; adekvat; **2** tilsvarende; **3** passende, skikket; brukbar.

adhere [əd'hɪə] *vi* **1** henge fast (el. sammen); **2** holde fast (*to* ved); holde seg (*to* til). **adherence** [əd'hɪərəns] *sb* **1** det å holde fast (*to* ved); **2** troskap (*to* mot). **adherent** [əd'hɪərənt] **1** *adj* fasthengende; klebende; **2** *sb* tilhenger (av parti etc). **adhesion** [əd'hiːʒn] *sb* **1** adhesjon; **2** fastklebing; **3** støtte; tilslutning. **adhesive** [əd'hiːsɪv] *adj* klebrig. **adhesive tape** *sb* limbånd.

adjacent [ə'dʒeɪsənt] *adj* nærliggende, tilgrensende. **adjoining** [ə'dʒɔɪnɪŋ] *adj* til|grensende, -støtende; nærliggende.

adjourn [ə'dʒɜːn] *vb* **1** avbryte, heve (møte); **2** oppsette, utsette; **3** begi seg (*to* til); flytte.

adjunct ['ædʒʌŋkt] *sb* **1** tilføyelse; **2** *a)* hjelpemiddel; *b)* medhjelper.

adjure [ə'dʒʊə] *vt* besverge; be innstendig/inntrengende; bønnfalle.

adjust [ə'dʒʌst] *vt* justere, regulere; tilpasse. **adjustable** [ə'dʒʌstəbl] *adj* regulerbar. **adjustment** [ə'dʒʌstmənt] *sb* justering, regulering; tilpasning.

ad lib [ˌæd'lɪb] **1** *adj* improvisert; **2** *adv* etter behag; **3** *vb* improvisere.

administer [əd'mɪnɪstə] *vb* **1** administrere; (be)styre, forvalte; ~ *to* ta seg av; ~ *the law* håndheve loven; **2** dele/porsjonere ut; gi. **administration** [əd,mɪnɪ'streɪʃn] *sb* administrasjon, administrering. **administrative** [əd'mɪnɪstrətɪv] *adj* administrativ. **administrator** [əd'mɪnɪstreɪtə] *sb* administrator.

admirable ['ædmərəbl] *adj* beundringsverdig. **admiration** [ˌædmə'reɪʃn] *sb* beundring (*of* for). **admire** [əd'maɪə] *vt* beundre.

admissible [əd'mɪsəbl] *adj* **1** tillatelig, tilstedelig; **2** adgangsberettiget. **admission** [əd'mɪʃn] *sb* **1** opptak (ved skole etc); adgang; **2** innrømmelse, tilståelse. **admit** [əd'mɪt] *vb* **1** gi adgang, slippe inn; **2** innrømme, vedgå; ~ *of (fig)* gi rom for; ~ *to* bekjenne. **admittance** [əd'mɪtəns] *sb* adgang. **admittedly** [əd'mɪtɪdlɪ] *adv* riktignok, utvilsomt.

admonish [əd'mɒnɪʃ] *vt* advare; formane. **admonition** [ˌædməʊ'nɪʃn] *sb* advarsel; formaning.

ado [ə'duː] *sb* oppstyr, ståhei; mas.

adolescence [ˌædəʊ'lesns] *sb* ungdom (dvs ungdomstid). **adolescent** [ˌædəʊ'lesnt] **1** *adj* ung; **1** *sb* ungdom (dvs ungt menneske).

adopt [ə'dɒpt] *vt* **1** adoptere, ta til seg; *fig* tilegne seg; **2** anta (bekjennelse, tro etc); gå over til. **adoption** [ə'dɒpʃn] *sb* adopsjon *etc*.

adorable [ə'dɔːrəbl] *adj* bedårende. **adoration** [ˌædə'reɪʃn] *sb* **1** tilbedelse; **2** forgudelse. **adore** [ə'dɔː] *vt* **1** dyrke, tilbe; **2** forgude.

adorn [ə'dɔːn] *vt* pryde, smykke.

adrift [ə'drɪft] *adj, adv* drivende, i drift.

adroit [ə'drɔɪt] *adj* **1** behendig; flink (*in* til); **2** smart.

adulation [ˌædjʊ'leɪʃn] *sb* (overdreven) smiger, smisking.

adult ['ædʌlt] **1** *adj* moden, voksen; **2** *sb* voksen (person).

adulterate [ə'dʌltəreɪt] *vt* forurense; forfalske (ved å blande opp, tynne ut etc). **adulteration** [əˌdʌltə'reɪʃn] *sb* forurensing *etc*. **adultery** [ə'dʌltərɪ] *sb* ekteskapsbrudd, hor.

advance [əd'vɑːns] **I** *sb* **1** fremrykning; *fl fig* tilnærmelser; **2** fremskritt; **3** (pris)stigning; *merk* avanse; **4** forskudd; *in* ~ på forskudd; **II** *vb* **1** gå/rykke frem; **2** gjøre fremskritt; ~*d* viderekommen; ~*d level* videregående trinn; **3** føre/sette frem; *fig* fremskynde; **4** legge/sette frem (forslag etc); **5** fremme, hjelpe frem; **6** forfremme; **7** legge på (priser etc); stige; **8** forskuttere.

advantage [əd'vɑːntɪdʒ] **I** *sb* **1** fordel; **2** overtak; **3** gagn, nytte; *take* ~ *of* benytte seg/dra nytte av (hendelser, ting etc); utnytte (personer); lure; **II** *vt* gagne, nytte. **advantageous** [ˌædvən'teɪdʒəs] *adj* fordelaktig.

advent ['ædvənt] *sb* ankomst.

adventitious [ˌædvən'tɪʃəs] *adj* tilfeldig.

adventure [əd'ventʃə] *sb* **1** eventyr, spennende opplevelse; **2** vågestykke; **3** fare, risiko; spenning. **adventurer** [əd'ventʃərə] *sb* eventyrer. **adventurous** [əd'ventʃərəs] *adj* **1** eventyrlysten; **2** farefull, risikabel.

adversary ['ædvəsərɪ] *sb* mot|part, -stander; fiende. **adverse** ['ædvɜːs] *adj* motsatt; fiendtlig; ugunstig. **adversity** [əd'vɜːsətɪ] *sb* motgang.

advertise ['ædvətaɪz] *vb* **1** avertere (*for* etter); **2** annonsere, kunngjøre. **advertisement** [əd'vɜːtɪsmənt] *sb* avertissement; annonse, kunngjøring. **advertising** ['ædvətaɪzɪŋ] *sb* reklame.

advice [əd'vaɪs] *sb* **1** råd; **2** melding, underretning; *merk* advis. **advisable** [əd'vaɪzəbl] *adj* (til)rådelig. **advise** [əd'vaɪz] *vt* **1** råde, tilrå; ~*r* rådgiver; **2** underrette; *merk* advisere. **advisory** [əd'vaɪzərɪ] *adj* rådgivende.

advocate **I** ['ædvəkət] *sb* **1** for|kjemper, -svarer; talsmann; **2** *skotsk* advokat; **II** ['ædvəkeɪt] *vt* **1** anbefale; **2** forsvare; **3** forfekte.

aerial ['eərɪəl] **I** *adj* **1** luftig, luft-; **2** fly-; **II** *sb* (luft)antenne.

afar [ə'fɑː] *adv* langt borte.

affable ['æfəbl] *adj* hyggelig, omgjengelig (og litt nedlatende).

affair [ə'feə] *sb* **1** affære; begivenhet, hending; **2** anliggende, sak; *fl* forretninger; **3** *(love ~)* forhold, kjærlighetshistorie; **4** *dgl* dings, greie.

affect [ə'fekt] *vt* **1** virke på; **2** bevege, gjøre inntrykk på; **3** angripe [om sykdom]; **4** foregi, late som;

5 like, ynde; 6 jåle seg til med. **affectation** [ˌæfək'teɪʃn] *sb* jåleri, tilgjorthet. **affection** [ə'fekʃn] *sb* 1 hengivenhet, kjærlighet; 2 lidelse, sykdom. **affectionate** [ə'fekʃnət] *adj* hengiven, kjærlig.

affidavit [ˌæfi'deɪvɪt] *sb* (skriftlig) beediget erklæring.

affiliate [ə'fɪlɪeɪt] *vb* affiliere; knytte til (seg); oppta (som kompanjong etc). **affiliation** [əˌfɪlɪ'eɪʃn] *sb* affiliering; til|knytning, -slutning; opptak.

affinity [ə'fɪnətɪ] *sb* 1 beslektet natur; 2 slektskap; svogerskap; 3 *kjemi* affinitet.

affirm [ə'fɜ:m] *vt* bekrefte; forsikre. **affirmation** [ˌæfə'meɪʃn] *sb* bekreftelse *etc*. **affirmative** [ə'fɜ:mətɪv] *adj, sb* bekreftende (svar); *answer in the ~* svare bekreftende.

affix I ['æfɪks] *sb* 1 vedheng; 2 forstavelse; 3 endelse; **II** [ə'fɪks] *vt* feste; tilføye.

afflict [ə'flɪkt] *vt* anfekte, plage. **affliction** [ə'flɪkʃn] *sb* anfektelse, plage.

affluence ['æfluəns] *sb* overflod, velstand. **affluent** ['æfluənt] *adj* rik, velstående. *the* **Affluent Society** velstandssamfunnet.

afford [ə'fɔ:d] *vt* 1 ha råd (*to* til); 2 skaffe; gi, yte.

affray [ə'freɪ] *sb* bråk, oppløp; slagsmål.

affright [ə'fraɪt] 1 *sb* frykt, skrekk; 2 *vt* skremme.

affront [ə'frʌnt] 1 *sb* fornærmelse; 2 *vt* fornærme.

afield [ə'fi:ld] *adv* 1 (ute) på jordet (el. i marken); *fig* på viddene; 2 langt borte.

afire [ə'faɪə] *adj, adv* i brann; *fig* i fyr og flamme.

aflame [ə'fleɪm] *adj, adv* i flammer; *fig* flammende, glødende (*with* av).

afloat [ə'fləʊt] *adj, adv* 1 flytende; *fig* med hodet over vannet; 2 til sjøs; 3 i omløp; i drift (gang, gjenge etc).

afoot [ə'fʊt] *adj, adv* 1 på beina, til fots; 2 i gang/gjenge; 3 *fig* i gjære.

afore [ə'fɔ:] 1 *adv, prep* foran; *sjø* forut; 2 *pref* foran(-); før(-). **afore|-mentioned** *adj* forannevnt, ovennevnt. **~-thought** *adj* overlagt, tilsiktet.

afraid [ə'freɪd] *adj* redd (*of* for; *that* for at; *to* for å).

afresh [ə'freʃ] *adv* (om) igjen, på ny(tt).

aft [ɑ:ft] *adv sjø* akterut. **after** ['ɑ:ftə] **I** *adj* (på)følgende, senere; **II** *adv* etter; etterpå; baketter, deretter; **III** *konj* etter at; **IV** *prep* 1 etter; *~ all* trass i/tross alt; 2 ifølge; *~ a fashion* på en måte (dvs ikke særlig vellykket etc). **after | image** *sb data* etterkopi. **~math** *sb* ettervirkning(er), følger. **~noon** *sb* ettermiddag [i engelsktalende land: etter kl. 12 middag]. **~wards** ['ɑ:ftəwədz] *adv* 1 etterpå, senere; 2 deretter.

again [ə'gen] *adv* (om) igjen, på ny(tt); *now and ~* av og til, nå og da.

against [ə'genst] *prep* (i)mot.

age [eɪdʒ] **I** *sb* 1 *a)* alder, alderstrinn; *be your ~!* vær ikke barnslig! *of ~* myndig; *under ~* mindreårig, umyndig; *b) (old ~)* alderdom; 2 *a)* menneskealder; *b)* tidsalder; *ages (dgl)* en hel evighet; **II** *vb* eldes; bli/gjøre gammel. **aged** *adj* 1 ['eɪdʒɪd] aldrende, gammel; 2 [eɪdʒd] *a boy ~ ten* en gutt på ti (år). **ageless** ['eɪdʒlɪs] *adj* tidløs.

agency ['eɪdʒənsɪ] *sb* 1 innflytelse, påvirkning; 2 *merk* byrå; agentur, representasjon. **agenda** [ə'dʒendə] *sb* dagsorden, (møte)program; sakliste. **agent** ['eɪdʒənt] *sb* 1 virkemiddel; 2 *merk* agent, representant; 3 *mil, pol* agent, spion.

aggravate ['ægrəveɪt] *vt* 1 forverre; *aggravating circumstances* skjerpende omstendigheter; 2 irritere. **aggravation** [ˌægrə'veɪʃn] *sb* 1 forverring, skjerpelse; 2 irritasjon.

aggregate I ['ægrɪgət] 1 *adj* (opp)samlet; sammensatt; 2 *sb* (opp)samlet masse/mengde; aggregat; **II** ['ægrɪgeɪt] *vb* hope (seg) opp. **aggregation** [ˌægrɪ'geɪʃn] *sb* ansamling, sammenhopning.

aggression [ə'greʃn] *sb* aggresjon. **aggressive** [ə'gresɪv] *adj* aggressiv, stridbar. **aggressor** [ə'gresə] *sb* aggressor, angriper.

aggrieved [ə'gri:vd] *adj* forurettet.

aghast [ə'gɑ:st] *adj* forferdet.

agile ['ædʒaɪl] *adj* livlig; smidig, spretten. **agility** [ə'dʒɪlətɪ] *sb* livlighet *etc*.

agitate ['ædʒɪteɪt] *vb* 1 riste, skake; 2 ryste, skake opp; *~d* oppskaket, rystet; 3 agitere. **agitation** [ˌædʒɪ'teɪʃn] *sb* risting *etc*; agitasjon, agitering.

aglow [ə'gləʊ] *adj, adv* glødende, skinnende; *fig* blussende (*with* av).

ago [ə'gəʊ] *adv* for ... siden; *a week (etc) ~* for en uke (etc) siden.

agonize ['ægənaɪz] *vb* 1 pine, plage; 2 lide kvaler.

agony ['ægənɪ] *sb* 1 angst, kval; dødskamp; 2 pine, smerte. **agony column** *sb* ≈ Personlig (dvs annonsespalte med etterlysninger etc).

agree [ə'gri:] *vb* 1 bli/være enige (*on* om; *that* om at; *to* om å; *with* med); 2 samtykke (*to* i å); 3 passe (sammen)/stemme overens (*with* med). **agreeable** [ə'grɪəbl] *adj* behagelig; 2 imøtekommende; 3 overensstemmende (*to* med). **agreement** [ə'gri:mənt] *sb* 1 enighet; 2 avtale, overenskomst; forlik; 3 overensstemmelse, samsvar.

agricultural [ˌægrɪ'kʌltʃərəl] *adj* jordbruks-. **agriculture** ['ægrɪˌkʌltʃə] *sb* jordbruk.

aground [ə'graʊnd] *adj, adv* grunnstøtt, på grunn.

ague ['eɪgju:] *sb* koldfeber; *især* malaria.

ahead [ə'hed] *adj, adv* forover, fremover; *go ~* gå i gang; 2 foran; *sjø* forut; *~ of* foran; forut for; 3 *(om vær og vind)* imot, kontrari; mot-.

aid [eɪd] 1 *sb* hjelp (og hjelpemiddel, hjelpetiltak); assistanse, støtte; 2 *vt* hjelpe, støtte.

ail [eɪl] *vb* 1 plage; 2 skrante, være syk(elig); feile noe. **ailment** ['eɪlmənt] *sb* plage, sykdom.

aim [eɪm] **I** *sb* 1 sikte; 2 forsett, hensikt; 3 (for)mål; **II** *vb* 1 rette (*at* mot); sikte (*at* på); *fig* mynte (*at* på); 2 strebe/trakte (*at* etter); 3 *(US) ~ at* ha som mål/til hensikt.

air [eə] **I** *sb* 1 luft; *som adj, pref* fly-, luft-; 2 luftning; 3 melodi, strofe; 4 mine, utseende; *put on ~s* gjøre seg til, skape seg; **II** *vt* 1 lufte (ut); 2 *fig* lufte (dvs bringe på bane, slå frempå om); gi luft (for); slå om seg med. **air|borne** *adj* flybåren. **~craft** *sb* fly. **~field** *sb* (mindre) flyplass. **~force** *sb* fly|styrke, -våpen. **~-hostess** *sb* flyvertinne. **~line** *sb* flyrute; *fl* flyselskap. **~mail** *sb* luftpost. **~man** *sb* flyger. **~plane** *sb US* = *aeroplane*. **~port** *sb* lufthavn, (større) flyplass. **~-raid** *sb* flyangrep; *~-raid warning* flyalarm. **~ways** *sb* flyselskap.

airy ['eərɪ] *adj* **1** luftig; **2** flyktig; **3** lettlivet, munter; lettferdig; **4** jålet, tilgjort.

aisle [aɪl] *sb* **1** gang (og midtgang), passasje; **2** sideskip (i kirke).

ajar [ə'dʒɑ:] *adv* på gløtt, på klem.

akimbo [ə'kɪmbəʊ] *adv: (with) arms ~* med hendene i siden.

akin [ə'kɪn] *adj* **1** beslektet/i slekt (*to* med); **2** lik.

alacrity [ə'lækrətɪ] *sb* iver, villighet.

alarm [ə'lɑ:m] **I** *sb* **1** alarm, varsel; **2** forskrekkelse; frykt, uro; **II** *vt* **1** alarmere, varsle; **2** forskrekke, skremme. **alarm clock** *sb* vekkeklokke. **alarming** [ə'lɑ:mɪŋ] *adj* skremmende.

alas [ə'læs] *interj* akk! dessverre!

albeit [ɔ:l'bi:ɪt] *konj bokl* (en)skjønt.

alcohol ['ælkəhɒl] *sb* alkohol. **alcoholic** [ˌælkə'hɒlɪk] **1** *adj* alkoholholdig; alkoholisk; alkohol-; **2** *sb* alkoholiker.

alder ['ɔ:ldə] *sb* or.

alderman ['ɔ:ldəmən] *sb* **1** bystyremedlem, formannskapsmedlem; **2** rådmann; **3** oldermann.

ale [eɪl] *sb* (lyst, engelsk) øl.

alert [ə'lɜ:t] **I** *adj* **1** årvåken, på vakt; **2** kjapp, våken; **II** *sb* **1** alarm, varsel; **2** *on the ~* på vakt.

algebra ['ældʒɪbrə] *sb* algebra, bokstavregning. **algebraic** [ˌældʒɪ'breɪɪk] *adj* algebraisk.

algorithm ['ælgəʊrɪðəm] *sb data, mat* algoritme. **algorithmic** ['ælgəʊ'rɪθmɪk] *adj data, mat* algoritmisk.

alias ['eɪlɪəs] **1** *adv* alias; **2** *sb* alias, dekknavn, falskt navn.

alibi ['ælɪbaɪ] *sb* **1** alibi; **2** unnskyldning.

alien ['eɪlɪən] **I** *adj* **1** utenlandsk; **2** fremmed(artet), vesensfremmed; *~ to* fjernt fra; uforenelig med; **II** *sb* **1** utlending; **2** *a)* fremmed; *b)* romvesen (dvs fremmed vesen fra verdensrommet). **alienate** ['eɪlɪəneɪt] *vt* **1** fremmedgjøre; **2** skille seg av med; støte fra seg; **3** avhende; over|dra, -føre. **alienation** [ˌeɪlɪə'neɪʃn] *sb* fremmedgjøring *etc*.

alight [ə'laɪt] **A** *adj, adv* **1** brennende, i brann; **2** strålende (*with* av); **B** *vi* **1** lande, slå seg ned (om fugler etc); **2** *~ from* gå/stige av (buss etc); **3** *~ on* finne, komme over.

align [ə'laɪn] *vb* **1** rette inn; stille (og stille opp, stille seg etc) på linje; *fig* komme på linje med; **2** stikke ut (trasé etc).

alike [ə'laɪk] **1** *adj* ens, lik; **2** *adv* likedan, likt, på samme måte.

alimentary [ˌælɪ'mentərɪ] *adj* **1** nærende, nærings-; **2** fordøyelses-; *the ~ canal* fordøyelseskanalen.

alimony ['ælɪmənɪ] *sb* underholdsbidrag.

alive [ə'laɪv] *adj* **1** levende; *~ with* yrende full av; **2** virksom; **3** kvikk; *~ to* våken for.

all [ɔ:l] **I** *adj* **1** all, alt; alle; **2** hel, helt; hele; *~ ears* lutter øre; *in ~ seriousness* i fullt alvor; **II** *adv* aldeles, fullstendig, ganske, helt; *~ alike* alle sammen; *~ but* nesten; *~ in (dgl)* helt utkjørt; *~ the better* så mye (*bokl* meget desto) bedre; *~ the same* likevel; *it's ~ up with them (dgl)* det er ute med dem; **III** *pref* all-, alt-; full(-), hel(-); *~-out* gjennomført, total; *~-round* allsidig; altomfattende, universal; generell; *~time* heltids-; *dgl* alle tiders; *~-white* bare for hvite; **IV** *pron, sb* alle, alt; *~ she could do/hope for* alt (dvs det eneste) hun kunne gjøre/håpe på.

allay [ə'leɪ] *vt* **1** berolige; **2** dempe; dulme, lindre.

allegation [ˌælɪ'geɪʃn] *sb* påstand. **allege** [ə'ledʒ] *vt* **1** påstå; **2** anføre, hevde. **allegedly** [ə'ledʒɪdlɪ] *adv* angivelig.

allegiance [ə'li:dʒəns] *sb* **1** troskap; **2** lydighet.

allergic [ə'lɜ:dʒɪk] **I** *adj* allergisk (*to* mot); **2** overfølsom (*to* for); **II** *sb* allergiker. **allergy** ['ælədʒɪ] *sb* allergi.

alleviate [ə'li:vɪeɪt] *vt* lindre, mildne; lette. **alleviation** [əˌli:vɪ'eɪʃn] *sb* lindring.

alley ['ælɪ] *sb* **1** bakgate, smug; **2** allé.

alliance [ə'laɪəns] *sb* **1** allianse, forbund; **2** (familie)forbindelse. **allied** [ə'laɪd] *adj* alliert (*to/with* med).

allot [ə'lɒt] *vt* **1** tildele; **2** fordele, dele ut; **3** anvise. **allotment** [ə'lɒtmənt] *sb* **1** tildeling *etc*; **2** *(~ garden)* kolonihage.

allow [ə'laʊ] *vb* **1** tillate; *be ~ed to* få lov til (å); **2** bevilge; gi, tildele; **3** innrømme; *~ for* ta hensyn til; ta i betraktning; *~ of (fig)* gi rom for. **allowance** [ə'laʊəns] *sb* **1** tillatelse; **2** bevilgning (og bevilget sum, f.eks. lommepenger, kostgodtgjørelse, husholdningspenger); **3** *fig* innrømmelse; spillerom; *make ~(s) for* = *allow for*; **4** avslag, fradrag.

alloy **I** *sb* **1** ['ælɔɪ] legering; **2** *fig* [ə'lɔɪ] (forringende) tilsetning; **II** *vt* **1** legere; **2** forringe (ved oppblanding).

all-season oil *sb petro* helårsolje.

allspice ['ɔ:lspaɪs] *sb* allehånde.

allude [ə'lu:d] *vi* hentyde (*to* til).

allure [ə'ljʊə] *vt* forføre; friste, lokke.

allusion [ə'lu:ʒn] *sb* hentydning (jf *allude*). **allusive** [ə'lu:sɪv] *adj* forblommet.

ally **I** ['ælaɪ] *sb* alliert, (forbunds)felle; **II** [ə'laɪ] *vt* **1** alliere; **2** forbinde, forene.

almighty [ɔ:l'maɪtɪ] *adj* allmektig

almond ['ɑ:mənd] *sb* mandel.

almost ['ɔ:lməʊst] *adv* nesten.

alms [ɑ:mz] *sb* almisse(r).

aloft [ə'lɒft] *adj, adv* høyt oppe; *sjø* til værs (dvs oppe i masten/riggen).

alone [ə'ləʊn] **1** *adj* alene, ensom; **2** *adv* bare; *bokl* alene.

along [ə'lɒŋ] **I** *adv* **1** av sted; *bring ~* ha/ta med (seg); *come* ~ bli/være med; **2** videre; **II** *prep* **1** langs (med); **2** bortover; **3** ~ *with* (sammen) med. **alongside** [ə'lɒŋsaɪd] *adv, prep* langs (med); side om side (med); ved siden av.

aloof [ə'lu:f] *adj, adv* for seg selv, (langt) unna; *fig* kjølig, reservert.

aloud [ə'laʊd] *adv* **1** hørbart, høyt (nok til å høres); **2** høyt.

alphabet ['ælfəbɪt] *sb* alfabet. **alphabetic(al)** [ˌælfə'betɪk(l)] *adj* alfabetisk. **alphabetic | character** *sb data* alfabetisk tegn. ~ **key** *sb data* bokstavtast. **alphanumeric(al)** ['ælfənju:'merɪk(l)] *adj data* alfanumerisk.

already [ɔ:l'redɪ] *adv* allerede, alt.

Alsatian [æl'seɪʃn] *sb (~ dog)* schæfer(hund).

also ['ɔ:lsəʊ] *adv* også, dessuten.

altar ['ɔ:ltə] *sb* alter.

alter ['ɔ:ltə] *vb* endre(s), forandre (seg). **alteration** [ˌɔ:ltə'reɪʃn] *sb* endring, forandring.

altercation [ˌɔ:ltə'keɪʃn] *sb* uoverensstemmelse; krangel.

alternate A [ɔ:l'tɜ:nət] **I** *adj* (av)vekslende, skiftevis; *ofte* annenhver; **II** *US* **1** *adj* reserve-, vara-; **2** *sb* vara|kvinne, mann; **B** ['ɔ:ltəneɪt] *vb* alternere, veksle; skiftes (om); *alternating current (AC)* vekselstrøm. **alternate | function key** *sb data* vekslende funksjonsnøkkel. ~ **track** *sb data* alternativt spor. **alternation** [ˌɔ:ltə'neɪʃn] *sb* alternering, veksling; skifting. **alternative** [ɔ:l'tɜ:nətɪv] *adj, sb* alternativ.

although [ɔ:l'ðəʊ] *konj* skjønt.

altimeter ['æltɪmɪtə] *sb* høydemåler. **altitude** ['æltitju:d] *sb* høyde (over havet).

alto ['æltəʊ] *sb mus* alt(stemme).

altogether [ˌɔ:ltə'geðə] *adv* **1** fullstendig, helt; **2** alt i alt, stort sett; **3** *sb: in the* ~ splitter naken.

always ['ɔ:lweɪz] *adv* alltid, bestandig.

amalgamate [ə'mælgəmeɪt] *vb* **1** blande/smelte sammen, amalgamere(s); **2** forene(s), slutte (seg) sammen. **amalgamation** [əˌmælgə'meɪʃn] *sb* **1** sammen|blanding, -smelting; **2** forening, sammenslutning.

amass [ə'mæs] *vt* hope opp.

amateur ['æmətə] *sb* amatør. **amateurish** [ˌæmə'tɜ:rɪʃ] *adj* amatørmessig.

amaze [ə'meɪz] *vt* forbause (sterkt), forbløffe. **amazement** [ə'meɪzmənt] *sb* (stor) forbauselse/forundring.

ambassador [æm'bæsədə] *sb* ambassadør.

amber ['æmbə] **I** *adj* (rav)gul; *om trafikklys* gult; **II** *sb* **1** rav; **2** ravgult; *om trafikklys* gult.

ambiguity [ˌæmbɪ'gjuətɪ] *sb* tvetydighet. **ambiguous** [æm'bigjuəs] *adj* **1** tvetydig; **2** tvilsom.

ambition [æm'bɪʃn] *sb* ambisjon, ærgjerrighet. **ambitious** [æm'bɪʃəs] *adj* ambisiøs, ærgjerrig.

amble ['æmbl] **I** *sb* slentring; *om dyr* passgang; **II** *vi* **1** (gå og) drive, slentre; **2** gå/ri etc i passgang.

ambulance ['æmbjʊləns] *sb* ambulanse, sykebil.

ambush ['æmbʊʃ] **1** *sb* bakhold; **2** *vb* angripe/overfalle fra bakhold; ligge i bakhold (for).

ameliorate [ə'mi:lɪəreɪt] *vb* forbedre (seg); bedre(s), bli/gjøre bedre. **amelioration** [əˌmi:lɪə'reɪʃn] *sb* (for)bedring *etc*.

amenable [ə'mi:nəbl] *adj* **1** føyelig, medgjørlig; **2** mottakelig/åpen (*to* for); **3** ~ *to* ansvarlig for; underlagt.

amend [ə'mend] *vb* **1** forbedre (seg); **2** rette på. **amendment** [ə'mendmənt] *sb* **1** forbedring; **2** endring (og endringsforslag); **3** *US* grunnlovsendring, (tilleggs)lov. **amends** [ə'mendz] *sb fl* erstatning; oppreisning; *make* ~ gjøre godt igjen.

amenity [ə'mi:nətɪ] *sb* **1** behagelighet; *fl* bekvemmeligheter; fordeler, goder; **2** høflighet.

amiability [ˌeɪmɪə'bɪlətɪ] *sb* vennlighet *etc*. **amiable** ['eɪmɪəbl] *adj* vennlig; elskverdig, hyggelig.

amicability [ˌæmɪkə'bɪlətɪ] *sb* vennskapelighet *etc*. **amicable** ['æmɪkəbl] *adj* **1** vennskapelig; **2** *jur* minnelig.

amid(st) [ə'mɪd(st)] *prep* **1** midt i(blant); **2** under (dvs ledsaget/omgitt av).

amiss [ə'mɪs] *adj, adv* feil(aktig), galt; *take* ~ ta ille opp.

amity ['æmətɪ] *sb* **1** vennskap; **2** vennlighet.

ammo ['æməʊ] *slang = ammunition.*

ammonia [ə'məʊnɪə] *sb* ammoniakk; *liquid* ~ salmiakk.

ammunition [ˌæmjʊ'nɪʃn] *sb* ammunisjon.

amnesty ['æmnɪstɪ] **1** *sb* amnesti; **2** *vt* gi amnesti, benåde.

among(st) [ə'mʌŋ(st)] *prep* blant, mellom.

amorous ['æmərəs] *adj* **1** forelsket; **2** kjærlig, øm; kjælen.

amortization [əˌmɔ:tɪ'zeɪʃn] *sb* amortisering. **amortize** [ə'mɔ:taɪz] *vt* amortisere, avskrive; tilbakebetale (lån).

amount [ə'maʊnt] **I** *sb* **1** beløp, sum; **2** mengde; **3** betydning; **II** *vi:* ~ *to* **1** beløpe seg til, komme på; **2** bety, innebære.

amphibian [æm'fɪbɪən] *sb* amfibium; *mil etc* amfibiekjøretøy. **amphibious** [æm'fɪbɪəs] *adj* amfibisk, amfibie-.

ample ['æmpl] *adj* **1** rommelig, vid; **2** rik(elig), mer enn nok; **3** utførlig. **amplification** [ˌæmplɪfɪ'keɪʃn] *sb* forsterkning *etc*. **amplifier** ['æmplɪfaɪə] *sb* forsterker (for radio etc). **amplify** ['æmplɪfaɪ] *vb* **1** forsterke; forstørre, utvide, øke; **2** gå i detaljer; *dgl* utbre seg.

amputate ['æmpjʊteɪt] *vt* amputere. **amputation** [ˌæmpjʊ'teɪʃn] *sb* amputasjon.

amuck [ə'mʌk] *adv: run* ~ gå amok.

amuse [ə'mju:z] *vt* more, underholde. **amusement** [ə'mju:zmənt] *sb* moro, underholdning. **amusing** [ə'mju:zɪŋ] *adj* morsom.

anaemia [ə'ni:mɪə] *sb* anemi. **anaemic** [ə'ni:mɪk] *adj* anemisk; *fig også* blodfattig.

anaesth(a)esia [ˌænɪs'θi:zɪə] *sb* anestesi, følelsesløshet; *dgl med* bedøvelse; *general* ~ (full) narkose.

anaesthetic [ˌænɪsˈθetɪk] **I** *adj* **1** anestetisk, bedøvelses-; **2** følelsesløs; *fig* ufølsom; **II** *sb* bedøvelse (og bedøvelsesmiddel).

analog [ˈænəlɒg] *adj især data = analogous.* **analog | computer** *sb data* analogmaskin. **~ data** *sb fl data* analogdata. **analogous** [əˈnæləgəs] *adj* analog, samsvarende, tilsvarende. **analogy** [əˈnælədʒɪ] *sb* analogi, samsvar(ighet).

analyse [ˈænəlaɪz] *vt* analysere. **analysis** [əˈnæləsɪs] *sb* analyse. **analyst** [ˈænəlɪst] *sb* analytiker. **analytic** [ˌænəˈlɪtɪk] *adj* analytisk.

anarchist [ˈænəkɪst] *sb* anarkist. **anarchistic** [ˌænəˈkɪstɪk] *adj* anarkistisk. **anarchy** [ˈænəkɪ] *sb* anarki, lovløshet.

anatomical [ˌænəˈtɒmɪkl] *adj* anatomisk. **anatomist** [əˈnætəmɪst] *sb* anatom. **anatomy** [əˈnætəmɪ] *sb* **1** anatomi; **2** *fig* oppbygning; analyse; **3** *slang* beinrangel, skjelett.

ancestor [ˈænsɪstə] *sb* stam|far, -mor; *fl* for|fedre, -mødre. **ancestral** [ænˈsestrəl] *adj* **1** *a)* fars-, fedrene; *b)* mors-, mødrene; **2** nedarvet. **ancestry** [ˈænsɪstrɪ] *sb* **1** aner; for|fedre, mødre; **2** herkomst; slekt, ætt.

anchor [ˈæŋkə] **I** *sb* anker; **II** *vb* **1** ankre (opp); **2** forankre, feste. **anchorage** [ˈæŋkərɪdʒ] *sb* **1** ankring (og ankerplass, havn); *fig* forankring, feste; **2** havneavgift.

anchovy [ˈæntʃəvɪ] *sb* ansjos.

ancient [ˈeɪnʃənt] *adj* **1** fordums; fortids; oldtids-; **2** eldgammel; **3** gammeldags.

and [ænd] *konj* og.

anemone [əˈnemənɪ] *sb* anemone; *(white ~)* hvitveis; *blue ~* blåveis; *sea ~* sjøanemone.

anew [əˈnju:] *adv* om igjen, på ny(tt).

angel [ˈeɪndʒəl] *sb* engel. **angelic** [ænˈdʒelɪk] *adj* engleaktig.

anger [æŋgə] **1** *sb* sinne; **2** *vt* gjøre sint.

angle [ˈæŋgl] **A I** *sb* **1** vinkel; *fig* synsvinkel; **2** bøy, sving; **3** hjørne, krok; **II** *vt* **1** gi en bestemt vinkel/vinkling; sikte inn; **2** for|dreie, -vrenge; **B 1** *sb* angel, (fiske)krok; **2** *vi* angle, fiske (med snøre og krok). **angler** [ˈæŋglə] *sb* (sports)fisker.

Angles [ˈæŋglz] *sb fl* (folkeslaget) angler. **Anglican** [ˈæŋglɪkən] **1** *adj* anglikansk, høykirkelig; *the ~ Church* den engelske statskirke; **2** *sb* anglikaner. **Anglo-** [ˈæŋgləʊ-] *pref* angel-, anglo-; engelsk(-). **Anglo-Saxon** [ˌæŋgləʊˈsæksən] **1** *adj* angelsaksisk; **2** *sb* angelsakser.

angry [ˈæŋgrɪ] *adj* **1** sint (*about/at* for; *with* på); **2** *om sår* hissig, rødflammet; betent; **3** *om sjø* opprørt.

anguish [ˈæŋgwɪʃ] *sb* angst; kval, pine. **anguished** [ˈæŋgwɪʃt] *adj* forpint.

angular [ˈæŋgjʊlə] *adj* **1** vinkelformet, vinkel-; **2** med skarpe kanter/utspring *etc*; *fig* kantet, keitet; **3** knoklet, radmager.

animal [ˈænɪml] **1** *adj* animalsk, dyrisk, dyre-; **2** *sb* dyr. **animate I** [ˈænɪmət] *adj* **1** levende; **2** livlig; **II** [ˈænɪmeɪt] *vt* **1** gjøre levende; **2** *fig* bevege; **3** lage (tegninger til) tegnefilm; **4** live opp; **5** inspirere, oppmuntre. **animated** [ˈænɪmeɪtɪd] *adj* livlig, opprømt. **animation** [ˌænɪˈmeɪʃn] *sb* liv (og livaktighet, livlighet etc).

animosity [ˌænɪˈmɒsətɪ] *sb* fiendskap; motvilje, uvilje; hat, nag.

ankle [ˈæŋkl] *sb* ankel.

annals [ˈænlz] *sb fl* annaler, (år)bøker.

annex I [ˈænəks] *sb* **1** anneks, tilbygg; **2** tillegg, vedlegg; **II** [əˈneks] *vt* **1** annektere, innlemme; **2** knytte/legge til. **annexation** [ˌænekˈseɪʃn] *sb* annektering *etc.*

annihilate [əˈnaɪəleɪt] *vt* tilintetgjøre. **annihilation** [əˌnaɪəˈleɪʃn] *sb* tilintetgjøring.

anniversary [ˌænɪˈvɜ:sərɪ] *sb* **1** årsdag; **2** fødselsdag.

annotate [ˈænəʊteɪt] *vt* kommentere; forsyne med kommentarer (merknader, forklarende noter etc). **annotation** [ˌænəʊˈteɪʃn] *sb* kommentar(er), merknad(er), noter.

announce [əˈnaʊns] *vt* annonsere, kunngjøre; **2** melde; gi beskjed/si fra om; **3** bebude, forkynne. **announcer** [əˈnaʊnsə] *sb* hallo|dame, -mann. **announcement** [əˈnaʊnsmənt] *sb* kunngjøring *etc.*

annoy [əˈnɔɪ] *vt* ergre; plage, sjenere. **annoyance** [əˈnɔɪəns] *sb* ergrelse *etc.* **annoying** [əˈnɔɪɪŋ] *adj* plagsom, sjenerende.

annual [ˈænjʊəl] **I** *adj* **1** årlig, års-; **2** ettårig; **II** *sb* **1** årbok; årlig publikasjon; **2** ettårig plante. **annuity** [əˈnju:ətɪ] *sb* annuitet, livrente.

annul [əˈnʌl] *vt* annullere, oppheve; erklære ugyldig. **annulment** [əˈnʌlmənt] *sb* annullering *etc.*

anoint [əˈnɔɪnt] *vt* salve.

anomalous [əˈnɒmələs] *adj* avvikende, uregelmessig. **anomaly** [əˈnɒməlɪ] *sb* anomali; avvik, uregelmessighet.

anon [əˈnɒn] *adv gml* om litt, snart; *ever and ~* rett som det er.

anonymity [ˌænəˈnɪmətɪ] *sb* anonymitet. **anonymous** [əˈnɒnɪməs] *adj* anonym.

another [əˈnʌðə] *adj, pron* (en) annen; en ny; (en) til, enda en; *ofte* noe annet; noe nytt.

answer [ˈɑ:nsə] **I** *sb* **1** svar; *in ~ to* som svar på; **2** løsning (*to* på); **3** *jur* forsvarsinnlegg; **II** *vb* **1** (be)svare, svare på; *~ a charge* forsvare seg mot en anklage; *~ the phone* ta telefonen; *~ the purpose* svare til hensikten; **2** *med adv/prep:* **~ back** svare (uforskammet etc) igjen; **~ for** svare/gå god for; **~ to** svare på/til; etterkomme, lystre; *~ to treatment* reagere (positivt) på behandling. **answerable** [ˈɑ:nsərəbl] *adj* **1** som kan besvares; **2** ansvarlig; **3** fyllestgjørende, tjenlig.

ant [ænt] *sb* maur.

antagonism [ænˈtægənɪzəm] *sb* fiendskap, motsetningsforhold; antagonisme. **antagonist** [ænˈtægənɪst] *sb* motstander. **antagonistic** [ænˌtægəˈnɪstɪk] *adj* antagonistisk, fiendtlig(sinnet). **antagonize** [ænˈtægənaɪz] *vt* bekjempe, motsette seg.

antarctic [æntˈɑ:ktɪk] *adj* antarktisk.

antecedent [ˌæntɪˈsi:dənt] **I** *adj* forut (*to* for); forutgående; **II** *sb* **1** forutgående begivenhet *etc*; *fl* forhistorie; bakgrunn; **2** for|gjenger, -løper.

antedate [ˌæntɪ'deɪt] *vt* forutdatere; *fig* foregripe. **antediluvian** [ˌæntɪdɪ'lu:vɪən] **1** *adj* fra før syndfloden; *slang* fossil (dvs håpløst gammeldags); **2** *sb slang* fossil (dvs håpløst gammeldags person).

antenna [æn'tenə] *sb* **1** antenne; **2** følehorn.

anterior [æn'tɪərɪə] *adj* forut (*to* for); forutgående, tidligere.

anteroom ['æntɪrʊm] *sb* forværelse.

anthem ['ænθəm] *sb* hymne, salme.

ant-hill ['ænthɪl] *sb* maurtue.

antibiotic [ˌæntɪbaɪ'ɒtɪk] **1** *adj* antibiotisk; **2** *sb* antibiotikum.

anticipate [æn'tɪsɪpeɪt] *vt* **1** foregripe, komme i forkjøpet; *fig* ta på forskudd; **2** forutse; forvente; **3** glede seg/se frem til. **anticipation** [ænˌtɪsɪ'peɪʃn] *sb* foregripelse *etc*; forventning; *in* ~ på forhånd. **anticipatory** [æn'tɪsɪpeɪtərɪ] *adj* foregripende; forhånds-, på forhånd; forventningsfull.

antics ['æntɪks] *sb fl* ablegøyer, sprell.

antidote ['æntɪdəut] *sb* motgift.

anti|-freeze (solution) *sb petro* frostvæske. ~ **-knock (agent, component, compound)** *sb petro* antibankemiddel.

antipathy [æn'tɪpəθɪ] *sb* antipati.

antipodes [æn'tɪpədi:z] *sb fl* antipoder.

antiquarian [ˌæntɪ'kweərɪən] **I** *adj* **1** old-; oldsaks-; oldtids-; **2** antikvar-; **II** *sb* **1** oldgransker; oldsakssamler; **2** antikvar(bokhandler). **antiquary** ['æntɪkwərɪ] *sb* **1** antikvitetshandler; **2** antikvitetssamler. **antiquated** ['æntɪkweɪtɪd] *adj* foreldet, gammeldags; antikvert. **antique** [æn'ti:k] **I** *adj* **1** antikk; **2** foreldet, gammel; **II** *sb* **1** antikvitet; **2** oldtidslevning. **antiquity** [æn'tɪkwətɪ] *sb* **1** antikken; **2** oldsak; *fl også* antikviteter; fortidslevninger.

antler ['æntlə] *sb* gevir, (hjorte)horn.

anvil ['ænvɪl] *sb* ambolt.

anxiety [æŋ'zaɪətɪ] *sb* **1** engstelse, uro; frykt; **2** bekymring; **3** iver. **anxious** ['æŋkʃəs] *adj* **1** engstelig/urolig (*about* for); **2** bekymret (*about* for/over); **3** ivrig (*that/to* etter å); oppsatt/spent (*to* på å).

any [enɪ] **I** *adj, pron* **1** (ikke) noe/noen; (uten) noe/noen; **2** noe/noen (som helst); hva (hvem, hvilken, hvilket) som helst; **3** alle; enhver, ethvert; **4** eventuell(e), eventuelt; **II** *adv* **1** noe; *do you feel ~ better* føler du deg (noe) bedre; **2** det minste; det grann/spor. **anybody** ['enɪˌbɒdɪ] *pron* hvem som helst; noen som helst; alle (og enhver). **anyhow** ['enɪhaʊ] *adv* **1** på noen som helst måte; **2** i hvert fall; likevel, uansett; **3** tilfeldig; skjødesløst. **anyone** ['enɪwʌn] = *anybody*. **anything** ['enɪθɪŋ] *pron* **1** hva som helst; ~ *but* alt annet enn; *like* ~ som bare det; **2** noe (som helst). **anyway** ['enɪweɪ] = *anyhow*. **anywhere** ['enɪweə] *adv* **1** hvor som helst; overalt; **2** noesteds.

apace [ə'peɪs] *adv* (meget) raskt.

apart [ə'pɑ:t] *adv* **1** unna; til side; **2** fra hverandre; ~ *from* bortsett fra. **apartment** [ə'pɑ:tmənt] *sb* **1** rom, værelse; *fl også* leilighet; **2** *US* leilighet; ~ *building/house* leiegård.

apathetic [ˌæpə'θetɪk] *adj* apatisk. **apathy** ['æpəθɪ] *sb* apati, likegyldighet.

ape [eɪp] **1** *sb* (menneske)ape; *fig* apekatt; **2** *vi* ape/herme etter.

aperture ['æpətjʊə] *sb* åpning; hull; spalte, sprekk; *foto* blender(åpning).

apex ['eɪpeks] *sb* spiss, topp.

apiece [ə'pi:s] *adv* for hver, for stykket.

apocalypse [ə'pɒkəlɪps] *sb* apokalypse, dommedag. **apocalyptic** [əˌpɒkə'lɪptɪk] *adj* **1** apokalyptisk, dommedags-; **2** gåtefull.

apologetic [əˌpɒlə'dʒetɪk] *adj* **1** unnskyldende; **2** forsvars-. **apologize** [ə'pɒlədʒaɪz] *vi* be om unnskyldning. **apology** [ə'pɒlədʒɪ] *sb* **1** unnskyldning; **2** forsvar; **3** (dårlig) erstatning/unnskyldning; surrogat.

apostle [ə'pɒsl] *sb* apostel. **apostolic** [ˌæpə'stɒlɪk] *adj* apostolisk.

apostrophe [ə'pɒstrəfɪ] *sb* apostrof.

appal [ə'pɔ:l] *vt* forferde, slå med skrekk. **appalling** [ə'pɔ:lɪŋ] *adj* forferdelig, skrekkelig.

apparatus [ˌæpə'reɪtəs] *sb* **1** apparat; **2** innretning; **3** utstyr; redskaper *fl*; **4** system.

apparel [ə'pærəl] **1** *sb* antrekk, drakt; klær; **2** *vt* (i)kle, utstyre.

apparent [ə'pærənt] *adj* **1** (klart) synlig; **2** tydelig, åpenbar; **3** øyensynlig; tilsynelatende. **apparition** [ˌæpə'rɪʃn] *sb* **1** tilsynekomst; **2** fremtoning, skikkelse; **3** gjenferd, spøkelse; (ånde)syn.

appeal [ə'pi:l] **I** *sb* **1** (innstendig) bønn; *også jur* anke, appell; **2** tiltrekning (og tiltrekningskraft); **II** *vi* **1** appellere/henvende seg (*to* til); ~ *to the country* skrive ut (ny)valg; **2** be innstendig (*for* om); **3** *især jur* anke, appellere; **4** ~ *to* tiltale; virke tiltalende/tiltrekkende på.

appear [ə'pɪə] *vi* **1** komme til syne, vise seg; **2** møte frem; **3** opptre (på scene etc); **4** komme ut (om bøker etc); **5** se ut som. **appearance** [ə'pɪərəns] *sb* **1** tilsynekomst; **2** fremmøte; **3** opptreden; **4** utseende, ytre.

appease [ə'pi:z] *vt* **1** forsone; **2** berolige; dempe, stagge; bilegge. **appeasement** [ə'pi:zmənt] *sb* forsoning *etc*.

append [ə'pend] *vt* **1** tilføye; **2** henge på. **appendage** [ə'pendɪdʒ] *sb* **1** vedheng; **2** tilbehør. **appendicitis** [əˌpendɪ'saɪtɪs] *sb* blindtarmsbetennelse. **appendix** [ə'pendɪks] *sh* **1** til|føyelse, -legg; **2** vedheng; *med* blindtarm.

appertain [ˌæpə'teɪn] *vi:* ~ *to* **1** høre med til; **2** angå, vedrøre; gjelde/passe for.

appetite ['æpɪtaɪt] *sb* appetitt. **appetizer** ['æpɪtaɪzə] *sb* appetittvekker. **appetizing** ['æpɪtaɪzɪŋ] *adj* appetittvekkende; delikat, lekker.

applaud [ə'plɔ:d] *vb* **1** applaudere, klappe for; **2** bifalle, godkjenne. **applause** [ə'plɔ:z] *sb* applaus, bifall.

apple ['æpl] *sb* eple. **apple-pie** ['æpl,paɪ] *sb* eplekake; *in ~-pie order* i (sin) skjønneste orden.

appliance [ə'plaɪəns] *sb* **1** anvendelse, bruk; **2** (hjelpe)middel; *fl også* redskaper, verktøy; utstyr.

applicability [,æplɪkə'bɪlətɪ] *sb* anvendelighet *etc*. **applicable** ['æplɪkəbl] *adj* anvendelig/brukbar (*to* på/til). **applicant** ['æplɪkənt] *sb* (an)søker (*for* på/til); kandidat (*for* til). **application** [,æplɪ'keɪʃn] *sb* **1** anvendelse, bruk; praktisering; påføring (av maling etc); strøk; *hot ~s* varme omslag; **2** arbeidsomhet, flid; **3** ansøkning/søknad (*for* om/på); anmodning (*for* om). **application | language** *sb data* funksjonsspråk. **~ program** *sb data* brukerprogram. **~ software** *sb data* brukerprogramvare.

apply [ə'plaɪ] *vb* **1** anvende/bruke (*to* på); legge (smøre, stryke etc) på; *~ oneself to* gjøre seg flid med; **2** søke (*for* om/på); **3** *~ to* gjelde/passe for.

appoint [ə'pɔɪnt] *vt* **1** bestemme, fastsette; **2** peke ut; **3** velge; ansette, utnevne; **4** anvise, forordne. **appointment** [ə'pɔɪntmənt] *sb* **1** avtale; **2** ansettelse, utnevnelse; **3** stilling; **4** *fl* utstyr.

apportion [ə'pɔ:ʃn] *vt* fordele (likt), porsjonere ut; tildele.

apposite ['æpəuzɪt] *adj* rammende, treffende.

appraisal [ə'preɪzl] *sb* vurdering *etc*. **appraise** [ə'preɪz] *vt* vurdere; taksere, verdsette; evaluere.

appreciable [ə'pri:ʃəbl] *adj* merkbar. **appreciate** [ə'pri:ʃɪeɪt] *vb* **1** forstå (rett), være klar over; **2** verdsette; **3** sette pris på, være takknemlig for; **4** stige (i verdi). **appreciation** [ə,pri:ʃɪ'eɪʃn] *sb* forståelse *etc*. **appreciative** [ə'pri:ʃɪətɪv] *adj* **1** anerkjennende; forståelsesfull; **2** takknemlig.

apprehend [,æprɪ'hend] *vt* **1** (opp)fatte; begripe, forstå; **2** anta, gå ut fra; **3** frykte (for); **4** anholde, (på)gripe; arrestere. **apprehension** [,æprɪ'henʃn] *sb* **1** oppfatning *etc*; fatteevne; **2** engstelse, frykt; **3** anholdelse *etc*. **apprehensiv** [,æprɪ'hensɪv] *adj* **1** engstelig, fryktsom; urolig; **2** oppvakt.

apprentice [ə'prentɪs] **I** *sb* lærling; lære|gutt, -pike; **II** *vt* **1** sette i lære (*to* hos); **2** ta i lære. **apprenticeship** [ə'prentɪʃɪp] *sb* lære(tid).

apprise [ə'praɪz] *vt* underrette.

approach [ə'prəutʃ] **I** *sb* **1** tilnærming; *fig* fremgangsmåte; holdning, innstilling; *fl* (utilbørlige) tilnærmelser; **2** adgang; innkjørsel, innseiling *etc*; **II** *vb* **1** nærme seg; **2** bringe nærmere; **3** henvende seg til.

approbate ['æprəubeɪt] *US = approve*. **approbation** [,æprəu'beɪʃn] *sb* godkjenning.

appropriate I [ə'prəuprɪət] *adj* passende, tilbørlig; **II** [ə'prəuprɪeɪt] *vt* **1** tilegne seg; **2** tilvende seg; **3** bevilge, sette av (midler). **appropriation** [ə,prəuprɪ'eɪʃn] *sb* tilegnelse *etc*.

approval [ə'pru:vl] *sb* godkjenning *etc*. **approve** [ə'pru:v] *vb (~ of)* godkjenne; gå med på; bifalle.

approximate 1 [ə'prɒksɪmət] *adj* omtrentlig, tilnærmet; nær (*to* opp til); **2** [ə'prɒksɪmeɪt] *vb* nærme (seg). **approximately** [ə'prɒksɪmətlɪ] *adv* tilnærmelsesvis, tilnærmet; cirka, omtrent; om lag.

apricot ['eɪprɪkɒt] *sb* aprikos.

April ['eɪprəl] april. **April Fool** *sb* aprilsnarr.

apron ['eɪprən] *sb* **1** forkle; **2** skvettlær; **3** transportbånd; **4** oppstillingsplass (for fly).

apt [æpt] *adj* **1** slående, treffende; **2** passende, skikket; **3** flink (*at* til); **4** tilbøyelig (*to* til); utsatt (*to* for); *be ~ to* ha lett for (å). **aptitude** ['æptɪtju:d] *sb* **1** anlegg; dyktighet; **2** tilbøyelighet.

aquatic [ə'kwætɪk] **I** *adj* vann-; **II** *sb* **1** vanndyr, vannplante; **2** *fl* vannsport.

aquiline ['ækwɪlaɪn] *adj* ørne-.

arable ['ærəbl] *adj* **1** dyrkbar; **2** (opp)dyrket.

arbiter ['ɑ:bɪtə] *sb* **1** = *arbitrator*; **2** herre, hersker. **arbitrary** ['ɑ:bɪtrərɪ] *adj* **1** egenmektig, vilkårlig; **2** skjønnsmessig. **arbitrate** ['ɑ:bɪtreɪt] *vb* **1** megle; **2** avgjøre/dømme (ved voldgift). **arbitration** [,ɑ:bɪ'treɪʃn] *sb* voldgift (og voldgifts|avgjørelse, -dom); megling. **arbitrator** ['ɑ:bɪtreɪtə] *sb* voldgifts|dommer, -mann; megler, oppmann.

arbour ['ɑ:bə] *sb* lysthus.

arc [ɑ:k] *sb* (sirkel)bue.

arcade [ɑ:'keɪd] *sb* **1** arkade, buegang; **2** (innelukket) butikk|arkade, -gate; **3** ≈ (automat)spillehall.

arch [ɑ:tʃ] **A** *adj* skøyeraktig; **B 1** *sb (~way)* bue(gang), hvelv(ing); **2** *vb* bue/krumme (seg); hvelve (seg); **C** *(arch-) pref* erke-, hoved-.

archaic [ɑ:'keɪɪk] *adj* arkaisk; foreldet; gammelmodig.

arch|bishop [,ɑ:tʃ'bɪʃəp] *sb* erkebiskop. **~-enemy** [,ɑ:tʃ'enɪmɪ] *sb* erkefiende.

archer ['ɑ:tʃə] *sb* bueskytter. **archery** ['ɑ:tʃərɪ] *sb* bueskyting.

architect ['ɑ:kɪtekt] *sb* arkitekt. **architectonic** [,ɑ:kɪtek'tɒnɪk], **architectural** [,ɑ:kɪ'tektʃərəl] *adj* arkitektonisk. **architecture** ['ɑ:kɪtektʃə] *sb* arkitektur.

archives ['ɑ:kaɪvz] *sb fl* arkiv. **archivist** ['ɑ:kɪvɪst] *sb* arkivar.

arch-priest [,ɑ:tʃ'pri:st] *sb* overprest, yppersteprest.

archway ['ɑ:tʃweɪ] *sb* buegang, hvelv(ing).

Arctic ['ɑ:ktɪk] *adj* **1** arktisk; **2** *(med liten forbokstav)* iskald.

ardent ['ɑ:dənt] *adj* brennende; *fig også* lidenskapelig. **ardour** ['ɑ:də] *sb* glød, lidenskap.

arduous ['ɑ:djuəs] *adj* **1** anstrengende; vanskelig; **2** bratt.

area ['eərɪə] *sb* **1** *a)* område; *b) data* dataområde, lagerområde; **2** areal, flate(innhold); **3** lysgrav (især større, med inngang til kjelleretasje).

arena [ə'ri:nə] *sb* **1** scene, skueplass; **2** arena, kampplass.

argue ['ɑ:gju:] *vb* **1** argumentere; *~ away* bortforklare; *~ into* overtale til (å); **2** hevde/påstå (især i diskusjon); **3** bestride; **4** diskutere; krangle, trette. **argument** ['ɑ:gjumənt] *sb* **1** argument (også *data*); argumentering, bevis(føring); **2** påstand, resonnement;

3 diskusjon; krangel *etc*; **4** (innholds)sammendrag. **argumentation** [ˌɑ:gjʊmən'teɪʃn] *sb* argumentering *etc*; argumentasjon.

arid ['ærɪd] *adj* tørr; *fig også* gold. **aridity** [ə'rɪdətɪ] *sb* tørrhet.

aright [ə'raɪt] *adv* rett, riktig.

arise [ə'raɪz] *vi* **1** dukke opp, komme til syne; vise seg; ~ *from* komme/oppstå av; **2** reise seg; stå opp.

aristocracy [ˌærɪ'stɒkrəsɪ] *sb* **1** aristokrati, overklasse; **2** overklassestyre. **aristocrat** ['ærɪstəkræt] *sb* aristokrat. **aristocratic** [ˌærɪstə'krætɪk] *adj* aristokratisk.

arithmetic 1 *adj* [ˌærɪθ'metɪk] *især data* = *arithmetical*; **2** *sb* [ə'rɪθmətɪk] aritmetikk, regning. **arithmetical** [ˌærɪθ'metɪkl] *adj* aritmetisk, regne-. **arithmetic check** *sb data* aritmetisk kontroll.

arm [ɑ:m] **A** *sb* **1** arm; **2** erme; **3** gren, utløper; **B I** *sb* (især *fl*) våpen; *firearms* skytevåpen; *small-arms* håndvåpen; **II** *vb* **1** væpne (seg); ruste (opp); **2** armere, pansre.

armament ['ɑ:məmənt] *sb* **1** krigs|materiell, -utstyr; tungt skyts; **2** (opp)rustning.

arm|chair *sb* lenestol. **~ful** *sb* fange.

armistice ['ɑ:mɪstɪs] *sb* våpenstillstand.

armlet ['ɑ:mlɪt] *sb* armbind.

armour ['ɑ:mə] *sb* **1** *(suit of ~)* rustning; **2** armering, pansring; **3** panser(våpen) (dvs stridsvogner etc). **armoured** ['ɑ:məd] *adj* pansret, panser-. **armourer** ['ɑ:mərə] *sb* børsemaker; våpen|fabrikant, -smed. **armoury** ['ɑ:mərɪ] *sb* **1** (våpen)arsenal; **2** våpen|fabrikk, -smie.

armpit ['ɑ:mpɪt] *sb* armhule. **arm's length price** *sb petro* markedspris.

army ['ɑ:mɪ] *sb* **1** armé, hær; **2** hærskare.

aroma [ə'rəʊmə] *sb* aroma. **aromatic** [ˌærəʊ'mætɪk] *adj* aromatisk.

around [ə'raʊnd] *adv, prep* **1** rundt (omkring); **2** *US* i nærheten.

arouse [ə'raʊz] *vt* vekke (opp).

arraign [ə'reɪn] *vt* **1** anklage; **2** stevne (for retten).

arrange [ə'reɪndʒ] *vb* **1** arrangere, ordne; **2** forberede, planlegge; **3** avtale, komme til enighet; **4** bilegge. **arrangement** [ə'reɪndʒmənt] *sb* arrangering *etc*; arrangement.

arrant ['ærənt] *adj* notorisk, toppmålt.

array [ə'reɪ] **I** *sb* **1** fylking/oppstilling (til kamp); (slag)orden; **2** mønstring, samling; **3** antrekk, drakt; **4** antenne; **5** *data* datatabell; **II** *vt* **1** fylke/stille opp (til kamp); mobilisere; **2** (i)kle; pynte. **array | pitch** *sb data* linjeavstand. **~ processor** *sb data* serieprosessor.

arrears [ə'rɪəz] *sb fl* gjeld, rest(anser); ~ *of work* ugjort arbeid (som venter på en); *in ~ with* til rest med.

arrest [ə'rest] **I** *sb* **1** arrestasjon; **2** beslag(leggelse); **3** stans(ing), stopp; **II** *vt* **1** arrestere; **2** *fig* fengsle; fange (oppmerksomheten etc); **3** hemme, hindre; stanse, stoppe. **arresting** [ə'restɪŋ] *adj* fengslende; frapperende, slående.

arrival [ə'raɪvl] *sb* **1** ankomst; *bokl* komme; **2** (ny)ankommende, nykommer; **3** ankommet gods *etc*.

arrive [ə'raɪv] *vb* **1** (an)komme, komme (frem (*at/in* til); **3** nå/rekke (frem); *fig* nå frem, slå igjennom.

arrogance ['ærəgəns] *sb* arroganse *etc*. **arrogant** ['ærəgənt] *adj* arrogant; hoven, overlegen.

arrow ['ærəʊ] *sb* pil. **arrow|head** *sb* pilspiss. **~ key** *sb data* piltast.

arson [ɑ:sn] *sb* brannstiftelse; mordbrann.

art [ɑ:t] *sb* **1** kunst (og kunstart); *applied ~* brukskunst; **2** kunstgrep; list, påfunn; **3** menneskeverk [i motsetning til naturprodukt].

arterial [ɑ:'tɪərɪəl] *adj* **1** pulsåre-; **2** hoved-. **artery** ['ɑ:tərɪ] *sb* **1** arterie, pulsåre; **2** gjennomfartsvei, hovedtrafikkåre.

artful ['ɑ:tfʊl] *adj* listig, slu.

arthritic [ɑ:'θrɪtɪk] *adj* giktisk. **arthritis** [ɑ:'θraɪtɪs] *sb* (ledd)gikt.

article ['ɑ:tɪkl] **I** *sb* **1** artikkel, vare; **2** artikkel (i avis etc); **3** artikkel (dvs paragraf, post, punkt etc); *fl også* vedtekter; (lærling)kontrakt; **4** *gram* artikkel; **II** *vt* **1** anføre punkt for punkt; **2** sette i lære.

articulate I [ɑ:'tɪkjʊlət] *adj* **1** artikulert, tydelig (uttalt); **2** veltalende; **3** leddet, leddelt; **II** [ɑ:'tɪkjʊleɪt] *vb* **1** artikulere, snakke tydelig; **2** forbinde med ledd. **articulation** [ɑ:ˌtɪkjʊ'leɪʃn] *sb* artikulering *etc*; artikulasjon.

artifice ['ɑ:tɪfɪs] *sb* **1** list, snedighet; **2** knep, lureri; **3** ferdighet. **artificial** [ˌɑ:tɪ'fɪʃl] *adj* **1** kunstig; **2** kunslet, tilgjort. **artificial crude** *sb petro* syntetisk råolje.

artillery [ɑ:'tɪlərɪ] *sb* artilleri.

artisan [ˌɑ:tɪ'zæn] *sb* håndverker.

artist ['ɑ:tɪst] *sb* (billed)kunstner. **artiste** [ɑ:'ti:st] *sb* artist. **artistic** [ɑ:'tɪstɪk] *adj* artistisk, kunstnerisk.

artless ['ɑ:tlɪs] *adj* **1** enkel, naturlig; **2** endefrem, liketil.

as [æz] **I** *adv* (like)så, ~ *much* såpass; *I thought ~ much* jeg tenkte/kunne tenke meg det; ~ *well* også (jf II/4); ~ *yet* ennå; **II** *konj* **1** da; idet, mens; **2** da, ettersom, siden; **3** etter (hvert) som; **4** som; ~ *if/though* som om; ~ *well* ~ så vel som; ~ *it were* faktisk, så å si; ~ *you were! (mil)* (på stedet) hvil! **5** ~ *for/to*, ~ *regards* hva angår; med hensyn til; *so ~ to* for å; slik at; **III** *pron* som; *such ~* slik som.

asbestos [æz'bestəs] *sb* asbest.

ascend [ə'send] *vb* **1** gå opp, stige; **2** gå/klatre (oppover); **3** bestige. **ascend|ancy, ~ency** [ə'sendənsɪ] *sb* makt, (over)herredømme. **ascension** [ə'senʃn] *sb* oppstigning; *især rel* himmelfart. **ascent** [ə'sent] *sb* **1** motbakke, stigning; **2** oppstigning.

ascertain [ˌæsə'teɪn] *vt* **1** finne ut; **2** forvisse seg om; fastslå.

ascetic [ə'setɪk] **1** *adj* asketisk; ytterst enkel og nøysom; **2** *sb* asket. **asceticism** [ə'setɪsɪzəm] *sb* askese.

ascribe [ə'skraɪb] *vt* til|legge, -skrive; henføre (*to* til).

ash [æʃ] *sb* **A** ask; **B 1** aske (dvs bestemt slags); *cigar* ~ sigaraske; **2** *fl a)* aske (dvs generelt); *the house was burnt to ~es* huset brant ned til aske; *b)* aske, støv (dvs jordiske levninger).

ashamed [ə'ʃeɪmd] *adj* skamfull (*of* over).

ash-can *sb US* søppelbøtte.

ashen ['æʃən] *adj* **A** aske(tres)-; **B** aske-, askegrå.

ashore [ə'ʃɔ:] *adv* **1** i land; **2** på grunn.

ash|-pan *sb* askeskuffe. **~-tray** *sb* askebeger.

aside [ə'saɪd] **I** *adv* **1** til side; **2** avsides; ~ *from* bortsett fra; **II** *sb* avsides replikk (i skuespill).

ask [ɑ:sk] *vb* **1** spørre (om); ~ *about* forhøre seg/spørre om; ~ *if* spørre om; **2** be (om); ~ *for* be om (å få); **3** forlange/kreve (å få); **4** invitere; *dgl* be.

askance [ə'skæns] *adv* på skjeve; *look* ~ *(at)* skotte/*fig* se skjevt (på/til).

askew [ə'skju:] *adj, adv* skjev(t); på skjeve (skrå, snei etc); *look* ~ skjele.

aslant [ə'slɑ:nt] **1** *adv* skjevt; på skjeve (skrå, snei etc); **2** på skrå over.

asleep [ə'sli:p] *adj, adv* i søvn, sovende; *be* ~ sove; *fall* ~ falle i søvn, sovne.

asparagus [ə'spærəgəs] *sb* asparges.

aspect ['æspekt] *sb* **1** utseende; **2** (fremtids)utsikt; (utviklings)mulighet; **3** side (av sak); **4** beliggenhet.

aspen ['æspən] *sb* asp.

asperity [ə'sperətɪ] *sb* **1** barskhet; **2** strenghet.

aspersion [ə'spɜ:ʃn] *sb* bakvaskelse.

asphalt ['æsfælt] **1** *sb* asfalt; **2** *vb* asfaltere. **asphalt enamel** *sb petro* asfaltbelegg.

asphyxiate [əs'fɪksɪeɪt] *vt* kvele (ved mangel på oksygen); *ofte* røykforgifte; *~d (stundom)* skinndød. **asphyxiation** [əs,fɪksɪ'eɪʃn] *sb* kvelning, kvelningsdød.

aspirant [ə'spaɪərənt] *sb* aspirant, kandidat, søker. **aspiration** [,æspə'reɪʃn] *sb* **1** (inn)ånding; pusting; **2** lengsel; **3** ambisjon, streben. **aspire** [ə'spaɪə] *vi* **1** hige (strebe, trakte etc) etter (å); **2** stige. **aspiring** [ə'spaɪərɪŋ] *adj* ærgjerrig.

ass [æs] *sb* esel; *fig* [*ofte uttalt* ɑ:s] tosk.

assail [ə'seɪl] *vt* **1** angripe, overfalle; **2** plage. **assailant** [ə'seɪlənt] *sb* angriper, overfalls|kvinne, -mann.

assassin [ə'sæsɪn] *sb* (snik)morder. **assassinate** [ə'sæsɪneɪt] *vt* (snik)myrde. **assassination** [ə,sæsɪ'neɪʃn] *sb* (snik)mord.

assault [ə'sɔ:lt] **I** *sb* **1** (storm)angrep; **2** *jur (~ and battery)* (kriminelt) overfall; **II** *vt* angripe, overfalle; storme.

assay [ə'seɪ] **I** *sb* (analyse)prøve; **II** *vt* **1** prøve (finheten av metall); **2** forsøke.

assemblage [ə'semblɪdʒ] *sb* **1** (for)samling; **2** montering. **assemble** [ə'sembl] *vb* **1** (for)samles, møtes; komme/kalle sammen; **2** montere, sette sammen; **3** *data* assemblere. **assembler** [ə'semblə] *sb data* assembler. **assembly** [ə'semblɪ] *sb* **1** (for)samling; **2** møte; **3** montering; montasje. **assembly | language** *sb data* assemblerspråk. **~ line** *sb* samlebånd. **~ phase** *sb data* assembleringstrinn. **~ program** *sb data* assembler.

assent [ə'sent] **1** *sb* sanksjon; godkjenning, samtykke; **2** *vi* samtykke (*to* i); bifalle, godkjenne.

assert [ə'sɜ:t] *vt* **1** påstå; **2** forfekte, hevde; ~ *oneself* gjøre seg gjeldende. **assertion** [ə'sɜ:ʃn] *sb* påstand *etc.* **assertive** [ə'sɜ:tɪv] *adj* påståelig; (selv)sikker.

assess [ə'ses] *vt* **1** taksere, verdsette; **2** vurdere; **3** beskatte; **4** pålegge (især skatt). **assessment** [ə'sesmənt] *sb* taksering *etc.*

asset ['æset] *sb* **1** fordel, gode; aktivum; verdifull egenskap; **2** eiendom; *~s and liabilities* aktiva og passiva.

assiduity [,æsɪ'dju:ətɪ] *sb* **1** flid; **2** oppmerksomhet, påpasselighet. **assiduous** [ə'sɪdjuəs] *adj* arbeidsom, flittig; iherdig.

assign [ə'saɪn] *vt* **1** anvise, tildele; sette av (*to* til); *data* tilordne; **2** overdra; **3** beramme, fastsette (tid, sted); **4** oppnevne, utpeke; **5** anføre (angi, oppgi etc som grunn). **assignation** [,æsɪg'neɪʃn] *sb* **1** anvisning; **2** overdragelse; **3** avtale; (stevne)møte. **assignment** [ə'saɪnmənt] *sb* **1** anvisning, tildeling; **2** overdragelse (og overdragelsesdokument); **3** angivelse (av grunn); **4** oppdrag; (skole)lekse; **5** utnevnelse.

assimilate [ə'sɪmɪleɪt] *vb* **1** assimilere(s), oppta(s); gå opp i; **2** bli/gjøre lik (*to/with* med). **assimilation** [ə,sɪmɪ'leɪʃn] *sb* assimilering *etc*; assimilasjon.

assist [ə'sɪst] *vb* assistere, hjelpe; *ofte* være med på. **assistance** [ə'sɪstəns] *sb* assistanse, hjelp. **assistant** [ə'sɪstənt] **1** *adj* assisterende; hjelpe-, med-; **2** *sb* assistent, (med)hjelper. **assistant driller** *sb petro* boreassistent.

assizes [ə'saɪzɪz] *sb fl* ≈ (distrikts)|domstoler, -ting; (lokale) rettsmøter satt av High Court.

associate I [ə'səuʃɪət] **1** *adj* assosiert, tilknyttet; med-; **2** *sb* kollega, kompanjong; medlem; **II** [ə'səuʃɪeɪt] *vb* **1** assosiere, forbinde; **2** forene(s), slutte (seg) sammen; **3** ~ *with* omgås/være sammen med. **association** [ə,səusɪ'eɪʃn] *sb* **1** (idé)assosiasjon; **2** omgang, samvær; **3** forbund, forening; sammenslutning.

assorted [ə'sɔ:tɪd] *adj* **1** assortert, blandet; **2** tilpasset; som passer sammen. **assortment** [ə'sɔ:tmənt] *sb* **1** sortering; **2** assortiment, utvalg.

assume [ə'sju:m] *vt* **1** anta, formode, gå ut fra; **2** foregi, late som; *an ~d look* en påtatt mine; **3** overta, påta seg. **assuming** [ə'sju:mɪŋ] *adj* **1** innbilsk; **2** anmassende; overmodig. **assumption** [ə'sʌmpʃn] *sb* antakelse *etc.*

assurance [ə'ʃuərəns] *sb* **1** forvissning, sikkerhet; **2** (selv)sikkerhet; **3** forsikring, løfte; **4** (livs)forsikring (jf *insurance*). **assure** [ə'ʃuə] *vt* **1** forsikre; garantere; **2** (livs)forsikre.

aster ['æstə] *sb* asters.

astern [ə'stɜ:n] *adv* akterut; akterover.

asthma ['æsmə] *sb* astma. **asthmatic** [æs'mætɪk] **1** *adj* astmatisk; **2** *sb* astmatiker.

astir [ə'stɜ:] *adv* **1** på ferde; **2** i vigør.

astonish [ə'stɒnɪʃ] *vt* forbause (sterkt), forbløffe. **astonishment** [ə'stɒnɪʃmənt] *sb* (stor) forbauselse.

astound [ə'staʊnd] *vt* sjokkere.

astraddle [ə'strædl] *adj, adv* overskrevs.

astray [ə'streɪ] *adj, adv* på villspor/villstrå.

astride [ə'straɪd] **1** *adv* overskrevs; på tvers; **2** *prep* skrevs over; tvers over.

astute [ə'stju:t] *adj* **1** gløgg, skarp(sindig); **2** slu.

asunder [ə'sʌndə] *adv* **1** atskilt, fra hverandre; **2** i stykker.

asylum [ə'saɪləm] *sb* **1** asyl; **2** *a)* fristed, tilfluktssted; *b)* (politisk) asyl.

at [æt] *prep* **I** *om retning, sted etc* **1** på; i (om småsteder); hos, ved; ~ *home* hjemme; **2** mot, på, til (dvs i retning av); *dgl* etter; *look* ~ *me* se på meg; *he threw a stone* ~ *the dog* han kastet en stein etter hunden; **II** *om måte, tilstand etc* **1** i, ved (dvs opptatt av etc); ~ *war* i krig; **2** i, med; ~ *a single leap* med ett sprang/et eneste sprang; **3** ~ *a moment's notice* på et øyeblikks varsel; ~ *the request/suggestion of* etter anmodning/forslag av; ~ *the sight of* ved synet av; **4** ~ *all* i det hele tatt; ~ *best* i beste fall; ~ *worst* i verste fall; **III** *om tid og rekkefølge* i, ved; ~ *first* først, til å begynne med; ~ *last* til slutt; ~ *long last* endelig, omsider; ~ *least* minst, i det minste; ~ *length* (1) omsider; (2) omstendelig, utførlig; ~ *once* straks, med en gang; ~ *the age of* i en alder av.

athlete ['æθli:t] *sb* **1** (fri)idretts|kvinne, -mann; **2** atlet, kraftkar. **athletic** [æθ'letɪk] **I** *adj* **1** (fri)idretts-; **2** atletisk, kraftig, muskuløs; **II** *sb fl* (fri)idrett; gymnastikk.

atmosphere ['ætməsfɪə] *sb* atmosfære (også *fig*); luft. **atmospheric** ['ætməs'ferɪk] **1** *adj* atmosfærisk, luft-; **2** *sb fl* radiostøy; *dgl* forstyrrelser.

atom ['ætəm] *sb* atom; *fig også* fnugg, snev. **atomic** [ə'tɒmɪk] *adj* atomisk, atom-. **atomize** ['ætəmaɪz] *vt* **1** pulverisere; **2** forstøve. **atomizer** ['ætəmaɪzə] *sb* forstøver, sprayflaske.

atone [ə'təʊn] *vi* sone; bøte/lide (*for* for).

atrocious [ə'trəʊʃəs] *adj* **1** grusom; **2** *dgl* fæl, skrekkelig. **atrocity** [ə'trɒsətɪ] *sb* grusomhet *etc*.

attaboy ['ætəbɔɪ] *interj US* bravo! heia!

attach [ə'tætʃ] *vb* **1** feste (*to* på, til); ~ *oneself to* slutte seg til; **2** hefte/klebe (*to* fast på/til); **3** føye/knytte (*to* til); ~ *importance to* tillegge betydning; **4** beslaglegge, båndlegge. **attaché** [ə'tæʃeɪ] *sb* attaché. **attaché case** [ə'tæʃɪkeɪs] *sb* dokumentmappe.

attachment [ə'tætʃmənt] *sb* **1** fastgjøring/festing *etc*; tilknytning; *fig* hengivenhet; **2** tilføyelse, tillegg; *fl også* tilbehør, utstyr; **3** beslag(leggelse).

attack [ə'tæk] **I** *sb* angrep, overfall; *fig* (skarp) kritikk; **II** *vt* **1** angripe, overfalle; **2** kritisere skarpt; **3** ta fatt på.

attain [ə'teɪn] *vb* **1** (opp)nå; **2** nå (frem) til. **attainment** [ə'teɪnmənt] *sb* oppnåelse; prestasjon; resultat.

attempt [ə'tempt] **1** *sb* forsøk (*at* på); **2** *vt* forsøke, forsøke seg på.

attend [ə'tend] *vb* **1** møte frem/opp; være til stede; **2** være oppmerksom, høre etter; **3** (~ *to*) betjene, ekspedere; **4** ta seg av; pleie, stelle; **5** ledsage. **attendance** [ə'tendəns] *sb* fremmøte *etc*. **attendant** [ə'tendənt] **I** *adj* **1** tilstedeværende; **2** tjenestegjørende; **3** ledsagende, medfølgende; **II** *sb* **1** tilstedeværende (person); deltaker (i møte etc); **2** oppsynsmann, vakt(mann); **3** tjener; **4** ledsager. **attention** [ə'tenʃn] *sb* oppmerksomhet; ~! giv akt! ~, *please!* pass på! se opp! hør etter! *pay* ~ *to* legge merke til; merke seg. **attention key** *sb data* avbruddstast. **attentive** [ə'tentɪv] *adj* oppmerksom; påpasselig.

attenuate **I** [ə'tenjʊət] *adj* mager, tynn; (av)svekket; **II** [ə'tenjʊeɪt] *vt* **1** gjøre magrere/tynnere; fortynne; **2** dempe, svekke; redusere. **attenuation** [əˌtenjʊ'eɪʃn] *sb især* svekking; *som adj* dempings-, svekkings-.

attest [ə'test] *vb* **1** attestere, bekrefte, bevitne; **2** vise. **attestation** [ˌætə'steɪʃn] *sb* attestering *etc*.

attic ['ætɪk] *sb* kvist, loftsrom.

attire [ə'taɪə] **1** *sb* antrekk, drakt; **2** *vt* (i)kle, utstyre.

attitude ['ætɪtju:d] *sb* **1** holdning; **2** innstilling; **3** positur; *strike an* ~ gjøre seg til.

attorney [ə'tɜ:nɪ] *sb* **1** fullmektig; **2** *US* advokat; *district* ~ statsadvokat; **3** *General Attorney* regjeringsadvokat; *US* justisminister.

attract [ə'trækt] *vt* tiltrekke (seg). **attraction** [ə'trækʃn] *sb* **1** tiltrekning (og tiltrekningskraft); *fig* sjarm; **2** attraksjon. **attractive** [ə'træktɪv] *adj* attraktiv, tiltrekkende.

attribute **1** ['ætrɪbju:t] *sb* attributt, (spesiell) egenskap; *data også* billedattributt; **2** [ə'trɪbju:t] *vt:* ~ *to* henføre til; tillegge, tilskrive. **attribution** [ˌætrɪ'bju:ʃn] *sb* **1** henføring *etc*; **2** attributt.

auburn ['ɔ:bən] *adj* kastanjebrun.

auction ['ɔ:kʃn] **1** *sb* auksjon; **2** *vt* auksjonere. **auctioneer** [ˌɔ:kʃə'nɪə] *sb* auksjonarius.

audacious [ɔ:'deɪʃəs] *adj* **1** dristig, vågal; **2** dumdristig; **3** formastelig, frekk. **audacity** [ɔ:'dæsətɪ] *sb* dristighet *etc*.

audible ['ɔ:dəbl] *adj* hørbar, hørlig. **audience** ['ɔ:dɪəns] *sb* **1** *koll* tilhørere; *ofte* publikum (dvs kino- og teaterpublikum, radiolyttere, fjernsynsseere, lesekrets, tilskuere etc); **2** audiens.

audit ['ɔ:dɪt] **1** *sb* revisjon; **2** *vt* revidere (regnskap). **audition** [ɔ:'dɪʃn] **I** *sb* **1** hørsel; **2** prøve(synging etc før engasjement); **II** *vb* (la) prøvesynge *etc*. **auditor** ['ɔ:dɪtə] *sb* revisor. **auditorium** [ˌɔ:dɪ'tɔ:rɪəm] *sb* auditorium; konsertsal; teatersalong.

auger ['ɔ:gə] *sb* bor, navar.

aught [ɔ:t] *pron, sb* noe (som helst); *for* ~ *I know* for alt (hva) jeg vet.

augment [ɔ:g'mənt] *vb* (for)øke, vokse. **augmentation** [ˌɔ:gmən'teɪʃn] *sb* forøkelse; økning, vekst.

augur ['ɔ:gə] **I** *sb* spåmann, varseltyder; *gml*

augur; **II** *vb* **1** (inn)varsle; tyde på; **2** spå.

august [ɔ:'gʌst] *adj* majestetisk, opphøyd; **2** ærverdig. **auk** [ɔ:k] *sb* alke.

auld [ɔ:ld] *adj skotsk* gammel; ~ *lang syne* (de gode) gamle dager.

aunt, auntie, aunty ['ɑ:nt(ɪ)] *sb* tante.

auspices ['ɔ:spɪsiz] *sb fl* beskyttelse; (beskyttende) ledelse; auspisier. **auspicious** [ɔ:'spɪʃəs] *adj* lovende.

austere [ɒ'stɪə] *adj* **1** barsk, streng; **2** enkel, nøysom. **austerity** [ɒ'sterətɪ] *sb* **1** barskhet *etc*; **2** *som adj* krise-; spare-.

authentic [ɔ:'θentɪk] *adj* ekte, opprinnelig; autentisk.

author ['ɔ:θə] *sb* **1** forfatter; **2** opphavs|kvinne, -mann, -person; autor.

authoritarian [ˌɔ:θɒrɪ'teərɪən] *adj, sb* autoritær (person). **authoritative** [ɔ:'θɒrɪtətɪv] *adj* **1** bydende, myndig; **2** pålitelig; *ofte* ansett; toneangivende; **3** autoritativ, offisiell. **authority** [ɔ:'θɒrətɪ] *sb* **1** autoritet, myndighet; **2** fullmakt; **3** fag|kvinne, -mann, -person; **4** (pålitelig) kilde. **authorization** [ˌɔ:θəraɪ'zeɪʃn] *sb* autorisering *etc*; autorisasjon. **authorize** ['ɔ:θəraɪz] *vt* **1** autorisere, bemyndige; **2** godkjenne.

authorship ['ɔ:θəʃɪp] *sb* forfatterskap.

auto ['ɔ:təʊ] **1** *pref* auto-, egen-, selv-; **2** *sb* = *automobile*.

auto|biography [ˌɔ:təʊbaɪ'ɒgrəfɪ] *sb* selvbiografi. **~graph** ['ɔ:təgrɑ:f] **1** *sb* autograf, navnetrekk; **2** *vt* skrive navnet sitt i/på.

automatic [ˌɔ:tə'mætɪk] **1** *adj* automatisk; *fig* uvilkårlig; **2** *sb* automatpistol. **automatic | check** *sb data* automatisk kontroll. **~ coding** = ~ *programming*. **~ data processing** *sb data* automatisk databehandling. **~ programming** *sb data* automatisk programmering. **~ punch** *sb data* hullemaskin. **~ restart** *sb data* automatisk omstart.

automation [ˌɔ:tə'meɪʃn] *sb* automatisering; automasjon, datastyrt produksjon *etc*.

automaton [ɔ:'tɒmətən] *sb* automat.

automobile ['ɔ:təməʊbi:l] *sb gml* (automo)bil.

autopsy ['ɔ:təpsɪ] *sb* obduksjon.

autumn ['ɔ:təm] *sb* høst. **autumnal** [ɔ:tʌmnəl] *adj* høstlig, høst-.

auxiliary [ɔ:g'zɪlɪərɪ] **I** *adj* hjelpe-, støtte-; **II** *sb* **1** hjelper; *fl også* hjelpetropper; **2** hjelpeverb. **auxiliary storage** *sb data* hjelpelager.

avail [ə'veɪl] **I** *sb* gagn, hjelp, nytte; **II** *vb* **1** hjelpe; (være til) nytte; **2** ~ *oneself of* benytte seg/dra nytte av. **availability** [əˌveɪlə'bɪlətɪ] *sb* tilgjengelighet *etc*. **available** [ə'veɪləbl] *adj* **1** brukbar; **2** disponibel, tilgjengelig; for hånden; **3** til stede. **available time** *sb data* tilgjengelig tid.

avalanche ['ævəlɑ:nʃ] *sb* **1** lavine, snøskred; **2** *fig* flom, lavine, ras, skred.

avarice ['ævərɪs] *sb* griskhet *etc*. **avaricious** [ˌævə'rɪʃəs] *adj* grisk, grådig; gjerrig.

avenge [ə'vendʒ] *vt* hevne. **avenger** [ə'vendʒə] *sb* hevner.

avenue ['ævənju:] *sb* **1** aveny, bred gate; allé; **2** innkjørsel; *fig* adgang, vei.

aver [ə'vɜ:] *vt* bekrefte, forsikre; bevise.

average ['ævərɪdʒ] **I** *adj* **1** gjennomsnittlig; **2** middels; **II** *sb* **1** gjennomsnitt; *on an/the* ~ gjennomsnittlig; **2** *merk, sjø* havari; **III** *vt* **1** beregne gjennomsnittet av; **2** utgjøre gjennomsnittlig/i gjennomsnitt. **average adjuster** *sb merk, sjø* dispasjør.

averse [ə'vɜ:s] *adj* motvillig; ~ *from/to* uvillig/lite tilbøyelig til (å). **aversion** [ə'vɜ:ʃn] *sb* motvilje, uvilje; aversjon; *my (etc) pet* ~ det verste jeg (etc) vet.

avert [ə'vɜ:t] *vt* **1** vende bort; *fig* avlede; **2** avverge, hindre.

aviation [ˌeɪvɪ'eɪʃn] *sb* flyging, luftfart. **aviator** ['eɪvɪeɪtə] *sb* flyger.

avid ['ævɪd] *adj* **1** begjærlig/grådig (*for/of* etter); **2** ivrig. **avidity** [ə'vɪdətɪ] *sb* begjær(lighet), grådighet.

avocation [ˌævəʊ'keɪʃn] *sb* **1** bigeskjeft, fritidssyssel; **2** *(egtl vocation)* kall, yrke.

avoid [ə'vɔɪd] *vt* sky, unngå; holde seg unna. **avoidable** [ə'vɔɪdəbl] *adj* unngåelig, som kan unngås.

avouch [ə'vaʊtʃ] *vb* **1** erklære; påstå; **2** bekrefte; garantere.

avow [ə'vaʊ] *vt* innrømme, vedgå; tilstå. **avowal** [ə'vaʊəl] *sb* innrømmelse *etc*. **avowedly** [ə'vaʊɪdlɪ] *adv* uforbeholdent, åpent.

await [ə'weɪt] *vt* vente (på).

awake [ə'weɪk] **I** *adj* **1** våken; **2** ~ *to (fig)* våken for; klar over; **II** *vb* **1** våkne; ~ *to* våkne opp til; bli klar over; **2** vekke. **awaken** [ə'weɪkn] *vb* **1** våkne; **2** vekke; ~ *to* gjøre klar over. **awakening** [ə'weɪknɪŋ] *sb* (opp)våkning; *fig også* vekkelse.

award [ə'wɔ:d] **I** *sb* **1** belønning, premie; **2** (dommer)avgjørelse; **II** *vt* tildele; bevilge, tilkjenne.

aware [ə'weə] *adj* klar (*of* over); oppmerksom (*of* på). **awareness** [ə'weənɪs] *sb* oppmerksomhet; årvåkenhet.

awash [ə'wɒʃ] *adj* **1** overskyllet (av vann); (beliggende) i vannskorpen; **2** *sjø* synkende.

away [ə'weɪ] **I** *adj:* ~ *match* bortekamp; **II** *adv* **1** borte (og bortreist etc); vekk, unna; **2** bort, vekk; av sted; **3** i vei.

awe [ɔ:] **I** *sb* (ære)frykt; (overveldende) respekt; **II** *vt* **1** fylle med ærefrykt; **2** kue, skremme. **awe|-inspiring** *adj* (ære)fryktinngytende. **~some** *adj* (ære)-fryktinngytende; skremmende. **~-stricken, ~-struck** *adj* fylt/grepet av ærefrykt.

awful ['ɔ:fʊl] *adj* **1** = *awesome*; **2** forferdelig, grusom; **3** *slang* ['ɔ:fl] fæl, reddsom; fryktelig. **awfully** ['ɔ:fʊlɪ] *adv* **1** grusomt *etc*; **2** *slang* ['ɔ:flɪ] fryktelig, veldig; ~ *nice of you* fryktelig snilt av deg.

awhile [ə'waɪl] *adv* (i) en stund.

awkward ['ɔ:kwəd] *adj* **1** keitet, klosset; **2** kjedelig, pinlig; **3** brysom; ubekvem, ubeleilig; tungvint; vanskelig; lei. **awkwardness** ['ɔ:kwədnɪs] *sb* keitethet *etc.*

awl [ɔ:l] *sb* syl.

awning ['ɔ:nɪŋ] *sb* markise, solseil.

awry [ə'raɪ] *adj, adv* skakk; skakt, på skakke; skjev(t); *go ~* gå dårlig/skjevt.

ax(e) [æks] **I** *sb* **1** øks; *have an ~ to grind* (være ute for å) mele sin egen kake; **2** *fig* sparekniv; **II** *vt fig* bruke sparekniven, skjære ned på (utgifter).

axis ['æksɪs] *sb* akse. **axle** ['æksl] *sb* (hjul)aksel.

ay(e) [aɪ] **1** *adv, interj sjø* ja; *~ ~, sir!* javel! [sagt til overordnede ved parering av ordre]; **2** *sb pol etc* jastemme; *the ~s have it* forslaget *etc* er vedtatt.

B

babble ['bæbl] **I** *sb* pludring *etc;* **II** *vb* **1** bable; pludre; **2** plapre (ut med), skravle; **3** klukke (om bekk).

babe [beɪb] = *baby II.*

baboon [bə'bu:n] *sb* bavian.

baby ['beɪbɪ] **I** *adj* **1** baby-, spedbarns-; **2** mini-; **II** *sb* **1** baby, spedbarn; *fig* pattebarn; **2** *US slang* (søt) jente; kjæreste. **baby-sit** *vb* sitte/være barnevakt. **baby-sitter** *sb* barnevakt.

bachelor ['bætʃələ] *sb* **1** ungkar; **2** *Bachelor* person med laveste universitetseksamen (*of Arts* i humanistiske fag; *of Science* i realfag).

back [bæk] **I** *adj* **1** bakre, bak-; **2** rygg-; **II** *adv* **1** igjen, tilbake (om f.eks. vekslepenger); **2** *a few years ~* for noen (få) år siden; **III** *sb* **1** bakside, rygg; **2** *sjø* bakk; **3** back (i fotball); **4** *on the ~ of all that* på toppen av det hele; *get/put up his ~* ergre (irritere el. tirre ham; **IV** *vb* **1** bakke, rygge; *sjø* skåte; *~ down* trekke seg; frafalle krav *etc;* *~ out (of)* trekke seg (ut av); **2** *(~ up)* hjelpe, støtte; *dgl* bakke opp; **3** *~ a horse* holde (dvs satse penger) på en hest; **4** *merk* endossere.

back|bone *sb* ryggrad; *fig* karakterstyrke; *dgl også* tæl. **~fire** **1** *sb* tilbakeslag; **2** *vb* kutte ut (dvs stanse, om motor); *fig* slå feil.

background ['bækgraʊnd] *sb* bakgrunn. **background text** *sb data* ledetekst.

backing ['bækɪŋ] *sb* hjelp, støtte; *dgl* oppbakking.

back|lash *sb* **1** dødgang; **2** floke, vase (på fiskesnøre etc); **3** *fig* motstøt. **~log** *sb* ugjort arbeid (dvs arbeid en er kommet på etterskudd med). **~ number** *sb* gammelt nummer (av avis etc). **~ pay** *sb* etterbetaling. **~slider** *sb* frafallen (person). **~space** *vt data* tilbakeflytte. **~space character** *sb data* tilbaketegn. **~space key** *sb data* tilbaketast. **~stage** *adv* bak scenen; *fig* privat (om skuespillere). **~ talk** *sb* nesevist svar. **~track** *vi* følge spor tilbake. **~up** *sb data* oppbakking, sikkerhetskopiering.

backward [bækwəd] *adj* **1** tilbakeliggende, underutviklet; **2** tilbakestående, evneveik; **3** sky, tilbakeholden; **4** *~ glance* blikk bakover/tilbake. **backward(s)** ['bækwəd(z)] *adv* **1** bakover, tilbake; **2** baklengs; **3** bakvendt.

back|water *sb* (bak)evje. **~woods** *sb fl* villmark, ødemark; *fig* avkrok.

bad [bæd] **I** *adj* **1** dårlig, slem; **2** lei, ubehagelig; *feel ~ about* være lei (seg) for; **3** alvorlig, ondartet; **4** bedervet, skjemt; vond; *go ~* råtne; **II** *sb: go to the ~* gå i hundene. **bad | blood** *sb* ondt blod. **~ feeling(s)** *sb (fl)* misstemning. **~ language** *sb* banning, usømmelig språk/tale.

badge [bædʒ] *sb* **1** merke; *policeman's ~* politiskilt; **2** tegn.

badger ['bædʒə] **I** *sb* grevling; **II** *vt* **1** ergre, irritere; **2** plage.

badly ['bædlɪ] *adv* **1** dårlig, elendig; vondt; **2** *~ beaten* forslått; rundjult; *~ wounded* hardt såret; **3** *want ~* trenge sårt.

baffle ['bæfl] *vt* **1** forvirre; *~ all description* trosse enhver beskrivelse; **2** hindre.

bag [bæg] **I** *sb* **1** pose, sekk; veske; *fig* bytte, fangst; *~ and baggage* pikk og pakk; *~s of (dgl)* masser/massevis av; *in the ~* i orden; **2** *fl* bukser; **3** *slang* kvinnfolk; **II** *vb* **1** putte i en sekk *etc;* **2** pose seg; **3** sikre seg, snappe; *~s it!* fritt for den/det!

baggage ['bægɪdʒ] *sb* bagasje.

baggy ['bægɪ] *adj* poset, sekket; vid.

bag pipes *sb fl* sekkepipe(r).

bail [beɪl] **I** *sb* **1** kausjon; *go/put in ~ for* kausjonere/stille kausjon for; **2** *petro* skåk; **II** *vt* **1** *~ out* kausjonere for (anklaget, slik at han el. hun kan løslates inntil rettssaken tar til); **2** lense, øse (båt tom for vann); **3** = *bale C.*

bailiff ['beɪlɪf] *sb* **1** lensmannsbetjent; **2** rettsbetjent; stevnevitne; **3** forvalter.

bait [beɪt] **I** *sb* **1** agn, åte; **2** lokke|mat, -middel; **II** *vb* **1** agne; legge ut åte (for); **2** egge, sette opp; **3** sette (hest) på beite.

baize [beɪz] *sb* boi. **baize door** *sb* filtdør.

bake [beɪk] *vb* **1** bake(s), steke(s); **2** brenne(s) (om keramikk, teglstein etc). **baker** ['beɪkə] *sb* baker. **bakery** ['beɪkərɪ] *sb* bakeri. **baking** ['beɪkɪŋ] *sb* baking; bakst. **bakingpowder** *sb* bakepulver.

balance ['bæləns] **I** *sb* **1** (skål)vekt; **2** balanse, likevekt; **3** overskudd; *the ~* resten; **4** *merk* saldo; **II** *vb*

1 balansere; avveie; 2 *merk* saldere. **balance|-sheet** *sb merk* status(rapport).

balcony ['bælkənɪ] *sb* balkong; galleri.

bald [bɔ:ld] *adj* 1 skallet; 2 bar, naken; *fig* knapp, nødtørftig; gold.

balderdash ['bɔ:ldədæʃ] *sb* sludder, vrøvl.

bale [beɪl] **A** *sb* ondskap; **B** 1 *sb* (vare)balle; 2 *vt* pakke i baller; **C** *vi:* ~ *out* hoppe ut (i fallskjerm); **D** = *bail II/2.*

balk [bɔ:k] **I** *sb* 1 (bære)bjelke; 2 (for)hindring, hinder; **II** *vb* 1 forpurre, hindre; 2 narre; 3 refusere (dvs om hest: nekte å ta hinder).

ball [bɔ:l] **I** *sb* 1 ball; kule; nøste; 2 ball, danse|-fest, *dgl* -moro; 3 *(slang)* ~*s!* sludder; **II** *vb* 1 klumpe (seg) sammen; 2 ~*ed up* floket; forvirret.

ballad ['bæləd] *sb* (folke)vise. **ballade** [bə'lɑ:d] *sb* ballade.

ballast ['bæləst] *sb* 1 ballast; 2 kult/pukklag (i vei).

ball-bearing(s) *sb (fl)* kulelager.

balloon [bə'lu:n] 1 *sb* ballong; 2 *vi* ese/svelle opp (som en ballong).

ballot ['bælət] **I** *sb* 1 stemmeseddel; 2 (skriftlig) avstemning, valg; valgresultat; **II** *vi* 1 stemme (skriftlig); 2 trekke lodd. **ballot-box** ['bælətbɒks] *sb* valgurne.

ballroom ['bɔ:lrʊm] *sb* dansesal. **ballroom dancing** *sb* selskapsdans.

balm [bɑ:m] *sb* balsam; *fig* lindring; trøst, vederkvegelse. **balmy** ['bɑ:mɪ] *adj* balsamisk; mild; vederkvegende.

bamboo [bæm'bu:] *sb* bambus.

ban [bæn] **I** *sb* 1 bann(lysing); 2 fredløshet; 3 forbud; **II** *vb* 1 bannlyse; 2 forby.

banana [bə'nɑ:nə] *sb* banan.

band [bænd] **I** *sb* 1 bånd; 2 bord, kant; 3 band, orkester; 4 *data* sporgruppe; 5 bande, gjeng; **II** *vb* 1 binde sammen; 2 forene(s).

bandage ['bændɪdʒ] 1 *sb* bandasje, forbinding; 2 *vt* bandasjere, forbinde.

Band-Aid ['bænd,eɪd] *sb, registered trademark* ≈ kvikkplaster.

bandana [bæn'dɑ:nə], **bandanna** [bæn'dænə] *sb* halstørkle.

band|box *sb* hatteske; *just out of the* ~ elegant; lekker, smart (i klesveien). **~master** *sb* kapellmester, orkesterleder. **~ printer** *sb data* båndskriver. **~stand** *sb* podium. **~-waggon** *sb: join (climb/jump on) the ~-waggon* slutte seg til parti/sak etc som har vind i seilene

bandy ['bændɪ] **I** *adj* = *~-legged*; **II** *sb* bandy-(kølle); **III** *vt* 1 kaste (ball etc) frem og tilbake; 2 utveksle (især ukvemsord); *ofte* munnhugges; *have one's name bandied about* komme/være på folkemunne. **bandy-legged** *adj* hjulbeint.

bane [beɪn] *sb* 1 forderv, ulykke; 2 *rat's-~* rottegift. **baneful** ['beɪnfʊl] *adj* 1 fordervelig; ondsinnet; 2 giftig.

bang [bæŋ] **A I** *adv* pladask; **II** *interj* bang! pang! **III** *sb* brak, drønn, smell; *go over with a* ~ bli/gjøre dundrende suksess; **IV** *vb* 1 smelle (med); 2 banke/dundre (*at* på); **B** *sb, vt* (klippe) pannelugg.

bangle ['bæŋgl] *sb* 1 armbånd; 2 ankelring.

banish ['bænɪʃ] *vt* 1 landsforvise; 2 *fig* bannlyse, forvise (fra tankene). **banishment** ['bænɪʃmənt] *sb* forvisning *etc.*

banisters ['bænɪstəz] *sb fl* gelender, rekkverk.

bank [bæŋk] **A I** *sb* 1 (elve)bredd; 2 demning, dike; 3 skrent, skråning; veikant; 4 bakke, haug; 5 (sky)banke; (snø)drive; 6 sandbanke; 7 (roer)benk; 8 gruppe (av instrumenter etc); 9 dossering; 10 krengning; **II** *vb* 1 dynge sammen; drive/fyke sammen; hope (seg) opp; ~ *up* demme opp; 2 dossere; 3 krenge; **B I** *sb* 1 *(savings ~)* (spare)bank; 2 bank, pott (i hasardspill); **II** *vb* 1 ha (sette el. spare) penger i bank; 2 ~ *(up)on* regne med, stole på.

banker ['bæŋkə] *sb* 1 bankforbindelse; 2 bankier; banksjef; 3 bankør (i hasardspill).

bank-holiday *sb* bankfridag (som også er offentlig fridag). **banking** *sb* bankvirksomhet. **bank|-note** *sb* pengeseddel. **~-rate** *sb* (bank)diskonto.

bankrupt ['bæŋkrʌpt] 1 *adj* fallitt, konkurs; 2 *sb* fallent. **bankruptcy** ['bæŋkrəptsɪ] *sb* fallitt, konkurs.

banner ['bænə] *sb* banner, fane.

banns [bænz] *sb fl* (ekteskaps)lysing; *ask the* ~ ta ut lysing; *call (publish/put up/read) the* ~ *for* lyse (til ekteskap) for.

banquet ['bæŋkwɪt] 1 *sb* bankett, festmåltid; 2 *vb* arrangere/delta i bankett.

bant [bænt] *vi* slanke seg.

bantam ['bæntəm] **I** *adj* 1 liten, men kraftig; 2 lettvekts- (også *fig*); **II** *sb* 1 dverghøne; 2 plugg (dvs liten, men kraftig kar).

banter ['bæntə] 1 *sb* (godmodig) erting; fleip-(ing); 2 *vb* erte, fleipe (med).

baptism ['bæptɪzəm] *sb* dåp. **baptist** ['bæptɪst] *sb* (gjen)døper; *med stor forbokstav* baptist. **baptize** ['bæptaɪz] *vt* døpe.

bar [bɑ:] **I** *prep* bortsett fra, unntatt; ~ *none* uten unntak; **II** *sb* 1 stang; stolpe; bom, slå; sprosse; *fl* gitter, sprinkler; 2 bom, sperre; 3 hinder, hindring; 4 skranke (især i rettssal); *the Bar* advokatstanden; 5 disk; *især* bar(disk); 6 bar; kafé, kafeteria; 7 strime, stripe; 8 (avlangt) stykke, barre; *a* ~ *of chocolate* en sjokoladeplate; 9 tverr|ligger, -tre; bjelke (i våpenskjold etc); stolpe (på medaljebånd); 10 (sand)banke, rev; 11 *mus* takt(strek); **III** *vt* 1 sette slå for; sperre/stenge (med bom); 2 forby; hindre; stenge ute, utelukke.

barb [bɑ:b] 1 *sb* brodd, pigg; mothake; 2 *vt* sette brodder *etc* på.

barbarian [bɑ:'beərɪən] 1 *adj* barbarisk; 2 *sb* barbar. **barbarism** ['bɑ:bərɪzəm] *sb* barbari. **barbarity** [bɑ:'bærətɪ] *sb* umenneskelighet, umenneskelig grusomhet. **barbarous** ['bɑ:bərəs] *adj* 1 barbarisk, grusom; **2** usivilisert, vill; **3** grov/uslepen (om manerer etc).

barbecue ['bɑ:bɪkju:] *sb* **1** (hage)grill; **2** *US* hagefest etc med grillstekt mat.

barbed wire ['bɑ:bd,waɪə] *sb* piggtråd.

barber ['bɑ:bə] *sb* barber(er).

bar | code *sb data* strekkode. ~ **code label** *sb data* streketikett.

bard [bɑ:d] *sb* skald.

bare ['beə] **I** *adj* **1** bar, naken; **2** (nesten) tom; ~ *of furniture* sparsomt møblert; **3** *a* ~ *majority* et knapt flertall; **II** *vt* avdekke; blotte, blottlegge; ~ *one's teeth* flekke tenner.

bare|-faced ['beəfeɪst] *adj* skjeggløs; *fig* frekk, uforskammet. **~foot** ['beəfʊt] *adj, adv* barbeint, barfotet.

barely ['beəlɪ] *adv* **1** knapt, så vidt; **2** nødtørftig, sparsomt.

bargain ['bɑ:gɪn] **I** *sb* **1** (avsluttet) handel; (godt) kjøp; *into the* ~ på kjøpet; *dgl også* attpå; **2** *(~ sale)* (ut)salg; **II** *vb* (for)handle, kjøpslå (*with* med; *for* om); *more than ~ed for* mer enn ventet/regnet med.

bargain|-counter *sb* utsalgsdisk. ~ **sale** *sb* (ut)salg.

barge [bɑ:dʒ] **I** *sb* **1** (laste)pram, lekter; **2** (sjefs)-sjalupp; **3** klubbåt; **II** *vi* komme farende; støte (*against/into* mot); ~ *in* trenge (seg) inn; *dgl* komme busende (inn). **bargee** [bɑ:'dʒi:] = **bargeman** ['bɑ:dʒmən] *sb* lekteskipper. **~pole** ['bɑ:dʒpəʊl] *sb* båtshake.

bark [bɑ:k] **A I** *sb* bark (på tre); **II** *vt* **1** barke (tømmer); **2** skrubbe (seg opp); **B 1** *sb* gjøing, (hunde)glam; **1** *vb* gjø, gneldre; ~ *up the wrong tree* kritisere feil person etc; være (kommet) på villspor. **C** *sb* bark(skip).

barkeeper ['bɑ:,ki:pə] *sb* = *~tender.*

barker ['bɑ:kə] *sb* utroper.

barley ['bɑ:lɪ] *sb* (kornslaget) bygg.

barn [bɑ:n] *sb* **1** låve; *US* driftsbygning; **2** *slang* rønne. **barnyard** [,bɑ:n'jɑ:d] *sb* tun.

baron ['bærən] *sb* **1** baron; **2** *US slang* kakse, magnat.

bar printer *sb data* typestangskriver.

barrack ['bærək] **I** *sb* brakke; *fl* (militær)forlegning; brakker, kaserne(r); **II** *vt* **1** innkvartere i brakke(r); **2** komme med hånlige *etc* tilrop.

barrage [bə'rɑ:ʒ] *sb* **1** dam(anlegg); **2** sperre. **barrage | balloon** *sb* sperreballong. ~ **fire** *sb* sperreild.

barrel ['bærəl] **I** *sb* **1** fat, tønne; **2** beholder (f.eks. i fyllepenn); **3** trommel, valse; **4** (gevær)|løp, -pipe; **II** *vt* fylle på tønne(r); tappe på fat. **barrel|-organ** *sb* lirekasse. **~-printer** *sb data* trommelskriver.

barren ['bærən] **I** *adj* **1** gold, ufruktbar; **2** steril; **3** mager, skrinn; **II** *sb* ødemark.

barricade [,bærɪ'keɪd] **1** *sb* barrikade; **2** *vt* barrikadere.

barrier ['bærɪə] *sb* **1** barriere, hindring; **2** bom, skranke.

barring ['bɑ:rɪŋ] *prep* = *bar I.*

barrister ['bærɪstə] *sb* (skranke)advokat (jf *bar II, 4*).

barrow ['bærəʊ] *sb* **1** båre; *wheel-~* trillebår; **2** gravhaug; **3** galte.

barter ['bɑ:tə] **1** *sb* bytte(handel), tuskhandel; bytte, utveksling; **2** *vb* bytte(handle), drive tuskhandel; bytte; utveksle (*against/for* mot).

base [beɪs] **I** *adj* **1** simpel, ussel; **2** falsk, uekte; **3** ~ *metals* uedle metaller; **4** *US* = *bass A I*; **II** *sb* **1** basis; grunn|flate, -linje; fot, sokkel; **2** utgangspunkt; **3** *mil* base, støttepunkt; **4** *kjemi* base; **5** base (i baseball); **6** *US* = *bass A II*; **III** *vt* basere/grunnlegge (*upon* på). **baseless** *adj* grunnløs.

basement ['beɪsmənt] *sb* **1** grunnmur; **2** kjeller (etasje).

base | oil *sb petro* baseolje. ~ **text** *sb data* fast tekst.

bashful ['bæʃfʊl] *adj* blyg, unnselig.

basic ['beɪsɪk] *adj* elementær, grunnleggende. **basically** ['beɪsɪklɪ] *adv* egentlig, i bunn og grunn.

basin ['beɪsn] *sb* **1** bolle; *sugar* ~ sukker|kopp, -skål; **2** (vaskevanns)fat; servant, vask; kum; **3** basseng; **4** nedslagsdistrikt.

basis ['beɪsɪs] *sb* **1** basis, grunnlag; **2** hovedbestanddel.

bask [bɑ:sk] **1** *sb* solbad; **2** *vi* kose seg i solen, slikke sol.

basket ['bɑ:skɪt] *sb* kurv.

bass A [beɪs] **I** *adj* bass-; **II** *sb* **1** basstemme; **2** bassanger; **B** [bæs] *sb* **1** abbor; **2** (linde)bast.

bassoon [bə'su:n] *sb* fagott.

basswood ['bæswʊd] *sb US* lind, lindetre.

bastard ['bɑ:stəd] **I** *adj* bastard-, uekte; **II** *sb* **1** bastard, kjøter; **2** *gml* løsunge.

baste [beɪst] *vt* **A** tråkle; **B** dryppe (stek).

bastion ['bæstɪən] *sb* bastion, (be)festning.

bat [bæt] **I** *sb* **1** flaggermus; *~s in the belfry (slang)* bløt på pæra; *like a ~ on a sticky wicket (slang)* som lus på en tjærekost; **2** balltre; **3** råemne (for keramiker); **II** *vb* **1** slå (med balltre); **2** *US slang* blunke (med); *not ~ an eyelid* ikke få blund på øynene (dvs ligge søvnløs); ikke (så mye som) blunke (dvs ikke bli overrasket etc).

batch [bætʃ] *sb* **1** porsjon (av f.eks. bakst); **2** flokk, gruppe. **batching** *sb* dosering, porsjonering. **batch processing** *sb data* satsvis behandling.

bate [beɪt] **A** *vb: with ~d breath* i åndeløs spenning [egtl med tilbakeholdt pust]; **B** *sb slang* raseri(anfall).

bath [bɑ:θ] **I** *sb* **1** bad (især i badekar); **2** badevann; **3** bad (dvs badeanstalt); **4** *kjemi etc* bad; **II** *vt* bade (især spedbarn). **bathchair** [,bɑ:θ'tʃeə] *sb* rullestol. **bathe** [beɪð] **I** *sb* bad (utendørs, i sjøen etc); dukkert; **II** *vb* **1** bade (i sjøen etc); **2** bade (dvs vaske (seg), skylle etc). **bathing** ['beɪðɪŋ] *sb* bading. **bathing|-cap** *sb* badehette. **~-costume** = *~-suit.* **~-drawers** = *~-trunks.* **~-dress** = **~-suit** *sb* badedrakt. **~-trunks** *sb fl* badebukse(r). **bath|-robe** *sb* badekåpe. **~-room** *sb* bad (dvs badeværelse); toalett.

~**-tub** *sb* badekar.

batman ['bætmən] *sb* (offisers)oppasser.

baton ['bætən] *sb* **1** batong, kølle; **2** embetsstav; (militær) kommandostav; marskalkstav; **3** *mus* taktstokk.

battalion [bə'tæliən] *sb* bataljon.

batten ['bætn] **I** *sb* **1** labank; lekte, spikerslag; **2** *sjø* skalkelist; **II** *vb* **1** feste med lekter *etc*; **2** *sjø*: ~ *down the hatches* skalke lukene; **3** meske seg (*on* på); fråtse.

batter ['bætə] **1** *sb* røre (til pannekaker, vafler etc); **2** *vb* slå (i stykker); ramponere. **battering-ram** ['bætəriŋræm] *sb* murbrekker.

battery ['bætəri] *sb* **1** (akkumulator)batteri; **2** (kanon)batteri; **3** gruppe, sett; **4** legemsfornærmelse (jf *assault I 2*). **battery | charger** *sb* batterilader.

battle ['bætl] **1** *sb* kamp, slag; **2** *vb* (be)kjempe; kjempe (med/mot). **battle|field** *sb* slagmark. **~-ments** *sb fl* brystvern. **~ship** *sb* slagskip.

batty ['bæti] *adj slang* skrullet.

baud [bɔ:d] *sb data* baud.

baulk [bɔ:k] = *balk*.

bawl [bɔ:l] **I** *sb* skrik; **II** *vb* **1** belje, skrike; **2** *US slang*: ~ *out* skjelle ut.

bay [bei] **A** *sb* **1** (hav)bukt; **2** avdeling, fløy; **3** karnapp, lite rom; nisje; **4** fag (i murverk etc); **5** sidespor (med endestasjon); **B** *sb* **1** laurbær(tre); **2** *fl fig* laurbær (dvs heder, ære); **C I** *sb* **1** gjøing, (hunde)glam; **2** *hold/keep at* ~ holde fra livet; **II** *vi* gjø, halse; **D 1** *adj* rødbrun (om hest); **2** *sb* fuks (dvs rødbrun hest).

bayonet ['beiənit] **1** *sb* bajonett; **2** *vt* stikke med bajonett.

be [bi:] *vi* være (og bli; eksistere, leve, være til; befinne seg, ha det; komme på, koste; hende, skje etc); *she is writing* hun (sitter og) skriver; *they were sleeping* de (lå og) sov.

beach [bi:tʃ] **1** *sb* strand(bredd); **2** *vt* sette (båt) på grunn; trekke (båt) på land. **beach|-comber** *sb* (havne)boms. **~head** *sb* brohode.

beacon ['bi:kən] **I** *sb* **1** varde; **2** fyr(lykt); fyrtårn; **3** signallys; *især* blinklys (ved fotgjengerovergang); **II** *vt* **1** lyse for; **2** merke med fyrlykt *etc*.

bead [bi:d] **I** *sb* **1** perle (av glass, metall, tre etc); *fl også* rosenkrans: **2** blære, dråpe; **3** (sikte)korn; **4** (dekk)vulst; **II** *vt* **1** træ perler; **2** perlebrodere; pynte med perler.

beadle ['bi:dl] *sb* kirketjener.

beady ['bi:di] *adj* **1** perle|aktig, -lignende; perle-; **2** ~ *eyes* små (glitrende, stikkende) øyne.

beak [bi:k] *sb* **1** nebb; **2** *slang* politidommer; **3** lærer.

beam [bi:m] **I** *sb* **1** bjelke; **2** *sjø* dekksbjelke; skips|-bredde, -side; *on the port/starboard* ~ på babord/styrbord side; **3** bredde; *broad in the* ~ *(hum)* bred over baken; **4** bom; skinne; stang; **5** stråle; **II** *vb* **1** (ut)-stråle; *fig* smile *etc* strålende; **2** *radio* sende (i en bestemt retning).

bean [bi:n] *sb* **1** bønne; *fl slang* gryn (dvs penger); **2** *slang*: *full of* ~*s* full av tæl; **3** *slang* = **bean-feast** ['bi:nfi:st], **beano** ['bi:nəu] *sb slang* fest. **beanstalk** ['bi:nstɔ:k] *sb* bønnestengel; *dgl fig* langt rekel.

bear [beə] **A I** *sb* **1** bjørn; **2** *merk* baissespekulant; **II** *vb merk* spekulere i prisfall; **B** *vb* **1** bære (især *fig*); ~ *away the prize* hente/ta hjem seieren; ~ *oneself* (opp)-føre seg; **2** holde ut, tåle; ~ *up (well)* ta det kjekt; ~ *with* bære over med; **3** gi, yte; komme med; ~ *company* holde med selskap; ~ *witness to* vitne om; **4** føde; **5** dytte; presse, trykke; **6** støtte seg/hvile tungt (*on* på); **7** *med adv/prep* ~ **down** renne overende/i senk; ~ **down (up)on** (især *sjø*) stå (med kurs) ned mot; ~ **out** bekrefte, støtte; ~ **(up)on** angå, ha betydning for.

beard [biəd] **I** *sb* **1** skjegg; **2** snerp (på korn); **II** *vt* trosse, utfordre.

bearer [beərə] *sb* **1** bærer; **2** budbringer; **3** overbringer; *merk* ihendehaver. **bearing** ['beəriŋ] *sb* **1** holdning, oppførsel; **2** forbindelse (*on* med); (inn)-virkning (*on* på); **3** retning; *sjø* peiling; *take one's* ~ orientere seg; **4** *(child-~)* (barne)fødsel; **5** lager (jf *ball-bearing(s)*.

beast [bi:st] *sb* **1** dyr; ~ *of burden* lastedyr; ~ *of prey* rovdyr; **2** best, udyr. **beastly** ['bi:stli] *adj, adv* **1** dyrisk; **2** motbydelig.

beat [bi:t] **I** *adj* slått (ut), utkjørt; **II** *sb* **1** slag; *mus* takt(slag), rytme; **2** (patruljerings)distrikt, runde; *be off/out of one's* ~ være på gyngende grunn; **III** *vb* **1** banke, hamre, slå; ~ *off* avverge, slå tilbake; ~ *time* slå takten; ~ *up* denge, jule opp; **2** piske (egg, krem etc); **3** beseire, slå; **4** overgå; **5** *sjø* baute; **6** ~ *about the bush* gå som katten om den varme grøten, ~ *it (slang)* stikke av. **beating** ['bi:tiŋ] *sb* juling; *fig* nederlag.

beatitude [bi:'ætitju:d] *sb* (lykk)salighet.

beau [bəu] *sb* **1** beundrer, kavaler; **2** laps.

beautiful ['bju:təful] *adj* vakker. **beautify** ['bju:tifai] *vt* forskjønne, gjøre vakker. **beauty** ['bju:ti] *sb* **1** skjønnhet; *Sleeping Beauty* Tornerose; **2** *fig* perle (dvs prakt|eksemplar, stykke). **beauty-parlour** *sb* skjønnhetssalong.

beaver ['bi:və] *sb* bever; *fig* (arbeids)jern, (flittig) maur.

because [bi'kɒz] *konj* fordi; ~ *of (prep)* på grunn av.

beck [bek] *sb* vink; *be at her* ~ *and call* lystre hennes minste vink. **beckon** ['bekən] *vb* gjøre tegn til; vinke (på).

become [bi'kʌm] *vb* **1** bli (til); ~ *of* bli av, bli til med; gå med; **2** kle; *that hat* ~*s you* den hatten kler deg; **3** passe/sømme seg for. **becoming** [bi'kʌmiŋ] *adj* **1** kledelig; **2** passende, sømmelig.

bed [bed] **I** *sb* **1** seng; ~ *and board* kost og losji; **2** (blomster)bed; **3** leie; *river-~* elveleie; **4** fundament; **II** *vt* **1** legge (til sengs); **2** skaffe sengeplass til; **3** fundamentere; støpe ned; **4** plante i bed. **bedding** ['bediŋ] *sb* **1** sengeklær; *gml* (senge)halm; **2** fundament, underlag; *sjø* bedding.

bedlam ['bedləm] *sb* **1** galehus; **2** spetakkel.

bed|pan *sb* bekken (dvs potte for sengeliggende).

~post *sb* sengestolpe. **~-ridden** *adj* sengeliggende [pga sykdom]. **~rock** *sb* grunnfjell. **~room** *sb* soveværelse. **~side** *sb* sengekant. **~-sitter, ~-sitting-room** *sb* hybel. **~spread** *sb* sengeteppe. **~time** *sb* sengetid.

bee [bi:] *sb* **1** bie; *a ~ in one's bonnet* en fiks idé; **2** *US a)* dugnad; *b)* konkurranse (som selskapslek).

beech [bi:tʃ] *sb* bøk.

beef [bi:f] *sb* **1** oksekjøtt; **2** okse, storfe (som slaktedyr); okse(slakt); **3** *fig* kraft, styrke. **beef|eater** *sb* populær betegnelse på bl.a. vaktene i Tower of London. **~steak** *sb* biff. **~tea** *sb* (okse)buljong. **beefy** *adj* kraftig, velfødd.

bee|hive *sb* bikube. **~line** *sb* luftlinje (dvs rett linje mellom to punkter).

beer ['bɪə] *sb* øl. **beer-house** *sb* ølstue, kneipe.

beet [bi:t] *sb* bete, roe.

beetle ['bi:tl] **I** *sb* **1** bille; **2** broleggerjomfru; **3** *slang* (asfalt)boble (dvs liten bil, især av den gamle folkevogntypen); **II** *vb* **1** kravle; **2** stampe; **3** henge/rage utover. **beetle-browed** *adj* med buskete øyenbryn.

befall [bɪ'fɔ:l] *vb* hende; ramme, tilstøte.

befit [bɪ'fɪt] *vt* sømme seg for.

before [bɪ'fɔ:] **I** *adv* **1** før, tidligere; **2** i forveien; **II** *konj* før (enn); **III** *prep* **1** før; foran; **2** fremfor; **3** forut for; **4** i nærvær av. **beforehand** [bɪ'fɔ:hænd] *adv* på forhånd; *~ with* på forskudd med.

befriend [bɪ'frend] *vt* **1** være venn(er) med; **2** være hjelpsom/snill mot.

beg [beg] *vb* **1** be (om); *~ off* be (seg) fri; be (seg) fritatt for; **2** tigge; **3** *merk etc* tillate seg.

beget [bɪ'get] *vt* **1** avle, frembringe; **2** *fig* føre til, resultere i.

beggar ['begə] **I** *sb* tigger; **II** *vt* **1** bringe til tiggerstaven; **2** overgå; *~ description* trosse enhver beskrivelse. **beggarly** ['begəlɪ] *adj* armodslig, ynkelig. **beggary** ['begərɪ] *sb* fattigdom.

begin [bɪ'gɪn] *vb* begynne (på); *~ at* begynne på (dvs fra et bestemt sted); *~ on* begynne på/ta til med (noe). **beginner** *sb* (ny)begynner; *~'s luck* begynnerflaks. **beginning** *sb* begynnelse.

begone [bɪ'gɒn] *interj* forsvinn!

begrudge [bɪ'grʌdʒ] *vt* misunne.

beguile [bɪ'gaɪl] *vt* **1** lure, narre; **2** fordrive tiden for, underholde.

behalf [bɪ'hɑ:f] *sb: in/on ~ of* på vegne av; *in/on his (etc) ~* på hans (etc) vegne.

behave [bɪ'heɪv] *vr* oppføre seg; *well-behaved* veloppdragen. **behaviour** [bɪ'heɪvɪə] *sb* oppførsel.

behead [bɪ'hed] *vt* halshugge.

behind [bɪ'haɪnd] **I** *adv* **1** bak; *~ in/with* på etterskudd med; *fall/lag ~* sakke akterut; **2** igjen, tilbake; **II** *prep* bak(om); *~ time* forsinket; *~ the times* avleggs, foreldet; **III** *sb* bak(ende). **behindhand** [bɪ'haɪndhænd] *adv* bak(etter); *~ in* på etterskudd med.

behold [bɪ'həʊld] *vt* (be)skue, se (på). **beholden** [bɪ'həʊldən] *adj* forbunden, takknemlig; *~ to* takk skyldig.

behove [bɪ'həʊv] *vt* **1** påhvile, tilkomme; **2** anstå seg for, passe/sømme seg for.

being ['bi:ɪŋ] *sb* **1** eksistens, tilværelse; *come into ~* bli til; **2** skapning, vesen; *human ~s* mennesker.

belabour [bɪ'leɪbə] *vt* **1** (rund)jule, slå løs på; **2** *fig* bearbeide; gå løs på.

belated [bɪ'leɪtɪd] *adj* forsinket (især til etter mørkets frembrudd).

belch [beltʃ] **I** *sb* **1** oppstøt, rap; **2** sky (av røyk etc); **II** *vb* **1** rape; **2** spy ut (røyk etc).

beleaguer [bɪ'li:gə] *vt* beleire.

belfry ['belfrɪ] *sb* klokketårn, støpul.

belie [bɪ'laɪ] *vt* **1** fornekte; gjøre til skamme; **2** motsi; gi et falskt inntrykk av.

belief [bi'li:f] *sb* **1** (fast) tro, forvissning; overbevisning; *in my ~* etter min mening; **2** tillit; *~ in* tro på; tiltro til. **believable** [bi'li:vəbl] *adj* trolig (dvs som er til å tro); troverdig. **believe** [bɪ'li:v] *vb* **1** tro (fast og sikkert); *~ in* tro på; ha tiltro til, stole på; **2** anta, tro; mene. **believer** [bɪ'li:və] *sb* troende (dvs religiøst troende person).

belittle [bɪ'lɪtl] *vt* ned|sette, -vurdere; redusere; ringeakte.

bell [bel] **1** *sb* bjelle, klokke; *sjø* glass; **2** *vt* henge bjelle på. **bell|-bottomed** *adj* med sleng (dvs svært vide buksebein). **~boy** *sb* pikkolo. **~-buoy** *sb* klokkebøye.

belle [bel] *sb* (kvinnelig) skjønnhet.

bell-hop *sb US = bellboy*.

bellicose ['belɪkəʊs] *adj* krigersk, stridbar. **belligerent** [bɪ'lɪdʒərənt] *adj, sb* krigførende (land).

bellow ['beləʊ] **1** *sb* brøl; **2** *vi* belje; brøle. **bellows** ['beləʊz] *sb fl* belg.

bell|-pull *sb* klokkestreng. **~-push** *sb* ringeknapp.

belly ['belɪ] **1** *sb* mave, underliv; **2** *vb* (få til å) svulme opp. **belly|-ache** *sb* mave|knip, -pine. **~-acher** *sb slang* kverulant. **~ful** *sb* rikelig porsjon; *slang* omgang juling. **~-landing** *sb* buklanding.

belong [bi'lɒŋ] *vi* **1** *~ to* tilhøre; **2** høre hjemme. **belongings** [bɪ'lɒŋɪŋz] *sb fl* eiendeler, personlige effekter; tilbehør.

beloved [bɪ'lʌvd] **1** *adj* avholdt, (høyt) elsket; **2** *sb* elsket person, kjæreste.

below [bɪ'ləʊ] **I** *adv* **1** nede, nedenunder; *sjø* under dekk; **2** nedenfor; nederst (på brevark etc); lenger ute (i bok etc); **II** *prep* **1** nedenfor; **2** under.

belt [belt] **I** *sb* **1** belte; reim; **2** belte, område; **II** *vt* **1** feste med belte; **2** slå med belte. **belting** ['beltɪŋ] *sb* juling [især med belte eller lærreim].

bemoan [bɪ'məʊn] *vt* gråte over.

bemused [bɪ'mju:zd] *adj* forvirret, omtåket.

bench [bentʃ] *sb* benk, krakk; *sjø* tofte; *the Bench* dommersetet; *fig* dommerstanden; *be raised to the Bench* bli utnevnt til dommer/*også* til biskop. **benchmark** ['bentʃmɑ:k] *sb* standardverdi (som noe prøves mot).

bend [bend] **I** *sb* **1** bøy, krok; kurve, sving; **2** *sjø* stikk (dvs knute); **3** *fl* ≈ dykkersyke; **II** *vb* **1** bøye (seg); ~ *a bow* spenne en bue; ~ *a sail* beslå et seil; **2** snu, vende; dreie; **3** ~ *one's mind to* konsentrere seg om; rette oppmerksomheten mot; **4** ~ *to* føye seg for; underkaste seg.

beneath [bɪ'ni:θ] *adv, prep* (neden)under.

benediction [ˌbenɪ'dɪkʃn] *sb* velsignelse. **benefaction** [ˌbenɪ'fækʃn] *sb* velgjerning. **benefactor** ['benɪfæktə] *sb* velgjører.

beneficence [bɪ'nefɪsəns] *sb* godgjørenhet, veldedighet. **beneficent** [bɪ'nefɪsənt] *adj* **1** god, snill; **2** godgjørende, veldedig; **3** gunstig, velgjørende. **beneficial** [ˌbenɪ'fɪʃəl] *adj* fordelaktig. **beneficiary** [ˌbenɪ'fɪʃərɪ] *sb* begunstiget (person, i testamente).

benefit ['benɪfit] **I** *sb* **1** fordel; gagn; utbytte; *give her the* ~ *of doubt* la tvilen komme henne til gode; **2** stønad; hjelp, støtte; *unemployment* ~ arbeidsledighetstrygd; **II** *vb* gagne, hjelpe, nytte; ~ *by* dra nytte av; ha/høste fordel av.

benevolence [bɪ'nəvələns] *sb* velvilje *etc*. **benevolent** [bɪ'nəvələnt] *adj* velvillig; imøtekommende, vennlig.

benighted [bɪ'naɪtɪd] *adj* overrasket av nattemørket; *især fig* formørket, uvitende.

benign [bɪ'naɪn] *adj* **1** snill, vennlig; velvillig; **2** gunstig; **3** *med* godartet. **benignant** [bɪ'nɪgnənt] = *benign*.

bent [bent] *sb* **1** tilbøyelighet (*for* til); **2** anlegg (*for* for); **3** *a)* forkjærlighet; *to the top of one's* ~ av hjertens lyst *b) som adj:* ~ *on* oppsatt på.

benumb [bɪ'nʌm] *vt* gjøre følelsesløs.

bequeath [bɪ'kwi:ð] *vt* testamentere. **bequest** [bɪ'kwest] *sb* testamentarisk gave.

bereave [bɪ'ri:v] *vt* berøve; *bereft of reason/speech* berøvet forstanden/talens bruk. **bereaved** [bɪ'ri:vd]: *the* ~ (den/de) etterlatte/gjenlevende (etter en avdød); (den/de) sørgende. **bereavement** [bɪ'ri:vmənt] *sb* (smertelig) tap.

beret ['bereɪ] *sb* beret, (uniforms)alpelue.

berry ['berɪ] *sb* bær.

berth [bɜ:θ] **I** *sb* **1** køy(e); **2** kaiplass; *give a wide* ~ holde godt klar av; *fig* holde seg langt unna; **3** jobb; **II** *vb* fortøye ved kai.

beseech [bɪ'si:tʃ] *vt* bønnfalle.

beset [bɪ'set] *vt* angripe; kringsette; *især fig* besette, plage.

beside [bɪ'saɪd] *prep* ved siden av; ~ *oneself* ute av seg; ~ *the mark (point/question)* irrelevant, uten betydning (for saken). **besides** [bɪ'saɪdz] **1** *adv* dessuten; **2** *prep* foruten, i tillegg til.

besiege [bɪ'si:dʒ] *vt* beleire; *fig* bestorme, plage. **besieger** [bɪ'si:dʒə] *sb* beleirer.

bespeak [bɪ'spi:k] *vt* **1** bestille; **2** røpe, vise; vitne om.

best [best] **1** *adj* best; **2** *adv* best; **3** *vt slang* ta innersvingen på (dvs være bedre enn, vinne over, men også lure, utnytte etc).

bestir [bɪ'stɜ:] *vr:* ~ *oneself* få fart på seg, ta seg sammen.

best man *sb* forlover.

bestow [bɪ'stəʊ] *vt* **1** gi, skjenke; **2** anbringe. **bestowal** [bɪ'stəʊəl] *sb* (gave)overrekkelse; tildeling.

bestride [bɪ'straɪd] *vt* skreve over; ri på.

bet [bet] **I** *sb* **1** veddemål; **2** innsats (i veddemål); **II** *vb* vedde; *you* ~*!* vær sikker! det skal være sikkert!

betake [bɪ'teɪk] *vr:* ~ *oneself to* **1** begi seg til; **2** gå i gang med.

bethink [bɪ'θɪŋk] *vr* **1** ~ *oneself* tenke seg om; **2** ~ *oneself of* ta i betraktning.

betide [bɪ'taɪd] *vb gml* hende (med); times; *woe* ~ *you!* ve deg!

betimes [bɪ'taɪmz] *adv* i tide; tidlig.

betoken [bɪ'təʊkən] *vi* bety (dvs tyde på).

betray [bɪ'treɪ] *vt* **1** bedra, svike; **2** forråde, røpe. **betrayal** [bɪ'treɪəl] *sb* forræderi; svik.

betroth [bɪ'trəʊð] *vt* forlove, trolove. **betrothal** [bɪ'trəʊðl] *sb* forlovelse, trolovelse.

better [betə] **1** *adj* bedre; *the* ~ *part* mesteparten, størsteparten; *for* ~ *(f)or worse* i medgang og motgang; *be (all) the* ~ *for it* (bare) ha godt av det; **2** *adv* bedre; *you had* ~ det er best du; **3** *sb* overmann (især med tanke på klasse og stand); **4** *vb* bedre (seg), forbedre(s).

between [bɪ'twi:n] **1** *adv* innimellom; **2** *prep* mellom. **betwixt** [bɪ'twɪkst] = *between*.

bevel [bevl] **1** *sb* fas, skråkant; **2** *vt* avfase; skjære/slipe *etc* skrått.

beverage ['bevərɪdʒ] *sb* brygg, drikk.

bevy ['bevɪ] *sb* **1** flokk; **2** (fugle)sverm.

bewail [bɪ'weɪl] *vt* gråte over.

beware [bɪ'weə] *vb* passe seg (*of* for).

bewilder [bɪ'wɪldə] *vt* forvirre. **bewilderment** [bɪ'wɪldəmənt] *sb* forvirring.

bewitch [bɪ'wɪtʃ] *vt* forhekse.

beyond [bɪ'jɒnd] **1** *adv* bortenfor; **2** *prep* bortenfor; utenfor, (ut)over; *dgl* hinsides; ~ *me/my comprehension* over/hinsides min forstand; ~ *repair* som ikke kan repareres/*fig* gjøres godt igjen.

biannual [baɪ'ænjʊəl] **1** *adj* halvårlig; **2** *sb* halvårlig publikasjon.

bias ['baɪəs] **I** *sb* **1** skråretning/skråsnitt (på stoff); **2** ensidighet, partiskhet; **II** *vt* **1** skjære på skrå; **2** gi et skjevt bilde av. **bias(s)ed** ['baɪəst] *adj* forutinntatt, partisk; tendensiøs.

bib [bɪb] **1** *sb* smekke: *in one's best* ~ *and tucker (slang)* stivpyntet; **2** *vi* pimpe.

bible ['baɪbl] *sb* bibel. **biblical** ['bɪblɪkl] *adj* bibelsk.

bicker ['bɪkə] *vi* krangle.

bicycle ['baɪsɪkl] **1** *sb* sykkel; **2** *vi* sykle.

bid [bɪd] **I** *sb* **1** bud (på auksjon etc); **2** *US* anbud; **3** melding (i bridge); *no* ~ pass; **II** *vb* **1** by (*for* på); ~ *defiance* by tross, trosse; ~ *farewell* si/ta farvel; ~ *good morning* si/ønske god morgen; **2** *US* gi/komme med anbud; **3** melde (i bridge); **4** befale, (på)by; **5** ~

fair to se ut til å (bli). **bidding** ['bɪdɪŋ] *sb* befaling, (på)bud.

bide [baɪd] *vt* avvente; ~ *one's time* se tiden an; vente til rette øyeblikk.

bier ['bɪə] *sb* (lik)båre.

big [bɪg] *adj* **1** stor, svær; **2** *som adv: talk* ~ skryte.

bigamist ['bɪgəmɪst] *sb* bigamist. **bigamy** ['bɪgəmɪ] *sb* bigami.

big | game *sb* storvilt. ~ **shot** *sb slang* kakse. ~ **wig** *sb slang* blære, viktigper.

bike [baɪk] *dgl = bicycle.*

bilberry ['bɪlbərɪ] *sb* blåbær.

bile [baɪl] *sb* galle; *fig* dårlig humør.

bilge [bɪldʒ] **I** *sb* **1** tønnebuk; **2** *sjø* kimming/slag (dvs skipsbunnens runding og nederste del); **3** *slang* skrap; sludder; **II** *vb* **1** bue seg ut; **2** *sjø* springe lekk; **3** *slang* dumpe, stryke. **bilge|-pump** *sb sjø* lensepumpe. **~-water** *sb sjø* slagvann. **bilgy** ['bɪldʒɪ] *adj* råtten, stinkende.

bilious ['bɪlɪəs] *adj* galle-; *fig* gretten.

bill [bɪl] **A I** *sb* **1** regning; *merk* faktura, nota; **2** *US* pengeseddel; **3** plakat; (løpe)seddel; program(plakat); **4** fortegnelse, liste; **5** attest; **6** lovforslag; **II** *vt* **1** sette på regning(en); sende regning til; *merk* anføre, debitere; **2** kunngjøre (ved plakater etc); **B 1** *sb* nebb; **2** *vi:* ~ *and coo* kjæle (med hverandre); **C** *sb* **1** huggert, stridsøks; **2** (lue)skygge. **billboard** ['bɪlbɔ:d] *sb* oppslagstavle; *US* plakattavle, (stor) reklameplakat.

billet ['bɪlɪt] **1** *sb* (militær)forlegning; **2** *vt* innkvartere (soldater).

billfold ['bɪlfəʊld] *sb* lommebok.

billiards ['bɪlɪədz] *sb fl* biljard.

billion ['bɪlɪən] *sb* billion; *US* milliard.

bill of | exchange *sb merk* veksel. ~ ~ **fare** *sb* meny(seddel), spisekart. ~ ~ **health** *sb* helseattest. ~ ~ **lading** *sb merk* fraktbrev, konnossement.

billow ['bɪləʊ] **1** *sb* (stor) bølge; **2** *vi* bølge; svulme.

bill|-poster, ~-sticker *sb* plakatklistrer.

bin [bɪn] *sb* **1** binge, kasse; **2** silo.

binary ['baɪnərɪ] *adj data etc* binær. **binary | character** *sb data* binærtegn. ~ **code** *sb data* binærkode. ~ **digit** *sb data* bit. ~ **search** *sb data* binærsøk. ~ **variable** *sb data* logisk variabel.

bind [baɪnd] *vb* **1** binde, feste; (for)binde; binde inn (bøker); **2** stramme; hemme, hindre; **3** binde, forplikte. **binder** ['baɪndə] *sb* **1** bokbinder; **2** selvbinder. **binding** ['baɪndɪŋ] **1** *adj* bindende, obligatorisk; **2** *sb* (bok)bind, innbinding.

binoculars [bɪ'nɒkjʊləz] *sb fl* kikkert.

biodegradable ['baɪəʊ,dɪ'greɪdəbl] *adj* biologisk nedbrytbar (dvs som kan brytes ned på vanlig måte i naturen).

biographer [baɪ'ɒgrəfə] *sb* biograf. **biographic(al)** [,baɪəʊ'græfɪk(l)] *adj* biografisk. **biography** [baɪ'ɒgrəfɪ] *sb* biografi.

biologic(al) [,baɪəʊ'lɒdʒɪk(l)] *adj* biologisk. **biologist** [baɪ'ɒlədʒɪst] *sb* biolog. **biology** [baɪ'ɒlədʒɪ] *sb* biologi.

birch [bɜ:tʃ] **I** *sb* **1** bjerk; **2** (bjerke)ris; **II** *vt* rise. **birchen** ['bɜ:tʃən] *adj* bjerke-.

bird [bɜ:d] *sb* fugl; ~*s of a feather flock together* like barn leker best. **bird of | passage** *sb* trekkfugl. ~ ~ **prey** *sb* rovfugl. **bird's-eye view** *sb* fugleperspektiv.

birth [bɜ:θ] *sb* **1** fødsel; *give* ~ *to* føde; *fig* gi støtet til; **2** byrd, herkomst. **birth|day** *sb* fødselsdag; ~*day suit* Adams/Evas drakt (dvs nakenhet). **~place** *sb* fødested.

biscuit ['bɪskɪt] *sb* **1** kjeks; **2** *US også* ≈ bolle.

bishop ['bɪʃəp] *sb* **1** biskop; **2** løper (i sjakk). **bishopric** ['bɪʃəprɪk] *sb* bispedømme.

bison ['baɪsn] *sb* bison, bøffel(okse).

bit [bɪt] *sb* **1** bit(e); stump, (lite) stykke; *fig* grann, smule; ~ *by* ~ gradvis; **2** egg/krone (på bor etc); kjeft (på tang); skjær (på nøkkel); **3** bissel, (munn)bitt; **4** *data* bit, binærsiffer; **5** liten mynt (*GB hist* 3 pence; *US: two bits* = 25 cent). **bit | bearing** *sb petro* borkronelager.

bitch [bɪtʃ] *sb* tispe; *dgl* troll (dvs arg kjerring etc); *slang* hore; *son of a* ~ meget sterkt skjellsord (egtl tispe- el. horesønn). **bitchy** ['bɪtʃɪ] *adj dgl* gretten, sur; ondskapsfull.

bite [baɪt] **I** *sb* **1** bitt; napp (av fisk); stikk (av insekt); **2** (smerte)sting; *fig* snert; **3** bit(e); **II** *vb* **1** bite; nappe (om fisk); stikke (om insekt); ~ *the dust* bite i gresset; **2** bite seg fast/få tak (om f.eks. hjul på glatt føre); ta (om kulde/vind, bor, sag etc); etse (om kjemikalier). **biting** ['baɪtɪŋ] *adj* bitende *etc*; skarp.

bit | load *sb petro* borkronetrykk. ~ **manipulation** *sb data* bithåndtering. ~ **map** *sb data* punktmatrise. ~ **map graphics** *sb data* punktgrafikk. ~ **rate** *sb data* baud.

bitter ['bɪtə] **I** *adj* **1** besk, bitter; **2** bitende, skarp; **II** *sb* bitter [= slags øl].

bit | wear *sb petro* bor(krone)slitasje. ~ **weight** = ~ *load.*

bitumen ['bɪtjʊmɪn] *sb petro* asfalt, bitumen. **bituminous** [bɪ'tju:mɪnəs] *adj petro* asfaltholdig, asfalt-; bituminøs.

black [blæk] **I** *adj* svart; *fig* dyster, mørk, nifs; **II** *sb* **1** (fargen) svart; **2** neger; **3** *merk: in the* ~ med overskudd; **III** *vb* **1** sverte; **2** ~ *out* mørklegge; stryke ut; miste bevisstheten. **black|beetle** *sb* kakerlakk. **~berry** *sb* bjørnebær. **~bird** *sb* svarttrost. **~board** *sb* (vegg)tavle. **~-currant** *sb* solbær.

blacken ['blækn] *vb* **1** sverte; *fig også* baktale; **2** bli svart.

black | eye *sb* blått øye (etter slag etc). **~guard** ['blægɑ:d] *sb* kjeltring.

blacking ['blækɪŋ] *sb* sverte.

black|leg *sb, vb* (være) streikebryter. **~mail 1** *sb* (penge)utpressing; **2** *vt* presse (penger av). ~ **market** *sb* svartebørs. **~out** *sb* **1** blending, mørklegging; **2** (kortvarig) besvimelse/hukommelsestap; *dgl også* jernteppe. ~ **pudding** *sb* blodpølse. **~smith** *sb* (grov)smed.

bladder ['blædə] *sb* blære.

blade [bleɪd] *sb* **1** blad (på planter samt på kniv, sag, øks, åre etc); skulderblad; **2** skjær (på plog, skøyte, veihøvel etc); **3** (bryter)kniv; (propell)vinge; (sverd)klinge; (turbin)skovl; (veksel)tunge; **4** *slang* kjekkas, sprade.

blame [bleɪm] **1** *sb* feil, skyld; ansvar; **2** *vt* skylde på. **blameless** *adj* skyldfri; feilfri, uklanderlig.

blanch [blɑ:ntʃ] *vb* bleke(s); *~ed almonds* skåldede mandler.

bland [blænd] *adj* **1** imøtekommende; (nedlatende) vennlig; **2** behagelig, mild.

blandish ['blændɪʃ] *vt* smigre; smiske for. **blandishment** ['blændɪʃmənt] *sb* smiger; smisking.

blank [blæŋk] **I** *adj* blank; tom; ubeskrevet; **II** *sb* **1** tomrom; åpen plass; **2** blankett, skjema; **3** *data* blankfelt; **4** nite (dvs blankt lodd, uten gevinst); *fig* bomskudd; **5** blankett (dvs råemne til mynt etc).

blanket ['blæŋkɪt] **1** *sb* (ull)teppe; **2** *vb* dekke (som) med et teppe; *fig* dekke, skjule.

blare ['bleə] **1** *sb* brøl; (trompet)støt; **2** *vb* gjalle, skingre; tute.

blaspheme [blæs'fi:m] *vb* spotte (Gud); *dgl* banne, sverge. **blasphemous** ['blæsfəməs] *adj* blasfemisk, (guds)bespottelig. **blasphemy** ['blæsfəmɪ] *sb* blasfemi, (guds)bespottelse.

blast [blɑ:st] **I** *sb* **1** kraftig vindkast; *at/in full ~* med full styrke; i full fart (gang/sving etc); **2** eksplosjon; minering, sprengning; **3** ladning, (minerings)-skudd; **4** (luft)trykkbølge; **II** *vt* **1** minere, sprenge; **2** ruinere; skade, ødelegge; *~ it!* pokker ta (det)! **blasted** ['blɑ:stɪd] *adj dgl* forbasket, fordømt; pokkers. **blast-furnace** *sb* masovn.

blatant ['bleɪtənt] *adj* bråkende; høyrøstet; påtrengende.

blaze [bleɪz] **A I** *sb* **1** bluss, flamme; **2** brann; (flammende) bål; *~ of colour* glødende fargeprakt; **3** utbrudd; **II** *vb* **1** brenne (klart); *~ up* flamme opp; **2** skinne, stråle; **3** bryte ut; **4** utbasunere; **5** *~ away* fyre løs (med skytevåpen); **B I** *sb* **1** bles; **2** blink (dvs merke etter tømmerblinking); **II** *vt* blinke (tømmer); *~ a trail* merke en sti etc; rydde/*fig* bane vei.

blazon ['bleɪzn] **1** *sb* våpen(skjold); **2** = *blaze A II 4.* **blazonry** ['bleɪzənrɪ] *sb* heraldikk.

bleach [bli:tʃ] *vb* bleke(s). **bleaching agent** *sb* blekemiddel; *også* fargefjerner.

bleak [bli:k] *adj* **1** guffen, (rå)kald; **2** dyster; forblåst; gold.

blear ['blɪə] *adj, vt* (gjøre) tåket/uklar. **bleary** ['blɪərɪ], **bleary-eyed** *adj* surøyd, vassøyd.

bleat [bli:t] **1** *sb* breking *etc*; **2** *vi: om sau* breke; *om geit* mekre; *om kalv* raute.

bleed [bli:d] *vb* **1** blø; **2** årelate; såre til blods; **3** *a)* svette, skille ut vann/væske; *b) petro* skille/svette ut (olje fra smørefett); **4** *slang* (få til å) punge ut/betale i dyre dommer; *~ white* flå til skinnet.

blemish ['blemɪʃ] **1** *sb* flekk; *især fig* lyte, plett; **2** *vt* skjemme ut, vansire.

blench [blentʃ] *vi* fare sammen; vike tilbake; *without ~ing* uten å blunke.

blend [blend] **1** *sb* blanding, mikstur; **2** *vb* blande (seg). **blender** ['blendə] *sb* blander, blandeaggregat.

bless [bles] *vt* **1** velsigne; **2** love/prise (Gud etc); **3** *~ oneself* korse seg; *~ me/my soul!* bevares! bevare meg vel! **blessed** ['blesɪd] *adj* **1** velsignet; hellig; salig; **2** *slang* fordømt. **blessing** ['blesɪŋ] *sb* **1** velsignelse; **2** bordbønn.

blight [blaɪt] **I** *sb* **1** *om plantesykdommer* brann, meldugg, rust; **2** *fig* pest, plage; **II** *vt* **1** skade, ødelegge; **2** *fig* forpeste, plage. **Blighty** ['blaɪtɪ] *sb slang* (gode, gamle) England.

blimey ['blaɪmɪ] *interj vulg* jøss.

blimp [blɪmp] *sb* **1** lite luftskip; **2** tjukkas; **3** flokse; **4** (film)kassett; **5** *Colonel Blimp* (typen på en) trangsynt reaksjonær.

blind [blaɪnd] **I** *adj* blind (*in/of* på; *to* for); **II** *sb* **1** rullegardin; skodde; *Venetian ~* persienne; **2** bakhold, skjul; *fig* skalkeskjul; **3** blindspor; **III** *vt* **1** blinde; **2** *data* skjerme. **blind alley** *sb* blindgate. **blindfold** ['blaɪndfəʊld] **1** *adj, adv* med bind for øynene; **2** *vt* binde for øynene på. **blindman's buff** *sb* blindebukk (dvs leken).

blink [blɪŋk] **I** *sb* **1** blink, blunk; **2** glimt; **II** *vb* **1** blinke/blunke (med); **2** glimte; **3** lukke øynene for, overse. **blinkers** ['blɪŋkəz] *sb fl* skylapper. **blinking** ['blɪŋkɪŋ] *adj slang* jævlig.

bliss [blɪs] *sb* fryd, lykksalighet. **blissful** ['blisfʊl] *adj* lykksalig.

blister ['blɪstə] **I** *sb* **1** blemme, vable; blære; **2** *med* trekkplaster; **II** *vb* **1** få blemmer; danne blærer; **2** legge på trekkplaster.

blithe [blaɪð] *adj* glad(lynt), munter.

blizzard ['blɪzəd] *sb* snøstorm.

bloated ['bləʊtɪd] *adj* oppblåst, pløsen; fet; *fig* hoven.

bloc [blɒk] *sb* blokk (av stater). **block** [blɒk] **I** *sb* **1** blokk [f.eks. frimerkeblokk, hatteblokk, retterblokk, huggestabbe; *data også* datablokk]; **2** (bolig)blokk; (bygnings)kompleks; (by)kvartal; *~ of flats* leiegård; **3** kloss; **4** klisjé; **5** sperring; **6** (talje)blokk; *~ and tackle* talje; **II** *vt* **1** blokkere, sperre; **2** blokke (hatter, sko etc); **3** *data* blokke; **4** *~ in/out* skissere/streke opp.

blockade [blɒ'keɪd] **1** *sb* blokade; *raise/run the ~* heve/bryte blokaden; **2** *vt* blokkere.

block | character *sb data* blokksluttegn. *~* **check** *sb data* blokkontroll.

blockhead ['blɒkhed] *sb* tosk. **blockish** ['blɒkɪʃ] *adj* dum, innskrenket.

block letters *sb fl* blokkbokstaver.

bloke [bləʊk] *sb dgl* fyr, kompis.

blond(e) [blɒnd] *adj* blond, lys. **blonde** [blɒnd] *sb* blondine.

blood [blʌd] *sb* blod; *~-and-thunder story* røverhistorie; *in cold ~* med kaldt blod. **blood | bank** *sb* blodbank. **~-curdling** *adj* nifs [egtl som får blodet til å fryse/stivne i årene]. **~-donor** *sb* blodgiver. **~-group** *sb* = *~-type*. **~hound** *sb* blodhund. **~less** *adj* 1 blek, blodfattig; tander; 2 ublodig; 3 *fig* (følelses) kald. **~letting** *sb* årelating. **~poisoning** *sb* blodforgiftning. **~-pressure** *sb* blodtrykk. **~shed** *sb* blodsutgytelse; blodbad. **~shot** *adj* blodskutt. **~-stained** *adj* blodig, blod|flekket; *fig* -besudlet. **~thirsty** *adj* blodtørstig. **~-transfusion** *sb* blodoverføring. **~-type** *sb* blodtype. **~-vessel** *sb* blod|kar, -åre. **bloody** *adj* 1 blodig; 2 *slang* fordømt, helvetes.

bloom [blu:m] **I** *sb* 1 (pryd)blomst; *in the ~ of youth* i sin fagreste ungdom, i ungdommens vår; 2 blomst, blomstring; 3 dun (på fruktskall, hud etc); 4 fargespill, skinn (som f.eks. på olje); fluoresens; **II** *vi* blomstre; stå i (full) blomst. **bloomer** ['blu:mə] *sb* **A** flause, tabbe; **B** *fl* gammeldagse dame(under)bukser. **blooming** ['blu:mɪŋ] *adj* 1 blomstrende; 2 = *bloody 2.*

blossom ['blɒsəm] **I** *sb* 1 (frukt)blomst; 2 = *bloom I 2*; **II** = *bloom II.*

blot [blɒt] **I** *sb* flekk; *fig* lyte; **II** *vt* 1 bruke trekkpapir på; *~ out* (ut)slette.

blotch [blɒtʃ] *sb* 1 blemme; (fø)flekk; kvise; 2 = *blot I.*

blotter ['blɒtə] *sb* løsjer, trekkpapir(mappe); kladdebok. **blotting-paper** ['blɒtɪŋ,peɪpə] *sb* trekkpapir.

blouse [blauz] *sb* bluse.

blow [bləu] **A** *sb* slag, støt; *fl også* slagsmål; 2 sjokk, slag; **B** = *bloom I 2*; **C I** *sb* 1 blåst; 2 vind|kast, -kule, -støt; 3 luftetur; frisk luft; **II** *vb* 1 blåse (og blåse på; fløyte, pipe, tute; pese, pruste etc); *~ in* komme fykende; *~ off steam* slippe ut damp; *fig* avreagere; *~ over* drive over; *~ out* blåse ut; *~ up* blåse/pumpe opp; sprenge/bli sprengt i luften; *dgl* forstørre (f.eks. fotografi); *fig* over|dimensjonere, -drive; *~ one's lid/top* fly i flint; *~ one's own trumpet* skryte (av seg selv); 2 *slang: ~ money* sløse med penger; *~ the expense* blåse i utgiftene. **blow|lamp** *sb* blåselampe. **~out** *sb* utblåsing; *petro især* utblåsing av olje fra borehull; *~out preventer* utblåsingssikring. **~torch** *sb* = *~ lamp.*

blubber ['blʌbə] 1 *sb* (hval)spekk; 2 *vi* grine, tute; *~ out* hikste frem.

bludgeon ['blʌdʒən] 1 *sb* klubbe, kølle; 2 *vt* slå med klubbe *etc.*

blue [blu:] **I** *adj* 1 blå; 2 melankolsk, nedfor; 3 *once in a ~ moon* en sjelden gang; **II** *sb* 1 blått; 2 *fl* blues (= melankolsk melodi/vise etc); *have got the ~s* være/føle seg melankolsk *etc*; **III** *vt* 1 farge blå; 2 *slang* sløse bort. **blue|bell** *sb skotsk* blåklokke. **~berry** *sb* skinntryte. **~-blooded** *adj* adelig, med blått blod. **~bottle** *sb* spyflue. **~ gas** *sb petro* vanngass. **~print** *sb* blåkopi; *at the ~ stage (fig)* på tegnebrettet.

bluff [blʌf] **A** 1 *sb* bløff; 2 *vb* bløffe; **B I** *adj* 1 bratt; 2 barsk (men real); **II** *sb* skrent.

blunder ['blʌndə] **I** *sb* flause, tabbe; **II** *vi* 1 gjøre en tabbe; 2 *~ into* ramle/komme farende inn i; dumpe opp i.

blunt [blʌnt] **I** *adj* 1 sløv, stump; butt; 2 avvisende, barsk; **II** *vt* sløve.

blur [blɜ:] 1 *sb* tåke (dvs uklarhet); 2 *vb* dimme, sløre; bli/gjøre uklar.

blurb [blɜ:b] *sb* omslagstekst (på bok).

blurt [blɜ:t] *vt: ~ out* plumpe ut med.

blush [blʌʃ] *sb, vi* rødme.

bluster ['blʌstə] **I** *sb* 1 bråk, mas; 2 skryt; **II** *vi* 1 bråke; bruke seg; 2 skryte.

boar [bɔ:] *sb* 1 villsvin; 2 galte.

board [bɔ:d] **I** *sb* 1 planke (og bord, brett, plate, tavle etc); 2 (spise)bord (og kost, dvs mat); *~ and lodgings* kost og losji; 3 (råds)bord (og råd; direksjon, styre; komité, nemnd, utvalg etc); 4 (spille)bord; 5 *sjø* baut, slag; skipsside; *go by the ~* gå over bord; *fig* gå i vasken; 6 *the ~s* de skrå bredder (dvs teateret); **II** *vb* 1 bordkle, panele; 2 ha i kosten; ha losjerende; *~ at/with* losjere hos; 3 *sjø* borde, entre; gå om bord (i). **boarder** ['bɔ:də] *sb* 1 leieboer, pensjonær; 2 kostskoleelev; 3 *sjø* entregast. **boarding** ['bɔ:dɪŋ] *sb* 1 bordkledning, panel(ing); 2 pensjon. **boarding|-house** *sb* pensjonat. **~-school** *sb* kostskole. **board|-room** *sb* styrerom. **~-wages** *sb fl* kostpenger.

boast [bəust] **I** *sb* 1 skryt; 2 noe å skryte av; **II** *vb* 1 skryte; 2 nevne med stolthet; rose seg av (å ha/være etc).

boat [bəut] 1 *sb* båt; 2 *vi* reise med båt. **boatswain** ['bəusn] *sb* båtsmann.

bob [bɒb] **I** *sb* 1 kniks; nikk; 2 kortklipt hår; stusset hale; 3 dobbe; dupp; (lite) lodd; pendelskive; 4 *slang = shilling*; **II** *vb* 1 knikse; nikke; 2 kortklippe; stusse; 3 duppe; rykke; *~ up* dukke opp.

bobbin ['bɒbɪn] *sb* spole.

bobby ['bɒbɪ] *sb gml dgl* (engelsk) politimann.

bode [bəud] *vb* bære bud om, (inn)varsle. **bodeful** ['bəudful] *adj* illevarslende.

bodice ['bɒdɪs] *sb* (kjole)liv.

bodily ['bɒdɪlɪ] 1 *adj* kroppslig, legemlig; 2 *adv* i samlet tropp. **body** ['bɒdɪ] *sb* 1 kropp (og person; legeme, lik; hoveddel som f.eks. karosseri, skrog, stamme); 2 gruppe, korps; (for)samling; *in a ~* alle som en. **bodyguard** ['bɒdɪgɑ:d] *sb* livvakt.

bog [bɒg] 1 *sb* myr; 2 *vt: be/get ~ged down* kjøre seg fast (f.eks. i myr, men også *fig*). **boggy** ['bɒgɪ] *adj* myrlendt.

bog(e)y ['bəugɪ] *sb* buse(mann); skrømt, spøkelse.

bogus ['bəugəs] *adj* humbug-, svindel-.

boil [bɔɪl] **A** *sb* byll; **B** 1 *sb* kok; 2 *vb* koke; *~ down* koke inn; *fig* redusere. **boiler** ['bɔɪlə] *sb* 1 kjel(e); 2 varmtvannsbeholder. **boilerplate** ['bɔɪləpleɪt] *sb data* standardtekst.

boisterous ['bɔɪstərəs] *adj* bråkende; voldsom.

bold [bəuld] *adj* 1 djerv, modig; 2 *(~faced)* freidig, frekk; 3 dristig (i linjeføring, snitt, utførelse etc); klar, tydelig; *om skrift* fet. **boldface** ['bəuldfeɪs] *adj,* *sb* (halv)fet (skrift).

bole [bəul] *sb* (tre)stamme.

bollard ['bɒləd] *sb* **1** *sjø* puller; **2** blinkfyr (e.l. til markering av kjørefelt etc).

bolster ['bəulstə] **1** *sb* (under)pute; **2** *vt (~ up)* støtte (opp) med puter; *fig* sy puter under armene på.

bolt [bəult] **I** *adv: ~ upright* rett opp og ned; **II** *sb* **1** bolt, (maskin)skrue; **2** rigel, skåte; **3** pil (især til armbrøst); **4** lyn; *thunder~* tordenkile; *~ from the blue* lyn fra klar himmel; *make a ~ for it* stikke av; **5** (tøy)rull; **III** *vb* **1** bolte (fast); **2** sette bom/slå for; **3** løpe løpsk; stikke av; **4** sluke (mat).

bomb [bɒm] *sb, vt* bombe. **bombard** [bɒm'bɑ:d] *vt* bombardere. **bombardment** [bɒm'bɑ:dmənt] *sb* bombardement. **bomber** ['bɒmə] *sb* bombefly. **bombshell** ['bɒmʃel] *sb fig* bombe (dvs stor overraskelse etc).

bonanza [bəu'nænzə] *sb US* rik gull- el. sølvåre; *fig* gullgruve.

bond [bɒnd] **I** *sb* **1** bånd; *fl fig* lenker; **2** forpliktelse; **3** *merk* obligasjon; **4** (mursteins)forband; **5** *merk* frilager; **II** *vt merk* legge på frilager. **bondage** ['bɒndɪdʒ] *sb* livegenskap; *også fig* slaveri.

bone [bəun] **I** *sb* **1** bein, knokkel; **2** *~ of contention* stridens eple; *make no ~s about* ikke komme med innvendinger; ikke legge skjul på; *også* ikke betenke seg; **II** *vt* rense for bein.

bonfire ['bɒn,faɪə] *sb* (fest)bål.

bonnet ['bɒnɪt] *sb* **1** kyse(hatt); **2** skottelue; **3** (bil)panser.

bonnie, bonny ['bɒnɪ] *adj* **1** kjekk; **2** frodig, lubben.

bony ['bəunɪ] *adj* knoklet, radmager.

boo [bu:] **1** *interj* fy!; **2** *vb* pipe (ut).

boob [bu:b] *US* = **booby** ['bu:bɪ] *sb* tosk. **booby-trap** ['bu:bɪtræp] *sb* (mine)felle.

book [buk] **I** *sb* bok; *bring to ~* trekke til ansvar; *by the ~* korrekt [egtl etter/i samsvar med boken]; **II** *vb* **1** bokføre; **2** notere [f.eks. for parkeringsforseelse]; **3** bestille (billetter etc, *for* til); *~ed up* bortbestilt, utsolgt. **bookcase** *sb* bok|hylle, -skap. **booking | clerk** *sb* billettselger. **~ office** *sb* billettkontor.

bookie ['bukɪ] *slang = bookmaker.*

bookish ['bukɪʃ] *adj* boklig; pedantisk.

book|-keeper *sb* bokholder. **~let** *sb* brosjyre, hefte. **~maker** *sb* veddeløpsagent. **~seller** *sb* bok|-handler, -selger. **~shop** *sb* bokhandel. **~-stall** *sb* (avis)kiosk. **~store** *sb US = ~shop.*

boom [bu:m] **A** *sb* **1** *sjø* bom; **2** lense; **B 1** *sb* brak, drønn; (kanon)torden; **2** *vi* drønne, tordne; **C I** *sb merk* høykonjunktur; oppsving; **II** *vb* **1** oppreklamere; drive opp (salg etc); **2** stige/øke sterkt; *fig* blomstre.

boon [bu:n] **I** *adj: ~ companion* god kamerat; **II** *sb* **1** fordel; **2** gave; gratiale; *fig* velsignelse.

boor ['buə] slamp; simpel fyr. **boorish** ['buərɪʃ] *adj* grov, ubehøvlet; simpel.

boost [bu:st] **I** *sb fig* **1** innsprøytning, oppstrammer (især om reklamekampanje etc); **2** oppstiver; puff (i oppmuntrende retning); **II** *vt* **1** drive opp (salg ved kraftig reklame etc); **2** oppmuntre; *fig* skyve på; stive opp; **3** forsterke/øke (effekt, spenning etc). **booster** ['bu:stə] *sb* forsterker; *petro også* pumpestasjon; kompressor, trykkforsterker.

boot [bu:t] **A I** *sb* støvel; *get/give the ~ (slang)* få/gi sparken; **II** *vt* **1** sparke (dvs avskjedige); **2** *data* starte opp; **B** *sb* bagasjerom (i bil etc); **C 1** *sb* gagn, nytte; *to ~* på kjøpet; **2** *vt* gagne, nytte. **boot|black** *sb* skopusser. **~ button** *sb data* oppstartingstast. **~ diskette** *sb data* oppstartingsdiskett.

booth [bu:θ] *sb* **1** (salgs)bod; **2** stemmeavlukke; **3** (restaurant)bås; **4** *US* (telefon)kiosk.

boot|lace *sb* skolisse. **~legger** *sb US* (brennevins)smugler; (sprit)gauk. **~less** *adj* fåfengt. **~licker** *sb* spyttslikker. **~strap I** *sb* **1** støvelstropp; **2** *data* primærlaster; **II** *vt data* primærlaste.

booty ['bu:tɪ] *sb* bytte, rov; hærfang.

booze [bu:z] *dgl* **1** *sb* børst (dvs brennevin); **2** *vi* børste (dvs drikke brennevin); rangle, ture.

border [bɔ:də] **I** *sb* **1** bord, kant, rand; **2** grense(område); **II** *vb* **1** grense til; **2** avgrense; begrense.

bore [bɔ:] **A I** *sb* **1** borehull; **2** borevidde; kaliber; løp (på skytevåpen); **II** *vt* bore; **B 1** *sb* kjedelig person; *fig* plage; **2** *vt* kjede; *be ~d* kjede seg. **boredom** ['bɔ:dəm] *sb* kjedsom(melig)het. **boring** ['bɔ:rɪŋ] *adj* kjedelig. **boring oil** *sb petro etc* boreolje.

borough ['bʌrə] *sb* by, bykommune, kjøpstad (med rett til representasjon i Parlamentet); valgkrets; *rotten ~* valgkrets som, enda den kanskje bare eksisterte på papiret, hadde slik rett frem til reformen av 1832.

borrow ['bɒrəu] *vb* låne (av andre).

Borstal ['bɔ:stl] *sb (~ Institution)* skolehjem (for unge lovovertredere).

bosom ['buzəm] *sb* barm, bryst; *fig også* skjød.

boss [bɒs] **A** *dgl* **1** *sb* bas, sjef; **2** *vb* dominere; styre, stå for; **B** *sb* **1** knapp, knott; **2** (hjul)nav. **bossy** ['bɒsɪ] *adj* **A** *dgl* dominerende, herskesyk; sjefete; **B** bulket.

botanic(al) [bə'tænɪk(l)] *adj* botanisk. **botanist** ['bɒtənɪst] *sb* botaniker. **botany** ['bɒtənɪ] *sb* botanikk.

both [bəuθ] **1** *adj, adv, pron* begge; *have it ~ ways* få i både pose og sekk; **2** *konj: both ... and* både ... og.

bother ['bɒðə] **1** *sb* bry(deri); plage; mas; **2** *vb* bry (seg med); gidde; mase på, plage.

bottle ['bɒtl] **1** *sb* flaske; **2** *vt* fylle/tappe på flaske(r). **bottleneck** *sb* flaskehals.

bottom ['bɒtəm] *sb* **1** bunn; underside; *fig* innerste vesen; *at the ~ (of)* nederst (i/på); på bunnen (av); *at ~ (fig)* i bunn og grunn, på bunnen; **2** *fl petro etc* bunnprodukter; *~s cut, ~s fraction* restfraksjon; **3** sete; *slang* bak(ende). **bottom|-hole pressure** *sb petro* bunntrykk. **~ margin** *sb data etc* bunnmarg.

bough [bau] (hoved)gren.

boulder ['bəuldə] *sb* kampestein, rullestein.

bounce [baʊns] **I** *sb* **1** hopp, sprett; **2** bråk; skryt; **II** *vb* **1** hoppe; (få til å) sprette; **2** bykse, jumpe; dumpe, humpe; ~ *into* komme brasende (farende, settende etc) inn. **bouncing** ['baʊnsɪŋ] *adj* bumset; kraftig.

bound [baʊnd] **A** *sb, vb* (be)grense; *out of ~s* adgang forbudt (*to* for); **B** *sb, vb* byks(e), hopp(e), jump(e); sprett(e); **C** *adj:* ~ *for* bestemt for; på vei til; **2** ~ *to* (forut)bestemt/nødt til (å); ~ *up in* fordypet i; sterkt interessert i/opptatt av; ~ *up with* nøye forbundet med. **boundary** ['baʊndərɪ] *sb* grense(linje). **boundary function** *sb data* grensefunksjon. **bounden** ['baʊndən] *adj: your ~ duty* din simple plikt.

bounteous ['baʊntɪəs], **bountiful** ['baʊntɪfʊl] *adj* gavmild, rundhåndet; rikelig. **bounty** ['baʊntɪ] *sb* **1** gavmildhet; **2** gave; **3** bonus; premie.

bouquet [bʊ'keɪ] *sb* **1** bukett; **2** bouquet.

bourbon ['bɜ:bən] *sb* (type *US*) whisky.

bourgeois ['bʊəʒwɑ:] *adj, sb* bursjoa(-). **bourgeoisie** [ˌbʊəʒwɑ:'zi:] *sb* bursjoasi.

bout [baʊt] *sb* **1** anfall, ri; raptus; **2** omgang, runde, tørn.

bow [baʊ] **A 1** *sb* bukk; **2** *vb* bukke; ~ *to* bøye seg for; **B** [baʊ] *sb sjø* baug; **C** [bəʊ] *sb* **1** bue; **2** kurve; **3** løkke, sløyfe.

bowel ['baʊəl] *sb* tarm; *fl* innvoller; *fig* indre. **bowel movement** *sb* avføring.

bower ['baʊə] *sb* **1** lysthus; **2** karnapp; jomfrubur.

bowl [bəʊl] **A I** *sb* bowlingkule; kjeglekule; **II** *vb* **1** bowle; spille kjegler; **2** kaste/spille ball; ~ *over* kaste over ende; *fig* gjøre målløs; **3** rulle; trille; **B** *sb* **1** bolle, skål; **2** pipehode; **3** skjeblad. **bowler** ['bəʊlə] *sb* **1** kaster (i cricket); **2** skalk, stivhatt.

bow-legged ['bəʊlegd] *adj* hjulbeint.

bowling alley ['bəʊlɪŋˌælɪ] *sb* bowlingbane; kjeglebane.

bow|sprit ['bəʊsprɪt] *sb* baugspryd. **~-tie** [ˌbəʊ'taɪ] *sb* flue, sløyfe, tversoverslips. **~-window** [ˌbəʊ'wɪndəʊ] *sb* karnappvindu.

box [bɒks] **A I** *sb* **1** boks, eske, kasse; **2** losje (i teater etc); **3** skilderhus; vaktstue; (liten) hytte; **4** bås, spiltau; **II** *vt* legge i boks *etc*; ~ *up* stenge inne; **B 1** *sb* ørefik; **2** *vb* bokse; fike til; **C** *sb* = *~wood*; **D** *Boxing Day* 2. juledag. **box | office** *sb* billettkontor. **~-office success** *sb* kassestykke (dvs teaterstykke etc som går godt). **~wood** *sb* buksbom.

boy [bɔɪ] *sb* **1** gutt; **2** (innfødt) tjener.

boycott ['bɔɪkət] *sb, vb* boikott(e).

boy|-friend *sb* (jentes) kjæreste/venn. **~hood** *sb* guttedager, (gutts) barndom. **~ish** *adj* gutteaktig. **~ scout** *sb* guttespeider, speidergutt.

bra [brɑ:] *sb dgl* behå, brystholder [jf *brassière*].

brace [breɪs] **A I** *sb* **1** støtte(bjelke etc); knekt; **2** klamp; strammer; *fl* klammer; **3** stag; *sjø* bras; **4** borvinde; **5** *fl* (bukse)seler; **II** *vt* **1** avstive, styrke, støtte; **2** stramme; spenne (inn); ~ *oneself*, ~ *up* stramme (seg) opp; **3** *sjø* brase; **B** *sb* par (om fugler og hunder). **bracelet** ['breɪslɪt] *sb* armbånd; *fl slang* håndjern. **bracer** ['breɪsə] *sb slang* hjertestyrker. **bracing** ['breɪsɪŋ] *adj* forfriskende, styrkende.

bracken ['brækn] *sb* bregne.

bracket ['brækɪt] **I** *sb* **1** (hylle)knekt; konsoll; lampettarm; **2** (hake)parentes; klamme(r); **3** gruppe, klasse; **II** *vt* **1** sette i parentes; **2** ~ *together* sette i samme klasse (båt, gruppe etc).

brackish ['brækɪʃ] *adj* brakk(-).

brad [bræd] *sb* stift. **bradawl** ['brædɔ:l] *sb* syl.

brag [bræg] *vi* skryte. **braggart** ['brægət] *sb* skrythals.

braid [breɪd] **I** *sb* **1** flette; **2** snor, tresse; **II** *vt* **1** flette; **2** besette med snorer *etc*.

brain [breɪn] **1** *sb* hjerne; *fl* forstand, vett; *rack one's ~(s)* vri hjernen; **2** *vt* slå skallen inn på. **brain-wave** *sb* lys idé. **brainy** *adj* intelligent, skarp.

brake [breɪk] *sb, vb* brems(e).

bramble ['bræmbl] *sb* **1** klunger; tornebusk, tornekratt; **2** bjørnebær(busk).

branch [brɑ:ntʃ] **I** *sb* **1** gren; *fig også* arm, utløper; **2** *merk* bransje; avdeling, filial; **II** *vi* skyte grener; *fig* forgrene seg.

brand [brænd] **I** *sb* **1** brann; glo; fakkel; **2** svijern; svimerke; *fig* skamplett; **3** *merk* varemerke; fabrikat, kvalitet; **II** *vt* brennemerke; *fig* stemple. **branding-iron** *sb* svijern.

brandish ['brændɪʃ] *vt* svinge (især sverd).

brand-new *adj* splinter ny.

brandy ['brændɪ] *sb* konjakk.

brass [brɑ:s] **I** *sb* **1** messing; **2** messinginstrumenter; **II** *sb dgl* **1** = *~-hat*; **2** *slang* gryn (dvs penger); **3** frekkhet. **brass | band** *sb* hornorkester. **~ check** *sb* bestikkelse, smøring. **~-hat** *sb dgl* høyere offiser.

brassière ['bræsɪə] *sb* brystholder.

brass tack *sb* **1** messingstift; **2** *get down to ~ ~s* komme til saken. **brassy** ['brɑ:sɪ] **I** *adj* **1** messingaktig, messing-; **2** skingrende, skurrende; **3** *slang* frekk; **II** *sb* golfkølle.

brat [bræt] *sb* (uskikkelig etc) unge.

bravado [brə'vɑ:dəʊ] *sb* **1** dumdristighet; **2** kjekkaseri, skryt. **brave** [breɪv] **1** *adj* modig, tapper; **2** *vt* trosse; utfordre. **bravery** ['breɪvərɪ] *sb* mot, tapperhet.

brawl [brɔ:l] **I** *sb* **1** krangel, trette; **2** slagsmål; **3** bråk, spetakkel; **II** *vi* **1** bråke; **2** krangle, trette.

brawn [brɔ:n] *sb* **1** muskler; styrke; **2** (grise)sylte. **brawny** ['brɔ:nɪ] *adj* muskuløs.

bray [breɪ] **A I** *sb* **1** eselskryt; **2** trompetstøt; **II** *vi* **1** skryte (som et esel); **2** skratte (som en trompet); **B** *vt* støte; finknuse, male.

brazen ['breɪzn] **1** *adj* = *brassy I*; **2** *vt:* ~ *it out* frekt late som ingeng ting.

brazier ['breɪzɪə] *sb* **1** fyrfat; **2** gjørtler.

breach [bri:tʃ] **I** *sb* **1** brudd (på lov, løfte etc); **2** bresje; gjennombrudd (i frontlinje/mur etc); **II** *vt* bryte gjennom.

bread [bred] **1** *sb* brød [i sin alminnelighet, dvs som produkt eller næringsmiddel]; *loaf of ~* brød (dvs om det enkelte brød); **2** *vt* griljere, panere.

breadth [bredθ] *sb* bredde; *fig* vidde.

bread-winner *sb* (familie)forsørger.

break [breɪk] **I** *sb* **1** brudd; revne, rift; lekkasje; **2** avbrudd, avbrytelse; brudd (også *data*); pause; friminutt; **3** omslag, skifte; overgang (i jazz); **4** *dgl* sjanse; *rotten* ~ uflaks; **5** *US* flause; **II** *vb* **1** brekke (og knekke, knuse; bryte ned; gå/slå i stykker; *data* bryte; *fig* bryte, overtre; degradere (offiser); ruinere, ødelegge etc); **2** *med adv/prep* ~ **down** bryte(s) ned; ta fra hverandre; bryte sammen; *fig også* analysere; spesifisere; ~ **in** *(horses etc)* temme; ri/kjøre in (hester etc); ~ **in (up)on** avbryte; trenge seg på; ~ **loose** bryte/rive seg løs; ~ **through** bryte *etc* igjennom; ~ **up** bryte *etc* opp; splitte (folkemasse); *fig* gå/reise fra hverandre, skille(s); begynne på (skole)ferie etc; bryte ned, ødelegge(s); falle fra hverandre; forfalle, falle sammen; klarne (om vær); **3** ~ *the back of* få unna det tyngste/vanskeligste; ~ *even* spille *etc* uavgjort; holde det så vidt gående; *merk* gå i balanse (dvs verken tjene eller tape noe); ~ *a fall* ta av for et fall; ~ *the news* meddele (sørgelig) nyhet så skånsomt som mulig.

breakage ['breɪkɪdʒ] *sb* **1** brudd(sted): **2** brekkasje. **breakdown** *sb* sammenbrudd; driftsstans, motorstopp; *fig* analyse, spesifikasjon. **breaker** *sb* brottsjø. **break|fast** ['brekfəst] *sb, vb* (spise) frokost. ~ **key** *sb data* stopptast. ~**neck** *adj* halsbrekkende. ~**point** *sb data* avbruddspunkt. ~**-through** *sb* gjennombrudd. ~**-up** *sb* oppbrudd *etc*; skoleslutt (før ferie); forfall, oppløsning. ~**water** *sb* bølgebryter.

bream [bri:m] **A** *sb* brasme; **B** *vt* skrape (båt).

breast [brest] **I** *sb* **1** bryst; **2** *make a clean* ~ *of* tilstå åpent og ærlig; **II** *vt* **1** sette brystet mot; **2** stevne mot (strøm, vind etc); *fig* trosse; utfordre. **breasting dolphin** *sb petro* fender. **breastwork** *sb* brystvern.

breath [breθ] *sb* pust, åndedrag; *below/under one's* ~ hviskende. **breathe** ['bri:ð] *vb* **1** puste; **2** hviske; **3** *petro etc* (av)lufte. **breathless** ['breθlɪs] *adj* andpusten; *fig* åndeløs.

breech [bri:tʃ] *sb* bakstykke, kammer, laderom (på skytevåpen). **breeches** ['brɪtʃɪz] *sb fl* (kne)bukser; *riding-*~ ridebukser.

breed [bri:d] **I** *sb* (husdyr)rase; **II** *vb* **1** avle, føde; *fig* frembringe; forårsake; **2** ale opp, oppdrette; **3** fostre, oppdra; *well-bred* veloppdragen. **breeding** *sb* **1** oppdrett; **2** (gode) manerer. **breeding fire** *sb petro* stikkflamme.

breeze [bri:z] **I** *sb* **1** bris, luftning; **2** *dgl* småkrangel; utidighet; **II** *vi* **1** blåse (lett); **2** fare, feie, fyke. **breezy** ['bri:zɪ] *adj* **1** frisk; luftig; **2** jovial; livlig.

brethren ['breðrɪn] *sb fl gml* brødre.

brevity ['brevətɪ] *sb* korthet.

brew [bru:] **I** *sb* brygg, drikk; **II** *vb* **1** brygge (øl); trakte (te etc); **2** *fig* brygge på. **brewer** ['bruə] *sb* (øl)brygger. **brewery** ['bruərɪ] *sb* bryggeri.

briar ['braɪə] *sb* briar(pipe).

bribe [braɪb] **1** *sb* bestikkelse [om pengene etc]; **2** *vt* bestikke. **bribery** ['braɪbərɪ] *sb* bestikkelse [om handlingen].

brick [brɪk] **I** *sb* **1** murstein, teglstein; **2** liten blokk; (bygge)kloss; **3** *slang* kjekk kar; **II** *vt* mure (*in/up* igjen). **brick|bats** *sb fl* mur(steins)|biter, -rester. ~**-field** *sb* teglverk. ~**-kiln** *sb* teglovn. ~**-layer** *sb* murer.

bridal ['braɪdl] **1** *adj* brude-, bryllups-; **2** *sb* bryllup. **bride** [braɪd] *sb* brud. **bridegroom** ['braɪdgrum] *sb* brudgom. **bridesmaid** ['braɪdzmeɪd] *sb* brudepike.

bridge [brɪdʒ] **A I** *sb* **1** bro (også *data*); **2** stol (på fiolin); **3** neserygg; **II** *vt* slå bro over; **B** *sb* (kortspillet) bridge. **bridge | plug** *sb petro* broplugg. ~**wall** *sb petro* flamme|bro, -vegg.

bridle ['braɪdl] **I** *sb* beksel; tøyle; **II** *vb* **1** beksle; *også fig* tøyle; **2** kneise med nakken.

brief [bri:f] **A I** *adj* kort (dvs kortfattet, kortvarig); **II** *sb* sammendrag; (advokats) saksfremstilling; *fl* (retts)saker; saksdokumenter; **III** *vt* **1** engasjere advokat; **2** instruere, orientere; *også* briefe; **B** *sb* truse.

brig [brɪg] *sb sjø* **1** brigg; **2** arrest.

brigand ['brɪgənd] *sb* (landeveis)røver.

bright [braɪt] *adj* **1** klar, lys; **2** munter; **3** gløgg, oppvakt. **brighten** ['braɪtn] *vb* **1** lysne; lyse opp; **2** (blank)pusse; **3** kvikne til; live opp. **brightness** ['braɪtnɪs] *sb* klarhet *etc*; (lys)|skinn, -skjær.

brilliance ['brɪlɪəns] *sb* **1** (stråle)glans; **2** overlegen dyktighet; strålende begavelse. **brilliant** ['brɪlɪənt] *adj* **1** glitrende, strålende; **2** glimrende; **3** strålende begavet.

brim [brɪm] **I** *sb* **1** kant, rand; **2** brem; **II** *vb* **1** fylle til randen; **2** renne over. **brimful** ['brɪmful] *adj* breddfull.

brimstone ['brɪmstən] *sb* svovel.

brindle(d) ['brɪndl(d)] *adj* brannet, stripet.

brine [braɪn] *sb* saltlake; *petro også* lut.

bring [brɪŋ] *vb* **1** bringe; hente; ha/ta med (seg); komme med; **2** *med adv/prep* ~ **about** forårsake, få i stand; *sjø* vende; ~ *an action/a charge* **against** reise sak/ tiltale mot; ~ **back** bringe *etc* tilbake; få til å huske (på); ~ **down** hente/ta ned; felle (= skyte ned); *fig* få ned på jorden igjen; ~ **forward** legge frem (især *fig*); *merk* overføre; ~ **in** bringe *etc* inn; *fig* innbringe; ~ *in a verdict* avsi en (jury)kjennelse; ~ **off** gjennomføre; lykkes med; ~ **on** fremkalle; føre til; ~ **out** få (klart) frem; utgi (bøker); innføre (døtre) i selskapslivet; ~ **over** omvende; ~ **round** få til bevissthet; overtale; ~ **to** få til bevissthet; *sjø* dreie bi; ~ *home to* få til å begripe; ~ **through** få/gjøre frisk (igjen); ~ **under** undertrykke; ~ **up** oppdra; bringe på bane; fremstille (for retten); (få til å) stanse; *slang* kaste opp.

brink [brɪŋk] *sb* kant, rand; *fig* pynt, stup. **brinkmanship** ['brɪŋkmənʃɪp] *sb fig* (farlig) balansegang.

briny ['braɪnɪ] **1** *adj* salt; **2** *sb: the* ~ blåmyra (dvs havet).

brisk [brɪsk] *adj* frisk; kvikk; livlig; sprek.

bristle ['brɪsl] **I** *sb* bust; **II** *vi* **1** ~ *up* reise bust; **2**

stritte. **bristly** ['brɪslɪ] *adj* stiv, strittende.

Britain ['brɪtn] *sb: Great* ~ Storbritannia. **Britannic** [brɪ'tænɪk], **British** ['brɪtɪʃ] *adj* britisk. **Britisher** ['brɪtɪʃə], **Briton** ['brɪtn] *sb* brite.

brittle ['brɪtl] *adj* skjør, sprø.

broach [brəʊtʃ] *vt* **1** anstikke, ta hull på (fat, tønne etc); **2** *fig* bringe på bane.

broad [brɔ:d] **I** *adj* **1** bred; *også fig* vid; *in* ~ *outline* i store trekk; **2** ~ *awake* lys våken; ~ *daylight* høylys dag; *a* ~ *hint* et tydelig vink; **3** grov; **II** *sb US vulg* kvinnfolk. **broad|band** *sb data etc* bredbånd. **~cast 1** *adj* kringkastet; **2** *sb* kringkasting; (radio)sending; **3** *vb* kringkaste. **~cloth** *sb* (fint) klede. **broaden** *vb* utvide(s). **broad|-gauge(d)** *adj sb* bredspor(et). **~-minded** *adj* vidsynt; frisinnet. **~sheet** *sb* **1** plakat; **2** skillingsvise. **~side** *sb sjø* bredside.

brogue [brəʊg] *sb* **1** (solid) tursko; **2** dialekt (især irsk uttale av engelsk).

broil [brɔɪl] **A** *sb* bråk; krangel; **B** *vb* steke(s) (på spidd el. rist over åpen varme).

broke [brəʊk] *adj* blakk, pengelens. **broken** ['brəʊkən] *adj* **1** brutt ned; ruinert, ødelagt; **2** gebrokken; **3** kupert; humpet, ujevn. **broken|down** *adj* nedbrutt. **~-hearted** *adj* sønderknust. **~winded** *adj* andpusten, stakkåndet.

broker ['brəʊkə] *sb* megler. **brokerage** ['brəʊkərɪdʒ] *sb* meglerprovisjon.

bronchitis [brɒŋ'kaɪtɪs] *sb* bronkitt.

bronco ['brɒŋkəʊ] *sb US* (halv)vill hest.

bronze [brɒnz] *sb* bronse.

brooch [brəʊtʃ] *sb* brosje, (bryst)nål.

brood [bru:d] **1** *sb* kull (især om fugleunger); *slang* avkom, yngel; **2** *vi* ruge; *fig* gruble, sture. **broody** ['bru:dɪ] *adj* **1** liggesjuk (om høne); **2** sturen.

brook [brʊk] **A** *sb* bekk; **B** *vt* tillate; tåle; finne seg i. **brooklet** ['brʊklɪt] *sb* liten bekk.

broom 1 [bru:m] *sb* gyvel; **2** [brʊm] feiekost, (sope)lime. **broomstick** ['brʊmstɪk] *sb* kosteskaft.

broth [brɒθ] *sb* (kjøtt)suppe.

brothel ['brɒθl] *sb* bordell, horehus.

brother ['brʌðə] *sb* bror; *fig* (embets)bror; (fag)felle, kollega. **brother|hood** ['brʌðəhʊd] *sb* brorskap. **~-in-law** ['brʌðərɪnlɔ:] *sb* svoger. **~ly** ['brʌðəlɪ] *adj, adv* broderlig.

brow [braʊ] *sb* **1** panne; **2** (øyen)bryn; **3** bryn, kam, pynt. **browbeat** ['braʊbi:t] *vt* hundse.

brown [braʊn] **I** *adj, sb* brun(t); **II** *vb* **1** brune(s); **2** *slang:* ~ *off* skjelle ut; *~ed off* grinet; kei og lei. **brownie** ['braʊnɪ] *sb* **1** nisse; **2** meise (dvs småpikespeider).

browse [braʊz] *vb* **1** beite, gnage; **2** kikke/titte på; smålese her og der i bøker.

bruise [bru:z] **1** *sb* skramme, skrubbsår; blått merke; **2** *vb* slå; skrubbe opp. **bruiser** ['bru:zə] *sb* (proff)bokser; bølle, slåsskjempe.

brunt [brʌnt] *sb: bear the* ~ bære hovedbyrden; ta støyten.

brush [brʌʃ] **I** *sb* **1** børste (og børsting); kost, pensel; **2** revehale; **3** buskas, kratt; **4** basketak; sammenstøt; **II** *vb* **1** børste, feie; ~ *aside/away* feie *etc* vekk; *fig* avfeie; ~ *off* feie *etc* av; *fig* avvise; ~ *up* pusse opp; *fig* friske opp; **2** streife. **brushwood** ['brʌʃwʊd] *sb* krattskog, småskog.

brute [bru:t] **I** *adj* dyrisk, rå; **II** *sb* **1** dyr; **2** best, udyr.

bubble ['bʌbl] **1** *sb* boble; *fig* luftig foretagende; svindel; **2** *vi* boble.

buccaneer [ˌbʌkə'nɪə] *sb* sjørøver.

buck [bʌk] **I** *sb* **1** bukk; hann (av hjortedyr, hare og kanin); **2** bukk (f.eks. til gymnastikk); sagkrakk; **3** *slang* laps, sprade; sjarmør; **4** *US slang* indianer; neger; menig (soldat); dollar; *a fast* ~ lettjente (men som oftest tvilsomt fortjente) penger; *pass the* ~ skyve fra seg ansvaret; **II** *vb* **1** gjøre bukkesprang; *om hest* skyte rygg; sparke bakut; *fig også* slå seg vrang; **2** *slang:* ~ *up* få fart på seg; stramme seg opp. **buck|skin** *sb* hjorteskinn. **~shot** *sb* dyrehagl. **~teeth** *sb fl* utstående tenner.

bucket ['bʌkɪt] *sb* bøtte, spann.

buckle ['bʌkl] **I** *sb* spenne; **II** *vb* **1** spenne fast; stramme med spenne; ~ *on* spenne på (seg); ~ *(down) to* ta fatt på; **2** bulke; gi/krølle seg; sige sammen. **buckle | arrestor** *sb petro* bulestopper. ~ **detector** *sb petro* buledetektor. **buckling** *sb* solslyng.

buckram ['bʌkrəm] **1** *adj* stiv; *fig også* stram; **2** *sb* buckram [= slags bokbindermateriale].

bud [bʌd] **1** *sb* knopp; **2** *vi* spire; skyte knopp(er). **budding** ['bʌdɪŋ] *adj* spirende; *fig også* gryende, vordende.

buddy ['bʌdɪ] *sb US slang* kamerat, kompis.

budge [bʌdʒ] **A** *vb* rikke/røre (seg); **B** *dgl* = **budgerigar** ['bʌdʒərɪgɑ:] *sb* undulat.

budget ['bʌdʒɪt] **I** *sb* **1** budsjett; **2** bunke/haug (med brev etc); **II** *vi:* ~ *for* budsjettere (med); *slang* regne med.

buff [bʌf] **I** *adj* **1** bøffellærs-; semsket; **2** gulbrun; **II** *sb* **1** bøffellær; semsklær; **2** polérpute; **3** gulbrun(t); **III** *vt* **1** semske; **2** polere.

buffalo ['bʌfələʊ] sb bøffel.

buffer ['bʌfə] **I** *sb* **1** buffer, støtdemper; **2** *data* buffer; **3** *petro* buffer(tank), mellomtank; stopper; **4** *slang* (gammel) knark; stabeis; **II** *vb data* bufre. **buffer | management** *sb data* bufferbehandling. ~ **pool** *sb data* bufferområde. ~ **storage** *sb data* bufferlager.

buffet ['bʌfɪt] **A I** *sb* slag, støt (også *fig*); **II** *vt* **1** slå; dra til; **2** kjempe mot; **B** *sb* anretningsbord; **C** ['bʊfeɪ] *sb* serveringsdisk; (jernbane)restaurant. **buffet | car** *sb* spisevogn. ~ **supper** *sb* stående buffet.

bug [bʌg] **A I** *sb* **1** (vegge)lus; *fl* utøy; **2** *US* insekt; *~-eyed (slang)* med øynene på stilk; stirrende; **II** *vt* sprøyte mot utøy; **B** *slang* **I** *sb* **1** basill (især *fig*); dille, mani; *som endelse* -idiot; **2** feil, mangel; *data* programfeil; **3** tyverialarm; **4** skjult mikrofon; **5** *US* gærning; **6** *big* ~ kakse, pamp; **II** *vt* **1** avlytte (med skjult mikrofon); **2** *what's ~ging you?* hva går det av/feiler det deg?

bugaboo ['bʌgəbu:], **bugbear** ['bʌgbeə] *sb* busemann.

buggy ['bʌgɪ] **A** *adj* **1** befengt med utøy; **2** *US slang* gal; **B** *sb* **1** tralle, vogn; vagg; **2** gigg; *US* trille.

bugle ['bju:gl] *sb* (signal)horn, trompet. **bugle-call** *sb* hornsignal. **bugler** *sb* hornblåser.

build [bɪld] **I** *sb* **1** byggemåte, konstruksjon; *stundom* struktur; **2** (kropps)bygning; fasong, figur; **II** *vb* bygge. **building** ['bɪldɪŋ] *sb* **1** bygging; **2** bygning. **building | association, ~ society** *sb* bolig(bygge)lag.

bulb [bʌlb] *sb* **1** (lys)pære; **2** kolbe; kule; **3** (blomster)løk, knoll. **bulbous** ['bʌlbəs] *adj* pære- (el. kuppel- el. løk)formet.

bulge [bʌldʒ] **I** *sb* **1** bule, bulk; kul; **2** topp (på kurve etc); **II** *vb* (få til å) bule ut.

bulk [bʌlk] **I** *sb* **1** masse, mengde; omfang; *the ~ of* mesteparten av; **2** (stor) kropp; **3** *sjø* last, parti; **II** *vi* ruve. **bulk | cargo** *sb sjø* massegods. **~head** *sb sjø* skott. **~ oil** *sb petro* bulkolje. **~ storage** *sb data* masselager. **bulky** *adj* ruvende, svær.

bull [bʊl] **A I** *sb* **1** okse; hann (av elefant, hval og andre store dyr); **2** *merk* haussespekulant; **3** *slang* skryt; *Irish ~* nonsens, tull(prat); **4** *slang* purk (dvs politimann); **II** *vb* **1** spekulere i prisstigning; **2** *slang* bløffe; skryte; sludre; **B** *sb* (pave)bulle.

bullet ['bʊlɪt] *sb* (gevær)kule. **bullet-proof** *adj* skuddsikker.

bull|fight *sb* tyrefektning. **~finch** *sb* dompap.

bullion ['bʊlɪən] *sb* barre (av gull el. sølv); umyntet gull/sølv.

bull|nose *sb petro* slangehode. **~ring** *sb* tyrefekterarena. **bull's-eye** *sb* **1** blink (på målskive); **2** (skips)-ventil; **3** slags sukkertøy.

bully ['bʊlɪ] **I** *adj, interj* flott, (kjempe)fint; **II** *sb* **1** bølle, tyrann; **2** hermetisk oksekjøtt; **III** *vt* hundse, tyrannisere.

bulrush ['bʊlrʌʃ] *sb* dunkjevle.

bulwark ['bʊlwək] *sb* **1** bastion, bolverk; *fig* vern; **2** *sjø* skansekledning.

bum [bʌm] **I** *adj* elendig, ynkelig; **II** *sb* **1** lasaron; **2** *slang* rumpe; **III** *vi* gå på bommen.

bumblebee ['bʌmblbi:] *sb* humle.

bump [bʌmp] **I** *adv* bums; **II** *sb* **1** dunk, støt, slag; **2** kul; **3** dump, hump; lufthull (som fly dumper gjennom); **4** (egen) evne; *~ of locality* stedsans; **III** *vb* **1** dunke, skumpe, støte; **2** *slang: ~ off* ekspedere (dvs drepe); krepere (dvs dø). **bumper** ['bʌmpə] **A** *sb* **1** støtfanger; **2** *fl* oppmerking (langs fotgjengerovergang); **B 1** *adj slang* rekord-; **2** *sb* breddfullt glass.

bumpkin ['bʌm(p)kɪn] *sb* naiv fyr, slamp.

bumptious ['bʌmpʃəs] *adj* hoven, innbilsk, overlegen.

bumpy ['bʌmpɪ] *adj* dumpet, humpet.

bun [bʌn] *sb* **1** (hvete)bolle; **2** (hår)topp.

bunch [bʌntʃ] **I** *sb* **1** bunt, knippe; *~ of flowers* blomsterbukett; **2** klase, klynge; kvast; **3** flokk, gjeng; **4** hevelse; kul; pukkel; **II** *vb* bunte(s) (sammen).

bundle ['bʌndl] **I** *sb* bunt, bylt; pakke; **II** *vb* **1** *~ up* bunte *etc* sammen; **2** *~ off* sende/komme seg vekk.

bung [bʌŋ] **1** *sb* propp, spuns; **2** *vt* spunse; *~ up* tette igjen.

bungle ['bʌŋgl] **1** *sb* lappverk; makkverk; **2** *vb* forkludre; slurve (med). **bungler** ['bʌŋglə] *sb* **1** klossmajor; rotebukk; **2** slurvekopp.

bunk [bʌŋk] **I** *sb, vi* køye; **II** *slang* **1** *sb* flukt; **2** *vi: ~ off* stikke av; **III** = *bunkum*. **bunker** ['bʌŋkə] **I** *sb* **1** bunker (dvs rom for kull el. olje); **2** bunker (dvs sandgrop på golfbane); *fig* hindring; **3** bunker (dvs beskyttelsesrom); **II** *vb* **1** *sjø* bunkre; **2** *be ~ed* være i vanskeligheter. **bunker fuel** *sb petro* bunkerolje.

bunkum ['bʌŋkəm] *sb* sludder, tøv.

bunny ['bʌnɪ] *sb* kanin(pus).

bunting ['bʌntɪŋ] *sb* **1** buskspurv; **2** flaggduk; *fig* flagging; **3** babypose.

buoy [bɔɪ] **1** *sb* bøye; **2** *vt* merke med bøye(r); *~ up* holde flytende; *fig* oppmuntre; stramme opp. **buoyancy** ['bɔɪənsɪ] *sb* oppdrift; *fig* overskudd; tiltakslyst. **buoyant** ['bɔɪənt] *adj* **1** flytende; med oppdrift; **2** *merk* stigende (om marked); **3** *fig* lett, spenstig; optimistisk.

bur [bɜ:] *sb* borre.

burden ['bɜ:dn] **I** *sb* **1** byrde; **2** *sjø* drektighet, lasteevne; **3** refreng; **II** *vt* bebyrde; lesse på. **burdensome** ['bɜ:dnsəm] *adj* byrdefull, tung.

burdock ['bɜ:dɒk] = *bur*.

bureau ['bjʊərəʊ] *sb* **1** kontor (især offentlig); **2** skatoll; skrivebord; **3** *US* kommode. **bureaucracy** [bjʊə'rɒkrəsɪ] *sb* byråkrati. **bureaucrat** ['bjʊərəʊkræt] *sb* byråkrat. **bureaucratic** [ˌbjʊərəʊ'krætɪk] *adj* byråkratisk.

burg [bɜ:g] *sb US slang* by.

burgeon ['bɜ:dʒən] **1** *sb* knopp, spire; **2** *vi* knoppes, spire (især *fig* og *poet*).

burgess ['bɜ:dʒɪs] *sb* borger.

burgh ['bʌrə] *skotsk* = *borough*.

burglar ['bɜ:glə] *sb* innbruddstyv (især en som opererer om natten, jf *house-breaker*). **burglary** ['bɜ:glərɪ] *sb* innbrudd. **burgle** ['bɜ:gl] *vb* begå innbrudd (i).

burial ['berɪəl] *sb* begravelse.

burlap ['bɜ:læp] *sb* sekkestrie.

burlesque [bɜ:'lesk] **I** *adj* burlesk; **II** *sb* **1** parodi (især som revynummer); **2** *US* (annenrangs) varieté; **III** *vt* parodiere.

burly ['bɜ:lɪ] *adj* røslig; bastant, svær; sterk.

burn [bɜ:n] **A 1** *sb* brannsår; **2** *vb* brenne; svi; etse; **B** [bɜ:rn] *skotsk* (liten) bekk. **burner boom** *sb petro* avbrenningsbom. **burn(ing) point** *sb petro* tennings|punkt, -temperatur. **~ property** *sb petro* brennverdi. **~ quality** *sb petro* brenn|egenskap, -kvalitet.

burnish ['bɜ:nɪʃ] *vb* polere (metall).

burp [bɜ:p] *sb, vb US slang* rap(e). **burp gun** *sb*

slang maskinpistol.

burr ['bɜ:] **I** *sb* **1** surr, surring (av maskiner etc); **2** grat/skjegg (på metalldeler); **3** skarring; **4** = *bur*; **II** *vb* skarre.

burrow ['bʌrəʊ] **1** *sb* jordhull; (revs etc) gang, hi, hule; **2** *vb* grave (seg ned).

bursar ['bɜ:sə] *sb* **1** kasserer; kvestor (ved universitet); **2** (universitets)stipendiat; student med stipendium. **bursary** ['bɜ:sərɪ] *sb* **1** kasse, kassererkontor; *især* kvestur; **2** stipendium.

burst [bɜ:st] **I** *sb* **1** eksplosjon, sprengning (og brak, smell; brudd, revne, sprekk etc); **2** utbrudd; *fig* anfall; **3** salve, skuddserie; **II** *vb* **1** eksplodere, sprenge(s); **2** briste, revne, sprekke; ~ *into* briste/ bryte ut i; sette i (å); ~ *out* utbryte; ~ *up* eksplodere, sprenge(s); *slang* gå i vasken; ~*-up* fiasko; ~*ing with* sprekkeferdig/struttende av; **3** *data* løsrive; **4** fare, styrte; ~ *in upon* komme stormende inn til; (trenge seg på og) forstyrre. **burst | mode** *sb data* blokkmodus. ~ **transmission** *sb data* avbruddsoverføring.

bury ['berɪ] *vt* begrave. **burying-ground** ['berɪɪŋgraʊnd] *sb* gravplass, kirkegård.

bus [bʌs] **I** *sb* **1** buss; **2** *data* (data)buss; **3** *slang* kjerre (om bil, fly etc); **II** *vi* busse, ta bussen. **bus|-driver, ~man** *sb* bussjåfør. **~-stop** *sb* bussholdeplass.

bush [bʊʃ] **A** *sb* **1** busk; *US* kratt; **2** utmark, villmark; (ur)skog (især i Australia); *the* ~ landsbygda; **B** *sb* **1** bøssing, fôring; **2** *vt* fôre (ut); **C** = *bushel.*

bushel [bʊʃl] *sb* skjeppe, se midtsidene.

bush|-fighter *sb* geriljasoldat. **~man** *sb* **1** buskmann; **2** nybygger (i Australia). **~ranger** *sb* nybygger; skogskar; *tidl også* fredløs; røver, stimann. ~ **telegraph** *sb dgl* jungeltelegraf. **bushy** *adj* busket.

business ['bɪznɪs] *sb* **1** forretning(er), handel; bransje; **2** butikk, forretning; forretningsforetagende; *on* ~ i forretninger; **3** gjøremål, yrke; **4** oppgave, plikt; ærend; *come/get (down) to* ~ komme til saken; *mean* ~ mene det alvorlig; *that's no* ~ *of yours/none of your* ~ det har ikke De (el. du) noe med; *dgl* det raker deg ikke; **5** *dgl* affære, sak; greie. **business|-like** *adj* forretningsmessig; praktisk, saklig. **~man** *sb* forretningsmann.

bus network *sb data* bussnett.

bust [bʌst] **A** *sb* byste; **B** *dgl, slang* **I** *adj* blakk; ruinert; *go* ~ gå dukken; **II** *sb* **1** slag, støt; **2** fiasko; konkurs; degradering; **3** rangel; **III** *vb* **1** knuse, ødelegge; *fig* degradere; ruinere; **2** gå konkurs; **3** ~ *away* stikke av; ~ *out* kaste ut; stryke (til eksamen). **buster** ['bʌstə] *sb slang* **1** brande, kraftkar; **2** *i tiltale* kamerat, kompis; **3** kraftig bombe *etc.*

bustle ['bʌsl] **A 1** *sb* mas; travelhet; geskjeftighet; **2** *vb* kjase, skynde seg; mase (på); **B** *sb* kø (på gammeldags kjole).

bust-up ['bʌstʌp] *sb dgl* krangel, slagsmål.

busy ['bɪzɪ] **1** *adv* travel; (travelt) opptatt; **2** *vr:* ~ *oneself about (in/with)* beskjeftige seg/være (travelt) opptatt med. **busybody** *sb* geskjeftig person.

but [bʌt] **1** *adv* bare; *had I* ~ *known* hadde jeg bare visst; **2** *konj* men; uten at; **3** *prep* unntatt; uten; ~ *for (him, that etc)* uten (ham, det etc); hadde det ikke vært for (ham, det etc); *I cannot* ~ jeg kan ikke annet enn; *who* ~*?* hvem annen enn? *last* ~ *one* nest sist; **4** *pron* som ikke; **5** *sb* innvending, men.

butane ['bju:teɪn] *sb petro* butan.

butcher ['bʊtʃə] **1** *sb* slakter; **2** *vt* slakte. **butchery** ['bʊtʃərɪ] *sb* **1** slakting; myrderier, nedslakting; **2** slakteri.

butler ['bʌtlə] *sb* hovmester.

butt [bʌt] **A** *sb* **1** tykkende (som f.eks. kolbe, skaft, (økse)hammer); **2** (sigarett)stump; *slang* sigarett; **B** *sb* **1** *fl* skytebane; **2** *fig* skyteskive (*of* for); **C** *vb* renne/ stange hodet (*against* mot); ~ *in* avbryte; legge seg borti; **D** *sb* **1** vinfat; øltønne; **2** butt, (regnvanns)-tønne.

butter ['bʌtə] **1** *sb* smør; **2** *vt* smøre smør på; ~ *up* smigre; smiske for. **butter|cup** *sb* smørblomst. **~fly** *sb* sommerfugl. **~fly valve** *sb petro* strupeventil. ~ **-fingered** *adj* slipphendt. **~milk** *sb* kjernemelk. **~-scotch** *sb* (slags) karamell, knekk.

buttocks ['bʌtəks] *sb fl* bak(ende).

button ['bʌtn] **I** *sb* **1** knapp; knott; **2** *fl* pikkolo; **II** *vb* knappe(s). **buttonhole 1** *sb a)* knapphull; *b)* knapphullsblomst; **2** *vt* gripe fatt i (og oppholde med snakk).

buttress ['bʌtrɪs] **1** *sb* strebepilar; *fig også* støtte; **2** *vt:* ~ *up* støtte (opp); holde oppe; *fig* underbygge.

buxom ['bʌksəm] *adj* ferm, trivelig; ~ *blonde* yppig blondine.

buy [baɪ] **I** *sb* handel, kjøp; **II** *vb* **1** kjøpe; ~ *off* kjøpe (seg) fri; kjøpe ut; ~ *over* bestikke, kjøpe; **2** *US* godta, tro på; *do you* ~ *that?* biter du på den?

buzz [bʌz] **I** *sb* summing, surring; *give a* ~ slå på tråden (dvs telefonere); **II** *vb* **1** summe, surre; *om rykter* svirre; **2** vimse. **buzzard** ['bʌzəd] *sb* **1** (mus)våk; **2** gribb; **3** *slang* knark, stabeis.

by [baɪ] **A** *adv* i nærheten; (like) ved; forbi; til side; *stand* ~ stå ved (løfte etc); holde seg klar; stå ferdig; ~ *and* ~ etter hvert; om litt; ~ *and large* stort sett; ~ *the* ~*(e),* ~ *the way* apropos, forresten; **B** *prep* **I** *om sted, retning etc* **1** hos; (like) ved; ved siden av; ~ *oneself* alene; *have* ~ *one* ha på seg/i lommen etc; **2** forbi; gjennom; langs (med); over, via; ~ *land* til lands; ~ *sea* sjøveien; *go* ~ *air* (ta) fly; *north* ~ *northeast* nord til nordøst; **II** *om middel og måte* **1** av, på, ved; etter, ifølge; *know* ~ *sight/*~ *the voice* kjenne av utseende/på stemmen; **2** med; ved hjelp av; ~ *chance* tilfeldigvis; *four* ~ *eight* fire ganger åtte; **3** for; *merk* pr.; ~ *degrees* gradvis; ~ *twos and threes* to og tre om gangen; **4** *made etc* ~ laget etc av; **5** ~ *all means* ja visst; for all del; ~ *no means* langt ifra, på ingen måte; *better* ~ *far* langt bedre; *lawyer* ~ *profession* advokat av yrke; **III** *om tidspunkt* om, på, til; innen, senest; ~ *night* om natten, ved nattetider; ~ *the end of the day* mot kveld, ved dagens slutt.

bye-bye [ˌbaɪ'baɪ] **I** *slang* = *good-bye*; **II** ['baɪ-

baɪ] *sb* **1** *a)* søvn; *b)* vuggesang; **2** *go (to)* ~ bye (dvs sovne, sove).

by(e)-law ['baɪlɔ:] *sb* (lokal) forordning, forskrift; (politi)vedtekt.

by-election ['baɪɪˌlekʃn] *sb* suppleringsvalg.

bygone ['baɪgɒn] *adj* fordums, tidligere; *let ~s be ~s* la gjemt være glemt. **byname** ['baɪneɪm] *sb* oppnavn, økenavn. **bypass** ['baɪpɑ:s] **I** *sb* **1** omkjøring, ringvei; **2** *petro* omføringsrør, omledning, shuntledning; ~ *valve* omledningsventil, shuntventil; **II** *vt* kjøre forbi/utenom. **by-product** *sb* biprodukt. **bystander** *sb* tilskuer.

byte [baɪt] *sb data* byte. **byte | address** *sb data* byteadresse. **~mode** *sb data* bytemodus.

byword ['baɪwɜ:d] *sb* **1** munnhell; **2** (dårlig) eksempel.

C

cab [kæb] *sb* **1** drosje; **2** førerhus.

cabbage ['kæbɪdʒ] *sb* (hode)kål.

cabby ['kæbɪ] *sb* = *cabman.*

cabin ['kæbɪn] *sb* **1** *sjø* lugar; **2** førerhus, kabin; **3** *(log ~)* (tømmer)hytte. **cabinet** ['kæbɪnɪt] *sb* **1** skap; montre; **2** *the Cabinet* kabinettet, regjeringen. **cabinet-maker** *sb* møbelsnekker.

cable ['keɪbl] **I** *sb* **1** kabel; *sjø* (anker)kjetting; trosse; kabellengde (et lengdemål, se midtsidene); **2** (telegraf)kabel; **3** *(~gram)* (kabel)telegram; **II** *vt* **1** feste med kabel; **2** telegrafere (til).

cab|man ['kæbmən] *sb* drosjesjåfør. **~rank** ['kæbræŋk], **~stand** ['kæbstænd] *sb* drosjeholdeplass.

cackle ['kækl] **1** *sb* kakling, snadring; skravling; *cut the ~ (dgl)* hold munn; **2** *vi* kakle, snadre; skravle.

cad [kæd] *sb* pøbel, simpel fyr.

cadaver [kə'dɑɪvə] *sb* kadaver, lik. **cadaverous** [kə'dævərəs] *adj* dødningaktig, likblek.

cadet [kə'det] *sb* **1** kadett; **2** yngre sønn.

caesarean [si:'zeərɪən] *adj*: ~ *operation/section* keisersnitt.

cage [keɪdʒ] **I** *sb* **1** bur; *slang* fengsel; **2** krigsfangeleir; **3** heisestol (i gruveheis); **4** kurv (i kurvball); **II** *vt* sette i bur; sperre inne. **cagey** ['keɪdʒɪ] *adj slang* **1** forsiktig, tilbakeholden; **2** slu.

cajole [kə'dʒəʊl] *vt* smigre; snakke rundt. **cajolery** [kə'dʒəʊlərɪ] *sb* smiger; overtalelse.

cake [keɪk] **I** *sb* **1** kake; **2** (liten) blokk; klatt, klump; stykke; **II** *vb* klumpe (seg) sammen; kline (til); skorpe seg.

calamitous [kə'læmɪtəs] *adj* katastrofal *etc.* **calamity** [kə'læmətɪ] *sb* elendighet; katastrofe, ulykke.

calculate ['kælkjʊleɪt] *vb* **1** beregne, kalkulere; ~ *(up)on* regne med; stole på; **2** *US* anta, gå ut fra. **calculated** ['kælkjʊleɪtɪd] *adj* **1** beregnet (*to* på å); **2** bevisst, overlagt. **calculating** ['kælkjʊleɪtɪŋ] *adj* **1** beregnende, slu; **2** forsiktig, omtenksom. **calculation** [ˌkælkjʊ'leɪʃn] *sb* beregning *etc.* **calculator** ['kælkjʊleɪtə] *sb* kalkulator; (elektronisk) lommeregner.

calf [kɑ:f] **A** *sb* kalv; *fig* grønnskolling; **B** *sb* (tykk)legg.

calibration [ˌkælɪ'breɪʃn] *sb* kalibrering *etc.* **calibre** ['kælɪbə] *sb* kaliber (også *fig*); boring.

call [kɔ:l] **I** *sb* **1** rop, skrik (*for* om); anrop, kalling; opp|kall, -ringning; (navne)opprop; *fig* dragning, kall(else); **2** (kort) besøk/opphold; (skips)anløp; **3** fordring, krav; **4** anmodning (*for* om); oppfordring (*for* til); **5** foranledning, grunn; **6** melding (i kortspill); **II** *vb* **1** rope/skrike (*for* om); anrope, kalle opp; purre, vekke; sende bud på; ~ *a meeting* beramme et møte; ~ *a strike* erklære streik; ~ *the roll* foreta navneopprop; **2** kalle (for); betegne (som); **3** *(~ at/on)* besøke; stanse (i/ved, f.eks. om tog); anløpe (havn); **4** melde (i kortspill); **5** *med adv/prep* ~ **for** spørre etter; komme for å hente; forlange; forutsette; nødvendiggjøre; ~ **forth** forårsake; fremkalle; *fig* mobilisere (energi, krefter etc); ~ **off** kalle/trekke tilbake; *fig også* avlyse; få slutt på; ~ **over** rope opp; ~ **up** ringe opp; gjenkalle i erindringen; innkalle til militærtjeneste; ~ **(up)on** appellere til; henvende seg til. **call|-box** ['kɔ:lbɒks] *sb* telefonkiosk. **caller** ['kɔ:lə] *sb* besøkende. **calling** ['kɔ:lɪŋ] *sb* **1** (opp)kalling *etc*; **2** yrke; **3** kall.

ca(l)iper | log, ~ pig *sb petro* kaliberlogg. **cal(l)ipers** ['kælɪpəz] *sb fl* **1** (krum)passer; **2** (tømmer)klave.

callosity [kæ'lɒsətɪ] *sb* trell (dvs hard hud); *fig* hardhudethet, ufølsomhet. **callous** ['kæləs] *adj* med treller; hard; *fig også* hardhudet, ufølsom.

callow ['kæləʊ] *adj* **1** fjærløs; bar, naken; **2** *fig* grønn, uerfaren.

calm [kɑ:m] **I** *adj* behersket, rolig; **II** *sb* **1** ro, stillhet; **2** (vind)stille; **III** *vb* berolige; falle til ro.

calumniate [kə'lʌmnɪeɪt] *vt* baktale, bakvaske. **calumny** ['kæləmnɪ] *sb* baktalelse, bakvaskelse.

camel ['kæməl] *sb* kamel.

camera ['kæmərə] *sb* foto(grafi)apparat, kamera. **camera-man** ['kæmərəmən] *sb* (film)fotograf.

camouflage ['kæmʊflɑ:ʒ] **1** *sb* kamuflasje; **2** *vt* kamuflere.

camp [kæmp] **1** *sb* leir; **2** *vi* kampere, ligge i leir; slå leir. **campaign** [kæm'peɪn] **1** *sb* felttog; *fig også* kampanje; **2** *vi* delta i felttog/kampanje; drive kampanje. **campaigner** [kæm'peɪnə] *sb* kriger *etc.*

camphor ['kæmfə] *sb* kamfer.

campus ['kæmpəs] *sb US* universitet, universitetsområde.

can [kæn] **A I** *sb* **1** kanne; dunk, spann; **2** (hermetikk)boks; **3** *slang* bak(ende); do; fengsel; **II** *vt* **1** hermetisere; **2** *slang* holde opp med; kaste ut; gi sparken; **B** *vi pres* kan, er i stand til.

canal [kə'næl] *sb* **1** (kunstig) kanal; **2** gang; renne; rør.

canary [kə'neərɪ] **1** *adj (~-coloured)* kanarigul; **2** *sb (~-bird)* kanarifugl.

cancel ['kænsl] *vb* **1** annullere, oppheve, tilbakekalle; avlyse; avbestille; **2** (makulere ved å) stryke ut *etc*; *~led stamps* brukte/stemplede frimerker; **3** forkorte (brøk). **cancel character** *sb data* annulleringstegn, slettetegn. **cancellation** [ˌkænsə'leɪʃn] *sb* annullering *etc.*

cancer ['kænsə] *sb* kreft. **cancerous** ['kænsərəs] *adj* kreftsyk, kreft-.

candid ['kændɪd] *adj* oppriktig, ærlig (ofte på en litt naiv måte).

candidate ['kændɪdeɪt] *sb* kandidat. **candidature** ['kændɪdətʃə] *sb* kandidatur.

candied ['kændɪd] *adj* kandisert; *fig* sukkersøt.

candle ['kændl] *sb* **1** (stearin)lys; **2** = **candle | power** ['kændlˌpaʊə] *sb* (normal)lys. **~stick** ['kændlstɪk] *sb* lysestake.

candour ['kændə] *sb* oppriktighet; (ofte litt naiv) ærlighet.

candy ['kændɪ] **I** *sb* **1** kandis(sukker); **2** *US* konfekt, sukkertøy; *ofte* godter (herunder også sjokolade); **II** *vb* kandisere (frukt etc).

cane [keɪn] **I** *sb* **1** rør (dvs spanskrør, sukkerrør etc); **2** spaserstokk; **II** *vt* pryle (med spanskrør). **cane chair** *sb* kurvstol.

canine I ['keɪnaɪn] **1** *adj* hundelignende, hunde-; **2** *sb* hund; dyr av hundefamilien; **II** ['kænaɪn] *sb (~ tooth)* hjørnetann.

canister ['kænɪstə] *sb* **1** blikkboks, dåse; **2** *(~ shot)* kardesk.

canker ['kæŋkə] *sb* kreft(skade). **cankerous** ['kæñkərəs] *adj* kreftsyk, kreft-; skadelig, ødeleggende.

canned [kænd] *adj især* hermetisert. **canned music** *sb* musikk på bånd/plate. **cannery** ['kænərɪ] *sb* hermetikkfabrikk.

cannon ['kænən] *sb* **1** maskinkanon (i f.eks. krigsfly); **2** gammeldags kanon; **3** artilleri, skyts.

canny ['kænɪ] *adj* **1** forsiktig, omtenksom (især i pengesaker); **2** listig, lur; utspekulert.

canoe [kə'nu:] *sb, vb* (padle i) kano.

canon ['kænən] *sb* **1** kanon (om Bibelens kanoniske skrifter); *fig* rettesnor; **2** kanon (dvs kjedesang); **3** kannik. **canonical** [kə'nɒnɪkl] *adj* kanonisk; kirkelig.

canopy ['kænəpɪ] *sb* baldakin, kalesje.

cant [kænt] **A** *sb* **1** hykleri; uoppriktighet; tomme fraser; **2** sjargong; **B 1** *sb* helling, skråning; **2** *vb* helle, skråne; tippe.

cantankerous [kæn'tæŋkərəs] *adj* gretten; kranglet.

canteen [kæn'ti:n] *sb* **1** kantine, messe; **2** feltflaske; kokekar (til feltbruk).

canter ['kæntə] **1** *sb* kort (dvs langsom) galopp; **2** *vb* ri/sette i kort galopp.

canvas ['kænvəs] *sb* lerret; presenning; seil(duk); telt(duk). **canvass** ['kænvəs] *vb* **1** agitere (især politisk, ved husbesøk); **2** diskutere, drøfte.

canyon ['kænjən] *sb* dalsluk, slukt; fjellkløft.

cap [kæp] **I** *sb* **1** lue; *skull ~* kalott; **2** hette, kappe; deksel; (flaske)kapsel; *screw ~* skrulokk; **3** *(percussion ~)* tennhette; kruttlapp; **4** *sjø* eselhode; **II** *vb* **1** sette lue *etc* på; dekke, tekke; **2** overgå; *to ~ it all* for å sette kronen på verket.

capability [ˌkeɪpə'bɪlətɪ] *sb* dyktighet *etc.* **capable** ['keɪpəbl] *adj* **1** dyktig, flink; **2** i stand (*of* til); kapabel. **capacious** [kə'peɪʃəs] *adj* rommelig, vid. **capacitate** [kə'pæsɪteɪt] *vt* sette i stand (*to* til). **capacitor** ['kə'pæsɪtə] *sb elec, petro etc* kondensator. **capacity** [kə'pæsətɪ] *sb* **1** kapasitet, evne (til å fatte, gripe, holde, lære, romme etc); **2** evne (*for* til); dyktighet; **3** egenskap (*as* av); stilling (*as* som).

cape [keɪp] **A** *sb* (ermeløs) kappe, slengkappe; **B** *sb* kapp, nes, odde.

caper ['keɪpə] **A 1** *sb* (gledes)hopp, krumspring; **2** *vi* hoppe og sprette; **B** *sb fl* kapers.

capital ['kæpɪtl] **I** *adj* **1** hoved-, størst, viktigst; **2** kapital-; **3** døds- (dvs som medfører dødsstraff); **4** *dgl* fantastisk, kjempefin; **II** *sb* **1** hovedstad; **2** = *~ letter*; **3** kapital; *make ~ of* utnytte, slå mynt på; **4** kapitél, søylehode. **capitalize** ['kæpɪtəlaɪz] *vt* **1** kapitalisere; **2** skrive med stor(e) bokstav(er); **3** *(~ on)* utnytte, slå mynt på. **capital letter** *sb* stor bokstav; majuskel, versal. **capitulate** [kə'pɪtjuleɪt] *vi* kapitulere, overgi seg. **capitulation** [kəˌpɪtju'leɪʃn] *sb* kapitulasjon.

caprice [kə'pri:s] *sb* innfall, lune. **capricious** [kə'prɪʃəs] *adj* lunefull, vimset.

capsize [kæp'saɪz] *vb* kantre, velte.

capstan ['kæpstən] *sb sjø* gangspill.

capsule ['kæpsju:l] *sb* **1** kapsel; **2** *fig* konsentrat.

captain ['kæptɪn] **1** *sb* kaptein (og anfører, leder; feltherre; høvding etc); *sjø* skipsfører; **2** *vt* lede; være kaptein for.

caption ['kæpʃn] **1** (kapittel)overskrift; **2** billedtekst; **3** filmtekst.

captivate ['kæptɪveɪt] *vt* fange; *fig* fengsle, sjarmere. **captive** ['kæptɪv] **I** *adj* **1** fanget; *fig* fengslet; **2** fortøyd (om ballong); **II** *sb* fange. **captivity** [kæp'tɪvətɪ] *sb* fangenskap. **capture** ['kæptʃə] **I** *sb* **1** fanging; *sjø* kapring; **2** bytte, fangst; *sjø* prise, **II** *vt* fange; erobre, kapre.

car [kɑ:] *sb* **1** bil; **2** (jernbane)vogn; **3** kupé (i personheis); **4** gondol, kurv (under ballong og luftskip).

caravan ['kærəvən] *sb* **1** karavane; **2** campingvogn; sirkusvogn; sigøynervogn.

caraway ['kærəweɪ] *sb* karve.

carbine ['kɑ:baɪn] *sb* karabin.

carbolic [kɑ:'bɒlɪk] *adj* karbol-.

carbon ['kɑ:bən] *sb* **1** karbon; **2** *(~-paper)* karbonpapir. **carbon | copy** *sb* gjenpart. **~ value** *sb petro* karbon|tall, -verdi. **carburettor** [ˌkɑ:bjʊ'retə] *sb* forgasser.

carcase, carcass ['kɑ:kəs] *sb* kadaver, skrott (av dyr).

card [kɑ:d] **A** *sb* **1** kort; *(playing-~)* (spill)kort; **2** *slang* gøyal fyr; **B** *sb, vb* karde.

cardamom ['kɑ:dəməm] *sb* kardemomme.

card|board ['kɑ:dbɔ:] *sb* kartong. **~ code** *sb data* kortkode. **~ deck** *sb data* (kort)bunke. **~ feed** *sb data* kortmater. **~ field** *sb data* kortfelt. **~ hopper** *sb data* kortkasse.

cardigan ['kɑ:dɪgən] *sb* strikkejakke.

cardinal ['kɑ:dɪnl] **I** *adj* hoved-, viktigst; **II** *sb* **1** kardinal; **2** grunntall. **cardinal number** *sb* grunntall.

card | jam *sb data* kortklemme. **~ pack** *sb data* (kort)bunke. **~ path** *sb data* kortbane. **~ punch** *sb data* korthuller. **~-sharper** *sb* falskspiller. **~ sorter** *sb data* kortsorterer. **~ stacker** *sb data* kortstabler.

care [keə] **I** *sb* **1** forsiktighet, omtanke, påpasselighet; *take ~* være forsiktig; **2** omsorg; pass, pleie, stell; varetekt; *take ~ of* passe på; sørge for; ta seg av; *take ~ of yourself!* vær forsiktig! *ofte* ha det bra/godt! **3** bekymring; **II** *vi* **1** bry seg om; *I don't ~ if I do* (jeg vil) gjerne det; *for all I ~* gjerne for meg; **2** like; kunne tenke seg; *~ about* ha lyst til; interessere seg for; *~ for* bry seg om; være glad i; passe, pleie, stelle; ta seg av.

career [kə'rɪə] **I** *sb* **1** kurs, løpebane; **2** yrke; **3** karriere; **4** full fart; vilt løp; **II** *vi* fare, styrte. **careerist** [kə'rɪərɪst] *sb* karrierejeger, streber. **career woman** *sb* yrkeskvinne.

care|free ['keəfri:] *adj* sorgløs, ubekymret. **~ful** ['keəfʊl] *adj* **1** forsiktig, påpasselig; **2** omhyggelig. **~-laden** ['keəˌleɪdn] = *~worn.* **~less** ['keəlɪs] *adj* likegyldig; uvøren; nonchalant.

caress [kə'res] **1** *sb* kjærtegn; **2** *vt* kjærtegne; kjæle for/med.

caretaker ['keəˌteɪkə] *sb* oppsynsmann, vakt(mester). **caretaker government** *sb* forretningsministerium.

careworn ['keəwɔ:n] *adj* sorg(be)tynget.

carfare ['kɑ:feə] *sb US* **1** billett (på buss, trikk etc); **2** billettpris, takst.

cargo ['kɑ:gəʊ] *sb fly, sjø* last.

caricature ['kærɪkəˌtjʊə] **1** *sb* karikatur; **2** *vt* karikere, tegne karikatur av. **caricaturist** ['kærɪkəˌtjʊərɪst] *sb* karikaturtegner.

carnage ['kɑ:nɪdʒ] *sb* blodbad, massakre. **carnal** ['kɑ:nl] *adj* kjødelig, sanselig. **carnal abuse** *sb* sedelighetsforbrytelse. **carnation** [kɑ:'neɪʃn] *sb* **1** nellik; **2** kjøttfarge. **carnivorous** [kɑ:'nɪvərəs] *adj* kjøttetende.

carol ['kærəl] **1** *sb* (lov)sang; *Christmas ~* julesang; **2** *vi* juble, (lov)synge.

carouse [kə'raʊz] *vi* rangle, ture.

carp [kɑ:p] **A** *sb* karpe; **B** *vi* kritisere (smålig); *~ at* hakke på.

carpenter ['kɑ:pɪntə] *sb* (bygnings)snekker, tømmermann. **carpentry** ['kɑ:pɪntrɪ] *sb* tømmermannsarbeid.

carpet ['kɑ:pɪt] **1** *sb* (gulv)teppe; **2** *vt* legge teppe på. **carpet|bag** *sb* vadsekk. **~ slippers** *sb fl* filttøfler.

carriage ['kærɪdʒ] *sb* **1** kjøretøy, vogn; **2** passasjervogn; **3** transport; *merk* frakt; **4** *(gun-~)* (kanon)lavett; **5** slede (på verktøymaskin); vogn (på skrivemaskin); **6** holdning, måte å føre seg på. **carriage|-drive** *sb* oppkjørsel. **~ return** *sb data* vognretur; *~-return character* vognreturtegn. **~-way** *sb* kjørebane; *dual ~-way* motorvei. **carrier** ['kærɪə] *sb* **1** bærer *etc;* speditør, transportfirma; bud; *US* postbud; **2** transportmiddel; *aircraft-~* hangarskip; **3** bagasjebrett; **4** understell; **5** smittebærer. **carrier | gas** *sb petro* bæregass. **~-pigeon** *sb* brevdue.

carrion ['kærɪən] *sb* åtsel.

carrot ['kærət] *sb* gulrot.

carry ['kærɪ] **I** *sb* **1** grep, tak; bæring, løft; **2** rekkevidde; **3** *mat* menteoverføring; **II** *vb* **1** bære; bringe; frakte, føre, transportere; *~ oneself* (opp)føre seg; **2** bære; holde oppe, (under)støtte; *fig* tåle; **3** gå med/ha på seg (av f.eks. klær); ha med seg; *~ in one's head* ha i hodet (dvs huske); **4** inkludere, medføre; **5** gjennomføre; (opp)nå; *~ one's point* få medhold; **6** vinne; rive med seg; *~ by assault* ta med storm; *carried by a vote of 67 to 43* vedtatt med 67 mot 43 stemmer; **7** *med adv/prep* *~* **away** bære/føre med seg; *fig* rive med; *~* **forward** *merk* overføre, transportere; *~* **off** bære *etc* bort; *fig* gjennomføre; vinne; *carried off one's feet* revet/slått over ende; *fig* revet med; *~* **on** drive/praktisere (*as* som); fortsette/drive på (*with* med); bære seg; ta på vei; *~ings-on* bråk; upassende oppførsel; *~* **on with** *også* stå i med; *~* **out** utføre; fullbyrde; oppfylle; *~* **over** *merk* overføre, transportere; *~* **through** gjennomføre.

cart [kɑ:t] **1** *sb* kjerre, (arbeids)vogn; **2** *vt* kjøre (bort med) kjerre; slepe (på). **cartage** ['kɑ:tɪdʒ] *sb* (betaling for) kjøring. **carter** ['kɑ:tə] *sb* kjørekar.

cartilage ['kɑ:tɪlɪdʒ] *sb* brusk.

cartload ['kɑ:tləʊd] *sb* kjerrelass.

carton ['kɑ:tn] *sb* kartong, (papp)eske. **cartoon** [kɑ:'tu:n] **I** *sb* **1** karikatur, vittighetstegning (især politisk); **2** tegneserie; **3** *(animated ~)* tegnefilm; **II** *vt* karikere. **cartoonist** [kɑ:'tu:nɪst] *sb* vittighetstegner.

cartridge ['kɑ:trɪdʒ] *sb* **1** patron; **2** film|rull, (-)spole; **3** pickuphode; **4** *data* (magnetbånd)kassett. **cartridge | disk** *sb data* platekassett. **~ ribbon** *sb data* kassettfargebånd.

cartwright ['kɑ:traɪt] *sb* vognmaker.

carve [kɑ:v] *vb* **1** hugge/skjære (inn, til, ut); meisle; **2** skjære opp. **carving** ['kɑ:vɪŋ] *sb* **1** oppskjæring *etc*; **2** treskjæring. **carving-knife** *sb* forskjærkniv.

cascade [kæs'keɪd] **1** *sb* foss, vannfall; kaskade; **2** *vi* flomme, fosse.

case [keɪs] **A** *sb* **1** tilfelle; *in ~ of* i tilfelle av; *in any ~* i hvert fall, uansett; *in no ~* ikke i noe tilfelle, under ingen omstendighet; *in that/this ~* i så fall; *(just) in ~* for alle tilfelles skyld; **2** (retts)sak; *have a strong ~* stå sterkt; **3** kasus; **B I** *sb* **1** eske; etui, futteral; skrin; **2** boks; kasse; montre; **3** hylse; hylster, kapsel; slire; **4** mappe, veske; **II** *vt* **1** kle; bygge inn; **2** legge i eske *etc*.

casement ['keɪsmənt] *sb* vindu (sidehengslet, i motsetning til skyvevindu).

cash [kæʃ] **I** *sb* **1** kontanter, (rede) penger; **2** *merk* kasse; *~ on delivery* kontant ved levering; mot oppkrav; **II** *vb* **1** heve penger (på sjekk etc); *~ in on* tjene (penger) på; **2** utbetale penger (på sjekk etc). **cash-account** *sb* kassakonto. **cashier A** [kæ'ʃɪə] *sb* kasserer; **B** [kə'ʃɪə] *vt* kassere, vrake; avskjedige (i unåde, med vanære). **cash register** *sb* kassaapparat.

casing ['keɪsɪŋ] *sb* **1** hylster; kapsel, innkapsling; omslag; (over)trekk; futteral; *petro* fôringsrør; **2** løpegang (til snøring, strikk etc). **casing | hanger** *sb petro* røroppheng. **~-head gas** *sb petro* våtgass.

cask [kɑ:sk] *sb* (vin)fat, tønne. **casket** ['kɑ:skɪt] *sb* **1** skrin (til smykker etc); **2** *US* likkiste.

casserole ['kæsərəʊl] *sb* **1** ildfast form; **2** mat tilberedt i ildfast form; ≈ gryterett.

cast [kɑ:st] **I** *sb* **1** kast; **2** (støpe)form; avstøpning; *fig* form, preg; **3** anstrøk, tilbøyelighet; **4** rollebesetning; **5** *petro etc* fargespill, skinn; **II** *vb* **1** kaste (og hive, slenge; kassere etc); *~ a vote* avgi stemme; **2** støpe; **3** fordele roller (i et skuespill); tildele rolle; **4** *med adv/prep ~* **about** spekulere; tenke frem og tilbake; *~* **about for** se seg om etter; *be ~* **away** lide skibbrudd; *~* **down** nedfor; *~* **on** legge opp (masker); *~* **off** felle av (masker); *~* **up** beregne; slå sammen.

castaway ['kɑ:stəweɪ] *adj/sb* skibbrudden; *fig* forstøtt, fortapt (person).

caste [kɑ:st] *sb* kaste.

cast-iron [ˌkɑ:st'aɪən] *adj* støpejerns-; *fig* urokkelig.

castle ['kɑ:sl] *sb* borg, slott; tårn (i sjakk); *~ in Spain* luftslott.

castor ['kɑ:stə] *sb* **1** trinse; **2** bøsse, strødåse. **castor|-oil** *sb* lakserolje. **~-sugar** *sb* strøsukker.

castrate [kæ'streɪt] *vt* kastrere. **castration** [kæ'streɪʃn] *sb* kastrasjon, kastrering.

casual ['kæʒjʊəl] *adj* **1** tilfeldig; **2** ledig, utvungen; **3** skjødesløs. **casualty** ['kæʒjʊəltɪ] *sb* **1** ulykke, ulykkestilfelle; **2** *fl* ofre (dvs døde og/eller sårede ved ulykker, i krig etc).

cat [kæt] **I** *sb* **1** katt; **2** *sjø* (anker)katt; **II** *vb* **1** *sjø* katte (anker); **2** *slang* kaste opp, spy.

catalog(ue) ['kætəlɒg] *sb* katalog; fortegnelse, register.

catalyst ['kætəlɪst] *sb* katalysator. **catalytic** [ˌkætə'lɪtɪk] *adj* katalytisk.

catastrophe [kə'tæstrəfɪ] *sb* katastrofe. **catastrophic** [ˌkætə'strɒfɪk] *adj* katastrofal.

catch [kætʃ] **I** *sb* **1** grep, tak; **2** bytte, fangst; *fig* fordel; *slang* godt parti; **3** (sperre)hake; (dør)stopper; (smekk)lås; haspe; klinke; **4** aber, hake; *there's a ~ in it* det er en hake ved det; **II** *vb* **1** fange (opp); gripe; ta (fatt i); få tak; henge/sitte fast; hekte/henge seg opp; *~ oneself* ta seg i det; *~ on* slure mot; *fig* oppfatte; slå an; *~ on to* oppdage; komme under vær med; *~ up* rive til seg; *fig* snappe opp; *caugt up in* oppslukt av; rotet opp i; **2** fange; **3** fange/samle opp; **4** overraske/ta (på fersk gjerning); *~ out* avsløre; gripe i feil *etc*; **5** begripe, oppfatte; **6** nå, rekke; *~ up (on/with)* innhente; komme à jour (med); **7** få, pådra seg; *~ (a) cold* bli forkjølet; *~ fire* begynne å brenne, ta fyr; *~ it* få kjeft/juling *etc*; **8** treffe; ramme, råke; *~ him a clip* gi ham en lusing. **catching** ['kætʃɪŋ] *adj* smittsom; *fig* fengende, smittende. **catchment** ['kætʃmənt] *sb: ~-area, ~-basin* nedslagsdistrikt. **catchword** ['kætʃwɜ:d] sb slagord. **catchy** ['kætʃɪ] *adj* **1** fengende; ørefallende, øynefallende; **2** lumsk, vrien.

categorical [ˌkætɪ'gɒrɪkl] *adj* kategorisk. **category** ['kætɪgərɪ] *sb* kategori.

cater ['keɪtə] *vi* **1** levere mat (*for* til); **2** *~ for* skaffe, tilgodese (især med underholdning etc); *~ to* sørge for, ta seg av. **caterer** ['keɪtərə] *sb* ferdigmatleverandør; selskapsarrangør.

caterpillar ['kætəpɪlə] **I** *adj* belte- (dvs med beltetrekk); **II** *sb* **1** kålorm, larve; **2** *fl* larveføtter; belter, beltetrekk.

cathead ['kæthed] *sb petro* nokk.

cathedral [kə'θi:drəl] *sb* katedral, domkirke.

cathode ['kæθəʊd] *sb* katode. **cathode | ray** *sb fysikk* katodestråle. **~ ray tube** *sb data* katodestrålerør, CRT-skjerm. **~ ray unit** *sb data* monitor(enhet).

catholic ['kæθəlɪk] **I** *adj* **1** alminnelig, omfattende; **2** frisinnet; **II** *(Roman) Catholic* **1** *adj* (romersk-) katolsk; **2** *sb* katolikk.

catkin ['kætkɪn] *sb* rakle. **cat|-nap, ~-sleep** *sb* høneblund, (liten) lur. **cat's-paw** *sb fig* redskap. **cattish** ['kætɪʃ] *adj* katteaktig; *fig* intrigant; ondskapsfull.

cattle ['kætl] *sb* (stor)fe, kveg.

cat-walk *sb* gang|bro, -planke; *petro også* rørbro.

Caucasian [kɔ:'keɪzɪən] **I** *adj* **1** kaukasisk; **2** indoeuropeisk; *US* hvit (i huden); **II** *sb* **1** kaukasier; **2** indoeuropeer; *US* hvit (person).

cauldron ['kɔ:ldrən] *sb* gryte, (stor) kjele.

cauliflower ['kɒlɪflaʊə] *sb* blomkål.

cause [kɔ:z] **I** *sb* **1** opphav/årsak (*of* til); **2** grunn (*of* til); **3** (for)mål; sak; *common ~* felles sak; **II** *vt* forårsake.

causeway ['kɔ:zweɪ] *sb* (vei)fylling; vei på demning over myr etc; chaussé.

caustic ['kɔ:stɪk] *adj* kaustisk; *fig* bitende, skarp.

caustic soda *sb* kaustisk soda, lut. **cauterization** [ˌkɔ:təraɪ'zeɪʃn] *sb* kauterisering *etc.* **cauterize** ['kɔ:təraɪz] *vt* kauterisere, etse; brenne ut (f.eks. et sår).

caution [kɔ:ʃn] **I** *sb* **1** forsiktighet; **2** advarsel; **3** *US* kausjon; **4** *slang* raring; **II** *vt* advare. **cautionary** ['kɔ:ʃnərɪ] *adj* advarende. **cautious** ['kɔ:ʃəs] *adj* forsiktig.

cavalcade [ˌkævl'keɪd] *sb* (rytter)opptog; *også fig* kavalkade. **cavalier** [ˌkævə'lɪə] **I** *adj* **1** feiende, flott; **2** overlegen; hensynsløs; **II** *sb* **1** ridder, rytter; **2** kavaler; *hist* rojalist. **cavalry** ['kævlrɪ] *sb* kavaleri.

cave [keɪv] **I** *sb* **1** hule; **2** (parti)fraksjon; **II** *vb* hule ut; ~ *in* falle (rase el. styrte) sammen. **cave-in** [ˌkeɪv'ɪn] *sb petro* brønnerosjon; utrasing, utvasking. **cavern** ['kævən] *sb* hule. **cavernous** ['kævənəs] *adj* hul, uthult.

cavity ['kævətɪ] *sb* hulrom; hull (i tann).

cease [si:s] **1** *sb* opphør, stans; **2** *vb* holde opp/ slutte (med). **cease|-fire** *sb* våpen|hvile, -stillstand. **~less** *adj* uavbrutt.

cedar ['si:də] *sb* seder(tre).

cede [si:d] *vt* **1** avstå, oppgi; levere fra seg; **2** innrømme.

ceiling ['si:lɪŋ] *sb* **1** (innvendig) tak; himling; **2** *fig* tak (dvs øverste grense).

celebrate ['selɪbreɪt] *vb* **1** feire; **2** gjøre ære på. **celebrated** ['selɪbreɪtɪd] *adj* berømt. **celebration** [ˌselɪ'breɪʃn] *sb* feiring. **celebrity** [sɪ'lebrətɪ] *sb* berømthet, berømt person.

celery ['selərɪ] *sb* (stang)selleri.

celestial [sɪ'lestɪəl] *adj* himmelsk, himmel-. **celestial body** *sb* himmellegeme.

celibacy ['selɪbəsɪ] sølibat.

cell [sel] *sb* celle.

cellar ['selə] *sb* kjeller. **cellar deck** *sb petro* kjellerdekk.

cement [sɪ'ment] **1** *sb* bindemiddel (som sement, kitt, lim etc); *fig* bånd; **2** *vt* sementere (og kitte, lime etc); *fig* forene, styrke.

cemetery ['semɪtrɪ] *sb* gravlund, gravplass (uten kirke).

censor ['sensə] **I** *sb* sensor; **II** *vt* **1** sensurere; **2** kritisere strengt. **censorial** [sen'sɔ:rɪəl] *adj* sensor-. **censorious** [sen'sɔ:rɪəs] *adj* dømmesyk. **censorship** ['sensəʃɪp] *sb* **1** sensur; **2** sensorstilling. **censure** ['senʃə] **1** *sb* mishag, misnøye; kritikk; **2** *vt* klandre, kritisere.

census ['sensəs] *sb* folketelling.

cent [sent] *sb* **1** *US* cent (= 1/100 dollar); **2** hundredel; *per* ~ prosent. **centenarian** [ˌsentɪ'neərɪən] **1** *adj* hundreårig; hundreårs-; **2** *sb* hundreåring; *slang* jubelolding. **centenary** [sen'ti:nərɪ], **centennial** [sen'tenɪəl] **1** *adj* = *centenarian 1*; **2** *sb a)* hundreårsdag; *b)* hundreårsperiode.

centigrade ['sentɪgreɪd] *adj, sb* celsius(grader). **centiped** ['sentɪped] *sb* tusenbein.

central ['sentrəl] **1** *adj* sentral(-); viktig(st); **2** *sb US* (telefon)sentral. **centralization** [ˌsentrəlaɪ'zeɪʃn] *sb* sentralisering *etc.* **centralize** ['sentrəlaɪz] *vb* sentralisere; sentrere; konsentrere; samle (seg). **central | processing unit** (fork **CPU**), ~ **processor** *sb data* (sentral) prosessorenhet.

centre ['sentə] **1** *adj* senter-; sentral(-), sentrums-; kjerne-, midt-; **2** *sb* sentrum; *fig også* kjerne, midtpunkt; **3** *vb* sette/stå i sentrum; ~ *about* samle (seg) om.

century ['sentʃərɪ] *sb* århundre.

ceramic [sɪ'ræmɪk] **1** *adj* keramisk; **2** *sb: ceramics* keramikk. **ceramist** ['serəmɪst] *sb* keramiker.

cereal ['sɪərɪəl] **1** *adj* korn-; **2** *sb* korn; *fl* kornprodukter; *især* frokostgryn (o.a. retter laget av kornblandinger eller kornprodukter); *ofte* grøt.

ceremonial [ˌserɪ'məʊnɪəl] *adj, sb* seremoniell. **ceremonious** [ˌserɪ'məʊnɪəs] *adj* seremoniøs; (overdrevent) høytidelig. **ceremony** ['serɪmənɪ] *sb* seremoni; *stand on* ~ holde på formene.

certain ['sɜ:tn] *adj* **1** sikker, viss (*about, of* på; *that* på at); *be* ~ *to* forvisse seg om (at); huske/passe på å; sikkert komme til å; **2** pålitelig, sikker; **3** bestemt, viss. **certainly** ['sɜ:tnlɪ] *adv* **1** sikkert, utvilsomt; **2** *som svar* ja visst, selvsagt. **certainty** ['sɜ:tntɪ] *sb* sikkerhet, visshet.

certificate **1** [sə'tɪfɪkət] *sb* attest, vitnemål; sertifikat; **2** [sə'tɪfɪkeɪt] *vt* gi/utstede attest *etc.* **certification** [ˌsɜ:tɪfɪ'keɪʃn] *sb* attest(ering) *etc.* **certified** ['sɜ:tɪfaɪd] *adj, pp* attesteret (etc, jf *certify*). **certified public accountant** *sb især US* statsautorisert revisor. **certify** ['sɜ:tɪfaɪ] *vb* attestere, bevitne; sertifisere; *også* autorisere.

certitude ['sɜ:tɪtju:d] *sb* visshet.

cessation [se'seɪʃn] *sb* opphør, stans.

cession ['seʃn] *sb* avståelse.

cesspit ['sespɪt], **cesspool** ['sespu:l] *sb* kloakkkum, septiktank; *fig* kloakk, pøl.

chafe [tʃeɪf] **I** *sb* gnagsår; *fig* irritasjon; **II** *vb* **1** gni (for å varme); **2** gnage; skrape/skrubbe (opp); **3** *fig* ergre, irritere; ergre seg (*at* over).

chaff [tʃɑ:f] **A I** *sb* **1** agner; **2** hakkels(e); **3** avfall; **II** *vt* hakke (halm etc); **B 1** *sb* (godmodig) erting; **2** *vt* erte (godmodig); fleipe/drive gjøn (med).

chaffinch ['tʃæfɪntʃ] *sb* bokfink.

chain [tʃeɪn] **I** *sb* **1** kjetting, lenke; kjede; **2** rekke, serie; **3** *fl sjø* røst(jern); **II** *vt* lenke (fast). **chain|-armour, ~-mail** *sb* ringbrynje. ~ **printer** *sb data* kjedeskriver. ~ **reaction** *sb* kjedereaksjon.

chair ['tʃeə] **I** *sb* **1** stol; **2** forsete (og formann, ordstyrer, president etc, både om plassen, vervet og personen); **3** lærestol, professorat; **4** bærestol; **II** *vt* **1** lede forhandlinger/møte etc; **2** bære på gullstol. **chair|man** *sb* formann (etc, jf *~person*). **~person** *sb* for|kvinne, -mann; leder; ord|fører, -styrer; president. **~woman** *sb* forkvinne (etc, jf *~person*).

chalk [tʃɔ:k] **1** *sb* kritt; **2** *vb* kritte (opp); ~ *out* skissere/streke opp; ~ *up* notere (opp); skrive på regning(en).

challenge ['tʃælɪndʒ] **I** *sb* **1** utfordring; **2** (vaktposts) anrop; **3** (rettslig) innsigelse/protest; **II** *vt* **1** trosse, utfordre; **2** bestride; **3** anrope.

chamber ['tʃeɪmbə] *sb* **1** værelse; kammer; lite rom; *fl også* leilighet; (kontor)lokaler; advokatkontor; **2** møtesal (og fremmøtt forsamling); **3** kammer (i nasjonalforsamling); **4** kammer (i skytevåpen). **chamber|lein** *sb* kammerherre; *Lord C~ (of the Household)* hoffmarskalk (som bl.a. også var teatersensor); *town ~* kemner. **~maid** *sb* kammerpike; værelsespike (på hotell). **Chamber of Commerce** *sb* ≈ handelskammer. **chamberpot** *sb* nattpotte.

chameleon [kə'mi:lɪən] *sb* kameleon.

chamois ['ʃæmwɑ:] *sb* **1** gemse; **2** = **chamois leather** *sb* **1** semsklær, semsket skinn; **2** pusseskinn.

champ ['tʃæmp] **A** *vb* tygge (på bekselet); *fig* være utålmodig; **B** = *champion II 2.* **champion** ['tʃæmpɪən] **I** *adj* mester-, vinner-; **II** *sb* **1** forkjemper (*of* for); forsvarer (*of* av); **2** mester, vinner; **III** *vt* forsvare. **championship** ['tʃæmpɪənʃɪp] *sb* mesterskap.

chance [tʃɑ:ns] **I** *adj* tilfeldig; **II** *sb* **1** tilfeldighet, tilfelle; slump, (slumpe)treff; **2** anledning; mulighet, sjanse; *stand a fair/good ~* ha rimelige/gode utsikter; **III** *vb* **1** hende; falle seg; slumpe til; *~ upon* komme over; finne tilfeldig; **2** risikere, våge.

chancellor ['ʃɑ:nsələ] *sb* **1** kansler; **2** førstesekretær (ved ambassade etc); **3** *C~ of the Exchequer* finansminister; **4** *Lord (High) C~* lordkansler (Overhusets president og Englands høyeste juridiske embetsmann).

chandelier [ˌʃændə'lɪə] *sb* lysekrone.

change [tʃeɪndʒ] **I** *sb* **1** forandring; (om)bytte, skifte; *for a ~* til en avveksling/forandring; **2** vekslepenger; småpenger; **II** *vb* **1** forandre (seg) (*into* til); bytte/skifte (*for* ut med); *~ down/up* gire ned/opp; *~ hands* skifte eier; *~ one's mind* ombestemme seg; skifte mening; **2** veksle (penger); gi igjen. **changeable** ['tʃeɪndʒəbl] *adj* foranderlig. **changeling** ['tʃeɪndʒlɪŋ] *sb* bytting.

channel ['tʃænl] **I** *sb* **1** kanal (fortrinnsvis naturlig); strede, sund; **2** (skips)lei, rute; **3** elveleie; **4** kanal (for radio/TV); **5** *fig* kanal, vei; **II** *vt* **1** grave ut (kanal); **2** kanalisere. **channel capacity** *sb data* kanalkapasitet. **channelling** *sb petro* kanaldannelse.

chant [tʃɑ:nt] **I** *sb* **1** messing; monoton sang; **2** (gammel) melodi/sang; **II** *vb* messe.

chaos ['keɪɒs] *sb* kaos, forvirring. **chaotic** [keɪ'ɒtɪk] *adj* kaotisk.

chap [tʃæp] **A 1** *sb* sprekk; sprukken hud; **2** *vb* (få til å) sprekke/bli sår; **B** *sb fl* kjaker, kjever (især på dyr); **C** *sb slang* fyr, kar.

chapel ['tʃæpl] *sb* **1** kapell, slottskirke; **2** bedehus; *som adj også* dissenter- frikirke- (i motsetning til *Church of England*). **chapel-of-ease** *sb* annekskirke.

chaperon ['ʃæpərəun] *sb, vb* (være) anstandsdame/*dgl* forkle (for).

chap-fallen *adj* lang i ansiktet (av skuffelse etc).

chaplain ['tʃæplɪn] *sb* prest (især ved institusjon, f.eks. fengselsprest, garnisonsprest, sykehusprest); feltprest, skipsprest.

chapter ['tʃæptə] *sb* kapittel.

char [tʃɑ:] **A** *vb* forkulle(s); **B 1** *sb (~woman)* rengjøringshjelp, vaskekone; **2** *vi* gjøre rent; skure, vaske; **C** *sb* røye; **D** *sb slang* te.

character ['kærɪktə] *sb* **1** karakter, natur; **2** skussmål; særpreg; **3** person(lighet); *quite a ~ (dgl)* litt av en type; **4** person (i roman etc); **5** bokstav, (skrift)-tegn. **character | check** *sb data* tegnkontroll. **~ density** *sb data* tegntetthet. **characteristic** [ˌkærɪktə'rɪstɪk] **1** *adj* karakteristisk; **2** *sb* eiendommelighet; særpreg. **characterization** [ˌkærɪktəraɪ'zeɪʃn] *sb* karakterisering. **characterize** ['kærɪktəraɪz] *vt* karakterisere. **character | log** *sb petro* karakterlogg. **~ printer** *sb data* tegnskriver. **~ reader** *sb data* tegnleser.

charcoal ['tʃɑ:kəul] sb trekull; *petro også* aktivkarbon.

charge [tʃɑ:dʒ] **I** *sb* **1** anklage, beskyldning; tiltale; **2** (storm)angrep; **3** omkostning, utgift; pris(krav); gebyr; **4** ladning (av sprengstoff, elektrisk strøm etc); **5** belastning; byrde; *fig* ansvar; *in ~* ansvarlig (*of* for); tjenestegjørende, vakthavende; **6** oppdrag, oppgave; pålegg; **7** omsorg, varetekt (og om det en har i varetekt, som f.eks. pasient, pleiebarn, protegé); **8** instruks; oppfordring; direktiv(er), ordre; **9** *petro* (inn)-sats; **II** *vb* **1** anklage, beskylde; sikte/tiltale (*with* for); **2** angripe, storme; **3** forlange; ta (i pris); *merk* anføre, debitere; *~ it to my account* før det på min konto; **4** (be)laste; fylle (opp); lade; **5** pålegge; *fig* betro; **6** formane; instruere; oppfordre; beordre. **charge|-account** *sb US* konto (i forretning). **~ gas** *sb petro* rågass. **charger** *sb* **A** stridshest; **B** stort fat. **charge stock** *sb petro* råstoff.

chariot ['tʃærɪət] *sb* (strids)vogn.

charitable ['tʃærətəbl] *adj* godgjørende, veldedig; snill. **charity** ['tʃærətɪ] *sb* **1** (neste)kjærlighet; **2** godgjørenhet, veldedighet; **3** veldedig stiftelse *etc.*

charlatan ['ʃɑ:lətən] *sb* kvakksalver; humbugmaker, svindler; sjarlatan.

charm [tʃɑ:m] **I** *sb* **1** amulett; **2** trolldom; tryllemiddel; *fig* fortryllelse; **3** sjarm; **II** *vb* **1** forhekse, fortrylle; **2** sjarmere.

chart [tʃɑ:t] **I** *sb* **1** *sjø* draft, (sjø)kart; **2** diagram; skjema; tabell; **3** *data* flytskjema; **II** *vt* **1** kartlegge; **2** stikke ut kurs; **3** vise ved diagram *etc.* **charter** ['tʃɑ:tə] **I** *sb* **1** dokument; *the C~ of the United Nations* FN-pakten; **2** fribrev; privilegium; **3** *fly, sjø* befraktning; befraktningskontrakt; **II** *vt* **1** privilegere; **2** *merk* autorisere; **3** *fly, sjø* befrakte, chartre. **chartered accountant** *sb* statsautorisert revisor. **charter-party** *sb fly, sjø* certeparti.

chary ['tʃeərɪ] *adj* **1** forsiktig, var(som); **2** påholden, sparsom.

chase [tʃeɪs] **A I** *sb* **1** forfølgelse, jakt; *in ~ of* på jakt etter; **2** forfulgt (person); jaget (dyr); **II** *vb* **1** forfølge; **2** jage (etter); jakte på; *~ down* oppspore (og innhente); **3** *slang* fly/løpe etter; **B** *vt* siselere. **chaser**

sb **A 1** forfølger, jager; jeger; **2** slurk øl (e.l. etter en dram); **B** siselør.

chasm ['kæzəm] *sb* dyp kløft; avgrunn, svelg.

chassis ['ʃæsɪ] *sb* chassis, understell.

chaste [tʃeɪst] *adj* **1** kysk, ren, ærbar; **2** enkel, (stil)ren. **chasten** ['tʃeɪsn] *vt* **1** refse, tukte; **2** rense. **chastise** [tʃæ'staɪz] *vt* straffe strengt, tukte. **chastity** ['tʃæstətɪ] *sb* kyskhet, renhet; uskyld, ærbarhet.

chat [tʃæt] *sb, vi* prat(e), snakk(e).

chattels ['tʃætlz] *sb fl* løsøre.

chatter ['tʃætə] **I** *sb* skravling *etc*; **II** *vi* **1** skravle; **2** *især om fugler* skvaldre, skvatre; *om skrivemaskin etc* klapre; *om automatvåpen etc* skratte, smatre; **3** hakke (tenner). **chatterbox** *sb* skravlebøtte.

chauffeur ['ʃəufə] *sb* (privat)sjåfør.

cheap [tʃi:p] *adj* **1** billig, godtkjøps(-); **2** lettkjøpt; dårlig, simpel, tarvelig; *hold* ~ forakte, se ned på. **cheapen** ['tʃi:pən] *vb* **1** bli/gjøre billig(ere); **2** forsimple.

cheat [tʃi:t] **I** *sb* **1** bedrag *etc*; **2** bedrager, svindler; **II** *vb* bedra, lure; snyte, svindle.

check [tʃek] **A I** *sb* **1** hindring; stans, stopp; demper; **2** kontroll (og kontrollpost, kontrollpunkt, kontrollør); **3** (kontroll)undersøkelse; **4** hake, kryss *etc* (som tegn på at noe er kontrollert); **5** kontrollmerke (som f.eks. billett, bong, garderobeskilt, kassalapp, kvittering, talong); **II** *vb* **1** hemme, hindre; stanse, stoppe; holde tilbake; dempe; **2** kontrollere, undersøke; *dgl* sjekke; ~ *off* hake/krysse av; ~ *up* undersøke (nærmere); **3** irettesette; **B I** *interj* **1** sjakk! **2** *slang* det stemmer! **II** *sb* sjakk (dvs situasjonen, jf *chess*); **III** *vt* sette sjakk; **C 1** *adj (~ed)* rutet; **2** *sb* rute(r); rutet stoff; **D** *US* **I** *sb* **1** *merk* sjekk; **2** nota, regning; **3** spillemerke; **II** *vb* **1** registrere, skrive inn (bagasje etc); levere (f.eks. yttertøy mot kontrollmerke i garberobe); **2** ~ *in* melde seg inn; stemple inn (på arbeidsplass); ta inn (på hotell); ~ *out* melde seg ut *etc*. **check | bit** *sb data* kontrollbit. ~ **card** *sb data* kontrollkort. ~ **digit** *sb data* kontrollsiffer.

checker ['tʃekə] **1** *sb* kontrollør *etc*; **2** *US* = *chequer*.

checkers ['tʃekəz] *sb fl US* dam (dvs spillet).

check | key *sb data* kontrollnøkkel. ~**mate 1** *interj, sb* sjakkmatt; **2** *vt* gjøre/sette sjakkmatt; *fig* slå ut. ~ **point** *sb* kontroll|punkt, -post. ~ **problem** *sb data* kontrolleksempel. ~**-up** *sb* kontroll, undersøkelse. ~ **valve** *sb petro* prøveventil.

cheek [tʃi:k] **I** *sb* **1** kinn; ~ *by jowl* tett sammen; **2** bakke, kjeft (etc, på verktøy); nebb; **3** frekkhet; **II** *vt* være frekk mot. **cheeky** ['tʃi:kɪ] *adj* frekk; nebbet, oppkjeftig.

cheer ['tʃɪə] **I** *(interj) cheers!* skål! **II** *sb* **1** (godt) humør; (høy) stemning; **2** bevertning, traktement; **3** hurra(rop); **III** *vb* **1** glede; oppmuntre, trøste; ~ *up!* friskt mot! opp med humøret! **2** hylle; rope hurra (for); **3** heie (for/på). **cheerful** *adj* **1** glad; lystig, munter; **2** gledelig. **cheerio** [ˌtʃɪərɪ'əu] *interj dgl* **1** hei (på deg)! ha det! **2** skål! **cheer|-leaders** *sb fl US* heiagjeng. ~**less** *adj* bedrøvelig, sørgelig; nedtrykt, trist; uglad.

cheese [tʃi:z] *sb* ost. **cheese-parings** ['tʃi:zˌpeərɪŋgz] *sb fl* osteskorper; *fig* smuler, småtteri(er); bagateller.

chemical ['kemɪkl] **1** *adj* kjemisk; **2** *sb fl* kjemikalier. **chemist** ['kemɪst] *sb* **1** kjemiker; **2** apoteker. **chemistry** ['kemɪstrɪ] *sb* kjemi. **chemist's (shop)** apotek.

cheque [tʃek] *sb merk* sjekk. **cheque-book** *sb* sjekkhefte. **chequer** ['tʃekə] **I** *sb* **1** rute; firkantet felt; **2** rutemønster; **3** dambrett; **4** *fl = draughts*; **II** *vt* **1** dele opp i ruter; **2** variere, gjøre broket/skiftende. **chequered** ['tʃekəd] *adj* **1** rutet; **2** broket; skiftende; variert.

cherish ['tʃerɪʃ] *vt* **1** skatte; sette høyt; **2** fostre, nære (f.eks. håp, ønske); holde levende.

cherry ['tʃerɪ] **1** *adj* kirsebærrød; **2** *sb* kirsebær(tre). **cherry picker** *sb petro* heiskurv.

chess [tʃes] *sb* (spillet) sjakk. **chess|board** *sb* sjakkbrett. ~**man** *sb* sjakkbrikke.

chest [tʃest] *sb* **1** kiste; kasse; skrin; **2** bryst(kasse); *get it off one's* ~ lette sitt hjerte for det. **chestnut** ['tʃestnʌt] **I** *adj* kastanjebrun; **II** *sb* **1** kastanje(tre); **2** *slang* gammel vits. **chest-of-drawers** *sb* kommode.

chevron ['ʃevrən] *sb* vinkel (dvs distinksjon som angir militær etc befalingsmanns grad).

chew [tʃu:] **I** *sb* **1** tygging; **2** munnfull, tygge (dvs noe å tygge på); **II** *vb* tygge (på); *fig* gruble (over).

chick [tʃɪk] *sb* **1** kylling; fugleunge; **2** smårolling; **3** *US slang* ungjente. **chicken** [tʃɪkɪn] **I** *adj* **1** kylling-; *især US også* hønse-; **2** *slang* = *~-hearted*; **II** *sb* **1** kylling; *især US også* høne; **2** smårolling; *fig* grønnskolling; **3** *slang* feiging; **III** *vi slang* bli redd; ~ *out* trekke seg (av feighet). **chicken|-feed** *sb slang* bagateller; småpenger. ~**-hearted** *adj slang* feig. ~**-pox** *sb* vannkopper.

chide [tʃaɪd] *vb* klage, mase; skjenne (på).

chief [tʃi:f] **I** *adj* **1** viktigst; hoved-; **2** først; størst; høyest, øverst-; **II** *sb* **1** leder, sjef; hersker; høvding; **2** *in* ~ = **chiefly** ['tʃi:flɪ] *adv* **1** hovedsakelig, stort sett; **2** især, først og fremst. **Chief of Staff** *sb* stabssjef. **chieftain** ['tʃi:ftən] *sb* høvding.

child [tʃaɪld] *sb* barn. **child|bed** *sb* barselseng. ~**birth** *sb* (barne)fødsel. ~**hood** *sb* barndom; *be in one's second* ~ gå i barndommen. **childish** ['tʃaɪldɪʃ] *adj* barnaktig, barnslig. **childlike** ['tʃaɪldlaɪk] *adj* barnlig; uskyldig (som et barn).

chill [tʃɪl] **1** *adj* kald, kjølig; **2** *sb* kjølighet, kulde; *ofte* kuldegysning; *cast a ~ over (fig)* legge en demper på; **2** *vb* bli/gjøre kald; *fig* legge en demper på; ta motet fra. **chilling** ['tʃɪlɪŋ] *adj* kjølig (dvs avvisende, udeltagende etc). **chilly** ['tʃɪlɪ] *adj* (nokså) kjølig; *fig* kjølig (dvs avvisende etc).

chime [tʃaɪm] **I** *sb* **1** klokkeklang; kiming, ringing; **2** *fl* klokkespill; **3** harmoni, samklang; **II** *vb* **1** kime, ringe; **2** harmonere; ~ *in* stemme i; erklære seg enig.

chimney ['tʃɪmnɪ] *sb* **1** pipe, skorstein; **2** grue, ildsted; **3** lampeglass; **4** bergskorte. **chimney|-corner** *sb* peiskrok. **~-piece** *sb* kaminhylle. **~-sweep(er)** *sb* (skorsteins)feier.

chin [tʃɪn] *sb* hake (dvs ansiktsdelen).

china ['tʃaɪnə] **1** *adj* porselens-; **2** *sb* porselen.

chink [tʃɪŋk] **A** *sb* revne, sprekk; **B 1** *sb* klirr(ing); skrangling; **2** *vb* klirre/skrangle (med); **C** *sb slang: Chink* kineser.

chip [tʃɪp] **I** *sb* **1** flis, spon; ~ *of the old block (fig)* alen av samme stykke; **2** hakk, skår; skall; **3** skive (av eple, potet etc stekt i smult); **4** spillemerke; **5** *data* brikke (med integrerte kretser); chip; **II** *vb* **1** hugge/telgje (til); **2** flise (seg) opp; få/slå hakk i; **3** skjære i skiver.

chirp [tʃɜ:p] **1** *sb* kvitring, kvitter; **2** *vb* kvitre. **chirpy** ['tʃɜ:pɪ] *adj* livlig, munter. **chirrup** ['tʃɪrəp] = *chirp*.

chisel ['tʃɪzl] **I** *sb* huggjern, meisel; **II** *vt* **1** hugge/meisle ut; **2** *slang* snyte, svindle.

chivalrous ['ʃɪvlrəs] *adj* **1** ridder-; **2** ridderlig. **chivalry** ['ʃɪvlrɪ] *sb* **1** ridderskap; **2** ridderlighet.

chives [tʃaɪvz] *sb fl* gressløk.

chock [tʃɒk] **I** *sb* klamp, (tre)kloss; kile; **II** *vt (~ up)* **1** klosse opp; støtte opp (med klosser etc); **2** feste (med klamp etc); kile fast; **3** fylle (opp).

chocolate ['tʃɒklət] *sb* sjokolade.

choice [tʃɔɪs] **I** *adj* utsøkt; **II** *sb* **1** valg [både om det å velge og det en velger]; *by/for* ~ fortrinnsvis, helst; **2** utvalg.

choir ['kwaɪə] *b* **1** (sang)kor; **2** kor (dvs del av kirke).

choke [tʃəʊk] **I** *sb* **1** kvelning (og kvelningsanfall); klump i halsen; **2** choke, startspjeld (i forbrenningsmotor); **II** *vb* **1** kveles; *~d with sobs* gråtkvalt; **2** kvele, strupe; ~ *back/down* svelge; *især* bite i seg; ~ *up* fylle (opp); tette igjen; **3** bruke choke (på).

choose [tʃu:z] *vb* **1** velge (*between* mellom; *from* blant); velge ut; kåre/velge til; **2** foretrekke.

chop [tʃɒp] **A I** *sb* **1** hugg; kutt; hakk; **2** avhugd stykke; **3** kotelett; **II** *vb* hugge, kappe; kutte (av/opp); hakke (opp); **B** *vi:* ~ *about/round* slå om (dvs skifte retning, om vind); ~ *and change* vingle, være ustadig; **C** = *chap B*. **chop-house** *sb* kafé, spiseforretning. **chopper** ['tʃɒpə] *sb* **I** (mindre) øks, kjøttøks; **II** *US slang* helikopter; **2** billettkontrollør; **3** kulesprøyte; **4** gangster. **choppy** ['tʃɒpɪ] *adj* krapp (om sjø). **chopsticks** ['tʃɒpstɪks] *sb fl* spisepinner.

chord [kɔ:d] *sb* **1** bånd, streng; **2** akkord; *fig* tone; **3** korde (i en sirkel).

chores [tʃɔ:z] *sb fl* (hus)arbeid; jobbing.

chorus ['kɔ:rəs] **1** *sb* kor; omkved, refreng; **2** *vb* rope/synge *etc* i kor.

chow [tʃaʊ] *sb US slang* mat.

christen ['krɪsn] *vt* døpe, gi navn. **christening** ['krɪsnɪŋ] *sb* (barne)dåp. **Christian** ['krɪstʃən] *adj*, *sb* kristen (person). **Christian name** *sb* døpenavn, fornavn.

Christmas ['krɪsməs] *sb* jul; *Father* ~ julenissen. **Christmas | Box** *sb* julegave. ~ **Day** *sb* 1. juledag. ~ **Eve** *sb* julaften. ~ **tree** *sb* **1** juletre; **2** *petro* ventiltre.

chromium ['krəʊmɪəm] *adj*, *sb* krom(-). **chromium|-plated** *adj* forkrommet. ~ **plating** *sb* forkromning, *dgl* krom.

chronic ['krɒnɪk] *adj* **1** kronisk; **2** *vulg* forferdelig, fæl.

chronicle ['krɒnɪkl] **1** *sb* historie, krønike(bok); **2** *vt* berette om; *især* skrive ned.

chubby ['tʃʌbɪ] *adj* lubben.

chuck [tʃʌk] **A** *sb* bakker/chuck (på dreiebenk etc); **B I** *sb* **1** klukk(ing); **2** smatt(ing); **II** *vi* **1** klukke (som høne); **2** smatte (som på hest); **C** *dgl* **I** *sb* **1** kast (og kasting); *get/give the* ~ få/gi sparken; **2** klapp, klask; **3** dikk(ing); **II** *vt* **1** hive/slenge (vekk); **2** klappe, klaske; **3** dikke (under haken); **D** *slang* **1** *sb US* mat; **2** *vt:* ~ *it!* hold opp!

chuckle ['tʃʌkl] **1** *sb* klukking; klukklatter; **2** *vi* klukke; klukkle, godte seg.

chuck wagon *sb US* feltkjøkken.

chug [tʃʌg] **1** *sb* dunk(ing); tøff(ing); **2** *vi* dunke, tøffe (som f.eks. motorbåt).

chum [tʃʌm] *dgl* **I** *sb* (rom)kamerat; **II** *vi:* ~ *up with* **1** bli/være godvenner med; **2** *US* dele rom med. **chummy** ['tʃʌmɪ] *dgl* **I** *adj* kameratslig; **II** *sb* **1** kamerat; **2** feiergutt.

chunk [tʃʌŋk] *sb* klump, tykk skive.

church [tʃɜ:tʃ] *sb* kirke. **church | service** *sb* gudstjeneste. **~warden** *sb* kirkeverge. **~yard** *sb* kirkegård.

churlish ['tʃɜ:lɪʃ] *adj* gretten, tverr.

churn [tʃɜ:n] **I** *sb* **1** (smør)kjerne; **2** (stort) melkespann; **II** *vb* **1** kjerne (smør); **2** kverne, male; virvle; ~ *up* piske opp.

chute [ʃu:t] **I** *sb* **1** (transport)renne, (-)sjakt, (-)slisk; **2** (elve)stryk; **3** akebakke; rutsjebane; **4** *(para~)* (fall)skjerm; **II** *vb* sende/sette utfor (transport)renne *etc*.

cider ['saɪdə] *sb* (eple)sider.

cigar [si'gɑ:] *sb* sigar. **cigarette** [ˌsigə'ret] *sb* sigarett.

cinder ['sɪndə] *sb* **1** glo; **2** *især fl* sinders.

Cinderella [ˌsɪndə'relə] Askepott.

cinema ['sɪnəmə] *sb* **1** kino; **2** film(kunst).

cinnamon ['sɪnəmən] *sb* kanel.

cipher ['saɪfə] **I** *sb* **1** null; **2** siffer, talltegn; **3** monogram; **4** chiffer, siffer(skrift); kode; **II** *vb* **1** *dgl* regne (ut); **2** skrive i kode; sifrere.

circle ['sɜ:kl] **I** *sb* **1** ring, sirkel; **2** bane; omløp, runde; **3** gruppe; krets/ring (av mennesker); **4** *dress/upper* ~ første/annen losjerad (el. balkong) i teater; **II** *vb* **1** kretse, sirkle; **2** omringe.

circuit ['sɜ:kɪt] *sb* **1** omkrets; **2** runde; **3** kretsløp; *elek* strømkrets; **4** rettskrets; tingreise. **circuitous** [sə'kju:ɪtəs] *adj* indirekte, omsvøpsfull. **circuit switching** *sb data* linjeveksling. **circular** ['sɜ:kjʊlə] **1** *adj* (sirkel)rund; ring-, rund-; **2** *sb* rundskriv, sirkulære. **circulate** ['sɜ:kjʊleɪt] *vb* **1** sirkulere, være i omløp; **2** sende rundt; sette i omløp. **circulation** [ˌsɜ:kjʊ'leɪʃn] *sb* **1** omløp, sirkulasjon; kretsløp; **2** opplag (av avis etc).

circum|cise ['sɜ:kəmsaɪz] *vt* omskjære. **~cision** [ˌsɜ:kəm'sɪʒn] *sb* omskjæring. **~ference** [sə'kʌmfərəns] *sb* omkrets; *dgl ofte* område. **~navigate** [ˌsɜ:kəm'nævɪgeɪt] *vt* seile rundt (jorden). **~-navigation** ['sɜ:kəmˌnævɪ'geɪʃn] *sb* (jord)omseiling. **~spect** ['sɜ:kəmspekt] *adj* forsiktig, omtenksom.

circumstance ['sɜ:kəmstəns] *sb* kjensgjerning; *især fl* forhold, omstendighet(er); (økonomiske) kår. **circumstantial** [ˌsɜ:kəm'stænʃl] *adj* **1** detaljert, omstendelig; **2** *~ evidence* indisium, indisier.

circumvent [ˌsɜ:kəm'vent] *vt* **1** omgå (bestemmelser etc); **2** lure, overliste. **circumvention** [ˌsɜ:kəm'venʃn] *sb* omgåelse *etc*.

circus ['sɜ:kəs] *sb* **1** sirkus; **2** rund plass/rundt torg (i by); *ofte* rundkjøring.

cistern ['sɪstən] *sb* sisterne, vanntank.

cite [saɪt] *vt* **1** sitere; anføre, påberope seg; **2** stevne (for retten).

citizen ['sɪtɪzn] *sb* **1** (by)borger, by|kvinne, -mann; **2** innbygger, (stats)borger. **citizenship** ['sɪtɪznʃɪp] *sb* **1** (stats)borgerskap; **2** samfunnsånd. **city** ['sɪtɪ] *sb* (større) by; *(the) City* Londons (og andre storbyers) forretningssentrum (og/eller gamleby). **city hall** *sb US* ≈ rådhus.

civic ['sɪvɪk] **I** *adj* **1** borgerlig, borger-; by-; **2** kommunal, kommune-; **3** samfunns-; **II** *sb: ~s* samfunnslære. **civil** ['sɪvl] *adj* **1** sivil; borgerlig, borger-; **2** samfunns-, stats-; **3** dannet, kultivert; høflig; hyggelig, vennlig. **civilian** [sɪ'vɪlɪən] **1** *adj* sivil; **2** *sb* sivilist, sivilperson. **civility** [sɪ'vɪlətɪ] *sb* dannelse; høflighet. **civilization** [ˌsɪvɪlaɪ'zeɪʃn] *sb* sivilisasjon; *ofte* kultur. **civilize** ['sɪvɪlaɪz] *vt* sivilisere. **civil servant** *sb* embets|kvinne, -mann; statstjeneste|kvinne, mann. *the* **Civil Service** statsadministrasjonen. **civil war** *sb* borgerkrig.

clad [klæd] *adj gml* dekket; iført, (i)kledd.

claim [kleɪm] **I** *sb* **1** fordring, krav; påstand; **2** erstatningskrav (til forsikringsselskap); *dgl* skade; **3** skjerp (i gruve etc); lodd; **II** *vt* **1** fordre, forlange, kreve; **2** hevde, påstå. **claimant** ['kleɪmənt] *sb* fordringshaver.

clam [klæm] **1** *sb* (spiselig) skjell; *close as a ~* stum som en østers; **2** *vi* sanke skjell.

clamber ['klæmbə] klatre/klyve (på alle fire); kravle.

clammy ['klæmɪ] *adj* klam, rå.

clamorous ['klæmərəs] *adj* bråkende *etc*. **clamour** ['klæmə] **1** *sb* bråk, leven; skrik, skrål (især for å oppnå noe); **2** *vb* skrike, skråle; forlange, protestere *etc* høylytt.

clamp [klæmp] **1** *sb* klamp, klemme; krampe; (skru)tvinge; **2** *vb* spenne fast (med tvinge etc); *~ down on* legge/øve press på.

clan [klæn] *sb* **1** klan, stamme; **2** klikk.

clandestine [klæn'destɪn] *adj* hemmelig, skjult; i smug.

clang [klæŋ] **1** *sb* (metall)klang, klirr(ing); **2** *vb* klinge; klirre (med). **clangour** ['klæŋgə] *sb* (metall)-klang; larm. **clank** [klæŋk] **1** *sb* klirr(ing) *etc*; **2** *vb* klirre; rasle/skramle (med).

clap [klæp] **A I** *sb* **1** brak, skrall, smell; **2** klapp, klask; **II** *vb* klappe; klaske, smakke; kyle, slenge; *~ up* smøre sammen; sperre inne; **B** *sb vulg* dryppert.

claret ['klærət] *sb* rødvin; *slang* blod.

clarification [ˌklærɪfɪ'keɪʃn] *sb* (av)klaring *etc*. **clarify** ['klærɪfaɪ] *vb* **1** avklare(s); oppklare(s); **2** klare (væske for grums). **clarity** ['klærətɪ] *sb* klarhet.

clash [klæʃ] **I** *sb* **1** skramling *etc*; **2** kollisjon, sammenstøt; *fig* konflikt; **II** *vb* **1** skramle, skrangle; **2** kollidere; *fig* falle sammen (dvs i tid: hende samtidig); **3** støte sammen; ryke uklar.

clasp [klɑ:sp] **I** *sb* **1** hekte, lås, spenne; **2** grep; (fast) tak; håndtrykk; omfavnelse; **II** *vb* **1** folde (hekte, huke etc) sammen; **2** gripe; ta (et fast) tak i; holde fast.

class [klɑ:s] **I** *sb* **1** (skole)klasse (og kull, parti, årgang, årsklasse, kursus, time etc); **2** (samfunns)-klasse; **3** *fig* klasse (dvs kvalitet, stil etc); **II** *vt* **1** klassifisere; sette i klasse. **class-conscious** *adj* klassebevisst. **classic** ['klæsɪk] **I** *adj* **1** førsteklasses; **2** klassisk; **3** tradisjonsrik; **II** *sb* **1** klassiker (om forfatter, bok etc); **2** klassisk filolog. **classical** ['klæsɪkl] *adj* klassisk. **classification** [ˌklæsɪfɪ'keɪʃn] *sb* klassifisering *etc*. **classify** ['klæsɪfaɪ] *vt* **1** klassifisere; arrangere, gruppere; **2** gradere (dvs hemmeligstemple, om dokumenter etc).

clatter ['klætə] **I** *sb* **1** skramling *etc*; **2** skravling; **II** *vb* **1** skramle, skrangle; slamre; **2** skravle.

clause [klɔ:z] *sb* **1** (ledd)setning; **2** avsnitt, paragraf; **3** klausul.

claw [klɔ:] **1** *sb* klo; **2** *vt* gripe/krafse (etter); klore.

clay [kleɪ] *sb* **1** leire; **2** *(~ pipe)* krittpipe; **3** *fig* støv (dvs jordiske levninger).

clean [kli:n] **I** *adj* **1** ren; *fig* anstendig; uskyldig; *come ~ (dgl)* tilstå; **2** jevn, regelmessig; **II** *adv* fullstendig, helt; **III** *vb (~ down/out)* gjøre ren(t); pusse, rense, vaske; *~ed out (dgl)* blakk, pengelens; *~ up* gjøre ren(t); rydde opp. **clean-cut** *adj* klar; tydelig (avgrenset); velskapt. **cleaner** ['kli:nə] *sb* **1** renser(i); *dry ~* kjemisk renseri; **2** rensemiddel; **3** vasker/vaskehjelp *etc*. **cleaning pig** *sb petro* rensepigg. **cleanliness** ['klenlɪnɪs] *sb* renslighet; *~ is next to godliness* rent skinn gir rent sinn. **cleanly** **1** *adj* ['klenlɪ] renslig; **2** *adv* ['kli:nlɪ] rent. **cleanse** [klenz] *vt* **1** rense, vaske; **2** *fig* rense *(from/of* for). **clean-shaven** *adj* glattbarbert.

clear ['klɪə] **I** *adj* **1** klar; blank; lys; **2** *a)* ren; *~ of* fri for; *b) petro* blyfri; **3** klar, tydelig: **4** gjennomsiktig, klar; **5** fullstendig, hel; **6** *all ~* faren over (dvs signalet etter flyalarm etc); **II** *adv* **1** fullstendig, helt; **2**

klart, tydelig; **III** *vb* **1** renske/rydde (opp (i)); **~ away** rydde unna; *fig* rydde av veien; **~ off** få/gjøre unna; forsvinne; **~ out** renske/rydde opp (i); *dgl* fordufte; *~ed out (dgl)* blakk, pengelens; **~ up** rydde opp; oppklare; klarne (opp); **2** klare (hinder etc); gå *etc* klar av; **3** *sjø* klarere; **4** *data* slette; **5** *dgl* tjene (netto). **clearance** ['klɪərəns] *sb* **1** klaring, spillerom; **2** *sjø* klarering; **3** *slum* **~** (slum)sanering. **clear|-cut** *adj* renskåren; klar, tydelig. **~-headed** *adj* klartenkt. **clearing** ['klɪərɪŋ] *sb* **1** rydding *etc*; **2** rydning; ryddet/åpen plass; **3** *merk* avregning; clearing. **clearness** ['klɪənɪs] *sb* klarhet. **clear-sighted** *adj* klarsynt.

cleavage ['kli:vɪdʒ] *sb* kløft; spalte, spaltning; *fig* brudd. **cleave** [kli:v] **A** *vb* kløyve; spalte, splitte; **B** *vi* klebe/*fig* holde fast (*to* ved). **cleft** [kleft] *sb* kløft; spalte.

clemency ['klemənsɪ] *sb* **1** barmhjertighet, nåde; **2** mildhet.

clench [klentʃ] *vb* **1** klemme/presse sammen; **~** *one's teeth/jaws* bite tennene sammen; **2** ta et fast tak; **3** = *clinch II.*

clergy ['klɜ:dʒɪ] *sb* geistlighet, presteskap. **clergyman** ['klɜ:dʒɪmən] *sb* prest.

clerical ['klerɪkl] *adj* **1** geistlig, preste-; **2** kontor(ist)-. **clerk** [klɑ:k] *sb* **1** kontorist; *ofte* fullmektig, sekretær; *chief* **~** kontorsjef; *junior* **~** kontorist; *også* kontorlærling, volontør; **2** *US* [klɜ:k] (butikk)ekspeditør; *desk* **~** portier; **3** *gml* klerk, skriver; geistlig.

clever ['klevə] *adj* **1** klok (især på en litt lur måte); durkdreven, smart; **2** dyktig/flink (*at* til). **cleverness** ['klevənɪs] *sb* klokskap *etc.*

clew [klu:] *sb* (garn)nøste; *fig* ledetråd.

click [klɪk] *sb, vb* klikk(e), knepp(e).

client ['klaɪənt] *sb* klient, kunde. **clientèle** [ˌkli:ɑ:n'tel] *sb* klientell, kundekrets.

cliff [klɪf] *sb* (fjell)skrent; klippe. **cliff-hanger** *sb* filmserie/føljetong (etc med avsnitt som slutter på et særlig spennende sted).

climate ['klaɪmɪt] *sb* klima, værlag; *fig* himmelstrøk. **climatic** [klaɪ'mætɪk] *adj* klimatisk.

climax ['klaɪmæks] **1** *sb* klimaks, høydepunkt; **2** *vb* nå/bringe til toppen.

climb [klaɪm] **1** *sb* klatring *etc*; klatretur; **2** *vb* klatre/klyve (opp (i/på); over); bestige; gå opp(over); **~** *down (fig)* gi seg; innrømme feil etc; *~-down (fig)* tilbaketog.

clinch [klɪntʃ] **I** *sb* clinch; *dgl* omfavnelse; **II** *vb* **1** klinke (nagler etc); **2** gå i clinch; omfavne (hverandre); **3** avgjøre, slå fast. **clincher** ['klɪntʃə] *sb dgl* avgjørende argument.

cling [klɪŋ] *vi* klynge seg (*to* til). **clinging** ['klɪŋɪŋ] *adj* ettersittende (om klær).

clinic ['klɪnɪk] *sb* klinikk. **clinical** ['klɪnɪkl] *adj* **1** klinisk; **2** syke(hus)-; **~** *thermometer* syketermometer.

clink [klɪŋk] **A 1** *sb* ringling *etc*; **2** *vb* ringle (med); single; **B** *sb slang* kasjott (dvs fengsel).

clip [klɪp] **A I** *sb* klipping *etc*; avklipp; (ut)klipp; **II** *vt* **1** klippe; stekke, stusse; **2** sluke (endestavelser); **B I** *sb* **1** klemme, klype; binders; **2** (øre)klips; **II** *vt* hefte sammen; holde fast; **C** *slang* **I** *sb* **1** lusing, ørefik; **2** *US* (stor) fart; **II** *vt* slå, dra til. **clipper** *sb* **1** klipper (om skip og fly); **2** *fl* klipper, klippemaskin; saks. **clipping** *sb* **1** (ut)klipp; **2** *data* klipping.

clique [kli:k] *sb* klikk, gruppe.

cloak [kləʊk] **1** *sb* kappe (uten ermer); *fig* skalkeskjul; dekke, skinn; **2** *vt* dekke til, skjule. **cloak|-and--dagger** *adj* kappe-og-dolk [betegnelse på en type røverromaner]. **~room** *sb* garderobe.

clock [klɒk] **I** *sb* **1** klokke; **2** *data* taktenhet; **II** *vb* ta tiden (for/på); **~** *in/out* stemple inn/ut (på arbeidsplass). **clock | drive** *sb data* taktdriver. **~ing** *sb data* taktstyring. **~-maker** *sb* klokkemaker, urmaker. **~ pulse** *sb data* taktsignal. **~-puncher** *sb dgl* lønnsslave. **~wise** *adj* med urviserne. **~work** *sb* urverk.

clod [klɒd] *sb* jordklump.

clog [klɒg] **I** *sb* **1** klamp, kloss; *fig* hemsko; **2** tresko; **II** *vb* **1** tette(s) igjen; hemme, hindre; **2** bebyrde.

cloister ['klɔɪstə] **I** *sb* **1** buegang(er); søylegang; **2** kloster; *fig* avsondrethet; **II** *vt* sette i kloster.

clone [kləʊn] *sb, vb* klone.

close I [kləʊs] *adj* **1** nær(-); *a* **~** *call (shave/thing)* noe en bare så vidt slipper unna; *at* **~** *quarter* på nært hold; **2** inngående; nærgående; nøyaktig; påpasselig; **3** (inne)lukket; tett; trang; *fig* innesluttet; **4** innestengt; lummer; **5** hemmelig, skjult; **6** = *~-fisted*; **II** [kləʊs] *adv* like/nær/tett (ved); kloss (innpå); snau-, tett-; **III** *sb* **A** [kləʊs] inngjerding; (stor, lukket) gårdsplass; **B** [kləʊz] opphør, slutt; *draw to a* **~** li mot/nærme seg slutten; **IV** [kləʊz] *vb* **1** *(~ down/up)* lukke(s), stenge(s); **2** (av)slutte; *closing date* siste frist (for søknad etc); **3** **~** *in (up)on* nærme seg (truende); omringe; **~** *up* lukke, stenge; tette igjen; følge på, slutte rekkene; **~** *with* få kontakt med (fiende etc); gå med på (avtale etc); slå til. **closed | loop** *sb data* lukket sløyfe. **~ shop** *sb data* lukket drift. **close|-fisted** *adj* gjerrig, påholden. **~ season** *sb* fredningstid. **closet** ['klɒzɪt] **I** *sb* **1** kott; (innbygd) skap; **2** (vann)klosett; **3** *gml* kammers; **II** *vt: be ~ed with* være/tale i enerom med. **close-up** *sb* nærbilde.

clot [klɒt] **1** *sb* klatt/klump (især av levret blod); **2** *vb* klumpe/levre (seg); størkne.

cloth [klɒθ] *sb* **1** klede, stoff; klut; tøy(stykke); **2** prestekjole, *the Cloth* geistligheten. **cloth cap** *sb* sikspens(lue). **clothe** [kləʊð] *vt* **1** kle (på); **2** holde/utstyre med klær; **3** *fig* (i)kle. **clothes** [kləʊðz] *sb fl* klær, tøy. **clothes|-horse** *sb* tørkestativ. **~-line** *sb* klessnor. **~-peg, ~-pin** *sb* (kles)klype. **~-rack** = *~-horse.* **clothing** ['kləʊðɪŋ] *sb* klær, tøy; *fig* drakt.

cloud [klaʊd] **I** *sb* **1** sky; **2** sverm; **3** uklarhet; **4** skygge; **II** *vb* **1** skye over; **2** fordunkles; bli/gjøre uklar; **3** *fig* formørke(s); kaste skygge over. **cloud|-burst** *sb* skybrudd. **cloudy** *adj* **1** (over)skyet; **2** grumset, uklar.

clout [klaut] **I** *sb* **1** fille, klut; **2** lusing, ørefik; **II** *vt* slå, dra til.

clove [kləuv] **A** *sb* (krydder)nellik; **B** *sb* kløft (av hvitløk).

clover ['kləuvə] *sb* kløver(plante).

clown [klaun] **I** *sb* **1** bajas, klovn; **2** *gml* slamp; **II** *vi* klovne; spille bajas.

cloy [klɔɪ] *vb* bli/gjøre matlei.

club [klʌb] **A 1** *sb* klubbe, kølle; **2** *vt* slå med klubbe/kølle; **B 1** *sb* forening, klubb; klubblokale(r); **2** *vi* gå/slå seg sammen; gjøre felles sak; **C** *sb fl* kløver (i kort). **club-foot** *sb* klumpfot.

cluck [klʌk] *sb, vi* klukk(e).

clue [klu:] *sb* **1** ledetråd; nøkkel, spor; **2** nøkkelord (i kryssord); **3** stikkord (til skuespiller).

clump [klʌmp] **A 1** *sb* klynge, gruppe; **2** *vt* plante tett (sammen); **B** *vi* klampe, trampe; gå tungt.

clumsy ['klʌmzɪ] *adj* **1** kluntet, tung; **2** klosset, klønet.

cluster ['klʌstə] **I** *sb* **1** klase; **2** flokk, klynge; **II** *vb* **1** vokse i klase(r); **2** flokke seg; ligge i klynge omkring. **cluster drilling** *sb petro* boring i flere hull samtidig.

clutch [klʌtʃ] **A I** *sb* **1** grep; (fast) tak; *fl fig* klør (dvs makt, vold); **2** kløtsj, kobling; **II** *vb* gripe/ta (*at* etter); **B** *sb* kull (kyllinger).

clutter ['klʌtə] **1** *sb* rot, virvar; **2** *vb:* ~ *up* rote til, urydde.

coach [kəutʃ] **A** *sb* **1** (stor) vogn; **2** *(motor-~)* fjernbuss, rutebuss (i motsetning til bybuss); (turist)buss; **3** jernbanevogn; **B I** *sb* **1** instruktør, trener; **2** manuduktør, privatlærer; **II** *vb* **1** instruere, trene; **2** manudusere, lese privat (med). **coach|-man** *sb* kusk, vognmann. **~work** *sb* karosseri.

coagulate [kəu'ægjuleɪt] *vb* koagulere, størkne. **coagulation** [kəu,ægju'leɪʃn] *sb* koagulering *etc.*

coal [kəul] **1** *sb* kull; **2** *vb* bunkre; forsyne med/ta inn kull.

coalesce [,kəuə'les] *vb* **1** forenes; smelte/vokse sammen; **2** *data* samle. **coalescence** [,kəuə'lesns] *sb* sammensmeltning *etc.*

coalfish ['kəulfɪʃ] *sb* sei.

coalition [,kəuə'lɪʃn] *sb* forbund, koalisjon.

coal|-mine, ~-pit *sb* kullgruve. **~-scuttle** *sb* kullboks. **~ tar** *sb* kulltjære.

coaming ['kəumɪŋ] *sb sjø* lukekarm.

coarse [kɔ:s] *adj* **1** grov, ru; **2** grov, ubearbeidet; **3** rå, ubehøvlet; vulgær.

coast [kəust] **I** *sb* kyst; **II** *vb* **1** seile langs kysten; **2** ake (kjøre, trille etc) utforbakke. **coastal** ['kəustl] *adj* kyst-.

coat [kəut] **I** *sb* **1** frakk, kappe, kåpe; (drakt)jakke; ~ *and skirt* (spaser)drakt; ~ *of arms* våpenskjold; *great-~, over-~, top~* (vinter)frakk, ytterfrakk; **2** (dyre)ham; (fjær)drakt; **3** hinne; lag/strøk (maling etc); **II** *vt* dekke; (be)kle, trekke; stryke (maling etc). **coat-hanger** *sb* kleshenger. **coating** ['kəutɪŋ] *sb* **1** stoff (til kappe etc); **2** belegg, hinne; lag; trekk; strøk; *petro etc* kappe, kledning. **coat-tail** *sb* frakkeskjøt.

coax [kəuks] *vb* lokke, overtale.

cob [kɒb] *sb* **1** hannsvane; **2** (liten, kraftig) ridehest; **3** *(corn-~)* maiskolbe; **4** klump; stump; (brød)-skalk.

cobble ['kɒbl] **A 1** *sb (~stone)* kuppelstein, (rund) brostein; **2** *vt* brolegge (med kuppelstein); **B** *vt* flikke/lappe (sko). **cobbler** ['kɒblə] *sb* (lappe)skomaker; *fig* fusker (i faget).

cob-web ['kɒbweb] *sb* spindelvev.

cock [kɒk] **A I** *sb* **1** hane; hann(fugl); **2** bas, leder; **3** kran, tapp; **4** hane (på skytevåpen); **II** *vt* **1** *(~ up)* brette opp; heve, løfte, reise; ~ *one's ears* spisse ører; ~ *one's eye* skotte; **2** spenne (hanen på skytevåpen); **B 1** *sb* (høy)|såte, (-)stakk; **2** *vt* såte (høy). **cockade** [kɒ'keɪd] *sb* kokarde. **cock|-and-bull story** *sb* røverhistorie. **~-crow** *sb* hanegal; *fig* daggry. **~-eyed** *adj slang* **1** blingset; **2** pussa; **3** skrudd; skrullet, tåpelig. **~-fight** *sb* hanekamp.

cockle ['kɒkl] *sb* (hjerte)musling, (saue)skjell. **cockleshell** ['kɒklʃel] *sb* muslingskall, skjell; *fig* nøtteskall (dvs liten båt).

cockney ['kɒknɪ] **1** *adj, sb* (østkant)londonsk; **2** (østkant)londoner.

cockpit ['kɒkpɪt] *sb* cockpit, fører|hus, -kabin.

cockroach ['kɒkrəutʃ] *sb* kakerlakk.

cockscomb ['kɒkskəum] *sb* **1** hanekam; **2** narrelue; *fig* narr. **cocksure** [,kɒk'ʃuə] *adj* skråsikker.

coco ['kəukəu] *sb (~-palm, ~nut palm)* kokos(palme). **cocoa** ['kəukəu] *sb* kakao. **coconut** ['kəukənʌt] *sb* kokosnøtt.

cocoon [kə'ku:n] *sb* kokong.

cod [kɒd] *sb (~-fish)* torsk.

coddle ['kɒdl] *vt* degge med/for.

code [kud] **I** *sb* **1** kodeks, lovsamling; *fig* regler; (uskrevne) lover; **2** kode; **II** *vt* **1** (skrive i) kode; **2** = *codify*. **code | converter** *sb data* kode|omformer, -omsetter. **~ table** *sb data* kodetabell. **codify** ['kɒdɪfaɪ] *vt* kodifisere.

codling ['kɒdlɪŋ] *sb* småtorsk. **cod-liver oil** *sb* (torskelever)tran.

co-ed [,kəu'ed] *sb US dgl* skolepike; kvinnelig student. **coeducation** [,kəuedju:'keɪʃn] *sb* undervisning i blandede klasser.

coerce [kəu'ɜ:s] *vt* presse/tvinge (frem). **coercion** [kəu'ɜ:ʃn] *sb* press, tvang. **coercive** [kəu'ɜ:sɪv] *adj* tvangs-, tvingende.

coexist [,kəuɪg'zɪst] *vi* eksistere/finne sted *etc* samtidig. **coexistence** [,kəuɪg'sɪstəns] *sb* sameksistens; *peaceful* ~ fredelig sameksistens.

coffee ['kɒfɪ] *sb* kaffe. **coffe|-bar** *sb* kaffebar; kafé, kafeteria. **~-bean** *sb* kaffebønne. **~-cup** *sb* kaffekopp. **~-grounds** *sb fl* kaffegrut. **~-house** *sb gml* = *~-bar.* **~-mill** *sb* kaffekvern. **~-pot** *sb* kaffekjele.

coffer ['kɒfə] *sb* **1** (penge)skrin; bankboks; **2** *fl* (bank)hvelv; *fig* (økonomiske) midler; **3** *(~-dam)* kofferdam, senkekasse.

coffin ['kɒfɪn] *sb* (lik)kiste.

cog [kɒg] *sb* tann (i tannhjul); kam, knast.

cogency ['kəʊdʒənsɪ] *sb* overbevisningskraft; tyngde, vekt. **cogent** ['kəʊdʒənt] *adj* overbevisende (om argument).

cogitate ['kɒdʒɪteɪt] *vb* grunne/spekulere (på); tenke (ut). **cogitation** [ˌkɒdʒɪ'teɪʃn] *sb* tankevirksomhet, tenking; overveielse. **cognizance** ['kɒgnɪzəns] *sb* **1** kjennskap (*of* til); kunnskap (*of* om); **2** kompetanse(område). **cognizant** ['kɒgnɪzənt] *adj*: *be ~ of* ha kjennskap til, være vitende om.

cogwheel ['kɒgwi:l] *sb* tannhjul.

cohabit [kəʊ'hæbɪt] *vi* bo/leve sammen (især uten å være gift). **cohabitant** [kəʊ'hæbɪtənt] *sb* samboer. **cohabitation** [ˌkəʊhæbɪ'teɪʃn] *sb* samboerskap.

cohere [kəʊ'hɪə] *vi* henge sammen; *fig* stemme overens. **coherence** [kəʊ'hɪərəns] *sb* sammenheng. **coherent** [kəʊ'hɪərənt] *adj* sammenhengende.

coil [kɔɪl] **I** *sb* **1** kveil, rull; spiral; **2** spole; vikling; **II** *vb* **1** kveile (seg) opp; **2** spole (opp); vikle.

coin [kɔɪn] **I** *sb* mynt, pengestykke; **II** *vt* **1** mynte; prege (mynt); **2** *fig* finne opp; *~ a phrase/a word* lage et (nytt) uttrykk/ord. **coinage** ['kɔɪnɪdʒ] *sb* **1** mynting, preging; **2** myntsystem; **3** nydannet ord *etc*; nydannelse.

coincide [ˌkəʊɪn'saɪd] *vi* falle sammen (i tid og/eller rom); hende samtidig; *fig* stemme overens (*with* med). **coincidence** [kəʊ'ɪnsɪdəns] *sb* sammentreff; overensstemmelse.

coke [kəʊk] **A 1** *sb* koks; **2** *vt* forkokse; **B** *sb US dgl* **1** kola(drikk); **2** kokain. **coke | deposition** *sb petro* koks|avleiring, -utskilling. **~ formation** *sb petro* koksdannelse. **coker** *sb petro* forkoksingsanlegg, koksverk. **coker | gas** *sb petro* koksgass. **coking** *sb petro* forkoksing.

colander ['kʌləndə] *sb* dørslag.

cold [kəʊld] **I** *adj* kald; *leave one ~* ikke gjøre inntrykk på en; **II** *sb* **1** kulde; *be left out in the ~* bli frosset ut; gå for lut og kaldt vann; **2** forkjølelse; *catch (a) ~/take ~* bli forkjølet.

collaborate [kə'læbəreɪt] *vi* samarbeide. **collaboration** [kəˌlæbə'reɪʃn] *sb* samarbeid. **collaborator** [kə'læbəreɪtə] *sb* **1** medarbeider; **2** kollaboratør (dvs en som samarbeider med fienden).

collapse [kə'læps] **1** *sb* sammenbrudd; fiasko; **2** *vb* bryte/falle sammen. **collapsible** [kə'læpsəbl] *adj* sammenleggbar; til å slå ned/sammen.

collar ['kɒlə] **I** *sb* **1** krave; **2** snipp; **3** halsbånd; klave; **4** hylse; mansjett, muffe; ring; **II** *vt* **1** ta i kraven; gripe; dra/hale med seg; **2** *slang* kvarte, rappe. **collar|-bone** *sb* kravebein. **~-stud** *sb* skjorteknapp.

collate [kɒ'leɪt] *vb* **1** sammenholde; kontrollere; *data også* kollatere; **2** kalle (til prest).

colleague ['kɒli:g] *sb* kollega.

collect A [kə'lekt] *vb* **1** samle (på); samle/sanke (inn/sammen); *~ stamps* samle på frimerker; **2** forsamle(s), komme sammen; samle seg; **3** hente; innkassere, kreve inn; *~ oneself* ta seg sammen; **B** ['kɒlekt] *sb* kollekt, kort bønn. **collected** [kə'lektɪd] *adj* *fig* fattet, samlet. **collection** [kə'lekʃn] *sb* **1** (penge)-innsamling; *rel* kollekt; *merk* inkasso; **2** (an)samling, flokk; **3** samling (av kunst etc). **collective** [kə'lektɪv] **I** *adj* felles(-), kollektiv(-); **II** *sb* **1** fellesskap, kollektiv; kollektivbruk; **2** *gram (~ noun)* kollektiv (dvs mengdesord som har entallsform, f.eks. engelske ord som *audience, cattle, crowd*). **collectivization** [kəˌlektɪvaɪ'zeɪʃn] *sb* kollektivisering. **collectivize** [kə'lektɪvaɪz] *vt* kollektivisere. **collector** [kə'lektə] *sb* **1** samler *etc*; *merk* inkassator, *tax-~* skatteoppkrever; **2** strøm|avtaker, -samler.

college ['kɒlɪdʒ] *sb* **1** college, høyere skole; *junior ~ (US)* ≈ videregående skole; **2** akademi, høyskole; **3** universitet; fakultet, universitetsavdeling; **4** kollegium.

collide [kə'laɪd] *vi* kollidere.

collier ['kɒlɪə] *sb* **1** kullgruvearbeider; **2** kullbåt. **colliery** ['kɒlɪərɪ] *sb* kullgruve.

collision [kə'lɪʒn] *sb* kollisjon.

colloquial [kə'ləʊkwɪəl] *adj* dagligdags (om ord og uttrykk); *ofte* folkelig; muntlig, samtale-. **colloquialism** [kə'ləʊkwɪəlɪzəm] *sb* ord/uttrykk fra dagligtalen.

collusion [kə'lu:ʒn] *sb* hemmelig avtale (forståelse, sammensvergelse etc).

colonial [kə'ləʊnɪəl] **1** *adj* koloni-; **2** *sb* innbygger i koloni. **colonialism** [kə'ləʊnɪəlɪzəm] *sb* kolonialisme. **colonist** ['kɒlənɪst] *sb* kolonist, nybygger (i koloni). **colonization** [ˌkɒlənaɪ'zeɪʃn] *sb* kolonisering. **colonize** ['kɒlənaɪz] *vt* kolonisere. **colony** ['kɒlənɪ] *sb* koloni.

colossal [kə'lɒsl] *adj* kolossal, (kjempe)diger. **colossus** [kə'lɒsəs] *sb* koloss, kjempe(statue).

colour [kʌlə] **I** *sb* **1** farge, fargestoff; kulør; **2** ansiktsfarge; *off ~* nedfor, utilpass; **3** *fl* fane(r); (skips)-flagg; **4** anstrøk, skinn; *under ~ of* under påskudd av; **II** *vb* **1** farge(s); få/ta farge; rødme; **2** *fig* farge(legge) (dvs overdrive, pynte på). **colour|bar** *sb* raseskille. **~fast** *adj* fargeekte. **~ful** *adj* fargerik. **~ing** *sb* **1** farge(stoff); farger; **2** koloritt. **~less** *adj* fargeløs.

colt [kəʊlt] *sb* unghest; *fig* jypling.

column ['kɒləm] *sb* **1** søyle; *petro også* kolonne, tårn; **2** kolonne (også *data*); (tall)rekke; **3** spalte (i avis etc). **columnist** ['kɒləmnɪst] *sb* spaltist (dvs journalist med fast spalte i en eller flere aviser). **column still** *sb petro* destillasjonstårn.

comb [kəʊm] **I** *sb* **1** kam; **2** karde; **3** *(honey~)* bikake, vokskake; **II** *vb* **1** gre, kjemme; *fig* finkjemme; *~ out (fig)* renske ut; *~-out* utrenskning; **2** karde; **3** bryte (om bølge).

combat ['kɒmbæt] **1** *sb* kamp, strid; **2** *vb* kjempe (mot), slåss (med). **combatant** ['kɒmbətənt] *adj/sb* stridende (part, person).

combination [ˌkɒmbɪ'neɪʃn] *sb* kombinering *etc*; kombinasjon, sammenslutning. **combine I** ['kɒmbaɪn] *sb* sammenslutning; konsortium, syndikat; **2** *(~-harvester)* skurtresker; **II** [kəm'baɪn] *vb* kombinere(s); forene(s), gå/slutte seg sammen.

combustible [kəm'bʌstəbl] **I** *adj* **1** brennbar; **2** *fig* lettfengelig (dvs irritabel, snarsint etc); **II** *sb fl* brensel. **combustion** [kəm'bʌstʃn] *sb* forbrenning. **combustion | engine** *sb* forbrenningsmotor. ~ **plant** *sb petro* forbrenningsanlegg.

come [kʌm] *vi* **1** komme (og gå, dra/reise, nå/rekke etc); ~ *spring* til våren; *the years to* ~ årene som kommer; **2** bli, være; falle (seg); utvikle seg; ~ *cheap* være billig; ~ *easy* falle/være lett; *she's coming ten* hun går i sitt tiende (år); **3** *dgl* agere, spille; ~ *it* gjøre seg til; ~ *the great man* spille den store mann; **4** *som interj* nå! nå, nå! nåda! ~ *now!* gi deg (litt nå)! **5** *med adv/prep* ~ **about** hende, gå for seg; *sjø* gå baut; *om vind* springe om; ~ **across** komme over; finne *etc* tilfeldig; vekke interesse *etc*; gjøre lykke/suksess; *US slang* punge ut; plapre, røpe; ~ **at** komme til; få tak i; angripe; ~ **away** gå/komme seg unna; falle av, løsne; ~ **by** komme med; komme *etc* forbi (innom, over/via etc); finne, komme over; få tak i; ~ **down** komme *etc* ned; falle ned/sammen; *fig* forfalle; gå i arv; ~ *down handsomely (dgl)* bidra/betale generøst; ~ **down (up)on** *fig* kaste seg over; ~ **down with** *dgl* punge ut med; bli angrepet av (sykdom); ~ **forward** komme *etc* frem; melde seg; ~ **in** komme in (frem, opp, i bruk, på mote, til makten etc); ~ **in for** bli utsatt for; ~ *in handy/useful* komme godt med; ~ **into** komme (inn) i; bli/få (etter hvert); ~ *into being/existence* bli til; ~ *into money* arve/komme til penger; ~ **loose** løsne; ~ **off** løsne, falle av; *fig* gå av stabelen; gå i orden; ~ *off it!* hold opp (med det der)! ~ **on** komme inn (frem, opp, over etc); møte, treffe på; ~ *on!* kom igjen! sett i gang! ~ **out** komme *etc* ut; bryte/slå ut; blomstre, spire; bli kjent; debutere (i selskapslivet); gå til streik; ~ **out against/for** erklære seg (åpent) mot/for; ~ **out with** komme (frem) med; *dgl* kramme ut med, røpe; ~ **over** komme *etc* over; *dgl* (begynne å) bli; ~ **round** komme igjen (rundt, tilbake etc); komme *etc* innom; komme til seg selv; la seg overtale/overbevise; ~ **to** komme *etc* til; komme til å; komme til seg selv; resultere i; komme på; *sjø* legge bi; *(now that I)* ~ *to think of it* (nå) når jeg tenker på det; ved nærmere ettertanke; ~ *to this/that* for den saks skyld; *they had it coming to them (dgl)* det kan de takke seg selv for; det har de (bare) godt av; ~ **under** komme (falle/høre) inn under; ~ **up** komme frem/opp *etc*; komme inn (til byen, universitetet etc); ~ **up against** støte på (som hindring); ~ **up with** komme *etc* med; foreslå; legge frem; innhente; ~ **upon** komme over; finne tilfeldig; ta på fersk gjerning; ~ **within** = ~ *under*.

comedian [kə'mi:dɪən] *sb* gjøgler, komiker. **comedy** [kɒmədɪ] *sb* komedie, lystspill.

comely [kʌmlɪ] *adj* (nokså) pen.

comfort ['kʌmfət] **I** *sb* **1** komfort; velvære; **2** trøst; støtte; **II** *vt* trøste; oppmuntre. **comfortable** ['kʌmfətəbl] *adj* behagelig, komfortabel; hyggelig; sorgløs. **comforter** ['kʌmfətə] *sb* **1** trøster *etc*; **2** (ull)skjerf; **3** narresmokk. **comfy** ['kʌmfɪ] *dgl* = *comfortable*.

comic ['kɒmɪk] **I** *adj* komedie-; morsom, underholdende; **II** *sb* **1** komiker; **2** *fl* tegneserie(r). **comical** ['kɒmɪkl] *adj* **1** morsom; **2** komisk, latterlig. **comic | book,** ~ **paper** *sb* (tegne)seriehefte. **strip** *sb* tegneserie.

command [kə'ma:nd] **I** *sb* **1** befaling, (på)bud; **2** myndighet; *be in* ~ *of* ha kommandoen over; **3** herredømme; *have a good* ~ *of English* beherske engelsk godt; **4** disposisjon; *at* ~ til rådighet; **5** *a) data* kommando; *b) mil* kommando, militæravdeling; **II** *vb* **1** befale, påby; **2** kommandere; **3** beherske, rå(de) over; **4** forlange, kreve; ~ *respect* avtvinge/inngyte respekt. **command code** *sb data* kommandokode. **commandeer** [ˌkɒmən'dɪə] *vt* rekvirere. **commander** [kə'ma:ndə] *sb* **1** kommandant, sjef; **2** *sjø mil* kommandørkaptein; **3** kommandør (av en orden). **commander-in-Chief** *sb mil* øverstkommanderende. **commandment** [kə'ma:ndmənt] *sb* (på)bud; *the ten* ~*s* de ti bud. **command | menu** *sb data* kommandomeny. ~ **mode** *sb data* direktestyrt modus. **commando** [kə'ma:ndəu] *sb* **1** kommandosoldat; **2** kommando(styrke).

commemorate [kə'meməreɪt] *vt* feire (minnet om); være til minne om. **commemoration** [kəˌmemə'reɪʃn] *sb* **1** jubileum, minnefest; **2** minnegudstjeneste. **commemorative** [kə'memərətɪv] *adj* jubileums-, minne-.

commence [kə'mens] *vi* begynne (med/på). **commencement** [kə'mensmənt] *sb* (på)begynnelse.

commend [kə'mend] *vt* **1** rose; **2** anbefale; **3** betro, overgi til. **commendable** [kə'mendəbl] *adj* prisverdig, rosverdig; **2** anbefalelsesverdig.

comment ['kɒment] **1** *sb* (ofte kritisk) bemerkning; kommentar (også *data*); **2** *vi* bemerke (*on* til); kommentere. **commentary** ['kɒməntrɪ] *sb* kommentar(er). **commentator** ['kɒmənteɪtə] *sb* kommentator.

commerce ['kɒmɜ:s] *sb* handel. **commercial** [kə'mɜ:ʃl] **I** *adj* handels-, merkantil(-); *også* kommersiell; *petro etc* drivverdig; **II** *sb* **1** *(~ traveller)* handelsreisende; **2** *US* reklame (dvs reklameinnslag i radio- el. fjernsynsprogram). **commercialization** [kəˌmɜ:ʃəlaɪ'zeɪʃn] *sb* kommersialisering *etc*. **commercialize** [kə'mɜ:ʃəlaɪz] *vt* kommersialisere, utnytte kommersielt; *dgl* tjene/slå mynt på.

commingle [kɒ'mɪŋgl] *vb* blande (seg).

commiserate [kə'mɪzəreɪt] *vb* føle med, synes synd på. **commiseration** [kəˌmɪzə'reɪʃn] *sb* medfølelse, medynk.

commissar [ˌkɒmɪ'sa:] *sb* kommissær. **commissary** ['kɒmɪsərɪ] *sb* **1** representant, utsending; **2** intendant; **3** kommissær.

commission [kə'mɪʃn] **I** *sb* **1** fullmakt; **2** bestilling; oppdrag; **3** (offisers)utnevnelse; *in* ~ i aktiv tjeneste; **4** nemnd; ~ *of inquiry* undersøkelseskommisjon; **5** begåelse (av forbrytelse, dumhet etc); **6** *merk* kommisjon, provisjon; **II** *vt* **1** gi fullmakt til; **2** gi i oppdrag; **3** utnevne (til offiser). **commissionaire** [keˌmɪʃə'neə] *sb* dørvakt, portier. **commissioner**

[kə'mɪʃnə] *sb* **1** medlem av en nemnd *etc*; **2** kommissær [om forskjellige høyere embetsmenn, bl.a. Londons politimester].

commit [kə'mɪt] *vt* begå (forbrytelse, dumhet etc); **2** betro, overlate; ~ *to memory* lære (seg) utenat; **3** ~ *oneself* vise farge; ~ *oneself to* forplikte seg til. **commitment** [kə'mɪtmənt] *sb* engasjement, forpliktelse. **committee** [kə'mɪtɪ] *sb* komité, nemnd.

commodity [kə'mɒdətɪ] *sb* **1** *fl* varer; **2** *gml* nyttegjenstand.

common ['kɒmən] **I** *adj* **1** felles; offentlig; **2** alminnelig, vanlig; ~ *sense* sunt vett; **3** simpel; **II** *sb* **1** allmenning; friareal; løkke; **2** *in* ~ (til) felles; **3** *out of the* ~ utenom det vanlige. **commoner** ['kɒmənə] *sb* **1** borger; **2** *UK* underhusmedlem. **commonplace** ['kɒmənpleɪs] **1** *adj* dagligdags; **2** *sb* alminnelighet. **commons** ['kɒmənz] *sb fl* **1** *the* ~ allmennheten; **2** *the (House of) C~* Underhuset (i det britiske parlament). **commonwealth** ['kɒmənwelθ] *sb* **1** statssamfunn; *the (British) C~ (of Nations)* Det britiske samveldet; **2** *hist* republikk.

commotion [kə'məʊʃn] *sb* bråk, oppstyr.

communal ['kɒmjʊnl] *adj* **1** offentlig; **2** felles(-). **commune 1** ['kɒmju:n] *sb* kommune; **2** [kə'mju:n] *vi* omgås (nært og fortrolig). **communicate** [kə'mju:nɪkeɪt] *vb* **1** meddele; overføre; **2** kommunisere; stå i forbindelse (med hverandre). **communication** [kə,mju:nɪ'keɪʃn] *sb* meddelelse *etc*; kommunikasjon. **communicative** [kə'mju:nɪkətɪv] *adj* meddelsom, åpen(hjertig). **communion** [kə'mju:nɪən] *sb* **1** fellesskap; **2** rådslagning; samtale; **3** trossamfunn; **4** *Holy C~* altergang, nattverd. **community** [kə'mju:nətɪ] *sb* **1** samfunn; **2** fellesskap; **3** *(religious ~)* trossamfunn. **community | centre** *sb* samfunnshus, velhus. ~ **singing** *sb* allsang.

commute [kə'mju:t] *vb* **1** forandre; **2** bytte, skifte (ut); **3** *især US* reise (daglig mellom bosted og arbeidsplass); ≈ pendle. **commuter** [kə'mju:tə] *sb* lokalreisende, pendler; *ofte* drabantby- el. forstadsboer.

compact I [kəm'pækt] *adj* kompakt, tett (sammenpakket); **II** ['kɒmpækt] *sb* **1** etui; *især* pudderdåse; **2** overenskomst, pakt.

companion [kəm'pænɪən] **A** *sb* **1** kamerat, ledsager; **2** motstykke; **3** håndbok; **B** *sb sjø* = *~ladder*, *~way*. **companion|able** [kəm'pænɪənəbl] *adj* omgjengelig. **~ladder** *sb sjø* lugartrapp. **~ship** [kəm'pænɪənʃɪp] *sb* **1** kameratskap; **2** selskap. **~way** *sb* = *~ladder*. **company** ['kʌmpənɪ] *sb* **1** samvær; *keep* ~ holde/være sammen; *part* ~ *with* skilles fra; **2** flokk, følge; gjester, selskap; besetning; kompani; **3** *merk* kompani, selskap.

comparable ['kɒmprəbl] *adj* sammenlignbar. **comparative** [kəm'pærətɪv] **1** *adj* forholdsvis, sammenlignings-; **2** *sb* komparativ. **comparatively** [kəm'pærətɪvlɪ] *adv* forholdsvis, relativt. **compare** [kəm'peə] **I** *sb: beyond (past/without)* ~ uten sammenligning; **II** *vb* **1** sammenligne(s) (*to* med); **2** gradbøye(s).

compartment [kəm'pɑ:tmənt] *sb* avdeling; (jernbane)kupé; *sjø* skott.

compass ['kʌmpəs] **I** *sb* **1** kompass; **2** omfang, rekkevidde; **3** *(pair of) ~s* passer; **II** *vt* **1** omgi; **2** *fig* fatte.

compassion [kəm'pæʃn] *sb* medfølelse, medlidenhet, medynk. **compassionate** [kəm'pæʃnət] *adj* medfølende, medlidende.

compatible [kəm'pætəbl] *adj* forenelig/overensstemmmende (*with* med); *også* kompatibel.

compatriot [kəm'pætrɪət] *sb* landsmann.

compel [kəm'pel] *vt* tvinge (frem).

compensate ['kɒmpənseɪt] *vb* kompensere, oppveie; erstatte. **compensation** [,kɒmpən'seɪʃn] *sb* kompensasjon *etc*.

compere ['kɒmpeə] **1** *sb* konferansier; **2** *vb* opptre som/være konferansier (for).

compete [kəm'pi:t] konkurrere. **competence** ['kɒmpɪtəns] *sb* kompetanse *etc*. **competent** ['kɒmpɪtənt] *adj* **1** kompetent, sakkyndig; **2** dyktig, flink; **3** passende; tilstrekkelig; (vel) skikket. **competition** [,kɒmpɪ'tɪʃn] *sb* konkurranse. **competitive** [kəm'petətɪv] *adj* konkurrerende, konkurranse-, **competitor** [kəm'petɪtə] *sb* konkurrent; (konkurranse)deltaker.

compile [kəm'paɪl] *vt* **1** skrive/utarbeide (på grunnlag av innsamlet materiale); **2** *data* kompilere. **compiler** [kəm'paɪlə] *sb data* kompilator.

complacence [kəm'pleɪsəns] *sb* selvgodhet *etc*. **complacent** [kəm'pleɪsənt] *adj* selvgod; (selv)tilfreds.

complain [kəm'pleɪn] *vi* beklage seg/klage (*of* over); *merk* reklamere (dvs klage på en vare). **complainant** [kəm'pleɪnənt] *sb* klager, saksøker. **complaint** [kəm'pleɪnt] *sb* **1** klage; *merk* reklamasjon; **2** lidelse, plage; sykdom.

complaisance [kəm'pleɪzəns] *sb* omgjengelighet *etc*. **complaisant** [kəm'pleɪzənt] *adj* omgjengelig, imøtekommende; snill.

complement I ['kɒmplɪmənt] *sb* **1** komplettering *etc*; **2** fullt antall; **3** komplement; **II** ['kɒmplɪment] *vt* komplettere, supplere.

complementary [,kɒmplɪ'mentərɪ] *adj* **1** tilleggs-, utfyllende; **2** komplementær(-). **complete** [kəm'pli:t] **I** *adj* **1** fullstendig, hel, komplett; **2** fullført; **3** *gml* fullendt; **II** *vt* **1** fullføre; **2** komplettere. **completion** [kəm'pli:ʃn] *sb* fullføring *etc*.

complex ['kɒmpleks] **I** *adj* **1** innviklet, komplisert; **2** sammensatt, kompleks. **complexion** [kəm'plekʃn] *sb* **1** (ansikts)farge; **2** utseende, ytre.

compliance [kəm'plaɪəns] *sb* **1** føyelighet; **2** overensstemmelse, samsvar. **compliant** [kəm'plaɪənt] *adj* **1** føyelig; **2** overensstemmende.

complicate ['kɒmplɪkeɪt] *vt* komplisere. **complicated** ['kɒmplɪkeɪtɪd] *adj* floket, innviklet. **complication** [,kɒmplɪ'keɪʃn] *sb* forvikling, komplikasjon.

complicity [kəm'plɪsətɪ] *sb* delaktighet (i forbrytelse).

compliment I ['kɒmplɪmənt] *sb* **1** kompliment, ros; **2** *fl* (nokså formell) hilsen; *my ~s to your mother* hils Deres mor (fra meg); **II** ['kɒmplɪment] *vt* **1** komplimentere (*on* med); rose; **2** gratulere (*on* med). **complimentary** [ˌkɒmplɪ'mentrɪ] *adj* **1** rosende; **2** fri-, gratis-; gave-. **complimentary ticket** *sb* fribillett.

comply [kəm'plaɪ] *vi* imøtekomme; innvilge; *~ with* etterkomme.

component [kəm'pəunənt] **1** *adj* del-; **2** *sb* (bestand)del, løs del; komponent.

comport [kəm'pɔ:t] **1** *vr: ~ oneself* (opp)føre seg; **2** *vb* stemme overens (*with* med).

compose [kəm'pəuz] *vb* **1** lage; sette sammen; komponere; forfatte; sette (bokstaver); **2** arrangere, ordne; *~ one's thoughts* samle tankene; **3** berolige; bilegge; **4** *be ~d of* bestå av. **composed** [kəm'pəuzd] *adj* behersket, fattet, rolig. **composer** [kəm'pəuzə] *sb* komponist. **composite log** *sb petro* sammensatt logg.

composition [ˌkɒmpə'zɪʃn] *sb* **1** sammensetning; beskaffenhet, natur; **2** komposisjon; artikkel, skrift; (skoˌ)stil; **3** (typografisk) sats; **4** ordning; overenskomst; *merk* akkord. **compositor** [kəm'pɒzɪtə] *sb* setter. **composure** [kəm'pəuʒə] *sb* fatning, sinnsro.

compound A ['kɒmpaund] **I** *adj* sammensatt; **II** *sb* **1** blanding; sammensetning; sammensatt ord; **2** (inngjerdet) område/tomt; **B** [kəm'paund] *vb* **1** blande (sammen); sette sammen; **2** bilegge; *~ a felony* se gjennom fingrene med en forbrytelse. **compound | interest** *sb* rentesrente. **~ larceny** *sb* grovt tyveri. **~ oil** *sb petro* blandingsolje.

comprehend [ˌkɒmprɪ'hend] *vt* **1** fatte/forstå (fullt ut); **2** omfatte. **comprehensible** [ˌkɒmprɪ'hensəbl] *adj* fattbar, forståelig. **comprehension** [ˌkɒmprɪ'henʃn] *sb* **1** fatteevne; **2** omfang. **comprehensive** [ˌkɒmprɪ'hensɪv] *adj* (alt)omfattende. **comprehensive school** *sb* skole som omfatter videregående undervisning i alle eller de fleste fag.

compress I ['kɒmpres] *sb* kompress; **II** [kəm'pres] *vt* **1** komprimere; presse/trenge sammen; **2** forkorte. **compression** [kəm'preʃn] *sb* kompresjon *etc*. **compressor** [kəm'presə] *sb* kompressor.

comprise [kəm'praɪz] *vt* omfatte.

compromise ['kɒmprəmaɪz] **I** *sb* kompromiss; **II** *vb* **1** inngå kompromiss; **2** kompromittere; **3** utsette for fare.

compulsion [kəm'pʌlʃn] *sb* tvang. **compulsory** [kəm'pʌlsərɪ] *adj* obligatorisk, tvungen; tvangs-.

compunction [kəm'pʌŋkʃn] *sb* samvittighetsnag; skrupler *(fl)*.

compute [kəm'pju:t] *vb* anslå, (be)regne. **compute mode** *sb data* operasjonsmodus. **computer** [kəm'pju:tə] *sb* **1** regnemaskin; **2** *data* datamaskin. **computer | graphic** *sb data* infografi. **~ instruction** *sb data* maskininstruksjon. **~ language** *sb data* maskinspråk. **~ program** *sb data* (data)program. **~ science** *sb data* informatikk. **~ time** *sb data* maskintid. **~ utility** *sb data* datakraft. **~ word** *sb data* maskinord.

comrade ['kɒmreɪd] *sb* kamerat.

con [kɒn] **A 1** *adv* kontra; *pro and ~* for og imot; **2** *sb* motargument; **B** *vt (~ over)* pugge, studere; **C** *vb slang* bløffe, svindle; *som adj* bløff-; jf *confidence 4*.

conceal [kən'si:l] *vt* gjemme, skjule. **concealment** [kən'si:lmənt] *sb* **1** gjemmested, skjul; **2** hemmeligholdelse.

concede [kən'si:d] *vt* **1** innrømme; **2** avstå; gi etter.

conceit [kən'si:t] *sb* **1** innbilskhet; **2** vittig bemerkning/formulering. **conceited** [kən'si:tɪd] *adj* innbilsk.

conceivable [kən'si:vəbl] *adj* mulig, tenkelig. **conceive** [kən'si:v] *vb* **1** forestille/tenke seg; komme (til å tenke) på; finne på; **2** unnfange, bli svanger.

concentrate ['kɒnsəntreɪt] *vb* konsentrere/samle seg (*on/upon* om). **concentration** [ˌkɒnsən'treɪʃn] *sb* konsentrasjon.

concept ['kɒnsept] *sb* = *conception 1*. **conception** [kən'sepʃn] *sb* **1** begrep, forestilling, idé; **2** oppfatning; måte å se tingene på; **3** befruktning, unnfangelse. **conceptual** [kən'septjuəl] *adj* begrepsmessig, begreps-.

concern [kən'sɜ:n] **I** *sb* **1** anliggende, sak; **2** konsern, (større) firma; **3** andel; **4** bekymring, engstelse; **II** *vt* **1** angå; *~ oneself about (in/with)* beskjeftige seg med; interessere seg for; *as far as I am ~ed* for min egen del; **2** bekymre, gjøre bekymret; uroe. **concerning** [kən'sɜ:nɪŋ] *prep* angående, om.

concert I ['kɒnsət] *sb* **1** konsert; *~ grand* konsertflygel; **2** samstemmighet; **II** [kən'sɜ:t] *vt* arrangere, ordne. **concerted** [kən'sɜ:tɪd] *adj* forent, samlet.

concession [kən'seʃn] innrømmelse; **2** avståelse, oppgivelse; **3** konsesjon. **concessionary** [kən'seʃnərɪ] *sb petro* rettighetshaver.

conciliate [kən'sɪlɪeɪt] *vt* for|like, -sone; vinne (for seg). **conciliation** [kənˌsɪlɪ'eɪʃn] *sb* forsoning *etc*.

concise [kən'saɪs] *adj* konsis; kort.

conclude [kən'klu:d] *vb* **1** (av)slutte; **2** konkludere, slutte (seg til); **3** *især US* beslutte. **conclusion** [kən'klu:ʒn] *sb* konklusjon, slutning; slutt; *in ~* til slutt. **conclusive** [kən'klu:sɪv] *adj* avgjørende.

concoct [kən'kɒkt] *vt* **1** brygge/koke sammen; **2** finne på; spekulere ut. **concoction** [kən'kɒkʃn] *sb* brygg, drikk; *fig* oppspinn, sammenkok.

concord ['kɒŋkɔ:d] *sb* enighet, samstemmighet; samsvar. **concordance** [kən'kɔ:dəns] *sb* **1** = *concord*; **2** konkordans. **concordant** [kən'kɔ:dənt] *adj* samstemmig.

concourse ['kɒnkɔ:s] *sb* **1** sammenstimling; **2** sammenfall; **3** *US* stasjonshall (o.a. større samlingssteder).

concrete A ['kɒnkri:t] **I** *adj* konkret; **II** *sb* **1** konkret (ting); **2** betong; **III** *vt* dekke med betong; **B** [kən'kri:t] størkne.

concur [kən'kɜ:] *vi* **1** istemme, være enig; **2** hende samtidig; **3** *~ to* bidra/medvirke til. **concurrence**

[kən'kʌrəns], **concurrency** [kən'kʌrənsɪ] *sb* enighet; sammenfall; samtidighet. **concurrent** [kən'kʌrənt] **I** *adj* **1** enig, samstemmig; **2** samtidig (også *data*); **3** medvirkende; **II** *sb* medvirkende årsak.

concussion [kən'kʌʃn] *sb* **1** (~ *of the brain)* hjernerystelse; **2** risting.

condemn [kən'dem] fordømme; **2** dømme; **3** beslaglegge (især smuglergods); **4** kondemnere. **condemnation** [ˌkɒndem'neɪʃn] *sb* fordømmelse *etc*. **condemned cell** *sb* dødscelle.

condensate [kən'denseɪt] *sb* kondensat. **condensate | stripper** *sb petro* kondensatrenser. ~ **well** *sb petro* kondensatbrønn. **condensation** [ˌkɒnden'seɪʃn] *sb* **1** kondens; **2** sammendrag. **condense** [kən'dens] *vb* **1** fortette, kondensere; **2** forkorte, trekke sammen. **condenser** [kən'densə] *sb* kondensator. **condenser oil** *sb petro* kondensatorolje.

condescend [ˌkɒndɪ'send] *vi* **1** nedlate seg (*to* til); **2** velvilligst gå med på. **condescension** [ˌkɒndɪ'senʃn] *sb* nedlatenhet *etc*.

condiment ['kɒndɪmənt] *sb* krydder.

condition [kən'dɪʃn] **I** *sb* **1** betingelse, vilkår; **2** (til)stand; form, kondisjon; **3** *fl* forhold, omstendigheter; **II** *vt* **1** bestemme; betinge; ~*ed by* avhengig av; **2** forberede; legge til rette; kondisjonere; gjøre egnet. **conditional** [kən'dɪʃənl] *adj* betinget, betingelses-. **condition code** *sb data* statuskode.

condole [kən'dəul] *vi* kondolere. **condolences** [kən'dəulənsɪz] *sb fl* kondolanse(r); *please accept my* ~*s* (jeg) kondolerer.

condone [kən'dəun] *vt* **1** overse; tilgi; **2** oppveie.

conduce [kən'dju:s] *vi* bidra, føre, tjene (*to* til). **conducive** [kən'dju:sɪv] *adj* medvirkende. **conduct** **I** ['kɒndʌkt] *sb* **1** oppførsel; **2** føring, ledelse; **II** [kən'dʌkt] *vb* **1** føre, lede; ~ *oneself* (opp)føre seg; **2** dirigere, styre; **3** lede (elektrisitet etc). **conduction** [kən'dʌkʃn] *sb* ledning; (over)føring. **conductor** [kən'dʌktə] *sb* **1** fører, leder; dirigent; **2** billettør; **3** leder (av elektrisitet etc); *lightning* ~ lynavleder. **conductress** [kən'dʌktrɪs] *sb* konduktør (om kvinne).

conduit ['kɒndɪt] *sb* rør(ledning).

cone [kəun] *sb* **1** kongle; **2** kjegle; **3** kremmerhus (især av kjeks, til iskrem).

confection [kən'fekʃn] *sb* **1** syltetøy; søt kake etc; *fl* søtsaker; **2** blanding; **3** (dame)konfeksjon. **confectioner** [kən'fekʃnə] *sb* konditor. **confectionery** [kən'fekʃənrɪ] *sb* godter, slikkeri; godtebutikk.

confederacy [kən'fedərəsɪ] *sb* forbund; (kon)føderasjon. **confederate A** [kən'federət] **I** *adj* alliert; konføderert; **II** *sb* **1** forbundsfelle; **2** medskyldig; **B** [kən'fedəreɪt] *vb* forene(s), slutte (seg) sammen. **confederation** [kən,fedə'reɪʃn] *sb* allianse, forbund, union; (kon)føderasjon.

confer [kən'fɜ:] *vb* **1** overdra; skjenke, tildele; **2** konferere. **conference** ['kɒnfərəns] *sb* konferanse, samtale. **conferment** [kən'fɜ:mənt] *sb* overdragelse *etc*.

confess [kən'fes] *vb* bekjenne (synd); innrømme (feil); tilstå (forbrytelse). **confession** [kən'feʃn] *sb* bekjennelse *etc; rel især* trosbekjennelse. **confessor** [kən'fesə] *sb* skriftefar.

confide [kən'faɪd] *vb* **1** stole (*in* på); **2** betro seg (*to* til). **confidence** ['kɒnfɪdəns] *sb* **1** tillit, tiltro (*in* til); **2** fortrolighet; **3** selvtillit; **4** *som adj* bløff-. **confidence | game** = ~ *trick*. ~ **man** *sb* bløffmaker; sjarlatan, svindler; bondefanger. ~ **trick** *sb* bløff; svindel; bondefangeri. ~ **trickster** = ~ *man*. **confident** ['kɒnfɪdənt] *adj* (selv)sikker; tillitsfull. **confidential** [ˌkɒnfɪ'denʃl] *adj* **1** fortrolig, konfidensiell; **2** betrodd.

configuration [kən,fɪgju'reɪʃn] *sb* fasong; skikkelse; fremtoning. **configuration chart** *sb data* konfigurasjonsskjema.

confine **I** ~*s* ['kɒnfaɪnz] *sb fl* grense(r); **II** [kən'faɪn] *vt* **1** begrense; innskrenke; **2** sperre inne; **3** *be* ~*d* ligge i barsel(seng). **confinement** [kən'faɪnmənt] *sb* **1** innesperring; *solitary* ~ enecelle; **2** barsel(seng).

confirm [kən'fɜ:m] *vt* **1** bekrefte; **2** konfirmere; **3** ~*ed (fig)* inkarnert, inngrodd. **confirmation** [ˌkɒnfə'meɪʃn] *sb* **1** bekreftelse; **2** konfirmasjon; **3** *data* klarsvar.

confiscate ['kɒnfiskeɪt] *vt* beslaglegge, konfiskere. **confiscation** [ˌkɒnfɪs'keɪʃn] *sb* beslag(leggelse).

conflagration [ˌkɒnflə'greɪʃn] *sb* (stor)brann.

conflict **I** ['kɒnflɪkt] *sb* **1** konflikt, motsetning; **2** kamp; **II** [kən'flɪkt] *vi* stride(s).

confluence ['kɒnfluəns] *sb* sammenløp (av elver); møte; sammenstimling.

conform [kən'fɔ:m] *vb* **1** føye/rette seg (*to* etter); **2** tilpasse seg (*to* til); **3** ensrette(s), konformere(s). **conformity** [kən'fɔ:mətɪ] *sb* **1** likhet; **2** overensstemmelse; **3** ensrettethet, konformitet.

confound [kən'faund] *vt* **1** forbløffe, gjøre målløs; **2** forveksle; **3** *gml* kullkaste; ødelegge; **4** *dgl:* ~ *it!* pokker ta det! **confounded** [kən'faundɪd] *adj dgl* fordømt, pokkers.

confront [kən'frʌnt] *vt* **1** konfrontere; *ofte* sammenligne; **2** møte (dristig); trosse. **confrontation** [ˌkɒnfrən'teɪʃn] *sb* konfrontering *etc*; konfrontasjon.

confuse [kən'fju:z] *vt* **1** forvirre, gjøre forfjamset; **2** forveksle. **confusion** [kən'fju:ʒn] *sb* forvirring *etc*.

confutation [ˌkɒnfju:'teɪʃn] *sb* tilbakevisning *etc*. **confute** [kən'fju:t] *vt* gjendrive, tilbakevise; motbevise.

congeal [kən'dʒi:l] *vb* (stiv)fryse; stivne, størkne.

congenial [kən'dʒi:nɪəl] *adj* (ånds)beslektet; **2** behagelig, tiltalende; gunstig. **congeniality** [kən,dʒi:nɪ'ælətɪ] *sb* ånds|fellesskap, -slektskap.

congenital [kən'dʒenɪtl] *adj* medfødt.

congested [kən'dʒestɪd] *adj* **1** overfylt; **2** overbefolket; **3** blokkert. **congestion** [kən'dʒestʃn] *sb* **1** opphopning; sterk tilstrømning; *traffic* ~ trafikkork; **2** overbefolkning.

conglomerate **I** [kən'glɒmərət] **1** *adj* sammensatt; uensartet; **2** *sb* konglomerat; **II** [kən'glɒməreɪt] *vb* klumpe (seg) sammen. **conglomeration** [kən,glɒmə'reɪʃn] *sb* **1** sammenhop(n)ing; sammenhopet masse; **2** konglomerat.

congratulate [kən'grætʃʊleɪt] *vt* gratulere, lykkønske (*on* med). **congratulation** [kən,grætʃʊ'leɪʃn] *sb* gratulasjon *etc*. **congratulatory** [kən,grætʃʊ'leɪtərɪ] *adj* gratulasjons-.

congregate ['kɒŋgrɪgeɪt] *vb* forsamle(s), samle (seg). **congregation** [,kɒŋgrɪ'geɪʃn] *sb* (for)samling; menighet. **congregational** [,kɒŋgrɪ'geɪʃənl] *adj* (fri)kirkelig, menighets-. **congress** ['kɒŋgres] *sb* **1** kongress, møte(serie); **2** *the C~* Kongressen (dvs nasjonalforsamlingen) i USA. **congressional** [kən'greʃənl] *adj* kongress-.

conic(al) ['kɒnɪk(l)] *adj* konisk, kjegle-. **coniferous** [kə'nɪfərəs] *adj* konglebærende.

conjectural [kən'dʒektʃərəl] *adj* formodet; teoretisk; tvilsom. **conjecture** [kən'dʒektʃə] **1** *sb* antakelse *etc*; **2** *vb* anta, formode, gjette.

conjugal ['kɒndʒʊgəl] *adj* ekteskapelig. **conjugate** ['kɒndʒʊgeɪt] *vt* konjugere, bøye (verb). **conjugation** [,kɒndʒʊ'geiʃn] *sb* konjugering *etc*; konjugasjon. **conjunction** [kən'dʒʌŋkʃn] *sb* **1** forbindelse, sammenheng; **2** konjunksjon.

conjure A ['kʌndʒə] *vb* trylle; *~ up* mane frem; **B** [kən'dʒʊə] *vb* besverge; bønnfalle. **conjurer** ['kʌndʒərə] *sb* tryllekunstner.

conk [kɒŋk] **A** *sb slang* snyteskaft; **B** *vb dgl: ~ out* fuske, streike (om motor etc).

connect [kə'nekt] *vb* **1** forbinde, knytte sammen; **2** korrespondere (om kommunikasjonsmidler). **connection, connexion** [kə'nekʃn] *sb* **1** forbindelse *etc*; tilkobling; **2** korresponderende (buss, tog etc); **3** kundekrets; tilhengere.

connivance [kə'naɪvəns] *sb* det å se gjennom fingrene med noe; ≈ overbærenhet. **connivant** [kə'naɪvənt] *adj* ≈ ovebærende. **connive** [kə'naɪv] *vi: ~ at* lukke øynene for; se gjennom fingrene med; *også* bære over med.

connotation [,kɒnəʊ'teɪʃn] *sb* bibetydning, konnotasjon. **connote** [kə'nəʊt] *vt (om ord)* ha som bibetydning; *ofte* innebære.

conquer ['kɒŋkə] *vt* erobre; **2** beseire, overvinne. **conquest** ['kɒŋkwest] *sb* erobring.

conscience ['kɒnʃəns] *sb* samvittighet. **conscientious** [,kɒnʃɪ'enʃes] *adj* **1** samvittighetsfull; **2** samvittighets-. **conscientious objector** *sb* militærnekter (dvs en som nekter å gjøre militærtjeneste av samvittighetsgrunner). **conscious** ['kɒnʃəs] *adj* **1** ved bevissthet; våken; **2** bevisst, vitende; *~ of* klar over. **consciousness** ['kɒnʃəsnɪs] *sb* bevissthet.

conscript 1 ['kɒnskrɪpt] *sb* vernepliktig (soldat); **2** [kən'skrɪpt] *vt* utskrive (til militærtjeneste). **conscription** [kən'skrɪpʃn] *sb* utskrivning (til militærtjeneste.

consecrate ['kɒnsɪkreɪt] *vt* innvie, vigsle; hellige. **consecration** [,kɒnsɪ'kreɪʃn] *sb* innvielse, vigsling.

consecutive [kən'sekjʊtɪv] *adj* fortløpende, sammenhengende; *data* etterfølgende. **consecutive operation** *sb data* sekvensiell operasjon.

consensus [kən'sensəs] *sb* (alminnelig) enighet. **consent** [kən'sent] **1** *sb* samtykke; **2** *vi* samtykke (*to* i).

consequence ['kɒnsɪkwəns] *sb* **1** konsekvens, resultat; *in ~ of* som følge av; **2** betydning. **consequent** ['kɒnsɪkwənt] *adj* følgende, som følger (av). **consequential** [,kɒnsɪ'kwenʃl] *adj* **1** = *consequent*; **2** innbilsk; overlegen. **consequently** ['kɒnsɪkwəntlɪ] *adv* altså, følgelig.

conservation [,kɒnsə'veɪʃn] *sb* bevaring *etc*. **conservative** [kən'sɜ:vətɪv] **I** *adj* **1** bevarende *etc*; **2** konservativ; **3** måteholden; *a ~ estimate* et forsiktig overslag; **II** *sb* konservativ (person, politiker). **conservatory** [kən'sɜ:vətrɪ] *sb* **1** drivhus; **2** konservatorium. **conserve** [kən'sɜ:v] **I** *sb fl* syltetøy; **II** *vt* **1** bevare; frede; konservere; **2** spare på (så det varer lenger).

consider [kən'sɪdə] *vt* **1** overveie, tenke på; **2** ta hensyn til; *all things ~ed* alt tatt i betraktning; **3** betrakte som. **considerable** [kən'sɪdərəbl] *adj* betraktelig, betydelig. **considerate** [kən'sɪdərət] *adj* hensynsfull, omtenksom. **consideration** [kən,sɪdə'reɪʃn] *sb* **1** overveielse; **2** hensyn, hensynsfullhet; omtanke; oppmerksomhet; *take into ~* ta i betraktning; **3** betydning; betydningsfull faktor; **4** godtgjørelse. **considering** [kən'sɪdərɪŋ] *prep* i betraktning av; med tanke på.

consign [kən'saɪn] *vt* **1** sende (varer etc); **2** levere; overlate. **consignment** [kən'saɪnmənt] *sb* (vare)sending.

consist [kən'sɪst] *vi* **1** bestå (*in* i; *of* av); **2** *~ with* stemme (overens) med. **consistence** [kən'sɪstəns] *sb* konsistens. **consistency** [kən'sɪstənsɪ] *sb* **1** konsekvens; (indre) sammenheng; **2** = *consistence*. **consistent** [kən'sɪstənt] *adj* **1** konsekvent; sammenhengende; **2** forenelig/overensstemmende (*with* med).

consolation [,kɒnsə'leɪʃn] *sb* trøst. **console A** ['kɒnsəʊl] *sb* **1** (hylle)knekt; konsoll; **2** *a)* (radio)kabinett; *b) data* konsoll; **3** styrepult; **B** [kən'səʊl] *vt* trøste.

consolidate [kən'sɒlɪdeɪt] *vb* konsolidere(s); styrke(s); samle (krefter etc). **consolidation** [kən,sɒlɪ'deɪʃn] *sb* konsolidering *etc*.

consonant ['kɒnsənənt] **1** *adj* harmonisk, samstemmig; **2** *sb* konsonant.

consort I ['kɒnsɔ:t] *sb* **1** gemal(inne); **2** ledsager; **II** [kən'sɔ:t] *vi: ~ with* omgås, være sammen med; gå/passe sammen med.

conspicuous [kən'spɪkjʊəs] *adj* iøynefallende; påfallende; *make oneself ~* vekke oppsikt.

conspiracy [kən'spɪrəsɪ] *sb* konspirasjon, sammensvergelse. **conspire** [kən'spaɪə] *vb* konspirere, sammensverge (seg).

constable ['kʌnstəbl] *sb* (politi)konstabel; *Chief Constable* ≈ politimester. **constabulary** [kən'stæbjʊlərɪ] **1** *adj* politi-; **2** *sb: the Constabulary* politiet.

constant ['kɒnstənt] *adj* **1** stadig; *dgl* evinnelig; **2**

konstant, stabil; **3** standhaftig, trofast.

constellation [ˌkɒnstəˈleɪʃn] *sb* stjernebilde; *fig* konstellasjon; gruppe(ring).

consternation [ˌkɒnstəˈneɪʃn] *sb* bestyrtelse, forferdelse.

constipate [ˈkɒnstɪpeɪt] *vt: ~d* med treg mave. **constipation** [ˌkɒnstɪˈpeɪʃn] *sb* **1** forstoppelse, treg mave; **2** *data* vranglås (forårsaket av for stor mengde inndata).

constituency [kənˈstɪtjʊənsɪ] *sb* valgkrets. **constituent** [kənˈstɪtjʊənt] **I** *adj* **1** grunnlovgivende; **2** velger-; **3** *(~ part)* bestanddel; **II** *sb* **1** velger; **2** bestanddel. **constitute** [ˈkɒnstɪtju:t] *vt* **1** konstituere, utnevne; **2** etablere, stifte; **3** danne, utgjøre. **constitution** [ˌkɒnstɪˈtju:ʃn] *sb* **1** forfatning, grunnlov; **2** konstitusjon, helse; **3** beskaffenhet, natur; sammensetning. **constitutional** [ˌkɒnstɪˈtju:ʃənl] **I** *adj* **1** forfatningsmessig, grunnlovsmessig; **2** konstitusjonell, medfødt; **II** *sb dgl* (daglig) spasertur; mosjonstur.

constrain [kənˈstreɪn] *vt* presse/tvinge (frem). **constrained** [kənˈstreɪnd] *adj* anstrengt, unaturlig; hemmet. **constraint** [kənˈstreɪnt] *sb* press, tvang; *fig* forlegenhet.

constrict [kənˈstrɪkt] *vt* stramme; snøre sammen; *fig* innsnevre. **constriction** [kənˈstrɪkʃn] *sb* sammensnøring.

construct [kənˈstrʌkt] *vt* konstruere; bygge, reise (byggverk etc). **constructing** [kənˈstrʌktɪŋ] *sb data* blokking. **construction** [kənˈstrʌkʃn] *sb* **1** konstruksjon *etc*; **2** fortolkning, mening (jf *construe*). **constructive** [kənˈstrʌktɪv] *adj* byggende; *fig også* konstruktiv. **construe** [kənˈstru:] *vb* **1** fortolke; **2** analysere (setning); **3** kombinere (ord etc).

consul [ˈkɒnsl] *sb* konsul. **consular** [ˈkɒnsjʊlə] *adj* konsulær, konsul-. **consulate** [ˈkɒnsjʊlət] *sb* konsulat. **consult** [kənˈsʌlt] *vb* **1** konsultere, rådspørre; *~ with* rådføre seg med; **2** ta hensyn til. **consultant** [kənˈsʌltənt] *sb* konsulent, rådgiver. **consultation** [ˌkɒnsəlˈteɪʃn] *sb* konsultering *etc*; konsultasjon.

consume [kənˈsju:m] *vb* **1** (for)bruke; **2** (for)tære, ødelegge; **3** *be ~d with (fig)* være oppslukt av. **consumer** [kənˈsju:mə] *sb* forbruker. **consuming** [kənˈsju:mɪŋ] *adj* som legger beslag på tid og krefter; ≈ altoppslukende. **consummate I** [kənˈsʌmət] *adj* fullendt, perfekt; **II** [ˈkɒnsəmeɪt] *vt* **1** fullbyrde; **2** fullende, fullføre. **consummation** [ˌkɒnsəˈmeɪʃn] *sb* fullbyrdelse *etc*. **consumption** [kənˈsʌmpʃn] *sb* **1** forbruk; **2** fortæring; **3** tæring (dvs lungetuberkulose). **consumptive** [kənˈsʌmptɪv] **1** *adj* (for)tærende; **2** *adj, sb* tæringssyk (person).

contact 1 [ˈkɒntækt] *sb* kontakt; berøring; forbindelse; **2** [kənˈtækt] *vt* kontakte; sette (seg) i forbindelse med. **contagion** [kənˈteɪdʒn] *sb* smitte (ved kontakt). **contagious** [kənˈteɪdʒəs] *adj* smittefarlig, smittsom; *fig* smittende.

contain [kənˈteɪn] *vt* **1** inneholde; romme; **2** beherske, holde på. **container** [kənˈteɪnə] *sb* beholder.

contaminate [kənˈtæmɪneɪt] *vt* forurense; (be)-smitte. **contamination** [kənˌtæmɪˈneɪʃn] *sb* forurens(n)ing; smitte.

contemplate [ˈkɒntempleɪt] *vt* **1** meditere (over); **2** overveie, tenke på; **3** betrakte. **contemplation** [ˌkɒntemˈpleɪʃn] *sb* kontemplasjon. **contemplative** *adj* **1** [ˈkɒntəmpleɪtɪv] tankefull; **2** [kənˈtemplətɪv] kontemplativ.

contemporaneous [kənˌtempəˈreɪnɪəs] *adj* samtidig. **contemporary** [kənˈtemprərɪ] *adj, sb* samtidig (både om fortid og nåtid); *ofte* moderne (foreteelse, person etc).

contempt [kənˈtempt] *sb* **1** forakt; **2** respektløshet. **contemptible** [kənˈtemptəbl] *adj* foraktelig, ynkelig. **contemptuous** [kənˈtemptjʊəs] *adj* foraktelig, hånlig.

contend [kənˈtend] *vb* **1** kjempe; konkurrere; **2** hevde, påstå. **contending** [kənˈtendɪŋ] *adj* (mot)-stridende.

content A [kənˈtent] **I** *adj* **1** fornøyd, tilfreds; **2** rede; villig; **II** *sb* tilfredshet; **III** *vt* tilfredsstille; *~ oneself with* nøye seg med; **B** [ˈkɒntənt] *sb, oftest fl* innhold.

contention [kənˈtenʃn] *sb* **1** påstand; **2** diskusjon; **3** konflikt; *dgl* krangel. **contentious** [kənˈtenʃəs] *adj* **1** kranglevoren; **2** omtvistet.

contentment [kənˈtentmənt] *sb* tilfredshet; tilfredsstillelse.

contest I [ˈkɒntest] *sb* **1** kamp; **2** konkurranse; **II** [kənˈtest] *vb* **1** bestride; **2** konkurrere/slåss om. **contestant** [kənˈtestənt] *sb* **1** kjemper; **2** konkurransedeltaker.

contiguous [kənˈtɪgjʊəs] *adj* nær(liggende); tilstøtende.

continence [ˈkɒntɪnəns] *sb* måtehold; (seksuell) avholdenhet. **continent** [ˈkɒntɪnənt] **I** *adj* **1** måteholden; **2** (seksuelt) avholdende; **II** *sb* kontinent, verdensdel. **continental** [ˌkɒntɪˈnentl] *adj* kontinental(-), fastlands-; *ofte* europeisk (dvs sett fra De britiske øyer).

contingency [kənˈtɪndʒənsɪ] *sb* tilfelle, (tilfeldig) omstendighet; *stundom* krise-, unntaks-. **contingent** [kənˈtɪndʒənt] **I** *adj* **1** tilfeldig; **2** avhengig (*upon* av); **II** *sb mil etc* kontingent, (troppe)styrke.

continual [kənˈtɪnjʊəl] *adj* **1** uavbrutt; **2** stadig. **continuance** [kənˈtɪnjʊəns] *sb* **1** varighet; **2** fortsettelse; fortsatt opphold *etc*. **continuation** [kənˌtɪnjʊˈeɪʃn] *sb* fortsettelse *etc*. **continue** [kənˈtɪnju:] *vb* **1** fortsette; *(to be) ~d* fortsettes (i neste nummer etc); **2** (for)bli; vare ved. **continuity** [ˌkɒntɪˈnju:ətɪ] *sb* **1** kontinuitet, ubrutt rekke/sammenheng; **2** handlingsforløp (i film); **3** annonsering, sammenbindende kommentarer (i radio/TV). **continuous** [kənˈtɪnjʊəs] *adj* **1** kontinuerlig, sammenhengende; **2** stadig, uavbrutt.

contort [kənˈtɔ:t] *vt* fordreie, vri. **contortion** [kənˈtɔ:ʃn] *sb* fordreining *etc*. **contortionist** [kənˈtɔ:ʃnɪst] *sb* slangemenneske.

contour [ˈkɒntʊə] **1** *sb* kontur, omriss; **2** *vt* streke opp. **contour map** *sb* konturkart.

contraband ['kɒntrəbænd] **1** *adj* ulovlig; *især* smugler-; **2** *sb* kontrabande; smugling; smuglergods.

contraception [ˌkɒntrə'sepʃn] *sb* prevensjon. **contraceptive** [ˌkɒntrə'septɪv] **1** *adj* befruktningshindrende; **2** *sb* preventiv(middel).

contract I ['kɒntrækt] *sb* kontrakt; **II** [kən'trækt] *vb* **A 1** inngå avtale/kontrakt; kontrahere; **2** pådra/skaffe seg; bli ansvarlig for; **B** trekke (seg) sammen; forkorte. **contraction** [kən'trækʃn] *sb* sammentrekning. **contractor** [kən'træktə] *sb* kontrahent; leverandør; entreprenør.

contradict [ˌkɒntrə'dɪkt] *vt* benekte; motsi. **contradiction** [ˌkɒntrə'dɪkʃn] *sb* motsigelse; ~ *in terms* selvmotsigelse. **contradictory** [ˌkɒntrə'dɪktərɪ] *adj* (selv)motsigende.

contraption [kən'træpʃn] *sb dgl* innretning; dings, greie.

contrary I ['kɒntrərɪ] **1** *adj* motsatt; *sjø* kontrari; imot, mot-; ~ *to* i strid med; **2** *sb* det motsatte; *on the* ~ tvert imot; **II** [kən'treərɪ] *adj dgl* sta; vrang, vrien. **contrast I** ['kɒntrɑ:st] *sb* kontrast; (sterk) motsetning; **2** [kən'trɑ:st] *vb* kontrastere; *ofte* sammenligne.

contravene [ˌkɒntrə'vi:n] *vt* **1** gå imot; stå i strid med; **2** overtre; **3** bestride. **contravention** [ˌkɒntrə'venʃn] *sb* imøtegåelse *etc.*

contribute [kən'trɪbju:t] *vb* **1** bidra (med); **2** bidra (*to* til). **contribution** [ˌkɒntrɪ'bju:ʃn] *sb* **1** bidrag; **2** medvirkning; **3** krigsskatt. **contributor** [kən'trɪbjʊtə] *sb* bidragsyter. **contributory** [kən'trɪbjʊtərɪ] *adj* **1** bidrags-; **2** medvirkende.

contrite ['kɒntraɪt] *adj* angrende; sønderknust (av anger). **contrition** [kən'trɪʃn] *sb* anger.

contrivance [kən'traɪvəns] *sb* **1** oppfinnsomhet; **2** påfunn; innretning, mekanisme. **contrive** [kən'traɪv] *vb* **1** finne på; klekke ut; **2** klare (å få endene til å møtes).

control [kən'trəʊl] **I** *sb* **1** kontroll (og kontroll|stasjon, tiltak); regulering; ledelse, styring; *birth-*~ fødselsregulering, prevensjon; *be in/take* ~ ha/(over)ta makten (ledelsen, styringen etc); *be out of* ~ være uten styring; *get out of* ~ løpe løpsk; *lose* ~ *(of)* miste kontrollen (over); **2** *fl* [*også* 'kɒntrəʊlz] styreinnretning (som ratt, spak, stikke); kontrollpanel; **II** *vt* **1** kontrollere; styre; **2** beherske; **3** regulere. **controllable** [kən'trəʊləbl] *adj* kontrollerbar. **control | area,** ~ **block** *sb data* styrelagerområde. ~ **break** *sb data* styrt avbrudd. ~ **function** *sb data* styreoperasjon. **controller** [kən'trəʊlə] *sb* **1** kontrollør *etc*; **2** *merk* ≈ regnskapssjef, revisjonssjef; (økonomi)direktør; **3** *data* ytre styreenhet. **control | mode** *sb data* styremodus. ~ **standard** *sb data* integritetsstandard. ~ **total** *sb data* nonsenssum. ~ **valve** *sb petro* kontrollventil, styringsventil.

controversial [ˌkɒntrə'vɜ:ʃl] *adj* kontroversiell, omtvistet. **controversy** [kən'trɒvəsɪ] *sb* kontrovers, uenighet.

contusion [kən'tu:ʒn] *sb* blått merke (etter slag, støt etc).

convalescence [ˌkɒnvə'lesns] *sb* bedring, rekonvalesens. **convalescent** [ˌkɒnvə'lesnt] **1** *adj* på bedringens vei; *2 sb* rekonvalesent.

convene [kən'vi:n] *vb* møte(s); samle (seg); kalle sammen.

convenience [kən'vi:nɪəns] *sb* **1** passende anledning; *at your (earliest)* ~ når/så snart det passer/måtte passe Dem; **2** bekvemmelighet; fordel, nytte; *fl også* komfort; *public* ~*s* offentlig toalett. **convenient** [kən'vi:nɪənt] *adj* **1** beleilig, passende; **2** fordelaktig; nyttig.

convent ['kɒnvənt] *sb* (nonne)kloster.

convention [kən'venʃn] *sb* **1** kongress, møte; **2** avtale, overenskomst; **3** skikk og bruk. **conventional** [kən'venʃənl] *adj* konvensjonell; tradisjonell; vanlig.

converge [kən'vɜ:dʒ] *vb* konvergere; (få til å) løpe sammen/nærme seg hverandre.

conversant [kən'vɜ:sənt] *adj* fortrolig (*with* med). **conversation** [ˌkɒnvə'seɪʃn] *sb* **1** konversasjon, samtale; **2** omgang, samvær. **conversational** [ˌkɒnvə'seɪʃənl] *adj* konversasjons-, samtale-. **conversational | language** *sb data* dialogspråk. ~ **mode** *sb data* dialogform. **converse A** ['kɒnvɜ:s] **1** *adj* motsatt, omvendt; **2** *sb* motsetning; omvendt forhold *etc*; **B** [kən'vɜ:s] *vi* **1** konversere, (sam)tale; **2** omgås, vanke sammen.

conversion [kən'vɜ:ʃn] *sb* forandring; *merk* konvertering; *rel* omvendelse. **convert 1** ['kɒnvɜ:t] *sb* konvertitt, (ny)omvendt; **2** [kən'vɜ:t] *vt* forandre, omdanne; *data, merk etc* konvertere, omsette, veksle; *rel* omvende. **converter** [kən'vɜ:tə] *sb* omformer. **convertible** [kən'vɜ:təbl] **1** *adj* foranderlig *etc*; *merk* konvertibel; **2** *sb* kabriolet.

convey [kən'veɪ] *vt* **1** bære; (over)føre; transportere; **2** formidle; meddele; **3** overdra, overføre. **conveyance** [kən'veɪəns] *sb* **1** transport (og transport|middel, -måte); **2** overdragelse, skjøte. **conveyer** [kən'veɪə] *sb* **1** overbringer; tilbringer; **2** speditør, transportør. **conveyer belt** *sb* transportbånd. **conveyor** [kən'veɪə] *sb* = *conveyer.*

convict I ['kɒnvɪkt] *sb* straffange; domfelt (person); **II** [kən'vɪkt] *vt* **1** ~ *of (a crime)* finne skyldig i (en forbrytelse); **2** ~ *of (an error etc)* overbevise om (en feil etc). **conviction** [kən'vɪkʃn] *sb* **1** dom(fellelse); **2** overbevisning; *carry* ~ virke overbevisende.

convince [kən'vɪns] *vt* overbevise (*of* om; *that* om at).

convivial [kən'vɪvɪəl] *adj* lystig, munter; selskapelig (anlagt).

convocation [ˌkɒnvə'keɪʃn] *sb* **1** sammenkalling; **2** (kirke)møte. **convoke** [kən'vəʊk] *vt* innkalle/sammenkalle (til møte).

convolution [ˌkɒnvə'lu:ʃn] *sb* kveil, oppkveiling; vinding.

convoy ['kɒnvɔɪ] *sb, vt* konvoi(ere).

convulse [kən'vʌls] *vt* **1** ryste, skake; **2** fremkalle krampe(trekninger). **convulsed** [kən'vʌlst] *adj* fortrukket (*with* av). **convulsion** [kən'vʌlʃn] *sb* **1** rystelse; *fig* omveltning; **2** krampe(trekning). **convulsive** [kən'vʌlsɪv] *adj* **1** rystende, skakende; **2** krampaktig.

coo [ku:] **1** *sb* kurring; **2** *vb* kurre.

cook [kuk] **I** *sb* kokk(e); **II** *vb* **1** lage mat; **2** *dgl* fikse (dvs forfalske etc); ~ *up* brygge sammen; pønske ut. **cooker** ['kukə] *sb* **1** koke|apparat, -plate; komfyr; **2** sylte|bær, -frukt. **cookery** ['kukərɪ] *sb* matlaging. **cookery book** *sb* kokebok. **cookie** ['kukɪ] *sb* småkake. **cooking** ['kukɪŋ] = *cookery*. **cooky** ['kukɪ] = *cookie*.

cool [ku:l] **1** *adj* kjølig; sval; *fig* kald, likegyldig; rolig; *dgl* freidig; **2** *sb* kjølighet; **3** *vb* (av)kjøle; kjølne; ~ *down/off* (av)kjøle; *fig* hisse (seg) ned. **coolant** ['ku:lənt] *sb petro etc* kjøle|middel, -væske. **cooler** ['ku:lə] sb kjøler; *petro etc også* kondensator.

coolie ['ku:lɪ] *sb* kuli.

coop [ku:p] **1** *sb* (kylling)bur; **2** *vt* sette i bur; ~*ed in/up* innesperret.

co-op ['kəuɒp] *sb dgl* samvirkelag.

cooper ['ku:pə] *sb* bøkker.

co-operate [kəu'ɒpəreɪt] *vi* **1** samarbeide; **2** medvirke. **cooperation** [kəuˌɒpə'reɪʃn] *sb* **1** samarbeid; **2** medvirkning; **3** kooperasjon, samvirke. **co-operative** [kəu'ɒpərətɪv] **I** *adj* **1** samarbeidende *etc*; **2** kooperativ(-), samvirke(lags)-; **II** *sb* kooperativ, samvirkelag. **co-operative | society** *sb* samvirkelag (dvs laget). ~ **store** *sb* samvirkelag (dvs butikken).

co-opt [kəu'ɒpt] *vt* velge inn (*to a committee* i en komité). **co-optation** [ˌkəuɒp'teɪʃn] *sb* selvsupplering.

co-ordinate I [ˌkəu'ɔ:dənət] **1** *adj* koordinert *etc*; **2** *sb* koordinat; **II** [ˌkəu'ɔ:dɪneɪt] *vt* koordinere, samordne; sideordne. **co-ordination** [ˌkəuˌɔ:dɪ'neɪʃn] *sb* koordinering *etc*.

cop [kɒp] **A** *sb* spole; **B** *slang* **I** *sb* **1** purk (dvs politimann); **2** *a fair* ~ lønn/straff som fortjent; **II** *vt* **1** fakke, huke; **2** snappe, sikre seg.

cope [kəup] **A** *sb* korkåpe; kappe; **B** *vi:* ~ *with* klare, mestre; hamle opp med.

copious ['kəupɪəs] *adj* rikelig.

copper ['kɒpə] **A** **1** *adj* kobber-; **2** *sb* kobber (og ting av kobber, som f.eks. kjeler og mynter); **3** *vt* = ~ *-bottom*; **B** = *cop I 1*. **copper|-bottom** *vt* kobberforhude. ~**plate** *sb* kobberstikk.

coppice ['kɒpɪs] *sb* kratt.

co-product ['kəuˌprɒdʌkt] *sb* biprodukt.

copse [kɒps] = *coppice*.

copulate ['kɒpjuleɪt] *vi* pare seg. **copulation** [ˌkɒpju'leɪʃn] *sb* paring.

copy ['kɒpɪ] **I** *sb* **1** etterligning, kopi; avskrift; **2** eksemplar (av bok etc); **3** forskrift, mønster; **4** manuskript, *dgl* manus; (avis)stoff; (annonse-/reklame)-tekst; *fair* ~ renskrevet manuskript; *rough* ~ kladd; **II** *vb* etterligne, kopiere; skrive av. **copy|book** *sb* skrivebok. ~**cat** *sb* apekatt (dvs en som aper/plaprer etter andre). ~**right** *sb* forlagsrett; opphavsrett. ~ **writer** *sb* (reklame)tekstforfatter.

coral ['kɒrəl] **I** *adj* korallrød, korall-; **II** *sb* **1** korall; **2** bitering (til spedbarn).

cord [kɔ:d] **I** *sb* **1** snor, (tykk) hyssing; **2** = *chord 1*; **3** (ved)favn; **II** *vt* **1** snøre; binde fast; **2** besette med snorer. **cordage** ['kɔ:dɪdʒ] *sb* tauverk.

cordial ['kɔ:dɪəl] **I** *adj* **1** hjertelig; **2** (hjerte)styrkende; **II** *sb* hjertestyrker. **cordiality** [ˌkɔ:dɪ'ælətɪ] *sb* hjertelighet.

cordon ['kɔ:dn] **I** *sb* **1** kjede/ring (av politimenn etc); **2** ordensbånd; **3** pyntesnor; **II** *vt:* ~ *off* sperre av.

corduroy ['kɔ:dərɔɪ] *sb* kordfløyel; *dgl* kord.

core [kɔ:] **I** *sb* **1** kjerne(hus); *fig* kjerne; **2** *data, elek* (magnet)kjerne; **II** *vt* stikke/ta ut kjernehuset av. **core | drilling** *sb petro* kjerneboring. ~ **sample** *sb petro* kjerneprøve.

cork [kɔ:k] **1** *sb* kork; **2** *vt* korke. **corker** ['kɔ:kə] *sb slang* **1** siste ord; slående argument; **2** bløff; diger skrøne; **3** bløffmaker; kjekkas. **cork-screw** *sb* korketrekker.

cormorant ['kɔ:mərənt] *sb* skarv.

corn [kɔ:n] **A** *sb* korn (især hvete, i Skottland havre); *US* mais; **B** *sb* liktorn; **C** *vt* (lett)salte, salte ned.

corner ['kɔ:nə] **I** *sb* **1** hjørne; krok; avkrok; **2** *merk* oppkjøp (i spekulasjonsøyemed); **II** *vb* **1** runde et hjørne; **2** drive opp i et hjørne; sette til veggs; **3** *merk* kjøpe opp (i spekulasjonsøyemed).

cornet ['kɔ:nɪt] *sb* **1** kornett; **2** kremmerhus.

cornice ['kɔ:nɪs] *sb* **1** gesims; taklist; **2** gardinbrett.

corny ['kɔ:nɪ] *adj* **1** kornet; **2** med liktorner; **3** *slang* forslitt; rar, skrullet, sprø.

corollary [kə'rɒlərɪ] *sb* naturlig følge/resultat.

corona [kə'rəunə] *sb* **1** korona; **2** krans; rosett; krone. **coronation** [ˌkɒrə'neɪʃn] *sb* kroning. **coroner** ['kɒrənə] *sb* embetsmann som forestår **coroner's inquest** *sb* rettslig likskue. **coronet** ['kɒrənət] *sb* liten adelskrone.

corporal ['kɔ:prəl] **1** *adj* korporlig, legemlig; **2** *sb* korporal. **corporate** ['kɔ:pərət] *adj* **1** korporasjons-; *US* (aksje)selskaps-; **2** felles, samlet. **corporation** [ˌkɔ:pə'reɪʃn] *sb* **1** korporasjon; *US* (aksje)selskap; **2** bystyre; *som adj* kommunal, kommune-. **corporeal** [kɔ:'pɔ:rɪəl] *adj* **1** fysisk, legemlig; **2** materiell. **corps** [kɔ:] *sb* korps. **corpse** [kɔ:ps] *sb* lik. **corpulence** ['kɔ:pjuləns] *sb* korpulens. **corpulent** ['kɔ:pjulənt] *adj* korpulent, tykk(fallen). **corpuscle** ['kɔ:pʌsl] *sb* blodlegeme.

corral [kə'rɑ:l] *US* [kə'ræl] **I** *sb* **1** innhegning, kve; hestehage; **2** *US* vognborg; **II** *vt* **1** drive sammen; **2** stille opp i vognborg.

correct [kə'rekt] **I** *adj* **1** nøyaktig, riktig, sann; **2** korrekt, passende; **II** *vt* **1** rette; beriktige, korrigere; *stand* ~*ed* innrømme (og beklage) feil; **2** irettesette. **correction** [kə'rekʃn] *sb* rettelse *etc*. **corrective** [kə'rektɪv] **I** *adj* forbedrings-; **II** *sb* **1** korrektiv; **2** botemiddel.

correlate ['kɒrəleɪt] *vb* **1** bringe i samsvar (med hverandre); **2** svare til (hverandre). **correlation** [ˌkɒrɪ'leɪʃn] *sb* korrelasjon, samsvar; vekselvirkning.

correspond [ˌkɒrɪ'spɒnd] *vi* **1** svare (*to* til); **2** brevveksle, korrespondere (*with* med). **correspondence** [ˌkɒrɪ'spɒndəns] *sb* **1** overensstemmelse, samsvar; **2** brevveksling, korrespondanse. **correspondent** [ˌkɒrɪ'spɒndənt] **I** *adj* overensstemmende, samsvarende, tilsvarende; **II** *sb* **1** korrespondent; **2** *(newspaper ~)* (avis)korrespondent; **3** *merk* (forretnings)forbindelse. **corresponding** [ˌkɒrɪ'spɒndɪŋ] *adj* tilsvarende.

corroborate [kə'rɒbəreɪt] *vt* bekrefte, støtte.

corrode [kə'rəud] *vb* korrodere, ruste; tære(s), ødelegge(s); *om syre etc* etse(s). **corrosion** [kə'rəuʒn] *sb* korrosjon, rust(skade). **corrosive** [kə'rəusɪv] **1** *adj* korroderende *etc*; **2** *sb især* etsende middel.

corrugated ['kɒrugeɪtɪd] *adj* bølget; foldet, rynket; riflet. **corrugated | iron** *sb* bølgeblikk. **~ road** *sb dgl* vaskebrett (dvs humpet vei).

corrupt [kə'rʌpt] **I** *adj* **1** korrupt; (moralsk) fordervet; **2** bedervet; forurenset; **3** forvansket; **II** *vb* **1** korrumpere(s); ødelegge(s) moralsk; **2** bederve(s), råtne; forurense; **3** forvanske (betydning/uttale av ord, innhold i tekst etc). **corruptible** [kə'rʌptəbl] *adj* **1** korrupt, lett å bestikke; **2** *gml* forfengelig. **corruption** [kə'rʌpʃn] *sb* **1** korrupsjon *etc*; **2** *data* magnetlus.

corsage [kɔ:'sɑ:ʒ] *sb* **1** *US* blomst/liten blomsterbukett til kjolepynt etc; **2** kjoleliv.

cosmetic [kɒz'metɪk] **1** *adj* kosmetisk; **2** *sb fl* kosmetikk. **cosmetician** [ˌkɒzmə'tɪʃn] *sb* skjønnhetsekspert, sminkør.

cosmopolitan [ˌkɒzmə'pɒlɪtən] **1** *adj* kosmopolitisk; **2** *sb* kosmopolitt.

cost [kɒst] **1** *sb* omkostning, utgift; kost, (kost)pris; *fig* bekostning; *at all ~s* for enhver pris; *at the ~ of* på bekostning av; **2** *vb* koste; *merk* kostnadsberegne.

coster ['kɒstə], **costermonger** ['kɒstəmʌŋgə] *sb* gateselger (med fruktkjerre).

costly ['kɒstlɪ] *adj* kostbar, verdifull; *fig* dyrebar.

cost | of living *sb* leveomkostninger. **~ sheet** *sb merk* kalkyle.

costume ['kɒstju:m] **I** *sb* **1** kostyme; **2** drakt (dvs jakke og skjørt); **II** *vt* kostymere; kle.

cosy ['kəuzɪ] *adj* koselig; hyggelig; **2** *sb* tevarmer.

cot [kɒt] **A** *sb* (barne)seng; køye; **B** *sb* bu; (saue)fjøs; **2** *poet = cottage.*

cote [kəut] *sb* lite hus (for dyr); *dove-~* dueslag; *sheep-~* sauefjøs.

cottage ['kɒtɪdʒ] *sb* lite hus (på landet); landsted.

cotton ['kɒtn] **I** *sb* bomull (og bomulls|plante, -stoff, tråd, -varer etc); **II** *vi* **1** *~ up* bli venner; **2** *slang: ~ on (to)* begripe/forstå (etter hvert); gå med på. **cotton | mill** *sb* bomullsspinneri. **~ wool** *sb* (syke)bomull, vatt.

couch [kautʃ] **A I** *sb* benk, sofa; *gml* leie; **II** *vb* **1** legge seg; **2** krype sammen (på lur, i dekning etc); **3** kle (tanker) i ord; uttrykke; **B** = **couch-grass** *sb* kveke.

cough [kɒf] *sb, vb* hoste.

council ['kaunsl] *sb* **1** råd (dvs råds|forsamling, -møte); *rel* konsil, kirkemøte; **2** styre; *city (borough, county, town etc) ~* by-, herreds-, kommunestyre, formannskap etc; **3** *som adj ofte* kommunal, kommune-. **councillor** ['kaunsələ] *sb* **1** rådsmedlem; **2** (by)styremedlem *etc*.

counsel [kaunsl] **I** *sb* **1** rådslagning; *hold/take ~ with* rådføre seg med; *take ~ (together)* rådslå (sammen); **2** forslag; råd; mening; **3** juridisk bistand; **4** *Counsel* juridisk rådgiver (især om advokat engasjert i rettssak); *Counsel for the Crown/for the Prosecution* aktor (dvs anklager i straffesak); *Counsel for the Defence* forsvarer (i straffesak); *Counsel for the Defendant/Plaintiff* saksøktes/saksøkerens prosessfullmektig (i sivil sak); **II** *vt* råde; tilrå. **counsellor** ['kaunsələ] *sb* **1** rådgiver; **2** *US og Irland* advokat.

count [kaunt] **A I** *sb* **1** (opp)telling; (opp)regning; **2** beregning; **3** anklagepunkt; **II** *vb* **1** telle (opp); regne (sammen); *~ up* summere (opp); **2** inkludere; *~ in* regne/telle med; *~ out* ikke regne med; sette ut av betraktning; *~ (up)on* regne med; stole på; *every little ~s* alle monner drar; **3** anse/betrakte (som); **B** *sb* greve (i land utenom England). **countable** ['kauntəbl] **1** *adj* tellelig, som kan telles; **2** *sb* = **countable noun** *sb* (engelske) substantiv som kan brukes med *a* eller *an* foran, og i flertall med *many* eller et tallord foran. **count-down** *sb* nedtelling.

countenance ['kauntɪnəns] **I** *sb* **1** ansikt; mine, uttrykk; **2** godkjenning; støtte; **II** *vt* godkjenne; oppmuntre, støtte.

counter ['kauntə] **A** *sb* disk, skranke; (ekspedisjons)luke; **B** *sb* **1** telleverk, (-)teller; **2** spillemerke; **C 1** *adv* (i)mot; motsatt; *~ to* i strid med; **2** *pref* kontra-, mot-; **3** *vb* gå/kjempe *etc* (i)mot; *fig* imøtegå.

counter|act *vt* motvirke. **~balance 1** *sb* motvekt; **2** *vt* oppveie. **~feit 1** *adj* forfalsket, uekte; **2** *sb* forfalskning; **3** *vt* forfalske. **~feiter** *sb* falskmyntner. **~foil** *sb* talong (i sjekkhefte etc). **~mand 1** *sb* tilbakekalling; **2** *vt* oppheve; tilbakekalle. **~measure** *sb* mottiltak. **~pane** *sb* sengeteppe. **~part** *sb* motstykke. **~poise 1** *sb* likevekt; motvekt; **2** *vt* oppveie. **~sign 1** *sb* feltrop, passord; **2** *vt* kontrasignere. **~sink** *vt* forsenke (skruehode etc).

countess ['kauntɪs] *sb* grevinne (i England om *earl's* hustru, jf *count B*).

countless ['kauntlɪs] *adj* talløs, utallig.

country ['kʌntrɪ] *sb* **1** land (og folk, nasjon, stat); *the ~* folket, nasjonen; velgerne; *appeal to the ~* gå til valg; utskrive (ny)valg; **2** land, landsbygd; **3** = *~side.* **country | cousin** *sb dgl* gudsord fra landet. **~ gentleman** *sb* godseier. **~-house** *sb* **1** gods; **2** landsted. **~man** *sb* **1** mann fra landet; ≈ bonde; **2** landsmann. **~-seat** *sb* gods. **~side** *sb* **1** landskap, terreng; **2** distrikt. **~woman** *sb* **1** kvinne fra landet; ≈ bondekvinne; 2 landskvinne.

county ['kaʊntɪ] *sb* grevskap [nærmest tilsvarende norsk fylke].

coup [ku:] *sb* kupp; ~ *d'état* statskupp.

couple ['kʌpl] **I** *sb* **1** par; **2** kobbel; **II** *vb* **1** forene (seg); koble (sammen); **2** pare (seg) (om dyr).

coupon ['ku:pɒn] *sb* **1** kupong; *football* ~ tippekupong; **2** rasjoneringsmerke.

courage ['kʌrɪdʒ] *sb* mot, tapperhet. **courageous** [kə'reɪdʒəs] *adj* modig, tapper.

courier ['kʊrɪə] *sb* kurér, ilbud.

course [kɔ:s] **I** *sb* **1** (for)løp, gang; kurs, retning; bane; *in the* ~ *of* under, i løpet av; *in (the)* ~ *of time* omsider; *in due* ~ i sin tid; i tur og orden; *of* ~ naturligvis; *a matter of* ~ en selvfølge; **2** rekke, serie; kurs(us); **3** lag, skifte (av murstein etc): **4** (mat)rett; *main* ~ hovedrett; **5** *golf* ~ golfbane; *race-*~ veddeløpsbane; **II** *vb* **1** forfølge, jage; **2** flomme, rennne; styrte.

court [kɔ:t] **I** *sb* **1** *jur* rett (både om rettssalen og rettens medlemmer); ~ *of justice/law* domstol; *in* ~ i retten; *in the* ~ i rettssalen; *settle out of* ~ ordne i minnelighet; **2** hoff; *at* ~ ved hoffet; **3** (gårds)plass, gård; *tennis-*~ tennisbane; **4** kur, oppvartning; *pay* ~ *to* gjøre kur til; **II** *vb* **1** kurtisere; beile til; **2** søke; strebe etter; **3** utfordre; ~ *danger* leke med faren. **courteous** ['kɜ:tɪəs] *adj* **1** elskverdig; høflig; **2** høvisk. **courtesy** ['kɜ:tɪsɪ] *sb* **1** elskverdighet; høflighet; **2** høviskhet. **court-house** *sb* rettssal, tinghus. **courtier** ['kɔ:tɪə] *sb* hoffmann. **courtly** ['kɔ:tlɪ] *adj* høvisk. **court|-martial** *sb, vb* (stille for) krigsrett. **~ship** *sb* kurtise. **~yard** *sb* gårdsplass.

cousin ['kʌzn] *sb* **1** søskenbarn; fetter, kusine; *second* ~ tremenning; **2** *dgl* slektning.

cove [kəʊv] *sb* **A** bukt, liten vik; **B** *slang* fyr, kar.

covenant ['kʌvənənt] *sb, vb* (slutte) pakt.

Coventry ['kɒvəntrɪ]: *send to* ~ boikotte, fryse ut.

cover ['kʌvə] **I** *sb* **1** dekning, ly; skjulested; **2** beskyttelse; *air* ~ flydekning; **3** dekke; deksel, lokk; hette, kapsel; **4** sengeteppe, (ull)teppe; **5** innpakning, omslag; *under separate* ~ (med) separat (post); **6** innbinding; bind, perm; **7** skalkeskjul; *under* ~ *of* under dekke/foregivende av; **8** kuvert; **9** dekning (av gjeld, utlegg etc); **II** *vt* **1** dekke (over/til); kle, trekke; sette bind på; *fig* dekke (dvs betale gjeld etc); *om bussruter etc* betjene; *om journalister etc* referere; ~ *up* skjule; kle (godt) på; **2** beskytte; *~ed against* dekket (dvs forsikret) mot; **3** holde dekket (med skytevåpen etc); **4** inkludere, omfatte; ~ *a wide field* spenne over et vidt felt; **5** tilbakelegge. **cover address** *sb* dekkadresse. **coverage** ['kʌvərɪdʒ] *sb* dekning (og beskyttelse, forsikring, reportasje etc). **covering** ['kʌvərɪŋ] *sb* dekke (og deksel, lokk; futteral, trekk; hette, kapsel etc). **coverlet** ['kʌvəlɪt] *sb* sengeteppe.

covert **1** ['kʌvət] *adj* fordekt, hemmelig; **2** ['kʌvə(t)] *sb* dekning, skjulested; kratt.

covet ['kʌvɪt] *vt* begjære. **covetous** ['kʌvɪtəs] *adj* begjærlig (*of* etter).

cow [kaʊ] **I** *sb* **1** ku; **2** hunn (av f.eks. elefant, hval, sjiraff); **II** *vt* kue. **coward** ['kaʊəd] *sb* feiging. **cowardice** ['kaʊədɪs] *sb* feighet. **cowardly** ['kaʊədlɪ] *adj* **1** feig; **2** ynkelig. **cowbane** *sb* selsnepe.

cower ['kaʊə] *vi* krype sammen.

cow|hand *sb* fjøsrøkter, sveiser. **~herd** *sb* gjeter. **~house** *sb* fjøs.

cowl [kaʊl] *sb* **1** (munke)kutte; **2** (munke)hette; **3** (damp)hette, (røyk)hatt; (kjøler)kappe; (motor)panser.

cow|pox *sb* (ku)kopper. **~shed** *sb* (sommer)fjøs. **~slip** *sb* marianøkleband.

coxcomb ['kɒkskəʊm] *sb* **1** narrelue; **2** laps, snobb; viktigper.

coxswain ['kɒksweɪn, *blant sjøfolk* 'kɒksn] *sb* **1** kvartermester (i marinen); **2** cox (= rormann på kapproingsbåt).

coy [kɔɪ] *adj* blyg, unnselig (ofte på en skjelmsk måte); kokett.

CPU time *sb data* prosessortid (jf *central processing unit*).

crab [kræb] **I** *sb* **1** krabbe; **2** løpekatt (på kranutligger); **3** = *~-apple*; **II** *vt dgl* rakke ned på. **crab-apple** *sb* villeple. **crabbed** ['kræbɪd] *adj* **1** gretten, sur; **2** innviklet, vanskelig; **3** gnidret (om skrift). **crab-pot** *sb* teine.

crack [kræk] **I** *sb* **1** revne, sprekk; brudd; skår; **2** brak, drønn; **3** knall, (skarpt) smell; smekk; *fig* snert; **4** *dgl* øyeblikk; ~ *of dawn/day* daggry; **5** *dgl* mester; *som adj* elite-, topp-; **6** forsøk (*at* på); **7** *slang: wise-*~ vits; spydighet; **II** *vb* **1** knekke, knuse; slå i stykker; sprekke; **2** knalle, smelle; smekke; **3** *petro* krakke, spalte; **4** *dgl, slang:* ~ *a crib* begå (et) innbrudd; ~ *a joke* rive av seg en vits; ~ *up* ødelegge(s); krasje; *fig* bryte sammen. **cracked | gas** *sb petro* spaltet gass. ~ **gasoline** *sb petro* spaltet bensin. ~ **residue** *sb petro* spaltet (destillasjons)rest. **cracker** ['krækə] *sb* **1** (slags) kjeks; **2** *(fire-~)* kinaputt; **3** *(nut~s)* nøtteknekker. **cracking plant** *sb petro* spaltingsanlegg.

crackle ['krækl] **1** *sb* knitring *etc*; **2** *vi* knitre, sprake; smatre; knake.

cradle ['kreɪdl] **1** *sb* vugge; **2** *vt* vugge; legge (som) i vugge.

craft [krɑ:ft] *sb* **1** fag, håndverk; **2** dyktighet, evne; *ofte* (-)kunst; **3** knep, list; **4** fartøy(er), skip. **craftsman** ['krɑ:ftsmən] *sb* fagmann, håndverker. **crafty** ['krɑ:ftɪ] *adj* listig, slu.

crag [kræg] *sb* (berg)hammer, knaus; klippe. **craggy** ['krægɪ] *adj* forreven; klippefull.

cram [kræm] *vb* **1** proppe, stappe; **2** pugge.

cramp [kræmp] **A I** *sb* krampe(trekning); **II** *vt* **1** hemme, hindre; ~ *somebody's style (dgl)* hindre en i å utfolde seg; **2** forårsake krampe; **B** *sb, vt* (feste med) krampe(r). **cramped** [kræmpt] *adj* **1** krampaktig; **2** sammentrengt, trang; **3** gnidret (om skrift); **4** hemmet, hindret.

cranberry ['krænbərɪ] *sb* tranebær. **crane** [kreɪn] **I** *sb* **1** trane; **2** (heise)kran; **II** *vb* strekke hals. **crane operator** *sb* kranfører.

crank [kræŋk] **A 1** *sb* sveiv; **2** *vt* sveive (i gang etc); dreie (på); **B** *sb* original, særling. **crankshaft** ['kræŋkʃɑ:ft] *sb* veivaksel. **cranky** ['kræŋkɪ] *adj* **1** falleferdig, vaklevoren; **2** forskrudd, rar.

cranny ['krænɪ] *sb* revne, sprekk.

crape [kreɪp] *sb* sørgeflor, svart krepp.

craps [kræps] *sb slang* **1** *(crap-shooting)* terningspill; **2** *US* sludder, tøv.

crash [kræʃ] **A I** *sb* **1** kollisjon, sammenstøt; krasj, nedstyrtning; **2** brak; splintrende lyd; **3** sammenbrudd; konkurs, krakk; **II** *vb* **1** kollidere; krasje, styrte (ned); **2** bryte sammen; styrte sammen; gå over ende (dvs gå konkurs); **B** *sb* (håndkle)dreil. **crash-helmet** *sb* styrthjelm.

crass [kræs] *adj:* ~ *ignorance* grov uvitenhet; ~ *ingratitude* svart utakknemlighet.

crate [kreɪt] *sb* **1** pakkasse; (sprinkel)kasse; **2** *slang* skranglekasse.

crave [kreɪv] *vb* kreve; be om; ~ *for* lengte etter.

craven ['kreɪvn] **1** *adj* feig; **2** *sb* feiging.

craving ['kreɪvɪŋ] *sb* (indre) forlangende; trang.

crawl [krɔ:l] **I** *sb* **1** krabbing *etc*; **3** *the* ~ crawl (ing); **II** *vi* **1** krabbe, krype; kravle; snegle seg (av sted); ~ *to* krype (dvs smiske) for; **2** crawle; **3** kry/ myldre (*with* av); *it makes my flesh* ~ jeg får gåsehud av det.

crayfish ['kreɪfɪʃ] *sb* kreps.

crayon [kreɪən] *sb, vt* (tegne med) fargeblyant/ tegnekritt.

craze [kreɪz] *sb* galskap; mani; *dgl* dille; *the latest* ~ siste skrik. **crazy** ['kreɪzɪ] *adj* **1** (sinns)forvirret; **2** gal/tullet (*about* etter); vilt begeistret (*about* for); **3** sinnssvak, tåpelig; **4** forvirrende, rotet; **5** skakk, skjev; falleferdig.

creak [kri:k] **1** *sb* knirk(ing); **2** *vi* knirke.

cream [kri:m] **I** *sb* fløte, krem; *fig* elite; **II** *vt* **1** skumme fløten av; **2** tilsette fløte. **creamery** ['kri:mərɪ] *sb* meieri; melkebutikk. **creamy** ['kri:mɪ] *adj* fløteaktig; kremgul; *fig* glatt, myk.

crease [kri:s] **I** *sb* **1** brett, (presse)fold; **2** fure, rynke; **II** *vt* brette(s), krølle(s); presse(s). **crease|-less, ~proof** *adj* krøllfri.

create [krɪ'eɪt] *vt* **1** skape, frembringe; **2** *data* opprette; **3** forårsake; **4** utnevne til. **creation** [krɪ'eɪʃn] *sb* skapelse *etc.* **creative** [krɪ'eɪtɪv] *adj* skapende, kreativ. **creativity** [ˌkrɪə'tɪvətɪ] *sb* skaperevne. **creator** [krɪ'eɪtə] *sb* skaper. **creature** ['kri:tʃə] *sb* **1** skapning, vesen; **2** krøtter; **3** *fig* redskap; håndlanger.

credence ['kri:dəns] = *credit I 1.* **credentials** [krɪ'denʃəlz] *sb fl* (ak)kreditiver; anbefalingsbrev. **credibility** [ˌkredɪ'bɪlətɪ] *sb* troverdighet. **credible** ['kredəbl] *adj* troverdig. **credit** ['kredɪt] **I** *sb* **1** tillit, (til)tro; *give* ~ *to/place* ~ *in* feste lit til; **2** anerkjennelse; poeng (for deleksamen etc); *be/add to one's* ~ tale/ tjene til ens fordel; **3** anseelse; (godt) skussmål; **4** *merk* kredit(postering); kreditt; **II** *vt* **1** (til)tro; tro på; **2** godskrive; tillegge; *merk også* kreditere. **creditable** ['kredɪtəbl] *adj* aktverdig; fortjenstfull. **creditor** ['kredɪtə] *sb* kreditor. **credulity** [krɪ'dju:lətɪ] *sb* godtroenhet. **credulous** ['kredjuləs] *adj* godtroende, lettroende.

creed [kri:d] *sb* tro, trosbekjennelse.

creek [kri:k] *sb* 1 bukt, vik; **2** *US* bekk; bielv.

creep [kri:p] **I** *sb* **1** kryping *etc*; *fig* krypinn; smutthull; *the* ~*s* frysninger, gåsehud; **2** kryp, usling; **II** *vi* krype; liste/snike seg; *om planter* slynge seg. **creeper** ['kri:pə] *sb* **1** kryper (om forskjellige dyr og planter); slyngplante; **2** transportbånd; **3** *fl* (is)brodder, kramponger; lekedrakt, sparkebukse. **creepy** ['kri:pɪ] *adj* nifs, uhyggelig.

cremate [krɪ'meɪt] *vt* kremere. **cremation** [krɪ'meɪʃn] *sb* kremering; kremasjon. **crematorium** [ˌkremə'tɔ:rɪəm], **crematory** ['kremətərɪ] *sb* krematorium.

crescent ['kresnt] **I** *adj* **1** halvmåneformet; **2** tiltakende, voksende; **II** *sb* månesigd.

cress [kres] *sb* karse.

crest [krest] *sb* **1** kam, (fjær)topp; fjærbusk; våpen(merke); **2** kam (dvs bølgetopp, åsrygg etc). **crestfallen** ['krest,fɔ:lən] *adj* motfallen, nedtrykt.

crevasse [krɪ'væs] *sb* (bre)sprekk.

crevice ['krevɪs] *sb* (fjell)sprekk, revne.

crew [kru:] *sb* besetning, mannskap; flokk, gjeng.

crib [krɪb] **A I** *sb* **1** barneseng; **2** krybbe; **3** binge; **II** *vt* sperre/stenge inne; **B I** *sb* **1** plagiat; **2** fuskelapp (især kopiert oversettelse); **II** *vb* **1** plagiere; **2** fuske.

cricket ['krɪkɪt] *sb* **A** siriss; **B** cricket; *not* ~ *(dgl)* urealt, usportslig.

crime [kraɪm] *sb* forbrytelse. **criminal** ['krɪmɪnl] **1** *adj* forbrytersk, kriminell; **2** *sb* forbryter.

crimp [krɪmp] *vt* kruse, krølle. **crimping tool** *sb* avisoleringstang.

crimson ['krɪmzn] **1** *adj, sb* høyrød(t), karmosinrød(t); **2** *vb* farge høyrød(t); rødme.

cringe [krɪndʒ] *vi* krype (sammen); *fig* krype/ smiske (*before/to* for).

crinkle ['krɪŋkl] **1** *sb* krøll; rynke; **2** *vb* krølle (seg); rynke(s); sno.

cripple ['krɪpl] **1** *sb* krøpling; **2** *vt* forkrøple; lamme; helseslå.

crisis ['kraɪsɪs] *sb* **1** krise; **2** nødstilstand.

crisp [krɪsp] **I** *adj* **1** sprø; **2** frisk, skarp (om vind og vær); **3** småkruset; **4** fyndig; klar, konsis; **II** *sb fl* franske poteter; **III** *vb* bli/gjøre sprø *etc.*

criss-cross ['krɪskrɒs] **1** *adj* kryss-; **2** *adv, vb* (gå/ slå streker etc) på kryss og tvers.

criterion [kraɪ'tɪərɪən] *sb* kriterium.

critic ['krɪtɪk] *sb* kritiker. **critical** ['krɪtɪkl] *adj* kritisk. **criticism** ['krɪtɪsɪzəm] *sb* kritkkk. **criticize** ['krɪtɪsaɪz] *vb* kritisere.

croak [krəuk] **I** *sb* kvekk(ing) *etc*; **II** *vb* **1** kvekke; skrike (hest); **2** varsle ulykke; **3** *slang* krepere.

crochet ['krəuʃeɪ] **1** *sb* hekling, hekletøy; **2** *vb* hekle. **crochet-hook** *sb* heklenål.

crock [krɒk] **A** *sb* krukke; **B** *dgl* **I** *sb* **1** øk; **2** stakkar; **3** skranglekasse; **II** *vb:* ~ *up* knekke; ødelegge; bryte sammen; ~*ed up* skrøpelig; slått ut.

crony ['krəʊnɪ] *sb* kamerat, nær venn.

crook [krʊk] **I** *sb* **1** hake, krok; krumstav; **2** bøy, sving; **3** *slang* kjeltring; **II** *vb* bøye (seg); krøke(s). **crooked** ['krʊkɪd] *adj* kroket; *fig* uhederlig. **crooked hole** *sb petro* skjev brønn.

croon [kru:n] **1** *sb* nynning; **2** *vb* nynne, (små)-synge. **crooner** ['kru:nə] *sb* (slager)sanger, vokalist.

crop [krɒp] **A I** *sb* **1** avling; **2** mengde; flokk; **II** *vb* **1** beplante, tilså; **2** bære (avling); **3** ~ *up/out* dukke opp; **B I** *sb* snauklipt hår; **II** *vt* **1** snauklippe; **2** beite (av), (snau)gnage; **3** beskjære; kupere; stusse; **C** *sb* **1** (fugle)kro; *dgl* mave; **2** svepeskaft. **cropper** ['krɒpə] *sb* **1** *good* ~ vekst som gir god avling; **2** *dgl* fall; *fig* fiasko; *come a* ~ falle/styrte (ned); *fig* mislykkes; dumpe, stryke.

cross [krɒs] **I** *adj* **1** kryssende; skrå-, tverr-; **2** motsatt; mot- (om vind); **3** *dgl* gretten, sint; **II** *pref* kors-, kryss-, tverr-; **III** *sb* **1** kors; *fig* plage; **2** kryss, tverrstrek; *fig* strek i regningen; **3** krysning, mellomting; **IV** *vb* **1** krysse; gå *etc* (tvers) over; korse, legge i/over kors; ~ *my heart* kors på halsen; **2** motarbeide; **3** = ~-*-breed.* **cross|-country** *adj* terreng- (dvs som går på tvers av vei og sti); ~*-country race* terrengløp; *ofte* langrenn; ~*-country skiing* langrenn (på ski); *også* skiløping (i motsetning til hopp og alpine grener). ~**cut** *sb* snarvei. ~**-eyed** *adj* skjeløyd. **crossing** *sb* **1** kryssing *etc;* **2** (gate)kryss; **3** *(pedestrian* ~*)* fotgjengerovergang. **cross|patch** *sb* grinebiter, tverrpomp- ~**road** *sb* korsvei; *fl* veikryss. ~**walk** *sb* = *crossing 3.* ~**word** *sb* kryssord.

crotch [krɒtʃ] *sb* **1** kløft (mellom f.eks. gren og stamme); **2** skrev, skritt.

crouch [kraʊtʃ] **1** *sb* sammenkrøpet stilling; **2** *vi* krype sammen.

crow [krəʊ] **I** *sb* **1** kråke; **2** hanegal; **3** pludring; **II** *vi* **1** gale; **2** pludre; **3** godte seg. **crowbar** ['krəʊbɑ:] *sb* brekkjern; *dgl* kubein.

crowd [kraʊd] **I** *sb* **1** (folke)masse; **2** *dgl* flokk, gjeng; klikk; **3** haug; **II** *vb* **1** flokke seg; stimle sammen; **2** stue sammen; overlesse. **crowded** ['kraʊdɪd] *adj* overfylt, stappfullt.

crown [kraʊn] **I** *sb* **1** krone; *the Crown* kronen (dvs kongemakten); *jur* påtalemyndigheten; **2** krans (som seierstrofé etc); **3** (fjell)topp; (hatte)pull; isse; **II** *vt* **1** krone; bekranse; **2** avslutte; toppe. **crown | block** *sb petro etc* kronblokk, toppblokk. ~ **gear** *sb* kron|drev, -hjul. ~ **land** *sb* statsallmenning. **crow's|-feet** *sb fl* smilerynker (rundt øynene). ~**-nest** *sb sjø* utkikkstønne.

crucial ['kru:ʃl] *adj* avgjørende. **crucial | component** *sb* nøkkelkomponent. ~ **moment** *sb* kritisk øyeblikk.

crucible ['kru:səbl] *sb* smeltedigel; *fig* ildprøve.

crucifixion [ˌkru:sɪ'fɪkʃn] *sb* korsfestelse. **crucify** ['kru:sɪfaɪ] *vt* korsfeste.

crude [kru:d] **I** *adj* **1** rå, uraffinert; *fig* grov, primitiv; ~ *facts* nakne fakta; **2** uferdig; *fig* umoden; **II** *sb petro* = ~ *oil.* **crude | gas** *sb petro* rågass (dvs urenset gass). ~ **oil,** ~ **petroleum** *sb petro* råolje. ~ **tar** *sb petro* råtjære.

cruel ['krʊəl] *adj* grusom. **cruelty** ['krʊəltɪ] *sb* grusomhet.

cruet ['kru:ɪt] *sb* flaske (til kryddersaus etc). **cruet-stand** ['kru:ɪtstænd] *sb* bordoppsats.

cruise [kru:z] **I** *sb* kryss(tokt); cruise, sjøreise; seiltur; **II** *vi* **1** krysse; være på cruise (seiltur/sjøreise); **2** gå med marsjfart; *cruising speed* marsjfart. **cruiser** ['kru:zə] *sb* krysser; *cabin-*~ (større) motorbåt.

crumb [krʌm] *sb* smule. **crumble** ['krʌmbl] *vb* **1** smuldre (opp); falle fra hverandre; **2** forfalle, synke i grus. **crumple** ['krʌmpl] *vb* **1** krølle (seg); rynke(s); **2** ~ *up* falle (rase, synke etc) sammen.

crunch [krʌntʃ] **1** *sb* knasing *etc;* **2** *vb* knase, knuse; knitre, sprake.

crusade [kru:'seɪd] *sb, vb* (føre) korstog. **crusader** [kru:'seɪdə] *sb* korsfarer.

crush [krʌʃ] **I** *sb* **1** knusing; pressing; (presset) fruktsaft; **2** trengsel; **3** *dgl* forelskelse, svermeri; *have a* ~ *on* sverme for, være forelsket i; **II** *vb* **1** knuse(s); presse(s); *fig* undertrykke; **2** krølle (seg); rynke(s).

crust [krʌst] **1** *sb* (hardt) skall; skorpe; skare; **2** *vb (~ over)* skorpe seg; danne skare. **crustacean** [krʌ'steɪʃən] *sb* skalldyr. **crusty** ['krʌstɪ] *adj* skorpet (etc, jf *crust*); *fig* gretten, irritabel.

crutch [krʌtʃ] *sb* **1** krykke; **2** = *crotch 2.*

crux [krʌks] *sb* problem, problematisk punkt; springende punkt.

cry [kraɪ] **I** *sb* **1** rop, skrik; *a far/long cry from* langt fra; **2** gråt; *have a good* ~ (få) gråte ordentlig ut; **II** *vb* **1** rope, skrike; ~ *down* rakke ned på; ~ *off* sende avbud; trekke seg; ~ *up* slå stort opp; **2** gråte. **cry-baby** *sb* skrikerunge; *fig* sippe.

crypt [krɪpt] *sb* krypt. **cryptic** ['krɪptɪk] *adj* kryptisk, gåtefull.

crystal ['krɪstl] *sb* krystall; *US også* urglass. **crystalline** ['krɪstəlaɪn] *adj* krystallinsk; krystallklar, krystall-. **chrystallize** ['krɪstəlaɪz] *vb* krystallisere(s).

cub [kʌb] *sb* unge (av bjørn, rev, ulv, løve, tiger etc); valp; *fig* grønnskolling.

cube [kju:b] **I** *sb* **1** terning; **2** kubikktall; **II** *vt* opphøye i tredje potens. **cubic** ['kju:bɪk] *adj* **1** terningformet; **2** kubikk-. **cubicle** ['kju:bɪkl] *sb* lite avlukke/rom; kammers, kott.

cuckold ['kʌkəʊld] **1** *sb* hanrei; **2** *vt* bedra/sette horn på (ektemann).

cuckoo ['kʊku:] *sb* gjøk.

cucumber ['kju:'kʌmbə] *sb* agurk.

cud [kʌd] *sb: chew the* ~ tygge drøv; *især fig* diskutere/prate i det uendelige.

cuddle ['kʌdl] **I** *sb* kjæling *etc;* **II** *vb* **1** kjæle (med); omfavne; **2** ~ *up* krype sammen/inntil hverandre; (ligge og) kose seg.

cudgel ['kʌdʒəl] **1** *sb* klubbe, kølle; **2** *vt* slå med klubbe *etc*; ~ *one's brain* vri hjernen.

cue [kju:] *sb* **A** hint, vink; *på scenen* stikkord; **B 1** (biljard)kø; **2** hårpisk.

cuff [kʌf] **A I** *sb* **1** mansjett; *off the* ~ *(dgl)* improvisert; **2** *US* (bukse)oppbrett; **B 1** *sb* slag, (øre)fik; **2** *vt* fike til, slå. **cuff-link** ['kʌflɪŋk] *sb* mansjettknapp.

culminate ['kʌlmɪneɪt] *vi* kulminere. **culmination** [ˌkʌlmɪ'neɪʃn] *sb* kulminering; høydepunkt, kulminasjon.

culpable ['kʌlpəbl] *adj* (straff)skyldig; *fig* syndig. **culprit** ['kʌlprɪt] *sb* skyldig (person); forbryter; *fig* synder.

cult [kʌlt] *sb* kult(us), (guds)dyrkelse. **cultivate** ['kʌltɪveɪt] *vt* **1** dyrke (jord); **2** *fig* (ren)dyrke, utvikle; **3** *fig* dyrke, ha sterk og aktiv interesse for. **cultivated** ['kʌltɪveɪtid] *adj* dannet, kultivert. **cultivation** [ˌkʌltɪ'veɪʃn] *sb* dyrking *etc*. **cultivator** ['kʌltɪveɪtə] *sb* **1** jordbruker, (åker)dyrker; **2** kultivator(harv). **cultural** ['kʌltʃərəl] *adj* kulturell, kultur-. **culture** ['kʌltʃə] *sb* kultur (og (opp)dyrking, rendyrking, foredling, dannelse etc); sivilisasjon. **cultured** ['kʌltʃəd] *adj* kulturell; kultivert.

cumbersome ['kʌmbəsəm] *adj* besværlig, brysom; tungvint.

cumulative ['kju:mjʊlətɪv] *adj* kumulativ; (stadig) økende.

cunning ['kʌnɪŋ] **I** *adj* **1** listig, slu; **2** *dgl* flink; **3** *US* tiltrekkende; **II** *sb* **1** list, sluhet; **2** *gml* dyktighet.

cup [kʌp] **I** *sb* **1** kopp; beger (og *fig* vin); *in one's* ~ beruset; **2** *sport* pokal; **II** *vt* **1** forme (hendene) til en kopp; **2** koppe, koppsette. **cupboard** ['kʌbəd] *sb* skap. **cupboard-love** *sb* matfrieri.

cupidity [kju:'pɪdətɪ] *sb* grådighet, (penge)griskhet.

cupola ['kju:pələ] *sb* kuppel.

cuppa ['kʌpə] *sb (dgl = cup of tea)* kopp te.

cup-tie ['kʌptaɪ] *sb sport* cupkamp.

cur [kɜ:] *sb* kjøter.

curable ['kjʊərəbl] *adj* helbredelig. **curate** ['kjʊərət] *sb* kapellan. **curator** [kjʊə'reɪtə] *sb* konservator; bestyrer/direktør (for museum etc).

curb [kɜ:b] **I** *sb* **1** tøyle; **2** = *kerb*; **II** *vt* tøyle; *fig* holde i tømme; legge bånd på.

curd [kɜ:d] *sb (fl)* dravle, ostemasse. **curdle** ['kɜ:dl] *vb* (få melk etc til å) løpe sammen eller skille/skjære seg.

cure ['kjʊə] **I** *sb* **1** helbredelse; **2** hehandling, kur; **3** *data* kall; **II** *vb* **1** helbrede, kurere (*of* for); **2** avhjelpe; råde bot på; **3** konservere (ved å røyke, salte, speke, tørke etc).

curfew ['kɜ:fju] *sb* portforbud.

curio ['kjʊərɪəʊ] *sb* kuriositet, sjeldenhet; raritet. **curiosity** [ˌkjʊərɪ'ɒsətɪ] *sb* nysgjerrighet. **curious** ['kjʊərɪəs] *adj* **1** nysgjerrig; **2** merkverdig; uvanlig.

curl [kɜ:l] **1** *sb* krøll; ~ *of smoke* røykspiral; **2** *vb* kruse/krølle (seg); ~ *up* falle sammen; ~ *(oneself) up* rulle seg (dvs krype godt) sammen.

curlew ['kɜ:lju:] *sb* spove.

curling-pin *sb* krøllspenne.

curly ['kɜ:lɪ] *adj* krøllet, kruset.

currant ['kʌrənt] *sb* **1** *(red* ~*)* rips; **2** korint.

currency ['kʌrənsɪ] *sb* **1** myntsort, valuta; penger; **2** omløp, utbredelse; **3** gangbarhet; *data også* aktualitet; *gain* ~ bli alminnelig akseptert. **current** ['kʌrənt] **I** *adj* **1** gangbar, gjengs; akseptert; **2** aktuell, nåværende; løpende; ~ *affairs* ≈ aktuelt (i radio/TV); ~ *issue* siste nummer/utgave etc; **II** *sb* **1** strøm (også elektrisk); strømdrag; strømning; **2** (for)løp, gang; retning; tendens. **currently** ['kʌrəntlɪ] *adv* **1** for tiden *etc*; **2** stadig.

curriculum [kə'rɪkjʊləm] *sb* pensum.

curry ['kʌrɪ] **A 1** *sb* (matrett med) karri; **2** *vt* krydre/tilberede med karri; **B** *vt* **1** strigle; **2** berede (lær og skinn); **3** ~ *favour with* innynde seg hos.

curse [kɜ:s] **I** *sb* **1** forbannelse; **2** ed; **II** *vb* (for)banne.

cursor ['kɜ:sə] *sb data* markør. **cursory** ['kɜ:sərɪ] *adj* flyktig; overfladisk.

curt [kɜ:t] *adj* kort (og avvisende).

curtail [kɜ:'teɪl] *vt* korte av/inn på; beskjære; forkorte.

curtain ['kɜ:tn] **I** *sb* **1** gardin; forheng; *fig* slør; teppe; **2** *a)* (scene)teppe; *b)* teppefall; **II** *vt* henge gardin *etc* foran; ~ *off* dele av med forheng.

curtsey, curtsy ['kɜ:tsɪ] **1** *sb* kniks; neiing; *drop/make a* ~ neie; **2** *vi* neie.

curvature ['kɜ:vətʃə] *sb* krumning; bue. **curve** [kɜ:v] **1** *sb* kurve, sving; bue, bøy; krumning; **2** *vb* svinge; krumme (seg).

cushion ['kʊʃn] **I** *sb* **1** (sofa)pute; *fig* (støt)demper; **2** vant (på biljardbord); **II** *vt* støtte opp *etc* med puter; *fig* avbøte, dempe. **cushy** ['kʊʃɪ] *adj dgl* behagelig, lett.

cuss [kʌs] *slang* **1** *sb, vb = curse*; **2** *sb* fyr, kar. **cussed** ['kʌsɪd] *adj dgl* **1** forbannet; **2** gretten; vrang, vrien.

custard ['kʌstəd] *sb* **1** (slags) eggekrem; **2** vanilje|pudding, -saus.

custodian [kʌ'stəʊdɪən] *sb* oppsynsmann; vakt(mann), vokter; bestyrer. **custody** ['kʌstədɪ] *sb* **1** forvaring, varetekt; oppbevaring; **2** varetekt, varetektsfengsel.

custom ['kʌstəm] *sb* **1** skikk (og bruk); **2** regel, (sed)vane; **3** søkning; (fast) kundeforhold; **4** *fl* toll; *the Customs* tollvesenet, tollen; ~*s officer* tollfunksjonær, toller; **5** *US som pref* spesial|bestilt, -laget; bestillings-. **customary** ['kʌstəmərɪ] *adj* alminnelig, vanlig; hevdvunnen. **customer** ['kʌstəmə] *sb* **1** kunde; **2** *dgl* fyr, kar. **customize** ['kʌstəmaɪz] *vt* brukertilpasse; *dgl fig* skreddersy.

cut [kʌt] **I** *sb* **1** skjæring *etc*; **2** flenge, kutt, sår; **3** hugg, slag; **4** hakk, skår; **5** (av)klipp, utklipp; skive, stykke; (an)del, part; **6** *petro* fraksjon, utsnitt; **7** beskjæring, kutt(ing); nedsettelse; **8** fasong, snitt; utseende; **9** hipp, stikk; fornærmelse; *give her the* ~

overse henne; **10** (gjennom)skjæring; sti, tråkk; *short ~* snarvei; **11** klisjé, trykkplate; **II** *vb* **1** skjære (og hugge, kappe, klippe, kutte) av/opp/over; hugge (og klippe, skjære) til/ut; spikke/telgje (til); file/slipe (til); grave/hule (ut); felle; meie, slå; **2** skjære (seg); kastrere; såre (især *fig*); **3** begrense; beskjære; sløyfe; **4** løpe, stikke (av); *~ class/school* skulke skolen; *~ the red light* kjøre/gå mot rødt lys; **5** *~ the cards* ta av (i kortspill); *~ dead* behandle som luft; *~ a figure* gjøre inntrykk; opptre flott; *~ it fine* beregne (tiden) hårfint; *~ a friend* slå hånden av en venn; *~ no ice (with)* ikke komme noen vei (med); ikke forslå (duge/nytte) (mot); **6** *med adv/prep* ~ **across** skrå/ta en snarvei over; ~ **after** sette/skynde seg etter; ~ **at** hugge *etc* etter; *fig* forpurre, hindre; ~ **away** skjære *etc* vekk; stikke av; ~ **back** beskjære; ~ **down** hugge *etc* ned; beskjære; redusere; ~ **in** avbryte; kjøre brått inn (foran nettopp passert bil); ~ **into** gjøre innhugg i; avbryte; ~ **off** hugge *etc* av; koble ut; *fig* avskjære, isolere; slå hånden av; ~ **out** klippe (og hugge/skjære) ut; *dgl* kutte ut [dvs slutte med]; ~ **short** avbryte; stanse; forkorte; ~ **up** skjære *etc* opp; *fig* såre; *~ up rough* bli sint; slå seg vrang; **III** *pret og pp av II: ~ and dried* fiks og ferdig; *~ out for* bestemt for; egnet til; *(badly) ~ up, ~ to pieces (fig)* (sterkt) opprevet.

cutaway *sb* **1** sjakett, snippkjole; **2** røntgentegning (dvs tegning som viser det indre av maskiner etc).

cute [kju:t] *adj* **1** gløgg, skarp; **2** *US* nydelig, søt.

cut glass *sb* krystall(glass).

cutlass ['kʌtləs] *sb* huggert.

cutler ['kʌtlə] *sb* knivsmed. **cutlery** ['kʌtlərɪ] *sb* kniver; knivsmedarbeid.

cutlet ['kʌtlɪt] *sb* **1** kotelett; **2** filet.

cut | price *sb* lavpris. **~rate** *adj* rabatt-. **~throat** *sb* knivstikker; snikmorder; *som adj* morder-.

cutting ['kʌtɪŋ] **I** *adj* skjærende *etc* (jf *cut II*); *fig* sårende; **II** *sb* **1** skjæring *etc*; *press ~s* (avis)utklipp; **2** avlegger; **3** *fl petro* bor|kaks, -kutt.

cycle ['saɪkl] **I** *sb* **1** syklus; **2** sykkel; **II** *vi* **1** gå rundt; gå i ring; **2** sykle. **cyclic** ['saɪklɪk] *adj* syklisk. **cyclist** ['saɪklɪst] *sb* syklist. **cyclone** ['saɪkləun] *sb* syklon.

cylinder ['sɪlɪndə] *sb* sylinder. **cylindrical** [sɪ'lɪndrɪkl] *adj* sylindrisk.

cynic ['sɪnɪk] *sb* kyniker. **cynical** ['sɪnɪkl] *adj* kynisk. **cynicism** ['sɪnɪsɪzəm] *sb* kynisme.

czar [zɑ:] *sb* tsar.

D

dab [dæb] **I** *sb* **1** dask, klaps; **2** klatt, (liten) smule; **II** *vb* **1** berøre lett; daske, klapse; **2** klatte, skvette; **3** drive/pusle (*at/in* med).

dad [dæd], **daddy** ['dædɪ] *sb dgl* pappa.

daffodil ['dæfədɪl] *sb* påskelilje.

dagger ['dægə] *sb* dolk.

daily ['deɪlɪ] **I** *adj, adv* daglig; **II** *sb* **1** *(~ newspaper)* (dags)avis; **2** daghjelp.

dainty ['deɪntɪ] **I** *adj* **1** elegant; lekker; **2** kresen; **II** *sb* delikatesse, godbit.

dairy ['deərɪ] *sb* **1** meieri; melkebutikk; **2** melkebu. **dairymaid** ['deərɪmeɪd] *sb* budeie; meierske.

dais ['deɪɪs] *sb* podium, plattform.

daisy ['deɪzɪ] *sb* **1** tusenfryd; *push up the daisies (dgl)* ligge under torva (dvs være død); **2** *dgl* knupp, perle; prakteksemplar. **daisywheel** *sb data* typehjul. **daisywheel printer** *sb data* typehjulsskriver.

dally ['dælɪ] *vb* **1** flørte; kjæle; **2** *~ with* leke med (i tankene).

dam [dæm] **A** **1** *sb* dam, demning; **2** *vt: ~ up* demme opp; **B** *sb* (dyre)mor.

damage ['dæmɪdʒ] **I** *sb* **1** skade (på ting); **2** tap (på grunn av skade); *fl* (skades)erstatning; **II** *vt* skade.

dame [deɪm] *sb* **1** dame, frue; **2** *US slang* jente, kvinnfolk.

damn [dæm] **I** *interj slang* fordømt! pokker! **II** *sb slang: I don't care a ~* jeg gir blaffen/pokker; **III** *vt* **1** dømme (til evig fortapelse); **2** forbanne, fordømme; **3** *slang: ~ it all!* pokker ta hele greia! **damnable** ['dæmnəbl] *adj* **1** fordømmelig, forkastelig; **2** *dgl* elendig, fæl. **damnation** [dæm'neɪʃn] **I** *interj* fordømt! pokker (også)! **II** *sb* **1** fortapelse; **2** forbannelse.

damp [dæmp] **I** *adj* fuktig, klam, rå; **II** *sb* **1** fuktighet; **2** *fig* demper; **III** *vt* **1** fukte; **2** dempe/legge en demper på. **dampen** ['dæmpən] **1** = *damp III*; **2** bli fuktig.

damsel ['dæmzl] *sb gml* jomfru, ungpike.

dance [dɑ:ns] **I** *sb* dans (og dansemoro); **II** *vb* **1** danse; **2** = *dandle*. **dancer** ['dɑ:nsə] *sb* danser(inne).

dandelion ['dændɪlaɪən] *sb* løvetann.

dandle ['dændl] *vt* huske (opp og ned, f.eks. på fanget); ride ranke med.

dandy ['dændɪ] **1** *adj dgl* kjempefint, flott; **2** *sb* laps, snobb.

danger ['deɪndʒə] *sb* **1** fare (og faresignal); *in ~ (of)* i fare (for); **2** risiko. **dangerous** ['deɪndʒərəs] *adj* farlig; farefull, risikabel.

dangle ['dæŋgl] *vb* dingle (med); henge og dingle.

dank [dæŋk] *adj* klam, rå.

dapper ['dæpə] *adj* pertentlig.

dappled ['dæpld] *adj, pp* droplet, flekket.

dare ['deə] **I** *sb* utfordring; **II** *vb* **1** tore, våge; **2** driste seg til (å); **3** trosse; utfordre. **dare-devil** ['deədevl] *sb* våghals. **daring** ['deərɪŋ] **I** *adj* **1** dristig, vågal; **2** frekk; **II** *sb* vågemot.

dark [dɑ:k] **1** *adj* mørk (og dunkel; dyster, hemmelig(hetsfull), mystisk etc); **2** *sb fig (~ness)* mørke; uvitenhet. **darken** ['dɑ:kn] *vb* mørkne; *fig* formørke(s). **dark oil** *sb petro* mørk (smøre)olje.

darling ['dɑ:lɪŋ] **1** *adj dgl* henrivende, yndig; søt; **2** *sb* kjæreste; *dgl* skatten/vennen min *etc*.

darn [dɑ:n] **A 1** *sb* stopp; **2** *vb* stoppe (strømper etc); **B** *(= damned)* **1** *især adv* fordømt, pokkers; **2** *interj (~ it)* søren (også)!

dart [dɑ:t] **I** *sb* **1** sett; (plutselig) sprang; **2** kastepil; *fl* (pilkastspillet) darts; **II** *vb* **1** fare, pile, styrte; **2** kaste, slenge, slynge.

dash [dæʃ] **A I** *sb* **1** brå bevegelse; sprang; fremstøt; futt (og fart); **2** sprint, spurt; **3** dråpe, skvett; *fig også* anelse, tanke; **4** skvalp(ing), skvulp(ing); **5** klask, slag; **6** (penne)strøk; (tanke)strek; **II** *vb* **1** fare, styrte; sprinte, spurte; **2** slenge, slynge; *~ off* få unna i en fei; rable ned; **3** plaske; skvette; **4** knuse; **B** = *darn B 2*. **dashing** ['dæʃɪŋ] *adj* **1** (feiende) flott; **2** dristig.

dastard ['dæstəd] *sb* feiging; (feig) bølle. **dastardly** ['dæstədlɪ] *adj* feig; simpel.

data ['deɪtə] *sb fl* **1** informasjon, opplysninger; fakta; **2** *data (som oftest med vb i ent)* data (for elektronisk behandling). **data | bank** *sb data* databank. **~ base** *sb data* database. **~ card** *sb data* hullkort. **~ entry** *sb data* datainngang. **~ item** *sb data* dataelement. **~ processing** *sb data* databehandling. **~ safety** *sb data* datasikkerhet. **~ security** *sb data* datavern; ≈ personvern. **~ transfer/transmission** *sb data* dataoverføring.

date [deɪt] **A I** *sb* **1** dato, datum; *out of ~* avleggs; *to ~* (inn)til nå; **2** årstall; tidspunkt; periode; **2** *dgl, især US* stevnemøte; fast følge, kjæreste; **II** *vb* **1** datere; **2** tidfeste; *~ back to/from* skrive seg fra; **3** foreldes; **4** *dgl, især US* avtale stevnemøte; ha (fast) følge/gå ut (med); **B** *sb* daddel(palme). **dated** ['deɪtɪd] *adj* avleggs, foreldet.

daub [dɔ:b] **I** *sb* smøreri; **II** *vb* **1** smøre på (maling etc); klatte, skvette; **2** kline til.

daughter ['dɔ:tə] *sb* datter. **daughter-in-law** ['dɔ:trɪn,lɔ:] *sb* svigerdatter.

daunt [dɔ:nt] *vt* kue; ta motet fra. **dauntless** *adj* uforferdet; ukuelig.

dawdle ['dɔ:dl] *vb* somle/søle (*away* bort); drive dank. **dawdler** ['dɔ:dlə] *sb* somlekopp.

dawn [dɔ:n] **1** *sb* daggry; **2** *vi* demre, gry; *~ (up)on* demre/gå opp for.

day [deɪ] *sb* **1** *(~-time)* dag; *~-by-~, ~-to-~* daglig; *one of these (fine) ~s* en vakker dag; med det første; *some ~* en dag (i fremtiden); *the other ~* forleden (dag); *to a ~* (akkurat) på dagen; **2** *(~ and night)* døgn; **3** *fl* periode, tid; *in ~s to come* i dagene/tiden som kommer.

daze [deɪz] **1** *sb* forvirring, ørske; **2** *vt* gjøre fortumlet (forvirret, ør etc); bedøve. **dazzle** ['dæzl] **1** *sb* glitring; blendende glans/lysskjær etc; **2** *vt* blende; forvirre.

deacon ['di:kən] *sb* **1** diakon; **2** hjelpeprest.

dead [ded] **I** *adj* **1** død (og livløs; utdødd; følelsesløs; matt, vissen, ugyldig; *dgl, slang* dau, kjip, trøtt); *~ body* lik; **2** *dgl* akkurat, nøyaktig; *in ~ earnest* på ramme alvor; **II** *adv* **1** dødsens; død(s)-; **2** fullstendig; absolutt; *~ against* stikk imot; *~ ahead* rett forut; *~ calm* blikk stille; *~ certain* skråsikker; *~ set on* fast bestemt på; **III** *sb* **1** *the ~* de døde; **2** *in the ~ of night/winter* midt på natten/vinteren. **deaden** ['dedn] *vt* **1** dempe; (av)svekke; **2** døyve; sløve. **dead | end** *sb* blindgate. **~ heat** *sb* dødt løp. **~line** *sb* siste frist. **~lock** *sb fig* vranglås (også *data*); blindgate; stampe. **~ly** *adj, adv* dødelig (og dødbringende); livsfarlig; drepende. **~ oil** *sb petro* avgasset olje. **~pan** *dgl* **1** *adj* uttrykksløs; **2** *sb (~pan face)* pokerfjes; uttrykksløst ansikt. **~ race** = *dead heat*. **~ well** *sb petro* død brønn.

deaf [def] *adj* døv, tunghørt. **deaf-aid** ['defeɪd] *sb* høreapparat. **deafen** ['defn] *vt* **1** gjøre døv; **2** lydisolere. **deafening** ['defnɪŋ] *adj* øredøvende. **deaf-mute** [,def'mju:t] *adj* døvstum.

deal [di:l] **A** *sb* mengde; *a good/great ~* en hel del, temmelig mye; **B I** *sb* **1** forretning, handel; *fair/square ~* real behandling; *it's a ~* det er en avtale; **2** tur til å gi (i kortspill); *new ~* ny sjanse; **II** *vb* **1** fordele; gi, tildele; **2** handle (*in* med; *at/with* hos); **3** *~ with* behandle; ta seg av; handle om; **C** *sb* furu (og gran, som materiale). **dealer** ['di:lə] *sb* handelsmann, (-)handler.

dean [di:n] *sb* **1** (dom)prost; **2** dekan(us).

dear ['dɪə] **I** *adj* **1** kjær; *dgl* søt (og snill); **2** dyrebar, verdifull; *for ~ life (dgl)* for bare livet; **3** dyr, kostbar; **II** *adv (~ly)* **1** dyrt, dyrekjøpt; **2** dyrt, kostbart; **3** inderlig; **III** *interj: ~ me! oh ~!* du slette tid! **IV** *sb dgl* elskede, kjære(ste).

dearth [dɜ:θ] *sb* knapphet, nød.

death [deθ] *sb* død, dødsfall; døden; *be bored to ~* (holde på å) kjede livet av seg. **death|-bed** *sb* dødsleie. **~-blow** *sb, også fig* dødsstøt; (drepende) slag. **~ly** *adj, adv* dødelig; dødsens; døds-. **~-rate** *sb* dødelighetsprosent, dødelighet. **~-roll** *sb* (liste over) drepte/omkomne. **~sentence** *sb* dødsdom. **~-warrant** *sb fig* dødsdom.

debar [dɪ'bɑ:] *vt* utelukke/stenge ute (*from* fra); hindre (*from* i).

debase [dɪ'beɪs] *vt* **1** forringe; **2** fornedre.

debate [dɪ'beɪt] **1** *sb* debatt; **2** *vb* debattere, diskutere (især offentlig). **debatable** [dɪ'beɪtəbl] *adj* diskutabel, omtvistet.

debauch [di'bɔ:tʃ] **1** *sb* utskeielse; **2** *vt* forderve; forlede til umoral etc. **debauched** [dɪ'bɔ:tʃt] *adj* ryggesløs, utsvevende. **debauchery** [dɪ'bɔ:tʃərɪ] *sb* ryggesløshet; *fl også* orgier.

debonair [ˌdebə'neə] *adj* munter, sorgløs; beleven.

debris ['deɪbrɪ] *sb* ruiner; rester.

debt [det] *sb* gjeld; *out of* ~ gjeldfri; *get/run into* ~ pådra seg/sette seg i gjeld. **debtor** ['detə] *sb* debitor, skyldner.

debug [dɪ'bʌg] *vt* avluse (også *data*).

decay [dɪ'keɪ] **1** *sb* forfall; forråtnelse, oppløsning; **2** *vi* forfalle; morkne, råtne; gå i oppløsning.

decease [dɪ'si:s] **1** *sb* død; **2** *vi* dø; *the ~d* (den) avdøde; de døde.

deceit [dɪ'si:t] *sb* bedrag(eri); falskhet, svik. **deceitful** [dɪ'si:tfʊl] *adj* falsk, svikefull. **deceive** [dɪ'si:v] *vt* **1** bedra; narre; *~d into* forledet/lurt til (å); **2** skuffe; *~d in* skuffet over.

decency ['di:sənsɪ] *sb* anstendighet *etc*. **decent** ['di:sənt] *adj* **1** anstendig, sømmelig; ærbar; **2** rett, riktig; respektabel; **3** *dgl* grei, real; skikkelig.

deception [dɪ'sepʃn] *sb* **1** bedrag(eri); **2** skuffelse. **deceptive** [dɪ'septɪv] *adj* **1** bedragersk; villedende; **2** skuffende.

decide [dɪ'saɪd] *vb* **1** avgjøre; **2** beslutte; bestemme seg; *what ~d you to* hva fikk deg til å.

deciduous [dɪ'sɪdjʊəs] *adj* som feller (bladene om høsten). **deciduous trees** *sb fl* løvtrær.

decimal ['desɪml] *adj* desimal-. **decimal | digit** *sb data etc* desimalsiffer. ~ **notation** *sb data* desimalnotasjon. ~ **numeral** *sb* desimaltall.

decimate ['desɪmeɪt] *vt* desimere; utrydde et meget stort antall [egentlig hver tiende person i en gruppe].

decision [dɪ'sɪʒn] *sb* **1** avgjørelse; beslutning; **2** besluttsomhet, fasthet. **decisive** [dɪ'saɪsɪv] *adj* **1** avgjørende; **2** bestemt; endelig.

deck [dek] **I** *sb* **1** (båt)dekk; **2** *især US (~ of cards)* (kort)stokk; **II** *vt* **1** dekorere, pynte; **2** legge dekk på.

declaim [dɪ'kleɪm] *vb* **1** deklamere; **2** ~ *against* ta kraftig til orde mot. **declamation** [ˌdeklə'meɪʃn] *sb* deklamering *etc*.

declaration [ˌdeklə'reɪʃn] *sb* **1** proklamasjon; **2** erklæring, uttalelse; **3** angivelse; (toll)deklarasjon; ~ *of income* lønnsoppgave. **declare** [dɪ'kleə] *vb* **1** proklamere; kunngjøre, offentliggjøre; ~ *war* erklære krig; **2** erklære, uttale; hevde, påstå; **3** deklarere; angi, oppgi; *have you anything to* ~ har De noe å fortolle; **4** melde (i kortspill).

decline [dɪ'klaɪn] **I** *sb* forfall; nedgang, tilbakegang; *også* svekkelse; **II** *vb* **1** nekte; **2** avslå; avstå fra; **3** redusere(s); minke; **4** helle; skråne (utfor); dale, synke; gå ned; *declining years* siste leveår; **5** forfalle; svekke(s); **6** *gram* bøye (substantiv). **declivity** [dɪ'klɪvətɪ] *sb* helling.

decode [dɪ'kəʊd] *vt* dechiffrere, tyde; *data også* dekode.

decompose [ˌdi:kəm'pəʊz] *vb* **1** bryte(s) ned; spalte(s); **2** råtne; gå i oppløsning. **decomposition** [di:ˌkɒmpə'zɪʒn] *sb* **1** nedbrytning *etc*; **2** forråtnelse.

decorate ['dekəreɪt] *vt* **1** dekorere; pynte, (ut)smykke; pusse opp; **2** dekorere (med orden). **decoration** [ˌdekə'reɪʃn] *sb* dekorasjon *etc*. **decorative** ['dekrətɪv] *adj* dekorativ. **decorator** ['dekəreɪtə] *sb* dekoratør; *interior ~ (ofte)* interiørarkitekt. **decorous** ['dekərəs] *adj* anstendig, sømmelig, tekkelig. **decorum** [dɪ'kɔ:rəm] *sb* anstendighet *etc*.

decoy ['di:kɔɪ] **1** *sb* lokkefugl; **2** *vt* lokke/lure (i felle).

decrease **1** ['di:kri:s] *sb* nedgang; reduksjon; svinn; **2** [dɪ'kri:s] *vb* forminske, redusere; avta, minke.

decree [dɪ'kri:] **I** *sb* **1** dekret, forordning; **2** *jur* kjennelse; **II** *vb* dekretere, forordne; påby.

decrepit [dɪ'krepɪt] *adj* avfeldig; skrøpelig. **decrepitude** [dɪ'krepɪtju:d] *sb* avfeldighet; skrøpelighet.

decry [dɪ'kraɪ] *vt* **1** rakke ned på; **2** nedvurdere.

dedicate ['dedɪkeɪt] *vt* **1** hellige, vigsle; **2** vie; ~ *oneself to* gå helt (og fullt) inn for; **3** dedisere, tilegne; **4** *data etc* reservere. **dedication** [ˌdedɪ'keɪʃn] *sb* **1** innvielse *etc*; **2** dedikasjon, tilegnelse; **3** målbevissthet; plikttroskap.

deduce [dɪ'dju:s] *vt* avlede/slutte (seg til, *from* av, fra). **deduct** [dɪ'dʌkt] ta bort; trekke fra. **deduction** [dɪ'dʌkʃn] *sb* **1** konklusjon, slutning; **2** fradrag, rabatt.

deed [di:d] *sb* **1** dåd; handling; **2** *jur* dokument; *især* skjøte.

deem [di:m] anse; anslå; mene.

deep [di:p] **1** *adj* dyp; dyptliggende; **2** *adv (~ly)* dypt; **3** *sb* dybde; (hav)dyp. **deepen** ['di:pən] *vb* fordype(s); bli/gjøre dypere. **deep|-freeze** **1** *sb* dypfryser, fryseboks; **2** *vt* dypfryse. **~-rooted** *adj* rotfestet. **~-seated** **~-set** *adv* dyptliggende, rotfestet.

deer ['dɪə] *sb* hjort, (hjorte)dyr.

deface [dɪ'feɪs] *vt* skamfere, vansire; ødelegge (innskrift etc).

defamation [ˌdefə'meɪʃn] *sb* ærekrenkelse. **defamatory** [dɪ'fæmətərɪ] *adj* ærekrenkende. **defame** [dɪ'feɪm] *vt* ærekrenke; vanære.

default [di'fɔ:lt] **I** *sb* **1** uteblivelse; *win by* ~ vinne ved walkover; **2** (plikt)forsømmelse; **3** *data* normal-, standard-; **II** *vi* **1** utebli (især fra retten); **2** forsømme seg. **default | option** *sb data* normalbetingelse. ~ **value** *sb data* normalverdi.

defeat [dɪ'fi:t] **1** *sb* nederlag, tap; skuffelse, tilbakeslag; **2** *vt* overvinne; slå (tilbake).

defect [dɪ'fekt] **1** *sb* feil, lyte, mangel; **2** *vi* svikte; *pol* hoppe av. **defective** [dɪ'fektɪv] *adj* mangelfull; manglende. **defector** [dɪ'fektə] *sb* avhopper, overløper.

defence [dɪ'fens] *sb* forsvar (og forsvars|verk(er), -våpen); *the ~ (jur)* forsvaret. **defend** [dɪ'fend] *vt* forsvare, verge. **defendant** [dɪ'fendənt] *sb jur: the* ~

(den) anklagede/saksøkte. **defense** [dɪ'fens] *US* = *defence*. **defensible** [dɪ'fensəbl] *adj* forsvarlig. **defensive** [dɪ'fensɪv] *adj* defensiv, forsvars-.

defer [dɪ'fɜ:] **A** *vt* utsette; vente med; **B** *vi: ~ to* bøye seg for; respektere. **deference** ['defərəns] *sb: in ~ to* av respekt for. **deferential** [ˌdefə'renʃl] *adj* respektfull; ærbødig. **deferment** [dɪ'fɜ:mənt] *sb* utsettelse.

defiance [dɪ'faɪəns] *sb* trass, tross; forakt; *bid ~ to* trasse, trosse; utfordre; gjøre/yte motstand mot; *in ~ of* stikk imot; trass i, til tross for. **defiant** [dɪ'faɪənt] *adj* trassig; utfordrende.

deficiency [dɪ'fɪʃənsɪ] *sb* mangel; manko, underskudd. **deficient** [dɪ'fɪʃənt] *adj* mangelfull. **deficit** ['defɪsɪt] *sb* mangel; manko, underskudd.

defile A ['dɪfaɪl] **1** *sb* (trangt) pass; **2** *vi* defilere; **B** [dɪ'faɪl] *vt* forurense, skitne til.

define [dɪ'faɪn] *vt* **1** definere; **2** avgrense, begrense. **definite** ['definɪt] *adj* bestemt; nøyaktig (avgrenset etc). **definitely** ['definɪtlɪ] *adv, især dgl* avgjort; javisst; sikkert. **definition** [ˌdefɪ'nɪʃn] *sb* **1** definisjon; **2** avgrensning; **3** tydelighet.

deflate [dɪ'fleɪt] *vt* **1** ta luften ut av (ballong etc); **2** deflatere. **deflation** [dɪ'fleɪʃn] *sb* **1** tømming for luft; **2** deflasjon.

deflect [dɪ'flekt] *vb* (få til å) bøye av; *fig også* avvike.

defoam [dɪ'fəʊm] *vt petro etc* (av)skumme.

deform [dɪ'fɔ:m] *vt* forkrøple, misdanne. **deformed** [dɪ'fɔ:md] *adj* forkrøplet, misdannet, vanskapt. **deformity** [dɪ'fɔ:mətɪ] *sb* misdannethet, vanskapthet.

defraud [dɪ'frɔ:d] *vt* bedra, snyte.

defray [dɪ'freɪ] *vt* bestride (betaling, utlegg); betale.

deft [deft] *adj* fingernem; dyktig, flink; (be)hendig.

defunct [dɪ'fʌŋkt] *adj* **1** død; **2** avleggs; ugyldig.

defy [dɪ'faɪ] *vt* **1** trasse, trosse; gjøre/yte motstand mot; **2** utfordre; *I ~ you to* du klarer aldri i verden å; **3** vise forakt (for).

degas [dɪ'gæs] *vt petro* avgasse, (av)lufte.

degenerate 1 [dɪ'dʒenərət] *adj, sb* degenerert (person); **2** [dɪ'dʒenəreɪt] *vi* degenerere; utarte. **degeneration** [dɪˌdʒenə'reɪʃn] *sb* degenerering *etc*; degenerasjon.

degradation [ˌdegrə'deɪʃn] *sb* **1** degradering; **2** forfall; fornedrelse. **degrade** [dɪ'greɪd] *vt* **1** degradere; **2** fornedre; nedverdige.

degree [dɪ'gri:] *sb* **1** grad; *by ~s* gradvis; *to a ~ (dgl)* til de grader; **2** rang; trinn; **3** (akademisk) grad.

deify ['di:ɪfaɪ] *vt* opphøye til gud; forherlige.

deign [deɪn] *vt* verdige(s); nedlate seg (*to* til å).

deity ['deɪətɪ] *sb* guddommelighet; gud, guddom.

dejected [dɪ'dʒektɪd] *adj* motløs; nedslått. **dejection** [dɪ'dʒekʃn] *sb* motløshet.

delay [dɪ'leɪ] **I** *sb* forsinkelse *etc*; **II** *vb* **1** forsinke, oppholde; **2** utsette; **3** nøle; vente med.

delectable [dɪ'lektəbl] *adj* behagelig; *ofte iron* deilig.

delegate I ['delɪgət] *adj* delegert, utsending; representant; **II** ['delɪgeɪt] *vt* **1** oppnevne (som representant); **2** betro (oppgave etc); delegere/overdra (ansvar etc). **delegation** [ˌdelɪ'geɪʃn] *sb* **1** delegering *etc*; **2** delegasjon.

delete [dɪ'li:t] *vt* stryke (ut), (ut)slette; *~ as required* stryk det som ikke passer. **deletion** [dɪ'li:ʃn] *sb* (ut)stryking, strykning.

deliberate I [dɪ'libərət] *adj* **1** overlagt; *nå ofte* bevisst; **2** sindig, veloverveid; **II** [dɪ'lɪbəreɪt] *vb* **1** overveie; tenke (grundig) igjennom; **2** rådslå. **deliberation** [dɪˌlɪbə'reɪʃn] *sb* **1** forsett, overlegg; **2** overveielse, rådslagning; **3** omhu, sindighet.

delicacy ['delɪkəsɪ] *sb* **1** finhet *etc*; **2** delikatesse. **delicate** ['delɪkət] *adj* **1** fin; **2** bløt, myk; **3** *især fig* hårfin; **4** forfinet; **5** fintfølende; sart; **6** skrøpelig, svak(elig) syk(elig); **7** prippen; pyset; **8** kinkig, vanskelig; **9** delikat, lekker. **delicious** [dɪ'lɪʃəs] *adj* deilig, lekker; herlig. **delight** [dɪ'laɪt] **1** *sb* fryd/glede (*in* over, ved); **2** *vb* fryde/glede seg (*in* over, ved). **delighted** [dɪ'laɪtɪd] *adj, pp* henrykt, svært glad; *I shall be ~* det skal være meg en (stor) fornøyelse/glede. **delightful** [dɪ'laɪtfʊl] *adj* deilig, festlig; bedårende, fortryllende.

delineate [dɪ'lɪnɪeɪt] *vt* skissere; streke opp.

delinquency [dɪ'lɪŋkwənsɪ] *sb* **1** (plikt)forsømmelse; **2** forseelse, lovovertredelse; *juvenile ~* ungdomskriminalitet. **delinquent** [dɪ'lɪŋkwənt] **1** *adj* forsømmelig; skyldig; **2** *sb* forbryter, lovovertreder; *dgl* synder.

delirious [dɪ'lɪrɪəs] *adj* **1** forvirret, omtåket; delirisk; **2** *dgl* himmelhenrykt, vilt begeistret.

deliver [dɪ'lɪvə] *vt* **1** (av)levere, overlevere; rette/slå (slag); fremføre/holde (tale); **2** (be)fri; frelse, redde; **3** forløse; *be ~ed of* nedkomme med (dvs føde). **deliverance** [dɪ'lɪvərəns] *sb* befrielse, frelse *etc*. **delivery** [dɪ'lɪvərɪ] *sb* **1** (av)levering *etc*; (post)ombæring; **2** fremføring (av f.eks. tale); **3** forløsning, nedkomst (dvs fødsel). **delivery van** *sb* varebil.

delude [dɪ'lu:d] *vt* lure, narre.

deluge ['delju:dʒ] **1** *sb* flom; syndflod; **2** *vt* oversvømme.

delusion [dɪ'lu:ʒn] *sb* (selv)bedrag; illusjon. **delusive** [dɪ'lu:sɪv] *adj* bedragersk; villedende.

delve [delv] *vb, nå især fig* grave.

demand [dɪ'mɑ:nd] **I** *sb* **1** krav; *også* nota, regning; *on ~* på forlangende; **2** etterspørsel; *in (great) ~* (sterkt) etterspurt; **II** *vt* forlange (å få vite); kreve.

demarcate ['di:mɑ:keɪt] *vt* trekke opp grense(linje); avgrense, begrense. **demarcation** [ˌdi:mɑ:'keɪʃn] *sb* avgrensing; demarkasjon.

demean [dɪ'mi:n] *vt: ~ oneself* skjemme seg ut; nedverdige seg. **demeanour** [dɪ'mi:nə] *sb* oppførsel; holdning.

demented [dɪ'mentɪd] *adj* gal; (sinns)forvirret; *dgl* fra seg, ute av seg.

demise [dɪ'maɪz] **I** *sb* **1** bortgang, død; **2** overdragelse; **II** *vt* overdra.

demob [dɪ'mɒb] *dgl* = *demobilize*. **demobilization** [dɪˌməʊbəlaɪ'zeɪʃn] *sb* demobilisering. **demobilize** [dɪ'məʊbɪlaɪz] *vt* demobilisere, dimittere.

democracy [dɪ'mɒkrəsɪ] *sb* demokrati. **democrat** ['deməkræt] *sb* **1** demokrat; **2** *US: Democrat* medlem av Det demokratiske parti. **democratic** [ˌdemə'krætɪk] *adj* demokratisk.

demolish [dɪ'mɒlɪʃ] *vt* rive ned; rasere, ødelegge. **demolition** [ˌdemə'lɪʃn] *sb* (ned)riving *etc*; rivning.

demon ['di:mən] *sb* demon, djevel. **demoniac** [dɪ'məʊnɪæk] **1** *adj* demonisk, djevelsk; **2** *sb* besatt (person).

demonstrate ['demənstreɪt] *vb* demonstrere, påvise; vise frem. **demonstration** [ˌdemən'streɪʃn] *sb* demonstrasjon *etc*.

demur [dɪ'mɜ:] **1** *sb* nøling; **2** ~ *at/to* nøle med (å); gjøre innsigelser/komme med innvendinger mot (å).

demure [dɪ'mjʊə] *adj* **1** kokett, skjelmsk; **2** (ofte tilgjort) alvorlig, beskjeden; stillferdig.

den [den] *sb* **1** hi; *dgl* hule (også om lite arbeidsrom etc); **2** bule, reir.

denial [dɪ'naɪəl] *sb* (be)nektelse *etc* (jf *deny*).

denizen ['denɪzn] *sb* **1** innbygger (også om stedegne dyr og planter); **2** (samfunns)borger; **3** naturalisert statsborger.

denomination [dɪˌnɒmɪ'neɪʃn] *sb* **1** betegnelse; benevnelse, navn; **2** kategori; klasse; gruppe; (tros)samfunn; **3** (måle)enhet; **4** pålydende (verdi). **denominator** [dɪ'nɒmɪneɪtə] *sb* nevner (i brøk).

denote [dɪ'nəʊt] *vt* **1** bety, innebære; **2** betegne; indikere.

denounce [dɪ'naʊns] *vt* **1** anklage; fordømme; ta sterkt avstand fra; **2** angi; **3** si opp (avtale).

dense [dens] *adj* **1** tett, tykk; tettpakket; **2** dum, innskrenket. **density** ['densətɪ] *sb* tetthet *etc*. **density log** *sb petro* tetthetslogg.

dent [dent] *sb*, *vb* bulk(e).

denture ['dentʃə] *sb* gebiss, (tann)protese.

denunciation [dɪˌnʌnsɪ'eɪʃn] *sb* anklage *etc* (jf *denounce*).

deny [dɪ'naɪ] *vt* **1** (be)nekte; **2** fornekte; ikke ville kjennes ved; **3** avslå.

deoil [dɪ'ɔɪl] *vb* fjerne olje (fra).

depart [dɪ'pɑ:t] *vb* **1** (av)gå, (av)reise; dra; forlate; **2** avvike, fravike; **3** *gml* gå bort (dvs dø).

department [dɪ'pɑ:tmənt] *sb* **1** departement; **2** avdeling (i forretning); **3** domene; felt, område; fag. **department store** *sb* (stor)magasin, varehus. **departure** [dɪ'pɑ:tʃə] *sb* avreise *etc*.

depend [dɪ'pend] *vi* **1** ~ *(up)on* avhenge av; stole på; **2** *gml* henge (ned). **dependable** [dɪ'pendəbl] *adj* pålitelig. **dependant** [dɪ'pendənt] *sb* avhengig/*især* forsørget (person). **dependence** [dɪ'pendəns] *sb* **1** avhengighet; **2** tillit. **dependency** [dɪ'pendənsɪ] *sb* besittelse, koloni. **dependent** [dɪ'pendənt] **I** *adj* **1** avhengig (især av forsørger); forsørget; **2** underordnet; **3** *gml* (ned)hengende; **II** *sb* = *dependant*.

depict [dɪ'pɪkt] *vt* beskrive/skildre (ved hjelp av bilder); avbilde, illustrere; skissere.

deplete [dɪ'pli:t] *vt* tappe (ut), tømme; bruke opp. **depletion** [dɪ'pli:ʃn] *sb* tømming *etc*; rovdrift.

deplorable [dɪ'plɔ:rəbl] *adj* beklagelig. **deplore** [dɪ'plɔ:] *vt* beklage.

deport [dɪ'pɔ:t] *vt* **A** deportere, landsforvise; **B** (opp)føre seg. **deportation** [ˌdi:pɔ:'teɪʃn] *sb* deportasjon, landsforvisning. **deportment** [dɪ'pɔ:tmənt] *sb* holdning; oppførsel.

depose [dɪ'pəʊz] *vb* **1** avsette; **2** vitne. **deposit** [dɪ'pɒzɪt] **I** *sb* **1** depositum, (bank)innskudd; **2** avleiring, bunnfall; forekomst (av malm etc); **II** *vt* **1** plassere; legge/sette fra seg; **2** deponere; (inn)betale (som bankinnskudd, del av kjøpesum etc); **3** avleire, bunnfelle. **deposition** [ˌdepə'zɪʃn] *sb* **1** avsettelse; **2** avleiring; **3** vitneforklaring. **depositor** [dɪ'pɒzɪtə] *sb* innskyter.

depot ['depəʊ] *sb* **1** (militær)depot, magasin; lager, opplag; **2** lager|bygning, -lokale; **3** *US* ['di:pəʊ] (større) bussterminal, jernbanestasjon.

depraved [dɪ'preɪvd] *adj* fordervet, lastefull. **depravity** [dɪ'prævətɪ] *sb* lastefullhet.

deprecate ['deprɪkeɪt] *vt* beklage; fordømme, misbillige.

depreciate [dɪ'pri:ʃɪeɪt] *vb* **1** forringe(s); sette ned/synke (i verdi); **2** nedvurdere; snakke nedsettende om. **depreciation** [dɪˌpri:ʃɪ'eɪʃn] *sb* (verdi)forringelse *etc*.

depredations [ˌdeprɪ'deɪʃnz] *sb fl* herjing(er), plyndring.

depress [dɪ'pres] *vt* **1** trykke (ned); **2** undertrykke; **3** deprimere; **4** presse/trykke (marked, priser etc). **depression** [dɪ'preʃn] *sb* **1** fordypning; **2** depresjon; **3** lavtrykk.

deprivation [ˌdeprɪ'veɪʃn] *sb* berøvelse; tap. **deprive** [dɪ'praɪv] *vt:* ~ *of* berøve, ta fra. **deprived** [dɪ'praɪvd] *adj*, *ofte* underprivilegert.

depth [depθ] *sb* dybde, dyp.

deputation [ˌdepjʊ'teɪʃn] *sb* deputasjon, utsending(er). **depute** [dɪ'pju:t] *vt* delegere, overdra. **deputize** ['depjʊtaɪz] **1** *vi* være stedfortreder for; **2** *US vt* oppnevne til stedfortreder. **deputy** ['depjʊtɪ] *sb* stedfortreder, varaperson; *som adj* vara-.

derail [dɪ'reɪl] *vt* (få til å) spore av. **derailleur** [dɪ'reɪlə] *sb* kjedegir (på sykkel). **derailment** [dɪ'reɪlmənt] *sb* avsporing.

derange [dɪ'reɪndʒ] *vt* forstyrre; kullkaste, ødelegge; *mentally* ~*d* sinnsforvirret.

derelict ['derɪlɪkt] **1** *adj* forlatt, herreløs; **2** *sb* forlatt skip; herreløst gods; *også fig* vrak. **dereliction** [ˌderɪ'lɪkʃn] *sb* **1** oppgivelse (av land etc); **2** (plikt)forsømmelse.

deride [dɪ'raɪd] *vt* latterliggjøre; spotte. **derision** [dɪ'rɪʒn] *sb* hån(latter), spott. **derisive** [dɪ'raɪsɪv] *adj* **1** hånlig, spottende; **2** latterlig.

derivation [ˌderɪ'veɪʃn] *sb* **1** avledning; **2** opprinnelse. **derivative** [dɪ'rɪvətɪv] **1** *adj* avledet; **2** *sb* avledning. **derive** [dɪ'raɪv] *vb* **1** få, oppnå; utvinne; **2** avlede, utlede; **3** ~ *from* komme av; stamme fra.

derogatory [dɪ'rɒgətrɪ] *adj* nedsettende.

derrick ['derɪk] *sb* **1** kran(bom); **2** *petro* boretårn. **derrick man** *sb petro* tårn|arbeider, -mann.

desalt [dɪ'sɔ:lt] *vt petro etc* avsalte.

descend [dɪ'send] *vb* **1** komme ned; gå ned(over); dale, synke; lande; **2** gå/stige av; **3** gå i arv; **4** *be ~ed from* stamme fra. **descendant** [dɪ'sendənt] *sb* etterkommer. **descent** [dɪ'sent] *sb* **1** nedstigning *etc*; landing; **2** utforbakke; **3** avstamning, herkomst.

describe [dɪ'skraɪb] *vt* beskrive, skildre. **description** [dɪ'skrɪpʃn] *sb* beskrivelse *etc*. **descriptive** [dɪ'skrɪptɪv] *adj* beskrivende.

desecrate ['desɪkreɪt] *vt* vanhellige. **desecration** [ˌdesɪ'kreɪʃn] *sb* vanhelligelse.

desert A [dɪ'zɜ:t] **I** *vb* **1** forlate; desertere/rømme (fra); **2** late i stikken; svikte; **II** *sb fl* lønn (dvs straff) som fortjent; **B** ['dezət] **1** *adj* gold; ubebodd, øde; **2** *sb* ødemark; ørken. **deserted** [dɪ'zɜ:tɪd] *adj* **1** forlatt; sveket; **2** øde. **desertion** [dɪ'zɜ:ʃn] *sb* desertering. **deserve** [dɪ'zɜ:v] *vb* fortjene; ha krav på. **deserved** [dɪ'zɜ:vd] *adj, pp* (vel)fortjent; berettiget.

desiccate ['desɪkeɪt] *vt* tørke (ut). **desiccation** [ˌdesɪ'keɪʃn] *sb* uttørking, tørke.

design [dɪ'zaɪn] **I** *sb* **1** mønster, tegning; **2** skisse, utkast; plan(tegning); **3** konstruksjon; design, form(givning); **4** hensikt; *by ~* med forsett (hensikt/vilje); **II** *vb* **1** tegne; **2** planlegge; tenke ut; ha til hensikt. **designate I** ['dezɪgnət] *adj* utpekt; **II** ['dezɪgneɪt] *vt* **1** peke ut; benevne, kalle; betegne som; **2** angi (tydelig); markere. **designation** [ˌdezɪg'neɪʃn] *sb* utpeking *etc*. **designation hole** *sb data* styrehull. **designer** [dɪ'zaɪnə] *sb* designer, formgiver; konstruktør; tegner.

desirable [dɪ'zaɪərəbl] *adj* ønskelig. **desire** [dɪ'zaɪə] **I** *sb* **1** ønske; begjær; **2** anmodning; **II** *vt* **1** ønske; begjære; **2** anmode, be. **desirous** [dɪ'zaɪərəs] *adj* begjærlig/ivrig (*of* etter).

desist [dɪ'zɪst] *vi: ~ from* avholde seg/avstå fra; holde opp med.

desk [desk] *sb* skrivebord; kateter; pult. **desk top publishing** *sb data* skrivebordssetting

desolate I ['desələt] *adj* **1** (lagt) øde; **2** forlatt; ensom; **3** dyster; trist; **II** ['desəleɪt] *vt* **1** legge øde; **2** herje; avfolke. **desolation** [ˌdesə'leɪʃn] *sb* forlatthet *etc*.

despair [dɪ'speə] **1** *sb* fortvilelse; håpløshet; **2** *vi* fortvile. **despairing** [dɪ'speərɪŋ] *adj* fortvilet.

despatch [dɪ'spætʃ] = *dispatch*.

despicable ['despɪkəbl] *adj* foraktelig, ynkelig. **despise** [dɪ'spaɪz] *vt* forakte, se ned på.

despite [dɪ'spaɪt] *prep* til tross for, trass i.

despoil [dɪ'spɔɪl] *vt* plyndre.

despond [dɪ'spɒnd] *vi* fortvile; tape motet. **despondency** [dɪ'spɒndənsɪ] *sb* motløshet. **despondent** [dɪ'spɒndənt] *adj* motløs; nedfor; fortvilet.

destination [ˌdestɪ'neɪʃn] *sb* **1** bestemmelse, skjebne; **2** bestemmelsessted, mål. **destine** ['destɪn] *vt: ~d to* (forut)bestemt til (å). **destiny** ['destɪnɪ] *sb* skjebne.

destitute ['destɪtju:t] *adj* fattig, nødlidende; ~ *of* blottet for. **destitution** [ˌdestɪ'tju:ʃn] *sb* fattigdom, nød.

destroy [dɪ'strɔɪ] *vt* ødelegge; rasere, rive ned. **destruction** [dɪ'strʌkʃn] *sb* ødeleggelse *etc*. **destructive** [dɪ'strʌktɪv] *adj* ødeleggende; nedbrytende, skadelig; destruktiv.

desultory ['desəltrɪ] *adj* planløs, springende, usystematisk.

detach [dɪ'tætʃ] *vt* **1** koble fra; løsne; ta av; **2** *mil* detasjere, ta ut (til spesialoppdrag). **detached** [dɪ'tætʃt] *adj* **1** fritt|liggende, -stående; **2** objektiv; uengasjert, upartisk; **3** reservert. **detachment** [dɪ'tætʃmənt] *sb* **1** frakobling *etc*; **2** objektivitet *etc*; **3** *mil* detasjement, (spesial)avdeling.

detail ['di:teɪl] **I** *sb* **1** detalj; **2** = *detachment 3*; **II** *vt* **1** fortelle detaljert; **2** = *detach 2*.

detain [dɪ'teɪn] *vt* **1** forsinke, hefte, oppholde; **2** anholde; holde i varetekt; internere.

detect [dɪ'tekt] *vt* oppdage; finne ut. **detection** [dɪ'tekʃn] *sb* oppdagelse. **detective** [dɪ'tektɪv] *sb* detektiv, oppdager.

detention [dɪ'tenʃn] *sb* **1** forsinkelse; **2** arrest; varetekt.

deter [dɪ'tɜ:] *vt* avholde (*from* fra); avskrekke; hindre. **detergent** [dɪ'tɜ:dʒənt] **1** *adj* rensende; **2** *sb* rensemiddel; vaske|middel, -pulver *etc*.

deteriorate [dɪ'tɪərɪəreɪt] *vb* **1** gjøre dårligere/verre; skade; **2** bli dårligere/verre; forverres. **deterioration** [dɪˌtɪərɪə'reɪʃn] *sb* forringelse; forverring.

determination [dɪˌtɜ:mɪ'neɪʃn] *sb* **1** beslutsomhet; **2** avgjørelse, bestemmelse; **3** fastsettelse. **determine** [dɪ'tɜ:mɪn] *vb* **1** avgjøre, bestemme; fastsette; **2** bestemme seg for; beslutte.

deterrent [dɪ'terənt] *adj, sb* avskrekkende (middel).

detest [dɪ'test] *vt* avsky. **detestable** [dɪ'testəbl] *adj* avskyelig. **detestation** [ˌdɪtes'teɪʃn] *sb* **1** avsky; **2** vederstyggelighet; noe motbydelig.

detonate ['detəneɪt] *vb* detonere; (få til å) eksplodere. **detonation** [ˌdetə'neɪʃn] *sb* detonasjon *etc*.

detour ['di:tuə] *sb* omvei; *US* omkjøring.

detract [dɪ'trækt] *vb* ta vekk; ~ *from* trekke fra; minske, nedsette. **detraction** [dɪ'trækʃn] *sb* reduksjon; *især fig* forkleinelse; nedsettende omtale.

detriment ['detrɪmənt] *sb* skade. **detrimental** [ˌdetrɪ'mentl] *adj* skadelig.

devastate ['devəsteɪt] *vt* herje; legge øde. **devastation** [ˌdevə'steɪʃn] *sb* herjing; (store) ødeleggelser; ruin.

develop [dɪ'veləp] *vb* **1** utvikle (seg *into* til); utfolde (seg); **2** få/pådra seg (sykdom etc); legge seg til (vane etc); danne seg; **3** bygge ut; opparbeide, regulere; **4** fremkalle (film). **development** [dɪ'veləpmənt] *sb* utvikling *etc*; (film)fremkalling.

deviate ['di:vɪeɪt] *vi* avvike/bøye av (*from* fra). **deviation** [ˌdi:vɪ'eɪʃn] *sb* avvik(else); *sjø etc* deviasjon, misvisning; avdrift.

device [dɪ'vaɪs] *sb* **1** plan, påfunn; knep; *leave them to their own ~s* la dem klare seg selv/seile sin egen sjø; **2** innretning; oppfinnelse; *dgl* dings, greie; **3** *data* utstyrsenhet; **4** devise, valgspråk.

devil [devl] **I** *sb* **1** djevel; **2** slave (dvs underordnet sliter); lærling, løpegutt; **II** *vb* **1** tilberede med mye krydder; **2** jobbe, slite. **devilish** ['devlɪʃ] *adj* djevelsk; *dgl* pokkers.

devious ['di:vɪəs] *adj* **1** avvikende; kroket, slynget; *~ route* omvei; **2** snedig; som går krokveier.

devise [dɪ'vaiz] *vt* **1** planlegge; klekke/tenke ut; **2** testamentere bort.

devoid [dɪ'vɔɪd] *adj* blottet/tom (*of* for).

devote [dɪ'vəut] *vt* hellige, vie; ofre. **devoted** [dɪ'vəutɪd] *adj* hengiven; oppofrende; trofast. **devotee** [ˌdevəu'ti:] *sb* dyrker, ivrig tilhenger. **devotion** [dɪ'vəuʃn] *sb* **1** hengivelse; oppofrelse; **2** hengivenhet, (dyp) kjærlighet; **3** fromhet; *fl* andaktsøvelser, andakt; bønner.

devour [dɪ'vauə] *vt* sluke.

devout [dɪ'vaut] *adj* **1** from; **2** inderlig; oppriktig.

dew [dju:] *sb* dugg. **dewy** ['dju:ɪ] *adj* dugget, duggvåt; duggfrisk.

dewater [dɪ'wɔ:tə] *vt petro etc* dehydrere, fjerne vann fra.

dewax [dɪ'wæks] *vt petro* avparafinere, fjerne parafin/voks fra.

dexterity [dek'sterətɪ] *sb* dyktighet. **dext(e)rous** ['dekstrəs] *adj* (be)hendig; dyktig, flink.

dial ['daɪəl] **I** *sb* **1** tallskive, urskive; **2** nummerskive (på telefonapparat); **3** skala (på radioapparat etc); **4** *slang* fjes; **II** *vt* **1** slå (telefon)nummer; **2** stille inn på (radiostasjon etc).

diamond ['daɪəmənd] *sb* **1** diamant; **2** glasskjærer; **3** rombe; ruter (i kortspill).

diaper ['daɪəpə] *sb* **1** bleie; **2** dreil.

diaphragm ['daɪəfræm] *sb* **1** hinne; (skille)vegg; membran (i høyttaler etc); **2** mellomgulv; **3** *foto* (iris)blender.

diarrhoea [ˌdaɪə'rɪə] *sb* diaré.

diary ['daɪərɪ] *sb* dagbok.

dice [daɪs] **I** *sb fl* terninger; *no ~ (US dgl)* niks; (det) nytter ikke; **II** *vb* **1** spille terninger; **2** skjære i terninger.

dictate **I** ['dɪkteɪt] *sb, oftest fl* diktat; ordre, påbud; **II** [dɪk'teɪt] *vb* **1** foreskrive; **2** diktere; forordne, påby; kommandere. **dictation** [dɪk'teɪʃn] *sb* diktat *etc*. **dictator** [dɪk'teɪtə] *sb* diktator. **dictatorial** [ˌdɪktə'tɔ:rɪəl] *adj* diktatorisk. **dictatorship** [dɪk'teɪtəʃɪp] *sb* diktatur.

diction ['dɪkʃn] *sb* diksjon.

dictionary ['dɪkʃənrɪ] *sb* **1** ordbok; **2** *data* (data) katalog.

die [daɪ] **A** *sb* **1** terning; **2** matrise, pregeplate; (mynt)stempel; (gjenge)bakke; **B** *vi* dø, omkomme, miste livet. **diehard** ['daɪhɑ:d] *sb* hardhaus; stabeis.

diesel (oil) ['di:zl] *sb petro* diesel(olje).

diet ['daɪət] **A I** *sb* **1** kosthold; **2** diett; *be on a ~* leve/være på diett; *dgl* slanke seg; **II** *vb* sette (leve, være) på diett; *dgl* slanke seg; **B** *sb* møte(serie); forsamling; riksdag. **dietary** ['daɪətrɪ] **1** *adj* dietetisk, diett-; **2** *sb* forpleining; diett, kost; kostregulativ.

differ ['dɪfə] *vi* **1** være forskjellig (*from* fra); være ulik(e); **2** være uenig (*from/with* med). **difference** ['dɪfrəns] *sb* **1** forskjell, ulikhet; **2** uenighet; uoverensstemmelse. **different** ['dɪfrənt] *adj* forskjellig, ulik. **differentiate** [ˌdɪfə'renʃɪeɪt] *vb* differensiere/skjelne (mellom).

difficult ['dɪfɪkəlt] *adj* vanskelig. **difficulty** ['dɪfɪkəltɪ] *sb* vanskelighet.

diffidence ['dɪfɪdəns] *sb* nøling *etc*. **diffident** ['dɪfɪdənt] *adj* **1** nølende, usikker; **2** sky, tilbakeholden; fryktsom.

diffuse **I** [dɪ'fju:s] *adj* **1** diffus, spredt, uklar; **2** ordrik, utflytende; **II** [dɪ'fju:z] *vb* **1** blande(s); diffundere, trenge gjennom; **2** spre; sende ut. **diffusion** [dɪ'fju:ʒn] *sb* diffusjon *etc*; spredning; utbredelse.

dig [dɪg] **I** *sb dgl* **1** utgravning; **2** dytt, puff; hint, stikk; **3** *fl slang* hybel; **II** *vb* **1** grave; *~ (oneself) in* grave (seg) ned; *fig* klore seg fast; *~ into (dgl)* gå løs på; kaste seg over; *~ out/up* grave ut (opp, frem); **2** dytte (til); **3** *dgl* jobbe, slite; **4** *US slang* forstå/skjønne (seg på); like; digge.

digest **I** ['daɪdʒest] *sb* sammendrag; **II** [daɪ'dʒest] *vb* **1** fordøye; svelge (dvs tåle, finne seg i); **2** forstå; tilegne seg (fullt ut); **3** gjengi i sammendrag. **digestion** [daɪ'dʒestʃn] *sb* fordøyelse. **digestive** [daɪ'dʒestɪv] *adj* fordøyelses-.

digit ['dɪdʒɪt] *sb* **1** finger (og fingerbredde); **2** tå; **3** siffer; (ensifret) tall. **digital** ['dɪdʒɪtl] *adj* digital(-).

dignified ['dɪgnɪfaɪd] *adj* verdig; høytidelig. **dignify** ['dɪgnɪfaɪ] *vt* hedre; gjøre ære på. **dignitary** ['dɪgnɪtrɪ] *sb* rangsperson. **dignity** ['dɪgnətɪ] *sb* anstand, verdighet; høy stilling.

digress [daɪ'gres] *vi* digresjonere, komme bort fra saken. **digression** [daɪ'greʃn] *sb* digresjon, sidesprang.

dike [daɪk] *sb* **1** (drenerings)grøft; **2** dike; dam, demning.

dilapidated [dɪ'læpɪdeɪtɪd] *adj* falleferdig; (ned)slitt.

dilate [daɪ'leɪt] *vb* **1** utvide (seg); sperre/spile opp; **2** *~ upon* dvele ved; utbre seg om.

diligence **A** [dɪlɪdʒəns] *sb* arbeidsomhet, flid; **B** ['dɪlɪʒɑ:ns] *sb* diligence. **diligent** ['dɪlɪdʒənt] *adj* arbeidsom, flittig.

dilly-dally ['dɪlidælɪ] *vi* nøle, være ubesluttsom; somle.

dilute [daɪ'lju:t] **1** *adj* fortynnet, oppspedd; **2** *vt* fortynne, spe (opp, ut); svekke. **dilution** [daɪ'lju:ʃn] *sb* oppløsning.

dim [dɪm] **I** *adj* **1** sløret, uklar; **2** dunkel, mørk; **3** *dgl* sløv, treg; **II** *vb* **1** sløre, gjøre uklar *etc*; **2** blende (ned).

dime [daɪm] *sb US dgl* ticent.

dimension [dɪ'menʃn] *sb* **1** dimensjon, mål; utstrekning; **2** *fl* dimensjoner, størrelse.

diminish [dɪ'mɪnɪʃ] *vb* **1** forminske, redusere; **2** avta, minke. **diminution** [ˌdɪmɪ'nu:ʃn] *sb* forminskelse *etc*. **diminutive** [dɪ'mɪnjʊtɪv] **1** *adj* diminutiv, ørlite(n); **2** *sb* diminutiv.

dimple ['dɪmpl] **I** *sb* **1** smilehull; **2** fordypning; (liten) grop; **II** *vb* få/vise smilehull.

dim|-wit ['dɪmwɪt] *sb* tosk. **~-witted** [ˌdɪm'wɪtɪd] *adj* dum, tåpelig.

din [dɪn] **1** *sb* bråk, larm; dur; **2** *vb* bråke, larme; dure.

dine [daɪn] *vb* **1** spise middag; **2** servere middag; spandere middag på. **diner** ['daɪnə] *sb* **1** middagsgjest; **2** spisevogn.

dingey, dinghy ['dɪŋgɪ] *sb* **1** jolle; **2** *(rubber ~)* (oppblåsbar) gummiflåte.

dingy ['dɪndʒɪ] *adj* skitten, uvasket; lurvet, snusket; mørk.

dining|-car *sb* spisevogn. **~-room** *sb* spisestue. **~-table** *sb* middagsbord, spisebord. **dinner** ['dɪnə] *sb* middag (og middagsmat). **dinner|-jacket** *sb* smoking. **~-party** *sb* (større) middag, middagsselskap.

dint [dɪnt] *sb* **1** = *dent*; **2** *by ~ of* ved hjelp av.

diocese ['daɪəsɪs] *sb* bispedømme.

dip [dɪp] **I** *sb* **1** dypp(ing); *dgl* dukkert; **2** bad (dvs farge etc som ting dyppes ned i); **3** helling; fordypning, søkk; **4** prås, talglys; **II** *vb* **1** dyppe (og senke ned i; dukke; dyppe seg; døpe); **2** øse *(out/up* opp); **3** helle; skråne (utfor); dale, synke; *~ the headlights* blende lyset (dvs billyskasterne).

diploma [dɪ'pləʊmə] *sb* diplom; (avgangs)vitnemål. **diplomacy** [dɪ'pləʊməsɪ] *sb* **1** diplomati; **2** takt(følelse). **diplomat** ['dɪpləmæt] *sb* diplomat. **diplomatic** [ˌdɪplə'mætɪk] *adj* diplomatisk, taktfull. **diplomatist** [dɪ'pləʊmətɪst] = *diplomat*.

dipper ['dɪpə] *sb* øse(kar). **dip-stick** ['dɪpstɪk] *sb* peilestav.

dire ['daɪə] *adj* forferdelig, skrekkelig; *ofte* desperat.

direct [dɪ'rekt] **I** *adj* **1** direkte, rett; **2** likefrem; umiddelbar; **II** *adv* direkte; **III** *vb* **1** rettlede, veilede; vise; **2** adressere, stile; sende; **3** (hen)lede, (hen)vende; rette; **4** dirigere, lede, styre; **5** beordre, pålegge; kommandere. **direct | current** *sb* likestrøm. **~ hit** *sb* fulltreffer. **direction** [dɪ'rekʃn] *sb* **1** kurs, retning; **2** *fl* adresse; **3** instruks; ordre; *~s for use* bruksanvisning; **4** ledelse; (over)oppsyn; **5** direksjon, styre. **directional drilling** *sb petro* retningsboring. **directly** [dɪ'rektlɪ] **I** *adv* direkte, like, rett, umiddelbart; **2** [*også* 'dreklɪ] straks; **II** *konj* [*oftest* 'dreklɪ] så snart (som). **directness** [dɪ'rektnɪs] *sb fig* åpenhet. **director** [dɪ'rektə] *sb* **1** styremedlem; **2** direktør; leder, styrer; **3** (film)instruktør, regissør. **directory** [dɪ'rektərɪ] **I** *adj* veiledende; **II** *sb* **1** adressekalender; **2** *data* adressekatalog, dokumentregister; **3** *(tele) phone ~* telefonkatalog.

dirge [dɜ:dʒ] *sb* gravsalme.

dirt [dɜ:t] **I** *som adv: ~ cheap* latterlig billig; *~ poor* lutfattig; **II** *sb* **1** møkk, skitt; griseprat; **2** søle; **3** *US* jord. **dirt road** *sb US* grusvei. **dirty** ['dɜ:tɪ] **I** *adj* **1** møkket, skitten; sølet; griset, uanstendig; **2** dårlig (om vær); **3** *dgl* gemen, simpel; **II** *vb* skitne (seg) til.

disability [ˌdɪsə'bɪlətɪ] *sb* **1** udyktighet; inkompetanse; **2** uførhet. **disable** [dɪs'eɪbl] *vt* **1** gjøre udyktig; **2** invalidisere; gjøre ufør. **disabled** [dɪs'eɪbld] *adj, pp* invalidisert, ufør.

disadvantage [ˌdɪsəd'vɑ:ntɪdʒ] *sb* ulempe; skade.

disagree [ˌdɪsə'gri:] *vi* være uenig. **disagreeable** [ˌdɪsə'gri:əbl] *adj* ubehagelig. **disagreement** [ˌdɪsə'gri:mənt] *sb* uenighet; uoverensstemmelse.

disappear [ˌdɪsə'pɪə] *vi* forsvinne, bli borte. **disappearance** [ˌdɪsə'pɪərəns] *sb* forsvinning.

disappoint [ˌdɪsə'pɔɪnt] *vt* skuffe. **disappointment** [ˌdɪsə'pɔɪntmənt] *sb* skuffelse.

disapproval [ˌdɪsə'pru:vl] *sb* misbilligelse; motvilje, uvilje. **disapprove** [ˌdɪsə'pru:v] *vb* misbillige, mislike.

disarm [dɪs'ɑ:m] *vb* **1** avvæpne; **2** nedruste. **disarmament** [dɪs'ɑ:məmənt] *sb* **1** avvæpning; **2** nedrustning.

disaster [dɪ'zɑ:stə] *sb* katastrofe, (forferdelig) ulykke. **disastrous** [dɪ'zɑ:strəs] *adj* katastrofal; sørgelig.

disband [dɪs'bænd] *vb* oppløse (især militær enhet); spre (seg).

disc [dɪsk] *sb* **1** (rund) skive; **2** diskus; *slipped ~* diskusprolaps; **3** se også *disk*.

discard I ['dɪskɑ:d] *sb* kassering *etc*; **II** [dɪs'kɑ:d] *vt* **1** kassere, vrake; avskjedige; **2** sake (kort).

descern [dɪ'sɜ:n] *vb* skjelne; (kunne) se. **discerning** [dɪ'sɜ:nɪŋ] *adj* skjønnsom; skarp(sindig). **discernment** [dɪ'sɜ:nmənt] *sb* innsikt; klarsyn; dømmekraft.

discharge [dɪs'tʃɑ:dʒ] **I** *sb* **1** lossing *etc*; utladning; avlastning; **2** utsendelse; utsondring (og puss, verk etc); utslipp; *petro også* utløp; **3** (skudd)salve; **4** avskjed; løslatelse; utskrivelse; **5** innfrielse; **II** *vt* **1** losse; tømme; lade ut; **2** avlaste, lette; **3** avgi, utsondre; utstråle; sende ut; **4** avfyre/løsne (skudd); **5** avskjedige; løslate (fra fengsel); utskrive (fra sykehus etc); sende fra seg; **6** innfri/oppfylle (forpliktelse); dekke (gjeld).

disciple [dɪ'saɪpl] *sb* disippel. **discipline** ['dɪsɪplɪn] **I** *sb* **1** disiplin; **2** (disiplinær)straff; tukt; **3** fag, (vitenskaps)gren; **II** *vt* **1** disiplinere; oppdra; **2** tukte.

disclose [dɪs'kləʊz] *vt* **1** avdekke; avsløre, røpe; **2** åpenbare. **disclosure** [dɪs'kləʊʒə] *sb* avsløring *etc*.

disco ['dɪskəʊ] *sb dgl* = *discotheque*.

disconcert [ˌdɪskən'sɜ:t] *vt* **1** forstyrre; gjøre flau/

forlegen; **2** forpurre. **disconcerted** [ˌdɪskən'sɜ:tɪd] *adj* bestyrtet.

disconsolate [dɪs'kɒnsələt] *adj* **1** utrøstelig; **2** trøstesløs.

discontent [ˌdɪskən'tent] **1** *adj* = *discontented*; **2** *sb* misnøye. **discontented** [ˌdɪskən'tentɪd] *adj* mis(for)nøyd.

discord I ['dɪskɔ:d] *sb* **1** uoverensstemmelse; krangel, trette; **2** disharmoni, dissonans; **II** [dɪs'kɔ:d] *vi* ikke harmonere/stemme overens med. **discordant** [dɪs'kɔ:dənt] *adj* disharmonisk.

discotheque ['dɪskətek] *sb* diskotek.

discount I ['dɪskaʊnt] *sb* **1** diskonto; **2** avslag, rabatt; *at a* ~ lite etterspurt; lavt i kurs; **II** [dɪs'kaʊnt] *vt* **1** diskontere; **2** gi rabatt; **3** trekke fra (for overdrivelser etc).

discourage [dɪs'kʌrɪdʒ] *vt* **1** gjøre motløs, ta motet fra; **2** avskrekke, skremme. **discouragement** [dɪs'kʌrɪdʒmənt] *sb* **1** motløshet; **2** fraråding; motvirking; avskrekkende faktor/forhold.

discourse [dɪs'kɔ:s] **I** *sb* **1** avhandling; forelesning; **2** *gml* samtale; **II** *vi* forelese (*upon* over).

discover [dɪs'kʌvə] oppdage, finne ut; avsløre, åpenbare; **2** (plutselig) forstå/skjønne. **discovery** [dɪs'kʌvərɪ] *sb* oppdagelse *etc*.

discredit [dɪs'kredɪt] **I** *sb* **1** vanry; skam; **2** mistro, tvil; **II** *vt* **1** bringe skam over; bringe i vanry (*with* hos); **2** tvile på; ikke feste lit til. **discreditable** [dɪs'kredɪtəbl] *adj* vanærende.

discreet [dɪs'kri:t] *adj* diskret, taktfull; forsiktig, omtenksom.

discrepancy [dɪs'krepənsɪ] *sb* diskrepans, misforhold.

discretion [dɪs'kreʃn] *sb* **1** diskresjon, takt(fullhet); **2** omdømme, skjønn; (god) forstand; *age/years of* ~ skjells år og alder; *at* ~ som en selv synes; etter behag; når det måtte passe.

discriminate I [dɪs'krɪmɪnət] = *discriminating 1*; **II** [dɪs'krɪmɪneɪt] *vb* **1** skjelne (*between* mellom); se forskjell på; **2** ~ *against* diskriminere; gjøre forskjell på. **discriminating** [dɪs'krɪmɪneɪtɪŋ] *adj* **1** kresen, kritisk; skjønnsom; **2** diskriminerende; **3** differensiert. **discrimination** [dɪsˌkrɪmɪ'neɪʃn] *sb* diskriminering *etc*.

discuss [dɪs'kʌs] *vt* diskutere, drøfte. **discussion** [dɪs'kʌʃn] *sb* diskusjon *etc*.

disdain [dɪs'deɪn] **1** *sb* forakt, ringeakt; **2** *vt* forakte, ringeakte; forsmå. **disdainful** [dɪs'deɪnfʊl] *adj* hånlig, ringeaktende.

disease [dɪ'zi:z] *sb* sykdom, syke. **diseased** [dɪ'zi:zd] *adj* syk(elig).

disfigure [dɪs'fɪgə] *vt* vansire; skjemme.

disgorge [dɪs'gɔ:dʒ] *vt* gulpe opp; spy (ut); gi fra seg.

disgrace [dɪs'greɪs] **I** *sb* **1** vanære; skam, skjensel; **2** unåde; **II** *vt* **1** vanære; være en skam for; **2** la falle i unåde. **disgraceful** [dɪs'greɪsfʊl] *adj* vanærende; skammelig.

disgruntled [dɪs'grʌntld] *adj* mis(for)nøyd; utilfreds.

disguise [dɪs'gaɪz] **I** *sb* **1** forkledning; *fig også* maske; **2** forstillelse; **II** *vt* **1** forkle; **2** skjule. **disguised** [dɪs'gaɪzd] *adj* forkledd; *fig* fordekt.

disgust [dɪs'gʌst] **1** *sb* avsky, vemmelse; **2** *vt* virke frastøtende på. **disgusted** [dɪs'gʌstɪd] *adj* opprørt; fylt av vemmelse. **disgusting** [dɪs'gʌstɪŋ] *adj* frastøtende, motbydelig; vemmelig.

dish [dɪʃ] **I** *sb* **1** fat; *fl* servise; *do the ~es (US)* vaske opp; **2** (mat)rett; porsjon; **II** *vt* **1** legge på fat; servere; ~ *up* diske/varte opp med; **2** *dgl* sette en stopper for; ta innersvingen på. **dish-cloth** *sb* oppvaskklut.

dishearten [dɪs'hɑ:tn] *vt* ta motet fra.

dishevelled [dɪ'ʃevld] *adj* bustet, ustelt (på håret); sjusket, uordentlig.

dish|-washer *sb* **1** tallerkenvasker; **2** oppvaskmaskin. **~-water** *sb* oppvaskvann; *fig også* skvip.

disillusion [ˌdɪsɪ'lu:ʒn] **1** *sb* desillusjonering; skuffelse; **2** *vt* desillusjonere; skuffe.

disinfect [ˌdɪsɪn'fekt] *vt* desinfisere. **disinfectant** [ˌdɪsɪn'fektənt] *adj, sb* desinfiserende (middel).

disinherit [ˌdɪsɪn'herɪt] *vt* **1** gjøre arveløs; **2** *the ~ed masses* de underprivilegerte masser.

disintegrate [dɪs'ɪntɪgreɪt] *vb* gå i oppløsning, løse (seg) opp. **disintegration** [dɪsˌɪntə'greɪʃn] *sb* oppløsning *etc*.

disinterested [dɪs'ɪntrɪstɪd] *adj* uhildet, upartisk.

disjointed [dɪs'dʒɔɪntɪd] *adj* usammenhengende, springende.

disk [dɪsk] *sb* **1** *sb data* disk(ett), (magnet)plate; **2** = *disc*. **disk drive** *sb data* diskettstasjon, platedrev. **diskette** *sb data* diskett. **diskette cover** *sb data* diskettkonvolutt.

dislike [dɪs'laɪk] **1** *sb* motvilje; antipati; **2** *vt* mislike.

dislodge [dɪs'lɒdʒ] *vt* **1** fjerne; **2** fordrive, tvinge ut.

dismal ['dɪzməl] *adj* bedrøvelig, trist; dyster, mørk; guffen.

dismantle [dɪs'mæntl] *vt* **1** rydde (ut av); *sjø* avtakle, rigge ned; **2** avvikle; legge ned; sløyfe; **3** demontere, ta fra hverandre. **dismay** [dɪs'meɪ] **1** *sb* forferdelse; skrekk; **2** *vt* forferde; slå med skrekk.

dismember [dɪs'membə] *vt* lemleste; rive fra hverandre.

dismiss [dɪs'mɪs] *vt* **1** sende bort (ut, fra seg etc); avvise; skyve fra seg; **2** gi lov til å gå; gi fri (etter skole, tjeneste etc); dimittere; **3** avskjedige. **dismissal** [dɪs'mɪsl] *sb* **1** bortsending; hjemsending; dimittering; **2** avvisning; **3** avskjed.

dismount [dɪs'maʊnt] *vb* **1** gå/stige (ned) av; **2** kaste av hesten; **3** demontere, ta ned.

disorder [dɪs'ɔ:də] **I** *sb* **1** rot, uorden; forvirring; **2** ordensforstyrrelse; uro(ligheter); **3** (fysisk) uregelmessighet; sykdom; **II** *vt* bringe uorden i; rote til; forstyrre. **disorderly** [dɪs'ɔ:dəlɪ] *adj* **1** rotet, uordentlig; **2** ulovlig; opprørsk.

disown [dɪs'əʊn] *vt* fornekte, ikke (ville) kjennes ved.

disparage [dɪs'pærɪdʒ] *vt* rakke ned på; redusere. **disparagement** [dɪs'pærɪdʒmənt] *sb* nedrakking *etc.*

dispatch [dɪs'pætʃ] **I** *sb* **1** (rask) ekspedering; **2** hurtighet, raskhet; **3** depesje, melding; **II** *vt* **1** ekspedere; sende ut/av sted etc; **2** få unna; **3** ekspedere, gjøre det av med (dvs drepe). **dispatch|-case** *sb* dokumentmappe. **~-rider** *sb* ordonnans.

dispel [dɪs'pel] *vt* spre; fordrive, drive vekk.

dispensary [dɪ'spensərɪ] *sb* **1** reseptur; *dgl* apotek, bedriftslegekontor (etc, hvor man kan få medisiner og ambulant behandling); **2** *US* vinhandel. **dispensation** [ˌdɪspen'seɪʃn] *sb* **1** tildeling; **2** (for)ordning; tilskikkelse; **3** dispensasjon, fritakelse. **dispense** [dɪ'spens] *vb* **1** tildele; (gjøre i stand og) dele ut; ekspedere resept; **2** håndheve; **3** *~ from* frita for; **4** *~ with* (kunne) unnvære; gjøre overflødig. **dispenser** [dɪ'spensə] *sb* **1** (be)holder; **2** farmasøyt, reseptar.

dispersal [dɪ'spɜ:sl] *sb* spredning *etc.* **disperse** [dɪ'spɜ:s] *vb* spre (seg); splitte(s).

dispirited [dɪ'spɪrɪtɪd] *adj* nedfor; motløs, nedslått.

displace [dɪs'pleɪs] *vt* **1** (for)flytte; fordrive; fjerne; **2** fortrenge; erstatte. **displaced person** *sb* tvangsforflyttet person; flyktning. **displacement** [dɪs'pleɪsmənt] *sb* **1** forflytning *etc*; **2** fortrengning; deplasement.

display [dɪ'spleɪ] **1** *sb* fremvisning; utstilling; *data* skjermvisning; *fashion ~* moteoppvisning; **2** *vt* vise (frem); stille ut; demonstrere; utfolde; legge for dagen. **display | device** *sb data* (data)skjerm. **~ image** *sb data* bilde. **~ point** *sb data* grafisk element. **~ tube** *sb data* billedrør.

disport [dɪs'pɔ:t] *vr: ~ oneself* boltre/tumle seg; more seg.

disposal [dɪ'spəʊzl] *sb* **1** arrangering; inndeling; oppstilling; **2** disposisjon, rådighet; **3** avhending, salg; **4** kassering, kasting. **dispose** [dɪ'spəʊz] *vb* **1** inndele, ordne; stille opp; **2** disponere/forføye (over); **3** gjøre stemt/tilbøyelig; **4** *~ of* anbringe; fordele; få unna; kvitte seg med; *merk* avhende, selge. **disposition** [ˌdɪspə'zɪʃn] *sb* **1** arrangement, plan; **2** disposisjon, rådighet; **3** legning; tilbøyelighet.

dispossess [ˌdɪspə'zes] *vt: ~ of* berøve for; ta fra, *også* fordrive fra (gård og grunn).

disprove [dɪs'pru:v] *vt* motbevise.

disputable [dɪ'spju:təbl] *adj* omstridt; tvilsom. **dispute** [dɪ'spju:t] **I** *sb* diskusjon; disputt; **II** *vb* **1** diskutere; disputere; **2** krangle (om); **3** bestride; **4** motsette seg.

disregard [ˌdɪsrɪ'gɑ:d] **1** *sb* mangel på respekt; ringeakt; tilsidesettelse; **2** *vt* ikke bry seg om (vise oppmerksomhet, respekt etc); neglisjere, overse; se bort fra.

disrepair [ˌdɪsrɪ'peə] *sb* forfall; ustand.

disreputable [dɪs'repjʊtəbl] *adj* beryktet; redselsfull; fæl.

disrupt [dɪs'rʌpt] *vt fig* splitte, sprenge. **disruption** [dɪs'rʌpʃn] *sb* splittelse, sprengning; oppløsning, sammenbrudd.

dissect [dɪ'sekt] *vt* dissekere.

dissemble [dɪ'sembl] *vb* **1** forstille seg, hykle; **2** skjule.

disseminate [dɪ'semɪneɪt] *vt* spre, utbre.

dissension [dɪ'senʃn] *sb* splid, strid. **dissent** [dɪ'sent] **I** *sb* dissens; avvikende mening; uenighet; **II** *vi* **1** dissentere; **2** være dissenter.

dissipate ['dɪsɪpeɪt] *vb* **1** oppløse(s); spre (seg); drive bort/vekk; **2** kaste (skusle, søle, ødsle etc) bort; **3** leve utsvevende; *~d* forranglet, herjet. **dissipation** [ˌdɪsɪ'peɪʃn] *sb* **1** oppløsning *etc*; **2** ødsling *etc*; **3** utsvevelse(r).

dissociate [dɪ'səʊʃɪeɪt] *vt* holde fra hverandre; skille (at); *~ oneself from* distansere seg fra.

dissolute ['dɪsəlju:t] *adj* utsvevende. **dissolution** [ˌdɪsə'lu:ʃn] *sb* oppløsning *etc.* **dissolv** [dɪ'zɒlv] *vb* løse (seg) opp; smelte(s); *fig også* oppløse(s).

dissuade [dɪ'sweɪd] *vt* fraråde; *~ them from it* få dem fra (å gjøre) det. **dissuasion** [dɪ'sweɪʒn] *sb* fraråding *etc.*

distaff ['dɪstɑ:f] *sb* tein (på rokk). *the* **distaff side** *sb* spinnesiden (dvs kvinnene i familien/slekten).

distance ['dɪstəns] **I** *sb* **1** avstand; distanse, strekning; *in the ~* i det fjerne; **2** tidsrom; **II** *vt (out~)* distansere; legge bak seg. **distant** ['dɪstənt] *adj* fjern; *two miles ~* to miles borte.

distaste [dɪs'teɪst] *sb* avsmak; motvilje, ulyst. **distasteful** [dɪs'teɪstfʊl] *adj* usmakelig; ubehagelig.

distend [dɪ'stend] *vb* utvide (seg); ese, svulme (opp).

distil [dɪ'stɪl] *vb* **1** destillere; **2** utskille; dryppe (ned). **distillation** [ˌdɪstɪ'leɪʃn] *sb* destillering *etc.* **distillation | column** = *~ tower.* **~ plant** *sb petro* destillasjonsanlegg. **~ tower** *sb petro* destillasjonstårn. **distillery** [dɪ'stɪlərɪ] *sb* destilleri; brenneri.

distinct [dɪ'stɪŋkt] *adj* **1** klar, tydelig; distinkt; **2** forskjellig; **3** atskilt. **distinction** [dɪ'stɪŋkʃn] *sb* **1** forskjell; skille; skjelning; **2** fremragende dyktighet; anseelse, ry; **3** distinksjon; utmerkelse. **distinctive** [dɪ'stɪŋktɪv] *adj* karakteristisk, særegen; markant, tydelig. **distinguish** [dɪ'stɪŋgwɪʃ] *vb* **1** skjelne (*between* mellom); **2** fremheve; markere; særprege; *~ oneself* utmerke seg. **distinguished** [dɪ'stɪŋgwɪʃt] *adj* fremragende; særpreget; berømt; distingvert.

distort [dɪs'tɔ:t] *vt* for|dreie, -vanske, -vrenge; vri. **distortion** [dɪs'tɔ:ʃn] *sb* fordreining *etc.*

distract [dɪs'trækt] *vt* for|styrre, -virre; distrahere. **distraction** [dɪs'trækʃn] *sb* **1** forstyrrelse *etc*; (sinns)forvirring; **2** atspredelse, tidsfordriv. **distraught** [dɪs'trɔ:t] *adj* for|styrret, -virret; forrykt.

distress [dɪ'stres] **I** *sb* **1** fortvilelse; nød; **2** dyp bekymring; smerte; sorg; **II** *vt* smerte; bekymre, engste; plage. **distressed** [dɪ'strest] *adj* nødlidende.

distribute [dɪs'trɪbju:t] *vt* **1** distribuere, fordele; dele (gi, sende etc) ut; spre; **2** gruppere; klassifisere. **distribution** [ˌdɪstrɪ'bju:ʃn] *sb* distribuering *etc.*

district ['dɪstrɪkt] *sb* distrikt, område; krets, strøk. **district | attorney** *sb US* statsadvokat. **~ heating** *sb* fjernvarme. **~ nurse** *sb* distriktssykepleier, hjemmesykepleier.

distrust [dɪs'trʌst] **1** *sb* mistro; **2** *vt* mistro, ikke stole på.

disturb [dɪ'stɜ:b] *vt* **1** forstyrre, uroe; **2** urydde. **disturbance** [dɪ'stɜ:bəns] *sb* (ordens)forstyrrelse; uro.

disuse 1 [dɪs'ju:s] *sb: fall into ~* gå av bruk; **2** [dɪs'ju:z] *vt: ~d* avlagt, kassert; nedlagt; ubenyttet.

ditch [dɪtʃ] **I** *sb* grøft; grav, grop; **II** *vb* **1** grøfte; drenere (ved grøfting); **2** *dgl* kjøre utfor (veien); *om fly* nødlande; **3** *US* kassere; *slang* skulke; lure seg unna/stikke av (fra).

ditty ['dɪtɪ] *sb* vise(stump).

dive [daɪv] **I** *sb* **1** stup (i sjøen etc); **2** *dgl, slang* kjeller(lokale); *US* bule, kneipe; **II** *vi* **1** stupe; fare/pile (ned i); **2** dykke. **diver** ['daɪvə] *sb* dykker.

diverge [daɪ'vɜ:dʒ] *vi* avvike, være forskjellig. **divergence** [daɪ'vɜ:dʒəns] *sb* **1** avvik(else); **2** divergens, (menings)forskjell. **divergent** [daɪ'vɜ:dʒənt] *adj* avvikende. **divers** ['daɪvɜ:z] *adj gml* flere (forskjellige). **diverse** [daɪ'vɜ:s] *adj* forskjellig(artet). **diversify** [daɪ'vɜ:sɪfaɪ] *vt* variere. **diversion** [daɪ'vɜ:ʃn] *sb* **1** avledning; avledende manøver etc; **2** *a)* omdirigering; *b) US (traffic ~)* omkjøring; **2** tidsfordriv; underholdning. **diversity** [daɪ'vɜ:sətɪ] *sb* mangfold; variasjon. **divert** [daɪ'vɜ:t] *vt* **1** avlede; omdirigere; **2** more, underholde.

divest [daɪ'vest] *vt* **1** *~ of* kle av; *~ oneself of* kvitte seg med; legge av; **2** berøve (*of* for).

divide [dɪ'vaɪd] **I** *sb* dele; (vann)skille; **II** *vb* **1** dele (seg); dele av (inn, opp etc); **2** dividere; (kunne) dividere(s); **3** skille(s); skille lag; splitte (og *fig* så splid etc); **4** fordele; dele ut; **5** votere.

divination [ˌdɪvɪ'neɪʃn] *sb* forutsigelse, spådom; gjetning. **divine** [dɪ'vaɪn] **A I** *adj* **1** guddommelig, guds-; **2** *dgl* bedårende, skjønn; **II** *sb* geistlig; teolog; **B** *vb* **1** forutsi, spå; gjette (seg til); **2** gå med ønskekvist.

diving|-bell, ~-capsule *sb petro etc* dykkerklokke. **~-deck** *sb petro* dykkerdekk. **~-dress** = *~-suit.* **~-helmet** *sb* dykkerhjelm. **~-suit** *sb* dykkerdrakt.

divinity [dɪ'vɪnətɪ] *sb* **1** guddom(melighet); **2** teologi.

divisible [dɪ'vizəbl] *adj* delelig. **division** [dɪ'vɪʒn] *sb* **1** (inn)deling; divisjon; **2** dele, skille(linje); **3** del; avdeling; distrikt, krets; **4** gruppe(ring); *mil* divisjon; **5** splid, uenighet; **6** avstemning, votering.

divorce [dɪ'vɔ:s] **1** *sb* skilsmisse; **2** *vt* skille seg (fra).

divulge [daɪ'vʌldʒ] *vt* avsløre, røpe.

dizziness ['dɪzɪnɪs] *sb* svimmelhet, ørske. **dizzy** ['dɪzɪ] *adj* **1** svimmel, ør; **2** svimlende.

do [du:] **A** *vb* **I** *som hjelpeverb* **1** *(i spørsmål og nektelser) ~ you want to go?* vil du (gjerne) gå? *you want to go, don't you?* du vil gjerne gå, ikke sant? *you don't want to go, ~ you?* du vil (helst) ikke gå, vil du vel? *I don't want to go* jeg vil ikke gå; **2** *(til understrekning) I ~ hope that* jeg håper virkelig at; **II** *som hovedverb* **1** gjøre (og lage, utføre; fremføre, oppføre; spille (rolle); arbeide/drive etc med; lese/studere (et fag); arrangere, ordne; få/gjøre etc i stand; tilberede; lage i stand; stelle (hus etc); avslutte; fullføre; tilbakelegge); *~ well* gjøre det godt; *well-to-~* velstående; *~ to death* drepe; *nothing ~ing (dgl)* niks; ikke tale om; **2** passe; være nok; *that will ~* det klarer seg; *that wont ~* det forslår ikke; *dgl* den går ikke; **3** befinne seg; ha det; **4** *med adv/prep* **~ away** *with* avskaffe; fjerne; rydde av veien; **~ by** behandle; **~ for** stelle (huset) for; strekke til for; *done for (dgl)* utslitt; ferdig, fortapt; **~ in** *slang* drepe; **~ out** gjøre rent; rydde opp (i); **~ up** pusse opp; fikse/pynte på; hefte opp; knappe igjen; pakke inn; **~ with** *oneself* ta seg til; *I could ~ with a drink* jeg kunne tenke meg/trenge en drink; *be/have done with* være (bli/gjøre seg) ferdig med; *make ~ with* greie/klare seg med; **~ without** klare seg uten; **B** *slang* **1** *sb* svindel; **2** *vt (~ over)* snyte; svindle; *~ out of* lure/narre fra; **C** *sb dgl* fest.

docile ['dəusaɪl] *adj* føyelig; lærevillig. **docility** [dəu'sɪlətɪ] *sb* føyelighet; lærevillighet.

dock [dɒk] **A I** *sb* **1** dokk; **2** *fl* brygge(r); kai(anlegg); **II** *vb* **1** dokksette; **2** gå i dokk; **B I** *sb* kupert hale; **II** *vt* **1** kupere, stusse; **2** redusere; kutte ned på; **C** *sb* anklagebenk. **dockyard** *sb* (skips)verft.

doctor ['dɒktə] **I** *sb* **1** doktor; **2** lege; **II** *vt* **1** behandle (sykdom); *dgl* doktorere, reparere; **2** blande opp; spe ut; **3** forfalske.

document 1 ['dɒkjumənt] *sb* dokument (også *data*); **2** ['dɒkjument] *vt* dokumentere. **documentary** [ˌdɒkju'mentərɪ] **1** *adj* dokumentarisk; dokument-; **2** *sb, især fl* dokumentarfilm. **documentation** [ˌdɒkjumən'teɪʃn] *sb* dokumentering; *data etc* dokumentasjon; ≈ bruksanvisning.

dodge ['dɒdʒ] **I** *sb* **1** unnvikende bevegelse/manøver; **2** knep, krumspring; **II** *vb* unngå; smette unna; lure seg unna (ved knep).

doe [dəu] *sb* då, kolle; hind, hunn (av hjortedyr, hare og kanin). **doeskin** *sb* hjorteskinn.

doff [dɒf] *vt gml* ta av seg (f.eks. lue).

dog [dɒg] **I** *sb* **1** hund; **2** hann (av rev og ulv); **3** *dgl* fyr, kar; **4** griper, klo; **II** *vt* forfølge. **dog-eared** *adj* med eselører (om bok). **dogged** ['dɒgɪd] *adj* sta, stivnakket. **dog tag** *sb mil* identifikasjonsmerke.

dole [dəul] **A I** *sb* **1** almisse; *dgl* (sosial)trygd; *on the ~ (dgl)* på sosialen; **2** *dgl* (arbeidsledighets)trygd; **II** *vt: ~ out* dele ut (i små porsjoner); **B** *sb gml* smerte; sorg. **doleful** ['dəulful] *adj* smertelig; trist.

doll [dɒl] **1** *sb* dukke; **2** *vb dgl: ~ up* fiffe/pynte seg; dolle (seg) opp; spjåke/stase (seg) ut.

dolorous ['dɒlərəs] *adj* **1** sørgmodig, trist; **2** jammerlig, smertelig, sørgelig.

dolphin ['dɒlfɪn] *sb* delfin.

dolt [dəult] *sb* dust, tosk.

domain [dəu'meɪn] *sb* **1** domene, (makt)område; **2** (over)herredømme; **3** (fag)område, felt; **4** *data* kontrollområde.

dome [dəum] *sb* **1** kuppel; hvelving; **2** (prakt)-bygning.

domestic [də'mestɪk] **I** *adj* **1** hjemlig, hjemme-; huslig, hus-; **2** innenlandsk, innenriks(-); **3** hus-, tam(-); ~ *animal* husdyr; **II** *sb* (~ *servant*) hushjelp, tjener. **domesticate** [də'mestɪkeɪt] *vt* temme; ~*ed* (*også*) huslig; hus-, tam-.

domicile ['dɒmɪsaɪl] **I** *sb* bosted; hjemsted; **II** *vb* **1** være bosatt; **2** bosette seg.

dominance ['dɒmɪnəns] *sb* dominans; (over)herredømme. **dominant** ['dɒmɪnənt] *adj* **1** dominerende, fremherskende; **2** *mus også sb* dominant. **dominate** ['dɒmɪneɪt] *vb* dominere, (be)herske. **domination** [,dɒmɪ'neɪʃn] *sb* herredømme. **domineer** [,dɒmɪ'nɪə] *vi* dominere, regjere. **dominion** [də'mɪnɪən] *sb* **1** herredømme; **2** dominion, koloni med selvstyre.

don [dɒn] **A** *sb* **1** universitetslærer; **2** *slang* ekspert, kløpper; **B** *vt gml* ta på seg (f.eks. lue).

donate [dəu'neɪt] *vt* donere; gi/skjenke (især penger). **donation** [dəu'neɪʃn] *sb* donasjon.

donkey ['dɒŋkɪ] *sb* **1** esel; **2** (~-*engine*) donkey-(maskin).

donor ['dəunə] *sb* donor; donator, giver.

doom [du:m] **1** *sb* dom; straff; **2** *vt* (for)dømme.

door [dɔ:] *sb* dør; *fig også* åpning; *back* ~ bakdør; *front* ~ gatedør, port. **door|-bell** *sb* dørklokke. **~-keeper** *sb* dør|vakt, vokter. **~-mat** *sb* dørmatte. **~-plate** *sb* dørskilt, navneskilt. **~post** *sb* dørstolpe. **~-step** *sb* dør|stokk, -trinn; trappestein. **~way** *sb* døråpning.

dope [dəup] **I** *sb* **1** (slags) ferniss; impregnering, smurning; **2** *dgl* dop, narkotisk stoff; **3** *slang* (stall)-tips; **II** *vt* **1** fernissere; impregnere, smøre; **2** *dgl* bedøve; dope, gi narkotisk el. stimulerende middel; narkotisere.

dormant ['dɒmənt] *adj* **1** sovende; **2** hvilende, i ro (inntil videre); latent. **dormitory** ['dɔ:mɪtrɪ] *sb* sovesal.

dose [dəus] **1** *sb* dosis; dose, porsjon; **2** *vt* gi/porsjonere ut (medisin).

dot [dɒt] **A I** *sb* prikk, punkt; flekk, plett; **II** *vt* **1** sette prikk over; **2** prikke; ~*ted about* spredd omkring/utover; ~*ted with* overstrødd med; **B** *sb* medgift.

dotage ['dəutɪdʒ] *sb* (alderdoms)sløvhet, senilitet. **dote** [dəut] *vi* **1** ~ *on* forgude, elske blindt; **2** gå i barndommen.

dot matrix *sb data* punkt(matrise).

double ['dʌbl] **I** *adj* dobbelt(-); *fig også* tvetydig; **II** *adv* **1** dobbelt(-), to ganger (så mange/mye); **2** parvis, to og to; **III** *sb* **1** det dobbelte; **2** dobbeltgjenger; dublett; stedfortreder; *film* stand-in; **3** *mil* forsert marsj, *on the* ~ i springmarsj; **IV** *vb* **1** doble; fordoble(s); **2** brette (folde, legge etc) dobbelt; ~ *back* brette etc tilbake; snu og løpe i motsatt retning; ~ *up* brette etc sammen; krøke seg (*fig* bryte, knekke etc) sammen; **3** være stedfortreder for; *film, teater* dublere. **double|-barrelled** *adj* dobbeltløpet; *fig* tvetydig. **~-breasted** *adj* dobbelt|knappet, spent. **~-cross** *vt* bedra, svindle: jukse, lure. **~-dealing** **1** *adj* falsk; som spiller dobbeltspill; **2** *sb* dobbeltspill, falskhet; juks, svindel. **~-decker** *sb* dobbeltdekker; *især* toetasjes buss. **~-edged** *adj* tveegget. **~-faced** *adj* tosidig; *fig* tvetydig.

doublet ['dʌblɪt] *sb* **1** dublett; **2** *hist* vams.

doubt [daut] **1** *sb* tvil, usikkerhet; *no* ~ utvilsomt; **2** *vi* betvile, tvile (på); være usikker. **doubtful** ['dautful] *adj* **1** tvilende; **2** tvilsom. **doubtless** ['dautlɪs] *adj, adv* utvilsom(t).

dough [dəu] *sb* **1** deig; **2** *slang* gryn (dvs penger). **dough|boy** *sb* smultbolle; *US slang* (menig) soldat. **~nut** *sb* smult|bolle, -ring.

doughty ['dautɪ] *adj* drabelig; *gml* djerv.

dove [dʌv] *sb* due (også *fig* og *poet*). **dove|-colour(ed)** *adj, sb* duegrå(tt). **~-cot(e)** *sb* dueslag. **~tail** **1** *sb* sinking; **2** *vb* sinke; føye/passe sammen.

dowager ['dauɪdʒə] *sb* (fornem) enke.

dowdy ['daudɪ] *adj, sb* **1** sjusket (kvinne); **2** umoderne kledd (kvinne).

down [daun] **A I** *adj* ned-; ned(ad)gående; **II** *adv* **1** ned (og nede; nedover; ned (bort, frem) til etc); ut (fra London etc); *cash/money* ~ kontant betaling; *be* ~ *(in spirits)* være nede (*især fig* deprimert, sliten etc); *close* ~ stenge; **2** ~ *and out (dgl)* slått ut; *også* = ~*cast,* ~*hearted*; **3** ~ **for** for/på tur til; ~ **on** *one's luck* uheldig; *get* ~ **to** *business/work* komme til saken; *come* ~ **(up)on** kaste seg over; skjelle ut; *be* ~ **with** *(influenza etc)* ligge til sengs (med influensa etc); **III** *prep* nede i, ned(over); ~ *the river* nedover elven; **IV** *sb* **1** loddrett (i kryssord); **2** *ups and* ~*s* medgang og motgang; **V** *vt dgl* legge ned; slå ned; ~ *tools* legge ned arbeidet (dvs form for streik); **B** *sb* dun; **C** *sb* **1** klitt, (sand)-dyne; **2** *fl* høydedrag, ås(er). **down | arrow key** *sb data* nedtast. **~cast** *adj* ned|slått, -trykt; deprimert. **~fall** *sb* **1** nedfall; nedbør; **2** fall; undergang. **~-hearted** *adj* = ~*cast.* **~hill** *adv* nedover, utfor (bakke). **~ payment** *sb* kontant betaling; kontantbeløp (ved avbetaling). **~pour** *sb* regnskyll. **~right** *adj* **1** enkel, liketil; **2** oppriktig, ærlig; **3** *dgl også adv* gjennomført; regulær(t); åpenbar(t); ganske enkelt; rett og slett. **~stairs** *adv* ned (trappen); nede, nedenunder. **~ time** *sb petro* borestans, dødtid. **~to-earth** *adj* jordnær, nøktern. **~town** *adv, især US* (i) sentrum; inn/ned til sentrum; sentrums-. **~ train** *sb* avgående tog (dvs fra London til forstedene etc). **~-trodden** *adj* undertrykt. **~ward** *adj* nedover-, utfor-; fallende. **~wards** *adv* ned(over); utfor.

downy ['daunɪ] *adj* dunet.

dowry ['dauərɪ] *sb* medgift.

doze [dəuz] **1** *sb* blund, døs; **2** *vi* døse, (små)-blunde.

dozen ['dʌzn] *sb* dusin.

drab [dræb] *adj* **1** *også sb* skittenbrun(t); **2** grå; kjedelig, monoton.

draft [drɑ:ft] **I** *sb* **1** kladd, konsept; utkast; **2** *mil* innkalling; **3** *mil* detasjement, (mindre) avdeling; **4** *merk* tratte; **5** *US* = *draught*; **II** *vt* **1** kladde, konsipere; lage utkast (til); **2** innkalle (til militærtjeneste); ta ut (mannskaper) til.

drag [dræg] **I** *sb* **1** drag; **2** bremse(kloss); belastning; motstand; hemsko, hindring; **3** harv, slodd (og annen redskap som slepes); (sokne)dregg; **II** *vb* **1** dra (på); dra (hale, slepe, trekke) etter seg; **2** harve, slodde; **3** sokne (i). **drag bit** *sb petro* skrapekrone (på bor). **draggle** ['drægl] *vb* trekke (etter seg) i sølen; **2** sjokke, subbe.

dragon ['drægən] *sb* drage. **dragonfly** ['drægənflaɪ] *sb* øyenstikker.

dragoon [drə'gu:n] *sb* dragon, kavalerist.

drain [dreɪn] **I** *sb* **1** avløp, sluk; *fl* kloakk; **2** (av)-tapping, (ut)tømming; belastning, påkjenning (ved svinn, tap etc); **3** drenering (og dreneringsǀgrøft, -kanal, -renne, -rør etc); **4** slurk, tår; munnfull; **II** *vb* drenere (og grøfte; tappe/tømme (for vann); tørrlegge; tørke (inn, opp, ut); lense; tømme til bunns etc). **drainǀage** ['dreɪnɪdʒ] *sb* **1** drenering *etc*; **2** kloakk(system); **3** kloakkvann. **~-pipe** *sb* drenrør.

drake [dreɪk] *sb* andrik, (ande)stegg.

dram [dræm] *sb* **1** vektenhet, se midtsidene; **2** (whisky)dram.

drape [dreɪp] **I** *sb, især US* forheng, portière; gardin; **II** *vt* **1** drapere; arrangere i folder; **2** dekorere (med draperier etc); hylle (inn i). **draper** ['dreɪpə] *sb* manufakturhandler. **drapery** ['dreɪpərɪ] *sb* **1** draperi; drapering; **2** manufakturhandel.

drastic ['dræstɪk] *adj* drastisk.

draught [drɑ:ft] *sb* **1** trekk; **2** slep(ing), trekk(ing); **3** (fiske)fangst, varp; **4** *sjø* dypgående; **5** tapping (og dram, slurk, tår etc); *at a ~* i ett drag; *on ~* på fat; **6** *fl* dam(spill). **draughtsman** ['drɑ:ftsmən] *sb* **I** dambrikke; **II 1** tegner; **2** konsipist.

draw [drɔ:] **I** *sb* **1** trekning *etc*; *quick on the ~* rask på avtrekkeren; **2** uavgjort kamp/konkurranse etc; **3** tiltrekning (og tiltrekningskraft); trekkplaster; **4** drag (av sigarett etc); *dgl* blås; **II** *vb* **1** trekke (frem, opp, til, ut); dra/trekke (for, fra, ned); trekke (lodd, *for* om); *~ (a) blank* mislykkes; **2** trekke (til seg); fremkalle, vekke; provosere; **3** hente; skaffe (seg); heve (penger, lønn etc); tappe (øl etc); **4** tegne; *(~ up* streke/trekke opp; skissere; *~ a distinction* skjelne; *~ out* rentegne; *fig* utpensle; **5** skrive ut, utstede; **6** spille uavgjort; **7** *sjø* stikke (dypt i sjøen); **8** *med adv/prep ~* **away** *from* trekke (seg) unna; løpe etc fra; *~* **back** trekke (seg) tilbake; *~* **down** *fig* nedkalle; forårsake, medføre; *~* **in** trekke etc inn; begrense (seg); *~* **off** trekke (seg) unna (ut, vekk etc); tappe (av); *~* **on** dra/trekke på (seg); nærme seg; *merk* trassere (*fig, dgl også* trekke) på; resultere i; trekke med seg; *~* **out** (se også 4) trekke (seg) ut; tøye (seg); bli lengre; *fig* provosere; pumpe, uteske; få til å røpe etc; *~* **up** (se også 4) hale (heise, trekke etc) opp; komme nærmere; (kjøre frem og) stanse; *~ oneself up* rette/stramme seg opp. **drawǀback** *sb* mangel, ulempe. **~bridge** *sb* klaffebro, vindebro. **drawer 1** ['drɔ:ə] *sb* tegner; **2** [drɔ:] *sb* skuff; *chest of ~s* kommode; **3** *~s* [drɔ:z] *sb fl* underbukse(r). **drawing** ['drɔ:ɪŋ] *sb* tegning. **drawingǀ-board** *sb* tegnebrett. **~-pin** *sb* tegnestift. **~--room** *sb* salong, (daglig)stue.

drawl [drɔ:l] **1** *sb* langsom (ofte affektert) tale; **2** *vb* si/snakke slepende (el. affektert langsomt).

dread [dred] **1** *sb* frykt, redsel (*of* for); **2** *vb* frykte/være (svært) redd (for). **dreadful** ['dredfʊl] *adj* forferdelig, fryktinngytende.

dream [dri:m] **1** *sb* drøm; **2** *vb* drømme; *~ up* dikte opp.

dreary ['drɪərɪ] *adj* ensformig, kjedelig; trist.

dredge [dredʒ] **A 1** *sb* (bunn)skraper; mudderapparat; **2** *vb* skrape opp (fra bunnen av elver etc); mudre opp; **B** *vt* drysse, strø.

dregs [dregz] *sb fl* bunnfall; berme, utskudd.

drench [drentʃ] **1** *sb* gjennombløting; **2** *vt* gjennombløte, gjøre klissvåt.

dress [dres] **I** *sb* **1** kjole; **2** klær; (kles)drakt; antrekk; **II** *vb* **1** kle (på); kle (på) seg; kle seg om; holde/utstyre med klær; *~ out/up* pynte (seg); kle (seg) ut; pynte på; stase opp; **2** arrangere, ordne; sette opp (hår); *~ down* strigle (hest); skjelle ut; jule opp; **3** dekorere, pynte; **4** gjøre/stelle i stand til; tilberede (mat); berede (skinn); **5** bandasjere, forbinde; **6** *mil* rette inn; stille på linje. **dress ǀ circle** *sb* balkong (i teatersalong). **~-coat** *sb* (snipp)kjole. **dresser A** *sb* påkleder(ske); **B** *sb* **1** (benke)skap; **2** *US* toalettbord. **dressing** *sb* **1** påkledning; **2** dekorasjon, pynt; **3** dressing, (salat)saus; fyll; **4** bandasje(r), forbindingssaker. **dressǀmaker** *sb* dameskredder; (kjole)-syerske, sydame. *~* **rehearsal** *sb* generalprøve, kost og mask. *~* **suit** *sb* = *~ coat*. *~* **uniform** *sb* gallauniform.

dribble ['drɪbl] *vb* **1** dryppe; sive; sikle; **2** drible (i fotball).

drift [drɪft] **I** *sb* **1** bevegelse (og bevegelsesretning); drift; **2** strøm; **3** (for)mål; innhold, mening; tendens; **4** (snø)drive; haug; **II** *vb* **1** drive, flyte; **2** (gå og) drive, slentre: **3** drive (sammen); fløte (tømmer); hope (seg) opp. **drift-wood** *sb* drivved.

drill [drɪl] **A 1** *sb* bor, drill; **2** *vb* bore, drille; **B 1** *sb* drill, eksersis; (inn)øving; **2** *vb* drille, eksersere; øve (inn); **C 1** *sb* fure, rad; **2** *vt* radså; **D** *sb* drill (dvs kraftig bomullsstoff). **drill(ing) ǀ bit** *sb petro etc* borkrone. *~* **column** *sb petro* borestreng. *~* **floor** *sb petro* boregulv. *~* **fluid** = *~ mud*. *~* **line** *sb petro* borevaier. *~* **mast** *sb petro* boremast. *~* **mud** *sb petro* boreslam. *~* **platform** *sb petro* boreplattform. *~* **rig** *sb petro* borerigg. *~* **vessel** *sb petro* borefartøy. **drill ǀ pipe** *sb petro* borerør. *~* **shaft** *sb petro* boreskaft. *~* **stem, ~ string** *sb petro* borestreng.

drink [drɪŋk] **1** *sb* drikk(e); dram, drink; *også*

drukkenskap, fyll; **2** *vb* drikke; ~ *to* skåle for. **drinking** ['drɪŋkɪŋ] **1** *som adj* drikk-; **2** *sb* drikk(ing). **drinking-bout** *sb* rangel.

drip [drɪp] **1** *sb* drypp(ing); **2** *vb* dryppe; *~ping wet* dryppende våt.

drive [draɪv] **I** *sb* **1** kjøretur; kjøring; **2** *US (~-way)* oppkjørsel; **3** driftighet; driv(kraft), energi; fremdrift, pågangsmot; **4** aksjon, (innsamlings)kampanje; **5** drivverk; **II** *vb* **1** drive; presse, tvinge; **2** kjøre (dvs selv føre kjøretøyet, jf *ride II 3*); **3** ~ *at* hentyde/sikte til; ~ *away at* drive på/henge i med; *let ~ at* lange ut mot; sende av sted mot. **drive door** *sb data* diskettklaff.

drivel ['drɪvl] **I** *sb* **1** sludder, tøv; pjatt; **2** sikl(ing); **II** *vi* **1** sludre, tøve; **2** sikle.

driver ['draɪvə] *sb* **1** (-)driver, driftekar; **2** sjåfør, (vogn)fører. **driver's license** *US* = **driving licence** *sb* førerkort.

drizzle ['drɪzl] *sb, vb* duskregn(e).

droll [drəul] *adj* komisk; pussig.

dromedary ['drɒmədərɪ] *sb* dromedar.

drone [drəun] **I** *sb* **1** drone; lathans; snylter; **2** brum(ming), dur; **II** *vb* brumme; dure; kverne; lire av seg.

droop [dru:p] **I** *sb* hengende/lutende stilling; slapphet; **II** *vi* **1** henge (slapt ned); lute; **2** visne.

drop [drɒp] **I** *sb* **1** dråpe; *acid ~s* syrlige drops/ sukkertøy; *ear-~s* øredobber; **2** fall (og fallhøyde); fallem; **II** *vb* **1** dryppe; **2** falle (ned); falle om; la seg falle; *ready to ~* falleferdig, segneferdig; **3** la falle; miste, slippe (ned); gi slipp/*fig* avkall på; *dgl* droppe (også = sløyfe, utelate); ~ *a letter* sende et brev; ~ *her at the station* sette/slippe henne av ved stasjonen; **4** felle, skyte (ned); **5** dale, synke; **6** *med adv/prep* ~ **astern** = ~ *behind*; ~ **away** *(off/out)* falle fra; bli borte (en etter en); ~ **behind** sakke akterut; ~ **in** *on* stikke innom (hos); ~ **off** tape seg; blunde, småsove; falle i søvn; sovne (inn) (dvs dø); ~ **out** bryte løp/ studier etc; bryte over tvert/ut; gi opp; slutte (med); ~ **through** falle igjennom; gjøre fiasko. **dropper** ['drɒpə] *sb* dråpeteller.

drought [draut] *sb* tørke(periode).

drown [draun] *vb* **1** drukne; *they were all ~ed* de druknet alle sammen; **2** oversvømme.

drowsy ['drauzɪ] *adj* døsig.

drudge [drʌdʒ] **1** *sb* (arbeids)trell, sliter; **2** *vi* slave, slite. **drudgery** ['drʌdʒərɪ] *sb* slit; kjedelig arbeid.

drug [drʌg] **I** *sb* **1** apotekervare, legemiddel; **2** rusgift; *fl især* narkotika; **3** *merk* uselgelig vare; **II** *vb* **1** bedøve; forgifte; **2** bruke narkotika. **druggist** ['drʌgɪst] *sb* legemiddelforhandler; *US* innehaver av **drug-store** *sb* ≈ apotek (som også fører en mengde andre varer, f.eks. toalettartikler, blader og bøker, og også fungerer som kafeteria, sodabar, tesalong etc).

drum [drʌm] **I** *sb* **1** tromme; **2** trommel, valse; **3** fat, fustasje; **4** trommehinne; **II** *vb* **1** tromme; ~ *up* tromme sammen; **2** banke, dundre. **drummer** *sb* trommeslager.

drunk [drʌŋk] **I** *adj* beruset, full; **II** *sb* **1** fyllik; **2** fyllekalas. **drunkard** ['drʌŋkəd] *sb* dranker, fyllik. **drunken** ['drʌŋkən] *adj* (for)drukken; (stadig) beruset/full. **drunken driving** *sb* fyllekjøring. **drunkenness** *sb* drukkenskap.

dry [draɪ] **1** *adj* tørr (og tørrlagt etc); **2** *vb* tørke; tørre; ~ *up* tørke inn; *som interj* hold kjeft! **dry | facts** *sb fl* nakne fakta. ~ **gas** *sb petro* tørrgass. ~ **goods** *sb fl* korn; *US* manufakturvarer. ~ **hole** *sb petro* tørt hull.

dual ['dju:əl] *adj* dobbelt(-); todelt.

dub [dʌb] *vt* **1** slå til ridder; **2** gi (øke)navn; **3** *film* dubbe; **4** impregnere, smøre.

dubious ['dju:bɪəs] *adj* tvilsom; usikker, uviss; **2** tvilsom.

ducal ['dju:kl] *adj* hertugelig. **duchess** ['dʌtʃɪs] *sb* hertuginne. **duchy** ['dʌtʃɪ] *sb* hertugdømme.

duck [dʌk] **A** *sb* **1** and; *lame ~* stakkar; handikappet etc person; politiker som ikke kommer til å bli gjenvalgt; **2** amfibiekjøretøy; **B I** *sb* dukkert; dukking; **II** *vb* **1** dukke; **2** dukke (unna); **C** *sb* seilduk; grovt lerret; *fl* lerretsbukser.

dud [dʌd] **I** *adj* falsk, uekte; **II** *sb* **1** *mil* blindgjenger; *fig* falsum; fiasko; **2** *fl* gamle klær; filler og bein.

due [dju:] **I** *adj* skyldig; betalbar, forfallen; *be ~ to* skyldes; *become/fall ~* forfalle (til betaling); **2** passende, tilbørlig; **3** ventet (ifølge avtale, rute etc); **II** *adv sjø: ~ east/west etc* rett (mot) øst/vest etc; **III** *sb* rett; tilgodehavende; skyldighet; *fl* avgifter; kontingent.

duffer ['dʌfə] *sb* **1** dust, tosk; **2** klossmajor, kløne.

dug [dʌg] *sb* spene; jur.

dugout ['dʌgaut] *sb* **1** beskyttelsesgrav, skyttergrop; **2** kano (av uthult trestamme).

duke [dju:k] *sb* hertug.

dull [dʌl] **I** *adj* **1** matt, uklar; ~ *weather* gråvær; **2** treg, tungnem; **3** kjedelig, langtekkelig; **4** sløv, stump; **II** *vb* **1** bli/gjøre matt *etc*; **2** sløve(s); dulme, lindre.

duly ['dju:lɪ] *adv* passende; tilbørlig; rettelig.

dumb [dʌm] *adj* **1** målløs, stum; **2** *US dgl* dum. **dumbfound** [dʌm'faund] *vt* forbløffe; slå med forvirring.

dummy ['dʌmɪ] **I** *adj* uekte; **II** *sb* **1** prøve (som ser ut som den ferdige vare etc); attrapp; imitasjon; **2** prøve|byste, -dukke; utstillingsfigur; **3** blindemann; *fig* stråmann. **dummy pig** *sb petro* inspeksjonspigg.

dump [dʌmp] **I** *sb* **1** fylling, søppelhaug; **2** *mil* (midlertidig) depot, lager(plass); **3** *data* dump; **4** *slang* avkrok, hull; kneipe; **II** *vt* **1** dumpe (også *data*); kaste/slenge fra seg; kassere; **2** *merk* dumpe.

dun [dʌn] **A 1** *adj* gråbrun; mørk; **2** *sb* gråbrunt; **B I** *sb* **1** inkassobud; **2** rykkerbrev; **II** *vt* purre (på innbetaling); rykke.

dunce [dʌns] *sb* sinke, tosk.

dune [dju:n] *sb* (sand)dyne.

dung [dʌŋ] *sb* gjødsel, møkk.

dungarees [ˌdʌŋgə'ri:z] *sb fl* dongeribukse(r).

dungeon ['dʌndʒən] *sb* fangehull, fengsel.

dunghill ['dʌŋhɪl] *sb* dynge, gjødselhaug.

dupe [dju:p] **A 1** *sb* (godtroende) fjols; tosk; **2** *vt* lure, narre; **B** *dgl, især foto* = **duplicate I** ['dju:plɪkət] **1** *adj* dobbelt(-), dublett-; **2** *sb* dublett; gjenpart, kopi; **II** ['dju:plɪkeɪt] *vt* duplisere; kopiere, ta gjenpart/kopi av. **duplicity** [dju:'plɪsətɪ] *sb* dobbeltspill, falskhet; lureri.

durable ['djʊərəbl] *adj* holdbar, varig. **duration** [djʊ'reɪʃn] *sb* varighet; *for the* ~ inntil videre.

duress(e) [djʊ'res] *sb* press, tvang.

during ['djʊərɪŋ] *prep* under, i løpet av.

dusk [dʌsk] *sb* skumring, tusmørke.

dust [dʌst] **I** *sb* **1** støv; **2** avfall, søppel; **II** *vt* **1** støve (av); tørre støv av; **2** strø. **dust|bin** *sb* søppelkasse. **~-chute** *sb* søppelsjakt. **~-coat** *sb* støvfrakk. **duster** *sb petro* tørt borehull. **dust|man** *sb* søppelmann. **~pan** *sb* feiebrett. **dusty** *adj* støvet; *fig også* knusktørr.

Dutch [dʌtʃ] *adj, sb* **1** nederlandsk (se midtsidene); **2** *dgl:* ~ *comfort/consolation* mager trøst; *double* ~ labbelensk; *go* ~ spleise; *...then I'm a ~man* ...så kan du kalle meg en krakk.

dutiable ['dju:tɪəbl] *adj* avgiftspliktig, tollpliktig.

dutiful ['dju:tɪfʊl] *adj* pliktoppfyllende; lydig. **duty** ['dju:tɪ] **I** *adj* **1** plikt-; **2** tjenestegjørende, vakthavende; **II** *sb* **1** plikt, skyldighet; *sense of* ~ pliktfølelse; **2** (plikt)tjeneste, vakt; oppgave, verv; *do ~ for* gjøre tjeneste som; *off* ~ (tjeneste)fri; *on* ~ i tjeneste, på vakt; **3** avgift, gebyr; toll. **duty-free** *adj* avgiftsfri, tollfri.

dwarf [dwɔ:f] **I** *sb* dverg **II** *vt* **1** hindre/stanse i veksten; forkrøple; **2** få til å se liten ut (ved sammenligning); dominere; overskygge; ta luven fra.

dwell [dwel] *vi* **1** bo, oppholde seg (*at* i, ved; *in* i); **2** ~ *(up)on* dvele/oppholde seg ved. **dwelling-house** *sb* bolig(hus), våningshus.

dwindle ['dwɪndl] *vi* svinne (inn).

dye [daɪ] **1** *sb* farge(stoff); **2** *vb* farge(s); *~d-in-the-wool (fig)* (vaske)ekte; *også* erke-.

dyke [daɪk] = *dike.*

dynamic [daɪ'næmɪk] **I** *adj* **1** dynamisk; **2** energisk; **II** *sb fl* dynamikk; *fig også* drivkraft.

dynamite ['daɪnəmaɪt] *sb, vt* (sprenge med) dynamitt.

dynastic [dɪ'næstɪk] *adj* dynastisk, dynasti-. **dynasty** ['dɪnəstɪ] *sb* dynasti.

dysentery ['dɪsəntrɪ] *sb* dysenteri.

E

each [i:tʃ] **1** *adj* hver (enkelt); **2** *pron* (en)hver; ~ *other* hverandre (især når det dreier seg om to, jf *one 6: one another*).

eager [i:gə] *adj* ivrig (*for/to* etter (å)); oppsatt/spent (*to* på (å)).

eagle ['i:gl] *sb* ørn. **eagle-owl** *sb* hubro.

ear [ɪə] **A** *sb* **1** øre (og hørsel, gehør); **2** (gryte)øre; hank; **B** *sb* aks.

earl [з:l] *sb* jarl; greve. **earldom** ['з:ldəm] *sb* jarls|dømme, -verdighet; grevskap.

ear|lobe *sb* øreflipp. **~shot** *sb* hørevidde.

early ['з:lɪ] *adj, adv* tidlig.

earn [з:n] *vt* **1** tjene; ~ *one' living/livelihood* tjene til livets opphold; **2** fortjene; **3** innbringe; skaffe; **4** få; oppnå.

earnest ['з:nɪst] **A 1** *adj* alvorlig; **2** *sb* alvor; **B** *sb* **1** forsmak; ~ *of* tegn på; løfte om; **2** *(~-money)* håndpenger.

earnings ['з:nɪŋz] *sb fl* inntekt(er); fortjeneste.

earth [з:θ] **I** *sb* **1** jord (og jordbunn; landjord; jordklode(n), verden); **2** hi, jordhule; **II** *vt* **1** ~ *up* kaste igjen (grav/grop); dekke med jord; hyppe (poteter); **2** jorde (elektrisk utstyr). **earthen** ['з:θən] *adj* jord-; leir(e)-. **earthenware** ['з:θənweə] *sb* steintøy.

earthly ['з:θlɪ] *adj* jordisk; verdslig. **earth|quake** ['з:θkweɪk] *sb* jordskjelv. **~worm** ['з:θwз:m] *sb* meitemark.

ease [i:z] **I** *sb* **1** letthet; **2** ledighet, utvungenhet; **3** komfort; velvære; *at* ~ avslappet, hvilende; i ro og mak; *ill at* ~ utilpass; ille til mote; *put at* ~ få til å slappe av/føle seg (som) hjemme etc; **4** lettelse; lindring; **II** *vb* **1** *(~ off)* lette; lindre; ~ *of* befri for; **2** løse/slakke på; ~ *off/up* slappe av; ta det (mer) med ro.

easel ['i:zl] *sb* staffeli.

easily ['i:zɪlɪ] *adv* **1** lett, lettvint *etc* (jf *easy 1*); **2** ~ *the best etc* avgjort/opplagt den beste etc.

east [i:st] **I** *adj* øst-, østre; østlig, østa-; **II** *adv* **1** østover; ~ *of* øst for; **2** østpå; **III** *sb* øst; *to the ~ of* øst for.

Easter ['i:stə] *sb* påske.

easterly ['i:stəlɪ] *adj, adv* **1** østlig; fra øst; østa-; **2** mot øst. **eastern** ['i:stən] *adj* østlig; østre- øst-; *Eastern (også)* orientalsk. **eastward** ['i:stwəd] *adj* østlig (dvs mot øst). **eastwards** ['i:stwədz] *adv* østover, mot øst.

easy ['i:zɪ] **I** *adj* **1** lett; lettvint, ubesværet; ~ *money* lettjente penger; **2** *(~-going)* grei, liketil; **3** behagelig, passende; trygg; **4** bekvem, makelig; **II** *adv* lett; ~ *does it!* forsiktig (nå)! ta det rolig! *go* ~ ta det med ro; *go ~ on* spare på, være forsiktig med; *stand ~ (mil)* stå/ta på stedet hvil; *take it ~* ta det rolig. **easy|-chair** *sb* lenestol. **~-going** *adj* avslappet, uforstyrrelig; munter, sorgløs; likeglad.

eat [i:t] **I** *sb fl slang* mat; **II** *vb* **1** spise; **2** fortære; etse/tære (på). **eatable** ['i:təbl] *adj* spiselig.

eaves [i:vz] *sb fl* takskjegg. **eavesdrop** ['i:vzdrɒp] *vb* smuglytte.

ebb [eb] **1** *sb (~-tide)* ebbe/fjære (sjø); *fig* manko; forfall, nedgang; **2** *vb* ebbe; minke, synke; (for)-svinne.

ebony ['ebənɪ] *sb* ibenholt.

eccentric [ɪk'sentrɪk] **1** *adj* eksentrisk; forskrudd, rar; **2** *sb* eksentriker; (underlig) skrue. **eccentricity** [ˌeksən'trɪsətɪ] *sb* eksentrisitet *etc.*

ecclesiastic [ɪˌkli:zɪ'æstɪk] *adj, sb* geistlig (person). **ecclesiastical** [ɪˌkli:zɪ'æstɪkl] *adj* geistlig, kirkelig.

echo ['ekəʊ] **1** *sb* ekko, gjenlyd; gjenklang; **2** *vb* gi gjenlyd; kaste/bli kastet tilbake; ape/herme etter. **echo-sounder** *sb* ekkolodd.

eclipse [ɪ'klɪps] **1** *sb* formørkelse; **2** *vt* formørke; *fig* overskygge.

economic [ˌi:kə'nɒmɪk] **1** *adj* økonomisk, økonomi-; **2** *sb fl* (sosial)økonomi. **economical** [ˌi:kə'nɒmɪkl] *adj* sparsommelig; økonomisk. **economist** [i:'kɒnəmɪst] *sb* **1** (sosial)økonom; **2** sparsommelig person. **economize** [i:'kɒnəmaɪz] *vb* spare; økonomisere. **economy** [i:'kɒnəmɪ] *sb* **1** sparsommelighet; økonomisering; (god) økonomi; **2** *political ~* (sosial)-økonomi.

ecstasy ['ekstəsɪ] *sb* ekstase. **ecstatic** [ek'stætɪk] *adj* ekstatisk; (som) i ekstase.

eczema ['eksɪmə] *sb* eksem.

eddy ['edɪ] **1** *sb* (strøm)virvel; (bak)evje; **2** *vi* virvle (rundt).

edge [edʒ] **I** *sb* **1** kant; rand, utkant; bredd; bord, (kant)list; *on ~* på (høy)kant; irritabel; **2** *(cutting ~)* egg; skjær; *give/put an ~ to* skjerpe; *fig også* sette (en) spiss på; *take the ~ off* sløve; *fig* ta brodden av; **3** skarphet (især *fig*); **4** *slang* forsprang; overtak; **II** *vb* **1** kante; **2** skjerpe; **3** lirke (på plass etc); ake (skubbe, skyve) seg; *~ nearer* trekke (seg) nærmere. **edge|-ways, ~wise** ['edʒweɪz, -waɪz] *adv* på (høy)kant. **edging** ['edʒɪŋ] *sb* bord, kant.

edible ['edəbl] **1** *adj* spiselig (dvs ikke giftig, skadelig etc); matnyttig; **2** *sb fl* mat(varer).

edifice ['edɪfis] *sb* (stor) bygning, byggverk. **edify** ['edɪfaɪ] *vt* oppbygge; belære (moralsk). **edifying** ['edɪfaɪɪŋ] *adj* oppbyggelig.

edit ['edɪt] *vt* redigere; *film* klippe. **edition** [ɪ'dɪʃn] *sb* utgave; opplag. **edit mode** *sb data* redigeringsmodus. **editor** ['edɪtə] *sb* redaktør. **editorial** [ˌedɪ'tɔ:rɪəl] **1** *adj* redaksjonell; redaksjons-; redaktør-; **2** *sb* leder(artikkel), redaksjonell artikkel. **editor program** *sb data* redigeringsprogram.

educate ['edjʊkeɪt] *vt* utdanne; undervise; instruere; lære opp; oppdra. **education** [ˌedjʊ'keɪʃn] *sb* utdannelse *etc.* **educational** [ˌedjʊ'keɪʃənl] *adj* utdannelses-, undervisnings-.

eel [i:l] *sb* ål.

eerie, eery ['ɪərɪ] *adj* nifs.

efface [ɪ'feɪs] *vt* utslette; stryke ut.

effect [ɪ'fekt] **I** *sb* **1** resultat, virkning; inntrykk; *bring/carry into ~* gjennomføre; virkeliggjøre; sette i kraft/verk; *take ~* gjøre (sin) virkning; tre i kraft; **2** betydning, (menings)innhold; *(letter/proposal etc) to the ~ that* (brev/forslag etc) som går ut på at; **3** *fl* effekter, eiendeler; **II** *vt* bevirke, forårsake; besørge, effektuere; utvirke, få i stand. **effective** [ɪ'fektɪv] *adj* **1** aktiv; effektiv; **2** gyldig; virksom; **3** *mil* stridsdyktig. **effectual** [ɪ'fektʃʊəl] *adj* kraftig, virkningsfull; probat.

effeminate [ɪ'femɪnət] *adj* feminin [sagt om menn]; bløtaktig, kvinnfolkaktig.

effervescent [ˌefə'vesnt] *adj* boblende, brusende, musserende; overstrømmende, sprudlende.

efficiency [ɪ'fɪʃənsɪ] *sb* effektivitet *etc.* **efficient** [ɪ'fɪʃənt] *adj* effektiv; dyktig, flink.

effigy ['efɪdʒɪ] *sb* bilde.

effort ['efət] *sb* **1** anstrengelse, krafttak; energisk forsøk; **2** prestasjon.

effrontery [ɪ'frʌntərɪ] *sb* frekkhet, uforskammethet.

effusion [ɪ'fju:ʒn] *sb* utgytelse; *fig også* flom. **effusive** [ɪ'fju:sɪv] *adj* overstrømmende.

egg [eg] **A** *sb* **1** egg; **2** *slang* fyr, kar; **B** *vt: ~ on* egge, tilskynde. **egg-head** *sb slang* superintellektuell person.

egoism ['egəʊɪzəm] *sb* egoisme (i nøytral, filosofisk betydning). **egoist** ['egəʊɪst] *sb* egoist. **egoistic** [ˌegəʊ'ɪstɪk] *adj* egoistisk, selvsentrert. **egotism** ['egəʊtɪzəm] *sb* egoisme (oftest i nedsettende betydning); innbilskhet, selvopptatthet. **egotist** ['egəʊtɪst] *sb* egoist. **egotistic** [ˌegəʊ'tɪstɪk] *adj* egoistisk; innbilsk, selvopptatt.

egregious [ɪ'gri:dʒəs] *adj* grov, hårreisende; toppmålt.

eider ['aɪdə] *sb* ærfugl.

either ['aɪðə] **I** *adj, pron* **1** den/det ene eller den/det andre; hvilken/hvilket som helst (av to); **2** hver sin/sitt; *on ~ side* på hver (sin) side; på begge sider; **3** *etter nektelse* noen (av to); **II** *adv: etter nektelse* heller; **III** *konj: ~ ... or* enten ... eller.

ejaculate [ɪ'dʒækjʊleɪt] *vt* **1** ejakulere, sprøyte ut; **2** utbryte. **ejaculation** [ɪˌdʒækjʊ'leɪʃn] *sb* ejakulering *etc.*

ejct [ɪ'dʒekt] *vt* **1** fordrive, kaste ut; **2** sende (slynge, sprøyte, spy) ut. **ejection** [ɪ'dʒekʃn] *sb* utkasting *etc.*

eke [i:k] *vt: ~ out* drøye; få til å vare/strekke til.

elaborate I [ɪ'læbərət] *adj* innviklet; detaljert, omstendelig (utarbeidet); **II** [ɪ'læbəreɪt] *vt* utarbeide (omhyggelig); **2** utdype; forklare nærmere; gå i detalj. **elaboration** [ɪˌlæbə'reɪʃn] *sb* utdypelse *etc.*

elapse [ɪ'læps] *vi* gå (om tiden).

elastic [ɪ'læstɪk] **1** *adj* elastisk; fjærende; smidig; tøyelig; **2** *sb* strikk. **elasticity** [ˌelæ'stɪsətɪ] *sb* elastisitet *etc.*

elated [ɪ'leɪtɪd] *adj* opprømt (*at* over). **elation** [ɪ'leɪʃn] *sb* opprømthet; jublende glede.

elbow ['elbəʊ] **I** *sb* **1** albue; **2** kne (dvs vinkelforbindelse); **II** *vt:* ~ *one's way* albue/trenge seg frem.

elder ['eldə] **A I** *adj* eldre/eldst (av to); **II** *sb* **1** eldre (person); **2** eldste(bror) (i kirkesamfunn); **B** *sb* hyll. **elderly** ['eldəlɪ] *adj* eldre.

elect [ɪ'lekt] **I** *adj* kåret, (ut)valgt; **II** *vt* **1** kåre, velge (ut); **2** bestemme seg for; foretrekke. **election** [ɪ'lekʃn] *sb* **1** valg; **2** kåring, utvelgelse.

electric [ɪ'lektrɪk] *adj* elektrisk (drevet, ladet etc). **electrical** [ɪ'lektrɪkl] *adj* elektrisk; elektrisitets-, elektro-. **electrician** [ˌɪlek'trɪʃn] *sb* elektriker. **electricity** [ˌɪlek'trɪsətɪ] *sb* elektrisitet. **elektrification** [ɪˌlektrifɪ'keɪʃn] *sb* elektrisering *etc.* **electrify** [ɪ'lektrɪfaɪ] *vt* **1** elektrisere, gjøre elektrisk; **2** elektrifisere, gjøre elektrisk drevet. **electrocute** [ɪ'lektrəkju:t] *vt* avlive/drepe med elektrisitet; *US* henrette i den elektriske stol. **electrocution** [ɪˌlektrə'kju:ʃn] *sb* avliving med elektrisitet. **electronic** [ˌɪlek'trɒnɪk] **1** *adj* elektronisk; **2** *sb fl* elektronikk. **electronic | data processing** *sb data* elektronisk databehandling. ~ **funds transfer** *sb data* elektronisk betalingsoverføring.

elegance ['elɪgəns] *sb* eleganse. **elegant** ['elɪgənt] *adj* elegant.

element ['elɪmənt] *sb* **1** grunstoff; (bestand)del; **2** *fl* begynnelsesgrunner, grunnleggende kunnskaper. **elemental** [ˌelɪ'mentl] *adj* element-, natur-. **elementary** [ˌelɪ'mentrɪ] *adj* elementær(-), grunnleggende.

elephant ['elɪfənt] *sb* elefant.

elevate ['elɪveɪt] *vt* **1** heve, løfte; **2** høyne; forfremme, opphøye; (opp)løfte. **elevated railway** *sb* høybane. **elevation** [ˌelɪ'veɪʃn] *sb* **1** heving; **2** høyning; forfremmelse, opphøyelse; opphøyethet, verdighet; løftet stemning; **3** stigning; høyde (over havet); **4** elevasjon; **5** oppriss. **elevator** ['elɪveɪtə] *sb* **1** *US* heis; **2** høyderor (på fly); **3** *a)* (korn)transportør; *b) især US* kornsilo; **4** *petro* klave.

elf [elf] *sb* alv.

elicit [ɪ'lɪsɪt] *vt* få (bringe, kalle, lokke etc) frem.

eligible ['elidʒebl] *adj* **1** valgbar; **2** passende, tilfredsstillende.

eliminate [ɪ'lɪmɪneɪt] *vt* eliminere, fjerne; kvitte seg med. **elimination** [ɪˌlɪmɪ'neɪʃn] *sb* eliminering *etc.*

elm [elm] *sb* alm.

elocution [ˌelə'kjuʃn] *sb* foredrag (dvs måte å fremføre tale etc på); talekunst.

elongate ['i:lɒŋgeɪt] *vb* forlenge; strekke (seg).

elope [ɪ'ləʊp] *vt* flykte, rømme.

eloquence ['eləʊkwəns] *sb* veltalenhet. **eloquent** ['eləʊkwənt] *adj* veltalende; *fig også* megetsigende, talende.

else [els] *adv* **1** ellers; for øvrig; **2** annen, annet; andre. **elsewhere** [ˌels'weə] *adv* annensteds, annetsteds; et annet sted; andre steder.

elucidate [ɪ'lu:sɪdeɪt] *vt* belyse *(fig)*; forklare (nærmere). **elucidation** [ɪˌlu:sɪ'deɪʃn] *sb* belysning *(fig)*; klargjøring.

elude [ɪ'lu:d] *vt* unngå, unnvike; slippe/smette unna. **elusive** [ɪ'lu:sɪv] *adj* unnvikende; vanskelig å få tak i/på.

emaciated [ɪ'meɪʃɪeɪtɪd] *adj* utmagret; (skinn)-mager. **emaciation** [ɪˌmeɪʃɪ'eɪʃn] *sb* utmagring *etc.*

emanate ['eməneɪt] *vi* strømme (frem); stråle (ut); utgå. **emanation** [ˌemə'neɪʃn] *sb* utstrømming *etc.*

emancipate [ɪ'mænsɪpeɪt] *vt* emansipere, frigjøre; frigi. **emancipation** [ɪˌmænsɪ'peɪʃn] *sb* emansipering *etc.*

emasculate 1 [ɪ'mæskjʊlət] *adj* kastrert; kjønnsløs; svak, svekket; **2** [ɪ'mæskjʊleɪt] *vt* kastrere; svekke.

embalm [ɪm'bɑ:m] *vt* balsamere.

embankment [ɪm'bæŋkmənt] *sb* demning; dike (langs elv); kai.

embark [ɪm'bɑ:k] *vb* **1** innskipe (seg); gå/ta om bord; **2** ~ *(up)on* legge ut på; gi seg i kast med. **embarkation** [ˌembɑ:'keɪʃn] *sb* innskipning *etc.*

embarrass [ɪm'bærəs] *vt* gjøre forlegen/forvirret; sette i forlegenhet; **2** hemme, hindre. **embarrassment** [ɪm'bærəsmənt] *sb* forlegenhet.

embassy ['embəsɪ] *sb* ambassade.

embellish [ɪm'belɪʃ] *vt* forskjønne; pynte; (ut)-smykke. **embellishment** [em'belɪʃmənt] *sb* forskjønnelse *etc.*

embers ['embəz] *sb fl* glør.

embezzle [ɪm'bezl] *vt* underslå.

embitter [ɪm'bɪtə] *vt* forbitre, gjøre bitter.

emblem ['embləm] *sb* emblem, merke; symbol, tegn.

embodiment [ɪm'bɒdɪmənt] *sb* legemliggjøring *etc.* **embody** [ɪm'bɒdɪ] *vt* **1** legemliggjøre; personifisere; **2** kle/uttrykke i ord; utforme; **3** innbefatte, omfatte; romme.

embolden [ɪm'bəʊldən] *vt* gi mot, gjøre dristig; oppflamme.

embrace [ɪm'breɪs] **I** *sb* omfavnelse; **II** *vb* **1** omfavne (hverandre); **2** gripe (ivrig); **3** (an)ta, godta; slutte seg til; **4** innbefatte, omfatte.

embroider [ɪm'brɔɪdə] *vb* brodere; *fig også* utbrodere. **embroidery** [ɪm'brɔɪdərɪ] *sb* broderi.

embroil [ɪm'brɔɪl] *vt* innvikle; blande/trekke inn i; implisere; **2** forstyrre; bringe uorden i.

emend [i:'mend] *vt* rette (feil etc); forbedre (tekst). **emendation** [ˌi:mən'deɪʃn] *sb* rettelse; forbedring.

emerald ['emərəld] *sb* smaragd.

emerge [ɪ'mɜ:dʒ] *vi* komme frem (opp, ut, til syne etc); dukke opp; vise seg.

emergency [ɪ'mɜ:dʒənsɪ] *sb* **1** krise(situasjon);

nøds|situasjon, -tilstand; *state of* ~ unntakstilstand; **2** *som adj* krise-, nød(s)-; beredskaps-; reserve-. **emergency | area** *sb* katastrofeområde. ~ **landing** *sb* nødlanding. ~ **plan** *sb* beredskapsplan. ~ **room** *sb* skadestue.

emery ['emərɪ] *sb* smergel.

emigrant ['emɪgrənt] *sb* emigrant. **emigrate** ['emɪgreɪt] *vi* emigrere. **emigration** [ˌemɪ'greɪʃn] *sb* emigrering, emigrasjon.

eminence ['emɪnəns] *sb* **1** forhøyning, høyde(drag); **2** opphøyethet; anseelse, fremtredende posisjon. **eminent** ['emɪnənt] *adj* fremragende; fremtredende; høytstående.

emissary ['emɪsərɪ] *sb* utsending; (hemmelig) agent. **emission** [ɪ'mɪʃn] *sb* **1** (ut)sending *etc*; **2** utstedelse. **emit** [ɪ'mɪt] *vt* **1** sende (ut); kaste (slynge, sprøyte, stråle etc) ut; gi fra seg; komme med; sette i; **2** utstede.

emolument [ɪ'mɒljʊmənt] *sb* (bi)inntekt; avkastning, utbytte.

emotion [ɪ'məʊʃn] *sb* (sinns)bevegelse; (sterk) følelse. **emotional** [ɪ'məʊʃənl] *adj* **1** følelsesmessig, følelses-; **2** følsom; (lett)bevegelig.

emperor ['empərə] *sb* keiser.

emphasis ['emfəsɪs] *sb* (etter)trykk; tyngde, vekt. **emphasize** ['emfəsaɪz] *vt* legge trykk/vekt på; *fig* understreke. **emphatic** [ɪm'fætɪk] *adj* ettertrykkelig.

empire ['empaɪə] *sb* **1** keiserrike; imperium, verdensrike; **2** (over)herredømme.

employ [ɪm'plɔɪ] **I** *sb* ansettelse; tjeneste; **II** *vt* **1** beskjeftige, sysselsette; ha i arbeid; **2** anvende, bruke; (ut)nytte. **employee** [ˌemplɔɪ'i:] *sb* arbeidstaker. **employer** [ɪm'plɔɪə] *sb* arbeidsgiver. **employment** [ɪm'plɔɪmənt] *sb* ansettelse; beskjeftigelse, sysselsetting; arbeid.

empower [ɪm'paʊə] *vt* **1** bemyndige; **2** sette i stand (*to* til).

empress ['emprɪs] *sb* keiserinne.

empty ['emptɪ] **1** *adj* tom; **2** *sb fl* tomgods (dvs tomflasker, tomkasser etc); **3** *vb* tømme(s).

emulate ['emjʊleɪt] *vt* **1** kappes/konkurrere med; (forsøke å) etterligne/overgå; **2** *data* emulere.

enable [ɪ'neɪbl] *vt* sette i stand (*to* til (å)). **enabled** [ɪ'neɪbld] *adj* **1** (satt) i stand til; **2** *data* avbruddssikker.

enact [ɪ'nækt] *vt* **1** bestemme, forordne; vedta; lovfeste; **2** oppføre/spille (en scene etc). **enactment** [ɪ'næktmənt] *sb* **1** vedtakelse av lov; **2** forordning, lov.

enamel [ɪ'næml] **I** *sb* **1** emalje; **2** glasur; **3** (emalje)lakk; **II** *vt* **1** emaljere; **2** glas(s)ere; **3** lakkere (med emaljelakk).

enamoured [ɪ'næməd] *adj* forelsket (*of* i); henrykt (*of* over).

encase [ɪn'keɪs] *vt* innkapsle; pakke inn; sette trekk på.

enchant [ɪn'tʃɑ:nt] *vt* **1** fryde, henrykke; **2** forhekse; (be)dåre, sjarmere. **enchantment** [ɪn'tʃɑ:ntmənt] *sb* forheksing *etc*; fortryllelse.

encircle [ɪn'sɜ:kl] *vt* omgi; innringe, omringe; gå rundt (om).

enclose [ɪn'kləʊz] *vt* **1** omgi (med gjerde etc); gjerde inn; **2** legge i omslag (konvolutt, pakke etc). **enclosed** [ɪn'kləʊzd] *adj* vedlagt. **enclosure** [ɪn'kləʊʒə] *sb* **1** inngjerding, kve; gjerde; **2** bilag, vedlegg.

encode [ɪn'kəʊd] *vt data* (om)kode.

encompass [ɪn'kʌmpəs] *vt* omgi, omslutte; *fig* omfatte.

encore [ɒŋ'kɔ:] **1** *adv, interj* dakapo (dvs om igjen); **2** *sb, vb* (forlange) ekstranummer.

encounter [ɪn'kaʊntə] **I** *sb* **1** møte (især plutselig og uventet); **2** (ofte fiendtlig) sammenstøt; **II** *vt* møte; støte/treffe på.

encourage [ɪn'kʌrɪdʒ] *vt* sette mot i; **2** oppmuntre; inspirere; **3** støtte. **encouragement** [ɪn'kʌrɪdʒmənt] *sb* oppmuntring *etc*.

encroach [ɪn'krəʊtʃ] *vi:* ~ *upon* trenge inn på; *fig også* trenge seg på; legge (utilbørlig) beslag på.

encumber [ɪn'kʌmbə] *vt* **1** bebyrde, tynge; plage; hemme, hindre; hefte; **2** fylle opp. **encumbered** [ɪn'kʌmbəd] *adj* nedlesset, overlesset; *merk* beheftet; *fig også* belemret.

encyclop(a)edia [enˌsaɪkləʊ'pi:dɪə] *sb* (konversasjons)leksikon.

end [end] **I** *sb* **1** ende (og endestykke); stump; tamp; ~ *on, on* ~ på ende/høykant; på rad; i trekk; **2** avslutning, opphør; slutt; *at an* ~ oppbrukt, slutt; *at one's wit's* ~ opprådd; *in the* ~ til slutt; i lengden; **3** (for)mål, hensikt; ~*s and means* mål og midler; **II** *vb* (av)slutte, ende; ~ *in* ende med; ~ *off* avslutte; ~ *up* (av)slutte.

endanger [ɪn'deɪndʒə] *vt* utsette for fare; sette på spill.

endear [ɪn'dɪə] *vt:* ~ *oneself to* gjøre seg elsket/ godt likt av. **endearing** [ɪn'dɪərɪŋ] *adj* inntagende, vinnende. **endearment** [ɪn'dɪəmənt] *sb* kjærtegn; uttrykk for hengivenhet/ømhet.

endeavour [ɪn'devə] **1** *sb* anstrengelse; (iherdig) forsøk; **2** *vi* anstrenge/bestrebe seg; streve.

ending ['endɪŋ] *sb* (av)slutning, slutt; ende. **endless** ['endlɪs] *adj* endeløs, uendelig.

endorse [ɪn'dɔ:s] *vt* **1** *merk* endossere, påtegne; *fig* garantere, godkjenne; **2** støtte, gi sin tilslutning. **endorsement** [ɪn'dɔ:smənt] *sb* påtegning *etc*.

endow [ɪn'daʊ] *vt* gi, skjenke (pengemidler); ~*ed with* begavet med. **endowment** [ɪn'daʊmənt] *sb* legat, stiftelse.

endurable [ɪn'djʊərəbl] *adj* til å holde ut. **endurance** [ɪn'djʊərəns] *sb* **1** utholdenhet; motstandskraft, seighet; **2** varighet. **endure** [ɪn'djʊə] *vi* **1** holde ut, tåle; gjennomgå; **2** vare.

enema ['enɪmə] *sb* klyster.

enemy ['enəmɪ] *sb* fiende.

energetic [ˌenə'dʒetɪk] *adj* energisk. **energy**

['enədʒɪ] *sb* energi; handlekraft, styrke.

enervate ['enəveɪt] *vt* svekke, utmatte. **enervating** ['enəveɪtɪŋ] *adj* helseskadelig, nedbrytende.

enfeeble [ɪn'fi:bl] *vt* avkrefte, svekke.

enfold [ɪn'fəuld] *vt* **1** innhylle, omslutte; **2** omfavne.

enforce [ɪn'fɔ:s] *vt* **1** håndheve; gjennomføre, sette i verk; **2** bestyrke, forsterke; **3** tvinge (frem); tiltvinge seg. **enforcement** [ɪn'fɔ:smənt] *sb* håndhevelse *etc.*

enfranchise [ɪn'fræntʃaɪz] *vt* **1** gi stemmerett (og andre politiske rettigheter og forpliktelser); **2** frigi (slaver).

engage [ɪn'geɪdʒ] *vb* **1** engasjere; ansette, feste; ~ *(oneself) in* beskjeftige seg med; **2** påta seg; innlate seg på; **3** forplikte (seg til); garantere, love; *~d (to be married)* (ring)forlovet; **4** oppta; legge beslag på; **5** *mil* innlate seg i kamp (med); **6** koble inn; gripe inn i hverandre. **engagement** [ɪn'geɪdʒmənt] *sb* **1** engasjering *etc*; engasjement; **2** forpliktelse *etc*; avtale; løfte; forlovelse; **3** *mil* kamp, trefning; **4** innkobling *etc.* **engaging** [ɪn'geɪdʒɪŋ] *adj fig* tiltrekkende, vinnende.

engender [ɪn'dʒendə] *vt* **1** frembringe; *fig* vekke; **2** *fig* avle.

engine ['endʒɪn] *sb* **1** (kraft)maskin, motor; *gml også* redskap; **2** *(railway ~)* lokomotiv. **engine-driver** *sb* lokomotivfører. **engineer** [ˌendʒɪ'nɪə] **I** *sb* **1** ingeniør; **2** maskinist; *chief ~ (sjø)* maskinsjef; **3** *US* lokomotivfører; **4** *mil: the Engineers* Ingeniørvåpenet; **II** *vb* **1** arbeide som ingeniør; lede anleggs-/byggearbeid; **2** arrangere, få i stand. **engine | fuel** *sb petro* motor|brensel, -drivstoff. **~ oil** *sb petro* motorolje.

engrave [ɪn'greɪv] *vt* **1** gravere; **2** *(~ (up)on)* prege; *fig* innprente i. **engraver** [ɪn'greɪvə] *sb* gravør. **engraving** [ɪn'greɪvɪŋ] *sb* gravering; (kobber)stikk; (tre)snitt).

engross [ɪn'grəus] *vt: ~ed in* fordypet i; fengslet av.

engulf [ɪn'gʌlf] *vt* oppsluke.

enhance [ɪn'hɑ:ns] *vt* forhøye, forsterke, (for)øke.

enigma [ɪ'nɪgmə] *sb* gåte, mysterium. **enigmatic** [ˌenɪg'mætɪk] *adj* gåtefull, mystisk.

enjoin [ɪn'dʒɔɪn] *vt* **1** *(~ on)* påby; pålegge; **2** formane; nøde; **3** *US jur* forby.

enjoy [ɪn'dʒɔɪ] *vt* nyte; (kunne) glede seg over; ~ *oneself* ha det hyggelig. **enjoyment** [ɪn'dʒɔɪmənt] *sb* glede; nytelse.

enlarge [ɪn'lɑ:dʒ] *vb* forstørre(s); bli/gjøre større; **2** ~ *(up)on* utbre seg om. **enlargement** [ɪn'lɑ:dʒmənt] *sb* forstørrelse. **enlarger** [ɪn'lɑ:dʒə] *sb foto* forstørrelsesapparat.

enlighten [ɪn'laɪtn] *vt, især fig* opplyse. **enlightenment** [ɪn'laɪtnmənt] *sb* opplysning.

enlist [ɪn'lɪst] *vb* **1** (la seg) rekruttere, verve; **2** sikre seg. **enlistment** [ɪn'lɪstmənt] *sb* verving *etc.*

enliven [ɪn'laɪvn] *vt* live opp; gjøre livlig(ere).

enmity ['enmətɪ] *sb* fiendskap, uvennskap.

ennoble [ɪ'nəubl] *vt* adle; *fig* foredle.

enormity [ɪ'nɔ:mətɪ] *sb* uhyrlighet; grov forbrytelse etc. **enormous** [ɪ'nɔ:məs] *adj* enorm, uhyre stor; veldig.

enough [ɪ'nʌf] *adj, adv* nok, tilstrekkelig; *som sb* tilstrekkelig antall/mengde *etc*; ~ *and to spare* mer enn nok; *be good ~ to* vær(e) så snill å; *sure ~* ganske riktig.

enquire *etc* [ɪn'kwaɪə], se *inquire* etc.

enrage [ɪn'reɪdʒ] *vt* gjøre rasende.

enraptured [ɪn'ræptʃəd] *adj* henrykt; *også* full av beundring.

enrich [ɪn'rɪtʃ] *vt* **1** berike; **2** pryde, utsmykke.

enrol(l) [ɪn'rəul] *vt* innrullere; melde/skrive (seg) inn; verve. **enrollment** [ɪn'rəulmənt] *sb* innrullering *etc.*

ensign ['ensaɪn, *sjø* 'ensn] *sb* **1** fane, flagg (i den britiske marine: *red ~* på handelsskip, *white ~* på krigsskip); **2** distinksjon; merke/tegn (på grad, verdighet etc).

enslave [ɪn'sleɪv] *vt* slavebinde.

ensue [ɪn'sju:] *vi: ~ from/on* følge/komme (som en følge) av. **ensuing** [ɪn'sju:ɪŋ] *adj* (på)følgende; neste.

ensure [ɪn'ʃuə] *vt* **1** sikre/trygge *(against/from* mot); garantere; **2** forvisse (seg).

entail [ɪn'teɪl] **I** *sb* stamgods; **II** *vt* **1** medføre, nødvendiggjøre; **2** opprette stamgods.

entangle [ɪn'tæŋgl] *vt* fange; filtre/vikle inn i; *fig* besnære. **entangled** [ɪn'tæŋgld] *adj* floket, innviklet. **entanglement** [ɪn'tæŋglmənt] *sb* vase; *fig* floke, forvikling(er).

enter ['entə] *vb* **1** *a)* komme inn (i); *b)* bli medlem av/i; bli opptatt (som elev/medlem etc) av (i/på/ved); **2** *a)* gå (kjøre, reise etc) inn (i); *b)* gå/melde seg etc inn (i); begynne (som elev etc) i (på/ved); **3** føre/skrive inn; *merk* bokføre, postere; **4** *data* entre; **5** *med adv/prep* ~ **for** melde (seg) på til; ~ **into** inngå (i); innlate seg i/på; leve/sette seg inn i; begynne på; ~ **(up)on** begynne/ta fatt på; gi seg ut på; slå inn på; overtra, tiltre.

enterprise ['entəpraɪz] *sb* **1** (dristig) foretagende; *også merk* bedrift, virksomhet; **2** energi, foretaksomhet; initiativ. **enterprising** ['entəpraɪzɪŋ] *adj* energisk, foretaksom.

entertain [ˌentə'teɪn] *vt* underholde; **2** holde selskap for; beverte, traktere; **3** nære, overveie; ha i tankene; *merk* reflektere på. **entertainer** [ˌentə'teɪnə] *sb* underholdningsartist. **entertainment** [ˌentə'teɪnmənt] *sb* underholdning *etc.*

enthral(l) [ɪn'θrɔ:l] *vt* **1** fengsle, trollebinde; **2** slavebinde.

enthrone [ɪn'θrəun] *vt* sette på tronen; innsette (især biskop) i embete; *fig* høyakte.

enthusiasm [ɪn'θju:zɪæzəm] *sb* begeistring, entusiasme. **enthusiastic** [ɪnˌθju:zɪ'æstɪk] *adj* begeistret, entusiastisk.

entice [ɪn'taɪs] *vt* forføre *(into* til); lokke *(from* bort fra); friste. **enticement** [ɪn'taɪsmənt] *sb* forførelse *etc*.

entire [ɪn'taɪə] *adj* fullstendig; hel, udelt; *fig også* fullkommen, komplett. **entirety** [ɪn'taɪətɪ] *sb* helhet, hele.

entitle [ɪn'taɪtl] *vt* **1** benevne, navngi; sette tittel på; **2** berettige (*to* til). **entitlement** [ɪn'taɪtlmənt] *sb* benevnelse *etc*.

entity ['entətɪ] *sb* (innerste) vesen; eksistens.

entrails ['entreɪlz] *sb fl* innvoller; *fig* indre.

entrance A ['entrəns] *sb* **1** inngang (og inngangsdør; innkjørsel, innseiling etc); **2** inntreden (og innmarsj, inntog etc); entré (på scene etc); **3** adgang; **B** [ɪn'trɑ:ns] *vt* henrykke.

entreat [ɪn'tri:t] *vt* bønnfalle. **entreaty** [ɪn'tri:tɪ] *sb* bønnfallelse.

entrench [ɪn'trentʃ] *vt* forskanse (seg); befeste, styrke.

entrust [ɪn'trʌst] *vt* betro; overgi, overlate (til).

entry ['entrɪ] *sb* **1** inngang (også *data*); **2** inntreden; påmelding; *fl også* (påmeldte) deltakere; **3** innføring, notat; (regnskaps)post; *merk også* bokføring; **4** *(dictionary ~)* oppslagsord.

enumerate [ɪ'nju:məreɪt] *vt* regne, telle opp. **enumeration** [ɪ,nju:mə'reɪʃn] *sb* oppregning.

enunciate [ɪ'nʌnsɪeɪt] *vb* **1** erklære, forkynne; **2** uttale (ord). **enunciation** [ɪ,nʌnsɪ'eɪʃn] *sb* erklæring *etc*.

envelop [ɪn'veləp] *vt* dekke (til); innhylle. **envelope** ['envələʊp] *sb* konvolutt; omslag.

enviable ['envɪəbl] *adj* misunnelsesverdig. **envious** ['envɪəs] *adj* misunnelig.

environment [ɪn'vaɪərənmənt] *sb* omegn; omgivelser; miljø; *fig også* forhold, omstendigheter. **environmental** [ɪn,vaɪərən'mentl] *adj* miljø-. **environs** [ɪn'vaɪərənz] *sb fl* omegn, omgivelser.

envisage [ɪn'vɪzɪdʒ] *vt* **1** se i øynene; **2** betrakte, se på; **3** imøtese; forestille seg; regne med.

envoy ['envɔɪ] *sb* **1** sendebud, utsending; **2** sendemann.

envy ['envɪ] **1** *sb* misunnelse (og gjenstand for misunnelse); **2** *vt* misunne.

epidemic [,epɪ'demɪk] **1** *adj* epidemisk; **2** *sb* epidemi.

epithet ['epɪθet] *sb* (beskrivende) tilnavn.

epitome [ɪ'pɪtəmɪ] *sb* **1** eksempel, mønster; **2** sammendrag.

epoch ['i:pɒk] *sb* epoke.

equable ['ekwəbl] *adj* uforstyrrelig; jevn, likevektig. **equal** ['i:kwəl] **I** *adj* **1** ens(artet); lik; jevnbyrdig; **2** *~ to (fig)* på høyde med; **3** jevn; rolig; **II** *sb* like(mann); **III** *vt* ligne, være lik; kunne måle seg med. **equality** [ɪ'kwɒlətɪ] *sb* ensartethet *etc*; likhet. **equalization** [,i:kwəlaɪ'zeɪʒn] *sb* likestilling *etc*. **equalize** ['i:kwəlaɪz] *vt* likestille, jevnstille; utligne. **equanimity** [,ekwə'nɪmətɪ] *sb* likevekt, (sinns)ro; fatning. **equation** [ɪ'kweɪʃn] *sb* **1** ligning; **2** utligning. **equator** [ɪ'kweɪtə] *sb* ekvator. **equatorial** [,ekwə'tɔ:rɪəl] *adj* ekvatorial, ekvator-.

equestrian [ɪ'kwestrɪən] **1** *adj* rytter-; ride-; **2** *sb* rytter.

equilibrium [,i:kwɪ'lɪbrɪəm] *sb* balanse, likevekt.

equinox ['i:kwɪnɒks] *sb* jevndøgn.

equip [ɪ'kwɪp] *vt* utruste, utstyre. **equipment** [ɪ'kwɪpmənt] *sb* utrustning, utstyr; tilbehør.

equitable ['ekwɪtəbl] *adj* rettferdig, rimelig. **equity** ['ekwətɪ] *sb* rettferd(ighet), rimelighet; *jur også* billighet. **equity crude** *sb petro* eierolje. **equivalence** [ɪ'kwɪvələns] *sb* likeverd(ighet). **equivalent** [ɪ'kwɪvələnt] **1** *adj* likeverdig; tilsvarende; **2** *sb* motstykke; noe tilsvarende. **equivocal** [ɪ'kwɪvəkl] *adj* tvetydig; tvilsom.

era ['ɪərə] *sb* era, tidsalder.

eradicate [ɪ'rædɪkeɪt] *vt* utrydde, ødelegge; rykke opp med rot. **eradication** [ɪ,rædɪ'keɪʃn] *sb* utryddelse *etc*.

erase [ɪ'reɪz] *vt* radere (stryke/viske) ut; utslette; *data især* slette. **erase head** *sb data* slettehode. **eraser** [ɪ'reɪzə] *sb* viskelær.

erect [ɪ'rekt] **1** *adj* oppreist; rak, rett; **2** *vt* oppføre; reise, sette opp; montere; bygge, konstruere. **erection** [ɪ'rekʃn] *sb* **1** oppføring *etc*; **2** byggverk; konstruksjon.

ermine ['ɜ:mɪn] *sb* **1** røyskatt; **2** hermelin (og hermelinskåpe etc); **3** dommerkappe.

erode [ɪ'rəud] *vt* erodere, tære på. **erosion** [ɪ'rəuʒn] *sb* erosjon.

erotic [ɪ'rɒtɪk] **1** *adj* erotisk; **2** *sb* erotiker.

err [ɜ:] *vi* **1** gjøre/ta feil; **2** synde.

errand ['erənd] *sb* ærend; (mindre) oppdrag.

errant ['erənt] *adj* **1** (om)vandrende; **2** villfarende). **erratic** [ɪ'rætɪk] *adj* **1** springende, uregelmessig; **2** uberegnelig. **erroneous** [ɪ'rəunɪəs] *adj* feilaktig, uriktig. **error** ['erə] *sb* feil, feiltakelse. **error | condition** *sb data* feiltilstand. **~ control** *sb data* feilsikring. **~ message** *sb data* feilmelding. **~ recovery** *sb data* feilretting.

erudite ['erudaɪt] *adj* lærd. **erudition** [,eru'dɪʃn] *sb* lærdhet, stor lærdom.

erupt [ɪ'rʌpt] *vi* bryte frem/ut; *om vulkan* ha/være i utbrudd. **eruption** [ɪ'rʌpʃn] *sb* utbrudd.

escalate ['eskəleɪt] *vb* opptrappe, øke trinnvis. **escalation** [,eskə'leɪʃn] *sb* opptrapping. **escalator** ['eskəleɪtə] *sb* rulletrapp.

escapade [,eskə'peɪd] *sb* eskapade, sidesprang. **escape** [ɪ'skeɪp] **I** *sb* **1** flukt; **2** (nød)utvei; redning; **3** avløp; *fig også* utløp; **II** *vb* **1** flykte, komme (seg) unna; **2** unngå, holde seg unna; **3** *her name ~s me* jeg kommer ikke på navnet hennes. **escape | capsule** *sb petro etc* redningsklokke. **~ valve** *sb* sikkerhetsventil.

eschew [ɪs'tʃu:] *vt* sky, unngå.

escort I ['eskɔ:t] *sb* **1** eskorte; **2** kavaler; **II** [ɪ'skɔ:t] *vt* eskortere, ledsage (for å beskytte).

especial [ɪ'speʃl] *adj* spesiell, særlig. **especially** [ɪ'speʃlɪ] *adv* især.

espionage ['espɪənɑ:ʒ] *sb* spionasje.

espouse [ɪ'spaʊz] *vt* **1** støtte; gå inn for; **2** *gml* ekte, gifte seg med.

esquire [ɪ'skwaɪə] *sb* **1** *hist* væpner; **2** (etter navn i adresse etc, *fork* til *Esq*) herr.

essay 1 ['eseɪ] *sb* artikkel, essay; *også* (skole)stil, skriftlig oppgave; **2** [e'seɪ] *vb gml* forsøke.

essence ['esns] *sb* **1** (innerste) vesen; kjerne; **2** ekstrakt, essens. **essential** [ɪ'senʃl] **I** *adj* **1** (absolutt) nødvendig; **2** grunnleggende, vesentlig; **II** *sb* nødvendig (bestand)del.

establish [ɪ'stæblɪʃ] *vt* **1** grunnlegge, opprette; innsette; ~ *oneself (merk)* etablere/nedsette seg; begynne/åpne forretning; **2** (be)vise, godtgjøre; fastslå. **established** [ɪ'stæblɪʃt] *adj* etablert; grunnfestet. **establishment** [ɪ'stæblɪʃmənt] *sb* **1** grunnleggelse *etc*; **2** etablissement; organisasjon; **3** *the Establishment* de samfunnsbevarende institusjoner (især kongehuset, hæren og kirken).

estate [ɪ'steɪt] *sb* **1** eiendom (især *real* ~ fast eiendom); gods; **2** (samfunns)klasse, stand; **3** *gml* (til)-stand. **estate car** *sb* stasjonsvogn.

esteem [ɪ'sti:m] **I** *sb* aktelse; respekt; **II** *vt* **1** (høy)akte; respektere; **2** anse/betrakte (som). **estimable** ['estɪməbl] *adj* aktverdig. **estimate 1** ['estɪmət] *sb* overslag; skjønn; vurdering; **2** ['estɪmeɪt] *vb* anslå, beregne; vurdere.

estrange [ɪ'streɪndʒ] *vt* gjøre fremmed for; støte fra seg.

estuary ['estjʊərɪ] *sb* (især lang) elvemunning.

etch [etʃ] *vb* etse, gravere, radere; *fig også* prege. **etching** ['etʃɪŋ] *sb* radering.

eternal [ɪ'tɜ:nl] *adj* **1** evig(varende); **2** *dgl* evinnelig. **eternity** [ɪ'tɜ:nətɪ] *sb* evighet(en).

ether ['i:θə] *sb* eter. **ethereal** [i:'θɪərɪəl] *adj* **1** eterisk, overjordisk; **2** flyktig.

ethical ['eθɪkl] *adj* etisk. **ethics** ['eθɪks] *sb fl* etikk, (moral)lære.

etiquette ['etɪket] *sb* etikette; god tone.

eulogy ['ju:lədʒɪ] *sb* lovtale.

eunuch ['ju:nək] *sb* eunukk.

evacuate [ɪ'vækjʊeɪt] *vt* **1** evakuere; trekke seg tilbake fra/ut av; **2** *dgl* evakuere, (for)flytte; **3** tømme. **evacuation** [ɪˌvækjʊ'eɪʃn] *sb* evakuering *etc*. **evacuee** [ɪˌvækju:'i:] *sb* evakuert (person).

evade [ɪ'veɪd] *vt* **1** unngå; **2** holde/lure seg unna.

evaluate [ɪ'væljʊeɪt] *vt* bedømme; evaluere, vurdere; verdsette. **evaluation** [ɪˌvæljʊ'eɪʃn] *sb* bedømmelse *etc*.

evanescent [ˌi:və'nesnt] *adj* flyktig; forgjengelig; kortvarig.

evangelic [ˌi:væn'dʒelɪk] *adj* evangelisk, evangelie-. **evangelical** [ˌi:væn'dʒelɪkl] **1** *adj* evangelisk; *især* lavkirkelig; pietistisk; **2** *sb* (lavkirkelig) protestant; pietist. **evangelist** [ɪ'vændʒəlɪst] *sb* **1** evangelist; **2** emissær, predikant.

evaporate [ɪ'væpəreɪt] *vb* **1** (få til å) fordampe/fordunste; *fig* fordufte; **2** dampe/koke inn. **evaporation** [ɪ'væpə'reɪʃn] *sb* fordamp(n)ing.

evasion [ɪ'veɪʒn] *sb* **1** unngåelse, unnvikelse; **2** omgåelse; *fig* påskudd; utflukt. **evasive** [ɪ'veɪsɪv] *adj* unnvikende.

eve [i:v] *sb* **1** *poetisk* aften; **2** (hellig)aften; dag (og især kveld) før høytid (el. stor begivenhet); *on the* ~ *of* på terskelen til.

even [i:vn] **A I** *adj* **1** plan, slett; glatt; **2** jevn, regelmessig; **3** jevn(byrdig); lik; *be/get* ~ *with* gjøre/få gjort opp med; *dgl* være/bli skuls med; **4** likevektig, stø; **II** *adv* **1** endog, selv; til og med; ~ *if/though* selv om; ~ *if I have to* om jeg så skal (måtte); *not* ~ ikke engang; **2** akkurat, nettopp; ~ *as* (akkurat) idet; nettopp som; **3** ~ *better (etc)* enda bedre (etc); **III** *vt* **1** ~ *out* jevne (ut); *fig også* fordele likt; **2** ~ *up* oppveie, utligne; **B** *sb poetisk* aften.

evening ['i:vnɪŋ] *sb* aften, kveld.

event [ɪ'vent] *sb* **1** begivenhet, (viktig) hending; **2** *a)* (idretts)øvelse; *b)* (program)innslag; **3** forhold, omstendighet; *at all* ~*s* i ethvert tilfelle; *in any* ~ uansett; i alle tilfeller; **4** mulighet; *in the* ~ *of* i tilfelle av; *in that* ~ i så fall. **eventful** [ɪ'ventfʊl] *adj* **1** begivenhetsrik; **2** betydningsfull. **eventual** [ɪ'ventʃʊəl] *adj* endelig (og nærmest uunngåelig). **eventually** [ɪ'ventʃʊəlɪ] *adv* omsider; til slutt; med tiden.

ever ['evə] *adv* **1** noen gang; *hardly* ~ neppe noensinne; nesten aldri; **2** stadig; hele tiden; *for* ~ for alltid/evig; *for* ~ *and* ~ i all evighet; **3** *gml* alltid; **4** *dgl, slang:* ~ *so much* massevis; ~ *so nice* veldig hyggelig; *did you* ~*!* har du hørt etc på maken! *how/what (etc)* ~ hvordan/hva (etc) i all verden; *the greatest* ~ *etc* alle tiders største etc; **5** *i brev: Yours* ~ (alltid) din. **evergreen** ['evəgri:n] *adj, sb* eviggrønn (plante); *fig* (alltid) populær (slager); ≈ gjenganger. **everlasting** [ˌevə'lɑ:stɪŋ] *adj* **1** evigvarende; **2** evinnelig. **evermore** [ˌevə'mɔ:] *adv* (for) evig.

every ['evrɪ] *adj* (en)hver; hver eneste; all(e); ~ *bit as good (etc) as* (minst) like god (etc) som; ~ *little helps* alle monner drar; ~ *now and again/then* rett som det er/var; ~ *other* annenhver. **every|body** ['evrɪbɒdɪ] *pron* enhver; alle. **~day** ['evrɪdeɪ] *adj* hverdagslig, hverdags-; dagligdags, daglig-. **~one** ['evrɪwʌn] = *everybody*. **~thing** ['evrɪθɪŋ] *pron* alt. **~where** ['evrɪweə] *adv* overalt.

evict [ɪ'vɪkt] *vt jur* kaste ut (av hus, leilighet etc). **eviction** [ɪ'vɪkʃn] *sb* utkastelse.

evidence ['evɪdəns] **I** *sb* **1** bevis(materiale); vitne (og vitneprov); *give* ~ vitne (i retten); **2** tegn; spor; *be in* ~ forekomme, opptre; gjøre seg gjeldende; *bear* ~ *of* vise tegn til/spor etter; **II** *vt* (be)vise. **evident** ['evɪdənt] *adj* klar, tydelig; åpenbar. **evidently** ['evɪdəntlɪ] *adv* tydeligvis, åpenbart.

evil ['i:vl] **I** *adj* ond, slett; syndig; **II** *sb* **1** ond handling; synd; **2** onde; ulykke; **3** skade.

evince [ɪ'vɪns] *vt* røpe, vise; legge for dagen.

evoke [ɪ'vəʊk] *vt* bringe/kalle frem; påkalle; vekke.

evolution [ˌi:və'lu:ʃn] *sb* **1** evolusjon, utvikling; **2**

utfoldelse; **3** *mil* manøver. **evolve** [ɪ'vɒlv] *vb* utvikle ((seg) gradvis); utfolde (seg).

ewer ['ju:ə] *sb* (vaskevanns)mugge.

exact [ɪg'zækt] **1** *adj* eksakt, nøyaktig; presis; **2** *vt* forlange, kreve; inndrive. **exacting** [ɪg'zæktɪŋ] *adj* fordringsfull, krevende. **exactitude** [ɪg'zæktɪtju:d] *sb* nøyaktighet.

exaggerate [ɪg'zædʒəreɪt] *vb* overdrive. **exaggeration** [ɪg,zædʒə'reɪʃn] *sb* overdrivelse.

exalt [ɪg'zɔ:lt] *vt* **1** heve; opphøye; **2** (lov)prise; heve til skyene. **exaltation** [,egzɔ:l'teɪʃn] *sb* **1** opphøyelse *etc*; **2** overspenthet. **exalted** [ɪg'zɔ:ltɪd] *adj* **1** opphøyet, høytstående; **2** verdig; **3** *fig* eksaltert; oppstemt; overspent.

exam [ɪg'zæm] *fork* for **examination** [ɪg,zæmɪ'neɪʃn] *sb* **1** gransking, undersøkelse; **2** inspeksjon, kontroll; **3** eksaminering; eksamen, prøve; **4** avhør, forhør. **examine** [ɪg'zæmɪn] *vt* **1** granske, undersøke; **2** eksaminere, spørre (ut); avhøre, forhøre. **examiner** [ɪg'zæmɪnə] *sb* eksaminator.

example [ɪg'zɑ:mpl] *sb* **1** eksempel; forbilde, mønster; **2** prøve(eksemplar).

exasperate [ɪg'zɑ:spəreɪt] *vt* ergre, irritere; (opp)hisse. **exasperation** [ɪg,zɑ:spə'reɪʃn] *sb* harme, raseri; irritasjon.

excavate ['ekskəveɪt] *vt* grave (ut); *fig også* avdekke.

exceed [ɪk'si:d] *vt* **1** overgå; **2** overskride. **exceedingly** [ɪk'si:dɪŋlɪ] *adv* umåtelig, ytterst.

excel [ɪk'sel] *vb* **1** overgå; overstråle; **2** utmerke seg (fremfor andre). **excellence** ['eksələns] *sb* **1** overlegenhet (dvs fremragende dyktighet); **2** fortrinn. **excellent** ['eksələnt] *adj* fremragende, utmerket.

except [ɪk'sept] **1** *konj gml* med mindre; uten (at); **2** *prep* unntatt; uten; ~ *for/that* bortsett fra; om det ikke hadde vært for (at); **3** *vt* unnta, utelate. **excepting** [ɪk'septɪŋ] = *except 1/2*. **exception** [ɪk'sepʃn] *sb* **1** unntak(else); utelatelse; **2** innvending; *take ~ to* innvende/protestere mot; ta avstand fra. **exceptional** [ɪk'sepʃənl] *adj* u(sed)vanlig.

excerpt ['eksɜ:pt] *sb* utdrag.

excess [ɪk'ses] **I** *sb* **1** overmål; overskudd; *in ~ of* mer enn; ut over; **2** overdrivelse; *fl* utskeielse(r); **II** *som adj* [*også* 'ekses] mer-; overskudds-. **excessive** [ɪk'sesɪv] *adj* **1** overdreven; ublu, urimelig; **2** tøylesløs.

exchange [ɪks'tʃeɪndʒ] **I** *sb* **1** bytte; (ut)veksling; *in ~ for* i bytte for; til gjengjeld for; **2** *a)* pengeveksling, valutaveksling; *b)* innveksling (og vekslekontor); *c)* børs; **3** *(telephone ~)* sentralbord; telefonsentral; **II** *vb* **1** bytte (og byttehandle); skifte, utveksle; **2** *mil* bli overført.

exchequer [ɪks'tʃekə] *sb* **1** *the Exchequer* det britiske finansdepartement; *Chancellor of the Exchequer* finansminister; **2** kasse, pengebeholdning; fond.

excise I ['eksaɪz] *sb* (forbruks)avgift; **II** [ɪk'saɪz] *vt* klippe/skjære ut. **excision** [ɪk'sɪʒn] *sb* utskjæring.

excite [ɪk'saɪt] *vt* **1** hisse opp; **2** fremkalle, vekke; pirre, stimulere; **3** irritere; **4** magnetisere. **excited** [ɪk'saɪtɪd] *adj* opphisset; *ofte* ivrig, spent. **excitement** [ɪk'saɪtmənt] *sb* opphisselse *etc*; opphissende/spennende *etc* begivenhet. **exciting** [ɪk'saɪtɪŋ] *adj* spennende.

exclaim [ɪks'kleɪm] *vb* utbryte; rope (ut). **exclamation** [,eksklə'meɪʃn] *sb* utbrudd, utrop. **exclamation mark** *sb* utropstegn.

exclude [ɪks'klu:d] *vt* utelukke; holde ute/utenfor. **exclusion** [ɪks'klu:ʒn] *sb* utelukkelse; *to the ~ of* til fortrengsel for. **exclusive** [ɪks'klu:sɪv] *adj* **1** eksklusiv; fornem, snobbet; **2** enestående (i kvalitet etc); utsøkt; **3** ~ *attention* udelt oppmerksomhet; ~ *right(s)* enerett; **4** ~ *of* fraregnet.

excommunicate [,ekskə'mju:nɪkeɪt] *vt* bannlyse, ekskommunisere. **excommunication** [,ekskəmju:nɪ'keɪʃn] *sb* bannlysing.

excrement ['ekskrəmənt] *sb* ekskrement. **excrete** [ɪk'skri:t] *vt* utskille, utsondre. **excretion** [ɪks'kri:ʃn] *sb* utskilling *etc*.

excruciating [ɪk'skru:ʃɪeɪtɪŋ] *adj* pinefull.

excursion [ɪk'skɜ:ʃn] *sb* (liten) tur; *også fig* avstikker, utflukt.

excuse I [ɪk'skju:s] *sb* **1** unnskyldning; *in ~ of* som unnskyldning for; **2** påskudd; (unnskyldende) grunn; *without ~* uten (gyldig) grunn; **II** [ɪk'skju:z] *vb* **1** unnskylde; **2** frita, unnta; *be ~d* bli fritatt; få slippe; få (lov til å) gå.

execute ['eksɪkju:t] *vt* **1** utføre; sette i verk; **2** fullbyrde; *merk* effektuere; **3** henrette; **4** foredra, oppføre; utøve. **execution** [,eksɪ'kju:ʃn] *sb* **1** utførelse; *carry/put into ~* sette i verk; **2** henrettelse; **3** (kunstnerisk) foredrag; teknikk; utøvelse; **4** *mil* (ødeleggende) virkning. **executioner** [,eksɪ'kju:ʃnə] *sb* bøddel. **executive** [ɪg'zekjʊtɪv] **I** *adj* **1** administrativ; *ofte* ledende, overordnet; **2** utøvende; **II** *sb* **1** utøvende makt/myndighet; **2** overordnet (funksjonær); leder, sjef. **executive program** *sb data* styreprogram. **executor** [ɪg'zekjʊtə] *sb* **1** utøver; **2** *jur* eksekutør.

exemplary [ɪg'zemplərɪ] *adj* eksemplarisk. **exemplification** [ɪg,zemplɪfɪ'keɪʃn] *sb* eksemplifisering. **exemplify** [ɪg'zemplɪfaɪ] *vi* **1** eksemplifisere; belyse/vise ved eksempel; ta/tjene som eksempel; **2** *jur* ta rettskjent avskrift/utskrift av.

exempt [ɪg'zempt] **1** *adj* fritatt; unntatt; **2** *vt* frita (*from* for); unnta (*from* fra).

exercise ['eksəsaɪz] **I** *sb* **1** anvendelse, bruk; beskjeftigelse; utøvelse; **2** mosjon, trening; *fl mil* eksersis; **3** oppgave; prøve; øvelse; **II** *vb* **1** anvende, bruke; (ut)øve; utvise; legge for dagen; **2** mosjonere, trene; *mil* eksersere; **3** *~d about* bekymret over; opptatt av.

exert [ɪg'zɜ:t] *vt* anvende; sette inn; *~ one's influence* gjøre sin innflytelse gjeldende; *~ oneself* anstrenge seg. **exertion** [ɪg'zɜ:ʃn] *sb* anvendelse; utøvelse; anstrengelse.

exhalation [,eksə'leɪʃn] *sb* utånding *etc*. **exhale** [eks'heɪl] *vb* **1** puste/ånde ut; **2** gi fra seg; spy ut.

exhaust [ɪg'zɔ:st] **I** *sb* eksos; **II** *vt* **1** bruke (helt) opp; **2** tømme (helt); *fig* behandle uttømmende; **3** *fig* utmatte; slite ut. **exhausting** [ɪg'zɔ:stɪŋ] *adj* anstrengende; trettende, utmattende. **exhaustion** [ɪg'zɔ:stʃən] *sb* utmattelse. **exhaustive** [ɪg'zɔ:stɪv] *adj* fullstendig, uttømmende.

exhibit [ɪg'zɪbɪt] **I** *sb* **1** utstilling; **2** utstillingsgjenstand; **3** *jur* (fremlagt) bevis; **II** *vt* **1** stille ut; vise (frem); **2** røpe; legge for dagen. **exhibition** [ˌeksɪ'bɪʃn] *sb* **1** utstilling; **2** demonstrasjon; tilkjennegivelse; **3** stipendium.

exhilarate [ɪg'zɪləreɪt] *vt* sette i godt humør. **exhilarated** [ɪg'zɪləreɪtɪd] *adj* opprømt. **exhilaration** [ɪgˌzɪlə'reɪʃn] *sb* opprømthet.

exhort [ɪg'zɔ:t] *vt* formane; tilskynde; legge (innstendig) på hjertet. **exhortation** [ˌeksɔ:'teɪʃn] *sb* formaning; tilskyndelse.

exigency [ɪg'zɪdʒənsɪ] *sb* krise, nødstilstand; vanskelighet.

exile ['egzaɪl] **I** *sb* **1** eksil, (lands)forvisning; **2** landsforvist (person); **II** *vt* landsforvise.

exist [ɪg'zɪst] *vi* eksistere; leve, være til; finnes, forekomme. **existence** [ɪg'zɪstəns] *sb* eksistens, tilvære(lse).

exit ['eksɪt] **1** *sb* utgang; **2** *vb* gå ut (fra scene, av dataprogram etc).

exodus ['eksədəs] *sb* (masse)utreise.

exorbitant [ɪg'zɔ:bɪtənt] *adj* overdreven; ublu; uhørt.

expand [ɪk'spænd] *vb* **1** strekke/utvide (seg); bli/gjøre større; **2** folde (seg) ut; åpne (seg); *fig* tø opp; utfolde seg. **expanse** [ɪk'spæns] *sb* (ut)strekning; flate, vidde. **expansion** [ɪk'spænʃn] *sb* **1** ekspansjon, utvidelse; **2** utbredelse; **3** utstrekning. **expansive** [ɪk'spænsɪv] *adj* **1** ekspansiv, voksende; som utvider/kan utvide seg; **2** utstrakt, vid; omfattende, rommelig; *fig* generøs; åpen(hjertig).

expatriate 1 [eks'pætrɪət] *adj, sb* utvandrer(-); **2** [eks'pætrɪeɪt] *vb* utvandre.

expect [ɪk'spekt] *vt* **1** vente (seg); forvente, regne med; **2** *dgl* anta, gå ut fra. **expectant** [ɪk'spektənt] *adj* **1** (av)ventende; **2** forventningsfull. **expectation** [ˌekspek'teɪʃn] *sb* **1** forventning; **2** *fl* (gode) fremtidsutsikter.

expedient [ɪk'spi:dɪənt] **1** *adj* formålstjenlig; hensiktsmessig; **2** *sb* (virke)middel; tilflukt; utvei.

expedition [ˌekspɪ'dɪʃn] *sb* **1** ekspedisjon, ferd, tokt; **2** *mil* felttog; **3** raskhet. **expeditious** [ˌekspɪ'dɪʃəs] *adj* rask, snar; ekspeditt.

expel [ɪk'spel] *vt* utvise; fordrive, utstøte.

expend [ɪk'spend] *vt* bruke (opp), forbruke. **expenditure** [ɪk'spendɪtʃə] *sb* **1** (for)bruk; **2** utgift(er), utlegg. **expense** [ɪk'spens] *sb* utgift(er); *at the ~ of* på bekostning av. **expense account** *sb merk* omkostningskonto. **expensive** [ɪk'spensɪv] *adj* dyr, kostbar.

experience [ɪk'spɪərɪəns] **I** *sb* **1** erfaring; **2** opplevelse; **II** *vt* **1** erfare, oppleve; føle, kjenne; sanse; **2** gjennomgå; møte. **experienced** [ɪk'spɪərɪənst] *adj* **1** erfaren; **2** rutinert, øvet.

experiment 1 [ɪk'sperɪmənt] *sb* eksperiment, forsøk; **2** [ɪk'sperɪment] *vi* eksperimentere. **experimental** [ɪkˌsperɪ'mentl] *adj* eksperimentell, forsøks-. **experimentation** [ɪkˌsperɪmen'teɪʃn] *sb* eksperimentering.

expert ['ekspɜ:t] **1** *adj* fagmessig, sakkyndig; ekspert-; **2** *sb* ekspert, fagmann; spesialist.

expiration [ˌekspɪ'reɪʃn] *sb* **1** opphør, utløp; *merk* forfall; **2** utånding. **expire** [ɪk'spaɪə] *vi* **1** utløpe; *merk* forfalle; **2** puste ut; *især fig* utånde.

explain [ɪk'spleɪn] *vt* forklare; gjøre rede for. **explanation** [ˌeksplə'neɪʃn] *sb* forklaring; redegjørelse. **explanatory** [ɪk'splænətrɪ] *adj* forklarende. **explicable** [ek'splɪkəbl] *adj* forklarlig. **explicit** [ɪk'splɪsɪt] *adj* bestemt; klar, utvetydig.

explode [ɪk'spləʊd] *vb* **1** eksplodere; detonere, sprenge; **2** *fig* avsløre, torpedere.

exploit I ['eksplɔɪt] *sb* bedrift, dåd; **II** [ɪk'splɔɪt] *vt* **1** bruke, drive; utnytte; **2** utbytte. **exploitation** [ˌeksplɔɪ'teɪʃn] *sb* **1** utnyttelse; **2** utbytting.

exploration [ˌeksplə'reɪʃn] *sb* (ut)forskning *etc*; forskningsferd, oppdagelsesreise. **exploration | drilling** *sb petro* leteboring. **~ licence** *sb petro* letetillatelse. **explore** [ɪk'splɔ:] *vt* (ut)forske; granske, undersøke; dra på forskningsferd gjennom *etc*. **explorer** [ɪk'splɔ:rə] *sb* oppdagelsesreisende.

explosion [ɪk'spləʊʒn] *sb* eksplosjon. **explosive** [ɪk'spləʊsɪv] **1** *adj* eksplosiv; **2** *sb* eksplosiv, sprengstoff.

exponent [ɪk'spəʊnənt] *sb* eksponent (også *mat*); (typisk) eksempel/representant; talsmann.

export I ['ekspɔ:t] *sb* **1** eksport, utførsel; **2** *fl* eksport|artikler, -varer; **II** [ɪk'spɔ:t] *vt* eksportere, utføre. **exportation** [ˌekspɔ:'teɪʃn] *sb* eksport(ering).

expose [ɪk'spəʊz] *vt* **1** utsette (*to* for); **2** stille ut; vise (frem); **3** avsløre; blotte, blottlegge; **4** *foto* eksponere. **exposition** [ˌekspə'zɪʃn] *sb* (orienterende) fremstilling; utredning; **2** utstilling. **exposure** [ɪk'spəʊʒə] *sb* **1** utsatthet; *weak from ~* forkommen, medtatt; utmattet; **2** fremvisning; *også fig* blottelse; **3** *fig* avsløring; **4** *foto* eksponering; *dgl* bilde.

expound [ɪk'spaʊnd] *vt* forklare; fortolke, utlegge.

express [ɪk'spres] **I** *adj* **1** bestemt; uttrykkelig; utvetydig; **2** uttrykt (dvs om likhet); **3** *også adv* omgående; ekspress-, il-; *send ~* sende (som) ekspress; **II** *sb* **1** *(~ train)* ekspress(tog); **2** *(~ messenger)* ilbud; **3** transportbyrå; *som adj* spedisjons-, vare-; **4** (post)ombæring; utkjøring (av gods etc); **III** *vt* **1** si, uttrykke; vise; **2** sende (som) ekspress. **expression** [ɪk'spreʃn] *sb* uttrykk; beskrivelse. **expressive** [ɪk'spresɪv] *adj* uttrykksfull.

expulsion [ɪk'spʌlʃn] *sb* forvisning (etc. jf *expel*).

exquisite [ek'skwɪzɪt] *adj* **1** utsøkt; fremragende; raffinert; **2** intens (om smerte); **3** fintfølende.

extant [ek'stænt] *adj* (stadig) eksisterende; (fremdeles) bevart.

extend [ɪk'stend] *vb* **1** forlenge; strekke/tøye (seg); utvide (seg); ~ *oneself* anstrenge seg (til det ytterste); **2** rekke (frem/ut); *fig* by, gi; vise. **extension** [ɪk'stenʃn] *sb* **1** forlengelse; utvidelse; utstrekning; **2** forlengelse, utsettelse; **3** tilbygg, utvidelse; **4** linje (under sentralbord); biapparat; hustelefon. **extensive** [ɪk'stensɪv] *adj* **1** utstrakt, vid; **2** omfattende. **extent** [ɪk'stent] *sb* **1** utstrekning; omfang; **2** grad.

extenuate [ɪk'stenjʊeɪt] *vt* forminske, redusere; avsvekke, mildne; unnskylde; *extenuating circumstances* formildende omstendigheter.

exterior [ɪk'stɪərɪə] **I** *adj* **1** utvendig, ytre; **2** utenriks-; **II** *sb* eksteriør, ytre; utseende.

exterminate [ɪk'stɜ:mɪneɪt] *vt* utrydde. **extermination** [ɪk,stɜ:mɪ'neɪʃn] *sb* utryddelse.

external [ɪk'stɜ:nl] **I** *adj* **1** utvortes; utvendig, ytre; **2** = *exterior 2*; **II** *sb fl* ytre (former; forhold, omstendigheter; seremonier etc).

extinct [ɪk'stɪŋkt] *adj* (ut)slokt; utdødd; død. **extinction** [ɪk'stɪŋkʃn] *sb* **1** (ut)slokking; **2** utryddelse; utslettelse; **3** opphør. **extinguish** [ɪk'stɪŋgwɪʃ] *vt* **1** slokke; **2** utrydde; utslette.

extol [ɪk'stəʊl] *vt* (lov)prise; heve til skyene.

extort [ɪk'stɔ:t] *vt:* ~ *from* fravriste; tvinge (tilståelse etc) ut av. **extortion** [ɪk'stɔ:ʃn] *sb* tvang; press, utpressing.

extra ['ekstrə] **I** *adj* ekstra(-); tilleggs-; reserve-; **II** *adv* ekstra; særlig; u(sed)vanlig; **III** *sb* **1** ekstrautgift(er); tillegg; **2** *teater* statist.

extract I ['ekstrækt] *sb* **1** ekstrakt, essens; utkok; **2** utdrag; sitat; **II** [ɪk'strækt] *vt* **1** ta/trekke ut; **2** ekstrahere, trekke ut (essens etc); presse; **3** sitere (i utdrag). **extraction** [ɪk'strækʃn] *sb* **1** uttrekning *etc*; **2** opprinnelse; avstamning, ætt.

extradite ['ekstrədaɪt] *vt* utlevere (forbryter til et annet land). **extradition** [,ekstrə'dɪʃn] *sb* utlevering.

extraneous [ɪk'streɪnɪəs] *adj* fremmed; uvedkommende.

extraordinary [ɪk'strɔ:dnrɪ] *adj* ekstraordinær, u(sed)vanlig; merkelig, påfallende.

extravagance [ɪk'strævəgəns] *sb* råflotthet *etc*; skrullet oppførsel; (sært) påfunn. **extravagant** [ɪk'strævəgənt] *adj* **1** råflott; ødsel; **2** (svært) overdreven; urimelig.

extreme [ɪk'stri:m] **I** *adj* **1** ytterst, ytter-; endelig, ende-; **2** ekstrem, ytterliggående; overdreven; **II** *sb* **1** ytterlighet; grense; **2** fare; nød. **extremity** [ɪk'streməti] *sb* **1** ytter|punkt, -grense *etc*; ytterlighet; **2** *fl* ekstremiteter, lemmer.

extricate ['ekstrɪkeɪt] *vt* få (lirke, trekke etc) løs; befri.

exuberance [ɪg'zju:bərəns] *sb* yppighet *etc*. **exuberant** [ɪg'zju:bərənt] *adj* **1** yppig; frodig; **2** overstrømmende.

exude [ɪg'zju:d] *vb* avsondre, utskille; svette.

exult [ɪg'zʌlt] *vi* fryde seg/juble (*at/in* over). **exultant** [ɪg'zʌltənt] *adj* frydefull, jublende; triumferende. **exultation** [,egzʌl'teɪʃn] *sb* fryd, jubel.

eye [aɪ] **I** *sb* **1** øye (og blikk; oppfatning, syn; (nål)øye; hempe, løkke; malje etc); **2** *be all ~s* gjøre store øyne; *by* ~ etter øyemål; *see ~ to ~* være enig; *set/clap ~ on* få øye på; *with an ~ to* med henblikk på; **II** *vt* betrakte, mønstre; se/stirre på. **eye|ball 1** *sb* øyeeple; **2** *slang* fiksere, stirre på. **~brow** *sb* øyenbryn. **~-catcher** *sb* blikkfang. **~lash** *sb* øyenvippe. **~let** *sb* snørehull; hempe; malje. **~lid** *sb* øyenlokk. **~sight** *sb* syn, synsevne. **~sore** *sb* stygt syn; *fig* torn i øyet.

F

fable ['feɪbl] *sb* **1** fabel; legende; **2** skrøne. **fabled** ['feɪbld] *adj* legendarisk.

fabric ['fæbrɪk] *sb* **1** stoff; tøy; **2** konstruksjon, (opp)bygning; sammensetning, struktur. **fabricate** ['fæbrɪkeɪt] *vt* sette opp; sette sammen; fabrikkere (dvs dikte opp, finne på, forfalske).

fabulous ['fæbjʊləs] *adj* fabelaktig, fantastisk; legendarisk.

face [feɪs] **I** *sb* ansikt (og fasade, forside, front; (ytter)side, (over)flate etc); *også* (ur)skive; *on the ~ of it* umiddelbart; ved første øyekast; **II** *vb* **1** vende (ansiktet, forsiden etc) mot; stå *etc* vendt mot; *about (left/right) ~!* helt (venstre/høyre) om! **2** møte (dristig/tillitsfullt); se i øynene; **3** overflatebehandle; avrette; pusse; slipe; **4** kle, trekke. **facet** ['fæsɪt] *sb* fasett.

facetious [fə'si:ʃəs] *adj* spøkefull, vittig (især på en anstrengt måte).

face value *sb* pålydende (verdi); *take it at ~ ~* ta det for hva det er.

facile ['fæsaɪl] *adj* **1** lett; *især* lettvint, lettkjøpt; **2** rask (og noe overfladisk); **3** føyelig, omgjengelig. **facilitate** [fə'sɪlɪteɪt] *vt* gjøre lett(ere); fremme, lette. **facility** [fə'sɪlətɪ] *sb* **1** letthet; **2** (lett) adgang; (rik) anledning; *fl* muligheter; hjelpemidler; utstyr.

fact [fækt] *sb* **1** faktum, kjensgjerning; *as a matter of ~/in point of ~* faktisk, i virkeligheten; **2** gjerning, handling.

faction ['fækʃn] *sb* fraksjon, klikk; (parti)gruppe; **2** splid, uenighet.

factor ['fæktə] *sb* **1** bestanddel, faktor; **2** forhold, omstendighet; **3** agent, megler; **4** *skotsk* forvalter. **factory** ['fæktərɪ] *sb* **1** fabrikk; **2** *gml* handelsstasjon. **factual** ['fæktʃuəl] *adj* faktisk, virkelig.

faculty ['fækəltɪ] *sb* **1** anlegg/evne (*for/of* for/til (å)); sans; **2** fakultet (og lærerstab).

fad [fæd] *sb* mani; påfunn.

fade [feɪd] *vb* **1** visne; tape seg; (få til å) falme; **2** (for)svinne; dø/svinne hen; *film, radio etc* fade, tone (ut).

fag [fæg] **I** *sb* **1** jobbing, slit; **2** *slang* sigarett; **II** *vb* **1** jobbe, slite; slave; **2** gjøre sliten.

fail [feɪl] **I** *sb: without ~* helt sikkert **II** *vb* **1** mislykkes; slå feil; stryke (til eksamen etc); **2** stryke (dvs la dumpe til eksamen etc); **3** svikte; (for)svinne; tape seg; **4** forsømme, unnlate; glemme; **5** gå konkurs. **failing** ['feɪlɪŋ] **1** *prep* i mangel av; **2** *sb* = **failure** ['feɪljə] *sb* **1** feil, mangel; svikt; fiasko; **2** forsømmelse, utelatelse; forglemmelse; **3** konkurs.

faint [feɪnt] **I** *adj* **1** svak (og matt, slapp; uklar, vag etc); **2** forsagt, fryktsom; **II** *sb* besvimelse, uvett; **III** *vi* **1** svekkes, bli svakere; **3** (for)svinne; tape seg.

fair [feə] **I** *adj* **1** real, rettferdig; **2** passende, rimelig; noenlunde; **3** fint/pent (om været); **4** lovende; tilfredsstillende; **5** lys(håret); *gml* fager, pen; **6** klar, ren; feilfri; **II** *adv* **1** realt, ærlig; **2** direkte, rett; **III** *sb* marked; torg; utstilling, (vare)messe. **fairly** ['feəlɪ] *adv* **I** nokså, temmelig (jf *rather*); **II 1** realt, rettferdig; **2** fullstendig; helt (og holdent). **fair play** *sb* ærlig spill; real opptreden *etc*.

fairy ['feərɪ] **I** *adj* alve-, fe-; eventyr-; **II** *sb* **1** alv, fe; **2** *US slang* homse. **fairytale** ['feərɪteɪl] *sb* eventyr.

faith [feɪθ] *sb* **1** tro (*in* på); tillit (*in* til); **2** troskap; **3** løfte; **4** trossamfunn. **faithful** ['feɪθful] *adj* **1** tro(fast); **2** pålitelig. **faithfully** ['feɪθfulɪ] *adv* trofast *etc*; *Yours ~* med vennlig hilsen (dvs som avslutning på brev). **faithless** ['feɪθlɪs] *adj* troløs.

fake [feɪk] **I** *sb* **1** forfalskning; etterligning; **2** bløff (og bløffmaker); **II** *vt* forfalske *etc*.

falcon ['fɔ:lkn] *sb* falk.

fall [fɔ:l] **I** *sb* **1** fall (og fallhøyde; helling, skråning; nedfall, nedbør; *fig* nedgang); *fl* foss, (vann)fall; **2** *US* høst; **II** *vi* **1** falle (ned, over ende etc); **2** helle/skråne (*away from* nedover fra); **3** avta, minke; dale, synke; **4** falle seg; hende, inntreffe; **5** bli; *~ an easy prey to* bli et lett bytte for; *~ asleep* falle i søvn; **6** *med adv/prep* ~ **across** møte; støte/treffe på; ~ **among** falle/havne blant; ~ **apart** falle fra hverandre; ~ **astern** sakke akterut; ~ **away** falle av (bort/fra etc); svikte; bli borte, forsvinne; ~ **back** vike; gi plass; falle/trekke seg tilbake; *~ back on (også)* ty til; ~ **behind** sakke akterut; komme på etterskudd; ~ **in** falle/rase *etc* sammen; *mil* mønstre; stille opp; ~ **into** falle (flyte, renne) ut i; *fig* henfalle til; ~ **off** falle av; bli dårligere; tape seg; minke; ~ **on** = *~ (up)on*; ~ **out** falle *etc* ut; *om hår* falle av; *mil* tre av; ~ **out with** ryke uklar med; ~ **over** falle over ende; velte; ~ **short** ikke komme (gå, nå, rekke) langt nok; komme til kort; ~ **through** falle igjennom; *fig* gå over styr; mislykkes; ~ **to** falle (ned) på; ta fatt på; ~ **under** falle (høre, komme) inn under; ~ **(up)on** falle *etc* over; falle (ned) på; overfalle; ~ **within** = *~ under*.

fallacious [fə'leɪʃes] *adj* villedende. **fallacy** ['fæləsɪ] *sb* feil(slutning); villfarelse.

fall-out ['fɔ:laut] *sb* (radioaktivt) nedfall.

fallow ['fæləu] **I** *adj* **1** brakk, udyrket; **2** gulbrun; **II** *sb* brakkmark. **fallow-deer** *sb* dådyr.

false [fɔ:ls] *adj* **1** feilaktig, uriktig; gal; **2** bedragersk; **3** falsk, uekte; **4** *som adv: play ~* bedra, svike. **falsehood** ['fɔ:lshud] *sb* falskhet; løgn, usannhet. **falsify** ['fɔ:lsɪfaɪ] *vt* **1** forfalske; **2** gjøre til skamme; motbevise.

falter ['fɔ:ltə] *vb* **1** nøle; stamme, stotre; **2** vakle.

fame [feɪm] *sb* berømmelse, ry. **famed** [feɪmd] *adj* berømt.

familiar [fə'mɪlɪə] **I** *adj* **1** fortrolig/vel kjent (*with* med); **2** vanlig, velkjent; **3** familiær, påtrengende; **II** *sb* omgangsvenn. **familiarize** [fə'mɪlɪəraɪz] *vt* **1** *~ oneself with* gjøre seg kjent med; **2** gjøre kjent. **family** ['fæmlɪ] *sb* familie, slekt; *have a large ~ (også)* ha mange barn.

famine ['fæmɪn] *sb* mangel; *især* hungersnød. **famish** ['fæmɪʃ] *vb* sulte (ut); lide hungersnød. **famished** ['fæmɪʃt] *adj* utsultet. **famishing** ['fæmɪʃɪŋ] *adj dgl* skrubbsulten.

famous ['feɪməs] *adj* **1** berømt; **2** storartet, utmerket.

fan [fæn] **A I** *sb* vifte; **II** *vb* **1** vifte; blåse/puste (på, til); **2** (få til å) spre seg i vifteform; **B** *sb dgl* **1** (ivrig) beundrer/tilhenger; fan; **2** entusiast, fanatiker.

fanciful ['fænɪful] *adj* **1** fantasifull; **2** innfallsrik; impulsiv, ustadig; **3** fantastisk, fantasi-. **fancy** ['fænsɪ] **I** *adj* **1** fargerik; (sterkt) mønstret; (ut)brodert; mote-, pynte-; **2** hemningsløs; overdreven; **3** innbilt; fantasi-; **4** *US merk* førsteklasses, kvalitets-; luksus-; **II** *sb* **1** fantasi; innbilning; **2** innfall, påfunn; **3** forkjærlighet; *take a ~ to* legge sin elsk på; **4** (flyktig) forelskelse; svermeri; **III** *vt* **1** (kunne) forestille (innbille, tenke) seg; **2** like; foretrekke; *~ oneself* være innbilsk; *dgl* føle seg. **fancy ball** *sb* kostymeball.

fan fold paper *sb data* listepapir.

fang [fæŋ] *sb* **1** huggtann; **2** hake; klo.

fantastic [fæn'tæstɪk] *adj* **1** fantastisk; **2** uvirkelig. **fantasy** ['fæntəsɪ] *sb* fantasi (og især fantasiprodukt; innbilning, fantastisk historie etc).

far [fɑ:] **I** *adj boklig* **1** fjern; langt borte/unna etc; **2** bortre; lengst borte/unna etc; **II** *adv* langt; *~ and away* absolutt, overlegent; *~ and wide* vidt og bredt; *as ~ as I am concerned* hva meg angår; for mitt vedkommende; *in so ~ as* for så vidt/i den utstrekning som; *so ~* foreløpig; hittil; **III** *sb: by ~* langt; *by ~ the best (etc)* uten sammenligning (el. langt) den beste (etc). **far|-away** *adj* fjern. **~-famed** *adj* vidgjeten; vidt berømt. **~-fetched** *adj* søkt, unaturlig. **~-off** = *~-away*.

farce [fɑ:s] *sb* farse, komedie. **farcical** ['fɑ:sɪkl] *adj* farseaktig, latterlig.

fare [feə] **I** *sb* **1** billett(pris), takst; **2** passasjer; **3** kost, mat; **II** *vi* **1** klare seg; **2** *gml* fare, reise. **farewell** [ˌfeə'wel] **1** *adj* avskjeds-; **2** *interj* farvel; **3** *sb* avskjed, farvel.

farm [fɑ:m] **I** *sb* **1** (bonde)gård, gårdsbruk; **2** = *~house*; **II** *vb* **1** bruke/dyrke (jord); drive gårdsbruk; **2** forpakte; *~ out* forpakte bort; sette bort (arbeid). **farmer** ['fɑ:mə] *sb* gårdbruker. **farm|hand** *US* = *~ worker*. **~house, ~stead** *sb* bondegård; våningshus (på gård). **~ worker** *sb* gårdsarbeider. **~yard** *sb* (gårds)tun.

farthing ['fɑ:ðɪŋ] *sb* **1** tidligere brukt mynt, se midtsidene; **2** *fig* døyt, grann.

fascinate ['fæsɪneɪt] *vt* **1** fascinere; *fig* fengsle; **2** hypnotisere (om slanger). **fascinating** ['fæsɪneɪtɪŋ] *adj* fascinerende; fengslende; henrivende, fortryllende.

fashion ['fæʃn] **I** *sb* **1** måte; maner; *after/in a ~* på sett og vis; **2** mote; *set the ~* angi moten; **II** *vt* forme; lage (til). **fashionable** ['fæʃnəbl] *adj* elegant; moteriktig.

fast [fɑ:st] **A I** *adj* **1** fast(gjort); **2** trofast; **3** holdbar; (farge)ekte; **II** *adv* fast; sikkert, trygt; *~ asleep* i dyp søvn; **B I** *adj* **1** hurtig, rask; *be ~* gå for fort (om klokke); **2** hektisk, lettlivet; råflott, ødsel; **II** *adv* **1** hurtig, raskt; **2** hektisk, rastløst; vilt; **3** *gml* like, rett; **C** *sb, vb* faste. **fasten** [fɑ:sn] *vb* **1** feste; gjøre/sette *etc* fast; **2** *~ (up)on* gripe tak i; *fig* feste seg ved.

fastidious [fə'stɪdɪəs] *adj* kresen, nøye på det.

fast line *sb petro* løpevaier; hurtigboreline.

fat [fæt] **I** *adj* **1** fet; **2** *slang: a ~ lot* ikke noe større/særlig; snarere lite; **II** *sb* fett (og fedme); **III** *vt* fete (opp); gjø. **fat-head** *sb dgl* tosk.

fatal ['feɪtl] *adj* **1** dødelig; **2** ødeleggende; **3** skjebnebestemt, uavvendelig; skjebnesvanger. **fatality** [fə'tælətɪ] *sb* **1** ulykke; (ulykkes)dødsfall; **2** dødelighet; **3** skjebne(bestemthet). **fate** [feɪt] **1** *sb* skjebne; **2** *vt: ~d to* forutbestemt til (å). **fateful** ['feɪtful] *adj* skjebnesvanger.

father ['fɑ:ðə] **I** *sb* **1** far; *fig* grunnlegger, opphavsmann; *fl* (for)fedre; **2** pater; **II** *vt* **1** avle, fostre; være far (*fig* opphavsmann) til; **2** *~ (up)on* tillegge farskap *etc*. **father|hood** ['fɑ:ðəhud] *sb* farskap. **~-in-law** ['fɑ:ðerˌɪn'lɔ:] *sb* svigerfar. **fatherly** ['fɑ:ðəlɪ] *adj* faderlig.

fathom ['fæðəm] **1** *sb* favn (som lengdemål, se midtsidene); **2** *vt* lodde; *fig* fatte, utgrunne. **fathomless** ['fæðəmlɪs] *adj* bunnløs; uutgrunnelig.

fatigue [fə'ti:g] **I** *sb* **1** utmattelse; **2** strabaser; **3** *mil* kjøkkentjeneste, leirtjeneste; **II** *vt* utmatte.

fat oil *sb petro* fet/mettet olje.

fatten ['fætn] *vb* **1** fete (opp); gjø; **2** bli fet; legge på seg.

fatuous ['fætjuəs] *adj* narraktig, tåpelig.

faucet ['fɔ:sɪt] *sb* (tappe)kran.

fault [fɔ:lt] *sb* **1** feil, mangel; **2** skyld; *be in ~* ha skylden; **3** forkastning (i jordskorpen). **fault time** *sb data* feiltid. **faulty** ['fɔ:ltɪ] *adj* mangelfull.

favour ['feɪvə] **I** *sb* **1** gunst; velvilje; **2** vennlighet; (vennlig) tjeneste; **3** støtte; begunstigelse; *in ~ of* stemt for; **4** favorisering; **5** merke; *især* rosett, sløyfe etc; **II** *vt* **1** godkjenne, støtte; **2** begunstige, favorisere; beskytte; **3** være fordelaktig/gunstig for; **4** stå til tjeneste; **5** ligne (mest på). **favourable** ['feɪvrəbl] *adj* fordelaktig, gunstig (stemt). **favourite** ['feɪvrɪt] *adj, sb* favoritt(-).

fawn [fɔ:n] **A 1** *adj* (*~-coloured*) gulbrun; **2** *sb* dåkalv; **B** *vi* **1** *~ (up)on* logre/smiske for.

fear [fɪə] **1** *sb* engstelse, frykt; *for/from ~ of* av frykt for; **2** *vb* frykte (for); være engstelig/redd for. **fear|ful** ['fɪəful] *adj* **1** engstelig, redd; **2** forferdelig, fryktelig. **~less** ['fɪəlɪs] *adj* fryktløs, uredd.

feasible ['fi:zəbl] *adj* (praktisk) gjennomførlig, mulig.

feast [fi:st] **I** *sb* **1** fest(dag); høytid; **2** fest(måltid); **II** *vb* **1** feste; delta i fest; **2** *~ (up)on* fryde seg ved; glede seg over.

feat [fi:t] *sb* prestasjon.

feather ['feðə] **1** *sb* (fugle)fjær; **2** *vt* forsyne/utstyre *etc* med fjær; *~ one's nest* være om seg.

feature ['fi:tʃə] **I** *sb* **1** trekk (og ansiktstrekk; sær|drag, -preg; kjenne|merke, -tegn etc); *fl* ansikt; mine, uttrykk; **2** hoveddel, viktigste del; (hoved)attraksjon; **3** (*~ article*) hovedoppslag (i avis etc); kronikk; spissartikkel; **II** *vt* **1** fremheve; lansere/vise som hovedattraksjon *etc*; **2** prege, særmerke.

federal ['fedrəl] *adj* føderal, forbunds-. **federation** [ˌfedə'reɪʃn] *sb* forbundsstat(er); føderasjon.

fee [fi:] **I** *sb* **1** betaling; avgift, gebyr; honorar, salær; kontingent; **2** (nedarvet) gods; len; **II** *vt* betale (avgift etc); (be)lønne.

feeble [fi:bl] *adj* svak; matt, slapp. **feeble-minded** [ˌfi:bl'maɪndɪd] *adj* tosket; åndssvak.

feed [fi:d] **I** *sb* **1** føde (især til spedbarn); (dyre)fôr; **2** *petro etc* råmaterialer, råstoff; mating, tilførsel; **3** (*~ pipe, ~er*) materør, tilførselsledning; **II** *vb* **1** (er)nære; fø; fôre, mate; *~ on* spise; leve av; fôre med; *fed up with (dgl)* (lut) lei av; **2** *dgl* beite; spise; **3** forsyne, mate, tilføre. **feedback** *sb* tilbakeføring; *fig* tilbakemelding. **feedback system** *sb data* tilbakemeldingssystem. **feeder** *sb petro etc* doseringsapparat, mater. **feed hole** *sb data* styrehull. **feeding-bottle** *sb* tåteflaske. **feed | pitch** *sb data* hullavstand. **~ track** *sb data* styrespor.

feel [fi:l] **I** *sb* fornemmelse, følelse; **II** *vb* **1** føle, ha på følelsen; merke; *~ for/with* føle med; **2** føle (kjenne, ta) på; *~ how/whether* kjenne (etter) hvordan/om; **3** føle/kjenne seg; *~ equal (dgl up) to* føle seg opplagt/i stand til; *~ like* føle seg som; ha lyst på/til; *~ low* føle seg elendig/nedfor etc; **4** føles/kjennes (*as* *if/though* som om); **5** forstå, innse; oppfatte; **6** mene, synes. **feeler** ['fi:lə] *sb* følehorn; *fig* føler. **feeling** ['fi:lɪŋ] **1** *adj* følsom; medfølende; **2** *sb* fornemmelse, følelse.

feign [feɪn] *vt* foregi; late som; simulere. **feint** [feɪnt] *sb* **1** påskudd; simulering; **2** finte; *mil* skinnangrep.

felicitate [fə'lɪsɪteɪt] *vt* gratulere. **felicity** [fə'lɪsətɪ] *sb* **1** tilfredshet; lykke; **2** velvalgte ord *etc*.

feline ['fi:laɪn] **1** *adj* katteaktig, katte-; **2** *sb* katt, kattedyr.

fell [fel] *vt* felle; hugge (ned).

fellow ['feləʊ] *sb* **1** (fag)felle, kollega; kamerat; *som adj* med-; **2** *a)* medlem (av akademi, fakultet, brorskap, forening etc); *b)* (universitets)stipendiat; **3** *dgl* fyr, kar. **fellowship** ['feləʊʃɪp] *sb* **1** kameratskap *etc*; **2** (universitets)stipendium.

felon ['felən] *sb* forbryter. **felony** ['felənɪ] *sb* (grov) forbrytelse.

felt [felt] *sb* filt; *roofing* ~ takpapp.

female ['fi:meɪl] **I** *adj* **1** hunn-, hunkjønns-; **2** kvinnelig, kvinne-; **II** *sb* **1** hunn(dyr); **2** *vulg* kvinnfolk.

fen [fen] *sb* myr(strekning), sump.

fence [fens] **A 1** *sb* gjerde; **2** *vt* gjerde inn; sette opp gjerde (mellom, rundt etc); **B** *vb* **1** fekte; ~ *off* avverge, parere; **2** omgå; komme med utflukter; **C** *sb* heler. **fend** [fend] *vb* **1** ~ *off* avverge, parere; **2** ~ *for* kjempe (streve, sørge) for; ~ *for oneself* klare seg selv; klare seg på egen håd. **fender** ['fendə] *sb* **1** gnistfanger (foran ildsted); **2** kufanger (på lokomotiv); støtfanger; **3** *sjø* fender; **4** *US* (bil)skjerm.

ferment I ['fɜ:mənt] *sb* **1** gjær(stoff); **2** *fig* gjæring; (politisk etc) uro; **II** [fə'ment] *vb* **1** (få til å) gjære; **2** *fig* hisse opp. **fermentation** [,fɜ:mən'teɪʃn] *sb* gjæring.

fern [fɜ:n] *sb* bregne.

ferocious [fə'rəʊʃəs] *adj* grusom, vill. **ferocity** [fə'rɒsətɪ] *sb* grusomhet, villskap.

ferret ['ferɪt] **I** *sb* fritte; hvit jaktilder; **II** *vb* **1** drive jakt med fritte; **2** ~ *out* oppspore; fritte ut.

ferry ['ferɪ] **I** *sb* **1** ferje(sted); **2** = *~-boat*; **II** *vb* ferje; ta ferje. **ferry-boat** *sb* ferje.

fertile ['fɜ:taɪl] *adj* fruktbar. **fertility** [fə'tɪlətɪ] *sb* fruktbarhet. **fertilize** ['fɜ:tɪlaɪz] *vt* **1** gjødsle; **2** befrukte. **fertilizer** ['fɜ:tɪlaɪzə] *sb* kunstgjødsel.

fervent ['fɜ:vənt], **fervid** ['fɜ:vɪd] *adj fig* brennende, glødende; ivrig. **fervour** ['fɜ:və] *sb* glød, lidenskap; iver.

fester ['festə] **I** *sb* materie, verk; **II** *vb* **1** bli/være betent; verke; **2** *fig* nage, ulme.

festival ['festɪvl] **I** *adj* fest-; festival-; **II** *sb* **1** fest, høytid; **2** festival, stevne(dager). **festive** ['festɪv] *adj* **1** festlig, fest-; **2** munter. **festivity** [fə'stɪvətɪ] *sb* fest(lighet). **festoon** [fə'stu:n] **1** *sb* festong, girlande; **2** *vt* festonere.

fetch [fetʃ] *vb* **1** hente; **2** bringe; innbringe; **3** frembringe; produsere; skaffe; **4** *dgl* gi, tildele (slag).

fetter ['fetə] **1** *sb* fot|jern, (-)lenke; **2** *vt* legge i (fot)jern; *fig* hemme, hindre.

feud [fju:d] **A** *sb* feide, bitter strid; **B** *sb hist* len.

fever ['fi:və] *sb* feber. **feverish** ['fɪvərɪʃ] *adj* febril; *fig* febrilsk.

few [fju:] *adj, sb* (bare noen) få; *every ~ minutes* med få minutters mellomrom; rett som det er; *the ~* minoriteten; de få; **2** *a ~* en del; noen; *quite a ~* en god del; ganske mange.

fiancé(e) [fɪ'ɑ:nseɪ] *sb* forlovede (*fiancé* om mann, *fiancée* om kvinne).

fib [fɪb] *sb, vb dgl* skrøne.

fibre ['faɪbə] *sb* fiber. **fibre grease** *sb petro* fibersmørefett. **fibrous** ['faɪbrəs] *adj* fiberaktig, fiber-.

fickle ['fɪkl] *adj* skiftende, ustadig; upålitelig.

fiction ['fɪkʃn] *sb* **1** oppdiktet historie *etc*; oppspinn, påfunn; **2** skjønnlitteratur. **fictional** ['fɪkʃənl] *adj* **1** oppdiktet; **2** skjønnlitterær. **fictitious** [fɪk'tɪʃəs] *adj* oppdiktet; fiktiv.

fiddle ['fɪdl] **I** *sb* **1** fele; **2** felespill; **II** *vb* **1** spille fele; **2** drive/slenge (*about* omkring); **3** fikle/tukle (*with* med); **4** *slang* fikse (på) (dvs forfalske). **fiddler** ['fɪdlə] *sb* felespiller, spillemann. **fiddle-sticks** ['fɪdlstɪks] *interj* sludder.

fidelity [fɪ'delətɪ] *sb* **1** troskap; **2** nøyaktighet.

fidget ['fɪdʒɪt] **I** *sb* **1** rastløshet; (utålmodig) uro; **2** rastløs *etc* person; **II** *vb* sitte *etc* urolig; vri på seg (av nervøsitet etc); ~ *with* fikle/tukle med; plukke på.

field [fi:ld] **I** *sb* **1** jorde, åker; (inn)mark; **2** flate, vidde; felt; *take the ~* dra i felten; *fig* dra til felts; **3** *a)* (idretts)|bane, -plass; *b)* (konkurranse)deltakere; *c)* (ute)lag; *d)* felt (i løp); **4** felt, område; **II** *vb* **1** spille ute/på utelaget; **2** mønstre/sette opp lag; sende (lag) på banen. **field|-day** *sb mil* manøverdag; *fig* stor dag. **~ events** *sb fl* tekniske øvelser (i friidrett). **~-glasses** *sb fl* (felt)kikkert. **~ joint** *sb petro* feltskjøt. **~ label** *sb data* feltmerke. **~ name** *sb data* feltnavn. **~ order** *sb data* feltrekkefølge. **~ potential** *sb petro* (et felts) produksjonskapasitet. **~ type** *sb data* felttype.

fiend [fi:nd] *sb* **1** djevel; **2** udyr; **3** *dgl: dope ~* narkoman; *football ~* fotballidiot.

fierce ['fɪəs] *adj* **1** voldsom; vill; **2** heftig, intens.

fiery ['faɪərɪ] *adj* **1** flammende, glødende; **2** hissig, ildfull.

fig [fɪg] *sb* **1** fiken(tre); **2** døyt, grann.

fight [faɪt] **I** *sb* **1** kamp, strid; slagsmål; **2** kampånd; **II** *vb* **1** bekjempe; kjempe (mot); slåss (med); ~ *shy of* holde seg unna; **2** *sjø mil* manøvrere (skip i kamp). **fighter** ['faɪtə] *sb* **1** kjemper *etc*; **2** jager(fly); *som adj* jager-.

figurative ['fɪgjʊrətɪv] *adj* billedlig, figurlig. **figure** ['fɪgə] **I** *sb* **1** siffer; (ensifret) tall; beløp, pris; *fl* aritmetikk, regning; **2** diagram, figur; mønster; **3** bilde; avbildning, gjengivelse; **4** fasong, form; skikkelse; **5** person; (fremtredende) skikkelse; **6** tur (i dans); **II** *vb* **1** dekorere (med figurer etc); **2** forestille; betegne, symbolisere; **3** forestille/tenke seg; mene, synes; **4** figurere, opptre; **5** beregne; regne (ut); *it ~s* det stemmer. **figure|-head** *sb* gallionsfigur; *fig* toppfigur (uten virkelig innflytelse). **~ of speech** *sb* billedlig uttrykk; talefigur. **~-skating** *sb* kunstløp (på skøyter).

filament ['filəmənt] *sb* fiber, trevl; (tynn) tråd; (gløde)tråd.

filch [filtʃ] *vt* naske.

file [faıl] **A 1** *sb* fil (også *data*); **2** *vt* file; *filings* filspon; **B 1** *sb* brevordner; arkiv (og arkiv|skap, -skuff etc); *fl* kartotek, register; *on ~* arkivert; **2** *vt* arkivere; *filing clerk* arkivar; **C I** *sb* **1** rad, rekke; linje; *mil* geledd; *single ~* gåsegang; **2** (kjøre)felt, fil; **II** *vi* gå i gåsegang; marsjere (på rekke, etter hverandre). **file | creation** *sb data* filoppretting. **~ directory** *sb data* filkatalog; dokumentregister. **~ management, ~ processing** *sb data* filbehandling. **~ protection** *sb data* filsikring. **~ separator** *sb data* filskilletegn.

filial ['filıəl] *adj* datterlig, sønnlig.

fill [fil] **I** *sb* fylde (og fylling, (på)fyll; avpasset porsjon; (tilstrekkelig) mengde etc); **II** *vb* **1** fylle; *~ in* fylle ut (skjema etc); komplettere, supplere; *~ up* fylle opp; fylle på; **2** fylles; bli full; *~ out* legge på seg; legge seg ut; **3** (opp)fylle; **4** utføre; effektuere, ekspedere. **filler | gas** *sb petro* fyllgass. **~ pass** *sb petro* oppfyllingslag.

fillet ['filıt] **A 1** *sb* filet; **2** *vb* filetere; **B** *sb* hårbånd, pannebånd.

filling ['filıŋ] *sb* (tann)plombe, **filling station** *sb* bensinstasjon.

film [film] **I** *sb* **1** hinne; **2** (fotografisk) film; **3** film(forestilling); **II** *vb* **1** *(~ over)* dekke(s) med en hinne; **2** filme; filmatisere.

filter ['filtə] **1** *sb* filter; **2** *vb* filtrere(s); sive.

filth [filθ] *sb* griseri, skitt; *fig* slibrighet. **filthy** ['filθı] *adj* griset, skitten; *fig* slibrig, uanstendig.

fin [fin] *sb* finne.

final ['faınl] **I** *adj* **1** sist, slutt-; **2** endelig; avgjørende; avsluttende, avslutnings-; **II** *sb (fl)* (avgangs)eksamen; finale(kamp etc). **final character** *sb data* sluttegn. **finally** ['faınəlı] *adv* endelig, omsider; til slutt.

finance ['faınæns] **1** *sb* finansvesen; økonomi; *fl* finanser; penger; **2** *vt* finansiere. **financial** [faı'nænʃl] *adj* finansiell; finans-; økonomisk. **financier** [faı'nænsıə] *sb* finansmann.

find [faınd] **I** *sb* funn; oppdagelse; **II** *vt* **1** finne (og finne igjen; finne ut; finne på etc); *~ them out* avsløre dem; **2** skaffe; utstyre; *~ (oneself) in* holde (seg) med; **3** *jur* avgi kjennelse; *~ guilty* erklære/finne skyldig. **finder** ['faındə] *sb* **1** (-)finner; **2** *(view-~)* søker (på kamera etc). **finding** ['faındıŋ] *sb* **1** funn; oppdagelse; resultat (av leting etc); **2** *jur* kjennelse.

fine [faın] **A I** *adj* **1** fin (og pen, vakker; deilig, delikat, lekker; fremragende, god etc); **2** fin, forfinet; klar; ren(set); **3** fin, (ør)liten; slank, tynn; **4** fin, skarp; kresen; **II** *adv* **1** *dgl* bra, fint; **2** fin-, ren-; **B 1** *sb* bot, mulkt; **2** *vt* bøtlegge; **C** *sb: in ~* kort sagt.

finery ['faınərı] *sb* pynt, stas; finklær. **finesse** [fı'nes] *sb* **1** finfølelse, takt; **2** finesse; *ofte* lureri.

finger ['fıŋgə] **1** *sb* finger; **2** *vt* berøre; ta på. **fingerprint 1** *sb* fingeravtrykk; **2** *vb* ta fingeravtrykk av.

finish ['finıʃ] **I** *sb* **1** avslutning, slutt; fullføring; (inn)spurt; sluttkamp; **2** sluttbehandling; *især* finpuss(ing), polering; **II** *vb* **1** fullføre; (av)slutte; gjøre (seg) ferdig; *~ off/up* gjøre (seg) ferdig; gjøre rent bord; ekspedere/kvitte seg med (dvs drepe); **2** sluttbehandle; *især* (fin)pusse, polere. **finishing touch** *sb især fig* siste strøk; siste hånd på verket.

fir [fɜ:] *sb* furu(tre).

fire ['faıə] **I** *sb* **1** ild, varme; *fig* glød, hete; **2** varme (i ovn, på ildsted etc); bål; **3** brann; **4** *mil* ild(givning); skudd(salve); **II** *vb* **1** sette fyr/tenne på; *fig* oppildne; *~ up* tenne (dvs bli hissig, ivrig etc); **2** brenne (leirvarer etc); (varme)tørke; **3** fyre (opp i); **4** *mil* (av)fyre; skyte (med); **5** *dgl* gi sparken. **fire | alarm** *sb* brannalarm. **~arm** *sb* skytevåpen. **~ brigade** *sb* brann|korps, -vesen. **~-cracker** *sb* kinaputt. **~-engine** *sb* brannbil. **~-escape** *sb* brannstige; nødutgang. **~-extinguisher** *sb* brannslokningsapparat. **~guard** *sb* gnistfanger (foran ildsted); kamingitter. **~-hose** *sb* brannslange. **~-irons** *sb fl* glokarer og ildtang. **~man** *sb* brannmann. **~place, ~side** *sb* ildsted (som kamin, ovn, peis etc); ovnskrok. **~proof** *adj* **1** ildfast; **2** brann|fast, herdig. **~ station** *sb* brannstasjon. **~wood** *sb* (ved som) brensel. **~works** *sb* fyrverkeri. **firing-squad** *sb* eksekusjonspelotong.

firm [fɜ:m] **I** *adj* **1** fast, hard; **2** sikker, stø; solid; **2** *adv: stand ~* stå fast; **III** *sb* firma, forretning. **firmware** *sb data* fastvare.

first [fɜ:st] **I** *adj* først; forrest; fremst; **II** *adv* **1** først; **2** for første gang; **III** *sb* **1** begynnelse; **2** førsteplass; beste karakter. **first | aid** *sb* førstehjelp. **~born** *adj* førstefødt. **~ class** *sb* første klasse. **~-class** *adj* førsteklasses. **~ name** *sb* fornavn. **~ night** *sb* première(forestilling). **~ officer** *sb sjø* (første)styrmann. **~-rate** *adj* førsteklasses.

firth [fɜ:θ] *sb* fjord; *skotsk* elvemunning.

fish [fıʃ] **I** *sb* **1** fisk; **2** *dgl* fyr, kar; type; **II** *vb* **1** fiske (i); **2** *~ for* fiske etter (dvs forsøke å oppnå/hale ut av etc); *~ out/up* fiske (dra, hale etc) frem/opp. **fisher** ['fıʃə] *sb gml* = **fisherman** ['fıʃəmən] *sb* fisker. **fishery** ['fıʃərı] *sb* fiske. **fishing** ['fıʃıŋ] *sb* fiske, fisking. **fishing|-rod** *sb* fiskestang. **~-tackle** *sb* fiske|redskap, -saker, -utstyr. **fish|monger** ['fıʃmʌŋgə] *sb* fiskehandler (især med kjerre). **~wife** ['fıʃwaıf] *sb* fiskekone (på torg eller med kjerre). **fishy** ['fıʃı] *adj* **1** fiskeaktig, fiske-; **2** tvilsom; mistenkelig.

fission ['fıʃn] *sb* (atom)spaltning. **fissure** ['fıʃə] *sb* revne, sprekk.

fist [fist] *sb* (knytt)neve.

fit [fit] **A** *sb* **1** anfall, ri; **2** raptus; *by ~s (and starts)* i rykk og napp; **B I** *adj, adv* **1** passende; skikket; sømmelig; *see/think ~ to* finne det formålstjenlig (passende, riktig etc) å; *dgl* finne det for godt å; **2** sprek; i (god) form; **3** *dgl: ~ to* ferdig til å; **II** *sb* passform;

(til)pasning; *be an excellent/tight* ~ sitte som støpt; **III** *vb* **1** passe (til/sammen med); **2** tilpasse; innstille; ~ *in* føye/passe inn (i); **3** gjøre/sette i stand (til); ~ *out* ruste ut; utstyre. **fit|ful** ['fɪtful] *adj* rykkvis; ujevn. **~ness** ['fɪtnɪs] *sb* **1** skikkethet *etc*; dugelighet; **2** sprekhet; (god) form. **fittings** ['fɪtɪŋz] *sb fl* (især fast) innredning; inventar, utstyr; armatur; installasjon(er).

fix [fɪks] **I** *sb dgl* knipe; vrien situasjon; **II** *vb* **1** feste; gjøre/sette fast; festne (seg); **2** bestemme, fastsette; fastslå; ~ *(up)on* feste seg ved; bestemme seg for; **3** arrangere; ordne; ~ *up* ordne opp (med); stelle i stand; **4** fikse, reparere; **5** *foto* fiksere. **fixation** [fɪk'seɪʃn] *sb* **1** festing *etc*; **2** *foto* fiksering. **fixed** [fɪkst] *adj* fast; avgjort, bestemt; fastslått. **fixed | disk** *sb data* hard|disk, -plate. ~ **form** *sb data* fast format. **fixture** ['fɪkstʃə] *sb* (fast) innredning/inventar.

fizz [fɪz] **1** *sb* brusing *etc*; *dgl* sjampis, skum (dvs champagne); **2** *vi* bruse, sprudle; skumme.

flabbergast ['flæbəgɑ:st] *vt dgl* forbløffe, sjokkere.

flabby ['flæbɪ] *adj* pløsen; slapp.

flag [flæg] **A I** *sb* flagg; **II** *vt* **1** flaggsmykke; **2** signalisere (især med flagg); ~ *(down) a taxi* praie en drosje; **B** *vi* **1** henge (ned); henge med hodet (især om blomster); **2** *fig* dabbe av; tape seg; **C** *sb (~stone)* (stein)helle.

flagon ['flægən] *sb* **1** vin|kanne, -karaffel; **2** vinflaske (især liten og tykkmavet).

flagrant ['fleɪgrənt] *adj* utfordrende; skammelig, skjendig.

flair [fleə] *sb* sans, teft; medfødt anlegg.

flak [flæk] *sb* antiluftskyts.

flake [fleɪk] **1** *sb* flak; spon; fnugg; **2** *vi:* ~ *off* flasse; skalle av.

flamboyant [flæm'bɔɪənt] *adj* **1** fargesprakende; **2** gloret, prangende; brautende.

flame [fleɪm] **I** *sb* **1** flamme; **2** *dgl* kjæreste; **II** *vi* flamme; ~ *up* bli/komme i fyr og flamme. **flame arrestor** *sb petro* flammefelle.

flange [flændʒ] *sb* flens, kant.

flank [flæŋ] **1** *sb* flanke, fløy; side; **2** *vt* flankere; *mil* omgå, utflankere.

flannel ['flænl] *sb* flanell; *fl* flanellsbukser; *dgl* (langt ull)undertøy.

flap [flæp] **I** *sb* **1** klask; slag, smekk; **2** klaff (på bord, konvolutt etc); **II** *vb* **1** daske, slå; smekke (med); **2** flakse (med); **3** *slang* kjase, mase.

flare [fleə] **I** *sb* **1** bluss; (kort) oppblussing/oppflamming; *fig* utbrudd; **2** nødbluss; signalrakett; *mil* lysbombe; **3** *petro* fakkel; **4** volang; utskrådd stoffstykke (buksebein, skjørt etc); **II** *vi* **1** blusse, skinne; ~ *up* blusse/flamme opp; *fig* fare opp; **2** *petro* brenne av. **flare | boom** *sb petro* avbrenningsbom. ~ **platform** *sb petro* avbrenningsplattform. ~ **tower** *sb petro* avbrenningstårn.

flash [flæʃ] **I** *sb* **1** blink, (lys)glimt; blunk; **2** *foto* = *~lamp*; **3** *(news-~)* kort nyhetsmelding; **4** (uniforms)-merke; **II** *vb* **1** blinke; glimte (til); lyne; *fig* fare; **2** sende/stråle ut. **flash|back** *sb* tilbake|blikk, -glimt (især i film). **~gun** *sb* = *~lamp*. **~light** *sb* lommelykt. **~lamp** *sb foto* blitz(lampe).

flask [flɑ:sk] *sb* **1** *(hip-~)* (lomme)lerke; **2** (tykkmavet) vinflaske; **3** *kjemi* kolbe.

flat [flæt] **A I** *adj* **1** flat, jevn; rett; *fig* ens(artet); **2** ens|formig, -tonig; kjedelig; flau, vammel; *om øl etc* doven; **3** avgjort, endelig; kategorisk; **4** *mus* med fortegnet ♭; **II** *adv* **1** *fall* ~ falle til jorden *(fig)*; mislykkes; *lay* ~ jevne med jorden; slå ned; **2** direkte, ubetinget; **3** ~ *out* av alle krefter; helt utkjørt; **III** *sb* **1** flate; lavland, (lav)slette; **2** *mus* (note med) fortegnet ♭; **3** *dgl* punktering; **B** *sb* leilighet. **flat|foot** *sb* plattfot; *US slang* purk. **~-footed** *adj* plattfot(et); *dgl* håndfast; liketil. **~-heeled** *adj* lavhælt. **~let** *sb* hybel(leilighet). ~ **rate** *sb* enhets|pris, -tariff. ~ **refusal** *sb* blankt avslag. **flatten** ['flætn] *vb* planere; jevne (ut); bli/gjøre (seg) flat. **flat tyre** *sb* flatt (dvs punktert) dekk; punktering.

flatter ['flætə] *vt* smigre. **flattery** ['flætərɪ] *sb* smiger.

flaunt [flɔ:nt] *vb* svinge/vaie (med); briske seg/skilte med.

flavour ['fleɪvə] **I** *sb* **1** arma; duft; velsmak; **2** smak; *fig* anstrøk, snev; **II** *vt* smake til; sette smak på. **flavouring** ['fleɪvərɪŋ] *sb* smaksstoff; krydder.

flaw [flɔ:] *sb* feil, lyte; mangel. **flawless** ['flɔ:lɪs] *adj* feilfri, lyteløs.

flax [flæks] *sb* lin(plante). **flaxen** ['flæksn] *adj* hørgul; linhåret; lys blond.

flay [fleɪ] *vt* flå; **2** hudflette; kritisere nådeløst.

flea [fli:] *sb* loppe. **fleabag** ['fli:bæg] *sb* **1** loppekasse (dvs seng); **2** (billig) losjihus. **fleabite** *sb* loppebitt; *fig også* nålestikk.

fleck [flek] **I** *sb* **1** flekk, plett; **2** fnugg; **II** *vt* flekke, plette.

fledged [fledʒd] *adj* flygeferdig; *full-~* fullbefaren; *newly~* nybakt. **fledg(e)ling** ['fledʒlɪŋ] *sb* flygeferdig fugleunge; *fig* nybegynner.

flee [fli:] *vi* flykte, rømme.

fleece [fli:s] **1** *sb* pels, skinn; ull; *dgl* lugg, manke (dvs hodehår); **2** *vt* klippe; *fig* flå; plyndre til skinnet. **fleecy** ['fli:sɪ] *adj* lodden, ullen.

fleet [fli:t] **A** *sb* flåte (av fly, skip etc); **B** *adj poet* hastig, ilende; snar. **fleeting** ['fli:tɪŋ] *adj* flyktig, kortvarig.

flesh [fleʃ] *sb* kjøtt; *put on* ~ legge på seg. **fleshy** ['fleʃɪ] *adj* kjøttfull; tykk.

flex [fleks] **A** *sb* (elektrisk) kabel, ledning; **B** *vt* bøye. **flexible** ['fleksəbl] *adj* bøyelig, fleksibel; føyelig, smidig. **flexible disk** *sb data* diskett.

flick [flɪk] **1** *sb* smekk, snert; knips(ing); **2** *vt* smekke/snerte til; knipse (med); knipse til. **flicker** ['flɪkə] **I** *sb* **1** blafring *etc*; **II** *vi* **1** blafre, flakke; **2** spille med tungen (som en slange).

flight [flaɪt] **A** *sb* **1** flyging, flytur; flukt; **2** (fugle)-trekk, **3** skur, sverm; **4** *(~ of stairs)* trapp (mellom to etasjer); **5** *fly mil* ving; **B** *sb* flukt; *put to* ~ jage på flukt. **flighty** ['flaɪtɪ] *adj* ustadig, vinglet.

flimsy ['flɪmsɪ] **I** *adj* **1** (tynn og) gjennomsiktig; **2** spinkel, skrøpelig; **II** *sb* **1** gjennomslagspapir; **2** *fl slang* gjennomsiktig nattøy/undertøy etc.

flinch [flɪntʃ] *vi* vike tilbake/unna; vegre seg.

fling [flɪŋ] **I** *sb* kast(ing); sleng; **II** *vb* **1** kyle; hive, kaste; slenge; **2** fare, storme, styrte.

flip [flɪp] **I** *sb* **1** knips; snert; **2** flytur; svipptur; **3** (slags) punsj; toddi; **II** *vb* **1** knipse (til); **2** rappe/snerte (til).

flippancy ['flɪpənsɪ] *sb* nesevishet *etc*. **flippant** ['flɪpənt] *adj* **1** nesevis; nebbet; **2** rappmunnet.

flirt [flɜ:t] *sb, vb* flørt(e). **flirtation** [flɜ:'teɪʃn] *sb* flørt(ing).

flit [flɪt] *vi* **1** fare, pile; flagre (som en sommerfugl etc); **2** flytte (især i smug, for å slippe unna husleien); stikke av.

float [fləut] **I** *sb* **1** flyter (og flåte; flottør, pongtong; dupp, garnblåse; redningsvest, svømmeblære etc); **2** blokkvogn; flatvogn; **II** *vb* **1** flyte (i vann); sveve (i luft); drive; gli; **2** fløte; holde flytende; **3** oversvømme; **4** *merk* få/hjelpe i gang. **flo(a)tation method** *sb petro* fløtemetode. **floating | head** *sb petro* flytehode. **~ hose** *sb petro* flyteslange.

flock [flɒk] **A 1** *sb* flokk (især av fugler og småfe); (folke)mengde; *rel* forsamling, menighet; hjord; **2** *vi* flokke/samle seg; **B** *sb* dott (av hår eller ull).

flog [flɒg] *vt* piske; slå.

flood [flʌd] **I** *sb* **1** flom, oversvømmelse; **2** = *~ tide*; **II** *vb* **1** oversvømme; **2** (få til å) flomme/flyte over. **flood | gate** *sb* sluseport. **~light** *sb* flombelysning. **~ tide** *sb* flo, høyvann.

floor [flɔ:] **I** *sb* **1** gulv (og sal i motsetning til galleri); *take the ~* ta ordet (i debatt etc); **2** etasje; **3** bunn (dvs nederste grense); **II** *vt* **1** legge gulv i; **2** slå ned/ut; slå i bakken/gulvet; **3** sette i beit. **floorwalker** *sb* inspektør (i stormagasin).

flop [flɒp] **I** *sb* **1** dunk; plask, plump; **2** *slang* fiasko; **II** *vb* **1** dumpe, dunke; **2** klaske, plaske; daske; **3** *slang* gjøre fiasko; dumpe, stryke. **floppy (disk)** *sb data* diskett.

floral ['flɔ:rəl] *adj* blomster-. **florid** ['flɒrɪd] *adj* **1** blomstrende *(fig)*; overlesset; **2** rødmusset. **florist** ['flɒrɪst] *sb* blomster|forretning, -gartneri; blomster|-handler, -selger(ske).

floss [flɒs] *sb* **1** dun(hår); **2** flokksilke.

flotsam ['flɒtsəm] *sb* (drivende) vrakgods.

flounce [flauns] **1** *sb* kappe, volang; **2** *vt* sette kappe(r) på; pynte med volanger.

flounder ['flaundə] **A** *vi* **1** bakse, kave; mase; **2** klusse, rote; **3** hakke, stamme; **B** *sb* skrubbe; *US* flyndre.

flour ['flauə] **1** *sb* mel; **2** *vt* mele; drysse/strø mel over/på.

flourish ['flʌrɪʃ] **I** *sb* **1** feiende/flott bevegelse; **2** slyng, sløyfe(r); snirkler; **3** fanfare; **II** *vb* **1** blomstre *(fig)*; trives; **2** svinge (med); vifte med.

flow [fləu] **I** *sb* **1** flyt(ing); (elve)løp, strøm; **2** flo; *også fig* flom; **3** overflod, strøm; **II** *vi* flyte, renne, strømme; *også fig* bølge, flomme. **flowchart** *sb data etc* flytskjema. **flowing well** *sb petro* selvproduserende (olje)brønn.

flower ['flauə] **1** *sb* blomst; **2** *vi* blomstre.

flow schedule *sb petro* produksjonsprogram.

flu [flu:] *sb dgl* influensa.

fluctuate ['flʌktjueɪt] *vi* skifte, variere; fluktuere; *~ between* vakle mellom. **fluctuation** [ˌflʌktju'eɪʃn] *sb* skifting *etc*.

flue [flu:] *sb* (ovns)rør, pipe, skorstein; røykrør.

fluency ['flu:ənsɪ] *sb* flytende tilstand; flyt (i tale). **fluent** ['flu:ənt] *adj* flytende (især om tale).

fluff [flʌf] **I** *sb* **1** dun; lo; **2** fadese, flause, tabbe; **II** *vt* **1** *~ out* purre opp i; riste (opp) (pute etc); **2** forkludre, ødelegge; rote til. **fluffy** ['flʌfɪ] *adj* bløt, dunet; loet.

fluid ['flu:ɪd] **I** *adj* **1** flytende; *fig* skiftende, ustadig; **2** gass|aktig, -formig; **II** *sb* **1** væske; **2** gass(art).

fluke [flu:k] **A** *sb* flaks, hell; **B** *sb* ankerfligg; mothake.

flurry ['flʌrɪ] **I** *sb* **1** byge; (regn)skur; (vind)kule; **2** forfjamselse; oppskjørtethet; **II** *vt* gjøre forfjamset *etc*.

flush [flʌʃ] **A I** *sb* **1** rødme, rødming; **2** flom, strøm; **3** skylling; spyling; **4** begeistring, opprømthet; **II** *vb* **1** rødme; *fig* gløde; **2** oppgløde; oppmuntre; **3** flomme/strømme (*out* ut); **4** skylle; spyle; **B** *adj* **1** jevn, plan; **2** (bredd)full; fylt til randen; **C** *vb* **1** skremme opp (fugler); **2** fly opp (om fugler).

fluster ['flʌstə] **1** *sb* befippelse, forfjamselse; **2** *vt* forvirre; gjøre forfjamset.

flute [flu:t] **A 1** *sb* fløyte; **2** *vi* spille fløyte; **B** *vt* kannelere, rifle.

flutter ['flʌtə] **I** *sb* **1** flagring *etc*; *fig* nervøsitet, uro; **2** rystelse; vibrasjon; **3** *dgl* (liten) spekulasjon; veddemål; **II** *vb* **1** flagre, flakse; **2** blafre, flakke; vifte; skjelve.

flux [flʌks] *sb* **1** flyt(ing); strøm; (ut)strømning; **2** fluss(middel).

fly [flaɪ] **A 1** *sb* flue; **II** *vb* **1** fly (og ta fly, reise/sende med fly, sende til værs etc); **2** fare, styrte; *let ~ (at)* fare/gå løs på; **3** flykte/rømme (fra); **4** føre/heise (flagg); vaie; **B** *sb* flik, klaff; buksesmekk, gylf; **C** *adj slang* skarp, smart. **flyer** ['flaɪə] *sb* flyger. **flying** ['flaɪɪŋ] *adj* flygende, fly(ge)-; flyger-; *fig* lyn-. **flying squad** *sb* utrykningspatrulje.

foal [fəul] **1** *sb* fole, føll; **2** *vi* følle.

foam [fəum] **1** *sb* fråde, skum; **2** *vi* fråde, skumme. **foamrubber** *sb* skumgummi.

fob [fɒb] *vt* lure; *~ him off with* avspise ham med; *~ it off on them* prakke det på dem.

focus ['fəukəs] **I** *sb* brennpunkt, fokus; **II** *vb* **1** fokusere, samle (seg) i brennpunktet; **2** (skarp)innstille (kamera, kikkert etc); **3** *fig* konsentrere (seg).

fodder ['fɒdə] **1** *sb* (dyre)fôr; **2** *vt* fôre.

foe [fəu] *sb poet* fiende.

fog [fɒg] **1** *sb* tåke; **2** *vb* tåkelegge; omtåke, (til)-

sløre; dugge. **foggy** ['fɒgɪ] *adj* tåket, uklar.

fogey ['fəugɪ] *sb* knark, stabeis.

foible ['fɔɪbl] svakhet (dvs svakt punkt etc); (sær)egenhet.

foil [fɔɪl] **A I** *sb* **1** folie; tynt belegg/lag; **2** kontrast; motstykke; **II** *vt* **1** foliere; dekke med folie; **2** forpurre, hindre; **C** *sb* florett, korde.

fold [fəuld] **A I** *sb* brett, fold; **II** *vb* **1** brette/folde (sammen); ~ *up* klappe/legge sammen; bryte sammen; gå konk(urs); **2** (~ *up*) hylle/pakke inn; **B I** *sb* **1** kve; **2** flokk; *gml rel* fold (dvs forsamling, menighet); hjord; **II** *vt* sette i kve. **folding** ['fəuldɪŋ] *som adj* sammenleggbar. **folding seat** *sb* klappsete.

foliage ['fəulɪɪdʒ] *sb* bladverk, løv.

folk [fəuk] *sb* **1** folk (og folkeslag, nasjon); **2** *fl dgl a)* familie, slekt; *b)* folkens. **folk-tale** *sb* folkeeventyr.

follow ['fɒləu] **I** *sb* følge; (opp)følging; **II** *vb* **1** følge (og forfølge; følge etter (i); følge med (i); *fig* rette seg etter etc); ~ *up* forfølge *(fig)*, følge opp; følge på; *as* ~*s* som følger; **2** praktisere; drive med. **follower** ['fɒləuə] *sb* **1** forfølger; **2** følgesvenn; ledsager; **3** tilhenger; **4** (fast) følge; kavaler. **following** ['fɒləuɪŋ] **I** *adj* følgende; ledsagende; **II** *sb* **1** følge; **2** støtte, tilhengere.

folly ['fɒlɪ] *sb* dumhet, dårskap; tåpelighet.

foment [fəu'ment] *vt* hisse opp til; nøre opp under.

fond [fɒnd] *adj* **1** kjærlig, snill; ~ *of* glad i; **2** dumsnill; godfjottet; **3** ~ *hope* forfengelig håp; ~*ly imagine* være så dum å tro. **fondle** ['fɒndl] *vt* kjærtegne.

font [fɒnt] *sb* **1** (døpe)font; **2** typesnitt (også *data*); **3** = *fount*.

food [fu:d] *sb* føde, næring; mat.

fool [fu:l] **A I** *adj* dum, tåpelig; **II** *sb* **1** fjols, tosk; **2** narr; **III** *vb* **1** oppføre seg som en tosk; ~ *around* tulle, tøyse; vimse; ~ *away* kaste (somle, sløse etc) bort; **2** ~ *out of* lure/narre fra; **B** *sb* fruktkrem. **fool|-hardy** ['ful:ha:dɪ] *adj* dumdristig. ~**ish** ['fu:lɪʃ] *adj* dum, tåpelig; fjollet. ~**proof** ['fu:lpru:f] *adj* idiotsikker.

foot [fut] **I** *sb* **1** fot (og (fot)trinn; fotstykke, sokkel; basis, underlag; *mil* fotfolk, infanteri); *my* ~*!* sludder! vrøvl! *on* ~ stående; på beina; til fots; *fig* i gang; i gjære; *put one's* ~ *down* opptre (protestere, si fra etc) bestemt; *put one's* ~ *into it* blamere seg; tråkke i spinaten; **2** fot (som lengdemål, se midtsidene); **II** *vb* **1** ~ *up* addere/legge sammen (tallkolonne); ~ *the bill* betale regningen; **2** *dgl* (~ *it*) gå, traske; danse; ta seg en svingom. **footbridge** *sb* gangbro. **footer** *sb data* bunntekst. **foot|fall** *sb* (lyden av) fottrinn. ~**hold** *sb* fotfeste. **footing** ['futɪŋ] *sb* **1** fotfeste; **2** stilling; situasjon; *on a friendly* ~ på vennskapelig fot. **foot|lights** *sb fl* rampelys. ~**path** *sb* (gang)sti. ~**print** *sb* fotspor. ~**sore** *adj* sårbeint. ~**step** = ~*fall*. ~**sure** *adj* sikker på foten. ~**wear** *sb* fottøy, skotøy. ~**worn** *adj* ned|-slitt, -tråkket; sliten.

fop [fɒp] *sb* snobb. **foppish** ['fɒpɪʃ] *adj* snobbet.

for [fɔ:] **A** *konj boklig* for; **B** *prep* **I 1** for (dvs til beste for; til fordel for; istedenfor; på vegne av; for ... skyld etc); **2** etter (dvs for å hente, skaffe etc); **3** (dvs bestemt for etc); mot (dvs i retning av etc); **4** som (dvs i egenskap av etc); **II** *om formål, hensikt, årsak etc* **1** ~ *joy* av glede; ~ *love* av kjærlighet/lyst etc; for moro skyld (dvs ikke for penger etc); *hard up* ~ vanskelig stilt med hensyn til; *marry* ~ *money* gifte seg for pengenes skyld; *meant* ~ *a joke* ment som (en) spøk; **2** *hope* ~ håpe (på); *it is not* ~ *me to* det er ikke min sak/det sømmer seg ikke for meg å; **3** ~ *this reason* derfor; av den grunn; ~ *want of* av mangel på; i mangel av; *what* ~ hvorfor; **III** *om forhold, sammenheng etc* **1** *as* ~ hva angår; med hensyn til; *as* ~ *me/*~ *my part/I* ~ *one* for mitt vedkommende; hva meg angår; jeg for min del; **2** ~ *all that* likevel; tross alt; **IV** *om tid og rom* **1** ~ *a few days* (i) et par dager; ~ *the present/the time being* for tiden; for øyeblikket; **2** *walk* ~ *several miles* gå flere *miles*.

forage ['fɒrɪdʒ] **1** *sb* fôr; furasje, furasjering; **2** *vi* furasjere; hente/skaffe fôr; ~ *for (dgl)* gå på jakt etter.

foray ['fɒreɪ] **1** *sb* innfall, streiftog; **2** *vi* herje, plyndre; gjøre streiftog.

forbear 1 ['fɔ:beə] *sb* stamfar; *især fl* forfedre; **2** [fɔ:'beə] *vb* avholde seg (*from* fra); unnlate. **forbearance** [fɔ:'beərəns] *sb* **1** unnlatelse *etc*; **2** overbærenhet; tålmodighet. **forbearing** [fɔ:'beərɪŋ] *adj* overbærende, tolerant; tålmodig.

forbid [fə'bɪd] *vt* forby. **forbidding** [fə'bɪdɪŋ] *adj* avvisende, utilnærmelig; skremmende.

force [fɔ:s] **I** *sb* **1** makt; kraft, styrke; *join* ~*s with* gjøre felles sak med; *join the Forces* gå inn i det militære; **2** virkning; gyldighet; *come/put into* ~ tre/sette i kraft; **II** *vt* tvinge (og drive, presse, tvinge frem; tiltvinge seg); *fig* forsere; overanstrenge. **forceful** ['fɔ:sful] *adj* kraftig, sterk; myndig.

forceps ['fɔ:seps] *sb* tang.

forcible ['fɔ:səbl] *adj* **1** kraftig, sterk; voldsom; **2** overbevisende; virkningsfull.

ford [fɔ:d] **1** *sb* vadested; **2** *vt* vade (over).

fore [fɔ:] **A I** *adj* forrest, for-, frem-; **II** *adv sjø* forut; ~ *and aft* (fra) for til akter; **III** *sb* **1** *sjø* (~*body*) forskip; **2** *to the* ~ i forgrunnen; ledende; **B** *pref* **1** for-, frem-; **2** forut-; på forhånd; **3** *sjø* fokke-; for-.

fore|arm 1 ['fɔ:ra:m] *sb* underarm; **2** [fɔ:r'a:m] *vt a)* ruste/væpne på forhånd; *b)* forberede. ~**bode** [fɔ:'bəud] *vt* bebude, (inn)varsle. ~**bodings** [fɔ:'bəudɪŋgz] *sb fl* (bange) anelser. ~**cast** ['fɔ:ka:st] **1** *sb* forutsigelse, prognose; (for)varsel; **2** *vt* forutsi; varsle (om). ~**castle** ['fəuksl] *sb sjø* bakk, fordekk (især på eldre seilskip); ruff. ~**court** ['fɔ:kɔ:t] *sb* forgård. ~**fathers** ['fɔ:fa:ðəz] *sb fl* forfedre. ~**finger** ['fɔ:fɪŋgə] *sb* pekefinger. ~**front** ['fɔ:frʌnt] *sb*: *the* ~ forreste linje. ~**going** [fɔ:'gəuɪŋ] *adj* foregående; forutgående. ~**gone** ['fɔ:gɒn] *adj*: ~*gone conclusion* gitt (el. uavvendelig) resultat (dvs noe som er gitt på forhånd). ~**ground** ['fɔ:graund] *sb* forgrunn. ~**head** ['fɒrɪd] *sb* panne.

foreign ['fɒrən] *adj* **1** uten|landsk, -riks; *(the) Foreign Office* utenriksdepartementet; *(the) Foreign Secretary* utenriksministeren; **2** fremmed(artet); *~ to* fjernt fra; uforenelig med. **foreigner** ['fɒrənə] *sb* utlending.

fore|man ['fɔ:mən] *sb* formann. **~mast** ['fɔ:mɑ:st] *sb sjø* fokkemast. **~most** ['fɔ:məʊst] *adj, adv* forrest; fremst, ledende. **~name** ['fɔ:neɪm] *sb* fornavn. **~runner** ['fɔ:rʌnə] *sb* forløper. **~running** *sb petro* førstefraksjon. **~sail** ['fɔ:seɪl] *sb sjø* fokk. **~see** [fɔ:'si:] *vt* forutse. **~seeable** [fɔ:'si:əbl] *adj* som kan forutses; *in the ~seeable future* i overskuelig fremtid. **~shadow** [fɔ:'ʃædəʊ] *vt* bebude, (inn)varsle. **~shore** ['fɔ:ʃɔ:] *sb* strand(belte). **~shorten** [fɔ:'ʃɔ:tn] *vt* forkorte; gjengi mindre (i perspektivisk tegning etc). **~sight** ['fɔ:saɪt] *sb* forutseenhet. **~skin** ['fɔ:skɪn] *sb* forhud.

forest ['fɒrɪst] *sb* **1** skog (og skogområde); **2** jaktterreng.

forestall [fɔ:'stɔ:l] *vt* komme i forkjøpet; avverge, hindre.

forester ['fɒrɪstə] *sb* **1** forstmann; skog|forvalter, -vokter; **2** skogsarbeider; **3** skogsdyr, skogsfugl. **forestry** ['fɒrɪstrɪ] *sb* **1** forstvesen, skogbruk; **2** skog.

fore|taste ['fɔ:teɪst] *sb* forsmak. **~tell** [fɔ:'tel] *vt* forutsi; varsle om. **~thought** ['fɔ:θɔ:t] *sb* fremsyn; omtanke. **~warn** [fɔ:'wɔ:n] *vt* advare (på forhånd). **~woman** ['fɔ:wʊmən] *sb* forkvinne. **~word** ['fɔ:wɜ:d] *sb* forord.

forfeit ['fɔ:fɪt] **I** *sb* **1** pris (en må betale for å ha forbrutt seg, forspilt sine sjanser etc); bot, mulkt; *pay the ~ of one's life* betale/bøte med livet; **2** *(game of) ~s* pantelek; **II** *vt* forlise, forspille; gå glipp av; miste, tape. **forfeiture** ['fɔ:fɪtʃə] *sb* forbrutt eiendom *etc*.

forge [fɔ:dʒ] **I** *sb* **1** esse; smie; **2** (metall)verksted; **II** *vt* **1** smi; *fig* forme, skape; **2** forfalske; **3** *~ ahead* arbeide (kjempe, presse etc) seg frem. **forgery** ['fɔ:dʒərɪ] *sb* falskneri; forfalskning.

forget [fə'get] *vb* glemme. **forgetful** [fə'getfʊl] *adj* glemsom. **forget-me-not** [fə'getmɪnɒt] *sb* forglemmegei.

forgive [fə'gɪv] *vb* tilgi; forlate (synd); ettergi (gjeld). **forgiveness** [fə'gɪvnɪs] *sb* tilgivelse *etc*. **forgiving** [fə'gɪvɪŋ] *adj* overbærende.

fork [fɔ:k] **I** *sb* **1** gaffel; greip; høygaffel; **2** avgrening, kløft (mellom to grener etc); vei|dele, skille; **II** *vb* **1** bruke/ta med (høy)gaffel *etc*; **2** dele/kløyve (seg); **3** *slang: ~ out/up* punge ut (med). **fork-lift (truck)** *sb* gaffeltruck.

forlorn [fə'lɔ:n] *adj* **1** forlatt; (ensom og) ulykkelig; **2** *~ hope* halsløst foretagende; *mil ofte* selvmords|oppdrag, -patrulje.

form [fɔ:m] **I** *sb* **1** ytre (form); fasong, skikkelse; **2** form; oppbygning, struktur; **3** art, slag(s), sort, type; *she ran true to ~ (dgl)* hun fornektet sèg ikke; **4** måte; system; **5** (dannet) opptreden; manerer, oppførsel; *it is bad ~* det er ikke god tone; **6** formulering, ordlyd; **7** *(printed ~)* blanket, formular, skjema; **8** (fysisk) form; **9** benk (uten rygg); **10** klasse (især i videregående skole); **II** *vb* **1** danne, forme; lage; utvikle; bygge opp; **2** utgjøre; **3** *mil* formere; danne formasjon. **formal** ['fɔ:ml] *adj* **1** formell; **2** regelmessig; **3** utvendig; overfladisk. **formality** [fɔ:'mælətɪ] *sb* **1** formell opptreden *etc*; formellhet; **2** formalitet, formsak. **format** ['fɔ:mæt] *især data* **1** *sb* format; **2** *vt* formatere. **formation** [fɔ:'meɪʃn] *sb* **1** forming *etc*; **2** formasjon; formering (= oppstilling).

former ['fɔ:mə] *adj* tidligere; forhenværende; *the ~* førstnvnte. **formerly** ['fɔ:məlɪ] *adv* før (i tiden); tidligere.

form feed *sb data* blankettmating.

formidable ['fɔ:mɪdəbl] *adj* fryktelig, skremmende; avskrekkende; imponerende; formidabel.

formula ['fɔ:mjʊlə] *sb* **1** *a)* formular; *b)* talemåte, uttrykk; **2** resept; **3** formel. **formulate** ['fɔ:mjʊleɪt] *vt* formulere, uttrykke. **formulation** [ˌfɔ:mjʊ'leɪʃn] *sb* formulering *etc*.

forsake [fə'seɪk] *vt* **1** forlate, svikte; **2** oppgi.

forth [fɔ:θ] *adv* **1** frem, ut; **2** videre. **forthcoming** [fɔ:θ'kʌmɪŋ] *adj* **1** (nær) forestående; kommende; ventet; **2** imøtekommende. **forthwith** [fɔ:θ'wɪθ] *adv* omgående, straks.

fortification [ˌfɔ:tɪfɪ'keɪʃn] *sb* forsterkning *etc*; *fl mil* befestning(er). **fortify** ['fɔ:tɪfaɪ] *vt* forsterke, styrke; *mil* befeste; *fig* underbygge. **fortitude** ['fɔ:tɪtju:d] *sb* (indre) styrke; fasthet.

fortnight ['fɔ:tnaɪt] *sb* fjorten dager; to uker.

fortress ['fɔ:trɪs] *sb* festning; befestet by/område etc.

fortuitous [fɔ:'tju:ɪtəs] *adj* tilfeldig. **fortunate** ['fɔ:tʃnət] *adj* heldig. **fortunately** ['fɔ:tʃnətlɪ] *adv* heldigvis. **fortune** ['fɔ:tʃən] *sb* **1** hell, lykke; **2** skjebne; **3** fremgang, suksess; **4** formue, rikdom. **fortune-teller** *sb* spå|kone, -mann.

forward ['fɔ:wəd] **I** *adj* **1** fremadrettet; frem-; **2** forrest; for-; frem-; **3** fremmelig; tidlig ute; **4** imøtekommende; ivrig; **5** frempå, ubeskjeden; **II** *adv (~s)* **1** fremad, fremover; forover; **2** frem, ut; **3** *sjø* ['fɒrəd] forut; **III** *sb sport* forward, løper; **IV** *vt* **1** fremme, hjelpe frem; **2** ekspedere; sende (og sende etter, til ny adresse).

fossil ['fɒsl] *adj, sb* fossil(-). **fossil fuel** *sb petro* fossilt brennstoff (som kull, olje og naturgass).

foster ['fɒstə] **I** *adj* foster-, pleie-; **II** *vt* **1** fostre, oppdra; **2** pleie; *fig* nære, omgås; **3** fremme; (under)støtte.

foul [faʊl] **I** *adj* **1** skitten; sjofel, slibrig; stygg; **2** ekkel, vemmelig; vond; **3** *sport etc* ureal, ureglementert; **4** floket, rotet; **5** tett, tilstoppet; **6** *fall/run ~ of* renne/seile på; kollidere med; *fig* ryke uklar med; **II** *sb* **1** *sport (~ play)* foul, ureglementert spill; juks; **2** *through fair and ~* gjennom tykt og tynt; **III** *vb* **1** forurense; grise (skitne, svine) til; **2** floke seg; vikle seg inn (i); **3** kollidere (med). **foul play** *sb* juks; *også* forbrytelse.

found [faʊnd] *vt* **1** etablere, grunnlegge; opprette/

stifte (især ved pengegave); **2** bygge, reise; **3** bygge/ være basert (*on* på). **foundation** [faʊn'deɪʃn] *sb* **1** etablering *etc*; stiftelse; fond, legat; **2** *(fl)* fundament, grunnmur; *fig* grunnvoll; **3** grunnlag/underlag (også for sminke etc samt figurfremhevende klesplagg). **founder** ['faʊndə] **I** *sb* grunnlegger, stifter; **II** *vb* **1** *sjø* forlise, gå til bunns; **2** falle/segne sammen; snuble.

foundling ['faʊndlɪŋ] *sb* hittebarn.

foundry ['faʊndrɪ] *sb* støperi.

fount [faʊnt] *sb poet* kilde. **fountain** ['faʊntɪn] *sb* **1** kilde; fontene, springvann; **2** *fig* kilde; opphav, opprinnelse. **fountain|head** *sb* kilde, utspring. **~-pen** *sb* fyllepenn.

four [fɔ:] *adj, sb* fire(tall); firer. **four|-poster** *sb* himmelseng. **~some** *sb* firemannslag; kortlag (med fire personer).

fowl [faʊl] **I** *sb* **1** (-)fugl; **2** høner, høns; **II** *vi* gå/ dra på fuglejakt. **fowler** ['faʊlə] *sb* fugle|fanger, -jeger.

fox [fɒks] *sb* rev. **foxhole** ['fɒkshəʊl] *sb mil* dekningsgrav, skyttergrop. **foxy** ['fɒksɪ] *adj* reverød; *fig* sleip, slu; lur.

fraction ['frækʃn] *sb* brøk; *fig* brøkdel. **fracture** ['fræktʃə] **1** *sb* brudd (og bruddsted); **2** *vb* brekke, knekke; bryte/gå i stykker. **fragile** ['frædʒaɪl] *adj* skjør; skrøpelig; svak(elig); spinkel. **fragment** ['frægmənt] *sb* brudd(stykke); del. **fragmentary** ['frægməntərɪ] *adj* fragmentarisk; oppstykket.

fragrance ['freɪgrəns] *sb* duft, vellukt; aroma. **fragrant** ['freɪgrənt] *adj* duftende, velluktende; aromatisk.

frail [freɪl] skrøpelig, svak(elig); skjør; spinkel.

frame [freɪm] **I** *sb* **1** ramme (til bilde etc); karm (til dør, vindu etc); innfatning; bord, kant; **2** *(~work)* ramme(verk); reisverk; spant (og spantekonstruksjon); *fig* (opp)bygning; skjelett; struktur; *~ of mind* sinns|stemning, -tilstand; **II** *vb* **1** ramme inn; **2** bygge (opp); reise; konstruere; danne/forme (seg); **3** finne på; tenke ut; **4** arte/utvikle seg; tegne til å bli; **5** *slang: ~ up* forfalske, *især US* fabrikere falsk anklage/ falske bevis etc. **frame | house** *sb US* trehus. **~-up** *sb* (inkriminerende) felle; falsk anklage etc.

franchise ['fræntʃaɪz] *sb* **1** rettighet; borgerrett; **2** stemmerett; **3** *US a)* bevilling; (offentlig) tillatelse; *b) som vb* gi slik bevilling/tillatelse.

frank [fræŋk] **A** *adj* likefrem, åpen; oppriktig; **B** *vt* frankere.

frantic ['fræntɪk] *adj* hektisk, oppjaget; vill; voldsom.

fraternal [frə'tɜ:nl] *adj* broderlig; brorskaps-. **fraternity** [frə'tɜ:nətɪ] *sb* **1** brorskap; forening/selskap (i USA især av studenter etc); laug; stand; **2** broderlighet.

fraud [frɔ:d] *sb* **1** bedrag(eri), svindel; svik; **2** bedrager, humbug(maker); svindler. **fraudulent** ['frɔ:djʊlənt] *adj* bedragersk *etc*.

fraught [frɔ:t] *adj: ~ with* full av; fylt/ladet med.

fray [freɪ] **A** *sb* kamp, strid; **B** *vb* bli frynset/loslitt etc; frynse (seg).

freak [frik] **I** *sb* **1** innfall, lune; kuriositet, raritet; **2** avviker, original; raring; tulling; *slang også* frik; *Jesus ~* Jesus-frik; *pill ~* pillenarkoman; **3** misfoster, vanskapning; **II** *vi (~ out)* frike ut (dvs oppføre seg sterkt avvikende, asosialt etc). **freakish** ['fri:kɪʃ] *adj* **1** lunefull *etc*; **2** original; rar; sær; *slang* frikete.

freckle ['frekl] **1** *sb* fregne; **2** *vb* få fregner; bli/ gjøre fregnet.

free [fri:] **I** *adj* **1** fri, uavhengig; **2** befridd, fri(gitt); **3** fritatt (*of* for); **4** løs, ubundet; **5** fri(gjort); tvangfri, utvungen; **6** uhemmet, uhindret; *~ of* kvitt; fri for; **7** familiær, freidig; **8** *(~-handed)* raus, rundhåndet; *be ~ with* ikke spare på; **9** ledig; tilgjengelig, åpen; **II** *adj, adv* fri(tt), gratis; fri-; **III** *vt* befri, sette/slippe fri; frigjøre. **free|born** *sb* fribåren. **~dom** ['fri:dəm] *sb* frihet *etc*. **~-for-all** *sb* åpen konkurranse etc; alminnelig slagsmål. **~ form** *sb data* fritt format. **~holder** *sb* selveier; *især* ≈ odelsbonde. **~mason** *sb* frimurer. **~-spoken** *adj* frittalende, åpenhjertig. **~ trade** *sb* frihandel. **~way** *sb* motorvei.

freeze [fri:z] **I** *sb* **1** frost; kulde(periode); **2** *(deep ~)* fryseboks; **3** *fig* (fast)frysing, stopp; **II** *vb* **1** fryse (og dypfryse; fryse på, fryse til (is); fryse fast/inne etc); *~ over* fryse på; fryse til is; **2** *fig, merk* (fast)fryse (dvs begrense, sperre, stanse etc); **3** *fig* stivne (av redsel etc); bli stående *etc* urørlig. **freezer** ['fri:zə] *sb* (dyp)fryser, fryseboks.

freight [freɪt] **1** *sb* frakt (og frakt|avgift, -omkostninger); last; *US også* gods; **2** *vt* befrakte; laste (med). **freighter** ['freɪtə] *sb* lastebåt; transportfly. **freight-train** *sb* godstog.

French [frentʃ] *adj, sb* fransk (og franskmann, se også midtsidene); *take ~ leave* fordufte, stikke av. **French | frie(d)s** *sb fl* franske (smultstekte) poteter. **~ horn** *sb* valthorn. **~ letter** *sb* kondom. **~ polish** *sb* (møbel)politur, skjellakk.

frenzied ['frenzɪd] *adj* hektisk, oppjaget; opphisset, rasende. **frenzy** ['frenzɪ] *sb* opphisselse, raseri.

frequency ['fri:kwənsɪ] *sb* **1** hyppighet; **2** frekvens. **frequent 1** ['fri:kwənt] *adj* alminnelig, vanlig; hyppig; **2** [fri:'kwent] *vt* besøke ofte; omgås. **frequentation** [ˌfri:kwən'teɪʃn] *sb* hyppig(e) besøk; søkning.

fresh [freʃ] *adj* **1** ny; fersk, frisk; *fig* nybakt, uerfaren; *som adv* ny-; **2** frisk (især av utseende: rødmusset, sunn etc); opplagt, uthvilt; **3** forfriskende; **4** *US* frekk, nærgående. **fresh | ground** *sb* jomfruelig grunn/mark. **~man** *sb* første års student; grønnskolling. **~ oil** *sb petro* friskolje. **~ water** *sb* ferskvann.

fret [fret] **A I** *sb* **1** ergrelse, irritasjon; **2** bekymring, uro; **II** *vb* **1** ergre (seg); irritere; **2** bekymre (seg); uroe; **2** gnage/tære (på); **B** *vt* dekorere med utskjæringer; **C** *sb* bånd (på gitars etc gripebrett). **fret|ful** ['fretfʊl] *adj* grinet, irritabel. **~saw** *sb* løvsag. **~work** *sb* løvsagarbeid; utskjæringer.

friar ['fraɪə] *sb* (tigger)munk.

friction ['frɪkʃn] *sb* friksjon.

fridge [frɪdʒ] *sb dgl* kjøleskap.

fried *adj dgl data* brutt sammen.

friend [frend] *sb* **1** venn; **2** *Friend* kveker. **friendliness** ['frendlɪnɪs] *sb* vennlighet *etc.* **friendly** ['frendlɪ] *adj* vennlig; vennskapelig. **friendship** ['frendʃɪp] *sb* vennskap.

fright [fraɪt] *sb* frykt, skrekk; redsel; *look a* ~ se fæl/redselsfull *etc* ut. **frighten** ['fraɪtn] *vt* skremme. **frightful** ['fraɪtfʊl] *adj* forferdelig, skrekkelig; redselsfull.

frigid ['frɪdʒɪd] *adj* kald, kjølig; frigid; *fig* avvisende.

frill [frɪl] *sb* rynke|kant, -kappe; rysj; *fig* dikkedarer, jåleri; tøys; *put on ~s* gjøre seg viktig; skape seg.

fringe [frɪndʒ] *sb* **1** (ut)kant; *som adj* perifer; utkant-, ytter-; **2** frynse(r); **3** pannelugg. **fringe benefits** *sb fl* frynsegoder; tilleggs|goder, -ytelser.

frisk [frɪsk] **A** *vi* hoppe og sprette; boltre seg; **B** *vt* kroppsvisitere, ransake.

frivolity [frɪ'vʌlətɪ] *sb* lettsindighet *etc.* **frivolous** ['frɪvələs] *adj* lettsindig, overfladisk; frivol.

fro [frəʊ] *adv: to and* ~ frem og tilbake; til og fra.

frock [frɒk] *sb* **1** kjole; **2** kappe, kutte; kittel.

frog [frɒg] *sb* **1** frosk; **2** agraman. **frogman** *sb* froskemann.

frolic ['frɒlɪk] **1** *sb* lystighet; spillopper; **2** *vi* gjøre spillopper; more seg. **frolicsome** ['frɒlɪksəm] *adj* lystig, munter.

from [frɒm] *prep* fra (og av; etter; som følge av; på grunn/grunnlag av etc); ~ *memory* etter hukommelsen; ~ *necessity* av nødvendighet; ~ *what I hear* etter hva jeg hører.

front [frʌnt] **I** *adj* forrest, først; for-, første-; front-; **II** *sb* **1** fasade, forside; *fig* forgrunn; *in* ~ *of* foran; på forsiden av; **2** *mil* front (og frontlinje); **3** *(water~)* sjøside; strandpromenade; **4** *(shirt-~)* skjortebryst; **5** *poet* panne; ansikt, åsyn; **6** frekkhet; **III** *vb* **1** vende (ut) mot; stå *etc* vendt mot, stå overfor; **2** fasadekle. **frontage** ['frʌntɪdʒ] *sb* fasade, forside. **frontal** ['frʌntl] *adj* frontal(-), front-. **front door** *sb* gatedør. **frontier** ['frʌntɪə] *sb* grense (og især grense|land, -område, strøk). **front | rank** *sb* forreste/fremste rekke. **~-rank** *adj* betydelig, fremstående. **~ room** *sb* rom mot/til gate.

frost [frɒst] **I** *sb* **1** frost, kulde; rim; *black* ~ barfrost; **2** *dgl* fiasko; skuffelse; **II** *vb* **1** frostskade; fryse på/til; **2** glassere (kake); **3** mattere (glass). **frost|-bite** *sb* frost(skade), forfrysning. **~-bitten** *adj* frostskadet. **~-bound** *adj* med tele. **frosted** ['frɒstɪd] *adj* frossen; rimet; *også fig* kjølig; *om hår* gråsprengt. **frosting** ['frɒstɪŋ] *sb* (melis- el. sukker)glasur. **frosty** ['frɒstɪ] *adj* frossen, (is)kald; *fig* avvisende, utilnærmelig.

froth [frɒθ] **I** *sb* **1** fråde, skum; **2** *fig* fraser, tomt snakk; **II** *vi* fråde, skumme.

frown [fraʊn] **1** *sb* rynket panne; **2** *vi* rynke pannen; se morsk ut; ~ *(up)on* misbillige; se med ublide øyne på.

frowzy ['fraʊzɪ] *adj* **1** innestengt, kvalm (om luft); **2** sjusket, uordentlig.

frugal ['fru:gl] *adj* enkel, nøysom; sparsom(melig). **frugality** [fru:'gælətɪ] *sb* enkelhet *etc.*

fruit [fru:t] **1** *sb* frukt; *fl* avling, grøde; *fig* resultat(er); utbytte; **2** *vi* bære frukt; gi frukter. **fruiterer** ['fru:tərə] *sb* frukthandler. **fruitful** ['fru:tfʊl] *adj* fruktbar; *fig* fruktbringende. **fruition** [fru:'ɪʃn] *sb* oppnåelse, realisering. **fruitless** ['fru:tlɪs] *adj* ufruktbar; *fig* fruktesløs, resultatløs; mislykket. **fruity** ['fru:tɪ] *adj* **1** fruktig; med fruktsmak; frukt-; **2** fulltonende, rik; **3** saftig; *fig især* folkelig, grov(kornet).

frustrate [frʌ'streɪt] *vt* **1** (for)hindre; krysse, komme i veien for; **2** skuffe. **frustration** [frʌ'streɪʃn] *sb* (følelse av) nederlag; skuffelse; fortvilelse; frustrasjon.

fry [fraɪ] **A** *vb* steke(s); **B** *sb* fiskeyngel; *small* ~ småfisk; *især fig* (små)kryp, ubetydeligheter. **frying-pan** *sb* stekepanne.

fuel ['fju:əl] **I** *sb* **1** brensel; **2** drivstoff; **II** *vb* forsyne med/ta inn brensel/drivstoff. **fuel | additive** *sb petro* drivstofftilsetning. **~ dope** *sg petro* antibankemiddel, oktantallforbedrer. **~ oil** *sb petro* brenselolje, fyringsolje.

fugitive ['fju:dʒɪtɪv] **I** *adj* **1** flyktende; **2** flyktig; **II** *sb* **1** flyktning; **2** rømling.

fulcrum ['fʌlkrəm] *sb* (om)dreiningspunkt; anlegg/støtte (for vektstang etc); *også fig* fast punkt.

fulfil [fʊl'fɪl] *vt* full|byrde, -føre; (opp(fylle, tilfredsstille. **full** [fʊl] **A I** *adj* **1** full, fylt; *dgl (~ up)* (stapp)mett; **2** full(stendig); hel, komplett; **3** fyldig; *om klær* vid; **4** rik(elig); **II** *adv* fullt, helt; full-, hel-; **III** *sb* fylde; helhet; fullstendighet; *in* ~ fullstendig; i (sin) helhet; **B** *vt* stampe, valke (ull). **full|-blown** *adj* (fullt) utsprunget; *fig* moden; velutviklet. **~-dress** *adj* fullstendig, komplett; general-. **~-length** *adj* **1** i full/normal lengde; **2** i full/normal størrelse. **~ moon** *sb* fullmåne. **~-page** *adj* helsides-. **~ stop** *sb* punktum. **~-time** *adj* fulltids- heldags-. **~ word** *sb data* maskinord.

fulminate ['fʌlmɪneɪt] *vi* eksplodere (især *fig*); ~ *against* rase/tordne mot; fordømme i drøye ordelag.

fulsome ['fʊlsəm] *adj* overdreven; vammel. **fulsome praise** *sb* skamros(ing).

fumble ['fʌmbl] *vb* famle (*for* etter); fomle, klusse; ~ *with* fingre/tukle med.

fume [fju:m] **I** *sb* **1** røyk; damp, dunst; **2** opphisselse, raseri; **II** *vb* **1** ryke; dampe, dunste; **2** rase; skumme (av raseri); **3** røykbeise.

fun [fʌn] *sb* moro; *for/in* ~ for moro skyld; for/på spøk.

function ['fʌŋkʃn] **I** *sb* **1** funksjon (og gjøremål, oppgave, virksomhet; virkemåte, virkning etc); **2** fest(lighet); (offisiell) høytidelighet, seremoni; **II** *vi* fungere, virke; funksjonere. **functional** ['fʌŋkʃənl] *adj* **1** funksjonell; funksjons-; **2** offisiell. **functionary**

['fʌŋkʃnərɪ] *sb* (offentlig) funksjonær (især brukt i nedsettende betydning). **function key** *sb data* funksjonstast.

fund [fʌnd] **I** *sb* **1** forråd, lager; **2** *især fl* (penge)-fond; **3** *fl* (penge)midler; (økonomiske) ressurser; **II** *vt* **1** anbringe penger i statsobligasjoner; **2** kapitalisere. **fundamental** [ˌfʌndə'mentl] **1** *adj* fundamental, grunnleggende; vesentlig; **2** *sb, især fl* grunnprinsipp(er).

funeral ['fju:nərəl] *sb* begravelse. **funeral parlour** *sb US* begravelsesbyrå. **funereal** [fju:'nɪərɪəl] *adj* dyster, mørk; begravelses-; nifs.

fungus ['fʌŋgəs] *sb* sopp (som art).

funk [fʌŋk] **I** *sb dgl* **1** panikk; redsel, skrekk; **2** reddhare; **II** *vi dgl* krype sammen/vike unna (av skrekk).

funnel ['fʌnl] **I** *sb* **1** trakt; **2** (ventilasjons)|kanal, -rør, sjakt; røykrør, (skips)skorstein; **II** *vt* kanalisere, lede.

funny ['fʌnɪ] *adj* **1** gøyal, morsom; komisk; **2** pussig, snodig; merkelig, underlig.

fur [fɜ:] **I** *sb* **1** pels (og pelsverk); **2** belegg (på tungen etc); **II** *vb* **1** pelsfôre; besette/kante med skinn; **2** få pels; bli lodden; **3** danne belegg. **fur-coat** *sb* pels(kåpe), skinnkåpe.

furbish ['fɜ:bɪʃ] *vt* polere, pusse; ~ *up* pusse opp; *fig* friske opp.

furious ['fjʊərɪəs] *adj* rasende; vill, voldsom.

furl [fɜ:l] *vb* folde/rulle (seg) sammen; slå sammen; slå ned (paraply etc).

furlong ['fɜ:lɒŋ] *sb* et lengdemål, se midtsidene.

furnace ['fɜ:nɪs] *sb* **1** (sentral)fyr; ildsted; **2** masovn; smelteovn.

furnish ['fɜ:nɪʃ] *vt* **1** levere, skaffe; ~ *with* forsyne/utstyre med; **2** møblere. **furniture** ['fɜ:nɪtʃə] *sb* inventar, møbler; utstyr; tilbehør.

furrow ['fʌrəʊ] **I** *sb* **1** fure, rille; spor; (plog)får; **2** (dyp) rynke; **II** *vt* fure, rynke; pløye.

furry ['fɜ:rɪ] *adj* pelskledd, pels-.

further ['fɜ:ðə] **A I** *adj* **1** fjernere; **2** ytterligere; *till/until* ~ *notice* inntil videre; **II** *adv* **1** *(~more)* dessuten; **2** *dgl: wish them* ~ ønske dem dit pepperen gror; **B** *vt* fremme; hjelpe (frem). **furthermore** [ˌfɜ:ðə'mɔ:] *adv* = *further A II 1*. **furthermost** ['fɜ:ðəməʊst] *adj* lengst borte.

furtive ['fɜ:tɪv] *adj* hemmelig(hetsfull); fordekt; stjålen.

fury ['fjʊərɪ] *sb* **1** raseri; **2** furie, heks.

fuse [fju:z] **A I** *sb elek* sikring; **II** *vb* **1** smelte; brenne av; **2** fusjonere; gå/slutte seg sammen; **B** *sb* lunte; *mil* brannrør, tennrør.

fuselage ['fju:zɪlɑ:ʒ] *sb* (fly)kropp.

fusion ['fju:ʒn] *sb* **1** (sammen)|blanding, -smelting; **2** fusjon, sammenslutning; **3** (termonukleær) fusjon.

fuss [fʌs] **I** *sb* **1** oppskjørtethet; bekymring, engstelse (især over småting); **2** oppstyr, ståhei; mas; *make a ~ of* gjøre krus på/vesen av; **II** *vb* mase (på); gjøre/være oppskjørtet; ~ *about* vimse omkring; ~ *over* dulle med. **fussy** ['fʌsɪ] *adj* **1** oppskjørtet; nervøs, urolig; irritabel; **2** geskjeftig, maset; **3** pirket.

futile ['fju:taɪl] *adj* forgjeves; nytteløs; **2** intetsigende. **futility** [fju:'tɪlətɪ] *sb* nytteløshet *etc*.

future ['fju:tʃə] **1** *adj* fremtidig, fremtids-; **2** *sb* fremtid; *gram* futurum.

fuzzy ['fʌzɪ] *adj* **1** dunet; loet; lodden; **2** uklar, utydelig.

G

gab [gæb] *sb dgl* prat, snakk; *have the gift of the ~* ha snakketøyet i orden.

gabble ['gæbl] **I** *sb* **1** skravling; **2** rør, vrøvl; **II** *vb* plapre, skravle; røre, vrøvle.

gable ['geɪbl] *sb* gavl.

gadget ['gædʒɪt] *sb dgl* (fiks) innretning; dings, greie, sak.

gag [gæg] **I** *sb* **1** knebel; *fig* munnkurv; **2** *teater* (improvisert) blødme/vits etc; **II** *vb* **1** kneble, stoppe munnen på; **2** *teater* improvisere vitser *etc*.

gage [geɪdʒ] **A** *sb* **1** pant, sikkerhet; **2** *fig* hanske (dvs utfordring); **B** = *gauge I*.

gaiety ['geɪətɪ] *sb* lystighet, munterhet; fest(ing).

gain [geɪn] **I** *sb* **1** *fl* fortjeneste; gevinst, vinning; **2** økning, vekst; **II** *vb* **1** oppnå, skaffe seg; ~ *ground* vinne terreng; **2** nå/rekke (frem til); **3** (for)øke; vokse; *(~ weight)* legge på seg; **4** fortne (om klokke); ~ *(up)on* ta/vinne innpå. **gainful** ['geɪnfʊl] *adj* innbringende.

gainsay [geɪn'seɪ] *vt* (be)nekte; motsi.

gait [geɪt] *sb* gange; måte å gå på. **gaiter** ['geɪtə] *sb* gamasje.

galaxy ['gæləksɪ] *sb* galakse, stjernetåke; *fig* strålende forsamling etc; stjerneparade.

gale [geɪl] *sb* kuling; storm; *moderate ~* stiv kuling; *fresh ~* sterk kuling; *strong ~* liten storm; *whole ~* full storm.

gall [gɔ:l] **A** *sb* **1** galle; **2** bitterhet; **3** *US dgl* frekkhet, uforskammethet; **B I** *sb* gnagsår; hudløst sted; *fig* irritasjon; ømt punkt; **II** *vt* **1** gnage, skave; **2** irritere; ergre, plage.

gallant ['gælənt] **I** *adj* **1** tapper; **2** (feiende) flott; **3** beleven, galant; **II** *sb* kavaler. **galantry** ['gæləntrɪ] *sb* tapperhet.

gallery ['gælərɪ] *sb* **1** galleri; *teater især* balkong; *fig* tilhørere, tilskuere; **2** *(shooting-~)* (innendørs) skytebane; **3** (smal) gang/korridor; stoll (= vannrett gruvegang); **4** svalgang, søylegang. **gallery rifle** *sb* salong|gevær, -rifle.

galley ['gælɪ] *sb* **1** *sjø* galei; **2** *sjø* bysse; **3** (sats)-skiff; **4** = **galley|-proof** *sb* spaltekorrektur. **~ range** *sb sjø* skipskomfyr.

gallon [gælən] *sb* et hulmål, se midtsidene.

gallop ['gæləp] **I** *sb* galopp; **II** *vb* **1** (la/få til å) galoppere; **2** fare, styrte.

gallows ['gæləuz] *sb* galge.

galore [gə'lɔ:] *adv* i massevis.

galoshes [gə'lɒʃɪz] *sb fl* kalosjer.

galvanize ['gælvənaɪz] *vt* galvanisere; *fig* anspore; (opp)ildne; fjetre.

gambit ['gæmbɪt] *sb* gambit (i sjakk); innledende trekk; *fig* utspill, åpning.

gamble ['gæmbl] **1** *sb* (sjanse)spill; hasard(spill); **2** *vb* spille (hasard/høyt spill); ta (store) sjanser; spekulere.

gambol ['gæmbl] **1** *sb (fl)* hopp, sprett; **2** *vi* hoppe, sprette.

game [geɪm] **A I** *adj* **1** kjekk, modig; standhaftig, uforferdet; **2** rede, villig; **~** *for* opplagt/rede til; med på; **II** *sb* **1** lek, spill (også om det en leker/spiller med: brett, brikker etc); sport (og *fl* idretts|begivenhet, -konkurranse; (-)leker; game (i tennis); omgang, parti; **~** *of cards* slag kort; *play the* **~** følge spillets regler; være med på leken; **2** (listig) plan; knep, lureri; **3** (jakt)bytte, vilt; **B** *vb* spille (hasard); **C** *adj: have a* **~** *leg* halte på det ene beinet. **game|-keeper** *sb* skogvokter. **~-licence** *sb* jakt|kort, -tillatelse. **~-master** *sb* gymnastikklærer; idrettsinstruktør. **~ reserve** *sb* viltreservat.

gamut ['gæmət] *sb mus* register; skala; *fig* (fullt) omfang; rekkevidde.

gander ['gændə] *sb* gasse.

gang [gæŋ] **1** *sb* flokk; (arbeids)|gjeng, -lag; (forbryter)|bande, -gjeng; *dgl* klikk; pakk, sleng; **2** *vi* angripe/jage i flokk; **~** *up* rotte seg sammen.

gangrene ['gæŋgri:n] **1** *sb* koldbrann; **2** *vb* forårsake/bli angrepet av koldbrann.

gangway ['gæŋweɪ] *sb* **1** *sjø* landgang; **2** gang/ passasje (mellom benkerader).

gaol [dʒeɪl] **1** *sb* fengsel; **2** *vt* fengsle. **gaolbird** ['dʒeɪlbɜ:d] *sb* fengselsfugl.

gap [gæp] *sb* **1** hull, åpning; **2** sprekk; gap, kløft; slukt; *fig* avstand. **gap | character, ~ digit** *sb data* utfyllingstegn.

garage ['gærɑ:ʒ] **1** *sb* garasje; *ofte* bensinstasjon; (mindre) bilverksted, serviceverksted; **2** *vt* sette i garasje.

garb [gɑ:b] **1** *sb* antrekk, drakt; **2** *vt:* **~***ed in* iført; kledd i.

garbage ['gɑ:bɪdʒ] *sb* **1** skyller; avfall, søppel; **2** *data* (data)søppel. **garbage | can** *sb US* søppel|bøtte, -kasse, -spann. **~ collection** *sb data* datasanering.

garble ['gɑ:bl] *vt* forvanske; gjengi feilaktig/misvisende etc.

garden [gɑ:dn] *sb* hage; *især fl* park; husrekke med forhager; *market-***~** handelsgartneri. **gardener** ['gɑ:-dnə] *sb* gartner. **gardening** ['gɑ:dnɪŋ] *sb* hagearbeid.

gargle ['gɑ:gl] **1** *sb* gurglevann; **2** *vb* gurgle (seg).

garish ['geərɪʃ] *adj* gloret grell, skrikende; skjærende.

garland ['gɑ:lənd] **1** *sb* krans (av blomster, løv etc); **2** *vt* bekranse.

garlic ['gɑ:lɪk] *sb* hvitløk.

garment ['gɑ:mnt] *sb* (kles)plagg; *fl* klær.

garnish ['gɑ:nɪʃ] **1** *sb* garnering, pynt; **2** *vt* dekorere, pynte; garnere. **garniture** ['gɑ:nɪtʃə] *sb* **1** garnityr; **2** pynt (og pynte|gjenstander, -sett); **3** = *garnish 1.*

garret ['gærət] *sb* kvist(værelse), takkammer; loft.

garrison ['gærɪsn] *mil* **I** *sb* garnison; **II** *vt* **1** (for)-legge garnison/tropper i; **2** garnisonere; legge (tropper) i garnison.

garrulous [gæruləs] *adj* snakkesalig (især på en litt plagsom måte).

garter ['gɑ:tə] *sb* strømpebånd; *US* armstrikk; sokkeholder; strømpestropp.

gas [gæs] **I** *sb* **1** gass; **2** *US dgl* bensin; *også* gass-(pedal); **3** *dgl* tomt snakk; skryt; **II** *vb* **1** forsyne med (lys)gass; **2** gasse, gassforgifte; **3** *dgl* skvaldre; skryte. **gas|-bag** *sb* gass|ballong, beholder; *fig* pratmaker. **~ cleaning, ~ conditioning** *sb petro* gassrensing. **~-cooker** *sb* gasskomfyr. **~ drying** *sb petro* gasstørking. **gaseous** ['gæsɪəs] *adj* gass|aktig, -formig. **gas | eruption** *sb petro* gassutbrudd. **~ field** *sb petro* gassfelt. **~ fire** *sb* gasskamin. **~-fittings** *sb fl* gassarmatur. **~light** *sb* gass|lys; lampe, -lykt. **~ log** *sb petro* gasslogg. **~-mask** *sb* gassmaske. **~meter** *sb* gassmåler. **~-oven** *sb* gasstekeovn. **~ phase** *sb petro* gassfase. **~-ring** *sb* gass|bluss, -apparat. **~ scrubbing** = **~** *washing.* **~-station** *sb US* bensinstasjon. **~-stove** = **~***-cooker.* **~ washing** *sb petro* gassvasking. **~-works** *sb* gassverk.

gash [gæʃ] **1** *sb* flenge, kutt; dypt/gapende sår; **2** *vt* flenge (og skjære, sprette etc) opp.

gasket ['gæskət] *sb* **1** pakning (og pakningsring etc); **2** *sjø* (beslag)seising.

gasolene, gasoline ['gæsəli:n] *sb US* bensin.

gasp [gɑ:sp] **1** *sb* gisp(ing); stønn; **1** *vb* gispe; snappe etter pusten; stønne.

gate [geɪt] *sb* port (og (større) ytterdør; grind; bom, le; (dam)luke, sluseport; *fig* innfallsport etc); *data* port. **gate|crasher** *sb dgl* ubedt eller uventet gjest [≈ en som ramler inn med døren]. **~-house** *sb* portstue; portner|bolig, -stue. **~-keeper** *sb* portvakt, portner. **~-post** *sb* portstolpe. **~way** *sb* (inngangs)-portal; (port)åpning; *fig* innfallsport.

gather ['gæðə] *vb* **1** forsamle(s); samle (seg); **2** samle/sanke (opp, sammen etc); plukke; **3** vokse, øke; tilta (etter hvert); **4** gå ut fra; slutte (seg til); **5** rynke; trekke sammen. **gathering** ['gæðərıŋ] *sb* (for)samling. **gathering line** *sb petro* samle(rør)ledning.

gaudy ['gɔ:dı] *adj* gloret, prangende.

gauge [geıdʒ] **I** *sb* **1** mål (og målestokk; måleinstrument, måler etc); **2** kaliber (og boring; dimensjon; (tråd)tykkelse etc); **3** sporvidde; **II** *vt* **1** måle; **2** ta mål av (dvs bedømme, vurdere etc).

gaunt [gɔ:nt] *adj* **1** (rad)mager, tynn; utmagret; **2** dyster; gold, naken; øde.

gauntlet ['gɔ:ntlıt] *sb* **A** *hist* stridshanske; *nå især* kjøre-, ridehanske; fektehanske; **B** *run the ~* løpe spissrot.

gauze [gɔ:z] *sb* gas; *også fig* slør; *surgical ~* gasbind; *wire ~* (metall)trådduk.

gavel ['gævl] *sb* (formanns)klubbe; (auksjons)|-hammer, -klubbe.

gawky ['gɔ:kı] *adj* klosset, klønet; ulenkelig.

gay [geı] *adj* **1** glad; lystig, munter; **2** lettsindig; **3** *dgl* homoseksuell.

gaze [geız] **1** *sb* stirring; stirrende blikk; **2** *vi* stirre (*at/(up)on* på).

gazette [gə'zet] **1** *sb* lysingsblad; *som del av egennavn* avis, blad; **2** *vt: be ~d* bli kunngjort/utlyst *etc*; *mil* bli beordret/overført *etc.*

gear [gıə] **I** *sb* **1** tannhjuls|forbindelse, -overføring, (-)utveksling; *også* gir(kasse); **2** apparat; innretning; mekanisme; *landing-~* landingshjul, understell; **3** utstyr; (ut)rustning; seletøy; *dgl* greier, saker; **4** *dgl* klær; **II** *vb* **1** gire (*down* ned; *up* opp); sette i gir; stå/være i gir; **2** *~ed to* tilpasset (til); innrettet/innstilt på. **gear|-box** *sb* gir(kasse). **~-lever, -shift, -stick** *sb* gir|spak, -stang. **~-wheel** *sb* tannhjul.

gem [dʒem] **1** *sb* edelstein; juvel, perle; *fig også* praktstykke; **2** *vt* juvelpryde.

gender ['dʒendə] *sb gram* kjønn.

general ['dʒenərəl] **I** *adj* **1** allmenn(-); generell, hoved-; *in ~* i alminnelighet; i hovedtrekkene; **2** ordinær, vanlig; alminnelig; **3** generell, vag; uspesifisert; **II** *sb mil* general, se også midtsidene. **general election** *sb* parlamentsvalg. **generality** [ˌdʒenə'rælətı] *sb* **1** alminnelighet; **2** allmennhet, flertall; største|del, -part; **3** allmenngyldighet. **generalize** ['dʒenrəlaız] *vb* **1** generalisere; **2** gjøre allment kjent/tilgjengelig *etc.* **generally** ['dʒenrəlı] *adv* **1** vanligvis; **2** allment; **3** stort sett. **general practitioner** *sb* allmennpraktiserende lege.

generate ['dʒenəreıt] *vt* **1** produsere; frembringe; utvikle; **2** *data* generere; **3** avle. **generation** [ˌdʒenə'reıʃn] *sb* **1** produksjon (og produsering etc); avling; **2** generasjon, slektledd; mannsalder. **generator** ['dʒenəreıtə] *sb* generator; dynamo.

generosity [ˌdʒenə'rɒsətı] *sb* gavmildhet *etc*; storsinn. **generous** ['dʒenərəs] *adj* gavmild; raus, rundhåndet; **2** rikelig; **3** storsinnet; edel(modig).

genesis ['dʒenəsıs] *sb* opprinnelse; skapelse.

genial ['dʒi:nıəl] *adj* **1** hyggelig, vennlig; omgjengelig; **2** gunstig; *om klima* behagelig, mild.

genius ['dʒi:nıəs] *sb* **1** geni; *~ for* begavelse/talent for; **2** skytsengel; god fe/ånd; **3** *fig* atmosfære, ånd.

gent [dʒent] *(vulg fork* for *gentleman)* herre(mann); *fl* herretoalett. **genteel** [dʒen'ti:l] *adj gml* dannet; fornem; *nå især iron* affektert, tertefin.

gentile ['dʒentaıl] **1** *adj* hedensk; *Gentile* ikkejødisk; **2** *sb* hedning; *Gentile* ikke-jøde.

gentility [dʒen'tılətı] *sb* affektasjon (etc, jf *genteel*).

gentle ['dʒentl] *adj* **1** forsiktig, varsom; hensynsfull; øm; **2** snill, vennlig; **3** lett, mild, svak; jevn; **4** fornem, velbåren. **gentleman** ['dʒentlmən] *sb* **1** herre; *dgl* hedersmann; **2** *hist* mann av god ætt; **3** *gml* økonomisk uavhengig mann. **gentlewoman** ['dʒentlˌwumən] *sb* **1** dame; **2** *hist* hoff|dame, -frøken. **gently** ['dʒentlı] *adv* forsiktig *etc.*

gentry ['dʒentrı] *sb* **1** lavadel; *the landed ~* godseierstanden; **2** *dgl* folk.

genuine ['dʒenjuın] *adj* autentisk, ekte; sann.

geographer [dʒı'ɒgrəfə] *sb* geograf. **geographical** [ˌdʒıə'græfıkl] *adj* geografisk. **geography** [dʒı'ɒgrəfı] *sb* geografi. **geologist** [dʒı'ɒlədʒıst] *sb* geolog. **geological** [ˌdʒıə'lɒdʒıkl] *adj* geologisk. **geology** [dʒı'ɒlədʒı] *sb* geologi. **geometric(al)** [ˌdʒıə'metrık(l)] *adj* geometrisk. **geometry** [dʒı'ɒmətrı] *sb* geometri.

germ [dʒɜ:m] *sb* **1** kim, spire; *fig* begynnelse; **2** (sykdomsfremkallende) bakterie.

germane [dʒɜ:'meın] *adj* aktuell, relevant.

germinate ['dʒɜ:mıneıt] *vb* spire; *også fig* gro, utvikle seg. **germination** [ˌdʒɜ:mı'neıʃn] *sb* spiring *etc*

gesticulate [dʒe'stıkjuleıt] *vi* gestikulere. **gesticulation** [ˌdʒestıkju'leıʃn] *sb* gestikulering. **gesture** ['dʒestʃə] **1** *sb* håndbevegelse, tegn; geberde; *også fig* gest(us); **2** *vi* gjøre tegn (fakter, geberder etc); gestikulere.

get [get] *vb* **1** få (og få seg; få med seg; få tak i; skaffe (seg); finne; (gå og) hente etc); **2** fullføre; oppnå; nå, rekke; tjene; vinne; *~ anywhere/somewhere* få gjort/utrettet noe; komme noen vei; **3** (an)komme (se især 10); **4** bli (og begynne/komme til å bli, gå bort og bli etc); begynne/komme i gang med; *~ even (dgl)* bli skuls; *~ going* komme av gårde; komme i gang; **5** forstå; (opp)fatte; skjønne (etter hvert); tilegne seg; *~ wind of/US slang: ~ wise to* komme under vær med; få snusen i; *I don't ~ you* jeg skjønner deg ikke (riktig); *I've got it* nå har jeg det; **6** forårsake; få til (å); sørge for (at/å); *~ one's hair cut* få klippet håret sitt; *have got (to)* måtte; være nødt til; *they've got to wait* de må/*dgl* får vente; **7** få has/ram på; overmanne; sette til veggs; **8** forbløffe; **9** ergre, irritere; plage; **10** *med adv/prep ~* **about** komme (seg) ut; reise (omkring); *fig* bli kjent; ~ **abroad** komme ut (dvs bli kjent); ~ **across** få (gå, komme seg etc) over; *fig* bli/gjøre seg forstått; fenge, slå an; ~ **ahead** komme *etc* foran; komme (seg) frem; gjøre fremskritt; ~ **along** komme (seg) av gårde; klare seg; komme overens; ~ **around** = ~ *about*; *fig også* omgå; lure, overliste; ~ **at** få tak i/fatt på; komme til; komme til livs; komme frem til; komme under vær med; *what are you ~ting at* hva sikter du til; ~ **away** flykte; komme (seg)/slippe unna; ~ **back** komme/vende tilbake; få igjen; ~ **back at** ta igjen med; hevne seg på; ~ **by** komme/slippe *etc* forbi; passere; ~ **down** få (gå, komme seg etc) ned; gå/stige av; ~ **down to** begynne med; ta fatt på; ~ **in** (an)komme; få (gå, komme seg etc) inn; bli (inn)-valgt; ~ **into** få (gå, komme seg etc) inn/opp i; ~ **off** få av; få (gå, komme seg etc) av sted; komme (seg) unna/vekk; slippe (løs); gå av (buss, tog etc); ~ *off cheaply* slippe billig fra det; ~ **on** gå (komme, stige etc) på; legge/sette på; få på seg; komme (seg) videre; *fig* komme seg frem; ~ **on to** komme under vær med; avsløre; oppdage; ~ **on with** fortsette med; komme overens med; *how are you ~ting on* hvordan har du det; hvordan klarer du deg; ~ **out** få (gå, komme seg etc) ut; få/komme frem; *fig* bli kjent; ~ *out of hand* komme ut av kontroll; løpe løpsk; bli uregjerlig/ustyrlig etc; ~ **over** komme over; fullføre; bli/gjøre seg ferdig med; *fig* over|komme, -vinne; ~ *it over (with)* få det overstått; ~ **round** = ~ *about/around*; *fig også* overtale; ~ **through** få (gå, komme seg etc) igjennom; bli/gjøre seg ferdig med; komme/nå frem; gjennomføre; klare (seg); ~ **to** komme/nå frem til; begynne/ta fatt på; komme i gang med; ~ **together** møtes; komme sammen; (for)samle; be (få, *dgl* tromme) sammen; ~ **under** undertrykke; underlegge seg; ~ **up** få (gå, komme seg etc) opp; reise seg; stå opp; stige (opp); arrangere, ordne; pynte (på); få (gjøre, stelle etc) i stand; rigge til; ruste ut; ~ **up to** gå (komme, rekke etc) frem til. **get-up** *sb dgl* antrekk; utrustning, utstyr; *fig* fremtoning; personlighet.

geyser ['gi:zə] *sb* **1** geysir, varm kilde; **2** varmtvannsbereder.

ghastly ['gɑ:stlɪ] *adj* **1** dødlignende; likblek; **2** nifs, uhyggelig; skrekkelig; **3** *dgl* fæl, redselsfull. **ghost** [gəʊst] *sb* ånd; gjenferd, spøkelse; *fig* skygge; *the Holy Ghost* Den hellige ånd. **ghostly** ['gəʊstlɪ] *adj især* spøkelsesaktig. **ghost-writer** *sb* en som skriver bøker for andre personer og i deres navn.

giant ['dʒaɪənt] **1** *adj* kjempe|messig, -stor; kjempe-; **2** *sb* kjempe, monstrum.

gibber ['dʒɪbə] *vi* plapre; snøvle. **gibberish** ['dʒɪbərɪʃ] *sb* sludder, tøv.

gibbet ['dʒibɪt] **1** *sb* galge; *også fig* gapestokk; **2** *vt* henge (i galge); *fig* henge ut; sette/stille i gapestokk.

gibe [dʒaɪb] *vi* håne, spotte; gjøre narr (*at* av).

giddy ['gɪdɪ] *adj* **1** svimmel, ør; svimlende; **2** tankeløs, ustadig.

gift [gɪft] *sb* **1** gave, presang; **2** begavelse; anlegg, evne. **gifted** ['gɪftɪd] *adj* begavet.

gig [gɪg] *sb* gigg (både om båt og kjøretøy).

gigantic [dʒaɪ'gæntɪk] *adj* kjempe|messig, -stor; gigantisk, veldig.

giggle ['gɪgl] *sb, vi* knis(e).

gild [gɪld] *vt* forgylle.

gill *sb* **A** [gɪl] gjelle; **B** [dʒɪl] et hulmål, se midtsidene.

gilt [gɪlt] **1** *adj* forgylt; **2** *sb* forgylling. **gilt-edged** *adj* gullkantet.

gimcrack ['dʒɪmkræk] **1** *adj* forloren, uekte; godtkjøps-; **2** *sb* jugl, kram; nips.

gimlet ['gɪmlɪt] *sb* (spiker)bor, vridbor.

gimmick ['gɪmɪk] *sb dgl* **1** knep; juks, lureri; **2** egenhet; maner, vane; **3** reklamepåfunn; **4** dings, greie.

gin [dʒɪn] **A I** *sb* **1** felle, snare; **2** (bomulls)rensemaskin; **II** *vt* **1** fange i felle/snare; **2** rense (bomull); **B** *sb* gin.

ginger ['dʒɪndʒə] **I** *adj* rødblond; **II** *sb* **1** ingefær; **2** *dgl* fart, futt; **III** *vt (~ up)* sette fart i.

gingerly ['dʒɪndʒəlɪ] *adj, adv* forsiktig, varsom(t).

gipsy ['dʒɪpsɪ] *sb* sigøyner.

gird [gɜ:d] *vt* **1** spenne på seg (belte etc); **2** omgi, omslutte.

girder ['gɜ:də] *sb* (bære)bjelke.

girdle ['gɜ:dl] **I** *sb* **1** belte; **2** hofteholder; **II** *vt (~ about, in, round)* omgi, omslutte.

girl [gɜ:l] *sb* jente, pike. **girl|friend** *sb* (gutts) kjæreste, venninne. **~hood** *sb* (pikes) barndom. **~ish** ['gɜ:lɪʃ] *adj* jentete, jenteaktig.

girth [gɜ:θ] *sb* **1** (buk)gjord, salgjord; **2** omfang, omkrets; livvidde.

gist [dʒɪst] *sb* (hoved)innhold; kjerne(punkt).

give [gɪv] **I** *sb* elastisitet, fjæring; spenst; *fig* ettergivenhet, smidighet; **II** *vb* **1** gi (og skjenke; bidra (med); yte; avgi, (av)levere; forsyne (med); skaffe etc); **2** forårsake, vekke, volde; ~ *them to believe that* la dem tro at; **3** gi seg (og gi etter; fjære, svikte; falle sammen etc); ~ *way* vike; gi tapt; trekke seg (tilbake/unna etc); gi seg (og gi etter; briste, knekke; svikte etc); ~ *way to* vike plassen for; *fig* gi etter for; **4** innrømme; gå med på; **5** frembære (takk etc); foreslå/utbringe (f.eks. skål); *I ~ you Mrs Jones* skål for fru Jones; **6** utstøte; komme med; legge/sette frem; **7** *med adv/prep* ~ **away** gi bort; utlevere; forråde, røpe; ~ **back** gi/levere tilbake; gi igjen; *fig også* gjengjelde; ~ **forth** avgi; utstøte; ~ **in** levere/sende inn; gi opp (og gi seg, gi tapt etc); ~ **in to** gi etter for; ~ **off** avgi, gi fra seg; sende ut; ~ **on to** føre *etc* inn/ut til; ~ **out** dele/sende ut; meddele, tilkjennegi; svikte; gi seg; gå i stykker; slippe opp (for); ~ **over** avlevere; over|gi, -levere; *dgl* holde opp/slutte med; ~ **up** avlevere; over|gi, -levere; utlevere; gi opp (og gi seg, gi tapt etc); holde opp/slutte med; gi avkall på; ~ *oneself up* overgi seg; *fig* hengi seg (*to* til); ~ **(up)on** vende (inn/ut) mot. **given** ['gɪvn] *adj* **1** gitt (og angitt, oppgitt etc); **2** nærmere avtalt (bestemt, fastsatt, spesifisert etc); **3** forutsatt; **4** ~ *(over) to* henfallen til; tilbøyelig til. **giveaway** *sb petro* kvalitetsmargin. **given name** *sb* døpenavn, fornavn.

gizzard ['gɪzəd] *sb* krås; *fig* hals.

glacial ['gleɪsɪəl] *adj* **1** *a)* isbre-; *b)* istids-; **2** iskald, isnende. **glacier** ['gleɪsɪə] *sb* isbre.

glad [glæd] *adj* **1** glad (*about/of* for; *that* for/over at); **2** gledelig. **gladden** ['glædn] *vt* glede. **gladly** ['glædlɪ] *adv* gladelig; med glede.

glamorous ['glæmərəs] *adj* (som tar seg) romantisk, strålende (ut); forførende; fortryllende. **glamour** ['glæmə] *sb* romantisk skjær; stråleglans; fortryllelse; sjarm.

glance [glɑ:ns] **I** *sb* **1** blikk, øyekast; **2** glimt; blink(ing); **II** *vb* **1** kikke/kaste et blikk (*at* på); **2** blinke, glimte; **3** ~ *off* prelle av (på).

gland [glænd] *sb* kjertel. **glandular** ['glændjʊlə] *adj* kjertel-.

glare [gleə] **I** *sb* **1** blendende/skarpt lys(skjær); glans, skinn; **2** skuling; olmt blikk; **II** *vb* **1** glitre; skinne (sterkt); skjære i øynene; **2** skule/stirre olmt (*at* på). **glaring** ['gleərɪŋ] *adj* **1** skarp, skjærende; blendende; **2** skulende; olm; **3** skrikende *(fig)*; iøynefallende.

glass [glɑ:s] **1** *sb* glass (og ting helt eller delvis av glass, som barometer, langkikkert, leseglass, speil, glasservise, glasstøy, i *fl* især briller og (dobbelt)kikkert); **2** *vt* sette glass(ruter) i. **glass|-blower** *sb* glassblåser. **~-cutter** *sb* glasskjærer. **glassy** ['glɑ:sɪ] *adj* glassaktig. **glaze** [gleɪz] **I** *sb* glasur; **II** *vb* **1** sette glass(ruter) i; **2** glassere; **3** bli glassaktig. **glazier** ['gleɪzɪə] *sb* glassmester.

gleam [gli:m] **1** *sb* (lys)stråle; glimt, streif; **2** *vi* skinne, stråle; glitre.

glean [gli:n] *vb* plukke (korn); samle/sanke (sammen). **gleanings** ['gli:nɪŋz] *sb fl* innsamlet stoff etc.

glee [gli:] *sb* glede, lystighet; (skade)fryd. **gleeful** ['gli:fʊl] *adj* opprømt.

glen [glen] *sb* trang dal.

glib [glɪb] *adj* glatt, sleip *(fig)*; rappmunnet.

glide [glaɪd] **I** *sb* glidning; glidende bevegelse; glideflukt; **II** *vi* **1** gli, skli; **2** seile, sveve; fly i glideflukt. **glider** ['glaɪdə] *sb* glidefly.

glimmer ['glɪmə] **1** *sb* flakkende (svakt, usikkert etc) lys; *fig* glimt, skimt; **2** *vi* glimte; skimre; skinne svakt/usikkert etc.

glimpse [glɪmps] **1** *sb* glimt; **2** *vt* skimte; få et glimt av.

glint [glɪnt] **1** *sb* glimt, streif; **2** *vi* blinke, glimte; funkle.

glisten ['glɪsn] *vi* glinse, skinne; glitre.

glitter ['glɪtə] **1** *sb* (stråle)glans; glitring; *fig* prakt; **2** *vi* funkle, glitre; stråle (klart).

gloat [gləʊt] *vi* fryde/godte seg/triumfere (*over/upon* over).

globe [gləʊb] *sb* **1** kule (og kuleformede ting, især av glass, som glass|ballong, -bolle, -kuppel etc); **2** globus; klode.

gloom [glu:m] *sb* **1** (halv)mørke; dysterhet; **2** tristhet; tungsinn. **gloomy** ['glu:mɪ] *adj* mørk; dyster; trist; nedstemt.

glorification [ˌglɔ:rɪfɪ'keɪʃn] *sb* forherligelse *etc.* **glorify** ['glɔ:rɪfaɪ] *vt* **1** forherlige; lovprise; **2** forskjønne; kaste glans over. **glorious** ['glɔ:rɪəs] *adj* **1** glimrende, praktfull, strålende; **2** berømmelig, ærefull. **3** *dgl* deilig, herlig, vidunderlig. **glory** ['glɔ:rɪ] **I** *sb* **1** berømmelse; ære; **2** glans, prakt; **3** salighet; himmelsk herlighet; **4** *rel* lovprising; **II** *vi:* ~ *in* fryde/glede seg over; være stolt av.

gloss [glɒs] **1** *sb* glans; polering; *især fig* ferniss, politur; **2** *vt* blankpusse, polere.

glossary ['glɒsərɪ] *sb* glossar.

glossy ['glɒsɪ] *adj* blank(polert), skinnende.

glove [glʌv] *sb* hanske.

glow [gləʊ] **1** *sb* glød, varme; **2** *vi* gløde; *fig* blusse. **glower** ['glaʊə] *vi* skule/stirre olmt (*at* på). **glow-worm** *sb* sankthansorm.

glue [glu:] **1** *sb* klister, lim; **2** *vt* klebe, klistre, lime.

glum [glʌm] *adj* dyster, trist.

glut [glʌt] **1** *sb* overflod; **2** *vt* over|fylle, -mette; stappe (full). **glutton** ['glʌtn] *sb* **1** slukhals, storeter; **2** jerv. **gluttonous** ['glʌtənəs] *adj* forsluken, grådig. **gluttony** ['glʌtənɪ] *sb* forslukenhet, grådighet; fråtsing.

gnarled [nɑ:ld] *adj* knortet, knudret; forvridd, kroket.

gnash [næʃ] *vt* skjære (tenner).

gnat [næt] *sb* knott, (stikk)mygg.

gnaw [nɔ:] *vb* **1** gnage (på); **2** tære (på); nage.

gnome [nəʊm] *sb* dverg; nisse.

go [gəʊ] **I** *sb dgl* **1** driv, energi; fart, futt; tæl; **2** forsøk; kule, omgang; *have a* ~ *at* forsøke seg på; **3** travelhet, virksomhet; *on the* ~ på farten; **II** *vb* **1** gå (og dra, kjøre, reise etc (omkring)); ~ *fishing* dra på fisketur; ~ *for a walk* ta (seg) en spasertur; ~ *on a journey* reise bort; dra/legge ut på (en) reise; **2** gå; være i gang; *fig* være i vigør etc; **3** gå (dvs forløpe; arte/utvikle seg etc); *as teachers* ~ som lærere flest; *as things* ~ som forholdene *etc* (nå engang) er; **4** gå (og føre, lede, strekke seg etc (til)); ~ *far* gå (nå, rekke etc) langt; *fig* drive det langt/vidt; **5** gå/dra sin vei; gå ut; *fig* gå av bruk/mote; svikte; gi etter; gi seg; *be gone* være ferdig/*dgl* gåen; **6** gå (dvs bli akseptert, trodd, tolerert etc); *anything* ~*es* alt gjelds (går, er lov/mulig etc); *what she says* ~*es* hennes ord er lov; **7** bli; ~ *bad* bli dårlig (råtten, sur etc); tape seg; **8** bidra; ~ *halves/shares* dele likt; **9** *be* **going** *to* skulle (til å); komme til å; være i ferd med å; **10** *med adv/prep* ~ **about** gå *etc* omkring; sirkulere; være i omløp; *sjø* stagvende; ~ *about it* gripe det an; ~ **about with** ha (mer eller mindre fast) følge med; ~ **after** gå *etc* etter; *fig* legge seg/være ute etter; ~ **against** gå/stride mot; ~ **ahead** gå *etc* i forveien; gå videre; gå i gang; ~ **along** bli/være med; gå *etc* videre; ~ **along with** gå med på; være enig i/med; ~ **at** gå løs på; ~ **away** gå (sin vei);

reise *etc* bort; ~ **back** gå/vende *etc* tilbake; ~ **back (up)on** gå tilbake på (løfte etc); late i stikken; svikte; ~ **before** gå *etc* foran; gå/komme før(e); møte/komme opp for (f.eks. domstol); bli forelagt/innkalt til; ~ **behind** gå *etc* bak; gå/komme etter; ~ **between** gå/legge seg imellom; *~-between* mellommann, megler; ~ **beyond** over|gå, -stige; gå/sette seg ut over; ~ **by** gå (om tiden); gå *etc* forbi; reise *etc* med (over, via); *fig* følge; bygge på; holde seg til; (inn)rette seg etter; ~ **down** gå *etc* ned; løye/spakne (om vind); dra/reise (ut) fra (London eller annen storby eller fra universitetet); *fig* gli ned (dvs bli akseptert, trodd etc); ~ **for** gå (legge seg, være ute) etter; (gå og) hente; gå (passere, bli solgt etc) for; gjelde (for); *dgl* gå løs på; ~ **forward** gå *etc* frem(over); gjøre fremskritt; ~ **in** gå *etc* inn; gå bak en sky (om f.eks. solen); ~ **in for** engasjere/interessere seg for; støtte; ~ **into** gå *etc* inn i; *fig* begynne med; sette seg inn i; ~ **off** gå/dra sin vei (fra); forløpe/gå (især bra); gå av (dvs eksplodere); forsvinne; stikke av; *om varer etc* gå unna; *fig* bli borte (dvs sovne, miste bevisstheten); tape seg (i kvalitet); ~ **on** fortsette/gå *etc* videre; gå (om tiden); foregå; bråke; bære seg; *nothing to ~ on* ingenting å bygge på/holde seg til; *gone on (dgl)* (håpløst) forelsket i; ~ **out** gå *etc* ut; gå av bruk/mote; gå ut (dvs gå mot slutten); ~ *all out* anstrenge seg til det ytterste; ~ **out for** legge seg etter (*fig*); ~ **over** gå/klatre *etc* over; *fig* granske, undersøke; overhale; ~ *over (big)* gjøre (stormende) lykke; ~ **round** gå *etc* rundt; sirkulere; være i omløp; rekke/strekke til; ~ **through** gå *etc* igjenom; bli vedtatt; *fig også* gjennomgå; ~ **through with** gjennomføre; ~ **to** dra/reise til; bidra/gå til; henvende seg til; ~ **together** gå *etc* sammen; *fig* passe sammen; ~ **under** gå *etc* under; gå konkurs; ~ **up** gå *etc* opp; dra/reise (inn) til (London eller annen storby eller til universitetet); *om hus etc* bli oppført; ~ **with** gå *etc* med; følge (med); ledsage; ha (mer eller mindre fast) følge med; ~ **without** gå/klare seg etc uten; *it ~es without saying* det sier seg selv.

goad [gəʊd] **1** *sb* piggstav; *fig* spore; **2** *vt* drive (frem, især med piggstav); *fig* anspore, egge.

goal [gəʊl] *sb* mål. **goal-keeper** *sb* mål|mann, -vokter.

goat [gəʊt] *sb* geit.

gobble ['gɒbl] **A** *vb* sluke; jafse i seg; slurpe; **B 1** *sb* buldring; **2** *vi* buldre (som en kalkun).

goblet ['gɒblɪt] *sb* **1** beger, pokal; *rel* kalk; **2** stettglass.

goblin ['gɒblɪn] *sb* nisse.

god [gɒd] *sb* gud; *tin ~* kakse, småpave. **goddess** ['gɒdɪs] *sb* guddinne. **god|fearing** *adj* gudfryktig. **~forsaken** *adj* gudsforlatt; *dgl* gudsforgåen, ryggesløs. **~less** *adj* gudløs. **~like** *adj* guddommelig. **~ly** *adv* from, gudfryktig; gudelig.

goggle ['gɒgl] **1** *sb fl* beskyttelsesbriller; **2** *vi* stirre stivt; stå på stilk (om øyne).

going ['gəʊɪŋ] *sb* gang(e); fart; føre, terreng; *get ~* komme (seg) av sted; komme i gang; *while the ~ is good* mens leken er god; *rough ~* hard kjøring *etc*; hardkjør(ing).

gold [gəʊld] *sb* gull. **gold-digger** *sb* **1** gullgraver; **2** *slang* vamp. **golden** ['gəʊldən] *adj* gull-; gyllen. **gold|field** *sb* gullfelt. **~fish** *sb* gullfisk. **~mine** *sb* gullgruve. **~-rush** *sb* gullfeber. **~smith** *sb* gullsmed.

golf [gɒlf] *sb, vb* (spille) golf. **golf|-course, -links** *sb* golfbane.

gong [gɒŋ] *sb* gongong.

good [gʊd] **I** *adj, adv* **1** god (= passende, tjenlig); bra, fin(t); utmerket; **2** god (= frisk; nærende, sunn; gagnlig, nyttig etc); **3** god (= behagelig, deilig, velsmakende etc); *have a ~ time* ha det hyggelig; **4** dyktig/flink (*at* til); **5** god(hjertet); snill, vennlig; **6** anstendig, dydig: *dgl* ordentlig, skikkelig; **7** pålitelig, sikker; **8** gyldig; *hold ~* holde stikk; stemme; **9** betraktelig, betydelig; **10** grundig; solid; **II** *sb* **1** (det) gode; gagn, nytte; *common ~* felles beste; *it's no ~* det nytter ikke; **2** *fl* gods, varer; effekter, eiendeler. **good|-bye** *interj, sb* adjø, farvel; avskjed. **~-for-nothing** *adj* udugelig; ubrukelig, verdiløs. **~-humoured** *adj* godlynt; hyggelig, snill. **~-looking** *adj* kjekk, pen. **goodly** *adj* **1** kjekk, pen; **2** betraktelig, betydelig. **good|-natured** *adj* gemyttlig, godmodig; snill. **~ness** *sb* **1** godhet; vennlighet; *have the ~ to* være så snill å; **2** kraft (i kjøtt etc); **3** *dgl: ~ knows* gud(ene) vet; *thank ~* gudskjelov. **~ sense** *sb* (sunn) fornuft; sunt vett. **~-sized** *adj* velvoksen. **~-tempered** *adj* godlynt, godmodig; snill. **~will** *sb* **1** godvilje; velvilje; **2** godt omdømme; **3** *merk* klientell, kundekrets.

goose [gu:s] *sb* gås. **goose|berry** *sb* stikkelsbær. **~-flesh** *sb* gåsehud. **~-step** *sb, vb* (gå i) hanemarsj.

gore [gɔ:] **1** *sb bokl* blod (især tykt og levret, fra sår); **2** *vt* gjennombore, spidde.

gorge [gɔ:dʒ] **I** *sb* **1** gjel, skar, slukt; **2** mave(innhold); hals, strupe; **3** fråtsing; overdådig måltid; **II** *vb* sluke/stappe i seg (mat); fråtse.

gorgeous ['gɔ:dʒəs] *adj* praktfull, storslagen; flott, glimrende.

gory ['gɔ:rɪ] *adj* blodig.

gosh [gɒʃ] *interj slang* jøss.

gospel ['gɒspl] *sb* evangelium.

gossamer ['gɒsəmə] *sb* **1** spindelvev; **2** flor.

gossip ['gɒsɪp] **I** *sb* **1** folkesnakk; sladder (og person som farer med sladder; ≈ sladretaske); **2** (små)prating; skravling (og skravlebøtte); **II** *vi* sladre; prate, skravle.

Gothic ['gɒθɪk] *adj, sb* gotisk. **Gothic novel** *sb* grøsser, skrekkroman.

gouge [gaʊdʒ] **1** *sb* huljern; **2** *vt: ~ out* grave/hule ut; rive ut.

gout [gaʊt] *sb* gikt.

govern ['gʌvən] *vb* **1** regjere, styre; **2** beherske; dirigere; kontrollere; **3** bestemme; *gram* styre. **governess** ['gʌvnɪs] *sb* guvernante. **government** ['gʌvnmənt] *sb* **1** regjering; **2** ledelse; styre (og styreform); **3** guvernement; provins. **government | bonds, ~**

securities *sb fl* statsobligasjoner. **governor** ['gʌvənə] *sb* **1** guvernør; stattholder; **2** bestyrer, direktør (især for offentlig institusjon); **3** styremedlem (især ved skoler, sykehus o.l.); **4** *dgl* bas, sjef; **5** *mek* regulator.

gown [gaʊn] **I** *sb* **1** kjole (især til penbruk); **2** (embets)kappe; **II** *vt:* ~*ed* antrukket; kledd (i).

grab [græb] **I** *sb* **1** (raskt) grep; **2** grabb; **II** *vb* gripe tak i; slå kloen i.

grace [greɪs] **I** *sb* **1** eleganse, ynde; *fl* pene manerer; **2** anstendighet, sømmelighet(ssans); *with a good* ~ elskverdig, vennlig; **3** godvilje, velvilje; imøtekommenhet; *merk* henstand; **4** bordbønn; **5** (Guds) nåde; **II** *vt* **1** beære; kaste glans over; **2** pryde, smykke. **graceful** ['greɪsfʊl] *adj* grasiøs, ledig, smidig; elegant, yndig. **graceless** ['greɪslɪs] *adj* **1** keitet, klosset; **2** fordervet; gudsforgåen. **gracious** ['greɪʃəs] *adj* **1** imøtekommende, velvillig; snill; *gml rel* nådig; **2** *som interj: Good(ness)* ~! (du) gode/store Gud!

gradation [grə'deɪʃn] *sb* gradering; gradvis overgang (nyansering, sjattering etc). **grade** [greɪd] **I** *sb* **1** grad, trinn; kvalitet, sortering; **2** *US* (skole)klasse; **3** *US* karakter (for skolearbeid etc); *make the* ~ *(dgl)* tilfredsstille kravene; klare seg bra; **4** *US* stignings|forhold, -grad; *down* ~ fall; utforbakke; *fig* nedgang, retur; *up* ~ stigning; *fig* oppgang; **II** *vt* **1** gradere, sortere (etter kvalitet, størrelse etc); **2** planere, regulere; **3** *(~ up)* foredle (ved avl). **grade | crossing** *sb* plan|kryss, -overgang. ~ **school** *sb US* grunnskole. **gradient** ['greɪdɪənt] *sb* **1** stignings|forhold, -grad; **2** *(downward ~)* fall; **3** *(upward ~)* stigning. **gradual** ['grædjʊəl] *adj* gradvis. **graduate I** ['grædʒʊət] *sb* **1** kandidat (dvs person med eksamen fra universitet, i USA også videregående skole eller fagskole); **2** måleglass; **3** *som adj* ≈ akademisk; *US også* (fag)utdannet; (fullt) utlært; autorisert; **II** ['grædjʊeɪt] *vb* **1** gradere; dele inn i grader; **2** klassifisere; sortere; **3** avlegge akademisk eksamen; **4** *US* avlegge (især videregående) eksamen; **5** *især US* uteksaminere.

graft [grɑ:ft] **A I** *sb* **1** podning (og podekvist); **2** *med* transplantering (og transplantat); **II** *vb* **1** pode; **2** *med* transplantere; **B** *sb* korrupsjon, nepotisme.

grain [greɪn] *sb* **1** kor; **2** frø; *fig også* kjerne; **3** korn; grann, smule; **4** fiber(retning); struktur; årring(er); narv (på lær); *against the* ~ mot veden; *fig* mot ens natur (instinkter, tilbøyeligheter etc); **5** en vektenhet, se midtsidene.

grammar ['græmə] *sb* grammatikk; språk(bruk); *bad* ~ dårlig (dvs især ukorrekt) språk. **grammar school** *sb* videregående skole (mest sammenfallende med norsk: allmennfaglig studieretning). **grammatical** [grə'mætɪkl] *adj* grammatikalsk; grammatisk.

granary ['grænərɪ] *sb* korn|låve, -magasin.

grand [grænd] **I** *adj* **1** stor (og storartet, stor|slagen, -slått); imponerende; praktfull, prektig; **2** betydelig, fremragende; **3** hoved-, stor-; **4** fornem; hoven, storsnutet; **5** *dgl* flott, kjempefin; festlig; **II** *sb* **1** *(~ piano)* flygel; **2** *US slang* tusenlapp (dvs tusen dollar).

grand|children *sb fl* barnebarn. ~**dad** *sb* bestepappa. ~**daughter** *sb* datterdatter, sønnedatter. ~**father** *sb* bestefar. ~**ma** *sb* bestemamma. ~**mother** *sb* bestemor. ~**pa** = ~*dad*. ~**parents** *sb fl* besteforeldre. ~**son** *sb* dattersønn, sønnesønn.

grange [greɪndʒ] *sb* **1** (herre)gård; landsted med gårdsbruk; **2** *gml* = *granary*.

grant [grɑ:nt] **I** *sb* **1** bevilgning; bidrag, tilskudd; stipendium; gave; **2** overdragelse; **II** *vt* **1** bevilge; gi, tildele; innvilge; *fig* innrømme; *take for ~ed* ta for gitt; *~ed/~ing (that)* forutsatt/under forutsetning av (at); **2** over|dra, -føre.

grape [greɪp] *sb* drue. **grapevine** ['greɪpvaɪn] *sb* vin|ranke, -stokk; *US slang* jungeltelegraf.

graph [græf] *sb* diagram, kurve; graf. **graphic** ['græfɪk] *adj* **1** grafisk; **2** *fig* levende/malende (skildret etc). **graphic | character** *sb data etc* grafisk tegn. ~ **display device** *sb data* grafisk skjerm. ~ **language** *sb data* grafisk språk.

grapple ['græpl] *vb* gripe (tak i); huke seg fast (i); ~ *with* kjempe/slåss med; hanskes med.

grasp [grɑ:sp] **1** *sb* fast grep/tak; rekkevidde; *fig* fatteevne; **2** *vb* gripe (tak i); *fig* begripe, (opp)fatte; ~ *at* gripe etter.

grass [grɑ:s] *sb* gress; *at* ~ på beite.

grate [greɪt] **A** *sb* **1** rist; gitter; **2** ildsted; **B** *vb* **1** raspe, rive; skrape (opp); **2** gnisse, knirke; skurre; *fig* irritere.

grateful ['greɪtfʊl] *adj* **1** takknemlig; **2** behagelig, kjærkommen. **gratification** [ˌgrætɪfɪ'keɪʃn] *sb* **1** glede; tilfredsstillelse; **2** *gml* belønning. **gratify** ['grætɪfaɪ] *vt* **1** glede; **2** tilfredsstille; **3** *gml* belønne.

grating ['greɪtɪŋ] **A** *adj* skurrende; *fig* irriterende; **B** *sb* rist; gitter, sprinkler.

gratitude ['grætɪtju:d] *sb* takknemlighet. **gratuitous** [grə'tju:ɪtəs] *adj* **1** fri, gratis; **2** ukallet; uberettiget, unødig. **gratuity** [grə'tju:ətɪ] *sb* **1** bonus; gratiale, gratifikasjon; dusør, finnerlønn; drikkepenger; **2** gave.

grave [greɪv] **A** *adj* **1** alvorlig; **2** høytidelig; verdig; **B** *sb* grav; **C** *vt* gravere/skjære (inn); *fig* prege. **grave|stone** *sb* gravstein. ~**yard** *sb* gravlund.

gravel ['grævl] **I** *sb* grus; **II** *vt* **1** gruse; **2** *dgl* sette i beit.

gravitate ['grævɪteit] *vi* gravitere/bevege seg *(to(wards))* mot). **gravitation** [ˌgrævɪ'teɪʃn] *sb* gravitering *etc*; gravitasjon. **gravity** ['grævətɪ] *sb* **1** gravitasjon, tyngdekraft; **2** tyngde, vekt; **3** alvor; høytidelighet, verdighet.

gravy ['greɪvɪ] *sb* kjøttkraft, sjy; saus.

graze [greɪz] **A** *vb* (la) beite/gresse (på); **B I** *sb* **1** skrubbsår; **2** *(grazing shot)* streifskudd; **II** *vb* **1** skrubbe (opp); **2** streife; berøre (så vidt).

grease [gri:s] **1** *sb* (smøre)fett; **2** *vt* smøre (med fett); ~ *his palms* smøre (dvs bestikke) ham. **grease | additive** *sb petro* smørefettilsetning. ~**-gun** *sb* fettpresse. ~**-paint** *sb* (teater)sminke. ~ **separator** *sb petro* fettutskiller. ~ **worker** *sb petro* smørefettvalker.

greasy ['gri:sɪ] *adj* fet (og fettet); fett-; glatt, sleip.

great [greɪt] **I** *adj* **1** stor (især *fig* = betydelig, fremragende, viktig etc); stor-; *Great Britain* Storbritannia (= England, Wales og Skottland); *live to a ~ age* oppnå en høy alder; **2** *dgl* deilig, fin, hyggelig; *have a ~ time* ha det storartet *etc*; **3** *~ at* flink/svær til; *~ on* flink i/til; *US slang fig* besatt av; vill etter; **II** *adv: things are going ~* det går glimrende *etc*. **great|-coat** *sb* (tykk) frakk; vinterfrakk. **~-grandchildren** *sb fl* barnebarnsbarn. **~-grandparents** *sb fl* oldeforeldre.

greed [gri:d] *sb* begjærlighet; griskhet, grådighet. **greedy** ['gri:dɪ] *adj* **1** grisk, grådig; **2** begjærlig.

green [gri:n] **I** *adj* **1** grønn; **2** umoden; *fig også* uerfaren; **II** *sb* **1** grønn (farge); grønt; **2** eng, voll; gressplen; **3** *fl* grønnsaker etc. **green | belts** *sb fl* friarealer (rundt by). **~ crude** *sb petro* grønn råolje. **~grocer** *sb* grønnsakhandler. **~horn** *sb* grønnskolling.

greet [gri:t] *vt* **1** hilse (og hilse på, hilse velkommen etc); **2** *fig* møte. **greeting** ['gri:tɪŋ] *sb* hilsen, hilsning.

gregarious [grɪ'geərɪəs] *adj* selskapelig (anlagt); som gror (lever, opptrer etc) i flokk (klynge, gruppe etc).

grenade [grɪ'neɪd] *sb* granat.

grey [greɪ] **1** *adj* grå; **2** *sb* grå (farge); grått; **3** *vb* gråne(s); farge/male grå. **grey | hen** *sb* orrhøne. **~hound** *sb* mynde. **~lag** *sb* grågås.

grid [grɪd] *sb* **1** nett (og nettverk; ledningsnett, lysnett, samkjøringsnett; gradnett, rutenett etc); **2** gitter, rist.

grief [gri:f] *sb* **1** (dyp) sorg; **2** ulykke; **3** *US dgl: good ~!* bevare meg vel! **grievance** ['gri:vəns] *sb* klage(mål); urett (som gir grunn til klage). **grieve** [gri:v] *vb* bedrøve; volde sorg; **2** sørge. **grievous** ['gri:vəs] *adj* **1** beklagelig, sørgelig, trist; **2** alvorlig; hard, vond.

grill [grɪl] **I** *sb* **1** grill (og grillrom); **2** grillrett; **II** *vb* **1** grille(s), grillsteke(s); **2** kryssforhøre; *dgl* grille; ta under (hard, hensynsløs etc) behandling; la gjennomgå.

grim [grɪm] *adj* **1** barsk, morsk; **2** hard, ukuelig; **3** fryktelig, skrekkelig.

grimace [grɪ'meɪs] **1** *sb* grimase; **2** *vi* gjøre grimaser; skjære ansikter.

grime [graɪm] **1** *sb* skitt; **2** *vt* skitne til. **grimy** ['graɪmɪ] *adj* skitten.

grin [grɪn] **I** *sb* bredt smil; glis; **II** *vb* **1** smile bredt; **2** si smilende.

grind [graɪnd] **I** *sb* (daglig) kjør/mas; tredemølle (*fig*); **II** *vb* **1** knuse; male (opp); pulverisere; **2** gni; skure, skrape; **3** plage, tyrannisere; **4** kvesse, skjerpe, slipe; **5** dreie; sveive på; *dgl* kverne (rundt); **6** (få til å) jobbe/slite; *~ (away) at* pugge/terpe på. **grinder** ['graɪndə] *sb* **1** knuser *etc*; jeksel; kvern; møllestein; **2** sliper *etc*; slipestein. **grindstone** *sb* slipestein.

grip [grɪp] **I** *sb* **1** grep, tak; *be at ~s with* kjempe (bakse, tumle etc) med; *come/get to ~s with* komme/ryke opp å slåss med; *fig* gi seg i kast med; **2** håndtak, spak; **3** griper; **4** *US* (reise)|koffert, -veske; **II** *vb* gripe (tak i); holde fast (i/på).

grisly ['grɪzlɪ] *adj* fæl, nifs, uhyggelig.

grist [grɪst] *sb* korn (især *fig*); *~ to one's mill* vann på mølla.

grit [grɪt] **I** *sb* **1** grus, småstein; sand; **2** grovmalt/knust korn; grøpp, gryn; **3** mot, standhaftighet; *dgl* tæl; **II** *vt* **1** gruse; strø grus/sand på; **2** skrape, skure; knase; *~ one's teeth* bite tennene sammen.

grizzled ['grɪzld] *adj* grånet, grå(sprengt). **grizzly** ['grɪzlɪ] *sb US (~ bear)* gråbjørn.

groan [grəʊn] **I** *sb* **1** stønn(ing); sukk; **2** knaking; knirking; **II** *vb* **1** stønne; klage høylytt; **2** knake, knirke; gi seg.

grocer ['grəʊsə] *sb* dagligvarehandler; *dgl* kjøpmann; *gml* kolonialhandler. **grocery** ['grəʊsərɪ] *sb* dagligvare|butikk, forretning, -handel; *fl også* dagligvarer.

groin [grɔɪn] *sb* lyske, skritt.

groom [gru:m] **I** *sb* **1** stallkar; **2** = *bridegroom*; **II** *vt* **1** stelle/strigle (hest); **2** pleie/stelle (seg); **3** *dgl* forberede; gjøre ferdig/rede; trimme.

groove [gru:v] **I** *sb* **1** fure, rille; spor; **2** *fig* tralt, vane; **II** *vt* lage spor *etc* i. **groovy** ['gru:vɪ] *adj* **1** ensporet; ensidig, transynt; **2** *slang* fantastisk, flott: inne, moderne; ålreit.

grope [grəʊp] *vb* famle/føle seg frem (*after/for* etter).

gross [grəʊs] **A** *adj* **1** grov; simpel, vulgær; **2** sløv, treg; **3** grov, åpenbar; skamløs; **4** frodig, tykk; **5** fet, tykk (om personer); **6** *merk* brutto(-); **B** *sb merk* gross.

ground [graʊnd] **I** *sb* **1** jord (og jordbunn; bakke, mark; grunn; grunne; (sjø)bunn etc); *touch ~* ta/gå på grunn; grunnstøte; **2** felt (og mark, terreng; område; *fig* materiale, stoff etc); eiendom, tomt; plass; *cover much ~* reise langt; tilbakelegge (en) lang strekning; fare over (nå, rekke; *fig* omfatte) mye; **3** grunnlag, underlag; (bak)grunn; bunn; **4** (bak)-grunn, motiv; årsak; **5** *fl* bunnfall; grut; **II** *vb* **1** *sjø* gå/sette på grunn; **2** *fly* gi startforbud; sette på bakken; **3** bygge (og grunne, grunnlegge *on* på); **4** *~ in* innføre i (dvs undervise i begynnelsesgrunnene); **5** *elek* jorde. **ground | crew** *sb* bakkemannskap. **~ floor** *sb* første etasje. **~less** *adj* grunnløs, ubegrunnet. **~ sheet** *sb* teltunderlag. **~ staff** = *~ crew*.

group [gru:p] **1** *sb* gruppe; flokk; klase, klynge; **2** *vb* gruppere (seg); danne/samle i grupper. **group | item** *sb data* gruppeelement. **~ separator** *sb data* gruppeskilletegn.

grouse [graʊs] **A** *sb* fugl (dvs fuglevilt); *især* rype(r); *black ~* orr|fugl, -hane, -høne; *hazel ~* jerpe; *white ~* fjellrype; *willow ~* lirype; *wood ~* storfugl, tiur; **B** *dgl* **1** *sb* klage; **2** *vi* klage, syte; brumme.

grouting ['graʊtɪŋ] *sb petro* ballast, steinfylling

grove [grəʊv] *sb* skogholt; lund.

grovel [grɒvl] *vi* krype/smiske (*before/to* for).

grow [grəu] *vb* **1** vokse, øke; gro, spire; utvikle seg; ~ *out of* vokse fra; *fig* stamme/utvikle seg fra; ~ *up* vokse (opp); bli voksen; **2** dyrke/produsere (grønnsaker etc); **3** bli (etter hvert).

growl [graul] **I** *sb* knurring; rumling; **II** *vb* **1** knurre; **2** rumle.

growth [grəuθ] *sb* **1** avling, (års)vekst; **2** (ut)vekst; byll, svulst; **3** utvikling.

grub [grʌb] **A** *vb:* ~ *out/up* grave/rote frem/opp *etc*; **B** *sb* **I** larve; **II** *slang* **1** mat; **2** slave, sliter. **grubby** ['grʌbɪ] *adj* **1** skitten; uflidd, ustelt; **2** full av larver/ mark.

grudge [grʌdʒ] **1** *sb* motvilje, uvilje; *bear/owe a* ~ bære nag; **2** *vt* misunne; gi *etc* motvillig. **grudgingly** ['grʌdʒɪŋlɪ] *adj* motvillig.

gruel ['gruəl] *sb* velling. **gruelling** ['gruəlɪŋ] *adj* amstrengende, hard, streng.

gruesome ['gru:səm] *adj* fæl; makaber, nifs; uhyggelig.

gruff [grʌf] *adj* avvisende; barsk, brysk; røff.

grumble ['grʌmbl] **I** *sb* knurring *etc*; **II** *vb* **1** knurre (dvs beklage seg grettent og surmulende); protestere; sutre, syte; **2** rumle.

grumpy ['grʌmpɪ] *adj* gretten, sur.

grunt [grʌnt] **1** *sb* grynt(ing); **2** *vb* grynte.

guarantee [ˌgærən'ti:] **I** *sb* garanti, sikkerhet; *(guaranty)* kausjon; *(guarantor)* kausjonist; **II** *vt* **1** garantere, kausjonere; innestå (*for* for; *that* for at); **2** *dgl* love (sikkert). **guarantor** [ˌgærən'tɔ:] *sb jur* garantist; kausjonist. **guaranty** ['gærəntɪ] *sb jur* garanti; kausjon; sikkerhet.

guard [gɑ:d] **I** *sb* **1** aktpågivenhet, vaktsomhet; *off one's guard* uoppmerksom; *on* ~ på post/vakt; **2** beskyttelse, forsvar; beskytter; **3** vakt(post); *the Guards* Garden; **4** fangevokter, fengselsbetjent; **5** beskyttelse (i form av bøyle, plate, skjerm etc); **6** overkonduktør (på tog); *US* billettkontrollør, konduktør; **II** *vb* **1** beskytte, skjerme, verne; **2** vokte; holde vakt (over); vokte (seg). **guard|boat** *sb* patruljebåt. **~-duty** *sb* vakt(tjeneste). **guarded** ['gɑ:dɪd] *adj* **1** beskyttet; bevoktet; **2** forsiktig; forbeholden. **guardhouse** *sb* vaktstue. **guardian** ['gɑ:dɪən] *sb* **1** beskytter; vokter; formynder, verge. **guardian | angel** *sb* skytsengel. **~ship** *sb* formynderskap, vergemål. **guard|-rail** *sb* rekkverk. ~ **room** *sb* vakt|lokale, -rom, -stue. **guardsman** ['gɑ:dzmən] *sb* gardist.

guess [ges] **I** *sb* gjetning; antakelse, formodning; **II** *vb* **1** gjette; anta, formode; **2** *nå især US* mene, synes; tro.

guest [gest] *sb* gjest. **guest|house** *sb* gjestgiveri, pensjonat. **~room** *sb* gjesteværelse.

guffaw [gʌ'fɔ:] **1** *sb* knegging (dvs kneggende latter); **2** *vi* knegge; gaple, skoggerle.

guidance ['gaɪdəns] *sb* førerskap, ledelse. **guide** [gaɪd] **I** *sb* **1** fører, leder; reiseleder; **2** rådgiver, veileder; **3** håndbok (også = *~book*); ~ *to* innføring/veiledning i (dvs veiledende bok etc); **4** *girl* ~ speiderpike; **5** *mek* føring, styring; *som adj* styre-; **II** *vt* **1** føre lede; **2** være reiseleder (for); **3** råde; rettlede, veilede. **guidebook** *sb* reisehåndbok, turistfører; guide; *også* (utstillings etc)katalog. **guide edge** *sb data* styrekant. **guided | missile** *sb mil* (fjern)styrt rakett. ~ **tour** *sb* pakketur, selskapsreise. **guide-post** *sb* veiviser(stolpe), veiskilt.

guild [gɪld] *sb* laug.

guile [gaɪl] *sb* list, sluhet; svik(efullhet). **guileless** ['gaɪllɪs] *adj* troskyldig; ærlig; uten svik.

guilt [gɪlt] *sb* skyld (og skyldfølelse, skyldighet etc). **guiltless** ['gɪltlɪs] *adj* skyldfri, uskyldig. **guilty** ['gɪltɪ] *adj* skyldig (*of* i); skyld|betynget, -bevisst; straffskyldig.

guinea ['gɪnɪ] *sb gml* en myntenhet, se midtsidene. **guineapig** ['gɪnɪpɪg] *sb* marsvin; *fig* forsøkskanin.

guise [gaɪz] *sb* forkledning; foregivende, skinn; påskudd.

gulf [gʌlf] *sb* **1** golf; vid/åpen bukt; **2** avgrunn, svelg.

gull [gʌl] **A** *sb* måke; **B** **1** *sb* (godtroende) fjols; tosk; **2** *vt* lure (opp i stry); bedra, snyte. **gullible** ['gʌləbl] *adj* godtroende, lettlurt.

gullet ['gʌlɪt] *sb* spiserør; hals, svelg; strupe.

gully ['gʌlɪ] *sb* **1** kløft; **2** (vann)renne; rennestein; (kloakk)avløp.

gulp [gʌlp] **1** *sb* gulp(ing); slurk; **2** *vb:* ~ *down* gulpe ned.

gum [gʌm] **A I** *sb* gummi (og gummi|plante, -saft; (gummi)lim, solusjon; *US* også ting av gummi, som gummistøvel, kalosje og *(chewing-~)* tyggegummi); **II** *vt* **1** gummiere; **2** lime (med gummilim); **3** *US slang (~ up)* forkludre, ødelegge; sabotere; **B** *sb fl* tannkjøtt.

gumption ['gʌmpʃn] *sb dgl* foretaksomhet, pågangsmot, tæl; omløp i hodet; sunt vett.

gun [gʌn] **I** *sb* **1** skytevåpen (som gevær, rifle, pistol, revolver; kanon etc); *fl også* skyts; *stand/stick to one's ~s* holde stand/stillingen; **2** skytter; jeger; **II** *vb dgl* **1** skyte (på); **2** *be/go ~ning for* for ute etter/på jakt etter. **gun|-barrel** *sb* geværløp *etc*. **~-boat** *sb* kanonbåt. **~-fire** *sb* geværild *etc*; skyting. **~man** *sb US* revolvermann; gangster. **gunner** ['gʌnə] *sb* **1** *mil* artillerist; artillerikvartermester/kanoner (i marinen); maskingeværskytter (i bombefly etc); **2** skytter; jeger. **~powder** *sb* krutt. **~-runner** *sb* våpensmugler. **~shot** *sb* skudd (og skuddvidde). **~shy** *adj* skuddredd. **~smith** *sb* børsemaker. **~stock** *sb* geværkolbe. **~wale** *sb* (båt)ripe, reling.

gurgle ['gɜ:gl] **1** *sb* klukking *etc*; pludring; **2** *vi* klukke (og klukkle etc); boble, risle; pludre.

gush [gʌʃ] **I** *sb* utbrudd; flom, strøm; *fig* utgytelse; sentimentalitet; **II** *vi* **1** flomme, strømme, velle; bruse, fosse; **2** utgyte seg; flomme/svømme over (av). **gusher** ['gʌʃə] *sb* **1** *petro* (særlig kraftig og rik) oljekilde; **2** sentimental skravlebøtte.

gust [gʌst] *sb* byge (med nedbør eller vind); vind|-

kast, -kule, -støt.

gut ['gʌt] **I** *sb, især fl* **1** tarmer; *dgl* innvoller; mave; *(cat~)* tarmsnor; *især* fortom; fiolin-/racketstreng etc; **2** innhold; *fig* marg; kraft, saft; nerve; **3** mot; besluttsomhet, fasthet; karakter(styrke); **II** *vt* **1** rense/sløye (fisk); ta ut innvollene av; **2** plyndre; tømme for innhold; rasere, ruinere.

gutter ['gʌtə] *sb* **1** takrenne; nedløpsrenne; **2** rennestein. **guttersnipe** ['gʌtəsnaɪp] *sb* rennesteinsunge.

guy [gaɪ] **A I** *sb* **1** (stor) fille|dukke, -mann; fugleskremsel (også *fig*); bajas, klovn; **2** laps, pyntedukke; **3** *US dgl* gutt; kar, mann; **II** *vt (~ at)* gjøre narr av; **B** *sb sjø* bardun; stag; gitau.

guzzle ['gʌzl] *vb* **1** fråtse; lange/sette i seg; **2** pimpe; tylle i seg.

gymnasium [dʒɪm'neɪzɪəm] *sb* gymnastikksal; idrettshall. **gymnastic** [dʒɪm'næstɪk] **1** *adj* gymnastisk, gymnastikk-; **2** *sb fl* gymnastikk.

gypsy ['dʒipsɪ] = *gipsy*.

H

haberdasher ['hæbədæʃə] *sb* **1** manufakturhandler; **2** *US* (innehaver av) herreekviperingsforretning. **haberdashery** ['hæbədæʃərɪ] *sb* **1** manufaktur|forretning, -varer; **2** *US* herreekvipering (og herreekviperingsforretning).

habit [hæbɪt] *sb* **1** vane (og uvane); bruk, praksis; sedvane; **2** (kles)drakt, habitt. **habitable** ['hæbɪtəbl] *adj* beboelig. **habitation** [ˌhæbɪ'teɪʃn] *sb* bolig (og beboelse). **habit-forming** ['hæbɪt'fɔ:mɪŋ] *adj* vanedannende. **habitual** [hə'bɪtjʊəl] *adj* (sed)vanlig; vane-. **habituate** [hə'bɪtjʊeɪt] *vt* venne (*to* til).

hack [hæk] **A I** *sb* **1** øk; **2** leie|hest, -vogn; (heste)drosje; **3** grovarbeider, sliter; **II** *vb* **1** leie ut (arbeidskraft, hest og vogn etc); **2** leie (arbeidskraft etc); kjøre drosje; **B** *vb* **1** hakke/kutte opp; **2** hoste (gneldrende); bjeffe, gjø. **hacker** ['hækə] *sb data* datasnok. **hackneyed** ['hæknɪd] *adj* banal, forslitt. **hack|saw** ['hæksɔ:] *sb* baufil. **~work** ['hækwɜ:k] *sb* grovarbeid; (litterært) dusinarbeid. **~-writer** ['hækraɪtə] *sb* bladsmører.

haddock ['hædək] *sb* hyse, kolje.

hag [hæg] *sb* heks; gammel kjerring.

haggard ['hægəd] *adj* hulkinnet, mager; uttært.

haggle ['hægl] krangle (især om pris etc); prute.

hail [heɪl] **A 1** *sb* hagl (og haglvær); **2** *vb* hagle; *fig* (la det) hagle/regne (med); **B I** *sb* **1** anrop, praiing; *within ~* på praiehold; innen hørevidde; **2** hilsen, hilsing; **II** *vb* **1** anrope, praie; **2** hilse (velkommen); hylle; **3** *dgl: ~ from* komme/stamme fra. **hail|stone** *sb* hagl. **~storm** *sb* haglbyge.

hair [heə] *sb* hår (og hårstrå). **hair|cut** *sb* hårklipp(ing). **~-do** *sb* frisering; frisyre, hårfasong. **~dresser** *sb* frisør. **~pin** *sb* hårnål. **~-splitting** *sb* ordkløveri. **hairy** ['heərɪ] *adj* håret, hår-; lodden.

hale [heɪl] *adj* frisk, sunn; *~ and hearty* rask og rørig.

half [hɑ:f] **1** *adj* halv(-); *~ and ~* halv (el. like mye) av hver; *~-seas over (dgl)* på en snurr (dvs beruset); **2** *adv* halvt, halvveis; *not ~ bad (dgl)* slett ikke så verst; **2** *sb* halv|del, part; halvår (og semester, termin etc). **half|-baked** *adj* halvstekt; *fig* uferdig; umoden. **~-bred, ~-breed, ~-caste** *adj, sb* halv|blods(-), -kaste(-). **~-cock** *sb* halvspenn. **~crown** *sb* en myntenhet, se midtsidene. **~-done** *adj* halv|ferdig, -stekt. **~hearted** *adj* halvhjertet. **~-measures** *sb fl* halve forholdsregler/tiltak. **~penny** *sb* en myntenhet, se midtsidene. **~time** *sb* **1** halv(gått) tid; **2** pause (mellom omgangene i f.eks. fotball). **~-tracks** *sb fl* halvbelter (på traktor etc). **~way** *adj* halvveis, halv. **~-wit** *sb* tomsing. **~-witted** *adj* halv|skrullet, tomset.

halibut ['hælɪbət] *sb* hellefisk, kveite.

hall [hɔ:l] *sb* **1** bygning (især offentlig og/eller med møtelokaler etc); **2** gods; herre|gård, -sete; **3** forsamlingssal; spisesal (især på studenthjem); **4** entré, hall, vestibyle; *US også* korridor; **5** *(guild ~)* laugsbygning. **hallmark** ['hɔ:lmɑ:k] *sb, vb* (forsyne især gull- og sølvvarer med garanti)|merke, -stempel; *fig* garanti (og garantere); kjenne|merke, -tegn.

hallow ['hæləʊ] **1** *sb gml* helgen; **2** *vt* hellige, vigsle. **Hallowe'en** [ˌhæləʊ'i:n] *sb* allehelgensaften.

halo ['heɪləʊ] *sb* glorie.

halt [hɔ:lt] **A 1** *sb* stans, stopp (og holdeplass, stoppested); pause; hvil, rast; *mil* holdt; **2** *vb* stanse, stoppe; ta (en) pause; *mil* gjøre/kommandere holdt; **B** *vi* **1** halte; **2** nøle, vakle. **halter** ['hɔ:ltə] *sb* **1** grime (til hest); **2** løkke; *hangman's ~* (bøddel)strikke.

halve [hɑ:v] *vt* halvere; dele likt.

halyard ['hæljəd] *sb sjø* fall.

ham [hæm] *sb* **1** skinke; **2** lår (især baksiden av låret); **2** *slang* (radio)amatør; tredjerangs skuespiller. **ham-handed** [ˌhæm'hændɪd] *adj* klosset, trehendt.

hamlet ['hæmlɪt] *sb* landsby (især mindre og uten kirke); grend, husklynge.

hammer ['hæmə] **1** *sb* hammer; (auksjons)-klubbe; *sport.* slegge; **2** *vb* hamre (og banke, dundre, slå etc).

hammock ['hæmək] *sb* hengekøye.

hamper ['hæmpə] **A** *sb* (mat- el. niste)kurv; **B** *vt* hemme, hindre.

hamstring ['hæmstrıŋ] **1** *sb* (kne)hase; **2** *vt* skjære hasene over på; *fig* lamme, stekke.

hand [hænd] **I** *sb* **1** hånd (og håndfull; (hånd)-grep, tak; håndlag; håndsrekning; håndsbredd (= 4 *inches*); (hånd)skrift etc); *også* bunt, klase; *merk* 5 stk.; **at ~** for hånden; nær (forestående); **by ~** med/ved håndkraft; personlig (dvs personlig el. med bud); **in ~** i bakhånd; i reserve; under arbeid/behandling; under kontroll; **off ~,** se *~hand*; *get it off one's ~s* bli kvitt det; få det unna(gjort)/fra hånden; **on ~** for hånden; til rådighet; *have it on one's ~s* ha ansvaret for det; ha det hvilende på seg; **out of ~** på stående fot; uten videre; utenfor kontroll; **to ~** i hende; for hånden; til rådighet; **under ~** under kontroll; underhånden; *~ over fist/hand* jevnt/støtt og sikkert; *be a good ~ at* ha (et) godt håndlag med; være flink til; *have no ~ in* ikke ha (hatt) noe å gjøre med; *win ~s down* vinne overlegent; **2** (arbeids)mann, (kropps)arbeider; *fl* mannskaper; *old ~* veteran; *dgl* gammel (ring)rev; **3** applaus; *a big ~* (en) kraftig applaus; **4** viser; **5** *fig* kant, side; *on the one/the other ~* på den ene/den andre siden; **6** kortspiller (samt kort (på hånden) og slag kort etc); *show one's ~* vise farge; tone flagg; **II** *vt* (over)|gi, (-)levere, (-)rekke; **~ down** hente/ta ned; hjelpe ned (liten trapp etc); gi videre; (la) gå i arv; *~-me-down* ferdigsydd (og av heller dårlig kvalitet); konfeksjons-; avlagt, brukt; **~ in** levere/sende inn; **~ on** gi (sende, la gå etc) videre; **~ out** dele/levere ut; *~-out* utdeling (og tildeling); erklæring, pressemelding; **~ over** over|gi, -levere, -rekke; utlevere; **~ round** = *~ out.* **hand|bag** *sb* håndveske. **~ball** *sb* håndball. **~bill** *sb* løpeseddel. **~brake** *sb* håndbrems. **~cart** *sb* håndkjerre. **~cuffs** *sb fl* håndjern. **~ful** *sb* håndfull; *quite a ~ful* noe uhåndterlig (el. uregjerlig).

handicraft ['hændıkra:ft] *sb* håndverk (og håndlag, håndverksmessig dyktighet etc).

handkerchief ['hæŋkətʃi:f] *sb* lommetørkle.

handle ['hændl] **I** *sb* **1** håndtak, skaft; hank; sveiv; *fly off the ~ (dgl)* fly i flint; **2** *fig* fin/fordelaktig tittel; **II** *vt* **1** holde i; bruke, håndtere; **2** behandle; lede, styre; **3** greie, klare; **4** *merk* (lager)føre; handle med.

handlebar ['hændlba:] *sb, især fl* (sykkel)styre.

hand-out ['hændaut] *sb, se hand II.*

hand|-made *adj* håndlaget. **~-organ** *sb* lirekasse. **~-picked** *adj* håndplukket. **~rail** *sb* gelender, rekkverk. **~shake** *sb* håndtrykk.

handsome [hænsəm] *adj* **1** kjekk; pen, vakker; tiltrekkende; **2** klekkelig; raus, rundhåndet.

handwriting ['hænd,raıtıŋ] *sb* håndskrift.

handy ['hændı] *adj* **1** hendig; fingernem; **2** nyttig; *come in ~* komme godt med; **3** for hånden; i nærheten. **handyman** ['hændımən] *sb* altmuligmann.

hang [hæŋ] **I** *sb* **1** fall (dvs måten stoff etc faller på); **2** *dgl* sammenheng; virkemåte; *get the ~ of* få tak i fremgangsmåten (teknikken, meningen etc); **3** *dgl: I don't care a ~* jeg gir blaffen; **II** *vb* **1** henge (og henge ned (fra); henge opp; dekorere, drapere; bli hengt etc); *~ it!* pokker (ta det)! **2** *med adv/prep* **~ about/***US* **(a)round** (gå og) drive/slenge; **~ back** holde seg tilbake; betenke seg; nøle; **~ by** *(a rope etc)* henge i (et tau etc); **~ on** henge i (på, ved etc); være avhengig av; *sagt i telefonen* et øyeblikk (dvs ikke legg på røret); **~ on to** holde fast på/*fig* ved; huke (klamre, klore etc) seg fast i; **~ out** henge ut; *slang* bo; holde til; **~ together** henge/holde sammen; **~ up** henge opp; legge på (telefonrøret); *be hung up* bli oppholdt; bli/være forsinket; **~ upon** = *~ on.* **hangman** ['hæŋmən] *sb* bøddel. **hangover** ['hæŋəuvə] *sb* bakrus; *be hungover* ha tømmermenn.

hanker ['hæŋkə] *vi: ~ for* hige (lengte, trakte etc) etter.

hansom ['hænsəm] *sb (~-cab)* (tohjuls) hestedrosje.

haphazard [hæp'hæzəd] **1** *adj/adv* tilfeldig; på måfå/slump; **2** *sb* slump, tilfelle. **happen** ['hæpn] *vi* **1** hende, skje; finne sted; **2** hende (tilfeldigvis); falle seg; *~ upon* komme over (dvs finne/støte på etc ved en tilfeldighet); *as it ~s* tilfeldigvis. **happening** ['hæpnıŋ] *sb* **1** begivenhet, hending; **2** *teater etc* improvisert forestilling etc. **happiness** ['hæpınıs] *sb* lykke. **happy** ['hæpı] *adj* **1** glad, lykkelig (*at* for/over; *that* for/over at); **2** gledelig; god, heldig; **3** fornøyd, tilfreds; **4** beleilig; treffende. **happy-go-lucky** *adj* sorgløs, ubekymret; likesæl.

harangue [hə'ræŋ] **1** *sb* (lang, kjedelig) preken; tirade; **2** *vb* holde slik preken (for).

harass ['hærəs] *vt* plage, trakassere.

harbinger ['ha:bındʒə] *sb* for|løper, (-)varsel; bud(bærer).

harbour ['ha:bə] **I** *sb* **1** havn; **2** ly, skjulested; **II** *vb* **1** huse; gi ly; skjule; **2** *fig* nære, omgås med (planer etc).

hard [ha:d] **I** *adj* **1** hard (og fast, solid, stiv etc); **2** vanskelig; *~ of hearing* tunghørt; **3** anstrengende; streng, strid; *~ and fast* fast, ubøyelig; uforanderlig; **II** *adv* **1** hardt *etc*; **2** energisk, flittig; **3** anstrengt; med vanskelighet; *be ~ up* sitte hardt (trangt, vanskelig etc) i det; **4** sterkt, voldsomt; **5** like; straks. **hard | cash** *sb* kontanter. **~ disk** *sb data* hard|disk, -plate; (fast) platelager. **~ drugs** *sb fl* (vanedannende) narkotika. **~-earned** *adj* hardt (for)tjent; surt ervervet; dyrekjøpt. **~en** ['ha:dn] *vb* bli/gjøre hard; herde(s); forherde(s). **~-headed** *adj* **1** sta, strid; **2** nøktern, praktisk. **hardihood** ['ha:dıhud] *sb* dristighet (etc, jf *hardy*). **hard | liquor** *sb* (sterkt) brennevin. **~ luck** *sb* uhell. **~ly** ['ha:dlı] *adv* **1** knapt, neppe; snaut; så vidt; *~ ever* nesten aldri; **2** hardt, strengt (etc, jf *hard I 3*). **~ paraffin** *sb petro* hard|parafin, -voks. **~ship**

['hɑ:dʃɪp] *sb* motgang; vanskelighet; *fl* strabaser. ~ **tack** *sb* beskøyt, skipskjeks. ~**ware** ['hɑ:dweə] *sb* **1** isenkram, jernvarer; **2** *data* maskinvare. ~ **wax** *sb petro* = ~ *paraffin*. ~**-wired** *adj data etc* fastkoblet. ~**wood** *sb* hardved, løvtre(virke). **hardy** ['hɑ:dɪ] *adj* **1** dristig; **2** hardfør, sterk.

hare [heə] *sb* hare. **hare-brained** [ˌheə'breɪnd] *adj* tankeløs.

hark [hɑ:k] *vb* **1** høre (på); lytte (til); **2** ~ *back (to)* gå/vende tilbake (til).

harlot ['hɑ:lət] *sb gml* skjøge.

harm [hɑ:m] **1** *sb* skade; *mean no* ~ ikke mene noe vondt (med det); **2** *vt* skade. **harm|ful** ['hɑ:mfʊl] *adj* skadelig. ~**less** ['hɑ:mlɪs] *adj* uskadelig; harmløs, ufarlig.

harmonious [hɑ:'məʊnɪəs] *adj* harmonisk. **harmonize** ['hɑ:mənaɪz] *vb* **1** harmonere; (få til å) stemme overens; **2** *musikk* harmonisere. **harmony** ['hɑ:mənɪ] *sb* harmoni; samklang; overensstemmelse.

harness ['hɑ:nɪs] **I** *sb* sele(tøy); (ut)rustning; *in* ~ i (fullt) arbeid; **II** *vt* **1** sele på; spenne for); **2** *fig* temme, tøyle; utnytte (især vannkraft).

harp [hɑ:p] **I** *sb* harpe; **II** *vi* **1** spille harpe; **2** ~ *on* gnåle/terpe på.

harpoon ['hɑ:'pu:n] *sb, vt* harpun(ere).

harrow ['hærəʊ] **I** *sb* harv; **II** *vt* **1** harve; **2** *fig* såre; rive opp. **harrowing** ['hærəʊɪŋ] *adj* opprivende.

harsh [hɑ:ʃ] *adj* **1** grov, ru; **2** skjærende, skurrende; **3** barsk, streng; hard, uforsonlig.

harvest ['hɑ:vɪst] **I** *sb* **1** høst (og især høstarbeid, innhøstning; (innhøstet) avling etc); **2** avkastning, resultat, utbytte; frukt; **II** *vt* høste (inn). **harvester** ['hɑ:vɪstə] *sb* **1** høstarbeider (og onnekar etc); **2** skurtresker.

hash [hæʃ] **1** *sb* hakkemat, lapskaus; *fig* rot, sammensurium; **2** *vt:* ~ *up* hakke/kutte opp; *fig* forkludre, rote til.

haste [heɪst] *sb* hast(verk); travelhet; ~ *is waste* hastverk er lastverk; *make* ~ skynde seg. **hasten** ['heɪsn] *vb* **1** skynde seg; **2** skynde på; forsere, fremskynde. **hasty** ['heɪstɪ] *adj* **1** rask, snar; **2** forhastet, overilt; **3** brå; hissig, snarsint; ubesindig.

hat [hæt] *sb* hatt.

hatch [hætʃ] **A** *sb* **1** luke; *sjø* (dekks)luke; **2** lem; (nederste) halvdør; *sjø* lukelem; **B I** *sb* **1** (ut)ruging; **2** kull (kyllinger etc); **II** *vb* klekke(s) (ut); ruge(s) ut; ~ *out* klekke/pønske ut. **hatchway** ['hætʃweɪ] *sb sjø* luke(åpning).

hatchet ['hætʃɪt] *sb* **1** håndøks, liten øks; **2** stridsøks.

hate [heɪt] **I** *sb* **1** avsky, motvilje; **2** hat; **II** *vt* **1** *dgl* mislike; ikke (kunne) fordra (like, holde ut etc); **2** avsky, hate. **hateful** ['heɪtfʊl] *adj* motbydelig; forhatt. **hatred** ['heɪtrɪd] *sb* hat.

hatter ['hætə *sb* hattemaker.

haughty ['hɔ:tɪ] *adj* hoven, hovmodig; kaut, overlegen.

haul [hɔ:l] **I** *sb* **1** haling, slep; buksering; **2** frakt, transport; **3** fangst; kupp, varp; **II** *vb* hale; dra, trekke; buksere, slepe; frakte, transportere. **haulage** ['hɔ:lɪdz] *sb* bukserpenger; frakt(omkostninger), transport.

haunch [hɔ:ntʃ] *sb* hofte(parti); bak|ende, -part; *dgl* bak, ende.

haunt [hɔ:nt] **1** *sb* tilholdssted; **2** *vt* besøke (hyppig og/eller regelmessig); vanke i; *fig* hjemsøke; forfølge, plage; *a ~ed house* et hus det spøker i.

have [hæv] *vt* **I** *som hjelpeverb* **1** ha, være; ~ *done/finished with* ha gjort seg/være ferdig med; **2** ~ *(got) to* måtte; være nødt til; **II** *som hovedverb* **1** ha (og eie; få, ha fått; få/ta seg = innta, nyte, drikke, spise etc); ~ *you got/(US ofte) do you ~?* har du? *(også) ~ you got?* har du (nå, i dette øyeblikk)? *do you ~?* har du (som regel, vanligvis)? ~ *had enough* ha fått nok; være forsynt/mett; *let them ~ it* la dem ha (få etc) den/det; *dgl også* gi dem inn; la dem (få) gjennomgå; **2** ha kjennskap til/kunnskaper om; **3** få/ha til (å gjøre etc); la (gjøre etc); **4** *dgl* dupere; lure; *you've been had* du er blitt lurt/snytt; **5** *med adv/prep* ~ **at** gå løs på; lange ut etter; ~ **back** få igjen/tilbake; ~ **down** få/ha ned; få/ha ut (dvs på besøk fra London eller annen større by); ~ **in** ha (i huset); ~ **on** ha på (seg); ~ *something on them* ha noe på (dvs vite noe (ufordelaktig) om) dem; ~ **out** få (ha, ta etc) ut; ~ *it out with* få snakket ut/gjort opp med; ~ **up** få/ha opp; få/ha inn (dvs på besøk fra landet).

haven ['heɪvn] *sb* havn; *især fig* ly, tilfluktssted.

haversack ['hævəsæk] *sb* ryggsekk; skulderveske (især til militær bruk].

havoc ['hævək] *sb* (omfattende) ødeleggelse; *make ~ of/play ~ among/with* rasere, ruinere, ødelegge.

haw [hɔ:] **A 1** *sb* kremt(ing); **2** *vi* kremte; ~ *and hum* hakke og stamme; **B** *sb* = ~*thorn*.

hawk [hɔ:k] *sb* **A** *sb* hauk; **B** *vt* selge (på gaten, ved dørene etc); *fig* spre, utbre; *no ~ers or beggars* salg og betling forbudt.

hawser ['hɔ:sə] *sb* trosse.

hawthorne ['hɔ:θɔ:n] *sb* hagtorn.

hay [heɪ] *sb* høy. **hay|cart** *sb* høyvogn. ~**cock** *sb* høysåte. ~ **fever** *sb* høy|feber, -snue. ~**field** *sb* eng. ~**-fork** *sb* høygaffel. ~**maker** *sb* slåttekar. ~**rick,** ~**stack** *sb* høystakk. ~**wire** *sb* hesjetråd; *som adj dgl* floket; forvirret, skrullet.

hazard ['hæzəd] **I** *sb* **1** fare, risiko; **2** slump, slumpetreff; tilfelle; **3** hasard(spill); **II** *vt* **1** utsette for fare; **2** driste seg til; våge. **hazardous** ['hæzədəs] *adj* risikabel, vågsom; hasardiøs.

haze [heɪz] *sb* dis; tåke, uklarhet.

hazel ['heɪzl] **I** *adj* **1** hassel-; **2** nøttebrun; **II** *sb* **1** hassel(busk); **2** nøttebrunt.

hazy ['heɪzɪ] *adj* disig; tåket, uklar.

head [hed] **I** *adj, pref* **1** hode-; **2** hoved-, over-; første-; **3** forrest, først; for-; **4** mot-; **II** *sb* **1** hode (og individ, person; *dgl* snute); *om dyr* stykke(r); **2** hode (dvs forstand, intelligens; tanker etc); *keep one's ~*

holde hodet kaldt; *off one's* ~ fra forstanden/*dgl* vettet; **3** overhode; hersker, leder; overlærer (etc, jf ~*master etc*); *dgl* bas, sjef; **4** topp (og toppunkt); skum (på øl etc); *fig* høydepunkt, krise; **5** hovedavsnitt; overskrift, tittel; forside, front; ~*s or tails* krone eller mynt; ~*-on collision* frontkollisjon; *at the* ~ *of* forrest i; øverst på/ved; i spissen/teten for; **6** begynnelse, opprinnelse; kilde, utspring; bunn/innerste del (av fjord); **7** kurs, retning; fremskritt; **8** *(~land)* nes, odde, pynt; **9** fallhøyde; trykk (på vann, damp etc); **10** *sjø mil slang* toalett; **III** *vb* **1** danne hode; sette hode på; **2** heade, nikke, skalle (ball); **3** stevne/stå (*for* mot); ha/sette kurs (*for* mot); **4** føre, lede; gå/stå i spissen (for); stå først/øverst (på liste etc). **head|-ache** *sb* hodepine; *dgl fig* problem. ~ **clerk** *sb* fullmektig, kontorsjef. **~-dress** = ~*-gear*. **header** ['hedə] *sb* **1** hodestups fall; stup; **2** *data* topptekst; **3** *petro* samle|ledning, -stokk; manifold. **head-gear** *sb* hodeplagg; hodelag (på sele). **heading** ['hedɪŋ] *sb* **1** overskrift, tittel; **2** kurs, retning. **head|land** *sb* nes, odde, pynt. **~less** *adj* hodeløs. **~light** *sb* front|lykt, -lys(kaster). **~line** *sb* overskrift. **~long** *adj, adv* hodestups; *fig* hodekulls. ~ **loss** *sb petro etc* trykktap. **~man** *sb* leder, sjef. **~master** = ~*teacher* (om mann). **~mistress** = ~*teacher* (om kvinne). **~phones** *sb fl* øretelefoner. **~piece** *sb* hjelm. **~quarters** *sb fl* hovedkvarter. **~rest** *sb* hodestøtte. **~room** *sb* takhøyde; fri høyde; klaring. **~-sea** *sb* stampesjø. **~set** = ~*phones*. **~spring** *sb* kilde, utspring. **~stone** *sb* (hoved)hjørnestein; gravstein. **~strong** *adj* egen(sindig), sta; strid. **~teacher** *sb* overlærer, rektor, skole(be)styrer. ~ **waiter** *sb* hovmester. **~waters** *sb* = ~*spring*. **~way** *sb* fremgang. **~-wind** *sb* motvind.

heal [hi:l] *vb* kurere; helbrede(s), lege(s); ~ *up* gro. **health** [helθ] *sb* helse, sunnhet; *your* ~*!* skål! **health resort** *sb* kursted. **healthy** ['helθɪ] *adj* helsebringende; frisk, sunn.

heap [hi:p] **1** *sb* dynge, haug; mengde; ~*s of (dgl)* masser av; **2** *vt:* ~ *together* dynge sammen; ~ *up* hope opp; ~ *with* overdynge/overøse med.

hear [hɪə] *vb* **1** høre (og høre på); **2** *jur:* ~ *a case* behandle en (retts)sak. **hearing** ['hɪərɪŋ] *sb* **1** hørsel; **2** *a)* (over)høring; påhør; avhør; *b)* høring; *jur* saksbehandling; **3** lydhørhet; **4** hørevidde. **hearken** ['hɑ:kn] *vi boklig* høre (*to* på); lytte (*to* til). **hearsay** ['hɪəseɪ] *sb* (folke)snakk, sladder; rykte(r).

hearse [hɜ:s] *sb* båre; lik|bil, -vogn.

heart [hɑ:t] *sb* hjerte; *fig også* kjerne; midte, midtpunkt; *at* ~ på hjertet; *by* ~ utenat; *lose* ~ miste motet; *set one's* ~ *on* være ivrig etter/oppsatt på; *take* ~ fatte mot. **heart|ache** *sb* hjertesorg. **~-breaker** *sb* hjerteknuser. **~-breaking** *adj* hjerteskjærende; *dgl* dødsens kjedelig. **~-broken** *adj* nedbrutt, sønderknust. **hearten** ['hɑ:tn] *vt* oppmuntre; sette mot i. **heart|felt** *adj* inderlig; dypt følt. **~less** *adj* hjerteløs. **~-rending** *adj* hjerteskjærende. **~sick** = ~*-broken*. **~-strings** *sb* hjerterøtter.

hearth [hɑ:θ] *sb* arne, grue.

hearty ['hɑ:tɪ] *adj* hjertelig, oppriktig; **2** frisk, sunn; kraftig, sterk; glupende (om appetitt); solid (om måltid).

heat [hi:t] **I** *sb* **1** hete, varme; **2** glød, lidenskap; **3** brunst, løpetid; **4** *sport* heat; **II** *vb* varme (*up* opp); bli het/varm. **heated** ['hi:tɪd] *adj* heftig; opphisset. **heating oil** *sb petro* fyringsolje.

heath [hi:θ] *sb* **1** lyng; **2** hei, (lyng)mo.

heathen ['hi:ðn] **1** *adj* hedensk, hedning(e)-; **2** *sb* hedning.

heather ['heðə] *sb* **1** (røss)lyng; **2** hei, (lyng)mo. **heathery** ['heðərɪ] *adj* lyngbevokst; lyngfarget.

heave [hi:v] **I** *sb* hiv, løft *etc*; **II** *vb* **1** heve (og heve seg); løfte; heise opp; ~ *to* dreie/legge bi; **2** hive på seg; bølge, svulme; **3** *dgl* hive, kyle, slenge; **4** utstøte; ~ *a sigh* sukke (tungt).

heaven ['hevn] *sb* himmel (i religiøs forstand, jf *sky*). **heavenly** ['hevnlɪ] *adj* himmelsk.

heaviness ['hevɪnɪs] *sb* tyngde *etc*. **heavy** ['hevɪ] **1** *adj* tung (og kraftig, massiv, solid; *fig også* trykkende, tyngende; trettende; tungnem etc); **2** *adv (heavily)* tungt; *time lay* ~ *on their hands* tiden falt dem svært lang. **heavy|-duty** *adj* ekstra kraftig/solid. ~ **fuel oil** *sb petro* tung fyringsolje. **~-handed** *adj* hardhendt, håndfast; klosset. **~-hearted** *adj* tung om hjertet.

heckle ['hekl] *vt* avbryte (taler) med plagsomme spørsmål; forstyrre med tilrop.

hectic ['hektɪk] *adj* hektisk; forkavet, oppskjørtet.

hedge [hedʒ] **I** *sb (~row)* hekk; **II** *vb* **1** gjerde inn; sette opp hekk (rundt); *fig* begrense; hemme, hindre; **2** beskytte, verne; gardere (seg); **3** komme med utflukter; vri seg unna.

heed [hi:d] **1** *sb* oppmerksomhet; **2** *vt* ense, vøre; gi akt på. **heedless** ['hi:dlɪs] *adj* uaktsom, uvøren.

heel [hi:l] **A I** *sb* **1** hæl; *at (on/upon) their* ~*s* i hælene på dem; *bring to* ~ kuste; få til å føye seg; *come to* ~ føye/jenke seg; falle til fote; *down at* ~*s* nedtrådt, utgått; sjusket; forhutlet, forkommen; *under the* ~ under hælen (dvs undertrykt); **2** *petro* tankrest; **3** *slang* stymper, usling; **II** *vt* hæle, hælflikke; **B** *vb sjø* (få til å) krenge.

hefty ['heftɪ] *adj dgl* røslig, svær.

heifer ['hefə] *sb* kvige.

height [haɪt] *sb* høyde; høydepunkt, toppunkt. **heighten** ['haɪtn] *vb* **1** heve, høyne; opphøye; **2** forøke; øke(s); forstørre(s); forsterke, intensivere.

heinous ['heɪnəs] *adj* avskyelig; grufull, skrekkelig.

heir [eə] *sb* arving. **heiress** ['eərɪs] *sb* (kvinnelig) arving. **heirloom** ['eəlu:m] *sb* arvestykke.

helicopter ['helɪkɒptə] *sb* helikopter. **helicopter deck, helipad** ['helɪpæd] *sb petro etc* helikopterdekk.

hell [hel] *sb* helvete; ~ *for leather* (alt) hva remmer og tøy kan holde. **hell|-bent** *adj* fandenivoldsk. **~-cat** *sb* furie, heks.

helm [helm] **A** *sb* ror|kult, -pinne; (skips)ratt; styre, styring; *fig også* ror; *at the* ~ til rors; ved roret; **B** *sb gml* = **helmet** ['helmɪt] *sb* hjelm. **helmsman**

['helmzmən] *sb* ror|gjenger, mann.

help [help] **I** *sb* **1** hjelp; assistanse, bistand, støtte; **2** (med)hjelper; hjelp (i huset etc); assistent; **3** (hjelpe)middel; **II** *vb* **1** hjelpe; assistere, bistå, støtte; **2** servere (for); betjene; forsyne (med mat); **3** (for)-hindre; hjelpe (for); *we couldn't ~ it* vi kunne ikke noe for det; **4** unngå; la være. **help|ful** *adj* **1** hjelpsom; **2** nyttig. **~ing** *sb* (mat)porsjon; forsyning. **~less** *adj* hjelpeløs. **~ menu** *sb data* hjelpemeny.

helter-skelter [ˌheltə'skeltə] *adv* hulter til bulter; hodekulls.

hem [hem] **A I** *sb* fald, kant(ing); **II** *vt* **1** falde, kante; **2** *~ in (about/round)* omgi, omringe, omslutte; hemme, hindre; **B 1** *interj* hm; **2** *vi* kremte.

hemisphere ['hemɪsfɪə] *sb* halvkule.

hemorrhage ['hemərɪdʒ] *sb* blødning.

hemp [hemp] *sb* **1** hamp; **2** cannabis, hasj(isj).

hen [hen] *sb* høne; hunn(fugl). **hen-pecked** *adj* hundset; *~-pecked husband* tøffelhelt.

hence [hens] *adv* **1** herfra; **2** fra nå av; **3** derfor; av den(ne) grunn. **henceforth, henceforward** *adv* heretter; for fremtiden.

henchman ['hentʃmən] *sb* følgesvenn, tilhenger; leiesvenn, medløper.

herald ['herəld] **I** *sb* **1** herold, utroper; **2** budbærer; forløper; **II** *vt* forkynne; innvarsle; bære bud (om). **heraldic** [he'rældɪk] *adj* heraldisk. **heraldry** ['herəldrɪ] *sb* heraldikk.

herb [hɜ:b] *sb* urt; plante. **herbage** ['hɜ:bidʒ] *sb* **1** urter; planter; **2** *gml* beiterett.

herd [hɜ:d] **I** *sb* **1** buskap, bøling; **2** (-)gjeter; *gml* (-)hyrde; **3** horde, masse; **II** *vb* **1** gjete; drive sammen; **2** flokke seg (sammen). **herdsman** ['hɜ:dzmən] *sb* gjeter.

here [hɪə] *adv* **1** her; *~'s how!* skål! *~'s to John* skål for John! *~ you are* vær så god (dvs her er det du/De har bedt om, sett etter etc); **2** hit. **hereabouts** [ˌhɪərə'baʊts] *adv* her omkring; her i nærheten. **hereafter** [ˌhɪər'ɑ:ftə] **1** *adv* heretter; **2** *sb: the ~* fremtiden; livet etter dette. **hereby** ['hɪəbaɪ] *adv* herved.

hereditary [hɪ'redɪtrɪ] *adj* **1** arvelig; arve-; **2** nedarvet. **heredity** [hɪ'redətɪ] *sb* **1** arvelighet; **2** *gml* slektsarv.

heresy ['herəsɪ] *sb* kjetteri. **heretic** ['herətɪk] **1** *adj = heretical*; **2** *sb* kjetter. **heretical** [hɪ'retɪkl] *adj* kjettersk.

hereupon [ˌhɪərə'pɒn] *adv* heretter; derpå, så. **herewith** [ˌhɪə'wɪð] *adv* hermed.

heritage ['herɪtɪdʒ] *sb* arv.

hermit ['hɜ:mɪt] *sb* eneboer, eremitt.

hernia ['hɜ:nɪə] *sb* brokk.

hero ['hɪərəʊ] *sb* helt. **heroic** [hɪ'rəʊɪk] **I** *adj* heltemodig, helte-; heroisk; **II** *sb* **1** heltedikt; **2** *fl* høyttravende stil; storslagne fakter; heltepositur. **heroine** ['herəʊɪn] *sb* heltinne. **heroismn** ['herəʊɪzəm] *sb* heltemot, heroisme.

heron ['herən] *sb* hegre.

herring ['herɪŋ] *sb* sild.

hesitant ['hezɪtənt] *adj* nølende, ubesluttsom. **hesitate** ['hezɪteɪt] *vi* nøle; betenke seg; være ubesluttsom. **hesitation** [ˌhezɪ'teɪʃn] *sb* nøling *etc.*

hew [hju:] *vb* hugge (og hugge til/ut); *~ down* felle; hugge ned.

hey [heɪ] *interj* hei; *~ presto!* hokus pokus! simsalabim! vips! **heyday** ['heɪdeɪ] *sb* glanstid; høydepunkt.

hibernate ['haɪbəneɪt] *vi* overvintre; gå/ligge i dvale/hi. **hibernation** [ˌhɪbə'neɪʃn] *sb* overvintring; dvale.

hiccough, hiccup ['hɪkʌp] **1** *sb* hikk; hikke, hikking; **2** *vi* hikke.

hide [haɪd] **A 1** *sb: (~-away, ~-out)* gjemmested, skjul; dekning; **2** *vb* gjemme/skjule (seg); gå/ligge i dekning; *(play at) ~-and-seek* (leke) gjemsel; **B 1** *sb* hud, skinn; **2** *vt* flå; banke, denge. **hidden layer** *sb petro* blindsone; skjult lag.

hideous ['hɪdɪəs] *adj* avskyelig; fæl, grusom; skrekkelig.

hiding ['haɪdɪŋ] *sb* **1** gjemmested; dekning, skjul; **2** (omgang) juling.

high [haɪ] **I** *adj* **1** høy (og lang, stor; kraftig, sterk; intens, skingrende; fornem, høytstående; utrert, ytterliggående; *slang* høy = beruset, narkotisert etc); *~ and dry* på grunn (om skip); *fig* på bar bakke; isolert; (satt) utenfor; *~ and mighty* mektig; arrogant, storsnutet; *have a ~ old time (dgl)* ha det veldig gøy; **2** (lett) bedervet/skjemt *etc*; **II** *adv* høyt *etc*; høy-; **III** *sb* høydepunkt (og høyeste posisjon/punkt; *dgl* høygir, høytrykk, høyere/videregående skole, høyeste kort etc); *on ~* i det høye (dvs himmelen). **high|ball** *sb, især US* (whisky)pjolter. **~-born** *adj* høybåren; av fornem ætt. **~brow** *adj, sb* intellektuell (person); åndssnobb(et). **~-class** *adj* førsteklasses. **~ command** *sb mil* overkommando. **~-falutin(g), ~-flown** *adj* høyttravende; bombastisk, svulstig. **~-handed** *adj* arrogant; egen|mektig, -rådig; hensynsløs, vilkårlig. **~ hat** *sb* floss(hatt). **~ jump** *sb sport* høydesprang. **Highlander** *sb* (skotsk) høylender. **highlight 1** *sb, især fl* høylys; *fig* høydepunkt; **2** *vt* kaste lys/*fig* glans over; fremheve. **highly** *adv* høylig (og høyst; i høy(este) grad; meget, svært; sterkt etc); *speak ~ of* snakke pent/rosende om; *think ~ of* ha høye tanker om. **high|-minded** *adj* høysinnet. **~-necked** *adj* høyhalset. **~ness** *sb* høyhet. **~-octane** *adj petro* høyoktan(-). **~powered** *adj* dynamisk, energisk; meget kraftig. **~-ranking** *adj* høy (dvs av høy rang); høytstående. **~-rise** *sb* høyhus. **~road** = *~way*. **~-run** *adj petro = ~-octane*. **~ school** *sb* høyere/videregående skole; høyskole. **~-sounding** *adj* rungende; bombastisk, svulstig; hul. **~ spirits** *sb fl* strålende humør. **~ street** *sb* hovedgate. **~strung** *adj* (over)|nervøs, (-)anspent. **~-tail** *vb US slang* følge hakk i hæl; rømme; stikke av. **~ tide** *sb* flo, høyvann. **~ treason** *sb* høyforræderi. **~way** *sb* hovedvei, riksvei; allfarvei (også *fig*); direkte rute/vei; *the Highway Code* veitrafikkloven. **~ words** *sb fl* harde ord; trette.

hike [haɪk] *dgl* **1** *sb* (fot)tur, vandring: **2** *vi* dra/gå på fottur. **hiker** ['haɪkə] *sb* fotturist, vandrer.

hilarious [hɪ'leərɪəs] *adj* lystig, løssluppen; (overstadig) munter. **hilarity** [hɪ'lærətɪ] *sb* lystighet *etc*.

hill [hɪl] *sb* **1** høyde; kolle, ås; *go over the ~ (US slang)* rømme; *mil* ta tjuvperm; **2** bakke; **3** haug. **hill-billy** ['hɪlbɪlɪ] *sb US* fjellbonde. **hillock** ['hɪlək] *sb* (liten) haug; tue. **hillside** ['hɪlsaɪd] *sb* li, åsside.

hilt [hɪlt] *sb* hjalt, håndtak; *up to the ~* fullstendig; helt og holdent.

hind [haɪnd] **A** *adj* bakre-, bak-; **B** *sb* hind; **C** *sb gml* gårds|arbeider, -gutt.

hinder ['hɪndə] *vt* (for)hindre; forsinke, hefte; hemme. **hindrance** ['hɪndrəns] *sb* (for)hindring.

hindsight ['haɪndsaɪt] *sb* etterpåklokskap.

hinge [hɪndʒ] **I** *sb* hengsel; **II** *vb* **1** hengsle; sette hengsel/hengsler på; **2** *~ (up)on* avhenge av; dreie seg om.

hint [hɪnt] **1** *sb* antydning, hentydning; råd, vink; **2** *vb* antyde; ymte (om); *~ at* hentyde til.

hip [hɪp] **A** *sb* hofte; **B** *sb* nype; **C** *adj slang* med (på leken/notene etc); ukonvensjonell; obs(ervant), våken. **hip-flask** *sb* (lomme)lerke.

hippo ['hɪpəʊ] *dgl fork* for **hippopotamus** [ˌhɪpə'pɒtəməs] *sb* flodhest.

hire ['haɪə] **I** *sb* **1** (ut)leie; *for ~* til leie; **2** leie(avgift), vederlag; lønn; **II** *vt* ansette, feste; (for)hyre; leie. **hire|ling** ['haɪəlɪŋ] *sb* leiesvenn. **~-purchase** *sb* avbetaling.

hiss [hɪs] **1** *sb* fresing *etc*; **2** *vb* frese, hvese; visle; *~ off* pipe ut.

historian [hɪ'stɔ:rɪən] *sb* historiker. **historic** [hɪ'stɒrɪk] *adj* historisk (dvs av historisk betydning); berømt, viktig. **historical** [hɪ'stɒrɪkl] *adj* historisk, historie-. **history** ['hɪstərɪ] *sb* historie.

hit [hɪt] **I** *sb* **1** slag; treff; *fig* fulltreffer; lykketreff; suksess; *happy ~* lykkelig innfall/påfunn; treffende bemerkning etc; **2** hipp, stikk; **II** *vb* **1** slå; ramme, treffe; *~ off* ta på kornet (dvs etterligne etc treffende); **2** passe; *~ it off* komme (godt) overens; **3** *~ (up)on* finne; komme over; råke/treffe på.

hitch [hɪtʃ] **I** *sb* **1** rykk; **2** hake (især *fig*); (for)hindring; **3** *sjø* stikk; **II** *vb* **1** *~ up* hale (dra, heise etc) opp; **2** feste; binde, knyte; hekte/henge (seg) opp; **3** *dgl* = **hitch-hike** ['hɪtʃhaɪk] *vi dgl* haike.

hither ['hɪðə] *adv gml* hit. **hitherto** [ˌhɪðə'tu:] *adv* hittil.

hive [haɪv] **I** *sb* **1** *(bee~)* (bi)kube (og bisverm); **2** mylder, vrimmel; **II** *vb* sette i (bi)kube; bo/leve i samfunn (som bier).

hoard [hɔ:d] **1** *sb* forråd, lager; *fig* fond, skatt; **2** *vb* lagre; legge (seg) opp; hamstre. **hoarding** ['hɔ:dɪŋ] *sb* **A** lagring; hamstring; **B** (planke)gjerde.

hoarfrost ['hɔ:frɒst] *sb* rim(frost).

hoarse [hɔ:s] *adj* hes.

hoary ['hɔ:rɪ] *adj* rimet; *fig* grå(håret), hvithåret; eldgammel.

hoax [həʊks] **I** *sb* **1** juks, lureri; **2** bløff; skrøne; **3** puss, skøyerstrek; **II** *vt* **1** jukse, lure; bløffe; **2** spille et puss.

hobble ['hɒbl] **1** *sb* halting; **2** *vb* halte; hinke, humpe.

hobby ['hɒbɪ] *sb* hobby. **hobby-horse** *sb* gyngehest; *også fig* kjepphest.

hobnail ['hɒbneɪl] *sb* sko|besparer, (-)nudd.

hobnob ['hɒbnɒb] *vi* omgås familiært.

hoe [həʊ] **1** *sb* hakke; **2** *vb* hakke, hyppe.

hog [hɒg] *sb* **1** galte; **2** grobian.

hoist [hɔɪst] **1** *sb* heiseinnretning, vinsj; **2** *vt* heise.

hold [həʊld] **A I** *sb* **1** grep, tak; **2** feste, hold; holdepunkt; **II** *vb* **1** holde (og holde fast (ved); holde på etc); **2** holde (oppe); bære, (under)støtte; **3** (inne)holde, romme; **4** holde (stilling etc); bekle (embete); (inne)ha, eie; fastholde; *~ office* ha/sitte med (regjerings)makten; *~ one's ground/one's own* hevde/klare seg; holde stand; **5** ha (i hodet/tankene); nære; omgås (med); *~ in contempt* nære/vise forakt for; **6** anse/holde for; mene; fremholde, hevde; **7** stanse, stoppe; holde igjen/tilbake; beherske/holde seg; *~ it!* hold an! stopp/vent litt! *~ one's peace/tongue* holde fred/munn; **8** arrangere; (av)holde; **9** holde (seg); vare (ved); ikke gå i stykker *etc*; *~ good/true* holde stikk; gjelde; **10** *med adv/prep ~ it* **against** *him etc* kritisere ham etc for det; legge ham etc det til last; *~ (oneself)* **aloof** holde seg for seg selv; *~* **back** hindre, stanse; holde igjen/tilbake; holde seg tilbake; *~* **by** holde fast ved; holde seg til; *~* **down** holde ned(e); beholde; holde på; *~* **forth** fortsette; fremholde, hevde; *~* **in** holde inn(e); holde i tømme; beherske/holde seg; *~* **off** holde (seg) borte (unna/vekk); hefte, oppholde; *~* **on** holde fast (*to* på/ved); stanse, vente; *~* **out** holde (og holde stand, holde ut; vare; rekke/strekke til etc); holde/rekke frem; *fig* forespeile; *~* **over** utsette; *~* **to** holde fast på/ved; *~* **up** holde opp(e); holde frem (som eksempel etc); hefte, oppholde; overfalle, rane; *~* **with** holde/være enig med; **B** *sb sjø* (laste)rom. **hold-all** ['həʊldɔ:l] *sb* bag; koffert; (reise)veske. **holder** ['həʊldə] *sb* holder (og håndtak, skaft; feste, klemme; eier, innehaver; ihendehaver etc). **holding** ['həʊldɪŋ] *sb* **1** avholdelse; **2** (fast) eiendom; **3** aksje (og aksjepost). **hold | mode** *sb data* holdemodus. *~* **range** *sb data* holdeområde. **~-up** ['həʊldʌp] *sb* overfall, ran.

hole [həʊl] **I** *sb* **1** hull; åpning; hule; **2** *dgl* knipe, vanskelighet; **II** *vb* gjennomhulle; lage/slå hull i.

holiday ['hɒlədɪ] *sb* **1** helligdag, helg; **2** *fl* fridager; ferie. **holiday|-maker** *sb* feriegjest, ferierende. *~* **resort** *sb* feriested. **holiness** ['həʊlɪnɪs] *sb* hellighet.

hollow ['hɒləʊ] **I** *adj* **1** (inn)hul, tom; **2** inn|fallen, sunken; **II** *sb* fordypning; uthulning; hull; **III** *vt: ~ out* hule ut.

holly ['hɒlɪ] *sb* kristtorn.

holster ['həʊlstə] *sb* (pistol)hylster.

holy ['həʊlɪ] *adj* hellig.

homage ['hɒmɪdʒ] *sb* **1** hyllest; *pay ~ to* hylle; **2**

hist troskapsed (til føydalherre).

home [həʊm] **I** *som adj* **1** hjemlig; hjem-, hjemme-; **2** innenlands, innenriks(-); *Home Office* innenriksdepartementet; *Home Rule* selvstyre; **II** *adv* **1** hjem (og *dgl* hjemme); **2** hjemme-; **3** *fig* i blinken; i mål; *bring ~ to* overbevise; gjøre det klart for; *drive ~* innprente; slå fast; **III** *sb* **1** hjem (og hjem|by, -land, stavn, -sted etc); *make oneself at ~* finne seg til rette; late som man er hjemme; **2** hjem (dvs internat, pensjonat, aldershjem, sykehjem etc); institusjon; **3** *sport* (eget) mål; **IV** *vb* **1** finne veien hjem; sette kursen hjemover; **2** *mil, om raketter etc* finne målet; (mål)-styre. **home|coming** *sb* hjemkomst. **~ computer** *sb data* hjemmedatamaskin. **~-grown** *adj* hjemmeavlet. **~ help** *sb* hjemmehjelp. **~land** *sb* hjemland. **~less** *adj* hjemløs. **~ly** ['həʊmlɪ] *adj* **1** enkel, folkelig; dagligdags; *især US* lite pen; **2** hjemlig. **~-made** *adj* hjemmelaget. **~sick** *adj* syk av hjemlengsel. **~-spun** *adj* hjemmespunnet; *dgl* hjemmelaget, tarvelig. **~stead** *sb* (selvstendig) gårdsbruk. **~ team** *sb sport* hjemmelag. **~ truth** *sb* ubehagelig sannhet. **~ward** ['həʊmwəd] *adj* hjem-; *~ bound* på hjemvei; med kurs hjemover. **~wards** ['həʊmwədz] *adv* hjemover. **~work** *sb* hjemme|arbeid, -lekse.

homicide ['həʊmɪsaɪd] *sb* **1** drap, mord; **2** drapsmann, morder.

homogeneous [ˌhəʊmə'dʒi:nɪəs] *adj* ensartet, homogen.

hone [həʊn] *sb, vt* bryne.

honest ['ɒnɪst] *adj* **1** ærlig; hederlig, oppriktig; **2** *gml* ærbar. **honestly** ['ɒnɪstlɪ] *adv* ærlig *etc*; oppriktig/ærlig talt. **honesty** ['ɒnəstɪ] *sb* ærlighet *etc*.

honey ['hʌnɪ] *sb* **1** honning; **2** *dgl, i tiltale* kjæreste; *oftest* søta, vesla; vennen min *etc*. **honey|comb** *sb* bikake, vokskake. **~combed** *adj* gjennomhullet (som en bikake); underminert; gjennomsyret. **~moon** *sb, vi* **1** (feire) hvetebrødsdager; **2** (dra på) bryllupsreise. **~suckle** *sb* kaprifolium.

honorary ['ɒnrərɪ] *adj* honorær, æres-. **honour** ['ɒnə] **I** *sb* **1** ære; oppriktighet; sømmelighetssans; *~ bright!* (på) æresord! *in ~ bound* æresforpliktet; *word of ~* æresord; **2** respekt, ærbødighet; honnør, æresbevisning; *in ~ of* til ære for; **3** heder (og hederstegn); utmerkelse(r); **4** pryd, stolthet; **5** *Your Honour* form for tiltale til visse embetspersoner; på norsk kan brukes «ærede» eller «herr» pluss yrkestittel, ofte bare tittel og navn; **II** *vt* **1** hedre, ære; respektere; **2** *merk* honorere, innfri; betale. **honourable** ['ɒnrəbl] *adj* **1** hederlig, rettskaffen; **2** ærefull; **3** (høy)aktet, æret (især brukt i tiltale eller formell omtale, jf *honour I 5*).

hood [hʊd] **I** *sb* **1** hette (og damp-, røykhette; kappe etc); **2** *US* (bil)panser; **II** *vt: ~ed* med hette *etc*.

hoodlum ['hu:dləm] *US slang = hooligan.*

hoodwink ['hʊdwɪŋk] *vt* bedra; føre bak lyset.

hoof [hu:f] *sb* hov; klov.

hook [hʊk] **I** *sb* krok (og hake, hekte; knagg; sigd etc); *~s and eyes* hekter (og maljer); *by ~ or by crook* med det gode eller det onde; *swallow ~, line, and sinker (fig)* sluke rått; **II** *vb* **1** feste (med hekte, krok etc); *~ up* hake/hekte sammen; **2** ta (med krok); *fig* få på kroken; **3** krumme, krøke. **hooker** ['hʊkə] *sb* hore. **hook-up** *sb* sammenkobling, tilknytning; samkjøring; forbindelse, samband; allianse.

hooligan ['hu:lɪgən] *sb* bølle, ramp.

hoop [hu:p] **A I** *sb* **1** ring; *især* tønnebånd; trillehjul; **2** bøyle; **II** *vt* beslå med tønnebånd; **B** = *whoop.*

hoot [hu:t] **I** *sb* **1** tuting, uling; piping; **2** *slang* døyt, grann; **II** *vb* tute, ule. **hooter** ['hu:tə] *sb* sirene; (damp)fløyte; (bil)horn.

hop [hɒp] **A I** *sb* **1** hopp(ing); sprang; hink(ing), hump(ing); **2** (etappe av) flytur; **3** *slang* dans, svingom; **II** *vb* hoppe, springe (og hoppe/springe over); hinke, humpe; **B 1** *sb bot* humle; **2** *vi* plukke humle.

hope [həʊp] **1** *sb* håp; *beyond/past ~* hinsides håp/redning; **2** *vb* håpe (*for* på); *~ against ~* håpe tross alt; klamre seg til håpet. **hope|ful** ['həʊpfʊl] *adj* forhåpningsfull, håpefull. **~less** ['həʊplɪs] *adj* håpløs.

hopper ['hɒpə] **A** *sb* **1** hopper (etc, jf *hop A II*); **2** losse|sjakt, -slisk; **3** binge; (samle)kasse; **B** *sb* humleplukker.

hopscotch ['hɒpskɒtʃ] *sb* paradis(hopping).

horde [hɔ:d] *sb* **1** (nomade)stamme; **2** flokk, horde.

horizon [hə'raɪzn] *sb* horisont. **horizontal** [ˌhɒrɪ'zɒntl] *adj, sb* horisontal (linje, stilling etc).

horn [hɔ:n] **I** *sb* horn; *fog-~* tåkelur; **II** *vt* **1** sette horn på; **2** stange; ta på hornene. **horn|less** *adj* hornløs, kollet. **~owl** *sb* hornugle. **~-rimmed spectacles** *sb fl* hornbriller.

hornet ['hɔ:nɪt] *sb* geitehams, veps. **hornet's nest** *sb* vepsebol.

horny ['hɔ:nɪ] *adj* **1** hornaktig; hard; med treller; **2** *dgl* kåt.

horrible ['hɒrəbl] *adj* **1** gruoppvekkende; grusom, skrekkelig; **2** *dgl* fæl, gyselig, reddsom. **horrid** ['hɒrɪd] *adj* **1** forferdelig, skrekkelig; **2** ekkel; gyselig. **horrify** ['hɒrɪfaɪ] *vt* forferde; fylle/slå med redsel. **horror** ['hɒrə] *sb* **1** gru, skrekk; **2** avsky; avskyelig/fælt syn *etc*. **horror|-stricken, ~-struck** *adj* redselsslagen, skrekkslagen.

horse [hɔ:s] **I** *sb* **1** hest; *mil koll* kavaleri; *dark ~* outsider; uberegnelig faktor; *on ~back* ridende; til hest; **2** bukk, stativ; **II** *vb* **1** ri; *~ around (slang)* husere; holde leven; **2** forsyne med hester. **horse|-chestnut** *sb* hestekastanje. **~fly** *sb* klegg. **~man** *sb* (dyktig) rytter (om mann). **~manship** *sb* ridekunst. **~-play** *sb* grov spøk. **~power** *sb* hestekraft. **~race** *sb* hesteveddeløp. **~-radish** *sb* pepperrot. **~-sense** *sb* sunt vett. **~shoe** *sb* hestesko. **~whip** *sb, vt* (slå med) ridepisk. **~woman** *sb* (dyktig) rytter (om kvinne).

hose [həʊz] **A 1** *sb* (vann)slange; **2** *vt* spyle; **B** *sb* **1** *hist* hoser (= bukser); **2** *koll merk* strømper, strømpevarer. **hose | float** *sb petro* slangeflottør. **~ line** *sb petro* produksjonsslange. **hosier** ['həʊzɪə] *sb* trikotasjehandler. **hosiery** ['həʊzɪərɪ] *sb* trikotasje(varer);

strømper (og strømpevarer); trikotasje|fabrikk, -forretning.

hospitable ['hɒspɪtəbl] *adj* gjestfri. **hospital** ['hɒspɪtl] *sb* hospital, sykehus. **hospitality** [ˌhɒspɪ'tælətɪ] *sb* gjestfrihet. **hospitalize** ['hɒspɪtəlaɪz] *vt US* legge inn på sykehus.

host [həʊst] *sb* **A** flokk, mengde; hær(skare); **B 1** vert; *fl* vertskap; **2** (hotell)vert; vertshusholder; **C** *(rel) Host* hostie, nattverdsbrød. **hostess** ['həʊstɪs] *sb* vertinne.

hostage ['hɒstɪdʒ] *sb* gissel.

hostel ['hɒstəl] *sb* **1** *gml* gjestgiveri, herberge; **2** hospits, internat; studenthjem *etc*; *youth* ~ ungdomsherberge.

hostile ['hɒstaɪl] *adj* fiendtlig(sinnet). **hostility** [hɒ'stɪlətɪ] *sb* fiendskap; fiendtlighet.

hot [hɒt] **I** *adj* **1** het; (svært og især ubehagelig) varm; **2** brennende (især *fig* = heftig, intens; ivrig, lidenskapelig etc); *om krydder etc* skarp, sterk; **3** oppfarende; hissig, snarsint; voldsom; **4** (rykende) fersk; ~ *on the track/trail of* like i hælene på; **5** farlig, risikabel; vanskelig, vrien; **6** *elek* strømførende; **7** radioaktiv; *dgl* varm; **II** *adv* hett, varmt *etc*. **hot | air** *sb* varmluft; *fig* skryt; tomt prat. **~bed** *sb* mistbenk; *fig* arnested. **~-blooded** *adj* varmblodig; *fig* hetlevret, hissig. **~head** *sb* hissigpropp. **~-headed** *adj* hissig. **~ dog** *sb* pølse med lumpe. **~house** *sb* drivhus. **~ line** *sb* direkte (telefon)linje (især mellom statsoverhoder). **~ news** *sb fl* fersk(e) (og især sensasjonell(e)) nyhet(er). **~ spot** *sb dgl* knipe, vanskelighet. **~ water** *sb* varmt vann; *især fig* vanskeligheter. **~-water bottle** *sb* varmeflaske.

hound [haʊnd] **I** *sb* **1** jakthund (især revehund, støver); **2** kjøter, usling; **II** *vt* jage/drive jakt på (med hunder); forfølge, jage.

hour ['aʊə] *sb* time; klokkeslett, tidspunkt; stund, øyeblikk; *fl* arbeidstid, kontortid, åpningstid; *after ~s* etter stengetid; *at all ~s (of the day)* til alle døgnets tider; *by the ~* for timen; per time; *for ~s (and ~s)* i timevis; *within the ~* i løpet av/innen en time. **hourly** ['aʊəlɪ] *adj, adv* **1** (som skjer etc) en gang i timen/hver time; **2** (som skjer etc) stadig; **3** (som kan skje etc) når som helst.

house I [haʊs] *sb* **1** hus (og bygning, (by)gård; bolig, hjem; *fig* familie, husholdning etc); *like a ~ on fire (dgl)* glimrende, utmerket; **2** (handels)hus; firma, selskap; **3** familie, slekt; **4** kammer (i nasjonalforsamling); ting; *the House (dgl)* parlamentet, tinget (og *fork* for *the House of Commons* Underhuset; *the House of Lords* Overhuset; *the House of Representatives (US)* Representantenes hus); **5** sal; (teater)salong; *fig* forestilling; publikum; *bring down the ~* gjøre stormende lykke; **II** [haʊz] *vt* **1** huse; gi husly; romme; **2** lagre, oppbevare. **house|-agent** *sb* eiendomsmegler. **~boat** *sb* husbåt. **~-breaker** *sb* innbruddstyv (som opererer om dagen (jf *burglar*). **~-broken** *adj* renslig, stueren (om f.eks. katt). **~hold** *sb* husholdning; husstand; *som adj* husholdnings-. **~holder** *sb* huseier; familie|far, -overhode; forsørger. **~hold word** *sb* begrep (dvs velkjent ord, uttrykk, også om ting). **~keeper** *sb* husholder(ske). **~maid** *sb* stuepike, tjenestepike. **~master** *sb* lærer ved internatskole som også har oppsyn med et (av) internat(ene). **~mother** *sb* (hus)mor ved internatskole etc. **~top** *sb* hustak. **~wife A** ['haʊswaɪf] *sb* husmor; **B** ['hʌzɪf] *sb* syetui, sysaker. **~work** *sb* husarbeid. **housing** ['haʊzɪŋ] **I** *adj* bolig-; bygnings-; **II** *sb* **1** hus(rom); bolig(er); **2** innlosjering.

hovel ['hɒvl] *sb* rønne, skur.

hover ['hɒvə] *vi* **1** sveve; **2** vente; holde seg i nærheten. **hovercraft** ['hɒvəkrɑ:ft] *sb* luftputefartøy.

how [haʊ] *adv* **1** hvordan; ~ *about?* hva med? *how are you?* hvordan går det/har du det/står det til? ~ *come (US dgl)* hvorfor; hvordan kan det ha seg; ~ *do you do* (sies stort sett bare når man blir presentert for en fremmed, og er da nærmest ≈) goddag/det gleder meg *etc*; *here's ~! (US dgl)* skål! **2** hvor; ~ *many/much* hvor mange/mye; ~ *nice* (nei) så hyggelig! **3** *US dgl* hva (for noe). **however** [haʊ'evə] **I** *adv* **1** hvor(dan) ... enn; uansett hvor(dan); ~ *hard she works* hvor hardt hun enn arbeider; **2** hvordan i all verden; **II** *konj* **2** dog, enda, likevel; **2** men; imidlertid.

howl [haʊl] *sb, vb* hyl(e), ul(e). **howler** ['haʊlə] *sb* **1** hyler *etc*; **2** *dgl* brøler, tabbe. **howling** ['haʊlɪŋ] *adj* **1** hylende *etc*; **2** *slang* dundrende; forrykende; fenomenal.

hub [hʌb] *sb* nav; midtpunkt, sentrum. **hub-cap** *sb* hjulkapsel.

hubhub ['hʌbʌb] *sb* skrål(ing); leven, spetakkel; hurlumhei.

huckleberry ['hʌklberɪ] *sb* skinntryte.

huddle ['hʌdl] **I** *sb* flokk, klynge; **II** *vb* **1** flokke (klumpe, klynge) seg sammen; stue sammen; **2** ~ *up* krype sammen (med knærne oppunder seg).

hue [hju:] *sb* **A** farge; nyanse, skjær; **B** ~ *and cry* alarm, anskrik.

huff [hʌf] *sb* humørsyke; surhet. **huffy** ['hʌfɪ] *adj* gretten, sur.

hug [hʌg] **I** *sb* klem; omfavnelse; **II** *vt* **1** klemme, omfavne; holde/trykke inn til seg; **2** klamre/klynge seg til; **3** *sjø* holde seg/seile tett inn til/opp mot.

huge [hju:dʒ] *adj* diger, enorm, kolossal, veldig.

hulk [hʌlk] *sb* **1** holk; gammelt skip (og skipsskrog); **2** bamse, rusk; brande. **hulking** ['hʌlkɪŋ] *adj* diger; tung (og klosset).

hull [hʌl] **A** *sb* (skips)skrog; **B 1** *sb* hams, skall; **2** *vt* skrelle.

hum [hʌm] **I** *interj* hm; **II** *sb* **1** nynning; **2** summing, surring; **3** kremt(ing); **III** *vb* **1** nynne, småsynge; **2** summe, surre; **3** ~ *and haw* harke og kremte; rømme seg.

human ['hju:mən] **I** *adj* **1** menneskelig, menneske-; **2** = *humane 1*; **II** *sb (~ being)* menneske; menneskelig vesen. **humane** [hju:'meɪn] *adj* **1** human, (med)menneskelig; hensynsfull; **2** = **humanistic** [ˌhju:mə'nɪstɪk] *adj* humanistisk; human-. **humani-**

tarian [hju:ˌmænɪ'teərɪən] **1** *adj* humanitær; menneske(venn)lig; **2** *sb* menneskevenn; filantrop; humanist. **humanity** [hju:'mænətɪ] *sb* **1** menneskehet(en); menneskene; **2** humanitet, (med)menneskelighet; **3** *the Humanities* de humanistiske fag/vitenskaper. **humanize** ['hju:mənaɪz] *vb* humanisere; bli/gjøre menneskelig.

humble ['hʌmbl] **I** *adj* **1** beskjeden, tilbakeholden; ydmyk; **2** enkel, ringe; fattig; **II** *vt* fornedre; ydmyke.

humbug ['hʌmbʌg] **I** *interj* sludder! **II** *sb* **1** juks; bedrag, svindel; **2** humbugmaker, juksemaker; svindler.

humdrum ['hʌmdrʌm] *adj* ensformig, monoton; kjedelig.

humid ['hju:mɪd] *adj* fuktig. **humidity** [hju:'mɪdətɪ] *sb* fuktighet.

humiliate [hju:'mɪlɪeɪt] *vt* ydmyke. **humiliation** [hju:ˌmɪlɪ'eɪʃn] *sb* ydmykelse. **humility** [hju:'mɪlətɪ] *sb* ydmykhet; underdanighet.

hummock ['hʌmək] *sb* haug, høyde.

humorous ['hju:mərəs] *adj* humoristisk. **humour** ['hju:mə] **I** *sb* **1** *(sense of ~)* humor (og humoristisk sans); **2** humør; (sinns)stemning; **3** innfall, lune; **II** føye; gi etter for.

hump [hʌmp] *sb* kul, pukkel; klump. **humpback** ['hʌmpbæk] *sb* pukkelrygg (og pukkelrygget person). **humpbacked** ['hʌmpbækt] *adj* pukkelrygget.

Hun [hʌn] *sb* **1** hunner; *fig* vandal; **2** *slang* tysker (især tysk soldat).

hunch [hʌntʃ] **I** *sb* **1** kul, pukkel; klump; **2** klump; tykk skive; tykt stykke; **3** *oppr US slang* (forut)anelse, varsel; mistanke; **II** *vt (~ one's back)* skyte rygg; gjøre seg skutrygget. **hunch-back(ed)** ['hʌntʃbæk(t)] = *hump-back(ed)*.

hundredweight ['hʌndrədweɪt] *sb* en vektenhet, se midtsidene.

hunger ['hʌŋgə] **1** *sb* hunger, sult; **2** *vi* sulte; *også fig* hungre (*for* etter). **hungry** ['hʌŋgrɪ] *adj* sulten.

hunt [hʌnt] **I** *sb* **1** jakt (i England især parforsejakt, revejakt til hest, samt jaktdistrikt og jaktselskap); **2** leting; **II** *vb* **1** drive jakt/jakte på; jage; ~ *down* (jage og) fange; (oppspore og) innhente; **2** lete (*for* etter); ~ *out/up* lete frem; snuse opp. **hunter** ['hʌntə] *sb* **1** jeger; **2** jakthest. **huntsman** ['hʌntsmən] *sb* **1** jeger; **2** pikør.

hurdle ['hɜ:dl] **I** *sb* **1** (flyttbart) risgjerde; **2** hekk (til hekkeløp); hinder; *fig* (for)hindring; **3** *fl* = *~-race*; **II** *vt* gjerde inn. **hurdle-race** *sb* hekkeløp; hinder|løp, -ritt.

hurl [hɜ:l] *vt* slynge; kaste, kyle, slenge.

hurrah [hʊ'rɑ:], **hurray** [hʊ'reɪ] **1** *interj, sb* hurra; **2** *vi* rope hurra.

hurricane ['hʌrɪkən] *sb* orkan. **hurricane|-lamp, ~-lantern** *sb* stormlykt.

hurried ['hʌrɪd] *adj* **1** drevet, (opp)jaget; forkavet; **2** rask; hastig, skyndsom; **3** flyktig. **hurry** ['hʌrɪ] **I** *sb* hast(verk); travelhet; *fig* lettvinthet; *in a ~* i en fart; *be in a ~* ha det travelt; *there's no ~* det haster ikke; **II** *vb* **1** skynde seg; **2** forsere; drive (jage, skynde etc) på.

hurt [hɜ:t] **I** *adj* **1** skadet; **2** *fig* såret; krenket, støtt; **II** *sb* skade; **III** *vb* **1** skade; **2** *fig* såre; fornærme, krenke; **3** smerte; gjøre vondt.

hurtle ['hɜ:tl] *vb* **1** fare, rase, styrte, suse; *gml* kollidere; **2** kaste, kyle, slenge; slynge.

husband ['hʌzbənd] **1** *sb* (ekte)mann; husbond; **2** *vt* husholderere/økonomisere med; spare på. **husbandry** ['hʌzbəndrɪ] *sb* **1** husholderering, økonomisering; sparsommelighet; **2** *gml* jordbruk.

hush [hʌʃ] **I** *interj* hysj! **II** *sb* stillhet; taushet; **III** *vb* **1** hysje (på); bringe til taushet; ~ *up* dysse ned; **2** tie (stille); være stille. **hush-money** *sb* bestikkelse (dvs betaling for å holde tett).

husk [hʌsk] **1** *sb* hams, skall; *fl* agner; **2** *vt* ta hamsen *etc* av. **husky** ['hʌskɪ] **I** *adj* **1** med hams *etc*; **2** *fig* tørr; hes, ru; rusten; **3** *dgl* røslig, svær; **II** *sb* brande, rusk; kraftkar.

hussy ['hʌsɪ] *sb* **1** flyfille, tøyte; **2** nebbe(nose).

hustle ['hʌsl] **I** *sb* **1** dytting *etc*; trengsel; **2** livlighet; travelhet; fart, kjør; **II** *vb* dytte, skubbe; kjase, mase.

hut [hʌt] *sb* hytte; skjul, skur; *mil* brakke.

hutch [hʌtʃ] *sb* **1** bur (til kaniner etc); **2** binge, bøle; kasse, kiste; **3** skjul, skur; rønne.

hydrogen ['haɪdrədʒən] *sb* hydrogen, vannstoff. **hydrogen bomb** *sb* hydrogenbombe.

hymn [hɪm] **1** *sb* hymne, lovsang; salme; **2** *vt* lovsynge.

hyphen ['haɪfn] **1** *sb* bindestrek; **2** *vt* = **hyphenate** ['haɪfəneɪt] *vt* forsyne med bindestrek; sette bindestrek mellom. **hyphenation** [ˌhaɪfə'neɪʃn] *sb* orddeling (med bindestrek). **hyphenation program** *sb data* orddelingsprogram.

hypnotic [hɪp'nɒtɪk] **I** *adj* hypnotisk, søvndyssende; **II** *sb* **1** hypnotisert person; **2** sovemiddel. **hypnotize** ['hɪpnətaɪz] *vt* hypnotisere.

hypo ['haɪpəʊ] *sb* **1** *foto dgl* fiks (= fikser|bad, -væske); **2** *slang* = *hypodermic syringe*. **hypocrisy** [hɪ'pɒkrəsɪ] *sb* hykleri, hykling. **hypocrite** ['hɪpəkrɪt] *sb* hykler. **hypodermic** [ˌhaɪpəʊ'dɜ:mɪk] **I** *adj* (som gis) under huden; **II** *sb* **1** = ~ *syringe*; **2** = ~ *needle*. **hypodermic | needle** *sb* injeksjonsnål, kanyle. ~ **syringe** *sb* (injeksjons)sprøyte (og injeksjon, innsprøytning, sprøyte; *fig* opp|kvikker, -strammer; stimulans etc). **hypothesis** [haɪ'pɒθɪsɪs] hypotese, teori; formodning. **hypothetic(al)** [ˌhaɪpəʊ'θetɪk(l)] *adj* hypotetisk, teoretisk; formodet, tenkt.

hysteria [hɪ'stɪərɪə] *sb* hysteri. **hysteric(al)** [hɪ'sterɪk(l)] *adj* hysterisk. **hysterics** [hɪ'sterɪks] *sb fl* hysterisk(e) anfall; hysteri.

I

ice [aɪs] **I** *sb* **1** is; **2** iskrem; **II** *vb* **1** fryse (til); islegge(s); **2** (av)kjøle; **3** glassere (med sukkerglasur). **ice|-age** *sb* istid. **~berg** *sb* isfjell. **~-bound** *adj* islagt, tilfrosset; innefrosset. **~-breaker** *sb* isbryter. **~-cream** *sb* iskrem. **~-floe** *sb* isflak. **~-pack** *sb* pakkis. **icicle** ['aɪsɪkl] *sb* istapp. **icy** ['aɪsɪ] *adj* (is)kald, is-.

idea [aɪ'dɪə] *sb* **1** begrep, forestilling; idé; **2** formodning; (vag) anelse; **3** idé, tanke; innfall, påfunn; **4** hensikt, mening. **ideal** [aɪ'dɪəl] **I** *adj* **1** ideal(-); idémessig, idé-; **2** ideell; **II** *sb* ideal; forbilde, mønster.

identical [aɪ'dentɪkl] *adj* **1** identisk (*to/with* med); (selv)samme; **2** helt lik. **identical twins** *sb fl* eneggede tvillinger. **identification** [aɪˌdentɪfɪ'keɪʃn] *sb* **1** identifisering *etc*; identifikasjon; *fl* kjenne|merker, -tegn; **2** legitimering; *som adj* legitimasjons-. **identify** [aɪ'dentɪfaɪ] *vt* **1** identifisere; kjenne igjen; **2** *~ oneself* legitimere seg. **identity** [aɪ'dentətɪ] *sb* identitet; *som adj* identitets-; identifikasjons-, legitimasjons-.

idle ['aɪdl] **I** *adj* **1** uvirksom; (arbeids)ledig; **2** doven, lat; **3** forgjeves; intetsigende, tom; *~ reports* løse rykter; **II** *vb* **1** *(~ about)* drive dank; *~ away* kaste/sløse bort; **2** gå på tomgang. **idle | character** *sb date* tomgangstegn. **~ time** *sb data* ubenyttet tid. **idler** ['aɪdlə] *sb* dagdriver.

idol ['aɪdl] *sb* avgud. **idolatry** [aɪ'dɒlətrɪ] *sb* avgudsdyrking; forguding; blind/nesegrus beundring.

if [ɪf] *konj* **1** hvis; dersom, om; *as ~* som om; **2** *(even ~)* om så; selv om; **3** *dgl* om; *ask ~* spørre om.

ignite [ɪg'naɪt] *vb* **1** fenge; ta fyr; **2** tenne (på). **ignition** [ɪg'nɪʃn] *sb* antennelse; tenning. **ignition | flame** *sb petro* tenningsflamme. **~ point** *sb petro* tenningspunkt. **~ quality** *sb petro* tenningsegenskap.

ignominous [ˌignə'mɪnɪəs] *adj* vanærende; skammelig, skjendig; *dgl* forsmedelig. **ignominy** ['ɪgnəmɪnɪ] *sb* **1** skam, skjensel; **2** vanære; æreløs handling/oppførsel.

ignorance ['ɪgnərəns] *sb* uvitenhet. **ignorant** ['ɪgnərənt] *adj* **1** uvitende; uopplyst; **2** *~ of* ukjent med; uvitende om. **ignore** [ɪg'nɔ:] *vt* ignorere, overse; ikke kjenne til/vite om; ikke bry seg om. **ignore character** *sb data* annulleringstegn.

ill [ɪl] **I** *adj* **1** dårlig, syk; *fall/be taken ~* bli syk; **2** dårlig, ille; ond (og ondsinnet, slem, stygg etc); **II** *adv* dårlig, ille; ondt; stygt; *~ at ease* uvel; ille til mote; **III** *sb* onde; ulykke. **ill|-advised** *adj* ubesindig; uoverlagt. **~-disposed** *adj* uvennlig (stemt); gretten, sur.

illegibility [ɪˌledʒə'bɪlətɪ] *sb* uleselighet. **illegible** [ɪ'ledʒəbl] *adj* uleselig; utydelig (skrevet etc).

illegitimate [ˌɪlɪ'dʒɪtɪmət] *adj* illegitim, lovstridig; u(lov)hjemlet; **2** født utenfor ekteskap.

ill-fated *adj* skjebnesvanger; ulykksalig.

illicit [ɪ'lɪsɪt] *adj* ulovlig.

illiteracy [ɪ'lɪtərəsɪ] *sb* analfabetisme; uvitenhet. **illiterate** [ɪ'lɪtərət] **1** *adj* uvitende; *især* som verken kan lese eller skrive; **2** *sb* analfabet.

ill|-judged *adj* feilbedømt; uoverlagt. **~-mannered** *adj* udannet. **~-natured** *adj* grinet, sur. **~ness** *sb* sykdom. **~-omened** *adj* illevarslende; ulykksalig. **~-tempered** *adj* gretten; hissig. **~timed** *adj* ubeleilig; malplassert. **~-treat** *vt* mishandle; behandle dårlig.

illuminate [ɪ'lu:mɪneɪt] *vt* **1** illuminere; **2** belyse, lyse opp; belyse; opplyse; kaste lys over. **illumination** [ɪˌlu:mɪ'neɪʃn] *sb* illuminering *etc*. **illumination gas** *sb petro* lysgass.

illusion [ɪ'lu:ʒn] *sb* illusjon; innbilning. **illusory** [ɪ'lu:sərɪ] *adj* illusorisk; uvirkelig.

illustrate ['ɪləstreɪt] *vt* **1** illustrere; **2** belyse/forklare (ved hjelp av eksempler). **illustration** [ˌɪlə'streɪʃn] *sb* **1** illustrasjon; **2** forklaring/illustrering (ved hjelp av eksempler). **illustrious** [ɪ'lʌstrɪəs] *adj* **1** lysende; strålende; **2** berømt; fremragende.

image ['ɪmɪdʒ] **I** *sb* **1** bilde; **2** speilbilde; **3** (sinn)-bilde; **4** (slående) likhet; **II** *vt* **1** gjenspeile, reflektere; **2** = *imagine*. **imagery** ['ɪmɪdʒrɪ] *sb* **1** *koll* bilder; **2** billed|bruk, -språk. **imaginable** [ɪ'mædʒɪnəbl] *adj* tenkelig. **imaginary** [ɪ'mædʒɪnrɪ] *adj* innbilt, uvirkelig. **imagination** [ɪˌmædʒɪ'neɪʃn] *sb* **1** fantasi; innbilnings|evne, -kraft; **2** innbilning **imaginative** [ɪ'mædʒinətɪv] *adj* fantasi|full, -rik; oppfinnsom. **imagine** [ɪ'mædʒɪn] *vt* **1** forestille/innbille seg; **2** anta, tro; tenke.

imitate ['ɪmɪteɪt] *vt* imitere; etterligne, kopiere. **imitation** [ˌɪmɪ'teɪʃn *sb* etterligning, kopi. **imitative** ['ɪmɪtətɪv] *adj* som etterligner.

immaculate [ɪ'mækjʊlət] *adj* **1** ren, ubesmittet; **2** feilfri, ulastelig.

immaterial [ˌɪmə'tɪərɪəl] *adj* **1** immateriell, ulegemlig; uvirkelig; **2** uvesentlig.

immeasurable [ɪ'meʒərəbl] *adj* som ikke kan måles; umåtelig; uoverskuelig.

immediate [ɪ'mi:dɪət] *adj* **1** direkte, umiddelbar; **2** omgående, øyeblikkelig. **immediate | cancel** *sb data* direkteavbrudd. **immediately** [ɪ'mi:dɪətlɪ] *adv* **1** umiddelbart; like; **2** straks; omgående; øyeblikkelig.

immemorial [ˌɪmɪ'mɔ:rɪəl] *adj* **1** uminnelig; **2** eldgammel.

immense [ɪ'mens] *adj* kolossal; veldig (stor etc).

immensity [ɪ'mensətɪ] *sb* kolossal størrelse *etc.*

immerse [ɪ'mɜ:s] *vt* dyppe/senke ned (i vann etc); **2** ~ *oneself in* fordype seg i. **immersion** [ɪ-'mɜ:ʃn] *sb* neddypping *etc.*

immersion heater *sb* dyppkoker, varmekolbe.

immigrant ['ɪmɪgrənt] *sb* innvandrer. **immigrate** ['ɪmɪgreɪt] *vi* innvandre. **immigration** [ˌɪmɪ'greɪʃn] *sb* innvandring.

imminent ['ɪmɪnənt] *adj* nær (forestående); overhengende; truende.

immortalize [ɪ'mɔ:təlaɪz] *vt* gjøre udødelig; bevare for bestandig/for ettertiden.

imp [ɪmp] *sb* **1** djevelunge; **2** skøyer|fant, -unge. **impish** ['ɪmpɪʃ] *adj* skøyeraktig; trollet.

impact ['ɪmpækt] *sb* **1** (sammen)støt; (an)slag; treff; **2** (inn)virkning, inntrykk; slagkraft. **impact printer** *sb data* slagskriver.

impair [ɪm'peə] *vt* skade; forringe, svekke.

impale [ɪm'peɪl] *vt* spidde.

impart [ɪm'pɔ:t] *vt* gi (videre); meddele (videre).

impasse [æm'pɑ:s] *sb* **1** blindgate; **2** dødpunkt; vranglås.

impassioned [ɪm'pæʃnd] *adj* glødende, lidenskapelig.

impassive [ɪm'pæsɪv] *adj* uttrykksløs; uanfektet; ufølsom.

impatience [ɪm'peɪʃns] *sb* utålmodighet. **impatient** [ɪm'peɪʃnt] *adj* utålmodig.

impeach [ɪm'pi:tʃ] *vt* **1** anklage (især for embetsforbrytelse); stille for riksrett; **2** mistenkeliggjøre; dra i tvil. **impeachment** [ɪm'pi:tʃmənt] *sb* anklage *etc.*

impeccable [ɪm'pekəbl] *adj* feilfri; ulastelig.

impecunious [ˌɪmpɪ'kju:nɪəs] *adj* fattig, ubemidlet.

impede [ɪm'pi:d] *vt* hemme, hindre. **impediment** [ɪm'pedɪmənt] *sb* hindring; (sjenerende) feil/ lyte; *ofte* stamming.

impel [ɪm'pel] *vt* drive/presse/tvinge (frem); tilskynde.

impend [ɪm'pend] *vi* være i anmarsj/nær forestående *etc.* **impending** [ɪm'pendɪŋ] *adj* kommende; overhengende, truende.

impenetrable [ɪm'penɪtrəbl] *adj* ugjennomtrengelig; *fig* uutgrunnelig.

imperative [ɪm'perətɪv] **I** *adj* **1** bydende; **2** tvingende nødvendig; **II** *sb gram* imperativ.

imperial [ɪm'pɪərɪəl] **I** *adj* **1** keiserlig, keiser-; **2** imperie, samvelde-; **3** britisk (især om mål og vekt, se midtsidene); **II** *sb* fippskjegg.

imperil [ɪm'perəl] *vt* bringe i/utsette for fare.

impersonate [ɪm'pɜ:səneɪt] *vt* **1** fremstille (på scene); spille (rolle som); **2** utgi seg for (å være); **3** etterligne; **4** personifisere. **impersonation** [ɪmˌpɜ:sə'neɪʃn] *sb* personifisering *etc.*

impertinence [ɪm'pɜ:tɪnəns] *sb* nesevishet *etc.* **impertinent** [ɪm'pɜ:tɪnənt] *adj* **1** nesevis, uforskammet; **2** uvedkommende.

imperturbable [ˌɪmpə'tɜ:bəbl] *adj* uforstyrrelig; urokkelig.

impervious [ɪm'pɜ:vɪəs] *adj* **1** ugjennomtrengelig; (vann)tett; **2** *fig* utilgjengelig; uimottakelig.

impetuosity [ɪmˌpetʃʊ'ɒsətɪ] *sb* heftighet *etc.*

impetuous [ɪm'petʃʊəs] *adj* **1** heftig; oppfarende, snarsint; **2** impulsiv; umiddelbar.

impetus ['ɪmpɪtəs] *sb* **1** (driv)kraft; fart (fremover); **2** insitament, stimulans.

impious ['ɪmpɪəs] *adj* ugudelig; uærbødig.

implacable [ɪm'plækəbl] *adj* uforsonlig; hard, ubøyelig.

implement **1** ['ɪmplɪmənt] *sb* redskap, verktøy; **2** ['ɪmplɪment] *vt* realisere, virkeliggjøre; fullføre, gjennomføre; oppfylle.

implicate ['ɪmplɪkeɪt] *vt* **1** implisere; inn|blande, -vikle; **2** bety, innebære. **implication** [ˌɪmplɪ-'keɪʃn] *sb* **1** implisering; innblanding; **2** implikasjon; underforstått mening *etc.* **implicit** [ɪm'plɪsɪt] *adj* **1** implisitt; forutsatt, underforstått; **2** absolutt, ubetinget; blind *(fig)*.

implore [ɪm'plɔ:] *vt* bønnfalle/trygle (om).

imply [ɪm'plaɪ] *vt* **1** bety, innebære; **2** antyde; insinuere.

import **I** ['ɪmpɔ:t] *sb* **1** *fl* import(varer); **2** betydning; konsekvens; **3** viktighet; **II** [ɪm'pɔ:t] *vt* **1** importere, innføre; **2** bety, innebære; **3** ha/være av betydning for. **importance** [ɪm'pɔ:təns] *sb* betydning, viktighet. **important** [ɪm'pɔ:tənt] *adj* betydningsfull, viktig. **importation** [ˌɪmpɔ:'teɪʃn] *sb* import (og importering); innførsel.

importunate [ɪm'pɔ:tʃʊnət] *adj* **1** pågående; innpåsliten, plagsom; **2** påtrengende. **importune** [ɪm-'pɔ:tʃu:n] *vt* plage, sjenere; mase på. **importunity** [ˌɪmpɔ:'tju:nətɪ] *sb* påtrengenhet; mas.

impose [ɪm'pəuz] *vb* **1** pålegge (avgift, plikt etc); ilegge (bot, straff etc); **2** påtvinge; *dgl* prakke på; **3** ~ *(up)on* dupere; utnytte; bedra, lure. **imposing** [ɪm-'pəuzɪŋ] *adj* imponerende; overveldende. **imposition** [ˌɪmpe'zɪʃn] *sb* **1** påleggelse (og pålegg = avgift/skatt; bot; pålagt plikt/straff etc); **2** lureri, svindel; opptrekkeri.

impossibility [ɪm'pɒsə'bɪlətɪ] *sb* umulighet. **impossible** [ɪm'pɒsəbl] *adj* **1** umulig; **2** *dgl* utålelig, uutholdelig.

impostor [ɪm'pɒstə] *sb* bedrager, svindler. **imposture** [ɪm'pɒstʃə] *sb* bedrageri, svindel.

impotence ['ɪmpətəns] *sb* **1** avmektighet, maktesløshet; **2** impotens. **impotent** ['ɪmpətənt] *adj* **1** avmektig, maktesløs; **2** impotent.

impoverish [ɪm'pɒverɪʃ] *vt* gjøre fattig; **2** utarme; svekke.

impracticable [ɪm'præktɪkəbl] *adj* **1** ugjennomførlig; umulig; **2** ufarbar; **3** umedgjørlig.

imprecation [ˌɪmprɪ'keɪʃn] *sb* forbannelse.

impregnable [ɪm'pregnəbl] *adj* uinntakelig; *fig* uangripelig.

impress **I** ['ɪmpres] *sb* avtrykk, merke; preg, stempel; **II** [ɪm'pres] *vt* **1** merke, prege; innprente; **2**

imponere; gjøre inntrykk på. **impression** [ɪm'preʃn] *sb* **1** (av)trykk, merke; inntrykk; **2** opplag (av bok etc); trykning; **3** fornemmelse, følelse; inntrykk. **impressive** [ɪm'presɪv] *adj* virkningsfull; slående; imponerende; som gjør inntrykk.

imprint I ['ɪmprɪnt] *sb* (av)trykk, merke; preg; **II** [ɪm'prɪnt] *vt* **1** prege, trykke; **2** innprente.

imprison [ɪm'prɪzn] *vt* fengsle; kaste/sette i fengsel. **imprisonment** [ɪm'prɪznmənt] *sb* fengsling.

improbable [ɪm'prɒbəbl] *adj* usannsynlig; lite trolig.

improper [ɪm'prɒpə] *adj* **1** upassende; **2** feilaktig; **3** uanstendig, usømmelig.

improve [ɪm'pru:v] *vb* **1** bedre(s); bli/gjøre bedre; ~ *(up)on* forbedre; **2** utnytte. **improvement** [ɪm'pru:vmənt] *sb* forbedring.

improvise ['ɪmprəvaɪz] *vb* improvisere.

imprudent [ɪm'pru:dənt] *adj* ubetenksom, uklok; overilt.

impudence ['ɪmpjʊdəns] *sb* uforskammethet *etc.* **impudent** ['ɪmpjʊdənt] *adj* uforskammet; frekk, nesevis.

impulse ['ɪmpʌls] *sb* **1** impuls, innskytelse; *a man of* ~ en impulsiv mann; **2** oppmuntrig, tilskyndelse; puff. **impulsive** [ɪm'pʌlsɪv] *adj* impulsiv.

impunity [ɪm'pju:nətɪ] *sb* straffrihet.

imputation [ˌɪmpjʊ'teɪʃn] *sb* beskyldning; bebreidelse; *fig* lyte. **impute** [ɪm'pju:t] *vt* **1** tillegge (ansvar, skyld etc); **2** anklage, beskylde; bebreide.

in [ɪn] **I** *adj* **1** inn- (dvs ankommende, inngående etc); **2** inne-; hjemme-; *pol* regjerings- (om det parti som har regjeringsmakten); **II** *adv* **1** inn; hjemme, inne; *pol* med (regjerings)makten; **2** *dgl* aktuell; på mote; **3** ~ *for* påmeldt til; for/på tur til; *be* ~ *for* ha i vente; kunne vente seg; **III** *prep* **1** *om sted og retning* i (og inni, nedi, oppi, uti etc); på (jf *at, on*); hos; ~ *the open* i friluft; under åpen himmel; ~ *the sky* på himmelen; **2** *om forhold og tilstand* i, på; blant; under; ~ *love* forelsket; ~ *these circumstances* under disse omstendigheter; *one* ~ *ten* én av ti; **3** *om middel og måte* med, ved; i, på; ~ *answer to* som svar på; ~ *her defence* til hennes forsvar; ~ *my opinion* etter min mening; **4** *om tid* om; i, på; ~ *an hour* om en time; ~ *the end* til slutt; **5** *(for øvrig)* ~ *as/so far as* for så vidt som; ~ *that* ettersom, siden; fordi; derved at; for så vidt som; **IV** *sb* **1** *the* ~*s (pol)* regjeringspartiet; *sport* innelaget; *dgl* de som er inne/med (dvs som vanker på de rette stedene, følger moten, kjenner sjargongen etc); **2** *know the* ~*s and outs of* kjenne ut og inn.

inadvertent [ˌɪnəd'vɜ:tənt] *adj* uaktsom, uoppmerksom. **inadvertently** [ˌɪnəd'vɜ:təntlɪ] *adv* av vanvare.

inalienable [ɪn'eɪlɪənəbl] *adj* uavhendelig; umistelig; som ikke kan tas fra en.

inane [ɪ'neɪn] *adj* **1** intetsigende, tom; **2** meningsløs; tåpelig.

inasmuch [ˌɪnəz'mʌtʃ] *adv:* ~ *as* ettersom, siden; for så vidt som.

inaugural [ɪ'nɔ:gjʊrəl] **1** *adj* innvielses, åpnings-; tiltredelses-; **2** *sb* åpningstale; tiltredelsesforelesning. **inaugurate** [ɪ'nɔ:gjʊreɪt] *vt* **1** innsette i embete; **2** innvie; åpne (utstilling etc); **3** inn|lede, -varsle (ny epoke etc).

incandescent [ˌɪnkæn'desnt] *adj* **1** hvitglødende; **2** skinnende, strålende.

incapacitate [ˌɪnkə'pæsɪteɪt] *vt* gjøre udyktig; sette ut av drift/virksomhet etc; diskvalifisere.

incarcerate [ɪn'kɑ:səreɪt] *vt* fengsle; kaste/sette i fengsel. **incarceration** [ɪnˌkɑ:sə'reɪʃn] *sb* fengsling.

incarnate I [ɪn'kɑ:neɪt] *adj* inkarnert, legemliggjort; personifisert; **II** ['ɪnkɑ:neɪt] *vt* **1** inkarnere, legemliggjøre; **2** gi konkret form. **incarnation** [ˌɪnkɑ:'neɪʃn] *sb* inkarnering *etc*; inkarnasjon.

incendiary [ɪn'sendɪərɪ] **I** *adj* **1** brann-; **2** *fig* (opp)flammende; oppviglersk; **II** *sb* **1** brannstifter; *fig* oppvigler; **2** *mil* brannbombe. **incense 1** ['ɪnsens] *sb* røkelse; **1** [ɪn'sens] *vt* opphisse, tirre. **incentive** [ɪn'sentɪv] **1** *adj* ansporende, oppmuntrende; **2** *sb* spore, tilskyndelse; oppmuntring.

incessant [ɪn'sesnt] *adj* uavlatelig, ustanselig; uavbrutt, uopphørlig.

inch [ɪntʃ] **I** *sb* **1** tomme, se midtsidene; **2** *dgl* bit(e); ørlite stykke etc; *within an* ~ *of* like ved/på nippet til (å); **II** *vb* snegle/snike seg (frem).

incidence ['ɪnsɪdəns] *sb* **1** forekomst; hyppighet, utstrekning; **2** virkning, utslag. **incident** ['ɪnsɪdənt] **1** *adj:* ~ *to* forbundet med; knyttet til; **2** *sb* (tilfeldig) hending; opptrinn, scene; episode. **incidental** [ˌɪnsɪ'dentl] *adj* **1** ledsagende; tilhørende; **2** tilfeldig; uvesentlig. **incidentally** [ˌɪnsɪ'dentəlɪ] *adv* tilfeldigvis; *stundom* apropos, forresten.

incinerate [ɪn'sɪnəreɪt] *vt* forbrenne; brenne (helt) opp. **incineration** [ɪnˌsɪnə'reɪʃn] *sb* forbrenning. **incinerator** [ɪn'sɪnəreɪtə] *sb* forbrenningsovn, (søppel)forbrenner. **incinerator plant** *sb petro etc* forbrenningsanlegg.

incipient [ɪn'sɪpɪənt] *adj* begynnende; gryende, spirende.

incision [ɪn'sɪʒn] *sb* snitt; kutt. **incisive** [ɪn'saɪsɪv] *adj* skjærende, skarp. **incisor** [ɪn'saɪzə] *sb* fortann.

incite [ɪn'saɪt] *vt* egge (til); anspore/tilskynde (til). **incitement** [ɪn'saɪtmənt] *sb* spore, tilskyndelse.

inclement [ɪn'klemənt] *adj* barsk, streng (især om klima); ublid.

inclination [ˌɪnklɪ'neɪʃn] *sb* **1** bøyning; bukk, nikk; **2** = *incline I*; **3** tilbøyelighet, tendens; forkjærlighet. **incline** [ɪn'klaɪn] **I** *sb* helling, skråning; **II** *vb* **1** bøye (seg); **2** helle, skråne; **3** gjøre tilbøyelig (*to* til); **4** ha (en) tendens/være tilbøyelig (*to* til); *feel* ~*d to* ha lyst til (å).

include [ɪn'klu:d] *vt* innbefatte, omfatte; inkludere. **inclusive** [ɪn'klu:sɪv] *adj* **1** innbefattet, medregnet; inklusive; **2** samlet; brutto(-); alt inklusive.

income ['ɪnkʌm] *sb* inntekt(er). **income tax return** *sb* selvangivelse.

inconclusive [ˌɪnkən'klu:sɪv] *adj* resultatløs; uten avgjørende betydning/virkning etc.

incongruous [ɪn'kɒŋgruəs] *adj* **1** uoverensstemmende (*to/with* med); *mat* inkongruent; **2** avstikkende, upassende; **3** urimelig.

inconsequent [ɪn'kɒnsɪkwənt] *adj* selvmotsigende, ulogisk; inkonsekvent. **inconsequential** [ɪnˌkɒnsɪ'kwenʃl] *adj* **1** = *inconsequent*; **2** ubetydelig, uvesentlig.

inconvenience [ˌɪnkən'vi:nɪəns] **1** *sb* bry(deri), uleilighet; ulempe; **2** *vt* bry, uleilige. **inconvenient** [ˌɪnkən'vi:nɪənt] *adj* brysom, ubeleilig.

incorporate I [ɪn'kɔ:pərət] *adj* innlemmet, opptatt; forent; **II** [ɪn'kɔ:pəreɪt] *vb* **1** inkorporere, innlemme; innarbeide; **2** forene(s); slutte (seg) sammen; *merk* danne aksjeselskap; **3** legemliggjøre.

incorrigible [ɪn'kɒrɪdʒəbl] *adj* uforbederlig.

increase I ['ɪnkri:s] *sb* økning; stigning; (til)-vekst; **II** [ɪn'kri:s] *vb* **1** øke; stige; vokse; **2** forøke, utvide; forhøye, forstørre.

incredible [ɪn'kredəbl] *adj* utrolig. **incredulity** [ˌɪnkrə'dju:lətɪ] *sb* vantro; skepsis. **incredulous** [ɪn'kredjuləs] *adj* tvilende, vantro; skeptisk.

increment ['ɪnkrɪmənt] *sb* (til)vekst, økning; *data også* inkrement. **incremental** [ˌɪnkrɪ'mentl] *adj* (trinnvis) voksende.

incriminate [ɪn'krɪmɪneɪt] *vt* inkriminere; anklage/beskylde (for forbrytelse). **incrimination** [ɪnˌkrɪmɪ'neiʃn] *sb* inkriminering. **incriminatory** [ɪn'krɪmɪnətərɪ] *adj* belastende, inkriminerende.

inculcate ['ɪnkʌlkeɪt] *vt* inn|plante, -pode; -prente. **inculcation** [ˌɪnkʌl'keɪʃn] *sb* innpoding *etc*.

incur [ɪn'kɜ:] *vt* pådra seg; ~ *debts* sette seg i gjeld.

incurable [ɪn'kjuərəbl] *adj* uhelbredelig.

incursion [ɪn'kɜ:ʃn] *sb* plutselig angrep/innfall; raid.

indebted [ɪn'detɪd] *adj* **1** forgjeldet; i gjeld; **2** *be ~ to* stå i (takknemlighets)gjeld til.

indeed [ɪn'di:d] **I** *adv* **1** virkelig; sannelig; **2** riktignok, visstnok; **II** *interj* (nei) jaså! (så) sannelig!

indefatigable [ˌɪndɪ'fætɪgəbl] *adj* utrettelig.

indefinite [ɪn'definət] *adj* ubestemt, vag. **indefinitely** [ɪn'definətlɪ] *adv* på ubestemt tid.

indelible [ɪn'deləbl] *adj* uutslettelig.

indemnify [ɪn'demnɪfaɪ] *vt* **1** erstatte; holde skadesløs; **3** sikre/trygge (*against/from* mot). **indemnity** [ɪn'demnətɪ] *sb* **1** erstatningsbeløp; **2** straffrihet.

indent I ['ɪndent] *sb* **1** *a)* = *indentation*; *b) data* automatisk innrykk; **2** *merk* eksportordre; **3** rekvisisjon; **II** [ɪn'dent] *vt* **1** lage/skjære *etc* hakk i; **2** bulke; lage fordypninger i; **3** bestille, rekvirere; **4** rykke inn (dvs begynne ny linje med innrykning). **indentation** [ˌɪnden'teɪʃn] *sb* **1** hakk; innskjæring; **2** bulk; **3** innrykning.

independence [ˌindɪ'pendəns] *sb* uavhengighet *etc*. **independent** [ˌɪndɪ'pendənt] *adj* uavhengig; fri, selvstendig.

indeterminate [ˌɪndɪ'tɜ:mɪnət] *adj* ubestemt; uklar, vag.

index ['ɪndeks] **I** *sb* **1** viser; *fig* pekepinn; **2** = ~ *finger*: **3** indeks, (stikkord)register; *data* innholdsliste; **4** *mat* eksponent; **II** *vt* **1** registrere; **2** forsyne med register. **index | card** *sb* kartotekkort. **~ finger** *sb* pekefinger. **~ level** *sb data* indeksnivå. **~ record** *sb data* indekspost. **~ word** *sb data* indeksord.

Indian ['ɪndɪən] **I** *adj* **1** indisk; **2** indiansk; **II** *sb* **1** inder; **2** *(Red ~)* indianer. **Indian | corn** *sb US* mais. **~ file** *sb* gåsegang. **~ ink** *sb* tusj.

indicate ['ɪndɪkeɪt] *vt* **1** vise (til); peke/*fig* tyde på; **2** antyde; indikere. **indication** [ˌɪndɪ'keɪʃn] *sb* **1** tegn, tilkjennegivelse; indikasjon; **2** antydning, indikering.

indict [ɪn'daɪt] *vt* anklage; reise tiltale mot. **indictment** [ɪn'daɪtmənt] *sb* anklage; tiltale.

indifference [ɪn'dɪfrəns] *sb* likegyldighet *etc*. **indifferent** [ɪn'dɪfrənt] *adj* **1** likegyldig; **2** likeglad; **3** middels; ordinær.

indigence ['ɪndɪdʒəns] *sb* fattigdom, nød.

indigenous [ɪn'dɪdʒɪnəs] *adj* innfødt; hjemmehørende, stedegen.

indigent ['ɪndɪdʒənt] *adj* fattig, nødlidende; trengende.

indigestion [ˌɪndɪ'dʒestʃn] *sb* dårlig fordøyelse; *dgl* dårlig mave; vondt i maven.

indignant [ɪn'dɪgnənt] *adj* indignert; harm, sint. **indignation** [ˌɪndɪg'neɪʃn] *sb* indignasjon *etc*. **indignity** [ɪn'dɪgnətɪ] *sb* dårlig/skammelig behandling; krenkelse; nedverdigelse.

indispensable [ˌɪndi'spensəbl] *adj* uunnværlig; (absolutt) nødvendig.

individual [ˌɪndɪ'vidjuəl] **1** *adj* individuell; enkelt(stående); egen(artet); **2** *sb* individ; enkelt|person, vesen. **individuality** [ˌɪndɪˌvɪdʒu'ælətɪ] *sb* individualitet; sær|drag, -preg.

indolence ['ɪndələns] *sb* dorskhet *etc*. **indolent** ['ɪndələnt] *adj* dorsk, treg; doven, lat.

indomitable [ɪn'dɒmɪtəbl] *adj* ukuelig; ubendig.

indubitable [ɪn'dju:bɪtəbl] *adj* utvilsom; unektelig.

induce [ɪn'dju:s] *vt* forårsake; frem|bringe, -kalle; *elek* indusere; **2** få til; bevege, formå. **inducement** [ɪn'dju:smənt] *sb* spore, tilskyndelse. **induction** [ɪn'dʌkʃn] *sb* indusering *etc*; induksjon. **induction log** *sb petro* induksjonslogg.

indulge [ɪn'dʌldʒ] *vb* **1** tilfredsstille (især litt for ofte); ~ *in* unne seg; hengi seg til; **2** føye; gi etter for; skjemme bort. **indulgence** [ɪn'dʌldʒəns] *sb* ettergivenhet *etc*. **indulgent** [ɪn'dʌldʒənt] *adj* (altfor) ettergivende/føyelig; overbærende; lemfeldig, svak.

industrial [ɪn'dʌstrɪəl] *adj* **1** industriell, industri-; **2** fag-, yrkes-. **industrious** [ɪn'dʌstrɪəs] *adj* arbeidsom, flittig. **industry** ['ɪndəstrɪ] *sb* **1** industri(gren); næringsvei; **2** arbeidsomhet, flittighet; flid.

inebriate I [ɪ'ni:brɪət] **1** *adj* beruset, full; **2** *sb* dranker, fyllik; **II** [ɪ'ni:brɪeɪt] *vt* beruse.

ineffable [ɪn'efəbl *adj* ubeskrivelig, usigelig.

inept [ɪ'nept] *adj* **1** dum, tåpelig; **2** malplassert; **3** klosset; uskikket.

inert [ɪ'nɜ:t] *adj* **1** *fys* inert, treg; **2** dorsk, treg; doven. **inertia** [ɪ'nɜ:ʃə] *sb* **1** *fys* inerti, treghet; **2** dorskhet, treghet; dovenskap.

inestimable [ɪn'estɪməbl] *adj* uvurderlig.

inevitable [ɪn'evɪtəbl] *adj* uunngåelig.

inexorable [ɪn'eksərəbl] *adj* ubønnhørlig; hard, steil.

infallible [ɪn'fæləbl] *adj* ufeilbarlig; usvikelig (sikker etc).

infamous ['ɪnfəməs] *adj* **1** skamløs, skjendig; **2** æreløs; beryktet, nederdrektig. **infamy** ['ɪnfəmɪ] *sb* skam, skjensel; æreløshet.

infancy ['ɪnfənsɪ] *sb* (tidlig) barndom; *jur* mindreårighet. **infant** ['ɪnfənt] **I** *adj* barne-; spedbarns-; *jur* mindreårig; **II** *sb* **1** (lite) barn; **2** *jur* mindreårig. **infantile** ['ɪnfəntaɪl] *adj* barnslig, barne-.

infatuate [ɪn'fætjʊeɪt] *vt* (be)dåre; forblinde. **infatuated** [ɪn'fætjʊeɪtɪd] *adj* *især* blindt/vilt forelsket. **infatuation** [ɪnˌfætjʊ'eɪʃn] *sb* forblindelse (især blind forelskelse etc).

infect [ɪn'fekt] *vt* infisere; smitte. **infection** [ɪn'fekʃn] *sb* infeksjon (og infeksjonssykdom); smitte. **infectious** [ɪn'fekʃəs] *adj* **1** smittefarlig; **2** smittende, smittsom.

infer [ɪn'fɜ:] *vt* slutte (seg til); utlede. **inference** ['ɪnfərəns] *sb* konklusjon, slutning.

inferior [ɪn'fɪərɪə] **I** *adj* **1** lav (og lavtstående; lavere, nedre, undre; under- etc); **2** dårlig (og dårligere; mindreverdig, underlegen etc); **3** underordnet; **II** *sb* underordnet *etc* person. **inferiority** [ɪnˌfɪərɪ'ɒrətɪ] *sb* underlegenhet; underordnet stilling etc. **inferiority complex** *sb* mindreverdskompleks.

infest [ɪn'fest] *vt* herje (i); oversvømme (især om skadedyr); hjemsøke, plage.

infidel ['ɪnfɪdəl] *adj, sb* vantro (person); gudløs, hedning. **infidelity** [ˌɪnfɪ'delətɪ] *sb* **1** vantro; **2** troløshet, utroskap.

infiltrate ['ɪnfɪltreɪt] *vb* infiltrere; sige (sive, trenge etc) inn (gjennom, nedi etc).

infinite ['ɪnfɪnɪt] *adj* uendelig; endeløs, grenseløs; ubegrenset. **infinity** [ɪn'fɪnətɪ] *sb* uendelighet(en).

infirm [ɪn'fɜ:m] *adj* skrøpelig, svak(elig). **infirmary** [ɪn'fɜ:mərɪ] *sb* sykehus (og sykestue; aldershjem, pleiehjem etc). **infirmity** [ɪn'fɜ:mətɪ] *sb* skrøpelighet *etc*.

inflame [ɪn'fleɪm] *vb* **1** sette fyr på; flamme opp; ta fyr; **2** oppflamme; opphisse; **3** bli/gjøre betent. **inflammable** [ɪn'flæməbl] *adj* **1** brennbar; brannfarlig; lettantennelig; **2** lett|bevegelig, -fengelig. **inflammation** [ˌɪnflə'meɪʃn] *sb* **1** antennelse; oppflamming; brann, **2** opphisselse; **3** betennelse; inflammasjon. **inflammation point** *sb petro* flammepunkt, tenningspunkt.

inflate [ɪn'fleɪt] *vt* **1** blåse/pumpe opp; fylle med luft *etc*; **2** *merk* inflatere. **inflated** [ɪn'fleɪtɪd] *adj* oppblåst; *fig også* blæret, hoven; svulstig. **inflation** [ɪn'fleɪʃn] *sb* **1** oppblåsing *etc*; *fig* oppblåsthet; **2** *merk* inflasjon.

inflection, inflexion [ɪn'flekʃn] *sb* **1** bøyning; **2** *gram* bøyning (samt bøyningsendelse og bøyd form).

inflict [ɪn'flɪkt] *vt* til|dele, -føye; påføre; forårsake, volde. **infliction** [ɪn'flɪkʃn] *sb* **1** tildeling *etc*; **2** hjemsøkelse, plage; straff(edom).

influence ['ɪnflʊəns] **1** *sb* innflytelse; virkning (og invirkning, påvirkning); **2** *vt* influere (på); ha/øve innflytelse på; påvirke. **influential** [ˌɪnflʊ'enʃl] *adj* innflytelsesrik. **influx** ['ɪnflʌks] *sb* tilstrømming.

inform [ɪn'fɔ:m] *vb* **1** informere; fortelle, meddele; opplyse, underrette; **2** ~ *against* angi, (an)melde. **informant** [ɪn'fɔ:mənt] *sb* hjemmelsmann, kilde. **informatics** [ɪn'fɔ:mətɪks] *sb data* informatikk. **information** [ˌɪnfə'meɪʃn] *sb* informering *etc*; informasjon, opplysning(er). **information | bit** *sb data* informasjonsbit. ~ **channel** *sb data* informasjonskanal. ~ **feedback** *sb data* tilbakemelding. ~ **interchange** *sb data* informasjonsutveksling. ~ **processing** *sb data* databehandling. ~ **separator** *sb data* grensetegn.

infraction [ɪn'frækʃn] *sb* (lov)|brudd, (-)overtredelse.

infringe [ɪn'frɪndʒ] bryte/overtre (lov etc); ~ *upon* krenke. **infringement** [ɪn'frɪndʒmənt] *sb* (lov)-overtredelse; krenkelse (*upon* av); overgrep (*upon* mot).

infuriate [ɪn'fjʊərɪeɪt] *vt* gjøre rasende.

infuse [ɪn'fju:z] *vt* **1** ~ *with* fylle med; tilføre; **2** (la) trekke (om te etc).

ingenious [ɪn'dʒi:nɪəs] *adj* **1** kløktig, skarpsindig; **2** oppfinnsom; **3** kunstferdig; sinnrik. **ingenuity** [ˌɪndʒɪ'nju:ətɪ] *sb* kløkt, skarpsinn; oppfinnsomhet.

ingenuous [ɪn'dʒenjʊəs] *adj* likefrem, åpen; troskyldig. **ingenuousness** [ɪn'dʒenjʊəsnɪs] *sb* åpenhet *etc*.

ingot ['ɪŋgət] *sb* barre, metallblokk.

ingratiate [ɪn'greɪʃɪeɪt] *vt:* ~ *oneself with* innsmigre/innynde seg hos.

ingredient [ɪn'gri:dɪənt] *sb* (bestand)del, ingrediens.

inhabit [ɪn'hæbɪt] *vt* bebo; bo/holde til i. **inhabitable** [ɪn'hæbɪtəbl] *adj* beboelig. **inhabitant** ['ɪn'hæbɪtənt] *sb* **1** beboer; **2** innbygger.

inhalation [ˌɪnhə'leɪʃn] *sb* innånding *etc*. **inhale** [ɪn'heɪl] *vb* inhalere; puste/ånde inn.

inherent [ɪn'hɪərənt] *adj* iboende; medfølgende; medfødt.

inherit [ɪn'herɪt] *vb* arve. **inheritable** [ɪn'herɪtəbl] *adj* **1** arvelig; **2** arveberettiget. **inheritance** [ɪn'herɪtəns] *sb* arv. **inherited error** *sb data* arvefeil.

inhibit [ɪn'hɪbɪt] *vt* hemme, hindre; holde igjen/tilbake. **inhibited | mud** *sb petro* hemmet slam. ~ **oil** *sb petro* stabil olje. **inhibiting signal** *sb data* sperresignal. **inhibition** [ˌɪnhɪ'bɪʃn] *sb* hemning *etc*. **inhibitor** [ɪn'hɪbɪtə] *sb petro* hemmer, stabilisator.

inimical [ɪ'nɪmɪkl] *adj* **1** fiendtlig, uvennlig; **2** ugunstig, skadelig.

inimitable [ɪ'nɪmɪtəbl] *adj* uforlignelig, makeløs.

iniquitous [ɪ'nɪkwɪtəs] *adj* urettferdig; skammelig, skjendig. **iniquity** [ɪ'nɪkwətɪ] *sb* **1** grov urett(ferdighet); **2** ondskap; syndefullhet; **3** ugjerning.

initial [ɪ'nɪʃl] **1** *adj* først, innledende; begynnelses-, åpnings-; initial-; **2** *sb* forbokstav, initial; **3** *vt* parafere/undertegne *etc* med initialer. **initiate I** [ɪ'nɪʃɪət] *adj, sb* innviet (person); nyopptatt (medlem, ordens|bror, -søster etc); **II** [ɪ'nɪʃɪeɪt] *vt* **1** begynne, innlede, åpne; **2** innføre, innvie; gjøre delaktig i; **3** oppta (som medlem etc). **initiative** [ɪ'nɪʃɪətɪv] **I** *adj* = *initial 1*; **II** *sb* **1** initiativ; innledende skritt; **2** foretaksomhet; tiltak(slyst).

inject [ɪn'dʒekt] *vt* sprøyte inn. **injection** [ɪn'dʒekʃn] *sb* injeksjon, innsprøytning; *dgl* sprøyte. **injection well** *sb petro* injeksjonsbrønn.

injunction [ɪn'dʒʌŋkʃn] *sb* pålegg; befaling, ordre.

injure ['ɪndʒə] *vt* skade; såre. **injurious** [ɪn'dʒʊərɪəs] *adj* **1** skadelig; **2** krenkende, sårende. **injury** ['ɪndʒərɪ] *sb* **1** skade; kvestelse, lesjon; **2** krenkelse; fornærmelse; urett.

ink [ɪŋk] **I** *sb* **1** blekk; **2** *(printer's ~)* (trykk)sverte; **II** *vt* få blekk/sverte på; *(~ in)* streke/trekke opp med blekk/tusj. **inking** ['ɪŋkɪŋ] *sb data* streking. **ink | jet printer** *sb data* blekkstråleskriver. **~pad** *sb* stempelpute. **~pot** *sb* blekkhus.

inkling ['ɪŋklɪŋ] *sb* anelse; antydning, vink.

inland I ['ɪnlənd] **1** *adj* innenlandsk, innenlands-; **2** *sb* innland; **II** [ɪn'lænd] *adv* inn (inne, innover) i landet.

in-laws [ɪn'lɔ:z] *sb fl dgl* svigerfamilie.

inlet ['ɪnlet] *sb* **1** kil, vik; innløp; **2** strede, sund; **3** innlegg, kile.

inmate ['ɪnmeɪt] *sb* beboer (især om pasienter på sykehus, innsatte i fengsel etc).

inmost ['ɪnməʊst] *adj* innerst; dypest/lengst inne.

inn [ɪn] *sb* **1** gjestgiveri, vertshus; kro; **2** *Inns of Court* fellesbetegnelse for de fire institusjoner som utdanner jurister og utsteder sakførerbevilling i England. **innkeeper** ['ɪn,ki:pə] *sb* vertshusholder; krovert.

innate [ɪ'neɪt] *adj* medfødt.

inner ['ɪnə] *adj* indre, innvendig. **innermost** ['ɪnəməʊst] = *inmost*. **innings** ['ɪnɪŋz] *sb* **1** *sport* inneomgang (dvs den tiden et lag i baseball eller cricket spiller inne); **2** *fig* glanstid, høydepunkt.

innocence ['ɪnəsns] *sb* uskyld(ighet) *etc*. **innocent** ['ɪnəsnt] **I** *adj* **1** uskyldsren; **2** uskyldig (*of* i); **3** harmløs, uskadelig; **4** naiv, troskyldig; **5** *dgl: ~ of* blottet for; komplett uvitende om; **II** *sb* uskyldig *etc* person.

innocuous [ɪ'nɒkjʊəs] *adj* harmløs, uskadelig.

innovate ['ɪnəʊveɪt] *vb* fornye; forandre, forbedre (ved å bringe inn noe nytt). **innovation** [,ɪnəʊ'veɪʃn] *sb* fornyelse; nyhet, nyskapning.

innuendo [,ɪnju:'endəʊ] *sb* insinuasjon; (forblommet/tvetydig etc) antydning.

innumerable [ɪ'nju:mərəbl] *adj* talløs, utallig.

inoculate [ɪ'nɒkjʊleɪt] *vt* **1** vaksinere; **2** *fig* innpode.

inordinate [ɪ'nɔ:dɪnət] *adj* overdreven; uforholdsmessig.

input ['ɪnpʊt] *sb* **1** *a)* inngang; *b)* inntak; *c)* tilførsel; **2** *data* inndata. **input | channel** *sb data* innkanal. **~ data** *sb data* inndata. **~ device** *sb data* innenhet. **~ gas** *sb petro* injisert gass. **~ process** *sb data* innmating. **~ stream** *sb data* jobbstrøm.

inquest ['ɪnkwest] *sb* granskning, undersøkelse; *(coroner's ~)* (rettslig) likskue. **inquire** [ɪn'kwaɪə] *vb* **1** forhøre seg (om); *(~ for)* be om; spørre etter; **2** *~ into* granske, undersøke; (etter)forske (i). **inquiry** [ɪn'kwaɪərɪ] *sb* **1** forespørsel; spørsmål; **2** granskning, undersøkelse; (etter)forskning. **inquisition** [,ɪnkwɪ'zɪʃn] *sb* grundig undersøkelse. **inquisitive** [ɪn'kwɪzətɪv] *adj* spørrelysten, vitebegjærlig; (især litt for påtrengende) nysgjerrig.

inroad ['ɪnrəʊd] (plutselig) angrep, overfall; *fig* inngrep.

insane [ɪn'seɪn] *adj* gal, sinnssyk. **insanity** [ɪn'sænətɪ] *sb* galskap, sinnssykdom.

insatiable [ɪn'seɪʃɪəbl], **insatiate** [ɪn'seɪʃɪət] *adj* umettelig; grådig.

inscribe [ɪn'skraɪb] *vt* **1** skrive (gravere, hugge etc) inn; **2** dedisere, tilegne; **3** føre inn; registrere. **inscription** [ɪn'skrɪpʃn] *sb* **1** innskrivning *etc*; **2** innskrift, inskripsjon.

inscrutable [ɪn'skru:təbl] *adj* uutgrunnelig; uransakelig.

insect ['ɪnsekt] *sb* insekt.

insensate [ɪn'senseɪt] *adj* livløs; følelsesløs; *fig* ufølsom. **insensible** [ɪn'sensəbl] *adj* **1** bevisstløs; **2** uvitende (*of* om); **3** følelsesløs; **4** følelseskald; ufølsom; **5** umerkelig.

insert [ɪn'sɜ:t] *vt* legge (skyte, sette, stikke etc) inn; rykke/sette inn (annonse etc); føye/legge til. **insertion** [ɪn'sɜ:ʃn] *sb* innlegging *etc*; innlegg, innstikk; tilføyelse, tillegg.

inside [,ɪn'saɪd] **I** *adj* **1** innvendig; indre(-); inner-; **2** fortrolig; førstehånds-; **II** *adv* **1** inn (og inne, inni); innenfor; på innsiden; **2** *dgl: ~ of* innen; **III** *prep* innenfor; inni; inne i; **2** innen; **IV** *sb* **1** innside, innerside; *~ out* vrengt; *know ~ out* kjenne ut og inn; *turn ~ out* vrenge; endevende; **2** *dgl* indre (dvs innvoller, mave etc).

insidious [ɪn'sɪdɪəs] *adj* lumsk, snikende.

insight ['ɪnsaɪt] *sb* innblikk; innsikt; dyp/grundig forståelse.

insignia [ɪn'sɪgnɪə] *sb fl* verdighetstegn; *~ of rank (mil)* distinksjoner.

insinuate [ɪn'sɪnjʊeɪt] *vt* **1** *~ oneself* innsmigre/innynde seg; **2** insinuere. **insinuation** [ɪn,sɪnjʊ'eɪʃn] *sb* **1** innsmigring *etc*; **2** insinuering; insinuasjon.

insipid [ɪn'sɪpɪd] **I** *adj* **1** emmen, flau; kjedelig, utvannet.

insist [ɪn'sɪst] *vb* insistere (*upon* på); fastholde; hevde, påstå. **insistence** [ɪn'sɪstəns] *sb* insistering *etc*; påståelighet. **insistent** [ɪn'sɪstənt] *adj* fast (bestemt); påståelig.

insolence ['ɪnsələns] *sb* uforskammethet *etc*. **insolent** ['ɪnsələnt] *adj* uforskammet; frekk, utfordrende; fornærmende.

insomnia [ɪn'sɒmnɪə] *sb* søvnløshet. **insomniac** [ɪn'sɒmnɪæk] *sb* søvnløs person.

insomuch [ˌɪnsəʊ'mʌtʃ] *adv* **1** ~ *as* for så vidt som; **2** ~ *that* i den grad/utstrekning at; slik at.

inspect [ɪn'spekt] *vt* **1** granske/undersøke nøye; **2** inspisere, overvåke; **3** *mil* inspisere, mønstre. **inspection** [ɪn'spekʃn] *sb* inspisering *etc*; inspeksjon; granskning, undersøkelse. **inspector** [ɪn'spektə] *sb* **1** inspektør; **2** (i politiet nærmest) førstebetjent; *chief* ~ (politi)overbetjent.

inspiration [ˌɪnspə'reɪʃn] *sb* **1** inspirering *etc*; inspirasjon (og inspirasjonskilde etc); **2** *dgl* innskytelse; lys idé. **inspire** [ɪn'spaɪə] *vt* **1** inspirere; animere, stimulere, vekke; **2** fylle, inngyte.

install [ɪn'stɔ:l] *vt* **1** etablere; innsette (i stilling etc); **2** installere, montere; legge inn; sette opp. **installation** [ˌɪnstə'leɪʃn] *sb* **1** innsettelse *etc*; **2** installering *etc*; installasjon. **instalment** [ɪn'stɔ:lmənt] *sb* **1** del (av f.eks. føljetong); porsjon; **2** *merk* avdrag, rate. **instalment plan** *sb* avbetalings|ordning, -system; *dgl også* avbetaling.

instance ['ɪnstəns] **I** *sb* **1** eksempel; **2** (enkelt)tilfelle; *in the first* ~ først; i første instans/omgang; til å begynne med; **3** *at the* ~ *of* etter anmodning/på foranledning av; **II** *vt* anføre som eksempel. **instant** ['ɪnstənt] **I** *adj* **1** omgående, øyeblikkelig; **2** pressende, påtrengende; **II** *sb* øyeblikk, stund. **instantaneous** [ˌɪnstən'teɪnɪəs] *adj* momentan, øyeblikkelig.

instead [ɪn'sted] *adv* **1** heller, isteden; **2** ~ *of* istedenfor.

instep ['ɪnstep] *sb* vrist.

instigate ['ɪnstɪgeɪt] *vt* egge/hisse opp (til); oppfordre/tilskynde til. **instigation** [ˌɪnstɪ'geɪʃn] *sb* oppfordring, tilskyndelse.

instil [ɪn'stɪl] *vt* inngi, inngyte; bibringe.

instinct 1 [ɪn'stɪŋkt] *adj* fylt; besjelet, gjennomsyret; **2** ['ɪnstɪŋkt] *sb* instinkt; medfødt sans (evne, tendens etc).

institute ['ɪnstɪtju:t] **I** *sb* institutt; **II** *vt* **1** etablere (og innlede/opprette; instituere etc); **2** innsette; utnevne. **institution** [ˌɪnstɪ'tju:ʃn] *sb* **1** etablering *etc*; **2** institusjon; institutt; **3** sedvane, skikk (og bruk). **institutional** [ˌɪnstɪ'tju:ʃənl] *adj* institusjons-; institusjonell.

instruct [ɪn'strʌkt] *vt* **1** undervise; lære (opp); **2** instruere; veilede, vise; **3** meddele, underrette. **instruction** [ɪn'strʌkʃn] *sb* **1** undervisning *etc*; **2** instruering; instruksjon; instruks; ~*s for use* bruksanvisning. **instructive** [ɪn'strʌktɪv] *adj* instruktiv; opplysende; veiledende. **instructor** [ɪn'strʌktə] *sb* instruktør; lærer; veileder.

instrument I ['ɪnstrʊmənt] *sb* **1** instrument, redskap; **2** *(musical* ~*)* (musikk)instrument; **3** *jur* dokument; **II** ['ɪnstrʊment] *vt* instrumentere. **instrumental** [ˌɪnstrʊ'mentl] *adj* **1** medvirkende (*in* til); **2** instrumental(-); instrument-.

insubordinate [ˌɪnsəb'ɔ:dnət] *adj* oppsetsig, ulydig; opprørsk. **insubordination** ['ɪnsəˌbɔ:dɪ'neɪʃn] *sb* oppsetsighet etc; *mil* ordrenekt(ing).

insular ['ɪnsjʊlə] *adj* **1** øy-; **2** avsondret, isolert; *fig* provinsiell, trangsynt. **insularity** [ˌɪnsjʊ'lærətɪ] *sb* avsondret/isolert beliggenhet; *fig* trangsynthet. **insulate** ['ɪnsjʊleɪt] *vt* isolere. **insulating oil** *sb petro* transformatorolje. **insulation** [ˌɪnsjʊ'leɪʃn] *sb* isolering; isolasjon.

insult 1 ['ɪnsʌlt] *sb* fornærmelse; **2** [ɪn'sʌlt] *vt* fornærme, krenke.

insurance [ɪn'ʃʊərəns] *sb* **1** (skade)forsikring; **2** *(~ policy)* forsikring, (forsikrings)polise. **insure** [ɪn'ʃʊə] *vt* forsikre (især ting, jf *assure*).

insurgent [ɪn'sɜ:dʒənt] **1** *adj* opprørsk; **2** *sb* opprører; mytterist; opprørsk soldat etc. **insurrection** [ˌɪnsə'rekʃn] *sb* oppstand; mytteri; opprør.

intact [ɪn'tækt] *adj* intakt; uberørt; ubeskåret; uskadd.

integral ['ɪntɪgrəl] **I** *adj* **1** integrerende; nødvendig, vesentlig; **2** komplett; hel, udelt; **II** *sb mat* integral. **integrate** ['ɪntɪgreɪt] *vt* integrere; samordne (i et hele). **integrity** [ɪn'tegrətɪ] *sb* integritet; fullstendighet, helhet; *fig* helstøpthet; rettskaffenhet.

intellect ['ɪntəlekt] *sb* **1** intellekt; forstand; **2** intelligens (dvs intelligent person); *koll* intelligentsia. **intellectual** [ˌɪntɪ'lektjʊəl] *adj, sb* intellektuell (person). **intelligence** [ɪn'telɪdʒəns] *sb* **1** intelligens; **2** nyhet(er); opplysning(er); *mil* etterretning(er). **intelligence | officer** *sb* etterretningsoffiser. ~ **service** *sb* etterretnings|tjeneste, -vesen. **intelligent** [ɪn'telɪdʒənt] *adj* intelligent; klok, oppvakt. **intelligent | pig** *sb petro* inspeksjonspigg, sonde. ~ **terminal** *sb data* programmerbar terminal. **intelligible** [ɪn'telɪdʒəbl] *adj* klar, tydelig; forståelig.

intend [ɪn'tend] *vt* mene; akte, tilsikte; ha til hensikt; ~*ed for* bestemt for/til. **intens** [ɪn'tens] *adj* intens; heftig, voldsom. **intensify** [ɪn'tensɪfaɪ] *vb* intensivere; forsterke, utdype. **intensity** [ɪn'tensətɪ] *sb* intensitet *etc*. **intensive** [ɪn'tensɪv] *adj* intens (og intensiv); forsterkende. **intent** [ɪn'tent] **I** *adj* **1** ivrig; (an)spent; **2** ~ *(up)on* oppsatt på; **II** *sb* forsett, hensikt; plan; *to all* ~*s and purposes* praktisk talt; i enhver henseende. **intention** [ɪn'tenʃn] *sb* hensikt, intensjon; mening, tanke; plan; (for)mål. **intentional** [ɪn'tenʃənl] *adj* forsettlig, tilsiktet.

inter [ɪn'tɜ:] *vt* begrave, jordfeste.

intercede [ˌɪntə'si:d] *vi* gå imellom; opptre som mellommann; megle; gå i forbønn (*with* hos; *for/on behalf of* for).

intercept [ˌɪntə'sept] *vt* **1** avskjære; avbryte, stanse; **2** fange/snappe opp.

intercession [ˌɪntəˈseʃn] *sb* mellomkomst (etc, jf *intercede*).

interchange [ˌɪntəˈtʃeɪndʒ] **1** *sb* utveksling; **2** *vt* utveksle; bytte/skifte ut; la bytte plass etc. **interchangeable** [ˌintəˈtʃeɪndʒəbl] *adj* utbyttbar, utskiftbar.

intercom [ˈɪntəkɒm] *fork* for *intercommunication system*. **intercommunicate** [ˌɪntəkəˈmju:nɪkeɪt] *vi* kommunisere; ha/stå i forbindelse (med hverandre). **intercommunication** [ˈɪntəkəˌmju:nɪˈkeɪʃn] *sb* forbindelse, samband. **intercommunication system** *sb* (høyttalende) hustelefonanlegg; internt samtaleanlegg.

intercourse [ˈɪntəkɔ:s] *sb* **1** forbindelse; omgang, samkvem; **2** *(sexual ~)* samleie.

interdict I [ˈɪntədɪkt] *sb* forbud; *rel* interdikt; **II** [ˌɪntəˈdɪkt] *vt* **1** forby; **2** hindre; holde tilbake.

interest [ˈɪntrɪst] **I** *sb* **1** interesse; *take an ~ in* interessere seg for; ha (fatte, få etc) interesse for; **2** (egen) fordel; gode; **3** (an)del, part; interesse; **4** *merk* rente(r); *at ~* mot rente(r); *bear (carry, return) ~* forrentes; gi/kaste av seg renter; **II** *vt* interessere; gjøre interessert. **interested** [ˈɪntrɪstɪd] *adj* **1** interessert *etc*; **2** forutinntatt; **3** egennyttig, selvisk. **interesting** [ˈɪntrɪstɪŋ] *adj* interessant.

interface [ˈɪntəfeɪs] *sb data* grensesnitt. **interface unit** *sb data* tilpasser.

interfere [ˌɪntəˈfɪə] *vi* **1** gå/legge seg imellom; ~ *with* forstyrre, sjenere; blande/legge seg oppi; **2** komme/legge seg i veien for. **interference** [ˌɪntəˈfɪərəns] *sb* innblanding *etc*; forstyrrelse, inngrep; interferens.

interior [ɪnˈtɪərɪə] **I** *adj* **1** innvendig; indre(-); innendørs(-); interiør-; **2** innlands; **3** innenlandsk; innenlands-, innenriks-; **II** *sb* **1** indre; interiør; **2** *US: Department of the Interior* innenriksdepartementet.

interjection [ˌɪntəˈdʒekʃn] *sb* interjeksjon, utropsord.

interlock [ˌɪntəˈlɒk] *vb* **1** gripe inn i hverandre; koble/låse sammen; **2** *data* stenge.

interloper [ˈɪntələʊpə] *sb* påtrengende person; ubuden gjest.

interlude [ˈɪntəlu:d] *sb* mellomspill; opphold, pause.

intermediary [ˌɪntəˈmi:dɪərɪ] **I** *adj* **1** formidlende, megler-; **2** mellom-; overgangs-; **II** *sb* **1** formidler, megler; mellommann; **2** mellom|ledd, -stadium; **3** overgang (og overgangsstadium). **intermediate** [ˌɪntəˈmi:dɪət] **I** *adj* **1** foreløpig, midlertidig; **2** mellomliggende; **II** *sb* = *intermediary II*. **intermediate | character** *sb data* mellomtegn. **~ system** *sb data* mellomliggende system.

interment [ɪnˈtɜ:mənt] *sb* begravelse, jordfestelse.

interminable [ɪnˈtɜ:mɪnəbl] *adj* endeløs; uendelig (lang etc).

intermission [ˌɪntəˈmɪʃn] *sb* opphold, pause. **intermittent** [ˌɪntəˈmɪtənt] *adj* periodisk; som opptrer *etc* med visse mellomrom; avbrutt, skiftende.

intern 1 [ˈɪntɜ:n] *sb US* kandidat (på sykehus); **2** [ɪnˈtɜ:n] *vt* internere. **internal** [ɪnˈtɜ:nl] *adj* **1** indre; innvendig. **internal | block** *sb data* intern blokk. **~ combustion engine** *sb* forbrenningsmotor. **~ label** *sb data* internetikett. **~ procedure** *sb data* intern prosedyre. **~ reader** *sb data* intern leser. **~ storage** *sb data* indre lager. **internment** [ɪnˈtɜ:nmənt] *sb* internering.

interpose [ˌɪntəˈpəʊz] *vb* **1** avbryte (med protest, spørsmål etc); **2** komme imellom; legge/stille (seg) imellom; blande/legge seg oppi; **3** gå imellom; megle.

interpret [ɪnˈtɜ:prɪt] *vb* **1** (for)tolke; belyse, klargjøre; tyde; **2** oversette, tolke; opptre som tolk. **interpretation** [ɪnˌtɜ:prɪˈteɪʃn] *sb* fortolkning *etc*; tolking. **interpreter** [ɪnˈtɜ:prɪtə] *sb* **1** tolk; **2** *data* kortskriver; tolkeprogram.

interrogate [ɪnˈterəʊgeɪt] *vt* spørre (ut); eksaminere, forhøre. **interrogation** [ɪnˌterəʊˈgeɪʃn] *sb* (ut)spørring *etc*; forhør. **interrogative** [ˌɪntəˈrɒgətɪv] **1** *adj* spørrende, spørre-; **2** *sb gram* spørre|-ord, -pronomen.

interrupt [ˌɪntəˈrʌpt] *vt* avbryte; stanse, stoppe. **interruption** [ˌɪntəˈrʌpʃn] *sb* avbrytelse *etc*.

intersect [ˌɪntəˈsekt] *vb* krysse/skjære (hverandre); skjære igjennom. **intersection** [ˌɪntəˈsekʃn] *sb* skjæringspunkt; krysning (og krysningspunkt); *især US* veikryss.

interval [ˈɪntəvəl] *sb* mellomrom; opphold, pause; *mus* intervall.

intervene [ˌɪntəˈvi:n] *vi* **1** komme imellom/i veien; gå/legge seg imellom; **2** intervenere; gripe inn; ta affære. **intervention** [ˌɪntəˈvenʃn] *sb* mellomkomst *etc*; intervensjon; innblanding; inngrep.

interview [ˈɪntəvju:] **I** *sb* **1** intervju; **2** konferanse (f.eks. i forbindelse med ny stilling); møte; **II** *vt* **1** intervjue; **2** ha konferanse *etc* med.

intestines [ɪnˈtestɪnz] *sb fl* tarmer, innvoller.

intimacy [ˈɪntɪməsɪ] *sb* intimitet *etc*. **intimate A** [ˈɪntɪmət] **I** *adj* **1** intim, privat; **2** nær(stående); fortrolig; **3** grundig, inngående; **II** *sb* fortrolig/nær venn; **B** [ˈɪntɪmeɪt] *vt* tilkjennegi; antyde; slå frempå om; slå på.

intimidate [ɪnˈtɪmɪdeɪt] *vt* skremme, terrorisere; intimidere. **intimidation** [ɪnˌtɪmɪˈdeɪʃn] *sb* skremsel *etc*.

into [ˈɪntʊ] *prep* **1** inn (og ned, opp, over, ut etc) i; *far ~ the night* (til) langt utover/utpå natten; **2** til; *persuade (translate, turn etc) ~* overtale (oversette, forvandle etc) til.

intolerable [ɪnˈtɒlərəbl] *adj* utålelig, uutholdelig; ufordragelig.

intonation [ˌɪntəʊˈneɪʃn] *sb* **1** intonasjon; tonefall; **2** *rel* messing.

intoxicant [ɪnˈtɒksɪkənt] **1** *adj* berusende; **2** *sb* rusdrikk. **intoxicate** [ɪnˈtɒksɪkeɪt] *vt* beruse. **intoxication** [ɪnˌtɒksɪˈkeɪʃn] *sb* beruselse, rus.

intrepid [ɪnˈtrepɪd] *adj* fryktløs, uredd; dristig.

intricacy ['ɪntrɪkəsɪ] *sb* innviklethet *etc; fl* forviklinger. **intricate** ['ɪntrɪkət] *adj* innviklet; vanskelig å finne ut av; intrikat.

intrigue [ɪn'tri:g] **I** *sb* **1** intrigering, renkespill; **2** intrige, sammensvergelse; **3** (hemmelig) kjærlighetsforhold; **II** *vb* **1** intrigere; smi renker; **2** fengsle; gjøre nysgjerrig.

intrinsic [ɪn'trɪnsɪk] *adj* iboende; indre. **intrinsic value** *sb* egenverdi.

introduce [ˌɪntrə'dju:s] *vt* **1** introdusere; bringe på bane; komme *etc* med; **2** begynne; innlede, åpne; **3** føre/sette inn; **4** forestille, presentere. **introduction** [ˌɪntrə'dʌkʃn] *sb* introdusering *etc*; introduksjon; innføring (også = elementær lærebok etc); presentasjon; *letter of* ~ anbefalingsbrev.

intrude [ɪn'tru:d] *vb* trenge (seg) (*into* inn i; *upon* på). **intruder** [ɪn'tru:də] *sb* inntrenger; ubuden gjest etc. **intrusion** [ɪn'tru:ʒn] *sb* inntrengning. **intrusive** [ɪn'tru:sɪv] *adj* påtrengende.

inundate ['ɪnʌndeɪt] *vt* oversvømme; neddynge; overvelde.

inure [i'njʊə] *vt* **1** ~ *to* herde mot; **2** ~*d to* vant til.

invade [ɪn'veɪd] *vt* **1** invadere; angripe, overfalle; trenge inn i; **2** krenke; gjøre inngrep i.

invalid A ['ɪnvəlɪd] **1** *adj* (arbeids)ufør, sykelig; **2** *sb* handikappet/ufør (person); invalid; **II** ['ɪnvəli:d] *vt* **1** sykmelde; *mil* sykepermittere; kjenne tjenesteudyktig (pga sykdom etc); **2** invalidisere; **B** [ɪn'vælɪd] *adj* **1** ugyldig; **2** grunnløs. **invalidate** [ɪn'vælɪdeɪt] *vt* annullere; gjøre ugyldig. **invalid data** *sb fl data* ugyldige data. **invalidity** [ˌɪnvə'lɪdətɪ] *sb* **1** ugyldighet; **2** invaliditet, uførhet. **invaluable** [ɪn'væljʊəbl] *adj* uvurderlig.

invasion [ɪn'veɪʒn] *sb* invasjon.

invent [ɪn'vent] *vt* **1** finne opp; **2** finne på; klekke/tenke ut. **invention** [ɪn'venʃn] *sb* oppfinnelse. **inventive** [ɪn'ventɪv] *adj* oppfinnsom. **inventor** [ɪn'ventə] *sb* oppfinner.

inventory ['ɪnvəntrɪ] *sb* **1** fortegnelse/liste (over beholdninger, inventar etc); *annual* ~ årlig vareopptelling; **2** (lager)beholdning.

inverse [ɪn'vɜ:s] *adj* omvendt. **inverse video** *sb data* negativt bilde. **inversion** [ɪn'vɜ:ʃn] *sb* **1** omvending; inversjon; *gram* omvendt ordstilling; **2** (især seksuelt) avvik; *ofte* homofili. **invert I** ['ɪnvɜ:t] **1** *adj* omvendt; motsatt; invertert; **2** *sb* avviker; homofil (person); **II** [ɪn'vɜ:t] *vt* snu (opp ned); vende (om på); ~*ed commas* anførselstegn, gåseøyne.

invertebrate [ɪn'vɜ:tɪbrət] **1** *adj* virvelløs; **2** *sb* virvelløst dyr.

inverted | directory *sb data* invertert katalog. ~ **file** *sb data* invertert fil. ~ **list** *sb data* invertert liste.

invest [ɪn'vest] *vb* **1** *merk* investere; plassere (penger); ~ *in (dgl)* kjøpe; spandere på seg; **2** ~ *with* iføre, ikle; utstyre med; **3** ~ *with* gi, skjenke, tildele; **4** beleire, omringe.

investigate [ɪn'vestɪgeɪt] *vt* undersøke; etterforske; granske, **investigation** [ɪnˌvestɪ'geɪʃn] *sb* undersøkelse *etc*. **investigator** [ɪn'vestɪgeɪtə] *sb* etterforsker.

investiture [ɪn'vestɪtʃə] *sb* (embets)innsettelse, investitur. **investment** [ɪn'vestmənt] *sb* **1** investering; **2** = *investiture*.

inveterate [ɪn'vetərət] *adj* inngrodd; kronisk, uforbederlig.

invidious [ɪn'vɪdɪəs] *adj* forargelig, støtende; urettferdig; uheldig (dvs som vekker misunnelse, nag etc).

invigorate [ɪn'vɪgəreɪt] *vt* styrke. **invigorating** [ɪn'vɪgəreɪtɪŋ] *adj* forfriskende, oppkvikkende, stimulerende.

invincible [ɪn'vɪnsəbl] *adj* uovervinnelig.

inviolable [ɪn'vaɪələbl] *adj* ukrenkelig.

invitation [ˌɪnvɪ'teɪʃn] *sb* innbydelse *etc*. **invite** [ɪn'vaɪt] *vt* **1** innby, invitere; **2** be om (å få etc); utbe seg; **3** invitere (oppfordre, oppmuntre etc) til.

invocation [ˌɪnvəʊ'keɪʃn] *sb* påkallelse.

invoice ['ɪnvɔɪs] *merk* **1** *sb* faktura; **2** *vt* fakturere.

invoke [ɪn'vəʊk] *vt* **1** anrope (også *data*); påkalle; appellere til; **2** besverge; mane frem.

involve [ɪn'vɒlv] *vt* **1** engasjere, innvikle; blande/trekke inn; implisere, involvere; **2** innebære, medføre; nødvendiggjøre. **involvement** [ɪn'vɒlvmənt] *sb* engasjement.

inward ['ɪnwəd] **1** *adj* indre; innvendig; inner-; **2** *adv* innover, innad; ~ *bound* (for) inngående; med kurs innover. **inwardly** ['ɪnwədlɪ] *adv* innover; i sitt indre (sitt hjerte, sitt stille sinn etc). **inwards** ['ɪnwədz] = *inward 2*.

iodine ['aɪəʊdi:n] *sb* jod.

I O U [ˌaɪəʊ'ju:] *sb* gjeldsbrev [egtl *I owe you* jeg skylder Dem/deg].

irascible [ɪ'ræsəbl] *adj* hissig, oppfarende.

iridescence [ˌɪrɪ'desns] *sb* regnbueglans. **iridescent** [ˌɪrɪ'desnt] *adj* strålende *etc* i alle regnbuens farger. **iris** ['aɪərɪs] *sb* **1** iris, regnbuehinne; **2** *bot* iris, sverdlilje. **iris diaphragm** *sb* irisblender.

iron ['aɪən] **I** *sb* **1** jern (og redskap, våpen etc av jern); *som adj* jernhard; jern-, stål-; **2** *(flat-~)* strykejern; **3** *dgl* golfkølle; **4** *US slang* skytejern/skyter (dvs skytevåpen); **II** *vb* stryke(s); ~ *out* glatte/jevne (ut). **iron|-bound** *adj* jernbeslått; *om kystfarvann* forreven, klippefull; *fig* ubøyelig. **~-clad** *adj* jernkledd; pansret, panser-. **~monger** *sb* jernvarehandler. **~smith** *sb* (grov)smed. **~work** *sb* jernarbeid; jernbeslag; smijernsarbeid. **~works** *sb fl* jernverk.

irrefutable [ɪ'refjʊtəbl] *adj* ugjendrivelig; uimotsigelig.

irregular [ɪ'regjʊlə] *adj* uregelmessig, irregulær. **irregularity** [ɪˌregjʊ'lærətɪ] *sb* uregelmessighet *etc*.

irresistible [ˌɪrɪ'sɪstəbl] *adj* uimotståelig.

irrespective [ˌɪrɪ'spektɪv] *adj:* ~ *of* uansett; uten hensyn til; uavhengig av.

irrigate ['ɪrɪgeɪt] *vt* **1** vanne; overrisle; irrigere; **2** *med* skylle ut. **irrigation** [ˌɪrɪ'geɪʃn] *sb* (kunstig) vanning *etc*. **irrigation cooler** *sb petro etc* overrislingskjøler.

irritable ['ırıtəbl] *adj* irritabel, pirrelig. **irritate** ['ırıteıt] *vt* irritere, pirre; ergre. **irritation** [ˌırı'teıʃn] *sb* irritering; irritasjon.

island ['aılənd] *sb* **1** øy; **2** *(street ~)* trafikkøy. **isle** [aıl] *sb* øy. **isolate** ['aısəleıt] *vt* isolere; avskjære/avsondre (fra omverdenen). **isolation** [ˌaısə'leıʃn] *sb* isolering; isolasjon.

issue ['ıʃu:] **I** *sb* **1** flom; strøm (og utstrømning); utflod; **2** ut|deling, (-)levering; tildeling; (tildelt) porsjon/rasjon; **3** utstedelse; utgivelse; publisering (og publikasjon); **4** opplag; nummer/utgave (av avis, blad); **5** emne, sak; (strids)spørsmål; *at* ~ under debatt; om|stridt, -tvistet; **6** resultat; *await the* ~ vente og se (hvordan det går); **7** *jur* avkom, etterkommer; **II** *vb* **1** flomme/strømme ut; velle frem; **2** gå/komme *etc* ut; ~ *from* komme (som en følge) av; **3** dele (gi, sende etc) ut; ut|gi, -levere; ut|skrive, -stede; *be ~d with* bli tildelt; få utlevert.

isthmus ['ısməs] *sb* eid.

italic [ı'tælık] **1** *adj* kursiv(ert); **2** *sb fl* kursiv; kursivert skrift; *my ~s/the ~s are mine* uthevelsene er mine/er foretatt av meg.

itch [ıtʃ] **1** *sb* kløe; *fig* brennende lyst/trang; *(an)* ~ *to write* skrivekløe; **2** *vi* kløe; *be ~ing to* klø (i fingrene) etter (å).

item ['aıtəm] **I** *adv* likeså; enn videre; **II** *sb* **1** detalj; enhet, stykke; *collector's* ~ samlerobjekt; **2** post/punkt (i liste, oversikt etc); **3** *data* (data)element; **4** emne, sak; *news* ~ nyhet (i avis etc).

itinerant [aı'tınərənt] *adj* om|reisende, (-)vandrende. **itinerary** [aı'tınərərı] *sb* reiserute; rutebeskrivelse; reise|beskrivelse, -håndbok.

ivory ['aıvərı] *adj*. *sb* elfenbein(s-).

ivy ['aıvı] *sb* eføy.

J

jab [dʒæb] **I** *sb* **1** slag *etc*; **2** *dgl* sprøyte(stikk); **II** *sb* slå; dulte, dytte; stikke.

jabber ['dʒæbə] **1** *sb* skravl(ing) *etc*; **2** *vb* skravle; snadre; lire av seg.

jack [dʒæk] **I** *adj, sb* hann(-); **II** *sb* **1** *dgl* fyr, kar; kamerat, kompis; (arbeids)mann (også med stor forbokstav, av *Jack* = *John*, jf bruken av Ola på norsk); **2** knekt (i kortspill); **3** donkraft, jekk; brekk|jern, -stang; håndtak, sveiv; **4** *elek* jakk, (veksel)plugg; **5** *sjø* gjøs; **III** *vt (~ up)* jekke opp.

jackal ['dʒækɔ:l] *sb* sjakal.

jackass ['dʒækæs] *sb* **1** (hann)esel; **2** tosk; dust, tulling.

jack-boots ['dʒækbu:ts] *sb fl* kravestøvler.

jacket ['dʒækıt] *sb* **1** jakke; **2** kappe, mantel; **3** *petro* fagverksunderstell; plattformfot; **4** varetrekk; (smuss)omslag; **5** skall, skrell.

jack|-knife *sb* (stor) follekniv. ~ **leg** *sb US petro* overløpsledning. **~-of-all-trades** *sb* altmuligmann, tusenkunstner. **~pot** *sb* (slags) poker; *fig* storgevinst; uventet hell.

jade [dʒeıd] **A** *sb* jade; **B I** *sb* **1** øk; **2** (grepa) jente, kvinnfolk; **3** merr; heks, hurpe; **II** *vt: ~d* trett, utslitt; *fig* (for)slitt.

jag [dʒæg] **A 1** *sb* pigg, spiss, takk; **2** *vt* flenge (hakke, rive etc) opp; **B** *sb US slang* rangel. **jaggy** ['dʒægı] *adj* forreven; takket.

jail [dʒeıl], se *gaol*.

jam [dʒæm] **A** *sb* syltetøy; **B I** *sb* **1** klynge, mølje; trengsel; *traffic* ~ trafikkork; **2** blokkering, forstoppelse; stans; **3** *slang* klemme, knipe; **II** *vb* **1** knuse, mase; klemme (presse, stappe, stue etc) sammen; **2** blokkere; stanse; forstyrre (radiosending); **3** kjøre/sette seg fast; henge seg opp; ~ *the brakes* panikkbremse (egtl så hjulene blokkeres). **jammer** ['dʒæmə] *sb* støysender.

jangle ['dʒæŋgl] **I** *sb* skramling *etc*; **II** *vi* **1** skramle, skrangle; skurre; **2** krangle (høyrøstet).

janitor ['dʒænıtə] *sb* **1** dørvakt; **2** *US* portner, vaktmester.

jar [dʒɑ:] **A I** *sb* **1** risting, skaking; støt (fulgt av skurrende etc lyd); skraping, skurring; **2** rystelse; (lettere) sjokk; **3** mislyd, skurring (dvs mindre uoverensstemmelser); **II** *vb* **1** riste, skake; **2** skrape; skurre; raspe; **3** ryste; skake opp; sjokkere; **4** forstyrre; skjemme, ødelegge; **5** krangle, trette; **B** *sb* krukke; kar.

jargon ['dʒɑ:gən] *sb* sjargong, fagspråk; **2** uforståelig snakk; kaudervelsk.

jaundice ['dʒɔ:ndıs] **1** *sb* gulsott; *fig* misunnelse; **2** *vt: ~d* misunnelig, sjalu.

jaunt [dʒɔ:nt] **1** *sb* tripp; (liten) tur/utflukt; **2** *vi* dra på tur/utflukt.

jaunty ['dʒɔ:ntı] *adj* **1** kaut, kry; selvsikker; **2** lystig.

javelin ['dʒævlın] *sb sport* (kaste)spyd.

jaw [dʒɔ:] **I** *sb* **1** kjeve; *koll* hake(parti), kjaker; **2** *fl* kjeft; bakker/kjever (på skrustikke etc); **3** *dgl* oppkjeftighet; kjefting; **II** *vb* **1** skravle, sludre; **2** kjefte, bruke seg.

jay [dʒeɪ] *sb* **1** nøtteskrike; *fig* kjeftesmelle; **2** *dgl* fommel. **jay-walker** *sb* rågjenger, (trafikk)svime.

jazz [dʒæz] **I** *sb* **1** jass(musikk); **2** futt, pepp; **II** *vb* **1** danse/spille jass; **2** jasse opp; *fig* sprite opp; sette fart i.

jealous ['dʒeləs] *adj* **1** sjalu, skinnsyk; **2** misunnelig; **3** påpasselig; *især rel* nidkjær. **jealousy** ['dʒeləsɪ] *sb* sjalusi *etc*.

jeer ['dʒɪə] **1** *sb* hån(flir), spott; **2** *vb* (*~ at*) hånflire; håne, spotte.

jelly ['dʒelɪ] **1** *sb* gelé; **2** *vb* bli til/lage gelé. **jelly-fish** ['dʒelɪfɪʃ] *sb* manet.

jemmy ['dʒemɪ] *sb* kubein (= brekkjern).

jeopardize ['dʒepədaɪz] *vt* utsette for fare; risikere; sette på spill. **jeopardy** ['dʒepədɪ] *sb* fare, risiko.

jerk [dʒɜ:k] **I** *sb* **1** rykk(ing) *etc*; kast, sleng; **2** (muskel)trekning; rykning; **3** *US slang* dust; skrulling, tomsing; **II** *vb* nappe/rykke (til); dytte; kaste, slenge. **jerky** ['dʒɜ:kɪ] *adj* rykkvis; ujevn.

jerry ['dʒerɪ] *sb* **1** *mil slang: Jerry* tysker; tysk soldat; **2** *slang* potte. **jerry-built** *adj* smurt opp (dvs sjusket oppført av dårlige materialer).

jersey ['dʒɜ:zɪ] *sb* **1** jersey(stoff); **2** *(Jersey)* jerseyku; **3** genser.

jest [dʒest] **I** *sb* **1** spøk; vits, vittighet; **2** skyteskive (for andres spøk); offer; **II** *vi* spøke. **jester** ['dʒestə] *sb* **1** spøkefugl; *hist* narr.

jet [dʒet] **A I** *sb* **1** strøm, stråle; **2** sprut; **3** dyse, spreder, strålerør; munnstykke, tut; **4** *(jet plane)* jet (fly); *som adj* jet-; reaksjonsdrevet, reaksjons-; **II** *vb* strømme (stråle, sprute, sprøyte etc) ut; **B** *sb* gagat, jett. **jet | bit** *sb petro* spylekrone. **~-black** ['dʒetblæk] *adj, sb* beksvart. **~ dredging** *sb petro* spylegraving. **~ fuel** *sb petro* jetdrivstoff. **~ nozzle** *sb petro etc* spyledyse. **~ pod** *sb petro* spylerør.

jetsam ['dʒetsəm] *sb sjø* gods som er kastet over bord. **jetison** ['dʒetɪzn] *vt sjø* kaste (gods) over bord for å lette skipet.

jetty ['dʒetɪ] *sb* molo.

Jew [dʒu] *sb* jøde.

jewel ['dʒu:əl] **1** *sb* edelstein; juvel; smykke; *fig også* skatt; **2** *vt* juvelpryde. **jeweller** ['dʒu:ələ] *sb* juvelér; gullsmed; *US også* urmaker. **jewelry, jewellery** ['dʒu:əlrɪ] *sb* juveler; smykker.

Jewess ['dʒu:ɪs] *sb* jødinne. **Jewish** ['dʒu:ɪʃ] *adj* jødisk.

jib [dʒɪb] **I** *sb* **1** *sjø* klyver; **2** (kran)utligger; **II** *vi* **1** *sjø* jibbe; **2** bli være sta; slå seg vrang; *~ at* steile over; vike tilbake for.

jibe [dʒaɪb] = gibe.

jiffy ['dʒɪfɪ] *sb dgl* øyeblikk.

jig [dʒɪg] **A I** *sb* gigg (dvs dansen); **II** *vb* **1** danse gigg; **2** huske/vippe (opp og ned); riste; **B** *sb mek* jigg, holder; stativ. **jig|saw** *sb* dekupørsak, løvsag. **~saw puzzle** *sb* puslespill (av uregelmessig formede biter som skal settes sammen til et bilde).

jilt [dʒɪlt] **1** *sb* flørt; svikefull/ustadig jente; **2** *vt* svike (i kjærlighet); gi kurven.

jingle ['dʒɪŋgl] **1** *sb* ringling *etc*; bjelleklang; **2** *vb* ringle, skrangle; single. **jingle bells** *sb fl* dombjeller.

job [dʒɒb] **I** *sb* **1** arbeid (og især kortere arbeidsoppgave); **2** *dgl* jobb (dvs arbeid, post, stilling); **3** *dgl* affære, sak; **II** *vb* **1** (små)jobbe; **2** *dgl* jobbe (= spekulere etc); fikse, ordne. **job | control language** *sb data* styrespråk. **~ control statement** *sb data* styresetning. **~ input file** *sb data* jobbfil. **~ output file** *sb data* utskriftsfil. **~ scheduler** *sb data* (jobb)fordeler. **~ statement** *sb data* jobbsetning.

jockey ['dʒɒkɪ] **I** *sb* **1** jockey; **2** *disc ~* plate|annonsør, prater; **II** *vb* lure, svindle.

jocose [dʒəʊ'kəʊs] *adj* (anstrengt) morsom/spøkefull. **jocosity** [dʒəʊ'kɒsətɪ] *sb* (anstrengt) spøk/spøkefullhet. **jocular** ['dʒɒkjʊlə] *adj* spøkefull, morsom.

jog [dʒɒg] **I** *sb* **1** dytt(ing) *etc*; risting; **2** luntetrav; jogging; **II** *vb* **1** dytte, puffe; riste, skumpe; *~ her memory* friske på hukommelsen hennes; **2** lunte, småtrave; jogge.

join [dʒɔɪn] **I** *sb = joint II 1*; **II** *vb* **1** forbinde (og skjøte; føye/sette sammen etc); **2** forene(s); gå (komme, slutte seg etc) sammen; **3** gå/melde seg inn (i); bli medlem (av); *~ in* delta; bli/være med; *~ up (dgl mil)* verve seg. **joiner** ['dʒɔɪnə] *sb* (møbel)snekker. **joint** [dʒɔɪnt] **I** *adj* forent, samlet; felles; **II** *sb* **1** forbindelse; sammenføyning, skjøt; fuge; **2** ledd (og leddforbindelse); *out of ~* ut(e) av ledd; **3** *(~ of meat)* stek; **4** *US slang* bule, kneipe; **III** *vt* **1** skjøte; føye/sette sammen; **2** partere; dele (kutte, skjære etc) opp. **jointly** ['dʒɔɪntlɪ] *adv* i fellesskap; sammen.

joke [dʒəʊk] **1** *sb* spøk; vits, vittighet; *practical ~* pek, puss; skøyerstrek; **2** *vi* spøke. **joker** ['dʒəʊkə] *sb* **1** spøkefugl; **2** *US slang* fyr, kar; type; **3** joker.

jolly ['dʒɒlɪ] **I** *adj* **1** lystig, munter; **2** *dgl* finfin, super; festlig, hyggelig; **II** *adv* svært, veldig; *~ good* flott, supert.

jolt [dʒəʊlt] **1** *sb* rykk, støt; **2** *vb* rykke; riste, skake; skumpe.

jostle ['dʒɒsl] *vb* dytte/skumpe til; mase/trenge seg frem.

jot [dʒɒt] **1** *sb* døyt, grann; **2** *vt: ~ down* rable/skrive ned.

journal ['dʒɜ:nl] *sb* **1** magasin, tidsskrift; avis; **2** journal; *sjø etc* logg(bok), (skips)dagbok. **journalism** ['dʒɜ:nəlɪzəm] *sb* journalistikk. **journalist** ['dʒɜ:nəlɪst] *sb* journalist. **journey** ['dʒɜ:nɪ] **1** *sb* reise; **2** *vi* reise (især til lands).

jovial ['dʒəʊvɪəl] *adj* gemyttlig, hyggelig; lystig, munter.

jowl [dʒaʊl] *sb* hake(parti), kjake; kinn; *cheek by ~* side om side; tett sammen.

joy [dʒɔɪ] *sb* fryd, glede; *wish one ~* ønske en alt godt/lykke til. **joy|ful** ['dʒɔɪfʊl] *adj* glad, lykkelig. **~less** ['dʒɔɪlɪs] *adj* gledesløs, trist. **~ous** ['dʒɔɪəs] *adj* glad; lystig, munter. **~ stick** *sb data etc* styrespak.

jubilant ['dʒu:bɪlənt] *adj* jublende; frydefull, gledestrålende. **jubilation** [ˌdʒu:bɪ'leɪʃn] *sb* jubel; festing, festligheter. **jubilee** ['dʒu:bɪlɪ] *sb* jubileum (især femtiårs).

judge ['dʒʌdʒ] **I** *sb* **1** *jur* dommer; **2** *sport* dommer, oppmann; **3** kjenner; (smaks)dommer; **II** *vb* **1** *jur* dømme/være dommer (i rettssak); **2** dømme/være dommer (oppmann etc i/mellom); **3** anslå, bedømme; mene, synes; *to ~ from* å dømme etter. **judgement** ['dʒʌdʒmənt] *sb* **1** *jur* dom (og domfelling, straff etc): **2** bedømmelse; avgjørelse, dom; **3** anslag, overslag, skjønn; **4** dømmekraft, vurderingsevne. **judicial** [dʒu:'dɪʃl] *adj* **1** dommer-; **2** juridisk, rettslig; retts-. **judiciary** [dʒu:'dɪʃɪərɪ] **1** *adj* = *judicial*; **2** *sb koll: the ~* domstolene; *pol* den dømmende makt. **judicious** [dʒu:'dɪʃəs] *adj* klok; forsiktig, skjønnsom.

jug [dʒʌg] *sb* **1** mugge; **2** *slang* kasjott, fengsel.

juggernaut ['dʒʌgənɔ:t] *sb* molok; veldig (altoppslukende, uimotståelig etc) makt.

juggle ['dʒʌgl] *vb* **1** sjonglere; trylle; bløffe, lure; **2** fikse (dvs forfalske, svindle med etc). **juggler** ['dʒʌglə] *sb* **1** sjonglør; **2** tryllekunstner; **3** bedrager, svindler.

juice [dʒu:s] *sb* **1** saft; *meat ~* kjøttkraft; *tobacco ~* tobakkssaus; **2** *slang* (elektrisk) strøm. **juicy** ['dʒu:sɪ] *adj* saftig.

jumble ['dʒʌmbl] **1** *sb* forvirring; rot, røre; sammensurium; **2** *vb* rote sammen; ligge og flyte (utover). **jumble market** *sb* loppe|marked, -torg.

jump [dʒʌmp] **I** *sb* **1** hopp, sprang; **2** rykk, sett; **II** *vb* **1** hoppe/springe (over, på etc); *dgl* bykse, jumpe; *~ at (dgl)* hoppe på (dvs akseptere, gå med på etc med iver); *~ to conclusions* trekke forhastede slutninger; **2** kvekke; fare sammen; **3** fare/fyke i været (om f.eks. priser). **jumper** ['dʒʌmpə] *sb* **1** hopper *etc*; **2** genser, jumper; bluse; **3** *især US* ermeløs kjole (over bluse etc). **jump | instruction** *sb data* hoppinstruksjon. **~over** *sb petro* overføringsrør; tverrforbindelse mellom rørledninger. **~ scrolling** *sb data* rykkvis rulling. **jumpy** ['dʒʌmpɪ] *adj* skvetten.

junction ['dʒʌŋkʃn] *sb* **1** forbindelse, sammenføyning; skjøt; **2** møtested; *især* jernbaneknutepunkt; (større) veikryss; **3** forening, møte. **juncture** ['dʒʌŋktʃə] *sb* **1** møte; sammenfall; **2** omstendighet(er); (kritisk) stadium/tidspunkt.

junior ['dʒu:nɪə] **I** *adj* **1** yngre; junior(-); **2** underordnet; lavere (i grad/rang etc); **II** *sb* **1** yngre person; *she is my ~* hun er yngre enn jeg; **2** junior (= sønn); *merk* junior(sjef); juniorpartner; yngre kollega; **3** *US* elev/student i sitt tredje studieår (av i alt fire). **junior high school** *sb US* ungdomsskole.

juniper ['dʒu:nɪpə] *sb* einer.

junk [dʒʌŋk] **A** *sb* **1** skrap, skrot; søppel; **2** *slang* narkotika (især heroin); **B** *sb sjø* djunke. **junk food** *sb* søppelmat (dvs især fettrik og næringsfattig mat fra gatekjøkken etc). **junkie, junky** ['dʒʌŋkɪ] *sb* narkotiker, narkovrak. **junk | man** *sb* skraphandler. **~ shop** *sb* skraphandel; *sjø* skipshandel. **~ yard** *sb* skraphandlertomt.

jurisdiction [ˌdʒuərɪs'dɪkʃn] *sb* jurisdiksjon; doms|makt, myndighet; rettsdistrikt; rettspleie. **juror** ['dʒuərə] *sb* jurymedlem, lagrettemedlem. **jury** ['dʒuərɪ] *sb* jury, lagrette.

just [dʒʌst] **A** *adv* **1** akkurat, like; nettopp, nylig; **2** bare; (bare) så vidt; **3** nøyaktig, presis; *~ the opposite* akkurat motsatt; det stikk motsatte; *~ the same* likevel; **4** *~ about* sånn omtrent; *~ tell med* si meg engang; *~ who owns that house* hvem eier egentlig det huset; **5** *dgl* simpelthen; *~ fine!* flott! kjempefin(t)! **B** *adj* rettferdig; (rett og) riktig; **2** rett|skaffen, -sindig; **3** berettiget, rimelig. **justice** ['dʒʌstɪs] *sb* **1** rett, rettferd(ighet); **2** berettigelse; riktighet; **3** (høyesteretts)dommer; *Justice of the Peace* fredsdommer. **justification** [ˌdʒʌstɪfɪ'keɪʃn] *sb* berettigelse *etc*. **justify** ['dʒʌstɪfaɪ] *vt* **1** berettige; **2** forsvare, rettferdiggjøre; **3** *data* innpasse, stille. **justly** ['dʒʌstlɪ] *adv* med rette.

jut [dʒʌt] *vi* stritte/strutte (ut); *~ out* stikke frem; stå ut.

juvenile ['dʒu:vɪnaɪl] **1** *adj* ung(dommelig); ungdoms-; **2** *sb* ungdom (dvs ungt menneske). **juvenile | delinquency** *sb* ungdomskriminalitet. **~ delinquent** *sb* ungdomsforbryter.

juxtaposition [ˌdʒʌkstəpə'zɪʃn] *sb* sidestilling; plassering ved siden av hverandre.

K

kangaroo [ˌkæŋgə'ru:] *sb* kenguru.

keel [ki:l] **1** *sb* kjøl; *on an even ~* på rett kjøl; sikkert, støtt; **2** *vb: ~ over* kantre, krenge; vende (med) kjølen i været.

keen [ki:n] *adj* **1** bitende, skarp; kvass; **2** dyp (og dyptfølt); intens, sterk; **3** følsom; fin; *a ~ eye* et skarpt blikk; **4** ivrig (*on* etter; *to* etter å); (svært) interessert (*on* i); energisk.

keep [ki:p] **I** *sb* **1** underhold; forpleining, kost; **2** *dgl: for ~s* for bestandig; for godt; **II** *vb* **1** holde (og beholde; holde på; holde fast ved; (opp)bevare, gjemme (på) etc); *~ in mind* huske (på); *~ your seats!* bli sittende! **2** forsinke, hefte; oppholde; holde igjen/tilbake; **3** holde (seg); forholde/oppføre seg; opprettholde; ~ *quiet* være stille; **4** (over)holde; feire, helligholde; følge (skikk etc); **5** eie, (inne)ha; ~ *pigs* holde griser; **6** drive; (be)styre; stelle (hus etc); ~ *books* føre bøker/regnskap etc; **7** forsørge, underholde; holde (forsynt) med; **8** forbli; fortsette/holde frem (med); ~ *straight on* fortsette rett frem; **9** holde seg; vare (ved); **10** *med adv/prep* ~ **at** holde til; mase på; ~ **away** unngå; holde (seg) unna; ~ **back** holde igjen/tilbake; fortie; ~ **down** holde nede; ~ **from** (av)holde fra; fortie/skjule for; ~ **in** holde hjemme/inne etc; holde igjen (i sjakk, i tømme etc); ~ *in touch* holde kontakten; ~ *in with* holde seg inne med; ~ *one's hand in* holde ferdigheten/øvelsen ved like; ~ **off** holde (seg) unna; ~ **on** beholde (hatt etc) på; fortsette/holde frem (med); ~ **out** holde (seg) ute; ~ **up** opprettholde; holde ved like; holde (det) gående; ~ *up with* holde følge/tritt med; holde seg/være på høyde med. **keeper** ['ki:pə] *sb* **1** (-)oppsynsmann; (-)vakt, (-)vokter; **2** (-)eier, (-)innehaver; (-)holder. **keeping** ['ki:pɪŋ] *sb* **1** forvaring, varetekt; **2** underhold; **3** overensstemmelse, samsvar. **keepsake** ['ki:pseɪk] *sb* (ting til) erindring/minne; suvenir.

keg [keg] *sb* kagge; lite fat.

kelly ['kelɪ] *sb petro* drivrør, medbringerstang.

ken [ken] *sb* kunnskapsområde; kunnskaper.

kerb [kɜ:b] *sb (~-stone)* fortauskant.

kernel ['kɜ:nl] *sb* kjerne.

kerosene, kerosine ['kerəsi:n] *sb* parafin.

kettle ['ketl] *sb* gryte, kjele; *a pretty ~ of fish (dgl)* en nydelig suppe(das). **kettle-drum** ['ketldrʌm] *sb* pauke.

key [ki:] **I** *som adj* nøkkel-; **II** *sb* **1** nøkkel *(for/of/to* til); **2** nøkkel (dvs fasit, løsning, svar etc); **3** (skru)nøkkel; **4** blei, kile; splint; **5** *mus etc* klaff, ventil; knapp; tangent, tast; **6** *mus* toneart; grunntone; *off ~* falsk; **III** *vt* **1** feste (med blei etc); kile fast; **2** ~ *up* spenne; stramme inn/opp; *mus* stemme; *fig* stimulere; stramme opp; *~ed-up* oppspilt. **key | bed** *sb petro* nøkkellag. **~board I** *sb* **1** tangentbord, tastatur; *data også* tastbord; **2** *mus a)* klaviatur; *b)* klaviatur- el. tangentinstrument; **II** *vt data* taste inn. **~board punch** *sb data* kort|huller, -punch. **~click** *sb data* tasteklikk. ~ **entry** *sb data* inntasting. ~ **field** *sb data* nøkkelfelt. ~ **fraction** *sb petro* nøkkelfraksjon. **~hole** *sb* nøkkelhull. ~ **matching** *sb data* nøkkelkontroll. **~note** *sb mus, fig* grunntone. **~pad** *sb data* tastgruppe. ~ **position** *sb* nøkkel|posisjon, -stilling. ~ **stroke** *sb data* **1** tastetrykk; **2** inntasting (av det enkelte tegn). ~ **transformation** *sb data* nøkkeltransformering.

kick [kɪk] **I** *sb* **1** spark, spenn; *ved skyting* rekyl; **2** *petro* tilløp til utblåsning; **3** *dgl* futt, smell; tæl; **4** *dgl* gøy, moro; spenning: **II** *vb* sparke, spenne; *om skytevåpen* slå (dvs rekylere); ~ *against* protestere (vilt) mot; stritte imot; ~ *at* kritisere; ~ *back* slå/virke tilbake; slå/ta igjen; ~ *off (sport)* foreta avspark; *~-off* avspark; ~ *up a fuss/row etc* lage/stelle i stand bråk.

kid [kɪd] **A** *sb* **1** (geite)|kje, -killing; **2** *(~skin)* geiteskinn, sjevrå; **3** *dgl (~dy)* barn; *fl* (små)unger; **B** *vt* lure, narre; erte; *you're ~ding* du (bare) tøyser; det er bare noe du sier. **kid | brother** *sb* lillebror. ~ **gloves** *sb fl* glacéhansker; *fig* silkehansker. **~skin** *sb* geiteskinn, sjevrå. ~ **sister** *sb* lillesøster.

kidney ['kɪdnɪ] *sb* nyre.

kill [kɪl] **I** *sb* **1** *(~ing)* drap; **2** (jakt)bytte; **II** *vb* **1** drepe; slakte; ~ *time* fordrive/slå i hjel tiden; **2** *petro* kvele (tilløp til utblåsning); **3** spolere, ødelegge. **kill|-joy** *sb* gledesdreper. ~ **line** *sb petro* kveleledning, slamslange. ~ **mud** *sb petro* kveleslam.

kiln [kɪl(n)] *sb* tørkeovn.

kin [kɪn] *sb* familie, slekt; *next of ~* nærmeste pårørende. **kins|folk** *sb koll* slekt(ninger). **~man** *sb* (mannlig) slektning. **~woman** *sb* (kvinnelig) slektning.

kind [kaɪnd] **A** *sb* **1** slag(s), sort; art, type; gruppe, klasse; ~ *of [dgl* 'kaɪndə] liksom; på en måte; **2** naturalier, varer; *repay in ~* betale/gjengjelde med samme mynt, **B** *adj* god, snill; vennlig; *will you be ~ enough to* vil De/du være så snill (å). **kind|-hearted** *adj* godhjertet, snill. **~ly** ['kaɪndlɪ] *adj, adv* elskverdig, vennlig: *will you ~* vil De/du være så snill (å). **~ness** *sb* godhet, vennlighet.

kindergarten ['kɪndə,gɑ:tn] *sb* barnehage, førskole.

kindle [kɪndl] *vb* **1** ta fyr; **2** tenne/sette fyr på; nøre/tenne opp; **3** oppflamme(s). **kindling** ['kɪndlɪŋ] *sb* opptenningsved. **kindling point** *sb petro etc* flammepunkt.

kindred ['kɪndrɪd] **I** *adj* **1** beslektet; **2** *dgl* lignende, maken; **II** *sb* **1** slektskap; **2** slekt(ninger).

king [kɪŋ] *sb* konge. **kingdom** ['kɪŋdəm] *sb* **1** konge|dømme, rike; **2** rike; domene, område; **3** (Guds) rike; ~ *come (dgl)* det hinsidige; *wait till ~ come (dgl)* vente til dommedag. **king's evidence** *sb* kronvitne.

kink [kɪŋk] **I** *sb* **1** bukt, løkke, krøll, slyng; **2** floke; **3** grille, innfall; fiks idé; **II** *vb* slå bukt på; slå krøll på seg; floke seg (til).

kinship ['kɪnʃɪp] *sb* slektskap.

kipper ['kɪpə] *sb* røykesild.

kiss [kɪs] **1** *sb* kyss; ~ *of life* munn-mot-munn-metoden (for livredning); *fig* livgivende impuls etc; **2** *vb* kysse (hverandre); ~ *the dust/ground* bite i gresset.

kit [kɪt] *sb* **1** utstyr; *mil også* effekter; **2** (håndverkers) verktøy|(kasse, -sett etc). **kit-bag** *sb* pakksekk.

kitchen [kɪtʃɪn] *sb* kjøkken. **kitchenette** [,kɪtʃɪ'net] *sb* tekjøkken.

kite [kaɪt] *sb* **1** glente; **2** (papir)drage; **3** prøveballong.

kith [kɪθ] *sb: ~ and kin* slekt og venner.

kit inspection *sb mil* pussvisitasjon.

kitten ['kɪtn] *sb* kattunge.

knack [næk] *sb* håndlag; *get the ~ of it* få taket på det.

knapsack ['næpsæk] *sb* ryggsekk.

knave [neɪv] *sb* **1** kjeltring, skurk; slyngel; **2** knekt (i kortspill). **knavish** ['neɪvɪʃ] *adj* kjeltringaktig; upålitelig.

knead [ni:d] *vt* elte, kna.

knee [ni:] kne. **knee-cap** *sb* kneskjell; *dgl* kneskål. **kneel** [ni:l] *vi* knele; bøye kne.

knell [nel] *sb* (klokke)klemt; klemting/ringing (med klokker, især ved dødsfall).

knickerbockers ['nɪkəbɒkəz] *sb fl* nikkers. **knickers** ['nɪkəz] *sb fl* **1** dameunderbukser; **2** = *knickerbockers.*

knife [naɪf] **1** *sb* kniv; **2** *vt* bruke kniv (på); stikke/ såre med kniv; *fig* dolke; falle i ryggen.

knight [naɪt] **I** *sb* **1** ridder; **2** *GB* tittel som gir rett til *Sir* foran (for)navnet; **3** ridder (av losje, orden etc); **4** springer (i sjakk); **II** *vt* slå til ridder. **knighthood** ['naɪthʊd] *sb* ridder|rang, -skap, -verdighet.

knit [nɪt] *vb* **1** strikke; **2** sammen|føye, -sveise; *closely ~ted* fast oppbygd/sammentømret; **3** *~ the brows* rynke (øyen)brynene. **knitting** ['nɪtɪŋ] *sb* **1** strikking; **2** strikketøy. **knitting-needle** *sb* strikkepinne.

knob [nɒb] *sb* **1** (rundt) håndtak; knapp/knott (til dør, skuff etc); **2** klump, knort; kul. **knobbly** ['nɒblɪ] *adj* knortet.

knock [nɒk] **I** *sb* **1** *(~ing)* bank(ing) *etc*; **2** slag; støt; **II** *vb* **1** banke (*at/on* på); dundre, hamre; **2** slå; *~ on the head* slå i hodet; **3** *med adv/prep* ~ **about** rundjule, skamslå; mishandle; *dgl* farte omkring; ~ **back** *dgl* gi baksmell; *slang* helle/slå i seg (dram etc); ~ **down** rive/slå ned; *dgl* sette ned (pris); rive (ned); ta fra hverandre; *~-down price* bunnpris, gibortpris; ~ **off** slå av; slå av på; gjøre seg ferdig med; *dgl* ta kvelden; rive av seg (vits etc); skylle ned (dram etc); *slang* krepere (dvs dø); kverke (dvs drepe); ~ **out** banke ut (av); slå ned/ut; ~ **over** velte; slå over ende; ~ **together** *dgl* flikke (slå, smøre etc) sammen; ~ **up** rundjule; slå i stykker; sette en stopper for; *dgl* smøre opp/sammen; *slang* sette unge på. **knock-back** *sb* baksmell. **knocker** *sb* dørhammer.

knot [nɒt] **I** *sb* **1** knute, stikk; *sjø* knop (også = 1 nautisk mil); **2** rosett, sløyfe; **3** floke, innviklet problem; **4** klynge; flokk, gruppe; **5** kvist (i trevirke); knast, knort; **II** *vb* **1** knyte; lage knute(r); slå knute (på); **2** binde/knytte (sammen). **knotty** ['nɒtɪ] *adj* **1** floket, innviklet; **2** kvistrik; knortet, knudret.

know [nəʊ] **I** *sb dgl: in the ~* innviet, underrettet; **II** *vb* **1** vite; kjenne til; være klar over; *~ about/of* kjenne til; vite om; **2** forstå (og forstå seg på); kunne; *~ how to* kunne; vite hvordan (en skal); **3** kjenne (og kjenne igjen). **know-how** *sb* fagkunnskap; faglig dyktighet/erfaring; sakkunnskap; ekspertise, kompetanse. **knowing** *adj* **1** vitende *etc*; **2** dyktig; erfaren; innsiktsfull; **3** forslagen, utspekulert; *a ~ing look* et megetsigende blikk. **knowledge** ['nɒlɪdʒ] *sb* **1** kunnskap(er), lærdom; viten; *common ~* (allment) kjent sak; noe alle vet; **2** kjennskap (*of* til); forståelse. **knowledgeable** ['nɒlɪdʒəbl] *adj dgl* vel|informert, underrettet.

knuckle ['nʌkl] **1** *sb* knoke; ledd; **2** *vi: ~ under* gi seg; gi tapt.

knurl [nɜ:l] **I** *sb* **1** knast, knort; **2** rifling; riflet mønster/rand etc; **II** *vt* rifle, rulettere.

Kraut [kraʊt] *sb US slang* tysker; tysk soldat.

L

label ['leɪbl] **I** *sb* **1** etikett, (merke)lapp; kjenne|-merke, tegn; betegnelse; **2** *data* etikett (og båndslutt-, filslutt-, internetikett); **II** *vt* sette (merke)lapp på; betegne, karakterisere. **label | check** *sb data* etikettkontroll. ~ **variable** *sb data* merkevariabel.

laboratory [lə'bɒrətərɪ] *sb* laboratorium. **laborious** [lə'bɔ:rɪəs] *adj* arbeidsom, strevsom; **2** anstrengende, tung; **3** møysommelig; omstendelig. **labour** ['leɪbə] **I** *sb* **1** (kropps)arbeid; jobbing, slit; strev; **2** jobb; (stykke) arbeid; **3** *koll* arbeidere (især = arbeidskraft); *pol* arbeiderklassen; *Labour = the Labour Party* det britiske arbeiderparti; **4** (fødsels)-veer; **II** *vb* **1** arbeide (hardt); jobbe, slite; **2** *~ under* lide under; være plaget av; **3** bearbeide; utarbeide; gå (for mye) i detalj; **4** ha veer. **laboured** ['leɪbəd] *adj* **1** anstrengt, tung; **2** omstendelig; kunstlet, oppstyltet. **labourer** ['leɪbərə] *sb* (kropps)arbeider. **labour exchange** *sb* arbeids(formidlings)kontor.

lace [leɪs] **I** *sb* **1** bånd, lisse; reim, snor; (uniforms)tresse; **2** blonde(r), knipling(er); **II** *vb* **1** snøre(s); **2** besette med snorer *etc*; **3** kante/pynte med blonder *etc*; **4** *dgl: ~ into* slå løs på; **5** *dgl* sprite opp; *~d coffee* kaffedokter. **lace boots** *sb fl* snørestøvler.

lacerate ['læsəreɪt] *vt* **1** flenge opp; rive i stykker; **2** såre; *især fig* såre dypt. **lacerated** ['læsəreɪtɪd] *adj*, *især fig* opprevet. **laceration** [ˌlæsə'reɪʃn] *sb* oppflenging *etc*.

lack [læk] **I** *sb* mangel, skort; savn; *for ~ of* av mangel på; **II** *vb* **1** mangle, savne; trenge; **2** mangle (dvs ikke være til stede el. for hånden). **lack-lustre** ['lækˌlʌstə] *adj* glansløs, matt.

lacquer ['lækə] *sb, vt* lakk(ere).

lad [læd] *sb* (ung)gutt; kar; *dgl* kjekkas; *skotsk* kjæreste.

ladder ['lædə] **I** *sb* **1** stige; *sjø* fallreip, leider; **2** raknet (strømpe)maske; **II** *vb* rakne; *~ed* raknet. **ladder-proof** *adj* raknefri.

laddie ['lædɪ] *sb* gutt(unge).

laden ['leɪdn] *adj* lastet; (be)lesset; bebyrdet, tynget; fylt/mettet med. **lading** ['leɪdɪŋ] *sb* last; frakt.

ladle ['leɪdl] **1** *sb* sleiv, øse; **2** *vt* øse; *~ out* øse opp; dele/øse ut.

lady ['leɪdɪ] **I** *som adj* kvinnelig; hunn-; **II** *sb* **1** dame; *the old ~ (hum)* kona, madammen; **2** *Lady (som tittel)* lady; *Your Ladyship* Deres høyhet/nåde; **3** *rel: Our Lady* Vår Frue (= jomfru Maria). **lady|bird** *sb* marihøne. **~-killer** *sb* kvinnebedårer, skjørtejeger. **~like** *adj* damemessig; fornem; *om menn* feminin, jålet.

lag [læg] **A 1** *sb* somling *etc*; forsinkelse; **2** *vi (~ behind)* somle; komme/ligge etter; sakke akterut; **B I** *sb* **1** (tønne)stav; **2** isolasjon; **II** *vt* (varme)isolere (kjeler, rør etc); **C** *slang* **1** *sb* forbryter; straffange; **2** *vt* fengsle; deportere. **laggard** ['lægəd] *sb* etternøler; somlekopp. **lagging** ['lægɪŋ] *sb* isolasjon, isolasjonsmateriale.

lager ['lɑ:gə] *sb* pils.

lair [leə] *sb* hi, hule; (dyrs) leie.

laity ['leɪətɪ] *sb* legfolk.

lake [leɪk] *sb* (inn)sjø, vann.

lamb [læm] **I** *sb* **1** lam (og lamme|kjøtt, -skinn etc); **2** lam (dvs søtt, veloppdragent barn); sau (dvs dum, troskyldig person); **II** *vi* lamme (dvs få lam).

lame ['leɪm] **I** *adj* **1** halt (*in* på); **2** tam (dvs lite overbevisende etc); *~ excuse* dårlig (begrunnet, fremført etc) unnskyldning; **II** *vt* helseslå, skamslå; gjøre/slå halt.

lament [lə'ment] **I** *sb* jammer, klage(sang); **II** *vb* **1** jamre/klage (over); sørge over; **2** beklage; klage over. **lamentable** ['læməntəbl] *adj* **1** beklagelig, sørgelig; **2** elendig, ynkelig. **lamentation** [ˌlæmən'teɪʃn] *sb* jammer, jamring; klage|(rop), -sang.

lamp [læmp] *sb* lampe, lykt. **lamp | kerosene** *sb petro* lampeolje, parafin. **~-post** *sb* lyktestolpe. **~-shade** *sb* lampeskjerm.

lance [lɑ:ns] **I** *sb* lanse; **II** *vt* **1** angripe med lanse; **2** snitte opp med: **lancet** ['lɑ:nsɪt] *sb* lansett.

land [lænd] **I** *sb* **1** (fast)land, landjord; **2** (dyrkings)jord; jordeiendom; grunn (og grunneiendom); **3** land, rike; **II** *vb* **1** lande; gå/komme i land; *be ~ed in* befinne seg/være havnet i; **2** landsette, losse; **3** hale i land (dvs sikre seg, få tak i etc); **4** *slang* lange til; *~ him one on the jaw* gi ham en på kjaken.

land-agent *sb* eiendomsmegler.

landing ['lændɪŋ] **I** *adj* **1** landings-; **2** *mil* landgangs-; **II** *sb* **1** landing; landsetting, lossing; landgang (under invasjon); **2** landingsplass; **3** *sport* ned|-slag, -sprang; **4** repos, trappeavsats. **landing|-craft** *sb* landgangsfartøy. **-~field** *sb* (mindre) flyplass. **~-force** *sb* landgangsstyrke. **~-gear** *sb* (fly)understell. **~-ground** *sb* = *~-field*. **~-party** *sb* = *~-force*. **~ platform** *sb petro* lasteplattform. **~ shoulder** *sb petro* forankringsskulder. **~-strip** *sb* rullebane; (mindre) flyplass.

land|lady ['lænˌleɪdɪ] *sb* **1** vertinne (på hotell etc); hybelvertinne; **2** kvinnelig godseier. **~locked** ['lændlɒkt] *adj* (helt eller delvis) omgitt av land. **~lord** ['lænlɔ:d] *sb* **1** vert (på hotell etc); husvert; krovert; hotelleier; **2** (mannlig) godseier. **~lubber** ['lænˌlʌbə] *sb* landkrabbe. **~mark** ['lændmɑ:k] *sb* **1** grense|merke, -skjell; **2** landingsmerke (for fly); sjømerke (for skip); **3** kjenne|merke, -tegn; landemerke; milepæl. **~owner** ['lændˌəʊnə] *sb* grunneier; godseier. **~scape** ['lænskeɪp] *sb* landskap. **~slide** ['lændslaɪd] *sb* **1** ras, skred; jordfall; **2** (valg)skred. **~ward** ['lændwəd] **1** *adj* land-; **2** *adv* mot land.

lane [leɪn] *sb* **1** vei (især smal landevei med gjerde/hekk på begge sider); **2** smug; smal/trang gate; **3** (gang)vei; passasje; **4** (kjøre)felt (på motorvei etc); **5** rute; (skips)led; (fly)korridor; **6** bane/felt (på idrettsplass).

language ['læŋgwɪdʒ] *sb* språk.

languid ['læŋgwɪd] *adj* **1** matt, slapp; **2** apatisk, likegyldig; **3** treg. **languish** ['læŋgwɪʃ] *vi* bli slapp; dø/sykne hen. **languishing** ['læŋgwɪʃɪŋ] *adj* hen|døende, -syknende; lengselsfull; (van)smektende. **languor** ['læŋgə] *sb* **1** matthet, slapphet; **2** apati, likegyldighet; **3** treghet; **4** trykkende stillhet.

lank [læŋk] *adj* **1** (rad)mager; lang og tynn; **2** pistret (om hår). **lanky** ['læŋkɪ] *adj* (rad)mager; hengslet, oppløpen, ulenkelig.

lantern ['læntən] *sb* lanterne, lykt. **lantern-jawed** *adj* langkjaket; hulkinnet.

lanyard ['lænjəd] *sb* **1** snor (til fløyte, kniv, revolver etc); avtrekkersnor (til kanon); **2** taljereip.

lap [læp] **A** *sb* fang, skjød; **B I** *sb* **1** overlapping; flik, fold; **2** omgang, tørn; **3** etappe; del (av reise etc); **4** *sport* runde (i løpskonkurranse); **II** *vb* **1** overlappe; legge/ligge over (hverandre); **2** brette/folde over; **3** innhylle, svøpe; **C I** *sb* **1** lepjing, slikking; **2** skvalping; (bølge)skvulp; **3** skvip; **II** *vb* **1** lepje/slikke (i seg); **2** skvalpe/skvulpe (om småbølger); **D I** *sb* polérskive; **II** *vt* **1** polere; **2** slipe sammen. **lap-dog** *sb* skjødehund.

lapel [lə'pel] *sb* slag (på jakke etc).

lapse [læps] **I** *sb* **1** forseelse, forsømmelse; lapsus; **2** flyt, sig; forløp (av tid); **3** nedgang; (gradvis) bortfall/opphør; utløp; **II** *vi* **1** feile; forse seg; synde i det små; **2** flyte, sige; forløpe, gå; *~ into* falle/gå tilbake til; henfalle til; slå over i; **3** gå (gradvis) av bruk; **4** bortfalle; utløpe.

lap | time *sb sport* rundetid. **~-top** *adj data* bærbar (dvs egentlig til å ha på fanget).

larceny ['lɑ:sənɪ] *sb* tyveri.

larch [lɑ:tʃ] *sb* lerk.

lard [lɑ:d] **I** *sb* **1** matfett, smult; **2** spekk; **II** *vt* spekke. **larder** ['lɑ:də] *sb* matbod, spiskammer.

large [lɑ:dʒ] **I** *adj* **1** stor; **2** rommelig, vid; **3** omfattende, vidtrekkende; **4** rikelig; **5** storsinnet; liberal; vidsynt; **II** *adv* stort; *talk* ~ skryte; slå stort på det; **III** *sb* **1** *at* ~ på frifot; **2** *people at* ~ folk flest/i sin alminnelighet; **3** *talk/write at* ~ snakke/skrive i det vide og brede. **large|-handed** *adj* raus, rundhåndet. **~-hearted** *adj* godhjertet. **largely** ['lɑ:dʒlɪ] *adv* **1** overveiende; stort sett; **2** i (temmelig) stor grad/utstrekning; **3** rundhåndet; rikelig. **large|-minded** *adj* raus, storsinnet; liberal; vidsynt. **~-scale integration** *sb data* storskalaintegrasjon.

lark [lɑ:k] **A** *sb* lerke; **B 1** *sb* leven, moro; *for* ~ for moro skyld; **2** *vi* tulle, tøyse; holde leven.

lascivious [lə'sɪvɪes] *adj* **1** kåt, lysten; (erotisk) eggende; forførerisk.

laser ['leɪzə] *sb* laser. **laser | printer** *sb data* laserskriver. ~ **storage** *sb data* laserlager.

lash [læʃ] **I** *sb* **1** pisk (og piskeslag, -straff); (piske)snert; flengende kritikk *etc*; **2** *(eye-~)* (øyen)-vippe; **II** *vb* **1** piske (med); peise på; rappe til; **2** piske (mot); **3** piske (dvs egge, hisse) opp; **4** hudflette (dvs irettesette/kritisere etc strengt); **5** laske/surre (sammen). **lash-up** *sb* sammenflikking; provisorisk sammenkobling etc.

lass [læs] *sb skotsk* (ung)jente: kjæreste. **lassie** ['læsɪ] *sb* jentunge, (små)jente.

lassitude ['læsɪtju:d] *sb* tretthet, utmattelse; slapphet.

last [lɑ:st] **A I** *adj* **1** *om rekkefølge* sist; bakerst; **2** *om tid* forrige (dvs nærmest foregående); senest, sist; ~ *night* i går kveld; ~ *year* i fjor; **3** *om gradering* høyest, størst, ytterst; **II** *adv* sist; siste gang; til sist/slutt; **III** *sb* den (det, de) siste; **IV** *vi* holde (seg); vare (ved); **2** holde (ut); **3** strekke til; **4** (fortsette å) leve; *he won't ~ long* han har ikke lenge igjen; **B** *sb* (sko)lest. **lasting** ['lɑ:stɪŋ] *adj* varig *etc*; drøy, holdbar. **lastly** ['lɑ:stlɪ] *adv* endelig; til sist/slutt. **last running** *sb petro* haleheng (= siste del av destillasjonen).

latch [lætʃ] **I** *sb* **1** (dør)klinke; skåte; slå; **2** smekklås; **II** *vb* **1** lukke med skåte/slå; **2** låse med smekklås; smekke igjen. **latch|key** *sb* (gatedørs)nøkkel, portnøkkel. ~ **pin** *sb petro etc* låsepinne.

late [leɪt] **I** *adj* **1** sen; **2** (for) sen; forsinket; **3** sen- (dvs på slutten av); **4** forhenværende; forrige, siste; tidligere; **5** nylig; *om sykdom* nettopp overstått; **6** (nylig) avdød; **II** *adv* sent; *~r on* senere; *of* ~ nylig; i det siste/den senere tid. **lately** ['leɪtlɪ] *adj* nylig; *only* ~ først i den senere tid.

latency ['leɪtənsɪ] *sb* **1** latens; **2** *data* ventetid. **latent** ['leɪtənt] *adj* latent.

lath [lɑ:θ] *sb* lekte, list; sprosse. **lath fence** *sb* stakitt(gjerde).

lathe [leɪð] *sb* dreiebenk.

lather ['læðə] **I** *sb* **1** (såpe)skum; **2** fråde, skum-(svette); **II** *vb* **1** såpe inn; **2** fråde, skumme; **3** *slang* denge/jule (opp).

latitude ['lætɪtju:d] *sb* **1** bredde(grad); **2** (bevegelses)frihet, spillerom.

latter ['lætə] *adj* **1** *the* ~ (den) sistnevnte (av to); den andre; denne/dette (av to personer/ting); disse (av to flokker/grupper); **2** nyere; senere. **latterly** ['lætəlɪ] *adv* i det siste; i våre dager; nå for tiden.

lattice ['lætɪs] *sb* gitter(verk); sprinkler. **lattice column** *sb petro* fagverksøyle.

laud [lɔ:d] *vt* rose. **laudable** ['lɔ:dəbl] *adj* rosverdig.

laugh [lɑ:f] **1** *sb* latter; *it's a* ~ det er til å le av; **2** *vb* le (*at* av); ~ *up one's sleeve* le i skjegget (dvs triumferende etc for seg selv). **laughing-stock** ['lɑ:fɪŋstɒk] *sb: be the* ~ *of* være til latter/spott for. **laughter** ['lɑ:ftə] *sb* latter.

launch [lɔ:ntʃ] **A I** *sb* **1** sjøsetting, stabelavløpning; (rakett)utskytning; *fig* lansering; **2** bedding, slipp; **II** *vb* **1** sende (og især kaste, slynge etc) av sted (opp/ut etc); ~ *(out) into* kaste seg ut i; **2** sjøsette; **3** skyte ut (rakett/torpedo etc); **4** lansere; sette i gang; **B** *sb* motor|båt, -ferje; *mil* barkasse. **launch chamber** *sb petro* avsenderkammer. **launching|-pad** ['lɔ:ntʃɪŋpæd] *sb* (rakett)utskytningsrampe. ~ **trap** *sb petro* rørskraperfelle.

launder ['lɔ:ndə] *vb* **1** vaske (og rulle, stryke) tøy; **2** kunne vaskes; tåle vask. **launderette** [ˌlɔ:ndə'ret] *sb* selvbetjeningsvaskeri, vaske(ri)automat. **laundress** ['lɔ:ndrɪs] *sb* vaskeri|arbeider(ske), -hjelp. **laundry** ['lɔ:ndrɪ] *sb* **1** vaskeri; vaskerom; **2** (tøy til) vask.

laureate I ['lɔ:rɪət] *adj* **1** laurbærkranset; **2** *sb (Poet Laureate)* hoffdikter; **II** ['lɔ:rɪeɪt] *vt* **1** laurbærkranse; **2** utnevne til hoffpoet.

lav [læv] *fork* for **lavatory** ['lævətərɪ] *sb* **1** toalett (og toalettrom, vaskerom; (vaske)servant, bad etc); **2** vannklosett.

lavender ['lævɪndə] *adj, sb* lavendel(-).

lavish ['lævɪʃ] **I** *adj* **1** flott; (altfor) raus/rundhåndet; **2** overdådig, ødsel; **II** *vt* ødsle (med); øse ut.

law [lɔ:] *sb* **1** lov (og lov|regel, -regler, -samling etc); *the* ~ loven; *dgl* myndighetene, øvrigheten; politiet; **2** jus (og rettsvitenskap; retts|pleie, -praksis; (lov og) rett etc). **law|-abiding** ['lɔ:əˌbaɪdɪŋ] *adj* lovlydig. **~-court** ['lɔ:ˌkɔ:t] *sb* **1** domstol; **2** rettslokale. **~ful** ['lɔ:fʊl] *adj* **1** lovlig; **2** rettmessig. **~less** ['lɔ:lɪs] *adj* **1** lovløs; **2** rettsløs; **3** ulovlig.

lawn [lɔ:n] *sb* (gress)plen. **lawn-mower** ['lɔ:nˌməʊə] *sb* gressklipper.

law-suit ['lɔ:su:t] *sb* rettssak; prosess, søksmål. **lawyer** ['lɔ:jə] *sb* advokat, jurist.

lax [læks] *adj* **1** løs, slakk; **2** avslappet; **3** likegyldig; giddeløs, slapp. **laxity** ['læksətɪ] *sb* slapphet *etc*.

lay [leɪ] **A** *adj* leg, ulærd; **B** *sb* **1** vise; **2** (fugle)-sang; **C I** *sb* **1** beliggenhet, plassering; retning; **2** *sjø* andel, part; lott; **3** *slang* bransje, (spesial)felt; **II** *vb* **1** legge (og sette, stille; legge *etc* frem/til rette; legge (smøre, stryke etc) på; *fig* forelegge etc); ~ *claim to* gjøre krav på; ~ *hold of* få tak i; sikre seg; ~ *siege to* beleire; ~ *the table* dekke bordet; **2** glatte/jevne (ut); **3** stille (dvs dempe, fordrive; mane bort/ned; få til å legge seg); **4** vedde; satse, sette; ~ *a wager* inngå et veddemål; **5** *med adv/prep* ~ **about** *(one)* gå løs på; slå om seg; ~ **bare** blotte; avsløre, blottlegge; ~ **by** legge *etc* til side; *sjø* legge bi; ~ **down** legge *etc* ned; legge opp (en plan); sette opp (en regel); stikke ut (en kurs); ~ *down the law* gi klar beskjed; uttale seg autoritativt/bestemt; ~ **for** *US* ligge på lur etter; ~ **in** legge *etc* i; forsyne seg med; lagre; *dgl* legge i seg; ~ **into** gå løs på; ~ **low** slå ned; ~ **off** holde seg (*dgl* ligge) unna; holde opp (en stund); permittere (midlertidig); ~ **on** legge *etc* på; smøre/stryke på; legge inn (gass, vann etc); ~ **open** = ~ *bare*; ~ **out** legge *etc* ut; arrangere, ordne; skissere; tegne ut; ~ *out cold* slå ut (dvs slå bevisstløs); ~ **to** legge *etc* til; *sjø* legge bi; ~ **up** legge *etc* opp; gjemme unna; legge til side. **lay barge** *sb petro* legge|fartøy, -lekter. **lay-by** ['leɪbaɪ] *sb* **1** parkeringsfelt (langs (motor)vei); **2** møteplass (for biler). **layer** ['leɪə] **I** *sb* **1** (-)legger *etc*; **2** lag, sjikt; belegg, hinne; **3** avlegger; **II** *vb* **1** lagdele; **2** sette avlegger(e). **lay|man** ['leɪmən] *sb* legmann. **~-off** ['leɪɒf] *sb* (kortere) arbeidsstans/permittering. **~-out** ['leɪaʊt] *sb* **1** arrangement; innredning, planløsning; **2** layout, uttegning; oppsetning; **3** (verktøy)|sett, -utstyr. **~-out character** *sb data* redigeringstegn. **~-spread** *sb petro* leggerigg. ~ **vessel** *sb petro* legge|fartøy, -skip.

laziness ['leɪzɪnɪs] *sb* dovenskap *etc*. **lazy** ['leɪzɪ] *adj* doven, lat. **lazy-bones** ['leɪzɪˌbəʊnz] *sb* dovenpels, lathans.

lead A [led] *sb* **1** bly (og lodd, plombe, søkke etc av bly); **2** *(black-~)* grafitt; **B** [li:d] **I** *sb* **1** ledelse; førerskap, føring; **2** forsprang (*of* på); **3** hovedrolle (og hovedrolleinnehaver); **4** (hunde)|halsbånd, -reim; **5** kabel, ledning; **6** kanal, (vann)renne; **7** utspill (i kort); **II** *vb* **1** føre, lede; gå i spissen/teten (for); ~ *off* begynne, innlede; ~ *(up) to* føre til; resultere i; *that's what I'm ~ing up to* det er det jeg vil frem til; **2** dirigere, styre; **3** føre (liv, tilværelse etc); leve; (la) gjennom|gå, leve; **4** spille ut (kort). **lead** [led] **additive** *sb petro* blytilsetning. **leaded** ['ledɪd] *adj* **1** bly-; blyinnfattet; **2** *petro etc* blytilsatt. **leaden** ['ledn] *adj* bly|grå, -tung; bly-. **leader** ['li:də] *sb* **1** fører, leder; **2** (an)fører, sjef; **3** leder(artikkel). **leadership** ['li:dəʃɪp] *sb* førerskap; ledelse; lederstilling. **lead-free** ['ledfri:] *adj petro* blyfri. **leading** ['li:dɪŋ] **1** *adj* førende, ledende; viktigst; hoved-; **2** *sb* føring, ledelse. **leading lady** *sb* førstedame; primadonna. **leadless** ['ledlɪs] *adj petro* blyfri. **lead** [led] **pencil** *sb* blyant. **leadsman** ['ledzmən] *sb sjø* loddhiver.

leaf [li:f] *sb* **1** blad; *koll* løv(verk); **2** ark, blad; (bok)side; *turn over a new ~* begynne på et nytt blad; **3** folie; *gold ~* bladgull; **4** forlengelses|klaff, -plate (til bord); (dør)fløy. **leaflet** ['li:flɪt] *sb* **1** lite blad; **2** flygeblad; **3** brosjyre, folder.

league [li:g] **A** **1** *sb* forbund, forening; *sport etc* liga; **2** *vb* forene(s); gå/slutte seg sammen; **B** *sb gml* en lengdenhet, se midtsidene.

leak [li:k] **1** *sb* brudd; lekk, lekkasje; hull, utetthet; **2** *vb* lekke (*out* ut); (la) lekke/sive ut. **leakage** ['li:kɪdʒ] *sb* lekkasje.

lean [li:n] **A I** *adj* **1** mager, tynn; **2** skrinn; **II** *vb* magert kjøtt; **B** *vb* **1** helle, skråne; ~ *backwards* helle/lute bakover; lene seg bakover; **2** ~ *against/on* lene/støtte (seg) mot/på; **3** ~ *upon* forlate/støtte seg på; være avhengig av; **4** ~ *towards* tendere mot; ha en tendens/tilbøyelighet til (å). **lean gas** *sb petro* mager gass. **leaning** ['li:nɪŋ] *sb* tendens, tilbøyelighet. **lean oil** *sb petro* mager (= mindreverdig) olje. **lean-to** ['li:ntu:] *sb* halvtak; tilbygd skur etc.

leap [li:p] **1** *sb* hopp, sprang; *by ~s and bounds* med stormskritt; **2** *vi* hoppe/springe (over). **leapfrog** ['li:pfrɒg] *sb: play ~* hoppe bukk. **leapyear** ['li:pjɜ:] *sb* skuddår.

learn [lɜ:n] *vb* **1** lære (seg); **2** erfare; få høre/vite. **learned** ['lɜ:nɪd] *adj* lærd; kunnskapsrik. **learning** ['lɜ:nɪŋ] *sb* **1** (inn)læring; **2** lærdom, kunnskaper.

lease [li:s] **1** *sb* leie(forhold); leiekontrakt; bygsling; forpaktning; *new ~ of life* forlenget livsfrist; ny (livs)sjanse; **2** *vt* leie; bygsle; forpakte. **lease-hold** ['li:shəʊld] **I** *adj* bygslet; forpaktet; **II** *sb* **1** bygsling; forpaktning; **2** bygslet grunn; forpaktet eiendom.

leash [li:ʃ] **1** *sb* kobbel; hunde|lenke, -reim; **2** *vt* holde i bånd; binde (sammen).

least [li:st] **1** *adj, adv* minst; ~ *of all* aller minst; minst av alt; **2** *som sb* det minste; *to say the ~ (of it)* mildest talt.

leather ['leðə] **I** *sb* lær; **II** *vt* **1** fôre/kle med lær; **2** *slang* denge/jule (opp). **leathern** ['leðən] *adj* **1** lær-(dvs av lær); **2** = *leathery*. **leatherneck** ['leðənek] *sb US slang* **1** hardhaus; **2** *mil* marine|infanterist, -soldat. **leathery** ['leðərɪ] *adj* læraktig, seig.

leave [li:v] **I** *sb* **1** lov; adgang, tillatelse; **2** *(~ of absence)* permisjon; *(shore ~)* landlov; **3** avskjed, farvel; *take ~ of* ta avskjed/farvel med; si adjø/farvel til; *take ~ of one's senses* gå fra forstanden/vettet; **II** *vb* **1** gå (og dra, reise etc fra); gå *etc* sin vei; ~ *school* slutte (på) skolen; **2** forlate (og reise, rømme, stikke etc fra); ~ *go/hold (of)* gi slipp (på); slippe (taket i); **3** over|late, -levere (*to* til); legge (sette, stille etc) fra seg; legge *etc* igjen (*with* hos); ~ *them to their own devices* overlate dem til seg selv; **4** etterlate (seg); levne; gå *etc* fra; ~ *it at that* la det bli med det; **5** *med adv/prep ~ (lying)* **about** la ligge og flyte; ~ **alone** la ligge; la være i fred; ikke forstyrre (røre, bry seg om etc); holde seg unna; ~ **aside** sette ut av betraktning; ~ **behind** etterlate (seg); ikke ta med (seg); gå *etc* fra; la bli hjemme; ~ **for** dra/reise til; ~ **off** holde opp/slutte (med); ~ **open** la stå (åpen)/åpent; ~ **out** ute|-late, -lukke; ikke regne med/ta hensyn til; ~ **over** levne; utsette.

leaven ['levn] **I** *sb* **1** surdeig; **2** impuls, spore; **II** *vt* syre; *fig* gjennomsyre.

lecherous ['letʃərəs] *adj* vellystig; lidderlig.

lecture ['lektʃə] **I** *sb* **1** forelesning, foredrag; **2** irettesettelse, reprimande; skjennepreken; **II** *vt* **1** forelese; holde foredrag; **2** irettesette; skjenne på. **lecturer** ['lektʃərə] *sb* foreleser; foredragsholder; ≈ universitetslektor.

ledge [ledʒ] *sb* (smal) hylle; avsats/fremspring (i fjellside etc).

ledger ['ledʒə] *sb* protokoll; register; *merk* hovedbok.

lee [li:] *adj, sb* le(side).

leech [li:tʃ] *sb* igle.

leek [li:k] *sb* purre(løk).

leer ['lɪə] **I** *sb* **1** ondt (foraktelig, hånlig etc) blikk; **2** lystent/vellystig glis; **3** fjollet flir; **II** *vi* **1** skule (ondt *etc*); **2** glise lystent *etc*; **3** kope, måpe; flire fjollet.

leeward ['li:wəd; *sjø* 'lu:əd] **1** *adj* le; **2** *adv* i le; **3** *sb* leside. **leeway** ['li:weɪ] *sb* avdrift; *fig* forsinkelse; *make up* ~ ta igjen det forsømte.

left [left] *adj, sb* venstre(-); *the Left (Wing) (pol)* venstre(fløyen). **left | arrow key** *sb data* venstretast. **~-hand** ['lefthænd] *adj* venstrehånds-; venstre(-). **~-handed** [ˌleft'hændɪd] *adj* keivhendt; *fig* kløntet. **Leftish** ['leftɪʃ] *adj pol* venstre|orientert, -vridd; radikal. **Leftist** ['leftɪst] **1** *adj* = *Leftish*; **2** *sb* venstre|-politiker, -radikaler. **left-justify** *vt data* venstreinnpasse.

left-overs ['left,əʊvəz] *sb fl* levninger, rester.

leg [leg] *sb* **1** bein (og buksebein; strømpe|legg, -skaft; bordbein etc); *on one's last* ~ på siste verset; på stumpene; *pull his (etc)* ~ drive gjøn/holde leven med ham (etc); **2** etappe.

legacy ['legəsɪ] *sb* legat; testamentarisk gave; *også fig* arv.

legal [li:gl] *adj* lov|formelig, -hjemlet; legal, lovlig; **2** juridisk, rettslig. **legality** [li:'gælətɪ] *sb* lovlighet *etc*.

legend ['ledʒənd] *sb* **1** legende; **2** inskripsjon, (inn)skrift; **3** (billed)tekst; tegnforklaring (på kart etc). **legendary** ['ledʒəndərɪ] *adj* legendarisk, legende-.

legerdemain [ˌledʒədə'meɪn] *sb* fingerferdighet; taskenspillerkunster.

legible ['ledʒəbl] *adj* leselig; klar, tydelig.

legion ['li:dʒən] *sb* **1** legion; **2** hærskare, mengde.

legislate ['ledʒɪsleɪt] *vi* gi/lage lover. **legislation** [ˌledʒɪ'sleɪʃn] *sb* **1** lovgivning; **2** lovverk. **legislative** ['ledʒɪslətɪv] *adj* lovgivende. **legislator** ['ledʒɪsleɪtə] *sb* **1** lovgiver; **2** medlem av: **legislature** ['ledʒɪsleɪtʃə] *sb* lovgivende forsamling. **legitimacy** [lɪ'dʒɪtɪməsɪ] *sb* legitimitet; lovlighet *etc*. **legitimate I** [lɪ'dʒɪtɪmət] *adj* **1** legitim, lovlig; rettmessig; **2** ektefødt; arveberettiget; **3** berettiget, rimelig; **II** [lɪ'dʒɪtɪmeɪt] *vt* legitimere; erklære legitim *etc*.

leisure ['leʒə] *sb* fritid; *at one's* ~ i ro og mak; når det passer; når en har tid. **leisurely** ['leʒəlɪ] *adj, adv* bedagelig, makelig.

lemming ['lemɪŋ] *sb* lemen.

lemon ['lemən] *adj* **1** sitron (og sitrontre); **2** *dgl* fadese, fiasko; dårlig (mangelfullt, mislykket etc) eksemplar. **lemonade** [ˌlemə'neɪd] *sb* limonade; (sitron)brus.

lend [lend] *vt* **1** låne (ut); ~ *a hand* gi en håndsrekning; **2** gi; bidra med/til.

length [leŋθ] *sb* **1** lengde; distanse, strekning; **2** lengde (dvs stump, stykke etc); (stoff)kupong. **lengthen** ['leŋθən] *vt* forlenge(s); bli/gjøre lengre. **lengthways** ['leŋθweɪz], **lengthwise** ['leŋθwaɪz] *adv* på langs. **lengthy** ['leŋθɪ] *adj* lang|dryg, tekkelig.

leniency ['li:nɪənsɪ] *sb* overbærenhet *etc*. **lenient** [li:nɪənt] *adj* overbærende; lemfeldig, mild; tolerant.

lens [lens] *sb* **1** (optisk) linse; **2** *foto etc* objektiv. **lens | aperture** *sb* blender(åpning), lysstyrke. **~ hood** *sb* motlysblender, solblender.

Lent [lent] *sb* faste(tid); fasten.

leper ['lepə] *sb* spedalsk (person). **leprosy** ['leprəsɪ] *sb* lepra, spedalskhet. **leprous** ['leprəs] *adj* spedalsk.

less [les] **1** *adj, sb* mindre (antall, mengde, størrelse etc); færre; *none the* ~ ikke desto mindre; **2** *adv* mindre; ikke (fullt) så; **3** *prep* minus. **lessen** ['lesn] *vb* **1** avta, minke; forminskes; **2** forminske, redusere; sette ned. **lesser** ['lesə] *adj* **1** *bokl* mindre (betydelig etc); **2** minst (av to).

lesson ['lesn] **I** *sb* **1** (undervisnings)time; leksjon; **2** lekse; *prepare one's ~s* gjøre/lese lekser; **3** advarsel, lærepenge; **4** lektie; **II** *vt dgl* irettesette; lese (en) teksten.

lest [lest] *konj* **1** for at (...) ikke; for ikke å; **2** at; for at; *we were afraid* ~ *they should* vi var redd (for at) de skulle.

let [let] **I** *sb* (ut)leie; **II** *vb* **1** la (og tillate; gi/la få lov etc); ~ *drive/fly at* kaste seg over; fare/gyve løs på; ~ *go (of)* gi/la gå fra seg; gi slipp på; slippe (taket i); ~ *oneself go* slippe/slå seg løs; **2** *(~ out)* leie ut; *to* ~ til leie; **3** *med adv/prep* ~ **alone** la være (alene/i fred etc); *fig* for ikke å nevne (si, snakke om etc); langt mindre; ~ **by** (la) slippe forbi; ~ **down** slippe *etc* ned; legge ned (skjørt etc); *fig* skuffe, svikte; late i stikken; ~ **in** lukke/(la) slippe inn; ~ **in on** innvie/gjøre delaktig i; ~ **into** (la) slippe inn i; felle/føye inn i; *fig* = ~ *in on*; ~ **loose** slippe løs; slippe/slå seg løs; gi utløp for; ~ **off** slippe løs/ut; la slippe; avfyre; sende *etc* opp/ut; ~ **on** *dgl* gi inntrykk av; late som; ymte/slå frempå (om); røpe; sladre (om); ~ **out** (se også 2) (la) slippe ut; legge ut (for trange klær); *fig* røpe; ~ **through** (la) slippe igjennom; ~ **up** *dgl* avta, minke; gi seg; holde opp; ta (en) pause.

lethal ['li:θl] *adj* dødelig, dødbringende; drepende.

letter ['letə] *sb* **1** bokstav; (skrift)type; **2** brev; **3** *fl* boklig lærdom; litteratur. **letter|-box** *sb* brevkasse, postkasse. **~-perfect** *adj* ordrett; pinlig nøyaktig (gjengitt); perfekt. **~ quality** *sb data* brevkvalitet.

lettuce ['letɪs] *sb* (blad)salat.

let-up ['letʌp] *sb* opp|hold, -lett; pause; pusterom.

level ['levl] **I** *adj* **1** horisontal, vannrett; **2** jevn, slett; flat, plan; **3** lik; *som adv* jevnt, likt; *draw* ~ *with* komme likt med; **4** (av)balansert, likevektig; sindig, stø; nøktern; *do one's* ~ *best* gjøre sitt (aller) beste; **II** *sb* **1** (vannrett) flate; nivå, plan, trinn; *on a* ~ *with* på høyde med; *on the* ~ *(dgl)* grei, skvær; til å stole på; **2**

(spirit-~) libelle, vaterpass; **III** *vt* **1** flate/jevne ut; **2** gjøre lik(e); jevne ut; **3** rasere; jevne med jorden; **4** ~ *at* rette (sikte, stille etc inn) mot; sikte på; **5** *dgl* snakke rett ut (av posen). **level|-crossing** *sb* plan|-kryss, overgang. **~-headed** *adj* nøktern, sindig; klar i hodet. **~ race** *sb* dødt løp.

lever ['li:və] **I** *sb* **1** vektstang; *især* brekkjern, spett; brekkstang; **2** spak, stang; håndtak; **II** *vt* heve/løfte (ved hjelp av vektstang etc). **leverage** ['li:vər-ɪdʒ] *sb* **1** vektstangs|forhold, -virkning; utveksling; **2** (over)tak; innflytelse, makt; fordel.

levity ['levətɪ] *sb* **1** letthet; **2** lettsindighet, overfladiskhet; (sorgløs) munterhet.

levy ['levɪ] **I** *sb* **1** skatt (og utskrivning samt oppkreving av skatt); **2** oppbud (og mobilisering/utskrivning av mannskaper); **II** *vt* **1** ilegge/pålegge skatt; utskrive (skatt); **2** inndrive/oppkreve (skatt); **3** innkalle/utskrive (mannskaper); mobilisere; **4** ~ *war* erklære/føre krig.

lewd [lu:d] *adj* lidderlig, slibrig; uanstendig; lysten.

liability [ˌlaɪə'bɪlətɪ] *sb* **1** ansvar (og ansvars|forhold, (-)forpliktelse, (-)plikt etc); byrde; hemsko, ulempe; **2** tendens, tilbøyelighet. **liable** ['laɪəbl] *adj* **1** ansvarlig (*for* for); ansvars|forpliktet, (-)pliktig; **2** tilbøyelig; *make/render oneself* ~ *to* utsette seg for (å).

liaison [lɪ'eɪzn] *sb* **1** *mil* forbindelse, samband; **2** (især illegitimt kjærlighets)forhold.

liar ['laɪə] *sb* løgner.

libel ['laɪbl] **I** *sb* **1** injurie(r), ærekrenkelse(r); bakvaskelse(r); smedeskrift; **2** anklage(skrift); siktelse; **3** *dgl* krenkelse (*on* av); fornærmelse; **II** *vt* injuriere, ærekrenke; bakvaske. **libellous** ['laɪbləs] *adj* injurierende; ære|krenkende, ærig.

liberal ['lɪbərəl] **I** *adj* **1** raus, rundhåndet; gavmild, generøs; **2** rikelig; **3** frisinnet; vidsynt; liberal; tolerant; **4** *(pol) Liberal* liberal, venstre-; **II** *sb* frilynt/frisinnet (person); liberaler; *Liberal* medlem av *the Liberal Party* det liberale parti i Storbritannia. **liberality** [ˌlɪbə'rælətɪ] *sb* **1** rundhåndethet *etc*; **2** frisinn *etc*. **liberate** ['lɪbəreɪt] *vt* befri; fri|gi, -gjøre. **liberation** [ˌlɪbə'reɪʃn] *sb* befrielse *etc*. **liberator** ['lɪbəreɪtə] *sb* befrier. **liberty** ['lɪbətɪ] *sb* **1** frihet; *at* ~ fri; på frifot; **2** privilegium; rett(ighet); **3** (fri) adgang; tillatelse; *be at* ~ *to* fritt kunne; ha frihet til å; **4** landlov.

librarian [laɪ'breərɪən] *sb* bibliotekar. **library** ['laɪbrərɪ] *sb* **1** bibliotek, boksamling; **2** (leie)bibliotek.

licence ['laɪsəns] *sb* **1** (skriftlig) tillatelse; bevilling, lisens; sertifikat; *ofte* skjenkerett; **2** (handle)frihet; **3** tøylesløshet. **licence fee** *sb* lisens|avgift, -gebyr. **license** ['laɪsəns] **1** *sb US* = *licence*; **2** *vt* gi bevilling *etc* til; *fully* ~*d* (med) alle rettigheter (dvs for salg av øl, vin og brennevin). **licensee** [ˌlaɪsn'si:] *sb* lisensinnehaver; rettighetshaver; innehaver av bevilling; *især* krovert (med skjenkerett). **license plate** *sb US* nummerskilt (på bil). **licentious** [laɪ'senʃəs] *adj* tøylesløs; utsvevende.

lichen [laɪkn] *sb* lav.

lick [lɪk] **I** *sb* slikk(ing); ~ *and a promise* kattevask; overfladisk behandling etc; **II** *vb* **1** slikke (og slikke på, slikke opp/i seg etc); ~ *the dust* bite i gresset; **2** *dgl* denge, slå; ~ *into shape* få skikk på.

lid [lɪd] *sb* **1** lokk; dekke, deksel; **2** *(eye~)* øyelokk.

lie [laɪ] **A I** *sb* = *lay C I 1*; **II** *vi* **1** ligge; være (senge)liggende; befinne seg; være beliggende/plassert *etc*; **2** *gml* overnatte; **3** *jur* bli tatt/kunne tas til følge; **4** *med adv/prep* ~ **about** ligge og flyte/slenge; ~ **ahead** ligge foran (en); ligge forut; ~ **back** ligge tilbakelent; ligge/lene seg bakover; ~ **by** ligge ubrukt/uvirksom; *sjø* ligge bi/på været; ~ **down** legge seg; ligge; ~ **down under** finne seg i; ta imot/tåle (uten å kny); ~ **in** ligge lenge (om morgenen); ligge i barsel(seng); ligge i (dvs bero på, skyldes); ~ **low** ligge på bakken/nede; ligge lavt/i dekning; gå stille i dørene; holde seg i bakgrunnen; ~ **off** ha/holde pause; holde seg (*dgl* ligge) unna; ~ **on** ligge på; hvile (tungt) på; ~ **over** ligge over (dvs krenge); stå over (dvs vente (med)/være utsatt til en senere anledning); ~ **up** ligge til sengs; være sengeliggende; **B 1** *sb* løgn, usannhet; **2** *vi* lyve. **lie-down** *sb* hvil.

lieu [lju:] *sb*: *in* ~ *of* istedenfor; i stedet for.

life [laɪf] *sb* liv; livlighet; *bring to* ~ bringe/vekke til live; *come to* ~ bli levende; komme til bevissthet/til seg selv; *for (dear)* ~ for (bare) livet. **life|belt** *sb* livbelte. **~blood** *sb* hjerteblod; livsnerve. **~boat** *sb* livbåt, redningsbåt. **~buoy** *sb* redningsbøye. **~ force** *sb* livskraft. **~guard** *sb* **1** livgarde; **2** *US* livredder (dvs vakt på badestrand). **~-jacket** *sb* redningsvest. **~less** *adj* livløs. **~like** *adj* livaktig; naturtro, virkelighetstro; levende, realistisk. **~-line** *sb* livline, redningstau. **~long** *adj* livs|lang, -varig. **~-preserver** *sb* batong, kølle; *US* redningsvest. **~ raft** *sb* redningsflåte. **~-size(d)** *adj, sb* (i) full størrelse; (i) legemsstørrelse. **~-span** *sb* (normal) levetid. **~time** *sb* levetid, livstid; menneskealder. **~work** *sb* livsverk.

lift [lɪft] **I** *sb* **1** løft(ing); heving; **2** hjelp; støtte, understøttelse; *give her a* ~ gi henne en håndsrekning; la henne få sitte på (dvs gi henne skyss); **3** heis; **II** *vb* **1** *(~ up)* løfte; heve, reise; **2** heve/løfte seg; lette (om tåke etc); **3** grave/ta opp (poteter etc); **4** (opp)heve; **5** *slang* lette, stjele. **lifting costs** *sb fl petro* utvinningskostnader.

light [laɪt] **A I** *adj* lys; **II** *sb* **1** lys (og lysning, lysskjær; lyskilde etc); *(day~)* dagslys; *bring to* ~ bringe for dagen; *come to* ~ komme for dagen/for en dag; **2** belysning; opplysning; **3** (stearin)lys; lampe, lykt; lanterne; **4** bluss; flamme; *også* = *~house*; **5** vindu (og vindusrute); fag; **6** innsikt; opplysning(er); kunnskap(er); **III** *vb* **1** tenne lys; tenne/bli tent (på); ~ *up* tenne (på) lyset; belyse; lyse opp; lysne; **2** lyse opp; lyse (for); **B 1** *adj* lett (og fin, mild, svak, tynn; uanselig, ubetydelig; lettsindig; overfladisk etc); **2** *adv* lett; *travel* ~ reise med lite bagasje; **C** *vi* **1** komme over (dvs finne/støte på etc ved en tilfeldighet); **2** *gml*

= *alight II.* **light|-bodied** *adj petro etc* tyntflytende. ~ **button** *sb data* lysknapp. ~ **crude** *sb petro* lett råolje. ~**-emitting diode** *sb* lysemitterende diode. **lighten** ['laɪtn] *vb* **A 1** bli/gjøre lys(ere); belyse; lyse opp; lysne; **2** glimte; lyne; **B** bli/gjøre lett(ere); lette; letne; live opp. **light end** *sb petro* lettkomponent. **lighter** ['laɪtə] *sb* **A** tenner; **B** *sjø* lekter.

light|-fingered *adj* **1** fingernem; **2** langfingret (dvs tyvaktig). ~**-footed** *adj* lettbeint, rappfotet. ~ **fuel oil,** ~ **heating oil** *sb petro* lett fyringsolje. ~ **gun** *sb data* = ~ *pen.* ~**handed** *adj* **1** netthendt; lett på hånden; **2** *sjø etc* underbemannet. ~**-headed** *adj* **1** svimmel, ørsken; **2** lettsindig, tankeløs; **3** overstadig. ~**-hearted** *adj* lettlivet, munter; sorgløs. ~**house** *sb* fyr|hus, -lys, -tårn; ~*house keeper* fyrvokter.

lighting ['laɪtɪŋ] *sb* belysning.

light | lubricating oil *sb petro* lett smøreolje. ~**-minded** *adj* lettsindig; ustadig. ~**ness** *sb* letthet *etc.*

lightning ['laɪtnɪŋ] *sb* lyn; ~ *conductor,* ~ *rod* lynavleder. **light | pen** *sb data* lyspenn. ~**ship** *sb* fyrskip. ~**weight 1** *adj* lettvekts-; **2** *sb* lettvekter.

likable ['laɪkəbl] *adj* likende(s); sympatisk, tiltalende. **like** [laɪk] **A I** *adj* **1** lignende; (svært) lik; ~ *that* slik; på den måten; ~ *this* slik; på denne måten; *be* ~ ligne; være lik; *feel* ~ føle seg som; ha lyst til; kunne tenke seg; *look* ~ ligne; se ut som; *that's more* ~ *it* det er/var bedre; sånn skal det være; **2** ens; (helt) lik; **II** *adv* **1** (på samme måte) som; ~ *as (gml)* (like)-som; **2** ~ *enough* sannsynligvis, trolig; **III** *konj, prep* **1** *dgl* som om; **2** (slik/i samme grad etc) som; **IV** *sb* make(n); en/noe lignende; *the* ~*s of us* sånne som oss; **B I** *sb fl* forkjærlighet, hang; ~*s and dislikes* sympatier og antipatier; **II** *vt* **1** like; synes om; være glad i; **2** foretrekke; ønske; *I should* ~ *to* jeg skulle/ville gjerne. **likelihood** ['laɪklɪhʊd] *sb* sannsynlighet *etc.* **likely** ['laɪklɪ] **1** *adj* sannsynlig, trolig; rimelig; **2** *adv* sannsynligvis; *as* ~ *as not* formodentlig; (høyst) sannsynlig. **liken** ['laɪkn] *vt:* ~ *to* sammenligne med. **likeness** ['laɪknɪs] *sb* **1** likhet; **2** *dgl* bilde (dvs portrett). **likewise** ['laɪkwaɪz] *adv* **1** like|dan, -ledes, -så; på samme måte; **2** *US dgl* (takk) det samme/i like måte. **liking** ['laɪkɪŋ] *sb* forkjærlighet; tilbøyelighet; *have a* ~ *for* ha til overs for.

lilac ['laɪlək] **I** *adj* lilla(farget); **II** *sb* **1** syrin; **2** lilla (farge).

lilt [lɪlt] **1** *sb* trall; munter melodi/sang; **2** *vb* tralle.

lily ['lɪlɪ] *sb* lilje. **lily of the valley** *sb* liljekonvall.

limb [lɪm] *sb* **1** lem; arm; bein; **2** gren.

lime [laɪm] **A 1** *sb* kalk; *slaked* ~ lesket kalk; **2** *vt* kalke; **B** *sb* **1** limett (= slags sitron); **2** = ~*tree.* **lime | juice** *sb* sitronsaft. ~**light** *sb* rampelys. ~**stone** *sb* kalkstein. ~**-treated mud** *sb petro* kalkhemmet slam. ~**tree** *sb* lind.

limit ['lɪmɪt] **1** *sb* grense; **2** *vt* begrense; innskrenke. **limitation** [,lɪmɪ'teɪʃn] *sb* begrensning; innskrenkning. **limited** ['lɪmɪtɪd] *adj* **1** begrenset; innskrenket; **2** *merk:* ~ *(liability) company* aksjeselskap (med begrenset ansvar). **limit | check** *sb data* grensekontroll. ~ **test** *sb data* grenseprøve

limp [lɪmp] **A 1** *sb* halting; **2** *vi* halte; humpe (av sted etc); **B** *adj* sjasket, slapp; bløt.

limpet ['lɪmpɪt] *sb* **1** albuskjell; *fig* igle; **2** *mil* limpet (= slags sugemine).

limpid ['lɪmpɪd] *adj* gjennomsiktig; (krystall)-klar.

linden ['lɪndən] *sb* lind, lindetre.

line [laɪn] **A I** *sb* **1** linje; grense(linje); kant; **2** linje, strek; kontur, (om)riss; fure, rynke; trekk; **3** line, snor, snøre; streng; kabel, ledning (til telegraf, telefon etc); *fl US* tøyler; *give him enough* ~ la ham løpe linen ut; **4** rad, rekke; kø; *bring (come/fall) into* ~ *with* bringe (komme) på linje med; **5** linje (av bokstaver, ord etc); *fl teater* replikk; *(marriage)* ~*s* vielsesattest; *get/have a* ~ *on (dgl)* få/ha opplysninger om; (få) vite noe om; **6** (slekts)linje; familie; **7** linje, rute; skinnegang, skinner; spor; **8** kurs; retning (og retningslinje); fremgangsmåte; metode; prinsipp; **9** bransje, fag; felt, område; spesialitet; **10** varer; (vare)parti; vare|slag, -sort; *a cheap* ~ en billig kvalitet; **11** *fl* forhold, omstendigheter; *hard* ~*s (dgl)* uflaks; **II** *vb* **1** linjere; tegne/trekke (opp) streker; **2** ~ *up* plassere/stille (opp) på linje/i rekke; stille seg på linje/rekke; **3** fure, rynke; **B** *vt* fôre; kle (innvendig). **lineage** ['lɪnɪɪdʒ] *sb* herkomst, ætt; famile; slekt (slinje). **lineal** ['lɪnɪəl] *adj* **1** direkte; i rett (nedstigende) linje; **2** = *linear.* **lineament** ['lɪnɪəmənt] *sb* (ansikts)|drag, -trekk. **linear** ['lɪnɪə] *adj* lineær (også *data*); linje-, strek-. **line | deletion character** *sb data* linjeslettetegn. ~ **feed character** *sb data* linjeflyttetegn. ~ **drawing** *sb* strektegning. ~ **graphics** *sb data* linjegrafikk.

linen ['lɪnɪn] **1** *adj* lin-; **2** *sb* lin (og lintøy; dekketøy, sengetøy etc; *gml* linnet; undertøy); (lin)lerret; *fl* hvitevarer; *dirty* ~ skittentøy. **linen draper** *sb* hvitevarehandler.

line | pack *sb petro* rørpakning. ~ **printer** *sb data* linjeskriver.

liner ['laɪnə] *sb* **A** rute|fly, -skip; **B** fôring; *især* avtakbart fôr. **liner hanger** *sb petro* røroppheng.

line | switching *sb data* linjeveksling. ~**-up** *sb petro* tilpasning.

linger ['lɪŋgə] *vi* somle; trekke ut; vare (ved). **lingering** ['lɪŋgərɪŋ] *adj* langvarig, vedvarende.

lingo ['lɪŋgəʊ] *sb* kråkemål, labbelensk; *dgl neds* språk.

lining ['laɪnɪŋ] *sb* **1** fôr (og fôring, fôrstoff etc); (be)kledning; **2** kant (og kanting, kantebånd etc).

link [lɪŋk] **I** *sb* **1** kjetting|ledd, (-)lekk; **2** ledd (og bindeledd, forbindelsesledd; overgang, overgangsledd etc); *missing* ~ manglende mellomledd; **II** *vb* forbinde(s); forene (seg); *data* kjede, lenke; ~*ed list (data)* kjedet liste; ~ *up* kjede (lenke, binde, knytte, koble etc) sammen; henge sammen. **linkage** ['lɪŋkɪdʒ] *sb data* lenke. **linkage editor** *sb data* lenkeredigerer. **link-up** ['lɪŋkʌp] *sb* forbindelse; (sammen)-kobling.

links [lɪŋks] *sb fl* golfbane.

linseed ['lɪnsi:d] *sb* linfrø. **linseed oil** *sb* linolje.

lintel ['lɪntl] *sb* overligger (over dør, vindu etc); dørbjelke, vindusbjelke.

lion ['laɪən] *sb* **1** løve; **2** berømt/fetert person; selskapsløve. **lioness** ['laɪənɪs] *sb* hunnløve, løvinne.

lip [lɪp] *sb* **1** leppe; *keep a stiff upper ~* ikke fortrekke en mine; ikke la seg merke med noe; **2** (helle)-kant, tut; brem, rand; **3** *dgl* uforskammethet. **lip|-reading** *sb* munnavlesning. **~-service** *sb* slesking, smiger; munnsvær. **~-stick** *sb* leppestift.

liqueur [lɪ'kjʊə] *sb* likør. **liquid** ['lɪkwɪd] **I** *adj* **1** flytende; væskeformig; **2** blank (pga fuktighet, især om øyne); **3** bløt, myk; **4** smektende, smeltende; **5** *merk* likvid; lett omsettelig; **II** *vb* væske. **liquidate** ['lɪkwɪdeɪt] *vb* **1** *merk* avvikle, likvidere; **2** betale (gjeld); bringe (mellomværende) ut av verden; **3** likvidere (dvs drepe, utrydde). **liquor** ['lɪkə] *sb* brennevin.

lisp [lɪsp] **1** *sb* lesping; **2** *vb* lespe.

list [lɪst] **A 1** *sb* fortegnelse, liste; kartotek; **2** *vt* listeføre, registrere; føre/skrive opp *etc* (på liste); **B** *sb* **1** grense, (ut)kant; **2** strime, stripe; (tøy)|remse, -strimmel; (tetnings)list; **C** *sjø* **1** *sb* slagside; **2** *vi* krenge (over); få/ha slagside. **list slippers** *sb fl* (fille)tøfler, tøysko.

listen ['lɪsn] *vi* lytte (*for* etter; *to* til); *~ in* høre (på) radio; *~ in to* høre på (et bestemt radioprogram). **listener** ['lɪsnə] *sb* tilhører; (radio)lytter.

listless ['lɪstlɪs] *adj* likeglad, skjødeløs; apatisk, sløv.

literacy ['lɪtərəsɪ] *sb* lese- og skrivekyndighet. **literal** ['lɪtərəl] *adj* **1** bokstavelig; bokstav-; **2** ordrett. **literally** ['lɪtərəlɪ] *adv* **1** bokstavelig talt; **2** ordrett; *dgl* til punkt og prikke. **literary** ['lɪtərərɪ] *adj* litterær; litteratur-. **literate** ['lɪtərət] *adj, sb* lese- og skrivekyndig (person). **literature** ['lɪtərətʃə] *sb* litteratur.

lithe [laɪð] *adj* bøyelig; myk, smidig; spenstig.

litigate ['lɪtɪgeɪt] *vb* prosedere; gå rettens vei. **litigation** [ˌlɪtɪ'geɪʃn] *sb* prosess; retts|trette, -tvist.

litter ['lɪtə] **I** *sb* **1** søppel; skrammel, skrot; **2** rot; **3** halm, strå; torvstrø; **4** (unge)kull; **5** bærestol; **6** båre; **II** *vb* **1** søple (grise, rote etc) til; **2** dekke/strø med halm *etc*; **3** få unger. **litter|-bug, ~-lout** *sb* natursvin (dvs en som forsøpler sine omgivelser).

little ['lɪtl] **I** *adj* **1** liten, lille-; kort(-); små(-); smålig; ubetydelig; **2** kort(varig); *a ~ while ago* for litt/en liten stund siden; **3** litt; **II** *adv* litt; *~ short of* nesten, nærmest; praktisk talt; **III** *sb* litt (og liten bite/stykke; liten stund; *fig* liten smule/tanke etc); *~ by ~* litt etter litt; *every ~ counts* alle monner drar.

live I [laɪv] *adj* **1** levende; *ofte* ordentlig, virkelig; **2** brennende, glødende; strømførende; ladd; ueksplodert; **II** [lɪv] *vb* **1** leve; **2** bo; oppholde seg; **3** levendegjøre; praktisere; leve opp til; **4** *med adv/prep ~* **by** leve av; *~* **down** komme over (med tiden); overvinne; gjøre til skamme; *~* **fast** leve sterkt/vilt; *~* **high** leve godt (fett, høyt etc); *~* **in** bo på (arbeids)stedet; *~* **on** leve på; leve (videre); *~* **out** bo ute (dvs utenfor arbeidsstedet); *ofte* bo hjemme; *~* **over** *again* gjenoppleve; *~* **through** gjennomleve; oppleve; *~* **up to** leve opp til; levendegjøre; praktisere. **livelihood** ['laɪvlɪhʊd] *sb* levebrød, utkomme. **lively** ['laɪvlɪ] *adj* **1** lystig, munter; livlig; livat, sprelsk, vilter; **2** energisk; frisk, kjapp; **3** levende.

liver ['lɪvə] *sb* lever.

liveried ['lɪvərɪd] *adj* livrékledd. **livery** ['lɪvərɪ] *sb* **1** livré; **2** drakt; *især* laugs|drakt, -uniform. **livery | company** *sb* laug (i London City). **~ stable** *sb* leiestall.

livestock [laɪvstɒk] *sb* besetning, buskap.

livid ['lɪvɪd] *adj* blå|grå, -svart; blygrå; **2** *slang* (*~ with rage*) rasende.

living ['lɪvɪŋ] **I** *adj* **1** levende; **1** livaktig, naturtro; **II** *sb* **1** levebrød, utkomme; (preste)kall; **2** liv (dvs leve|måte, -sett, vis etc); *cost of ~* leveomkostninger; *standard of ~* levestandard. **living room** *sb* (daglig)stue, oppholdsrom.

lizard ['lɪzəd] *sb* firfisle, øgle.

load [ləʊd] **I** *sb* **1** byrde, bør; lass; **2** ladning, last; belastning; **II** *vb* **1** belaste; (*~ down*) belesse; tynge (ned); **2** (*~ up*) laste (opp); lesse (på); **3** fylle; *især* lade (skyte)våpen; sette film i (kamera); **4** *data* laste (inn); *~ and go* last og kjør. **loader** ['ləʊdə] *sb data* laster. **loading | buoy** *sb petro* lastebøye. **~ hose** *sb petro* lasteslange. **~ platform** *sb petro* lasteplattform. **~ procedure** *sb data* lasteprosedyre. **loadline** ['ləʊdlaɪn] *sb* laste|linje, -merke. **load | map** *sb data* adresseliste. **~ point** *sb data* skrivestartpunkt. **~ time** *sb data* lastetid.

loaf [ləʊf] **A** *sb* (*~ of bread*) brød; *slang* knoll/kuppel (dvs hode); **B** *vi* drive dank. **loafer** ['ləʊfə] *sb* dagdriver.

loam [ləʊm] *sb* **1** fet/leirholdig jord; **2** mager leire.

loan [ləʊn] **I** *sb* **1** lån; **2** utlån; **II** *vt US* låne (bort, ut). **loaner** ['ləʊnə] *sb* (penge)utlåner. **loan-office** *sb* lånekontor.

loath [ləʊθ] *adj* uvillig. **loathe** [ləʊð] *vt* avsky; ikke kunne fordra. **loathsome** ['ləʊðsəm] *adj* avskyelig, motbydelig.

lobby ['lɒbɪ] **I** *sb* **1** hall, vestibyle; lobby; **2** korridor; **II** *vb* drive korridorpolitikk; ≈ påvirke. **lobbyist** ['lɒbɪɪst] *sb* korridorpolitiker.

lobe [ləʊb] *sb* **1** flik, lapp; **2** (*ear ~*) øreflipp.

lobster ['lɒbstə] *sb* hummer.

local ['ləʊkl] **I** *adj* **1** lokal, stedlig; stedegen; **2** ≈ kommunal(-), kommune-; **II** *sb dgl* **1** *the ~* lokalen (dvs lokalavisen, lokaltoget etc); stam|kroen, -puben; **2** *the ~s* lokalbefolkningen. **local | anaesthetic** *sb* lokalbedøvelse. *the ~* **authorities** *sb fl* de lokale/stedlige myndigheter. **~ colour** *sb* lokalkoloritt. **~ election** *sb* ≈ kommunevalg. **~ government** *sb* ≈ kommunalt selvstyre. **locality** [ləʊ'kælətɪ] *sb* **1** sted (og især hjemsted, voksested, åsted etc); distrikt, område; strøk; **2** beliggenhet. **localization** [ˌləʊkəlaɪ'zeɪʃn] *sb* lokalisering *etc*. **localize** ['ləʊkəlaɪz] *vt* **1** lokalisere, stedfeste; **2** begrense, innskrenke; **3** gi lokalt preg etc. **locate** [ləʊ'keɪt] *vt* **1** finne; lokalisere, stedfeste; **2** bestemme/fastsette beliggenheten av; legge/plassere (i landskapet etc). **location** [ləʊ'keɪʃn] *sb* **1** lokalisering *etc*; beliggenhet; **2** *film* opptakssted (utenfor studio); *on* ~ utendørs. **locator** [ləʊ'keɪtə] *sb data* posisjonsindikator.

loch [lɒχ] *sb skotsk* 1 (inn)sjø, vann; **2** fjordarm; (trang) fjord.

lock [lɒk] **A I** *sb* **1** lås; lås|anordning, -mekanisme; (fast)låsing; beknip, klemme; ~, *stock and barrel* rubb og rake; **2** sluse (og slusekammer); **II** *vb* **1** låse; falle/gå i lås; (kunne) låses; være til å låse; henge seg opp; låse seg; **2** gripe; holde fast; om|favne, -slutte; **3** *med adv/prep* ~ **away** låse ned; gjemme (bort); ~ **in** låse (sperre, stenge etc) inne; ~ **out** låse (stenge etc) ute; ~ **up** låse; lukke, stenge; låse (sperre, stenge etc) inne; låse ned; **B** *sb* (hår)lokk. **locker** ['lɒkə] *sb* **1** (låsbart) skap; garderobeskap; **2** oppbevarings|boks, -rom; kott. **locker room** *sb* (idretts)garderobe. **locket** ['lɒkɪt] *sb* medaljong. **lock|-gate** *sb* sluseport. **~-keeper** *sb* slusevokter. **~out** *sb* utestengning; lockout. **~smith** *sb* låsesmed. **~-up** *sb* **1** arrest(lokale), fengsel; **2** stengetid.

locomotion [ˌləʊkə'məʊʃn] *sb* bevegelse (fra et sted til et annet); befordring. **locomotive** [ˌləʊkə'məʊtɪv] **1** *adj* bevegelses-; **2** *sb* lokomotiv.

lode [ləʊd] *sb* malmåre. **lodestar** ['ləʊdstɑ:] *sb* ledestjerne.

lodge [lɒdʒ] **I** *sb* **1** hytte; *ofte* stue (= lite hus); *caretaker's ~, porter's ~* portner|bolig, -stue; **2** *(freemasons' ~)* (frimurer)losje; **3** hi, hule; **II** *vb* **1** huse; ha boende; inn|kvartere, -losjere; **2** bo/losjere (*at* hos/i; *in* i; *with* hos); **3** anbringe; legge, sette; ~ *a complaint with* inngi/sende (en) klage til; **4** deponere/plassere (*with* hos/i); **5** sette seg fast. **lodger** ['lɒdʒə] *sb* leieboer, losjerende. **lodging** ['lɒdʒɪŋ] *sb* innlosjering *etc*; *fl* losji. **lodging-house** *sb* losjihus.

loft [lɒft] *sb* **1** loft; **2** galleri. **lofty** ['lɒftɪ] *adj* **1** høy (ikke om mennesker, skjønt *Lofty* kan brukes som oppnavn på lang, hengslet person); **2** elevert, opphøyet; edel; **3** overlegen, stolt.

log [lɒg] **A** *sb* tømmerstokk; kabbe, kubbe; **B I** *sb* **1** logg; **2** *data etc* journal; **II** *vb* **1** føre inn i loggbok etc; **2** *data etc* logge (*off* ut; *on* inn). **log|-book** *sb* loggbok; skips|dagbok, journal. **~-cabin** *sb* tømmerhytte. **~ file** *sb petro* journal. **~ger** *sb* tømmerhugger. **~ging** *sb* tømmerhugst.

logic ['lɒdʒɪk] *sb* logikk. **logical** ['lɒdʒɪkl] *adj* logisk.

loins [lɔɪnz] *sb fl* lender; korsrygg; *på slakt* nyrestykke. **loincloth** *sb* lendeklede.

loiter [lɔɪtə] *vi* (gå og) drive, slenge; slentre; ~ *away* somle bort. **loiterer** ['lɔɪtərə] *sb* dagdriver; somlekopp.

loll [lɒl] *vb* **1** ligge henslengt; (stå og) henge; **2** henge ut; la (især tungen) henge ute.

lone [ləʊn] *adj bokl* enslig; ensom. **loneliness** ['ləʊnlɪnɪs] *sb* ensomhet. **lonely** ['ləʊnlɪ], **lonesome** ['ləʊnsəm] *adj* **1** enslig; ensom; **2** ensom; (ene og) forlatt; **2** ensom; øde (og forlatt).

long [lɒŋ] **1** *adj* lang (og langvarig); lang-; lengde-; *merk* langsiktig; *fig* drøy; **2** *adv* lenge (og lang-, langt-, lenge-); for lengst; ~ *ago* for lenge siden; *be ~ in* være lenge om å; bruke lang tid på (å); *take ~* ta lang tid; **3** *sb* lang periode/tid; langt tidsrom; *before ~* om ikke lenge; snart; *for ~* lenge; i lang tid; *the ~ and the short of it* saken i et nøtteskall; summen av det (hele); **4** *vi* lengte (*for* etter; *to* etter å). **long-distance** *adj* **1** langdistanse-; **2** fjern-; *~-distance call* rikstelefon(samtale). **longevity** [lɒn'dʒevətɪ] *sb* lang levetid. **longhand** *sb* vanlig skrift (i motsetning til stenografi = *shorthand*). **longing** ['lɒŋɪŋ] **1** *adj* lengtende; lengselsfull; **2** *sb* lengsel. **longitude** ['lɒndʒɪtju:d] *sb* lengde(grad). **long | memory** *sb* god hukommelse. ~ **odds** *sb fl* små sjanser. **~-range** *adj* langdistanse-; *mil også* langtrekkende. **~shoreman** *sb* **1** kystfisker; **2** havnearbeider. ~ **shot** *sb dgl* slumpetreff. ~ **standing** *sb* gammel dato; godt renommé. **~-suffering** *adj* langmodig, tålmodig. **~-winded** *adj* lang|dryg, tekkelig; omstendelig; kjedelig.

look [lʊk] **I** *sb* **1** blikk; *dgl* kikk, titt; *have a ~ at* kaste et blikk/*dgl* ta en titt på; **2** utseende; mine, uttrykk; *fl* (især pent) utseende; **II** *vb* **1** se; *dgl* kikke/titte (*at* på); se etter; undersøke; ~ *(here)!* se her! *dgl* hør her! **2** synes; late til (å); se ut (*as if* som om; *like* som); se ... ut; *it ~s like rain* det ser ut til å bli regn; **3** *med adv/prep* ~ **about** *(one)* se seg om(kring); ~ **about for** se seg om etter; ~ **after** se etter; følge med blikket/øynene; passe på; ta seg av; ~ **ahead** se fremover; være forutseende; ~ **alive!** (la det gå litt) kvikt nå! ~ **around** se seg om(kring); lete (rundt omkring); ~ **at** se på; betrakte; overveie; ~ **away** se bort (vekk, til en annen kant etc); ~ **back** se seg tilbake; minnes; ~ **elsewhere** lete/se et annet sted/andre steder; *dgl* se seg om etter noe annet; ~ **for** lete/se etter; regne med; vente seg; ~ **forward** *to* glede seg/se frem til; ~ **in** se (kikke, stikke etc) innom (*on* hos); se på (fjernsyn); ~ **into** se nærmere på; undersøke; ~ **on** betrakte; se på; ~ **out** se ut; se opp (dvs se seg for, være forsiktig); ~ **out on** = ~ *upon*; ~ **over** se igjennom/over; gjennomgå; ~ **sharp** = ~ *alive*; ~ **through** se gjennom; synes gjennom; gjennomskue; ~ **to** se på (som forbilde); se hen til; vende seg til; regne med; ~ *to it* passe på (sørge for, ta seg av) det; ~ **towards** se mot; *også* = ~ *upon*; ~ **up** se opp; slå opp (i leksikon, ordbok etc); besøke, oppsøke; bedres; ta seg opp; ~ *up!* opp med humøret! ~ **(up)on** se på; vende (ut) mot; ha beliggenhet/utsikt (ut) mot. **looking-glass** *sb* speil.

look-out ['lʊkaʊt] *sb* **1** utkikk, vakt(post); **2** utkikks|post, -sted; **3** (fremtids)utsikter.

loom [lu:m] **A** *sb* vev(stol); **B** *vi* dukke frem/ komme til syne (især uklart og illevarslende); reise seg truende.

loop [lu:p] **I** *sb* **1** løkke, sløyfe; slyng; **2** hempe, stropp; øye; **3** krusedull, krøll; **4** *data* sløyfe; **II** *vb* **1** lage/slå løkke(r) (på); feste med/knyte i sløyfe(r); **2** bevege seg i slyng/sløyfer etc; bukte seg (om larver etc); loope (om fly). **loop | control** *sb data* sløyfekontroll. **~hole** ['lu:phəʊl] *sb* liten åpning; *især* kikkhull; luftehull; skyteskår; smutthull. **looping** ['lu:pɪŋ] *sb data* sløyfebehandling.

loose [lu:s] **I** *adj* **1** løs, ubundet; ledig; fri, ubunden; *be at a ~ end* ikke vite hva en skal gjøre; **2** løselig; utflytende; usammenhengende; **3** løsaktig; lett på tråden; **II** *vt* **1** slippe løs *etc*; løsne (på); *poet, rel* (for)løse; **2** løsne/fyre av (skudd); **3** kaste loss. **loosen** ['lu:sn] *vb* **1** løse (opp); løsne (på); slippe løs; sette fri; **2** *(~ up)* slakke på; slappe av (på); tø opp. **loose|-fitting** *adj* løstsittende. **~-limbed** *adj* oppløpen, ulenkelig.

loot [lu:t] **1** *sb* bytte, rov; **2** *vb* herje, plyndre; røve.

lop [lɒp] **A** *vt* hugge (kappe, kutte etc) av; **B** *vi* henge ned; (henge og) slenge. **lop|-eared** *adj* med hengeører. **~-sided** *adj* skjev; usymmetrisk; skakk.

loquacious [ləʊ'kweɪʃəs] *adj* pratsom, snakkesalig.

lord [lɔ:d] **I** *sb* **1** herre, hersker; mester; **2** *Lord (som tittel)* lord; *My Lord* [mɪ'lɔ:d] Deres høyhet/ nåde; *jur* [*ofte* mɪ'lʌd] herr dommer; *Your Lordship* Deres høyhet/nåde; *the Lord Mayor of London* borgermesteren i London; **3** adelsmann, lord; medlem av *the House of Lords* Overhuset i det britiske parlament; **4** *the Lord* Gud, Herren; *Our Lord* Vårherre; *the Lord's Prayer* Fadervår; **II** *vt:* *~ it over* herske/spille herre (og mester) over. **lordly** [lɔ:dlɪ] *adj* **1** adelig, fornem; **2** prektig, stor|slagen, slått; **3** overlegen, storsnutet.

lore [lɔ:] *sb* kjennskap (til bestemt emne); kunnskaper (basert på tradisjon); overlevering(er).

lorry ['lɒrɪ] *sb* lastebil.

lose [lu:z] *vb* **1** miste; tape; *~ one's temper* miste besinnelsen; *~ one's way* gå seg bort; gå (seg) vill; *~ sight of* miste/tape av syne; **2** tape; bli overvunnet; lide nederlag; *~ by (in, on)* tape på/ved (å); *~ ground* tape terreng; *~ out (US)* tape; *~ a motion* bli nedstemt; **3** berøve; få til å miste; *it will ~ you your job* det kommer til å koste deg jobben (din); **4** spille; kaste bort; **5** saktne (om klokke); **6** komme for sent til; ikke nå/ rekke; gå glipp av. **loser** ['luzə] *sb* taper. **losing returns** *sb fl petro* sirkulasjonssvikt; slamtap. **loss** [lɒs] *sb* tap; mangel, manko; (assuranse)skade; *især* skadebeløp; *sjø* havari; *fig* savn; *at a ~* med tap *etc*; *fig* rådvill; i villrede; *be at a ~ for* mangle, savne; være opprådd for. **lost** [lɒst] *adj* **1** mistet, tapt; for|spilt, -tapt; *~ in* fordypet/hensunket i; *be ~ to (all sense of shame etc)* være blottet for (all skamfølelse etc); ikke eie (skam etc) i livet; *be ~ (up)on* være bortkastet/spilt på; **2** bortkommet; villfaren(de); opprådd, rådvill; i villrede; *be completely ~* verken vite ut eller inn; **3** forsvunnet; (meldt) savnet; død, omkommet (etter ulykke etc); forlist, havarert. **lost | cause** *sb* håpløs sak (dvs som er tapt på forhånd). **~ circulation** *sb petro* sirkulasjonssvikt.

lot [lɒt] **I** *sb* **1** lodd (og loddtrekning); **2** lodd (= skjebne); *it fell to my ~ to* det falt på meg å; det ble min oppgave å; **3** lott, part; parti (varer etc); **4** *US* jord|lodd, -stykke; teig; tomt; **5** *dgl: a bad ~* en dårlig/tvilsom person; **II** *sb dgl* **1** flokk, gjeng; sleng; **2** *a ~* en god del; temmelig mange/mye; *the ~* alt sammen; **3** *som adv: a ~ better (etc)* en god del bedre (etc).

loth [ləʊθ] = *loath.*

lotion ['ləʊʃn] *sb* vann (til kosmetisk etc bruk: ansiktsvann, hudvann, rensevann etc).

loud [laʊd] **I** *adj* **1** høy (og høylytt); kraftig/sterk (om lyd); **2** høyrøstet; bråkende, støyende; **3** grell, skrikende; gloret; **II** *adv (~ly)* høyt. **loud-speaker** *sb* høyttaler.

lounge [laʊndʒ] **I** *sb* **1** (hotell)salong; hall, vestibyle; **2** (daglig)stue, salong; **II** *vi* **1** slentre; (gå og) drive/slenge; **2** ligge henslengt. **lounge-chair** *sb* dyp (lene)stol.

louse [laʊs] **1** *sb* lus; **2** *vt US: ~ up* forkludre, spolere, ødelegge. **lousy** ['laʊzɪ] *adj* **1** luset; **2** *dgl* dårlig, elendig; **3** *dgl US: ~ with* smekkfull (stappfull, stinn etc) av.

lout [laʊt] *sb* **1** kloss(major), kløne; **2** slamp.

lovable ['lʌvəbl] *adj* elskelig, kjær. **love** [lʌv] **I** *sb* **1** kjærlighet; elskov, forelskelse; *~ for* kjærlighet til (især mennesker); *~ of* kjærlighet til (især dyr og ting); forkjærlighet for; lyst til; *in ~ with* forelsket/ glad i; *be in ~ with* være forelsket/glad i; *fall in ~ with* forelske seg/bli forelsket i; *make ~* elske (dvs ha samleie); *make ~ to* elske (dvs ha samleie) med; **2** kjæreste; **3** elskede; *dgl* jenta/snuppa mi (etc, sagt i fleng til venninner, kvinnelig betjening etc); **4** (kjærlig) hilsen; *give/send one's ~* sende (sin) hilsen; *give her my ~* hils henne fra meg; **5** *isn't he a ~!* han er vel søt! **6** *sport* null (poeng etc); **II** *vt* elske; være (svært) glad i; ha lyst på/til; *I should/I'd ~ to* jeg skulle/ville gjerne; *som svar på innbydelse etc* svært gjerne. **love|-affair** *sb* kjærlighets|forhold, -historie. **~-letter** *sb* kjærlighetsbrev. **loveliness** *sb* skjønnhet (etc, jf *lovely*). **love|-lock** *sb* dårelokk. **~lorn** *adj* elskovssyk; *især* ulykkelig forelsket. **lovely** ['lʌvlɪ] *adj* **1** skjønn, yndig; henrivende, nydelig; **2** *dgl* deilig, herlig; morsom; storartet; **3** *US* elskelig. **love|-making** *sb* kurtise(ring); elskov; intim kjærlighet; samleie. **~-match** *sb* kjærlighetsekteskap. **~-philtre, ~-potion** *sb* elskovsdrikk, kjærlighetsdrikk. **lover** ['lʌvə] *sb* **1** elsker, kjæreste (især om mann); **2** -elsker, -venn; *~ of animals* dyrevenn. **love|sick** *adj* elskovssyk, kjærlighetssyk. **~-song** *sb* kjærlighets|dikt, -sang. **~-story** *sb* kjærlighetshistorie. **~-token** *sb* kjærlighetspant. **loving** ['lʌvɪŋ] *adj* kjærlig; hengiven; øm.

low [ləʊ] **A I** *adj* **1** lav (og lavt|liggende, -stående; lavere|liggende, -stående; lavbygd, liten etc); grunn (om vannstand); dyp (om stemme, tone); **2** ringe, ubetydelig; *have a ~ opinion of* ha små tanker om; **3** nedrig, simpel, tarvelig; vulgær; **4** nedfor, nedtrykt; redusert, svak; **II** *adv* lavt *etc* (samt dypt og dypt/langt nede etc); *bring ~* redusere; nedverdige; ydmyke; *burn ~* brenne svakt; *run ~* minke; slippe opp (*on* for); **III** *sb* lavmål (og lavpunkt; laveste posisjon/punkt; *dgl* lavgir, lavtrykk etc); **B 1** *sb* raut(ing); **2** *vi* raute. **low|-born** *adj* lavættet. **~-bred** *adj* udannet, uoppdragen. **~-brow** *adj, sb* uintellektuell (person). **~ current** *sb* svakstrøm. **~-down** *adj* gemen, nederdrektig. **lower** ['ləʊə] **I** *adj* lavere *etc*; **II** *vb* **1** fire, senke; *~ away* låre; **2** minke; minske, redusere; sette/slå ned; dempe, svekke; **3** forringe; ydmyke; *~ oneself* nedlate/nedverdige seg. **lower | case** *sb koll* minuskler; små bokstaver. **~ deck** *sb sjø* banjer(dekk); *fig* underoffiserer og mannskaper. **low|-grade** *adj* mindreverdig. **~-key(ed)** *adj* lavmælt, stillferdig; reservert. **~lands** *sb fl* lavland. **~-necked** *adj* nedringet, utringet. **~ pressure** *sb* **1** lavt trykk; **2** lavtrykk. **~-spirited** *adj* ned|slått, -trykt. **~ tide, ~ water** *sb* lavvann.

loyal ['lɔɪəl] *adj* tro (og trofast); lojal; lovlydig. **loyalty** ['lɔɪəltɪ] *sb* troskap *etc*; lojalitet.

lube [lu:b] *sb dgl petro* smøreolje.

lubricant ['lu:brɪkənt] *sb* smøremiddel; (smøre)|-fett, (-)olje. **lubricate** ['lu:brɪkeɪt] *vt* smøre. **lubrication** [ˌlu:brɪ'keɪʃn] *sb* smøring.

lucid ['lu:sɪd] *adj* lys (og lysende, skinnende etc); klar. **lucidity** [lu:'sɪdətɪ] *sb* klarhet *etc*.

luck [lʌk] *sb* **1** lykke(n); skjebne(n); tilfelle(t); *dgl* slump(en); slumpetreff(et); *bad/hard ~* uhell; motgang; *dgl* uflaks; *good ~*! lykke til! *be down on one's ~* være uheldig; sitte i uhell; *be in/out of ~* være heldig/uheldig; *dgl* ha flaks/uflaks; **2** hell; lykke; medgang. **luckless** ['lʌklɪs] *adj* uheldig. **lucky** ['lʌkɪ] *adj* heldig; lykkebringende, lykke-; *a ~ chance* et lykketreff; *be ~ in/with* være heldig med.

lucrative ['lu:krətɪv] *adj* innbringende, lønnsom; lukrativ.

ludicrous ['lu:dɪkrəs] *adj* latterlig; (ufrivillig) komisk.

lug [lʌg] **A 1** *sb* strabasiøst slep *etc*; **2** *vt* hale, slepe; dra, trekke; rykke; **B** *sb* **1** kam, knast; **2** hank, øre; **C** *sb* = *~sail*. **luggage** ['lʌgɪdʒ] *sb* bagasje. **luggage|-carrier** *sb* bagasje|brett, -bærer. **~-rack** *sb* bagasje|hylle, -nett. **lugsail** *sb* luggerseil.

lukewarm ['lu:kwɔ:m] *adj* lunken; *fig også* halvhjertet, valen.

lull [lʌl] **I** *sb* opphold, pause; stille periode; vindstille; **II** *vb* **1** berolige, roe; bysse (i søvn); dulme, døyve; **2** stilne; *om vind* løye, spakne. **lullaby** ['lʌləbaɪ] *sb* vugge|sang, -vise.

lumber ['lʌmbə] **I** *sb* **1** trelast, tømmer; **2** skrammel, skrot, tral; **II** *vi* **1** traske (tungt); klampe, trampe; **2** ramle, rumle; **3** hugge tømmer. **lumber|-jack, ~-man** *sb* tømmerhugger; skogsarbeider. **~mill** *sb* sagbruk. **~room** *sb* pulterkammer. **~yard** *sb* trelasttomt.

luminosity [ˌlu:mɪ'nɒsətɪ] *sb* **1** glans, skinn; klarhet; **2** lysstyrke. **luminous** ['lu:mɪnəs] *adj* **1** (selv)lysende; skinnende; **2** klar, lysende.

lump [lʌmp] **A I** *sb* **1** klump; (uregelmessig) bite/stykke; *in the ~* alt i alt; alt under ett; ; **2** hevelse, kul; **3** *dgl* dråk, slamp; rugg; deise, dundre; **II** *vt* **1** klumpe (seg) sammen; slå sammen (beløp etc); se/ta under ett; **2** *~ along* humpe/lunte av sted; **B** *vt: if you don't like it you can/may ~ it* det får du (bare) finne deg i.

lunacy ['lu:nəsɪ] *sb* sinnssykdom; *dgl* galskap, vanvidd. **lunar** ['lu:nə] *adj* måne-. **lunatic** ['lu:nətɪk] **I** *adj* **1** sinnssyk; sinnssyke-; **2** *dgl* sinnssvak, vanvittig; **II** *sb* sinnssyk (person).

lunch [lʌntʃ] **I** *sb* lunsj; *dgl* formiddagsmat; **II** *vb* **1** lunsje; spise lunsj; **2** servere lunsj (til). **lunch | box** *sb* matdåse. **~break** *sb* lunsjpause. **luncheon** ['lʌntʃn] *sb bokl* = *lunch*. **lunch | packet** *sb* matpakke. **~room** *sb* lunsjrom; (bedrifts)|kantine, (-)messe. **~time** *sb* = *~break*. **~ voucher** *sb* lunsjbillett (som gir rett til lunsj på arbeidsgiverens bekostning).

lung [lʌŋ] *sb* lunge.

lunge [lʌndʒ] **1** *sb* utfall; plutselig kast (sett, støt etc); **2** *vi* kaste seg/styrte frem; gjøre (et) utfall.

lurch [lɜ:tʃ] **A I** *sb* sjangling *etc*; krengning; **II** *vi* **1** sjangle; ta en overhaling; **2** *sjø* krenge; **B** *sb: leave in the ~* late i stikken.

lure ['ljʊə] **1** *sb* agn; lokke|mat, -middel; åte; **2** *vt* forføre, lokke; besnære.

lurid ['ljʊərɪd] *adj* **1** flammerød; flammende, glødende; **2** nifs, skummel, uhyggelig.

lurk [lɜ:k] *vi* ligge på lur; ligge og lure/vente. **lurking** ['lɜ:kɪŋ] *adj* lurende; truende.

luscious ['lʌʃes] *adj* **1** saftig; søt; **2** søtlaten; vammel; **3** frodig, yppig.

lush [lʌʃ] *adj* frodig, yppig (om vegetasjon); saftig.

lust [lʌst] **I** *sb* **1** begjær, (sterk) lyst; **2** lystenhet; vellyst; **II** *vi: ~ after/for* begjære.

lustre ['lʌstə] *sb* glans, skinn, skjær. **lustrous** ['lʌstrəs] *adj* skinnende (blank); glitrende, strålende.

lusty ['lʌstɪ] *adj* **1** kraftig; energisk; kjekk, staut; **2** før, svær; korpulent.

luxuriance [lʌg'zʊərɪəns] *sb* frodighet *etc*. **luxuriant** [lʌg'zʊərɪənt] *adj* frodig, yppig; kraftig, rik. **luxuriate** [lʌg'zʊərɪeɪt] *vi* **1** vokse frodig *etc*; stå i fullt flor; **2** leve i luksus/overflod; *~ in* fråtse/*dgl* velte seg i. **luxurious** [lʌg'zʊərɪəs] *adj* luksuriøs, luksus-; overdådig. **luxuriously** [lʌg'zʊərɪəslɪ] *adv* med velbehag. **luxury** ['lʌkʃərɪ] *sb* **1** luksus (og luksusartikkel etc); luksustilværelse; **2** overdådighet; overflod.

lye [laɪ] *sb* lut.

lymph [lɪmf] *sb* lymfe(væske).

lynch [lɪntʃ] *vt* lynsje. **lynch law** *sb* lynsjjustis.

lynx [lɪnks] *sb* gaupe. **lynx-eyed** *adj* skarp|synt, -øyd.

lyric ['lɪrɪk] **I** *adj* lyrisk; **II** *sb* **1** lyrisk dikt; **2** *fl* tekst (til sang, vise etc). **lyrical** ['lɪrɪkl] *adj* **1** = *lyric I*; **2** stemningsfull. **lyric poet** *sb* lyriker.

M

ma [mɑ:] *fork* for *mamma 1.*

ma'am [mæm] *fork* for *madam.*

mac [mæk] *fork* for *mackintosh.*

macadam ['mə'kædəm] *sb* fast veidekke.

mace [meɪs] *sb* **1** septer; **2** *hist* klubbe, kølle.

machinations [ˌmæki'neɪʃnz] *sb fl* intriger(ing); renker, renkespill. **machine** [mə'ʃi:n] **I** *sb* **1** maskin; **2** maskin(menneske); automat, robot; **3** apparat, organisasjon; (parti)maskin; **II** *vt* maskin(be)arbeide. **machine | address** *sb data* absolutt adresse. **~ code** *sb data* instruksjonskode. **~-gun** *sb, vb* (skyte med) maskingevær. **~ instruction** *sb data* maskininstruksjon. **~-made** *adj* maskin|fremstilt, -laget, -produsert. **~ oil** *sb petro* maskinolje. **machinery** [mə'ʃi:nərɪ] *sb* maskineri; mekanisme. **machinery deck** *sb petro* maskindekk. **machine | time** *sb data* maskintid. **~ tool** *sb* arbeidsmaskin, verktøymaskin. **~ word** *sb data* maskinord.

mackintosh ['mækɪntɒʃ] *sb* regnfrakk.

mad [mæd] *adj* **1** sinnssyk; *dgl* gal, sprø; **2** *dgl* opphisset; vill; fra seg; **~ about/after** gal/vill *etc* etter; **~ for** *(water etc)* vanvittig (av tørst etc); **~ with** *(fear, pain etc)* gal av (frykt, smerte etc); **3** *US* rasende, sint; *dgl* forbannet (*at/on* på).

madam ['mædəm] *sb (i tiltale)* **1** fru(e), frøken; **2** Deres Majestet/Kongelige Høyhet.

madden ['mædn] *vt* **1** gjøre sinnssyk *etc*; **2** ergre, irritere; *US* gjøre rasende *etc*. **mad|house** *sb dgl* galehus (også *fig*). **~ness** *sb* **1** sinnssykdom; *dgl* galskap, vanvidd; **2** *US* raseri, sinne.

maelstrom ['meɪlstrɒm] *sb* malstrøm, virvelstrøm; *fig* heksegryte.

magazine [ˌmægə'zi:n] *sb* **1** lager(bygning), magasin; **2** kammer, magasin (i skytevåpen); **3** magasin, tidsskrift; blad.

maggot ['mægət] *sb* larve, mark.

magic ['mædʒɪk] **I** *adj (~al)* magisk; **II** *sb* **1** magi; hekseri, trolldom; **2** trylling. **magician** [mə'dʒɪʃn] *sb* **1** magiker, trollmann; **2** tryllekunstner. **magic wand** *sb* tryllestav.

magisterial [ˌmædʒɪs'tɪərɪəl] *adj* bydende, myndig; dominerende; **2** magistrat(s)-; øvrighets-; **3** magister-. **magistrate** ['mædʒɪstreɪt] *sb* **1** magistrat; *især* (forhørs)dommer, fredsdommer; **2** øvrighetsperson.

magnanimity [ˌmægnə'nɪmətɪ] *sb* storsinn *etc*. **magnanimous** [mæg'nænɪməs] *adj* storsinnet; generøs; edel, høysinnet.

magnet ['mægnɪt] *sb* magnet. **magnetic** [mæg'netɪk] *adj* magnetisk; *fig også* tiltrekkende. **magnetic | pig** *sb petro* magnetisk pigg. **~ survey** *sb petro* magnetisk undersøkelse.

magnificence [mæg'nɪfɪsns] *sb* storhet *etc*. **magnificent** [mæg'nɪfɪsnt] *adj* stor (og især stor|artet, -slagen, -slått); praktfull. **magnifier** ['mægnɪfaɪə] *sb* **1** forstørrelsesglass; **2** forsterker(rør). **magnify** ['mægnɪfaɪ] *vt* **1** forstørre; forsterke; **2** overdrive; **3** *gml rel* forherlige; opphøye. **magnitude** ['mægnɪtju:d] *sb* **1** størrelse (og størrelsesorden); omfang; **2** storhet; *fig* betydning.

magpie ['mægpaɪ] *sb* **1** skjære; **2** pratmaker, skravlebøtte.

mahogany [mə'hɒgənɪ] *sb* mahogni(tre).

maid [meɪd] *sb* **1** hushjelp; tjeneste|jente, -pike; *nurse* **~** barnepike; **2** *gml* frøken, jomfru; **3** *bokl* pike. **maiden** ['meɪdn] **1** *adj* ugift; frøken-; jomfruelig, jomfru-; **2** *sb = maid 2, 3.* **maiden|head** *sb* **1** hymen, møydom; **2** frøkenstand. **~hood** *sb = ~head 2.* **~ name** *sb* pikenavn. **~ speech** *sb* jomfrutale. **maid | of honour** *sb* **1** hoffdame; **2** (brudens) forlover. **~-servant** *sb = maid 1.*

mail [meɪl] **A 1** *sb* post (og post|forsendelse, -sending etc); **2** *vt* poste; sende i/med posten; **B** *hist* **1** *sb* panser; *coat of* **~** panserskjorte, (ring)brynje; **2** *vi* pansre. **mail|bag** *sb* postsekk. **~box** *sb US* postkasse. **~ coach** *sb* postvogn; *hist* diligence. **~ing list** *sb* adresseliste, kundeliste. **~ order** *sb* postordre.

maim [meɪm] *vt* kveste, lemleste; skade, såre; skamfere.

main [meɪn] **I** *adj* viktigst; vesentlig(st); hoved-; stor-; **II** *sb* **1** *fl* hovedledning (for elektrisitet, gass, vann etc); **2** kraft, styrke; **3** storpart; *fig* hovedsak; *in the* **~** hovedsakelig; stort sett; **4** *poet* hav. **main | column** *sb petro* hovedtårn. **~ control unit** *sb data* hovedstyreenhet. **~file** *sb data* hovedfil. **~ flow** *sb data* hovedflyt. **~ fraction** *sb petro* hovedfraksjon. **~frame** *sb data* prosessorenhet. **~ header** *sb petro* hovedsamledning. **mainland** ['meɪnlənd] *sb* **1** fastland; **2** hovedland; hjemland, moderland. **main line** *sb* hovedlinje; stambane. **mainly** ['meɪnlɪ] *adv* hovedsakelig; (alt) vesentlig; overveiende. **main | part** *sb = main II 3.* **~ point** *sb* hoved|punkt, -sak. **~ program** *sb data* hovedprogram. **mains | receiver, ~ set** *sb* nettmottaker (i motsetning til batteriradio). **main | storage** *sb* hovedlager (også *data*). **~ stream** *sb petro* hovedfraksjon. **~ street** *sb* hoved|gate, -vei. **mains system** *sb* ledningsnett. **~ voltage** *sb* nettspenning.

maintain [meɪn'teɪn] *vt* **1** håndheve, (opprett)holde; bevare, vedlikeholde; **2** forsørge, underholde; støtte, *mil* forsyne; **3** fremholde, hevde; påstå; **4** forsvare; rettferdiggjøre. **maintenance** ['meɪntənəns] *sb* **1** håndhevelse *etc*; bevaring, vedlikehold; **2** støtte; underhold; *jur* underholdsbidrag; *mil* forsyning(er); **3** opprettholdelse (av mening, påstand etc); forsvar.

maize [meɪz] *sb* mais. **maize-cob** *sb* maiskolbe.

majestic [mə'dʒestɪk] *adj* majestetisk. **majesty** ['mædʒəstɪ] *sb* majestet.

major ['meɪdʒə] **I** *adj* **1** større (av to); *især* viktigere; hoved-; **2** eldre (av to brødre); eldst; **3** større (dvs temmelig stor); stor-; **4** *mus* dur-; **II** *vi US:* ~ *in* studere (*dgl* ha/ta) som hovedfag. **majority** [mə'dʒɒrətɪ] *sb* **1** flertall, majoritet; største|del, -part; **2** myndighetsalder. **major | key** *sb mus* dur(toneart). ~ **pool** *sb petro* stor forekomst.

make [meɪk] **I** *sb* **1** (opp)bygning; konstruksjon; **2** produksjon, tilvirkning; *in the* ~ under arbeid; i produksjon; *on the* ~ ærgjerrig; på vei oppover (i samfunnet etc); **3** fasong, form; *fig* støpning; **4** merke, modell; type; fabrikat; **II** *vb* **1** lage (og bygge (opp); fabrikkere, fremstille, produsere; tilberede; gjøre/lage i stand etc); **2** gjøre (og gjøre seg); foreta (seg); handle; (ut)virke; gjennomføre, utføre; (av)slutte; ~ *a call* ta en telefon (dvs ringe); ~ *love* elske (intimt); *dgl* ligge sammen; ~ *love to* kurtisere; elske (intimt); *dgl* ligge med; ~ *a remark* komme med en bemerkning; ~ *a speech* holde en tale; ~ *war* føre krig; **3** oppnå; få/skaffe (seg); nå/rekke (frem til); greie, klare; prestere, yte; *dgl* gjøre, holde; ~ *money* tjene penger; ~ *one's fortune* gjøre (sin) lykke; ~ *ten knots* gjøre (dvs holde en fart av) ti knop; **4** forårsake; bevirke, utvirke; få i stand; få til (å bli etc); gjøre/utnevne til; la (bli etc); ~ *believe* innbille (seg); foregi, late som (om); ~ *do* få til å rekke/strekke til; ~ *do with* greie/klare seg med; ~ *a fool of* gjøre narr av; ~ *a fool of oneself* dumme seg ut; *can you* ~ *it work* kan du få den/det til å gå/virke; *don't* ~ *me laugh* få meg ikke til å le; **5** anslå (beregne/sette etc) til; ~ *it out to be* anslå det til å være; få det til å bli; *what do you* ~ *of it* hva får du ut av det; hva mener du om det; **6** (vise seg å) bli/være; utgjøre; **7** en del stående uttrykk: ~ **bold to** driste seg til å; ~ **certain/sure of** forvisse seg om; ~ **eyes at** blunke/skotte til; (øyen)flørte med; ~ **faces** gjøre grimaser; skjære ansikter; ~ **free of** gi fri adgang *etc* til; ~ **free with** benytte/forsyne seg (fritt) av; ta seg friheter med; ~ **friends** bli venner; ~ **fun/game of** gjøre narr av; ha moro/holde leven med; ~ **good** gjøre det godt (dvs ha suksess etc); gjennomføre; greie, klare; erstatte, gjenopprette; gjøre godt (igjen); bevise, godtgjøre; ~ **head(way)** avansere; gå/rykke frem; ~ **head(way) against** holde stand/stå seg mot; ~ **light of** bagatellisere; gjøre lite vesen av; ~ **little of** gjøre lite ut av; *også* = ~ *light of*; ~ **much of** gjøre mye ut av; slå stort opp; ~ **oneself scarce** *(dgl)* fordufte, stikke av; ~ **sure** sikre, trygge; forvisse seg (om); **to** ~ **sure** for sikkerhets skyld; for å være på den sikre siden; **8** *med adv/prep* ~ **after** løpe/sette etter; ~ **against** hindre, motvirke; ~ **(as if)** gjøre/late som (om); gi det skinn/utseende av; ~ **at** fare mot; gå løs på; ~ **away** skynde seg unna/vekk; ~ **away with** stikke av med; *dgl* gjøre ende på; søle bort; rydde av veien (dvs drepe); ~ **for** begi seg til; sette kursen mot; fare/gå løs på; bidra/tjene til; ~ **from** lage av (især mht råmaterialer); ~ **into** forvandle (gjøre, lage etc om) til; ~ **of** lage av (især mht halvfabrikata); få/gjøre ut av; ~ **off (with)** = ~ *away (with)*; ~ **on** fortsette/skynde seg videre; *dgl* gjøre (dvs tjene) på; ~ **out** skimte, skjelne; forstå, oppfatte; finne ut av; bli klar over; hevde, påstå; *US* greie/klare seg; ~ **over** over|dra, -føre (*to* til); forandre; ~ **to** gå i gang; gjøre mine til; ~ **towards** gå *etc* mot; styre/sette kursen mot; ~ **up** lage; sette sammen; sette/stille opp; skrive ut; finne på; dikte opp; sminke; kle ut; pakke inn; utgjøre, være; representere; ~ **up for** erstatte; innhente/ta igjen (det forsømte etc); ~ **up to** styre mot; nærme seg; flørte med; smigre; sleske for; ~ **up with** gjøre opp med; forlike/forsone seg med. **make-believe** **1** *adj, adv* påtatt; skinn-; på liksom; **2** *sb* foregivende, skinn. **maker** ['meɪkə] *sb* **1** bygger *etc*; fabrikant, produsent, tilvirker; **2** skaper. **makeshift** ['meɪkʃɪft] **1** *adj* provisorisk; **2** *sb* nødhjelp, provisorium; midlertidig ordning *etc*. **make-up** ['meɪkʌp] *sb* **1** sminke(saker); *teat også* maske(ring); **2** sammensetning; beskaffenhet, natur; **3** arrangement; design, utseende; *ofte* emballasje, (inn)pakning; **4** *petro* påfyll(ing), tilsetning; **5** påfunn; skrøne. **make-up time** *sb data* omkjøringstid.

malady ['mælədɪ] *sb* sykdom.

malcontent ['mælkən,tent] *adj, sb* misfornøyd/utilfreds (person).

male [meɪl] **I** *adj* **1** hann-, hannkjønns-; **2** mannlig, manns-; **3** mandig, maskulin; **II** *sb* **1** hann(dyr); **2** mann(folk).

malevolent [mə'levələnt] *adj* ondsinnet, ondskapsfull; skadefro. **malice** ['mælɪs] *sb* ondskap; ondsinnethet, ondskapsfullhet; *bear* ~ bære nag; *(with)* ~ *aforethought* med forsett/overlegg. **malicious** [mə'lɪʃəs] *adj* ondsinnet, ondskapsfull. **malicious | damage,** ~ **mischief** *sb* hærverk. **malign** [mə'laɪn] **1** *adj* skadelig; **2** *vt* baktale; rakke ned på. **malignant** [mə'lɪgnənt] *adj* **1** ondartet, livstruende; skadelig; **2** ondsinnet, ondskapsfull.

malinger [mə'lɪŋgə] *vi* **1** simulere (sykdom); late som om man er syk; **2** skulke. **malingering** [mə'lɪŋgərɪŋ] *sb, adj* skulkesyk(e).

mallard ['mæləd] *sb* stokkand.

malleable ['mælɪəbl] *adj* hammerbar, smibar, valsbar; *fig* føyelig, medgjørlig. **mallet** ['mælɪt] *sb* (tre)klubbe, kølle.

malnutrition [,mælnju:'trɪʃn] *sb* underernæring.

malt [mɔ:lt] **1** *sb* malt; **2** *vb* malte(s).

maltreat [mæl'tri:t] *vt* mishandle; maltraktere. **maltreatment** [mæl'tri:tmənt] *sb* mishandling.

mamma *sb* **1** [mə'mɑ:] mamma; **2** ['mæmə] bryst(kjertel). **mammal** ['mæməl] *sb* pattedyr.

mammoth ['mæməθ] *sb* mammut.

mammy ['mæmɪ] *sb* **1** = *mamma 1*; **2** *US* negerdadda; farget barnepike.

man [mæn] **I** *sb* **1** menneske (og mennesket; menneskeheten, menneskene); **2** mann; ~ *about town* herre på byen; *to a* ~*/to the last* ~ til siste mann; **3**

(ekte)mann; elsker, kjæreste; **4** (kammer)tjener; **5** *fl* besetning, mannskap(er); menige (soldater); **6** (-)mann; *sjø* -farer (dvs -fartøy, -skip); **II** *vt* **1** bemanne; **2** ~ *oneself* manne/stramme seg opp.

manacle ['mænəkl] **1** *sb fl* håndjern; fot|jern, -lenker; **2** *vt* sette håndjern på; legge i jern/lenker.

manage ['mænɪdʒ] *vb* **1** administrere, (be)styre, lede; **2** behandle, håndtere; mestre; **3** greie/klare (seg). **management** ['mænɪdʒmənt] *sb* **1** administrasjon, ledelse; **2** behandling, håndtering. **manager** ['mænɪdʒə] *sb* bestyrer (og leder, sjef; direktør, disponent, forretningsfører, impressario etc).

mandate ['mændeɪt] **1** *sb* mandat (og *pol* mandat|område, -stat); fullmakt, oppdrag; **2** *vt pol* sette/stille under mandat. **mandatory** ['mændətərɪ] *adj* **1** fullmakt(s)-; mandat-; **2** *US* obligatorisk, påbudt; **3** bydende, myndig.

mane [meɪn] *sb* man, manke.

manger ['meɪndʒə] *sb* krybbe.

mangle ['mæŋgl] **A I** *sb* **1** rulle; **2** vrimaskin; **II** *vt* **1** rulle (tøy); **2** vri (i vrimaskin); **B** *vt* lemleste; mishandle, skamfere.

man|handle ['mæn,hændl] *vt* **1** bruke håndkraft på; **2** mishandle; overfalle, rane. **~head** *sb petro* mannhull.

manhood ['mænhʊd] *sb* **1** manndom (og manndoms|alder, -kraft, styrke etc); mandighet; **2** menn; mannlig befolkning.

mania ['meɪnɪə] *sb* galskap, vanvidd; mani. **maniac** ['meɪnɪæk] *adj, sb* gal/vanvittig (person); *sex* ~ sedelighetsforbryter.

manifest ['mænɪfest] **I** *adj* åpenbar; klar, tydelig; **II** *sb sjø* ladnings|angivelse, -manifest; **III** *vb* **1** manifestere (seg); vise/åpenbare (seg); komme til uttrykk; **2** *sjø* føre opp på ladningsangivelsen. **manifestation** [,mænɪfes'teɪʃn] *sb* manifestering *etc*; manifestasjon. **manifesto** [,mænɪ'festəʊ] *sb* manifest.

manifold ['mænɪfəʊld] **1** *adj* mangfoldig(e); **2** *sb* forgreningsrør, grenrør; manifold; *petro* rørstokk; **3** *vt* mangfoldiggjøre.

manikin ['mænɪkɪn] *sb* **1** dverg, mannsling; **2** leddedukke; **3** = *mannequin 2*.

manipulate [mə'nɪpjʊleɪt] *vt* **1** manipulere (med); behandle, håndtere. **manipulation** [mə,nɪpjʊ'leɪʃn] *sb* manipulering etc; manipulasjon; *data* håndtering.

mankind *sb* **1** [mæn'kaɪnd] menneskeheten, menneskene; **2** ['mænkaɪnd] mannkjønnet, mennene.

manly ['mænlɪ] *adj* mandig.

mannequin ['mænɪkɪn] *sb* **1** mannekeng; **2** utstillings|dukke, figur.

manner ['mænə] *sb* **1** fremgangs)måte; sett, vis; **2** oppførsel; manerer; **3** sed, skikk; bruk, vane; **4** slags; *by no ~ of means* ikke på noen (som helst) måte. **mannered** ['mænəd] *adj* **1** manerlig; maniert, tilgjort; **2** med ... manerer; *ill-~* udannet, uoppdragen; *well-~* dannet, veloppdragen. **mannerism** ['mænərɪzəm] *sb* maner (og manerlighet); *dgl* jåleri. **mannerly** ['mænəlɪ] *adj* dannet, høflig.

mannish ['mænɪʃ] *adj* mannfolkaktig, mannhaftig; som en mann.

manoeuvre [mə'nu:və] **I** *sb* (militær)manøver; **II** *vb* **1** holde manøver; **2** manøvrere; jenke/lirke (til).

man|-of-war *sb* krigsskip.

manor ['mænə] *sb* gods, herregård.

man-power *sb* håndkraft; arbeidskraft; menneskemateriell.

mansion ['mænʃn] *sb* **1** (større) privatbolig, villa; **2** *fl* (finere betegnelse for) leiegård.

man|-sized *adj* fullvoksen. **~-slaughter** *sb* (uaktsomt) drap.

mantel ['mæntl] = **mantelpiece** ['mæntlpi:s] *sb* kamin|gesims, -hylle.

mantle ['mæntl] *sb* **1** kappe; **2** dekke, teppe; **3** gløde|hette, nett (til parafinlampe etc).

manual ['mænjʊəl] **I** *adj* manuell; hånd-, kropps-; **II** *sb* **1** håndbok; **2** manual. **manual | calling** *sb data* manuell oppkalling. ~ **operation** *sb data* manuell behandling. ~ **system** *sb data* manuelt system.

manufacture [,mænjʊ'fæktʃə] **I** *sb* **1** fabrikkering *etc*; fabrikasjon; **2** *fl* (industri)|produkter, -varer; **II** *vt* **1** fabrikkere (og fremstille, produsere etc); **2** dikte opp; finne på. **manufactured gas** *sb petro* lysgass. **manufacturer** [,mænjʊ'fæktʃərə] *sb* fabrikant (og fabrikk); produsent.

manure [mə'njʊə] **1** *sb* gjødsel; *dgl* møkk; **2** *vt* gjødsle.

many ['menɪ] **1** *adj* mange; **2** *sb* mengde; *a good/great ~* en hel del.

map [mæp] **I** *sb* (land)kart; **II** *vt* **1** kartlegge; lage (et) kart over; *data også* avbilde; **2** ~ *out* planlegge. **map file** *sb* avbildingsfil.

maple ['meɪpl] *sb* lønn, lønnetre. **maple-syrup** *sb* lønnesirup.

mar [mɑ:] *vt* skade; **2** skjemme, spolere; ødelegge.

maraud [mə'rɔ:d] *vi* gå på rov; herje, plyndre. **marauder** [mə'rɔ:də] *sb* plyndrer; marodør.

marble ['mɑ:bl] *sb* marmor (og marmor|blokk, -plate etc); *fl* (marmor)skulpturer.

march [mɑ:tʃ] **1** *sb* marsj; **2** *vb* (la) marsjere; ~ *on* marsjere videre; marsjere mot (for å angripe, innta etc).

marchioness ['mɑ:ʃənɪs] *sb* markise (dvs markis hustru, jf *marquess, marquis*).

mare ['meə] *sb* hoppe; *dgl* merr.

margin ['mɑ:dʒɪn] *sb* **1** marg; kant, rand; **2** margin, spillerom. **marginal** ['mɑ:dʒɪnl] *adj* kant-, rand-; marginal(-).

marguerite [,mɑ:gə'ri:t] *sb* prestekrave.

marine [mə'ri:n] **I** *adj* marine-, skips-; marin(-), hav-; **II** *sb* **1** flåte, marine; **2** *mil* marine|infanterist, -soldat; *the Marines, the Marine Corps (US)* marineinfanteriet. **marine insurance** *sb* sjøforsikring. **mariner** ['mærɪnə] *sb bokl* sjømann. **marine riser** *sb petro* slamstigerør.

marital ['mærɪtl] *adj* ekteskapelig; **2** ektemanns-; som ektemann.

maritime ['mærɪtaɪm] *adj* **1** maritim; sjø-; skips-; **2** kyst-.

mark [mɑ:k] **I** *sb* **1** merke; flekk, plett; **2** hakk, skår; skramme; **3** merke (dvs bumerke, kjennemerke, varemerke etc); **4** preg, stempel (især *fig*); **5** (skole)-karakter; poeng; *også* anmerkning; **6** indikasjon; (kjenne)tegn; uttrykk; **7** avmerket/oppmerket sted etc; (grense)|merke, -skjell; *sport* startgrop; *on your ~s!* innta plassene! **8** mål(skive); blink; *beside/wide of the ~* utenfor (blinken *etc*); *fig* langt fra målet; (saken) uvedkommende; *make one's ~* gjøre det godt; nå målet; **9** standard(nivå); *above/below the ~* over/under gjennomsnittet; **II** *vt* **1** merke (og merke av/opp; sette merke i/på/ved etc); **2** rette (skoleoppgaver etc); gi karakter(er)/poeng; gi/sette anmerkning-(er); **3** karakterisere, kjennetegne; prege, utmerke; **4** indikere; betegne; markere; *~ time* gjøre/ta på stedet marsj; *fig også* se tiden an; **5** *med adv/prep* **~ down** redusere/sette ned (pris); **~ in** merke (av); **~ off/out** merke av/opp; stikke ut; merke (peke, plukke etc) ut; *~ed out for* (forut)bestemt til; **~ up** forhøye/sette opp (pris). **mark-down** *sb* (pris)nedsettelse. **marked** [mɑ:kt] *adj* **1** merket *etc*; **2** markert; klar, tydelig; **3** påfallende, mistenkelig. **marker** ['mɑ:kə] *sb data* indikator. **marker crude** *sb petro* basisråolje.

market ['mɑ:kɪt] **I** *sb* **1** marked (og markedsplass); torg (og torghall); **2** (stor)magasin; (større) butikk/forretning; **3** marked (dvs handel, handelsmuligheter etc); *som adj* handels-, markeds-; **II** *vb* **1** markedsføre; falby, selge; **2** (for)handle; drive (torg)-handel; **3** kjøpe/*dgl* handle (på torget); *go ~ing* gå på torget. **market-house** *sb* markedshall, torghall; (stor)magasin; (større) butikk/forretning. **marketing** ['mɑ:kɪtɪŋ] *sb* markedsføring, salg. **market-place** *sb* marked, markedsplass, torg(hall).

mark | reader *sb data* merkeleser. **~ scanning** *sb data* merkeavsøking. **~ sensing** *sb data* merkelesing.

marksmamn ['mɑ:ksmən] *sb* (skarp)skytter. **marksmanship** ['mɑ:ksmənʃɪp] *sb* (god) skyteferdighet.

mark-up *sb* (pris)forhøyelse.

maroon [mə'ru:n] **A** *adj, sb* rødbrun(t); **B** *vt* etterlate på øde øy etc; **C** *sb* maron(neger), rømt negerslave.

marquess, marquis ['mɑ:kwɪs] *sb* marki.

marriage ['mærɪdʒ] *sb* ekteskap, giftermål. **marriage|able** ['mærɪdʒəbl] *adj* gifteferdig. **~ lines** *sb* vielsesattest.

marrow ['mærəʊ] *sb* **1** marg; **2** kjerne; (livs)kraft.

married couple *sb* ektepar. **marry** ['mærɪ] *vb* **1** gifte seg (med); **2** gifte bort; **3** forene; føye (binde, koble etc) sammen.

marsh [mɑ:ʃ] *sb* myr(land), sump.

marshal ['mɑ:ʃl] **I** *sb* **1** *mil etc* marskalk; **2** seremonimester; **3** *US: Marshall* marshal(l); ≈ politimester; *(fire ~)* brannmester; **II** *vt* **1** arrangere, ordne; stille opp; rangere (jernbanevogner); **2** føre/lede (seremonielt); geleide.

marten ['mɑ:tn] *sb* mår.

martial ['mɑ:ʃl] *adj* krigersk. **martial law** *sb* (militær) unntakstilstand.

martin ['mɑ:tn] *sb* (tak)svale.

marvel ['mɑ:vl] **I** *sb* **1** under (og underverk, vidunder etc); mirakel; **2** *gml* undring; **II** *vi* (for)undre seg (*at* over). **marvellous** ['mɑ:vələs] *adj* vidunderlig; *dgl* fantastisk; kjempefin(t); storartet.

mash [mæʃ] **I** *sb* **1** mos, stappe; **2** bløtfôr, mask; **3** sammensurium, smørje; **II** *vt* mose (sammen); lage stappe (av).

mask [mɑ:sk] **1** *sb* maske; *fig også* dekke, skjul; **2** *vt* maskere/*fig* skjule (seg).

mason ['meɪsn] *sb* **1** murer; **2** *(free~)* frimurer. **masonic** [mə'sɒnɪk] *adj* frimurerisk, frimurer-. **masonry** ['meɪsənrɪ] *sb* **1** mur (og murer|arbeid, -håndverk, murverk etc); **2** frimureri.

masquerade [ˌmæskə'reɪd] **1** *sb* maskeball, maskerade; **2** *vi* opptre/være forkledd; *~ as* opptre som; utgi seg for (å være).

mass [mæs] **A 1** *sb* masse; haug, mengde; **2** *vb* hope (seg) opp; samle (i store mengder); **B** *sb rel (Mass)* messe.

massacre ['mæsəkə] **1** *sb* massakre; blodbad, nedslakting; **2** *vt* massakrere.

massage ['mæsɑ:ʒ] **1** *sb* massasje, massering; **2** *vt* massere.

massiv ['mæsɪv] *adj* **1** massiv; solid, tett; tung; **2** *dgl* diger, svær, veldig.

mass storage *sb data* masselager.

mast [mɑ:st] *sb* mast; stang; *petro* boremast. **masthead** ['mɑ:sthed] *sb* (maste)topp.

master ['mɑ:stə] **I** *adj* **1** mesterlig, mester-; **2** hoved-, moder-; **II** *sb* **1** eier, innehaver; (hus)herre; **2** (håndverks)mester; arbeidsgiver, sjef; *dgl* bas; *også* = *~ mariner)*; **3** herre, hersker; *Master Tom (Smith)* unge herr (Tom) Smith; **4** mester (dvs overlegent dyktig fagmann etc); **5** *(school~)* lærer (især ved videregående skole); *gml* skolemester; *(head~)* overlærer, rektor, skole(be)styrer; **6** *(Master of Arts/Science)* magister (i humanistiske fag/realfag); **III** *vt* **1** mestre (og overvinne; få bukt med; beherske, dominere; *dgl* greie, klare etc); **2** lære/tilegne seg (grundig); forstå/mestre (til bunns). **master | builder** *sb* byggmester. **~ clock** *sb data* hovedtaktenhet. **~ console** *sb data* hovedkonsoll. **~ copy** *sb* original(eksemplar); masterkopi. **~ key** *sb* hovednøkkel. **masterly** ['mɑ:stəlɪ] *adj* mesterlig; overlegent dyktig/flink. **master | mariner** *sb* kaptein/skipsfører (i handelsflåten). **~-mind** *sb* geni; hjerne (bak foretagende); *som vt* være hjernen bak. **~ of ceremonies** *sb* konferansier, toastmaster; seremonimester. **~piece** *sb* mester|stykke, -verk. **mastership** ['mɑ:stəʃɪp] *sb* **1** mesterskap *etc*; **2** herredømme; **3** lærerstilling *etc*. **~ station** *sb data* sentralstasjon. **~-stroke** *sb* mesterstykke; *dgl* genistrek. **mastery** ['mɑ:stərɪ] *sb* **1** mestring *etc*; overtak;

2 = *mastership 1, 2.*

mat [mæt] **A I** *sb* **1** matte; løper, teppe; **2** brikke, serviett; bordskåner; **3** floke, vase; sammenfiltret (hår)masse; **II** *vb* **1** dekke med matte(r) *etc;* **2** floke seg *etc;* **B** *(matt)* **1** *adj* glansløs, matt; **2** *vt* mattere.

match [mætʃ] **A I** *sb* **1** (idretts)kamp, (-)konkurranse, (-)match; **2** like(mann); jevnbyrdig (motstander); **3** make(n); motstykke, sidestykke; **4** ekteskap, giftermål; *a good* ~ et godt parti; **II** *vb* **1** sette opp mot (i konkurranse); matche; **2** (kunne) måle seg med; være jevnbyrdig med/maken til; **3** passe/stå til; **4** gifte (bort); *slang* spleise; **B** *sb* fyrstikk. **match|box** *sb* fyrstikkeske. **~less** ['mætʃlɪs] *adj* makeløs, uforlignelig. **~maker** *sb* giftekniv. **~wax** *sb petro* fyrstikkparafin. **~wood** *sb* fyrstikkved; *fig* pinneved.

mate [meɪt] **I** *sb* **1** (arbeids)kamerat, kollega; *dgl* kompis; **2** assistent, (med)hjelper; *sjø* mat; **3** *sjø (chief/first ~)* (første)styrmann; overstyrmann; **4** make (især om fugler); parkamerat; **5** ektefelle; **II** *vb* **1** pare (seg); **2** gifte seg (med); gifte bort.

material [mə'tɪərɪəl] **I** *adj* **1** legemlig; fysisk; konkret; materiell; **2** vesentlig, viktig; **II** *sb* materiale, stoff; *dgl* (-)saker.

maternal [mə'tɜ:nl] *adj* **1** moderlig, mors-; **2** på morssiden. **maternity** [mə'tɜ:nətɪ] **1** *som adj* barsel-; føde-, fødsels-; **2** *sb* moderskap; morsverdighet. **maternity|-clothes** *sb fl* mammaklær. ~ **hospital** *sb* fødselsklinikk. ~ **ward** *sb* føde|avdeling, -stue; barselstue.

maths [mæθs] *sb dgl* matte (dvs matematikk).

mating season *sb* parings|sesong, -tid.

matriculate [mə'trɪkjʊleɪt] *vb* **1** immatrikulere(s); **2** ta (examen) artium. **matriculation** [məˌtrɪkjʊ'leɪʃn] *sb* immatrikulering *etc.* **matrimonial** [ˌmætrɪ'məʊnɪəl] *adj* ekteskapelig, ekteskaps-. **matrimony** ['mætrɪmənɪ] *sb* ekteskap. **matron** ['meɪtrən] *sb* **1** frue, kone; matrone; *som adj* frue-, kone-; **2** (hus)mor (ved institusjon, internat etc); bestyrerinne, forstanderinne; oldfrue; **3** over|sykepleier, -søster. **matrix** ['meɪtrɪks] *sb* **1** matrise (også *data*); støpeform; **2** gangart. **matrix | printer** *sb data* matriseskriver. ~ **storage** *sb data* matriselager.

matt [mæt] = *mat B.*

matted ['mætɪd] *adj* floket, sammenfiltret; tovet.

matter ['mætə] **I** *sb* **1** materie, stoff; **2** *(subject-~)* emne, tema; **3** sak, ting; *fl* forhold(ene), omstendighetene; situasjonen; *for that ~/for the ~ of that* for den sak(en)s skyld; **4** betydning, viktighet; anliggende; *no ~!* det gjør ingen ting/spiller ingen rolle! *no ~ what (who etc)* likegyldig/uansett hva (hvem etc); **5** brysom/vanskelig sak; *what's the ~ (with)* hva er i veien (med); **6** materie, puss, verk; **7** (typografisk) sats; *printed ~* trykksak(er); **II** *vi* **1** bety/gjøre noe; være av betydning; *it doesn't ~* det gjør ikke noe/spiller ingen rolle; **2** væske; avsondre materie. **matter | of course** *sb* selvfølge(lighet); *~-of-course* selv|følgelig, -sagt; tilforlatelig. ~ **of fact** *sb* faktum, kjensgjerning; *~-of--fact* nøktern, saklig, prosaisk; *as a ~ of fact* egentlig, faktisk; i virkeligheten. ~ **of form** *sb* formsak. ~ **of opinion** *sb* smakssak.

matress ['mætrɪs] *sb* madrass.

mature [mə'tjʊə] **I** *adj* **1** moden; **2** *merk* forfalt (til betaling etc); **3** veloverveid; **II** *vb* **1** modne(s); **2** *merk* forfalle (til betaling etc). **maturity** [mə'tjʊərətɪ] *sb* modenhet *etc.*

maudlin ['mɔ:dlɪn] *adj* sentimental; tåredryppende, -kvalt.

maul [mɔ:l] *vt* maltraktere, mishandle, skamfere.

mauve [mɔ:v] *adj, sb* (grå)lilla.

maxim ['mæksɪm] *sb* fyndord; (grunn)setning; (leve)regel; maksime. **maximum** ['mæksɪməm] **1** *som adj* maksimal-; **2** *sb* maksimum; høydepunkt, toppunkt.

may [meɪ] **A** *vb pres* **1** kan; kan få (lov til å); kan kanskje/muligens; ~ **be** kan være; kanskje, muligens; *however that ~ be* hvordan det nå (enn) forholder seg (med det); *come what ~* komme hva som (komme) vil; hva som enn skjer; *if I ~ say so* om jeg får lov (til) å si det; om jeg så må si; *you ~ just as well (go etc)* du kan like gjerne (gå etc); **2** skal kunne; **3** gid, må(tte); *~ they be happy!* gid de blir/måtte de bli lykkelige! **B** *sb May* mai. **maybe** ['meɪbɪ] *adv, især US* kanskje, muligens. **may-beetle, ~-bug** *sb* oldenborre. **~day** *sb* **1** *May Day* maidag(en) (dvs 1. mai: arbeidets dag); **2** *radio* internasjonalt nødsignal. **~fly** *sb* døgnflue.

mayhem ['meɪhem] *sb US* **1** (grov) legemsbeskadigelse; mishandling; **2** overfall.

mayor ['meə] *sb* borgermester, (by)ordfører.

maze [meɪz] *sb* **1** labyrint; **2** floke, forvirring.

mead [mi:d] *sb poet* = **meadow** ['medəʊ] *sb* eng, gresslette.

meagre ['mi:gə] *adj* **1** mager; **2** skral, skrinn; utilstrekkelig.

meal [mi:l] *sb* **A** (mat)mål, måltid; **B** (grovmalt) mel. **mealticket** *sb* matbillett. **mealy** ['mi:lɪ] *adj* melet; *fig* blek.

mean [mi:n] **A** *vb* **1** tenke (på); ha i tankene; mene; sikte til; **2** akte; ha til hensikt; *~ business (dgl)* mene det alvorlig; ha alvorlige hensikter; *meant for* eslet til; *she meant no harm* hun mente ikke noe vondt med det; **3** bety, innebære; ha (som) betydning; **B** *adj* **1** fattigslig, ringe; **2** dårlig; *dgl* elendig, ynkelig; **3** *(~--minded)* simpel, tarvelig; lumpen; ondskapsfull; gemen; **4** smålig; gjerrig; *dgl* gnien, lusen; **5** *US* flau, skamfull; **6** *US* indisponert, uvel; nedfor; **C 1** *adj* gjennomsnittlig; middels, middel-; **2** *sb* gjennomsnitt (og gjennomsnittsverdi etc; middel|tall, -verdi etc); *the golden/happy ~* den gylne middelvei; **D** *sb* **1** *fl* middel; (fremgangs)måte; vis; *by ~s of* ved hjelp av; *by all (manner of) ~s* på alle (mulige) måter; for enhver pris; *især fig* absolutt; avgjort; selvsagt; for all del; *by no (manner of) ~s* ikke på noen (som helst) måte; på ingen (som helst) måte; *by some ~s (or other)* på en eller annen måte; *ways and ~s* måter og midler; *især* økonomiske virkemidler; **2** *fl* midler (dvs penger eller pengers verdi); *beyond/within one's ~s* over/etter evne.

meander [mɪ'ændə] *vi* **1** bukte (slynge, sno) seg; **2** komme bort fra saken; fortape seg i digresjoner.

meaning ['mi:nɪŋ] **I** *adj* megetsigende, talende; **II** *sb* **1** hensikt, mening; **2** betydning. **meaning|ful** ['mi:nɪŋfʊl] *adj* **1** meningsfull; betydningsfull; **2** = *meaning I.* **~less** ['mi:nɪŋlɪs] *adj* meningsløs *etc*; intetsigende.

means test *sb* behovsprøve.

meantime ['mi:ntaɪm], **meanwhile** ['mi:nwaɪl] **1** *adv* imens; i mellomtiden; imidlertid; **2** *sb* mellomtid; mellomliggende periode/tid.

measles ['mi:zlz] *sb* meslinger; *German* ~ røde hunder. **measly** ['mi:zlɪ] *adj* **1** med meslinger; **2** *dgl* ussel, ynkelig.

measure ['məʒə] **I** *sb* **1** mål (og målestokk; måle|-enhet, -system; måle|bånd, -glass, -kar etc); ~ *for* ~ like for like; *to* ~ etter mål; **2** grad, utstrekning; *beyond* ~ over all måte; over alle grenser; **3** måte(hold); **4** forholdsregel, tiltak; (virke)middel; **5** versemål; rytme, takt; **II** *vb* **1** måle (og måle opp/ut; ta mål av etc); registrere; ~ *out* måle/porsjonere ut; ~ *up to/with* passe med/til; holde mål/kunne måle seg med; **2** bedømme, taksere, vurdere; **3** avpasse (*by/to* etter). **measurement** ['meʒəmənt] *sb* mål (dvs høyde, lengde etc); måling, måltaking.

meat [mi:t] *sb* **1** kjøtt (og kjøttmat); **2** *fig* (vektig) innhold. **meat | ball** *sb* kjøttbolle. ~ **grinder** *sb* kjøttkvern. **~pie** *sb* kjøtt|pai, -postei.

mechanic [mɪ'kænɪk] *sb* mekaniker; maskin|arbeider, (-)montør. **mechanical** [mɪ'kænɪkl] *adj* **1** mekanisk; (maskin)teknisk; maskinell; maskin-; **2** maskinmessig; automatisk, mekanisk. **mechanical | cutter,** ~ **trencher** *sb petro etc* mekanisk graver. **mechanics** [mɪ'kænɪks] *sb* mekanikk; (maskin)teknikk. **mechanism** ['mekənɪzəm] *sb* mekanisme; mekanikk, verk; maskineri. **mechanize** ['mekənaɪz] *vt* **1** mekanisere; *mil også* motorisere; **2** automatisere.

medal ['medl] *sb* medalje.

medium ['mi:dɪəm] *sb* **1** *a)* hjelpemiddel, redskap; *b)* formidler, mellommann; **2** meningsbærer; uttrykksmiddel; medium; **3** gjennomsnitt; mellomting; middel; **4** (spiritistisk etc) medium. **medium | distillate** *sb petro* mellomdestillat. **~-scale integration** *sb data* mellomskalaintegrasjon.

meddle ['medl] *vi:* ~ *in/with* blande seg opp i/legge seg bort i (ting som ikke angår en). **meddlesome** ['medlsəm] *adj* geskjeftig.

mediate ['mi:dɪeɪt] *vb* megle; formidle ved mellomkomst. **mediation** [ˌmi:dɪ'eɪʃn] *sb* megling *etc.*

medic ['medɪk] *sb US dgl* **1** lege, medisiner; **2** sanitetssoldat. **medical** [medɪkl] **I** *adj* **1** (indre)medisinsk; **2** legevitenskapelig; lege-; **II** *sb dgl* **1** *(~ man)* lege(student), medisiner; **2** = *medical examination.* **medical | attendance** *sb* legetilsyn; (syke)pleie. ~ **care** *sb* lege|behandling, -hjelp; sykepleie. ~ **certificate** *sb* legeattest. ~ **examination** *sb* legeundersøkelse. ~ **officer** *sb* sanitetslege. ~ **officer of health** *sb* distriktslege. ~ **practitioner** *sb* lege. ~ **service** *sb* legetjeneste; sanitetstjeneste. **medication** [ˌmedɪ'keɪʃn] *sb* **1** legebehandling; **2** medikamentering. **medicine** ['medsɪn] *sb* **1** legevitenskap, medisin; **2** medisin (dvs legemiddel). **medicine|-cabinet** *sb* medisinskap. **~-chest** *sb* medisin|kasse, -kiste; *især* skipsapotek. **~-cupboard** *sb* = *~-cabinet.* **~-man** *sb* medisinmann; *hum* lege.

medieval [ˌmedɪ'i:vəl] *adj* middelaldersk, middelalder-.

mediocre [ˌmi:dɪ'əʊkə] *adj* middelmåtig.

meditate ['medɪteɪt] *vb* **1** meditere; ~ *upon* grunne på; reflektere over; **2** overveie; tenke på. **meditation** [ˌmedɪ'teɪʃn] *sb* meditering *etc*; meditasjon.

medium ['mi:dɪəm] **I** *adj* gjennomsnittlig; middels, middel-; mellom-; **II** *sb* **1** (hjelpe)middel; redskap; (menings)bærer; uttrykksmiddel; formidler; medium; **2** element; materiale, stoff; **3** gjennomsnitt, middel; mellomting; *the happy* ~ den gylne middelvei.

medley ['medlɪ] *sb* (broket) blanding; potpurri.

meek [mi:k] *adj* ydmyk; mild, saktmodig; forsagt.

meet [mi:t] **A I** *sb* **1** samling (til revejakt); **2** *US* møte; *især sport* stevne; **II** *vb* **1** møte, treffe; støte/treffe på; ~ *with* erfare, oppleve; komme ut for; **2** møtes, treffes; komme sammen; **3** bli presentert for; ~ *my wife* hils på (= dette er) min kone; **4** imøtekomme; oppfylle, tilfredsstille; *merk* dekke, honorere, innfri; **B** *adj gml* passende, sømmelig. **meeting** ['mi:tɪŋ] *sb* møte, sammenkomst *etc.*

mellow ['meləʊ] **I** *adj* **1** moden; fyldig, rik; saftig; **2** bløt, myk; søt; **3** mild(net), overbærende; **II** *vb* **1** modne(s); **2** bløtgjøre(s); mildne(s).

melodious [mɪ'ləʊdɪəs] *adj* melodiøs, velklingende; melodisk. **melody** ['melədɪ] *sb* melodi, tone; sang.

melt [melt] *vb* **1** smelte; **2** bråne, tine; **3** formilde(s); mykne; tø opp; **4** løse seg opp; forsvinne; ~ *into* smelte sammen med; gå (gradvis) over i.

member ['membə] *sb* **1** medlem; *pol også* representant; **2** del; ledd; **3** *gml* lem. **Member | of Congress** *sb US* kongressmedlem. ~ **of Parliament** *sb GB* parlamentsmedlem. **membership** ['membəʃɪp] *sb* medlemskap (og medlemstall). **membership | badge** *sb* medlemsmerke. ~ **card** *sb* medlemskort. ~ **subscription** *sb* medlemskontingent.

memo ['meməʊ] *fork* for *memorandum.* **memoirs** ['memwa:z] *sb fl* erindringer, memoarer. **memorable** ['memərəbl] *adj* minneverdig. **memorandum** [ˌmemə'rændəm] *sb* notat, opptegnelse; referat, resymé; memorandum; promemoria. **memorial** [mɪ'mɔ:rɪəl] **I** *adj* minne-; **II** *sb* **1** minnesmerke (og minne|bauta, -hall, -stein etc); minnegudstjeneste; *war* ~ krigsminnesmerke; **2** *bokl* andragende, ansøkning; betenkning, utredning; **3** *fl* opptegnelser. **Memorial Day** *US* De falnes dag (vanligvis 30. mai). **memorize** ['meməraɪz] *vt* lære (seg) utenat; memorere; *fig* notere (seg). **memory** ['memərɪ] *sb* **1**

erindring, hukommelse; *within living* ~ i manns minne; **2** minne; påminnelse; *in* ~ *of* til minne om; **3** *data* lager(enhet); **4** ettermæle. **memory | extension** *sb data* tilleggslager. ~ **protection** *sb data* lagersikring.

menace ['menəs] **1** *sb:* ~ *to* trussel mot; *dgl* fare for; **2** *vt* true (med).

mend [mend] **I** *sb* **1** reparasjon/utbedring (dvs reparert etc sted); bot, lapp; stopp; **2** bedring; *on the* ~ på bedringens vei; **II** *vb* **1** reparere (og utbedre; gjøre/sette i stand; bøte, lappe; stoppe etc); **2** bli bedre (etter sykdom); komme seg; **3** forbedre (seg); ~ *one's ways* begynne et (nytt og) bedre liv.

mendacious [men'deɪʃəs] *adj* løgnaktig, usannferdig. **mendacity** [men'dæsətɪ] *sb* løgnaktighet.

menial ['mi:nɪəl] **I** *adj* **1** mindreverdig; simpel; nedverdigende; **2** underdanig; krypende, slesk, servil; slave-; **II** *sb* **1** tjener; **2** *fig* slave; krypende/slesk person.

mental ['mentl] **I** *adj* **1** mental(-); sinns-; sjels-; **2** hode- (dvs utført i hodet); hjerne-; *make a* ~ *note of* merke seg; notere/skrive (seg) bak øret; **II** *sb dgl* = ~ *patient.* **mental | cruelty** *sb* åndelig grusomhet. ~ **deficiency** *sb* åndssvakhet. ~ **home** *sb* psykiatrisk klinikk. **mentality** [men'tælətɪ] *sb* mentalitet; sinn (og sinnelag). **mental patient** *sb* sinnssyk (person).

mention ['menʃn] **1** *sb* omtale; **2** *vt* nevne, omtale; fortelle/snakke om; *don't* ~ *it!* ingen årsak! å, jeg ber!

menu ['menju:] *sb* **1** meny, spise|kart, -seddel; **2** *data* meny. **menu-driven** *adj data* menystyrt.

mercenary ['mɜ:sənrɪ] **I** *adj* **1** leid, leie-; **2** grådig, kremmeraktig; beregnende; **II** *sb* leiesvenn; *især* leiesoldat; *fl* leietropper.

merchandise ['mɜ:tʃəndaɪz] *sb koll* varer. **merchant** ['mɜ:tʃənt] *sb* handelsmann; grosserer, (stor)|kjøpmann, -handler; *som adj* handels-. **merchant|man** *sb* handelsskip. ~ **marine** *sb* handelsflåte.

merciful ['mɜ:sɪful] *adj* barmhjertig, nådig; mild. **merciless** ['mɜ:sɪlɪs] *adj* nådeløs, ubarmhjertig.

mercury ['mɜ:kjurɪ] *sb* kvikksølv.

mercy ['mɜ:sɪ] *sb* **1** barmhjertighet; medfølelse; *at his* ~ i hans vold; *have* ~ *on* ha medlidenhet med; **2** *rel* miskunn, nåde.

mere [mɪə] **A** *adj* ren; *a* ~ *pretext* bare et påskudd; **B** *sb* tjern. **merely** ['mɪəlɪ] *adv* bare; rett og slett.

meretricious [ˌmerɪ'trɪʃəs] *adj* gloret, prangende; forloren, uekte.

merge [mɜ:dʒ] *vb* **1** forene(s); slutte (seg) sammen; fusjonere; ~ *into* gå opp i; smelte sammen med; **2** *data* flette, samsortere. **merger** ['mɜ:dʒə] *sb* fusjon; sammen|slutning, -smeltning. **merge sort** *sb data* fletteprogram, samsorteringsprogram.

merit ['merɪt] **I** *sb* **1** fortjeneste; god egenskap/side; **2** *fl* lønn (som fortjent); **II** *vt* fortjene; gjøre seg fortjent til. **meritorious** [ˌmerɪ'tɔ:rɪəs] *adj* fortjenstfull.

mermaid ['mɜ:meɪd] *sb* havfrue.

merriment ['merɪmənt] *sb* lystighet, munterhet; moro. **merry** ['merɪ] *adj* lystig, munter; glad; ~ *Christmas!* gledelig/god jul! **merry-go-round** ['merɪgəuˌraund] *sb* karusell.

mesh [meʃ] **I** *sb* maske (i garn, nett etc); *fl* garn, nett; *fig også* snare; **II** *vb* **1** fange (i garn, nett, snare etc); **2** gripe inn i hverandre (om tannhjul etc).

mess [mes] **A** **1** *sb* forvirring, rot; søl; **2** *vb* rote/søle (til); ~ *about* (drive og) fomle/rote med; klusse med; ~ *up* forkludre, spolere, ødelegge; **B** *mil, sjø* **I** *sb* **1** bakk, bord (dvs personer som skaffer (dvs spiser) sammen); **2** = ~*-room*; **II** *vi* skaffe/spise sammen.

message ['mesɪdʒ] *sb* budskap; meddelelse; melding (også *data*). **messenger** ['mesɪndʒə] *sb* bud (og bud|bærer, -bringer etc). **messenger boy** *sb* løpegutt, visergutt.

mess-room ['mesrum] *sb mil, sjø etc* kantine, messe.

messy ['mesɪ] *adj* rotet, sølet.

metal ['metl] **I** *sb* **1** metall; *fl* (jernbane)skinner; **2** *(~ling, road-~)* kult, pukk (og pukk|lag, -stein); **II** *vt* **1** metallisere; kle med metall; **2** kulte. **metallic** [mɪ'tælɪk] *adj* metallisk, metall-.

meter ['mi:tə] *sb* måler (og måle|apparat, -instrument, -redskap etc). **metering | area** *sb petro* måle|område, -stasjon. ~ **deck** *sb petro* måledekk. ~ **pump** *sb petro* doseringspumpe.

methane ['mi:θeɪn] *sb* metan.

method ['meθəd] *sb* **1** metode, system; **2** (fremgangs)måte. **methodical** [mɪ'θɒdɪkl] *adj* metodisk, planmessig, systematisk.

methyl ['meθɪl] *sb* metyl.

meticulous [mɪ'tɪkjuləs] *adj* omhyggelig; pinlig nøyaktig; omstendelig, pirket.

metre ['mi:tə] *sb* **1** metrum, versemål; **2** meter. **metric** ['metrɪk] *adj* metrisk, meter-. **metrical** ['metrɪkl] *adj* **1** i bunden form; på vers; **2** = *metric.* **metrication** [ˌmetrɪ'keɪʃn] *sb* overgang til: *the* **metric system** *sb* det metriske system (for mål og vekt, basert på meter, liter og kilogram, se midtsidene).

metropolis [mɪ'trɒpəlɪs] *sb* **1** hovedstad; **2** storby, verdensby; metropol. **metropolitan** [ˌmetrə'pɒlɪtən] **I** *adj* **1** hovedstads-; storby-, verdensby-; **2** *rel (Metropolitan)* metropolitt-; **II** *sb* **1** hovedstadsboer; storbyboer; **2** *rel (Metropolitan)* metropolitt.

mettle ['metl] iherdighet, standhaftighet, utholdenhet; fyrighet, temperament; stoff, to; tæl. **mettlesome** ['metlsəm] *adj* energisk, livlig; fyrig, temperamentsfull.

mew [mju:] **A** *sb* **1** *fl gml* stallbygninger; **2** *Mews* del av gatenavn (især der det ligger/lå slike stallbygninger, som nå er bygget om til garasjer eller leiligheter); **B** *vt:* ~ *up* sperre/stenge inne.

mica ['maɪkə] *sb* glimmer; *dgl* kråkesølv.

micro- ['maɪkrəu] *pref* mikro-. **micro|chip** *sb data* mikrobrikke. **~computer** *sb data* mikro(data)maskin. **~disk** *sb data* kassettdiskett. **~fiche** *sb data* mikrokort. **~form** *sb data* mikromedium. ~ **log** *sb* *petro* mikrologg. ~ **processor** *sb data* mikroprosessor. **~wave oven** *sb* mikrobølgeovn.

mid [mɪd] **1** *('mid) bokl, gml = amid*; **2** *adj, pref* midt-; i/på midten; midt i/på; *in ~-air* (høyt oppe) i luften; mellom himmel og jord. **midbarrel** *sb petro* mellomdestillat. **midday** ['mɪddeɪ] *adj, sb* middag(s-). **middle** ['mɪdl] **I** *adj* midt- (og midtre; midterst; i midten); mellom-; middel-; **II** *sb* **1** midte; *in the ~ of* midt i/på; (midt) under; **2** mellomting, middel; **3** liv, midje. **middle-aged** *adj* middelaldrende. *the* **Middle Ages** *sb fl* Mellomalderen, Middelalderen. **middle finger** *sb* langfinger. **~man** *sb* mellommann; formidler; mellomledd. **middling** ['mɪdlɪŋ] **1** *adj* middels, passelig; *dgl* passe; *fair to ~* ikke så verst; sånn passe; **2** *adv* middels, noenlunde; ganske, nokså, temmelig.

midge [mɪdʒ] *sb* **1** knott, mygg; **2** pusling, spjæling. **midget** ['mɪdʒɪt] **1** *som adj* dverg-, lilleputt-; mini-; **2** *sb* dverg.

midland ['mɪdlənd] *adj, sb* innland(s-); *the Midlands* de sentrale grevskaper i England.

midnight *adj, sb* midnatt(s-).

midship *adj, sb* midtskip(s-). **midshipman** *sb* sjøkadett.

midst [mɪdst] **1** *('midst) = amidst*; **2** *sb* midte; *in the ~ of* midt i/under; midt (i)blant; midt i(mellom).

mid|summer *adj, sb* midtsommer(s-). **~winter** *adj, sb* midtvinter(s-). **~way** *adj, adv* halvveis, midtveis; på halvveien.

midwife ['mɪdwaɪf] *sb* jordmor.

might [maɪt] *sb* makt, styrke; kraft. **mighty** ['maɪtɪ] **I** *adj* **1** mektig; sterk; **2** svær, veldig; **II** *adv dgl* veldig.

migrate [maɪ'greɪt] *vi* flytte; (ut)vandre; *om fugler* trekke. **migration** [maɪ'greɪʃn] *sb* **1** flytting; (ut)vandring; (fugle)trekk. **migratory** ['maɪgrətrɪ] *adj* **1** (om)vandrende; nomade-; **2** trekk-. **migratory birds** *sb fl* trekkfugler.

mike [maɪk] *sb dgl* mikk (= mikrofon).

mild [maɪld] *adj* mild; varsom; bløt, dempet; *om smak* lett, linn; svak. **mildness** ['maɪldnɪs] *sb* mildhet *etc*.

mildew ['mɪldju:] *sb* meldugg; *dgl* jordslag, mugg. **mildewed** ['mɪldju:d] *adj* jordslått, muggen.

mile [maɪl] *sb* engelsk mil, se midtsidene. **milestone** ['maɪlstəʊn] *sb mile*|stein, -stolpe; ≈ kilometer|stein, -stolpe; *fig* milepæl. **mil(e)age** ['maɪlɪdʒ] *sb* avstand/tilbakelagt distanse (i *miles*).

militant ['mɪlɪtənt] *adj* militant, stridende; krigersk, stridbar; aggressiv. **military** ['mɪlɪtərɪ] **1** *adj* militær(-); **2** *sb: the ~* militæret. **military | academy** *sb* krigsskole, militærakademi. **~ college** *sb* befalsskole. **~ service** *sb* militærtjeneste, verneplikt. **militia** [mɪ'lɪʃə] *sb* milits.

milk [mɪlk] **I** *sb* **1** melk; *come home with the ~* komme hjem utpå morgensiden (etter fest etc); **2** melkesaft; **II** *vb* melke; *a good ~er* en god melkeku. **milk|-and-water 1** *adj* tynn, utvannet; flau; **2** *sb fig* melkepapp. **~-bar** *sb* melkebar. **~-bottle** *sb* melkeflaske. **~-can, ~-churn** *sb* melkespann. **~-glass** *sb* melkeglass. **milking** *sb* **1** melking; **2** (melke)mål (dvs den melkemengde en ku gir når den melkes). **milking machine** *sb* melkemaskin. **milk|maid** *sb* **1** budeie; **2** meieriarbeider (om kvinne). **~man** *sb* **1** sveiser; **2** meieriarbeider (om mann); **3** melke|handler, -mann. **~-powder** *sb* melkepulver, tørrmelk. **~-round** *sb* melke|runde, -rute. **~-run** *sb* melkerute; *fig, især mil* rutine|oppdrag, -tokt. **~sop** *sb* mammadalt, pyse. **~-tooth** *sb* melketann. **~-white** *adj* melkehvit. **milky** *adj* melkehvit; melkeaktig, melke-. *the* **Milky Way** Melkeveien.

mill [mɪl] **I** *sb* **1** kvern (nå især håndkvern); mølle (og mølle|bruk, -bygning etc); *put through the ~* la gjennomgå (en hard skole); **2** fabrikk; bruk; verk (især valseverk); verksted; *steel ~* stålverk; **3** maskin (især fres, stanse etc); **4** *slang* slagsmål; **II** *vb* **1** kverne, virvle; gå i ring; gå rundt; **2** knuse/male (i kvern etc); **3** valse (metall); **4** stampe, valke; **5** frese (ut); forme; **6** rifle, rille; rande (mynt); **7** stanse (ut); prege; **8** piske (til krem/skum etc); *slang* denge, slå. **mill|board** *sb* (bokbinder)papp. **~-dam** *sb* **1** mølledemning; **2** = *~-pond*. **~-hand** *sb* fabrikkarbeider. **~-pond** *sb* mølledam. **~-race** *sb* møllerenne. **~stone** *sb* møllestein. **~-stream** *sb* mølle|bekk, -elv. **~-wheel** *sb* møllehjul.

millenium [mɪ'lenɪəm] *sb* **1** årtusen; **2** tusenårig periode; tusenårsrike.

miller ['mɪlə] *sb* **1** møller; **2** freser.

millet ['mɪlɪt] *sb* hirse.

milliard ['mɪljɑ:d] *sb GB* milliard.

milliner ['mɪlɪnə] *sb* modist, motehandler(ske). **millinery** ['mɪlɪnərɪ] *sb* mote|artikler, -varer; damehatter.

milling ['mɪlɪŋ] *sb* **1** (for)maling; mølle|drift, -virksomhet; **2** valsing (etc, jf *mill II, 3-7*); rifling (dvs riflet rand etc). **milling | cutter** *sb = ~ tool*. **~ machine** *sb* fres, fresemaskin. **~ tool** *sb* fres(er), frese|hode, -stål, -verktøy.

million ['mɪlɪən] *sb* million. **millionaire** [,mɪlɪə'neə] *sb* millionær.

mime [maɪm] **I** *sb* **1** (panto)mime; **2** pantomimeskuespiller; mimiker; **II** *vb* mime. **mimic** ['mɪmɪk] **I** *adj* **1** imiterende *etc*; parodierende; **2** foregitt, simulert; skinn-; **II** *sb* imitator, parodiker; **III** *vb* **1** imitere; etter|ape, -ligne; herme/ta etter; parodiere; **2** ligne (til forveksling). **mimicry** ['mɪmɪkrɪ] *sb* **1** etter|aping, -herming, -ligning; **2** beskyttelseslikhet, mimikry; **3** mimikk.

mince [mɪns] **I** *sb* finhakket kjøtt; hakkemat; **II** *vb* **1** finhakke; **2** snakke jålet/tilgjort; *not ~ matters* snakke rett ut; ikke legge fingrene mellom. **mincemeat** ['mɪnsmi:t] *sb* **1** fyll av tørket frukt, nyrefett og krydder, brukt i: **mince-pai** ['mɪnspaɪ] *sb* (slags) frukt|pai, -terte (som også er tilsatt konjakk). **mincing** ['mɪnsɪŋ] *adj* affektert, jålet; tertefin.

mind [maɪnd] **I** *sb* **1** hukommelse; erindring,

minne; *bear in ~* huske/tenke på; ta i betraktning; *bring/call to ~* minne om; (få til å) huske/tenke på; gjenkalle i erindringen; *put in ~ of* minne om; få til å huske/tenke på; *(since) time out of ~* (i) uminnelige tider; **2** mening, oppfatning; tanker (og især tankegang; tenke|måte, -sett); *in my ~* etter min mening; *in two ~s* tvilrådig, usikker; *of one ~* enig(e); av samme mening; *make up one's ~* bestemme seg; **3** innstilling, sinnelag; lyst, tilbøyelighet; *have a (good/great) ~ to* ha (god) lyst til å; **4** forstand, intellekt, tenkeevne; sinn; *state of ~* sinnstilstand; *in one's right ~* ved sine fulle fem; *dgl også* vel bevart; *out of one's ~* fra seg; ute av seg; fra forstanden/*dgl* vettet; *have (got) something on one's ~* ha noe på hjertet/noe som plager/trykker en; **5** sjel; ånd (= intellektuell personlighet); **II** *vb* **1** passe (på); se etter; ta seg av; **2** passe seg (for); være forsiktig (med); *~ (out)!* se opp! (vær) forsiktig! *~ the step (etc)* se opp for trinnet (etc); *~ you!* så vidt du vet det! *~ you don't forget* glem (nå) endelig ikke; pass på at du ikke glemmer; **3** ense, vøre; bry seg om; legge merke til; *US* adlyde, lystre; rette seg etter; *~ your own business* pass dine egne saker; ikke bry deg; **4** ha/være imot; innvende mot; *do you ~ my smoking* har De/du noe imot at jeg røyker; *I don't ~* gjerne for meg; jeg har ingenting imot det; *I don't ~ admitting that* jeg innrømmer gjerne at; *I don't ~ if I do* ja, takk; gjerne det, takk; *would you ~ shutting the door* vil De/du være så snill (har De/du noe imot/kunne De/du tenke Dem/deg) å lukke døren. **-minded** ['maındıd] *adj* innstilt (på); tilbøyelig (til); -bevisst, -sinnet; ... i hu/til sinns. **mindful** ['maındfʊl] *adj* oppmerksom; påpasselig; hensynsfull. **mind reader** *sb* tankeleser.

mine [maın] **I** *sb* **1** gruve (og gruveanlegg); bergverk; *fig* gullgruve; fond, vell; **2** *mil* mine; **II** *vb* **1** bryte/utvinne (kull, malm etc); drive bergverk/gruvedrift; *~ for* grave etter; **2** minere, sprenge; minelegge; *fig* underminere. **miner** ['maınə] *sb* gruvearbeider. **mine|-field** *sb* minefelt. **~-layer** *sb* minelegger. **~sweeper** *sb* minesveiper.

mineral ['mınərəl] *adj, sb* mineral(-). **mineral | jelly** *sb petro* vaselin. **~ oil** *sb petro* mineralolje. **~ turpentine** *sb petro* mineralterpentin, white spirit.

mingle ['mıŋgl] *vb* blande (seg).

mini ['mını] *pref* mini-; kort-, lille-, små-. **mini-computer** *sb data* mikro(data)maskin. **miniature** ['mınıətʃə] *adj, sb* miniatyr(-). **miniature railway** *sb* modelljernbane. **mini-car** *sb* småbil. **minimize** ['mınımaız] *vt* **1** minske/redusere (til et minimum); **2** bagatellisere; undervurdere.

minion ['mınıən] *sb* **1** favoritt, yndling; **2** *neds* håndlanger, lakei.

mini-skirt *sb* miniskjørt.

minister ['mınıstə] **I** *sb* **1** minister (også i utenrikstjenesten); statsråd; **2** (dissenter-/frikirke)prest; *skotsk* sogneprest; **II** *vi: ~ to* hjelpe; ta seg av. **ministry** ['mınıstrı] *sb* **1** departement; statsrådsstilling; **2** ministerium, regjering; preste|embete, -gjerning, -kall, -stand.

minnow ['mınəʊ] *sb* ørekyte.

minor ['maınə] **I** *adj* **1** mindre; *især* mindre betydningsfull etc; underordnet, under-; **2** yngre (av to brødre); yngst; mindreårig, umyndig; **3** mindre (dvs temmelig liten); bagatellmessig, uvesentlig; **4** *mus* moll; **II** *sb* mindreårig/umyndig (person). **minority** [maı'nɒrətı] *sb* **1** mindretall, minoritet; **2** mindreårighet, umyndighet. **minor key** *sb mus* moll(toneart).

minster ['mınstə] *sb* domkirke; *oppr* klosterkirke.

minstrel ['mınstrəl] *sb* musiker; sanger; *hist* minnesanger, trubadur.

mint [mınt] **A I** *sb* **1** mynt(verk); **2** *dgl* masse, mengde; formue; **3** kilde; opphav (og opphavssted); *(in) ~ condition* fabrikkny; *dgl* som ny; **II** *vb* **1** mynte; prege/slå mynt; **2** fabrikkere *(fig)*; finne på; **B** *sb* mynte.

minute A [maı'nju:t] *adj* **1** ørliten; bitte liten; ubetydelig; **2** detaljert; nitid, nøyaktig; **B** ['mınıt] *sb* **1** minutt; *fig* øyeblikk; *in a ~* om et øyeblikk; *to the ~* presis; på minuttet; **2** memorandum, notat; departementsskriv; **3** *fl* (møte)referat. **minute|-book** *sb* møteprotokoll. **~-hand** *sb* langviser, minuttviser.

minx [mıŋks] *sb* nebbenose; nesevis jente/jentunge; *hum* skøyerjente; villkatt.

miracle ['mırəkl] *sb* mirakel, under. **miraculous** [mı'rækjʊləs] *adj* **1** mirakuløs, overnaturlig; mirakel-; **2** *dgl* fantastisk. **mirage** [mı'rɑ:ʒ] *sb* luftspeiling; illusjon.

mire ['maıə] *sb* gjørme, søle.

mirror ['mırə] **I** *sb* **1** speil; **2** (av)speiling; (speil)bilde; **2** *vt* (av)speile, gjenspeile.

mirth [mɜ:θ] *sb* lystighet, munterhet. **mirthful** ['mɜ:θfʊl] *adj* lystig, munter.

misadventure [,mısəd'ventʃə] *sb* uhell; ulykke(stilfelle).

misbegotten [,mısbı'gɒtn] *adj* **1** født utenfor ekteskap; **2** *dgl* elendig; motbydelig.

miscarriage [mıs'kærıdʒ] *sb* **1** dårlig/uheldig utfall; **2** bortkomst, tap; **3** abort. **miscarriage of justice** *sb* justismord. **miscarry** [mıs'kærı] *vi* **1** mislykkes; gå galt; slå feil; **2** komme bort; **3** abortere.

miscellaneous [,mısı'leınıəs] *adj* blandet; forskjellig(artet); assortert, variert. **miscellany** [mı'selənı] *sb* blanding (især skrifter av blandet innhold); diverse.

mischief ['mıstʃıf] *sb* **1** onde (og ondskap, ondsinnethet, ondskapsfullhet etc); skade; *dgl* rampestreker, ugagn; *get into ~* komme på gale veier; *make ~* gjøre ugagn; lage/stelle i stand bråk; **2** skøyeraktighet; *koll* skøyerstreker, spillopper; **3** = **mischief-maker** *sb* **1** rampunge; ugagnskråke; **2** skøyer. **mischievous** ['mıstʃıvəs] *adj* **1** ond (og ondsinnet, ondskapsfull etc); **2** skadelig; **3** uskikkelig; *dgl* rampet; **4** skøyeraktig.

misconduct I [mıs'kɒndʌkt] *sb* **1** upassende oppførsel; **2** ekteskapsbrudd, utroskap; **3** vanskjøtsel; forsømmelse, mislighet; misligholdelse; **II** [,mıskən-

'dʌkt] *vb* **1** oppføre seg dårlig (lumpent, upassende etc); ~ *oneself with* stå i (utenomekteskapelig) forhold til; **2** vanskjøtte; misligholde.

misconstrue [ˌmɪskən'stru:] *vt* tolke/tyde galt; misforstå, oppfatte.

misdeed [mɪs'di:d] *sb* forbrytelse, ugjerning; *gml* misgjerning. **misdemeanour** [ˌmɪsdɪ'mi:nə] *sb* forseelse.

miser ['maɪzə] *sb* gjerrigknark, gnier. **miserable** ['mɪzərəbl] *adj* **1** ulykkelig; ussel, ynkelig; bedrøvelig; **2** elendig; jammerlig, kummerlig. **misery** ['mɪzərɪ] *sb* elendighet; ulykke; *fl* lidelser.

misfire [ˌmɪs'faɪə] **I** *sb* klikk(ing) *etc*; **II** *vi* **1** klikke (om skytevåpen); feiltenne/fuske (om forbrenningsmotor); **2** mislykkes; slå feil; falle til jorden (om spøk etc).

misfit ['mɪsfɪt] *sb* **1** dårlig passform/snitt; plagg som passer/sitter dårlig; **2** mislykket/mistilpasset person; utskudd.

misfortune [mɪs'fɔ:tʃn] *sb* uhell; ulykke; *dgl* uflaks.

misgiving [mɪs'gɪvɪŋ] *sb* mistanke, tvil; *fl* bange anelser.

mishap ['mɪshæp] *sb* uhell; ulykke; *dgl* uflaks.

misinterpret [ˌmɪsɪn'tɜ:prɪt] *vt* feiltolke; mistyde.

misjudge [mɪs'dʒʌdʒ] *vb* feilbedømme; ta feil (av).

mislay [mɪs'leɪ] *vt* forlegge.

mislead [mɪs'li:d] *vt* villede; *fig også* forføre.

misnomer [ˌmɪs'nəʊmə] *sb* feilaktig/misvisende betegnelse; galt navn (ord, uttrykk etc).

miss [mɪs] **A I** *sb* **1** feil (og især feil|kast, -slag, -spark etc); *dgl* bom (og bomskudd); *that was a lucky/ near* ~ det var på hengende håret; **2** *give her a* ~ unngå henne; *give it a* ~ holde seg unna/borte fra det; **II** *vb* **1** ikke nå (rekke, treffe; finne, oppdage etc); gå glipp av; komme for sent til; *dgl* bomme på; *you can't* ~ *it* du kan ikke unngå å se det etc; **2** unngå; slippe unna; **3** savne; *badly/greatly* ~*ed* dypt savnet; **4** forsømme, unnlate; utelate; ~ *out on (US)* gå glipp av; **B** *sb* **1** *Miss* frøken; **2** *dgl: miss* småfrøken, ungpike.

misshapen [ˌmɪs'ʃeɪpn] *adj* misdannet, deformert; vanskapt.

missile ['mɪsaɪl, *US* 'mɪsl] *sb* kastevåpen; prosjektil; missil, rakett. **missile fuel** *sb petro* rakettbrennstoff.

mission ['mɪʃn] *sb* **1** delegasjon, utsending; misjon; *rel også* misjons|stasjon, -virksomhet *etc*; **2** kall, misjon; oppgave; **3** *mil* oppdrag, tokt. **missionary** ['mɪʃnərɪ] **1** *adj* misjons-; **2** *sb* misjonær.

missing ['mɪsɪŋ] *adj* savnet; borte, mistet.

missis ['mɪsɪz] *sb* **1** *hum* kone; **2** *dgl* frue, matmor.

mist [mɪst] **I** *sb* **1** dis, tåke; dugg (på vindusrute etc); uklarhet; **2** duskregn, yr; **II** *vb* **1** (~ *over)* dugge; bli tåket/uklar; **2** duskregne, yre.

mistake [mɪs'teɪk] **I** *sb* **1** feil(takelse), mistak; *by* ~ ved en feil; **2** misforståelse; **II** *vt* **1** ta feil; **2** forveksle (*for* med); misforstå; *a case of* ~*n identities* en forveksling (av personer).

mister ['mɪstə] *sb* **1** (i skrift alltid *fork* til *Mr*) herr (som tiltaleform); **2** *vulg* mester.

mistletoe ['mɪsltəʊ] *sb* misteltein.

mistress ['mɪstrɪs] *sb* **1** frue (tiltaleformen fru blir i skrift alltid *fork* til *Mrs*, uttalt 'mɪsɪz); husmor, matmor; **2** hersker(inne); herre *(fig)*; **3** lærer (om kvinne); **4** ekspert/mester (om kvinne); **5** elskerinne; **6** *gml* kjæreste (om kvinne).

misty ['mɪstɪ] *adj* disig, tåket; dugget (om vindusrute etc); uklar.

mite [maɪt] *sb* **1** liten mynt; skilling, øre; skjerv; **2** (lite) krek/kryp; nor, nurk; **3** grann, smule; **4** midd.

mitigate ['mɪtɪgeɪt] *vt* lindre, mildne; dempe; redusere. **mitigation** [ˌmɪtɪ'geɪʃn] *sb* lindring *etc*.

mitre ['maɪtə] *sb* **A** *(~-joint)* gjæring, gjæringsskjøt; **B** *sb* bispelue, mitra. **mitre block,** ~ **box** *sb* gjær(ings)kasse.

mitt [mɪt] *sb* **1** baseballhanske; **2** *dgl* boksehanske; **3** = **mitten** ['mɪtn] *sb* **1** vott; **2** halvhanske.

mix [mɪks] *vb* blande/*dgl* mikse (sammen); blandes; blande seg (med); omgås. **mixed** [mɪkst] *adj, pp* blandet; assortert, variert; ~ *up* blandet (sammen); *dgl* forvirret; ~ *up in/with* blandet inn/opp i; innblandet i. **mixer** ['mɪksə] *sb* **1** blande|maskin, -verk; blander; kjøkkenmaskin, mikser; **2** *fig* omgjengelig person. **mixing | hopper** *sb petro etc* blandekar. ~ **jet** *sb* blandedyse. ~ **plant** *sb petro* blandeanlegg. ~ **ratio** *sb* blandingsforhold. **mixture** ['mɪkstʃə] *sb* blanding, mikstur.

moan [məʊn] **1** *sb* jammer *etc*; **2** *vi* jamre, klage; stønne.

moat [məʊt] *sb* vollgrav.

mob [mɒb] **I** *sb* (folke)|masse, -mengde; flokk, gjeng; pakk, pøbel; mobb; **II** *vt* **1** flokke seg/stimle sammen om; **2** angripe/storme (i flokk); **3** mobbe.

mobile ['məʊbaɪl] *adj* **1** bevegelig, mobil; **2** skiftende. **mobility** [məʊ'bɪlətɪ] *sb* bevegelighet *etc*. **mobilization** [ˌməʊbɪlaɪ'zeɪʃn] *sb* mobilisering. **mobilize** ['məʊbɪlaɪz] *vb* mobilisere.

mock [mɒk] **I** *adj* falsk, uekte; narre-; **II** *vb* **1** håne, spotte; latterliggjøre; **2** ape/herme etter. **mockery** ['mɒkərɪ] *sb* **1** forhånelse; hån, spott; latterliggjøring; **2** gjenstand for hån/latter; skyteskive; **3** parodi, vrengebilde.

mode [məʊd] *sb* **1** måte; **2** fasong, mote; **3** *data etc* modus.

model ['mɒdl] **I** *adj* mønstergyldig, mønster-; **II** *sb* **1** modell; **2** eksempel, forbilde; mønster; **3** (foto)-modell, mannekeng; **4** *(artist's ~)* (kunstners) modell; **III** *vb* **1** forme, modellere; **2** ~ *(up)on* etterligne, kopiere; ta etter; **3** arbeide som (foto)modell/mannekeng; **4** stå modell.

moderate I ['mɒdərət] *adj* moderat, måteholden; rimelig; *som sb* moderat *etc* person/*især* politiker; **2** middels, måtelig; middelmåtig; **II** ['mɒdəreɪt] *vb* **1**

moderere (seg); dempe, mildne; **2** redusere; sette ned. **moderation** [ˌmɒdəˈreɪʃn] *sb* moderering *etc*; moderasjon.

modern [ˈmɒdn] *adj* **1** moderne: **2** nåtids-; *som sb* nåtidsmenneske. **modernity** [məˈdɜːnətɪ] *sb* modernitet; motepreg; *som adj* mote-. **modernize** [ˈmɒdənaɪz] *vt* modernisere.

modest [ˈmɒdɪst] *adj* **1** beskjeden, tilbakeholden; **2** tekkelig, sømmelig; ærbar. **modesty** [ˈmɒdɪstɪ] *sb* beskjedenhet *etc*; **2** tekkelighet *etc*.

modification [ˌmɒdɪfɪˈkeɪʃn] *sb* modifisering *etc*; modifikasjon. **modify** [ˈmɒdɪfaɪ] *vt* **1** modifisere (også *data*); til|lempe, -passe; endre; **2** moderere; (av)dempe, mildne.

modulate [ˈmɒdjʊleɪt] *vt* modulere; avpasse, tilpasse. **modulation** [ˌmɒdjʊˈleɪʃn] *sb* modulering *etc*; modulasjon.

moist [mɔɪst] *adj* fuktig, rå. **moisten** [ˈmɔɪsn] *vb* fukte; bli/gjøre fuktig. **moisture** [ˈmɔɪstʃə] *sb* fuktighet, væte; råme.

molar [ˈməʊlə] *sb* jeksel.

molasses [məˈlæsɪz] *sb fl* fôrsirup, melasse; mørk sirup.

mole [məʊl] *sb* **A** føflekk; **B** muldvarp; **C** molo. **mole|-hill** *sb* muldvarp|haug, -skudd. **~-skin** *sb* muldvarpskinn; engelsk skinn; *fl* mollskinnsbukser.

molest [məˈlest] *vt* forulempe, plage; molestere.

mollify [ˈmɒlɪfaɪ] *vt* bløtgjøre; formilde.

molly [ˈmɒlɪ] *sb* pyse. **mollycoddle** [ˈmɒlɪkɒdl] **1** *sb* = *molly*; **2** *vt* forkjæle; degge med (især *oneself* seg selv).

mom [mɒm] *sb US mamma 1.*

moment [ˈməʊmənt] *sb* **1** øyeblikk; **2** betydning, viktighet; viktig faktor/moment; **3** = *momentum*. **momentary** [ˈməʊməntərɪ] *adj* betydningsfull, viktig. **momentum** [məˈmentəm] *sb* (driv)kraft; fart; *fys* moment.

monarch [ˈmɒnək] *sb* hersker, monark; *især* konge. **monarchist** [ˈmɒnəkɪst] *sb* monarkist. **monarchy** [ˈmɒnəkɪ] *sb* monarki.

monastery [ˈmɒnəstərɪ] *sb* (munke)kloster.

monetary [ˈmʌnɪtrɪ] *adj* penge-; monetær, mynt-. **money** [ˈmʌnɪ] *sb* penger. **money|-bag** *sb* pengesekk; *fig* pengemann, riking; *fl også* massevis av penger. **~-box** *sb* pengeskrin; sparebøsse. **~-changer** *sb* pengeveksler; valutaveksler. **~-grubber** *sb* gnier, pengepuger. **~-lender** *sb* pengeutlåner; *især* ågerkar. **~order** *sb* postanvisning.

monger [ˈmʌŋgə] *sb* (-)handler, (-)kremmer, (-)selger.

mongrel [ˈmɒŋgrəl] *sb* blanding(srase); bastard, kjøter.

monitor [ˈmɒnɪtə] **I** *sb* **1** ordensmann/tillitsmann (især i skoleklasse); **2** (radio-/telefon)avlytter; **3** *TV* (*~ screen*) (billed)monitor, skjerm; **II** *vb* **1** kontrollere, overvåke; **2** avlytte (fiendtlig, utenlandsk radiosending etc).

monk [mɒŋk] *sb* munk.

monkey [ˈmʌŋkɪ] **I** *sb* ape(katt); skøyer, spilloppmaker; **II** *vb* **1** gjøre ablegøyer (skøyerstreker, spillopper etc); holde leven; **2** *~ with* fingre (klusse, tukle etc) med; plukke på. **monkey | board** *sb petro* tårnplattform. *~* **business** *sb* lureri, svindel; tull, tøys. **~-wrench** *sb* skiftenøkkel.

monopolize [məˈnɒpəlaɪz] *vt* monopolisere; få (ha, tilta seg etc) eneretten til; legge beslag på (all oppmerksomhet etc). **monopoly** [məˈnɒpəlɪ] *sb* enerett, monopol. **monorail** [ˈmɒnəʊreɪl] *sb* (*~ track*) enskinnebane. **monotonous** [məˈnɒtənəs] *adj* monoton; ens|formig, -tonig; kjedelig. **monotony** [məˈnɒtənɪ] *sb* monotoni *etc*.

monsoon [mɒnˈsuːn] *sb* monsun (og monsun|tid, -vind); *(wet ~)* regntid.

monster [ˈmɒnstə] *sb* monstrum, uhyre; misfoster, vanskapning. **monstrosity** [mɒnˈstrɒsətɪ] *sb* **1** = *monster*; **2** uhyrlighet. **monstrous** [ˈmɒnstrəs] *adj* **1** kjempe|diger, -svær; kolossal, uhyre; **2** misdannet, vanskapt; **3** uhyrlig; opprørende.

month [mʌnθ] *sb* måned. **monthly** [ˈmʌnθlɪ] **I** *adj* månedlig, måneds-; **II** *adv* månedlig; hver måned; **2** månedsvis; **III** *sb* måneds|blad, -(tids)skrift.

mood [mud] sb humør, (sinns)stemning; lune; *in the ~* opplagt (*for* på, til; *to* til å). **moody** [ˈmuːdɪ] *adj* **1** humørsyk; lunefull, lunet; **2** nedtrykt, tungsindig; **3** gretten.

moon [mun] **1** *sb* måne; *poet* måned; *once in a blue ~ (dgl)* en sjelden gang (iblant); **2** *vb: ~ about/around* flakke/irre omkring; *fig* drømme seg bort; *~ away* kaste (sløse, somle etc) bort. **moon|beam** *sb* månestråle. **~calf** *sb* idiot; åndssvak (person); mehe, naut. **~less** *adj* uten måne. **~light** *sb* måneskinn. **~lit** *adj* månebelyst; i måneskinn. *~* **pool** *sb petro* kjellerdekks|hull, -åpning. **~shine** *sb* måneskinn; *dgl* sludder, tøv; *US slang* hjemmebrent; smuglerbrennevin. **~shiner** *sb* hjemmebrenner; (sprit)|gauk, -smugler. **~struck** *adj* månesyk; forvirret, tomset.

moor [ˈmʊə] **A** *sb* hei, (lyng)mo; myr; **B** *vt sjø* **1** fortøye; **2** ligge fortøyd. **moor|cock** *sb* rypestegg. **~fowl, ~-game** *sb koll* ryper. **~-land** *sb* hei, (lyng)moer. **mooring base** *sb petro* bunnfundament. **moorings** [ˈmʊərɪŋz] *sb fl* fortøyning(er).

moose [muːz] *sb* (nordamerikansk) elg.

moot [muːt] **1** *adj: a ~ point* et omstridt punkt/spørsmål; **2** *sb hist* forsamling, møte; ting; **3** *vt* reise (dvs bringe på bane, ta opp til diskusjon etc).

mop [mɒp] **I** *sb* **1** *a)* mopp, svaber; *b)* oppvask|-børste, -kost; **2** (hår)tjafs; flusk, lugg; manke; **II** *vt* moppe, svabre; *~ one's brow* tørke svetten (av pannen); *~ up* tørke opp; *især dgl* rydde/*mil* renske opp; få unna; gjøre seg ferdig med.

mope [məʊp] *vi* være nedtrykt/sturen; synes synd på seg selv.

moral [ˈmɒrəl] **I** *adj* moralsk, moral-; sedelig; **II** *sb* **1** moral (i historie etc); **2** *fl* moral (dvs moralsk holdning, moralske prinsipper etc); seder; sed og skikk. **morale** [mə'rɑ:l] *sb mil* moral, (kamp)ånd. **morality** [mə'rælətɪ] *sb* **1** moral(itet); dyd, sedelighet; moral|bud, -lære, -prinsipp; **2** *(~ play)* moralitet (middelalderskuespill med moraliserende tendens). **moralize** ['mɒrəlaɪz] *vi* moralisere.

morbid ['mɔ:bɪd] *adj* sykelig; (sjelelig) usunn; morbid.

more [mɔ:] **I** *adj* mer; flere; større (i antall, mengde etc); *som sb* større antall/mengde etc; *all the ~* desto flere/mer; så mange flere; så mye (*bokl* meget desto) mer; *(the) ~'s the pity* så mye (*bokl* meget desto) verre; *the ~ reason there is to* desto større grunn er det til (å); **II** *adv* **1** mer; *ved gradbøyning også* -(e)re; *~ difficult (useful etc)* vanskeligere (nyttigere etc); *~ often than not* som oftest; *the ~ so as* så mye (*bokl* meget desto) mer som; **2** *om antall/mengde* ytterligere; *five ~ days* fem dager til; *once ~* en gang til; om igjen; **3** *om tid* lenger, mer; *no ~ war* aldri mer krig. **moreover** [mɔ:'rəuvə] *adv* dessuten.

morgue [mɔ:g] *sb* likhus.

morn [mɔ:n] *sb poet* = **morning** ['mɔ:nɪŋ] *sb* morgen; formiddag; *the ~ after (the night before)* dagen derpå; *this ~* i dag morges. **morning|-coat** *sb* sjakett. **~-dress** *sb* formiddags|antrekk, -kjole. **~-gown** *sb* morgen|kjole, -kåpe. **~ sickness** *sb* morgenkvalme, svangerskapskvalme.

morose [mə'rəus] *adj* grinet, sur; gretten, tverr.

morphia ['mɔ:fɪə], **morphine** ['mɔ:fi:n] *sb* morfin.

morrow ['mɒrəu] *sb* **1** *bokl* morgendag; dagen (der)etter; **2** *gml* = *morning.*

morsel ['mɔ:sl] *sb* (mat)bit, smule.

mortal ['mɔ:tl] **I** *adj* **1** dødelig (dvs som ikke lever evig); *dgl* menneskelig; **2** dødbringende, dødelig, døds-; **3** *dgl* dødsens (dvs forferdelig, skrekkelig etc); ytterst; **II** *sb* dødelig (person); *dgl* menneske; *hum* skapning, vesen; levende sjel. **mortal | combat** *sb* kamp på liv og død. **~ enemy** *sb* dødsfiende. **~ fight** *sb* = *~ combat.* **mortality** [mɔ:'tælətɪ] *sb* dødelighet *etc.* **mortal | remains** *sb fl* jordiske levninger. **~ sin** *sb* dødssynd.

mortar ['mɔ:tə] **I** *sb* **1** mørtel; **2** morter; **3** *mil* mortér, mørser; **II** *vt* binde (med mørtel); mure (opp). **mortar-board** *sb* **1** mørtelbrett; **2** *hum* studentlue (av den typen med flat pull som er vanlig i engelsktalende land).

mortgage ['mɔ:gɪdʒ] **1** *sb* pant (især i fast eiendom); pantelån; pantobligasjon; *first/second ~* første-/annenprioritet; **2** *vt* pantsette. **mortgage | bank** *sb* hypotektbank. **~ bond** *sb* pantobligasjon. **~ loan** *sb* pantelån.

mortician [mɔ:'tɪʃn] *sb US* innehaver/leder av begravelsesbyrå; ≈ begravelses|agent, -entreprenør. **mortification** [,mɔ:tɪfɪ'keɪʃn] *sb* ergrelse *etc.* **mortify** ['mɔ:tɪfaɪ] *vb* **1** ergre; plage; **2** ydmyke; krenke, såre; **3** forårsake (bli angrepet av, utvikle seg til etc) koldbrann; **4** *rel: ~ one's flesh* speke sitt kjøtt (dvs søke å vinne bukt med sine syndige lyster ved å leve ytterst nøysomt og endog plage seg selv).

mortice, mortise ['mɔ:tɪs] **1** *sb* tapphull; **2** *vt* felle/tappe sammen. **mortice | chisel** *sb* huggjern, stemjern; lokkebeitel. **~ joint** *sb* tappforbindelse (også *~-and-tenon joint*).

mortuary ['mɔ:tʃʊrɪ] *sb* lik|hus, (-)kapell.

mosaic [məu'zeɪɪk] **I** *adj* **1** mosaikk-; **2** *Mosaic* mosaisk; **II** *sb* mosaikk(arbeid).

mosque [mɒsk] *sb* moské.

mosquito [mə'ski:təu] *sb* moskito; (malaria)mygg. **mosquito net** *sb* moskitonett.

moss [mɒs] *sb* mose. **mossy** ['mɒsɪ] *adj* mosegrodd; moselignende; mose-.

most [məust] **I** *adj* mest; flest; størst (i antall/mengde etc); *som sb* det meste; de fleste; storparten; størstedelen; *at (the) ~* høyst; i høyden; *for the ~ part* for det meste; **II** *adv* **1** mest; *ved gradbøyning også* -(e)st; *~ difficult (useful etc)* vanskeligst (nyttigst etc); **2** meget, svært; særdeles, særs; *~ certainly!* absolutt! ja visst! *~ interesting* høyst/virkelig interessant. **mostly** ['məustlɪ] *adv* for det meste; stort sett.

mote [məut] *sb* fnugg, grann.

moth [mɒθ] *sb* **1** møll; **2** nattsvermer. **moth|-bag** *sb* møllpose. **~-ball** *sb* møllkule. **~-eaten** *adj* møllspist. **~-proof** *adj* møllsikker.

mother ['mʌðə] **1** *sb* mor; *fig* kilde, opphav; **2** *vt* være (som en) mor for; ta seg moderlig av. **mother | board** *sb data* moderkort. **~ country** *sb pol etc* moderland; *også* fedreland. **~hood** *sb* moderskap. **~-in-law** *sb* svigermor. **motherly** ['mʌðəlɪ] *adj* moderlig; moder-, mors-. **mother|-of-pearl** *sb* perlemor. **~ oil** *sb petro* utgangsolje. **~ tongue** *sb* morsmål.

motif [məu'ti:f] *sb* motiv, tema. **motion** ['məuʃn] **I** *sb* **1** bevegelse; **2** tegn, vink; **3** forslag; **II** *vb* **1** gjøre en bevegelse; **2** gjøre tegn til. **motion|less** ['məuʃnlɪs] ubevegelig. **~ picture** *sb* (kino)film, kinostykke. **motivate** ['məutɪveɪt] *vt* motivere. **motive** ['məutɪv] **I** *adj* bevegende; bevegelses-, driv-; **II** *sb* **1** (beveg)grunn, motiv; *fig* drivkraft; **2** = *motif.* **motive | force, ~ power** *sb* drivkraft.

motley ['mɒtlɪ] **I** *adj* broket, spraglet; mangefarget; uensartet; **II** *sb* **1** (broket) blanding; **2** *hist* narredrakt.

motor ['məutə] **I** *adj* **1** motor-; bil-; **2** bevegelses-; motorisk; **II** *sb* **1** motor; (kraft)maskin; **2** bil; motor|-kjøretøy, -vogn; **3** bevegelses|muskel, -nerve; **III** *vt* **1** bile; kjøre bil; **2** frakte/transportere *etc* med bil. **motor|-bicycle** *sb* moped: (lett) motorsykkel. **~bike** *sb dgl* = *~cycle.* **~-boat** *sb* motorbåt. **~cade** *sb US* bil|-kolonne, -kortesje. **~-car** *sb* bil; motor|kjøretøy, -vogn. **~-coach** *sb* buss (også skinnebuss); motorvogn. **~cycle** *sb* motorsykkel. **motorist** ['məutərɪst] *sb* bilfører, bilist. **motorize** ['məutəraɪz] *vt* motorisere. **motor|-launch** *sb* motorbarkasse; (større) motorbåt. **~-man** *sb* motor|mann, -passer; togfører, vognfører. **~ race** *sb* billøp. **~-scooter** *sb* scooter, skuter. **~vehicle** *sb* motor|kjøretøy, -vogn. **~way** *sb* motorvei.

mottled ['mɒtld] *adj* broket, spraglet; flekket, spettet.

mould [məʊld] **A I** *sb* **1** (støpe)form; mal, sjablon; modell, mønster; *fig* preg, støpning; karakter; **2** form (til matlaging); *om matrett* form, rand; pudding; **3** *(~ing)* (profil)list, pyntelist; **II** *vt* **1** støpe; **2** forme, modellere; **B** *sb* muld(jord); **C** *sb* mugg. **moulder** ['məʊldə] *vi* smuldre; falle i grus; morkne. **moulding** ['məʊldɪŋ] *sb* = *mould A I 3*. **mould oil** *sb petro* formolje, skallolje. **mouldy** ['məʊldɪ] *adj* muggen; *fig* mosegrodd; møllspist; forslitt.

moult [məʊlt] **1** *sb* myting; fjær-/hamskifte; **2** *vi* skifte fjær|drakt, -ham.

mound [maʊnd] *sb* (jord)haug; forhøyning, høyde; *mil* voll.

mount [maʊnt] **I** *sb* **1** *bokl* berg/fjell (især som del av egennavn); **2** (monterings)|ramme, -underlag; billed|mappe, -ramme (av kartong); passepartout; **3** affutasje, (kanon)lavett; **4** ridehest; **5** *hum* sykkel; **II** *vb* **1** bestige; gå/klatre opp (i/på); **2** stige (opp); heve/reise seg; **3** montere; klebe/sette *etc* opp; **4** stige til hest; utstyre/*mil* sette opp med (ride)hester; *~ed police* ridende politi; **5** *mil: ~ guard* gå/holde vakt; *~ an offensive* gå til angrep; ta offensiven. **mountain** ['maʊntɪn] *sb* berg, fjell. **mountaineer** [ˌmaʊntɪ'nɪə] *sb* fjellklatrer, tindebestiger. **mountainous** ['maʊntɪnəs] *adj* fjellrik. **mountain range** *sb* fjellkjede. **mountebank** ['maʊntɪbæŋk] *sb* kvakksalver, sjarlatan.

mourn [mɔ:n] *vb* sørge (over); bære/ha sorg. **mournful** ['mɔ:nfʊl] *adj* bedrøvet, nedtrykt; sorgfull; trist. **mourning** ['mɔ:nɪŋ] **I** *adj* sørgende, sørge-; **II** *sb* **1** sorg; **2** sørgedrakt; *go into ~* anlegge sorg.

mouse I [maʊs] *sb* **1** mus; *field-~* markmus, skogmus; *house ~* husmus; **2** *data* mus, skjermpilot; **3** *fig* forsagt/forskremt *etc* person; **II** [maʊz] *vi* gå på musejakt (om katter etc). **mouse|coloured** *adj* musegrå. **~-hole** *sb* musehull. **~trap** *sb* musefelle.

mouth [maʊθ] **I** *sb* **1** munn; *have a big ~ (slang)* være svær i kjeften; *it made my ~ water* det fikk tennene mine til å løpe i vann; **2** inngang, åpning; munning; **II** *vb* **1** uttale, ytre; si (frem); **2** tygge. **mouth|-ful** *sb* munnfull. **~-organ** *sb* munnspill. **~piece** *sb* munnstykke; *fig* talerør.

movable ['mu:vəbl] *adj* bevegelig; flyttbar, transportabel. **move** [mu:v] **I** *sb* **1** bevegelse; *især* flytning, oppbrudd; *get a ~ on (dgl)* få fart på seg; *on the ~ (dgl)* i bevegelse; på farten; **2** trekk (i sjakk etc); *fig* initiativ, skritt; *make a ~ to* gjøre mine/tilløp til; **II** *vb* **1** bevege (seg); flytte/røre (på) seg; *~ along/on* fortsette/gå videre; **2** flytte (på); *data* overføre; **3** *(~ house)* flytte; skifte bopel; **4** bevege, drive; sette i bevegelse/gang; **5** influere, påvirke; få til (å); **6** bevege/røre (f.eks. *to tears* til tårer); **7** foreslå; legge frem forslag om. **movement** ['mu:vmənt] *sb* bevegelse *etc* (også *fig*); flytning, transport; *mek* (gang)verk, *mus* sats; *fig* retning, tendens. **movie** ['mu:vɪ] *adj, sb dgl* film(-); *fl* kino(-); *go to the ~s* gå på kino. **moving** ['mu:vɪŋ] *adj* gripende, rørende.

mow [məʊ] **I** *sb* **1** høy|stakk, -såte; kornstakk; **2** høyloft; kornloft; **II** *vt* skjære (korn); slå (gress, høy); *~ down* meie ned. **mower** ['məʊə] *sb* **1** slåttekar; **2** gress|klipper, -klippemaskin; slåmaskin.

much [mʌtʃ] **I** *adj, sb* meget, mye; *not ~ (left etc)* ikke stort (igjen etc); **II** *adv* meget, mye; *~ better (etc)* mye bedre (etc); *~ the best (etc)* avgjort/langt det beste (etc); **2** stort, svært; *~ the same* stort sett den/det samme; *~ to my surprise* til min store forbauselse.

muck [mʌk] **I** *sb* **1** møkk, (natur)gjødsel; **2** *dgl* skitt, søppel; **II** *vb* **1** skitne (*dgl* grise/rakke) til; *(~ up)* spolere, ødelegge; **2** *~ about* gå og drive/slenge. **muck-rake 1** *sb* gjødselgreip; **2** spa møkk; *fig* rote/rydde opp i skandaler *etc*. **muck-raker** *sb* møkkgraver; *især fig* journalist som avdekker skandaløse *etc* forhold; *ofte* ≈ skandale|jeger, -journalist.

mucus ['mju:kəs] *sb* slim.

mud [mʌd] *sb* søle; gjørme, leire; dynn, slam; mudder. **mud|bath** *sb* gytjebad. **~ cake** *sb petro* slamkake. **~ circulation** *sb petro* slamsirkulasjon. **~ cup** *sb petro* slamkopp. **muddle** ['mʌdl] **I** *sb* forvirring, rot; uklarhet; **II** *vb* **1** forvirre; skape uklarhet; **2** forkludre; rote til; *~ along/through* hangle igjennom; *~ away* rote (somle, søle etc) bort. **muddy** ['mʌdɪ] *adj* **1** sølet *etc*; **2** grumset, uklar. **mud | filtrate** *sb petro* slamfiltrat. **~-flap** *sb* skvettlapp. **~guard** *sb* (skvett)-skjerm. **~ hose** *sb petro* slamslange. **~lark** *sb* gategutt, rennesteinsunge. **~ line** *sb petro* slamledning, kveleledning. **~ log** *sb petro* slamlogg. **~-off** *sb petro* slamtetning. **~-pie** *sb* sølekake.

muff [mʌf] **A** *sb* muffe; *mek også* holk, hylse; **B 1** *sb* kloss(major), kløne; tosk, tulling; **2** *vb* forkludre, spolere; bomme (på).

muffin ['mʌfɪn] *sb* slags stor bolle (som er mer mat enn kake og ikke det samme som kalles muffin på norsk).

muffle ['mʌfl] **A** *sb* surre, vikle; svøpe/*dgl* tulle inn; *~ up well* pakke godt inn/på seg (med klær, skjerf etc); **2** dempe (lyd). **muffler** ['mʌflə] *sb* **1** halstørkle, skjerf; **2** lydpotte (på bil); lyddemper.

mufti ['mʌftɪ] *sb* **1** *mil: in ~* i sivil; sivilkledd; **2** mufti.

mug [mʌg] **A** *sb* krus, seidel; **B** *dgl, slang* **I** *sb* **1** kjeft, munn; **2** fjes, tryne; **3** dust, fjols; tulling; **4** forbryter, gangster; **II** *vt* **1** pugge, terpe; *~ up* repetere (i form av nilesing like før eksamen); **2** *US* overfalle, rane.

mulberry ['mʌlbərɪ] *sb* morbær(tre).

mule [mju:l] *sb* muldyr; *fig* stabeis. **mulish** ['mju:lɪʃ] *adj* sta (som et esel); gjenstridig, vrang.

multi- ['mʌltɪ] *pref* multi-; fler-, mange-. **multi|-copy form** *sb data* flerkopipapir. **~list** *sb data* multiliste. **multiple** ['mʌltɪpl] **1** *adj* fler-, multippel(-); sammensatt; **2** *sb* multiplum; *least common ~* fellesnevner; minste felles multiplum. **multi|plex** ['mʌltɪpleks] *vt data* multiplekse. **~ply** ['mʌltɪplaɪ] *vb* **1**

multiplisere; *dgl* gange; **2** vokse/øke (i antall); formere seg (raskt); mangfoldiggjøre(s). **~plying punch** *sb data* hullkortregner. **~point** ['mʌltɪpɔɪnt] *adj data etc* flerpunkts-. **~-programming** *sb data* multiprogramkjøring. **~tude** ['mʌltɪtju:d] *sb* hærskare; masse, mengde. **~tudinous** [ˌmʌltɪ'tju:dɪnəs] *adj* tallrik; mangfoldig. **~-user computer** *sb data* flerbrukermaskin. **~-user system** *sb data* flerbrukersystem. **~-well cluster** *sb petro* brønnklynge.

mum [mʌm] **A** *sb dgl = mamma 1*; **B 1** *adj* taus; *keep ~* holde tett; **2** *interj* hysj! stille! **3** *sb* taushet; *~'s the word* nå gjelder det å holde munn.

mumble ['mʌmbl] **1** *sb* mumling; **2** *vb* mumle; snakke lavt/utydelig *etc*.

mummify ['mʌmɪfaɪ] *vb* mumifisere(s); skrumpe/tørke inn; balsamere(s). **mummy** ['mʌmɪ] *sb* **A** mumie; **B** = *mamma 1*.

mumps [mʌmps] *sb* kusma.

munch [mʌntʃ] *vb* gomle/knaske (på).

mundane ['mʌndeɪn] *adj* verdslig; jordisk, verdens-.

municipal [mju:'nɪsɪpl] *adj* kommunal(-), kommune-. **municipality** [mju:ˌnɪsɪ'pæləti] *sb* **1** (by)-kommune; **2** bystyre.

munificence [mju:'nɪfɪsns] *sb* gavmildhet *etc*. **munificent** [mju:'nɪfɪsnt] *adj* gavmild; raus, rundhåndet.

munition [mju:'nɪʃn] **1** *sb fl* krigsmateriell; **2** *vt* forsyne/utruste (med våpen og ammunisjon).

mural ['mjʊərəl] **1** *adj* mur-, vegg-; **2** *sb (~ painting)* freske; freskomaleri, veggmaleri.

murder ['mɜ:də] **I** *sb* mord; **II** *vt* **1** myrde; **2** *dgl* drepe (dvs ødelegge totalt); mishandle, radbrekke. **murderer** ['mɜ:dərə] *sb* morder. **murderous** ['mɜ:dərəs] *adj* morderisk; drepende, ødeleggende.

murky ['mɜ:kɪ] *adj* mørk; dyster, skummel.

murmur ['mɜ:mə] **I** *sb* summing *etc*; **II** *vb* **1** summe, suse; klukke, sildre; **2** hviske, snakke lavt; **3** knurre, mukke; murre (om svake smerter).

muscle ['mʌsl] **1** *sb* muskel; **2** *vi dgl* bruke makt; *~ in* trenge seg inn; tvinge seg på. **muscular** ['mʌskjʊlə] *adj* muskuløs, muskel-.

muse [mju:z] *vi* **1** fundere, grunne; sitte *etc* i dype tanker; drømme (seg bort).

mush [mʌʃ] *sb* grøt, velling; sørpe; *US især* maisgrøt; *fig* kliss.

mushroom ['mʌʃrʊm] **I** *sb* **1** (spiselig) sopp; **2** paddehatt; **II** *vi* **1** plukke sopp; **2** gro opp/skyte i været som paddehatter.

music ['mju:zɪk] *sb* **1** musikk; *face the ~* ta følgene/konsekvensene (av det en har gjort etc); **2** *koll* noter. **musical** ['mju:zɪkl] **I** *adj* **1** musikalsk; musikk-; **2** melodiøs, velklingende; **II** *sb* **1** *(~ comedy)* musikal, syngespill; operette; **2** musikkfilm. **musical instrument** *sb* musikkinstrument. **music|-hall** *sb* varieté; *US* vaudeville(teater). **~-stand** *sb* notestativ. **~-stool** *sb* pianokrakk. **musician** [mju:'zɪʃn] *sb* musiker; musikant.

musk [mʌsk] *sb* moskus. **musk|-ox** *sb* moskusokse. **~-rat** *sb* bisamrotte, moskusrotte.

muslin ['mʌzlɪn] *sb* musselin.

mussel ['mʌsl] *sb* blåskjell; musling.

must [mʌst] **A 1** *sb dgl* nødvendighet; **2** *vb pres* må; er nødt til; **B** *sb* most; **C** *sb* mugg (og muggenhet).

mustang ['mʌstæŋ] *sb* mustang; (vill eller halvvill) hest.

mustard ['mʌstəd] *sb* sennep.

muster ['mʌstə] **1** *sb* (for)samling; mønstring; **2** *vb* mønstre; kalle sammen; møte frem/opp; samle (seg); *~ one's courage* ta mot til seg.

musty ['mʌstɪ] *adj* innestengt, muggen; *fig* mosegrodd.

mute [mju:t] **I** *adj* **1** stum; **2** taus; **II** *sb* **1** stum (person); **2** *mus* sordin; **III** *vt* dempe.

mutilate ['mju:tɪleɪt] *vt* **1** lemleste, skamfere; mishandle; **2** forvrenge. **mutilation** [ˌmju:tɪ'leɪʃn] *sb* lemlestelse *etc*.

mutineer [ˌmju:tɪ'nɪə] *sb* mytterist, opprører. **mutinous** ['mju:tɪnəs] *adj* opprørsk. **mutiny** ['mju:tɪnɪ] **1** *sb* mytteri, opprør; **2** *vi* gjøre mytteri/opprør.

mutter ['mʌtə] **I** *sb* mumling *etc*; **II** *vb* **1** mumle (frem); snakke/si lavt (utydelig etc); **2** brumme, mukke.

mutton ['mʌtn] *sb* fårekjøtt, sauekjøtt. **mutton|-chop** *sb* fårekotelett. **~-head** *sb dgl* dumskalle, tosk.

mutual ['mju:tʃʊəl] *adj* **1** gjensidig; **2** delt, felles.

muzzle ['mʌzl] **I** *sb* **1** mule; nese, snute; **2** munning; dyse, strålerør; **3** munnkurv; **II** *vt* sette munnkurv på; *især fig* kneble; stoppe munnen på.

myrtle ['mɜ:tl] *sb* myrt.

mysterious [mɪ'stɪərɪəs] *adj* gåtefull, mystisk. **mystery** ['mɪstərɪ] *sb* **1** mysterium; gåte, hemmelighet; **2** mystikk, hemmelighetsfullhet. **mystic** ['mɪstɪk] **I** *adj* **1** = *mysterious*; **2** mystisk, okkult; mysterie-; **3** hemmelighetsfull; **II** *sb* mystiker. **mystification** [ˌmɪstɪfɪ'keɪʃn] *sb* mystifisering *etc*; mystifikasjon. **mystify** ['mɪstɪfaɪ] *vt* mystifisere; forvirre.

myth [mɪθ] *sb* **1** myte; fabel; (gude)sagn; **2** usannhet; oppdiktet historie. **mythical** ['mɪθɪkl] *adj* **1** mytisk, myte-; **2** oppdiktet. **mythology** [mɪ'θɒlədʒɪ] *sb* mytologi. **mythological** [ˌmɪθə'lɒdʒɪkl] *adj* mytologisk.

N

nag [næg] *vb* **1** kjefte/skjenne (*at* på); **2** gnåle/mase (på); plage.

nail [neɪl] **I** *sb* **1** negl; klo; **2** spiker, stift; nagle; **II** *vt* nagle/spikre (fast); *fig* slå fast: ~ *down* spikre igjen.

naked ['neɪkɪd] *adj* **1** naken; **2** bar, udekket; avdekket, blottet; *the* ~ *eye* det blotte øye.

name [neɪm] **I** *sb* **1** navn (og benevnelse); **2** berømmelse, ry; rykte; **II** *vt* **1** kalle (og oppkalle); benevne; **2** nevne, oppgi; **3** utnevne, velge; nominere. **nameless** ['neɪmlɪs] *adj* **1** navnløs; **2** unevnelig. **namely** ['neɪmlɪ] *adv* nemlig; det vil si. **namesake** ['neɪmseɪk] *sb* navne; navne|bror, -søster.

nanny ['nænɪ] *sb* barnepike, dadda.

nap [næp] **A 1** *sb* blund, lur; **2** *vi* blunde; ta seg en blund/lur; **B** *sb* lo (på ullstoff etc); floss, napp.

nape [neɪp] *sb (~ of the neck)* nakke(grop).

napkin ['næpkɪn] *sb* **1** *(table-~)* serviett; **2** bleie; **3** *(sanitary ~)* (sanitets)bind. **nappy** ['næpɪ] *sb* bleie.

narcissus [nɑ:'sɪsəs] *sb* narsiss; *(white ~)* pinselilje.

narcosis [nɑ:'kəusɪs] *sb* narkose. **narcotic** [nɑ:'kɒtɪk] **1** *adj* narkotisk; **2** *sb* narkotikum, narkotisk middel.

narrate [næ'reɪt] *vt* berette, fortelle. **narrative** ['nærətɪv] **1** *adj* fortellende, forteller-; **2** *sb* beretning, fortelling. **narrator** [næ'reɪtə] *sb* forteller.

narrow ['nærəu] **I** *adj* **1** begrenset, liten; **2** smal; trang; **3** snau, snever; knepen; *have a ~ escape* så vidt slippe unna; **4** inngående; nøyaktig, nøye; nitid; **5** *(~-hearted, ~-minded)* smålig, småskåren; trangsynt; **II** *sb fl* (smalt) sund; (trangt) skar; **III** *vb* gjøre smalere/trangere; begrense; innsnevre. **narrow | cut, ~ fraction** *sb petro* smal fraksjon. **~-gauge** *adj* smalsporet.

nasty ['nɑ:stɪ] *adj* **1** skitten; ekkel, vemmelig; **2** lei, ubehagelig; **3** farlig; ond (og ondartet etc).

natal ['neɪtl] *adj* fødsels-, føde-. **nation** ['neɪʃn] *sb* nasjon; folk; stat. **national** ['næʃənl] **I** *adj* **1** nasjonal; **2** landsomfattende; lands-; stats-; **II** *sb* (stats)borger. **national | anthem** *sb* nasjonalsang. **~ service** *sb* (tvungen) verneplikt. **nationality** [ˌnæʃə'nælətɪ] *sb* nasjonalitet. **native** ['neɪtɪv] **I** *adj* **1** innfødt; hjemmehørende (*to* i, på); stedegen (*to* for); **2** medfødt; **II** *sb* innfødt (person). **native country** *sb* fedreland. **nativity** [nə'tɪvətɪ] *sb* **1** fødsel; **2** horoskop.

natural ['nætʃrəl] **I** *adj* **1** naturlig, natur-; **II** *sb dgl* **1** (natur)begavelse; **2** tomsing, tulling. **natural | child** *sb gml* kjærlighetsbarn (dvs barn født utenfor ekteskap). **~ history** *sb* natur|fag, -historie. **naturalize** ['nætʃrəlaɪz] *vt* **1** naturalisere; gi (stats)borgerskap; **2** oppta (i seg); *be ~d* få/vinne innpass; slå rot. **naturally** ['nætʃrəlɪ] *adv* naturlig(vis). **natural science** *sb* natur|fag, -vitenskap. **nature** ['neɪtʃə] *sb* **1** natur (dvs naturen, naturkreftene etc, *aldri* i betydningen landskap, flora etc); **2** beskaffenhet, vesen; **3** lynne, sinnelag; natur; **4** art, slag(s).

naught [nɔ:t] *sb* ingenting; *bring to ~* forpurre; kullkaste. **naughty** ['nɔ:tɪ] *adj* uskikkelig; slem.

nausea ['nɔ:sɪə] *sb* kvalme. **nauseate** ['nɔ:sɪeɪt] *vt* gjøre kvalm. **nauseous** ['nɔ:sɪəs] *adj* kvalmende; ekkel, motbydelig.

nautical ['nɔ:tɪkl] *adj* nautisk, skips-. **naval** ['neɪvl] *adj* flåte-, marine-; nautisk, skips-. **nave** [neɪv] *sb* midtskip (i kirke).

navel ['neɪvl] *sb* navle.

navigable ['nævɪgəbl] *adj* **1** farbar; **2** styrbar. **navigate** ['nævɪgeɪt] *vt* navigere (og styre; føre, kjøre, seile etc). **navigation** [ˌnævɪ'geɪʃn] *sb* navigering *etc*; navigasjon. **navigator** ['nævɪgeɪtə] *sb* navigatør; *hist* sjøfarer. **navvy** ['nævɪ] *sb* anleggsarbeider, rallar. **navy** ['neɪvɪ] *sb* marine, (skips)flåte. **navy blue** *adj, sb* marineblå(tt).

near ['nɪə] **I** *adj* **1** nær (og nærliggende etc); *GB også* venstre (i forbindelse med kjøretøy og veitrafikk); **2** nærig, påholden; gjerrig; **II** *adv, prep* like/nær ved; i nærheten (av); **III** *vb* nærme seg; bringe/komme nærmere. **nearby** ['nɪəbaɪ] *adj* nærliggende; i nærheten. **nearly** ['nɪəlɪ] *adv* nesten; *not ~* langt fra; på langt nær.

neat [ni:t] *adj* **1** nett; pen, pyntelig; ordentlig; ryddig, velordnet; **2** treffende; velturnert; **3** ren, u(opp)blandet.

nebulous ['nebjuləs] *adj* tåket.

necessarily [ˌnesə'serəlɪ] *adv* nødvendigvis. **necessary** ['nesəsrɪ] *adj* nødvendig, påkrevet. **necessitate** [nɪ'sesɪteɪt] *vt* nødvendiggjøre; tvinge. **necessity** [nɪ'sesətɪ] *sb* nødvendighet; behov, trang; *in ~* nødlidende, trengende.

neck [nek] **I** *sb* **1** hals; *risk/save one's ~* våge/redde skinnet; *stick one's ~ out (dgl)* våge seg frempå; stikke seg frem; **2** flaskehals; *også* smalt sund *etc*; **II** *vi slang* kjæle, kline. **neck|lace** *sb* halskjede. **~line** *sb* utringning. **~tie** *sb* slips.

need [ni:d] **I** *sb* **1** nødvendighet; behov, trang; mangel; *there's no ~ to* det er ingen grunn til (å); **2** nød(lidenhet); **II** *vb* **1** trenge (til); ha behov for; mangle; **2** behøve, måtte.

needle ['ni:dl] **I** *sb* nål; *også* (grammofon)stift; (instrument)viser; *(knitting-~)* (strikke)pinne; **II** *vt* **1** sy; **2** punktere; stikke hull i/på; **3** smyge/smøye (seg) forbi/gjennom *etc*; **4** *dgl* egge; sette opp; erte, irritere. **needlework** *sb* håndarbeid, søm.

needy ['ni:dɪ] *adj* nødlidende, trengende.

negation [nɪ'geɪʃn] *sb* nektelse; *også data* negasjon. **negative** ['negətɪv] **I** *adj* **1** nektende; **2** negativ; minus-; **II** *sb* **1** negativ; **2** nektelse; *in the* ~ (be)-nektende; **III** *vt* **1** motbevise; **2** forkaste; **3** oppheve; gjøre virkningsløs. **negative response** *sb data* negativt svar.

neglect [nɪ'glekt] **I** *sb* **1** forsømmelse; *(state of* ~*)* forfall, forsømthet; **2** likegyldighet, neglisjering; **II** *vt* **1** forsømme; van|røkte, -skjøtte; **2** neglisjere, overse; vise likegyldighet overfor. **negligence** ['neglɪdʒəns] *sb* forsømmelighet *etc.* **negligent** ['neglɪdʒənt] *adj* forsømmelig; likegyldig; likeglad, skjødesløs. **negligible** ['neglɪdʒəbl] *adj* bagatellmessig, ubetydelig.

negotiable [nɪ'gəʊʃɪəbl] *adj* **1** omsettelig; **2** farbar, fremkommelig; overkommelig. **negotiate** [nɪ'gəʊʃɪeɪt] *vb* **1** forhandle/underhandle (om); **2** arrangere, formidle; omsette; avhende, selge; **3** *dgl* klare/overvinne (vanskelighet etc); komme (seg) forbi/frem. **negotiation** [nɪˌgäʊʃɪ'eɪʃn] *sb* forhandling *etc.*

negress ['ni:grɪs] *sb (Negress)* negresse. **negro** ['ni:grəʊ] *sb (Negro)* neger.

neigh [neɪ] **1** *sb* vrinsk(ing); knegging; **2** *vi* vrinske, knegge.

neighbour ['neɪbə] *sb* nabo; side|kvinne, -mann; *rel* neste. **neighbourhood** ['neɪbəhʊd] *sb* **1** nabo|-lag, -skap; omegn; **2** distrikt, strøk; **3** nærhet. **neighbouring** ['neɪbərɪŋ] *adj* til|grensende, -støtende; nærliggende.

neither ['naɪðə] **I** *adv, konj* **1** verken; ~ ... *nor* verken ... eller; **2** *dgl* heller ikke; ~ *do we* (det gjør) ikke vi heller; **II** *pron* ingen/ingenting (især av to).

nephew ['nevju:] *sb* nevø.

nerve [nɜ:v] **I** *sb* **1** nerve; *gml* sene; **2** kraft, styrke; **3** *dgl* dristighet; (selv)sikkerhet; *have the* ~ *to* driste seg/være frekk nok til å; **II** *vt* styrke; stålsette. **nervous** ['nɜ:vəs] *adj* **1** nerve-; **2** nervøs.

nest [nest] **A I** *sb* **1** rede; **2** bol; **3** sett; **II** *vi* bygge rede; **B** *vt data* neste. **nestle** ['nesl] *vb* krype sammen; ligge godt/lunt; ~ *down* legge/sette (seg) godt til rette (*against* inn til).

net [net] **A I** *sb* nett (og nettverk); garn; **II** *vt* **1** fange/ta i garn; **2** sette garn i; **B 1** *adj* netto(-); **2** *vt* tjene (netto); *dgl* gjøre. **netback** ['netbæk] *sb petro* nettoverdi.

nether ['neðə] *adj gml* nedre, nederst; neder-; undre, underst; under-.

net | pay zone *sb petro* effektiv produksjonssone. **value** *sb petro etc* nettoverdi.

nettle ['netl] **1** *sb* nesle; **2** *vt* ergre, irritere; terge.

network ['netwɜ:k] *sb* nett(verk) (også *data*). **network | architecture** *sb data* nettarkitektur. ~ **chart** *sb data* nettverksdiagram. ~ **interface** *sb data* nettgrensesnitt. ~ **planning** *sb data* nettverksplanlegging. ~ **security** *sb data* nettverkssikring.

neuter ['nju:tə] **I** *adj* **1** ukjønnet; *dgl* kjønnsløs; **2** intetkjønns-; **II** *sb* **1** ukjønnet plante/dyr; *dgl* kastrert dyr (især katt); **2** intetkjønn. **neutral** ['nju:trəl] *adj, sb* nøytral (person, stat etc).

never ['nevə] *adv* aldri; ~ *mind!* ingen årsak! det gjør ingen ting! blås i det! pytt! **nevermore** [ˌnevə'mɔ:] *adv* aldri mer. **nevertheless** [ˌnevəðə'les] *adj, konj* dog, likevel; ikke desto mindre; til tross for det.

new [nju:] *adj* ny(-); fersk, frisk; moderne; *som adv* nylig, ny-. **new|-born** *adj, sb* nyfødt (barn etc). **~-comer** *sb* nykommer. ~ **deal** *sb* nytt (ut)spill; ny sjanse. **~-fangled** *adj* nymotens. ~ **line key** *sb data* linjeskifttast. **newly** ['nju:lɪ] *adv* nettopp, nylig; ny-. **newly-wed(s)** *sb (fl)* nygift(e); nygift ektepar. **news** [nju:z] *sb fl* nyhet(er), nytt. **news | agency** *sb* pressebyrå, telegrambyrå. **~agent** *sb* avisselger. **~-boy** *sb* avis|bud, -gutt. **~flash** *sb* (korte) nyheter (i radio). **~letter** *sb* meldingsblad; forenings-, klubb-, medlemssirkulære etc. **~paper** *sb* avis. **~print** *sb* avispapir. **~reel** *sb* filmavis. **~-stall, ~-stand** *sb* aviskiosk. **~worthy** *adj* som har nyhetsverdi.

newt [nju:t] *sb* salamander.

next [nekst] **I** *adj* **1** neste (dvs nærmeste, nærmest følgende; første, førstkommende i en rekke/serie etc); *the* ~ *man (dgl)* den første, den beste; hvem som helst; **2** nabo-, side-; ~ *door* ved siden av (vårt hus etc); ~ *door to* = *II 3*; **II** *adv* **1** der|etter, nest, -på; *what* ~*?* hva nå/så? **2** *(~ time)* neste gang; **3** ~ *to* nesten; nærmest; så godt som; **III** *prep (~ to)* nærmest; ved siden av; **IV** *sb* neste(mann).

nib [nɪb] *sb* pennesplitt.

nibble ['nɪbl] **I** *sb* **1** bitt/napp (på krok); **2** *data* nibbel; **II** *vb (~ at)* **1** bite/nappe (etter); bite på; *fig* hakke på; **2** gnage/småspise (på).

nice [naɪs] *adj* **1** behagelig, hyggelig; *dgl* pen; sympatisk, tiltalende; *iron* fin, nydelig; **2** deilig, god; **3** fin (= fint|følende, -merkende etc); sart, ømtålig; **4** pirket; kresen; nøye (på det); **5** hårfin; spissfindig, subtil. **nicety** ['naɪsətɪ] *sb* **1** nøyaktighet, presisjon; *to a* ~ på en prikk; **2** kresenhet; **3** spissfindighet.

niche [nɪtʃ] *sb* nisje; *the right* ~ den rette hylle/plass.

nick [nɪk] **I** *sb* **1** hakk, skår; **2** *in the* ~ *of time* i siste liten; **II** *vt* skjære hakk *etc* i.

nickel ['nɪkl] **I** *sb* **1** nikkel; **2** *US dgl* femcent(stykke), **II** *vt (~-plate)* fornikle.

nickname ['nɪkneɪm] **1** *sb* økenavn; klengenavn, oppnavn; **2** *vt* kalle (dvs sette økenavn etc på).

niece [ni:s] *sb* niese.

niggard ['nɪgəd] *sb* gjerrigknark, gnier. **niggardly** ['nɪgədlɪ] *adj* gjerrig, gnien, lusen.

nigh [naɪ] *adv, prep gml* nær (ved); nesten.

night [naɪt] *sb* **1** natt; aften, kveld; **2** *som adj* natt(e)-; aftens-, kvelds-. **night|cap** *sb* **1** nattlue; **2** kveldsdrink. **~dress** *sb* nattkjole. **~fall** *sb* skumring; mørkets frembrudd. **~gown** *sb* natt|drakt, -kjole. **nightie** ['naɪtɪ] *sb dgl* natt|drakt, kjole. **nightingale** ['naɪtɪŋgeɪl] *sb* nattergal. **nightly** ['naɪtlɪ] *adj, adv* **1** om kvelden/natten; **2** hver kveld/natt. **night|mare** *sb* mareritt. **~shirt** *sb* nattskjorte. **~-spot** *sb dgl* nattklubb. **~-things** *sb fl dgl* nattøy. **~-walker** *sb* **1** søvngjenger; **2** nattevandrer.

nil [nɪl] *sb* ingenting; null.

nimble ['nɪmbl] *adj* **1** rask, vever; **2** kvikk; rask (i oppfatningen).

nincompoop ['nɪŋkəmpu:p] *sb* tosk.

nine [naɪn] *adj, sb* ni; nier, nitall. **nine-days' wonder** *sb* (kortvarig) sensasjon.

nip [nɪp] **A I** *sb* bitt; bite, klype; **II** *vb* **1** bite; klype; knipe (*off* av); nappe; **~** *in the bud* kvele i fødselen; **2** fare; smette, smutte; **B** *sb* dram; knert, støyt.

nipple ['nɪpl] *sb* **1** brystvorte; **2** (smøre)nippel.

nitrate ['naɪtreɪt] *sb* nitrat, salpeter. **nitric acid** *sb* salpetersyre.

no [nəʊ] **I** *adj, pron* ingen, intet; **~** *one* ingen; *in* **~** *time* på et øyeblikk; **II** *adv* **1** nei; **2** ikke (det grann/spor etc); **~** *farther* ikke lenger (om avstand); **~** *further* ikke lenger; ikke mer; ingen flere; **~** *longer/more* ikke lenger/mer; **III** *sb* avslag; nei(stemme); *the* **~***es have it* forslaget (etc) er nedstemt.

nobility [nəʊ'bɪlətɪ] *sb* **1** edelhet *etc*; høysinn; **2** adel(skap); *GB* (høy)adelen. **noble** ['nəubl] **I** *adj* **1** *(~-minded)* edel; høysinnet, nobel; prektig; **2** adelig, adels-; fornem; **II** *sb* adelsmann.

nobody ['nəubədɪ] *pron, sb* ingen; ingenting/null (dvs ubetydelig person).

nocturnal [nɒk'tɜ:nl] *adj* nattlig.

nod [nɒd] **I** *sb* **1** nikk; **2** blund, dupp; **II** *vb* **1** nikke (med); *have a ~ding acquaintance with* være på nikk med; kjenne flyktig; **2** blunde; duppe (dvs småsove).

node [nəud] *sb* knute(punkt) (også *data etc*).

noise [nɔɪz] *sb* (forstyrrende/ubehagelig) lyd; bråk, larm, støy; ulyd. **noiseless** ['nɔɪzlɪs] *adj* lydløs; støyfri.

noisome ['nɔɪsəm] *adj* ubehagelig; ekkel, vemmelig.

noisy ['nɔɪzɪ] *adj* bråkende, larmende; høyrøstet.

no-load loss *sb petro* tomgangstap.

nominal ['nɒmɪnl] *adj* nominell; i navnet bare; navne-; *ofte* symbolsk. **nominal bore** *sb petro* nominell diameter. **nominate** ['nɒmɪneɪt] *vt* nominere; stille som (valg)kandidat; **2** utnevne. **nominee** [,nɒmɪ'ni:] *sb* (valg)kandidat.

non [nɒn] *pref* **1** ikke(-), u-; non-; **2** *som norsk suff* -fri. **non|-alcoholic** *adj* alkoholfri. **~-cladded** *adj petro* ikke-isolert. **~-combatant** *adj, sb mil* ikke-stridende (person). **~-com(missioned officer)** *sb mil* befal(ingsmann), underoffiser. **~-committal** *adj* forbeholden, umeddelsom; uforbindtlig. **~conformist** *sb rel* dissenter; *GB* nonkonformist (dvs medlem av kirkesamfunn utenfor den engelske statskirke). **~-descript** *adj, sb* ubestemmelig/ubestemt (person, ting).

none [nʌn] **I** *adv* ikke (det spor); **~** *the less* ikke desto mindre; **~** *the wiser* like klok (dvs ikke særlig klokere); **~** *too (clever etc)* ikke noe større/særlig (smart etc); **II** *pron* **1** ingenting, intet; **2** ingen.

non|-erasable storage *sb data* leselager. **~-return damper** *sb petro* tilbakeslagsspjeld. **~-escaping key** *sb data* dødtast. **~sealed bit** *sb petro* åpen borkrone.

nonplus [nɒn'plʌs] *vt* forbløffe; forvirre; sette fast; bringe/sette i knipe etc.

nonsense ['nɒnsəns] *sb* nonsens, sludder, tøv, vås.

nonsensical [nɒn'sensɪkl] *adj* meningsløs; fjollet, tøvet; dum.

non|-stick *adj* klebefri (især om stekepanne etc med teflonbelegg etc som gjør at maten ikke henger ved). **~-union** *adj* uorganisert (dvs ikke fagorganisert).

nook [nuk] *sb* hjørne, krok; avsides/bortgjemt sted.

noon [nu:n] *sb* middag (dvs midt på dagen). **noon|day, ~tide** *sb* = *noon*.

noose [nu:s] *sb* renne|løkke, -snare.

nope [nəup] *adv US slang* nei, niks.

nor [nɔ:] *konj* **1** eller (jf *neither*); **2** heller ikke; **~** *do I* (det gjør) ikke jeg heller.

normal ['nɔ:ml] **I** *adj* **1** normal, regulær; ordinær; **2** *mat* loddrett, perpendikulær; **II** *sb* **1** *mat* normal; **2** *petro* normallogg. **normalize** ['nɔ:məlaɪz] *vt* normalisere (også *data*).

Norman [nɔ:mən] *adj, sb* normanner(-); normannisk. **Norse** [nɔ:s] **1** *adj* (gammel)norsk, norrøn; nordisk; **2** *sb* (gammel)norsk, norrønt. **Norseman** ['nɔ:smən] *sb* nordmann (især fra norrøn tid).

north [nɔ:θ] **I** *adj* nord(-); nordre(-); nordlig; norda-; **II** *adv* **1** nordover; **~** *of* nord for; **2** nordpå; **III** *sb* nord; *to the* **~** *of* nord for. **northerly** ['nɔ:ðəlɪ] *adj, adv* **1** nordlig, fra nord; norda-; **2** mot nord. **northern** ['nɔ:ðən] *adj* nordlig, nordre, nord. **northerner** ['nɔ:ðənə] *sb* nordbo; *US ofte* norskamerikaner. **northward** ['nɔ:θwəd] *adj* nordlig (dvs med nordlig retning). **northwards** ['nɔ:θwədz] *adv* nordover; mot nord.

nose [nəuz] **I** *sb* **1** nese, snute; teft; *pay through the* **~** bli snytt (dvs betale overpris); *turn up one's* **~** *at* rynke på nesen av; **2** spiss, tut; munning; for|part, -stavn; **II** *vb* **1** lukte; snuse; **2** **~** *one's way* famle/føle *etc* seg frem. **nose|cone** *sb* rakett|nese, -spiss. **~gay** ['nəuzgeɪ] *sb* blomster|bukett, -kvast. **~-wheel** *sb* nesehjul (på fly). **nos(e)y** ['nəuzɪ] *dgl* **1** *adj* nysgjerrig; **2** *sb (Nosey Parker)* nysgjerrigper. **nostril** ['nɒstrɪl] *sb* nesebor.

not [nɒt] *adv* ikke.

notability [,nəutə'bɪlətɪ] *sb* **1** fremragende egenskap *etc*; **2** notabilitet; fremstående person. **notable** ['nəutəbl] *adj* **1** bemerkelsesverdig; **2** fremtredende; klar, tydelig; **3** (vel)kjent. **notary** ['nəutərɪ] *sb (~ public)* notar(ius publicus). **notation** [nəu'teɪʃn] *sb* **1** (-)skrift; tegnsystem; *data, mus etc* notasjon; note|-skrift, -system; **2** *US* = *note I 1*.

notch [nɒtʃ] **1** *sb* hakk, skår; merke; **2** *vt* gjøre/skjære hakk *etc* i; skåre.

note [nəut] **I** *sb* **1** notat, notis; *make a* **~** *of* notere/skrive ned; merke/notere seg; **2** (kort) brev; **3** merknad, note; *også data* kommentar; **4** (penge)seddel;

nota, regning; **5** tone (og tone|fall, -lag); *mus også* note; **6** tangent; **7** merke; (skille)tegn; ~ *of exclamation/interrogation* utrops-/spørsmålstegn; **8** oppmerksomhet; *take ~ of* merke seg; **9** anseelse, betydning; berømmelse, ry; **II** *vt* **1** notere (seg); notere/skrive ned; **2** merke seg; legge merke til. **noted** ['nəutɪd] *adj* ansett; fremragende; berømt, (vel)kjent. **noteworthy** ['nəutwɜ:ðɪ] *adj* bemerkelsesverdig.

nothing ['nʌθɪŋ] **1** *adv* (slett) ikke; ~ *near* på langt nær; **2** *pron, sb* ingenting, intet; ikke noe; ~ *doing! (dgl)* ikke tale om! *there's ~ to it* det er ikke noe i det (dvs det er ikke sant); det er så lett som bare det; *that's ~ to you* det angår/raker ikke deg.

notice ['nəutɪs] **I** *sb* **1** meddelelse, underretning; **2** (nyhets)|melding, -notis; **3** varsel (især om oppsigelse etc); *a month's ~* én måned oppsigelse; *at short ~* på kort varsel; *give ~* si opp; **4** oppmerksomhet; *take no ~ of* ikke ense/vøre; ikke bry seg om; **II** *vb* **1** få øye på; legge merke til; se; **2** bemerke, nevne. **noticeable** ['nəutɪsəbl] *adj* merkbar. **notifiable** [ˌnəutɪ'faɪəbl] *adj* meldepliktig (dvs som må meldes, rapporteres etc). **notification** [ˌnəutɪfɪ'keɪʃn] *sb* kunngjøring *etc.* **notify** ['nəutɪfaɪ] *vt* **1** kunngjøre, meddele; melde; **2** underrette, varsle.

notion ['nəuʃn] *sb* **1** begrep, forestilling, idé; *dgl* anelse; mening; **2** *fl US* småtteri(er); *merk* kortevarer. **notoriety** [ˌnəutə'raɪətɪ] *sb* beryktethet *etc.* **notorious** [nəu'tɔ:rɪəs] *adj* **1** beryktet; vidkjent (for dårlige egenskaper etc); **2** alminnelig kjent; notorisk, vitterlig.

notwithstanding [ˌnɒtwɪð'stændɪŋ] **1** *adv* likevel; ikke desto mindre; **2** *konj* enda, skjønt; **3** *prep* til tross for.

nought [nɔ:t] *sb* **1** null; **1** = *naught.*

noun [naʊn] *sb* substantiv.

nourish ['nʌrɪʃ] *vt* (er)nære, fø; nære; gi næring til. **nourishing** ['nʌrɪʃɪŋ] *adj* nærende, sunn. **nourishment** ['nʌrɪʃmənt] *sb* (er)næring; føde, mat.

novel ['nɒvl] **1** *adj* ny (dvs hittil ukjent; ny og usedvanlig/uvant etc); **2** *sb* roman. **novelette** [nɒv'let] *sb* kortroman. **novelist** ['nɒvlɪst] *sb* (roman)forfatter. **novelty** ['nɒvəltɪ] *sb* nyhet (dvs ny ting, nytt påfunn etc); *fl også* nyheter, nyhetsartikler (især billig kram, leketøy etc). **novice** ['nɒvɪs] *sb* (ny)begynner; *også rel* novise.

now [naʊ] **1** *adv* nå; ~ *and again,* ~ *and then* nå og da; av og til; *every ~ and then* rett som det er/var; stadig vekk; **2** *konj:* ~ *that* nå da; *dgl* nå som. **nowadays** ['naʊədeɪz] *adv* nå til dags; nå for tiden.

nowhere ['nəuweə] *adv* ingensteds.

noxious ['nɒkʃəs] *adj* skadelig.

nozzle ['nɒzl] *sb* munnstykke; spiss, tut; dyse, strålerør; *spray ~* sprededyse, spreder.

nuclear ['nju:klɪə] *adj* kjerne-, nukleær(-); *dgl også* atom-. **nuclear | bomb** *sb* atombombe. ~ **disarmament** *sb* kjernefysisk nedrustning. ~ **energy** *sb* kjerne|energi, -kraft; *dgl* atomkraft. ~ **physics** *sb* kjernefysikk. ~ **power** *sb* **1** kjernekraft; *dgl* atomkraft; **2** atommakt (dvs stat som disponerer kjernevåpen). **~-powered** *adj* atomdrevet. ~ **reactor** *sb* atomreaktor. ~ **warfare** sb kjernefysisk krig(føring); *dgl* atomkrig(føring). ~ **weapons** *sb fl* kjernevåpen; *dgl* atomvåpen. **nucleus** ['nju:klɪəs] *sb* **1** kjerne, nukleus; **2** *data* kjerneprogram.

nude [nju:d] **1** *adj* naken; avkledd, bar; **2** *sb* **1** naken person; *især* akt(maleri etc); **2** nakenhet; *in the ~* naken.

nudge [nʌdʒ] **1** *sb* puff *etc;* **2** *vt* puffe (dulte, dytte, skubbe etc) til med albuen.

nudity ['nju:dətɪ] *sb* nakenhet.

nugget ['nʌgɪt] *sb* klump (især av gull); liten bit(e); lite stykke; *~s of wisdom (fig)* gullkorn.

nuisance ['nju:sns] *sb* **1** plage, ulempe; **2** ubehagelig person.

nuke [n(j)u:k] *sb US slang* atom|bombe, -våpen; *ban the ~s* forby atomvåpen.

null [nʌl] *adj* ugyldig (især *jur* = ~ *and void* ugyldig og maktesløs; uten rettskraft). **null character** *sb data* tomtegn. **nullify** ['nʌlɪfaɪ] *vt* annullere, oppheve; omstøte. **null | line** *sb data* nullinje. ~ **set** *sb data* tom mengde. ~ **statement** *sb data* nullsetning. ~ **string** *sb data* tomstreng.

numb [nʌm] **1** *adj* nummen, valen; følelsesløs; **2** *vt* gjøre nummen *etc.*

number ['nʌmbə] **I** *sb* **1** *a)* nummer; *b)* tall(ord); **2** antall, mengde; **3** nummer/størrelse (i klær etc); **4** eksemplar/nummer (av tidsskrift etc); **II** *vt* **1** telle (og regne/telle opp; regne sammen etc); nummerere; ~ *among* regne(s) (med) blant; **2** telle (dvs bli/utgjøre til sammen etc). **number plate** *sb* nummerskilt. **numeral** ['nju:mərəl] *sb* tall (og tall|ord, -tegn). **numerator** ['nju:məreɪtə] *sb mat* teller. **numeric(al)** [nju:'merɪk(l)] *adj* numerisk; tallmessig, tall-. **numeric character** *sb data* siffer. ~ **control** *sb data* numerisk styring. ~ **pad** *sb data* talltastatur. ~ **shift** *sb data* numerisk skift. ~ **word** *sb data* numerisk ord. **numerous** ['nju:mərəs] *adj* tallrik.

nun [nʌn] *sb* nonne. **nunnery** ['nʌnərɪ] *sb* (nonne)kloster.

nuptial ['nʌpʃəl] *bokl* **1** *adj* brude-, bryllups-; **2** *sb fl* bryllup.

nurse ['nɜ:s] **I** *sb* **1** *(hospital ~, sick ~)* sykepleier; syke|pleierske, (-)søster; **2** *(children's ~)* barne|pike, pleierske; **3** *(wet-~)* amme; **4** arnested, vugge; **II** *vt* **1** pleie/stelle (syke); passe (på); ta seg av; **2** amme; **3** (opp)fostre; fø (opp); **4** (er)nære. **nurse-maid** *sb* barne|pike, pleierske. **nursery** ['nɜ:sərɪ] *sb* **1** barneværelse; *day ~* dag|hjem, -institusjon; **2** = ~ *garden*; **3** arnested, utklekkingsanstalt. **nursery | garden** *sb* planteskole. ~ **rhyme** *sb* barne|regle, -rim. ~ **school** *sb* barnehage. ~ **slope** *sb* begynnerbakke (ved skiskole etc). **nursing-home** *sb* pleiehjem; (privat)klinikk. **nurture** ['nɜ:tʃə] **I** *sb* (er)næring *etc;* **II** *vt* **1** (er)nære, fø; **2** (opp)fostre; **3** oppdra, utdanne.

nut [nʌt] *sb* **1** nøtt; *dgl også* knoll/kuppel (dvs hode); **2** mutter; **3** (vrient) problem. **nut-crackers** *sb* nøtteknekker. **nutmeg** ['nʌtmeg] *sb* muskatnøtt. **nutriment** ['nju:trɪmənt] *sb* næring; nærings|-middel, -stoff. **nutrition** [nju:'trɪʃn] *sb* (er)næring. **nutritious** [nju:'trɪʃəs] *adj* nærende, næringsrik; sunn.

nuts [nʌts] *US slang* **1** *adj* gal, sprø; ~ *about/on* gal/tullet etter; **2** *interj* sludder! vrøvl!. **nutshell** *sb* nøtteskall (også *fig*). **nutty** ['nʌtɪ] *adj* **1** nøtte|aktig, -lignende; nøtte-. **2** skrullet, sprø.

O

oak [əʊk] *sb* eik. **oaken** ['əʊkən] *adj* eike-.

oakum ['əʊkəm] *sb* drev, (dytte)stry.

oar [ɔ:] *sb* **1** åre; **2** = **oars|man** ['ɔ:zmən], **~woman** ['ɔ:zwʊmən] *sb* roer.

oasis [əʊ'eɪsɪs] *sb* oase.

oath [əʊθ] *sb* ed; *især fl* banning, bannskap.

oatmeal ['əʊtmi:l] *sb* **1** havremel; **2** = **oatmeal porridge** *sb* havregrøt. **oats** [əʊts] *sb fl* havre.

obdurate ['ɒbdjʊrət] *adj* sta, stivsinnet, strid; hardnakket.

obedience [ə'bi:dɪəns] *sb* lydighet. **obedient** [ə'bi:dɪənt] *adj* lydig (*to* mot). **obeisance** [əʊ-'beɪsns] *sb* ærbødig hilsen.

obese [əʊ'bi:s] *adj* (svært) fet/tykk; korpulent, svær. **obesity** [əʊ'bi:sətɪ] *sb* fedme, korpulens.

obey [ə'beɪ] *vb* adlyde, lystre; ~ *orders* parere ordre.

obituary [ə'bɪtjʊərɪ] *sb* nekrolog.

object I ['ɒbdʒɪkt] *sb* **1** ting; *også fig* gjenstand; **2** fenomen, syn; **3** (for)mål, hensikt; *money no* ~ på prisen ses ikke (dvs pengene/prisen spiller ingen rolle); **4** *gram* objekt; **II** [əb'dʒekt] *vi* innvende/protestere (*to* mot). **objection** [əb'dʒekʃn] *sb* innvending; innsigelse, protest. **objective** [əb'dʒektɪv] **I** *adj* **1** objektiv, saklig; **2** *gram* objekt(s)-; **II** *sb* **1** *mil* mål; **2** objektiv (til fotoapparat, kikkert etc); **3** *(~ case)* avhengighetsform, objektsform. **objector** [əb'dʒektə] *sb* en som innvender/protesterer; motdebattant, motstander. **object study** *sb data etc* målstudie.

obligation [ˌɒblɪ'geɪʃn] *sb* **1** forpliktelse, plikt; ansvar; *under ~ to* forpliktet til (å); **2** takknemlighetsgjeld; **3** obligasjon. **obligatory** [ə'blɪgətrɪ] *adj* bindende; obligatorisk. **oblige** [ə'blaɪdʒ] *vt* **1** forplikte, tvinge; **2** hjelpe; gjøre en tjeneste. **obliged** [ə'blaɪdʒd] *adj* **1** forpliktet, tvunget; **2** takknemlig; *(I'm) much ~ (to you)* jeg skylder Dem stor takk; jeg er (Dem) meget takknemlig/*gml* meget forbunden. **obliging** [ə'blaɪdʒɪŋ] *adj* imøtekommende; tjenestevillig.

oblique [ə'bli:k] *adj* **1** skrå (og skrånende etc); skjev; **2** indirekte; forblommet.

obliterate [ə'blɪtəreɪt] *vt* utslette; tilintetgjøre.

oblivion [ə'blɪvɪən] *sb* glemsel *etc*. **oblivious** [ə'blɪvɪəs] *adj* glemsom; som glemmer/har glemt; ~ *of* likegyldig med; ~ *of/to* uvitende om.

oblong ['ɒblɒŋ] **1** *adj* avlang; rektangulær; **2** *sb* avlang figur/form etc; rektangel.

obnoxious [əb'nɒkʃəs] *adj* motbydelig; ekkel, vemmelig; støtende.

obscene [əb'si:n] *adj* obskøn, uanstendig; rå. **obscenity** [əb'senətɪ] *sb* obskønitet *etc*.

obscure [əb'skjʊə] **I** *adj* **1** mørk; **2** dunkel, uklar; **3** ubemerket, upåaktet; ukjent; **4** obskur; (heller) tvilsom; **II** *vt* **1** formørke; fordunkle; **2** skjule. **obscurity** [əb'skjʊərətɪ] *sb* **1** mørke *etc*; **2** uklarhet.

obsequies ['ɒbsɪkwɪz] *sb fl* begravelse (og især begravelses|ritual, -seremoni). **obsequious** [əb'si:-kwɪəs] *adj* krypende, underdanig; servil.

observance [əb'zɜ:vns] *sb* **1** overholdelse; **2** skikk (og bruk); praksis; **3** seremoni; **4** = *observation 1*. **observant** [əb'zɜ:vnt] *adj* **1** aktpågivende, våken; observant; **2** påpasselig; nøye. **observation** [ˌɒbzə-'veɪʃn] *sb* **1** iakttakelse *etc*; observering; observasjon; **2** bemerkning *etc*; **3** = *observance 1*. **observatory** [əb'zɜ:vətrɪ] *sb* konservatorium. **observe** [əb'zɜ:v] *vb* **1** iaktta, observere; se; legge merke til; **2** feire/holde (helligdager etc); (over)holde (lover etc); følge (skikk og bruk); **3** bemerke, si; ytre.

obsess [əb'ses] *vt* anfekte, plage. **obsessed** [əb-'sest] *adj* (som) besatt. **obsession** [əb'seʃn] *sb* **1** anfektelse, plage; besettelse; **2** fiks idé.

obsolescence [ˌɒbsə'lesns] *sb* foreldelse (dvs det å bli foreldet etc). **obsolescent** [ˌɒbsə'lesnt] *adj* (i ferd med å bli) foreldet; gammeldags, umoderne.

obstacle ['ɒbstəkl] *sb* (for)hindring; *sport etc* hinder.

obstinacy ['ɒbstɪnəsɪ] *sb* gjenstridighet *etc*. **obstinate** ['ɒbstɪnət] *adj* gjenstridig, oppsetsig; stivsinnet, strid; hardnakket.

obstruct [əb'strʌkt] *vt* **1** (for)hindre; hemme, vanskeliggjøre; obstruere; drive obstruksjon; **2** sperre (for); blokkere.

obtain [əb'teɪn] *vb* **1** få (og få kjøpt, få tak i etc); oppnå; skaffe (seg); **2** *bokl* gjelde (og ha gyldighet, være gyldig etc). **obtainable** [əb'teɪnəbl] *adj* oppnåelig; som kan fås/skaffes *etc*.

obtrude [əb'tru:d] *vb* ~ *(up)on* trenge (seg) på. **obtrusive** [əb'tru:sɪv] *adj* påtrengende.

obtuse [əb'tju:s] *adj* **1** butt, stump; sløv; **2** tungnem; dum.

obvious ['ɒbvɪəs] *adj* innlysende; klar, tydelig; åpenbar. **obviously** ['ɒbvɪəslɪ] *adv* tydeligvis; åpenbart.

occasion [ə'keɪʒn] **I** *sb* **1** anledning, leilighet; *on* ~ leilighetsvis, stundom; *profit by the* ~ benytte seg av/utnytte anledningen; *take* ~ *to* benytte anledningen til å; **2** begivenhet; spesiell anledning; *in honour of the* ~ til ære for dagen *etc*; **3** (for)anledning; grunn, årsak; **II** *vt* foranledige, forårsake; få til. **occasional** [ə'keɪʒənl] *adj* leilighets-; tilfeldig. **occasionally** [ə'keɪʒnəlɪ] *adv* leilighetsvis; nå og da.

occupant ['ɒkjʊpənt] *sb* **1** beboer (av hus, leilighet etc); **2** eier, innehaver; **3** okkupant. **occupation** [ˌɒkjʊ'peiʃn] *sb* **1** besittelse; (eiendoms)overtakelse; **2** beskjeftigelse, sysselsetting; stilling, yrke; næringsvei; **3** okkupering; besettelse, okkupasjon. **occupation efficiency** *sb data* utnyttelsesgrad. **occupier** ['ɒkjʊpaɪə] *sb især* leieboer. **occupy** ['ɒkjʊpaɪ] *vt* **1** eie, (inne)ha; bebo, bo i; **2** ta i besittelse; besette, okkupere; **3** beskjeftige, sysselsette; **4** engasjere, oppta; legge beslag på (tid); ta (tid); strekke seg over.

occur [ə'kɜ:] *vi* **1** hende, skje; finne sted; **2** forekomme, opptre; eksistere, finnes; **3** *it* ~*s to me* det forekommer/slår meg; *it never* ~*red to them* det falt dem aldri (el. ikke) inn. **occurence** [ə'kʌrəns] *sb* begivenhet, hendelse; forekomst.

ocean ['əʊʃn] *sb* osean, (verdens)hav; ~*s of* masser/massevis av; *også* (et) hav av.

ochre ['əʊkə] *sb* oker (og oker|farge, -gult etc).

octopus ['ɒktəpəs] *sb* (åttearmet) blekksprut.

oculist ['ɒkjʊlɪst] *sb* øyenlege.

odd [ɒd] *adj* **1** merkelig, underlig; rar; påfallende; **2** tilfeldig; uregelmessig; løs (og løsrevet); **3** overskytende; ekstra(-), tilleggs-; *sixty-odd* noenogseksti; **4** enkelt(-); umake, upar; **5** odde(-), ulike. **oddball** ['ɒdbɔ:l] *sb US slang* raring. **oddity** ['ɒdətɪ] *sb* merkverdighet, raritet; egenhet, særhet; *om personer* raring. **odd jobs** *sb fl* leilighetsjobber, småjobber. **oddments** ['ɒdmənts] *sb fl* **1** levninger, rester; **2** = *odds and ends*, se *odds 4*. **odd parity** *sb data* ulik paritet. **odds** [ɒdz] *sb fl* **1** odds (dvs forskjell mellom innsats og gevinst i veddemål etc); ulikhet; **2** mulighet/sannsynlighet (uttrykt i tall); sjanse (dvs mulig utfall); *fight against heavy* ~ kjempe mot stor overmakt; **3** uoverensstemmelse; uenighet; *at* ~ *with* på kant med; **4** ~ *and ends* småting, småtteri(er); saker og ting.

odious ['əʊdɪəs] *adj* avskyelig, motbydelig; forhatt.

odour ['əʊdə] *sb* **1** lukt (og duft, odør, stank); **2** anstrøk, snev; **3** omdømme, rykte.

of [əv] *prep* **1** *om opprinnelse og sammenheng* av, fra; etter (= etterlatt av); til (= tilhørende); ~ *good family* av god familie; *the love* ~ *a mother* en mors kjærlighet; **2** *om egenskaper og materialer* av; med; over; på; *a girl* ~ *three* en pike på tre (år); *a woman* ~ *ideas* en kvinne med ideer; en idérik kvinne; **3** *om tid* i; om, på; fra; ~ *an evening* om kvelden(e); ~ *a Sunday* (på) søndag(ene); ~ *late* nylig; ~ *this date (US)* fra dags dato; fra i dag (av); per i dag; *ten minutes* ~ *three (US)* ti (minutter) på tre; **4** *om sted* av; for (= i forhold til); fra; ved; *the Battle* ~ *Hastings* slaget ved Hastings; *the City* ~ *Tromsø* Tromsø by; **5** *i adverbialer etc* av; etter; for; med; om; på; *cure (etc)* ~ helbrede (etc) for; *dream (etc)* ~ drømme (etc) om; *in search* ~ på jakt/leting etter; *lover* ~ -elsker (etc, se *lover 2*); *maker* ~ -maker (etc, se *maker*); *proud (etc)* ~ stolt (etc) av; *sure* ~ sikker på; *smell/taste* ~ lukte/smake (av); *think* ~ tenke på; *what* ~ hva med; hvordan er det med.

off [ɒf] **I** *adj, adv* **1** av (= falt etc av; frakoblet; slått av; løs, løsnet etc); av gårde/sted; bort, borte; unna, vekk; *teater* avsides; bak/utenfor scenen; ~ *and on* av og på; av og til; *be* ~ komme seg av sted; *hands* ~! fingrene fra fatet! *it's only a month* ~ det er bare en måned til; *where are you* ~ *to* hvor skal du hen; **2** avlyst; (av)brutt, hevet; forbi, over; slutt; **3** bortre, bort-; ytre, ytter-; ut- (og utenfor(-), utenom(-); utvendig etc); *GB også* høyre (i forbindelse med kjøretøy og veitrafikk); *US fig* utenfor (= desorientert etc); **4** fri (og fri-, fritids- etc); *have/take a day* ~ ha/ta (seg) en fridag; **5** situert, stilt; **6** avsides; fjern (= lite sannsynlig etc); **7** død (dvs stille, uvirksom etc); *som sb* = ~*-season*; **8** skjemt; (lett) anløpet/bedervet; **II** *prep* **1** av (og ned/ut etc av); fra (og bort(e)/vekk fra; ned/ut fra); unna; ~ *Main Street* (i en sidegate) til Storgaten; ~ *the mark/point* utenfor; irrelevant; uaktuelt; **2** (like/rett) utenfor; *sjø også* av (= på høyde med; ut for); **3** fri for/fra; **4** på; *live* ~ *the tourists* leve på turistene (dvs av turisttrafikken).

offal ['ɒfl] *sb* avfall, søppel.

off|-beat *adj dgl* ukonvensjonell; utenom det vanlige. **~-chance** *sb* svak/ørliten mulighet. **~-colour** *adj* **1** falmet, misfarget; **2** nedfor, uopplagt.

offence [ə'fens] *sb* **1** forseelse; lovovertredelse; (mindre) forbrytelse; **2** fornærmelse, krenkelse; *no* ~ *(meant)* det var ikke vondt ment; godt ord igjen; **3** forargelse, harme; *give* ~ vekke anstøt/forargelse; *take* ~ bli forarget *etc*; **4** angrep, offensiv; *som adj* angreps-. **offend** [ə'fend] *vb* **1** forse/forgå seg; **2** fornærme, krenke; såre; **3** forarge, støte; **4** ergre, irritere. **offender** [ə'fendə] *sb* lovovertreder; (mindre) forbryter; *hum* synder. **offense** [ə'fens] *sb* = *offence*. **offensive** [ə'fensɪv] **I** *adj* **1** angreps-; offensiv, pågående; **2** frastøtende; ubehagelig; **3** forargelig, støtende; **II** *sb* angrep, offensiv.

offer ['ɒfə] **I** *sb* tilbud (*of* om); bud; **II** *vb* **1** fremby/tilby (seg); utby, (ut)love; falby; ~ *an apology* komme med en unnskyldning; ~ *resistance* by (gjøre, yte etc) motstand; **2** foreslå, fremsette.

off-hand [ˌɒf'hænd] *adj, adv* **1** på stående fot; improvisert, uforberedt; **2** (lett) henkastet; tilfeldig; **3** nonchalant, skjødesløs(t).

office ['ɒfɪs] *sb* **1** kontor; **2** departement; direktorat, etat; **3** (be)stilling, embete; regjerings|makt, -posisjon; **4** plikt(er); gjøremål, oppgaver; arbeid; **5** *fl* oppmerksomhet; hjelp, tjeneste(r); **6** *fl* riter, ritual(er); gudstjeneste. **office | bearer** *sb* = *official II 1*. ~ **boy** *sb* internbud, kontorbud; volontør. ~ **hours** *sb fl* kontortid, åpningstid. **officer** ['ɒfɪsə] *sb* **1** = *official II 1*; **2** *mil* offiser; **3** *(police ~)* konstabel (NB i tiltale til og omtale av politi|kvinne, -mann); **4** styremedlem (i forening etc). **official** [ə'fɪʃl] **I** *adj* **1** offisiell; **2** embets-; tjeneste-; ~ *capacity* embets medfør; **II** *sb* **1** embets|kvinne, -mann; -person; (offentlig) tjeneste|-kvinne, -mann; (høyere) funksjonær; *government* ~ statstjeneste|kvinne, -mann; *ofte* tals|kvinne, -mann for regjeringen; **2** *sport etc* funksjonær, leder. **officiate** [ə'fɪʃɪeɪt] *vi* fungere, virke; *rel* forrette (*at* ved). **officious** [ə'fɪʃəs] *adj* **1** geskjeftig; **2** offisiøs (= halvoffisiell).

offing ['ɒfɪŋ] *sb* rom sjø; *in the* ~ i farvannet; under oppseiling.

offish ['ɒfɪʃ] *adj* reservert, utilnærmelig.

off|-licence *sb* bevilling for salg av brennevin ut av huset (dvs ikke bare til nytelse på stedet). **~-line** *adj data* frakoblet. **~-plot** *adj petro* = *~-site*. **~-season** *sb* dødperiode (utenfor sesongen). **~set** ['ɒfset] **I** *adj* **1** forskjøvet; **2** fremhevet, uthevet; **II** *sb* **1** erstatning, motvekt; **2** *(~ process)* offset(metode, -trykk); **3** *data* forskyvning; **III** *vt* **1** balansere, oppveie; **2** = *set off*. **~-shore** *adj, adv* **1** kyst- (dvs langs/utenfor kysten); **2** fralands. **~shore drilling** *sb petro* olje|boring/utvinning til havs. **~shore installations** *sb fl petro* oljeinstallasjoner til havs. **~shore loading** *sb data* oljelasting til havs; bøyelasting. **~shore manager** *sb petro* feltsjef. **~-side** *sb GB* høyreside (i forbindelse med kjøretøy og veitrafikk); *sport* offside. **~-site** *adj petro* utenfor anleggsområdet. **~spring** ['ɒfsprɪŋ] *sb* **1** avkom, etterkommere; barn; **2** produkt, resultat. **~-stage** *adj, adv* avsides; bak/utenfor scenen; i kulissene.

oft [ɒft] *gml, poet* = **often** ['ɒfn] *adv* ofte; *more ~ than not* som oftest.

off|-one *adj* ene-, engangs- (dvs som finnes i bare ett eksemplar, eller som foregår bare én gang). **~-taste** *sb* bismak, usmak. **~-white** *adj* antikkhvit, kremfarget.

ogle ['əugl] **1** *sb* (forelsket etc) øyekast; **2** *vb* kaste forelskede (forføreriske, kokette etc) blikk på; øyenflørte (med).

ogre ['əugə] *sb* uhyre; troll.

oil [ɔɪl] **1** *sb* olje, petroleum; *fig* smøring (= bestikkelse, smiger etc); *fl* oljehyre; oljemalerier; **2** *vt* olje, smøre (*fig også* = bestikke, smigre etc). **oil | (base) mud** *sb petro* oljeboreslam. ~ **boom** *sb petro* oljelense. **~-can** *sb* oljekanne. **~cloth** *sb* oljelerret; voksduk. ~ **colours** *sb fl* oljefarger. ~ **deposit** *sb petro* olje|rest, -slam. **~-derrick** *sb petro* boretårn, oljetårn. **~-drum** *sb petro* oljefat. **~-field** *sb petro* oljefelt. ~ **film** *sb* oljefilm. ~ **in bulk** *sb petro* bulkolje. ~ **in place** *sb petro* tilstedeværende olje. **~-lamp** *sb* oljelampe, parafinlampe. ~ **mud** *sb petro* oljeslam; *også* = ~ *deposit*. ~ **painting** *sb* oljemaleri. ~ **pipeline** *sb petro* olje(rør)ledning. ~ **platform** *sb petro* (olje)boreplattform. ~ **product** *sb petro* (rå)oljeprodukt. ~ **refinery** *sb petro* (rå)oljeraffineri. ~ **refining** *sb petro* (rå)oljeraffinering. ~ **reservoir** *sb petro* oljereservoar. **~-rig** *sb petro* oljerigg. ~ **separation** *sb petro* oljeseparering. **~skin** *sb* oljelerret; *fl* oljehyre. ~ **slick** *sb* oljeflak (etter søl eller utslipp i sjøen). **~-tanker** *sb* oljetanker. ~ **sludge** *sb petro* = ~ *mud*. ~ **spill** *sb* **1** oljesøl; **2** oljeflak. ~ **(storage) tank** *sb petro* oljetank. **~-well** *sb petro* oljekilde.

ointment ['ɔɪntmənt] *sb* salve; (hud)krem.

old [əuld] **1** *adj* gammel (og alderssstegen; aldrende, eldet etc); **2** *sb: days/times of* ~ gamle dager. **old | age** *sb* alderdom. **~-age pension** *sb* alderstrygd. *the* ~ **country** *sb* gamlelandet.

olden ['əuldən] *adj bokl* fordums.

old|-fashioned *adj* **1** gammeldags; **2** gammel|-klok, -modig. ~ **hand** *sb* gammel rev (dvs erfaren person); veteran. ~ **hat** *sb US slang* gammelt nytt; *som adj* foreldet, gammeldags. ~ **maid** *sb* gammel jomfru. ~ **offender** *sb* tilbakefallsforbryter. ~ **salt** *sb* (gammel) sjøulk. **~-timer** *sb* veteran.

olive ['ɒlɪv] **I** *adj* oliven|farget, -grønn; **II** *sb* **1** oliven(tre); **2** oliven|farge, -grønt.

omen ['əumən] *sb* (for)varsel, tegn. **ominous** ['ɒmɪnəs] *adj* illevarslende; truende.

omission [ə'mɪʃn] *sb* forsømmelse *etc*. **omit** [ə'mɪt] *vt* **1** forsømme, unnlate; **2** utelate; hoppe over.

omnibus ['ɒmnɪbəs] **1** *adj* samle- (især om omfattende samleverk); **2** *sb gml* buss. **omnipotent** [ɒm'nɪpətənt] *adj* allmektig. **omniscient** [ɒm'nɪsɪənt] *adj* allvitende.

on [ɒn] **A** *adv* **1** frem (og fremad, fremover etc); videre; *from that day* ~ fra den dagen (av); **2** på (= tilkoblet; skrudd/slått etc på; i gang; på programmet/ *dgl* tapetet); ~ *and off* = *off and* ~; *I'm* ~ *(dgl)* jeg er med (dvs enig, interessert, klar over hva det dreier seg om etc); **3** på (= på plass etc); *have nothing* ~ ikke ha noe på (seg); *put the kettle* ~ sette over (kaffe- eller te)kjelen; **B** *prep* **I** *om retning, sted etc* **1** på (og opp(e) på; oppå, utenpå); langsmed, ved; hos, i; ~ *land* på land; til lands; ~ *the coast* på (langs, ved etc) kysten; ~ *the house* gratis (dvs huset = eieren/verten etc spanderer); ~ *the side* utenom; *dgl* på si; **2** mot; *smile* ~ smile mot/til; *take vengeance* ~ ta hevn over; **II** *om forhold og tilstand* angående, om; *lecture* ~ forelese om/ over; holde foredrag om; **2** for (= overfor; i forhold til); *it is not fair* ~ *them* det er ikke riktig/realt mot dem; **3** ~ *fire* i brann; ~ *loan* til låns; ~ *sale* på salg; til salgs; ~ *the cheap (dgl)* billig; ~ *the sly (dgl)* fordektig; i smug; **III** *om middel, måte etc* **1** etter, ifølge; ~ *good authority* fra pålitelig kilde; på velunderrettet hold; **2** med; ~ *purpose* med hensikt/vilje; forsettlig; **3** ved (jf *IV 2*); ~ *thinking it over* ved nærmere ettertanke; **4** av (og på grunn av; som følge av etc); med risiko for; **IV** *om rekkefølge og tid* **1** om, på; ~ *Sunday* (om) søndagene; (på) søndag; *on time* presis; **2** ved; ~ *her arrival* ved hennes ankomst; da hun kom; ~ *my asking* på min forespørsel; da jeg spurte.

once [wʌns] **I** *adv* **1** én gang; *for* ~ for en gangs skyld; **2** en gang (i fortiden); ~ *upon a time* det var en gang; **II** *konj* når ... først; ~ *inside, we'll be safe* kommer vi først innenfor, er vi trygge; **III** *sb* én gang; *this time* (for) denne ene gangen.

one [wʌn] *adj, pron* én, ett; **2** en bestemt; en viss; *that* ~ den der; *this* ~ denne her; **3** en eller annen; ~ *of these days* en av dagene; en vakker dag; **2** en, man; **5** *the good* ~*s* de gode/snille; *the young* ~*s* barna; ungdommen; **6** ~ *another* hverandre (især om flere enn to); *I for* ~ jeg for min del; *it's all* ~ *to me* det er det samme for meg. **one-way | list** *sb data* enveisliste. ~ **street** *sb* enveisgate. ~ **transmission** *sb data* enveisoverføring.

onion ['ʌnɪən] *sb* løk.

on-line *adj data* direktekoblet, tilkoblet. **on-line system** *sb data* direktestyrt system.

onlooker ['ɒn,lʊkə] *sb* tilskuer.

only ['əʊnlɪ] **I** *adj* eneste; **II** *adv* **1** alene; **3** ~ *then* først da; ~ *when* først da/når; ~ *yesterday* først (dvs så sent som) i går; **III** *konj* (~ *that*) om ... bare ikke; bortsett fra at. **only|begotten** *adj* enbåren. ~ **child** *sb* enebarn.

onset ['ɒnset] *sb* **1** angrep; **2** begynnelse; frembrudd, utbrudd; komme. **onsite** ['ɒnsaɪt] *sb petro* prosessområde. **onslaught** ['ɒnslɔ:t] *sb* storm(angrep). **onto** ['ɒntə] *prep* **1** frem (og ned, opp, ut etc) på; frempå *etc*; **2** *slang: they're* ~ *me* de har (fått) mistanke til meg. **onward** ['ɒnwəd] **1** *adj* fremadskridende, frem; **2** *adv* fremad, fremover; frem; fremme.

on-the-fly printer *sb data* fluktskriver.

ooze [u:z] **1** *sb* dynn, slam; **2** *vi* dryppe; sile; sive, tyte.

opaque [əʊ'peɪk] *adj* ugjennomsiktig; matt, uklar; mørk; **2** sløv, treg.

open ['əʊpən] **1** *adj* åpen (og oppslått; ut|brettet, -foldet; *fig* åpen|bar, -lys; oppriktig, åpenhjertig etc); **2** *sb* åpent område/terreng etc; *in the* ~ under åpen himmel; *come out into the* ~ tre åpent frem; **3** *vb* åpne (og åpne seg; slå opp; brette/folde ut; *fig* begynne, innlede etc); ~ **into** føre inn til; ~ **on (to)** føre inn/ut til; vende (ut) mot; ha utsikt mot; ~ **out** brette/folde (seg) ut; bre seg ut; ligge utbredt; ~ **up** åpne (seg); ligge oppslått; *fig* gjøre tilgjengelig. **open|-and-shut** *adj* opplagt (dvs nærmest avgjort på forhånd). ~**-handed** *adj* raus, rundhåndet. ~ **hole** *sb petro* åpen brønn. ~ **hole completion** *sb petro* åpen avslutning. ~**ing** *sb* åpning *etc.* ~**-minded** *adj* fordomsfri.

operand ['ɒpərənd] *sb data* operand. **operate** ['ɒpəreɪt] *vb* **1** virke; gå (dvs være i gang); arbeide; **2** drive (og holde i gang); betjene/passe (maskin etc); føre, kjøre; **3** bevirke, forårsake; **4** operere. **operate mode** *sb data* operasjonsmodus. **operating | company** *sb petro* operatørselskap. ~ **hours** *sb fl petro etc* driftstid. ~ **line** *sb petro* driftslinje. ~ **platform** *sb petro* driftsplattform. ~ **pressure** *sb petro* driftstrykk. ~ **ratio** *sb data* tilgjengelighet. ~ **space** *sb data* billedområde. ~ **system** *sb data* operativsystem. ~ **time** *sb data* nyttet tid. **operation** [,ɒpə'reɪʃn] *sb* **1** drift, gang; funksjon; **2** betjening; kjøring; **3** (inn)virkning; **4** operasjon. **operation | code** *sb data* operasjonskode. ~ **manager** *sb petro* driftsleder. ~ **manual** *sb petro etc* driftshåndbok. **operative** ['ɒprətɪv] **I** *adj* **1** effektiv, virksom; gyldig; **2** operativ; operasjons-; **II** *sb* (fabrikk)arbeider. **operator** ['ɒpəreɪtə] *sb* **1** maskinist; maskin|passer; -fører, -kjører; operatør; *US også* driftsbestyrer; eier, innehaver; **2** *a)* telefonist; sentralbord|dame, -mann; *b)* telegrafist; **3** *data* operator, operatør; **4** *petro* operatør(selskap); **5** kirurg; opererende lege; **6** spekulant. **operator | command** *sb data* operatørkommando. ~ **console** *sb data* konsoll. ~ **control panel** *sb data* styrepanel. ~ **message** *sb data* operatørmelding.

opinion [ə'pɪnɪən] *sb* **1** mening, oppfatning; *in my* ~ etter min mening; **2** betenkning, utredning. **opinionated** [ə'pɪnɪəneɪtɪd] *adj* påståelig, sta; dogmatisk.

opponent [ə'pəʊnənt] **1** *adj* fiendtlig (*to* mot); motsatt (*to* av); **2** *sb* mot|part, -spiller; -stander.

opportune ['ɒpətju:n] *adj* beleilig, gunstig. **opportunity** [,ɒpə'tju:nətɪ] *sb* (gunstig) anledning/leilighet; mulighet, sjanse.

oppose [ə'pəʊz] *vb* **1** bekjempe; kjempe/slåss mot; motstå; motsette seg; opponere/gjøre motstand (mot); **2** ~ *to* sette opp mot. **opposite** ['ɒpəzɪt] **I** *adj* **1** motsatt; **2** motstående; *som prep også* (rett) overfor; **II** *sb* motsetning; *the* ~ *of* det motsatte av. **opposition** [,ɒpə'zɪʃn] *sb* **1** motstand; *the Opposition (pol)* opposisjonen; **2** motsetning.

oppress [ə'pres] *vt* **1** undertrykke; **2** tynge. **oppression** [ə'preʃn] *sb* undertrykkelse *etc.* **oppressed** [ə'prest] *adj* beklemt; ned|trykt, (-)tynget. **oppressive** [ə'presɪv] *adj* **1** undertrykkende; tyrannisk; **2** tyngende; trykkende; deprimerende. **oppressor** [ə'presə] *sb* undertrykker; tyrann.

opt [ɒpt] *vi* bestemme seg (for); velge; ~ *for* stemme for; ~ *out (dgl)* trekke seg; ikke ville uttale seg *etc.*

optic ['ɒptɪk] *adj* optisk; syns-, øye-. **optics** ['ɒptɪks] *sb* optikk. **optical** ['ɒptɪkl] *adj* optisk. **optical | character** *sb data* optisk tegn. ~ **character reader** *sb data* optisk leser. ~ **character reading/ recognition** *sb data* optisk lesning. ~ **disk** *sb data* optisk plate. ~ **memory** *sb data* optisk lager. ~ **reader** *sb data* = ~ *character reader.* ~ **reading** *sb data* = ~ *character reading.* ~ **scanner** *sb data* optisk (av)søker. ~ **storage** *sb data* videoplatelager. **optician** [ɒp'tɪʃn] *sb* optiker.

option ['ɒpʃn] *sb* valg (og især mulighet/rett til å velge, og det en foretrekker/velger); forkjøpsrett (*on* til); opsjon (*on* på); *at* ~ etter (fritt) valg. **optional**

['ɒpʃənl] *adj* valgfri; frivillig.

opulence ['ɒpjuləns] *sb* overflod; rikdom, velstand. **opulent** ['ɒpjulənt] *adj* (svært) rik; velstående.

or [ɔ:] *konj* eller; ~ *else* ellers.

oral ['ɔ:rəl] **1** *adj* muntlig; munn-; **2** *sb dgl* muntlig (dvs muntlig eksamen).

orange ['ɒrɪndʒ] **I** *adj* oransje(farget); **II** *sb* **1** oransje; **2** appelsin.

oration [ɔ:'reɪʃn] *sb* (høytidelig) tale. **orator** ['ɒrətə] *sb* taler. **oratory** ['ɒrətrɪ] *sb* talekunst; veltalenhet.

orb [ɔ:b] **I** *sb* **1** klode; kule; **2** krets, sirkel; **II** *vt* omgi, (om)kranse. **orbit** ['ɔ:bɪt] **I** *sb* **1** kretsløp; (omløps)bane; **2** område, sfære; **3** øyenhule; **II** *vi* gå (kretse, sirkle) i bane.

orchard ['ɔ:tʃəd] *sb* frukthage.

orchestra ['ɔ:kɪstrə] *sb* orkester. **orchestral** [ɔ:'kəstrəl] *adj* orkester-.

orchid ['ɔ:kɪd] *sb* orkidé.

ordain [ɔ:'deɪn] *vt* **1** bestemme; forordne; **2** ordinere, prestevie.

ordeal [ɔ:'di:l] *sb* hard prøve; *fig* ildprøve, prøvelse.

order ['ɔ:də] **I** *sb* **1** orden (og arrangement, oppstilling; rang, rekkefølge; regelmessighet; system etc); *mil også* formasjon; **2** forfatning, (til)stand; *out of* ~ i ustand; **3** (ro og) orden; ordnede forhold; **4** orden (= ordensregler, vedtekter etc); *især* dagsorden, forretningsorden; **5** befaling, ordre; instruks; (på)bud; *be under ~s to* ha ordre om å; *by ~ of* etter ordre av; **6** bestilling, ordre; leveranse, levering; *(made etc) to ~* (laget etc) etter/på bestilling; *postal ~* postanvisning; **7** hensikt; *in ~ that* for at; *in ~ to* for å; **8** gruppe; slag(s); *biol* orden; **9** orden (dvs munkeorden, ridderorden etc); selskap; **10** orden (= ordenstegn etc); **11** *fl* geistlig embete/kall; *take (holy) ~s* la seg prestevie; **II** *vt* **1** arrangere/ordne (især i rekkefølge); sortere; systematisere; **2** befale, beordre; påby; **3** dirigere; forordne, ordinere; **4** bestille, rekvirere. **order code** *sb data* operasjonskode. **orderly** ['ɔ:dəlɪ] **I** *adj* **1** ordentlig, velordnet; regelmessig; systematisk; **2** høflig, veloppdragen; skikkelig; **II** *sb mil* **1** (offisers)oppasser; ordonans; **2** sykepasser. **ordinal** ['ɔ:dɪnl] **1** *adj* ordens-; **2** *sb* ordenstall. **ordinance** ['ɔ:dɪnəns] *sb* bestemmelse, forordning. **ordinary** ['ɔ:dɪnrɪ] *adj* **1** alminnelig, vanlig; normal, regelmessig; **2** gjennomsnittlig, gjennomsnitts-; *ofte* ubetydelig. **ordination** [ˌɔ:dɪ'neɪʃn] *sb* ordinasjon. **ordnance** ['ɔ:dnəns] *sb* **1** artilleri; (tungt) skyts; **2** våpenteknisk materiell. **Ordnance Survey** *sb* ≈ Statens kartverk.

ore [ɔ:] *sb* erts, malm.

organ ['ɔ:gən] *sb* **1** organ (og legemsdel, lem; avis, publikasjon; stemme/*fig* talerør etc); **2** utøvende myndighet etc; *ofte* organisasjon; *fig* redskap; **3** orgel. **organ grinder** *sb* lirekassemann. **organic** [ɔ:'gænɪk] *adj* organisk. **organization** [ˌɔ:gənaɪ'zeɪʃn] *sb* organisering *etc*; organisasjon, **organize** ['ɔ:gənaɪz] *vt* **1** arrangere, ordne; systematisere; **2** organisere; etablere, opprette.

orientate ['ɔ:rɪənteɪt] *vt* **1** plassere/rette inn *etc* mot øst; **2** bestemme/orientere (i forhold til kompassretningene); ~ *oneself* orientere seg. **orientation** [ˌɔ:rɪən'teɪʃn] *sb* **1** bestemt beliggenhet/plassering *etc*; **2** orientering.

orifice ['ɒrɪfɪs] *sb* munning; hull, åpning.

origin ['ɒrɪdʒɪn] *sb* **1** opphav, opprinnelse; kilde, rot; **2** *data* startpunkt. **original** [ə'rɪdʒənl] *adj, sb* original(-). **originality** [əˌrɪdʒɪ'nælətɪ] *sb* originalitet. **originally** [ə'rɪdʒɪnəlɪ] *adv* originalt; opprinnelig. **originate** [ə'rɪdʒɪneɪt] *vb* **1** forårsake; frembringe, skape; **2** ~ *from* komme/oppstå av; utgå fra.

ornament **1** ['ɔ:nəmənt] *sb* pryd(else); forskjønnelse, utsmykning; pynt; dekorasjon, ornament; **2** ['ɔ:nəment] *vt* pryde; forskjønne, (ut)smykke; pynte; dekorere, ornamentere. **ornamental** [ˌɔ:nə'mentl] *adj* dekorasjons-, pryd; ornamental(-). **ornate** [ɔ:'neɪt] *adj* (rikt) prydet/(ut)smykket; *neds* over|brodert, lesset; snirklet.

orphane ['ɔ:fn] **1** *adj* foreldreløs; **2** *sb* foreldreløst barn; **3** *vt* gjøre foreldreløs. **orphanage** ['ɔ:fnɪdʒ] *sb* barnehjem.

oscillate ['ɒsɪleɪt] *vb* **1** svinge; vibrere; bevege (seg)/gå frem og tilbake; **2** skifte, variere; vakle.

ostensible [ɒ'stənsəbl] *adj* angivelig, foregitt; tilsynelatende, øyensynlig. **ostentation** [ˌɒsten'teɪʃn] *sb* brautende opptreden; brask og bram; *ofte* praktutfoldelse. **ostentatious** [ˌɒsten'teɪʃəs] *adj* brautende, skrytende; prangende.

ostrich ['ɒstrɪtʃ] *sb* struts.

other ['ʌðə] **1** *adj, pron* annen, annet; andre; *the ~ day* forleden (dag); **2** *adv (~wise)* annerledes. **otherwise** ['ʌðəwaɪz] *adj, adv* annerledes; ellers.

otter ['ɒtə] *sb* oter.

ought [ɔ:t] *vb pres:* ~ *to* burde, bør.

ounce [aʊns] *sb* en vektenhet, se midtsidene.

oust [aʊst] *vt* drive/jage ut (bort, vekk etc); for|-drive, -trenge.

out [aʊt] **I** *adv* **1** ut (og bort, vekk, frem, opp etc); ute (og utenfor; borte; fremme, oppe etc); *US også prep* ut av/gjennom; ~ **of** ut/ute av *etc*; utenfor; uten(-); på grunn/som følge av; ~ *of breath* andpusten; ~ *of curiosity (etc)* av nysgjerrighet (etc); ~ *of fashion* avleggs, umoderne; ~ *of money* pengelens; *~-of--the-way* avsides; *fig* usedvanlig; påfallende, søkt; ~ *of wedlock* utenfor ekteskap; ~ *of work* arbeidsløs; **2** omme, over, slutt; til ende; oppbrukt; **3** ~ *and away the best (etc)* langt den/det beste (etc); ~ *and* ~ helt/tvers igjennom; *be* ~ være i streik; streike; *be* ~ *in* ta feil i; *be* ~ *with* være på kant/være uenig med; **II** *pref* **1** ut-, ute-; uten-; borte-; **2** opp-; over-; ut-; **III** *sb* **1** *the ~s (pol)* opposisjonen; *sport* utelaget; **2** *at ~s with* på kant/uvenner med; **3** *ins and ~s*, se *in IV 2*; **IV** *vt dgl* drive/kaste ut; fortrenge.

out|bid *vt* overby. **~board** *adj* utenbords(-). **~bound** *adj sjø* (for) utgående. **~brave** *vt* trasse, trosse; overgå i tapperhet. **~break** *sb* **1** utbrudd; **2** opp|rør, -stand; reisning. **~burst** *sb* utbrudd (især av følelser). **~cast** *adj, sb* fordrevet/utstøtt (person); hjemløs (person). **~class** *vt* utklasse; vinne overlegent over. **~come** *sb* følge, resultat. **~crop** *sb* utløper; *især fig* følge, resultat. **~cry** *sb* **1** (an)skrik; (ut)rop; **2** (rama)skrik; brudulje, bråk. **~distance** *vt* distansere; gå/løpe fra; overgå. **~do** *vt* over|gå, -treffe. **~door** *adj* utendørs(-); frilufts-. **~doors** *adv* ute, utendørs; utenfor.

outer ['autə] *adj* ytre, ytter-. **outer|most** *adj* ytterst. **~ space** *sb* (verdens)rommet.

out|fit I *sb* **1** utrustning, utstyr; **2** gruppe, lag; *US mil* avdeling; **3** organisasjon; virksomhet; **II** *vt* = *fit out*. **~fitter** *sb* (innehaver av) herreekviperingsforretning. **~fox** *vt* = *~smart*. **~going** *adj* utgående; fratredende; *fig* utadvendt. **~grow** *vt* vokse fra.

outing ['autɪŋ] *sb* (land)tur, utflukt.

out|landish *adj* fremmed(artet); rar; utenlandsk. **~last** *vt* leve/vare lenger enn. **~law I** *sb* fredløs (person); banditt, røver; **II** *vt* **1** erklære/lyse fredløs; **2** *US* erklære/gjøre ulovlig. **~lay 1** *sb* utlegg; **2** *vt* legge ut (penger). **~let** *sb* avløp, utløp. **~let gas** *sb petro* utløpsgass. **~line I** *sb* **1** kontur, omriss; *fl* grunntrekk, hovedtrekk; **2** skisse, utkast; **II** *vt* streke/trekke opp; resymere/skissere (i store trekk). **~live** *vt* overleve (dvs leve lenger enn). **~look** *sb* **1** utkikk; utkikkspost; **2** utsikt; **3** innstilling, tankegang; livssyn. **~lying** *adj* avsidesliggende. **~moded** *adj* umoderne; avleggs, foreldet. **~number** *vt* overgå (i antall). **~patient** *sb* dagpasient. **~put** *sb* **1** produksjon, produkt; ytelse; **2** avkastning, utbytte; **3** *data* utmating; *som adj* utgående; **4** effekt. **output | channel** *sb data* utkanal. **~ data** *sb data* utdata. **~ device** *sb data* utenhet. **~ process** *sb data* utmating. **~ stream** *sb data* utskriftsstrøm.

out|rage ['autreɪdʒ] **I** *sb* **1** vold (og voldsomhet; volds|forbrytelse, -handling; voldtekt etc); **2** grov fornærmelse/krenkelse; **II** *vt* fornærme/krenke grovt; voldta. **~rageous** [aut'reɪdʒəs] *adj* **1** opprørende, sjokkerende; skjendig; **2** voldsom.

out|right I *adj* fullstendig, gjennomført; direkte; **II** *adv* **1** straks, øyeblikkelig; **2** fullstendig; helt (og holdent). **~set** *sb* begynnelse. **~shine** *vt* overstråle. **~side I** *adj* **1** utvendig; ytre, ytter-; utenforstående; *ofte* ekstra(-); **2** fjern; **II** *adv* **1** ut; ute, utenfor; utenpå; *~side of (US)* utenfor; unntatt; **2** oppå; ovenpå; **III** *prep* **1** utenfor; utenpå; **2** oppå; **IV** *sb* **1** utside, ytterside; eksteriør, ytre; **2** (ytter)grense; *at the ~side* høyst (regnet); maksimalt. **~size** *adj, sb* (av/i) stor størrelse. **~skirts** *sb fl* utkant(er); omegn. **~smart** *vt* lure, overliste. **~spoken** *adj* frittalende; oppriktig, åpen(hjertig). **~standing** *adj* **1** fremragende; **2** gjenstående; *merk* utestående; **3** utstående. **~ward I** *adj* **1** utvendig, utvortes; ytre; **2** utgående; **II** *adv* ut (og utad, utetter, utover etc); *~ward bound (sjø)* for utgående. **~wardly** *adv* **1** utenpå; i det ytre; **2** utadtil; tilsynelatende, øyensynlig. **~wards** *adv* = *~ward II*. **~weigh** *vt* oppveie. **~wit** *vt* overliste.

oven ['ʌvn] *sb* ovn.

over ['əuvə] **I** *adv* **1** over; *all ~* over (det) hele; **2** over (dvs forbi, omme, slutt etc); *get it ~ with (US)* få det overstått; **3** *(~ again)* om igjen; **4** *(left ~)* igjen, tilbake; til overs; **5** over ende; **6** *især som pref* altfor; over-; **II** *prep* **1** over; ovenpå; **2** over (= mer enn); *~ and above* (ut) over; mer enn; dessuten, ytterligere; foruten; **3** *~ a period of years* gjennom en årrekke.

over|act *vb* over|drive, -spille. **~all I** *adv* over (det) hele; **II 1** *adj* allmenn, generell; **2** *sb fl* overall, kjeledress. **~bearing** *adj* hoven, overlegen. **~board** *adv* over bord. **~cast** *adj* overskyet. **~come** *vb* **1** beseire, overvinne; overvelde; **2** seire/vinne til slutt. **~do** *vb* overdrive; koke/steke *etc* for lenge. **~draft** *sb* overtrekk (av bankkonto); overtrukket beløp. **~draw** *vb* **1** overtrekke (bankkonto); overskride; **2** overdrive. **~dress** *vb* kle seg for fint (overlesset, påpyntet etc). **~due** *adj* forsinket; *merk* forfalt. **~eat** *vr* forspise seg. **~flow I** *sb* **1** flom, oversvømmelse; *fig* overflod; **2** *data* overflyt; **II** *vb* oversvømme. **~flow check** *sb data* overflytkontroll. **~flow storage** *sb data* overflytlager. **~grown** *adj* forvokst; gjengrodd, tilgrodd. **~haul I** *sb* **1** forbikjøring; **2** ettersyn; overhaling; **II** *vt* **1** hale inn på; (ta igjen og) kjøre forbi; **2** etterse (grundig); overhale. **~head I** *adv* over; ovenpå; **II 1** *adj* over-; topp-; *ofte* luft-; **2** *sb fl (~ cost)* administrasjonsomkostninger, generalomkostninger. **~head door** *sb* vippeport. **~head operation** *sb data* administrativ operasjon. **~head railway** *sb* høybane. **~hear** *vt* overhøre (dvs få høre noe det ikke er meningen at en skal høre). **~joyed** *adj* overlykkelig. **~land** *adj, adv* over land; landverts; til land. **~lap 1** *sb* overlapping; overlappet skjøt etc; **2** *vb* overlappe. **~load** *vt* overbelaste. **~look** *vt* **1** ha utsikt over; beherske/kontrollere (pga høy beliggenhet); **2** overse (dvs ikke legge merke til etc); **3** se gjennom fingrene med. **~night I** *adj* nattlig, natt(e)-; **II** *adv* **1** natten over; **2** i løpet av natten; **3** kvelden i forveien. **~pass** *sb* bro (over motorvei etc). **~power** *vt* over|manne, -velde. **~rate** *vt* **1** overvurdere; **2** overbeskatte. **~rule** *vt* avvise; oppheve; stemme ned. **~run** *vt* **1** løpe/renne ned; *fig også* oversvømme; **2** overskride (tidsfrist etc). **~seas 1** *adj* oversjøisk; **2** *adv* på den andre siden av havet. **~see** *vt* overvåke; kontrollere. **~seer** *sb* oppsynsmann, vakt; overvåker. **~sight** *sb* **1** (over)oppsyn, tilsyn; **2** uaktsomhet; forglemmelse. **~sleep** *vr* forsove seg. **~statement** *sb* overdrivelse. **~step** *vt* overskride. **~stock** *vb* ta inn for mye på lager. **~strung** *adj* overspent. **~-subscribed** *adj merk* overtegnet.

overt ['əuvɜ:t] *adj* åpen (og åpen|bar, -lys etc); utilslørt.

over|take *vt* **1** innhente/ta igjen (og kjøre forbi); passere; **2** over|raske, -rumple; *fig* ramme. **~tax** *vt* overbeskatte. **~throw 1** *sb* (om)styrting *etc*; fall, nederlag; **2** *vt* styrte; beseire, overvinne; kullkaste. **~time** *adj, adv, sb* overtid(s-). **~ture** *sb* **1** innledning, åpning; ouverture; **2** forslag; tilnærmelse. **~turn** *vb* kantre, velte. **~weight** *adj, sb* overvekt(ig). **~whelm** *vt* **1** over|skylle, -svømme; **2** over|manne; -velde. **~work I** *sb* ekstraarbeid, overtidsarbeid; **II** *vb* **1** arbeide for mye; overanstrenge seg; **2** bearbeide *etc* for mye. **~wrought** *adj* **1** over|anstrengt, -arbeidet; **2** over(be)arbeidet; utbrodert, utpenslet; **3** over|nervøs, -spent.

owe [əʊ] *vb* skylde; være (en) skyldig. **owing** ['əʊɪŋ] *adj* **1** skyldig; ubetalt, utestående; **2** ~ *to* på grunn av.

owl [aʊl] *sb* ugle.

own [əʊn] **I** *adj, pron* egen, eget; egne; *hold one's ~* holde stand; klare seg (på egen hånd); *on one's ~* selvstendig, uavhengig; på egen hånd; **II** *vb* **1** eie, inneha; **2** innrømme; (an)erkjenne. **owner** ['əʊnə] *sb* eier, innehaver. **ownership** ['əʊnəʃɪp] *sb* eie (og eiendomsrett).

ox [ɒks] *sb* **1** okse (især gjeldokse); stut; **2** *(oxen)* kveg, storfe.

oxide ['ɒksaɪd] *sb* oksid. **oxygen** ['ɒksɪdʒən] *sb* oksygen, surstoff.

oyster [ɔɪstə] *sb* østers.

P

pa [pɑ:] *fork* for *papa.*

pace [peɪs] **I** *sb* **1** skritt; **2** gang|art, -lag; *om hest* passgang; **3** fart, tempo; *set the ~* bestemme farten; *fig also* slå an tonen; **II** *vb* **1** *a)* skritte (opp); *b)* marsjere; **2** bestemme farten (for).

pacific [pə'sɪfɪk] **1** *adj* fredelig, rolig; fredsommelig; **2** *sb the Pacific (Ocean)* Stillehavet. **pacify** ['pæsɪfaɪ] *vt* bilegge; pasifisere; berolige, stille.

pack [pæk] **I** *sb* **1** bunt, bylt; bør, oppakning, pakning; *~ of cards* kort|leik, -stokk; *~ of lies* løgn fra ende til annen; **2** *a) US* pakke; *b) data* pakke; **3** *a)* flokk, gjeng; pakk, sleng; *b)* flokk, (hunde)kobbel; **II** *vb* **1** pakke (også *data)*; *~ off* ekspedere; sende av sted/fra seg; *~ up* pakke (sakene sine); pakke sammen (dvs gi opp etc); **2** pakke/stue sammen; flokkes; flokke seg; **3** pakke, tette; isolere; **4** hermetisere; legge ned (sardiner etc); **5** *US* bære/slepe på. **package** ['pækɪdʒ] *sb* **1** bunt, bylt; **2** pakke, pakning; **3** emballasje, innpakning. **packaged program** *sb data* programpakke. **pack-animal** *sb* lastedyr, pakkdyr. **packed column/tower** *sb petro* fylt tårn. **packer** ['pækə] *sb* **1** pakker; **2** hermetikkarbeider; **3** = **packery** ['pækərɪ] *sb* hermetikkfabrikk. **packet** ['pækɪt] *sb* **1** pakke (også *data)*; **2** = *~-boat*; **3** *slang* bråte, haug; god slump (f.eks. penger). **packet-boat** *sb* postbåt. **packhorse** *sb* kløvhest. **packing** *sb* **1** pakking; **2** emballasje, (inn)pakning. **packing|-case** *sb* pakkasse. **~ density** *sb data* pakkingstetthet. **pack-saddle** *sb* kløvsal.

pact [pækt] *sb* pakt; avtale, overenskomst [især høytidelig inngått i skriftlig form].

pad [pæd] **A I** *sb* **1** pute [*især* støtpute, salpute, tredepute etc]; *sjø* skamfilingsmatte; **2** underlag, underlagsmatte; **3** *(writing ~)* skriveblokk; **4** tampong; **5** *(launching ~)* utskytnings|plattform, -rampe [for raketter]; **II** *vt* polstre, vattere; fôre/stoppe ut; **B 1** *sb* sti, tråkk; vei; **2** *vi* labbe; traske, tråkke; *~ it* ta beina fatt. **padding** ['pædɪŋ] *sb* polstring; *data* utfylling; *fig* fyllekalk.

paddle ['pædl] **A I** *sb* **1** paddel, padleåre; **2** hjulskovl; **3** luffe; **4** rørepinne, tvare; **II** *vb* padle; **B 1** *sb* vassing; **2** *vi* vasse. **paddle|-steamer** *sb* hjuldamper. **~-wheel** *sb* skovlhjul.

paddock ['pædək] *sb* hestehage, paddock.

padlock ['pædlɒk] *sb, vt* (låse med) hengelås.

pagan ['peɪgən] **1** *adj* hedensk; **2** *sb* hedning.

page [peɪdʒ] **A 1** *sb* side (i bok etc); **2** *vt* paginere; forsyne med sidetall; **B I** *sb* **1** pasje; **2** hotellbud, pikkolo; **II** *vt* kalle på/sende bud på (ved hjelp av pikkolo). **page alignment** *sb data* sideinnstillling.

pageant ['pædʒənt] *sb* opptog (især historisk, med praktfulle drakter etc). **pageantry** ['pædʒəntrɪ] *sb* praktutfoldelse; pomp og prakt.

page | formatting *sb data* sideformatering. **~ layout** *sb data* sideutforming. **~ printer** *sb data* sideskriver.

pail [peɪl] *sb* bøtte, spann; pøs.

pain [peɪn] **I** *sb* **1** smerte; lidelse(r), pine; *fl* veer; *~ and suffering* tort og svie; *~ in the neck* plageånd; plagsomt problem etc; **2** *fl* bryderi; møye, umak; **II** *vt* gjøre vondt; pine, smerte. **pain|ful** *adj* smertefull. **~killer** *sb* smertestillende middel. **~less** ['peɪnlɪs] *adj* smertefri.

paint [peɪnt] **I** *sb* **1** maling (og malerfarge); *wet ~!* nymalt! **2** sminke. **paint|-box** *sb* fargeskrin; malerkasse. **~-brush** *sb* maler|kost, -pensel. **painstaking** ['peɪnsteɪkɪŋ] *adj* nøyaktig, omhyggelig. **painter** ['peɪntə] *sb* maler. **painting** ['peɪntɪŋ] *sb* **1** maling; **2** maleri; **3** malerkunst.

pair [peə] **I** *sb* **1** par (og ektepar etc); **2** parkamerat; motstykke, pendant; **II** *vb* pare (seg); *~ off* ordne (seg) parvis.

pal [pæl] *dgl* **1** *sb* kamerat, kompis; **2** *vi: ~ up (with)* bli godvenner (med).

palace ['pælɪs] *sb* palass, slott.

palatable ['pælətəbl] *adj* velsmakende; behagelig, tiltalende. **palate** ['pælɪt] *sb* gane.

pale [peɪl] **A I** *adj* **1** blek; **2** blass; lys; **II** *vi* blekne; **B** *sb* **1** pæl, stake, stolpe; **2** (inngjerdet) område, kve. **pale-face** *sb* blekansikt. **palisade** [ˌpælɪ'seɪd] **I** *sb* **1** palisade, pæleverk; **2** *fl især US* høy, bratt elvebredd/ strandskrent; **II** *vt* omgi med palisade(r).

pall [pɔ:l] **A** *sb* teppe; *især* likklede; **B** *vi* tape sin tiltrekning. **pall-bearer** *sb* marskalk (ved begravelse); *US* kistebærer.

pallid ['pælɪd] *adj* gusten; (sykelig) blek. **pallor** ['pælə] *sb* (sykelig) blekhet.

palm [pɑ:m] **A 1** *sb* håndflate; **2** *vt* palmere; skjule i hånden; ~ *it off upon them* prakke det på dem; **B** *sb* palme.

palpable ['pælpəbl] *adj* **1** håndpåtakelig, konkret; **2** følbar, merkbar; tydelig. **palpitate** ['pælpɪteɪt] *vi* banke raskt (om hjerte).

palsy ['pɔ:lzɪ] **1** *sb* lamhet, lammelse; **2** *vt* lamme.

paltry ['pɔ:ltrɪ] *adj* ussel, ynkelig.

pamper ['pæmpə] *vt* forkjæle; degge/dulle med; skjemme bort.

pamphlet ['pæmflɪt] *sb* brosjyre, hefte; *fl* småskrifter.

pan [pæn] **I** *sb* panne (og gryte, kasserolle, kokekar etc); sjeide|brett, -kar, -panne; (krutt)panne; **II** *vb* **1** ~ *off/out* vaske ut (gull etc); ~ *out* gi gull *etc* (ved utvasking); *fig* forløpe heldig; gi utbytte; **2** *film* panorere.

panacea [ˌpænə'sɪə] *sb* universal|medisin, -middel; patentmedisin.

pane [peɪn] *sb* (vindus)rute.

panel ['pænl] **I** *sb* **1** panel (og paneling); (firkantet) felt/flate; (dør)|fylling, -speil; (instrument)|bord, -brett, tavle; **2** liste/oppgave (især over jurymedlemmer og trygdekasseleges pasienter); **3** (bedømmelses)komité; jury; (diskusjons)|gruppe, -lag; **II** *vt* panele. **panel doctor** *sb* trygdekasselege.

pang [pæŋ] *sb* smerte(stikk); ~*s of conscience* samvittighetsnag.

panic ['pænɪk] **1** *adj* panisk; **2** *sb* panikk; **3** *vi* få panikk. **panic-stricken** *adj* panikkslagen. **panicky** ['pænɪkɪ] *adj* oppskaket, skremt.

panoply ['pænəplɪ] *sb* **1** full rustning; **2** fullt/stort oppbud.

pant [pænt] **I** *sb* **1** gisp, stønn; **2** pesing; **II** *vb* **1** gispe, stønne; **2** pese; **3** hige/tørste (*after/for* etter).

panties ['pæntɪz] *sb fl dgl* truse(r).

pantry ['pæntrɪ] *sb* **1** *gml* spiskammer; **2** anretning; matvarelager (i storhusholdning); **3** *sjø* penteri.

pants [pænts] *sb fl* bukse(r).

pap [pæp] *sb* **A** melke|papp, -velling; barnemat (også *fig*); **B** *gml* brystvorte.

papa [pə'pɑ:] *sb* pappa.

papacy ['peɪpəsɪ] *sb* pave|dømme, -velde. **papal** ['peɪpl] *adj* pavelig, pave-.

paper ['peɪpə] **I** *sb* **1** papir; *fl* papirer (til legitimering etc); dokumenter, verdipapirer; **2** *(news~)* avis, blad; **3** artikkel; avhandling, essay; (skole)stil; **4** *(examination ~)* oppgave/prøve (til eksamen etc); **5** *(wall~)* tapet; **6** = *~-money)*; **7** *især US* (fri)billett; gratistilskuer *etc* (dvs en med fribillett); **II** *vt* tapetsere. **paper|-back** *sb* heftet bok; billigbok. **~-backed** *adj* heftet (om bok). **~-bag** *sb* (papir)pose. **~-basket** *sb* papirkurv. **~clip** *sb* binders; papir|klemme, -klype. **~ extractor** *sb data* arkmater. **~-hanger** *sb* tapetserer. **~-knife** *sb* papirkniv. **~-mill** *sb* papirfabrikk. **~-money** *sb* papirpenger; (penge)|seddel, -sedler. **~-pulp** *sb* papirmasse. **~ tape** *sd data* hullbånd. **~-work** *sb* papirarbeid; *fig* papirmølle.

par [pɑ:] *sb* **1** *on ~ with* jevngod/på høyde med; på like fot med; **2** *fig* & *merk* pari; *above/below ~* over/ under pari.

parachute ['pærəʃu:t] *sb, vb* (hoppe ut i) fallskjerm. **parachutist** ['pærəʃu:tɪst] *sb* fallskjermhopper.

parade [pə'reɪd] **I** *sb* **1** parade (og paradering); mønstring, oppstilling; (troppe)revy; appell, parole; **2** oppvisning; **3** opptog; demonstrasjonstog; **4** promenade, spaservei; **II** *vb* **1** (la) paradere *etc*; **2** vise (frem); skilte med; skryte av; vise seg. **parade ground** *sb* paradeplass.

paragon ['pærəgən] *sb* forbilde, mønster; eksempel (til etterfølgelse).

paragraph ['pærəgrɑ:f] **I** *sb* **1** avsnitt; paragraf (og paragraftegn); **2** (avis-, nyhets)notis; **II** *vt* **1** dele inn i avsnitt; **2** skrive om (i avis).

parallel ['pærələl] **I** *adj* parallell (*to/with* med); **II** *sb* **1** parallell (linje etc); *fig* sidestykke; **2** bredde-(grad); **3** sammenligning; **III** *vt* **1** parallellisere; sammenligne; **2** fremby/oppvise maken; **3** *især US* gå/ løpe parallelt med. **parallel bars** *sb fl* skranke (til turn).

paralyse ['pærəlaɪz] *vt* **1** lamme, paralysere; **2** fjetre, lamslå. **paralysis** [pə'rælɪsɪs] *sb* lammelse, paralyse (også *fig*).

parameter [pə'ræmɪtə] *sb data, mil etc* parameter.

paramount ['pærəmaʊnt] *adj* høyst, størst; ytterst viktig *etc*.

parapet ['pærəpɪt] *sb* **1** brystvern; **2** gjerde, rekkverk.

parasite ['pærəsaɪt] *sb* parasitt, snyltedyr; *fig* snylter.

para|trooper ['pærətru:pə] *sb* fallskjerm|jeger, -soldat. **~troops** ['pærətru:ps] *sb fl* fallskjermtropper.

parcel ['pɑ:sl] **I** *sb* **1** pakke; **2** *gml* (jord)stykke, teig; parsell; **3** *part and ~ of* fast bestanddel av; **II** *vt* **1** *~ out* porsjonere (parsellere, stykke etc) ut; **2** *(~ up)* bunte sammen; pakke inn.

parch [pɑ:tʃ] *vt* (av)svi; brenne (opp). **parched** [pɑ:tʃt] *adj* avsvidd; tørr, uttørket.

parchment ['pɑ:tʃmənt] *sb* pergament.

pardon ['pɑ:dn] **1** *sb* forlatelse, tilgivelse; *I beg your) ~!* unnskyld (= jeg oppfattet ikke hva De sa)! **2** *vt* unnskylde; forlate, tilgi; benåde. **pardonable**

['pɑ:dnəbl] *adj* tilgivelig; forståelig, unnskyldelig.

pare [peə] *vt* skrelle; (be)skjære; skjære vekk.

parent ['peərənt] *sb* **1** forelder (dvs far eller mor); *fl* foreldre; **2** *fig* opphav, rot. **parentage** ['peərəntɪdʒ] *sb* foreldreforhold; byrd, ætt. **parental** [pə'rentl] *adj* foreldre- (og faderlig, fars-; moderlig, mors-).

parenthesis [pə'renθɪsɪs] *sb* parentes.

parenthood ['peərənthud] *sb* foreldreskap.

parings ['peərɪŋz] *sb fl* skall, skrell; flis(er), spon.

parish ['pærɪʃ] *sb* (kirke)sogn, prestegjeld; *især US* menighet. **parish clerk** *sb* klokker. **parishioner** [pə'rɪʃənə] *sb* sognebarn. **parish register** *sb* kirkebok.

parity ['pærətɪ] *sb* **1** likhet; **2** *merk* paritet. **parity | bit** *sb data* paritetsbit. **~ check** *sb data* paritetskontroll.

park [pɑ:k] **I** *sb* **1** park (og parkanlegg; *US også* idretts|park, -plass); **2** *(car-~)* parkeringsplass; **II** *vb* parkere. **parking** ['pɑ:kɪŋ] *sb* parkering; *no ~!* parkering forbudt! **parking | lane** *sb* parkeringsfelt. **~ light** *sb* park(erings)lys. **~ lot** *sb* parkeringsplass. **~ meter** *sb* parkometer. **~ ticket** *sb* rød lapp (for parkeringsforseelse).

parlance ['pɑ:ləns] *sb* (sam)tale; språkbruk; *common ~* (vanlig) dagligtale. **parley** ['pɑ:lɪ] **1** *sb* konferanse; **2** *vi* diskutere; konferere. **parliament** ['pɑ:ləmənt] *sb* parlament, nasjonalforsamling; *Parliament* Parlamentet (dvs det britiske). **parliamentarian** [,pɑ:ləmən'teərɪən] **1** *adj* parlamentariker-; parlaments-; **2** *sb* parlamentariker. **parliamentary** [,pɑ:lə'mentərɪ] *adj* parlamentarisk; parlaments-. **parlour** ['pɑ:lə] *sb* **1** (daglig)stue, salong; **2** besøksrom, mottakelsesværelse; **3** skjenkestue; **4** *US (parlor)* salong (f.eks. *beauty ~* skjønnhetssalong; *hairdresser's ~* frisersalong; *photographer's ~* fotoatelier). **parlo(u)r car** *sb* salongvogn (på jernbane). **parlour | maid** *sb* stuepike. **~ pink** *sb* salongradikaler.

parody ['pærədɪ] *sb, vt* parodi(ere).

parole [pə'rəul] **I** *sb* **1** æresord; **2** *US: release on ~* betinget benådning; prøveløslatelse; **II** *vt US* prøveløslate.

parquet ['pɑ:keɪ] *sb* parkett.

parrot ['pærət] *sb* **1** papegøye; **2** apekatt (dvs etterplaprer).

parry ['pærɪ] *sb* parering; **2** *vt* avverge, parere.

parsimonious [,pɑ:sɪ'məunɪəs] *adj* gjerrig, knuslet, smålig.

parsing ['pɑ:sɪŋ] *sb data* spalting.

parsley ['pɑ:slɪ] *sb* (krus)persille.

parsnip ['pɑ:snɪp] *sb* pastinakk.

parson ['pɑ:sn] *sb dgl* (sogne)prest. **parsonage** ['pɑ:snɪdʒ] *sb* prestegård.

part [pɑ:t] **I** *adv* dels, delvis; **II** *sb* **1** del (og andel, part; bit(e), stykke etc); *in ~* dels, delvis; *take in good ~* ta (opp) i beste mening; **2** distrikt, strøk; *in these ~s* på disse kanter; her omkring; **3** rolle; andel, part; *take ~ (in)* ta del (i); være med (på); **4** parti, side; *for my (etc) ~* for min (etc) del; **5** *mus* stemme; **6** *gml* evner, talent(er); begavelse; **III** *vb* dele (seg); skille(s); skille lag; gå fra hverandre; splitte(s); *~ company (with)* bli uenige; skille lag (med); *~ friends* skilles som venner; *~ with* skille seg av med; gi avkall på; gi opp; slutte med. **partake** [pɑ:'teɪk] *vb* **1** delta (*in* i); *~ in/of* ta del i; være med på; **2** *~ of* ha en snev/et anstrøk av. **partial** ['pɑ:ʃl] *adj* **1** delvis; ufullstendig; **2** partisk; *be ~ to* ha (en) forkjærlighet for. **participant** [pɑ:'tɪsɪpənt] **1** *adj* deltakende; **2** *sb* deltaker. **participate** [pɑ:'tɪsɪpeɪt] *vi* **1** delta (*in* i); være med (*in* på); **2** = *partake 2.* **participation** [pɑ:,tɪsɪ'peɪʃn] *sb* deltakelse. **participation interest** *sb petro* deltakerandel. **participle** [pɑ:'tɪsɪpl] *sb* partisipp. **particle** ['pɑ:tɪkl] *sb* partikkel; (liten) bit(e); del; grann. **particoloured** ['pɑ:tɪ,kʌləd] *adj* broket, mangefarget. **particular** [pə'tɪkjulə] **I** *adj* **1** (sær)egen, særskilt; enestående, spesiell; **2** fordringsfull; kresen, nøye(regnende); **II** *sb* **1** detalj, enkelthet; **2** *in ~* især, særlig. **particularly** [pə'tɪkjuləlɪ] *adv* især, særlig; spesielt. **parting** ['pɑ:tɪŋ] **I** *adj* avskjeds-; **II** *sb* **1** avskjed; skilsmisse (dvs ikke oppløsning av ekteskap, men det å gå fra hverandre, skille lag); **2** skill (i håret). **partition** [pɑ:'tɪʃn] **I** *sb* **1** (av)deling, oppdeling; *data* partisjon; **2** skillevegg; **II** *vt (~ off)* dele av. **partly** ['pɑ:tlɪ] *adv* delvis; (til) dels. **partner** ['pɑ:tnə] *sb* **1** felle, (par)kamerat; kompanjong, partner; makker, medspiller; **2** deltaker. **partnership** ['pɑ:tnəʃɪp] *sb* **1** kompaniskap; **2** delaktighet. **part|-singing, ~-song** *sb* flerstemmig sang(stykke). **~-time** *adj* deltids-. **~-timer** *sb* deltidsarbeider.

partridge ['pɑ:trɪdʒ] *sb* rapphøne.

party ['pɑ:tɪ] *sb* **1** parti; **2** *jur* part; **3** med|ansvarlig, skyldig; *be a ~ to* være delaktig i; **4** avdeling; gruppe; lag; *mil også* kommando, pelotong; *petro* målelag; **5** selskap; fest, lag; **6** *hum* personasje, type. **party | chief** *sb petro* lagleder. **~ line** *sb* **1** partstelefon; **2** *pol* parti|linje; -liste, -program.

pass [pɑ:s] **I** *sb* **1** bestått (eksamen, også om karakteren); **2** forhold, tilstand; (kinkig/kritisk) situasjon; **3** passerseddel; permisjonsseddel (og permisjon); adgangstegn; (fri)billett; **4** fremstøt; tilnærmelse; støt/utfall (i fektning); pasning (i fotball etc); *make a ~/~es at* lange ut etter; slå an med; **5** (magisk) håndbevegelse/strykning; **6** passasje, vei; (skips)lei; **7** fjellovergang, pass; **8** *data* rundgang; **II** *vb* **1** passere (og gå/komme, dra/reise, gli, kjøre, seile etc forbi, gjennom, ned, over, ut etc); forløpe/gå (om tid); *fig* overgå; *~ in the street* møte(s) på gaten; **2** (gjennomgå og) greie, klare; bestå (eksamen etc); *~ muster* holde mål; **3** (gjennomgå og) godkjenne; la bestå (eksamen etc); vedta (lovforslag); **4** la passere (etc, jf *II 1*); slippe frem; **5** gi (og rekke/sende; kaste/slenge/ sparke etc videre/fra seg); (la) sirkulere; sette i omløp; *~ one's eye over* fare over (med øynene); **6** føre; kjøre, sende; renne, stikke; *~ a rope round* slå et tau rundt; **7** forkynne; erklære, si; uttale, ytre; *~ sentence (up)on* avsi/felle dom over; *~ the time of day with* hilse på; **8** foregå; finne sted; **9** forsvinne; bli borte; gå bort (dvs dø); gi seg; gå over; **10** *om tid* fordrive; få til å gå; **11** melde pass (i kortspill); **12** *med adv, prep* **~ along** fortsette; gå *etc* videre; sende *etc* videre; **~ away** = *II 9*; **~ by** passere; gå *etc* forbi; *fig* gi seg; gå over; forbigå, overse; **~ for** gå (dvs bli solgt, tatt etc) for; **~ in** levere/sende *etc* inn; **~ into** forandres/forvandles til; bli/gå over til; **~ off** forløpe, gå; avverge, parere; *fig* gi seg; gå over; **~ off as** utgi (seg) for (å være); **~ off on** lure/prakke på; **~ on** fortsette; gå *etc* videre; gå bort (dvs dø); sende *etc* videre; **~ out** *dgl* besvime; *slang* pigge av (dvs dø); **~ over** dra/reise over; *fig* hoppe over; ignorere, overse; **~ round** sende rundt; **~ through** dra/reise gjennom; kjøre/sende gjennom; renne/stikke gjennom; *fig* gjennomgå; **~ up** *US dgl* gi/la gå fra seg.

passable ['pɑ:səbl] *adj* **1** farbar; **2** (noenlunde) akseptabel; brukbar. **passage** ['pæsɪdʒ] *sb* **1** passering (etc, jf *pass II*); **2** gjennomfart (og overfart, reise, tur etc samt billett, frakt); **3** passasje; gang, korridor; **4** utdrag; (kort) avsnitt/sitat; **5** vedtakelse (av lovforslag); **6** *fl* ordskifte; dyst, holmgang. **passenger** ['pæsɪndʒə] *sb* passasjer. **passer-by** [ˌpɑ:sə'baɪ] *sb* forbipasserende (person). **passing** ['pɑ:sɪŋ] **I** *adj* forbigående; flyktig; **II** *sb* **1** bortgang (dvs død); **2** = *passage 5*.

passion ['pæʃn] *sb* **1** lidenskap; glød, heftighet; **2** pasjon; mani; **3** lidelse; *the Passion* Jesu lidelseshistorie. **passionate** ['pæʃənət] *adj* lidenskapelig; glødende, heftig.

passive ['pæsɪv] *adj, sb* passiv. **passivity** [pə'sɪvətɪ] *sb* passivitet.

pass|key ['pɑ:ski:] *sb* gatedørsnøkkel; hovednøkkel. **~-mark** *sb* laveste ståkarakter (ved eksamen, prøve etc). **Passover** ['pɑ:sˌəʊvə] *sb* (jødenes) påske.

passport ['pɑ:spɔ:t] *sb* (politi)pass.

password ['pɑ:swɜ:d] *sb* feltrop; stikkord.

past [pɑ:st] **I** *adj* for|gangen, -løpen; *for the ~ few days/weeks* (i) de siste par dager/uker; *the ~ century* (det) forrige århundre; *the ~ tense (gram)* fortid; **2** full|endt, -kommen; **II** *adv* fordi; **III** *prep* **1** etter (om tid); *five ~ ten* fem over ti; *half ~ three* halv fire; **2** bortenfor; forbi; **3** over; utenfor; hinsides; *~ bearing/endurance* uutholdelig; *~ belief* utrolig; *~ comprehension* ufattelig; **IV** *sb* fortid; *in the ~* i gamle dager.

paste [peɪst] **I** *sb* **1** deig; masse, pasta; farse, postei; **2** klister; **3** strass (til fremstilling av kunstige edelsteiner); *som adj* simili-, strass-; **II** *vt* klistre; *~ up* klistre opp; klebe/klistre igjen. **paste|board** *sb* papp. **~-up** *sb* oppklebning.

past generations *sb fl* tidligere generasjoner.

pastime ['pɑ:staɪm] *sb* tidsfordriv; fritidsbeskjeftigelse.

past master *sb* fullbefaren (anerkjent, suveren etc) mester.

pastry ['peɪstrɪ] *sb* **1** (kake)deig; butterdeig; **2** *koll* (konditor)kaker. **pastry-cook** *sb* konditor.

pasture ['pɑ:stʃə] **1** *sb* beite(mark); **2** *vb* beite; sette på beite.

pasty I ['peɪstɪ] *adj* **1** deiget; **2** = *~-faced*; **II** ['pæstɪ] *sb* (kjøtt)pai, postei. **pasty-faced** *adj* blekfet, kvapset.

pat [pæt] **A I** *sb* **1** klapp, klaps; smekk; **2** klatt; **II** *vb* klappe/slå (lett); klapse; *~ down* glatte ut (med små, lette slag); **B I** *adj* **1** fiks og ferdig; **2** slående, treffende; **II** *adv* **1** parat, rede; **2** beleilig.

patch [pætʃ] **1** *sb* lapp (og bot samt plasterlapp, åkerlapp etc); flekk, plett; flik; dott, tott; **2** *vt* bøte, flikke, lappe; reparere; *~ up* bøte/flikke på; lappe sammen; *~ed-up* sammenflikket.

pate [peɪt] *sb dgl* **1** hode, skolt; **2** isse, skalle.

patent ['peɪtənt] **I** *adj* **1** åpenbar; innlysende, klar; **2** patent-; *letters ~* patentbrev; **II** *sb* patent (*for* på); patentrett(ighet); **III** *vt* patentere; ta patent på. **patent leather shoes** *sb fl* lakksko.

pater ['peɪtə] *sb slang* far (især husfar på internatskole etc). **paternal** [pə'tɜ:nl] *adj* **1** faderlig, fars-; **2** på farssiden. **paternity** [pə'tɜ:nətɪ] *sb* **1** farskap; **2** opphav, opprinnelse.

path [pɑ:θ] *sb* **1** (*~way*) sti, tråkk; vei; **2** bane, rute; *in her ~* i hennes fotspor/kjølvann; **3** *data* bane, vei. **path|finder** *sb* stifinner; *fig* foregangs|kvinne, -mann; -person; pioner. **~less** *adj* uveisom, veiløs.

patience ['peɪʃens] *sb* **1** tålmod(ighet); **2** (kort)kabal. **patient** ['peɪʃənt] **1** *adj* tålmodig; **2** *sb* pasient.

patrimony ['pætrɪmənɪ] *sb* **1** farsarv; **2** kirkegods.

patrol [pə'trəʊl] **1** *sb* patrulje (og patruljetjeneste, patruljering etc); **2** *vb* (av)patruljere. **patrolman** *sb* patruljerende konstabel.

patron ['peɪtrən] *sb* **1** beskytter; *hist* skytsherre; **2** (fast) kunde; stamgjest. **patronage** ['pætrənɪdʒ] *sb* **1** beskyttelse; **2** kundekrets; **3** kallsrett, utnevnelsesrett. **patronize** ['pætrənaɪz] *vt* **1** beskytte; støtte; favorisere; **2** være (fast) kunde hos; **3** behandle nedlatende/overlegent. **patronizing** ['pætrənaɪzɪŋ] *adj* nedlatende. **patron saint** *sb* skytshelgen.

patter ['pætə] **A 1** *sb* (lett) klapring/tripping; tromming (som av regndråper etc); **2** *vi* klapre *etc*; **B I** *sb* **1** kakling, plapring; oppramsing (og ramse, regle etc); **2** (fag)sjargong; røverspråk; **II** *vb* kakle, plapre, skravle; lire av seg (rivende fort).

pattern ['pætən] **I** *sb* **1** eksempel, forbilde; **2** mønster (og mønstertegning); **3** (stoff)prøve; **II** *vb* bruke som/ta til forbilde *etc*. **pattern recognition** *sb data* mønstergjenkjenning.

paunch [pɔ:ntʃ] *sb* svær mave.

pauper ['pɔ:pə] *sb* fattiglem, stakkar.

pause [pɔ:z] **1** *sb* pause; opphold, stans; avbrytelse; *give ~ to* vekke til ettertanke; **2** *vi* holde/ta pause.

pave [peɪv] *vt* brolegge. **pavement** ['peɪvmənt] *sb* fortau. **pavilion** [pə'vɪlɪən] *sb* **1** paviljong; **2** klubbhus (på idrettsbane etc); **3** stort telt.

paving ['peɪvɪŋ] *sb* brolegning.

paw [pɔ:] **I** *sb* labb, pote; **II** *vb* **1** klore/skrape (på); stampe (på); **2** klå/plukke på.

pawn [pɔ:n] **A** *sb* **1** bonde (i sjakk); **2** *fig* brikke; (viljeløst) redskap; **B** *vt* pantsette; *dgl* stampe. **pawn|broker** *sb* pantelåner. **~shop** *sb* pantelånerforretning.

pay [peɪ] **I** *sb* **1** betaling, godtgjørelse; **2** lønn; **3** tjeneste (og tjenesteforhold); **II** *vb* **1** betale; gasjere, lønne; betale/lønne seg; **~** *down* betale kontant(beløp); **~** *off* (ut)betale; gi (arbeidere etc) sluttoppgjør; **~** *out* (ut)betale; **~** *up* punge ut; **2** gi, skjenke; **~** *a call/visit on* besøke; avlegge (et) besøk/(en) visitt hos; **~** *out (sjø)* gi ut (på tauende etc); slakke (på). **pay|able** ['peɪəbl] *adj* **1** betalbar; for|fallen, -falt; **2** *dgl* overkommelig (i pris). **~back period** *sb petro* inntjeningsperiode. **~day** *sb* lønningsdag. **~load** *sb* nyttelast. **~master** *sb* (lønnings)kasserer. **~ment** *sb* **1** betaling *etc*; **2** gasje, lønn. **~-off** *sb* avregning, utbetaling; *fig* regnskapets dag. **~-packet** *sb* lønnings|-konvolutt, -pose. **~-phone** *sb US* telefonautomat (med myntinnkast); ≈ mynttelefon. **~-roll, ~-sheet** *sb* lønningsliste. **~slip** *sb* lønnsslipp. **~ zone** *sb petro* produksjonssone; produserende brønn/lag.

pea [pi:] *sb* ert. **pea-soup** sb erte(r)suppe.

peace [pi:s] *sb* **1** fred; **2** ro, stillhet; **~** *of mind* sinnsro, sjelefred. **peaceable** ['pi:səbl] *adj* fredsommelig, fredelig. **peaceful** ['pi:sful] *adj* **1** fredelig; fredfull; rolig, stille; **2** fredsommelig; fredselskende.

peach [pi:tʃ] *sb* **1** fersken (og ferskentre); **2** *fig* perle, skatt; kjernekar, knupp.

peacock ['pi:kɒk] *sb* påfugl(hane).

peak [pi:k] *sb* **1** topp; nut, tind; spiss; *som adj* topp-; **2** høydepunkt; klimaks, toppunkt; **3** (lue)-skygge. **peaked** [pi:kt] *adj* = *peaky*. **peak hours** *sb fl* rushtid. **peaky** ['pi:kɪ] *adj* **A** spiss; toppet; **B** mager, uttæret.

peal [pi:l] **I** *sb* **1** kiming, (klokke)ringing; **2** klokkespill; **3** brak, smell; brus(ing); **~***s of laughter* lattersalver; **~***s of thunder* torden|brak, -skrall; **II** *vb* **1** kime/ringe (med); **2** brake, drønne; skralle; runge.

pear [peə] *sb* pære (og pæretre).

pearl [pɜ:l] *sb* **1** perle; *mother-of-~* perlemor; **2** (perle)gryn. **pearl-diver** *sb* perledykker. **pearly** ['pɜ:lɪ] *adj* **1** perlelignende *etc*; perle-; **2** perle|brodert, -smykket.

peasant ['peznt] *sb* bonde (især som klassebetegnelse, jf *farmer*). **peasantry** ['pezntrɪ] *sb koll* bondestand, bønder.

peat [pi:t] *sb* torv.

pebble ['pebl] *sb* (små)stein.

peck [pek] **A I** *sb* **1** hakking *etc*; **2** (lett) kyss; **3** *slang* mat; **II** *vb* **1** hakke (med nebb); pikke, plukke; knerte, (små)banke; **~** *at* hakke etter; hakke på (dvs stadig kritisere etc); **2** kysse (lett, på kinnet etc); **3** småspise; **~** *at one's food* pirke i maten; være matlei; **B** *sb a)* en måleenhet, se midtsidene; *b)* bråte, mengde. **peckish** ['pekɪʃ] *adj dgl* (små)sulten.

peculiar [pɪ'kju:lɪə] *adj* **1** merkelig, rar; eiendommelig, påfallende; **2** særegen (*to* for); særlig, særskilt; spesiell. **peculiarity** [pɪˌkju:lɪ'ærətɪ] *sb* særegenhet *etc*.

pecuniary [pɪ'kju:nɪərɪ] *adj* pengemessig, penge-; pekuniær.

pedal ['pedl] **1** *sb* pedal; **2** *vb* bruke pedaler; drive med pedal(er); trå (sykkel etc).

peddle ['pedl] *vb* falby/selge (ved dørene, på gaten etc). **peddler** ['pedlə] *sb* kramkar, kremmer; dør-/gateselger.

pedestal ['pedɪstl] *sb* fotstykke, sokkel; pidestall. **pedestrian** [pɪ'destrɪən] **I** *adj* **1** fotgjenger-; **2** alminnelig, ordinær; kjedelig, snusfornuftig; **II** *sb* fotgjenger. **pedestrian crossing** *sb* fotgjengerovergang.

pedigree ['pedɪgri:] *sb* stamtavle.

pedlar ['pedlə] *sb* = *peddler*.

peek [pi:k] **1** *sb* kikk, titt; **2** *vi* kikke/titte (*at* på).

peel [pi:l] **I** *sb* skall, skrell; skinn; **II** *vb* **1** skrelle; flekke/flå (*off* av); **2** flasse/skalle (av); **3** *slang: keep one's eyes ~ed* holde øynene stive. **peelings** ['pi:lɪŋz] *sb fl* skall, skrell; avskalling; flass.

peep [pi:p] **A I** *sb* **1** glimt; kikk, titt; **2** = *~hole*; **II** *vi* kikke/titte (*at* på); **~** *out* titte frem; *Peeping Tom* kikker; **B 1** *sb* kvitring *etc*; **2** *vi* kvitre, pipe. **peephole** ['pi:phəʊl] *sb* kikkhull.

peer [pɪə] **A** *vi:* **~** *at/into* granske, mønstre; se nærmere/nøye på; **B** *sb* **1** likemann; jevnbyrdig (person); **2** *(~ of the realm)* lord; (høy) adelsmann (med rett til sete i Overhuset). **peer|age** ['pɪərɪdʒ] *sb* **1** adelsstand, høyadel; **2** adelskalender. **~ess** ['pɪərɪs] *sb* (høy) adelsdame; lords hustru. **~less** ['pɪəlɪs] *adj* makeløs, uforlignelig.

peevish ['pi:vɪʃ] *adj* gretten, grinet; sur.

peg [peg] **I** *sb* **1** plugg; pinne, stift; spuns, tapp; *(clothes-~)* (kles)klype; *(hat-~)* (hatte-/kles)knagg; *(tent-~)* teltplugg; **2** *dgl* pinne (dvs dram, drink); **II** *vb* **1** feste (med plugger etc); **~** *down* plugge *etc* fast; binde/tjore (fast); **~** *out* merke opp (med pæler); stikke ut; *dgl* pigge av (dvs dø); **2** stabilisere (kurs, pris etc).

pellet ['pelɪt] *sb* pille; liten ball/kule.

pelt [pelt] **A I** *sb* **1** pisking (av regn); slag; **2** *at full ~* i full fart; **II** *vb* **1** bombardere; kaste, kyle; over|-dynge, -øse; **2** piske (om regn); hølje/pøse ned; **B** *sb* (uberedt) skinn; hud.

pelvis ['pelvɪs] *sb* bekken.

pen [pen] **A 1** *sb* penn (og pennesplitt); **2** *vt* skrive/tegne med penn; **B 1** *sb* kve; **2** *vt:* **~** *in/up* sperre/stenge inne; *fig* demme opp. **pen|-case** *sb* pennal. **~-holder** *sb* penneskaft. **~ name** *sb* forfatternavn, pseudonym.

penal ['pi:nl] *adj* straff(e)-; straffbar; straffskyldig. **penalize** ['pi:nəlaɪz] *vt* **1** erklære/gjøre straffbar; sette straff for; **2** gi straffepoeng *etc*; handikappe. **penal servitude** *sb* straffarbeid. **penalty** ['penltɪ] *sb* **1** straff; **2** bot, mulkt; **3** straffepoeng; handikap. **penalty kick** *sb* straffespark. **penance** ['penəns] *sb* bot (og botsøvelse).

pencil ['pensl] **1** *sb* blyant; **2** *vt* skrive/tegne med blyant.

pendant ['pendənt] **I** *adj* = *pendent*; **II** *sb* **1** øredobb (og andre slags hengesmykker); anheng; **2** hengelampe; **3** = *pennant*. **pendent** ['pendənt] *adj* **1** hengende; **2** uavgjort. **pending** ['pendıŋ] **I** *adj* uavgjort; *jur* verserende; **II** *prep* **1** i påvente av; **2** under.

pendulum ['pendjʊləm] *sb* pendel.

penetrate ['penıtreıt] *vb* **1** bryte/trenge gjennom; **2** ~ *into* trenge inn i; **3** gjennom|syre, -trenge; **4** vinne innsikt i; **5** gjennomskue. **penetration** [,penı'treıʃn] *sb* **1** gjennomtrengning *etc*; **2** innsikt; kløkt, skarpsinn.

penguin ['peŋgwın] *sb* pingvin.

peninsula [p'nınsjʊlə] *sb* halvøy.

penitence ['penıtəns] *sb* anger; bot (og botsøvelse). **penitent** ['penıtənt] **1** *adj* angrende; botferdig; **2** *sb* botferdig synder; skriftebarn. **penitentiary** [,penı'tenʃərı] *sb* **1** *især US* fengsel; **2** forbedringsanstalt.

pennant ['penənt] *sb* stander, vimpel. **pennant line** *sb petro* bøyeline.

penniless ['penılıs] *adj* pengelens. **penny** ['penı] *sb* **1** en myntenhet, se midtsidene; **2** pennystykke; pengestykke, skilling; *US dgl* cent; *spend a* ~ gå på et visst sted (dvs toalettet).

pension ['penʃn] **1** *sb* pensjon; **2** *vt* (~ *off*) pensjonere. **pensionable** ['penʃnəbl] *adj* pensjonsberettiget. **pensioner** ['penʃnə] *sb* pensjonist. **pension | plan, ~ scheme** *sb* pensjonsordning.

pensive ['pensıv] *adj* tankefull; tenksom.

pent [pent] *adj*: ~ *in/up* innestengt/oppdemmet (især *fig*).

pentagon ['pentəgən] *sb* **1** femkant; **2** *(the) Pentagon* forsvarsdepartementet i USA. **pentagon platform** *sb petro* pentagonplattform.

Pentecost ['pentıkɒst] *sb* (jødenes) pinse.

penthouse ['penthaʊs] *sb* **1** halvtak; (le)skur; **2** *især US* takleilighet (ofte påkostet og attraktiv).

penultimate [pen'ʌltımət] *adj* nest sist.

penury ['penjʊrı] *sb* armod, fattigdom.

people ['pi:pl] **I** *sb* **1** *koll* folk, mennesker; **2** familie, slekt; **3** befolkning; **4** folk(eslag), nasjon; **5** *US: the People* påtalemyndigheten(e); **II** *vt* befolke.

pep [pep] *sb slang* futt, pepp, tæl. **pep talk** *sb* oppmuntrende/stimulerende *etc* tale; *ofte* opp|stiver, -strammer.

pepper ['pepə] **I** *sb* pepper; **II** *vt* **1** pepre; *fig* krydre; **2** bombardere/la det hagle (*with* med); **3** drysse, strø; overså.

per [pɜ:] *prep* per, pr.; ~ *cent* prosent; ~ *thousand* promille; *as* ~ *agreement* etter/ifølge avtale. **percentage** [pə'sentıdʒ] *sb* prosent(andel).

perambulator [pə'ræmbjʊleıtə] *sb* barnevogn.

perceive [pə'si:v] *vt* **1** oppfatte (med sansene); legge merke til; **2** forstå, (inn)se. **perceptible** [pə'septəbl] *adj* merkbar. **perception** [pə'sepʃn] *sb* oppfatning (dvs oppfatningsevne); sansning. **perceptive** [pə'septıv] *adj* (sanse)var, våken.

perch [pɜ:tʃ] **A I** *sb* **1** vagle; **2** høy beliggenhet; høyt stade; **3** lengdeenhet, se midtsidene; **II** *vb* **1** vagle seg; sitte/sette seg på vagle; **2** kneise/ligge (høyt og fritt) over; **B** *sb* abbor.

percolate ['pɜ:kəleıt] *vb* **1** filtrere(s); **2** (la) sive gjennom. **percolator** ['pɜ:kəleıtə] *sb* kaffetrakter.

percussion [pə'kʌʃn] *sb* **1** (an)slag; (sammen)støt; **2** (~ *instruments*) slag|instrumenter, -verk; trommer.

perdition [pə'dıʃn] *sb* ruin(ering); undergang; ødeleggelse.

peremptory [pə'remptərı] *adj* bydende; bestemt, myndig.

perennial [pə'renıəl] **I** *adj* **1** varig; konstant, stadig; evig(varende); **2** flerårig (om planter); **II** *sb* staude.

perfect A ['pɜ:fıkt] **I** *adj* **1** fullkommen, perfekt; **2** fullendt; fullstendig; **3** perfektum-; **II** *sb* perfektum; **B** [pə'fekt] *vt* full|ende, -føre; fullkommengjøre, perfeksjonere. **perfection** [pə'fekʃn] *sb* fullkommenhet *etc*; perfeksjon.

perfidious [pə'fıdıəs] *adj* troløs; falsk, svikefull. **perfidy** ['pɜ:fıdı] *sb* troløshet *etc*.

perforate ['pɜ:fəreıt] *vb* **1** (gjennom)hulle, perforere; **2** gjennomtrenge. **perforation** [,pɜ:fə'reıʃn] *sb* (gjennom)hulling, perforering; tagging (på frimerker). **perforator** ['pɜ:fəreıtə] *sb* perforator, hullemaskin; *data* huller.

perform [pə'fɔ:m] *vb* **1** utføre; foreta; *dgl* gjøre; *rel* forrette; **2** oppføre, spille; opptre. **performance** [pə'fɔ:məns] *sb* **1** utførelse *etc*; **2** oppføring *etc*; forestilling; **3** *data etc* yteevne. **performer** [pə'fɔ:mə] *sb* (utøvende) kunstner etc.

perfume 1 ['pɜ:fju:m] *sb* parfyme; **2** [pə'fju:m] *vi* parfymere.

perfunctory [pə'fʌŋktərı] *adj* likegyldig, skjødesløs; mekanisk, overfladisk.

perhaps [pə'hæps] *adv* kanskje.

peril ['perəl] *sb* (stor) fare. **perilous** ['perələs] *adj* farlig; farefull; risikofylt.

perimeter [pə'rımıtə] *sb* (om)krets; ytre forsvarsverker.

period ['pıərıəd] *sb* **1** (tids)periode; tid, tidsrom; **2** periode, setningsgruppe; **3** punktum. **periodic** [,pıərı'ɒdık] *adj* periodisk. **periodical** [,pıərı'ɒdıkl] **1** *adj* = *periodic*; **2** *sb* tidsskrift.

peripheral [pə'rıfərəl] *adj* perifer(isk), ytre. **peripheral device** *sb data* ytre enhet.

perish ['perıʃ] *vb* **1** omkomme; **2** forgå; gå til grunne; gå under; bli ødelagt; **3** gå (for)tapt; **4** *gml* ødelegge. **perishable** ['perıʃəbl] *adj* forgjengelig; *om matvarer* (lett) bedervelig.

perjure ['pɜ:dʒə] *vt*: ~ *oneself* begå mened; avgi falsk forklaring/sverge falsk (i retten). **perjury** ['pɜ:dʒərı] *sb* mened *etc*.

perk [pɜ:k] *vb*: ~ *up* komme seg; kvikne til. **perky** ['pɜ:kı] *adj 1* kaut, kry; **2** livlig.

permanence ['pɜ:mənəns] *sb* varighet. **permanent** ['pɜ:mənənt] **1** *adj* permanent, varig; **2** *sb* (~

wave) permanent (i håret).

permeate ['pɜ:mɪeɪt] *vb* trenge gjennom; gjennom|syre, trenge.

permissible [pə'mɪsəbl] *adj* tillatelig. **permission** [pə'mɪʃn] *sb* lov, tillatelse. **permissive** [pə'mɪsɪv] *adj* (litt for) frisinnet (overbærende, tolerant etc). **permit 1** ['pɜ:mɪt] *sb* lov, tillatelse (især skriftlig); adgangstegn, passerseddel *etc*; **2** [pə'mɪt] *vb* tillate; gi lov/tillatelse; ~ *of* gi adgang til/rom for; åpne mulighet(er) for.

pernicious [pə'nɪʃəs] *adj* skadelig; ondartet, pernisiøs.

peroxide [pə'rɒksaɪd] **1** *adj:* ~ *hair* (vannstoff)-bleket hår; **2** *sb* peroksid.

perpetrate ['pɜ:pɪtreɪt] *vt* begå/forøve (især forbrytelse). **perpetrator** ['pɜ:pɪtreɪtə] *sb* gjernings|-kvinne, -mann.

perpetual [pə'petʃʊəl] *adj* **1** evig(varende); **2** uopphørlig; *dgl* evinnelig, konstant, stadig. **perpetuate** [pə'petʃʊeɪt] *vt* opprettholde (bevare, sikre etc) (for all fremtid).

perplex [pə'pleks] *vt* forvirre; sette i forlegenhet.

persecute ['pɜ:sɪkju:t] *vt* forfølge (for politiske meninger, religiøs tro etc). **persecution** [,pɜ:sɪ'kju:ʃn] *sb* forfølgelse. **persecutor** [,pɜ:sɪ'kju:tə] *sb* forfølger; plageånd.

perseverance [,pɜ:sɪ'vɪərəns] *sb* standhaftighet *etc*. **persevere** [,pɜ:sɪ'vɪə] *vi* være standhaftig; ~ *in/at/with* fortsette (bli ved, holde frem etc) med. **persevering** [,pɜ:sɪ'vɪərɪŋ] *adj* standhaftig; utholdende; iherdig.

persist [pə'sɪst] *vi* **1** ~ *in* fortsette (drive på, ture frem etc) med; holde fast ved; **2** (ved)vare; holde (seg). **persistence** [pə'sɪstəns] *sb* hardnakkethet *etc*. **persistent** [pə'sɪstənt] *adj* **1** hardnakket; iherdig, seig; strid; **2** stadig, vedvarende.

person ['pɜ:sn] *sb* **1** person; individ; *in* ~ personlig; **2** utseende; skikkelse. **personable** ['pɜ:snəbl] *adj* likende(s); pen, tiltrekkende. **personage** ['pɜ:snɪdʒ] *sb* personlighet (dvs fremragende, kjent etc person). **personal** ['pɜ:snl] **I** *adj* **1** personlig; privat(-); egen(-); **2** kropps-; **II** *sb fl US* personlig(spalte). **personal | computer (PC)** *sb data* personlig datamaskin (PD). ~ **data** *sb fl data* persondata. **personality** [,pɜ:sə'nælətɪ] *sb* **1** personlighet (dvs personlige egenskaper); **2** *fl* personligheter (dvs nærgående, uforskammede etc bemerkninger); **3** = *personage*. **personification** [pə,sɒnɪfɪ'keɪʃn] *sb* personifisering *etc*. **personify** [pə'sɒnɪfaɪ] *vt* personifisere, legemliggjøre. **personnel** [,pɜ:sə'nel] *sb* personale, stab; mannskap(er); *mil* personell. **personnel | manager, ~ officer** *sb* personalsjef.

perspective [pə'spektɪv] **I** *adj* perspektivisk, perspektiv-; **II** *sb* **1** perspektiv; **2** fremtids|perspektiv(er), (-)utsikter.

perspicacious [,pɜ:spɪ'keɪʃəs] *adj* klarsynt, skarp(synt). **perspicacity** [,pɜ:spɪ'kæsətɪ] *sb* klarsyn; skarp|sindighet, -sinn. **perspicuous** [pə'spɪkjʊəs] *adj* klar, lettfattelig.

perspiration [,pɜ:spə'reɪʃn] *sb* svette; svetting. **perspire** [pə'spaɪə] *vi* svette.

persuade [pə'sweɪd] *vt* **1** overtale; **2** overbevise; *~d of* overbevist om; sikker på. **persuasion** [pə'sweɪʒn] *sb* **1** overtalelse (og overtalelsesevne); **2** overbevisning; (livs)syn, tro. **persuasive** [pə'sweɪsɪv] *adj* overtalende *etc*; veltalende.

pert [pɜ:t] *adj* nebbet, nesevis.

pertain [pə'teɪn] *vi:* ~ *to* **1** høre med til; være forbundet med; **2** angå, vedrøre.

pertinacious [,pɜ:tɪ'neɪʃəs] *adj* hardnakket, iherdig. **pertinacity** [,pɜ:tɪ'næsətɪ] *sb* hardnakkethet etc.

pertinent ['pɜ:tɪnənt] *adj* aktuell; relevant; treffende.

perturb [pə'tɜ:b] *vt* forstyrre, uroe; gjøre engstelig.

pervade [pə'veɪd] *vt* gjennom|strømme, -trenge; gjennomsyre. **pervasion** [pə'veɪʃn] *sb* gjennomtrenging *etc*. **pervasive** [pə'veɪsɪv] *adj* gjennomtrengende.

perverse [pə'vɜ:s] *adj* **1** fordervet, skakkjørt; ond; **2** forstokket; slem, vrang(villig). **perversion** [pə'vɜ:ʃn] *sb* **I** (jf *perverse*) fordervethet *etc*; **II** (jf *pervert II*) **1** forvanskning *etc*; **2** pervertering; perversjon. **perversity** [pə'vɜ:sətɪ] *sb* perversitet. **pervert I** ['pɜ:vɜ:t] *sb* pervers person; **II** [pə'vɜ:t] *vt* **1** forvanske; for|dreie, -vrenge; **2** for|derve, -kvakle; pervertere. **perverted** [pə'vɜ:tɪd] *adj* pervers; abnorm, unormal.

pest [pest] *sb* **1** plage(ånd); *fig også* pest; **2** skadedyr. **pester** ['pestə] *vt* bry, plage; trakassere. **pestilence** ['pestɪləns] *sb* (far)sott, pest.

pet [pet] **A 1** *adj* kjæle-; yndlings-; **2** *sb* kjæle|-degge, -dyr; **3** *vt* kjærtegne; kjæle (intimt) med; **B** *sb* grettenhet.

petal ['petl] *sb* kronblad.

peter ['pi:tə] *vi:* ~ *out* ebbe ut; løpe ut i sanden.

petition [pɪ'tɪʃn] **I** *sb* **1** (skriftlig) andragende/anmodning; bønnskrift, petisjon; **2** *(election ~)* valgprotest; **II** *vt* anmode (be, søke etc) om.

petrified ['petrɪfaɪd] *adj* forsteinet; *fig* lamslått; skrekkslagen. **petrify** ['petrɪfaɪ] *vb* forsteine(s).

petrochemical [,petrəʊ'kemɪkl] *adj* petrokjemisk. **petrol** ['petrəl] *sb* bensin. **petroleum** [pɪ'trəʊljəm] *sb* mineralolje, petroleum. **petroleum | coke** *sb petro* petroleumskoks. ~ **gas** *sb petro* petroleumsgass. ~ **jelly** *sb petro* vaselin. **petrol station** *sb* bensinstasjon.

petticoat ['petɪkəʊt] *sb* under|kjole, -skjørt.

pettish ['petɪʃ] *adj* gretten, grinet; vranten.

petty ['petɪ] *adj* **1** liten, ubetydelig; **2** smålig, tarvelig; **3** lavere (grad, rang etc); under-. **petty| cash** *sb* småpenger. ~ **larceny** *sb* nasking.

petulance ['petjʊləns] *sb* grinethet *etc*. **petulant** ['petjʊlənt] *adj* grinet; gretten, irritabel.

pew [pju:] *sb* kirkestol.

pewter ['pju:tə] *sb* tinn(saker).

phantasy ['fæntəsɪ] *sb* = *fantasy*. **phantom** ['fæntəm] *sb* fantom; spøkelse; ånd (og åndesyn). **phantom space** *sb data* usynlig mellomrom.

phase [feɪz] *sb* stadium, trinn; fase.

pheasant ['feznt] *sb* fasan.

phenomenal [fə'nɒmɪnəl] *adj* **1** fenomen-; **2** fenomenal. **phenomenon** [fə'nɒmɪnən] *sb* **1** fenomen; foreteelse; **2** *dgl* mirakel, viduner(barn).

philander [fɪ'lændə] *vi* flørte; kurtisere (uten alvorlige hensikter).

phlegm [flem] *sb* **1** slim; **2** flegma.

phone [fəʊn] *fork* for *telephone* **1** *sb* telefon; **2** *vb* ringe, telefonere. **phone | booth, ~ box** *sb* telefon|boks, -kiosk.

phoney ['fəʊnɪ] *dgl, slang* **I** *adj* forloren, uekte; jukse-, svindel-; *også* liksom-; **II** *sb* **1** juks; humbug, lureri; svindel; bløff; **2** bløffmaker, svindler.

phosphorescent [ˌfɒsfə'resnt] *adj* fosforescerende, selvlysende.

photo ['fəʊtəʊ] *sb dgl* foto(grafi). **photograph** ['fəʊtəgrɑ:f] *sb* fotografi. **photographer** [fə'tɒgrəfə] *sb* fotograf. **photographic** [ˌfəʊtə'græfɪk] *adj* fotografisk. **photography** [fə'tɒgrəfɪ] *sb* **1** fotografi (som håndverk/kunst); **2** fotografering.

phrase [freɪz] **1** *sb* ordforbindelse; (kortere) uttrykk, vending; **2** *vt* formulere; uttrykke (i ord). **phrase | book** *sb* parlør. **~-monger** *sb* frasemaker.

physic ['fɪzɪk] *sb dgl* medisin. **physical** ['fɪzɪkl] *adj* **1** fysisk; **2** håndgripelig, materiell; ytre; **3** legemlig; **4** kjødelig, sanselig. **physical | layer** *sb data* fysisk lag. **~ level** *sb data* fysisk nivå. **~ record** *sb data* fysisk post. **~ training** *sb* kroppsøving. **physician** [fɪ'zɪʃn] *sb* lege. **physicist** ['fɪzɪsɪst] *sb* fysiker. **physics** ['fɪzɪks] *sb fl* fysikk (som fag).

pick [pɪk] **A I** *sb* **1** valg (dvs anledning/rett etc til å velge); utvalg; utplukk; elite; *fig også* blomst, krem; **2** pirker; stikke(r); pigg, spiss; **II** *vt* **1** plukke, sanke; samle inn (opp, sammen etc); **~** *up* plukke/ta *etc* opp; finne; få tak i; hente (og *slang* hekte = arrestere); skaffe (og lære/tilegne) seg; *fig* komme seg; ta seg opp; **~** *up courage* fatte mot; **~** *up with* bli kjent med; slå an med; **2** *(~ out)* plukke ut; søke/velge (seg) ut; bestemme seg for; hakke på (dvs stadig kritisere etc); **~** *(up) sides (sport)* velge lag; **3** plukke (og pille, pirke etc) på; pille/pirke (seg) i/på; **~** *at* pirke *etc* i/på; hakke på (dvs stadig kritisere etc); **4** rappe, stjele; **B 1** *sb (~axe)* (pigg)hakke; **2** *vb* hakke (opp); bruke hakke (på). **picket** ['pɪkɪt] **I** *sb* **1** (gjerde)sprosse; (tjor)pæl; stake, stang; **2** pikett; vakt|avdeling, -patrulje, post; **3** streikevakt; **II** *vt* **1** gjerde inn; **2** binde, tjore; **3** bevokte; passe (på); avpatruljere; **4** blokkere (streikerammet bedrift etc); gå (som) streikevakt foran.

pick device *sb data* pekeenhet.

pickle ['pɪkl] **I** *sb* **1** (salt)lake; **2** knipe, vanskelighet; **II** *vt* (lake)salte; legge ned i lake; sylte.

pick|lock *sb* dirk. **~pocket** *sb* lommetyv. **~up** *sb* **1** oppsamling (etc, jf *pick A II 1*); **2** *a)* (grammofon)-pickup; *b)* strømavtaker; **3** (mindre) varebil; **4** tilfeldig bekjentskap; gatepike; **5** *fig* fremgang, oppgang; økning. **pickup boat** *sb petro* redningsbåt.

picnic ['pɪknɪk] **I** *sb* **1** (land)tur, utflukt; **2** *dgl* bare barnemat/blåbær; ren lek; **II** *vi* dra på (land)-tur/utflukt.

pictorial [pɪk'tɔ:rɪəl] **I** *adj* **1** billedmesig; billed-; **2** malerisk; **II** *sb* billedblad. **picture** ['pɪktʃə] **I** *sb* **1** bilde; *data* mønster; **2** *fig* (uttrykt) bilde/likhet; **3** *fig* (vakkert) syn; **4** *gml* (spille)film; *go to the ~s* gå på kino; **II** *vt* **1** male; *fig også* skildre; **2** forestille seg. **picture | element** *sb data* billedelement. **~ palace** *sb* kino. **~ postcard** *sb* prospektkort; *fig* glansbilde. **picturesque** [ˌpɪktʃə'resk] *adj* **1** malerisk; **2** *fig* levende, malende. **picture theatre** *sb* = *~ palace*.

pidgin ['pɪdʒɪn] *sb (Pidgin English)* pidginengelsk [slags blandingsengelsk som især snakkes i asiatiske og visse afrikanske havnestrøk].

pie [paɪ] *sb* pai, postei.

piece [pi:s] **I** *sb* **1** bit(e), del, stykke; **~** *by* **~** stykke for stykke; stykkevis; *by the* **~** per stykke; enkeltvis, stykkevis; *come/go to ~s* falle fra hverandre; gå i stykker; bryte/falle sammen; *take to ~s* ta fra hverandre; **2** eksemplar; eksempel (på); tilfelle (av); **~** *of evidence* bevis; **~** *of furniture* møbel; **~** *of (good) advice* (godt) råd; **~** *of good luck* hell; **~** *of impudence* uforskammethet (dvs uforskammet bemerkning etc); **~** *of information* opplysning; **~** *of news* nyhet (dvs nyhetsmelding); **3** (avis)artikkel *etc*; (musikk)stykke; (teater)stykke; **4** (penge)stykke; **5** kanon, skyts; gevær; **6** brikke (til brettspill); **II** *vt* **1** lappe (sammen); **2** **~** *together* sette sammen (av småbiter); *dgl* flikke sammen. **piecemeal** ['pi:smi:l] *adv* stykkevis; stykke for stykke.

pier ['pɪə] *sb* **1** (brygge)utstikker; (landings)-brygge; molo; **2** (bro)pilar.

pierce ['pɪəs] *vt* gjennombore; bore hull i; trenge inn (i). **piercing** ['pɪəsɪŋ] *adj* gjennom|borende, -trengende.

piety ['paɪətɪ] *sb* fromhet, gudfryktighet.

pig [pɪg] *sb* **1** gris; *fig også* svin; **2** råjernsblokk; **3** *petro* pigg; rørskrape; skyttel.

pigeon ['pɪdʒɪn] *sb* **1** due; **2** godfjott. **pigeon house** *sb* due|hus, -slag.

piggish ['pɪgɪʃ] *adj* **1** griset, skitten; **2** grisk, grådig. **piggy** ['pɪgɪ] **1** *adj dgl* = *piggish 2*; **2** *sb* smågris. **piggy|back** *sb petro* ekstraanker. **~ bank** *sb* sparegris. **pig|-headed** *adj* sta. **~ iron** *sb* råjern (i blokker). **~ receiver** *sb petro* piggsluse. **~skin** *sb* svinelær. **~sty** *sb* grisehus.

pike [paɪk] **A** *sb* **1** pigg, spiss; spidd; **2** lanse; **3** *(turn~)* veibom (og bomvei); *US* (større, avgiftsbelagt) motorvei; **B** *sb* gjedde. **pikestaff** ['paɪkstɑ:f] *sb* lanseskaft.

pile [paɪl] **A** *sb* pæl, påle; **B I** *sb* **1** dynge, haug; bunke, stabel; masse; **2** (større) bygning; (bygnings)-kompleks; **3** batteri, tørrelement; **4** *(atomic ~)* atomreaktor; **II** *vt* dynge/hauge/stable (*up* opp/sammen);

~ *on* bygge/stable opp; lesse på; ~ *up* bygge/stable opp; hope (seg) opp; kollidere, krasje; krasjlande; **C** *sb* lo (på ullstoff etc); hår, pels. **pile | driver** *sb* rambukk. **~up** *sb* kjedekollisjon; (kraftig) kollisjon; krasjlanding.

pilfer ['pɪlfə] *vb* naske, rappe; stjele

pill [pɪl] *sb* pille, tablett; *the Pill* pillen (dvs p-pillen); *be/go on the* ~ bruke p-piller (regelmessig).

pillage ['pɪlɪdʒ] **1** *sb* plyndring *etc*; **2** *vb* plyndre, herje.

pillar ['pɪlə] *sb* **1** søyle; stolpe; **2** pilar, støtte. **pillarbox** *sb GB* postkasse (i form av en søyle).

pillion ['pɪlɪən] *sb* baksete (på motorsykkel); *ride* ~ sitte bakpå.

pillory ['pɪlərɪ] **1** *sb* gapestokk; **2** *vt* sette/stille i gapestokk.

pillow ['pɪləʊ] *sb* (hode)pute. **pillow|-case, ~-slip** *sb* putevar.

pilot ['paɪlət] **I** *som adj* **1** for-, forløper-; **2** forsøks-, prøve-; **II** *sb* **1** fører, guide; kjentmann; los; **2** pilot; **III** *vt* **1** føre; lose; **2** navigere, styre. **pilot | flame** *sb petro* beredskapsflamme, sikringsflamme. ~ **scheme** *sb* prøvedrift.

pimp [pɪmp] **1** *sb* hallik; **2** *vi* drive hallikvirksomhet.

pimple ['pɪmpl] *sb* filipens, kvise.

pin [pɪn] **I** *sb* **1** nål (og knappenål, pyntenål. sikkerhetsnål etc); **2** stift; bolt; (stemme)skrue; plugg, tapp; **3** *(rolling-~)* kjevle; **II** *vt* feste (hefte, sette fast etc) med nål(er); ~ *down* holde/klemme *etc* fast; holde nede; ~ *up* stifte (sette, slå etc) opp.

pinafore ['pɪnəfɔ:] *sb* (barne)forkle.

pinboard ['pɪnbɔ:d] *sb data* pluggbord.

pincers ['pɪnsəz] *sb fl* **1** *(pair of ~)* (knipe)tang; **2** klo, saks.

pinch [pɪntʃ] **I** *sb* **1** klyp (og klyping etc); **2** klype; ~ *of snuff* pris snus; **3** klemme, knipe(tak); *at a* ~ i et knipetak; **II** *vb* **1** klype, knipe; klemme; stramme; **2** knipe (på); **3** *dgl* rappe, stjele; **4** *slang* hekte, huke. **pinchpenny** *sb dgl* gnier.

pin-cushion ['pɪnkʊʃn] *sb* nålepute.

pine [paɪn] **A** *sb* furu(tre); **B** *vi* **1** *(~ away)* tæres hen; vantrives; **2** ~ *after/for* lengte (sukke, vansmekte etc) etter. **pineapple** ['paɪn,æpl] *sb* ananas.

pin|head *sb* knappenålshode. **~hole** *sb* ørlite hull.

pinion ['pɪnɪən] **A** *sb* drev; (lite) tannhjul; **B I** *sb* **1** vinge(spiss); **2** svingfjær; **II** *vt* binde armene (fast til kroppen) på.

pink ['pɪŋk] **A I** *adj* **1** lyserød; rødmusset; **2** radikal; sosialistisk; *US ofte* kommunistisk; **II** *sb* **1** lyserødt, lyserød farge; **2** nellik; **3** radikaler; sosialist; *US ofte* kommunist; **B** *vt* gjennom|bore, -hulle; perforere; **C** *vi* banke (om motorbank).

pinnacle ['pɪnəkl] *sb* **1** spir, tårn; (mur)tind; **2** topp.

pin-point ['pɪnpɔɪnt] *sb* nålespiss; *fig også* knappenålshode; *som vt* lokalisere; presisere; sette fingeren på. **pin-prick** ['pɪnprɪk] *sb* nålestikk.

pint [paɪnt] *sb* **1** et hulmål, se midtsidene; **2** *dgl a)* ≈ halvflaske (melk etc); *b)* halvliter (øl).

pioneer [,paɪə'nɪə] **1** *sb* pioner; kolonist, nybygger; banebryter, foregangs|kvinne, -mann; **2** *vb* være pioner *etc*; bane vei (for).

pious ['paɪəs] *adj* from.

pip [pɪp] *sb* **A** (frukt)|kjerne, -stein; **B 1** øye (på terning); **2** tegn (på spillkort); **3** stjerne (i distinksjon); **C** blipp (i radarsignal); pipp (i tidssignal etc).

pipe [paɪp] **I** *sb* **1** rør(ledning); **2** pipe; fløyte; **3** *dgl* luftrør; **4** *(tobacco ~)* (tobakks)pipe; **5** (vin)fat (se for øvrig midtsidene om ~ som hulmål); **II** *vb* **1** føre/lede gjennom rør; **2** pipe (dvs blåse på pipe etc); ~ *down (dgl)* hisse seg ned; ~ *up* spille opp; stemme i; *dgl* diske/varte opp med; **3** tute; hvine, plystre; **4** besette/pynte med snorer. **pipe | bowl** *sb* pipehode. ~ **cleaner** *sb* piperenser. ~ **deck** *sb petro* rørdekk. **~dream** *sb* ønskedrøm; luftslott. **~line** *sb petro* rørledning. **~line plug** *sb petro* rørplugg. **piper** ['paɪpə] *sb* piper; *især* sekkepiper (= sekkepipeblåser); *pay the ~ (dgl)* betale fornøyelsen/moroa. **pipe | section** *sb petro* rørstrekk. ~ **string** *sb petro* rørstreng. ~ **trench** *sb petro* rørgate. **piping** ['paɪpɪŋ] **I** *adj* pipende *etc*; **II** *adv:* ~ *hot* skåldende het; **III** *sb* **1** *koll* rør; rør|opplegg, -system; **2** piping *etc*. **pipe|line** *sb* rørledning; *især* oljeledning; *fig* direkte forbindelse. ~ **rack** *sb* pipestativ. ~ **stem** *sb* pipemunnstykke.

piquant ['pi:kənt] *adj* pikant; skarp. **pique** [pi:k] **I** *sb* fornærmelse; ergrelse, irritasjon; **II** *vb* **1** fornærme, krenke; såre; **2** egge; pirre; **3** ~ *oneself on* smigre seg med; være stolt av.

piracy ['paɪərəsɪ] *sb* piratvirksomhet, sjørøveri. **pirate** ['paɪərət] **I** *sb* **1** pirat, sjørøver; **2** fribytter/hai (dvs person som stjeler og utnytter andres rettigheter); *også* pirat; **II** *vb* **1** drive sjørøveri; **2** drive piratvirksomhet (jf *I 2*). **pirate | edition** *sb* piratutgave (av bok etc). ~ **transmitter** *sb* piratsender.

pistol ['pɪstl] *sb, vi* (skyte med) pistol.

piston ['pɪstən] *sb* **1** stempel (i forbrenningsmotor etc); **2** ventil (i messingblåseinstrument); pistong. **piston rod** *sb* stempelstang.

pit [pɪt] **A I** *sb* **1** avgrunn, svelg; **2** utgravning (og grav, grop, gruve, (gruve)sjakt etc); **3** fordypning; hulhet, hull; **4** kopparr; **5** *teater* parterre(publikum); **6** *merk* avdeling/seksjon (av børs); **7** depot (under bilveddeløp); **II** *vb* **1** merke (med fordypninger etc); **2** ~ *against* sette/stille opp mot; **B** *sb US* (frukt)|-kjerne, -stein. **pitfall** *sb* dyregrav; fallgruve, felle.

pitch [pɪtʃ] **A I** *sb* **1** kast; **2** (fast) plass/stand; **3** helling (og hellingsvinkel); reisning/skråning (på tak); stigning (på propellblad etc); **4** høyde (og høydepunkt, topp); *mus* tonehøyde; **5** *data* tegn per tomme; **6** *sjø* stamping; **II** *vb* **1** kaste; hive, kyle, slenge; ~ *and toss* kaste på stikka; knipse (krone eller mynt); *(game of)* ~*-and-toss* sjansespill; ~ *in* ta fatt; **2** falle; stupe, styrte; *sjø* stampe; ~ *into* kaste seg over; fare/gyve *etc* løs på; ~ *upon* slå ned på; **3** reise; sette/slå opp (telt); **4** helle, skråne; gi helling; **5** *mus* bestemme tonehøyde; *dgl* slå an tonen; **6** *mil: ~ed battle* regulært slag; **B 1** *sb* bek; **2** *vt* beke. **pitch|-black** *adj* beksvart. **~-dark** *adj* bekmørk(t). **pitcher** ['pɪtʃə] *sb* **A** kaster (især i baseball etc); **B** krukke; (stor) mugge. **pitchfork I** *sb* høygaffel; **II** *vt* **1** ta med/på høygaffel; **2** *mil etc* kaste/sette inn (mannskaper, materiell etc). **pitchpine** ['pɪtʃpaɪn] *sb* (bek)furu.

pith [pɪθ] *sb* **1** marg; **2** kjerne; *fig* kraft, saft. **pith-helmet** *sb* (slags) tropehjelm; ≈ korkhjelm. **pithy** ['pɪθɪ] *adj* margfull; kraftig, saftig; fyndig.

pitiable ['pɪtɪəbl] *adj* = *pitiful 2/3*. **pitiful** ['pɪtɪful] *adj* **1** medfølende; **2** elendig, ussel; medynkvekkende; **3** foraktelig, ynkverdig. **pitiless** ['pɪtɪlɪs] *adj* ubarmhjertig, nådeløs.

pittance ['pɪtəns] *sb* bagatell/smule (især hva penger angår); nødtørftig underhold.

pity ['pɪtɪ] **I** *sb* **1** med|følelse, -lidenhet, -ynk; **2** synd (dvs noe leit etc); **II** *vt* ha medfølelse *etc* med; synes synd på.

pivot ['pɪvət] **1** *sb* akse; omdreinings|akse, -punkt; **2** *vi* dreie (seg)/svinge (*on* om).

pixie, pixy ['pɪksɪ] *sb* alv, fe.

placard ['plækɑ:d] **1** *sb* oppslag, plakat; **2** *vt* sette opp plakat(er) på.

placate [plə'keɪt] *vt* berolige, stagge; formilde.

place [pleɪs] **I** *sb* **1** plass, rom; **2** (bestemt) sted; *ofte* bosted, hjemsted; åsted; *at my ~* hjemme hos meg; *in ~* på plass; *in ~ of* i stedet for; *in the first ~* for det første; i første omgang; til å begynne med; *også* i utgangspunktet; *in the first/second (etc) ~* for det første/andre (etc); *out of ~* ikke på plass; *fig* malplassert, upassende; *take ~* finne sted; **3** (større) sted; distrikt, område, strøk; *go ~s* farte/reise omkring (i verden); **4** post, stilling; stand; **II** *vt* **1** plassere (og legge, sette etc på et bestemt sted); finne en plass til; deponere; anbringe, investere; *~ confidence in* feste/sette (sin) lit til; **2** *fig* plassere (dvs kjenne igjen etc).

placid ['plæsɪd] *adj* rolig, uforstyrrelig; (like) blid.

plague [pleɪg] **I** *sb* **1** (far)sott; *(bubonic ~)* (bylle)pest; **2** plage; **II** *vt* ergre, plage.

plaice [pleɪs] *sb* rødspette.

plaid [plæd] *sb* (skotsk) pledd; tartan.

plain [pleɪn] **I** *adj* **1** klar, tydelig; lettfattelig; **2** ordinær, vanlig; enkel, liketil; **3** alminnelig (av utseende); *ofte* lite pen; **4** endefrem, likefrem; **5** flat; jevn, slett; **II** *sb* slette(land); vidde; flate, flatland. **plain | clothes** *sb fl* daglig antrekk; *især* sivilklær (i motsetning til uniform); *~-clothes man* sivilkledd politimann. **~ knitting** *sb* rettstrikking. **~ ring** *sb* glatt ring. *the ~* **truth** *sb* den nakne sannhet.

plaintiff ['pleɪntɪf] *sb* saksøker; *find for the ~* ta saksøkerens påstand til følge. **plaintive** ['pleɪntɪv] *adj* klagende; vemodig, vemods|full, -fylt.

plait [plæt] *sb, vt* flette.

plan [plæn] **I** *sb* **1** plan(tegning); (oversikts)tegning; riss; **2** plan; prosjekt; **3** metode; system; **4** fremgangsmåte; **II** *vt* **1** planlegge; **2** *US dgl* akte; ha i sinne; tenke (på å gjøre); regne med.

plane [pleɪn] **A I** *adj* **1** flat, plan; **2** jevn, slett; **II** *sb* **1** (plan) flate; **2** plan; nivå, stadium; **3** bære|flate, -plan; **4** *(aero~, air~)* fly; **5** høvel; **III** *vb* **1** *om fly* plane (ut); *~ down* gå ned i glideflukt; **2** høvle (og planhøvle, sletthøvle; pusse/rette av etc); **B** *sb (~-tree)* platan.

plank [plæŋk] **I** *sb* **1** planke; **2** *pol* program|punkt, -post; **II** *vt* **1** kle med planker; **2** smelle; slenge.

plant [plɑ:nt] **I** *sb* **1** plante, vekst; **2** (anleggs)utstyr; (fabrikk)inventar; maskiner(i); **3** fabrikk; verksted; anlegg; **II** *vt* **1** plante, sette; så; **2** plante *(fig)*; anbringe, plassere; **3** etablere, grunnlegge, opprette. **plantation** [plæn'teɪʃn] *sb* plantasje; (be)plantning; plantefelt. **planter** ['plɑ:ntə] *sb* **1** plantasjeeier; **2** planter (og plantemaskin).

plaque [plɑ:k] *sb* **1** plakett; (minne)plate; **2** plakk (dvs. belegg på tennene).

plaster ['plɑ:stə] **I** *sb* **1** *(~ of Paris)* (brent) gips; **2** (mur)puss; **3** plaster; **II** *vt* **1** gipse; (gips)pusse; **2** plastre; **3** *dgl* kline/smøre på; over|dynge, -øse. **plaster | cast** *sb* **1** gipsavstøpning; **2** gipsbandasje. **~ saint** *sb dgl* helgen(figur); *fig* dydsmønster.

plastic ['plæstɪk] **I** *adj* **1** formbar; plastisk; myk, smidig; **2** plast-; **II** *sb fl* plast (og plast|masse, -stoff etc). **plasticine** ['plæstɪsi:n] *sb* modeller|leire, -masse; plastilin. **plastic surgery** *sb* plastisk kirurgi.

plate [pleɪt] **I** *sb* **1** (flat) tallerken (og kuvert, porsjon; (mat)rett etc); fat; **2** *koll* sølvtøy (og plettvarer); **3** *sport* pokal; **4** plate (av glass, metall etc); *(dental ~)* plate, tannprotese; *(name ~)* navne|plate, -skilt; **5** plansje; (helsides) illustrasjon; **II** *vt* **1** kle med (metall)plater; pansre; **2** plettere (og for|gylle, -nikle, -sølve, -tinne etc). **plateau** ['plætəu] *sb* platå. **plate|-ful** *sb* tallerken(full); porsjon. **~glass** *sb* speilglass. **~layer** *sb* skinnelegger. **~-rack** *sb* tallerkenhylle. **~ shears** *sb fl* platesaks.

platform ['plætfɔ:m] *sb* **1** plattform (og perrong; tribune, talerstol etc); **2** *pol* partiprogram; *især* valgprogram. **platform manager** *sb petro* plattformsjef.

plating ['pleɪtɪŋ] *sb* plettering (etc, jf *plate II 2*); plett(varer).

platitude ['plætɪtju:d] *sb* platthet; selvfølgelighet; floskel.

platoon [plə'tu:n] *sb mil* tropp.

platter ['plætə] *sb* bakke, brett; fat (især av tre).

play [pleɪ] **I** *sb* **1** lek; kapplek, konkurranse; (selskaps)spill; *~ on words* ordspill; lek med ord; **2** moro, spøk; *in ~* for moro skyld; for/på spøk; **3** skuespill, (teater)forestilling; **4** spill (på musikkinstrument); foredrag, fremføring; **5** drift, virksomhet; gang; **6** (bevegelses)frihet, spillerom; slark; **7** spill (av farger, lys etc); **II** *vb* **1** leke (med); leke/more seg; spille (selskapsspill etc); **2** spille (golf, tennis etc); spille/la spille (mot); sette opp (på lag etc mot); spille ut (mot); *~ ball* spille ball; *fig* være med på leken; *~ cricket* spille cricket; *fig* følge spillereglene; *~ fair* spille rent/ærlig spill; *~ foul* spille urent etc; *~ the game* være med på leken; følge spillereglene; *især* være real/skvær etc; ~ *safe* gardere seg; holde seg på den sikre siden; **3** spille ((på) musikkinstrument); foredra, fremføre; **4** spille (teater); oppføre (skuespill); opptre (som); spille (rolle som); oppføre seg som; ~ *hard to get* gjøre seg/spille kostbar; **5** utføre; handle; virke; ~ *a (practical) joke on* gjøre (en) en skøyerstrek; spille (en) et puss; ~ *a trick (up)on* gjøre (en) et pek; misbruke, utnytte; **6** bevege seg (fritt); ha fritt spillerom; **7** spille (om farger, lys etc); **8** rette (lys-, vannstråle etc); la spille (om farger, lys etc); **9** *med adv, prep* ~ **about** (løpe omkring og) leke; ~ **about with** fikle/tukle med; leke med; ~ **along with** holde seg inne/på god fot med; ~ **around** fjase, tøyse; flørte; ~ **at** *(Indians, war etc)* leke (indianere, krig etc); ~ **away** spille bort; *fig* forspille; *sport* spille borte/på bortebane; ~ **back** spille om igjen/tilbake etc; ~ **down** bagatellisere; gjøre lite vesen av; nedvurdere; ~ **for** spille om; ~ *for time* forsøke å vinne tid; ~ **off** prakke på; drive (gjøn) med; *sport* spille omkamp; ~ **off against** spille ut mot; ~ **on** spille på; spille videre; ~ **out** spille ferdig/til ende; utspille (sin rolle); ~ *out a rope* gi ut (et) tau; ~ *out time* trekke ut tiden; ~ **over** spille igjennom; spille om igjen; ~ **to** spille for; ~ **up** gå i gang; spille opp; oppreklamere; ~ **upon** spille på (især *fig*); ~ **up to** snakke etter munnen; spille opp til; smigre; ~ **with** leke/spille (sammen) med; overveie, tenke på.

play|-acting *sb* (komedie)spill; simulering. **~-back** *sb* tilbakespill; avspilling (av båndopptak etc); *fig* motspill, reaksjon. **~bill** *sb* teaterplakat. **~boy** *sb* laps, sprade; velstående dagdriver.

player ['pleɪə] *sb* spiller.

play|fellow *sb* lekekamerat. **~ful** ['pleɪfʊl] *adj* leken, lekelysten. **~goer** *sb* teatergjenger. **~ground** *sb* lekeplass; skolegård; *også fig* tumleplass. **~group** *sb* førskole|gruppe, -klasse. **~house** *sb* teater.

playing|-cards *sb fl* spillkort. ~ **field** *sb* idretts|bane, -plass; lekeplass.

play|mate *sb* = *~fellow*. **~-off** *sb sport* omkamp. **~-pen** *sb* lekegrind. **~room** *sb* leke|rom, -stue. **~-school** *sb* førskole. **~suit** *sb* lekedrakt. **~thing** *sb* leke(tøy). **~wright** *sb* dramatiker, skuespillforfatter.

plea [pli:] *sb* **1** (inntrengende) anmodning/bønn (*for* om); **2** påskudd, unnskyldning; **3** *jur* rettssak; påstand; (saks)innlegg. **plead** [pli:d] *vb* **1** be (inntrengende); bønnfalle/trygle (*for* om); **2** påberope seg; unnskylde seg med; **3** *jur a)* føre sak; pledere (i retten); *b)* erklære/påstå seg; ~ *guilty* erkjenne/erklære seg skyldig.

pleasant ['pleznt] *adj* behagelig, deilig; hyggelig, omgjengelig; vennlig. **pleasantry** ['plezntrɪ] *sb* spøk (og spøkefullhet). **please** [pli:z] *vb* **1** behage, glede; tilfredsstille; gjøre til lags; **2** finne for godt; lyste, ønske; ~ *yourself* gjør som du vil; **3** *(if you) ~!* vær så snill! *coffee for two, ~!* to kaffe, takk! *yes, ~!* ja, takk! **pleased** [pli:zd] *adj* fornøyd, tilfreds; glad. **pleasure** ['pleʒə] *sb* **1** fornøyelse, glede; *find/take ~ in* finne glede i/ved; glede seg over; *have the ~ of* ha gleden av (å); **2** ønske; lyst; *at ~* etter behag/ønske; **3** *som adj* fornøyelses-, lyst-. **pleasure | craft** *sb* lyst|båt, -fartøy. **~-loving, ~-seeking** *adj* nytelsessyk.

pleat [pli:t] **1** *sb* fold, brett; **2** *vt* folde, plissere.

pledge [pledʒ] **I** *sb* **1** pant (og håndpant); garanti, sikkerhet; **2** høytidelig løfte; ~ *of secrecy* taushetsløfte; *sign the ~* undertegne avholdsløfte; *dgl* gå inn i losjen; **II** *vt* **1** pantsette; gi i/som pant; ~ *one's word* gi sitt ord; **2** forplikte seg (til); love; **3** skåle (for).

plentiful ['plentɪfʊl] *adj* rikelig. **plenty** ['plentɪ] *sb* **1** masse; overflod, rikelighet; ~ *of* massevis/rikelig av; *dgl* fullt opp av; **2** *som adv US dgl* svært, veldig.

pliable ['plaɪəbl] *adj* **1** bøyelig; myk, smidig; **2** ettergivende, føyelig. **pliers** ['plaɪəz] *sb fl (pair of ~)* (flat)tang, nebbtang.

plight [plaɪt] *sb* forfatning, tilstand.

plod [plɒd] *vi* **1** slite, streve; jobbe; **2** traske.

plot [plɒt] **I** *sb* **1** jord|stykke, (-)teig, (-)tomt; **2** grunn|plan, -riss; **3** handling (i roman etc); intrige; **4** komplott, sammensvergelse; **II** *vb* **1** kartlegge; avsette (plotte, merke av/opp) på et kart; *data* plotte; **2** *US* parsellere/stykke ut (land); **3** tegne grunnplan *etc*; **4** planlegge; pønske/tenke ut; **5** konspirere/legge opp råd (*against* mot). **plotter** ['plɒtə] *sb* grafskriver. **plotting head** *sb data* plottehode.

plough [plaʊ] **1** *sb* plog; **2** *vt* pløye; ~ *back* pløye ned; *fig* pløye tilbake (dvs investere fortjeneste i nye forretninger etc).

plover ['plʌvə] *sb* brokkfugl, lo; *(golden ~)* heilo; *(ringed ~)* sandlo.

plow [plaʊ] *US* = *plough*.

pluck [plʌk] **I** *sb* **1** napp, rykk; **2** *fl* innmat (av slakt); **3** mot (og pågangsmot); energi, tæl; **II** *vb* plukke, ribbe (fugl); ~ *at* nappe/rykke i; ~ *up courage* ta mot til seg. **plucky** ['plʌkɪ] *adj dgl* modig; kjekk.

plug [plʌg] **I** *sb* **1** plugg (og propp, spuns, tapp etc); **2** *(electric ~)* støpsel; **3** *(spark~, sparking-~)* tennplugg; **II** *vb* **1** plugge/tette igjen; **2** ~ *in* plugge inn (støpsel etc); **3** *dgl: ~ away at* pugge/terpe på. **plugboard** ['plʌgbɔ:d] *sb data* pluggbord. **plugboard chart** *sb data* koblingsskjema. **plugging** ['plʌgɪŋ] *sb petro* plugging (dvs avstenging av borehull/brønn). **plug-in unit** *sb data* innpluggingsenhet.

plum [plʌm] *sb* **1** plomme (og plommetre); **2** rosin; godbit, lekkerbisken.

plumage ['plʌmɪdʒ] *sb* fjærdrakt.

plumb [plʌm] **I** *adj* **1** loddrett; **2** ~ *nonsense* det rene/skjære nonsens; *dgl* loddrett tøv; **II** *adv* **1** akkurat, nøyaktig; **2** *US dgl* fullstendig, helt; **III** *sb* (bly)-lodd; **IV** *vt* lodde (opp). **plumber** ['plʌmə] *sb* rørlegger. **plumbing** ['plʌmɪŋ] *sb* sanitær|anlegg, installasjoner; røropplegg; rørleggerarbeid. **plumb-line** *sb* loddline.

plume [plu:m] **I** *sb* fjær (og fjærbusk, hjelmbusk etc); **II** *vt* **1** glatte (pusse, pynte etc) fjærene sine; **2** pynte (seg) med fjær; ~ *oneself on* rose seg av; smigre seg med.

plummet ['plʌmɪt] **1** *sb* (bly)lodd; søkke; **2** *vi* falle (bratt); styrte.

plump [plʌmp] **A** *adj* buttet, lubben; velnært; **B I** *adv* brått; med ett; *som interj* pladask, plump; **II** *vb* **1** dumpe/falle (*down upon* ned på); **2** la falle; **~** *(oneself) down in a chair* dumpe/kaste seg ned i en stol; **3** **~** *for* gå inn for; stemme for/på.

plunder ['plʌndə] **1** *sb* (ut)plyndring; bytte, rov; **2** *vb* plyndre, røve; herje.

plunge [plʌndʒ] **I** *sb* stup; *take the* **~** våge (det store) spranget; **II** *vb* **1** stupe; kaste/styrte seg (hodestups); **2** kjøre/stikke (*into* inn/ned i).

plural ['plʊərəl] **1** *adj* flertalls-, fler-; **2** *sb* flertall.

plush [plʌʃ] **I** *adj* **1** plysj-; **2** *fig* elegant, smart; behagelig; **II** *sb* plysj.

ply [plaɪ] **A** *sb* **1** (enkelt) lag (i bildekk, finérplate etc); kordel; (enkelt) tråd (i garn, snor etc); *three-*~ tre|slått, trådet; **B** *vb* **1** bruke (flittig); **2** arbeide med; drive/utøve (håndverk etc); **3** forsyne (regelmessig); **4** gå i fast rute/regelmessig fart. **plywood** ['plaɪwʊd] *sb* kryssfiner.

pneumonia [nju:'məʊnɪə] *sb* lungebetennelse.

poach [pəʊtʃ] **A** *vb* drive ulovlig fiske/jakt; fiske/skyte ulovlig; **B** *vt* pochere (egg). **poacher** ['pəʊtʃə] *sb især* krypskytter.

pock [pɒk] *sb* pustel. **pock-marked** ['pɒkma:kt] *adj* kopparret.

pocket ['pɒkɪt] **I** *sb* lomme; **II** *vt* **1** legge (putte, stikke etc) i lommen; stikke til seg; **2** finne seg i (uten å kny). **pocket|-book** *sb* **1** lommebok; **2** billigbok. **~ edition** *sb* billigutgave (av bok). **~ expenses** *sb fl* småutgifter. **~handkerchief** *sb* lommetørkle. **~-money** *sb* lommepenger.

pod [pɒd] **I** *sb* belg, skolm; **II** *vb* **1** danne/sette belg; **2** pille/skolme (erter etc).

poem ['pəʊɪm] *sb* dikt. **poet** ['pəʊɪt] *sb* dikter, poet. **poetic** [pəʊ'etɪk] **1** *adj* poetisk; **2** *sb fl* poetikk, verslære. **poetry** ['pəʊɪtrɪ] *sb* poesi; dikterkunst, diktning.

poingnant ['pɔɪnənt] *adj* **1** skarp; bitende; bitter; **2** intens.

point [pɔɪnt] **I** *sb* **1** spiss (og *fig* brodd, skarphet); odd (og spiss ende, spisst redskap etc); flik, snipp; *(~ of land)* nes, odde; **2** prikk, punkt; merke/strek (på gradestokk, kompassrose etc); *(decimal ~)* (desimal)-komma; *(full ~)* punktum; **3** *(~ of time)* tidspunkt; stund, øyeblikk; *be on the ~ of* være på nippet/skulle til (å); **4** sted; posisjon, post; stadium, trinn; *~ of departure* utgangspunkt; *~ of view* synspunkt; **5** (hoved)|poeng, (-)punkt; (-)sak; emne, tema; moment (i stil etc); *beside the ~* saken uvedkommende; irrelevant; usaklig; *come to the ~* komme til saken; *make/score a ~* bevise en påstand etc; *to the ~* til saken; saklig; **6** formål, hensikt; *dgl* vits; *there's no ~ in* det har ingen hensikt/*dgl* er ingen vits i (å); **7** egenskap; (oftest god) side; **8** henblikk, henseende; hensyn; *in ~ of fact* egentlig, faktisk; ærlig talt; **9** poeng; **10** *fl* pens, (spor)veksel; **II** *vb* **1** peke (og peke/sikte med); **~ at** peke/sikte på; rette mot; **~ out** peke ut; påpeke; fremheve; **~ to** peke mot (på, i retning av etc); (hen)vise til; tyde på; **~ up** *US* fremheve; påvise; **2** spisse; kvesse, skjerpe; tilspisse; **3** sette (skille)tegn; **4** markere, poengtere. **pointblank** [ˌpɔɪnt'blæŋk] *adj, adv* **1** *mil* flat(banet); rett(linjet); på kloss hold; **2** likefrem; uten omsvøp. **pointed** ['pɔɪntɪd] *adj* **1** spiss *etc*; bitende, skarp; **2** poengtert; klar, utpreget. **pointer** ['pɔɪntə] *sb* **1** pekestokk; viser (på klokke, vekt etc); *fig* hint, pekepinn; **2** pointer.

poise [pɔɪz] **I** *sb* **1** balanse, likevekt; **2** fatning; (sinns)likevekt; **II** *vb: ~d* (av)balansert; *~d for* på spranget til; klar (parat, rede etc) til.

poison ['pɔɪzn] **1** *sb* gift; **2** *vt* forgifte. **poisonous** ['pɔɪznəs] *adj* giftig.

poke [pəʊk] **A I** *sb* **1** dytt (og dytting etc); **2** karing; pirk(ing); **II** *vb* **1** dytte, puffe, skubbe; **2** stikke, støte; kare/pirke (med finger, pinne etc); *~ fun at* holde leven med; gjøre narr av; **3** *~ about/around* snuse omkring; **B** *sb gml* pose, sekk. **poker** ['pəʊkə] *sb* **A** ildraker; **B** poker.

polar ['pəʊlə] *adj* polar(-). **polar | bear** *sb* isbjørn. **~ cap** *sb* polkalott. **pole** [pəʊl] **A** *sb* pol; **B I** *sb* **1** pæl, påle; mast, stang, stolpe; **2** en lengdeenhet, se midtsidene; **II** *vb* stake (seg) frem. **pole|-jumping** *sb* = *~-vault*. **~-star** *sb* pol(ar)stjerne; *fig* ledestjerne. **~-vault** *sb* stavsprang.

police [pə'li:s] **1** *sb* politi (og politi|etat, -korps, styrke, -vesen etc); **2** *vt* avpatruljere/overvåke (med politi); holde/sørge for ro og orden. **police | commissioner** *sb* politimester (i London og enkelte andre større byer). **~ constable** *sb* politi|konstabel; -kvinne, -mann. **~ cordon** *sb* politi(av)sperring. **~-court** *sb* politirett. **~-dog** *sb* politihund. **~ force** *sb* politi|korps, -styrke, -vesen. **~ headquarters** *sb* hovedpolitistasjon. **~-magistrate** *sb* politidommer. **~man** *sb* politimann. **~ officer** *sb* politi|konstabel; -kvinne, -mann. **~ regulation(s)** *sb* politivedtekt(er). **~ reporter** *sb* kriminalreporter. **~ sergeant** *sb* politioverbetjent. **~ station** *sb* politistasjon. **~ superintendent** *sb* visepolitisjef; avdelings/stasjonssjef (i politiet). **~ woman** *sb* politikvinne. **policy** ['pɒləsɪ] *sb* **A 1** politikk (dvs fremgangsmåte; holdning, innstilling; plan etc); **2** klokskap; kløkt; **B** *(insurance ~)* (forsikrings)-polise. **policy holder** *sb* forsikringstaker.

polish ['pɒlɪʃ] **I** *sb* **1** polering *etc*; finpuss(ing); **2** poler(ings)middel; (møbel)|politur, -puss; **3** glans; *fig* ferniss, politur (dvs pene manerer etc); **II** *vb* **1** polere; (blank)pusse; bone (gulv); **2** perfeksjonere; polere; *~ed manners* avslepne manerer. **polite** [pə'laɪt] *adj* høflig; dannet, kultivert. **politenss** [pə'laɪtnɪs] *sb* høflighet *etc*.

political [pə'lɪtɪkl] *adj* politisk; stats-. **political science** *sb* statsvitenskap. **politician** [ˌpɒlɪ'tɪʃn] *sb* politiker. **politics** ['pɒlɪtɪks] *sb fl* politikk.

poll [pəʊl] **I** *sb* **1** avstemning; valg; *fl* valg|lokale, -sted; *go to the ~s* gå til valg; *head the ~* få flest stemmer (ved et valg); **2** stemmeopptelling; valgdeltakelse; *declare the ~* offentliggjøre valgresultatet; **3** *(opinion ~)* meningsmåling, opinionsundersøkelse; **4** *gml* hode; *fig* individ, person; **II** *vb* **1** (avgi) stemme; **2** telle opp stemmer; **3** få/oppnå stemmer; **4** intervjue (under meningsmåling). **polling** ['pəulɪŋ] *sb* avstemning *etc*; *data* avspørring. **polling|-booth** *sb* stemme|avlukke, -bås. **~day** *sb* valgdag. **~-station** *sb* valg|lokale, -sted.

pollute [pə'lu:t] *vt* **1** forurense; grise/søle til; **2** besmitte; profanere, vanhellige. **pollution** [pə'lu:ʃn] *sb* forurensning *etc*.

pomp [pɒmp] *sb* prakt(utfoldelse); glitter, stas; *~ and circumstance* pomp og prakt. **pompous** ['pɒmpəs] *adj* **1** blæret, innbilsk; **2** praktfull, storslagen.

pond [pɒnd] *sb* dam.

ponder ['pɒndə] *vb* overveie; grunne/tenke (på). **ponderous** ['pɒndərəs] *adj* **1** svær, uhåndterlig; tung; **2** tungtveiende, vektig; **3** anstrengt, omstendelig; tung.

poniard ['pɒnɪəd] *sb* dolk, stilett.

pontoon [pən'tu:n] *sb* pongtong. **pontoon bridge** *sb* pongtongbro.

pony ['pəunɪ] *sb* ponni (også om andre, fortrinnsvis små hester og om unghester]. **pony-tail** *sb* hestehale(frisyre).

pool [pu:l] **A** *sb* basseng; dam; kulp; pytt; *petro* (petroleums)forekomst; **B I** *sb* **1** omgang/pulje (i spill); *dgl* kule; **2** fellestiltak; sammenskudd (av penger, materiell etc); *merk* pool, ring; *dgl* spleis; *machine ~* maskin-/traktorstasjon; *typing/typists' ~* sekretær|byrå, -service; ≈ skrivestue; **3** *(football) ~s* (fotball)tipping; *do (play/go in for) the ~s* tippe; **4** (slags) biljard; **II** *vb* gjøre felles sak; gå/slutte seg sammen; *merk* danne pool/ring; *dgl* spleise; *~ one's resources* forene sine krefter/ressurser. **pool-room** *sb* biljard|rom, -salong. **pools | coupon** *sb* tippekupong. **~ dividend, ~ prize** *sb* tippepremie.

poor ['puə] *adj* **1** fattig; nødlidende, trengende; pengelens; **2** stakkars; ussel, ynkelig; *~ dear (etc)!* stakkars liten! arme kroken! **3** mangelfull; dårlig, elendig; **4** mager, skrinn; skral. **poorly** ['puəlɪ] **1** *adj dgl* dårlig, uvel; **2** *adv* fattigslig; *~ off* dårlig stilt.

pop [pɒp] **A I** *sb* **1** knall; (lite) smell; snert; **2** skudd; **3** *dgl* brus, selters; **II** *vb* **1** knalle, smelle; **2** skyte (*at* etter/på); **3** fare, smette, smutte, stikke, svippe; *~ a question* fyre av et spørsmål; *~ the question* fri; *~* **in** stikke innom, *~* **off** stikke av; *~* **out** blåse ut (f.eks. et lys); *~* **round** stikke bortom/innom; *~* **up** dukke opp; **4** *US* poppe (= riste mais, popkorn etc); **5** *slang* stampe (dvs pantsette); **B** *sb dgl* pappa, paps; **C** *adj, sb (dgl fork* for *popular* og *popular music etc)* pop(-); popmusikk *etc*.

pope [pəup] *sb* pave.

popgun ['pɒpgʌn] *sb* luftgevær; *også* korkpistol, leketøyspistol.

poplar ['pɒplə] *sb* poppel.

poppy ['pɒpɪ] *sb* valmue.

populace ['pɒpjuləs] *sb: the ~* befolkningen; (de brede lag av) folket. **popular** ['pɒpjulə] *adj* **1** populær(-); folkelig, folke; **2** populær (*among* blant; *with* hos); avholdt; (godt) likt; yndet; utbredt. **popular | feature** *sb* attraksjonsnummer. *~* **front** *sb* folkefront. *~* **government** *sb* folkestyre. *~* **science** *sb* populærvitenskap. **populate** ['pɒpjuleɪt] *vt* befolke. **population** [,pɒpju'leɪʃn] *sb* befolkning; *koll* innbyggere. **populous** ['pɒpjuləs] *adj* folkerik; tett befolket.

porch [pɔ:tʃ] *sb* **1** bislag, vindfang; **2** *US* veranda.

porcupine ['pɔ:kjupaɪn] *sb* pinnsvin.

pore [pɔ:] **A** *sb* pore; **B** *vi: ~ over (a book etc)* henge over (en bok etc).

pork [pɔ:k] *sb* flesk, svinekjøtt.

porous ['pɔ:rəs] *adj* porøs.

porpoise ['pɔ:pəs] *sb* nise.

porridge ['pɒrɪdʒ] *sb* (havre)grøt.

port [pɔ:t] **A** *sb* havn (og havneby); ly, tilfluktssted; *~ of arrival/entry* ankomsthavn; *~ of call* anløps|havn, -sted; *~ of discharge* lossehavn; *~ of loading* lastehavn; *~ of registry* registreringshavn, hjemsted; **B** *sb* **I** *skotsk* port; **II 1** skipsport (som f.eks. kanonport, lasteport); **2** = *~hole*; **C 1** *adj, sb* babords(-); **2** *vt* dreie (til) babord; *~ the helm* legge roret babord; **D** *sb* portvin. **porthole** ['pɔ:thəul] *sb* kuøye, ventil.

portable ['pɔ:təbl] *adj* bærbar, transportabel. **portable radio** *sb* reiseradio.

portend [pɔ:'tend] *vt* bebude; varsle (om). **portent** ['pɔ:tənt] *sb* omen, varsel (især om ulykke). **portentous** [pɔ:'tentəs] *adj* illevarslende; uhellvarslende.

porter ['pɔ:tə] *sb* **A 1** *(railway ~)* bærer; **2** havnearbeider; *coal ~* kullemper; **3** *US* sovevognskonduktør; **B** dørvakt, portner, portvakt; *(hall ~)* (hotell)portier; **C** porter (= slags mørkt, sterkt øl).

portfolio [pɔ:t'fəulɪəu] *sb* **1** (dokument)mappe, veske; **2** mappe; (akt)omslag; *merk etc* portefølje; *pol også* ministerpost; **3** (samling dokumenter, fotografier, tegninger etc i en) presentasjonsmappe.

portion ['pɔ:ʃn] **I** *sb* **1** (an)del, part; del/lodd (dvs skjebne); **2** porsjon; mål (dvs tilmålt mengde); **II** *vt* dele opp (i porsjoner); fordele; dele/porsjonere ut.

portly ['pɔ:tlɪ] *adj* **1** korpulent; før, tykk; **2** statelig, verdig.

portrait ['pɔ:trɪt] *sb* portrett. **portray** [pɔ:'treɪ] *vt* portrettere. **portrayal** [pɔ:'treɪəl] *sb* portrettering.

pose [pəuz] **I** *sb* stilling; attityde; positur; **II** *vb* **1** posere; sitte/stå *etc* modell; *~ in the nude* stå nakenmodell; **2** skape seg; stille (seg) i positur; *~ as* opptre som; gi seg ut for (å være); **3** legge/sette frem. **poser** ['pəuzə] *sb* **1** vanskelig problem/spørsmål; *dgl* (hard) nøtt; **2** = **poseur** [pəu'zɜ:] *sb* posør.

posh [pɒʃ] *adj dgl* elegant, flott; snobbet.

position [pə'zɪʃn] **I** *sb* **1** (fast) plass/sted; beliggenhet, posisjon; *mil* post, stilling; **2** posisjon (i samfunnet etc); **3** post/stilling (i yrkeslivet); **4** holdning, (inn)stilling; **5** forhold, omstendighet(er); *in a ~ to* i stand til (å); **II** *vt* plassere; sette *etc* på plass; sette opp. **positioning** [pə'zɪʃnɪŋ] *sb data* posisjonering.

positive ['pɒzətɪv] **I** *adj* **1** overbevist (*that* om at); sikker (*that* på at); **2** uttrykkelig; utvilsom; **3** reell, virkelig; *dgl* direkte, likefrem; **4** byggende, konstruktiv; positiv; pluss-; **II** *sb foto* positiv.

posse ['pɒsɪ] *sb* oppbud (som f.eks. letemannskaper, manngard, utrykningskolonne etc).

possess [pə'zes] *vt* eie, (inne)ha; besitte; være i besittelse av; ~ *oneself of* bemektige seg; ta i besittelse; *be ~ed of* eie; være i besittelse av; *like one ~ed* som besatt. **possession** [pə'zeʃn] *sb* **1** besittelse, eiendom; *fl* eiendeler; *take ~ of* ta i besittelse; **2** besettelse; **3** *self-~* selv|beherskelse, -kontroll. **possessive** [pə'zesɪv] **I** *adj* **1** eiendoms-; **2** besittende; besitter-, eier-; eie-; **3** eieglad; sjalu; **II** *sb (the ~ case)* eieform, genitiv.

possibility [ˌpɒzə'bɪlətɪ] *sb* mulighet *etc.* **possible** ['pɒzəbl] *adj* mulig; tenkelig.

possum ['pɒsəm] *sb: play ~* ligge som/spille død (når en blir angrepet etc).

post [pəʊst] **A I** *sb* **1** post; posisjon, stilling; *remain at one's ~* bli på (sin) post; **2** handelsstasjon; utpost; **3** post, stilling (i yrkeslivet); **II** *vt* postere, stasjonere; plassere; ~ *sentries* sette ut vakt(post)er; **B I** *sb* post (og post|fører, kusk, -rytter, -vogn etc; poststasjon; skysstasjon); post|hus, kontor; post|gang, -vesen; *by ~* i/med posten; **II** *vb* **1** poste; sende med posten; **2** *(~ up)* postere; føre inn (i protokoll etc); **3** *be/keep ~ed* være/holde underrettet; **C 1** *sb* stolpe; *bed-~* sengestolpe; *gate-~* portstolpe; *lamp-~* lyktestolpe; **2** *vt (~ up)* kunngjøre, meddele; melde; slå opp plakater (om); ~ *no bills!* plakater forbudt! **D** *sb mil* hornsignal; **E** *pref* etter-, post-. **postage** ['pəʊstɪdʒ] *sb* porto. **postage | rates** *sb fl* portotakster. ~ **stamp** *sb* frimerke. **post|-bag** *sb* **1** postsekk; **2** leserbrevspalte (i ukeblad etc). **~box** *sb* postboks. **~card** *sb* brevkort, postkort. **~-chaise** *sb* diligence; postvogn. **~code** *sb* postnummer. **~date** *vt* etterdatere. **posted price** *sb petro* referansepris. **poster** ['pəʊstə] *sb* **1** plakat; **2** *(bill-~)* plakatklistrer.

posterior [pɒs'tɪərɪə] **I** *adj* **1** bakre, bak-; **2** senere; **II** *sb* bak(ende). **posterity** [pɒs'terətɪ] *sb koll* **1** etterkommere; **2** ettertid(en).

post|-free *adj, adv* franko, portofri(tt). **~-graduate 1** *adj* videregående (om forskning/studier etter BA-eksamen); **2** *sb* person som driver slike studier; ≈ forsker. **~-haste** *adv* i hui og hast. **~man** *sb* postbud. **~mark** *sb* poststempel. **~master, ~mistress** *sb* post|mester, -åpner (om henholdsvis mann og kvinne). ~ **meridiem** *adv* etter kl 12 middag (se midtsidene, dag og tid). ~ **mortem (examination)** *sb* obduksjon. **~-office** *sb* post|hus, -kontor; post|departement, -verk, -vesen; poststyre. **~-office box** *sb* postboks. **~-office savings bank** *sb* postsparebank. ~ **officer** *sb* postfunksjonær. **~-paid** *adj, adv* franko, portofri(tt).

postpone [pəʊst'pəʊn] *vt* oppsette, utsette.

postscript ['pəʊstskrɪpt] *sb* etterskrift.

posture ['pɒstʃə] **1** *sb* holdning, (inn)stilling; positur; **2** *vi* posere; stille seg opp; stille seg i positur.

post-war [ˌpəʊst'wɔ:] *adj* etterkrigs-.

posy [pəʊzɪ] *sb* **1** (liten) blomsterbukett; **2** innskrift, inskripsjon (især i ring); devise, motto.

pot [pɒt] **I** *sb* **1** gryte (og gryterett); kasserolle, kjele; *take ~-luck* ta til takke (med det huset har å by på); **2** beger, krus; (premie)pokal; **3** kanne, mugge; krukke; potte; **4** *slang* marihuana; **II** *vt* **1** hermetisere; legge ned; **2** potte (dvs plante i potte); **3** *dgl* sette på potte; **4** *dgl* plaffe/skyte ned. **pot|-boiler** *sb* kommersielt masseprodukt (om bok, film etc). **~-hole** *sb* **1** hull (i veidekke); **2** jettegryte. **~sherd** *sb* potteskår. **~-shot** *sb* slengeskudd, slumpeskudd.

potato [pə'teɪtəʊ] *sb* potet.

potent ['pəʊtənt] *adj* **1** kraftig, sterk; mektig; **2** potent. **potential** [pəʊ'tenʃl] **1** *adj* mulig, potensiell; potensial-; **2** *sb* potensial, potensiell; kapasitet, (yte)-evne.

potion ['pəʊʃn] *sb* brygg, drikk.

potter ['pɒtə] **A** *sb* pottemaker, keramiker; **B** *vi* pusle/stulle (*at* med); ~ *about* rusle/tusle rundt; ~ *away* somle bort. **potter's wheel** *sb* pottemaker|hjul, -skive. **pottery** ['pɒtərɪ] *sb* **1** pottemakeri, pottemakerverksted; **2** keramikk, steintøy.

pouch [paʊtʃ] **1** *sb* (skinn)|pose, (-)pung; taske, veske; **2** *vb* pose seg; bule ut.

poultice ['pəʊltɪs] *sb* (grøt)omslag.

poultry ['pəʊltrɪ] *sb koll* fjærfe; *især* høns. **poultry|-farm** *sb* hønseri. **~-yard** *sb* hønsegård.

pounce [paʊns] **1** *sb* (rovfugls) nedslag; **2** *vi: ~ on* slå ned på; fare løs på; kaste seg over.

pound [paʊnd] **A** *sb* pund (mynt- og vektenhet, se midtsidene); **B** *vb* **1** *(~ at/on)* banke (dundre, hamre etc) (på); **2** knuse, støte; pulverisere; **C** *sb* innhegning, kve.

pour [pɔ:] **I** *sb (down~)* regnskyll, øsregn; **II** *vb* **1** flomme, strømme; *dgl* hølje, pøse; helle (skjenke, øse etc) (opp); utøse (seg); **3** strømme/velte (om menneskemasser etc).

pout [paʊt] **1** *sb* geip, trutmunn; furting; **2** *vb* lage/sette trutmunn; geipe; furte, surmule.

poverty ['pɒvətɪ] *sb* fattigdom. **poverty-stricken** *adj* utarmet; (svært) fattig.

powder [paʊdə] **I** *sb* **1** pulver; **2** *(face-~)* pudder; **3** *(gun~)* krutt; **II** *vb* **1** pulverisere; **2** pudre (seg). **powder|-keg** *sb* kruttønne; *fig også* hissigpropp. **~-magazine** *sb* krutt|hus, magasin. **~-puff** *sb* pudderkvast. **~-room** *sb* dame|garderobe, toalett. **~-stained** *adj* kruttsvertet.

power ['paʊə] **I** *sb* **1** myndighet (og myndighetsområde etc); makt; ~ *of attorney* fullmakt; **2** stat, (stor)makt; **3** evne; *fl* begavelse; (ånds)evner; *intellectual ~s (også)* intellektuell styrke; **4** energi, kraft; *som adj* kraft-; motordrevet, motor-; elektrisk; **5** styrke; **6** *mat* potens; **II** *vt* drive (med elektrisitet, motor etc). **power|ful** *adj* kraftig, sterk; mektig. **~-house** *sb* **1** = *~-station*; **2** *fig* kraft, maktfaktor (dvs dynamisk, sterk person). **~less** *adj* kraftløs, svak; avmektig, maktesløs. **~-plant** *sb* = *~-station.* **~-point** *sb* stikkontakt. **~-station** *sb* kraftstasjon. **~-supply** *sb* kraft|forsyning, -tilførsel. **~-switch** *sb* hovedbryter.

practicable ['præktıkəbl] *adj* **1** (praktisk) gjørlig, mulig; gjennomførbar; **2** anvendelig, brukbar; **3** farbar. **practical** ['præktıkl] *adj* praktisk. **practical joke** *sb* skøyerstrek. **practically** ['præktıklı] *adv* **1** praktisk; **2** praktisk talt; så godt som. **practice** ['præktıs] **I** *sb* **1** praksis (i motsetning til teori); **2** praksis, (sed)vane; bruk, fremgangsmåte; **3** trening, øvelse; *out of ~* ute av trening; **4** praksis (dvs praktisering, advokat/leges etc virksomhet); **II** = **practise** ['præktıs] *vb* **1** øve (og øve seg i/på); trene; **2** praktisere; gjennomføre; utøve; drive (som). **practitioner** [præk'tıʃnə] *sb* **1** praktiserende advokat/lege etc; **2** praktiker.

prairie ['preərı] *sb* prærie.

praise [preız] **1** *sb* pris, ros; lovord; **2** *vt* prise, rose.

pram *sb* **1** [præm] *fork* for *perambulator* barnevogn; **2** [prɑ:m] pram.

prance [prɑ:ns] *vi* steile (om hest); danse på bakbeina; **2** hoppe/danse (av glede); **3** spankulere, sprade.

prank [præŋk] *sb* skøyerstrek, spikk; *fl også* spillopper.

prattle ['prætl] **I** *sb* babling *etc*; **II** *vb* **1** bable, pludre; **2** skravle.

prawn [prɔ:n] *sb* (slags stor) reke.

pray [preı] *vb* **1** be (til Gud); *~ for* be for; be om (å få); *~ to* be til; **2** anmode/be (*for* om; *to* om å); **3** *gml* vær så snill/vennlig; *~, be seated* vær så god, ta plass. **prayer** ['preə] *sb* **1** bønn (til Gud); **2** andakt.

pre- [pri:-, prı-, pre-] *pref* for-, foran(-), forut-, før-, pre-.

preach [pri:tʃ] *vb* preke, holde en preken; forkynne; *~ down* rakke ned på; *~ up* rose opp i skyene. **preacher** ['pri:tʃə] *sb* predikant.

precarious [prı'keərıəs] *adj* risikabel, utsatt; usikker, ustø; prekær.

precaution [prı'kɔ:ʃn] *sb* forsiktighet (og forsiktighetsregel); omtanke. **precautionary** [prı'kɔ:ʃnərı] *adj* forsiktighets-; sikkerhets-, verne-.

precede [prı'si:d] *vb* føre, (inn)lede; gå foran/forut (for), **precedence** [prı'si:dəns] *sb* forrang; *take ~ of/over* ha forrang (frem)for; gå/komme forut for; gå foran. **precedent 1** [prı'si:dənt] *adj: ~ to* forut/forutgående for; tidligere enn; **2** ['presıdənt] *sb* presedens.

precept ['pri:sept] *sb* **1** forskrift; **2** regel, rettesnor.

precinct ['pri:sıŋkt] *sb* **1** inngjerding; inngjerdet område; *også* grense; **2** distrikt, område; *US* ≈ bydel; *fl* omgivelser; enemerker.

precious ['preʃəs] *adj* **1** kostbar, verdifull; **2** dyrebar, kostelig; kjær; **3** affektert; utpenslet, utstudert; presiøs.

precipice ['presıpıs] *sb* stup; bratt skrent; avgrunn. **precipitate I** [prə'sıpıtət] **1** *adj* hodekulls; forhastet, overilt; **2** [*også* prə'sıpıteıt] *sb* bunnfall; **II** [prə'sıpıteıt] *vt* **1** kaste (seg) nedover/utfor; slenge/slynge ned(over); **2** styrte av sted; skynde seg (især nedover); stupe; **3** fortette(s), kondensere(s); bunnfelle(s). **precipitation** [prı,sıpı'teıʃn] *sb* **1** styrting *etc*; **2** hastverk; **3** fortetning *etc*; nedbør. **precipitous** [prə'sıpıtəs] *adj* **1** stupbratt; **2** = *precipitate I 1.*

précis ['preısı] *sb* resymé, sammendrag.

precise [prı'saıs] *adj* **1** nøyaktig, presis; **2** korrekt; nøye, pertentlig. **precision** [prı'sıʒn] *sb* nøyaktighet *etc*; presisjon.

preclude [prı'klu:d] *vt* ute|lukke, -stenge; (for)hindre.

precocious [prı'kəuʃəs] *adj* bråmoden, fremmelig; *stundom* veslevoksen.

preconceive [,pri:kən'si:v] *vt* (opp)fatte/tenke ut på forhånd. **preconceived** [,pri:kən'si:vd] *adj* forutfattet. **preconception** [,pri:kən'sepʃn] *sb* forutfattet mening/oppfatning; forhåndsinntrykk.

precursor [,pri:'kɜ:sə] *sb* for|gjenger, -løper.

predatory ['predətərı] *adj* plyndrende; rov-, røver-.

predecessor ['pri:dısesə] *sb* forgjenger; *fl ofte* forfedre.

predicament [prı'dıkəmənt] *sb* forlegenhet; *dgl* knipe.

predict [prı'dıkt] *vt* forutsi. **predictable** [prı'dıktəbl] *adj* forutsigelig. **prediction** [prı'dıkʃn] *sb* forutsigelse, spådom.

predispose [,pri:dı'spəuz] *vt* (pre)disponere; gjøre mottakelig/stemt (*to* for) på forhånd. **predisposition** ['pri:,dıspə'zıʃn] *sb* anlegg, legning; tendens.

predominance [prı'dɒmınəns] *sb* dominans *etc.* **predominant** [prı'dɒmınənt] *adj* dominerende, fremherskende; overlegen. **predominate** [prı'dɒmıneıt] *vt* dominere; være fremherskende.

preen [pri:n] *vt* **1** *om fugler* pusse/pynte (fjærene); **2** *~ oneself* kroe seg.

prefab ['pri:fæb] **1** *adj* ferdigbygd, prefabrikkert; **2** *sb* ferdighus. **prefabricate** [pri:'fæbrikeıt] *vt* prefabrikkere.

preface ['prefıs] **1** *sb* forord; **2** *vt* innlede (med forord); skrive forord til. **prefatory** ['prefətərı] *adj* innledende.

prefect ['pri:fekt] *sb* **1** ordenselev, tillitselev (på skole); **2** *hist* prefekt.

prefer [prı'fɜ:] *vt* **1** foretrekke (*to* fremfor); heller ville (ha); **2** fremsette (krav etc); **3** befordre, forfremme. **preferable** ['prefərəbl] *adj* som er å foretrekke. **preferably** ['prefərəblı] *adv* fortrinnsvis, helst. **preference** ['prefərəns] *sb* **1** valg (dvs det en foretrekker/velger); forkjærlighet; *in ~ to* fremfor; **2** begunstigelse; **3** fortrinnsrett; preferanse. **preferential** [,prefə'renʃl] *adj* fortrinnsberettiget; privilegert; preferanse-.

prefix ['pri:fiks] *sb* forstavelse; *data* innledningstegn. **prefix notation** *sb data* prefiks notasjon.

pregnancy ['pregnənsɪ] *sb* graviditet *etc.* **pregnant** ['pregnənt] *adj* **1** gravid, svanger; *om dyr* drektig; **2** betydningsfull, vektig; innholdsmettet.

prejudice ['predʒʊdɪs] **I** *sb* **1** fordom; *ofte* antipati, motvilje; **2** skade, ulempe; *to the ~ of* til skade/ugunst for; **II** *vt* **1** influere, påvirke; inngi fordommer; **2** skade; volde ulempe *etc.*

preliminary [prɪ'lɪmɪnər] **1** *adj* forberedende; innledende; **2** *sb* forberedelse; innledning; *fl* forhåndsundersøkelser; innledende skritt/tiltak.

prelude ['prelju:d] **1** *sb* innledning, åpning; forspill, preludium; **2** *vb* innlede, åpne; preludere.

premature ['premətʃə] *adj* for tidlig (moden etc); forhastet, overilt.

premeditate [pri:'medɪteɪt] *vt* planlegge/tenke ut (på forhånd). **premeditated** [pri:'medɪteɪtɪd] *adj* forsettlig, overlagt. **premeditation** [pri:,medɪ'teɪʃn] *sb* forsett, overlegg.

premier ['premɪə] **1** *adj* først; fremst; best, fornemst; **2** *sb* statsminister.

premise ['premɪs] *sb* **1** forutsetning, premiss(e); **2** *fl* lokale(r), lokaliteter; hus; (fast) eiendom; tomt.

premium ['pri:mɪəm] *sb* **1** (forsikrings)premie; **2** bonus; belønning, godtgjørelse; premie; **3** *merk* kursgevinst; *at a ~* høyt i kurs (også *fig*).

premonition [,premə'nɪʃn] *sb* (for)varsel, tegn; **2** (forut)|anelse, -følelse.

preoccupation [,pri:,ɒkjʊ'peɪʃn] *sb* opptatthet *etc.* **preoccupied** [pri:'ɒkjʊpaɪd] *adj* i (andre) tanker; tankefull, åndsfraværende; *~ with* opptatt av. **preoccupy** [pri'ɒkjʊpaɪ] *vt* oppta/legge beslag på *etc* (i forveien eller før alle andre).

prep [prep] *sb dgl, slang* **1** lekselesing; **2** = *preparatory school.*

prepaid [,pri:'peɪd] *adj* betalt på forhånd.

preparation [,prepə'reɪʃn] *sb* **1** forberedelse *etc*; **2** preparat. **preparatory** [prɪ'pærətərɪ] *adj* forberedende; innledende. **preparatory school** *sb* forberedelsesskole, forskole. **prepare** [prɪ'peə] *vb* forberede (seg); gjøre/lage (i stand); klargjøre (også *data*); tilberede; ut|arbeide, -ferdige; preparere. **prepared** [prɪ'peəd] *adj* (for)beredt *etc*; *~ to* klar (rede, villig etc) til (å).

preponderant [prɪ'pɒndərənt] *adj* fremherskende, overveiende.

prepossessing [,pri:pə'zesɪŋ] *adj* tiltalende; vinnende.

preposterous [prɪ'pɒstərəs] *adj* meningsløs, urimelig; *dgl* latterlig.

prerogative [prɪ'rɒgətɪv] *sb* privilegium, rett(ighet).

prerequisite [,pri:'rekwɪzɪt] *adj, sb* nødvendig (forutsetning/krav); forutsetning; betingelse, vilkår.

prescribe [prɪ'skraɪb] *vb* **1** forordne, foreskrive; *med især* forskrive, ordinere; **2** dekretere, påby. **prescription** [prɪ'skrɪpʃn] *sb* **1** forordning *etc*; *med* resept; **2** dekret, påbud.

presence ['prezns] *sb* nærvær, tilstedeværelse; *(~ of mind)* åndsnærværelse. **present A** ['preznt] **I** *adj* **1** nærværende, tilstedeværende; **2** nåværende; **II** *sb* **1** *the ~ (time)* nåtiden; **2** *the ~ (tense)* nåtid, presens; **B I** ['preznt] *sb* gave; foræring, presang; **II** [prɪ'zent] *vt* **1** gi; forære, skjenke; (til)by; (inn)levere; over|levere, -rekke; **2** legge (sette, stille etc) frem; *~ oneself* fremstille/melde seg; møte frem; **3** frem|by, ()vise; **4** forestille, presentere. **presentable** [prɪ'zentəbl] *adj* presentabel. **presentation** [,prezən'teɪʃn] *sb* **1** over|levering, -rekkelse; gave; **2** fremstilling (og fremstillings|form, -måte); fremføring, oppføring; **3** presentasjon; forevisning. **presently** ['prezntlɪ] *adv* **1** om litt; snart (etter); **2** *US* for tiden/øyeblikket.

presentiment [prɪ'zentɪmənt] *sb* (forut)|anelse, -følelse.

preservation [,prezə'veɪʃn] *sb* **1** bevaring *etc*; vedlikehold; *(state of ~)* forfatning, (til)stand; **2** konservering *etc.* **preservative** [prɪ'zɜ:vətɪv] **1** *adj* bevarende; konserverings-; **2** *sb* konserveringsmiddel. **preserve** [prɪ'zɜ:v] **I** *sb* **1** reservat; **2** *fl* syltetøy; **II** *vt* **1** bevare, vedlikeholde; beskytte, verne; frede; **2** konservere (og hermetisere, sylte etc); **3** opprettholde.

preset ['pri:set] *vt data* forhåndssette.

preside [prɪ'zaɪd] *vi* presidere; *~ at/over a meeting* lede et møte. **presidency** ['prezɪdənsɪ] *sb* **1** president|skap, -stilling, tid; **2** førerskap, ledelse. **president** ['prezɪdənt] *sb* president; (general)direktør; formann, leder (i forening/klubb, i styre etc); *US også* (universitets)rektor. **presidential** [,prezɪ'denʃl] *adj* president- *etc.*

press [pres] **A I** *sb* **1** pres (og pressing); trykk; **2** *a)* presse; trykkeri; *(printing ~)* trykkpresse; *the ~* pressen (dvs avisene etc); *b)* forlag (især som del av navn); **3** skap (især innebygget); **II** *vb* **1** presse (og klemme, knuge, kryste etc); trykke (på); **2** drive/presse (på); nøde; innskjerpe; insistere (på); tvinge; *~ the point/question* gå hardt på; forlange/kreve en avgjørelse/et avgjørende svar; *be ~ed for* ha det vanskelig (dårlig, knapt etc) med; være opprådd for; **3** presse seg frem; trenge (seg) på; dytte, mase; **4** haste; være presserende; **B** *vt* presse (= tvangs|forhyre, -verve). **press | agent** *sb* = *~ secretary.* **~-cutting** *sb* avisutklipp. **~-gang** *sb* pressgjeng. **~ notice, ~ release** *sb* pressemelding. **~ secretary** *sb* pressesekretær. **pressure** ['preʃə] *sb* **1** press, trykk; **2** press, påtrykk; travelhet; nød, vanskelighet. **pressure|-cooker** *sb* trykkoker. **~-gauge** *sb* manometer, trykkmåler. **~-group** *sb* pressgruppe.

prestore ['pri:stɔ:] *vt data* forhåndslagre.

presumable [prɪ'zju:məbl] *adj* formentlig. **presumably** [prɪ'zju:məblɪ] *adv* formodentlig; antakelig, trolig. **presume** [prɪ'zju:m] *vb* **1** anta, forutsette; tro; **2** våge; driste seg til; tillate seg; **3** *~ upon* misbruke, utnytte. **presumption** [prɪ'zʌmpʃn] *sb* **1** antakelse, formodning; **2** anmasselse, frekkhet. **presumptive** [prɪ'zʌmptɪv] *adj* antatt, formodet; presumptiv. **presumptuous** [prɪ'zʌmptʃuəs] *adj* anmassende, frekk; innbilsk, overmodig.

pretence [prɪ'tens] *sb* **1** foregivende, skinn; påskudd; **2** fordring, krav; pretensjon. **pretend** [prɪ'tend] *vb* **1** foregi; late som; hykle, simulere; **2** ~ *to* fordre, kreve; gjøre krav på. **pretender** [prɪ'tendə] *sb* **1** (tvilsom) fordringshaver; **2** (tron)pretendent. **pretension** [prɪ'tenʃn] *sb* **1** foregivende; **2** fordring, krav; **3** innbilskhet. **pretentious** [prɪ'tenʃəs] *adj* fordringsfull, kravstor; innbilsk; prangende, pretensiøs.

pretext ['pri:tekst] *sb* påskudd; (tom) unnskyldning.

pretty ['prɪtɪ] **1** *adj* (ganske) pen; *ofte* småpen; *især iron* fin, nydelig; **2** *adv dgl* ganske, temmelig.

prevail [prɪ'veɪl] *vi* **1** seire, vinne; få/ha overtaket; **2** herske/råde (dvs være fremherskende/rådende); ~ *upon* overtale; bevege/få til (å). **prevalence** ['prevələns] *sb* (alminnelig) forekomst; utbredelse. **prevalent** ['prevələnt] *adj* alminnelig, vanlig; (frem)herskende, rådende; gjengs; utbredt.

prevaricate [prɪ'værɪkeɪt] *vi* komme med utflukter; svare unnvikende. **prevarication** [prɪ,værɪ'keɪʃn] *sb* unnvikende svar; *fl* utflukter.

prevent [prɪ'vent] *vt* forebygge; avverge, (for)hindre. **prevention** [prɪ'venʃn] *sb* forebygging; forhindring. **preventive** [prɪ'ventɪv] *adj* forebyggende, preventiv.

previous ['pri:vɪəs] *adj* foregående, tidligere; ~ *to* forut for; før. **previously** ['pri:vɪəslɪ] *adv* før, tidligere.

pre-war [,pri:'wɔ:] *adj* førkrigs-.

prey [preɪ] **I** *sb* rov; bytte/offer (*to* for); **II** *vi:* ~ *upon* **1** jage (som bytte); **2** knuge, nage; tære på.

price [praɪs] **1** *sb* pris; **2** *vt* prise; pris|merke, -sette. **price | bracket** *sb* pris|klasse, -leie. **~less** *adj* uvurderlig; kostelig. **~ range** *sb* = ~ *bracket*.

prick [prɪk] **I** *sb* **1** prikk(ing); stikk; sting (av smerte); **2** spiss; brodd, tagg; torn; **II** *vb* **1** stikke (hull i/på); ~ *one's finger* stikke seg i fingeren; **2** prikke, stikke; gjøre vondt; **3** ~ *up one's ears* spisse ører. **prickle** ['prɪkl] **1** *sb* nål; pigg, tagg; torn; **2** *vb* prikke, stikke; krible. **prickly** ['prɪklɪ] *adj* **1** pigget, tagget; tornet; **2** prikkende, stikkende; kriblende.

pride [praɪd] **I** *sb* **1** stolthet; *take* ~ *in* være kry/stolt av; **2** hovmod, overlegenhet; **II** *vt:* ~ *oneself (up)on* være kry/stolt av; (kunne) rose seg av.

priest [pri:st] *sb* prest (især anglikansk eller katolsk samt i fremmede religioner). **priestess** ['pri:stɪs] *sb* prestinne. **priesthood** ['pri:sthʊd] *sb* presteskap; preste|stand. -stilling.

prig [prɪg] *sb* narr; innbilsk/selvgod person. **priggish** ['prɪgɪʃ] *adj* narraktig; innbilsk, selvgod.

prim [prɪm] *adj* **1** formell, stiv; pertentlig; **2** prippen, snerpet.

primacy ['praɪməsɪ] *sb* **1** førsteplass, ledelse; over|høyhet, -legenhet; **2** erkebiskopverdighet. **primary** ['praɪmərɪ] *adj* **1** først, opprinnelig; fremst; primær-; **2** elementær-. **primary | file** *sb data* primærfil. ~ **function** *sb data* primærfunksjon. ~ **school** *sb* grunnskole. ~ **text** *sb data* fast tekst.

prime [praɪm] **I** *adj* **1** først, første-; hoved-; **2** førsteklasses, prima; **II** *sb* **1** begynnelse; **2** høydepunkt; beste periode/tid; **III** *vb* forberede, klargjøre; *især* armere; forsyne med tenn|ladning, -sats. **prime | key** *sb data* primærnøkkel. ~ **minister** *sb* statsminister. ~ **number** *sb* primtall. **primer** ['praɪmə] *sb* begynnerbok. **primeval** [praɪ'mi:vl] *adj* forhistorisk, ur(tids)-; opprinnelig. **primitive** ['prɪmɪtɪv] *adj* **1** primitiv; opprinnelig; ur(tids)-; **2** enkel, gammeldags. **primrose** ['prɪmrəuz] *sb* marianøklebånd.

prince [prɪns] *sb* **1** fyrste; **2** prins. **Prince Consort** *sb* prinsgemal. **princely** ['prɪnslɪ] *adj* fyrste-, prinse-; *fig* fyrstelig-. **princess** [prɪn'ses] *sb* **1** fyrstinne; **2** prinsesse. **principal** ['prɪnsəpl] **I** *adj* fremst, viktigst; hoved-; **II** *sb* **1** overhode; prinsipal, sjef; *ofte* rektor, (skole)styrer; **2** (investert) kapital. **principality** [,prɪnsɪ'pælətɪ] *sb* fyrstedømme. **principle** ['prɪnsəpl] *sb* **1** grunn|element, -prinsipp; **2** prinsipp, rettesnor; (leve)regel; *on* ~ av prinsipp.

print [prɪnt] **I** *sb* **1** trykk (og trykning; trykt materiale; skrift, trykksak; trykkskrift; blokkskrift; trykte bokstaver etc); *in* ~ på trykk; *om bøker etc* på lager; *out of* ~ utsolgt (fra forlaget); **2** blad (dvs reproduksjon, stikk etc); *foto* bilde, kopi; **3** avtrykk, spor; merke, preg; **4** mønstret/trykt bomullsstoff (til sommerkjoler etc); **II** *vt* **1** trykke (bøker etc); skrive (med blokkbokstaver/trykte bokstaver); *også* offentliggjøre/publisere (på trykk); **2** reprodusere; ta avtrykk/kopi(er) av; *foto* kopiere; **3** *data* skrive ut. **printable** ['prɪntəbl] *adj* trykk|ferdig, -klar. **printed | circuit board** *sb data* kretskort. ~ **matter** *sb* trykksak(er). **printer** ['prɪntə] *sb* **1** trykker; **2** *data* skriver. **printer's | error** *sb* trykkfeil. ~ **ink** *sb* trykksverte. **printing | office** *sb* = ~ *shop*. ~ **press** *sb* trykkpresse; trykkeri. ~ **shop** *sb* trykkeri. **printout** *sb data* utskrift. **print | position** *sb data* skriveposisjon. ~ **queue** *sb data* utskriftskø. ~ **wheel** *sb data* skrivehjul.

prior ['praɪə] **A 1** *adj* forutgående, tidligere; **2** *adv:* ~ *to* før; forut for; **B** *sb* prior. **prioress** ['praɪərɪs] *sb* priorinne. **priority** [praɪ'ɒrətɪ] *sb* forrang, førsterett; prioritet. **priory** ['praɪərɪ] *sb* prior(inne)-kloster.

prison ['prɪzn] *sb* fengsel. **prisoner** ['prɪznə] *sb* fange; ~ *of war* krigsfange.

privacy ['prɪvəsɪ] *sb* **1** tilbaketrukkenhet; enerom, ensomhet; **2** fortrolighet, hemmelighet. **privacy protection** *sb data etc* personvern. **private** ['praɪvɪt] **I** *adj* **1** tilbaketrukket; alene, avsondret; **2** privat; **3** fortrolig, hemmelig; **4** *mil* menig; **II** *sb* **1** *(~ soldier)* menig (soldat); **2** *fl* kjønnsdeler; **3** *in* ~ fortrolig, hemmelig; under fire øyne. **privateer** [,praɪvə'tɪə] *sb* kaper (og kaper|gast, -kaptein, -skip). **private | enterprise** *sb* privat initiativ. ~ **eye** *sb slang* privatdetektiv. ~ **member** *sb* vanlig parlamentsmedlem (dvs som ikke er medlem av regjeringen). **privation** [praɪ'veɪʃn] *sb* berøvelse; mangel, savn; nød.

privilege ['prɪvɪlɪdʒ] *sb* privilegium, rett(ighet). **privileged** ['prɪvɪlɪdʒd] *adj* privilegert.

privy ['prɪvɪ] *adj gml, jur* hemmelig, privat; ~ *to* innviet i. **Privy Council** *sb* geheimråd, riksråd.

prize [praɪz] **A I** *sb* **1** premie, pris; gevinst; belønning; *som adj* premie-, pris-; **2** (krigs)bytte; prise; **3** klenodium, skatt; **II** *vt* skatte; verdsette (høyt); **B** *vt:* ~ *open/up* brekke/bryte opp. **prize|-fighter** *sb* proffbokser. **~-money** *sb* prisepenger.

pro [prəʊ] **A 1** *pref* for; i favør av; pro(-); **2** *sb:* ~*s and cons* argumenter for og imot; **B** *sb dgl* profesjonell (idrettsutøver etc).

probability [ˌprɒbə'bɪlətɪ] *sb* sannsynlighet. **probable** ['prɒbəbl] *adj* sannsynlig, trolig. **probably** ['prɒbəblɪ] *adv* sannsynligvis. **probation** [prə'beɪʃn] *sb* prøve; *især* prøvetid; *on* ~ (løslatt) på prøve. **probe** [prəʊb] **1** *sb* sonde; sondering; gransking, undersøkelse; **2** *vt* sondere; granske, undersøke.

procedure [prə'si:dʒə] *sb* **1** fremgangsmåte, metode; forretningsorden; rettergang; **2** *data etc* prosedyre. **proceed** [prə'si:d] *vi* **1** gå/rykke frem (*to* til); **2** fortsette; gå videre; **3** ~ *from* komme/utgå fra; **4** ~ *against* anlegge/gå til sak mot. **proceeding** [prə'si:dɪŋ] *sb* fremgangsmåte *etc*; *(legal ~s)* rettergang, rettergangsordning; rettssak. **proceeds** ['prəʊsi:dz] *sb fl* avkastning, utbytte. **process A** ['prəʊsəs] **I** *sb* **1** (fremstillings)|metode, (-)prosess; **2** (for)løp, gang; utvikling; **3** prosess, (retts)sak; **4** *data* prosess; **II** *vt* bearbeide/behandle (på en bestemt måte); *ofte* foredle; *data* kjøre, prosessere; *foto* fremkalle; kopiere; reprodusere; **B** [prə'ses] *vi gml* gå i prosesjon/tog. **process control** *sb data* prosesstyring. **procession** [prə'seʃn] *sb* prosesjon, (opp)tog. **processor** [prə'sesə] *sb data* prosessor.

proclaim [prə'kleɪm] *vt* proklamere; erklære, forkynne; kunngjøre, utrope. **proclamation** [ˌprɒklə'meɪʃn] *sb* proklamering *etc*; proklamasjon.

procure [prə'kjʊə] *vt* anskaffe/skaffe (seg).

prod [prɒd] **I** *sb* **1** pigg(stav); **2** stikk; *fig* dytt/puff (i en bestemt retning); **II** *vb (~ at)* pirke (på); stikke (i); drive (frem med spisst redskap); egge, oppildne.

prodigal ['prɒdɪgl] **1** *adj* ødsel (*of* med); *the ~ son* den fortapte sønn; **2** *sb* ødeland.

prodigious [prə'dɪdʒəs] *adj* **1** fabelaktig, fantastisk; vidunderlig; **2** kolossal, veldig. **prodigy** ['prɒdɪdʒɪ] *sb* **1** mirakel, vidunder; **2** monstrum, uhyre.

produce I ['prɒdju:s] *sb* produksjon; *især* avkastning, avling; (landbruks)produkter; **II** [prə'dju:s] *vt* **1** ta (legge, vise etc) frem; skaffe (frem); **2** fabrikkere; frem|bringe, -stille; lage, produsere; **3** bære (avling); gi, yte; kaste av seg; **4** bevirke, forårsake, volde. **producer** [prə'dju:sə] *sb* **1** produsent *etc*; **2** iscenesetter (oftest også med økonomisk ansvar); *radio/TV* producer. **product** ['prɒdʌkt] *sb* produkt. **production** [prə'dʌkʃn] *sb* fremstilling *etc*; produksjon. **production | facilities** *sb* produksjonsutstyr. ~ **licence** *sb* *petro* utvinningstillatelse. ~ **platform** *sb petro* produksjonsplattform. ~ **program** *sb data* produksjonsprogram. ~ **time** *sb data* produksjonstid. ~ **well** *sb petro* produksjonsbrønn.

profane [prə'feɪn] **I** *adj* **1** profan, verdslig; **2** blasfemisk; ugudelig; vanhellig; **II** *vt* profanere, vanhellige. **profanity** [prə'fænətɪ] *sb* blasfemi; *især* banning.

profess [prə'fes] *vt* **1** bekjenne/erklære (åpent); **2** påstå (om seg selv); gi seg ut for/gjøre krav på (å kunne, være etc); **3** praktisere/virke som. **professedly** [prə'fesɪdlɪ] *adv* angivelig. **profession** [prə'feʃn] *sb* **1** profesjon, yrke; **2** erklæring/påstand (som ikke nødvendigvis er riktig). **professional** [prə'feʃənl] **1** *adj* profesjonell, yrkes-; **2** *sb* profesjonell (idrettsutøver, kunstner etc). **professor** [prə'fesə] *sb* professor. **professorship** [prə'fesəʃɪp] *sb* professorat.

proffer ['prɒfə] **1** *sb* tilbud; **2** *vt* tilby (og tilby seg).

proficiency [prə'fɪʃnsɪ] *sb* dyktighet *etc*. **proficient** [prə'fɪʃnt] **1** *adj* (anerkjent) dyktig/flink; **2** *sb* ekspert, sakkyndig.

profit ['prɒfɪt] **I** *sb* **1** fordel; **2** *fl* fortjeneste, profitt; avkastning, utbytte; **II** *vb* **1** gagne, nytte; ~ *by* dra/ha nytte av; **2** profittere/tjene (*by* på). **profitable** ['prɒfɪtəbl] *adj* innbringende, lønnsom; fordelaktig, gunstig. **profiteer** [ˌprɒfɪ'tɪə] **1** *sb* (krigs)profitør; **2** *vi* drive som profitør.

profligate ['prɒflɪgət] **1** *adj* ryggesløs; lastefull, utsvevende; **2** *sb* libertiner.

profound [prə'faʊnd] *adj* dyp (især = dypsindig; dypt|gående, -pløyende; gjennomgripende, grundig etc). **profoundly** [prə'faʊndlɪ] *adv* dypt, inderlig. **profundity** [prə'fʌndətɪ] *sb* dyp (og dypsindighet etc); dybde.

profusion [prə'fju:ʒn] *sb* overdådighet.

progeny ['prɒdʒənɪ] *sb* avkom.

program ['prəʊgræm] **1** *sb* program; **2** *vt* programmere. **program | card** *sb data* programkort. **programmable** *adj data* programmerbar. **programmer** *sb data* programmerer. **programming** *sb data* programmering. **program | release** *sb data* programutgave. ~ **run** *sb data* programkjøring. ~ **unit** *sb data* programmodul.

progress I ['prəʊgres] *sb* **1** fremrykning; **2** frem|gang, -skritt; bedring; utvikling; gang; **II** [prə'gres] *vi* **1** avansere; gå fremover; gå sin gang; **2** bedres; gjøre fremskritt. **progressive** [prə'gresɪv] **I** *adj* **1** fremadskridende, fremad-; *ofte* stigende, økende; **2** fremskrittsvennlig, progressiv; *ofte* radikal; **II** *sb* progressiv *etc* person/politiker.

prohibit [prə'hɪbɪt] *vt* forby (ved lov); hindre. **prohibition** [ˌprəʊɪ'bɪʃn] *sb* forbud; *især* brennevinsforbud. **prohibitive** [prə'hɪbɪtɪv] *adj* **1** forbuds-; **2** prohibitiv; *dgl, om pris* ublu.

project I ['prɒdʒekt] *sb* plan, prosjekt; utkast; **II** [prə'dʒekt] *vb* **1** planlegge, prosjektere; **2** rage frem; stikke frem/ut; **3** kaste (frem); skyte/slynge (ut); projisere. **project control** *sb data* prosjektstyring. **projection** [prə'dʒekʃn] *sb* **1** planlegging, prosjektering; prosjekt; **2** projisering. **projector** [prə'dʒektə] *sb* **1** planlegger; *iron* prosjektmaker; **2** (film)fremviser; lysbilledapparat; pro(s)jektør. **project planning** *sb data* prosjektplanlegging.

prolific [prə'lɪfɪk] *adj* frodig, fruktbar; produktiv.

prolong [prə'lɒŋ] *vt* forlenge, prolongere; fornye. **prolongation** [ˌprəulɒŋ'geɪʃn] *sb* forlengelse *etc.*

prom [prɒm] *sb dgl* **1** promenadekonsert; **2** *US* = *promenade I 2.* **promenade** [ˌprɒmɪ'nɑ:d] **I** *sb* **1** promenade (og promenade|gate, strøk); **2** *US* skoleball, studentball; **II** *vb* promenere, spasere.

prominence ['prɒmɪnəns] *sb* **1** fremspring *etc*; **2** betydning (og betydningsfullhet *etc*). **prominent** ['prɒmɪnənt] *adj* **1** frem|springende, -stikkende; utstående; **2** iøynefallende; frem|skutt, -tredende; **3** betydelig, fremragende.

promiscuity [ˌprɒmɪs'kjuətɪ] *sb* **1** (sammen)-blanding *etc*; **2** promiskuitet. **promiscuous** [prə'mɪskjuəs] *adj* **1** blandet (sammen); *ofte* rotet, tilfeldig; **2** promiskuøs; løsaktig, utuktig.

promise ['prɒmɪs] **1** *sb* løfte (*of* om); **2** *vb* forsikre; love; gi håp/løfte om. **promising** ['prɒmɪsɪŋ] *adj* lovende, løfterik.

promontory ['prɒməntrɪ] *sb* nes, odde, pynt.

promote [prə'məut] *vt* **1** oppmuntre; fremme, støtte; stimulere/øke (salg etc); **2** forfremme; flytte opp (elev). **promoter** [prə'məutə] *sb* **1** forretningsfører; manager, promotor; **2** *merk* kontakt|person, -skaper; initiativtaker. **promotion** [prə'məuʃn] *sb* **1** fremme, støtte; hjelp; **2** forfremmelse; opp|flytning, -rykk.

prompt [prɒmpt] **I** *adj* omgående, øyeblikkelig; kontant; **II** *sb* **1** tilskyndelse *etc*; **2** *data* DOS-tegn, klartegn; **III** *vt* **1** bevege, tilskynde; drive; **2** sufflere. **prompter** ['prɒmptə] *sb* sufflør. **promptitude** ['prɒmptɪtju:d] *sb* raskhet.

prone [prəun] *adj* **1** utstrakt (på maven); nesegrus; **2** tilbøyelig (*to* til); *accident-~* stadig utsatt for ulykker.

prong [prɒŋ] *sb* **1** (gaffel)|tann, -tind; *ofte* stift; **2** gaffel; greip.

pronoun ['prəunaun] *sb* pronomen. **pronounce** [prə'nauns] *vb* **1** uttale; **2** uttale seg (*on* om); erklære, si. **pronounced** [prə'naunst] *adj* erklært; ut|preget, -talt. **pronunciation** [prəˌnʌnsɪ'eiʃn] *sb* uttale.

proof [pru:f] **I** *adj* ugjennomtrengelig; *som suff* -fast, -sikker, -tett, -trygg; **II** *sb* **1** bevis; **2** (kvalitets)|-prøve, (-)prøving; **3** prøve (= prøve|bilde, -avtrykk etc); *især* korrektur; **4** enhet for alkoholinnhold = 57,1 volumprosent (*75 degrees ~* = 75 prosent av 57,1 = en alkoholprosent på ca 43). **proof-reader** *sb* korrekturleser.

prop [prɒp] **I** *sb* **1** (av)stiver, støtte(bjelke); *fig* støtte; **2** *fl film/teat slang* rekvisitter; **II** *vt (~ up)* avstive, støtte (opp).

propagate ['prɒpəgeɪt] *vb* **1** formere/forplante (seg); **2** spre, utbre. **propagation** [ˌprɒpə'geɪʃn] *sb* **1** forplantning; **2** spredning, utbredelse.

propane ['prəupeɪn] *sb* propan.

propel [prə'pel] *vt* drive (frem). **propellent** [prə'pelənt] **1** *adj* drivende, driv-; **2** *sb (propellant)* driv|-kraft, -stoff. **propeller** [prə'pelə] *sb* propell.

propensity [prə'pensətɪ] *sb* hang/tilbøyelighet (*for/to* til (å)).

proper ['prɒpə] *adj* **1** korrekt, riktig; passende, sømmelig; **2** egentlig, virkelig; **3** *dgl* ordentlig, skikkelig; real. **proper name** *sb* egennavn. **property** ['prɒpətɪ] *sb* (fast) eiendom; *ofte* formue, midler; **2** (spesiell) egenskap; egenhet, eiendommelighet; **3** *fl film/teat* rekvisita.

prophecy ['prɒfɪsɪ] *sb* profeti *etc.* **prophesy** ['prɒfɪsaɪ] *vt* profetere; forutsi, spå.

proportion [prə'pɔ:ʃn] **I** *sb* **1** forhold; *fl* proporsjon(er); *ofte* størrelse (og størrelses|forhold, -orden); **2** (an)del; **II** *vt* **1** avpasse (*to* etter/til); proporsjonere; **2** dele (i et bestemt forhold); porsjonere (ut).

proposal [prə'pəuzl] *sb* **1** forslag *etc*; **2** frieri. **propose** [prə'pəuz] *vb* **1** foreslå; *~ a toast* utbringe en skål; **2** akte; ha i sinne/i tankene; **3** fri (*to* til). **proposition** [ˌprɒpə'zɪʃn] **I** *sb* **1** forslag; *pol også* proposisjon; **2** erklæring, uttalelse; **3** (lære)setning, tese; **4** *dgl* affære, sak; foretagende; **II** *vt US* komme med et (tvilsomt) forslag.

proprietary [prə'praɪətərɪ] *adj* **1** besittende; eiendoms-, eier-; **2** mønsterbeskyttet, patentert; *~ articles* merkevarer. **proprietor** [prə'praɪətə] *sb* eier, innehaver. **propriety** [prə'praɪətɪ] *sb* korrekthet; anstendighet, sømmelighet.

propulsion [prə'pʌlʃn] *sb* (frem)drift.

prose [prəuz] *sb* prosa.

prosecute ['prɒsɪkju:t] *vt* **1** drive/holde på med; forfølge (dvs følge opp, jf *persecute*); **2** anklage, tiltale; anlegge sak/reise tiltale mot. **prosecution** [ˌprɒsɪ'kju:ʃn] *sb* **1** oppfølging; utførelse; utøvelse; **2** anklage, tiltale; rettsforfølgelse, straffeforfølgning; *ofte* anklager (dvs anklagemyndighet, aktorat). **prosecutor** ['prɒsɪkju:tə] *sb* aktor, anklager; saksøker; *public ~* offentlig anklager.

prospect I [prɒspekt] *sb* **1** utsikt, utsyn; **2** forventning; (fremtids)|perspektiv, (-)utsikt; *ofte* mulighet; **3** skjerp; **II** [prə'spekt] *vb* lete (især etter malm); grave gull. **prospector** [prə'spektə] *sb* malmleter, skjerper; gullgraver.

prosper ['prɒspə] *vb* **1** trives; gjøre det godt; ha fremgang; **2** begunstige; hjelpe; gi fremgang/hell. **prosperity** [prɒs'perətɪ] *sb* fremgang, suksess; trivsel. **prosperous** ['prɒspərəs] *adj* fremgangsrik; *ofte* velstående.

prostitute ['prɒstɪtju:t] **1** *sb* prostituert (person); **2** *vt* prostituere.

prostrate I ['prɒstreɪt] *adj* **1** utstrakt (på maven); **2** (liggende) utmattet; nedbrutt, sønderknust; **3** nesegrus; **II** [prɒ'streɪt] *vt* **1** kaste/velte over ende; **2** utmatte; knekke, kue.

protagonist [prəʊ'tægənɪst] *sb* hovedperson (i roman etc).

protect [prə'tekt] *vt* beskytte (*against/from* mot); skjerme, verne; sikre, trygge. **protection** [prə'tekʃn] *sb* beskyttelse *etc*; *data især* sikring. **protective** [prə'tektɪv] *adj* beskyttende *etc*; beskyttelses-, verne-. **protector** [prə'tektə] *sb* beskytter.

protest I ['prəʊtest] *sb* protest; inn|sigelse, -vending; **II** [prə'test] *vb* **1** protestere (og *US* protestere mot); **2** erklære; fremholde, hevde; påstå.

protract [prə'trækt] *vt* forhale/trekke ut (tiden).

protrude [prə'tru:d] *vb* rage (skyte, stikke etc) frem.

proud [praʊd] *adj* **1** kry/stolt (*of* av); **2** hoven; overmodig; kaut; **3** flott; praktfull, prektig.

prove [pru:v] *vb* **1** bevise, godtgjøre; **2** vise (og påvise); **3** bekrefte; bringe på det rene; forvisse seg om; **4** prøve (og etterprøve, utprøve etc); sette på prøve; **5** (~ *to be*) vise seg (å være).

proverb ['prɒvɜ:b] *sb* ord|språk, -tak; fyndord. **proverbial** [prə'vɜ:bɪəl] *adj* **1** fyndig (som et ordtak); **2** legendarisk; som det går frasagn om; *også* (vel)kjent.

provide [prə'vaɪd] *vb* **1** forsyne (med); levere; skaffe; yte; ~ *for* forsørge; **2** forberede seg; ~ *against* ta (sine) forholdsregler mot; treffe tiltak mot; **3** bestemme, fastsette; forordne; foreskrive. **provided** [prə'vaɪdɪd] *konj* (~ *that*) forutsatt (at); under forutsetning av (at). **providence** ['prɒvɪdəns] *sb* forsyn(et), skjebne(n). **provident** ['prɒvɪdənt] *adj* forsiktig, omtenksom; forutseende. **providential** [,prɒvɪ'denʃl] *adj* skjebnebestemt.

province ['prɒvɪns] *sb* **1** landsdel, provins; **2** felt, område; (virke)gren. **provincial** [prə'vɪnʃl] **1** *adj* provins-; *fig* provinsiell (= bornert, trangsynt etc); **2** *sb* provinsboer.

provision [prə'vɪʒn] *sb* **1** anskaffelse; **2** forråd, forsyning; *fl også* mat, proviant; **3** forsørgelse, underhold; omsorg; **4** foranstaltning; forholdsregel, tiltak; **5** *jur* bestemmelse, forordning. **provisional** [prə'vɪʒənl] *adj* foreløpig, midlertidig; provisorisk.

provocation [,prɒvə'keɪʃn] *sb* provosering *etc*; provokasjon. **provocative** [prə'vɒkətɪv] *adj* provoserende *etc*; (opp)hissende; utfordrende. **provoke** [prə'vəʊk] *vt* **1** provosere; (an)spore, egge; utfordre; **2** ergre, irritere; terge, tirre; hisse (opp).

prow [praʊ] *sb* baug, forstavn.

prowl [praʊl] **1** *sb* lur(ing); lusking; *ofte* streiftog; **2** *vi* luske; lure/snike seg (omkring); patruljere, spane. **prowl car** *sb US* patruljebil.

proximity [prɒk'sɪmətɪ] *sb* nærhet; naboskap; beslektethet, slektskap.

proxy ['prɒksɪ] *sb* **1** fullmektig; stedfortreder; **2** fullmakt.

prude [pru:d] *sb* dydsmønster, snerpe.

prudence ['pru:dns] *sb* forsiktighet *etc*. **prudent** ['pru:dnt] *adj* forsiktig, omtenksom; forutseende. **prudential** [pru:'denʃl] **1** *adj* forsiktig *etc*; forsiktighets-; **2** *sb fl* fornuftshensyn.

prune [pru:n] **A** *sb* sviske; **B** *vt* (~ *away/down*) beskjære; skjære ned på.

pry [praɪ] **A** *vi*: ~ *into* snuse i; legge nesen (sin) opp i (andres/andre folks affærer); **B** *vt* (~ *open*) bryte opp.

psalm [sɑ:m] salme.

psychiatric [,saɪkɪ'ætrɪk] *adj* psykiatrisk. **psychiatrist** [saɪ'kaɪətrɪst] *sb* psykiater. **psychiatry** [saɪ'kaɪətrɪ] *sb* psykiatri. **psychic** ['saɪkɪk] **I** *adj* **1** psykisk; **2** *dgl* okkult, overnaturlig; mystisk; **II** *sb* **1** *dgl* medium; person med psykiske (overnaturlige, spiritistiske etc) evner; **2** *slang* skrulling, skrulle. **psychological** [,saɪkə'lɒdʒɪkl] *adj* psykologisk. **psychologist** [saɪ'kɒlədʒɪst] *sb* psykolog. **psychology** [saɪ'kɒlədʒɪ] *sb* psykologi. **psychopath** ['saɪkəʊpæθ] *sb* psykopat. **psychosis** [saɪ'kəʊsɪs] *sb* psykose. **psychotherapist** [,saɪkəʊ'θerəpɪst] *sb* psykoterapeut. **psychotherapy** [,saɪkəʊ'θerəpɪ] *sb* psykoterapi.

ptarmigan ['tɑ:mɪgən] *sb* fjellrype.

pub [pʌb] *sb* (*fork* for *public house*) kro, vertshus. **public** ['pʌblɪk] **1** *adj* offentlig (og allmenn(-), felles(-); folke-; *ofte* kommunal(-), kommune-; stats- etc); **2** *sb*: *the* ~ offentligheten, publikum; *in* ~ offentlig, åpenlyst. **publication** [,pʌblɪ'keɪʃn] *sb* bekjentgjøring *etc*; publisering (og publikasjon). **public | convenience** *sb* offentlig toalett. ~ **domain** *sb* ≈ offentlig eie (*data* især om programmer som mot en nominell avgift er frigitt til allmenn benyttelse). ~ **house** *sb* se *pub*. **publicity** [pʌb'lɪsətɪ] *sb* **1** offentlighet; **2** publisitet; (offentlig) omtale *etc*; reklame. **publicize** ['pʌblɪsaɪz] *vt* gi publisitet. **public | opinion** *sb* folkemening(en). ~ **opinion poll** *sb* (offentlig) meningsmåling/opinionsundersøkelse. ~ **school** *sb* **1** *GB* (eksklusiv, kostbar) kostskole; **2** *US* offentlig skole. ~ **spirit** *sb* samfunnsånd. **publish** ['pʌblɪʃ] *vt* bekjentgjøre, kunngjøre; offentliggjøre, publisere; *om bøker etc* utgi. **publisher** ['pʌblɪʃə] *sb* forlegger. **publishing | firm,** ~ **house** *sb* forlag.

pucker ['pʌkə] **1** *sb* nyve; (liten) rynke; **2** *vb* rynke (seg); snurpe (sammen).

puddle ['pʌdl] *sb* søle|dam, -pytt.

puff [pʌf] **I** *sb* **1** pust (og blaff, drag, gufs; blås, blåst etc); ~*s of smoke* små røykskyer; **2** krembolle; **II** *vb* **1** puste; blåse *etc* støtvis; dampe, ryke; tøffe; ~ *and blow* puste og pese; ~ *at (a pipe etc)* dampe/patte på (en pipe etc); ~ *out* blåse ut; ~ *up* blåse opp; skape blest om; slå (stort) opp; ~*ed-up* oppblåst *etc*; **2** (~ *out*) få til å heve seg/svulme. **puffy** ['pʌfɪ] *adj* **1** andpusten; kortpustet; **2** oppblåst; blæret, hoven; viktig.

pugnacious [pʌg'neɪʃəs] *adj* stridbar, stridslysten; kranglet.

pug-nose ['pʌgnəʊz] *sb* oppstoppernese.

puke [pju:k] *vb* kaste opp.

pull [pʊl] **I** *sb* **1** drag (dvs det å dra/trekke etc); trekk|evne, -kraft; *fig* innflytelse; tiltrekning (og tiltrekningskraft); **2** håndtak; (dør)|grep, -vrier; snor/

streng (til å trekke i); **3** *dgl* drag (av sigarett etc); slurk (især av flaske); **II** *vb* **1** dra (og hale, slepe, trekke samt dra *etc* i/på); ~ *faces* gjøre grimaser; skjære ansikter; ~ *a fast one (US dgl)* overrumple; ta innersvingen (på); slå en plate; fortelle en våget historie; ~ *his leg* drive gjøn/holde leven med ham; ~ *one's weight* legge seg i selen; ta sin tørn; ~ *(the) strings/wires* trekke i trådene; **2** plukke, sanke; rense; **3** rive/slite (i/i stykker); **4** *(~ an oar)* ro; **5** *med adv, prep* ~ **about** herje/herse med; ~ **down** rive ned; redusere, svekke; ~ **off** klare; lykkes med; ~ **round** komme seg (etter sykdom etc); hjelpe gjennom (vanskeligheter etc); ~ **through** klare/slå seg igjennom; hjelpe gjennom (vanskeligheter etc); ~ *oneself* **together** ta seg sammen; ~ **up** dra/rykke opp; stanse, stoppe.

pullet ['pʊlɪt] *sb* unghøne.

pulley ['pʊlɪ] *sb* reimskive. **pulley-block** *sb* (skive)blokk, talje.

pulp [pʌlp] **1** *sb* bløt masse (som f.eks. papirmasse, tremasse); *dgl* grøt, mos; velling; *også* fruktkjøtt; *beat to a* ~ slå sønder og sammen; **2** *vb* bli/forvandle til en bløt masse; *dgl* mase (sammen); mose.

pulpit ['pʊlpɪt] *sb* prekestol.

pulsate [pʌl'seɪt] *vi* pulsere, vibrere; banke, slå.

pulse [pʌls] **1** *sb* puls (og pulsslag); rytme; **2** *vi* banke/slå (om pulsen); pulsere, vibrere.

pumice ['pʌmɪs] *sb* pimpestein.

pummel ['pʌml] *vt* slå løs på.

pump [pʌmp] **A** *sb, vb* pumpe; **B** *sb* dansesko.

pumpkin ['pʌmpkɪn] *sb* gresskar.

pun [pʌn] *sb, vi* (lage) ordspill.

punch [pʌntʃ] **A 1** *sb* neveslag; bokse|slag, -støt; **2** *vt* dra til; slå (hardt); **B 1** *sb* punsel, stanse; dor, kjørner; *data etc* hulle|maskin, -stanser; *(hollow ~)* lokk|-beitel, -meisel; *(ticket ~)* billett|saks, -tang; hulltang; **2** *vt* klippe (slå, stanse etc) hull i; perforere, punche; **C** *sb* punsj. **punch | card** *sb data* hullkort. ~ **tape** *sb data* hullbånd.

punctilious [pʌŋk'tɪlɪəs] *adj* (altfor) nøyaktig/nøye; (ytterst) korrekt; pedantisk. **punctual** ['pʌŋktʃʊəl] *adj* presis, punktlig. **punctuate** ['pʌŋktʃʊeɪt] *vt* **1** sette skilletegn; **2** poengtere, understreke. **punctuation** [,pʌŋktʃʊ'eɪʃn] *sb* tegnsetning. **puncture** ['pʌŋktʃə] **1** *sb* gjennomboring *etc*; stikk; punktering; **2** *vb* gjennom|bore, -hulle; gå/stikke hull på; punktere.

pungent ['pʌndʒənt] *adj* **1** skarp (om lukt, smak etc); **2** bitende; kvass, spydig.

punish ['pʌnɪʃ] *vt* **1** straffe; **2** maltraktere, mishandle. **punishment** ['pʌnɪʃmənt] *sb* straff.

punt [pʌnt] **1** *sb* flatbunnet elvebåt; **2** *vb* stake (seg frem med) elvebåt.

puny ['pju:nɪ] *adj* ørliten; puslet, ynkelig.

pup [pʌp] *fork* for ***puppy***.

pupil ['pju:pl] *sb* **A** (skole)elev; **B** pupill.

puppet ['pʌpɪt] *sb* **1** dukke (til dukketeater); marionett; **2** *fig* nikkedukke, stråmann. **puppet show** *sb* dukketeater.

puppy ['pʌpɪ] *sb* **1** (hunde)valp; **2** laps, sprade; sprett.

purchase ['pɜ:tʃəs] **I** *sb* **1** handel, (inn)kjøp; anskaffelse, ervervelse; innkjøpt vare; **2** godt tak; hold (og holdepunkt); (fot)feste; fordel, overtak; **II** *vt* kjøpe (inn); skaffe seg (for penger).

pure ['pjʊə] *adj* **1** ren; uskyldig, uskyldsren; kysk; **2** klar, tydelig; **3** ekte, uforfalsket; uoppblandet; **4** ren (og skjær); fullstendig, total. **purely** ['pjʊəlɪ] *adv* rent (og fullstendig, totalt; bare, utelukkende etc). **purgatory** ['pɜ:gətrɪ] *sb* skjærsild(en). **purge** [pɜ:dʒ] **I** *sb* **1** rensing; *pol etc* opprenskning, utrenskning; **2** avføringsmiddel; **II** *vt* **1** rense (*of/from* for); *rel* lutre; *(~ out)* utrenske (politiske motstandere etc); **2** gi avføringsmiddel; rense/skylle (tarmene med klyster). **purging** *sb petro* gasspyling. **purification** [,pjʊərɪfɪ'keɪʃn] *sb* renselse *etc*. **purify** ['pjʊərɪfaɪ] *vt* rense (*of/from* for); gjøre/vaske ren; klare (væske); *rel* lutre.

purloin [pɜ:'lɔɪn] *vt bokl* stjele.

purple ['pɜ:pl] *adj, sb* purpur(-).

purpose ['pɜ:pəs] **I** *sb* **1** hensikt; mening, plan; **2** formål; *to the* ~ formålstjenlig; relevant; til saken; **3** forsett; *on* ~ med forsett (hensikt, vilje etc); **4** besluttsomhet; **II** *vt* akte; ha til hensikt. **purposeful** *adj* meningsfylt; målbevisst; formålsbestemt. **purposeless** *adj* formålsløs; unyttig. **purposely** *adv* forsettlig.

purr [pɜ:] **I** *sb* maling *etc*; **II** *vi* **1** *om katt* male; **2** *om maskiner etc* summe, surre; dure.

purse [pɜ:s] **1** *sb* (penge)pung; *også* (hånd)veske; *fig* penger (og pengesum; fond, kasse; budsjett, finanser etc); **2** *vt* *(~ up)* snurpe (sammen); rynke. **purse-strings** *sb fl: hold the* ~ sitte på pengesekken (dvs bestemme hvem som skal få penger og hva de skal brukes til).

pursuance [pə'sjʊəns] *sb* oppfølging; *in* ~ *of* = *pursuant to*. **pursuant** [pə'sjʊənt] *adj:* ~ *to* etter, ifølge; i samsvar med; i tilknytning til. **pursue** [pə'sju:] *vt* **1** forfølge, jage; **2** følge (forelesning, kurs etc); praktisere; (stadig) drive med; **3** strebe etter. **pursuit** [pə'sju:t] *sb* forfølgelse *etc*; *in* ~ *of* på jakt etter.

purvey [pɜ:'veɪ] *vb* forsyne med; levere/skaffe (forsyninger, især av matvarer); være leverandør (*for/to* til). **purveyor** [pɜ:'veɪə] *sb* leverandør.

pus [pʌs] *sb* materie, puss; verk.

push [pʊʃ] **I** *sb* **1** dytt(ing); puff, støt; press, trykk; påtrykk; **2** driv (og driftighet); iherdighet, pågåenhet; **3** fremstøt, offensiv; **4** krise, nødstilfelle; *at a* ~ i et knipetak; **II** *vb* **1** dytte/skyve (på); puffe/skubbe (til); mase/trenge seg frem; **2** trykke (på); **3** drive, tvinge; forsere, presse; nøde; **4** *med adv, prep* ~ **ahead** rykke/trenge frem; mase/trenge seg frem; ~ **along** fortsette/gå videre; ~ **aside** skyve til side; ~ **away** skyve unna; skyve/støte fra seg; ~ **forward** = ~ *ahead*; ~ **off** sende av sted/fra seg; legge fra land; *også* = ~ *along*; ~ **out** skyve ut; ~ **over** velte; dytte/skyve over ende; ~ **through** bryte/trenge (seg) igjennom;

drive/tvinge igjennom; ~ **up** drive opp/i været; ~ *up the daisies (dgl)* ligge under torva (dvs være død). **push|-button** *sb* trykknapp. **~-cart** *sb* dragkjerre, håndkjerre; trille|bag, -kurv; *US også* = **~-chair** *sb* (barne)kjerre, sportsvogn. **pusher** ['pʊʃə] *sb slang* narkotika|hai, (-)langer. **pushing** ['pʊʃɪŋ] *adj* pågående; innpåsliten, påtrengende. **push-over** *sb* lett oppgave; svak motstander. **~-through** *sb* gjennombrudd.

puss [pʊs], **pussy** ['pʊsɪ] *sb* pus, (puse)katt.

put [pʊt] **I** *sb* kast; *især* (kule)støt; **II** *vb* **1** legge (og putte, sette, stille; anbringe, plassere etc); ~ *it here/there (dgl)* kom med handa/labben; **2** sende; kjøre, renne; stikke; **3** kaste; ~ *the weight (shot, stone)* støte kule; **4** *sjø* seile; gå, løpe; **5** (frem)|sette, -stille; komme med; legge/sette frem; **6** forårsake; gjøre (til); ~ *right/straight* få orden/skikk på; rette, rettlede; ~ *wise (dgl)* orientere; underrette (om); **7** formulere; uttrykke (seg); *to ~ it mildly* for å si det mildt; **8** *med adv, prep* ~ **about** sette i omløp; *sjø* (stag)vende; *fig* forurolige; ~ **across** ferje/sette over; lykkes (med); få til å forstå *etc*; *dgl* prakke på; innbille; ~ **ashore** sette i land; losse; ~ **aside** legge/*fig* skyve til side; ~ **away** legge *etc* til side; gjemme/spare (på); *dgl* sperre inne (på asyl etc); rydde av veien (= drepe); ~ **back** legge *etc* tilbake; forsinke, hemme; *sjø* gjøre vendereis; ~ **by** legge *etc* til side; ~ **down** sette *etc* fra seg; hente/ta ned; sette ned; slå ned; notere (seg); skrive ned; ~ *it* **down to** *(the cold etc)* gi (kulden etc) skylden for det; ~ **forth** rekke/sette frem; gi/sende ut; skyte (knopper/skudd etc); (la) kunngjøre/meddele; *fig* mobilisere, oppby; ~ **forward** legge *etc* frem; komme med (forslag etc); ~ **in** legge *etc* inn (samt installere, montere etc); ha/helle i; til|føye, -sette; legge/skyte inn (et ord etc); legge/sette frem (forslag etc); legge (arbeid etc) i; anvende/bruke (krefter etc) på; ~ *in an appearance* møte frem/opp; vise seg; ~ **in at/to** *sjø* gå/løpe inn til; legge til ved; ~ **in for** anmode/søke om; fremme/komme med krav om; ~ **inside** *dgl* sette inn (dvs i fengsel); ~ **into** legge *etc* (inn) i; kle/uttrykke i (ord); oversette til; ~ **off** legge *etc* vekk; kvitte seg med; *sjø* skyve fra land; stikke til sjøs; *fig* utsette; avvise; skyve/støte fra seg; forstyrre; få fra (dvs hindre etc); ~ **off on** nøde/prakke på; ~ **on** legge *etc* på; smøre/stryke på; kle/ta på (seg); sette over (gryte etc); satse/sette (penger) på; sette på (avisartikkel etc); sette opp (teaterstykke etc); anspore, egge; ~ **on to** sette over (telefonsamtale) til; henvise til; ~ *them on to it* sette dem på det (dvs gjøre dem oppmerksom på det; få dem til å huske/tenke på det); ~ **out** legge *etc* ut; sette *etc* frem; gi/sende ut; stikke ut (øyne); slukke (lys/varme etc); bringe/få ut av fatning; ergre, irritere; ~ *out (to sea)* gå (legge, løpe, stå etc) ut; stikke til sjøs; ~ **over** = ~ *across*; *I wouldn't ~ it* **past** *her* det tror jeg så gjerne om henne; hun er troendes til det; ~ **through** sende igjennom; la gjennomgå; *fig* avslutte; gjennomføre; utføre; ~ **through to** sette over til (dvs gi (telefon)forbindelse med); ~ **to** *death* drepe; ~ *to expenses* påføre utgifter; ~ *to flight* jage på flukt; ~ *to sea* stikke til sjøs; ~ *to shame* gjøre til skamme; ~ *to silence* bringe til taushet; ~ **together** sette *etc* sammen; addere; legge sammen; ~ **under** legge *etc* under; ~ **up** legge *etc* opp; oppføre; reise (og føre, sette etc) opp; slå opp; legge på (pris); komme med; legge/sette frem (forslag etc); gi husly (til); legge unna/til side; pakke inn/sammen; arrangere, etablere; ~*up (money etc)* skaffe/skyte inn (penger etc); ~ **up to** egge (hisse, sette opp) til; informere (orientere, underrette etc) om; fremlegge (for); ~ **up with** tåle; finne seg i; ~ **upon** = ~ *on*. **put-off** *sb* påskudd; utsettelse. **put-on** *adj* påtatt, tilgjort.

putrefaction [ˌpju:trɪ'fækʃn] *sb* forråtnelse *etc*; råttenhet, råttenskap. **putrefy** ['pju:trɪfaɪ] *vb* (få til å) råtne/gå i forråtnelse. **putrescence** [pju:'tresns] *sb* forråtnelse. **putrescent** [pju:'tresnt] *adj* råtnende. **putrid** ['pju:trɪd] *adj* råtten.

putty ['pʌtɪ] **1** *sb* kitt; **2** *vt* kitte.

put-up *adj* avtalt på forhånd; fingert.

puzzle ['pʌzl] **I** *sb* **1** problem; gåte, hodebry; *også* puslespill; **2** forvirring; rådvillhet, villrede; **II** *vb* **1** forvirre; sette fast/på prøve etc; sette i forlegenhet; **2** grunne; bry hjernen; ~ *out* spekulere ut. **puzzling** ['pʌzlɪŋ] *adj* forvirrende; gåtefull.

pylon ['paɪlən] *sb* (kraft)ledningsmast.

python ['paɪθn] *sb* pyton(slange).

Q

quack [kwæk] **A I** *sb* **1** kvekk(ing) *etc*; **2** gakk-gakk (dvs and etc); **II** *vi* kvekke, snadre; **B** *sb* kvakksalver, sjarlatan.

quad [kwɒd] *dgl fork* for *quadrangle/quadruplet*. **quadrangle** ['kwɒdræŋgl] *sb* **1** (rettvinklet) firkant; **2** firkantet gårdsplass. **quadrate I** ['kwɒdrət] **1** *adj* kvadratisk; **2** *sb* kvadrat; **II** [kwə'dreɪt] *vb* kvadrere(s). **quadruped** ['kwɒdrʊped] *sb* firbeint dyr. **quadruplets** ['kwɒdrʊplɪts] *sb fl* firlinger.

quagmire ['kwægmaɪə] *sb* hengemyr; *fig* gyngende grunn; vanskelig situasjon.

quail [kweɪl] **A** *sb* vaktel; **B** *vi* bli engstelig/redd;

bøye/vike unna.

quaint [kweınt] *adj* artig, snodig; gammel|dags, -modig (og derfor spennende, tiltrekkende etc).

quake [kweık] **1** *sb (earth~)* jordskjelv; **2** *vi* ryste, skake, skjelve. **Quaker** ['kweıkə] *sb* kveker.

qualification [ˌkwɒlıfı'keıʃn] *sb* **1** kvalifisering *etc*; kvalifikasjon; **2** betingelse, vilkår; forutsetning; **3** begrensning, forbehold; modifikasjon. **qualified** ['kwɒlıfaıd] *adj* kvalifisert *etc*; fag|lært, (-)utdannet; autorisert. **qualify** ['kwɒlıfaı] *vb* **1** kvalifisere (seg); forberede/utdanne (seg); gjøre (seg) egnet/skikket; **2** autorisere, bemyndige; gi rett; gjøre berettiget; **3** begrense, innskrenke; modifisere; spesifisere (nærmere); **4** beskrive; *gram* bestemme; **5** mildne; dempe, moderere. **qualitative** ['kwɒlıtətıv] *adj* kvalitativ. **quality** ['kwɒlətı] *sb* **1** kvalitet; *som adj* kvalitets-; **2** beskaffenhet; egenskap; **3** *gml* stand. **quality printer** *sb data* skjønnskriver.

qualm [kwɑ:m] *sb* tvil, uro; *fl* skrupler.

quandary ['kwɒndərı] *sb* forlegenhet, knipe; pinlig/vanskelig situasjon.

quantitative ['kwɒntıtətıv] *adj* kvantitativ. **quantity** ['kwɒntətı] *sb* kvantitet; antall, mengde; omfang, volum; *in quantities* i (store) mengder.

quarantine ['kwɒrənti:n] *sb, vt* (holde/sette etc i) karantene.

quarrel ['kwɒrəl] **I** *sb* **1** krangel, trette; **2** ankepunkt; innvending; **II** *vi* kjekle, krangle, trette. **quarrelsome** ['kwɒrəlsəm] *adj* kranglevoren.

quarry ['kwɒrı] **A** *sb* (jakt)bytte, rov; **B I** *sb* steinbrudd; **II** *vb* **1** bryte (stein); **2** *fig* grave frem; forske, granske.

quart [kwɔ:t] *sb* et hulmål, se midtsidene. **quarter** ['kwɔ:tə] **I** *sb* **1** fjerde|del, -part; kvart (og kvartal, kvarter); fjerding; *US* 25 cent; *som adj* fjerdings(-), kvart(als)-; **2** distrikt, strøk; bydel; kvartal, kvarter; *from that ~* fra den kanten; *in the highest ~s* på høyeste hold; **3** *fl* hus|rom, -være; losji; *mil* forlegning, kvarter; **4** *sjø* låring; **5** *sjø mil* post, stilling; **6** *mil* nåde (mot beseiret fiende); **7** *om mål og vekt* se midtsidene; **II** *vt* **1** dele i fire; *gml* partere (forbryter); **2** *mil* forlegge, innkvartere. **quarter|-deck** *sb* akterdekk, skanse. **~-final** *sb* kvartfinale. **quarterly** ['kwɔ:təlı] **1** *adj* fjerdedels-, kvartals-; **2** *adv* kvartalsvis; **3** *sb* kvartalstidsskrift. **quarter|master** *sb mil* kvartermester. **~master general** *sb mil* generalintendant. **~ platform** *sb petro* boligplattform.

quaver ['kweıvə] **I** *sb* **1** skjelving *etc*; **2** *mus* åttendedelsnote; **II** *vb* **1** skjelve; dirre, sitre; **2** trille (dvs slå *etc* triller).

quay [ki:] *sb* brygge, kai.

queasy ['kwizı] *adj* **1** sart, ømtålig; disponert for kvalme; **2** kvalm; **3** kvalmende.

queen [kwi:n] **I** *sb* **1** dronning; **2** dame (i kortspill); **II** *vt: ~ it (over)* herske (over, som en dronning); spille dronning (for/over). **queen's evidence** *sb* kronvitne.

queer ['kwıə] **I** *adj* **1** underlig; *dgl* unormal; rar (av seg); **2** fordektig, mistenkelig; mystisk; **3** *dgl* uvel; **4** *dgl* homo(fil); **II** *sb slang* homse (dvs homofil mann).

quell [kwel] *vt bokl, poet* knuse; kue, undertrykke; dempe.

quench [kwentʃ] *vt* **1** slokke (varme); **2** slokke (tørste); **3** kue, undertrykke; dempe, stille; **4** avkjøle (i/med vann).

querulous ['kweruləs] *adj* gretten, irritabel; kranglvoren, trettekjær.

query ['kwıərı] **I** *sb* **1** spørsmål; *også data* forespørsel; **2** tvil; **II** *vt* **1** spørre (*whether* om); **2** bestride, betvile; tvile på. **quest** [kwest] **1** *sb* leting/søking (*for* etter); *in ~ of* på jakt/leting etter; **2** *vi* lete/søke (*for* etter). **question** ['kwestʃən] **I** *sb* **1** spørsmål; *pol* interpellasjon; **2** tvil; innvending; *beyond (past, without etc) ~* utvilsomt; hevet over (hinsides, uten etc) tvil; *call in ~* bestride; dra/trekke i tvil; **3** problem; emne, tema; sak; *come into ~* komme på tale; *out of the ~* umulig; ikke på tale; *put the ~* ta saken opp til votering; **4** *gml* tortur; *put to the ~* underkaste pinlig forhør; **II** *vt* **1** spørre; **2** forhøre; spørre ut; **3** bestride; dra/trekke i tvil. **questionable** ['kwestʃənəbl] *adj* tvilsom, usikker. **questionaire** [ˌkwestʃə'neə] *sb* enquête, rundspørring. **questioner** ['kwestʃənə] *sb* spørsmålsstiller. **question|-mark** *sb* spørsmålstegn. **~ time** *sb pol etc* spørretime.

queue [kju:] **I** *sb* **1** kø; **2** hårpisk; **II** *vi (~ up)* stå/stille seg i kø.

quibble ['kwıbl] **1** *sb* ordkløveri, spissfindighet; utflukt; **2** *vi* vri (på ord etc); bruke/komme med utflukter.

quick [kwık] **I** *adj* **1** hurtig (og kjapp, rask, snar etc); **2** kvikk, livlig; **3** gløgg, oppvakt; **4** *gml* levende; **II** *adv dgl* **1** *(~ly)* fort, kjapt; **2** *som pref* hurtig-, snar-; **III** *sb* (levende) kjøtt; *fig* ømt punkt; *cut him to the ~* såre ham dypt; ramme ham på hans ømmeste punkt. **quicken** ['kwıkn] *vb* **1** påskynde; jage/skynde på; **2** kvikke/live opp; anspore, stimulere; **3** kvikne til. **quick|sand** *sb* kvikksand. **~silver** *sb* kvikksølv. **~ start** *sb data* varmstart. **~-tempered** *adj* oppfarende, snarsint. **~-witted** *adj* slagferdig; snarrådig.

quid [kwıd] *sb* pund (dvs myntenheten, se midtsidene); **2** (tobakks)buss.

quiet ['kwaıət] **I** *adj* **1** rolig; stille, stillferdig; fredelig; **2** dempet/diskret (især om farger); **3** hemmelig(holdt), skjult; undertrykt; **II** *sb* **1** ro, stillhet; **2** hemmelighet; *on the ~* i all stillhet; i det skjulte; **III** *vb* = **quieten** ['kwaıətn] *vb* berolige, stagge; dempe; roe (seg); *(~ down)* falle til ro. **quietness** ['kwaıətnıs], **quietude** ['kwaııtju:d] *sb* ro, stillhet.

quill [kwıl] *sb* **1** *a) (~-feather)* (hale)fjær, svingfjær; *b)* fjærpenn; **2** pigg (på pinnsvin).

quilt [kwılt] **1** *sb* vatteppe; **2** *vt* matelassere, vattere.

quinine [kwı'ni:n] *sb* kinin.

quintessence [kwın'tesns] *sb* kvintessens, innbegrep.

quintet, quintette [kwɪn'tet] *sb* kvintett.

quintuplets ['kwɪntjuplɪts] *sb fl* femlinger.

quip [kwɪp] **I** *sb* **1** spissfindighet; dobbeltbunnet/tvetydig vittighet; **2** sarkasme, spydighet; **II** *vi* være sarkastisk/spydig; raljere, spotte; spøke.

quirk [kwɜ:k] *sb* **1** innfall, lune; egenhet; **2** = *quip I.*

quit [kwɪt] **I** *adj:* ~ *of* fri for; kvitt; **II** *vt* **1** forlate; flytte (fra); gå (dra, reise etc) fra; **2** nedlegge, oppgi; ~ *hold of* gi slipp på; **3** *US* holde opp/slutte (med); ~ *smoking* slutte å røyke; **4** betale tilbake; ~ *scores* kvitte, utligne; **5** *gml* = *acquit.*

quite [kwaɪt] *adv* **1** fullstendig, helt; ~ *another story* en ganske/helt annen sak; **2** virkelig; absolutt, ubetinget; ~ *so* javisst; ganske riktig; ~ *the thing* siste mote/skrik; **3** ganske, nokså, temmelig.

quits [kwɪts] *adj* kvitt; *be* ~ *with* være kvitt/skuls med; *double or* ~ dobbelt eller kvitt.

quiver ['kwɪvə] **A** *sb* (pile)kogger; **B** **1** *sb* skjelving *etc*; **2** *vb* (få til å) skjelve; dirre, sitre.

quiz [kwɪz] **I** *sb* **1** spørrekonkurranse; **2** fiksering; nærgående *etc* blikk; **II** *vt* **1** eksaminere; spørre ut; **2** *gml* erte, spotte; drive gjøn med; **3** *gml* fiksere; stirre nærgående (overlegent, uforskammet etc) på. **quizzical** ['kwɪzɪkl] *adj* **1** komisk, snurrig; **2** ertende, spotsk; **3** spørrende; tvilende, vantro.

quoit [kwɔɪt] *sb* **1** (kaste)ring; **2** ringspill.

quorum ['kwɔ:rəm] *sb* beslutningsdyktig antall.

quota ['kwəutə] *sb* kvote, part; del.

quotation [kwəu'teɪʃn] *sb* **1** sitat; **2** *merk* pris (og pris|liste, -notering); anbud, overslag. **quotation marks** *sb fl* anførselstegn. **quote** [kwəut] **I** *vt* **1** sitere; gjengi/gjenta (ordrett); *også* jeg siterer; anførselstegn begynner; *un*~ anførselstegn slutter; sitat slutt; **2** oppgi (som eksempel etc); **3** *merk* nevne/si en pris; gi/komme med et (pris)tilbud; **II** *sb dgl* sitat; *fl* anførselstegn. **quoth** [kwəuθ] *vt gml pret* sa.

quotient ['kwəuʃənt] *sb mat* kvotient.

qwerty keyboard *sb data* ≈ (standard)tastatur (med bokstavene q-w-e-r-t-y plassert som på en vanlig skrivemaskin).

R

rabbit ['ræbɪt] *sb* kanin.

rabble ['ræbl] *sb* mobb, pakk. **rabble-rouser** *sb* oppvigler.

rabid ['ræbɪd] *adj* **1** gal (av hundegalskap); **2** rasende, vill; rabiat. **rabies** ['reɪbi:z] *sb* hundegalskap.

race [reɪs] **A** *sb* rase (og folkeferd, stamme; familie, slekt); **B** **I** *sb* **1** kappløp (og kapp|kjøring, -ritt, -seilas etc); renn; **2** *(~s, ~-meeting)* hesteveddeløp; **II** *vb* **1** løpe *etc* om kapp; delta i løp/renn *etc*; **2** drive hestesport; **3** fare (jage, rase etc av sted); **4** ruse (motor). **race|-course** *sb* veddeløpsbane. **~-horse** *sb* veddeløpshest. **~-track** *sb* = *~-course.* **racial** ['reɪʃl] *adj* rasemessig, rase-. **racing** ['reɪsɪŋ] *sb* **1** hestesport; veddeløpssport; **2** = *race B I 1.*

rack [ræk] **A** **I** *sb* **1** oppsats, stativ; ramme, rekke; *hat-~* hattehylle; **2** tannstang; **II** *vt* sette i stativ *etc*; **B** **I** *sb* pinebenk; **II** *vt* **1** pine, torturere; ~ *one's brain* vri hjernen; **2** plage; undertrykke; ut|pine, -suge; **C** *sb* **1** drivende sky(banke); **2** *go to ~ and ruin* forfalle; gå den veien høna sparker. **racket** ['rækɪt] **A** **I** *sb* **1** bråk, spetakkel; **2** festing; *on the* ~ på rangel; **3** geskjeft; *US især* forbrytersk/lyssky virksomhet; **II** *vi* feste, rangle; **B** *sb* (tennis)racket. **racketeer** [ˌrækɪ'tɪə] *sb* kjeltring, gangster.

racy ['reɪsɪ] *adj* **1** kraftig; livlig; **2** karakteristisk; sær|egen, -preget; **3** drøy, saftig; pikant.

radiance ['reɪdɪəns] *sb* (stråle)glans; (ut)stråling. **radiant** ['reɪdɪənt] *adj* **1** (ut)strålende, skinnende; **2** strålende. **radiate** ['reɪdɪeɪt] *vb* **1** (ut)stråle; **2** stråle ut; spre seg i vifteform. **radiation** [ˌreɪdɪ'eɪʃn] *sb* (ut)stråling. **radio** ['reɪdɪəu] **I** *(radio-) som pref* **1** radio-; **2** radium-, røntgen-; stråle-; **II** *sb* radio(apparat); **III** *vb* kringkaste; sende over radio. **radio|active** *adj* radioaktiv. **~-therapy** *sb* strålebehandling.

radish ['rædɪʃ] *sb* reddik.

raffle ['ræfl] **1** *sb* (veldedighets)basar; tombola; **2** *vt* lodde ut.

raft [rɑ:ft] **I** *sb* (tømmer)flåte; *rubber* ~ (oppblåsbar) gummiflåte; **II** *vb* **1** fløte (tømmer); **2** seile på flåte. **rafter** ['rɑ:ftə] *sb* **1** tak|bjelke, -sperre; **2** (tømmer)fløter.

rag [ræg] **A** *sb* fille, klut; *dgl* blekke (om ubetydelig avis etc); **B** *dgl* **1** *sb* bråk, leven; skøyerstreker; **2** *vb* erte; holde leven med. **ragamuffin** ['rægəmʌfɪn] *sb gml* fillefrans. **rag paper** *sb* klutepapir.

rage [reɪdʒ] **I** *sb* **1** raseri; villskap, voldsomhet; **2** *dgl* (mote)galskap; dille, mani; *all the* ~ siste skrik; **II** *vi* rase.

ragged ['rægɪd] *adj* **1** fillet; lurvet; **2** forreven, takket; **3** ujevn, uregelmessig.

raid [reɪd] **I** *sb* **1** (plutselig) angrep/overfall; innfall, raid; **2** plyndringstokt; ran, røveri; **3** rassia; **II** *vb* **1** overfalle; plyndre; **2** gjøre rassia (i).

rail [reɪl] **A I** *sb* **1** gjerde; gelender, rekkverk; *sjø* rekke, reling; **2** stang, tverrtre; *fl* tverrpinner; **3** skinne; *fl* skinnegang, spor; *by ~* med jernbane(n)/ *dgl* tog(et); *off the ~s* avsporet; **II** *vt* sette opp rekkverk *etc*; *~ in* gjerde inn; **B** *vi* bruke seg (*against* på); *~ at* skjelle ut. **rail|-car** *sb* skinnebuss. **~road, ~way** *sb* jernbane.

rain [reɪn] **1** *sb* regn (og regnvær); **2** *vb* regne, strømme; *fig* la det regne (med); *~ cats and dogs* høljregne; *it never ~s but it pours* skal det være, så skal det være; en ulykke kommer sjelden alene. **rain|bow** *sb* regnbue. **~coat** *sb* regn|frakk, -kappe. **~proof** *adj* vanntett. **rainy** ['reɪnɪ] *adj* regnfull; regnværs-.

raise [reɪz] **I** *sb US* forhøyelse; *især* (lønns)pålegg; **II** *vt* **1** heve; (få til å) heve seg; løfte (og heise, trekke etc opp); *~ a blockade/siege* heve en blokade/beleiring; **2** forhøye, høyne; (for)øke; **3** (for)bedre, forfremme; *~ to the peerage* adle; **4** oppføre, reise; sette opp; bygge; **5** jage/vekke opp; fremkalle, provosere; **6** samle (inn/ sammen); *~ an army* stable på beina en hær; *~ money/a loan* reise penger/et lån; **7** oppdra; fø frem; *fig* bringe på bane; **8** ale opp; oppdrette; dyrke; **9** *sjø: ~ land* få land i sikte. **raiser** ['reɪzə] *sb US* oppdretter, produsent.

raisin ['reɪzn] *sb* rosin.

rake [reɪk] **A I** *sb* rive; **II** *vb* **1** rake (*together/up* sammen); *~ in* sope inn; *~ up* skrape sammen; **2** *sjø* bestryke; beskyte langskips; **B 1** *sb* helling, skråstilling (om skipsmaster etc); **2** *vb* stille/stå skrått; **C** *sb* fyllik; frekkas; uthaler. **rakish** ['reɪkɪʃ] *adj* **A** *sjø* elegant, smekker; fartspreget; med sterkt hellende master etc); **B** frekk.

rally ['rælɪ] **I** *sb* **1** (for)samling, stevne; (større) møte; rally; **2** bedring; **II** *vb* **1** møtes; samle (seg) igjen; **2** oppmuntre; sette (nytt) håp/mot i; **3** bli bedre; komme seg.

ram [ræm] **I** *sb* **1** saubukk, vær; **2** rambukk; *sjø* vedder; **II** *vt* **1** drive/ramme (ned); *dgl* dytte (kjøre, stappe etc) (ned); kyle, slenge; **2** *sjø* vedre; renne i senk.

ramble ['ræmbl] **I** *sb* tur/vandring (uten bestemt mål); **II** *vi* **1** drive (rusle, slentre etc) (omkring); **2** gjøre sidesprang (i tale); la innfallene råde; **3** *om planter* klatre/slynge seg. **rambling** ['ræmblɪŋ] *adj* **1** planløs, rotet; tilfeldig (oppført etc); krinklet; **2** springende, usammenhengende.

ramification [ˌræmɪfɪ'keɪʃn] *sb* forgrening; *fl også* utløpere. **ramify** ['ræmɪfaɪ] *vi* forgrene (seg); danne utløpere.

ramp [ræmp] **I** *sb* **1** rampe; skråplan; **2** *petro = stinger*; **II** *vb* **1** skråne; **2** forsyne med rampe(r). **rampant** ['ræmpənt] *adj* **1** vill, voldsom; ustyrlig; *be ~* florere; ta overhånd; rase; **2** frodig, yppig; **3** steilende (om løve på våpenskjold etc).

rampart ['ræmpɑ:t] *sb* **1** festningsvoll; **2** beskyttelse, vern.

ramrod ['ræmrɒd] *sb* ladestokk, pussestokk; *stiff as a ~* stiv som en pinne; stiv og strunk.

ramshackle ['ræmʃækl] *adj* falleferdig, skrøpelig.

ranch [rɑ:ntʃ, *US* ræntʃ] *US* **1** *sb* kvegfarm; **2** *vb* drive kvegfarm. **rancher** [rɑ:ntʃə, *US* ræntʃə] *sb* kvegfarmer.

rancid ['rænsɪd] *adj* harsk; **2** ram, stram; *fig* bitter. **rancour** ['ræŋkə] *sb* bitterhet, nag; hat.

random ['rændəm] **1** *adj* tilfeldig, vilkårlig; **2** *sb: at ~* på måfå/slump. **random | access memory, ~ access storage** *sb data* direktelager, internhukommelse. **~ file** *sb data* direktefil. **~ number** *sb data* slumptall. **~ sample** *sb* stikkprøve.

range [reɪndʒ] **I** *sb* **1** linje, rekke; kjede; **2** gruppe, klasse; serie; *~ of colours* fargeskala; **3** område, felt; *(shooting ~)* skytebane; **4** avstand; utstrekning; (rekke)vidde; spillerom; *at long/short ~* på langt/kort hold; **5** *US* beite, havnegang; **6** komfyr; **II** *vb* **1** arrangere, ordne; gruppere, klassifisere; rangere; **2** rette (sikte, stille etc) inn; **3** strekke seg (*from* fra; *to* til); *fig* inkludere, omfatte; **4** *US* (la) beite. **range-finder** *sb* avstandsmåler. **ranger** ['reɪndʒə] *sb* **1** (skog)oppsynsmann; **2** (fjell)vandrer; **3** kommandosoldat.

rank [ræŋk] **A I** *sb* **1** rad, rekke; geledd, linje; **2** gruppe, klasse; posisjon, rang; (militær) grad; *the ~s (dgl)* militæret; *other ~s* korporaler og menige; *the ~ and file = other ~s; fig også* menigmann; *take ~ of* ha rang foran; **II** *vb* **1** rangere; gi/ha rang; gruppere, klassifisere; plassere; *~ among/with* høre med til; regne(s) med blant; **2** *US: ~ing officer* rangeldste; høyeste (tilstedeværende) offiser; **B** *adj* **1** ram, stram; **2** grov, krass; åpenbar; *~ poison* ren og skjær gift.

rankle ['ræŋkl] *vi* nage, pine, plage; svi.

ransack ['rænsæk] *vt* **1** ransake; **2** plyndre, røve.

ransom ['rænsəm] **I** *sb* **1** løsepenger; *a king's ~* en (hel) formue; *hold to ~* (holde fanget og) kreve løsepenger for; **2** løskjøping; **II** *vt* **1** kjøpe fri; **2** frigi mot løsepenger.

rant [rænt] **1** *sb* fraser, (ord)skvalder; **2** *vb* skravle løs; skvaldre.

rap [ræp] **A I** *sb* **1** (lett) banking; **2** rapp, smekk; *fig* kritikk; *take the ~* få skylden; **II** *vb* **1** banke (lett); **2** slå; rappe til; **B** *sb: not a ~* ikke det grann; ikke en døyt.

rapacious [rə'peɪʃəs] *adj* grisk, grådig. **rapacity** [rə'pæsətɪ] *sb* griskhet *etc*.

rape [reɪp] **1** *sb* voldtekt; **2** *vt* voldta.

rapid ['ræpɪd] **I** *adj* **1** hurtig, rask; **2** bratt; **II** *sb fl* stryk.

rapt [ræpt] *adj* henført, henrykt. **rapture** ['ræptʃə] *sb* henførthet, henrykkelse. **rapturous** ['ræptʃərəs] *adj* **1** henrykt; **2** henrivende.

rare [reə] **A** *adj* **1** sjelden, uvanlig; **2** utsøkt; ypperlig; **3** tynn (om luft); **B** *adj US* råstekt.

rascal ['rɑ:skl] *sb* kjeltring, skurk, slyngel.

rash [ræʃ] **A** *adj* forhastet, overilt; **B** *sb* utslett. **rashness** ['ræʃnɪs] *sb* ubesindighet.

rasher ['ræʃə] *sb* tynn skive bacon etc.

rasp [rɑ:sp] **I** *sb* **1** rasp; **2** raspende/skurrende *etc* lyd; **II** *vb* **1** raspe; **2** file; gnikke, gnisse; skrape/skure *etc* (om forskjellige ulyder); *også* gå på nervene løs; **3** snakke skurrende.

raspberry ['rɑ:zbərɪ] *sb* **1** bringebær; **2** *slang* (forskjellige former ufine lyder) ≈ mislyd, ulyd; *give him a ~* pipe ham ut.

rat [ræt] **I** *sb* **1** rotte; *fig* overløper; angiver, tyster; *smell a ~* ane uråd; **2** *slang: Rats!* Nonsens! Sludder! **II** *vi* **1** gå på rottejakt; **2** *~ on* angi; sladre/tyste på.

ratch [rætʃ] = **ratchet** ['rætʃɪt] *sb* **1** sperre(verk); **2** = **ratchet wheel** *sb* sperrehjul.

rate [reɪt] **A I** *sb* **1** *om fart, mengde, størrelse etc* (-)grad, (-)målestokk; (-)prosent, (-)rate, (-)sats, (-)tariff; (-)pris, (-)takst; (-)hyppighet, (-)takt; (-)fart, (-)tempo; *at a/the ~ of* med en fart av; til en kurs/pris av; **2** *om måte etc: at any ~* i hvert fall; under enhver omstendighet; *at that/this ~* (om det fortsetter) på den/denne måten; i så fall; **3** (kommune) skatt; (kommunal) særskatt; **4** gruppe, klasse; *first-~* førsteklasses; **5** gang (om klokke); **II** *vb* **1** anslå, bedømme; *~ among* regne (med) blant; *~ highly* sette høyt; **2** taksere, vurdere; evaluere; ligne; tariffere; **3** *sjø* klassifisere; **4** *US* fortjene; ha krav på; være berettiget til; **B** *vb* kjefte; bruke seg på. **rate | of exchange** *sb* valutakurs. **~ of interest** *sb* rentefot. **~ of penetration** *sb petro* borehastighet. **~ of taxation** *sb* skattøre. **~-payer** *sb* skattebetaler.

rather ['rɑ:ðə] *adv* **1** heller, snarere; *~ not* helst ikke; *I had/would ~ that* jeg så/ville helst at; **2** ganske, nokså, temmelig; *~ a failure* nærmest en fiasko; *~ well* ikke så verst; *I ~ think* jeg tror nesten; **3** *dgl* [ˌrɑ:'ðɜ:] absolutt; javisst; (svært) gjerne.

ratification [ˌrætɪfɪ'keɪʃn] *sb* ratifisering; ratifikasjon. **ratify** ['rætɪfaɪ] *vt* ratifisere.

rating ['reɪtɪŋ] *sb* **A 1** bedømmelse, vurdering; **2** taksering; tariffering; **3** gradering; karaktersetting, karaktersystem; evaluering; **4** *sjø* klassifisering; bemanningsskala; **B** kjeft, overhøvling.

ratio ['reɪʃɪəʊ] *sb* forhold. **ration** ['ræʃn] **I** *sb* rasjon; **II** *vt* **1** rasjonere (på); **2** sette på rasjon. **rational** ['ræʃənl] *adj* **1** fornufts-; **2** fornuftig, rasjonell; **3** fornuftig, rimelig; vettig. **rationalistic** [ˌræʃnə'lɪstɪk] *adj* rasjonalistisk. **rationalize** ['ræʃnəlaɪz] *vt* rasjonalisere. **rationalization** [ˌræʃnəlaɪ'zeɪʃn] *sb* rasjonalisering. **ration card** *sb* rasjoneringskort.

ratlin(e)s ['rætlɪnz] *sb fl sjø* vevlinger.

rat race *sb* tredemølle (*især* = det daglige kjøret/maset). **ratter** ['rætə] *sb* rottefanger. **ratsbane** ['rætsbeɪn] *sb* rottegift.

rat(t)an [rə'tæn] *sb* spanskrør(palme).

rattle ['rætl] **I** *sb* **1** skrangling *etc*; (baby)|rangle, (-)skrangle; *(death-~)* (døds)ralling; **2** plapring, skravling; **II** *vb* **1** skramle/skrangle (med); klapre/rasle (med); ralle; **2** plapre, skravle; *~ off* lire av seg. **rattled** ['rætld] *adj* forvirret, usikker.

raucous [rɔ:kəs] *adj* hes.

ravage ['rævɪdʒ] **1** *sb* ødeleggelse; *fl også* herjing(er); **2** *vt* ødelegge; herje, plyndre.

rave [reɪv] *vi* rase (og skrike; bære seg; fantasere, snakke over seg; snakke begeistret/henført etc).

ravel ['rævl] *vb* **1** trevle(s) opp; **2** gjøre forvirret (floket, ugrei etc).

raven ['reɪvn] *sb* ravn; *som adj* ravnsvart. **ravenous** ['rævənəs] *adj* **1** skrubbsulten; **2** forsluken, grådig; glupsk.

ravine [rə'vi:n] *sb* kløft, slukt.

raving ['reɪvɪŋ] **mad** *adj* ravgal; splitter gal.

ravish ['rævɪʃ] *vt* **1** henrykke; gjøre begeistret; **2** *gml* bortføre, rane; skjende, voldta. **ravishing** ['rævɪʃɪŋ] *adj* fortryllende, henrivende.

raw [rɔ:] *adj* **1** rå; **2** fersk, umoden; uerfaren; **3** ubearbeidet, uferdig; **4** rå(kald), sur; **5** hudløs, sår; øm; **6** *dgl* brutal, hard. **raw|-boned** *adj* skinnmager. **~ data** *sb fl data* rådata. **~ deal** *sb* urettferdig behandling. **~hide** *adj, sb* (av) ugarvet lær.

ray [reɪ] **A 1** *sb* stråle; *fig* glimt, snev; **2** *vb* stråle (ut); **B** *sb* rokke.

raze [reɪz] *vt* rasere, ødelegge (fullstendig); jevne med jorden. **razor** ['reɪzə] *sb* barberkniv; *(safety ~)* barberhøvel. **razor|-blade** *sb* barberblad. **~edge** *sb* knivsegg; *fig* skillelinje; kritisk punkt.

re [ri:] *prep* ad, angående. **re-** [rɪ-, ri:-] *pref* gjen-, om-, tilbake- *etc* (som f.eks. i *~conquer* gjenerobre; *~group* omgruppere; *~pay* tilbakebetale).

reach [ri:tʃ] **I** *sb* **1** utstrekning (av hånd etc); **2** (hånd)grep; rekkevidde; omfang, spenn; evne, makt; *within/out of ~* innenfor/utenfor rekkevidde; **3** strekning; strøk, trakt; *sjø* baut, strekk; *fig* felt, område; **II** *vb* **1** rekke (*out* ut); strekke seg (*for* etter); *~ down* rekke/ta ned; **2** (opp)nå; rekke (frem/opp etc til). **reach-me-down** *adj* ferdigsydd, konfeksjons-.

react [rɪ'ækt] *vi* **1** reagere (*against* mot; *to* på); **2** innvirke (*on* på). **reaction** [rɪ'ækʃn] *sb* **1** reaksjon, tilbakevirkning; **2** (inn)virkning; **3** bakstreveri, reaksjon. **reactionary** [rɪ'ækʃənərɪ] *adj, sb* reaksjonær (person). **reactor** [rɪ'æktə] *sb* reaktor.

read [ri:d] **I** *sb* lesning; **II** *vb* **1** lese; forstå/tyde (vanskelig skrift etc); **2** lese (et fag); studere; **3** forelese. **readable** ['ri:dəbl] *adj* leselig; leseverdig. **reader** ['ri:də] *sb* **1** (person el. f.eks. datamaskin som) leser; oppleser; *(publisher's ~)* forlagskonsulent; **2** foreleser, (universitets)lektor; **3** lesebok.

readdress [ˌri:ə'dres] *vt* omadressere.

read head *sb data* lesehode.

readily ['redɪlɪ] *adv* **1** (bered)villig, rede; gjerne; **2** omgående, raskt; **3** lett, uten vanskelighet(er). **readiness** ['redɪnɪs] *sb* **1** villighet; **2** raskhet; **3** beredskap.

reading ['ri:dɪŋ] *sb* **1** lesing (og lesning, opplesning; lesestoff; lesemåte, (tekst)forståelse; (for)tolkning etc); *wide ~* omfattende lesning (dvs kunnskaper en har lest seg til); **2** behandling (av lovforslag). **reading|-glasses** *sb* lesebriller. **~lamp** *sb* leselampe. **~-room** *sb* lese|sal, -værelse.

readjust [ˌri:ə'dʒʌst] *vt* (om)justere; endre, revidere.

read-only | memory, ~ storage *sb data* leselager.

ready ['redɪ] *adj* **1** ferdig, rede; i (ferdig) stand; **2** (bered)villig; **3** rask, snar; ~ *answer* svar på rede hånd; ~ *wit* slagferdighet; **4** for hånden; ~ *money* rede penger. **ready-made** *adj* ferdig|laget, -sydd *etc.*

real ['rɪəl] *adj* **1** reell, virkelig; *in* ~ *life* i det virkelige liv; i virkeligheten; **2** ekte; *in* ~ *earnest* i fullt alvor; **3** *dgl, som adv:* ~ *fine* virkelig fin. **real estate** *sb* fast eiendom. **realistic** [ˌrɪə'lɪstɪk] *adj* realistisk; virkelighetstro. **reality** [rɪ'ælətɪ] *sb* realitet, virkelighet. **realization** [ˌrɪəlaɪ'zeɪʃn] *sb* **1** (full) forståelse; **2** realisering, virkeliggjøring; **3** realisasjon, (ut)salg. **realize** ['rɪəlaɪz] *vt* **1** forstå (fullt ut); innse; **2** realisere, virkeliggjøre; **3** realisere; selge (ut). **really** ['rɪəlɪ] *adv* **1** egentlig, faktisk; i virkeligheten; **2** *som interj* jaså; (nei) virkelig; sier du/De det.

realm [relm] *sb* **1** (konge)rike; **2** felt, område, sfære.

real time *sb data* sanntid.

realtor ['rɪəltə] *sb US* eiendomsmegler. **realty** ['rɪəltɪ] *sb US* (fast) eiendom.

reap [ri:p] høste (inn). **reaper** ['ri:pə] *sb* **1** selvbinder; **2** *fl* skurfolk. **reaping-hook** *sb* sigd.

reappear [ˌri:ə'pɪə] *vi* dukke opp/komme til syne igjen.

rear ['rɪə] **I** *sb* **1** bak|del, -part; -side; *slang* do; *vulg* bak(ende); *at the* ~ *of* på baksiden av; *in the* ~ *of* bakerst/innerst (i); **2** = ~*guard*; **3** *som adj* bakre, bakerst; bak-; **II** *vb* **1** ale opp; dyrke; **2** (opp)fostre, oppdra; **3** heve, løfte; ~ *up* steile. **rearguard** *sb mil* baktropp.

rearrange [ˌri:ə'reɪndʒ] *vt* om|gruppere, -ordne; flytte (omkring) på.

reason [ri:zn] **I** *sb* **1** grunn/årsak (*for* til); *the* ~ *why* årsaken til (at); *for that* ~ av den grunn; *with* ~ med rette; **2** forstand, tenkeevne; fornuft; rimelighet; *in* ~ innenfor rimelighetens grenser; *out of all* ~ hinsides all fornuft; *dgl* helt bort i veggene; *stand to* ~ være innlysende/fullstendig klart; **II** *vb* **1** argumentere, diskutere; **2** slutte (seg til); tenke; resonnere; **3** overbevise; ~ *away* bortforklare; ~ *into* få til (å); ~ *out of* få fra (å). **reasonable** ['ri:znəbl] *adj* **1** fornuftig; rimelig; **2** akseptabel, moderat. **reasonin** ['ri:znɪŋ] *sb* **1** begrunnelse; resonnement; **2** tankegang.

reassurance [ˌri:ə'ʃʊərəns] *sb* beroligelse *etc.* **reassure** [ˌri:ə'ʃʊə] *vt* **1** berolige; **2** gjenforsikre, reassurere.

rebel I ['rebl] *sb* opprører; *som adj* opprørs-; **II** [rɪ'bel] *vi* gjøre opprør. **rebellion** [rɪ'belɪən] *sb* opprør. **rebellious** [rɪ'belɪəs] *adj* **1** opprørsk; **2** oppsetsig, uregjerlig.

rebirth [ˌri:'bɜ:θ] *sb* gjenfødelse. **reborn** [ˌri:'bɔ:n] *adj rel* gjenfødt.

rebound [rɪ'baʊnd] **1** *sb* (tilbake)sprett; *fig* reaksjon, tilbakeslag; **2** *vi* sprette/springe (tilbake); *fig* slå tilbake.

rebuff [rɪ'bʌf] **1** *sb* avslag; avvisning; **2** *vt* irettesette; klandre, kritisere.

rebuild [ˌri:'bɪld] *vt* gjenoppbygge.

recalcitrant [rɪ'kælsɪtrənt] *adj* gjenstridig; oppsetsig, ulydig.

recall [rɪ'kɔ:l] **I** *sb* tilbakekalling *etc*; *beyond/past* ~ ugjenkallelig; **II** *vt* **1** kalle tilbake; gjenkalle (i erindringen); huske, minnes; **2** ta tilbake (dvs annullere, oppheve; fornekte).

recant [rɪ'kænt] *vb* ta i seg igjen (noe en har sagt); fornekte.

recapitulate [ˌri:kə'pɪtjʊleɪt] *vb* gjenta; gå gjennom (hovedpunktene) på nytt; oppsummere, sammenfatte.

recapture [ri:'kæptʃə] *vt* gjenerobre.

recede [rɪ'si:d] *vi* **1** vike; gå/trekke seg tilbake; *fig* ta avstand; **2** skråne bakover. **receding prices** *sb fl* fallende priser.

receipt [rɪ'si:t] **I** *sb* **1** mottakelse; *be in* ~ *of* ha (mottatt); være i besittelse av; **2** kvittering; **3** oppskrift; **II** *vt* kvittere for. **receive** [rɪ'si:v] *vb* **1** motta (og ta imot); **2** få, oppebære; ~ *hospitality* nyte gjestfrihet; **3** gi adgang; oppta (som elev, medlem etc); **4** ha (som) gjest(er). **received** [rɪ'si:vd] *adj* akseptert, godtatt; gjengs; *Received Pronunciation* ≈ normaluttale (dvs den uttale av britisk engelsk som har fått hevd som den mest korrekte); *Received (Standard) English* ≈ normalengelsk (dvs den normgivende form for britisk engelsk). **receiver** [rɪ'si:və] *sb* **1** mottaker; *især* heler; **2** *(official* ~*)* bobestyrer; **3** mottaker(apparat); **4** = *receptacle.*

recent ['ri:snt] *adj* ny; av ny/sen dato; nåtids-; *in* ~ *years* i de senere år. **recently** ['ri:sntlɪ] *adv* nylig.

receptacle [rɪ'septəkl] *sb* (be)holder; (samle)kar. **reception** [rɪ'sepʃn] *sb* mottakelse (etc, jf *receive*). **receptive** [rɪ'septɪv] *adj* mottakelig. **reception | clerk** *sb US* (hotell)portier. ~ **desk** *sb* (hotell)resepsjon. **receptionist** [rɪ'sepʃnɪst] *sb* forværelsesdame; (leges etc) kontorsøster; portier.

recess [rɪ'ses] *sb* **1** opphold; pause; (retts)ferie; **2** alkove; nisje; *fig* avkrok; fristed. **recession** [rɪ'seʃn] *sb* **1** tilbaketrekning; **2** (økonomisk) tilbakeslag; lavkonjunktur.

recipe ['resɪpɪ] *sb* oppskrift/resept (*for* på).

recipient [rɪ'sɪpɪənt] *sb* mottaker.

reciprocal [rɪ'sɪprəkəl] *adj* gjensidig. **reciprocate** [rɪ'sɪprəkeɪt] *vb* **1** gjengjelde; utveksle; utligne; **2** bevege (seg) avvekslende frem og tilbake/opp og ned etc.

recital [rɪ'saɪtl] *sb* **1** (omstendelig) beretning; **2** *mus* resitasjon. **recitation** [ˌresɪ'teɪʃn] *sb* opplesning *etc; US* (lekse)høring. **recite** [rɪ'saɪt] *vb* **1** lese opp; deklamere, foredra, fremsi; **2** berette/fortelle (detaljert); **3** regne opp; **4** *US* høre/bli hørt (i lekser).

reckless ['reklɪs] *adj* uvøren; likeglad (*of* med).

reckon ['rekən] *vb* **1** regne (og beregne; regne sammen/ut; telle); ~ **in** regne med; ta i betraktning; ~ **up** regne/telle sammen; ~ **(up)on** gjøre regning med; ~ **with** gjøre opp med; regne med; stole på; **2** anse/betrakte (som); **3** anta, mene; (skulle) tro.

reckoning ['rekənɪŋ] *sb* (be)regning; regnskap; *sjø* bestikk; *day of* ~ regnskapets dag; dommedag.

reclamation [ˌreklə'meɪʃn] *sb* gjenvinning *etc*. **reclaim** [rɪ'kleɪm] *vb* **1** gjen(inn)vinne (f.eks. jord til dyrking); **2** redde; reformere; rehabilitere (forbryter); attføre; **3** kreve (å få) tilbake; *jur* vindisere.

recline [rɪ'klaɪn] hvile; lene (seg); ligge (bakover).

recognition [ˌrekəg'nɪʃn] *sb* gjenkjennelse *etc*. **recognize** ['rekəgnaɪz] *vt* **1** kjenne igjen; **2** anerkjenne, påskjønne; *merk* erkjenne (mottakelsen av); svare på (brev); **3** akseptere, godta; innrømme; gå med på.

recoil [rɪ'kɔɪl] **I** *sb* **1** det å vike *etc* tilbake; *fig* motvilje; **2** rekyl; *fig* tilbakeslag; **II** *vi* **1** vike (springe, trekke seg etc) tilbake; **2** slå tilbake; *fig* falle tilbake (*upon* på); **3** rekylere.

recollect [ˌrekə'lekt] *vb* **1** huske, minnes. **recollection** [ˌrekə'lekʃn] *sb* erindring, hukommelse.

recommend [ˌrekə'mend] *vt* **1** anbefale; **2** betro, over|gi, late. **recommendation** [ˌrekəmən'deɪʃn] *sb* anbefaling *etc*.

recompense ['rekəmpens] **1** *sb* belønning; vederlag; (tilbake)betaling; gjengjeld; **2** *vt* belønne; gi i vederlag; betale (tilbake); gjengjelde.

reconcile ['rekənsaɪl] *vt* **1** forsone; forlike; bilegge; **2** *data* avstemme. **reconciliation** [ˌrekənsɪlɪ'eɪʃn] *sb* forsoning *etc*.

reconnaissance [rɪ'kɒnɪsəns] *sb* rekognosering. **reconnaissance licence** *sb petro* letetillatelse. **reconnoitre** [ˌrekə'nɔɪtə] *vi* rekognosere, speide; undersøke.

reconstruct [ˌri:kən'strʌkt] *vt* **1** bygge opp igjen; **2** rekonstruere.

record I ['rekɔ:d] *sb* **1** (offisiell) fortegnelse/opptegnelse; protokoll; register; *fl også* arkiv; *off (the)* ~ *(dgl)* uoffisiell; *on* ~ nedskrevet, protokollert; *go on* ~ *as saying that* erklære åpent at; **2** vitnesbyrd; (nedskrevet) beretning/rapport; dokument; *clean* ~ rent rulleblad; *person with a* ~ tidligere straffet person; **3** *(grammophone* ~*)* (grammofon)plate; **4** *data* post; **5** *sport etc* rekord; **II** [ri:'kɔ:d] *vt* **1** notere; skrive ned; protokollere; føre inn; **2** ta opp (på film, lydbånd, plate etc); **3** registrere, vise. **recorder** [ri'kɔ:də] *sb* **1** registreringsapparat; (-)skriver; **2** (by)dommer; **3** blokkfløyte. **recording** [rɪ'kɔ:dɪŋ] *sb især* innspilling, opptak. **record | gap** *sb data* postmellomrom. **~-player** *sb* platespiller. **~ type** *sb data* posttype.

recount [ri'kaunt] *vt* berette, fortelle.

recourse [rɪ'kɔ:s] *sb* tilflukt.

recover [rɪ'kʌvə] *vb* **1** gjenvinne; få/ta igjen; finne igjen; berge; ~ *(one's) expenses* få utgiftene (sine) dekket; **2** bli frisk/komme seg (igjen); **3** *data* gjenopprette. **recovery** [rɪ'kʌvərɪ] *sb* **1** berging; **2** bedring; **3** *data* gjenoppretting; **4** *petro* utvinning. **recovery vehicle** *sb* kranvogn, servicebil.

recreation [ˌrekrɪ'eɪʃn] *sb* avkobling, rekreasjon. **recreational** [ˌrekrɪ'eɪʃənl] *adj* rekreasjons-. **recreation ground** *sb* lekeplass.

recrimination [rɪˌkrɪmɪ'neɪʃn] *sb* (mot)beskyldning.

recruit [rɪ'kru:t] **I** *sb* rekrutt; **II** *vb* **1** rekruttere, verve; **2** bringe opp i full styrke/fullt antall *etc*; supplere; *fig* styrke(s); komme seg.

rectification [ˌrektɪfɪ'keɪʃn] *sb* beriktigelse *etc*; rektifisering. **rectify** ['rektɪfaɪ] *vt* **1** beriktige; rette (på); **2** rektifisere, rense. **rectitude** ['rektɪtju:d] *sb* rettskaffenhet.

rector ['rektə] *sb* **1** sogneprest (i *Church of England*); **2** rektor, skole(be)styrer. **rectory** ['rektərɪ] *sb* prestegård.

recumbent [rɪ'kʌmbənt] *adj* tilbakelent; liggende (bakover); hvilende.

recuperate [ri'kju:pəreɪt] *vb* komme seg; komme til krefter (igjen); styrke(s). **recuperation** [rɪˌkju:pə'reɪʃn] *sb* bedring; gjenvinning av kreftene. **recuperative** [rɪ'kju:pərətɪv] *adj* helbredende, styrkende.

recur [rɪ'kɜ:] *vi* **1** gjenta seg; **2** ~ *to* gå (komme, vende etc) tilbake til. **recurrence** [rɪ'kʌrəns] *sb* **1** gjentakelse; **2** tilbakevending. **recurrent** [rɪ'kʌrənt] *adj* tilbakevendende.

recycle [ˌri:'saɪkl] *vt* resirkulere; (gjenvinne og) bruke om igjen.

red [red] **I** *adj* rød; **II** *sb* **1** rødt; **2** *merk: in the* ~ med underskudd. **red|breast** *sb* rødstrupe. **~-brick university** *sb* nyere universitet (i motsetning til de tradisjonsrike universitetene i Cambridge og Oxford). **~ carpet** *sb* rød løper. **~coat** *sb gml* rødjakke (dvs britisk soldat). **~ deer** *sb* kronhjort.

redden ['redn] *vb* **1** farge/male rød; **2** rødme.

redeem [rɪ'di:m] *vt* **1** innløse; kjøpe igjen/tilbake; **2** innfri, (over)holde; **3** redde; forløse, frelse; **4** oppveie; gjøre godt igjen. **redemption** [rɪ'dempʃn] *sb* innløsning *etc*; redning; *beyond/past* ~ redningsløst fortapt.

red|-handed *adj: catch ~-handed* ta på fersk gjerning. **~ herring** *sb* røykesild; *især fig* blindspor; avledende manøver etc. **~-hot** *adj* rødglødende. **Red Indian** *sb* indianer. **red|-letter day** *sb fig* heldig dag; lykkedag.

redolent ['redələnt] *adj* duftende; *be* ~ *of (fig)* minne om.

redoubtable [rɪ'dautəbl] *adj* **1** fryktinngytende; **2** drabelig.

redress [rɪ'dres] **1** *sb* oppreisning; erstatning; *beyond* ~ uopprettelig; **2** *vt* gjenopprette; erstatte; avhjelpe, bøte på.

red|skin *sb* rødhud (= indianer). **~ tape** *sb* formaliteter, papirmølle. **~-tape** *adj* byråkratisk.

reduce [rɪ'dju:s] *vb* **1** minske, redusere; sette ned; *dgl* slanke seg; **2** bringe/sette (i en bestemt tilstand); ~ *to order* få orden på (igjen); **3** forandre; gjøre om; forkorte (brøk); smelte (malm). **reduction** [rɪ'dʌkʃn] *sb* reduksjon *etc*; avslag, rabatt.

redundancy [rɪ'dʌndənsɪ] *sb* **1** overflod, overflødighet; **2** arbeidsløshet. **redundant** [rɪ'dʌndənt] *adj* **1** (altfor) rikelig; **2** overflødig, overskytende; **3** (overflødig/til overs og dermed) arbeidsløs.

redwood *sb* rødtre; (kalifornisk) kjempegran.

reed [ri:d] *sb* **1** siv, (tak)rør; *fig* halmstrå; **2** *poet* (rør)fløyte; **3** flis, rørblad (til klarinett etc); **4** vevskje.

reef [ri:f] **A** *sb* (klippe)rev; **B 1** *sb* rev (i seil); **2** *vb* reve (seil). **reef-knot** *sb* båtsmannsknop.

reek [ri:k] **I** *sb* **1** stank; **2** *bokl, skotsk* os; (tykk) røyk; **II** *vi* **1** stinke; **2** dampe, ose; *~ing with* dampende av.

reel [ri:l] **A 1** *sb* trommel, valse; snelle, spole; (garn)vinde; *data etc* båndspole; **2** *vt* spole (hespe, rulle, sveive, vinde etc) opp; *~ off (dgl)* lire av seg; **B I** *sb* sjangling *etc*; **II** *vi* **1** rave, sjangle; svaie; **2** snurre/*dgl* seile rundt; virvle; **C** *sb skotsk* (dansen) reel.

refer [rɪ'fɜ:] **to** *vb* **1** henvise/(over)sende til; **2** hentyde/(hen)vise til; **3** angå, berøre; sette/stå i forbindelse med; **4** slå opp (i bok etc). **referee** [ˌrefə'ri:] *sb* (idretts)dommer, oppmann. **reference** ['refrəns] *sb* **1** henvisning *etc*; **2** referanse (dvs attest, garantist etc). **reference | book** *sb* oppslagsbok. **~ library** *sb* håndbibliotek. **~ manual** *sb* brukerhåndbok.

referendum [ˌrefə'rendəm] *sb* folkeavstemning.

refine [rɪ'faɪn] *vb* foredle, forfine; raffinere. **refined** [rɪ'faɪnd] *adj* (dannet og) elegant; forfinet, raffinert. **refinery** [rɪ'faɪnərɪ] *sb* raffineri. **refinement** [rɪ'faɪnmənt] *sb* **1** foredling *etc*; raffinering; **2** (dannelse og) eleganse; raffinement.

reflect [rɪ'flekt] *vb* (av)speile, gjenspeile; *~ upon* falle tilbake på; kaste skygge over; så mistanke/tvil *etc* om; **2** reflektere; overveie; tenke (etter). **reflection** [rɪ'flekʃn] *sb* **1** (av)speiling *etc*; refleks; **2** refleksjon, ettertanke; *on ~* ved nærmere ettertanke. **reflective** [rɪ'flektɪv] *adj* (etter)tenksom; tankefull. **reflector** [rɪ'flektə] *sb* reflektor; katteøye, refleks. **reflexion** [rɪ'flekʃn] *sb = reflection.*

reflux ['ri:flʌks] *sb petro* refluks, tilbakeløp.

reform [rɪ'fɔ:m] **I** *sb* **1** reform; **2** *= reformation 1*; **II** *vb* **1** reformere; forbedre; **2** forbedre seg. **reformation** [ˌrefə'meɪʃn] *sb* **1** reformering; forbedring; **2** reformasjon. **reformatory** [rɪ'fɔ:mətərɪ] **1** *adj* reformerende; forbedrings-; reform-; **2** *sb* spesialskole. **reformer** [rɪ'fɔ:mə] *sb* reformator.

refract [rɪ'frækt] *vt* bryte (lys). **refractory** [rɪ'fræktərɪ] *adj* gjenstridig; uregjerlig; sta; *om sykdom* hardnakket; *om materiale* uhåndterlig.

refrain [rɪ'freɪn] **A** *vi* avholde seg (*from* fra); la være; **B** *sb* omkved, refreng.

refresh [rɪ'freʃ] *vt* **1** forfriske, oppkvikke; styrke; *~ oneself* ta en forfriskning; spise (og især drikke) litt; **2** friske opp; *~ one's memory* friske på hukommelsen. **refreshing** [rɪ'freʃɪŋ] *adj* forfriskende; stimulerende. **refreshments** [rɪ'freʃmənts] *sb fl* forfriskninger.

refrigerate [rɪ'frɪdʒəreɪt] *vt* (av)kjøle. **refrigerator** [rɪ'frɪdʒəreɪtə] *sb* kjøleskap.

refuel [ˌri:'fju:əl] *vi* bunkre/tanke opp (igjen).

refuge ['refju:dʒ] *sb* **1** tilfluktssted; beskyttelse, ly; *take ~ in* ta sin tilflukt til; ty til; **2** *(street-~)* refuge, trafikkøy. **refugee** [ˌrefjʊ'dʒi:] *sb* flyktning.

refund 1 ['ri:fʌnd] *sb* tilbakebetaling; **2** [rɪ'fʌnd] *vb* betale tilbake.

refurbish [rɪ'fɜ:bɪʃ] *vt* pusse opp.

refusal [rɪ'fju:zl] *sb* **1** avslag; **2** forkjøpsrett. **refuse 1** ['refju:s] *sb* avfall, søppel; **2** [rɪ'fju:z] *vb* avslå, nekte; vegre (seg).

refutation [ˌrefjʊ'teɪʃn] *sb* gjendrivelse *etc.* **refute** [rɪ'fju:t] *vt* gjendrive, motbevise; tilbakevise.

regain [rɪ'geɪn] *vt* få (ta, vinne etc) tilbake.

regal ['rɪ:gl] *adj* kongelig.

regard [rɪ'gɑ:d] **I** *sb* **1** *bokl, gml* blikk; **2** henblikk; *in ~ of/to, with ~ to* med henblikk på; med hensyn til; *in this ~* i denne henseende; **3** (det å ta) hensyn; *~less* likeglad (*of* med); uten å ta hensyn (*of* til); *out of ~ for* av hensyn til; **4** aktelse; *hold in ~* akte, respektere; **5** *fl* hilsen(er); **II** *vt* **1** *bokl, gml* betrakte; se (nøye) på; **2** anse/betrakte (*as* som); **3** angå, vedkomme; *as ~s = regarding*; **4** ense, vøre; akte. **regarding** [rɪ'gɑ:dɪŋ] *prep* angående; med hensyn til; *også* hva angår.

regency ['ri:dʒənsɪ] *sb* regentskap.

regenerate I [rɪ'dʒenərət] *adj* gjenfødt; **II** [rɪ'dʒenəreɪt] *vb* **1** fornye(s) (åndelig); bli født på ny; **2** regenerere(s). **regeneration** [rɪˌdʒenə'reɪʃn] *sb* gjenfødelse *etc.*

regent ['ri:dʒənt] **1** *adj* regjerende; regent-; **2** *sb* regent. **regime** [reɪ'ʒi:m] *sb* regime, styre(form). **regiment 1** ['redʒɪmənt] *sb* regiment; **2** ['redʒɪment] *vt* disiplinere; organisere. **regimental** [ˌredʒɪ'mentl] **I** *adj* **1** regiments-; **2** militær(-); **II** *sb fl* regimentsfarger; uniform(er).

region ['ri:dʒən] *sb* distrikt, område, strøk; felt, sfære. **regional** ['ri:dʒənl] *adj* regional(-).

register ['redʒɪstə] **I** *sb* **1** register (og journal, liste, protokoll etc); **2** register (dvs stemmeleie, toneområde); **3** telleverk; *cash ~* kasseapparat; **4** spjeld; **II** *vb* **1** (inn)registrere (og føre/skrive (seg) inn; notere (seg) etc); **2** (registrere og) vise; **3** rekommandere (postsending). **registration** [ˌredʒɪ'streɪʃn] *sb* registrering *etc.* **registry** ['redʒɪstrɪ] *sb* **1** register (dvs arkiv, registreringskontor etc); **2** *= registration.* **registry office** *sb* byfogdkontor.

regret [rɪ'gret] **I** *sb* **1** savn; vemod; sorg; **2** beklagelse (*at* over); anger; *we have no ~s* vi angrer ikke; **II** *vt* **1** savne; minnes med vemod; sørge over; **2** beklage (*that* at; *to* å (måtte)); **3** angre. **regrettable** [rɪ'gretəbl] *adj* beklagelig. **regretful** [rɪ'gretfʊl] *adj* angrende, angerfull.

regular ['regjʊlə] **I** *adj* **1** jevn, regelmessig; **2** fast, regulær, vanlig; **3** korrekt; ordentlig, skikkelig; **4** *dgl* ren, veritabel; erke-; **5** *US* standard(-); vanlig; **II** *sb* **1** *(~ soldier)* (yrkes)soldat; **2** *(~ customer)* fast kunde; stamgjest *etc.* **regularity** [ˌregjʊ'lærətɪ] *sb* regelmessighet *etc.* **regulate** ['regjʊleɪt] *vt* **1** kontrollere, regulere: **2** arrangere, ordne; standardisere. **regulation**

[ˌregjʊ'leɪʃn] *sb* **1** regulering *etc*; **2** bestemmelse; forskrift; (ordens)regel; **3** *som adj* foreskreven, reglementert.

rehabilitate [ˌri:hə'bɪlɪteɪt] *vt* rehabilitere, restaurere; attføre. **rehabilitation** [ˌri:həˌbɪlɪ'teɪʃn] *sb* rehabilitering *etc*.

rehearsal [rɪ'hɜ:sl] *sb* **1** (teater)prøve; **2** repetisjon. **rehearse** [rɪ'hɜ:s] *vb* **1** innstudere (rolle etc); prøve (teateroppsetning etc); **2** repetere.

reign [reɪn] **1** *sb* regjering (og regjeringstid); styre; **2** *vi* regjere, styre; bestemme; råde.

rein [reɪn] **1** *sb (fl)* tømme(r), tøyle(r); **2** *vt* tøyle, styre; holde i tømme.

reindeer ['reɪndɪə] *sb* rein (og reinsdyr).

reinforce [ˌri:ɪn'fɔ:s] *vt* forsterke, styrke. **reinforced concrete** *sb* armert betong. **reinforcement** [ˌri:ɪn'fɔ:smənt] *sb* forsterkning.

reinstate [ˌri:ɪn'steɪt] *vt* gjeninnsette (i embete etc).

reinsure [ˌri:ɪn'ʃʊə] *vt* gjenforsikre, reassurere.

reject I ['ri:dʒekt] *sb* utskuddsvare; **II** [rɪ'dʒekt] *vt* **1** (for)kaste; kassere; **2** avslå, forsmå, vrake; avvise. **rejection** [rɪ'dʒekʃn] *sb* kassering *etc*.

rejoice [rɪ'dʒɔɪs] *vb* juble; fryde/glede seg (*in* over; *that* over at). **rejoicing** [rɪ'dʒɔɪsɪŋ] *sb* (stor) glede; *fl* festligheter; jubel.

rejoin [rɪ'dʒɔɪn] **A** *vb* svare; **B** *vt* slutte seg til (militæravdeling, skipsmannskap etc) igjen. **rejoinder** [rɪ'dʒɔɪndə] *sb* svar; *jur* duplikk.

rejuvenate [rɪ'dʒu:vɪneɪt] *vb* forynges.

relapse [rɪ'læps] **1** *sb* tilbakefall; frafall; **2** *vi* falle fra/tilbake; *med* få tilbakefall.

relate [rɪ'leɪt] *vb* **1** berette, fortelle; **2** sette i forbindelse (*to/with* med); *be ~d to (også)* være beslektet/i slekt med; **3** angå; ha/stå i forbindelse (*to* med). **relation** [rɪ'leɪʃn] *sb* **1** beretning, skildring; **2** forbindelse, sammenheng; forhold; *in/with ~ to* med hensyn til; **3** *data etc* relasjon; **4** = *~ship 1, 2*. **relational data base** *sb data* relasjonsdatabase. **relationship** [rɪ'leɪʃnʃɪp] *sb* **1** slektskap; **2** slektning; **3** = *relation 2*. **relative** ['relətɪv] **I** *adj* **1** forholdsvis, relativ; **2** *~ to* angående; **II** *sb* **1** slektning; **2** relativt pronomen *etc*. **relatively** ['relətɪvlɪ] *adv* forholdsvis, relativt.

relax [rɪ'læks] *vb* **1** løsne; slippe (tak); lempe/slappe av på; **2** slappe av. **relaxation** [ˌri:læk'seɪʃn] *sb* **1** lempelse *etc*; **2** avslapning, hvile; rekreasjon.

relay ['ri:leɪ] **I** *sb* **1** (arbeids)skift; nytt lag (kobbel, spann etc); ny forsyning etc; *work by/in ~s* arbeide (i/på) skift; **2** *(~ race)* stafett(løp); **3** *radio, TV* relé (og relésender); **II** [rɪ'leɪ] *vt radio, TV* relésende.

release [rɪ'li:s] **I** *som adj* utløser-; **II** *sb* **1** *a)* frigivelse *etc*; utløsning; (ut)slipp; *b)* utløser; **2** ettergivelse; **3** overdragelse; **III** *vt* **1** *a)* frigi, løslate; slippe (løs); *b)* utløse; **2** la gå; slippe (taket i); slippe ut (nyheter, opplysninger etc); sende ut (på markedet); **3** oppgi; overdra.

relegate ['relɪgeɪt] *vt* **1** henvise; overlate; **2** degradere; flytte ned (i ligafotball); **3** relegere, utvise. **relegation** [ˌrelɪ'geɪʃn] *sb* henvisning *etc*; utvisning.

relent [rɪ'lent] *vi* gi etter; mykne; tø opp. **relentless** [rɪ'lentlɪs] *adj* hard, ubøyelig.

relevance ['reləvəns] *sb* relevans. **relevant** ['reləvənt] *adj* relevant; som angår saken.

reliability [rɪˌlaɪə'bɪlətɪ] *sb* pålitelighet *etc*; *om maskiner etc også* (funksjons)stabilitet. **reliable** [rɪ'laɪəbl] *adj* pålitelig, troverdig. **reliance** [rɪ'laɪəns] *sb* tillit, tro; *place/put ~ in/(up)on* feste lit til; stole/tro på. **reliant** [rɪ'laɪənt] *adj* tillitsfull.

relic ['relɪk] *sb* **1** *fl* (oldtids)|levninger, -rester; **2** relikvie.

relief [rɪ'li:f] **A I** *som adj* hjelpe-, støtte-; **2** ekstra-, reserve-; **II** *sb* **1** hjelp, støtte; lettelse, lindring; trøst; *gml* forsorg, understøttelse; **2** (behagelig) avveksling; **3** forsterkning; unnsetning; *mil også* avløsning; **B** *sb* relieff; *fig* tydelighet. **relief well** *sb petro* avlastningsbrønn. **relieve** [rɪ'li:v] **A** *vt* **1** lindre; *~ of* befri/lette for; hjelpe av med; *~ one's feelings* få utløsning for sine følelser; *~d to hear etc* lettet over å høre etc; **2** (av)hjelpe; (under)støtte; **3** befri, unnsette; **4** *mil* avløse; **5** frita (for ansvar, plikter etc); **B** *vt* sette i relieff.

religion [rɪ'lɪdʒən] *sb* religion. **religious** [rɪ'lɪdʒəs] *adj* religiøs (og from, gudfryktig etc); *også* samvittighetsfull.

relinquish [rɪ'lɪŋkwɪʃ] *vt* avstå, oppgi; gi avkall på.

relish ['relɪʃ] **I** *sb* **1** (vel)smak; **2** appetitt, matglede; velbehag; **3** krydder, smakstilsetning; **4** anelse, anstrøk; bismak; **II** *vt* **1** nyte; like; sette pris på; glede seg over; **2** krydre; smake til.

relocate [ˌri:ləʊ'keɪt] *vt* (for)flytte; omplassere.

reluctance [rɪ'lʌktəns] *sb* motvilje, ulyst. **reluctant** [rɪ'lʌktənt] *adj* mot|villig, ~strebende; uvillig; *be ~ to* kvie seg for (å).

rely [rɪ'laɪ] *vi: rely (up)on* stole på; regne med (når det gjelder hjelp etc).

remain [rɪ'meɪn] **I** *sb fl* levninger, rester; etterlatte skrifter, *(mortal ~s)* jordiske levninger; lik; **II** *vi* **1** bli/være igjen; **2** forbli; fortsette å være. **remainder** [rɪ'meɪndə] *sb* rest.

remake [ˌri:'meɪk] *vt* gjøre/lage om (igjen).

remand [rɪ'mɑ:nd] **1** *sb* (begjæring om) varetekt; forlenget/ny fengslingskjennelse; **2** *vt* begjære satt i varetekt; avsi (ny) fengslingskjennelse over. **remand home** *sb* ≈ sikringsanstalt; *også* skolehjem.

remark [rɪ'mɑ:k] **I** *sb* **1** bemerkning; **2** *worthy of ~* verd å legge merke til; **II** *vb* **1** bemerke, si; kommentere; **2** legge merke til. **remarkable** [rɪ'mɑ:kəbl] *adj* bemerkelsesverdig; påfallende; uvanlig.

remarry [ˌri:'mærɪ] *vb* gifte (seg) igjen/på nytt.

remedial [rɪ'mi:dɪəl] *adj* hjelpe-, støtte-. **remedy** ['remɪdɪ] **1** *sb* (hjelpe)|middel, (-)råd; *past ~* uhelbredelig; **2** *vt* (av)hjelpe; helbrede; utbedre; rette på.

remember [rɪ'membə] *vb* **1** huske (på); minnes; **2**

~ me to her hils henne fra meg; **3** betenke/huske på (med gave etc). **remembrance** [rɪ'membrəns] *sb* erindring, hukommelse; minne; *in ~ of* til minne om; **2** minne(gave); **3** *fl* hilsen(er).

remind [rɪ'maɪnd] *vt* minne om. **reminder** [rɪ'maɪndə] *sb* påminnelse; purring.

reminisce [ˌremɪ'nɪs] *vi* minnes. **reminiscence** [ˌremɪ'nɪsns] *sb* erindring, minne; (på)minnelse; *fl* (livs)erindringer. **reminiscent** [ˌremɪ'nɪsnt] *adj*: ~ *of* som minner om.

remiss [rɪ'mɪs] *adj* forsømmelig, likegyldig. **remission** [rɪ'mɪʃn] *sb* ettergivelse, tilgivelse; fritakelse. **remit** [rɪ'mɪt] *vb* **1** tilgi; frita; **2** sende (især penger) med post; remittere; **3** henvise; (over)sende. **remittance** [rɪ'mɪtəns] *sb* remittering (og remisse).

remnant ['remnənt] *sb* levning, rest.

remonstrance [rɪ'mɒnstrəns] *sb* protest(ering). **remonstrate** ['remənstreɪt] *vi* innvende, protestere.

remorse [rɪ'mɔ:s] *sb* anger; samvittighetsnag; dyp beklagelse. **remorse|ful** *adj* angerfull, angrende. **~less** *adj* forherdet; hjerteløs; ubarmhjertig.

remote [rɪ'məʊt] *adj* avsides; langt unna; fjern; svak, utydelig. **remote | control** *sb* fjern|kontroll, -styring. **~ terminal** *sb data* fjernterminal. **~ user** *sb data* fjernbruker.

removable [rɪ'mu:vəbl] *adj* flyttbar; til å fjerne/ta av *etc*. **removal** [rɪ'mu:vl] *sb* flytting *etc*; fjerning. **remove** [rɪ'mu:v] *vb* **1** fjerne; flytte (på); ta bort (vekk, ut etc); ta av (seg); **2** avsette; kvitte seg med; **3** flytte opp (i høyere klasse); **4** *first cousin once (twice) ~d* fetters/kusines barn (barnebarn). **remover** [rɪ'mu:və] *sb* flyttemann; *(fl)* flyttebyrå.

remunerate [rɪ'mju:nəreɪt] *vt* (be)lønne. **remuneration** [rɪˌmju:nə'reɪʃn] *sb* betaling, godtgjørelse; belønning. **remunerative** [rɪ'mju:nərətɪv] *adj* innbringende, lønnsom.

renaissance [rɪ'neɪsns] *sb* **1** fornyelse, gjenfødelse; **2** *the Renaissance* renessansen. **renascence** [rɪ'næsns] *sb* = *renaissance 1*. **renascent** [rɪ'næsnt] *adj* gjenoppvåknende; på vei mot ny suksess.

rend [rend] *vt* rive (i stykker); spjære, sønderrive.

render ['rendə] *vt* **1** gjengjelde; gi igjen/tilbake; **2** (av)gi, yte; (over)|levere, -sende; *~ an account* presentere en regning; avlegge rapport/regnskap; *~ up* overgi; **3** forårsake; gjøre (til); *~ null and void* erklære/kjenne død og maktesløs; **4** gjengi (på scene, i kunstnerisk form etc); (for)tolke. **rendering** ['rendərɪŋ] *sb især* gjengivelse, tolkning.

renew [rɪ'nju:] *vt* **1** fornye; reparere; **2** forynge; gjenopplive; **3** gjenta; **4** forlenge, prolongere; fornye; **5** erstatte/skifte ut (med nytt). **renewable** [rɪ'nju:əbl] *adj* fornybar. **renewal** [rɪ'nju:əl] *sb* fornyelse *etc*.

renounce [rɪ'naʊns] *vt* **1** avsverge; fornekte; ikke ville kjennes ved; **2** frasi seg; gi avkall på.

renovate ['renəveɪt] *vt* modernisere; overhale, reparere; restaurere. **renovation** [ˌrenə'veɪʃn] *sb* modernisering *etc*; restaurering.

renown [rɪ'naʊn] *sb* berømmelse, ry. **renowned** [rɪ'naʊnd] *adj* berømt, navngjeten.

rent [rent] **A I** *sb* (leie)avgift; (hus)leie; **II** *vb* **1** leie (hus/leilighet); forpakte (jord); **2** leie ut; forpakte bort; **3** *(be ~ed)* leies ut; være til leie; **B** *sb* revne, spjære; sprekk; brudd, splittelse. **rental** ['rentl] *sb* leie(inntekt).

renunciation [rɪˌnʌnsɪ'eɪʃn] *sb* avkall, fornektelse (etc, jf *renounce*).

reopen [ri:'əʊpən] *vb* gjenåpne; åpne igjen.

reorganize [ri:'ɔ:gənaɪz] *vb* omorganisere, reorganisere.

repair [rɪ'peə] **A I** *sb* **1** reparering, utbedring; reparasjon; **2** forfatning, (til)stand; *in good ~* godt vedlikeholdt; *out of ~* i ustand; **II** *vt* **1** reparere, utbedre; avhjelpe; erstatte; (gjen)opprette; **2** beriktige; rette (på); **B** *vi* begi seg; dra, reise. **repairable** [rɪ'peərəbl] *adj* som kan repareres. **repair time** *sb data* feilrettingstid. **reparable** ['repərəbl] *adj* **1** (gjen)opprettelig; som kan erstattes; **2** = *repairable*. **reparation** [ˌrepə'reɪʃn] *sb* **1** erstatning, oppreisning; *fl især* krigsskadeerstatning(er); **2** reparasjon, utbedring.

repartee [ˌrepɑ:'ti:] *sb* **1** kjapt/vittig svar; **2** slagferdighet.

repast [rɪ'pɑ:st] *sb bokl* måltid.

repatriate [ri:'pætrɪeɪt] *vt* repatriere. **repatriation** [ˌri:pætrɪ'eɪʃn] *sb* repatriering.

repay [ri:'peɪ] *vb* **1** betale tilbake; **2** gjengjelde; (be)lønne; straffe. **repayment** [ri:'peɪmənt] *sb* **1** tilbakebetaling; erstatning; **2** gjengjeld(else).

repeal [rɪ'pi:l] **1** *sb* opphevelse *etc*; **2** *vt* annullere, oppheve; tilbakekalle.

repeat [rɪ'pi:t] **I** *sb* gjentakelse (og *mus* gjentakelsestegn); *teat* reprise; **II** *vb* **1** gjenta; gjøre (om) igjen; **2** gjenta, repetere; si (om) igjen; si videre. **repeatedly** [rɪ'pi:tɪdlɪ] *adv* gjentatte ganger; stadig (vekk).

repel [rɪ'pel] *vt* **1** drive (slå, trenge etc) tilbake; **2** frastøte. **repellent** [rɪ'pelənt] *adj* frastøtende, motbydelig.

repent [rɪ'pent] *vb* angre (*of* på). **repentance** [rɪ'pentəns] *sb* anger. **repentant** [rɪ'pentənt] *adj* angrende.

repercussion [ˌri:pə'kʌʃn] *sb* **1** tilbake|slag, -støt; **2** ekko, gjenlyd; **3** *fl* ettervirkninger, følger; konsekvens(er).

repertoire ['repətwɑ:] *sb* repertoar. **repertory** ['repətərɪ] *sb* **1** = *repertoire*; **2** fond, lager *(fig)*.

repetition [ˌrepə'tɪʃn] *sb* gjentakelse, repetisjon.

replace [rɪ'pleɪs] *vt* **1** sette tilbake (på plass); **2** gjeninnsette; **3** avløse; erstatte. **replacement** [rɪ'pleɪsmənt] *sb især* avløsning; erstatning.

replenish [rɪ'plenɪʃ] *vt* fornye (lagerbeholdning etc); etterfylle; supplere. **replete** [rɪ'pli:t] *adj* **1** full; velforsynt; **2** stappfull; (over)mett. **repletion** [rɪ'pli:ʃn] *sb* overfylthet; overmål.

reply [rɪ'plaɪ] **1** *sb* svar; *in ~ to* som svar på; **2** *vb* svare.

report [rɪ'pɔ:t] **I** *sb* **1** beretning (og melding; rapport, referat; utredning etc); 2 forlydende; (folke)-snakk; *fl også* rykter; 3 omdømme, rykte; 4 drønn/smell (av skudd); II *vb* 1 melde, rapportere; melde seg (*at* ved; *to* for); ~ *(up)on* avgi melding/rapportere om; 2 notere (seg); referere; 3 melde (til øvrighet); rapportere (til foresatt etc). **reported speech** *sb* indirekte tale. **reporter** [rɪ'pɔ:tə] *sb* (nyhets)journalist, reporter.

repose [rɪ'pəʊz] I *sb* 1 hvile, søvn; fred, ro; II *vb* 1 ligge; 2 hvile; *fig* bero (*on* på). **repository** [rɪ'pɒzɪtrɪ] *sb* oppbevaringssted; lager.

reprehend [ˌreprɪ'hend] *vt bokl* misbillige; irettesette, klandre. **reprehensible** [ˌreprɪ'hensəbl] *adj* klanderverdig.

represent [ˌreprɪ'zent] *vt* 1 forestille (å være); gjengi; være (et) uttrykk *etc* for; ~ *oneself as* gi seg ut for (å være); 2 representere; opptre for/på vegne av; 3 fremstille/spille (på scene etc). **representation** [ˌreprɪzen'teɪʃn] *sb* 1 gjengivelse; skildring; 2 fremstilling; forklaring; forestilling (dvs formell protest); 3 *pol* representasjon. **representative** [ˌreprɪ'sentətɪv] I *adj* representativ/typisk (*of* for); II *sb* 1 representant; *the House of Representatives* Representantenes Hus (i den amerikanske kongress); 2 typisk eksempel.

repress [rɪ'pres] *vt* undertrykke; *psykol* fortrenge. **repression** [rɪ'preʃn] *sb* undertrykkelse *etc*. **repressive** [rɪ'presɪv] *adj* undertrykkelses-; tvangs-.

reprieve [rɪ'pri:v] I *sb* 1 benådning; 2 henstand, utsettelse; II *vt* benåde; utsette (fullbyrdelse av dødsstraff); *fig* gi henstand.

reprimand ['reprɪmɔ:nd] *sb, vt* (gi) reprimande/(offentlig) irettesettelse.

reprisal [rɪ'praɪzl] *sb* gjengjeld(else); *fl* represalier.

reproach [rɪ'prəʊtʃ] 1 *sb* bebreidelse; 2 *vt* bebreide/klandre (*for/with* for). **reproachful** [rɪ'prəʊtʃful] *adj* bebreidende.

reproduce [ˌri:prə'dju:s] *vb* 1 gjengi (som kopi); reprodusere; *også data* duplisere; 2 formere/forplante seg; 3 regenerere; frembringe igjen. **reproduction** [ˌri:prə'dʌkʃn] *sb* reprodusering *etc*; reproduksjon; kopi.

reproof [rɪ'pru:f] *sb* 1 misbilligelse; 2 bebreidelse, irettesettelse. **reprove** [rɪ'pru:v] *vt* bebreide, irettesette; klandre.

reptile ['reptaɪl] *sb* krypdyr.

republic [rɪ'pʌblɪk] *sb* republikk. **republican** [rɪ'pʌblɪkən] I *adj* republikansk; II *sb* 1 republikaner; 2 *Republican* medlem av Det republikanske parti (i USA).

repudiate [rɪ'pju:dɪeɪt] *vt* 1 fornekte; forstøte (f.eks. hustru); 2 avvise, forkaste. **repudiation** [rɪˌpju:dɪ'eɪʃn] *sb* fornektelse *etc*.

repugnance [rɪ'pʌgnəns] *sb* avsky; (sterk) motvilje/ulyst. **repugnant** [rɪ'pʌgnənt] *adj* frastøtende, motbydelig.

repulse [rɪ'pʌls] I *sb* 1 tilbakeslag; 2 avslag; avvisning; II *vt* 1 drive/slå tilbake; 2 avslå; avvise; støte fra seg. **repulsion** [rɪ'pʌlʃn] *sb* 1 motvilje, ulyst; 2 frastøting. **repulsive** [rɪ'pʌlsɪv] *adj* frastøtende.

reputable ['repjʊtəbl] *adj* aktet, aktverdig; velrenommert; vel ansett. **reputation** [ˌrepjʊ'teɪʃn] *sb* omdømme; *be held in* ~ ha godt ord på seg. **repute** [rɪ'pju:t] I *sb* anseelse, omdømme, rykte; II *vt: be* ~*d* være ansett/betraktet (*as* som; *to be* for å være). **reputedly** [rɪ'pju:tɪdlɪ] *adj* angivelig, formentlig.

request [rɪ'kwest] I *sb* 1 anmodning, bønn; *også data* fordring; ordre; *on* ~ etter/på anmodning; etter forlangende; 2 etterspørsel; *in* ~ etterspurt; II *vt* anmode/be om.

require [rɪ'kwaɪə] *vt* 1 behøve, trenge; 2 forlange, kreve. **requirement** [rɪ'kwaɪəmənt] *sb* behov krav. **requisite** ['rekwɪzɪt] 1 *adj* nødvendig, påkrevet; 2 *sb* nødvendighet (og nødvendighetsartikkel). **requisition** [ˌrekwɪ'zɪʃn] I *sb* 1 rekvirering; 2 rekvisisjon; II *vt* rekvirere; beslaglegge; forlange/kreve (å få utlevert).

rerun ['ri:rʌn] *data etc* 1 *sb* omkjøring; 2 *vt* kjøre om igjen. **rerunning** ['ri:rʌnɪŋ] *sb petro* omproduksjon.

rescue ['reskju:] 1 *sb* befrielse; redning; 2 *vt* befri; redde. **rescue | basket** *sb petro etc* redningskurv. ~ **equipment** *sb petro etc* redningsutstyr. **rescuer** ['reskju:ə] *sb* befrier; rednings|kvinne, -mann; -redder.

research [rɪ'sɜ:tʃ] 1 *sb* forskning *etc*; 2 *vi* forske, granske; ~ *into* utforske. **researcher** [rɪ'sɜ:tʃə] *sb* forsker.

resemblance [rɪ'zembləns] *sb* likhet. **resemble** [rɪ'zembl] *vt* ligne.

resent [rɪ'zent] *vt* være sint for; føle seg/være krenket over; ta ille opp; *I* ~ *interruptions* jeg kan ikke fordra avbrytelser/å bli avbrutt. **resentful** [rɪ'zentful] *adj* sint. **resentment** [rɪ'zentmənt] *sb* ergrelse, harme; sinne.

reservation [ˌrezə'veɪʃn] *sb* 1 forbehold, reservasjon; 2 *især US* reservering; bestilling av plass/hotellrom etc; 3 *US* reservat. **reserve** [rɪ'zɜ:v] I *sb* 1 reserve; forråd, lager; 2 forbehold, innskrenkning; 3 reserverthet, tilbakeholdenhet; 4 reservat; II *vt* 1 holde tilbake; legge til side; 2 reservere/sikre seg; *all rights* ~*d* ettertrykk *etc* forbudt; 3 bestille. reservere; holde av; legge beslag på. **reservoir** ['rezəvwa:] *sb* beholder (og beholdning); reservoar.

reset [ri'set] *vt* tilbake|føre, -stille; nullstille.

reside [rɪ'zaɪd] *vi* bo/residere (*at/in* i). **residence** ['rezɪdəns] *sb* 1 opphold; 2 bolig, hjem; residens. **resident** ['rezɪdənt] I *adj* 1 bosatt; bofast, fastboende; *om dyr/planter etc* stedegen; 2 *data* lagringsfast; II *sb* 1 beboer; fastboende (person); 2 *(~ bird)* stamfugl. **residential** [ˌrezɪ'denʃl] *adj* beboelses-, bolig-. **residual** [rɪ'zɪdjʊəl] *adj* gjenværende, rest-. **residue** ['rezɪdju:] *sb* 1 levning(er), rest; *petro* destillasjonsrest; 2 *kjemi* bunnfall.

resign [rɪ'zaɪn] *vb* 1 avstå (fra); oppgi; si fra seg;

si opp (medlemskap, stilling etc); ta avskjed/trekke seg tilbake (*from* fra); **2** over|gi, -late; betro; **3** ~ *oneelf to* resignere/bøye seg for; finne seg i. **resignation** [ˌrezɪg'neɪʃn] *sb* **1** fratredelse *etc*; avskjed; **2** resignasjon.

resilience [rɪ'zɪlɪəns] *sb* elastisitet *etc*. **resilient** [rɪ'zɪlɪənt] *adj* elastisk, fjærende; *fig* spenstig; seig, ukuelig.

resin ['rezɪn] *sb* harpiks, kvae.

resist [rɪ'zɪst] *vb* motstå; gjøre motstand mot; motsette seg. **resistance** [rɪ'zɪstəns] *sb* motstand (og motstandsevne); resistens. **resistant** [rɪ'zɪstənt] *adj* motstandsdyktig; resistent.

resolute ['rezəlu:t] *adj* beslutsom. **resolution** [ˌrezə'lu:ʃn] *sb* **1** *a)* avgjørelse, beslutning; *b)* besluttsomhet; **2** erklæring, resolusjon; **3** *data etc* oppløsning. **resolve** [rɪ'zɒlv] *sb* = *resolution 1*; **II** *vb* **1** beslutte; bestemme seg for/til; **2** erklære; vedta (i resolusjons form); **3** oppklare, (opp)løse. **resolved** [rɪ'zɒlvd] *adj* beslutsom, bestemt; resolutt.

resonance ['rezənəns] *sb* gjen|lyd, -klang; resonans. **resonant** ['rezənənt] *adj* gjenlydende; rungende.

resort [rɪ'zɔ:t] **I** *sb* **1** tilholdssted; **2** utfluktssted; **3** tilflukt (og tilfluktssted); utvei; *last* ~ siste instans; **II** *vi*: ~ *to* benytte (seg av); ty til.

resound [rɪ'zaʊnd] *vb* gjenlyde; gjalle, runge.

resource [rɪ'sɔ:s] *sb* **1** (hjelpe)middel, utvei; *fl også* ressurser; **2** fritidsbeskjeftigelse; tidsfordriv; **3** rådsnarhet. **resourceful** [rɪ'sɔ:sfʊl] *adj* rådsnar.

respect [rɪ'spekt] **I** *sb* **1** aktelse, respekt; **2** oppmerksomhet; *gml* oppvartning; *fl* hilsen(er); **3** henseende; *in* ~ *of/with* ~ *to* med hensyn til; *in every* ~ i enhver henseende; på alle måter; **II** *vt* **1** akte; ha aktelse/respekt for; **2** (over)holde, respektere; ta hensyn til; **3** angå, vedrøre. **respectable** [rɪ'spektəbl] *adj* **1** aktverdig, respektabel; **2** anstendig; bra, skikkelig; **3** betydelig. **respectful** [rɪs'pektfʊl] *adj* ærbødig. **respective** [rɪ'spektɪv] *adj* respektiv. **respectively** [rɪ'spektɪvlɪ] *adv* henholdsvis, respektive; især.

respiration [ˌrespə'reɪʃn] *sb* pust(ing), åndedrett; respirasjon.

respite ['respaɪt] *sb* **1** hvil, (hvile)pause; **2** utsettelse; frist, henstand; respitt.

resplendence [rɪ'splendəns] *sb* glans; prakt. **resplendent** [rɪ'splendənt] *adj* glimrende, strålende; prektig.

respond [rɪ'spɒnd] *vi* **1** svare; **2** reagere (*to* på). **response** [rɪ'spɒns] *sb* **1** svar; **2** reaksjon. **responsibility** [rɪˌspɒnsə'bɪlətɪ] *sb* ansvar (og den/det en har ansvaret for). **responsible** [rɪ'spɒnsəbl] *adj* **1** ansvarlig (*for* for; *to* overfor); **2** pålitelig; ansvarsbevisst; **3** ansvarsfull. **responsive** [rɪ'spɒnsɪv] *adj* **1** svarende, svar-; **2** mottakelig, åpen; lydhør.

rest [rest] **A I** *sb* **1** hvil(e); ro; *come to* ~ falle til ro; **2** anlegg, støtte; underlag; **3** *mus* pause(tegn); **II** *vb* **1** hvile; raste; ta (seg en) hvil; **2** (la) hvile; **3** ~ *(up)on* bygge/stole på; være avhengig av; **4** være; forbli; ~ *assured* (kunne) være trygg (på); (kunne) stole på; *it* ~*s with you* det påhviler deg; **B** *sb* rest.

restart ['ri:stɑ:t] **1** *sb* omstart; **2** *vt* starte på nytt.

restitution [ˌrestɪ'tju:ʃn] *sb* **1** erstatning; oppreisning; **2** tilbakelevering (av tyvegods).

restive ['restɪv] *adj* **1** utålmodig; rastløs (om personer); **2** sta (om hester).

rest|less ['restlɪs] *adj* hvileløs, rastløs.

restoration [ˌrestə'reɪʃn] *sb* **1** tilbakelevering *etc*; **2** gjenoppbygging, gjenreising; restaurering; **3** helbredelse, restitusjon; **4** gjeninnsettelse (i embete etc). **restore** [rɪ'stɔ:] *vt* **1** gi/levere tilbake; **2** sette på plass (igjen); **3** gjenreise; bygge opp (igjen); restaurere; **4** rekonstruere; *data* gjenopprette; **5** reparere; gjøre i stand (igjen); helbrede, lege; **6** fornye; gjen|innføre, -opplive, -opprette; **7** gjeninnsette (i embete etc).

restrain [rɪ'streɪn] *vi* **1** beherske, undertrykke; begrense, innskrenke; **2** hindre; holde igjen/tilbake. **restraint** [rɪ'streɪnt] *sb* **1** (selv)beherskelse; tilbakeholdenhet; undertrykkelse; **2** begrensning, innskrenkning; **3** bånd, tvang; **4** *jur* sikring.

restrict [rɪ'strɪkt] *vt* begrense, innskrenke; legge bånd/restriksjoner på. **restriction** [rɪ'strɪkʃn] *sb* begrensning, innskrenkning. **restrictive** [rɪ'strɪktɪv] *adj* innskrenkende; restriktiv; hemmende, hindrende.

rest room *sb* venteværelse; *US især* (offentlig) toalett.

result [rɪ'zʌlt] **I** *sb* følge, konsekvens; resultat; **II** *vi* **1** komme som en følge/et resultat (*from* av); resultere (*in* i); **2** ende, slutte. **resultant** [rɪ'zʌltənt] *adj* (på)følgende, resulterende.

resume [rɪ'zju:m] *vt* gjenoppta; begynne/fortsette med igjen. **resumption** [rɪ'zʌmpʃn] *sb* gjenopptakelse *etc*.

resurgence [rɪ'sɜ:dʒəns] *sb* (gjen)oppblussing. **resurgent** [rɪ'sɜ:dʒənt] *adj* (gjen)oppblussende; fornyet, nytt.

resurrect [ˌrezə'rekt] *vb* **1** gjenoppstå/gjenoppvekke (fra de døde); **2** gjenopplive; ta i bruk igjen etc; **3** *dgl* grave frem/opp. **resurrection** [ˌrezə'rekʃn] *sb* gjenopplivelse *etc*; *the Resurrection* Oppstandelsen (dvs Jesu oppstandelse fra de døde).

resuscitate [rɪ'sʌsɪteɪt] *vb* gjenopplive; vekke av bevisstløshet. **resuscitation** [rɪ'sʌsɪ'teɪʃn] *sb* gjenoppliving *etc*.

retail I ['ri:teɪl] **1** *adj* detalj-; **2** *adv* i detalj/smått; **3** *sb* detalj(salg); **II** [ri:'teɪl] *vb* **1** selge/bli solgt i detalj; **2** bringe/fortelle videre.

retain [rɪ'teɪn] *vt* **1** bevare, holde på; holde igjen/tilbake *etc*; **2** engasjere (især advokat); ~*ing fee* forskuddshonorar (til advokat). **retainer** [rɪ'teɪnə] *sb* **1** = *retaining fee*; **2** *gml* tjener; *family* ~ tyende.

retake [ˌri:'teɪk] **I** *sb film* nytt opptak; **II** *vt* **1** gjenerobre; ta tilbake; **2** *film* ta (fotografere, skyte) om igjen.

retaliate [rɪ'tælɪeɪt] *vi* gjengjelde, slå igjen; hevne seg; straffe. **retaliation** [rɪˌtælɪ'eɪʃn] *sb* gjengjeld(else) *etc*.

retard [rɪ'tɑ:d] forsinke, hefte; hemme, hindre; sette tilbake; *mentally ~ed* mentalt utviklingshemmet.

retch [retʃ] *vi* brekke seg.

retell [ˌri:'tel] *vt* gjenta; fortelle om igjen.

retention [rɪ'tenʃn] *sb* tilbakeholdelse (etc, jf *retain*).

reticence ['retɪsəns] *sb* tilbakeholdenhet *etc*. **reticent** ['retɪsənt] *adj* tilbakeholden; innesluttet, taus.

retinue ['retɪnju:] *sb* følge; tilhengere.

retire [rɪ'taɪə] **1** *sb* retrett(signal); **2** *vb* trekke seg tilbake; *(~ to bed)* gå til sengs; *~ on a pension* gå av med pensjon. **retired** [rɪ'taɪəd] *adj* **1** tilbaketrukket *etc*; **2** avsides(liggende); ensom; **3** pensjonert. **retirement** [rɪ'taɪəmənt] *sb* **1** retrett, tilbaketrekning; **2** tilbaketrukkenhet; avsondrethet, ensomhet; **3** ensomt sted *etc*; **4** fratredelse, pensjonering.

retort [rɪ'tɔ:t] **I** *sb* gjenmæle, motmæle; svar (på tiltale); **II** *vb* **1** svare (skarpt igjen; ta til gjenmæle/motmæle; **2** gjengjelde, utligne; ta igjen/bli skuls med.

retouch [ˌri:'tʌtʃ] *vt* retusjere.

retrace [rɪ'treɪs] *vt* følge (spor etc) tilbake; gjenkalle (i erindringen).

retract [rɪ'trækt] *vb* **1** tilbakekalle; ta i seg igjen; **2** trekke inn (opp, tilbake etc).

retreat [rɪ'tri:t] **I** *sb* **1** retrett (og retrettsignal); tilbaketrekning; **2** tilbaketrukkenhet; ensomhet; **3** tilfluktssted; **II** *vi* **1** trekke seg tilbake; retirere, vike; **2** skråne bakover.

retrench [rɪ'trentʃ] *vb* skjære ned (forbruk, utgifter etc); innskrenke; økonomisere. **retrenchment** [rɪ'trentʃmənt] *sb* innskrenkning; økonomisering; sparepolitikk.

retribution [ˌretrɪ'bju:ʃn] *sb* gjengjeldelse, straff.

retrieval [rɪ'tri:vl] *sb* **1** gjen|ervervelse, -vinning; *data* gjenfinning; **2** redning. **retrieve** [rɪ'tri:v] *vb* **1** gjenvinne; finne/få igjen; *data også* gjenfinne; **2** apportere, hente.

retrograde ['retrəgreɪd] **I** *adj* **1** tilbakegående; (som er) i tilbakegang/på retur; **2** som blir verre; **II** *vi* **1** gå/trekke seg tilbake; **2** bli verre.

retrogression [ˌretrə'greʃn] *sb* tilbake|fall, -gang; forverring. **retrogressive** [ˌretrə'gresɪv] *adj* som er i tilbakegang; degenererende.

retrospect ['retrəspekt] *sb* tilbakeblikk; *in ~* i tilbakeblikk; når en ser/tenker tilbake. **retrospective** [ˌretrə'spektɪv] *adj* retrospektiv; som minnes/ser seg tilbake; minne-; **2** (med) tilbakevirkende (kraft).

return [rɪ'tɜ:n] **I** *adj* retur-, tilbake-; **II** *sb* **1** retur (og returnering); tilbake|komst, -reise, -tur; **2** returnering, tilbake|levering, -sending; retur (og retur|-gods, -varer); *by ~ (of post)* omgående; **3** tilbakebetaling; gjengjeld; kompensasjon, motytelse; *in ~ (for)* i stedet/til gjengjeld (for); **4** *many happy ~s of the day* gratulerer med dagen; **5** *(fl)* avkastning, utbytte; fortjeneste; **6** (til)svar; *in ~ to* som svar på; **7** innberetning, rapport; melding; oppgave; **8** valg (dvs det å bli valgt); *election ~s* valgresultat(er); **III** *vb* **1** returnere; dra (gå, komme, reise, vende etc) hjem/tilbake; **2** returnere; bringe (gi, levere, sende, sette etc) tilbake; **3** betale tilbake; gjengjelde; gi igjen (som motytelse etc); *~ a blow* slå igjen; *~ interest/a profit* gi rente(r)/fortjeneste; *~ a service* gjøre en gjentjeneste; **4** besvare; svare igjen; **5** erklære; innberette, melde, oppgi, rapportere; *~ a verdict* avgi en kjennelse; **6** velge. **return | fare** *sb* = *~ ticket*. *~* **match** *sb* returkamp. *~* **ticket** *sb* returbillett. *~* **visit** *sb* gjenvisitt.

reunion [ˌri:'ju:nɪən] *sb* gjenforening; (ny) samling. **reunite** [ˌri:ju:'nait] *vb* gjenforene(s); komme sammen/møtes (igjen); bringe sammen (igjen).

rev [rev] *vb dgl (~ up)* gi gass.

reveal [rɪ'vi:l] *vt* avsløre, røpe; åpenbare; *også* vise.

revel ['revl] **I** *sb* fest(ing); *fl også* rangel; **II** *vi* **1** feste; more seg; slå seg løs; rangle; **2** *~ in* nyte; fryde/glede seg over; gasse seg i. **revelry** ['revlrɪ] *sb* rangel.

revelation [ˌrevə'leɪʃn] *sb* avsløring (etc, jf *reveal*); åpenbaring.

revenge [rɪ'vendʒ] **I** *sb* **1** gjengjeld(else); hevn; **2** *sport* revansj; **II** *vt: ~ oneself on* hevne seg på; *be ~ed on* få/ta hevn over. **revengeful** [rɪ'vendʒfʊl] *adj* hevngjerrig.

revenue ['revənju:] *sb* (stats)inntekter; *især* avgifter, skatter, toll. **revenue | officer** *sb* toller. *~* **stamp** *sb* stempelmerke.

reverberate [rɪ'vɜ:bəreɪt] *vt* gjalle, runge; gi/kaste gjenlyd. **reverberation** [rɪˌvɜ:bə'reɪʃn] *sb* gjenlyd *etc*.

revere [rɪ'vɪə] *vt* (høy)akte, ære; ha (dyp) ærbødighet for. **reverence** ['revərəns] **I** *sb* **1** (dyp) respekt/ærbødighet; **2** ærbødig hilsen; reverens; **3** velærverdighet; **II** *vt* (høy)akte, vise ærbødighet. **reverend** ['revərənd] **1** *adj* ærverdig; **2** *som sb, om geistlige: the Reverend* pastor, prest; *the Very Reverend* (dom)prost; *the Right Reverend* biskop; *the Most Reverend* erkebiskop. **Reverend Mother** *sb* abbedisse. **reverent** ['revərənt], **reverential** [ˌrevə'renʃl] *adj* ærbødig.

reverie ['revərɪ] *sb* dagdrøm(mer), drømmer.

reversal [rɪ'vɜ:sl] *sb* **1** (om)|bytting, -vending; reversering; **2** bytte, skifte; *fig* omslag; **3** annullering, omstøtelse. **reverse** [rɪ'vɜ:s] **I** *adj* motsatt, omvendt; **II** *sb* **1** motsetning; det motsatte/omvendte; **2** bakside, vrange; revers; **3** reversering, rygging; *(~ gear/mechanism)* revers (på bil); reverseringsmekanisme; **4** omslag, skifte; **5** tilbakeslag; nederlag; **III** *vb* **1** forandre; (ende)vende; vrenge; kullkaste; **2** reversere, rygge; sette i revers; *sjø* slå bakk; **3** *jur* annullere, tilbakekalle; omstøte, underkjenne. **reverse | print** *sb data* negativ skrift. *~* **video** *sb data* negativt bilde.

reversible [rɪ'vɜ:səbl] *adj* **1** reverserbar; **2** vendbar.

reversion [rɪ'vɜ:ʃn] *sb* **1** tilbake|fall, -vending; **2** reversering; om|kastning, stilling; omslag, skifte; **3** hjemfall (og hjemfallsrett); arverett. **revert** [rɪ'vɜ:t] *vi* gå (komme, vende etc) tilbake; hjemfalle.

review [rɪ'vju:] **I** *sb* **1** tilbakeblikk; *pass in* ~ la passere revy; **2** gransking, undersøkelse; anmeldelse/kritikk (av bøker etc); **3** magasin, tidsskrift; **4** mønstring, parade; (troppe)revy; **II** *vb* **1** revidere; gå igjennom (på ny); **2** granske, undersøke; anmelde (bøker etc); inspisere/mønstre (tropper). **review copy** *sb* anmeldereksemplar. **reviewer** [rɪ'vju:ə] *sb* (bok)anmelder, kritiker.

revile [rɪ'vaɪl] *vt* (for)håne; overhøvle; skjelle ut; rakke ned på.

revise [rɪ'vaɪz] *vt* **1** revidere; gjennomgå/granske (på ny); **2** korrigere/rette (på). **revision** [rɪ'vɪʒn] *sb* (ny) gjennomgåelse; revisjon; korrigering, retting.

revitalize [ri:'vaɪtəlaɪz] *vt* gjenopplive; bringe/sette nytt liv i.

revival [rɪ'vaɪvl] *sb* **1** gjenopplivning *etc*; **2** *rel* vekkelse. **revivalist** [rɪ'vaɪvəlɪst] *sb* vekkelsespredikant. **revive** [rɪ'vaɪv] *vb* **1** gjenopp|live, -vekke; gjeninnføre; komme/ta i bruk (igjen); **2** komme seg (igjen); kvikne til.

revocation [ˌrevə'keɪʃn] *sb* tilbakekalling *etc*. **revoke** [rɪ'vəuk] *vt* tilbakekalle; annullere, oppheve.

revolt [rɪ'vəult] **I** *sb* **1** opprør, oppstand; reisning; **2** avsky, vemmelse; **II** *vb* **1** gjøre opprør/oppstand; protestere (sterkt); **2** opprøre(s); fylle(s) med vemmelse (*at* over). **revolting** [rɪ'vəultɪŋ] *adj* frastøtende, motbydelig.

revolution [ˌrevə'lu:ʃn] *sb* **1** omdreining *etc*; **2** revolusjon. **revolutionary** [ˌrevə'lu:ʃnərɪ] *adj, sb* revolusjonær (person). **revolutionize** [ˌrevə'lu:ʃənaɪz] *vt* revolusjonere. **revolve** [rɪ'vɒlv] *vb* rotere; dreie/snurre *etc* rundt; (få til å) gå rundt.

revulsion [rɪ'vʌlʃn] *sb* **1** (plutselig) forandring; omslag, skifte; **2** reaksjon (*against* mot).

reward [rɪ'wɔ:d] **1** *sb* belønning; godtgjørelse, vederlag; dusør; *in ~ for* som lønn/til takk for; **2** *vt* (be)lønne. **rewarding** [rɪ'wɔ:dɪŋ] *adj* givende, utbytterik; verdifull.

rewrite [ˌri:'raɪt] *vt* omskrive.

rheumatic [ru:'mætɪk] **1** *adj* revmatisk; **2** *sb* revmatiker. **rheumatism** ['ru:mətɪzəm] *sb* revmatisme.

rhino ['raɪnəu] *fork* for **rhinoceros** [raɪ'nɒsərəs] *sb* neshorn.

rhubarb ['ru:ba:b] *sb* rabarbra.

rhyme [raɪm] **I** *sb* **1** rim (og rimord); **2** rimet vers; regle (som går på rim); **II** *vb* rime (*with* på).

rhythm ['rɪðəm] *sb* rytme. **rhythmic(al)** ['rɪðmɪk(l)] *adj* rytmisk.

rib [rɪb] **I** *sb* **1** ribbein; ribbe (på slakt); **2** ribbe; kant, rand; fure, stripe; vrangbord; **3** (blad)nerve; (grat)bue; (paraply)spile; *sjø* (skips)spant; **II** *vt* ribbe; forsyne/forsterke *etc* med ribber.

ribald ['rɪbəld] **1** *adj* grov (og grovkornet); uanstendig, vulgær; **2** *sb* pøbel; råtamp.

riband ['rɪbənd] *sb* = **ribbon** ['rɪbən] *sb* **1** bånd (og ordensbånd); lisse, strimmel; **2** fille, lase; **3** *fl* (kjøre)tømmer.

rice [raɪs] *sb* ris (og risengryn).

rich [rɪtʃ] *adv* **1** rik (*in* på); **2** kostelig, verdifull; rikt smykket/utstyrt *etc*; **3** fruktbar; rik(holdig); ~ *soil* rik jord; **4** kraftig; nærende, næringsrik; **5** dyp (om farge); fulltonende, fyldig; **6** *dgl* komisk; festlig, morsom. **riches** ['rɪtʃɪz] *sb fl* rikdom(mer). **rich gas** *sb petro* våt gass. **richness** ['rɪtʃnɪs] *sb* rikdom.

rick [rɪk] **A 1** *sb* (høy)stakk; **2** *vt* stakke; sette i stakk; **B** = *wrick*.

rickets ['rɪkɪts] *sb fl* rakitt, engelsk syke. **rickety** ['rɪkɪtɪ] *adj* gebrekkelig, skrøpelig; **2** rakittisk (dvs med engelsk syke).

rid [rɪd] *vt* (be)fri/rense (*of* for); ~ *oneself/get ~ of* bli kvitt; kvitte seg med. **riddance** ['rɪdəns] *sb: good ~ (of/to bad rubbish)!* godt/gudskjelov *etc* at jeg/vi ble kvitt det *etc*.

ridden ['ridn] *adj* besatt; *fear-~* angstreden.

riddle ['rɪdl] **A 1** *sb* gåte; **2** *vt* løse (gåte); **B I** *sb* sikt, såld; grusharpe, skakebrett; **II** *vt* **1** sikte, sile; **2** gjennomhulle.

ride [raɪd] **I** *sb* **1** ridetur, ritt; **2** (motor)sykkeltur; **3** (kjøre)tur (med offentlig transportmiddel etc); **4** *slang: take for a ~* lure, snyte; **II** *vb* **1** ri (og ri på; sitte skrevs over, høyt oppe på etc); **2** kjøre (motor)sykkel; sykle; **3** kjøre med (offentlig transportmiddel etc, jf *drive II 2*); **4** bære/bli båret oppe; hvile på; **5** stå/sveve (høyt på himmelen); **6** flyte; seile; *let it/matters ~* la saken/tingene *etc* gå sin gang; stille det/saken *etc* i bero. **rider** ['raɪdə] *sb* **1** rytter (og sykkelrytter etc); **2** påtegning; tilleggs|bestemmelse, -klausul.

ridge [rɪdʒ] **1** *sb* kam (= bølgekam etc); rabbe, ås(rygg); høydedrag; møne, takrygg; **2** *vt* danne ryggen av; kamme opp.

ridicule ['rɪdɪkju:l] **1** *sb* latter (dvs latterliggjøring); spott; **2** *vt* latterliggjøre; spotte; gjøre narr av. **ridiculous** [rɪ'dɪkjuləs] *adj* latterlig; komisk.

rife [raɪf] *adj* **1** alminnelig, gjengs, vanlig; **2** full (*with* av).

riff-raff ['rɪfræf] *sb* berme, pøbel.

rifle ['raɪfl] **A 1** *sb* rifle; *fl* geværtropper, infanteri; **2** *vt* fure, rifle; **B** *vt* endevende, gjennomrote. **rifle-range** *sb* **1** skytebane; **2** skudd|hold, -vidde.

rift [rɪft] *sb* revne, sprekk; kløft (og *fig* splid, uenighet etc).

rig [rɪg] **A I** *sb* **1** *petro, sjø* rigg; **2** redskaper, utstyr; **3** *dgl* antrekk, klær; **II** *vb* **1** *sjø* rigge; **2** ~ *out* ruste (ut); utstyre; ~ *up* montere; sette opp/sammen; *petro* klargjøre (for boring) *dgl* rigge opp/til; **3** *dgl: ~ out* kle opp; **B** *vt* fikse, ordne; manipulere.

right [raɪt] **A I** *adj* **1** rett (og rettferdig); riktig; **2** akkurat; korrekt, riktig; *be ~* ha rett; være riktig; *get ~* forstå/oppfatte på riktig måte; bringe/komme i orden; få skikk på; **3** passende, riktig; *that's all ~* det er i orden; *også* ingen årsak; **4** normal, riktig; frisk, sunn; **II** *adv* **1** rett, riktig; *(it) serves them ~* det er til pass for dem; det har de (bare) godt av; **2** direkte, like, rett; ~ **along** *US* straks; hele tiden; ~ **away** omgående, straks; *I'll be ~* **back** *US* jeg er/kommer straks tilbake; ~ **in** *the middle of* midt oppi; akkurat midt i; ~ **now** *US dgl* akkurat nå; for øyeblikket; ~ **off** omgående, straks; på stående fot; ~ **on** rett frem; ~ **out** like (rent, rett etc) ut; fullstendig; **3** fullstendig, helt; ~ **about** helt om; ~ **through** tvers igjennom; **III** *sb* **1** rett(ferd); (det som er) rett/riktig; *be in the* ~ ha rett; *by* ~ *of* i kraft av; *by* ~*s* med rette; egentlig; ærlig talt; om alt går/gikk riktig for seg; **2** rett (og rettighet; rettmessighet, rettmessig krav etc); berettigelse; ~ *of way* forkjørsrett; veirett; hevd; *assert/stand on one's* ~*s* hevde/stå på sin rett; *be (well) within one's* ~*s* være i sin (fulle) rett; *in one's own* ~ som sin egen eiendom; selvstendig; på egen hånd; **3** skyldighet; *do them* ~ gjøre rett (og skjell) mot dem; **IV** *vt* **1** rette (opp); bringe/få på rett kjøl; **2** beriktige; rette (på); skaffe rett; **B 1** *adj* høyre; **2** *adv* på høyre side *etc*; til høyre; **3** *sb* høyre (side etc). **right arrow key** *sb data* høyretast. **rightdown** *adj, adv* gjennomført; ordentlig; virkelig. **righteous** ['raɪtʃəs] *adj* **1** rett|ferdig, -skaffen; **2** gudfryktig, rettferdig. **right|ful** *adj* **1** rettmessig; **2** berettiget; rettferdig. **~-hand** *adj* høyre, høyrehånds-. **~-handed** *adj* høyrehendt. **rightists** *sb fl* høyrefolk. **right-justify** *vt data* høyrestille (dvs justere for rett høyremarg). **rightly** *adv* **1** med rette; **2** rett, riktig. **right|-minded** *adj* rettsindig, rettenkende. ~ **shift** *sb data* høyreskift. ~ **side** *sb* rette, rettside. **~-thinking** *adj* rettenkende. **~-turn** *sb* høyre|sving, -vending. *the* ~ **wing** *sb pol* høyrefløyen.

rigid ['rɪdʒɪd] *adj* **1** stiv, ubøyelig; **2** fast, streng.

rigmarole ['rɪgmərəʊl] *sb* sludder, tøv; harang, tirade.

rigorous ['rɪgərəs] *adj* **1** hard, streng; rigorøs; **2** barsk, streng. **rigour** ['rɪgə] *sb* barskhet, strenghet.

rile [raɪl] *vt dgl* ergre, irritere.

rim [rɪm] **I** *sb* **1** kant, rand; brem; **2** felg; flens; **II** *vt* innfatte; kante; danne/forsyne med kant *etc*.

rind [raɪnd] *sb* skall, skrell; (oste)skorpe; (fleske)-svor.

ring [rɪŋ] **A I** *sb* ring (og krets, kretsløp; arena, manesje; (bokse)ring; (veddeløps)bane; *fig* klikk, krets etc); **II** *vb* **1** innringe, omringe; slå ring rundt; ringe, ringmerke; sette ring på; **3** gå *etc* i ring; **B I** *sb* **1** ringing (og ringelyd); *give a* ~ ringe opp; slå på tråden; **2** klang, lyd; *fig* preg, tone(fall); **II** *vb* **1** ringe (med/på); ~ *for* ringe etter; ~ *off* ringe av; ~ *up* ringe opp; telefonere til; **2** klinge, lyde, låte; ~ *a bell (dgl)* få en klokke til å ringe (dvs høres/virke kjent etc); **2** (gjen)lyde, runge. **ring|-leader** *sb* anfører; (opprørs)leder. **~let** *sb* (hår)lokk. ~ **network** *sb data* ringnett.

rink [rɪŋk] *sb* (rulle)skøytebane.

rinse [rɪns] **I** *sb* **1** (ut)skylling (og skyllevann); **2** (hår)tonemiddel; **II** *vt (~ out)* skylle (ut); ~ *down* skylle ned.

riot ['raɪət] **I** *sb* **1** opp|rør, -stand; *fl* opptøyer; *the Riot Act* opprørsloven; **2** (voldsomt) utbrudd; eksplosjon *(fig)*; *run* ~ løpe løpsk; **3** bråk, leven, spetakkel; **II** *vi* **1** gjøre opprør; delta i opptøyer *etc*; **2** ~ *in* fråtse/velte seg i (dvs overdrive etc sterkt). **riotous** ['raɪətəs] *adj* **1** opprørsk; **2** bråkende; løssluppen, vill.

rip [rɪp] **A I** *sb* flenge, revne, rift; **II** *vb* **1** flenge/rive (opp etc); sprette opp; rakne; revne, spjære(s); kløyve/sage (opp på langs); ~ *off* rive/sprette av; *dgl* rappe, stjele; overfalle, rane; ~ *out* rive av/ut; *dgl* rive av seg (dvs ramse opp, si etc); **2** rykke/trekke (i); **3** fare, styrte, suse; ~ *into* fare/gyve løs på; **B** *sb dgl* rundbrenner, uthaler. **rip-cord** *sb* utløsersnor (til fallskjerm).

ripe [raɪp] *adj* **1** moden; (fullt) utviklet; **2** ~ *for* klar for; parat/rede til. **ripen** ['raɪpən] *vb* modne(s).

rip-off *sb dgl* overfall, ran.

ripple ['rɪpl] **1** *sb* krusning; (bølge)skvulp; **2** *vb* kruse (seg); skvulpe; *fig* bølge.

rip-saw *sb* kløyvsag.

rise [raɪz] **I** *sb* **1** oppgang, (-)stigning; *om fisk* napp(ing); vaking; *fig* forfremmelse; fremgang; **2** bakke (og bakketopp; haug, høyde, kolle etc); stigning; skråning (oppover); **3** vekst, økning; (lønns)-pålegg; (pris)stigning; *om deig etc* esing, heving; *om elv etc* (opp)svulming; **4** kilde, utspring; begynnelse, årsak; *give* ~ *to* for|anledige, -årsake; **II** *vi* **1** reise seg; stå opp; stige (opp); *om fisk* nappe; sprette, vake; *early* ~ morgenfugl; **2** stige; skråne (oppover); **3** avansere; gjøre fremskritt; stige; bli forfremmet; ~ *from the ranks* gå gradene; ~ *in the world* komme seg frem i verden; bli til noe; ~ *to the occasion* vokse med oppgaven(e); vise seg å være situasjonen voksen; **4** reise seg (dvs gjøre opprør, *against* mot); **5** vokse, øke; ese, heve seg; svulme (opp); tilta; bli høyere (kraftigere, sterkere etc); **6** ha sitt utspring (i); komme fra. **riser** ['raɪzə] *sb petro* (slam)stigerør. **rising** ['raɪzɪŋ] **1** *adj* stigende *etc*; **2** *sb* opp|rør, -stand.

risk [rɪsk] **1** *sb* fare/risiko (*of* for); *at the* ~ *of* med fare for (å); *take a* ~ ta en sjanse; **2** *vt* risikere; utsette for fare/risiko; våge. **risky** ['rɪskɪ] *adj* risikabel.

rite [raɪt] *sb* rite, ritus; *fl* ritual; (religiøs) seremoni. **ritual** ['rɪtʃʊəl] **1** *adj* rituell, ritual-; **2** *sb* ritual.

rival ['raɪvl] **1** *adj* konkurrerende; rivaliserende; **2** *sb* konkurrent; rival, medbeiler; motstander; **3** *vt* kappes (konkurrere, måle seg) med; rivalisere. **rivalry** ['raɪvlrɪ] *sb* kappestrid, konkurranse; rivalisering.

river ['rɪvə] *sb* elv; *også fig* flod; flom, strøm; *sell him down the* ~ forråde ham. **riverside** *sb* elvebredd.

rivet ['rɪvɪt] **I** *sb* nagle; **II** *vt* **1** klinke; nagle; **2** ~ *one's eyes on* nagle blikket i.

rivulet ['rɪvjʊlɪt] *sb* bekk, liten elv.

road [rəʊd] *sb* **1** vei; *high/main* ~ hovedvei, riksvei; *the high* ~ allfarveien; *rel* den brede vei; *rules of the* ~ trafikkregler; sjøveisregler; *on the* ~ underveis; på farten; på turné; *one for the* ~ *(dgl)* avskjedsdrink *etc*; **2** *sjø (~s, ~stead)* red; **3** *US (rail~)* (jern)bane; skinnegang. **road|-block** *sb* veisperring. **~-hog** *sb* bilbølle, råkjører. **~-house** *sb* veikro. **~map** *sb* bilkart, veikart. ~ **safety** *sb* trafikksikkerhet. **~-sense** *sb* trafikkvett. **~side** *sb* vei|grøft, -kant. **~-sign** *sb* trafikkskilt.

roadster ['rəʊdstə] *sb* **1** *hist* skysshest; **2** *især* liten toseter; sportsbil.

roam [rəʊm] *vb* flakke (streife, vandre etc) omkring (i, på).

roan [rəʊn] **1** *adj* (rød)skimlet; **2** *sb* skimmel.

roar [rɔ:] **I** *sb* **1** brøl; **2** brak, drønn; **3** bråk; sterk brusing; **II** *vb* **1** brøle; **2** brake, drønne; tordne; bruse sterkt. **roaring** ['rɔ:rɪŋ] *adj* **1** brølende *etc*; **2** strykende; ~ *success* knallsuksess; *dgl* dundrende suksess.

roast [rəʊst] **1** *adj* stekt; ~ *beef* (ferdigstekt) oksestek; **2** *sb* stek (og steking); ~ *of beef* oksestek; **3** *vb* steke (og bake, riste etc).

rob [rɒb] *vt* plyndre (*of* for); ~ *of (også)* fra|rane, -røve. **robber** ['rɒbə] *sb* overfallsmann, ransmann; røver. **robbery** ['rɒbərɪ] *sb* overfall, ran; røveri.

robe [rəʊb] **I** *sb* **1** (især fotsid) kappe/kåpe; (embets)|drakt, -kappe; *(bath-~)* badekåpe; *US* morgenkåpe; slåbrok; **2** kjole (i butikk- og motesjargong); robe; **II** *vb: ~d in* iført; kledd i.

robin ['rɒbɪn] *sb (~ redbreast)* rødstrupe.

rock [rɒk] **A** *sb* **1** *(bed~)* (grunn)fjell; **2** (fjell)knaus, klippe; *i sjøen* skjær; **3** (kampe)stein, (klippe)blokk; *US* (små)stein; **B** *vb* gynge, vugge; riste/rugge (på). **rock | bit** *sb petro* rullekrone. **~-bottom** *adj, især fig* bunn-, lav-. **rockery, rock-garden** *sb* steinbed.

rocket ['rɒkɪt] **1** *sb* rakett; **2** *vi dgl* fare opp/stige til værs *etc* (som en rakett).

rocking-chair *sb* gyngestol.

rocky ['rɒkɪ] *adj* **A** forreven, klippefull; steinet; **B** *dgl* ustø, vaklevoren.

rod [rɒd] *sb* **1** stang; **2** stokk; kjepp, stav; **3** en måleenhet, se midtsidene; **4** *US slang* skyter (dvs skytevåpen).

rodent ['rəʊdənt] *adj, sb* gnager(-).

roe [rəʊ] *sb* **A** (fiske)rogn; **B** rå(dyr).

Roger ['rɒdʒə] **1** *interj* javel; oppfattet; skal bli; **2** *sb (Jolly ~)* sjørøverflagg.

rogue [rəʊg] *sb* **1** kjeltring, slyngel; skøyer; **2** *gml* landstryker. **roguish** ['rəʊgɪʃ] *adj* **1** kjeltringaktig; **2** skøyeraktig.

role, rôle [rəʊl] *sb* rolle.

roll [rəʊl] **I** *sb* **1** rull; *(~ of fat)* (fett)valk; **2** rundstykke; rulade; **3** rulling; rullende bevegelse; **4** rumling; rumlende lyd; (tromme)virvel; **5** fortegnelse, liste; rulle; **II** *vb* **1** rulle (og rulle/velte seg); trille; ~ *by/on* gå (om tid); ~ *in* rulle (strømme, velte etc) inn; ~ *over* velte (over ende); ~ *up* rulle opp/sammen; hope seg opp; **2** kjevle/valse (ut); **3** bølge; vagge; vugge (med); **4** rumle; slå en (tromme)virvel. **roll-collar** *sb* rullekrave. **roller** ['rəʊlə] *sb* **1** rulle, trommel, valse; (gardin)stokk; (rulle)bandasje; **2** dønning; lang bølge. **roller|-coaster** *sb US* rutsjebane. **~-skates** *sb fl* rulleskøyter.

rollicking ['rɒlɪkɪŋ] *adj* livlig; lystig; løssluppen.

rolling ['rəʊlɪŋ] *sb* rulling *etc*. **rolling|-mill** *sb* valsemølle. **~-pin** *sb* kjevle. **~-stock** *sb* rullende materiell. **rolltop desk** *sb* sjalusipult.

Roman ['rəʊmən] **I** *adj* romersk (og romersk-katolsk); romer-; **II** *sb* **1** romer; **2** (romersk) katolikk. **romance** [rəʊ'mæns] **I** *sb* **1** eventyrlig/romantisk fortelling; *gml* ridderroman; **2** fantasifull/fantastisk historie/opplevelse *etc*; **3** romantikk; romantisk stemning; romanse; svermeri; **4** *Romance (især som adj)* romansk; **II** *vi* romantisere; overdrive. **romantic** [rəʊ'mæntɪk] **I** *adj* romantisk; **II** *sb* **1** romantiker; **2** romantikk.

romp [rɒmp] **I** *sb* **1** leven; tumling; (vilter) lek; **2** galneheie, villkatt; villstyring; **II** *vi* boltre/tumle seg; leke (viltert og støyende).

roof [ru:f] **1** *sb* (utvendig) tak; hvelv(ing); *(~ of the mouth)* gane; *raise the ~* sette huset på ende; **2** *vt* legge tak på.

rook [rʊk] **A** *sb* (korn)kråke; **B** **1** *sb* falskspiller, (kort)svindler; **2** *vt* bedra, snyte, svindle (især i kortspill); **C** *sb* tårn (i sjakk). **rookery** ['rʊkərɪ] *sb* **1** kråke|koloni, -flokk; **2** fuglefjell; yngleplass (især for pingviner og sel); **3** *dgl* rottereir (om forfallen, overbefolket leiegård etc).

room [rʊm] **I** *sb* **1** rom, værelse; *fl* (ungkars)leilighet; **2** plass, rom; **3** anledning, mulighet; armslag; **II** *vi* bo (i); ~ *with* bo sammen med. **room-mate** *sb* værelseskamerat. **-roomed** [-rʊmd] *som suff* -roms. **roomy** ['rʊmɪ] *adj* rommelig, vid.

roost [ru:st] **1** *sb* vagle; **2** *vi* vagle seg (opp); *dgl* sove. **rooster** ['ru:stə] *sb* hane.

root [ru:t] **A** **1** *sb* rot; *fl* rotfrukter, røtter; ~ *and branch* helt og holdent; rubb og stubb; *strike/take ~* slå rot; **2** *vb* slå rot; **B** *vb* **1** grave/rote (*out* frem; *up* opp); ~ *out (også)* utrydde; ~ *up (også)* rykke opp/ta (opp) med rot; **2** *US slang* heie (på idrettslag etc). **rooted** ['ru:tɪd] *adj* rotfestet; *be ~ to the spot* stå som (fast)naglet (til stedet).

rope [rəʊp] **1** *sb* tau (og reip, kabel, line, snor etc); *fl* tauverk; *know the ~s (dgl)* kjenne fremgangsmåten/knepene; være inne i sakene; **2** *vt* binde (med tau); ~ *in* huke; få tak i; ~ *off* sperre av (med tauer). **rope|-dancer** *sb* linedanser. **~-ladder** *sb* taustige. **~-walk** *sb = ~-yard*. **~-walker** *sb = ~-dancer*. **~-yard** *sb* reperbane.

rosary ['rəʊzərɪ] *sb* rosenkrans. **rose** [rəʊz] *sb* **1** rose (og rosenbusk); **2** rosa (farge); **3** rosett, sløyfe; **4** dyse/spreder (på vannkanne etc). **rose|-bed** *sb* rosenbed. **~-bud** *sb* rosenknopp. **~-leaf** *sb* rosenblad. **rosemary** ['rəʊzmərɪ] *sb* rosmarin. **rose|-red** *adj* rosen|farget, -rød. **~wood** *sb* rosentre.

rosin ['rɒzɪn] *sb, vt* (gni med) harpiks.

roster ['rɒstə] *sb* vaktliste; turnusliste.

rostrum ['rɒstrəm] *sb* podium, talerstol.

rosy ['rəʊzɪ] *adj* **1** rosa(farget); *fig* rosenrød; **2** blussende, rødkinnet.

rot [rɒt] **I** *sb* **1** forråtnelse, råte; **2** *slang (tommy-~)* sludder, tull, vrøvl; **II** *vb* **1** råtne, gå i forråtnelse; la ligge og råtne; **2** *be ~ting* vrøvle, prate tull.

rota ['rəʊtə] *sb* omgang; turnus (og turnusliste). **rotary** ['rəʊtərɪ] *adj* roterende; rotasjons-. **rotary**

drilling *sb petro* roterende boring. **rotate** [rəʊ'teɪt] *vb* **1** rotere; gå rundt; **2** bytte/veksle (på); gå på omgang/runde.

rote [rəʊt] *sb: by* ~ utenat; på rams.

rotten ['rɒtn] *adj* **1** råtten; bedervet, fordervet; morken; **2** *slang* dårlig, elendig. **rotten luck** *sb dgl* uflaks.

rough [rʌf] **I** *adj* **1** humpet, ujevn; grov, knudret, ru; **2** bustet; ragget; strid, strittende; **3** opprørt; **4** barsk; brutal; hard(hendt), ublid; uregjerlig; vanskelig (å mestre/holde styr på etc); **5** ubehøvlet; grov, rå; primitiv; **6** ubearbeidet; skissemessig; foreløpig, løselig; omtrentlig; **II** *adv* **1** = *~ly*; **2** *cut up* ~ bli ubehagelig; *play/treat* ~ være/behandle hardhendt; **III** *sb* **1** ujevnhet *etc*; **2** uferdig stand; *in the* ~ grovt regnet; løselig anslått; **3** = *~-neck*; **4** = ~ *draft*; **IV** *vt* **1** *(~ up)* gjøre ujevn *etc;* ~ *it* leve primitivt/strabasiøst *etc;* ~ *up* buste til; flosse opp; maltraktere; **2** ~ *in* grovhugge *etc*; skissere; ~ *out* lage utkast (til). **rough|-and--ready** *adj* enkel og grei; primitiv, men effektiv. ~ **copy,** ~ **draft** *sb* kladd, utkast. ~ **house** *sb* bråk, slagsmål. **roughly** ['rʌflɪ] *adv* **1** ujevnt *etc*; **2** barskt; primitivt; brutalt, hardhendt; **3** anslagsvis; grovt regnet; stort sett. **roughneck** *sb* **1** hardhaus; **2** *petro* (bore)dekksarbeider, oljeriggarbeider; *fl* boregjeng; **3** bølle, ramp.

round [raʊnd] **I** *adj* **1** rund; (av)rundet; rund-; runde-; **2** lubben, trinn; **3** full, hel; komplett; ~ *sum* rund sum; pent beløp; **II** *adv, prep* **1** rundt; om (og omkring); **2** *(~ about)* rundt (regnet); omkring; om lag; **III** *sb* **1** rund skive *etc*; rundt stykke *etc*; **2** fylde, rundhet; **3** runde (og rund|dans, -sang, -tur etc); krets(gang), omløp; omgang; *stand a ~ (of drinks)* rive i en omgang (drinker); **4** *mil (~ of ammunition)* skudd; **5** (stige)trinn; **IV** *vb* **1** runde(s), avrunde(s); ~ *off* avrunde; **2** ~ *up* drive/jage sammen; *data etc* avrunde oppover. **round|about** ['raʊndəbaʊt] **I** *adj* omstendelig, omsvøpsfull; indirekte; **II** *sb* **1** karusell; **2** rundkjøring. **~-up** *sb* **1** sammen|driving, -jaging; **2** (fe)drift; bøling, flokk; **3** massearrestasjon; rassia.

rouse [raʊz] *vb* **1** jage/vekke (opp); *sjø* purre; **2** hisse opp; irritere; vekke *(fig)*; stimulere; ~ *oneself* ta seg sammen.

roustabout ['raʊstəbaʊt] *sb petro* (bore)dekksarbeider, oljeriggarbeider. **roustabout pusher** *sb petro* arbeidsleder.

rout [raʊt] **A 1** *sb* sammenbrudd; totalt nederlag; *put to* ~ jage på (vill) flukt; **2** *vt:* ~ *out/up* jage/vekke opp; rote frem.

route [ru:t] **1** *sb* kurs, rute, vei; *mil* marsjordre; **2** *vt data* dirigere, rute.

rove [rəʊv] *vb* flakke/streife (omkring i/på).

row A [rəʊ] **I** *sb* kø; rad, rekke; linje; **II 1** *sb* rotur; **2** *vb* ro; **B** [raʊ] *sb dgl* krangel, trette; bråk, spetakkel.

rowan ['raʊən] *sb* rogn.

row|-boat *sb* robåt.

rowdy ['raʊdɪ] **1** *adj* bråket, kranglevoren; **2** *sb slang* bølle; bråkmaker.

rowing-boat *sb* robåt. **rowlock** ['rɒlək] *sb* tollegang, åregaffel.

row pitch *sb data* linjeavstand, radavstand.

royal ['rɔɪəl] **I** *adj* **1** kongelig, konge-; **2** *dgl* flott, storartet; **II** *sb sjø* røyl. **royalty** ['rɔɪəltɪ] *sb* **1** kongelig person; *koll* de kongelige; kongefamilien; **2** kongeverdighet; **3** royalty (dvs prosentavgift til forfatter, oppfinner etc for rettighet).

rub [rʌb] **I** *sb* **1** gnidning *etc*; **2** aber, hake; hindring; vanskelighet; **II** *vb* gni (og frottere, skrubbe; massere, stryke; polere, pusse, slipe etc); ~ **along** *dgl* humpe og gå; (så vidt) klare seg; ~ **down** frottere; massere; ~ *it* **in** gni (massere, smøre etc) inn; *fig* banke det inn; gi det inn med (te)skje; ~ **off/out** pusse/ viske ut; skrape/skrubbe *etc* vekk; ~ **out** gni/smøre *etc* ut; *fig* kverke, utrydde; ~ **up** polere; pusse opp; *fig* friske opp; ~ *elbows/shoulders* **with** omgås (nært og ofte); vanke (sammen) med.

rubber ['rʌbə] **A 1** *sb* gummi (og ting av gummi, som gummistøvel, kalosje, kondom, viskelær etc); **2** *vt* gummiere; **B** *sb* en/noe som gnir (etc, jf *rub II*); frotter|håndkle, -klut; massør; polerhanske; **C** *sb* robber (omgang i kortspill). **rubber | band** *sb* gummistrikk. ~ **cement,** ~ **solution** *sb* (gummi)solusjon. ~ **stamp** *sb* (gummi)stempel; *fig* (offisiell) godkjenning. **~-stamp** *vt* stemple; *fig* godkjenne.

rubbish ['rʌbɪʃ] *sb* **1** avfall, søppel; **2** sludder, tøv.

rubble ['rʌbl] *sb koll* mur|brokker, -rester; stein (i haug, røys, ur etc).

rub-down ['rʌbdaʊn] *sb* frottering; massering.

rubicund ['ru:bɪkənd] *adj* rødmusset. **ruby** ['ru:bɪ] **1** *adj* rubinrød; **2** *sb* rubin.

rub-out character *sb data* slettetegn.

rucksack ['rʊksæk] *sb* ryggsekk.

rudder ['rʌdə] *sb* ror.

ruddy ['rʌdɪ] *adj* **1** rød (og rød|lett, -musset etc); **2** = *bloody 2*.

rude [ru:d] *adj* **1** uforskammet; udannet, uhøflig; **2** uanstendig, upassende; **3** kraftig, voldsom; **4** robust; **5** grov, primitiv.

rue [ru:] **1** *sb* anger, sorg; **2** *vt* angre (på); være lei (seg) for. **rueful** ['ru:fʊl] *adj* anger|full, -given; angrende.

ruff [rʌf] **A** *sb* **1** fjær|krans, -krave; **2** pipekrave; prestekrave; **B 1** *sb* trumfing (i kortspill); **2** *vb* trumfe.

ruffian ['rʌfiən] *sb* kjeltring, skurk; voldsforbryter.

ruffle ['rʌfl] **I** *sb* **1** pipestrimmel, rynkekrave; rysj; **2** krus; krusning (på vannflate); **3** bestyrtelse; oppstyr, røre; **II** *vb* **1** kruse; rynke; **2** bringe i ulage; buste/pjuske til; rote/rufse opp i; bruse med fjær; **3** irritere (seg); bringe/komme i ulage.

rug [rʌg] *sb* **1** (lite) gulvteppe; rye; **2** pledd.

rugged ['rʌgɪd] *adj* **1** kupert, ujevn; ulendt; forreven, takket; **2** furet, rynket; **3** barsk; rusket, stormfull; **4** rufset, maskulin; **5** robust, solid.

rugger ['rʌgə] *sb dgl* rugby(fotball).

ruin ['ru:ɪn] **I** *sb* **1** ruinering; total ødeleggelse; **2**

ruin (dvs ruinert bygning etc); *fall in(to)* ~*s* synke i grus; **II** *vt* ruinere; legge i ruin(er). **ruinous** ['ru:ɪnəs] *adj* ruinerende, ødeleggende.

rule [ru:l] **I** *sb* **1** regel; forskrift; norm; *fl også* reglement, vedtekter; *jur* rettsregler; **2** regel, vane; **3** avgjørelse, bestemmelse; *jur* kjennelse; **4** makt, myndighet; regjering (og regjeringstid); styre; **5** = ~*er*; **II** *vb* **1** beherske; herske over; lede, styre; regjere; **2** avgjøre; bestemme; beslutte, vedta; erklære; ~ *out* utelukke; sette ut av betraktning; **3** linjere; trekke strek(er); ~ *off* skille med en strek; *fig* utelukke; **4** ligge/stå (om kurs, pris etc). **ruler** ['ru:lə] *sb* **1** hersker; leder; **2** linjal. **ruling** ['ru:lɪŋ] **I** *adj* **1** herskende; regjerende; **2** fremherskende; **II** *sb* **1** herredømme; kommando; **2** *jur* kjennelse.

rum [rʌm] **A** *adj dgl* pussig, snodig; rar; **B** *sb* rom; *US også* brennevin.

rumble ['rʌmbl] **I** *sb* **1** bulder/buldring *etc*; **2** *US* bagasjerom (i bil); åpent baksete; *dgl* svigermorsete; **II** *vb* buldre; ramle, skramle; rulle, rumle.

ruminant ['ru:mɪnənt] **1** *adj* drøvtyggende; **2** *sb* drøvtygger. **ruminate** ['ru:mɪneɪt] *vi* **1** tygge drøv; **2** overveie, spekulere; gruble (lenge og vel over); grunne (på).

rummage ['rʌmɪdʒ] **I** *sb* **1** gjennomroting; ransaking; grundig leting; **2** *(~ sale)* opprydningssalg; loppemarked; **II** *vb* endevende; gjennom|rote, -støve, -søke; ransake.

rumour ['ru:mə] **I** *sb* **1** rykte; ~ *has it that* det fortelles/går rykter om at; **2** *vt: be ~ed* ryktes; bli fortalt.

rump [rʌmp] *sb* **1** bakdel (på slakt); halestykke (på fugl); **2** *hum* bak(ende), rumpe; **3** rest, slump.

rumple ['rʌmpl] *vt* krølle, rynke; buste/pjuske til.

run [rʌn] **I** *sb* **1** løp (og løpetur, springmarsj; kappløp, renn etc); *on the* ~ på farten; på flukt; **2** (for)løp, gang; tendens; **3** rift; sterk pågang/etterspørsel (*(up)on* etter);run/stormløp (*(up)on* på); **4** (snar)tur, tripp; (kort) besøk/visitt; *test/trial* ~ prøve|kjøring, -tur; **5** (tilbakelagt) strekning; (dags)tur; seilas; **6** rekke, serie; (lengre) periode; (fortløpende) drift/produksjon etc; **7** kurs; lei, rute; spor, tråkk; sti, vei; (bekke)far; (elve)|leie, -løp; akebakke, bob(sleigh)bane; *the usual* ~ den daglige tralten; **8** *data etc* kjøring (av maskiner, program etc); **9** vanlig art (slag, type etc); **10** adgang (*of* til); rett (*of* til å bruke etc); **11** beite(mark), havning; løpegård; **12** par, sett; **13** (fiske)stim; **II** *vb* **1** løpe (og fare, fly, renne, springe etc samt delta i (kapp)løp, renn etc); rakne; ~ *for it* løpe for å nå/rekke; stikke av; ~ *like wildfire* gå/spre seg som ild i tørt gress; ~ *straight (dgl)* holde seg på matta; være lovlydig; **2** drive, jage; få til å løpe etc; la delta i (kapp)løp etc; ~ *him hard* drive/kjøre ham hardt; ~ *to earth/ground* finne, oppspore; innhente; ta igjen; **3** gå (ligge, strekke seg etc i en bestemt retning/fra ... til ... etc); *it ~s in the family* det ligger til familien (dvs det er arvelig); **4** føre/strekke (kabel, ledning, rør etc); dra, trekke; træ; **5** tendere; vise tegn/tendens; ~ *a temperature* ha feber; ~ *to fat* (ha lett for å) legge på seg; være tykkfallen; ~ *to ruin* forfalle; ~ *to waste* gå til spille; **6** møte; pådra seg; utsette seg for; ~ *the risk of* ta risikoen/sjansen på (å); **7** (la seg) nominere; stille (seg) til valg; ~ *for President* være presidentkandidat; **8** flyte (og flomme, renne, strømme etc); flyte *etc* utover; lekke; dryppe (om stearinlys); ~ *short* gå/løpe tom; slippe opp (*of* for); **9** la flomme *etc*; helle (vann etc) utover; ~ *her a bath* tappe i badekaret for henne; **10** *a)* gå (dvs funksjonere, virke; fungere; være i gang; kjøre, rulle, trille; ake, gli, skli; flyte, renne; drive, seile etc); *fig* forløpe, gå; gjelde, være gyldig; *b) data etc* kjøre (maskiner, program etc); **11** drive (dvs få til å bevege seg, funksjonere, virke etc); kjøre, seile; dirigere, manøvrere, styre; holde i gang; ~ *a film* kjøre/vise en film; **12** administrere, (be)styre; drive, lede; føre (varer); ~ *liquor* smugle brennevin; ~ *the show (dgl)* stå for styre og stell; **13** *med adv, prep* ~ **about** løpe *etc* omkring; ~ **across** støte på (dvs finne, møte etc tilfeldig); ~ **after** løpe *etc* etter; *fig* stå/trakte etter; ~ **against** gå imot; komme ut for; *også* = ~ *across*; ~ **aground,** ~ **ashore** renne (seile, sette etc) på grunn; ~ **away** løpe sin vei; flykte, rømme, stikke av; *don't let him ~ away with you* la ham ikke bløffe/dupere deg; ~ **back** løpe *etc* tilbake; *fig* tenke (la tankene gå/løpe) tilbake; ~ **down** løpe *etc* ned; kjøre ned; (jage og) innhente; ta igjen; fange; felle; gå ned (om urverk); lades ut (om batteri); innskrenke (drift etc); sette ned (produksjonstempo etc); *fig* nedvurdere; rakke ned på; *også* = ~ *round; be/feel ~ down* være/føle seg nedkjørt (sliten, nedfor etc); ~ **in** reise *etc* inn (især på kort besøk); arrestere; sette inn (i fyllearrest, varetektsfengsel etc); ~ **into** løpe *etc* på; kollidere med; pådra seg; utsette seg for; *også* = ~ *across*; ~ **off** flykte (etc, jf ~ *away*); tappe (av/ut); tømme (for); la renne *etc* vekk; skylle (spyle, vaske etc) vekk; *fig* lire av seg; ramse opp; ~ **on** fortsette (uten avbrekk); drive på (især skravle) i ett kjør; henge sammen; dreie seg/handle om; ~ **out** gå/løpe ut (samt forfalle til betaling etc); rage/stikke ut; jage/kaste ut; slippe opp (*of* for); ta slutt; ~ **out on** *slang* late i stikken; svikte; ~ **over** flomme *etc* over; kjøre *etc* over, fare over (dvs gjennomgå, lese *etc* flyktig); *også* = ~ *round*; ~ **round** komme/stikke bortom/innom etc; ~ **through** løpe *etc* gjennom; fare/gå igjennom (dvs gjennomgå *etc* flyktig); gjennombore; streke/stryke ut; gjennomføre; ~ **to** (jf *II 5*) løpe/nå opp i; beløpe seg til; komme på (i pris); rekke/strekke til; ~ **up** løpe *etc* opp; kjøre *etc* frem; heve; heise (opp); sette opp (pris); føre/sette opp (især provisorisk bygning etc); legge sammen (tallkolonne); *også* = ~ *round;* ~ *up a bill* sette seg i gjeld; ~ **up against** = ~ *against*; ~ **(up)on** løpe/støte på; dreie seg/handle om; ~ **with** flomme (flyte, strømme etc) av; kry (vrimle, yre etc) av. **run-away** **1** *adj* flyktet, rømt; **2** *sb* rømling. **run-down** *sb* innskrenkning; ned|skjæring, -trapping. **run-down line** *sb petro* produktledning.

rung [rʌŋ] *sb* trinn (på stige); tverrtre.

runner ['rʌnə] *sb* **1** *a)* løper (etc, jf *run II*); *b)* løpegutt; bud, viser|gutt, -pike; *c)* løper (på bord eller gulv); *d)* utløper (av plante); **2** mei(e); skøyte|-jern, -skjær. **runner-up** *sb* nummer to (i idrettskonkurranse etc). **running** ['rʌnɪŋ] **1** *adj* løpende (etc, jf *run II*); **2** *sb* løp (og løping, renn etc). **running|-board** *sb* stigbrett. **~ costs** *sb fl* løpende utgifter. **~ knot** *sb* løpeknute; renneløkke. **~ time** *sb data* kjøretid. **run-over** *sb* overgang (dvs fortsettelse av artikkel etc lenger ute i blad el. tidsskrift). **runway** ['rʌnweɪ] *sb* **1** rullebane (på flyplass); **2** kjørebane, veibane; **3** renne, slisk; **4** sti, tråkk.

rupture ['rʌptʃə] **I** *sb* **1** brudd; splittelse; uenighet; **2** brokk; **II** *vb* briste, revne; brekke, knekke; sprenge(s).

rural ['ru:rəl] *adj* landlig; landsens.

ruse [ru:z] *sb* list, lureri; knep.

rush [rʌʃ] **A I** *sb* **1** travelhet; jag, kjør, mas; **2** rift, sterk pågang (*for* etter); **II** *vb* **1** fare, jage; storme, styrte; suse; **2** drive; jage/skynde på; sende *etc* i all hast; forsere; *don't ~ me* ikke mas (på meg); **B** *sb* **1** siv; **2** døyt, grann, smule. **rush-hours** *sb fl* rushtid.

russet ['rʌsɪt] **I** *adj* **1** rustrød; rødbrun; **2** hjemme|laget, vevd; **II** *sb* **1** rustrødt; rødbrunt; **2** (slags grovt, hjemmevevd)vadmel.

rust [rʌst] **1** *sb* rust; *green ~* irr; **2** *vb* ruste; anløpe, irre; *fig* sløves, svekkes.

rustic ['rʌstɪk] **I** *adj* **1** landlig, landsens; bonde-; land-; **2** enkel, naturlig, opprinnelig; **3** bondsk; grov, primitiv; **II** *sb* bonde.

rustle ['rʌsl] **I** *sb* rasling; susing; **II** *vb* **1** rasle (og rasle med); få til å rasle; **2** *dgl: ~ up* fikse/orge (dvs skaffe, samle sammen); **3** *US dgl* stjele. **rustler** ['rʌslə] *sb US dgl* hestetyv, kvegtyv.

rusty ['rʌstɪ] *adj* **1** rusten, rust-; anløpet; **2** medtatt; sløvet, svekket; hes (om stemme); *be ~* være ute av trening/øvelse.

rut [rʌt] **A 1** *sb* hjulspor; *fig* rutine, vane; daglig kjør/tralt; **2** *vb* lage hjulspor; **B 1** *sb* brunst (og brunsttid); **2** *vi* være brunstig. **rutted** ['rʌtɪd] *adj* med hjulspor. **rutting** ['rʌtɪŋ] *adj* brunstig.

ruthless ['ru:θlɪs] *adj* grusom, nådeløs, ubarmhjertig; hensynløs.

rye [raɪ] *sb* **1** rug; **2** (amerikansk el. irsk) whisky (laget på rug); **3** = **rye-bread** *sb* rugbrød.

S

sable ['seɪbl] *sb* sobel (og sobelpels); *som adj, sb bokl* svart (farge).

sabotage ['sæbətɑ:ʒ] **1** *sb* sabotasje; **2** *vt* sabotere; forøve sabotasje mot/på. **saboteur** [,sæbə'tɜ:] *sb* sabotør.

sabre ['seɪbə] *sb* sabel.

sack [sæk] **A I** *sb* **1** sekk; **2** *dgl: get/give the ~* få/gi sparken; **3** *dgl* køye, seng; *hit the ~* gå til køys; **II** *vt* **1** legge/putte i sekk(er); **2** *dgl* gi sparken; **B 1** *sb* plyndring *etc*; **2** *vt* plyndre; herje. **sack-cloth** *sb* sekke|lerret, -strie.

sacrament ['sækrəmənt] *sb* sakrament. **sacred** ['seɪkrɪd] *adj* **1** helliget; hellig; *dgl* ukrenkelig; **2** guddommelig; *også* kirkelig, kirke-; religions-; **3** høytidelig. **sacrifice** ['sækrɪfaɪs] **I** *sb* **1** offer (og offer|-gave, -handling); *fig* oppofrelse; **2** *merk: at a ~* med tap; **II** *vb* **1** ofre; **2** *merk* selge med tap. **sacrificial** [,sækrɪ'fɪʃl] *adj* offer-. **sacrilege** ['sækrɪlɪdʒ] *sb* helligbrøde.

sad [sæd] *adj* nedfor; lei (seg); bedrøvet, trist. **sadden** ['sædn] *vb* bli/gjøre nedfor *etc*.

saddle ['sædl] **I** *sb* **1** (ride)sal; **2** sykkelsete; **II** *vt* **1** sale; legge sal på; **2** *fig* bebyrde (*with* med).

sadness ['sædnɪs] *sb* bedrøvelse, tristhet; nedtrykthet; vemod.

safe [seɪf] **I** *adj* **1** sikker, trygg; *better ~ than sorry* bedre føre var enn etter snar; **2** pålitelig; *ofte* forsiktig; **3** uskadd; *~ and sound* i god behold; **4** ufarlig; **II** *sb* **1** pengeskap, safe; **2** matskap; *især* flueskap. **safe|-conduct** *sb* **1** fritt leide; **2** leidebrev. **~-deposit** *sb* bankboks. **~guard I** *sb* **1** beskyttelse, vern; **2** eskorte, (sikkerhets)vakt; **II** *vt* beskytte. **~-keeping** *sb* (trygg) forvaring/oppbevaring. **~ seat** *sb pol* sikker plass (på nominasjonsliste el. stemmeseddel). **safety** [seɪftɪ] *sb* sikkerhet *etc*. **safety | belt** *sb* sikkerhets|-belte, -sele. **~ catch** *sb* **1** sikkerhetslås; **2** sikring (på skytevåpen). **~ delegate** *sb* verneombud. **~-hook** *sb* karabinkrok. **~ lock** *sb* = *~ catch*. **~ pin** *sb* sikkerhetsnål. **~ razor** *sb* barberhøvel. **~ valve** *sb* sikkerhetsventil; *petro også* slangebruddsventil.

sag [sæg] **I** *sb* sig *etc*; **II** *vi* **1** henge (ned); sige (sammen); *fig* dale, synke; **2** gi seg, svikte.

sagacious [sə'geɪʃəs] *adj* skarp(sindig); klok, kløktig. **sagacity** [sə'gæsətɪ] *sb* skarpsinn *etc*.

sage [seɪdʒ] **A 1** *adj* vis; *ofte* forsiktig; (snus)fornuftig; **2** *sb* vismann; **B** *sb* salvie.

sail [seɪl] **I** *sb* **1** seil; **2** seil|båt, -skip, -skute; seiler; **3** seilas, seiltur; båt|reise, -tur; **4** (mølle)vinge; **II** *vb* **1** seile; *fig også* duve, sveve; **2** reise med båt; be|fare, -seile; **3** navigere. **sailor** ['seɪlə] *sb* sjømann.

saint [seɪnt] *sb* helgen. **saintly** ['seɪntlɪ] *adj* helgenaktig, hellig; from; (meget) gudfryktig.

sake [seɪk] *sb* **1** *for my (etc)* ~ for min (etc) skyld; **2** *for the* ~ *of* av hensyn til.

salable ['seɪləbl] *adj* salgbar, selgelig; kurant.

salacious [sə'leɪʃəs] *adj* **1** slibrig, uanstendig; **2** lidderlig. **salacity** [sə'læsətɪ] *sb* slibrighet *etc*.

salad ['sæləd] *sb* salat (som rett); *in our* ~*-days* i vår grønne ungdom.

salaried ['sælərɪd] *adj* (fast)lønnet, gasjert. **salary** ['sælərɪ] *sb* (fast) gasje/lønn; månedslønn.

sale [seɪl] *sb* **1** salg; *også* avsetning, omsetning; *for/on* ~ til salgs; **2** (billig)salg, utsalg; **3** *(~ by auction)* auksjon. **saleable** ['seɪləbl] *adj* = *salable*. **sales | department** *sb* salgsavdeling. **~man** *sb* salgsrepresentant/selger (om mann). **~manship** *sb* selger|-egenskaper, -evner; -virksomhet. **~ talk** *sb* salgsargumenter; selgerprat. **~ tax** *sb* omsetningsavgift. **~woman** *sb* salgsrepresentant/selger (om kvinne).

salient ['seɪlɪənt] **I** *adj* **1** fremspringende; utstående; **2** *fig* fremtredende, iøynefallende; **II** *sb* fremspring. **salient point** *sb* springende punkt.

saline 1 ['seɪlaɪn] *adj* saltholdig, salt-; **2** [sə'laɪn] *sb* salt|gruve; -kilde, -sjø.

saliva [sə'laɪvə] *sb* spytt. **salivary** ['sælɪvərɪ] *adj* spytt-. **salivate** ['sælɪveɪt] *vi* utsondre (for mye) spytt; sikle.

sallow ['sæləʊ] **1** *adj* gulblek, gusten; **2** *vb* bli/gjøre gulblek.

sally ['sælɪ] **I** *sb* **1** *mil* utfall (for å bryte omringning); **2** streiftog; tur, utflukt; **3** vittig bemerkning/utbrudd; *sallies of wit* sprudlende vidd; **II** *vi* **1** *mil* gjøre utfall; **2** ~ *forth/out* dra av sted/ut (på tur etc).

salmon ['sæmən] *sb* laks. **salmon trout** *sb* sjøørret.

salon ['sælɒn] *sb* salong; *især* kunst|salong, -utstilling. **saloon** [sə'lu:n] *sb* **1** salong (på hotell, skip etc); sal; **2** *US* bar, kneipe; vertshus (med skjenkerett); saloon; **3** salongvogn; **4** *(~-car)* sedan. **saloon bar** *sb* bar (på hotell etc).

salt [sɔ:lt] **I** *adj* salt(-), saltholdig; *fig* drøy, (ram)-salt; **II** *sb* **1** salt; *(common ~)* bordsalt, kjøkkensalt; *fl* luktesalt; **2** *slang: old* ~ (gammel) sjøulk; **III** *vt* **1** salte; **2** salte ned (også *fig* = gjemme/spare på etc). **salt-cellar** *sb* saltkar. **salty** ['sɔ:ltɪ] *adj* = *salt I*.

salubrious [sə'lu:brɪəs] *adj* helsebringende, sunn. **salutary** ['sæljʊtrɪ] *adj* **1** gagnlig, velgjørende; **2** = *salubrious*. **salutation** [ˌsælјʊ'teɪʃn] *sb* hilsing *etc*; hilsen. **salute** [sə'lu:t] **1** *sb* hilsen; *mil* honnør; salutt-(ering); **2** *vb* hilse (og hilse på, hilse velkommen etc); *mil* gjøre honnør/saluttere (for).

salvage ['sælvɪdʒ] **I** *sb* **1** berging (især til sjøs); **2** berget last/skip; **3** bergingslønn; **4** avfall, skrap (og især utnytting av avfall etc); **II** *vt* **1** berge (last/skip etter havari; innbo etc etter brann etc); *også* redde; **2** utnytte (avfall). **salvation** [sæl'veɪʃn] *sb* frelse, redning. **Salvation Army** Frelsesarmeen.

salve [sælv] *sb, vt* salve.

salver ['sælvə] *sb* (presenter)brett.

salvo ['sælvəʊ] *sb* (skudd)salve.

same [seɪm] *adj, pron* samme; *all/just the* ~ likevel; *be all/just the* ~ *to* være akkurat det samme for; *amount/come to the* ~ *thing* bli det samme; komme ut på ett; *(and) the* ~ *to you* (takk) det samme.

sample ['sæmpl] **I** *sb* **1** (prøve)eksemplar, (stikk)-prøve; **2** *data* utvalg; **II** *vt* prøve (og prøvesmake etc).

sanctify ['sæŋktɪfaɪ] *vt* helliggjøre; hellige, vigsle. **sanctimonious** [ˌsæŋktɪ'məʊnɪəs] *adj* skinnhellig.

sanction ['sæŋkʃn] **1** *sb* godkjenning, sanksjon; stadfesting; **2** *vt* godkjenne, sanksjonere.

sanctuary ['sæŋktʃʊərɪ] *sb* **1** helligdom; **2** tilfluktssted; **3** fredet område; reservat.

sand [sænd] *sb* sand; *fl også* sand|strand, -strekning.

sandal ['sændl] *sb* sandal.

sand|bag *sb* sandsekk. **~bank, ~bar** *sb* sand|banke, -grunne; rev. **~-blast** *vt* sandblåse. **~ dune** *sb* sanddyne, klitt. **~-glass** *sb* timeglass. *the* **Sandman** ≈ Ole Lukkøye. **sand|paper 1** *sb* sandpapir; **2** *vt* pusse med sandpapir. **~piper** *sb* snipe. **~-pit** *sb* sandkasse. **~stone** *sb* sandstein.

sandwich ['sænwidʒ] **1** *sb* smørbrød (dvs dobbelt, med pålegg imellom); **2** *vb* legge/stikke imellom; legge lagvis.

sandy ['sændɪ] *adj* **1** sandet, sand-; **2** sandfarget; *især om hår* rødblond.

sane [seɪn] *adj* **1** (mentalt) sunn; tilregnelig; **2** fornuftig.

sanitary ['sænɪtrɪ] *adj* **1** hygienisk; **2** helse-, sunnhets-. **sanitary | napkin, ~ towel** *sb* (sanitets)-bind. **sanitation** [ˌsænɪ'teɪʃn] *sb* helsestell, sunnhetsvesen; hygiene.

sanity ['sænətɪ] *sb* **1** (mental) sunnhet; tilregnelighet; **2** sunn fornuft.

Santa Claus [ˌsæntə'klɔ:z] *sb* julenissen.

sap [sæp] **A 1** *sb mil* løpegrav; **2** *vb mil* lage løpegraver; underminere; **B I** *sb* **1** sevje; **2** (livs)kraft, (-)mot; saft, tæl: **II** *vi* tappe for krefter; svekke, tære på. **sapling** ['sæplɪŋ] *sb* ungtre.

sarcasm ['sɑ:kæzəm] *sb* sarkasme. **sarcastic** [sɑ:-'kæstɪk] *adj* sarkastisk, spydig.

sash [sæʃ] *sb* **A** *(~ window)* skyvevindu (til å skyve opp og ned); **B** *mil etc* skulderskjerf (til uniform); geheng.

satchel ['sætʃəl] *sb* skoleveske; skulderveske; ransel.

sate [seɪt] = **satiate** ['seɪʃɪeɪt] *vt* overmette; proppe, stappe; fylle/tilfredsstille til overmål. **satiety** [sə'taɪətɪ] *sb* (over)metthet; lede.

satellite ['sætəlaɪt] *sb* satellitt. **satellite | computer** *sb data* satellittmaskin. **~ tree** *sb petro* satellittre. **~ wells** *sb fl petro* satellittbrønner.

satire ['sætaɪə] *sb* satire. **satirical** [sə'tɪrɪkl] *adj* satirisk. **satirist** ['sætərɪst] *sb* satiriker.

satisfaction [ˌsætɪs'fækʃn] *sb* **1** tilfredshet; tilfredsstillelse; **2** godtgjørelse; oppreisning. **satisfactory** [ˌsætɪs'fæktərɪ] *adj* tilfredsstillende *etc*. **satisfied** ['sætɪsfaɪd] *adj* **1** tilfreds *etc*; mett; **2** overbevist.

satisfy ['sætɪsfaɪ] *vt* **1** tilfredsstille; gjøre fornøyd/ tilfreds *etc*; mette; **2** møte/oppfylle (krav etc); være nok/tilfredsstillende; **3** overbevise.

saturate ['sætʃəreɪt] *vt* mette; gjennom|bløte, -væte; *fig* gjennom|syre, -trenge. **saturation** [ˌsætʃə'reɪʃn] *sb* metning *etc*; *kjemi også* saturasjon.

sauce [sɔ:s] *sb* saus; **2** *dgl* frekkhet, uforskammethet. **saucepan** ['sɔ:spən] *sb* gryte, kasserolle. **saucer** ['sɔ:sə] *sb* skål, tallerken. **saucy** ['sɔ:sɪ] *adj* frekk, uforskammet.

saunter ['sɔ:ntə] *vi* slentre.

sausage ['sɒsɪdʒ] *sb* pølse.

savage ['sævɪdʒ] **I** *adj* **1** primitiv, usivilisert; **2** rasende, vill; barbarisk, grusom; **II** *sb* vill(mann); *fl* naturfolk; *især fig* barbar. **savagery** ['sævɪdʒrɪ] *sb* villskap; barbari, grusomhet.

save [seɪv] **I** *konj, prep* unntatt; ~ *for* bortsett fra; **II** *vb* **1** frelse, redde; **2** spare (*up* sammen); legge til side; **3** *data* arkivere, lagre; **4** skåne/spare (for); **5** slippe, unngå. **saving** ['seɪvɪŋ] **A I** *adj* frelsende *etc*; *ofte* forsonende; ~ *grace* forsonende trekk; **II** *sb* **1** sparing *etc*; **2** *fl* sparepenger; **B** = *save I*. **savings | account** *sb* sparekonto. **~-bank** *sb* sparebank. **saviour** ['seɪvɪə] *sb* frelser *etc*; *the Saviour, Our Saviour* Frelseren, Vår Frelser.

savour ['seɪvə] **1** *sb* smak; *fig også* anstrøk, antydning; påminnelse; **2** *vi:* ~ *of* smake (av); *fig* ha et anstrøk av; minne om. **savoury** ['seɪvərɪ] *adj* velsmakende; *især* velkrydret.

saw [sɔ:] *sb, vb* sag(e). **saw|dust** *sb* sag|flis, -mugg. **~mill** *sb* sagbruk. **sawyer** ['sɔ:jə] *sb* sager.

Saxon ['sæksn] *(Anglo-~)* **1** *adj* (angel)saksisk; **2** *sb* (angel)sakser.

say [seɪ] **I** *sb* mening; uttalelse, ytring; *have a ~* ha noe å si (dvs være meningsberettiget); *have one's ~* si/få sagt det en har å si; **II** *vb* **1** si, ytre; uttale (seg); ~ *grace* be (lese, si frem) bordbønn; *it goes without ~ing* det sier seg selv; *that is to ~* det vil si; **2** mene, synes; **3** *som interj etc* hør (her); si meg (en gang). **saying** ['seɪɪŋ] *sb* **1** bemerkning; **2** ordtak.

scab [skæb] *sb* **1** skorpe (på sår); **2** uorganisert arbeider; streikebryter.

scabbard ['skæbəd] *sb* skjede, slir(e).

scaffold ['skæfəld] *sb* **1** stillas; **2** skafott.

scald [skɔ:ld] **I** *sb* skålding (og især brannsår etc etter skålding); **II** *vt* **1** skålde; **2** varme (melk) til oppunder kokepunktet.

scale [skeɪl] **A I** *sb* **1** *a)* skala; *b)* målestokk; *on a large ~* i stor målestokk; **2** måle|instrument, -redskap; **II** *vt* **1** bestige; klatre opp (på); **2** tegne i (nærmere angitt) målestokk; **3** justere/regulere (verdi, etter nærmere angitt skala); *data* skalere; **B I** *sb* **1** (vekt)skål; **2** *(pair of ~s)* (skål)vekt; **II** *vi* veie; **C I** *sb* **1** (fiske)skjell; **2** flak, skall; **II** *vb* **1** rense (fisk); **2** fjerne flak/skall *etc; dgl* skrape; **3** flasse/skalle (av);

scalp [skælp] **1** *sb* hodehud, skalp; **2** *vt* skalpere.

scamper ['skæmpə] **1** *sb* kort/rask løpetur; **2** *vi* løpe; ~ *off* fare/styrte av sted.

scan [skæn] *vb* **1** granske; la øynene gli undersøkende over; *data* avsøke; **2** skandere (vers). **scanning** ['skænɪŋ] *sb* gransking; *data* avsøking. **scansion** ['skænʃn] *sb* skandering.

scant [skænt] *adj* knapp, knepen; ubetydelig. **scanty** ['skæntɪ] *adj* knapp; snau; mager, skrinn.

scapegoat ['skeɪpgəʊt] *sb* syndebukk.

scar [skɑ:] *sb, vb* arr(e); merke.

scarce ['skeəs] *adj* knapp; sjelden; uvanlig; *make oneself ~ (dgl)* for|dufte, -svinne. **scarcely** ['skeəslɪ] *adv* knapt, neppe. **scarcity** ['skeəsətɪ] *sb* knapphet/ mangel (*of* på).

scare ['skeə] **1** *sb* redsel, skrekk; *ofte* panikk; **2** *vt* skremme. **scare|crow** ['skeəkrəʊ] *sb* fugleskremsel. **~monger** ['skeəmʌŋgə] *sb* panikkmaker.

scarf [skɑ:f] **A** *sb* skjerf; **B 1** *sb (~ joint)* lasking, skarving; **2** *vt* laske, skarve.

scarlet ['skɑ:lət] **1** *adj* skarlagensrød; **2** *sb* skarlagensrødt. **scarlet fever** *sb* skarlagensfeber.

scary ['skeərɪ] *adj* foruroligende; nifs, skremmende.

scathing ['skeɪðɪŋ] *adj* bitende/flengende (om bemerkning, kritikk etc).

scatter ['skætə] *vb* **1** drysse/strø (ut); spre (utover); **2** splitte(s); spre (seg). **scatter-brained** *adj* vimset. **scattered** ['skætəd] *adj* spredt.

scavenge ['skævɪndʒ] *vb* grave etter (i søppel). **scavenger** ['skævɪndʒə] *sb* **1** åtseldyr; **2** en som roter i avfall og søppel; renovasjonsarbeider, søppelkjører.

scene [si:n] *sb* **1** scene (dvs del av skuespill etc); *også* opptrinn; *fl især* kulisser; **2** skueplass; **3** syn (dvs det en ser); *stundom* landskap; omgivelser. **scenery** ['si:nərɪ] *sb* landskap; natur; omgivelser. **scenic** ['si:nɪk] *adj* naturskjønn.

scent [sent] **I** *sb* **1** lukt (og især dyrs luktesans); *også fig* teft; **2** duft, godlukt; **3** parfyme; **II** *vt* **1** lukte; få teften av; *fig* få mistanke om; **2** parfymere.

sceptic ['skeptɪk] *sb* skeptiker. **sceptical** ['skeptɪkl] *adj* skeptisk. **scepticism** ['skeptɪsɪzəm] *sb* skepsis.

sceptre ['septə] *sb* septer.

schedule ['ʃedju:l] **I** *sb* liste; rute|plan, -tabell; *ofte* plan; **II** *vt* **1** bestemme/fastsette tidspunkt for; **2** legge/utarbeide en (time)plan for; *as ~d* som planlagt; **3** *data* fordele.

schematic [ski:'mætɪk] *adj* skjematisk. **scheme** [ski:m] **I** *sb* **1** system; orden, rekkefølge; *fig* skjema; **2** plan, utkast; *fig også* mønster; **3** intrige, renke; ondsinnet plan; **II** *vb* **1** planlegge; **2** intrigere; smi renker.

schism ['s(k)ɪzəm] *sb* skisma; brudd, splittelse.

scholar ['skɒlə] *sb* **1** lærd (person); vitenskaps|kvinne, -mann (især innen humanistiske fag, jf *scientist*); *ofte* filolog; **2** student (med stipendium); **3** *gml* disippel, elev; *nå især* energisk/flink elev/student. **scholarly** ['skɒləlɪ] *adj* lærd. **scholarship** ['skɒləʃɪp] *sb* **1** lærdom; **2** stipendium. **school** [sku:l] **A 1**

sb skole; *fig også* lærdom, utdannelse; **2** *vt* lære (opp); undervise; skolere; trene; **B** *sb* (fiske)stim; flokk. **school|-bag** *sb* skoleveske. **~-book** *sb gml* skolebok. **~boy** *sb* skolegutt. **~ days** *sb fl* skole|dager, -tid. **~girl** *sb* skolepike. **~house** *sb* skole(bygning, -hus, -stue). **schooling** ['sku:lɪŋ] *sb* **1** skolegang; **2** opplæring, skolering, undervisning. **school|ma'am, ~marm** *sb dgl* frøken, lærerinne. **~master** *sb* lærer. **~mate** *sb* skolekamerat. **~mistress** *sb* lærer(inne). **~ report** *sb* karakterer (og karakter|bok), -kort); (skole)vitnemål. **~room** *sb* klasseværelse, skolestue. **~teacher** *sb* lærer.

schooner ['sku:nə] *sb* skonner(t).

science ['saɪəns] *sb* **1** vitenskap (og vitenskapsgren); *især* naturvitenskap; **2** naturfag, realfag; **3** *dgl* dyktighet (især i sport). **scientific** [ˌsaɪən'tɪfɪk] *adj* vitenskapelig *etc.* **scientist** ['saɪəntɪst] *sb* vitenskaps|kvinne, -mann (især innen realfag, jf *scholar*); naturvitenskaps|kvinne, -mann.

scissors ['sɪzəz] *sb fl (pair of ~)* saks.

scoff [skɒf] **1** *sb* hån (og hånsord); spott; **2** *vb (~ at)* håne, spotte.

scold [skəʊld] **1** *sb* kjeftesmelle; **2** *vb* kjefte/bruke munn (på).

scone [skəʊn] *sb* scone (slags flat tekake).

scoop [sku:p] **I** *sb* **1** skuffe; sleiv; **2** *dgl* kupp, varp (dvs det å ha sikret seg godt (avis)stoff); **3** *merk* kupp (dvs heldig transaksjon); **II** *vt* **1** grave; skovle; skyfle; *~ out/up* skuffe inn; måke/sope opp; **2** *dgl* gjøre et kupp/varp.

scope [skəʊp] *sb* synsvidde; *især fig* rekkevidde (og område, sfære; spillerom, (utviklings)muligheter etc).

scorch [skɔ:tʃ] *vb* **1** brenne; svi (av); **2** *dgl* fare (fyke, suse etc) av sted; *ofte* råkjøre.

score [skɔ:] **A I** *sb* **1** kutt, skår; (inn)snitt; merke (især til avregning, kontroll etc); **2** regning, regnskap; *run up a ~* sette seg i/stifte gjeld; *settle an old ~ (fig)* gjøre opp et gammelt mellomværende; **3** (antall) mål, poeng (etc i konkurranse); *ofte* situasjon, stilling); **4** motiv, årsak; *on that ~* på det punktet; hva det angår; **5** *mus* partitur; *dgl* noter; **II** *vb* **1** merke (med hakk *etc*); kutte, skåre, snitte; **2** notere (opp); føre regnskap (især over poeng etc i konkurranse); **3** vinne poeng *etc*; score/*dgl* skyte (mål); *~ off* få overtaket på; **4** *mus* arrangere, instrumentere; **B** *sb* snes.

scorn [skɔ:n] **I** *sb* forakt; hån; *også* gjenstand for forakt; **II** *vt* **1** forakte; håne, spotte; **2** avvise med forakt. **scornful** ['skɔ:nfʊl] *adj* foraktfull, hånlig; foraktelig.

Scot [skɒt] *sb skotsk* skotte. **Scotch** [skɒtʃ] **I** *adj* skotsk; **II** *sb* **1** skotsk (språk); **2** (skotsk) whisky; **3** *koll* skotte. **Scots** [skɒts] *skotsk* **I** *adj* skotsk; **II** *sb* **1** skotsk (språk); **2** *koll* skotter. **Scottish** ['skɒtɪʃ] *adj* skotsk.

scoundrel ['skaʊndrəl] *sb* kjeltring, skurk.

scour ['skaʊə] **A I** *sb* **1** skuring *etc*; **2** *petro* erosjon, undergraving (rundt installasjoner på havbunnen); **II** *vt* skure (rent); skrubbe; skrape (rust etc); **B** *vt* gjennom|støve, -søke; ransake.

scourge [skɜ:dʒ] **1** *sb* pisk, svolk; *nå især fig* svøpe; **2** *vt især fig* hjemsøke, plage.

scouring ['skaʊrɪŋ] *sb petro* erosjon, undergraving (jf *scour A I 2*).

scout [skaʊt] **I** *sb* **1** speider; **2** *(Boy Scout)* speider(gutt); **II** *vi* speide/*dgl* være på utkikk (*for* etter).

scowl [skaʊl] **1** *sb* morskt/skulende blikk; **2** *vi* skule; se morsk/sint ut.

scrabble ['skræbl] *vi* krafse/rote (*about for* rundt etter).

scraggy ['skrægɪ] *adj* radmager; knoklet, skranglet.

scram [skræm] *vi imperativ* forsvinn!

scramble ['skræmbl] **I** *sb* **1** klatring *etc*; **2** *dgl* (vilt) kappløp/slagsmål; **II** *vi* **1** klatre, klyve; krabbe, kravle; **2** mase, streve; *~ for* slåss om (dvs for å få tak i etc); krafse etter; **3** kaste om (telefonsamtale etc, dvs gjøre den uforståelig for uvedkommende). **scrambled eggs** *sb (fl)* eggerøre.

scrap [skræp] **A** *sb* **1** bite, smule; *fl også* (avis)-utklipp; **2** skrap, søppel; avfall; **B** *sb dgl* slagsmål. **scrap|-book** *sb* utklippsbok. **~-iron** *sb* skrapjern.

scrape [skreɪp] **I** *sb* **1** skraping *etc*; **2** knipe, vanskelighet; **II** *vb* **1** skrape (og skrape med; raspe/rive opp; skrape/skrubbe (seg) opp etc); *~ a living* så vidt livberge seg; **2** *med adv, prep* ~ **off** skrape av; ~ **out** krafse/skrape ut; ~ **past/through** så vidt berge/klare seg (igjennom); ~ **together/up** skrape (= spare) sammen; *~ (up) an acquaintance with* gjøre seg kjent med (på en innpåsliten måte). **scraper** *sb* skrape(r); *petro* rørskrape.

scratch [skrætʃ] **I** *adj* sammen|rasket, -skrapet; tilfeldig; **II** *sb* **1** skraping (dvs skrapende/rispende lyd); **2** merke, ripe; **3** risp; (lite) sår; *også fig* skramme; **4** startstrek; *også* mål(linje); *come up to ~* holde mål; innfri forventningene; *start from ~* begynne på bar bakke; **III** *vb* **1** ripe (og rispe; klore, krasse; risse, skrape etc); rive hull (i); *~ along* hangle igjennom; *~ out/through* radere/stryke ut; *~ up* skrape (= spare) sammen; **2** klø (og klø seg (i/på)); **3** rable ned; **4** trekke (seg) fra konkurranse etc; **5** *data* slette, stryke. **scratcher** ['skrætʃə] *sb petro* = *scraper*. **scratch | file** *sb data* midlertidig fil. **~pad storage** *sb data* kladdelager.

scrawl [skrɔ:l] **1** *sb* rabbel (og rabling); **2** *vb* rable; skrive slurvet/utydelig.

scrawny ['skrɔ:nɪ] *adj* radmager

scream [skri:m] **1** *sb* hyl, skrik; hvin; **2** *vb* hyle, (ill)skrike; hvine.

screech [skri:tʃ] **1** *sb* hvin, hyl; **2** *vb* hvine (om f.eks. bremser); skrike (om f.eks. usmurt dør); hyle, remje.

screen [skri:n] **I** *sb* **1** skjerm(brett); *fig også* beskyttelse, vern; *smoke ~* røykteppe; *wire ~* tråd|duk, (-)netting; *også* fluenetting; **2** *data, TV* skjerm; billedflate; **3** (grus)harpe, skakebrett; sikt, såld; **3** film|-

duk, (-)lerret; **II** *vt* **1** skjerme; beskytte, verne; ~ *off* avskjerme; **2** harpe, sikte; **3** vise (film) på lerretet. **screen | image** *sb data* (skjerm)bilde. **~-play** *sb* filmmanuskript; *også* film, kinostykke. **~-test** *sb* prøvefilming.

screw [skru:] **I** *sb* **1** skrue; **2** propell; **3** press, tvang; *fig* tommeskrue; **II** *vb* **1** skru; ~ *down* skru igjen/til; ~ *off/on* skru av/på; ~ *up one's courage* ta mot til seg; ~ *up one's eyes* knipe sammen øynene; myse; **2** presse, tvinge. **screwdriver** *sb* skrutrekker.

scribble ['skrɪbl] **1** *sb* rabbel, skribling; **2** *vb* rable, skrible. **scribe** [skraɪb] *sb* **1** skriver; **2** skriftlærd. **script** [skrɪpt] *sb* **1** (hånd)skrift; **2** *fork* for *manuscript* manuskript. **scripture** ['skrɪptʃə] *sb: the Holy Scripture* Skriften (dvs Bibelen). **script-writer** *sb* manuskriptforfatter; tekstforfatter.

scroll [skrəʊl] **I** *sb* **1** bokrulle, skriftrulle; **2** spiral; krusedull, snirkel; **II** *vi data, TV* rulle.

scrub [skrʌb] **A 1** *sb* skrubbing; **2** *vb* skrubbe, skure; **B** *sb* kratt(skog). **scrubber** ['skrʌbə] *sb petro* (gass)vasker, skrubber. **scrubbing|-board** *sb* skurebrett, vaskebrett. **~-brush** *sb* skure|børste, -kost.

scruple ['skru:pl] *sb* skruppel. **scrupulous** ['skru:pjʊləs] *adj* meget nøye; samvittighetsfull; skrupuløs.

scrutinize ['skru:tɪnaɪz] *vt* granske (inngående). **scrutiny** ['skru:tɪnɪ] *sb* (inngående) granskning.

scuffle ['skʌfl] **1** *sb* basketak, slagsmål; **2** *vi* slåss.

scullery ['skʌlərɪ] *sb* grovkjøkken.

sculptor ['skʌlptə] *sb* billedhugger. **sculpture** ['skʌlptʃə] **I** *sb* **1** skulptur; **2** billedhuggerkunst; **II** *vb* hugge (meisle, skjære etc) ut; forme, modellere.

scum [skʌm] *sb* skum; *især fig* avskum; berme, pakk.

scurrilous ['skʌrɪləs] *adj* sjofel, uanstendig; grov.

scurry ['skʌrɪ] **I** *sb* **1** (rask) løping; **2** byge, skur; **II** *vi* fare, pile, renne, styrte.

scurvy ['skɜ:vɪ] *sb* skjørbuk.

scythe [saɪð] *sb, vt* (slå med) ljå.

sea [si:] *sb* **1** hav, sjø; **2** (stor) bølge; *også* sjø, sjøgang; *choppy/short* ~ krapp sjø; *hard/heavy* ~ svær/tung sjø; sterk sjøgang; **3** *fl* farvann. **sea|bed** *sb* havbunn. **~bird** *sb* sjøfugl. **~board** *sb* kyst. **~-eagle** *sb* havørn. **~farer** *sb* sjø|farer, -mann. **~faring** *adj* sjøfarende. **~food** *sb* fisk og skalldyr (som mat). **~front** *sb* strandpromenade. **~-going** *adj* havgående. **~-gull** *sb* havmåke.

seal [si:l] **A I** *sb* **1** segl (og forsegling); *fig* garanti; løfte (især om taushet); **2** signet; **II** *vt* **1** forsegle (og lakke, plombere; klebe/lukke igjen; stoppe/tette igjen etc); *on ~ed orders* med forseglede ordre; **2** sette (sitt) segl på/under; *fig* besegle; **B** *sb* sel. **sealing** [si:lɪŋ] *sb* selfangst. **sealing-wax** *sb* lakk (til forsegling).

sea|legs *sb fl* sjøbein. **~ level** *sb* hav(over)flate.

seam [si:m] **I** *sb* **1** fuge, søm; sammenføyning; **2** sjikt/tynt lag (av kull etc); gang, åre; **II** *vt; ~ed with* furet av.

sea|man *sb* sjømann. **~manship** *sb* sjømannskap.

seamstress ['semstrɪs] *sb* sydame, syerske. **seamy** ['si:mɪ] *adj* med søm(mer); *the ~ side* vrangen; *fig* skyggesiden.

sea|port *sb* havneby. **~-power** *sb* sjømakt; sjømilitær makt.

sear ['sɪə] *vt* **1** brenne, svi; **2** forherde.

search [sɜ:tʃ] **I** *sb* leting *etc; data* søk; *in ~ of/on the ~ for* på jakt/leting etter; **II** *vb* **1** lete (*for* etter); ransake; *data også* søke; **2** granske, undersøke; *~ me (dgl)* neimen om jeg vet; spør ikke meg. **searching** ['sɜ:tʃɪŋ] *adj* granskende, undersøkende. **search | key** *sb data* søkenøkkel. **~light** *sb* søkelys. **~-party** *sb* letemannskaper. **~-warrant** *sb* ransakingsordre.

sea|-shell *sb* strandskjell; musling(skall). **~shore** *sb* kyst; strand|kant, -linje. **~sick** *adj* sjøsyk. **~side** *sb* kyst; *~side resort* badested.

season ['si:zn] **I** *sb* årstid; *også* sesong; **II** *vb* **1** modne(s) (især ved henging, lagring, tørking etc); **2** krydre; sette smak på. **seasonal** ['si:znəl] *adj* årstids-; som angår årstiden(e); sesong-. **seasoning** ['si:znɪŋ] *sb* krydder.

seat [si:t] **I** *sb* **1** sete, sitteplass; stol; *take a ~* sette seg; ta plass; **2** buksebak; bak(ende); **3** (bo)sted; *country ~* (større) landsted; **II** *vt* ha/skaffe (sitte)plass til; ~ *oneself* sette seg. **seat-belt** *sb* sikkerhets|belte, -sele (i bil, fly etc).

sea|-urchin *sb* sjøpinnsvin. **~-wall** *sb* dike. **~ward(s)** *adj, adv* sjø-; (som vender) mot sjøen/sjøsiden; til havs/sjøs. **~-water** *sb* havvann, sjøvann. **~weed** *sb* sjøgress, tang. **~worthy** *adj* sjødyktig.

secateurs [ˌsekə'tɜ:z] *sb fl (pair of ~)* hagesaks.

secede [sɪ'si:d] *vi* tre/trekke seg ut. **secession** [sɪ'seʃn] *sb* uttredelse.

seclude [sɪ'klu:d] *vt* avsondre; stenge inne/ute. **seclusion** [sɪ'kluʃn] *sb* avsondrethet *etc*.

second ['sekənd] **I** *adj* annen(-); nummer to; andre; nest-, neste(-); **II** *sb* **1** annenmann; nummer to; *også* nestemann; etterfølger; **2** annenplass; annen|fiolin, -stemme; **3** sekund; **4** sekundant; **5** *fl* sekundavarer; **III** *vt* sekundere, støtte. **secondary** ['sekəndrɪ] *adj* sekundær, underordnet. **secondary | school** *sb* videregående skole. ~ **storage** *sb data* hjelpelager. **second|-best** *adj* nest best. ~ **chamber** *sb* annetkammer (i nasjonalforsamling etc). ~ **childhood** *sb* senilitet; *be in one's ~ childhood* gå i barndommen. **~-class** *adj* annenklasses. ~ **cousin** *sb* tremenning. **~hand 1** *adj* annenhånds, brukt; **2** *sb* sekundviser. ~ **name** *sb* etternavn. ~ **nature** *sb* (inngrodd) vane. **~-rate** *adj* annen|klasses, -rangs; mindreverdig. ~ **thoughts** *sb fl* nærmere ettertanke.

secrecy ['si:krəsɪ] *sb* hemmelighet; *især* hemmelighetsfullhet. **secret** ['si:krɪt] **I** *adj* **1** hemmelig, skjult; **2** avsondret, bortgjemt; **3** hemmelighetsfull; **II** *sb* hemmelighet. **secretary** ['sekrətrɪ] *sb* **1** sekretær (ofte med høyere posisjon og større myndighet og ansvar enn hva den norske tittelen vanligvis tilsier); **2** for|kvinne, -mann (i forening, institusjon etc). **secret | ballot** *sb* hemmelig valg. ~ **service** *sb* hemmelig etterretningsvesen. **Secretary | General** *sb* generalsekretær. **~ of State** *sb* **1** minister, statsråd; departementssjef; **2** *US* utenriksminister. **secrete** [sɪ'kri:t] *vt* **1** gjemme (bort); skjule; **2** ut|skille, -sondre. **secretion** [sɪ'kri:ʃn] *sb* **1** (bort)gjemming; **2** utskilling; sekresjon, sekret. **secretive** ['si:krətɪv] *adj* hemmelighetsfull; innesluttet, taus.

sect [sekt] *sb* sekt. **sectarian** [sek'teərɪən] *adj* sekterisk, sekt-. **section** ['sekʃn] **1** *sb* avsnitt, del; avsnitt, gruppe; seksjon; *cross* **~** (tverr)snitt; **2** *vt* (inn)dele/ordne i avsnitt etc. **sector** ['sektə] *sb* sektor; avsnitt, del.

secular ['sekjʊlə] *adj* **1** verdslig; **2** leg(-).

secure [sɪ'kjʊə] **I** *adj* **1** sikker, trygg; trygt forvart etc; **2** fast, stabil; solid (festet, forankret etc); **II** *vt* **1** sikre, trygge; befeste; **2** feste/lukke *etc* forsvarlig; **3** sikre seg; få fatt/tak i. **security** [sɪ'kjʊərətɪ] *sb* **1** sikkerhet *etc; merk etc også* garanti; kausjon (og kausjonist); pant; **2** beskyttelse, vern; sikring. **security level** *sb data* sikkerhets|grad, -nivå.

sedate [sɪ'deɪt] *adj* rolig; sindig, uforstyrrelig; sedat. **sedative** ['sedətɪv] *adj, sb* beroligende (middel). **sedentary** ['sedəntərɪ] *adj* (stille)sittende.

sedition [sɪ'dɪʃn] *sb* opprørskhet; oppvigleri. **seditious** [sɪ'dɪʃəs] *adj* opprørsk.

seduce [sɪ'dju:s] *vt* for|føre, -lede; lokke. **seducer** [sɪ'dju:sə] *sb* forfører. **seduction** [sɪ'dʌkʃn] *sb* **1** forføring; **2** besnærende/forførende egenskap; *ofte* sjarm. **seductive** [sɪ'dʌktɪv] *adj* forførende, forførerisk; besnærende, (for)lokkende; sjarmerende, vinnende.

see [si:] **A** *vb* **1** se; **~** *for oneself* se selv; få syn for sagn; **~** *into* granske, undersøke; **~** *over* bese, inspisere; **~** *through* gjennomskue; **~** *them through* hjelpe dem **~** *the back of* bli kvitt; **2** se for (gjennom, over etc); seg; forestille/tenke seg; *let me* **~** la meg (nå) se; **3** innse; forstå, oppfatte; **~** *the light (US dgl)* forstå/innse (feil, tabber etc); *(you)* **~***?* skjønner (du)? *you* **~** *(også)* nemlig; **~***ing (that)* ettersom, siden; da; **4** erfare, oppleve; møte; treffe (på); **5** besøke; se innom hos/til; **6** ta imot/snakke med (besøkende etc); **7** følge, ledsage; **~** *her home* følge henne hjem; **~** *off* se av sted; følge (til stasjon etc); **~** *out* følge ut/til døren etc; **8** *(***~** *about)* påse; sørge for; ta seg av; **~** *about it* tenke på det; tenke over saken; **~** *after* passe (på); se til; ta seg av; **~** *to it* ta seg av det; **~** *(to it) that* påse/sørge for at; **B** *sb* **1** bispestol; *the Holy See* pavestolen; **2** bispe|dømme, -sete; -embete.

seed [si:d] **I** *sb* frø; *fl også* såkorn, sæd; *fig* spire; *go/run to* **~** gå i frø; **II** *vb* **1** sette frø; **2** ta frøene ut av; **3** *sport* seede. **seedling** ['si:dlɪŋ] *sb* frøplante. **seedy** ['si:dɪ] *adj* **1** loslitt; **2** *dgl* uvel.

seek [si:k] *vb* **1** lete (etter); *data også* søke; **~** *after* jage/strebe etter; **~** *for* se etter; *sought after* etter|-spurt, -søkt; **2** søke (om/på); **3** (for)søke/prøve (å gjøre etc). **seek time** *sb data* søketid.

seem [si:m] *vi* synes; se ut (som/som om); **~** *to* late til/synes å. **seeming(ly)** ['si:mɪŋ(lɪ)] *adj (adv)* tilsynelatende. **seemly** ['si:mlɪ] *adj* anstendig, sømmelig; tilbørlig.

seep [si:p] *vi* sive, tyte.

seer ['sɪə] *sb* seer, profet.

seesaw ['si:sɔ:] *sb, vb* (huske på) dumphuske/vippe(brett).

seethe [si:ð] *vi* koke, syde; boble; *seething with rage* frådende/skummende av raseri.

segment ['segmənt] *sb* segment; del, part; snitt. **segregate 1** ['segrɪgət] *adj* avsondret, isolert; **2** ['segrɪgeɪt] *vt* skille (og skille ut/fra hverandre etc). **segregation** [ˌsegrɪ'geɪʃn] *sb* skille; *især* raseskille.

seize [si:z] *vb* **1** gripe, snappe; **~** *(up)on* kaste seg over; slå kloen i; **2** arrestere, (på)gripe; ta; **3** beslaglegge; ta (i besittelse); **4** angripe (om sykdom). **seizure** ['si:ʒə] *sb* **1** griping *etc*; **2** arrest, pågripelse; **3** beslag(leggelse); **4** anfall; *ofte* slag.

seldom ['seldəm] *adv* sjelden.

select [sɪ'lekt] **1** *adj* ut|søkt, -valgt; *ofte* eksklusiv; **2** *vt* velge (plukke, ta etc) ut. **selecting** [sɪ'lektɪŋ] *sb data* utvelging. **selection** [sɪ'lekʃn] *sb* **1** valg, velging; utvalg; **2** den/det en velger. **selection | check** *sb data* utvelgingskontroll. **~ signal** *sb data* kallesignal. **selective** [sɪ'lektɪv] *adj* selektiv, (ut)velgende. **selector** [sɪ'lektə] *sb data* lyspenn.

self [self] **1** *pref* egen-, selv-; **2** *sb* jeg(et), selv(et); *my poor* **~** min ringe person; *one's better* **~** ens bedre jeg. **self|absorbed** *adj* selvopptatt. **~-assertive** *adj* selvhevdende; overlegen. **~-centred** *adj* selv|opptatt, -sentrert. **~-confidence** *sb* selvtillit. **~-conscious** *adj* forlegen; keitet; sjenert. **~contained** *adj* selvstendig, uavhengig; tilbakeholden. **~-defence** *sb* selvforsvar. **~-denial** *sb* selvfornektelse. **~-determination** *sb* selvbestemmelse (og især selvbestemmelsesrett); *pol* selvråderett. **~-evident** *adj* (selv)innlysende. **~-government** *sb* selvstyre. **~important** *adj* innbilsk, viktig. **~-imposed** *adj* selvpålagt. **~indulgent** *adj* nytelsessyk. **~-interest** *sb* egeninteresse. **~ish** ['selfɪʃ] *adj* selvisk; egen|kjærlig, -nyttig; egoistisk. **~less** ['selflɪs] *adj* uselvisk, uegennyttig. **~-made** *adj* selvlært; som er kommet seg frem (i verden) på egen hånd. **~-ordained** *adj* selvbestaltet. **~-pity** *sb* selvmedlidenhet. **~-possessed** *adj* behersket, fattet; rolig. **~-possession** *sb* selvbeherskelse. **~praise** *sb* selvros. **~-preservation** *sb* selvoppholdelsesdrift. **~--propelled** *adj* motordrevet, motor-; motorisert. **~-protection** *sb* egenbeskyttelse. **~-reliance** *sb* selvsikkerhet. **~-reliant** *adj* selvsikker. **~-reproach** *sb* selvbebreidelse. **~-respect** *sb* selvrespekt. **~-restraint** *sb* selvbeherskelse. **~-righteous** *adj* egenrettferdig, selvgod. **~-rule** *sb* selvstyre. **~-sacrifice** *sb* selvoppofrelse. **~-same** *adj* selvsamme. **~-satisfied** *adj* selvtilfreds. **~-seeking** *adj* **1** egoistisk; **2** *sb* egoisme. **~-service** *sb* selvbetjening. **~-starter** *sb* selvstarter. **~-styled** *adj* påstått; selv|-bestaltet, -oppnevnt. **~-sufficient** *adj* selv|forsynt, -hjulpen; innbilsk, selvtilfreds. **~-supporting** *adj* selv|ervervende, -forsørgende. **~-taught** *adj* selvlært.

~-willed *adj* egenrådig, sta.

sell [sel] *vb* **1** selge; **~** *off/out* realisere; selge ut; **~** *up* selge ved tvangsauksjon; **2** lure, snyte; *(~ down the river)* forråde, svike. **seller** ['selə] *sb* **1** selger; **2** vare som går godt; *best-~* bestselger. **sell-out** *sb* forræderi.

selvage, selvedge ['selvɪdʒ] *sb* jare (og jarekant).

semblance ['sembləns] skikkelse; likhet, skinn.

semen ['si:mn] *sb* sæd.

semi- ['semɪ-] *pref* halv-, semi-. **semi|-annual** *adj* halvårlig. **~-circle** *sb* halvsirkel. **~-circular** *adj* halvsirkelformet. **~-conductor** *sb* halvleder. **~-conscious** *adj* halvt bevisstløs. **~-detached** *adj* vertikalt delt (dvs om hus som henger delvis sammen med nabohuset). **~-final** *sb* semifinale. **~-skilled** *adj* delvis faglært.

seminar ['semɪnɑ:] *sb* seminar. **seminary** ['semɪnərɪ] *sb* (katolsk) preste|seminar, -skole.

semi-submersible *adj petro etc* halvt nedsenket.

sempstress ['sempstrɪs] *sb* = *seamstress.*

senate ['senət] *sb* senat. **senator** ['senətə] *sb* senator. **senatorial** [,senə'tɔ:rɪəl] *adj* senator-.

send [send] *vb* **1** sende (og sende av sted/ut etc); **~ about** *one's business* avfeie; be ryke og reise; **~ along** sende av sted/videre; **~ away** sende bort/vekk; **~ down** utvise fra skole/universitet; *merk* sette ned priser; **~ for** sende bud etter/på; bestille, rekvirere; **~ forth** sende/skyte *etc* ut; ut|bre, -sende; utstøte; **~ in** sende inn; oversende; **~ off** sende av gårde (av sted, ut etc); avgi, utsondre; **~ round** by/sende rundt; la sirkulere; **~ up** sende inn; melde (seg) på; melde opp/på (til eksamen); *merk* sette opp priser; *dgl* dømme til/sende i fengsel; **2** drive/gjøre til; **~** *him crazy* drive ham fra vettet. **sender** ['sendə] *sb* (av)-sender.

senile ['si:naɪl] *adj* senil. **senility** [sɪ'nɪlətɪ] *sb* senilitet. **senior** ['si:nɪə] **I** *adj* **1** eldre (*to* enn); eldst; senior-; **2** høyere (*to* enn) i rang; overordnet, sjef-; *ofte* avdelings-; **II** *sb* **1** eldstemann, senior; **2** overordnet, sjef; **3** *US* fjerde/siste års elev/student. **senior citizen** *sb* alderstrygdet (person). **seniority** [,si:nɪ'ɒrətɪ] *sb* **1** høyere alder/rang *etc*; **2** ansiennitet.

sensation [sen'seɪʃn] *sb* **1** følelse; sanse|fornemmelse, -inntrykk; sansning; **2** sensasjon; oppsikt, røre. **sensational** [sen'seɪʃənl] *adj* sensasjonell. **sense** [sens] **I** *sb* **1** sans (og sanseevne); sansning; **2** sans (dvs egenskap, evne; bevissthet, forståelse etc); følelse, kjensle; **~** *of duty* pliktfølelse; **~** *of humour* humoristisk sans; **3** fornuft; fatteevne, forståelse; sunn sans; *fl også* tilregnelighet; sans og samling; *dgl* vett; *bring/come to one's ~s* bringe/komme til fornuft; *common ~* sunt vett; *have ~ enough to* ha vett nok til å; *a man of ~* en vettig mann; *out of one's ~s* fra sans og samling; *dgl* fra vettet; *recover one's ~s* gjenvinne fatningen, **4** betydning, mening; *in more than one ~* i mer enn én forstand; *it doesn't make ~* det gir ingen mening; jeg *etc* skjønner det ikke; **II** *vt US* fornemme, sanse; føle, merke; skjønne. **senseless** ['senslɪs] *adj* **1** bevisstløs; sanseløs; **2** vettløs, uvettig. **sensibility** [,sensɪ'bɪlətɪ] *sb især* følsomhet. **sensible** ['sensəbl] *adj* **1** fornuftig; *dgl* vettig; **2 ~** *of* klar over; oppmerksom på; **3** merkbar, sansbar; **4** = *sensitive.* **sensing station** *sb data* lesestasjon. **sensitive** ['sensɪtɪv] *adj* **1** følsom; sart, ømfintlig; nærtagende; **2** mottakelig; *foto* lysømfintlig. **sensitivity** [,sensɪ'tɪvətɪ] *sb* følsomhet *etc.* **sensitize** ['sensɪtaɪz] *vt* gjøre (mer) følsom/mottakelig *etc.* **sensor** ['sensə] *adj data etc* sensor. **sensory** ['sensərɪ] *adj* føle-, sanse-. **sensual** ['senʃʊəl] *adj* sanselig, sensuell. **sensuality** [,senʃʊ'ælətɪ] *sb* sanselighet *etc.* **sensuous** [senʃʊəs] *adj* sanselig, sanse-.

sentence ['sentəns] **I** *sb* **1** setning; **2** dom; **II** *vt* dømme (*to* til). **sententious** [sen'tenʃəs] *adj* **1** fyndig; **2** pompøs.

sentiment ['sentɪmənt] *sb* **1** bevegelse, følelse; stemning; **2** holdning, innstilling; mening. **sentimental** [,sentɪ'mentl] *adj* sentimental; romantisk, svermerisk. **sentimentality** [,sentimen'tælətɪ] *sb* sentimentalitet etc.

sentinel ['sentɪnl] *sb* **1** (skilt)vakt; **2** *data* flagg.

sentry ['sentrɪ] *sb* (skilt)vakt, vaktpost. **sentry-box** *sb* skilderhus.

separable ['seprəbl] *adj* atskillelig; delelig. **separate I** ['seprət] *adj* **1** atskilt, isolert; separert; **2** særskilt; **II** ['sepəreɪt] *vb* skille/skjelne fra hverandre; skilles; gå fra hverandre; separere(s). **separation** [,sepə'reɪʃn] *sb* atskillelse; deling, skilling; separasjon.

septic ['septɪk] *adj* betent, infisert, septisk.

sepulchre ['sepəlkə] *sb* gravkammer.

sequel ['si:kwəl] *sb* **1** etterspill, følge; **2** fortsettelse.

sequence ['si:kwəns] **1** *sb* rekke(følge); *data også* sekvens; **2** *data etc* sekvensere. **sequential** [sɪ'kwenʃl] *adj data etc* sekvensiell; *også* serie-.

serene [sɪ'ri:n] *adj* **1** rolig, uforstyrrelig; *ofte* opphøyd; **2** klar, ren. **serenity** [si'renətɪ] *sb* (opphøyd) ro; klarhet.

serf [sɜ:f] *sb* livegen; slave, trell. **serfdom** ['sɜ:fdəm] *sb* livegenskap; slaveri, trelldom.

sergeant ['sɑ:dʒənt] *sb* sersjant.

serial ['sɪərɪəl] **I** *adj* **1** periodisk, serie-; **2** føljetong-; **II** *sb* **1** *(~ story)* fortsettelsesfortelling, føljetong; **2** seriemagasin; tidsskrift; ukeblad. **serial interface** *sb data* seriegrensesnitt. **serialize** ['sɪərɪəlaɪz] *vt* produsere (skrive, sende etc) som serie. **serializer** *sb data* serieomkoder. **serial | number** *sb* serienummer. **~ printer** *sb data* seriell skriver. **~ processing** *sb data* seriebehandling. **~ transfer, ~ transmission** *sb data* serieoverføring. **series** ['sɪərɪz] *sb* orden, rekkefølge; **2** rekke(følge), serie.

serious ['sɪərɪəs] *adj* **1** alvorlig, høytidelig; **2** betenkelig, farlig. **seriousness** ['sɪərɪəsnɪs] *sb* alvor.

sermon ['sɜ:mən] *sb* preken.

serpent ['sɜ:pənt] *sb* slange. **serpentine** ['sɜ:pəntaɪn] *adj* slangeaktig; buktet, slynget; *fig* listig, troløs.

servant ['sɜ:vənt] *sb* **1** tjener (og tjeneste|jente, -pike; hushjelp etc); **2** embets|kvinne, -mann; (stats)-tjeneste|kvinne, -mann. **serve** ['sɜ:v] **I** *sb sport* serve, serving; **II** *vb* **1** arbeide (for); tjene/være tjener (hos); tjene/tjenestegjøre (*as* som); (av)tjene (verneplikt); sone (straff); ~ *on a committee* sitte i en komité; ~ *one's apprenticeship* gå i lære; stå ut læretiden; ~ *one's time* sitte inne (dvs i fengsel); **2** forslå; greie/klare seg; ~ *as* fungere (og opptre/virke; gjøre nytte/tjeneste etc) som; *it ~s my turn* det klarer seg/holder for meg/for mitt formål/til min bruk; **3** gagne, hjelpe, nytte; fremme; *(it) ~s you right* det er til pass for deg; det har du godt av; *may I ~ you in any way?* er det noe jeg kan hjelpe Dem/stå til tjeneste med? **4** betjene, ekspedere; servere (for); ~ *out* dele/porsjonere ut; *dgl* gi inn; **5** gi; overlevere, presentere; ~ *a trick* spille et puss; ~ *with* forsyne med; **6** *(US: ~ notice)* meddele, underrette; varsle; *jur* forkynne (dom, stevning etc); **7** behandle; oppføre seg mot; **8** *sport* serve. **service** ['sɜ:vɪs] **I** *sb* **1** arbeid, tjeneste; *(domestic ~)* husarbeid; *at your ~* til (Deres) tjeneste; *go into ~* ta seg huspost; **2** tjeneste (og tjenestegjøring); embete; offentlig stilling/tjeneste; krigs-/militærtjeneste; forsvars/tjenestegren; *(divine ~)* gudstjeneste; *som adj* tjeneste-; forsvars, militær-; *active ~* krigstjeneste; *burial ~* begravelsesritual; *marriage ~* bryllupsseremoni; *secret ~* etterretningstjeneste; *see ~* gjøre krigstjeneste; **3** etat, verk, vesen; stell; *health ~* helse|stellet, -tjenesten; **4** (service)organisasjon, system; *bus ~* buss|forbindelse, -rute; **5** fordel, gagn, nytte; hjelp; *merk også* tjenesteytelse(r); **6** (kunde)betjening, ekspedering; servering; **7** servise; **8** service (dvs ettersyn, pass, stell, vedlikehold etc); **9** kunngjøring, meddelelse; *jur* forkynnelse; **10** *sport* serve, serving; **II** *vb* **1** passe, stelle, vedlikeholde; **2** betjene; ta seg av. **serviceability** [ˌsɜ:vɪsə'bɪlətɪ] *sb data* tilgjengelighet. **serviceable** ['sɜ:vɪsəbl] *adj* **1** brukbar, tjenlig; **2** holdbar, solid. **service | book** *sb* alterbok, bønnebok ~ **capsule** *sb petro* vedlikeholdsklokke. ~ **charge** *sb* drikkepenger. ~ **contract** *sb petro* entreprenøravtale. ~ **door** *sb* = ~ *entrance.* ~ **dress** *sb* = ~ *uniform.* ~ **elevator** *sb* kjøkkenheis, matheis. ~ **entrance** *sb* personalinngang. ~ **flat** *sb* tjenesteleilighet. ~ **hatch** *sb* serveringsluke. ~ **industry** *sb* service|industri, -næring; tjeneste|industri, -næring. ~ **lift** *sb* = ~ *elevator.* ~ **record** *sb mil etc* rulleblad. ~ **routine** *sb data* hjelperutine. ~ **station** *sb* bensinstasjon. ~ **uniform** *sb* tjenesteuniform. **serviette** [ˌsɜ:vɪ'et] *sb* serviett. **servile** ['sɜ:vaɪl] *adj* servil; krypende, underdanig; slave-. **servility** [sɜ:'vɪlətɪ] *sb* servilitet *etc.* **servitude** ['sɜ:vɪtju:d] *sb* slaveri, trelldom.

session ['seʃn] *sb* **1** møte, sesjon; **2** *skotsk* semester.

set [set] **I** *som adj, jf III* **1** anbrakt, plassert; (be)liggende; satt (og nedsatt, oppsatt etc); *deeply ~* dyptliggende; *well-~* vel|bygd, -skapt; velplassert; **2** bestemt; berammet, fastsatt; foreskrevet, forordnet; **3** fast (bestemt etc); beslutsom; *især US* sta, steil, strid; ~ *on* oppsatt på; **4** fast (dvs festet etc); ubevegelig; permanent, uforanderlig; ~ *stare* stivt blikk; **5** formell; regulær; **6** *dgl: all ~* alt i orden; (alt er) klappet og klart; **II** *sb* **1** (an)samling; *om personer* gruppe, lag; omgangskrets; *dgl* klikk; *neds også* bande, gjeng; *om ting* sett; bestikk, garnityr; servise; *dgl* (-)greier, (-)saker; **2** apparat; *TV ~* TV-apparat; **3** beliggenhet, plassering; holdning, (inn)stilling; *the ~ of her head* måten hun holder hodet på; **4** retning; tendens, tilbøyelighet; **5** fasong, snitt; fall; **6** angrep; sett; *dead ~* kraftig angrep; målbevisst forsøk; *be dead ~ on* gå målbevisst inn for; **7** stikling; **8** *film* dekorasjon(er), kulisse(r); opptakssted; **9** *sport* sett (i tennis etc); **III** *vb* **1** sette (og sette fra seg/på plass etc); anbringe, plassere; feste (og sette fast); legge/sette ut; plante/sette (ut); satse/sette (på); ~ *one's cap at* legge an på; legge seg etter; ~ *at ease/rest* berolige; ~ *an edge to* lage/sette egg på; *fig* skjerpe; sette (en) spiss på; ~ *eyes on* få øye på; ~ *one's face against* sette seg bestemt imot; ~ *fire/light to* sette fyr på; ~ *one's hand/name to* sette navnet sitt under; ~ *one's heart to* bli/være oppsatt på; ~ *right/straight* bringe i orden; få/sette i stand; sette på rett spor; ~ *a trap for* legge en felle for; **2** bestemme; beramme, fastsette; foreskrive, forordne; angi/anslå (tone etc); ~ *an example* gi/foregå med et eksempel; ~ *the fashion* angi/sette moten; ~ *the pace* angi/bestemme farten; ~ *a problem/task* gi en oppgave/et arbeid; **3** forårsake; forberede; gjøre/sette i stand; ~ *thinking* få til å tenke; ~ *to work* sette i arbeid; **4** arrangere, ordne; *mus* tonesette; **5** stille (og stille inn); justere, regulere; **6** feste; spenne, stramme; ~ *one's jaw/teeth* bite tennene sammen; **7** festne seg; *om planter* slå rot; sette blomst/frukt; **8** stivne, størkne; sette seg (dvs stivne etc); **9** dale, synke; gå ned; **10** besette/overså (*with* med); pynte; **11** gå/stå (om strøm, tidevann etc); **12** *med adv, prep* ~ **about** gå i gang (med); ta fatt (på); ~ **back** sette *etc* tilbake; bremse, stanse; hemme, hindre; ~ **down** sette *etc* ned/fra seg; sette/slippe av; notere/sette ned (på papir etc); anslå, vurdere; sette på plass (dvs irettesette etc); ~ **forth** dra av sted; legge i vei; fremsette (forslag etc); fremholde, hevde; ~ **in** sette *etc* inn (og *fig* bryte løs; sette inn med); gå mot land (om strøm, tidevann etc); ~ **off** dra av sted; legge i vei; sette i gang; avfyre, detonere; fremheve, utheve; sette i relieff; ~ **off against** sette i relieff/sette opp mot; ~ **on** *(jf III 3)* hisse/pusse (hund etc) på; ~ **on to** anspore (egge, hisse etc) til; ~ **out** sette *etc* ut (også om rykte etc); legge/sette frem; dra av sted; legge i vei; ~ **to** gå i gang med/ta fatt på (å); ~ **up** sette *etc* opp; montere; oppføre, reise; arrangere, forberede, utruste; starte; sette i gang; ~ **up as** *merk* etablere/nedsette seg som; ~ **upon** angripe, overfalle; gå løs på; kaste seg over; *også* = ~ *on.* **set|-back** *sb* tilbakeslag; hemsko, hindring. ~ **books** *sb fl* pensumbøker. **~-down** *sb* irettesettelse, skrape. **~-off** *sb* flatterende *etc* bakgrunn; kontrast. ~ **phrase** *sb* stående vending. ~ **square** *sb* vinkelhake. ~ **subject** *sb* oppgitt emne.

settee [se'ti:] *sb* (liten) sofa.

setting ['setɪŋ] *sb* **1** plassering *etc*; innfatning; omgivelser. bakgrunn; **2** (sol)nedgang.

settle ['setl] *vb* **1** anbringe, plassere; legge/sette til rette; installere; **2** (*~ down*) bosette seg; slå seg ned; *merk* etablere/nedsette seg; *~ down to* begynne med; ta fatt på; **3** bebygge, kolonisere; **4** avgjøre; bestemme, fastsette; beslutte; *~ on* bestemme seg for; bli enig om; **5** betale/gjøre opp (gjeld etc); *~ an account* gjøre opp et mellomværende; **6** synke (til bunns); bunnfelle(s); *~ (down) on* avsette seg/slå seg ned på; **7** falle/komme til ro; legge seg/stilne (om vind etc); *~ for* nøye seg med; slå seg til ro/til tåls med; **8** (*~ down*) berolige; bilegge; stille; **9** over|dra/-føre (*upon* til). **settlement** ['setlmənt] *sb* **1** anbringelse *etc*; **2** bebyggelse; koloni, nybyggergrend; **3** avgjørelse; bestemmelse; ordning; **4** betaling, oppgjør; bileggelse; **5** overdragelse. **settler** ['setlə] *sb* **1** nybygger; **2** *petro* skilletank.

set|-to *sb* krangel, slagsmål. **~up, ~-up** *sb* oppstilling; arrangement, ordning, system; situasjon, stilling; *data etc* oppsett(ing). **setup mode** *sb data* startmodus.

sever ['sevə] *vb* **1** bryte(s); brekke, knekke; hugge av/over; **2** skille(s); splitte(s). **several** ['sevrəl] **I** *adj* **1** atskillige, flere; noen; **2** særskilt; enkelt, respektive; **II** *pron* en del; noen.

severe [sɪ'vɪə] *adj* barsk, streng (også om klima etc); lei, slem. **severity** [sɪ'verətɪ] *sb* barskhet *etc*.

sew [səʊ] *vb* sy; *~ up* sy sammen. **sewing** ['səʊɪŋ] *sb* sying, søm. **sewing-machine** *sb* symaskin.

sewage ['sju:ɪdʒ] *sb* kloakk (dvs kloakk|avfall, -slam, -vann etc). **sewer** ['sju:ə] *sb* kloakk|anlegg, -system.

sex [seks] *sb* **1** kjønn; **2** erotikk, kjønnsliv; sex; *have ~ with* ha samleie med; ligge med.

sexton ['sekstən] *sb* kirketjener; graver; ringer.

sexual ['sekʃʊəl] *adj* seksuell, seksual-; kjønns-. **sexual intercourse** *sb* (seksuelt) samleie. **sexuality** [ˌsekʃʊ'ælətɪ] *sb* seksualitet. **sexy** ['seksɪ] *adj* erotisk utfordrende/tiltrekkende; sexig, sexy.

shabby ['ʃæbɪ] *adj* **1** loslitt, lurvet; **2** sjofel, tarvelig.

shack [ʃæk] *sb* (liten/provisorisk) hytte; (arbeids)brakke; koie; skjul, skur.

shackle ['ʃækl] **1** *sb* (den ene halvdelen av) håndjern, fotjern; *fl fig* jern, lenker; **2** *vb* lenke(binde).

shade [ʃeɪd] **I** *sb* **1** skygge (dvs skyggefullt sted, skyggelagt parti etc); **2** skjær; nyanse, sjattering; **3** skjerm; (lue)skygge; **4** *US* persienne; rullegardin; **II** *vb* **1** skygge (for); kaste skygge (over/på); skyggelegge, sjattere; **2** beskytte, dekke; (av)skjerme. **shadow** ['ʃædəʊ] **I** *sb* **1** (slag)skygge; skyggebilde; **2** *dgl* skygge (dvs forfølger etc); **3** *fig* anelse, antydning; *without a ~ of* uten skygge/spor av; **II** *vt* **1** formørke; kaste skygge (over/på); **2** *dgl* skygge (dvs (for)følge som en skygge); **3** (*fore~*) antyde; *~ forth* innvarsle; bære bud om. **shadowy** ['ʃædəʊɪ] *adj* **1** skyggefull, skygge-; **2** skyggeaktig; tåket, uklar. **shady** [ʃeɪdɪ] *adj* skyggefull, skygge-; **2** som befinner seg på skyggesiden; **3** *dgl* lyssky, tvilsom.

shaft [ʃɑ:ft] *sb* **1** skaft; **2** stengel, stilk; (søyle)skaft; **3** pil; lanse, spyd; *~ of sunlight* sol|strime, -stripe, -stråle; **4** akse, aksel; **5** sjakt; *air ~, ventilating ~* luftsjakt, ventilasjonssjakt. **shafted** ['ʃɑ:ftɪd] *adj* -skaftet; med skaft. **shafting** ['ʃɑ:ftɪŋ] *sb* akselledning.

shaggy ['ʃægɪ] *adj* **1** ragget, stridhåret; **2** bustet, uflidd.

shake [ʃeɪk] **I** *sb* **1** rystelse, skjelving; **2** støt; *især fig* sjokk; **3** (*hand~*) håndtrykk; **II** *vb* **1** riste; ryste, skake; skjelve; *~ one's head* riste på hodet; *~ a leg (dgl)* danse; *~ off* riste av seg; kvitte seg med; *~ up* riste (godt); **2** skake (opp); sjokkere, skremme; **3** *~ hands* håndhilse (*with* på); *~! (dgl)* kom med handa! (det er en) avtale! **shake-up** *sb* omkalfatring, omveltning; (radikal) forandring. **shaky** ['ʃeɪkɪ] *adj* skjelvende, ustø; gebrekkelig; skranten.

shale [ʃeɪl] *sb* (leir)skifer. **shale base** *sb petro* skiferbasis.

shall [ʃæl] *vb pres* **1** skal, vil; *I ~ be back by tomorrow* jeg er tilbake (igjen) i morgen; *you ~ repent this* dette skal du komme til å angre på; *I shouldn't do that* jeg ville ikke gjøre/ha gjort det (om jeg var deg); **2** *jur: every person should be liable to pay* enhver er/skal være forpliktet til å betale.

shallow ['ʃæləʊ] **1** *adj* grunn; *fig også* overfladisk; **2** *sb* grunne; **3** *vb* bli/gjøre grunnere.

sham [ʃæm] **1** *adj* falsk, forstilt; imitert, uekte; skinn-; **2** *sb* humbug; etterligning, imitasjon; forstillelse; bløff, juks; **3** *vb* foregi; late som; forstille seg; hykle, simulere.

shamble ['ʃæmbl] **1** *sb* sjokking, subbing; **2** *vi* sjokke, subbe; sjangle.

shambles ['ʃæmblz] *sb* **1** slakter|bu, -hus; **2** nedslakting; blodbad, massakre.

shame [ʃeɪm] **I** *sb* **1** skam, vanære; *~ on you!* skam deg! *for ~!* fy (for skam)! **2** skam(følelse), skamfullhet; *to my ~ I must confess that* jeg må med skam bekjenne at; **3** skam (= skammelig handling/hending etc); *it's a ~* det er (stor) skam; **II** *vt* gjøre skamfull; skamme/skjemme ut; vanære; bringe skam over. **shamefaced** ['ʃeɪmfeɪst] *adj* **1** blyg, unnselig; **2** flau, forlegen; skamfull. **shameful** ['ʃeɪmfʊl] *adj* **1** skamelig, skjendig; **2** motbydelig. **shameless** ['ʃeɪmlɪs] *adj* skamløs; frekk.

shampoo [ʃæm'pu:] **1** *sb* (hår)sjampo; sjamponering; **2** *vt* sjamponere; vaske (håret med sjampo).

shamrock ['ʃæmrɒk] *sb* kløverblad, trekløver (især som Irlands nasjonalsymbol).

shank [ʃæŋk] *sb* **1** legg, (skinne)bein; **2** strømpe|-legg, -skaft; **3** *mek* skaft, stang; *petro* borkroneskaft; **4** stett; stilk.

shanty ['ʃæntɪ] *sb* **A** (planke)skur; (primitiv) hytte; **B** *sjø* oppsang, sjanti. **shanty-town** *sb* brakkeby; slumstrøk med bordhytter og bølgeblikkskur.

shape [ʃeɪp] **1** *sb* fasong, form; figur, skikkelse; **2**

vb forme; gi/ta form; danne (seg); ~ *up (dgl)* gi/ta (fast) form; utvikle seg gunstig. **shapeless** ['ʃeɪplɪs] *adj* formløs, uformelig. **shapely** ['ʃeɪplɪ] *adj* velskapt.

share ['ʃeə] **A I** *sb* **1** del; part, porsjon; *go ~s* dele likt; spleise; **2** andel, lodd; *do one's ~* gjøre sitt/sin del; *it fell to my ~* det falt på meg/falt i min lodd; **3** *merk* aksje; **II** *vb* **1** (for)dele; dele ut; **2** dele; ha felles/ sammen; være felles/sammen om; ~ *and ~ alike* dele likt; **3** delta; ta del i; være med på; **B** *sb* (plog)skjær. **shared memory** *sb data* felleslager. **share|holder** *sb* aksjeeier. **~ware** *sb data* ≈ frigitt programvare (som en bare betaler en nominell pris for).

shark [ʃɑ:k] *sb* hai.

sharp [ʃɑ:p] **I** *adj* **1** skarp (og kvass, skjærende, spiss etc); **2** sterk, voldsom; glupende (om appetitt); **3** bitende; skarp (i smak etc); stram; streng; **4** gløgg, smart; **5** *mus* med (fortegnet) kryss; *D ~* diss; **II** *adv* skarpt (etc, jf *I*); *om klokkeslett* presis; *look ~!* (la det gå litt) kvikt nå! **III** *sb* **1** *mus* (note med fortegnet) kryss; **2** *dgl* ekspert, kløpper; **IV** *vb* **1** *mus* forhøye (med en halv tone); **2** *dgl* lure, snyte. **sharpen** ['ʃɑ:pən] *vb* kvesse(s); skjerpe(s); spisse(s). **sharper** ['ʃɑ:pə] *sb* svindler; bondefanger; *card-~* falskspiller, kortsvindler. **sharpshooter** ['ʃɑ:p,ʃu:tə] *sb* skarpskytter.

shatter ['ʃætə] **1** *sb: in(to) ~s* i filler; i stumper og stykker; **2** *vb* knuse (og splintre, sprenge, ødelegge, bryte ned etc); knuses *etc.* **shattering** ['ʃætərɪŋ] *adj* **1** knusende *etc*; **2** øredøvende.

shave [ʃeɪv] **I** *sb* **1** barbering; **2** (avskavet) flis/ spon; **3** *that was a close ~* det var på nære nippet; **II** *vb* **1** barbere (seg); **2** høvle/skave (*off* av); skrape; **3** streife/stryke innpå. **shaver** ['ʃeɪvə] *sb* **1** barber; **2** barbermaskin. **shaving** ['ʃeɪvɪŋ] *sb* **1** barbering; **2** *fl* (høvel)|flis, -spon. **shaving | brush** *sb* barberkost. **~ cream** *sb* barberkrem. **~ lotion** sb etterbarberingsvann. **~ mirror** *sb* barberspeil. **~ stick** *sb* barbersåpe.

shawl [ʃɔ:l] *sb* sjal.

sheaf [ʃi:f] **1** *sb* korn|bånd, (-)nek; **2** *vt* binde i nek.

shear ['ʃɪə] **I** *sb* **1** avklipp (især avklipt ull etc); **2** klipt sau etc; **3** *fl* (saue)saks; *garden ~s* hagesaks; hekksaks; *tailor's ~* skreddersaks; *tinners ~s* blikksaks; **II** *vb* klippe (især sauer); skjære (korn); beskjære (planter).

sheath [ʃi:θ] *sb* skjede, slire. **sheathe** [ʃi:ð] *vt* **1** stikke i skjede/slire; **2** *mek, sjø* forhude, trekke. **sheathing** ['ʃi:ðɪŋ] *sb sjø* forhudning.

sheave [ʃi:v] **A** *sb* (blokk)skive; **B** *vt* binde i nek.

shebang [ʃɪ'bæŋ] *sb US* **1** hytte; kåk, skur; **2** bule, kneipe; sjapp(e); **3** *the whole ~* hele sulamitten.

shed [ʃed] **A** *sb* hytte, skur; **B** *sb* skille, skjell; *water~* vannskille; **C** *vt* **1** felle (blad, fjær, tårer etc); skifte (hud); skyte (ham); **2** spre; sende ut; utgyte; *~ light on* kaste lys over.

sheen [ʃi:n] *sb* glans; skinn, skjær.

sheep [ʃi:p] *sb* sau (og sauer, saueflokk); *black ~* (*fig*) familiens sorte får. **sheep|dog** *sb* fårehund (især collie). **~fold** *sb* sauekve. **~ish** ['ʃi:pɪʃ] *adj* flau, forlegen; (med et) fåret/tåpelig (uttrykk i ansiktet). **~skin** *sb* saueskinn.

sheer ['ʃɪə] **I** *adj* **1** klar; ren, skjær; *fig også* pur; blott (og bar); **2** (stup)bratt; loddrett; **3** flortynn; gjennomsiktig; **II** *adv* **1** bratt; brått; **2** fullstendig, helt; **III** *sb sjø (fl)* spring (i dekkslinje); **IV** *vb sjø* dreie/falle av; *~ off* vike unna (fra).

sheet [ʃi:t] **I** *sb* **1** laken; *(winding ~)* lik|laken, -svøp; **2** (papir)ark; blad, (mindre) avis; **3** (metall)-plate; **4** (vann)|flate, -speil; **5** flak, lag; *~ of fire* flammehav; *the rain fell in ~s* regnet stod som en vegg; **6** *sjø* skjøte (på seil); *three ~s in the wind (slang)* kanonfull; **7** *sjø: fore~s* forende; *stern~s* akterende; **II** *vt* **1** svøpe i laken; **2** kle med plater. **sheeted** ['ʃi:tɪd] *adj* plate|belagt, -kledd. **sheeting** ['ʃi:tɪŋ] *sb* laken|lerret, -staut.

shelf [ʃelf] *sb* **1** hylle; *(set of shelves)* reol; *on the ~* (lagt) på hylla (dvs avleggs, ute av bruk etc); **2** avsats, fjellhylle; **3** rev, sandbanke; grunne; *continental ~* kontinentalsokkel.

shell [ʃel] **I** *sb* **1** skall (og konkylie, sneglehus; skjell; ertebelg, nøttehams; hylse, hylster; (over)trekk etc); **2** bombe, granat; patron; **3** (bygnings)skjelett; skallkonstruksjon; **II** *vb* **1** ta skallet *etc* av; **2** bombardere (med granater); beskyte. **shell|fish** *sb* skalldyr. **~proof** *adj* bombesikker, granatsikker; splintsikker. **~shock** *sb* granatsjokk.

shelter ['ʃeltə] **I** *sb* **1** beskyttelse, ly; deknings|-grav, -grop; tilfluktsrom; **2** leskur; tilfluktssted; *fig også* tilflukt; **II** *vb* gi/søke dekning/ly; beskytte, skjerme, verne; skjule (seg). **shelterhalf** *sb mil* teltduk (som også kan brukes som regnslag etc).

shelve [ʃelv] *vb* **1** sette opp hylle(r); **2** legge i/på hylle(r); *fig* legge på hylla; skrinlegge; **3** helle/skråne (især jevnt, f.eks. om havbunn).

shepherd ['ʃepəd] **1** *sb* (saue)gjeter; *gml* og *poet* (fåre)hyrde; **2** *vt* gjete, røkte, vokte; våke over. **shepherdess** ['ʃepədɪs] *sb* gjeterjente; *gml* og *poet* hyrdinne.

sherd [ʃɜ:d] *sb* potteskår.

sheriff ['ʃerɪf] *sb* sheriff; *GB* = høy embetsmann med især representative oppgaver; *skotsk* = dommer i et *county; US* = folkevalgt politimester/underdommer; *ofte* ≈ lensmann.

shield [ʃi:ld] **1** *sb* skjold; *fig* beskyttelse, vern; **2** *vt* skjerme; beskytte, verne. **shielding** ['ʃi:ldɪŋ] *sb data* skjerming.

shift [ʃɪft] **I** *sb* **1** ombytte, skifte; forandring; **2** (arbeids)skift; *work in ~s* arbeide (i/på) skift; **3** råd, utvei; *make ~ to* så vidt greie (å); **4** påskudd, utflukt; knep; **5** under|trøye, -tøy; linnet, serk; **II** *vb* bytte (på); skifte (og skiftes); veksle; flytte (på seg); forskyve seg (om last); forandre retning; *om vind også* slå om; *~ one's ground* skifte holdning/standpunkt; *~ one's lodgings* flytte; skifte bopel; *~ the helm* legge om roret; *she was ~ing about* hun snudde og vendte på seg; *they*

~ed the blame on to him de la (skjøv, veltet etc) skylden (over) på ham. **shift character** *sb data* skifttegn. **shiftless** ['ʃɪftlɪs] *adj* slapp, udugelig. **shifty** ['ʃɪftɪ] *adj* upålitelig, ustadig; falsk, uærlig.

shilling ['ʃɪlɪŋ] *sb* myntenhet, se midtsidene.

shimmer ['ʃɪmə] **1** *sb* skimmer, skjær; **2** *vi* skinne svakt; skimre.

shin [ʃɪn] **I** *sb (~bone)* skinnebein; **II** *vb* **1** sparke på leggen/skinnebeinet; **2** klatre opp (i/over).

shine [ʃaɪn] **I** *sb* glans, skinn; (lys)skjær; *take a ~ to* legge sin elsk på; *take the ~ out of* ta glansen av; **II** *vb* **1** skinne (og la skinne); stråle; **2** *fig* briljere, glimre; **3** pusse (især sko).

shingle ['ʃɪŋgl] **A I** *sb* **1** (tak)spon; **2** sjingel(frisyre); **3** *US* butikkskilt; *hang out one's ~* åpne forretning/praksis; **II** *vt* **1** tekke med spon; **2** sjingle (hår); **B** *sb* grus; grov singel.

shiny ['ʃaɪnɪ] *adj* skinnende (blank).

ship [ʃɪp] **I** *sb* fartøy, skip; *US også* fly; luft|fartøy, -skip; **II** *vb* **1** innskipe (seg); mønstre på; gå/ta om bord, laste (inn); **2** sende/transportere sjøveien; **3** *~ water/a sea* ta inn vann/få en sjø over seg; **4** hekte/huke på plass; gjøre klar. **ship|board** *sb* skipsside; *on ~board* om bord. **~-broker** *sb* skipsmegler. **~builder** *sb* skipsbygger. **~-chandler** *sb* skipshandler. **~load** *sb* skipslast. **~master** *sb* skips|fører, (-)kaptein. **~mate** *sb* skipskamerat. **~ment** *sb* utskiping; (skips)last; sending, (vare)parti. **~owner** *sb* skipsreder. **shipping** ['ʃɪpɪŋ] **I** *adj* **1** sjøfarts-; skips-, skipsfarts-; shippping-; **II** *sb* **1** *a)* sjøfart, skipsfart; shipping; *b) koll* skip, tonnasje; **2** forsendelse, sending. **shipping | agent** *sb* skipsmegler; befrakter; forhyrer; speditør. **~ articles** *sb fl* hyre(kontrakt). **~ clerk** *sb* spedisjonsassistent; *US* pakker. **~ company** *sb* (skips)rederi. **~ list** *sb* skipsliste. **~ master** *sb* forhyringssjef, hyrebas. **~ office** *sb* rederikontor. **~ opportunity** *sb* skipsleilighet. **~ trade** *sb* sjøfart, skipsfart. **ship|-rigged** *adj* fullrigget. **~shape** *adj, adv* klart skip (dvs alt i orden og på plass); *dgl* i fin/tipp topp stand. **~type rig** *sb petro* boreskip. **~wreck I** *sb* forlis, skibbrudd; *make ~ of* ruinere, ødelegge; **II** *vb* **1** forlise, lide skibbrudd; **2** få til å lide skibbrudd; *også fig* kjøre/renne i senk. **~wright** *sb* skipsbygger. **~yard** *sb* skipsverft.

shire ['ʃaiä; *som del av navn ofte* -ʃiä, ʃä] *sb* grevskap; ≈ fylke.

shirk [ʃɜ:k] *vb* skulke; lure seg unna.

shirt [ʃɜ:t] *sb* skjorte; *keep one's ~ on* beherske seg; holde hodet kaldt; *put one's ~ on* sats (alt) på. **shirting** ['ʃɜ:tɪŋ] *sb* **1** skjortestoff; **2** shirting. **shirt|-front** *sb* skjortebryst. **~sleeve** *sb* skjorteerme. **~tail** *sb* skjorteflak.

shist [ʃɪst] *sb petro* (leir)skifer.

shiver ['ʃɪvə] **A 1** *sb* hutring, skjelving; *fl* kuldegysninger; *it gives me the ~s/sends a cold ~ down my back* det får det til å gå kaldt nedover ryggen på meg; **2** *vb* hutre, skjelve; gyse; **B 1** *sb* flis, splint, stump; **2** *vb* splintre(s). **shivery** ['ʃɪvərɪ] *adj* skjelvende; kulsen.

shoal [ʃəʊl] **A 1** *sb* (fiske)stim; **2** *vi* stime (især om fisk); **B 1** *sb* (sand)banke, grunne; **2** *vi* bli grunnere.

shock [ʃɒk] **A I** *sb* **1** rystelse, støt; *fig* sjokk, slag; **2** sammenstøt; storm(angrep); **II** *vt* **1** ryste, skake; *fig* sjokkere; **2** støte/tørne mot; kollidere med; **B 1** *sb* (korn)stakk; **2** *vt* sette i stakk; **C** *sb: a ~ of hair* en kraftig (hår)manke; en frodig lugg. **shock | absorber** *sb* støtdemper. **~-headed** *adj* med masse tykt hår; bustet, lurvet. **~ing** *adj* rystende, sjokkerende. **~ resistant** *adj* støtsikker. **~ therapy, ~ treatment** *sb* sjokkbehandling. **~ troops** *sb fl* støttropper. **~ wave** *sb* sjokkbølge.

shoddy ['ʃɒdɪ] **I** *adj* **1** sjoddi-; **2** simpel, tarvelig; **II** *sb* sjoddi (dvs ull av opprevne filler).

shoe [ʃu:] **I** *sb* **1** sko (og skoning, skotøy; støvel, støvlett etc); *rubber ~s* kalosjer; **2** doppsko; holk, hylse; beslag, skoning; **II** *vt* **1** sko; utstyre med sko; skaffe sko til; **2** beslå. **shoe|black** *sb* = *~shine*. **~horn** *sb* sko|horn, -jern. **~lace** *sb* skolisse. **~maker** *sb* skomaker. **~shine** *sb* skopusser. **~string** *sb gml* skolisse; *happily married on a ~string* fattig, men lykkelig gift.

shoo [ʃu:] **I** *interj* **1** husj! vekk (med deg)! **2** *US* puh! pøh! **II** *vt* jage/skremme vekk; føyse unna.

shoot [ʃu:t] **I** *sb* **1** (plante)skudd; **2** jakt (og jaktrett, selskap, -tur etc); **3** fylling; losseplass (for søppel etc); **4** rutsjebane; styrtrenne, slisk; **II** *vb* **1** skyte (= avfyre skudd); **2** jage; drive/gå på jakt; **3** slenge, slynge; kyle; **4** losse, tømme; helle/styrte ut; **5** fare, pile; **6** skyte (i været); gro/spire (fort); **7** *dgl* fotografere, filme (dvs ta opp film); *dgl* skyte; **8** *slang: ~ out!* kom med det! syng ut! **9** *med adv, prep* **~ along** ekspedere kvikt; fare av sted; **~ at** skyte på; *fig* ta sikte på; **~ away** fyre løs; skyte bort; **~ down** skyte ned; **~ off** fyre av; fare/fyke av sted; stikke av; **~ out** skyte/stikke frem; jage/kaste ut; **~ up** skyte i været; vokse raskt. **shooting** ['ʃu:tɪŋ] **I** *adj* **1** skyte-; **2** jakt; **3** ilende, jagende; **II** *sb* **1** skyting, skuddveksling; **2** jakt; **3** smertesting. **shooting | gallery** *sb* (innendørs) skytebane. **~ match** *sb* skytekonkurranse. **~ range** *sb* (utendørs) skytebane. **~ pain** *sb* ilende/stikkende smerte. **~ party** *sb* **1** jaktselskap; **2** eksekusjonspelotong. **~ script** *sb film* dreiebok. **~ star** *sb* stjerneskudd. **~ war** *sb* (regulær) krig (i motsetning til kald krig).

shop [ʃɒp] **I** *sb* **1** butikk, forretning; **2** verksted (og *fl* fabrikk); arbeids|plass, -sted; *også* fag, yrke; *talk ~* prate fag/forretninger; **II** *vb* handle, gå i butikken/butikker; gjøre innkjøp; *go ~ping* gå og handle. **shop | assistant** *sb* (butikk)|ekspeditrise, -ekspeditør. **~ committee** *sb* klubbstyre/tillitsmannsutvalg (ved bedrift). **~ drawing** *sb* arbeidstegning. **~ foreman** *sb* verksmester. **~keeper** *sb* kjøpmann. **~lifter** *sb* butikktyv. **shopping** ['ʃɒpɪŋ] *sb* handel, innkjøp; handling. **shopping | bag, ~ basket** *sb* handle|veske, -kurv. **~ centre** *sb* butikksentrum, kjøpesenter. **~ list** *sb* handleliste, innkjøpsliste; *også* huskeliste. **shop|-soiled** *adj* skitten; ≈ demonstrasjons-, utstillings- (om vare som selges til nedsatt pris etter å ha vært brukt til demonstrasjon el. utstilling). **~ steward** *sb* klubbleder, (faglig) tillitsperson. **~walker** *sb* inspektør (i stormagasin etc).

shore [ʃɔ:] **A 1** *sb* kyst, strand; land (i motsetning til hav); *on ~* i/på land; *off ~* utenfor kysten, utaskjærs (se også *off-~*); **2** *vb* gå/sette i land; sette på grunn; **B 1** *sb* støtte(bjelke), (skrå)stiver; **2** *vt (~ up)* (av)stive; støtte (opp). **shore approach** *sb petro* landingssone. **shoring** ['ʃɔ:rɪŋ] *sb* avstivning, forstøtning.

short [ʃɔ:t] **I** *adj* **1** kort (og kortvokst, stutt; kortfattet; kortvarig; lav, lavvokst; liten; knapp, snau etc); *~ of* bortsett fra; med unntak av; *come/face ~ of* ikke nå opp til; *go ~* mangle, savne; *in ~* kort sagt; *little ~ of* nesten; *nothing ~ of* intet mindre enn; *run ~ of* slippe opp for; **2** skjør, sprø; **3** ren, ublandet (om drikkevarer); bar, sterk; **II** *adv* brått, plutselig; *stop ~* bråstoppe; **III** *sb* **1** kort vokal/stavelse; kort note; **2** *fl* kortbukse, shorts. **shortage** ['ʃɔ:tɪdʒ] *sb* knapphet, mangel, skort. **short|bread** *sb* mørdeigkake. **~-circuit 1** *sb* kortslutning; **2** *vb* kortslutte. **~coming** *sb* mislykket forsøk etc; feil, lyte, mangel; handikap. **~cut 1** *sb* beinvei, snarvei; **2** *vi* ta beinveien *etc*. **shorten** ['ʃɔ:tn] *vb* forkorte(s); forminske(s), redusere(s); skrumpe inn. **shortening** ['ʃɔ:tnɪŋ] *sb* **1** forkortelse *etc*; **2** matfett, smult. **short|hand 1** *adj* stenografisk; *~ note* stenogram; **2** *sb* stenografi; **3** *vb* stenografere. **~handed** *adj* underbemannet. **~legged** *adj* kortbeint, lavbeint. **~-lived** *adj* kortvarig. **shortly** ['ʃɔ:tlɪ] *adv* **1** kort *etc*; **2** *~ north (etc) of* litt nord (etc) for; **3** snart; om litt; om ikke lenge; i løpet av kort tid. **short | memory** *sb* dårlig hukommelse. **~ notice** *sb* kort varsel. **~-range** *adj* kortdistanse-. **~ sea** *sb* krapp sjø. **~-sighted** *adj* nærsynt; *fig* kortsynt. **~-spoken** *adj* kort (dvs avvisende, brysk; ordkarg etc). **~ story** *sb* novelle. **~-tempered** *adj* hissig, oppfarende. **~-term** *adj* korttids-. **~-wave** *adj* kortbølge-. **~-winded** *adj* andpusten.

shot [ʃɒt] **I** *adj* isprengt; *~ with gold* gullinnvirket; **II** *sb* **1** skudd (og hagl, kule, patron, prosjektil samt skudd|kraft, -vidde etc); *også* kuler, prosjektiler *etc; have a ~ at* forsøke seg på; *like a ~* som et lyn/skudd; **2** skytter; *dead ~* mesterskytter; **3** kule (især til spill og sport); *put the ~* støte kule; **4** *dgl* bilde, fotografi; (film)opptak; **5** *slang* dram, drink; skudd/sprøyte (dvs innsprøytning); *a ~ in the arm* en opp|kvikker/-strammer. **shot|gun** *sb* hagle (= hagl|børse, -gevær). **~proof** *adj* skuddsikker.

shoulder ['ʃəʊldə] **I** *sb* skulder, aksel; bog (på slakt); **II** *vb* **1** skuldre; ta på skulderen; aksle; **2** dytte unna med skulderen. **shoulder|-blade** *sb* skulderblad. **~-strap** *sb* **1** skulderklaff; **2** skulder|reim, -stropp.

shout [ʃaʊt] **1** *sb* rop, skrik; brøl; **2** *vb* rope, skrike; brøle.

shove [ʃʌv] **1** *sb* dytt, puff; **2** *vb* dytte, puffe, skubbe; *~ off* legge ut (dvs fra land); stikke av.

shovel ['ʃʌvl] **1** *sb* skuffe, skyffel; skovl; **2** *vt* skuffe, skyfle; måke; *~ in (dgl)* sope inn.

show [ʃəʊ] **I** *sb* **1** fremvisning, utstilling; *cattle ~* fesjå; *puppet ~* dukketeater; *by ~ of hands* ved håndsopprekning; *make a ~* vise seg; *make a ~ of* vise (stolt) frem; prale med; *make a good ~* ta seg godt ut; *on ~* utstilt; på utstilling; *be on ~* bli vist; være utstilt/på utstilling; la seg vise frem; **2** oppvisning; revy(forestilling), show; **3** utseende, ytre; skinn; *put on a ~* forstille seg; late som; **4** skue, syn; *a beautiful/magnificent ~* et vakkert/praktfullt syn; **5** *dgl* affære, greie, sak; *give the ~ away* røpe alt; sladre; tilstå; *run the whole ~* stå for styre og stell; *sick of the whole ~* lei hele greia; *steal the ~* stikke seg frem (på andres bekostning); ta all oppmerksomhet; **6** *dgl: good ~!* flott! godt gjort! *put up a good ~* gjøre en god innsats; **II** *vb* **1** vise (frem); stille ut; *~ off* bære/stille til skue; vise (skrytende) frem; *~ through* skinne igjennom; **2** vise seg; synes, vises; bli/være synlig; komme til syne; *~ to advantage* ta seg ut til sin fordel; *~ up* (an)komme; vise seg; synes godt; komme til sin rett; *it doesn't ~* det syns ikke; **3** vise; avsløre, røpe. **show|-bill** *sb* (reklame)plakat. **~-board** *sb* oppslagstavle; reklameplakat. **~-boat** *sb* teaterbåt. **~-business** *sb* underholdnings|bransje(n), -industri(en). **~-case** *sb* utstillings|monter, -skap. **~down** *sb* det å legge kortene på bordet; *fig* oppgjør, styrkeprøve.

shower ['ʃaʊə] *sb* **I** *sb* **1** byge/skur (med regn el. hagl); *fig* regn; flom, strøm; *there was a ~ of complaints* klagene strømmet inn; **2** *(~bath)* dusj; **II** *vb* **1** (la det) strømme/styrte ned; *~ gifts (etc) on* overøse med gaver (etc); **2** dusje; ta dusj.

show|girl *sb* revypike, sparkepike. **~-jumping** *sb* sprangridning. **~man** *sb* underholdningsartist, (revy)skuespiller, varietéartist. **~-number** *sb* revynummer. **~-off** *sb* skryt; blærethet, viktigmakeri. **~-piece** *sb* utstillingsgjenstand. **~-place** *sb* severdighet, turistattraksjon. **~-room** *sb* demonstrasjonsrom. **~window** *sb* utstilllingsvindu. **showy** ['ʃəʊɪ] *adj* prangende, iøynefallende.

shrapnel ['ʃræpnl] *sb* granatkardesk, shrapnel(granat).

shred [ʃred] **1** *sb* fille, strimmel; *in ~s* fillet; **2** *vb* rive/trevle opp; bli revet/trevlet opp.

shrew [ʃru:] *sb* **1** *(~mouse)* spissmus; **2** hespetre, kjeftesmelle. **shrewish** ['ʃru:ɪʃ] *adj* arrig.

shrewd [ʃru:d] *adj* **1** gløgg, skarp(sindig); klok; **2** lur, slu: **3** bitende/gjennomtrengende (om vind).

shriek [ʃri:k] *sb, vi* hyl(e), skrik(e).

shrill [ʃrɪl] **1** *adj* skingrende; skarp, skjærende; **2** *vi* skingre, skrike.

shrimp [ʃrɪmp] **I** *sb* **1** reke; **2** *dgl* pusling; **II** *vb* fange/fiske reker.

shrine [ʃraɪn] *sb* **1** helgenskrin, relikvieskrin; **2** helgengrav; *fig* helligdom; alter.

shrink [ʃrɪŋk] **I** *sb US slang* psykiater, psykolog; **II** *vb* **1** (få til å) krympe/skrumpe (inn/sammen); **2** vike tilbake (*from* fra). **shrinkage** ['ʃrɪŋkɪdʒ] *sb* (inn)skrumpning, krympning; svinn.

shrivel ['ʃrɪvl] *vb* (få til å) krympe/skrumpe (inn/sammen); visne.

shroud [ʃraʊd] **I** *sb* **1** lik|laken, -svøp: **2** *fl sjø* vant; **II** *vt* hylle/svøpe (inn).

shrub [ʃrʌb] *sb* busk. **shrubbery** ['ʃrʌbərɪ] *sb* buskas, kratt.

shrug [ʃrʌg] **1** *sb* skuldetrekning; **2** *vb* (*~ one's shoulders*) trekke på skuldrene.

shrunken ['ʃrʌŋkən] *adj* (*pp* av *shrink*) innskrumpet; rynket, vissen.

shudder ['ʃʌdə] **1** *sb* grøss(ing), gys; **2** *vi* grøsse, gyse.

shuffle ['ʃʌfl] **I** *sb* **1** sjokking *etc*; *walk with a ~* (gå og) sjokke; gå og subbe med føttene; **2** (kort)|blanding, -stokking; **3** krumspring, unnaluring; utflukter; **II** *vb* **1** (gå og) sjokke; slepe/subbe med føttene; *~ one's feet* sitte/stå urolig; stå og trippe (av nervøsitet etc); **2** blande/stokke (kort); **3** lure seg unna; komme med utflukter; **4** skyve (fra seg); *~ away/off* kvitte seg med; *~ through* fare gjennom. **shuffling** ['ʃʌflɪŋ] **1** *adj* unnvikende; **2** *sb data* (data)sanering.

shun [ʃʌn] *vt* sky, unngå; holde seg unna.

shunt [ʃʌnt] **I** *sb* **1** rangering (av jernbanevogner); (spor)skifting; **2** parallell|kobling, -krets; shunt; **II** *vb* **1** rangere; pense (tog inn på sidespor); **2** parallellkoble, shunte. **shunter** ['ʃʌntə] *sb* rangermann, sporskifter. **shunting yard** *sb* ranger-/skifte|stasjon, -tomt.

shut [ʃʌt] *vb* **1** lukke(s), stenge(s); kunne lukkes/stenges; *~ the mouth of* stoppe munnen på; **2** *med adv, prep* *~* **away** gjemme bort; isolere; sperre inne; *~* **down** lukke, stenge; stanse arbeid; *~* **in** sperre/stenge inne; *~* **off** slå/stenge av; sperre av; utelukke; *~* **out** stenge ute; utelukke; *~* **up** lukke, stenge; sperre/stenge inne; *~ up!* hold kjeft! **shut|-down** *sb* (midlertidig) lukking/stenging; (kortere) arbeidsstans. **~-down system** *sb petro* avstengningssystem. **~-eye** *sb dgl* blund.

shutter ['ʃʌtə] **I** *sb* **1** vindus|lem, (-)skodde; **2** (kamera)lukker; **II** *vt* sette lemmer/skodder for.

shuttle ['ʃʌtl] **I** *sb* **1** skyttel; **2** ferge/tog *etc* i skytteltrafikk; *space ~* romferge; **II** *vb* **1** bevege (seg) som en skyttel; **2** pendle; gå i pendelfart/skytteltrafikk. **shuttle|cock** *sb* badmintonball. *~* **pig** *sb petro* skyttel|pigg, -sonde. *~* **service** *sb* skytteltrafikk. *~* **valve** *sb petro* skyttelventil.

shy [ʃaɪ] **A 1** *adj* blyg, unnselig; sjenert; sky; engstelig; skvetten, var; *~ of* sjenert for; *fight ~ of* (forsøke å) unngå; **2** *sb* skvetting; plutselig sett/sprang; **3** *vi* skvette; **B I** *sb* **1** kast; **2** *dgl* forsøk; *have a ~ at* prøve seg på; **II** *vb* kaste; kyle, slenge.

sick [sɪk] **I** *adj* **1** syk; dårlig, uvel; *reported ~* sykmeldt; **2** kvalm; *air~* luftsyk; *car~* bilsyk; *sea~* sjøsyk; *be ~* være kvalm; brekke seg; kaste opp; *it makes me ~* det er til å bli kvalm av; **3** sykelig; **4** kei/lei (*of* av); **II** *sb* syk (person); *the ~* de syke. **sick|bay** *sb* syke|lugar, -stue. **~bed** *sb* syke|leie, -seng. **sicken** ['sɪkn] *vb* bli/gjøre syk *etc*. **sickening** ['sɪknɪŋ] *adj* kvalmende, motbydelig. **sick | humour** *sb* makaber humor. **~-leave** *sb* sykepermisjon.

sickle ['sɪkl] *sb* sigd.

sick-list *sb* sykeliste; *on the ~-list* sykmeldt.

sick|ly ['sɪklɪ] **I** *adj* sykelig (og blek, gusten, matt, slapp etc); **2** kvalm (og kvalmende); **II** *adv* sykelig (etc, jf *sick I*). **~ness** ['sɪknɪs] *sb* **1** sykdom; **2** kvalme. **~-nurse** *sb* sykepleier. **~pay** *sb* sykepenger. **~-room** *sb* syke|sal, -stue.

side [saɪd] **I** *sb* side (og side|linje, -stykke, bredd, kant; grense, linje; retning; lag, parti etc); *by my ~* ved siden av meg; *from all ~s* fra alle kanter; *on all ~s* på alle kanter; fra alle kanter/sider; *on both ~s* på begge sider; *on either ~* på hver (sin) side; på begge sider; *on my ~* på min side; (jeg) for min del; *on the ~* ved siden av; *dgl* på si; *on the safe ~* på den sikre siden; *change ~s* skifte side (lag, parti etc); *pick up ~s* velge lag (dvs deltakere som til sammen skal utgjøre laget); *take ~s* ta parti; **2** *dgl* overlegenhet, viktighet; innbilskhet; *put on ~* blære seg; **II** *vi: ~ with* ta parti for. **side|-arms** *sb fl* (sidevåpen som f.eks.) bajonett, sabel; pistol. **~board** *sb* **1** anretningsbord; buffet, skjenk; **2** sidekarm (på vogn). **~-burns** *sb fl* bakkenbarter, kinnskjegg. **~car** *sb* sidevogn. *~* **door** *sb* side|dør, -inngang. *~* **effect** *sb* bivirkning. **~-glance** *sb* sideblikk. *~* **issue** *sb* biting; underordnet sak/spørsmål. *~* **judge** *sb* meddommer. **~light** *sb* sidelys; side|lampe, -lykt; *fig* streiflys. **~line I** *sb* **1** sidelinje; **2** biartikkel; **3** bistilling; **II** *vt sport* sette/ta ut av spillet. **~long 1** *adj* sidelengs, side-; skrå(nende), skrå-; *fig* indirekte; **2** *adv* sidelengs; skrått, på skrå. **~-look** *sb* sideblikk. **~-note** *sb* randbemerkning. **~-on** *adv* fra siden; i profil. *~* **saddle** *sb* damesal. **~show** *sb* mindre forestilling/nummer (ved siden av hovedattraksjon etc). **~-step 1** *sb* skritt til siden; **2** *vb* ta et skritt til siden; *fig* omgå, unngå. **~-track 1** *sb* sidespor; **2** *vb* kjøre inn/sette på et sidespor; *fig* avspore, distrahere. **~tracking** *sb petro* sideboring. **~walk** *sb US* fortau. **~ways** *adj, adv* sidelengs; fra/på siden; skrått, på skrå; på tvers. **~-wind** *sb* sidevind; *fig* indirekte angrep/metode etc. **siding** ['saɪdɪŋ] *sb* sidespor. **sidle** ['saɪdl] *vb* føre/gå sidelengs; *~ up to* nærme seg nølende/ydmykt.

siege [si:dʒ] *sb* beleiring; *lay ~ to* beleire.

sieve [si:v] **1** *sb* sil; sikt, såld; **2** *vt* sikte, sile. **sieve plate** *sb petro* hullplate, silplate. **sift** [sɪft] *vb* sikte, sile; *fig* finsikte; granske (nøye); *~ out* skille ut. **sifter** ['sɪftə] *sb* sikt, såld.

sigh [saɪ *sb, vb* sukk(e).

sight [saɪt] **I** *sb* **1** syn (dvs syns|evne, -sans); **2** syn (og synsvidde); sikte; *at first ~* ved første blikk/øyekast; *come into ~* komme til syne; *get ~ of* få øye på; *in ~* i sikte; innenfor synsvidde; *lose ~ of* tape av syne; *out of ~* ute av syne; *within ~ = in ~*; **3** sikt(barhet); **4** syn (dvs noe å se på/som er verd å se på etc); severdighet; *a ~ for sore eyes* en fryd for øyet; **5** inspisering; inspeksjon; undersøkelse; *(fl)* observasjoner; **6** *dgl* masse, mengde; **7** sikte (på skytevåpen);

fl siktemidler; **8** inspeksjons|hull, -åpning; kikkhull; siktehull; **II** *vb* se; få øye på; sikte på. **sight|less** *adj* blind. **~ly** *adj* statelig; som tar seg godt ut; pen. **~read** *vb* ekstemporere; lese/synge fra bladet. **~seer** *sb* skuelysten person; turist. **~worthy** *adj* severdig.

sign [saɪn] **I** *sb* **1** tegn; merke, symbol; *mus* fortegn; *fig* (jær)tegn, varsel; **2** (uthengs)skilt; **3** signal; **II** *vb* **1** gjøre tegn; angi (fremstille, merke, vise etc) med tegn; merke opp; **3** sette opp skilt etc; **3** under|skrive, -tegne; **~** *away* fraskrive seg; **~** *on* ansette, engasjere; *sjø* (for)hyre; mønstre på; ta hyre; **~** *over* overdra; **~** *up* melde seg på (*for* til); la seg verve. **signal** ['sɪgnl] **I** *adj* **1** enestående; fremragende, glimrende; **2** signal- (etc, jf *II*); **II** *sb* **1** signal (og tegn, varsel; merke etc); **2** *fl mil (=* **~** *troops)* sambandstropper; **III** *vb* signalere (og signalisere); gi/gjøre tegn. **signal | book** *sb* signalbok. **~-box** *sb* signal|boks, -hytte; *også* = **~**-*tower*. **~ character** *sb data* fortegn. *the* **Signal Corps** *sb mil* hærens samband. **signal | man** *sb mil* sambands|mann, -soldat. **~ service** *sb mil* sambandstjeneste; *dgl* samband. **~-tower** *sb* stillverk. **signatory** ['sɪgnətrɪ] **1** *adj* signatar-; **2** *sb* underskriver. **signatory power** *sb pol* signatar(makt). **signature** ['sɪgnətʃə] *sb* **1** underskrift, signatur; **2** *mus* fortegn; **3** = **signature | song, ~ theme, ~ tune** *sb* kjenningsmelodi. **signboard** *sb* (uthengs)skilt. **signet** ['sɪgnɪt] *sb* segl, signet. **significance** [sɪg'nɪfɪkəns] *sb* betydning (og betydningsfullhet etc); *data* vekt. **significant** [sɪg'nɪfɪkənt] *adj* **1** betydningsfull, viktig; betydelig; **2** betegnende; uttrykksfull; megetsigende, talende. **signification** [ˌsɪgnɪfɪ'keɪʃn] *sb* **1** tilkjennegivelse; **2** betydning (av ord); mening. **signify** ['sɪgnɪfaɪ] *vb* **1** tilkjennegi; **2** bety, innebære; stå for. **sign | language** *sb* tegnspråk. **~ painter** *sb* skiltmaler.

silence ['saɪləns] **I** *sb* **1** stillhet; **~**! stille! **2** taushet; *put to* **~** bringe til taushet; **II** *vt* få til å være stille; bringe til taushet. **silencer** ['saɪlənsə] *sb* lyddemper. **silent** ['saɪlənt] *adj* stille; **2** taus; **3** stum (især om bokstaver); **II** *sb* = **silent film/movie** *sb* stumfilm.

silhouette [ˌsɪlu:'et] **1** *sb* silhuett, skyggebilde; **2** *vt* avtegne seg/stå i silhuett.

silicon ['sɪlɪkən] *sb* silisium, silikon. **silicon chip** *sb data* silisiumbrikke.

silk [sɪlk] *sb* silke (og silke|garn, -tråd; *fl* -klær, -varer etc); silkekappe. **silken** ['sɪlkən] *adj* silke|bløt, -myk; silke-. **silkworm** ['sɪlkwɜ:m] *sb* silkeorm. **silky** ['sɪlkɪ] *adj* silkeaktig (og silke|lignende; -bløt, -fin, -myk; -glinsende etc); silke-; *fig* katte|myk, -vennlig.

sill [sɪl] *sb* **1** bunnstokk, svill(e), syllstokk; **2** dør|stokk, -terskel; **3** vindus|karm, -post.

silly ['sɪlɪ] **1** *adj* fjollet, tåpelig; dum; *the* **~** *season* agurktiden (dvs om stille (avis)sesong, i sommerferietiden etc); **2** *sb* fjols, tosk; dumrian; dustemikkel.

silver ['sɪlvə] **1** *sb* sølv (og sølv|penger, -tøy etc); *som adj* sølv- (og sølv|blank, -glinsende etc); *born with a* **~**-*spoon in one's mouth* født med en sølvskje i munnen (dvs av velstående foreldre); **2** *vt* forsølve; foliere. **silver | anniversary** *sb* 25|årsdag, -jubileum. **~-coated** *adj* forsølvet; foliert. **~-haired** *adj* med (sølv)grått hår; med sølvstenk (i håret). **~ jubilee** *sb* = **~** *anniversary*. **~-mounted** *adj* sølv|beslått, -innrammet. **~plate** *sb* (sølv)plett; sølv(tøy). **~-smith** *sb* sølvsmed. **~-tongued** *adj* (forførerisk) veltalende. **~ware** *sb* sølvtøy. **~ wedding** *sb* sølvbryllup. **silvery** ['sɪlvərɪ] *adj* sølv|blank, -glinsende, skinnende; *fig* sølvklar; klokkeren.

similar ['sɪmɪlə] *adj* lik (og likeartet; *mat* -dannet); lignende. **similarity** [ˌsɪmɪ'lærətɪ] *sb* likhet. **similarly** ['sɪmɪləlɪ] *adv* likeledes; på samme måte. **simile** ['sɪmɪlɪ] *sb* lignelse. **similitude** [sɪ'mɪlɪtju:d] *sb* likhet; *in the* **~** *of* i skikkelse av.

simmer ['sɪmə] **1** *sb* småkoking *etc*; **2** *vb* (la) småkoke; syde; putre.

simper ['sɪmpə] **1** *sb* affektert *etc* smil; **2** *vi* smile affektert (dumt, fjollet etc).

simple ['sɪmpl] **I** *adj* **1** enkel; naturlig, ukunstlet; **2** enkel, usammensatt; *også* = **~**-*hearted* og **~**-*minded*. **3** enkel, ukomplisert; liketil; *as* **~** *as pie* (så lett) som fot i hose; *pure and* **~** *(gml)* ganske enkelt; **II** *sb* **1** person av enkel opprinnelse; **2** bestandel, element; **3** legeurt. **simple | equation** *sb* førstegradsligning. **~ fraction** *sb* enkel/ubrudden brøk. **~-hearted** *adj* troskyldig; endefrem, likefrem. **~-minded** *adj* enfoldig, naiv. **simpleton** ['sɪmpltən] *sb* dumrian, tosk. **simplex operation** *sb data* enveisdrift. **simplicity** [sɪm'plɪsətɪ] *sb* enkelhet (etc, jf *simple I*). **simplify** ['sɪmplɪfaɪ] *vt* forenkle; *mat* forkorte (brøk). **simply** ['sɪmplɪ] *adv* **1** enkelt (etc, jf *simple I*); **2** ganske enkelt; simpelthen; **3** bare; **~** *and solely* ene og alene.

simulate ['sɪmjʊleɪt] *vb* **1** simulere; foregi, late som; **2** etterligne, imitere. **simulation** [ˌsɪmjʊ'leɪʃn] *sb* simulering *etc*.

simultaneity ['sɪməltə'nɪətɪ] *sb* samtidighet. **simultaneous** [ˌsɪml'teɪnɪəs] *adj* samtidig; simultan-.

sin [sɪn] **1** *sb* synd; *deadly* **~** dødssynd; **2** *vb* synde (*against* mot). **sin|ful** *adj* syndefull, syndig. **~less** *adj* syndfri. **~ner** *sb* synder.

since [sɪns] **I** *adv* siden; deretter, senere; *ever* **~** helt fra/siden; **II** *konj* **1** siden; **~** *last I saw them* siden sist jeg så dem; **2** da, ettersom, fordi, siden; **~** *the car has broken down we shall have to walk* ettersom bilen er gått i stykker, må vi gå; **III** *prep* siden.

sincere [sɪn'sɪə] *adj* oppriktig, uforstilt; ekte. **sincerely** [sɪn'sɪəlɪ] *adv* oppriktig *etc; Yours* **~** ≈ ærbødigst/med vennlig hilsen (i brev). **sincerity** [sɪn'serətɪ] *sb* oppriktighet.

sinew ['sɪnju:] *sb* sene; *fl ofte* kraft, styrke. **sinewy** ['sɪnjʊɪ] *adj* senesterk, senet.

sing [sɪŋ] *vb* **1** synge (og besynge, synge om etc); **~** *in tune* synge rent; **~** *out* synge ut (også *fig*); **~** *small (fig)* stemme ned tonen; **2** kunne synges; være sangbar; **3** suse/synge (om tekjele etc); **4** kvitre/pipe (om fugler); synge. **singer** ['sɪŋə] *sb* sanger. **singing**

['sɪŋɪŋ] *sb* sang (dvs det å synge); synging.

singe [sɪndʒ] **1** *sb* sviing (og svimerke; lite brannsår etc); **2** *vb* svi(s); brenne(s); *be ~d (fig)* brenne/svi fingrene/fingertuppene (sine).

single ['sɪŋgl] **I** *adj* **1** enkel(-), enkelt(-); en-, ene-; eneste; **2** alene, enslig; **3** enslig (dvs ugift); **4** enkel; oppriktig, åpen; ærlig; **II** *sb* **1** (enkelt)individ; enkelt person/ting etc; *in ~s and pairs* enkeltvis og parvis; **2** singleplate; **III** *vb* **1** *~ out* skille ut; peke (plukke, velge etc) ut; **2** tynne (ut). **single|-breasted** *adj* enkelt|knappet, -spent. *~* **combat** *sb* tvekamp. **~-family house** *sb* enebolig. *~* **gentleman** *sb* ungkar. **~-grade oil** *sb petro* engradsolje. **~-handed** *adj* **1** enhånds; som bruker/har bare én hånd; **2** egenhendig; på egenhånd. **~-hearted, ~-minded** *adj* ensporet (dvs med bare én ting for øyet); målbevisst. **singlet** ['sɪŋglɪt] *sb* (under)trøye. **single | ticket** *sb* enveisbillett (i motsetning til returbillet). *~* **track** *sb* enkeltspor. **~-track** *adj* enkeltsporet; *fig* ensporet. **~-user system** *sb data* enbrukersystem. **singly** ['sɪŋglɪ] *adv* **1** enkeltvis; **2** alene; på egenhånd.

sing-song ['sɪŋsɒŋ] **I** *adj* messende, monoton; ens|formig, -tonig; kjedelig; **II** *sb* **1** messing; monoton sang etc; **2** visekveld; **III** *vi* messe; synge/tale enstonig.

singular ['sɪŋgjʊlə] **I** *adj* **1** enkelt(-); separat(-); **2** enestående; sjelden, uvanlig; **3** egen, egenartet; eiendommelig, påfallende; merkelig, underlig; **II** *sb gram* entall. **singularity** [ˌsɪŋgjʊ'lærətɪ] *sb* **1** egenhet, eiendommelighet; **2** særhet.

sinister ['sɪnɪstə] **I** *adj* **1** illevarslende, uhellsvanger; dyster, truende; skummel; **2** lyssky; fordervelig, ond; **3** *gml* venstre (side av våpenskjold etc).

sink [sɪŋk] **I** *sb* **1** *a)* oppvaskkum; *b)* (utslags)-vask; **2** avløp, kloakk; **II** *vb* **1** synke (og senke seg; dale, falle; gå ned/under; helle, skråne utfor etc); **2** senke; bore/skyte *etc* i senk; få til å synke; la synke; *~ one's nails/teeth into* sette neglene/tennene i; *~ a post in(to)* ramme ned en pæl/stolpe i; **3** grave (ut); *~ roots* slå rot/røtter; *~ a well* grave en brønn; **4** ødelegge; **5** *dgl: ~ money in(to)* sette penger i; satse penger på.

sinuous ['sɪnjʊəs] *adj bokl* buktet, slynget; snodd.

sip [sɪp] **1** *sb* liten slurk/tår; knert, nipp; **2** *vb* smådrikke; nippe (*at* til).

siphon ['saɪfn] **I** *sb* **1** hevert; **2** sifong; **II** *vb* stikke(s) om med hevert.

sir [sɜ:] **I** *sb* **1** herr (som høflig tiltaleord oversettes *~* som oftest ikke, eller med herr samt tittel/stillingsangivelse, eventuelt bare tittel; til kongen: *Sir* Deres majestet; i møter, f.eks. i parlamentet: *Sir* herr president (formann, ordstyrer etc); på skolen: *Sir* lærer; i brev: *Dear Sir* Kjære og fullt navn eller Kjære med tittel og etternavn; *stundom* Herr samt tittel; i leserbrev: Herr redaktør; til militært befal: *yes, ~* ja(vel) samt militær grad); **2** (som *baronet's* og *knight's* tittel i forbindelse med fullt navn eller bare fornavn) *Sir Walter Scott* eller *Sir Walter*; **II** *vt* si *sir* til; *ofte ≈* dise; si De til. **sire** ['saɪə] **I** *sb* **1** opphav, (stam)far; **2** herre (brukt i tiltale); *især* herre konge; **II** *vb: ~d by* falt etter (dvs avlet av; avkom av/etter).

siren ['saɪərən] *sb* sirene.

sirloin ['sɜ:lɔɪn] *sb* mørbrad(stek).

sis [sɪs] *sb (US fork* for *sister)* søster. **sissy** ['sɪsɪ] *sb* mammadalt, pyse. **sister** ['sɪstə] *sb* **1** søster (og nonne, sykesøster etc og om kvinne i søsters sted); **2** (yrkes)søster, kollega; medlem av søsterskap. **sister|-hood** *sb* søster|forhold, -skap; -orden. **~-in-law** *sb* svigerinne. **~ly** *adj* søsterlig.

sit [sɪt] *vb* **1** sitte (og sitte i/på; ha sete; sitte sammen; være (for)samlet; holde (retts)møte etc); **2** ligge (og om fugler især ruge); være beliggende/plassert; **3** sitte (dvs om klærs passform); **4** ha/skaffe sitteplass til; benke; **5** *med adv, prep ~* **back** lene seg tilbake; *fig* forholde seg avventende; sitte med hendene i fanget; *~* **by** sitte ved siden av; sitte hos/ved; *~* **down** sette seg; *~ down to* sette seg til med/å; konsentrere seg om (å); *~ down under* finne seg i; *~* **for** sitte (modell) for; sitte som/være representant for; *~ for an examination* være oppe til eksamen; *~* **in** delta; være med/til stede; sitte/være barnevakt; demonstrere ved å okkupere rom el. bygning og ikke flytte seg før visse krav er innfridd; *~* **on** sitte på; *fig* kue; holde nede; *~ on a board/a committee* sitte i et styre/en komité; *~ on a case* holde (retts)møte i en sak; *~ heavily on* hvile tungt på; *~* **out** sitte til ende/til det er slutt; sitte lenger enn; *~* **through** bli sittende (til det er slutt); *~* **tight** sitte fast; bli sittende (hvor man er); ikke rikke seg; *~* **up** sitte; sitte oppe; reise (rette, sette etc) seg (opp); *fig* spisse ører; stusse; *~ up for* sitte oppe og vente på; *~* **with** sitte hos (for å passe på). **sit-down strike** *sb* streik, især av kortere varighet, hvor de streikende blir på arbeidsplassen. **sit-in** *sb* form for demonstrasjon (jf *sit in*).

site [saɪt] *sb* beliggenhet; sted; tomt.

sitter ['sɪtə] *sb* en som sitter (etc, jf *sit*); *baby-~* barnevakt; *bed-~* hybel. **sitting** ['sɪtɪŋ] **I** *adj* sittende, sitte- (etc, jf *sit*); **II** *sb* sitting/det å sitte (etc, jf *sit*); *at one/a single ~* i ett strekk (dvs uten pauser); **2** (tilstrekkelig) sitteplass; **3** sammenkomst; møte (i nasjonalforsamling etc). **sitting | duck** *sb dgl* takknemlig offer. *~* **member** *sb* parlamentsmedlem på gjenvalg. **~-room** *sb* **1** (daglig)stue, oppholdsrom; **2** sitteplass.

situated ['sɪtjʊeɪtɪd] *adj* beliggende; anbrakt, plassert; *fig* stedt, stilt; *comfortably ~* velsituert. **situation** [ˌsɪtjʊ'eɪʃn] *sb* **1** beliggenhet; **2** situasjon; forhold, omstendigheter; *have the ~ well in hand* ha situasjonen under full kontroll; **3** post, stilling (dvs arbeid).

six [sɪks] *adj, sb* seks(tall); sekser; *at ~es and sevens* hulter til bulter. **six|-footer** *sb* person som er seks fot (= 1,83 m) høy; *dgl* røslig/svær kar. **~-shooter** *sb* seksløper; revolver med seks skudd.

sizable ['saɪzəbl] *adj* temmelig stor; anselig, betraktelig, betydelig. **size** [saɪz] **A I** *sb* størrelse (og dimensjon(er), format, kaliber, mål, nummer etc); *of* *a* ~ av samme størrelse; like store; *that's about the* ~ *of it* sånn omtrent ligger det an; *try on for* ~ prøve (på) (dvs om klesplagg, for å se om størrelsen passer); **II** *vb* **1** ordne/sortere etter størrelse; ~ *up* ta mål av; taksere, vurdere; **2** lage i en bestemt størrelse; *small-~d* i liten størrelse/små nummer; **B 1** *sb* limvann; **2** *vt* limstryke; behandle/bestryke med limvann; lime. **sizing pig** *sb petro* kaliberpigg.

sizzle ['sɪzl] **1** *sb* fresing, putring; **2** *vi* frese/putre (ved steking etc).

skate [skeɪt] **A 1** *sb* skøyte; *ofte* rulleskøyte; **2** *vi* gå på skøyter; **B** *sb* rokke, skate. **skate-board 1** *sb* rullebrett; **2** *vi* ake (kjøre, renne, stå etc) på rullebrett. **skater** ['skeɪtə] *sb* (rulle)skøyteløper. **skating** ['skeɪtɪŋ] *sb* (rulle)skøyteløp(ing); *som adj* (rulle)skøyte-; *figure* ~ kunstløp på (is)skøyter; *speed* ~ hurtigløp på (is)skøyter. **skating-rink** *sb* skøytebane.

skein [skeɪn] *sb* **1** dukke (med garn, tråd etc); *fig* floke; **2** flokk (især av svaner, vill|ender og -gjess).

skeletal ['skelɪtl] *adj* skjelett-. **skeleton** ['skelɪtn] *sb* skjelett (og bein|bygning, -grind; rammeverk, spant(er); (om)riss, utkast; skjema etc). **skeleton | army** *sb* spøkelseshær. ~ **dance** *sb* dødningdans. ~ **key** *sb* hovednøkkel. ~ **steps** *sb* jerntrapp (med åpne opptrinn).

sketch [sketʃ] **I** *sb* **1** skisse, utkast; **2** sketsj; **II** *vt* (~ *out*) skissere; streke/trekke opp; gjøre/lage utkast til. **sketchy** ['sketʃɪ] *adj* skissemessig; skissert; (lett) henkastet; overfladisk, flyktig.

skewer ['skjʊə] **I** *sb* **1** steke|pinne, -spidd; **2** blokkeringshendel (på sykkelhjulnav); **II** *vt* feste med stekepinne.

ski [ski:] *sb, vb* (gå på) ski.

skid [skɪd] **I** *sb* **1** bremse|kloss, -sko; **2** skrens(ing); **II** *vi* skrense; gli/skli (ut).

skier ['ski:ə] *sb* skiløper. **skiing** ['ski:ɪŋ] *sb* skiløping. **ski|-jump** *sb* hoppbakke, skibakke.

skilful ['skɪlfʊl] *adj* dyktig, flink; kyndig.

ski-lift *sb* ski|heis, -trekk.

skill [skɪl] *sb* dyktighet; ferdighet, kyndighet. **skilled** [skɪld] *adj* dyktig, flink; *især* fag|lært, -utdannet.

skillet ['skɪlɪt] *sb* liten kasserolle (med skaft og vanligvis tre bein).

skim [skɪm] *vb* **1** skumme (av); **2** dekke/bli dekket med et tynt lag; **3** gli/stryke (bort)over; **4** fare over (især *fig*); ~ *through a book* fare gjennom en bok. **skim(med) milk** *sb* skummet melk. **skimmer** *sb petro* olje|opptaker, -skummer.

skimp [skɪmp] **1** *adj* knapp, snau; mager, skrinn; **2** *vb* være gjerrig/gnien (med); knusle med; spare/spinke (på). **skimpy** ['skɪmpɪ] *adj* **1** gjerrig, gnien, knegen; **2** snau, trang.

skin [skɪn] **I** *sb* **1** hud, skinn (og beholder av hud el. skinn, f.eks. lærflaske, skinnsekk); ~ *and all* (med) hud og hår; *by the* ~ *of one's teeth* med nød og neppe; *get under one's* ~ ergre/irritere en; interessere/oppta en sterkt; *have a thick* ~ være tykkhudet; *in one's* ~ i Adams/Evas drakt (dvs naken); **2** hinne; snerk; **3** skall, skrell; skinn; **4** forhudning (og hud); kledning, trekk; **5** *dgl, slang* gnier; svindler; krøkke/øk (= gammel hest); **II** *vb* **1** flå (og *fig* snyte, svindle); skrelle; flenge/vrenge av; pille/plukke (av); ~ *by/through* så vidt knipe seg forbi/gjennom; ~ *a flint* være gnien; være om seg; ~ *one's knee* skrubbe (seg opp på) kneet; **2** dekke(s) med hud; ~ *over* gro, (til)heles. **skin|-deep** *adj* overfladisk; som ikke stikker særlig dypt. **~-diver** *sb* froske|kvinne, -mann. ~ **dresser** *sb* buntmaker, pelsbereder. **~flint** *sb dgl* gnier. **~-food** *sb* ansiktskrem etc. **~ful** *sb* det en lærflaske etc kan holde; *fig* rikelig (å drikke); drøy omgang/porsjon. ~ **grafting** *sb* hudtransplantasjon. **~less** *adj* husløs. **skinned** [skɪnd] *adj* **1** flådd; *fig* plyndret til skinnet; **2** *-skinned* -hudet, -kledd. **skinner** ['skɪnə] *sb* buntmaker, pelsbereder. **skinny** ['skɪnɪ] *adj* (skinn)mager. **skin|tight** *adj* ettersittende, åletrang.

skip [skɪp] **1** *sb* hopp, sprang; det å hoppe/springe over noe (især når man leser); **2** *vb a)* hoppe/springe over; ~ *it* stikke av; *b)* hoppe tau.

skipper ['skɪpə] **I** *sb* **1** skipper, (skips)kaptein; **2** *sport* (lag)kaptein; **3** *dgl* bas, sjef; **II** *vt sport* være (lag)kaptein for.

skipping-rope ['skɪpɪŋ,rəʊp] *sb* hoppetau.

skirmish ['skɜ:mɪʃ] **1** *sb* forpostfektning; (lett) sammenstøt/trefning; skuddveksling; **2** *vi* kjempe i spredte fektninger.

skirt [skɜ:t] **I** *sb* **1** skjørt (og *slang* kvinnfolk); *fl* (frakke)skjøter; **2** *fl* utkant(er); **II** *vb* **1** gå/ligge langs med (langs kanten/randen av); **2** (~ *round*) gå/kjøre etc utenom; *fig* liste/lure seg utenom; **3** så vidt streife; være en hårsbredd fra. **skirt-chaser** *sb* skjørtejeger.

skittish ['skɪtɪʃ] *adj* **1** livlig, lystig; leken; **2** sky/urolig (om hest); skvetten.

skittles ['skɪtlz] *sb fl* kjegler; kjeglespill; *life is not all beer and ~s* livet er ikke bare (en) dans på roser. **skittle-alley** *sb* kjeglebane.

skulduggery [skʌl'dʌgərɪ] *sb* fanteri, lureri; svindel.

skulk [skʌlk] *vb* gjemme seg; lure seg/luske unna; skulke. **skulking** ['skʌlkɪŋ] *adj* unnalurende; feig.

skull [skʌl] *sb* (hjerne- el. hode)skalle; kranium, *fig* hode; *have an empty* ~ være tomhjernet; *have a thick* ~ være tykkhodet. **skullcap** *sb* kalott.

skunk [skʌŋk] *sb* **1** stinkdyr; **2** *vulg* drittsekk.

sky [skaɪ] **1** *sb* himmel (dvs himmelvelv, jf *heaven*); *fl* himmelstrøk; **2** *vb* sende/skyte opp (mot himmelen); henge høyt. **sky|-blue** *adj, sb* himmelblå(tt). **~-high** *adj, adv* himmelhøy(t), skyhøy(t). **~lark 1** *sb* lerke; **2** *vi* fjase, tøyse; holde leven. **~light** *sb* overlysvindu, takvindu *sjø* skylight. **~line** *sb* **1** horisont, synskrets; **2** silhuett (av hus, trær etc mot himmelen el. horisonten). **~rocket 1** *sb* rakett; **2** *vi* fare/fyke i været (som en rakett). **~scraper** *sb* skyskraper. **~ward(s)** *adj, adv* mot himmelen; til himmels; oppover; til værs.

slab [slæb] **I** *sb* **1** plate, skive; helle, steinflis; flat blokk; **2** bakhun(ved); **II** *vb* **1** dele opp i plater etc; **2** dekke med heller/plater etc.

slack [slæk] **I** *adj* **1** langsom, treg; **2** forsømmelig, slurvet; slapp; **3** død, *dgl* dau (dvs kjedelig, stille) etc); flau, laber; **4** løs; slakk, slapp; **5** dårlig stekt (om bakverk); med rårand; **II** *sb* **1** slakk (dvs hengende/ løs bukt, tauende etc); **2** dødgang; slark, sluring; **3** dødperiode; pause, stans; stillstand; **III** *vb* **1** *(~ off/ out)* slakke (på); fire/gi ut på; *~ off (også)* løsne (på); **2** slappe av; bli slappere; *~ around* gå og daffe; **3** *(~ up) = slacken 3.* **slacken** ['slækn] *vb* **1** slakke (på); gjøre slakkere; **2** dabbe/slappe av; kjølne; **3** minske; saktne; avta; løye, spakne; stilne.

slag [slæg] **1** *sb* slagg; **2** *vb* slagge(s).

slake [sleɪk] **I** *sb* leirvelling, slikk; **II** *vt* **1** slokke (tørste); **2** leske (kalk).

slam [slæm] **I** *sb* **1** smell; **2** slem (i kortspill); **II** *vb* smelle (med); *~ the door* smelle igjen døren; *~ on the brakes* hugge bremsene i.

slander ['slɑ:ndə] **1** *sb* bakvaskelse; ærekrenkelse; **2** *vt* bak|tale, -vaske; ærekrenke. **slanderous** ['slɑ:ndərəs] *adj* baktalersk; ærekrenkende.

slang [slæŋ] *adj, sb* slang(-).

slant [slɑ:nt] **I** *sb* **1** skråning (og skrå retning, strime, stripe etc); *on the ~* diagonalt; skrått; på skrå; **2** syns|punkt, -vinkel; **II** *vb* **1** helle, skråne; gi/ha skrå retning etc; falle skrått/på skrå; **2** gi bestemt retning/ tendens; *~ed news* fargede/tendensiøse nyheter.

slap [slæp] **I** *adv* bardus, bums; like, rett; **II** *sb* dask; slag (med flat hånd); klaps, klask, smekk; *a ~ in the face* et slag i ansiktet (dvs en stor skuffelse etc); **III** *vt* **1** daske, klaske; slå (med flat hånd); *get ~ped* få en smekk; **2** *(~ together/up)* smøre sammen/opp. **slap|dash** ['slæpdæʃ] **1** *adj* hastverks-, slurvet; **2** *adv* likeglad, uvørent. **~happy** *adj* likesæl, sorgløs. **~stick** ['slæpstɪk] **1** *adj* lavkomisk; **2** *sb (~ comedy)* grov farse; bløtkakekomedie. **~-up** *adj dgl* førsteklasses, super.

slash [slæʃ] **I** *sb* **1** flenge; dypt sår; (piske)slag; **2** splitt (i kjole/skjørt); **II** *vb* **1** flenge/snitte opp; piske, slå; *fig* kritisere sønder og sammen; **2** splitte opp (kjole/skjørt). **slashing** ['slæʃɪŋ] *adj fig* flengende.

slat [slæt] *sb* **1** sprinkel, sprosse; **2** list; ribbe, spile.

slate [sleɪt] **I** *sb* **1** skifer (og skifergrått); skiferstein; **2** tavle; a clean ~ et rent rulleblad (dvs en uplettet fortid); *start with a clean ~* begynne på et nytt blad (dvs et nytt og bedre liv); **II** *vt* **1** skifertekke; **2** *(US)* føre opp på dagsorden/program; foreslå; nominere.

slaughter ['slɔ:tə] **1** *sb* slakting; blodbad, nedslakting; **2** *vt* slakte (ned); drepe, massakrere. **slaughterer** ['slɔ:tərə] *sb* **1** slakter; **2** massemorder. **slaughter-house** *sb* slaktehus, slakteri.

slave [sleɪv] **1** *sb* slave, trell; **2** *vi* slave, trelle; *~ away at* slite/jobbe hardt med. **slave|-driver** *sb* slave|-driver (nå især *fig*). **~-market** *sb* slavemarked.

slaver ['slævə] **1** *sb* savl, sikkel; **2** *vb* savle/sikle (på). **slavery** ['sleɪvərɪ] *sb* slaveri, trelldom. **slave|-ship** *sb* slaveskip. **~-trade, ~-traffic** *sb* slavehandel. **slavish** ['sleɪvɪʃ] *adj* slavisk; slave-.

slay [sleɪ] *vt gml* slå i hjel; drepe. **slayer** ['sleɪə] *sb gml* banemann, drapsmann.

sleazy ['sli:zɪ] *adj* sjusket, slusket.

sled [sled] = *sledge A.* **sledge** [sledʒ] **A 1** *sb* kjelke; (mindre) slede); **2** *vb* ake; kjøre/trekke på kjelke etc; **B** *sb* = **sledge-hammer** ['sledʒ,hæmə] *sb* slegge.

sleek [sli:k] **1** *adj* glatt; blank, glinsende; *fig* sleip; **2** *vt* glatte; *~ oneself* fiffe seg (opp). **sleeky** ['sli:kɪ] *adj* glatt; sleip, slesk.

sleep [sli:p] **I** *sb* søvn; blund, lur; *go to ~* sovne; *in one's ~* i søvne; *put to ~* legge (for å få til å sove); få til å falle i søvn; **II** *vb* **1** sove; **~ in** bo på arbeidsstedet (dvs slik at man også sover der); forsove seg; sove lenge; **~ off** sove av seg; **~ out** ligge ut; overnatte utenfor hjemmet; *~ the clock* **round** sove rundt; **~ with** ligge (dvs ha samleie) med; **2** innkvartere; skaffe sengeplass til. **sleep-drugged** *adj* søvn|drukken, (-)ørsken. **sleeper** ['sli:pə] *sb* **1** sovende person; **2** sove|kupé, -vogn; **3** (jernbane)sville; *petro* rørsville. **sleeping** ['sli:pɪŋ] *adj* sovende, sove-. **sleeping|-accomodation** *sb* sove|plass; -kupé, -lugar. **~-bag** *sb* sovepose. **~-car** *sb* sovevogn. **~-compartment** *sb* sovekupé. **~-draught** *sb* sovedrikk. **~ partner** *sb* passiv deltaker/kompanjong. **~-pill** *sb* sovepille. **~-sickness** *sb* sovesyke. **sleep|less** *adj* søvnløs. **~-walker** *sb* søvngjenger. **sleepy** ['sli:pɪ] *adj* søvnig.

sleet [sli:t] *sb, vb* sludd(e). **sleety** ['sli:tɪ] *adj* sluddet; slapset, sørpet.

sleeve [sli:v] *sb* **1** erme; *have something up one's ~* ha noe/en trumf i bakhånden; *laugh up one's ~* le i skjegget; *turn up one's ~s* brette opp (skjorte)ermene; **2** hylse, muffe; mansjett; bøssing; **3** plateomslag (dvs til grammofonplate). **sleeve-link** *sb* mansjettknapp.

sleigh [sleɪ] **1** *sb* slede (især en som trekkes av hest); (større) kjelke; **2** *vb* frakte/kjøre med slede; ake. **sleigh-bells** *sb fl* dombjeller. **sleighing** ['sleɪɪŋ] *sb* slede|kjøring, -tur; kanefart.

sleight [slaɪt] *sb: ~-of-hand* knep, trick; fingerferdighet, taskenspilleri.

slender ['slendə] *adj* **1** slank; **2** *fig* spinkel; skrøpelig, svak.

slice [slaɪs] **I** *sb* **1** skive, plate; leiv; *~ of bread* brød|skive, -stykke; **2** andel, stykke; **3** spatel; *fish ~* fiskespade; **II** *vb* **1** *(~ up)* skjære i skiver; *~ off* flekke/ skrelle (av); **2** partere; dele opp; stykke ut.

slick [slɪk] **I** *adj* **1** glatt; *fig også* sleip; **2** elegant, flott; smart; **3** behendig, flink; **II** *sb* glatt flate/flekk etc; **III** *vt (~ up)* glatte (på); fiffe/pynte seg.

slide [slaɪd] **I** *sb* **1** glidning (og skrens; glide|bane, (-)renne; slisk; rutsjebane; akebakke, sklie; skliing etc); *land~* (jord)ras; *snow~* snøskred; **2** skyver; slede, sleid; glider; **3** lysbilde, slide; **4** hår|klemme, -spenne; **II** *vb* **1** gli (og la/få til å gli); skyve bortover; **2** ake; rutsje, skli; *let things ~* la det skure/stå til; **3** smyge, smøye; liste seg; *~ over* gå lett over. **slide |**

caliper *sb* skyvelære. ~ **fastener** *sb* glidelås. ~ **gauge** *sb* = ~ *caliper*. ~ **rule** *sb* regnestav. **sliding** ['slaɪdɪŋ] *som adj* glidende *etc*; skyve-. **sliding | bar** *sb* skyve|bom, (-)slå. ~ **bolt** *sb* skåte. ~ **caliper** *sb* = *slide caliper*. ~ **door** *sb* skyvedør. ~ **gauge** *sb* = *slide caliper*. ~ **rule** *sb* = *slide rule*. ~ **scale** *sb* glideskala.

slight [slaɪt] **I** *adj* **1** sped (og spedlemmet); spinkel; tynn; skrøpelig; **2** ubetydelig; lett, svak; liten; *not the ~est* ikke det ringeste/aller minste; **II** *sb* forbigåelse, tilsidesettelse; neglisjering; ringeakt; uhøflighet; **III** *vt* forbigå, overse; neglisjere; fornærme; ringeakte.

slim [slɪm] **I** *adj* **1** slank, tynn; **2** liten; svak, ubetydelig; **II** *vi* slanke seg. **slimming** ['slɪmɪŋ] *sb* slanking; slankekur.

slime [slaɪm] *sb* slim; dynn, gjørme. **slimy** ['slaɪmɪ] *adj* slimet.

sling [slɪŋ] **I** *sb* **1** slynge; *også* = *~shot*; **2** *a)* reim (især til å bære i, f.eks. skulderreim til veske); *gun~* geværreim; *b)* (kjetting)lenge; stropp; **3** armbind, fatle; **II** *vb* **1** slynge; kaste, slenge; **2** henge opp; *sjø* heise (opp). **slingshot** ['slɪŋʃɒt] *sb* sprettert.

slink [slɪŋk] *vi* (gå og) luske (lure, snike etc); smyge (seg).

slip [slɪp] **I** *sb* **1** glidning (og utglidning; (mindre) ras/skred; skrens, sluring etc); *give them the ~* lure seg/smette unna dem; **2** glipp; feil (og feiltrinn); lapsus; *~ of the pen* skrivefeil; *~ of the tongue* forsnakkelse; **3** (dyne)trekk; putevar; **4** under|kjole, -skjørt; **5** (papir)lapp, seddel; slipp; remse, strimmel; korrektur|flak, -spalte; **6** stikling; **7** *(~way)* (opphalings)|-bedding, (-)slipp; **8** leirvelling, slikker; **II** *vb* **1** gli (og skli, skrense, slure etc); glippe; smette, smutte; smyge; liste/snike seg; **2** feile; begå/gjøre en bommert/en (mindre) feil; **3** stikke til (dvs gi ubemerket); liste/smugle (til); **4** unn|gå, -slippe; *it has ~ped my attention* det har unngått min oppmerksomhet; *it has ~ped my mind* jeg har glemt det; **5** slippe (løs); **6** *med adv, prep* ~ **across** prakke på; *let* ~ **at** fare/gyve løs på; ~ **away** liste seg bort/vekk; slippe ubemerket unna; ~ **by** = ~ *past*; ~ **in** *the clutch* slippe (opp) clutchen; ~ **into** gli inn/ut i; smette inn/ut i; ~ *into one's clothes* hoppe i/kaste på seg klærne; ~ **off** *one's clothes* slenge/smøye av seg klærne; ~ **on** slenge/smøye på seg; *it just ~ped* **out** det bare glapp ut (av meg); ~ **over** fare/gli (lett) over; ~ *over on* = ~ *across*; ~ **past** smette forbi; *the years ~ped past* årene gikk (fort og umerkelig); *it ~ped* **through** *their fingers* det forsvant mellom fingrene/hendene på dem; ~ **up** gli (og miste fotfestet); begå/gjøre en bommert/en (mindre) feil. **slip|-bend** *sb* = *~-knot*. **~-cover** *sb* vare|bind, (-)trekk. **slip-knot** *sb* slippestikk. **~over** *sb* slippover. **slipper** [slɪpə] *sb* tøffel. **slippery** ['slɪpərɪ] *adj* glatt, sleip (også *fig*). **slip|-road** *sb* avkjøringsvei. **~shod** ['slɪpʃɒd] *adj* sjokkende, subbende; nedtrådt; sjusket, (til)sjasket. **~-stream** *sb* propellstrøm. **~-up** *sb* bommert, (mindre) feil.

slit [slɪt] **1** *sb* splitt; spalte, sprekk; revne, rift; **2** *vb* flenge (og klippe, skjære, snitte etc (opp)); flenges *etc* opp. **slit|-eyed** *adj* med smale øyne. **~-trench** *sb* skytter|grav, -grop.

slither ['slɪðə] *vi* gli, skli. **slithery** ['slɪðərɪ] *adj* glatt.

sliver ['slɪvə] **1** *sb* flis, splint; remse, strimmel; **2** *vb* flise(s) opp; skjære/bli skåret i remser etc.

slobber ['slɒbə] **I** *sb* savl, sikkel; *fig* sentimentalitet; rør, vrøvl; **II** *vb* **1** savle/sikle (på, utover etc); **2** skvalpe, skvulpe; søle.

slog [slɒg] *vb* **1** slå (hardt); **2** jobbe, slite. **slogger** ['slɒgə] *sb* sliter.

slogan ['sləʊgən] *sb* slagord; devise, motto.

sloop [slu:p] *sb sjø* slupp.

slop [slɒp] **A I** *sb* **1** søle|dam, -pytt; **2** skvett, tår; rest, slatt; **3** oppvaskvann; skyllevann; sølevann; **4** skyller; *fl* skvip, søl; **II** *vb* **1** spille, søle; skvalpe, skvulpe; skvette; **2** sjokke, subbe; **B** *sb* løstsittende klesplagg; *fl* sjømanns|klær, -utstyr; **C** *sb slang* purk (dvs politimann). **slop|-basin, ~-bowl** *sb* avfalls|-bolle, -skål; skyllebolle. **~-chest** *sb sjø* slappkiste (dvs kasse med klær etc som stuerten selger til mannskapet). **~-pail** *sb* skyllebøtte; toalettbøtte. **~-shop** *sb* klesbutikk (især for sjøfolk). **~-sink** *sb* utslagsvask.

slope [sləʊp] **I** *sb* helling, skråning; **II** *vb* **1** (la) helle/skråne; **2** ~ *off (dgl)* lure/luske seg unna; stikke av. **sloping** ['sləʊpɪŋ] *adj* skrånende.

slop oil *sb petro* sloppolje.

sloppy ['slɒpɪ] *adj* **1** gjørmet, sølet; **2** tynn, vassen; *fig* røret, sentimental; **3** sjusket, slurvet.

sloptank *sb petro* slopptank.

slosh [slɒʃ] **I** *sb* **1** skvalping, skvulping; **2** (vassing i) slaps/søle; **II** *vb* **1** skvalpe, skvulpe; søle; **2** *slang* delje/dra til.

slot [slɒt] **I** *sb* sprekk; sliss, spalte; spor (i skruehode); åpning; *data* (diskett)åpning; *put a coin in the ~* legge en mynt på automaten (jf *~-machine*); **II** *vb* **1** lage spalte/sprekk *etc* i; **2** bevege (seg) langs en sliss/et spor etc.

sloth [sləʊθ] *sb* **1** dovendyr; **2** dorskhet, treghet.

slot-machine *sb* (salgs- el. spille)automat.

slouch [slaʊtʃ] **I** *sb* **1** slapp holdning; *walk with a ~* gå og sjokke/subbe; **2** slamp, slappfisk; slask; **II** *vb* **1** gå/sitte slapt; sjokke, subbe; **2** henge slapt ned.

sloughing ['slʌfɪŋ] *sb petro* utvasking.

sloven ['slʌvn] *sb* slamp, slask; sjusket/slurvet person. **slovenly** ['slʌvnlɪ] *adj* sjusket, slurvet.

slow [sləʊ] **I** *adj* **1** langsom, sakte; sen; *be ~ to* være sen med (om, til etc) å; *my watch is ten minutes ~* klokken min går ti minutter for sakte; **2** lang|dryg, -tekkelig; **3** *fig* flau, laber; død; stille; **II** *adv* langsomt, sakte; sent; *go ~* ta det med ro; gå forsiktig til verks; gå sakte (især: sette ned (arbeids)|tempo, ytelse som middel i arbeidskonflikt); **III** *vb (~ down)* bli/gjøre langsommere; saktne/sette ned farten (på); forsinke, hefte. **slow|-down** *sb* nedsatt (arbeids)|tempo, (-)ytelse. **~-footed** *adj* som går langsomt/tungt.

~-going *adj* som tar det med knusende ro. ~ **motion** *sb* langsom kino; sakte film. ~ **train** *sb* somletog. ~-**witted** *adj* tungnem; dorsk, treg. ~**worm** *sb* stålorm.

sludge [slʌdʒ] *sb* **1** gjørme; slaps, sørpe; søle; **2** (olje)slam.

slug [slʌg] *sb* **A** snegle; *fig* lathans; **B** kule (til skytevåpen); **3** *vb US* delje/dra til; slå ned. **sluggard** ['slʌgəd] *sb* dovenpels, lathans. **slugger** ['slʌgə] *sb især US* **1** slåsskjempe; bølle; **2** proffbokser. **sluggish** ['slʌgɪʃ] *adj* dorsk, treg; doven, lat.

sluice [slu:s] **I** *sb* **1** sluse (og sluse|port, -renne, -vann etc); **2** mølle|bekk, -renne; tømmerrenne; **II** *vb* **1** sluse; føre/gå gjennom et sluseanlegg; **2** skylle, spyle; ~ *ore* vaske ut erts/malm; ~ *one's worries* drukne sorgene (sine). **sluice-gate** *sb* sluseport.

slum [slʌm] **1** *sb* fattigkvarter, slum|(distrikt, -strøk); **2** *vi: go ~ming* besøke slumdistriktene (av nysgjerrighet eller i veldedig øyemed). **slum clearance** *sb* (slum)|rehabilitering, (-)sanering.

slumber ['slʌmbə] **1** *sb* slummer, lett søvn; **2** *vi* slumre.

slump [slʌmp] **I** *sb* (plutselig) kurs-/prisfall; krakk; depresjon, nedgangs|periode, -tider; **II** *vi* **1** falle (og la seg falle el. sette seg) tungt; **2** falle brått (om kurser, priser etc).

slur [slɜ:] **I** *sb* **1** utydelig skrift/(ut)tale; **2** *mus* bindebue (i noteskrift); **3** *fig* flekk, plett; **II** *vb* **1** skrive/snakke utydelig; ~ *over* fare/gå lett over; **2** spille/synge legato; forsyne (noter) med bindebue; **3** rakke ned på.

slush [slʌʃ] *sb* **1** gjørme; slaps, sørpe; søle; **2** sentimentalt sludder; føleri.

slut [slʌt] *sb* **1** sjuske, slumse; **2** ludder.

sly [slaɪ] *adj* **1** lur; snedig, utspekulert; sleip, slu; **2** hemmelig (og hemmelighetsfull); *on the* ~ i smug.

smack [smæk] **A I** *adv* rett; like, lukt; bardus; **II** *sb* **1** dask, klask, smekk; smell; **2** smellkyss; **III** *vb* smekke/smelle med; dra (slå, smelle etc) til; ~ *one's lips* smatte (med leppene); **B 1** *sb* smak (og bismak, forsmak; smaksprøve); antydning, snev; **2** *vi* smake (*of* av); **C** *sb* fiske|skøyte, -smakke.

small [smɔ:l] **I** *adj* **1** liten (og kort, lav, små-; ubetydelig, dårlig, ringe etc); *fl* små; *feel* ~ føle seg liten (flat, flau etc); *in a* ~ *way* i all beskjedenhet; *not the ~est* ikke den/det minste/ringeste; *on the* ~ *side* i minste laget; **2** lav(mælt), spak; **3** = *~-minded*; **II** *adv* **1** smått; **2** lavt, lavmælt; spakt; **3** *think* ~ *of* ikke ha (særlig) høye tanker om; **III** *sb* **1** *the* ~ *of the back* korsryggen; *the* ~ *of the leg* smalleggen; **2** *fl* småting, småtteri(er); småplagg. **small** | **arms** *sb fl* hånd(skyte)våpen. ~ **beer** *sb* tynt øl; *fig* bagatell(er). ~ **change** *sb koll* skillemynt, småpenger; vekslepenger; *fig* bagateller. ~-**chequered** *adj* smårutet. ~ **craft** *sb koll* småbåter. ~-**holder** *sb* småbruker. *in the* ~ **hours** i de små timer. ~-**minded** *adj* smålig, småskåren. ~ **people** *sb koll* haugfolk, underjordiske. ~ **potatoes** *sb fl US dgl* bagateller. ~**pox** *sb* (sykdommen) kopper. ~-**scale** *adj, adv* i liten målestokk. ~**shot** *sb* null/ubetydelighet (dvs ubetydelig person). ~ **talk** *sb* småprating. ~**time** *adj dgl* ubetydelig; av dårlig kvalitet.

smart [smɑ:t] **I** *adj* **1** gløgg; skarp, smart; dyktig/flink (om enn ikke alltid helt hederlig); **2** oppvakt, våken; kjapp, rask, snar; **3** skarp, sviende; kraftig, sterk; heftig; **4** elegant; flott; fiks, smart; velkledd; **II** *sb* svie (og sviende smerte etc); *fig* lidelse, smerte; **III** *vi* svi; føle smerte; *fig* lide; *you shall* ~ *for this* dette skal du få svi for. **smarten** ['smɑ:tn] *vb (~ up)* fiffe (pynte, stelle etc) seg; fikse på. **smart** | **alec** *sb US dgl* blære, viktigper; *~-alec (adj)* blæret, viktig; oppesen.

smash [smæʃ] **I** *adv* med et brak; **II** *sb* **1** brak, smell; (voldsomt) slag; *go to* ~ gå i knas/i stykker; **2** knusing, ødeleggelse; ruin; **III** *vb* **1** gå/slå i stykker; (~ *up)* knuse, smadre; sprenge(s); *merk* gå konkurs; ~ *in* knuse; slå inn; ~ *into* brase (fare, smelle etc) inn i; **2** kaste (så noe knuses); kyle, slenge. **smash hit** *sb* knallsuksess. **smashing** ['smæʃɪŋ] *adj* **1** knusende (etc, jf *smash III*); **2** overveldende; fantastisk, flott, strålende; *dgl* dundrende. **smash-up** *sb* (kraftig) kollisjon/sammenstøt; sammenbrudd; *merk* konkurs.

smattering ['smætərɪŋ] *sb* overfladisk kjennskap/kunnskap (*of* om, til).

smear ['smɪə] **1** *sb* (fett)flekk; til|grising, -smøring; *fig* bakvaskelse; nedrakking, tilsvining; **2** *vt* kline/smøre utover: grise/skitne til; *fig* bakvaske; rakke ned (på); svine til. **smeary** ['smɪərɪ] *adj* fettet, klissen; tilsmurt.

smell [smel] **I** *sb* lukt (og luktesans); **II** *vb* **1** lukte, være; få teften av; ~ *at* lukte på; ~ *out* snuse frem/opp; *dgl* røyke ut; **2** (~ *of)* lukte (av). **smelling**|-**bottle** *sb* lukteflaske. ~-**salt** *sb* luktesalt. **smelly** ['smelɪ] *adj* (ille)luktende, stinkende.

smelt [smelt] *vt* smelte (jern etc).

smile [smaɪl] **1** *sb* smil; **2** *vb* smile (*at* til).

smirk [smɜ:k] **1** *sb* fett *etc* smil; **2** *vi* smile fett (selvtilfreds, sleskt, smørret etc).

smite [smaɪt] *vb gml* slå; *fig* hjemsøke/ramme (med plager etc); **2** drepe; slå i hjel.

smith [smɪθ] *sb* smed.

smithereens [ˌsmɪðə'ri:nz] *sb fl* småbiter; *blow (in)to* ~ sprenge i stumper og stykker.

smithy ['smɪðɪ] *sb* smie.

smock [smɒk] *sb* forkle/kittel *især med* **smocking** ['smɒkɪŋ] *sb* vaffelsøm.

smog [smɒg] *sb* røykblandet tåke (ordet er en sammentrekning av *smoke* og *fog*).

smoke [sməuk] **I** *sb* **1** røyk; *end in/vanish into* ~ gå opp i røyk; **2** røyk (dvs det å røyke, noe å røyke på); **II** *vb* **1** ryke; dampe, ose; **2** *a)* røyke (matvarer); *b)* røyke (tobakk etc); ~ *out* røyke ut; **3** røyk|beise, -sverte; sote (til); **4** *mil* røyklegge; *fig* tåkelegge. **smoke**|-**bomb** *sb* røykbombe. ~-**curtain** *sb* røykteppe. ~-**dried** *adj* røykt (om matvarer). ~-**grimed** *adj* røyksvertet. ~-**laden** *adj* røyk|full, -mettet. ~**less** *adj* røykfri. ~**point** *sb petro* røykpunkt. ~**proof** *adj* røyktett. **smoker** ['sməʊkə] *sb* **1** røyker; *heavy* ~ storrøyker; **2** røyke|kupé, -vogn. **smoke|-room** *sb* røyke|rom, -salong. **~-screen** *sb* røykteppe. **~stack** *sb* pipe, skorstein. **~-stand** *sb* pipestativ. **~tight** *sb* røyktett. **smoking** ['sməʊkɪŋ] **1** *adj a)* rykende; dampende, osende; *b)* røykende; røyke-; **2** *sb* røyking; *no* ~ røyking forbudt. **smoking|-car, ~ carriage** *sb* røykevogn. **~-compartment** *sb* røykekupé. **~-jacket** *sb* røykejakke. **~-room** *sb* røyke|rom, -salong. **smoky** ['sməʊkɪ] *adj* **1** rykende; dampende, osende; **2** røyk|full; -svart, -svertet; **3** tåket, tåke-.

smooth [smu:ð] **I** *adj* **1** glatt (og glattpolert, -slipt etc); jevn, slett; flat; *sjø* smul; **2** glatt (om tale); flytende; tungerapp; **2** *adv* glatt, jevnt *etc*; **III** *sb* **1** jevn/slett strekning; *sjø* smult farvann; **2** glatting; *give one's hair a* ~ glatte på håret; **IV** *vb* **1** (~ *down/out)* jevne, glatte (og jevne/glatte ut, glatte på etc); ~ *over* glatte over; **2** dempe, lette, mildne; berolige. **smooth|-shaven** *adj* glattbarbert. **~-spoken** *adj* **1** beleven; **2** *neds* = **~-tongued** *adj* glattunget; sleip, slesk.

smother ['smʌðə] **1** *sb* kvelende røyk(sky)/støvsky; **2** *vb* kvele (og kveles, holde på å bli kvalt); *fig* bekjempe, undertrykke.

smoulder ['sməʊldə] **1** *sb* ulming; ulmende ild; **2** *vi* ulme.

smudge [smʌdʒ] **I** *sb* **1** flekk (som er gnidd/klint utover); kluss(ing); **2** *US (~-fire)* osende/rykende bål; **II** *vb* **1** kline til; gni/smøre utover; **2** få til å ose/ryke.

smug [smʌg] *adj* selv|god, -tilfreds; dydsiret.

smuggle ['smʌgl] *vb* smugle. **smuggler** ['smʌglə] *sb* smugler. **smuggling** ['smʌglɪŋ] *sb* smugling.

smut [smʌt] **I** *sb* **1** sot|flak, -flekk; skitt, smuss; **2** griseprat, uanstendighet(er); **3** brann/rust (på planter); **II** *vb* **1** skitne til (især med sot); **2** *om planter* angripes av brann/rust; frembringe brann/rust. **smutty** ['smʌtɪ] *adj* **1** skitten, sotet; **2** griset, uanstendig; **3** *om planter* angrepet av brann/rust.

snack [snæk] **1** *sb* matbit (dvs lett måltid etc); **2** *vi* få seg en matbit.

snag [snæg] *sb* **1** gren/rot (etc som sitter fast i elvebunn etc og kan være farlig for mindre fartøyer); **2** *fig* aber, ulempe; hindring.

snail [sneɪl] **1** *sb* snegl; *at (a) ~'s pace* i/med sneglefart; **2** *vi* snegle seg (av sted).

snake [sneɪk] **1** *sb* slange, snok; *a ~ in the grass* en slange i paradiset (dvs en lurende fare/fiende); **2** *vi* sno seg (av sted). **snaky** ['sneɪkɪ] *adj* **1** slangeaktig, buktet; **2** listig, slu.

snap [snæp] **I** *adj* **1** brå, plutselig; overrumplende, overrumplings-; **2** forhastet, overilt; uoverlagt; **II** *sb* **1** glefs(ing); biting, bitt; napp(ing); **2** brudd, knekk; smekk, smell; klikk; **3** = *~-lock*; **4** kort periode; **5** lett jobb; **6** *dgl* fart, futt; tæl; **III** *vb* **1** bite/glefse (etter); ~ *at* gripe (nappe, snappe etc) etter; *fig også* knurre/snerre mot; ~ *up* rive til seg; snappe opp; **2** brekke, knekke; *dgl* ryke (dvs briste, gå i stykker); **3** knalle/smelle (med); klikke/smekke (med); knipse (med); ~ *to attention* slå hælene sammen (og stå i givakt); **4** *dgl:* ~ *(into) it* få opp farten; skynde seg. **snap|-fastener** *sb* trykknapp, trykklås. **~-hook** *sb* karabinkrok. **~-lock** *sb* smekklås; sneppert. **snappish** ['snæpɪʃ] *adj* barsk, morsk; bisk. **snappy** ['snæpɪ] *adj* **1** fiende, flott; kvikk, rask; smart; *make it* ~ la det gå litt kvikt; **2** = *snappish*. **snapshot** ['snæpʃɒt] *sb* **1** slengeskudd; **2** *foto* øyeblikksbilde.

snare [sneə] *sb, vt* (fange i) snare.

snarl [snɑ:l] **A 1** *sb (~ing)* knurring, snerring; **2** *vi* knurre/snerre (*at* mot); **B** *sb* floke, vase; rot, ugreie.

snatch [snætʃ] **I** *sb* **1** grep; snapping; *make a ~ at* gripe/snappe etter; **2** bit(e); *især* bruddstykke, stubb; *by/in ~es* rykkvis, stykkevis; *dgl* i rykk og (harde) napp; **II** *vb* gripe/snappe (*at* etter); *he was ~ed away* han ble revet bort (dvs av døden).

sneak [sni:k] **I** *sb* **1** lusking *etc*; **2** snik, usling; sladderhank; **3** *sport* markkryper; **II** *vb* **1** luske; liste seg; lure/snike seg; **2** ~ *it from them* lure det fra dem. **sneakers** ['sni:kəz] *sb fl* tennissko, turnsko.

sneer ['snɪə] **1** *sb* hånflir, kaldflir; hånlig/spydig bemerkning etc; **2** *vi* håne, spotte; ~ *at* flire hånlig av.

sneeze [sni:z] **1** *sb* nys(ing); **2** *vi* nyse; *not to be ~d at* ikke å forakte/forsmå.

snide [snaɪd] *adj* hånlig, nedsettende.

sniff [snɪf] *sb, vb* **1** snufs(e), snøft(e); **2** sniff(e).

snigger ['snɪgə] *sb, vb* knis(e).

snip [snɪp] **I** *sb* **1** (avklipt) bit/stykke; **2** *dgl* kupp, varp; **II** *vb* klippe/kutte (*off* av).

sniper ['snaɪpə] *sb* snikskytter.

snippet ['snɪpɪt] *sb* (avklipt) bit/stykke; *fl* små|biter, -stykker; *fig* brokker, bruddstykker.

snivel ['snɪvl] **1** *sb* snufs(ing); *dgl* snørr og tårer; **2** *vi* snufse; klynke, sutre.

snob [snɒb] *sb* snobb. **snobbery** ['snɒbərɪ] *sb* snobberi, snobbethet. **snobbish** ['snɒbɪʃ] *adj* snobbet.

snoop [snu:p] *vi* snoke; ~ *into* stikke nesen sin opp i. **snooper** ['snu:pə] *sb data* datasnok.

snooty ['snu:tɪ] *adj* snobbet, overlegen.

snooze [snu:z] **1** *sb* blund, lur; **2** *vi* ta seg en blund/lur.

snore [snɔ:] *sb, vb* snork(e).

snort [snɔ:t] **1** *sb* prust(ing) *etc*; **2** *vi* pruste; blåse, fnyse.

snot [snɒt] *sb vulg* snørr. **snotty** ['snɒtɪ] *adj vulg* snørret; *også* = *~-nosed* (snørr)hoven, overlegen.

snout [snaʊt] *sb* snute, tryne.

snow [snəʊ] **1** *sb* snø (og snø|fall, -vær etc); **2** *vb* snø; *fig* drysse/falle (som snø); *~ed in/up* innesnødd, nedsnødd; *we are ~ed under with letters* vi drukner/holder på å drukne i brev. **snow|ball** *sb* snøball. **~bank** *sb* snø|fonn, -kant; brøytekant. **~blind** *adj* snøblind. **~bound** *adj* innesnødd. **~-bunting** *sb* snøspurv. **~-capped, ~-clad, ~-covered** *adj* snø|dekt, -kledd; med snø på toppen(e). **~drift** *sb* snø|drive, -fonn. **~drop** *sb* snøklokke. **~fall** *sb* snø|fall, -vær. **~-fence**

sb snøgjerde, skjerm. **~field** *sb* snøvidde. **~flake** *sb* snøfnugg. **~-goggles** *sb fl* snøbriller. **~house** *sb* snø|-hus, -hytte. **~line** *sb* snøgrense. **~man** *sb* snømann. **~-mouse** *sb* snømus. **~-owl** *sb* snøugle. **~-plough** *sb* snøplog; *~-plough turn* (snø)plogsving. **~-removal** *sb* snørydding. **~-shoes** *sb fl* truger. **~slide** *sb* snøskred. **~storm** *sb* snøstorm (betyr på engelsk som oftest bare snø|fall, -vær). **~-white** *adj* snøhvit. **snowy** ['snəuɪ] *adj* snø|dekt, -hvit; snø-.

snub [snʌb] **A 1** *sb* irettesettelse; *dgl* overhaling, skrape, smekk; **2** *vt* bite av (dvs avbryte bryskt); sette på plass; gi en overhaling/skrape. **snub-nose** *sb* oppstoppernese; *~d* med oppstoppernese.

snuff [snʌf] **A 1** *sb* tanne; utbrent veke; **2** *vt* pusse lys (dvs trimme veken); *~ out* slokke/snyte (lys); *fig* kverke, ødelegge; **B I** *sb* **1** snus(tobakk); pris (snus); **2** snøft(ing); **3** *dgl: up to ~* i førsteklasses stand; i god form; **II** *vb* **1** snuse; bruke/ta snus; **2** snøfte; puste (inn) gjennom nesen. **snuff|-box** *sb* snusdåse. **~-coloured** *adj* snusbrun. **snuffers** ['snʌfəz] *sb fl* lysesaks. **snuffle** ['snʌfl] **1** *sb* snøvling; **2** *vi* snøvle; snufse.

snug [snʌg] **I** *adj* **1** koselig, lun; *be as ~ as a bug (in a rug) (dgl)* ha det som lusa i en skinnfell/som plommen i egget; **2** gjemt, skjult; trygt forvart; *keep it ~* holde det hemmelig; **3** ordentlig, skikkelig; ryddig; **4** stram, tettsittende; **II** *vi* = **snuggle** ['snʌgl] *vb* legge seg/ligge godt (koselig, lunt etc); krype sammen; *~ up to* krype (godt) inn til.

so [səu] **I** *adv* **1** *om grad, utstrekning etc* så; i den grad; *dgl ofte* sånn; *it was ~ kind of you* det var *så* snilt av deg; *why did you laugh ~?* hvorfor lo du/dere sånn? **2** *om måte etc* så (dvs sådan); slik (og slik som); sånn; på den/denne måten; *~ it is* slik er det; *ofte* det er riktig; det stemmer; *~ we have* det har vi; *ofte* det er riktig; det stemmer; *and ~ am I* det er jeg også; *I hope ~* jeg håper det; *it ~ happened that* det falt/traff seg slik at; **3** *en del uttrykk* **~ as to** for (på den måten) å; **~ far** så langt/vidt; *~ far, ~ good* (så langt er/var alt) vel og bra; *and* **~ forth** = *and ~ on*; **~ long!** ha det (bra så lenge)! **~ long as** så lenge som; når (hvis, om etc) bare; såfremt; *it's all* **~ much** *rubbish* det er bare tull alt sammen; *and* **~ on** og så videre; **~ that** slik at; **~ to say/speak** så å si; **~ what** hva så; **even ~** enda, likevel; **ever ~** *happy (etc)* hoppende glad (etc); **just ~** akkurat slik (og ikke annerledes); *the* **more** *~ as* så meget/mye mer som; *an hour* **or** *~* en times tid; en time eller så; **II** *konj* **1** derfor; av den grunn; så (= altså, ergo, følgelig etc); *it was late, ~ we went home* det var sent, (så) derfor gikk vi hjem; **2** så (...) altså; *~ you don't like it* (så) du liker den altså ikke.

soak [səuk] **I** *sb* **1** bløtning (og gjennombløtning, utbløtning etc); bløyte; **2** *dgl* skyllebøtte (dvs kraftig regnskur); **II** *vb* **1** (gjennom)|bløte(s), -væte(s); legge/ligge i bløt; bløte(s) ut; **2** *(~ up)* suge (opp); **3** sive/trenge (*into* inn/ned i; *through* gjennom).

so-and-so ['səunsəu] *sb* den og den (om person en ikke nevner navnet på); *you old ~!* din noksagt!

soap [səup] **1** *sb* såpe; **2** *vt* såpe inn; *fig* smigre; sleske for. **soap|-box** *sb* såpekasse (især som improvisert talerstol). **~bubble** *sb* såpeboble. **~-flakes** *sb fl* såpespon. **~-powder** *sb* såpepulver. **~-suds** *sb* såpe|-skum, -vann. **soapy** ['səupɪ] *adj* såpe- (og såpe|aktig, -lignende, -glatt etc); *fig* sleip, slesk.

soar [sɔ:] *vi* **1** sveve høyt; **2** stige (raskt, sterkt etc, f.eks. også om priser).

sob [sɒb] **1** *sb* hikst, hulk; **2** *vb* hikste/hulke (frem). **sob|story** *sb* rørende/sentimental historie. **~-stuff** *sb* tåredryppende artikkel/historie etc.

sober ['səubə] **I** *adj* **1** edru; **2** nøktern; rolig, sindig; edruelig; **3** dempet, diskret; *om farger etc også* mørk; **II** *vb (~ down)* bli/gjøre edru. **sobriety** [sə'braɪətɪ] *sb* beherskelse; nøkternhet.

so-called ['səukɔ:ld] *adj* såkalt.

soccer ['sɒkə] *dgl (fork* for *association fotball)* (vanlig) fotball.

sociability [ˌsəuʃə'bɪlətɪ] *sb* omgjengelighet *etc*. **sociable** ['səuʃəbl] *adj* omgjengelig; selskapelig (anlagt); selskaps- (dvs med evne til å omgås folk). **social** ['suʃl] **I** *adj* **1** samfunns-, sosial(-); *from a ~ point of view* samfunnsmessig sett; *of ~ importance* samfunns|gagnlig, -viktig; **2** selskapelig, selskaps-; *~ conventions* omgangsformer; *meet ~ly/in a ~ way* ha selskapelig omgang med; **II** *sb* (selskapelig) sammenkomst. **Social Democrat** *sb* sosialdemokrat. **social | science** *sb* samfunns|fag, -vitenskap. **~ security** *sb* sosialtrygd; ≈ folke|pensjon, -trygd. **~ worker** *sb* sosialarbeider. **socialism** ['səuʃelɪzəm] *sb* sosialisme. **socialist** ['səuʃəlɪst] **1** *adj* sosialistisk; **2** *sb* sosialist. **socialistic** [ˌsəuʃə'lɪstɪk] *adj* sosialistisk. **socialization** [ˌsəuʃəlaɪ'zeɪʃn] *sb* sosialisering. **socialize** ['səuʃəlaɪz] *vt* sosialisere. **society** [sə'saɪətɪ] *sb* **1** samfunn (og samfunnet); *class of ~* samfunnsklasse; *pillars of ~* samfunnsstøtter; **2** selskap (dvs omgang, samvær etc); *Society* sosieteten; **2** forening; forbund, selskap; *co-operative ~* andels|lag, -selskap; samvirkelag. **sociological** [ˌsəusɪə'lɒdʒɪkl] *adj* sosiologisk. **sociologist** [ˌsəusɪ'ɒlədʒɪst] *sb* sosiolog. **sociology** [ˌsəusɪ'ɒlədʒɪ] *sb* sosiologi.

sock [sɒk] **A** *sb* **1** sokk; kort strømpe; *pull one's ~s up* ta seg sammen; **2** innleggssåle; **B** *slang* **1** *adv* dønn, rett; *~ in the eye* rett i øyet; **2** *sb* slag, teve; **3** *vt* dra til (dvs slå hardt).

socket ['sɒkɪt] *sb* **1** holder; sokkel; hylse, hylster; kapsel; **2** stikkontakt; **3** øyenhule; hofteskål, leddhule.

sod [sɒd] *sb* (gress)torv.

soda ['səudə] *sb* soda (og sodavann); *baking ~* bakepulver. **soda|-fountain** *sb* (soda)sifong; *især US* isbar. **~-water** *sb* soda(vann), selters.

sodden ['sɒdn] *adj* **1** gjennom|bløt, -våt; **2** *om brød etc* deiget; med rårand; tung.

sodium ['səudɪəm] *sb* natrium.

soft [sɒft] **I** *adj* **1** bløt, myk; **2** blid, mild, nennsom; dempet, svak; **3** svak, veik; pyset, ømskinnet; **4** lett (å behandle, utføre etc); **5** alkoholfri; **II** *som adv* bløtt, mykt; **III** *sb* = *~ness*. **soft|-boiled** *adj* bløtkokt. **~ copy** *sb data* skjermbilde. **~ currency** *sb* bløt valuta. **~ data** *sb fl data* mykdata. **~ drink** *sb* (alkoholfri) drikk; fruktsaft; mineralvann. **soften** ['sɒfn] *vb* **1** bli/gjøre bløt (etc, jf *soft I*); **2** blidgjøre, formilde; mildne; *~ up* myke opp (især *fig*). **soft | error** *sb data* mykfeil. **~-footed** *adj* stillfarende. **~-headed** *adj* dum(snill); tosket, tåpelig. **~-hearted** *adj* godhjertet; snill; varm. **~ hyphen** *sb data* myk bindestrek. **~ job** *sb* lett/makelig jobb. **~ key** *sb data* programmerbar tast. **~ light** *sb* dempet (bløtt, mildt etc) lys. **~ music** *sb* dempet/svak musikk. **~ness** ['sɒftnɪs] *sb* bløthet (etc, jf *soft I*). **~ option** *sb* behagelig alternativ; ≈ minste motstands vei. **~ palate** *sb* bløt gane. **~-pedal** *sb* spille (piano) med demperpedal/moderator; *fig* moderere seg; uttale seg forsiktig/med forbehold. **~ soap** *sb* grønnsåpe; *fig* smiger. **~-soap** *vt* smigre; smiske for. **~-spoken** *adj* lavmælt; blid, vennlig. **~ spot** *sb* ømt punkt (især *fig*). **~ware** *sb data* program(vare). **~ware compatible** *adj data* programkompatibel. **~ware package** *sb data* programpakke. **~wood** *sb* (bløte tresorter som) furu, gran.

soggy ['sɒgɪ] *adj* vasstrukken; rå, tung.

soil [sɔɪl] **A** *sb* jord (og jordbunn, jordsmonn etc); *set foot on Norwegian ~* sette foten på norsk jord; **B 1** *sb* møkk, skitt; ekskrementer; gjødsel; **2** *vb* bli/gjøre skitten; grise/rakke til.

sojourn ['sɒdʒn] *bokl* **1** *sb* (kort) opphold; **2** *vi* gjøre et (kort) opphold; oppholde seg (for en tid).

solace ['sɒlɪs] **1** *sb* trøst; **2** *vt* trøste.

solar ['səʊlə] *adj* solar(-), sol-; *the ~ system* solsystemet.

solas equipment ['səʊləs] *sb petro etc* redningsutstyr (*solas* står for *safety of life at sea*).

solder ['sɒldə] **1** *sb* lodde|metall, -tinn; **2** *vt* lodde. **soldering-iron** *sb* loddebolt.

soldier ['səʊldʒə] **1** *sb* soldat; *også fig* kriger, stridsmann; *~ of fortune* lykkeridder; *~'s pay* sold, soldatlønn; **2** *vi* tjene som/være soldat. **soldiering** ['səʊldʒərɪŋ] *sb* militær|liv, -tjeneste; krigerliv. **soldierlike** ['səʊldʒəlaɪk], **soldierly** ['səʊldʒəlɪ] *adj* **1** soldat-, soldater-; kriger-; militær(-); **2** kjekk, tapper. **soldiery** ['səʊldʒərɪ] *sb* krigsfolk, militære.

sole [səʊl] **A** *adj* **1** ene, eneste; *for the ~ purpose of* ene og alene/utelukkende for å; **2** ene-, eneste; **B 1** *sb* såle (dvs fotsåle, skosåle etc); **2** *vt* (halv)såle; **C** *sb* tunge(flyndre). **solely** ['səʊlɪ] *adv* alene; ene og alene; utelukkende. **sole | right** *sb* enerett. **~ risk** *sb petro* egenrisiko. **~ woman** *sb* enslig kvinne.

solemn ['sɒləm] *adj* alvorlig, alvorsfull; høytidelig. **solemnity** ['sə'lemnətɪ] *sb* **1** høytidelighet; **2** seremoniell; høytidelige seremonier. **solemnize** ['sɒləmnaɪz] *vt* feire (høytidelig); forestå høytidelighet; forrette (ved).

solicit [sə'lɪsɪt] *vb* **1** anmode/be (inntrengende) om; utbe seg; **2** antaste/slå an med (især om prostituertes gatetrafikk); *også* trekke. **solicitation** [sə,lɪsɪ'teɪʃn] *sb* anmodning/bønn (etc, jf *solicit*). **soliciting** [sə'lɪsɪtɪŋ] *sb* (prostituertes) gatetrafikk. **solicitor** [sə'lɪsɪtə] *sb* **1** *GB* advokat; juridisk rådgiver; *Solicitor General* ≈ regjeringsadvokat, riksadvokat; **2** *US* kunde|besøker, -verver; *pol* stemmeverver; agitator. **solicitous** [sə'lɪsɪtəs] *adj* **1** bekymret/engstelig (*about/for* for); **2** ivrig (*to* etter å). **solicitude** [sə'lɪsɪtju:d] *sb* bekymring, engstelse; omsorg.

solid ['sɒlɪd] **I** *adj* **1** fast (dvs i fast form); **2** massiv; bastant; tung; *om metaller etc også* gedigen; **3** solid; kraftig, sterk; holdbar; **4** pålitelig; velfundert; vektig; *også* solid; **5** sammenhengende; ubrutt, udelt; *three ~ hours* tre hele/stive (klokke)timer; **6** enstemmig; **7** *fys, mat* fast, tredimensjonal; kubikk-; **II** *sb* fast legeme/stoff. **solidarity** [,sɒlɪ'dærətɪ] *sb* solidaritet. **solid | fuel** *sb* fast brensel/drivstoff. **~ gold** *sb* rent gull. **solidify** [sə'lɪdɪfaɪ] *vb* bli/gjøre fast (etc, jf *solid I*); (få til å) stivne/størkne; *fig* konsolidere. **solidity** [sə'lɪdətɪ] *sb* fasthet (etc, jf *solid I*); soliditet. **solid | measure** *sb* kubikkmål (for f.eks. tømmer). **~ propellant** *sb* fast drivstoff. **~ vote** *sb* enstemmighet.

soliloquize [sə'lɪləkwaɪz] *vb* snakke med seg selv; *teat* holde enetale/monolog. **soliloquy** [sə'lɪləkwɪ] *sb* enetale, monolog. **solitaire** [,sɒlɪ'teə] *sb US* og *gml GB* kabal. **solitary** ['sɒlɪtərɪ] *adj* **1** eneste; en (enkelt); enkelt-; *a ~ case* et enkelttilfelle; **2** alene, enslig; ensom; **3** ensomt beliggende; *også* øde. **solitary confinement** *sb* enecelle, isolat. **solitude** ['sɒlɪtju:d] *sb* ensomhet; ensom beliggenhet. **solo** ['səʊləʊ] **1** *adj, adv* solo(-); **2** *sb* solo (og solo|forestilling, -opptreden etc). **soloist** ['səʊləʊɪst] *sb* solist.

solstice ['sɒlstɪs] *sb* solverv.

solubility [,sɒlju'bɪlətɪ] *sb* oppløselighet. **soluble** ['sɒljʊbl] *adj* **1** oppløselig; **2** = *solvable*. **solution** [sə'lu:ʃn] *sb* **1** *kjemi* (opp)løsning (både om prosessen og produktet); **2** *fig* løsning (på oppgave etc). **solvable** ['sɒlvəbl] *adj* som kan løses (forklares, oppklares etc). **solve** [sɒlv] *vt* løse (oppgave etc); oppklare. **solvency** ['sɒlvənsɪ] *sb merk* solvens. **solvent** ['sɒlvənt] **I** *adj* **1** oppløsende, oppløsnings-; **2** *merk* solvent; **II** *sb* løsemiddel, (opp)løsningsmiddel.

sombre ['sɒmbə] *adj* dyster, mørk.

some [sʌm, səm] **I** *adj, pron* **1** noe (og noen; enkelte, somme, visse; litt, en del etc); **2** en (eller annen); et (eller annet); *~ other day/time* en annen dag/gang; *in ~ way or other* på en eller annen måte; **3** nokså mange/mye; en god del; *of ~ importance* av en viss betydning; **4** *US* ordentlig, skikkelig; real; *~ woman* litt av et kvinnfolk; **II** *adv* cirka, omtrent; rundt regnet; *~ ten years ago* for om lag ti år siden. **some|body** ['sʌmbədɪ] *pron* **1** noen; en (eller annen); **2** noe til jente/kar etc; *he thinks he is (a) ~body* han tror han er noe. **~how** ['sʌmhaʊ] *adv* **1** på en (eller annen) måte; **2** (*~how or other*) av en eller annen grunn. **~one** ['sʌmwʌn] = *somebody*. **~place** ['sʌmpleɪs] *adv US dgl* et (eller annet) sted.

somersault ['sʌməsɔ:lt] *sb, vb* (slå) kollbøtte/saltomortale.

some|thing ['sʌmθɪŋ] *adv, pron* noe; et (ellet annet); *~thing like* noe i likhet med; *~thing of a hero* litt/noe av en helt; *tell me ~thing* si meg en ting; *you've got ~thing there* du er inne på noe der. **~time** ['sʌmtaɪm] **1** *adj gml* forhenværende, tidligere; **2** *adv* en (eller annen) gang. **~times** ['sʌmtaɪmz] *adv* av og til; iblant, stundom. **~way** ['sʌmweɪ] *adv* = *~how*. **~what** ['sʌmwɒt] **1** *adv* litt, noe; ganske, nokså; *~what surprised* en smule overrasket; **2** *pron* noe. **~where** ['sʌmweə] *adv* et (eller annet) sted; etsteds, noesteds; *~where about/around* et sted i nærheten av (dvs cirka, omtrent, om lag).

son [sʌn] *sb* sønn. **son-in-law** *sb* svigersønn.

song [sɒŋ] *sb* sang; *også* vise; dikt, vers; *buy/sell for a ~* kjøpe/selge for en slikk og en ingenting; *nothing to make a ~ about (dgl)* ingenting å skrive hjem om (dvs gjøre noe vesen av). **song|bird** *sb* sangfugl. **~-book** *sb* sangbok. **songster** ['sɒŋstə] *sb* **1** sanger; **2** sangfugl.

sonic ['sɒnɪk] *adv* sonisk, lyd-. **sonic bang, ~ boom** *sb* brak som høres når fly går gjennom lydmuren.

sonnet ['sɒnɪt] *sb* sonette.

sonny ['sɒnɪ] *sb* lillegutt, småen.

sonorous ['sɒnərəs] *adj* fulltonende, klangfull; sonor.

soon [su:n] *adv* **1** snart; *~ after* like etter; *~er or later* før eller senere/siden; *as/so ~ as* så snart som; *no ~er ... than* ikke før ... så; *the ~er the better* jo før jo heller; **2** tidlig; **3** *(just) as ~* heller, snarere; like gjerne.

soot [su:t] **1** *sb* sot; **2** *vt* sote (ned/til).

sooth [su:θ] *sb bokl, gml* sannhet; *in ~* i sannhet. **soothe** [su:ð] *vt* **1** berolige; **2** lindre, mildne. **soother** ['su:ðə] *sb (baby ~)* narresmokk. **soothsayer** ['su:θseɪə] *sb* sannsiger(ske); spå|kone, -mann.

sooty ['su:tɪ] *adj* **1** sotet, sotsvart; **2** svartsmusket.

sop [sɒp] **I** *sb* **1** oppbløtt brød(bit); **2** godbit (især som bestikkelse/smøring); **3** *(milk~)* pyse, spjæling; **II** *vt* bløte (ved å dyppe i melk, suppe etc); *~ up* suge/tørke opp.

sophisticated [sə'fɪstɪkeɪtɪd] *adj* **1** fin (og især forfinet); **2** raffinert, sofistikert; verdens|erfaren, -vant; **3** affektert, tilgjort.

sopping wet ['sɒpɪŋ], **soppy** ['sɒpɪ] *adj* klissvåt, søkkvåt.

sorcerer ['sɔ:sərə] *sb* trollmann. **sorceress** ['sɔ:sərəs] *sb* heks, trollkvinne. **sorcery** ['sɔ:sərɪ] *sb* hekseri, trolldom.

sordid ['sɔ:dɪd] *adj* **1** skitten, snusket; dyster, skummel; **2** simpel, smålig.

sore [sɔ:] **I** *adj* **1** sår, øm; *have a ~ throat* være sår i halsen; **2** pinlig, smertelig; **3** sår (til sinns); *with a ~ heart* med tungt hjerte; **4** ergerlig, forurettet; sur; **5** *gml (også* som *adv)* svare, såre; *in ~ distress* i bitter/dyp nød; **II** *sb* sår (og sårt sted, ømt punkt etc). **sorely** ['sɔ:lɪ] *adv* **1** sårt (etc, jf *sore I*); **2** sterkt, svært (jf *sore I 5*). **sorehead** *sb* grinebiter.

sorority [sə'rɒrətɪ] *sb* **1** søsterskap; *rel* nonneorden; **2** *US* (akademisk) kvinneforening.

sorrel ['sɒrl] *sb* **A** **1** *adj* fuksrød, rødbrun; **2** *sb* fuks (= fuksrød hest); **B** *sb* gaukesyre.

sorrow ['sɒrəʊ] **1** *sb* sorg; **2** *vi* sørge. **sorrowful** *adj* sorg|full, -tung; sørgelig. **sorry** ['sɒrɪ] *adj* **1** bedrøvet, lei (seg); *som interj* beklager! dessverre! unnskyld! *be ~ for* være lei seg for; synes synd på; *feel ~ for* føle med; synes synd på; *he'll be ~ for this* dette skal han få angre på; *I'm ~ to hear that* det gjør meg vondt å høre at; *I'm ~ to say that* jeg beklager å måtte si at; **2** elendig, ynkelig; bedrøvelig, jammerlig.

sort [sɔ:t] **I** *sb* **1** slags, sort; type; *all ~s of* alle slags; *nothing of the ~* ikke tale om; langt ifra; slett ikke; *of a ~/~ of (dgl)* en/et slags; *that ~ of people* den slags folk/mennesker; *this ~ of thing/these ~ of things* den slags ting; **2** måte, vis; *I ~ of thought that (dgl)* jeg tenkte nærmest at; jeg tenkte på en måte at; **3** *dgl* type; *a decent ~* en skikkelig (bra, hyggelig etc) fyr; **4** *dgl: out of ~s* i dårlig humør; ute av lage; **II** *vb* **1** *(~ over/out)* sortere (og sortere fra, ut etc); **2** passe; *~ with* omgås; vanke sammen med; *~ ill/well with* passe (gå, stå etc) dårlig/godt til. **sort | key** *sb data* sorteringsnøkkel. **~ pass** *sb data* sorteringstrinn.

soul [səʊl] *sb* sjel; *heart and ~* (med) liv og lyst; *keep body and ~ together* (så vidt) opprettholde livet; få endene til å møtes.

sound [saʊnd] **A** *adj* **1** sunn (og frisk); *a ~ mind in a ~ body* en sunn sjel i et sunt legeme; *safe and ~* i god behold; **2** grunnfestet, solid; vederheftig; **3** omhyggelig; dyktig, flink; **4** grundig; ordentlig, skikkelig; *a ~ beating* en real omgang juling; **5** *også adv: be ~ asleep* sove dypt/trygt; **B I** *sb* lyd; *it has a suspicious ~* det lyder mistenkelig; **II** *vb* **1** klinge; gi lyd; høres, lyde; *dgl* låte; **2** få til å klinge *etc*; la lyde; *~ a bell* ringe med en klokke; *~ a gong* slå på en gongong; *~ a trumpet* blåse på en trompet; **3** uttale; si, ytre; *you don't ~ the h in hour* man uttaler ikke h-en i *hour*; **4** prøve/teste (ved å slå på og lytte til klangen); **C** *vb* **1** lodde; peile (dybden av); **2** sondere, undersøke; *~ out* spørre ut; **B** *sb* **1** strede, sund; **2** svømmeblære. **sound | barrier** *sb* lydmur. **~ effects** *sb fl* lyd|effekter, kulisser; kontentum. **~-film** *sb* lydfilm. **sounding** ['saʊndɪŋ] *sb* lodding (jf *sound C 1*); *fl a)* loddefarvann; *b)* dybdeforhold; loddet dybde. **sounding|-line** *sb* lodd(e)line. **~-rod** *sb* peilestav. **sound | intensity** *sb* lydstyrke. **~less** *adj* **A** lydløs; **B** bunnløs (dvs loddet når ikke bunnen (jf *C 1*). **~proof** *adj* lyd|isolert, tett. **~-track** *sb* lydspor (på film etc). **~-wave** *sb* lydbølge.

soup [su:p] *sb* suppe; *in the ~ (dgl)* i klisteret (dvs i vanskeligheter). **soup|-kitchen** *sb* suppekjøkken (f.eks. som ledd i hjelp til katastroferammede). **~-plate** *sb* dyp tallerken.

sour ['saʊə] **I** *adj* sur; *fig også* gretten, grinet; **II** *vb* **1** bli/gjøre sur; surne; **2** for|bitre, -sure.

source [sɔ:s] *sb* **1** kilde, utspring; **2** kilde, opphav; *~ of information* (informasjons)kilde. **source | code** *sb data* kildekode. **~ language** *sb* kildespråk (dvs det språket noe opprinnelig er uttrykt på eller oversettes fra, jf *target language*). ~ **listing** *sb data* programliste. ~ **program** *sb data* kildeprogram.

sour crude *sb petro* høysvovelråolje.

souse [saus] *vb* **1** *a)* over|skylle, -sprøyte (med vann); *b)* legge i vann; **2** legge (ned) i (salt)lake.

south [sauθ] **I** *adj* sør(-), søndre(-); sørlig; sønna-; **II** *adv* **1** sørover; ~ *of* sør for; **2** sørpå; **III** *sb* sør; *the South* Syden; *US* sørstatene; *to the* ~ *of* sør for. **southerly** ['sʌðəlı] *adj, adv* **1** sørlig; fra sør; sønna-; **2** mot sør. **southern** ['sʌðən] *adj* sørlig; søndre, sør-. **southerner** ['sʌðənə] *sb* **1** sydlending; **2** *US: Southerner* sørstatsamerikaner. **southward** ['sauθwəd] *adj* sørlig (dvs mot sør). **southwards** ['sauθwədz] *adv* sørover; mot sør. **sou(th)-wester** *sb* **1** [sau(θ)'westə] sørvestvind; **2** [sau'westə] sydvest (dvs regnværsplagget).

sovereign ['sɒvrın] **I** *adj* **1** suveren; enerådende; uovertruffen; **2** effektiv, probat; **II** *sb* **1** suveren (hersker); monark; **2** sovereign (= gammel gullmynt, se midtsidene). **sovereignty** ['sɒvrəntı] *sb* suverenitet *etc.*

sow A [səu] *vb* så (og så ut, tilså etc); **B** [sau] *sb* purke. **sower** ['səuə] *sb* såmann. **sowing-machine** *sb* såmaskin.

space [speıs] **I** *sb* **1** *fys* rom; (verdens)rommet; *som adj* rom-; **2** plass, rom; *i avis* spalteplass; *leave* ~ *for* sette av plass til; la det stå (igjen) et åpent rom for; **3** avstand, mellomrom; *empty* ~ tomrom; **4** tidsrom; periode, stund; **II** *vt* anbringe (ordne, plassere etc) med visse mellomrom. **space|-bar** *sb* mellomromstast, ordskiller (på skrivemaskin etc). ~ **character** *sb data* mellomromstegn. **~-capsule** *sb* romkapsel. **~-craft** *sb* = *~-ship.* ~ **key** *sb data* = ~ *bar.* **~-probe** *sb* rakettsonde, romsonde. **~-rocket** *sb* romrakett. **~-ship** *sb* romskip. **~-station** *sb* romstasjon. **~-suit** *sb* romdrakt. ~ **travelling** *sb* romfart. **spacing** ['speısıŋ] *sb* mellomrom; (innbyrdes) avstand. **spacious** ['speıʃəs] *adj* rommelig; vid; vidstrakt, utstrakt.

spade [speıd] **A 1** *sb* spade; *call a ~ a ~* kalle en spade for en spade (dvs nevne tingene ved deres rette navn); **2** *vt* spa (og spa løs, opp etc); **B** *sb* spar (i kort); *ace of* ~ sparess. **spadework** *sb* (forberedende) grovarbeid.

span [spæn] **I** *sb* **1** spann (= ca 9 tommer, dvs 23 cm, egtl avstanden mellom spissen av tommelen og lillefingeren når de strekkes ut); **2** spenn(vidde); brospenn; **3** spann (av tid); tidsrom; **4** *især US* spann (av okser etc); **II** *vt* **1** måle i spann (jf *I 1*); **2** spenne om/over; strekke seg over/rundt.

spangle ['spæŋgl] **1** *sb* paljett; **2** *vt* besette/pynte med paljetter; *star-~d* stjerne|besatt, -bestrødd, -(be)sådd.

spaniel ['spænıəl] *sb* (hunderasen) spaniel.

spank [spæŋk] **I** *sb (~ing)* bank, juling (især om en enkelt dask etc); **II** *vt* **1** klaske/slå (med flat hånd); denge, jule; **2** skyte god fart; strekke godt ut. **spanking** ['spæŋkıŋ] **1** *adj dgl* (feiende) flott; lekker, smart; **2** *sb* juling.

spanner ['spænə] *sb* skrunøkkel.

spar [spɔ:] **A** *sb sjø* rundholt (til master, rær etc); **B** *vi* **1** sparre (i boksing); **2** krangle, trette.

spare [speə] **I** *adj* **1** ekstra(-), reserve-; **2** mager; tynn (og senet); **3** knapp, snau; sparsom; **II** *vb* **1** skåne (og skåne for); forskåne; ~ *their lives* spare livet deres; **2** spare på; bruke forsiktig; være forsiktig med; ~ *no expense/pains* ikke sky noen utgifter/anstrengelse; *she doesn't ~ herself* hun sparer seg ikke; **3** avse, unnvære; *to* ~ til overs; *enough/plenty and to* ~ mer en nok. **spare | bed** *sb* ekstraseng, gjesteseng. ~ **bedroom** *sb* gjesteværelse. ~ **parts** *sb fl* reservedeler. **~-rib** *sb* ≈ (mager) ribbe. **~time** *sb* fritid; ledige stunder. ~ **tyre,** ~ **wheel** *sb* reserve|dekk, -hjul. **sparing** ['speərıŋ] *adj* sparsom(melig), økonomisk; nøysom; ~ *of words* fåmælt, ordknapp; *use ~ly* bruke forsiktig/med måte.

spark [spɑ:k] **1** *sb* gnist; **2** *vi* gnistre; slå gnister; *om forbrenningsmotor* tenne; ~ *off (fig)* starte, utløse; sette i gang. **spark(ing)-plug** *sb* tennplugg. **sparkle** ['spɑ:kl] **1** *sb* gnist(ring); (lys)glimt; **2** *vi* gnistre; glimte, glitre; lyne; *om musserende vin* perle, skumme, sprudle.

sparrow ['spærəu] *sb* spurv.

sparse [spɑ:s] *adj* glissen/spredt (om befolkning, vegetasjon etc); sparsom; tynn.

spasm ['spæzəm] *sb* **1** krampe, spasme; **2** anfall, ri. **spasmodic** [spæz'mɒdık] *adj* krampaktig, spasmodisk. **spastic** ['spæstık] **1** *adj* spastisk; **2** *sb* spastiker.

spate [speıt] *sb* **1** sterk strøm; plutselig flom/oversvømelse; **2** *fig* flom, vell.

spatial ['speıʃl] *adj* romlig, rom-.

spatter ['spætə] **1** *sb* skvett(ing); sprut, stenk; **2** *vb* skvette/sprute (på); søle (til).

spawn [spɔ:n] **I** *sb* **1** (fiske)rogn; (froske)egg; **2** (fiske)yngel; *fig, især neds* unger; avkom, yngel; **II** *vb* **1** gyte; yngle; *om fisk også* leke; **2** *især neds* yngle; frembringe/produsere i store mengder; klekke ut.

speak [spi:k] *vb* **1** snakke; *mer bokl* tale; **2** uttale seg; si, ytre; ~ *one's mind/piece* snakke rett ut/rett fra leveren; si meningen sin; *so to* ~ så å si; **3** tale (dvs holde foredrag/tale); **4** *med adv, prep* ~ **about** snakke/tale om; ~ **for** uttale seg i favør av/til fordel for; tale for; vitne om; ~ *for oneself* snakke for seg selv; ~ **of** snakke/tale om; *nothing to ~ of* ikke noe å snakke om (dvs uten betydning); ~ **out** snakke ut; snakke høyt (høyere, tydelig(ere) etc); ~ **to** snakke med; henvende seg/snakke til; ~ **up** gripe/ta ordet; snakke høyt/høyere; ~ *up for* ta til orde for; ~ **well** snakke godt (for seg); ha en behagelig stemme. **speakeasy** ['spi:kˌi:zı] *sb US* smugler|bar, -kneipe (dvs som selger/solgte smuglerbrennevin). **speaker** ['spi:kə] *sb* **1** taler; den som snakker/sier noe; **2** ordstyrer; *parl etc* for|kvinne, -mann; president. **speaking** ['spi:kıŋ] **I** *adj* **1** talende (etc, jf *speak*); tale-; ~ *for myself* jeg for min del; *be on ~ terms with* være på talefot med; *gene-*

rally ~ stort sett; i det store og hele; *roughly* ~ grovt sagt; *seriously* ~ alvorlig talt; *strictly* ~ strengt tatt; *within* ~ *range (især sjø)* på praiehold; **2** *(i telefonen) Could I* ~ *to Mrs Smith, please? - Speaking.* Kunne jeg få snakke med Mrs Smith? - Det er meg. *John Brown* ~ Det(te) er John Brown. **II** *sb* **1** snakk(ing), tale; *in a manner of* ~ på en (viss) måte; så å si; **2** (politisk) møte.

spear ['spɪə] **I** *sb* **1** spyd; lanse; **2** lyster, lystregaffel; **II** *vt* **1** gjennombore/spidde (med spyd etc); **2** lystre. **spearhead** ['spɪəhed] **I** *sb* **1** spyd|blad, -odd, -spiss; **2** *mil* angrepsspiss, støttropper; **II** *vt* danne/være angrepsspiss for; gå i brodden/spissen for.

special ['speʃl] **1** *adj* spesiell; særlig, sær-; ekstra(-), spesial-; **2** *sb* noe ekstra/spesielt (som f.eks. ekstra|nummer, tog, -utgave); *today's* ~ dagens rett. **special delivery** *som adj, adv US* ekspress-, il-. **specialist** ['speʃəlɪst] *sb* spesialist; *som adj* spesialist-; spesial-. **speciality** [ˌspeʃɪ'ælətɪ] *sb* **1** spesiale/spesialitet (dvs spesiell vare, virksomhet etc); **2** sær|egenhet, -kjenne, -merke. **specialization** [ˌspeʃəlaɪ'zeɪʃn] *sb* spesialisering. **specialize** ['speʃəlaɪz] *vb* spesialisere seg (*in* i/på); utvikle(s) i en bestemt retning. **special license** *sb* kongebrev. **specialty** ['speʃltɪ] *sb* = *speciality 1.* **specie** ['spi:ʃɪ] *sb koll* mynt; *in* ~ i klingende mynt. **species** ['spi:ʃi:z] *sb* **1** (biologisk) art; **2** *dgl* slag(s). **specific** [spə'sɪfɪk] *adj* **1** spesiell; særlig, sær-; ~ *to* særegen for; **2** spesifikk; uttrykkelig (spesifisert). **specifically** [spə'sɪfɪklɪ] *adv* spesielt, spesifikt. **specification** [ˌspesɪfɪ'keɪʃn] *sb* spesifisering; spesifikasjon. **specify** ['spesɪfaɪ] *vt* spesifisere; angi (beskrive, definere etc) nærmere. **specimen** ['spesɪmən] *sb* eksemplar; prøve (og prøve|eksemplar, -stykke etc). **specimen page** *sb* prøveside.

specious ['spi:ʃəs] *adj bokl* tilsynelatende riktig/sann etc; besnærende, bestikkende; *også* skinn-.

speck [spek] *sb* **1** flekk; **2** fnugg, prikk. **speckle** ['spekl] *sb* flekk, merke. **speckled** ['spekld] *adj, pp* flekket; broket, spettet; droplet. **speckless** ['speklɪs] *adj* flekkfri; *fig* plettfri.

specks [speks] *sb fl dgl* briller. **spectacle** ['spektəkl] *sb* **1** syn (dvs noe å se på/som er verd å se på); skue; ut|sikt, -syn; *make a* ~ *of oneself* blamere seg; gjøre skandale; **2** flott opptog/seremoni etc; **3** *fl* briller. **spectacled** ['spektəkld] *adj* bebrillet, med briller. **spectacular** [spek'tækjʊlə] *adj* flott, imponerende; prangende. **spectator** [spek'teɪtə] *sb* tilskuer. **spectre** ['spektə] *sb* spøkelse, ånd (og åndesyn). **spectral** ['spektrəl] *adj* **1** spektral(-), spektrums-; **2** spøkelsesaktig, spøkelses-. **spectrum** ['spektrəm] *sb* spektrum; *fig også* spekter.

speculate ['spekjʊleɪt] *vi* **1** spekulere (*about/(up)on* over/på); **2** spekulere (*in* i). **speculation** [ˌspekjʊ'leɪʃn] *sb* spekulering; spekulasjon. **speculative** ['spekjʊlətɪv] *adj* spekulativ. **speculator** ['spekjʊleɪtə] *sb* spekulant.

speech [spi:tʃ] *sb* **1** tale (dvs evnen til å tale, måten å tale på); ~ *is silver but silence is golden* tale er sølv, men taushet er gull; *bereft of* ~ berøvet taleevnen/talens bruk; *part of* ~ ordklasse; **2** tale (dvs foredrag, forelesning etc). **speech|day** *sb* eksamensfest, årsavslutning (med taler og utdeling av vitnemål). ~ **defect** *sb* talefeil. **~less** *adj* målløs/stum (især av bevegelse etc). ~ **marks** *sb fl* anførselstegn. ~ **recognition** *sb data* talegjenkjenning. ~ **synthesis** *sb data* talesyntese.

speed [spi:d] **I** *sb* **1** fart, hastighet; *full* ~ full fart; toppfart; *more haste, less* ~ ≈ hastverk er lastverk; **2** (ulovlig) stor fart/hastighet; **3** *gml: wish them good* ~ ønske dem hell og lykke; **4** *slang* stoff (især amfetamin etc); **II** *vb* **1** skynde seg; fare/ile av sted; **2** få til å bevege seg raskt; sende (raskt); ~ *up* skynde på; fremskynde, påskynde; **3** *gml: God* ~ *you!* Gud være med deg! **speed|-boat** *sb* speedbåt, hurtiggående motorbåt. **~-cop** *sb dgl* trafikkonstabel (i utrykningspolitiet). **speeding** ['spi:dɪŋ] *sb* overtredelse av fartsgrensen; ≈ råkjøring; *he was fined £50 for* ~ han fikk en bot på 50 pund for å ha kjørt for fort. **speed|-limit** *sb* fartsgrense. **~-skating** *sb* skøyteløp (dvs hurtigløp på skøyter). **~-track, ~-way** *sb* speedway|bane, -løype. **speedy** ['spi:dɪ] *adj* hurtig, rask.

spell [spel] **A** *vb* **1** bokstavere(s), stave(s); *how do you* ~ *your name* hvordan staver du navnet ditt; **2** bety, innebære; *his refusal* ~*s ruin to our plans* avslaget hans innebærer at planene våre går i vasken; **B** *sb* trylle|formular, -ord; *cast a* ~ *over/put a* ~ *on* forhekse; kaste trolldom på; *under a* ~ forhekset, tryllebundet; **C I** *sb* **1** (kort) periode/stund; ~ *of cold* kuldeperiode; **2** tur/tørn (til å arbeide etc); *take a* ~ *at* ta (en) tørn ved; **II** *vt US* avløse; skiftes på/ta tørn med. **spellbound** *adj* for|hekset, -tryllet; tryllebundet; bergtatt, fjetret. **spelling** ['spelɪŋ] *sb* bokstavering, staving. **spelling|-book** *sb* ABC-bok. ~ **check** *sb data* stavekontroll. ~ **mistake** *sb* stavefeil.

spend [spend] *vt* **1** bruke/gi ut penger (*on* på); bruke opp; forbruke; ~ *oneself* slite seg ut; **2** sløse/søle (bort); ødsle (med). **spender** ['spendə] *sb* en som bruker (især for mange) penger; ≈ ødeland. **spending** ['spendɪŋ] *sb* (penge)forbruk (især for stort). **spending money** *sb* lommepenger. ~ **power** *sb* kjøpekraft. **spendthrift** ['spendθrɪft] *sb* ødeland. **spent** [spent] *adj, pp* oppbrukt; ut|kjørt, -slitt.

sperm [spɜ:m] *sb* sperma, sæd.

spew [spju:] *vb* spy; kaste opp.

sphere ['sfɪə] *sb* **1** kule; klode, planet; *petro* kule(tank); **2** fag (og fag|krets, -område etc); feil (og erfaringsfelt, virkefelt etc); sfære; ~ *of interest* interessesfære. **spherical** ['sferɪkl] *adj* sfærisk; kuleformet, kule-. **spherical tank** *sb petro* kuletank.

spice [spaɪs] **1** *sb* krydder; *fig også* spiss; **2** *vt* krydre (også *fig*); (~ *up*) sette (en) spiss på. **spicy** ['spaɪsɪ] *adj* **1** krydret, skarp; **2** *om historie, vits etc* dristig, våget; på kanten.

spick [spɪk] *adj:* ~ *and span* splinter ny; (skinnende) blank og velholdt.

spider ['spaɪdə] *sb* edderkopp. **spidery** ['spaɪdərɪ] *adj* **1** edderkoppaktig; **2** spindelvev|aktig, -tynn.

spigot ['spɪgət] *sb* **1** spuns, tapp; **2** kran.

spike [spaɪk] **I** *sb* **1** brodd, pigg, spiss; stor nagle/spiker; **2** aks; **II** *vt* **1** forsyne/utstyre med brodder *etc*; sette pigger på; **2** spidde; drive nagler/spiker gjennom; fornagle (kanon); ~ *their guns* forpurre planene deres; velte spillet for dem. **spiked** | **crude** *sb petro* anriket råolje. ~ **(running-)shoes** *sb fl* piggsko. **spike heel** *sb* stiletthæl.

spill [spɪl] *vb* **1** søle (ut); spille(s); renne over; ~ *the beans (slang)* plapre ut; røpe hemmelighet(er); **2** kaste (rytter av hesten). **spill oil** *sb petro* avfallsolje, spillolje.

spin [spɪn] **I** *sb* **1** snurring, virvling; *om ball* skru; *om fly* spinn; **2** svipptur, tripp; *trial* ~ (kort) prøvetur; **II** *vb* **1** rotere; snurre (rundt); virvle; *om ball* skru (dvs gi skru); *om fly* gå i spinn; *my head is* ~*ning* det går rundt for meg; **2** spinne; **3** ~ *out* dra/trekke ut; trekke i langdrag; **4** ~ *a yarn* spinne en ende (dvs fortelle en god historie).

spinach ['spɪnɪdʒ] *sb* spinat.

spinal ['spaɪnl] *adj* rygg(rads)-, spinal-.

spindle ['spɪndl] *sb* **1** spindel/tapp (på dreiebenk, platespiller etc); **2** rokkehode, tein; spole. **spindle|-legged, ~shanked** *adj* med lange, tynne bein. **~-shanks** *sb* (langt, tynt) rekel.

spin|-drier, -dryer *sb* sentrifuge, tørketrommel (til vask). **~-dry** *vt* sentrifugere (vasket tøy for å tørke det).

spine [spaɪn] *sb* **1** rygg|rad, -søyle; **2** bokrygg; **3** pigg, torn. **spineless** ['spaɪnlɪs] *adj* uten ryggrad; *fig* holdningsløs. **spiny** ['spaɪnɪ] *adj* pigget, tornet.

spinning|-jenny *sb* spinnemaskin; **~-wheel** *sb* (spinne)rokk.

spin-off *sb* biprodukt (ofte uforutsett).

spinster ['spɪnstə] *sb* ugift kvinne; *dgl* gammel jomfru.

spiral ['spaɪərəl] **1** *adj, sb* spiral(-); **2** *vi* sno seg (i spiraler). **spiral|-bit** *sb* spiralbor. **~-spring** *sb* spiralfjær. ~ **stairs** *sb fl* vindeltrapp.

spire ['spaɪə] *sb* **1** (kirke)spir; spisst tårn; **2** spiss, topp.

spirit ['spɪrɪt] **I** *sb* **1** ånd (i motsetning til materie); **2** ånd (dvs gjenferd, spøkelse); *an evil* ~ en ond ånd; **3** person (især med tanke på personligheten); *ofte* sjel; *også* åndsmenneske; *congenial* ~*s* beslektede ånder; *guiding* ~*s* ledende (bærende, drivende etc) krefter; *a noble* ~ en nobel sjel; **4** (pågangs)mot; energi; livslyst; *dgl* fart, liv(lighet); *that's the* ~*!* sånn, ja! sånn skal det være! **5** *fl* humør, lune; *in high* ~*s* i godt humør; *in low* ~*s* i dårlig humør; **6** innstilling; sinnelag; ånd; **7** ånd (dvs egentlig innhold, mening etc); *the* ~ *of the law* lovens ånd (i motsetning til dens bokstav/ordlyd); **8** alkohol, sprit, *fl* brennevin; **II** *vt* **1** *(~ up)* oppmuntre; animere, inspirere; stimulere; stramme opp; **2** ~ *away* trylle bort; få til å forsvinne. **spirited** ['spɪrɪtɪd] *adj* **1** energisk, kraftig; livlig; modig; **2** *som ending* i ... humør; *high-/low-~* i dårlig/godt humør. **spirit|lamp** *sb* spritlampe. **~-level** *sb* libelle, vaterpass. **~-stove** *sb* spritapparat. **spiritual** ['spɪrɪtʃʊəl] **I** *adj* **1** åndelig (i motsetning til materiell); ånds-; **2** religiøs, åndelig; geistlig; *the Lords Spiritual* biskopene og erkebiskopene i det britiske overhus; **II** *sb (Negro Spiritual)* ≈ neger|salme, -sang. **spiritualism** ['spɪrɪtʃʊəlɪzəm] *sb* spiritisme; **2** spiritualisme. **spiritualist** ['spɪrɪtʒʊəlɪst] *sb* **1** spiritist; **2** spiritualist.

spit [spɪt] **A 1** *sb* spytt; **2** *vb* spytte; **B I** *sb* **1** landtunge, nes; **2** (steke)spidd; **II** *vt* spidde; sette på spidd; **C** *sb* spadedybde.

spite [spaɪt] **I** *sb* **1** ondskap (og ondskapsfullhet); *have a* ~ *against* bære nag mot; nære hat til; **2** *in* ~ *of* til tross for; trass i; **II** *vt* plage, sjikanere. **spiteful** ['spaɪtful] *adj* ondsinnet, ondskapsfull.

spittle ['spɪtl] *sb* spytt. **spittoon** [spɪ'tu:n] *sb* spyttebakke.

splash [splæʃ] **I** *interj* plask; **II** *sb* **1** plask(ing); skvalp(ing), skvulp(ing); **2** skvett, sprut, sprøyt; **3** affekt, oppstyr; *make a* ~ vekke oppstyr; skape sensasjon; **III** *vb* plaske (skvette, sprute etc) på; søle til.

spleen [spli:n] *sb* **1** milt; **2** livstretthet; melankoli; humørsyke.

splendid ['splendɪd] *adj* flott, prektig; strålende; stor|artet, -slagen. **splendour** ['splendə] *sb* glans, prakt; storslagenhet.

splice [splaɪs] **1** *sb* spleis(ing); skjøt(ing); **2** *vt* spleise (tauverk); skjøte (f.eks. film); ~ *the mainbrace (sjø)* dele ut ekstra rasjon av rom til mannskapet); *get ~d (slang)* bli spleiset (dvs gift).

splint [splɪnt] *sb* skinne (til spjelking); *put into* ~*s* spjelke. **splinter** ['splɪntə] **1** *sb* splint; flis, spon; **2** *vb* splintre(s). **splinter** | **group,** ~ **party** *sb* utbrytergruppe. **~-proof** *adj* splintsikker.

split [splɪt] **I** *adj, pp* kløvd/spaltet (etc, jf *III*); **II** *sb* **1** sprekk; revne, rift; spalte; **2** *fl* spagat; *do the* ~*s* gå ned i spagat(en); **III** *vb* **1** sprekke; briste, revne; ~ *one's sides (with laughter)* holde på å revne/sprekke av latter; ~ *up* revne, sprekke; spalte(s); bryte opp (etter selskap etc); gå fra hverandre/hver til sitt; bli uenige; **2** kløyve, splintre; ~ *hairs* drive ordkløyveri; *hair-splitting* ordkløyveri; **3** dele (likt); halvere; ~ *the cost/expenses* dele utgiftene; **4** *slang* sladre, tyste. **split** | **screen** *sb data* delt skjerm. ~ **mind,** ~ **personality** *sb* spaltsinn; spaltet personlighet. ~ **second** *sb* brøkdelen av et sekund. **splitting headache** *sb* sterk (*dgl* dundrende) hodepine.

splutter ['splʌtə] **1** *sb* sprut(ing); (opphisset) stemmesurr; **2** *vb* sprute; spytte; *især* snakke ivrig/opphisset; hakke, stamme.

spoil [spɔɪl] **I** *sb (fl)* bytte, rov; **II** *vb* **1** ødelegge; forderve, ruinere; spolere; skjemme bort; **2** *be* ~*ing for* være ivrig etter/oppsatt på. **spoilsport** ['spɔɪlspɔ:t] *sb* gledesdreper, lyseslokker.

spoke [spəʊk] *sb* **1** eike (i hjul); **2** trinn (i stige).

spokes|man ['spəʊksmən], **~woman** ['spəʊkswumən] *sb* tals|kvinne, -mann; foregangs|kvinne, mann.

sponge [spɒndʒ] **I** *sb* **1** svamp; *pass the ~ over* stryke ut; *throw in/up the ~* gi opp; gi seg; gi tapt; **2** = *~-cake*; **II** *vb* **1** *(~ down)* vaske (med svamp); *(~ off/ out)* pusse (stryke, viske etc) ut; **2** *~ on (dgl)* snylte på. **sponge-cake** ['spɒndʒkeɪk] *sb* ≈ sukkerbrød-(bunn). **sponger** ['spɒndʒə] *sb* snylter, snyltegjest. **spongy** ['spɒndʒɪ] *adj* svampaktig, svampet; porøs.

sponsor ['spɒnsə] **1** *sb* garantist, kausjonist; *radio, TV, sport etc* sponsor; **2** *vt* garantere/kausjonere for; være sponsor for; *dgl* sponse.

spontaneity [ˌspɒntə'neɪətɪ] *sb* spontanitet *etc.* **spontaneous** [spɒn'teɪnɪəs] *adj* spontan; umiddelbar; uvilkårlig. **spontaneous combustion** *sb* selvantennelse.

spook [spu:k] *sb* spøkelse. **spooky** ['spu:kɪ] *adj* spøkelsesaktig; nifs, uhyggelig.

spool [spu:l] *sb* spole, snelle. **spooling** ['spu:lɪŋ] *sb data* spoling. **spool piece** *sb petro* rørpasstykke, skjøterør.

spoon [spu:n] **1** *sb* skje; **2** *vb* bruke skje; spise/øse opp *etc* med skje. **spoon|-bait** *sb* skjesluk. **~-feed** *vt* mate med skje; *fig* gi inn med skjeer. **~ful** *adj* skjefull.

sporadic [spə'rædɪk] *adj* sporadisk.

spore [spɔ:] *sb bot* spore.

sporran ['spɒrən] *sb* belte|pung, -veske (som bæres i forbindelse med skotsk kilt).

sport [spɔ:t] **I** *sb* **1** lek, moro; atspredelse, tidsfordriv; *(ofte fl)* idrett, sport; idrettsstevne; sportsbegivenhet; *som adj* idretts-, sports-; *athletic ~s* friidrett; *country ~s* jakt, fiske og hesteveddeløp; friluftsliv; **2** leven, moro, spøk; *in ~* for moro skyld; på spøk; *make ~ of* drive ap/gjøn med; holde leven med; **3** *dgl (~sman)* (god) idretts|kvinne, -mann; *især* grei (real, skvær etc) gutt/jente; *be a good ~* være grei *etc*; ikke være lumpen/ureal etc; **II** *vb* **1** leke; ha det moro; drive idrett/sport; sporte; **2** *dgl* gå med (for å vise seg); flotte seg/prange med; *he ~ed a moustache* han hadde/gikk med bart. **sporting** ['spɔ:tɪŋ] *adj* **1** idretts-, sports-; **2** grei, real, skvær; sportig, sporty; **3** *a ~ chance* en fair/reell sjanse. **sportive** ['spɔ:tɪv] *adj* leken, lystig; spøkefull. **sports|car** *sb* sportsbil. **~man** *sb* **1** idrettsmann; *også* grei/real kar; **2** friluftsmann (især jeger, sportsfisker, hestekar). **~manship** *sb* (god) sportsånd. **~ shirt** *sb* sportsskjorte. **~woman** *sb* idrettskvinne (etc, jf *sportsman*).

spot [spɒt] **I** *sb* **1** flekk, merke; *fig også* plett; **2** fregne, (fø)flekk; filipens, kvise; utslett; **3** plass, sted; *også* punkt; *bright ~ (fig)* lyspunkt; *in a tight ~* i knipe/vanskeligheter; *on the ~* på stedet; *soft (tender, weak) ~* svakt/ømt punkt; **II** *vb* **1** flekke; sette flekk-(er) på; bli flekket; **2** oppdage; få øye på; kjenne igjen. **spot | cash** *sb* betaling på stedet (dvs ved mottakelse av varen). **~ check** *sb* stikkprøve. **~less** *adj* flekkfri, plettfri (også *fig*). **~light 1** *sb* prosjektør(lys), søkelys; **2** *vt* bringe i søkelyset; sette søkelys på. **spotted** ['spɒtɪd] *adj, pp* flekket. **spotty** ['spɒtɪ] *adj* **1** flekket, uren; **2** ujevn (dvs av ujevn kvalitet). **spot | test** *sb* = *~ check.* **~ welding** *sb* punktsveising.

spouse [spaʊz] *sb gml* ektefelle.

spout [spaʊt] **I** *sb* **1** tut; **2** sprut, stråle; **3** *up the ~ (slang)* i knipe/vanskeligheter; **II** *vb* **1** sprute, sprøyte; **2** *dgl* deklamere, forkynne.

sprain [spreɪn] **1** *sb* forstuing, vrikking; **2** *vt* forstue, vrikke.

sprat [spræt] *sb* brisling.

sprawl [sprɔ:l] *vi* **1** ligge/sitte (makelig) henslengt; **2** (ligge og) kave/sprelle; **3** bre/spre seg planløst og uregelmessig; gro/vokse (vilt) utover.

spray [spreɪ] **1** *sb* dusj; sprut, sprøyt; **2** *vt* dusje; sprute, sprøyte. **sprayer** ['spreɪə] *sb* **1** sprutflaske; **2** sprøyte(pistol), (-)sprøyter. **~-gun** *sb* sprøytepistol. **~-head, ~-nozzle** *sb* (sprøyte)dyse.

spread [spred] **I** *sb* **1** ut|bredelse, -strekning; **2** omfang, spenn(vidde); **3** *i avis etc* oppslag; annonse/ artikkel etc over to sider; **4** *dgl* bugnende (fest)bord; **II** *vb* **1** spre; ut|bre, -spre; bre/smøre (utover); *~ the table* dekke bordet; **2** bre/spre seg; strekke seg ut; *~ oneself* spre seg (for mye); ha (for) mange jern i ilden. **spread|-eagle** [ˌspred'i:gl] *vi* ligge med sprikende/ utstrakte armer og bein. **~sheet** *sb data* regneark.

spree [spri:] *sb dgl* leven, moro; rangel.

sprig [sprɪg] *sb* **1** liten kvist; *også* dusk, kvast; **2** *neds* jypling, sprett.

sprightly ['spraɪtlɪ] *adj* livlig, lystig, munter.

spring [sprɪŋ] **I** *sb* **1** vår; *poet* forår; *in the ~* om våren; **2** kilde (og kildevell); *fig også* opphav, utspring; **3** hopp, sprett; sprang; **4** elastisitet, fjæring; spennkraft; spenst(ighet), sprett; **5** (spring)fjær; **6** driv|fjær, -kraft (dvs drivende kraft); **II** *vb* **1** hoppe, sprette; *~ down/out etc* springe (fare, styrte etc) ned/ut etc; *~ to one's feet* springe (fare, sprette etc) opp; **2** *(~ up)* bryte (skyte, springe, velle etc) frem/opp; oppstå plutselig; **3** *~ from* komme av; stamme fra; ha (sitt) utspring i; **4** detonere, sprenge; utløse; **5** meddele/ røpe plutselig; *~ a question* stille et overrumplende/ uventet spørsmål; *~ a surprise* komme med en overraskelse; **6** bruke/spandere (i stor stil); *~ eighty quid* spenne åtti pund; **7** knekke, splintre; sprekke; *~ a leak* springe lekk. **spring|-balance** *sb* fjærvekt. **~-bed** *sb* = *~-mattress.* **~-board** *sb* springbrett, trampoline; stupebrett. **~-catch** *sb* smekklås; sneppert. **~-cleaning** *sb* vårrengjøring. **~-clip** *sb* fjær|bøyle, holder, -klemme. **~-cushion** *vb* fjære. **~ fever** *sb* **1** vårfornemmelser; **2** vårslapphet. **~head** *sb* kilde; *fig også* utspring. **~-hook** *sb* karabinkrok. **~like** *adj* vårlig. **~-loaded** *adj* fjærbelastet. **~ suspension** *sb* fjæropphengning. **~tide** *sb* **1** vår(tid); **2** springflo. **~time** *sb* = *~tide 1.* **springy** *adj* fjærende, spenstig.

sprinkle ['sprɪŋkl] **1** *sb* dusj; lett regn; **2** *vb* dusje; skvette/sprute vann på; småregne. **sprinkler** ['sprɪŋklə] *sb* **1** (vann)spreder; **2** sprinkler(anlegg). **sprinkling** ['sprɪŋklɪŋ] *sb* dryss, stenk; lite antall.

sprint [sprɪnt] *sb, vi* sprint(e), spurt(e).

sprite [spraɪt] *sb* alv, fe.

sprocket ['sprɒkɪt] *sb* kjede(tann)hjul. **sprocket | hole** *sb data* styrehull. ~ **track** *sb data* styrespor.

sprout [spraʊt] **1** *sb* skudd, spire; *Brussels ~s* rosenkål; **2** *vb* spire.

spruce [spru:s] **A** *sb* gran(tre); **B 1** *adj* fiks, smart; velkledd; **2** *vb* fikse/pynte (seg).

spry [spraɪ] *adj* sprek; kvikk, livlig.

spud [spʌd] *sb slang* potet.

spudding-in *sb petro* borestart.

spume [spju:m] *sb* fråde, skum.

spunk [spʌŋk] *sb dgl* mot; tæl.

spur [spɜ:] **1** *sb* spore; *fig også* ansporing; *on the ~ of the moment* etter et øyeblikks innskytelse; på stående fot; **2** *vt* spore; sette sporene i; *fig* anspore.

spurious ['spjʊərɪəs] *adj* falsk, uekte.

spurn [spɜ:n] *vt* avvise (med forakt); vrake.

spurt [spɜ:t] **I** *sb* **1** sprut, sprøyt; stråle; *~ of flame* stikkflamme; **2** utbrudd; **3** spurt; **II** *vi* **1** sprute, sprøyte; stråle; **2** spurte.

sputter ['spʌtə] **I** *sb* **1** spruting; fresing, spraking; **2** opphisset snakk; stamming og stotring; **II** *vb* **1** sprute; frese, sprake; **2** spytte; snakke ivrig og opphisset; stamme og stotre.

spy [spaɪ] **I** *sb* spion; **II** *vb* **1** spionere; *~ on* spionere på; utspionere; **2** oppdage; få øye på. **spy|-glass** *sb* (liten) kikkert. **~-hole** *sb* judasøye (= kikkhull i celledør etc).

squabble ['skwɒbl] **1** *sb* krangel; **2** *vi* krangle.

squad [skwɒd] *sb især mil* lag; *firing ~* eksekusjonspelotong. **squad car** *sb US* politibil, patruljebil.

squadron ['skwɒdrən] *sb mil* eskadron (i hæren); eskadre (i marinen); skvadron (i flyvåpenet). **squadron leader** *sb* major (i flyvåpenet).

squalid ['skwɒlɪd] *adj* skitten, ustelt; elendig, ussel.

squall [skwɔ:l] **I** *sb* **1** skrik, vræl; **2** (regn)|byge, -skur; kastevind, vindkule; **II** *vi* skrike, vræle.

squalor ['skwɒlə] *sb* skitt; elendighet, ussel|dom, -het.

squander ['skwɒndə] *vt* søle/ødsle bort; sløse med.

square ['skweə] **I** *adj* **1** firkantet, kvadratisk; kvadrat-; **2** rettvinklet; rett avskåret etc; avrettet, kant|-hugget, -skåret; *om personer = ~-built*; **3** *mat* kvadrat-; **4** *fig* rett|linjet, skaffen; ordentlig, skikkelig; real, skvær; **5** avgjort/oppgjort (dvs betalt); *dgl* skværet opp; *~ with* kvitt/skuls med; **6** uavgjort (dvs likt stilt); **7** *slang* firkanta (dvs dum, treg; dogmatisk etc); **II** *adv (~ly) især* **1** vinkelrett (*on* på); i rett vinkel (*to* med); **2** like, rett; *dgl, slang* dønn; **III** *sb* **1** firkant, kvadrat; rute; firkantet/kvadratisk felt/plass etc; karré; kvartal; torg; *back to ~ one* tilbake til utgangspunktet; **2** vinkel|hake, -linjal; -mål; **3** *mat* kvadrat; annen potens; **4** *on the ~* ærlig og redelig; likefrem, åpen(t); real(t); **IV** *vb* **1** gjøre firkantet (kvadratisk, rettvinklet etc); avrette; kant|hugge, -skjære; *sjø* skvære; *the ~d circle* bokseringen; **2** *mat* kvadrere; opphøye i annen (potens); **3** *(~ up)* ordne, utligne; dekke; gjøre/*dgl* skvære opp; *he ~d up and left* han betalte (regningen) og gikk; **4** få til å stemme/gå opp; *~ with* bringe i samsvar med; **5** *dgl* bestikke, smøre. **square|-bashing** *sb mil slang* drill (i sluttet orden). **~-built** *adj* firskåren, undersetsig. ~ **brackets** *sb fl* hakeparentes(er); skarpe klammer. ~ **deal** *sb* real/ skikkelig behandling. **~head** *sb US* **1** skandinav; *især* svenske; **2** dumskalle. ~ **jaw** *sb* kraftig hake. ~ **meal** *sb* solid måltid. ~ **measure** *sb* flatemål. **~-rigged** *adj* skværrigget. **~-rigger** *sb* skværrigger. ~ **root** *sb* kvadratrot. **~-sail** *sb* råseil, skværseil. **~-shouldered** *adj* bredskuldret. **~-toed** *adj* **1** *om skotøy* bredsnutet; **2** *fig* gammeldags; treg.

squash [skwɒʃ] **A I** *sb* **1** trengsel; (sammenpakket) menneskemasse; **2** klask(ing), svupp(ing); **3** fruktdrikk, squash; **II** *vb* **1** presse; **2** bli klemt/presset; **3** presse/trenge seg; **4** *dgl* lukke munnen på; ta knekken på; **5** *dgl* slå ned; (under)kue; **B** *sb* squash (slags gresskar); **C** *sb* (ballspillet) squash.

squat [skwɒt] **I** *adj* undersetsig; liten og tykk; **II** *vi* **1** sitte på huk; **2** *om dyr* krype sammen; **3** *dgl* sitte; **4** okkupere (ubebodd hus). **squatter** ['skwɒt] *sb* husokkupant.

squaw [skwɔ:] *sb* squaw (dvs indiansk hustru/ kvinne).

squawk [skwɔ:k] **I** *sb* **1** (fugle)skrik; **2** *dgl* skrik, vræl; **II** *vi* **1** skrike, vræle; **2** *slang* sladre, tyste.

squeak [skwi:k] **I** *sb* **1** hvin; knistring, pip(ing); knirk(ing); **2** *it was a narrow ~* det var på nippet/på hengende hår; **II** *vb* **1** hvine; knistre, pipe; *om hengsler etc* knirke; **2** *dgl* sladre, tyste. **squeaky** ['skwi:kɪ] *adj* knirkende.

squeal [skwi:l] **I** *sb* hyl(ing), skrik(ing); *~ing brakes* hvinende bremser; **II** *vb* **1** hyle, skrike; hvine; **2** *dgl* sladre, tyste. **squealer** ['skwi:lə] *sb* **1** dyr som skriker; **2** *slang* sladrehank, tyster.

squeamish ['skwi:mɪʃ] *adj* **1** som (lett) blir kvalm; **2** prippen, snerpet; pyset; **3** kresen.

squeeze [skwi:z] **I** *sb* **1** press(ing), trykk; *fig* utpressing (og om resultatet: bestikkelse, smøring, løsepenger etc); *the ~ of a lemon* saften av en (presset) sitron; **2** håndtrykk; klem, omfavnelse; **3** trengsel; tettpakket forsamling etc; **II** *vb* **1** presse/trykke (sammen); kryste; *fig* legge press på; tvinge; *~ money out of* presse penger av; *~ (the juice out of) a lemon* presse (saften av) en sitron; **2** *(~ through)* presse/tvinge (seg) frem; *~ one's way* trenge seg frem; *how can you all ~ in* hvordan får dere plass alle sammen; **3** klemme, omfavne.

squelch [skweltʃ] **1** *sb* svupp(ing); svuppende lyd; **2** *vb* svuppe; gå/vasse med en svuppende lyd; surkle.

squid [skwɪd] *sb* (liten) blekksprut.

squiggle ['skwɪgl] *sb* krusedull.

squint [skwɪnt] **I** *sb* **1** skjeling, skjeløydhet; *have a ~ in the left eye* skjele på venstre øye; **2** raskt øyekast; *take a ~ at* ta en titt på; **II** *vi* skjele; *vulg* blingse. **squint-eyed** *adj* skjeløyd; *vulg* blingset.

squire ['skwaɪə] **I** *sb* **1** godseier, storbonde; **2** *hist* ridderslvenn, væpner; **3** *hum* kavaler; **II** *vt* opptre som/være kavaler for.

squirm [skwɜ:m] *vi* krympe/vri seg; sno seg.

squirrel ['skwɪrl] *sb* ekorn.

squirt [skwɜ:t] **I** *sb* **1** sprut; (liten, tynn) stråle; **2** *dgl* pusling, spjæling; **II** *vb* sprute, stråle.

stab [stæb] **I** *sb* **1** stikk (og stikksår); støt (med kniv etc); ~ *in the back* dolkestøt i ryggen; *fig også* bakholdsangrep; **2** iling/sting (av smerte etc); **3** *dgl* forsøk; **II** *vb* stikke (med kniv etc); dolke. **stabbing** ['stæbɪŋ] *adj især* gjennomborende. **stabbing-board** *sb petro* monteringsplattform.

stability [stə'bɪlətɪ] *sb* stabilitet. **stabilization** [ˌsteɪbəlaɪ'zeɪʃn] *sb* stabilisering. **stabilize** ['steɪbəlaɪz] *vt* stabilisere. **stable** ['steɪbl] **A 1** *sb* stall; **2** *vt* ha/sette på stallen; **B** *adj* stabil; fast; varig. **stable|-boy** *sb* stall|gutt, kar, -knekt. ~ **tip** *sb* stalltips.

stack [stæk] **I** *sb* **1** stabel (av torv, ved etc); (høy)|-stakk, -såte; *mil* (gevær)|kobbel, -pyramide; *dgl* dynge, haug; **2** *(chimney-~)* pipe, skorstein; **3** *data* stakk|lager, -liste; **II** *vt* **1** sette i stakk *etc; dgl* dynge/hauge sammen; hope opp; **2** *mil* koble (geværer); sette (geværer) i pyramide.

stadium ['steɪdɪəm] *sb* stadion.

staff [stɑ:f] **I** *sb* **1** stav, stokk; stang; *flag~* flaggstang; **2** personale; *også mil* stab; *som adj* personal-, personell-; *mil* stabs-; *be on the ~ of* være ansatt i/ved; **3** *mus* noteplan; *the ~* de fem notelinjene; **II** *vt* bemanne; forsyne med personell. **staff | dance** *sb* firmafest. ~ **entrance** *sb* personalinngang. ~ **officer** *sb* stabsoffiser.

stag [stæg] *sb* **1** hannhjort, (kron)hjort; **2** mann (som er på dans/fest uten dame). **stag-party** *sb dgl* herreselskap; *ofte* utdrikkingslag.

stage [steɪdʒ] **I** *sb* **1** plattform, podium; *på teater* scene; *fig også* arena, skueplass, åsted; **2** (arbeids)-plattform, stillas; **3** stadium, trinn; *a three-~ rocket* en tretrinnsrakett; **4** etappe; *gml også* skysskifte, skysstasjon; *også = ~-coach; advance by easy ~s* rykke frem i små etapper; **II** *vb* oppføre/sette opp teaterstykke; *fig* arrangere; få/sette i stand/i verk. **stage|-coach** *sb* diligence, postvogn. **~craft** *sb* scene|kunst, -teknikk. ~ **direction** *sb* sceneanvisning. ~ **door** *sb* skuespillerinngang. ~ **driver** *sb* diligencekusk; post|fører, -kusk. ~ **effects** *sb fl* teatereffekter. ~ **fright** *sb* lampefeber; sceneskrekk. **~-hand** *sb* scenearbeider. ~ **manager** *sb* regissør, sceneinstruktør. **~-struck** *adj* teatergal. ~ **version** *sb* scene|utgave, -versjon. ~ **whisper** *sb* teaterhvisking.

stagger ['stægə] **I** *sb* raving, sjangling; **II** *vb* **1** rave, sjangle; vakle; **2** ryste, sjokkere; forbløffe. **staggering** ['stægərɪŋ] *adj* rystende *etc.*

staging ['steɪdʒɪŋ] *sb* **1** (arbeids)plattform; (henge)stillas; **2** iscenesetting.

stagnant ['stægnənt] *adj* stillestående. **stagnate** [stæg'neɪt] *vi* stagnere; stanse (i utvikling, vekst etc). **stagnation** [stæg'neɪʃn] *sb* stagnering, stagnasjon.

staid [steɪd] *adj* adstadig; sedat; stø.

stain [steɪn] **I** *sb* **1** flekk; *fig også* plett; *a ~ on his honour* en (skam)plett på hans ære; **2** farge, kulør; *især* beis; **II** *vb* **1** flekke; søle til; *~ed with nicotine* nikotinflekket; *blood~ed* blodflekket; **2** sette en (skam)plett på; skjemme ut; vanære; **3** beise, farge. **stained glass** *sb* kulørt glass; *stained-glass window* ≈ glassmaleri.

stainless ['steɪnlɪs] *adj* **1** flekkfri; *fig* plettfri, uplettet; **2** rustfri. **stainless steel** *sb* rustfritt stål. **stain remover** *sb* flekkfjerner.

stair ['steə] *sb* trapp (og især trappetrinn); *fl* trapp, trappeløp; (trappe)oppgang; *flight of ~s* trapp (og trappeløp). **stair|case, ~way** *sb* trapp (og trappe|løp, -oppgang). **~-well** *sb* trappe|brønn, -hus, -sjakt.

stake [steɪk] **I** *sb* **1** pæl (og påle; stang, stolpe; staur etc); marterpæl, skampæl; *hist* heksebål, kjetterbål; *condemned to the ~* dømt til (å bli brent på) bålet; **2** innsats (i veddemål etc); *at ~* på spill; *her life was at ~* det stod om livet for henne; *play for high ~s* spille (et) høyt spill; **II** *vt* **1** støtte opp med pæler etc; *(~ out)* merke av/opp (med pæler etc); stake ut; *~ a claim* merke opp/stake ut et skjerp etc; *også fig* markere sin interesse(sfære); *~ off* gjerde inn (med pæler etc); **2** risikere/satse (*on* på); *~ everything on one throw* satse alt på ett kast/kort.

stale [steɪl] *adj* foreldet; ikke lenger fersk/frisk; ufrisk; *om øl* dovent; *om luft* dårlig, innestengt; *om historie/vits etc* forslitt; *om idrettsmann* overtrenet. **stalemate** ['steɪlmeɪt] **1** *sb* dødpunkt; *i sjakk* patt; **2** *vt* sette patt.

stalk [stɔ:k] **A** *sb* stengel, stilk; **B** *vb* **1** liste (lure, snike etc) seg inn på; **2** spankulere, sprade. **stalking** ['stɔ:kɪŋ] *sb* snikjakt.

stall [stɔ:l] **I** *sb* **1** bås, spiltau; **2** utsalgs|bod, -bord, -sted; markeds|bod, -plass; torgplass; **3** *teat* orkester-(plass), parterre; **II** *vb* **1** holde/sette på bås(en); *ofte* fôre opp; gjø; **2** stanse; gå i stå; få motorstopp; *om fly* stalle; **3** *fig* komme med utflukter; *~ for time* svare unnvikende (for å vinne tid).

stallion ['stælɪən] *sb* (avls)hingst.

stalwart ['stɔ:lwət] **1** *adj* drabelig; kraftig, sterk; solid, stø; **2** *sb* kraftkar; kjernekar; pålitelig/trofast tilhenger.

stamina ['stæmɪnə] *sb* motstandkraft, utholdenhet; seighet; to, tæl.

stammer ['stæmə] **1** *sb* stamming, stamhet; **2** *vb* stamme (frem).

stamp [stæmp] **I** *sb* **1** stamping (og stampe|maskin, -verk etc); tramp(ing); tråkking; **2** stempel (og stempelavtrykk); stanse (og stanseverktøy); *fig også* merke, preg; *leave one's ~ on* sette sitt preg/stempel på; **3** *(postage ~)* frimerke (som i GB også brukes som stempelmerke); **4** slag(s), type; karakter; **II** *vb* **1** stampe; trampe/tråkke (*on* på); knuse; pukke (stein); *~ one's foot* stampe med foten; trampe i bakken/gulvet; **2** stemple; prege, presse; stanse; *~ out* stanse ut; *også* trampe/tråkke ut (og *fig* knuse; ut|rydde, -slette, jf *II 1*); *it was ~ed on him* det hadde satt sitt preg/

stempel på ham; det stod skrevet utenpå ham; **3** frankere; sette frimerke/stempelmerke på. **stamp|-act** *sb* stempellov(en). **~-album** *sb* frimerkealbum. **~ battery** *sb* pukkverk. **~-collection** *sb* frimerkesamling. **~-collector** *sb* frimerkesamler. **~-duty** *sb* stempelavgift.

stampede [stæm'pi:d] **1** *sb* panikk, stormløp; **2** *vb* flykte i panikk; drive/skremme på (vill) flukt.

stamp | hammer *sb* fallhammer. **~-hinge** *sb* frimerkehengsel. **~machine** *sb* frimerkeautomat. **~ mill** *sb* **1** stampemølle; **2** pukkverk. **~-mount** *sb* = *~-hinge.* **~-pad** *sb* stempelpute.

stance [stæns] *sb* **1** plass, posisjon, post (især i cricket og golf); **2** holdning, innstilling.

stand [stænd] **I** *sb* **1** stans(ing), stopp; opphold; holdt; *teat* forestilling (under turné); *bring to a ~* stanse/stoppe (dvs få til å stanse etc); *come to a ~* stanse/stoppe (dvs gjøre holdt); **2** plass, posisjon, post; *også = ~point; cab-~* drosjeholdeplass; *I hope I have made my ~ clear* jeg håper jeg har gjort det klart hvor jeg står (dvs hva jeg mener etc); *make a ~* (stanse og) ta kampen opp; *take one's ~* ta oppstilling/plass; *fig* ta standpunkt/stilling; **3** plattform, podium; tribune; *US jur* vitneboks; *put on the ~* føre som vitne; *take the ~* ta plass i vitneboksen; møte/opptre som vitne; **4** bod, kiosk; (utstillings)stand; markedsplass, torgplass; **5** holder, stativ; *umbrella ~* paraplystativ; **6** (skog)bestand; **II** *vb* **1** stå (og stå som); reise seg (og bli stående); stanse (og bli stående); *om bygninger etc* ligge (dvs være beliggende/plassert); *~ a head higher than* rage/være et hode høyere enn; *~ six feet* være seks fot høy; *as it/matters stood* som saken(e) stod; *the church ~s on a river* kirken ligger ved en elv; **2** bestå; gjelde; stå ved lag/ved makt; *does the offer still ~* står tilbudet fremdeles ved makt; **3** stå fast; holde stand; *~ one's ground* holde stillingen; **4** gjennomgå; *~ accused* stå/være anklaget; *~ (one's) trial* stå for retten; **5** tåle; finne seg i; ut|holde, -stå; *~ closer scrutiny* tåle nærmere gransking; **6** sette/stille opp; reise (opp); få til å stå; *~ the bottle on the table* sette (fra seg) flasken på bordet; **7** *sjø* holde/stå (dvs seile i bestemt retning); *~ inshore* stå (inn) mot land; **8** rive i/spandere (på); *~ a round of drinks* rive i en omgang (drinker); **9** *en del uttrykk: ~ a good/poor chance* ha store/små sjanser; *~ corrected* innrømme (og beklage) feil; *~ for Parliament* stille til valg som parlamentsmedlem; *~ for re--election* stille til gjenvalg; *~ in great danger* bringe i/utsette for stor fare; *~ in need of help* trenge hjelp; *~ on ceremony* holde på formene; *~ on one's rights* hevde (holde, stå på) sin rett; *~ to lose* risikere å tape; *~ to win* ha sjanse til å vinne; *I wont ~ for it* jeg finner meg ikke/vil ikke finne meg i det; *it ~s to reason* det sier seg selv; **10** *med adv, prep ~* **about** stå omkring (i grupper); *~ about idly* stå og henge; *~* **again** stille til gjenvalg; *~* **aloof** holde seg/stå for seg selv; *fig* forholde seg avventende (passiv, reservert etc); *~* **apart** stå et stykke unna; *også = ~ aloof*; *~* **aside** gå/tre til side; *~* **at** stå på/ved (f.eks. om skalaviser). *~* **away** = *~ aside*; *~ away from (sjø)* holde/stå ut fra (f.eks. kysten); *~* **back** gå (rykke, trekke seg etc) tilbake; gå av veien/til side; *også = ~ aloof*; *~* **by** stå hos; stå ved siden av; holde seg klar (parat, rede etc); *fig* bistå, hjelpe, støtte; *~ by one's word* stå ved sitt ord; *~* **clear** holde seg unna; *~* **fast,** *~* **firm** stå fast; *~* **first** stå først/som nummer én; *~* **for** stå for (dvs betegne, bety; representere, symbolisere etc); gjøre tjeneste som; *~* **good** gjelde; være gyldig; *~* **idle** stå (uvirksom); være ute av drift; *~* **in** plassere (sette, stille etc) i; *sjø* holde/stå innover (dvs mot land); *~* **in for** vikariere/være stedfortreder for; *~* **in with** delta med; stå i ledtog med; *~* **off** holde seg unna/på avstand; holde unna/fra livet; tre frem (på bakgrunn av); *sjø* holde/stå utover (dvs fra land); *~* **on** stå på; *fig* basere seg/være basert på; bero på; insistere på; *~* **out** stå ut; rage (springe, tre etc) frem; skille seg ut; holde stand; holde ut; *~* **out against** gjøre (seig) motstand mot; avtegne seg (i silhuett) mot; *~* **out for** gå i bresjen for; holde fast på/ved; *~* **out with** holde ut med; holde stand mot; *~* **over** stå over (for å passe på); overvåke; bero, utstå; *~* **pat** stå (urokkelig) på sitt; være sta/standhaftig; *~* **to** fortsette (å arbeide etc); stå fast; holde/stå fast ved; *mil* holde seg klar/i beredskap; *~* **together** holde/stå sammen; *~* **up** reise seg; stå (opp); holde seg/vare (i bruk, mot slitasje etc); *US* svikte; holde for narr; *~ her up* la henne stå og vente (forgjeves); *~* **up against** forsvare/klare seg mot; *~* **up for** gå i bresjen for; slå et slag for; *~* **up to** møte (i kamp); forsvare/klare seg mot; *fig* motstå, tåle; *~* **up well** klare seg bra; *~* **upon** stå på; *fig* insistere/legge vekt på; *~ well* **with** stå seg godt med; komme godt ut av det med.

standard ['stændəd] **I** *adj* standard(-); normal(-); gjengs, vanlig; **II** *sb* **1** banner, fane; standart; *the ~ of revolt* opprørsfanen; **2** standard; målestokk, norm; myntfot; **3** nivå, trinn; (grunnskole)klasse; **4** stolpe, støtte(bjelke); mast; stander. **standard|-bearer** *sb* fanebærer. **~ candle** *sb* normallys. **standardization** [ˌstændədaɪ'zeɪʃn] *sb* standardisering. **standardize** ['stændədaɪz] *vt* standardisere. **standard | lamp** *sb* stålampe. **~ of living** *sb* levestandard. **~ rate** *sb* normalsats.

stand|-by *sb* **1** beredskap; **2** (pålitelig) hjelpemiddel; **~-in** *sb* stedfortreder (især for filmstjerne under farlig opptak); vikar.

standing ['stændɪŋ] **I** *adj* **1** stående (etc, jf *stand II*); **2** stille (og stillestående); ubevegelig; **3** varig; fast, stadig; **II** *sb* **1** stilling (dvs måte å stå etc på); **2** posisjon, stilling, stand; status; anseelse; *of high ~* av høy rang; *også* stands-; **3** varighet; *of long ~* av gammel dato/lang varighet; *også* mangeårig. **standing--room** *sb* ståplass.

stand|-offish *adj* kjølig, reservert. **~pipe** *sb petro* slamrør. **~point** *sb* standpunkt; holdning, innstilling.

standstill ['stænstɪl] *sb* stans; stillstand; *come to a ~* stanse; gå i stå.

stand|-to *sb* (alarm)beredskap. **~-up** *adj* stående (dvs som gjøres mens en står).

stanza ['stænzə] *sb* strofe, vers.

staple ['steɪpl] **A** *sb* hoved|vare, -produkt; stapelvare; **B 1** *sb a)* (hefte)stift; *b)* bøyle (på hengelås); krampe; **2** *vt* stifte (sammen). **stapler** ['steɪplə] *sb* = **stapling-machine** *sb* stiftemaskin.

star [stɑ:] **I** *sb* **1** stjerne; *Stars and Stripes* Stjernebanneret (USAs nasjonalflagg); *shooting ~* stjerneskudd; **2** *film etc* stjerne; **II** *vb film etc* **1** opptre i hovedrolle; **2** lansere i hovedrolle; *~ring Charles Chaplin* med Charles Chaplin i hovedrollen.

starboard 1 *adj, adv* styrbord-, styrbords(-); **2** *sb* styrbord; **3** *vt: ~ the helm* legge roret styrbord.

starch [stɑ:tʃ] **1** *sb* stivelse; *fig* stivhet; **2** *vt* stive (tøy); gjøre stiv. **starchy** ['stɑ:tʃɪ] *adj* **1** stivelsesholdig; **2** stivet; *fig* stiv, formell.

stardom *sb* (film)stjerneverdenen.

stare ['steə] **1** *sb* stirring; stirrende/stivt blikk; **2** *vb* stirre (*at* på; *in* inn i).

starfish *sb* korstroll, sjøstjerne..

staring ['steərɪŋ] *adj* **1** stirrende (jf *stare 2*); *it was ~ me in the face* den/det lå rett for nesen på meg; **2** grell, skrikende.

stark [stɑ:k] **1** *adj* stiv (og stivnet); **2** *adv* fullstendig, helt, komplett; *~ naked* splitter naken; *~ staring mad* splitter pine gal.

starling ['stɑ:lɪŋ] *sb* stær.

star|let *sb* ung filmstjerne. **~light** *sb* stjerne|skinn, -skjær. **~lit** *adj* stjerneklar. **starry** ['stɑ:rɪ] *adj* (glitrende) stjerneklar; stjerne|(be)sådd, -glitrende. **starry-eyed** *adj* romantisk; livsfjern, virkelighetsfjern. **star-spangled** *adj* stjerne|besådd, -glitrende.

start [stɑ:t] **I** *sb* **1** start (og startsted, utgangspunkt); begynnelse, innledning, åpning; *from ~ to finish* fra først til sist; *make a fresh ~* begynne på nytt/på et nytt blad; **2** for|del, -sprang; *they had a ~ of/over us* de hadde et forsprang/overtak på oss; **3** rykk; sett, støkk; *by fits and ~s* i rykk og napp; **II** *vb* **1** starte; begynne (og begynne med/på); innlede, åpne; sette i gang; *~ a baby (dgl)* bli med barn; *~ the fire* tenne opp/på; *it ~ed me thinking* det fikk meg til å tenke; *tears ~ed to his eyes* han fikk (plutselig) tårer i øynene; **2** jage (opp); skremme; **3** fare sammen; rykke til; **4** løsne; gå opp (i sammenføyningene); gi/slå seg; **5** *med adv, prep ~* **afresh** begynne forfra (på nytt, på et nytt blad etc); *~* **at** begynne med/på (i f.eks. lønn); *~* **from** begynne/starte fra; gå ut fra; *~* **off** *on* begynne/starte med; *~* **out** *to* begynne å; sette seg fore å; *~* **up** sette i gang/starte (motor); fare/springe opp; fare sammen; *to ~* **with** for det første; til å begynne med. **starter** ['stɑ:tə] *sb* **1** (selv)starter; startmotor; **2** (konkurranse)deltaker; **3** forrett; **4** *US* begynnelse. **starting|-point** *sb* utgangspunkt. **~-post** *sb* startplass.

startle ['stɑ:tl] *vt* **1** skremme; skake opp; **2** for|bløffe, -skrekke.

start-up *sb petro* oppstarting.

starvation [stɑ:'veɪʃn] *sb* hunger (og hungersnød); sult. **starve** [stɑ:v] *vb* sulte; lide hungersnød; (*~ out)* sulte ut; *~ for* hungre/lengte etter; *~ to death* sulte i hjel; *be starving (for food) dgl* holde på å sulte i hjel (dvs være svært sulten); *be ~d of* være underernært på.

state [steɪt] **A** *sb* **1** stand (og tilstand); *biol etc* stadium; *in a (terrible) state* i en sørgelig forfatning; *fig* opphisset; fra seg; ute av seg; **2** rang, stilling; stand; *single/unmarried ~* enslig/ugift (stand); **3** seremoniell; prakt; *som adj* galla-; prakt-, stas-; parade-; *lie in ~* ligge på lit de parade; *receive in ~* motta med fullt seremoniell; **4** *(State)* stat; (selvstendig) land/nasjon; *som adj* offisiell, stats-; *US også* som angår den enkelte delstat; *the States = the United States of America* De forente stater, Sambandsstatene; *the State of Maryland (etc)* (del)staten Maryland (etc); *the Department of State/State Department (US)* utenriksdepartementet; *Secretary of State (GB)* minister, statsråd; *US* utenriksminister; **B** *vt* uttrykke (i ord); redegjøre for; erklære, uttale; si (frem); *~ a fact* konstatere (et) faktum; *~ one's name* oppgi/si navnet sitt; *as ~d* som oppgitt/spesifisert; *the witness ~d that* vitnet erklærte at. **state | appartment(s)** *sb (fl)* representasjons|leilighet, lokale(r). *~* **coach** *sb* gallavogn. **~craft** *sb* stats(manns)kunst. **State Department** *sb*, se *state A 4*. **state|-directed** *adj* stats|dirigert, -styrt; *~-directed funeral* statsbegravelse (begravelse på statens bekostning). **~less** *adj* statsløs. **stately** ['steɪtlɪ] *adj* verdig; prektig, statelig. **statement** ['steɪtmənt] *sb* erklæring (og uttalelse; beretning, fremstilling, redegjørelse; meddelelse, melding etc); *data* setning; *make a ~* avgi/komme med en erklæring/uttalelse; *jur* avgi forklaring. **state | of affairs** *sb* situasjon, stilling; tingenes tilstand. *~* **of health** *sb* helsetilstand. *~* **of play** *sb* stilling (i diskusjon, konkurranse etc). *~* **of war** *sb* krigstilstand. **~-operated** *adj* statsdrevet. *~* **police** *sb* statspoliti. **~room** *sb* representasjons|lokale, -rom; salong, stasstue; *især sjø* lugar; *US også* kupé. **statesman** ['steɪtsmən] *sb* statsmann. **statesman|like** *adj* statsmannsmessig, statsmanns-. **~ship** *sb* stats(manns)kunst.

static ['stætɪk] **1** *adj* statisk; stillestående, ubevegelig; **2** *sb fl* radiostøy; *dgl* forstyrrelser, spraking.

station ['steɪʃn] **I** *sb* **1** bestemt plass/sted; *ofte* (-)post, (-)stasjon; *som adj* stasjons-; *broadcasting ~* radiostasjon, kringkastingsstasjon; *disk ~* diskettstasjon; *fire ~* brannstasjon; *police ~* politistasjon; *railway ~* jernbanestasjon; **2** posisjon; rang, stand; stilling (i livet); *marry above one's ~* gifte seg over sin stand; **3** (australsk) sauefarm; **II** *vt* plassere; postere, stasjonere. **stationary** ['steɪʃnrɪ] *adj* stasjonær; fast montert. **stationer** ['steɪʃənə] *sb* papirhandler. **stationery** ['steɪʃnrɪ] *sb* skrive|papir, -saker; papirvarer. **station | master** *sb* stasjonsmester. **~-wagon** *sb* stasjons|bil, -vogn.

statistical [stə'tɪstɪkl] *adj* statistisk. **statistician** [ˌstætɪ'stɪʃn] *sb* statistiker. **statistics** [stə'tɪstɪks] *sb* *fl* statistikk (og statistisk materiale etc).

statue ['stætʃu:] *sb* statue. **statuesque** [ˌstætʃu'esk] *adj* statue|aktig, -lignende; prektig, statelig. **statuette** [ˌstætʃu'et] *sb* statuett. **stature** ['stætʃə] *sb* (legems)høyde; *short of* ~ kort/liten a vekst. **status** ['steɪtəs] *sb* status; posisjon, stilling. **status | field** *sb data* meldingsfelt. ~ **line** *sb data* statuslinje. ~ **symbol** *sb* statussymbol. **statute** ['stætʃu:t] *sb* statutt, vedtekt; (nedskrevet) lov. **statutory** ['stætʃutrɪ] *adj* lov|festet, -messig; lov-.

staunch [stɔ:ntʃ] **A** *adj* lojal, trofast; solid, stø; **B** *vt* stemme/stanse (blod).

stave [steɪv] **I** *sb* **1** stav (især tønne|stav og -staver); sprosse, stang; **2** (stige)trinn; **3** *mus* note|linje, -plan; strofe; **II** *vt* **1** ~ *in* slå inn (stavene i en tønne); knuse, smadre; **2** ~ *off* avverge; holde unna/fra livet; holde stangen.

stay [steɪ] **A I** *sb* **1** opphold; stans, stopp; **2** *jur* utsettelse; **3** *dgl* tæl, utholdenhet; **II** *vb* **1** bli (dvs forbli; bli boende/værende; bli sittende/stående etc); ~ *for dinner* bli til middag; ~ *overnight/the night* bli natten over; overnatte; *it has come to* ~ den/det er kommet for å bli; **2** hefte, oppholde; stanse (dvs få til å stanse/stoppe); *jur* utsette; ~ *one's hand* forholde seg avventende/passiv; unnlate å gripe inn; **3** holde ut; vise utholdenhet; ~ *the course* gjennomføre løpet; stå distansen *etc* (ut); **4** stagge/stille (sult etc); **5** *med adv, prep* ~ **at** bo på (hos, ved etc); oppholde seg på (hos, ved etc); ~ **away** utebli; holde seg borte/unna; ~ **for** se *A II 1*; ~ **in** holde seg inne/innendørs; ~ *in bed* holde sengen; ~ *in bed late* ligge lenge (om morgenen); ~ **on** bli (lenger enn forutsatt/ventet etc); ~ **out** bli ute/utendørs; ~ **put** *dgl* bli sittende/stående *etc*; bli hvor man er; ~ **up** bli/være oppe (dvs ikke gå og legge seg); ~ *up late* være lenge oppe (om kvelden); ~ **with** bo/overnatte *etc* hos; **B I** *sb* **1** *sjø* stag; bardun; *fig* støtte; *quick/slack in* ~*s* rask/sen i vendingen; **2** *fl* korsett, snøreliv; **II** *vb* støtte; stive av; holde oppe. **staysail** *sb* stagseil.

stead [sted] *sb* **1** plass, sted; *også* -sted; -gård, -plass; *in her* ~ i hennes sted; **2** *it will stand him in good* ~ det vil være nyttig/til god hjelp for ham. **steadfast** ['stedfəst] *adj* fast; standhaftig, urokkelig; stø. **steady** ['stedɪ] **I** *adj* **1** stabil, stø; (be)sindig, rolig; **2** jevn, regelmessig; *go* ~ *(dgl)* ha (fast) følge; *keep her* ~*! (sjø)* støtt så! hold henne (dvs båten) på rett kurs! **II** *sb dgl* fast følge; kjæreste; **III** *vb* bli/gjøre stø; stive av; støtte (opp); *fig* berolige, roe. **steady job** *sb* fast arbeid.

steak [steɪk] *sb* biff.

steal [sti:l] *vb* **1** stjele; liste/lure (*from* fra); ~ *a march on* komme i forkjøpet; (ubemerket) skaffe seg et forsprang på; ~ *the scene/the show* stjele forestillingen/ *dgl* showet (dvs sørge for å få all oppmerksomhet henledet på seg); **2** liste/lure seg (dvs bevege seg stille, stjålent etc); ~ *away/off* lure seg unna; stikke av (i all stillhet). **stealth** [stelθ] *sb: by* ~ i smug; i stillhet. **stealthy** ['stelθɪ] *adj* listende, lurende; *a* ~ *glance* et stjålent øyekast.

steam [sti:m] **I** *sb* **1** damp (og fuktighet, råme; dugg på vindusrute etc; os; dunst, utdunstning); **2** *dgl* fart, futt; tæl; *let off* ~ slippe ut damp; *især fig* få utløp for ergrelse/sinne etc; avreagere; **II** *vb* dampe (og damp|koke, -tørre; ose, ryke; dugge; dunste etc); ~ *open* dampe opp (f.eks. en gjenklebet konvolutt); ~ *up* sette fart i; *fig* hisse opp. **steam|boat** *sb* dampbåt. **~-boiler** *sb* dampkjel(e). **~-engine** *sb* dampmaskin. **~er** *sb* damper (= **1** dampskip; **2** dampkoker). ~ **hammer** *sb* damphammer. **~powered** *adj* dampdrevet. **~-roller** *sb* dampveivals(e). **~ship** *sb* dampskip. ~ **whistle** *sb* dampfløyte. ~ **winch** *sb* dampvinsj. **steamy** ['sti:mɪ] *adj* dampende, dampfylt; damp-; dugget, tåket; rå.

steed [sti:d] *sb bokl/poet* ganger (dvs hest).

steel [sti:l] **1** *sb* stål (og ting av stål, især om redskaper og våpen); *som adj* stål-; **2** *vt* (stål)herde; *især fig* stålsette. **steel | band** *sb* calypsoband. **~-blue** *adj* stålblå. **~-clad** *adj* stål|kledd, (-)pansret. **~-grey** *adj* stålgrå. ~ **mill** *sb* stålverk. **~-plated** *adj* = ~*-clad.* ~ **wool** *sb* stålull. **~works** *sb fl* = ~ *mill.* **steely** ['sti:lɪ] *adj* stålhard, stål-; *fig* hard, ubøyelig; urokkelig.

steep [sti:p] **A I** *adj* **1** bratt, steil; **2** *dgl* drøy, urimelig; ublu; ~ *price* stiv pris; **II** *sb bokl* skrent; stup; **B** *vb* **1** bløte (ut); gjennombløte; **2** *fig:* ~*ed in* gjennomsyret av; fordypet/hensunket i. **steepen** ['sti:pn] bli/gjøre bratt(ere). **steeple** ['sti:pl] *sb* spisst tårn; kirketårn. **steeple|chase** *sb* terreng|løp, -ritt (med hinder). **~-jack** *sb* blikkslager (som arbeider på kirketårn etc).

steer ['stɪə] **A** *vb* styre; lose, navigere; *hum* geleide; ~ *clear of* gå/styre klar av; **B** *sb* ungstut. **steerage** ['stɪərɪdʒ] *sb* **1** tredjeklasse/turistklasse (på skip); *også* dekksplass; **2** styring. **steering** ['stɪərɪŋ] *sb* styring. **steering|-column** *sb* rattstamme. **~-gear** *sb* styring; styre|mekanisme, -snekke; -innretning, -maskin. **~-rod** *sb* styrestang. **~-wheel** *sb* ratt, styrehjul. **steersman** ['stɪəzmən] *sb* ror|gjenger, -mann.

stellar ['stelə] *adj* stjerne-; stellar(-).

stem [stem] **A I** *sb* **1** stamme (også *fig*, f.eks. om ordstamme); **2** stengel, stilk (også om f.eks. pipe|-munnstykke, -stilk); stett (på glass); *mus* (note)hals; **3** stavn, stevn; *from* ~ *to stern* fra for til akter; **4** *(~ turn)* stemsving (på ski); ; **II** *vi US:* ~ *from* komme/stamme fra; skrive seg fra; **B** *vt* **1** stanse, stemme; demme opp for (også *fig*); **2** ~ *the current/the tide* gå mot strømmen (også *fig*). **stem | Christie, ~ Christiania** *sb* Kristianiasving (på ski). **stemmed** [stemd] *adj* -stilket; *long-*~ langstilket.

stench [stentʃ] *sb* stank.

stencil ['stensl] **1** *sb* sjablon, stensil; **2** *vt* stensilere; male (prege, trykke etc) ved hjelp av sjabloner/stensiler.

steno ['stenəu] *sb*, *US fork* for **stenographer** [stə'nɒgrəfə] *sb* stenograf. **stenographic** [ˌstenəu'græfik] *adj* stenografisk. **stenography** [stə'nɒgrəfɪ] *sb* stenografi.

step [step] **A I** *sb* **1** skritt, steg; trinn; *~ by ~* skritt for skritt; gradvis, trinnvis; *take a ~* ta et skritt; *take ~s to* ta skritt (dvs gjøre noe, ta sine forholdsregler etc) for å; *watch one's ~* se seg for; være forsiktig; **2** *(foot~)* fot|trinn, (-)spor; *follow in his ~s* følge i hans (fot)spor; **3** takt, tritt; *break ~* bryte/komme ut av takt(en); *in/out of ~* i/ute av takt; *keep ~ with* gå i takt med; holde tritt med; **4** trinn (i stige, trapp etc); *pair of ~s* gardintrapp, trappestige; **5** *fig* trinn (på rangstige etc); *get one's ~* bli forfremmet; **II** *vb* **1** skritte (dvs gå/komme etc et par skritt); tre, trå; *fig* skride; *~ this way, please* (vennligst kom) denne vei; **2** steppe; *~ it (dgl)* danse; **3** *med adv, prep: I must ~* **along** jeg må (se å) komme meg av sted/komme (meg) videre; *~* **aside** *fig* gå/tre til side; *~* **back** gå tilbake; *fig* trekke seg/tre tilbake; *~* **between** gå/legge seg imellom; *~* **down** gå (komme, stige etc) ned; trekke seg/tre tilbake; sette ned gradvis; *~* **in** gå (komme, tre etc) inn; gripe/skride inn; *~* **inside** gå (komme, tre etc) innenfor; *~* **into** *a fortune* arve en formue; *dgl* komme til penger; *~* **on** trå på; *~ on it* gi (full) gass; få opp farten; *~* **out** gå (komme, tre etc) ut; lange ut; skritte opp; *~ out on (US)* være utro mot; *~* **up** øke gradvis/trinnvis; fremskynde; **B** *pref* ste-. **step|child** *sb* stebarn. **~daughter** *sb* stedatter. **~father** *sb* stefar. **~ladder** *sb* gardintrapp, trappestige. **~mother** *sb* stemor. **stepping-stone** *sb* **1** vadestein; **2** *fig* skritt/trinn (på veien); springbrett. **stepson** *sb* stesønn.

stereo ['sterɪəʊ] **1** *adj = stereophonic*; **2** *dgl* stereo (dvs stereo|anlegg, -radio etc). **stereophonic** [ˌsterɪəʊ'fɒnɪk] *adj* stereofonisk. **stereoscope** ['sterɪəʊskəʊp] *sb* stereoskop. **stereoscopic** [ˌsterɪəʊ'skɒpɪk] *adj* stereoskopisk. **stereotype** ['sterɪəʊtaɪp] *sb* klisjé; *fig også* forslitt frase/uttrykk. **stereotyped** ['sterɪəʊtaɪpt] *adj* stereotyp; klisjé|aktig, -preget; forslitt.

sterile ['steraɪl] *adj* steril; gold, ufruktbar. **sterility** [stə'rɪlətɪ] *sb* sterilitet *etc*. **sterilization** [ˌsterɪlaɪ'zeɪʃn] *sb* sterilisering. **sterilize** ['sterɪlaɪz] *vt* sterilisere.

sterling ['stɜ:lɪŋ] **I** *adj* **1** full|verdig, -lødig; **2** *fig* helstøpt; ekte, opprinnelig; (bunn)solid, traust; **II** *sb* britisk mynt/valuta; *payable in ~* betalbar i britisk valuta.

stern [stɜ:n] **A** *adj* **1** krevende; **2** hard, streng; barsk; **B** *sb* **1** *sjø* akterende, hekk; **2** bak|del, -part; ende. **sternsheets** ['stɜ:nʃi:ts] *sb fl* akter|plikt, -rom; -tofter.

stevedore ['sti:vədɔ:] *sb* bryggearbeider, stuer.

stew [stju:] **I** *sb* **1** ragu, stuing; ≈ lapskaus; **2** *dgl: in a ~* nervøs, oppjaget; **II** *vb* (små)koke, (-)putre; lage ragu *etc* av; *let him ~ in his own juice* la ham steke i sitt eget fett (dvs la ham selv ordne opp i sine problemer etc).

steward ['stju:əd] *sb* **1** (hus)hovmester; intendant, økonom; *hist* godsforvalter; **2** *fly, sjø* steward, stuert; **3** *(shop ~)* klubbleder, (faglig) tillitsperson; **4** seremonimester; stevne|arrangør, -leder; ordensvakt; **5** veddeløpsleder. **stewardess** ['stju:ədɪs] *sb* kvinnelig steward/stuert *etc*; *især* flyvertinne; *sjø* lugarpike, trise.

stick [stɪk] **A 1** *sb* stokk (og kjepp, påk, stav; kvist, pinne etc); stykke (av kritt, såpe etc); *sport* kølle; kø (til biljard); *sjø* stake/stang (dvs del av mast); *fly (joy-~)* stikke; styre|pinne, -spak; *dgl* tørrpinne; tverrpomp; *~s (of furniture) dgl* innbo, møbler; *get hold of the wrong end of the ~* misforstå; komme på feil spor; *give the ~/take a ~ to* pryle; *not a ~* ikke en flis; **2** *vt* støtte opp med stokker etc; *~ peas* stenge erter; **B** *vb* **1** stikke; gjennombore, spidde; *~ a pig* stikke (dvs slakte) en gris; **2** feste; klebe/lime (sammen); *~ a poster* sette/slå opp en plakat; *~ no bills* plakater forbudt; **3** henge/sitte fast; bli hengende/sittende (fast); *make ~* få til å sitte (fast); *fig* gjøre effektiv/gyldig; *the door ~s* døren går trått; **4** *dgl* plassere (og legge, putte, sette, stikke, stille etc); *just ~ it there* bare sett den/det der; **5** tåle; holde ut; *~ it* finne seg i det; **6** *med adv, prep ~* **around** bli/holde seg i nærheten; *~* **at** holde fast ved; klebe ved; *~ at nothing* ikke vike tilbake for noen ting; *don't ~ at trifles* heng deg ikke opp i bagateller; *~* **by** stå ved; holde fast ved; være tro mot; *~* **down** klebe/klistre igjen; *dgl* legge/sette fra seg; rable/skrive ned; *~* **in** stikke *etc* inn; *~ in the mud* sitte fast i leiren; *især fig* holde fast ved foreldede meninger etc; *~-in-the-mud* stabeis; ultrakonservativ (person); *~* **on** klebe/klistre på; sette/ta på (seg); *~ it on (slang)* smøre tykt på; ta kraftig i; *~* **out** rage/stikke frem; stikke seg frem; holde ut (jf *B 5*); *~ out for* holde fast ved; stå fast på (krav etc); *~ out one's neck* våge seg (for) langt frem; våge skinnet; *it ~s out a mile* det er synlig på lang avstand; det er ikke til å ta feil av; *~* **to** henge/klebe (fast) ved; stå ved; *~ to one's bush/last* bli ved sin lest (dvs holde seg til det en kan og har greie på); *~ to one's promise* stå ved sitt løfte; *~* **together** holde sammen; *~* **up** rage/stikke opp; klistre (sette, slå etc) opp; *dgl* overfalle, rane; *~ up for* gå i bresjen for; ta i forsvar; *~ up to* gjøre motstand mot; sette seg imot; *~ 'em up!* opp med hendene! **sticker** ['stɪkə] *sb* **1** stikkeredskap; brodd, pigg; torn; **2** en som stikker (etc, jf *stick B*); griseslakter; **3** (gummiert) etikett; klebemerke, oblat; **4** en påhengelig (iherdig, sta etc) person. **sticking-plaster** *sb* heftplaster.

stickler ['stɪklə] *sb* pedant, petimeter; *be a ~ for* være meget nøye med.

stick-up *sb* overfall, ran.

sticky ['stɪkɪ] *adj* **1** klebrig; klissen, seig; **2** klam, lummer; trykkende; **3** ubehagelig; vanskelig, vrang, vrien; *come to a ~ end (slang)* ende med forferdelse; dø en ubehagelig død.

stiff [stɪf] **I** *adj* **1** stiv; hard, ubøyelig (også *fig*); *~ as a poker* stiv som en pinne; **2** hard; streng, strid; vanskelig, vrien; sterk (om brennevin, vind etc); **3** *dgl: bore ~* kjede livet av; *scare ~* skremme vettet av; **II** *sb dgl* kadaver, lik. **stiffen** ['stɪfn] *vb* bli/gjøre stiv(ere) etc.

stifle ['staɪfl] *vb* kvele(s); undertrykke. **stifling** ['staɪflɪŋ] *adj* kvelende; lummer.

stigma ['stɪgmə] *sb* brennemerke; skamplett; *også rel* stigma. **stigmatize** ['stɪgmətaɪz] *vt* brennemerke; *også rel* stigmatisere.

stile [staɪl] *sb* klyveled.

stiletto [stɪ'letəʊ] *sb* stilett. **stiletto heel** *sb* stiletthæl.

still [stɪl] **A I** *adj, adv* **1** rolig, stille; *om vin* ikke musserende; **2** dempet, stille; **3** taus; **II** *sb* **1** *poet* dyp ro/stillhet; **2** *film* stillbilde; (vanlig) fotografi; **III** *vt* **1** berolige; **2** dempe; bringe til taushet; **B** *adv* **1** fremdeles, stadig; ennå; **2** enda; ~ *another (example etc)* enda et (eksempel etc); ~ *better* enda bedre; **3** likevel, dog; **C I** *sb* **1** destillasjonsapparat; **2** destilleri; brenneri; **II** *vt* destillere. **still|-birth** *sb* dødfødsel. **~-born** *adj* dødfødt. **~-life** *sb* stilleben.

stilt [stɪlt] *sb, især fl (a pair of~s)* (et par) stylte(r). **stilted** ['stɪltɪd] *adj* oppstyltet; stiv, unaturlig.

stimulant ['stɪmjʊlənt] **1** *adj* oppkvikkende, stimulerende; **2** *sb* stimulans; oppkvikkende/stimulerende middel. **stimulate** ['stɪmjʊleɪt] *vt* stimulere; egge, oppirre. **stimulus** ['stɪmjʊləs] *sb* stimulans; ansporing, spore.

sting [stɪŋ] **I** *sb* **1** stikk; smerte|stikk, (-)sting; **2** brodd; nesle|hår, -tråd; **II** *vb* **1** stikke (med brodd etc); brenne, svi; **2** *fig* såre; *stung by remorse* naget av anger.

stinger ['stɪŋə] *sb petro* pongtongbro, rampe.

stingy ['stɪndʒɪ] *adj* **1** gjerrig; gnien, smålig; **2** knuslet; ynkelig lite etc.

stink [stɪŋk] **I** *sb* **1** stank; *fl, skoleslang* kjemi (dvs faget); **2** *dgl* bråk, spetakkel; *public* ~ offentlig skandale; *raise a* ~ lage bråk; **II** *vi* stinke; *fig* være berykket.

stint [stɪnt] **I** *sb* **1** *without* ~ rikelig; uten å være knuslet/smålig; **2** *do one's* ~ gjøre sin daglige dont/gjerning; **II** *vb* knipe inn/spare på.

stipend ['staɪpend] *sb* gasje, lønn (især til prester).

stipple ['stɪpl] *vt* stiple.

stipulate ['stɪpjʊleɪt] *vb* stille som betingelse/vilkår; ~ *for* betinge seg; forutsette; **2** avtale; bli enig/komme overens om; stipulere. **stipulation** [ˌstɪpjʊ'leɪʃn] *sb* betingelse, vilkår; bestemmelse.

stir [stɜː] **I** *sb* **1** *(~ring)* røring *etc*; **2** oppstyr, røre; *create a* ~ vekke oppstyr; **II** *vb* **1** bevege (seg); røre (og røre på seg; røre i; røre opp/rundt i etc); **2** vekke; ruske opp i; ~ *the blood* begeistre; hisse opp. **stirring** ['stɜːrɪŋ] *adj* opphissende; spennende.

stirrup ['stɪrəp] *sb* stigbøyle.

stitch [stɪtʃ] **I** *sb* **1** sting (i søm); maske (i hekling, strikking etc); *a* ~ *in time saves nine* ≈ bedre føre var enn etter snar; *drop a* ~ miste en maske; **2** *med* hold, sting (i siden etc); **3** *dgl* fille, klut; *sjø* seil; *he hasn't got a (dry)* ~ *on* han har ikke en (tørr) tråd på kroppen; *with every* ~ *of sail set* med alle kluter (= seil) satt; **II** *vb* sy (sammen); hefte/neste (sammen).

stoat [stəʊt] *sb* røyskatt.

stock [stɒk] **I** *som adj* **1** lager-; **2** fast, stående; standard; *også* forslitt, stereotyp; *he had three* ~ *jokes* han hadde tre stående vitser (på repertoaret sitt); **II** *sb* **1** forråd, lager; beholdning, bestand; *(live~)* besetning, buskap; fe, kveg; *in* ~ på lager; *out of* ~ utolgt; ikke på lager; *take* ~ holde vareopptelling; gjøre opp status; *take* ~ *of* vurdere; **2** *(fl)* investert kapital; *især* (stats)obligasjoner; *US* aksjer; *~s and shares* aksjer og obligasjoner; *take* ~ *in (US)* kjøpe aksje(r) i; *dgl* feste lit/tiltro til; **3** herkomst; slekt, ætt; *of peasant* ~ av bondeætt; **4** (tre)stamme, (-)stokk; hovedstamme; rotstokk; *~s and stones* livløse ting; **5** underlag; blokk, stokk; *fl* bedding, slipp; *hist* gapestokk; **6** håndtak; skaft, skjefte; *rifle* ~ geværkolbe; **7** (rå)materiale; kraft, sjy; buljong; *film* ~ råfilm; **8** levkøy; **9** *hist* halsbind; **III** *vt* **1** forsyne/utstyre (*with* med); ~ *up* supplere lagerbeholdningen; **2** føre; ha på lager; *well-~ed* vel|assortert, -forsynt. **stockade** [stɒ'keɪd] **I** *sb* **1** palisade(verk); **2** *mil slang* kakebu; straffeleir; **II** *vt* befeste med palisader. **stock|-book** *sb* **2** aksjeprotokoll; **2** = *~-ledger*. **~breeder** *sb* kvegoppdretter. **~broker** *sb* aksjemegler. **~car** *sb* krøttervogn, kuvogn. **~car racing** *sb* billøp med vanlige biler (ikke racerbiler). ~ **company** *sb US* aksjeselskap. **~-cube** *sb* buljongterning. ~ **exchange** *sb* (fonds)børs. **~fish** *sb* stokkfisk, tørrfisk. ~ **goods** *sb fl* lagervarer. **~-holder** *sb* aksjeeier, aksjonær.

stocking ['stɒkɪŋ] *sb* strømpe.

stock|-in-trade *sb* **1** vare|beholdning, (-)lager; **2** driftsmidler; (nødvendig) utrustning/utstyr; *fig* fast repertoar. **~-jobber** *sb* børsspekulant. ~ **keeper** *sb* lagerarbeider. **~-ledger** *sb* lagerprotokoll. ~ **list** *sb* kursliste. ~ **market** *sb* fonds|børs, marked. **~pile 1** *sb* (reserve)|lager, (-)opplag; forråd; *mil* beredskapslager; **2** *vt* bygge opp (reserve)lager av; *også* dynge sammen; hope opp; *neds* hamstre. **~room** *sb* lager(rom). **~-still** *adj* dørgende stille. **~-taking** *sb* vareopptelling; status.

stocky ['stɒkɪ] *adj* tettbygd, undersetsig; kort/liten og tykk.

stockyard *sb* **1** krøtter|inngjerding, -kve; *US også* kjøtthall; **2** lagertomt.

stodge [stɒdʒ] *sb* tung kost. **stodgy** ['stɒdʒɪ] *adj: om mat* solid, tung; *om stil* tung, uinspirerende; *om personer* kjedelig.

stoic ['stəʊɪk] **1** *adj* = *stoical*; **2** *sb* stoiker. **stoical** ['stəʊɪkl] *adj* stoisk. **stoically** ['stəʊɪklɪ] *adv* med stoisk ro.

stoke [stəʊk] *vb* fyre; passe fyr(en); være fyrbøter. **stoker** ['stəʊkə] *sb* fyrbøter.

stole [stəʊl] *sb* stola.

stolid ['stɒlɪd] *adj* dorsk, treg; tungnem.

stomach ['stʌmək] **1** *sb* mave; *fig* appetitt, (mat)lyst; *have no* ~ *for* ikke ha noe lyst til; ikke kunne noe med; *it nearly turned my* ~ jeg holdt på å kaste opp av det; **2** *vt* fordøye (især *fig*); *I can't* ~ *it* jeg greier (klarer, orker etc) det ikke; jeg holder det ikke ut.

stomp [stɒmp] *vi* stampe, trampe.

stone [stəʊn] **I** *som adj, adv* **1** stein-; **2** *fig* fullstendig, helt; **II** *sb* **1** stein (og brostein, gatestein; grav|stein, -støtte; edelstein; gallestein etc); *not leave a ~ standing* ikke la det bli stein tilbake på stein (dvs jevne med jorden; rasere fullstendig); *leave no ~ unturned* ikke la noe middel/noen utvei være uprøvd; **2** vektenhet, se midtsidene; **3** brikke (især til domino); **III** *vt* **1** steine; kaste stein på; **2** fjerne stein(er) fra; ta stein(ene) ut av. *the* **Stone Age** steinalderen. **stone|-blind** *adj* stærblind. **~-breaker, ~ crusher** *sb* stein|pukker; *mek* -knuser. **~cutter, -dresser** *sb* steinhugger.

stoned [stəʊnd] *adj slang* døddrukken; neddopet, narkotisert. **stone|-dead** *adj* steindød. **~-deaf** *adj* stokkdøv. **~ fruit** *sb* steinfrukt. **~ hammer** *sb* steinslegge. **~mason** *sb* gråsteinsmurer. **~pit** *sb* steinbrudd. **~ sober** *adj* klinkende edru. **~-wall 1** *sb* stein|gjerde, -mur; **2** *vt fig* drive filibuster/obstruksjon. **~ware** *sb* steintøy. **~work** *sb* gråsteinsmur.

stony ['stəʊnɪ] *adj* **1** steinet; *on ~ ground* på steingrunn; **2** *fig* hard; kald. **stony|-broke** *adj slang* raka fant. **~ glare** *sb* = *~ stare*. **~ silence** *sb* isnende taushet. **~ stare** *sb* kaldt (hardt, uforsonlig etc) blikk.

stool [stu:l] *sb* **1** stol (uten rygg); krakk, taburett; skammel; **2** avføring, stolgang. **stool-pigeon** *sb* lokkedue.

stoop [stu:p] **I** *sb* **1** luting; lutende gange/holdning; *walk with a ~* gå lutrygget; **2** (rovfugls) nedslag, stup; **II** *vb* **1** lute; være dukknakket/lutrygget; **2** bøye seg (ned); *fig* nedverdige seg; **3** slå/stupe ned (på) (om rovfugl).

stop [stɒp] **I** *sb* **1** stopp (og stoppested etc); *bus-~* bussholdeplass; *come to a ~* stanse; *dead ~* brå|stans, -stopp; **2** avbrytelse, stans, stopp; opphør, slutt; *bring to a ~* stanse; sette en stopper for; **3** stopper (og stoppe|kloss, -knast); kork; plugg, propp; hindring; *put a ~ to* sette en stopper for; **4** skilletegn; *især (full ~)* punktum; **5** *mus* klaff, ventil (på blåseinstrument); register (på orgel); **6** *foto* blender|trinn, åpning; **7** lukkelyd; **II** *vb* **1** (få til å) stanse/stoppe; *~ a blow* (av)parere/fange opp et slag; *~ a bullet* bli truffet av en kule; **2** stanse/stoppe (dvs gjøre holdt); **3** (for)hindre; sperre (veien for); stanse; **4** holde opp; slutte med; ta (en) pause; *~ payment* innstille betalingen; **5** stoppe (igjen); fylle/tette igjen; *~ his mouth* stoppe munnen på ham; *~ one's ears* lukke ørene (dvs ikke ville høre); **6** *dgl* stanse/gjøre et opphold (underveis); **7** *mus* registrere (f.eks. orgel); **8** *foto* blende (*down* ned); **9** *med adv, prep* **~ at** *(a hotel)* ta inn (på et hotell); *~ at nothing* ikke vike tilbake for noe; **~ away** holde seg borte/unna; **~ dead** bråstoppe; **~ down** se *II 8*; **~ from** = *~ out of*; **~ off** *US* gjøre et kort opphold (underveis); *~ £30* **out of** *his wages* holde tilbake 30 pund av lønnen hans; trekke ham for 30 pund i lønnen; **~ over** *(at)* stanse/gjøre opphold (hos/ved); ligge over (hos); **~ short** = *~ dead*; **~ up** fylle/tette igjen; *~ up (late)* være lenge oppe (om kvelden). **stop|-cock** *sb* stoppekran. **~ code** *sb data* stoppkode. **~gap 1** *adj* midlertidig; krise-, nødhjelps-; **2** *sb* nødhjelp; (midlertidig) erstatning; surrogat; *use it as a ~gap* bruke den/det i mangel av noe bedre. **~ key** *sb data* stopptast. **~-over** *sb* (kortere) opphold/stans (underveis). **stoppage** ['stɒpɪdʒ] *sb* **1** stans (og driftsstans; avbrudd, avbrytelse etc); **2** tilbakehold (av utbetaling); (lønns)trekk; **3** fylling; tilstopping; **4** hindring, sperring; **5** *foto* blender(innstilling). **stopper** ['stɒpə] **I** *sb* **1** stans, stopper; *put a ~ on* sette en stopper for; **2** kork; plugg, propp; **3** *sjø (chain ~)* (kjetting)stopper; **II** *vt* **1** korke; plugge/tette igjen; **2** *sjø* legge en stopper på. **stopping** ['stɒpɪŋ] *sb* fylling; *især* plombe. **stop-press (news)** *sb fl* siste nytt (dvs som kommer idet avisen skal gå i trykken). **~-sign** *sb* stopp|signal, -skilt. **~-watch** *sb* stoppeklokke.

storage ['stɔ:rɪdʒ] *sb* **1** lagring, oppbevaring; **2** lager(plass); *også* = *~ house*; **3** lagerleie; oppbevaringsavgift; **4** *elek* oppladning. **storage | battery** *sb* akkumulator(batteri). **~ block** *sb data* lagerblokk. **~ control** *sb data* lagerstyring. **~ heater** *sb* varmemagasin. **~ house** *sb* lager; magasin, pakkhus. **~ map** *sb data* lagerliste. **~ protection** *sb data* lagersikring. **~ size** *sb data* lagerkapasitet. **~ tank** *sb petro* lagertank. **store** [stɔ:] **I** *sb* **1** lager(beholdning); beholdning(er), forsyning(er); forråd; opplag; *~s of* hauger/mengder av; *in ~* på lager; *have in ~ (fig)* ha i vente; **2** lager(bygning); magasin, pakkhus; *mil* depot; **3** *GB fl* varemagasin; *US ent* butikk, forretning; *chain ~* kjedeforretning; *department ~* stormagasin, varemagasin; *general ~* land|handel, -handleri; **4** *set great ~ by/on* sette stor pris på; legge stor vekt på; **II** *vt* **1** *(~ up)* lagre; legge til side; hope opp; **2** forsyne; fylle; *~ with provisions* utruste med proviant. **store|house** *sb* lager(bygning); magasin, pakkhus. **~-keeper** *sb* **1** lagersjef; materialforvalter; **2** *US* butikkinnehaver, kjøpmann. **~room** *sb* lager(rom).

stor(e)y ['stɔ:rɪ] *sb* etasje. **storeyed, storied** ['stɔ:rɪd] *adj* -etasjes (dvs med ... etasjer); *multi-~ car park* bilparkering i flere etasjer; ≈ parkeringshus.

stork [stɔ:k] *sb* stork.

storm [stɔ:m] **I** *sb* **1** storm; *oftere* uvær, uværsbyge; *thunder~* torden|byge, -vær; *ride out a ~* ri av en storm (også *fig*); **2** (følelses)|storm, (-)utbrudd; *~ in a teacup* storm i et vannglass; *~ of applause* bifallsbrus; *~ of protest* proteststorm; **3** *mil* storm(angrep); *take by ~* ta med storm; **II** *vb* **1** storme; blåse sterkt; **2** rase; *~ and rage* skjelle og smelle; **3** *mil* storme; (inn)ta med storm. **storm|-beaten** *adj* stormpisket. **~-bound** *adj* værfast. **~ centre** *sb* stormsenter, uværssentrum. **~-cloud** *sb* uværssky. **~ful** *adj* stormfull. **~ lamp, ~ lantern** *sb* stormlykt. **~ petrel** *sb* havsvale; *fig* urokråke. **~ porch** *sb* vindfang. **~-proof** *adj* uværssikker. **~-tossed** *adj* omtumlet av storm/uvær. **~-troops** *sb fl* stormtropper. **~wind** *sb* stormvind. **stormy** ['stɔ:mɪ] *adj* stormende/stormfull (også *fig*); storm-, uværs-.

story ['stɔ:rɪ] **A I** *sb* **1** historie; **2** beretning, fortelling; anekdote, skrøne; *short* ~ novelle; **3** *dgl* skrøne (dvs usann historie); *tell stories (også)* lyve, skrøne; **4** handling/intrige (i roman etc); **5** folkesnakk, rykte; *the* ~ *goes that* det fortelles/ryktet vil ha det til at; **II** *vt: storied* sagnomsust; *a storied past* en minnerik fortid; **B** se *stor(e)y*. **story|-book** *sb* eventyrbok, fortellingsbok; *også* novellesamling; *~-book ending* lykkelig slutt. **~-teller** *sb* (eventyr)forteller; skrønemaker. **~-writer** *sb* (novelle)forfatter; *også* historieskriver (jf *1*).

stout [staʊt] **I** *adj* **1** røslig; kraftig, sterk; **2** modig, tapper; standhaftig; **3** svær, tykk; før, korpulent; **II** *sb* (slags) sterkt øl. **stout-hearted** *adj* kjekk, modig; *gml* behjertet.

stove [stəʊv] *sb* ovn; kokeapparat, komfyr. **stove-pipe** *sb* ovnsrør, pipe; *~-pipe (hat)* flosshatt.

stow [stəʊ] *vt* pakke (ned); stue (bort); *sjø* beslå (køye, seil etc); ~ *away* pakke bort/ned; legge vekk/til side. **stowaway** *sb* blindpassasjer.

straddle ['strædl] **1** *sb* skreving; *fig* tvetydig/uforpliktende holdning; **2** *vb* skreve/sitte skrevs (over); *fig* innta en vaklende/tvetydig holdning; *dgl* sitte på gjerdet.

strafe [streɪf] *vt dgl* **1** beskyte/bombardere (fra fly i lav høyde); **2** straffe; gi en overhaling.

straggle ['strægl] *vi* **1** flakke/streife omkring; forville seg; gå seg bort; *om ting* bre/spre seg utover; **2** bli etter; ikke kunne holde følge. **straggler** ['stræglə] *sb* etternøler.

straight [streɪt] **I** *adj* **1** rett (og rettlinjet; rak, strak etc); *om hår* glatt, slett; *om tankegang* klar; *dead* ~ snorrett; **2** rank, rett (i ryggen); **3** ordentlig; korrekt, riktig; *get/put* ~ bringe i orden; få orden/skikk på; *set* ~ rettlede; **4** rettskaffen; pålitelig, ærlig; skikkelig; **5** likefrem; oppriktig, åpenhjertig; *a* ~ *answer* et greit/realt svar; **6** *dgl* bar (dvs om brennevin: ren, ublandet); **7** *keep a* ~ *face* bevare masken (dvs alvoret etc); gjøre gode miner til slett spill; *vote the* ~ *ticket* følge partilinjen (i sin stemmegivning); **II** *adv* **1** rett (etc, jf *I 1* og *2*); **2** *(~ away/off)* like, rett; omgående, straks; *come* ~ *to the point* gå rakt/rett på sak; *tell them* ~ *out* si dem det like/rett ut; **3** *go/run* ~ leve et lovlydig liv; *også* = *keep* ~ holde seg klar av loven; **III** *sb* **1** rett linje (stykke, veistrekning etc); oppløpsside (på idrettsbane); *out of* ~ kroket; (vind)skjev; **2** *be on the* ~ holde seg på den rette siden av loven; **3** straight (i poker). **straight | angle** *sb* like vinkel (dvs på 180 grader). **~-backed** *adj* rakrygget, rettrygget; *om stol også* høyrygget. ~ **combed** *adj* glattkjemmet. **straighten** ['streɪtn] *vb* rette (opp, ut etc); ~ *one's face* legge ansiktet i de rette folder; ~ *out* rette ut; *om bulket bil* rette opp; *fig* ordne seg; ordne opp i; glatte over; jevne ut; ~ *up* rette (seg) opp; rydde opp (i). **straight | fight** *sb* (politisk) valgkamp mellom (bare) to kandidater. **straightforward** [streɪt'fɔ:wəd] *adj* **1** endefrem, likefrem; åpenhjertig; **2** enkel, liketil; real, skvær; ærlig. **straight | play** *sb* tale|drama, -stykke. ~ **tip** *sb* stalltips. **straightway** ['streɪtweɪ] *adv* omgående, straks.

strain [streɪn] **A I** *sb* **1** spent/strammet tilstand; *under* ~ under belastning; **2** (sterk) påkjenning; (over)anstrengelse; press, stress; ~ *on the nerves* nervepåkjenning; *it is a* ~ *on the eyes* det tar på øynene; **3** *med* forstrekning; **II** *vb* **1** spenne; stramme, strekke; *fig* anspenne; (over)anstrenge; ~ *after* hige/jage etter; ~ *at* (se også *5*) nære betenkeligheter ved; nøle; ~ *at the leash* slite i kobbelet; være utålmodig etter å komme i gang; **2** for|vanske, -vri; overdrive; ~ *the law* bøye loven; ~ *the truth* tøye sannheten; **3** *med* forstrekke; **4** *bokl* knuge, presse; **5** filtrere(s), sile(s); ~ *at a gnat* hefte seg i småting; gjøre opphevelser for bagateller; **B** *sb* **1** slekt, ætt; herkomst; **2** rase; art, type; **3** (karakter)|drag, (-)trekk; *også* anlegg; element, spor; snev; **4** tone(fall); grunntone; **5** *fl poet* melodi; strofer, toner; musikk. **strained** [streɪnd] *adj, pp* (an)spent; anstrengt; *også* forsert, søkt. **strainer** ['streɪnə] *sb* filter; sikt, sil.

strait [streɪt] **I** *adj gml* smal, trang; **II** *sb* **1** *(fl)* strede, sund; **2** *fl* klemme, knipe(tak); vanskelighet(er). **straiten** ['streɪtn] *vt* inn|skrenke, -snevre (især *fig*). **straitened** ['streɪtnd] *adj* trang; *in* ~ *circumstances* i trange/vanskelige kår. **strait|-jacket** *sb* tvangstrøye. **~-laced** *adj* snerpet; (moralsk) streng.

strand [strænd] **A** *sb* **1** fiber (i tråd etc); dukt, kordel; snor, streng; *fig* bånd; **2** hår(strå); lokk, tjafs; **B 1** *sb bokl* bredd, strand; **2** *vb* strande; *be (left) ~ed* bli stående (igjen) hjelpeløs/på bar bakke etc.

strange [streɪndʒ] *adj* **1** fremmed(artet); ukjent; *be* ~ *to something* være ukjent med noe; **2** merkelig, underlig; rar; ~ *to say* merkelig/underlig nok. **stranger** ['streɪndʒə] *sb* fremmed (person).

strangle ['strægl] *vt* **1** kvele, strupe; **2** undertrykke. **stranglehold** ['stræŋglhəʊld] *sb* kvele(r)tak, strupetak (især *fig*). **strangulation** [ˌstræŋgjʊ'leɪʃn] *sb* kveling, struping.

strap [stræp] **I** *sb* (lær)reim, stropp; **II** *vt* **1** spenne fast (med reimer, stropper etc); **2** denge/jule (med reim etc). **strap|hanger** *sb* ståpassasjer (dvs passasjer som står og holder seg fast i stroppen på buss etc). **~ping** *adj* røslig, svær; kraftig, sterk. **~less** *adj*, *sb* (kjole) uten skulderstropper.

stratagem ['strætədʒəm] *sb* (krigs)list, lureri. **strategic** [strə'ti:dʒɪk] **1** *adj* strategisk; **2** *sb fl* strategi (dvs som fag/vitenskap). **strategist** ['strætɪdʒɪst] *sb* strateg. **strategy** ['strætɪdʒɪ] *sb* strategi (dvs fremgangsmåte, plan etc).

stratosphere ['strætəsfɪə] *sb* stratosfære. **stratospheric** [ˌstrætəs'ferɪk] *adj* stratosfærisk. **stratum** ['streɪtəm] *sb* **1** lag, stratum; **2** befolkningslag, klasse.

straw [strɔ:] *sb* strå (og ting av strå, især sugerør og *gml* stråhatt); *koll* halm; *catch (grasp, seize)/clutch at a* ~ gripe etter/klynge seg til et halmstrå; *I don't care a* ~ jeg gir blaffen (i det); *the last* ~ *(that breaks the camel's back)* ≈ dråpen som får begeret til å flyte over. **straw|berry** *sb* jordbær. **~-chopper** *sb* hakkelsmaskin. **~-coloured** *adj* strå|farget, -gul.

stray [streɪ] **I** *adj* **1** bortkommet; herreløs, hjemløs; **2** spredt, tilfeldig; sporadisk; **II** *sb* hjemløst/omflakkende barn; herreløst dyr; **III** *vi* flakke/vandre omkring; komme på avveie/villspor. **stray dog** *sb* løsbikkje.

streak [stri:k] **I** *sb* **1** strek; strime, stripe; *like a ~ (of lightning)* som en strek/(et lyn); **2** drag, trekk; anstrøk, snev; **3** *have a ~ of luck/bad luck* ha (forbigående) flaks/uflaks; sitte i hell/uhell; **II** *vb* **1** streke opp, merke med streker/striper; **2** *dgl* fare/suse (av sted). **streaky** ['stri:kɪ] *adj* stripet; broket, variabel; *fig* usikker, upålitelig.

stream [stri:m] **I** *sb* **1** strøm; *go with the ~* følge med strømmen; **2** bekk; elv, vassdrag; **II** *vi* flyte, strømme; *om flagg* vaie; *om hår* flagre (i vinden). **stream day** *sb petro* driftsdøgn. **streamer** ['stri:mə] *sb* **1** vimpel; **2** konfetti, serpentin; **3** *data* strømmer. **streaming tape** *sb data* = *streamer 3.* **streamlined** ['stri:mlaɪnd] *adj* strømlinjeformet, strømlinjet.

street [stri:t] *sb* gate; *~s ahead of* langt forut for; *~s apart* vidt forskjellige; *the man in the ~* mannen i gata (dvs gjennomsnitts|mannen, -mennesket). **street arab** *sb* gategutt. **~car** *sb US* sporvogn, trikk. **~ cleaner** *sb* gatefeier. **~ door** *sb* gatedør. **~-girl** *sb* gatepike, prostituert. **~-lamp** *sb* gate|lampe, -lykt. **~ organ** *sb* lirekasse. **~ peddler** *sb* gateselger. **~ sweeper** *sb* gatefeier; feiebil.

strength [streŋθ] *sb* **1** kraft, styrke; *go from ~ to ~* vokse seg stadig sterkere; *try one's ~ on* prøve kreftene (sine) på; **2** styrke (dvs sterk egenskap/side etc); **3** *on the ~ of* i kraft av; i tillit til; **4** (mannskaps)styrke; *bring up to ~* bringe opp i full styrke; *in (great) ~* mannsterk(t), tallrik(e). **strengthen** ['streŋθn] *vb* forsterke(s), styrke(s); bli/gjøre sterk(ere). **strengthening** ['streŋθnɪŋ] *sb* forsterkning, styrking.

strenuous ['strenjʊəs] *adj* **1** energisk; iherdig, ivrig; **2** anstrengende, tung.

stress [stres] **I** *sb* **1** *mek* spenning; **2** belastning; press, trykk; *times of ~* harde/vanskelige tider; **3** ettertrykk, vekt; *lay ~ on* fremheve, understreke; legge vekt på; **4** betoning, (etter)trykk; aksent; **5** *med* stress; (mental) påkjenning; **II** *vt* aksentuere, betone; legge trykk/vekt på. **stressed** [strest] *adj, pp* **1** (an)spent, stresset; **2** betont, trykksterk. **stress-mark** *sb* aksent(tegn).

stretch [stretʃ] **I** *sb* **1** *(~ing)* strekk(ing); *give a ~* strekke (på) seg; **2** anspennelse, anstrengelse; *by a ~ of imagination* med litt fantasi/*ofte* godvilje; *også* ved å tøye fantasien (litt); **3** distanse, strekning; langside (på idrettsbane); *sjø* baut, strekk; **4** periode, tidsrom; *at a ~* i ett strekk; *do a ~ (slang)* sitte inne (dvs sone fengselsstraff); **II** *vb* **1** strekke, tøye; spenne/strekke ut; rekke (ut); *~ a point* strekke seg litt lenger enn regler etc gir adgang til; *ofte* gjøre en innrømmelse/et unntak; *~ one's power* gjøre en (kraft)anstrengelse; *~ one's principles* slakke på prinsippene (sine); **2** strekke/tøye seg. **stretcher** ['stretʃə] *sb* **1** strekker (etc, jf *stretch II 1*); **2** (syke)båre. **stretcher-bearer** *sb* portør, sykebærer.

strew [stru:] *vt* (be)strø; strø/så ut.

stricken ['strɪkn] *adj, pp* slått (især *fig*); hjemsøkt, plaget; *terror-~* skrekkslagen.

strict [strɪkt] *adj* **1** nøye, omhyggelig; nøyeregnende, streng; *in ~ confidence* i dypeste fortrolighet; **2** nøyaktig, presis; *in the ~ sense of the word* i ordets egentlige betydning. **strict accuracy** *sb* pinlig nøyaktighet. **strictly | confidential** *adj* strengt fortrolig. **~ speaking** *adv* strengt tatt. **stricture** ['strɪktʃə] *sb* **1** *med* forsnevring; **2** (streng) kritikk.

stride [straɪd] **I** *sb* langt skritt/steg; *get into one's ~* komme i gang/i gjenge; *take it in one's ~* ta det i samme vendingen/*dgl* slengen; **II** *vb* **1** skritte (godt ut); skride; **2** skreve/sitte skrevs over.

strife [straɪf] *sb* bråk, krangel; strid, ufred.

strike [straɪk] **I** *sb* **1** streik; *be on ~* streike; *call a ~* erklære streik; *come/go out on ~* gå til streik; *general ~* generalstreik; **2** funn (av gull, olje etc); *make a ~* gjøre et rikt funn/*fig* et godt varp; være heldig; **3** *mil* (fly)angrep; bombe|angrep, -tokt; **II** *vb* **1** slå (og slå i, mot, på, til etc; *fig, mus* slå an); ramme, råke, treffe; *~ a blow for* slå et slag for; *~ a rock* gå/støte på en klippe; *~ fire* slå ild; *~ (the) ground* gå på grunn; *~ terror into them* slå dem med skrekk; *~ while the iron is hot* smi mens jernet er varmt; *the hour has struck* klokken/timen er slagen; tiden er inne; **2** finne; komme over; støte på; *~ oil* finne olje; *fig* gjøre et kupp/et varp; **3** prege/slå (mynt etc); *fig* slå (dvs gjøre et bestemt inntrykk på); *he doesn't ~ me as particularly bright* han virker ikke særlig oppvakt (på meg); *how does it ~ you* hva synes du om den/det; *the idea just struck me that* det slo meg nettopp at; jeg kom akkurat til å tenke på at; **4** angripe; slå til; *om orm* hugge (til); *~ at the very roots of* undergrave; angripe innenfra; **5** begi seg; gå; *~ for home* (be)gi seg på hjemvei; sette kursen hjemover; *~ into the wood* begi seg inn i skogen; **6** *sjø* fire, låre; *~ one's flag/the colours* stryke flagget (dvs overgi seg); **7** streike; *(~ work)* legge ned arbeidet; **8** *en del uttrykk: ~ a balance* gjøre opp status; *fig* komme frem til et kompromiss; *~ a bargain* (av)slutte en handel; *~ a light* tenne et lys; *~ a match* tenne en fyrstikk; *~ an attitude* stille seg i positur; gjøre seg til; *~ an average* ta et gjennomsnitt; *~ blind/deaf* slå med blindhet/døvhet; *~ it lucky* gjøre sin lykke; *~ root* slå rot; *it struck home* den satt (dvs virket som den skulle); **9** *med adv, prep* **~ against** slå/støte mot; gå/støte på; ramme, treffe; **~ at** hugge/slå etter; angripe; **~ back** slå igjen/tilbake; **~ down** felle; slå ned; **~ for** streike for (å oppnå); kjempe/slå et slag for; **~ in** slå inn (om sykdom etc); *~ in with a remark* falle inn med/skyte inn en bemerkning; **~ into** slå/svinge *etc* inn på (en vei etc); slå over i; **~ inwards** = *~ in*; **~ off** slette/stryke (ut); hugge/kappe av; **~ on** slå/støte mot; gå/støte på; treffe (på); *fig* falle på; **~ out** slette/stryke (ut); slå fra seg/om seg; lange ut; *~ out a plan* komme med/sette frem en plan; **~ out for** begi seg/legge i vei mot;

~ out into begi seg inn/ut i; slå inn på; **~ through** slå/trenge (i)gjennom; **~ up** slå/spille opp; sette/stemme i; begynne; **~** *up a friendship* innlede/slutte vennskap; **~ upon** slå/støte mot (etc, jf **~** *on*); **~** *upon a plan* finne/hitte på en plan. **strike|-bound** *adj* streikerammet. **~-breaker** *sb* streikebryter. **~ fund** *sb* streikekasse. **~-leader** *sb* streikeleder. **~-pay** *sb* streike|bidrag, -lønn. **striker** ['straɪkə] *sb især* streikende (person). **striking** ['straɪkɪŋ] *adj* slående; frapperende, påfallende; *~ly beautiful* oppsiktvekkende/usedvanlig vakker.

string [strɪŋ] **I** *sb* **1** snor (og line, snøre; hyssing, tråd; bånd, lisse; fiber, trevl; sene etc); (blad)nerve; slyngtråd; *data, mus* streng; *the ~s* strykerne (dvs strykeinstrumentene i et orkester); **~** *of beads/pearls* perlekjede; *harp on the same* **~** gnåle på den samme (gamle) leksen; *have on a* **~** dominere; ha full kontroll over; *pull (the) ~s* trekke i trådene (dvs øve innflytelse); *with no ~s attached* uten betingelser/forbehold; **2** rad, rekke; kø; bunt, knippe; **~** *of words* ramse, regle; **II** *vb* **1** forsyne med snor *etc*; *især* strenge; sette streng(er) på; **2** træ (perler etc) på en snor; **3** henge (opp) i en snor *etc*; **4** strekke (snorer); stramme; *mus* stemme (strengeinstrument); *fig* anspenne; *strung up* anspent; (over)nervøs; **5** *med adv, prep* **~ along** gjøre narr av; holde leven med; **~ along with** slå følge med; *fig* være enig med; **~ out** spre (seg); stille (seg) på rad/rekke; **~ together** bunte/knytte sammen; **~ up** *dgl* klynge opp (dvs henge, henrette ved hengning). **string | band** *sb* = **~** *orchestra*. **~ bean** *sb* brekkbønne, snittebønne. **stringed** *adj, pp mus* -strenget; strenge-, stryke-. **string | instrument** *sb* strengeinstrument, strykeinstrument. **~ manipulation** *sb data* strenghåndtering. **~ orchestra** *sb* strykeorkester. **~ quartet** *sb* strykekvartett. **stringy** ['strɪndʒɪ] *adj* **1** senet; senesterk; **2** trevlet; treen, treet.

stringency ['strɪndʒənsɪ] *sb* strenghet *etc*; stringens. **stringent** ['strɪndʒənt] *adj* streng; knapp/stram (om økonomiske forhold); stringent.

strip [strɪp] **I** *sb* **1** remse, strimmel; stripe; **2** *(comic ~)* tegneserie **II** *vb* **1** kle av (seg); *(~ off)* skrelle (flekke, flå etc) av; *(~ down)* demontere; ta fra hverandre; *~ped to the skin* naken til skinnet; *~ped to the waist* med bar overkropp; **2 ~** *of* berøve; røve/ta fra; *~ped of everything* ribbet for alt. **strip cartoon** *sb* tegneserie. **stripe** [straɪp] **I** *sb* **1** stripe; strime; **2** *mil etc* (ermedistinksjon i form av) stripe, vinkel; *get one's ~s* bli forfremmet; *lose one's ~s* bli degradert; **3** *US* slag(s), sort; **II** *vt* stripe. **striped** [straɪpt] *adj* stripet. **stripper** *sb især* stripteasedanserinne. **strip|-show, ~-tease** *sb* avkledningsǀakt, scene, -show; striptease.

strive [straɪv] *vi* kjempe (*against* mot; *with* med; streve/stri (*for* for); strebe (*after/for* etter).

stroke [strəʊk] **A I** *sb* **1** slag; hugg, støt; *at a/one* **~** med ett slag; *at/on the* **~** *of (twelve etc)* på slaget (tolv etc); **2** *med* slag(anfall); *have a* **~** bli rammet av/få slag; **3** prestasjon; **~** *of genius* genialt innfall/tiltak; *også* genistrek; **~** *of luck* lykketreff; *he hasn't done a* **~** *of work* han har ikke gjort et slag arbeid; *finishing* **~** siste hånd på verket; **4** tak (i roing, svømming etc); **5** strøk (med penn, pensel etc); **6** *mus* taktslag; *give/set the* **~** angi takten; **7** *sport* stroke; bakerste roer; **II** *vt* stryke (dvs kjærtegne/klappe lett).

stroll [strəʊl] **1** *sb* (spaser)tur, vandring; **2** *vi* spasere; streife/vandre omkring.

strong [strɒŋ] *adj* sterk (og kraftig, mektig; robust, solid; sunn etc); **~** *arguments* vektige argumenter; **~** *eyes* gode øyne; godt syn; **~** *language* banning, kraftuttrykk; **~** *measures* drastiske tiltak; *come/go it a bit* **~** gå lovlig (dvs litt for) langt/vidt; *still going* **~** (fremdeles) i full vigør; *there is some* **~** *feelings about it* det er stor uenighet/sterk diskusjon om det. **strong|-arm** *vt* overfalle, rane; bruke vold mot. **~-box** *sb* pengeǀ-skap, -skrin. **~ breeze** *sb* liten kuling. **~ cheese** *sb* skarp ost. **~ gale** *sb* liten storm. **~hold** *sb* (be)festning, borg; (befestet) tilfluktssted; *fig* høyborg. **~-minded** *adj* karakterfast, viljesterk. **~point** *sb* befestet stilling; forsvarsstilling; støttepunkt; motstandsrede. **~-room** *sb* (bank)hvelv. **~-willed** *adj* viljesterk.

structural ['strʌktʃərəl] *adj* bygnings-, konstruksjons-; strukturell, struktur-. **structure** ['strʌktʃə] *sb* **1** (opp)bygning; byggemåte, konstruksjon; struktur; **2** bygning, konstruksjon.

struggle ['strʌgl] **1** *sb* kamp, strid; slit, strev; *the* **~** *for existence* kampen for tilværelsen; **2** *vi* kjempe, stri(de); slite, streve; **~** *free* kjempe seg fri; **~** *through* kjempe seg (i)gjennom.

strum [strʌm] **1** *sb* klimpring; **2** *vb* klimpre (på).

strut [strʌt] **A 1** *sb* spankulering, sprading; **2** *vi* spankulere, sprade; **~** *in borrowed feathers* smykke seg med lånte fjær; **B** *sb* stiver, støtte(bjelke).

stub [stʌb] **I** *sb* **1** stump; **2** *US* talong (i sjekkhefte); **II** *vt* **1 ~** *out a cigarette* stumpe en sigarett; **2 ~** *one's toe* støte tåen (sin). **stubble** ['stʌbl] *sb* **1** (korn)-stubb; stubbmark; **2** *(~ of beard)* skjeggstubb.

stubborn ['stʌbən] *adj* **1** egenrådig, sta; **2** halsstarrig; hardnakket; ukuelig.

stubby ['stʌbɪ] *adj* firskåren, undersetsig; stumpet, stump-; kort og tykk; *om skjegg* kort og stritt.

stuck [stʌk] *adj, pp: be/get* **~** bli hengende/sittende (fast); gå i stå; *be* **~** *for* være i beit for; slippe opp for; *be* **~** *on* være (håpløst/svermerisk) forelsket i; *be* **~** *with* bli sittende igjen med (det ingen andre vil ha). **stuck-up** *adj dgl* blæret, innbilsk.

stud [stʌd] **A I** *sb* **1** (pynte)ǀnagle, -stift; **2** kraveknapp, skjorteknapp; **II** *vt* beslå med (pynte)ǀnagle, -stift; *~ded with (også)* bestrødd/oversådd med; **B** *sb* (veddeløps)stall; avlshester; stutteri.

student ['stju:dənt] *sb* student; *også* forsker, gransker; praktikant; elev; **~** *of music* musikkstudent; *law* **~** jusstudent; *medical* **~** legestudent. **student teacher** *sb* (lærer)kandidat.

stud | farm *sb* (heste)stutteri. **~ fee** *sb* bedekningsavgift, springpenger. **~ horse** *sb* avlsǀhest, -hingst.

studied ['stʌdɪd] *adj, pp* **1** kunnskapsrik, lærd; *well* ~ *in* vel bevandret i; **2** tilsiktet, velberegnet; utstudert; *with* ~ *calm* med tilkjempet ro. **studio** ['stju:dɪəʊ] *sb* **1** studio (for film, fjernsyn, radio etc); **2** atelier. **studio | appartment** *sb* atelierleilighet. ~ **couch** *sb* sovesofa. ~ **flat** *sb* = ~*appartment.* **studious** ['stju:dɪəs] *adj* leselysten, lærelysten; **2** flittig; grundig, omhyggelig; **3** utstudert; ~ *effort* bevisst anstrengelse; ~ *politeness* utstudert høflighet. **study** ['stʌdɪ] **I** *sb* **1** studering(er); studium; **2** (studie)|emne, (-)fag; *make a* ~ *of it* studere/undersøke det; *her face was a* ~ ansiktet hennes var et studium verdt; **3** *a)* avhandling, studie; *mus* etyde; *b)* (for)studie, skisse; **4** arbeids|rom, -værelse; studerværelse; (hjemme)kontor; *stundom* bibliotek; **5** fundering(er); grubling; *in a brown* ~ i dype funderinger/tanker; **II** *vb* **1** studere (og studere på/til; lese på/til; forske, granske, undersøke etc); ~ *out* tenke ut; *she is* ~*ing to be a vet* hun studerer til dyrlege; **2** innstudere (en rolle).

stuff [stʌf] **I** *sb* **1** emne, materiale(r), stoff; *dgl* (saker og) ting; *doctor's* ~ medisiner; *food-*~ mat(varer); *green* ~ grønnsaker; *household* ~ husholdningsredskaper, kjøkkenutstyr; *he's got the right* ~ *in him* han er av det rette slaget; *that's the* ~ sånn skal det være; **2** *(*~*ing)* fyll (til kake, postei etc); farse; **3** skrap, skrot; søppel; ~ *and nonsense* sludder og vrøvl; **4** *gml* ull(stoff); **II** *vt* **1** proppe, stappe; stoppe (møbler etc); stoppe ut (dyr); *(*~ *up)* stoppe til; tette igjen; **2** ~ *oneself* ete seg stappmett; forspise seg; **3** farsere; fylle (med farse etc); **4** *dgl* innbille; lure (til å tro etc). **stuffing** ['stʌfɪŋ] *sb* polstring, stopp; fyll; *også* innmat; *knock the* ~ *out of (dgl)* jekke ned; ta pippen fra. **stuffy** ['stʌfɪ] *adj* **1** kvalm, lummer; inne|lukket, -stengt; **2** *dgl* gretten, grinet; fornærmet; **3** *dgl* snerpet; blæret, hoven.

stultify ['stʌltɪfaɪ] *vt bokl* latterliggjøre; få til å virke komisk/latterlig.

stumble ['stʌmbl] **I** *sb (stumbling)* snubling *etc*; **II** *vi* **1** snuble; ~ *across/(up)on* snuble over (dvs finne ved et tilfelle); ~ *along* tumle av sted; **2** stamme, stotre. **stumbling-block** *sb* anstøtsstein; hindring.

stump [stʌmp] **I** *sb* **1** stubb, stump; (tre)stubbe; **2** *dgl* bein; *stir one's* ~*s* røre på/bruke beina; **3** *dgl* (improvisert) talerstol; **II** *vb* **1** humpe (*about* omkring; *along* av sted); **2** *dgl* sette fast/til veggs; forvirre; gjøre perpleks; **3** *dgl* reise rundt som folketaler; **4** *slang:* ~ *up* punge ut. **stumper** ['stʌmpə] *sb dgl* hard nøtt (dvs vanskelig oppgave etc). **stumpy** ['stʌmpɪ] *adj* kortvokst; liten og tykk.

stun [stʌn] *vt* **1** slå bevisstløs; svimeslå; **2** lamslå, sjokkere. **stunning** ['stʌnɪŋ] *adj* **1** lammende, sjokkerende; **2** overveldende.

stunt [stʌnt] **A** *vt* hindre/stanse i veksten; forkrøple; **B** *sb* **1** akrobatstykke; kraftprestasjon; **2** kunststykke, nummer; *pull a* ~ gjøre et pek. **stunt man** *sb* stuntmann (= stedfortreder for f.eks. skuespiller under særlig farlig opptak).

stupefaction [ˌstju:pɪ'fækʃn] *sb* sløvhet *etc.* **stupefy** ['stju:pɪfaɪ] *vt* **1** sløve; bedøve, døyve; **2** lamme, lamslå. **stupendous** [stju:'pendəs] *adj* overveldende. **stupid** ['stju:pɪd] **1** *adj* dum, tosket; tåpelig; sløv(et); **2** *sb* tosk. **stupidity** [stju:'pɪdətɪ] *sb* dumhet *etc.* **stupor** ['stju:pə] *sb* sløvhet, sløvsinn; *med* stupor.

sturdy ['stɜ:dɪ] *adj* kraftig, solid; hardfør, robust.

sturgeon ['stɜ:dʒən] *sb* stør.

stutter ['stʌtə] **1** *sb* stamming, stotring; **2** *vb* stamme, stotre.

sty [staɪ] *sb* **A** *(pig-*~*)* grise|binge, -hus; **B** sti (på øyet).

style [staɪl] **I** *sb* **1** stil (dvs fremstillingsform, skrivemåte etc); *fl* stilarter; **2** stil (dvs formell, fornem etc opptreden); ~ *of life* livs|stil; -form, -førsel; *in bad* ~ smakløs(t); *live in (grand)* ~ leve flott/på stor fot; **3** (kles)|stil, (-)mote; **4** tittel; *he had no right to the* ~ *of colonel* han hadde ingen rett til å kalle seg oberst; **5** griffel, skrivestift; stylus; **II** *vt* **1** benevne, kalle; titulere; **2** formgi/tegne (i en bestemt stil); gi bestemt stilpreg. **stylish** ['staɪlɪʃ] *adj* elegant; stilig, stilfull. **stylist** ['staɪlɪst] *sb* stilist. **stylistic** [staɪ'lɪstɪk] *adj* stilistisk. **stylus** ['staɪləs] *sb* **1** stylus; griffel, skrivestift; **2** *data* posisjonspeker. **stylus printer** *sb data* matriseskriver.

suave [swɑ:v] *adj* beleven, elskverdig; høflig.

sub- [sʌb-] *pref* **1** under-; **2** undergrunns; **3** halv-, sub- (se for øvrig de enkelte oppslagsord på *sub-*).

subaltern ['sʌbltən] *sb* offiser av lavere grad enn kaptein.

sub-committee ['sʌbkə'mɪtɪ] *sb* underkomité.

subconscious [sʌb'kɒnʃəs] **1** *adj* underbevisst; **2** *sb: the* ~ underbevisstheten.

subdivide [ˌsʌbdɪ'vaɪd] *vb* underinndele; viderefordele. **subdivision** [ˌsʌbdɪ'vɪʒn] *sb* underinndeling.

subdue [səb'dju:] *vt* **1** under|kue, -trykke, -tvinge; overvinne; **2** dempe, mildne; redusere.

subhuman [ˌsʌb'hju:mən] *adj* umenneskelig.

subject ['sʌbdʒɪkt] **I** *adj* **1** avhengig (*to* av); ~ *to (også)* under|gitt, -kastet, -lagt; **2** ~ *to* utsatt for; tilbøyelig til (å få, pådra seg etc); **3** ~ *to* med forbehold om; *all quotations are* ~ *to revision without notice* med forbehold om prisendringer uten varsel; **II** *sb* **1** undersått; statsborger (i monarki); **2** *(*~ *matter)* emne, tema; (skole)fag; *om kunst* motiv, sujett; *be the* ~ *of* være gjenstand for; *change the* ~ skifte (samtale)-emne; *on the* ~ *of* angående; i anledning av; **3** *gram* subjekt; **III** *vt* **1** under|kaste, kue, -tvinge; -legge seg; **2** ~ *to* gjøre til gjenstand for; ~ *to torture* underkaste tortur. **subjection** [səb'dʒekʃn] *sb* **1** underkastelse *etc*; **2** avhengighet. **subjective** [səb'dʒektɪv] *adj* **1** subjektiv; **2** *gram* nominativ(-), subjekt-; *the* ~ *case* nominativ. **subject matter** *sb* se *subject II 2.*

subjugate ['sʌbdʒʊgeɪt] *vt* under|kue, -trykke, -tvinge; legge seg. **subjugation** [ˌsʌdʒʊ'geɪʃn] *sb* underkuelse *etc.*

subjunctive [səb'dʒʌŋktɪv] *gram* **1** *adj* konjunktiv-; **2** *sb (the ~ mood)* konjunktiv.

sublease [ˌsʌb'li:s] *sb, vb* fremleie. **sublet** [ˌsʌb'let] *vb* leie ut (på fremleie).

sublimate I ['sʌblɪmət] **1** *adj* sublimert; sublimat-; **2** *sb* sublimat; **II** ['sʌblɪmeɪt] *vt* sublimere. **sublimation** [ˌsʌblɪ'meɪʃn] *sb* sublimering; sublimasjon. **sublime** [sə'blaɪm] *adj* **1** opphøyd; edel, nobel; **2** enestående, storslagen; sublim.

submarine [ˌsʌbmə'ri:n] **1** *adj* undersjøisk, undervanns-; **2** *sb* undervannsbåt.

submerge [səb'mɜ:dʒ] *vb* **1** dyppe/senke ned (i vann etc); dukke, dykke; **2** oversvømme; sette under vann. **submerged** [səb'mɜ:dʒd] *adj* ned|dykket, -senket. **submergence** [səb'mɜ:dʒəns] *sb* = *submersion*. **submersible** [səb'mɜ:səbl] *adj* nedsenkbar. **submersible platform,** *sb petro* nedsenkbar plattform. **submersion** [səb'mɜ:ʃn] *sb* neddykking *etc*; oversvømmelse.

submission [səb'mɪʃn] *sb* **1** underkastelse; overgivelse; **2** underdanighet, ydmykhet; ærbødighet; **3** *jur* anførsel; frem|føring, -legging; innlegg. **submissive** [səb'mɪsɪv] *adj* føyelig, lydig; underdanig, ydmyk. **submit** [səb'mɪt] *vb* **1** underkaste (*oneself* seg); *~ to one's lot* finne seg i sin skjebne; *~ to the inevitable* bøye seg for det uunngåelige; **2** legge/sette frem; forelegge; sende inn; **3** *jur* foreslå; gjøre gjeldende; *I ~ that* jeg tillater meg å foreslå (antyde, mene etc) at.

subnormal [səb'nɔ:ml] *adj* under normalt/normalen.

subordinate I [sə'bɔ:dɪnət] **1** *adj* underordnet; *gram* bi-, ledd-; *~ clause* bisetning, leddsetning; **2** *sb* underordnet (funksjonær etc); **II** [sə'bɔ:dɪneɪt] *vt* underordne. **subordination** [səˌbɔ:dɪ'neɪʃn] *sb* underordning; underordnet forhold/stilling *etc*; lydighet.

subpoena [səb'pi:nə] *jur* **1** *sb (writ of ~)* stevning (av vitne etc); **2** *vt* (inn)stevne; innkalle (som vitne etc).

subprogram ['sʌbˌprəugrəm] *sb data* delprogram.

sub|scribe [səb'skraɪb] *vb* **1** under|skrive, -tegne; *~ to* godkjenne, tiltre; abonnere/subskribere på; **2** tegne seg for (et bidrag på). **~script** ['sʌbskrɪpt] *sb data* halvsteg ned. **~scripting** [səb'skrɪptɪŋ] *sb data* indeksering. **~scription** [səb'skrɪpʃn] *sb* **1** under|skrift, -tegning; *især* abonnement, subskripsjon; **2** (tegnet) bidrag.

subsea | completion [səb'si:] *sb petro* bunninstallasjon(er). **~ engineer** *sb petro* undervannstekniker.

subsequent ['sʌbsɪkwənt] *adj* (etter)følgende, påfølgende; senere. **subsequently** ['sʌbsɪkwəntlɪ] *adv* der|etter, -på; siden; *også* følgelig.

subservient [səb'sɜ:vɪənt] *adj* underdanig.

subside [səb'saɪd] *vi* **1** bunnfelles; synke (til bunns etc); *om fundament etc* sette seg; **2** løye, spakne, stilne; gi/legge seg; bli rolig(ere). **subsidence** [səb'saɪdəns] *sb* bunnfelling *etc*.

subsidiary [səb'sɪdɪərɪ] **1** *adj* hjelpe-, støtte-; **2** *sb* hjelper; *merk* datterselskap; *fl mil* hjelpetropper.

subsidize ['sʌbsɪdaɪz] *vt* (stats)understøtte, subsidiere. **subsidy** ['sʌbsədɪ] *sb* (stats)|støtte, -tilskudd; *fl* subsidier.

subsist [səb'sɪst] *vi* bestå, eksistere, finnes; leve. **subsistence** [səb'sɪstəns] *sb* **1** eksistens; liv; tilværelse; **2** underhold, utkomme; livsnødvendigheter.

subsoil ['sʌbsɔɪl] *sb* undergrunn; dypere jordlag.

substance ['sʌbstəns] *sb* **1** stoff, substans; **2** hoved|bestanddel, -innhold; kjerne; vesen; *også* virkelighet; *in ~* faktisk; i hovedsak(en); i realiteten; **3** fasthet; soliditet; *også* gehalt, kvalitet; **4** midler (dvs eiendom, formue etc); *a man of ~* en holden (formuende, velstående etc) mann. **substantial** [səb'stænʃl] *adj* **1** legemlig; materiell; virkelig; **2** vesentlig, virkelig(st); **3** solid; kraftig, sterk; **4** betraktelig, betydelig. **substantiate** [səb'stænʃɪeɪt] *vt* underbygge; bevise, godtgjøre; dokumentere.

substitute ['sʌbstɪtju:t] **1** *sb* erstatning, surrogat; stedfortreder, vikar; **2** *vt* sette i stedet (for); *~ plastic for rubber* erstatte gummi med plast. **substitute character** *sb data* erstatningstegn. **substitution** [ˌsʌbstɪ'tju:ʃn] *sb* erstatning, surrogat.

substring ['sʌbstrɪŋ] *sb data* delstreng.

substructure ['sʌbstrʌktʃə] *sb* fundament, underlag.

subterfuge ['sʌbtəfju:dʒ] *sb* påskudd, utflukt.

subterranean [ˌsʌbtə'reɪnɪən] *adj bokl* underjordisk; undergrunns-.

subtitle ['sʌbtaɪtl] *sb* **1** undertittel; **2** tekst(ing) (til spillefilm).

subtle ['sʌtl] *adj* **1** (hår)fin, subtil; **2** listig, slu; smart, snedig; **3** raffinert; skarpsindig; spissfindig; **4** innviklet, intrikat. **subtlety** ['sʌtlɪ] *sb* subtilitet *etc*.

subtract [səb'trækt] *vt* subtrahere, trekke fra. **subtraction** [səb'trækʃn] *sb* subtrahering; subtraksjon.

subtropical [ˌsʌb'trɒpɪkl] *adj* subtropisk.

suburb ['sʌbɜ:b] *sb* drabantby, forstad. **suburban** [sə'bɜ:bən] **1** *adj* drabantby-, forstads-; **2** *sb* drabantbyboer, forstadsboer. **suburbia** [sə'bɜ:bɪə] *sb* (typisk) drabantby (især nedsettende om holdninger, miljø etc).

subversion [səb'vɜ:ʃn] *sb* om|styrtning, -veltning; undergravningsvirksomhet. **subversive** [səb'vɜ:sɪv] *adj* (samfunns)|nedbrytende, (-)ødeleggende; *også* undergravnings-. **subvert** [səb'vɜ:t] *vt* om|styrte, -velte; nedbryte, undergrave.

subway ['sʌbweɪ] *sb* **1** (fotgjenger)|tunnel, -undergang; **2** *US* tunnelbane, undergrunnsbane.

succeed [sək'si:d] *vb* **1** lykkes; *~ in* ha hell/lykkes med; *did you ~* lyktes det (for deg); *også* fikk du det til; klarte du det; *they ~ed in* det lyktes dem å; de klarte å; **2** avløse, (etter)følge; **3** *~ to the throne* arve tronen. **success** [sək'ses] *sb* fremgang, suksess; gunstig resultat/utfall; hell; *be a ~* være en suksess; gjøre lykke/suksess. **successful** [sək'sesful] *adj* fremgangsrik; vellykket; heldig. **succession** [sək'seʃn] *sb* **1** rekke, rekkefølge; *in ~* på rad/rekke; **2** arve|følge,

-gang; tronfølge. **successive** [sək'sesɪv] *adj* (etter)-følgende; på rad/rekke; suksessiv; *~ly (også)* gradvis; litt etter litt. **successor** [sək'sesə] *sb* etterfølger; avløser; tronfølger.

succinct [sək'sɪŋkt] *adj* kort(fattet); fyndig, konsis; knapp.

succour ['sʌkə] *bokl* **1** *sb* hjelp, unnsetning; **2** *vt* hjelpe, unnsette.

succulent ['sʌkjʊlənt] *adj* saftig.

succumb [sə'kʌm] *vi* **1** *~ to* bukke under/gi etter for; **2** dø.

such [sʌtʃ] *adj, pron* **1** slik(e), sånn(e); *~ as* slik(e) som; *også* som for eksempel; *~ as it is* som den/det nå engang er (dvs ikke noe særlig å skryte av); *~ is life* sånn er livet; *as ~* som sådan; *on ~ an occasion* ved en slik anledning; **2** slikt; den slags; sånt noe; *drinking, gambling and ~* drikk, spill og den slags; *Smith or some ~ name* Smith eller noe i den retning (dvs et navn av den typen); **3** så; *he was ~ a nice fellow* han var *så* hyggelig; *in ~ a fine weather* i (et) så fint vær.

suck [sʌk] **1** *sb (~ing)* sug(ing); drag; **2** *vt* suge (og suge på); die, patte; *~ up* suge opp; *~ up to* klenge/kline seg inn på; sleske/smigre for. **sucker** ['sʌkə] *sb* **1** suger *etc*; suge|skive, skål; sugerør; **2** rotskudd, villskudd; **3** *US* (godtroende) fjols/tosk; *play him for a ~* lure ham; få ham til å gå på limpinnen. **suckle** ['sʌkl] *vt* amme; gi bryst. **suckling** ['sʌklɪŋ] *sb* diebarn, spedbarn; *om dyr* dielam, spedkalv etc; *fig* grønnskolling, pattebarn. **suction** ['sʌkʃn] *sb* suging (og innsuging, oppsuging etc); *som adj* suge-.

sudden ['sʌdn] *adj* brå, plutselig; *all of a ~* brått, plutselig; *it is (all) so ~* det kommer så plutselig/brått på. **suddenly** ['sʌdnlɪ] *adv* brått, plutselig; uventet.

suds [sʌdz] *sb fl* såpe|skum, -vann.

sue [su:] *vb* **1** saksøke; anlegge/reise sak (mot); *~ for damages* reise erstatnings|krav/-søksmål (mot); **2** be (*for* om).

suede [sweɪd] *sb* semsket skinn.

suet ['su:ɪt] *sb* talg.

suffer ['sʌfə] *vb* **1** lide; *~ from* lide av/under; **2** gjennomgå; *~ damage* lide tap; **3** tillate; finne seg i. **sufferance** ['sʌfərəns] *sb især* (stilltiende) tillatelse. **suffering** ['sʌfərɪŋ] **1** *adj* lidende; **2** *sb* lidelse, smerte.

suffice [sə'faɪs] *vb* strekke til; være nok; *~ it (to say) that* det får være nok (å si) at; *også* kort sagt. **sufficiency** [sə'fɪʃnsɪ] *sb* tilstrekkelig mengde *etc*. **sufficient** [sə'fɪʃnt] *adj* nok, tilstrekkelig.

suffix ['sʌfɪks] **1** *sb gram* endelse/ending; suffiks; **2** *vt* føye/legge til (en ending); *også* henge på.

suffocate ['sʌfəkeɪt] *vb* kvele(s). **suffocation** [ˌsʌfə'keɪʃn] *sb* kvelning.

suffrage ['sʌfrɪdʒ] *sb* stemme (og stemmerett). **suffragette** [ˌsʌfrə'dʒet] *sb* stemmerettskvinne (dvs forkjemper for kvinnelig stemmerett); suffragette.

sugar ['ʃʊgə] **1** *sb* sukker; *fig* kliss(prat); smiger; **2** *vt* sukre; *fig* smigre. **sugar|-basin** *sb* sukkerskål. **~-beet** *sb* sukker|bete, -roe. **~-bowl** *sb* = *~-basin*. **~-cane** *sb* sukkerrør. **~ daddy** *sb dgl* eldre elsker (eller kavaler som spanderer på ungjenter). **~loaf** *sb* sukkertopp. **~ maple** *sb* sukkerlønn. **~-plum** *sb* sukkertøy. **~-refinery** *sb* sukkerraffineri. **~-tongs** *sb fl* sukkerklype. **sugary** ['ʃʊgərɪ] *adj* sukret, søt; *fig også* innsmigrende; søtlaten.

suggest [sə'dʒest] *vt* **1** foreslå; henstille; **2** antyde; slå frempå (om); **3** henlede tanken på; tyde på; *what does this figure ~ to you* hva minner denne figuren deg om; hva får denne figuren deg til å tenke på. **suggested price** *sb* veiledende pris. **suggestible** [sə'dʒestəbl] *adj* suggestibel; lett påvirkelig. **suggestion** [sə'dʒestʃn] *sb* **1** forslag; henstilling; *offer a ~* komme med et forslag; **2** antydning; hint, ymt; snev; påminnelse; **3** suggestion. **suggestive** [sə'dʒestɪv] *adj* **1** tankevekkende (og assosiasjonsvekkende, stemnings|skapende, -vekkende; suggestiv etc); stimulerende; *be ~ of* minne om; **2** *neds* tvetydig; lummer, slibrig; uanstendig.

suicidal [ˌsu:ɪ'saɪdl] *adj* selvmorderisk (også *fig*); selvmords-. **suicide** ['su:ɪsaɪd] *sb* **1** selvmord; **2** selvmorder.

suit [su:t] **I** *sb* **1** (*~ of clothes)* sett klær; *især (man's ~)* (herre)dress; *(woman's ~)* drakt; *~ of armour* rustning; *bathing ~* badedrakt; *dress ~* snippkjole; *gym ~* gym(nastikk)drakt; *space ~* romdrakt; **2** an|modning, -søkning; begjæring; **3** beiling, frieri; **4** *jur (law~)* prosess, rettssak; saksanlegg, søksmål; *bring a ~* anlegge/reise sak; **5** farge/kulør (i kortspill); **II** *vt* **1** passe (*for* til); tilfredsstille; *om klær også* kle; være kledelig for; *~ yourself* gjør som det passer deg/som du vil; **2** *~ to* avpasse/innrette etter; tilpasse til; *~ the action to the word(s)* la handling følge på ord (dvs gjøre alvor av det en sier); **3** *be ~ed for/to* være egnet for/til; egne seg/passe (for/til). **suitable** [su:təbl] *adj* passende; egnet, skikket. **suite** [swi:t] *sb* **1** (høytstående persons) følge; **2** gruppe, sett; serie; rad, rekke; *mus etc* suite; *~ of furniture* møblement; **3** suite (på hotell etc); *the bridal ~* brudesuiten. **suitor** [su:tə] *sb* **1** (an)søker; **2** beiler, frier.

sulk [sʌlk] **1** *sb: in the ~* furten; **2** *vi* furte, surmule. **sulky** ['sʌlkɪ] **A** *adj* furten, surmulende; **B** *sb* sulky (= lett travervogn).

sullen ['sʌlən] *adj* **1** gretten, grinet; sur; tverr; **2** dyster, mørk.

sully ['sʌlɪ] *vt* flekke; skitne til; *fig* besudle, tilsvine.

sulphate ['sʌlfeɪt] *sb* sulfat. **sulphur** ['sʌlfə] *sb* svovel.

sultry ['sʌltrɪ] *adj* lummer, trykkende (varm).

sum [sʌm] **I** *sb* **1** sum; total|beløp, -sum; *in ~* i korthet; kort sagt; **2** summering; addisjonsstykke; regne|oppgave, -stykke; *do a ~* gjøre et regnestykke; **II** *vb* **1** *~ up* addere, summere; legge sammen; **2** *~ up* oppsummere, resymere; *jur* gi rettsbelæring. **summarize** ['sʌməraɪz] *vt* oppsummere, resymere. **summary** ['sʌmərɪ] **1** *adj* kort(fattet); sammenfattet;

summarisk; **2** *sb* oppsummering, resymé, sammendrag. **summation** [sʌ'meɪʃn] *sb* **1** addisjon, sammenlegging; **2** oppsummering, resymé.

summer ['sʌmə] **1** *sb* sommer; *som adj* sommer-; **2** *vi* tilbringe sommeren. **summer|-cholera** *sb* sommerdiaré. **~ holidays** *sb fl* sommerferie. **~-school** *sb* sommerskole. **~time** *sb* sommer(tid); *som adj* sommerlig, sommer-. **~ time** sommertid (dvs forskjøvet tid). **summery** ['sʌmərɪ] *adj* sommerlig.

summing-up *sb* oppsummering; *jur* rettsbelæring.

summit ['sʌmɪt] *sb* topp. **summit | meeting** *sb* toppmøte. **~ talk** *sb* toppkonferanse.

summon ['sʌmən] *vt* **1** innkalle (og sammenkalle, tilkalle etc); sende bud etter/på; *jur* stevne; **~** *as a witness* stevne som vitne; **2** **~** *up* oppby/samle (krefter, mot etc). **summoner** ['sʌmənə] *sb* stevnevitne. **summons** ['sʌmənz] **1** *sb* inn|kalling, (-)stevning; *mil* oppfordring, tilsigelse; **2** *vt jur (serve a ~)* (inn)-stevne.

sumptuous ['sʌmptʃʊəs] *adj* overdådig; flott, praktfull.

sum total *sb* samlet beløp/sum; totalsum.

sun [sʌn] **I** *sb* **1** sol (og solskinn); **2** (fiks)stjerne; **II** *vb* sole (seg). **sun|-bath** *sb* solbad. **~-bathe** *vi* sole seg; ta solbad. **~beam** *sb* solstråle. **~-blind** *sb* markise. **~-bonnet** *sb* solhatt. **~burn** *sb* solbrenthet. **~burned, ~burnt** *adj* sol|brent, (-)brun.

sundae ['sʌndɪ] *sb* fruktis(krem).

sunder ['sʌndə] *vt bokl* splitte; skille (fra hverandre).

sun|-dial *sb* solur. **~down** *sb dgl* solnedgang. **~-dried** *adj* soltørket.

sundries ['sʌndrɪz] *sb fl* diverse (utgifter etc). **sundry** ['sʌndrɪ] *adj* diverse, forskjellig(e); *all and ~* Gud og hvermann.

sun|flower *sb* solsikke. **~-glasses** *sb fl* solbriller. **~-hat** *sb* solhatt. **~-lamp** *sb* **1** høyfjellssol; **2** filmsol (dvs sterkt prosjektørlys til bruk under filmopptak). **~light** *sb* sol(skinn). **~lit** *adj* sol|belyst, -lys.

sunny ['sʌnɪ] *adj* **1** sol|belyst, -blank, -fylt, -lys, -rik; solskinns-; *a ~ day* en solskinnsdag; **2** glad, munter; strålende; lys til sinns.

sun|ray *sb* solstråle. **~rise** *sb* soloppgang. **~set** *sb* solnedgang. **~shade** *sb* solskjerm; markise; parasoll. **~shine** *sb* solskinn. **~-spot** *sb* solflekk. **~stroke** *sb* heteslag, solstikk. **~struck** *adj* rammet av heteslag/solstikk. **~tan** *sb* sol|brenthet, (-)brunhet. **~-up** *sb dgl* soloppgang.

sup [sʌp] **A** *vb* **1** spise aftens(mat); **2** servere aftens(mat) (for/til); **B 1** *sb* munnfull; nipp, tår; *neither bite nor ~* verken vått eller tørt (dvs verken noe å spise eller drikke); **2** *vb* nippe (til).

super ['su:pə] **1** *adj, adv* flott, kjempefin(t), super(t); **2** *pref* super-; *også* ekstra(-); over-; hyper-; **3** *sb (~numerary)* statist.

superabundance [ˌsu:pərə'bʌndəns] *sb* overflod. **superabundant** [ˌsu:pərə'bʌndənt] *adj* rikelig; i overflod.

superannuated [ˌsu:pər'ænjʊeɪtɪd] *adj* pensjonert; *også* overårig; *dgl* avdanket. **superannuation** [ˌsu:pərˌænjʊ'eɪʃn] *sb* pensjon(ering), trygd(ing).

superb [su:pɜ:b] *adj* stor|artet, -slagen; ypperlig; superb.

supercilious [ˌsu:pə'sɪlɪəs] *adj* hoven, overlegen.

superficial [ˌsu:pə'fɪʃl] *adj* overfladisk; overflate-.

superfluous [su:'pɜ:flʊəs] *adj* overflødig.

superhuman [ˌsu:pə'hju:mən] *adj* overmenneskelig.

superimpose [ˌsu:pərɪm'pəʊz] *vt* legge over (ovenpå, oppå etc).

superintend [ˌsu:pərɪn'tend] *vb* lede; overvåke; føre/ha tilsyn med. **superintendence** [ˌsu:pərɪn'tendəns] *sb* (over)oppsyn; kontroll, overvåking. **superintendent** [ˌsu:pərɪn'tendənt] *sb* leder; (over)oppsyns|kvinne, -mann; inspektør, kontrollør (og om andre personer i kontrollerende/ledende stilling, f.eks. byggeleder, direktør, disponent, distriktssjef, forstander, forvalter, intendant, overingeniør, overlege, tilsynsfører); *i politiet* avdelingsjef, stasjonssjef; visepolitimester.

superior [sə'pɪərɪə] **I** *adj* overlegen (dvs bedre, finere, flinkere; flere, mer; høyere, større etc enn); over-; **II** *sb* **1** foresatt, overordnet; overmann; **2** *Father Superior* abbed; *Mother Superior* abbedisse. **superiority** [səˌpɪərɪ'ɒrətɪ] *sb* overlegenhet; overlegen dyktighet *etc*.

superlative [su:'pɜ:lətɪv] **1** *adj* superlativ-; enestående, glimrende, ypperlig; **2** *sb gram (the ~ degree)* superlativ.

supermarket ['su:pəmɑ:kɪt] *sb* kjøpesenter, supermarked.

supernatural [ˌsu:pə'nætʃrəl] *adj* overnaturlig.

supernumerary [ˌsu:pə'nju:mərərɪ] **1** *adj* overtallig; reserve-; **2** *sb* overtallig person; *mil* surnumerær offiser; *film/teater* statist.

superscript ['su:pəskrɪpt] *sb data* halvsteg opp.

supersede [ˌsu:pə'si:d] *vt* avløse, erstatte; fortrenge.

supersonic [ˌsu:pə'sɒnɪk] *adj* overlyds-, supersonisk.

superstition [ˌsu:pə'stɪʃn] *sb* overtro. **superstitious** [ˌsu:pə'stɪʃəs] *adj* overtroisk.

superstructure ['su:pəstrʌktʃə] *sb* overbygning.

supervise ['su:pəvaɪz] *vt* overvåke; føre/ha tilsyn med; kontrollere. **supervision** [ˌsu:pə'vɪʒn] *sb* over|oppsyn, -våking; tilsyn; kontroll. **supervisor** ['su:pəvaɪzə] *sb* oppsyns|kvinne, -mann; kontrollør, overvåker. **supervisory routine** *sb data* styrerutine.

supine ['sju:paɪn] *adj* **1** (liggende) på ryggen; **2** doven, dvask.

supper ['sʌpə] *sb* aftens(mat), kvelds(mat); *rel* nattverd.

supplant [sə'plɑ:nt] *vt* erstatte, fortrenge.

supple ['sʌpl] *adj* elastisk; bøyelig, myk; spenstig; *fig også* ettergivende, føyelig.

supplement 1 ['sʌplɪmənt] *sb* supplement, tillegg; bilag; **2** ['sʌplɪment] *vt* supplere, utfylle; komplettere. **supplemental** [ˌsʌplɪ'mentl], **supplementary** [ˌsʌplɪ'mentərɪ] *adj* supplerende; ekstra(-), tilleggs-. **supplementation** [ˌsʌplɪmən'teɪʃn] *sb* supplering.

suppliant ['sʌplɪənt] **1** *adj* (ydmykt) bønnfallende/bønnlig; bønn-; **2** *sb* ydmyk (an)søker; bedende/bønnfallende person; supplikant. **supplicant** ['sʌplɪkənt] *sb* = *suppliant 2.* **supplicate** ['sʌplɪkeɪt] *vb* bønnfalle/trygle (*for* om). **supplication** [ˌsʌplɪ'keɪʃn] *sb* ydmyk bønn *etc.* **supplicatory** ['sʌplɪkətərɪ] *adj* bedende, bønnlig; ydmyk.

supplier [sə'plaɪə] *sb* leverandør. **supply** [sə'plaɪ] **I** *sb* **1** leveranse, levering; forsyning, tilførsel; ~ *and demand* tilbud og etterspørsel; **2** *fl* forråd, lager; forsyninger; materiell; **3** *fl pol* bevilgninger; **II** *vt* **1** levere, skaffe; forsyne (*with* med); **2** (ut)fylle; ~ *a deficiency* avhjelpe et savn; ~ *a demand* dekke et behov; tilfredsstille en etterspørsel. **supply | boat, ~ vessel** *sb petro etc* forsynings|båt, -fartøy.

support [sə'pɔ:t] **I** *sb* **1** hjelp, støtte; *data* systemstøtte; *in ~ (mil)* i reserve; *in ~ of* til hjelp/støtte for; **2** forsørgelse, underhold; understøttelse; **3** fundament, underlag; **4** støtte(bjelke); stolpe; **II** *vt* **1** bære; holde oppe; støtte (opp); **2** hjelpe, støtte; *også data* understøtte; **3** forsørge, underholde; *have a large family to ~* ha (en) stor familie å forsørge; **4** tåle, utstå; finne seg i. **supporter** [sə'pɔ:tə] *sb* **1** hjelper, støtte (dvs en som hjelper/støtter etc); (noe som) bærer/understøtter; støtte; **2** supporter, tilhenger. **support | program** *sb data* systemprogramvare. **~ vessel** *sb petro etc* moderskip.

suppose [sə'pəʊz] *vt* **1** anta, formode; mene, tro; **2** innebære, forutsette; *supposing (that)* sett at; *you're not ~d to* det er ikke meningen at du. **supposition** [ˌsʌpə'zɪʃn] *sb* antakelse, formodning.

suppository [sə'pɒzɪtrɪ] *sb* stikkpille.

suppress [sə'pres] *vt* **1** under|kue, -trykke; slå ned; **2** undertrykke; fortie; *fig også* kvele. **suppresion** [sə'preʃn] *sb* undertrykkelse *etc.* **suppressor** [sə'presə] *sb* **1** undertrykker; **2** *radio etc* støydemper.

supremacy [sʊ'preməsɪ] *sb* overhøyhet; herredømme. **supreme** [sʊ'pri:m] *adj* høyest, øverst(-).

surcharge ['sɜ:tʃɑ:dʒ] **I** *sb* **1** gebyr, tilleggsavgift; **2** overbelastning; **II** *vt* **1** forlange tilleggsavgift; **2** overbelaste.

sure ['ʃʊə] *adj* **1** sikker (*of* på; *that* på at); *be ~ to* glem (nå) ikke å; husk (nå) på å; *know for ~* vite sikkert; *make ~* forvisse seg om; *to be ~!* ja visst! sikkert! **2** pålitelig; trygg; **3** ~ *enough!* ganske riktig! **surely** ['ʃʊəlɪ] *adv* **1** sikkert *etc*; **2** *dgl* vel (dvs forhåpentlig etc). **surety** ['ʃʊərətɪ] *sb* **1** sikkerhet, garanti; **2** garantist.

surf [sɜ:f] **1** *sb* brenning; **2** *vi* surfe. **surf-board** *sb* surfebrett.

surface ['sɜ:fɪs] **I** *sb* overflate; utside, ytterside; **II** *vb* **1** overflatebehandle; **2** *om ubåt* gå/komme opp i overflatestilling. **surface mail** *sb* vanlig post (i motsetning til luftpost).

surfeit ['sɜ:fɪt] **1** *sb* overmål (især av mat og drikke); forspisthet; **2** *vt* gjøre overmett/*fig* matlei.

surge [sɜ:dʒ] *sb, vi* bølge; *fig* brus(e).

surgeon ['sɜ:dʒən] *sb* kirurg. **surgery** ['sɜ:dʒərɪ] *sb* **1** kirurgi, kirurgisk behandling; *dgl* operasjon; **2** operasjons|sal, stue; **3** legekontor; *GB også* tannlegekontor. **surgical** ['sɜ:dʒɪkl] *adj* kirurgisk; *også* sykehus-; bandasje-, sår-.

surly ['sɜ:lɪ] *adj* grinet, sur.

surmise 1 ['səmaɪz] *sb* antakelse *etc*; **2** [sə'maɪz] *vb* anta, formode; gjette.

surmount [sə'maʊnt] *vt* heve seg/rage over; *be ~ed by* ha på toppen; være kronet med.

surname ['sɜ:neɪm] *sb* etternavn, familienavn.

surpass [sɜ:'pɑ:s] *vt* over|gå, -stige, -treffe. **surpassing** [sɜ:'pɑ:sɪŋ] *adj* blendende (*fig*); overveldende, uovertruffet.

surplus ['sɜ:pləs] *sb* overskudd; *som adj* overskudds-.

surprise [sə'praɪz] **I** *sb* overraskelse; *take by ~* overraske, overrumple; komme overraskende/overrumplende på; **II** *vt* **1** overraske; for|bause, -bløffe; **2** ta på fersk gjerning. **surprising** [sə'praɪzɪŋ] *adj* forbausende, overraskende.

surrender [sə'rendə] **I** *sb* overgivelse *etc*; **II** *vt* **1** kapitulere; overgi seg; **2** oppgi; gi/levere fra seg; **3** ~ *oneself to* hengi seg til.

surreptitious [ˌsʌrəp'tɪʃəs] *adj bokl* hemmelig, skjult.

surround [sə'raʊnd] *vt* om|gi, -ringe. **surrounding** [sə'raʊndɪŋ] **1** *adj* om(kring)liggende; **2** *sb fl* omegn, omgivelser; miljø.

surveillance [sə'veɪləns] *sb* overvåking; oppsikt, oppsyn.

survey I ['sɜ:veɪ] *sb* **1** over|sikt, -syn; **2** (geografisk) oppmåling; kartlegging; *også* undersøkelse; **II** [sə'veɪ] *vt* **1** overskue; se (utover) på; **2** besiktige; måle opp (land). **surveying** [sə'veɪɪŋ] *sb* landmåling. **surveyor** [sə'veɪə] *sb* **1** inspektør, oppsyns|-kvinne, -mann; **2** landmåler. **survey ship** *sb petro* leteskip.

survival [sə'vaɪvl] *sb* **1** over|levelse, -leving; **2** (fortids)levning. **survival capsule** *sb petro etc* redningsklokke. **survive** [sə'vaɪv] *vb* **1** overleve (dvs berge livet); **2** *a)* overleve (dvs leve lenger enn); *b)* bestå, vare; være igjen. **survivor** [sə'vaɪvə] *sb* overlevende (person etc).

susceptibility [səˌseptə'bɪlətɪ] *sb* **1** følsomhet, mottakelighet; **2** *fl* følelser. **susceptible** [sə'septəbl] *adj* **1** følsom/mottakelig (*to* for); (lett)påvirkelig; **2** ømfintlig (*to* for).

suspect I ['sʌspekt] **1** *adj* mistenkelig, suspekt; mistenkt; **2** *sb* mistenkelig/mistenkt (person); **II** [sə'spekt] *vt* **1** mistenke (*of* for); **2** mistro; tvile på; **3** ane; ha (en) anelse om; *også* frykte; være redd for.

suspend [sə'spend] *vt* **1** henge (opp); la henge/sveve etc; **2** utsette; ~ *payment* innstille betalingen; **3**

suspendere. **suspenders** [sə'spendəz] *sb fl* sokkeholdere; *US* bukseseler. **suspense** [sə'spens] *sb* spenning; usikkerhet, uvisshet. **suspension** [sə'spenʃn] *sb* opphengning (etc, jf *suspend*). **suspension bridge** *sb* hengebro.

suspicion [sə'spɪʃn] *sb* mistanke (etc, jf *suspect II*); *above ~* hevet over mistanke; *under ~ (of)* mistenkt (for (å)). **suspicious** [sə'spɪʃəs] *adj* **1** mistenksom; **2** mistenkelig.

sustain [sə'steɪn] *vt* **1** bære; holde oppe; *fig* opprettholde, støtte; **2** underholde; forsyne/forsørge (med mat); **3** lide, tåle; **4** *jur* anerkjenne, godkjenne; gi medhold. **sustenance** ['sʌstɪnəns] *sb* underhold; *især* mat, næring.

swab [swɒb] *sb* **1** svaber; **2** vattpinne (e.l. til å pensle/rense sår etc eller til å ta prøver med, også om selve prøvene); **2** *vt* pensle.

swaddle ['swɒdl] *vt* reive (spedbarn).

swagger ['swægə] **I** *sb* **1** spankulering, sprading; **2** brauting, skryt; **II** *vi* spankulere, sprade.

swallow ['swɒləʊ] **A 1** *sb* svelg; *dgl* hals; **2** *vt* svelge; **B** *sb* svale.

swamp [swɒmp] **I** *sb* myr, sump; **II** *vt* **1** oversvømme; fylle med vann; **2** *fig* overvelde, nedsylte. **swampy** ['swɒmpɪ] *adj* myrlendt, sumpig.

swan [swɒn] *sb* svane.

swap [swɒp] *vb* **1** *data* veksle (*in* inn; *out* ut); **2** = *swop*. **swapping** ['swɒpɪŋ] *sb data* lagerveksling.

swarm [swɔ:m] **A 1** *sb* sverm; **2** *vi* sverme (om bier etc); myldre/yre *(with* av); **B** *vb* klatre (med hender og føtter); kravle.

swarthy ['swɔ:ðɪ] *adj* mørkhudet, svartsmusket.

swathe [sweɪð] *vt* bandasjere, forbinde; hylle/svøpe inn.

sway [sweɪ] **I** *sb* **1** svai(ing) *etc*; **2** makt, (over)herredømme; *under the ~ of* under innflytelse av; **II** *vb* **1** svaie; svinge (med); **2** beherske, kontrollere; influere, lede; **3** *sjø (~ up)* heise/hive (opp).

swear [sweə] *vb* **1** sverge; *~ by (dgl)* sverge til (dvs tro fullt og fast på); *~ in (jur)* ta (vitne) i ed; *~ him to secrecy* få ham til å sverge på at han skal holde tett; **2** banne. **swearwords** *sb fl* bannord, eder; banning.

sweat [swet] **I** *sb* svette; svetting; *dgl* slit; hardt arbeid; **II** *vb* **1** svette; *dgl* jobbe/slite hardt; *~ it out (US)* slite seg gjennom det; vente tålmodig på det; **2** la svette; *især* drive hardt (for ussel betaling); ≈ utbytte. **sweater** ['swetə] *sb* genser. **sweat shirt** *sb* trenings|genser, -trøye. **sweaty** ['swetɪ] *adj* svett; *især* som en blir svett av; *også* slitsom; hard, tung.

swede [swi:d] *sb* kålrot.

sweep [swi:p] **I** *sb* **1** feiing *etc*; tak med feiekost *etc*; strøk/sving (med div redskap); *make a clean ~ of* gjøre rent bord; **2** *(chimney-~)* (skorsteins)feier; **3** (rekke)-vidde; strekning; **II** *vb* **1** feie, sope; *~* **along** feie/rive med seg; *~* **away** feie unna/vekk; *~* **down on** slå ned på; *~* **up** feie/sope opp; **2** *sjø, mil* sveipe (miner); **3** bevege seg/komme feiende; **4** bølge/strekke seg (foran en, især om landskap etc med myke linjer og kurver). **sweeping** ['swi:pɪŋ] *adj* **1** feiende (flott etc); **2** gjennomgripende, omfattende; **3** bred, rund (dvs riktig i store trekk, om enn ikke i alle detaljer). **sweepstake** ['swi:psteɪk] *sb* hesteveddeløp (kombinert med lotteri).

sweet [swi:t] **I** *adj* **1** søt (og *fig* deilig, yndig; blid, bløt, melodisk etc); *have a ~ tooth* like søtsaker; være en slikkmunn; **2** *petro* svovelfattig, søt; **II** *sb* **1** dessert; **2** sukkertøy; *fl også* godter, søtsaker. **sweet crude** *sb petro* lavsvovelråolje. **sweeten** ['swi:tn] *vb* **1** sukre, søte; **2** bli søt(ere). **sweetening** ['swi:tnɪŋ] *sb* søtnings|middel, -stoff. **sweet|heart** *sb* kjæreste. **~-meat** *sb koll* sukkertøy, søtsaker; gotter, slikkeri. **~ness** *sb* sødme, søthet; *fig* ynde *etc*. **~-scented** *adj* (søtt) duftende, velluktende. **~shop** *sb* godtebutikk. **~-tempered** *adj* blid, elskelig.

swell [swel] **I** *adj* **1** elegant/smart (i klesveien); lapset, snobbet; **2** *US* finfin, flott; super; **II** *sb* **1** svulming *etc*; **2** dønning; **3** *dgl* elegant/smart (kledd) person; laps, snobb; **III** *vb* svulme; hovne (opp); trutne; vokse, øke; stige. **swelling** ['swelɪŋ] *sb især* hevelse, kul.

swelter ['sweltə] *vi: be ~ing* holde på å forgå av varme; *~ing hot* stekende het.

swerve [swɜ:v] *vb* bøye av; svinge/vike unna.

swift [swɪft] **A** *adj* rask, snar; **B** *sb* tårnsvale. **swiftness** ['swɪftnɪs] *sb* hurtighet, raskhet.

swill [swɪl] **I** *sb* **1** (ut)skylling; spyling; **2** skyller; **3** slurk; **II** *vb* **1** skylle (ut); **2** *dgl* helle (skylle, *dgl* tylle) i seg.

swim [swɪm] **I** *sb* svømme, svømmetur; *go for/have a ~* få/ta seg en svømmetur/et (sjø)bad; **II** *vb* **1** svømme (og svømme i/over; flomme/svømme over (av); *fig* være badet (i) etc); **2** *my head is ~ming* det går rundt for meg. **swimmer** ['swɪmə] *sb* svømmer; *be a good ~* være flink til å svømme. **swimming | bath** *sb* svømme|bad, basseng. *~* **costume** *sb* badedrakt. *~* **pool** *sb* svømmebasseng. **~trunks** *sb fl* badebukse(r). **swim-suit** *sb* badedrakt.

swindle ['swɪndl] **1** *sb* bedrag, lureri; svindel; **2** *vb* bedra, lure; snyte; svindle. **swindler** ['swɪndlə] *sb* bedrager, svindler.

swine [swaɪn] *sb (koll)* svin.

swing [swɪŋ] **I** *sb* **1** sving(ing) *etc; dgl* svingom (dvs dans); **2** plass til å svinge seg på; *især* bevegelsesfrihet, spillerom; **3** travelhet; fart, futt; *in full ~* i full gang; **4** huske; **II** *vb* **1** svinge (og svinge seg; svinge med/på etc); dreie, snu, vende; **2** (henge og) dingle; *dgl* bli hengt.

swirl [swɜ:l] **1** *sb* virvel; **2** *vb* virvle (og virvle opp/rundt etc).

swish [swɪʃ] **I** *sb* sus(ing) *etc*; susende rapp/slag; **II** *vb* **1** suse, visle; **2** la suse *etc*; **3** slå/svinge (med noe) så det hviner/suser; *dgl* peise på; rappe til; denge, slå.

switch [swɪtʃ] **I** *sb* **1** *elek etc* bryter; **2** pens, (spor)-veksel; **3** *data* omkoblingspunkt; **4** (ride)pisk, svolk; **5** løsflette; **II** *vb* **1** *elek* sette/slå over (*to* til); *~ off* slå av; ~ *on* slå på; **2** pense; skifte (til et annet) spor; *også* rangere; **3** piske (og piske/slå med; slå/svinge med); peise på; rappe til. **switch|-board** *sb* **1** fordelingstavle; **2** sentralbord.

swivel ['swɪvl] **1** *sb* sving|bolt, (-)tapp; **2** *vt* dreie/svinge (rundt). **swivel-chair** *sb* svingstol.

swollen ['swəulən] *adj* hoven, oppsvulmet.

swoon [swu:n] **1** *sb bokl* besvimelse; *også* avmakt; **2** *vi* besvime.

swoop [swu:p] **1** *sb* nedslag; **2** *vi:* ~ *down on* slå ned på (om rovfugl etc).

swop [swɒp] **1** *sb* bytte(handel); **2** *vb dgl* bytte (med); ~ *places with* bytte plass med; ~ *stamps* bytte frimerker.

sword [sɔ:d] *sb* sverd; *put to the* ~ drepe/henrette med sverd. **sword|-dance** *sb* sverddans. **~fish** *sb* sverdfisk.

syllabic [sɪ'læbɪk] *adj* stavelses-. **syllable** ['sɪləbl] *sb* stavelse. **syllabus** ['sɪləbəs] *sb* leseplan, studieplan; pensum.

sylph [sɪlf] *sb* sylfide.

symbol ['sɪmbl] *sb* symbol, tegn. **symbolic** [sɪm'bɒlɪk] *adj* symbolsk. **symbolize** ['sɪmbəlaɪz] *vt* symbolisere.

symmetric(al) [sɪ'metrɪk(l)] *adj* symmetrisk. **symmetry** ['sɪmətrɪ] *sb* symmetri.

sympathetic [ˌsɪmpə'θetɪk] *adj* deltagende, medfølende; velvillig (innstilt). **sympathetic strike** *sb* sympatistreik. **sympathize** ['sɪmpəθaɪz] *vi:* ~ *with* føle med; være velvillig innstilt til. **sympathy** ['sɪmpəθɪ] *sb* deltakelse, medfølelse; velvilje.

symphonic [sɪm'fɒnɪk] *adj* symfonisk, symfoni-.

symphony ['sɪmfənɪ] *sb* symfoni.

symptom ['sɪmptəm] *sb* symptom, tegn. **symptomatic** [ˌsɪmptə'mætɪk] *adj* symptomatisk.

synagogue ['sɪnəgɒg] *sb* synagoge.

synchronize ['sɪŋkrənaɪz] *vb* synkronisere(s); sam|kjøre(s), -ordne(s). **synchronous** ['sɪŋkrənəs] *adj* synkron. **synchronous | computer** *sb data* synkron(data)maskin. ~ **device** *sb data* synkronutstyr. ~ **transmission** *sb data* synkronoverføring.

syndicate **1** ['sɪndɪkət] *sb* syndikat; **2** ['sɪndɪkeɪt] *vt* syndikalisere.

syndrome ['sɪndrəum] *sb* syndrom, sykdomsbilde.

synonym ['sɪnənɪm] *sb* synonym. **synonymous** [sɪ'nɒnɪməs] *adj* synonym(-).

syntax ['sɪntæks] *sb* syntaks. **syntax error** *sb data* syntaksfeil.

synthesis ['sɪnθəsɪs] *sb* syntese. **synthetic** [sɪn'θetɪk] *adj* syntetisk; kunstig, uekte.

syphon ['saɪfn] = *siphon.*

syringe ['sɪrɪndʒ] *sb* (injeksjons)sprøyte.

syrup ['sɪrəp] *sb* sirup.

sysop ['sɪsɒp] *sb data* = *system operator.* **system** ['sɪstəm] *sb* system; orden, plan; rutine; *the* ~ *(også)* opplegget, organismen; (samfunns)systemet. **system analyst** *sb data* systemplanlegger. **systematic** [ˌsɪstə'mætɪk] *adj* systematisk. **system | board** *sb data* systemkort. ~ **manager** *sb data* systemleder. ~ **operator** *sb data* systemoperatør. ~ **restart** *sb data* varmstart. ~ **software** *sb data* systemprogramvare. ~ **disk** *sb data* systemdiskett.

T

ta [tɑ:] *interj dgl* takk.

tab [tæb] *sb* **1** merkelapp; *fig* kjennemerke; *keep ~s/a ~ on* føre kontroll/regnskap med; holde øye med; **2** hempe; **3** tabulator.

tabby ['tæbɪ] *adj, sb* brannet (katt).

tab character *sb data* tabulatortegn.

tabernacle ['tæbənækl] *sb rel hist* tabernakel; *dgl* bedehus, (dissenter)kirke.

tab key *sb data* tabulatortast.

table ['teɪbl] **I** *sb* **1** bord; *fig* kost, mat; **2** tabell; fortegnelse, liste; **3** *(~ land)* platå, taffelland; **II** *vt* legge/sette på bordet; *især fig* sette på dagsordenen; *også* utsette; *dgl* legge på hyllen/på is. **table|cloth** *sb* (bord)duk. **~knife** *sb* bordkniv. **~-linen** *sb* dekketøy. **~-mat** *sb* kuvertbrikke. **~spoon** *sb* spiseskje. **tablet** ['tæblɪt] *sb* **1** (minne)|plate, -tavle; plakett; **2** notis|blokk, -bok; **3** pille, tablett. **table|-talk** *sb* bordkonversasjon. ~ **tennis** *sb* bordtennis. **~-ware** *sb* (spise)bestikk.

tabloid ['tæblɔɪd] *sb* tabloidavis; middagsavis i tabloidformat; *også* bulevardavis.

taboo, tabu [tə'bu] **1** *adj, sb* tabu(-); **2** *vt* belegge med tabu; *dgl* bannlyse, forby. **taboo word** *sb* tabuord.

tab stop *sb data* tabulatorstopp.

tabular ['tæbjulə] *adj* tabellarisk, tabell-. **tabulate** ['tæbjuleɪt] *vt* tabellarisere; sette opp i tabellform. **tabulation** [ˌtæbju'leɪʃn] *sb* tabellarisering.

tacit ['tæsɪt] *adj* stilltiende, underforstått. **taciturn** ['tæsɪtɜ:n] *adj* fåmælt, ordknapp; taus.

tack [tæk] **A I** *sb* **1** nudd, stift; (liten) nagle; *(thumb ~)* tegnestift; **2** nest, (hefte)sting; **3** *sjø* hals (og halsbarm samt baut, slag; strekk, strekning; kurs, retning etc); *on the port/starboard ~* for babords/styrbords halser; *on the right/wrong ~* på rett spor/villspor; **II** *vb* **1** stifte (hefte, neste etc) fast; **2** *sjø* baute, krysse; stagvende; *fig* legge om kursen; **B** *sb sjø (hard ~)* beskøyter, skipskjeks.

tackle ['tækl] **I** *sb* **1** talje; **2** *sjø* rigg, takkelasje; tauverk; **3** utstyr; *dgl* greier, saker; **4** *sport* angrep, takling; **II** *vt* angripe; gå løs på; *dgl* fikse, klare; løse; ordne (opp med); *sport også* takle.

tact [tækt] *sb* takt (dvs diskresjon, finfølelse etc). **tact|ful** *adj* taktfull. **~less** *adj* taktløs.

tactical ['tæktɪkl] *adj* taktisk. **tactician** [tæk'tɪʃn] *sb* taktiker. **tactics** ['tæktɪks] *sb fl* taktikk.

tadpole ['tædpəʊl] *sb* rumpetroll.

taffrail ['tæfreɪl] *sb sjø* **1** hakkebrett; **2** akterreling.

tag [tæg] **I** *sb* **1** (løs) ende; stump, tamp; flik; *også* dott, tjafs; slintre; **2** (lisse)nebb, (snøre)dopp; **3** (merke)lapp; **4** forslitt frase/sitat; omkved, refreng; **5** *(game of ~)* sisten; **II** *vb* **1** feste/hefte/henge (*on/on to* på); tilføye; **2** *~ along (after, behind)* følge i hælene på; *dgl* henge etter; **3** merke; feste merkelapp på.

tail [teɪl] **I** *sb* **1** hale; *(coat)~s* (frakke)skjøter; *dgl også* snippkjole; *hum* snibel; **2** *fl* revers (på mynt etc); *dgl* mynt (dvs myntside i motsetning til kroneside); **II** *vb* følge i hælene på; *dgl* henge etter; *slang* skygge. **tail|-end** *sb* ende, slutt. **~gate** *sb* bakdør (på varebil etc). **~-light** *sb* baklys.

tailor ['teɪlə] **1** *sb* skredder; **2** *vb* skreddersy; *også* lage *etc* etter mål/på bestilling. **tailor-made** *adj* skreddersydd.

taint [teɪnt] **I** *sb* flekk; lyte, mangel; skamplett; **II** *vb* **1** bederve(s), forderve(s); råtne; **2** besmitte, besudle; plette.

take [teɪk] **I** *sb* **1** fangst (især av fisk); **2** *US* avkastning, utbytte; inntekt(er); **II** *vb* **1** ta (og ta fatt (i); gripe/holde (fast) etc); **2** (inn)ta; *~ the chair* lede debatten/møtet; *~ the floor* gripe/ta ordet (i debatt); *~ a stand* (inn)ta et standpunkt; **3** (på)gripe; fakke, fange, ta; *fig* pådra seg; *~ cold* bli forkjølet; *~ fire* ta fyr; *~ ill/sick* bli dårlig; *~ prisoner* ta til fange; **4** ha/ta med seg; **5** følge, ledsage; *~ her home* følge henne hjem; **6** ta (seg); innta/nyte (mat, drikke etc); **7** skaffe/tilegne seg; få; ha; holde; *~ a fancy/liking to* begynne å like; få til overs for; *~ (an) interest in* fatte/nære interesse for; *~ pleasure in* glede seg over/ved; *~ pride in* være stolt av/over; **8** leie; holde (dvs abonnere på); **9** (an)ta; gå ut fra; *~ for granted* ta for gitt; *I ~ it that* jeg formoder/går ut fra at; *I ~ it to mean that* jeg oppfatter det derhen/slik at; **10** *~ it easy* ta det rolig; *~ one's leave (of)* ta avskjed/farvel (med); *~ place* finne sted; **11** *med adv, prep ~* **after** ta etter (dvs etterligne, herme etter etc); *~* **apart** ta fra hverandre; *fig* mishandle, ødelegge; *~* **away** ta bort/vekk; *~ oneself away* fjerne seg; *~* **back** ta igjen/tilbake; *~* **by** *storm* ta med storm; *~* **down** slå/ta ned; demontere, rive ned; *fig* notere, skrive ned; *dgl også* jekke ned; redusere (dvs få til å virke liten, ubetydelig etc); *~* **for** ta for (dvs forstå/oppfatte som); *~* **in** ta inn (*også* = redusere livvidde etc på klesplagg); huse; gi hus|ly, -rom; *fig* forstå, oppfatte; *dgl også* dupere; lure, svindle; *~* **into** *one's head* sette seg i hodet (dvs bestemme seg for etc); *~* **off** ta av/vekk; fjerne, ta bort; ta sats; lette/starte (om fly); *fig* parodiere; ape/herme etter; *~ oneself off* fjerne seg; *~* **on** ta på (seg); ansette (arbeidere etc); *fig* påta seg; slå an; ta på vei; *~* **out** ta ut (frem, opp etc); ta med (seg) ut; fjerne (især flekker); bestille/ta ut (lysing etc); dekke/tegne (forsikring etc); *~ it* **out of** slite/ta på; *~ it* **out on** *him* la det gå ut over ham; la ham få unngjelde for det; *~* **over** overta; *~* **to** begynne/ta til med; gå inn for; ta/ty til; *dgl* slå seg på (f.eks. flasken); *~* **up** ta opp; oppta (og gjenoppta); innta (stilling); begynne med; gå inn for; slå seg på; *~ up arms* gripe til våpen; *~ up (one's) lodgings* bosette seg; slå seg ned; *~ him* **up on** *it* ta ham på ordet; *~* **up with** gi seg i lag med; innlate seg med; *~* **upon** *oneself* påta seg. **take|-in** *sb dgl* lureri, svindel. **~-off** *sb* sats; start (om fly). **~-over** *sb* overtakelse. **taker** *sb* **1** (-)taker; (-)holder; **2** en som aksepterer/inngår et veddemål etc. **taking-down** *sb dgl* dukkert, nesestyver.

talc [tælk], **talcum** ['tælkəm] *sb* talk(um).

tale [teɪl] *sb* fortelling, historie; *(fairy ~)* eventyr; *tell ~s* fortelle eventyr/skrøner; *især* fare med sladder/løst snakk.

talent ['tælənt] *sb* begavelse, talent. **talented** ['tæləntɪd] *adj* begavet, talentfull.

talk [tɔ:k] **I** *sb* **1** samtale (og samtaleemne); konversasjon; *small ~* (små)prating; **2** kåseri; (lettere) foredrag; **II** *vb* **1** prate, snakke; samtale; *~ it over* snakke om/drøfte det; *~ them out of it* snakke dem fra det; **2** kåsere; holde foredrag. **talkative** ['tɔ:kətɪv] *adj* pratsom, snakkesalig. **talkie** ['tɔ:kɪ] *sb* talefilm. **talking-to** ['tɔ:kɪŋtu:] *sg dgl* irettesettelse, skrape.

tall [tɔ:l] *adj* **1** høy (av vekst); lang, stor; **2** *dgl* overdreven; utrolig, drøy; *~ story/tale* (diger) skrøne. **tallish** ['tɔ:lɪʃ] *adj* nokså/temmelig høy.

tallow ['tæləʊ] *sb* talg.

tame [teɪm] **I** *adj* tam, temmet; **II** *vt* **1** temme; **2** kue.

tamper ['tæmpə] *vi: ~ with* fingre (klusse, tukle etc) med; plukke på.

tan [tæn] **I** *adj* (gyllen)brun, solbrun; **II** *sb (sun-~)* brun|farge, -het (som følge av soling); **III** *vb* **1** bli/gjøre (sol)brun; *~ oneself* sole seg; **2** garve; *~ his hide (dgl fig)* garve ryggstykkene hans (dvs gi ham en omgang juling).

tang [tæŋ] *sb* (gjennomtrengende) lukt, smak; eim, tev.

tangent ['tændʒənt] *sb geom* tangent; *fly/go off at a ~ (fig)* komme (ut) på viddene (dvs komme bort fra emnet/saken).

tangible ['tændʒəbl] *adj* håndgripelig; til å ta og føle på. **tangle** ['tæŋgl] **1** *sb* floke, vase; rot, uorden; **2** *vb* filtre/floke (seg) sammen.

tank [tæŋk] *sb* **1** tank; stor beholder; **2** *mil* stridsvogn; *dgl* tank. **tankard** ['tæŋkəd] *sb* (øl)krus, (-)seidel. **tanker** ['tæŋkə] *sb* tankskip; *dgl* tanker. **tank top** *sb* topp (dvs kort, ermeløs bluse etc).

tanner ['tænə] *sb* garver. **tannery** ['tænərı] *sb* garveri.

tantamount ['tæntəmaunt] *adj:* ~ *to* ensbetydende med.

tantrum ['tæntrəm] *sb* (raseri)anfall; ri, tokt.

tap [tæp] **A I** *sb* kran; *især* øl|kran, -tapp; *også* drikkevarer, øl; *(~-house, ~-room)* bar; *on* ~ på fat; **II** *vt* **1** tappe (fra fat, kran etc) **2** *dgl* bomme (dvs låne, især penger); **3** tyvlytte (ved å koble seg inn på telefonlinje etc); **B 1** *sb* lett slag; **2** *vb* gi et lett slag; slå lett. **tap|-dance, ~-dancing** *sb* steppdans, stepping.

tape [teıp] **I** *sb* **1** bånd (og bendelbånd, lydbånd, målebånd etc); *red* ~ byråkrati; *dgl* papirmølle; **2** *sport* målsnor; **II** *vt* **1** feste med bånd; **2** måle med målebånd. **tape | deck** *sb* bånd|opptaker, -spiller. ~ **drive** *sb data* (magnet)bånddrev. **~measure** *sb* målebånd.

taper ['teıpə] **1** *sb* veke; vokslys; **2** *vb* smalne (av).

tape | recorder *sb* båndopptaker. ~ **reader** *sb data* hullbåndleser. ~ **station** *sb data* (magnet)båndstasjon. ~ **storage** *sb data* (magnet)båndlager.

tapestry ['tæpıstrı] *sb* billedteppe, gobelin.

tape-worm *sb* bendelorm.

tar [tɑ:] **1** *sb* tjære; *old* ~ *(slang)* sjø|gutt, (-)ulk; **2** *vt* tjærebre.

target ['tɑ:gıt] *sb* **1** mål; sikte|mål, -punkt; **2** mål(skive), skyteskive. **target | language** *sb* målspråk (dvs det språket noe oversettes til, jf *source language*). **~-practice** *sb (mil)* skiveskyting, skyteøvelse. ~ **study** *sb data etc* målstudie.

tariff ['tærıf] *sb* **1** tariff; *især* tolltariff; **2** prisliste.

tarmac ['tɑ:mæk] *sb* asfalt(dekke).

tarnish ['tɑ:nıʃ] *vb* sette flekker/*fig* pletter på; skitne/smusse til; ta glansen av.

tarpaulin [tɑ:'pɔ:lın] *sb* presenning.

tarry 1 ['tɑ:rı] *adj* tjære|aktig, -holdig; **2** ['tærı] *vi* nøle, somle.

tartan ['tɑ:tən] *sb* skotskrutet stoff.

task [tɑ:sk] *sb* **1** (især) hardt arbeid; slit, strev; **2** oppgave, verv; *mil* oppdrag; **3** *take to* ~ irettesette; skjenne på. **task|-force** *sb mil* kampgruppe; spesialstyrke. **~-master, ~mistress** *sb* en som pålegger oppgaver; *også* tuktemester.

tassel ['tæsl] *sb* dusk.

taste [teıst] **1** *sb* smak (og smakssans); smakebit; *fig* behag, lyst; *have a ~ for* ha sans for; *in bad* ~ smakløs(t); *in good* ~ smakfull(t); *to my* ~ etter min smak; *there's no accounting for ~s* ≈ smak og behag kan ikke diskuteres; **2** *vb* smake (på); *fig* erfare, oppleve; få smak(en) på; ~ *of* smake av. **taste|ful** *adj* velsmakende; *fig* smakfull. **~less** *adj* uten smak; *også fig* smakløs, usmakelig. **tasty** ['teıst **I** *sb* **1**] *adj* = *tasteful.*

tattered ['tætəd] *adj* fillet. **tatters** ['tætəz] *sb fl* filler.

tatto [tæ'tu:] **A** *sb* **1** banking, dundring; tromming; **2** *mil* tappenstrek; **3** (militær) drilloppvisning; **B 1** *sb* tatovering; **2** *vt* tatovere.

taunt [tɔ:nt] *sb, vt* hån(e), spott(e).

taut [tɔ:t] *adj* spent, stram.

tavern ['tævən] *sb hist* kro, vertshus.

tax [tæks] **I** *sb* **1** skatt; *især* statsskatt; *også* toll; avgift, gebyr; **2** byrde; anstrengelse, påkjenning; prøve (og prøvelse); **II** *vt* **1** beskatte, skattlegge; **2** utsette for anstrengelse/påkjenning; bebyrde; **3** anklage; dadle/klandre (*with* for). **tax|able** ['tæksəbl] *adj* skattbar. **~ation** [tæk'seıʃn] *sb* beskatning, skattlegging. ~ **free** *adj* **1** skattefri; **2** fritatt for skatt. **~-collector** *sb* skatteoppkrever.

taxi ['tæksı] **I** *sb (~-cab)* drosje(bil); **II** *vb* **1** drosje (dvs kjøre med/ta drosje); **2** takse (= kjøre fly på bakken). **taxi rank** *sb* drosjeholdeplass.

tax-payer *sb* skattebetaler.

tea [ti:] *sb* te. **tea | bag** *sb* tepose. **~-break** *sb* tepause. **~caddy** *sb* teboks.

teach [ti:tʃ] *vb* undervise (i); instruere; lære (opp); være lærer. **teacher** ['ti:tʃə] *sb* lærer. **teaching** ['ti:tʃıŋ] *sb* undervisning; lærervirksomhet.

tea|cloth *sb* kjøkkenhåndkle. **~-cosy** *sb* tevarmer. **~cup** *sb* tekopp; *storm in a ~cup* ≈ storm i et vannglass. **~-kettle** *sb* = *~pot.*

team [ti:m] **I** *sb* **1** (for)spann; **2** *sport* lag, parti; **II** *vb:* ~ *up* danne lag; slutte seg/slå seg sammen (i lag). **team|-mate** *sb* lagkamerat. ~ **spirit** *sb* lagånd. **~-work** *sb* gruppearbeid, samarbeid.

tea|-party *sb* teselskap. **~pot** *sb* te|kanne, -kjele.

tear A ['tıə] *sb* tåre; *fl* gråt; *in ~s* gråtende; **B** [teə] **I** *sb* revne/rift (i klær etc); **II** *vb* **1** rive (og rive av, opp, over, ut etc); *(~ up)* rive i stykker; *be torn between* slites/vakle mellom (dvs ikke kunne bestemme seg for det ene eller det andre); **2** fare (storme, styrte etc) (*along* av sted). **tear|-drop** *sb* tåre. **~ful** *adj* tåre|fylt, -våt; gråtende. **~-gas** *sb* tåregass. **~less** *adj* tåreløs, tørr.

tearoom *sb* tesalong.

tease [ti:z] **1** *sb dgl* = *teaser 1*; **2** *vt* erte; irritere, plage. **teaser** ['ti:zə] *sb* **1** ertekrok; **2** *fig* nøtt (dvs vanskelig problem etc).

tea|-service, ~-set *sb* teservise. **~spoon** *sb* teskje. **~strainer** *sb* tesil.

teat [ti:t] *sb* patte, spene.

tea|-things *sb fl* teservise. **~-time** *sb* tetid. **~-tray** *sb* te|brett, -brikke. **~-urn** *sb* samovar.

technical ['teknıkl] *adj* **1** teknisk; **2** industri-. **technicality** [ˌteknı'kælətı] *sb* teknisk detalj (punkt, side etc); *stundom* formalitet. **technical | section leader, ~ supervisor** *sb petro etc* teknisk sjef. **technician** [tek'nıʃn] *sb* tekniker. **technique** [tek'ni:k] *sb* **1** teknikk; **2** teknisk dyktighet; ferdighet, håndlag. **technological** [ˌteknə'lɒdʒıkl] *adj* teknologisk. **technologist** [tek'nɒlədʒıst] *sb* teknolog. **technology** [tek'nɒlədʒı] *sb* teknologi.

tedious ['ti:dıəs] *adj* kjedelig, trettende.

teem [ti:m] *vi* kry, myldre, vrimle, yre (*with* av). **teenager** ['ti:n,eɪdʒə] *sb* tenåring. **teeth** [ti:θ] **1** *sb fl* av *tooth*; **2** *vi* få (sine første) tenner. **teething troubles** *sb fl* barnesykdommer (dvs begynnervansker). **teetotaller** [ti:'təʊtlə] *sb* (total)avholds|kvinne, -mann. **tele|communications** [,telɪkə,mju:nɪ'keɪʃnz] *sb fl* telekommunikasjoner. **~gram** ['telɪgræm] *sb* telegram. **~graph** ['telɪgrɑ:f] **1** *sb* telegraf; **2** *vb* telegrafere. **~graphic** [,telɪ'græfɪk] *adj* telegrafisk. **~graphist** [tɪ'legrəfɪst] *sb* telegrafist. **~graph wire** *sb* telegraftråd. **~graphy** [tɪ'legrəfɪ] *sb* telegrafi. **~pathy** [tɪ'lepəθɪ] *sb* telepati. **~pathic** [,telɪ'pæθɪk] *adj* telepatisk. **~phone** ['telɪfəʊn] **1** *sb* telefon (og telefonapparat); **2** *vb* telefonere. **~phone | booth** *sb* telefonkiosk. **~phone directory** *sb* telefonkatalog. **~phone exchange** *sb* telefonsentral. **~phone operator** *sb* telefonist. **~scope** ['telɪskəʊp] *sb* teleskop; *især* (astronomisk) kikkert. **~scopic** [,telɪ'skɒpɪk] *adj* **1** teleskopisk, teleskop-; kikkert; **2** sammenskyvbar (dvs med deler som kan skyves inn i hverandre); *også* uttrekkbar. **~text** *sb* tekst-tv. **~vise** ['telɪvaɪz] *vt* sende i fjernsyn. **~vision** ['telɪ,vɪʒn] *sb* fjernsyn. **~vision set** *sb* fjernsynsapparat.

tell [tel] *vb* **1** berette/fortelle (*about/of* om); *også* røpe, tilstå; **~** *tales* sladre; fortelle (usanne) historier; skrøne; **2** underrette (om); fortelle/si (til); *can you* **~** *me* kan De/du si meg; **3** instruere; be|fale, -ordre; påby; **~** *him to go away* be ham gå (sin vei); *do as you are told* gjør som du er (blitt) bedt om; **4** skjelne (*from* fra); **~** *apart* skjelne fra hverandre; **5** *dgl* virke; leite/ta (*on* på); **6** *gml* regne, telle; *all told* alt medregnet. **teller** ['telə] *sb* **1** forteller *etc*; **2** (bank)kasserer. **telling** ['telɪŋ] **1** *adj* effektiv, virkningsfull; **2** *sb* fortelling *etc*; *især* sladring. **telltale** ['telteɪl] **I** *adj* **1** sladder-; **2** megetsigende, talende; **2** *sb* sladderhank.

telly ['telɪ] *sb dgl (fork* for *television)* fjernsyn.

temper ['tempə] **I** *sb* **1** temperament; **2** gemytt, lynne; humør; **3** selvberskelse, (sinns)ro; *keep/lose one's* **~** bevare/miste fatningen; *out of* **~** *with (dgl)* forbannet/sint på; **4** *om metaller* hardhet, herdningsgrad; **II** *vb* **1** modifisere; dempe, mildne; **2** *om metaller* herde(s). **temperament** ['temprəmənt] *sb* temperament; gemytt, lynne; natur; *også* hissighet, sinne; lidenskap. **temperamental** [,temprə'mentl] *adj* temperamentsfull; *dgl også* hissig, lidenskapelig; inngrodd, intens. **temperance** ['tempərəns] *sb* moderasjon, måtehold; forsiktighet. **temperate** ['temprət] *adj* moderat, måteholden; forsiktig, **temperature** ['temprətʃə] *sb* temperatur; *have/run a* **~** ha feber.

tempest ['tempɪst] *sb* storm. **tempestuous** [tem'pestʃʊəs] *adj* stormfull; *fig også* rasende, voldsom.

temple ['templ] *sb* **A** tempel; **B** tinning.

temporary ['tempərərɪ] *adj* foreløpig, midlertidig; kortvarig.

tempt [tempt] *vt* forføre, friste. **temptation** [temp'teɪʃn] *sb* fristelse. **tempter** ['temptə] *sb* frister. **temptress** ['temptrɪs] *sb* fristerinne.

tenacious [tɪ'neɪʃəs] *adj* fast; vedholdende; sta, strid; seig. **tenacity** [tɪ'næsətɪ] *sb* fasthet *etc*.

tenancy ['tenənsɪ] *sb* **1** forpaktning; **2** leie|forhold, -mål. **tenant** ['tenənt] *sb* **1** forpakter; **2** beboer, leieboer.

tend [tend] **A** *vt* **1** gjete, røkte; vokte; passe på; **2** pleie, stelle; se etter; ta seg av; **B** *vi* tendere (*to* mot); ha en tendens/tilbøyelig (*to* til (å)). **tendency** ['tendənsɪ] *sb* tendens, tilbøyelighet; hang. **tender** ['tendə] **A I** *sb* **1** anbud; tilbud; **2** *jur: legal* **~** lovlig betalingsmiddel; **3** *petro a)* hjelpemann; *b)* = **~** *vessel*; **II** *vb* gi/sende inn anbud (*for* på); **B** *adj* **1** øm|fintlig, -skinnet. -tålig; skjør; **2** følsom, sart; fintfølende; **3** kjærlig, øm; **4** *om kjøtt* mør; **C** *sb* **1** gjeter (etc, jf *tend A*); **2** tender (og tender|skip, -vogn); depotskip; hjelpefartøy; **3** (-)holder; varetaker. **tender|-hearted** *adj* varmhjertet, ømhjertet. **~loin** *sb* mørbrad(stek). **~ vessel** *sb petro* hjelpefartøy.

tenement ['tenɪmənt] *sb* **1** *jur* bolig, leilighet; **2** *(~-house)* leiegård.

tenor ['tenə] **A** *adj, sb* tenor(-); **B** *sb* mening, tankegang; (hoved)innhold.

tense [tens] **A** *adj* **1** stram; (stramt) strukket; **2** *fig* (an)spent; **B** *sb gram* tid (og tidsform). **tension** ['tenʃn] *sb* **1** stramming; stramhet; **2** anspenthet; spenning; spent forhold etc.

tent [tent] *sb* telt.

tentacle ['tentəkl] *sb* fang|arm, -tråd; tentakel.

tentative ['tentətɪv] *adj* forsøks-, prøve-; tentativ.

tepid ['tepɪd] *adj* lunken.

term [tɜ:m] **I** *sb* **1** periode, tidsrom; termin; *også* tidsfrist; *ved skole og universitet* semester, termin; **2** (fag)|ord, -uttrykk; *også* vending; *in no uncertain ~s* i utvetydige ordelag/vendinger; med all ønskelig tydelighet; *scientific ~s* vitenskapelig terminologi; *technical ~s* teknisk terminologi; **3** *fl* betingelser, vilkår; *merk ofte* priser; *come to/make ~s with* komme overens/til enighet med; bli enig med; *on good ~s with* på god/vennskapelig fot med; *on speaking ~s* på talefot; **4** *mat etc* ledd; **II** *vt* kalle; be|nevne, -tegne. **terminable** ['tɜ:mɪnəbl] *adj* oppsigelig; som kan bringes til avslutning/opphør. **terminal** ['tɜ:mɪnl] **I** *adj* avslutnings-, termin-; **2** endelig; ende-, slutt-; **II** *sb* **1** endestasjon, terminal; *petro også* mottakerstasjon; **2** *data* terminal (dvs skjerm og tastbord); **3** *elek* (pol)-klemme. **terminal cancer** *sb* kreft i siste (uhelbredelige og dødelige) stadium. **terminate** ['tɜ:mɪneɪt] *vb* **1** avgrense, begrense; avslutte; **2** ende, slutte; stanse, stoppe; sette en stopper for. **termination** [,tɜ:mɪ'neɪʃn] *sb* avslutning, slutt. **terminology** [,tɜmɪ'nɒlədʒɪ] *sb* terminologi. **terminus** ['tɜ:mɪnəs] *sb* endestasjon, terminal.

termite ['tɜ:maɪt] *sb* termitt(maur).

terrace ['terəs] **I** *sb* **1** terrasse; **2** tribune(r) (på idrettsplass); **3** (sammenhengende) husrekke/rekkehus; **II** *vt* terrassere.

terrible ['terəbl] *adj* forferdelig, fryktelig, grusom, skrekkelig. **terrific** [tə'rɪfik] *adj* fryktinngytende, skrekkinnjagende; forferdelig, skrekkelig; *dgl* fabelaktig, fantastisk; fenomenal; veldig. **terrified** ['terɪfaɪd] *adj, pp* skrekkslagen, vettskremt. **terrify** ['terɪfaɪ] *vt* skremme; slå med redsel/skrekk.

territorial [ˌterɪ'tɔ:rɪəl] *adj* territorial-. **territory** ['terɪtrɪ] *sb* (land)område, territorium; distrikt, strøk.

terror ['terə] *sb* redsel, skrekk; terror. **terrorism** ['terərɪzəm] *sb* terrorisme. **terrorist** ['terərɪst] *sb* terrorist. **terrorize** ['terəraɪz] *vt* terrorisere.

terse [tɜ:s] *adj* fyndig; kort og klar.

test [test] **1** *sb* prøve, test; utprøving; *intelligence* ~ intelligensprøve; *put to the* ~ sette på prøve; **2** *vt* prøve (dvs sette på prøve); teste, utprøve; undersøke.

testament ['testəmənt] *sb* testament(e); *the New/Old Testament* Det nye/Det gamle testamente.

test | case *sb jur* prøvesak. ~ **data** *sb data* prøvedata. ~ **drive** *sb* prøvekjøring. ~ **flight** *sb* prøveflyging.

testicle ['testɪkl] *sb* testikkel. **testify** ['testɪfaɪ] *vb* **1** vitne (i retten); **2** *(~ to)* attestere; be|krefte, -vitne. **testimonial** [ˌtestɪ'məunɪəl] *sb* anbefalingsbrev, attest; bevitnelse, vitnemål, vitnesbyrd. **testimony** ['testɪmənɪ] *sb* vitne|erklæring, -utsagn; vitnesbyrd.

test | pilot *sb* prøveflyger. **~-probe** *sb petro etc* prøve|sonde, -stav. **~-tube** *sb* prøverør.

tether ['teðə] **1** *sb* tjor; *at the end of one's* ~ på bristepunktet; **2** *vt* tjore.

text [tekst] *sb* tekst. **text | area** *sb data* tekstområde. **~book** ['tekstbʊk] *sb* lærebok. ~ **editor** *sb data* tekstredigeringsprogram.

textile ['tekstaɪl] *adj, sb* tekstil(-).

text | processing *sb data* tekstbehandling. ~ **processor** *sb data* tekstbehandlingsmaskin.

texture ['tekstʃə] *sb* tekstur; oppbygning, struktur; sammensetning.

than [ðæn] *konj* enn.

thank [θæŋk] *vt* takke; ~ *God* gudskjelov; ~ *you* takk (skal De/du ha). **thankful** ['θæŋkfʊl] *adj* takknemlig. **thankfulness** ['θæŋkfʊlnɪs] *sb* takknemlighet. **thankless** ['θæŋklɪs] *adj* utakknemlig. **thanks** [θæŋks] *interj, sb fl* takk; ~ *to* takket være.

that [ðæt] **I** *adv dgl* så; ~ *far* så langt; **II** *konj* at; *so* ~ slik/så at; for at; **III** *pron* **1** den/det (der); ~ *is* det vil si; *~'s a dear* så er du snill/søt; *~'s it* (det er) akkurat/nettopp (det det er); ~ *which* det som; *at* ~ attpåtil; til og med; enda; **2** *relativt pron* som (både om personer og ting).

thatch [θætʃ] **1** *sb* halmtak, stråtak (og tak|halm, -strå); **2** *vt* halmtekke, stråtekke.

thaw [θɔ:] **1** *sb* tøvær, mildvær; **2** *vb* tø (og bråne, smelte, tine etc); *fig også* tine/tø opp.

theatre ['θɪətə] *sb* **1** teater; **2** skueplass; *mil* krigsskueplass; *med (operating ~)* operasjonssal.

thee [ði:] *pron gml* deg.

theft [θeft] *sb* tyveri.

theme [θi:m] *sb* tema. **theme song** *sb* gjennomgangsmelodi, kjenningsmelodi.

then [ðen] **I** *adj dgl* daværende; **II** *adv* **1** da (og dengang, den gangen); ~ *and there/there and* ~ der og da; straks, uoppholdelig, øyeblikkelig; **2** deretter, så; *what* ~ hva så; **3** dessuten; (og) så; **4** (i) så (fall); **5** altså; *now,* ~ nå (og nåda, hva nå etc).

theologian [ˌθi:ə'ləudʒɪən] *sb* teolog. **theological** [ˌθi:ə'lɒdʒɪkl] *adj* teologisk. **theology** [θi:'ɒlədʒɪ] *sb* teologi.

theoretic(al) [θɪə'retɪk(l)] *adj* teoretisk. **theory** ['θɪərɪ] *sb* teori. **theorist** ['θɪərɪst] *sb* teoretiker.

therapeutic [ˌθerə'pju:tɪk] *adj* terapeutisk. **therapist** ['θerəpɪst] *sb* terapeut. **therapy** ['θerəpɪ] *sb* terapi.

there [ðeə] **1** *adv* der, dit; *som foreløpig sb* det; *bokl* der; ~ *are many who* det er mange som; ~ *were cries for help* det hørtes/var rop om hjelp; *~'s a good boy* så er du snill (gutt); *~'s no saying/telling* det er ikke godt/mulig å si; ~ *you are* vær så god (dvs der/her har du det du har bedt om); *også* der kan du (bare) se; **2** *som interj* så! nå! nåda! **thereabouts** ['ðeərəbaʊts] *adv* deromkring. **thereafter** [ðeər'ɑ:ftə] *adv* deretter. **thereby** [ðeə'baɪ] *adv* derved. **therefore** ['ðeəfɔ:] *adv* derfor. **thereupon** [ˌðeərə'pɒn] *adv* der|etter, -på.

thermal ['θɜ:ml] *adj* termisk, varme-. **thermal | cracking** *sb petro* termisk krakking/spalting. ~ **printer, thermographic printer** *sb data* varmeskriver. **thermometer** [θə'mɒmɪtə] *sb* termometer.

thesis ['θi:sɪs] *sb* **1** påstand, tese; teori; **2** avhandling.

thick [θɪk] **I** *adj* **1** tykk; **2** tett (og grumset, grøtet, uklar etc); **3** tett(pakket); tettsatt; tett besatt; ~ *with (også)* pakkfull av; **II** *adv* tykt; tett; *come* ~ *and fast* komme/opptre *etc* tett etter hverandre; *også* komme slag i slag; **III** *som sb: in the* ~ *of* midt i/under; *through* ~ *and thin* gjennom tykt og tynt. **thicken** ['θɪkən] *vb* tykne/tetne (til). **thicket** ['θɪkɪt] *sb* kratt, (skog)tykning. **thick|-headed** *adj* tykkhodet. **~-set** *adj* tettbygd, undersetsig; firskåren. **~-skinned** *adj* tykkhudet (også *fig*).

thief [θi:f] *sb* tyv. **thieve** [θi:v] *vb* stjele.

thigh [θaɪ] *sb* lår.

thimble ['θɪmbl] *sb* fingerbøl.

thin [θɪn] **I** *adj* **1** tynn (og mager, skrinn; slank; sped etc); **2** sparsom, spredt; **3** tynn, utvannet; **II** *adv* tynt; **III** *som sb* se *thick III*; **IV** *vb* **1** bli/gjøre tynn; **2** fortynne, tynne ut.

thine [ðaɪn] *pron gml* din, ditt; dine.

thing [θɪŋ] *sb* **1** ting; *fl også* saker; *dgl især* klær; effekter, løsøre; *the same* ~ den/det samme; *the very* ~ akkurat den/det en trenger/snakker om etc; *have a* ~ *about (dgl)* være besatt (dvs svært opptatt) av; *see ~s* se syner (dvs innbille seg ting); **2** *fl* forhold, omstendigheter; *the way ~s are* slik forholdene (situasjonen, stillingen etc) er.

think [θɪŋk] **I** *sb dgl: then you've (got) another* ~ *coming* da/så må du tenke om igjen; **II** *vb* **1** tenke (og betenke; tenke over; tenke seg om etc); ~ *about* tenke på; ~ *of* tenke på (dvs planlegge/ha planer om); huske, minnes; finne/hitte på; ~ *better of it* ombestemme seg; ~ *out* tenke ut; ~ *over* tenke over; ~ *it over* overveie/tenke over det; **2** anse; mene, tro; synes; ~ *highly of* ha høye tanker om; sette (stor) pris på; ~ *lightly of* blåse av; ~ *nothing of* ikke ense/høre; ikke ha noe til overs for. **thinker** ['θɪŋkə] *sb* tenker; ≈ filosof. **thinking** ['θɪŋkɪŋ] **1** *adj* tenkende; **2** *sb* tenk(n)ing.

thinner ['θɪnə], **thinning agent** *sb* tynner. **thin-skinned** *adj* tynnhudet; *fig* ømskinnet.

third [θɜ:d] **1** *adj* tredje(-); **2** *sb* tredje|del, -part. **third | party** *sb jur* tredjemann. **~rate** *adj* tredjerangs.

thirst [θɜ:st] **1** *sb* tørst(s); **2** *vi især fig* tørste (*for* etter). **thirsty** ['θɜ:stɪ] *adj* tørst; *fig også* begjærlig.

this [ðɪs] **1** *adv dgl* så; ~ *much* så mye (som dette); **2** *pron* denne/dette (her); ~ *day* i dag; dags dato; dagen i dag; ~ *day month/week* en måned/uke (fra) i dag.

thistle ['θɪsl] *sb* tistel.

thong [θɒŋ] *sb* (lær)|reim. -stropp.

thorn [θɔ:n] *sb* torn. **thorny** ['θɔ:nɪ] *adj* tornet, tornefull.

thorough ['θʌrə] *adj* **1** fullstendig, hel; **2** grundig, omhyggelig. **thorough|bred** *adj, sb* fullblods (og fullblodshest). **~fare** *sb* gjennomfarts|vei, -åre. **~ly** *adv* fullstendig; ganske, helt.

thou [ðaʊ] *pron gml* du.

though [ðəʊ] **1** *adv* likevel; **2** *konj* (en)skjønt; selv om; enda; om (...) enn; *even* ~ selv om; *young* ~ *he was* ung som han var (dvs enda så ung han var).

thought [θɔ:t] *sb* **1** tenkning (og tenkeevne; ettertanke, omtanke etc); *on first* ~*s* i første omgang; ved første øyekast; *on second* ~*s* ved nærmere ettertanke; **2** forestilling, idé; hensikt, plan; *have no* ~*s of* ikke ha planer om/til hensikt (å). **thought|ful** *adj* **1** tankefull, tenksom; **2** omtenksom; hensynsfull. **~less** *adj* **1** tankeløs; ubesindig, ubetenksom; **2** hensynsløs.

thrash [θræʃ] *vb* **1** denge, jule; slå; **2** ~ *out a problem* gjennomdiskutere et problem; **3** = *thresh.* **trashing** ['θræʃɪŋ] *sb* juling.

thread [θred] **I** *sb* **1** tråd; **2** (skrue)gjenge; **II** *vt* **1** træ (i, på etc); **2** ~ *one's way* sno seg (frem). **threadbare** ['θredbeə] *adj* loslitt.

threat [θret] *sb* trussel. **threaten** ['θretn] *vb* true (og true med).

three [θri:] *adj, sb* tre(tall); treer. **three|-cornered** *adj* tre|kantet, -sided; *om hatt* tresnutet. **~-D, ~-dimensional** *adj* tredimensjonal. **~-piece** *adj* som består av tre deler (om dress, sofagruppe etc). **~ply** *adj* tre|slått, -trådet; *om kryssfinér* med tre lag.

thresh [θreʃ] *vb* treske. **threshing-machine** *sb* treske|maskin, -verk.

threshold ['θreʃəʊld] *sb* terskel, treskel.

thrift [θrɪft] *sb* sparsommelighet. **thrifty** ['θrɪftɪ] *adj* sparsommelig, økonomisk.

thrill [θrɪl] **I** *sb* spenning; *også* kribling, grøssing; **II** *vb* **1** sitre/skjelve (især av spenning; **2** bli begeistret (*at* over); bli betatt (*with* av). **thriller** ['θrɪlə] *sb* spennende film/roman; thriller; *ofte* grøsser. **thrilling** ['θrɪlɪŋ] *adj* spennende.

thrive [θraɪv] *vi* blomstre, trives; ha fremgang/hell. **thriving** ['θraɪvɪŋ] *adj fig* blomstrende.

throat [θrəʊt] *sb* hals, strupe; svelg. **throaty** ['θrəʊtɪ] *adj* hals-, strupe-; guttural.

throb [θrɒb] **1** *sb* banking; (puls)slag; **2** *vi* banke/slå (om hjerte etc); pulsere.

throne [θrəʊn] *sb* trone.

throng [θrɒŋ] **1** *sb* (menneske)|masse, (-)stimmel; trengsel; **2** *vb* stimle sammmen; flokke/trenge seg (sammen etc).

throttle ['θrɒtl] **I** *sb* trottel; *dgl* struper; **II** *vb* **1** kvele, strupe; **2** trotle (dvs regulere tilførsel av drivstoff til motor).

through [θru:] **I** *adj (om tog etc)* gjennom|gående, -gangs-; direkte(-); **II** *adv* **1** gjennom (og igjennom); *put* ~ sette over (telefonsamtale); **2** ferdig; ~ *and* ~ tvers igjennom; *fig* gjennomført; *be* ~ være ferdig/*fig* utkjørt; *carry* ~ fullføre; gjøre seg ferdig med; **III** *prep* gjennom; over, via; *live* ~ *the night* leve natten over; **2** *om årsak* ved (og ved hjelp av; på grunn av); *it hap pened* ~ *no fault of yours* det var ikke din skyld (at det hendte). **throughout** [θru:'aʊt] **1** *adv* helt igjennom; **2** *prep* gjennom hele.

throw [θrəʊ] **I** *sb* kast; **II** *vb* **1** kaste; *dgl* hive, kyle, slenge; **2** ~ *a bridge over* slå (en) bro over; ~ *a fit* få (et) anfall; ~ *a party* arrangere/holde (et) selskap; **3** *med adv, prep* ~ **about** kaste *etc* omkring; slå om seg (med); ~ **about for** lete etter; *fig* spekulere på; ~ **away** kaste bort; *fig* forspille; sløse bort; ~ **back** kaste *etc* tilbake; ~ **by** kassere; ~ **down** kaste/styrte ned; ~ **in** kaste *etc* inn; gi attpå; skyte inn (penger); kaste/skyte inn (et ord etc); ~ *in one's lot with* gjøre felles sak med; ~ **into** kaste *etc* inn i; forvandle (omdanne, skape (om) etc) til; *fig også* hensette i; ~ *into the bargain* gi attpå/på kjøpet; ~ *into gear* sette i gir; ~ **off** kaste av (seg); *fig* befri seg for; ~ **on** kaste/legge *etc* på; kaste/slenge på seg (klær etc); ~ **open** slå opp (dør etc); åpne på vidt gap; ~ **out** kaste (helle, slå etc) ut; sende ut; *fig også* kaste frem; slå frempå (om); ~ *out of gear* sette ut av gir; *dgl* sette i fri; ~ *out of work* gjøre (plutselig) arbeidsløs; ~ **over** forlate, oppgi; gå fra; svikte; slå hånden av; slå opp med; ~ **together** føre sammen; ~ **up** kaste *etc* opp; slå opp; *dgl* slenge/smøre opp (dvs bygge raskt og slurvet). **throw|-back** *sb fig* tilbakeslag. **~-down** *sb fig* **1** avslag; **2** nederlag.

thru [θru:] *US* = *through.*

thrush [θrʌʃ] *sb* (mål)trost.

thrust [θrʌst] **1** *sb* støt *etc*; **2** *vb* støte (og drive, kjøre, renne, stikke; dytte, puffe; trykke etc); ~ *upon* påtvinge.

thud [θʌd] *sb, vi* dunk(e), klask(e).

thug [θʌg] *sb* **1** bølle; **2** gangster, (volds)forbryter.

thumb [θʌm] **I** *sb* tommel(finger); *dgl* tommeltott; *Tom Thumb* Tommeliten; **II** *vt* **1** fingre med; bla i (især her og der, med tommelen); ~ *through (også)* tomle gjennom; **2** ~ *a lift* haike.

thump [θʌmp] *sb, vb* dunk(e).

thunder ['θʌndə] **1** *sb* torden (og torden|brak, drønn; -vær); **2** *vb* tordne (og brake, buldre, drønne, dundre etc). **thunder|bolt** *sb* lyn (og torden); *gml* tordenkile. **~clap** *sb* tordenbrak. **~storm** *sb* tordenvær. **~struck** *adj* lamslått.

thus [ðʌs] *adv* slik; så (og så|dan, -ledes); *også* derfor.

thwart [θwɔ:t] **A** *vt* komme i veien for/krysse (planer etc); **B** *sb sjø* tofte.

thy [ðaɪ] *pron gml* din, ditt; dine.

thyme [taɪm] *sb* timian.

tic [tɪk] *sb* (muskel)|rykning, -trekning.

tick [tɪk] **A I** *sb* **1** tikk(ing); *halv a ~ (dgl)* et blunk/øyeblikk; **2** hake/merke *etc* (ved noe som er kontrollert); **3** *dgl* nota, regning; *on ~* på krita (dvs kreditt); **II** *vb* **1** tikke (som klokke etc); **2** sette hake/merke ved (ting som er kontrollert etc); *~ off* hake (krysse, merke etc) av; **3** *~ him off* irettesette ham; skjelle ham ut; **B** *sb* bolster; (dyne)trekk; (pute)var; **C** *sb* (blod)midd, flått.

ticket ['tɪkɪt] *sb* **1** billett; **2** lodd(seddel); **3** *(party ~)* partiprogram; *også* stemmeseddel. **ticket | collector** *sb* billettør. **~ punch** *sb* billettang.

tickle ['tɪkl] **I** *sb* kiling *etc*; **II** *vb* **1** kile; *fig også* kildre, pirre; **2** klø; **3** *dgl* more; *she was ~d* hun hadde moro av det. **ticklish** ['tɪklɪʃ] *adj* **1** kilen; **2** *fig* kilden; kinkig, vanskelig.

tidal ['taɪdl] *adj* tidevanns-. **tide** [taɪd] **I** *sb* **1** tidevann (og tidevannsstand); *ofte* flo, høyvann; **2** *fig* bølge; strøm/strømning (om folkemening, moter etc); **II** *vt: ~ over* hjelpe (over en vanskelighet); gi en håndsrekning (i et knipetak). **tidings** ['taɪdɪŋz] *sb fl* nyhet(er); *gml* tidende(r).

tidy ['taɪdɪ] **1** *adj* nett, pen; ordentlig, skikkelig; **2** *vb (~ up)* rydde (opp).

tie [taɪ] **I** *sb* **1** bånd (især *fig*); *~s of friendship* vennskapsbånd; **2** forpliktelse; *ofte* byrde; (tung) plikt; **3** *sport etc* uavgjort kamp/stilling; dødt løp; **II** *vb* **1** binde; feste (med bånd etc); *~ down* binde (på hender og føtter); *dgl* baste og binde; *~ up* binde; feste, fortøye; *ofte* pakke inn (og slå hyssing om); **2** knyte; knytte; **3** forplikte; **4** *sport etc (~ with)* spille *etc* uavgjort (med); stå likt (med). **tie-in spread** *sb petro* sammenkoblingsrigg.

tier ['tɪə] *sb* (benke)rad.

tie-up ['taɪʌp] *sb* forbindelse, tilknytning; sammenslutning.

tiger ['taɪgə] *sb* tiger.

tight [taɪt] **I** *adj* **1** tett (og tettpakket; tett|sittende, -sluttet; tett|bygd, -vokst etc); *også* fast; *fig* taus; **2** strammet; spent, stram; **3** trang; *fig også* snever; *in a ~ corner (spot, squeeze etc)* i klemme/knipe; **4** *dgl* full/pussa (dvs beruset); **5** *dgl US = ~-fisted*; **II** *adv (~ly)* stramt; tett. **tighten** ['taɪtn] *vb (~ up)* stramme(s). **tight|-fisted** *adj* gjerrig, påholden. **~-laced** *adj* snerpet. **~-lipped** *adj* fåmælt, ordknapp. **~-rope** *sb* stram (balanse)line. **tights** [taɪts] *sb fl* **1** strømpebukse(r); **2** trikot(bukser).

tigress ['taɪgrɪs] *sb* hunntiger.

tile [taɪl] **I** *sb* **1** takstein; **2** (vegg)flis; **II** *vt* **1** tekke med (tak)stein; **2** legge fliser.

till [tɪl] **A** *konj, prep* (inn)til; *not ~* ikke før; **B** *sb* pengeskuff (i kassaapparat); **C** *vt* dyrke (jord); dyrke opp. **tiller** ['tɪlə] *sb* **A** (jord)dyrker; **B** *sjø* rorkult.

tilt [tɪlt] **1** *sb* helling, skråstilling; **2** *vb* helle, tippe; sette/stille på skrå.

timber ['tɪmbə] **I** *sb* **1** tømmer (og tømmerstokk); tre (og trematerialer); ved; *også* skog; **2** dekksbjelke; (skips)spant; **II** *vt* tømre (opp). **timbered** ['tɪmbəd] *adj, pp* (opp)tømret, -tømret.

time [taɪm] **I** *sb* **1** tid (og tiden; tidspunkt; gang, stund; anledning, sesong etc); *også* levetid; *fl især* tids|avsnitt, (-)periode; *~ and ~ again* gang på gang; gjentatte ganger; *(the) ~'s up* tiden er omme/ute; det er stengetid; *at a ~* av/om gangen; *at no ~* aldri; *at one ~* en gang (i tiden); *at the ~* da, dengang, den gangen; *at the same ~* samtidig; *at ~s* av og til; en gang iblant; til sine tider; *for the ~ being* for tiden/øyeblikket; *in no ~ (dgl)* omgående, straks; om/på et øyeblikk; *on ~* presis, punktlig; *some ~* en gang (i fremtiden); en eller annen gang; *what's the ~* hvor mange er klokken; **2** *six ~s four* seks ganger fire; **3** *mus* takt, tempo; *in/out of ~* i/ute av takt; *keep ~* holde takten; **II** *vt* **1** bestemme tiden for; **2** ta tiden for/på. **time | bomb** *sb* tidsinnstilt bombe. **~-card** *sb* stemplingskort. **~honoured** *adj* ærverdig. **~-keeper** *sb* **1** timeskriver; **2** tidtaker; tidtakerur. **~-lag** *sb* tidsforskjell (mellom ulike tidssoner). **~less** *adj* tidløs; evig. **~-limit** *sb* tids|begrensning, (-)frist. **~ly** ['taɪmlɪ] *adj, adv* i rett(e) tid; betimelig, tidsnok. **~-piece** *sb gml* klokke. **timer, time | register** *sb data* taktregister. **~sanctioned** *adj* hevdvunnen; *også = ~-honoured.* **~-saving** *adj* tidsbesparende. **~-server** *sb* opportunist. **~ sharing** *sb data* tidsdeling. **~-sheet** *sb = ~-card.* **~-signal** *sb* tidssignal. **~-switch** *sb* tidsbryter. **~-table** *sb* timeplan; tempoplan, tidsplan; *især* togtabell. **~-worn** *adj* (ned)slitt; utslitt.

timid ['tɪmɪd] *adj* engstelig, fryktsom, redd. **timidity** [tɪ'mɪdətɪ] *sb* engstelighet *etc.* **timorous** ['tɪmərəs] *adj = timid.*

tin [tɪn] **I** *sb* **1** blikk (dvs hvitblikk, jernblikk etc); **2** blikk|boks, -eske; *især* hermetikkboks; **II** *vt* **1** *(~-plate)* fortinne; **2** hermetisere. **tinfoil** ['tinfɔɪl] *sb* tinnfolium, sølvpapir.

tinge [tɪndʒ] **1** *sb* (farge)skjær, (-)tone; anstrøk; **2** *vt* tone; farge (svakt) *fig* gi et anstrøk/skjær.

tin-opener ['tɪnəupənə] *sb* bokseåpner, hermetikkopptaker.

tinkle ['tɪŋkl] **1** *sb* ringling *etc*; **2** *vb* ringle (med); klirre, single; klinge, skrangle.

tinsel ['tɪnsl] **1** *sb* glitter; (flitter)stas; **2** *vt* pynte med glitter *etc.*

tinsmith ['tɪnsmɪθ] *sb* blikk(en)slager; tinnsmed

tint [tɪnt] **1** *sb* farge|nyanse, (-)tone; **1** *vb* farge/bli farget (svakt); tone(s).

tiny ['taɪnɪ] *adj* ørliten.

tip [tɪp] **A I** *sb* (ytter)ende; spiss, tipp, tupp; *også* holk; **II** *vt* **1** forsyne med spiss *etc*; **2** danne (utgjøre, være etc) spissen *etc* på; **B I** *sb* avfallsplass, fylling; **II** *vb* **1** tippe, velte; bikke, vippe; **II** *vb* **1** ~ *over* tippe over ende; ~ *up* tippe opp; **2** tømme (avfall etc); *dgl* tippe; **C I** *sb* **1** lett slag; **2** drikkepenger; dusør; tipp; *dgl* tips; **3** råd; *især (~-off)* hint, vink; tipp; *dgl* tips; **II** *vt* **1** slå lett; **2** *dgl (~ off)* gi et vink; holde underrettet.

tipple ['tɪpl] *sb* drink.

tipster ['tɪpstə] *sb* en som gir/selger (veddeløps)-tips. **tipsy** ['tɪpsɪ] *adj dgl* pussa (dvs lettere beruset).

tiptoe ['tɪptəʊ] **1** *adv* på tærne; på tå; **2** *vi* gå på tærne/på tå; *også* liste seg.

tire ['taɪə] **A** *sb* = *tyre*; **B** *vb* **1** trette, utmatte; gjøre sliten/trett; **2** tretne; bli sliten/trett. **tired** ['taɪəd] *adj* ut|mattet, -slitt; sliten, trett. **tireless** ['taɪəlɪs] *adj* utrettelig. **tiresome** ['taɪəsəm] *adj* trettende; *også* byrdefull. **tiring** ['taɪərɪŋ] *adj* slitsom, trettende.

tiro ['taɪərəʊ] *sb* nybegynner.

tissue ['tɪʃu:] *sb* **1** (organisk) vev; **2** stoff (især fint og tynt); *også* = *~-paper*; **3** *fig* nett(verk), vev. **tissue-paper** *sb* silkepapir; papirlommetørkle; renseserviett (av papir).

tit [tɪt] *sb* **A** meise; **B** ~ *for tat* like for like; **C** *vulg* (bryst)vorte; pupp. **titbit** ['tɪtbɪt] *sb* lekkerbisken.

titillate ['tɪtɪleɪt] *vt* kile; *især fig* kildre, pirre. **titillation** [ˌtɪtɪ'leɪʃn] *sb* kiling *etc*.

title ['taɪtl] *sb* **1** tittel (også adelstittel etc); benevnelse, navn; overskrift; **2** rett(ighet); krav (*to* på); *også* atkomst|brev, -dokument; skjøte. **titled** ['taɪtld] *adj* med tittel *etc; især* adelig. **title page** *sb* tittelside. **titular** ['tɪtjʊlə] *adj* titulær.

to I [tu:] *adv* **1** igjen (dvs lukket); *push/put* ~ skyve igjen/inntil; **2** ~ *and fro* til og fra; frem og tilbake; **II** [tə] **1** *inf merke* å; **2** *(in order ~)* for å; **III** [tʊ] *prep* **1** til (og bort, frem, opp etc til); mot (dvs i retning av; ~ *the end* til siste slutt; *a quarter ~ five* kvart på fem; *give it ~ them* gi det til dem; *go ~ sleep* legge seg (for) å sove; *here's ~ you!* skål (for deg)! **2** mot (dvs i forhold til; sammenlignet med etc); *prefer* ~ foretrekke fremfor; *win by five ~ three* vinne (med) fem mot tre.

toad [təʊd] *sb* padde. **toadstool** ['təʊdstu:l] *sb* fluesopp.

toast [təʊst] **A 1** *sb* ristet brød(skive); **2** *vb* riste (brød etc); ~ *oneself* bake/steke seg (i solen, ved varmen etc); **B 1** *sb* skål; **2** *vt* skåle/utbringe en skål for.

tobacco [tə'bækəʊ] *sb* tobakk.

toboggan [tə'bɒgən] **1** *sb* kjelke, slede; **2** *vi* ake/kjøre med kjelke.

today [tə'deɪ] **1** *adv* i dag; **2** *sb* dagen i dag; denne dagen; *fig* nåtiden; vår tid.

toddle ['tɒdl] *vi* stabbe (som et lite barn); gå ustøtt. **toddler** ['tɒdlə] *sb* (små)|rolling, (-)tass; pjokk; tulle.

toe [təʊ] **1** *sb* tå; **2** *vt* berøre med en tå/med tærne; *dgl* sparke; ~ *the line* stå/vente på startstreken; *fig* følge spillets regler; være med på notene.

toffee ['tɒfɪ] *sb* slags konfekt; ≈ karamell.

together [tə'geðə] *adv* sammen; *come* ~ møtes; komme sammen; *get* ~ samle(s); få/*dgl* tromme sammen; komme sammen.

toggle *vt* bryte/slutte strøm ved hjelp av **toggle key, ~ switch** *sb* vippebryter.

togs [tɒgz] *sb fl dgl* klær.

toil [tɔɪl] **1** *sb* slit, strev; hardt/tungt arbeid; **2** *vi* slite, streve; arbeide hardt/tungt.

toilet ['tɔɪlɪt] *sb* **1** antrekk, påkledning; klær; *også* toalett; **2** toalett, WC. **toilet-paper** *sb* toalettpapir.

toils [tɔɪlz] *sb fl fig* garn, nett; snarer.

token ['təʊkən] *sb* tegn, varsel; symbol; *ofte* bevis; *som adj* symbolsk; *in ~ of* som/til tegn på.

tolerable ['tɒlərəbl] *adv* utholdelig; **2** *dgl* tålelig; noenlunde bra (god, stor etc); passabel. **tolerance** ['tɒlərəns] **sb** toleranse *etc*. **tolerant** ['tɒlərənt] *adj* tolerant, tålsom; overbærende. **tolerate** ['tɒləreɪt] *vt* tolerere, tåle, utholde; tillate. **toleration** [ˌtɒlə'reɪʃn] *sb* fordragelighet, toleranse.

toll [təʊl] **A** *sb* **1** avgift, gebyr; skatt; toll; **2** *fig* beskatning, innhugg; *the ~ of the road(s)* trafikk|døden, ulykkene; *også* -ofrene; *take ~ of* gjøre innhugg i; **B 1** *sb* (klokke)ringing; **2** *vb* ringe (med). **toll|-bar, ~-gate** *sb* bom (eller bomstasjon på avgiftsbelagt vei). **~-keeper** *sb* bomvokter. **~ road** *sb* (avgiftsbelagt) bomvei.

tomahawk ['tɒməhɔ:k] *sb* indianerøks.

tomato [tə'mɑ:təʊ] *sb* tomat.

tomb [tu:m] *sb* grav (og grav|kammer), -mæle, -sted etc).

tomboy ['tɒmbɔɪ] *sb* villkatt (dvs vilter jente); galneheie, guttejente.

tombstone ['tu:mstəʊn] *sb* gravstein.

tomcat ['tɒmkæt] *sb* hannkatt.

tome [təʊm] *sb* bind (især om større bok); foliant.

tommy ['tɒmɪ] *sb dgl mil* (menig) soldat. **tommy-gun** *sb* maskinpistol.

tomorrow [tə'mɒrəʊ] **1** *adv* i morgen; ~ *morning* i morgen tidlig; **2** *sb* morgendagen; *the day after* ~ i overmorgen.

ton [tɒn] *sb* **1** vektenhet, se midtsidene; **2** *dgl: ~s of* dynger/hauger av; massevis av; **3** *slang* 100 *miles* i timen; *~up (ofte)* råkjøring (især med motorsykkel); *~-up boys* motorsykkelfantomer.

tone [təʊn] **I** *sb* **1** tone; klang, lyd; **2** tone|fall, -lag; betoning; **3** holdning; stemning; preg; retning, tendens; **4** (farge)|nyanse, (-)tone; **II** *vb* **1** tone; ~ *down* dempe; tone ned; ~ *up* friske opp; **2** ~ *with* harmonere med/stå til (især om farger). **toneless** ['təʊnlɪs] *adj* tonløs; kjedelig, monoton.

tongs [tɒŋz] *sb fl (pair of ~)* tang; *sugar* ~ sukkerklype.

tongue [tʌŋ] *sb* tunge (også om flammetunge, landtunge etc); **2** språk; *gml* tunge(mål); *mother* ~

morsmål. **tongue|-tied** *adj* målbundet. **~-twister** *sb* tungebrekker (dvs ord eller setning som er vanskelig å uttale).

tonic ['tɒnɪk] **1** *adj* oppkvikkende, styrkende; **2** *sb* styrke|drikk, -middel; oppkvikker; oppkvikkende middel; tonikum; *(~ water)* tonic.

tonight [tə'naɪt] **I** *adv* **1** i natt; **2** i aften; *dgl* i kveld; **II** *sb* denne natten *etc; ~'s paper* aftenavisen for i dag.

tonnage ['tɒnɪdʒ] *sb* tonnasje (og tonnasjeavgift).

too [tu:] *adv* **1** også; dessuten; i tillegg; **2** altfor, for.

tool [tu:l] **I** *sb* **1** (hånd)verktøy; redskap; **2** *fig* (lydig) instrument/redskap; *også* stråmann; II *vt dgl* bearbeide (med håndverktøy). **tool | box** *sb* verktøykasse. **~ joint** *sb petro* rørkobling. **~ kit** *sb* verktøysett. **~ pusher** *sb dgl petro* boresjef. **~ shed** *sb* redskapsskur. **~ string** *sb petro* verktøystreng.

toot [tu:t] **1** *sb* tut(ing); **2** *vb* tute (med horn etc); blåse (på).

tooth [tu:θ] *sb* **1** tann; *by the skin of one's teeth* med nød og neppe; *fight ~ and nail* kjempe/slåss med nebb og klør; *have a sweet ~* være glad i søtsaker; tann (på tannhjul etc); kam, knast; tagg, takk, tind. **tooth|-ache** *sb* tann|pine, -verk. **~brush** *sb* tannbørste. **~less** *adj* tannløs. **~paste** *sb* tann|krem, -pasta. **~pick** *sb* tannpirker. **~some** *adj* deilig, velsmakende.

top [tɒp] **A I** *som adj* topp-; høyest, øverst; ytterst, ytter-; best, størst; **II** *sb* **1** topp (og toppunkt); høyeste punkt; største høyde; *fig også* høydepunkt; *at the ~* på toppen; øverst; *on (the) ~ of* på toppen av; *fig også* i tillegg til; **2** topp (dvs topplate etc); over|del, -flate, -side; **3** *dgl* sjef; bestemann; nummer én; **III** *vb* **1** toppe; danne/utgjøre toppen *etc* av; *~ off* avrunde; fullende; **2** rage opp; **3** nå toppen; nå opp; **4** toppskjære; beskjære (i toppen); **B** *sb* snurrebass. **top|-boots** *sb fl* langstøvler, skaftestøvler. **~ brass** *sb dgl* toppledelse. **~-coat** *sb* (ytter)frakk. **~ dog** *sb dgl* bas, sjef. **~ drawer** *sb dgl* sosialgruppe én. **~-flight** *adj* = *~-notch.* **~-hat** *sb* flosshatt. **~heavy** *adj* overtung.

topic ['tɒpɪk] *sb* (samtale)emne, tema; *også* sak. **topical** ['tɒpɪkl] *adj* aktuell

top|less *adj* toppløs. **~ margin** *sb data* toppmarg. **~most** *adj* høyest, øverst. **~notch** *adj dgl* førsteklasses, topp-.

topple ['tɒpl] *vb* (få til å) vakle/ta overbalanse; styrte; velte; falle/*dgl* ramle over ende.

top|-ranking *adj* meget høytstående. **~ secret** *adj* topphemmelig.

topsy-turvy ['tɒpsɪ'tɜ:vɪ] *adj, adv* opp-ned; kaotisk, rotet; hulter til bulter.

torch [tɔ:tʃ] *sb* **1** fakkel; **2** *(electric ~)* lommelykt.

torment 1 ['tɔ:mənt] *sb* pine, pinsel; **2** [tɔ:'ment] *vt* pine; *fig også* plage. **tormentor** [tɔ:'mentə] *sb* piner; *især* plageånd.

tornado [tɔ:'neɪdəʊ] *sb* tornado; skypumpe, virvelstorm.

torpedo [tɔ:'pi:dəʊ] **1** *sb* torpedo; **2** *vt* torpedere; *fig også* kjøre i senk; sette en stopper for; ødelegge.

torrent ['tɒrənt] *sb* strøm (i elv etc); *~s of rain* regn i stride strømmer; regnskyll, skybrudd. **torrential** [tə'renʃl] *adj* strid(-), *~ rain* skybrudd.

torrid ['tɒrɪd] *adj* glovarm, (stekende) het.

tortoise ['tɔ:təs] *sb* skilpadde.

tortuous ['tɔ:tʃʊəs] *adj* kroket, vridd; buktet; snirklet, snodd; *fig* underfundig; intrigant, renkefull-.

torture ['tɔ:tʃə] **I** *sb* tortur; pine, pinsel; **II** *vt* **1** pine, torturere; **2** for|vanske, -vrenge; *fig* radbrekke; gjøre vold på. **torturer** ['tɔ:tʃərə] *sb* torturist.

Tory ['tɔ:rɪ] *adj, sb pol* konservativ(-).

toss [tɒs] **I** *sb* kast *etc*; knipsing (jf *II 2*); **II** *vb* **1** tumle/velte seg; **2** kaste, slenge; *~ off (dgl)* helle/skylle i seg; rive av seg; *~ one's head* kneise med nakken; *~ (up) a coin* kaste/knipse mynt og krone. **toss-up** *sb dgl* usikker (tvilsom, uavgjort etc) sak.

tot [tɒt] **A** *sb* **1** pjokk, tass; (små)rolling; **2** dram, knert; *også fig* anelse, smule; grann; **B** *vb dgl: ~ up* summere; legge sammen; bli/utgjøre (til sammen).

total ['təʊtl] **1** *adj* full(stendig), hel; total; **2** *sb (sum ~)* total|beløp, -sum; **3** *vt* beløpe seg til; bli/utgjøre til sammen. **totalitarian** [,təʊ,tælɪ'teərɪən] *adj, sb* totalitær (person). **totality** [təʊ'tælətɪ] *sb* helhet, hele; totalitet. **total line** *sb data* sumlinje.

totter ['tɒtə] *vi* vakle; holde på å falle (over ende); rave, sjangle.

touch [tʌtʃ]ɪ **I** *sb* **1** berøring, kontakt; **2** forbindelse; (gjensidig) forståelse; *be in ~ with* ha (stå, være i etc) forbindelse med; *get into ~ with* komme/sette seg i forbindelse med; *keep in ~* holde kontakten; holde forbindelsen (*with* med); *lose ~ with* miste forbindelsen/kontakten med; *within ~* innenfor rekkevidde; **3** følelse (dvs følesans); *rough/soft to the ~* grov/myk å ta på; **4** (pensel)strøk; *finishing ~* avsluttende/siste strøk; siste finpuss; **5** grann, smule, snev; anstrøk; antydning; **6** drag, trekk; preg; **7** *(~ and run)* sisten; **8** *mus* anslag; **II** *vb* **1** (be)røre; røre ved; ta på; *dgl også* ta sine fingre i (dvs ha med å gjøre); *~ one's cap* hilse til luen; *~ wood* bank i bordet; *not ~* ikke røre; *især fig* avstå fra; holde seg unna; **2** berøre (hverandre); tangere; komme nær; grense til; *~ and go (sjø)* berøre sjøbunnen uten å komme til skade; *dgl* streife; komme (så vidt) nær; *fig* greie/klare så vidt; *~ bottom* berøre/ta bunnen; *fig* nå bunnen; sette bunnrekord; **3** nå/rekke (opp, ned etc til); *fig* kunne måle seg med; komme opp mot; **4** bevege, gripe, røre; **5** angå, vedrøre; *~ deeply* gjøre dypt inntrykk på; *~ one's honour* gå på æren løs (for en); **6** berøre (dvs komme inn på; nevne løselig etc); **7** slå an (streng, tangent etc); **8** *med adv, prep* **~ at** berøre, streife; komme nær; grense til; komme inn på (dvs nevne); *sjø* anløpe (havn); **~ down** lande (om fly); **~ down at** mellomlande i/på; **~ for** *dgl* bomme (dvs låne av); *slang* rappe/stjele fra; **~ off** skildre treffende; ta på kornet; *også* skissere; *US* utløse; sette i gang; **~ on** grense til; angå; komme inn på (dvs nevne); **~ to** føre (hånden etc) til; *~ a* *match to the paper* sette en fyrstikk (bort)til papiret; ~ **up** friske opp; pynte på; streke/trekke opp; retusjere; ~ *up his memory* friske på hukommelsen hans; ~ **upon** = ~ *on* ~ **with** berøre med; ~*ed with* angrepet av (sykdom etc); med en snev av. **touch|-and-go** *adj* (lett) henkastet; rask, springende; risikabel, sjansepreget; farlig. **~-down** *sb* landing (med fly). **touched** [tʌtʃt] *adj* (be)rørt *etc*; **2** *dgl* rar, skrullet; sprø. **touching** ['tʌtʃɪŋ] *adj* gripende, rørende. **touch screen** *sb data* berøringsskjerm. **touchy** ['tʌtʃɪ] *adj* irritabel; nærtagende.

tough [tʌf] *adj* **1** hard, seig; *dgl også* tøff; **2** kraftig, sterk; *dgl, slang* barsk; **3** vanskelig, vrien; **4** bøllet, voldsom. **toughen** ['tʌfn] *vb* bli/gjøre seig *etc*. **tough luck** *sb* uflaks.

tour ['tʊə] **1** *sb* (rund)|reise, (-)tur; **2** *vb* reise (rundt i); *også* turnere. **tourism** ['tʊərɪzəm] *sb* turisme, turisttrafikk. **tourist** ['tʊərɪst] *sb* turist. **tournament** ['tʊənəmənt] *sb hist* turnering.

tow [təʊ] **A 1** *sb* slep (og slept fartøy); tauing; *on* ~ på slep; slept; **2** *vt* slepe, taue; **B** *sb* drev, (dytte)stry.

toward(s) [tə'wɔ:d(z), tɔ:d(z)] *adv, prep* mot, til (dvs i retning av); vendt mot; *fig* bortimot, henimot; nesten.

towel ['taʊəl] *sb* håndkle.

tower ['taʊə] **I** *sb* **1** tårn; **2** borg(tårn), festning; **3** *fig* tilflukt, vern; støtte; **II** *vi* rage opp; tårne seg opp. **towering** ['taʊərɪŋ] *adj* tårnhøy; kneisende; *fig* veldig; ubendig.

town [taʊn] *sb* by; *som adj* by-, stads-; *man about* ~ herre på byen. **town | centre** *sb* (by)sentrum. ~ **clerk** *sb* byskriver; rådmann. ~ **council** *sb* bystyre. ~ **councillor** *sb* bystyremedlem. ~ **hall** *sb* rådhus. **~ship** *sb* by|kommune, -samfunn; *US* ≈ herred, kommune. **townspeople** *sb koll* byfolk.

toxic ['tɒksɪk] *adj* giftig.

toy [tɔɪ] **1** *sb* leke(tøy); **2** *vi* leke (*with* med). **toyshop** *sb* leketøysbutikk.

trace [treɪs] **I** *sb* **1** (fot)spor; *også* merke; **2** grann, smule; **3** antydning, snev; **II** *vt* **1** risse (streke, trekke etc) opp; **2** kalkere, overføre; tegne av; kopiere; **3** etterspore; oppspore; følge sporet av/etter. **traceable** ['treɪsəbl] *adj* som kan etterspores/oppspores. **trace program** *sb data* sporeprogram. **tracing** ['treɪsɪŋ] *sb* kalkering, overføring.

track [træk] **I** *sb* **1** spor (og fotspor, hjulspor etc); *sjø* kjølvann; *også* farvann; *keep* ~ *of* føre/ha oppsyn med; ha føling med; holde seg à jour med; *make* ~*s for (dgl)* sette kursen mot; *også* stikke av til; *on the* ~ *of* på sporet av/etter; **2** sti, tråkk; løype, spor; *off the* ~ utenfor allfarvei; på villspor; *the beaten* ~ den slagne landevei; **3** kurs, retning; bane (især for løp og andre friidrettsøvelser); **4** spor (dvs skinnegang, skinner); linje; **5** belte (på beltekjøretøy); **II** *vt* **1** følge sporet av/etter; ~ *down/out* etterspore, oppspore; finne; **2** hale, slepe, trekke. **track | density** *sb data* sportetthet. ~ **event** *sb* friidrettskonkurranse *især* løp. **~ing** *sb data* sporfølging. ~ **pitch** *sb data* sporavstand. ~ **suit** *sb* treningsdrakt.

tract [trækt] *sb* **A** egn, område, strøk, trakt; **B** (små)skrift, traktat. **tractable** ['træktəbl] *adj* føyelig, medgjørlig. **traction** ['trækʃn] *sb* drag; trekk (og trekk|evne, -kraft); *som adj* trekk-; driv-. **tractor** ['træktə] *sb* traktor. **tractor feed** *sb data* traktormater.

trade [treɪd] **I** *sb* **1** handel (og forretning; forretnings|liv, -virksomhet; næring, nærings|liv, -vei; industri etc); **2** fag, håndverk; yrke; bransje; **3** *the Trades* passaten; **II** *vb* **1** handle (*in* med, dvs med varer; *with* med, dvs med handelspartnere); **2** bytte(handle); *she* ~*d in her car (for a new one)* hun byttet inn bilen sin (mot en ny); **3** ~ *(up)on* utnytte. **trade|-in** *sb* innbytte (og bytteobjekt). **~mark** *sb* varemerke; *fig* merke, preg. ~ **name** *sb* handelsnavn. ~ **price** *sb* engrospris. **trader** *sb* handelsmann, (-)handler; *også* handelsskip. **tradesman** *sb* detaljist, (små)kjøpmann. **trade(s)|-school** *sb* yrkesskole. **~-union** *sb* fagforening. **~-unionist** *sb* fagforeningsmedlem. **trade-wind** *sb* passat(vind). **trading** *sb* handel; *som adj* handels-; *også* drifts-.

tradition [trə'dɪʃn] *sb* tradisjon. **traditional** [trə'dɪʃənl] *adj* tradisjonell, tradisjons-.

traffic ['træfɪk] **I** *sb* **1** trafikk; **2** trafikkering; **3** handel; *især neds* trafikk (dvs lyssky handel/transaksjon); **II** *vi* handle (*in* med, dvs med varer); *især* drive lyssky handel/transaksjon. **trafficator** ['træfɪkeɪtə] *sb* = **traffic | indicator** *sb* blinklys. ~ **island** *sb* refuge, trafikkøy. ~ **jam** *sb* trafikkork. ~ **lights** *sb fl* trafikk|fyr, -lys. ~ **warden** *sb* parkometervakt.

tragedy ['trædʒɪdɪ] *sb* **1** *teater* tragedie; **2** tragedie (dvs sørgelig etc hendelse). **tragic** ['trædʒɪk] *adj* tragisk, sørgelig.

trail [treɪl] **I** *sb* **1** merke/spor (etter); tråkk; *også* rute; **2** fotspor; **3** sti/vei (i villmark); **4** hale, slep; ~ *of smoke* røykhale; **II** *vb* **1** slepe/trekke (etter seg, med seg); **2** klatre; krype; *om planter* slynge seg; **3** slepe seg frem; **4** *US* følge sporet av/etter; *hum* dilte etter. **trailer** ['treɪlə] *sb* **1** *(~-car)* tilhenger(vogn); trailer; *ofte* campingvogn; **2** slyngplante; kryper; **3** trailer (dvs klipp fra film etc som skal settes opp senere).

train [treɪn] **I** *sb* **1** (opp)tog, prosesjon; *(railway ~)* (jernbane)tog; *by* ~ med tog(et); **2** følge; tilhengere; **3** hale, slep; **4** rekke, serie; rad; ~ *of thoughts* tankerekke; **II** *vb* **1** lære (trene, øve etc) opp; utdanne (seg); **2** drille, eksersere; **3** sikte/stille inn (*(up)on* mot); gi bestemt retning. **trainee** [treɪ'ni:] *sb* **1** lærling; **2** praktikant. **trainer** ['treɪnə] *sb* **1** trener; **2** dressør; domptør, dyretemmer. **training** ['treɪnɪŋ] *sb* trening *etc; som adj* trenings-; skole-, undervisnings-; utdannelses-. **training college** *sb* lærerskole, seminar.

trait [treɪt] *sb* drag, trekk (og ansikts|drag, -trekk etc).

traitor ['treɪtə] *sb* forræder. **traitorous** ['treɪtərəs] *adj* forrædersk.

tram [træm] *sb* = **tram|car** *sb* sporvogn, trikk.

~way *sb* sporvognslinje, trikkelinje; trikkeskinner.

tramp [træmp] **I** *sb* **1** tramp(ing); **2** (fot)tur; **3** landstryker, tramp; **II** *vb* **1** trampe, traske; **2** gå (fottur); vandre. **trample** ['træmpl] *vb* trampe/tråkke (ned, på).

tranquil ['træŋkwɪl] *adj* rolig; fredelig. **tranquility** [træŋ'kwɪlətɪ] *sb* ro; fred(elighet). **tranquilize** ['træŋkwɪlaɪz] *vt* berolige. **tranquilizer** ['træŋkwɪlaɪzə] *sb* beroligende middel.

trans- [trænz-] *pref* trans-; gjennom(-), over(-).

transcribe [træn'skraɪb] *vt* transkribere. **transcript** ['trænskrɪpt] *sb* avskrift, utskrift. **transcription** [træn'skrɪpʃn] *sb* transkribering; transkripsjon.

transfer I ['trænsfɜ:] *sb* over|dragelse, -føring *etc*; **II** [træns'fɜ:] *vb* **1** over|dra, -føre; **2** (over)flytte; **3** oversette. **transfer rate** *sb data* overføringshastighet.

transform [træns'fɔ:m] *vt* forvandle (*into* til); transformere. **transformation** [ˌtrænsfə'meɪʃn] *sb* forvandling *etc*. **transformer** [træns'fɔ:mə] *sb* transformator.

transient ['trænzɪənt] *adj* flyktig, forbigående, kortvarig; *data* lagringsflyktig. **transient error** *sb data* forbigående feil.

transistor [træn'zɪstə] *sb* **1** transistor; **2** transistorradio. **transit** ['trænsɪt] *sb* transitt; gjennom|fart, -gang, -reise; *som adj* transitt-; gjennomgangs-. **transition** [træn'zɪʃn] *sb* overgang. **transitory** ['trænsɪtrɪ] *adj* = *transient*.

translate [trænz'leɪt] *vt* **1** oversette; **2** tolke. **translater** [trænz'leɪtə] *sb data* = *translation program*. **translation** [trænz'leɪʃn] *sb* oversettelse. **translation program** *sb data* oversettingsprogram. **translator** [trænz'leɪtə] *sb* oversetter; *data også* = *translater*.

translucent [trænz'lu:snt] *adj* gjennomskinnelig; (delvis) gjennomsiktig.

transmission [trænz'mɪʃn] *sb* overføring *etc*. **transmission line** *sb data etc* overføringslinje. **transmit** [trænz'mɪt] *vt* **1** overføre; kringkaste/sende (i radio); **2** levere/sende (videre); sende fra seg; la gå i arv; **3** overføre, smitte; **4** (over)føre; lede; slippe igjennom. **transmitter** [trænz'mɪtə] *sb* (radio)sender.

transparency [træn'spærənsɪ] *sb* **1** gjennomsiktighet; **2** lysbilde. **transparent** [træn'spærənt]] *adj* **1** gjennomsiktig **2** gjennomskuelig; **3** klar, lettfattelig.

transpire [træn'spaɪə] *vb* **1** komme for en dag; vise seg; **2** *gml* hende.

transplant [træns'plɑ:nt] **I** *sb* **1** transplantering, transplantasjon **2** transplantat (dvs transplantert organ); **II** *vb* **1** plante om **2** transplantere; **3** *fig* flytte (på). **transplantation** [ˌtrænsplɑ:n'teɪʃn] *sb* = *transplant I 1*.

transport ['trænspɔ:t] **I** *sb* **1** transport(ering); *som adj* transport-; **2** = *~ ship, ~ vessel*; **3** begeistring (og *især* begeistringsrus); henførelse, transe; **II** *vt* **1** frakte, transportere; flytte; føre; **2** *hist* deportere, landsforvise. **transportation** [ˌtrænspɔ:'teɪʃn] *sb* transport(ering); *hist* deportering, deportasjon. **transported** [træn'spɔ:tɪd] *adj, pp* **1** transportert *etc*; **2** begeistret; hen|ført, -revet. **transport | ship, ~ vessel** *sb* troppetransport(skip).

trap [træp] **1** *sb* felle (også *fig*); **2** *vt* fange/ta (i felle); *især fig* legge (en) felle for; få til å gå i en felle. **trapdoor** ['træpˌdɔ:] *sb* lem (i gulv); luke (i tak etc). **trapper** ['træpə] *sb* (pels)jeger.

trapeze [trə'pi:z] *sb* trapes.

trappings ['træpɪŋz] *sb fl* **1** utstyr; *især* (flott) ridetøy; stassele; **2** utstaffering; pynt, stas.

trash [træʃ] *sb* avfall, søppel. **trashy** ['træʃɪ] *adj* verdiløs.

travel ['trævl] **I** *sb* reise (og reising); *især fl* utenlandsreiser; **II** *vb* **1** reise; **2** gå (dvs bevege seg); **3** gå (på beina); vandre. **travel | agency, ~ bureau** *sb* reisebyrå. **travelled** ['trævld] *adj* **1** bereist; **2** *a)* trafikkert; *b)* besøkt. **traveller** ['trævlə] *sb* **1** reisende; veifarende; landstryker; **2** *(commercial ~)* (reisende) salgsrepresentant; handelsreisende. **traveller's cheque** *sb* reisesjekk. **travelling salesman** *sb* handelsreisende; (reisende) salgsrepresentant.

travesty ['trævɪstɪ] **1** *sb* parodi, travesti; **2** *vt* parodiere.

trawl [trɔ:l] **I** *sb* trål; **II** *vb* **1** tråle; *~ for (fig)* fiske etter; **2** fiske med trål. **trawler** ['trɔ:lə] *sb* tråler.

tray [treɪ] *sb* **1** bakke, brett; fat; **2** flat skuff/skål; (brev)kurv.

treacherous ['tretʃərəs] *adj* forrædersk. **treachery** ['tretʃərɪ] *sb* forræderi; svik, troløshet.

tread [tred] **I** *sb* **1** gange (og gang|art, -lag; måte å gå på); **2** skritt, trinn; **3** (slite)bane (på dekk, skotøy etc); **II** *vb* **1** gå (på beina); **2** trampe/tråkke (på); *~ a path* tråkke (en) sti. **treadle** ['tredl] **1** *sb* fot|brett, (-)skammel; *især* tråbrett (på tråsymaskin etc); **2** *vt* trå (dvs drive med fotkraft/pedaler). **treadmill** ['tredmɪl] *sb* tredemølle.

treason ['tri:zn] *sb* (høy)forræderi. **treasonable** ['tri:znəbl], **treasonous** ['tri:znəs] *adj* forrædersk, troløs.

treasure ['treʒə] **I** *sb* skatt; (store) rikdommer; **II** *vt* **1** skatte; sette stor pris på; **2** *(~ up)* ta vare på (som et klenodium). **treasurer** ['treʒərə] *sb* **1** kasserer; **2** *gml* skattmester. **treasure|-house** *sb* skattkammer. **~-trove** *sb* nedgravd skatt; skattefunn. **treasury** ['treʒərɪ] *sb* **1** skattkammer; **2** finanser; kasse. *the* **Treasury** *sb* ≈ finansdepartementet; *the ~ Bench* regjeringsbenken i det britiske underhus.

treat [tri:t] **I** *sb* **1** traktement, traktering; underhold; **2** fryd; nytelse; **II** *vb* **1** behandle (dvs håndtere etc); oppføre seg mot; **2** *(~ of)* behandle (som emne/tema, dvs handle om etc); **3** behandle (for sykdom etc); passe, pleie, stelle; ta seg av; **4** *~ to* traktere med; gi (som en spesiell glede/oppmerksomhet etc); glede med; **5** forhandle, underhandle; **6** anse, betrakte. **treatise** ['tri:tɪz] *sb* avhandling. **treatment** ['tri:tmənt] *sb* behandling *etc*. **treaty** ['tri:tɪ] *sb* avtale, overenskomst; pakt, traktat.

treble ['trebl] **A 1** *adj* tredobbelt; **2** *vb* tredoble(s); **B** *adj, sb* diskant(-); sopran(-).

tree [tri:] *sb* **1** tre; **2** *slang* galge. **tree|less** ['tri:lɪs] *adj* trebar. **~ structure** *sb data* trestruktur.

trellis ['trelɪs] **1** *sb* sprinkler, tremmeverk; espalier; **2** *vt* forsyne/støtte opp med sprinkler *etc*.

tremble ['trembl] **1** *sb* skjelving; **2** *vi* skjelve; dirre; riste, skake.

tremendous [trɪ'mendəs] *adj* enorm, veldig; voldsom.

tremor ['tremə] *sb* skjelving; dirring, sitring. **tremulous** ['tremjʊləs] *adj* skjelvende *etc*; fryktsom, nervøs.

trench [trentʃ] **1** *sb* grav, grøft; grop; *mil* skyttergrav; **2** *vb* grave grøft(er); *mil* beskytte/omgi med skyttergraver. **trenchant** ['trentʃənt] *adj* skarp, skjærende; *især fig* gjennom|borende, -trengende; inntrengende.

trend [trend] **1** *sb* retning, tendens; trend; *set the ~* bestemme retningen/tendensen; være retningsbestemmende; **2** *vi* gå/strekke seg (*towards* mot). **trend-setter** *sb* trendsetter (dvs begivenhet eller person som påvirker/skaper en viss mote, stil, trend etc). **trendy** ['trendɪ] *adj* motepreget; *neds også* nymotens.

trespass ['trespəs] **I** *sb* overtredelse *etc*; **II** *vi* **1** *~ (up)on* trenge seg inn (hos/på) uten lov; *fig* trenge seg på; trekke for store veksler på; *No ~ing!* Ingen adgang! **2** *gml* forgå/forse seg. **trespasser** ['trespəsə] *sb* uvedkommende (dvs person som uten lov trenger seg inn på andres eiendom etc).

tress [tres] *sb* flette; (hår)lokk.

trestle ['tresl] *sb* (tre)bukk.

trial ['traɪəl] *sb* **1** forsøk; **2** prøve, test; *on ~* på prøve; **3** *jur* retts|forhandling, -sak; *on ~* for retten; **4** prøvelse; lidelse, plage.

triangle ['traɪæŋgl] *sb* trekant; *også mus* triangel. **triangular** [traɪ'æŋgjʊlə] *adj* trekantet.

tribal ['traɪbl] *adj* stamme-. **tribe** [traɪb] *sb* (folke)stamme.

tribunal [traɪ'bju:nl] *adj* domstol, tribunal.

tributary ['trɪbjʊtərɪ] **1** *adj, om elv* bi-, side-; **2** *sb især* bielv, sideelv. **tribute** ['trɪbju:t] *sb* **1** skatt; **2** anerkjennelse, hyllest; tributt.

trice [traɪs] *sb: in a ~* i en håndvending; på et øyeblikk.

trick [trɪk] **I** *sb* **1** pek, spikk; (skøyer)strek; *play a ~ on* spille (en) et puss; **2** *(conjuring ~)* tryllekunst; *også* trikk, triks; **3** knep, kunststykke; egen fremgangsmåte; **4** egenhet, særdrag; **5** stikk (i kortspill); **II** *vt* lure, narre; jukse, svindle; *~ into* lure/narre til (å); *~ out of* lure/narre fra. **trickery** ['trɪkərɪ] *sb* lureri; svindel; fanteri. **trickster** ['trɪkstə] *sb* skøyer. **tricky** ['trɪkɪ] *adj* **1** listig, lur **2** innviklet, vanskelig.

trickle ['trɪkl] **1** *sb* drypp(ing); sildring; **2** *vb* dryppe; sildre. **trickle-bed reactor** *sb petro* rislereaktor.

tricycle ['traɪsɪkl] *sb* trehjulssykkel.

trifle ['traɪfl] **I** *sb* **1** bagatell; grann, smule; *fl også* småting, småtterier; *a ~* litt; en smule; **2** (slags) dessert(kake); **II** *vb* leke (fjase, tøyse etc) (*with* med). **trifling** ['traɪflɪŋ] **1** *adj* bagatellmessig, ubetydelig, uvesentlig; **2** *sb* fjas, tant, tøys.

trigger ['trɪgə] **1** *sb* avtrekker (på skytevåpen etc); utløser; **2** *vt (~ off)* utløse; gi støtet til. **trigger-happy** *adj* skyte|gal, -glad.

trill [trɪl] **1** *sb* trille; **2** *vb* slå triller.

trim [trɪm] **I** *adj* **1** nett, pen, pyntelig; ordentlig, skikkelig; velordnet; **2** elegant, (vel)soignert; smart; **II** *sb* **1** stand (og tilstand; orden); *get into ~* komme i form; *in good ~* i god stand; i god form; *også* velopplagt; *out of ~* i ustand; i dårlig form; *også* uopplagt; **2** antrekk, klær; utstyr; **III** *vb* **1** ordne; gjøre/sette i stand; justere, stille; **2** beskjære, stusse; trimme; **3** pynte; garnere, kante; **4** *sjø* trimme; **5** *dgl* skjelle ut; gi en overhaling. **trim cooler** *sb petro* trimmekjøler. **trimming** ['trɪmɪŋ] *sb* kanting (og kantebånd); besetning, pynt.

trinity ['trɪnətɪ] *sb* treenighet.

trinkets ['trɪŋkɪts] *sb fl* (ikke særlig verdifulle) smykker; bijouteri, tingel-tangel.

trip [trɪp] **I** *sb* **1** (kort) reise; (snar)tur, tripp; utflukt; **2** fall, snubling; *fig* feiltrinn; **II** *vb* **1** trippe; **2** snuble (og falle); **3** sparke/spenne bein på/under; **4** *(~ up)* begå en feil; gjøre en tabbe.

tripe [traɪp] *sb* **1** innmat; **2** *slang* skrap, søppel; sludder.

triple ['trɪpl] **1** *adj* tre|dobbelt, -foldig; tre-, trippel-; **2** *vb* tredoble(s). **triplets** ['trɪplɪts] *sb fl* trillinger. **triplicate I** ['trɪplɪkət] **1** *adj, adv* i tre eksemplarer; **2** *sb* triplikat; **II** ['trɪplɪkeɪt] *vt* lage/utstede i tre eksemplarer. **tripod** ['traɪpɒd] *sb* trefot; trebeint stativ; *især* fotostativ.

trite [traɪt] *adj* for|slitt, -tersket; banal.

triumph ['traɪəmf] **1** *sb* triumf; **2** *vi* triumfere/vinne (*over* over). **triumphal** [traɪ'ʌmfl] *adj* triumferende, triumf-. **triumphant** [traɪ'ʌmfənt] *adj* triumferende.

trivial ['trɪvɪəl] *adj* triviell; hverdagslig. **triviality** [ˌtrɪvɪ'ælətɪ] *sb* trivialitet *etc*; banalitet.

trolley ['trɒlɪ] *sb* **1** kjerre, vogn; tralle; trillebord; **2** dressin; **3** kontakttrinse. **trolley-bus** *sb* strømbuss, trolleybuss.

troop [tru:p] **I** *sb* **1** flokk, gruppe; **2** *mil* avdeling, enhet; *ofte* eskadron; *fl* tropper, troppestyrke(r); **II** *vi* **1** flokke (seg); stimle (sammen); **2** marsjere (i tropp). **trooper** ['tru:pə] *sb* soldat; *især* kavalerist; *US også* (ridende) politimann.

trophy ['trəʊfɪ] *sb* trofé.

tropic ['trɒpɪk] *sb* **1** vende|krets, -sirkel; *the Tropic of Cancer/of Capricorn* Krepsens/Steinbukkens vendekrets; **2** *the ~s* tropene.

trot [trɒt] **I** *sb* trav(ing); **II** *vb* **1** trave (og la trave; sette i trav); **2** dilte, lunte; småløpe.

trouble ['trʌbl] **I** *sb* **1** vanskelighet(er); forstyrrelse, uro; *ofte* feil/mangel (som volder forstyrrelse etc); *dgl* bråk, mas; kluss, trøbbel; *ask for ~* være ute etter bråk; *get into* ~ komme i vanskeligheter *etc; it got me into a lot of* ~ det skaffet meg en bråte vanskeligheter; **2** bry(deri); besvær, møye; uleilighet, umak(e); *no* ~ *(at all)* ≈ bare hyggelig (dvs det er/var bare en fornøyelse å hjelpe Dem etc); *put to* ~ uleilige; være til bry for; *take the* ~ *to* ta bryet med å; uleilige/umake seg med å; **II** *vb* **1** forstyrre; bry, uleilige, umake; volde bry(deri)/uleilighet; ~ *oneself about* bry seg med; *don't* ~ *yourself on my account* (gjør Dem) ikke noe bryderi for min skyld; *may I* ~ *you for the salt* tør jeg be Dem sende meg saltet; **2** bekymre, engste, uroe; plage; ~*d about* bekymret/urolig over; **3** opprøre; sette i opprør; bringe uro i; ~*d waters* opprørt/urolig sjø; *fig* rørt vann. **trouble|-maker** *sb* bråkmaker, urostifter. **~shooter** *sb* feil|finner, -søker; -retter; *fig* freds|stifter; (-)megler. **~some** *adj* brysom, vanskelig; lei. **~ spot** *sb* urosenter.

trough [trɒf] *sb* **1** trau; **2** bølgedal.

troupe [tru:p] *sb* trupp.

trousers ['traʊzəz] *sb fl (pair of* ~*)* (lange) bukser.

trousseau ['tru:səʊ] *sb* brudeutstyr.

trout [traʊt] *sb* ørret.

trowel ['traʊəl] *sb* **1** murskje; *lay on with a* ~ smøre tykt på (dvs overdrive sterkt); **2** *(garden* ~*)* planteskje.

truancy ['tru:ənsɪ] *sb* skulk(ing). **truant** ['tru:ənt] *sb* skulker; *play* ~ skulke; lure seg unna.

truce [tru:s] *sb* **1** våpen|hvile, -stillstand; **2** pause, stans.

truck [trʌk] **A** *sb* **1** lastebil; **2** åpen godsvogn; **3** godstralle; **B** *sb* bytte(handel); tuskhandel, tusking; *have no* ~ *with* ikke ha noen befatning med/noe å gjøre med.

trudge [trʌdʒ] **1** *sb* trasking; **2** *vi* traske.

true [tru:] **I** *adj* **1** sann(ferdig); riktig; *come* ~ gå i oppfyllelse; slå til; bli til virkelighet; **2** oppriktig, ærlig; **3** tro(fast) (*to* mot); lojal; pålitelig; **4** korrekt, riktig; **5** ekte, virkelig; **II** *adv* sant *etc*. **truism** ['tru:ɪzəm] *sb* banalitet; selvfølgelighet; truisme. **truly** ['tru:lɪ] *adv* **1** sant; **2** oppriktig, ærlig; *Yours* ~ *(i brev)* ≈ Med vennlig hilsen; **3** sannelig; **4** virkelig. **true|-blue** *adj* god som gull. **~-love** *sb* hjertenskjær.

trumpet ['trʌmpɪt] **1** *sb* trompet; **2** *vb* blåse på trompet; *også* trompetere, utbasunere. **trumpet|-call** *sb* trompetstøt. **trumpeter** ['trʌmpɪtə] *sb* trompetist.

truncheon ['trʌntʃən] *sb* kølle.

trunk [trʌŋk] **I** *som adj* hoved-, stam-; **II** *sb* **1** (tre)stamme; **2** torso; *dgl* kropp; **3** hoveddel; **4** (stor) koffert; **5** snabel; **7** *fl* badebukse; turnbukse. **truncate** [trʌŋ'keɪt] *vt data* avkutte, trunkere. **truncation** [trʌŋ'keɪʃn] *sb data* avkutting, trunkering. **trunk|-call** *sb* rikstelefon(samtale). **~-line** *sb* hoved|ledning, -linje; *jernb* stambane; *petro* hovedrørledning; ilandføringsrør. **~road** *sb* hovedvei.

truss [trʌs] *sb* fagverksøyle.

trust [trʌst] **I** *sb* **1** ~ *in* tillit til; tro på; *on* ~ på kreditt; *put one's trust in* sette sin lit til; stole på; **2** forvaring, varetekt; forvaltning (og forvaltet gods, forvaltede midler etc); *jur også* vergemål; *(position of* ~*)* tillitsverv; *hold in* ~ forvalte; **3** legat; **4** *merk* sammenslutning, trust; **II** *vb* **1** ~ *in* stole/tro på; ha tillit til; ~ *her to do it* regne med/stole på at hun gjør det; **2** håpe (på); **3** betro, overlate; ~ *him with it* overlate den/det i hans varetekt; **4** gi kreditt. **trustee** [trʌs'ti:] *sb* **1** tillitsperson; **2** formynder, verge; **3** bestyrer; *fl også* forstanderskap, styre. **trusteeship** [trʌs'ti:ʃɪp] *sb* forvaltning; vergemål. **trustful** ['trʌstfʊl], **trusting** ['trʌstɪŋ] *adj* tillitsfull. **trustworthy** ['trʌst,wɜ:ðɪ] *adj* pålitelig. **trusty** ['trʌstɪ] *adj bokl* = *trustworthy*.

truth [tru:θ] *sb* **1** sannhet; *to tell the* ~ for å si det som det er; sant å si; **2** sannferdighet. **truthful** *adj* sann(ferdig); oppriktig. **truthless** *adj* usann; troløs.

try [traɪ] **I** *sb dgl* forsøk; *give it a* ~*/have a* ~ *at it* forsøke seg/gjøre et forsøk på det; **II** *vb* **1** forsøke/prøve (på); **2** granske, undersøke; teste, (ut)prøve; ~ *for* forsøke å få/oppnå etc; *ofte* søke på; ~ *on* prøve på (om klær etc); ~ *one's hand at* forsøke seg på; ~ *out* gjennomprøve; ut|eksperimentere, -prøve; **3** *jur* prøve (sak) for retten; forhøre; *be tried* komme/bli stilt for retten; **4** prøve (dvs utsette for motgang/prøvelser etc). **trying** ['traɪɪŋ] *adj* anstrengende, prøvsom; plagsom.

tub [tʌb] *sb* **1** balje, stamp; **2** *(bath*~*)* badekar; *også* karbad.

tubby ['tʌbɪ] *adj* fet; (liten og) tykk.

tube [tju:b] *sb* **1** rør (og rørledning); **2** tube; hylse, kapsel; **3** tunnelbane (i rørformet tunnel, som den i London); **4** *US* (radio)rør. **tube bundle** *sb petro* rørsats.

tuber ['tju:bə] *sb* (rot)knoll. **tubercular** [tju:'bɜ:kjʊlə] *adj* = *tuberculous*. **tuberculosis** [tju:,bɜ:kjʊ'ləʊsɪs] *sb* tuberkulose. **tuberculous** [tju:'bɜ:kjʊləs] *adj* tuberkuløs, tuberkulose; tuberkel-.

tubing ['tju:bɪŋ] *sb koll* rør; slanger. **tubing hanger** *sb petro* røroppheng. **tubular** ['tju:bjʊlə] *adj* rørformet, rør-.

tuck [tʌk] **I** *sb* **1** brett (og innbrett, oppbrett etc); legg; **2** *slang* godter, søtsaker; kaker; **II** *vb* **1** brette (inn/opp); plissere; sy legg; **2** ~ *in/up* pakke (svøpe, tulle etc) inn; **3** *dgl:* ~ *in* lange/legge i seg; helle/tylle i seg. **tuck-shop** *sb* godtebutikk.

tuft [tʌft] *sb* dott, kvast; dusk; tust. **tufted** ['tʌftɪd] *adj* tustet; som har (eller gror i) dusker/kvaster etc.

tug [tʌg] **I** *sb* **1** rykk (*at* i); **2** hardt tak; **3** haling, slep(ing); **4** slepebåt; **II** *vb* **1** dra, hale; slepe, taue; **2** slite, streve; jobbe hardt. **tug of war** *sb* dragkamp, tautrekking.

tuition [tju:'ɪʃn] *sb* opplæring, undervisning; manuduksjon; *også* skolepenger.

tulip ['tju:lɪp] *sb* tulipan.

tumble ['tʌmbl] **I** *sb* fall; rundkast, velt; **II** *vb* **1** falle (og ramle, styrte, tumle etc) over ende; velte; gjøre rundkast; ~ *across* komme over (dvs finne, møte etc tilfeldig); ~ *down* ramle/styrte ned; ~ *in (dgl)* tørne inn (dvs gå til sengs); ~ *to* gå i gang med; tafatt på; *fig* snuble over (dvs uforvarende finne løsningen på problem etc); **2** kaste/slenge over ende. **tumble|-down** *adj* falleferdig. **~-drier, ~-dryer** *sb* tørketrommel. **tumbler** *sb* **1** akrobat; **2** (drikke)glass.

tummy ['tʌmɪ] *sb dgl* mave.

tumour ['tju:mə] *sb* svulst.

tumult ['tju:mʌlt] *sb* **1** bråk; oppløp, tumult(er); **2** (sinns)opprør; forvirring, virvar. **tumultuous** [tju:'mʌltʃʊəs] *adj* larmende, støyende; opprørt, voldsom.

tune [tju:n] **I** *sb* **1** melodi; **2** harmoni, samklang; *også* enighet; *in ~* harmonisk; rent; *in ~ with* i samsvar med; *out of ~* falsk, ustemt; *fig* nedfor; uopplagt; **II** *vb* **1** stemme (instrument); **2** *~ in to* stille inn på (radiostasjon etc). **tuneful** *adj* harmonisk, melodiøs; musikalsk. **tuneless** *adj* umelodiøs. **tuner** ['tju:nə] *sb* **1** -stemmer; *piano-~* pianostemmer; **2** *radio etc* avstemmer; kanalvelger.

tunic ['tju:nɪk] *sb* **1** *mil* uniformsjakke; *ofte* uniform (i motsetning til sivilt antrekk); **2** bluse; kittel; tunika; *også* gym(nastikk)drakt for piker.

tunnel ['tʌnl] **1** *sb* tunnel; **2** *vi* bygge (lage, sprenge etc) tunnel.

turbid ['tɜ:bɪd] *adj* **1** grumset; **2** *fig* forvirret, uklar.

turbulence ['tɜ:bjʊləns] *sb* turbulens *etc*. **turbulent** ['tɜ:bjʊjənt] *adj* turbulent; opprørt, urolig; stormende.

tureen [tjʊ'ri:n] *sb* (suppe)terrin.

turf [tɜ:f] **I** *sb* **1** (gress)torv; **2** gress (og gresslette; gress|plen, -voll etc); **3** *sport* veddeløpsbane, galoppbane; **4** hesteveddeløp; **II** *vt* torvtekke.

turgid ['tɜ:gɪd] *adj* **1** hoven, oppsvulmet; **2** *fig* oppblåst, svulstig.

turkey ['tɜ:kɪ] *sb* kalkun.

turmoil ['tɜ:mɔɪl] *sb* forvirring; bråk, uro; ufred.

turn [tɜ:n] **I** *sb* **1** om|dreining, -løp: runde; **2** omgang, runde; periode; tur, tørn; nummer (i revy, på sirkus etc); *(~ and) ~ about = by ~s* etter tur; på omgang/skift; skiftevis, vekselvis; *in ~* i sin tur; i tur og orden; *også* etter tur *etc; out of ~* utenfor tur; *take a ~* ta (i) et tak; *take ~s at* skiftes/veksle om (å gjøre noe); *take ~s with* skiftes/veksle med; **3** forandring, omslag, skifte; vending; *(new ~)* ny retning; *~ of the tide* tidevannsskifte; *fig også* omslag, (strøm)kentring; *at the ~ of the century* ved århundreskiftet; *favourable ~* gunstig vending; **4** sving (og svingning, dreining, vridning etc); **5** runde/slag (dvs kort spasertur etc); *go for a ~* slå et slag; **6** anledning; *fair ~* rimelig sjanse; **7** anlegg, evner; hang, lyst; tendens, tilbøyelighet; *~ of mind* tankegang; innstilling; *have a practical ~* være praktisk anlagt; **8** gjerning, handling; *bad ~* pek; (stygg) strek; *evil ~* bjørnetjeneste; *good ~* (god) tjeneste; **9** fasong, form; **10** formål, hensikt; *done to a ~* passe kokt/stekt etc; *serve one's ~* gjøre sin nytte; svare til forventningene; *to a ~* glimrende; **11** *dgl* forskrekkelse; sjokk, støkk; **12** *dgl* anfall; raptus, ri, tokt; **II** *vb* **1** (få til å) gå rundt; dreie/svinge (om/rundt); snu/vende (seg); *mil* omgå; *~ a corner* runde (dreie/svinge om) et hjørne; *fig* komme over en kneik; klare seg gjennom en krise; klare brasene; *~ her head* fordreie hodet på henne; gjøre henne innbilsk/tummelumsk etc; *~ his brain* gjøre ham svimmel/*fig* forstyrret; *dgl* drive ham fra vettet; *~ one's back on* vende ryggen mot; *fig* vende (en) ryggen; *~ one's stomach* få det til å vrenge seg i en; gjøre en kvalm; *~ tail (dgl)* flykte, rømme; stikke av; **2** sveive/svinge (på); dreie/vri (på); **3** bøye (og av|bøye, -lede etc); **4** (hen)|lede, (-)vende; rette; *~ one's hand to* gå i gang med; ta fatt på; greie, klare; *~ one's steps to* rette/styre skrittene (sine) mot; **5** *~ into* forandre/forvandle til; bli forandret/forvandlet til; **6** *~ into* gjøre til; få til (å bli/være etc); *~ loose* sette/slippe løs; sette fri; **7** *~ into* omdanne til; overføre/oversette til; **8** bli (gradvis); vise seg å bli/være etc; utvikle seg til; *the milk has ~ed* melken er blitt sur; **9** passere/runde (dvs nå et vendepunkt); *~ fifty* runde femti (år); **10** dreie (dvs forme ved dreiing); *fig* turnere (replikk etc); **11** *med adv, prep ~* **about** snu/vende (seg); snu seg (rundt); *mil* gjøre helomvending/helt om; *fig* overveie; *About ~!* Helt om! *~* **against** snu/vende (seg) mot; hisse/sette opp mot; *~* **away** snu/vende (seg) bort; drive/jage etc bort; av|vende, -vise; *~* **back** snu; vende tilbake; vise (drive, jage etc) tilbake; brette tilbake/til side etc; *~* **down** svinge ned (sidegate etc); brette/slå ned (krave etc); skru/slå ned (gassflamme etc); *fig* avslå; avvise, forkaste; *~* **from** snu/vende seg (bort, vekk etc) fra; få bort/vekk fra; drive/jage etc vekk fra; *~* **in** slå/svinge inn (på sidevei etc); brette inn; levere/sende inn; *dgl* tørne inn (dvs køye, gå til sengs); *~* **into** bli/gjøre til (etc, jf *II 5-7*); *~* **off** svinge/ta av (fra hovedvei etc); skru/slå av (lys, radio etc); avvise; drive/jage etc vekk; få til å miste interesse/lyst etc; *~* **on** sette (skru, slå etc) på (lys, radio etc); snu/vende (seg) mot; hisse/sette opp mot; gjøre begeistret (ivrig, lysten, opphisset etc); dreie/svinge om; *fig* dreie seg/handle om; avhenge av; *~* **out** rykke/tørne ut; snu/vende (seg) ut; sende ut; drive/jage ut; forvise, utvise; kaste ut; slokke (især levende lys); fremstille, produsere; prestere, yte; utstyre; *fig* arte/utvikle seg; vise seg å bli/være etc; *~ out as expected* gå som ventet; *~* **over** bla/vende om; brette/snu (rundt); velte; over|dra, -føre, -gi; gi/levere fra seg; omsette; henvise; *fig* overveie; *~* **round** gå rundt; dreie/vikle rundt; snu (seg); vende om; *~* **to** snu/vende (seg) mot; begynne/ta fatt (på); gå i gang (med); gripe/ty til; forvandle/gjøre til; *~ to account* dra nyutte av; bli/komme til nytte; *~* **up** brette opp; legge (snu, vende etc) opp (f.eks. om kort); møte frem/opp; komme; *fig* hende; dukke opp; vise seg (å bli, være etc); *~* **upon** snu/vende (seg) mot; kaste seg over; hisse/sette opp mot; drive/kaste (tilbake) mot; *~* **upside down** snu opp ned (på). **turn|around** *sb petro* driftspause. **~around time** *sb data* omløpstid. **~coat** ['tɜ:nkəʊt] *sb* vendekåpe (dvs ustadig person); vinglefant, værhane. **turning** ['tɜ:nɪŋ] *sb* dreining *etc*. **turning-**

-point *sb* vendepunkt, omslag. **turn(ing)table** *sb* dreieskive.

turnip ['tɜ:nɪp] *sb* **1** turnips; nepe; **2** *(~ cabbage)* kål|rabi, -rot; **3** *slang* tambak (dvs stort lommeur).

turn|key ['tɜ:nki:] *sb* fangevokter, slutter. **~-out** *sb* **1** utrykning; **2** fremmøte, oppmøte; **3** fremtoning, utseende; **4** resultat. **~-over** *sb* **1** overdragelse; **2** omsetning; **3** produksjon. **~pike** ['tɜ:npaɪk] *sb* veibom; *også* bomvei. **~stile** ['tɜ:nstaɪl] *sb* korsbom. **~-up** *sb* **1** opp|brett, -slag; **2** *fig* slumpetreff.

turpentine ['tɜ:pəntaɪn] *sb* terpentin.

turquoise ['tɜ:kwɔɪz] *adj, sb* turkis(-).

turret ['tʌrɪt] *sb* (lite) tårn; *mil* kanontårn.

turtle ['tɜ:tl] *sb* skilpadde. **turtle graphics** *sb data* sporgrafikk.

tusk [tʌsk] *sb* støttann.

tussle ['tʌsl] **1** *sb* basketak, håndgemeng; slagsmål; **2** *vi* slåss (*with* med).

tut [tʌt] *interj* **1** hysj; **2** nånå.

tutelage ['tju:tɪlɪdʒ] *sb* formynderskap; vergemål. **tutor** ['tju:tə] **I** *sb* **1** studie(vei)leder; manuduktør; **2** huslærer, privatlærer; **3** formynder; **II** *vb* instruere, lære; manudusere; gi privatundervisning. **tutorial** [tju:'tɔ:rɪəl] **1** *adj* privat(lærer)-; **2** *sb* manuduksjon; *stundom* håndbok, lærebok.

tux [tʌks] *dgl fork* for **tuxedo** [tʌk'si:dəu] *sb US* smoking.

twain [tweɪn] *adj, sb gml* to.

twang [twæŋ] **I 1** *sb* klang (fra streng som slås an); klimprelyd; **2** *(nasal ~)* nasalklang; lett snøvling; **II** *vb* **1** klimpre (på); klinge; **2** snakke i nesen; snøvle.

tweak [twi:k] *sb, vt* klyp(e).

tweezers ['twi:zəz] *sb fl (pair of ~)* pinsett.

twice [twaɪs] *adv* to ganger.

twiddle ['twɪdl] *vb* dreie (og sno, tulle, tvinne etc) (rundt).

twig [twɪg] *sb* kvist.

twilight ['twaɪlaɪt] *sb* halv|lys, -mørke; demring, skumring.

twin [twɪn] **1** *adj* dobbelt(-), to-; tvilling-; **2** *sb* tvilling. **twin | beds** *sb* dobbeltseng. **~-set** *sb* cardigansett. **~ towns** *sb fl* tvillingbyer; vennskapsbyer.

twine [twaɪn] *sb* **1** *sb* hyssing, snor; **2** *vb* slynge/sno seg; tvinne.

twinge [twɪndʒ] *sb* sting (av smerte); *~ of conscience* stikk i samvittigheten; ≈ samvittighetsnag.

twinkle ['twɪŋkl] **1** *sb* blink(ing) *etc*; **2** *vb* blinke, glimte; funkle. **twinkling** ['twɪŋklɪŋ] *sb* blink(ing), glimt(ing); funkling; *~ of an eye* blunk, øyeblikk.

twirl [twɜ:l] *vb* snurre/virvle (seg) rundt.

twist [twɪst] **I** *sb* **1** vrid (og vridning etc); vrikk; **2** sving, slyng; **3** drag, (karakter)trekk; egenhet; **4** (dansen) twist; **II** *vb* **1** vri (rundt); dreie seg; slynge/sno seg; *~ somebody round one's little finger* tvinne en om lillefingeren (sin); *~ somebody's arm/elbow* legge/øve press på en (for å oppnå noe); **2** skru; vri (rundt); **3** for|dreie, -vri; vri/vrenge (på); **4** twiste (dvs danse twist). **twister** ['twɪstə] *sb* **1** nøtt, problem; **2** *a)* ordkløver, vriompeis; *b)* kjeltring, svindler.

twitch [twɪtʃ] **1** *sb* napp, rykk; trekning; **2** *vb* nappe/rykke (i); rykke til.

twitter ['twɪtə] **I** *sb* kvitring, kvitter; *in a ~* forkavet, oppspilt; **II** *vi* **1** kvitre; **2** fnise/knise nervøst; være (og *især* pludre, snakke etc) oppspilt.

'twixt [twɪkst] = *betwixt.*

two [tu:] *adj, sb* to(tall); toer. **two|-faced** *adj* falsk, uoppriktig. **~fold** *adj, adv* dobbelt. **~-piece** *adj* todelt (om plagg som består av to deler). **~-time** *vb slang* lure; snyte, svindle. **~-timing** *adj slang* bedragersk. **~-way** *adj* **1** dobbelt; **2** toveis; **3** med trafikk i begge retninger.

tycoon [taɪ'ku:n] *sb dgl* finansfyrste, industrileder.

type [taɪp] **I** *sb* **1** type; modell, mønster; **2** art, slag; gruppe; **3** (skrift)type; *koll* sats, skrift, trykk; **II** *vb* skrive på (skrive)maskin. **type|cast 1** *adj* som skapt for (oppgave, rolle etc); **2** *vt* tildele (skuespiller) rolle som passer til typen. **~font** *sb data etc* typesnitt. **~script** *sb* (maskinskrevet) manuskript. **~wheel** *sb data* typehjul. **~write** *vb* = *type II.* **~writer** *sb* skrivemaskin.

typhoid ['taɪfɔɪd] *sb (~ fever)* tyfoid(feber); *dgl også* = *typhus.*

typhoon [taɪ'fu:n] *sb* tyfon.

typhus ['taɪfəs] *sb* (flekk)tyfus.

typical ['tɪpɪkl] *adj* typisk. **typify** ['tɪpɪfaɪ] *vt* representere; være typen på/typisk for. **typing** *sb* maskinskriv(n)ing. **typist** *sb* skrivemaskinoperatør. **typographer** [taɪ'pɒgrəfə] *sb* typograf. **typographic** [,taɪpə'græfɪk] *adj* typografisk. **typography** [taɪ'pɒgrəfɪ] *sb* typografi.

tyrannical [tɪ'rænɪkl] *adj* tyrannisk. **tyrannize** ['tɪrənaɪz] *vb (~ over)* tyrannisere. **tyrannous** ['tɪrənəs] *adj* = *tyrannical.* **tyranny** ['tɪrənɪ] *sb* tyranni. **tyrant** ['taɪrənt] *sb* tyrann.

tyre [taɪə] *sb* dekk (til bilhjul etc).

tyro ['taɪərəu] *sb* = *tiro.*

U

ubiquitous [ju:'bɪkwɪtəs] *adj bokl* allestedsnærværende.

udder ['ʌdə] *sb* jur.

ugly ['ʌglɪ] *adj* **1** stygg; fæl, heslig; **2** truende; dyster, skummel; **3** ond(skapsfull), slem; **4** ubehagelig; lei.

ulcer ['ʌlsə] *sb (gastric ~)* mavesår.

ulterior [ʌl'tɪərɪə] *adj* **1** bortre, fjernere; *gml* hinsidig; *fig også* bakenforliggende, underliggende; *~ motives* baktanker; **2** fremtidig, senere. **ultimate** ['ʌltɪmət] *adj* **1** endelig, sist; ytterst; **2** grunn-. **ultimately** ['ʌltɪmətlɪ] *adv* i siste instans. **ultimatum** [ˌʌltɪ'meɪtəm] *sb* ultimatum.

umbilical [ʌm'bɪlɪkl] *adj: ~ cord* navlestreng. **umbilical | cable** *sb petro* navlestrengskabel. **~ (hose)** *sb petro* navle|slange, -streng.

umbrella [ʌm'brelə] *sb* paraply; *fig* beskyttelse; ly, vern.

umpire ['ʌmpaɪə] **1** *sb* oppmann; *især sport* dommer; **2** *vb* dømme; være dommer/oppmann.

umpteenth [ˌʌmp'ti:nθ] *adj dgl, slang: for the ~ time* for ørtende (eller jeg vet ikke hvilken) gang.

un- [ʌn-] *pref* u- (eller av-, fra-, ikke-, mis-; -fri, -løs etc, se de enkelte oppslagsord på *un-*).

unabated [ˌʌnə'beɪtɪd] *adj* uforminsket, usvekket.

unable [ʌn'eɪbl] *adj: ~ to* ute av stand til (å).

unaccountable [ˌʌnə'kaʊntəbl] *adj* ubegripelig, uforklarlig.

unaccustomed [ˌʌnə'kʌstəmd] *adj* **1** uvant (*to* med (å)); **2** uvanlig.

unadulterated [ˌʌnə'dʌltəreɪtɪd] *adj* ren, uoppblandet; uforfalsket.

unadvised [ˌʌnəd'vaɪzd] *adj* utilrådelig; forhastet, overilt.

unaffected [ˌʌnə'fektɪd] *adj* **1** ekte, oppriktig, uforstilt; **2** uberørt, upåvirket.

unalienable [ʌn'eɪlɪənəbl] *adj* uavhendelig, umistelig.

unanimity [ju:nə'nɪmətɪ] *sb* enstemmighet. **unanimous** [ju:'nænɪməs] *adj* enstemmig.

unannounced [ˌʌnə'naʊnst] *adj* uanmeldt, uannonsert.

unapproachable [ˌʌnə'prəʊtʃəbl] *adj* utilnærmelig.

unarmed [ʌn'ɑ:md] *adj* u(be)væpnet.

unassuming [ˌʌnə'sju:mɪŋ] *adj* beskjeden, fordringsløs.

unavailing [ˌʌnə'veɪlɪŋ] *adj* fånyttig, resultatløs.

unavoidable [ˌʌnə'vɔɪdəbl] *adj* uunngåelig.

unaware [ˌʌnə'weə] *adj* uvitende (*of* om). **unawares** [ˌʌnə'weəz] *adv* uforvarende; uten å vite det/være klar over det.

unbearable [ʌn'beərəbl] *adj* uutholdelig, utålelig.

unbecoming [ˌʌnbɪ'kʌmɪŋ] *adj* ukledelig.

unbelievable [ˌʌnbɪ'li:vəbl] *adj* utrolig; ubegripelig, ufattelig.

unbend [ʌn'bend] *vb* løsne/slakke (på); slappe av.

unbias(s)ed [ʌn'baɪəst] *adj* uhildet, upartisk; fordomsfri.

unblock *vb data* avblokke.

unborn [ʌn'bɔ:n] *adj* ufødt.

unbounded [ʌn'baʊndɪd] *adj* grenseløs, ubegrenset.

unbreakable [ʌn'breɪkəbl] *adj* **1** uknuselig; **2** uslåelig. **unbroken** [ʌn'brəʊkn] *adj* **1** sammenhengende, u(av)brutt; **2** utemmet; ikke innkjørt/innridd.

unburden [ʌn'bɜ:dn] *vt* lesse av; *fig* lette.

uncalled-for [ʌn'kɔ:ldfɔ:] *adj* upåkalt; unødvendig; *også* anmassende, påtrengende.

uncanny [ʌn'kænɪ] *adj* nifs, uhyggelig.

uncared-for [ʌn'keədfɔ:] *adj* forsømt.

unceasing [ʌn'si:sɪŋ] *adj* uavlatelig, uopphørlig, ustanselig.

uncertain [ʌn'sɜ:tn] *adj* **1** usikker, uviss; **2** upålitelig, utrygg. **uncertainty** [ʌn'sɜ:tntɪ] *sb* usikkerhet, uvisshet; tvil.

unclaimed [ʌn'kleɪmd] *adj* uavhentet (især om post); *også* herreløs.

uncle ['ʌŋkl] *sb* onkel; (også *slang* om pantelåner); *cry/say ~ (slang)* be om nåde; overgi seg.

unclouded [ʌn'klaʊdɪd] *adj* skyfri (også *fig*).

uncomfortable [ʌn'kʌmfətəbl] *adj* **1** ubehagelig, ubekvem; **2** utilpass; ille til mote.

uncommon [ʌn'kɒmən] *adj* u(sed)vanlig; ualminnelig.

uncompromising [ʌn'kɒmprəmaɪzɪŋ] *adj* kompromissløs.

unconcerned [ˌʌnkən'sɜ:nd] *adj* like|glad, -gyldig; ubekymret.

unconditional [ˌʌnkən'dɪʃənl] *adj* betingelsesløs.

unconscionable [ʌn'kɒnʃnəbl] *adj* urimelig; ublu.

unconscious [ʌn'kɒnʃəs] **I** *adj* **1** bevisstløs; **2** ubevisst; intetanende; **II** *sb: the ~* underbevisstheten.

unconsidered [ˌʌnkən'sɪdəd] *adj* uoverlagt, uoverveid.

unconstitutional ['ʌnˌkɒnstɪ'tju:ʃənl] *adj* forfatningsstridig, ukonstitusjonell.

uncountable [ʌn'kaʊntəbl] *adj* talløs, utallig; utellelig.

uncouth [ʌn'ku:θ] *adj* **1** keitet, klosset; **2** grov, ubehøvlet.

uncover [ʌn'kʌvə] *vt* **1** ta deksel/lokk *etc* av; **2** *fig* avdekke.

unction ['ʌŋkʃn] *sb* **1** salving; **2** salvelse (og salvelsesfullhet). **unctuous** ['ʌŋktjuəs] *adj* salvelsesfull.

undamaged [ʌn'dæmɪdʒd] *adj* uskadd.

undaunted [ʌn'dɔ:ntɪd] *adj* fryktløs, uforferdet.

undecided [ˌʌndɪ'saɪdɪd] *adj* ubesluttsom.

undeniable [ˌʌndɪ'naɪəbl] *adj* ubestridelig. **undeniably** [ˌʌndɪ'naɪəblɪ] *adv* unektelig.

under ['ʌndə] **1** *adv* under; *go* ~ *(sjø)* forlise; gå ned/under; **2** *pref* under-; **3** *prep* under (og bortunder, innunder, nedenunder, oppunder etc); *fig* lavere/mindre enn.

underbrush ['ʌndəbrʌʃ] *sb* underskog; kratt(skog).

undercarriage ['ʌndəkærɪdʒ] *sb* understell.

underclothes ['ʌndəkləʊðz] *sb fl*, **underclothing** ['ʌndəkləʊðɪŋ] *sb* undertøy.

undercover [ˌʌndə'kʌvə] *adj* hemmelig.

undercurrent ['ʌndəkʌrənt] *sb* understrøm.

undercut [ˌʌndə'kʌt] *vt* under|by, -selge.

underdeveloped [ˌʌndədɪ'veləpt] *adj* underutviklet.

underdog ['ʌndədɒg] *sb fig* svakere part; taper.

underdone [ˌʌndə'dʌn] *adj* for lite kokt/stekt; råstekt.

underestimate [ˌʌndər'estɪmeɪt] *vt* undervurdere.

underfed [ˌʌndə'fed] *adj* underernært.

undergo [ˌʌndə'gəʊ] *vt* gjennomgå.

undergraduate [ˌʌndə'grædʃʊət] *sb* (universitets)student.

underground A ['ʌndəgraʊnd] **I** *adj* **1** underjordisk; undergrunns-; ~ *blowout* undergrunnsutblåsing (på oljefelt); **2** *fig* undergrunns- (dvs hemmelig, illegal etc); **II** *sb (~ railway)* undergrunnsbane, tunnelbane; **B** [ˌʌndə'graʊnd] *adv* under jorden; *fig også* illegalt; i det skjulte; i hemmelighet.

undergrowth ['ʌndəgrəʊθ] *sb* underskog; kratt(skog).

underhand [ˌʌndə'hænd] *adj, adv* falsk(t), svikefull(t); hemmelig.

underline [ˌʌndə'laɪn] *vt* streke under; *også fig* understreke; fremheve, utheve. **underline key** *sb data* understrekingstast.

underling ['ʌndəlɪŋ] *sb* underordnet, undersått.

undermine [ˌʌndə'maɪn] *vt* under|grave, -minere; svekke.

underneath [ˌʌndə'ni:θ] *adv, prep* (neden)under.

undernourished [ˌʌndə'nʌrɪʃt] *adj* underernært.

underpants ['ʌndəpænts] *sb fl* underbukse(r).

underpass ['ʌndəpɑ:s] *sb* undergang (under jernbane, vei etc).

underpay [ˌʌndə'peɪ] *vt* underbetale.

underprivileged [ˌʌndə'prɪvɪlɪdʒd] *adj* underprivilegert.

underrate [ˌʌndə'reɪt] *vt* undervurdere.

undersecretary [ˌʌndə'sekrətərɪ] *sb: Parliamentary U~* minister uten statsrådsrang; ≈ departementssjef, statssekretær.

undersell [ˌʌndə'sel] *vt* underselge (dvs ta lavere pris for en vare enn konkurrentene gjør).

the **undersigned** [ˌʌndə'saɪnd] *sb* undertegnede.

undersized [ˌʌndə'saɪzd] *adj* underdimensjonert; liten.

underskirt ['ʌndəskɜ:t] *sb* underskjørt.

understaffed [ˌʌndə'stɑ:ft] *adj* underbemannet.

understand [ˌʌndə'stænd] *vb* forstå; begripe, oppfatte; skjønne; *give to* ~ gi forståelsen av; la forstå; *også* belære (om). **understandable** [ˌʌndə'stændəbl] *adj* forståelig. **understanding** [ˌʌndə'stændɪŋ] *sb* **1** forståelse *etc*; forståelsesfullhet; **2** enighet, overenskomst; **3** forutsetning.

understate [ˌʌndə'steɪt] *vt* underdrive (dvs heller si for lite enn for mye). **understatement** [ˌʌndə'steɪtmənt] *sb* underdrivelse.

understudy ['ʌndəstʌdɪ] *sb* reserve, stedfortreder.

undertake [ˌʌndə'teɪk] *vt* **1** gå i gang med; gå inn for; **2** påta seg (ansvar); garantere; stå inne for. **undertaker** ['ʌndəˌteɪkə] *sb US* innehaver/leder av begravelsesbyrå. **undertaking** [ˌʌndə'teɪkɪŋ] *sb* foretagende.

underwater ['ʌndəwɔ:tə] *adj* undervanns-.

underwear ['ʌndəweə] *sb* undertøy.

underworld ['ʌndəwɜ:ld] *sb* underverden; *dgl* forbryterverden.

undesirable [ˌʌndɪ'zaɪərəbl] *adj, sb* uønsket (person).

undeterred [ˌʌndɪ'tɜ:d] *adj* uskremt; uforknytt, uforsagt.

undeveloped [ˌʌndɪ'veləpt] *adj* ubebygd; uoppdyrket; uutviklet.

undies ['ʌndɪz] *sb fl dgl* (dame)undertøy.

undo [ʌn'du:] *vt* **1** løsne; løse/pakke *etc* opp; knyte opp; **2** annullere, omstøte; gjøre ugjort; **3** ødelegge; rasere, ruinere. **undo key** *sb data* angretast. **undoing** [ʌn'du:ɪŋ] *sb* ruin, ødeleggelse; ulykke. **undone** [ʌn'dʌn] *adj* **1** løsnet (etc, jf *undo*); **2** ugjort.

undoubted [ʌn'daʊtɪd] *adj* utvilsom.

undress [ʌn'dres] **1** *vr, vt* kle av (seg); **2** *sb: in a state of* ~ avkledd, naken.

undue [ʌn'dju:] *adj* utilbørlig; urimelig.

undulate ['ʌndjʊleɪt] *vi* bølge.

undying [ʌn'daɪɪŋ] *adj* udødelig, uvisnelig.

unearned [ʌn'ɜ:nd] *adj* ikke tjent; *især fig* ufortjent.

unearth [ʌn'ɜ:θ] *vt* grave frem; avdekke. **unearthly** [ʌn'ɜ:θlɪ] *adj* **1** overjordisk; **2** overnaturlig; nifs, uhyggelig.

uneasy [ʌn'i:zɪ] *adj* rastløs, urolig; engstelig.

unemployed [ˌʌnɪm'plɔɪd] *adj* arbeids|ledig, -løs. **unemployment** [ˌʌnɪm'plɔɪmənt] *sb* arbeids|ledighet, -løshet. **unemployment | benefit, ~ insurance** *sb* (arbeids)ledighetstrygd.

unending [ʌn'endɪŋ] *adj* endeløs, uendelig.

unendurable [ˌʌnɪn'djʊərəbl] *adj* uutholdelig.

unenlightened [ˌʌnɪn'laɪtnd] *adj* uopplyst, uvitende.

unequal [ʌn'i:kwəl] *adj* **1** ulik(e); **2** utilstrekkelig. **unequalled** [ʌn'i:kwəld] *adj* uforlignelig; uovertruffet.

unequivocal [ˌʌnɪ'kwɪvəkl] *adj* utvetydig.

unerring [ʌn'ɜ:rɪŋ] *adj* ufeilbarl(lig); *fig* usvikelig.

unexampled [ˌʌnɪg'zɑ:mpld] *adj* enestående, makeløs.

unfailing [ʌn'feɪlɪŋ] *adj* ufeilbar(lig); aldri sviktende; *også* årviss. **unfair** [ʌn'feə] *adj* urettferdig, ureal.

unfaithful [ʌn'feɪθful] *adj* **1** utro; **2** troløs.

unfamiliar [ˌʌnfə'mɪlɪə] *adj* ukjent.

unfasten [ʌn'fɑ:sn] *vt* knyte/løse opp; løsne.

unfathomable [ʌn'fæðəməbl] *adj* bunnløs; *fig* uutgrunnelig.

unfavourable [ʌn'feɪvrəbl] *adj* ugunstig.

unfeeling [ʌn'fi:lɪŋ] *adj* **1** følelsesløs; **2** ufølsom.

unfit [ʌn'fit] *adj* uskikket.

unfold [ʌn'fəuld] *vb* brette (folde, rulle etc) ut.

unforeseen [ˌʌnfɔ:'si:n] *adj* uforutsett.

unforgettable [ˌʌnfə'getəbl] *adj* uforglemmelig.

unfortunate [ʌn'fɔ:tʃunət] *adj* **1** uheldig; **2** ulykkelig. **unfortunately** [ʌn'fɔ:tʃunətlɪ] *adv* uheldigvis; dessverre.

unfounded [ʌn'faundɪd] *adj* grunnløs, u(be)grunnet.

unfriendly [ʌn'frendlɪ] *adj* uvennlig; fiendtlig; *fig* ugjestmild.

unfurl [ʌn'fɜ:l] *vt* folde/rulle ut.

ungainly [ʌn'geɪnlɪ] *adj* klønet, klosset.

ungenerous [ʌn'dʒenərəs] *adj* smålig, småskåren.

ungodly [ʌn'gɒdlɪ] *adj* ugudelig.

ungovernable [ʌn'gʌvənəbl] *adj* uregjerlig, ustyrlig.

ungrateful [ʌn'greɪtful] *adj* utakknemlig.

unguarded [ʌn'gɑ:dɪd] *adj* ubevoktet.

unhappy [ʌn'hæpɪ] *adj* ulykkelig; nedfor; lei seg.

unheard-of [ʌn'hɜ:dəv] *adj* uhørt; enestående.

unhinged [ʌn'hɪndʒd] *adj dgl* (gått) av hengslene (dvs ellevill, skrullet, sprø etc).

unhook [ʌn'huk] *vt* hekte av/opp.

unhoped-for [ʌn'həuptfɔ:] *adj* uventet (fordi en ikke har våget håpe på det).

unhurt [ʌn'hɜ:t] *adj* uskadd.

unicorn ['ju:nɪkɔ:n] *sb* enhjørning.

unidentified [ˌʌnaɪ'dentɪfaɪd] *adj* uidentifisert.

unification [ˌju:nɪfɪ'keɪʃn] *sb* forening, samling; sammenslutning. **uniform** ['ju:nɪfɔ:m] **I** *adj* **1** ens(artet); uforanderlig; konstant; **2** samstemmig; **II** *sb* uniform; **III** *vt* uniformere; ensrette; gjøre ens(artet). **uniformity** [ˌju:nɪ'fɔ:mətɪ] *sb* ensartethet, uniformitet. **unify** ['ju:nɪfaɪ] *vt* forene, samle; *også* gjøre ensartet.

unilateral [ˌju:nɪ'lætərəl] *adj* ensidig, unilateral.

unimaginative [ˌʌnɪ'mædʒɪnətɪv] *adj* fantasiløs.

unimpeachable [ˌʌnɪm'pi:tʃəbl] *adj* uangripelig, upåklagelig.

uninformed [ˌʌnɪn'fɔ:md] *adj* uinformert, uvitende.

uninhabited [ˌʌnɪn'hæbɪtɪd] *adj* ubebodd.

uninhibited [ˌʌnɪn'hɪbɪtɪd] *adj* hemningsløs.

uninjured [ʌn'ɪndʒəd] *adj* uskadd.

uninspired [ˌʌnɪn'spaɪəd] *adj* uinspirert.

uninterested [ʌn'ɪntrɪstɪd] *adj* uinteressert.

union ['ju:nɪən] *sb* **1** forening, union; sammenslutning; **2** enighet, samstemmighet; **3** ekteskap(elig forening); **4** = **Union Jack** *sb* det britiske nasjonalflagg.

unique [ju:'ni:k] *adj* enestående, uforlignelig; unik.

unisex ['ju:nɪseks] *adj* unisex- (dvs som er ens/ felles etc for begge kjønn). **unison** ['ju:nɪzn] *sb* enighet; samklang; *in* ~ samstemmig, unisont.

unit ['ju:nɪt] *sb* enhet; *mil også* avdeling, gruppe. **unite** [ju:'naɪt] *vb* forene (seg); gå/slutte (seg) sammen. *the* **United Kingdom** *sb* kongeriket Storbritannia og Nord-Irland. **unit separator** *sb data* dataskilletegn. **unity** ['ju:nətɪ] *sb* **1** enhet; **2** enighet, harmoni; **3** fellesskap.

universal [ˌju:nɪ'vɜ:sl] *adj* **1** universell, verdensomfattende; **2** alminnelig, generell; altomfattende, universal-. **universe** ['ju:nɪvɜ:s] *sb* univers. **university** [ˌju:nɪ'vɜ:sətɪ] *sb* universitet.

unjust [ʌn'dʒʌst] *adj* urettferdig; uberettiget, urettmessig.

unkempt [ʌn'kempt] *adj* uflidd, ustelt.

unkind [ʌn'kaɪnd] *adj* uvennlig; hardhjertet, ufølsom.

unknowing [ʌn'nəuɪŋ] *adj* uvitende. **unknown** [ʌn'nəun] *adj* ukjent.

unleash [ʌn'li:ʃ] *vt* slippe løs (især *fig*).

unless [ʌn'les] *konj* med mindre; om ikke.

unlikely [ʌn'laɪklɪ] *adj* usannsynlig; lite trolig.

unload [ʌn'ləud] *vt* losse; lesse av; *fig* lette (seg) (*of* for).

unlock [ʌn'lɒk] *vt* låse opp.

unlooked-for [ʌn'luktfɔ:] *adj* uforutsett, uventet.

unlucky [ʌn'lʌkɪ] *adj* uheldig; sørgelig.

unmanned [ʌn'mænd] *adj* ubemannet.

unmask [ʌn'mɑ:sk] *vb* demaskere.

unmatched [ʌn'mætʃt] *adj* makeløs, enestående.

unmentionable [ʌn'menʃnəbl] *adj* unevnelig.

unmindful [ʌn'maɪndful] *adj* uoppmerksom; ~ *of* uten tanke for/på.

unmistakable [ˌʌnmɪs'teɪkəbl] *adj* umiskjennelig, åpenbar; påtakelig.

unmitigated [ʌn'mɪtɪgeɪtɪd] *adj* ren(dyrket), u(opp)blandet.

unnatural [ʌn'nætʃərəl] *adj* unaturlig.

unnecessary [ʌn'nesɪsərɪ] *adj* unødvendig, overflødig.

unnerved [ˌʌn'nɜ:vd] *adj* lammet, maktesløs; motløs.

unnoticed [ʌn'nəutɪst] *adj* ubemerket.

unnumbered [ʌn'nʌmbəd] *adj* **1** unummerert **2**

talløs, utallig.

unobtrusive [ˌʌnəb'tru:sɪv] *adj* beskjeden, tilbakeholden.

unofficial [ˌʌnə'fɪʃl] *adj* uoffisiell; *om streik* ulovlig.

unpack [ʌn'pæk] *vt* pakke opp.

unparalleled [ʌn'pærələld] *adj* makeløs; uten sidestykke.

unpleasant [ʌn'pleznt] *adj* ubehagelig.

unprecedented [ʌn'presɪdentɪd] *adj* uten presedens; uhørt.

unprejudiced [ʌn'predʒʊdɪst] *adj* fordomsfri, uhildet.

unpretentious [ˌʌnprɪ'tenʃəs] *adj* beskjeden, fordringsløs.

unprincipled [ʌn'prɪnsəpld] *adj* prinsippløs.

unprofessional [ˌʌnprə'feʃənl] *adj* uprofesjonell.

unprovoked [ˌʌnprə'vəukt] *adj* uprovosert; *også* umotivert.

unqualified [ʌn'kwɒlɪfaɪd] *adj* **1** ukvalifisert; **2** ubetinget; forbeholdsløs, uforbeholden.

unquestionable [ʌn'kwestʃenəbl] *adj* sikker, utvilsom.

unquote [ʌn'kwəut] *vb* avslutte sitat; sette/si anførselstegn slutt.

unravel [ʌn'rævl] *vb* **1** trevle(s) opp; **2** løse opp (floke etc); greie ut; **3** løse (opp); oppklare.

unreal [ʌn'rɪəl] *adj* uvirkelig.

unreasonable [ʌn'ri:znəbl] *adj* urimelig.

unrelenting [ˌʌnrɪ'lentɪŋ] *adj* ubøyelig, uforsonlig.

unreliable [ˌʌnrɪ'laɪəbl] *adj* upålitelig.

unremitting [ˌʌnrɪ'mɪtɪŋ] *adj* uavlatelig, uopphørlig; usvekket.

unrequited [ˌʌnrɪ'kwaɪtɪd] *adj* ubesvart; ikke gjengjeldt.

unrest [ʌn'rest] *sb* uro.

unrestrained [ˌʌnrɪ'streɪnd] *adj* hemningsløs, tøylesløs.

unrestricted [ˌʌnrɪ'strɪktɪd] *adj* ubegrenset, uinnskrenket; uten restriksjoner; *om veitrafikk* uten fartsbegrensning.

unrivalled [ʌn'raɪvld] *adj* uforlignelig, uovertruffet.

unruffled [ʌn'rʌfld] *adj* uanfektet, uforstyrrelig.

unruly [ʌn'ru:lɪ] *adj* uregjerlig; vill, vilter.

unsaid [ʌn'sed] *adj* unevnt, usagt.

unsatisfied [ˌʌn'sætɪsfaɪd] *adj* utilfreds(stilt).

unsaturated [ˌʌn'sætʃəreɪtɪd] *adj* umettet.

unsavoury [ʌn'seɪvərɪ] *adj* smakløs; ekkel, vemmelig; uhumsk.

unscathed [ʌn'skeɪðd] *adv* uskadd.

unscrupulous [ʌn'skru:pjʊləs] *adj* samvittighetsløs, skruppelløs.

unseemly [ʌn'si:mlɪ] *adj* upassende, usømmelig.

unselfish [ʌn'selfɪʃ] *adj* uegennyttig, uselvisk.

unsettle [ʌn'setl] *vt* forstyrre, uroe; rokke. **unsettled** [ʌn'setld] *adj* **1** urolig, utrygg; **2** usikker, ustø; ustadig; **3** ubebodd; **4** uavgjort; uoppgjort.

unsightly [ʌn'saɪtlɪ] *adj* stygg.

unskilled [ʌn'skɪld] *adj* ufaglært; uøvd.

unsophisticated [ˌʌnsə'fɪstɪkeɪtɪd] *adj* naiv, troskyldig.

unsound [ʌn'saund] *adj* **1** (mentalt) sykelig/usunn; **2** feilaktig, uriktig; uholdbar.

unsparing [ʌn'speərɪŋ] *adj* som ikke sparer seg/holder noe tilbake; generøs.

unspeakable [ʌn'spi:kəbl] *adj* ubeskrivelig, unevnelig; usigelig. **unspoken** [ʌn'spəukən] *adj* usagt, uuttalt.

unsteady [ʌn'stedɪ] *adj* ustø.

unstuck [ʌn'stʌk] *adj: come* ~ løsne; falle av.

unstudied [ʌn'stʌdɪd] *adj* **1** utilsiktet; **2** ulært, ustudert.

unsuccessful [ˌʌnsək'sesfʊl] *adj* feilslått, mislykket.

unsuitable [ʌn'sju:təbl] *adj* upassende, uegnet.

unsurpassed [ˌʌnsə'pɑ:st] *adj* uovertruffet.

unswerving [ʌn'swɜ:vɪŋ] *adj* urokkelig; usvikelig.

unthinkable [ʌn'θɪŋkəbl] *adj* utenkelig. **unthinking** [ˌʌn'θɪŋkɪŋ] *adj* tankeløs, ubetenksom.

untidy [ʌn'taɪdɪ] *adj* **1** uordentlig, ustelt; **2** rotet, uryddig.

untie [ˌʌn'taɪ] *vt* knyte/løse opp; løsne, løse.

until [ən'tɪl] *konj, prep* (inn)til (om tiden); *not* ~ ikke før (enn); først da/når.

untimely [ʌn'taɪmlɪ] *adj* **1** ubeleilig; utenfor sesongen/årstiden etc; **2** *his* ~ *death* hans altfor tidlige død.

untiring [ʌn'taɪərɪŋ] *adj* utrettelig.

unto ['ʌntʊ] *prep gml* til.

untold [ʌn'təuld] *adj* ufortalt, unevnt, usagt.

untoward [ʌn'təuəd] *adj* ubeleilig, uheldig.

unused [ʌn'ju:st] *adj:* ~ *to* uvant med. **unusual** [ʌn'ju:ʒʊəl] *adj* uvanlig.

unveil [ʌn'veɪl] *vt* av|dekke, -duke, -sløre.

unwieldy [ʌn'wi:ldɪ] *adj* uhåndterlig.

unwilling [ʌn'wɪlɪŋ] *adj* uvillig; motvillig.

unwind [ʌn'waɪnd] *vb* **1** nøste (spole, vikle etc) opp; **2** spenne av (en fjær); *fig* slappe av.

unwrap [ʌn'ræp] *vb* pakke opp.

unzip [ʌn'zɪp] *vt* åpne glidelås.

up [ʌp] **I** *adj* opp-; opp(ad)gående, stigende; **II** *adv* opp (og oppe; oppover; opp (bort, frem etc) til etc); inn (til London etc, jf ~ *train*); *også* for retten; *fig* på tapetet; i gang/gjære; på ferde; forbi, over, slutt; ~ *and about/around* oppe/på beina (etter sykdom etc); *blow* ~ eksplodere; *dgl* fly/gå i luften; *hard* ~ vanskelig stilt; *hurry* ~ skynde seg; *lock* ~ låse; sperre inne; *pack* ~ pakke (sammen); *stand* ~ reise seg; stå (opp); *the game is* ~ spillet er ute; slaget er tapt; *time is* ~ tiden er ute; *også* (det er) stengetid; *what's* ~ hva er på ferde; **2** ~ **against** ansikt til ansikt med; overfor; ute for; *be* ~ **before** være (oppe) til behandling *etc* hos/i; ~ **for** *election* på valg; ~ **from** *the ground* fra bunnen/grunnen av; ~ **in** *arms* under våpen; *fig* i harnisk (*against* mot); ~ **to** bort/frem *etc* til; (inn)til; *be ~ to* holde på med; føle seg/være i stand til; *it's ~ to you* det avhenger av/står til deg; ~ **with** *dgl* på høyde med (dvs like god etc som); **III** *prep* opp (og især oppover; opp langs etc).

up-and-coming *adj* kommende, lovende (dvs med gode fremtidsutsikter).

upbraid [ʌp'breɪd] *vt* bebreide, irettesette; skjenne på.

upbringing ['ʌpbrɪŋɪŋ] *sb* opp|dragelse, -fostring.

update [ʌp'deɪt] *vt* oppdatere; bringe/føre à jour.

upgrade 1 ['ʌpgreɪd] **1** *sb: on the ~* i fremgang; på fremmarsj; **2** [ʌp'greid] *vt* oppgradere; forfremme.

upheaval [ʌp'hi:vl] *sb* omveltning.

uphill [ʌp'hɪl] **1** *adj* vanskelig; hard, strid, tung; **2** *adv* oppfor/oppover (en bakke).

uphold [ʌp'həuld] *vt* holde oppe; *især fig* opprettholde, støtte.

upholster [ʌp'həulstə] *vt* polstre, stoppe

upkeep ['ʌpki:p] *sb* vedlikehold (og vedlikeholdsutgifter); underhold.

upland ['ʌplənd] *sb* høyland.

uplift 1 ['ʌplɪft] *sb* opp|byggelse, -løftelse; oppmuntring; **2** [ʌp'lɪft] *vt* heve, høyne; løfte.

upon [ə'pɒn] *prep* = *on* (stundom for å understreke betydningen ytterligere, eller i mer formelle sammenhenger).

upper ['ʌpə] *adj* øvre, øverst(-); over-; *get/have the ~ hand* få/ha overtaket. **upper | case** *sb koll* majuskler; store bokstaver. ~ **class** *sb* overklasse. **~most** ['ʌpəməust] *adj, adv* øverst(-).

upright A ['ʌpraɪt] *adj* rettskaffen; redelig, ærlig; **B 1** [ʌp'raɪt] *adj* opprettstående; rank, rett; **2** ['ʌpraɪt] *sb* stander, stang, stolpe; *dgl også (~ piano)* piano (i motsetning til flygel).

uprising [ʌp'raɪzɪŋ] *sb* opprør, oppstand.

uproar ['ʌprɔ:] *sb* bråk, leven, spetakkel. **uproarious** [ʌp'rɔ:rɪəs] *adj* stormende, voldsom; støyende.

uproot [ʌp'ru:t] *vt* rykke opp med rot.

upset I ['ʌpset] *sb* velt (og velting etc); forstyrrelse; **II** [ʌp'set] *vb* **1** velte; *fig* kullkaste; **2** forstyrre, uroe; opprive, ryste. **upsetting** [ʌp'setɪŋ] *adj* foruroligende; opprivende.

upshot ['ʌpʃɒt] *sb* resultat, utfall; slutt (og sluttsum).

upside ['ʌpsaɪd] *sb* overside. **upside-down** [ˌʌpsaɪd'daun] *adv* opp ned; på hodet.

upstairs [ʌp'steəz] *adj, adv* ovenpå; i etasjen over.

upstanding [ʌp'stændɪŋ] *adj* **1** rank, sterk; **2** hederlig, rettskaffen.

upstart ['ʌpstɑ:t] *sb* oppkomling.

upsurge ['ʌpsɜ:dʒ] *sb* oppstand, reisning; *også* bølge.

uptight [ʌp'taɪt] *adj slang* anspent, nervøs.

uptown *adv, især US* i utkanten av/oppe i byen (i motsetning til i sentrum); ut fra sentrum.

up train *sb* ankommende/inngående tog (især om tog fra forstedene/provinsen inn til London).

upturn ['ʌptɜ:n] *sb* **1** stigning; **2** oppsving.

upward ['ʌpwəd] *adj* oppover-, oppfor-; stigende.

upwards ['ʌpwədz] *adv* oppover; ~ *of* over (dvs mer enn).

urban ['ɜ:bən] *adj* bymessig, by-; urban(-). **urbane** [ɜ:'beɪn] *adj* beleven, høflig; dannet. **urban guerilla** *sb* bygerilja (og medlem av bygerilja).

urchin ['ɜ:tʃɪn] *sb* gategutt; skøyer(gutt).

urge [ɜ:dʒ] **I** *sb* (indre) drift/trang; tilskyndelse; **II** *vt* **1** drive (*onward* frem, videre etc); **2** anspore, tilskynde; **3** nøde; *ofte* mase/trenge (seg) inn på; ~ *upon* legge en sterkt på hjertet; understreke kraftig overfor.

urgency ['ɜ:dʒənsɪ] *sb* press *etc*; tvingende nødvendighet; *ofte* nøds|fall, -tilfelle; *matter of ~* hastesak.

urgent ['ɜ:dʒənt] *adj* presserende *etc*; inntrengende; ivrig; påtrengende; *Urgent!* Haster!

urinate ['juərɪneɪt] *vi* urinere. **urine** ['juərɪn] *sb* urin.

urn [ɜ:n] *sb* **1** urne; **2** kaffe|maskin, -trakter; **3** samovar, temaskin.

usage ['ju:zɪdʒ] *sb* **1** behandling, håndtering; **2** (sed)vane, skikk; bruk; *ofte* språkbruk, usus. **use I** [ju:s] *sb* **1** anvendelse; bruk (og bruksområde); *ofte* formål, nytte; *come into ~* komme/bli tatt i bruk; *fall/get out of ~* gå av bruk; *is this of any ~ to you* har du bruk for denne/dette; *it's of no ~ (fig)* det har ingen hensikt/tjener ikke til noe; det nytter ikke; *what's the ~* hva skal det tjene til; *dgl* hva er vitsen med det; **2** bruksrett; *have the ~ of* ha adgang til; **3** bruk; (sed)vane, skikk; **II** [ju:z] *vb* **1** anvende, bruke, nytte; **2** behandle, håndtere; **3** bruke (dvs pleie, ha for vane); *get ~d to* bli vant til; venne seg til. **use|ful** ['ju:sful] *adj* brukbar, tjenlig; nyttig. **~less** ['ju:slɪs] *adj* ubrukelig; unyttig; nytteløs. **user** ['ju:zə] *sb* bruker. **user|-friendly** *adj* brukervennlig. ~ **guide** *sb* brukerveiledning. ~ **interface** *sb data* brukersnitt. ~ **manual** *sb* brukerhåndbok.

usher ['ʌʃə] **I** *sb* **1** dør|vakt, -vokter; *på kino/teater* kontrollør, plassanviser; **2** rettstjener; **3** seremonimester; **II** *vt* melde; ~ *in* føre/vise inn; *fig* inn|lede, -varsle. **usherette** [ˌʌʃə'ret] *sb* plassanviserske (på kino, teater etc).

usual ['ju:ʒuəl] *adj* alminnelig; (sed)vanlig. **usually** ['ju:ʒuəlɪ] *adv* vanligvis; i alminnelighet.

usurer ['ju:ʒərə] *sb* ågerkar.

usurp [ju:'zɜ:p] *vt* rane/rive til seg; usurpere. **usurper** [ju:'zɜ:pə] *sb* (makt)raner, usurpator. **usurpation** [ˌju:zɜ:'peɪʃn] *sb* (makt)ran, usurpering; usurpasjon.

usury ['ju:ʒərɪ] *sb* åger (og ågerrente); ublu/ulovlig rente.

utensil [ju:'tensl] *sb* (kjøkken)redskap.

utilitarian [ˌju:tɪlɪ'teərɪən] **1** *adj* nytte-; bruks-; **2** *sb* utilitarianer. **utility** [ju:'tɪlətɪ] *sb* **1** nytte (og nyttegjenstand); **2** offentlig bekvemmelighet/gode; *især* offentlig toalett; **3** *data* hjelpeprogram. **utility |**

equipment *sb petro* hjelpeutstyr. ~ **function** *sb data* hjelpefunksjon. ~ **routine** *sb data* hjelperutine. **utilization** [ˌju:tɪlaɪ'zeɪʃn] *sb* utnyttelse *etc.* **utilize** ['ju:tɪlaɪz] *vt* utnytte; anvende, ta i bruk; nyttiggjøre seg.

utmost ['ʌtməʊst] **1** *adj* ytterst (dvs mest, høyest, størst etc); **2** *sb* det/ens ytterste.

utter ['ʌtə] **A** *adj* fullstendig, total; absolutt, ubetinget; **B** *vt* ytre; si, uttale. **utterance** ['ʌtərəns] *sb* ytring *etc.* **utterly** ['ʌtəlɪ] *adv* fullstendig, totalt.

uvula ['ju:vjʊlə] *sb* drøpel. **uvular** ['ju:vjʊlə] *adj* drøpel-; skarrende, skarre-.

V

vac [væk] *sb dgl* = *vacation.* **vacancy** ['veɪkənsɪ] *sb* **1** tomhet; tomrom; *fig* tanketomhet; **2** ledighet; ledig stilling. **vacant** ['veɪkənt] *adj* **1** tom (også *fig*); **2** ledig, ubesatt; ubebodd. **vacate** [və'keɪt] *vt* **1** oppgi; gi fra seg; flytte fra; *også* rømme (fra); **2** *gml* annullere. **vacation** [və'keɪʃn] *sb* **1** rettsferie; universitetsferie; **2** *US* ferie.

vaccinate ['væksɪneɪt] *vt* vaksinere. **vaccination** [ˌvæksɪ'neɪʃn] *sb* vaksinering; vaksinasjon. **vaccine** ['væksi:n] *sb* vaksine.

vacillate ['væsɪleɪt] *vi* vakle; *især fig* nøle; være ustadig/vankelmodig. **vacillation** [ˌvæsɪ'leɪʃn] *sb* vakling *etc.*

vacuum ['vækjʊəm] *sb* vakuum; *dgl* tomrom. **vacuum | cleaner** *sb* støvsuger. ~ **flask** *sb* termosflaske.

vagabond ['vægəbɒnd] **1** *adj* om|flakkende, -streifende; landstryker-; **2** *sb* landstryker, omstreifer. **vagary** ['veɪgərɪ] *sb* innfall; lune, grille. **vagrancy** ['veɪgrənsɪ] *sb* landstrykerliv; *jur* løsgjengeri. **vagrant** ['veɪgrənt] **1** *adj* = *vagabond 1*; **2** *sb* landstryker, omstreifer; *jur* løsgjenger.

vague [veɪg] *adj* uklar, utydelig; vag; ubestemt; svevende.

vain [veɪn] *adj* **1** forgjeves; nytteløs; *in* ~ forgjeves, fåfengt; **2** innbilsk. **vainglorious** [veɪn'glɔ:rɪəs] *adj* forfengelig; pralende.

vale [veɪl] *sb bokl, poet* = *valley.*

valentine ['væləntaɪn] *sb* **1** valentinkort (som en sender til den en helst vil ha som kjæreste på valentinsdagen, 14. februar); **2** kjæreste (på valentinsdagen).

valet ['vælɪt] **1** *sb* (kammer)tjener; **2** *vt* være (kammer)tjener for/hos.

valiant ['vælɪənt] *adj* tapper.

valid ['vælɪd] *adj* **1** effektiv; *især jur* (retts)|gyldig, -kraftig; **2** holdbar; (vel)begrunnet. **validate** ['vælɪdeɪt] *vt* godkjenne; gi gyldighet; *data også* validere. **validation test** [ˌvælɪ'deɪʃn] *sb data* gyldighetsprøve. **validity** [və'lɪdətɪ] *sb* gyldighet *etc.* **validity check** *sb data* validitetskontroll.

valise [və'li:z] *sb* koffert; reiseveske, vadsekk.

valley ['vælɪ] *sb* dal.

valorous ['vælərəs] *adj* tapper. **valour** ['vælə] *sb* tapperhet.

valuable ['væljʊəbl] **1** *adj* verdifull; **2** *sb fl* verdisaker. **valuation** [ˌvæljʊ'eɪʃn] *sb* **1** taksering *etc*; **2** takst(pris); verdi. **valuator** ['væljʊeɪtə] *sb data* verdisetter. **value** ['væljʊ] **I** *sb* verdi; *merk, fig* valuta *mus etc* valør; *fig også* betydning, nytte; *face* ~ pålydende; **II** *vt* **1** taksere, verdsette, vurdere **2** skatte; sette (stor) pris på. **valuer** ['væljʊə] *sb* takst|kvinne, -mann.

valve [vælv] *sb* **1** ventil; klaff (og *anat* klapp); spjeld; **2** (radio)rør.

vampire ['væmpaɪə] *sb* vampyr.

van [væn] **A** *sb* **1** vare|bil, -vogn; **2** (innelukket) godsvogn; **B** *sb* front/spiss (især av flåte, hæravdeling etc). **vanguard** ['væŋgɑ:d] *sb* fortropp; *også fig* avantgarde.

vandal ['vændl] *sb* vandal. **vandalism** ['vændəlɪzəm] *sb* vandalisme.

vanilla [və'nɪlə] *sb* vanilje.

vanish ['vænɪʃ] *vi* forsvinne.

vanity ['vænətɪ] *sb* **1** forfengelighet; **2** tomhet.

vanquish ['væŋkwɪʃ] *vt* beseire, overvinne.

vapid ['væpɪd] *adj* doven (om øl etc); emmen, flau; smakløs.

vaporize ['veɪpəraɪz] *vb* fordampe. **vapour** ['veɪpə] *sb* **1** damp; **2** dunst (og utdunstning).

variable ['veərɪəbl] **I** *adj* **1** foranderlig, skiftende, variabel; **2** ustadig; **II** *sb* variabel; *data* programvariabel. **variance** ['veərɪəns] *sb* **1** forandring; **2** uenighet, splid; strid; *at* ~ *with* i splid/strid med. **variant** ['veərɪənt] **1** *adj* forskjellig; avvikende; *ofte* alternativ; **2** *sb* variant. **variation** [ˌveərɪ'eɪʃn] *sb* **1** avvik(else), forskjell; **2** (av)veksling, forandring; variasjon. **varicoloured** ['veərɪkʌləd] *adj* broket, mangefarget. **varicose veins** [ˌværɪkəʊs'veɪnz] *sb fl* åreknuter. **varied** ['veərɪd] *adj* forskjelligartet; mangfoldig; variert. **variegated** ['veərɪgeɪtɪd] *adj* broket, mangefarget. **variegation** [ˌveərɪ'geɪʃn] *sb* brokethet. **variety** [və'raɪətɪ] *sb* **1** (av)veksling, forskjellig(artet)het; forandring, variasjon; **2** mangfoldighet;

variert utvalg; **3** variant, varietet; avart; **4** *(~ show/ theatre)* varietē (og varieté|forestilling, -teater etc).
various ['veərɪəs] *adj* **1** forskjellig(artet); skiftende; **2** flere (forskjellige); *dgl* diverse; *for ~ reasons* av forskjellige grunner.

varnish ['vɑ:nɪʃ] **1** *sb* ferniss, politur; *fig* ytre glans; **2** *vt* fernissere, polere.

varsity ['vɑ:sətɪ] *sb dgl* universitet.

vary ['veərɪ] *vb* **1** forandre (seg); variere; **2** avvike (fra det normale); skifte, veksle.

vase [vɑ:z] *sb* vase.

vat [væt] *sb* kar; fat, tønne.

vast [vɑ:st] *adj* enorm; (uhyre) stor; veldig.

vault [vɔ:lt] **A** *sb* **1** velving; **2** kjeller, (kjeller)velv; **B 1** *sb* hopp, sprang; **2** *vb* hoppe (og især hoppe, springe, svinge seg etc opp/over med støtte av hendene etc); *pole-vaulter* stavhopper. **vaulting-horse** *sb* hest (som turnapparat).

veal [vi:l] *sb* kalvekjøtt.

veer ['vɪə] *vi* skifte/springe om (dvs skifte retning, især om vind).

vegetable ['vedʒɪtəbl] **1** *adj* vegetabilsk, plante-; **2** *sb fl* grønnsaker. **vegetarian** [ˌvedʒɪ'teərɪən] **1** *adj* vegetarisk, vegetar-; **2** *sb* vegetarianer. **vegetate** ['vedʒɪteɪt] *vi* vegetere. **vegetation** [ˌvedʒɪ'teɪʃn] *sb* vegetasjon.

vehemence ['vi:əməns] *sb* voldsomhet *etc*. **vehement** ['vi:əmənt] *adj* voldsom; heftig, lidenskapelig.

vehicle ['vi:ɪkl *sb* kjøretøy; **2** middel, redskap.

veil [veɪl] **1** *sb* slør; *fig også* slørethet; **2** *vt* (til)sløre; tilhylle; skjule.

vein [veɪn] *sb* **1** blodåre, vene; **2** nerve (i blad etc); **3** (malm)|gang, (-)åre; stripe; **4** *fig* humør, sinnstilstand; stemning; **5** *fig* tendens.

velocity [vɪ'lɒsətɪ] *sb* fart, hastighet.

velvet ['velvɪt] *sb* fløyel. **velvety** ['velvɪtɪ] *adj* fløyels|aktig, -myk.

venal ['vi:nl] *adj* bestikkelig, korrumpert; korrupt.

vendor ['vendɔ:] *sb* selger.

veneer [vɪ'nɪə] **I** *sb* **1** finér; **2** *fig* ferniss, tynt lag; **II** *vt* finere.

venerable ['venərəbl] *adj* ærverdig. **venerate** ['venəreɪt] *vt* ære; (høy)akte. **veneration** [ˌvenə'reɪʃn] *sb* aktelse, ærbødighet.

venereal [vɪ'nɪərɪəl] *adj* venerisk. **venereal disease** *sb* kjønnssykdom.

Venetian blind [vɪ'ni:ʃən 'blaɪnd] *sb* persienne.

vengeance ['vendʒəns] *sb* hevn; *with a ~* så det forslår/monner. **vengeful** ['vendʒful] *adj* hevngjerrig.

venison ['venzn] *sb* vilt; *især* dyrekjøtt.

venom ['venəm] *sb* **1** (slange)gift; **2** *fig* giftighet (dvs hatefullhet, ondskap etc). **venomous** ['venəməs] *adj* giftig (især *fig*).

vent [vent] **I** *sb* **1** luftehull, trekkhull **2** avløp, utløp; **3** *fig* utløp; *give ~ to* gi (fritt) utløp for; **II** *vt* lufte; gi luft/utløp for. **ventilate** ['ventɪleɪt] *vt* ventilere; *også fig* lufte (dvs bringe på bane etc). **ventilation** [ˌventɪ'leɪʃn] *sb* ventilering; ventilasjon. **ventilator** ['ventɪleɪtə] *sb* ventilator, vifte.

ventriloquist [ven'trɪləkwɪst] *sb* buktaler.

venture ['ventʃə] **I** *sb* **1** risiko, vågestykke; *at a ~* på lykke og fromme; **2** (sjansepreget) foretagende; spekulasjon; **II** *vb* **1** risikere; ta sjansen (på); **2** våge; driste seg til; **3** komme med/legge frem (forslag etc). **venturesome** ['ventʃəsəm] *adj* dristig, vågsom.

veracious [və'reɪʃəs] *adj* sannferdig. **veracity** [və'ræsətɪ] *sb* sannferdighet.

verb [vɜ:b] *sb* verb(um). **verbal** ['vɜ:bl] *adj* **1** muntlig; ord; **2** ordrett; **3** verbal(-). **verbalize** ['vɜ:bəlaɪz] *vt* verbalisere; uttrykke i ord. **verbatim** [vɜ:'beɪtɪm] *adj, adv* ordrett. **verbose** [vɜ:'bəus] *adj* ordrik. **verbosity** [vɜ:'bɒsətɪ] *sb* ordrikhet.

verdict ['vɜ:dɪkt] *sb* **1** (jury)kjennelse; **2** avgjørelse, dom.

verge [vɜ:dʒ] **A** *sb* (embets)stav; **B 1** *sb* kant, rand; *on the ~ of (fig)* på randen av/nippet til; **2** *vi* helle, skråne; dale, synke; *~ upon (fig)* gå mot; nærme seg. **verger** ['vɜ:dʒə] *sb* **1** kirketjener; **2** marskalk.

verifiable ['verɪfaɪəbl] *adj* beviselig, kontrollerbar; verifiserbar. **verification** [ˌverɪfɪ'keɪʃn] *sb* bekreftelse *etc*; verifisering; verifikasjon. **verifier** ['verɪfaɪə] *sb data* kontrollenhet. **verify** ['verɪfaɪ] *vt* **1** bekrefte; bevise, (under)støtte; verifisere; **2** (etter)prøve; forvisse seg om; *be verified (også)* gå i oppfyllelse. **verily** ['verɪlɪ] *adv gml* sannelig. **verisimilitude** [ˌverɪsɪ'mɪlɪtju:d] *sb* sannsynlighet. **veritable** ['verɪtəbl] *adj* virkelig; riktig, sann; veritabel. **verity** ['verətɪ] *sb* sannhet.

vermin ['vɜ:mɪn] *sb* skadedyr, utøy.

versatile ['vɜ:sətaɪl] *adj* allsidsig, mangesidig. **versatility** [ˌvɜ:sə'tɪlətɪ] *sb* allsidighet

verse [vɜ:s] *sb* **1** vers; *også* dikt, poesi; **2** *a)* verselinje; *b)* strofe.

versed [vɜ:st] *adj: ~ in* (vel) bevandret i.

version ['vɜ:ʃn] *sb* utgave, versjon.

versus ['vɜ:səs] *prep* mot.

vertebrate ['vɜ:tɪbreɪt] **1** *adj* virvel; **2** *sb* virveldyr.

vertical ['vɜ:tɪkl] **1** *adj* loddrett, vertikal; **2** *sb* loddrett linje; vertikal. **vertical step** *sb data* høydesteg.

very ['verɪ] **I** *adj* **1** (selv)samme; *this ~ day* den dag i dag; **2** ekte; sann, virkelig; **II** *adv* **1** meget, svært; *~ well* meget bra; *som svar* javel; (det) skal bli; **2** *my ~ best friend* min aller beste venn.

vespers ['vespəz] *sb fl* aftensang, vesper.

vessel ['vesl] *sb* **1** beholder, kar; **2** far|kost, -tøy; skip; **3** kanal, rør; (blod)|kar, -åre.

vest [vest] **A** *sb* **1** (under)trøye; **2** *US* vest; **B** *vt: ~ with* forlene med; overdra til. **vested interests** *sb fl* eierinteresse(r); kapitalinteresse(r).

vestige ['vestɪdʒ] *sb* spor (også *fig*).

vestment ['vestmənt] *sb* drakt, kledning; *især, oftest fl* messe|drakt, klær; ornat.

vestry ['vestrɪ] *sb* **1** sakristi; **2** bønnerom; menighetssal.

vet [vet] *dgl fork* for *veterinary 2.*

veteran ['vetərən] *sb* veteran.

veterinary ['vetrɪnərɪ] **1** *adj* veterinær-; **2** *sb (~ surgeon)* dyrlege, veterinær.

veto ['vi:təʊ] **1** *sb* veto (og vetorett); **2** *vt* nedlegge veto mot.

vex [veks] *vt* ergre, irritere; plage. **vexation** [vek'seɪʃn] *sb* **1** ergrelse *etc*; **2** sjikane(ring). **vexatious** [vek'seɪʃəs] *adj* plagsom, sjikanøs. **vexed** [vekst] *adj* lei, plagsom; *jur etc også* omstridt.

viable ['vaɪəbl] *adj* gjennomførlig, mulig; levedyktig.

viaduct ['vaɪədʌkt] *sb* viadukt, bro.

vibes [vaɪbz] *sb fl dgl = vibration 2.* **vibrate** [vaɪ'breɪt] *vi* **1** vibrere, svinge; **2** dirre, riste; skjelve. **vibration** [vaɪ'breɪʃn] *sb* **1** vibrering *etc* vibrasjon; **2** *fl dgl* vibrasjoner (dvs atmosfære, miljø, ånd etc).

vicar ['vɪkə] *sb* (sogne)prest. **vicarage** ['vɪkərɪdʒ] *sb* **1** prestegård; **2** prestekall. **vicarious** [vɪ'keərɪəs] *adj* stedfortredende, vikarierende; som erstatter noe annet.

vice A [vaɪs] **A** *sb* last (og lastefullhet); **2** lyte, mangel (især ved hest); **B 1** *sb* skrustikke; filklo; **2** *vt* holde (som) i en skrustikke etc; **C** *pref* vise- (dvs stedfortredende, vikarierende etc); **II** ['vaɪsɪ] *prep* istedenfor. **vice|-president** [vaɪs-] *sb* visepresident. **~roy** [vaɪs-] *sb* visekonge. **~ versa** [ˌvaɪsɪ'vɜ:sə] *adv* omvendt; vice versa.

vicinity [vɪ'sɪnətɪ] *sb* nabolag, nærhet.

vicious ['vɪʃəs] *adj* **1** ond(sinnet), ondskapsfull; **2** lastefull; dårlig, slett.

victim ['vɪktɪm] *sb* offer; *fall a ~ to* falle som offer for. **victimize** ['vɪktɪmaɪz] *vt* ofre; gjøre til offer; *dgl især* la unngjelde; la det gå ut over.

victor ['vɪktə] *sb* seierherre. **victorious** [vɪk'tɔ:rɪəs] *adj* seierrik, seirende; seiers-. **victory** ['vɪktərɪ] *sb* seier.

view [vju:] **I** *sb* **1** syn (og over|syn; -blikk, -sikt etc); besiktigelse; *come into ~* komme til syne; bli synlig; vise seg; **2** utsikt, utsyn (også *fig*); **3** plan, tanke; hensikt; *with a ~ to* med tanke på; **4** mening; anskuelse, betraktning; *in ~ of* i betraktning av; **II** *vt* **1** se på; besiktige; ta i øyesyn; **2** betrakte (dvs ta i betraktning; undersøke, vurdere etc). **viewer** ['vjuə] *sb* seer (og især fjernsynsseer). **view|data** *sb data* teledata. **~-finder** *sb* (kamera)søker. **~point** *sb* synspunkt.

vigil ['vɪdʒɪl] *sb* natte|vakt, -våking. **vigilance** ['vɪdʒɪləns] *sb* vaktsomhet, årvåkenhet. **vigilance committee** *sb* ≈ borgervern(gruppe). **vigilant** ['vɪdʒɪlənt] *adj* vaktsom, årvåken. **vigilante** [ˌvɪdʒɪ'læntɪ] *sb* ≈ medlem av borgervern(gruppe).

vigorous ['vɪgərəs] *adj* energisk, kraftig. **vigour** ['vɪgə] *sb* energi, kraft, styrke.

viking ['vaɪkɪŋ] *sb* viking.

vile [vaɪl] *adj* **1** skammelig, skjendig; sjofel; **2** *dgl* dårlig, elendig. **vilify** ['vɪlɪfaɪ] *vt* bakvaske; rakke ned på.

village ['vɪlɪdʒ] *sb* landsby; *ofte* småby; stasjonsby; tettsted. **villager** ['vɪlɪdʒə] *sb* landsbyboer *etc.*

villain ['vɪlən] *sb* skurk (især i roman etc); kjeltring. **villainous** ['vɪlənəs] *adj* skurkaktig. **villainy** ['vɪlənɪ] *sb* skurkaktighet; skurkestreker.

vindicate ['vɪndɪkeɪt] *vt* rettferdiggjøre, forsvare. **vindication** [ˌvɪndɪ'keɪʃn] *sb* rettferdiggjøring *etc.* **vindictive** [vɪn'dɪktɪv] *adj* hevngjerrig.

vine [vaɪn] *sb* vin|ranke, -stokk. **vinegar** ['vɪnɪgə] *sb* eddik. **vinery** ['vaɪnərɪ] *sb* **1** vinhus; **2** drivhus for drueodling. **vineyard** ['vɪnjəd] *sb* vin|gård, -mark, -slott.

vintage ['vɪntɪdʒ] *sb* **1** vin|høst, -årgang; *som adj* årgangs-; av edel/utsøkt årgang; *om biler* veteran- (dvs fra tiden 1916–1930).

violate ['vaɪəleɪt] *vt* **1** bryte, overtre; krenke; **2** voldta; øve vold mot; **3** profanere, vanhellige. **violation** [ˌvaɪə'leɪʃn] *sb* **1** brudd, overtredelse *etc*; **2** voldtekt. **violence** ['vaɪələns] *sb* **1** vold (og voldsomhet etc); *(act of ~)* voldshandling; *do ~ to* øve vold mot; **2** (gate)opptøyer; **3** voldtekt. **violent** ['vaɪələnt] *adj* **1** voldsom; voldelig; **2** *dgl* intens, kraftig.

violet ['vaɪələt] **I** *adj* **1** fiolblå; **2** fiolett; **II** *sb* **1** fiol (og fiolblått); **2** fiolett.

violin [ˌvaɪə'li:n] *sb* fiolin. **violinist** ['vaɪəlɪnɪst] *sb* fiolinist.

viper ['vaɪpə] *sb* huggorm; (gift)slange.

virgin ['vɜ:dʒɪn] **I** *adj* **1** jomfruelig, jomfru; **2** *a)* ren, uberørt; *b)* ubrukt; *petro etc* ubehandlet; **II** *sb* jomfru. **virginal** ['vɜ:dʒɪnl] *adj* jomfruelig, jomfru-. **virginity** [və'dʒɪnətɪ] *sb* jomfrudom; jomfruelighet.

virile ['vɪraɪl] *adj* viril; mandig, maskulin. **virility** [vɪ'rɪlətɪ] *sb* virilitet *etc.*

virtual ['vɜ:tʃʊəl] *adj* faktisk, virkelig. **virtue** ['vɜ:tʃu] *sb* **1** dyd (i motsetning til last); *patience is a ~* tålmodighet er en dyd; **2** dyd (i kjønnslig sammenheng); *of easy ~* lett på tråden; **3** effekt, evne, kraft; *by/in ~ of* i kraft av; **4** fordel, fortrinn. **virtuous** ['vɜ:tʃʊəs] *adj* **1** (moralsk) rett(sindig)/riktig; **2** dydig.

virus ['vaɪərəs] *sb* virus.

visa ['vi:zə] **1** *vt* visere; **2** *sb* visum.

viscosity [vɪ'skɒsətɪ] *sb* viskositet.

visibility [ˌvɪzɪ'bɪlətɪ] *sb* sikt(barhet). **visible** ['vɪzəbl] *adj* **1** synbar, synlig; **2** åpenbar; klar, tydelig. **vision** ['vɪʒn] *sb* **1** syn (dvs syns|evne, -sans); **2** *(range of ~)* syns|felt, -vidde; **3** (ånde)syn, åpenbaring; visjon; **4** (indre) syn; forutseenhet. **visionary** ['vɪʒnərɪ] *adj* synsk/visjonær (person).

visit ['vɪzɪt] **I** *sb* besøk, visitt; *pay a ~* besøke/avlegge et besøk; **II** *vb* **1** besøke; avlegge besøk/visitt (hos); **2** inspisere, visitere; **3** *rel* hjemsøke, plage. **visitation** [ˌvɪzɪ'teɪʃn] *sb* hjemsøkelse, plage. **visitor** ['vɪzɪtə] *sb* besøkende; *have ~s* ha fremmede/gjester; *you have a ~* det er besøk til deg. **visor** ['vaɪzə] *sb* (lue)skygge. **visual** ['vɪʒuəl] *adj* **1** syns-; visuell; **2** synlig. **visual display unit** *sb data* (data)-

skjerm. **visualize** ['vɪʒuəlaɪz] *vt* gjøre synlig/*især fig* anskuelig; *dgl* se for seg; *merk etc også* visualisere. **visual aids** *sb* visuelle hjelpemidler. **visualizing** ['vɪʒuälaɪzɪŋ] *sb* synliggjøring; visualisering.

vital ['vaɪtl] *adj* **1** livs|nødvendig, -viktig; **2** livskraftig, vital. **vitality** [vaɪ'tælətɪ] *sb* livskraft, vitalitet. **vital statistics** *sb fl* vitale mål (dvs målene rundt især kvinnes bryst, liv og hofter).

vivacious [vɪ'veɪʃəs] *adj* livlig. **vivacity** [vɪ'væsətɪ] *sb* livlighet.

vocabulary [və'kæbjulərɪ] *sb* **1** ordforråd, vokabular; **2** glossar, ordliste. **vocabulary program** *sb data* ordboksprogram. **vocal** ['vəukl] *adj* stemme-.

vocation [vəu'keɪʃn] *sb* **1** kall; **2** begavelse, evne; legning.

voice [vɔɪs] **I** *sb* **1** stemme; **2** stemme (dvs rett til å uttale seg etc); *have no ~ in* ikke ha noe å si (dvs ikke være meningsberettiget) om; **II** *vt* **1** sette stemme til; **2** gi uttrykk for. **voiced** [vɔɪst] *adj* stemt. **voiceless** ['vɔɪslɪs] *adj* stemmeløs, ustemt. **voice | recognition** *sb data* stemmegjenkjenning. **~ synthesis** *sb data* talesyntese.

void [vɔɪd] **I** *adj* **1** tom; *~ of* blottet for; **2** *jur (null and ~)* maktesløs, ugyldig; **II** *sb* tomrom; **III** *vt jur* erklære maktesløs/ugyldig.

volatile ['vɒlətaɪl] *adj* flyktig.

volcanic [vɒl'kænɪk] *adj* vulkansk. **volcano** [vɒl'keɪnəu] *sb* vulkan.

voluble ['vɒljubl] *adj* munnrapp; ordrik; *også* omstendelig.

volume ['vɒlju:m] *sb* **1** volum; *dgl også* størrelse; *fig* omfang; **2** bok(bind); enkelt|bind, -bok. **voluminous** [və'lu:mɪnəs] *adj* voluminøs; *dgl* omfangsrik, svær; *om bokserie* bindsterk.

voluntary ['vɒləntərɪ] *adj, sb* frivillig (soldat etc). **volunteer** [ˌvɒlən'tɪə] *sb* frivillig (især om soldater og andre som melder seg til farefulle oppdrag); **II** *vb* **1** melde seg (som) frivillig; tilby (seg); **2** si/ytre uoppfordret; komme med (bemerkning etc).

voluptuous [və'lʌptʃuəs] *adj* **1** yppig; **2** vellystig.

vomit ['vɒmɪt] **1** *sb* oppkast **2** *vb* kaste opp; *dgl, fig* spy ut.

voracious [və'reɪʃəs] *adj* glupsk, grådig; forsluken.

vortex ['vɔ:teks] *sb* virvel (og virvel|strøm, -vind); *også fig* malstrøm.

vote [vəut] **I** *sb* **1** stemme (og stemme|rett, -seddel); votum; *~ of confidence* tillitsvotum; **2** avstemning, valg; *put to ~* sette under avstemning; **3** valgdeltaker; **II** *vb* **1** stemme (*against* mot; *for* for/på); votere; *~ down* nedvotere; stemme ned; avvise, forkaste; *~ in* stemme/velge inn; **2** vedta; **3** *dgl* erklære for; **4** bevilge.

vouch [vautʃ] *vi* be|krefte, -vitne; *~ for* garantere (gå god, stå inne etc) for. **vouchsafe** [vautʃ'seɪf] *vt* nedlate seg (til å gi, yte etc); *også* unne.

vow [vau] **1** *sb* (høytidelig) løfte; *take the ~* avlegge klosterløfte; *dgl* gå i kloster; **2** *vt* love (høytidelig); *dgl* sverge på.

vowel ['vauəl] *sb* vokal.

voyage ['vɔɪɪdʒ] **1** *sb* (sjø)reise; **2** *vi* reise (med skip). **voyager** ['vɔɪədʒə] *sb* sjøfarer.

vulgar ['vʌlgə] *adj* **1** simpel, udannet, vulgær; **2** smakløs; gloret. **vulgar fraction** *sb* alminnelig brøk (i motsetning til desimalbrøk). **vulgarity** [vʌl'gærətɪ] *sb* **1** vulgaritet *etc*; **2** vulgarisme.

vulnerable ['vʌlnərəbl] *adj* sårbar.

vulture ['vʌltʃə] *sb* gribb.

W

wabble ['wɒbl] = *wobble*.

wad [wɒd] **I** *sb* **1** stopp (som fôring, isolasjon, mellomlegg etc); **2** (seddel)|bunke, -bunt; **II** *vt* **1** stoppe, vattere; fôre ut; **2** bunte sammen. **wadding** ['vɒdɪŋ] *sb* stopp *etc*.

waddle ['wɒdl] **1** *sb* vralting; **2** *vi* vralte.

wade [weɪd] *vb* vade; *~ through (fig)* pløye/slite seg igjennom. **wader** ['weɪdə] *sb* **1** vadefugl; **2** *fl* vadere (dvs lange gummistøvler). **wading bird** *sb* vadefugl.

wafer ['weɪfə] *sb* **1** (is)kjeks; **2** *rel* hostie, oblat. **wafer thin** *adj* løvtynn.

waffle ['wɒfl] **A** *sb* vaffel; **B** *dgl* **1** *sb* tøv, vrøvl; **2** *vi* røre, vrøvle.

waft [wɑ:ft] *vt* bære/føre (gjennom luften).

wag [wæg] **A 1** *sb* logring *etc*; **2** *vb* logre (med); *let one's tongue ~* fare med løst snakk; *dgl* la skravla gå; **B** *sb* skøyer, spøkefugl.

wage [weɪdʒ] **I** *sb, især fl* (arbeids)lønn, ukelønn; **II** *vt* **1** *~ war* føre krig; **2** = *wager 2*. **wage|-earner** *sb* lønnsmottaker. **~-freeze** *sb* lønnsstopp. **wager** ['weɪdʒə] **I** *sb* **1** veddemål; **2** innsats (i veddemål); **II** *vb* vedde; satse; risikere, våge.

waggish ['wægɪʃ] *adj* spøkefull, skøyeraktig.

waggle ['wægl] = *wag A*.

wag(g)on ['wægən] *sb* **1** vogn (især med fire hjul); **2** (åpen) godsvogn. **wag(g)oner** ['wægənə] *sb* kjørekar, vognmann.

waif [weɪf] *sb* **1** bortkommet/hjemløst barn; **2**

bortkommet/herreløst dyr; **3** hittegods.

wail [weɪl] **1** *sb* jammer *etc*; **2** *vb* jamre/klage (over).

waist [weɪst] *sb* liv, midje. **waist|coat** ['weɪskəut] *sb* vest. **~line** *sb* liv|linje; -vidde.

wait [weɪt] **I** *sb* **1** venting (og ventetid); **2** *in ~ (for)* på lur (etter); **II** *vb* **1** vente (*for* på); **2** utsette; vente med; **3** *~ at table* servere (ved bordet); *~ (up)on* varte opp. **waiter** ['weɪtə] *sb* servitør; *gml* kelner. **waiting | list** *sb* venteliste. **~ room** *sb* venteværelse. **waitress** ['weɪtrɪs] *sb* (kvinnelig) servitør; *gml* serveringsdame, servitrise.

waive ['weɪv] *vt* frafalle; avstå fra; gi avkall på. **waiver** ['weɪvə] *sb, især jur* (skriftlig) frafallelse/tilbakekallelse.

wake [weɪk] **A I** *sb poet* vake, våking; **II** *vb (~ up)* **1** vekke (opp); **2** våkne (opp); **B** *sb sjø* kjølvann. **wakeful** ['weɪkful] *adj* **1** våken, våke-; søvnløs; **2** (år)våken. **waken** ['weɪkən] *vb* = *wake A II.*

walk [wɔ:k] **I** *sb* **1** (spaser)tur; **2** spaservei; gang|sti, -vei; **3** gangart, gange; **4** *fig* (livs)|bane, -vei; opp|førsel, -treden; *~ of life* livsstilling; samfunns|-klasse, -lag; sosial posisjon etc; **II** *vb* **1** gå (på beina); spasere; **2** *med adv, prep* **~ away** gå sin vei; **~ away from** vinne overlegent over; **~ away with** *dgl* stikke av med; **~ into** *dgl* gjøre innhugg i; gå løs på; **~ off (with)** = *~ away (with)*; **~ on** gå videre; *også* = *~ over*; **~ out** gå ut; *dgl* streike; **~ out on** *dgl* svikte; late i stikken; **~ over** trampe/tråkke på. **walk-out** *sb dgl* streik.

wall [wɔ:l] **1** *sb* vegg; gjerde, mur; voll; *fig også* vern; *go to the ~* bli knekt/slått ut (især økonomisk); *go up the ~ (slang)* gå på veggen (av sinne etc); **2** *vt* omgi med mur/vegg *etc*; **~ in** gjerde inn; **~ off** avskjære; **~ up** mure igjen; mure/stenge inne.

wallaby ['wɒləbɪ] *sb* (slags liten) kenguru; *slang* australier.

wallcake ['wɔ:lkeɪk] *sb petro* slamkake, veggkake.

wallet ['wɒlɪt] *sb* **1** lommebok; **2** *gml* (niste)-skreppe.

wallflower ['wɔ:lflauə] *sb* **1** gyllenlakk; **2** *fig* veggpryd.

wallop ['wɒləp] *hum, slang* **I** *sb* **1** lusing; slag, smell; **2** øl; **II** *vt* slå (hardt); smelle til; denge.

wallow ['wɒləu] *vi: ~ in* rulle/velte seg i; *fig også* vasse i.

wallpaper ['wɔ:lpeɪpə] *sb* tapet.

walnut ['wɔ:lnʌt] *sb* valnøtt.

walrus ['wɔ:lrəs] *sb* hvalross.

waltz [wɔ:ls] *sb, vi* (danse) vals; vals(e).

wan [wɒn] *adj* blek, sykelig; matt.

wand [wɒnd] *sb* **1** taktstokk; **2** tryllestav.

wander ['wɒndə] *vi* **1** vandre; flakke (omkring); **2** *fig* komme bort (fra saken); *også* fantasere; snakke over seg. **wanderer** ['wɒndərə] *sb* vandrer. **wanderings** ['wɒndərɪŋz] *sb fl* vandringer; *fig* (feber)fantasier, villelser.

wane [weɪn] **I** *sb* minking *etc*; nedgang; *on the ~* i nedgang; på retur; avtagende; **II** *vi* **1** avta (især om månen); minke, bli mindre; **2** *fig* stilne; blekne; svinne; forta seg.

wangle ['wæŋgl] *vt dgl* fikse, ordne; skaffe (seg).

want [wɒnt] **I** *sb* **1** behov; *ofte* ønske; **2** knapphet, mangel; *be in ~ of* mangle, trenge; *for ~ of* av mangel på; **3** armod, fattigdom; **II** *vb* **1** mangle, savne; **2** trenge; ha behov for; *~ for nothing* ha alt en trenger; **3** ønske (seg); ville (ha). **wanted** ['wɒntɪd] *adj* **1** etterspurt; **2** ettersøkt (av politiet). **wanting** ['wɒntɪŋ] *prep* minus, uten.

wanton ['wɒntən] **I** *adj* **1** kåt, vilter; **2** overdådig, yppig; **3** formålsløs, meningsløs; *ofte* ondsinnet; **4** løsaktig, usedelig; **II** *sb* flokse, gatejente.

war [wɔ:] **1** *sb* krig; *declare ~ (on)* erklære krig (mot); **2** *vi* krige; føre krig; *fig også* stride(s). **war-baby** *sb* krigsbarn.

warble ['wɔ:bl] **1** (fugle)|sang, (-)triller; **2** *vi, om fugler* synge/slå triller. **warbler** ['wɔ:blə] *sb* sangfugl.

war-cry ['wɔ:kraɪ] *sb* krigsrop; hær|rop, -skrik.

ward [wɔ:d] **I** *sb* **1** vakt (og bevoktning, vakthold etc); **2** beskyttelse; *jur* formynderskap, vergemål; *også* myndling; **3** bydel, rode; distrikt; **4** avdeling (ved institusjon); sal/stue (på sykehus); *også* rom, værelse; **II** *vt* **1** vokte; våke over; beskytte, verge; **2** parere; *~ off* av|parere, -verge.

war-dance ['wɔ:dɑ:ns] *sb* krigsdans.

warden [wɔ:dn] *sb* vakt(mester), vokter; bestyrer (især ved herberge); forstander, oppsynsmann; *især US* fengselsdirektør; *church ~* kirkeverge. **warder** ['wɔ:də] *sb* slutter; (fange)vokter, fengselsbetjent. **wardress** ['wɔ:drɪs] *sb* kvinnelig slutter *etc*. **wardrobe** ['wɔ:drəub] *sb* garderobe (både om klær og klesskap etc). **wardroom** ['wɔ:dru:m] *sb sjø mil* offisersmesse.

ware ['weə] *sb* **1** *fl* varer; **2** *som suff* -tøy, -varer; *iron-~* isenkram, jernvarer. **warehouse 1** ['weəhaus] *sb* lager(bygning), pakkhus; **2** ['weəhauz] *vt* lagre (især møbler).

war|fare ['wɔ:feə] *sb* krig(føring]. **~-god** *sb* krigsgud. **~head** *sb* stridshode. **~like** *adj* **1** krigslignende; **2** krigersk. **~-lord** *sb* (øverste) krigsherre.

warm [wɔ:m] **1** *adj* varm; **2** *sb dgl* (opp)varming; *have a ~* varme seg; **3** *vb (~ up)* varme/varmes (opp). **warm|-blooded** *adj* varmblodig. **~-hearted** *adj* varmhjertet. **warmth** [wɔ:mθ] *sb* varme.

war-monger ['wɔ:mʌŋgə] *sb* krigshisser.

warn [wɔ:n] *vt* advare; varsle (om). **warning** ['wɔ:nɪŋ] *sb* (ad)varsel.

warp [wɔ:p] **I** *sb* **1** vindskjevhet; **2** renning (i vev); **II** *vb* **1** bøye; (for)vri; (få til å) slå seg; gjøre (vind)-skjev; **2** *fig* for|dreie, -vri, forkvakle.

war-path ['wɔ:pɑ:θ] *sb: on the ~* på krigsstien.

warrant ['wɒrənt] **I** *sb* **1** hjemmel; *dgl* rett; **2** (skriftlig) fullmakt/ordre; *jur især* arrestordre; **3** garanti, sikkerhet; **4** *mil* beskikkelse/utnevnelse (til *~-officer*); **II** *vt* **1** hjemle; bemyndige; gi rett til; **2** forsikre; garantere/innestå for. **warrant-officer** ['wɒrənt,ɒfisə] *sb mil* gradsbetegnelse for personell mellom befal og offiserer; ≈ underoffiser. **warranty** ['wɒrəntɪ] *sb* (skriftlig) garanti.

warring ['wɔ:rɪŋ] *adj* **1** krigførende; **2** *fig* motstridende. **warrior** ['wɒrɪə] *sb* kriger.

warship ['wɔ:ʃɪp] *sb* krigsskip.

wart [wɔ:t] *sb* vorte. **warthog** ['wɔ:thɒg] *sb* vortesvin.

war|-widow *sb* krigsenke. **~-worn** *adj* krigstrett.

wary ['weərɪ] *adj* forsiktig, var(som); omtenksom.

wash [wɒʃ] **I** *sb* **1** vask(ing) *etc*; **2** vask (dvs tøy til vask; klesvask, storvask etc); **3** bølgeslag; skvalp(ing), skvulp(ing); **4** lavering; lag/strøk (med vannfarge etc); **5** (-)vann (til skylling etc); *neds* skvip, søl; **II** *vb* **1** vaske (og vaske seg); **~** *away* vaske bort/vekk; **~** *down* vaske (godt); *ofte* spyle (ren); *også* skylle ned; **~** *off* vaske av/vekk; **~** *out* skylle/vaske ut; **~***ed out (dgl)* medtatt; slått ut; **~** *up* vaske opp; **2** tåle vask; *fig* duge; holde mål; **3** skylle; skvalpe, skvulpe; **~** *against* skylle/vaske mot; **~** *ashore* skylle i land; **~** *over* skylle over; **~** *overboard* skylle over bord; **~***ed up on the beach* skyllet opp på stranden; **4** lavere (dvs legge på et tynt lag/strøk med vannfarge etc); *også* hvitte, kalke. **wash|able** *adj* vaskbar, vaskeekte. **~-basin** *sb* vaske(vanns)fat; *også* håndvask; (vaske)servant. **washer** ['wɒʃə] *sb* **A 1** vasker, vaskeriarbeider; **2** vaskemaskin; *dish-~* oppvaskmaskin; **B** stopp|ring, -skive. **washing** ['wɒʃɪŋ] *sb* vask(ing) *etc*; vask (og vasketøy) etc); *som adj* vaske-. **washing|-machine** *sb* vaskemaskin. **~-powder** *sb* vaskepulver. **~-up** *sb* oppvask (også *fig*). **~-up liquid** *sb* (flytende) oppvaskmiddel. **~-up machine** *sb* oppvaskmaskin. **wash|-out** *sb* **1** (bort)skylling; sted som er skylt vekk (av f.eks. flom); **2** *dgl* fiasko; mislykket/ubrukelig person. **~room** *sb* toalett, vaskerom. **~-stand** *sb* (vaske)servant. **~-tub** *sb* vaskebalje. **washy** ['wɒʃɪ] *adj* tynn, utvannet; vassen; **2** utvasket; blek, falmet; **3** svak.

wasp [wɒsp] *sb* veps.

wastage ['weɪstɪdʒ] *sb* spill, svinn. **waste** [weɪst] **I** *adj* **1** øde(lagt); vill, ødslig; **2** unyttig, verdiløs; *især* avfalls-, søppel-; spill-; **II** *sb* **1** ødemark, ørken; **2** spill, svinn; ødsling; **~** *of time* bortkastet tid; *go/run to* **~** gå til spille; **3** avfall, søppel; *(cotton ~)* pussegarn, tvist; **III** *vb* **1** ødelegge; legge (land) øde; **2** kaste bort; sløse (med); **3** *(~ away)* svinne/tæres bort; for|falle, -komme. **waste|ful** *adj* ødsel. **~land** *sb* **1** uoppdyrket mark; ødemark; *også fig* brakkmark. **~ oil** *sb petro* avfallsolje, spillolje. **~-paper basket** *sb* papirkurv. **~pipe** *sb* avløpsrør.

watch [wɒtʃ] **I** *sb* **1** vakt(hold); **2** vakt(post); *koll* vaktmannskap; **3** *sjø (~ duty)* vakt(tjeneste); **4** (armbånds)ur; (lomme)klokke; **II** *vb* **1** betrakte, iaktta; se på; **2** speide/holde utkikk (*for* etter); **3** bevokte; passe på; holde (et) øye med; *gml også* våke over; **4** holde/stå vakt. **watch|dog** *sb* vakthund. **~ful** *adj* påpasselig; vaktsom, (år)våken; på vakt. **~-maker** *sb* urmaker. **~man** *sb* **1** vakt(mann); nattvakt; **2** *gml* vekter. **~room** *sb* vakt|rom, stue. **~word** *sb* feltrop, løsen.

water ['wɔ:tə] **I** *sb* **1** vann; hav, sjø; *fl* vannmasser; *hold* **~** holde vann; *fig også* stå for kritikk *etc; hot* **~** *(fig)* knipe, vanskeligheter; *troubled* **~***s* opprørt/urolig sjø; *(fig)* rørt vann; **2** tidevann (og tidevannsstand); **3** *fl* farvann; **4** *som suff* -vann; **II** *vb* **1** vanne; forsyne med/gi vann; **2** ta inn vann; **3** (vass)renne; fylles med vann/væske; *make her mouth* **~** få tennene hennes til å løpe i vann. **water|bird** *sb* sjøfugl; svømmefugl; vadefugl. **~-biscuit** *sb* smørbrødkjeks. **~-borne** *adj* transportert sjøveien. **~-buffalo** *sb* vannbøffel. **~-bus** *sb* sjøbuss. **~-closet** *sb* vannklosett. **~-colour** *sb* **1** akvarellfarge, vannfarge; **2** akvarell(maleri). **~course** *sb* vannvei (dvs kanal etc). **~cress** *sb* brønnkarse. **~fall** *sb* foss, vannfall. **~front** *sb* sjøside (av by etc); *også* brygge(r), havnestrøk. **~-level** *sb* vann|flate, -skorpe, -speil. **~-lily** *sb* vannlilje. **~-logged** *adj* oversvømmet; myrlendt, sumpet; vasstrukken. **~-main** *sb* hovedvannledning. **~mark** *sb* **1** vannmerke; **2** høyvannsmerke, vannstandsmerke. **~-meter** *sb* vannmåler. **~-pipe** *sb* vann|ledning, -rør. **~-power** *sb* vannkraft. **~proof** **1** *adj* vanntett; **2** *sb* regn|frakk, -kappe; **3** *vt* impregnere. **~-repellent** *adj* vannavstøtende. **~shed** *sb* vannskille. **~-ski** *sb, vi* (stå på) vannski. **~-supply** *sb* vannforsyning. **~tight** *adj* vanntett (også *fig*). **~way** *sb* = **~***course.* **~ well** *sb petro* vannbrønn. **~-wheel** *sb* vannhjul. **~works** *sb fl* vannverk. **watery** ['wɔ:tərɪ] *adj* **1** våt; vassen; **2** tynn, utvannet; svak.

wave [weɪv] **I** *sb* **1** vink(ing) *etc*; **2** bølge; **II** *vb* **1** vinke (og vinke med, til etc); svinge/vifte (med); **2** bølge; gå *etc* i bølger/bølgegang; **3** gjøre bølget; ondulere/*dgl* legge (håret). **wave|band** *sb* bølgebånd. **~length** *sb* bølgelengde. **waver** ['weɪvə] *vi* **1** blafre, flakke; **2** rave, sjangle; **3** vakle; (begynne å) gi etter; **4** nøle; være vinglet. **wavy** ['weɪvɪ] *adj* bølgende; bølget; bølge-.

wax [wæks] **A I** *sb* **1** voks; *(bees~)* bivoks; **2** *(cobbler's ~)* (skomaker)bek; **3** *(sealing ~)* (segl)lakk; **II** *vt* vokse; bone/polere (med voks); **B** *vi* **1** tilta/vokse (om månen etc); **2** *gml* bli; **C** *sb slang* raserianfall. **waxen** ['wæksən] *adj* voks- (og voks|blek, gul, -myk etc). **wax|work** *sb* voksarbeid; voks|dukke, -figur. **~works** *sb fl* vokskabinett.

way [weɪ] **A** *sb* **1** vei (jf *high~, rail~* etc); **~** *in* inngang; **~** *out* utgang; *fig* utvei; mulighet, sjanse; *ask one's* **~** spørre om veien; spørre seg for; *by* **~** *of* gjennom, via; *fig* i ferd med (å); tilbøyelig til (å); *by* **~** *of reply* som/til svar; *by the* **~** langs veien; underveis; *fig* forresten; apropos; *give* **~** vike; gi etter; *go one's* **~** gå sin vei; *go out of one's* **~** anstrenge seg; gjøre seg umak; *in one's* **~** i veien (for en); *lose one's* **~** gå seg bort/vill; *make* **~** gi plass; gå av veien; *right of* **~** atkomstrett; forkjørsrett; **2** retning; *fig* henseende; *in a fair* **~** *of* på god vei til (å); *in the* **~** *of* hva angår; med hensyn til; *the other* **~** *round* omvendt; (stikk) motsatt; *this* **~** *and that* hit og dit; **3** avstand; vei (= vei|strekning, -stykke); *go a long* **~** forslå/monne godt; **4** (fremgangs)måte; *især fl* opptreden, vesen;

manérer; ~ *of living* leve|sett, -vis; ~ *of thinking* tenkesett; ~*s and means* midler; metode, utvei; *get/have one's* ~ få viljen sin; *have it both* ~*s* få i både pose og sekk; *in a* ~ på en måte; *in a bad* ~ dårlig/uheldig stilt; *in a small* ~ i all beskjedenhet; *in no* ~ på ingen måte; *in some* ~*s* i visse henseender; på enkelte områder; *in the family* ~ gravid; *mend one's* ~*s* forbedre seg; bli et (nytt og) bedre menneske; **5** *fl* praksis, vane; skikk (og bruk); **6** *sjø etc* fart, gang; *gather* ~ få opp farten; *get under* ~ lette anker; komme av sted/*fig* i gang; **7** (bygge)bedding, stabel; **B** *US dgl (= away):* ~ *back in* langt tilbake i (tiden); ~ *up in* høyt oppe i. **way|-farer** *sb* veifarende. **~lay** [weɪ'leɪ] *vt* overfalle/rane (fra bakhold); ligge på lur etter. **~side** *sb* vei|kant, -side. **~ward** ['weɪwəd] *adj* egen(sindig); sta, strid. **~-warden** *sb* veivokter.

weak [wi:k] *adj* **1** svak (og svakelig); veik; kraftløs; **2** tynn (dvs oppblandet; ut|spedd, -vannet etc); emmen, flau. **weaken** ['wi:kən] *vb* svekke(s). **weakling** [wi:klɪŋ] *sb* svekling. **weakly** ['wi:klɪ] **1** *adj* svak(elig), tander; **2** *adv* svakt *etc*. **weakness** ['wi:knɪs] *sb* svakhet *etc*.

weal [wi:l] *sb* strime/stripe (etter piskeslag etc); pløse. **wealth** [welθ] *sb* rikdom, velstand; velståenhet. **wealthy** ['welθɪ] *adj* rik, velstående.

wean [wi:n] *vt* **1** avvenne (spedbarn fra brystføde); **2** venne (en person) av (med noe).

weapon ['wepən] *sb* våpen. **weaponry** ['wepənrɪ] *sb* rustninger, våpen.

wear ['weə] **I** *sb* **1** bruk (av klær); **2** klær; især som *suff* -klær, -tøy; **3** *(~ and tear)* slitasje; **II** *vb* **1** gå med (klesplagg etc); ha på (seg); *fig også* bære, ha; ~ *a troubled look* se bekymret ut; **2** *(~ away/out)* slite/slites (ut); slite/tære på; ~ *off* slites av; *fig* forta/gi seg; gå over (etter hvert); **3** holde (dvs tåle bruk/slitasje etc); ~ *well* holde (seg) godt. **wearer** ['weərə] *sb* bærer; bruker.

wearisome ['wɪərɪsəm] *adj* kjedelig, trettende. **weary** ['wɪərɪ] **I** *adj* **1** sliten, trett; **2** slitsom, trettende; møysommelig; **II** *vb* bli/gjøre trett; utmatte(s). **wearying** ['wɪərɪɪŋ] *adj* trettende; *også* kjedelig.

weasel ['wi:zl] *sb* røyskatt; snømus.

weather ['weðə] **I** *sb* **1** vær; **2** *sjø* lo(side), lovart(side); *også (~ side)* vindside; **II** *vb* **1** greie/klare (vanskeligheter etc); komme igjennom/ri av (krise, storm etc); **2** utsette(s) for vind og vær. **weather|-beaten** *adj* værbitt. **~-bound** *adj* værfast. **~cock** *sb* værhane. **~ed** *adj* værbitt; falmet; forvitret. **~ forecast, ~ report** *sb* værvarsel. **~-ship** *sb* vær(varslings)skip. **~-station** *sb* vær(varslings)stasjon. **~-vane** *sb* vindfløy, værhane.

weave [wi:v] *vb* **1** veve (sammen); **2** flette (og flette, tvinne etc sammen). **weaver** ['wi:və] *sb* vever.

web [web] *sb* stoff, tøy; vev; **2** nett(verk); **3** *(cob~, spider's ~)* (edderkopp)spinn, spindelvev; **4** svømmehud. **webbed** [webd] *adj = web-footed.* **web | equipment** *sb mil* webutstyr; ≈ reimtøy. **~-footed** *adj* svømme- (dvs med svømmehud).

wed [wed] *vb* (gi/ta til) ekte; gifte seg (med); ~*ded to* gift med; *fig også* (sterkt) knyttet til/opptatt av. **wedding** ['wedɪŋ] *sb* bryllup; *som adj* bryllups-, gifte-. **wedding|-cake** *sb* bryllupskake. **~-ring** *sb* giftering.

wedge [wedʒ] **1** *sb* blei, kile; *the thin edge of the* ~ den lille tuen (som kan velte stort lass); **2** *vt* kile fast.

wedlock ['wedlɒk] *sb* ekteskap.

wee [wi:] *adj* bitte liten; ørliten; *a* ~ *bit* en (liten) smule; litegrann.

weed [wi:d] **1** *sb* ugress(plante), ukrutt; **2** *vb* luke, renske; ~ *out* luke ut; *også* fjerne.

week [wi:k] *sb* uke; *this day* ~ en uke (fra) i dag. **week|day** *sb* hverdag, ukedag. **~end** *sb* helg, ukeslutt; weekend. **weekly** ['wi:klɪ] **1** *adj* ukentlig, uke-; **2** *adv* ukentlig; **3** *sb* uke|blad, -magasin, -skrift.

weep [wi:p] *vb* gråte (*for* av/over; *over* over); begråte; gråte over. **weep hole** *sb petro* dreneringshull.

weigh [weɪ] *vb* **1** veie; ~ **against** (av)veie mot (dvs sammenligne etc med); ~ **down** knuge/tynge (ned); ~ **in** (la seg) veie; ~ **upon** hvile/trykke på; ~ **with** ha betydning for; telle for; *også =* ~ *against*; **2** overveie; bedømme, vurdere; **3** *sjø:* ~ *anchor* heise/lette anker. **weight** [weɪt] **I** *sb* **1** tyngde, vekt; *også* lodd; *by* ~ etter vekt; **2** *fig* betydning; *carry* ~ ha betydning; veie (tungt); **II** *vt* belaste, tynge; ~ *down* tynge (ned) trykke (på). **weight|-coating** *sb petro* vekt|kappe, -kledning. **~-lifting** *sb* vektløfting. **~less** *adj* vektløs. **weighty** [weɪtɪ] *adj* vektig.

weird ['wɪəd] *adj* **1** nifs, uhyggelig; **2** *dgl* selsom; merkelig, underlig.

welcome ['welkəm] **1** *adj* kjærkommen, velkommen; *som interj* velkommen! *you're* ~! *(US)* ingen årsak! **2** *sb, vt* (hilse/ønske) velkommen.

weld [weld] *vb* sveise (og la seg sveise).

well [wel] **A I** *sb* **1** kilde, oppkomme; brønn; *især fig* vell; **2** lyssjakt; trappe|rom, -sjakt; heisesjakt; **II** *vi* strømme/velle (*out/up* frem/opp); **B I** *adj* bra, frisk; **2** fordelaktig, gunstig; **II** *adv* **1** bra, godt; vel; *think* ~ *of* synes godt om; **2** ordentlig, skikkelig; ~ *along/on (for)* langt på vei (til); ~ *off* velstående; ~ *over* godt og vel (over); **3** nok, vel; *be just as* ~ være like bra; *you may* ~ *be angry* du kan nok være sint (dvs det har du god grunn til); *you may as* ~ *go* du kan like gjerne gå; **III** *interj* godt (og vel)! vel (og bra)! nå, nåja; javel; **IV** *pref* vel(-); **V** *sb: wish them* ~ ønske dem (alt) godt. **well|-advised** *adj* klok, veloverveid. **~-appointed** *adj* velutstyrt. **~-balanced** *adj* avbalansert, likevektig. **~-behaved** *adj* veloppdragen. **~-being** *sb* velvære. **~-born** *adj* av fin/god familie; *gml* velbåren. **~-bred** *adj* veloppdragen; dannet; *om dyr* av god rase. **~ capacity** *sb petro* brønnkapasitet. **~-chosen** *adj* velvalgt. **~ cluster** *sb petro* brønnklynge. **~ completion** *sb petro* klargjøring (av brønn) for produksjon (etter boring). **~-conditioned** *adj* i god stand. **~conducted** *adj* velledet, velorganisert. **~-connected** *adj* med gode forbindelser; *ofte =* ~*-born*. **~-dis-**

posed *adj* velvillig (innstilt). **~-earned** *adj* velfortjent. **~-favoured** *adj* pen. **~-found** *adj* velforsynt; godt utstyrt; *fig* vel bevandret. **~-founded, ~-grounded** *adj* velbegrunnet. **~-grown** *adj* velvoksen. **~head** *sb petro* brønnhode. **~head equipment** *sb petro* brønnhodeutstyr. **~head pressure** *sb petro* brønnhodetrykk. **~-heeled** *adj slang* velbeslått (dvs temmelig rik). **~-informed** *adj* velunderrettet.

wellingtons ['welɪŋtənz] *sb fl* gummistøvler, slagstøvler.

well|-intentioned *adj* vel|menende, -ment. **~-known** *adj* velkjent. **~ log** *sb petro* brønnhullslogg. **~-mannered** *adj* dannet. **~-marked** *adj* godt oppmerket. **~-meaning** *adj* vel|menende, -ment. **~-meant** *adj* velment. **~-nigh** *adv* nesten. **~-proportioned** *adj* velproporsjonert. **~-read** *adj* belest. **~-seasoned** *adj* vellagret; *fig* erfaren. **~ service** *sb petro* brønnvedlikehold. **~-set** *adj* velbygd. **~-spoken** *adj* veltalende; vel talt. **~-stocked** *adj* godt forsynt (med varer etc). **~-timed** *adj* vel|beregnet, -valgt (med hensyn til tidspunkt). **~-to-do** *adj* velstående. **~-tried** *adj* velprøvd. **~-turned** *adj* velturnert; elegant formulert/uttrykt. **~wisher** *sb* en som vil/ønsker en vel. **~-worn** *adj* velbrukt; *ofte* forslitt.

werewolf ['wɪəwulf] *sb* varulv.

west [west] **I** *adj* vest(-), vestre(-); vestlig; **II** *adv* **1** vestover; **~** *of* vest for; **2** vestpå; **III** *sb* vest; *to the* **~** *of* vest for. **westerly** ['westəlɪ] *adj, adv* **1** vestlig; fra vest; vesta-; **2** mot vest. **western** ['westən] *adj* vestlig, vest-; *som sb* = **westerner** ['westənə] *sb* vesterlending; *US* vestamerikaner (dvs person fra vestsatene). **westward(s)** ['westwəd(z)] *adv* vestover.

wet [wet] **I** *adj* **1** fuktig, våt; rå; **2** regnfull; regnværs-; **II** *sb* **1** fuktighet, væte; **2** regn (og regn|tid, -vær etc); **III** *vt* væte; gjøre våt. **wet | blanket** *sb dgl* gledesdreper, lyseslokker. **~ gas** *sb petro* våt gass.

whack [wæk] *dgl* **I** *sb* **1** rapp, smekk; dask; **2** andel, part; **II** *vt* slå; klaske (rappe, smekke, smelle etc) til.

whale [weɪl] **I** *sb* **1** hval; **2** *US dgl: a* **~** *of* massevis av; **II** *vi* drive hvalfangst. **whaler** ['weɪlə] *sb* hval|-fanger, -fangstskute. **whaling** ['weɪlɪŋ] *sb* hvalfangst.

wharf [wɔ:f] *sb* brygge, kai.

what [wɒt] *adj, pron* **1** hva (og hva for en; hva for noe/noen; hva slags; hvilken, hvilket; hvilke); **~** *about/of* hva med; **~** *for* hvorfor; hva ... for; **~** *if* hva om; sett at; **~** *of it* hva så; **2** (nei) for en/noe *etc*; **~** *fools!* for noen tosker! **3** *vulg* (den/de) som. **whatever** [wɒt'evə] *adj, pron* **1** hva (...) enn; **2** hva *etc* som helst; *også* alt som; **3** *dgl* hva i all verden. **whatsoever** [ˌwɒtsəu'evə] *adj, pron* = *whatever*.

wheat [wi:] *sb* hvete.

wheedle ['wi:dl] *vt* godsnakke med; smigre, smiske for.

wheel [wi:l] **I** *sb* **1** hjul; **2** *(steering* **~***)* ratt; *at the* **~** ved rattet/*sjø* roret; **II** *vb* **1** rulle, trille; **2** dreie, svinge. **wheel|barrow** *sb* trillebår. **~base** *sb* hjulavstand. **~chair** *sb* rullestol. **~wright** *sb* hjulmaker.

wheeze [wi:z] *vi* hvese; snakke anstrengt/med hvesende/pipende stemme. **wheezy** ['wi:zɪ] *adj* hvesende; *især* astmatisk.

whelp [welp] *sb* **1** valp; *fig, dgl* (gutte)valp; **2** unge (av større rovdyr).

when [wen] *adv, konj* da, når; *også* enda, skjønt; *he walks* **~** *he can take a taxi* han går enda han kan ta drosje; *say* **~***!* si stopp (dvs når en har fått nok i glasset)!

whence [wens] *adv* hvorfra; hvor ... fra.

whenever [wen'evə] *adv, konj* **1** når (...) enn; **2** når som helst; *også* hver gang; **3** *dgl* når i all verden.

where ['weə] *adv* hvor; hvorhen; *også* der (hvor); dit (hvor); *that's* **~** *it is* der er det; det er der det er. **whereabouts 1** [ˌweərə'bauts] *adv* hvor (omtrent); **2** ['weərəbauts] *sb* oppholdssted, tilholdssted. **whereas** [weər'æz] *konj* mens (...) (derimot); *jur også* ettersom, siden. **whereby** [weə'baɪ] *adv* hvorved. **wherefore** ['weəfɔ:] **1** *konj dgl* hvorfor; **2** *sb fl* grunn(er), årsak(er). **wherein** [weər'ɪn] *adv* hvori. **whereof** [weər'ɒv] *adv gml* hvorav. **whereon** [weər'ɒn] *adv gml* hvorpå. **wheresoever** [ˌweəsəu'evə] *adv* = *wherever*. **whereto** [weə'tu:] *adv gml* hvortil. **whereunder** [weər'ʌndə] *adv gml* hvorunder. **whereupon** [weərə'pɒn] *adv* hvor|etter, -på. **wherever** [weər'evə] *adv* **1** hvor/hvorhen (...) enn; **2** hvor som helst; *også* overalt hvor; **3** *dgl* hvor/hvorhen i all verden. **wherewithal** ['weəwɪðɔ:l] **1** *adv gml* hvormed; **2** *sb* (det som skal til av) penger.

whet [wet] *vt* **1** kvesse, slipe; **2** *fig* skjerpe. **whetstone** ['wetstəun] *sb* bryne(stein); slipestein.

whether ['weðə] *konj* om, hvorvidt; **~** *... or no(t)* om ... eller ikke.

which [wɪtʃ] **1** *adj, pron* hvilken (og hvilket, hvilke; hva for en; hva for noe/noen); **2** *pron* hva, hvem; **3** *relativt pron* som (om ting). **whichever** [wɪtʃ'evə] *adj, pron* **1** hvilken (...) enn; **2** hvilken *etc* som helst; *også* den (det/de) som; **3** *dgl* hva/hvilken i all verden.

whiff [wɪf] **1** *sb* pust; drag, gufs; **2** *vb* blåse/puste (ut); gufse.

while [waɪl] **I** *konj* **1** mens; *også* så lenge (som); **2** enda, skjønt; **II** *sb* tid (og tidsrom); stund; *all this* **~** hele (denne) tiden; *for a* **~** for en stund/tid; *(every) once in a* **~** en gang iblant; *også* rett som det er; *worth (one's)* **~** møyen/umaken verd; **III** *vt:* **~** *away* fordrive/korte (tiden). **whilst** [waɪlst] *konj* mens.

whim [wɪm] *sb* innfall, lune.

whimper ['wɪmpə] **1** *sb* sutring *etc*; **2** *vb* sutre; klynke; jamre.

whimsical ['wɪmzɪkl] *adj* rar, snodig.

whine [waɪn] **I** *sb* jammer *etc*; **II** *vb* **1** jamre; hvine, ule; **2** klage; klynke, sutre.

whinny ['wɪnɪ] **1** *sb* knegg(ing); vrinsk(ing); **2** *vi* knegge, vrinske.

whip [wɪp] **I** *sb* pisk, svepe; *pol* innpisker, partipisk; *fig* snert; **II** *vb* **1** piske (på); bruke pisk/svepe (på); banke (denge, peise etc) på; *fig* drive; jage (på); **2** piske (egg, krem etc); **3** rive, rykke; snappe; slenge; **~** *off* rive av seg; **~** *out* rive frem (f.eks. skytevåpen).

whip|-cord *sb* piskesnor; *også* (slags) sterkt stoff. **~ hand** *sb fig* overtak. **~-handle** *sb* piskeskaft. **~-lash** *sb* piskeslag; *især fig* (piske)snert; *~-lash effect, ~-lash syndrome* piskesnert|skade, -virkning; -syndrom (dvs skade oppstått ved at hodet slynges voldsomt frem og tilbake som f.eks. under en bilkollisjon); nakkesleng-(skade). **~ping** *sb* pisking; juling. **~ping boy** *sb* syndebukk. **~-stitch** *sb* kastesting.

whirl [wɜ:l] **I** *sb* virvel, virvling; **II** *vb* **1** virvle; spinne, snurre; *også* snurre/virvle rundt med; **2** *~ away* fare/suse av sted (med). **whirl|pool** *sb* strømvirvel; virvelstrøm; malstrøm. **~wind** *sb* virvelvind.

whir(r) [wɜ:] **1** *sb* dur; summing; surr(ing); **2** *vi* dure; summe; surre.

whisk [wɪsk] **I** *sb* **1** (krem)pisker, -visp; **2** strøk; feiende bevegelse; **II** *vb* **1** feie/vifte med; **2** dra av sted (med); føre bort (plutselig og raskt); *~ away/off* feie/få unna; **3** piske (egg, krem etc). **whiskers** ['wɪskəz] *sb fl* **1** bakkenbarter, kinnskjegg; **2** værhår (på katt etc).

whisper ['wɪspə] **1** *sb* hvisking; *in a ~* hviskende; **2** *vb* hviske.

whistle ['wɪsl] **II** *vb* **1** plystring; fløyt(ing); **2** (signal)fløyte; **II** *vb* **1** plystre; *~ for* plystre etter; *fig* avskrive; skyte en hvit pinn(e) etter; **2** fløyte; pipe (med fløyte).

white [waɪt] **1** *adj* hvit; *fig* ren, uskyldig; uskyldshvit; *US* hederlig, real; **2** *sb* hvitfarge, hvitt; *også* (egge)hvite. **white | ant** *sb* termitt. **~-collar worker** *sb* hvitsnipparbeider (dvs funksjonær, kontorist etc). **~ elephant** *sb fig* gave det følger mer bryderi og utgifter med enn glede. **~ grouse** *sb* fjellrype. **Whitehall** ['waɪthɔ:l] *sb fig* den britiske regjering (fordi så mange av regjeringskontorene ligger i en gate i London med dette navnet). *the* **White House** Det hvite hus (= presidentboligen i USA); *fig* den amerikanske president/regjering. **white | lie** *sb* hvit løgn; nødløgn. **~ lime** *sb* kalk(maling). **~-limed** *adj* hvittet, kalket. **~-livered** *adj dgl* feig. **whiten** ['waɪtn] *vb* **1** (gjøre hvit ved å) hvitte, kalke, kritte; **2** blekne, hvitne; **3** *fig* hvitvaske, renvaske. **white | nights** *sb fl* søvnløse netter. **~ rage** *sb* (hvit)glødende raseri. **~-robed** *adj* hvitkledd. **~wash** **1** *sb* (hvitte)kalk; kalk|maling, -velling; **2** *vt* hvitte; kalke, kalkvaske; *fig* renvaske. **whiting** ['waɪtɪŋ] *sb* (hvitte)kalk; (slemme)kritt.

Whitsun ['wɪtsn] *sb* **1** *(Whit Sunday)* (første) pinsedag; **2** *(~tide)* pinse.

whittle ['wɪtl] *vb: ~ away/down* kutte/skjære ned (på).

whiz(z) [wɪz] **1** *sb* visling; **2** *vi* visle; fare av sted/forbi med vislende lyd; *også* suse. **whizz-kid** *sb dgl* vidunderbarn.

who [hu:] *pron* **1** hvem; *~ goes there* hvem (går) der; **2** *relativt pron* som (om personer); de/den som. **whodunit** [hu:'dʌnɪt] *sb dgl (= who done it)* kriminalroman. **whoever** [hu'evə] *pron* **1** hvem (...) enn; den/de som; *også* alle/enhver som; **3** *dgl* hvem i all verden.

whole [həʊl] **I** *adj* **1** hel (og helt, hele; hel og full etc); *som pref* hel-; **2** hel (dvs uskadd etc); **3** frisk, sunn; **II** *sb* hele, helhet; *the ~* alt; alle (sammen); *the ~ of her money* alle pengene hennes; *(up)on the ~* alt i alt; i det hele (tatt); stort sett. **whole|food** *sb* uraffinerte matvarer uten tilsetninger; *ofte* ≈ helsekost. **~-hearted** *adj* helhjertet. **~-length** *adj* helfigurs-. **~-meal** *sb* sammalt mel. **~-meal bread** *sb* helkornbrød. **~sale** *sb* engrossalg, *som adj* engros-; *fig også* masse-. **~some** ['həʊlsəm] *adj* helse|bringende, -gagnlig; sunn. **~-time** *adj* heldags(-), heltids-. **wholly** ['həʊlɪ] *adv* helt; fullstendig, ganske.

whom [hu:m] *pron* (avhengighetsform av *who*) **1** hvem; **2** som (og den/dem som).

whoop [hu:p] **I** *sb* hyl; høyt skrik; **II** *vb* **1** hyle; skrike høyt; **2** gispe (etter pusten); kike. **whooping-cough** *sb* kikhoste.

whop [wɒp] *vt slang* slå; vinne over. **whopper** ['wɒpə] *sb* **1** brande, kraftkar; **2** (kjempe)skrøne; **3** prakt|eksemplar, -stykke. **whopping** ['wɒpɪŋ] *dgl* **1** *adj* diger; **2** *adv* veldig.

whore [hɔ:] *sb, vi* hore.

whose [hu:z] *pron* (eieform av *which* og *who*) hvis; *dgl stundom* hvem sin (sitt, sine).

why [waɪ] **1** *adv* hvorfor; *that's ~* derfor (er det); det er grunnen (til at); *the reason ~* grunnen (til at); **2** *interj etc* hva! åh! (men ...) jo; nå (... da); *~, sure!* ja visst! selvsagt! *~, yes!* ja visst! jo visst!

wick [wɪk] *sb* veke.

wicked ['wɪkɪd] *adj* ond (og ond|skapsfull, -sinnet etc); forbrytersk; syndefull; slem, uskikkelig; dårlig. **wickedness** ['wɪkɪdnɪs] *sb* ondskap *etc.*

wicker ['wɪkə] **1** *adv* kurv- (og kurvfletnings- etc); **2** kurv (og kurvarbeid etc). **wicker|-chair** *sb* kurvstol. **~-work** *sb* kurv|arbeid, -fletning.

wicket *sb* **1** *a)* grind; *b)* halvdør; liten dør/port (innsatt i en større); **2** (skyve)luke; luke/taleåpning (ved skranke etc); **3** gjerde (i cricket). **wicket|-door, ~-gate** *sb = wicket 1.*

wide [waɪd] **I** *adj* **1** vid (og vidstrakt, vidtfavnende; rommelig, stor; *fig* omfattende etc); bred; **2** fjern; *~ of (the mark)* langt fra/langt utenfor (mål etc); **II** *adv* vidt *etc*; *~ apart* med store/vide mellomrom; *~ awake* lys våken; *~ open* vidåpen; *dgl* på vidt gap; *far and ~* vidt og bredt. **widely** ['waɪdlɪ] *adv* **1** vidt (og bredt); *fig* i stor/vid utstrekning; **2** spredt; med store mellomrom. **widen** ['waɪdn] *vb* utvide(s); bli/gjøre videre *etc.* **widespread** ['waɪdspred] *adj* vidstrakt; (vidt) ut|bredt, -strakt.

widow ['wɪdəʊ] *sb* enke. **widowed** ['wɪdəʊd] *adj* gjort til enke(mann); *ofte* gjenlevende. **widower** ['wɪdəʊə] *sb* enkemann. **widowhood** ['wɪdəʊhʊd] *sb* enkestand.

width [wɪdθ] *sb* **1** vidde; bredde (og stoffbredde etc); **2** *fig* spenn (og spennvidde).

wield [wi:ld] *vt* behandle/håndtere (redskap); føre/svinge (også om våpen); *~ power* utøve makt.

wife [waɪf] *sb* hustru; *dgl* kone; *gml* kvinne.

wig [wɪg] *sb* parykk.

wiggle ['wɪgl] *vb* sprelle/vrikke (med).

wild [waɪld] **I** *adj* **1** *om landskap, natur etc* uberørt; barsk, vill; *også* natur-; **2** *om mennesker* usivilisert, vill; barbarisk, primitiv; ~ *tribes* ville (folke)stammer; **3** *om dyr* utemmet, vill; ~ *animals* ville dyr; **4** *fig a)* rasende; stormende, stormfull; voldsom; ~ *with anger* vill av raseri; *driven* ~ drevet til vanvidd; *b)* hemningsløs; tankeløs; *dgl også* forrykt; ~ *about* gal/vill etter; ~ *schemes* ville planer; *c)* uregjerlig, vilter; **II** *adv* vilt *etc*; *go* ~ bli rabiat/vill; slå seg løs; **III** *sb* villmark; *fl også* ødemark(er). **wild | card** *sb data* jokersymbol. ~ **cat** *sb* villkatt. **~-cat** *adj (om streik)* ulovlig. **~-cat well** *sb petro* undersøkingsbrønn, utforskingsbrønn. **wilderness** ['wɪldənɪs] *sb* villmark, ødemark; ørken. **wild|-fire** *sb: spread like ~-fire* gå/spre seg som ild i tørt gress. **~fowl** *sb* fuglevilt. **~-goose chase** *sb fig* håpløst foretagende etc. **~-life** *sb* naturen (dvs dyre- og plantelivet).

wiles [waɪlz] *sb fl* list, renker.

wilful ['wɪlfʊl] *adj* **1** egen(sindig) sta; egenrådig, selvrådig; stiv|nakket, -sinnet; **2** forsettlig, overlagt; *også* bevisst.

will [wɪl] **I** *sb* **1** vilje; *at* ~ etter (eget) ønske; **2** *good* ~ godvilje, velvilje; *ill* ~ motvilje, uvilje; nag; **3** *(last* ~*)* testamente; **II** *vb* **1** ville (og som hjelpeverb *også* skal, vil); ~ *you come* kommer du; **2** *he would sit at the fire* han pleide å sitte ved varmen (ovnen, peisen etc); **3** befale, (på)by; **4** ønske; **5** testamentere. **willing** ['wɪlɪŋ] *adj* villig. **willingness** ['wɪlɪŋnɪs] *sb* villighet.

willow ['wɪləʊ] *sb* pil, piletre.

will-power ['wɪl,paʊə] *sb* viljestyrke.

wilt [wɪlt] *vb* **1** tørke inn; visne; **2** *fig* sykne (hen).

win [wɪn] **I** *sb dgl* seier; **II** *vb* **1** vinne (seier); **2** oppnå; få (tak i); skaffe seg; **3** nå; vinne frem til; **4** ~ *over* overtale; få over på sin side.

wince [wɪns] **1** *sb* grimase/trekning (av smerte etc); **2** *vb* krympe seg.

winch [wɪntʃ] **1** *sb* gangspill, vinsj; **2** *vt* vinsje; bevege (flytte, løfte etc) med gangspill/vinsj.

Winchester disk ['wɪntʃɪstə] *sb data* fast platelager; harddisk.

wind A [wɪnd] **I** *sb* **1** vind; **2** pust; **3** teft, vær; *get ~ of* få nyss om; komme under vær med; **4** (tarm)-gass, vind; *break* ~ fise; **5** *the* ~ blåserne (dvs blåseinstrumentene i et orkester); *the wood~* treblåserne; **II** *vt* **1** gjøre andpusten; ta pusten fra; **2** gi pusterom; la puste på; **3** blåse (på horn, trompet etc); **B** [waɪnd] **I** *sb* **1** bøy(ning), sving; **2** vikling, vinding; **II** *vb* **1** slynge/sno (seg); vikle/vinde (opp); hespe/nøste (opp); flette, tvinne; **2** sveive (og sveive i gang/opp etc); trekke opp (klokke etc); ~ *up* heise opp; **3** *fig: wound up* anspent, opphisset. **wind|bag** *sb fig* blære, skrythals. **~break** *sb* vind|fang, -skjerm. **~-cheater** *sb* vindjakke. **~fall** *sb* **1** vindfall; **2** nedfallsfrukt; **3** *fig* uventet hell. **~-instrument** *sb* blåseinstrument. **~lass** *sb* vinsj; (anker)spill. **~mill** *sb* vindmølle.

window ['wɪndəʊ] *sb* vindu. **window|-box** *sb* blomsterkasse. **~catch** *sb* vindus|haspe, -krok; *også* stormkrok. **~-pane** *sb* vindusrute. **~-sash** *sb* vindus|-karm, -ramme. *go* **~-shopping** *vb* (gå og) se i butikkvinduer. **~-sill** *sb* vindus|karm, -post.

wind|pipe *sb* luftrør. **~screen, ~ shield** *sb* front|-glass, rute (på f.eks. bil). **~-screen wiper** *sb* vindusvisker. **~swept** *adj* forblåst. **~ward** **1** *adj, adv* mot vinden; til lovart; **2** *sb* lovart, vindside. **windy** ['wɪndɪ] *adj* blåsende; vindfull (også om tarmgass).

wine [waɪn] *sb* vin.

wing [wɪŋ] **I** *sb* **1** vinge; **2** *mil* ving (dvs taktisk enhet bestående av to eller flere skvadroner); **3** fløy; **4** *teater* (side)kulisse; **II** *vb* **1** gi vinger; **2** bygge på/utstyre med fløyer. **wing|-chair** *sb* ørelappstol. **~ed** *adj* bevinget; med vinger. **~-span, ~-spread** *sb* vinge|-fang, -spenn. **~-tip** *sb* vingespiss.

wink [wɪŋk] **1** *sb* blunk *etc; fig* øyeblikk; *have forty ~s (dgl)* ta seg en høneblund; **2** *vb* blunke (med); blinke; ~ *at (fig)* lukke øynene for.

winner ['wɪnə] *sb* sierherre, vinner.

winter ['wɪntə] *sb* vinter. **wint(e)ry** ['wɪntrɪ] *adj* vinterlig, vinter; *fig* iskald.

wipe [waɪp] **1** *sb* (av)tørking *etc*; **2** *vb* tørke (av, bort etc); stryke (ut); pusse (f.eks. nesen); ~ *away* utslette; ~ *out* stryke ut; *fig* ut|radere, -rydde, -slette; tilintetgjøre.

wire ['waɪə] **I** *sb* **1** (metall)|streng, -tråd; ståltråd (og (ståltråd)|kabel, -trosse etc); *ofte* telefontråd, telegraftråd; **2** telegram; **II** *vb* **1** strekke/sette opp (metall)tråd *etc; især* legge opp/montere elektriske ledninger; *dgl ofte* koble; **2** telegrafere. **wire|-cutters** *sb fl* avbiter(tang). **~-haired** *adj* ruhåret. **~less** ['waɪəlɪs] **1** *adj* trådløs; *især* telegraf-; **2** *sb* (trådløs) telegrafi; **3** *vb* telegrafere; sende telegram. ~ **printer** *sb data* matriseskriver. **wiry** ['waɪərɪ] *adj fig* senesterk; kraftig, seig.

wisdom ['wɪzdə] *sb* visdom; fornuft, klokskap. **wise** [waɪz] *adj* vis; fornuftig, klok; *none the ~er* like klok (dvs ikke klokere eller bedre informert enn før).

wish [wɪʃ] **1** *sb* ønske; *også* hilsen (i brev etc); **2** *vb* ønske (seg); (gjerne) ville (ha); ~ *for* ønske noe (især noe nærmest uoppnåelig); ~ *them well* ønske dem (alt) godt; *I* ~ jeg skulle ønske. **wishful** ['wɪʃfʊl] *adj* lengselsfull, lengtende; ønske-. **wishful thinking** *sb* ønsketenkning.

wisp [wɪsp] *sb* dott; tjafs, tust. **wispy** ['wɪspɪ] *adj* pjusket; mager, spjælet.

wistful ['wɪstfʊl] *adj* lengselsfull, lengtende; vemodig.

wit [wɪt] **1** *sb, især fl* forstand, vett; vidd; *be at one's ~'s end* være opprådd; *have/keep one's ~s about one* holde hodet kaldt/klart; *live by one's ~s* leve av å bløffe/lure folk; **2** *vt: to* ~ nemlig.

witch [wɪtʃ] *sb* heks. **witch|craft** ['wɪtʃkrɑ:ft] *sb* heksekunst, hekseri; trolldom. **~-doctor** *sb* heksedoktor. **~-hunt** *sb* heksejakt (nå især *fig*).

with [wɪð] *prep* **1** med; **2** blant, hos; **3** *om årsak etc* av, for, på; *lie* ~ bero på. **withdraw** [wɪð'drɔ:] *vb* **1** trekke (seg) tilbake; **2** tilbakekalle; **3** ta tilbake; *især* ta ut (penger av banken). **withdrawal** [wɪð'drɔ:əl] *sb* tilbaketrekning *etc*.

wither ['wɪðə] *vb (~ away/up)* visne; få til å tørke inn/visne.

withhold [wɪð'həuld] *vt* holde igjen/tilbake. **within** [wɪð'ɪn] **I** *adv* **1** inne, innendørs; *også* hjemme; **2** innvendig; **II** *prep* inne i; innenfor; *om tid* innen; ~ *my memory* så vidt jeg kan huske. **without** [wɪð'aut] **I** *adv* ute, utendørs; **II** *prep* **1** (for)uten; *do/go* ~ klare seg uten; **2** *gml* utenfor. **withstand** [wɪð'stænd] *vb* motstå; gjøre motstand mot.

witless ['wɪtlɪs] *adj* dum; tåpelig, uforstandig.

witness ['wɪtnɪs] **I** *sb* **1** tilskuer, (øyen)vitne; **2** vitnesbyrd; *bear* ~ *to* vitne om; **II** *vb* **1** bevitne; se; legge merke til; *også* oppleve; **2** vitne om. **witness-box** *sb* vitne|boks, skranke.

witticism ['wɪtɪsɪzəm] *sb* vittighet; vits. **witty** ['wɪtɪ] *adj* vittig; morsom, spøkefull.

w. tingly ['wɪtɪŋlɪ] *adj* vitende; med forsett; med (vitende og) vilje.

wizard ['wɪzəd] *sb* trollmann.

wizened ['wɪznd] *adj* inn|skrumpet, -tørket.

wobble ['wɒbl] **I** *sb* ustøhet, vakling; ustadighet; **II** *vb* **1** slingre; vakle; være ustø/*fig* ustadig; **2** rokke/rugge (på). **wobbly** ['wɒblɪ] *adj* ustø; vaklende, vaklevoren; ustadig.

woe [wəu] *sb* ve, vånde; kval, smerte. **woeful** ['wəuful] *adj* sorgfull; *især hum* bedrøvelig, begredelig.

wolf [wulf] **1** *sb* ulv; **2** *vb dgl* sluke (mat); spise grådig.

wolverine ['wulvəri:n] *sb* jerv.

woman ['wumən] *sb* kvinne. **woman|hood** ['wumənhud] *sb* **1** modenhet (som kvinne); kvinnelighet (dvs det å være kvinne). **~kind** *sb koll* kvinner, kvinnekjønnet. **womenfolk** *sb koll* kvinner, kvinnfolk.

womb [wu:m] *sb* livmor; *også fig* skjød.

wonder ['wʌndə] **I** *sb* **1** forbauselse; (for)undring; **2** under(verk), vidunder; *no ~, small ~* intet under; ikke så underlig (dvs det er/var ikke så rart, merkelig, underlig etc); *work ~s* utrette mirakler; **II** *vi* undre(s), undre seg; *dgl* lure/spekulere (på); *I ~* mon tro. **wonder|ful** *adj* **1** vidunderlig; **2** *gml* merkelig. **~land** *sb* eventyr|land, -verden; vidunderland. **wondrous** ['wʌndrəs] *adj poet = wonderful 1.*

wont [wəunt] **1** *adj: be ~ to* være vant til/pleie (å); **2** *sb* (sed)vane. **wonted** ['wəuntɪd] *adj* (til)vant; vanlig.

woo [wu:] *vt* beile/fri til; strebe etter.

wood [wud] **I** *sb* **1** skog; **2** tre (og især tre|materialer, virke; tresort etc); ved; *også* brenne, brensel; *touch* ~ bank i bordet; **3** *fl* treblåseinstrumenter, treblåsere; **II** *vb* forsyne(s) med brensel/ved. **wood|-bird** *sb* skogsfugl. **~-carver** *sb* treskjærer. **~-carving** *sb* treskjæring. **~-cut** *sb* tresnitt. **~-cutter** *sb* tømmerhugger; vedhugger. **~-cutting** *sb* tømmerhugst; vedhugst. **wooded** ['wudɪd] *adj* skog|bevokst, -rik; skog-. **wooden** ['wudn] *adj* av tre; tre-. **wood|land** *sb* skog|distrikt, -område. **~pecker** *sb* hakkespett. **~pulp** *sb* tremasse. **~stack** *sb* tømmer|lunne, -stabel; vedstabel. **~work** *sb* treverk. **woody** ['wudɪ] *adj* **1** skogbevokst; **2** treaktig, tre-.

wool [wul] *sb* ull (og ull|garn, -stoff, -tråd etc). **woolgathering** *fig* **1** *adj* drømmende; distré, tankefull; **2** *sb* drømmer, fantasier. **wool(l)en** [wulən] **1** *adj* av ull; ull-; **2** *sb fl* ull|stoff; -klær, -plagg. **wool(l)y** ['wulɪ] **I** *adj* **1** ullaktig, ullen; ull-; **2** *fig* ullen ; **II** *sb* ullplagg; *især* (ull)genser. **wool sack** *sb* ullsekk (især om puten på presidentstolen i det britiske Overhus, og i overført betydning Overhusets president).

word [wɜ:d] **1** *sb* ord (også æresord samt erklæring; beskjed, melding; ordveksling, samtale; ord|duell, -strid; ordlyd, tekst etc); *in a ~* kort sagt; med ett ord; *have ~s with* krangle/trette med; *send ~ (for)* sende bud (etter/på); **2** *vb* ordlegge (seg); avfatte, formulere; uttrykke. **word-division** *sb* orddeling. **wording** ['wɜ:dɪŋ] *sb* ordlyd; tekst. **word|less** *adj* ordløs, stum. **~-perfect** *adj* ordrett. **~-play** *sb* ordspill. **~-power** *sb* ordforråd; evne til å ordlegge/uttrykke seg (godt). **~ processor** *sb data* tekstbehandler, tekstbehandlingsprogram. **~ processing** *sb data* tekstbehandling. **~ splitting** *sb* ordkløveri.

work [wɜ:k] **I** *sb* **1** arbeid (og verk, virksomhet; gjerning, yrke; maskins prestasjon/ytelse etc); *~ of art* kunstverk; *at ~* i arbeid; i gang; *fall/set to ~* gå i gang; ta fatt; begynne å arbeide; *make short ~ of* gjøre kort prosess med; *out of ~* arbeidsløs; **2** *(~ing)* (gang)verk; maskineri, mekanikk; **3** *fl (~shop)* verksted; bedrift, fabrikk; **II** *vb* **1** arbeide (og arbeide/drive med; behandle, håndtere, betjene; bevirke, forårsake, volde; fungere, funksjonere, virke etc); **2** bearbeide; forme, smi; **3** *med adv, prep ~* **away at** holde på (å arbeide) med; *~ something* **in/into** innarbeide noe i; legge noe inn (i); *~* **off** arbeide av (seg); avreagere; *~* **on** arbeide på; *fig* influere/virke på; *~* **out** iverksette, utføre; regne ut; *fig* virke; *~* **up** opparbeide; *~* **up to** arbeide (seg) opp til. **work|bench** *sb* arbeidsbenk. **~book** *sb* arbeidsbok. **~day** *sb* arbeidsdag. **worker** *sb* arbeider *etc*. **work | file** *sb data* arbeidsfil. **~ force** *sb* arbeids|stokk, -styrke. **~house** *sb* arbeidsanstalt. **working** **1** *adj* arbeidende *etc*; arbeider-; **2** *sb* arbeid *etc*. **working | area** *sb data* arbeidsområde. **~-class** *adj* arbeider-. *the ~* **classes** *sb fl* arbeiderne, arbeiderklassen(e). **~ day** *sb* arbeidsdag, virkedag. **~ order** *sb* driftsklar stand. **~ party** *sb* **1** arbeids|gjeng, -lag; **2** komité. **work|man** *sb* (kropps)arbeider. **~manship** *sb* fagkunnskap; faglig/fagmessig dyktighet. **~-out** *sb* **1** utprøving (i praksis); **2** *sport* trening; treningsøkt. **~room** *sb* arbeids|rom, -stue. **~shop** *sb* (jf *work I 3*) **1** fabrikk, verksted; **2** kurs, seminar. **~shy** *adj* arbeidssky. **~ station** *sb data* arbeidsstasjon. **~table** *sb* arbeidsbord; *ofte* sybord.

world [wɜ:ld] *sb* verden; *a ~ of (dgl)* en uendelighet av; *for (all) the ~* for alt i verden; *think the ~ of* ha svært høye tanker om. **world-famous** *adj* verdensberømt. **worldly** ['wɜ:ldlɪ] *adj* jordisk; *rel også* verdslig. **world|-power** *sb* verdensmakt, stormakt. **~-weary** *adj* livstrett. **~-wide** *adj* verdens|omfattende, omspennende.

worm [wɜ:m] **1** *sb* mark, orm; larve; *fig* stakkar, stymper; **2** *vb* sno (seg); lirke, lure.

worn [wɔ:n] *adj:* ~ *out* (ut)slitt.

worried ['wʌrɪd] *adj* bekymret, engstelig, urolig; *også* nervøs. **worrisome** ['wʌrɪsəm] *adj* bekymringsfull; engstelig, nervøs. **worry** ['wʌrɪ] **I** *sb* bekymring, engstelse, uro; **II** *vb* **1** være urolig; *især* bekymre/engste seg; **2** plage (og plage seg).

worse [wɜ:s] *adj, adv* verre; ~ *off* verre stilt; *be (all) the ~ for* ha/ta skade av; *none the ~ for* uskadd; like god; *the ~ for wear* nedslitt, utslitt. **worsen** ['wɜ:sn] *vb* forverre(s); bli/gjøre verre.

worship ['wɜ:ʃɪp] **I** *sb* **1** tilbedelse *etc*; **2** *Your Worship* Deres nåde (sagt til dommere etc); **II** *vt rel* dyrke, tilbe. **worshipper** ['wɜ:ʃɪpə] *sb rel* (-)dyrker.

worst [wɜ:st] *adj, adv* verst, *get the ~ of it* lide nederlag; få svi (for det).

worsted ['wu:stɪd] *adj, sb* kamgarn(s-).

worth [wɜ:θ] **1** *adj* verd(t); ~ *(one's) while* = *~while*; **2** *sb* verdi; *fig især* verd. **worth|less** *adj* verdiløs. **~while** *adj* møyen (strevet, umaken etc) verdt. **worthy** ['wɜ:ðɪ] *adj* **1** verdig (*of* til); *hum, iron ofte* ærverdig; *som suff* -dyktig; -verdig; *praise~* rosverdig; *sea~* sjødyktig.

wound [wu:nd] **1** *sb* sår; **2** *vt* såre.

wow [waʊ] **1** *interj* ah! oi! **2** *sb fig* blinkskudd, fulltreffer.

wrangle ['ræŋgl] **1** *sb* krangel; **2** *vi* krangle.

wrap [ræp] **1** *sb* sjal; kast, tørkle; *også* pledd; *fl* ytter|klær, -tøy; **2** *vt* (inn)hylle; *(~ up)* pakke/tulle inn. **wrapper** ['ræpə] *sb* **1** (bok)omslag; **2** *a)* (stort) sjal; *b)* kimono. **wrapping** ['ræpɪŋ] *sb* emballasje, innpakning. **wrapping-paper** *sb* innpakningspapir.

wrath [rɔ:θ] *sb* raseri, vrede.

wreath [ri:θ] *sb* krans. **wreathe** [ri:ð] *vt* (be)-kranse.

wreck [rek] **I** *sb* **1** ruin(ering), ødeleggelse; **2** *a)* forlis, havari, skibbrudd; *b)* vrak (ikke bare av skip); **II** *vt* **1** ruinere, ødelegge; rive ned; **2** *be ~ed* forlise, havarere; lide skibbrudd. **wrecking-crew** *sb* nedrivningsgjeng. **wreckage** ['rekɪdʒ] *sb* vrak(rester).

wren [ren] *sb* gjerdesmutt.

wrench [rentʃ] **I** *sb* **1** vri (og vridning, forvridning); **2** (brått/kraftig) rykk; **3** skiftnøkkel; **II** *vb* **1** (for)vri; ~ *from* fravriste; **2** rive, slite; rykke (brått, kraftig etc).

wrest [rest] *vt* vri, vriste; tvinge; ~ *from* fravriste.

wrestle ['restl] *vi sport* bryte (med); *fig* kjempe, streve. **wrestler** ['restlə] *sb* bryter.

wretch [retʃ] *sb* **1** stakkar, stymper; tufs; **2** kjeltring, usling. **wretched** ['retʃɪd] *adj* **1** elendig, ussel, ynkelig; **2** kjeltringaktig, skurkaktig.

wrick [rɪk] **1** *sb* forstuing; **2** *vt* forstue, vrikke.

wriggle ['rɪgl] **I** *sb* vrikk(ing) *etc*; sprell; **II** *vb* **1** vri/vrikke på seg; sno/åle seg; sprelle; **2** vri (på); sprelle (med).

wright [raɪt] *sb* -bygger, -maker.

wring [rɪŋ] *vb* **1** vri (seg); **2** pine, plage. **wringer** ['rɪŋə] *sb* vrimaskin.

wrinkle ['rɪŋkl] *sb, vb* rynke (seg). **wrinkled** ['rɪŋkld] *adj* rynket.

wrist [rɪst] *sb* håndledd. **wristwatch** ['rɪstwɒtʃ] *sb* armbåndsur.

writ [rɪt] *sb* skriv(else). **write** [raɪt] *vb* skrive; *også* avfatte, forfatte; *(~ down)* notere/skrive ned; ~ *in/off for* skrive etter noe (dvs bestille det skriftlig); ~ *off* skrive (og sende av sted); *fig* avskrive; ~ *out* renskrive; skrive ut; ~ *up* skrive opp (også *fig*). **write | head** *sb data* skrivehode. **~-off** *sb* avskrivning, tap. **~ protection** *sb data* skrivebeskyttelse. **writer** *sb* skriver; *især* forfatter.

writhe [raɪð] *vi, vr* krympe/vri (seg).

writing ['raɪtɪŋ] *sb* skriv(n)ing; skrift. **writing|-pad** *sb* skrive|mappe, -underlag. **~-paper** *sb* skrivepapir. **written** ['rɪtn] *adj* skrevet; skriftlig.

wrong [rɒŋ] **1** *adj, adv* feil(aktig), gal(t); urett, uriktig; *be (in the) ~* ha urett; ta feil; **2** *sb* urett; forurettelse; *do them ~* gjøre dem urett; **3** *vt* gjøre urett; forurette. **wrong|doer** *sb* en som gjør noe galt; forbryter, synder. **~doing** *sb* urett; forbrytelse, ugjerning; synd. **~ful** *adj* ulovlig; urettferdig.

wrought *pret, pp* av *work II 2* bearbeidet; formet, smidd. **wrought-up** *adj* (over)opphisset.

wry [raɪ] *adj* skjev, vridd.

Xmas ['krɪsməs] *fork* for *Christmas.*

X-ray ['eks,reɪ] **I** *sb* **1** røntgen(apparat); **2** røntgenbilde; **II** *vt* røntgen|behandle, -undersøke.

Y

yacht [jɒt] *sb* lyst|båt, (-)yacht.

yank [jæŋk] *vt* rykke, røske. **Yank** [jæŋk] *slang* = **Yankee** ['jæŋkɪ] **1** *adj* yankee-; *dgl* amerikansk; **2** *sb* yankee; *dgl* amerikaner; *hist* nordstatsamerikaner.

yap [jæp] *sb, vi* bjeff(e).

yard [jɑ:d] **A** *sb* **1** *sjø* rå; **2** lengdeenhet, se midtsidene; **B** *sb* **1** gård (dvs gårds|plass, -rom); *(farm-~)* (gårds)tun; **2** tomt; (inngjerdet/utendørs) arbeidsplass; *(dock~)* verft. **yard|-arm** *sb sjø* rånokk. **~stick** *sb* tommestokk; *især fig* målestokk.

yarn [jɑ:n] **I** *sb* **1** tråd, (ull)garn; **2** *dgl* ende (dvs god historie, skrøne); *spin a ~* spinne en ende (dvs fortelle en god historie/drøy skrøne); **II** *vi dgl* fortelle historier.

yawn [jɔ:n] **I** *sb* gjesp *etc*; **II** *vi* **1** gjespe; **2** gape (især stå åpen, på vidt gap etc).

year [jɜ:] *sb* **1** år; *~ by ~* år for år; *~s ago* for mange år siden; **2** årgang; års|klasse, (-)kull. **year|book** *sb* årbok. **~ling** *sb* åring (dvs årsgammelt dyr). **~ly** *adj, adv* årlig, års- hvert år.

yearn [jɜ:n] *vi* lengte (*for* etter; *to* etter å). **yearning** ['jɜ:nɪŋ] *sb* lengsel (*after/for* etter); *som adj* lengselsfull, lengtende.

yeast [ji:st] *sb* gjær.

yell [jel] *sb. vb* hyl(e), skrik(e).

yellow ['jeləʊ] **I** *adj* **1** gul; **2** *dgl* feig; **II** *sb* gult; **III** *vb* bli/gjøre gul. **yellow pages** *sb fl* fagfortegnelse, yrkesliste (i telefonkatalog etc).

yelp [jelp] *sb, vi* **1** bjeff(e); **2** hyl(e), vræl(e).

yen [jen] *vi US dgl = yearn.*

yeoman ['jəʊmən] *sb hist* fribonde.

yep [jep] *US dgl* = **yes** [jes] *adv, sb* ja.

yesterday ['jestədɪ] **1** *adv* i går; *~ morning* i går morges; **2** *sb* gårsdag(en); *the day before ~* i forgårs.

yesteryear ['jestəjɜ:] *poet* **1** *adv* i fjor; **2** *sb* fjorår(et); *the snow of ~* snøen som falt i fjor.

yet [jet] *adv, konj* **1** dog, likevel; **2** dessuten; enda, ytterligere; **3** foreløpig, ennå; enda/ennå en stund.

yew [ju:] *sb* barlind.

yield [ji:ld] **I** *sb* avling (og avkastning, utbytte etc); **II** *vb* **1** bære (avling); innbringe; kaste av seg; (av)gi, yte; **2** overgi (seg); gi etter/vike (*to* for).

yoke [jəʊk] **I** *sb* **1** bæretre, åk; *fig* slit, trelldom; **2** *(~ of oxen)* (okse)forspann; **II** *vt* **1** legge åk på; *fig* bringe under åket (dvs i trelldom); **2** *~d to* satt i spann med.

yokel ['jəʊkəl] *sb neds* bonde.

yolk [jəʊk] *sb* (egge)plomme.

yon [jɒn] *dial, gml* = **yonder** ['jɒndə] **1** *adj, pron* hin(t), hine; **2** *adv* dit; der borte; hist.

yore [jɔ:] *adv, sb bokl: of ~* fordum; i fordums tid; i gamle dager.

young [jʌŋ] **I** *adj* **1** ung, ungdoms-; *~ ones* avkom, unger; **2** *fig* fersk, ny; uerfaren; **II** *sb: the ~* de unge; ungdommen. **youngish** ['jʌŋɪʃ] *adj* ungdommelig; *dgl* yngre. **youngster** ['jʌŋstə] *sb* unggutt.

youth [ju:θ] *sb* **1** ungdom (dvs ungdomstid); **2** ungdom (dvs unge mennesker). **youth | centre** *sb* ungdoms|klubb, -senter. **~ employment officer** *sb* yrkesveileder. **~ful** ['ju:θfʊl] *adj* ungdommelig, ung; *dgl også* yngre. **~ hostel** *sb* ungdomsherberge.

yule [ju:l] *sb (~-tide)* jul, juletid.

Z

zane [zeɪn] *adj* skjør, sprø (dvs skrullet).

zeal [zi:l] *sb* glød, iver; nidkjærhet. **zealot** ['zelət] *sb* ivrig/nidkjær person; *især* fanatiker. **zealous** ['zeləs] *adv* ivrig, nidkjær; *ofte* fanatisk.

zebra ['zebrə] *sb* sebra. **zebra crossing** *sb* fotgjenger|felt, -overgang (merket med striper).

zenith ['zenɪθ] *sb* senit; *fig* høydepunkt.

zero ['zɪərəʊ] **1** *sb* null; **2** *vb:* ~ *in on* skyte seg inn på; *fig* konsentrere (seg) om.

zest [zest] *sb* **1** glede; fryd, lyst; **2** *fig* krydder (på tilværelsen etc).

Z-fold paper *sb data* listepapir.

zigzag ['zɪgzæg] **1** *adj* sikksakk-; **2** *adv* i sikksakk; **3** *sb, vi* (bevege seg, gå, løpe i) sikksakk. **zigzag-fold paper** *sb data* listepapir.

zinc [zɪŋk] *sb* sink.

zip [zɪp] **I** *sb* **1** visling; hvining/plystring (som av prosjektil); **2** skjærende lyd; **3** *dgl* futt, tæl; **4** = ~ *code*; **5** = *~-fastener*; **II** *vb* **1** visle; hvine, plystre; **2** fare/suse av sted; **3** lukke/åpne med glidelås. **zip | code** *sb US* postnummer. **~-fastener** *sb* glidelås. **zipper** ['zɪpə] *sb* = *~ fastener.*

zodiac ['zəʊdɪæk] *sb: the* ~ dyrekretsen.

zonal ['zəʊnl] *adj* sone- *etc.* **zone** [zəʊn] *sb* belte, sone; region, strøk.

zoo [zu:] *sb* (*fork* for *zoological garden*) dyre|hage, -park; zoologisk hage.